Official 2000
National Football League

Record & Fact Book

A National Football League Book.
Workman Publishing Co., New York.

NATIONAL FOOTBALL LEAGUE
280 Park Avenue, New York, N.Y. 10017 (212) 450-2000. NFL Internet Address: http://nfl.com

Printed in the United States of America.

A National Football League Book.

Compiled by the NFL Communications Department and Seymour Siwoff, Elias Sports Bureau.

Edited by Greg Solomon, NFL Communications Department, and Matt Marini, NFLP Publishing. Layout by William Tham. Proofread by Joe Velazquez, Chris McCloskey, and John Fawaz. Print managing by Dick Falk, Tina Dahl, and Lawson Desrochers. Cover design by Bill Madrid. Typesetting by Jill Franks.
Statistics by Elias Sports Bureau.
Produced by NFL Properties, Inc., Publishing Group, Los Angeles.

Cover photograph by Bill Stover.

Workman Publishing Co.
708 Broadway, New York, N.Y. 10003
Manufactured in the United States of America.
First printing, July 2000.
10 9 8 7 6 5 4 3 2 1

INDEX

2000 SCHEDULE AND NOTE CALENDAR

(All times local except American Bowl games, which are EDT.)
Nationally televised games indicated by network in parentheses.

	Saturday, July 29	Atlanta ____ at Indianapolis ____	7:00
		New Orleans ____ at New York Jets ____	8:00
	Sunday, July 30	Philadelphia ____ at Cleveland ____	8:00
		Pittsburgh ____ at Dallas ____	7:00
	Monday, July 31	AFC-NFC Pro Football Hall of Fame Game at Canton, Ohio	
		New England ____ vs. San Francisco ____	(ABC) 8:00
PRESEASON/FIRST WEEK	**Friday, August 4**	New England ____ at Detroit ____	7:00
Open Date:		Cincinnati ____ at Buffalo ____	7:30
Cleveland		Washington ____ at Tampa Bay ____	7:30
		Jacksonville ____ at Carolina ____	8:00
		New York Jets ____ at Green Bay ____	7:00
	Saturday, August 5	Miami ____ at Pittsburgh ____	7:30
		Chicago ____ at New York Giants ____	8:00
		Indianapolis ____ at Seattle ____	5:00
		Kansas City ____ at Tennessee ____	7:00
		New Orleans ____ at Minnesota ____	7:00
		Oakland ____ at St. Louis ____	7:00
		Philadelphia ____ at Baltimore ____	8:00
		San Diego ____ at San Francisco ____	6:00
		American Bowl at Tokyo, Japan	
		Atlanta ____ vs. Dallas ____	(ESPN) 10:00
		Denver ____ at Arizona ____	7:00
PRESEASON/SECOND WEEK	**Thursday, August 10**	Tampa Bay ____ at Miami ____	7:00
Open Date:		Carolina ____ at Pittsburgh ____	7:30
Philadelphia	**Friday, August 11**	Cincinnati ____ at Atlanta ____	7:30
		New England ____ at Washington ____	8:00
		New York Giants ____ at Jacksonville ____	(CBS) 8:00
	Saturday, August 12	Cleveland ____ at Chicago ____	7:00
		New Orleans ____ vs. Indianapolis ____ at W. Lafayette, Ind.	7:00
		New York Jets ____ at Baltimore ____	8:00
		Buffalo ____ at Detroit ____	(ESPN) 8:35
		Minnesota ____ at San Diego ____	6:00
		Seattle ____ at Arizona ____	7:00
	Sunday, August 13	Green Bay ____ at Denver ____	(FOX) 2:00
		Oakland ____ at Dallas ____	7:00
		San Francisco ____ at Kansas City ____	7:30
	Monday, August 14	St. Louis ____ at Tennessee ____	(ABC) 7:00
PRESEASON/THIRD WEEK	**Friday, August 18**	San Diego ____ at Atlanta ____	7:30
Open Date:		Tennessee ____ at Philadelphia ____	7:30
New Orleans		Baltimore ____ at Carolina ____	8:00
		New York Giants ____ at New York Jets ____	8:00
		Arizona ____ at Minnesota ____	(ESPN) 7:35
		Detroit ____ at Oakland ____	6:00
	Saturday, August 19	Chicago ____ at Cincinnati ____	7:30
		Washington ____ at Cleveland ____	7:30
		American Bowl at Mexico City, Mexico	
		Indianapolis ____ vs. Pittsburgh ____	(CBS) 8:00
		Buffalo ____ at St. Louis ____	7:00
		Jacksonville ____ at Kansas City ____	7:30
		Dallas ____ at Denver ____	7:00
		San Francisco ____ at Seattle ____	8:00
	Sunday, August 20	Tampa Bay ____ at New England ____	(FOX) 4:00
	Monday, August 21	Green Bay ____ at Miami ____	(ABC) 8:00

2000 SCHEDULE AND NOTE CALENDAR

PRESEASON/FOURTH WEEK
Open Date:
New York Jets

Thursday, August 24	Atlanta ____ at Jacksonville ____	7:30
	Buffalo ____ at Philadelphia ____	8:00
	Carolina ____ at New England ____	8:00
	Minnesota ____ at Indianapolis ____	7:00
	St. Louis ____ at Dallas ____	(ESPN) 7:35
	Seattle ____ at Oakland ____	6:00
Friday, August 25	Detroit ____ at Cincinnati ____	7:30
	Kansas City ____ at Tampa Bay ____	7:30
	Baltimore ____ at New York Giants ____	8:00
	Miami ____ at New Orleans ____	7:00
	Pittsburgh ____ at Washington ____	8:00
	Tennessee ____ at Chicago ____	7:00
	Denver ____ at San Francisco ____	6:00
	Arizona ____ at San Diego ____	7:00
Saturday, August 26	Cleveland ____ at Green Bay ____	4:00

KICKOFF WEEKEND
Open Date:
Cincinnati

Sunday, September 3 (CBS-TV National Weekend)	Arizona ____ at New York Giants ____	1:00
	Baltimore ____ at Pittsburgh ____	1:00
	Carolina ____ at Washington ____	1:00
	Chicago ____ at Minnesota ____	12:00
	Detroit ____ at New Orleans ____	12:00
	Indianapolis ____ at Kansas City ____	12:00
	Jacksonville ____ at Cleveland ____	1:00
	San Francisco ____ at Atlanta ____	1:00
	Tampa Bay ____ at New England ____	1:00
	Philadelphia ____ at Dallas ____	3:05
	New York Jets ____ at Green Bay ____	3:15
	San Diego ____ at Oakland ____	1:15
	Seattle ____ at Miami ____	4:15
	Tennessee ____ at Buffalo ____	(ESPN) 8:35
Monday, September 4	Denver ____ at St. Louis ____	(ABC) 8:00

SECOND WEEKEND
Open Date:
Pittsburgh

Sunday, September 10 (FOX-TV National Weekend)	Chicago ____ at Tampa Bay ____	1:00
	Cleveland ____ at Cincinnati ____	1:00
	Green Bay ____ at Buffalo ____	1:00
	Jacksonville ____ at Baltimore ____	1:00
	Kansas City ____ at Tennessee ____	12:00
	Miami ____ at Minnesota ____	12:00
	New York Giants ____ at Philadelphia ____	1:00
	Oakland ____ at Indianapolis ____	12:00
	Atlanta ____ at Denver ____	2:15
	Carolina ____ at San Francisco ____	1:15
	New Orleans ____ at San Diego ____	1:15
	St. Louis ____ at Seattle ____	1:15
	Washington ____ at Detroit ____	4:15
	Dallas ____ at Arizona ____	(ESPN) 5:35
Monday, September 11	New England ____ at New York Jets ____	(ABC) 9:00

THIRD WEEKEND
Open Dates:
Arizona, Indianapolis, Tennessee

Sunday, September 17 (FOX-TV National Weekend)	Atlanta ____ at Carolina ____	1:00
	Buffalo ____ at New York Jets ____	1:00
	Cincinnati ____ at Jacksonville ____	1:00
	Philadelphia ____ at Green Bay ____	12:00
	Pittsburgh ____ at Cleveland ____	1:00
	San Francisco ____ at St. Louis ____	12:00
	Tampa Bay ____ at Detroit ____	1:00
	Denver ____ at Oakland ____	1:05
	San Diego ____ at Kansas City ____	3:05
	Minnesota ____ at New England ____	4:15
	New Orleans ____ at Seattle ____	1:15
	New York Giants ____ at Chicago ____	3:15
	Baltimore ____ at Miami ____	(ESPN) 8:35
Monday, September 18	Dallas ____ at Washington ____	(ABC) 9:00

2000 SCHEDULE AND NOTE CALENDAR

FOURTH WEEKEND
Open Dates:
Buffalo, Carolina, Minnesota

Sunday, September 24
(CBS-TV National Weekend)

Cincinnati ____	at Baltimore ____	1:00
Detroit ____	at Chicago ____	12:00
New England ____	at Miami ____	1:00
Philadelphia ____	at New Orleans ____	12:00
St. Louis ____	at Atlanta ____	1:00
San Francisco ____	at Dallas ____	12:00
Tennessee ____	at Pittsburgh ____	1:00
Green Bay ____	at Arizona ____	1:05
Cleveland ____	at Oakland ____	1:15
Kansas City ____	at Denver ____	2:15
New York Jets ____	at Tampa Bay ____	4:15
Seattle ____	at San Diego ____	1:15
Washington ____	at New York Giants ____	(ESPN) 8:35

Monday, September 25

Jacksonville ____	at Indianapolis ____	(ABC) 8:00

FIFTH WEEKEND
Open Dates:
New Orleans, New York Jets, Oakland

Sunday, October 1
(FOX-TV National Weekend)

Baltimore ____	at Cleveland ____	1:00
Dallas ____	at Carolina ____	1:00
Indianapolis ____	at Buffalo ____	1:00
Minnesota ____	at Detroit ____	1:00
New York Giants ____	at Tennessee ____	12:00
Pittsburgh ____	at Jacksonville ____	1:00
San Diego ____	at St. Louis ____	12:00
Miami ____	at Cincinnati ____	4:05
New England ____	at Denver ____	2:05
Arizona ____	at San Francisco ____	1:15
Chicago ____	at Green Bay ____	3:15
Tampa Bay ____	at Washington ____	4:15
Atlanta ____	at Philadelphia ____	(ESPN) 8:35

Monday, October 2

Seattle ____	at Kansas City ____	(ABC) 8:00

SIXTH WEEKEND
Open Dates:
Dallas, Kansas City, St. Louis

Sunday, October 8
(CBS-TV National Weekend)

Buffalo ____	at Miami ____	1:00
Green Bay ____	at Detroit ____	1:00
Indianapolis ____	at New England ____	1:00
New Orleans ____	at Chicago ____	12:00
Pittsburgh ____	at New York Jets ____	1:00
Tennessee ____	at Cincinnati ____	1:00
Washington ____	at Philadelphia ____	1:00
New York Giants ____	at Atlanta ____	4:05
Cleveland ____	at Arizona ____	1:15
Denver ____	at San Diego ____	1:15
Oakland ____	at San Francisco ____	1:15
Seattle ____	at Carolina ____	4:15
Baltimore ____	at Jacksonville ____	(ESPN) 8:35

Monday, October 9

Tampa Bay ____	at Minnesota ____	(ABC) 8:00

SEVENTH WEEKEND
Open Dates:
Detroit, Miami, Tampa Bay

Sunday, October 15
(FOX-TV National Weekend)

Atlanta ____	at St. Louis ____	12:00
Baltimore ____	at Washington ____	1:00
Carolina ____	at New Orleans ____	12:00
Cincinnati ____	at Pittsburgh ____	1:00
Dallas ____	at New York Giants ____	1:00
Oakland ____	at Kansas City ____	12:00
San Diego ____	at Buffalo ____	1:00
Cleveland ____	at Denver ____	2:05
Indianapolis ____	at Seattle ____	1:05
New York Jets ____	at New England ____	4:05
Philadelphia ____	at Arizona ____	1:15
San Francisco ____	at Green Bay ____	3:15
Minnesota ____	at Chicago ____	(ESPN) 7:35

Monday, October 16

Jacksonville ____	at Tennessee ____	(ABC) 8:00

EIGHTH WEEKEND
Open Dates:
Green Bay, New York Giants, San Diego

Thursday, October 19

Detroit ____	at Tampa Bay ____	(ESPN) 8:35

Sunday, October 22 (FOX-TV National Weekend)

Arizona ____	at Dallas ____	12:00
Buffalo ____	at Minnesota ____	12:00
Chicago ____	at Philadelphia ____	1:00
Denver ____	at Cincinnati ____	1:00
New England ____	at Indianapolis ____	12:00
New Orleans ____	at Atlanta ____	1:00
St. Louis ____	at Kansas City ____	12:00
San Francisco ____	at Carolina ____	1:00
Tennessee ____	at Baltimore ____	1:00
Cleveland ____	at Pittsburgh ____	4:05
Seattle ____	at Oakland ____	1:05
Washington ____	at Jacksonville ____	4:15

Monday, October 23

Miami ____	at New York Jets ____	(ABC) 9:00

NINTH WEEKEND
Open Dates:
Chicago, Denver, New England

Sunday, October 29 (CBS-TV National Weekend)

Carolina ____	at Atlanta ____	1:00
Cincinnati ____	at Cleveland ____	1:00
Detroit ____	at Indianapolis ____	1:00
Green Bay ____	at Miami ____	1:00
Minnesota ____	at Tampa Bay ____	1:00
New York Jets ____	at Buffalo ____	1:00
Pittsburgh ____	at Baltimore ____	1:00
New Orleans ____	at Arizona ____	2:05
Philadelphia ____	at New York Giants ____	4:05
St. Louis ____	at San Francisco ____	1:05
Jacksonville ____	at Dallas ____	3:15
Kansas City ____	at Seattle ____	1:15
Oakland ____	at San Diego ____	(ESPN) 5:35

Monday, October 30

Tennessee ____	at Washington ____	(ABC) 9:00

TENTH WEEKEND
Open Date:
Jacksonville

Sunday, November 5 (CBS-TV National Weekend)

Baltimore ____	at Cincinnati ____	1:00
Buffalo ____	at New England ____	1:00
Dallas ____	at Philadelphia ____	1:00
Indianapolis ____	at Chicago ____	12:00
Miami ____	at Detroit ____	1:00
New York Giants ____	at Cleveland ____	1:00
Pittsburgh ____	at Tennessee ____	12:00
San Francisco ____	at New Orleans ____	12:00
Tampa Bay ____	at Atlanta ____	1:00
Washington ____	at Arizona ____	2:05
Denver ____	at New York Jets ____	4:15
Kansas City ____	at Oakland ____	1:15
San Diego ____	at Seattle ____	1:15
Carolina ____	at St. Louis ____	(ESPN) 7:35

Monday, November 6

Minnesota ____	at Green Bay ____	(ABC) 8:00

ELEVENTH WEEKEND
Open Date:
Washington

Sunday, November 12 (FOX-TV National Weekend)

Arizona ____	at Minnesota ____	12:00
Atlanta ____	at Detroit ____	1:00
Baltimore ____	at Tennessee ____	12:00
Chicago ____	at Buffalo ____	1:00
Cincinnati ____	at Dallas ____	12:00
New England ____	at Cleveland ____	1:00
New Orleans ____	at Carolina ____	1:00
Philadelphia ____	at Pittsburgh ____	1:00
Seattle ____	at Jacksonville ____	1:00
Kansas City ____	at San Francisco ____	1:05
Miami ____	at San Diego ____	1:05
Green Bay ____	at Tampa Bay ____	4:15
St. Louis ____	at New York Giants ____	4:15
New York Jets ____	at Indianapolis ____	(ESPN) 8:35

Monday, November 13

Oakland ____	at Denver ____	(ABC) 7:00

2000 SCHEDULE AND NOTE CALENDAR

TWELFTH WEEKEND
Open Date:
Seattle

Sunday, November 19 (FOX-TV National Weekend)	Arizona ____ at Philadelphia ____	1:00
	Buffalo ____ at Kansas City ____	12:00
	Carolina ____ at Minnesota ____	12:00
	Cincinnati ____ at New England ____	1:00
	Cleveland ____ at Tennessee ____	12:00
	Detroit ____ at New York Giants ____	1:00
	Indianapolis ____ at Green Bay ____	12:00
	Oakland ____ at New Orleans ____	12:00
	Tampa Bay ____ at Chicago ____	12:00
	New York Jets ____ at Miami ____	4:05
	San Diego ____ at Denver ____	2:05
	Atlanta ____ at San Francisco ____	1:15
	Dallas ____ at Baltimore ____	4:15
	Jacksonville ____ at Pittsburgh ____	(ESPN) 8:35
Monday, November 20	Washington ____ at St. Louis ____	(ABC) 8:00

THIRTEENTH WEEKEND
Open Date:
San Francisco

Thursday, November 23	New England ____ at Detroit ____	(CBS) 12:30
	Minnesota ____ at Dallas ____	(FOX) 3:05
Sunday, November 26 (CBS-TV National Weekend)	Buffalo ____ at Tampa Bay ____	1:00
	Chicago ____ at New York Jets ____	1:00
	Cleveland ____ at Baltimore ____	1:00
	Miami ____ at Indianapolis ____	1:00
	New Orleans ____ at St. Louis ____	12:00
	Philadelphia ____ at Washington ____	1:00
	Pittsburgh ____ at Cincinnati ____	1:00
	Atlanta ____ at Oakland ____	1:15
	Denver ____ at Seattle ____	1:15
	Kansas City ____ at San Diego ____	1:15
	Tennessee ____ at Jacksonville ____	4:15
	New York Giants ____ at Arizona ____	(ESPN) 6:35
Monday, November 27	Green Bay ____ at Carolina ____	(ABC) 9:00

FOURTEENTH WEEKEND
Open Date:
Baltimore

Thursday, November 30	Detroit ____ at Minnesota ____	(ESPN) 7:35
Sunday, December 3 (CBS-TV National Weekend)	Arizona ____ at Cincinnati ____	1:00
	Dallas ____ at Tampa Bay ____	1:00
	Denver ____ at New Orleans ____	12:00
	Miami ____ at Buffalo ____	1:00
	New York Giants ____ at Washington ____	1:00
	Oakland ____ at Pittsburgh ____	1:00
	St. Louis ____ at Carolina ____	1:00
	Seattle ____ at Atlanta ____	1:00
	Tennessee ____ at Philadelphia ____	1:00
	San Francisco ____ at San Diego ____	1:05
	Cleveland ____ at Jacksonville ____	4:15
	Indianapolis ____ at New York Jets ____	4:15
	Green Bay ____ at Chicago ____	(ESPN) 7:35
Monday, December 4	Kansas City ____ at New England ____	(ABC) 9:00

FIFTEENTH WEEKEND
Open Date:
Atlanta

Sunday, December 10 (FOX-TV National Weekend)	Arizona ____ at Jacksonville ____	1:00
	Carolina ____ at Kansas City ____	12:00
	Cincinnati ____ at Tennessee ____	12:00
	Detroit ____ at Green Bay ____	12:00
	Minnesota ____ at St. Louis ____	12:00
	New England ____ at Chicago ____	12:00
	Philadelphia ____ at Cleveland ____	1:00
	Pittsburgh ____ at New York Giants ____	1:00
	San Diego ____ at Baltimore ____	1:00
	Tampa Bay ____ at Miami ____	1:00
	Seattle ____ at Denver ____	2:05
	New Orleans ____ at San Francisco ____	1:15
	Washington ____ at Dallas ____	3:15
	New York Jets ____ at Oakland ____	(ESPN) 5:35
Monday, December 11	Buffalo ____ at Indianapolis ____	(ABC) 9:00

SIXTEENTH WEEKEND **Open Date:** **Philadelphia**	**Saturday, December 16**	Washington ____ at Pittsburgh ____	(FOX) 12:30
		Oakland ____ at Seattle ____	(CBS) 1:05
	Sunday, December 17 **(CBS-TV National Weekend)**	Atlanta ____ at New Orleans ____	12:00
		Denver ____ at Kansas City ____	12:00
		Detroit ____ at New York Jets ____	1:00
		Green Bay ____ at Minnesota ____	12:00
		Jacksonville ____ at Cincinnati ____	1:00
		New England ____ at Buffalo ____	1:00
		San Diego ____ at Carolina ____	1:00
		Tennessee ____ at Cleveland ____	1:00
		Chicago ____ at San Francisco ____	1:05
		Baltimore ____ at Arizona ____	2:15
		Indianapolis ____ at Miami ____	4:15
		New York Giants ____ at Dallas ____	(EPSN) 7:35
	Monday, December 18	St. Louis ____ at Tampa Bay ____	(ABC) 9:00

SEVENTEENTH WEEKEND **Open Date:** **Cleveland**	**Saturday, December 23**	Jacksonville ____ at New York Giants ____	(CBS) 12:30
		San Francisco ____ at Denver ____	(FOX) 2:15
		Buffalo ____ at Seattle ____	(ESPN) 5:35
	Sunday, December 24 **(FOX-TV National Weekend)**	Arizona ____ at Washington ____	1:00
		Chicago ____ at Detroit ____	1:00
		Cincinnati ____ at Philadelphia ____	1:00
		Kansas City ____ at Atlanta ____	1:00
		Miami ____ at New England ____	1:00
		New York Jets ____ at Baltimore ____	1:00
		St. Louis ____ at New Orleans ____	12:00
		Tampa Bay ____ at Green Bay ____	12:00
		Pittsburgh ____ at San Diego ____	1:05
		Carolina ____ at Oakland ____	1:15
		Minnesota ____ at Indianapolis ____	4:15
	Monday, December 25	Dallas ____ at Tennessee ____	(ABC) 8:00

Wild Card Playoff Games
Site Priorities
Three Wild Card teams (division non-champions with best three records) from each conference and the division champion with the third-best record in each conference will enter the first round of the playoffs. The division champion with the third-best record will play host to the Wild Card team with the third-best record. The Wild Card team with the best record will play host to the Wild Card team with the second-best record. There are no restrictions on intra-division games.

Saturday, December 30, 2000
American Football Conference
________________ at ________________ (ABC)
National Football Conference
________________ at ________________ (ABC)

Sunday, December 31, 2000
American Football Conference
________________ at ________________ (CBS)
National Football Conference
________________ at ________________ (FOX)

Divisional Playoff Games
Site Priorities
In each conference, the two division champions with the highest won-lost-tied percentage during the regular season will play host to the Wild Card winners. The division champion with the best record in each conference is assured of playing the lowest seeded Wild Card survivor. There are no restrictions on intra-division games.

Saturday, January 6, 2001
American Football Conference
________________ at ________________ (CBS)
National Football Conference
________________ at ________________ (FOX)

Sunday, January 7, 2001
American Football Conference
________________ at ________________ (CBS)
National Football Conference
________________ at ________________ (FOX)

Championship Games
Site Priorities for Championship Games
The home teams will be the surviving playoff winners with the best won-lost-tied percentage during the regular season. A Wild Card team cannot play host unless two Wild Card teams are in the game, in which case the Wild Card team that was seeded highest in the first round of the playoffs will be the home team.

Sunday, January 14, 2001

American Football Conference

________________ at ________________ (CBS)

National Football Conference

________________ at ________________ (FOX)

Super Bowl XXXV

Sunday, January 28, 2001

Super Bowl XXXV at Raymond James Stadium, Tampa, Florida

________________ vs. ________________ (CBS)

AFC-NFC Pro Bowl

Sunday, February 4, 2001

AFC-NFC Pro Bowl at Honolulu, Hawaii

AFC ______________ vs. NFC ______________ (ABC)

POSTSEASON GAMES

Saturday, December 30	AFC and NFC Wild Card Playoffs (ABC)
Sunday, December 31	AFC and NFC Wild Card Playoffs (CBS and FOX)
Saturday, January 6	AFC and NFC Divisional Playoffs (CBS and FOX)
Sunday, January 7	AFC and NFC Divisional Playoffs (CBS and FOX)
Sunday, January 14	AFC and NFC Championship Games (CBS and FOX)
Sunday, January 28	Super Bowl XXXV at Raymond James Stadium in Tampa, Florida (CBS)
Sunday, February 4	AFC-NFC Pro Bowl at Honolulu, Hawaii (ABC)

2000 NATIONALLY TELEVISED GAMES

Regular Season

Sunday, September 3	New York Jets at Green Bay (day, CBS) Tennessee at Buffalo (night, ESPN)
Monday, September 4	Denver at St. Louis (night, ABC)
Sunday, September 10	St. Louis at Seattle (day, FOX) Dallas at Arizona (night, ESPN)
Monday, September 11	New England at New York Jets (night, ABC)
Sunday, September 17	Minnesota at New England (day, FOX) Baltimore at Miami (night, ESPN)
Monday, September 18	Dallas at Washington (night, ABC)
Sunday, September 24	New York Jets at Tampa Bay (day, CBS) Washington at New York Giants (night, ESPN)
Monday, September 25	Jacksonville at Indianapolis (night, ABC)
Sunday, October 1	Tampa Bay at Washington (day, FOX) Atlanta at Philadelphia (night, ESPN)
Monday, October 2	Seattle at Kansas City (night, ABC)
Sunday, October 8	Oakland at San Francisco (day, CBS) Baltimore at Jacksonville (night, ESPN)
Monday, October 9	Tampa Bay at Minnesota (night, ABC)
Sunday, October 15	San Francisco at Green Bay (day, FOX) Minnesota at Chicago (night, ESPN)
Monday, October 16	Jacksonville at Tennessee (night, ABC)
Thursday, October 19	Detroit at Tampa Bay (night, ESPN)
Sunday, October 22	Washington at Jacksonville (day, FOX)
Monday, October 23	Miami at New York Jets (night, ABC)
Sunday, October 29	Jacksonville at Dallas (day, CBS) Oakland at San Diego (night, ESPN)
Monday, October 30	Tennessee at Washington (night, ABC)
Sunday, November 5	Denver at New York Jets (day, CBS) Carolina at St. Louis (night, ESPN)
Monday, November 6	Minnesota at Green Bay (night, ABC)
Sunday, November 12	Green Bay at Tampa Bay (day, FOX) New York Jets at Indianapolis (night, ESPN)
Monday, November 13	Oakland at Denver (night, ABC)
Sunday, November 19	Dallas at Baltimore (day, FOX) Jacksonville at Pittsburgh (night, ESPN)
Monday, November 20	Washington at St. Louis (night, ABC)
Thursday, November 23	New England at Detroit (day, CBS) Minnesota at Dallas (day, FOX)
Sunday, November 26	Tennessee at Jacksonville (day, CBS) New York Giants at Arizona (night, ESPN)
Monday, November 27	Green Bay at Carolina (night, ABC)
Thursday, November 30	Detroit at Minnesota (night, ESPN)
Sunday, December 3	Indianapolis at New York Jets (day, CBS) Green Bay at Chicago (night, ESPN)
Monday, December 4	Kansas City at New England (night, ABC)
Sunday, December 10	Washington at Dallas (day, FOX) New York Jets at Oakland (night, ESPN)
Monday, December 11	Buffalo at Indianapolis (night, ABC)
Saturday, December 16	Washington at Pittsburgh (day, FOX) Oakland at Seattle (day, CBS)
Sunday, December 17	Indianapolis at Miami (day, CBS) New York Giants at Dallas (night, ESPN)
Monday, December 18	St. Louis at Tampa Bay (night, ABC)
Saturday, December 23	Jacksonville at New York Giants (day, CBS) San Francisco at Denver (day, FOX) Buffalo at Seattle (night, ESPN)
Sunday, December 24	Minnesota at Indianapolis (day, FOX)
Monday, December 25	Dallas at Tennessee (night, ABC)

NATIONAL PRIMETIME TELEVISION GAMES AT A GLANCE

(All times local; Sunday on ESPN, Monday on ABC; also on CBS Radio)

Sunday, September 3	Tennessee at Buffalo (ESPN)	8:35
Monday, September 4	Denver at St. Louis (ABC)	8:00
Sunday, September 10	Dallas at Arizona (ESPN)	5:35
Monday, September 11	New England at New York Jets (ABC)	9:00
Sunday, September 17	Baltimore at Miami (ESPN)	8:35
Monday, September 18	Dallas at Washington (ABC)	9:00
Sunday, September 24	Washington at New York Giants (ESPN)	8:35
Monday, September 25	Jacksonville at Indianapolis (ABC)	8:00
Sunday, October 1	Atlanta at Philadelphia (ESPN)	8:35
Monday, October 2	Seattle at Kansas City (ABC)	8:00
Sunday, October 8	Baltimore at Jacksonville (ESPN)	8:35
Monday, October 9	Tampa Bay at Minnesota (ABC)	8:00
Sunday, October 15	Minnesota at Chicago (ESPN)	7:35
Monday, October 16	Jacksonville at Tennessee (ABC)	8:00
Thursday, October 19	Detroit at Tampa Bay (ESPN)	8:35
Monday, October 23	Miami at New York Jets (ABC)	9:00
Sunday, October 29	Oakland at San Diego (ESPN)	5:35
Monday, October 30	Tennessee at Washington (ABC)	9:00
Sunday, November 5	Carolina at St. Louis (ESPN)	7:35
Monday, November 6	Minnesota at Green Bay (ABC)	8:00
Sunday, November 12	New York Jets at Indianapolis (ESPN)	8:35
Monday, November 13	Oakland at Denver (ABC)	7:00
Sunday, November 19	Jacksonville at Pittsburgh (ESPN)	8:35
Monday, November 20	Washington at St. Louis (ABC)	8:00
Sunday, November 26	New York Giants at Arizona (ESPN)	6:35
Monday, November 27	Green Bay at Carolina (ABC)	9:00
Thursday, November 30	Detroit at Minnesota (ESPN)	7:35
Sunday, December 3	Green Bay at Chicago (ESPN)	7:35
Monday, December 4	Kansas City at New England (ABC)	9:00
Sunday, December 10	New York Jets at Oakland (ESPN)	5:35
Monday, December 11	Buffalo at Indianapolis (ABC)	9:00
Sunday, December 17	New York Giants at Dallas (ESPN)	7:35
Monday, December 18	St. Louis at Tampa Bay (ABC)	9:00
Saturday, December 23	Buffalo at Seattle (ESPN)	5:35
Monday, December 25	Dallas at Tennessee (ABC)	8:00

IMPORTANT DATES

2000

July 5	Claiming period of 24 hours begins in waiver system.
Mid-July	Preseason training camps open. Veteran players cannot be required to report earlier than 15 days prior to club's first preseason game or July 15, whichever is later.
July 15	Signing period ends at 4 P.M., Eastern Daylight Time, for Unrestricted Free Agents to whom June 1 tender was made by Old Club, and for Transition Players and Franchise Players who are eligible to receive Offer Sheets. After this date, and through 4 P.M., Eastern Standard Time, on November 7, Old Club has exclusive negotiating rights to these players.
July 31	Hall of Fame Game, Canton, Ohio: New England vs. San Francisco.
August 4	If a Drafted Rookie has not signed with his club by this date, he may not be traded to any other club in 2000.
August 5	American Bowl, Tokyo, Japan: Atlanta vs. Dallas.
August 22	Roster cutdown to maximum of 65 players on Active List by 4 P.M., Eastern Daylight Time.
August 27	Roster cutdown to maximum of 53 players on Active/Inactive List by 4 P.M., Eastern Daylight Time. NFL Europe League exemptions expire. Clubs may dress minimum of 42 and maximum of 45 players and third quarterback for each regular-season and postseason game.
August 28	After 4 P.M., Eastern Daylight Time, clubs may establish a Practice Squad of five players by signing free agents who do not have an accrued season of free agency credit or who were on the 45-player Active List for less than nine regular-season games during their only Accrued Season(s).
September 1	All clubs are required to identify their 49-player Active List by 7 P.M., Eastern Daylight Time, on this Friday and thereafter on each Friday before a regular-season Sunday game. No later than 1 hour and 30 minutes prior to kickoff, clubs must identify their 45-player Active List and third quarterback, if any.
September 3-4	Regular season opens.
September 19	Priority on multiple waiver claims is now based on the current season's standing.
October 10	All trading ends at 4 P.M., Eastern Daylight Time.
October 11	Players with at least four previous pension-credited seasons are subject to the waiver system for the remainder of the regular season and postseason.
November 7	Deadline for clubs to sign by 4 P.M., Eastern Standard Time, their unsigned Franchise and Transition players. If still unsigned after this date, such players are prohibited from playing in NFL in 2000.
November 7	Deadline for clubs to sign by 4 P.M., Eastern Standard Time, their Unrestricted and Restricted Free Agents to whom June 1 tender was made. If still unsigned after this date, such players are prohibited from playing in NFL in 2000.
November 7	Deadline for clubs to sign Drafted players by 4 P.M., Eastern Standard Time. If such players remain unsigned, they are prohibited from playing in NFL in 2000.
November 25	Deadline for reinstatement of players in Reserve List categories of Retired, Did Not Report, and Exclusive Rights, and of players who were placed on Reserve/Left Squad in a previous season.
December 22	Deadline for waiver requests in 2000, except for "special waiver requests" which have a 10-day claiming period, with termination or assignment delayed until after the Super Bowl.
December 26	Clubs may begin signing free-agent players for the 2001 season.
December 30-31	Wild Card Playoff Games.

2001

January 6-7	Divisional Playoff Games.
January 14	AFC and NFC Championship Games.
January 28	Super Bowl XXXV, Raymond James Stadium, Tampa, Florida.
February 4	AFC-NFC Pro Bowl, Honolulu, Hawaii.
February 5	Waiver system begins for 2001. Players with at least four previous pension-credited seasons that a club desires to terminate are not subject to the waiver system until after the trading deadline.
*February 15	Deadline at 4 P.M., Eastern Standard Time, for clubs to designate Franchise and Transition players.
*February 15	Expiration date of all player contracts due to expire in 2000.
*February 16	Free Agency period begins.
*February 16	Trading period begins for 2001 after expiration of all 2000 contracts.
February 22-26	Combine Timing and Testing, RCA Dome, Indianapolis, Indiana.
March 25-29	NFL Annual Meeting, Marriott Desert Springs, Palm Desert, California.
April 16	Deadline for signing of Offer Sheets by Restricted Free Agents.
April 21-22	Annual Player Selection Meeting, New York, N.Y.
June 1	Deadline for Old Club to send tender to its unsigned Restricted Free Agents or to extend Qualifying Offer, whichever is greater, in order to retain rights.
June 1	Deadline for Old Club to send tender to its unsigned Unrestricted Free Agents to retain rights if player is not signed by another club by July 15.

2002

*January 27	Super Bowl XXXVI, Louisiana Superdome, New Orleans, Louisiana.

2003

*January 26	Super Bowl XXXVII, Qualcomm Stadium, San Diego, California.

*Tentatively scheduled

The NFL is online to provide fans and media quick and easy access to all the latest professional football information.

NFL.COM—(http://nfl.com)

NFL.com, the league's year-round home page on the Internet, enters its fifth season in cyberspace. The site provides NFL information during the regular season, postseason, and offseason, including:

NEWS/STATS: Up-to-the-minute news from around the league, plus game previews, injury reports, and player and team stats.

TEAM AREAS: Customized areas for all 31 clubs featuring updated rosters, depth carts, and all the latest news from the teams.

GAMEDAY COVERAGE: Live game coverage with play-by-play, scores, and statistics, including graphical drive charts and comprehensive Java scoreboard that does not require reloading to get the latest information. Also includes "Player Tracker," which instantaneously updates individual player statistics.

VIDEO HIGHLIGHTS: The site will showcase NFL Films video highlights of the previous week's games as well as upcoming matchups. Video will also support feature stories and team highlight clips from every game last season.

SUPERBOWL.COM—(http://superbowl.com)

Look for superbowl.com in late December for complete coverage of the playoffs and Super Bowl XXXV. The multimedia site follows all postseason action and features audio and video clips of past Super Bowls.

During the week leading up to Super Bowl XXXV, the site will go 'live' from Tampa, providing coverage of events, press conferences, and chats with Super Bowl players and coaches.

On Super Bowl Sunday, superbowl.com will showcase a live Internet cybercast, complete with online commentators calling the action. The site also features digital photos from the game, live public address audio and press-box announcements, and live audio from foreign broadcasts.

NFLeurope.COM—(http://nfleurope.com)

The official site of NFL Europe League provides in-depth information on the six teams and their players, streaming video of one game each weekend, live audio broadcasts of all games, and weekly video highlights of game action. In addition, the site includes collectible online player trading cards of the league's Players of the Week, weekly player diaries from NFL allocated players, as well as a complete league stats package.

PLAYFOOTBALL.COM—(http://www.playfootball.com)

Play Football.com is the NFL's official web site for kids. It offers boys and girls an interactive sports destination where kids and their families can get actively involved with the NFL, including information on national youth football programs such as Punt, Pass & Kick, and NFL Flag. Youths also can find profiles on NFL players and people behind the scenes of the NFL, vote on weekly MVPs and Plays of the Week, play challenging games, and learn about football strategy and skill.

NFLhs.COM—(http://nflhs.com)

Part of the NFL's program to support youth football, nflhs.com features coaching tips from NFL personnel; scholarships, financial aid, and college eligibility information; stories of NFL players' high school experience; safety and nutrition facts, including proper tackling techniques and how to stay in shape; plus stories about the nation's top high school football teams. In addition, other features include insight into the world of officiating, an overview of NFL community programs, and a list of national high school football records.

NFL PLAYER SITES

Following are addresses for some current and former NFL players who have their own websites:

Reidel Anthony, Buccaneers (www.85rmp.com)
Darren Bennett, Chargers (www.nflaussie.com)
Doug Brien, Saints (www.kicking.com)
Derrick Brooks, Buccaneers (www.hit55.com)
Robert Brooks, Packers (www.robertbrooks.com)
Santana Dotson, Packers (www.santanadotson.com)
Jim Flanigan, Bears (www.jimflanigan.com)
Scott Frost, Jets (www.scottfrost.com)
Kent Graham, Giants (Kentgraham.com)
Mike Hollis, Jaguars (mikehollis.com)
Charlie Jones, Chargers (www.82mph.com)
Jim Kelly, Bills (www.jimkelly.com)
Shaun King, Buccaneers (www.shaunking.com)
Bronzell Miller, Chargers (www.bronzell.com)
Jerry Rice, 49ers (www.sportsline.com/u/jrice/)
Warren Sapp, Buccaneers (www.big99.com)
Junior Seau, Chargers (www.juniorseau.org/)
Jason Sehorn, Giants (www.sehornscorner.com)
Terrance Shaw, Chargers (www.run29.com)
Fran Tarkenton, Vikings-Giants (www.tarkenton.com)
Fred Taylor, Jaguars (www.run28.com)
Mike Utley, Lions (www.imageone.com/mikeutley/)

OFFICIAL NFL TEAM SITES

In addition to a dedicated area on NFL.COM, all 31 teams, including the new Houston franchise, have created their own Web sites, which have separate URLs, and are hot linked from NFL.COM.

Arizona Cardinals (www.azcardinals.com)
Atlanta Falcons (www.atlantafalcons.com)
Baltimore Ravens (www.baltimoreravens.com)
Buffalo Bills (www.buffalobills.com)
Carolina Panthers (www.cpanthers.com)
Cincinnati Bengals (www.bengals.com)
Chicago Bears (www.chicagobears.com)
Cleveland Browns (www.clevelandbrowns.com)
Dallas Cowboys (www.dallascowboys.com)
Denver Broncos (www.denverbroncos.com)
Detroit Lions (www.detroitlions.com)
Green Bay Packers (www.packers.com)
Houston NFL 2002 (www.nfl2002.com)
Indianapolis Colts (www.colts.com)
Jacksonville Jaguars (www.jaguars.com)
Kansas City Chiefs (www.kcchiefs.com)
Miami Dolphins (www.dolphinsendzone.com)
Minnesota Vikings (www.vikings.com)
New England Patriots (www.patriots.com)
New Orleans Saints (www.neworleanssaints.com)
New York Giants (www.giants.com)
New York Jets (www.newyorkjets.com)
Oakland Raiders (www.raiders.com)
Philadelphia Eagles (www.eaglesnet.com)
Pittsburgh Steelers (www.steelers.com)
San Diego Chargers (www.chargers.com)
St. Louis Rams (www.stlouisrams.com)
San Francisco 49ers (www.sf49ers.com)
Seattle Seahawks (www.seahawks.com)
Tampa Bay Buccaneers (www.buccaneers.com)
Tennessee Titans (www.titansonline.com)
Washington Redskins (www.redskins.com)

2000 SCHEDULING FORMULA

Each 2000 team schedule is based on a "common-opponent" formula initiated for the 1978 season, modified in 1995, and again in 1999 with the addition of Cleveland. Under the common-opponent format, all teams in a division play at least 10 of their 16 games the following season against common opponents. It is not a position scheduling format in which the strong play the strong and the weak play the weak.

In creating a schedule, the NFL seeks an easily understood and balanced formula that provides both competitive equality and a variety of opponents. Under the rotation scheduling system in effect from 1970-77, nondivision opponents were determined by a pre-set formula. This often resulted in competitive imbalances.

With common opponents as the basis for scheduling, a more competitive and equitable method of determining division champions and postseason playoff representatives has developed. Teams battling for a division title are playing approximately two-thirds of their games against common opponents.

In 1987, NFL owners passed a bylaw proposal designed to modify the common-opponent scheduling format and create greater equity. And in 1995, with the addition of two expansion teams, the 1987 changes were modified to include fifth-place teams in the common-opponent scheduling format for each division. The following chart shows a history of the pairings in non-division games within the conference since the change to a common-opponent format in 1978:

Prior Year's Finish in Division	Current Pairings in Non-Division Games Within Conference	Previous Pairings 1987-94	Previous Pairings 1978-86
1	1-1-2-3	1-1-2-3	1-1-4-4
2	1-2-2-4	1-2-2-4	2-2-3-3
3	1-3-3-5	1-3-3-4	2-2-3-3
4	2-4-4-5	2-3-4-4	1-1-4-4
5	3-4-5-5		

With the addition of Cleveland as the League's thirty-first franchise, some modifications to the scheduling formula were necessary to accomodate a new six-team division (AFC Central).

Under the common-opponent format, schedules of all NFL teams are figured according to the following formula. (The reference point for the figuring is the team's final division standing. Ties in divisions are broken according to the tie-breaking procedures outlined on page 25.)

A. Divisional Games

Each team will play home-and-home with the other teams in its division (8 games for all divisions except for teams in the AFC Central, which will each have 10 divisional games).

B. Intraconference Games

1. Each team in all divisions except the AFC Central will play four nondivision conference opponents based on the previous season's standings, as shown below.

2. Teams that finished first and second in the AFC Central in the previous season's standings will play two nondivision conference opponents, and teams that finished third, fourth, fifth, and sixth will each play three nondivision conference opponents, as shown below:

Prior Year's Finish in Division	NFC Teams	AFC East/West (alternating years)	AFC Central
1	1-1-2-3	1-1-2-3/1-1-2-4	1-1
2	1-2-2-4	1-2-2-5/1-2-2-3	2-2
3	1-3-3-5	2-3-3-4/1-3-3-5	3-3-4
4	2-4-4-5	1-4-4-6/3-4-4-5	3-4-4
5	3-4-5-5	4-5-5-6/2-5-5-6	3-5-5
6			4-5-5

C. Interconference Games

1. Continuing the current rotation, teams from each division of one conference will play teams from a division of the other conference, as follows:

1999	NFC-E vs. AFC-E	NFC-C vs. AFC-W	NFC-W vs. AFC-C
2000	NFC-E vs. AFC-C	NFC-C vs. AFC-E	NFC-W vs. AFC-W
2001	NFC-E vs. AFC-W	NFC-C vs. AFC-C	NFC-W vs. AFC-E

2. Each team in all divisions except the AFC Central will play four games against teams of a division of the other conference, as is done currently. The NFL will continue the rotation of interconference opponents, including rotation of home and away sites, for games between teams of the NFC and teams from the AFC East and AFC West that provides for all teams from NFC divisions to play all teams from the AFC East and AFC West four times in 15 years, two home and two away.

3. Teams that finish first and second in the AFC Central in the previous season will play four games against teams of a division of the other conference, and teams that finish third, fourth, fifth, and sixth will each play three games against teams of a division of the other conference, based on the standings from the previous season as shown below.

Prior Year's Finish In Division	AFC Central Schedule vs. NFC Division	NFC Division Schedule vs. AFC Central
1	1-2-3-4	1-2-3-4
2	1-2-3-5	1-2-3-5
3	1-2-4	1-2-4-6
4	1-3-5	1-3-5-6
5	2-4-5	2-4-5-6
6	3-4-5	

2000 NFL Standings

AFC

EAST (AE)

1 ________
2 ________
3 ________
4 ________
5 ________

CENTRAL (AC)

1 ________
2 ________
3 ________
4 ________
5 ________
6 ________

WEST (AW)

1 ________
2 ________
3 ________
4 ________
5 ________

NFC

EAST (NE)

1 ________
2 ________
3 ________
4 ________
5 ________

CENTRAL (NC)

1 ________
2 ________
3 ________
4 ________
5 ________

WEST (NW)

1 ________
2 ________
3 ________
4 ________
5 ________

A Team's 2001 Schedule

____
Team Name

OPPONENTS

1 ________
2 ________
3 ________
4 ________
5 ________
6 ________
7 ________
8 ________
9 ________
10 ________
11 ________
12 ________
13 ________
14 ________
15 ________
16 ________

2001 Non-Divisional Opponent Breakdown

Intraconference Games

American Football Conference

AFC East

	Home	Away
AE1	AW 1 AW 2	AC 1 AW 4
AE2	AW 2 AW 1	AC 2 AW 3
AE3	AW 3 AC 5	AC 3 AW 1
AE4	AW 4 AC 3	AC 4 AW 5
AE5	AW 5 AC 6	AC 5 AW 2

AFC Central

	Home	Away
AC1	AE 1	AW 1
AC2	AE 2	AW 2
AC3	AE 3	AW 3 AE 4
AC4	AE 4 AW 3	AW 4
AC5	AE 5	AW 5 AE 3
AC 6	AW 5 AW 4	AE 5

AFC West

	Home	Away
AW1	AC 1 AE 3	AE 1 AE 2
AW2	AC 2 AE 5	AE 2 AE 1
AW3	AC 3 AE 2	AE 3 AC 4
AW4	AC 4 AE 1	AE 4 AC 6
AW5	AC 5 AE 4	AE 5 AC 6

National Football Conference

NFC East

	Home	Away
NE1	NW 1 NC 3	NC 1 NW 2
NE2	NW 2 NC 1	NC 2 NW 4
NE3	NW 3 NC 5	NC 3 NW 1
NE4	NW 4 NC 2	NC 4 NW 5
NE5	NW 5 NC 4	NC 5 NW 3

NFC Central

	Home	Away
NC1	NE 1 NW 3	NW 1 NE 2
NC2	NE 2 NW 1	NW 2 NE 4
NC3	NE 3 NW 5	NW 3 NE 1
NC4	NE 4 NW 2	NW 4 NE 5
NC5	NE 5 NW 4	NW 5 NE 3

NFC West

	Home	Away
NW1	NC 1 NE 3	NE 1 NC 2
NW2	NC 2 NE 1	NE 2 NC 4
NW3	NC 3 NE 5	NE 3 NC 1
NW4	NC 4 NE 2	NE 4 NC 5
NW5	NC 5 NE 4	NE 5 NC 3

Interconference Games

BUF	NO CAR	SF ATL
IND	SF ATL	NO STL
MIA	ATL CAR	SF STL
NE	NO STL	ATL CAR
NYJ	SF STL	NO CAR

AC1	NC 2 NC 3	NC 1 NC 4
AC2	NC 1 NC 5	NC 2 NC 3
AC3	NC 1 NC 4	NC 2
AC4	NC 3	NC 1 NC 5
AC5	NC 2 NC 5	NC 4
AC6	NC 4	NC 3 NC 5

DEN	NYG WAS	DAL ARZ
KC	NYG PHL	ARZ WAS
OAK	DAL ARZ	NYG PHL
SD	ARZ WAS	DAL PHL
SEA	DAL PHL	NYG WAS

ARZ	KC DEN	SD OAK
DAL	SD DEN	OAK SEA
NYG	OAK SEA	KC DEN
PHL	SD OAK	KC SEA
WAS	KC SEA	SD DEN

NC1	AC 1 AC 4	AC 2 AC 3
NC2	AC 2 AC 3	AC 1 AC 5
NC3	AC 2 AC 6	AC 1 AC 4
NC4	AC 1 AC 5	AC 3 AC 6
NC5	AC 4 AC 6	AC 2 AC 5

ATL	NE BUF	MIA IND
CAR	NE NYJ	MIA BUF
NO	IND NYJ	NE BUF
STL	MIA IND	NE NYJ
SF	MIA BUF	IND NYJ

NFL PASSER RATING SYSTEM

The NFL rates its passers for statistical purposes against a fixed performance standard based on statistical achievements of all qualified pro passers since 1960. The current system replaced one that rated passers in relation to their position in a total group based on various criteria. The current system, which was adopted in 1973, removes inequities that existed in the former method and, at the same time, provides a means of comparing passing performances from one season to the next.

It is important to remember that the system is used to rate **passers,** not **quarterbacks.** Statistics do not reflect leadership, play-calling, and other intangible factors that go into making a successful professional quarterback. Four categories are used as a basis for compiling a rating:

—Percentage of completions per attempt
—Average yards gained per attempt
—Percentage of touchdown passes per attempt
—Percentage of interceptions per attempt

The **average** standard, is 1.000. The bottom is .000. To earn a 2.000 rating, a passer must perform at exceptional levels, i.e., 70 percent in completions, 10 percent in touchdowns, 1.5 percent in interceptions, and 11 yards average gain per pass attempt. The **maximum** a passer can receive in any category is 2.375.

For example, to gain a 2.375 in completion percentage, a passer would have to complete 77.5 percent of his passes. The NFL record is 70.55 by Ken Anderson (Cincinnati, 1982). To earn a 2.375 in percentage of touchdowns, a passer would have to achieve a percentage of 11.9. The record is 13.9 by Sid Luckman (Chicago, 1943). To gain 2.375 in percentage of interceptions, a passer would have to go the entire season without an interception. The 2.375 figure in average yards is 12.50, compared with the NFL record of 11.17 by Tommy O'Connell (Cleveland, 1957).

In order to make the rating more understandable, the point rating is then converted into a scale of 100. In rare cases, where statistical performance has been superior, it is possible for a passer to surpass a 100 rating. For example, take Steve Young's record-setting season in 1994 when he completed 324 of 461 passes for 3,969 yards, 35 touchdowns, and 10 interceptions. The four calculations would be:

—**Percentage of Completions**—324 of 461 is 70.28 percent. Subtract 30 from the completion percentage (40.28) and multiply the result by 0.05. The result is a point rating of **2.014**.
Note: If the result is less than zero (Comp. Pct. less than 30.0), award zero points. If the results are greater than 2.375 (Comp. Pct. greater than 77.5), award 2.375.

—**Average Yards Gained Per Attempt**—3,969 yards divided by 461 attempts is 8.61. Subtract three yards from yards-per-attempt (5.61) and multiply the result by 0.25. The result is **1.403**.
Note: If the result is less than zero (yards per attempt less than 3.0), award zero points. If the result is greater than 2.375 (yards per attempt greater than 12.5), award 2.375 points.

—**Percentage of Touchdown Passes**—35 touchdowns in 461 attempts is 7.59 percent. Multiply the touchdown percentage by 0.2. The result is **1.518**.
Note: If the result is greater than 2.375 (touchdown percentage greater than 11.875), award 2.375.

—**Percentage of Interceptions**—10 interceptions in 461 attempts is 2.17 percent. Multiply the interception percentage by 0.25 (0.542) and subtract the number from 2.375. The result is **1.833**.
Note: If the result is less than zero (interception percentage greater than 9.5), award zero points.

The sum of the four steps is (2.014 + 1.403 + 1.518 + 1.833) **6.768**. The sum is then divided by six (1.128) and multiplied by 100. In this case, the result is **112.8.** This same formula can be used to determine a passer rating for any player who attempts at least one pass.

The following is a list of qualifying passers who had a single-season passer rating of 100 or higher:

Player, Team	Season	Rating	Att.	Comp.	Pct.	Yds.	Avg.	TD	TD Pct.	Int.	Int. Pct.
Steve Young, San Francisco	1994	112.8	461	324	70.2	3,969	8.61	35	7.6	10	2.2
Joe Montana, San Francisco	1989	112.4	386	271	70.2	3,521	9.12	26	6.7	8	2.1
Milt Plum, Cleveland	1960	110.4	250	151	60.4	2,297	9.19	21	8.4	5	2.0
Sammy Baugh, Washington	1945	109.9	182	128	70.3	1,669	9.17	11	6.0	4	2.2
Kurt Warner, St. Louis	1999	109.2	499	325	65.1	4,353	8.72	41	8.2	13	2.6
Dan Marino, Miami	1984	108.9	564	362	64.2	5,084	9.01	48	8.5	17	3.0
Sid Luckman, Chicago Bears	1943	107.5	202	110	54.5	2,194	10.86	28	13.9	12	5.9
Steve Young, San Francisco	1992	107.0	402	268	66.7	3,465	8.62	25	6.2	7	1.7
Randall Cunningham, Minnesota	1998	106.0	425	259	60.9	3,704	8.72	34	8.0	10	2.4
Bart Starr, Green Bay	1966	105.0	251	156	62.2	2,257	8.99	14	5.6	3	1.2
Roger Staubach, Dallas	1971	104.8	211	126	59.7	1,882	8.92	15	7.1	4	1.9
Y.A. Tittle, N.Y. Giants	1963	104.8	367	221	60.2	3,145	8.57	36	9.8	14	3.8
Steve Young, San Francisco	1997	104.7	356	241	67.7	3,029	8.51	19	5.3	6	1.7
Bart Starr, Green Bay	1968	104.3	171	109	63.7	1,617	9.46	15	8.8	8	4.7
Ken Stabler, Oakland	1976	103.4	291	194	66.7	2,737	9.41	27	9.3	17	5.8
Joe Montana, San Francisco	1984	102.9	432	279	64.6	3,630	8.40	28	6.5	10	2.3
Charlie Conerly, N.Y. Giants	1959	102.7	194	113	58.2	1,706	8.79	14	7.2	4	2.1
Bert Jones, Baltimore	1976	102.5	343	207	60.3	3,104	9.05	24	7.0	9	2.6
Joe Montana, San Francisco	1987	102.1	398	266	66.8	3,054	7.67	31	7.8	13	3.3
Steve Young, San Francisco	1991	101.8	279	180	64.5	2,517	9.02	17	6.1	8	2.9
Len Dawson, Kansas City	1966	101.7	284	159	56.0	2,527	8.90	26	9.2	10	3.5
Vinny Testaverde, N.Y. Jets	1998	101.6	421	259	61.5	3,256	7.73	29	6.9	7	1.7
Steve Young, San Francisco	1993	101.5	462	314	68.0	4,023	8.71	29	6.3	16	3.5
Jim Kelly, Buffalo	1990	101.2	346	219	63.3	2,829	8.18	24	6.9	9	2.6
Steve Young, San Francisco	1998	101.1	517	322	62.3	4,170	8.07	36	7.0	12	2.3
Chris Chandler, Atlanta	1998	100.9	327	190	58.1	3,154	9.65	25	7.6	12	3.7
Jim Harbaugh, Indianapolis	1995	100.7	314	200	63.7	2,575	8.20	17	5.4	5	1.6

WAIVERS

The waiver system is a procedure by which player contracts or NFL rights to players are made available by a club to other clubs in the League. During the procedure, the 30 other clubs either file claims to obtain the players or waive the opportunity to do so—thus the term "waiver." Claiming clubs are assigned players on a priority based on the inverse of won-and-lost standing. The claiming period is three business days from the beginning of the League Year through April 30, 10 days from May 1 through the last business day before July 4, and 24 hours after July 4 through the conclusion of the regular season. If a player passes through waivers unclaimed, he becomes a free agent. All waivers are no recall and no withdrawal. Under the Collective Bargaining Agreement, from the beginning of the waiver system each year through the trading deadline (October 10, 2000), any veteran who has acquired four years of pension credit is not subject to the waiver system if the club desires to release him. After the trading deadline, such players are subject to the waiver system.

ACTIVE/INACTIVE LIST

The Active/Inactive List is the principal status for players participating for a club. It consists of all players under contract who are eligible for preseason, regular-season, and postseason games. Teams are permitted to open training camp with no more than 80 players under contract and thereafter must meet two mandatory roster reductions prior to the season opener. Teams will be permitted an Active List of 45 players and an Inactive List of eight players for each regular-season and postseason game. Provided that a club has two quarterbacks on its 45-player Active List, a third quarterback from its Inactive List is permitted to dress for the game, but if he enters the game during the first three quarters, the other two quarterbacks are thereafter prohibited from playing. Teams also are permitted to establish Practice Squads of up to five players who are eligible to participate in practice, but these players remain free agents and are eligible to sign with any other team in the league.

August 22 ....Roster reduction to 65 players
August 27 ....Roster reduction to 53 players
August 28 ....Teams establish a Practice Squad of up to five players

In addition to the squad limits described above, the overall roster limit of 80 players remains in effect throughout the regular season and postseason. The overall limit is applicable to players on a team's Active, Inactive, and Exempt Lists, players on the Practice Squad, and players on the Reserve List as Injured, Physically Unable to Perform, Non-Football Illness/Injury, and Suspended by Club.

RESERVE LIST

The Reserve List is a status for players who, for reasons of injury, retirement, military service, or other circumstances, are not immediately available for participation with a club. Players on Reserve/Injured are not eligible to practice or return to the Active/Inactive List in the same season that they are placed on Reserve. Players in the category of Reserve/Retired, Reserve/Did Not Report, Reserve/Exclusive Rights, and players who were placed in the category of Reserve/Left Squad in a previous season may not be reinstated during the period from 30 days before the end of the regular season through the postseason.

TRADES

Unrestricted trading between the AFC and NFC is allowed in 2000 through October 10, after which trading will end until 2001.

ANNUAL ACTIVE PLAYER LIMITS

NFL

Year(s)	Limit
1991-2000	45**
1985-90	45
1983-84	49
1982	45†-49
1978-81	45
1975-77	43
1974	47
1964-73	40
1963	37
1961-62	36
1960	38
1959	36
1957-58	35
1951-56	33
1949-50	32
1948	35
1947	35*-34
1945-46	33
1943-44	28
1940-42	33
1938-39	30
1936-37	25
1935	24
1930-34	20
1926-29	18
1925	16

**45 plus a third quarterback
† 45 for first two games
* 35 for first three games

AFL

Year(s)	Limit
1966-69	40
1965	38
1964	34
1962-63	33
1960-61	35

NFL FREE AGENCY MOVEMENT

The following chart details veteran free agents who signed with new teams:

	Unrestricted	Restricted	Transition	Franchise	TOTALS
1993	100	8	4	1	113
1994	104	7	4	0	115
1995	154	6	2	0	162
1996	100	4	2	0	106
1997	86	2	2	0	90
1998	112	4	1	2	119
1999	115	2	1	0	118

NFL ACTIVE STATISTICAL LEADERS

TOP ACTIVE PASSERS

1,000 or more attempts

	Yrs.	Att.	Comp.	Pct. Comp.	Yards	TD	Pct. TD	Had Int.	Pct. Int.	Rating Pts.
1. Brett Favre, G.B.	9	4,352	2,659	61.1	30,894	235	5.4	141	3.2	87.1
2. Brad Johnson, Wash.	6	1,456	898	61.7	10,468	68	4.7	42	2.9	87.0
3. Mark Brunell, Jax.	6	2,160	1,297	60.1	15,572	86	4.0	52	2.4	85.4
4. Troy Aikman, Dall.	11	4,453	2,742	61.6	31,310	158	3.5	127	2.9	82.6
5. Neil O'Donnell, Tenn.	9	3,057	1,766	57.8	20,408	114	3.7	62	2.0	82.0
6. Randall Cunningham, Minn.	14	4,075	2,301	56.5	28,557	198	4.9	128	3.1	81.4
7. Chris Chandler, Atl.	12	2,894	1,668	57.6	20,865	135	4.7	101	3.5	81.2
8. Steve Beuerlein, Car.	11	2,615	1,469	56.2	19,002	120	4.6	84	3.2	81.1
9. Warren Moon, K.C.	16	6,789	3,973	58.5	49,117	290	4.3	232	3.4	81.0
10. Jeff George, Wash.	10	3,731	2,162	57.9	26,045	147	3.9	104	2.8	81.0
11. Peyton Manning, Ind.	2	1,108	657	59.3	7,874	52	4.7	43	3.9	80.6
12. Jeff Blake, N.O.	7	2,230	1,244	55.8	15,174	93	4.2	63	2.8	79.1
13. Elvis Grbac, K.C.	6	1,431	855	59.8	9,572	56	3.9	49	3.4	78.5
14. Scott Mitchell, Cin.	9	2,147	1,208	56.3	14,688	92	4.3	70	3.3	78.2
15. Rich Gannon, Oak.	11	2,273	1,304	57.4	14,998	90	4.0	68	3.0	78.1
16. Steve McNair, Tenn.	5	1,461	821	56.2	9,838	50	3.4	36	2.5	78.1
17. Jim Harbaugh, S.D.	13	3,716	2,182	58.7	24,872	121	3.3	107	2.9	77.8
18. Erik Kramer, *	10	2,299	1,317	57.3	15,337	92	4.0	79	3.4	76.6
19.Drew Bledsoe, N.E.	7	3,921	2,192	55.9	25,966	147	3.7	123	3.1	75.7
20. Doug Flutie, Buff.	6	1,173	632	53.9	8,085	53	4.5	43	3.7	75.5
21. Vinny Testaverde, NYJ	13	4,613	2,569	56.0	32,575	205	4.4	191	4.1	75.5
22. Steve Bono, *	14	1,701	934	54.9	10,439	62	3.6	42	2.5	75.3
23. Gus Frerotte, Den.	6	1,710	919	53.7	11,886	57	3.3	51	3.0	74.5
24. Craig Erickson, *	7	1,092	591	54.1	7,625	41	3.8	38	3.5	74.3
25. John Friesz, N.E.	9	1,343	734	54.7	8,633	45	3.4	41	3.1	72.9
26. Rodney Peete, *	11	1,954	1,116	57.1	13,686	61	3.1	78	4.0	72.6
27. Tony Banks, Balt.	4	1,583	854	54.0	10,469	53	3.3	50	3.2	72.6
28. Bubby Brister, Minn.	13	2,192	1,197	54.6	14,363	81	3.7	77	3.5	72.6
29. Trent Dilfer, Balt.	6	2,038	1,117	54.8	12,969	70	3.4	80	3.9	69.4
30. Mike Tomczak, Det.	15	2,337	1,248	53.4	16,079	88	3.8	106	4.5	68.9

TOP ACTIVE SCORERS

(number in parentheses represents 2-point conversions scored)

	Yrs.	TD	FG	PAT	TP
1. Gary Anderson, Minn.	18	0	439	631	1,948
2. Morten Andersen, Atl.	18	0	416	592	1,840
3. Norm Johnson, *	18	0	366	638	1,736
4. Eddie Murray, *	18	0	344	531	1,563
5. Al Del Greco, Tenn.	16	0	320	506	1,466
6. Pete Stoyanovich, K.C.	11	0	267	394	1,195
7. Jerry Rice, S.F.	15	0	0	(4)	1,088
8. Steve Christie, Buff.	10	0	246	327	1,065
9. Jeff Jaeger, *	12	0	229	321	1,008
10. John Carney, S.D.	12	0	245	272	1,007
11. Chris Jacke, *	10	0	202	338	944
12. Emmitt Smith, Dall.	10	0	0	(1)	884
Matt Stover, Balt.	9	0	202	278	884
14. John Kasay, Car.	9	0	208	249	873
15. Jason Hanson, Det.	8	0	194	275	857
16. Jason Elam, Den.	7	0	186	288	846
17. Cris Carter, Minn.	13	0	0	(5)	700
18. Doug Pelfrey, Cin.	7	0	153	201	660
19. Cary Blanchard, Ariz.	6	0	149	170	617
20. Michael Husted, Oak.	7	0	137	181	592
21. Mike Hollis, Jax.	5	0	133	177	576
22. Todd Peterson, Sea.	6	0	128	181	565
23. Doug Brien, N.O.	6	0	122	186	552
24. Andre Reed, *	15	0	0	0	522
Thurman Thomas, Mia.	12	0	0	0	522
26. Jeff Wilkins, St.L.	6	0	107	188	509
27. Irving Fryar, Wash.	16	0	0	(2)	502
28. Ricky Watters, Sea.	8	0	0	(1)	488
29. Tim Brown, Oak.	12	1	0	(1)	476
30. Andre Rison, K.C.	11	0	0	(1)	470

TOP ACTIVE RUSHERS

	Yrs.	Att.	Yards	TD
1. Emmitt Smith, Dall.	10	3,243	13,963	136
2. Thurman Thomas, Mia.	12	2,849	11,938	65
3. Ricky Watters, Sea.	8	2,272	9,083	70
4. Jerome Bettis, Pitt.	7	2,106	8,463	41
5. Terry Allen, *	8	1,938	7,777	68
6. Chris Warren, Dall.	10	1,717	7,400	50
7. Marshall Faulk, St.L.	6	1,642	6,701	49
8. Terrell Davis, Den.	5	1,410	6,624	58
9. Curtis Martin, NYJ	5	1,694	6,550	45
10. Eddie George, Tenn.	4	1,360	5,365	28
11. Robert Smith, Minn.	7	1,116	5,297	25
12. Natrone Means, Car.	7	1,409	5,215	45
13. Adrian Murrell, Wash.	7	1,327	5,042	23
14. Garrison Hearst, S.F.	7	1,166	4,939	14
15. Randall Cunningham, Minn.	14	738	4,799	33
16. Gary Brown, *	8	1,032	4,300	21
17. Napoleon Kaufman, Oak.	5	885	4,293	12
18. Steve Young, S.F.	15	722	4,239	43
19. Jamal Anderson, Atl.	6	992	4,122	27
20. Edgar Bennett, *	7	1,115	3,992	21
21. Leroy Hoard, *	10	1,008	3,964	36
22. Errict Rhett, Cle.	6	1,103	3,885	29
23. Dorsey Levens, G.B.	6	885	3,548	25
24. Charlie Garner, S.F.	6	736	3,490	21
25. Corey Dillon, Cin.	3	758	3,459	19
26. Karim Abdul-Jabbar, *	4	1,003	3,413	33
27. Greg Hill, *	6	772	3,218	12
28. James Stewart, Det.	5	765	2,951	33
29. Mario Bates, Ariz.	6	810	2,921	36
30. Anthony Johnson, Car.	10	788	2,854	8

TOP ACTIVE PASS RECEIVERS

	Yrs.	No.	Yards	TD
1. Jerry Rice, S.F.	15	1,206	18,442	169
2. Andre Reed, *	15	941	13,095	86
3. Cris Carter, Minn.	13	924	11,688	114
4. Irving Fryar, Wash.	16	810	12,237	79
5. Tim Brown, Oak.	12	770	10,944	75
6. Michael Irvin, Dall.	12	750	11,904	65
7. Andre Rison, K.C.	11	702	9,599	78
8. Rob Moore, Ariz.	10	628	9,368	49
9. Herman Moore, Det.	9	626	8,664	59
10. Larry Centers, Wash.	10	604	5,083	22
11. Terance Mathis, Atl.	10	558	7,348	54
12. Shannon Sharpe, Balt.	10	552	6,983	44
13. Eric Metcalf, *	11	537	5,553	31
14. Tony Martin, Mia.	10	530	8,124	53
Carl Pickens, Cin.	8	530	6,887	63
16. Ben Coates, *	9	490	5,471	50
17. Ricky Proehl, St.L.	10	466	6,051	33
18. Quinn Early, *	12	460	6,448	40
19. Thurman Thomas, Mia.	12	456	4,341	22
20. Emmitt Smith, Dall.	10	442	2,728	11
21. Jeff Graham, S.D.	9	435	6,454	21
22. Mike Pritchard, Sea.	9	422	5,187	26
23. O.J. McDuffie, Mia.	7	401	4,931	29
24. Ricky Watters, Sea.	8	393	3,528	11
25. Keenan McCardell, Jax.	8	392	5,209	27
26. Isaac Bruce, St.L.	6	389	5,828	41
27. Jake Reed, N.O.	9	386	6,124	32
28. Marshall Faulk, St.L.	6	384	3,852	14
29. Chris Calloway, Atl.	10	381	5,402	30
Jimmy Smith, Jax.	6	381	5,674	28

TOP ACTIVE INTERCEPTORS

	Yrs.	No.	Yards	TD
1. Eugene Robinson, *	15	56	762	1
2. Rod Woodson, Balt.	13	54	1,163	9
3. Darrell Green, Wash.	17	50	586	6
4. Eric Allen, Oak.	12	47	662	5
5. Deion Sanders, Dall.	11	44	1,096	8
6. Cris Dishman, K.C.	12	42	550	3
7. James Hasty, K.C.	12	41	502	4
Aeneas Williams, Ariz.	9	41	551	6
9. Tim McDonald, *	13	40	640	4
10. Tyrone Braxton, *	13	36	617	4
LeRoy Butler, G.B.	10	36	508	1
12. Merton Hanks, *	9	33	410	3
13. Ray Buchanan, Atl.	7	32	590	4
Terrell Buckley, *	8	32	452	3
Eric Davis, Car.	10	32	414	4
Greg Jackson, S.D.	11	32	329	2
Darren Perry, N.O.	8	32	574	1
18. Mark Carrier, Wash.	10	31	340	1
Darryll Lewis, S.D.	9	31	549	5
20. Ray Crockett, Den.	11	29	421	2
Todd Lyght, St.L.	9	29	338	3
Troy Vincent, Phil.	8	29	562	3
Darryl Williams, Cin.	8	29	639	3
24. Willie Clay, *	8	27	437	2
Keith Lyle, St.L.	6	27	327	0
26. Tom Carter, Cin.	7	25	320	1
27. Ashley Ambrose, Atl.	8	24	208	1
Steve Atwater, *	11	24	408	1
Dwayne Harper, *	12	24	337	0
30. Mark McMillian, *	8	23	404	3
Charles Mincy, Oak.	8	23	379	3

TOP ACTIVE PUNT RETURNERS

40 or more punt returns

	Yrs.	No.	Yards	Avg.	TD
1. Darrien Gordon, Oak.	6	219	2,726	12.4	6
2. Karl Williams, T.B.	4	89	1,107	12.4	2
3. Jacquez Green, T.B.	2	53	657	12.4	1
4. Desmond Howard, *	8	182	2,189	12.0	7
5. Reggie Barlow, Jax.	4	117	1,381	11.8	2
6. Tiki Barber, NYG	3	44	506	11.5	1
7. Darrell Green, Wash.	17	51	576	11.3	0
8. Brian Mitchell, Wash.	10	317	3,476	11.0	7
9. Nate Jacquet, Mia.	3	41	447	10.9	0
10. Winslow Oliver, Atl.	4	122	1,325	10.9	2
11. Deion Sanders, Dall.	11	182	1,973	10.8	6
12. Jermaine Lewis, Balt.	4	153	1,633	10.7	4
13. Tamarick Vanover, *	5	181	1,930	10.7	4
14. Az-Zahir Hakim, St.L.	2	44	461	10.5	1
15. Jeff Burris, Ind.	6	100	1,045	10.5	0
16. Joey Galloway, Dall.	5	79	823	10.4	4
17. David Palmer, Minn.	6	152	1,577	10.4	2
18. Leon Johnson, NYJ	3	81	828	10.2	1
19. Tim Brown, Oak.	12	304	3,106	10.2	2
20. Troy Brown, N.E.	7	104	1,056	10.2	0
21. Glyn Milburn, Chi.	7	248	2,512	10.1	1
22. Kevin Williams, *	7	205	2,075	10.1	3
23. Amani Toomer, NYG	4	101	1,019	10.1	3
24. Iheanyi Uwaezuoke, *	4	52	523	10.1	0
25. Irving Fryar, Wash.	16	206	2,055	10.0	3
26. Eddie Kennison, Chi.	4	138	1,343	9.7	3
27. Terrell Buckley, *	8	76	736	9.7	1
28. Charles Jordan, *	6	63	609	9.7	0
29. Eric Metcalf, *	11	315	3,042	9.7	9
30. Dale Carter, Den.	8	83	787	9.5	2

TOP ACTIVE KICKOFF RETURNERS

40 or more kickoff returns

	Yrs.	No.	Yards	Avg.	TD
1. Tremain Mack, Cin.	3	96	2,547	26.5	2
2. Terry Fair, Det.	2	85	2,180	25.6	2
3. Tony Horne, St.L.	2	86	2,198	25.6	3
4. Ron Carpenter, *	5	42	1,066	25.4	0
5. Tim Brown, Oak.	12	49	1,235	25.2	1
6. Allen Rossum, Phil.	2	98	2,427	24.8	1
7. Michael Bates, Car.	7	256	6,333	24.7	4
8. Byron Hanspard, Atl.	2	40	987	24.7	2
9. Brock Marion, Mia.	7	84	2,067	24.6	0
10. John Avery, Den.	2	52	1,277	24.6	0
11. Derrick Cullors, N.E.	3	60	1,471	24.5	1
12. Glyn Milburn, Chi.	7	338	8,168	24.2	2
13. Duce Staley, Phil.	3	48	1,158	24.1	0
14. Tamarick Vanover, *	5	212	5,099	24.1	4
15. Tim Dwight, Atl.	2	80	1,917	24.0	1
16. Kevin Mathis, N.O.	3	43	1,029	23.9	0
17. Reggie Barlow, Jax.	4	59	1,410	23.9	1
18. Chris Watson, Den.	1	48	1,138	23.7	0
19. Mario Bates, Ariz.	7	53	1,251	23.6	0
20. Aaron Glenn, NYJ	6	108	2,527	23.4	1
21. Corey Harris, Balt.	8	188	4,386	23.3	1
22. Roell Preston, *	5	147	3,427	23.3	2
23. Reidel Anthony, T.B.	3	92	2,144	23.3	0
24. Kevin Williams, *	7	292	6,773	23.2	1
25. Deion Sanders, Dall.	11	154	3,524	22.9	3
26. Aaron Bailey, N.E.	5	153	3,501	22.9	2
27. David Dunn, Oak.	5	134	3,066	22.9	1
28. O.J. McDuffie, Mia.	7	92	2,103	22.9	0
29. Ahman Green, G.B.	2	63	1,438	22.8	0
30. Brian Mitchell, Wash.	10	421	9,586	22.8	2

TOP ACTIVE QUARTERBACK SACKERS

	Yrs.	No.
1. Bruce Smith, Wash.	15	171.0
2. Chris Doleman, *	15	150.5
3. Leslie O'Neal, K.C.	13	132.5
4. Clyde Simmons, Chi.	14	121.0
5. John Randle, Minn.	10	106.0
6. Neil Smith, *	12	104.5
7. Charles Haley, *	12	100.5
8. Henry Thomas, N.E.	13	89.0
9. Wayne Martin, *	11	82.5
10. Trace Armstrong, Mia.	11	82.0
11. Bryce Paup, Jax.	10	73.0
12. Cornelius Bennett, Ind.	13	68.5
13. Robert Porcher, Det.	8	66.5
Michael Sinclair, Sea.	8	66.5
15. Alfred Williams, *	9	59.5
16. Chuck Smith, Car.	8	58.5
17. Cortez Kennedy, Sea.	10	57.0
18. Rob Burnett, Balt.	10	56.5
Phil Hansen, Buff.	9	56.5
20. Michael McCrary, Balt.	7	55.0
21. Michael Strahan, NYG	7	52.5
22. Kevin Carter, St.L.	5	52.0
Tracy Scroggins, Det.	8	52.0
24. Chad Brown, Sea.	7	49.5
25. Bryant Young, S.F.	6	48.0
26. Chris Slade, N.E.	7	47.0
27. Anthony Pleasant, *	10	46.0
28. Bryan Cox, NYJ	9	45.5
Keith Hamilton, NYG	8	45.5
Eric Swann, Ariz.	9	45.5

TOP ACTIVE PUNTERS

50 or more punts

	Yrs.	No.	Avg.	LG
1. Darren Bennett, S.D.	4	432	44.5	66
2. Tom Rouen, Den.	7	470	44.2	76
3. Tom Tupa, NYJ	11	447	43.8	73
4. Matt Turk, Mia.	5	388	43.8	69
5. Sean Landeta, Phil.	15	1,033	43.4	74
6. Rick Tuten, St.L.	11	741	43.4	73
7. Craig Hentrich, Tenn.	6	448	43.4	78
8. Josh Miller, Pitt.	4	284	43.3	75
9. Kyle Richardson, Balt.	3	212	43.0	67
10. Leo Araguz, Oak.	4	280	42.9	64
11. Mitch Berger, Minn.	5	302	42.8	75
12. Toby Gowin, N.O.	3	244	42.8	72
13. Chris Gardocki, Cle.	9	618	42.7	72
14. Bryan Barker, Jax.	10	718	42.6	83
15. Mark Royals, T.B.	10	818	42.6	69
16. Hunter Smith, Ind.	1	58	42.5	61
17. Lee Johnson, N.E.	15	1,074	42.5	70
18. Brad Maynard, NYG	3	301	42.4	63
19. John Jett, Det.	7	489	42.3	62
20. Tommy Barnhardt, Wash.	13	811	42.3	65
21. Todd Sauerbrun, K.C.	5	328	42.2	72
22. Mike Horan, *	15	1,003	42.2	75
23. Tom Hutton, *	5	422	42.1	63
24. Scott Player, Ariz.	2	175	41.9	67
25. Daniel Pope, K.C.	1	101	41.8	64
26. Jeff Feagles, Sea.	12	980	41.7	77
27. Will Brice, Phi.	2	101	41.5	72
28. Louie Aguiar, *	9	706	41.4	71
29. Ken Walter, Car.	3	227	41.0	62
30. Chris Mohr, Buff.	10	758	40.7	80

** Free agent; subject to developments.*

COACHES RECORDS

ACTIVE COACHES' CAREER RECORDS (Order Based on Career Victories)

Start of 2000 Season

Coach	Team(s)	Regular Season Yrs.	Won	Lost	Tied	Pct.	Postseason Won	Lost	Tied	Pct.	Career Won	Lost	Tied	Pct.
Dan Reeves	Denver Broncos, New York Giants, Atlanta Falcons	19	167	128	1	.556	10	8	0	.556	177	136	1	.564
George Seifert	San Francisco 49ers, Carolina Panthers	9	106	38	0	.736	10	5	0	.667	116	43	0	.730
Jim Mora	New Orleans Saints, Indianapolis Colts	13	109	90	0	.548	0	5	0	.000	109	95	0	.534
Mike Holmgren	Green Bay Packers, Seattle Seahawks	8	84	44	0	.656	9	6	0	.600	93	50	0	.650
Dennis Green	Minnesota Vikings	8	81	47	0	.633	3	7	0	.300	84	54	0	.609
Bill Cowher	Pittsburgh Steelers	8	77	51	0	.602	5	6	0	.455	82	57	0	.590
Bobby Ross	San Diego Chargers, Detroit Lions	8	69	59	0	.539	3	5	0	.375	72	64	0	.529
Mike Shanahan	Los Angeles Raiders, Denver Broncos	7	61	39	0	.610	7	1	0	.875	68	40	0	.630
Tom Coughlin	Jacksonville Jaguars	5	49	31	0	.613	3	3	0	.500	52	34	0	.605
Jeff Fisher	Tennessee Titans	5	45	41	0	.523	3	1	0	.750	48	42	0	.533
Bruce Coslet	New York Jets, Cincinnati Bengals	8	47	74	0	.388	0	1	0	.000	47	75	0	.385
Norv Turner	Washington Redskins	6	42	53	1	.443	1	1	0	.500	43	54	1	.444
Dave Wannstedt	Chicago Bears, Miami Dolphins	6	40	56	0	.417	1	1	0	.500	41	57	0	.418
Wade Phillips	New Orleans Saints, Denver Broncos, Buffalo Bills	4	38	30	0	.559	0	3	0	.000	38	33	0	.535
Tony Dungy	Tampa Bay Buccaneers	4	35	29	0	.547	2	2	0	.500	37	31	0	.544
Bill Belichick	Cleveland Browns, New England Patriots	5	36	44	0	.450	1	1	0	.500	37	45	0	.451
Steve Mariucci	San Francisco 49ers	3	29	19	0	.604	2	2	0	.500	31	21	0	.596
Vince Tobin	Arizona Cardinals	4	26	38	0	.406	1	1	0	.500	27	39	0	.409
Jim Fassel	New York Giants	3	25	22	1	.531	0	1	0	.000	25	23	1	.520
Jon Gruden	Oakland Raiders	2	16	16	0	.500	0	0	0	.000	16	16	0	.500
Gunther Cunningham	Kansas City Chiefs	1	9	7	0	.563	0	0	0	.000	9	7	0	.563
Brian Billick	Baltimore Ravens	1	8	8	0	.500	0	0	0	.000	8	8	0	.500
Mike Riley	San Diego Chargers	1	8	8	0	.500	0	0	0	.000	8	8	0	.500
Dick Jauron	Chicago Bears	1	6	10	0	.375	0	0	0	.000	6	10	0	.375
Andy Reid	Philadelphia Eagles	1	5	11	0	.313	0	0	0	.000	5	11	0	.313
Chris Palmer	Cleveland Browns	1	2	14	0	.125	0	0	0	.000	2	14	0	.125
Dave Campo	Dallas Cowboys	0	0	0	0	.000	0	0	0	.000	0	0	0	.000
Al Groh	New York Jets	0	0	0	0	.000	0	0	0	.000	0	0	0	.000
Jim Haslett	New Orleans Saints	0	0	0	0	.000	0	0	0	.000	0	0	0	.000
Mike Martz	St. Louis Rams	0	0	0	0	.000	0	0	0	.000	0	0	0	.000
Mike Sherman	Green Bay Packers	0	0	0	0	.000	0	0	0	.000	0	0	0	.000

COACHES WITH 100 CAREER VICTORIES (Order Based on Career Victories)

Start of 2000 Season

Coach	Team(s)	Regular Season Yrs.	Won	Lost	Tied	Pct.	Postseason Won	Lost	Tied	Pct.	Career Won	Lost	Tied	Pct.
Don Shula	Baltimore Colts, Miami Dolphins	33	328	156	6	.676	19	17	0	.528	347	173	6	.665
George Halas	Chicago Bears	40	318	148	31	.671	6	3	0	.667	324	151	31	.671
Tom Landry	Dallas Cowboys	29	250	162	6	.605	20	16	0	.556	270	178	6	.601
Earl (Curly) Lambeau	Green Bay Packers, Chicago Cardinals, Washington Redskins	33	226	132	22	.624	3	2	0	.600	229	134	22	.623
Chuck Noll	Pittsburgh Steelers	23	193	148	1	.566	16	8	0	.667	209	156	1	.572
Chuck Knox	Los Angeles Rams, Buffalo Bills, Seattle Seahawks	22	186	147	1	.558	7	11	0	.389	193	158	1	.550
Dan Reeves	Denver Broncos, New York Giants, Atlanta Falcons	19	167	128	1	.556	10	8	0	.556	177	136	1	.564
Paul Brown	Cleveland Browns, Cincinnati Bengals	21	166	100	6	.621	4	8	0	.333	170	108	6	.609
Bud Grant	Minnesota Vikings	18	158	96	5	.620	10	12	0	.455	168	108	5	.607
Marv Levy	Kansas City Chiefs, Buffalo Bills	17	143	112	0	.561	11	8	0	.579	154	120	0	.562
Steve Owen	New York Giants	23	151	100	17	.595	2	8	0	.200	153	108	17	.581
Marty Schottenheimer	Cleveland Browns, Kansas City Chiefs	15	145	85	1	.630	5	11	0	.313	150	96	1	.609
Bill Parcells	New York Giants, New England Patriots New York Jets	15	138	100	1	.579	11	6	0	.647	149	106	1	.584
Joe Gibbs	Washington Redskins	12	124	60	0	.674	16	5	0	.762	140	65	0	.683
Hank Stram	Kansas City Chiefs, New Orleans Saints	17	131	97	10	.571	5	3	0	.625	136	100	10	.573
Weeb Ewbank	Baltimore Colts, New York Jets	20	130	129	7	.502	4	1	0	.800	134	130	7	.507
Mike Ditka	Chicago Bears, New Orleans Saints	14	121	95	0	.560	6	6	0	.500	127	101	0	.557
Sid Gillman	Los Angeles Rams, Los Angeles-San Diego Chargers, Houston Oilers	18	122	99	7	.550	1	5	0	.167	123	104	7	.541
George Allen	Los Angeles Rams, Washington Redskins	12	116	47	5	.705	2	7	0	.222	118	54	5	.681
Don Coryell	St. Louis Cardinals, San Diego Chargers	14	111	83	1	.572	3	6	0	.333	114	89	1	.561
George Seifert	San Francisco 49ers, Carolina Panthers	9	106	38	0	.736	10	5	0	.667	116	43	0	.730
John Madden	Oakland Raiders	10	103	32	7	.750	9	7	0	.563	112	39	7	.731
Jim Mora	New Orleans Saints, Indianapolis Colts	13	109	90	0	.548	0	5	0	.000	109	95	0	.534
Ray (Buddy) Parker	Chicago Cardinals, Detroit Lions, Pittsburgh Steelers	15	104	75	9	.577	3	1	0	.750	107	76	9	.581
Vince Lombardi	Green Bay Packers, Washington Redskins	10	96	34	6	.728	9	1	0	.900	105	35	6	.740
Tom Flores	Oakland-Los Angeles Raiders, Seattle Seahawks	12	97	87	0	.527	8	3	0	.727	105	90	0	.538
Bill Walsh	San Francisco 49ers	10	92	59	1	.609	10	4	0	.714	102	63	1	.617

Active coaches in bold.

The **Kansas City Chiefs** will play their 600th regular-season game in Week Four.

The **Oakland Raiders** need two victories for their 350th regular-season win.

The **San Francisco 49ers** need three victories to reach 400 regular-season wins.

The **Tennessee Titans** need two wins at Adelphia Coliseum to establish an NFL mark for victories to open a stadium. Tennessee was 8-0 in 1999, their inaugural season at Adelphia Coliseum. Three teams have opened stadiums with nine consecutive regular-season victories: Dallas (Texas Stadium, 1971), Akron Indians (League Park, 1920), Buffalo Bisons (Canisius Field, 1920).

Herman Moore, Detroit, needs 74 catches to become the eleventh player all-time with 700 career receptions. He has 626 in nine seasons.

Moore needs 336 receiving yards to reach 9,000. He has 8,664 receiving yards.

Cris Carter, Minnesota, needs 17 receptions to pass Art Monk, who is third all-time with 940. He needs 18 to pass Andre Reed (941) and move into second place with 941. Jerry Rice is the all-time leader with 1,139.

Andre Rison, Kansas City, needs 401 receiving yards to reach 10,000 in a career. In 11 seasons, Rison has 9,599 receiving yards.

Randy Moss, Minnesota, needs 1,000 receiving yards to become the second player all-time with 1,000-yard seasons in each of his first three years in the league. John Jefferson (San Diego 1978-1980) is the only other player to accomplish the feat.

Patrick Jeffers, Carolina, needs three straight 100-receiving yard games to break the NFL record of seven, which is currently held by three players. Jeffers has an active 5-game streak from the 1999 season.

Shannon Sharpe, Baltimore, needs 111 receptions and 998 yards to become the NFL's all-time leading tight end in catches and yards. Ozzie Newsome is the current leader with 662 receptions and 7,980 yards.

Tim Brown, Oakland, needs 30 receptions to become the eighth player all-time with 800 career receptions. In 12 seasons, Brown has 770.

Thurman Thomas, Miami, needs 802 rushing yards to pass Franco Harris (12,120), Marcus Allen (12,243), Jim Brown (12,312), and Tony Dorsett (12,739) to take over fifth all-time. Thomas has 11,938 career rushing yards in 12 seasons.

Thomas needs 214 rushing attempts to move past John Riggins (2,916), Tony Dorsett (2,936), Franco Harris (2,949), Eric Dickerson (2,996), Marcus Allen (3,022), and Barry Sanders (3,062) for third all-time. In 12 seasons, Thomas has 2,849 career rushing attempts, ninth on the NFL's all-time chart.

Thomas needs 1,376 total yards from scrimmage to move past Tony Dorsett (16,293) and Marcus Allen (17,654) for fourth all-time. Thomas has 16,279 career yards from scrimmage.

Curtis Martin, New York Jets, needs 1,000 rushing yards to become the third player in NFL history (Barry Sanders, Eric Dickerson) to rush for 1,000 yards in each of his first six seasons.

Eddie George, Tennessee, needs 1,200 rushing yards to join Eric Dickerson as the only two running backs in NFL history to rush for 1,200 yards in each of their first five NFL seasons.

Rod Woodson, Baltimore, needs one interception return for a touchdown to take sole possession of the all-time NFL lead. In 13 seasons, Woodson has 9, tied with Ken Houston for the most in league history.

Woodson has 54 career interceptions, tied for sixteenth on the NFL's all-time interception list. He needs three to move into a tie for tenth place.

Jason Elam, Denver, needs to connect on his first 38 extra-point attempts to pass Norm Johnson for first place all-time. Johnson's active streak is at 301. Elam's streak is at 264.

Morten Andersen, Atlanta, needs 24 field goals to pass all-time leader Gary Anderson (439). Andersen has 416 career field goals in 18 seasons.

Andersen needs to play in seven games to pass Clay Mathews (278), Gary Anderson (277) (see Anderson note), and Jim Marshall (282) to move into second place on the all-time career games played list.

Andersen has played in 276 career games. George Blanda is the all-time leader with 340.

Andersen needs 163 points to pass Gary Anderson (1,948) (see Anderson note) and George Blanda (2,002) to move into first on the NFL's all-time scorers list. Andersen has 1,840 career points.

Mike Vanderjagt, Indianapolis, needs to connect on his first 14 field-goal attempts to tie Gary Anderson (40), Minnesota, for most consecutive field goals made. Vanderjagt enters the season with a streak of 26 field goals made.

Gary Anderson, Minnesota, needs 55 points to pass George Blanda (2,002) to become the all-time leader for points scored in a career (see Andersen note). In 18 seasons, Anderson has scored 1,948 points.

Anderson needs to play in six games to pass Clay Mathews (278) and Jim Marshall (282) to move into second place on the all-time career games played list (see Andersen note). In 18 seasons, Anderson has played in 277 career games.

Leslie O'Neal, Kansas City, needs 10 sacks to pass Lawrence Taylor (132.5), Richard Dent (137.5), and Chris Doleman (142.5) for fourth all-time. In 13 seasons, O'Neal has 132.5 career sacks.

Cornelius Bennett, Indianapolis, needs three fumble recoveries to tie Rickey Jackson for second place all-time with 28. Bennett has 25 fumble recoveries in 13 seasons.

John Randle, Minnesota, needs 10 sacks for his ninth consecutive 10-sack season, which will tie him with Reggie White for first all-time.

Bryant Young, San Francisco, needs one safety to move into a tie with all-time leaders Doug English and Ted Hendricks, who have 4 safeties each.

Bruce Matthews, Tennessee, can tie Reggie White for second on the all-time list with his thirteenth Pro Bowl selection. Merlin Olsen was selected to 14 Pro Bowl games.

Matthews needs to play in 15 games to pass his older brother, Clay (278) to move into third place all-time in games played among nonkickers. In 17 seasons, Bruce has played in 264 games (see Andersen and Anderson notes).

DRAFT LIST FOR 2000

65th Annual NFL Draft, April 15-16, 2000
*Denotes Compensatory Selection

ARIZONA CARDINALS
1. Thomas Jones—7, RB, Virginia
2. Raynoch Thompson—41, LB, Tennessee
3. Darwin Walker—71, DT, Tennessee
4. David Barrett—102, DB, Arkansas
5. Mao Tosi—136, DT, Idaho
   *Jay Tant—164, TE, Northwestern
6. Jabari Issa—176, DT, Washington
7. Sekou Sanyika—215, LB, California

ATLANTA FALCONS
1. Choice to Baltimore
2. Travis Claridge—37, T, Southern California
3. Mark Simoneau—67, LB, Kansas State
4. Michael Thompson—100, T, Tennessee State
5. Anthony Midget—134, DB, Virginia Tech
6. Mareno Philyaw—172, WR, Troy State
7. Darrick Vaughn—211, DB, Southwest Texas State

BALTIMORE RAVENS
1. Jamal Lewis—5, RB, Tennessee, from Atlanta
   Travis Taylor—10, WR, Florida, from Denver
   Choice to Denver
2. Choice to Denver
3. Chris Redman—75, QB, Louisville
4. Choice to Minnesota
5. Richard Mercier—148, G, Miami, from San Diego
   Choice to San Francisco through Detroit, St. Louis, and Chicago
6. Adalius Thomas—186, DE, Southern Mississippi
   Cedric Woodard—191, DT, Texas, from Minnesota
7. Choice to Cleveland through St. Louis and Chicago

BUFFALO BILLS
1. Erik Flowers—26, DE, Arizona State
2. Travares Tillman—58, DB, Georgia Tech
3. Corey Moore—89, LB, Virginia Tech
4. Avion Black—121, WR, Tennessee State
5. Sammy Morris—156, RB, Texas Tech
6. Leif Larsen—194, DT, Texas-El Paso
7. Drew Haddad—233, WR, Buffalo
   *DaShon Polk—251, LB, Arizona

CAROLINA PANTHERS
1. Choice to New York Jets through Washington and San Francisco
   Rashard Anderson—23, DB, Jackson State, from Miami
2. Choice to Tampa Bay
   Deon Grant—57, DB, Tennessee, from Tampa Bay
3. Leander Jordan—82, G, Indiana, Pa.
4. Choice to Denver
   Alvin McKinley—120, DT, Mississippi State, from Tampa Bay
5. Gillis Wilson—147, DE, Southern
6. Jeno James—182, T, Auburn
7. Lester Towns—221, LB, Washington

CHICAGO BEARS
1. Brian Urlacher—9, LB, New Mexico
2. Mike Brown—39, DB, Nebraska
3. Dez White—69, WR, Georgia Tech
   Dustin Lyman—87, TE, Wake Forest, from Washington
4. Choice to St. Louis
   Reggie Austin—125, DB, Wake Forest, from St. Louis
5. Choice to Indianapolis through New Orleans
6. Frank Murphy—170, RB, Kansas State, from San Francisco
   Paul Edinger—174, K, Michigan State
7. Choice to Tennessee
   James Cotton—223, DE, Ohio State, from Cleveland
   Mike Green—254, DB, Northwestern State, La., from Cleveland

CINCINNATI BENGALS
1. Peter Warrick—4, WR, Florida State
2. Mark Roman—34, DB, Louisiana State
3. Ron Dugans—66, WR, Florida State
4. Curtis Keaton—97, RB, James Madison
5. Robert Bean—133, DB, Mississippi State
6. Neil Rackers—169, K, Illinois
7. Brad St. Louis—210, TE, Southwest Missouri State

CLEVELAND BROWNS
1. Courtney Brown—1, DE, Penn State
2. Dennis Northcutt—32, WR, Arizona
3. Travis Prentice—63, RB, Miami, Ohio
   JaJuan Dawson—79, WR, Tulane
4. Lewis Sanders—95, DB, Maryland
   Aaron Shea—110, TE, Michigan
5. Anthony Malbrough—130, DB, Texas Tech
   Lamar Chapman—146, DB, Kansas State
6. Choice to Miami
   Spergon Wynn—183, QB, Southwest Texas State
   Brad Bedell—206, G, Colorado
7. Manuia Savea—207, G, Arizona
   Eric Chandler—209, DE, Jackson State, from San Francisco through Chicago
   Choice to Chicago
   Rashidi Barnes—225, DB, Colorado, from Baltimore through St. Louis and Chicago
   Choice to Chicago

DALLAS COWBOYS
1. Choice to Seattle
2. Dwayne Goodrich—49, DB, Tennessee
3. Choice to Seattle
4. Kareem Larrimore—109, DB, West Texas A&M
5. Michael Wiley—144, WR, Ohio State
6. Mario Edwards—180, DB, Florida State
7. Orantes Grant—219, LB, Georgia

DENVER BRONCOS
1. Choice to Baltimore
   Deltha O'Neal—15, DB, California, from Baltimore
2. Ian Gold—40, LB, Michigan
   Kenoy Kennedy—45, DB, Arkansas, from Baltimore
3. Chris Cole—70, WR, Texas A&M
4. Jerry Johnson—101, DT, Florida State
   Cooper Carlisle—112, T, Florida, from Carolina
5. Choice to St. Louis
   Muneer Moore—154, WR, Richmond, from Washington through San Francisco and Seattle
6. Choice to Seattle
   Mike Anderson—189, RB, Utah, from Kansas City through St. Louis
7. Jarious Jackson—214, QB, Notre Dame
   *Leroy Fields—246, WR, Jackson State

DETROIT LIONS
1. Stockar McDougle—20, T, Oklahoma
2. Barrett Green—50, LB, West Virginia
3. Reuben Droughns—81, RB, Oregon
4. Choice to San Diego through Philadelphia
5. Todd Franz—145, DB, Tulsa
6. Quinton Reese—181, DE, Auburn
7. Choice to St. Louis
   *Alfonso Boone—253, DT, Mt. San Antonio JC (Calif.)

GREEN BAY PACKERS
1. Bubba Franks—14, TE, Miami
2. Chad Clifton—44, T, Tennessee
3. Steve Warren—74, DT, Nebraska
4. Na'il Diggs—98, LB, Ohio State, from San Francisco
   Anthony Lucas—114, WR, Arkansas
   *Gary Berry—126, DB, Ohio State
5. Kabeer Gbaja-Biamila—149, DE, San Diego State
   Joey Jamison—151, WR, Texas Southern, from Seattle
6. Choice to Seattle
7. Mark Tauscher—224, T, Wisconsin
   Ron Moore—229, DT, Northwestern Oklahoma, from Seattle
   *Charles Lee—242, WR, Central Florida
   *Eugene McCaslin—249, LB, Florida
   *Rondell Mealey—252, RB, Louisiana State

INDIANAPOLIS COLTS
1. Rob Morris—28, LB, Brigham Young
2. Marcus Washington—59, LB, Auburn
3. David Macklin—91, DB, Penn State
4. Josh Williams—122, DT, Michigan
5. Matt Johnson—138, C, Brigham Young, from Chicago through New Orleans
   Choice to New Orleans
6. Choice to New Orleans
7. Rob Renes—235, DT, Michigan
   Rodregis Brooks—238, DB, Alabama-Birmingham, from St. Louis through Oakland

JACKSONVILLE JAGUARS
1. R. Jay Soward—29, WR, Southern California
2. Brad Meester—60, C, Northern Iowa
3. T.J. Slaughter—92, LB, Southern Mississippi
4. Joey Chustz—123, T, Louisiana Tech
5. Kiwaukee Thomas—159, DB, Georgia Southern
6. Emanuel Smith—196, WR, Arkansas
7. Erik Olson—236, DB, Colorado State
   *Rob Meier—241, DE, Washington State
   *Shyrone Stith—243, RB, Virginia Tech
   *Danny Clark—245, LB, Illinois
   *Mark Baniewicz—247, T, Syracuse

KANSAS CITY CHIEFS
1. Sylvester Morris—21, WR, Jackson State
2. William Bartee—54, DB, Oklahoma
3. Greg Wesley—85, DB, Arkansas-Pine Bluff
4. Frank Moreau—115, RB, Louisville
5. Dante' Hall—153, RB, Texas A&M
   *Pat Dennis—162, DB, Louisiana-Monroe
6. Darnell Alford—188, T, Boston College, from Miami
   Choice to Denver through St. Louis
7. Desmond Kitchings—208, WR, Furman, from New Orleans
   Choice to New Orleans

MIAMI DOLPHINS
1. Choice to Carolina
2. Todd Wade—53, T, Mississippi
3. Ben Kelly—84, DB, Colorado
4. Deon Dyer—117, RB, North Carolina
5. Arturo Freeman—152, DB, South Carolina
6. Earnest Grant—167, DT, Arkansas-Pine Bluff, from Cleveland
   Choice to Kansas City
7. Choice to San Francisco
   Jeff Harris—232, DB, Georgia, from Minnesota through Cleveland and Chicago

MINNESOTA VIKINGS
1. Chris Hovan—25, DT, Boston College
2. Fred Robbins—55, DT, Wake Forest
   Michael Boireau—56, DE, Miami,
   from Washington
3. Doug Chapman—88, RB, Marshall
4. Antonio Wilson—106, LB,
   Texas A&M-Commerce, from Baltimore
   Tyrone Carter—118, DB, Minnesota
5. Choice to Washington
   *Troy Walters—165, WR, Stanford
6. Choice to Baltimore
7. Choice to Miami through Cleveland and Chicago
   *Mike Malano—240, C, San Diego State
   *Giles Cole—244, TE, Texas A&M-Kingsville
   *Lewis Kelly—248, G, South Carolina State

NEW ENGLAND PATRIOTS
1. Choice to San Francisco through New York Jets
2. Adrian Klemm—46, T, Hawaii
3. J.R. Redmond—76, RB, Arizona State
4. Choice Exercised in 1999 Supplemental Draft
   J'Juan Cherry, DB, Arizona State
   *Greg Robinson-Randall—127, T, Michigan State
5. Dave Stachelski—141, TE, Boise State
   Jeff Marriott—161, DT, Missouri, from St. Louis
6. Antwan Harris—187, DB, Virginia
   *Tom Brady—199, QB, Michigan
   *David Nugent—201, DT, Purdue
7. Casey Tisdale—226, DE, New Mexico
   *Patrick Pass—239, RB, Georgia

NEW ORLEANS SAINTS
1. Choice to Washington
2. Darren Howard—33, DE, Kansas State
3. Choice to Washington
4. Terrelle Smith—96, RB, Arizona State
5. Tutan Reyes—131, T, Mississippi
   Austin Wheatley—158, TE, Iowa,
   from Indianapolis
   *Chad Morton—166, RB, Southern California
6. Marc Bulger—168, QB, West Virginia
   Michael Hawthorne—195, DB, Purdue,
   from Indianapolis
   *Sherrod Gideon—200, WR, Southern Mississippi
7. Choice to Kansas City
   Kevin Houser—228, TE, Ohio State,
   from Kansas City

NEW YORK GIANTS
1. Ron Dayne—11, RB, Wisconsin
2. Cornelius Griffin—42, DT, Alabama
3. Ron Dixon—73, WR, Lambuth, Tenn.
4. Brandon Short—105, LB, Penn State
5. Ralph Brown—140, DB, Nebraska
6. Dhani Jones—177, LB, Michigan
7. Jeremiah Parker—217, DE, California

NEW YORK JETS
1. Shaun Ellis—12, DE, Tennessee, from Carolina
   through Washington and San Francisco
   John Abraham—13, LB, South Carolina,
   from San Diego through Tampa Bay
   Chad Pennington—18, QB, Marshall
   Anthony Becht—27, TE, West Virginia,
   from Tampa Bay
2. Choice to San Francisco
3. Laveranues Coles—78, WR, Florida State
4. Choice to San Francisco through Green Bay
5. Windrell Hayes—143, WR, Southern California
6. Tony Scott—179, DB, North Carolina State
7. Richard Seals—218, DT, Utah

OAKLAND RAIDERS
1. Sebastian Janikowski—17, K, Florida State
2. Jerry Porter—47, WR, West Virginia
3. Choice to Pittsburgh
4. Junior Ioane—107, DT, Arizona State
5. Shane Lechler—142, P, Texas A&M
6. Choice to Philadelphia
7. Mondriel Fulcher—227, TE, Miami
   Cliffton Black—231, DB, Southwest Texas State,
   from Washington through Denver and Seattle

PHILADELPHIA EAGLES
1. Corey Simon—6, DT, Florida State
2. Todd Pinkston—36, WR, Southern Mississippi
   Bobby Williams—61, G, Arkansas,
   from Tennessee
3. Choice to Tennessee
4. Gari Scott—99, WR, Michigan State
5. Choice to Tennessee
6. Thomas Hamner—171, RB, Minnesota
   John Frank—178, DE, Utah, from Oakland
   John Romero—192, C, California,
   from Washington
7. Choice to San Francisco through New England

PITTSBURGH STEELERS
1. Plaxico Burress—8, WR, Michigan State
2. Marvel Smith—38, T, Arizona State
3. Kendrick Clancy—72, DT, Mississippi
   Hank Poteat—77, DB, Pittsburgh, from Oakland
4. Danny Farmer—103, WR, UCLA
5. Clark Haggans—137, LB, Colorado State
   *Tee Martin—163, QB, Tennessee
6. Chris Combs—173, DT, Duke
   *Jason Gavadza—204, TE, Kent State
7. Choice to Washington

ST. LOUIS RAMS
1. Trung Canidate—31, RB, Arizona
2. Jacoby Shepherd—62, DB, Oklahoma State
3. John St. Clair—94, C, Virginia
4. Kaulana Noa—104, T, Hawaii, from Chicago
   Choice to Chicago
5. Brian Young—139, DE, Texas-El Paso,
   from Denver
   Choice to New England
6. Matt Bowen—198, DB, Iowa
7. Andrew Kline—220, G, San Diego State,
   from Detroit
   Choice to Indianapolis through Oakland

SAN DIEGO CHARGERS
1. Choice to New York Jets through Tampa Bay
2. Rogers Beckett—43, DB, Marshall
3. Damion McIntosh—83, T, Kansas State
4. Trevor Gaylor—111, WR, Miami, Ohio,
   from Detroit through Philadelphia
   Leonardo Carson—113, DE, Auburn
5. Choice to Baltimore
6. Shannon Taylor—184, LB, Virginia
   *Damen Wheeler—203, DB, Colorado
   *JaJuan Seider—205, QB, Florida A&M
7. Jason Thomas—222, G, Hampton

SAN FRANCISCO 49ERS
1. Choice to Washington
   Julian Peterson—16, LB, Michigan State,
   from New England through New York Jets
   Ahmed Plummer—24, DB, Ohio State,
   from Washington
2. John Engelberger—35, DE, Virginia Tech
   Jason Webster—48, DB, Texas A&M,
   from New York Jets
3. Giovanni Carmazzi—65, QB, Hofstra
   Jeff Ulbrich—86, LB, Hawaii,
   from Seattle
4. Choice to Green Bay
   John Keith—108, DB, Furman,
   from New York Jets through Green Bay
5. Paul Smith—132, RB, Texas-El Paso
   John Milem—150, DE, Lenoir-Rhyne,
   from Baltimore through Detroit, St. Louis,
   and Chicago
6. Choice to Chicago
7. Choice to Cleveland through Chicago
   Tim Rattay—212, QB, Louisiana Tech,
   from Philadelphia through New England
   Brian Jennings—230, TE, Arizona State,
   from Miami

SEATTLE SEAHAWKS
1. Shaun Alexander—19, RB, Alabama, from Dallas
   Chris McIntosh—22, T, Wisconsin
2. Ike Charlton—52, DB, Virginia Tech
3. Darrell Jackson—80, WR, Florida, from Dallas
   Choice to San Francisco
4. Marcus Bell—116, LB, Arizona
   Isaiah Kacyvenski—119, LB, Harvard,
   from Washington through San Francisco
5. Choice to Green Bay
6. James Williams—175, WR, Marshall,
   from Denver
   Tim Watson—185, DT, Rowan, from Green Bay
   John Hilliard—190, DT, Mississippi State
7. Choice to Green Bay

TAMPA BAY BUCCANEERS
1. Choice to New York Jets
2. Cosey Coleman—51, G, Tennessee,
   from Carolina
   Choice to Carolina
3. Nate Webster—90, LB, Miami
4. Choice to Carolina
5. James Whalen—157, TE, Kentucky
6. David Gibson—193, DB, Southern California
7. Joe Hamilton—234, QB, Georgia Tech

TENNESSEE TITANS
1. Keith Bulluck—30, LB, Syracuse
2. Choice to Philadelphia
3. Erron Kinney—68, TE, Florida, from Philadelphia
   Byron Frisch—93, DE, Brigham Young
4. Bobby Myers—124, DB, Wisconsin
   *Peter Sirmon—128, LB, Oregon
5. Aric Morris—135, DB, Michigan State,
   from Philadelphia
   Frank Chamberlin—160, LB, Boston College
6. Robaire Smith—197, DE, Michigan State
7. Mike Green—213, RB, Houston, from Chicago
   Wes Shivers—237, G, Mississippi State

WASHINGTON REDSKINS
1. LaVar Arrington—2, LB, Penn State,
   from New Orleans
   Chris Samuels—3, T, Alabama,
   from San Francisco
   Choice to San Francisco
2. Choice to Minnesota
3. Lloyd Harrison—64, DB, North Carolina State,
   from New Orleans
   Choice to Chicago
4. Choice to Seattle through San Francisco
   *Michael Moore—129, G, Troy State
5. Choice to Denver through San Francisco and
   Seattle
   Quincy Sanders—155, DB, Nevada-Las Vegas,
   from Minnesota
6. Choice to Philadelphia
   *Todd Husak—202, QB, Stanford
7. Delbert Cowsette—216, DT, Maryland,
   from Pittsburgh
   Choice to Oakland through Denver and Seattle
   *Ethan Howell—250, WR, Oklahoma State

DRAFT LIST

NUMBER OF PLAYERS DRAFTED—2000

BY POSITION:

Defensive Backs	52
Wide Receivers	34
Linebackers	31
Defensive Tackles	26
Running Backs	24
Defensive Ends	21
Tackles	19
Tight Ends	15
Quarterbacks	12
Guards	11
Centers	5
Kickers	3
Punters	1

BY COLLEGE:

Tennessee	9
Florida State	7
Michigan State	7
Arizona State	6
Michigan	6
Ohio State	6
Arizona	5
Arkansas	5
Florida	5
Kansas State	5
Miami	5
Southern California	5
Virginia Tech	5
Auburn	4
California	4
Colorado	4
Jackson State	4
Marshall	4
Mississippi State	4
Penn State	4
Southern Mississippi	4
Texas A&M	4
Virginia	4
West Virginia	4
Wisconsin	4
Alabama	3
Boston College	3
Brigham Young	3
Georgia	3
Georgia Tech	3
Hawaii	3
Mississippi	3
Nebraska	3
San Diego State	3
Southwest Texas State	3
Texas-El Paso	3
Utah	3
Wake Forest	3
Colorado State	2
Furman	2
Illinois	2
Iowa	2
Louisiana State	2
Louisiana Tech	2
Louisville	2
Maryland	2
Miami, Ohio	2
Minnesota	2
New Mexico	2
North Carolina State	2
Oklahoma	2
Oklahoma State	2
Oregon	2
Purdue	2
South Carolina	2
Stanford	2
Syracuse	2
Tennessee State	2
Texas Tech	2
Troy State	2
Washington	2
Alabama-Birmingham	1
Arkansas-Pine Bluff	1
Boise State	1
Buffalo	1
Central Florida	1
Duke	1
Florida A&M	1
Georgia Southern	1
Hampton	1
Harvard	1
Hofstra	1
Houston	1
Idaho	1
Indiana, Pa.	1
James Madison	1
Kent	1
Kentucky	1
Lambuth	1
Lenoir-Rhyne	1
Louisiana-Lafayette	1
Louisiana-Monroe	1
Missouri	1
Mt. San Antonio J.C. (Calif.)	1
Nevada-Las Vegas	1
North Carolina	1
Northern Iowa	1
Northwestern Oklahoma State	1
Northwestern	1
Notre Dame	1
Pittsburgh	1
Richmond	1
Rowan	1
South Carolina State	1
Southern	1
Southwest Missouri State	1
Texas	1
Texas A&M-Commerce	1
Texas A&M-Kingsville	1
Texas Southern	1
Tulane	1
Tulsa	1
UCLA	1
Washington State	1
West Texas A&M	1

BY CONFERENCE:

SEC	41
Big 10	36
Pac 10	28
Big 12	24
ACC	23
Big East	20
Mountain West	14
Conference USA	9
Independent	8
MAC	8
SWAC	8
WAC	7
Southland	6
North Central Intercollegiate Athletic	4
Lone Star	3
MEAC	3
Southern	3
Atlantic 10	2
Big West	2
Gateway	2
Ohio Valley	2
Ivy	1
Mid-South	1
New Jersey Athletic	1
Pennsylvania State Athletic	1
South Atlantic	1

UNDERCLASSMEN AND THE DRAFT

Year	Entered	Drafted	In Top 10
1989	25	12	3
1990	38	18	5
1991	33	22	2
1992	48	25	5
1993	46	24	5
1994	42	26	6
1995	42	22	2
1996	47	21	4
1997	44	27	7
1998	41	20	3
1999	35	27	5
2000	31	20	4

The following procedures will be used to break standings ties for postseason playoffs and to determine regular-season schedules. NOTE: Tie games count as one-half win and one-half loss for both clubs.

TO BREAK A TIE WITHIN A DIVISION

If, at the end of the regular season, two or more clubs in the same division finish with identical won-lost-tied percentages, the following steps will be taken until a champion is determined.

TWO CLUBS

1. Head-to-head (best won-lost-tied percentage in games between the clubs).
2. Best won-lost-tied percentage in games played within the division.
3. Best won-lost-tied percentage in games played within the conference.
4. Best won-lost-tied percentage in common games, if applicable.
5. Best net points in division games.
6. Best net points in all games.
7. Strength of schedule.
8. Best net touchdowns in all games.
9. Coin toss.

THREE OR MORE CLUBS

(Note: If two clubs remain tied after third or other clubs are eliminated during any step, tie breaker reverts to step 1 of the two-club format).

1. Head-to-head (best won-lost-tied percentage in games among the clubs).
2. Best won-lost-tied percentage in games played within the division.
3. Best won-lost-tied percentage in games played within the conference.
4. Best won-lost-tied percentage in common games.
5. Best net points in division games.
6. Best net points in all games.
7. Strength of schedule.
8. Best net touchdowns in all games.
9. Coin toss.

TO BREAK A TIE FOR THE WILD-CARD TEAM

If it is necessary to break ties to determine the three Wild-Card clubs from each conference, the following steps will be taken.

1. If the tied clubs are from the same division, apply division tie breaker.
2. If the tied clubs are from different divisions, apply the following steps.

TWO CLUBS

1. Head-to-head, if applicable.
2. Best won-lost-tied percentage in games played within the conference.
3. Best won-lost-tied percentage in common games, minimum of four.
4. Best average net points in conference games.
5. Best net points in all games.
6. Strength of schedule.
7. Best net touchdowns in all games.
8. Coin toss.

THREE OR MORE CLUBS

(Note: If two clubs remain tied after third or other clubs are eliminated, tie breaker reverts to step 1 of applicable two-club format.)

1. Apply division tie breaker to eliminate all but the highest ranked club in each division prior to proceeding to step 2. The original seeding within a division upon application of the division tie breaker remains the same for all subsequent applications of the procedure that are necessary to identify the three Wild-Card participants.
2. Head-to-head sweep. (Applicable only if one club has defeated each of the others or if one club has lost to each of the others.)
3. Best won-lost-tied percentage in games played within the conference.
4. Best won-lost-tied percentage in common games, minimum of four.
5. Best average net points in conference games.
6. Best net points in all games.
7. Strength of schedule.
8. Best net touchdowns in all games.
9. Coin toss.

When the first Wild-Card team has been identified, the procedure is repeated to name the second Wild-Card, i.e., eliminate all but the highest-ranked club in each division prior to proceeding to step 2, and repeated a third time, if necessary, to identify the third Wild Card. In situations where three or more teams from the same division are involved in the procedure, the original seeding of the teams remains the same for subsequent applications of the tie breaker if the top-ranked team in that division qualifies for a Wild-Card berth.

OTHER TIE-BREAKING PROCEDURES

1. Only one club advances to the playoffs in any tie-breaking step. Remaining tied clubs revert to the first step of the applicable division or Wild-Card tie breakers. As an example, if two clubs remain tied in any tie-breaker step after all other clubs have been eliminated, the procedure reverts to step one of the two-club format to determine the winner. When one club wins the tie breaker, all other clubs revert to step 1 of the applicable two-club or three-club format.
2. In comparing division and conference records or records against common opponents among tied teams, the best won-lost-tied percentage is the deciding factor since teams may have played an unequal number of games.
3. To determine home-field priority among division titlists, apply Wild-Card tie breakers.
4. To determine home-field priority for Wild-Card qualifiers, apply division tie breakers (if teams are from the same division) or Wild-Card tie breakers (if teams are from different divisions).

TIE-BREAKING PROCEDURE FOR SELECTION MEETING

If two or more clubs are tied in the selection order, the strength-of-schedule tie breaker is applied, subject to the following exceptions for playoff clubs:

1. The Super Bowl winner is last and the Super Bowl loser next-to-last.
2. Any non-Super Bowl playoff club involved in a tie shall be assigned priority within its segment below that of non-playoff clubs and in the order that the playoff clubs exited from the playoffs. Thus, within a tied segment a playoff club that loses in the Wild-Card game will have priority over a playoff club that loses in the Divisional playoff game, which in turn will have priority over a club that loses in the Conference Championship game. If two tied clubs exited the playoffs in the same round, the tie is broken by strength of schedule.

If any ties cannot be broken by strength of schedule, the divisional or conference tie breakers, whichever are applicable, are applied. Any ties that still exist are broken by a coin flip.

INSTANT REPLAY

For the 2000 season, the NFL will employ a system of Referee Replay Review to aid officiating.

Prior to the two-minute warning of each half, a Coaches' Challenge System will be in effect. After the two-minute warning, and throughout any overtime period, a Referee Review will be initiated by a Replay Assistant from a Replay Booth.

The following procedures will be used:

REVIEWS BY REFEREE: All Replay Reviews will be conducted by the Referee on a field-level monitor after consultation with the other covering official(s), prior to review. A decision will be reversed only when the Referee has *indisputable visual evidence* available to him that warrants the change.

COACHES' CHALLENGE: In each game, a team will be permitted a maximum of two challenges that will initiate Referee Replay reviews. Each challenge will require the use of a team time out. If a challenge is upheld, the time out will be restored to the challenging team. A challenge will never be restored. No challenges will be recognized from a team that has exhausted its time outs.

REPLAY ASSISTANT'S REQUEST FOR REVIEW: After the two-minute warning of each half, and throughout any overtime period, any review will be initiated by a Replay Assistant. There is no limit to the number of reviews that may be initiated by the Replay Assistant. His ability to initiate a review will be unrelated to the number of time outs that either team has remaining, and no time out will be charged for any review initiated by the Replay Assistant.

TIME LIMIT: Each review will be a maximum of 90 seconds in length, timed from when the Referee begins his review of the replay at the field-level monitor.

REVIEWABLE PLAYS: The Replay System will cover the following play situations only:

A) PLAYS GOVERNED BY SIDELINE, GOAL LINE, END ZONE, AND END LINE:

1. Scoring plays, including a runner breaking the plane of the goal line.
2. Pass complete/incomplete/intercepted at sideline, goal line, end zone, and end line.
3. Runner/receiver in or out of bounds.
4. Recovery of loose ball in or out of bounds.

B) PASSING PLAYS:

1. Pass ruled complete/incomplete/intercepted in the field of play.
2. Touching of a forward pass by an ineligible receiver.
3. Touching of a forward pass by a defensive player.
4. Quarterback (Passer) forward pass or fumble.
5. Illegal forward pass beyond line of scrimmage.
6. Illegal forward pass after change of possession.
7. Forward or backward pass thrown from behind line of scrimmage.

C) OTHER DETECTABLE INFRACTIONS:

1. Runner ruled not down by defensive contact.
2. Forward progress with respect to first down.
3. Touching of a kick.
4. Number of players on the field.

INSTANT REPLAY HISTORY

From 1986-1991, a limited system of Instant Replay was used on a year-by-year basis. Replay was also experimented with during the 1996 and 1998 preseasons.

Following are the results of both systems:

REGULAR SEASON, 1986-1991

Year	Games	Reversals	Plays Closely Reviewed
1986	224	38	374
1987	210	57	490
1988	224	53	537
1989	224	65	492
1990	224	73	504
1991	224	90	570
TOTAL	1,330	376	2,967

PRESEASON, 1996, 1998

Year	Games	Reversals	Challenges
1996	10	3	13
1998	10	3	10
TOTAL	20	6	23

VOTING SUMMARY, 1986-1992, 1997-2000

Year	Yes	No	Abstain	Votes Needed
1986	23	4	1	21 of 28
1987	21	7	0	21 of 28
1988	23	5	0	21 of 28
1989	24	4	0	21 of 28
1990	21	7	0	21 of 28
1991	21	7	0	21 of 28
1992	17	11	0	21 of 28
1997	20	10	0	23 of 30
1998	21	9	0	23 of 30
1999	28	3	0	24 of 31
2000	28	3	0	24 of 31

TEAMS VOTING AGAINST INSTANT REPLAY, 1997-2000

1997	1998	1999	2000
Arizona	Arizona	Arizona	Arizona
Buffalo	Buffalo	Cincinnati	Cincinnati
Chicago	Chicago	New York Jets	Kansas City
Cincinnati	Cincinnati		
Dallas	Kansas City		
Kansas City	New York Giants		
New York Giants	Oakland		
New York Jets	Tampa Bay		
Oakland	San Diego		
Tampa Bay			

The AFC

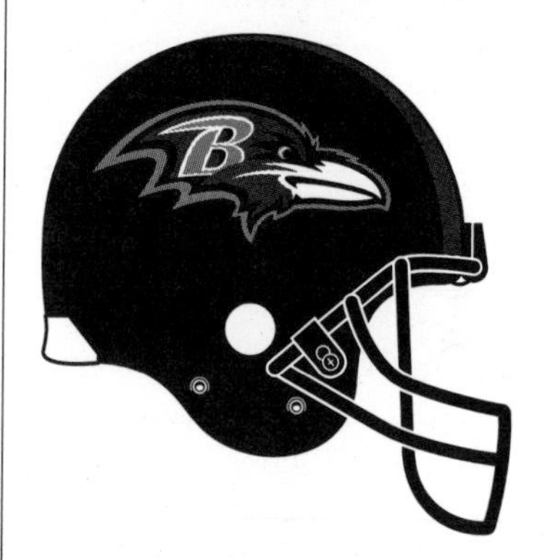

American Football Conference
Central Division
Team Colors: Black, Purple, and Metallic Gold
11001 Owings Mills Boulevard
Owings Mills, Maryland 21117
Telephone: (410) 654-6200

CLUB OFFICIALS

Owner: Arthur B. Modell
President: David Modell
Vice President/Public Relations: Kevin Byrne
Vice President/Business Development and Marketing: Dennis Mannion
Vice President/Player Personnel: Ozzie Newsome
Vice President/Administration: Pat Moriarty
Treasurer: Luis Perez
Senior Director of Broadcast and Corporate Partnerships: Mark Burdett
Senior Director of Communications and Development: Pam Malone
Director of Ticket Operations and Guest Services: Roy Sommerhof
Director of Operations/Information: Bob Eller
Director of Publications/Assistant Director of Public Relations: Francine Lubera
Director of Player Development: Earnest Byner
Director of Pro Personnel: James Harris
Director of College Scouting: Phil Savage
Director of Broadcasting and Video Production: Larry Rosen
Assistant Director of Pro Personnel: George Kokinis
Scouts: Eric DeCosta, Ron Marciniak, T.J. McCreight, Terry McDonough, Vince Newsome, Art Perkins
Head Trainer: Bill Tessendorf
Facilities Manager: Chuck Cusick
Equipment Manager: Ed Carroll
Video Director: Jon Dube
Stadium: PSINet Stadium • **Capacity:** 69,084
1101 Russell Street
Baltimore, Maryland 21230
Playing Surface: Natural Grass
Training Camp: Western Maryland College
2 College Hill
Westminster, Maryland 21157

RECORD HOLDERS

INDIVIDUAL RECORDS—CAREER

Category	Name	Performance
Rushing (Yds.)	Byron (Bam) Morris, 1996-97	1,511
Passing (Yds.)	Vinny Testaverde, 1996-97	7,148
Passing (TDs)	Vinny Testaverde, 1996-97	51
Receiving (No.)	Michael Jackson, 1996-98	183
Receiving (Yds.)	Michael Jackson, 1996-98	2,596
Interceptions	Rod Woodson, 1998-99	13
Punting (Avg.)	Kyle Richardson, 1998-99	43.4
Punt Return (Avg.)	Jermaine Lewis, 1996-99	10.7
Kickoff Return (Avg.)	Corey Harris, 1998-99	24.8
Field Goals	Matt Stover, 1996-99	94
Touchdowns (Tot.)	Michael Jackson, 1996-98	18
	Derrick Alexander, 1996-97	18
Points	Matt Stover, 1996-99	404

INDIVIDUAL RECORDS—SINGLE SEASON

Category	Name	Performance
Rushing (Yds.)	Priest Holmes, 1998	1,008
Passing (Yds.)	Vinny Testaverde, 1996	4,177
Passing (TDs)	Vinny Testaverde, 1996	33
Receiving (No.)	Michael Jackson, 1996	76
Receiving (Yds.)	Michael Jackson, 1996	1,201
Interceptions	Rod Woodson, 1999	7
Punting (Avg.)	Kyle Richardson, 1998	43.9
Punt Return (Avg.)	Jermaine Lewis, 1997	15.6
Kickoff Return (Avg.)	Corey Harris, 1998	27.6
Field Goals	Matt Stover, 1999	28
Touchdowns (Tot.)	Michael Jackson, 1996	14
Points	Matt Stover, 1999	116

INDIVIDUAL RECORDS—SINGLE GAME

Category	Name	Performance
Rushing (Yds.)	Priest Holmes, 11-22-98	227
Passing (Yds.)	Vinny Testaverde, 10-27-96	429
Passing (TDs)	Vinny Testaverde, 10-20-96	4
	Tony Banks, 12-5-99	4
Receiving (No.)	Priest Holmes, 10-11-98	13
Receiving (Yds.)	Qadry Ismail, 12-12-99	268
Interceptions	Many times	2
	Last time by Rod Woodson, 9-13-98	
Field Goals	Matt Stover, 9-21-97, 12-26-99	5
Touchdowns (Tot.)	Michael Jackson, 12-22-96	3
	Jermaine Lewis, 12-7-97	3
	Qadry Ismail, 12-12-99	3
Points	Michael Jackson, 12-22-96	18
	Matt Stover, 9-21-97	18
	Jermaine Lewis, 12-7-97	18
	Qadry Ismail, 12-12-99	18

2000 SCHEDULE

PRESEASON

Aug. 5	**Philadelphia**	8:00
Aug. 12	**New York Jets**	8:00
Aug. 18	at Carolina	8:00
Aug. 25	at New York Giants	8:00

REGULAR SEASON

Sept. 3	at Pittsburgh	1:00
Sept. 10	**Jacksonville**	1:00
Sept. 17	at Miami	8:35
Sept. 24	**Cincinnati**	1:00
Oct. 1	at Cleveland	1:00
Oct. 8	at Jacksonville	8:35
Oct. 15	at Washington	1:00
Oct. 22	**Tennessee**	1:00
Oct. 29	**Pittsburgh**	1:00
Nov. 5	at Cincinnati	1:00
Nov. 12	at Tennessee	12:00
Nov. 19	**Dallas**	4:15
Nov. 26	**Cleveland**	1:00
Dec. 3	Open Date	
Dec. 10	**San Diego**	1:00
Dec. 17	at Arizona	2:15
Dec. 24	**New York Jets**	1:00

PSINet STADIUM

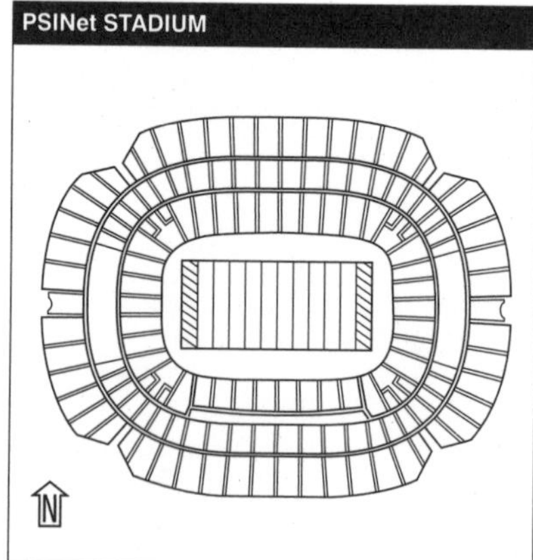

COACHING HISTORY

(24-39-1)

Years	Coach	Record
1996-98	Ted Marchibroda	16-31-1
1999	Brian Billick	8-8-0

1999 TEAM RECORD

PRESEASON (4-0)

Date	Result		Opponent
8/12	W	10-7	at Philadelphia
8/21	W	19-6	at Atlanta
8/28	W	28-24	Carolina
9/3	W	28-24	New York Giants

REGULAR SEASON (8-8)

Date	Result		Opponent	Att.
9/12	L	10-27	at St. Louis	62,100
9/19	L	20-23	Pittsburgh	68,965
9/26	W	17-10	Cleveland	68,803
10/3	W	19-13	at Atlanta (OT)	50,712
10/10	L	11-14	at Tennessee	65,486
10/21	L	8-35	Kansas City	68,771
10/31	L	10-13	Buffalo	68,673
11/7	W	41-9	at Cleveland	72,898
11/14	L	3-6	at Jacksonville	67,391
11/21	W	34-31	at Cincinnati	43,279
11/28	L	23-30	Jacksonville	68,428
12/5	W	41-14	Tennessee	67,854
12/12	W	31-24	at Pittsburgh	46,715
12/19	W	31-8	New Orleans	67,597
12/26	W	22-0	Cincinnati	68,036
1/2	L	3-20	at New England	50,263

(OT) Overtime

SCORE BY PERIODS

Ravens	64	84	85	85	6	—	324
Opponents	47	71	51	108	0	—	277

ATTENDANCE

Home 538,751 Away 478,031 Total 1,016,782
Single-game home record, 69,074 (12/13/98)
Single-season home record, 549,531 (1998)

1999 TEAM STATISTICS

	Ravens	Opp.
Total First Downs	259	260
Rushing	87	70
Passing	148	158
Penalty	24	32
Third Down: Made/Att.	65/229	86/252
Third Down Pct.	28.4	34.1
Fourth Down: Made/Att.	3/11	7/15
Fourth Down Pct.	27.3	46.7
Total Net Yards	4,778	4,222
Avg. Per Game	298.6	263.9
Total Plays	1,033	1,040
Avg. Per Play	4.6	4.1
Net Yards Rushing	1,754	1,231
Avg. Per Game	109.6	76.9
Total Rushes	431	392
Net Yards Passing	3,024	2,991
Avg. Per Game	189.0	186.9
Sacked/Yards Lost	56/336	49/291
Gross Yards	3,360	3,282
Att./Completions	546/270	599/328
Completion Pct.	49.5	54.8
Had Intercepted	20	21
Punts/Average	104/41.9	115/42.2
Net Punting Avg.	104/35.5	115/36.9
Penalties/Yards	125/1,010	122/1,118
Fumbles/Ball Lost	24/11	25/10
Touchdowns	34	31
Rushing	9	6
Passing	21	20
Returns	4	5
Avg. Time of Possession	29:24	30:36

1999 INDIVIDUAL STATISTICS

Passing	Att.	Comp.	Yds.	Pct.	TD	Int.	Tkld.	Rate
Banks	320	169	2,136	52.8	17	8	33/190	81.2
Case	170	77	988	45.3	3	8	17/116	50.3
S. Mitchell	56	24	236	42.9	1	4	6/30	31.5
Ravens	546	270	3,360	49.5	21	20	56/336	66.5
Opponents	599	328	3,282	54.8	20	21	49/291	67.1

SCORING	TD R	TD P	TD Rt	PAT	FG	Saf	PTS
Stover	0	0	0	32/32	28/33	0	116
Rhett	5	2	0	0/0	0/0	0	42
Ismail	0	6	0	0/0	0/0	0	36
Armour	0	4	0	0/0	0/0	0	24
Case	3	0	0	0/0	0/0	0	18
Johnson	0	3	0	0/0	0/0	0	18
Holmes	1	1	0	0/0	0/0	0	12
J. Lewis	0	2	0	0/0	0/0	0	12
Woodson	0	0	2	0/0	0/0	0	12
Evans	0	1	0	0/0	0/0	0	8
DeLong	0	1	0	0/0	0/0	0	6
Harris	0	0	1	0/0	0/0	0	6
Starks	0	0	1	0/0	0/0	0	6
Stokley	0	1	0	0/0	0/0	0	6
R. Lewis	0	0	0	0/0	0/0	1	2
Ravens	9	21	4	32/32	28/33	1	324
Opponents	6	20	5	26/27	19/25	0	277

2-Pt. Conversions: Evans.
Team 1-1, Opponents 4-4.

RUSHING	Att.	Yds.	Avg.	LG	TD
Rhett	236	852	3.6	52t	5
Holmes	89	506	5.7	72	1
Case	36	141	3.9	28	3
Evans	38	134	3.5	12	0
Banks	24	93	3.9	12	0
Johnson	1	12	12.0	12	0
J. Lewis	5	11	2.2	4	0
Ismail	1	4	4.0	4	0
S. Mitchell	1	1	1.0	1	0
Ravens	431	1,754	4.1	72	9
Opponents	392	1,231	3.1	31	6

RECEIVING	No.	Yds.	Avg.	LG	TD
Ismail	68	1,105	16.3	76t	6
Armour	37	538	14.5	54t	4
Evans	32	235	7.3	27	1
Johnson	29	526	18.1	76t	3
J. Lewis	25	281	11.2	46	2
Rhett	24	169	7.0	20t	2
Holmes	13	104	8.0	34t	1
DeLong	13	52	4.0	9	1
Pierce	11	102	9.3	26	0
Davis	6	121	20.2	73	0
Collins	4	62	15.5	28	0
Ofodile	4	25	6.3	9	0
Purnell	2	10	5.0	5	0
Stokley	1	28	28.0	28t	1
Ayanbadejo	1	2	2.0	2	0
Ravens	270	3,360	12.4	76t	21
Opponents	328	3,282	10.0	61	20

INTERCEPTIONS	No.	Yds.	Avg.	LG	TD
Woodson	7	195	27.9	66t	2
Starks	5	59	11.8	43t	1
McAlister	5	28	5.6	21	0
R. Lewis	3	97	32.3	60	0
Harris	1	24	24.0	24t	1
Ravens	21	403	19.2	66t	4
Opponents	20	220	11.0	56t	3

PUNTING	No.	Yds.	Avg.	In 20	LG
Richardson	103	4,355	42.3	39	63
Ravens	104	4,355	41.9	39	63
Opponents	115	4,854	42.2	24	59

PUNT RETURNS	No.	FC	Yds.	Avg.	LG	TD
J. Lewis	57	18	452	7.9	33	0
Woodson	2	2	0	0.0	7	0
Ravens	59	20	452	7.7	33	0
Opponents	43	28	468	10.9	86t	1

KICKOFF RETURNS	No.	Yds.	Avg.	LG	TD
Harris	38	843	22.2	66	0
J. Lewis	8	158	19.8	25	0
Ismail	4	55	13.8	19	0
McAlister	1	12	12.0	12	0
Washington	1	12	12.0	12	0
DeLong	1	11	11.0	11	0
Pierce	1	7	7.0	7	0
Ravens	54	1,098	20.3	66	0
Opponents	70	1,479	21.1	54	0

FIELD GOALS	1-19	20-29	30-39	40-49	50+
Stover	4/4	9/9	6/8	7/7	2/5
Ravens	4/4	9/9	6/8	7/7	2/5
Opponents	1/1	6/7	7/9	3/6	2/2

SACKS	No.
McCrary	11.5
Boulware	10.0
Burnett	6.5
Sharper	4.0
R. Lewis	3.5
Siragusa	3.5
Smith	2.0
Webster	2.0
Brown	1.0
Dalton	1.0
Harris	1.0
Jenkins	1.0
Trapp	1.0
Washington	1.0
Ravens	49.0
Opponents	56.0

2000 DRAFT CHOICES

Round	Name	Pos.	College
1	Jamal Lewis	RB	Tennessee
	Travis Taylor	WR	Florida
3	Chris Redman	QB	Louisville
5	Richard Mercier	G	Miami
6	Adalius Thomas	DE	Southern Mississippi
	Cedric Woodward	DT	Texas

BALTIMORE RAVENS

2000 VETERAN ROSTER

No.	Name	Pos.	Ht.	Wt.	Birthdate	NFL Exp.	College	Hometown	How Acq.	'99 Games/ Starts
95	Adams, Sam	DT	6-3	297	6/13/73	7	Texas A&M	Houston, Tex.	UFA(Sea)-'00	13/13*
88	# Armour, Justin	WR	6-4	215	1/1/73	6	Stanford	Manitou Springs, Colo.	FA-'99	15/7
57	# Atkins, James	G-T	6-6	330	1/28/70	7	Southwest Louisiana	Amite, La.	FA '98	2/1
30	Ayanbadejo, Obafemi	RB	6-2	235	3/5/75	2	San Diego State	Santa Cruz, Calif.	FA-'99	12/0
12	Banks, Tony	QB	6-4	225	4/5/73	5	Michigan State	San Diego, Calif.	T(StL)-'99	12/0
35	Bailey, Robert	CB	5-10	182	9/3/68	10	Miami	Miami, Fla.	UFA(Det)-'00	16/11*
76	Bobo, Orlando	G	6-3	300	2/9/74	4	Northeast Louisiana	West Point, Miss.	FA-'00	9/1*
58	Boulware, Peter	LB	6-4	255	12/18/74	4	Florida State	Columbia, S.C.	D1-'97	16/11
51	Brown, Cornell	LB	6-0	240	3/15/75	4	Virginia Tech	Lynchburg, Va.	D6-'97	16/5
90	Burnett, Rob	DE	6-4	270	8/27/67	11	Syracuse	Selden, N.Y.	D5-'90	16/16
10	# Case, Stoney	QB	6-3	201	7/7/72	6	New Mexico	Odessa, Tex.	FA-'99	10/4
92	Chase, Martin	DT	6-2	310	12/19/74	3	Oklahoma	Lawton, Okla.	D5a-'98	3/0
49	Collins, Ryan	TE	6-6	259	11/1/75	2	St. Thomas	Minneapolis, Minn.	FA-'99	4/3
91	Dalton, Lional	DT	6-1	320	2/21/75	3	Eastern Michigan	Detroit, Mich.	FA-'98	16/2
86	Davis, Billy	WR	6-1	205	7/6/72	6	Pittsburgh	El Paso, Tex.	FA-'99	16/0
85	DeLong, Greg	TE	6-4	255	4/3/73	6	North Carolina	Orefield, Pa.	UFA(Minn)-'99	16/7
61	Denson, Damon	G	6-4	310	2/8/75	3	Michigan	Aliquippa, Pa.	FA-'00	2/0*
8	Dilfer, Trent	QB	6-4	229	3/13/72	7	Fresno State	Aptos, Calif.	UFA(TB)-'00	10/10*
29	Evans, Chuck	RB	6-1	245	4/16/67	8	Clark	Augusta, Ga.	UFA(Minn)-'99	16/0
62	Flynn, Mike	G-T	6-3	295	6/15/74	3	Maine	Springfield, Mass.	FA-'97	12/0
71	Folau, Spencer	T	6-5	300	4/5/73	4	Idaho	Redwood City, Calif.	FA-'96	5/1
34	Graham, Jay	RB	5-11	215	7/14/75	4	Tennessee	Concord, N.C.	D3-'97	4/0
45	Harris, Corey	S	5-11	200	10/25/69	9	Vanderbilt	Indianapolis, Ind.	FA-'98	16/0
20	Herring, Kim	S	6-0	200	9/10/75	4	Penn State	Solon, Ohio	D2b-'97	16/16
33	† Holmes, Priest	RB	5-9	205	10/7/73	4	Texas	San Antonio, Tex.	FA-'97	9/4
87	Ismail, Qadry	WR	6-0	200	11/8/70	8	Syracuse	Wilkes-Barre, Pa.	FA-'99	16/16
50	Jackson, Brad	LB	6-0	230	1/11/75	2	Cincinnati	Akron, Ohio	FA-'98	13/0
83	Johnson, Patrick	WR	5-10	180	8/10/76	3	Oregon	Redlands, Calif.	D2-'98	10/6
84	Lewis, Jermaine	KR-WR	5-7	175	10/16/74	5	Maryland	Lanham, Md.	D5-'96	15/6
52	Lewis, Ray	LB	6-1	245	5/15/75	5	Miami	Lakeland, Fla.	D1b-'96	16/16
21	McAlister, Chris	CB	6-1	206	6/14/77	2	Arizona	Pasadena, Calif.	D1-'99	16/12
99	McCrary, Michael	DE	6-4	260	7/7/70	8	Wake Forest	Falls Church, Va.	UFA(Sea)-'97	16/16
60	Mitchell, Jeff	C	6-4	300	1/29/74	4	Florida	Clearwater, Fla.	D5-'97	16/16
64	Mulitalo, Edwin	G-T	6-3	340	9/1/74	2	Arizona	Daly City, Calif.	D4b-'99	10/8
11	Nash, Marcus	WR	6-3	195	2/1/76	3	Tennessee	Tulsa, Okla.	FA-'99	1/0
89	# Ofodile, A.J.	TE	6-6	260	10/9/73	5	Missouri	Detroit, Mich.	FA-'96	7/3
75	Ogden, Jonathan	G-T	6-8	335	7/31/74	5	UCLA	Washington, D.C.	D1a-'96	16/16
59	Payne, Rod	C	6-4	305	6/14/74	3	Michigan	Miami, Fla.	FA-'00	0*
53	Peters, Tyrell	LB	6-0	235	8/4/74	4	Oklahoma	Norman, Okla.	FA-'97	13/0
43	Poindexter, Anthony	S	6-0	210	7/28/76	2	Virginia	Jefferson Forest, Va.	D7-'99	0*
5	Richardson, Kyle	P	6-2	210	3/2/73	3	Arkansas State	Farmington, Mo.	FA-'98	16/0
2	Sharpe, Shannon	TE	6-2	230	6/26/68	11	Savannah State	Glennville, Ga.	UFA(Den)-'00	5/5*
55	† Sharper, Jamie	LB	6-3	240	11/23/74	4	Virginia	Richmond, Va.	D2a-'97	16/16
98	Siragusa, Tony	DT	6-3	340	5/14/67	11	Pittsburgh	Kenilworth, N.J.	UFA(Ind)-'97	14/14
22	Starks, Duane	CB	5-10	170	5/23/74	3	Miami	Miami Beach, Fla.	D1-'98	16/6
56	Stallings, Dennis	LB	6-0	240	5/25/74	4	Illinois	East St. Louis, Mo.	FA-'00	0*
80	Stokley, Brandon	WR	5-11	197	6/23/76	2	Southwest Louisiana	Comeaux, La.	D4a-'99	2/0
3	Stover, Matt	K	5-11	178	1/27/68	11	Louisiana Tech	Dallas, Tex.	PB(NYG)-'91	16/0
70	Swayne, Harry	T	6-5	295	2/2/65	14	Rutgers	Philadelphia, Pa.	UFA(Den)-'99	6/6
37	Thompson, Bennie	S	6-0	220	2/10/63	11	Grambling State	New Orleans, La.	UFA(NO)-'94	16/0
38	Trapp, James	CB	6-0	190	12/28/69	8	Clemson	Lawton, Okla.	UFA(Oak)-'99	16/0
77	Vickers, Kipp	G-T	6-2	298	8/27/69	5	Miami	Holiday, Fla.	UFA(Wash)-'00	11/0*
82	Wainright, Frank	TE	6-2	255	10/10/67	10	Northern Colorado	Arvada, Colo.	UFA(Mia)-'99	16/0
93	Washington, Keith	DE	6-4	270	12/18/72	6	Nevada-Las Vegas	Dallas, Tex.	FA-'97	16/0
72	Williams, Sammy	G-T	6-5	318	12/14/74	3	Oklahoma	Harvey, Ill.	FA-'99	0*
26	Woodson, Rod	CB	6-0	205	3/10/65	14	Purdue	Fort Wayne, Ind.	FA-'98	16/16

* Adams played 13 games with Seattle in '99; Bailey played 16 games with Detroit; Bobo played 9 games with Cleveland; Denson played 2 games with New England; Dilfer played 10 games with Tampa Bay; Payne last active with Cincinnati in '98; Poindexter was inactive for 4 games in '99; Sharpe played 5 games with Denver; Stallings last active with Tennessee in '95; Vickers played 11 games with Washington in '99; Williams was inactive for 8 games in '99.

† Restricted free agent; subject to developments.

Unrestricted free agent; subject to developments.

Players lost through free agency (5): CB DeRon Jenkins (SD; 16 games in '99); G Everett Lindsay (Cle; 16), QB Scott Mitchell (Cin; 2), RB Errict Rhett (Cle; 16), DE Fernando Smith (Minn; 15).

Also played with Ravens in '99—G Jeff Blackshear (16 games), S Stevon Moore (8), TE Aaron Pierce (10), TE Lovett Purnell (2), RB Tony Vinson (3), DT Larry Webster (16).

COACHING STAFF

Head Coach,
Brian Billick

Pro Career: First-year head coach Brian Billick, who was hired January 19, 1999, posted an 8-8 record last season, the most wins in franchise history, and a strong 6-3 finish (4-0 in December). Under Billick, the Ravens outscored their final nine opponents, 229-142. The offense averaged more than 25 points and 322 yards per game in the final nine games, after averaging slightly more than 13 points and 268 yards in the first seven contests. Billick and his staff helped groom quarterback Tony Banks, who threw a career-high 17 touchdown passes and a career-low eight interceptions in 10 starts. Wide receiver Qadry Ismail posted 1,105 yards on 68 catches and 6 touchdowns, while Justin Armour finished with 37 receptions for 538 yards and 4 touchdowns. Errict Rhett and Priest Holmes combined for six 100-yard rushing games, running behind a line led by three-time Pro Bowl starter Jonathan Ogden. Baltimore's defense finished second in the NFL in total yards allowed (263.9 yards per game) and first in fewest yards allowed per play (4.1) and opponent's average pass attempt (5.48). The defense did not allow a 100-yard rusher all season (along with St. Louis) and permitted only 38 plays of 20 or more yards, which ranked second in the league behind Buffalo (37). Baltimore finished 4-0 in December and was in contention for the postseason until week 16. Billick was the Minnesota offensive coordinator for five years (1994-98), orchestrating a Vikings' attack that set a variety of NFL and club records. The Minnesota offense broke the NFL record for most points scored in a season (556), surpassing the old mark (541) set by the 1983 Washington Redskins. Career record: 8-8.

Background: Prior to his appointment with the Vikings, Billick was a Stanford assistant from 1989-1991 under Vikings head coach Dennis Green. He spent three seasons as offensive coordinator at Utah State (1986-88). Billick coached receivers, tight ends, and quarterbacks at San Diego State from 1981-85 and held a dual responsibility as recruiting coordinator. He began his coaching career as an assistant at Redlands in 1977 and spent the following year (1978) as a graduate assistant at Brigham Young working with tight ends and the offensive line. Billick was assistant director of public relations for the San Francisco 49ers in 1979-1980.

Personal: Born February 28, 1954 in Fairborne, Ohio, Billick earned All-Western Athletic Conference honors and was a honorable mention All-America in 1976 as a tight end at Brigham Young. Played linebacker at Air Force as a freshman before transferring to Brigham Young. In 1977, Billick was drafted by the 49ers in the eleventh round, was released, and had a brief stint with the Dallas Cowboys, but did not play. He and his wife Kim have two daughters—Aubree and Keegan.

ASSISTANT COACHES

Matt Cavanaugh, offensive coordinator; born October 27, 1956, Youngstown, Ohio, lives in Owings Mills, Md. Quarterback Pittsburgh 1974-77. Pro quarterback New England Patriots 1978-1982, San Francisco 49ers 1983-85, Philadelphia Eagles 1986-89, New York Giants 1990-91. College coach: Pittsburgh 1993. Pro coach: Arizona Cardinals 1994-95, San Francisco 49ers 1996, Chicago Bears 1997-98, joined Ravens in 1999.

Jim Colletto, offensive line; born October 2, 1944, San Francisco, lives in Finksburg, Md. Fullback-linebacker UCLA 1964-67. No pro playing experience. College coach: UCLA 1967-68, Brown 1969, Xavier 1970-71, Pacific 1972-74, Cal State-Fullerton 1975-79 (head coach), UCLA 1980-1981, Purdue 1982-84, Arizona State 1985-87, Ohio State 1988-1990, Purdue 1991-96 (head coach), Notre Dame 1997-98. Pro coach: Joined Ravens in 1999.

Jack Del Rio, Jr., linebackers; born April 4, 1963, Castro Valley, Calif., lives in Reisterstown, Md. Linebacker Southern California 1981-84. Pro linebacker New Orleans Saints 1985-86, Kansas City Chiefs 1987-88, Dallas Cowboys 1989-1991, Minnesota Vikings 1992-95. Pro coach: New Orleans Saints 1997-98, joined Ravens in 1999.

Jeff Friday, strength and conditioning; born October 11, 1966, Milwaukee, Wis., lives in Ellicott City, Md. Attended Wisconsin-Milwaukee. No college or pro playing experience. College coach: Illinois State 1991-92, Northwestern 1992-95. Pro coach: Minnesota Vikings 1996-98, joined Ravens in 1999.

Wade Harman, tight ends-asst. offensive line; born October 1, 1963, Corydon, Iowa, lives in Reisterstown, Md. Linebacker Drake 1985, Utah State 1986. No pro playing experience. College coach: Utah State 1987-1991, Pacific 1992-95, Morningside 1996. Pro coach: Minnesota Vikings 1997-98, joined Ravens in 1999.

Donnie Henderson, secondary; born May 17, 1957, Baltimore, lives in Owings Mills, Md. Defensive back Utah State 1978-79. No pro playing experience. College coach: Utah State 1983-88, Idaho 1989-1990, California 1992-97, Houston 1998. Pro coach: Joined Ravens in 1999.

Milt Jackson, wide receivers; born October 16, 1943, Groesbeck, Texas, lives in Owings Mills, Md. Free safety Tulsa 1965-66. Pro defensive back San Francisco 49ers 1967. College coach: Oregon State 1973, Rice 1974, Califronia 1975-76, Oregon 1977-78, UCLA 1979. Pro coach: San Francisco 49ers 1980-82, Buffalo Bills 1983-84, Philadelphia Eagles 1985, Houston Oilers 1986-88, Indianapolis Colts 1989-1991, Los Angeles Rams 1992-93, Atlanta Falcons 1994-96, New York Giants 1997, Seattle Seahawks 1998, joined Ravens in 1999.

Marvin Lewis, defensive coordinator; born September 23, 1958, McDonald, Pa., lives in Finksburg, Md. Linebacker Idaho State 1977-1980. No pro playing experience. College coach: Idaho State 1981-84, Long Beach State 1985-86, New Mexico 1987-89, Pittsburgh 1990-91. Pro coach: Pittsburgh Steelers 1992-95, joined Ravens in 1996.

Chip Morton, asst. strength and conditioning; born November 27, 1962, Hamden, Conn., lives in Owings Mills, Md. Attended North Carolina. No college or pro playing experience. College coach: Ohio State 1985-86, Penn State 1987-1992. Pro coach: San Diego Chargers 1992-94, Carolina Panthers 1995-98, joined Ravens in 1999.

Russ Purnell, special teams; born June 12, 1948, Chicago, lives in Ellicott City, Md. Center Orange Coast (Calif.) J.C. 1966-67, Whittier College 1968-69. No pro playing experience. College coach: Whittier College 1970-71, Southern California 1982-84. Pro coach: Seattle Seahawks 1986-1994, Tennessee Oilers 1995, joined Ravens in 1999.

Rex Ryan, defensive line; born December 13, 1962, Ardmore, Okla., lives in Ellicott City, Md. Defensive end Southwest Oklahoma State 1983-86. No pro playing experience. College coach: Eastern Kentucky 1987-88, New Mexico Highlands 1989, Morehead State 1990-93, Cincinnati 1996-97, Oklahoma 1998. Pro coach: Arizona Cardinals 1994-95, joined Ravens in 1999.

Steve Shafer, defensive backs, asst. to the head coach; born December 8, 1940, Glendale, Calif., lives in Owings Mills, Md. Quarterback-defensive back Utah State 1961-62. Pro defensive back British Columbia Lions (CFL) 1963-67. College coach: San Mateo (Calif.) J.C. 1968-1974 (head coach 1973-74), San Diego State 1975-1982, 1994. Pro coach: Los Angeles Rams 1983-1990, Tampa Bay Buccaneers 1991-93, Oakland Raiders 1995-97, Carolina Panthers 1998, joined Ravens in 1999.

Matt Simon, running backs; born December 6, 1953, Akron, Ohio, lives in Columbia, Md. Linebacker Eastern New Mexico 1972-75. No pro playing experience. College coach: Washington 1982-1991, New Mexico 1992-94, North Texas 1994-97 (head coach). Pro coach: Denver Broncos 1998, joined Ravens in 1999.

Mike Smith, defensive assistant; born June 13, 1959, Chicago, lives in Eldersburg, Md. Linebacker East Tennessee 1977-1980. No pro playing experience. College coach: San Diego State 1982-85, Morehead State 1986, Tennessee Tech 1987-1998. Pro coach: Joined Ravens in 1999.

2000 FIRST-YEAR ROSTER

Name	Pos.	Ht.	Wt.	Birthdate	College	Hometown	How Acq.
Alfonzo, DeJuan	DB	6-0	205	1/2/77	Indiana State	Indianapolis, Ind.	FA
Arnaud, Robert	RB	5-11	206	10/3/76	Georgia	Morrow, Ga.	FA
Brookins, Jason	RB	6-0	224	1/5/76	Lane College	Mexico, Mo.	FA
Camacho, David	T	6-7	320	9/5/76	Oklahoma State	Compton, Calif.	FA
Clemons, Lloyd	RB	5-11	215	5/29/76	Michigan State	Detroit, Mich.	FA
Douglas, Marques (1)	DT	6-2	270	3/5/77	Howard	Greensboro, N.C.	FA-'99
Edison, Pedro	TE	6-3	250	1/28/76	East Tennessee State	Waynesboro, Va.	FA
Icsman, Don	P	6-1	190	12/5/72	Heidelberg	Sandusky, Ohio	FA
Jones, John	TE	6-4	240	4/4/75	Indiana, Pa.	Philadelphia, Pa.	FA
Kelly, Kenny	DB	6-0	207	12/7/77	Auburn	Winston Salem, N.C.	FA
Lewis, Jamal	RB	5-11	231	8/29/79	Tennessee	Atlanta, Ga.	D1a
Love, Clarence (1)	CB	5-10	181	6/16/76	Toledo	Jackson, Miss.	FA-'99
MacFarlane, Curtice (1)	G-T	6-4	310	11/4/74	San Jose State	Stockton, Calif.	FA
McGuire, Dan	PK	5-9	201	6/19/73	Boston College	Pennsauken, N.J.	FA
Mercier, Richard	G	6-3	295	5/13/75	Miami	Montreal, Quebec, Canada	D5
Mitchell, Anthony (1)	S	6-1	211	12/13/74	Tuskeegee	Atlanta, Ga.	FA-'99
Nord, Kendrick (1)	WR	6-2	210	4/28/72	Grambling State	Mobile, Ala.	FA-'99
Preston, Charles (1)	DE	6-5	270	4/19/75	Hampton	Washington, D.C.	FA-'99
Redman, Chris	QB	6-3	223	7/7/77	Louisville	Louisville, Ky.	D3
Robinson, Dan	QB	6-4	213	5/6/74	Hawaii	American Fork, Utah	FA
Smith, Jermaine	CB	5-11	195	11/10/77	Washington	Simi Valley, Calif.	FA
Taylor, Travis	WR	6-1	200	3/30/78	Florida	Jacksonville, Fla.	D1b
Thomas, Adalius	DE	6-2	270	8/17/77	Southern Mississippi	Equality, Ala.	D6a
Thompson, Germany	WR	6-2	208	10/12/76	New Mexico	Greenville, S.C.	FA
Washington, Lynde	CB	5-9	180	7/7/77	Hofstra	Largo, Md.	FA
Wilkinson, Calvin	DE	6-3	230	5/5/77	Temple	Vineland, N.J.	FA
Wittman, Ben	DE	6-1	242	8/10/76	Western Kentucky	Sarasota, Fla.	FA
Woodard, Cedric	DT	6-2	290	9/5/77	Texas	Sweeny, Tex.	D6b

The term NFL Rookie is defined as a player who is in his first season of professional football and has not been on the roster of another professional football team for any regular-season or postseason games. A Rookie is designated by an "R" on NFL rosters. Players who have been active in another professional football league or players who have NFL experience, including either preseason training camp or being on an Active List or Inactive List, or on Reserve/Injured or Reserve/Physically Unable to Perform for fewer than six regular-season games, are termed NFL First-Year Players. An NFL First-Year Player is designated by a "1" on NFL rosters. Thereafter, a player is credited with an additional year of experience for each season in which he accumulates six games on the Active List or Inactive List, or on Reserve/Injured or Reserve/Physically Unable to Perform.

BUFFALO BILLS

American Football Conference
Eastern Division
Team Colors: Royal Blue, Scarlet Red, and White
One Bills Drive
Orchard Park, New York 14127-2296
Telephone: (716) 648-1800

CLUB OFFICIALS

President: Ralph C. Wilson, Jr.
Executive Vice President/General Manager: John Butler
Corporate V.P.: Linda Bogdan
Treasurer: Jeffrey C. Littmann
Vice President/Player Personnel: Dwight Adams
Vice President/Communications: Scott Berchtold
Vice President/Business Development and Marketing: Russ Brandon
Vice President/Business Operations: Bill Munson
Vice President/Business Operations: Jim Overdorf
Director of Pro Personnel: A.J. Smith
Director of Merchandising: Christy Wilson Hofmann
Director of Marketing Communications: Marc Honan
Director of Marketing Partnerships: Jeff Fernandez
Director of Sales: Pete Guelli
Director of Merchandising: Julie Regan
Director of Ticket Sales: Jerry Foran
Director of Archives: Denny Lynch
Director of Stadium Operations: George Koch
Director of Guest Services & Event Management: Jan Eberle
Engineering and Operations Manager: Joseph Frandina
Director of Security: Bill Bambach
Ticket Director: June Foran
Media Relations Coordinator: Mark Dalton
Business Manager: Don Purdy
Equipment Manager: Dave Hojnowski
Asst. Equipment Manager: Randy Ribbeck
Strength/Conditioning Coordinator: Rusty Jones
Conditioning Assistant: Rich Gray
Trainers: Bud Carpenter, Corey Bennett, Greg McMillen
Video Director: Henry Kunttu
Asst. Video Director: Greg Estes
Scouts: Brad Forsyth, Tom Gibbons, Joe Haering, Doug Majeski, Buddy Nix, Bob Ryan, George (Chink) Sengel, David G. Smith, David W. Smith, Bob Williams
Stadium: Ralph Wilson Stadium
•**Capacity:** 73,840
One Bills Drive
Orchard Park, New York 14127-2296
Playing Surface: AstroTurf
Training Camp: St. John Fisher College
Rochester, New York 14618

RECORD HOLDERS

INDIVIDUAL RECORDS—CAREER

Category	Name	Performance
Rushing (Yds.)	Thurman Thomas, 1988-1999	11,938
Passing (Yds.)	Jim Kelly, 1986-1996	35,467
Passing (TDs)	Jim Kelly, 1986-1996	237
Receiving (No.)	Andre Reed, 1985-1999	941
Receiving (Yds.)	Andre Reed, 1985-1999	13,095
Interceptions	George (Butch) Byrd, 1964-1970	40
Punting (Avg.)	Paul Maguire, 1964-1970	42.1
Punt Return (Avg.)	Clifford Hicks, 1990-92	12.2
Kickoff Return (Avg.)	O.J. Simpson, 1969-1977	30.0
Field Goals	Steve Christie, 1992-99	208
Touchdowns (Tot.)	Andre Reed, 1985-1999	87
	Thurman Thomas, 1988-1999	87
Points	Steve Christie, 1992-99	902

INDIVIDUAL RECORDS—SINGLE SEASON

Category	Name	Performance
Rushing (Yds.)	O.J. Simpson, 1973	2,003
Passing (Yds.)	Jim Kelly, 1991	3,844
Passing (TDs)	Jim Kelly, 1991	33
Receiving (No.)	Andre Reed, 1994	90
Receiving (Yds.)	Eric Moulds, 1998	1,368
Interceptions	Billy Atkins, 1961	10
	Tom Janik, 1967	10
Punting (Avg.)	Billy Atkins, 1961	44.5
Punt Return (Avg.)	Keith Moody, 1977	13.1
Kickoff Return (Avg.)	Ed Rutkowski, 1963	30.2
Field Goals	Steve Christie, 1998	33
Touchdowns (Tot.)	O.J. Simpson, 1975	23
Points	Steve Christie, 1998	140

INDIVIDUAL RECORDS—SINGLE GAME

Category	Name	Performance
Rushing (Yds.)	O.J. Simpson, 11-25-76	273
Passing (Yds.)	Joe Ferguson, 10-9-83	419
Passing (TDs)	Jim Kelly, 9-8-91	6
Receiving (No.)	Andre Reed, 11-20-94	15
Receiving (Yds.)	Jerry Butler, 9-23-79	255
Interceptions	Many times	3
	Last time by Jeff Nixon, 9-7-80	
Field Goals	Steve Christie, 10-20-96	6
Touchdowns (Tot.)	Cookie Gilchrist, 12-8-63	5

2000 SCHEDULE

PRESEASON

Aug. 4	**Cincinnati**	7:30
Aug. 12	at Detroit	8:35
Aug. 19	at St. Louis	8:00
Aug. 24	at Philadelphia	8:00

REGULAR SEASON

Sept. 3	**Tennessee**	8:35
Sept. 10	**Green Bay**	1:00
Sept. 17	at New York Jets	1:00
Sept. 24	Open Date	
Oct. 1	**Indianapolis**	1:00
Oct. 8	at Miami	1:00
Oct. 15	**San Diego**	1:00
Oct. 22	at Minnesota	12:00
Oct. 29	**New York Jets**	1:00
Nov. 5	at New England	1:00
Nov. 12	**Chicago**	1:00
Nov. 19	at Kansas City	12:00
Nov. 26	at Tampa Bay	1:00
Dec. 3	**Miami**	1:00
Dec. 11	at Indianapolis (Mon.)	9:00
Dec. 17	**New England**	1:00
Dec. 23	at Seattle (Sat.)	5:35

COACHING HISTORY

(302-315-8)

1960-61	Buster Ramsey	11-16-1
1962-65	Lou Saban	38-18-3
1966-68	Joe Collier*	13-17-1
1968	Harvey Johnson	1-10-1
1969-70	John Rauch	7-20-1
1971	Harvey Johnson	1-13-0
1972-76	Lou Saban**	32-29-1
1976-77	Jim Ringo	3-20-0
1978-82	Chuck Knox	37-36-0
1983-85	Kay Stephenson***	10-26-0
1985-86	Hank Bullough****	4-17-0
1986-97	Marv Levy	123-78-0
1998-99	Wade Phillips	21-13-0

*Released after two games in 1968
**Resigned after five games in 1976
***Released after four games in 1985
****Released after nine games in 1986

RALPH WILSON STADIUM

1999 TEAM RECORD

PRESEASON (3-1)

Date	Result		Opponent
8/14	W	24-10	at Seattle
8/20	L	19-20	at Washington
8/28	W	30-3	at Cincinnati
9/4	W	16-14	Pittsburgh

REGULAR SEASON (11-5)

Date	Result		Opponent	Att.
9/12	L	14-31	at Indianapolis	56,238
9/19	W	17-3	New York Jets	68,839
9/26	W	26-0	Philadelphia	70,872
10/4	W	23-18	at Miami	74,073
10/10	W	24-21	Pittsburgh	71,038
10/17	L	14-20	Oakland	71,113
10/24	L	16-26	at Seattle	66,301
10/31	W	13-10	at Baltimore	68,673
11/7	W	34-17	at Washington	78,721
11/14	W	23-3	Miami	72,810
11/21	L	7-17	at New York Jets	79,285
11/28	W	17-7	New England	72,111
12/12	L	17-19	New York Giants	72,527
12/19	W	31-21	at Arizona	64,337
12/26	W	13-10	at New England (OT)	55,014
1/2	W	31-6	Indianapolis	61,959

(OT) Overtime

POSTSEASON (0-1)

Date	Result		Opponent	Att.
1/8	L	16-22	Tennessee	66,672

SCORE BY PERIODS

Bills	68	98	73	78	3	—	320
Opponents	66	80	23	60	0	—	229

ATTENDANCE

Home 562,499 Away 540,413 Total 1,102,912
Single-game home record, 80,368 (10/4/92)
Single-season home record, 635,889 (1991)

1999 TEAM STATISTICS

	Bills	Opp.
Total First Downs	313	244
Rushing	117	73
Passing	173	144
Penalty	23	27
Third Down: Made/Att	93/228	69/220
Third Down Pct.	40.8	31.4
Fourth Down: Made/Att	11/21	6/18
Fourth Down Pct.	52.4	33.3
Total Net Yards	5,333	4,045
Avg. Per Game	333.3	252.8
Total Plays	1,059	950
Avg. Per Play	5.0	4.3
Net Yards Rushing	2,040	1,370
Avg. Per Game	127.5	85.6
Total Rushes	519	407
Net Yards Passing	3,293	2,675
Avg. Per Game	205.8	167.2
Sacked/Yards Lost	27/185	37/214
Gross Yards	3,478	2,889
Att./Completions	513/290	506/269
Completion Pct.	56.5	53.2
Had Intercepted	16	12
Punts/Average	73/38.9	93/41.7
Net Punting Avg.	73/33.9	93/34.5
Penalties/Yards	97/789	97/790
Fumbles/Ball Lost	17/11	14/9
Touchdowns	35	23
Rushing	12	9
Passing	21	12
Returns	2	2
Avg. Time of Possession	32:12	27:48

1999 INDIVIDUAL STATISTICS

Passing	Att.	Comp.	Yds.	Pct.	TD	Int.	Tkld.	Rate
Flutie	478	264	3,171	55.2	19	16	26/176	75.1
Johnson	34	25	298	73.5	2	0	1/9	119.5
Van Pelt	1	1	9	100.0	0	0	0/0	104.2
Bills	513	290	3,478	56.5	21	16	27/185	78.1
Opponents	506	269	2,889	53.2	12	12	37/214	68.2

SCORING	TD R	TD P	TD Rt	PAT	FG	Saf	PTS
Christie	0	0	0	33/33	25/34	0	108
Moulds	0	7	0	0/0	0/0	0	42
Linton	5	1	0	0/0	0/0	0	38
A. Smith	6	0	0	0/0	0/0	0	36
Riemersma	0	4	0	0/0	0/0	0	24
P. Price	0	3	0	0/0	0/0	0	18
Collins	0	2	0	0/0	0/0	0	12
Gash	0	2	0	0/0	0/0	0	12
Flutie	1	0	0	0/0	0/0	0	6
Jones	0	0	1	0/0	0/0	0	6
Northern	0	0	1	0/0	0/0	0	6
Reed	0	1	0	0/0	0/0	0	6
Thomas	0	1	0	0/0	0/0	0	6
Bills	12	21	2	33/33	25/34	0	320
Opponents	9	12	2	22/22	23/31	0	229

2-Pt. Conversions: Linton.
Team 1-2, Opponents 0-1.

RUSHING	Att.	Yds.	Avg.	LG	TD
Linton	205	695	3.4	18	5
A. Smith	165	614	3.7	52t	6
Flutie	88	476	5.4	24t	1
Thomas	36	152	4.2	31	0
Johnson	8	61	7.6	25	0
Gordon	11	38	3.5	13	0
K. Williams	1	13	13.0	13	0
Moulds	1	1	1.0	1	0
Mohr	1	0	0.0	0	0
Van Pelt	1	-1	-1.0	-1	0
Hicks	1	-2	-2.0	-2	0
P. Price	1	-7	-7.0	-7	0
Bills	519	2,040	3.9	52t	12
Opponents	407	1,370	3.4	40	9

RECEIVING	No.	Yds.	Avg.	LG	TD
Moulds	65	994	15.3	54t	7
Reed	52	536	10.3	30	1
Riemersma	37	496	13.4	38	4
P. Price	31	393	12.7	45	3
K. Williams	31	381	12.3	35	0
Linton	29	228	7.9	28	1
Gash	20	163	8.2	31t	2
Collins	9	124	13.8	45	2
Loud	6	66	11.0	20	0
Jackson	4	34	8.5	16	0
Thomas	3	37	12.3	23t	1
A. Smith	2	32	16.0	23	0
Hicks	1	-6	-6.0	-6	0
Bills	290	3,478	12.0	54t	21
Opponents	269	2,889	10.7	50	12

INTERCEPTIONS	No.	Yds.	Avg.	LG	TD
Schulz	3	26	8.7	26	0
Winfield	2	13	6.5	10	0
Wiley	1	52	52.0	52	0
Holecek	1	35	35.0	35	0
T. Smith	1	29	29.0	29	0
Rogers	1	24	24.0	24	0
Irvin	1	1	1.0	1	0
Greer	1	0	0.0	0	0
Martin	1	0	0.0	0	0
Bills	12	180	15.0	52	0
Opponents	16	288	18.0	74t	1

PUNTING	No.	Yds.	Avg.	In 20	LG
Mohr	73	2,840	38.9	20	60
Bills	73	2,840	38.9	20	60
Opponents	93	3,875	41.7	22	60

PUNT RETURNS	No.	FC	Yds.	Avg.	LG	TD
K. Williams	33	17	331	10.0	27	0
P. Price	1	0	16	16.0	16	0
Bills	34	17	347	10.2	27	0
Opponents	23	25	226	9.8	26	0

KICKOFF RETURNS	No.	Yds.	Avg.	LG	TD
K. Williams	42	840	20.0	62	0
Porter	2	41	20.5	24	0
Loud	2	26	13.0	15	0
Jones	1	37	37.0	37t	1
P. Price	1	27	27.0	27	0
Gash	1	13	13.0	13	0
Gordon	1	11	11.0	11	0
Collins	1	6	6.0	6	0
Bills	51	1,001	19.6	62	1
Opponents	68	1,504	22.1	93	0

FIELD GOALS	1-19	20-29	30-39	40-49	50+
Christie	2/2	10/10	7/10	3/9	3/3
Bills	2/2	10/10	7/10	3/9	3/3
Opponents	0/0	8/8	9/11	6/9	0/3

SACKS	No.
B. Smith	7.0
Hansen	6.0
Wiley	5.0
Northern	3.5
Rogers	3.0
S. Price	2.5
Washington	2.5
P. Williams	2.5
Perry	1.5
Cowart	1.0
Cummings	1.0
Holecek	1.0
Moran	0.5
Bills	37.0
Opponents	27.0

2000 DRAFT CHOICES

Round	Name	Pos.	College
1	Erik Flowers	DE	Arizona State
2	Travares Tillman	DB	Georgia Tech
3	Corey Moore	LB	Virginia Tech
4	Avion Black	WR	Tennesse State
5	Sammy Morris	RB	Texas Tech
6	Leif Larsen	DT	Texas-El Paso
7	Drew Haddad	WR	Buffalo
	DaShon Polk	LB	Arizona

BUFFALO BILLS

2000 VETERAN ROSTER

No.	Name	Pos.	Ht.	Wt.	Birthdate	NFL Exp.	College	Hometown	How Acq.	'99 Games/ Starts
76	Albright, Ethan	G-T	6-5	278	5/1/71	6	North Carolina	Greensboro, N.C.	FA-'96	16/0
66	Allotey, Victor	G	6-3	320	4/8/75	3	Indiana	Brooklyn, N.Y.	D7-'98	0*
79	Brown, Ruben	G	6-3	304	2/13/72	6	Pittsburgh	Lynchburg, Va.	D1-'95	14/14
38	Bryson, Shawn	RB	6-1	233	8/26/76	2	Tennessee	Franklin, N.C.	D3-'99	0*
29	Carpenter, Keion	S	5-11	205	10/31/77	2	Virginia Tech	Baltimore, Md.	FA-'99	10/0
2	Christie, Steve	K	6-0	195	11/13/67	11	William & Mary	Oakville, Ontario, Canada	PB(TB)-'92	16/0
84	Collins, Bobby	TE	6-4	248	8/20/76	2	North Alabama	York, Ala.	D4b-'99	14/2
63	Conaty, Bill	G-T	6-2	300	3/8/73	3	Virginia Tech	Pennsauken, N.J.	FA-'97	7/1
56	Cowart, Sam	LB	6-2	245	2/26/75	3	Florida State	Jacksonville, Fla.	D2-'98	16/16
70	Fina, John	T	6-5	300	3/11/69	9	Arizona	Tucson, Ariz.	D1-'92	16/16
7	Flutie, Doug	QB	5-10	180	10/23/62	7	Boston College	Natick, Mass.	FA-'98	15/15
55	Foreman, Jay	LB	6-1	240	12/18/76	2	Nebraska	Eden Prairie, Minn.	D5-'99	7/0
31	Gordon, Lennox	RB	5-11	201	4/9/78	2	New Mexico	Higley, Ariz.	FA-'99	8/0
25	Greer, Donovan	DB	5-10	178	9/11/74	4	Texas A&M	Alief, Tex.	FA-'98	16/0
90	Hansen, Phil	DE	6-5	273	5/20/68	10	North Dakota State	Oakes, N.D.	D2-'91	14/14
77	Hicks, Robert	T	6-7	330	11/17/74	3	Mississippi State	Atlanta, Ga.	D3-'98	14/14
52	Holecek, John	LB	6-2	242	5/7/72	6	Illinois	Steger, Ill.	D5-'95	14/14
27	Irvin, Ken	CB	5-11	186	7/11/72	6	Memphis	Rome, Ga.	D4a-'95	14/14
88	Jackson, Sheldon	TE	6-3	250	7/24/76	2	Nebraska	Diamond Bar, Calif.	D7a-'99	13/4
11	Johnson, Rob	QB	6-4	212	3/18/73	6	Southern California	Newport Beach, Calif.	T(Jax)-'98	2/1
20	Jones, Henry	S	6-0	200	12/29/67	10	Illinois	St. Louis, Mo.	D1-'91	16/16
35	Linton, Jonathan	RB	6-1	234	11/7/74	3	North Carolina	Catasauqua, Pa.	D5-'98	16/2
9	Mohr, Chris	P	6-5	215	5/11/66	11	Alabama	Thomson, Ga.	FA-'91	16/0
80	Moulds, Eric	WR	6-2	204	7/17/73	5	Mississippi State	Lucedale, Miss.	D1-'96	14/14
74	Nails, Jamie	T	6-6	360	3/3/75	4	Florida A&M	Baxley, Ga.	D4-'97	16/3
53	Newman, Keith	LB	6-2	245	1/19/77	2	North Carolina	Tampa, Fla.	D4a-'99	3/0
60	Ostroski, Jerry	C	6-3	327	7/12/70	6	Tulsa	Collegeville, Pa.	FA-'93	15/15
72	Panos, Joe	G	6-3	300	1/24/71	7	Wisconsin	Brookfield, Ill.	FA-'98	0*
22	Porter, Daryl	CB	5-9	187	1/16/74	3	Boston College	Fort Lauderdale, Fla.	FA-'98	16/0
81	Price, Peerless	WR	6-0	190	10/27/76	2	Tennessee	Dayton, Ohio	D2-'99	16/4
91	Price, Shawn	DE	6-4	290	3/28/70	8	Pacific	Woodland Hills, Calif.	FA-'96	15/1
85	Riemersma, Jay	TE	6-5	254	5/17/73	5	Michigan	Zeeland, Mich.	D7b-'96	14/11
59	Rogers, Sam	LB	6-3	245	5/30/70	7	Colorado	Pontiac, Mich.	D2c-'94	16/16
23	Smith, Antowain	RB	6-2	228	3/14/72	4	Houston	Montgomery, Ala.	D1-'97	14/11
69	Spriggs, Marcus	T	6-3	315	5/17/74	4	Houston	Hattiesburg, Miss.	D6-'97	11/2
92	Washington, Ted	NT	6-5	330	4/13/68	10	Louisville	Tampa, Fla.	FA-'95	16/16
75	Wiley, Marcellus	DE	6-4	275	11/30/74	4	Columbia	Los Angeles, Calif.	D2-'97	16/1
93	Williams, Pat	DT	6-3	310	10/24/72	4	Texas A&M	Monroe, La.	FA-'97	16/0
26	Winfield, Antoine	CB	5-9	180	6/24/77	2	Ohio State	Akron, Ohio	D1-'99	16/2

* Allotey and Panos were inactive for 16 games in '99; Bryson missed '99 season because of injury.

Unrestricted free agent; subject to developments.

Players lost through free agency (4): DT Sean Moran (StL; 16 games in '99), S Kurt Schulz (Det; 16), CB Thomas Smith (Chi; 16), C Dusty Zeigler (NYG; 15).

Also played with Bills in '99—LB Dan Brandenburg (14 games), LB Joe Cummings (16), WR Kamil Loud (7), CB Emanuel Martin (7), LB Gabe Northern (16), LB Marlo Perry (16), WR Andre Reed (16), DE Bruce Smith (16), RB Thurman Thomas (5), QB Alex Van Pelt (1), WR Kevin Williams (16).

COACHING STAFF

Head Coach,
Wade Phillips

Pro Career: Became the eleventh head coach in Bills history on January 5, 1998, after having served as the club's defensive coordinator since 1995. In his first season, led the Bills to a 10-6 record and a return to the playoffs following a one-year hiatus. Enjoyed the best season of any first-year coach in Bills history, both in number of victories and turnaround in wins and losses. With an 11-5 mark in 1999, Phillips became just the fourteenth NFL coach since World War II to post 10 wins or more in each of his first two years as head coach. Throughout the last two seasons, only Jacksonville's Tom Coughlin and Minnesota's Dennis Green (25 each) have recorded more wins than Phillips's 21. Has been an NFL coach for 23 years, which includes a two-year stint as the head coach of the Denver Broncos in 1993-94. He led them to a wild-card playoff spot in 1993. Began his pro coaching career in 1976 with the Houston Oilers, where he remained until 1980. Then accepted the position of defensive coordinator for the New Orleans Saints (1981-85) and served as the head coach for the final four games of the 1985 season. Served as the defensive coordinator for the Philadelphia Eagles (1986-88) before joining the Broncos' staff in 1989 and serving as the defensive coordinator through the 1992 season. During the 1990 preseason, Phillips assumed the capacity of interim head coach. No pro playing experience. Career record: 27-27.

Background: Linebacker at Houston 1966-68. Coached at his alma mater in 1969. Served as the head coach at Orange (Texas) High in 1970-72. Moved to Oklahoma State as an assistant in 1973-74. Later served as an assistant at Kansas in 1975.

Personal: Born June 21, 1947. Is the son of former NFL coaching legend O.A. (Bum) Phillips. Has two children, daughter Tracy and a son Wesley, who plays quarterback at Texas-El Paso. He and his wife, Laurie, reside in East Amherst, New York.

ASSISTANT COACHES

Max Bowman, asst. to the head coach-tight ends; born September 18, 1945, Colorado Springs, Colo., lives in East Amherst, N.Y. Attended Nyack College. No college or pro playing experience. College coach: Westchester C.C. 1972-78, Lees McRae College 1979, Boston College 1980, Kent State 1981, Texas-El Paso 1982-85, Greenville College 1986-1993. Pro coach: West Virginia Rockets (AFL) 1981, joined Bills in 1998.

Bill Bradley, defensive backs; born January 14, 1947, Paletine, Texas, lives in Orchard Park, N.Y. Quarterback-defensive back-punter-kicker-returner-holder Texas 1966-68. Pro safety-punter-returner-holder Philadelphia Eagles 1969-1977, St. Louis Cardinals 1978. College coach: Texas 1987. Pro coach: San Antonio Gunslingers (USFL) 1983-84, Memphis Showboats (USFL) 1985, Calgary Stampeders (CFL) 1988-1990, San Antonio Riders (WLAF) 1991-92, Sacramento Gold Miners (CFL) 1993-94, San Antonio Texans (CFL) 1995, Toronto Argonauts (CFL) 1996-97, joined Bills in 1998.

Ted Cottrell, defensive coordinator; born June 13, 1947, Chester, Pa., lives in Orchard Park, N.Y. Linebacker Delaware Valley College 1966-68. Pro linebacker Atlanta Falcons 1969-1970, Winnipeg Blue Bombers (CFL) 1971. College coach: Rutgers 1973-1980, 1983. Pro coach: Kansas City Chiefs 1981-82, New Jersey Generals (USFL) 1983-84, Buffalo Bills 1986-89, Arizona Cardinals 1990-94, rejoined Bills in 1995.

Charlie Joiner, receivers; born October 14, 1947, Many, La., lives in Orchard Park, N.Y. Wide receiver Grambling 1965-68. Pro defensive back-wide receiver Houston Oilers 1969-1972, Cincinnati Bengals 1972-75, San Diego Chargers 1976-1986. Inducted into Pro Football Hall of Fame 1996. Pro coach: San Diego Chargers 1987-1991, joined Bills in 1992.

Ronnie Jones, special teams; born October 17, 1955, Dumar, Tex., lives in Buffalo. Running back Northwestern Oklahoma State 1974-77. No pro playing experience. College coach: Northeastern Oklahoma State 1979-1983, Tulsa 1984, Arizona State 1985-86, Texas-El Paso 1996-99. Pro coach: Philadelphia Eagles 1987-1990, Los Angeles Rams 1991, Los Angeles Raiders 1992, Houston Oilers 1993, Arizona Cardinals 1994-95, joined Bills in 2000.

Rusty Jones, strength and conditioning; born August 14, 1953, Berwick, Maine, lives in Hamburg, N.Y. Attended Springfield College. No college or pro playing experience. College coach: Springfield College 1978-79. Pro coach: Pittsburgh Maulers (USFL) 1983-84, joined Bills in 1985.

Chuck Lester, linebackers; born May 18, 1955, Chicago, lives in Orchard Park, N.Y. Linebacker Oklahoma 1974. No pro playing experience. College coach: Iowa State 1980-81, Oklahoma 1982-84. Pro coach: Kansas City Chiefs 1984-86 (scout), joined Bills in 1987.

John Levra, defensive line; born October 2, 1937, Arma, Kan., lives in Hamburg, N.Y. Guard-linebacker Pittsburg State 1963-65. No pro playing experience. College coach: New Mexico Highlands 1966-1970, Stephen F. Austin 1971-74, Kansas 1975-78, North Texas State 1979. Pro coach: British Columbia Lions (CFL) 1980, New Orleans Saints 1981-85, Chicago Bears 1986-1992, Denver Broncos 1993-94, Minnesota Vikings 1995, joined Bills in 1998.

Carl Mauck, offensive line; born July 7, 1947, McLeansboro, Ill., lives in Orchard Park, N.Y. Linebacker-center Southern Illinois 1966-68. Pro center Baltimore Colts 1969, Miami Dolphins 1970, San Diego Chargers 1971-74, Houston Oilers 1975-1981. Pro coach: New Orleans Saints 1982-85, Kansas City Chiefs 1986-88, Tampa Bay Buccaneers 1991, San Diego Chargers 1992-95, Arizona Cardinals 1996-97, joined Bills in 1998.

Joe Pendry, offensive coordinator; born August 5, 1947. Matheny, W. Va., lives in Orchard Park, N.Y. Tight end West Virginia 1966-67. No pro playing experience. College coach: West Virginia 1967-1974, 1976-77, Kansas State 1975, Pittsburgh 1978-79, Michigan State 1980-81. Pro coach: Philadelphia Stars (USFL) 1983, Pittsburgh Maulers (USFL) 1984 (head coach), Cleveland Browns 1985-88, Kansas City Chiefs 1989-1992, Chicago Bears 1993-94, Carolina Panthers 1995-97, joined Bills in 1998.

James Saxon, running backs; born March 23, 1966, Beaufort, S.C., lives in Buffalo. Running back American River J.C. (S.C.) 1985, San Jose State 1986-87. Pro running back Kansas City Chiefs 1988-1991, Miami Dolphins 1992-94, Philadelphia Eagles 1995. College coach: Rutgers 1997-98, Menlo College 1999. Pro coach: Joined Bills in 2000.

Turk Schonert, quarterbacks; born January 15, 1957, Torrance, Calif., lives in Lancaster, N.Y. Quarterback Stanford 1975-79. Pro quarterback Cincinnati Bengals 1980-85, Atlanta Falcons 1986, Cincinnati Bengals 1987-89. Pro coach: Tampa Bay Buccaneers 1992-95, joined Bills in 1998.

2000 FIRST-YEAR ROSTER

Name	Pos.	Ht.	Wt.	Birthdate	College	Hometown	How Acq.
Adams, Askari	DB	6-0	192	5/22/76	Penn State	Camp Hill, Pa.	FA
Black, Avion	WR	5-11	181	4/24/77	Tennessee State	Nashville, Tenn.	D4
Byrd, David	DB	5-11	193	11/15/77	Syracuse	Schenectady, N.Y.	FA
Carman, Jon	T	6-7	335	1/14/76	Georgia Tech	Waldorf, Md.	FA
Cavil, Kwame	WR	6-2	203	5/3/79	Texas	Waco, Tex.	FA
Cawley, Mike (1)	QB	6-1	210	8/28/72	James Madison	Pittsburgh, Pa.	FA
Cohen, Dustin	LB	6-3	236	12/22/76	Miami, Ohio	Oxford, Ohio	FA
Corle, Jason	RB	5-10	204	11/13/77	Towson	Barnegat, N.J.	FA
Crosby, Phillips	RB	6-0	243	11/11/76	Tennessee	Bessemer City, N.C.	FA
Durden, Reggie	CB	5-8	175	11/22/76	Florida State	Houston, Tex.	FA
Fisher, Bryce (1)	DT	6-3	263	5/12/77	Air Force	Renton, Wash.	D7b-'99
Flowers, Erik	DE	6-4	270	3/1/78	Arizona State	San Antonio, Tex.	D1
Giancola, Dan	K	5-10	200	1/28/70	Niagara College	St. Catherines, Ontario, Canada	FA
Gustafson, Ivan	TE	6-2	240	11/5/76	Whitworth	Tumwater, Wash.	FA
Haddad, Drew	WR	5-11	184	8/15/78	Buffalo	Westlake, Ohio	D7a
Hill, Jay	CB	6-0	185	3/16/75	Utah	Lehi, Utah	FA
Hill, Raion (1)	S	6-0	200	9/2/76	Michigan State	Marrero, La.	FA-'99
Hulsey, Corey (1)	G	6-5	358	7/26/77	Clemson	Lula, Ga.	FA
Jennings, John (1)	TE	6-3	243	7/2/75	Bellhaven College	Taylorsville, Miss.	FA
Jones, Corey	WR	5-10	170	1/22/77	Penn State	Lancaster, Pa.	FA
Jones, Fred	LB	6-2	246	10/18/77	Colorado	San Diego, Calif.	FA
Kelsey, Keith	LB	6-1	248	7/10/76	Florida	Newberry, Fla.	FA
Larsen, Leif	DT	6-4	295	4/3/75	Texas-El Paso	Tofte, Norway	D6
McDaniel, Jeremy (1)	WR	6-0	197	5/2/76	Arizona	New Bern, N.C.	FA-'99
Moore, Corey	LB	5-11	225	3/20/77	Virginia Tech	Brownsville, Tex.	D3
Morris, Sammy	RB	6-0	228	3/23/77	Texas Tech	San Antonio, Tex.	D5
Polk, DaShon	LB	6-2	235	3/13/77	Arizona	Pacoima, Calif.	D7b
Procell, Jarrett	DE	6-2	275	11/4/77	Louisiana Tech	Bossier City, L.A.	FA
Riley, Spencer	C	6-3	295	2/17/76	Tennessee	New Market, Tenn.	FA
Roth, Josh	RB	6-0	235	3/15/78	Buffalo	Conewango Valley, N.Y.	FA
Stambaugh, Phil	QB	6-3	217	8/10/78	Lehigh	Roseto, Pa.	FA
Sullivan, Corey	WR	6-2	190	8/13/77	Tennessee State	Miami, Fla.	FA
Tillman, Travares	S	6-1	190	10/8/77	Georgia Tech	Lyons, Ga.	D2
Tosaw, Mike	G	6-2	297	10/4/77	Missouri Southern	Aurora, Ill.	FA
Van Dyke, Jason	P	5-10	193	5/11/76	Adams State	Loveland, Colo.	FA
Williams, Nathaniel	DT	6-2	290	6/28/76	Virginia Tech	Jacksonville, Fla.	FA
Wright, Kenyatta	LB	6-0	238	2/19/78	Oklahoma State	Vian, Okla.	FA

The term NFL Rookie is defined as a player who is in his first season of professional football and has not been on the roster of another professional football team for any regular-season or postseason games. A Rookie is designated by an "R" on NFL rosters. Players who have been active in another professional football league or players who have NFL experience, including either preseason training camp or being on an Active List or Inactive List, or on Reserve/Injured or Reserve/Physically Unable to Perform for fewer than six regular-season games, are termed NFL First-Year Players. An NFL First-Year Player is designated by a "1" on NFL rosters. Thereafter, a player is credited with an additional year of experience for each season in which he accumulates six games on the Active List or Inactive List, or on Reserve/Injured or Reserve/Physically Unable to Perform.

NOTES

CINCINNATI BENGALS

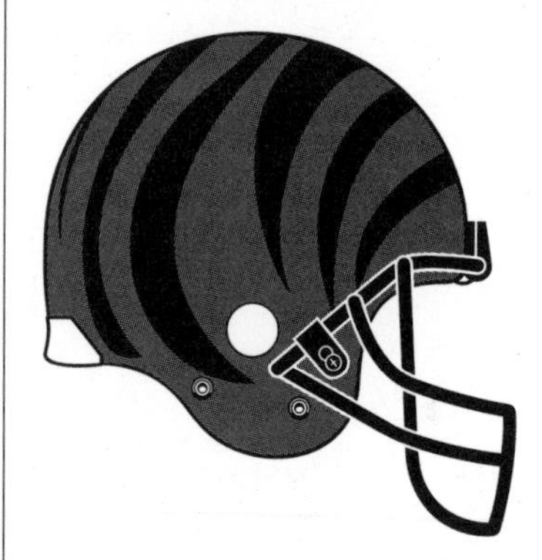

American Football Conference
Central Division
Team Colors: Black, Orange, and White
One Paul Brown Stadium
Cincinnati, Ohio 45202-3492
Telephone: (513) 621-3550
Ticket Office (513) 621-TDTD (8383)

CLUB OFFICIALS

President: Mike Brown
Senior Vice President: Pete Brown
Executive Vice President: Katie Blackburn
Vice President: Paul Brown
Vice President: John Sawyer
Business Development: Troy Blackburn
Business Manager: Bill Connelly
Chief Financial Officer: Bill Scanlon
Controller: Johanna Kappner
Managing Director of Paul Brown Stadium: Eric Brown
Director of Technology: Jo Ann Ralstin
Administration Assistant: Jan Sutton
Business Assistant: Terri Stewart
Receptionist: Teri Moratschek
Director of Sales and Community Affairs: Jeff Berding
Director of Corporate Sales and Marketing: Vince Cicero
Ticket Manager: Paul Kelly
Corporate Sales Executive: Tony Kountz
Corporate Sales Executive: Brian Sells
Corporate Sales Coordinator: Jennifer Benjamin
Premium Seating Sales Coordinator: Stephanie Mileham
Group Sales Manager: Kevin Lane
Merchandise Manager: Monty Montague
JungleVision Producer: Scott Simpson
Ticket Office: Tim Kelly, Bev Schmidt, Jason Williams
Public Relations Director: Jack Brennan
Assistant Public Relations Director: PJ Combs
Public Relations Assistant: Inky Studley
Internet Editor/Writer: Geoff Hobson
Director of Pro/College Personnel: Jim Lippincott
Scouting: Duke Tobin, Frank Smouse
Personnel Assistant: Debbie LaRocco
Athletic Trainer: Paul Sparling
Assistant Athletic Trainers: Billy Brooks, Brian Dykhuizen
Equipment Manager: Rob Recker
Assistant Equipment Manager: Jeff Brickner
Video Director: Travis Brammer
Assistant Video Director: TBA
Assistant to the Coaching Staff: Sandy Schick
Stadium: Paul Brown Stadium • **Capacity:** 65,600 est.
One Paul Brown Stadium
Cincinnati, Ohio 45202-3492
Playing Surface: Grass
Training Camp: Georgetown College
Georgetown, Kentucky 40324

RECORD HOLDERS

INDIVIDUAL RECORDS—CAREER

Category	Name	Performance
Rushing (Yds.)	James Brooks, 1984-1991	6,447
Passing (Yds.)	Ken Anderson, 1971-1986	32,838
Passing (TDs)	Ken Anderson, 1971-1986	197
Receiving (No.)	Carl Pickens, 1992-99	530
Receiving (Yds.)	Isaac Curtis, 1973-1984	7,101
Interceptions	Ken Riley, 1969-1983	65
Punting (Avg.)	Dave Lewis, 1970-73	43.8
Punt Return (Avg.)	Mitchell Price, 1990-93	10.4
Kickoff Return (Avg.)	Tremain Mack, 1997-99	26.5
Field Goals	Jim Breech, 1980-1992	225
Touchdowns (Tot.)	Pete Johnson, 1977-1983	70
Points	Jim Breech, 1980-1992	1,151

INDIVIDUAL RECORDS—SINGLE SEASON

Category	Name	Performance
Rushing (Yds.)	James Brooks, 1989	1,239
Passing (Yds.)	Boomer Esiason, 1986	3,959
Passing (TDs)	Ken Anderson, 1981	29
Receiving (No.)	Carl Pickens, 1996	100
Receiving (Yds.)	Eddie Brown, 1988	1,273
Interceptions	Ken Riley, 1976	9
Punting (Avg.)	Dave Lewis, 1970	46.2
Punt Return (Avg.)	Lemar Parrish, 1974	18.8
Kickoff Return (Avg.)	Tremain Mack, 1999	27.1
Field Goals	Doug Pelfrey, 1995	29
Touchdowns (Tot.)	Carl Pickens, 1995	17
Points	Doug Pelfrey, 1995	121

INDIVIDUAL RECORDS—SINGLE GAME

Category	Name	Performance
Rushing (Yds.)	Corey Dillon, 12-4-97	246
Passing (Yds.)	Boomer Esiason, 10-7-90	490
Passing (TDs)	Boomer Esiason, 12-21-86	5
	Boomer Esiason, 10-29-89	5
Receiving (No.)	Carl Pickens, 10-11-98	13
Receiving (Yds.)	Eddie Brown, 11-6-88	216
Interceptions	Many times	3
	Last time by David Fulcher, 12-17-89	
Field Goals	Doug Pelfrey, 11-6-94	6
Touchdowns (Tot.)	Larry Kinnebrew, 10-28-84	4
	Corey Dillon, 12-4-97	4
Points	Larry Kinnebrew, 10-28-84	24
	Corey Dillon, 12-4-97	24

2000 SCHEDULE

PRESEASON

Aug. 4	at Buffalo	7:30
Aug. 11	at Atlanta	7:30
Aug. 19	**Chicago**	7:30
Aug. 25	**Detroit**	7:30

REGULAR SEASON

Sept. 3	Open Date	
Sept. 10	**Cleveland**	1:00
Sept. 17	at Jacksonville	1:00
Sept. 24	at Baltimore	1:00
Oct. 1	**Miami**	4:05
Oct. 8	**Tennessee**	1:00
Oct. 15	at Pittsburgh	1:00
Oct. 22	**Denver**	1:00
Oct. 29	at Cleveland	1:00
Nov. 5	**Baltimore**	1:00
Nov. 12	at Dallas	12:00
Nov. 19	at New England	1:00
Nov. 26	**Pittsburgh**	1:00
Dec. 3	**Arizona**	1:00
Dec. 10	at Tennessee	12:00
Dec. 17	**Jacksonville**	1:00
Dec. 24	at Philadelphia	1:00

PAUL BROWN STADIUM

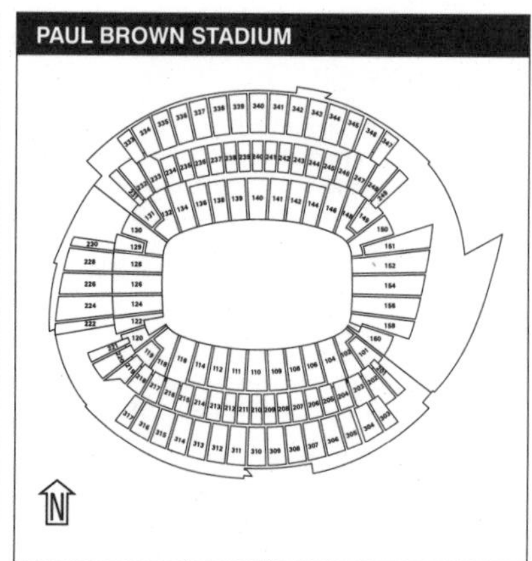

COACHING HISTORY

(215-264-1)

1968-75	Paul Brown	55-59-1
1976-78	Bill Johnson*	18-15-0
1978-79	Homer Rice	8-19-0
1980-83	Forrest Gregg	34-27-0
1984-91	Sam Wyche	64-68-0
1992-96	Dave Shula**	19-52-0
1996-99	Bruce Coslet	21-36-0

* Resigned after five games in 1978
** Released after seven games in 1996

1999 TEAM RECORD

PRESEASON (0-4)

Date	Result		Opponent
8/14	L	17-20	at Indianapolis
8/20	L	0-16	at Detroit
8/28	L	3-30	Buffalo
9/3	L	16-28	Atlanta

REGULAR SEASON (4-12)

Date	Result		Opponent	Att.
9/12	L	35-36	at Tennessee	65,272
9/19	L	7-34	San Diego	47,660
9/26	L	3-27	at Carolina	61,269
10/3	L	10-38	St. Louis	45,481
10/10	W	18-17	at Cleveland	73,048
10/17	L	3-17	Pittsburgh	59,669
10/24	L	10-31	at Indianapolis	55,996
10/31	L	10-41	Jacksonville	49,138
11/7	L	20-37	at Seattle	66,303
11/14	L	14-24	Tennessee	46,017
11/21	L	31-34	Baltimore	43,279
11/28	W	27-20	at Pittsburgh	50,907
12/5	W	44-30	San Francisco	53,463
12/12	W	44-28	Cleveland	59,972
12/26	L	0-22	at Baltimore	68,036
1/2	L	7-24	at Jacksonville	70,532

SCORE BY PERIODS

Bengals	91	70	58	64	0	—	283
Opponents	124	166	92	78	0	—	460

ATTENDANCE

Home 395,906 Away 519,108 Total 915,014
Single-game home record, 60,284 (10/17/71)
Single-season home record, 473,288 (1990)

1999 TEAM STATISTICS

	Bengals	Opp.
Total First Downs	293	316
Rushing	111	99
Passing	161	189
Penalty	21	28
Third Down: Made/Att	93/235	85/209
Third Down Pct.	39.6	40.7
Fourth Down: Made/Att	7/23	5/13
Fourth Down Pct.	30.4	38.5
Total Net Yards	5,277	5,497
Avg. Per Game	329.8	343.6
Total Plays	1,039	1,011
Avg. Per Play	5.1	5.4
Net Yards Rushing	2,051	1,699
Avg. Per Game	128.2	106.2
Total Rushes	442	454
Net Yards Passing	3,226	3,798
Avg. Per Game	201.6	237.4
Sacked/Yards Lost	49/278	35/229
Gross Yards	3,504	4,027
Att./Completions	548/300	522/312
Completion Pct.	54.7	59.8
Had Intercepted	18	12
Punts/Average	84/38.3	71/44.2
Net Punting Avg.	84/31.2	71/36.1
Penalties/Yards	126/1,027	105/835
Fumbles/Ball Lost	34/14	27/15
Touchdowns	33	53
Rushing	11	22
Passing	18	28
Returns	4	3
Avg. Time of Possession	29:59	30:01

1999 INDIVIDUAL STATISTICS

Passing	Att.	Comp.	Yds.	Pct.	TD	Int.	Tkld.	Rate
Blake	389	215	2,670	6.86	16	12	30/168	77.6
Smith	153	80	805	5.26	2	6	19/110	55.6
Covington	5	4	23	4.60	0	0	0/0	85.8
Pickens	1	1	6	6.00	0	0	0/0	91.7
Team	548	300	3,504	6.39	18	18	49/278	71.6
Opponents	522	312	4,027	7.71	28	12	35/229	92.3

SCORING	TD R	TD P	TD Rt	PAT	FG	Saf	PTS
Pelfrey	0	0	0	27/27	18/27	0	81
Scott	0	7	0	0/0	0/0	0	42
Dillon	5	1	0	0/0	0/0	0	36
Pickens	0	6	0	0/0	0/0	0	36
Jackson	0	2	0	0/0	0/0	0	14
Blake	2	0	0	0/0	0/0	0	12
McGee	0	2	0	0/0	0/0	0	12
Yeast	0	0	2	0/0	0/0	0	12
K. Carter	1	0	0	0/0	0/0	0	6
Groce	1	0	0	0/0	0/0	0	6
Heath	0	0	1	0/0	0/0	0	6
Mack	0	0	1	0/0	0/0	0	6
Shaw	1	0	0	0/0	0/0	0	6
Smith	1	0	0	0/0	0/0	0	6
Milne	0	0	0	0/0	0/0	0	2
Bengals	11	18	4	27/27	18/27	0	283
Opponents	22	28	3	49/50	29/32	1	460

2-Pt. Conversions: Jackson, Milne.
Team 2-6, Opponents 2-3

RUSHING	Att.	Yds.	Avg.	LG	TD
Dillon	263	1,200	4.6	50	5
Blake	63	332	5.3	16	2
Basnight	62	308	5.0	46	0
Smith	19	114	6.0	24	1
Milne	3	30	10.0	26	0
Williams	10	30	3.0	8	0
Groce	8	22	2.8	8	1
Shaw	4	20	5.0	10	1
K. Carter	6	15	2.5	8	1
Covington	2	-4	-2.0	-2	0
Yeast	2	-16	-8.0	-3	0
Bengals	442	2,051	4.6	50	11
Opponents	454	1,699	3.7	67t	22

RECEIVING	No.	Yds.	Avg.	LG	TD
Scott	68	1,022	15.0	76t	7
Pickens	57	737	12.9	75t	6
Jackson	31	369	11.9	29	2
Dillon	31	290	9.4	23	1
McGee	26	344	13.2	35	2
Groce	25	154	6.2	14	0
Basnight	16	172	10.8	47	0
Battaglia	14	153	10.9	30	0
Griffin	12	112	9.3	20	0
Williams	10	96	9.6	19	0
K. Carter	3	24	8.0	11	0
Yeast	3	20	6.7	8	0
Smith	1	6	6.0	6	0
Hundon	1	5	5.0	5	0
Bush	1	4	4.0	4	0
Shaw	1	-4	-4.0	-4	0
Bengals	300	3,504	11.7	76t	18
Opponents	312	4,027	12.9	73	28

INTERCEPTIONS	No.	Yds.	Avg.	LG	TD
Heath	3	72	24.0	58t	1
Copeland	2	16	8.0	12	0
Spikes	2	7	3.5	7	0
Bell	1	5	5.0	5	0
Blackmon	1	0	0.0	0	0
T. Carter	1	0	0.0	0	0
Hall	1	0	0.0	0	0
Myers	1	0	0.0	0	0
Bengals	12	100	8.3	58t	1
Opponents	18	305	16.9	44	1

PUNTING	No.	Yds.	Avg.	In 20	LG
Brice	60	2,475	41.3	12	72
Costello	22	744	33.8	1	44
Bengals	84	3,219	38.3	13	72
Opponents	71	3,136	44.2	25	70

PUNT RETURNS	No.	FC	Yds.	Avg.	LG	TD
Griffin	23	3	195	8.5	34	0
Yeast	10	6	209	20.9	86t	2
Jackson	2	1	6	3.0	8	0
Bengals	35	10	410	11.7	86t	2
Opponents	45	13	498	11.1	84t	1

KICKOFF RETURNS	No.	Yds.	Avg.	LG	TD
Mack	51	1,382	27.1	99t	1
Griffin	15	296	19.7	42	0
Williams	8	109	13.6	24	0
Jackson	6	179	29.8	46	0
Yeast	3	50	16.7	22	0
Dillon	1	4	4.0	4	0
Bengals	84	2,020	24.0	99t	1
Opponents	57	1,068	18.7	39	0

FIELD GOALS	1-19	20-29	30-39	40-49	50+
Pelfrey	1/1	9/11	7/12	0/2	1/1
Bengals	1/1	9/11	7/12	0/2	1/1
Opponents	3/3	11/12	6/8	7/7	2/2

SACKS	No.
Bankston	6.0
Gibson	4.5
Copeland	4.0
von Oelhoffen	4.0
Foley	3.5
Simmons	3.0
Spikes	3.0
Wilson	3.0
Bell	2.0
Curtis	1.0
Ross	1.0
Bengals	35.0
Opponents	49.0

2000 DRAFT CHOICES

Round	Name	Pos.	College
1	Peter Warrick	WR	Florida State
2	Mark Roman	DB	Louisiana State
3	Ron Dugans	WR	Florida State
4	Curtis Keaton	RB	James Madison
5	Robert Bean	DB	Mississippi State
6	Neil Rackers	K	Illinois
7	Brad St. Louis	TE-LS	Southwest Missouri State

CINCINNATI BENGALS

2000 VETERAN ROSTER

No.	Name	Pos.	Ht.	Wt.	Birthdate	NFL Exp.	College	Hometown	How Acq.	'99 Games/ Starts
71	Anderson, Willie	T	6-5	340	7/11/75	5	Auburn	Whistler, Ala.	D1-'96	14/14
33	Armour, JoJuan	S	5-11	220	7/10/76	2	Miami, Ohio	Toledo, Ohio	FA-'99	2/0
90	Bankston, Michael	DT	6-5	285	3/12/70	9	Sam Houston State	Elm Grove, Tex.	UFA(Ariz)-'98	16/9
93	Barndt, Tom	DT	6-3	293	3/14/72	5	Pittsburgh	Mentor, Ohio	UFA(KC)-'00	16/13*
35	Basnight, Michael	B	6-1	230	9/3/77	2	North Carolina A&T	Norfolk, Va.	FA-'99	13/1
89	Battaglia, Marco	TE	6-3	252	1/25/73	5	Rutgers	Queens, N.Y.	D2-'96	16/0
40	# Bell, Myron	S	6-0	210	9/15/71	7	Michigan State	Toledo, Ohio	UFA(Pitt)-'98	16/16
36	Bennett, Brandon	RB	5-11	220	2/3/73	2	South Carolina	Greer, S.C.	FA-'99	0*
37	Blackmon, Roosevelt	CB	6-1	185	9/10/74	3	Morris Brown	Belle Glade, Fla.	W(GB)-'98	5/3
96	Booker, Vaughn	DE	6-5	300	2/24/68	7	Cincinnati	Cincinnati, Ohio	UFA(GB)-'00	14/14*
74	Braham, Rich	C	6-4	305	11/6/70	7	West Virginia	Morgantown, W. Va.	W(Ariz)-'94	16/16
88	Bush, Steve	TE-LS	6-3	258	7/4/74	4	Arizona State	Paradise Valley, Ariz.	FA-'97	13/0
32	Carter, Ki-Jana	RB	5-10	222	9/12/73	6	Penn State	Westerville, Ohio	D1-'95	3/0
21	Carter, Tom	CB	6-0	190	9/5/72	8	Notre Dame	St. Petersburg, Fla.	W(Chi)-'99	14/8*
61	Coats, Tony	G	6-6	305	10/5/75	2	Washington	Port Orchard, Wash.	FA-'99	0*
92	Copeland, John	DE	6-3	280	9/20/70	8	Alabama	Lanett, Ala.	D1-'93	16/16
4	Covington, Scott	QB	6-2	217	1/17/76	2	Miami	Laguna Niguel, Calif.	D7b-'99	3/0
98	Curtis, Canute	LB	6-2	256	8/4/74	4	West Virginia	Amityville, N.Y.	FA-'98	15/0
73	DeMarco, Brian	G	6-7	323	4/9/72	6	Michigan State	Lorain, Ohio	UFA(Jax)-'99	7/7
28	† Dillon, Corey	RB	6-1	225	10/24/75	4	Washington	Seattle, Wash.	D2-'97	15/15
76	Doughty, Mike	T	6-7	315	2/18/75	2	Notre Dame	Lakeville, Minn.	FA-'98	0*
25	Fisher, Charles	CB	6-0	185	2/2/76	2	West Virginia	Aliquippa, Pa.	D2-'99	1/1
95	Foley, Steve	LB	6-3	260	9/9/75	3	Northeast Louisiana	Little Rock, Ark.	D3a-'98	16/16
99	Gibson, Oliver	DT	6-2	290	3/15/72	6	Notre Dame	Chicago, Ill.	UFA(Pitt)-'99	16/16
63	Goff, Mike	G	6-5	316	1/6/76	3	Iowa	Peru, Ill.	D3b-'98	12/1
91	Granville, Billy	LB	6-3	252	3/11/74	4	Duke	Trenton, N.J.	FA-'97	16/0
87	Griffin, Damon	WR-KR	5-9	186	6/14/76	2	Oregon	Los Angeles, Calif.	W(SF)-'99	13/0
46	Groce, Clif	RB	5-11	245	7/30/72	4	Texas A&M	College Station, Tex.	FA-'99	16/15
62	Gutierrez, Brock	C-G	6-3	304	9/25/73	4	Central Michigan	Charlotte, Mich.	FA-'98	16/0
26	Hall, Cory	S	6-0	205	12/5/76	2	Fresno State	Bakersfield, Calif.	D3-'99	16/12
27	Hawkins, Artrell	CB	5-10	190	11/24/75	3	Cincinnati	Johnstown, Pa.	D2-'98	14/13
22	Heath, Rodney	CB	5-10	170	10/29/74	2	Minnesota	Cincinnati, Ohio	FA-'99	16/9
20	Howard, Ty	CB	5-10	185	11/30/73	4	Ohio State	Columbus, Ohio	W(Ariz)-'99	12/3
85	Hundon, James	WR	6-1	173	4/9/71	4	Portland State	Daly City, Calif.	FA-'96	6/0
60	Jones, Rod	T	6-4	325	1/11/74	5	Kansas	Detroit, Mich.	D7-'96	16/15
15	Kresser, Eric	QB	6-2	223	2/6/73	2	Marshall	Palm Beach Gardens, Fla.	FA-'99	0*
94	Langford, Jevon	DE	6-3	290	2/16/74	5	Oklahoma State	Washington, D.C.	D4-'96	12/7
58	# Leeuwenburg, Jay	G-C	6-3	290	6/18/69	9	Colorado	St. Louis, Mo.	FA-'99	14/9
34	Mack, Tremain	S-KR	6-0	193	11/21/74	4	Miami	Tyler, Texas	D4-'97	12/0
24	Mathias, Ric	CB	5-10	180	12/10/75	3	Wisconsin-La Crosse	Monroe, Wis.	FA-'98	0*
82	McGee, Tony	TE	6-3	250	4/21/71	8	Michigan	Terre Haute, Ind.	D2-'93	16/16
19	Mitchell, Scott	QB	6-6	240	1/2/68	11	Utah	Springville, Utah	UFA(Balt)-'00	2/2*
23	Myers, Greg	S	6-1	202	9/30/72	5	Colorado State	Windsor, Colo.	D5-'96	12/4
72	O'Dwyer, Matt	G	6-5	300	9/1/72	6	Northwestern	Lincolnshire, Ill.	UFA(NYJ)-'99	16/16
9	Pelfrey, Doug	K	5-11	185	9/25/70	8	Kentucky	Edgewood, Ky.	D8-'93	16/0
81	Pickens, Carl	WR	6-2	206	3/23/70	9	Tennessee	Murphy, N.C.	D2-'92	16/14
97	Purvis, Andre	DT	6-4	310	7/14/73	4	North Carolina	Jacksonville, N.C.	D5-'97	5/0
79	Rehberg, Scott	G-T	6-8	330	11/17/73	4	Central Michigan	Kalamazoo, Mich.	FA-'00	15/13*
57	Ross, Adrian	LB	6-2	244	2/19/75	3	Colorado State	Elk Grove, Calif.	FA-'98	16/10
86	Scott, Darnay	WR	6-1	205	7/7/72	7	San Diego State	St. Louis, Mo.	D2-'94	16/16
39	Shaw, Sedrick	RB	6-0	214	11/16/73	4	Iowa	Austin, Tex.	W(Cle)-'99	4/0*
56	Simmons, Brian	LB	6-3	248	6/21/75	3	North Carolina	New Bern, N.C.	D1b-'98	16/16
11	Smith, Akili	QB	6-3	220	8/21/75	2	Oregon	San Diego, Calif.	D1-'99	7/4
51	Spikes, Takeo	LB	6-2	230	12/17/76	3	Auburn	Sandersville, Ga.	D1a-'98	16/16
70	Steele, Glen	DT	6-4	295	10/4/74	3	Michigan	Ligonier, Ind.	D4-'98	16/1
75	Stephens, Jamain	T	6-5	330	1/9/74	5	North Carolina A&T	Lumberton, N.C.	W(Pitt)-'99	7/2
59	# Truitt, Greg	LS	6-0	235	12/8/65	7	Penn State	Sarasota, Fla.	FA-'94	0*
53	Tumulty, Tom	LB	6-3	247	2/11/73	5	Pittsburgh	Pittsburgh, Pa.	D6-'96	0*
31	Williams, Darryl	S	6-0	202	1/8/70	9	Miami	Hialeah, Fla.	FA-'00	13/12*
30	Williams, Nick	RB	6-1	267	3/30/77	2	Miami	Farmington Hills, Mich.	D5-'99	11/0
55	Wilson, Reinard	DE	6-2	261	12/17/73	4	Florida State	Lake City, Fla.	D1-'97	15/0
42	Wright, Lawrence	S	6-1	211	9/6/73	3	Florida	Miami, Fla.	FA-'98	14/0
84	Yeast, Craig	WR-PR	5-7	160	11/20/76	2	Kentucky	Harrodsburg, Ky.	D4-'99	9/0

* Barndt played 16 games with Kansas City in '99; Bennett, Doughty, Mathias, Truitt, and Tumulty missed '99 season because of injury; Booker played 14 games with Green Bay; T. Carter played 12 games with Chicago and played 2 games with Cincinnati; Coats was inactive for 5 games; Kresser was inactive for 8 games; Mitchell played 2 games with Baltimore; Rehberg played 15 games with Cleveland; Shaw played 3 games with Cleveland and 1 game with Cincinnati; D. Williams played 13 games with Seattle.

Unrestricted free agent; subject to developments.

† Restricted free agent; subject to developments.

Players lost through free agency (2): QB Jeff Blake (NO; 14 games in '99), DT Kimo von Oelhoffen (Pitt; 16).

Also played with Cincinnati in '99—P Will Brice (11 games), CB Rico Clark (8), P Brad Costello (5), WR Willie Jackson (16), RB Brian Milne (1), LB Ben Peterson (3), LB Jimmy Sprotte (4).

COACHING STAFF

Head Coach,
Bruce Coslet

Pro Career: Coslet is entering his fourth full season as head coach of the Cincinnati Bengals. He was named the franchise's seventh head coach seven games into the 1996 season, leading the team to a 7-2 record during the final nine games after its 1-6 start. The Bengals started 1-7 in 1997, but again rebounded to finish 7-9. Cincinnati finished 3-13 in 1998. This is the second head coaching position held by Coslet, who was head coach of the New York Jets for four season from 1990-93. Coslet began his coaching career as an assistant coach with the San Francisco 49ers in 1980. He joined the Bengals as an assistant coach in 1981. Coslet coached with Cincinnati for nine seasons from 1981-89, including four as offensive coordinator from 1986-89, before becoming head coach of the Jets. After four seasons with the Jets, he again returned to Cincinnati as offensive coordinator in 1994, and retained that position until his promotion to head coach in 1996. Coslet played tight end for the Bengals for eight seasons from 1969-1976. Career record: 47-75.

Background: Coslet is a native of Oakdale, Calif., and played football for Joint H.S. He was a tight end for the University of the Pacific from 1965-67.

Personal: Born August 5, 1946, Coslet and his wife, Kathy, live in Cincinnati and have two children, son J.J., and daughter Amy.

ASSISTANT COACHES

Paul Alexander, offensive line; born February 12, 1960, Rochester, N.Y., lives in Cincinnati. Tackle Cortland State 1979-1981. No pro playing experience. College coach: Penn State 1982-84, Michigan 1985-86, Central Michigan 1987-1991. Pro coach: New York Jets 1992-93, joined Bengals in 1994.

Jim Anderson, running backs; born March 27, 1948, Harrisburg, Pa., lives in Cincinnati. Linebacker-defensive end California Western 1967-1970. No pro playing experience. College coach: California Western 1970-71, Scottsdale (Ariz.) Community College 1973, Nevada-Las Vegas 1974-75, Southern Methodist 1976-1980, Stanford 1981-83. Pro coach: Joined Bengals in 1984.

Ken Anderson, offensive coordinator; born February 15, 1949, Batavia, Ill., lives in Fort Mitchell, Ky. Quarterback Augustana (Ill.) 1967-1970. Pro quarterback Cincinnati Bengals 1971-1986. Pro coach: Joined Bengals in 1992.

Louie Cioffi, defensive staff assistant; born September 21, 1973, Greenlawn, N.Y., lives in Cincinnati. Attended SUNY-Stony Brook. No college or pro playing experience. College coach: C.W. Post 1995-96. Pro coach: New York Jets 1993-94, joined Bengals in 1997.

Mark Duffner, linebackers; born July 19, 1953, Annandale, Va., lives in Cincinnati. Defensive lineman William & Mary 1973-74. No pro playing experience. College coach: Ohio State 1975-76, Cincinnati 1977-1980, Holy Cross 1981-1991 (head coach 1986-1991), Maryland 1992-96 (head coach). Pro coach: Joined Bengals in 1997.

Ray Horton, defensive backs; born April 12, 1960, Tacoma, Wash., lives in Cincinnati. Defensive back Washington 1979-1982. Pro defensive back Cincinnati Bengals 1983-88, Dallas Cowboys 1989-1992. Pro coach: Washington Redskins 1994-96, joined Bengals in 1997.

Tim Krumrie, defensive line; born May 20, 1960, Menomonie, Wis., lives in Cincinnati. Defensive tackle Wisconsin 1979-1982. Pro defensive tackle Cincinnati Bengals 1983-1994. Pro coach: Joined Bengals in 1995.

Dick LeBeau, asst. head coach-defensive coordinator; born September 9, 1937, London, Ohio, lives in Cincinnati. Offensive-defensive back Ohio State 1954-57. Pro cornerback Detroit Lions 1959-1972. Pro coach: Philadelphia Eagles 1973-75, Green Bay Packers 1976-79, Cincinnati Bengals 1980-1991, Pittsburgh Steelers 1992-96, rejoined Bengals in 1997.

2000 FIRST-YEAR ROSTER

Name	Pos.	Ht.	Wt.	Birthdate	College	Hometown	How Acq.
Bean, Robert	CB	5-11	178	1/6/78	Mississippi State	Atlanta, Ga.	D5
Boies, Josh (1)	P	6-4	220	12/14/74	Temple	Santa Fe, N.M.	FA
Boyd, Lavelle	WR	6-3	215	9/12/76	Louisville	Louisville, Ky.	FA
Brown, Ricky	RB	5-11	225	12/6/76	Texas	Arlington, Texas	FA
Buckwalter, Alan	LB	6-1	235	6/2/77	Northwest Missouri State	Palmyra, Mo.	FA
Chalmers, Marvin	WR	6-2	210	5/23/77	Wake Forest	Richmond, Va.	FA
Costello, Brad (1)	P	6-1	230	12/12/74	Boston University	Moorestown, N.J.	FA-'99
Dorley, Doug	C	6-3	296	2/20/77	Bowling Green	Normal, Ill.	FA
Dugans, Ron	WR	6-2	205	4/27/77	Florida State	Tallahassee, Fla.	D3
Fleischhauer, Dave	DT	6-4	275	3/25/77	Penn State	Clemmons, N.C.	FA
Gray, Brian	FS	6-1	205	1/10/76	Brigham Young	Hawthorne, Calif.	FA
Hardaway, Eddie	WR	6-1	195	10/7/77	C.W. Post	Amityville, N.Y.	FA
Keaton, Curtis	RB	5-10	212	10/18/76	James Madison	Columbus, Ohio	D4
McDonald, Tariq	WR	6-0	190	8/8/78	Arizona State	Phoenix, Ariz.	FA
Pegues, Chad (1)	DT	6-0	304	12/13/76	Illinois State	Gainesville, Tex.	FA
Peterson, Ben (1)	LB	6-3	250	3/28/77	Pittsburg State	Clay Center, Kan.	FA
Rackers, Neil	K	6-0	205	8/16/76	Illinois	Florissant, Mo.	D6
Roesler, Roger	G	6-5	315	10/5/77	Texas	Round Rock, Tex.	FA
Roman, Mark	CB	5-11	188	3/26/77	Louisiana State	New Iberia, La.	D2
St. Louis, Brad	TE-LS	6-3	246	8/19/76	Southwest Missouri State	Belton, Mo.	D7
Spearman, Armegis	LB	6-1	254	4/5/78	Mississippi	Bruce, Miss.	FA
Thompkins, Gary	S	5-11	200	1/29/77	West Virginia	Miami, Fla.	FA
Vaughn, Damian (1)	TE	6-4	252	6/14/75	Miami, Ohio	Orrville, Ohio	FA
Warrick, Peter	WR-PR	5-11	195	6/19/77	Florida State	Bradenton, Fla.	D1
Willetts, Mike	DT	6-4	280	1/14/77	Boston College	Alexandria, Va.	FA

The term NFL Rookie is defined as a player who is in his first season of professional football and has not been on the roster of another professional football team for any regular-season or postseason games. A Rookie is designated by an "R" on NFL rosters. Players who have been active in another professional football league or players who have NFL experience, including either preseason training camp or being on an Active List or Inactive List, or on Reserve/Injured or Reserve/Physically Unable to Perform for fewer than six regular-season games, are termed NFL First-Year Players. An NFL First-Year Player is designated by a "1" on NFL rosters. Thereafter, a player is credited with an additional year of experience for each season in which he accumulates six games on the Active List or Inactive List, or on Reserve/Injured or Reserve/Physically Unable to Perform.

NOTES

Steve Mooshagian, wide receivers; born March 27, 1959, Downey, Calif., lives in Cincinnati. Wide receiver Cerritos College 1978-79, Fresno State 1980-81. No pro playing experience. College coach: Fresno State 1985-1994, Fresno City College 1995 (head coach), Nevada 1996, Pittsburgh 1997-98. Pro coach: Joined Bengals in 1999.

Al Roberts, special teams; born January 6, 1944, Fresno, Calif., lives in Cincinnati. Running back Washington 1964-65, Puget Sound 1967-68. No pro playing experience. College coach: Washington 1977-1982, 1996, Purdue 1986-87. Pro coach: Los Angeles Express (USFL) 1983-84, Houston Oilers 1984-85, Philadelphia Eagles 1988-1990, New York Jets 1991-93, Arizona Cardinals 1994-95, joined Bengals in 1997.

Frank Verducci, tight ends; born March 17, 1957, Glen Ridge, N.J., lives in Cincinnati. Tight end-fullback U.S. Merchant Marine Academy-Kings Port 1975. No pro playing experience. College coach: Colorado State 1980, Maryland 1981-83, Northern Illinois 1984, Iowa 1985-86, 1989-1998, Northwestern 1987-88. Pro coach: Joined Bengals in 1999.

Kim Wood, strength; born July 12, 1945, Barrington, Ill., lives in Cincinnati. Running back Wisconsin 1965-68. No pro playing experience. Pro coach: Joined Bengals in 1975.

CLEVELAND BROWNS

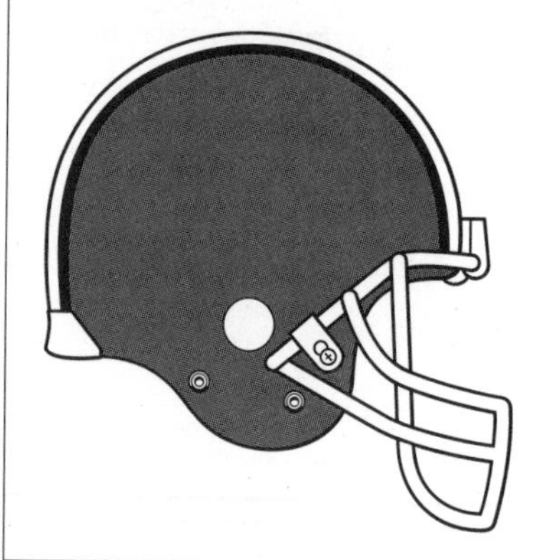

American Football Conference
Central Division
Team Colors: Brown, Orange, and White
76 Lou Groza Blvd.
Berea, Ohio 44017
Telephone: (440) 891-5000

CLUB OFFICIALS

Owner and Chairman: Alfred Lerner
President and Chief Executive Officer: Carmen Policy
Vice President, Director of Football Operations: Dwight Clark
Vice President, Business Operations and Chief Administrative Officer: Kofi Bonner
Vice President of Finance & Treasurer: Doug Jacobs
Vice President, Director of Stadium Operations and Security: Lew Merletti
Assistant Director of Football Operations & General Counsel: Lal Heneghan
Director of Player Personnel: Joe Collins
College Personnel Coordinator: Phil Neri
Pro Personnel Coordinator: Keith Kidd
Director of Operations: Bill Hampton
Executive Director of Marketing: Bruce Popko
Director of Ticket Operations: Mike Jennings
Manager of Stadium Operations: Diane Downing
Director, Cleveland Browns Foundation: Judge George White
Director of Publicity/Media Relations: Todd Stewart
Director of Publications/Internet: Dan Arthur
Director of Community Relations: HIllary Johnson
Coordinator of Publicity/Media Relations: Ken Mather
Coordinator of Publications/Internet: Amy Gretsinger
Browns Backers Coordinator: Krystal Thomas
Facilities Manager: Greg Hipp
Head Athletic Trainer: Mike Colello
Equipment Manager: Bobby Monica
Video Director: Pat Dolan
Head Groundskeeper: Chris Powell
Stadium: Cleveland Browns Stadium • **Capacity:** 73,300
1085 West 3rd Street
Cleveland, Ohio 44114
Playing Surface: Grass
Headquarters/Training Camp:
76 Lou Groza Boulevard
Berea, Ohio 44017

2000 SCHEDULE

PRESEASON

July 30	**Philadelphia**	8:00
Aug. 12	at Chicago	7:00
Aug. 19	**Washington**	7:30
Aug. 26	at Green Bay	4:00

REGULAR SEASON

Sept. 3	**Jacksonville**	1:00
Sept. 10	at Cincinnati	1:00
Sept. 17	**Pittsburgh**	1:00
Sept. 24	at Oakland	1:15
Oct. 1	**Baltimore**	1:00
Oct. 8	at Arizona	1:15
Oct. 15	at Denver	2:05
Oct. 22	at Pittsburgh	4:05
Oct. 29	**Cincinnati**	1:00
Nov. 5	**New York Giants**	1:00
Nov. 12	**New England**	1:00
Nov. 19	at Tennessee	12:00
Nov. 26	at Baltimore	1:00
Dec. 3	at Jacksonville	4:15
Dec. 10	**Philadelphia**	1:00
Dec. 17	**Tennessee**	1:00
Dec. 24	Open Date	

RECORD HOLDERS

INDIVIDUAL RECORDS—CAREER

Category	Name	Performance
Rushing (Yds.)	Jim Brown, 1957-1965	12,312
Passing (Yds.)	Brian Sipe, 1974-1983	23,713
Passing (TDs)	Brian Sipe, 1974-1983	154
Receiving (No.)	Ozzie Newsome, 1978-1990	662
Receiving (Yds.)	Ozzie Newsome, 1978-1990	7,980
Interceptions	Thom Darden, 1972-74, 1976-1981	45
Punting (Avg.)	Horace Gillom, 1950-56	43.8
Punt Return (Avg.)	Greg Pruitt, 1973-1981	11.8
Kickoff Return (Avg.)	Greg Pruitt, 1973-1981	26.3
Field Goals	Lou Groza, 1950-59, 1961-67	234
Touchdowns (Tot.)	Jim Brown, 1957-1965	126
Points	Lou Groza, 1950-59, 1961-67	1,349

INDIVIDUAL RECORDS—SINGLE SEASON

Category	Name	Performance
Rushing (Yds.)	Jim Brown, 1963	1,863
Passing (Yds.)	Brian Sipe, 1980	4,132
Passing (TDs)	Brian Sipe, 1980	30
Receiving (No.)	Ozzie Newsome, 1983	89
	Ozzie Newsome, 1984	89
Receiving (Yds.)	Webster Slaughter, 1989	1,236
Interceptions	Thom Darden, 1978	10
Punting (Avg.)	Gary Collins, 1965	46.7
Punt Return (Avg.)	Leroy Kelly, 1965	15.6
Kickoff Return (Avg.)	Billy Reynolds, 1954	29.5
Field Goals	Matt Stover, 1995	29
Touchdowns (Tot.)	Jim Brown, 1965	21
Points	Jim Brown, 1965	126

INDIVIDUAL RECORDS—SINGLE GAME

Category	Name	Performance
Rushing (Yds.)	Jim Brown, 11-24-57	237
	Jim Brown, 11-19-61	237
Passing (Yds.)	Bernie Kosar, 1-3-87	489
Passing (TDs)	Frank Ryan, 12-12-64	5
	Bill Nelsen, 11-2-69	5
	Brian Sipe, 10-7-79	5
Receiving (No.)	Ozzie Newsome, 10-14-84	14
Receiving (Yds.)	Ozzie Newsome, 10-14-84	191
Interceptions	Many times	3
	Last time by Frank Minnifield, 11-22-87	
Field Goals	Don Cockroft, 10-19-75	5
Touchdowns (Tot.)	Dub Jones, 11-25-51	*6
Points	Dub Jones, 11-25-51	36

*NFL Record

COACHING HISTORY

(387-299-10)

1950-62	Paul Brown	115-49-5
1963-70	Blanton Collier	79-38-2
1971-74	Nick Skorich	30-26-2
1975-77	Forrest Gregg*	18-23-0
1977	Dick Modzelewski	0-1-0
1978-84	Sam Rutigliano**	47-52-0
1984-88	Marty Schottenheimer	46-31-0
1989-90	Bud Carson***	12-14-1
1990	Jim Shofner	1-6-0
1991-95	Bill Belichick	37-45-0
1999	Chris Palmer	2-14-0

*Resigned after 13 games in 1977
**Released after eight games in 1984
***Released after nine games in 1990

CLEVELAND BROWNS STADIUM

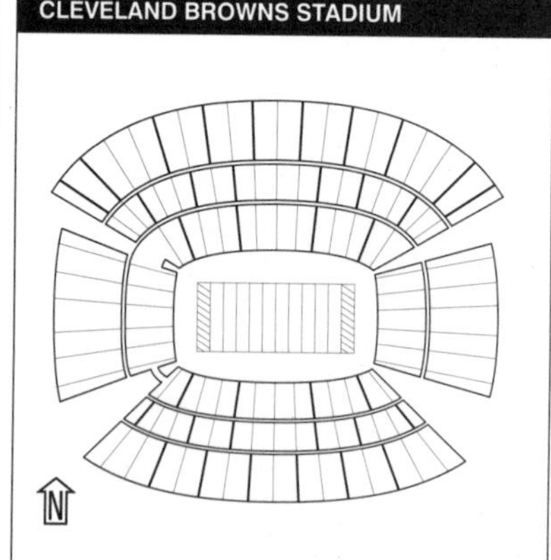

1999 TEAM RECORD

PRESEASON (2-3)

Date	Result		Opponent
8/9	W	20-17	vs. Dallas (OT)
8/14	L	3-30	at Tampa Bay
8/21	L	17-24	Minnesota
8/28	W	35-24	Chicago
9/2	L	17-30	at Philadelphia

REGULAR SEASON (2-14)

Date	Result		Opponent	Att.
9/12	L	0-43	Pittsburgh	73,138
9/19	L	9-26	at Tennessee	65,904
9/26	L	10-17	at Baltimore	68,803
10/3	L	7-19	New England	72,368
10/10	L	17-18	Cincinnati	73,048
10/17	L	7-24	at Jacksonville	62,047
10/24	L	3-34	at St. Louis	65,866
10/31	W	21-16	at New Orleans	48,817
11/7	L	9-41	Baltimore	72,898
11/14	W	16-15	at Pittsburgh	58,213
11/21	L	17-31	Carolina	72,818
11/28	L	21-33	Tennessee	72,008
12/5	L	10-23	at San Diego	53,147
12/12	L	28-44	at Cincinnati	59,972
12/19	L	14-24	Jacksonville	72,038
12/26	L	28-29	Indianapolis	72,618

(OT) Overtime

SCORE BY PERIODS

Browns	37	77	43	60	0	—	217
Opponents	75	146	99	117	0	—	437

ATTENDANCE

Home 569,380 Away 497,573 Total 1,066,953

Single-game home record, 85,073 (9/21/70)

Single-season home record, 620,496 (1980)

1999 TEAM STATISTICS

	Browns	Opp.
Total First Downs	220	368
Rushing	64	161
Passing	134	187
Penalty	22	20
Third Down: Made/Att	59/203	110/235
Third Down Pct.	29.1	46.8
Fourth Down: Made/Att	9/13	8/13
Fourth Down Pct.	69.2	61.5
Total Net Yards	3,762	6,046
Avg. Per Game	235.1	377.9
Total Plays	865	1,158
Avg. Per Play	4.3	5.2
Net Yards Rushing	1,150	2,736
Avg. Per Game	71.9	171.0
Total Rushes	313	610
Net Yards Passing	2,612	3,310
Avg. Per Game	163.3	206.9
Sacked/Yards Lost	60/385	25/147
Gross Yards	2,997	3,457
Att./Completions	492/271	523/331
Completion Pct.	55.1	63.3
Had Intercepted	15	8
Punts/Average	106/43.8	66/40.9
Net Punting Avg.	106/34.6	66/37.3
Penalties/Yards	92/714	88/776
Fumbles/Ball Lost	29/16	25/12
Touchdowns	28	49
Rushing	9	29
Passing	19	17
Returns	0	3
Avg. Time of Possession	23:38	36:22

1999 INDIVIDUAL STATISTICS

Passing	Att.	Comp.	Yds.	Pct.	TD	Int.	Tkld.	Rate
Couch	399	223	2,447	6.13	15	13	56/359	73.2
Detmer	91	47	548	6.02	4	2	4/26	75.7
Johnson	1	0	0	0.00	0	0	0/0	39.6
Kirby	1	1	2	2.00	0	0	0/0	79.2
Browns	492	271	2,997	6.09	19	15	60/385	73.5
Opponents	523	331	3,457	6.61	17	8	25/147	86.8

SCORING	TD R	TD P	TD Rt	PAT	FG	Saf	PTS
Kirby	6	3	0	0/0	0/0	0	54
Dawson	1	0	0	23/24	8/12	0	53
Johnson	0	8	0	0/0	0/0	0	48
Chiaverini	0	4	0	0/0	0/0	0	24
Edwards	0	2	0	0/0	0/0	0	12
Couch	1	0	0	0/0	0/0	0	8
Abdul-Jabbar	0	1	0	0/0	0/0	0	6
Detmer	1	0	0	0/0	0/0	0	6
I. Smith	0	1	0	0/0	0/0	0	6
Browns	9	19	0	23/24	8/12	0	217
Opponents	29	17	3	40/41	33/39	1	437

2-Pt. Conversions: Couch.
Team 1-4, Opponents 1-8.

RUSHING	Att.	Yds.	Avg.	LG	TD
Kirby	130	452	3.5	28	6
Abdul-Jabbar	115	350	3.0	21	0
Couch	40	267	6.7	40	1
Detmer	6	38	6.3	11	1
Edwards	6	35	5.8	28	0
G. Jones	8	15	1.9	9	0
Shepherd	1	5	5.0	5	0
Dawson	1	4	4.0	4t	1
Salaam	1	2	2.0	2	0
Shaw	3	2	0.7	3	0
Johnson	1	-6	-6.0	-6	0
Powell	1	-14	-14.0	-14	0
Browns	313	1,150	3.7	40	9
Opponents	610	2,736	4.5	52t	29

RECEIVING	No.	Yds.	Avg.	LG	TD
Johnson	66	986	14.9	64t	8
Kirby	58	528	9.1	78t	3
Chiaverini	44	487	11.1	28t	4
Edwards	27	212	7.9	27t	2
I. Smith	24	222	9.3	22	1
Shepherd	23	274	11.9	36	0
Abdul-Jabbar	13	59	4.5	21	1
Campbell	9	131	14.6	21	0
Davis	2	38	19.0	25	0
Shaw	2	8	4.0	7	0
Powell	1	45	45.0	45	0
Dav. Dunn	1	4	4.0	4	0
Bobo	1	3	3.0	3	0
Browns	271	2,997	11.1	78t	19
Opponents	331	3,457	10.4	54t	17

INTERCEPTIONS	No.	Yds.	Avg.	LG	TD
Pope	2	15	7.5	13	0
Barker	1	14	14.0	14	0
McCutcheon	1	12	12.0	12	0
Thierry	1	8	8.0	8	0
L. Jones	1	3	3.0	3	0
Abdullah	1	0	0.0	0	0
Little	1	0	0.0	0	0
Browns	8	52	6.5	14	0
Opponents	15	153	10.2	66t	1

PUNTING	No.	Yds.	Avg.	In 20	LG
Gardocki	106	4,645	43.8	20	61
Browns	106	4,645	43.8	20	61
Opponents	66	2,702	40.9	24	59

PUNT RETURNS	No.	FC	Yds.	Avg.	LG	TD
Johnson	19	10	128	6.7	15	0
Dav. Dunn	4	1	25	6.3	13	0
Gibson	2	2	9	4.5	8	0
Browns	25	13	162	6.5	15	0
Opponents	68	15	762	11.2	81t	2

KICKOFF RETURNS	No.	Yds.	Avg.	LG	TD
Powell	44	986	22.4	43	0
Kirby	11	230	20.9	28	0
Dav. Dunn	9	180	20.0	27	0
Hill	8	137	17.1	27	0
Saleh	5	43	8.6	14	0
Campbell	3	28	9.3	10	0
I. Smith	3	15	5.0	10	0
Chiaverini	2	35	17.5	22	0
Little	2	34	17.0	20	0
Johnson	1	25	25.0	25	0
G. Jones	1	12	12.0	12	0
Browns	89	1,725	19.4	43	0
Opponents	42	764	18.2	55	0

FIELD GOALS	1-19	20-29	30-39	40-49	50+
Dawson	0/0	2/2	3/5	3/5	0/0
Browns	0/0	2/2	3/5	3/5	0/0
Opponents	4/4	13/13	6/7	10/15	0/0

SACKS	No.
Thierry	7.0
J. Miller	4.5
Alexander	2.5
Barker	2.0
Holland	2.0
McCormack	2.0
Ball	1.0
McCutcheon	1.0
McNeil	1.0
A. Miller	1.0
Rainer	1.0
Browns	25.0
Opponents	60.0

2000 DRAFT CHOICES

Round	Name	Pos.	College
1	Courtney Brown	DE	Penn State
2	Dennis Northcutt	WR	Arizona
3	Travis Prentice	RB	Miami, Ohio
	JaJaun Dawson	WR	Tulane
4	Lewis Sanders	DB	Maryland
	Aaron Shea	TE	Michigan
5	Anthony Malbrough	DB	Texas Tech
	Lamar Chapman	DB	Kansas State
6	Spergon Wynn	QB	Southwest Texas State
	Brad Bedell	G	Colorado
7	Manuia Savea	G	Arizona
	Eric Chandler	DE	Jackson State
	Rashidi Barnes	DB	Colorado

CLEVELAND BROWNS

2000 VETERAN ROSTER

No.	Name	Pos.	Ht.	Wt.	Birthdate	NFL Exp.	College	Hometown	How Acq.	'99 Games/ Starts
53	Abdullah, Rahim	LB	6-5	233	3/22/76	2	Clemson	Jacksonville, Fla.	D2b-'99	16/13
94	Alexander, Derrick	DE	6-4	286	11/13/73	6	Florida State	Jacksonville, Fla.	UFA(Minn)-'99	16/16
77	Brown, Orlando	T	6-7	350	12/12/70	8	South Carolina State	Washington, D.C.	UFA(Balt)-'99	15/15
65	Bundren, Jim	C	6-3	303	10/6/74	3	Clemson	Wilmington, Del.	ED(NYJ)-'99	16/1
83	Campbell, Mark	TE	6-6	253	12/6/75	2	Michigan	Clawson, Mich.	FA-'99	14/4
84	Chiaverini, Darrin	WR	6-2	210	10/12/77	2	Colorado	Corona, Calif.	D5-'99	16/8
93	Colinet, Stalin	DE	6-6	288	7/17/74	4	Boston College	New York, N.Y.	T(Minn)-'99	11/9
2	Couch, Tim	QB	6-4	227	7/31/77	2	Kentucky	Hyden, Ky.	D1-'99	15/14
87	Davis, Zola	WR	6-0	185	1/16/75	2	South Carolina	Charleston, S.C.	FA-'99	6/1
4	Dawson, Phil	K	5-11	190	1/23/75	2	Texas	Dallas, Tex.	FA -'99	15/0
11	Detmer, Ty	QB	6-0	194	10/30/67	9	Brigham Young	San Antonio, Tex.	T(SF)-'99	5/2
62	Duff, Bill	DE-DT	6-3	285	2/24/74	2	Tennessee	Delran, N.J.	FA-'99	5/0
44	Edwards, Marc	RB	6-0	229	11/17/74	4	Notre Dame	Norwood, Ohio	T(SF)-'99	16/14
43	Ellsworth, Percy	S	6-2	225	10/19/74	5	Virginia	Drewryville, Va.	UFA(NYG)-'00	14/14*
24	Fuller, Corey	S	5-10	217	5/1/71	6	Florida State	Tallahassee, Fla.	UFA(Minn)-'99	16/16
17	Gardocki, Chris	P	6-1	200	2/7/70	10	Clemson	Stone Mountain, Ga.	UFA(Ind)-'99	16/0
73	Holland, Darius	DT	6-5	320	11/10/73	6	Colorado	Las Cruces, N.M.	UFA(Det)-'99	15/11
31	Jackson, Raymond	CB-S	5-10	189	2/17/73	5	Colorado State	Denver, Colo.	ED(Buff)-'99	14/0
85	Johnson, Kevin	WR	5-10	188	7/15/75	2	Syracuse	Hamilton Township, N.J.	D2a-'99	16/16
56	Jones, Lenoy	LB	6-1	235	9/25/74	5	Texas Christian	Marlin, Tex.	ED(Tenn)-'99	16/1
42	Kirby, Terry	RB	6-1	213	1/20/70	8	Virginia	Yorktown, Va.	UFA(SF)-'99	16/10
97	Kuehl, Ryan	DT	6-5	290	1/18/72	3	Virginia	Bethesda, Md.	FA-'99	16/0
57	Kyle, Jason	LB	6-3	242	5/12/75	6	Arizona State	Tempe, Ariz.	ED(Sea)-'99	0*
61	Lindsay, Everett	G-T	6-4	302	9/18/70	7	Mississippi	Burlington, Iowa	UFA(Balt)-'00	16/16*
20	Little, Earl	CB-S	6-0	191	3/10/73	3	Miami	Miami, Fla.	W(NO)-'99	9/0
50	McCombs, Tony	LB	6-2	256	8/24/74	3	Eastern Kentucky	Hopkinsville, Ky.	FA-'00	0*
33	McCutcheon, Daylon	CB	5-8	180	12/9/76	2	Southern California	La Puente, Calif.	D3a-'99	16/15
90	McKenzie, Keith	DE-DT	6-3	266	10/17/73	5	Ball State	Detroit, Mich.	UFA(GB)-'00	16/2*
22	McTyer, Tim	CB-S	5-11	181	12/14/75	4	Brigham Young	Los Angeles, Calif.	ED(Phil)-'99	2/2
98	Miller, Arnold	DE	6-3	239	1/3/75	2	Louisiana State	New Orleans, La.	FA-'99	9/0
95	Miller, Jamir	LB	6-5	266	11/19/73	7	UCLA	Oakland, Calif.	UFA(Ariz)-'99	15/15
55	Moore, Marty	LB	6-1	245	3/19/71	7	Kentucky	Phoenix, Ariz.	UFA(NE)-'00	15/2*
72	Oben, Roman	T	6-4	305	10/9/72	5	Louisville	Washington, D.C.	UFA(NYG)-'00	16/16*
59	Ogle, Kendall	LB	6-0	231	11/25/75	2	Maryland	Hillside, N.J.	D6b-'99	2/0
89	Palmer, Randy	TE	6-4	235	11/12/75	2	Texas A&M-Kingsville	Pleasanton, Tex.	W(Oak)-'99	3/0
82	Patten, David	WR	5-9	193	8/19/74	4	Western Carolina	Hopkins, S.C.	UFA(NYG)-'00	16/0*
80	Powell, Ronnie	WR	5-10	174	11/3/74	2	Northwestern State, La.	Hope, Ark.	FA-'99	14/0
71	Pyne, Jim	G	6-2	297	11/23/71	7	Virginia Tech	Wallingford, Conn.	ED(Det)-'99	16/16
58	Rainer, Wali	LB	6-2	235	4/19/77	2	Virginia	Charlotte, N.C.	D4-'99	16/15
23	Rhett, Errict	RB	5-11	211	12/11/70	6	Florida	West Hollywood, Fla.	UFA(Balt)-'00	16/10*
99	Roye, Orpheus	DE-DT	6-4	288	1/21/74	5	Florida State	Miami, Fla.	UFA(Pitt)-'00	16/16*
68	Ruhman, Chris	T	6-5	321	12/19/74	3	Texas A&M	Houston, Tex.	FA-'99	5/2
40	Saleh, Tarek	RB	6-0	240	11/7/74	4	Wisconsin	Fairfield, Conn.	ED(Car)-'99	16/0
21	Smith, Marquis	S	6-2	213	1/13/75	2	California	San Diego, Calif.	D3b-'99	16/2
91	Spriggs, Marcus	DT	6-4	314	7/26/76	2	Troy State	Washington, D.C.	D6a-'99	10/0
96	Thompson, Mike	DT	6-4	295	12/22/71	4	Wisconsin	Portage, Wis.	ED(Cin)-'99	10/0
64	Wohlabaugh, Dave	C	6-3	292	4/13/72	6	Syracuse	Hamburg, N.Y.	UFA(NE)-'99	15/15
75	Zahursky, Steve	G	6-6	305	9/2/76	2	Kent State	Euclid, Ohio	FA-'99	9/7

Ellsworth played 14 games with N.Y. Giants in '99; Kyle last active with Seattle in '98; Lindsay and Rhett played 16 games with Baltimore; McCombs last active with Arizona in '98; McKenzie played 16 games with Green Bay; Moore played 15 games with New England; Oben and Patten played 16 games with N.Y. Giants; Roye played 16 games with Pittsburgh.

Retired—Chris Spielman, 11-year linebacker, 0 games in '99.

Players lost through free agency (3): QB Jamie Martin (Jax; 0 games in '99), CB Ryan McNeil (Dall; 16), LB John Thierry (GB; 16).

Also played with Browns in '99—RB Karim Abdul-Jabbar (10 games), DT Jerry Ball (3), DE Roy Barker (12), G Orlando Bobo (9), T Lomas Brown (10), T Roger Chanoine (1), TE James Dearth (2), WR Damon Dunn (1), WR David Dunn (6), CB Marlon Forbes (16), WR Damon Gibson (2), RB Madre Hill (5), RB George Jones (6), DT John Jurkovic (10), DB Antonio Langham (13), DE Hurvin McCormack (13), S Marquez Pope (16), G-T Scott Rehberg (15), LB Tyrone Rogers (3), RB Rashaan Salaam (2), RB Sedrick Shaw (3), WR Leslie Shepherd (9), TE Irv Smith (13), LB James Williams (16).

COACHING STAFF

Head Coach,
Chris Palmer

Pro Career: Named head coach of Browns on January 21, 1999, coming to Cleveland from Jacksonville where he served as offensive coordinator and helped guide the Jaguars to the playoffs in each of the last two seasons. Jacksonville captured the AFC Central Division title with an 11-5 regular-season record in 1998 and defeated New England 25-10 in an AFC Wild Card Game. Jacksonville posted an identical 11-5 record in 1997 before losing at eventual Super Bowl XXXII champion Denver in a Wild Card Game. Palmer coached with the New England Patriots from 1993-96. He coached the team's wide receivers from 1993-95 and was the quarterbacks coach in 1996 when the Patriots captured the AFC championship and earned a berth in Super Bowl XXXI. Palmer served as wide receivers coach for the Houston Oilers from 1990-92 and helped Houston lead the NFL in passing offense each season. Palmer was the offensive line coach for the Canadian Football League's Montreal Concordes in 1983 and served as receivers coach in 1984 and quarterbacks coach/offensive coordinator in 1985 for the United States Football League's New Jersey Generals. Career record: 2-14.

Background: Quarterback at Southern Connecticut State 1968-1971. No pro playing experience. Began coaching career as assistant coaching the defensive line and wide receivers at the Connecticut from 1972-74. Wide receivers coach at Lehigh in 1975. Offensive coordinator at Colgate from 1976-1982. Head coach at the New Haven in 1986-87 and posted consecutive 8-2 marks. Head coach at Boston University in 1988-89. Career college head coaching record: 24-18.

Personal: Born September 23, 1949, Mt. Kisco, N.Y. Received bachelor's and master's degrees from Southern Connecticut State. Chris and his wife, Donna, reside in Cleveland. They have a son, Mark (2/24/77) and a daughter, Kristin (9/22/80).

ASSISTANT COACHES

Jerry Butler, wide receivers; born October 12, 1957, Ware Shoals, S.C., lives in Cleveland. Wide receiver Clemson 1975-78. Pro wide receiver Buffalo Bills 1979-1987. Pro coach: Joined Browns in 1999.

Keith Butler, linebackers; born May 16, 1956, Anniston, Ala., lives in Cleveland. Linebacker Memphis 1974-77. Pro linebacker Seattle 1978-1987. College coach: Memphis 1990-97, Arkansas State 1998. Pro coach: Joined Browns in 1999.

Pete Carmichael, offensive coordinator; born March 4, 1941, North Plainfield, N.J., lives in Cleveland. Quarterback Dayton 1961, Montclair State College 1962-63. No pro playing experience. College coach: Virginia Military 1965-66, New Hampshire 1967, Boston College 1968-1972, 1981-1993, Trenton State College 1973 (head coach), Columbia 1974-77, Merchant Marine Academy 1977-1980 (head coach). Pro coach: Jacksonville Jaguars 1995-99, joined Browns in 2000.

Pete Carmichael, Jr., offensive quality control; born October 6, 1971, Farmingham, Mass., lives in Cleveland. No college or pro playing experience. College coach: New Hampshire 1994, Louisiana Tech 1995-99. Pro coach: Joined Browns in 2000.

Romeo Crennel, defensive coordinator; born June 18, 1947, Lynchburgh, Va., lives in Cleveland. Offensive-defensive tackle, linebacker Western Kentucky 1966-69. No pro playing experience. College coach: Western Kentucky 1970-74, Texas Tech 1975-77, Mississippi 1978-79, Georgia Tech 1980. Pro coach: New York Giants 1981-1992, New England 1993-96, New York Jets 1997-99, joined Browns in 2000.

Jon Fabris, special teams-defensive assistant; born March 27, 1957, Chattanooga, Tenn., lives in Cleveland. Defensive back Mississippi 1976-79. No pro playing experience. College coach: Georgia Tech 1980, Washington State 1982-86, Iowa State 1987-1994, Notre Dame 1996, Kansas State 1997-98, South Carolina 1999. Pro coach: Joined Browns in 2000.

Jerry Holmes, defensive backfield; born December 22, 1957, Hampton, Va., lives in Cleveland. Defensive back Chowon (N.J.) J.C. 1976-77, West Virginia 1978-79. Pro defensive back New York Jets 1980-83, 1986-87, Pittsburgh Maulers (USFL) 1984, New Jersey Generals (USFL) 1985, Detroit Lions 1988-89, Green Bay Packers 1990-91. College coach: Hampton 1992-94, West Virginia 1995-98. Pro coach: Joined Browns in 1999.

John Hufnagel, quarterbacks; born September 13, 1951, Pittsburgh, lives in Cleveland. Quarterback Penn State 1969-1972. Pro quarterback Denver Broncos 1973-75, Calgary Stampeders (CFL) 1976-79, Saskatchewan Roughriders (CFL) 1980-83, 1987; Winnipeg Blue Bombers (CFL) 1984-85. Pro coach: Saskatchewan Roughriders (CFL) 1988, Calgary Stampeders (CFL) 1989-1995, New Jersey Red Dogs (Arena League) 1997-1998, joined Browns in 1999.

Tim Jorgensen, strength; born April 21, 1955, St. Louis, Mo., lives in Cleveland. Guard Southwest Missouri State 1974-76. No pro playing experience. College coach: Southwest Missouri State 1977-78, Alabama 1979, Louisiana State 1980-83. Pro coach: Philadelphia Eagles 1984-86, Atlanta Falcons 1987-1998, joined Browns in 1999.

Joe Kim, asst. strength; born June 18, 1969, Lakewood, Ohio, lives in Cleveland. No college or pro playing experience. Pro coach: Cleveland Browns 1991-95, Dallas (consultant) 1998, rejoined Browns in 2000.

Mark Michaels, special teams quality control; born August 15, 1963, Kingston, Pa., lives in Cleveland. Linebacker Connecticut 1982-85. No pro playing experience. College coach: New Haven 1987-1990, Brown 1994-97, Massachusetts 1998. Pro coach: Helsinki Roosters (Finnish Maple League) 1991, Utah Pioneers (Professional Spring Football League) 1992, joined Browns in 1999.

Ray Perkins, tight ends; born November 6, 1941, Mount Olive, Miss., lives in Cleveland. Wide receiver Alabama 1964-66. Pro wide receiver Baltimore Colts 1967-1971. College coach: Mississippi State 1973, Alabama 1983-86 (head coach), Arkansas State 1992 (head coach). Pro coach: New England Patriots 1974-77, 1993-1996, San Diego Chargers 1978, New York Giants 1979-1982 (head coach), Tampa Bay Buccaneers 1987-1990 (head coach), Oakland Raiders 1997, joined Browns in 1999.

Mike Pitts, defensive assistant; born September 25, 1960, Baltimore, lives in Cleveland. Defensive end Alabama 1980-83. Pro defensive lineman Atlanta Falcons 1983-86, Philadelphia Eagles 1987-1992, New England Patriots 1993-95. College coach: Morehouse College 1996-99. Pro coach: Joined Browns in 2000.

Tony Sparano, offensive quality control; born October 7, 1961, West Haven, Conn., lives in Cleveland. Center 1978-1981. No pro playing experience. College coach: New Haven 1984-87, 1994-98 (head coach 1994-98), Boston 1988-93. Pro coach: Joined Browns in 1999.

2000 FIRST-YEAR ROSTER

Name	Pos.	Ht.	Wt.	Birthdate	College	Hometown	How Acq.
Allamon, Kyle	TE	6-2	256	12/22/76	Texas Tech	Lubbock, Tex.	FA
Barnes, Rashidi	DB	5-11	200	6/26/78	Colorado	Berkeley, Calif.	D7c
Bedell, Brade	G-T	6-4	300	2/12/77	Colorado	Arcadia, Calif.	D6b
Brown, Courtney	DE	6-4	269	2/14/78	Penn State	Alvin, S.C.	D1a
Chandler, Eric	DE	6-6	285	6/6/77	Jackson State	Starkville, Miss.	D7b
Chanoine, Roger (1)	T	6-4	295	8/11/76	Temple	Newark, N.J.	FA-'99
Chapman, Lamar	DB	6-0	175	11/6/76	Kansas State	Liberal, Kan.	D5b
Dawson, JaJuan	WR	6-1	202	11/5/77	Tulane	Houston, Tex.	D3b
Dunn, Damon (1)	WR	5-9	182	3/15/76	Stanford	Arlington, Tex.	FA-'99
Dyra, Jeff	DT	6-4	290	7/17/77	Northwestern	Chicago, Ill.	FA
Estes, Steve	G-T	6-6	286	5/6/78	Colgate	Olean, N.Y.	FA
Gantous, Mike	DE	6-2	285	5/9/77	Louisville	Shaker Heights, Ohio	FA
Guilliams, Mike	G-T	6-5	298	3/28/77	Marshall	Beckley, W. Va.	FA
Gunn, Marcus	LB	6-3	255	8/11/77	Northeastern State, Okla.	Lawton, Okla.	FA
Hill, Madre (1)	RB	5-11	199	1/2/76	Arkansas	Malvern, Ark.	D7-'99
Jones, Dwaune	WR	6-0	189	7/11/77	Richmond	Washington, D.C.	FA
Jones, Michael	RB	6-1	240	12/21/78	Hampton	Ft. Washington, Md.	FA
Kerr, Jeff	LB	6-4	235	10/18/76	East Carolina	Salisbury, N.C.	FA
Klopf, Jeff	WR	5-10	177	10/27/75	Saginaw Valley State	Flint, Mich.	FA
Lamontagne, Noel	G-T	6-4	304	3/9/77	Virginia	Coopersburg, Pa.	FA
Lawless, Tramont	LB	6-3	254	10/9/76	Memphis	Nashville, Tenn.	FA
Lowe, Jeff	WR	5-11	196	3/10/77	Syracuse	Liverpool, N.Y.	FA
Malbrough, Anthony	DB	5-8	184	12/9/76	Texas Tech	Beaumont, Tex.	D5a
Matthews, Trevon	TE	6-2	249	10/8/76	South Carolina	Summerville, S.C.	FA
McKinney, Jeremy (1)	T	6-6	301	1/6/76	Iowa	Huntington Park, Colo.	FA-'99
Northcutt, Dennis	WR	5-10	175	12/22/77	Arizona	Los Angeles, Calif.	D2a
O'Hara, Shaun	C	6-3	285	6/23/77	Rutgers	Hillsborough, N.J.	FA
Prentice, Travis	RB	5-11	225	12/8/76	Miami, Ohio	Louisville, Ky.	D3a
Robinette, Greg	DT	6-2	285	2/4/77	West Virginia	Hampden, W. Va.	FA
Rogers, Tyrone (1)	DT	6-5	240	10/11/76	Alabama State	Montgomery, Ala.	FA-'99
Sanders, Lewis	DB	6-0	202	6/22/78	Maryland	Staten Island, N.Y.	D4a
Savea, Manuia	G-T	6-2	301	2/22/75	Arizona	Auto, American Samoa	D7a
Shea, Aaron	TE	6-3	256	12/5/76	Michigan	Ottawa, Ill.	D4b
Shuck, Kofi	WR	6-1	175	5/11/77	Wyoming	Park Forest, Ill.	FA
Simpson, Teto	DE	6-4	260	7/19/76	North Carolina	Greenville, N.C.	FA
Spikes, Rahshon	RB	5-10	212	10/16/77	North Carolina State	Meriden, N.C.	FA
Stiles, Caspor	LB	6-0	224	10/7/77	Memphis	Houston, Tex.	FA
Sudano, Nick	RB	6-1	244	3/19/77	Syracuse	Brook Park, Ohio	FA
Taylor, Ryan (1)	LB	6-2	230	12/11/76	Auburn	Dublin, Ga.	FA-'99
Terry, Nate	DB	6-3	185	10/5/76	West Virginia	Homestead, Fla.	FA
Thompson, Kevin	QB	6-5	222	7/27/77	Penn State	Damascus, Md.	FA
Turner, Lamont	LB	6-0	234	1/9/78	Vanderbilt	Franklin, Tenn.	FA
Wynn, Spergon	QB	6-3	229	8/10/78	Southwest Texas State	Houston, Tex.	D6a

The term NFL Rookie is defined as a player who is in his first season of professional football and has not been on the roster of another professional football team for any regular-season or postseason games. A Rookie is designated by an "R" on NFL rosters. Players who have been active in another professional football league or players who have NFL experience, including either preseason training camp or being on an Active List or Inactive List, or on Reserve/Injured or Reserve/Physically Unable to Perform for fewer than six regular-season games, are termed NFL First-Year Players. An NFL First-Year Player is designated by a "1" on NFL rosters. Thereafter, a player is credited with an additional year of experience for each season in which he accumulates six games on the Active List or Inactive List, or on Reserve/Injured or Reserve/Physically Unable to Perform.

DENVER BRONCOS

American Football Conference
Western Division
Team Colors: Orange, Broncos Navy Blue, and White
13655 Broncos Parkway
Englewood, Colorado 80112
Telephone: (303) 649-9000

CLUB OFFICIALS

President-Chief Executive Officer: Pat Bowlen
Vice President of Football Operations/Head Coach: Mike Shanahan
Vice President of Business Operations: Joe Ellis
Vice President of Administration: John Beake
General Manager: Neal Dahlen
Director of Pro Scouting: Rick Smith
Director of College Scouting: Ted Sundquist
Director of Salary Cap and Football Finance Administration: Dave Blando
Chief Financial Officer: Allen Fears
Senior Director of Ticket Operations/Business Development: Rick Nichols
Assistant to the President: Yolanda Saltus
Senior Director of Media Relations: Jim Saccomano
Director of Stadium Operations: Gail Stuckey
Senior Director of Operations: Bill Harpole
Senior Director of Marketing: Greg Carney
Director of Special Services: Fred Fleming
Director of Player Relations: Bill Thompson
Community Relations Coordinator: Steve Sewell
Trainer: Steve Antonopulos
Equipment Manager: Doug West
Video Director: Kent Erickson
Stadium: Denver Mile High Stadium
• **Capacity:** 76,082
1900 West Eliot
Denver, Colorado 80204
Playing Surface: Grass (PAT)
Training Camp: University of Northern Colorado
Greeley, Colorado 80639

2000 SCHEDULE

PRESEASON

Aug. 5	at Arizona	7:00
Aug. 13	**Green Bay**	2:00
Aug. 19	**Dallas**	7:00
Aug. 25	at San Francisco	6:00

REGULAR SEASON

Sept. 4	at St. Louis (Mon.)	8:00
Sept. 10	**Atlanta**	2:15
Sept. 17	at Oakland	1:05
Sept. 24	**Kansas City**	2:15
Oct. 1	**New England**	2:05
Oct. 8	at San Diego	1:15
Oct. 15	**Cleveland**	2:05
Oct. 22	at Cincinnati	1:00
Oct. 29	Open Date	
Nov. 5	at New York Jets	4:15
Nov. 13	**Oakland** (Mon.)	7:00
Nov. 19	**San Diego**	2:05
Nov. 26	at Seattle	1:15
Dec. 3	at New Orleans	12:00
Dec. 10	**Seattle**	2:05
Dec. 17	at Kansas City	12:00
Dec. 23	**San Francisco** (Sat.)	2:15

RECORD HOLDERS

INDIVIDUAL RECORDS—CAREER

Category	Name	Performance
Rushing (Yds.)	Terrell Davis, 1995-99	6,624
Passing (Yds.)	John Elway, 1983-1998	51,475
Passing (TDs)	John Elway, 1983-1998	300
Receiving (No.)	Shannon Sharpe, 1990-99	552
Receiving (Yds.)	Shannon Sharpe, 1990-99	6,983
Interceptions	Steve Foley, 1976-1986	44
Punting (Avg.)	Jim Fraser, 1962-64	45.2
Punt Return (Avg.)	Darrien Gordon, 1997-98	12.5
Kickoff Return (Avg.)	Abner Haynes, 1965-66	26.3
Field Goals	Jason Elam, 1993-99	186
Touchdowns (Tot.)	Terrell Davis, 1995-99	63
Points	Jim Turner, 1971-79	742

INDIVIDUAL RECORDS—SINGLE SEASON

Category	Name	Performance
Rushing (Yds.)	Terrell Davis, 1998	2,008
Passing (Yds.)	John Elway, 1993	4,030
Passing (TDs)	John Elway, 1997	27
Receiving (No.)	Lionel Taylor, 1961	100
Receiving (Yds.)	Steve Watson, 1981	1,244
Interceptions	Goose Gonsoulin, 1960	11
Punting (Avg.)	Tom Rouen, 1998	46.9
Punt Return (Avg.)	Floyd Little, 1967	16.9
Kickoff Return (Avg.)	Bill Thompson, 1969	28.5
Field Goals	Jason Elam, 1995	31
Touchdowns (Tot.)	Terrell Davis, 1998	23
Points	Terrell Davis, 1998	138

INDIVIDUAL RECORDS—SINGLE GAME

Category	Name	Performance
Rushing (Yds.)	Terrell Davis, 9-21-97	215
Passing (Yds.)	Frank Tripucka, 9-15-62	447
Passing (TDs)	Frank Tripucka, 10-28-62	5
	John Elway, 11-18-84	5
Receiving (No.)	Lionel Taylor, 11-29-64	13
	Bobby Anderson, 9-30-73	13
Receiving (Yds.)	Lionel Taylor, 11-27-60	199
Interceptions	Goose Gonsoulin, 9-18-60	*4
	Willie Brown, 11-15-64	*4
Field Goals	Gene Mingo, 10-6-63	5
	Rich Karlis, 11-20-83	5
	Jason Elam, 9-3-95	5
Touchdowns (Tot.)	Many times	3
	Last time by Terrell Davis, 11-24-97	
Points	Gene Mingo, 12-10-60	21

*NFL Record

COACHING HISTORY

(317-296-10)

1960-61	Frank Filchock	7-20-1
1962-64	Jack Faulkner*	9-22-1
1964-66	Mac Speedie**	6-19-1
1966	Ray Malavasi	4-8-0
1967-71	Lou Saban***	20-42-3
1971	Jerry Smith	2-3-0
1972-76	John Ralston	34-33-3
1977-80	Robert (Red) Miller	42-25-0
1981-92	Dan Reeves	117-79-1
1993-94	Wade Phillips	16-17-0
1995-99	Mike Shanahan	60-28-0

*Released after four games in 1964
**Resigned after two games in 1966
***Resigned after nine games in 1971

DENVER MILE HIGH STADIUM

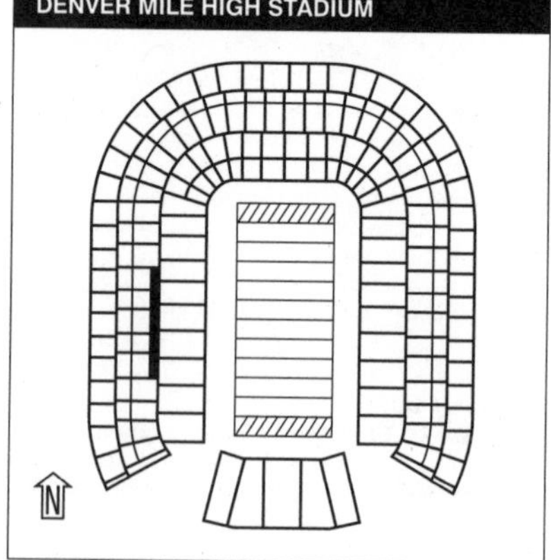

1999 TEAM RECORD

PRESEASON (3-2)

Date	Result		Opponent
8/7	W	20-17	vs. San Diego at Sydney, Australia
8/14	W	38-7	Arizona
8/23	L	12-27	vs. Green Bay at Madison, Wisconsin
8/29	L	12-22	at Dallas
9/3	W	34-3	San Francisco

REGULAR SEASON (6-10)

Date	Result		Opponent	Att.
9/13	L	21-38	Miami	75,623
9/19	L	10-26	at Kansas City	78,683
9/26	L	10-13	at Tampa Bay	65,297
10/3	L	13-21	New York Jets	74,181
10/10	W	16-13	at Oakland	55,704
10/17	W	31-10	Green Bay	73,352
10/24	L	23-24	at New England	60,011
10/31	L	20-23	Minnesota	75,021
11/7	W	33-17	at San Diego	61,204
11/14	L	17-20	at Seattle	66,314
11/22	W	27-21	Oakland (OT)	70,012
12/5	L	10-16	Kansas City	73,855
12/13	L	24-27	at Jacksonville	71,357
12/19	W	36-30	Seattle (OT)	65,987
12/25	W	17-7	at Detroit	73,158
1/2	L	6-12	San Diego	69,278

(OT) Overtime

SCORE BY PERIODS

Broncos	79	58	77	88	12	—	314
Opponents	34	115	62	107	0	—	318

ATTENDANCE

Home 593,811 Away 534,542 Total 1,128,353
Single-game home record, 76,089 (10/26/86)
Single-season home record, 598,224 (1981)

1999 TEAM STATISTICS

	Broncos	Opp.
Total First Downs	308	267
Rushing	107	88
Passing	168	154
Penalty	33	25
Third Down: Made/Att.	84/229	64/203
Third Down Pct.	36.7	31.5
Fourth Down: Made/Att.	6/14	5/11
Fourth Down Pct.	42.9	45.5
Total Net Yards	5,283	4,753
Avg. Per Game	330.2	297.1
Total Plays	1053	961
Avg. Per Play	5.0	4.9
Net Yards Rushing	1,864	1,737
Avg. Per Game	116.5	108.6
Total Rushes	465	440
Net Yards Passing	3,419	3,016
Avg. Per Game	213.7	188.5
Sacked/Yards Lost	34/227	50/283
Gross Yards	3,646	3,299
Att./Completions	554/319	471/273
Completion Pct.	57.6	58.0
Had Intercepted	18	15
Punts/Average	84/46.5	92/43.6
Net Punting Avg.	84/35.6	92/36.5
Penalties/Yards	114/872	114/1,016
Fumbles/Ball Lost	33/10	29/11
Touchdowns	32	35
Rushing	13	15
Passing	16	17
Returns	3	3
Avg. Time of Possession	31:06	28:54

1999 INDIVIDUAL STATISTICS

Passing	Att.	Comp.	Yds.	Pct.	TD	Int.	Tkld.	Rate
Griese	452	261	3,032	57.7	14	14	27/176	75.6
C. Miller	81	46	527	56.8	2	1	7/51	79.6
Brister	20	12	87	60.0	0	3	0/0	30.6
R. Smith	1	0	0	0.0	0	0	0/0	39.6
Broncos	554	319	3,646	57.6	16	18	34/227	73.6
Opponents	471	273	3,299	58.0	17	15	50/283	78.3

SCORING	TD R	TD P	TD Rt	PAT	FG	Saf	PTS
Elam	0	0	0	29/29	29/36	0	116
Gary	7	0	0	0/0	0/0	0	44
McCaffrey	0	7	0	0/0	0/0	0	42
R. Smith	0	4	0	0/0	0/0	0	24
Carswell	0	2	0	0/0	0/0	0	12
Chamberlain	0	2	0	0/0	0/0	0	12
Davis	2	0	0	0/0	0/0	0	12
Griese	2	0	0	0/0	0/0	0	12
Griffith	1	1	0	0/0	0/0	0	12
Cadrez	0	0	1	0/0	0/0	0	6
Loville	1	0	0	0/0	0/0	0	6
Romanowski	0	0	1	0/0	0/0	0	6
Watson	0	0	1	0/0	0/0	0	6
Pryce	0	0	0	0/0	0/0	1	2
Broncos	13	16	3	29/29	29/36	2	314
Opponents	15	17	3	31/32	25/29	0	318

2-Pt. Conversions: Gary.
Team 1-1, Opponents 1-3.

RUSHING	Att.	Yds.	Avg.	LG	TD
Gary	276	1,159	4.2	71	7
Davis	67	211	3.1	26	2
Loville	40	203	5.1	36t	1
Griese	46	138	3.0	23	2
Griffith	17	66	3.9	13	1
C. Miller	8	40	5.0	13	0
Avery	5	21	4.2	11	0
Brister	2	17	8.5	17	0
D. Smith	1	7	7.0	7	0
Lynn	2	2	1.0	1	0
Rouen	1	0	0.0	0	0
Broncos	465	1,864	4.0	71	13
Opponents	440	1,737	3.9	54	15

RECEIVING	No.	Yds.	Avg.	LG	TD
R. Smith	79	1,020	12.9	71	4
McCaffrey	71	1,018	14.3	78t	7
Chamberlain	32	488	15.3	88	2
Griffith	26	192	7.4	20	1
Carswell	24	201	8.4	20	2
Sharpe	23	224	9.7	24	0
Gary	21	159	7.6	21	0
Loville	11	50	4.5	15	0
Cooper	9	98	10.9	21	0
B. Miller	5	59	11.8	26	0
Avery	4	24	6.0	11	0
D. Smith	4	23	5.8	11	0
McGriff	3	37	12.3	15	0
Davis	3	26	8.7	10	0
Doering	3	22	7.3	9	0
Clark	1	5	5.0	5	0
Broncos	319	3,646	11.4	88	16
Opponents	273	3,299	12.1	67	17

INTERCEPTIONS	No.	Yds.	Avg.	LG	TD
James	5	59	11.8	45	0
Romanowski	3	35	11.7	18t	1
Carter	2	48	24.0	34	0
Crockett	2	14	7.0	10	0
E. Brown	1	13	13.0	13	0
Coghill	1	0	0.0	0	0
Pryce	1	0	0.0	0	0
Broncos	15	169	11.3	45	1
Opponents	18	231	12.8	60	1

PUNTING	No.	Yds.	Avg.	In 20	LG
Rouen	84	3,908	46.5	19	65
Broncos	84	3,908	46.5	19	65
Opponents	92	4,011	43.6	27	64

PUNT RETURNS	No.	FC	Yds.	Avg.	LG	TD
Watson	44	8	334	7.6	81t	1
McGriff	7	1	50	7.1	20	0
Coghill	3	1	25	8.3	10	0
Broncos	54	10	409	7.6	81t	1
Opponents	43	13	600	14.0	80t	1

KICKOFF RETURNS	No.	Yds.	Avg.	LG	TD
Watson	48	1,138	23.7	71	0
Avery	7	137	19.6	25	0
B. Miller	4	79	19.8	30	0
Loville	2	22	11.0	12	0
D. Smith	1	12	12.0	11	0
R. Smith	1	10	10.0	10	0
Broncos	63	1,398	22.2	71	0
Opponents	70	1,457	20.8	61	0

FIELD GOALS	1-19	20-29	30-39	40-49	50+
Elam	1/1	8/8	7/8	8/11	5/8
Broncos	1/1	8/8	7/8	8/11	5/8
Opponents	2/2	6/6	6/7	10/12	1/2

SACKS	No.
Pryce	13.0
Cadrez	7.0
Tanuvasa	7.0
N. Smith	6.5
Williams	4.0
Hasselbach	2.5
Crockett	2.0
Wayne	2.0
E. Brown	1.5
Traylor	1.5
Bowens	1.0
Braxton	1.0
Wilson	1.0
Broncos	50.0
Opponents	34.0

2000 DRAFT CHOICES

Round	Name	Pos.	College
1	Deltha O'Neal	DB	California
2	Ian Gold	LB	Michigan
	Kenoy Kennedy	DB	Arkansas
3	Chris Cole	WR	Texas A&M
4	Jerry Johnson	DT	Florida State
	Cooper Carlisle	T	Florida
5	Muneer Moore	WR	Richmond
6	Mike Anderson	RB	Utah
7	Jarious Jackson	QB	Notre Dame
	Leory Fields	WR	Jackson State

DENVER BRONCOS

2000 VETERAN ROSTER

No.	Name	Pos.	Ht.	Wt.	Birthdate	NFL Exp.	College	Hometown	How Acq.	'99 Games/ Starts
92	Archambeau, Lester	DE	6-5	275	6/27/67	11	Stanford	Montville, N.J.	UFA(Atl)-'00	15/15*
20	Avery, John	RB	5-9	190	1/11/76	3	Mississippi	Asheville, N.C.	T(Mia)-'99	6/0*
79	Banks, Chris	G	6-1	300	4/4/73	3	Kansas	Lexington, Mo.	FA-'98	16/1
9	Brohm, Jeff	QB	6-1	205	4/24/71	6	Louisville	Louisville, Ky.	FA-'99	0*
73	Brown, Cyron	DT	6-5	275	6/28/75	3	Western Illinois	Chicago, Ill.	FA-'98	7/0
26	Brown, Eric	S	6-0	210	3/20/75	3	Mississippi State	San Antonio, Tex.	D2-'98	10/10
59	Cadrez, Glenn	LB	6-3	240	1/2/70	9	Houston	El Centro, Calif.	FA-'95	16/15
89	Carswell, Dwayne	TE	6-3	260	1/18/72	6	Liberty	Jacksonville, Fla.	FA-'94	16/11
86	Chamberlain, Byron	TE	6-1	242	10/17/71	5	Wayne State	Fort Worth, Tex.	D7b-'95	16/0
88	Clark, Desmond	TE	6-3	255	4/20/77	2	Wake Forest	Lakeland, Fla.	D6a-'99	9/0
48	Coghill, George	S	6-0	210	3/30/70	4	Wake Forest	Fredricksburg, Va.	FA-'97	13/5
81	Cooper, Andre	WR	6-2	210	6/21/75	2	Florida State	Jacksonville, Fla.	FA-'98	10/1
39	Crockett, Ray	CB	5-10	184	1/5/67	12	Baylor	Dallas, Tex.	UFA(Det)-'94	16/16
74	Davis, Jerome	DE	6-4	275	3/4/74	2	Minnesota	Detroit, Mich.	FA-'00	0*
72	Davis, Nathan	DT	6-5	312	2/6/74	4	Indiana	Richmond, Ind.	FA-'00	5/0*
30	Davis, Terrell	RB	5-11	210	10/28/72	6	Georgia	San Diego, Calif.	D6b-'95	4/4
68	DeGraffenreid, Allen	T	6-5	305	6/3/74	2	Vanderbilt	Dunwoody, Ga.	FA-'00	0*
85	Doering, Chris	WR	6-4	195	5/19/73	2	Florida	Gainesville, Fla.	FA-'99	3/0
1	Elam, Jason	K	5-11	200	3/8/70	8	Hawaii	Ft. Walton Beach, Fla.	D3b-'93	16/0
12	Frerotte, Gus	QB	6-3	230	7/31/71	7	Tulsa	Ford City, Pa.	UFA(Det)-'00	9/6*
64	Friedman, Lennie	G	6-3	300	10/13/76	2	Duke	West Milford, N.J.	D2b-'99	0*
22	Gary, Olandis	RB	5-11	218	5/18/75	2	Georgia	Washington, D.C.	D4-'99	12/12
14	Griese, Brian	QB	6-3	215	3/18/75	3	Michigan	Miami, Fla.	D3-'98	14/13
29	Griffith, Howard	RB	6-0	230	11/17/67	8	Illinois	Chicago, Ill.	UFA(Car)-'97	16/16
67	Harrison, Chris	T	6-3	290	2/25/72	3	Virginia	Washington, D.C.	FA-'00	0*
96	Hasselbach, Harald	DE	6-6	285	9/22/67	7	Washington	Tsawassen, B.C., Canada	FA-'94	16/2
32	Jenkins, Billy	S	5-10	205	7/8/74	4	Howard	Albuquerque, N.M.	T(StL)-'00	16/16
60	Jones, K.C.	C	6-1	275	3/28/74	4	Miami	Midland, Tex.	FA-'97	0*
77	Jones, Tony	T	6-5	291	5/24/66	13	Western Carolina	Royston, Ga.	T(Balt)-'97	12/12
34	King, Carlos	RB	6-0	230	11/25/73	2	North Carolina State	Boonville, N.C.	FA-'00	0*
91	Kuberski, Bob	DT	6-4	300	4/5/71	6	Navy	Folson, Pa.	UFA(NE)-'00	5/0
78	Lepsis, Matt	T	6-4	290	1/13/74	3	Colorado	Conroe, Tex.	FA-'97	16/16
28	Lincoln, Jeremy	CB	5-10	182	10/26/70	9	Tennessee	Toledo, Ohio	UFA(NYG)-'00	15/7*
97	Lodish, Mike	DT	6-3	270	8/11/67	11	UCLA	Birmingham, Mich.	UFA(Buff)-'95	13/2
37	Lynn, Anthony	RB	6-3	230	12/21/68	7	Texas Tech	McKinney, Tex.	UFA(SF)-'97	16/0
87	McCaffrey, Ed	WR	6-5	215	8/17/68	10	Stanford	Allentown, Pa.	UFA(SF)-'95	15/15
83	McGriff, Travis	WR	5-8	185	6/24/76	2	Florida	Gainesville, Fla.	D3b-'99	14/0
82	Miller, Billy	WR-TE	6-3	215	4/24/77	2	Southern California	Westlake Village, Calif.	D7a-'99	10/0
51	Mobley, John	LB	6-1	236	10/10/73	5	Kutztown	Chester, Pa.	D1-'96	2/2
23	Moore, Jason	S	5-10	191	1/15/76	2	San Diego State	San Bernardino, Calif.	FA-'99	6/0
66	Nalen, Tom	C	6-3	286	5/13/71	7	Boston College	Foxboro, Mass.	D7c-'94	16/16
62	Neil, Dan	G	6-2	281	10/21/73	4	Texas	Cypress Creek, Tex.	D3-'97	15/15
95	Pittman, Kavika	DE	6-6	273	10/9/74	5	McNeese State	Leesville, La.	UFA(Dall)-'00	16/16*
31	Pounds, Darryl	CB	5-10	189	7/21/72	6	Nicholls State	Magnolia, Miss.	UFA(Wash)-'00	16/0*
93	Pryce, Trevor	DT	6-5	295	8/3/75	4	Clemson	Winter Park, Fla.	D1-'97	15/15
99	Reagor, Montae	DT	6-2	256	6/29/77	2	Texas Tech	Waxahachie, Tex.	D2a-'99	9/0
53	Romanowski, Bill	LB	6-4	245	4/2/66	13	Boston College	Vernon, Conn.	UFA(Phil)-'96	16/16
16	Rouen, Tom	P	6-3	225	6/9/68	8	Colorado	Hinsdale, Ill.	FA-'93	16/0
58	Russ, Steve	LB	6-4	245	9/16/72	4	Air Force	Stetsonville, Wisc.	FA-'99	8/0
69	Schlereth, Mark	G	6-3	287	1/25/66	12	Idaho	Anchorage, Alaska	UFA(Wash)-'95	16/16
42	Smith, Detron	RB	5-10	230	2/25/74	5	Texas A&M	Dallas, Tex.	D3a-'96	16/0
80	Smith, Rod	WR	6-0	200	5/15/70	6	Missouri Southern	Texarkana, Ark.	FA-'94	15/15
33	Spencer, Jimmy	CB	5-9	180	3/29/69	9	Florida	Belle Glade, Fla.	FA-'00	14/7*
35	Suttle, Jason	CB	5-10	182	12/2/74	2	Wisconsin	Burnsville, Minn.	FA-'99	5/0
98	Tanuvasa, Maa	DE	6-2	270	11/6/70	7	Hawaii	Mililani, Hawaii	FA-'95	16/16
70	Teague, Trey	T	6-5	285	12/27/74	3	Tennessee	Jackson, Tenn.	D7a-'98	16/4
13	Thomas, J.T.	WR	5-10	180	7/11/71	5	Arizona State	San Bernardino, Calif.	FA-'00	0*
94	Traylor, Keith	DT	6-2	304	9/3/69	9	Central State, Okla.	Little Rock, Ark.	UFA(KC)-'97	15/15
71	Tuten, Melvin	T	6-6	305	11/11/71	4	Syracuse	Washington, D.C.	FA-'99	2/0
21	Watson, Chris	CB	6-1	192	6/30/77	2	Eastern Illinois	Chicago, Ill.	D3a-'99	14/1
54	Wayne, Nate	LB	6-0	230	1/12/75	3	Mississippi	Macon, Miss.	D7b-'98	15/0
56	Wilson, Al	LB	6-0	240	6/21/77	2	Tennessee	Jackson, Tenn.	D1-'99	16/12

* Archambeau played in 15 games with Atlanta in '99; Avery played 1 game with Miami and 5 with Denver; Brohm last active with San Francisco in '97;J. Davis, DeGraffenreid, Friedman, Harrison, K.C. Jones, King missed '99 season because of injury; N. Davis played 5 games with Dallas; Frerotte played 9 games with Detroit; Jenkins played 16 games with St. Louis; Lincoln played 15 games with N.Y. Giants; Pittman played 16 games with Dallas; Pounds played 16 games with Washington; Spencer played 14 games with San Diego; Thomas last active with St. Louis in '98.

† Restricted free agent; subject to developments.

Unrestricted free agent; subject to developments.

Retired—Tyrone Braxton, 13-year safety, 16 games in '99.

Players last through free agency (3): DT Paul Grasmanis (Phil; 5 games in '99), CB Tory James (Oak; 16), TE Shannon Sharpe (Balt; 5).

Also played with Broncos in '99—QB Bubby Brister (2 games), CB Dale Carter (14), CB Darrius Johnson (16), RB Derek Loville (10), QB Chris Miller (3), DE Neil Smith (15).

COACHING STAFF

Head Coach,
Mike Shanahan

Pro Career: Became the eleventh head coach in Broncos history on January 31, 1995, coming to Denver from the 1994 world champion San Francisco 49ers, where he served as offensive coordinator from 1992-94. Mike Shanahan led the Broncos to back-to-back Super Bowl championships in 1997 and 1998, becoming just the fifth head coach to accomplish that feat. Shanahan led Denver to seven postseason wins in those two seasons, the highest two-year total in history. His 1997 Broncos became just the second Wild Card team to win the Super Bowl, and they became the first AFC team to capture the NFL crown in 14 years. In 1996 Shanahan led the Broncos to a 13-3 record and the AFC Western Division title, tying the club record for wins in a season and leading the NFL in total offense. In 1995 he improved the Broncos to an 8-8 mark. During his NFL career, Shanahan has been a part of teams that have played in nine AFC or NFC Championship Games, in addition to his six Super Bowl appearances, five with Denver and Super Bowl XXIX with San Francisco. In his 25 seasons coaching in the NFL and at the college level, Shanahan's teams have participated in postseason playoffs or bowl games 18 times. A driving force behind the Broncos' offense for all three of the team's Super Bowl appearances in the 1980s (following the '86, '87, and '89 seasons), he first came to Denver in 1984 as wide receivers coach. Shanahan was Broncos' offensive coordinator from 1985-87, and returned to Denver as quarterbacks coach on October 16, 1989, after serving as head coach of the Los Angeles Raiders in 1988 and through the first four games of the 1989 season. His record with the Raiders was 8-12. Career record: 68-40.

Background: Shanahan began his coaching career at Oklahoma in 1975-76, also coaching at Northern Arizona (1977), Eastern Illinois (1978), and Minnesota (1979), before moving on to Florida (1980-83). During his tenure on the college level, Shanahan's teams had a combined record of 77-29-3 (.720), including national championship seasons at Oklahoma in 1975 and at Eastern Illinois.

Personal: Shanahan was born in Oak Park, Illinois, on August 24, 1952. He attended East Leyden High School in Franklin Park and was a wishbone quarterback-defensive back at Eastern Illinois, graduating in 1974 with a degree in physical education and a master's degree in 1975. Mike and his wife, Peggy, have two children, son Kyle and daughter Krystal.

ASSISTANT COACHES

Frank Bush, nickel package/secondary; born January 10, 1963, Athens, Ga., lives in Englewood, Colo. Linebacker North Carolina State 1981-84. Pro linebacker Houston Oilers 1985-86. Pro coach: Houston Oilers 1992-94, joined Broncos in 1995.

Larry Coyer, linebackers; born April 19, 1943, Huntington, W. Va., lives in Englewood, Colo. Linebacker Marshall 1962-64. No pro playing experience. College coach: Marshall 1965-67, Iowa 1974-77, Oklahoma State 1978, Iowa State 1979-1983, 1995-96, UCLA 1987-89, Houston 1990, Ohio State 1991-92, East Carolina 1993, Pittsburgh 1997-99. Pro coach: Michigan Panthers (USFL) 1984-85, Memphis Showboats (USFL) 1986, New York Jets 1994, joined Broncos in 2000.

Rick Dennison, special teams; born June 22, 1958, in Kalispell, Mont., lives in Englewood, Colo. Tight end Colorado State 1976-79. Pro linebacker Denver Broncos 1982-1990. Pro coach: Joined Broncos in 1995.

Karl Dorrell, wide receivers; born December 18, 1968, Alameda, Calif., lives in Englewood, Colo. Wide receiver UCLA 1982-86. No pro playing experience. College coach: UCLA 1988, Central Florida 1989, Northern Arizona 1990-91, Colorado 1992-93, 1995-98, Arizona State 1994. Pro coach: Joined Broncos in 2000.

George Dyer, defensive line; born May 4, 1940, Alhambra, Calif., lives in Aurora, Colo. Center-linebacker U.C. Santa Barbara 1961-63. No pro playing experience. College coach: Humboldt State 1964-66, Coalinga (Calif.) J.C. 1967 (head coach), Portland State 1968-1971, Idaho 1972, San Jose State 1973, Michigan State 1977-79, Arizona State 1980-81. Pro coach: Winnipeg Blue Bombers (CFL) 1974-76, Buffalo Bills 1982, Seattle Seahawks 1983-1991, Los Angeles Rams 1992-94, joined Broncos in 1995.

Alex Gibbs, asst. head coach-offensive line; born February 11, 1941, Morganton, N.C., lives in Greenwood Village, Colo. Running back-defensive back Davidson College 1959-1963. No pro playing experience. College coach: Duke 1969-1970, Kentucky 1971-72, West Virginia 1973-74, Ohio State 1975-78, Auburn 1979-1981, Georgia 1982-83. Pro coach: Denver Broncos 1984-87, Los Angeles Raiders 1988-89, San Diego Chargers 1990-91, Indianapolis Colts 1992, Kansas City Chiefs 1993-94, rejoined Broncos in 1995.

Gary Kubiak, offensive coordinator-quarterbacks; born August 15, 1961, Houston, Tex., lives in Englewood, Colo. Quarterback Texas A&M 1979-1982. Pro quarterback Denver Broncos 1983-1991. College coach: Texas A&M 1992-93. Pro coach: San Francisco 49ers 1994, joined Broncos in 1995.

Pat McPherson, offensive assistant; born April 15, 1969, Santa Clara, Calif., live in Englewood, Colo. Linebacker Santa Clara 1991-92. No pro playing experience. Pro coach: Joined Broncos in 1998.

Ron Milus, defensive backs; born November 25, 1963, Tacoma, Wash., lives in Englewood, Colo. Defensive back Washington 1982-85. No pro playing experience. College coach: Washington 1991-98, Texas A&M 1999. Pro coach: Joined Broncos in 2000.

Brian Pariani, tight ends; born July 2, 1965, San Francisco, lives in Castle Pines, Colo. No college or pro playing experience. College coach: UCLA 1989. Pro coach: San Francisco 49ers 1991-94, joined Broncos in 1995.

Greg Robinson, defensive coordinator; born October 9, 1951, Los Angeles, Calif., lives in Aurora, Colo. Linebacker-tight end Pacific 1972-74. No pro playing experience. College coach: Pacific 1975-76, Cal State-Fullerton 1977-79, North Carolina State 1980-81, UCLA 1982-89. Pro coach: New York Jets 1990-94, joined Broncos in 1995.

Greg Saporta, asst. strength and conditioning; born February 2, 1957, New York, N.Y., lives in Englewood, Colo. Wide receiver Buffalo State 1977-79. No pro playing experience. College coach: Florida 1981-88, 1993-94, North Carolina 1989-1992. Pro coach: Joined Broncos in 1995.

John Teerlinck, pass rush specialist; born April 9, 1951, Rochester, N.Y., lives in Englewood, Colo. Defensive lineman Western Illinois 1970-73. Pro defensive tackle San Diego Chargers 1974-76. College coach: Iowa Lakes J.C. 1977, Eastern Illinois 1978-79, Illinois 1980-82. Pro coach: Chicago Blitz (USFL) 1983, Arizona Wranglers/Outlaws (USFL) 1984-85, Cleveland Browns 1989-1990, Los Angeles Rams 1991, Minnesota Vikings 1992-94, Detroit Lions 1995-96, joined Broncos in 1997.

Terry Tumey, defensive assistant; born October 29, 1965, Tulsa, Okla., lives in Parker, Colo. Defensive lineman UCLA 1983-1987. No pro playing experience. College coach: UCLA 1993-1998. Pro coach: joined Broncos in 1999.

Bobby Turner, running backs; born May 6, 1949, East Chicago, Ind., lives in Englewood, Colo. Defensive back Indiana State 1968-1971. No pro playing experience. College coach: Indiana State 1975-1982, Fresno State 1983-88, Ohio State 1989-1990, Purdue 1991-94. Pro coach: Joined Broncos in 1995.

Rich Tuten, strength and conditioning; born December 30, 1953, Columbia, S.C., lives in Englewood, Colo. Nose guard Clemson 1976-78. No pro playing experience. College coach: Florida 1979-1988, 1993-94, North Carolina 1989-1992. Pro coach: Joined Broncos in 1995.

2000 FIRST-YEAR ROSTER

Name	Pos.	Ht.	Wt.	Birthdate	College	Hometown	How Acq.
Anderson, Mike	RB	6-0	235	9/21/73	Utah	Winnsboro, S.C.	D6
Brown, DeAuntae (1)	CB	5-10	195	4/28/74	Central State, Ohio	Detroit, Mich.	FA
Buck, Steve (1)	QB	6-4	219	2/25/76	Weber State	Alta Loma, Calif.	FA
Butler, Hillary (1)	LB	6-2	244	1/5/71	Washington	Tacoma, Wash.	FA
Carlisle, Cooper	G-T	6-5	300	8/11/77	Florida	McComb, Miss.	D4b
Chorak, Jason (1)	DE	6-3	260	9/23/74	Washington	Vashon, Wash.	FA
Clark, Darius	S	5-10	204	4/13/77	Duke	Tampa, Fla.	FA
Cohens, Willie (1)	DE	6-2	264	11/21/76	Florida	Starke, Fla.	FA
Cole, Chris	WR	6-0	195	11/12/77	Texas A&M	Orange, Tex.	D3
Coleman, KaRon	RB	5-7	198	5/22/78	Stephen F. Austin	Missouri City, Tex.	FA
Fields, Leroy	WR	6-3	205	12/2/75	Jackson State	Monroe, La.	D7b
Gizzi, Chris (1)	LB	6-0	230	3/8/75	Air Force	Cleveland, Ohio	FA-'98
Gold, Ian	LB	6-0	223	8/23/78	Michigan	Ann Arbor, Mich.	D2a
Hampton, William (1)	CB	5-10	190	3/7/75	Murray State	Little Rock, Ark.	FA
Jackson, Jarious	QB	6-0	228	5/3/77	Notre Dame	Tupelo, Miss.	D7a
Johnson, Jerry	DT	6-0	292	7/11/77	Florida State	Ft. Pierce, Fla.	D4a
Jones, Chris (1)	LB	5-10	229	9/30/76	Clemson	Monroe, Ga.	FA
Jones, Toya (1)	S	6-1	199	10/28/76	Texas A&M	Refugio, Tex.	FA
Kennedy, Kenoy	S	6-1	203	11/15/77	Arkansas	Terrell, Tex.	D2b
Moore, Muneer	WR	6-1	200	3/15/77	Richmond	Eastville, Va.	D5
O'Neal, Deltha	CB	5-10	196	1/30/77	California	Milpitas, Calif.	D1
Rountree, Glenn (1)	G	6-3	304	11/24/73	Clemson	Suffolk, Va.	FA-'99
Trout, Brad (1)	S	6-2	209	1/22/75	Valdosta State	Miami, Fla.	FA-'99
Watts, Jason (1)	C	6-3	271	4/19/77	Kentucky	Oviedo, Fla.	FA-'99
Yamini, Bashir	WR	6-3	190	9/10/77	Iowa	Dolton, Ill.	FA

The term NFL Rookie is defined as a player who is in his first season of professional football and has not been on the roster of another professional football team for any regular-season or postseason games. A Rookie is designated by an "R" on NFL rosters. Players who have been active in another professional football league or players who have NFL experience, including either preseason training camp or being on an Active List or Inactive List, or on Reserve/Injured or Reserve/Physically Unable to Perform for fewer than six regular-season games, are termed NFL First-Year Players. An NFL First-Year Player is designated by a "1" on NFL rosters. Thereafter, a player is credited with an additional year of experience for each season in which he accumulates six games on the Active List or Inactive List, or on Reserve/Injured or Reserve/Physically Unable to Perform.

NOTES

INDIANAPOLIS COLTS

American Football Conference
Eastern Division
Team Colors: Royal Blue and White
P.O. Box 535000
Indianapolis, Indiana 46253
Telephone: (317) 297-2658

CLUB OFFICIALS

Owner and CEO: James Irsay
President: Bill Polian
Vice Chairman and COO: Michael G. Chernoff
Senior Vice President: Bob Terpening
Senior Vice President-Administration: Pete Ward
Vice President-Sales and Marketing: Ray Compton
Vice President-Finance: Kurt Humphrey
Vice President-Ticket Operations: Larry Hall
Vice President-Public Relations: Craig Kelley
Director of Football Operations: Dom Anile
Director of Pro Player Personnel: Clyde Powers
Director of College Scouting: Mike Butler
Director of Pro Scouting: Chris Polian
Director of Player Development: Steve Champlin
Director of Sponsorship Sales: Jay Souers
Director of Business Development: Tom Zupancic
Director of Ticket Sales: Greg Hylton
Director of Community Development/Player Relations: Bill Brooks
Director of Community Relations and Promotions: Nicole Duncan
Assistant Director of Public Relations: Ryan Robinson
Equipment Manager: Jon Scott
Video Director: Marty Heckscher
Head Trainer: Hunter Smith
Assistant Equipment Manager: Mike Mays
Assistant Trainers: Dave Hammer, Dave Walston
Assistant Video Director: John Starliper
Purchasing Administrator: Dave Filar
Stadium: RCA Dome • **Capacity:** 56,127
100 South Capitol Avenue
Indianapolis, Indiana 46225
Playing Surface: AstroTurf
Training Camp: Rose-Hulman Institute
5500 Wabash Avenue
Terre Haute, Indiana 47803

2000 SCHEDULE

PRESEASON

July 29	**Atlanta**	7:00
Aug. 5	at Seattle	5:00
Aug. 12	vs. New Orleans at West Lafayette, Indiana	7:00
Aug. 19	vs. Pittsburgh at Mexico City	8:00
Aug. 24	**Minnesota**	7:00

REGULAR SEASON

Sept. 3	at Kansas City	12:00
Sept. 10	**Oakland**	12:00
Sept. 17	Open Date	
Sept. 25	**Jacksonville** (Mon.)	8:00
Oct. 1	at Buffalo	1:00
Oct. 8	at New England	1:00
Oct. 15	at Seattle	1:05
Oct. 22	**New England**	12:00
Oct. 29	**Detroit**	1:00
Nov. 5	at Chicago	12:00
Nov. 12	**New York Jets**	8:35
Nov. 19	at Green Bay	12:00
Nov. 26	**Miami**	1:00
Dec. 3	at New York Jets	4:15
Dec. 11	**Buffalo** (Mon.)	9:00
Dec. 17	at Miami	4:15
Dec. 24	**Minnesota**	4:15

RECORD HOLDERS

INDIVIDUAL RECORDS—CAREER

Category	Name	Performance
Rushing (Yds.)	Lydell Mitchell, 1972-77	5,487
Passing (Yds.)	Johnny Unitas, 1956-1972	39,768
Passing (TDs)	Johnny Unitas, 1956-1972	287
Receiving (No.)	Raymond Berry, 1955-1967	631
Receiving (Yds.)	Raymond Berry, 1955-1967	9,275
Interceptions	Bob Boyd, 1960-68	57
Punting (Avg.)	Chris Gardocki, 1994-98	44.8
Punt Return (Avg.)	Ron Gardin, 1970-71	13.5
Kickoff Return (Avg.)	Jim Duncan, 1969-1971	32.5
Field Goals	Dean Biasucci 1984, 1986-1994	176
Touchdowns (Tot.)	Lenny Moore, 1956-1967	113
Points	Dean Biasucci, 1984, 1986-1994	783

INDIVIDUAL RECORDS—SINGLE SEASON

Category	Name	Performance
Rushing (Yds.)	Eric Dickerson, 1988	1,659
Passing (Yds.)	Peyton Manning, 1999	4,135
Passing (TDs)	Johnny Unitas, 1959	32
Receiving (No.)	Marvin Harrison, 1999	115
Receiving (Yds.)	Marvin Harrison, 1999	1,663
Interceptions	Tom Keane, 1953	11
Punting (Avg.)	Rohn Stark, 1985	45.9
Punt Return (Avg.)	Clarence Verdin, 1989	12.9
Kickoff Return (Avg.)	Jim Duncan, 1970	35.4
Field Goals	Cary Blanchard, 1996	36
Touchdowns (Tot.)	Lenny Moore, 1964	20
Points	Mike Vanderjagt, 1999	145

INDIVIDUAL RECORDS—SINGLE GAME

Category	Name	Performance
Rushing (Yds.)	Norm Bulaich, 9-19-71	198
Passing (Yds.)	Peyton Manning, 9-26-99	404
Passing (TDs)	Gary Cuozzo, 11-14-65	5
	Gary Hogeboom, 10-4-87	5
Receiving (No.)	Marvin Harrison, 12-26-99	14
Receiving (Yds.)	Raymond Berry, 11-10-57	224
Interceptions	Many times.	3
	Last time by Mike Prior, 12-20-92	
Field Goals	Many times.	5
	Last time by Cary Blanchard, 9-21-97	
Touchdowns (Tot.)	Many times.	4
	Last time by Eric Dickerson, 10-31-88	
Points	Many times.	24
	Last time by Eric Dickerson, 10-31-88	

COACHING HISTORY

BALTIMORE 1953-1983
(336-355-7)

1953	Keith Molesworth	3-9-0
1954-62	Weeb Ewbank	61-52-1
1963-69	Don Shula	73-26-4
1970-72	Don McCafferty*	26-11-1
1972	John Sandusky	4-5-0
1973-74	Howard Schnellenberger**	4-13-0
1974	Joe Thomas	2-9-0
1975-79	Ted Marchibroda	41-36-0
1980-81	Mike McCormack	9-23-0
1982-84	Frank Kush***	11-28-1
1984	Hal Hunter	0-1-0
1985-86	Rod Dowhower****	5-24-0
1986-91	Ron Meyer#	36-36-0
1991	Rick Venturi	1-10-0
1992-95	Ted Marchibroda	32-35-0
1996-97	Lindy Infante	12-21-0
1998-99	Jim Mora	16-17-0

*Released after five games in 1972
**Released after three games in 1974
***Resigned after 15 games in 1984
****Released after 13 games in 1986
#Released after five games in 1991

RCA DOME

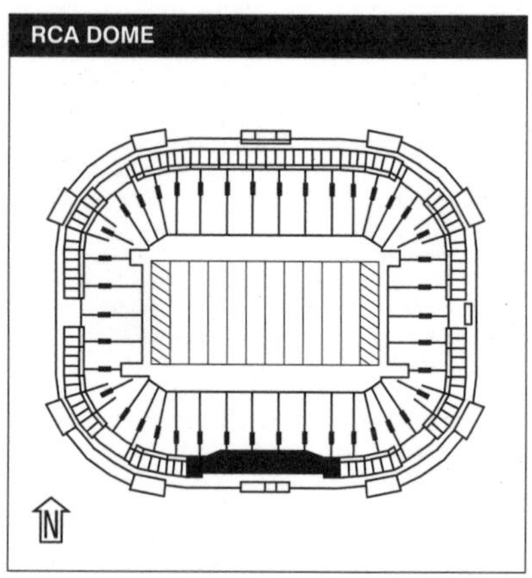

1999 TEAM RECORD

PRESEASON (3-1)

Date	Result		Opponent
8/7	L	6-9	at Chicago
8/14	W	20-17	Cincinnati
8/21	W	37-7	at New Orleans
9/2	W	31-28	Seattle

REGULAR SEASON (13-3)

Date	Result		Opponent	Att.
9/12	W	31-14	Buffalo	56,238
9/19	L	28-31	at New England	59,640
9/26	W	27-19	at San Diego	56,942
10/10	L	31-34	Miami	56,810
10/17	W	16-13	at New York Jets	78,112
10/24	W	31-10	Cincinnati	55,996
10/31	W	34-24	Dallas	56,860
11/7	W	25-17	Kansas City	56,689
11/14	W	27-19	at New York Giants	78,081
11/21	W	44-17	at Philadelphia	65,521
11/28	W	13-6	New York Jets	56,689
12/5	W	37-34	at Miami	74,096
12/12	W	20-15	New England	56,975
12/19	W	24-21	Washington	57,013
12/26	W	29-28	at Cleveland	72,618
1/2	L	6-31	at Buffalo	61,959

POSTSEASON (0-1)

Date	Result		Opponent	Att.
1/16	L	16-19	Tennessee	57,097

SCORE BY PERIODS

Colts	112	114	88	109	0	— 423
Opponents	51	109	63	110	0	— 333

ATTENDANCE

Home 426,012 Away 556,173 Total 982,185
Single-game home record, 61,139 (10/20/97)
Single-season home record, 481,305 (1984)

1999 TEAM STATISTICS

	Colts	Opp.
Total First Downs	327	304
Rushing	89	92
Passing	200	192
Penalty	38	20
Third Down: Made/Att	73/186	73/208
Third Down Pct.	39.2	35.1
Fourth Down: Made/Att	2/6	7/16
Fourth Down Pct.	33.3	43.8
Total Net Yards	5,726	5,221
Avg. Per Game	357.9	326.3
Total Plays	979	1,008
Avg. Per Play	5.8	5.2
Net Yards Rushing	1,660	1,715
Avg. Per Game	103.8	107.2
Total Rushes	419	406
Net Yards Passing	4,066	3,506
Avg. Per Game	254.1	219.1
Sacked/Yards Lost	14/116	41/269
Gross Yards	4,182	3,775
Att./Completions	546/338	561/328
Completion Pct.	61.9	58.5
Had Intercepted	17	10
Punts/Average	60/41.1	83/41.4
Net Punting Avg.	60/30.6	83/35.3
Penalties/Yards	81/683	130/1,093
Fumbles/Ball Lost	25/11	22/13
Touchdowns	46	36
Rushing	15	12
Passing	26	21
Returns	5	3
Avg. Time of Possession	30:45	29:15

1999 INDIVIDUAL STATISTICS

Passing	Att.	Comp.	Yds.	Pct.	TD	Int.	Tkld.	Rate
Manning	533	331	4,135	62.1	26	15	14/116	90.7
Walsh	13	7	47	53.8	0	2	0/0	22.4
Colts	546	338	4,182	61.9	26	17	14/116	88.5
Opponents	561	328	3,775	58.5	21	10	41/269	83.9

SCORING	TD R	TD P	TD Rt	PAT	FG	Saf	PTS
Vanderjagt	0	0	0	43/43	34/38	0	145
James	13	4	0	0/0	0/0	0	102
Harrison	0	12	0	0/0	0/0	0	74
Wilkins	0	4	3	0/0	0/0	0	42
Pollard	0	4	0	0/0	0/0	0	24
Dilger	0	2	0	0/0	0/0	0	12
Manning	2	0	0	0/0	0/0	0	12
Blevins	0	0	1	0/0	0/0	0	6
Cota	0	0	1	0/0	0/0	0	6
Colts	15	26	5	43/43	34/38	0	423
Opponents	12	21	3	31/31	26/29	2	333

2-Pt. Conversions: Harrison.
Team 1-3, Opponents 2-5.

RUSHING	Att.	Yds.	Avg.	LG	TD
James	369	1,553	4.2	72	13
Manning	35	73	2.1	13	2
Elias	13	28	2.2	8	0
Harrison	1	4	4.0	4	0
Wilkins	1	2	2.0	2	0
Colts	419	1,660	4.0	72	15
Opponents	406	1,715	4.2	28	12

RECEIVING	No.	Yds.	Avg.	LG	TD
Harrison	115	1,663	14.5	57t	12
James	62	586	9.5	54	4
Wilkins	42	565	13.5	80t	4
Dilger	40	479	12.0	30	2
Pollard	34	374	11.0	33	4
Green	21	287	13.7	50	0
Pathon	14	163	11.6	38	0
Shields	4	37	9.3	21	0
Elias	4	16	4.0	7	0
Jones	1	8	8.0	8	0
Greene	1	4	4.0	4	0
Colts	338	4,182	12.4	80t	26
Opponents	328	3,775	11.5	62	21

INTERCEPTIONS	No.	Yds.	Avg.	LG	TD
Poole	3	85	28.3	38	0
Blevins	2	115	57.5	74t	1
Burris	2	83	41.5	55	0
Wooten	1	4	4.0	4	0
Randolph	1	0	0.0	0	0
R. Thomas	1	0	0.0	0	0
Colts	10	287	28.7	74t	1
Opponents	17	189	11.1	37	2

PUNTING	No.	Yds.	Avg.	In 20	LG
Smith	58	2,467	42.5	16	61
Colts	60	2,467	41.1	16	61
Opponents	83	3,437	41.4	24	59

PUNT RETURNS	No.	FC	Yds.	Avg.	LG	TD
Wilkins	41	17	388	9.5	39t	1
Pathon	0	1	0	—	—	0
Colts	41	18	388	9.5	39t	1
Opponents	29	7	469	16.2	76	0

KICKOFF RETURNS	No.	Yds.	Avg.	LG	TD
Wilkins	51	1,134	22.2	97t	1
Pathon	6	123	20.5	31	0
Elias	5	82	16.4	21	0
Muhammad	2	41	20.5	22	0
Greene	1	14	14.0	14	0
Shields	1	3	3.0	3	0
Austin	1	0	0.0	0	0
Belser	0	0	—	—	0
Colts	67	1,397	20.9	97t	1
Opponents	83	1,822	22.0	50	0

FIELD GOALS	1-19	20-29	30-39	40-49	50+
Vanderjagt	2/2	10/10	11/13	10/11	1/2
Colts	2/2	10/10	11/13	10/11	1/2
Opponents	1/1	9/9	11/11	4/7	1/1

SACKS	No.
Bratzke	12.0
E. Johnson	7.5
Bennett	5.0
Peterson	3.0
M. Thomas	3.0
Burris	2.0
King	1.5
Belser	1.0
Berry	1.0
Blevins	1.0
Chester	1.0
Poole	1.0
Royal	1.0
Whittington	1.0
Colts	41.0
Opponents	14.0

2000 DRAFT CHOICES

Round	Name	Pos.	College
1	Rob Morris	LB	Brigham Young
2	Marcus Washington	LB	Auburn
3	David Macklin	DB	Penn State
4	Josh Williams	DT	Michigan
5	Matt Johnson	C	Brigham Young
7	Rob Renes	DT	Michigan
	Rodregis Brooks	DB	Alabama-Birmingham

INDIANAPOLIS COLTS

2000 VETERAN ROSTER

No.	Name	Pos.	Ht.	Wt.	Birthdate	NFL Exp.	College	Hometown	How Acq.	'99 Games/ Starts
47	Austin, Billy	CB-S	5-10	195	3/8/75	2	New Mexico	Washington, D.C.	FA-'98	16/0
83	Banta, Bradford	TE	6-6	260	12/14/70	7	Southern California	Baton Rouge, La.	D4-'94	16/0
29	Belser, Jason	S	5-9	196	5/28/70	9	Oklahoma	Kansas City, Mo.	D8a-'92	16/16
97	Bennett, Cornelius	LB	6-3	240	8/25/65	14	Alabama	Birmingham, Ala.	FA-'99	16/16
26	Blevins, Tony	CB-S	6-0	165	1/29/75	3	Kansas	Rockford, Ill.	W(SF)-'98	15/0
92	Bratzke, Chad	DE	6-5	275	9/15/71	7	Eastern Kentucky	Brandon, Fla.	UFA(NYG)-'99	16/16
20	Burris, Jeff	S	6-0	190	6/7/72	7	Notre Dame	Rock Hill, S.C.	UFA(Buff)-'98	16/16
64	Chester, Larry	DT	6-2	305	10/17/75	3	Temple	Hammond, La.	FA-'98	16/8
37	Cota, Chad	CB-S	6-1	198	8/8/71	6	Oregon	Ashland, Ore.	UFA(NO)-'99	15/15
85	Dilger, Ken	TE	6-5	259	2/2/71	6	Illinois	Mariah Hill, Ind.	D2-'95	15/15
78	Glenn, Tarik	T	6-5	335	5/25/76	4	California	Oakland, Calif.	D1-'97	16/16
10	Gonzalez, Pete	QB	6-1	216	7/24/74	3	Pittsburgh	Miami, Fla.	UFA(Pitt)-'00	1/0*
84	Green, E.G.	WR	5-11	190	6/28/75	3	Florida State	Ft. Walton Beach, Fla.	D3-'98	11/4
88	Harrison, Marvin	WR	6-0	181	8/25/72	5	Syracuse	Philadelphia, Pa.	D1-'96	16/16
13	Holcomb, Kelly	QB	6-2	212	7/9/73	4	Middle Tennessee State	Fayetteville, Tenn.	FA-'96	0*
79	Holsey, Bernard	DE-DT	6-2	285	10/10/73	5	Duke	Cave Spring, Ga.	UFA(NYG)-'00	16/0*
74	Jackson, Waverly	G	6-2	310	12/19/72	3	Virginia Tech	South Hill, Va.	FA-'98	16/16
32	James, Edgerrin	RB	6-0	216	8/1/78	2	Miami	Immokalee, Fla.	D1-'99	16/16
62	Johnson, Ellis	DT	6-2	292	10/30/73	6	Florida	Wildwood, Fla.	D1-'95	16/16
15	Jones, Isaac	WR	6-0	190	12/7/75	2	Purdue	Philadelphia, Pa.	FA-'99	1/1
7	Kight, Danny	K	6-0	200	8/18/71	2	Augusta State	Atlanta, Ga.	FA-'99	12/0
23	Lane, Fred	RB	5-10	205	9/6/75	4	Lane College	Franklin, Tenn.	T(Car)-'00	15/5*
18	Manning, Peyton	QB	6-5	230	3/24/76	3	Tennessee	New Orleans, La.	D1-'98	16/16
61	McCoy, Tony	DT	6-1	289	6/10/69	9	Florida	Orlando, Fla.	D4b-'92	10/0
76	McKinney, Steve	G	6-4	302	10/15/75	3	Texas A&M	Houston, Tex.	D4-'98	14/14
73	Meadows, Adam	T	6-5	299	1/25/74	4	Georgia	Powder Springs, Ga.	D2-'97	16/16
21	Miranda, Paul	CB-S	5-10	184	5/2/76	2	Central Florida	Thomasville, Ga.	D4-'99	5/0
50	Moore, Larry	C	6-2	312	6/1/75	3	Brigham Young	San Diego, Calif.	FA-'98	16/16
31	Muhammad, Mustafah	CB-S	5-10	180	10/19/73	2	Fresno State	Los Angeles, Calif.	FA-'99	11/1
91	Nwokorie, Chukie	DE	6-2	286	7/10/75	2	Purdue	Lafayette, Ind.	FA-'99	1/0
86	Pathon, Jerome	WR	6-0	187	12/16/75	3	Washington	Capetown, South Africa	D2-'98	10/2
52	Peterson, Mike	LB	6-2	229	6/17/76	2	Florida	Gainesville, Fla.	D2-'99	16/13
16	Plummer, Chad	WR	6-3	223	11/30/75	2	Cincinnati	Tallahassee, Fla.	FA-'99	1/0
81	Pollard, Marcus	TE	6-4	257	2/8/72	6	Bradley	Valley, Ala.	FA-'95	16/12
38	Poole, Tyrone	CB	5-8	188	2/3/72	6	Fort Valley State	Lagrange, Ga.	T(Car)-'98	15/14
63	Saturday, Jeff	C	6-2	298	6/8/75	2	North Carolina	Tucker, Ga.	FA-'99	11/2
99	Scioli, Brad	DE	6-3	277	9/6/76	2	Penn State	Bridgeport, Pa.	D5-'99	10/0
39	Shields, Paul	RB	6-1	238	1/31/76	2	Arizona	Mesa, Ariz.	FA-'99	13/3
17	Smith, Hunter	P	6-2	212	8/9/77	2	Notre Dame	Sherman, Tex.	D7a-'99	16/0
90	Thomas, Mark	DE	6-5	265	5/6/69	9	North Carolina State	Lilburn, Ga.	W(Chi)-'98	15/2
55	Thomas, Ratcliff	LB	6-0	240	1/2/74	3	Maryland	Alexandria, Va.	FA-'99	16/0
12	Vanderjagt, Mike	K	6-5	210	3/24/70	3	West Virginia	Oakville, Ontario, Canada	FA-'98	16/0
95	Whittington, Bernard	DE	6-5	280	8/20/71	7	Indiana	St. Louis, Mo.	FA-'94	15/15
80	Wilkins, Terrence	WR	5-8	179	7/29/75	2	Virginia	Washington, D.C.	FA-'99	16/11

* Gonzalez played 1 game with Pittsburgh in '99; Holcomb was inactive for 16 games; Holsey played 16 games with N.Y. Giants; Lane played 15 games with Carolina.

Also played with Colts in '99—LB Michael Barber (16 games), LB Bertrand Berry (16), DE-DT Shane Bonham (3), LB Jeff Brady (3), RB Keith Elias (14), RB Scott Greene (5), RB Darick Holmes (1), C Jason Johnson (16), DE Shawn King (9), CB-S Monty Montgomery (3), CB Thomas Randolph (15), LB Spencer Reid (12), LB Andre Royal (3), CB-S Eric Smedley (7), QB Steve Walsh (16), G-T Jamie Wilson (5), CB-S Tito Wooten (8).

COACHING STAFF

Head Coach,
Jim Mora

Pro Career: Jim Mora joined the Colts as their seventeenth head coach on January 12, 1998. Mora led the Colts to the AFC Eastern Division title and a 13-3 mark in 1999. Mora has a 16-17 record with the Colts following a 3-13 first season with the club. He joined the Colts after producing a 93-74 regular-season record with New Orleans from 1986-1996. Mora won more games than the previous nine Saints coaches combined. Mora is one of only 20 head coaches in NFL history who has had 10 or more consecutive seasons of service with the same team. Mora produced 91 victories during his first 10 seasons, a total exceeded by only eight other coaches in NFL history. Mora's 109 career wins rank third among active coaches, and he was the twenty-seventh coach to produce 100 career victories. Mora stands as the twenty-third-winningest coach in NFL history. His 1991 Saints squad went 11-5, earning the only division title in club history. Prior to his stint with New Orleans, Mora directed the Philadelphia/Baltimore Stars of the USFL from 1983-85. Mora forged a 48-13-1 record and led the Stars to two titles in three league-championship-game appearances. Mora began his pro coaching career in 1978 as defensive line coach with Seattle. In 1982, he was defensive coordinator at New England. Career record: 109-95.

Background: Played tight end and defensive end at Occidental College. Assistant coach at Occidental from 1960-63 and head coach from 1964-66. Linebacker coach at Stanford in 1967. Defensive assistant at Colorado from 1968-1973. Linebackers coach at UCLA in 1974. Defensive coordinator at Washington from 1975-77. Received bachelor's degree in physical education from Occidental in 1957. Also holds master's degree in education from Southern California.

Personal: Born May 24, 1935 in Glendale, Calif. Jim lives in Indianapolis and has three sons—Michael, Stephen, and Jim (defensive coordinator with San Francisco 49ers).

ASSISTANT COACHES

Bruce Arians, quarterbacks; born October 3, 1952, Paterson, N.J., lives in Indianapolis. Quarterback Virginia Tech 1971-74. No pro playing experience. College coach: Virginia Tech 1975-77, Mississippi State 1978-1980, 1993-95, Alabama 1981-82, 1997, Temple 1983-88 (head coach). Pro coach: Kansas City Chiefs 1989-1992, New Orleans Saints 1996, joined Colts in 1998.

George Catavolos, asst. head coach-defensive backs; born May 8, 1945, Chicago, lives in Indianapolis. Defensive back Purdue 1964-67. No pro playing experience. College coach: Purdue 1967-68, 1971-76, Middle Tennessee State 1969, Louisville 1970, Kentucky 1977-1981, Tennessee 1982-83. Pro coach: Indianapolis Colts 1984-1993, Carolina Panthers 1995-97, rejoined Colts in 1998.

Vic Fangio, defensive coordinator; born August 22, 1958, Dunmore, Pa., lives in Indianapolis. Attended East Stroudsburg. No pro playing experience. College coach: North Carolina 1993. Pro coach: Philadelphia/Baltimore Stars (USFL) 1984-85, New Orleans Saints 1986-1994, Carolina Panthers 1995-98, joined Colts 1999.

Todd Grantham, defensive line; born September 13, 1966, Pulaski, Va., lives in Indianapolis. Attended Virginia Tech. No college or pro playing experience. College coach: Virginia Tech 1990-95, Michigan State 1996-98. Pro coach: Joined Colts in 1999.

Richard Howell, asst. strength and conditioning; born February 19, 1972, Bladenboro, N.C., lives in Indianapolis. Quarterback Davidson 1990-93. No pro playing experience. College coach: Davidson 1994-98, North Carolina 1998-99. Pro coach: Barcelona Dragons (NFL Europe) 1999, joined Colts in 2000.

Gene Huey, running backs; born July 20, 1947, Uniontown, Pa., lives in Indianapolis. Defensive back-wide receiver Wyoming 1966-69. No pro playing experience. College coach: Wyoming 1970-74, New Mexico 1975-77, Nebraska 1978-1986, Arizona State 1987, Ohio State 1988-1991. Pro coach: Joined Colts in 1992.

Tony Marciano, tight ends; born June 14, 1956, Scranton, Pa., lives in Indianapolis. Attended Indiana (Pa.) No college or pro playing experience. College coach: Texas Christian 1978-1980, Southern Methodist 1981-86, Brown 1987-88, Richmond 1989-1990, Kent State 1991-92. Pro coach: Toronto Argonauts (CFL) 1994, Calgary Stampeders (CFL) 1995-97, joined Colts in 1998.

Tom Moore, offensive coordinator; born November 7, 1938, Owatanna, Minn., lives in Indianapolis. Quarterback Iowa 1957-1960. No pro playing experience. College coach: Iowa 1961-62, Dayton 1965-68, Wake Forest 1969, Georgia Tech 1970-71, Minnesota 1972-73, 1975-76. Pro coach: New York Stars (WFL) 1974, Pittsburgh Steelers 1977-1989, Minnesota Vikings 1990-93, Detroit Lions 1994-96, New Orleans Saints 1997, joined Colts in 1998.

Howard Mudd, offensive line; born February 10, 1942, Midland, Mich., lives in Indianapolis. Guard Hillsdale (Mich.) College 1960-63. Pro offensive lineman San Francisco 49ers 1964-69, Chicago Bears 1969-1970. College coach: California 1972-73. Pro coach: San Diego Chargers 1974-76, San Francisco 49ers 1977, Seattle Seahawks 1978-1982, 1993-97, Cleveland Browns 1983-88, Kansas City Chiefs 1989-1992, joined Colts in 1998.

Mike Murphy, linebackers; born September 25, 1944, New York, N.Y., lives in Indianapolis. Guard-linebacker Huron (S.D.) 1963-66. No pro playing experience. College coach: Vermont 1970-73, Idaho State 1974-76, Western Illinois 1977-78. Pro coach: Saskatchewan Roughriders (CFL) 1979-1983, Chicago Blitz (USFL) 1984, Detroit Lions 1985-89, Arizona Cardinals 1990-93, Seattle Seahawks 1995-97, joined Colts in 1998.

Jay Norvell, receivers; born March 28, 1963, Madison, Wis., lives in Indianapolis. Defensive back Iowa 1982-85. Pro defensive back Chicago Bears 1987. College coach: Iowa 1986, Northern Iowa 1988, Wisconsin 1989-1993, Iowa State 1995-97. Pro coach: Joined Colts in 1998.

John Pagano, defensive assistant; born March 30, 1967, Boulder, Colo., lives in Indianapolis. Linebacker Mesa State College 1985-88. No pro playing experience. College coach: Mesa State College 1989, Nevada-Las Vegas 1990-91, Louisiana Tech 1994, Mississippi 1995. Pro coach: New Orleans Saints 1996-97, joined Colts in 1998.

Kevin Spencer, special teams; born November 2, 1953, Queens, N.Y., lives in Indianapolis. Attended Springfield (Mass.) College. No college or pro playing experience. College coach: SUNY 1975-76, Cornell 1979-1980, Ithaca 1981-86, Wesleyan 1987-1990. Pro coach: Cleveland Browns 1991-94, Oakland Raiders 1995-97, joined Colts in 1998.

Jon Torine, strength and conditioning; born November 16, 1973, Livingston, N.J., lives in Indianapolis. Linebacker Springfield (Mass.) College 1991. No pro playing experience. Pro coach: Buffalo Bills 1995-97, joined Colts in 1998.

2000 FIRST-YEAR ROSTER

Name	Pos.	Ht.	Wt.	Birthdate	College	Hometown	How Acq.
Baker, John	P	6-3	223	4/22/77	North Texas	Beaumont, Tex.	FA
Brooks, Rodregis	DB	5-10	181	8/30/78	Alabama-Birmingham	Alexander City, Ala.	D7b
Daniels, Maurice	LB	6-0	237	5/8/77	Penn State	Alexandria, Va.	FA
Davis, Joel (1)	G-T	6-5	305	4/6/73	Army	Binghamton, N.Y.	FA
Finn, Jim (1)	RB	5-10	240	12/9/76	Penn	Teaneck, N.J.	FA
Freeman, Brad	DB	6-1	210	9/13/75	Mississippi State	Memphis, Tenn.	FA
Furrey, Mike	WR	5-10	179	5/12/77	Northern Iowa	Hilliard, Ohio	FA
Gentry, Josh	LB	6-1	240	6/3/78	Indianapolis	Remington, Ind.	FA
Gilbert, Ben	G	6-4	316	6/6/78	Ohio State	Lancaster, Ohio	FA
Gleason, Steve	DB	5-11	214	3/19/77	Washington State	Spokane, Wash.	FA
Gonzalez, Pete	QB	6-1	220	7/24/74	Pittsburgh	Miami, Fla.	FA
Green, Ibn	TE	6-2	215	6/3/76	Louisville	Louisville, Ky.	FA
Hall, Darran (1)	WR	5-10	170	8/9/75	Colorado State	San Diego, Calif.	FA
Insley, Trevor	WR	6-0	190	12/25/77	Nevada	San Clemente, Calif.	FA
Johnson, Matt	G	6-4	332	9/24/73	Brigham Young	Bluffton, Ind.	D5b
Kendra, Dan	RB	6-0	243	3/15/76	Florida State	Bethlehem, Pa.	FA
Keur, Josh (1)	TE	6-4	283	9/4/76	Michigan State	Muskegon, Mich.	FA
Lacoste, Paul (1)	LB	6-2	242	9/3/74	Mississippi State	Oxford, Miss.	FA
Macklin, David	DB	5-9	195	7/14/78	Penn State	Newport News, Va.	D3
McDougal, Kevin	RB	5-10	204	5/18/77	Colorado State	Denver, Colo.	FA
Merandi, John	C	6-2	293	2/23/78	Notre Dame	Blue Jay, Calif.	FA
Miller, Brandon	DT	6-1	299	11/27/75	Georgia	Greensboro, Ga.	FA
Miller, Craig (1)	DB	5-11	199	10/4/77	Utah State	Bakersfield, Calif.	FA
Moreira, Tom	G	6-3	331	6/16/77	Hofstra	Yonkers, N.Y.	FA
Morris, Rob	LB	6-2	250	1/18/75	Brigham Young	Nampa, Idaho	D1
Ornstein, Gus (1)	QB	6-3	232	11/23/74	Rowan	New York, N.Y.	FA
Reid, Ike	DE	6-4	250	12/21/75	Ohio Wesleyan	Hartford, Conn.	FA
Renes, Rob	DT	6-1	308	3/28/77	Michigan	Holland, Mich.	D7a
Ridder, Tim (1)	G-T	6-7	301	12/17/76	Notre Dame	Omaha, Neb.	FA
Robeen, Craig	T	6-6	306	4/26/77	Indiana	Hardin, Ill.	FA
Snellings, Paul (1)	T	6-4	295	11/5/75	Georgia	Lagrange, Ga.	FA
Snow, Justin	DE	6-3	232	12/21/76	Baylor	Abilene, Tex.	FA
Stimson, Nate (1)	LB	6-2	248	3/4/76	Georgia Tech	Palm Beach, Fla.	FA
Thomas, Scott (1)	DB	6-2	206	1/31/75	Azusa Pacific	Norwalk, Calif.	FA
Troy, Damon (1)	DB	6-1	203	8/27/76	Rowan	Whitesboro, N.J.	FA
Tucker, Josh	OT	6-4	294	8/5/78	Tennessee	Asheville, N.C.	FA
Washington, Marcus	LB	6-3	247	10/17/77	Auburn	Auburn, Ala.	D2
White, Jamel	RB	5-9	208	2/11/78	South Dakota-Vermillion	Los Angeles, Calif.	FA
Williams, Josh	T	6-3	284	8/9/76	Michigan	Houston, Tex.	D4
Williams, Payton	DB	5-7	170	11/19/78	Fresno State	Riverside, Calif.	FA
Wofford, Brian	WR	5-11	164	1/31/78	Clemson	Spartanburg, S.C.	FA

The term NFL Rookie is defined as a player who is in his first season of professional football and has not been on the roster of another professional football team for any regular-season or postseason games. A Rookie is designated by an "R" on NFL rosters. Players who have been active in another professional football league or players who have NFL experience, including either preseason training camp or being on an Active List or Inactive List, or on Reserve/Injured or Reserve/Physically Unable to Perform for fewer than six regular-season games, are termed NFL First-Year Players. An NFL First-Year Player is designated by a "1" on NFL rosters. Thereafter, a player is credited with an additional year of experience for each season in which he accumulates six games on the Active List or Inactive List, or on Reserve/Injured or Reserve/Physically Unable to Perform.

JACKSONVILLE JAGUARS

American Football Conference
Central Division
Team Colors: Teal, Black, and Gold
ALLTEL Stadium
One ALLTEL Stadium Place
Jacksonville, Florida 32202
Telephone: (904) 633-6000

CLUB OFFICIALS

Chairman and Chief Executive Officer: Wayne Weaver
Senior Vice President/Football Operations: Michael Huyghue
Senior Vice President/Marketing: Dan Connell
Vice President/Chief Financial Officer: Bill Prescott
Vice President, Administration/General Counsel: Paul Vance
Executive Director of Communications: Dan Edwards
Director of Player Personnel: Rick Reiprish
Director of Pro Scouting: Fran Foley
Director of College Scouting: Gene Smith
Director of Finance: Kim Dodson
Director of Facilities: Jeff Cannon
Director of Football Administration: Skip Richardson
Director of Information Technology: Bruce Swindell
Director of Broadcasting: Jennifer Kumik
Director of Corporate Sponsorship: Macky Weaver
Director of Brand Development: Roddy White
Director of Ticket Operations: Tim Bishko
Director of Ticket Sales: Steve Swetoha
Director of Player Administration/Community Affairs: Quentin Williams
Head Athletic Trainer: Michael Ryan
Video Director: Mike Perkins
Equipment Manager: Drew Hampton

Chair & Chief Executive Officer, Jaguars Foundation: Delores Barr Weaver
President, Jaguars Foundation: Dr. Gregory Gross
Stadium: ALLTEL Stadium • **Capacity:** 73,000
One ALLTEL Stadium Place
Jacksonville, Florida 32202
Playing Surface: Grass
Training Camp: ALLTEL Stadium
One ALLTEL Stadium Place
Jacksonville, Florida 32202

RECORD HOLDERS

INDIVIDUAL RECORDS—CAREER

Category	Name	Performance
Rushing (Yds.)	James Stewart, 1995-99	2,951
Passing (Yds.)	Mark Brunell, 1995-99	15,477
Passing (TDs)	Mark Brunell, 1995-99	86
Receiving (No.)	Jimmy Smith, 1995-99	381
Receiving (Yds.)	Jimmy Smith, 1995-99	5,674
Interceptions	Aaron Beasley, 1996-99	11
Punting (Avg.)	Bryan Barker, 1995-99	43.8
Punt Return (Avg.)	Reggie Barlow, 1997-99	11.8
Kickoff Return (Avg.)	Reggie Barlow, 1997-99	23.9
Field Goals	Mike Hollis, 1995-99	133
Touchdowns (Tot.)	James Stewart, 1995-99	38
Points	Mike Hollis, 1995-99	576

INDIVIDUAL RECORDS—SINGLE SEASON

Category	Name	Performance
Rushing (Yds.)	Fred Taylor, 1998	1,223
Passing (Yds.)	Mark Brunell, 1996	4,367
Passing (TDs)	Mark Brunell, 1998	20
Receiving (No.)	Jimmy Smith, 1999	116
Receiving (Yds.)	Jimmy Smith, 1999	1,636
Interceptions	Aaron Beasley, 1999	6
Punting (Avg.)	Bryan Barker, 1998	45.0
Punt Return (Avg.)	Reggie Barlow, 1998	12.9
Kickoff Return (Avg.)	Reggie Barlow, 1998	24.9
Field Goals	Mike Hollis, 1997, 1999	31
Touchdowns (Tot.)	Fred Taylor, 1998	17
Points	Mike Hollis, 1997	134

INDIVIDUAL RECORDS—SINGLE GAME

Category	Name	Performance
Rushing (Yds.)	Fred Taylor, 12-6-98	183
Passing (Yds.)	Mark Brunell, 9-22-96	432
Passing (TDs)	Mark Brunell, 11-29-98	4
Receiving (No.)	Keenan McCardell, 10-20-96	16
Receiving (Yds.)	Keenan McCardell, 10-20-96	232
Interceptions	Deon Figures, 8-31-97	2
	Aaron Beasley, 9-12-99	2
Field Goals	Mike Hollis, 12-1-96, 11-30-97	5
Touchdowns (Tot.)	James Stewart, 10-12-97	5
Points	James Stewart, 10-12-97	30

2000 SCHEDULE

PRESEASON

Aug. 4	at Carolina	8:00
Aug. 11	**New York Giants**	8:00
Aug. 19	at Kansas City	7:30
Aug. 24	**Atlanta**	7:30

REGULAR SEASON

Sept. 3	at Cleveland	1:00
Sept. 10	at Baltimore	1:00
Sept. 17	**Cincinnati**	1:00
Sept. 25	at Indianapolis (Mon.)	8:00
Oct. 1	**Pittsburgh**	1:00
Oct. 8	**Baltimore**	8:35
Oct. 16	at Tennessee (Mon.)	8:00
Oct. 22	**Washington**	4:15
Oct. 29	at Dallas	3:15
Nov. 5	Open Date	
Nov. 12	**Seattle**	1:00
Nov. 19	at Pittsburgh	8:35
Nov. 26	**Tennessee**	4:15
Dec. 3	**Cleveland**	4:15
Dec. 10	**Arizona**	1:00
Dec. 17	at Cincinnati	1:00
Dec. 23	at New York Giants (Sat.)	12:30

COACHING HISTORY

(53-35-0)

1995-99	Tom Coughlin	53-35-0

ALLTEL STADIUM

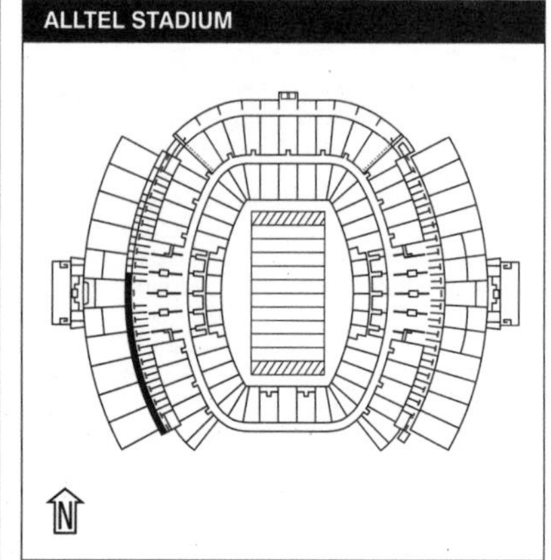

1999 TEAM RECORD

PRESEASON (3-1)

Date	Result		Opponent
8/13	W	35-10	Carolina
8/21	L	20-27	at New York Giants
8/26	W	31-6	Kansas City
9/2	W	27-6	at Dallas

REGULAR SEASON (14-2)

Date	Result		Opponent	Att.
9/12	W	41-3	San Francisco	68,678
9/19	W	22-20	at Carolina	64,261
9/26	L	19-20	Tennessee	61,502
10/3	W	17-3	at Pittsburgh	57,308
10/11	W	16-6	at New York Jets	78,216
10/17	W	24-7	Cleveland	62,047
10/31	W	41-10	at Cincinnati	49,138
11/7	W	30-7	at Atlanta	68,466
11/14	W	6-3	Baltimore	67,391
11/21	W	41-23	New Orleans	69,772
11/28	W	30-23	at Baltimore	68,428
12/2	W	20-6	Pittsburgh	68,806
12/13	W	27-24	Denver	71,357
12/19	W	24-14	at Cleveland	72,038
12/26	L	14-41	at Tennessee	66,641
1/2	W	24-7	Cincinnati	70,532

POSTSEASON (1-1)

Date	Result		Opponent	Att.
1/15	W	62-7	Miami	75,173
1/23	L	14-33	Tennessee	75,206

SCORE BY PERIODS

Jaguars	61	109	103	123	0	—	396
Opponents	44	81	40	52	0	—	217

ATTENDANCE

Home 552,823 Away 528,765 Total 1,081,588
Single-game home record, 74,143 (12/28/98)
Single-season home record, 561,472 (1998)

1999 TEAM STATISTICS

	Jaguars	Opp.
Total First Downs	331	248
Rushing	116	72
Passing	194	159
Penalty	21	17
Third Down: Made/Att.	92/230	72/215
Third Down Pct.	40.0	33.5
Fourth Down: Made/Att.	5/10	5/20
Fourth Down Pct.	50.0	25.0
Total Net Yards	5,586	4,334
Avg. Per Game	349.1	270.9
Total Plays	1,085	951
Avg. Per Play	5.1	4.6
Net Yards Rushing	2,091	1,444
Avg. Per Game	130.7	90.3
Total Rushes	514	373
Net Yards Passing	3,495	2,890
Avg. Per Game	218.4	180.6
Sacked/Yards Lost	36/221	57/373
Gross Yards	3,716	3,263
Att./Completions	535/320	521/291
Completion Pct.	59.8	55.9
Had Intercepted	11	19
Punts/Average	78/41.8	96/41.4
Net Punting Avg.	78/36.9	96/34.5
Penalties/Yards	90/755	93/728
Fumbles/Ball Lost	18/7	31/11
Touchdowns	42	24
Rushing	20	6
Passing	16	18
Returns	6	0
Avg. Time of Possession	31:57	28:03

1999 INDIVIDUAL STATISTICS

Passing	Att.	Comp.	Yds.	Pct.	TD	Int.	Tkld.	Rate
Brunell	441	259	3,060	58.7	14	9	29/174	82.0
Fiedler	94	61	656	64.9	2	2	7/47	83.5
Jaguars	535	320	3,716	59.8	16	11	36/221	82.3
Opponents	521	291	3,263	55.9	18	19	57/373	71.0

SCORING	TD R	TD P	TD Rt	PAT	FG	Saf	PTS
Hollis	0	0	0	37/37	31/38	0	130
J. Stewart	13	0	0	0/0	0/0	0	78
J. Smith	0	6	0	0/0	0/0	0	38
Taylor	6	0	0	0/0	0/0	0	36
McCardell	0	5	0	0/0	0/0	0	32
Jones	0	4	0	0/0	0/0	0	24
Beasley	0	0	2	0/0	0/0	0	12
Brady	0	1	0	0/0	0/0	0	8
Brunell	1	0	0	0/0	0/0	0	8
Barlow	0	0	1	0/0	0/0	0	6
Brackens	0	0	1	0/0	0/0	0	6
Craft	0	0	1	0/0	0/0	0	6
Whitted	0	0	1	0/0	0/0	0	6
Smeenge	0	0	0	0/0	0/0	1	2
Jaguars	20	16	6	37/37	31/38	3	396
Opponents	6	18	0	22/22	17/18	0	217

2-Pt. Conversions: Brady, Brunell, McCardell, J. Smith.
Team 4-5, Opponents 0-2.

RUSHING	Att.	Yds.	Avg.	LG	TD
J. Stewart	249	931	3.7	44t	13
Taylor	159	732	4.6	52	6
Brunell	47	208	4.4	15	1
Banks	23	82	3.6	21	0
Howard	13	55	4.2	22	0
Mack	7	40	5.7	19	0
Fiedler	13	26	2.0	15	0
Whitted	1	9	9.0	9	0
Barker	1	6	6.0	6	0
Shelton	1	2	2.0	2	0
Jaguars	514	2,091	4.1	52	20
Opponents	373	1,444	3.9	46	6

RECEIVING	No.	Yds.	Avg.	LG	TD
J. Smith	116	1,636	14.1	62	6
McCardell	78	891	11.4	49	5
Brady	32	346	10.8	30	1
J. Stewart	21	108	5.1	19	0
Jones	19	221	11.6	31	4
Barlow	16	202	12.6	31	0
Banks	14	137	9.8	38	0
Shelton	12	87	7.3	13	0
Taylor	10	83	8.3	41	0
Howard	1	8	8.0	8	0
Wiegert	1	-3	-3.0	-3	0
Jaguars	320	3,716	11.6	62	16
Opponents	291	3,263	11.2	65t	18

INTERCEPTIONS	No.	Yds.	Avg.	LG	TD
Beasley	6	200	33.3	93t	2
Darius	4	37	9.3	29	0
Thomas	2	36	18.0	36	0
Brackens	2	16	8.0	16t	1
Bryant	2	0	0.0	0	0
McElmurry	1	26	26.0	26	0
Marts	1	10	10.0	10	0
Boyer	1	5	5.0	5	0
Jaguars	19	330	17.4	93t	3
Opponents	11	149	13.5	43	0

PUNTING	No.	Yds.	Avg.	In 20	LG
Barker	78	3,260	41.8	32	83
Jaguars	78	3,260	41.8	32	83
Opponents	96	3,976	41.4	21	75

PUNT RETURNS	No.	FC	Yds.	Avg.	LG	TD
Barlow	38	17	414	10.9	74t	1
McCardell	6	4	41	6.8	19	0
Logan	1	0	7	7.0	7	0
Jaguars	45	21	462	10.3	74t	1
Opponents	37	12	259	7.0	36	0

KICKOFF RETURNS	No.	Yds.	Avg.	LG	TD
Barlow	19	396	20.8	56	0
Whitted	8	187	23.4	98t	1
Mack	6	112	18.7	32	0
Banks	5	78	15.6	20	0
Jackson	3	58	19.3	23	0
McCardell	2	19	9.5	10	0
Logan	1	25	25.0	25	0
Chamblin	1	6	6.0	6	0
Shelton	1	0	0.0	0	0
Jones	0	0	—	—	0
Jaguars	46	881	19.2	98t	1
Opponents	64	1,474	23.0	66	0

FIELD GOALS	1-19	20-29	30-39	40-49	50+
Hollis	0/0	12/13	8/9	10/15	1/1
Jaguars	0/0	12/13	8/9	10/15	1/1
Opponents	0/0	3/3	5/6	8/8	1/1

SACKS	No.
Brackens	12.0
Hardy	10.5
Walker	10.0
Smeenge	5.0
Boyer	4.0
Lake	3.5
L. Smith	3.0
Marts	2.0
Beasley	1.5
Payne	1.5
Wynn	1.5
Paup	1.0
Roberson	1.0
Curry	0.5
Jaguars	57.0
Opponents	36.0

2000 DRAFT CHOICES

Round	Name	Pos.	College
1	R. Jay Soward	WR	Southern California
2	Brad Meester	C	Northern Iowa
3	T.J. Slaughter	LB	Southern Mississippi
4	Joe Chustz	T	Louisiana Tech
5	Kiwaukee Thomas	DB	Georgia Southern
6	Emanuel Smith	WR	Arkansas
7	Erik Olson	DB	Colorado State
	Rob Meier	DE	Washington State
	Shyrone Stith	RB	Virginia Tech
	Danny Clark	LB	Illinois
	Mark Baniewicz	T	Syracuse

JACKSONVILLE JAGUARS

2000 VETERAN ROSTER

No.	Name	Pos.	Ht.	Wt.	Birthdate	NFL Exp.	College	Hometown	How Acq.	'99 Games/ Starts
22	Banks, Tavian	RB	5-10	208	2/17/74	3	Iowa	Bettendorf, Iowa	D4a-'98	8/1
4	Barker, Bryan	P	6-2	199	6/28/64	11	Santa Clara	Orinda, Calif.	UFA(Phil)-'95	16/0
84	Barlow, Reggie	WR	6-0	186	1/22/73	5	Alabama State	Montgomery, Ala.	D4-'96	14/2
21	Beasley, Aaron	CB	6-0	195	7/7/73	5	West Virginia	Pottstown, Pa.	D3-'96	16/16
71	Boselli, Tony	T	6-7	319	4/17/72	6	Southern California	Boulder, Colo.	D1a-'95	16/16
52	Boyer, Brant	LB	6-1	232	6/27/71	6	Arizona	Hooper, Utah	FA-'96	16/0
90	# Brackens, Tony	DE	6-4	257	12/26/74	5	Texas	Fairfield, Tex.	D2a-'96	16/15
80	Brady, Kyle	TE	6-6	274	1/14/72	6	Penn State	New Cumberland, Pa.	UFA(NYJ)-'99	13/12
8	Brunell, Mark	QB	6-1	216	9/17/70	8	Washington	Santa Maria, Calif.	T(GB)-'95	15/15
25	Bryant, Fernando	CB	5-10	174	3/26/77	2	Alabama	Murfreesboro, Tenn.	D1-'99	16/16
79	Cesario, Anthony	G	6-5	311	7/19/76	2	Colorado State	Pueblo, Colo.	D3-'99	0*
23	Chamblin, Corey	CB	5-10	188	5/29/77	2	Tennessee Tech	Birmingham, Ala.	FA-'99	11/0
62	# Coleman, Ben	G-T	6-5	323	5/18/71	8	Wake Forest	South Hill, Va.	W(Ariz)-'95	16/12
29	Craft, Jason	CB	5-10	178	2/13/76	2	Colorado State	Denver, Colo.	D5-'99	16/0
75	Curry, Eric	DE	6-6	277	2/3/70	8	Alabama	Thomasville, Ga.	FA-'98	5/0
20	Darius, Donovin	S	6-1	212	8/12/75	3	Syracuse	Camden, N.J.	D1b-'98	16/16
78	Fordham, Todd	G-T	6-5	303	10/9/73	4	Florida State	Tifton, Ga.	FA-'97	0*
85	Griffith, Rich	TE	6-5	260	7/31/69	7	Arizona	Tucson, Ariz.	FA-'95	16/0
51	Hardy, Kevin	LB	6-4	247	7/24/73	5	Illinois	Evansville, Ind.	D1-'96	16/16
1	Hollis, Mike	K	5-7	178	5/5/72	6	Idaho	Spokane, Wash.	FA-'95	16/0
24	Howard, Chris	RB	5-10	226	5/5/75	3	Michigan	River Ridge, La.	FA-'98	12/0
67	Ingram, Steve	G	6-4	315	5/8/71	5	Maryland	Greenbelt, Md.	FA-'99	6/0
83	Jackson, Lenzie	WR	6-0	187	6/17/77	2	Arizona State	Milpitas, Calif.	FA-'99	4/0
88	Jones, Damon	TE	6-5	266	9/18/74	4	Southern Illinois	Evanston, Ill.	D5-'97	15/8
37	Lake, Carnell	S	6-1	207	7/15/67	12	UCLA	Inglewood, Calif.	UFA(Pitt)-'99	16/16
93	Landolt, Kevin	DT	6-4	298	10/25/75	2	West Virginia	Burlington, N.J.	D4-'99	1/0
61	Leroy, Emarlos	DT	6-1	310	7/31/75	2	Georgia	Albany, Ga.	D6-'99	13/0
2	Lindsey, Steve	K	6-1	176	11/25/74	2	Mississippi	Hattiesburg, Miss.	FA-'99	16/0
32	Logan, Mike	DB	6-0	211	9/15/74	4	West Virginia	McKeesport, Pa.	D2-'97	2/0
34	Mack, Stacey	RB	6-1	237	6/26/75	2	Temple	Orlando, Fla.	FA-'99	12/0
10	Martin, Jamie	QB	6-2	206	2/8/70	6	Weber State	Arroyo Grande, Calif.	UFA(Cle)-'00	0*
58	Marts, Lonnie	LB	6-2	246	11/10/68	11	Tulane	New Orleans, La.	FA-'99	16/16
87	McCardell, Keenan	WR	6-1	185	1/6/70	9	Nevada-Las Vegas	Houston, Tex.	UFA(Balt)-'96	16/15
38	McElmurry, Blaine	S	6-0	192	10/23/73	2	Montana	Helena, Mont.	FA-'98	16/0
65	Neujahr, Quentin	C	6-4	294	1/30/71	6	Kansas State	Ulysses, Neb.	RFA(Balt)-'98	16/0
56	Nickerson, Hardy	LB	6-2	236	9/1/65	14	California	Compton, Calif.	UFA(TB)-'00	16/16*
95	Paup, Bryce	LB	6-5	250	2/29/68	11	Northern Iowa	Jefferson, Iowa	UFA(Buff)-'98	15/14
91	Payne, Seth	DT	6-4	289	2/12/75	4	Cornell	Victor, N.Y.	D4-'97	16/16
12	Quinn, Jonathan	QB	6-6	240	2/27/75	3	Middle Tennessee State	Nashville, Tenn.	D3-'98	0*
72	Searcy, Leon	T	6-4	315	12/21/69	9	Miami	Washington, D.C.	UFA(Pitt)-'96	16/16
31	Shelton, Daimon	RB	6-0	254	9/15/72	4	Sacramento State	Fresno, Calif.	D6-'97	16/9
99	Smeenge, Joel	DE	6-6	265	4/1/68	11	Western Michigan	Grand Rapids, Mich.	UFA(NO)-'95	15/7
82	Smith, Jimmy	WR	6-1	200	2/9/69	8	Jackson State	Jackson, Miss.	FA-'95	16/16
94	Smith, Larry	DT	6-5	282	12/4/74	2	Florida State	Folkston, Ga.	D2-'99	15/0
26	Stewart, Rayna	S	5-10	198	6/18/73	5	Northern Arizona	Chatsworth, Calif.	FA-'99	14/0
50	Storz, Erik	LB	6-2	240	6/24/75	2	Boston College	Rockaway, N.J.	FA-'98	7/0
28	Taylor, Fred	RB	6-1	227	1/27/76	3	Florida	Belle Glade, Fla.	D1a-'98	10/9
57	Terry, Corey	LB	6-3	246	3/6/76	2	Tennessee	Warrenton, N.C.	FA-'99	8/0
18	Twyner, Gunnard	WR	5-10	183	7/14/73	2	Western Illinois	Bettendorf, Iowa	FA-'00	0*
66	Wade, John	C-G	6-5	294	1/25/75	3	Marshall	Harrisonburg, Va.	D5-'98	16/16
96	Walker, Gary	DT	6-2	293	2/28/73	6	Auburn	Lavonia, Ga.	UFA(Tenn)-'99	16/16
86	Whitted, Alvis	WR	6-0	186	9/4/74	3	North Carolina State	Hillsborough, N.C.	D7a-'98	14/1
77	Wiegert, Zach	G	6-5	310	8/16/72	6	Nebraska	Fremont, Neb.	FA-'99	16/12
97	Wynn, Renaldo	DE	6-3	280	9/3/74	4	Notre Dame	Chicago, Ill.	D1-'97	12/10

* Cesario was inactive for 16 games in '99; Fordham missed '99 season because of injury; Martin was inactive 15 games with Cleveland; Nickerson played 16 games with Tampa Bay; Quinn was inactive for 15 games; Twyner last active with New Orleans in '97.

\# Unrestricted free agent; subject to developments.

Players lost through free agency (6): QB Jay Fiedler (Mia; 7 games in '99); T Joe Patton (SD; 0); RB James Stewart (Det; 14); CB Dave Thomas (NYG; 15); G Rich Tylski (Pitt; 10); DE Regan Upshaw (Oak; 6)

Also played with Jaguars in '99—LB Tom McManus (2), DE James Roberson (2), LB Bryan Schwartz (8).

COACHING STAFF

Head Coach,
Tom Coughlin

Pro Career: Under Tom Coughlin, the Jaguars became the only expansion team in NFL history to advance to the playoffs four times in their first five seasons. After a 4-12 inaugural season, Coughlin's team went 9-7 in year two on the way to the AFC Championship Game, and 11-5 and into the playoffs in both 1997 and 1998. Last year, Coughlin posted an NFL-best 14-2 mark in the regular season and a second AFC Championship Game appearance. Coughlin became the first head coach of the Jaguars on February 21, 1994, following a successful three seasons as head coach at Boston College. A veteran of 30 years in coaching, including 17 at the collegiate level and seven as an NFL assistant, Coughlin previously coached wide receivers for the Philadelphia Eagles (1984-85), Green Bay Packers (1986-87), and New York Giants (1988-1990). He was a member of the Giants' Super Bowl XXV champion coaching staff prior to being named head coach at Boston College in 1991. In three seasons at Boston College, he turned a struggling program into a top-20 team, posting a 21-13-1 record. His final season at Boston College was highlighted by eight consecutive wins, including a 41-39 victory over top-ranked Notre Dame, and a 9-3 finish. Despite an 0-2 start to the season, Boston College ranked thirteenth in the *Associated Press* poll and twelfth in the *USA Today/CNN* coaches poll at the end of the 1993 season. Coughlin's previous 14 seasons as a college coach were at Rochester Institute of Technology 1970-73 (head coach), Syracuse 1974-1980, and Boston College 1981-83. No pro playing experience. Career record: 53-35.

Background: Played wingback for Syracuse from 1965-67 under legendary coach Ben Schwartzwalder, along with teammates Larry Csonka and Floyd Little. Received Syracuse 1967 Orange Key Award as outstanding scholar athlete, and graduated in 1968 with bachelor's degree in education. Received master's degree in education from Syracuse in 1969.

Personal: Born August 31, 1947, Waterloo, N.Y. Was standout scholastic star for Waterloo Central High School. Tom and his wife, Judy, reside in Jacksonville. They have two daughters, Keli and Katie, and two sons, Tim and Brian.

ASSISTANT COACHES

John Bonamego, asst. special teams, born August 14, 1963, Waynesboro, Pa., lives in Jacksonville. Wide reciever-quarterback Central Michigan 1985-86. No pro playing experience. College coach: Maine 1988-1991, Lehigh 1992, Army 1993-98. Pro coach: Joined Jaguars in 1999.

Dom Capers, defensive coordinator; born August 5, 1950, Cambridge, Ohio, lives in Jacksonville. Defensive back Mount Union College 1968-1971. No pro playing experience. College coach: Kent State 1972-74, Hawaii 1975-76, San Jose State 1977, California 1978-79, Tennessee 1980-81, Ohio State 1982-83. Pro coach: Baltimore/Philadelphia Stars (USFL) 1984-85, New Orleans Saints 1986-1991, Pittsburgh Steelers 1992-94, Carolina Panthers 1995-98 (head coach), joined Jaguars in 1999.

Perry Fewell, secondary; born November 7, 1962, Gastonia, N.C., lives in Jacksonville. Defensive back Lenoir-Rhyne 1981-84. No pro playing experience. College coach: Army 1987, 1992-94, Kent State 1988-1991, Vanderbilt 1995-97. Pro coach: Joined Jaguars in 1998.

Greg Finnegan, asst. strength and conditioning; born February 21, 1969, Toledo, Ohio, lives in Jacksonville. Center Cornell 1988-1992. No pro playing experience. College coach: Kansas State 1993, Boston College 1994-97. Pro coach: Joined Jaguars in 1998.

Frank Gansz, special teams coordinator; born November 22, 1938, Altoona, Pa., lives in Jacksonville. Guard-linebacker Navy 1957-59. No pro playing experience. College coach: Air Force 1964-66, Colgate 1968, Navy 1969-1972, Oklahoma State 1973, 1975, Army 1974, UCLA 1976-77. Pro coach: San Francisco 49ers 1978, Cincinnati Bengals 1979-1980, Kansas City Chiefs 1981-82, 1986-88 (head coach 1987-88), Philadelphia Eagles 1983-85, Detroit Lions 1989-1993, Atlanta Falcons 1994-96, St. Louis Rams 1997-99, joined Jaguars in 2000.

Fred Hoaglin, tight ends; born January 28, 1944, Alliance, Ohio, lives in Jacksonville. Center Pittsburgh 1962-65. Pro center Cleveland Browns 1966-1972, Baltimore Colts 1973, Houston Oilers 1974-75, Seattle Seahawks 1976. Pro coach: Detroit Lions 1978-1984, New York Giants 1985-1992, New England Patriots 1993-96, joined Jaguars in 1997.

Jerald Ingram, running backs; born December 24, 1960, Beaver, Pa., lives in Jacksonville. Fullback Michigan 1979-1984. No pro playing experience. College coach: Ball State 1985-1990, Boston College 1991-93. Pro coach: Joined Jaguars in 1995.

Lane Kiffin, defensive quality control; born May 9, 1975, Lincoln, Neb., lives in Jacksonville. Quarterback Fresno State 1994-96. No pro playing experience. College coach: Fresno State 1997-98, Colorado State 1999. Pro coach: Joined Jaguars in 2000.

Mike Maser, offensive line; born March 2, 1947, Clayton, N.Y., lives in Jacksonville. Guard Buffalo 1967-1970. No pro playing experience. College coach: Marshall 1973, Bluefield State College 1974-78, Maine 1979-1980, Boston College 1981-1993. Pro coach: Joined Jaguars in 1995.

Garrick McGee, offensive quality control; born April 6, 1973, Kansas City, Mo., lives in Jacksonville. Quarterback Arizona State 1992, Northeast Oklahoma A&M 1993, Oklahoma 1994-95. No pro playing experience. College coach: Langston 1996-98, Northern Iowa 1999. Pro coach: Joined Jaguars in 2000.

John McNulty, wide receivers; born May 29, 1968, Scranton, Pa., lives in Jacksonville. Safety Penn State 1987-1990. No pro playing experience. College coach: Michigan 1991-94, Connecticut 1995-97. Pro coach: Joined Jaguars in 1998.

Jerry Palmieri, strength and conditioning; born October 30, 1958, Englewood, N.J., lives in Jacksonville. No college or pro playing experience. College coach: Oklahoma State 1984-87, Kansas State 1988-1992, Boston College 1993-94. Pro coach: Joined Jaguars in 1995.

John Pease, defensive line; born October 14, 1943, Pittsburgh, lives in Jacksonville. Wingback Utah 1963-64. No pro playing experience. College coach: Fullerton, Calif., J.C. 1970-73, Long Beach State 1974-76, Utah 1977, Washington 1978-1983. Pro coach: Philadelphia/Baltimore Stars (USFL) 1983-85, New Orleans Saints 1986-1994, joined Jaguars in 1995.

Bob Petrino, quarterbacks; born March 10, 1961, Lewiston, Mont., lives in Jacksonville. Quarterback Carroll College 1979-1982. No pro playing experience. College coach: Carroll College 1983, 1985-86, Weber State 1984, 1987-88, Idaho 1989-1991, Arizona State 1992-93, Nevada 1994, Utah State 1995-97, Louisville 1998. Pro coach: Joined Jaguars in 1999.

Lucious Selmon, outside linebackers; born March 15, 1951, Muskogee, Okla., lives in Jacksonville. Defensive tackle Oklahoma 1970-73. Pro defensive tackle Memphis Southmen (WFL) 1974-75. College coach: Oklahoma 1976-1994. Pro coach: Joined Jaguars in 1995.

Steve Szabo, inside linebackers; born September 11, 1943, Chicago, lives in Jacksonville. Halfback/defensive back Navy 1961-64. No pro playing experience. College coach: Johns Hopkins 1969, Toledo 1970, Iowa 1971-73, Syracuse 1974-76, Iowa State 1977-78, Ohio State 1979-1981, Western Michigan 1982-84, Edinboro 1985-87 (head coach), Northern Iowa 1988, Colorado State 1989-1990, Boston College 1991-93. Pro coach: Joined Jaguars in 1995.

2000 FIRST-YEAR ROSTER

Name	Pos.	Ht.	Wt.	Birthdate	College	Hometown	How Acq.
Baniewicz, Mark	T	6-6	303	3/24/77	Syracuse	Fairport, N.Y.	D7e
Battle, James (1)	WR	6-2	200	6/8/76	Oregon State	Pittsburg, Calif.	FA
Bollers, Trevor (1)	RB	6-0	260	9/24/74	Iowa	Edmonton, Alberta, Canada	FA
Burnett, Chester (1)	LB	5-10	238	4/15/75	Arizona	Denver, Colo.	FA
Christenson, Brandon	TE	6-5	249	5/10/77	Northwestern Oklahoma St.	Clinton, Okla.	FA
Chustz, Joe	T	6-7	304	1/18/77	Louisiana Tech	Denham Springs, La.	D4
Clark, Danny	LB	6-2	230	5/9/77	Illinois	Country Club Hills, Ill.	D7d
Collins, Leroy (1)	RB	5-11	200	4/5/76	Louisville	Hudson, N.Y.	FA
Feugill, John	T	6-7	308	12/20/75	Maryland	Methuen, Mass.	FA
Kempfert, David (1)	C	6-4	296	5/11/74	Montana	Missoula, Mont.	FA
Lethridge, Zebbie (1)	CB	6-0	201	1/31/75	Texas Tech	Lubbock, Tex.	FA
Meester, Brad	G-C	6-3	298	3/23/77	Northern Iowa	Parkersburg, Iowa	D2
Meier, Rob	DE	6-5	282	8/29/77	Washington State	West Vancouver, B.C., Canada	D7b
Olson, Erik	S	6-1	215	1/4/77	Colorado State	Ventura, Calif.	D7a
People, Kevin (1)	S	6-2	210	7/28/74	North Carolina Central	Fayetteville, N.C.	FA
Reilly, Ryan	DT	6-2	306	11/21/77	Arizona State	Placentia, Calif.	FA
Robinson, Roderick (1)	QB	6-2	230	5/17/76	Arkansas-Pine Bluff	Memphis, Tenn.	FA
Slaughter, T.J.	LB	6-0	247	2/20/77	Southern Mississippi	Birmingham, Ala.	D3
Smith, Emanuel	WR	6-1	219	2/3/76	Arkansas	Clinton, Miss.	D6
Southward, Brandon(1)	LB	6-4	249	12/3/76	Colorado	Colorado Springs, Colo.	FA
Soward, R. Jay	WR	5-11	177	1/16/78	Southern California	Rialto, Calif.	D1
Stith, Shyrone	RB	5-7	203	4/2/78	Virginia Tech	Chesapeake, Va.	D7c
Streater, Rahmaan (1)	DE	6-5	263	4/23/75	Richmond	Alexandria, Va.	FA
Thomas, Eric	C	6-3	282	11/5/77	Florida State	Miami, Fla.	FA
Thomas, Kiwaukee	CB	5-11	186	6/17/77	Georgia Southern	Perry, Ga.	D5
Waerig, John	TE	6-2	254	4/8/76	Maryland	Philadelphia, Pa.	FA
White, Chris (1)	DE	6-3	285	9/28/76	Southern	Shreveport, La.	D7b-'99
Williams, Kenneth	RB	6-1	248	4/15/77	Florida A&M	Baltimore, Md.	FA
Young, Donnie (1)	G	6-4	312	11/17/73	Florida	Osprey, Fla.	FA

The term NFL Rookie is defined as a player who is in his first season of professional football and has not been on the roster of another professional football team for any regular-season or postseason games. A Rookie is designated by an "R" on NFL rosters. Players who have been active in another professional football league or players who have NFL experience, including either preseason training camp or being on an Active List or Inactive List, or on Reserve/Injured or Reserve/Physically Unable to Perform for fewer than six regular-season games, are termed NFL First-Year Players. An NFL First-Year Player is designated by a "1" on NFL rosters. Thereafter, a player is credited with an additional year of experience for each season in which he accumulates six games on the Active List or Inactive List, or on Reserve/Injured or Reserve/Physically Unable to Perform.

NOTES

KANSAS CITY CHIEFS

American Football Conference
Western Division
Team Colors: Red, Gold, and White
One Arrowhead Drive
Kansas City, Missouri 64129
Telephone: (816) 920-9300

CLUB OFFICIALS

Founder: Lamar Hunt
Chairman of the Board: Jack Steadman
President: Carl Peterson
Executive Vice President, Assistant General Manager: Dennis Thum
Senior Vice President: Dennis Watley
Vice President of Football Operations: Lynn Stiles
Secretary: Jim Seigfreid
Director of Finance/Treasurer: Dale Young
Director of Public Relations: Bob Moore
Vice President of Sales and Marketing: Wallace Bennett
Vice President of Player Personnel: Terry Bradway
Director of Pro Personnel: Bill Kuharich
Director of College Scouting: Chuck Cook
Director of Operations: Steve Schneider
Director of Development: Ken Blume
Assistant Director of Public Relations: Pete Moris
Director of Corporate Sales: Anita Bailey
Director of Sales: Gary Spani
Community Relations Manager: Brenda Sniezek
Director of Ticket Operations: Doug Hopkins
Equipment Manager: Mike Davidson
Asst. Equipment Managers: Allen Wright, Chris Shropshire
Trainer: Dave Kendall
Assistant Trainers: Bud Epps, Don Sherwood
Director of Video Operations: John Wuehrmann
Manager of Video Operations: Mike Portz
Video Assistant: Todd Weger
Stadium: Arrowhead Stadium •**Capacity:** 79,451
One Arrowhead Drive
Kansas City, Missouri 64129
Playing Surface: Grass
Training Camp: University of
Wisconsin-River Falls
River Falls, Wisconsin 54022

2000 SCHEDULE

PRESEASON

Aug. 5	at Tennessee	7:00
Aug. 13	**San Francisco**	7:30
Aug. 19	**Jacksonville**	7:30
Aug. 25	at Tampa Bay	7:30

REGULAR SEASON

Sept. 3	**Indianapolis**	12:00
Sept. 10	at Tennessee	12:00
Sept. 17	**San Diego**	12:00
Sept. 24	at Denver	2:15
Oct. 2	**Seattle** (Mon.)	8:00
Oct. 8	Open Date	
Oct. 15	**Oakland**	12:00
Oct. 22	**St. Louis**	12:00
Oct. 29	at Seattle	1:15
Nov. 5	at Oakland	1:15
Nov. 12	at San Francisco	1:05
Nov. 19	**Buffalo**	12:00
Nov. 26	at San Diego	1:15
Dec. 4	at New England (Mon.)	9:00
Dec. 10	**Carolina**	12:00
Dec. 17	**Denver**	12:00
Dec. 24	at Atlanta	1:00

RECORD HOLDERS

INDIVIDUAL RECORDS—CAREER

Category	Name	Performance
Rushing (Yds.)	Christian Okoye, 1987-1992	4,897
Passing (Yds.)	Len Dawson, 1962-1975	28,507
Passing (TDs)	Len Dawson, 1962-1975	237
Receiving (No.)	Henry Marshall, 1976-1987	416
Receiving (Yds.)	Otis Taylor, 1965-1975	7,306
Interceptions	Emmitt Thomas, 1966-1978	58
Punting (Avg.)	Jerrel Wilson, 1963-1977	43.5
Punt Return (Avg.)	Noland Smith, 1967-69	11.1
Kickoff Return (Avg.)	Noland Smith, 1967-69	26.8
Field Goals	Nick Lowery, 1980-1993	329
Touchdowns (Tot.)	Otis Taylor, 1965-1975	60
Points	Nick Lowery, 1980-1993	1,466

INDIVIDUAL RECORDS—SINGLE SEASON

Category	Name	Performance
Rushing (Yds.)	Christian Okoye, 1989	1,480
Passing (Yds.)	Bill Kenney, 1983	4,348
Passing (TDs)	Len Dawson, 1964	30
Receiving (No.)	Carlos Carson, 1983	80
Receiving (Yds.)	Carlos Carson, 1983	1,351
Interceptions	Emmitt Thomas, 1974	12
Punting (Avg.)	Jerrel Wilson, 1965	46.0
Punt Return (Avg.)	Abner Haynes, 1960	15.4
Kickoff Return (Avg.)	Dave Grayson, 1962	29.7
Field Goals	Nick Lowery, 1990	34
Touchdowns (Tot.)	Abner Haynes, 1962	19
Points	Nick Lowery, 1990	139

INDIVIDUAL RECORDS—SINGLE GAME

Category	Name	Performance
Rushing (Yds.)	Barry Word, 10-14-90	200
Passing (Yds.)	Len Dawson, 11-1-64	435
Passing (TDs)	Len Dawson, 11-1-64	6
Receiving (No.)	Ed Podolak, 10-7-73	12
Receiving (Yds.)	Stephone Paige, 12-22-85	309
Interceptions	Bobby Ply, 10-16-62	*4
	Bobby Hunt, 12-4-64	*4
	Deron Cherry, 9-29-85	*4
Field Goals	Many times	5
	Last time by Nick Lowery, 9-21-93	
Touchdowns (Tot.)	Abner Haynes, 11-26-61	5
Points	Abner Haynes, 11-26-61	30

*NFL Record

COACHING HISTORY

DALLAS TEXANS 1960-62
(323-280-12)

1960-74	Hank Stram	129-79-10
1975-77	Paul Wiggin*	11-24-0
1977	Tom Bettis	1-6-0
1978-82	Marv Levy	31-42-0
1983-86	John Mackovic	30-35-0
1987-88	Frank Gansz	8-22-1
1989-98	Marty Schottenheimer	104-65-1
1999	Gunther Cunningham	9-7-0

*Released after seven games in 1977

ARROWHEAD STADIUM

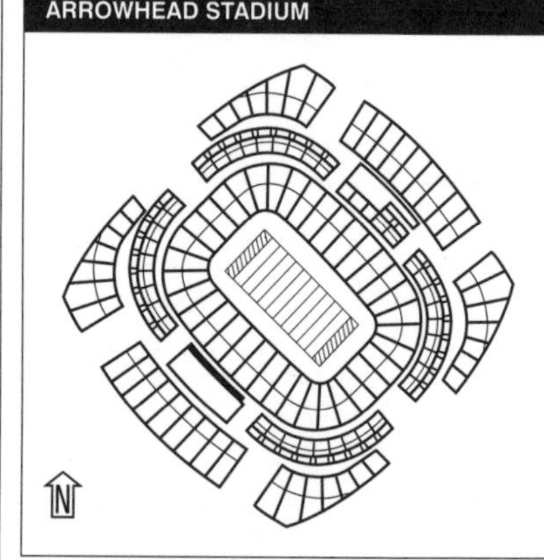

1999 TEAM RECORD

PRESEASON (2-2)

Date	Result		Opponent
8/15	W	22-20	Tennessee
8/21	L	7-17	Tampa Bay
8/26	L	6-31	at Jacksonville
9/3	W	34-27	at San Diego

REGULAR SEASON (9-7)

Date	Result		Opponent	Att.
9/12	L	17-20	at Chicago	58,381
9/19	W	26-10	Denver	78,683
9/26	W	31-21	Detroit	78,384
10/3	L	14-21	at San Diego	58,099
10/10	W	16-14	New England	78,636
10/21	W	35-8	at Baltimore	68,771
10/31	W	34-0	San Diego	78,473
11/7	L	17-25	at Indianapolis	56,689
11/14	L	10-17	at Tampa Bay	64,927
11/21	L	19-31	Seattle	78,714
11/28	W	37-34	at Oakland	48,632
12/5	W	16-10	at Denver	73,855
12/12	W	31-28	Minnesota	78,932
12/18	W	35-19	Pittsburgh	78,697
12/26	L	14-23	at Seattle	66,332
1/2	L	38-41	Oakland (OT)	79,026

(OT) Overtime

SCORE BY PERIODS

Chiefs	84	105	93	108	0	—	390
Opponents	50	133	74	62	3	—	322

ATTENDANCE

Home 629,569 Away 504,921 Total 1,134,490

Single-game home record, 82,094 (11/5/72)

Single-season home record, 629,569 (1999)

1999 TEAM STATISTICS

	Chiefs	Opp.
Total First Downs	282	281
Rushing	108	80
Passing	164	173
Penalty	10	28
Third Down: Made/Att	96/243	65/215
Third Down Pct.	39.5	30.2
Fourth Down: Made/Att	6/11	6/13
Fourth Down Pct.	54.5	46.2
Total Net Yards	5,321	5,039
Avg. Per Game	332.6	314.9
Total Plays	1,049	1,033
Avg. Per Play	5.1	4.9
Net Yards Rushing	2,082	1,557
Avg. Per Game	130.1	97.3
Total Rushes	521	415
Net Yards Passing	3,239	3,482
Avg. Per Game	202.4	217.6
Sacked/Yards Lost	26/170	40/286
Gross Yards	3,409	3,768
Att./Completions	502/295	578/317
Completion Pct.	58.8	54.8
Had Intercepted	15	25
Punts/Average	104/40.9	98/43.5
Net Punting Avg.	104/35.1	98/35.4
Penalties/Yards	126/982	107/787
Fumbles/Ball Lost	22/9	31/20
Touchdowns	47	38
Rushing	14	10
Passing	22	24
Returns	11	4
Avg. Time of Possession	30:20	29:40

1999 INDIVIDUAL STATISTICS

Passing	Att.	Comp.	Yds.	Pct.	TD	Int.	Tkld.	Rate
Grbac	499	294	3,389	58.9	22	15	26/170	81.7
Moon	3	1	20	33.3	0	0	0/0	57.6
Chiefs	502	295	3,409	58.8	22	15	26/170	81.5
Opponents	578	317	3,768	54.8	24	25	40/286	70.8

SCORING	TD R	TD P	TD Rt	PAT	FG	Saf	PTS
Stoyanovich	0	0	0	45/45	21/28	0	108
Gonzalez	0	11	0	0/0	0/0	0	66
Bennett	8	0	0	0/0	0/0	0	48
Horn	0	6	0	0/0	0/0	0	36
Alexander	1	2	0	0/0	0/0	0	18
Morris	3	0	0	0/0	0/0	0	18
Dishman	0	0	2	0/0	0/0	0	12
Edwards	0	0	2	0/0	0/0	0	12
Hasty	0	0	2	0/0	0/0	0	12
Lockett	0	2	0	0/0	0/0	0	12
Tongue	0	0	2	0/0	0/0	0	12
Vanover	0	0	2	0/0	0/0	0	12
Hicks	0	0	1	0/0	0/0	0	6
Johnson	0	1	0	0/0	0/0	0	6
Richardson	1	0	0	0/0	0/0	0	6
Shehee	1	0	0	0/0	0/0	0	6
Chiefs	14	22	11	45/45	21/28	0	390
Opponents	10	24	4	33/33	19/25	0	322

2-Pt. Conversions: None.
Team 0-2, Opponents 2-5.

RUSHING	Att.	Yds.	Avg.	LG	TD
Bennett	161	627	3.9	44	8
Morris	120	414	3.5	24	3
Richardson	84	387	4.6	26	1
Shehee	65	238	3.7	18	1
Anders	32	181	5.7	46	0
Cloud	35	128	3.7	14	0
Alexander	2	82	41.0	82t	1
Horn	2	15	7.5	9	0
Grbac	19	10	0.5	8	0
Pope	1	0	0.0	0	0
Chiefs	521	2,082	4.0	82t	14
Opponents	415	1,557	3.8	45	10

RECEIVING	No.	Yds.	Avg.	LG	TD
Gonzalez	76	849	11.2	73t	11
Alexander	54	832	15.4	86t	2
Horn	35	586	16.7	76t	6
Lockett	34	426	12.5	39t	2
Richardson	24	141	5.9	29	0
Rison	21	218	10.4	20	0
Shehee	18	136	7.6	17	0
Johnson	10	98	9.8	19	1
Bennett	10	41	4.1	12	0
Morris	7	37	5.3	9	0
Cloud	3	25	8.3	12	0
Anders	2	14	7.0	9	0
Jacoby	1	6	6.0	6	0
Chiefs	295	3,409	11.6	86t	22
Opponents	317	3,768	11.9	54	24

INTERCEPTIONS	No.	Yds.	Avg.	LG	TD
Hasty	7	98	14.0	56t	2
Dishman	5	95	19.0	47t	1
Edwards	5	50	10.0	28t	1
Warfield	3	0	0.0	0	0
Tongue	1	80	80.0	46t	1
McGlockton	1	30	30.0	30	0
Thomas	1	20	20.0	20	0
Woods	1	5	5.0	5	0
Patton	1	0	0.0	0	0
Chiefs	25	378	15.1	56t	5
Opponents	15	166	11.1	41	1

PUNTING	No.	Yds.	Avg.	In 20	LG
Pope	101	4,218	41.8	20	64
Stoyanovich	1	35	35.0	1	35
Chiefs	104	4,253	40.9	21	64
Opponents	98	4,260	43.5	34	62

PUNT RETURNS	No.	FC	Yds.	Avg.	LG	TD
Vanover	51	18	627	12.3	84t	2
L. Parker	5	1	51	10.2	35	0
Horn	1	0	18	18.0	18	0
Lockett	1	0	10	10.0	10	0
Chiefs	58	19	706	12.2	84t	2
Opponents	46	19	406	8.8	64t	1

KICKOFF RETURNS	No.	Yds.	Avg.	LG	TD
Vanover	44	886	20.1	29	0
Horn	9	165	18.3	28	0
Bennett	3	51	17.0	24	0
Cloud	2	28	14.0	18	0
Manusky	2	6	3.0	6	0
L. Parker	1	24	24.0	24	0
Johnson	1	11	11.0	11	0
Parten	1	11	11.0	11	0
Chiefs	63	1,182	18.8	29	0
Opponents	78	1,544	19.8	76t	1

FIELD GOALS	1-19	20-29	30-39	40-49	50+
Stoyanovich	1/1	7/7	5/6	7/13	1/1
Chiefs	1/1	7/7	5/6	7/13	1/1
Opponents	0/0	5/5	9/11	4/8	1/1

SACKS	No.
Thomas	7.0
Patton	6.5
O'Neal	5.5
D. Williams	5.0
Hicks	4.0
Edwards	3.0
Barndt	2.5
Tongue	2.0
McGlockton	1.5
Hasty	1.0
Ransom	1.0
Chiefs	40.0
Opponents	26.0

2000 DRAFT CHOICES

Round	Name	Pos.	College
1	Sylvester Morris	WR	Jackson State
2	William Bartee	CB	Oklahoma
3	Greg Wesley	S	Arkansas-Pine Bluff
4	Frank Moreau	RB	Louisville
5	Danté Hall	RB	Texas A&M
	Pat Dennis	CB	Louisiana-Monroe
6	Darnell Alford	T	Boston College
7	Desmond Kitchings	WR	Furman

KANSAS CITY CHIEFS

2000 VETERAN ROSTER

No.	Name	Pos.	Ht.	Wt.	Birthdate	NFL Exp.	College	Hometown	How Acq.	'99 Games/ Starts
82	Alexander, Derrick	WR	6-2	210	11/6/71	7	Michigan	Detroit, Mich.	UFA(Balt)-'98	16/15
38	Anders, Kimble	RB	5-11	226	9/10/66	10	Houston	Galveston, Tex.	FA-'91	2/2
35	Atkins, Larry	S	6-3	230	7/21/75	2	UCLA	Venice, Calif.	D3b-'99	9/0
30	Bennett, Donnell	RB	6-0	245	9/14/72	7	Miami	Ft. Lauderdale, Fla.	D2-'94	15/1
69	Blackshear, Jeff	G	6-6	323	3/29/69	8	Northeast Louisiana	Fort Pierce, Fla.	FA-'00	16/16*
93	Browning, John	DE	6-4	305	9/30/73	5	West Virginia	Miami, Fla.	D3-'96	0*
51	Bush, Lew	LB	6-2	245	12/2/69	8	Washington State	Atlanta, Ga.	FA-'00	16/14*
99	Clemons, Duane	DE	6-5	272	5/23/74	5	California	Riverside, Calif.	UFA(Minn)-'00	16/9*
34	Cloud, Mike	RB	5-10	205	7/1/75	2	Boston College	Portsmouth, R.I.	D2-'99	11/0
15	Collins, Todd	QB	6-4	228	11/5/71	6	Michigan	Walpole, Mass.	W(Buff)-'98	0*
11	Dar Dar, Kirby	WR	5-9	186	3/27/72	3	Syracuse	Morgan City, La.	FA-'00	0*
26	Dishman, Cris	CB	6-0	196	8/13/65	13	Purdue	Louisville, Ky.	FA-'99	16/16
59	Edwards, Donnie	LB	6-2	235	4/6/73	5	UCLA	Chula Vista, Calif.	D4-'96	16/16
83	Gammon, Kendall	TE	6-4	260	10/23/68	9	Pittsburg State	Wichita, Kan.	UFA(NO)-'00	16/0*
55	George, Ron	LB	6-2	247	3/20/70	8	Stanford	Heidelberg, Germany	FA-'98	16/0
88	Gonzalez, Tony	TE	6-4	251	2/27/76	4	California	Huntington Beach, Calif.	D1-'97	15/15
54	Graham, Aaron	C-G	6-4	301	5/22/73	5	Nebraska	Denton, Tex.	UFA(Ariz)-'00	16/16*
23	Gray, Carlton	CB	6-0	198	6/26/71	8	UCLA	Cincinnati, Ohio	FA-'99	16/0
18	Grbac, Elvis	QB	6-5	237	8/13/70	8	Michigan	Cleveland, Ohio	UFA(SF)-'97	16/16
61	Grunhard, Tim	C	6-2	311	5/17/68	11	Notre Dame	Chicago, Ill.	D2-'90	16/16
40	Hasty, James	CB	6-0	213	5/23/65	13	Washington State	Seattle, Wash.	UFA(NYJ)-'95	15/15
98	† Hicks, Eric	DE	6-6	278	6/17/76	3	Maryland	Erie, Pa.	FA-'98	16/16
85	Jacoby, Mitch	TE	6-4	260	12/8/73	4	Northern Illinois	Saukville, Wis.	T(StL)-'99	5/0
48	Kirby, Charles	RB	6-1	247	11/27/74	2	Virginia	Fayetteville, N.C.	FA-'99	0*
81	Lockett, Kevin	WR	6-0	187	9/8/74	4	Kansas State	Tulsa, Okla.	D2-'97	16/1
90	Martin, Steve	DT	6-4	303	5/31/74	5	Missouri	Jefferson City, Mo.	UFA(Phil)-'00	16/15*
57	Maslowski, Mike	LB	6-1	246	7/11/74	2	Wisconsin-La Crosse	Thorp, Wis.	FA-'99	15/0
75	McGlockton, Chester	DT	6-4	328	9/16/69	9	Clemson	Whiteville, N.C.	RFA(Oak)-'98	16/16
1	Moon, Warren	QB	6-3	218	11/18/56	17	Washington	Los Angeles, Calif.	FA-'99	1/0
91	O'Neal, Leslie	DE	6-4	281	5/7/64	15	Oklahoma State	Little Rock, Ark.	FA-'98	16/10
80	Parker, Larry	WR	6-1	200	7/14/76	2	Southern California	Bakersfield, Calif.	D4-'99	10/0
97	# Parten, Ty	DE	6-5	290	10/13/69	5	Arizona	Scottsdale, Ariz.	FA-'97	16/0
53	Patton, Marvcus	LB	6-2	243	5/1/67	11	UCLA	Lawndale, Calif.	UFA(Wash)-'99	16/16
13	Pope, Daniel	P	5-10	203	3/28/75	2	Alabama	Alpharetta, Ga.	FA-'99	16/0
95	Ransom, Derrick	DT	6-3	307	9/13/76	3	Cincinnati	Indianapolis, Ind.	D6-'98	10/0
49	Richardson, Tony	RB	6-1	235	12/17/71	6	Auburn	Daleville, Ala.	FA-'95	16/16
66	Riley, Victor	T	6-5	334	11/4/74	3	Auburn	Swansea, S.C.	D1-'98	16/16
89	Rison, Andre	WR	6-1	199	3/18/67	12	Michigan State	Flint, Mich.	FA-'97	15/14
5	Sauerbrun, Todd	P	5-10	204	1/4/73	6	West Virginia	Setauket, N.Y.	UFA(Chi)-'00	16/0*
29	Serwanga, Wasswa	CB	5-11	190	7/23/76	2	UCLA	Sacramento, Calif.	FA-'00	9/0*
22	Shehee, Rashaan	RB	5-10	210	6/20/75	3	Washington	Bakersfield, Calif.	D3-'98	9/5
68	† Shields, Will	G	6-3	321	9/15/71	8	Nebraska	Lawton, Okla.	D3-'93	16/16
65	Smith, Jeff	C-G	6-3	317	5/25/73	5	Tennessee	Decatur, Tenn.	D7b-'96	15/2
70	Spears, Marcus	T	6-4	320	9/28/71	7	Northwest State, La.	Scotlandville, La.	FA-'97	10/2
77	Stai, Brenden	G	6-4	310	3/30/72	6	Nebraska	Phoenix, Ariz.	FA-'00	16/16*
56	Stills, Gary	LB	6-2	235	7/11/74	2	West Virginia	Trenton, N.J.	D3a-'99	2/0
10	Stoyanovich, Pete	K	5-11	194	4/28/67	12	Indiana	Dearborn Heights, Mich.	T(Mia)-'96	16/0
79	Szott, Dave	G	6-4	289	12/12/67	11	Penn State	Clifton, N.J.	D7-'90	14/14
76	Tait, John	T	6-6	306	1/26/75	2	Brigham Young	Phoenix, Ariz.	D1-'99	12/3
50	Terry, Tim	LB	6-3	240	7/26/74	2	Temple	Hempstead, N.Y.	FA-'00	0*
27	Walker, Bracy	S	6-0	204	6/11/70	7	North Carolina	Fayetteville, N.C.	FA-'98	16/1
44	Warfield, Eric	CB	6-0	195	3/3/76	3	Nebraska	Texarkana, Ark.	D7a-'98	16/1
7	White, Ted	QB	6-2	225	5/29/76	2	Howard	Baton Rouge, La.	FA-'99	0*
92	Williams, Dan	DE	6-4	293	12/15/69	7	Toledo	Ypsilanti, Mich.	FA-'97	14/9
60	Willis, Donald	G	6-3	348	7/15/73	3	North Carolina A&T	Goleta, Calif.	FA-'00	0*
21	Woods, Jerome	S	6-2	202	3/17/73	5	Memphis	Memphis, Tenn.	D1-'96	15/15
96	Word, Mark	DE	6-4	270	11/23/75	2	Jacksonville State	Miami, Fla.	FA-'99	5/0

* Blackshear played 16 games with Baltimore in '99; Browning missed '99 season because of injury; Bush played 16 games with San Diego; Clemons played 16 games with Minnesota; Collins was inactive for 16 games; Dar Dar last active with Miami in '98; Gammon played 16 games with New Orleans; Graham played 16 games with Arizona; Kirby last active with Indianapolis in '98; Martin played 16 games with Philadelphia; Sauerbrun played 16 games with Chicago; Serwanga played 9 games with San Francisco; Stai played 16 games with Pittsburgh; Terry last active with Cincinnati in '97; White was inactive for 6 games in '99; Willis last active with New Orleans in '96.

† Restricted free agent; subject to developments.

Unrestricted free agent; subject to developments.

Players lost through free agency (4): DT Tom Barndt (Cin; 16 games in '99), WR Joe Horn (NO; 16), T Glenn Parker (NYG; 12), S Reggie Tongue (Sea; 16).

Also played with Chiefs in '99—K Jon Baker (2 games), K Scott Bentley (2), CB Juran Bolden (7), TE Lonnie Johnson (14), LB Greg Manusky (16), RB Byron (Bam) Morris (12), G Ralph Tamm (16), LB Derrick Thomas (16), WR Tamarick Vanover (14), DB Robert Williams (1), T Sammy Williams (1).

COACHING STAFF

Head Coach,
Gunther Cunningham

Pro Career: The Kansas City Chiefs ushered in a new era when Gunther Cunningham was named the eighth head coach in franchise history on January 22, 1999. In 1999, Cunningham guided the Chiefs to a 9-7 record, the best record of any rookie head coach in franchise history, making him the only one of the NFL's six first-year head coaches in 1999 with a winning record. Cunningham was promoted to head coach after four seasons (1995-98) as Kansas City's defensive coordinator. The Chiefs permitted an AFC-low 17.8 points per game over that span and twice led the NFL in scoring defense (1995 and 1997) during his tenure. He brought his expertise to the Chiefs after logging four seasons (1991-94) with the Raiders. He served as the Raiders' linebackers coach in 1991, as defensive coordinator the next two seasons, and defensive line coach in 1994. Prior to joining the Raiders, he spent six years (1985-1990) as the Chargers' defensive line coach. He began his NFL coaching career as the defensive line coach of the Baltimore Colts in 1982, staying there for three seasons. He originally entered the pro ranks in the CFL, coaching the defensive line and linebackers for the Hamilton Tiger-Cats in 1981. Career record: 9-7.
Background: Cunningham graduated from Oregon, where he was a linebacker and placekicker from 1966-68. He was a college assistant coach at Oregon (1969-1971), Arkansas (1972), Stanford (1973-76), and California (1977-1980).
Personal: Born June 19, 1946, in Munich, Germany, he is just the fourth foreign-born head coach in the NFL's 80-year history. Gunther and his wife, Rene, live in Leawood, Kansas, with their daughter, Natalie, and son, Adam.

ASSISTANT COACHES

Tom Clements, quarterbacks; born June 18, 1953, McKees Rocks, Pa., lives in Kansas City, Mo. Quarterback Notre Dame 1972-74. Pro quarterback: Ottawa Rough Riders (CFL) 1975-78, Saskatchewan Roughriders (CFL) 1979, Hamilton Tiger-Cats (CFL) 1979, 1981-83, Kansas City Chiefs 1980, Winnipeg Blue Bombers 1983-87. College coach: Notre Dame 1992-1995. Pro coach: New Orleans Saints 1997-99, joined Chiefs in 2000.
Jeff Fish, asst. strength and conditioning; born June 6, 1966, Ithaca, N.Y., lives in Lee's Summit, Mo. Wide receiver Western Carolina 1986-89. No pro playing experience. College coach: Western Michigan 1989-1991, Clemson 1991-93, Kent State 1993-95, Tulsa 1995-97. Pro coach: Tampa Bay Buccaneers 1997 (intern), joined Chiefs in 1998.
Jim Hostler, offensive assistant-quality control; born November 7, 1966, Bethel Park, Pa., lives in Blue Springs, Mo. Cornerback Indiana University (Pa.) 1986-89. No pro playing experience. College coach: Indiana University (Pa.) 1990-1992, 1994-99, Juniata College 1993. Pro coach: Joined Chiefs in 2000.
Jeff Hurd, strength and conditioning; born April 24, 1958, Pomona, Calif., lives in Overland Park, Kan. Attended Fort Hays State. No college or pro playing experience. College coach: Fort Hays State 1984, Delta State 1985, Clemson 1986, Western Michigan 1987-1993, Tulsa 1994. Pro coach: Jacksonville Jaguars 1995-97, joined Chiefs in 1998.
Bob Karmelowicz, defensive line; born July 22, 1949, New Britain, Conn., lives in Lenexa, Kan. Nose tackle Bridgeport 1968-1971. No pro playing experience. College coach: Arizona State 1974-78, Massachusetts 1979-1980, Texas-El Paso 1980-81, Illinois 1982-86, Washington State 1987-88, Miami 1989-1991. Pro coach: Cincinnati Bengals 1992-93, Washington Redskins 1994-96, joined Chiefs in 1997.
Al Lavan, running backs; born September 13, 1946, Pierce, Fla., lives in Overland Park, Kan. Defensive back Colorado State 1965-67. Pro defensive back Philadelphia Eagles 1968, Atlanta Falcons 1969-1970. College coach: Colorado State 1972, Louisville 1973, Iowa State 1974, Georgia Tech 1977-78, Stanford 1979, Washington 1992-95. Pro coach: Atlanta Falcons 1975-76, Dallas Cowboys 1980-88, San Francisco 49ers 1989-1990, Baltimore Ravens 1996-98, joined Chiefs in 1999.
Richard Mann, wide receivers; born April 20, 1947, Aliquippa, Pa., lives in Kansas City, Mo. Wide receiver Arizona State 1966-68. No pro playing experience. College coach: Arizona State 1974-79, Louisville 1980-81. Pro coach: Baltimore/Indianapolis Colts 1982-84, Cleveland Browns 1985-93, New York Jets 1994-96, Baltimore Ravens 1997-98, joined Chiefs in 1999.
Tom Pratt, asst. defensive line; born June 21, 1935, Edgerton, Wis., lives in Kansas City, Mo. Linebacker Miami 1953-56. No pro playing experience. College coach: Miami 1957-1960, Southern Mississippi 1961-62, U.S. Coast Guard Academy 1997. Pro coach: Kansas City Chiefs 1963-1977, 1989-1994, New Orleans Saints 1978-1980, Cleveland Browns 1981-88, Tampa Bay Buccaneers 1995, rejoined Chiefs in 2000.
Jimmy Raye, offensive coordinator; born March 26, 1946, Fayetteville, N.C., lives in Kansas City, Mo. Quarterback Michigan State 1965-67. Pro defensive back Philadelphia Eagles 1969. College coach: Michigan State 1971-75, Wyoming 1976. Pro coach: San Francisco 49ers 1977, Detroit Lions 1978-79, Atlanta Falcons 1980-82, 1987-89, Los Angeles Rams 1983-84, 1991, Tampa Bay Buccaneers 1985-86, New England Patriots 1990, joined Chiefs in 1992.
Keith Rowen, tight ends; born September 2, 1952, New York, N.Y., lives in Overland Park, Kan. Offensive tackle Stanford 1972-74. No pro playing experience. College coach: Stanford 1974-75, Long Beach State 1977-78, Arizona 1979-1982. Pro coach: Boston/New Orleans Breakers (USFL) 1983-84, Cleveland Browns 1984, Indianapolis Colts 1985-88, New England Patriots 1989, Atlanta Falcons 1990-93, Minnesota Vikings 1994-96, Oakland Raiders 1997-98, joined Chiefs in 1999.
Kurt Schottenheimer, defensive coordinator; born October 1, 1949, McDonald, Pa., lives in Leawood, Kan. Defensive back Miami 1969-1970. No pro playing experience. College coach: William Patterson 1974, Michigan State 1978-1982, Tulane 1983, Louisiana State 1984-85, Notre Dame 1986. Pro coach: Cleveland Browns 1987-88, joined Chiefs in 1989.
Willie Shaw, asst. head coach-defensive backs; born January 11, 1944, Glenmora, La., lives in Overland Park, Kan.. Cornerback New Mexico 1966-68. No pro playing experience. College coach: San Diego C.C. (Calif.) 1970-73, Stanford 1974-76, 1989-1991, Long Beach State 1977-78, Oregon 1979, Arizona State 1980-84. Pro coach: Detroit Lions 1985-88, Minnesota Vikings 1992-93, San Diego Chargers 1994, St. Louis Rams 1995-96, New Orleans Saints 1997, Oakland Raiders 1998-99, joined Chiefs in 2000.
Mike Solari, offensive line; born January 16, 1955, Daly City, Calif., lives in Leawood, Kan. Offensive lineman San Diego State 1975-76. No pro playing experience. College coach: Mira Vista (Calif.) J.C. 1977-78, U.S. International 1979, Boise State 1980, Cincinnati 1990-91. Pro coach: Dallas Cowboys 1987-88, Phoenix Cardinals 1989, San Francisco 49ers 1992-96, joined Chiefs in 1997.
Mike Stock, special teams; born September 29, 1939, Barberton, Ohio, lives in Overland Park, Kan. Fullback Northwestern 1957-1960. Pro running back Saskatchewan Roughriders (CFL) 1961. College coach: Northwestern 1961, Buffalo 1966-67, Navy 1968, Notre Dame 1969-1974, Wisconsin 1975-78, Eastern Michigan 1979-1983 (head coach), Notre Dame 1984-86, Ohio State 1992-94. Pro coach: Cincinnati Bengals 1987-1991, joined Chiefs in 1995.

2000 FIRST-YEAR ROSTER

Name	Pos.	Ht.	Wt.	Birthdate	College	Hometown	How Acq.
Alford, Darnell	T	6-4	334	6/11/77	Boston College	Fredericksburg, Va.	D6
Bartee, William	CB	6-1	190	6/25/77	Oklahoma	Daytona Beach, Fla.	D2
Bruce, Arland	WR	5-9	190	11/23/77	Minnesota	Olathe, Kan.	FA
Cloman, Scott (1)	WR	6-3	200	11/6/75	Southern	Bellflower, Calif.	FA
Crandell, Marcus (1)	QB	5-11	205	1/6/74	East Carolina	Charlotte, N.C.	FA
Dennis, Pat	CB	6-0	202	6/3/78	Louisiana-Monroe	Shreveport, La.	D5b
Gall, Chris (1)	RB	6-0	232	4/4/76	Indiana	Chicago, Ill.	FA
Gallery, Nick (1)	P	6-4	245	2/15/75	Iowa	Manchester, Iowa	FA
Garrett, Grant (1)	C	6-3	301	8/11/76	Arkansas	Fayetteville, Ark.	FA-'99
Hall, Dante	RB-KR	5-8	188	9/1/78	Texas A&M	Lufkin, Tex.	D5a
Hinton, Brian	CB	5-9	173	1/9/77	Southeast Missouri State	St. Louis, Mo.	FA
Jackson, Jonathan	LB	6-2	239	9/2/77	Oregon State	Las Vegas, Nev.	FA
Jackson, Ray (1)	CB	6-1	210	1/15/75	Washington State	Santa Ana, Calif.	FA
Jackson, Vershan (1)	RB	6-1	255	2/27/75	Nebraska	Omaha, Neb.	FA
King, Eric (1)	G	6-4	299	7/27/75	Richmond	Pittsburgh, Pa.	D7-'99
King, Percy	S	6-4	218	1/31/77	Ohio State	Columbus, Ohio	FA
Kitchings, Desmond	WR-KR	5-9	175	7/19/78	Furman	Columbia, S.C.	D7
Kirby, Charles (1)	FB	6-1	247	11/27/74	Virginia	Fayetteville, N.C.	FA-'99
Kubik, Brad (1)	G	6-3	292	3/31/75	Southwest Missouri State	Springfield, Mo.	FA-'98
Lindquist, Bill	QB	6-4	204	6/16/77	Benedictine	Kansas City, Mo.	FA
McGrew, Brock	WR	6-2	210	5/17/78	North Texas	Hearne, Tex.	FA
McMullen, Kirk	TE	6-4	250	7/19/77	Pittsburgh	Imperial, Pa.	FA
Moreau, Frank	RB	6-0	224	9/9/76	Louisville	Elizabethtown, Ky.	D4
Morris, Sylvester	WR	6-3	208	10/6/77	Jackson State	New Orleans, La.	D1
Murphy, Rob	G	6-5	305	1/18/77	Ohio State	Cincinnati, Ohio	FA
O'Neal, Andre	LB	6-1	235	12/1275	Marshall	Decatur, Ga.	FA
Pearsall, Melvin (1)	TE	6-2	245	2/3/75	Florida State	Wichita, Kan.	FA
Perez, Joe	WR	6-0	195	5/21/77	Murray State	Overland Park, Kan.	FA
Rawlings, Josh	T	6-3	314	4/11/77	Minnesota	Fort Gratiot, Mich.	FA
Riley, Earl	S	6-0	203	3/23/77	Washington State	Dos Palos, Calif.	FA
Shay, Brian (1)	RB	5-8	213	2/22/77	Emporia State	Paola, Kan.	FA
Sluder, Kevin	DT	6-3	270	9/20/77	Mississippi State	Pensacola, Fla.	FA
Stringer, Germaine	WR	5-7	170	1/4/76	Florida State	Atlanta, Ga.	FA
Waters, Brian (1)	C	6-3	293	2/18/77	North Texas	Waxahachie, Tex.	FA
Washington, Thomas	DT	6-3	310	12/12/76	Winston-Salem State	Charleston, S.C.	FA
Wesley, Greg	S	6-2	214	3/19/76	Arkansas-Pine Bluff	England, Ark.	D3

The term NFL Rookie is defined as a player who is in his first season of professional football and has not been on the roster of another professional football team for any regular-season or postseason games. A Rookie is designated by an "R" on NFL rosters. Players who have been active in another professional football league or players who have NFL experience, including either preseason training camp or being on an Active List or Inactive List, or on Reserve/Injured or Reserve/Physically Unable to Perform for fewer than six regular-season games, are termed NFL First-Year Players. An NFL First-Year Player is designated by a "1" on NFL rosters. Thereafter, a player is credited with an additional year of experience for each season in which he accumulates six games on the Active List or Inactive List, or on Reserve/Injured or Reserve/Physically Unable to Perform.

MIAMI DOLPHINS

American Football Conference
Eastern Division
Team Colors: Aqua, Coral, Blue, and White
7500 S.W. 30th Street
Davie, Florida 33314
Telephone: (954) 452-7000

CLUB OFFICIALS

Owner/Chairman of the Board: H. Wayne Huizenga
President/Chief Operating Officer: Eddie J. Jones
Head Coach: Dave Wannstedt
Senior Vice President-Business Operations: Bryan Wiedmeier
Senior Vice President-Finance & Administration: Jill R. Strafaci
Vice President-Player Personnel: Rick Spielman
Director of Football Operations: Bob Ackles
Director of Pro Personnel: Tom Heckert, Jr.
Director of College Scouting: Tom Braatz
Vice President-Media Relations: Harvey Greene
Director of Media Relations: Neal Gulkis
Director of Publications & Internet: Scott Stone
Senior Vice President-Sales and Marketing: Bill Galante
Vice President-Sales & Marketing: Jim Ross
Senior Director of Community & Alumni Relations: Fudge Browne
Head Athletic Trainer: Kevin O'Neill
Equipment Manager: Tony Egues
Video Director: Dave Hack
Stadium: Pro Player Stadium • **Capacity:** 75,192
2269 N.W. 199th Street
Miami, Florida 33056
Playing Surface: Grass (PAT)
Training Camp: Nova University
7500 S.W. 30th Street
Davie, Florida 33314

RECORD HOLDERS

INDIVIDUAL RECORDS—CAREER

Category	Name	Performance
Rushing (Yds.)	Larry Csonka, 1968-1974, 1979	6,737
Passing (Yds.)	Dan Marino, 1983-1999	*61,361
Passing (TDs)	Dan Marino, 1983-1999	*420
Receiving (No.)	Mark Clayton, 1983-1992	550
Receiving (Yds.)	Mark Duper, 1982-1992	8,869
Interceptions	Jake Scott, 1970-75	35
Punting (Avg.)	John Kidd, 1994-97	44.2
Punt Return (Avg.)	Freddie Solomon, 1975-77	11.4
Kickoff Return (Avg.)	Mercury Morris, 1969-1975	26.5
Field Goals	Pete Stoyanovich, 1989-1995	176
Touchdowns (Tot.)	Mark Clayton, 1983-1992	82
Points	Garo Yepremian, 1970-78	830

INDIVIDUAL RECORDS—SINGLE SEASON

Category	Name	Performance
Rushing (Yds.)	Delvin Williams, 1978	1,258
Passing (Yds.)	Dan Marino, 1984	*5,084
Passing (TDs)	Dan Marino, 1984	*48
Receiving (No.)	O.J. McDuffie, 1998	90
Receiving (Yds.)	Mark Clayton, 1984	1,389
Interceptions	Dick Westmoreland, 1967	10
Punting (Avg.)	John Kidd, 1996	46.3
Punt Return (Avg.)	Nate Jacquet, 1999	12.5
Kickoff Return (Avg.)	Duriel Harris, 1976	32.9
Field Goals	Olindo Mare, 1999	*39
Touchdowns (Tot.)	Mark Clayton, 1984	18
Points	Olindo Mare, 1999	144

INDIVIDUAL RECORDS—SINGLE GAME

Category	Name	Performance
Rushing (Yds.)	Mercury Morris, 9-30-73	197
Passing (Yds.)	Dan Marino, 10-23-88	521
Passing (TDs)	Bob Griese, 11-24-77	6
	Dan Marino, 9-21-86	6
Receiving (No.)	Jim Jensen, 11-6-88	12
Receiving (Yds.)	Mark Duper, 11-10-85	217
Interceptions	Dick Anderson, 12-3-73	*4
Field Goals	Olindo Mare, 10-17-99	6
Touchdowns (Tot.)	Paul Warfield, 12-15-73	4
	Mark Ingram, 11-27-94	4
Points	Paul Warfield, 12-15-73	24
	Mark Ingram, 11-27-94	24

*NFL Record

2000 SCHEDULE

PRESEASON

Aug. 5	at Pittsburgh	7:30
Aug. 10	**Tampa Bay**	7:00
Aug. 21	**Green Bay**	8:00
Aug. 25	at New Orleans	7:00

REGULAR SEASON

Sept. 3	**Seattle**	4:15
Sept. 10	at Minnesota	12:00
Sept. 17	**Baltimore**	8:35
Sept. 24	**New England**	1:00
Oct. 1	at Cincinnati	4:05
Oct. 8	**Buffalo**	1:00
Oct. 15	Open Date	
Oct. 23	at New York Jets (Mon.)	9:00
Oct. 29	**Green Bay**	1:00
Nov. 5	at Detroit	1:00
Nov. 12	at San Diego	1:05
Nov. 19	**New York Jets**	4:05
Nov. 26	at Indianapolis	1:00
Dec. 3	at Buffalo	1:00
Dec. 10	**Tampa Bay**	1:00
Dec. 17	**Indianapolis**	4:15
Dec. 24	at New England	1:00

COACHING HISTORY

(327-217-4)

1966-69	George Wilson	15-39-2
1970-95	Don Shula	274-147-2
1996-99	Jimmy Johnson	38-31-0

PRO PLAYER STADIUM

MIAMI DOLPHINS

1999 TEAM RECORD

PRESEASON (2-2)

Date	Result		Opponent
8/13	L	14-26	New Orleans
8/21	W	13-10	at San Diego
8/28	W	31-10	Detroit
9/2	L	17-25	at Green Bay

REGULAR SEASON (9-7)

Date	Result		Opponent	Att.
9/13	W	38-21	at Denver	75,623
9/19	W	19-16	Arizona	73,618
10/4	L	18-23	Buffalo	74,073
10/10	W	34-31	at Indianapolis	56,810
10/17	W	31-30	at New England	60,006
10/24	W	16-13	Philadelphia	73,975
10/31	W	16-9	at Oakland	61,556
11/7	W	17-0	Tennessee	74,109
11/14	L	3-23	at Buffalo	72,810
11/21	W	27-17	New England	74,295
11/25	L	0-20	at Dallas	64,328
12/5	L	34-37	Indianapolis	74,096
12/12	L	20-28	at New York Jets	78,246
12/19	W	12-9	San Diego	73,765
12/27	L	31-38	New York Jets	74,230
1/2	L	10-21	at Washington	78,106

POSTSEASON (1-1)

Date	Result		Opponent	Att.
1/9	W	20-17	at Seattle	66,170
1/15	L	7-62	at Jacksonville	75,173

SCORE BY PERIODS

Dolphins	50	106	58	112	0	—	326
Opponents	73	83	75	105	0	—	336

ATTENDANCE

Home 592,161 Away 538,805 Total 1,130,966
Single-game home record, 75,283 (10/27/96)
Single-season home record, 592,161 (1999)

1999 TEAM STATISTICS

	Dolphins	Opp.
Total First Downs	287	252
Rushing	81	79
Passing	188	145
Penalty	18	28
Third Down: Made/Att	80/236	60/208
Third Down Pct.	33.9	28.8
Fourth Down: Made/Att	8/14	8/16
Fourth Down Pct.	57.1	50.0
Total Net Yards	4,938	4,404
Avg. Per Game	308.6	275.3
Total Plays	1,071	936
Avg. Per Play	4.6	4.7
Net Yards Rushing	1,453	1,476
Avg. Per Game	90.8	92.3
Total Rushes	445	413
Net Yards Passing	3,485	2,928
Avg. Per Game	217.8	183.0
Sacked/Yards Lost	37/251	39/240
Gross Yards	3,736	3,168
Att./Completions	589/329	484/256
Completion Pct.	55.9	52.9
Had Intercepted	21	18
Punts/Average	81/41.0	85/41.1
Net Punting Avg.	81/34.8	85/34.4
Penalties/Yards	111/936	80/708
Fumbles/Ball Lost	23/13	19/10
Touchdowns	30	35
Rushing	8	6
Passing	20	19
Returns	2	10
Avg. Time of Possession	31:34	28:26

1999 INDIVIDUAL STATISTICS

Passing	Att.	Comp.	Yds.	Pct.	TD	Int.	Tkld.	Rate
Marino	369	204	2,448	55.3	12	17	9/66	67.4
Huard	216	125	1,288	57.9	8	4	28/185	79.8
Zolak	4	0	0	0.0	0	0	0/0	39.6
Dolphins	589	329	3,736	55.9	20	21	37/251	71.5
Opponents	484	256	3,168	52.9	19	18	39/240	71.0

SCORING	TD R	TD P	TD Rt	PAT	FG	Saf	PTS
Mare	0	0	0	27/27	39/46	0	144
Gadsden	0	6	0	0/0	0/0	0	36
Martin	0	5	0	0/0	0/0	0	30
Pritchett	1	4	0	0/0	0/0	0	30
Johnson	4	0	0	0/0	0/0	0	24
Collins	2	0	0	0/0	0/0	0	12
McDuffie	0	2	0	0/0	0/0	0	12
Madison	0	0	1	0/0	0/0	1	8
Abdul-Jabbar	1	0	0	0/0	0/0	0	6
Drayton	0	1	0	0/0	0/0	0	6
Konrad	0	1	0	0/0	0/0	0	6
Perry	0	1	0	0/0	0/0	0	6
Taylor	0	0	1	0/0	0/0	0	6
Dolphins	8	20	2	27/27	39/46	1	326
Opponents	6	19	10	33/35	31/40	0	336

2-Pt. Conversions: None.
Team 0-3, Opponents 0-0.

RUSHING	Att.	Yds.	Avg.	LG	TD
Johnson	164	558	3.4	34	4
Collins	131	414	3.2	25t	2
Pritchett	47	158	3.4	25	1
Huard	28	124	4.4	25	0
Denson	28	98	3.5	20	0
Abdul-Jabbar	28	95	3.4	12	1
Konrad	9	16	1.8	5	0
Jacquet	1	4	4.0	4	0
Zolak	2	-2	-1.0	-1	0
Marino	6	-6	-1.0	0	0
Martin	1	-6	-6.0	-6	0
Dolphins	445	1453	3.3	34	8
Opponents	413	1476	3.6	43	6

RECEIVING	No.	Yds.	Avg.	LG	TD
Martin	67	1,037	15.5	69t	5
Gadsden	48	803	16.7	62	6
McDuffie	43	516	12.0	34	2
Pritchett	43	312	7.3	30	4
Konrad	34	251	7.4	25	1
Drayton	32	299	9.3	26	1
Green	18	234	13.0	27	0
Johnson	15	100	6.7	17	0
Goodwin	8	55	6.9	14	0
Collins	6	32	5.3	12	0
Denson	4	28	7.0	10	0
Abdul-Jabbar	4	25	6.3	14	0
Perry	3	8	2.7	5	1
McKenzie	2	18	9.0	13	0
Jacquet	1	18	18.0	18	0
Huard	1	0	0.0	0	0
Dolphins	329	3,736	11.4	69t	20
Opponents	256	3,168	12.4	68t	19

INTERCEPTIONS	No.	Yds.	Avg.	LG	TD
Madison	7	164	23.4	42	1
Buckley	3	3	1.0	18	0
Marion	2	30	15.0	28	0
Surtain	2	28	14.0	28	0
Wilson	1	13	13.0	13	0
Rodgers	1	5	5.0	5	0
Taylor	1	0	0.0	0	0
Z. Thomas	1	0	0.0	0	0
Dolphins	18	243	13.5	42	1
Opponents	21	567	27.0	98t	7

PUNTING	No.	Yds.	Avg.	In 20	LG
Hutton	73	2,978	40.8	22	63
Bartholomew	7	308	44.0	1	51
Mare	1	36	36.0	0	36
Dolphins	81	3,322	41.0	23	63
Opponents	85	3,495	41.1	26	57

PUNT RETURNS	No.	FC	Yds.	Avg.	LG	TD
Jacquet	28	0	351	12.5	45	0
Buckley	8	5	13	1.6	8	0
McDuffie	7	8	62	8.9	21	0
Preston	1	0	6	6.0	6	0
Dolphins	44	13	432	9.8	45	0
Opponents	42	17	424	10.1	43	0

KICKOFF RETURNS	No.	Yds.	Avg.	LG	TD
Marion	62	1,524	24.6	93	0
Wilson	3	50	16.7	23	0
Avery	2	55	27.5	33	0
Johnson	2	26	13.0	19	0
Jacquet	1	26	26.0	26	0
McDuffie	1	17	17.0	17	0
Z. Thomas	1	15	15.0	15	0
Dolphins	72	1,713	23.8	93	0
Opponents	58	1,282	22.1	97t	1

FIELD GOALS	1-19	20-29	30-39	40-49	50+
Mare	1/1	9/9	17/17	9/14	3/5
Dolphins	1/1	9/9	17/17	9/14	3/5
Opponents	0/0	6/6	10/14	12/16	3/4

SACKS	No.
Owens	8.5
Armstrong	7.5
Bromell	5.0
Gardener	5.0
Wilson	3.0
Taylor	2.5
Surtain	2.0
Bowens	1.5
Buckley	1.0
Jackson	1.0
Marion	1.0
Z. Thomas	1.0
Dolphins	39.0
Opponents	37.0

2000 DRAFT CHOICES

Round	Name	Pos.	College
2	Todd Wade	T	Mississippi
3	Ben Kelly	DB	Colorado
4	Deon Dyer	RB	North Carolina
5	Arturo Freeman	DB	South Carolina
6	Earnest Grant	DT	Arkansas-Pine Bluff
7	Jeff Harris	DB	Georgia

MIAMI DOLPHINS

2000 VETERAN ROSTER

No.		Name	Pos.	Ht.	Wt.	Birthdate	NFL Exp.	College	Hometown	How Acq.	'99 Games/ Starts
93		Armstrong, Trace	DE	6-4	270	10/5/65	12	Florida	Birmingham, Ala.	T(Chi)-'95	16/2
2		Baker, Robert	WR	5-11	202	3/14/76	2	Auburn	Gainesville, Fla.	FA-'99	0*
60		Bock, John	G	6-3	295	2/11/71	6	Indiana State	Crystal Lake, Ill.	FA-'96	7/0
95		Bowens, Tim	DT	6-4	315	2/7/73	7	Mississippi	Okolona, Miss.	D1-'94	16/15
57	#	Brigance, O.J.	LB	6-0	236	9/29/69	5	Rice	Sugarland, Tex.	FA-'96	16/0
91		Bromell, Lorenzo	DE	6-6	270	9/23/75	3	Clemson	Georgetown, S.C.	D4-'98	15/1
76		Brown, James	T	6-6	325	11/30/70	8	Virginia State	Philadelphia, Pa.	T(NYJ)-'96	15/14
27	#	Buckley, Terrell	CB	5-10	180	6/7/71	9	Florida State	Pascagoula, Miss.	T(GB)-'95	16/11
21		Denson, Autry	RB	5-10	193	12/8/76	2	Notre Dame	Davie, Fla.	FA-'99	6/1
63		Dixon, Mark	G	6-4	300	11/26/70	3	Virginia	Jamestown, N.C.	FA-'98	13/13
65		Donnalley, Kevin	G	6-5	310	6/10/68	10	North Carolina	Raleigh, N.C.	UFA(Tenn)-'98	16/9
17		Doxzon, Todd	WR	6-0	190	3/28/75	2	Iowa State	Sioux City, Iowa	FA-'00	0*
16		Druckenmiller, Jim	QB	6-5	234	9/19/72	4	Virginia Tech	Northhampton, Pa.	T(SF)-'99	0*
9		Fiedler, Jay	QB	6-2	220	12/29/71	5	Dartmouth	Oceanside, N.Y.	UFA(Jax)-'00	7/1*
86		Gadsden, Oronde	WR	6-2	215	8/20/71	3	Winston-Salem State	Charleston, S.C.	FA-'98	16/7
58		Galyon, Scott	LB	6-2	245	3/23/74	5	Tennessee	Seymour, Tenn.	UFA(NYG)-'00	16/0*
92		Gardener, Daryl	DT	6-6	315	2/25/73	5	Baylor	Lawton, Okla.	D1-'96	16/15
83		Goodwin, Hunter	TE	6-5	270	10/10/72	5	Texas A&M	Bellville, Tex.	RFA(Minn)-'99	15/5
87		Green, Yatil	WR	6-2	205	11/25/73	4	Miami	Lake City, Fla.	D1-'97	8/1
28		Hill, Ray	CB	6-0	195	8/7/75	3	Michigan State	Detroit, Mich.	W(Buff)-'98	16/0
50	#	Hollier, Dwight	LB	6-2	242	4/21/69	9	North Carolina	Hampton, Va.	D4-'92	15/0
11		Huard, Damon	QB	6-3	215	7/9/73	4	Washington	Puyallup, Wash.	FA-'97	16/5
66		Irwin, Heath	G	6-4	300	6/27/73	5	Colorado	Boulder, Colo.	UFA(NE)-'00	15/13*
53		Izzo, Larry	LB	5-10	228	9/26/74	5	Rice	Houston, Tex.	FA-'96	16/0
38		Jackson, Calvin	CB	5-9	195	10/28/72	6	Auburn	Ft. Lauderdale, Fla.	FA-'95	16/10
88	†	Jacquet, Nate	WR	6-0	185	9/2/75	4	San Diego State	Duarte, Calif.	W(Ind)-'98	13/0
25		Jeffries, Greg	CB	5-9	195	10/16/71	8	Virginia	High Point, N.C.	UFA(Det)-'99	16/0
32		Johnson, J.J.	RB	6-1	230	4/20/74	2	Mississippi State	Mobile, Ala.	D2a-'99	13/4
52		Jones, Robert	LB	6-3	245	9/27/69	9	East Carolina	Blackstone, Va.	FA-'98	16/15
70		Jones, Willie	T	6-7	375	12/17/75	2	Grambling State	Belle Glade, Fla.	FA-'00	0*
44		Konrad, Rob	FB	6-3	255	11/12/76	2	Syracuse	Andover, Mass.	D2b-'99	15/9
29		Madison, Sam	CB	5-11	185	4/23/74	4	Louisville	Monticello, Fla.	D2-'97	16/16
10	†	Mare, Olindo	K	5-10	190	6/6/73	4	Syracuse	Cooper City, Fla.	FA-'97	16/0
31		Marion, Brock	S	5-11	205	6/11/70	8	Nevada	Bakersfield, Calif.	UFA(Dall)-'98	16/16
80		Martin, Tony	WR	6-1	175	9/5/65	11	Mesa College	Miami, Fla.	FA-'99	16/13
81		McDuffie, O.J.	WR	5-10	194	12/2/69	8	Penn State	Gate Mills, Ohio	D1-'93	12/10
79		Mixon, Kenny	DE	6-4	282	5/31/75	3	Louisiana State	Pineville, La.	D2b-'98	11/2
96		Owens, Rich	DE	6-6	275	5/22/72	6	Lehigh	Philadelphia, Pa.	UFA(Wash)-'99	16/14
89	†	Perry, Ed	TE	6-4	265	9/1/74	4	James Madison	Richmond, Va.	D6d-'97	16/1
59	†	Rodgers, Derrick	LB	6-1	230	10/14/71	4	Arizona State	New Orleans, La.	D3b-'97	16/15
61		Ruddy, Tim	C	6-3	300	4/27/72	7	Notre Dame	Dunmore, Pa.	D2b-'94	16/16
62		Ruegamer, Grey	C	6-5	310	6/1/76	2	Arizona State	Las Vegas, Nev.	D3-'99	0*
56		Russell, Twan	LB	6-1	220	4/25/74	4	Miami	Ft. Lauderdale, Fla.	FA-'00	9/0*
68		Sheldon, Mike	T	6-4	305	6/8/73	4	Grand Valley State	Villa Park, Ill.	FA-'97	9/0
98		Simpson, Antoine	DT	6-2	310	12/7/76	2	Houston	LaPorte, Tex.	FA-'99	4/0
74	†	Smith, Brent	T	6-5	315	11/21/73	4	Mississippi State	Pontotoc, Miss.	D3d-'97	13/4
26		Smith, Lamar	RB	5-11	225	11/29/70	7	Houston	Ft. Wayne, Ind.	FA-'00	13/2*
23		Surtain, Patrick	CB	5-11	190	6/19/76	3	Southern Mississippi	New Orleans, La.	D2a-'98	16/6
99	†	Taylor, Jason	DE	6-6	260	9/1/74	4	Akron	Woodland Hills, Pa.	D3a-'97	15/15
85		Thomas, Lamar	WR	6-1	170	2/12/70	8	Miami	Gainesville, Fla.	FA-'96	0*
34		Thomas, Thurman	RB	5-10	200	5/16/66	13	Oklahoma State	Missouri City, Tex.	FA-'00	5/3*
54		Thomas, Zach	LB	5-11	235	9/1/73	5	Texas Tech	Pampa, Tex.	D5c-'96	16/16
1	t-	Turk, Matt	P	6-5	235	6/16/68	6	Wisconsin-Whitewater	Greenfield, Wis.	T(Wash)-'00	14/0*
45		Walker, Brian	S	6-1	200	5/31/72	5	Washington State	Colorado Springs, Colo.	UFA(Sea)-'00	5/0*
78		Webb, Richmond	T	6-6	315	1/11/67	11	Texas A&M	Dallas, Tex.	D1-'90	15/14
24		Wilson, Jerry	CB	5-10	187	7/17/73	6	Southern	Lake Charles, La.	FA-'96	16/1
71		Wong, Joe	T	6-6	315	2/24/76	2	Brigham Young	Honolulu, Hawaii	D7b-'99	0*

* Baker, Doxzon, L. Thomas, and Wong missed '99 season because of injury; Druckenmiller was inactive for 14 games in '99; Fiedler played 7 games with Jacksonville; Galyon played 16 games with N.Y. Giants; Irwin played 15 games with New England; W. Jones was inactive for 16 games with St. Louis; Ruegamer was inactive for 15 games; Russell played 9 games with Washington; L. Smith played 13 games with New Orleans; T. Thomas played 5 games with Buffalo; Turk played 14 games with Washington; Walker played 5 games with Seattle.

† Restricted free agent; subject to developments.

Unrestricted free agent; subject to developments.

Retired—Dan Marino, 17-year quarterback, 11 games in '99.

t- Dolphins traded for Turk (Washington).

Players lost through free agency (2): RB Stanley Pritchett (Phil; 14 games in '99), S Shawn Wooden (Chi; 15).

Also played with the Dolphins in '99—RB Karim Abdul-Jabbar (3 games), RB John Avery (1), RB Kantroy Barber (2), RB Cecil Collins (8), TE Troy Drayton (14), G Kevin Gogan (16), LB Anthony Harris (5), P Tom Hutton (14), WR Kevin McKenzie (1), WR Roell Preston (1), WR Larry Shannon (2), QB Scott Zolak (1).

COACHING STAFF

Head Coach,
Dave Wannstedt

Pro Career: Was named the fourth head coach in Miami history on January 16, 2000. Begins his seventh season as an NFL head coach and his first with the Dolphins. Led the Chicago Bears to a regular-season record of 40-56 and a playoff mark of 1-1 in six seasons (1993-98) as head coach. Served as the Dolphins' assistant head coach in 1999. Began his NFL coaching career as linebackers coach with the Dolphins in 1989. Spent seven weeks in that post during the offseason before joining Jimmy Johnson in Dallas as the Cowboys' defensive coordinator prior to the 1989 season, and kept that spot through 1992. In Dallas, Wannstedt took over a defense that had ranked twentieth in the NFL the year prior to his arrival. By 1992, the Cowboys led the league in total defense as they went on to capture the first of two straight Super Bowl titles. Wannstedt took over the head coaching position with the Bears in 1993, and in his second year, he led Chicago to a 9-7 record and the team's first playoff win since the 1990 season as they advanced to the divisional round. In that 1994 playoff victory, the Bears defeated the NFC Central Division champion Minnesota Vikings at the Metrodome, the first road playoff win by Chicago since 1984. Wannstedt was named NFC coach of the year following the 1994 season. Career record: 41-57.
Background: Wannstedt began his coaching career in 1975 as defensive line coach at the University of Pittsburgh. He then served as defensive line coach at Oklahoma State for the 1979-1980 seasons before being promoted to defensive coordinator in 1981, a spot he held for two seasons. He moved on to Southern California in 1983 and was the Trojans' defensive line coach for the next three years. In 1986, Wannstedt took over as defensive coordinator at the University of Miami. In his three seasons in that post (1986-88), the Hurricanes' defense held opponents to a 2.2-yard average per carry, yielded an average of 10.9 points per game, and averaged 48 sacks a season. At Miami, Wannstedt's defenses produced 11 players who were drafted by the NFL, including five in the first two rounds. Wannstedt lettered three seasons (1971-73) as an offensive lineman at the University of Pittsburgh and was the team captain his senior season in 1973 on a club that featured future Heisman Trophy winning running back Tony Dorsett, then a freshman at Pitt. Following his collegiate career, Wannstedt was selected by Green Bay in the fifteenth round of the 1974 NFL draft. He spent the 1974 season on the Packers' injured reserve list with a neck injury.
Personal: Wannstedt was born in Pittsburgh, on May 21, 1952. He attended Baldwin High School in Pittsburgh. He and his wife, Jan, have two daughters, Keri and Jami.

ASSISTANT COACHES

Jim Bates, defensive coordinator; born May 31, 1946, Pontiac, Mich., lives in Miami. Linebacker Tennessee 1964-67. No pro playing experience. College coach: Tennessee 1968, Southern Mississippi 1972, Villanova 1973-74, Kansas State 1975-76, West Virginia 1977, Texas Tech 1978-1983, Tennessee 1989, Florida 1990. Pro coach: San Antonio Gunslingers (USFL) 1984-85 (head coach 1985), Arizona Outlaws (USFL) 1986, Detroit Drive (AFL) 1988, Cleveland Browns 1991-93, 1995, Atlanta Falcons 1994, Dallas Cowboys 1996-99, joined Dolphins in 2000.
Doug Blevins, kicking; born August 3, 1963, Abingdon, Va., lives in Vero Beach, Fla. No college or pro playing experience. College coach: Tennessee 1982-83, Emory & Henry College 1984-85, East Tennessee State 1986-87. Pro coach: World League kicking coordinator 1995-97, joined Dolphins in 1997.
Paul Boudreau, offensive line; born December 30, 1949, Arlington, Mass., lives in Miami. Offensive lineman Boston College 1971-73. No pro playing experience. College coach: Boston College 1974-75, Maine 1976-78, Dartmouth 1979-1981, Navy 1982. Pro coach: Edmonton Eskimos (CFL) 1983-86, New Orleans Saints 1987-1993, Detroit Lions 1994-96, New England Patriots 1997-98, joined Dolphins in 1999.
Clarence Brooks, defensive line; born May 20, 1951, New York, N.Y., lives in Miami. Guard Massachusetts 1970-73. No pro playing experience. College coach: Massachusetts 1976-1980, Syracuse 1981-89, Arizona 1990-92. Pro coach: Chicago Bears 1993-98, Cleveland Browns 1999, joined Dolphins in 2000.
Joel Collier, running backs; born December 25, 1963, Buffalo, lives in Plantation, Fla. Linebacker Northern Colorado 1984-87. No pro playing experience. College coach: Syracuse 1988-89. Pro coach: Tampa Bay Buccaneers 1990, New England Patriots 1991-93, joined Dolphins in 1994.
Robert Ford, wide receivers; born June 21, 1951, Belton, Texas, lives in Pembroke Pines, Fla. Wide receiver Houston 1970-72. No pro playing experience. College coach: Western Illinois 1974-76, New Mexico 1977-79, Oregon State 1980-1981, Mississippi State 1982-83, Kansas 1986, Texas Tech 1987-88, Texas A&M 1989-1990. Pro coach: Houston Gamblers (USFL) 1985, Dallas Cowboys 1991-97, joined Dolphins in 1998.
Chan Gailey, offensive coordinator; born January 5, 1952, Gainesville, Ga., lives in Miami. Quarterback Florida 1970-73. No pro playing experience. College coach: Florida 1974-75, Troy State 1976-78, 1983-84 (head coach), Air Force Academy 1979-1982, Samford 1993 (head coach). Pro coach: Denver Broncos 1985-1990, Birmingham Fire (World League) 1991-92 (head coach), Pittsburgh Steelers 1994-97, Dallas Cowboys 1998-99 (head coach), joined Dolphins in 2000.
Judd Garrett, offensive assistant; born June 25, 1967, Abington, Pa., lives in Miami. Running back Princeton 1987-89. Pro running back London Monarchs (WLAF) 1991-92, Dallas Cowboys 1993, Las Vegas Posse (CFL) 1994, San Antonio Texans (CFL) 1995. College coach: Princeton 1990. Pro coach: New Orleans Saints 1997-99, joined Dolphins in 2000.
John Gamble, strength and conditioning; born June 26, 1957, Richmond, Va., lives in Weston, Fla. Linebacker Hampton Institute 1975-78. No pro playing experience. College coach: Virginia 1982-1993. Pro coach: Joined Dolphins in 1994.
Pat Jones, tight ends; born November 4, 1947, Memphis, Tenn., lives in Ft. Lauderdale, Fla. Nose guard Arkansas Tech 1965, linebacker-nose guard Arkansas 1966-67. No pro playing experience. College coach: Arkansas 1974-75, Southern Methodist 1976-77, Pittsburgh 1978, Oklahoma State 1979-1994 (head coach 1984-1994). Pro coach: Joined Dolphins in 1996.
Bill Lewis, defensive nickel package; born August 5, 1941, Bristol, Pa., lives in Ft. Lauderdale, Fla. Quarterback East Stroudsburg State 1959-1962. No pro playing experience. College coach: East Stroudsburg State 1963-65, Pittsburgh 1966-68, Wake Forest 1969-1970, Georgia Tech 1971-72, 1992-94 (head coach), Arkansas 1973-76, Wyoming 1977-79, Georgia 1980-88, East Carolina 1989-1991 (head coach). Pro coach: Joined Dolphins in 1996.
Robert Nunn, defensive assistant; born June 10, 1965, Apache, Okla., lives in Miami. Linebacker Oklahoma State 1983-84 and 1986-87. No pro playing experience. College coach: Northeastern Oklahoma 1988, Tennessee 1989-1990, Georgia Military College 1991-99 (head coach 1992-99). Pro coach: Joined Dolphins in 2000.
Mel Phillips, secondary; born January 6, 1942, Shelby, N.C., lives in Miami Lakes, Fla. Defensive back-running back North Carolina A&T 1964-65. Pro defensive back San Francisco 49ers 1966-1977. Pro coach: Detroit Lions 1980-84, joined Dolphins in 1985.
Brad Roll, asst. strength and conditioning; born July 4, 1958, Houston, lives in Ft. Lauderdale, Fla. Center Blinn (Tex.) J.C. 1976-77, Stephen F. Austin 1978-79. No pro playing experience. College coach: Stephen F. Austin 1980, Southwestern Louisiana 1981-86, Kansas 1987-88, Miami 1989-1992. Pro coach: Tampa Bay Buccaneers 1993-95, joined Dolphins in 1996.
Randy Shannon, linebackers; born February 24, 1966, Miami, lives in Miami. Linebacker Miami 1985-88. Pro linebacker Dallas Cowboys 1989-1990. College coach: Miami 1991-97. Pro coach: Joined Dolphins in 1998.
Mike Shula, quarterbacks; born June 3, 1965, Baltimore, lives in Miami. Quarterback Alabama 1983-86. No pro playing experience. Pro coach: Tampa Bay Buccaneers 1988-1990, 1996-99, Miami Dolphins 1991-92, Chicago Bears 1993-95, rejoined Dolphins in 2000.
Mike Westhoff, special teams; born January 10, 1948, Pittsburgh, lives in Plantation, Fla. Center-linebacker Wichita State 1967-69. No pro playing experience. College coach: Indiana 1974-75, Dayton 1976, Indiana State 1977, Northwestern 1978-1980, Texas Christian 1981. Pro coach: Baltimore/Indianapolis Colts 1982-84, Arizona Outlaws (USFL) 1985, joined Dolphins in 1986.

2000 FIRST-YEAR ROSTER

Name	Pos.	Ht.	Wt.	Birthdate	College	Hometown	How Acq.
Adams, Ben (1)	G	6-5	315	12/27/75	Texas	La Mirada, Calif.	FA-'99
Alexander, Curtis (1)	RB	6-0	205	6/11/74	Alabama	Memphis, Tenn.	FA-'99
Connor, Rameel	DE	6-3	276	6/26/77	Illinois	Oak Park, Ill.	FA
Dyer, Deon	RB	5-11	264	10/2/77	North Carolina	Tidewater, Va.	D4
Edwards, Brian (1)	RB	6-1	220	6/6/76	East Tennessee State	Ocala, Fla.	FA-'99
Freeman, Arturo	S	6-0	196	10/27/76	South Carolina	Orangeburg, S.C.	D5
Gamble, Trent	CB	5-9	186	7/24/77	Wyoming	Parker, Colo.	FA
Grant, Ernest	DT	6-5	297	5/17/76	Arkansas-Pine Bluff	Atlanta, Ga.	D6
Gregory, Damian	DT	6-2	305	1/21/77	Illinois State	Lansing, Mich.	FA
Haley, Jermaine (1)	DT	6-4	270	2/23/73	Butte College	Fresno, Calif.	D7a-'99
Hamler, Tony	WR	6-0	187	8/13/75	Morehouse College	Miami, Fla.	FA
Hanson, Chris	P	6-1	214	10/25/76	Marshall	East Coweta, Ga.	FA
Harris, Jeff	CB	5-11	178	7/19/77	Georgia	Jacksonville, Fla.	D7
Hendricks, Tommy	LB	6-2	223	10/23/78	Michigan	Houston, Tex.	FA
Herndon, Steve	G	6-4	297	5/25/77	Georgia	LaGrange, Ga.	FA
Kelly, Ben	CB	5-10	191	9/15/78	Colorado	Cleveland, Ohio	D3
Leatherwood, Frank (1)	RB	6-2	260	8/15/77	Appalachian State	Clyde, N.C.	FA-'99
McKenzie, Kevin (1)	WR	5-9	187	9/20/75	Washington State	Long Beach, Calif.	FA-'99
Nuno, Carlos	TE	6-4	263	10/2/75	Brigham Young	Modesto, Calif.	FA
O'Donnell, Rich	TE	6-6	245	8/4/76	Weber State	Oroville, Calif.	FA
Ogunleye, Adewale	DE	6-4	253	8/9/77	Indiana	Staten Island, N.Y.	FA
Pope, O'Lester (1)	G	6-5	340	8/24/75	Southern Mississippi	Utica, Miss.	FA-'99
Shipley, Kyle	LB	6-1	234	11/19/76	Texas Tech	Arlington, Tex.	FA
Sigler, Kelvin	S	6-0	187	6/20/76	Alabama	Mobile, Ala.	FA
Snedegar, Jeff	LB	6-2	233	6/11/77	Kentucky	Salesville, Ohio	FA
Spotwood, Quinton	WR	5-11	184	12/13/77	Syracuse	Elizabeth, N.J.	FA
Steinauer, Orlondo	S	5-10	180	6/9/73	Western Washington	Seattle, Wash.	FA
Sylvester, Peter	RB	5-10	250	11/6/76	Drake	Chicago, Ill.	FA
Taylor, Jay	K	6-1	183	10/23/76	West Virginia	Hershey, Pa.	FA
Thomas, Corey	WR	5-11	169	6/6/75	Duke	Beddingfield, N.C.	FA
Wade, Todd	T	6-8	319	10/30/76	Mississippi	Jackson, Miss.	D2
Zimmerman, Scott	LB	6-0	237	4/29/77	Northern Colorado	Westminster, Colo.	FA

The term NFL Rookie is defined as a player who is in his first season of professional football and has not been on the roster of another professional football team for any regular-season or postseason games. A Rookie is designated by an "R" on NFL rosters. Players who have been active in another professional football league or players who have NFL experience, including either preseason training camp or being on an Active List or Inactive List, or on Reserve/Injured or Reserve/Physically Unable to Perform for fewer than six regular-season games, are termed NFL First-Year Players. An NFL First-Year Player is designated by a "1" on NFL rosters. Thereafter, a player is credited with an additional year of experience for each season in which he accumulates six games on the Active List or Inactive List, or on Reserve/Injured or Reserve/Physically Unable to Perform.

NEW ENGLAND PATRIOTS

American Football Conference
Eastern Division
Team Colors: Blue, Red, Silver, and White
Foxboro Stadium
60 Washington Street
Foxboro, Massachusetts 02035
Telephone: (508) 543-8200

CLUB OFFICIALS

Owner/Chief Executive Officer: Robert K. Kraft
Executive Vice President-Owner's Representative: Jonathan A. Kraft
Senior Vice President & Chief Operating Officer: Andrew Wasynczuk
Vice President of Corporate Marketing and Broadcast Sales: Daniel A. Kraft
Vice President-Finance: James Hausmann
Vice President of Player Development and Community Affairs: Donald Lowery
Vice President of Marketing & Special Events: Lou Imbriano
Assistant Director of Player Personnel: Scott Pioli
Director of Football Operations: Ken Deininger
Director of Media Relations: Stacey James
Controller: Jim Nolan
Director of Ticketing: Mike Nichols
General Manager of Foxboro Stadium: Dan Murphy
Building Services Manager: Bernie Reinhart
Head Trainer: Ron O'Neil
Equipment Manager: Don Brocher
Video Director: Jimmy Dee
Stadium: Foxboro Stadium • **Capacity:** 60,292
60 Washington Street
Foxboro, Massachusetts 02035
Playing Surface: Grass
Training Camp: Bryant College
Route 7
Smithfield, Rhode Island 02917

2000 SCHEDULE

PRESEASON

July 31	vs. San Francisco at Canton, Ohio	8:00
Aug. 4	at Detroit	7:00
Aug. 11	at Washington	8:00
Aug. 20	**Tampa Bay**	4:00
Aug. 24	**Carolina**	8:00

REGULAR SEASON

Sept. 3	**Tampa Bay**	1:00
Sept. 11	at New York Jets (Mon.)	9:00
Sept. 17	**Minnesota**	4:15
Sept. 24	at Miami	1:00
Oct. 1	at Denver	2:05
Oct. 8	**Indianapolis**	1:00
Oct. 15	**New York Jets**	4:05
Oct. 22	at Indianapolis	12:00
Oct. 29	Open Date	
Nov. 5	**Buffalo**	1:00
Nov. 12	at Cleveland	1:00
Nov. 19	**Cincinnati**	1:00
Nov. 23	at Detroit (Thu.)	12:30
Dec. 4	**Kansas City** (Mon.)	9:00
Dec. 10	at Chicago	12:00
Dec. 17	at Buffalo	1:00
Dec. 24	**Miami**	1:00

RECORD HOLDERS

INDIVIDUAL RECORDS—CAREER

Category	Name	Performance
Rushing (Yds.)	Sam Cunningham, 1973-79, 1981-82	5,453
Passing (Yds.)	Steve Grogan, 1975-1990	26,886
Passing (TDs)	Steve Grogan, 1975-1990	182
Receiving (No.)	Stanley Morgan, 1977-1989	534
Receiving (Yds.)	Stanley Morgan, 1977-1989	10,352
Interceptions	Raymond Clayborn, 1977-1989	36
Punting (Avg.)	Tom Tupa, 1996-97	44.7
Punt Return (Avg.)	Mack Herron, 1973-75	12.0
Kickoff Return (Avg.)	Allen Carter, 1975-76	27.2
Field Goals	Gino Cappelletti, 1960-1970	176
Touchdowns (Tot.)	Stanley Morgan, 1977-1989	68
Points	Gino Cappelletti, 1960-1970	1,130

INDIVIDUAL RECORDS—SINGLE SEASON

Category	Name	Performance
Rushing (Yds.)	Curtis Martin, 1995	1,487
Passing (Yds.)	Drew Bledsoe, 1994	4,555
Passing (TDs)	Vito (Babe) Parilli, 1964	31
Receiving (No.)	Ben Coates, 1994	96
Receiving (Yds.)	Stanley Morgan, 1986	1,491
Interceptions	Ron Hall, 1964	11
Punting (Avg.)	Tom Tupa, 1997	45.8
Punt Return (Avg.)	Mack Herron, 1974	14.8
Kickoff Return (Avg.)	Raymond Clayborn, 1977	31.0
Field Goals	Tony Franklin, 1986	32
Touchdowns (Tot.)	Curtis Martin, 1996	17
Points	Gino Cappelletti, 1964	155

INDIVIDUAL RECORDS—SINGLE GAME

Category	Name	Performance
Rushing (Yds.)	Tony Collins, 9-18-83	212
Passing (Yds.)	Drew Bledsoe, 11-13-94	426
Passing (TDs)	Vito (Babe) Parilli, 11-15-64	5
	Vito (Babe) Parilli, 10-15-67	5
	Steve Grogan, 9-9-79	5
Receiving (No.)	Terry Glenn, 10-3-99	13
Receiving (Yds.)	Terry Glenn, 10-3-99	214
Interceptions	Many times	3
	Last time by Roland James, 10-23-83	
Field Goals	Gino Cappelletti, 10-4-64	6
Touchdowns (Tot.)	Many times	3
	Last time by Curtis Martin, 11-3-96	
Points	Gino Cappelletti, 12-18-65	28

COACHING HISTORY

BOSTON 1960-1970
(282-322-9)

1960-61	Lou Saban*	7-12-0
1961-68	Mike Holovak	53-47-9
1969-70	Clive Rush**	5-16-0
1970-72	John Mazur***	9-21-0
1972	Phil Bengtson	1-4-0
1973-78	Chuck Fairbanks****	46-41-0
1978	Hank Bullough-Ron Erhardt#	0-1-0
1979-81	Ron Erhardt	21-27-0
1982-84	Ron Meyer##	18-16-0
1984-89	Raymond Berry	51-41-0
1990	Rod Rust	1-15-0
1991-92	Dick MacPherson	8-24-0
1993-96	Bill Parcells	34-34-0
1997-99	Pete Carroll	28-23-0

*Released after five games in 1961
**Released after seven games in 1970
***Resigned after nine games in 1972
****Suspended for final regular-season game in 1978
#Co-coaches
##Released after eight games in 1984

FOXBORO STADIUM

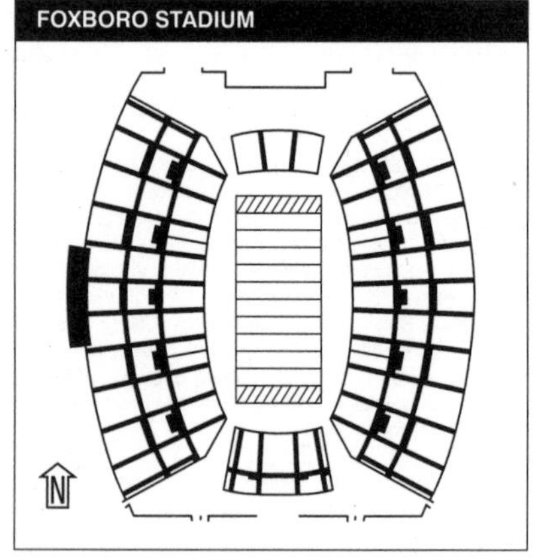

1999 TEAM RECORD

PRESEASON (1-3)

Date	Result		Opponent
8/13	L	14-20	Washington
8/21	W	34-14	Dallas
8/28	L	14-45	at Tampa Bay
9/2	L	20-23	at Carolina

REGULAR SEASON (8-8)

Date	Result		Opponent	Att.
9/12	W	30-28	at New York Jets	78,227
9/19	W	31-28	Indianapolis	59,640
9/26	W	16-14	New York Giants	59,169
10/3	W	19-7	at Cleveland	72,368
10/10	L	14-16	at Kansas City	78,636
10/17	L	30-31	Miami	60,006
10/24	W	24-23	Denver	60,011
10/31	W	27-3	at Arizona	55,830
11/15	L	17-24	New York Jets	59,077
11/21	L	17-27	at Miami	74,295
11/28	L	7-17	at Buffalo	72,111
12/5	W	13-6	Dallas	58,444
12/12	L	15-20	at Indianapolis	56,975
12/19	L	9-24	at Philadelphia	65,475
12/26	L	10-13	Buffalo (OT)	55,014
1/2	W	20-3	Baltimore	50,263

(OT) Overtime

SCORE BY PERIODS

Patriots	61	84	67	87	0	—	299
Opponents	70	101	56	54	3	—	284

ATTENDANCE

Home 479,056 Away 546,937 Total 1,025,993
Single-game home record, 61,457 (12/5/71)
Single-season home record, 482,572 (1986)

1999 TEAM STATISTICS

	Patriots	Opp.
Total First Downs	280	281
Rushing	72	106
Passing	184	154
Penalty	24	21
Third Down: Made/Att	79/223	81/231
Third Down Pct.	35.4	35.1
Fourth Down: Made/Att	4/13	5/18
Fourth Down Pct.	30.8	27.8
Total Net Yards	5,062	4,808
Avg. Per Game	316.4	300.5
Total Plays	1,021	1,048
Avg. Per Play	5.0	4.6
Net Yards Rushing	1,426	1,795
Avg. Per Game	89.1	112.2
Total Rushes	425	486
Net Yards Passing	3,636	3,013
Avg. Per Game	227.3	188.3
Sacked/Yards Lost	56/349	42/268
Gross Yards	3,985	3,281
Att./Completions	540/305	520/293
Completion Pct.	56.5	56.3
Had Intercepted	21	16
Punts/Average	90/41.5	95/41.2
Net Punting Avg.	90/34.6	95/33.7
Penalties/Yards	95/812	102/775
Fumbles/Ball Lost	27/12	29/15
Touchdowns	32	30
Rushing	9	6
Passing	19	23
Returns	4	1
Avg. Time of Possession	28:49	31:11

1999 INDIVIDUAL STATISTICS

Passing	Att.	Comp.	Yds.	Pct.	TD	Int.	Tkld.	Rate
Bledsoe	539	305	3,985	56.6	19	21	55/342	75.6
Brown	1	0	0	0.0	0	0	0/0	39.6
Warren	0	0	0	—	0	0	1/7	—
Patriots	540	305	3,985	56.5	19	21	56/349	75.4
Opponents	520	293	3,281	56.3	23	16	42/268	77.3

SCORING	TD R	TD P	TD Rt	PAT	FG	Saf	PTS
Vinatieri	0	0	0	29/30	26/33	0	107
Allen	8	1	0	0/0	0/0	0	54
Jefferson	0	6	0	0/0	0/0	0	36
Glenn	0	4	0	0/0	0/0	0	24
Coates	0	2	0	0/0	0/0	0	12
Faulk	1	1	0	0/0	0/0	0	12
Simmons	0	2	0	0/0	0/0	0	12
Bartrum	0	1	0	0/0	0/0	0	6
Brown	0	1	0	0/0	0/0	0	6
Eaton	0	0	1	0/0	0/0	0	6
Katzenmoyer	0	0	1	0/0	0/0	0	6
Law	0	0	1	0/0	0/0	0	6
McGinest	0	0	1	0/0	0/0	0	6
Warren	0	1	0	0/0	0/0	0	6
Patriots	9	19	4	29/30	26/33	0	299
Opponents	6	23	1	27/27	25/30	1	284

2-Pt. Conversions: None.
Team 0-2, Opponents 0-3.

RUSHING	Att.	Yds.	Avg.	LG	TD
Allen	254	896	3.5	39	8
Faulk	67	227	3.4	43	1
Warren	35	120	3.4	18	0
Bledsoe	42	101	2.4	25	0
T. Carter	6	26	4.3	9	0
Shaw	9	23	2.6	12	0
L. Johnson	2	13	6.5	13	0
Floyd	6	12	2.0	6	0
Ellison	2	10	5.0	8	0
Friesz	2	-2	-1.0	-1	0
Patriots	425	1,426	3.4	43	9
Opponents	486	1,795	3.7	60	6

RECEIVING	No.	Yds.	Avg.	LG	TD
Glenn	69	1,147	16.6	67	4
Jefferson	40	698	17.5	68t	6
Brown	36	471	13.1	37	1
Coates	32	370	11.6	27	2
Warren	29	262	9.0	21	1
T. Carter	20	108	5.4	20	0
Simmons	19	276	14.5	58t	2
Brisby	18	266	14.8	40	0
Allen	14	125	8.9	38	1
Faulk	12	98	8.2	19	1
Rutledge	7	66	9.4	13	0
Ellison	4	50	12.5	23	0
Shaw	2	31	15.5	29	0
Floyd	2	16	8.0	11	0
Bartrum	1	1	1.0	1t	1
Patriots	305	3,985	13.1	68t	19
Opponents	293	3,281	11.2	69t	23

INTERCEPTIONS	No.	Yds.	Avg.	LG	TD
Milloy	4	17	4.3	17	0
C. Carter	3	13	4.3	8	0
Serwanga	3	2	0.7	2	0
Law	2	20	10.0	27t	1
Katzenmoyer	1	57	57.0	57t	1
Bruschi	1	1	1.0	1	0
Israel	1	0	0.0	0	0
Slade	1	0	0.0	0	0
Patriots	16	110	6.9	57t	2
Opponents	21	299	14.2	84	1

PUNTING	No.	Yds.	Avg.	In 20	LG
L. Johnson	90	3,735	41.5	23	58
Patriots	90	3,735	41.5	23	58
Opponents	95	3,914	41.2	20	65

PUNT RETURNS	No.	FC	Yds.	Avg.	LG	TD
Brown	38	13	405	10.7	52	0
Faulk	10	4	90	9.0	20	0
Patriots	48	17	495	10.3	52	0
Opponents	36	20	345	9.6	45	0

KICKOFF RETURNS	No.	Yds.	Avg.	LG	TD
Faulk	39	943	24.2	95	0
Brown	8	271	33.9	54	0
Simmons	6	132	22.0	29	0
Jones	5	113	22.6	28	0
Warren	2	25	12.5	16	0
Ellison	1	13	13.0	13	0
Sullivan	1	1	1.0	1	0
Patriots	62	1,498	24.2	95	0
Opponents	64	1,441	22.5	58	0

FIELD GOALS	1-19	20-29	30-39	40-49	50+
Vinatieri	1/1	14/14	5/7	5/9	1/2
Patriots	1/1	14/14	5/7	5/9	1/2
Opponents	2/2	11/11	5/6	6/8	1/3

SACKS	No.
McGinest	9.0
Slade	4.5
Katzenmoyer	3.5
Eaton	3.0
Mitchell	3.0
Thomas	3.0
Whigham	3.0
Bruschi	2.0
Collons	2.0
T. Johnson	2.0
Milloy	2.0
C. Carter	1.0
Israel	1.0
Serwanga	1.0
Sullivan	1.0
Law	0.5
Spires	0.5
Patriots	42.0
Opponents	56.0

2000 DRAFT CHOICES

Round	Name	Pos.	College
2	Adrian Klemm	T	Hawaii
3	J.R. Redmond	RB	Arizona State
4	Greg Robinson-Randall	T	Michigan State
5	Dave Stachelski	TE	Boise State
	Jeff Marriott	DT	Missouri
6	Antwan Harris	DB	Virginia
	Tom Brady	QB	Michigan
	David Nugent	DT	Purdue
7	Casey Tisdale	DE	New Mexico
	Patrick Pass	RB	Georgia

NEW ENGLAND PATRIOTS

2000 VETERAN ROSTER

No.	Name	Pos.	Ht.	Wt.	Birthdate	NFL Exp.	College	Hometown	How Acq.	'99 Games/ Starts
67	Andersen, Jason	C	6-6	295	9/3/75	3	Brigham Young	San Jose, Calif.	D7-'98	9/1
18	Bailey, Aaron	WR	5-10	185	10/24/71	6	Louisville	Ann Arbor, Mich.	FA-'00	0*
7	Bishop, Michael	QB	6-2	217	5/15/76	2	Kansas State	Willis, Tex.	D7a-'99	0*
86	Bjornson, Eric	TE	6-4	236	12/15/71	6	Washington	Oakland, Calif.	UFA(Dall)-'00	16/6*
11	Bledsoe, Drew	QB	6-5	233	2/14/72	8	Washington State	Walla Walla, Wash.	D1-'93	16/16
82	Brisby, Vincent	WR	6-3	193	1/25/71	8	Northeast Louisiana	Houston, Tex.	D2c-'93	12/1
80	Brown, Troy	WR	5-10	190	7/2/71	8	Marshall	Blackville, S.C.	D8-'93	13/1
54	Bruschi, Tedy	LB	6-1	245	6/9/73	5	Arizona	Roseville, Calif.	D3-'96	14/14
42	Carter, Chris	S	6-2	209	9/27/74	4	Texas	Tyler, Tex.	D3b-'97	15/15
30	Carter, Tony	RB	6-1	232	8/23/72	7	Minnesota	Columbus, Ohio	UFA(Chi)-'98	16/14
90	Eaton, Chad	DT	6-5	300	4/6/72	4	Washington State	Puyallup, Wash.	FA-'97	16/16
47	Edwards, Robert	RB	5-11	218	10/2/74	2	Georgia	Tennille, Ga.	D1a-'98	0*
66	Ellis, Ed	T	6-7	330	10/13/75	4	Buffalo	Hamden, Conn.	D4b-'97	1/1
33	Faulk, Kevin	RB	5-8	197	6/15/76	2	Louisiana State	Carencro, La.	D2-'99	11/2
64	Fletcher, Derrick	G-T	6-6	348	9/9/75	2	Baylor	Aldine, Tex.	D5-'99	0*
37	Floyd, Chris	RB	6-2	235	6/23/75	3	Michigan	Detroit, Mich.	D3a-'98	13/0
17	Friesz, John	QB	6-4	223	6/19/67	11	Idaho	Missoula, Mont.	UFA(Sea)-'99	1/1
	Gaiter, Tony	WR-KR	5-8	170	7/15/74	2	Miami	Miami, Fla.	FA-'00	0*
41	George, Tony	S	5-11	200	8/10/75	2	Florida	Cincinnati, Ohio	D3-'99	16/1
88	Glenn, Terry	WR	5-11	185	7/23/74	5	Ohio State	Columbus, Ohio	D1-'96	14/13
91	Harris, Jon	DE	6-7	300	6/9/74	3	Virginia	Inward, N.Y.	FA-'00	0*
28	Harris, Raymont	RB	6-1	230	12/23/70	6	Ohio State	Lorain, Ohio	FA-'00	0*
10	Johnson, Lee	P	6-2	200	11/27/61	16	Brigham Young	Conroe, Tex.	FA-'99	16/0
52	Johnson, Ted	LB	6-4	250	12/4/72	6	Colorado	Alameda, Calif.	D2-'95	5/5
34	Jones, Tebucky	CB	6-2	219	10/6/74	3	Syracuse	New Britain, Conn.	D1b-'98	11/2
59	Katzenmoyer, Andy	LB	6-3	255	12/2/77	2	Ohio State	Westerville, Ohio	D1b-'99	16/11
68	Lane, Max	G	6-6	320	2/22/71	7	Navy	Norborne, Mo.	D6b-'94	16/6
24	Law, Ty	CB	5-11	200	2/10/74	6	Michigan	Aliquippa, Pa.	D1-'95	13/13
55	McGinest, Willie	DE	6-5	265	12/11/71	7	Southern California	Long Beach, Calif.	D1-'94	16/16
36	Milloy, Lawyer	S	6-1	208	11/14/73	5	Washington	Tacoma, Wash.	D2-'96	16/16
98	Mitchell, Brandon	DT	6-3	289	6/19/75	4	Texas A&M	Abbeville, La.	D2-'97	16/16
71	Rucci, Todd	G	6-5	296	7/14/70	8	Penn State	Upper Darby, Pa.	D2b-'93	16/15
83	Rutledge, Rod	TE	6-5	262	8/12/75	3	Alabama	Birmingham, Ala.	D2b-'98	16/2
63	Scott, Lance	C-G	6-3	295	2/15/72	6	Utah	Salt Lake City, Utah	UFA(NYG)-'00	0*
31	Serwanga, Kato	CB	6-1	198	7/23/76	2	California	Sacramento, Calif.	FA-'98	16/3
44	Shaw, Harold	RB	6-1	228	9/3/74	3	Southern Mississippi	Magee, Miss.	D6-'98	8/1
81	Simmons, Tony	WR	6-1	206	12/8/74	3	Wisconsin	Chicago, Ill.	D2a-'98	15/1
53	Slade, Chris	LB	6-5	245	1/30/71	8	Virginia	Newport News, Va.	D2a-'93	16/16
94	Spires, Greg	DE	6-1	265	8/12/74	3	Florida State	Cape Coral, Fla.	D3b-'98	11/1
95	Thomas, Henry	DT	6-2	277	1/12/65	14	Louisiana State	Houston, Tex.	FA-'97	16/16
4	Vinatieri, Adam	K	6-1	200	12/28/72	5	South Dakota State	Rapid City, S.D.	FA-'96	16/0
25	Whigham, Larry	S	6-2	205	6/23/72	7	Northeast Louisiana	Hattiesburg, Miss.	FA-'94	16/0
76	Williams, Grant	T	6-7	323	5/10/74	5	Louisiana Tech	Clinton, Miss.	UFA(Sea)-'00	16/15*
65	Woody, Damien	C	6-3	319	11/3/77	2	Boston College	Beaverdam, Va.	D1a-'99	16/16

* Bailey last active with Indianapolis in '98; Bishop and Fletcher were inactive for 15 games in '99; Bjornson played 16 games with Dallas in '99; Edwards and Scott (with N.Y. Giants) missed '99 season because of injury; Gaiter last active with San Diego in '98; J. Harris last active with Philadelphia in '98; R. Harris last active with Green Bay in '98; Williams played 16 games with Seattle in '99.

Players lost to free agency (8): RB Jerry Ellison (TB; 12 games); G Heath Irwin (Mia; 15), CB Steve Israel (NO; 13), WR Shawn Jefferson (Atl; 16), LB Jeff Kopp (Sea; 6), DT Bob Kuberski (Den; 5); LB Marty Moore (Cle; 15), DE-DT Chris Sullivan (Pitt; 16).

Also played with the Patriots in '99—RB Terry Allen (16 games), T Bruce Armstrong (16), TE Mike Bartrum (16), CB Terry Billups (2), DB Rico Clark (1), TE Ben Coates (16), DE Ferric Collons (14), LB Vernon Crawford (9), G Damon Denson (2), T Zefross Moss (13), LB Bernard Russ (6), RB Lamont Warren (16).

COACHING STAFF

Head Coach,
Bill Belichick

Pro Career: Bill Belichick became the fourteenth head coach of the Patriots on January 27, 2000. He is highly regarded as one of the NFL's premier defensive architects whose designs have consistently shut down some of the league's most potent offensive arsenals. Throughout the last 15 years, his defenses have contributed to the overall success of winning two Super Bowl titles, three conference titles, and five division titles. His impact was first felt in New England when he joined the Patriots in 1996. That year, the Patriots claimed their first division title in 10 years, rebounding from 6-10 in 1995 to 11-5, forced 34 turnovers, second in the AFC, and were among the stingiest defensive units in the league, allowing just 19.6 points per game—an improvement of four points per game from the prior year. In two playoff games, the defense allowed just 9 combined points, propelling the Patriots to victories over Pittsburgh (28-3) and Jacksonville (20-6) en route to Super Bowl XXXI against Green Bay. He rejoins the Patriots after three seasons as the assistant head coach and secondary coach of the New York Jets. In his first season in New York (1997), the Jets' defense limited opponents to 17.9 points per game, a 10.5-point improvement over the 1996 season, and played a key factor in the Jets' rise from 1-15 in 1996 to 9-7. In 1998, the Jets surrendered just 266 points, one point shy of Miami's league-leading 265, and defense was a critical factor in the team's ability to claim its first AFC East title with a franchise-best 12-4 regular-season record. The Jets advanced to the AFC Championship Game but lost to the eventual Super Bowl-champion Denver Broncos. In 1999, the Jets won seven of their final nine games, allowing only 18.4 points per game during that span. Belichick was just 23 years old when he began his NFL coaching career with the Baltimore Colts in 1975. He then coached the Detroit Lions (1976-77) and Denver Broncos (1978) before joining the New York Giants in 1979. He was named defensive coordinator in 1985, orchestrating a defensive unit that spurred the Giants to NFL titles in 1986 and 1990. Belichick was named the head coach of the Cleveland Browns in 1991. At the age of 37, he was the youngest head coach in the league. He inherited an aging squad whose 3-13 record in 1990 was the worst in franchise history. In his first year as head coach, the Browns set a franchise record by committing just 18 turnovers. In 1994, the Browns improved to 11-5, the second-best record in the AFC that year. The Browns eliminated the Patriots from the playoffs in a wild-card game, but were defeated by the Steelers in the divisional playoff round. The Browns defense allowed just 204 points all season, which was the lowest total in the NFL in 1994. Career record: 37-45.

Background: Belichick was a center/tight end at Wesleyan 1971-74.

Personal: Born April 16, 1952, Nashville. Bill and his wife, Debby, have three children—Amanda, Stephen, and Brian.

ASSISTANT COACHES

Jeff Davidson, asst. offensive line; born October 3, 1967, Akron, Ohio, lives in Franklin, Mass. Offensive lineman Ohio State 1986-89. Pro offensive lineman Denver Broncos 1990-92, New Orleans Saints 1994. Pro coach: New Orleans Saints 1995-96, joined the Patriots in 1997.

Ivan Fears, wide receivers; born November 15, 1954, Portsmouth, Va., lives in Foxboro, Mass. Running back William & Mary 1973-75. No pro playing experience. College coach: William & Mary 1977-1980, Syracuse 1981-1990. Pro coach: New England Patriots 1991-92, Chicago Bears 1993-98, rejoined Patriots in 1999.

Eric Mangini, defensive backs; born January 10, 1971, Hartford, Conn., lives in Medfield, Mass. Nose tackle Wesleyan (Conn.) 1989-1990, 1992-93. No pro playing experience. Pro coach: Cleveland Browns 1995, Baltimore Ravens 1996, New York Jets 1997-99, joined Patriots in 2000.

Randy Melvin, defensive line; born April 3, 1959, Aurora, Ill., lives in Foxboro, Mass. Defensive line Eastern Illinois 1978-1981. No pro playing experience. College coach: Eastern Illinois 1988-1994, Wyoming 1995-96, Purdue 1997-99. Pro coach: Joined Patriots in 2000.

Markus Paul, asst. strength and conditioning; born April 1, 1966, Orlando, Fla., lives in Plainville, Mass. Safety Syracuse 1984-88. Pro safety Chicago Bears 1989-1993, Tampa Bay Buccaneers 1993. Pro coach: New Orleans 1998-99, joined Patriots in 2000.

Dick Rehbein, quarterbacks; born November 22, 1955, Green Bay, lives in North Attleboro, Mass. Center Ripon College 1974-77. No pro playing experience. Pro coach: Green Bay Packers 1979-1983, Los Angeles Express (USFL) 1984, Minnesota Vikings 1984-1991, New York Giants 1992-99, joined Patriots in 2000.

Rob Ryan, linebackers, born December 13, 1962, Ardmore, Okla., lives in Franklin, Mass. Linebacker Oklahoma State 1984, Southwestern Oklahoma State 1985-86. No pro playing experience. College coach: Western Kentucky 1987, Ohio State 1988, Tennessee State 1989-1993, Hutchinson C.C. (Kan.) 1996, Oklahoma State 1997-99. Pro coach: Arizona Cardinals 1994-95, joined Patriots in 2000.

Dante Scarnecchia, asst. head coach-offensive line; born February 15, 1948, Los Angeles, lives in Wrentham, Mass. Center-guard California Western (now U.S. International) 1968-1970. No pro playing experience. College coach: California Western 1970-72, Iowa State 1973-74, Southern Methodist 1975-76, 1980-81, Pacific 1977-78, Northern Arizona 1979. Pro coach: New England Patriots 1982-88, Indianapolis Colts 1989-1990, rejoined the Patriots in 1991.

Brad Seely, special teams; born September 6, 1956, Vinton, Iowa, lives in Wrentham, Mass. Tackle-guard South Dakota State 1974-77. No pro playing experience. College coach: Colorado State 1980, Southern Methodist 1981, North Carolina State 1982, Pacific 1983, Oklahoma State 1984-88. Pro coach: Indianapolis Colts 1989-1993, New York Jets 1994, Carolina Panthers 1995-98, joined Patriots in 1999.

Mike Woicik, strength and conditioning; born September 26, 1956, Baltimore, lives in Foxboro, Mass. Attended Boston College. No college or pro playing experience. College coach: Springfield College 1978-79, Syracuse 1980-89. Pro coach: Dallas Cowboys 1990-96, New Orleans Saints 1997-99, joined Patriots in 2000.

Dewayne Walker, defensive assistant; born December 3, 1960, Los Angeles, lives in Foxboro, Mass. Cornerback Pasadena C.C. (Calif.) 1978-79, Minnesota 1980-81. Pro cornerback Edmonton Eskimos (CFL) 1982, Oakland Invaders (USFL) 1985. College coach: Mt. San Antonio C.C. (Calif.) 1988-1992, Utah State 1993, Brigham Young 1994, Oklahoma State 1995, California 1996-97. Pro coach: Joined Patriots in 1998.

Charlie Weis, offensive coordinator-running backs; born March 30, 1956, Trenton, N.J., lives in Cumberland, R.I. Attended Notre Dame. No college or pro playing experience. College coach: South Carolina 1985-88. Pro coach: New York Giants 1988-1992, New England Patriots 1993-96, New York Jets 1997-99, rejoined Patriots in 2000.

2000 FIRST-YEAR ROSTER

Name	Pos.	Ht.	Wt.	Birthdate	College	Hometown	How Acq.
Anderson, Maurice	DE-DT	6-3	290	1/19/75	Virginia	Blackstone, Va.	FA
Beadles, Terrance	G	6-3	315	4/27/76	Arkansas-Pine Bluff	Atlanta, Ga.	FA
Brady, Tom	QB	6-4	211	8/3/77	Michigan	San Mateo, Calif.	D6b
Bumgardner, Matt	WR	6-1	195	4/2/77	Texas A&M	Luling, Tex.	FA
Davis, Adam	G	6-4	310	1/11/77	Oklahoma State	Hobart, Okla.	FA
Davis, Shockmain	WR	6-0	201	8/20/77	Angelo State	Port Arthur, Tex.	FA
Eitzmann, Chris	TE	6-5	260	4/1/77	Harvard	Hardy, Neb.	FA
Eskridge, John	LB	6-3	230	5/3/76	SW Missouri State	Riverview, Fla.	FA
Gatrell, Rob	G	6-5	300	3/14/77	Fresno State	Brentwood, Calif.	FA
Grimes, Reggie	DE-DT	6-4	300	11/7/76	Alabama	Nashville, Tenn.	FA
Harris, Antwan	CB	5-9	186	5/29/77	Virginia	Raleigh, N.C.	D6a
Holleman, Chad	K	5-11	200	8/9/76	Georgia	Marietta, Ga.	FA
Howell, Evan	CB	5-11	186	10/14/77	Oklahoma State	Monroe, La.	FA
Johnson, Garrett (1)	DT	6-3	294	12/31/75	Illinois	Delleville, Ill.	FA-'99
Kibble, James	P	5-10	195	10/25/77	Virginia Tech	Manassas, Va.	FA
Klemm, Adrian	T	6-3	308	5/21/77	Hawaii	Santa Monica, Calif.	D2
Malveaux, Kelly	CB-S	5-9	176	5/11/76	Arizona	Bellflower, Calif.	FA
Marriott, Jeff	DL	6-4	301	3/3/77	Missouri	Chillicothe, Mo.	D5b
Megna, Marc (1)	LB	6-2	245	7/30/76	Richmond	Fall River, Mass.	FA-'99
Morey, Sean (1)	WR	5-11	190	2/26/76	Brown	Marshfield, Mass.	D7b-'99
Munch, John	LB	6-1	246	1/7/76	Illinois Wesleyan	Genoa, Ill.	FA
Nugent, David	DE-DT	6-4	303	10/27/77	Purdue	Collierville, Tenn.	D6c
Pass, Patrick	RB	5-10	208	12/31/77	Georgia	Tucker, Ga.	D7b
Paxton, Lonie	LS	6-2	274	3/13/78	Sacramento State	Corona, Calif.	FA
Pospisil, Scott	DE	6-2	280	11/30/76	Iowa	Mt. Vernon, Iowa	FA
Redmond, J.R.	RB	5-11	216	9/28/77	Arizona State	Carson, Calif.	D3
Rideau, Rodney	S	5-10	193	11/30/77	Oklahoma	Midwest City, Okla.	FA
Robinson-Randall, Greg	T	6-5	339	6/23/78	Michigan State	La Marque, Tex.	D4
Scarlett, Noel	DT	6-3	320	1/21/74	Langston	Ft. Lauderdale, Fla.	FA
Sheldon, Thad	LS	6-2	245	12/17/76	Iowa	Mason City, Iowa	FA
Smith, Jamel	LB	6-1	245	7/18/77	Virginia Tech	Columbia, S.C.	FA
Stachelski, Dave	TE	6-3	250	3/1/77	Boise State	Marysville, Wash.	D5a
Tardio, Robert	TE	6-5	245	3/17/77	Boston College	Franklin Lakes, N.J.	FA
Taylor, Kerry (1)	TE	6-2	252	1/24/77	Massachusetts	Mansfield, Mass.	FA
Tisdale, Casey	DE-LB	6-4	258	6/18/76	New Mexico	San Diego, Calif.	D7a
Tuitele, Maugaula	LB	6-2	260	5/26/78	Colorado State	San Bernardino, Calif.	FA
Tujague, Ryan	T	6-5	298	7/2/76	Washington State	Thousands Oaks, Calif.	FA
Williams, Martinez	WR	5-11	170	8/10/77	New Mexico	Montgomery, Ala.	FA
Woods, Mike	CB	5-9	189	9/23/76	Oklahoma	Del City, Okla.	FA

The term NFL Rookie is defined as a player who is in his first season of professional football and has not been on the roster of another professional football team for any regular-season or postseason games. A Rookie is designated by an "R" on NFL rosters. Players who have been active in another professional football league or players who have NFL experience, including either preseason training camp or being on an Active List or Inactive List, or on Reserve/Injured or Reserve/Physically Unable to Perform for fewer than six regular-season games, are termed NFL First-Year Players. An NFL First-Year Player is designated by a "1" on NFL rosters. Thereafter, a player is credited with an additional year of experience for each season in which he accumulates six games on the Active List or Inactive List, or on Reserve/Injured or Reserve/Physically Unable to Perform.

NEW YORK JETS

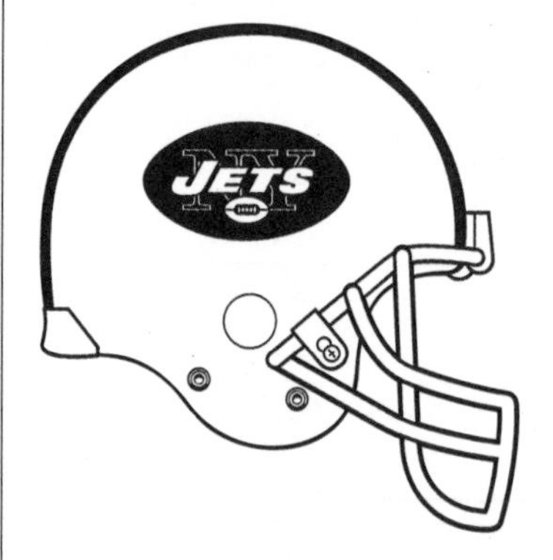

American Football Conference
Eastern Division
Team Colors: Green and White
1000 Fulton Avenue
Hempstead, New York 11550
Telephone: (516) 560-8100

CLUB OFFICIALS

Owner and CEO: Robert Wood Johnson IV
President: Steve Gutman
Director of Football Operations: Bill Parcells
Director of Player Personnel: Dick Haley
Director of Pro Player Development/Player Contract Negotiations: Mike Tannenbaum
Director of Player Development: Carl Banks
Director of Security: Steve Yarnell
Treasurer and Chief Financial Officer: Michael Gerstle
Executive Director of Business Operations: Bob Parente
Director of Public Relations: Frank Ramos
Director of Operations: Mike Kensil
Senior Manager Pro Player Development/AFC: JoJo Wooden
Manager of Pro Player Development/NFC: Brian Gaine
Talent Scouts: Trent Baalke, Joey Clinkscales, Michael Davis, Sid Hall, Jesse Kaye, Bob Schmitz
Director of Team Travel: Kevin Coyle
College Scouting Coordinator: John Griffin
Asst. Director of Public Relations: Douglas Miller
Public Relations Assistants: Sharon Czark, Danny Ferrauiloa
Coordinator of Special Projects: Ken Ilchuk
Controller: Mike Minarczyk
Senior Director of Marketing & Business Development: Mark Riccio
Accountant: Dawn Aponte
Manager of Football Computer Operations: Christine Haefling
Director of Information Technology: Thomas Murphy
Director of Ticket Operations: John Buschhorn
Assistant Director of Ticket Operations: Carol Anne Coppola
Assistant Director of Operations: Kathy Reade
Head Athletic Trainer: David Price
Assistant Athletic Trainer: John Mellody
Equipment Manager: Bill Hampton
Equipment Director: Clay Hampton
Assistant Equipment Manager: Gus Granneman
Video Director: John Seiter
Assistant Video Director: Jim Space
Digital Video Coordinator: Steve Piazza
Stadium: Giants Stadium • **Capacity:** 79,466
East Rutherford, New Jersey 07073
Playing Surface: Natural Grass
Training Center: 1000 Fulton Avenue
Hempstead, New York 11550

RECORD HOLDERS

INDIVIDUAL RECORDS—CAREER

Category	Name	Performance
Rushing (Yds.)	Freeman McNeil, 1981-1992	8,074
Passing (Yds.)	Joe Namath, 1965-1976	27,057
Passing (TDs)	Joe Namath, 1965-1976	170
Receiving (No.)	Don Maynard, 1960-1972	627
Receiving (Yds.)	Don Maynard, 1960-1972	11,732
Interceptions	Bill Baird, 1963-69	34
Punting (Avg.)	Curley Johnson, 1961-68	42.8
Punt Return (Avg.)	Dick Christy, 1961-63	16.2
Kickoff Return (Avg.)	Bobby Humphery, 1984-89	22.8
Field Goals	Pat Leahy, 1974-1991	304
Touchdowns (Tot.)	Don Maynard, 1960-1972	88
Points	Pat Leahy, 1974-1991	1,470

INDIVIDUAL RECORDS—SINGLE SEASON

Category	Name	Performance
Rushing (Yds.)	Curtis Martin, 1999	1,464
Passing (Yds.)	Joe Namath, 1967	4,007
Passing (TDs)	Vinny Testaverde, 1998	29
Receiving (No.)	Al Toon, 1988	93
Receiving (Yds.)	Don Maynard, 1967	1,434
Interceptions	Dainard Paulson, 1964	12
Punting (Avg.)	Curley Johnson, 1965	45.3
Punt Return (Avg.)	Dick Christy, 1961	21.3
Kickoff Return (Avg.)	Bobby Humphery, 1984	30.7
Field Goals	Jim Turner, 1968	34
Touchdowns (Tot.)	Art Powell, 1960	14
	Don Maynard, 1965	14
	Emerson Boozer, 1972	14
Points	Jim Turner, 1968	145

INDIVIDUAL RECORDS—SINGLE GAME

Category	Name	Performance
Rushing (Yds.)	Adrian Murrell, 10-27-96	199
Passing (Yds.)	Joe Namath, 9-24-72	496
Passing (TDs)	Joe Namath, 9-24-72	6
Receiving (No.)	Clark Gaines, 9-21-80	17
Receiving (Yds.)	Don Maynard, 11-17-68	228
Interceptions	Many times.	3
	Last time by Marcus Turner, 11-20-94	
Field Goals	Jim Turner, 11-3-68	6
	Bobby Howfield, 12-3-72	6
Touchdowns (Tot.)	Wesley Walker, 9-21-86	4
Points	Wesley Walker, 9-21-86	24

2000 SCHEDULE

PRESEASON

July 29	**New Orleans**	8:00
Aug. 4	at Green Bay	7:00
Aug. 12	at Baltimore	8:00
Aug. 18	**New York Giants**	8:00

REGULAR SEASON

Sept. 3	at Green Bay	3:15
Sept. 11	**New England** (Mon.)	9:00
Sept. 17	**Buffalo**	1:00
Sept. 24	at Tampa Bay	4:15
Oct. 1	Open Date	
Oct. 8	**Pittsburgh**	1:00
Oct. 15	at New England	4:05
Oct. 23	**Miami** (Mon.)	9:00
Oct. 29	at Buffalo	1:00
Nov. 5	**Denver**	4:15
Nov. 12	at Indianapolis	8:35
Nov. 19	at Miami	4:05
Nov. 26	**Chicago**	1:00
Dec. 3	**Indianapolis**	4:15
Dec. 10	at Oakland	5:35
Dec. 17	**Detroit**	1:00
Dec. 24	at Baltimore	1:00

COACHING HISTORY

New York Titans 1960-62
(266-335-8)

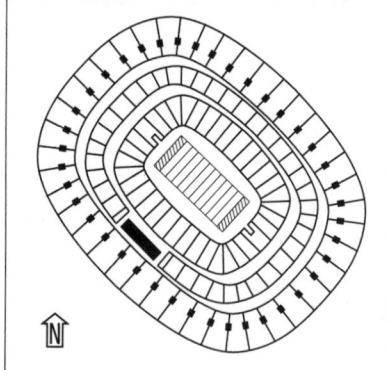

1960-61	Sammy Baugh	14-14-0
1962	Clyde (Bulldog) Turner	5-9-0
1963-73	Weeb Ewbank	73-78-6
1974-75	Charley Winner*	9-14-0
1975	Ken Shipp	1-4-0
1976	Lou Holtz**	3-10-0
1976	Mike Holovak	0-1-0
1977-82	Walt Michaels	41-49-1
1983-89	Joe Walton	54-59-1
1990-93	Bruce Coslet	26-39-0
1994	Pete Carroll	6-10-0
1995-96	Rich Kotite	4-28-0
1997-99	Bill Parcells	30-20-0

*Released after nine games in 1975
**Resigned after 13 games in 1976

GIANTS STADIUM

1999 TEAM RECORD

PRESEASON (3-1)

Date	Result		Opponent
8/14	L	16-27	at Green Bay
8/20	W	10-9	Philadelphia
8/28	W	16-10	at New York Giants
9/3	W	38-17	Minnesota

REGULAR SEASON (8-8)

Date	Result		Opponent	Att.
9/12	L	28-30	New England	78,227
9/19	L	3-17	at Buffalo	68,839
9/26	L	20-27	Washington	78,161
10/3	W	21-13	at Denver	74,181
10/11	L	6-16	Jacksonville	78,216
10/17	L	13-16	Indianapolis	78,112
10/24	L	23-24	at Oakland	47,326
11/7	W	12-7	Arizona	77,857
11/15	W	24-17	at New England	59,077
11/21	W	17-7	Buffalo	79,285
11/28	L	6-13	at Indianapolis	56,689
12/5	L	28-41	at New York Giants	78,200
12/12	W	28-20	Miami	78,246
12/19	W	22-21	at Dallas	64,271
12/27	W	38-31	at Miami	74,230
1/2	W	19-9	Seattle	78,154

SCORE BY PERIODS

Jets	55	101	48	104	0	—	308
Opponents	66	81	78	84	0	—	309

ATTENDANCE

Home 624,847 Away 519,699 Total 1,144,546
Single-game home record, 78,298 (11/21/99)
Single-season home record, 624,847 (1999)

1999 TEAM STATISTICS

	Jets	Opp.
Total First Downs	268	299
Rushing	111	97
Passing	139	180
Penalty	18	22
Third Down: Made/Att	78/226	90/221
Third Down Pct.	34.5	40.7
Fourth Down: Made/Att	11/25	6/13
Fourth Down Pct.	44.0	46.2
Total Net Yards	4,752	5,379
Avg. Per Game	297.0	336.2
Total Plays	999	1,030
Avg. Per Play	4.8	5.2
Net Yards Rushing	1,961	1,703
Avg. Per Game	122.6	106.4
Total Rushes	486	430
Net Yards Passing	2,791	3,676
Avg. Per Game	174.4	229.8
Sacked/Yards Lost	37/210	26/184
Gross Yards	3,001	3,860
Att./Completions	476/272	574/319
Completion Pct.	57.1	55.6
Had Intercepted	16	24
Punts/Average	82/45.0	78/40.9
Net Punting Avg.	82/38.1	78/34.8
Penalties/Yards	87/771	76/685
Fumbles/Ball Lost	22/6	24/11
Touchdowns	33	33
Rushing	7	16
Passing	22	16
Returns	4	1
Avg. Time of Possession	30:45	29:15

1999 INDIVIDUAL STATISTICS

Passing	Att.	Comp.	Yds.	Pct.	TD	Int.	Tkld.	Rate
Lucas	272	161	1,678	59.2	14	6	11/69	85.1
Mirer	176	95	1,062	54.0	5	9	22/102	60.4
Testaverde	15	10	96	66.7	1	1	0/0	78.8
Tupa	11	6	165	54.5	2	0	3/30	139.2
K. Johnson	1	0	0	0.0	0	0	1/9	39.6
Sowell	1	0	0	0.0	0	0	0/0	39.6
Jets	476	272	3,001	57.1	22	16	37/210	77.4
Opponents	574	319	3,860	55.6	16	24	26/184	68.3

SCORING	TD R	TD P	TD Rt	PAT	FG	Saf	PTS
Hall	0	0	0	27/29	27/33	0	108
K. Johnson	0	8	0	0/0	0/0	0	48
Martin	5	0	0	0/0	0/0	0	30
Anderson	0	3	0	0/0	0/0	0	18
Chrebet	0	3	0	0/0	0/0	0	18
Ward	0	3	0	0/0	0/0	0	18
Baxter	0	2	0	0/0	0/0	0	12
E. Green	0	2	0	0/0	0/0	0	12
Coleman	0	0	1	0/0	0/0	0	6
Cox	0	0	1	0/0	0/0	0	6
Lucas	1	0	0	0/0	0/0	0	6
Mirer	1	0	0	0/0	0/0	0	6
Ogbogu	0	0	1	0/0	0/0	0	6
Spence	0	1	0	0/0	0/0	0	6
Stoutmire	0	0	1	0/0	0/0	0	6
Jets	7	22	4	27/29	27/33	1	308
Opponents	16	16	1	33/33	26/31	0	309

2-Pt. Conversions: None.
Team 0-4, Opponents 0-0.

RUSHING	Att.	Yds.	Avg.	LG	TD
Martin	367	1,464	4.0	50	5
Lucas	41	144	3.5	21	1
Parmalee	27	133	4.9	18	0
Mirer	21	89	4.2	12	1
Anderson	16	84	5.3	16	0
Stone	2	27	13.5	36	0
Tupa	2	8	4.0	4	0
K. Johnson	5	6	1.2	12	0
Sowell	3	5	1.7	3	0
L. Johnson	1	2	2.0	2	0
Ward	1	-1	-1.0	-1	0
Jets	486	1,961	4.0	50	7
Opponents	430	1,703	4.0	36	16

RECEIVING	No.	Yds.	Avg.	LG	TD
K. Johnson	89	1,170	13.1	65	8
Chrebet	48	631	13.1	50t	3
Martin	45	259	5.8	34	0
Anderson	29	302	10.4	29	3
Ward	22	325	14.8	56t	3
Parmalee	15	113	7.5	23	0
Baxter	8	66	8.3	24	2
E. Green	7	37	5.3	10t	2
Early	6	83	13.8	24	0
Spence	3	15	5.0	9	1
Jets	272	3,001	11.0	65	22
Opponents	319	3,860	12.1	80t	16

INTERCEPTIONS	No.	Yds.	Avg.	LG	TD
Coleman	6	165	27.5	98t	1
V. Green	5	92	18.4	32	0
Glenn	3	20	6.7	12	0
Stoutmire	2	97	48.5	67t	1
Phifer	2	20	10.0	16	0
Wiltz	2	5	2.5	5	0
Mickens	2	2	1.0	2	0
Cox	1	27	27.0	27t	1
M. Jones	1	15	15.0	15	0
Jets	24	443	18.5	98t	3
Opponents	16	148	9.3	55	0

PUNTING	No.	Yds.	Avg.	In 20	LG
Tupa	81	3,659	45.2	25	69
Hall	1	34	34.0	1	34
Jets	82	3,693	45.0	26	69
Opponents	78	3,190	40.9	20	83

PUNT RETURNS	No.	FC	Yds.	Avg.	LG	TD
Ward	38	12	288	7.6	23	0
Sawyer	4	1	25	6.3	11	0
L. Johnson	1	1	6	6.0	6	0
Jets	43	14	319	7.4	23	0
Opponents	47	6	427	9.1	35	0

KICKOFF RETURNS	No.	Yds.	Avg.	LG	TD
Stone	28	689	24.6	50	0
Glenn	27	601	22.3	46	0
Williams	6	166	27.7	81	0
Farmer	4	84	21.0	30	0
L. Johnson	2	31	15.5	17	0
Jets	67	1,571	23.4	81	0
Opponents	63	1,589	25.2	95	0

FIELD GOALS	1-19	20-29	30-39	40-49	50+
Hall	0/0	3/4	17/17	7/12	0/0
Jets	0/0	3/4	17/17	7/12	0/0
Opponents	1/1	11/11	8/8	4/8	2/3

SACKS	No.
Lewis	5.5
Phifer	4.5
Logan	3.0
Farrior	2.0
Mickens	2.0
Pleasant	2.0
Ferguson	1.0
Gordon	1.0
M. Jones	1.0
Lyle	1.0
Ogbogu	1.0
Stoutmire	1.0
Wiltz	1.0
Jets	26.0
Opponents	37.0

2000 DRAFT CHOICES

Round	Name	Pos.	College
1	Shaun Ellis	DE	Tennessee
	John Abraham	LB	South Carolina
	Chad Pennington	QB	Marshall
	Anthony Becht	TE	West Virginia
3	Laveranues Coles	WR	Florida State
5	Windrell Hayes	WR	Southern California
6	Tony Scott	DB	North Carolina State
7	Richard Seals	DT	Utah

NEW YORK JETS

2000 VETERAN ROSTER

No.		Name	Pos.	Ht.	Wt.	Birthdate	NFL Exp.	College	Hometown	How Acq.	'99 Games/ Starts
20		Anderson, Richie	RB	6-2	230	9/13/71	8	Penn State	Sandy Spring, Md.	D6-'93	16/9
84		Baxter, Fred	TE	6-3	265	6/14/71	8	Auburn	Brundidge, Ala.	D5a-'93	14/8
97		Boose, Dorian	DE	6-5	292	1/29/74	3	Washington State	Tacoma, Wash.	D2-'98	12/0
98		Burton, Shane	DT-DE	6-6	305	1/18/74	5	Tennessee	Catawba, N.C.	UFA(Chi)-'00	15/0*
80		Chrebet, Wayne	WR	5-10	188	8/14/73	6	Hofstra	Garfield, N.J.	FA-'95	11/11
42		Coleman, Marcus	CB	6-2	210	5/24/74	5	Texas Tech	Dallas, Tex.	D5-'96	16/10
51		Cox, Brian	LB	6-4	250	2/17/68	10	Western Illinois	East St. Louis, Ill.	FA-'98	12/11
36		Crutchfield, Buddy	CB	6-0	196	3/7/76	3	North Carolina Central	Raleigh, N.C.	FA-'99	4/0
94		Dailey, Casey	LB	6-3	249	6/11/75	3	Northwestern	Covina, Calif.	D5a-'98	6/0
88	#	Early, Quinn	WR	6-0	190	4/13/65	13	Iowa	Great Neck, N.Y.	FA-'99	16/3
69		Fabini, Jason	T	6-7	312	8/25/74	3	Cincinnati	Ft. Wayne, Ind.	D4-'98	9/9
25		Farmer, Robert	RB	5-11	217	3/4/74	2	Notre Dame	Bolingbrook, Ill.	FA-'99	13/0
58		Farrior, James	LB	6-2	244	1/6/75	4	Virginia	Ettrick, Va.	D1-'97	16/4
72		Ferguson, Jason	DT	6-3	305	11/28/74	4	Georgia	Nettleton, Miss.	D7b-'97	9/9
47		Frost, Scott	S	6-3	219	1/4/75	3	Nebraska	Lincoln, Neb.	D3a-'98	14/0
67		Gisler, Mike	C-G	6-4	300	8/26/69	8	Houston	Runge, Tex.	UFA(NE)-'98	16/0
31		Glenn, Aaron	CB-KR	5-9	185	7/16/72	7	Texas A&M	Aldine, Tex.	D1-'94	16/16
54		Gordon, Dwayne	LB	6-1	245	11/2/69	8	New Hampshire	LaGrangeville, N.Y.	FA-'97	16/4
21		Green, Victor	S	5-11	210	12/8/69	8	Akron	Americus, Ga.	FA-'93	16/16
9		Hall, John	K	6-3	228	3/17/74	4	Wisconsin	Port Charlotte, Fla.	FA-'97	16/0
92	#	Hamilton, Bobby	DE-DT	6-5	280	1/7/71	6	Southern Mississippi	Columbia, Miss.	FA-'96	7/0
30		Hayes, Chris	S	6-0	206	5/7/72	4	Washington State	San Bernadino, Calif.	T(GB)-'97	15/0
65	#	Hudson, John	C-G	6-2	270	1/29/68	11	Auburn	Paris, Tenn.	UFA(Phil)-'96	16/0
71		Jenkins, Kerry	G-T	6-5	305	9/6/73	3	Troy State	Tuscaloosa, Ala.	FA-'97	16/16
32		Johnson, Leon	RB-KR	6-0	218	7/13/74	4	North Carolina	Morgantown, N.C.	D4b-'97	1/0
55		Jones, Marvin	LB	6-2	250	6/28/72	8	Florida State	Miami, Fla.	D1-'93	16/16
57		Lewis Mo	LB	6-3	258	10/21/69	10	Georgia	Peachtree, Ga.	D3-'91	16/16
93		Logan, Ernie	DT-DE	6-3	290	5/18/68	9	East Carolina	Fayetteville, N.C.	FA-'99	14/7
79		Loverne, David	G	6-3	299	5/22/76	2	San Jose State	Concord, Calif.	D3-'99	0*
6		Lucas, Ray	QB	6-3	214	8/6/72	3	Rutgers	Harrison, N.J.	FA-'97	9/9
95		Lyle, Rick	DE-DT	6-5	290	2/26/71	7	Missouri	Hickman Mills, Mo.	FA-'97	16/16
63		Machado, J.P.	G	6-4	300	1/6/76	2	Illinois	Monmouth, Ill.	FA-'00	5/0
73	#	Malamala, Siupeli	T	6-5	305	1/15/69	8	Washington	Kalaheo, Hawaii	FA-'99	6/1
28		Martin, Curtis	RB	5-11	210	5/1/73	6	Pittsburgh	Pittsburgh, Pa.	RFA(NE)-'98	16/16
68		Mawae, Kevin	C	6-4	305	1/23/71	7	Louisiana State	Leesville, La.	UFA(Sea)-'98	16/16
24		Mickens, Ray	CB-KR	5-8	184	1/4/73	5	Texas A&M	El Paso, Tex.	D3-'96	15/5
99		Ogbogu, Eric	DE	6-4	285	7/18/75	3	Maryland	Irvington, N.Y.	D6a-'98	14/0
34		Parmalee, Bernie	RB	5-11	210	9/16/67	9	Ball State	Jersey City, N.J.	FA-'99	16/0
56		Phifer, Roman	LB	6-2	248	3/5/68	10	UCLA	Pineville, N.C.	UFA(StL)-'99	16/12
98	#	Pleasant, Anthony	DE	6-5	280	1/27/68	11	Tennessee State	Century, Fla.	FA-'98	16/16
75		Rafferty, Ian	T	6-5	300	9/2/76	2	North Carolina State	Summerville, S.C.	FA-'99	5/0
45		Smith, Otis	CB	5-11	195	10/22/65	11	Missouri	New Orleans, La.	UFA(NE)-'97	1/1
33		Sowell, Jerald	RB	6-0	245	1/21/74	4	Tulane	Baker, La.	W(GB)-'97	16/0
82		Spence, Blake	RB	6-4	249	6/2/75	3	Oregon	San Juan Capistrano, Calif.	D5c-'98	10/0
83	#	Stone, Dwight	WR-KR	6-0	195	1/28/64	14	Middle Tennessee State	Florala, Ala.	FA-'99	16/0
26		Stoutmire, Omar	S	5-11	198	7/9/74	4	Fresno State	Long Beach, Calif.	FA-'99	12/5
50		Syvrud, J.J.	LB	6-3	255	5/10/77	2	Jamestown, N.D.	Rock Springs, Wyo.	D7b-'99	1/0
16		Testaverde, Vinny	QB	6-5	235	11/13/63	14	Miami	Floral Park, N.Y.	FA-'98	1/1
77		Thomas, Randy	G	6-4	301	1/19/76	2	Mississippi State	East Point, Ga.	D2-'99	16/16
7		Tupa, Tom	P-QB	6-4	225	2/6/66	12	Ohio State	Cleveland, Ohio	UFA(NE)-'99	16/0
89		Ward, Dedric	WR-KR	5-9	184	9/29/74	4	Northern Iowa	Cedar Rapids, Iowa	D3-'97	16/10
23		Williams, Kevin	CB-S	6-0	190	8/4/75	3	Oklahoma State	Pine Bluff, Ark.	D3b-'98	4/0
91		Wiltz, Jason	DT	6-4	300	11/23/76	2	Nebraska	New Orleans, La.	D4-'99	12/1
74		Young, Ryan	T	6-5	320	6/28/76	2	Kansas State	St. Louis, Mo.	D7a-'99	15/7

* Burton played 15 games with Chicago in '99; Loverne was inactive for 16 games.

Traded—WR Keyshawn Johnson (16 games in '99) to Tampa Bay.

Retired—John Elliott 12-year offensive tackle, 16 games in '99.

\# Unrestricted free agent, subject to developments.

Also played for Jets in '99—S Steve Atwater (12 games), LB Chad Cascadden (4), TE Eric Green (10), LB Olrick Johnson (3), DB Jermaine Jones (1), QB Rick Mirer (8), DB Corey Sawyer (5).

COACHING STAFF

Head Coach

Al Groh,

Pro Career: On January 24, 2000, Groh was named the Jets' twelfth full-time head coach. Groh took over control of the Jets after having served the previous three seasons (1997-99) as the team's linebackers coach under head coach Bill Parcells. With the Jets, Groh has been part of a team that won the AFC East in 1998 and played in the 1998 AFC Championship game. Groh came to the Jets after having served as the New England Patriots' defensive coordinator-linebackers coach from 1993-96. The 1996 Patriots faced the Green Bay Packers in Super Bowl XXXI. It was Groh's second appearance in a Super Bowl, having earned a ring as an assistant for the New York Giants' squad that defeated the Buffalo Bills in Super Bowl XXV. A football coach for 32 years, including 12 seasons in the NFL, Groh began his pro coaching career in 1987 with the Atlanta Falcons. After a season at South Carolina, he returned to the NFL ranks in 1989 with the New York Giants and served as the linebackers coach until taking over as the team's defensive coordinator in 1991. He then moved onto the Cleveland Browns in 1992 before beginning his stint with the Patriots.

Background: Defensive end at Virginia 1963-66. College assistant Army 1968-69, Virginia 1970-72, North Carolina 1973-77, Air Force 1978-79, Texas Tech 1980, Wake Forest 1981-86 (head coach), South Carolina 1988.

Personal: Born July 13, 1944, New York, N.Y. Al and his wife, Anne, live on Long Island and have three children—Michael, Ashley Anne, and Matthew.

ASSISTANT COACHES

Todd Bowles, secondary; born November 18, 1963, Elizabeth, N.J., lives on Long Island, N.Y. Defensive back Temple 1982-85. Pro defensive back Washington Redskins 1986-1990, San Francisco 49ers 1991, Washington Redskins 1991-92. Pro coach: Joined Jets in 2000.

Maurice Carthon, asst. head coach-running backs; born April 24, 1961, Chicago, lives on Long Island, N.Y. Running back Arkansas State 1979-1982. Pro running back New York Generals (USFL) 1983-85, New York Giants 1985-1991, Indianapolis Colts 1992. Pro coach: New England Patriots 1994-96, joined Jets in 1997.

Mike Groh, quality control-offensive assistant; born December 19, 1971, Charlottesville, Va., lives on Long Island, N.Y. Quarterback Virginia 1992-95. Pro quarterback Rhein Fire (World League of American Football) 1997. Pro coach: Joined Jets in 2000.

Todd Haley, wide receivers; born February 28, 1967, Atlanta, lives on Long Island, N.Y. Attended Florida and Miami. No college or pro playing experience. Pro coach: Joined Jets in 1996.

Ray Hamilton, defensive line; born January 20, 1951, Omaha, Neb., lives on Long Island, N.Y. Nose tackle Oklahoma 1969-1972. Pro nose tackle-defensive end New England Patriots 1973-1981. College coach: Tennessee 1992. Pro coach: New England Patriots 1985-89, Tampa Bay Buccaneers 1991, Los Angeles Raiders 1993-94, New York Jets 1995-96, New England Patriots 1997-99, rejoined Jets in 2000.

Dan Henning, offensive coordinator-quarterbacks; born June 21, 1942, Bronx, N.Y., lives on Long Island, N.Y. Quarterback William & Mary 1962-64. Pro quarterback San Diego Chargers 1964, 1966-67. College coach: Florida State 1968-1970, 1974, Virginia Tech 1971, 1973, Boston College 1994-96 (head coach). Pro coach: Houston Oilers 1972, New York Jets 1976-78, Miami Dolphins 1979-1980, Washington Redskins 1981-82, 1987-88, Atlanta Falcons 1983-86 (head coach), San Diego Chargers 1989-1991 (head coach), Detroit Lions 1992-93, Buffalo Bills 1997, rejoined Jets in 1998.

Pat Hodgson, offensive assistant for planning and research; born January 30, 1944, Columbus, Ga., lives on Long Island, N.Y. Tight end Georgia 1963-65. Pro tight end Washington Redskins 1966, Minnesota Vikings 1967. College coach: Georgia 1968-1970, 1972-77, Florida State 1971, Texas Tech 1978. Pro coach: San Diego Chargers 1978, New York Giants 1979-1987, Pittsburgh Steelers 1992-95, joined Jets in 1996.

John Lott, strength and conditioning; born May 9, 1964 Denton, Texas, lives on Long Island N.Y. Offensive lineman North Texas 1983-86. Offensive lineman Pittsburgh Steelers 1987. College coach: North Texas 1989, Houston 1990-96. Pro coach: Joined Jets in 1997.

Bill Muir, offensive line; born October 26, 1942, Pittsburgh, lives on Long Island, N.Y. Tackle Susquehanna 1962-64. No pro playing experience. College coach: Susquehanna 1965, Delaware Valley 1966-67, Rhode Island 1970-71, Idaho State 1972-73, Southern Methodist 1976-77. Pro coach: Orlando (Continental Football League) 1968-69, Houston-Shreveport Steamer (WFL) 1975, New England Patriots 1982-88, Indianapolis Colts 1989-1991, Philadelphia Eagles 1992-94, joined Jets in 1995.

Mike Nolan, defensive coordinator; born March 7, 1959, Baltimore, lives on Long Island, N.Y. No pro playing experience. College coach: Oregon 1981, Stanford 1982-83, Rice 1984-85, Louisiana State 1986. Pro coach: Denver Broncos 1987-1992, New York Giants 1993-96, Washington Redskins 1997-99, joined Jets in 2000.

William Roberts, asst. offensive line; born August 5, 1962 Miami, lives on Long Island, N.Y. Guard Ohio State 1980-83. Guard New York Giants 1984-1994, New England Patriots 1995-96, New York Jets 1997. Pro coach: Joined Jets in 1998.

Danny Rocco, defensive quality control/asst. special teams-linebackers; born July 16, 1960, Pittsburgh, lives on Long Island, N.Y. Linebacker Penn State 1979-1980, Wake Forest 1982-83. No pro playing experience. College coach: Wake Forest 1984-86, Colorado 1987, Tulsa 1988-1990, Boston College 1991-93, Texas 1994-97, Maryland 1998-99. Pro coach: Joined the Jets in 2000.

Bob Sutton, linebackers, born January 28, 1951, Ypsilanti, Mich., lives on Long Island, N.Y. Attended Eastern Michigan. No college or pro playing experience. College coach: Michigan 1972-73, Syracuse 1974, Western Michigan 1975-76, Illinois 1977-79, North Carolina State 1982, Army 1983-1999 (head coach 1991-99). Pro coach: Joined Jets in 2000.

Mike Sweatman, special teams; born October 23, 1947, Kansas City, Mo., lives on Long Island, N.Y. Linebacker Kansas 1964-67. No pro playing experience. College coach: Kansas 1973-74, 1979-1982, Tulsa 1977-78, Tennessee 1983. Pro coach: Minnesota Vikings 1984, New York Giants 1985-1992, New England Patriots 1993-96, joined Jets in 1997.

Ken Whisenhunt, tight ends; born February 28, 1962, Atlanta, lives in Cleveland. Tight end Georgia Tech 1980-84. Pro tight end Atlanta Falcons 1985-88, Washington Redskins 1990, New York Jets 1991-93. College coach: Vanderbilt 1995-96. Pro coach: Baltimore Ravens 1997-98, Cleveland Browns 1999, joined Jets in 2000.

2000 FIRST-YEAR ROSTER

Name	Pos.	Ht.	Wt.	Birthdate	College	Hometown	How Acq.
Abraham, John	LB	6-4	250	5/6/78	South Carolina	Timmonsville, S.C.	D1b
Becht, Anthony	TE	6-5	267	8/8/77	West Virginia	Drexel Hill, Pa.	D1d
Bristol, Mark	T	6-6	300	1/12/78	Mansfield	Philadelphia, Pa.	FA
Byrd, Anthony	T	6-5	295	8/12/77	Louisville	Bedford, Ohio	FA
Campbell, Brandon	WR	5-10	187	6/29/78	Eastern Michigan	Lakeview Terrace, Calif.	FA
Coles, Laveranues	WR	5-11	188	12/29/77	Florida State	Jacksonville, Fla.	D3
Coleman, Fred (1)	WR	6-1	190	1/31/75	Washington	Tyler, Tex.	FA-'99
Eaton, Jonathan	S	6-2	200	5/13/76	Akron	Wheelersburg, Ohio	FA
Ellis, Shaun	DE	6-5	280	6/24/77	Tennessee	Anderson, S.C.	D1a
Farmer, Matt	WR	6-0	190	3/4/74	Air Force	Pella, Iowa	FA
Gill, Brian	DE	6-3	282	10/14/77	McNeese State	Reserve, La.	FA
Hayes, Windrell	WR	5-11	204	12/14/76	Southern California	Stockton, Calif.	D5
Kubiak, Jim (1)	QB	6-2	211	5/12/72	Navy	Athol Springs, N.Y.	FA-'99
Lee, Del	CB	5-10	187	1/19/76	McNeese State	New Orleans, La.	FA-'99
Lotysz, Greg (1)	T	6-6	318	4/9/74	North Dakota	Thunder Bay, Ontario, Canada	FA-'99
Michals, Jon	DE	6-4	274	6/29/77	Minnesota	Oak Creek, Wis.	FA
Moreland, Jake	TE	6-3	227	1/18/77	Western Michigan	Milwaukee, Wis.	FA
Moses, Kelvin	LB	6-0	234	9/3/76	Wake Forest	Heartsville, S.C.	FA
Pennington, Chad	QB	6-3	229	6/26/76	Marshall	Knoxville, Tenn.	D1c
Peterson, Cory	WR	6-2	195	6/15/77	Mississippi	Germantown, Tenn.	FA
Pilon, Jeff	T	6-6	300	3/21/76	Syracuse	Nepean, Ontario, Canada	FA
Sanders, Vaughn	RB	5-11	210	3/19/77	Hofstra	Inwood, N.Y.	FA
Scott, Tony	CB	5-10	193	10/3/76	North Carolina State	Lawndale, N.C.	D6
Seals, Richard	DT	6-3	316	4/19/76	Utah	Houston, Tex.	D7
Short, Keith	C	6-2	285	4/19/77	Virginia Tech	Ashland, Va.	FA
Strohmeyer, Dax	LB	6-4	210	1/31/77	Rutgers	Upper Saddle River, N.J.	FA
Wiggins, Jermaine (1)	RB	6-2	255	1/18/75	Georgia	East Boston, Mass.	FA-'99

The term NFL Rookie is defined as a player who is in his first season of professional football and has not been on the roster of another professional football team for any regular-season or postseason games. A Rookie is designated by an "R" on NFL rosters. Players who have been active in another professional football league or players who have NFL experience, including either preseason training camp or being on an Active List or Inactive List, or on Reserve/Injured or Reserve/Physically Unable to Perform for fewer than six regular-season games, are termed NFL First-Year Players. An NFL First-Year Player is designated by a "1" on NFL rosters. Thereafter, a player is credited with an additional year of experience for each season in which he accumulates six games on the Active List or Inactive List, or on Reserve/Injured or Reserve/Physically Unable to Perform.

NOTES

OAKLAND RAIDERS

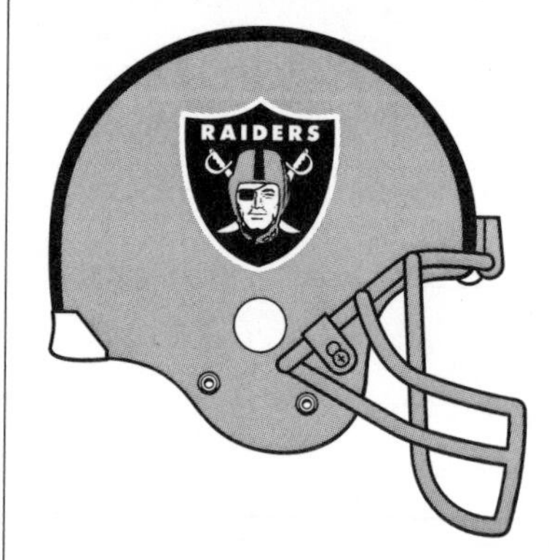

American Football Conference
Western Division
Team Colors: Silver and Black
1220 Harbor Bay Parkway
Alameda, California 94502
Telephone: (510) 864-5000

CLUB OFFICIALS

President of the General Partner: Al Davis
Chief Executive: Amy Trask
Executive Assistant: Al LoCasale
General Counsel: Jeff Birren
Senior Assistant: Bruce Allen
Personnel Executive: Mike Lombardi
Personnel Executive: Chet Franklin
Legal Affairs: Jeff Birren, Roxanne Kosarzycki
Finance: Marc Badain, Tom Blanda, Ron LaVelle, Derek Person
Special Projects: Jim Otto
Senior Administrator: Morris Bradshaw
Senior Executive: John Herrera
Public Relations Director: Mike Taylor
Public Relations: Craig Long
Broadcast and Multimedia: Billy Zagger
Ticket Operations: Peter Eiges
Head Trainer: H. Rod Martin
Assistant Trainer: Scott Touchet
Assistant Trainer: Mark Mayer
Equipment Manager: Bob Romanski
Video Director: Dave Nash
Stadium: Network Associates Coliseum
•**Capacity:** 63,132
Playing Surface: Grass
Training Camp: Napa Valley Marriott
Napa, California 94558

2000 SCHEDULE

PRESEASON

Aug. 5	at St. Louis	7:00
Aug. 13	at Dallas	6:00
Aug. 18	**Dallas**	6:00
Aug. 24	**Seattle**	6:00

REGULAR SEASON

Sept. 3	**San Diego**	1:15
Sept. 10	at Indianapolis	12:00
Sept. 17	**Denver**	1:05
Sept. 24	**Cleveland**	1:15
Oct. 1	Open Date	
Oct. 8	at San Francisco	1:15
Oct. 15	at Kansas City	12:00
Oct. 22	**Seattle**	1:05
Oct. 29	at San Diego	5:35
Nov. 5	**Kansas City**	1:15
Nov. 13	at Denver (Mon.)	7:00
Nov. 19	at New Orleans	12:00
Nov. 26	**Atlanta**	1:05
Dec. 3	at Pittsburgh	1:00
Dec. 10	**New York Jets**	5:35
Dec. 16	at Seattle (Sat.)	1:05
Dec. 24	**Carolina**	1:15

RECORD HOLDERS

INDIVIDUAL RECORDS—CAREER

Category	Name	Performance
Rushing (Yds.)	Marcus Allen, 1982-1992	8,545
Passing (Yds.)	Ken Stabler, 1970-79	19,078
Passing (TDs)	Ken Stabler, 1970-79	150
Receiving (No.)	Tim Brown, 1988-1999	770
Receiving (Yds.)	Tim Brown, 1988-1999	10,944
Interceptions	Willie Brown, 1967-1978	39
	Lester Hayes, 1977-1986	39
Punting (Avg.)	Leo Araguz, 1996-98	44.0
Punt Return (Avg.)	Claude Gibson, 1963-65	12.6
Kickoff Return (Avg.)	Jack Larscheid, 1960-61	28.4
Field Goals	Chris Bahr, 1980-88	162
Touchdowns (Tot.)	Marcus Allen, 1982-1992	98
Points	George Blanda, 1967-1975	863

INDIVIDUAL RECORDS—SINGLE SEASON

Category	Name	Performance
Rushing (Yds.)	Marcus Allen, 1985	1,759
Passing (Yds.)	Jeff George, 1997	3,917
Passing (TDs)	Daryle Lamonica, 1969	34
Receiving (No.)	Tim Brown 1997	104
Receiving (Yds.)	Tim Brown, 1997	1,408
Interceptions	Lester Hayes, 1980	13
Punting (Avg.)	Ray Guy, 1973	45.3
Punt Return (Avg.)	Claude Gibson, 1964	14.4
Kickoff Return (Avg.)	Harold Hart, 1975	30.5
Field Goals	Jeff Jaeger, 1993	35
Touchdowns (Tot.)	Marcus Allen, 1984	18
Points	Jeff Jaeger, 1993	132

INDIVIDUAL RECORDS—SINGLE GAME

Category	Name	Performance
Rushing (Yds.)	Napoleon Kaufman, 10-19-97	227
Passing (Yds.)	Jeff Hostetler, 10-31-93	424
Passing (TDs)	Tom Flores, 12-22-63	6
	Daryle Lamonica, 10-19-69	6
Receiving (No.)	Tim Brown, 12-21-97	14
Receiving (Yds.)	Art Powell, 12-22-63	247
Interceptions	Many times	3
	Last time by Terry McDaniel, 10-9-94	
Field Goals	Jeff Jaeger, 12-11-94	5
Touchdowns (Tot.)	Art Powell, 12-22-63	4
	Marcus Allen, 9-24-84	4
	Harvey Williams, 11-16-97	4
Points	Art Powell, 12-22-63	24
	Marcus Allen, 9-24-84	24
	Harvey Williams, 11-16-97	24

COACHING HISTORY

OAKLAND 1960-1981
LOS ANGELES 1982-1994
(369-252-11)

1960-61	Eddie Erdelatz*	6-10-0
1961-62	Marty Feldman**	2-15-0
1962	Red Conkright	1-8-0
1963-65	Al Davis	23-16-3
1966-68	John Rauch	35-10-1
1969-78	John Madden	112-39-7
1979-87	Tom Flores	91-56-0
1988-89	Mike Shanahan***	8-12-0
1989-94	Art Shell	56-41-0
1995-96	Mike White	15-17-0
1997	Joe Bugel	4-12-0
1998-99	Jon Gruden	16-16-0

*Released after two games in 1961
**Released after five games in 1962
***Released after four games in 1989

NETWORK ASSOCIATES COLISEUM

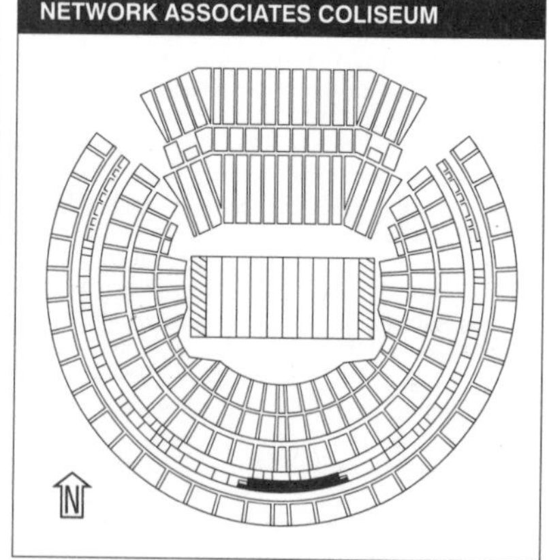

1999 TEAM RECORD

PRESEASON (3-1)

Date	Result		Opponent
8/7	W	18-17	at St. Louis
8/15	W	10-3	Dallas
8/30	L	8-16	San Francisco
9/3	W	43-7	at Arizona

REGULAR SEASON (8-8)

Date	Result		Opponent	Att.
9/12	L	24-28	at Green Bay	59,872
9/19	W	22-17	at Minnesota	64,080
9/26	W	24-17	Chicago	50,458
10/3	L	21-22	at Seattle	66,400
10/10	L	13-16	Denver	55,704
10/17	W	20-14	at Buffalo	71,113
10/24	W	24-23	New York Jets	47,326
10/31	L	9-16	Miami	61,556
11/14	W	28-9	San Diego	43,353
11/22	L	21-27	at Denver (OT)	70,012
11/28	L	34-37	Kansas City	48,632
12/5	W	30-21	Seattle	44,716
12/9	L	14-21	at Tennessee	66,357
12/19	W	45-0	Tampa Bay	46,395
12/26	L	20-23	at San Diego	63,846
1/2	W	41-38	at Kansas City (OT)	79,026

(OT) Overtime

SCORE BY PERIODS

Raiders	80	89	151	67	3	—	390
Opponents	64	81	71	107	6	—	329

ATTENDANCE

Home 386,664 Away 546,830 Total 933,494
Single-game home record, 61,523 (9/8/97)
Single-season home record, 398,915 (1996)

1999 TEAM STATISTICS

	Raiders	Opp.
Total First Downs	326	266
Rushing	110	85
Passing	196	161
Penalty	20	20
Third Down: Made/Att	85/216	70/212
Third Down Pct.	39.4	33.0
Fourth Down: Made/Att	7/8	7/14
Fourth Down Pct.	87.5	50.0
Total Net Yards	5,693	4,880
Avg. Per Game	355.8	305.0
Total Plays	1,057	981
Avg. Per Play	5.4	5.0
Net Yards Rushing	2,084	1,559
Avg. Per Game	130.3	97.4
Total Rushes	488	398
Net Yards Passing	3,609	3,321
Avg. Per Game	225.6	207.6
Sacked/Yards Lost	49/241	44/309
Gross Yards	3,850	3,630
Att./Completions	520/306	539/302
Completion Pct.	58.8	56.0
Had Intercepted	14	20
Punts/Average	77/39.5	82/43.2
Net Punting Avg.	77/32.3	82/37.6
Penalties/Yards	98/825	114/861
Fumbles/Ball Lost	22/15	26/13
Touchdowns	45	36
Rushing	18	10
Passing	24	22
Returns	3	4
Avg. Time of Possession	32:06	27:54

1999 INDIVIDUAL STATISTICS

Passing	Att.	Comp.	Yds.	Pct.	TD	Int.	Tkld.	Rate
Gannon	515	304	3,840	59.0	24	14	49/241	86.5
Hoying	5	2	10	40.0	0	0	0/0	47.9
Raiders	520	306	3,850	58.8	24	14	49/241	86.1
Opponents	539	302	3,630	56.0	22	20	44/309	75.0

SCORING	TD R	TD P	TD Rt	PAT	FG	Saf	PTS
Husted	0	0	0	30/30	20/31	0	90
Wheatley	8	3	0	0/0	0/0	0	66
Dudley	0	9	0	0/0	0/0	0	54
Brown	0	6	0	0/0	0/0	0	36
Crockett	4	1	0	0/0	0/0	0	30
Nedney	0	0	0	13/13	5/7	0	28
Kaufman	2	1	0	0/0	0/0	0	18
Jett	0	2	0	0/0	0/0	0	14
Gannon	2	0	0	0/0	0/0	0	12
Jordan	2	0	0	0/0	0/0	0	12
Johnstone	0	0	1	0/0	0/0	0	6
Ritchie	0	1	0	0/0	0/0	0	6
Shedd	0	0	1	0/0	0/0	0	6
D. Walker	0	1	0	0/0	0/0	0	6
Woodson	0	0	1	0/0	0/0	0	6
Raiders	18	24	3	43/43	25/38	0	390
Opponents	10	22	4	33/33	26/32	1	329

2-Pt. Conversions: Jett.
Team 1-2, Opponents 0-2.

RUSHING	Att.	Yds.	Avg.	LG	TD
Wheatley	242	936	3.9	30t	8
Kaufman	138	714	5.2	75t	2
Gannon	46	298	6.5	39	2
Crockett	45	91	2.0	7	4
Jordan	9	32	3.6	12	2
Ritchie	5	12	2.4	5	0
Brown	1	4	4.0	4	0
Hoying	2	-3	-1.5	-1	0
Raiders	488	2,084	4.3	75t	18
Opponents	398	1,559	3.9	52t	10

RECEIVING	No.	Yds.	Avg.	LG	TD
Brown	90	1,344	14.9	47	6
Ritchie	45	408	9.1	20t	1
Dudley	39	555	14.2	35	9
Jett	39	552	14.2	43	2
Wheatley	21	196	9.3	28	3
Mickens	20	261	13.1	30	0
Kaufman	18	181	10.1	50	1
Brigham	8	108	13.5	29	0
Jordan	8	82	10.3	30	0
Crockett	8	56	7.0	12t	1
D. Walker	7	71	10.1	21t	1
J. Williams	1	20	20.0	20	0
Woodson	1	19	19.0	19	0
Gannon	1	-3	-3.0	-3	0
Raiders	306	3,850	12.6	50	24
Opponents	302	3,630	12.0	73t	22

INTERCEPTIONS	No.	Yds.	Avg.	LG	TD
Gordon	3	44	14.7	28	0
Turner	3	43	14.3	24	0
Allen	3	33	11.0	31	0
Biekert	2	57	28.5	36	0
Mincy	2	23	11.5	21	0
Newman	2	16	8.0	16	0
Woodson	1	15	15.0	15t	1
K. Williams	1	14	14.0	14	0
Maryland	1	2	2.0	2	0
Johnstone	1	0	0.0	0	0
M. Walker	1	0	0.0	0	0
Raiders	20	247	12.4	36	1
Opponents	14	239	17.1	47t	2

PUNTING	No.	Yds.	Avg.	In 20	LG
Araguz	76	3,045	40.1	25	56
Raiders	77	3,045	39.5	25	56
Opponents	82	3,542	43.2	26	64

PUNT RETURNS	No.	FC	Yds.	Avg.	LG	TD
Gordon	42	14	397	9.5	78	0
Raiders	42	14	397	9.5	78	0
Opponents	38	15	479	12.6	84t	1

KICKOFF RETURNS	No.	Yds.	Avg.	LG	TD
Kaufman	42	831	19.8	48	0
Jordan	10	207	20.7	28	0
Branch	6	96	16.0	20	0
Treu	1	6	6.0	6	0
Ashmore	1	0	0.0	0	0
Mincy	1	0	0.0	0	0
Raiders	61	1140	18.7	48	0
Opponents	77	1626	21.1	93	0

FIELD GOALS	1-19	20-29	30-39	40-49	50+
Husted	2/2	3/3	7/11	8/12	0/3
Nedney	0/0	2/2	2/2	0/1	1/2
Raiders	2/2	5/5	9/13	8/13	1/5
Opponents	1/1	5/5	10/10	8/13	2/3

SACKS	No.
Johnstone	10.0
Russell	9.5
Bryant	4.5
Jackson	4.0
Barton	3.0
Ja. Harris	2.5
Biekert	2.0
Harvey	2.0
Maryland	1.5
Gordon	1.0
Osborne	1.0
Sword	1.0
M. Walker	1.0
K. Williams	1.0
Raiders	44.0
Opponents	49.0

2000 DRAFT CHOICES

Round	Name	Pos.	College
1	Sebastian Janikowski	K	Florida State
2	Jerry Porter	WR	West Virginia
4	Junior Ioane	DT	Arizona State
5	Shane Lechler	P	Texas A&M
7	Mondriel Fulcher	TE	Miami
	Cliffton Black	DB	Southwest Texas State

OAKLAND RAIDERS

2000 VETERAN ROSTER

No.	Name	Pos.	Ht.	Wt.	Birthdate	NFL Exp.	College	Hometown	How Acq.	'99 Games/ Starts
58	Alexander, Elijah	LB	6-2	235	8/2/70	8	Kansas State	Fort Worth, Tex.	FA-'00	0*
21	Allen, Eric	CB	5-10	185	11/22/65	13	Arizona State	San Diego, Calif.	T(NO)-'98	16/16
2	Araguz, Leo	P	5-11	190	1/18/70	4	Stephen F. Austin	Harlingen, Tex.	FA-'96	16/0
73	Ashmore, Darryl	G-T	6-7	310	11/1/69	9	Northwestern	Peoria, Ill.	FA-'98	16/2
50	Barton, Eric	LB	6-2	245	9/29/77	2	Maryland	Alexandria, Va.	D5-'99	16/3
54	Biekert, Greg	LB	6-2	255	3/14/69	8	Colorado	Longmont, Colo.	D7-'93	16/16
27	Branch, Calvin	S	5-11	195	5/8/74	4	Colorado State	Spring, Tex.	D6-'97	16/1
87	Brigham, Jeremy	TE	6-6	255	3/22/75	3	Washington	Scottsdale, Ariz.	D5-'98	16/2
81	Brown, Tim	WR	6-0	195	7/22/66	13	Notre Dame	Dallas, Tex.	D1-'88	16/16
94	Bryant, Tony	DE	6-6	275	9/3/76	2	Florida State	Marathon, Fla.	D2-'99	10/0
46	Burke, John	TE	6-4	240	9/7/71	6	Virginia Tech	Holmdel, N.J.	FA-'00	0*
30	Cherry, Je'Rod	S	6-1	205	5/30/73	5	California	Berkeley, Calif.	UFA(NO)-'00	16/0*
57	Coleman, Roderick	DE	6-2	265	8/16/76	2	East Carolina	Philadelphia, Pa.	D5-'99	3/0
79	Collins, Mo	T	6-4	325	9/22/76	3	Florida	Charlotte, N.C.	D1-'98	13/12
69	Colman, Doug	LB	6-2	250	6/4/73	5	Nebraska	Ocean City, N.J.	UFA(Tenn)-'00	16/0*
80	Copeland, Horace	WR	6-3	205	1/2/71	8	Miami	Orlando, Fla.	FA-'99	0*
32	Crockett, Zack	RB	6-2	240	12/2/72	6	Florida State	Pompano Beach, Fla.	UFA(Jax)-'99	13/1
64	DiNapoli, Gennaro	G	6-3	300	5/25/75	3	Virginia Tech	Cazenovia, N.Y.	D4-'98	11/9
33	Dorsett, Anthony	S	5-11	200	9/14/73	5	Pittsburgh	Aliquippa, Pa.	UFA(Tenn)-'00	16/1*
15	Drayton, Troy	TE	6-3	260	6/29/70	8	Penn State	Harrisburg, Pa.	FA-'00	14/13*
10	Driesbach, Scott	QB	6-3	210	12/16/75	2	Michigan	Mishawaka, Ind.	FA-'99	0*
83	Dudley, Rickey	TE	6-6	255	7/15/72	5	Ohio State	Henderson, Tex.	D1-'96	16/16
93	Duff, Jamal	DE	6-7	285	3/11/72	5	San Diego State	Tustin, Calif.	FA-'00	0*
88	Dunn, David	WR	6-3	210	6/10/72	6	Fresno State	San Diego, Calif.	UFA(Cle)-'00	6/0*
45	Fontenot, Chris	TE	6-4	250	7/11/74	2	McNeese State	Iota, La.	FA-'00	0*
12	Gannon, Rich	QB	6-3	210	12/20/65	13	Delaware	Philadelphia, Pa.	UFA(KC)-99	16/16
23	Gordon, Darrien	CB	5-11	190	11/14/70	8	Stanford	Shawnee, Okla.	FA-'99	16/2
93	# Harris, James	DE	6-6	285	5/13/68	7	Temple	East St. Louis, Ill.	FA-'98	16/16
14	Hoying, Bobby	QB	6-3	220	9/20/72	5	Ohio State	St. Henry, Ohio	T(Phil)-'99	2/0
5	Husted, Michael	K	6-0	195	6/16/70	8	Virginia	Hampton, Va.	FA-'99	13/0
90	Jackson, Grady	DT	6-2	325	1/21/73	4	Knoxville	Greensboro, Ala.	D6-'97	15/0
20	James, Tory	CB	6-2	185	5/18/73	5	Louisiana State	Marrero, La.	UFA(Den)-'00	16/4*
82	Jett, James	WR	5-10	170	12/28/70	8	West Virginia	Kearneysville, W. Va.	FA-'93	16/11
51	Johnstone, Lance	DE	6-4	250	6/11/73	5	Temple	Philadelphia, Pa.	D2-'96	16/16
28	Jordan, Randy	RB	5-11	215	6/6/70	7	North Carolina	Manson, N.C.	FA-'98	16/0
26	Kaufman, Napoleon	RB	5-9	185	6/7/73	6	Washington	Lompoc, Calif.	D1-'95	16/5
72	Kennedy, Lincoln	T	6-6	335	2/12/71	8	Washington	San Diego, Calif.	T(Atl)-'96	15/15
97	Lee, Shawn	DT	6-2	300	10/24/66	12	Northern Alabama	Brooklyn, N.Y.	FA-'00	0*
85	Mickens, Terry	WR	6-1	200	2/21/71	7	Florida A&M	Tallahassee, Fla.	UFA(GB)-'98	16/3
22	Mincy, Charles	S	6-0	200	12/16/69	10	Washington	Los Angeles, Calif.	FA-'99	16/6
31	Moore, Jerald	RB	5-9	230	11/20/74	4	Oklahoma	Houston, Tex.	FA-'00	0*
77	Myles, Toby	T	6-5	320	7/23/75	3	Jackson State	Jackson, Miss.	FA-'00	8/0*
6	Nedney, Joe	K	6-5	220	3/22/73	5	San Jose State	San Jose, Calif.	FA-'99	3/0
98	Osborne, Chuck	DT	6-2	290	11/2/73	4	Arizona	Canyon Country, Calif.	FA-'98	16/0
49	Pope, Marquez	S	5-11	190	10/29/70	9	Fresno State	Long Beach, Calif.	FA-'00	15/15*
42	Ray, Marcus	S	5-11	215	8/14/76	2	Michigan	Columbus, Ohio	FA-'99	8/0
40	Ritchie, Jon	RB	6-1	250	9/4/74	3	Stanford	Mechanicsburgh, Pa.	D3-'98	16/14
95	Robbins, Austin	DT	6-6	290	3/1/71	7	North Carolina	Washington, D.C.	UFA(NO)-'00	14/3*
63	Robbins, Barret	C	6-3	320	8/26/73	6	Texas Christian	Houston, Tex.	D2-'95	16/16
96	Russell, Darrell	DT	6-5	325	5/27/76	4	Southern California	San Diego, Calif.	D1-'97	16/16
84	Shedd, Kenny	WR	5-10	165	2/14/71	6	Northern Iowa	Davenport, Iowa	FA-'96	12/0
65	Sims, Barry	G-T	6-5	295	12/1/74	2	Utah	Park City, Utah	FA-'99	16/10
53	Smith, Travian	LB	6-4	240	8/26/75	2	Oklahoma	Tatum, Tex.	D5-'98	16/1
74	Stinchcomb, Matt	T	6-6	310	6/3/77	2	Georgia	Lilburn, Ga.	D1-'99	0*
66	Stokes, Barry	T	6-5	310	12/20/73	3	Eastern Michigan	Davison, Mich.	FA-'99	0*
56	Sword, Sam	LB	6-1	245	12/9/74	2	Michigan	Saginaw, Mich.	FA-'99	10/5
62	Treu, Adam	C	6-5	300	6/24/74	4	Nebraska	Lincoln, N.E.	D3-'97	16/0
91	Upshaw, Regan	DE	6-4	260	8/12/75	5	California	Pittsburg, Calif.	UFA(Jax)-'00	6/0*
38	Walker, Marquis	CB	5-10	175	7/6/72	5	Southeast Missouri State	St. Louis, Mo.	FA-'98	16/0
47	Wheatley, Tyrone	RB	6-0	235	1/19/72	6	Michigan	Inkster, Mich.	FA-'99	16/9
8	Whelihan, Craig	QB	6-5	220	4/15/71	5	Pacific	San Jose, Calif.	FA-'00	0*
34	Williams, Jermaine	RB	6-0	235	8/14/73	3	Houston	Greenville, N.C.	FA-'98	15/0
89	Williams, Rodney	WR	6-0	190	8/15/73	3	Arizona	Palmdale, Calif.	FA-'98	5/0
76	Wisniewski, Steve	G	6-4	305	4/7/67	12	Penn State	Houston, Tex.	D2-'89	16/16
24	Woodson, Charles	CB	6-1	205	10/7/76	3	Michigan	Fremont, Ohio	D1-'98	16/16
37	Woodson, Sean	S	6-1	205	8/27/74	2	Jackson State	Jackson, Miss.	FA-'00	0*

* Alexander last active with Indianapolis in '98; Burke and Whelihan last active with San Diego in '98; Cherry played 16 games with New Orleans in '99; Colman played 16 games with Tennessee; Copeland, Dreisbach, and S. Woodson were inactive for 16 games; Dorsett played 16 games with Tennessee; Drayton played 14 games with Miami; Duff last active with Washington in '97; Dunn played 6 games with Cleveland; Fontenot and S. Woodson last active with Philadelphia in '98; James played 16 games with Denver; Lee last active with Chicago in '98; Moore last active with St. Louis in '98; Myles played 8 games with N.Y. Giants; Pope played 15 games with Cleveland; Robbins played 14 games with New Orleans; Stinchomb was inactive for 3 games; Stokes was inactive for 1 game; Upshaw played 6 games with Jacksonville.

Unrestricted free agent; subject to developments.

Retired—Wade Wilson, 19-year quarterback, 0 games in '99.

Also played with Raiders in '99—LB Bobby Brooks (1 game), LB Richard Harvey (15), DT Russell Maryland (16), S Anthony Newman (16), T Nathan Parks (2), S Eric Turner (10), TE Derrick Walker (11), LB K.D. Williams (9).

COACHING STAFF

Head Coach,
Jon Gruden

Pro career: Became the twelfth head coach in Raiders history on January 22, 1998, after seven seasons as an NFL assistant coach. Guided Raiders to an 8-8 record in his second season as head coach. Gruden's teams reached the postseason five times during his assistant coaching tenure. Spent the last three years as offensive coordinator for the Philadelphia Eagles on Ray Rhodes's staff. The Eagles were 26-21-1 during this 1995-97 period, including playoff appearances after both the 1995 and 1996 seasons. In 1997, the Eagles ranked second in passing, fifth in rushing and third in total offense in the NFC. In 1996, they led the NFC in passing, were second in rushing and led the NFC in total offense. In 1995—his first season as an NFL offensive coordinator—the Eagles finished fourth in the league in rushing. He served as an offensive assistant to Green Bay Packers head coach Mike Holmgren in 1992, then spent the 1993 and 1994 campaigns as Green Bay's receivers coach. Gruden spent the 1991 season as wide receivers coach at the University of Pittsburgh under coach Paul Hackett. In 1990, he was an offensive assistant to head coach George Seifert with the San Francisco 49ers, working with offensive coordinator Holmgren. The 49ers were an NFL best 14-2 that season. Career record: 16-16.

Background: Quarterback at Dayton 1983-85, while earning bachelor's degree in communications. Won the prestigious Lt. Andy Zulli Memorial Award given annually "to the senior player who best exemplifies the qualities of sportsmanship and character." Dayton had a 24-7 record in Gruden's three varsity seasons there.

Personal: Born August 17, 1963, in Sandusky, Ohio. Gruden and his wife Cindy have two sons, Jon II, 4, and Michael, 1. His father, Jim, is a scout for the San Francisco 49ers and formerly served as an assistant coach under John McKay with the Tampa Bay Buccaneers from 1982-83. His brother Jay, who played in the Arena Football League, served as offensive coordinator of that league's Nashville team and is presently head coach of the Arena League's 1998 champion Orlando Predators.

2000 FIRST-YEAR ROSTER

Name	Pos.	Ht.	Wt.	Birthdate	College	Hometown	How Acq.
Akers, Jeremy (1)	G	6-5	305	1/9/74	Notre Dame	Washington, D.C.	FA
Black, Cliffton	S	6-0	195	4/11/77	Southwest Texas State	Fernando, Miss.	D7
Brooks, Bobby (1)	LB	6-2	240	3/3/76	Fresno State	Vallejo, Calif.	FA-'99
Buchanan, Shamari	WR	6-2	215	1/11/77	Alabama	Atlanta, Ga.	FA
Cannon, Rico (1)	WR	6-2	200	11/7/75	Newberry	Easley, S.C.	FA
Clements, Jimmy (1)	LB	6-2	235	12/28/73	Georgia Tech	Marietta, Ga.	FA
Cronshagen, Jeff	T	6-6	310	2/8/77	Stanford	Livermore, Calif.	FA
Day, Donnell	CB	5-9	180	7/19/76	Cal State-Northridge	San Diego, Calif.	FA
Fontenot, Chris (1)	TE	6-3	250	7/11/74	McNeese State	Iota, La.	FA
Fulcher, Mondriel	TE	6-3	250	10/15/76	Miami	Coffeyville, Kan.	D7
Hamilton, Joey	WR	6-1	200	8/12/78	Jacksonville State	Greenville, Ala.	FA
Harris, Johnnie (1)	S	6-2	210	8/21/72	Mississippi State	Chicago, Ill.	FA-'99
Ioane, Junior	DT	6-4	320	7/21/77	Arizona State	Mt. Pleasant, Utah	D4
Jackson, Jabari	RB	6-2	225	7/29/77	Southern California	San Francisco, Calif.	FA
Jackson, Julius	LB	6-1	245	11/7/76	Nebraska	Gainsville, Tex.	FA
Janikowski, Sebastian	K	6-1	255	3/2/78	Florida State	Daytona Beach, Fla.	D1
Jennings, Brandon	S	6-0	195	7/15/78	Texas A&M	Channelview, Tex.	FA
Johnson, Eric	S	6-0	215	4/30/76	Nebraska	Phoenix, Ariz.	FA
Knight, Marcus	WR	6-1	180	6/19/78	Michigan	Sylacauga, Ala.	FA
Lechler, Shane	P	6-2	230	8/7/76	Texas A&M	Sealy, Tex.	D5
Noah, Abdul Salaam	DT	6-4	280	9/14/78	San Jose State	Los Angeles, Calif.	FA
Porter, Jerry	WR	6-2	220	7/14/78	West Virginia	Washington, D.C.	D2
Shannon, Larry (1)	WR	6-4	210	2/2/75	East Carolina	Starke, Fla.	FA
Spann, Craig (1)	WR	6-0	180	8/8/75	Arizona State	Phoenix, Ariz.	FA
Taves, Josh (1)	DE	6-7	280	5/13/72	Northeastern	Yarmouth, Mass.	FA
White, Anthony	RB	6-0	195	5/1/77	Kentucky	Twinsburg, Ohio	FA

The term NFL Rookie is defined as a player who is in his first season of professional football and has not been on the roster of another professional football team for any regular-season or postseason games. A Rookie is designated by an "R" on NFL rosters. Players who have been active in another professional football league or players who have NFL experience, including either preseason training camp or being on an Active List or Inactive List, or on Reserve/Injured or Reserve/Physically Unable to Perform for fewer than six regular-season games, are termed NFL First-Year Players. An NFL First-Year Player is designated by a "1" on NFL rosters. Thereafter, a player is credited with an additional year of experience for each season in which he accumulates six games on the Active List or Inactive List, or on Reserve/Injured or Reserve/Physically Unable to Perform.

ASSISTANT COACHES

Fred Biletnikoff, wide receivers; born February 23, 1943, Erie, Pa., lives in San Ramon, Calif. Wide receiver Florida State 1962-64. Pro wide receiver Oakland Raiders 1965-1978, Montreal Alouettes (CFL) 1980. Inducted into Pro Football Hall of Fame in 1988. College coach: Palomar (Calif.) J.C. 1983, Diablo Valley (Calif.) J.C. 1984, 1986. Pro coach: Oakland Invaders (USFL) 1985, Calgary Stampeders (CFL) 1987-88, joined Raiders in 1989.

Chuck Bresnahan, defensive coordinator; born September 8, 1960, Springfield, Mass., lives in Alameda, Calif. Linebacker Navy 1979-1982. No pro playing experience. College coach: Navy 1983, 1986, Georgia Tech 1987-1991, Maine 1992-93. Pro coach: Cleveland Browns 1994-95, Indianapolis Colts 1996-97, joined Raiders in 1998.

Willie Brown, squad development; born December 2, 1940, Yazoo City, Miss., lives in Tracy, Calif. Defensive back Grambling 1959-1962. Pro defensive back Denver Broncos 1963-66, Oakland Raiders 1967-78. Inducted into Pro Football Hall of Fame in 1984. College coach: Long Beach State 1990-91 (head coach 1991). Pro coach: Oakland/Los Angeles Raiders 1979-1988, rejoined Raiders in 1995.

Bill Callahan, offensive coordinator-offensive line; born July 31, 1956, Chicago, lives in Danville, Calif. Quarterback Illinois-Benedictine 1975-77. No pro playing experience. College coach: Illinois 1980-86, Northern Arizona 1987-88, Southern Illinois 1989, Wisconsin 1990-94. Pro coach: Philadelphia Eagles 1995-97, joined Raiders in 1998.

Bob Casullo, special teams; born March 24, 1951, Little Falls, N.Y., lives in Alameda, Calif. Running back Brockport State College 1970-73. No pro playing experience. College coach: Syracuse 1985-1994, Georgia Tech 1995-98, Michigan State 1999. Pro coach: Joined Raiders in 2000.

Jim Erkenbeck, tight ends; born September 10, 1933, Los Angeles, lives in Alameda, Calif. Linebacker-end San Diego State 1949-1951. No pro playing experience. College coach: San Diego State 1961-63, Grossmont (Calif.) J.C. 1964-67 (head coach), Utah State 1968, Washington State 1969-1971, California 1972-76. Pro coach: Winnipeg Blue Bombers (CFL) 1977, Montreal Alouettes (CFL) 1978-1981, Calgary Stampeders (CFL) 1982, Philadelphia/Baltimore Stars (USFL) 1983-85, New Orleans Saints 1986, Dallas Cowboys 1987-88, Kansas City Chiefs 1989-1991, 1995-98, Los Angeles Rams 1992-94, joined Raiders in 1999.

Garrett Giemont, strength and conditioning; born August 31, 1957, Fullerton, Calif., lives in San Francisco. Attended Fullerton College. No college or pro playing experience. Pro coach: Los Angeles Rams 1990-91, joined Raiders in 1995.

Woodrow Lowe, defense; born June 9, 1954, Columbus, Ga., lives in Antioch, Calif. Linebacker Alabama 1973-75. Pro linebacker San Diego Chargers 1976-1986. Pro coach: Kansas City Chiefs 1995-98, joined Raiders in 1999.

Ron Lynn, defensive backs; born December 6, 1944, Youngstown, Ohio, lives in Pleasanton, Calif. Quarterback Mount Union College 1963-66. No pro playing experience. Pro coach: Oakland Invaders (USFL) 1983-85, San Diego Chargers 1986-1991, Cincinnati Bengals 1992-93, Washington Redskins 1994-96, New England Patriots 1997-99, joined Raiders in 2000.

Don Martin, quality control-defense; born September 17, 1949, Carrollton, Mo., lives Oakland. Running back Yale 1968-1970. Pro defensive back New England Patriots 1973, Kansas City Chiefs 1975, Tampa Bay Buccaneers 1976. College coach: Yale 1981-1996. Pro coach: Joined Raiders in 1998.

John Morton, offensive assistant; born September 24, 1969, Pontiac, Mich., lives in Castro Valley, Calif. Wide receiver Western Michigan 1991-92, Grand Rapids C.C. 1989-1990. Pro wide receiver Los Angeles Raiders 1993-94, Toronto Argonauts (CFL) 1995-96, Frankfurt Galaxy (WLAF) 1997. Pro coach: Joined Raiders in 1998.

Skip Peete, running backs, born January 30, 1963, Mesa, Ariz., lives in Alameda, Calif. Wide receiver Arizona 1981-82, Kansas 1984-85. Pro wide receiver New York Jets 1987. College coach: Pittsburgh 1988-92, Michigan State 1993-94, Rutgers 1995, UCLA 1996-97. Pro coach: Joined Raiders in 1998.

Robin Ross, linebackers; born August 17, 1954, Huntington Beach, Calif., lives in Alameda, Calif. Offensive lineman Rio Hondo C.C. 1973-74, Washington State 1975-76. No pro playing experience. College coach: Long Beach State 1977-1983, Cincinnati 1984-85, Washington State 1986, Iowa State 1987-1993, Western Washington 1994-95, Fresno State 1996, Oregon 1997-98. Pro coach: Joined Raiders in 1999.

David Shaw, quality control-offense; born July 31, 1972, San Diego, lives in Alameda, Calif. Wide receiver Stanford 1990-94. No pro playing experience. College coach: Western Washington 1995-96. Pro coach: Philadelphia Eagles 1997, joined Raiders in 1998.

Gary Stevens, quarterbacks; born March 19, 1943, Cleveland, lives in Alameda, Calif. Running back John Carroll 1963-65. No pro playing experience. College coach: Louisville 1971-74, Kent State 1975, West Virginia 1976-79, Miami 1980-88. Pro coach: Miami Dolphins 1989-1997, joined Raiders in 1998.

Mike Waufle, defensive line; born June 27, 1954, Hornell, N.Y., lives in Oakland. Defensive lineman Bakersfield J.C. 1975-76, Utah State 1977-78. No pro playing experience. College coach: Alfred 1979, Utah State 1980-84, Fresno State 1985-88, UCLA 1989, Oregon State 1990-91, California 1992-97. Pro coach: Joined Raiders in 1998.

PITTSBURGH STEELERS

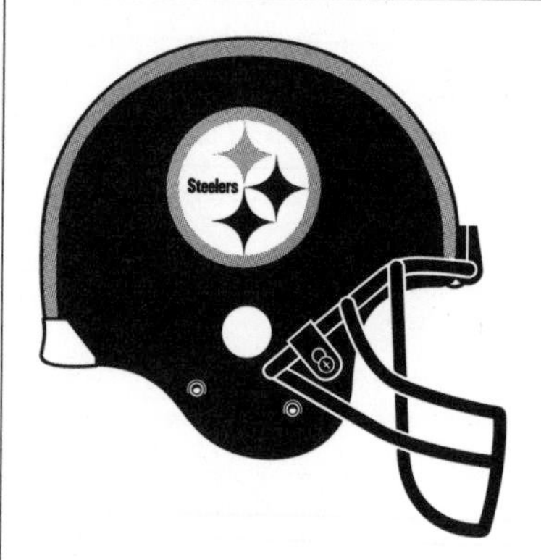

American Football Conference
Central Division
Team Colors: Black and Gold
Three Rivers Stadium
300 Stadium Circle
Pittsburgh, Pennsylvania 15212
Telephone: (412) 323-0300

CLUB OFFICIALS

President: Daniel M. Rooney
Vice President/General Counsel: Arthur J. Rooney II
Vice President: John R. McGinley
Vice President: Arthur J. Rooney, Jr.
Administration Advisor: Charles H. Noll
Communications Coordinator: Ron Wahl
Public Relations/Media Manager: David Lockett
Director of Business: Mark Hart
Business Relations Coordinator: TBA
Business Accounting Coordinator: Jim Ellenberger
Director of Football Operations: Kevin Colbert
College Personnel Coordinator: Bill Baker
Pro Personnel Coordinator: Doug Whaley
College Scouts: Mark Gorscak, Phil Kreidler, Bob Lane, Dan Rooney
Office/Ticket Coordinator: Geraldine R. Glenn
Ticket Manager: Brian Bonifate
Director of Marketingr: Tony Quatrini
Player Development Coordinator: Anthony Griggs
Trainers: John Norwig, Ryan Grove
Equipment Manager: Rodgers Freyvogel
Stadium: Three Rivers Stadium • **Capacity:** 59,600
300 Stadium Circle
Pittsburgh, Pennsylvania 15212
Playing Surface: AstroTurf
Training Camp: St. Vincent College
Latrobe, Pennsylvania 15650

2000 SCHEDULE

PRESEASON

July 30	at Dallas	7:00
Aug. 5	**Miami**	7:30
Aug. 10	**Carolina**	7:30
Aug. 19	vs. Indianapolis at Mexico City	8:00
Aug. 25	at Washington	8:00

REGULAR SEASON

Sept. 3	**Baltimore**	1:00
Sept. 10	Open Date	
Sept. 17	at Cleveland	1:00
Sept. 24	**Tennessee**	1:00
Oct. 1	at Jacksonville	1:00
Oct. 8	at New York Jets	1:00
Oct. 15	**Cincinnati**	1:00
Oct. 22	**Cleveland**	4:05
Oct. 29	at Baltimore	1:00
Nov. 5	at Tennessee	12:00
Nov. 12	**Philadelphia**	1:00
Nov. 19	**Jacksonville**	8:35
Nov. 26	at Cincinnati	1:00
Dec. 3	**Oakland**	1:00
Dec. 10	at New York Giants	1:00
Dec. 16	**Washington** (Sat.)	12:30
Dec. 24	at San Diego	1:05

RECORD HOLDERS

INDIVIDUAL RECORDS—CAREER

Category	Name	Performance
Rushing (Yds.)	Franco Harris, 1972-1983	11,950
Passing (Yds.)	Terry Bradshaw, 1970-1983	27,989
Passing (TDs)	Terry Bradshaw, 1970-1983	212
Receiving (No.)	John Stallworth, 1974-1987	537
Receiving (Yds.)	John Stallworth, 1974-1987	8,723
Interceptions	Mel Blount, 1970-1983	57
Punting (Avg.)	Bobby Joe Green, 1960-61	45.7
Punt Return (Avg.)	Bobby Gage, 1949-1950	14.9
Kickoff Return (Avg.)	Lynn Chandnois, 1950-56	29.6
Field Goals	Gary Anderson, 1982-1994	309
Touchdowns (Tot.)	Franco Harris, 1972-1983	100
Points	Gary Anderson, 1982-1994	1,343

INDIVIDUAL RECORDS—SINGLE SEASON

Category	Name	Performance
Rushing (Yds.)	Barry Foster, 1992	1,690
Passing (Yds.)	Terry Bradshaw, 1979	3,724
Passing (TDs)	Terry Bradshaw, 1978	28
Receiving (No.)	Yancey Thigpen, 1995	85
Receiving (Yds.)	Yancey Thigpen, 1997	1,398
Interceptions	Mel Blount, 1975	11
Punting (Avg.)	Bobby Joe Green, 1961	47.0
Punt Return (Avg.)	Bobby Gage, 1949	16.0
Kickoff Return (Avg.)	Lynn Chandnois, 1952	35.2
Field Goals	Norm Johnson, 1995	34
Touchdowns (Tot.)	Louis Lipps, 1985	15
Points	Norm Johnson, 1995	141

INDIVIDUAL RECORDS—SINGLE GAME

Category	Name	Performance
Rushing (Yds.)	John Fuqua, 12-20-70	218
Passing (Yds.)	Bobby Layne, 12-3-58	409
Passing (TDs)	Terry Bradshaw, 11-15-81	5
	Mark Malone, 9-8-85	5
Receiving (No.)	Courtney Hawkins, 11-1-98	14
Receiving (Yds.)	Buddy Dial, 10-22-61	235
Interceptions	Jack Butler, 12-13-53	*4
Field Goals	Gary Anderson, 10-23-88	6
Touchdowns (Tot.)	Ray Mathews, 10-17-54	4
	Roy Jefferson, 11-3-68	4
Points	Ray Mathews, 10-17-54	24
	Roy Jefferson, 11-3-68	24

*NFL Record

COACHING HISTORY

Pittsburgh Pirates 1933-1940
(452-479-20)

1933	Forrest (Jap) Douds	3-6-2
1934	Luby DiMelio	2-10-0
1935-36	Joe Bach	10-14-0
1937-39	Johnny (Blood) McNally*	6-19-0
1939-40	Walt Kiesling	3-13-3
1941	Bert Bell**	0-2-0
	Aldo (Buff) Donelli***	0-5-0
1941-44	Walt Kiesling****	13-20-2
1945	Jim Leonard	2-8-0
1946-47	Jock Sutherland	13-10-1
1948-51	Johnny Michelosen	20-26-2
1952-53	Joe Bach	11-13-0
1954-56	Walt Kiesling	14-22-0
1957-64	Raymond (Buddy) Parker	51-48-6
1965	Mike Nixon	2-12-0
1966-68	Bill Austin	11-28-3
1969-91	Chuck Noll	209-156-1
1992-99	Bill Cowher	82-57-0

*Released after three games in 1939
**Resigned after two games in 1941
***Released after five games in 1941
****Co-coach with Earle (Greasy) Neale in Philadelphia-Pittsburgh merger in 1943 and with Phil Handler in Chicago Cardinals-Pittsburgh merger in 1944

THREE RIVERS STADIUM

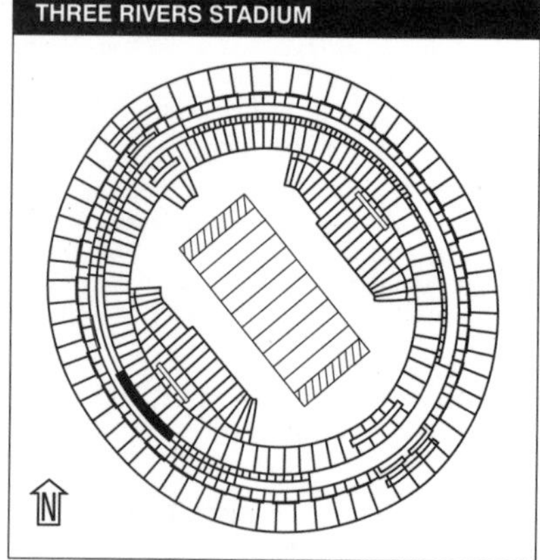

1999 TEAM RECORD

PRESEASON (1-3)

Date	Result		Opponent
8/13	W	30-23	Chicago
8/20	L	13-20	at Carolina
8/28	L	14-27	Washington
9/4	L	14-16	at Buffalo

REGULAR SEASON (6-10)

Date	Result		Opponent	Att.
9/12	W	43-0	at Cleveland	73,138
9/19	W	23-20	at Baltimore	68,965
9/26	L	10-29	Seattle	57,881
10/3	L	3-17	Jacksonville	57,308
10/10	L	21-24	at Buffalo	71,038
10/17	W	17-3	at Cincinnati	59,669
10/25	W	13-9	Atlanta	58,141
11/7	W	27-6	at San Francisco	68,657
11/14	L	15-16	Cleveland	58,213
11/21	L	10-16	at Tennessee	66,619
11/28	L	20-27	Cincinnati	50,907
12/2	L	6-20	at Jacksonville	68,806
12/12	L	24-31	Baltimore	46,715
12/18	L	19-35	at Kansas City	78,697
12/26	W	30-20	Carolina	39,428
1/2	L	36-47	Tennessee	48,025

SCORE BY PERIODS

Steelers	102	72	60	83	0	— 317
Opponents	100	102	59	59	0	— 320

ATTENDANCE

Home 471,886 Away 549,909 Total 1,021,795
Single-game home record, 60,608 (12/18/94)
Single-season home record, 471,886 (1999)

1999 TEAM STATISTICS

	Steelers	Opp.
Total First Downs	295	260
Rushing	111	92
Passing	159	142
Penalty	25	26
Third Down: Made/Att	90/234	64/203
Third Down Pct.	38.5	31.5
Fourth Down: Made/Att	7/24	8/16
Fourth Down Pct.	29.2	50.0
Total Net Yards	4,874	4,884
Avg. Per Game	304.6	305.3
Total Plays	1,067	953
Avg. Per Play	4.6	5.1
Net Yards Rushing	1,991	1,958
Avg. Per Game	124.4	122.4
Total Rushes	495	451
Net Yards Passing	2,883	2,926
Avg. Per Game	180.2	182.9
Sacked/Yards Lost	37/235	39/241
Gross Yards	3,118	3,167
Att./Completions	535/301	463/245
Completion Pct.	56.3	52.9
Had Intercepted	18	14
Punts/Average	84/45.2	92/40.6
Net Punting Avg.	84/38.1	92/34.3
Penalties/Yards	119/945	101/813
Fumbles/Ball Lost	19/7	29/14
Touchdowns	35	36
Rushing	14	10
Passing	19	20
Returns	2	6
Avg. Time of Possession	31:28	28:32

1999 INDIVIDUAL STATISTICS

Passing	Att.	Comp.	Yds.	Pct.	TD	Int.	Tkld.	Rate
Stewart	275	160	1,464	58.2	6	10	22/131	64.9
Tomczak	258	139	1,625	53.9	12	8	15/104	75.8
Bettis	1	1	21	100.0	1	0	0/0	158.3
Gonzalez	1	1	8	100.0	0	0	0/0	100.0
Steelers	535	301	3,118	56.3	19	18	37/235	71.1
Opponents	463	245	3,167	52.9	20	14	39/241	76.5

SCORING	TD R	TD P	TD Rt	PAT	FG	Saf	PTS
K. Brown	0	0	0	30/31	25/29	0	105
Huntley	5	3	0	0/0	0/0	0	48
Ward	0	7	0	0/0	0/0	0	44
Bettis	7	0	0	0/0	0/0	0	42
Edwards	0	5	0	0/0	0/0	0	30
Shaw	0	3	0	0/0	0/0	0	18
Stewart	2	1	0	0/0	0/0	0	18
Davis	0	0	1	0/0	0/0	0	6
Porter	0	0	1	0/0	0/0	0	6
Steelers	14	19	2	30/31	25/29	0	317
Opponents	10	20	6	34/35	20/26	5	320

2-Pt. Conversions: Ward.
Team 1-4, Opponents 0-1.

RUSHING	Att.	Yds.	Avg.	LG	TD
Bettis	299	1,091	3.6	35	7
Huntley	93	567	6.1	52	5
Stewart	56	258	4.6	21	2
Zereoue	18	48	2.7	8	0
Tomczak	16	19	1.2	17	0
Witman	6	18	3.0	7	0
Fuamatu-Ma'afala	1	4	4.0	4	0
Ward	2	-2	-1.0	3	0
Gonzalez	2	-3	-1.5	-1	0
Miller	2	-9	-4.5	0	0
Steelers	495	1,991	4.0	52	14
Opponents	451	1,958	4.3	82t	10

RECEIVING	No.	Yds.	Avg.	LG	TD
Edwards	61	714	11.7	41	5
Ward	61	638	10.5	42	7
Hawkins	30	285	9.5	23	0
Shaw	28	387	13.8	49	3
Huntley	27	253	9.4	25	3
Bettis	21	110	5.2	17	0
Blackwell	20	186	9.3	26	0
Bruener	18	176	9.8	29	0
Witman	12	106	8.8	38	0
Stewart	9	113	12.6	28	1
Lyons	8	81	10.1	25	0
Cushing	2	29	14.5	22	0
Johnson	2	23	11.5	18	0
Zereoue	2	17	8.5	14	0
Steelers	301	3,118	10.4	49	19
Opponents	245	3,167	12.9	88t	20

INTERCEPTIONS	No.	Yds.	Avg.	LG	TD
Shields	4	75	18.8	25	0
Washington	4	1	0.3	1	0
Kirkland	1	23	23.0	23	0
Emmons	1	22	22.0	22	0
Scott	1	16	16.0	16	0
Oldham	1	9	9.0	9	0
Roye	1	2	2.0	2	0
Davis	1	1	1.0	1	0
Steelers	14	149	10.6	25	0
Opponents	18	304	16.9	58t	3

PUNTING	No.	Yds.	Avg.	In 20	LG
Miller	84	3,795	45.2	27	75
Steelers	84	3,795	45.2	27	75
Opponents	92	3,737	40.6	32	78

PUNT RETURNS	No.	FC	Yds.	Avg.	LG	TD
Edwards	25	4	234	9.4	48	0
Hawkins	11	6	49	4.5	14	0
Shaw	4	3	53	13.3	17	0
Blackwell	1	1	39	39.0	39	0
Ward	1	0	2	2.0	2	0
Steelers	42	14	377	9.0	48	0
Opponents	39	13	392	10.1	94t	1

KICKOFF RETURNS	No.	Yds.	Avg.	LG	TD
Huntley	15	336	22.4	41	0
Blackwell	14	282	20.1	37	0
Edwards	13	234	18.0	44	0
Zereoue	7	169	24.1	35	0
Lyons	3	42	14.0	17	0
Cline	2	8	4.0	8	0
Ward	1	24	24.0	24	0
Fuamatu-Ma'afala	1	9	9.0	9	0
Vrabel	1	6	6.0	6	0
Steelers	57	1,110	19.5	44	0
Opponents	67	1,209	18.0	75	0

FIELD GOALS	1-19	20-29	30-39	40-49	50+
K. Brown	2/2	5/5	9/10	8/11	1/1
Steelers	2/2	5/5	9/10	8/11	1/1
Opponents	2/2	8/9	4/6	5/8	1/1

SACKS	No.
Gildon	8.5
Emmons	6.0
Flowers	5.0
Roye	4.5
Oldham	3.0
Steed	3.0
Kirkland	2.0
Porter	2.0
Vrabel	2.0
L. Brown	1.0
Henry	1.0
Shields	1.0
Steelers	39.0
Opponents	37.0

2000 DRAFT CHOICES

Round	Name	Pos.	College
1	Plaxico Burress	WR	Michigan State
2	Marvel Smith	T	Arizona State
3	Kendrick Clancy	DT	Mississippi
	Hank Poteat	DB	Pittsburgh
4	Danny Farmer	WR	UCLA
5	Clark Haggans	LB	Colorado State
	Tee Martin	QB	Tennessee
6	Chris Combs	DT	Duke
	Jason Gavadza	TE	Kent State

PITTSBURGH STEELERS

2000 VETERAN ROSTER

No.	Name	Pos.	Ht.	Wt.	Birthdate	NFL Exp.	College	Hometown	How Acq.	'99 Games/ Starts
27	Alexander, Brent	S	5-11	196	7/10/71	7	Tennessee State	Gallatin, Tenn.	FA-'00	16/16*
36	Bettis, Jerome	RB	5-11	250	2/16/72	8	Notre Dame	Detroit, Mich.	T(StL)-'96	16/16
89	Blackwell, Will	WR	6-0	190	7/6/75	4	San Diego State	Texarkana, Tex.	D2-'97	11/1
60	Brown, Anthony	T	6-5	315	11/6/72	6	Utah	Salt Lake City, Utah	UFA(Cin)-'99	16/11
3	Brown, Kris	K	5-10	204	12/23/76	2	Nebraska	Southlake, Tex.	D7c-'99	16/0
29	Brown, Lance	DB	6-2	203	2/2/72	5	Indiana	Jacksonville, Fla.	FA-'97	16/0
87	Bruener, Mark	TE	6-4	261	9/16/72	6	Washington	Aberdeen, Wash.	D1-'95	14/14
78	Conrad, Chris	T	6-6	310	5/27/75	3	Fresno State	Fullerton, Calif.	D3a-'98	11/3
80	Cushing, Matt	TE	6-3	258	7/2/75	2	Illinois	Chicago, Ill.	FA-'99	7/1
27	Davis, Travis	S	6-0	209	1/10/73	6	Notre Dame	Harbor City, Calif.	UFA(Jax)-'99	16/16
63	Dawson, Dermontti	C	6-2	292	6/17/65	13	Kentucky	Lexington, Ky.	D2-'88	7/7
62	Duffy, Roger	G-C	6-3	299	7/16/67	11	Penn State	Canton, Ohio	UFA(NYJ)-'98	16/11
81	Edwards, Troy	WR	5-9	192	4/7/77	2	Louisiana Tech	Shreveport, La.	D1-'99	16/6
66	Faneca, Alan	G	6-4	315	12/7/76	3	Louisiana State	New Orleans, La.	D1-'98	15/14
71	Farris, Kris	T	6-8	322	3/26/77	2	UCLA	Mission Viejo, Calif.	D3b-'99	0*
57	Fiala, John	LB	6-2	235	11/25/73	3	Washington	Kirkland, Wash.	FA-'98	16/0
41	Flowers, Lee	S	6-0	211	1/14/73	6	Georgia Tech	Columbia, S.C.	D5a-'95	15/15
45	Fuamatu-Ma'afala, Chris	RB	5-11	252	3/4/77	3	Utah	Honolulu, Hawaii	D6a-'98	10/0
72	Gandy, Wayne	T	6-5	310	2/10/71	7	Auburn	Haines City, Fla.	UFA(StL)-'99	16/16
92	Gildon, Jason	LB	6-3	255	7/31/72	7	Oklahoma State	Altus, Okla.	D3a-'99	16/16
11	Graham, Kent	QB	6-5	245	11/1/68	9	Ohio State	Wheaton, Ill.	UFA(NYG)-'00	9/9*
76	Henry, Kevin	DE	6-4	285	10/23/68	8	Mississippi State	Mound Bayou, Miss.	D4-'93	16/13
50	Holmes, Earl	LB	6-2	250	4/28/73	5	Florida A&M	Tallahassee, Fla.	D4a-'96	16/16
33	Huntley, Richard	RB	5-11	225	9/18/72	4	Winston-Salem State	Monroe, N.C.	FA-'98	16/2
83	Johnson, Malcolm	WR	6-5	215	8/27/77	2	Notre Dame	Washington, D.C.	D5b-'99	6/0
97	Kelsay, Chad	LB	6-2	252	4/9/77	2	Nebraska	Auburn, Neb.	D7b-'99	6/0
99	Kirkland, Levon	LB	6-1	270	2/17/69	9	Clemson	Lamar, S.C.	D2-'92	16/16
4	Miller, Josh	P	6-3	219	7/14/70	5	Arizona	East Brunswick, N.J.	FA-'96	16/0
61	Myslinski, Tom	G	6-3	293	12/7/68	8	Tennessee	Rome, N.Y.	FA-'00	10/2*
55	Porter, Joey	LB	6-2	240	3/22/77	2	Colorado State	Bakersfield, Calif.	D3a-'99	16/0
67	Pourdanesh, Shar	G-T	6-6	312	7/19/72	5	Nevada	Irvine, Calif.	T(Was)-'99	4/2
54	Schneck, Mike	LS	6-0	242	8/4/77	2	Wisconsin	Whitefish Bay, Wis.	FA-'99	16/0
30	Scott, Chad	CB-S	6-1	192	9/6/74	4	Maryland	Capitol Heights, Md.	D1-'97	13/12
82	Shaw, Bobby	WR	6-0	186	4/23/75	3	California	San Francisco, Calif.	UFA(Sea)-'98	15/1
47	Shields, Scott	S	6-4	228	3/29/76	2	Weber State	San Diego, Calif.	D2-'99	16/1
23	Simmons, Jason	CB	5-8	186	3/30/76	3	Arizona State	Inglewood, Calif.	D5-'98	16/0
91	Smith, Aaron	DE	6-5	281	4/9/76	2	Northern Colorado	Colorado Springs, Colo.	D4-'99	6/0
94	Staat, Jeremy	DE	6-5	300	10/10/76	3	Arizona State	Bakersfield, Calif.	D2-'98	16/2
93	Steed, Joel	NT	6-2	308	2/17/69	9	Colorado	Denver, Colo.	D3-'92	14/14
10	Stewart, Kordell	QB	6-1	211	10/16/72	6	Colorado	Marrero, La.	D2-'95	16/12
95	Sullivan, Chris	DE-DT	6-4	285	3/14/73	5	Boston College	North Attleboro, Mass.	UFA(NE)-'00	16/0*
79	Tharpe, Larry	T	6-4	305	11/19/70	8	Tennessee State	Macon, Ga.	FA-'00	0*
26	Townsend, Deshea	CB	5-10	175	9/8/75	3	Alabama	Batesville, Miss.	D4a-'98	16/4
84	Tuman, Jerame	TE	6-3	250	3/24/76	2	Michigan	Liberal, Kan.	D5a-'99	7/0
65	Tylski, Rich	G	6-5	308	2/27/71	5	Utah State	San Diego, Calif.	UFA(Jax)-'00	10/8*
69	von Oelhoffen, Kimo	DT	6-4	305	1/30/71	7	Boise State	Kaunakakai, Hawaii	UFA(Cin)-'00	16/5*
56	Vrabel, Mike	LB	6-4	250	8/14/75	4	Ohio State	Stow, Ohio	D3b-'97	10/0
86	Ward, Hines	WR	6-0	197	3/8/76	3	Georgia	Rex, Ga.	D3b-'98	16/14
20	Washington, Dewayne	CB	6-0	193	12/27/72	7	North Carolina State	Durham, N.C.	UFA(Minn)-'98	16/16
38	Witman, Jon	RB	6-1	240	6/1/72	5	Penn State	Wrightsville, Pa.	D3b-'96	16/11
2	Wright, Anthony	QB	6-1	195	2/14/76	2	South Carolina	Vanceboro, N.C.	FA-'99	0*
21	Zereoue, Amos	RB	5-8	202	10/8/76	2	West Virginia	Hempstead, N.Y.	D3c-'99	8/0

* Alexander played 16 games with Arizona in '99; Farris missed '99 season because of injury; Graham played 9 games with N.Y. Giants; Myslinski played 10 games with Dallas; Sullivan played 16 games with New England; Tharpe last active with Detroit in '98; Tylski played 10 games with Jacksonville; von Oelhoffen played 16 games with Cincinnati; Wright was inactive for 15 games.

Players lost through free agency (4): LB Carlos Emmons (Phil; 16 games in '99), S Chris Oldham (NO; 15), DE Orpheus Roye (Cle; 16), QB Mike Tomczak (Det; 16).

Also played with Steelers in '99—TE Tony Cline (2 games), S Travis Davis (16), QB Pete Gonzalez (1), DE Nolan Harrison (5), WR Courtney Hawkins (11), TE Mitch Lyons (14), G Brenden Stai (16), C Jim Sweeney (6).

COACHING STAFF

Head Coach,
Bill Cowher

Pro Career: Became the fifteenth head coach in Steelers history when he replaced Chuck Noll on January 21, 1992. In 1995, at age 38, he became the youngest coach to lead his team to a Super Bowl. Cowher is only the second coach in NFL history to lead his team to the playoffs in each of his first six seasons as head coach, the other coach is Pro Football Hall of Fame member Paul Brown. During Cowher's 14-year coaching career, teams he has been associated with have made the postseason 12 times. Began his NFL career as a free-agent linebacker with the Philadelphia Eagles in 1979, and then signed with the Cleveland Browns the following year. Cowher played three seasons (1980-82) in Cleveland before being traded back to the Eagles, where he played two more years (1983-84). Cowher began his coaching career in 1985 at age 28 under Marty Schottenheimer with the Browns. He was the Browns' special teams coach in 1985-86 and secondary coach in 1987-88 before following Schottenheimer to the Kansas City Chiefs in 1989 as defensive coordinator. Career record: 82-57.
Background: Excelled in football, basketball, and track for Carlynton High in Crafton, Pa. Was a three-year starter at linebacker for North Carolina State, serving as captain and earning team MVP honors as a senior. Graduated in 1979 with education degree.
Personal: Born in Pittsburgh, on May 8, 1957. His wife Kaye, also a North Carolina State graduate, played professional basketball for the New York Stars of the Women's Professional Basketball League with twin sister Faye. Bill and Kaye live in Pittsburgh and have three daughters—Meagan Lyn, Lauren Marie, and Lindsay Morgan.

ASSISTANT COACHES

Mike Archer, linebackers; born July 26, 1953, State College, Pa., lives in Pittsburgh. Safety/punter Miami 1972-75. No pro playing experience. College coach: Miami 1978-1983, Louisiana State 1984-1990 (head coach 1987-1990), Virginia 1991-92, Kentucky 1993-95. Pro coach: Joined Steelers in 1996.
Bob Bratkowski, receivers; born December 22, 1995, San Angelo, Tex., lives in Pittsburgh. Wide receiver Washington State. No pro playing experience. College coach: Missouri 1978-1980, Weber State 1981-85, Wyoming 1986, Washington State 1987-88, Miami 1989-1991. Pro coach: Seattle Seahawks 1992-98, joined Steelers in 1999.
Irv Eatman, offensive line assistant; born January 1, 1961, Birmingham, Ala., lives in Pittsburgh. Defensive end, offensive tackle UCLA 1979-1982. Pro offensive tackle Philadelphia/Baltimore Stars (USFL) 1983-85, Kansas City Chiefs 1986-1990, New York Jets 1991-92, Los Angeles Rams 1993, Atlanta Falcons 1994, Houston Oilers 1995-96. Pro coach: Green Bay Packers 1999, joined Steelers in 2000.
Kevin Gilbride, offensive coordinator; born August 27, 1951, North Haven, Conn., lives in Pittsburgh. Quarterback/tight end Southern Connecticut State 1971-73. No pro playing experience. College coach: Idaho State 1974-75, Tufts 1976-77, American International 1978-79, Southern Connecticut 1980-84, East Carolina 1987-88. Pro coach: Ottawa Rough Riders (CFL) 1985-86, Houston Oilers 1989-1994, Jacksonville Jaguars 1995-96, San Diego Chargers 1997-98, joined Steelers in 1999.
Jay Hayes, special teams, born March 3, 1960, South Fayette, Pa., lives in Pittsburgh. Defensive end Idaho 1980-81. Pro defensive end/linebacker Michigan Panthers (USFL) 1984, Memphis Showboats (USFL) 1985. College coach: Notre Dame 1988-1991, California 1992-94, Wisconsin 1995-98. Pro coach: Joined Steelers in 1999.
Dick Hoak, running backs; born December 8, 1939, Jeannette, Pa., lives in Greensburg, Pa. Halfback-quarterback Penn State 1958-1960. Pro running back Pittsburgh Steelers 1961-1970. Pro coach: Joined Steelers in 1972.
Tim Lewis, defensive coordinator; born December 18, 1961, Quakertown, Pa., lives in Pittsburgh. Defensive back Pittsburgh 1979-1982. Pro cornerback Green Bay Packers 1983-86. College coach: Texas A&M 1987-88, Southern Methodist 1989-1992, Pittsburgh 1993-94. Pro coach: Joined Steelers in 1995.
John Mitchell, defensive line; born October 14, 1951, Mobile, Ala., lives in Pittsburgh. Defensive end Eastern Arizona J.C. 1969-1970, Alabama 1971-72. No pro playing experience. College coach: Alabama 1973-76, Arkansas 1977-1982, Temple 1986, Louisiana State 1987-1990. Pro coach: Birmingham Stallions (USFL) 1983-85, Cleveland Browns 1991-93, joined Steelers in 1994.
Mike Mularkey, tight ends; born November 19, 1961, Ft. Lauderdale, Fla., lives in Pittsburgh. Tight end Florida 1979-1982. Pro tight end Minnesota Vikings 1983-88, Pittsburgh Steelers 1989-1991. College coach: Concordia 1993. Pro coach: Tampa Bay Buccaneers 1994-95, joined Steelers in 1996.
Willy Robinson, defensive backs; born February 10, 1956, Fort Carson, Colo., lives in Pittsburgh. Defensive back Fresno State 1976-77. No pro playing experience. College coach: San Jose State 1979, Fresno State 1980-1992, Miami 1993-94, Oregon State 1999. Pro coach: Seattle Seahawks 1995-98, joined Steelers in 2000.
Kent Stephenson, offensive line; born February 4, 1942, Anita, Iowa, lives in Pittsburgh. Guard-nose tackle Northern Iowa 1962-64. No pro playing experience. College coach: Wayne State 1965-68, North Dakota 1969-1971, Southern Methodist 1972-73, Iowa 1974-76, Oklahoma State 1977-78, Kansas 1979-1982. Pro coach: Michigan Panthers (USFL) 1983-84, Seattle Seahawks 1985-1991, joined Steelers in 1992.

2000 FIRST-YEAR ROSTER

Name	Pos.	Ht.	Wt.	Birthdate	College	Hometown	How Acq.
Atteberry, Kyle	P-K	5-11	169	4/27/76	Baylor	Kingwood, Tex.	FA
Battles, Ainsley	S	5-10	190	11/6/77	Vanderbilt	Lilbum, Ga.	FA
Brown, Ernie (1)	DT	6-3	295	3/14/71	Syracuse	Pittsburgh, Pa.	FA-'99
Brown, Demetrius	WR	6-3	209	4/10/76	Wisconsin	Milwaukee, Wis.	FA
Burress, Plaxico	WR	6-5	229	8/12/77	Michigan State	Virginia Beach, Va.	D1
Clancy, Kendrick	NT	6-1	280	9/17/78	Mississippi	Tuscaloosa, Ala.	D3a
Codie, Nakia (1)	S	6-2	208	1/20/76	Baylor	Cleburne, Tex.	FA
Combs, Chris	DE	6-6	310	5/27/75	Fresno State	Fullerton, Calif.	D6a
Curry, Sedrick	CB	6-1	193	11/23/76	Texas A&M	Houston, Tex.	FA
Farmer, Danny	WR	6-3	217	5/21/77	UCLA	Los Angeles, Calif.	D4
Foster, Jonathan	LB	6-1	246	4/11/77	Louisiana-Monroe	Amite, La.	FA
Fraley, Hank	G	6-2	300	9/21/77	Robert Morris	Gaithersburg, Md.	FA
Gavadza, Jason	TE	6-3	247	1/31/76	Kent	Toronto, Ont., Canada	D6b
Geason, Corey (1)	TE	6-3	255	8/12/75	Tulane	St. James, La.	FA
Goodspeed, Joey	RB	6-0	241	2/22/78	Notre Dame	Montgomery, Ill.	FA
Haggans, Clark	LB	6-3	250	1/10/77	Colorado State	Torrance, Calif.	D5a
Kreider, Dan	RB	5-11	242	3/11/77	New Hampshire	Mount Joy, Pa.	FA
Lowe, Reggie	LB	6-3	250	6/14/75	Troy State	Phenix City, Ala.	FA-'99
Lucas, Al	NT	6-1	294	9/1/78	Troy State	Macon, Ga.	FA
Martin, Tee	QB	6-1	221	7/25/78	Tennessee	Mobile, Ala.	D5b
McWashington, Shawn (1)	WR	5-9	180	1/24/75	Washington State	Seattle, Wash.	FA
Mitchell, Johnny	DE	6-4	312	10/20/76	Louisiana State	Marrero, La.	FA
Orlandini, Tony (1)	G	6-5	310	8/13/75	Pittsburgh	West Wyoming, Pa.	FA-'99
Poteat, Hank	CB	5-10	190	8/30/77	Pittsburgh	Harrisburg, Pa.	D3b
Sands, Mike	LB	6-4	235	12/16/77	Harvard	Cleveland Heights, Ohio	FA
Smith, Marvel	T	6-5	281	8/6/78	Arizona State	Oakland, Calif.	D2
Strickland, Timothy	CB	5-9	183	1/13/77	Mississippi	Memphis, Tenn.	FA
Thompson, Donnel	LB	5-11	234	2/17/78	Wisconsin	Madison, Wis.	FA
Wright, Destry	RB	5-11	208	7/9/77	Jackson State	Clarksdale, Miss.	FA

The term NFL Rookie is defined as a player who is in his first season of professional football and has not been on the roster of another professional football team for any regular-season or postseason games. A Rookie is designated by an "R" on NFL rosters. Players who have been active in another professional football league or players who have NFL experience, including either preseason training camp or being on an Active List or Inactive List, or on Reserve/Injured or Reserve/Physically Unable to Perform for fewer than six regular-season games, are termed NFL First-Year Players. An NFL First-Year Player is designated by a "1" on NFL rosters. Thereafter, a player is credited with an additional year of experience for each season in which he accumulates six games on the Active List or Inactive List, or on Reserve/Injured or Reserve/Physically Unable to Perform.

NOTES

SAN DIEGO CHARGERS

American Football Conference
Western Division
Team Colors: Navy Blue, White, and Gold
Qualcomm Stadium
P.O. Box 609609
San Diego, California 92160-9609
Telephone: (858) 874-4500

CLUB OFFICIALS

Chairman of the Board: Alex G. Spanos
President-Vice Chairman: Dean A. Spanos
Executive Vice President: Michael A. Spanos
Executive Vice President-Finance: Jeremiah T. Murphy
Vice President-Football Operations: Ed McGuire
Vice President & Chief Financial Officer: Jeanne M. Bonk
Vice President & Chief Operating Officer: Michael McNeely
Director of Player Personnel: Billy Devaney
Director of Pro Personnel: Greg Gaines
Head Athletic Trainer: James Collins
Director of Video Operations: Brian Duddy
Equipment Manager: Bob Wick
Director of Corporate Sales: John Covarrubias
Director of Ticket Operations: Mike Dougherty
Business Manager: John Hinek
Director of Public Relations: Bill Johnston
Director of Security: Dick Lewis
Director of Ticket and Premium Seat Sales: Jerry McBurney
Gameday and Special Events Manager: Sean O'Connor
Controller: Marsha Wells
Stadium: Qualcomm Stadium • **Capacity:** 71,000
9449 Friars Road
San Diego, California 92108
Playing Surface: Grass
Training Camp: University of California-San Diego
Third College
La Jolla, California 92037

2000 SCHEDULE

PRESEASON

Aug. 5	at San Francisco	6:00
Aug. 12	**Minnesota**	6:00
Aug. 18	at Atlanta	7:30
Aug. 25	**Arizona**	7:00

REGULAR SEASON

Sept. 3	at Oakland	1:15
Sept. 10	**New Orleans**	1:15
Sept. 17	at Kansas City	12:00
Sept. 24	**Seattle**	1:15
Oct. 1	at St. Louis	12:00
Oct. 8	**Denver**	1:15
Oct. 15	at Buffalo	1:00
Oct. 22	Open Date	
Oct. 29	**Oakland**	5:35
Nov. 5	at Seattle	1:15
Nov. 12	**Miami**	1:05
Nov. 19	at Denver	2:05
Nov. 26	**Kansas City**	1:15
Dec. 3	**San Francisco**	1:05
Dec. 10	at Baltimore	1:00
Dec. 17	at Carolina	1:00
Dec. 24	**Pittsburgh**	1:05

RECORD HOLDERS

INDIVIDUAL RECORDS—CAREER

Category	Name	Performance
Rushing (Yds.)	Paul Lowe, 1960-67	4,963
Passing (Yds.)	Dan Fouts, 1973-1987	43,040
Passing (TDs)	Dan Fouts, 1973-1987	254
Receiving (No.)	Charlie Joiner, 1976-1986	586
Receiving (Yds.)	Lance Alworth, 1962-1970	9,585
Interceptions	Gill Byrd, 1983-1992	42
Punting (Avg.)	Darren Bennett, 1995-99	44.5
Punt Return (Avg.)	Darrien Gordon, 1993-96	13.6
Kickoff Return (Avg.)	Leslie (Speedy) Duncan, 1964-1970	25.3
Field Goals	John Carney, 1990-99	243
Touchdowns (Tot.)	Lance Alworth, 1962-1970	83
Points	John Carney, 1990-99	995

INDIVIDUAL RECORDS—SINGLE SEASON

Category	Name	Performance
Rushing (Yds.)	Natrone Means, 1994	1,350
Passing (Yds.)	Dan Fouts, 1981	4,802
Passing (TDs)	Dan Fouts, 1981	33
Receiving (No.)	Tony Martin, 1995	90
Receiving (Yds.)	Lance Alworth, 1965	1,602
Interceptions	Charlie McNeil, 1961	9
Punting (Avg.)	Darren Bennett, 1996	45.6
Punt Return (Avg.)	Leslie (Speedy) Duncan, 1965	15.5
Kickoff Return (Avg.)	Keith Lincoln, 1962	28.4
Field Goals	John Carney, 1994	34
Touchdowns (Tot.)	Chuck Muncie, 1981	19
Points	John Carney, 1994	135

INDIVIDUAL RECORDS—SINGLE GAME

Category	Name	Performance
Rushing (Yds.)	Gary Anderson, 12-18-88	217
Passing (Yds.)	Dan Fouts, 10-19-80, 12-11-82	444
Passing (TDs)	Dan Fouts, 11-22-81	6
Receiving (No.)	Kellen Winslow, 10-7-84	15
Receiving (Yds.)	Wes Chandler, 12-20-82	260
Interceptions	Many times	3
	Last time by Dwayne Harper, 11-27-95	
Field Goals	John Carney, 9-5-93, 9-18-93	6
	Greg Davis, 10-5-97	6
Touchdowns (Tot.)	Kellen Winslow, 11-22-81	5
Points	Kellen Winslow, 11-22-81	30

COACHING HISTORY

Los Angeles 1960
(297-306-11)

1960-69	Sid Gillman*	83-51-6
1969-70	Charlie Waller	9-7-3
1971	Sid Gillman**	4-6-0
1971-73	Harland Svare***	7-17-2
1973	Ron Waller	1-5-0
1974-78	Tommy Prothro****	21-39-0
1978-86	Don Coryell#	72-60-0
1986-88	Al Saunders	17-22-0
1989-91	Dan Henning	16-32-0
1992-96	Bobby Ross	50-36-0
1997-98	Kevin Gilbride##	6-16-0
1998	June Jones	3-7-0
1999	Mike Riley	8-8-0

*Retired after nine games in 1969
**Resigned after 10 games in 1971
***Resigned after eight games in 1973
****Resigned after four games in 1978
#Resigned after eight games in 1986
##Released after six games in 1998

QUALCOMM STADIUM

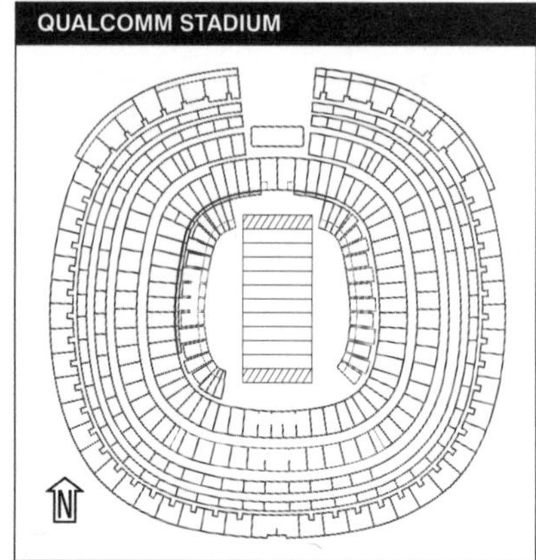

1999 TEAM RECORD

PRESEASON (0-5)

Date	Result		Opponent
8/7	L	17-20	vs. Denver at Sydney, Australia
8/12	L	24-31	at San Francisco
8/21	L	10-13	Miami
8/28	L	21-24	at St. Louis
9/3	L	27-34	Kansas City

REGULAR SEASON (8-8)

Date	Result		Opponent	Att.
9/19	W	34-7	at Cincinnati	47,660
9/26	L	19-27	Indianapolis	56,942
10/3	W	21-14	Kansas City	58,099
10/10	W	20-10	at Detroit	61,481
10/17	W	13-10	Seattle	59,432
10/24	L	3-31	Green Bay	68,274
10/31	L	0-34	at Kansas City	78,473
11/7	L	17-33	Denver	61,204
11/14	L	9-28	at Oakland	43,353
11/21	L	20-23	Chicago (OT)	56,055
11/28	L	27-35	at Minnesota	64,232
12/5	W	23-10	Cleveland	53,147
12/12	W	19-16	at Seattle	66,318
12/19	L	9-12	at Miami	73,765
12/26	W	23-20	Oakland	63,846
1/2	W	12-6	at Denver	69,278

(OT) Overtime

SCORE BY PERIODS

Chargers	40	112	46	71	0	—	269
Opponents	91	80	93	49	3	—	316

ATTENDANCE

Home 546,533 Away 503,838 Total 1,050,371
Single-game home record, 69,288 (11/7/99)
Single-season home record, 546,533 (1999)

1999 TEAM STATISTICS

	Chargers	Opp.
Total First Downs	262	279
Rushing	69	77
Passing	171	181
Penalty	22	21
Third Down: Made/Att	89/242	84/229
Third Down Pct.	36.8	36.7
Fourth Down: Made/Att	6/14	6/11
Fourth Down Pct.	42.9	54.5
Total Net Yards	4,589	4,905
Avg. Per Game	286.8	306.6
Total Plays	1,039	1,022
Avg. Per Play	4.4	4.8
Net Yards Rushing	1,246	1,321
Avg. Per Game	77.9	82.6
Total Rushes	410	432
Net Yards Passing	3,343	3,584
Avg. Per Game	208.9	224.0
Sacked/Yards Lost	46/284	41/263
Gross Yards	3,627	3,847
Att./Completions	583/332	549/315
Completion Pct.	56.9	57.4
Had Intercepted	24	15
Punts/Average	89/43.9	85/40.5
Net Punting Avg.	89/38.7	85/35.2
Penalties/Yards	104/823	117/909
Fumbles/Ball Lost	29/11	30/12
Touchdowns	25	34
Rushing	10	8
Passing	12	24
Returns	3	2
Avg. Time of Possession	30:00	30:00

1999 INDIVIDUAL STATISTICS

Passing	Att.	Comp.	Yds.	Pct.	TD	Int.	Tkld.	Rate
Harbaugh	434	249	2,761	57.4	10	14	37/208	70.6
Kramer	141	78	788	55.3	2	10	7/62	46.6
Moreno	7	5	78	71.4	0	0	1/3	108.0
Ricks	1	0	0	0.0	0	0	0/0	39.6
Reed	0	0	0	—	0	0	1/11	—
Chargers	583	332	3,627	56.9	12	24	46/284	65.2
Opponents	549	315	3,847	57.4	24	15	41/263	82.3

SCORING	TD R	TD P	TD Rt	PAT	FG	Saf	PTS
Carney	0	0	0	22/23	31/36	0	115
Means	4	1	0	0/0	0/0	0	30
Stephens	3	1	0	0/0	0/0	0	24
Bynum	1	2	0	0/0	0/0	0	18
Fazande	2	0	0	0/0	0/0	0	12
J. Graham	0	2	0	0/0	0/0	0	12
F. Jones	0	2	0	0/0	0/0	0	12
Lewis	0	0	2	0/0	0/0	0	12
Davis	0	1	0	0/0	0/0	0	6
Dixon	0	0	1	0/0	0/0	0	6
C. Jones	0	1	0	0/0	0/0	0	6
McCrary	0	1	0	0/0	0/0	0	6
Penn	0	1	0	0/0	0/0	0	6
Ricks	0	0	0	0/0	0/0	0	2
Chargers	10	12	3	22/23	31/36	1	269
Opponents	8	24	2	34/34	26/38	0	316

2-Pt. Conversions: Ricks.
Team 1-2, Opponents 0-0.

RUSHING	Att.	Yds.	Avg.	LG	TD
Fazande	91	365	4.0	54	2
Bynum	92	287	3.1	25	1
Means	112	277	2.5	15	4
Harbaugh	34	126	3.7	16	0
Fletcher	48	126	2.6	16	0
Stephens	24	61	2.5	9	3
Ricks	2	11	5.5	7	0
Kramer	5	1	0.2	3	0
Bennett	1	0	0.0	0	0
C. Jones	1	-8	-8.0	-8	0
Chargers	410	1,246	3.0	54	10
Opponents	432	1,321	3.1	26	8

RECEIVING	No.	Yds.	Avg.	LG	TD
J. Graham	57	968	17.0	54	2
F. Jones	56	670	12.0	36	2
Fletcher	45	360	8.0	25	0
Ricks	40	429	10.7	50	0
McCrary	37	201	5.4	38	1
Stephens	18	133	7.4	22	1
Penn	17	257	15.1	43	1
Bynum	16	209	13.1	80t	2
Davis	12	137	11.4	46	1
C. Jones	10	90	9.0	44t	1
Means	9	51	5.7	12t	1
Still	8	96	12.0	28	0
Pupunu	4	17	4.3	11	0
Seau	2	8	4.0	6	0
Reed	1	1	1.0	1	0
Chargers	332	3,627	10.9	80t	12
Opponents	315	3,847	12.2	81t	24

INTERCEPTIONS	No.	Yds.	Avg.	LG	TD
Lewis	4	9	2.3	5	0
Spencer	4	1	0.3	1	0
Dumas	2	92	46.0	68	0
Dimry	2	1	0.5	1	0
Seau	1	16	16.0	16	0
Simien	1	4	4.0	4	0
Harrison	1	0	0.0	0	0
Chargers	15	123	8.2	68	0
Opponents	24	196	8.2	38	1

PUNTING	No.	Yds.	Avg.	In 20	LG
Bennett	89	3,910	43.9	32	60
Chargers	89	3,910	43.9	32	60
Opponents	85	3,439	40.5	22	64

PUNT RETURNS	No.	FC	Yds.	Avg.	LG	TD
Penn	21	19	148	7.0	18	0
C. Jones	9	6	93	10.3	33	0
Reed	3	0	49	16.3	21	0
Turner	1	0	0	0.0	0	0
Chargers	34	25	290	8.5	33	0
Opponents	41	21	343	8.4	28	0

KICKOFF RETURNS	No.	Yds.	Avg.	LG	TD
Bynum	37	781	21.1	37	0
Stephens	18	335	18.6	28	0
Fletcher	7	112	16.0	22	0
Reed	5	72	14.4	21	0
Still	1	8	8.0	8	0
McCrary	1	4	4.0	4	0
Chargers	69	1,312	19.0	37	0
Opponents	67	1,550	23.1	49	0

FIELD GOALS	1-19	20-29	30-39	40-49	50+
Carney	2/2	13/13	6/8	9/12	1/1
Chargers	2/2	13/13	6/8	9/12	1/1
Opponents	0/0	7/7	9/13	7/12	3/6

SACKS	No.
Johnson	10.5
Parrella	5.5
Fontenot	5.0
Dixon	4.0
Hand	4.0
Seau	3.5
Dumas	2.0
Mohring	2.0
Bush	1.0
Harrison	1.0
Simien	1.0
Williams	1.0
Harden	0.5
Chargers	41.0
Opponents	46.0

2000 DRAFT CHOICES

Round	Name	Pos.	College
2	Rogers Beckett	DB	Marshall
3	Damion McIntosh	T	Kansas State
4	Trevor Gaylor	WR	Miami, Ohio
	Leonardo Carson	DE	Auburn
6	Shannon Taylor	LB	Virginia
	Damen Wheeler	DB	Colorado
	JaJuan Seider	QB	Florida A&M
7	Jason Thomas	G	Hampton

SAN DIEGO CHARGERS

2000 VETERAN ROSTER

No.		Name	Pos.	Ht.	Wt.	Birthdate	NFL Exp.	College	Hometown	How Acq.	'99 Games/ Starts
2		Bennett, Darren	P	6-5	235	1/9/65	6	No College	Perth, Australia	FA-'95	16/0
50		Binn, David	LS	6-3	250	2/6/72	7	California	San Mateo, Calif.	FA-'94	16/0
11		Bonner, Sherdrick	QB	6-4	238	10/18/68	2	California State-Northridge	Los Angeles, Calif.	FA-'00	0*
24		Brown, Fakhir	CB	5-11	192	9/21/77	2	Grambling	Mansfield, La.	FA-'99	9/3
43	†	Bynum, Kenny	RB	5-11	191	5/29/74	4	South Carolina State	Gainesville, Fla.	D5a-'97	16/5
3		Carney, John	K	5-11	175	4/20/64	11	Notre Dame	West Palm Beach, Fla.	FA-'90	16/0
32		Chancey, Robert	RB	6-0	252	9/7/72	4	No College	Millbrook, Ala.	RFA(Dall)-'00	1/0*
80		Conway, Curtis	WR	6-1	196	1/13/71	8	Southern California	Los Angeles, Calif.	UFA(Chi)-'99	9/8*
84		Davis, Reggie	TE	6-3	233	9/3/76	2	Washington	Huntington Beach, Calif.	FA-'99	16/3
87		Davis, Wendell	TE-HB	6-2	246	10/24/75	2	Temple	Escatawapa, Miss.	FA-'00	0*
90		Dingle, Adrian	DE	6-3	272	6/25/77	2	Clemson	Holly Hill, S.C.	D5a-'99	0*
51		Dixon, Gerald	LB	6-3	250	6/20/69	9	South Carolina	Rock Hill, S.C.	UFA(Cin)-'98	14/1
38		Dumas, Michael	S	6-0	198	3/18/69	9	Indiana	Lowell, Mich.	FA-'97	14/14
35		Fazande, Jermaine	RB	6-2	255	1/14/75	2	Oklahoma	Marrero, La.	D2-'99	7/3
41		Fletcher, Terrell	RB	5-8	196	9/14/73	6	Wisconsin	St. Louis, Mo.	D2b-'95	15/2
95		Fontenot, Al	DE	6-4	287	9/17/70	8	Baylor	Houston, Tex.	UFA(Ind)-'99	15/15
67		Fortin, Roman	C-G	6-5	297	2/26/67	11	San Diego State	Ventura, Calif.	FA-'98	16/16
71		Graham, DeMingo	G-T	6-3	310	9/10/73	3	Hofstra	Newark, N.J.	FA-'98	16/10
81		Graham, Jeff	WR	6-2	206	2/14/69	10	Ohio State	Dayton, Ohio	FA-'99	16/11
53	†	Hamilton, Michael	LB	6-2	245	12/3/73	4	North Carolina A&T	Greenville, S.C.	D3-'97	14/2
4		Harbaugh, Jim	QB	6-3	215	1/23/63	14	Michigan	Palo Alto, Calif.	T(Balt)-'99	14/12
92		Harden, Cedric	DE	6-6	260	10/19/74	3	Florida A&M	Atlanta, Ga.	D5-'98	5/0
33		Harris, Derrick	RB	6-0	252	9/18/72	4	Miami	Sugarland, Tex.	FA-'00	1/0*
37		Harrison, Rodney	S	6-1	207	12/15/72	7	Western Illinois	Chicago Heights, Ill.	D5b-'94	6/6
83		Heiden, Steve	TE	6-5	270	9/21/76	2	South Dakota State	Rushford, Minn.	D3-'99	11/0
54		Hill, Eric	LB	6-2	265	11/14/66	12	Louisiana State	Galveston, Tex.	UFA(StL)-'99	12/10
42		Jackson, Greg	S	6-1	217	8/20/66	12	Louisiana State	Miami, Fla.	FA-'99	14/9
65		Jackson, John	T	6-6	297	1/4/65	13	Eastern Kentucky	Cincinnati, Ohio	UFA(Pitt)-'98	15/15
64		Jacox, Kendyl	C-G	6-2	330	6/10/75	3	Kansas State	Dallas, Tex.	FA-'98	10/5
23		Jenkins, DeRon	CB	5-11	192	11/14/73	5	Tennessee	St. Louis, Mo.	UFA(Balt)-'00	16/15*
99		Johnson, Raylee	DE	6-3	272	6/1/70	8	Arkansas	Fordyce, Ark.	D4a-'93	16/16
82		Jones, Charlie	WR	5-8	175	12/1/72	5	Fresno State	Lemoore, Calif.	D4-'96	8/1
88		Jones, Freddie	TE	6-4	255	9/16/74	4	North Carolina	Landover, Md.	D2-'97	16/16
16		Leaf, Ryan	QB	6-5	235	5/15/76	3	Washington State	Great Falls, Mont.	D1-'98	0*
26		Lewis, Darryll	CB	5-9	188	12/16/68	10	Arizona	West Covina, Calif.	FA-'00	13/8
44		McCrary, Fred	RB	6-0	235	9/19/72	4	Mississippi State	Naples, Fla.	FA-'99	16/14
93		Mickell, Darren	DE	6-5	285	8/3/70	8	Florida	Miami, Fla.	FA-'00	1/0*
98		Mohring, Michael	DE-DT	6-5	295	3/22/74	3	Pittsburgh	West Chester, Pa.	FA-'97	16/1
13		Moreno, Moses	QB	6-1	205	9/5/75	3	Colorado State	Chula Vista, Calif.	FA-'99	1/0
70		Parker, Vaughn	T	6-3	300	6/5/71	7	UCLA	Buffalo, N.Y.	D2b-'94	15/15
97		Parrella, John	DT	6-3	290	11/22/69	8	Nebraska	Topeka, Kan.	FA-'94	16/16
68		Patton, Joe	G	6-4	310	1/5/72	6	Alabama A&M	Birmingham, Ala.	FA-'00	0*
31		Perry, Jason	S	6-0	200	8/1/76	2	North Carolina State	Passaic, N.J.	D4-'99	16/5
52		Reeves, John	LB	6-3	236	2/23/75	2	Purdue	Bradenton, Fla.	FA-'99	5/0
86		Ricks, Mikhael	WR	6-5	237	11/14/74	3	Stephen F. Austin	Anahuac, Tex.	D2-'98	16/15
74		Roundtree, Raleigh	T	6-4	295	8/31/75	4	South Carolina State	Augusta, Ga.	D4-'97	15/5
56		Ruff, Orlando	LB	6-3	247	9/26/76	2	Furman	Winnsboro, S.C.	FA-'99	14/0
25		Rusk, Reggie	CB	5-10	190	12/19/72	3	Kentucky	Texas City, Tex.	FA-'98	9/0
55		Seau, Junior	LB	6-3	250	1/19/69	11	Southern California	Oceanside, Calif.	D1-'90	14/14
34		Stephens, Tremayne	RB	5-11	206	4/16/76	3	North Carolina State	Greer, S.C.	FA-'98	11/2
21		Turner, Scott	CB	5-10	180	2/26/72	6	Illinois	Richardson, Tex.	FA-'98	15/0
28		Vance, Eric	S	6-2	218	7/14/75	3	Vanderbilt	Hurst, Tex.	FA-'00	6/0*
76		Williams, Jamal	DT	6-3	305	4/28/76	3	Oklahoma State	Washington, D.C.	D2(Supp)-'98	16/2
15		Williams, Stepfret	WR	6-0	175	6/14/73	4	Northeast Louisiana	Minden, La.	FA-'00	0*

* Bonner was inactive for 2 games in '99; Chancey played 1 game with Dallas; Conway played 9 games with Chicago; W. Davis last active with San Diego in '98; Dingle was inactive for 4 games; Harris played 1 game with St. Louis; Jenkins played 16 games with Baltimore; Leaf was inactive for 11 games; Mickell played 1 game with New Orleans; Patton was inactive for 2 playoff games with Jacksonville; Vance played 6 games with Tampa Bay; S. Williams last active with Cincinnati in '98.

† Restricted free agents; subject to developments.

Retired—Charles Dimry, 12-year cornerback, 12 games in '99; Aaron Taylor, 6-year guard, 14 games.

Players lost through free agency (2): DT Norman Hand (NO, 14 games in '99); CB Jimmy Spencer (Den, 14).

Also played with the Chargers in '99—LB Lew Bush (16 games), QB Erik Kramer (6), RB Natrone Means (7), DE Chris Mims (9), WR Chris Penn (16), TE Al Pupunu (8), CB Terrance Shaw (8), LB Tracy Simien (8), WR Bryan Still (4).

COACHING STAFF

Head Coach,
Mike Riley

Pro Career: Mike Riley was named the twelfth head coach in Chargers history on January 10, 1999. In his first season in San Diego, he led the Chargers to a record of 8-8, the team's best record since 1996. The 1999 Chargers had the best intra-division mark in the AFC West at 5-3, including one win each over Denver, Kansas City, and Oakland and a sweep of the two-game series over division champion Seattle. Riley has 25 years of coaching experience. He has spent nine seasons as a head coach, including two on the collegiate level (Oregon State 1997-98), four in the Canadian Football League (Winnipeg 1987-1990) and two in the World League (San Antonio 1991-92). Riley was named the CFL's coach of the year following the 1988 and 1990 seasons, winning the Grey Cup each of those seasons. He also spent three seasons (1983-85) as Winnipeg's secondary coach. Riley led the San Antonio Riders to a record of 11-9 in two World League seasons. His career professional record is 59-49. Career record: 8-8.

Background: Collegiately, Riley won two national championships, one as a player and one as a coach, and three bowl games. In two seasons (1997-98) as the head coach at Oregon State, he led the Beavers to their best record in 27 years. Riley served as an assistant coach at Southern California (1993-96), Northern Colorado (1986), Linfield College (1977-1982), Whitworth College (1976), and California (1975). In college, he played defensive back under Paul (Bear) Bryant at Alabama (1971-74), and won the 1973 national title. Riley graduated from Alabama with a bachelor's degree and earned his master's degree from Whitworth.

Personal: Born July 6, 1953 in Wallace, Idaho. Mike and his wife, Dee, have two children—Matthew and Kate.

ASSISTANT COACHES

DelVaughn Alexander, offensive assistant; born July 16, 1971, Los Angeles, lives in San Diego. Wide receiver Southern California 1993-94. No pro playing experience. College coach: Southern California 1995-97, Nevada-Las Vegas 1998. Pro coach: Joined Chargers in 1999.

Mark Banker, defensive assistant-secondary; born January 15, 1956, in Plymouth, Mass., lives in San Diego. Running back Springfield College 1975-77. No pro playing experience. College coach: Springfield 1978-1980, Cal State-Northridge 1981-1994, Hawaii 1995, Southern California 1996, Oregon State 1997-98. Pro coach: Joined Chargers in 1999.

Joe Bugel, offensive line; born March 10, 1940, Pittsburgh, lives in San Diego. Guard-linebacker Western Kentucky 1960-63. No pro playing experience. College coach: Western Kentucky 1964-68, Navy 1969-1972, Iowa State 1973, Ohio State 1974. Pro coach: Detroit Lions 1975-76, Houston Oilers 1977-1980, Washington Redskins 1981-89, Phoenix Cardinals 1990-93 (head coach), Oakland Raiders 1995-97 (head coach 1997), joined Chargers in 1998.

Geep Chryst, offensive coordinator; born June 25, 1962, Madison, Wisc., lives in San Diego. Linebacker Princeton 1981-84. Pro linebacker Orlando Thunder (World League) 1992. College coach: Wisconsin-Platteville 1987, Wisconsin 1988-1990. Pro coach: Orlando Thunder (World League) 1991, Chicago Bears 1991-95, Arizona Cardinals 1996-98, joined Chargers in 1999.

Paul Chryst, tight ends; born November 17, 1965, in Madison, Wisc., lives in San Diego. Quarterback-linebacker-tight end-holder Wisconsin 1986-88. No pro playing experience. College coach: West Virginia 1989-1990, Wisconsin-Platteville 1993, Illinois State 1995, Oregon State 1997-98. Pro coach: San Antonio Riders (World League) 1991-92, Edmonton Eskimos (CFL) 1993, Ottawa Rough Riders (CFL) 1994, Saskatchewan Roughriders (CFL) 1996, joined Chargers in 1999.

John Hastings, strength and conditioning; born July 5, 1964, in Newport News, Va., lives in San Marcos, Calif. No college or pro playing experience. Pro coach: Joined Chargers in 1990.

Mike Johnson, quarterbacks; born May 2, 1967, in Los Angeles, lives in San Diego. Quarterback Arizona State 1985-86, Akron 1988-89. Pro quarterback Arizona Cardinals 1990, San Antonio Riders (World League) 1991-92, British Columbia Lions (CFL) 1992-93, Shreveport Pirates (CFL) 1994-95. College coach: Oregon State 1997-99. Pro coach: Joined Chargers in 2000.

Andrew McClave, defensive assistant; born November 1, 1971, in Evanston, Ill., lives in San Diego. Linebacker UCLA 1990-93. No pro playing experience. College coach: Oregon State 1997-99. Pro coach: Joined Chargers in 2000.

Wayne Nunnely, defensive line; born March 29, 1952, Los Angeles, lives in San Diego. Fullback Nevada-Las Vegas 1972-75. No pro playing experience. College coach: Nevada-Las Vegas 1976, 1982-89 (head coach 1986-89), Cal Poly-Pomona 1977-78, Cal State-Fullerton 1979, Pacific 1980-81, Southern California 1991-92, UCLA 1993-94. Pro coach: New Orleans Saints 1995-96, joined Chargers in 1997.

Joe Pascale, defensive coordinator; born April 4, 1946, New York, N.Y., lives in San Diego. Linebacker Connecticut 1963-66. No pro playing experience. College coach: Connecticut 1967-68, Rhode Island 1969-1973, Idaho State 1974-76 (head coach 1976), Princeton 1977-79. Pro coach: Montreal Alouettes (CFL) 1980-81, Ottawa Rough Riders (CFL) 1982-83, New Jersey Generals (USFL) 1984-85, St. Louis/Phoenix Cardinals 1986-1993, Cincinnati Bengals 1994-96, joined Chargers in 1997.

Rod Perry, defensive backs; born September 11, 1953, Fresno, Calif., lives in San Diego. Defensive back Colorado 1972-74. Pro cornerback Los Angeles Rams 1975-1982, Cleveland Browns 1983-84. College coach: Columbia 1985, Fresno City College 1986, Fresno State 1987-88. Pro coach: Seattle Seahawks 1989-1991, Los Angeles Rams 1992-94, Houston Oilers 1995-96, joined Chargers in 1997.

Bruce Read, special teams; born January 26, 1962, in Santa Rosa, Calif., lives in San Diego. No college or pro playing experience. College coach: Oregon Institute of Technology 1980, Portland State 1981-84, Montana 1985-1996, Oregon State 1997-98. Pro coach: Joined Chargers in 1999.

Mike Sanford, wide receivers; born April 20, 1955, in Los Altos, Calif., lives in San Diego. Quarterback-safety Southern California 1973-76. No pro playing experience. College coach: Southern California 1977, 1989-1996, San Diego City College 1978, Army 1979-1980, Virginia Military Institute 1981-82, Long Beach State 1983-86, Purdue 1987-88, Notre Dame 1997-98. Pro coach: Joined Chargers in 1999.

Mike Schleelein, asst. strength and conditioning; born January 24, 1974, in Buffalo, lives in San Diego. Tight end Buffalo 1992-96. No pro playing experience. Pro coach: Joined Chargers in 1997.

Jim Vechiarella, linebackers; born February 20, 1937, Youngstown, Ohio, lives in San Diego. Linebacker Youngstown State 1955-57. No pro playing experience. College coach: Youngstown State 1964-1974, Southern Illinois 1976-77, Tulane 1978-1980. Pro coach: Charlotte (WFL) 1975, Los Angeles Rams 1981-82, Kansas City Chiefs 1983-85, New York Jets 1986-89, 1995-96, Cleveland Browns 1990, Philadelphia Eagles 1991-94, joined Chargers in 1997.

Ollie Wilson, running backs; born March 3, 1951, Worcester, Mass., lives in San Diego. Wide receiver Springfield 1971-73. No pro playing experience. College coach: Springfield 1975, Northeastern 1976-1982, California 1983-1990. Pro coach: Atlanta Falcons 1991-96, joined Chargers in 1997.

2000 FIRST-YEAR ROSTER

Name	Pos.	Ht.	Wt.	Birthdate	College	Hometown	How Acq.
Austin, Rick (1)	G	6-1	307	9/13/76	San Diego State	Rialto, Calif.	FA
Batteaux, Pat	WR	6-0	195	4/18/78	Texas Christian	Missouri City, Tex.	FA
Beckett, Rogers	S	6-3	205	1/31/77	Marshall	Apopka, Fla.	D2
Brown, Gregory	G	6-1	305	9/10/77	Houston	Hialeah, Fla.	FA
Brown, Wilbert (1)	G	6-2	310	5/9/77	Houston	Hooks, Tex.	FA-'99
Burton, Mike	QB	6-1	215	7/3/78	Trinity	La Jolla, Calif.	FA
Carson, Leonardo	DT	6-2	285	2/11/77	Auburn	Mobile, Ala.	D4b
Cooper, Robert	RB	5-10	205	11/29/76	Cincinnati	Bainbridge, Ga.	FA
Cortez, Jose (1)	K	5-11	205	5/27/75	Oregon State	Van Nuys, Calif.	FA
Criss, Shadwick	CB	5-10	185	1/11/76	Missouri	Denison, Tex.	FA
Curtis, Rico	S	6-1	217	6/1/77	San Diego State	San Bernardino, Calif.	FA
Darden, Tony (1)	CB	6-0	190	8/11/75	Texas Tech	San Antonio, Tex.	FA
Gaylor, Trevor	WR	6-3	195	11/3/77	Miami, Ohio	Hazelwood, Mo.	D4a
Gourdine, Damon	WR-KR	5-7	165	9/17/78	San Diego State	Rolling Hills, Calif.	FA
Grant, Gary	FB	6-2	248	4/15/78	Howard	Burtonsville, Md.	FA
Hampton, Wayne	DE	6-4	250	5/22/77	Rutgers	Paulsboro, N.J.	FA
Henry, Dwight (1)	CB	5-10	180	2/12/74	East Carolina	Plantation, Fla.	FA
Hogans, Richard (1)	LB	6-2	249	7/8/75	Memphis	Columbus, Ga.	FA
Jenkins, Ronney	RB	5-11	188	5/25/77	Northern Arizona	Oxnard, Calif.	FA
Jones, Reggie (1)	WR	6-0	195	5/8/71	Louisiana State	Kansas City, Mo.	FA
Knight, Seneca	DE	6-4	286	1/1/78	Grambling State	Alexander City, Ala.	FA
Matthews, Glenn	DT	6-3	295	1/26/77	North Dakota	Chicago, Ill.	FA
McCaskey, Terrence	TE	6-5	275	9/30/77	Mississippi State	Norcross, Ga.	FA
McIntosh, Damion	T	6-4	325	3/25/77	Kansas State	Hollywood, Fla.	D3
Nelson, Reginald (1)	T	6-4	310	6/23/76	McNeese State	Alexandria, La.	D5b-'99
Price, Durrell	RB	5-11	245	3/25/78	UCLA	Sylmar, Calif.	FA
Reed, Robert (1)	WR	6-1	203	1/14/75	Lambuth	Oxford, Miss.	FA-'99
Schexnayder, Calvin (1)	WR	6-0	195	11/19/69	Washington State	Magnolia, Ark.	FA
Seider, JaJuan	QB	6-1	230	4/16/77	Florida A&M	Belle Glade, Fla.	D6c
Sloan, Eric	CB	5-8	170	7/28/78	Troy State	College Park, Ga.	FA
Smart, Rod	RB	5-10	197	1/9/77	Western Kentucky	Lakeland, Fla.	FA
Stephens, Leonard	TE	6-3	245	7/9/78	Howard	Princeton, N.J.	FA
Swanson, Pete (1)	T	6-5	305	3/26/74	Stanford	San Bernito, Calif.	FA
Swayne, Kevin (1)	WR	6-2	195	1/17/75	Wayne State	Los Angeles, Calif.	FA
Talamaivao, Pene (1)	DT	6-4	305	6/14/75	Utah	Pomona, Calif.	FA
Taylor, Shannon	LB	6-3	247	2/16/75	Virginia	Roanoke, Va.	D6a
Thomas, Jason	G	6-3	300	6/10/77	Hampton	Savannah, Ga.	D7
Tuiaea, Mac	DT	6-6	300	5/29/77	Washington	Richmond, Wash.	FA
Wheeler, Damen	CB	5-9	170	9/3/77	Colorado	Sacramento, Calif.	D6b
White, Fred	S	5-10	205	3/18/77	Tennessee	Griffin, Ga.	FA

The term NFL Rookie is defined as a player who is in his first season of professional football and has not been on the roster of another professional football team for any regular-season or postseason games. A Rookie is designated by an "R" on NFL rosters. Players who have been active in another professional football league or players who have NFL experience, including either preseason training camp or being on an Active List or Inactive List, or on Reserve/Injured or Reserve/Physically Unable to Perform for fewer than six regular-season games, are termed NFL First-Year Players. An NFL First-Year Player is designated by a "1" on NFL rosters. Thereafter, a player is credited with an additional year of experience for each season in which he accumulates six games on the Active List or Inactive List, or on Reserve/Injured or Reserve/Physically Unable to Perform.

SEATTLE SEAHAWKS

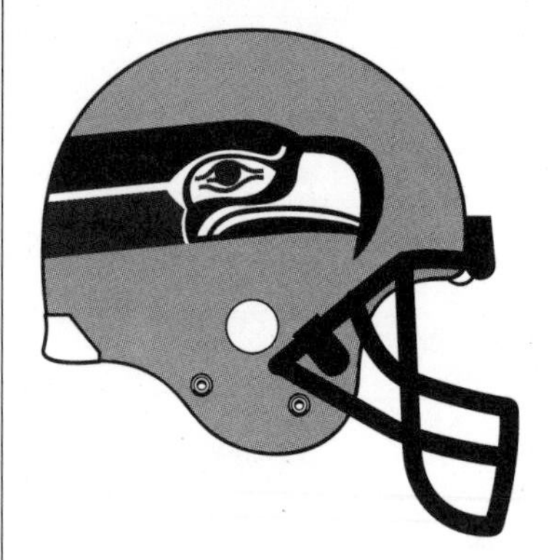

American Football Conference
Western Division
Team Colors: Blue, Green, and Silver
11220 N.E. 53rd Street
Kirkland, Washington 98033
Telephone: (425) 827-9777

CLUB OFFICIALS

Chairman: Paul Allen
President: Bob Whitsitt
Executive VP of Football Operations/
General Manager & Head Coach: Mike Holmgren
Sr. Vice President: Mike Reinfeldt
VP/CFO: Nathaniel (Buster) Brown
VP/Community Outreach, I.S., Facilities: Mike Flood
VP/General Counsel: Richard Leigh
Sr. VP/Marketing: Duane McLean
VP/Football Operations: Ted Thompson
VP/Corporate Sales: Scott Patrick
VP/Communications: Gary Wright
Director of Player Personnel: John Schneider
Director of College Scouting: Scot McCloughan
Director of Pro Scouting: Will Lewis
Director of Public Relations: Dave Pearson
Asst. Director of Public Relations: Steve Wright
Director of Community Outreach: Sandy Gregory
Director of Player Programs: Nesby Glasgow
Director of Publications: Vernon Cheek
Director of Corporate Sales: Doug Smith
Director of Broadcasting: Mike Wacker
Director of Vendor Sales: Kevin Williams
Director Ticket Operations/Customer Service:
Chuck Arnold
Assistant to the GM: Gary Reynolds
Administrative Assistant/Football Operations:
Bill Nayes
Video Director Football: Thom Fermstad
Head AthleticTrainer: Paul Federici
Equipment Manager: Erik Kennedy
Stadium: Husky Stadium • **Capacity:** 68,589
Montlake Boulevard
Seattle, Washington 98195
Playing Surface: Field Turf
Training Camp: Eastern Washington University
Cheney, Washington 99004

2000 SCHEDULE

PRESEASON

Aug. 5	**Indianapolis**	5:00
Aug. 12	at Arizona	7:00
Aug. 19	**San Francisco**	8:00
Aug. 24	at Oakland	6:00

REGULAR SEASON

Sept. 3	at Miami	4:15
Sept. 10	**St. Louis**	1:15
Sept. 17	**New Orleans**	1:15
Sept. 24	at San Diego	1:15
Oct. 2	at Kansas City (Mon.)	8:00
Oct. 8	at Carolina	4:15
Oct. 15	**Indianapolis**	1:05
Oct. 22	at Oakland	1:05
Oct. 29	**Kansas City**	1:15
Nov. 5	**San Diego**	1:15
Nov. 12	at Jacksonville	1:00
Nov. 19	**Open Date**	
Nov. 26	**Denver**	1:15
Dec. 3	at Atlanta	1:00
Dec. 10	at Denver	2:05
Dec. 16	**Oakland** (Sat.)	1:05
Dec. 23	**Buffalo** (Sat.)	5:35

RECORD HOLDERS

INDIVIDUAL RECORDS—CAREER

Category	Name	Performance
Rushing (Yds.)	Chris Warren, 1990-97	6,706
Passing (Yds.)	Dave Krieg, 1980-1991	26,132
Passing (TDs)	Dave Krieg, 1980-1991	195
Receiving (No.)	Steve Largent, 1976-1989	819
Receiving (Yds.)	Steve Largent, 1976-1989	13,089
Interceptions	Dave Brown, 1976-1986	50
Punting (Avg.)	Rick Tuten, 1991-97	43.8
Punt Return (Avg.)	Paul Johns, 1981-84	11.4
Kickoff Return (Avg.)	Steve Broussard, 1995-98	23.2
Field Goals	Norm Johnson, 1982-1990	159
Touchdowns (Tot.)	Steve Largent, 1976-1989	101
Points	Norm Johnson, 1982-1990	810

INDIVIDUAL RECORDS—SINGLE SEASON

Category	Name	Performance
Rushing (Yds.)	Chris Warren, 1994	1,545
Passing (Yds.)	Warren Moon, 1997	3,678
Passing (TDs)	Dave Krieg, 1984	32
Receiving (No.)	Brian Blades, 1994	81
Receiving (Yds.)	Steve Largent, 1985	1,287
Interceptions	John Harris, 1981	10
	Kenny Easley, 1984	10
Punting (Avg.)	Rick Tuten, 1995	45.0
Punt Return (Avg.)	Charlie Rogers, 1999	14.5
Kickoff Return (Avg.)	Steve Broussard, 1995	24.7
Field Goals	Todd Peterson, 1999	34
Touchdowns (Tot.)	Chris Warren, 1995	16
Points	Todd Peterson, 1999	134

INDIVIDUAL RECORDS—SINGLE GAME

Category	Name	Performance
Rushing (Yds.)	Curt Warner, 11-27-83	207
Passing (Yds.)	Dave Krieg, 11-20-83	418
Passing (TDs)	Dave Krieg, 12-2-84, 9-15-85, 11-28-88	5
	Warren Moon, 10-26-97	5
Receiving (No.)	Steve Largent, 10-18-87	15
Receiving (Yds.)	Steve Largent, 10-18-87	261
Interceptions	Kenny Easley, 9-3-84	3
	Eugene Robinson, 12-6-92	3
	Darryl Williams, 9-21-97	3
Field Goals	Norm Johnson, 9-20-87, 12-18-88	5
Touchdowns (Tot.)	Daryl Turner, 9-15-85	4
	Curt Warner, 12-11-88	4
Points	Daryl Turner, 9-15-85	24
	Curt Warner, 12-11-88	24

COACHING HISTORY

(176-204-0)

1976-82	Jack Patera*	35-59-0
1982	Mike McCormack	4-3-0
1983-91	Chuck Knox	83-67-0
1992-94	Tom Flores	14-34-0
1995-98	Dennis Erickson	31-33-0
1999	Mike Holmgren	9-8-0

*Released after two games in 1982

HUSKY STADIUM

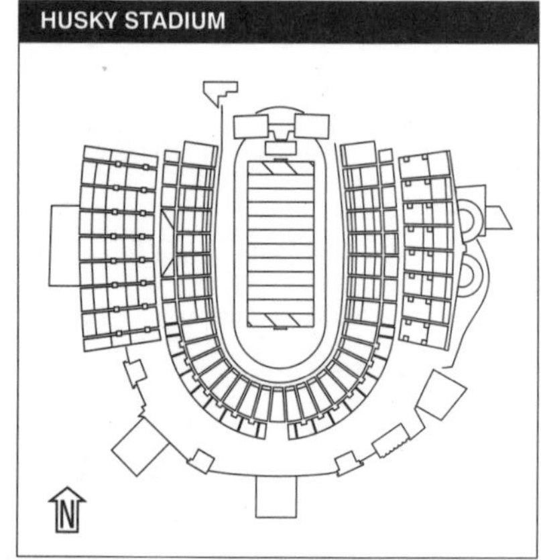

1999 TEAM RECORD

PRESEASON (1-3)

Date	Result		Opponent
8/14	L	10-24	Buffalo
8/19	L	23-24	at San Francisco
8/28	W	41-7	Arizona
9/2	L	28-31	at Indianapolis

REGULAR SEASON (9-7)

Date	Result		Opponent	Att.
9/12	L	20-28	Detroit	66,238
9/19	W	14-13	at Chicago	66,944
9/26	W	29-10	at Pittsburgh	57,881
10/3	W	22-21	Oakland	66,400
10/17	L	10-13	at San Diego	59,432
10/24	W	26-16	Buffalo	66,301
11/1	W	27-7	at Green Bay	59,869
11/7	W	37-20	Cincinnati	66,303
11/14	W	20-17	Denver	66,314
11/21	W	31-19	at Kansas City	78,714
11/28	L	3-16	Tampa Bay	66,314
12/5	L	21-30	at Oakland	44,716
12/12	L	16-19	San Diego	66,318
12/19	L	30-36	at Denver (OT)	65,987
12/26	W	23-14	Kansas City	66,332
1/2	L	9-19	at New York Jets	78,154

(OT) Overtime

POSTSEASON (0-1)

Date	Result		Opponent	Att.
1/9	L	17-20	Miami	66,170

SCORE BY PERIODS

Seahawks	86	104	70	78	0	—	338
Opponents	53	109	59	71	6	—	298

ATTENDANCE

Home 522,656 Away 526,787 Total 1,049,443

Single-game home record, 66,264 (10/26/97, 11/23/97)

Single-season home record, 522,656 (1999)

1999 TEAM STATISTICS

	Seahawks	Opp.
Total First Downs	276	313
Rushing	65	107
Passing	179	183
Penalty	32	23
Third Down: Made/Att.	68/210	89/239
Third Down Pct.	32.4	37.2
Fourth Down: Made/Att.	2/8	8/18
Fourth Down Pct.	25.0	44.4
Total Net Yards	4,805	5,426
Avg. Per Game	300.3	339.1
Total Plays	971	1,104
Avg. Per Play	4.9	4.9
Net Yards Rushing	1,408	1,934
Avg. Per Game	88.0	120.9
Total Rushes	408	484
Net Yards Passing	3,397	3,492
Avg. Per Game	212.3	218.3
Sacked/Yards Lost	38/232	38/252
Gross Yards	3,629	3,744
Att./Completions	525/288	582/320
Completion Pct.	54.9	55.0
Had Intercepted	16	30
Punts/Average	84/40.8	81/42.0
Net Punting Avg.	84/35.2	81/34.3
Penalties/Yards	98/883	128/985
Fumbles/Ball Lost	31/17	17/6
Touchdowns	34	30
Rushing	5	9
Passing	25	19
Returns	4	2
Avg. Time of Possession	27:48	32:12

1999 INDIVIDUAL STATISTICS

Passing	Att.	Comp.	Yds.	Pct.	TD	Int.	Tkld.	Rate
Kitna	495	270	3,346	54.5	23	16	32/198	77.7
Foley	30	18	283	60.0	2	0	6/34	113.6
Seahawks	525	288	3,629	54.9	25	16	38/232	79.8
Opponents	582	320	3,744	55.0	19	30	38/252	64.1

SCORING	TD R	TD P	TD Rt	PAT	FG	Saf	PTS
Peterson	0	0	0	32/32	34/40	0	134
Mayes	0	10	0	0/0	0/0	0	60
Dawkins	0	7	0	0/0	0/0	0	42
Watters	5	2	0	0/0	0/0	0	42
Pritchard	0	2	0	0/0	0/0	0	12
Bownes	0	1	0	0/0	0/0	0	6
R. Brown	0	1	0	0/0	0/0	0	6
Galloway	0	1	0	0/0	0/0	0	6
Hanks	0	0	1	0/0	0/0	0	6
Mili	0	1	0	0/0	0/0	0	6
C. Rogers	0	0	1	0/0	0/0	0	6
Springs	0	0	1	00/	0/0	0	6
W. Williams	0	0	1	0/0	0/0	0	6
Seahawks	5	25	4	32/32	34/40	0	338
Opponents	9	19	2	26/27	30/38	1	298

2-Pt. Conversions: None.
Team 0-2, Opponents 0-2.

RUSHING	Att.	Yds.	Avg.	LG	TD
Watters	325	1,210	3.7	45	5
Green	26	120	4.6	21	0
Kitna	35	56	1.6	10	0
R. Brown	14	38	2.7	9	0
Strong	1	0	0.0	0	0
Feagles	2	0	0.0	0	0
Foley	3	-1	-0.3	0	0
Galloway	1	-1	-1.0	-1	0
Bownes	1	-14	-14.0	-14	0
Seahawks	408	1,408	3.5	45	5
Opponents	484	1,934	4.0	71	9

RECEIVING	No.	Yds.	Avg.	LG	TD
Mayes	62	829	13.4	43t	10
Dawkins	58	992	17.1	45t	7
Watters	40	387	9.7	25	2
Fauria	35	376	10.7	25	0
R. Brown	34	228	6.7	26	1
Pritchard	26	375	14.4	51	2
Galloway	22	335	15.2	48	1
Mili	5	28	5.6	8	1
Bownes	4	68	17.0	49t	1
Jordan	1	6	6.0	6	0
Strong	1	5	5.0	5	0
Seahawks	288	3,629	12.6	51	25
Opponents	320	3,744	11.7	76t	19

INTERCEPTIONS	No.	Yds.	Avg.	LG	TD
Springs	5	77	15.4	42	0
W. Williams	5	43	8.6	40t	1
D. Williams	4	41	10.3	21	0
Bellamy	4	4	1.0	7	0
Joseph	3	82	27.3	40	0
Canty	3	26	8.7	19	0
Hanks	2	30	15.0	23t	1
Kennedy	2	12	6.0	7	0
Walker	1	21	21.0	21	0
Smith	1	0	0.0	0	0
Seahawks	30	336	11.2	42	2
Opponents	16	210	13.1	43	0

PUNTING	No.	Yds.	Avg.	In 20	LG
Feagles	84	3,425	40.8	34	59
Seahawks	84	3,425	40.8	34	59
Opponents	81	3,398	42.0	23	68

PUNT RETURNS	No.	FC	Yds.	Avg.	LG	TD
C. Rogers	22	18	318	14.5	94t	1
Jordan	5	3	47	9.4	15	0
Galloway	3	1	54	18.0	21	0
Joseph	0	2	0	—	—	0
Seahawks	30	24	419	14.0	94t	1
Opponents	36	18	370	10.3	81t	1

KICKOFF RETURNS	No.	Yds.	Avg.	LG	TD
Green	36	818	22.7	54	0
C. Rogers	18	465	25.8	49	0
Joseph	6	132	22.0	61	0
Jordan	3	62	20.7	24	0
Bownes	2	40	20.0	33	0
Fauria	2	15	7.5	8	0
Springs	1	15	15.0	15	0
Seahawks	68	1,547	22.8	61	0
Opponents	81	1,500	18.5	39	0

FIELD GOALS	1-19	20-29	30-39	40-49	50+
Peterson	1/1	10/10	8/11	14/16	1/2
Seahawks	1/1	10/10	8/11	14/16	1/2
Opponents	1/1	9/9	8/8	9/12	3/8

SACKS	No.
Daniels	9.0
Kennedy	6.5
Sinclair	6.0
C. Brown	5.5
Hanks	2.0
King	2.0
LaBounty	2.0
Parker	2.0
Adams	1.0
Smith	1.0
Seahawks	38.0
Opponents	38.0

2000 DRAFT CHOICES

Round	Name	Pos.	College
1	Shaun Alexander	RB	Alabama
	Chris McIntosh	T	Wisconsin
2	Ike Charlton	DB	Virginia Tech
3	Darrell Jackson	WR	Florida
4	Marcus Bell	LB	Arizona
	Isaiah Kacyvenski	LB	Harvard
6	James Williams	WR	Marshall
	Tim Watson	DT	Rowan
	John Hilliard	DT	Mississippi State

SEATTLE SEAHAWKS

2000 VETERAN ROSTER

No.		Name	Pos.	Ht.	Wt.	Birthdate	NFL Exp.	College	Hometown	How Acq.	'99 Games/ Starts
83		Bailey, Karsten	WR	5-10	201	4/26/77	2	Auburn	Newnan, Ga.	D3b-'99	2/0
63	#	Beede, Frank	G	6-4	296	5/1/73	5	Panhandle State	Antioch, Calif.	FA-'96	10/0
20		Bellamy, Jay	S	5-11	199	7/8/72	7	Rutgers	Aberdeen, N.J.	FA-'94	16/16
60		Bloedorn, Greg	C	6-6	278	11/15/72	4	Cornell	Elmhurst, Ill.	FA-'98	9/0
19		Bownes, Fabien	WR	5-11	192	2/29/72	4	Western Illinois	Aurora, Ill.	W(Chi)-'99	15/0
94		Brown, Chad	LB	6-2	240	7/12/70	8	Colorado	Altadena, Calif.	UFA(Pitt)-'97	15/15
34	#	Brown, Reggie	RB	6-0	244	6/26/73	5	Fresno State	Detroit, Mich.	D3b-'96	16/8
26		Canty, Chris	CB	5-9	185	3/30/76	4	Kansas State	Long Beach, Calif.	W(Chi)-'99	14/1
90		Cochran, Antonio	DE	6-4	297	6/21/76	2	Georgia	Montezuma, Ga.	D4-'99	4/0
81		Dawkins, Sean	WR	6-4	218	2/3/71	8	California	Sunnyvale, Calif.	UFA(NO)-'99	16/13
86		Fauria, Christian	TE	6-4	245	9/22/71	6	Colorado	Encino, Calif.	D2-'95	16/16
10		Feagles, Jeff	P	6-1	207	3/7/66	13	Miami	Anaheim, Calif.	UFA(Ariz)-'98	16/0
13		Foley, Glenn	QB	6-2	220	10/10/70	7	Boston College	Cherry Hill, N.J.	T(NYJ)-'99	3/1
62		Gray, Chris	G-C	6-4	305	6/19/70	8	Auburn	Birmingham, Ala.	UFA(Chi)-'98	16/10
11		Huard, Brock	QB	6-4	228	4/15/76	2	Washington	Puyallup, Wash.	D3a-'99	0*
71		Jones, Walter	T	6-5	300	1/19/74	4	Florida State	Aliceville, Ala.	D1b-'97	16/16
28		Joseph, Kerry	S	6-2	205	10/4/73	4	McNeese State	New Iberia, La.	FA-'98	16/4
66		Kendall, Pete	G	6-5	292	7/9/73	5	Boston College	Weymouth, Mass.	D1-'96	16/16
96		Kennedy, Cortez	DT	6-3	306	8/23/68	11	Miami	Wilson, Ark.	D1a-'90	16/16
92		King, Lamar	DE	6-3	294	8/10/75	2	Saginaw Valley State	Boston, Mass.	D1-'99	14/0
7		Kitna, Jon	QB	6-2	217	9/21/72	4	Central Washington	Tacoma, Wash.	FA-'96	15/15
59		Kopp, Jeff	LB	6-4	244	7/8/71	6	Southern California	Danville, Calif.	FA-'00	6/0*
99		LaBounty, Matt	DE	6-4	275	1/3/69	8	Oregon	Novato, Calif.	T(GB)-'96	16/1
56		Logan, James	LB	6-2	225	12/6/72	6	Memphis	Opp, Ala.	W(Cin)-'95	16/2
88		May, Deems	TE	6-4	263	3/6/69	9	North Carolina	Lexington, N.C.	UFA(SD)-'97	15/0
87		Mayes, Derrick	WR	6-0	205	1/28/74	5	Notre Dame	Indianapolis, Ind.	T(GB)-'99	16/15
89		Mili, Itula	TE	6-4	265	4/20/73	3	Brigham Young	Laie, Hawaii	D6-'97	16/1
44	#	Milne, Brian	RB	6-3	254	1/7/73	5	Penn State	Waterford, Pa.	FA-'99	11/1*
50		Myles, DeShone	LB	6-2	235	10/31/74	3	Nevada	Las Vegas, Nev.	D4-'98	5/0
97		Parker, Riddick	DT	6-3	274	11/20/72	4	North Carolina	Southampton, Va.	FA-'96	16/3
2		Peterson, Todd	K	5-10	177	2/4/70	6	Georgia	Valdosta, Ga.	FA-'95	16/0
85		Pritchard, Mike	WR	5-10	193	10/26/69	10	Colorado	Las Vegas, Nev.	FA-'96	14/5
31		Rogers, Charlie	RB	5-9	179	6/19/76	2	Georgia Tech	Cliffwood, N.J.	D5b-'99	12/0
51		Simmons, Anthony	LB	6-0	230	6/20/76	3	Clemson	Spartanburg, S.C.	D1-'98	16/16
70		Sinclair, Michael	DE	6-4	275	1/31/68	9	Eastern New Mexico	Beaumont, Tex.	D6-'91	15/15
24		Springs, Shawn	CB	6-0	195	3/11/75	4	Ohio State	Silver Springs, Md.	D1a-'97	16/16
38		Strong, Mack	RB	6-0	235	9/11/71	7	Georgia	Columbus, Ga.	FA-'93	14/1
61		Tobeck, Robbie	C-G	6-4	298	3/6/70	7	Washington State	Tarpon Springs, Fla.	UFA(Atl)-'00	16/16*
25		Tongue, Reggie	S	6-0	206	4/11/73	5	Oregon State	Fairbanks, Ark.	UFA(KC)-'00	16/16*
21	t-	Vinson, Fred	CB	5-11	180	4/2/77	2	Vanderbilt	North Augusta, S.C.	T(GB)-'00	16/1*
32		Watters, Ricky	RB	6-1	217	4/7/69	10	Notre Dame	Harrisburg, Pa.	UFA(Phil)-'98	16/16
69		Wedderburn, Floyd	T	6-5	333	5/5/76	2	Penn State	Upper Darby, Pa.	D5a-'99	0*
74		Weiner, Todd	T	6-4	300	9/16/75	3	Kansas State	Coral Springs, Fla.	D2-'98	11/1
27		Williams, Willie	CB	5-9	180	12/26/70	8	Western Carolina	Columbia, S.C.	UFA(Pitt)-'97	15/14

* Huard was inactive for 16 games in '99; Kopp played 6 games with New England; Milne played 1 game for Cincinnati and played 10 games with New England; Tobeck played 16 games with Atlanta; Tongue played 16 games with Kansas City; Vinson played 16 games with Green Bay; Wedderburn was inactive for 11 games.

t- Seahawks traded for CB Fred Vinson (Green Bay).

Traded—WR Joey Galloway (8 games in '99) to Dallas; RB Ahman Green (14) to Green Bay.

Players lost to free agency (5): DT Sam Adams (Balt; 13 games in '99), DE Phillip Daniels (Chi; 16), CB Fred Thomas (NO; 1), S Brian Walker (Mia; 5), T Grant Williams (NE; 16).

Also played with Seahawks in '99—LB Scott Fields (2 games), DB Randy Fuller (2), C Kevin Glover (6), G Brian Habib (16), S Merton Hanks (12), RB Dustin Johnson (1), WR Charles Jordan (4), C Mark Rodenhauser (8), LB Darrin Smith (15), DB Cordell Taylor (2), S Darryl Williams (13), DB Robert Williams (1), LB James Willis (16), WR Robert Wilson (2).

COACHING STAFF

Executive Vice President of Football Operations/ General Manager & Head Coach, Mike Holmgren

Pro Career: Named to his current position as the Seahawks' executive vice president of football operations/general manager and head coach on January 8, 1999. In addition to his coaching duties, Holmgren oversees all facets of the team's football operations, including scouting, personnel, salary cap, player negotiations, as well as regular coaching responsibilities. In his first season, Holmgren guided the Seahawks to their first postseason appearance since 1988. The Seahawks also won their first AFC West title since 1988, and hosted their first postseason game since 1984. Holmgren took control of the Seahawks following one of the most successful coaching stints in league history as the head coach of the Green Bay Packers (1992-98). By winning at least one game in five consecutive postseasons (1993-97) Holmgren joined John Madden (1973-77) as the only coaches in league history to accomplish that feat. In 14 NFL seasons (1999 head coach, 1992-98 head coach Green Bay, 1986-1991 assistant coach San Francisco) Holmgren's teams have posted a 155-68-1 (.694) record, hit double digits in the victory column 10 times, made the postseason 13 times, won three Super Bowls (XXIII, XXIV, and XXXI), and reached another (Super Bowl XXXII). Before becoming the Packers' head coach, Holmgren served as an assistant coach of the San Francisco 49ers from 1986-1991. Career record: 93-50.

Background: Quarterback at Southern California (1966-69) and was drafted by the St. Louis Cardinals in the eighth round of the 1970 NFL draft. He served as an assistant coach at San Francisco State (1981) and Brigham Young (1982-85). Earned his bachelor degree in business finance at Southern California.

Personal: Born June 15, 1948, in San Francisco. He and his wife, Kathy, live in Mercer Island, Wash. and have four daughters—Calla, Jenny, Emily, and Gretchen.

ASSISTANT COACHES

Larry Brooks, defensive line; born June 10, 1950, Prince George, Va., lives in Kirkland, Wash. Defensive lineman Virginia State 1968-1971. Pro defensive tackle Los Angeles Rams 1972-1982. College coach: Virginia State 1992-93. Pro coach: Los Angeles Rams 1983-1990, Green Bay Packers 1994-98, joined Seahawks in 1999.

Jerry Colquitt, offensive quality control; born June 28, 1972, Oak Ridge, Tenn., lives in Kirkland, Wash. Quarterback Tennessee 1991-94. Quarterback Frankfurt Galaxy (NFL Europe) 1997. College coach: Tennessee 1996-98. Pro coach: Joined Seahawks in 1999.

Nolan Cromwell, wide receivers; born January 30, 1955, Smith Center, Kan., lives in Bellevue, Wash. Quarterback-safety Kansas 1973-76. Pro defensive back Los Angeles Rams 1977-1987. Pro coach: Los Angeles Rams 1991, Green Bay Packers 1992-98, joined Seahawks in 1999.

Ken Flajole, linebackers; born October 4, 1954, Seattle, lives in Kirkland, Wash. Linebacker Wenatchee (Wash.) Valley C.C. 1973-74, Pacific Lutheran 1975-76. No pro playing experience. College coach: Pacific Lutheran 1977-78, Washington 1979, Montana 1980-85, Texas-El Paso 1986-88, Missouri 1989-1993, Richmond 1994, Hawaii 1995, Nevada 1996-97. Pro coach: Green Bay Packers 1998, joined Seahawks in 1999.

Gill Haskell, offensive coordinator; born September 24, 1943, San Francisco, lives in Kirkland. Defensive back San Francisco State 1961, 1963-65. No pro playing experience. College coach: Southern California 1978-1982. Pro coach: Los Angeles Rams 1983-1991, Green Bay Packers 1992-97, Carolina Panthers 1998-99, joined Seahawks in 2000.

Johnny Holland, asst. special teams-asst. strength & conditioning; born March 11, 1965, Belleville, Texas, lives in Kirkland. Linebacker Texas A&M 1983-86. Pro linebacker Green Bay Packers 1987-1993. Pro coach: Green Bay Packers 1995-99, joined Seahawks in 2000.

Kent Johnston, strength and conditioning; born February 21, 1956, Mexia, Texas, lives in Bellevue, Wash. Defensive back Stephen F. Austin 1974-77. No pro playing experience. College coach: Northwestern State (La.) 1979, Northeast Louisiana 1980-81, Alabama 1983-86. Pro coach: Tampa Bay Buccaneers 1987-1991, Green Bay Packers 1992-98, joined Seahawks in 1999.

Jim Lind, tight ends; born Novemeber 11, 1947, Isle, Minn., lives in Bellevue, Wash. Linebacker Bethel College 1965-66, defensive back Bemidji State 1971-72. No pro playing experience. College coach: St. Cloud State 1977-78, St. John's (Minn.) 1979-1980, Brigham Young 1981-82, Minnesota-Morris 1983-86 (head coach), Wisconsin-Eau Claire 1987-1991 (head coach). Pro coach: Green Bay Packers 1992-98, joined Seahawks in 1999.

Clayton Lopez, defensive quality control; born May 26, 1971, Los Angeles, lives in Kirkland, Wash. Safety Nevada 1991-94. No pro playing experience. College coach: Nevada 1995-98. Pro coach: Joined Seahawks in 1999.

Tom Lovat, asst. head coach-offensive line; born December 28, 1938, Bingham, Utah, lives in Bellevue, Wash. Guard-linebacker Utah 1958-1960. No pro playing experience. College coach: Utah 1967, 1972-76 (head coach 1974-76), Idaho State 1968-1970, Stanford 1977-79, Wyoming 1989. Pro coach: Saskatchewan Roughriders (CFL) 1971, Green Bay Packers 1980, 1992-98, St. Louis/Phoenix Cardinals 1981-84, 1990-91, Indianapolis Colts 1985-88, joined Seahawks in 1999.

Stump Mitchell, running backs; born March 15, 1959, St. Mary's, Ga., lives in Kirkland, Wash. Tailback The Citadel 1977-1980. Running back St. Louis/Phoenix Cardinals 1981-89. College coach: Morgan State 1995-98 (head coach 1996-98). Pro coach: San Antonio Rough Riders (WLAF) 1991, joined Seahawks in 1999.

Dick Roach, defensive backs; born August 23, 1937, Rapid City, S.D., lives in Kirkland. Defensive back Black Hills State 1952-55. No pro playing experience. College coach: Montana State 1966-69, Oregon State 1970, Wyoming 1971-72, Fresno State 1973, Washington State 1974-75. Pro coach: Montreal Alouettes (CFL) 1976-77, Kansas City Chiefs 1978-1980, New England Patriots 1981, Michigan Panthers (USFL) 1983-84, Tampa Bay Buccaneers 1985-86, Buffalo Bills 1987-1997, joined Seahawks in 1999.

Pete Rodriguez, special teams coordinator; born July 25, 1940, Chicago, lives in Kirkland, Wash. Guard-linebacker Denver 1959-1960, Western State (Colo.) 1961-63. No pro playing experience. College coach: Western State (Colo.) 1964, Arizona 1968-69, Western Illinois 1970-73, 1979-1982 (head coach), Florida State 1974-75, Iowa State 1976-78, Northern Iowa 1986. Pro coach: Michigan Panthers (USFL) 1983-84, Denver Gold (USFL) 1985, Jacksonville Bulls (USFL) 1986, Ottawa Rough Riders (CFL) 1987, Los Angeles Raiders 1988-89, Phoenix Cardinals 1990-93, Washington Redskins 1994-97, joined Seahawks in 1998.

Mike Sheppard, quarterbacks; born October 29, 1951, Tulsa, Okla., lives in Redmond, Wash. Wide receiver Cal Lutheran 1969-1972. No pro playing experience. College coach: Cal Lutheran 1974-76, Brigham Young 1977-78, U.S. International 1979, Idaho State 1980-81, Long Beach State 1982, 1984-86 (head coach), New Mexico 1987-1991 (head coach), California 1992. Pro coach: Cleveland Browns/Baltimore Ravens 1993-96, San Diego Chargers 1997-98, joined Seahawks in 1999.

Steve Sidwell, defensive coordinator; born August 30, 1944, Winfield, Kan., lives in Kirkland. Linebacker Colorado 1962-65. No pro playing experience. College coach: Colorado 1966-1973, Nevada-Las Vegas 1974-75, Southern Methodist 1976-1981. Pro coach: New England Patriots 1982-84, 1997-99, Indianapolis Colts 1985, New Orleans Saints 1986-1994, Houston Oilers 1995-96, joined Seahawks in 2000.

Rod Springer, asst. strength & conditioning; born September 19, 1960, Oklahoma City, Okla., lives in Kirkland. Attended Tarrleton State. No college or pro playing experience. College coach: Alabama 1985-86. Pro coach: Joined Seahawks in 1999.

2000 FIRST-YEAR ROSTER

Name	Pos.	Ht.	Wt.	Birthdate	College	Hometown	How Acq.
Alexander, Shaun	RB	5-11	218	8/30/77	Alabama	Florence, Ky.	D1a
Bell, Marcus	LB	6-1	237	7/19/77	Arizona	St. Johns, Ariz.	D4a
Burton, Kendrick (1)	DE	6-5	290	9/7/73	Alabama	Hartselle, Ala.	FA
Charlton, Ike	CB	5-11	205	10/6/77	Virginia Tech	Orlando, Fla.	D2
Conley, Tim	T	6-5	306	12/31/77	Sacramento State	Santa Monica, Calif.	FA
Eloms, Joey (1)	CB	5-10	183	4/4/76	Indiana	Fort Wayne, Ind.	FA
Epps, Dwan	LB	6-1	242	1/18/77	Texas Southern	Friendswood, Tex.	FA
Evans, Omar	CB	5-11	192	9/1/76	Howard	Silver Springs, Md.	FA
Feterik, Kevin	QB	5-11	207	9/14/77	Brigham Young	Los Alamitos, Calif.	FA
French, Rufus (1)	TE	6-3	257	3/15/78	Mississippi	Amory, Miss.	FA
Frier, T.J. (1)	DT	6-2	307	8/17/77	Memphis	Biloxi, Miss.	FA
Gilbert, Chris	C	6-2	305	7/4/76	Grand Valley State	Detroit, Mich.	FA
Green, Anthony	RB	6-1	243	5/13/77	West Virginia	Jersey City, N.J.	FA
Heppner, Kris	K	5-9	180	1/18/77	Montana	Helena, Mont.	FA
Herndon, Warner	S	6-1	210	2/9/78	Morgan State	Sacramento, Calif.	FA
Hill, James (1)	TE	6-4	246	10/25/74	Abileine Christian	Dallas, Tex.	FA
Hilliard, John	DT	6-2	285	4/16/76	Mississippi State	Houston, Tex.	D6c
Jackson, Darrell	WR	6-1	197	12/6/78	Florida	Dayton, Ohio	D3
Jenkins, Marcus (1)	G	6-4	302	9/12/75	Central Florida	Tampa, Fla.	FA
Kacyvenski, Isaiah	LB	6-1	250	10/3/77	Harvard	Endicott, N.Y.	D4b
Kehl, Ed (1)	LS-DT	6-4	305	8/3/72	Brigham Young	Sandy, Utah	FA
Kelly, Maurice	S	6-1	176	10/9/72	East Tennessee State	Orangebury, S.C.	FA
Keneley, Matt (1)	DT	6-5	284	12/1/73	Southern California	Mission Viejo, Calif.	FA
McIntosh, Chris	T	6-6	315	2/20/77	Wisconsin	Pewaukee, Wis.	D1b
Moorman, Brian (1)	P	5-11	180	2/8/76	Pittsburg State	Leesville, Kans.	FA
Morrison, Mac	LB	6-1	244	1/11/78	Penn State	Port Orchard, Wash.	FA
Osborne, Scot	LS	6-4	274	10/30/77	William & Mary	Asheville, N.C.	FA
Phillips, Rodnick	RB	5-11	205	11/17/77	Southern Methodist	Galveston, Tex.	FA
Swinton, Reginald (1)	WR	6-1	172	7/24/75	Murray State	Little Rock, Ark.	FA
Walker, Cory (1)	RB	5-10	188	6/4/73	Arkansas State	Memphis, Tenn.	FA
Watson, Tim	DT	6-4	290	12/23/74	Rowan	Williamstown, N.J.	D6b
Williams, James	WR	5-10	180	3/6/78	Marshall	Raymond, Miss.	D6a
Williams, Lamanzer (1)	DE	6-4	272	11/17/74	Minnesota	Ypsilanti, Mich.	FA

The term NFL Rookie is defined as a player who is in his first season of professional football and has not been on the roster of another professional football team for any regular-season or postseason games. A Rookie is designated by an "R" on NFL rosters. Players who have been active in another professional football league or players who have NFL experience, including either preseason training camp or being on an Active List or Inactive List, or on Reserve/Injured or Reserve/Physically Unable to Perform for fewer than six regular-season games, are termed NFL First-Year Players. An NFL First-Year Player is designated by a "1" on NFL rosters. Thereafter, a player is credited with an additional year of experience for each season in which he accumulates six games on the Active List or Inactive List, or on Reserve/Injured or Reserve/Physically Unable to Perform

TENNESSEE TITANS

American Football Conference
Central Division
Team Colors: Navy, Titans Blue, Red, Silver
460 Great Circle Road
Nashville, Tennessee 37228
Telephone: (615) 565-4000

CLUB OFFICIALS

Owner/Chairman of the Board: K.S. (Bud) Adams, Jr.
Executive Assistant to Owner/ Chairman of the Board: Thomas S. Smith
President/Chief Operating Officer: Jeff Diamond
Executive V.P./General Manager: Floyd Reese
Executive V.P: Don MacLachlan
Vice President/General Counsel: Steve Underwood
Asst. General Counsel: Elza Bullock
Vice President/Finance: Jackie Curley
Vice President/Community Affairs: Bob Hyde
Director of Player Personnel: Rich Snead
Director of College Scouting: Glenn Cumbee
Director of Sales and Operations: Stuart Spears
Asst. Dir. of Sales and Operations: Chad Bottorff
Director of Broadcasting: Mike Keith
Director of Marketing: Ralph Ockenfels
Director of Media Relations: Tony Wyllie
Asst. Dir. of Media Relations: Robbie Bohren
Director of Security: Steve Berk
Director of Ticket Operations: Marty Collins
Director of Player Programs: Al Smith
Director of Cheerleading and Entertainment: Meeka Gabriel
Director of Stadium Operations: Bill Dickerson
Suite and Club Services Manager: Bill Wainwright
Head Athletic Trainer: Brad Brown
Assistant Athletic Trainers: Don Moseley, Geoff Kaplan
Equipment Manager: Paul Noska
Video Coordinator: Ken Sparacino
Stadium: Adelphia Coliseum • **Capacity:** 67,000
One Titans Way
Nashville, Tennessee 37213
Playing Surface: Natural Grass
Training Camp: Baptist Sports Park
460 Great Circle Road
Nashville, Tennessee 37228
(615) 565-4000

2000 SCHEDULE

PRESEASON

Aug. 5	**Kansas City**	7:00
Aug. 14	**St. Louis**	7:00
Aug. 18	at Philadelphia	7:30
Aug. 25	at Chicago	7:00

REGULAR SEASON

Sept. 3	at Buffalo	8:35
Sept. 10	**Kansas City**	12:00
Sept. 17	Open Date	
Sept. 24	at Pittsburgh	1:00
Oct. 1	**New York Giants**	12:00
Oct. 8	at Cincinnati	1:00
Oct. 16	**Jacksonville** (Mon.)	8:00
Oct. 22	at Baltimore	1:00
Oct. 30	at Washington (Mon.)	9:00
Nov. 5	**Pittsburgh**	12:00
Nov. 12	**Baltimore**	12:00
Nov. 19	**Cleveland**	12:00
Nov. 26	at Jacksonville	4:15
Dec. 3	at Philadelphia	1:00
Dec. 10	**Cincinnati**	12:00
Dec. 17	at Cleveland	1:00
Dec. 25	**Dallas** (Mon.)	8:00

RECORD HOLDERS

INDIVIDUAL RECORDS—CAREER

Category	Name	Performance
Rushing (Yds.)	Earl Campbell, 1978-1984	8,574
Passing (Yds.)	Warren Moon, 1984-1993	33,685
Passing (TDs)	Warren Moon, 1984-1993	196
Receiving (No.)	Ernest Givins, 1986-1994	542
Receiving (Yds.)	Ernest Givins, 1986-1994	7,935
Interceptions	Jim Norton, 1960-68	45
Punting (Avg.)	Craig Hentrich, 1998-99	44.5
Punt Return (Avg.)	Billy Johnson, 1974-1980	13.2
Kickoff Return (Avg.)	Bobby Jancik, 1962-67	26.5
Field Goals	Al Del Greco, 1991-99	219
Touchdowns (Tot.)	Earl Campbell, 1978-1984	73
Points	Al Del Greco, 1991-99	942

INDIVIDUAL RECORDS—SINGLE SEASON

Category	Name	Performance
Rushing (Yds.)	Earl Campbell, 1980	1,934
Passing (Yds.)	Warren Moon, 1991	4,690
Passing (TDs)	George Blanda, 1961	36
Receiving (No.)	Charley Hennigan, 1964	101
Receiving (Yds.)	Charley Hennigan, 1961	1,746
Interceptions	Fred Glick, 1963	12
	Mike Reinfeldt, 1979	12
Punting (Avg.)	Craig Hentrich, 1998	47.2
Punt Return (Avg.)	Billy Johnson, 1977	15.4
Kickoff Return (Avg.)	Ken Hall, 1960	31.3
Field Goals	Al Del Greco, 1998	36
Touchdowns (Tot.)	Earl Campbell, 1979	19
Points	Al Del Greco, 1998	136

INDIVIDUAL RECORDS—SINGLE GAME

Category	Name	Performance
Rushing (Yds.)	Billy Cannon, 12-10-61	216
	Eddie George, 8-31-97	216
Passing (Yds.)	Warren Moon, 12-16-90	527
Passing (TDs)	George Blanda, 11-19-61	*7
Receiving (No.)	Charley Hennigan, 10-13-61	13
	Haywood Jeffires, 10-13-91	13
Receiving (Yds.)	Charley Hennigan, 10-13-61	272
Interceptions	Many times	3
	Last time by Samari Rolle, 12-26-99	
Field Goals	Roy Gerela, 9-28-69	5
Touchdowns (Tot.)	Billy Cannon, 12-10-61	5
Points	Billy Cannon, 12-10-61	30

*NFL Record

ADELPHIA COLISEUM

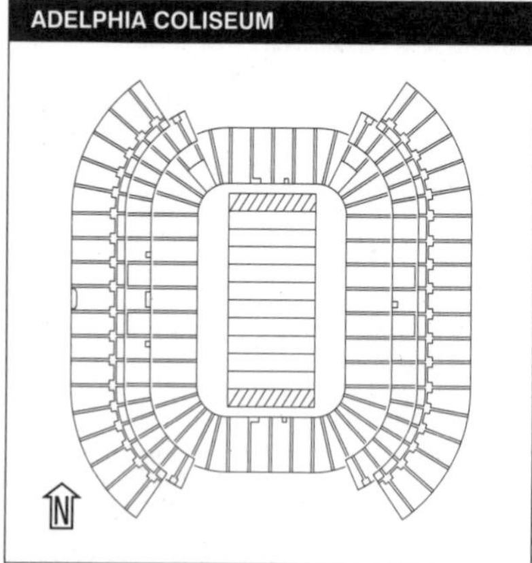

COACHING HISTORY

HOUSTON 1960-1996
(292-324-6)

1960-61	Lou Rymkus*	12-7-1
1961	Wally Lemm	10-0-0
1962-63	Frank (Pop) Ivy	17-12-0
1964	Sammy Baugh	4-10-0
1965	Hugh Taylor	4-10-0
1966-70	Wally Lemm	28-40-4
1971	Ed Hughes	4-9-1
1972-73	Bill Peterson**	1-18-0
1973-74	Sid Gillman	8-15-0
1975-80	O.A. (Bum) Phillips	59-38-0
1981-83	Ed Biles***	8-23-0
1983	Chuck Studley	2-8-0
1984-85	Hugh Campbell****	8-22-0
1985-89	Jerry Glanville	35-35-0
1990-94	Jack Pardee#	44-35-0
1994-99	Jeff Fisher	48-42-0

* Released after five games in 1961
** Released after five games in 1973
*** Resigned after six games in 1983
**** Released after 14 games in 1985
\# Released after 10 games in 1994

1999 TEAM RECORD

PRESEASON (1-3)

Date	Result		Opponent
8/15	L	20-22	at Kansas City
8/20	L	17-27	at Arizona
8/27	W	17-3	Atlanta
9/2	L	11-12	New Orleans

REGULAR SEASON (13-3)

Date	Result		Opponent	Att.
9/12	W	36-35	Cincinnati	65,272
9/19	W	26-9	Cleveland	65,904
9/26	W	20-19	at Jacksonville	61,502
10/3	L	22-24	at San Francisco	67,447
10/10	W	14-11	Baltimore	65,486
10/17	W	24-21	at New Orleans	51,875
10/31	W	24-21	St. Louis	66,415
11/7	L	0-17	at Miami	74,109
11/14	W	24-14	at Cincinnati	46,017
11/21	W	16-10	Pittsburgh	66,619
11/28	W	33-21	at Cleveland	72,008
12/5	L	14-41	at Baltimore	67,854
12/9	W	21-14	Oakland	66,357
12/19	W	30-17	Atlanta	66,196
12/26	W	41-14	Jacksonville	66,641
1/2	W	47-36	at Pittsburgh	48,025

POSTSEASON (3-1)

Date	Result		Opponent	Att.
1/8	W	22-16	Buffalo	66,672
1/16	W	19-16	at Indianapolis	57,097
1/23	W	33-14	at Jacksonville	75,206
1/30	L	16-23	vs. St. Louis, at Atlanta	72,625

SCORE BY PERIODS

Titans	113	97	85	97	0	—	392
Opponents	44	93	103	84	0	—	324

ATTENDANCE

Home 513,993 Away 492,838 Total 1,006,831
Single-game home record, 64,967 (12/26/99)
Single-season home record, 513,993 (1999)

1999 TEAM STATISTICS

	Titans	Opp.
Total First Downs	294	300
Rushing	109	81
Passing	167	193
Penalty	18	26
Third Down: Made/Att	83/217	70/200
Third Down Pct.	38.2	35.0
Fourth Down: Made/Att	7/12	4/14
Fourth Down Pct.	58.3	28.6
Total Net Yards	5,296	5,245
Avg. Per Game	331.0	327.8
Total Plays	1,011	994
Avg. Per Play	5.2	5.3
Net Yards Rushing	1,811	1,550
Avg. Per Game	113.2	96.9
Total Rushes	459	383
Net Yards Passing	3,485	3,695
Avg. Per Game	217.8	230.9
Sacked/Yards Lost	25/137	54/305
Gross Yards	3,622	4,000
Att./Completions	527/304	557/312
Completion Pct.	57.7	56.0
Had Intercepted	13	16
Punts/Average	90/42.5	80/42.9
Net Punting Avg.	90/38.1	80/37.2
Penalties/Yards	114/1,069	128/1,010
Fumbles/Ball Lost	17/9	39/24
Touchdowns	46	39
Rushing	19	8
Passing	23	26
Returns	4	5
Avg. Time of Possession	31:30	28:30

1999 INDIVIDUAL STATISTICS

Passing	Att.	Comp.	Yds.	Pct.	TD	Int.	Tkld.	Rate
McNair	331	187	2,179	56.5	12	8	16/74	78.6
O'Donnell	195	116	1,382	59.5	10	5	9/63	87.6
Wycheck	1	1	61	100.0	1	0	0/0	158.3
Titans	527	304	3,622	57.7	23	13	25/137	83.1
Opponents	557	312	4,000	56.0	26	16	54/305	82.3

SCORING	TD R	TD P	TD Rt	PAT	FG	Saf	PTS
Del Greco	0	0	0	43/43	21/25	0	106
E. George	9	4	0	0/0	0/0	0	78
McNair	8	0	0	0/0	0/0	0	48
Dyson	0	4	0	0/0	0/0	0	24
Thigpen	0	4	0	0/0	0/0	0	24
Neal	1	2	0	0/0	0/0	0	18
Roan	0	3	0	0/0	0/0	0	18
Byrd	0	2	0	0/0	0/0	0	12
Wycheck	0	2	0	0/0	0/0	0	12
Harris	0	1	0	0/0	0/0	0	8
Kearse	0	0	1	0/0	0/0	0	6
Mason	0	0	1	0/0	0/0	0	6
Mitchell	0	0	1	0/0	0/0	0	6
Sanders	0	1	0	0/0	0/0	0	6
Thomas	1	0	0	0/0	0/0	0	6
Walker	0	0	1	0/0	0/0	0	6
Thornton	0	0	0	0/0	0/0	1	2
Titans	19	23	4	43/43	21/25	4	392
Opponents	8	26	5	33/33	15/22	2	324

2-Pt. Conversions: Harris.
Team 1-3, Opponents 4-6

RUSHING	Att.	Yds.	Avg.	LG	TD
E. George	320	1,304	4.1	40	9
McNair	72	337	4.7	38	8
Thomas	43	164	3.8	22	1
Dyson	1	3	3.0	3	0
Hentrich	2	1	0.5	1	0
Neal	2	1	0.5	1t	1
O'Donnell	19	1	0.1	4	0
Titans	459	1,811	3.9	40	19
Opponents	383	1,550	4.0	72	8

RECEIVING	No.	Yds.	Avg.	LG	TD
Wycheck	69	641	9.3	35	2
Dyson	54	658	12.2	47t	4
E. George	47	458	9.7	54t	4
Thigpen	38	648	17.1	35	4
Harris	26	297	11.4	62t	1
Sanders	20	336	16.8	48t	1
Byrd	14	261	18.6	65t	2
Roan	9	93	10.3	24t	3
Thomas	9	72	8.0	26	0
Mason	8	89	11.1	31	0
Neal	7	27	3.9	8	2
Kent	3	42	14.0	25	0
Titans	304	3,622	11.9	65t	23
Opponents	312	4,000	12.8	78t	26

INTERCEPTIONS	No.	Yds.	Avg.	LG	TD
Rolle	4	65	16.3	30	0
Sidney	3	12	4.0	7	0
Holmes	2	17	8.5	19	0
Dorsett	1	43	43.0	43	0
Mitchell	1	42	42.0	42t	1
Bowden	1	29	29.0	29	0
Walker	1	27	27.0	27	0
Fisk	1	17	17.0	17	0
Robertson	1	3	3.0	3	0
Jackson	1	2	2.0	2	0
Titans	16	257	16.1	43	1
Opponents	13	227	17.5	47t	2

PUNTING	No.	Yds.	Avg.	In 20	LG
Hentrich	90	3,824	42.5	35	78
Titans	90	3,824	42.5	35	78
Opponents	80	3,435	42.9	25	72

PUNT RETURNS	No.	FC	Yds.	Avg.	LG	TD
Mason	26	15	225	8.7	65t	1
Preston	8	2	59	7.4	12	0
Byrd	2	0	8	4.0	8	0
S. George	1	0	18	18.0	18	0
Rolle	1	0	23	23.0	23	0
Sidney	1	0	4	4.0	4	0
Thigpen	1	0	21	21.0	21	0
Titans	40	17	358	9.0	65t	1
Opponents	45	22	335	7.4	32	0

KICKOFF RETURNS	No.	Yds.	Avg.	LG	TD
Mason	41	805	19.6	41	0
Preston	5	119	23.8	29	0
S. George	4	63	15.8	22	0
Kent	2	24	12.0	13	0
Byrd	2	16	8.0	9	0
Neal	2	15	7.5	14	0
Titans	56	1,042	18.6	41	0
Opponents	76	1,596	21.0	99t	2

FIELD GOALS	1-19	20-29	30-39	40-49	50+
Del Greco	1/1	8/8	7/9	4/6	1/1
Titans	1/1	8/8	7/9	4/6	1/1
Opponents	0/0	4/4	4/7	6/9	1/2

SACKS	No.
Kearse	14.5
Robinson	6.0
Ford	5.5
Thornton	4.5
Fisk	4.0
Holmes	4.0
Bowden	3.5
Evans	3.5
Rolle	3.0
Bishop	2.5
Jones	1.0
Frederick	0.5
Jackson	0.5
Robertson	0.5
Wortham	0.5
Titans	54.0
Opponents	25.0

2000 DRAFT CHOICES

Round	Name	Pos.	College
1	Keith Bulluck	LB	Syracuse
3	Erron Kinney	TE	Florida
	Byron Frisch	DE	Brigham Young
4	Bobby Myers	DB	Wisconsin
	Peter Sirmon	LB	Oregon
5	Aric Morris	DB	Michigan State
	Frank Chamberlin	LB	Boston College
6	Robaire Smith	DE	Michigan State
7	Mike Green	RB	Houston
	Wes Shivers	G	Mississippi State

TENNESSEE TITANS

2000 VETERAN ROSTER

No.	Name	Pos.	Ht.	Wt.	Birthdate	NFL Exp.	College	Hometown	How Acq.	'99 Games/ Starts
23	Bishop, Blaine	S	5-9	203	7/24/70	8	Ball State	Indianapolis, Ind.	D8-'93	15/15
84	Brown, Larry	TE	6-4	280	9/1/76	2	Georgia	Decatur, Ga.	FA-'99	9/0
83	Byrd, Isaac	WR	6-1	188	11/16/74	4	Kansas	St. Louis, Mo.	FA-'97	12/6
13	Daft, Kevin	QB	6-1	202	11/19/75	2	California-Davis	Tustin, Calif.	D5-'99	0*
3	Del Greco, Al	K	5-10	202	3/2/62	17	Auburn	Coral Gables, Fla.	FA-'91	16/0
87	Dyson, Kevin	WR	6-1	201	6/23/75	3	Utah	Clearfield, Utah	D1-'98	16/16
91	Evans, Josh	DT-DE	6-2	288	9/6/72	6	Alabama-Birmingham	West Shawmut, Ala.	FA-'95	11/10
51	Favors, Greg	LB	6-1	244	9/30/74	3	Mississippi State	Atlanta, Ga.	W(KC)-'99	15/0
97	Fisk, Jason	DT	6-3	295	9/4/72	6	Stanford	Davis, Calif.	UFA(Minn)-'99	16/16
92	Ford, Henry	DT	6-3	295	10/30/71	7	Arkansas	Ft. Worth, Tex.	D1-'94	12/9
94	# Frederick, Mike	DE	6-5	280	8/6/72	6	Virginia	Langhorne, Pa.	UFA(NYJ)-'99	13/0
27	George, Eddie	RB	6-3	240	9/24/73	5	Ohio State	Philadelphia, Pa.	D1-'96	16/16
26	George, Spencer	RB	5-9	200	10/28/73	3	Rice	Beaumont, Tex.	FA-'98	8/0
54	Glover, Phil	LB	5-11	241	12/17/75	2	Utah	Las Vegas, Nev.	D7-'99	1/0
56	Godfrey, Randall	LB	6-2	245	4/6/73	5	Georgia	Valdosta, Ga.	UFA(Dall)-'00	16/16*
15	Hentrich, Craig	P-K	6-3	205	5/18/71	7	Notre Dame	Alton, Ill.	UFA(GB)-'98	16/0
99	Holmes, Kenny	DE	6-4	270	10/24/73	4	Miami	Vero Beach, Fla.	D1-'97	14/7
72	Hopkins, Brad	T	6-3	305	9/5/70	8	Illinois	Moline, Ill.	D1-'97	16/16
96	Jones, Mike	DT-DE	6-4	280	8/25/69	10	North Carolina State	Columbia, S.C.	UFA(StL)-'99	11/3
90	Kearse, Jevon	DE	6-4	265	9/3/76	2	Florida	Ft. Myers, Fla.	D1-'99	16/16
86	Kent, Joey	WR	6-1	191	4/23/74	4	Tennessee	Huntsville, Ala.	D2-'97	8/0
50	Killens, Terry	LB	6-1	235	3/24/74	5	Penn State	Cincinnati, Ohio	D3-'96	16/1
60	Long, Kevin	C	6-5	295	5/2/75	3	Florida State	Summerville, S.C.	D7-'98	16/12
85	Mason, Derrick	WR	5-10	188	1/17/74	4	Michigan State	Detroit, Mich.	D4a-'97	13/0
76	Mathews, Jason	T	6-5	304	2/9/71	7	Texas A&M	Orange, Tex.	FA-'98	5/0
74	Matthews, Bruce	G-C	6-5	305	8/8/61	18	Southern California	Arcadia, Calif.	D1-'83	16/16
38	McCullough, George	CB	5-10	187	2/18/75	3	Baylor	Galveston, Tex.	D5-'97	5/0
9	McNair, Steve	QB	6-2	225	2/14/73	6	Alcorn State	Mt. Olive, Miss.	D1-'95	11/11
71	Miller, Fred	T	6-7	315	2/6/73	5	Baylor	Houston, Tex.	UFA(StL)-'00	16/16*
29	Mitchell, Donald	CB	5-9	185	12/14/76	2	Southern Methodist	Beaumont, Tex.	D4b-'99	16/0
41	Neal, Lorenzo	RB	5-11	240	12/27/70	8	Fresno State	Fresno, Calif.	UFA(TB)-'99	16/14
14	O'Donnell, Neil	QB	6-3	228	7/3/66	11	Maryland	Madison, N.J.	UFA(Cin)-'99	8/5
75	Olson, Benji	G	6-3	315	6/5/75	3	Washington	Port Orchard, Wash.	D5-'98	16/16
35	Phenix, Perry	S	5-11	210	11/14/74	3	Southern Mississippi	Dallas, Tex.	FA-'98	16/1
69	Piller, Zach	G	6-5	330	5/2/76	2	Florida	Tallahassee, Fla.	D3-'99	8/0
80	Roan, Michael	TE	6-3	250	8/29/72	6	Wisconsin	Iowa City, Iowa	D4-'95	11/1
31	Robertson, Marcus	S	5-11	205	10/2/69	10	Iowa State	Pasadena, Calif.	D4b-'91	15/15
55	Robinson, Eddie	LB	6-1	243	4/13/70	9	Alabama State	New Orleans, La	FA-'98	16/16
21	Rolle, Samari	CB	6-0	175	8/10/76	3	Florida State	Miami, Fla.	D2-'98	16/16
95	Salave'a, Joe	DT	6-3	290	3/23/75	3	Arizona	San Diego, Calif.	D4-'98	10/0
81	Sanders, Chris	WR	6-1	188	5/8/72	6	Ohio State	Denver, Colo.	D3a-'95	16/0
73	Sanderson, Scott	G-T	6-6	295	7/25/74	4	Washington State	Concord, Calif.	D3b-'97	3/3
37	Sidney, Dainon	CB	6-0	188	5/30/75	3	Alabama-Birmingham	Atlanta, Ga.	D3-'98	16/2
82	Thigpen, Yancey	WR	6-1	203	8/15/69	9	Winston-Salem State	Rocky Mount, N.C.	UFA(Pitt)-'98	10/10
22	Thomas, Rodney	RB	5-10	210	3/30/73	6	Texas A&M	Groveton, Tex.	D3b-'95	16/0
78	Thornton, John	DT	6-2	295	10/2/76	2	West Virginia	Philadelphia, Pa.	D2-'99	16/3
25	Walker, Denard	CB	6-1	190	8/9/73	4	Louisiana State	Garland, Tex.	D3a-'97	15/14
89	Wycheck, Frank	TE	6-3	250	10/14/71	8	Maryland	Philadelphia, Pa.	W(Wash)-'95	16/16

* Daft was inactive for 11 games in '99; Godfrey played 16 games with Dallas; Miller played 16 games with St. Louis.

† Restricted free agent; subject to developments.

\# Unrestricted free agent; subject to developments.

Players lost through free agency (5): LB Joe Bowden (Dall; 15 games in '99), LB Doug Colman (OaK; 16), S Anthony Dorsett (Oak; 16), TE Jackie Harris (Dall; 12), T Jon Runyan (Phil; 16).

Also played with Titans in '99—CB-S Steve Jackson (8 games), G Jason Layman (15), WR Roell Preston (2), LB Barron Wortham (16).

COACHING STAFF

Head Coach,
Jeff Fisher

Pro Career: Became the franchise's fifteenth head coach on January 5, 1995 after closing his first campaign as head coach/defensive coordinator. He replaced Jack Pardee on November 14, 1994, serving the remaining six games as head coach. Last season Fisher guided the team to a franchise-record 13 wins, ending a six-year playoff drought and earning the franchise's first AFC championship and Super Bowl appearance. Throughout the past two seasons, Fisher has guided Tennessee to a 16-2 record against AFC Central opponents, and he currently ranks second in franchise history in wins with 48. Fisher originally joined the Oilers in 1994 as the defensive coordinator after serving as defensive backs coach for the San Francisco 49ers (1992-93). Prior to heading up the 49ers' secondary, Fisher served as the defensive coordinator for the Los Angeles Rams (1991). He began his coaching career with the Philadelphia Eagles in 1986, where he handled defensive backs until becoming the NFL's youngest defensive coordinator in 1988. Drafted by Chicago in the seventh round in 1981, he spent five seasons as a cornerback and kick returner for the Bears (1981-85). Assisted defensive coordinator Buddy Ryan in Bears' 1985 Super Bowl championship season after being placed on injured reserve with ankle injury. Career record: 48-42.

Background: Played at Southern California (1977-1980) for John Robinson in a star-studded defensive backfield that included Ronnie Lott, Dennis Smith, and Joey Browner. Member of the USC team that won the national championship in 1978. Also served as the Trojans' backup placekicker and was a Pac-10 All-Academic selection in 1980.

Personal: Born February 25, 1958, in Culver City, Calif. Jeff and his wife, Juli, have three children, sons Brandon and Trenton, and daughter Tara. The family resides in Franklin, Tenn.

ASSISTANT COACHES

Jerry Gray, defensive backs; born December 16, 1962, Lubbock, Texas, lives in Franklin, Tenn. Defensive back Texas 1981-84. Pro safety-cornerback Los Angeles Rams 1985-1991, Houston Oilers 1992, Tampa Bay Buccaneers 1993. College coach: Southern Methodist 1995-96. Pro coach: Joined Titans/Oilers in 1997.

Mike Heimerdinger, offensive coordinator; born October 13, 1952, DeKalb, Ill., lives in Brentwood, Tenn. Wide receiver Eastern Illinois 1970-74. No pro playing experience. College coach: Florida 1980, Air Force 1981, North Texas State 1982, Florida 1983-87, Cal State-Fullerton 1988, Rice 1989-1993, Duke 1994. Pro coach: Denver Broncos 1995-99, joined Titans in 2000.

George Henshaw, asst. head coach; born January 22, 1948, Richmond, Va., lives in Nashville. Defensive tackle West Virginia 1967-69. No pro playing experience. College coach: West Virginia 1970-75, Florida State 1976-1982, Alabama 1983-86, Tulsa 1987 (head coach). Pro coach: Denver Broncos 1988-1992, New York Giants 1993-96, joined Titans/Oilers in 1997.

Craig Johnson, offensive assistant-quality control; born March 3, 1960, Rome, N.Y., lives in Nashville. Quarterback Wyoming 1978-1982. No pro playing experience. College coach: Wyoming 1983, Arkansas 1984, Army 1985, Rutgers 1986-88, Virginia Military Institute 1989-1991, Northwestern 1992-96, Maryland 1997-99. Pro coach: Joined Titans in 2000.

Alan Lowry, special teams; born November 21, 1950, Miami, Okla., lives in Franklin, Tenn. Defensive back-quarterback Texas 1970-72. No pro playing experience. College coach: Virginia Tech 1974, Wyoming 1975, Texas 1977-1981. Pro coach: Dallas Cowboys 1982-1990, Tampa Bay Buccaneers 1991, San Francisco 49ers 1992-95, joined Titans/Oilers in 1996.

Mike Munchak, offensive line; born March 5, 1960, Scranton, Pa., lives in Brentwood, Tenn. Guard-tackle Penn State 1979-1981. Pro guard Houston Oilers 1982-1993. Pro coach: Joined Titans/Oilers in 1994.

Jim Schwartz, linebackers; born June 2, 1966, Baltimore, lives in Nashville. Linebacker Georgetown 1984-88. No pro playing experience. College coach: Maryland 1989, Minnesota 1990, North Carolina Central 1991, Colgate 1992. Pro coach: Cleveland Browns/Baltimore Ravens 1995-98, joined Titans in 1999.

Sherman Smith, running backs; born November 1, 1954, Youngstown, Ohio, lives in Franklin, Tenn. Quarterback Miami (Ohio) 1972-75. Pro running back Seattle Seahawks 1976-1982, San Diego Chargers 1983-84. College coach: Miami (Ohio) 1990-91, Illinois 1992-94. Pro coach: Joined Titans/Oilers in 1995.

Ronnie Vinklarek, defensive assistant-quality control; born January 21, 1959, Weimer, Texas, lives in Nashville. Attended Southwest Texas State 1977-1981. No pro playing experience. College coach: Houston 1988-1993, Valdosta State 1997, Oklahoma State 1998-99. Pro coach: Birmingham Barracudas (CFL) 1995, joined Titans in 2000.

Steve Walters, wide receivers; born June 16, 1948, Jonesboro, Ark., lives in Nashville. Quarterback-defensive back Arkansas 1967-1970. No pro playing experience. College coach: Tampa 1973, Northeastern Louisana 1974-75, Morehead State 1976, Tulsa 1977-78, Memphis State 1979, Southern Methodist 1980-81, Alabama 1985. Pro coach: New England Patriots 1982-84, 1997-98, New Orleans 1986-1996, joined Titans in 1999.

Jim Washburn, defensive line; born December 2, 1949, Shelby, N.C., lives in Nashville. Offensive lineman Gardner-Webb 1969-1973. No pro playing experience. College coach: Southern Methodist 1976, Lees McRae J.C. 1977-78, Livingston 1979, New Mexico 1980-82, South Carolina 1983-88, Purdue 1989, Arkansas 1994-97, Houston 1998. Pro coach: London Monarchs (WLAF) 1991, Charlotte Rage (AFL) 1993, joined Titans in 1999.

Steve Watterson, strength and rehabilitation; born November 27, 1956, Newport, R.I., lives in Brentwood, Tenn. Attended Rhode Island. No college or pro playing experience. Pro coach: Philadelphia Eagles 1984-85, joined Titans/Oilers in 1986.

Gregg Williams, defensive coordinator; born July 15, 1958, Excelsior Springs, Mo., lives in Franklin, Tenn. Quarterback Northeast Missouri State 1976-79. No pro playing experience. College coach: Houston 1988-89. Pro coach: Joined Titans/Oilers in 1990.

2000 FIRST-YEAR ROSTER

Name	Pos.	Ht.	Wt.	Birthdate	College	Hometown	How Acq.
Arnold, Aaron	WR	6-1	185	12/27/77	California State-Northridge	Northridge, Calif.	FA
Brown, DeMario	RB	6-0	213	3/6/77	Utah State	Ridgecrest, Calif.	FA
Bulluck, Keith	LB	6-3	232	4/4/77	Syracuse	New City, N.Y.	D1
Chamberlin, Frank	LB	6-1	250	1/2/78	Boston College	Wahwah, N.J.	D5b
Clark, Kareem	CB	5-10	189	11/28/76	Arizona State	Yorba Linda, Calif.	FA
Coleman, Chris	WR	6-0	202	5/8/77	North Carolina State	Shelby, N.C.	FA
Davis, Wade	DB	5-11	185	7/20/77	Weber State	Aurora, Colo.	FA
Frisch, Byron	DE	6-5	267	12/17/76	Brigham Young	Bonita, Calif.	D3b
Gould, Garett	RB	6-2	238	5/30/76	Michigan State	Troy, Mich.	FA
Green, Mike	RB	6-0	249	9/2/76	Houston	Houston, Tex.	D7a
Griffin, Torrie	DT	6-5	275	7/21/76	Carson-Newman	Washington D.C.	FA
Harris, Gerald	WR	5-11	186	9/23/77	Washington	Kent, Wash.	FA
Heiner, Jamie	LB	6-1	236	9/6/75	Northern Colorado	Fort Collins, Colo.	FA
Hunt, Deon	LB	6-0	243	1/12/78	Hampton	Detroit, Mich.	FA
Kinney, Erron	TE	6-5	272	7/28/77	Florida	Ashland, Va.	D3a
Koch, Aaron	G	6-3	298	2/1/78	Oregon State	Keizer, Ore.	FA
Leach, Mike	TE	6-4	238	10/18/76	William & Mary	Lake Hopatcong, N.J.	FA
McDonald, Jason	G	6-6	320	5/26/77	Alabama	Theodore, Ala.	FA
McLemore, Brandon	S	6-3	205	5/2/77	Oregon	Torrance, Calif.	FA
Morris, Aric	S	5-10	208	7/22/77	Michigan State	Oak Park, Mich.	D5a
Myers, Bobby	S	6-1	189	11/10/76	Wisconsin	Hamden, Conn.	D4a
Page, Craig (1)	C	6-3	303	1/17/76	Georgia Tech	Jupiter, Fla.	FA-'99
Scarborough, Mike	WR	6-1	198	6/2/76	Texas Christian	Sugar Land, Tex.	FA
Shivers, Wes	T	6-5	318	3/8/77	Mississippi State	Benton, Miss.	D7b
Sirmon, Peter	LB	6-2	246	2/18/77	Oregon	Walla Walla, Wash.	D4b
Smith, Robaire	DE-DT	6-4	271	11/15/77	Michigan State	Flint, Mich.	D6
Umholtz, Tony	P-K	6-0	195	12/13/76	South Florida	Largo, Fla.	FA
Volek, Billy	QB	6-2	210	4/28/76	Fresno State	Fresno, Calif.	FA
Walker, Rod	DT	6-3	330	2/4/76	Troy State	Milton, Fla.	FA
Ware, Brad	S	6-1	205	3/26/78	Auburn	Powder Springs, Ga.	FA
Ware, Lenny	WR	6-1	195	5/5/77	Nevada-Las Vegas	Rancho Cucamonga, Calif.	FA
Warren, Jesse	DE	6-4	275	3/31/78	Colorado	Dallas, Tex.	FA
White, Jason	T	6-5	327	4/2/75	Oregon State	Discovery Bay, Calif.	FA
White, Jerard	FS	6-1	204	10/27/77	Massachusetts	Fort Washington, Md.	FA

The term NFL Rookie is defined as a player who is in his first season of professional football and has not been on the roster of another professional football team for any regular-season or postseason games. A Rookie is designated by an "R" on NFL rosters. Players who have been active in another professional football league or players who have NFL experience, including either preseason training camp or being on an Active List or Inactive List, or on Reserve/Injured or Reserve/Physically Unable to Perform for fewer than six regular-season games, are termed NFL First-Year Players. An NFL First-Year Player is designated by a "1" on NFL rosters. Thereafter, a player is credited with an additional year of experience for each season in which he accumulates six games on the Active List or Inactive List, or on Reserve/Injured or Reserve/Physically Unable to Perform.

NOTES

HOUSTON NFL 2002

American Football Conference
Houston NFL 2002
711 Louisiana Street
Suite 3300
Houston, Texas 77002
Telephone: (713) 336-7700

CLUB OFFICIALS

Chairman, President and CEO: Robert McNair
Vice Chairman: Philip Burguieres
Executive Vice President/General Manager: Charley Casserly
Executive Vice President: Steve Patterson
Senior Vice President/Sales & Marketing: Jamey Rootes
Vice President/General Counsel and Chief Administrative Officer: Suzanne Thomas
Vice President/Chief Financial Officer: Jimmy McDonald
Vice President/Corporate Finance: Scott Schwinger
Vice President/Corporate Sales: David Peart
Controller: Marilan Logan
Manager of Security: Ryan Reichert
Director of Pro Scouting: Chuck Banker
Associate Directors of Pro Scouting: Bobby Grier, Miller McCalmon
Coordinator of College Scouting: Mike Maccagnan
Manager of Player Information: Tom Halligan
National Scout: George Saimes
College Scouts: Larry Bryan, Don Deisch, Ralph Hawkins, Joel Patten, Pete Russell, Dave Sears
BLESTO Scout: Tom Throckmorton
Pro Scouting Assistant: Rob Kisiel
College Scouting Assistant: Jamaal Stephenson

The Houston NFL 2002 franchise will begin play in the AFC in 2002.

The NFC

ARIZONA CARDINALS

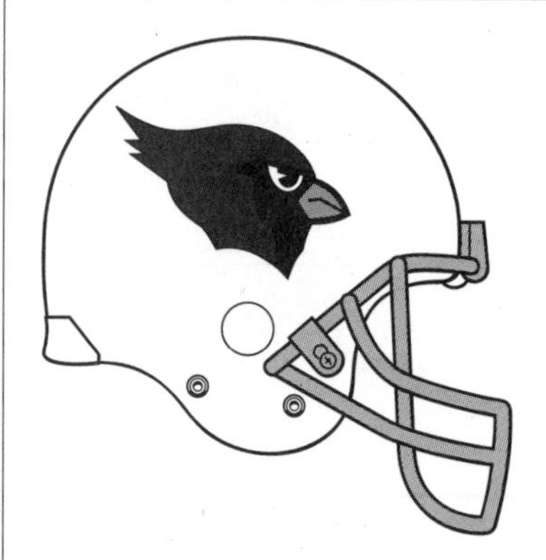

National Football Conference
Eastern Division
Team Colors: Cardinal Red, Black, and White
P.O. Box 888
Phoenix, Arizona 85001-0888
Telephone: (602) 379-0101

CLUB OFFICIALS

President: William V. Bidwill
Vice President: Larry Wilson
Vice Chairman: Thomas J. Guilfoil
Treasurer and Chief Financial Officer: Charley Schlegel
Vice President: William V. Bidwill, Jr.
Vice President/General Counsel: Michael Bidwill
Vice President/Sales and Marketing: Ron Minegar
General Manager: Bob Ferguson
Assistant to the President: Rod Graves
Public Relations Director: Paul Jensen
Media Coordinator: Greg Gladysiewski
Publications/Internet Coordinator: Luke Sacks
Director of Players Programs: Anthony Edwards
Director of Community Relations: Adele Harris
Director of Marketing: Joe Castor
Business Manager: Steve Walsh
Ticket Manager: Steve Bomar
Trainer: John Omohundro
Assistant Trainers: Jim Shearer, Jeff Herndon
Equipment Manager: Mark Ahlemeier
Assistant Equipment Manager: Steve Christensen
Stadium: Sun Devil Stadium • **Capacity:** 73,273
Fifth Street
Tempe, Arizona 85287
Playing Surface: Grass
Training Camp: Northern Arizona University
Flagstaff, Arizona 86011

2000 SCHEDULE

PRESEASON

Aug. 5	**Denver**	7:00
Aug. 12	**Seattle**	7:00
Aug. 18	at Minnesota	7:35
Aug. 25	at San Diego	7:00

REGULAR SEASON

Sept. 3	at New York Giants	1:00
Sept. 10	**Dallas**	5:35
Sept. 17	Open Date	
Sept. 24	**Green Bay**	1:05
Oct. 1	at San Francisco	1:15
Oct. 8	**Cleveland**	1:15
Oct. 15	**Philadelphia**	1:15
Oct. 22	at Dallas	12:00
Oct. 29	**New Orleans**	2:05
Nov. 5	**Washington**	2:05
Nov. 12	at Minnesota	12:00
Nov. 19	at Philadelphia	1:00
Nov. 26	**New York Giants**	6:35
Dec. 3	at Cincinnati	1:00
Dec. 10	at Jacksonville	1:00
Dec. 17	**Baltimore**	2:15
Dec. 24	at Washington	1:00

RECORD HOLDERS

INDIVIDUAL RECORDS—CAREER

Category	Name	Performance
Rushing (Yds.)	Ottis Anderson, 1979-1986	7,999
Passing (Yds.)	Jim Hart, 1966-1983	34,639
Passing (TDs)	Jim Hart, 1966-1983	209
Receiving (No.)	Larry Centers, 1990-98	535
Receiving (Yds.)	Roy Green, 1979-1990	8,497
Interceptions	Larry Wilson, 1960-1972	52
Punting (Avg.)	Jerry Norton, 1959-1961	44.9
Punt Return (Avg.)	Charley Trippi, 1947-1955	13.7
Kickoff Return (Avg.)	Ollie Matson, 1952, 1954-58	28.5
Field Goals	Jim Bakken, 1962-1978	282
Touchdowns (Tot.)	Roy Green, 1979-1990	70
Points	Jim Bakken, 1962-1978	1,380

INDIVIDUAL RECORDS—SINGLE SEASON

Category	Name	Performance
Rushing (Yds.)	Ottis Anderson, 1979	1,605
Passing (Yds.)	Neil Lomax, 1984	4,614
Passing (TDs)	Charley Johnson, 1963	28
	Neil Lomax, 1984	28
Receiving (No.)	Larry Centers, 1995	101
Receiving (Yds.)	Rob Moore, 1997	1,584
Interceptions	Bob Nussbaumer, 1949	12
Punting (Avg.)	Jerry Norton, 1960	45.6
Punt Return (Avg.)	John (Red) Cochran, 1949	20.9
Kickoff Return (Avg.)	Ollie Matson, 1958	35.5
Field Goals	Greg Davis, 1995	30
Touchdowns (Tot.)	John David Crow, 1962	17
Points	Jim Bakken, 1967	117
	Neil O'Donoghue, 1984	117

INDIVIDUAL RECORDS—SINGLE GAME

Category	Name	Performance
Rushing (Yds.)	LeShon Johnson, 9-22-96	214
Passing (Yds.)	Boomer Esiason, 11-10-96 (OT)	522
Passing (TDs)	Jim Hardy, 10-2-50	6
	Charley Johnson, 9-26-65, 11-2-69	6
Receiving (No.)	Sonny Randle, 11-4-62	16
Receiving (Yds.)	Sonny Randle, 11-4-62	256
Interceptions	Bob Nussbaumer, 11-13-49	*4
	Jerry Norton, 11-20-60	*4
	Kwamie Lassiter, 12-27-98	*4
Field Goals	Jim Bakken, 9-24-67	*7
Touchdowns (Tot.)	Ernie Nevers, 11-28-29	*6
Points	Ernie Nevers, 11-28-29	*40

*NFL Record

COACHING HISTORY

Chicago 1920-1959, St. Louis 1960-1987
(425-585-39)

1920-22	John (Paddy) Driscoll	17-8-4
1923-24	Arnold Horween	13-8-1
1925-26	Norman Barry	16-8-2
1927	Guy Chamberlin	3-7-1
1928	Fred Gillies	1-5-0
1929	Dewey Scanlon	6-6-1
1930	Ernie Nevers	5-6-2
1931	LeRoy Andrews*	0-1-0
1931	Ernie Nevers	5-3-0
1932	Jack Chevigny	2-6-2
1933-34	Paul Schissler	6-15-1
1935-38	Milan Creighton	16-26-4
1939	Ernie Nevers	1-10-0
1940-42	Jimmy Conzelman	8-22-3
1943-45	Phil Handler**	1-29-0
1946-48	Jimmy Conzelman	27-10-0
1949	Phil Handler-Buddy Parker***	2-4-0
1949	Raymond (Buddy) Parker	4-1-1
1950-51	Earl (Curly) Lambeau****	7-15-0
1951	Phil Handler-Cecil Isbell#	1-1-0
1952	Joe Kuharich	4-8-0
1953-54	Joe Stydahar	3-20-1
1955-57	Ray Richards	14-21-1
1958-61	Frank (Pop) Ivy##	17-29-2
1961	Chuck Drulis-Ray Prochaska-Ray Willsey###	2-0-0
1962-65	Wally Lemm	27-26-3
1966-70	Charley Winner	35-30-5
1971-72	Bob Hollway	8-18-2
1973-77	Don Coryell	42-29-1
1978-79	Bud Wilkinson####	9-20-0
1979	Larry Wilson	2-1-0
1980-85	Jim Hanifan	39-50-1
1986-89	Gene Stallings@	23-34-1
1989	Hank Kuhlmann	0-5-0
1990-93	Joe Bugel	20-44-0
1994-95	Buddy Ryan	12-20-0
1996-99	Vince Tobin	27-39-0

* Resigned after one game in 1931
** Co-coach with Walt Kiesling in Chicago Cardinals-Pittsburgh merger in 1944
*** Co-coaches for first six games in 1949
**** Resigned after 10 games in 1951
\# Co-coaches
\## Resigned after 12 games in 1961
\### Co-coaches
\#### Released after 13 games in 1979
@ Released after 11 games in 1989

SUN DEVIL STADIUM

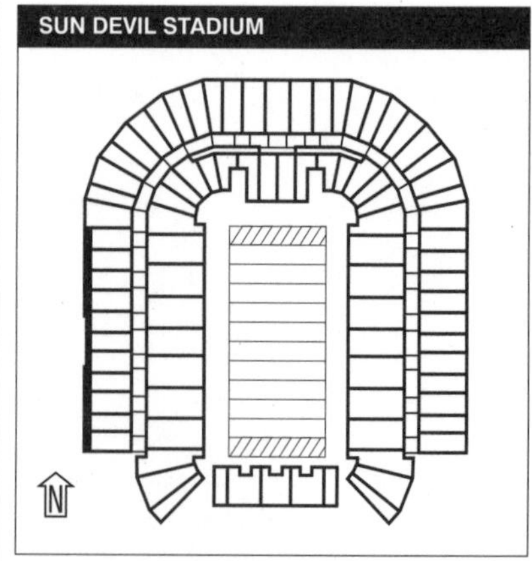

1999 TEAM RECORD

PRESEASON (1-3)

Date	Result		Opponent
8/14	L	7-38	at Denver
8/20	W	27-17	Tennessee
8/28	L	7-41	at Seattle
9/3	L	7-43	Oakland

REGULAR SEASON (6-10)

Date	Result		Opponent	Att.
9/12	W	25-24	at Philadelphia	64,113
9/19	L	16-19	at Miami	73,618
9/27	L	10-24	San Francisco	72,100
10/3	L	7-35	at Dallas	64,169
10/10	W	14-3	New York Giants	49,015
10/17	L	10-24	Washington	55,893
10/31	L	3-27	New England	55,830
11/7	L	7-12	at New York Jets	77,857
11/14	W	23-19	Detroit	49,600
11/21	W	13-9	Dallas	72,015
11/28	W	34-24	at New York Giants	77,809
12/5	W	21-17	Philadelphia	46,550
12/12	L	3-28	at Washington	75,851
12/19	L	21-31	Buffalo	64,337
12/26	L	14-37	at Atlanta	47,074
1/2	L	24-49	at Green Bay	59,818

SCORE BY PERIODS

Cardinals	19	97	50	79	0	—	245
Opponents	118	97	56	111	0	—	382

ATTENDANCE

Home 465,352 Away 539,603 Total 1,004,955
Single-game home record, 73,025 (9/19/93)
Single-season home record, 497,330 (1994)

1999 TEAM STATISTICS

	Cardinals	Opp.
Total First Downs	254	301
Rushing	77	128
Passing	150	157
Penalty	27	16
Third Down: Made/Att	72/221	94/232
Third Down Pct.	32.6	40.5
Fourth Down: Made/Att	4/17	4/15
Fourth Down Pct.	23.5	26.7
Total Net Yards	4,010	5,422
Avg. Per Game	250.6	338.9
Total Plays	999	1,068
Avg. Per Play	4.0	5.1
Net Yards Rushing	1,207	2,265
Avg. Per Game	75.4	141.6
Total Rushes	396	542
Net Yards Passing	2,803	3,157
Avg. Per Game	175.2	197.3
Sacked/Yards Lost	45/282	33/229
Gross Yards	3,085	3,386
Att./Completions	558/287	493/294
Completion Pct.	51.4	59.6
Had Intercepted	30	17
Punts/Average	94/42.0	89/42.4
Net Punting Avg.	94/36.7	89/34.2
Penalties/Yards	70/481	112/938
Fumbles/Ball Lost	31/10	28/10
Touchdowns	27	48
Rushing	13	17
Passing	11	25
Returns	3	6
Avg. Time of Possession	27:10	32:51

1999 INDIVIDUAL STATISTICS

Passing	Att.	Comp.	Yds.	Pct.	TD	Int.	Tkld.	Rating
Plummer	381	201	2,111	52.8	9	24	27/152	50.8
Da. Brown	169	84	944	49.7	2	6	18/130	55.9
Greisen	6	1	4	16.7	0	0	0/0	39.6
Pittman	1	1	26	100.0	0	0	0/0	118.8
Sanders	1	0	0	0.0	0	0	0/0	39.6
Cardinals	558	287	3,085	51.4	11	30	45/282	52.2
Opponents	493	294	3,386	59.6	25	17	33/229	82.9

SCORING	TD R	TD P	TD Rt	PAT	FG	Saf	PTS
Jacke	0	0	0	26/26	19/27	0	83
Bates	9	0	0	0/0	0/0	0	54
Moore	0	5	0	0/0	0/0	0	30
Boston	0	2	0	0/0	0/0	0	12
Pittman	2	0	0	0/0	0/0	0	12
Plummer	2	0	0	0/0	0/0	0	12
Cody	0	1	0	0/0	0/0	0	6
Fredrickson	0	0	1	0/0	0/0	0	6
Lassiter	0	0	1	0/0	0/0	0	6
Makovicka	0	1	0	0/0	0/0	0	6
McWilliams	0	1	0	0/0	0/0	0	6
Sanders	0	1	0	0/0	0/0	0	6
Swann	0	0	1	0/0	0/0	0	6
Cardinals	13	11	3	26/26	19/27	0	245
Opponents	17	25	6	44/45	16/24	1	382

2-Pt. Conversions: None.
Team 0-1, Opponents 0-3.

RUSHING	Att.	Yds.	Avg.	LG	TD
Murrell	193	553	2.9	22	0
Pittman	64	289	4.5	58t	2
Bates	72	202	2.8	16	9
Plummer	39	121	3.1	17	2
Da. Brown	13	49	3.8	10	0
Makovicka	8	7	0.9	7	0
Tillman	1	4	4.0	4	0
Boston	5	0	0.0	7	0
Player	1	-18	-18.0	-18	0
Cardinals	396	1,207	3.0	58t	13
Opponents	542	2,265	4.2	68t	17

RECEIVING	No.	Yds.	Avg.	LG	TD
Sanders	79	954	12.1	63	1
Murrell	49	335	6.8	23	0
Boston	40	473	11.8	43	2
Moore	37	621	16.8	71	5
Hardy	30	222	7.4	23	0
Pittman	16	196	12.3	46	0
McWilliams	11	71	6.5	11	1
Makovicka	10	70	7.0	15	1
Cody	6	60	10.0	16	1
Bates	5	34	6.8	18	0
McCullough	3	45	15.0	31	0
McKinley	1	4	4.0	4	0
Cardinals	287	3,085	10.7	71	11
Opponents	294	3,386	11.5	77t	25

INTERCEPTIONS	No.	Yds.	Avg.	LG	TD
Lassiter	2	110	55.0	78t	1
Fredrickson	2	57	28.5	34t	1
Knight	2	16	8.0	16	0
Tillman	2	7	3.5	6	0
Williams	2	5	2.5	8	0
Swann	1	42	42.0	42t	1
Wadsworth	1	23	23.0	23	0
Bennett	1	13	13.0	13	0
McCleskey	1	2	2.0	2	0
Chavous	1	1	1.0	1	0
Drake	1	0	0.0	0	0
McKinnon	1	0	0.0	0	0
Cardinals	17	276	16.2	78t	3
Opponents	30	336	11.2	59t	2

PUNTING	No.	Yds.	Avg.	In 20	LG
Player	94	3,948	42.0	18	60
Cardinals	94	3,948	42.0	18	60
Opponents	89	3,775	42.4	23	69

PUNT RETURNS	No.	FC	Yds.	Avg.	LG	TD
Cody	32	12	373	11.7	31	0
Boston	7	0	62	8.9	43	0
Pittman	4	0	16	4.0	7	0
Knight	3	1	38	12.7	27	0
McCleskey	1	0	0	0.0	0	0
Cardinals	47	13	489	10.4	43	0
Opponents	53	16	340	6.4	36	0

KICKOFF RETURNS	No.	Yds.	Avg.	LG	TD
Bates	52	1,231	23.7	68	0
Cody	4	76	19.0	29	0
Tillman	3	33	11.0	18	0
Pittman	2	31	15.5	22	0
Lassiter	1	13	13.0	13	0
Makovicka	1	10	10.0	10	0
Dishman	1	9	9.0	9	0
Cardinals	64	1,403	21.9	68	0
Opponents	59	1,224	20.7	88t	2

FIELD GOALS	1-19	20-29	30-39	40-49	50+
Jacke	0/0	5/5	10/12	4/7	0/3
Cardinals	0/0	5/5	10/12	4/7	0/3
Opponents	0/0	5/7	6/6	4/8	1/3

SACKS	No.
Rice	16.5
Swann	4.0
Burke	2.5
Fredrickson	2.0
Wadsworth	2.0
Drake	1.0
McKinnon	1.0
Ottis	1.0
Sapp	1.0
Swinger	1.0
Walz	1.0
Cardinals	33.0
Opponents	45.0

2000 DRAFT CHOICES

Round	Name	Pos.	College
1	Thomas Jones	RB	Virginia
2	Raynoch Thompson	LB	Tennessee
3	Darwin Walker	DT	Tennessee
4	David Barrett	DB	Arkansas
5	Mao Tosi	DT	Idaho
	Jay Tant	TE	Northwestern
6	Jabari Issa	DT	Washington
7	Sekou Sanyika	LB	California

ARIZONA CARDINALS

2000 VETERAN ROSTER

No.		Name	Pos.	Ht.	Wt.	Birthdate	NFL Exp.	College	Hometown	How Acq.	'99 Games/ Starts
24		Bates, Mario	RB	6-1	217	1/16/73	7	Arizona State	Tucson, Ariz.	UFA(NO)-'98	16/2
28	#	Bennett, Tommy	S	6-2	219	2/19/73	5	UCLA	San Diego, Calif.	FA-'96	15/15
15		Blanchard, Cary	K	6-1	232	11/5/68	8	Oklahoma State	Fort Worth, Tex.	UFA(NYG)-'00	10/0*
89		Boston, David	WR	6-2	210	8/19/78	2	Ohio State	Humble, Tex.	D1a-'99	16/8
66		Brooks, Ethan	G-T	6-6	299	4/27/72	4	Williams	Simsbury, Conn.	FA-'00	0*
7		Brown, Dave	QB	6-5	230	2/25/70	9	Duke	Summit, N.J.	UFA(NYG)-'98	8/5
83		Brown, Derek	TE	6-6	271	3/31/70	9	Notre Dame	Fairfax, Va.	UFA(Oak)-'99	15/0
95		Burke, Thomas	DE	6-3	261	10/12/76	2	Wisconsin	Poplar, Wisc.	D3-'99	16/3
25		Chavous, Corey	CB	6-0	204	1/15/76	3	Vanderbilt	Aiken, S.C.	D2a-'98	15/4
79		Clark, Jon	G-T	6-6	345	4/11/73	4	Temple	Philadelphia, Pa.	UFA(Chi)-'98	2/0
65		Clement, Anthony	T	6-7	355	4/10/76	3	Southwest Louisiana	Lafayette, La.	D2b-'98	16/14
82		Cody, Mac	WR	5-11	182	8/7/72	2	Memphis	St. Louis, Mo.	W(StL)-'99	13/0
64		Davidds-Garrido, Norberto	T	6-5	315	6/11/72	4	Southern California	La Puente, Calif.	UFA(Car)-'00	16/0*
62		Devlin, Mike	C	6-2	318	11/16/69	8	Iowa	Blacksburg, Va.	UFA(Buff)-'96	16/0
67		Dishman, Chris	G	6-3	320	2/27/74	4	Nebraska	Cozad, Neb.	D4-'97	13/10
76		Drake, Jerry	DT	6-5	310	7/9/69	5	Hastings College	Kingston, N.Y.	FA-'95	16/16
58		Folston, James	LB	6-3	240	8/14/71	7	Northeast Louisiana	Cocoa, Fla.	FA-'99	6/0
59		Fredrickson, Rob	LB	6-4	240	5/13/71	7	Michigan State	St. Joseph, Mich.	UFA(Oak)-'99	16/16
84		Gedney, Chris	TE	6-5	250	8/9/70	7	Syracuse	Liverpool, N.Y.	UFA(Chi)-'97	0*
60		Gruttadauria, Mike	C	6-3	297	12/6/72	5	Central Florida	Tarpon Springs, Fla.	UFA(StL)-'00	16/16*
80		Hardy, Terry	TE	6-4	266	5/31/76	3	Southern Mississippi	Montgomery, Ala.	D5-'98	16/16
70		Holmes, Lester	G	6-4	315	9/27/69	8	Jackson State	Tylertown, Miss.	UFA(Oak)-'98	13/13
19		Jenkins, Martay	WR	5-11	193	2/28/75	2	Nebraska-Omaha	Waterloo, Iowa	W(Dall)-'99	3/0
73		Joyce, Matt	G	6-7	313	3/30/72	5	Richmond	St. Petersburg, Fla.	FA-'96	15/15
86		Junkin, Trey	LS-TE	6-2	258	1/23/61	18	Louisiana Tech	North Little Rock, Ark.	W(Oak)-'96	16/0
22		Knight, Tom	CB	5-11	196	12/29/74	4	Iowa	Marlton, N.J.	D1-'97	16/11
42		Lassiter, Kwamie	S	6-0	202	12/3/69	6	Kansas	Newport News, Va.	FA-'95	16/16
53		Maddox, Mark	LB	6-1	233	3/23/68	10	Northern Michigan	Milwaukee, Wisc.	UFA(Buff)-'98	16/2
34		Makovicka, Joel	RB	5-11	246	10/6/75	2	Nebraska	Brainard, Neb.	D4-'99	16/10
44		McCleskey, J.J.	CB	5-8	184	4/10/70	7	Tennessee	Knoxville, Tenn.	W(NO)-'96	16/1
18		McCullough, Andy	WR	6-3	210	11/11/75	2	Tennessee	Dayton, Ohio	FA-'98	2/0
39		McKinley, Dennis	RB	6-2	245	11/3/76	2	Mississippi State	Weir, Miss.	D6b-'99	16/0
57		McKinnon, Ronald	LB	6-0	240	9/20/73	5	North Alabama	Elba, Ala.	FA-'96	16/16
85		Moore, Rob	WR	6-3	203	9/27/68	11	Syracuse	Hempstead, N.Y.	T(NYJ)-'95	14/10
74		Moten, Mike	DE	6-5	266	3/12/74	2	Florida	Daytona Beach, Fla.	FA-'98	0*
96		Ottis, Brad	DT	6-5	281	8/2/72	7	Wayne State, Neb.	Fremont, Neb.	FA-'96	14/7
32		Pittman, Michael	RB	6-0	214	8/14/75	3	Fresno State	San Diego, Calif.	D4-'98	10/2
10		Player, Scott	P	6-0	220	12/17/69	3	Florida State	St. Augustine, Fla.	FA-'98	16/0
16		Plummer, Jake	QB	6-2	197	12/19/74	4	Arizona State	Boise, Idaho	D2-'97	12/11
23		Rhinehart, Coby	CB	5-10	186	2/7/77	2	Southern Methodist	Dallas, Tex.	D6a-'99	16/0
97		Rice, Simeon	DE	6-5	260	2/24/74	5	Illinois	Chicago, Ill.	D1-'96	16/16
92		Rubio, Angel	DT	6-2	298	4/12/75	2	Southeast Missouri State	Los Angeles, Calif.	FA-'99	2/0
51		Rutledge, Johnny	LB	6-3	242	1/4/77	2	Florida	Belle Glade, Fla.	D2-'99	6/0
81		Sanders, Frank	WR	6-2	197	2/17/73	6	Auburn	Fort Lauderdale, Fla.	D2-'95	16/16
68		Scott, Yusuf	G	6-3	332	11/30/76	2	Arizona	La Porte, Tex.	D5b-'99	10/0
94		Sears, Corey	DT	6-3	300	4/15/73	3	Mississippi State	Converse, Tex.	W(StL)-'99	9/1
70		Shelton, L.J.	T	6-6	343	3/21/76	2	Eastern Michigan	Rochester Hills, Mich.	D1b-'99	9/7
93		Smith, Mark	DE	6-4	290	8/28/74	4	Auburn	Vicksburg, Miss.	D7-'97	2/0
98		Swann, Eric	DT	6-5	313	8/16/70	10	No college	Swann Station, N.C.	D1-'91	9/0
91		Swinger, Rashod	DT	6-2	286	11/27/74	3	Rutgers	Manalapan, N.J.	FA-'97	15/14
40		Tillman, Pat	S	5-11	204	11/6/76	3	Arizona State	San Jose, Calif.	D7c-'98	16/1
90		Wadsworth, Andre	DE	6-4	278	10/19/74	3	Florida State	Miami, Fla.	D1-'98	11/7
52		Walz, Zack	LB	6-4	228	2/13/76	3	Dartmouth	San Jose, Calif.	D6-'98	9/9
35		Williams, Aeneas	CB	5-11	202	1/29/68	10	Southern	New Orleans, La.	D3-'91	16/16

* Blanchard played 10 games with N.Y. Giants in '99; Brooks last active with St. Louis in '98; Davidds-Garrido played 16 games with Carolina; Gedney and Moten missed '99 season because of injury; Gruttadauria played 16 games with St. Louis.

Unrestricted free agent; subject to developments.

Players lost through free agency (3): T James Dexter (Car; 8 games in '99), C Aaron Graham (KC; 16), RB Adrian Murrell (Wash; 16).

Also played with Cardinals in '99—LB Melvin Bradley (1 game), QB Chris Greisen (2), K Chris Jacke (16), TE Johnny McWilliams (15), K Joe Nedney (1), LB Patrick Sapp (15).

COACHING STAFF

Head Coach,
Vince Tobin

Pro Career: Named Cardinals' head coach on February 7, 1996. Became thirty-third coach in the history of the franchise dating back to 1920. A 9-7 regular-season mark in 1998 translated into the team's first playoff appearance since 1982 and first postseason victory since 1947—a span of 51 years. The "Cardiac Cards" recorded seven victories by three points or less, won their first-round playoff contest 20-7 at Dallas, and logged eight wins against NFC opponents—the most by a Cardinals' team in 22 seasons. In his first season, Arizona rebounded from an 0-3 start to claim a 7-4 record in its final 11 games and remain in playoff contention until the final week of the season. Arizona improved from twenty-fourth (1995) to twelfth in offense, from twenty-sixth (1995) to twenty-first in defense, and forged the club's first winning November (3-1) since 1987. As a defensive coordinator of the Indianapolis Colts from 1994-95, oversaw a defense that was a principal reason Indianapolis finished 9-7 during the 1995 regular season before defeating San Diego (35-20) and Kansas City (10-7) in the first two rounds of postseason play. Tobin earned credit for rebuilding a Colts' defense he inherited that ranked last in overall defense in 1993. Tobin's first unit improved to twentieth in 1994 and tied for seventh with Carolina in 1995 at 314.2 yards per game. Tobin previously served as defensive coordinator of the Chicago Bears (1986-1992), tutoring a Bears' defense that set an NFL record for fewest points allowed in a 16-game season (187 in 1986). His 1986 Chicago unit topped the league by allowing just 258 yards per contest. The 1987 Bears surrendered the league's fewest points (215) and sported the best rushing defense (82.9). Tobin also earned victories over Tampa Bay and Washington as Chicago's interim head coach for Mike Ditka. Tobin's other coaching stops have been with the USFL Philadelphia/Baltimore Stars (1983-85), the CFL British Columbia Lions (1977-1982), and his alma mater, the University of Missouri (1967-1976). Tobin's defensive units in the CFL ranked second overall during his six seasons, while his defensive schemes in the USFL helped the Stars rank first defensively in 1983 and 1984 and second in 1985 while allowing the fewest points all three seasons. The Stars reached the league championship game each season, winning the final two times. Career record: 27-39.

Background: Tobin played defensive back at Missouri from 1961-64. He joined the Missouri coaching staff as a defensive assistant from 1967-1976, serving the final six years as defensive coordinator. Tobin owns a bachelor's degree in education and a master's degree in guidance and counseling.

Personal: Born September 29, 1943, in Burlington Junction, Missouri. He and his wife, Kathy, have two children—son Ryan and daughter Shannon.

ASSISTANT COACHES

Jeff FitzGerald, quality control; born April 18, 1960, Burbank, Calif., lives in Phoenix. Attended Oregon State. No college or pro playing experience. College coach: Cincinnati 1985-86, Alabama 1987-89, San Diego State 1994-97. Pro coach: Tampa Bay Buccaneers 1990-93, Washington Redskins 1998-99, joined Cardinals in 2000.

John Garrett, quarterbacks; born March 2, 1965, Danville, Pa., lives in Phoenix. Wide reciever Columbia 1983-84, Princeton 1987. Pro wide receiver Cincinnati Bengals 1989, San Antonio Riders (World League) 1991. Pro coach: Cincinnati Bengals 1995-98, joined Cardinals in 1999.

Joe Greene, defensive line; born September 24, 1946, Temple, Tex., lives in Phoenix. Defensive tackle North Texas State 1966-68. Pro defensive tackle Pittsburgh Steelers 1969-1981. Inducted into Pro Football Hall of Fame in 1987. Pro coach: Pittsburgh Steelers 1987-1991, Miami Dolphins 1992-95, joined Cardinals in 1996.

Hank Kuhlmann, special teams; born October 6, 1937, Webster Groves, Mo., lives in Phoenix. Running back Missouri 1956-59. No pro playing experience. College coach: Missouri 1962-1971, Notre Dame 1975-77. Pro coach: Green Bay Packers 1972-74, Chicago Bears 1978-1982, Birmingham Stallions (USFL) 1983-85, St. Louis/Phoenix Cardinals 1986-89, Tampa Bay Buccaneers 1991, Indianapolis Colts 1994-97, rejoined Cardinals in 1998.

Don Lawrence, tight ends; born June 4, 1937, Cleveland, lives in Phoenix. Offensive lineman Notre Dame 1957-58. Pro offensive lineman Washington Redskins 1959-1961. College coach: Notre Dame 1961-63, Kansas State 1964-65, Cincinnati 1966, Virginia 1970-73 (head coach 1971-73), Texas Christian 1974-75, Missouri 1976-77. Pro coach: British Columbia Lions (CFL) 1978-79, Kansas City Chiefs 1980-82, 1987-88, Buffalo Bills 1983-84, 1990-97, Tampa Bay Buccaneers 1985-86, Winnipeg Blue Bombers (CFL) 1989, joined Cardinals in 2000.

Larry Marmie, defensive backs; born October 17, 1942, Barnesville, Ohio, lives in Phoenix. Quarterback Eastern Kentucky 1962-65. No pro playing experience. College coach: Eastern Kentucky 1967-68, 1972-76, Morehead State 1968-1971, Tulsa 1977-78, North Carolina 1979-1982, Tennessee 1983-84, 1992-94, Arizona State 1988-1991 (head coach), UCLA 1995. Pro coach: Joined Cardinals in 1996.

Dave McGinnis, defensive coordinator; born August 7, 1951, Independence, Kan., lives in Phoenix. Defensive back Texas Christian 1970-72. No pro playing experience. College coach: Texas Christian 1973-74, 1982, Missouri 1975-77, Indiana State 1978-1981, Kansas State 1983-85. Pro coach: Chicago Bears 1986-1995, joined Cardinals in 1996.

Glenn Pires, linebackers; born September 13, 1958, New Bedford, Mass., lives in Phoenix. Linebacker Springfield College 1978-1980. No pro playing experience. College coach: Syracuse 1983-84, Dartmouth 1985-88, Michigan State 1989-1995. Pro coach: Joined Cardinals in 1996.

Vic Rapp, wide receivers; born December 23, 1935, Marionville, Mo., lives in Phoenix. Running back Southwest Missouri State 1954-57. No pro playing experience. Pro coach: Edmonton Eskimos (CFL) 1972-76, British Columbia Lions (CFL) 1977-1982 (head coach), Houston Oilers 1983, Los Angeles Rams 1984, Tampa Bay Buccaneers 1985-86, Detroit Lions 1987, Chicago Bears 1989-1992, joined Cardinals in 1996.

Bob Rogucki, strength and conditioning; born September 27, 1953, Clarksburg, W. Va., lives in Phoenix. No college or pro playing experience. College coach: Penn State 1981, Weber State 1982, Army 1983-89. Pro coach: Joined Cardinals in 1990.

Johnny Roland, running backs; born May 21, 1943, Corpus Christi, Tex., lives in Phoenix. Running back Missouri 1961-65. Pro running back St. Louis Cardinals 1966-1972, New York Giants 1973. College coach: Notre Dame 1975. Pro coach: Green Bay Packers 1974, Philadelphia Eagles 1976-78, Chicago Bears 1983-1992, New York Jets 1993-94, St. Louis Rams 1995-96, joined Cardinals in 1997.

Marc Trestman, offensive coordinator; born January 15, 1956, Minneapolis, Minn., lives in Phoenix. Quarterback Minnesota 1975-77, Moorhead (Minn.) State 1978. Pro quarterback Minnesota Vikings 1979. College coach: Miami 1981-84. Pro coach: Minnesota Vikings 1985-86, 1990-1991, Tampa Bay Buccaneers 1987, Cleveland Browns 1988-89, San Francisco 49ers 1995-96, Detroit Lions 1997, joined Cardinals in 1998.

George Warhop, offensive line; born September 19, 1961, Riverside, Calif., lives in Phoenix. Guard Mt. San Jacinto (Calif.) J.C. 1979-80. Pro center Cincinnati Bengals 1981-82. College coach: Cincinnati 1983, Kansas 1984-86, Vanderbilt 1987-89, New Mexico 1990, Southern Methodist 1993, Boston College 1994-95. Pro coach: London Monarchs (World League) 1991-92, St. Louis Rams 1996-97, joined Cardinals in 1998.

2000 FIRST-YEAR ROSTER

Name	Pos.	Ht.	Wt.	Birthdate	College	Hometown	How Acq.
Barrett, David	CB	5-10	195	12/22/77	Arkansas	Osceola, Ark.	D4
Bradley, Melvin (1)	LB	6-2	271	8/15/76	Arkansas	Barton, Ark.	D6b-'99
Broomfield, Donald	DT	6-3	295	6/10/76	Clemson	Olustee, Fla.	FA
Brown, Keith	RB	5-11	214	2/14/78	UCLA	Phoenix, Ariz.	FA
Cooper, Deke	S	6-2	215	10/18/77	Notre Dame	Evansville, Ind.	FA
Cox, Renard	CB	5-11	188	3/3/78	Maryland	Richmond, Va.	FA
DeBolt, Greg	P	5-11	184	9/23/76	Pittsburgh	Auburn, Wash.	FA
Gilmore, Bryan	WR	5-11	180	7/21/78	Midwestern State, Tex.	Lufkin, Tex.	FA
Issa, Jabari	DT	6-5	296	4/18/78	Washington	Foster City, Calif.	D6
Johnson, Paris (1)	S	6-3	223	1/18/76	Miami, Ohio	Chicago, Ill.	D5a-'99
Jones, Thomas	RB	5-10	205	8/19/78	Virginia	Big Stone Gap, Va.	D1
Keenan, Sean	QB	6-3	208	1/2/77	Williams College, Mass.	Rutland, Va.	FA
Keller, Matt	RB	5-11	235	12/2/76	Ohio State	Mason, Ohio	FA
Lane, Randall	WR	6-0	211	10/15/76	Purdue	Chicago, Ill.	FA
Love, Kelvin	WR	6-3	189	2/10/78	Mississippi State	Clarksdale, Miss.	FA
Lucas, Justin (1)	DB	5-10	187	7/15/76	Abilene Christian	Victoria, Tex.	FA-'99
Mitchell, Tywan (1)	WR-TE	6-5	220	12/10/75	Minnesota State-Mankato	Crete, Ill.	FA-'99
Sanyika, Sekou	LB	6-4	237	3/17/78	California	Hercules, Calif.	D7
Shoemaker, John	WR	6-2	185	1/4/77	Cal-Davis	Davis, Calif.	FA
Skapura, Robert	T	6-6	291	5/25/77	Louisiana Tech	Tucson, Ariz.	FA
Starkey, Jason	C	6-4	254	6/15/77	Marshall	Barboursville, W. Va.	FA
Tant, Jay	TE	6-3	252	12/4/77	Northwestern	Kettering, Ohio	D5b
Thompson, Ray	LB	6-3	220	11/21/77	Tennessee	New Orleans, La.	D2
Tosi, Mao	DT	6-5	291	12/12/76	Idaho	Anchorage, Alaska	D5a
Walker, Darwin	DT	6-1	280	6/17/77	Tennessee	Walterboro, S.C.	D3
Watton, Chris	G	6-2	290	10/6/77	Baylor	Foley, Ark.	FA
Williams, Clarence (1)	RB	5-9	196	5/16/77	Michigan	Detroit, Mich.	FA-'99
Younger, Jordan	CB	5-10	190	1/24/78	Connecticut	Trenton, N.J.	FA

The term NFL Rookie is defined as a player who is in his first season of professional football and has not been on the roster of another professional football team for any regular-season or postseason games. A Rookie is designated by an "R" on NFL rosters. Players who have been active in another professional football league or players who have NFL experience, including either preseason training camp or being on an Active List or Inactive List, or on Reserve/Injured or Reserve/Physically Unable to Perform for fewer than six regular-season games, are termed NFL First-Year Players. An NFL First-Year Player is designated by a "1" on NFL rosters. Thereafter, a player is credited with an additional year of experience for each season in which he accumulates six games on the Active List or Inactive List, or on Reserve/Injured or Reserve/Physically Unable to Perform.

ATLANTA FALCONS

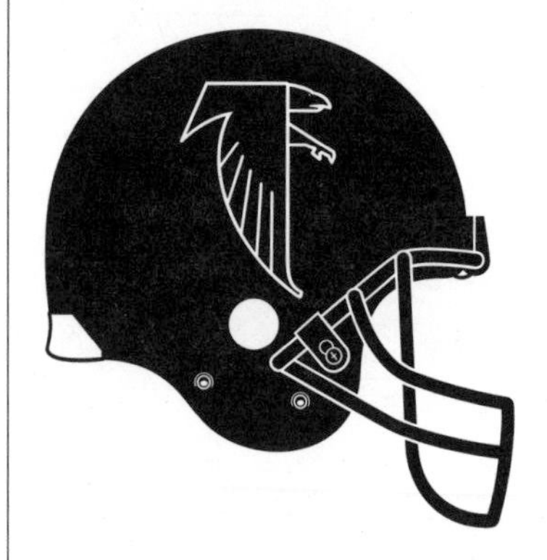

National Football Conference
Western Division
Team Colors: Black, Red, Silver, and White
4400 Falcon Parkway
Flowery Beach, Georgia 30542
Telephone: (770) 965-3115

CLUB OFFICIALS

President: Taylor Smith
Executive Vice President/Football Operations & Head Coach: Dan Reeves
Executive Vice President of Administration: Jim Hay
General Manager: Harold Richardson
Vice President of Football Operations: Ron Hill
Vice President of Finance, CFO: Kevin Anthony
Vice President of Corporate Development: Tommy Nobis
Controller: Wallace Norman
Administrative Asst./Finance: John Knox
Vice President/Marketing and Sales: Rob Jackson
Director of Corporate Development: Mark Fuhrman
Special Events: Spencer Treadwell
Director of Public Relations: Aaron Salkin
Asst. Director of Public Relations: Frank Kleha
Director of Ticket Operations: Jack Ragsdale
Assistant Director of Ticket Operations: Brent Coleman
Director of Community Relations: Carol Breeding
Player Programs Coordinator: Billy (White Shoes) Johnson
Director of Information Systems: Joseph Miller
Special Assistant to President: Jerry Rhea
Director of Player Personnel/Pro: Chuck Connor
Director of Player Personnel/College: Reed Johnson
Area Scouts: Ken Blair, Billy Campfield, Dick Corrick, Boyd Dowler, Elbert Dubenion, Bill Groman, Bob Harrison
National Scout: Mike Hagen
Regional Scout: Jeff Smith
Assistant to Vice President of Football Operations: Les Snead
Head Athletic Trainer: Ron Medlin
Assistant Athletic Trainers: Harold King, Thomas Reed
Video Director: Tom Atcheson
Assistant Video Director: Mike Crews
Equipment Manager: Brian Boigner
Senior Director/Gameday Coordinator: Horace Daniel
Stadium: Georgia Dome • **Capacity:** 71,228
One Georgia Dome Drive
Atlanta, Georgia 30313
Playing Surface: Artificial turf
Training Camp: Furman University
3300 Poinsett Highway
Greenville, South Carolina 29613

RECORD HOLDERS

INDIVIDUAL RECORDS—CAREER

Category	Name	Performance
Rushing (Yds.)	Gerald Riggs, 1982-88	6,631
Passing (Yds.)	Steve Bartkowski, 1975-1985	23,468
Passing (TDs)	Steve Bartkowski, 1975-1985	154
Receiving (No.)	Terance Mathis, 1994-99	465
Receiving (Yds.)	Alfred Jenkins, 1975-1983	6,257
Interceptions	Rolland Lawrence, 1973-1980	39
Punting (Avg.)	Rick Donnelly, 1985-89	42.6
Punt Return (Avg.)	Al Dodd, 1973-74	11.8
Kickoff Return (Avg.)	Tony Smith, 1992-94	24.9
Field Goals	Mick Luckhurst, 1981-87	115
Touchdowns (Tot.)	Andre Rison, 1990-94	56
Points	Mick Luckhurst, 1981-87	558

INDIVIDUAL RECORDS—SINGLE SEASON

Category	Name	Performance
Rushing (Yds.)	Jamal Anderson, 1998	1,846
Passing (Yds.)	Jeff George, 1995	4,143
Passing (TDs)	Steve Bartkowski, 1980	31
Receiving (No.)	Terance Mathis, 1994	111
Receiving (Yds.)	Alfred Jenkins, 1981	1,358
Interceptions	Scott Case, 1988	10
Punting (Avg.)	Billy Lothridge, 1968	44.3
Punt Return (Avg.)	Al Dodd, 1974	12.7
Kickoff Return (Avg.)	Sylvester Stamps, 1987	27.5
Field Goals	Morten Andersen, 1995	31
Touchdowns (Tot.)	Jamal Anderson, 1998	16
Points	Morten Andersen, 1995	122

INDIVIDUAL RECORDS—SINGLE GAME

Category	Name	Performance
Rushing (Yds.)	Gerald Riggs, 9-2-84	202
Passing (Yds.)	Steve Bartkowski, 11-15-81	416
Passing (TDs)	Wade Wilson, 12-13-92	5
Receiving (No.)	William Andrews, 11-15-81	15
Receiving (Yds.)	Terance Mathis, 12-13-98	198
Interceptions	Many times. Last time by Ray Buchanan, 12-5-99	2
Field Goals	Norm Johnson, 11-13-94	6
Touchdowns (Tot.)	Many times. Last time by Jamal Anderson, 11-1-98	3
Points	Norm Johnson, 11-13-94	20

2000 SCHEDULE

PRESEASON

July 29	at Indianapolis	7:00
Aug. 5	vs. Dallas at Tokyo, Japan	10:00
Aug. 11	**Cincinnati**	7:30
Aug. 18	**San Diego**	7:30
Aug. 24	at Jacksonville	7:30

REGULAR SEASON

Sept. 3	**San Francisco**	1:00
Sept. 10	at Denver	2:15
Sept. 17	at Carolina	1:00
Sept. 24	**St. Louis**	1:00
Oct. 1	at Philadelphia	8:35
Oct. 8	**New York Giants**	4:05
Oct. 15	at St. Louis	12:00
Oct. 22	**New Orleans**	1:00
Oct. 29	**Carolina**	1:00
Nov. 5	**Tampa Bay**	1:00
Nov. 12	at Detroit	1:00
Nov. 19	at San Francisco	1:15
Nov. 26	at Oakland	1:05
Dec. 3	**Seattle**	1:00
Dec. 10	Open Date	
Dec. 17	at New Orleans	12:00
Dec. 24	**Kansas City**	1:00

COACHING HISTORY

(205-312-5)

1966-68	Norb Hecker*	4-26-1
1968-74	Norm Van Brocklin**	37-49-3
1974-76	Marion Campbell***	6-19-0
1976	Pat Peppler	3-6-0
1977-82	Leeman Bennett	47-44-0
1983-86	Dan Henning	22-41-1
1987-89	Marion Campbell****	11-32-0
1989	Jim Hanifan	0-4-0
1990-93	Jerry Glanville	28-38-0
1994-96	June Jones	19-30-0
1997-99	Dan Reeves	28-23-0

*Released after three games in 1968
**Released after eight games in 1974
***Released after five games in 1976
****Retired after 12 games in 1989

GEORGIA DOME

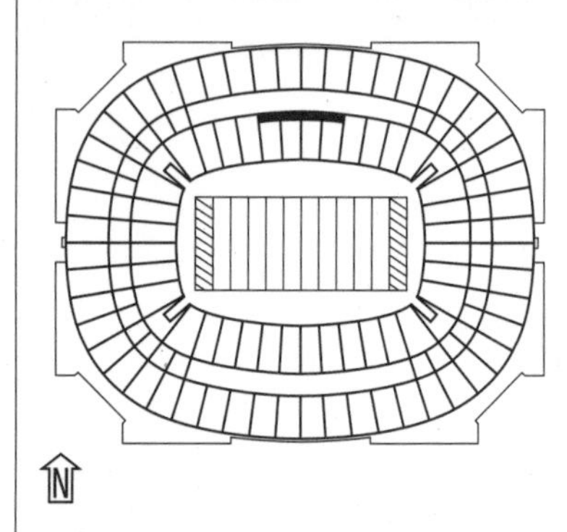

1999 TEAM RECORD

PRESEASON (2-2)

Date	Result		Opponent
8/13	W	35-31	Detroit
8/21	L	6-19	Baltimore
8/27	L	3-17	at Tennessee
9/3	W	28-16	at Cincinnati

REGULAR SEASON (5-11)

Date	Result		Opponent	Att.
9/12	L	14-17	Minnesota	69,555
9/20	L	7-24	at Dallas	63,663
9/26	L	7-35	at St. Louis	63,253
10/3	L	13-19	Baltimore (OT)	50,712
10/10	W	20-17	at New Orleans	57,289
10/17	L	13-41	St. Louis	51,973
10/25	L	9-13	at Pittsburgh	58,141
10/31	W	27-20	Carolina	52,594
11/7	L	7-30	Jacksonville	68,466
11/21	L	10-19	at Tampa Bay	65,158
11/28	L	28-34	at Carolina	55,507
12/5	W	35-12	New Orleans	62,568
12/12	L	7-26	at San Francisco	67,465
12/19	L	17-30	at Tennessee	66,196
12/26	W	37-14	Arizona	47,074
1/3	W	34-29	San Francisco	57,980

(OT) Overtime

SCORE BY PERIODS

Falcons	52	94	73	66	0	—	285
Opponents	75	156	59	84	6	—	380

ATTENDANCE

Home 458,627 Away 506,688 Total 965,315
Single-game home record, 70,089 (10/29/95)
Single-season home record, 553,979 (1992)

1999 TEAM STATISTICS

	Falcons	Opp.
Total First Downs	273	293
Rushing	68	111
Passing	179	149
Penalty	26	33
Third Down: Made/Att	68/196	86/220
Third Down Pct.	34.7	39.1
Fourth Down: Made/Att	5/14	8/18
Fourth Down Pct.	35.7	44.4
Total Net Yards	4,542	5,223
Avg. Per Game	283.9	326.4
Total Plays	931	995
Avg. Per Play	4.9	5.2
Net Yards Rushing	1,196	2,072
Avg. Per Game	74.8	129.5
Total Rushes	373	487
Net Yards Passing	3,346	3,151
Avg. Per Game	209.1	196.9
Sacked/Yards Lost	49/345	40/258
Gross Yards	3,691	3,409
Att./Completions	509/278	468/274
Completion Pct.	54.6	58.5
Had Intercepted	19	12
Punts/Average	80/39.5	72/39.9
Net Punting Avg.	80/37.1	72/33.1
Penalties/Yards	110/968	126/980
Fumbles/Ball Lost	24/16	16/6
Touchdowns	34	43
Rushing	9	18
Passing	22	20
Returns	3	5
Avg. Time of Possession	28:44	31:16

1999 INDIVIDUAL STATISTICS

Passing	Att.	Comp.	Yds.	Pct.	TD	Int.	Tkld.	Rate
Chandler	307	174	2,339	56.7	16	11	32/230	83.5
Graziani	118	62	759	52.5	2	4	12/78	64.2
Kanell	84	42	593	50.0	4	4	5/37	69.2
Falcons	509	278	3,691	54.6	22	19	49/345	76.7
Opponents	468	274	3,409	58.5	20	12	40/258	84.8

SCORING	TD R	TD P	TD Rt	PAT	FG	Saf	PTS
Andersen	0	0	0	34/34	15/21	0	79
Dwight	1	7	1	0/0	0/0	0	54
Christian	5	2	0	0/0	0/0	0	42
Mathis	0	6	0	0/0	0/0	0	36
German	0	3	0	0/0	0/0	0	18
Kozlowski	0	2	0	0/0	0/0	0	12
Oxendine	1	1	0	0/0	0/0	0	12
Buchanan	0	0	1	0/0	0/0	0	6
Calloway	0	1	0	0/0	0/0	0	6
Chandler	1	0	0	0/0	0/0	0	6
Hanspard	1	0	0	0/0	0/0	0	6
Oliver	0	0	1	0/0	0/0	0	6
Falcons	9	22	3	34/34	15/21	1	285
Opponents	18	20	5	40/40	26/35	1	380

2-Pt. Conversions: None.
Team 0-0, Opponents 1-2.

RUSHING	Att.	Yds.	Avg.	LG	TD
Oxendine	141	452	3.2	20	1
Hanspard	136	383	2.8	15	1
Christian	38	174	4.6	33t	5
Anderson	19	59	3.1	20	0
Chandler	16	57	3.6	14	1
Oliver	8	32	4.0	10	0
Dwight	5	28	5.6	9	1
Graziani	9	11	1.2	10	0
Mathis	1	0	0.0	0	0
Falcons	373	1,196	3.2	33t	9
Opponents	487	2,072	4.3	58	18

RECEIVING	No.	Yds.	Avg.	LG	TD
Mathis	81	1,016	12.5	52	6
Christian	40	354	8.9	36	2
Dwight	32	669	20.9	60t	7
Calloway	22	314	14.3	33	1
Oxendine	17	172	10.1	32	1
Santiago	15	174	11.6	46	0
German	12	219	18.3	62	3
Kozlowski	11	122	11.1	26	2
Harris	10	164	16.4	24	0
Hanspard	10	93	9.3	34	0
R. Kelly	8	146	18.3	50	0
Oliver	8	74	9.3	14	0
Baker	7	118	16.9	36	0
Anderson	2	34	17.0	32	0
Still	2	14	7.0	10	0
Monroe	1	8	8.0	8	0
Falcons	278	3,691	13.3	62	22
Opponents	274	3,409	12.4	90t	20

INTERCEPTIONS	No.	Yds.	Avg.	LG	TD
Buchanan	4	81	20.3	52t	1
Robinson	3	7	2.3	7	0
McBurrows	2	64	32.0	41	0
Booker	2	10	5.0	10	0
Carter	1	4	4.0	4	0
Falcons	12	166	13.8	52t	1
Opponents	19	365	19.2	91t	3

PUNTING	No.	Yds.	Avg.	In 20	LG
Stryzinski	80	3,163	39.5	27	55
Falcons	80	3,163	39.5	27	55
Opponents	72	2,875	39.9	15	60

PUNT RETURNS	No.	FC	Yds.	Avg.	LG	TD
Dwight	20	12	220	11.0	70t	1
Oliver	12	5	152	12.7	58t	1
Falcons	32	17	372	11.6	70t	2
Opponents	26	34	119	4.6	30	0

KICKOFF RETURNS	No.	Yds.	Avg.	LG	TD
Dwight	44	944	21.5	40	0
Oliver	24	441	18.4	28	0
E. Williams	3	37	12.3	18	0
Kozlowski	2	19	9.5	10	0
Harris	1	5	5.0	5	0
German	1	1	1.0	1	0
Marshall	1	-2	-2.0	-2	0
Falcons	76	1,445	19.0	40	0
Opponents	55	1,221	22.2	101t	2

FIELD GOALS	1-19	20-29	30-39	40-49	50+
Andersen	1/1	5/5	5/8	4/6	0/1
Falcons	1/1	5/5	5/8	4/6	0/1
Opponents	0/0	12/14	7/10	3/7	4/4

SACKS	No.
Smith	10.0
Dronett	6.5
Archambeau	5.5
Hall	4.5
Tuggle	3.5
Kerney	2.5
Brooking	2.0
Crockett	1.5
Buchanan	1.0
McBurrows	1.0
Sauer	1.0
Falcons	40.0
Opponents	49.0

2000 DRAFT CHOICES

Round	Name	Pos.	College
2	Travis Claridge	T	Southern California
3	Mark Simoneau	LB	Kansas State
4	Michael Thompson	T	Tennessee State
5	Anthony Midget	DB	Virginia Tech
6	Mareno Philyaw	WR	Troy State
7	Darrick Vaughn	DB	Southwest Texas State

ATLANTA FALCONS

2000 VETERAN ROSTER

No.	Name	Pos.	Ht.	Wt.	Birthdate	NFL Exp.	College	Hometown	How Acq.	'99 Games/ Starts
33	Ambrose, Ashley	CB	5-10	185	9/17/70	9	Mississippi Valley State	New Orleans, La.	UFA(NO)-'00	16/16*
5	Andersen, Morten	K	6-2	225	8/19/60	19	Michigan State	Struer, Denmark	FA(NO)-'95	16/0
32	Anderson, Jamal	RB	5-11	235	9/30/72	7	Utah	El Camino, Calif.	D7-'94	2/2
15	Baker, Eugene	WR	6-0	165	3/18/76	2	Kent	Monroeville, Pa.	FA-'99	3/1
20	Booker, Michael	CB	6-2	200	4/27/75	4	Nebraska	Oceanside, Calif.	D1-'97	13/1
23	Bradford, Ronnie	CB-S	5-10	198	10/1/70	8	Colorado	Minot, N.D.	UFA(Ariz)-'97	16/16
56	Brooking, Keith	LB	6-2	245	10/30/75	3	Georgia Tech	Senoia, Ga.	D1-'98	13/13
27	Brown, Omar	S	5-10	200	3/28/75	3	North Carolina	York, Pa.	D4-'98	13/0
34	Buchanan, Ray	CB	5-9	186	9/29/71	8	Louisville	Chicago, Ill.	UFA(Ind)-'97	16/16
52	Buckley, Marcus	LB	6-3	240	2/3/71	8	Texas A&M	Fort Worth, Tex.	FA-'00	12/0*
25	Carter, Marty	S	6-1	210	12/17/69	10	Middle Tennessee State	LaGrange, Ga.	UFA(Chi)-'99	11/11
35	Carty, Johndale	S	6-0	202	8/27/77	2	Utah State	Miami, Fla.	D4-'99	14/0
12	Chandler, Chris	QB	6-4	225	10/12/65	13	Washington	Everett, Wash.	T(Hous)-'97	12/12
44	Christian, Bob	RB	5-11	232	11/14/68	8	Northwestern	Florissant, Mo.	UFA(Car)-'97	16/14
68	Collins, Calvin	G-C	6-2	310	1/5/74	4	Texas A&M	Beaumont, Tex.	D6-'97	14/8
29	Cooks, Kerry	S	5-11	202	3/28/1974	2	Iowa	Irving, Tex.	FA-'00	0*
94	Crockett, Henri	LB	6-2	238	10/28/74	4	Florida State	Pompano Beach, Fla.	D4-'97	16/14
45	Downs, Gary	RB	6-1	210	6/6/72	7	North Carolina State	Columbus, Ga.	FA-'97	0*
54	Draft, Chris	LB	5-11	230	2/26/76	2	Stanford	Anaheim, Calif.	W(SF)-'00	7/0*
75	Dronett, Shane	DT	6-6	300	1/12/71	9	Texas	Orange, Tex.	FA-'97	16/16
83	Dwight, Tim	WR-KR	5-8	180	7/13/75	3	Iowa	Iowa City, Iowa	D4-'98	12/8
30	Gardner, Derrick	CB	6-0	185	3/10/77	2	California	Oakland, Calif.	FA-'99	7/0
87	German, Jammi	WR	6-1	192	7/4/74	3	Miami	Fort Myers, Fla.	FA-'99	14/0
7	Graziani, Tony	QB	6-2	215	12/23/73	4	Oregon	Modesto, Calif.	D7-'97	11/3
98	Hall, Travis	DT	6-5	297	8/3/72	6	Brigham Young	Kenai, Alaska	D6-'95	16/15
64	Hallen, Bob	C-G	6-4	305	3/9/75	3	Kent State	Cleveland, Ohio	D2-'98	16/14
24	Hanspard, Byron	RB	5-10	200	1/23/76	4	Texas Tech	Desoto, Tex.	D2-'97	12/4
82	Harris, Ronnie	WR	5-11	180	6/4/70	6	Oregon	Granada Hills, Calif.	FA-'98	13/0
91	Huff, Ben	DT	6-4	298	2/21/1975	2	Michigan	Charlotte, N.C.	FA-'99	0*
95	Jasper, Ed	DT	6-2	295	1/18/73	4	Texas A&M	Tyler, Tex.	FA-'99	13/0
84	Jefferson, Shawn	WR	5-11	180	2/22/69	10	Central Florida	Jacksonville, Fla.	UFA(NE)-'00	16/16*
13	Kanell, Danny	QB	6-3	220	11/21/73	5	Florida State	Fort Lauderdale, Fla.	FA-'99	3/1
51	Kelly, Jeff	LB	5-11	245	12/13/75	2	Kansas State	LaGrange, Tex.	D6-'99	16/1
89	Kelly, Reggie	TE	6-3	250	2/22/77	2	Mississippi State	Aberdeen, Miss.	D2-'99	16/2
97	Kerney, Patrick	DE	6-5	272	12/30/76	2	Virginia	Trenton, N.J.	D1-'99	16/2
85	Kozlowski, Brian	TE	6-3	250	10/4/70	7	Connecticut	Rochester, N.Y.	FA-'97	16/3
55	Marshall, Whit	LB	6-2	242	1/6/73	2	Georgia	Atlanta, Ga.	UFA-'99	15/0
81	Mathis, Terance	WR	5-10	186	6/7/67	11	New Mexico	Stone Mountain, Ga.	UFA(NYJ)-'94	16/16
22	McBurrows, Gerald	S	5-11	210	10/7/73	6	Kansas	Detroit, Mich.	UFA(StL)-'99	16/4
62	McClure, Todd	C	6-1	300	2/16/77	2	Louisiana State	Baton Rouge, La.	D7-'99	0*
77	McDaniels, Pellom	DE	6-3	280	2/21/68	8	Oregon State	San Jose, Calif.	UFA(KC)-'99	16/0
49	Monroe, Rod	TE	6-4	254	7/30/75	2	Cincinnati	Hearne, Tex.	FA-'98	2/0
26	Oliver, Winslow	RB	5-7	200	3/3/73	5	New Mexico	Houston, Tex.	FA-'99	14/0
28	Oxendine, Ken	RB	6-0	230	10/4/75	3	Virginia Tech	Chester, Va.	D7-'98	12/9
40	Paulk, Jeff	RB	6-0	240	4/26/76	2	Arizona State	Phoenix, Ariz.	D3-'99	1/0
63	Pilgrim, Evan	G	6-4	298	8/14/72	6	Brigham Young	Pittsburgh, Calif.	FA-'99	3/1
76	Portilla, Jose	T	6-6	315	9/11/72	3	Arizona	Houston, Tex.	FA-'98	4/0
14	Richardson, Wally	QB	6-4	225	2/11/74	3	Penn State	Orangeburg, S.C.	FA-'99	0*
74	Salaam, Ephraim	T	6-7	305	6/19/76	3	San Diego State	Sacramento, Calif.	D7-'98	16/16
88	Santiago, O.J.	TE	6-7	264	4/4/74	4	Kent State	Whitby, Ontario, Canada	D3-'97	14/14
91	Smith, Brady	DE	6-5	270	6/5/73	5	Colorado State	Barrington, Ill.	UFA(NO)-'00	16/16*
4	Stryzinski, Dan	P	6-2	205	5/15/65	11	Indiana	Vincennes, Ind.	UFA(TB)-'95	16/0
93	Swayda, Shawn	DT	6-5	294	9/4/74	3	Arizona State	Phoenix, Ariz.	FA-'99	4/0
58	Tuggle, Jessie	LB	5-11	232	4/4/65	14	Valdosta State	Spalding, Ga.	FA-'87	14/14
70	Whitfield, Bob	T	6-5	318	10/18/71	9	Stanford	Carson, Calif.	D1a-'92	16/16
21	Williams, Elijah	CB	5-10	180	8/20/75	3	Florida	Milton, Fla.	D6-'98	15/2

* Ambrose and Smith played 16 games with New Orleans in '99; Buckley last active with N.Y. Giants in '98; Cooks last active with Green Bay in '98; Downs and McClure missed '99 season because of injury; Draft played 7 games with San Francisco; Huff inactive for 1 game; Jefferson played 16 games with New England; Richardson last active with Baltimore in '98.

Players lost to free agency (4): DE Lester Archambeau (Den; 15 games in '99), LB Craig Sauer (Minn; 16), DE Chuck Smith (Car; 16), C Robbie Tobeck (Sea; 15).

Also played with Falcons in '99—T Greg Bishop (13 games), WR Chris Calloway (11), LB Lamont Green (1), LB Ruffin Hamilton (11), C Adam Schreiber (3), WR Bryan Still (3), CB Keith Thibodeaux (8), G Gene Williams (15).

COACHING STAFF

Head Coach,
Dan Reeves

Pro Career: Head coach Dan Reeves, the NFL's winningest active coach with 177 career victories, suffered through a 5-11 season on the heels of 1998's NFC championship season. Reeves led the Falcons to their first Super Bowl appearance after capturing the NFC championship in 1998, only his second season with Atlanta after taking over on January 20, 1997. Reeves led the Falcons to the NFC West title with a 14-2 record and a franchise-record 442 points. Reeves was named coach of the year in 1998 for the fifth time in his coaching career after the Falcons improved from a 7-9 finish in 1997. Reeves had been the head coach of the New York Giants from 1993-96. Prior to that, he compiled a 117-79-1 record as head coach of the Denver Broncos from 1981-1992, earning NFL coach of the year honors in 1982, 1988, and 1991. He led the Broncos to three Super Bowl berths, four AFC Championship Games, five AFC West Division titles, and eight winning seasons. In his first year in New York, he earned NFL coach of the year honors for a fourth time, taking the Giants from 6-10 to an 11-5 mark and a wild-card playoff victory. Overall, Reeves has accumulated 11 winning seasons as head coach and participated in 48 playoff games and nine Super Bowls as an NFL player, assistant coach, and head coach. Career record: 177-136-1.

Background: Prior to obtaining his first NFL head coaching job in 1981, Reeves had been a member of the Dallas Cowboys' coaching staff since 1970, spending a total of 16 years under Tom Landry as a player and coach. In 1977, he was named offensive coordinator of Landry's staff. Reeves began his pro career as a free agent running back for Dallas in 1965. Prior to that he was a quarterback at South Carolina from 1962-64, passing for 2,561 yards and 16 touchdowns. He totaled 3,376 yards during his career with the Gamecocks, leading to his induction into the school's hall of fame in 1978. Reeves later was inducted into the state of Georgia Sports Hall of Fame.

Personal: Born January 19, 1944, Americus, Ga. Dan and his wife, Pam, live in Atlanta, and have three children—Dana, Laura, and Lee.

ASSISTANT COACHES

Marvin Bass, asst. to head coach-pro personnel; born August 28, 1919, Norfolk, Va., lives in Suwanee, Ga. Tackle William & Mary 1940-42. No pro playing experience. College coach: William & Mary 1944-48, 1950-51 (head coach), North Carolina 1949, 1953-55, South Carolina 1956-59, 1961-65, Georgia Tech 1960, Richmond 1963. Pro coach: Washington Redskins 1952, Montreal Beavers (Continental League) 1966-67, Montreal Alouettes (CFL) 1968, Buffalo Bills 1969-71, Birmingham Americans (WFL) 1974-75, Denver Broncos 1982-92. Joined Falcons in 1997.

Don Blackmon, linebackers; born March 14, 1958, Pompano Beach, Fla., lives in Suwanee, Ga. Linebacker Tulsa 1977-80. Pro linebacker New England Patriots 1981-87. Pro coach: New England Patriots 1988-90, Cleveland Browns 1991-92, New York Giants 1993-96, joined Falcons in 1997.

Rich Brooks, asst. head coach-defensive coordinator; born August 10, 1941, Forest, Calif., lives in Duluth, Ga. Tailback, defensive back, and quarterback Oregon State 1959-62. No pro playing experience. College coach: Oregon State 1965-69, 1973, UCLA 1970, 1976, Oregon 1977-94 (head coach). Pro coach: Los Angeles Rams 1971-72, San Francisco 49ers 1974-75, St. Louis Rams 1995-96 (head coach), joined Falcons in 1997.

Greg Brown, secondary; born October 10, 1957, Denver, lives in Suwanee, Ga. Defensive back Texas-El Paso 1980. No pro playing experience. College coach: Wyoming 1987-88, Purdue 1989-1990, Colorado 1991-93. Pro coach: Tampa Bay Buccaneers 1984-86, Atlanta Falcons 1994, San Diego Chargers 1995-96, Tennessee Oilers 1997-98, San Francisco 49ers 1999, rejoined Falcons in 2000.

2000 FIRST-YEAR ROSTER

Name	Pos.	Ht.	Wt.	Birthdate	College	Hometown	How Acq.
Arians, Jake	K	5-10	203	1/26/78	Alabama-Birmingham	Blacksburg, Va.	FA
Belli, Adriano	DT	6-5	289	8/25/77	Houston	Toronto, Ontario, Canada	FA
Claridge, Travis	T	6-5	308	3/23/78	Southern California	Vancover, Wash.	D2
Doster, Reginald (1)	CB	5-9	185	1/2/76	Central Florida	Fort Lauderdale, Fla.	FA
Ekiyor, Emil (1)	DE	6-4	270	12/25/73	Central Florida	Daytona Beach, Fla.	FA-'99
Finneran, Brian (1)	WR	6-5	208	1/31/76	Villanova	Mission Viejo, Calif.	FA-'99
Hernandez, Adam (1)	G	6-3	310	11/14/76	Yale	Washington, D.C.	FA-'99
Johanningmeier, Ryan	T	6-6	304	1/22/77	Colorado	Fort Collins, Colo.	FA
Johnson, Doug	QB	6-2	226	10/27/77	Florida	Gainesville, Fla.	FA
Midget, Anthony	CB	5-11	193	2/22/78	Virginia Tech	Clewiston, Fla.	D5
Miller, Doug	DT	6-1	281	10/12/75	Howard	Tampa, Fla.	FA
Neil, Dallas	P	6-1	215	9/30/76	Montana	Great Falls, Mont.	FA
O'Neal, Matt	C	6-3	278	5/5/77	Oklahoma	San Diego, Calif.	FA
Philyaw, Mareno	WR	6-2	208	12/19/77	Troy State	Atlanta, Ga.	D6
Powell, Ozell (1)	T	6-4	302	11/17/73	Alabama	Greenville, Ala.	FA
Rackley, Derek	TE	6-4	260	7/18/77	Minnesota	Apple Valley, Minn.	FA
Simmons, Sam (1)	DE	6-6	272	1/2/75	Arkansas-Pine Bluff	Atlanta, Ga.	FA
Simoneau, Mark	LB	6-0	233	1/16/77	Kansas State	Smith Center, Kan.	D3
Smith, Brian (1)	LB	6-3	252	2/25/78	Alabama-Birmingham	Rome, Ga.	FA-'99
Smith, Maurice	RB	6-0	236	9/7/76	North Carolina A&T	Palmyra, N.C.	FA
Stukes, Charles	CB	5-9	185	1/24/77	Virginia	Baltimore, Md.	FA
Thompson, Michael	T	6-4	318	2/11/77	Tennessee State	Savannah, Ga.	D4
Vagedes, Steve	WR	6-2	217	9/2/76	Ohio Northern	Coldwater, Ohio	FA
Vaughn, Darrick	CB	5-11	190	10/2/78	Southwest Texas	Aldine, Tex.	D7
Wu, Jamie	G	6-2	328	9/18/77	Maryland	St. Charles, Ill.	FA

The term NFL Rookie is defined as a player who is in his first season of professional football and has not been on the roster of another professional football team for any regular-season or postseason games. A Rookie is designated by an "R" on NFL rosters. Players who have been active in another professional football league or players who have NFL experience, including either preseason training camp or being on an Active List or Inactive List, or on Reserve/Injured or Reserve/Physically Unable to Perform for fewer than six regular-season games, are termed NFL First-Year Players. An NFL First-Year Player is designated by a "1" on NFL rosters. Thereafter, a player is credited with an additional year of experience for each season in which he accumulates six games on the Active List or Inactive List, or on Reserve/Injured or Reserve/Physically Unable to Perform.

Jack Burns, wide receivers; born January 3, 1949, Tampa, Fla., lives in Suwanee, Ga. Safety Florida, 1967-70. No pro playing experience. College coach: Florida 1971-73, 1975, Louisville 1974, 1985-88, Texas 1976, Vanderbilt 1977-78, Auburn 1979-80. Pro coach: Tampa Bay Bandits (USFL) 1983, Washington Redskins 1989-91, Minnesota Vikings 1992-93, joined Falcons in 1997.

Rocky Colburn, asst. strength and conditioning; born May 24, 1963, Dallas, Ore., lives in Lawrenceville, Ga. Safety Alabama 1981-83. No pro playing experience. College coach: Alabama 1984, 1987-92, Samford 1986. Pro coach: Joined Falcons 1999.

James Daniel, asst. offensive line; born January 17, 1953, Wetumpka, Ala., lives in Suwanee, Ga. Offensive guard Alabama State 1970-73. No pro playing experience. College coach: Auburn 1981-92. Pro coach: New York Giants 1993-96, joined Falcons in 1997.

Joe DeCamillis, special teams; born June 29, 1965, Arvada, Colo., lives in Alpharetta, Ga. No college or pro playing experience. College coach: Wyoming 1988. Pro coach: Denver Broncos 1989, Miami Dolphins 1990, New York Giants 1993-96, joined Falcons in 1997.

Thom Kaumeyer, defensive quality control; born March 17, 1967, LaJolla, Calif., lives in Suwanee, Ga. Safety Paolmar J.C. (Calif). 1985-86, Oregon 1987-88. Pro safety Seattle Seahawks 1989-1990, New York Giants 1991-92. College coach: Palomar J.C. (Calif.) 1991, 1993-94, 1997-99. Pro coach: Joined Falcons in 2000.

Bill Kollar, defensive line; born November 27, 1952, Warren, Ohio, lives in Duluth, Ga. Defensive end Montana State 1971-74. Pro defensive end Cincinnati Bengals 1974-76, Tampa Bay Buccaneers 1977-81. College coach: Illinois 1985-87, Purdue 1988-89. Pro coach: Tampa Bay Buccaneers 1984, joined Falcons in 1990.

Al Miller, strength and conditioning; born August 29, 1947, El Dorado, Ark., lives in Alpharetta, Ga. Wide receiver Northeast Louisiana 1965-69. No pro playing experience. College coach: Northwestern State (La.) 1974-78, Mississippi State 1980, Northeast Louisiana 1981, Alabama 1982-84. Pro coach: Denver Broncos 1987-92, New York Giants 1993-96, joined Falcons in 1997.

Jerry Rhome, quarterbacks; born March 6, 1942, in Dallas, lives in Suwanee, Ga. Quarterback Southern Methodist 1960-61, Tulsa 1963-64. Pro quarterback Dallas Cowboys 1965-68, Cleveland Browns 1969, Houston Oilers 1970, Los Angeles Rams 1971-72. College coach: Tulsa 1973-75. Pro coach: Seattle Seahawks 1976-1982, Washington Redskins 1983-87, San Diego Chargers 1988, Dallas Cowboys 1989, Arizona Cardinals 1990-93, Minnesota Vikings 1994, Houston Oilers 1995-96, St. Louis Rams 1997-98, joined Falcons in 2000.

George Sefcik, offensive coordinator-running backs; born December 27, 1939, Cleveland, Ohio, lives in Suwanee, Ga. Halfback Notre Dame 1959-61. No pro playing experience. College coach: Notre Dame 1963-68, Kentucky 1969-1972. Pro coach: Baltimore Colts 1973-74, Cleveland Browns 1975-77, 1989-90, Cincinnati Bengals 1978-83, Green Bay Packers 1984-87, Kansas City Chiefs 1988, New York Giants 1991-96, joined Falcons in 1997.

Art Shell, offensive line; born November 26, 1946, Charleston, S.C., lives in Lawrenceville, Ga. Offensive-defensive tackle Maryland State 1965-67. Pro offensive tackle Oakland/Los Angeles Raiders 1968-82. Inducted into Pro Football Hall of Fame 1989. Pro coach: Los Angeles Raiders 1983-94 (head coach 1989-94), Kansas City Chiefs 1995-96, joined Falcons in 1997.

Warren "Rennie" Simmons, wide receivers; born February 25, 1942, Poughkeepsie, N.Y., lives in Gainesville, Ga. Center San Diego State 1961-65. No pro playing experience. College coach: Cal State-Fullerton 1974-78, Cerritos (Calif.) J.C. 1978-80, Vanderbilt 1995. Pro coach: Washington Redskins 1981-93, Los Angeles Rams 1994, Houston Oilers 1996, joined Falcons in 1997.

Ed West, offensive quality control; born August 2, 1961, Leighton, Ala., lives in Woodstock, Ga. Tight end Auburn 1980-83. Pro tight end Green Bay Packers 1984-1994, Philadelphia Eagles 1995-96, Atlanta Falcons 1997. Pro coach: Joined Falcons in 1998.

Brian Xanders, director of football systems; born April 10, 1971, East Stroudsburg, Pa., lives in Atlanta. Linebacker Florida State 1989-1992. No pro playing experience. Pro coach: Joined Falcons in 1997.

CAROLINA PANTHERS

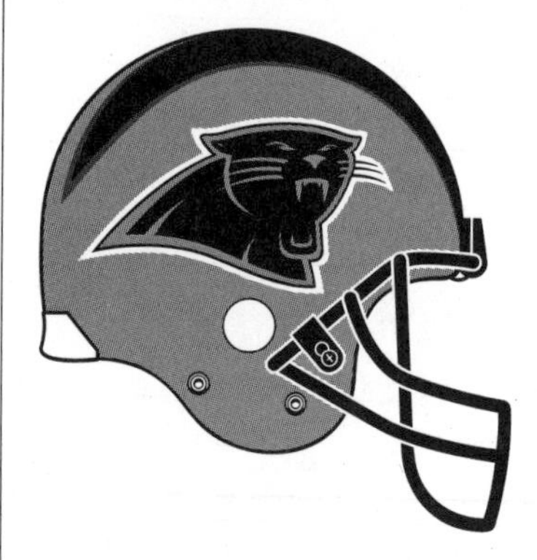

National Football Conference
Western Division
Team Colors: Black, Panther Blue, and Silver
800 South Mint Street
Charlotte, North Carolina 28202-1502
Telephone: (704) 358-7000

CLUB OFFICIALS

Founder/Owner: Jerry Richardson
President: Mark Richardson
President Carolina Stadium Corps.: Jon Richardson
Director of Player Personnel: Jack Bushofsky
Director of Football Operations: Marty Hurney
Director of Marketing and Sponsorships: Charles Waddell
Counsel: Richard M. Thigpen
Chief Financial Officer: Dave Olsen
Controller: Lisa Garber
Director of Pro Scouting: Mark Koncz
Pro Scouts: Hal Hunter, Ted Plumb
Director of College Scouting: Tony Softli
College Scouts: Hal Athon, Joe Bushofsky, Max McCartney, Jay Mondock, Jeff Morrow
Director of Communications: Charlie Dayton
Communications Assistant: Bruce Speight
Public Relations Assistant: Deedee Thomason
Director of Ticket Sales: Phil Youtsey
Director of Radio Broadcasting: Linda Ricca
Director of Television Broadcasting: Jerry Pelletier
Director of Player Relations: Donnie Shell
Director of Community Relations/Family Programs: B.J. Harrison Waymer
Director of Special Events: Leslie Matz
Director of Information Systems: Roger Goss
Football Systems: Rob Rogers
Video Director: Mark Hobbs
Assistant Video Director: Jeff Mueller
Head Trainer: John Kasik
Assistant Trainers: Al Shuford, Dan Ruiz
Equipment Manager: Jackie Miles
Assistant Equipment Manager: Don Toner
Director of Security: Gene Brown
Director of Facilities: Tom Fellows
Head Groundskeeper: Billy Ball
Office Manager: Jackie Jeffries
Stadium: Ericsson Stadium •**Capacity:** 73,250
Charlotte, North Carolina 28202-1502
Playing Surface: Grass
Training Camp: Wofford College
Spartanburg, South Carolina
29303

RECORD HOLDERS

INDIVIDUAL RECORDS—CAREER

Category	Name	Performance
Rushing (Yds.)	Fred Lane, 1997-99	2,001
Passing (Yds.)	Steve Beuerlein, 1996-99	8,960
Passing (Tds)	Steve Beuerlein, 1996-99	67
Receiving (No.)	Wesley Walls, 1996-99	231
Receiving (Yds.)	Muhsin Muhammad, 1996-99	2,918
Interceptions	Eric Davis, 1996-99	20
Punting (Avg.)	Ken Walter, 1997-99	41.0
Punt Return (Avg.)	Winslow Oliver, 1996-98	10.7
Kickoff Return (Avg.)	Michael Bates, 1996-99	26.5
Field Goals	John Kasay, 1995-99	126
Touchdowns (Tot.)	Wesley Walls, 1996-99	33
Points	John Kasay, 1995-99	532

INDIVIDUAL RECORDS—SINGLE SEASON

Category	Name	Performance
Rushing (Yds.)	Anthony Johnson, 1996	1,120
Passing (Yds.)	Steve Beuerlein, 1999	4,436
Passing (Tds)	Steve Beuerlein, 1999	36
Receiving (No.)	Muhsin Muhammad, 1999	96
Receiving (Yds.)	Muhsin Muhammad, 1999	1,253
Interceptions	Brett Maxie, 1995	6
Punting (Avg.)	Ken Walter, 1997	42.4
Punt Return (Avg.)	Winslow Oliver, 1996	11.5
Kickoff Return (Avg.)	Michael Bates, 1996	30.2
Field Goals	John Kasay, 1996	37
Touchdowns (Tot.)	Wesley Walls, 1999	12
	Patrick Jeffers, 1999	12
Points	John Kasay, 1996	145

INDIVIDUAL RECORDS—SINGLE GAME

Category	Name	Performance
Rushing (Yds.)	Fred Lane, 11-2-97	147
Passing (Yds.)	Steve Beuerlein, 12-12-99	373
Passing (Tds)	Steve Beuerlein, 1-2-00	5
Receiving (No.)	Muhsin Muhammad, 12-18-99	11
Receiving (Yds.)	Muhsin Muhammad, 9-13-98	192
Interceptions	Many times	2
	Last time by Jeff Brady, 9-27-98	
Field Goals	John Kasay, 9-1-96, 9-8-96	5
Touchdowns (Tot.)	Fred Lane, 11-2-97	3
	Tshimanga Biakabutuka, 10-3-99	3
	Muhsin Muhammad, 12-18-99	3
Points	Fred Lane, 11-2-97	18
	Tshimanga Biakabutuka, 10-3-99	18
	Muhsin Muhammad, 12-18-99	18

2000 SCHEDULE

PRESEASON

Aug. 4	**Jacksonville**	8:00
Aug. 10	at Pittsburgh	7:30
Aug. 18	**Baltimore**	8:00
Aug. 24	at New England	8:00

REGULAR SEASON

Sept. 3	at Washington	1:00
Sept. 10	at San Francisco	1:15
Sept. 17	**Atlanta**	1:00
Sept. 24	Open Date	
Oct. 1	**Dallas**	1:00
Oct. 8	**Seattle**	4:15
Oct. 15	at New Orleans	12:00
Oct. 22	**San Francisco**	1:00
Oct. 29	at Atlanta	1:00
Nov. 5	at St. Louis	7:35
Nov. 12	**New Orleans**	1:00
Nov. 19	at Minnesota	12:00
Nov. 27	**Green Bay** (Mon.)	9:00
Dec. 3	**St. Louis**	1:00
Dec. 10	at Kansas City	12:00
Dec. 17	**San Diego**	1:00
Dec. 24	at Oakland	1:15

ERICSSON STADIUM

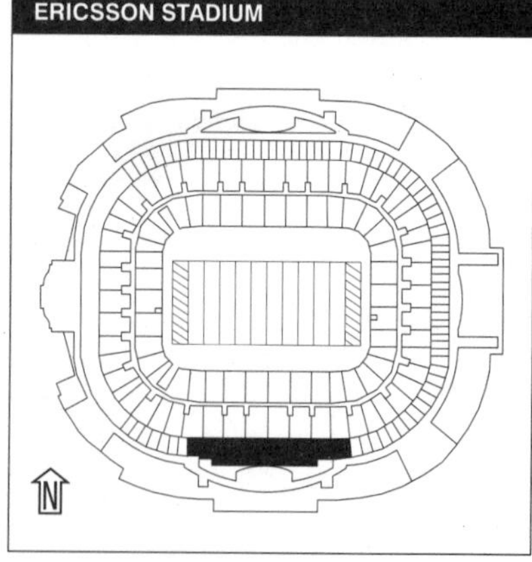

COACHING HISTORY

(39-43-0)

1995-98	Dom Capers	31-35-0
1999	George Seifert	8-8-0

1999 TEAM RECORD

PRESEASON (2-2)

Date	Result		Opponent
8/13	L	10-35	at Jacksonville
8/20	W	20-13	Pittsburgh
8/28	L	24-28	at Baltimore
9/2	W	23-20	New England

REGULAR SEASON (8-8)

Date	Result		Opponent	Att.
9/12	L	10-19	at New Orleans	58,166
9/19	L	20-22	Jacksonville	64,261
9/26	W	27-3	Cincinnati	61,269
10/3	L	36-38	at Washington	76,831
10/17	W	31-29	at San Francisco	68,151
10/24	L	9-24	Detroit	64,322
10/31	L	20-27	at Atlanta	52,594
11/7	W	33-7	Philadelphia	62,569
11/14	L	10-35	at St. Louis	65,965
11/21	W	31-17	at Cleveland	72,818
11/28	W	34-28	Atlanta	55,507
12/5	L	21-34	St. Louis	62,285
12/12	W	33-31	at Green Bay	59,869
12/18	W	41-24	San Francisco	62,373
12/26	L	20-30	at Pittsburgh	39,428
1/2	W	45-13	New Orleans	56,929

SCORE BY PERIODS

Panthers	90	155	89	87	0	—	421
Opponents	78	111	67	125	0	—	381

ATTENDANCE

Home 568,755 Away 503,076 Total 1,071,831
Single-game home record, 76,136 (12/10/95)
Single-season home record, 568,755 (1999)

1999 TEAM STATISTICS

	Panthers	Opp.
Total First Downs	307	331
Rushing	78	115
Passing	208	189
Penalty	21	27
Third Down: Made/Att	77/201	89/214
Third Down Pct.	38.3	41.6
Fourth Down: Made/Att	10/20	11/20
Fourth Down Pct.	50.0	55.0
Total Net Yards	5,686	5,503
Avg. Per Game	355.4	343.9
Total Plays	982	1,042
Avg. Per Play	5.8	5.3
Net Yards Rushing	1,525	1,898
Avg. Per Game	95.3	118.6
Total Rushes	356	450
Net Yards Passing	4,161	3,605
Avg. Per Game	260.1	225.3
Sacked/Yards Lost	51/286	35/235
Gross Yards	4,447	3,840
Att./Completions	575/345	557/327
Completion Pct.	60.0	58.7
Had Intercepted	15	15
Punts/Average	65/39.4	74/39.5
Net Punting Avg.	65/36.7	74/34.4
Penalties/Yards	106/857	109/877
Fumbles/Ball Lost	24/19	22/14
Touchdowns	50	47
Rushing	12	13
Passing	36	26
Returns	2	8
Avg. Time of Possession	29:23	30:37

1999 INDIVIDUAL STATISTICS

Passing	Att.	Comp.	Yds.	Pct.	TD	Int.	Tkld.	Rate
Beuerlein	571	343	4,436	60.1	36	15	50/280	94.6
Lewis	3	2	11	66.7	0	0	1/6	72.9
Bono	1	0	0	0.0	0	0	0/0	39.6
Panthers	575	345	4,447	60.0	36	15	51/286	94.3
Opponents	557	327	3,840	58.7	26	15	35/235	84.1

SCORING	TD R	TD P	TD Rt	PAT	FG	Saf	PTS
Kasay	0	0	0	33/33	22/25	0	99
Jeffers	0	12	0	0/0	0/0	0	72
Walls	0	12	0	0/0	0/0	0	72
Muhammad	0	8	0	0/0	0/0	0	48
Biakabutuka	6	0	0	0/0	0/0	0	36
Cunningham	0	0	0	13/14	3/3	0	22
Floyd	3	0	0	0/0	0/0	0	18
Bates	0	0	2	0/0	0/0	0	12
Beuerlein	2	0	0	0/0	0/0	0	12
Hayes	0	2	0	0/0	0/0	0	12
Kinchen	0	2	0	0/0	0/0	0	12
Lane	1	0	0	0/0	0/0	0	6
Panthers	12	36	2	46/47	25/28	0	421
Opponents	13	26	8	42/43	19/25	0	381

2-Pt. Conversions: None.
Team 0-3, Opponents 0-4.

RUSHING	Att.	Yds.	Avg.	LG	TD
Biakabutuka	138	718	5.2	67t	6
Lane	115	475	4.1	41t	1
Beuerlein	27	124	4.6	16	2
Floyd	35	78	2.2	16	3
Johnson	25	72	2.9	23	0
Metcalf	2	20	10.0	17	0
Jeffers	2	16	8.0	23	0
Bates	3	12	4.0	12	0
Hetherington	2	7	3.5	5	0
Carruth	1	4	4.0	4	0
Lewis	4	1	0.3	4	0
Bono	2	-2	-1.0	-1	0
Panthers	356	1,525	4.3	67t	12
Opponents	450	1,898	4.2	44t	13

RECEIVING	No.	Yds.	Avg.	LG	TD
Muhammad	96	1,253	13.1	60t	8
Jeffers	63	1,082	17.2	88t	12
Walls	63	822	13.0	37t	12
Biakabutuka	23	189	8.2	32	0
Lane	23	163	7.1	23	0
Floyd	21	179	8.5	25	0
Carruth	14	200	14.3	43	0
Johnson	13	103	7.9	22	0
Hayes	11	270	24.5	56t	2
Metcalf	11	133	12.1	33	0
Kinchen	5	45	9.0	26t	2
Mangum	1	6	6.0	6	0
Bates	1	2	2.0	2	0
Panthers	345	4,447	12.9	88t	36
Opponents	327	3,840	11.7	67t	26

INTERCEPTIONS	No.	Yds.	Avg.	LG	TD
Davis	5	49	9.8	16	0
Minter	3	69	23.0	44	0
Alexander	2	18	9.0	18	0
Evans	2	1	0.5	1	0
Richardson	1	27	27.0	27	0
Gilbert	1	4	4.0	4	0
Wells	1	1	1.0	1	0
Panthers	15	169	11.3	44	0
Opponents	15	267	17.8	57t	3

PUNTING	No.	Yds.	Avg.	In 20	LG
Walter	65	2,562	39.4	18	56
Panthers	65	2,562	39.4	18	56
Opponents	74	2,924	39.5	16	57

PUNT RETURNS	No.	FC	Yds.	Avg.	LG	TD
Metcalf	34	18	238	7.0	30	0
Johnson	1	0	3	3.0	3	0
Panthers	35	18	241	6.9	30	0
Opponents	32	21	158	4.9	27	0

KICKOFF RETURNS	No.	Yds.	Avg.	LG	TD
Bates	52	1,287	24.8	100t	2
Metcalf	4	56	14.0	31	0
Lane	3	58	19.3	22	0
Kinchen	3	29	9.7	15	0
Mangum	2	20	10.0	13	0
Hetherington	1	16	16.0	16	0
Johnson	1	9	9.0	9	0
Panthers	66	1,475	22.3	100t	2
Opponents	76	1,425	18.8	58	0

FIELD GOALS	1-19	20-29	30-39	40-49	50+
Kasay	1/1	8/8	6/6	5/6	2/4
Cunningham	0/0	2/2	0/0	1/1	0/0
Panthers	1/1	10/10	6/6	6/7	2/4
Opponents	0/0	5/5	8/11	6/8	0/1

SACKS	No.
Greene	12.0
Peter	4.5
Barrow	4.0
Rucker	3.0
Gilbert	2.5
E. Jones	2.5
Edwards	2.0
Minter	1.0
Richardson	1.0
Tuaolo	1.0
Wells	0.5
Panthers	35.0
Opponents	51.0

2000 DRAFT CHOICES

Round	Name	Pos.	College
1	Rashard Anderson	DB	Jackson State
2	Deon Grant	DB	Tennessee
3	Leander Jordan	G	Indiana, Pa.
4	Alvin McKinley	DT	Mississippi State
5	Gillis Wilson	DE	Southern
6	Jeno James	T	Auburn
7	Lester Towns	LB	Washington

CAROLINA PANTHERS

2000 VETERAN ROSTER

No.	Name	Pos.	Ht.	Wt.	Birthdate	NFL Exp.	College	Hometown	How Acq.	'99 Games/ Starts
24	Bates, Michael	RB	5-10	189	12/19/69	8	Arizona	Tucson, Ariz.	FA-'96	16/0
7	Beuerlein, Steve	QB	6-3	220	3/7/65	14	Notre Dame	Anaheim, Calif.	UFA(Jax)-'96	16/0
21	Biakabutuka, Tshimanga	RB	6-0	215	1/24/74	5	Michigan	Lonqueuil, Quebec, Canada	D1-'96	11/11
31	Booth, Tony	DB	6-1	195	8/3/75	2	James Madison	Richmond, Va.	D7-'99	0*
66	Campbell, Matt	G	6-4	300	7/14/72	6	South Carolina	North Augusta, S.C.	FA-'95	10/10
2	Craig, Dameyune	QB	6-1	200	4/19/74	2	Auburn	Prichard, Ala.	FA-'98	0*
72	Daniel, Robert	DE	6-6	275	10/19/75	2	Northwestern State, La.	Dallas, Tex.	D6-'99	0*
25	Davis, Eric	CB	5-11	185	1/26/68	11	Jacksonville State	Anniston, Ala.	UFA(SF)-'96	16/16
64	Dexter, James	G-T	6-7	320	3/3/73	5	South Carolina	Springfield, Va.	UFA(Ariz)-'00	8/5*
74	Dingle, Antonio	DT	6-2	315	10/7/76	2	Virginia	Hope Mills, N.C.	W(GB)-'99	3/00
33	Evans, Doug	CB	6-1	190	5/13/70	8	Louisiana Tech	Haynesville, La.	UFA(GB)-'98	16/16
40	Floyd, William	RB	6-1	242	2/17/72	7	Florida State	St. Petersburg, Fla.	UFA(SF)-'98	16/16
65	Garcia, Frank	C	6-2	302	1/28/72	6	Washington	Phoenix, Ariz.	D4-'95	16/16
94	Gilbert, Sean	DT	6-5	318	4/10/70	8	Pittsburgh	Aliquippa, Pa.	FA(Wash)-'98	16/16
14	Hankton, Karl	WR	6-2	202	7/24/70	3	Trinity College	New Orleans, La.	FA' 00	0*
81	Hayes, Donald	WR	6-4	208	7/13/75	3	Wisconsin	Madison, Wis.	D4-'98	13/1
44	Hetherington, Chris	RB	6-3	249	11/27/72	5	Yale	North Branford, Conn.	FA-'99	14/0
36	Hitchcock, Jimmy	CB	5-10	187	11/9/70	6	North Carolina	Concord, N.C.	UFA(Minn)-'00	16/16*
83	Jeffers, Patrick	WR	6-3	218	2/2/73	5	Virginia	Fort Worth, Tex.	RFA(Dall)-'99	15/10
23	Johnson, Anthony	RB	6-0	225	10/25/67	11	Notre Dame	South Bend, Ind.	W(Chi)-'95	16/0
75	Jones, Clarence	T	6-6	300	5/6/68	10	Maryland	Brooklyn, N.Y.	UFA(NO)-'99	16/16
54	Jones, Dontá	LB	6-2	235	8/27/72	6	Nebraska	Promfet, Md.	UFA(Pitt)-'99	16/0
59	# Jones, Ernest	DE	6-2	255	4/1/71	6	Oregon	Utica, N.Y.	W(NO)-'98	13/0
4	Kasay, John	K	5-10	198	10/27/69	10	Georgia	Athens, Ga.	UFA(Sea)-'95	13/0
88	Kinchen, Brian	TE	6-2	240	8/6/65	13	Louisiana State	Baton Rouge, La.	UFA(Balt)-'99	16/0
8	Lewis, Jeff	QB	6-2	211	4/17/73	4	Northern Arizona	Phoenix, Ariz.	T(Den)-'99	2/0
86	Mangum, Kris	TE	6-4	249	8/15/73	3	Mississippi	Magee, Miss.	D7-'97	11/0
20	Means, Natrone	RB	5-10	245	4/26/72	8	North Carolina	Concord, N.C.	UFA(SD)-'00	7/5*
82	# Metcalf, Eric	WR	5-10	190	1/23/68	12	Texas	Arlington, Va.	FA-'99	16/1
30	Minter, Mike	S	5-10	188	1/15/74	4	Nebraska	Lawton, Okla.	D2-'97	16/16
90	Morabito, Tim	DT	6-3	296	10/12/73	5	Boston College	Garnerville, N.Y.	W(Cin)-'97	16/16
87	Muhammad, Muhsin	WR	6-2	217	5/5/73	5	Michigan State	Lansing, Mich.	D2-'96	15/15
53	Navies, Hannibal	LB	6-2	240	7/19/77	2	Colorado	Oakland, Calif.	D4-'99	9/0
63	Nesbit, Jamar	C	6-4	330	12/17/76	2	South Carolina	Summerville, S.C.	FA-'99	7/0
97	Peter, Jason	DE	6-4	295	9/13/74	3	Nebraska	Locust, N.J.	D1-'98	9/0
56	t- Reid, Spencer	LB	6-1	247	2/8/76	3	Brigham Young	Pago Pago, American Samoa	T(Ind)-'99	12/0*
39	Richardson, Damien	S	6-1	210	4/3/76	3	Arizona State	Fresno, Calif.	D6-'98	15/0
93	Rucker, Micheal	DE	6-5	258	2/28/75	2	Nebraska	St. Joseph, Mo.	D2b-'99	16/0
11	Ryans, Larry	WR	5-11	182	7/28/71	2	Clemson	Greenwood, S.C.	FA-'00	0*
60	Shiver, Clay	G	6-4	300	1/22/72	4	Florida State	Tifton, Ga.	FA-'99	0*
91	Smith, Chuck	DE	6-2	262	12/21/69	9	Tennessee	Athens, Ga.	UFA(Atl)-'00	16/16*
67	Stoltenberg, Bryan	C	6-1	300	8/25/72	5	Colorado	Sugarland, Tex.	FA-'98	16/7
70	Terry, Chris	T	6-5	295	8/8/75	2	Georgia	Jacksonville, Fla.	D2a-'99	16/16
98	# Tuaolo, Esera	DT	6-2	281	7/11/68	10	Oregon State	Honolulu, Hawaii	FA-'99	12/0
80	Turner, Jim	WR	6-4	212	11/13/75	3	Syracuse	Jacksonville, Fla.	D7b-'98	0*
85	Walls, Wesley	TE	6-5	250	2/26/66	12	Mississippi	Pontotoc, Miss.	UFA(NO)-'96	16/16
13	Walter, Ken	P	6-1	195	8/15/72	4	Kent State	Euclid, Ohio	FA-'97	16/0
95	Wells, Dean	LB	6-3	248	7/20/70	8	Kentucky	Louisville, Ky.	UFA(Sea)-'99	16/10
37	# Wheeler, Leonard	CB	6-0	198	1/15/69	9	Troy State	Toccoa, Ga.	UFA(Minn)-'98	0*
99	Wiley, Chuck	DL	6-5	282	3/6/75	3	Louisiana State	Baton Rouge, La.	D3a-'98	16/16
96	Williams, Jay	DE	6-3	280	10/13/71	5	Wake Forest	Washington, D.C.	UFA(StL)-'00	16/0*
58	Woodall, Lee	LB	6-1	230	10/31/69	7	West Chester	Carlisle, Pa.	FA-'00	16/16*

* Booth, Daniel, Turner, and Wheeler missed '99 season because of injury; Craig was inactive for 16 games in '99; Dexter played 8 games with Arizona; Hankton last active with Philadelphia in '98; Hitchcock played 16 games with Minnesota; Means played 7 games with San Diego, Reid played 12 games with Indianapolis; Ryans last active with Tampa Bay in 1996; Shiver was inactive for 3 games; Smith played 16 games with Atlanta; Williams played 16 games with St. Louis; Woodall played 16 games with San Francicso.

\# Unrestricted free agent; subject to developments

Retired—Kevin Greene, 15-year linebacker, 16 games in '99.

Players lost through free agency (1): T Norberto Davidds-Garrido (Ariz; 16 games in '99).

Also played with Panthers in '99—S Brent Alexander (16 games), LB Micheal Barrow (16), QB Steve Bono (2), WR Rae Carruth (5), K Richie Cunningham (3), DE Antonio Edwards (14), RB Fred Lane (15), CB Steve Lofton (5), DT Viliami Maumau (1), DB Roderick Mullen (15), G Nate Newton (7), G Anthony Redmon (15), S Mike Scurlock (14), CB Michael Swift (15), DE Rick Terry (8), LB Steve Tovar (16).

COACHING STAFF

Head Coach,
George Seifert

Pro Career: Became the second coach in Carolina Panthers history on January 4, 1999. Ranks third all-time among NFL head coaches with a .730 winning percentage (behind Vince Lombardi and John Madden) and reached both 50 and 75 victories faster than any head coach in League history. One of eleven head coaches to win two or more Super Bowls. Coached on all five of San Francisco's Super Bowl championship teams, earning one ring as secondary coach (1981), two as defensive coordinator (1984, 1988), and two as head coach (1989, 1994). Ranks as 49ers' all-time leader with 98 regular-season victories and 108 total wins. Directed 49ers teams that boasted the NFL's best record in 1989, 1990, 1992, and 1994. Guided 49ers to club-record five NFC Championship Game appearances and tied Bill Walsh's club mark with six NFC West titles. Named 49ers head coach in 1989 and became second rookie head coach to win Super Bowl. Appointed San Francisco's defensive coordinator in 1983 after joining 49ers as secondary coach in 1980. No pro playing experience. Career record: 116-43.

Background: Linebacker at University of Utah (1960-62). Served a six-month tour of duty with the U.S. Army following graduation. Returned to Utah as a graduate assistant in 1964. Named head coach at Westminster College in Salt Lake City in 1965. Assistant at Iowa (1966), Oregon (1967-1971), and Stanford (1972-74). Left Stanford to become head coach at Cornell (1975-76). Joined Bill Walsh's staff at Stanford in 1977 and helped the Cardinal to a two-year mark of 17-7, including victories in the Sun and Bluebonnet Bowls. Received bachelor's degree in zoology (1963) and master's degree in physical education (1966) from Utah.

Personal: Born January 22, 1940, in San Francisco. He and his wife, Linda, have two children—Eve and Jason—and live in Los Altos, Calif.

2000 FIRST-YEAR ROSTER

Name	Pos.	Ht.	Wt.	Birthdate	College	Hometown	How Acq.
Anderson, Rashard	DB	6-2	204	6/14/77	Jackson State	Forest, Miss.	D1
Arndt, Bryan	TE	6-4	255	2/10/77	Boston College	Pittsburgh, Pa.	FA
Best, Dan (1)	T	6-5	290	6/2/76	Western Carolina	Faison, N.C.	FA
Beverly, Jim	G-T	6-4	304	12/20/76	East Tennessee State	Kingsport, Tenn.	FA
Blackshear, Cheston	G	6-3	289	8/12/77	Florida	Jacksonville, Fla.	FA
Burks, Dialleo (1)	WR	6-2	181	7/7/74	Eastern Kentucky	LaGrange, Ga.	FA
Crawford, Casey	TE	6-6	250	8/1/77	Virginia	Falls Church, Va.	FA
Dean, Michael	WR	6-2	170	5/18/77	Illinois	Key West, Fla.	FA
Fields, Haven	LB	6-1	223	7/4/78	Auburn	Miami, Fla.	FA
Foreman, Shawn (1)	WR	6-1	205	6/3/75	West Virginia	Chesapeake, Va.	FA
Grant, Deon	S	6-1	207	3/14/79	Tennessee	Augusta, Ga.	D2
Green, Lamont (1)	LB	6-3	230	7/10/76	Florida State	Miami, Fla.	FA
Green, Ray	S	6-3	187	3/22/77	South Carolina	Charleston, S.C.	FA
Harper, Deveron	CB	5-11	187	11/15/77	Notre Dame	Orangeburg, S.C.	FA
Hawkes, Michael	LB	6-1	231	4/11/77	Virginia Tech	Blackstone, Va.	FA
Hood, Kerry	WR	6-1	196	12/16/76	South Carolina	Atlanta, Ga.	FA
Hoover, Brad	RB	6-2	225	11/11/76	Western Carolina	Thomasville, N.C.	FA
Howard, Reggie	CB	6-1	191	5/17/77	Memphis State	Memphis, Tenn.	FA
James, Jeno	G	6-3	292	1/12/77	Auburn	Montgomery, Ala.	D6
Jones, Bryan	G	6-4	290	10/18/76	North Carolina	Valaparaiso, Fla.	FA
Jordan, Leander	G	6-3	333	9/15/77	Indiana, Pa.	Pittsburgh, Pa.	D3
Kale, Brandon	P	6-3	220	11/5/77	Wofford	Shelby, N.C.	FA
Kane, Morgan	RB	6-1	220	3/30/76	Wake Forest	Ottawa, Ontario, Canada	FA
Lenon, Paris	LB	6-2	220	11/26/77	Richmond	Lynchburg, Va.	FA
Lytle, Matt (1)	QB	6-4	225	9/4/75	Pittsburgh	Wyomissing Hills, Pa.	FA
McGee, Mike	DT	6-3	280	6/18/77	Illinois	Springfield, Ill.	FA
McKinley, Alvin	DT	6-3	292	6/9/78	Mississippi State	Weir, Miss.	D4
Meng, Eric	K	6-1	192	11/29/74	Georgia Southern	Jupiter, Fla.	FA
Mercer, Giradie	DT	6-2	285	3/19/76	Marshall	Washington, D.C.	FA
Minor, Kory (1)	LB	6-1	247	12/14/76	Notre Dame	La Puente, Calif.	FA
Mogridge, Allen	G	6-4	280	11/9/76	North Carolina	Sevierville, Tenn.	FA
Monroe, Kevin	CB	6-1	185	5/8/77	East Carolina	Greenville, N.C.	FA
Montgomery, Scottie	WR	6-1	195	5/26/78	Duke	Cherryville, N.C.	FA
Norman, Nathan	RB	6-1	234	3/20/78	Arkansas	Jackson, Mo.	FA
O'Neal, Derek	RB	6-1	205	12/8/75	South Carolina State	Gainesville, Fla.	FA
Parker, Sirr (1)	WR	5-11	196	10/31/77	Texas A&M	Los Angeles, Calif.	FA
Parmer, Jason	LB	6-2	230	5/16/77	James Madison	Manheim, Pa.	FA
Sanders, A'Jani	S	5-10	197	10/31/76	Notre Dame	Houston, Tex.	FA
Scott, Donald	P	6-5	210	1/31/76	Virginia	Rockville, Md.	FA
Simmons, Rasheed (1)	DE	6-5	244	9/17/75	Maryland	Edison, N.J.	FA
Snyder, Shawn	QB	6-3	225	5/13/76	Western Carolina	Knoxville, Tenn.	FA
Stull, Jim	T	6-6	301	1/19/77	Delaware	Finksburg, Md.	FA
Towns, Lester	LB	6-1	252	8/28/77	Washington	Pasadena, Calif.	D7
Weaver, Alton (1)	DT	6-3	276	10/2/75	Oklahoma State	Houston, Tex.	FA
Wilson, Gillis	DE	6-2	282	10/15/77	Southern	Patterson, La.	D5

The term NFL Rookie is defined as a player who is in his first season of professional football and has not been on the roster of another professional football team for any regular-season or postseason games. A Rookie is designated by an "R" on NFL rosters. Players who have been active in another professional football league or players who have NFL experience, including either preseason training camp or being on an Active List or Inactive List, or on Reserve/Injured or Reserve/Physically Unable to Perform for fewer than six regular-season games, are termed NFL First-Year Players. An NFL First-Year Player is designated by a "1" on NFL rosters. Thereafter, a player is credited with an additional year of experience for each season in which he accumulates six games on the Active List or Inactive List, or on Reserve/Injured or Reserve/Physically Unable to Perform.

ASSISTANT COACHES

Don Breaux, tight ends; born August 3, 1940, Jennings, La., lives in Charlotte. Quarterback McNeese State 1959-1961. Pro quarterback Denver Broncos 1963, San Diego Chargers 1964-65. College coach: Florida State 1966-67, Arkansas 1968-1971, 1977-1980, Florida 1973-74, Texas 1975-76. Pro coach: Houston Oilers 1972, Washington Redskins 1981-1993, New York Jets 1994, joined Panthers in 1995.

Jacob Burney, defensive line; born January 24, 1959, Chattanooga, Tenn., lives in Charlotte. Defensive tackle Tennessee-Chattanooga 1977-1980. No pro playing experience. College coach: New Mexico 1983-86, Tulsa 1987, Mississippi State 1988, Wisconsin 1989, UCLA 1990-92, Tennessee 1993. Pro coach: Cleveland Browns/Baltimore Ravens 1994-98, joined Panthers in 1999.

Chick Harris, running backs; born September 21, 1945, Durham, N.C., lives in Charlotte. Running back Northern Arizona 1966-69. No pro playing experience. College coach: Colorado State 1970-72, Long Beach State 1973-74, Washington 1975-1980. Pro coach: Buffalo Bills 1981-82, Seattle Seahawks 1983-1991, Los Angeles Rams 1992-94, joined Panthers in 1995.

Carlos Mainord, defensive backs, born August 26, 1944, Greenville, Texas, lives in Charlotte, N.C. Linebacker Navarro J.C. (Texas) 1962-63, McMurry College 1964-65. No pro playing experience. College coach: McMurry College 1966-68, Texas Tech 1969, 1983-85, 1987-1992, Ranger J.C. (Texas) 1970-71, 1972-77 (head coach), Rice 1978-1982, Miami 1986. Pro coach: Chicago Bears 1993-98, New Orleans Saints 1999, joined Panthers in 2000.

John Marshall, defensive coordinator-asst. head coach; born October 2, 1945, Arroyo Grande, Calif., lives in Charlotte. Linebacker Washington State 1964. No pro playing experience. College coach: Oregon 1970-76, Southern California 1977-79. Pro coach: Green Bay Packers 1980-82, Atlanta Falcons 1983-85, Indianapolis Colts 1986-88, San Francisco 49ers 1989-1998, joined Panthers in 1999.

Mike McCoy, offensive assistant; born April 1, 1972, San Francisco, lives in Charlotte. Quarterback Long Beach State 1990-91, Utah 1992-94. Pro quarterback Amsterdam Admirals (NFL Europe) 1997, Calgary Stampede (CFL) 1999. Pro coach: Joined Panthers in 1999.

Sam Mills, linebackers; born June 3, 1959, Neptune, N.J., lives in Charlotte. Linebacker Montclair State 1977-1980. Pro linebacker Philadelphia/Baltimore Stars (USFL) 1983-85, New Orleans Saints 1986-1994, Carolina Panthers 1995-97. Pro coach: Joined Panthers in 1999.

Bill Musgrave, offensive coordinator; born November 11, 1967, Grand Junction, Colo., lives in Charlotte. Quarterback Oregon 1987-1990. Pro quarterback San Francisco 49ers 1991-94, Denver Broncos 1995-96. Pro coach: Oakland Raiders 1997, Philadelphia Eagles 1998, joined Panthers in 1999.

Scott O'Brien, special teams; born June 25, 1957, Superior, Wis., lives in Charlotte. Defensive end Wisconsin-Superior 1975-78. Pro defensive end Green Bay Packers 1979, Toronto Argonauts (CFL) 1979. College coach: Wisconsin-Superior 1980-82, Nevada-Las Vegas 1983-85, Rice 1986, Pittsburgh 1987-1990. Pro coach: Cleveland Browns/Baltimore Ravens 1991-98, joined Panthers in 1999.

Alvin Reynolds, defensive quality control; born June 24, 1959, Pineville, La., lives in Charlotte. Safety Indiana State 1978-1981. No pro playing experience. College coach: Indiana State 1982-1992. Pro coach: Denver Broncos 1993-95, Baltimore Ravens 1996-98, joined Panthers in 1999.

Greg Roman, offensive quality control; born August 19, 1972, lives in Charlotte. Defensive line-linebacker John Carroll 1990-94. No pro playing experience. Pro coach: Joined Panthers in 1999.

Darrin Simmons, special teams quality control-asst. strength and conditioning; born April 9, 1973, Elkhart, Kan., lives in Charlotte. Punter Kansas 1993-95. No pro playing experience. College coach: Kansas 1996, Minnesota 1997. Pro coach: Baltimore Ravens 1998, joined Panthers in 1999.

Jerry Simmons, strength and conditioning; born June 15, 1954, Elkhart, Kan., lives in Charlotte. Linebacker Fort Hays State 1976-77. No pro playing experience. College coach: Fort Hays State 1978, Clemson 1980, Rice 1981-82, Southern California 1983-87. Pro coach: New England Patriots 1988-1990, Cleveland Browns/Baltimore Ravens 1991-98, joined Panthers in 1999.

Richard Williamson, wide receivers-asst. head coach offense; born April 13, 1941, Ft. Deposit, Ala., lives in Charlotte. Receiver Alabama 1961-62. No pro playing experience. College coach: Alabama 1963-67, 1970-71, Arkansas 1968-69, 1972-74, Memphis State 1975-1980 (head coach). Pro coach: Kansas City Chiefs 1983-86, Tampa Bay Buccaneers 1987-1991 (interim head coach final three games of 1990, head coach 1991), Cincinnati Bengals 1992-94, joined Panthers in 1995.

Tony Wise, offensive line, born December 28, 1951, Albany, N.Y., lives in Charlotte. Offensive lineman Ithaca College 1971-72. No pro playing experience. College coach: Albany State 1973, Bridgeport 1974, Central Connecticut State 1975, Washington State 1976, Pittsburgh 1977-78, Oklahoma State 1979-1983, Syracuse 1984, Miami 1985-88. Pro coach: Dallas Cowboys 1989-1992, Chicago Bears 1993-98, joined Panthers in 1999.

CHICAGO BEARS

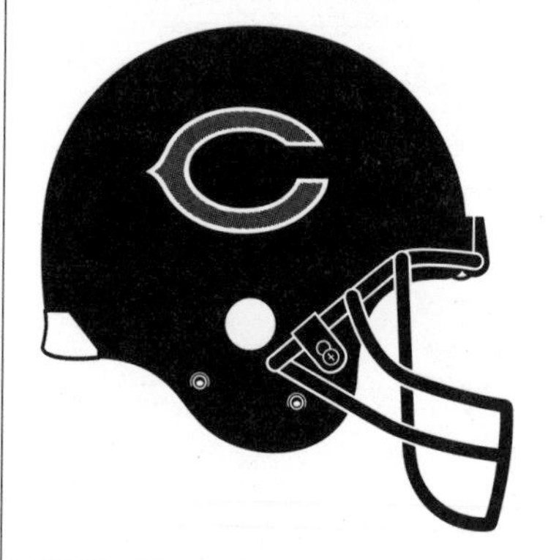

National Football Conference
Central Division
Team Colors: Navy Blue, Orange, and White
Halas Hall at Conway Park
1000 Football Drive
Lake Forest, Illinois 60045
Telephone: (847) 295-6600

CLUB OFFICIALS

Chairman Emeritus: Edward W. McCaskey
Chairman of the Board: Michael B. McCaskey
President and CEO: Ted Phillips
Secretary: Virginia H. McCaskey
Vice President: Tim McCaskey
Vice President of Player Personnel: Mark Hatley
Director of Pro Personnel: Scott Campbell
Director of College Scouting: Bill Rees
Director of Business Operations: Jim Miller
Director of Administration: Bill McGrane
Director of Player Development: Brian McCaskey
Director of Ticket Operations: George McCaskey
Director of Special Projects: Pat McCaskey
Director of Community Relations: John Bostrom
Manager of Sales and Development: Jack Trompeter
Director of Public Relations: Bryan Harlan
Asst. Director of Public Relations: Scott Hagel
Director of Information Services: Greg Gershuny
Controller: Karen Zust
Video Director: Dean Pope
Assistant Video Directors: Dave Hendrickson, Peter Taylor
Head Athletic Trainer: Tim Bream
Assistant Trainers: Eric Sugarman, Bobby Slater
Physical Development Coordinator: Russ Riederer
Asst. Physical Development Coordinator: Steve Little
Head Equipment Manager: Tony Medlin
Assistant Equipment Managers: Carl Piekarski, Jamal Nelson
Quality Control: Eric Studesville, Chuck Bullough
Scouts: Marty Barrett, Glenn Schembechler, George Paton, Jeff Shiver, Pat Roberts, Phil Emery, John Paul Young
Stadium: Soldier Field • **Capacity:** 66,944
425 McFetridge Place
Chicago, Illinois 60605
Playing Surface: Grass
Training Camp: University of Wisconsin-Platteville
Platteville, Wisconsin 53818

2000 SCHEDULE

PRESEASON

Aug. 5	at New York Giants	8:00
Aug. 12	**Cleveland**	7:00
Aug. 19	at Cincinnati	7:30
Aug. 25	**Tennessee**	7:00

REGULAR SEASON

Sept. 3	at Minnesota	12:00
Sept. 10	at Tampa Bay	1:00
Sept. 17	**New York Giants**	3:15
Sept. 24	**Detroit**	12:00
Oct. 1	at Green Bay	3:15
Oct. 8	**New Orleans**	12:00
Oct. 15	**Minnesota**	7:35
Oct. 22	at Philadelphia	1:00
Oct. 29	Open Date	
Nov. 5	**Indianapolis**	12:00
Nov. 12	at Buffalo	1:00
Nov. 19	**Tampa Bay**	12:00
Nov. 26	at New York Jets	1:00
Dec. 3	**Green Bay**	7:35
Dec. 10	**New England**	12:00
Dec. 17	at San Francisco	1:05
Dec. 24	at Detroit	1:00

RECORD HOLDERS

INDIVIDUAL RECORDS—CAREER

Category	Name	Performance
Rushing (Yds.)	Walter Payton, 1975-1987	*16,726
Passing (Yds.)	Sid Luckman, 1939-1950	14,686
Passing (TDs)	Sid Luckman, 1939-1950	137
Receiving (No.)	Walter Payton, 1975-1987	492
Receiving (Yds.)	Johnny Morris, 1958-1967	5,059
Interceptions	Gary Fencik, 1976-1987	38
Punting (Avg.)	George Gulyanics, 1947-1952	44.5
Punt Return (Avg.)	Ray (Scooter) McLean, 1940-47	14.8
Kickoff Return (Avg.)	Gale Sayers, 1965-1971	*30.6
Field Goals	Kevin Butler, 1985-1995	243
Touchdowns (Tot.)	Walter Payton, 1975-1987	125
Points	Kevin Butler, 1985-1995	1,116

INDIVIDUAL RECORDS—SINGLE SEASON

Category	Name	Performance
Rushing (Yds.)	Walter Payton, 1977	1,852
Passing (Yds.)	Erik Kramer, 1995	3,838
Passing (TDs)	Erik Kramer, 1995	29
Receiving (No.)	Johnny Morris, 1964	93
Receiving (Yds.)	Marcus Robinson, 1999	1,400
Interceptions	Mark Carrier, 1990	10
Punting (Avg.)	Bobby Joe Green, 1963	46.5
Punt Return (Avg.)	Harry Clark, 1943	15.8
Kickoff Return (Avg.)	Gale Sayers, 1967	37.7
Field Goals	Kevin Butler, 1985	31
Touchdowns (Tot.)	Gale Sayers, 1965	22
Points	Kevin Butler, 1985	144

INDIVIDUAL RECORDS—SINGLE GAME

Category	Name	Performance
Rushing (Yds.)	Walter Payton, 11-20-77	*275
Passing (Yds.)	Johnny Lujack, 12-11-49	468
Passing (TDs)	Sid Luckman, 11-14-43	*7
Receiving (No.)	Jim Keane, 10-23-49	14
Receiving (Yds.)	Harlon Hill, 10-31-54	214
Interceptions	Many times	3
	Last time by Mark Carrier, 12-9-90	
Field Goals	Roger LeClerc, 12-3-61	5
	Mac Percival, 10-20-68	5
Touchdowns (Tot.)	Gale Sayers, 12-12-65	*6
Points	Gale Sayers, 12-12-65	36

*NFL Record

SOLDIER FIELD

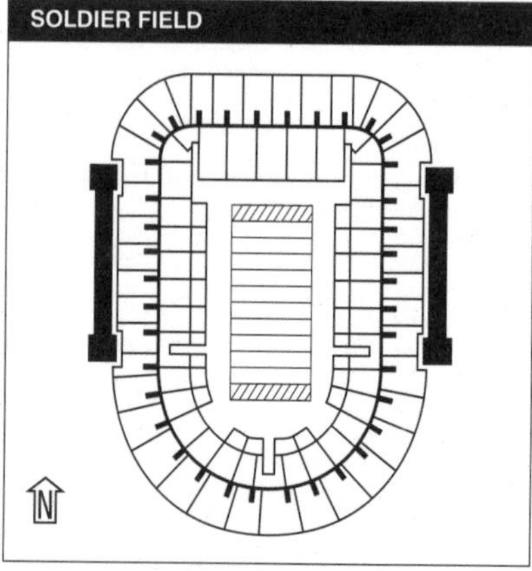

COACHING HISTORY

Decatur Staleys 1920, Chicago Staleys 1921 (626-442-42)

1920-29	George Halas	84-31-19
1930-32	Ralph Jones	24-10-7
1933-42	George Halas*	88-24-4
1942-45	Hunk Anderson-Luke Johnsos**	24-12-2
1946-55	George Halas	76-43-2
1956-57	John (Paddy) Driscoll	14-10-1
1958-67	George Halas	76-53-6
1968-71	Jim Dooley	20-36-0
1972-74	Abe Gibron	11-30-1
1975-77	Jack Pardee	20-23-0
1978-81	Neill Armstrong	30-35-0
1982-92	Mike Ditka	112-68-0
1993-98	Dave Wannstedt	41-57-0
1999	Dick Jauron	6-10-0

*Retired after five games to enter U.S. Navy
**Co-coaches

1999 TEAM RECORD

PRESEASON (2-2)

Date	Result		Opponent
8/7	W	9-6	Indianapolis
8/13	L	23-30	at Pittsburgh
8/21	W	38-24	St. Louis
8/28	L	24-35	at Cleveland

REGULAR SEASON (6-10)

Date	Result		Opponent	Att.
9/12	W	20-17	Kansas City	66,944
9/19	L	13-14	Seattle	66,944
9/26	L	17-24	at Oakland	50,458
10/3	W	14-10	New Orleans	66,944
10/10	W	24-22	at Minnesota	64,107
10/17	L	16-20	Philadelphia	66,944
10/24	L	3-6	at Tampa Bay	65,283
10/31	L	22-48	at Washington	77,621
11/7	W	14-13	at Green Bay	59,867
11/14	L	24-27	Minnesota (OT)	66,944
11/21	W	23-20	at San Diego (OT)	56,055
11/25	L	17-21	at Detroit	77,905
12/5	L	19-35	Green Bay	66,944
12/19	W	28-10	Detroit	66,944
12/26	L	12-34	at St. Louis	65,941
1/2	L	6-20	Tampa Bay	66,944

(OT) Overtime

SCORE BY PERIODS

Bears	52	69	84	64	3	—	272
Opponents	64	135	47	92	3	—	341

ATTENDANCE

Home 527,769 Away 525,495 Total 1,053,264
Single-game home record, 66,900 (9/5/93)
Single-season home record, 527,769 (1999)

1999 TEAM STATISTICS

	Bears	Opp.
Total First Downs	302	310
Rushing	82	89
Passing	203	196
Penalty	17	25
Third Down: Made/Att	91/247	93/229
Third Down Pct.	36.8	40.6
Fourth Down: Made/Att	11/27	2/11
Fourth Down Pct.	40.7	18.2
Total Net Yards	5,523	5,704
Avg. Per Game	345.2	356.5
Total Plays	1,118	1,058
Avg. Per Play	4.9	5.4
Net Yards Rushing	1,387	1,882
Avg. Per Game	86.7	117.6
Total Rushes	396	438
Net Yards Passing	4,136	3,822
Avg. Per Game	258.5	238.9
Sacked/Yards Lost	38/216	37/257
Gross Yards	4,352	4,079
Att./Completions	684/404	583/354
Completion Pct.	59.1	60.7
Had Intercepted	22	14
Punts/Average	85/40.9	80/38.9
Net Punting Avg.	85/35.4	80/32.1
Penalties/Yards	117/915	89/720
Fumbles/Ball Lost	32/15	29/19
Touchdowns	31	38
Rushing	4	11
Passing	25	23
Returns	2	4
Avg. Time of Possession	29:24	30:36

1999 INDIVIDUAL STATISTICS

Passing	Att.	Comp.	Yds.	Pct.	TD	Int.	Tkld.	Rate
Matthews	275	167	1,645	60.7	10	6	13/79	80.6
McNown	235	127	1,465	54.0	8	10	18/94	66.7
Miller	174	110	1,242	63.2	7	6	7/43	83.5
Bears	684	404	4,352	59.1	25	22	38/216	76.6
Opponents	583	354	4,079	60.7	23	14	37/257	85.0

SCORING	TD R	TD P	TD Rt	PAT	FG	Saf	PTS
M. Robinson	0	9	0	0/0	0/0	0	54
Boniol	0	0	0	17/18	11/18	0	50
Enis	3	2	0	0/0	0/0	0	30
Conway	0	4	0	0/0	0/0	0	24
Engram	0	4	0	0/0	0/0	0	24
Booker	0	3	0	0/0	0/0	0	18
Gowins	0	0	0	3/3	4/6	0	15
Jaeger	0	0	0	7/7	2/8	0	13
Allred	0	1	0	0/0	0/0	0	6
S. Harris	0	0	1	0/0	0/0	0	6
Holmes	0	0	0	0/0	2/2	0	6
Mayes	0	1	0	0/0	0/0	0	6
Milburn	1	0	0	0/0	0/0	0	6
Minter	0	0	1	0/0	0/0	0	6
Wetnight	0	1	0	0/0	0/0	0	6
McNown	0	0	0	0/0	0/0	0	2
Bears	4	25	2	27/28	19/34	0	272
Opponents	11	23	4	38/38	25/36	0	341

2-Pt. Conversions: McNown.
Team 1-3, Opponents 0-0.

RUSHING	Att.	Yds.	Avg.	LG	TD
Enis	287	916	3.2	19	3
McNown	32	160	5.0	18	0
Allen	32	119	3.7	13	0
Milburn	16	102	6.4	49t	1
Matthews	14	31	2.2	14	0
Bennett	6	28	4.7	15	0
Engram	2	11	5.5	9	0
Miller	3	9	3.0	9	0
Booker	1	8	8.0	8	0
Brooks	1	7	7.0	7	0
Conway	1	-2	-2.0	-2	0
Sauerbrun	1	-2	-2.0	-2	0
Bears	396	1,387	3.5	49t	4
Opponents	438	1,882	4.3	76t	11

RECEIVING	No.	Yds.	Avg.	LG	TD
Engram	88	947	10.8	56	4
M. Robinson	84	1,400	16.7	80t	9
Enis	45	340	7.6	28	2
Conway	44	426	9.7	30t	4
Wetnight	38	277	7.3	22	1
Milburn	20	151	7.6	22	0
Booker	19	219	11.5	57t	3
Brooks	14	160	11.4	30	0
Bennett	14	116	8.3	34	0
Allred	13	102	7.8	26	1
Allen	9	91	10.1	17	0
Mayes	8	82	10.3	24	1
Hallock	6	22	3.7	7	0
Bates	2	19	9.5	11	0
Bears	404	4,352	10.8	80t	25
Opponents	354	4,079	11.5	86t	23

INTERCEPTIONS	No.	Yds.	Avg.	LG	TD
Hudson	3	28	9.3	28	0
Minter	2	66	33.0	34t	1
Cousin	2	1	0.5	1	0
Parrish	1	41	41.0	41	0
Burton	1	37	37.0	37	0
Carter	1	36	36.0	36	0
Burns	1	15	15.0	15	0
Flanigan	1	6	6.0	6	0
S. Harris	1	0	0.0	0	0
W. Harris	1	-1	-1.0	-1	0
Bears	14	229	16.4	41	1
Opponents	22	359	16.3	88t	2

PUNTING	No.	Yds.	Avg.	In 20	LG
Sauerbrun	85	3,478	40.9	20	65
Bears	85	3,478	40.9	20	65
Opponents	80	3,115	38.9	20	66

PUNT RETURNS	No.	FC	Yds.	Avg.	LG	TD
Milburn	30	19	346	11.5	54	0
Bears	30	19	346	11.5	54	0
Opponents	36	15	266	7.4	35	0

KICKOFF RETURNS	No.	Yds.	Avg.	LG	TD
Milburn	61	1,426	23.4	93	0
Bennett	3	53	17.7	20	0
Hallock	2	10	5.0	7	0
Wiegmann	1	2	2.0	2	0
Tuinei	1	0	0.0	0	0
Bears	68	1,491	21.9	93	0
Opponents	57	948	16.6	56	0

FIELD GOALS	1-19	20-29	30-39	40-49	50+
Boniol	0/0	6/6	2/6	3/5	0/1
Jaeger	0/0	0/0	0/2	1/5	1/1
Gowins	0/0	3/3	0/0	1/2	0/1
Holmes	0/0	0/0	2/2	0/0	0/0
Bears	0/0	9/9	4/10	5/12	1/3
Opponents	0/0	12/14	8/11	3/6	2/5

SACKS	No.
Simmons	7.0
Flanigan	6.0
B. Robinson	5.0
Burton	3.0
Minter	3.0
Tuinei	2.5
Colvin	2.0
Davis	2.0
Holdman	2.0
W. Harris	1.0
Hudson	1.0
Smith	1.0
Wells	1.0
McDonald	0.5
Bears	37.0
Opponents	38.0

2000 DRAFT CHOICES

Round	Name	Pos.	College
1	Brian Urlacher	LB	New Mexico
2	Mike Brown	DB	Nebraska
3	Dez White	WR	Georgia Tech
	Dustin Lyman	TE	Wake Forest
4	Reggie Austin	DB	Wake Forest
6	Frank Murphy	RB	Kansas State
	Paul Edinger	K	Michigan State
7	James Cotton	DE	Ohio State
	Mike Green	DB	Northwestern State, La.

CHICAGO BEARS

2000 VETERAN ROSTER

No.		Name	Pos.	Ht.	Wt.	Birthdate	NFL Exp.	College	Hometown	How Acq.	'99 Games/ Starts
20		Allen, James	RB	5-10	215	3/28/75	3	Oklahoma	Wynnewood, Okla.	FA-'97	12/3
84		Allred, John	TE	6-4	249	9/9/74	4	Southern California	Del Mar, Calif.	D2-'97	16/5
70		Anderson, Ken	DT	6-3	310	10/4/75	3	Arkansas	Captain Shreveport, La.	FA-'98	2/0
36		Austin, Ray	S	5-11	204	12/21/74	4	Tennessee	Lawton, Okla.	W(NYJ)-'98	15/0
23		Azumah, Jerry	CB	5-10	195	9/1/77	2	New Hampshire	Worcester, Mass.	D5c-'99	16/2
12	t-	Bartholomew, Brent	P	6-2	220	10/22/76	2	Ohio State	Apopka, Fla.	T(Mia)-'00	2/0*
87		Bates, D'Wayne	WR	6-2	215	12/4/75	2	Northwestern	Aiken, S.C.	D3b-'99	7/1
86		Booker, Marty	WR	5-11	215	7/31/76	2	Northeast Louisiana	Jonesboro-Hodge, La.	D3c-'99	9/4
78		Brockermeyer, Blake	T	6-4	312	4/11/73	6	Texas	Arlington Heights, Tex.	UFA(Car)-'99	15/15
83		Brooks, Macey	WR	6-5	215	2/2/75	4	James Madison	Hampton, Va.	W(Dall)-'98	9/2
52		Burns, Keith	LB	6-2	245	5/16/72	7	Oklahoma State	Alexandria, Va.	UFA(Den)-'99	15/0
59		Colvin, Rosevelt	LB	6-3	260	9/5/77	2	Purdue	Indianapolis, Ind.	D4b-'99	11/0
21		Cousin, Terry	CB	5-9	182	4/11/75	4	South Carolina	Miami Beach, Fla.	FA-'97	16/9
93		Daniels, Phillip	DE	6-5	284	3/4/73	5	Georgia	Donalsonville, Ga.	UFA(Sea)-'00	16/16*
95		Davis, Russell	DE	6-4	295	3/28/75	2	North Carolina	Fayetteville, N.C.	D2-'99	11/8
81		Engram, Bobby	WR	5-10	192	1/7/73	5	Penn State	Camden, S.C.	D2-'96	16/14
44		Enis, Curtis	RB	6-1	240	6/15/76	3	Penn State	Union City, Ohio	D1-'98	15/12
99		Flanigan, Jim	DT	6-2	288	8/27/71	7	Notre Dame	Green Bay, Wis.	D3-'94	16/16
94		Hallock, Ty	RB	6-2	254	4/30/71	7	Michigan State	Greenville, Mich.	UFA(Jax)-'98	15/4
55		Harris, Sean	LB	6-3	252	2/25/72	6	Arizona	Magnet, Ariz.	D3a-'95	14/10
27		Harris, Walt	CB	5-11	195	8/10/74	5	Mississippi State	LaGrange, Ga.	D1-'96	15/15
74		Herndon, Jimmy	T	6-8	318	8/30/73	5	Houston	Baytown, Tex.	T(Jax)-'97	0*
68		Hills, Keno	G-T	6-6	305	6/13/73	5	Southwestern Louisiana	Tampa, Fla.	W(NO)-'99	0*
53		Holdman, Warrick	LB	6-1	238	11/22/75	2	Texas A&M	Alief, Tex.	D4a-'99	16/5
10		Holmes, Jaret	K	6-0	203	3/3/76	2	Auburn	Clinton, Miss.	W(Buff)-'99	3/0
26		Jones, Jermaine	CB	5-8	183	7/25/76	2	Northwestern State, La.	Morgan City, La.	W(NYJ)-'99	1/0
82	t-	Kennison, Eddie	WR	6-0	195	1/20/73	5	Louisiana State	Lake Charles, La.	T(NO)-'00	16/16
57		Kreutz, Olin	C	6-2	295	6/9/77	3	Washington	Honolulu, Hawaii	D3-'98	16/16
46		Levitt, Chad	RB	6-1	242	11/21/75	3	Cornell	Melrose Park, Pa.	W(StL)-'00	0*
65		Mannelly, Patrick	T-LS	6-5	285	4/18/75	3	Duke	Atlanta, Ga.	D6b-'98	16/0
9	#	Matthews, Shane	QB	6-3	196	6/1/70	7	Florida	Pascagoula, Miss.	UFA(Car)-'99	8/7
85		Mayes, Alonzo	TE	6-4	268	6/4/75	3	Oklahoma State	Oklahoma City, Okla.	D4-'98	16/9
8		McNown, Cade	QB	6-1	213	1/12/77	2	UCLA	West Linn, Ore.	D1-'99	15/6
24		Milburn, Glyn	RB-KR	5-8	174	2/19/71	8	Stanford	Santa Monica, Calif.	T(GB)-'98	16/1
15		Miller, Jim	QB	6-2	218	2/9/71	6	Michigan State	Waterford, Mich.	W(Det)-'98	5/3
76		Mims, Chris	DE	6-5	300	9/29/70	9	Tennessee	Los Angeles, Calif.	UFA(SD)-'00	9/0*
92		Minter, Barry	LB	6-2	245	1/28/70	8	Tulsa	Mt Pleasant, Tex.	T(Dall)-'93	16/16
73	†	Palmer, Dan	T	6-4	290	8/24/73	2	Air Force	Anderson, S.C.	FA-'98	0*
37		Parrish, Tony	S	5-10	206	11/23/75	3	Washington	Huntington Beach, Calif.	D2-'98	16/16
75		Perry, Todd	G	6-5	308	11/28/70	8	Kentucky	Elizabethtown, Ky.	D4a-'93	16/16
98		Robinson, Bryan	DE	6-4	295	6/22/74	4	Fresno State	Toledo, Ohio	W(StL)-'98	16/16
88		Robinson, Marcus	WR	6-3	215	2/27/75	4	South Carolina	Ft. Valley, Ga.	D4b-'97	16/11
91		Samuel, Khari	LB	6-3	242	10/14/76	2	Massachusetts	Framingham, Mass.	D5b-'99	13/1
96		Simmons, Clyde	DE	6-5	292	8/4/64	15	Western Carolina	Wilmington, N.C.	UFA(Cin)-'99	16/0
29		Smith, Frankie	S	5-9	182	10/8/68	8	Baylor	Groesbeck, Tex.	W(SF)-'98	15/0
25		Smith, Thomas	CB	5-11	190	12/5/70	8	North Carolina	Gates, N.C.	UFA(Buff)-'00	16/16*
33		Taylor, Cordell	CB	6-0	190	12/22/73	2	Hampton	Norfolk, Va.	W(Sea)-'99	0*
64		Tucker, Rex	G-T	6-5	300	12/20/76	2	Texas A&M	Midland, Tex.	D3a-'99	2/1
90		Tuinei, Van	DE	6-4	275	2/16/71	4	Arizona	Westminster, Calif.	W(Ind)-'99	16/8
58		Villarrial, Chris	G	6-4	310	6/9/73	5	Indiana, Pa.	Hershey, Pa.	D5-'96	15/15
67		Ward, Chris	DE	6-4	275	2/4/74	2	Kentucky	Decatur, Ga.	W(Tenn)-'00	0*
97		Wells, Mike	DT	6-3	315	1/6/71	7	Iowa	Arnold, Mo.	UFA(Det)-'98	16/16
89		Wetnight, Ryan	TE	6-2	236	11/5/70	8	Stanford	Fresno, Calif.	FA-'93	16/4
60		Wiegmann, Casey	C	6-3	295	7/20/75	5	Iowa	Parkersburg, Iowa	W(NYJ)-'97	16/0
71		Williams, James	T	6-7	340	3/29/68	10	Cheyney State, Pa.	Allerdice, Pa.	FA-'91	16/16
35		Williams, John	CB	5-7	180	7/26/74	2	Southern	Hammond, La.	W(Balt)-'00	0*
79		Wisne, Jerry	T	6-6	308	7/28/76	2	Notre Dame	Tulsa, Okla.	D5a-'99	7/1
22		Wooden, Shawn	S	5-11	205	10/23/73	5	Notre Dame	Abington, Pa.	UFA(Mia)-'00	15/6*

* Bartholomew played 2 games with Miami in '99; Daniels played 16 games with Seattle; Herndon missed '99 season because of injury; Hills and Taylor were inactive for 1 game; Levitt last active with Oakland in '97; Mims played 9 games with San Diego; Palmer was inactive for 16 games; T. Smith played 16 games with Buffalo; Ward last active with Baltimore in '97; Jo. Williams last active with Baltimore in '98; Wooden played 15 games with Miami.

† Restricted free agent; subject to developments.

Unrestricted free agent; subject to developments.

t- Bears traded for Bartholomew (Miami) and Kennison (New Orleans).

Players lost through free agency (3): DT Shane Burton (NYJ; 15 games in '99), WR Curtis Conway (SD; 9), P Todd Sauerbrun (KC; 16).

Also played with Bears in '99—RB Edgar Bennett (16 games), K Chris Boniol (10), CB Tom Carter (12), K Brian Gowins (2), S Chris Hudson (16), K Jeff Jaeger (3), LB Ricardo McDonald (16).

COACHING STAFF

Head Coach,
Dick Jauron

Pro Career: Named eleventh head coach in franchise history on January 24, 1999. Led Bears to six victories in rookie season and became only the third coach in franchise history to open tenure with a win (George Halas and Neill Armstrong are the others). Also became only the second Bears rookie head coach to collect wins at both Minnesota and Green Bay (Jim Dooley). As Jacksonville's inaugural defensive coordinator, he was instrumental in the success of the Jaguars, which included three playoff berths in the franchise's first four seasons and an appearance in the 1996 AFC Championship Game. Jauron coached defensive backs for nine years in Green Bay (1986-1994) before moving to Jacksonville. His coaching career started in Buffalo in 1985. Jauron played eight years as a defensive back in the NFL with the Detroit Lions and Cincinnati Bengals, earning a trip to the 1975 Pro Bowl. Career record: 6-10.
Background: Played running back at Yale from 1970-72 where he still holds the school's career rushing mark with 2,947 yards. Drafted by the Detroit Lions in the fourth round of the 1973 draft. Played defensive back for Detroit from 1973-77 and was named to the Pro Bowl after the 1974 season. Joined Cincinnati in 1978 and played with the Bengals until retiring in 1980. Spent several years away from NFL before joining the Buffalo Bills' coaching staff in 1985. Moved to Green Bay the following season and served as the defensive backs coach under three different head coaches (Forrest Greg, 1986-87; Lindy Infante, 1988-91; Mike Holmgren, 1992-94). Jauron accepted the defensive coordinator post with the expansion Jacksonville Jaguars in 1995 and helped lead the team to three consecutive playoff berths after their opening season.
Personal: Born October 7, 1950, Peoria, Ill. Dick and his wife Gail live in Lake Forest, Ill. and have two daughters—Kacy and Amy.

ASSISTANT COACHES

Keith Armstrong, special teams; born December 15, 1963, Trenton, N.J., lives in Round Lake Beach, Ill. Running back–defensive back Temple 1983-86. No pro playing experience. College coach: Temple 1986, Miami 1987-88, Akron 1989, Oklahoma State 1990-92, Notre Dame 1993. Pro coach: Atlanta Falcons 1994-96, joined Bears in 1997.
Vance Bedford, defensive backs; born August 20, 1958, Houston, Tex. Defensive back Texas 1977-79, 1981. Pro defensive back St. Louis Cardinals 1982, Oklahoma Outlaws (USFL) 1984. College coach: Navarro (Tex.) J.C. 1986, Colorado State 1987-1992, Oklahoma State 1993-94, Michigan 1995-98. Pro coach: Joined Bears in 1999.
Greg Blache, defensive coordinator; born March 9, 1949, New Orleans, lives in Lake Bluff, Ill. Attended Notre Dame. No college or pro playing experience. College coach: Notre Dame 1973-75, 1981-83, Tulane 1976-1980, Southern 1986, Kansas 1987. Pro coach: Jacksonville Bulls (USFL) 1984-85, Green Bay Packers 1988-1993, Indianapolis Colts 1994-98, joined Bears in 1999.
Jim Bollman, tight ends; born December 1, 1954, Ashtabula, Ohio, lives in Lake Bluff, Ill. Offensive lineman Ohio 1973-76. No pro playing experience. College coach: Miami (Ohio) 1977-1982, North Carolina State 1983-85, Youngstown State 1986-1990, Virginia 1991-94, Michigan State 1995-97. Pro coach: Philadelphia Eagles 1998, joined Bears in 1999.
Mike Borich, wide receivers; born December 8, 1966, South Jordan, Utah, lives in Grayslake, Ill. Wide receiver Snow J.C. 1986-87, Western Illinois 1988-89. No pro playing experience. College coach: New Hampshire 1989-1991, Northeastern 1992-94, Louisiana Tech 1995-98. Pro coach: Joined Bears in 1999.
Gary Crowton, offensive coordinator; born June 14, 1957, Provo, Utah, lives in Gurnee, Ill. Quarterback Snow J.C. 1975-77, Colorado State 1978. No pro playing experience. College coach: Brigham Young 1982, Snow J.C. 1983-86, Western Illinois 1987, New Hampshire 1988-1990, Boston College 1991-93, Georgia Tech 1994, Louisiana Tech 1995-98 (head coach 1996-98). Pro coach: Joined Bears in 1999.
Dale Lindsey, linebackers; born January 18, 1943, Bedford, Ind., lives in Lake Bluff, Ill. Linebacker Western Kentucky 1961-64. Pro linebacker Cleveland Browns 1965-1973. College coach: Southern Methodist 1988-89. Pro coach: Green Bay Packers 1986-87, New England Patriots 1990, Tampa Bay Buccaneers 1991, San Diego Chargers 1994-96, Washington Redskins 1997-98, joined Bears in 1999.
Earle Mosley, running backs; born December 20, 1946, Darby, Pa., lives in Buffalo Grove, Ill. Defensive back West Chester State 1970-72. No pro playing experience. College coach: West Chester State 1979, Rutgers 1980-83, Northwestern 1984-87, Temple 1988-1991, Notre Dame 1992-96, Stanford 1997-98. Pro coach: Joined Bears in 1999.
Rex Norris, defensive line; born December 10, 1939, Tipton, Ind., lives in Libertyville, Ill. Linebacker San Angelo (Tex.) J.C. 1959-1960, East Texas State 1961-62. No pro playing experience. College coach: Navarro (Tex.) J.C. 1970-71, Texas A&M 1972, Oklahoma 1973-1983, Arizona State 1984, Florida 1988-89, Tennessee 1990-91, Texas 1992-93. Pro coach: Detroit Lions 1985-87, Denver Broncos 1994, Tennessee Oilers 1995-98, joined Bears in 1999.
John Shoop, quarterbacks; born August 1, 1969, Pittsburgh, lives in Libertyville, Ill. Quarterback University of the South 1987-1990. No pro playing experience. College coach: Dartmouth 1991, Vanderbilt 1992-94. Pro coach: Carolina Panthers 1995-98, joined Bears in 1999.
Bob Wylie, offensive line; born February 16, 1951, West Warwick, R.I., lives in Lake Bluff, Ill. Linebacker Colorado 1969-1971. No pro playing experience. College coach: Brown 1980-82, Holy Cross 1983-84, Ohio 1985-87, Colorado State 1988-89, Cincinnati 1996. Pro coach: New York Jets 1990-91, Tampa Bay Buccaneers 1992-95, Cincinnati Bengals 1997-98, joined Bears in 1999.

2000 FIRST-YEAR ROSTER

Name	Pos.	Ht.	Wt.	Birthdate	College	Hometown	How Acq.
Austin, Reggie	CB	5-9	172	1/21/77	Wake Forest	Atlanta, Ga.	D4
Banks, Shawn (1)	LB	6-1	235	10/14/72	Texas Tech	Dallas, Tex.	FA
Barnes, Marlon (1)	RB	5-9	211	3/13/76	Colorado	Memphis, Tenn.	FA
Bridges, Corey (1)	WR	5-6	164	6/30/74	South Carolina	Newnan, Ga.	FA
Brown, Mike	S	5-10	202	2/13/78	Nebraska	Scottsdale, Ariz.	D2
Caldwell, Donnie (1)	S	5-11	185	10/26/77	Western Illinois	Lawton, Okla.	FA
Cantelupe, Jim (1)	S	6-1	195	3/12/74	West Point	Garfield Heights, Ohio	FA-'98
Cotton, James	DE	6-4	251	11/7/76	Ohio State	Cleveland, Ohio	D7a
Dolezel, Clint (1)	QB	6-4	205	3/25/70	East Texas State	Lorena, Tex.	FA
Donaldson, Cedric (1)	CB	5-9	180	2/12/76	Louisiana State	Jackson, Miss.	FA
Dragos, Scott (1)	RB	6-2	255	10/28/75	Boston College	Old Rochester, Mass.	FA-'99
Edinger, Paul	K	5-10	169	1/17/78	Michigan State	Lakeland, Fla.	D6b
Green, Mike	S	6-1	176	12/6/76	Northwestern State, La.	Ruston, La.	D7b
Hartsell, Mark (1)	QB	6-4	225	12/7/73	Boston College	Brockton, Mass.	FA
Jackson, Marlion	RB	6-1	242	10/11/77	Saginaw Valley State	Detroit, Mich.	FA
Langley, Aron (1)	P	6-1	185	5/31/76	Wyoming	Longwood, Col.	FA
Lyman, Dustin	TE	6-4	254	8/5/76	Wake Forest	Boulder, Col.	D3b
Mackey, Chad (1)	WR	6-2	200	3/21/74	Louisiana Tech	Spring Hill, Tex.	FA-'99
McMillon, Todd (1)	CB	5-10	183	9/9/73	Northern Arizona	Bellflower, Calif.	FA
Merritt, Ahmad	WR	5-10	188	2/5/77	Wisconsin	Chicago, Ill.	FA
Murphy, Frank	RB	6-1	206	2/11/77	Kansas State	Callahan, Fla.	D6a
Nivens, Damon	T	6-5	301	6/19/75	Southern	Bay Minette, Ala.	FA
Okeke, Uzooma (1)	G	6-2	310	9/3/70	Southern Methodist	Beaumont, Tex.	FA
Overhauser, Chad (1)	T	6-4	316	6/17/75	UCLA	Sacramento, Calif.	D7a-'98
Sanford, Sulecio (1)	WR	5-10	190	3/23/76	Middle Tennessee State	Milledgeville, Ga.	D7a-'99
Shepherd, Gannon	T	6-8	304	1/4/77	Duke	Atlanta, Ga.	FA
Urlacher, Brian	LB	6-3	249	5/25/78	New Mexico	Lovington, N.M.	D1
White, Dez	WR	6-1	219	8/23/79	Georgia Tech	Orange Park, Fla.	D3a
Williams, Brad	G	6-4	286	3/13/78	Notre Dame	Orange, Calif.	FA

The term NFL Rookie is defined as a player who is in his first season of professional football and has not been on the roster of another professional football team for any regular-season or postseason games. A Rookie is designated by an "R" on NFL rosters. Players who have been active in another professional football league or players who have NFL experience, including either preseason training camp or being on an Active List or Inactive List, or on Reserve/Injured or Reserve/Physically Unable to Perform for fewer than six regular-season games, are termed NFL First-Year Players. An NFL First-Year Player is designated by a "1" on NFL rosters. Thereafter, a player is credited with an additional year of experience for each season in which he accumulates six games on the Active List or Inactive List, or on Reserve/Injured or Reserve/Physically Unable to Perform.

NOTES

DALLAS COWBOYS

National Football Conference
Eastern Division
Team Colors: Royal Blue, Metallic Silver Blue, and White
Cowboys Center
One Cowboys Parkway
Irving, Texas 75063
Telephone: (972) 556-9900

CLUB OFFICIALS

Owner/President/General Manager: Jerry Jones
Executive Vice President-Player Personnel: Stephen Jones
Vice President/Marketing: George Hays
Vice President/Director of Charities and Special Events: Charlotte Anderson
Vice President/Legal/Director of Internet: Jerry Jones, Jr.
Public Relations Director: Rich Dalrymple
Assistant Director of Public Relations: Brett Daniels
Director of College and Pro Scouting: Larry Lacewell
Director of Operations: Bruce Mays
Director of Human Resources: Vincent Thompson
Treasurer: Robert Nunez
Ticket Manager: Carol Padgett
Trainer: Jim Maurer
Equipment Manager: Mike McCord
Video Director: Robert Blackwell
Cheerleader Director: Kelli Finglass
Stadium: Texas Stadium • **Capacity:** 65,675 Irving, Texas 75062
Playing Surface: Sportfield Turf
Training Camp: Midwestern State University Wichita Falls, Texas 76308

2000 SCHEDULE

PRESEASON

July 30	**Pittsburgh**	7:00
Aug. 5	vs. Atlanta at Tokyo, Japan	10:00
Aug. 13	**Oakland**	6:00
Aug. 19	at Denver	7:00
Aug. 24	**St. Louis**	7:35

REGULAR SEASON

Sept. 3	**Philadelphia**	3:05
Sept. 10	at Arizona	5:35
Sept. 18	at Washington (Mon.)	9:00
Sept. 24	**San Francisco**	12:00
Oct. 1	at Carolina	1:00
Oct. 8	Open Date	
Oct. 15	at New York Giants	1:00
Oct. 22	**Arizona**	12:00
Oct. 29	**Jacksonville**	3:15
Nov. 5	at Philadelphia	1:00
Nov. 12	**Cincinnati**	12:00
Nov. 19	at Baltimore	4:15
Nov. 23	**Minnesota** (Thu.)	3:05
Dec. 3	at Tampa Bay	1:00
Dec. 10	**Washington**	3:15
Dec. 17	**New York Giants**	7:35
Dec. 25	at Tennessee (Mon.)	8:00

RECORD HOLDERS

INDIVIDUAL RECORDS—CAREER

Category	Name	Performance
Rushing (Yds.)	Emmitt Smith, 1990-99	13,963
Passing (Yds.)	Troy Aikman, 1989-1999	31,310
Passing (TDs)	Troy Aikman, 1989-1999	158
Receiving (No.)	Michael Irvin, 1988-1999	750
Receiving (Yds.)	Michael Irvin, 1988-1999	11,904
Interceptions	Mel Renfro, 1964-1977	52
Punting (Avg.)	Mike Saxon, 1985-1992	41.5
Punt Return (Avg.)	Deion Sanders, 1995-99	13.3
Kickoff Return (Avg.)	Mel Renfro, 1964-1977	26.4
Field Goals	Rafael Septien, 1978-1986	162
Touchdowns (Tot.)	Emmitt Smith, 1990-99	147
Points	Emmitt Smith, 1990-99	884

INDIVIDUAL RECORDS—SINGLE SEASON

Category	Name	Performance
Rushing (Yds.)	Emmitt Smith, 1995	1,773
Passing (Yds.)	Danny White, 1983	3,980
Passing (TDs)	Danny White, 1983	29
Receiving (No.)	Michael Irvin, 1995	111
Receiving (Yds.)	Michael Irvin, 1995	1,603
Interceptions	Everson Walls, 1981	11
Punting (Avg.)	Sam Baker, 1962	45.4
Punt Return (Avg.)	Bob Hayes, 1968	20.8
Kickoff Return (Avg.)	Mel Renfro, 1965	30.0
Field Goals	Richie Cunningham, 1997	34
Touchdowns (Tot.)	Emmitt Smith, 1995	*25
Points	Emmitt Smith, 1995	150

INDIVIDUAL RECORDS—SINGLE GAME

Category	Name	Performance
Rushing (Yds.)	Emmitt Smith, 10-31-93	237
Passing (Yds.)	Don Meredith, 11-10-63	460
Passing (TDs)	Many times.	5
	Last time by Danny White, 10-30-83	
Receiving (No.)	Lance Rentzel, 11-19-67	13
Receiving (Yds.)	Bob Hayes, 11-13-66	246
Interceptions	Herb Adderley, 9-26-71	3
	Lee Roy Jordan, 11-4-73	3
	Dennis Thurman, 12-13-81	3
Field Goals	Chris Boniol, 11-18-96	*7
Touchdowns (Tot.)	Many times.	4
	Last time by Emmitt Smith, 9-4-95	
Points	Many times.	24
	Last time by Emmitt Smith, 9-4-95	

*NFL Record

COACHING HISTORY

(384-257-6)

1960-88	Tom Landry	270-178-6
1989-93	Jimmy Johnson	51-37-0
1994-97	Barry Switzer	45-26-0
1998-99	Chan Gailey	18-16-0

TEXAS STADIUM

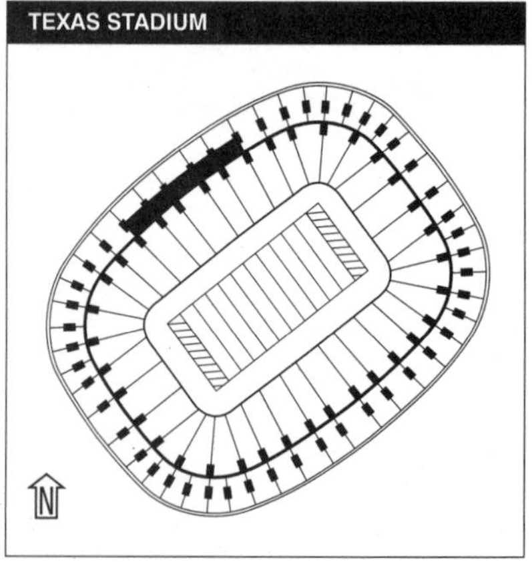

1999 TEAM RECORD

PRESEASON (1-4)

Date	Result		Opponent
8/9	L	17-20	vs. Cleveland at Canton, Ohio
8/15	L	3-10	at Oakland
8/21	L	14-34	at New England
8/29	W	22-12	Denver
9/2	L	6-27	Jacksonville

REGULAR SEASON (8-8)

Date	Result		Opponent	Att.
9/12	W	41-35	at Washington (OT)	79,237
9/20	W	24-7	Atlanta	63,663
10/3	W	35-7	Arizona	64,169
10/10	L	10-13	at Philadelphia	66,669
10/18	L	10-13	at New York Giants	78,204
10/24	W	38-20	Washington	64,377
10/31	L	24-34	at Indianapolis	56,860
11/8	L	17-27	at Minnesota	64,111
11/14	W	27-13	Green Bay	64,634
11/21	L	9-13	at Arizona	72,015
11/25	W	20-0	Miami	64,328
12/5	L	6-13	at New England	58,444
12/12	W	20-10	Philadelphia	64,086
12/19	L	21-22	New York Jets	64,271
12/24	L	24-31	at New Orleans	47,835
1/2	W	26-18	New York Giants	63,767

(OT) Overtime

SCORE BY PERIODS

Cowboys	87	92	80	87	6	—	352
Opponents	28	56	76	116	0	—	276

ATTENDANCE

Home 500,251 Away 517,963 Total 1,018,214
Single-game home record, 65,180 (11/12/95)
Single-season home record, 518,167 (1995)

1999 TEAM STATISTICS

	Cowboys	Opp.
Total First Downs	295	266
Rushing	129	81
Passing	139	154
Penalty	27	31
Third Down: Made/Att	77/219	71/221
Third Down Pct.	35.2	32.1
Fourth Down: Made/Att	6/17	4/9
Fourth Down Pct.	35.3	44.4
Total Net Yards	5,178	4,840
Avg. Per Game	323.6	302.5
Total Plays	1,024	997
Avg. Per Play	5.1	4.9
Net Yards Rushing	2,051	1,442
Avg. Per Game	128.2	90.1
Total Rushes	493	417
Net Yards Passing	3,127	3,398
Avg. Per Game	195.4	212.4
Sacked/Yards Lost	24/151	35/217
Gross Yards	3,278	3,615
Att./Completions	507/295	545/297
Completion Pct.	58.2	54.5
Had Intercepted	13	24
Punts/Average	81/43.2	93/41.2
Net Punting Avg.	81/35.1	93/34.2
Penalties/Yards	136/1,196	107/862
Fumbles/Ball Lost	22/10	23/9
Touchdowns	42	28
Rushing	16	6
Passing	20	19
Returns	6	3
Avg. Time of Possession	31:51	28:09

1999 INDIVIDUAL STATISTICS

Passing	Att.	Comp.	Yds.	Pct.	TD	Int.	Tkld.	Rate
Aikman	442	263	2,964	59.5	17	12	19/130	81.1
Garrett	64	32	314	50.0	3	1	5/21	73.3
Sanders	1	0	0	0.0	0	0	0/0	39.6
Cowboys	507	295	3,278	58.2	20	13	24/151	80.0
Opponents	545	297	3,615	54.5	19	24	35/217	68.4

SCORING	TD R	TD P	TD Rt	PAT	FG	Saf	PTS
E. Smith	11	2	0	0/0	0/0	0	78
Cunningham	0	0	0	31/31	12/22	0	67
Ismail	1	6	0	0/0	0/0	0	42
LaFleur	0	7	0	0/0	0/0	0	42
Murray	0	0	0	10/10	7/9	0	31
Irvin	0	3	0	0/0	0/0	0	18
Ellis	0	0	2	0/0	0/0	0	12
Teague	0	0	2	0/0	0/0	0	12
Tucker	0	2	0	0/0	0/0	0	12
Warren	2	0	0	0/0	0/0	0	12
Aikman	1	0	0	0/0	0/0	0	6
Bjornson	1	0	0	0/0	0/0	0	6
Coakley	0	0	1	0/0	0/0	0	6
Sanders	0	0	1	0/0	0/0	0	6
Hambrick	0	0	0	0/0	0/0	1	2
Cowboys	16	20	6	41/41	19/31	1	352
Opponents	6	19	3	24/24	26/33	0	276

2-Pt. Conversions: None.
Team 0-0, Opponents 3-4.

RUSHING	Att.	Yds.	Avg.	LG	TD
E. Smith	329	1,397	4.2	63t	11
Warren	99	403	4.1	25	2
Ismail	13	110	8.5	27t	1
Chancey	14	57	4.1	11	0
Thomas	8	35	4.4	10	0
Bjornson	1	20	20.0	20t	1
Garrett	6	12	2.0	9	0
Aikman	21	10	0.5	7	1
Tucker	1	8	8.0	8	0
Mills	1	-1	-1.0	-1	0
Cowboys	493	2,051	4.2	63t	16
Opponents	417	1,442	3.5	37	6

RECEIVING	No.	Yds.	Avg.	LG	TD
Ismail	80	1,097	13.7	76t	6
LaFleur	35	322	9.2	25	7
Warren	34	224	6.6	24	0
Mills	30	325	10.8	36	0
E. Smith	27	119	4.4	14t	2
Tucker	23	439	19.1	90t	2
Ogden	12	144	12.0	25	0
Irvin	10	167	16.7	37t	3
Bjornson	10	131	13.1	32	0
Thomas	10	64	6.4	13	0
McGarity	7	70	10.0	18	0
Brazzell	5	114	22.8	53	0
Lucky	5	25	5.0	8	0
Sanders	4	24	6.0	9	0
Lester	2	9	4.5	6	0
Johnston	1	4	4.0	4	0
Cowboys	295	3,278	11.1	90t	20
Opponents	297	3,615	12.2	71	19

INTERCEPTIONS	No.	Yds.	Avg.	LG	TD
Coakley	4	119	29.8	46t	1
Teague	3	127	42.3	95t	2
Reese	3	28	9.3	24	0
Sanders	3	2	0.7	2	0
Hawthorne	3	-2	-0.7	0	0
Hambrick	2	44	22.0	25	0
Woodson	2	5	2.5	5	0
Ellis	1	87	87.0	87t	1
K. Smith	1	16	16.0	16	0
Godfrey	1	10	10.0	10	0
Nguyen	1	6	6.0	6	0
Cowboys	24	442	18.4	95t	4
Opponents	13	100	7.7	30	0

PUNTING	No.	Yds.	Avg.	In 20	LG
Gowin	81	3,500	43.2	24	64
Cowboys	81	3,500	43.2	24	64
Opponents	93	3,836	41.2	17	59

PUNT RETURNS	No.	FC	Yds.	Avg.	LG	TD
Sanders	30	1	344	11.5	76	1
Ogden	4	2	28	7.0	10	0
Tucker	4	2	52	13.0	41	0
McGarity	3	4	16	5.3	9	0
Cowboys	41	9	440	10.7	76	1
Opponents	43	14	459	10.7	85t	1

KICKOFF RETURNS	No.	Yds.	Avg.	LG	TD
Tucker	22	613	27.9	79	0
Mathis	18	408	22.7	37	0
Ogden	12	252	21.0	29	0
Sanders	4	87	21.8	31	0
Noble	1	9	9.0	9	0
Coakley	1	3	3.0	3	0
Warren	0	0	—	—	0
Cowboys	58	1,372	23.7	79	0
Opponents	62	1,259	20.3	33	0

FIELD GOALS	1-19	20-29	30-39	40-49	50+
Cunningham	0/0	4/6	5/6	3/9	0/1
Murray	0/0	3/3	3/4	1/2	0/0
Cowboys	0/0	7/9	8/10	4/11	0/1
Opponents	0/0	8/8	11/11	7/13	0/1

SACKS	No.
Ellis	7.5
Hennings	5.0
Spellman	5.0
Noble	3.0
Pittman	3.0
Ekuban	2.5
Hambrick	2.5
Lett	1.5
Coakley	1.0
Godfrey	1.0
Nguyen	1.0
Woodson	1.0
Zellner	1.0
Cowboys	35.0
Opponents	24.0

2000 DRAFT CHOICES

Round	Name	Pos.	College
2	Dwayne Goodrich	DB	Tennessee
4	Kareem Larrimore	DB	West Texas A&M
5	Michael Wiley	WR	Ohio State
6	Mario Edwards	DB	Florida State
7	Orantes Grant	LB	Georgia

DALLAS COWBOYS

2000 VETERAN ROSTER

No.		Name	Pos.	Ht.	Wt.	Birthdate	NFL Exp.	College	Hometown	How Acq.	'99 Games/ Starts
76		Adams, Flozell	T	6-7	335	5/18/75	3	Michigan State	Bellwood, Ill.	D2-'98	16/16
8		Aikman, Troy	QB	6-4	220	11/21/66	12	UCLA	Henryetta, Okla.	D1-'89	14/14
29		Akins, Chris	S	5-11	195	11/29/76	2	Arkansas-Pine Bluff	Little Rock, Ark.	FA-'99	9/0
73		Allen, Larry	G	6-3	326	11/27/71	7	Sonoma State	Napa, Calif.	D2-'94	11/11
55	t-	Bordano, Chris	LB	6-1	241	12/30/74	3	Southern Methodist	San Antonio, Tex.	T(NO)-'00	15/12*
58		Bowden, Joe	LB	5-11	235	2/25/70	9	Oklahoma	Mesquite, Tex.	UFA(Tenn)-'00	15/15*
18		Brazzell, Chris	WR	6-2	193	5/22/76	2	Angelo State	Alice, Tex.	FA-'99	5/0
52		Coakley, Dexter	LB	5-10	228	10/20/72	4	Appalachian State	Mt. Pleasant, S.C.	D3a-'97	16/16
64		Diaz, Jorge	G	6-4	315	11/15/73	5	Texas A&M-Kingsville	Katy, Tex.	FA-'00	13/11*
96		Ekuban, Ebenezer	DE	6-3	265	5/29/76	2	North Carolina	Riverdale, Md.	D1-'99	16/2
98		Ellis, Greg	DE	6-6	286	8/14/75	3	North Carolina	Wendell, N.C.	D1-'98	13/13
69		Fricke, Ben	G-C	6-1	295	11/3/75	2	Houston	Austin, Tex.	FA-'99	3/0
84	t-	Galloway, Joey	WR	5-11	188	11/20/71	6	Ohio State	Bellaire, Ohio	T(Sea)-'00	8/4*
54		Hambrick, Darren	LB	6-2	227	8/30/75	3	South Carolina	Pasco, Fla.	D5a-'98	16/12
85		Harris, Jackie	TE	6-4	250	1/4/68	11	Northeast Louisiana	Pine Bluff, Ark.	UFA(Tenn)-'00	12/1*
38		Hawthorne, Duane	CB	5-10	175	8/26/76	2	Northern Illinois	St. Louis, Mo.	FA-'99	13/0
70	#	Hellestrae, Dale	G-C	6-5	291	7/11/62	16	Southern Methodist	Scottsdale, Ariz.	T(Raid)-'90	16/0
95		Hennings, Chad	DT	6-6	291	10/20/65	9	Air Force	Elberon, Iowa	D11-'88	16/16
66		Hutson, Tony	G-T	6-3	317	3/13/74	4	Northeast Oklahoma State	Houston, Tex.	FA-'97	2/2
88	#	Irvin, Michael	WR	6-2	207	3/5/66	13	Miami	Fort Lauderdale, Fla.	D1-'88	4/4
81		Ismail, Raghib	WR	5-11	190	11/18/69	8	Notre Dame	Wilkes Barre, Pa.	UFA(Car)-'99	16/14
48		Johnston, Daryl	RB	6-2	242	2/10/66	12	Syracuse	Youngstown, N.Y.	D2-'89	1/0
7		Justin, Paul	QB	6-4	211	5/19/68	6	Arizona State	Schaumburg, Ill.	UFA(StL)-'00	10/0*
89		LaFleur, David	TE	6-7	272	1/29/74	4	Louisiana State	Westlake, La.	D1-'97	16/16
78		Lett, Leon	DT	6-6	290	10/12/68	9	Emporia State	Fairhope, Ala.	D7-'91	8/1
86		Lucky, Mike	TE	6-6	273	11/23/75	2	Arizona	Antioch, Calif.	D7a-'99	14/4
83		McGarity, Wane	WR	5-8	197	9/30/76	2	Texas	San Antonio, Tex.	D4a-'99	5/1
82		McKnight, James	WR	6-1	198	6/17/72	7	Liberty	Apopka, Fla.	T(Sea)-'99	0*
47		McNeil, Ryan	CB	6-2	192	10/4/70	8	Miami	Westwood, Fla.	UFA(Cle)-'00	16/14*
94		Myers, Michael	DT-DE	6-2	288	1/20/76	3	Alabama	Vicksburg, Miss.	D4-'98	6/0
39		Neufeld, Ryan	RB	6-4	240	11/22/75	2	UCLA	Morgan Hill, Calif.	FA-'99	6/0
59		Nguyen, Dat	LB	5-11	231	9/25/75	2	Texas A&M	Rockport, Tex.	D3-'99	16/0
75		Noble, Brandon	DT	6-2	285	4/10/74	2	Penn State	Virginia Beach, Va.	FA-'99	16/0
2		Ogden, Jeff	WR	6-1	190	2/22/75	3	Eastern Washington	Snohomish, Wash.	FA-'98	16/0
77		Page, Solomon	T	6-4	321	2/27/76	2	West Virginia	Pittsburgh, Pa.	D2-'99	14/6
43		Reese, Izell	S	6-2	190	5/7/74	3	Alabama-Birmingham	Dothan, Ala.	D6-'98	8/4
80		Roche, Brian	TE	6-5	260	5/5/73	4	San Jose State	LaVerne, Calif.	FA-'00	0*
56		Russ, Bernard	LB	6-1	238	11/4/73	3	West Virginia	Utica, N.Y.	FA-'00	6/0*
22		Smith, Emmitt	RB	5-9	209	5/15/69	11	Florida	Escambia, Fla.	D1-'90	15/15
26		Smith, Kevin	CB	5-11	190	4/7/70	9	Texas A&M	Orange, Tex.	D1a-'92	8/8
90		Spellman, Alonzo	DT-DE	6-4	292	9/27/71	8	Ohio State	Mount Holly, N.J.	FA-'99	16/16
53		Stepnoski, Mark	C	6-2	265	1/20/67	12	Pittsburgh	Erie, Pa.	UFA(Tenn)-'99	15/15
31		Teague, George	S	6-1	196	2/18/71	8	Alabama	Montgomery, Ala.	FA-'98	14/14
44		Thomas, Robert	RB	6-1	252	12/1/74	3	Henderson State	Jacksonville, Ark.	FA-'98	16/7
50		Tolbert, Brandon	LB	6-3	230	4/6/75	2	Georgia	Villa Rica, Ga.	FA-'98	0*
87		Tucker, Jason	WR	6-1	182	6/24/76	2	Texas Christian	Waco, Tex.	FA-'99	15/4
42		Warren, Chris	RB	6-2	227	1/24/68	11	Ferrum	Burke, Va.	FA-'98	16/1
25		Williams, Charlie	CB	6-1	204	2/2/72	6	Bowling Green	Detroit, Mich.	D3-'95	16/8
79		Williams, Erik	T	6-6	311	9/7/68	10	Central State, Ohio	Philadelphia, Pa.	D3c-'91	14/14
28		Woodson, Darren	S	6-1	219	4/25/69	9	Arizona State	Phoenix, Ariz.	D2b-'92	15/15
57		Wortham, Barron	LB	5-11	245	11/1/69	7	Texas-El Paso	Everman, Tex.	FA-'00	16/15*
93		Zellner, Peppi	DE	6-5	257	3/14/75	2	Fort Valley State	Forsythe, Ga.	D4b-'99	13/0

* Bordano played 15 games with New Orleans in '99; Bowden played 15 games with Tennessee; Diaz played 13 games with Tampa Bay; Galloway played 8 games with Seattle; Harris played 12 games with Tennessee; Justin played 10 games with St. Louis; McKnight and Tolbert missed '99 season because of injury; McNeil played 16 games with Cleveland; Roche last active with Kansas City in '98; Russ played 6 games with New England; Wortham played 16 games with Tennessee.

\# Unrestricted free agent; subject to developments.

t- Cowboys traded for Bordano (New Orleans) and Galloway (Seattle).

Traded—CB Kevin Mathis (8 games in '99) to New Orleans.

Players lost through free agency (8): TE Eric Bjornson (NE; 16 games in '99), RB Robert Chancey (SD, 3), QB Jason Garrett (NYG; 5), LB Randall Godfrey (Tenn; 16), P Toby Gowin (NO; 16), LB Lemanski Hall (Minn; 10), G Tom Myslinski (Pitt; 10), DE Kavika Pittman (Den; 16).

Also played with Cowboys in '99—LB Quentin Coryatt (4 games), K Richie Cunningham (12), DT Nathan Davis (4), CB Wendell Davis (6), WR Alvin Harper (2), LB Nate Hemsley (6), RB Tim Lester (5), G Everett McIver (14), WR Ernie Mills (11), S Singor Mobley (16), K Eddie Murray (4), CB Deion Sanders (14), S Kenny Wheaton (5), RB Sherman Williams (1).

COACHING STAFF

Head Coach,
Dave Campo

Pro Career: Dave Campo became the fifth head coach in Cowboys history on January 26, 2000, after eleven seasons as an assistant with the club. Campo has participated in three Super Bowls, four NFC Championship Games, and won six division titles. He joins four NFL head coaches who have been a part of three or more Super Bowl titles in their coaching careers. That group includes George Seifert (five times), Mike Shanahan (three), and Mike Holmgren (three). For the last five seasons (1995-99), Campo has directed the Dallas defense. Campo previously directed the Cowboys' secondary (1991-94) and was a defensive assistant (1989-1990).

Background: Campo was a defensive back at Central Connecticut State from 1967-1970 and twice earned All-East honors at shortstop. He began his coaching career at Central Connecticut State, coaching linebackers (1971-72). He then moved to Albany State (1973), Bridgeport (1974), Pittsburgh (1975), Washington State (1976), Boise State (1977-79), Oregon State (1980), Weber State (1981-82), Iowa State (1983), Syracuse (1984-86), and Miami (1987-88).

Personal: Born in New London, Conn., on July 18, 1947. Was a standout at Robert E. Fitch High School in Groton, Conn. Dave and his wife, Kay, have six children—Angie, Eric, Becky, Tommy, Shelbie, and Michael.

ASSISTANT COACHES

Joe Avezzano, special teams; born November 17, 1943, Yonkers, N.Y., lives in Coppell, Texas. Guard Florida State 1961-65. Pro center Boston Patriots 1966. College coach: Florida State 1968, Iowa State 1969-1972, Pittsburgh 1973-76, Tennessee 1977-79, Oregon State 1980-84 (head coach), Texas 1985-88. Pro coach: Joined Cowboys in 1990.

Bill Bates, secondary; born June 6, 1961, Knoxville, Tenn., lives in Plano, Texas. Defensive back Tennessee 1979-1982. Pro defensive back Dallas Cowboys 1983-1997. Pro coach: Joined Cowboys in 1998.

Wes Chandler, wide receivers; born August 22, 1956, New Smyrna Beach, Fla., lives in Grapevine, Tex. Wide receiver Florida 1974-77. Pro wide receiver New Orleans Saints 1978-1981, San Diego Chargers 1981-87, San Francisco 49ers 1988. College coach: Central Florida 1994-95. Pro coach: Orlando Thunder (NFL Europe) 1992, Rhein Fire (NFLE) 1995-97, Frankfurt Galaxy (NFLE) 1998, Berlin Thunder (NFLE) 1999 (head coach), joined Cowboys in 2000.

George Edwards, linebackers; born January 16, 1967, Siler City, N.C., lives in Coppell, Texas. Linebacker Duke 1986-89. No pro playing experience. College coach: Florida 1990-91, Appalachian State 1992-95, Duke 1996, Georgia 1997. Pro coach: Joined Cowboys in 1998.

Wayne (Buddy) Geis, quarterbacks; born September 16, 1946, Altoona, Pa., lives in Irving, Texas. Wide receiver Northern Arizona 1965. No pro playing experience. College coach: Arizona 1974-76, Tulane 1977-1982, Memphis State 1986-87, Duke 1993, Tulane 1994. Pro coach: Jacksonville Bulls (USFL) 1984-85, Green Bay Packers 1988-1991, Memphis Mad Dogs (CFL) 1995, Indianapolis Colts 1996-97, joined Cowboys in 1998.

Steve Hoffman, kickers-quality control; born September 8, 1958, Camden, N.J., lives in Irving, Texas. Quarterback-running back-wide receiver Dickinson College 1979-1982. Pro punter Washington Federals (USFL) 1983. College coach: Miami 1985-87. Pro coach: Joined Cowboys in 1989.

Hudson Houck, offensive line; born January 7, 1943, Los Angeles, lives in Irving, Texas. Center Southern California 1962-64. No pro playing experience. College coach: Southern California 1970-72, 1976-1982, Stanford 1973-75. Pro coach: Los Angeles Rams 1983-1991, Seattle Seahawks 1992, joined Cowboys in 1993.

Jim Jeffcoat, defensive ends; born April 1, 1961, Cliffwood, N.J., lives in Irving, Texas. Defensive end Arizona State 1979-1982. Pro defensive end Dallas Cowboys 1983-1994, Buffalo Bills 1995-97. Pro coach: Joined Cowboys in 1998.

Joe Juraszek, strength and conditioning; born June 8, 1958, Chicago, lives in Coppell, Texas. Linebacker-defensive end New Mexico 1976-1980. No pro playing experience. College coach: Oklahoma 1981-86, 1993-96, Texas Tech 1987-1992. Pro coach: Joined Cowboys in 1997.

Les Miles, tight ends; born November 10, 1953, Elyria, Ohio, lives in Irving, Texas. Guard Michigan 1972-75. No pro playing experience. College coach: Colorado 1982-86, Michigan 1987-1994, Oklahoma State 1995-97. Pro coach: Joined Cowboys in 1998.

Dwain Painter, wide receivers; born February 13, 1942, Monroeville, Pa., lives in Coppell, Texas. Quarterback-defensive back Rutgers 1961-64. No pro playing experience. College coach: San Jose State 1971-72, College of San Mateo 1973, BYU 1974-75, UCLA 1976-78, Northern Arizona 1979-1981 (head coach), Georgia Tech 1982-85, Texas. 1986, Illinois 1987. Pro coach: Pittsburgh Steelers 1988-1991, Indianapolis Colts 1992-93, San Diego Chargers 1994-96, Denver Broncos 1997, joined Cowboys in 1998.

Andre Patterson, defensive tackles; born June 12, 1960, Camden, Ark., lives in Grapevine, Tex. Offensive lineman Contra Costa J.C. (Calif.) 1978-1980, Montana 1981. No pro playing experience. College coach: Montana 1982, Weber State 1988, Western Washington 1989, Cornell 1990, Washington State 1992-93, Cal Poly-San Luis Obispo 1994-96 (head coach). Pro coach: New England Patriots 1997, Minnesota Vikings 1998-99, joined Cowboys in 2000.

Clancy Pendergast, Nickel package; born November 29, 1967, Phoenix, lives in Irving, Texas. No college or pro playing experience. College coach: Mississippi State 1991, Southern California 1992, Oklahoma 1993-94. Pro coach: Houston Oilers 1995, joined Cowboys in 1996.

Jack Reilly, offensive coordinator; born May 22, 1945, Boston, lives in Coppell, Tex.. Quarterback Washington State 1963, Santa Monica J.C. (Calif.) 1964, Long Beach State 1965-66. No pro playing experience. College coach: El Camino J.C. (Calif.) 1980-84 (head coach 1981-84), Utah 1985-89. Pro coach: San Diego Chargers 1990-93, Los Angeles Raiders 1994, St. Louis Rams 1995-96, Dallas Cowboys 1997, New England Patriots 1998-99, rejoined Cowboys in 2000.

Tommie Robinson, offensive assistant; born April 4, 1963, Phenix City, Ala., lives in Fort Worth, Texas. Defensive back Troy State 1981-84. No pro playing experience. College coach: Arkansas 1991, Utah State 1992-93, Texas Christian 1994-97. Pro coach: Joined Cowboys in 1998.

Clarence Shelmon, running backs; born September 17, 1952, Bossier City, La., lives in Coppell, Texas. Running back Houston 1971-75. No pro playing experience. College coach: Army 1978-1980, Indiana 1981-83, Arizona 1984-86, Southern California 1987-1990. Pro coach: Los Angeles Rams 1991, Seattle Seahawks 1992-97, joined Cowboys in 1998.

Wade Wilson, quarterbacks; born February 1, 1959, Commerce, Texas, lives in Irving, Tex.. Quarterback East Texas State 1977-1980. Pro quarterback Minnesota Vikings 1981-1991, Atlanta Falcons 1992, New Orleans Saints 1993-94, Dallas Cowboys 1995-97, Oakland Raiders 1998-99. Pro coach: Joined Cowboys in 2000.

Mike Zimmer, defensive coordinator; born June 5, 1956, Peoria, Ill., lives in Colleyville, Texas. Quarterback-linebacker Illinois State 1974-76. No pro playing experience. College coach: Missouri 1979-1980, Weber State 1981-88, Washington State 1989-1993. Pro coach: Joined Cowboys in 1994.

2000 FIRST-YEAR ROSTER

Name	Pos.	Ht.	Wt.	Birthdate	College	Hometown	How Acq.
Anderson, Morris (1)	WR	6-1	194	2/22/77	Baylor	Tyler, Tex.	FA
Atkins, Corey	LB	6-0	235	11/11/76	South Carolina	Greenville, Md.	FA
Black, Michael (1)	RB	5-11	206	5/3/74	Washington State	Los Angeles, Calif.	FA
Brymer, Chris (1)	C-G	6-3	300	11/29/74	Southern California	Apple Valley, Calif.	FA-'99
Cantrell, Barry (1)	P	6-1	195	11/2/76	Fordham	Ft. Lauderdale, Fla.	FA
Chukwuma, Chrys	RB	6-1	229	5/12/78	Arkansas	Montgomery, Ala.	FA
Cone, Drew	WR	6-2	213	2/27/77	Southern Arkansas	Van Buren, Ark.	FA
Edwards, Mario	CB	6-0	191	12/1/75	Florida State	Pascagoula, Miss.	D6
Fields, Aaron	DE	6-4	243	1/9/76	Troy State	Notasulga, Ala.	FA
Garmon, Kelvin (1)	G	6-2	329	10/26/76	Baylor	Haltom, Tex.	D7-'99
Gholston, Kendrick (1)	DE	6-4	279	4/30/75	Louisville	Chicago, Ill.	FA-'99
Goodrich, Dwayne	CB	5-11	198	5/29/78	Tennessee	Oak Lawn, Ill.	D2
Grant, Orantes	LB	6-0	225	3/18/78	Georgia	Atlanta, Ga.	D7
Gray, Jonathan	T	6-4	335	1/17/76	Texas Tech	Lubbock, Tex.	FA
Hilbert, Jon	K	6-2	222	7/15/75	Louisville	Boonville, Ind.	FA
Hodge, Damon	WR	6-1	192	2/16/77	Alabama State	Thomaston, Ala.	FA
Hudson, George	G	6-4	311	11/10/76	New Mexico State	Vineland, Ontario, Canada	FA
Huggins, Johnny	TE	6-3	245	3/29/76	Alabama State	Zachary, La.	FA
Jackson, Al	G	6-3	306	5/18/77	Louisiana State	Moss Point, Miss.	FA
Jackson, Keith	DT	6-4	319	4/16/75	Cheyney University	Philadelphia, Pa.	FA
Kaiser, Jason (1)	S	6-0	190	11/9/73	Culver-Stockton	Highlands Ranch, Colo.	FA-'99
Key, Sean	S	5-11	185	6/25/77	Florida State	Miami, Fla.	FA
Knorr, Micah	P	6-2	193	1/9/75	Utah State	Orange, Calif.	FA
Larrimore, Kareem	CB	5-11	190	4/21/76	West Texas A&M	Los Angeles, Calif.	D4
Lindell, Rian	K	6-3	241	1/20/77	Washington State	Vancouver, Wash.	FA
Mitchell, Deon (1)	WR	5-10	180	4/30/76	Northern Illinois	Ft. Wayne, Ind.	FA-'99
Morgan, Beau (1)	S	5-10	203	8/4/75	Air Force	Carrollton, Tex.	FA-'99
Ortiz, Tony	LB	6-0	225	7/3/77	Nebraska	Waterbury, Conn.	FA
Phipps, Joe (1)	LB	6-1	220	11/1/75	Texas Christian	Diboll, Tex.	FA-'99
Pitts, Otis	DT	6-1	301	4/27/76	Louisiana Tech	Bossier City, La.	FA
Puleri, Charles	QB	6-2	215	3/1/70	New Mexico State	Bronx, N.Y.	FA
Rogers, Phillip	RB	6-1	226	3/15/77	Georgia Tech	East Point, Ga.	FA
Seder, Tim	K	5-9	180	9/17/74	Ashland University	Ashland, Ohio	FA
Shaw, Bryant	DE	6-3	287	7/17/78	Mississippi College	Ocean Springs, Miss.	FA
Slaughter, Chad	T	6-7	320	6/4/78	Alcorn State	Dallas, Tex.	FA
Stoerner, Clint	QB	6-2	210	12/29/77	Arkansas	Baytown, Tex.	FA
Tenner, James	G	6-2	345	1/24/76	Alcorn State	Little Rock, Ark.	FA
Tramel, Jasmine	S	5-11	198	7/17/76	Mississippi Valley State	Tampa, Fla.	FA
Underwood, Dimitrius (1)	DE	6-6	276	3/29/77	Michigan State	Fayetteville, N.C.	FA
Wiley, Michael	WR	5-11	189	1/5/78	Ohio State	Spring Valley, Calif.	D5
Wilkins, Greg (1)	DE-DT	6-4	305	11/1/73	Langston	Chicago, Ill.	FA-'99

The term NFL Rookie is defined as a player who is in his first season of professional football and has not been on the roster of another professional football team for any regular-season or postseason games. A Rookie is designated by an "R" on NFL rosters. Players who have been active in another professional football league or players who have NFL experience, including either preseason training camp or being on an Active List or Inactive List, or on Reserve/Injured or Reserve/Physically Unable to Perform for fewer than six regular-season games, are termed NFL First-Year Players. An NFL First-Year Player is designated by a "1" on NFL rosters. Thereafter, a player is credited with an additional year of experience for each season in which he accumulates six games on the Active List or Inactive List, or on Reserve/Injured or Reserve/Physically Unable to Perform.

DETROIT LIONS

National Football Conference
Central Division
Team Colors: Honolulu Blue and Silver
Pontiac Silverdome
1200 Featherstone Road
Pontiac, Michigan 48342
Telephone: (248) 335-4131

CLUB OFFICIALS

Chairman and President: William Clay Ford
Vice Chairman: William Clay Ford, Jr.
Executive Vice President and Chief Operating Officer: Chuck Schmidt
Vice President of Marketing and Sales: Steve Harms
Vice President of Player Personnel: Ron Hughes
Vice President of Communications, Sales and Marketing: Bill Keenist
Vice President of Football Administration: Larry Lee
Vice President of Finance and Chief Financial Officer: Tom Lesnau
Vice President of Stadium Development and Salary Cap: Tom Lewand
Secretary: David Hempstead
Director of Pro Personnel: Sheldon White
Director of College Scouting: Scott McEwen
Scouts: Russ Bollinger, Hessley Hempstead, Chad Henry, Lance Newmark, Charlie Sanders
Director of Media Relations: Steve Reaven
Director of Ticket Operations: Mark Graham
Director of Ticket Sales and Customer Service: Jennifer Manzo
Director of Broadcasting Services: Bryan Bender
Director of Detroit Lions Charities and Community Affairs: Tim Pendell
Head Athletic Trainer: Jay Shoop
Equipment Manager: Dan Jaroshewich
Video Director: Steve Hermans
Stadium: Pontiac Silverdome • **Capacity:** 80,311
1200 Featherstone Road
Pontiac, Michigan 48342
Playing Surface: AstroTurf
Training Camp: Saginaw Valley State University
University Center, Michigan 48710

2000 SCHEDULE

PRESEASON

Aug. 4	**New England**	7:00
Aug. 12	**Buffalo**	8:35
Aug. 18	at Oakland	6:00
Sept. 25	at Cincinnati	7:30

REGULAR SEASON

Sept. 3	at New Orleans	12:00
Sept. 10	**Washington**	4:15
Sept. 17	**Tampa Bay**	1:00
Sept. 24	at Chicago	12:00
Oct. 1	**Minnesota**	1:00
Oct. 8	**Green Bay**	1:00
Oct. 15	Open Date	
Oct. 19	at Tampa Bay (Thu.)	8:35
Oct. 29	at Indianapolis	1:00
Nov. 5	**Miami**	1:00
Nov. 12	**Atlanta**	1:00
Nov. 19	at New York Giants	1:00
Nov. 23	**New England** (Thu.)	12:30
Nov. 30	at Minnesota (Thu.)	7:35
Dec. 10	at Green Bay	12:00
Dec. 17	at New York Jets	1:00
Dec. 24	**Chicago**	1:00

RECORD HOLDERS

INDIVIDUAL RECORDS—CAREER

Category	Name	Performance
Rushing (Yds.)	Barry Sanders, 1989-1998	15,269
Passing (Yds.)	Bobby Layne, 1950-58	15,710
Passing (TDs)	Bobby Layne, 1950-58	118
Receiving (No.)	Herman Moore, 1991-99	626
Receiving (Yds.)	Herman Moore, 1991-99	8,664
Interceptions	Dick LeBeau, 1959-1972	62
Punting (Avg.)	Yale Lary, 1952-53, 1956-1964	44.3
Punt Return (Avg.)	Jack Christiansen, 1951-58	12.8
Kickoff Return (Avg.)	Pat Studstill, 1961-67	25.7
Field Goals	Eddie Murray, 1980-1991	243
Touchdowns (Tot.)	Barry Sanders, 1989-1998	109
Points	Eddie Murray, 1980-1991	1,113

INDIVIDUAL RECORDS—SINGLE SEASON

Category	Name	Performance
Rushing (Yds.)	Barry Sanders, 1997	2,053
Passing (Yds.)	Scott Mitchell, 1995	4,338
Passing (TDs)	Scott Mitchell, 1995	32
Receiving (No.)	Herman Moore, 1995	*123
Receiving (Yds.)	Herman Moore, 1995	1,686
Interceptions	Don Doll, 1950	12
	Jack Christiansen, 1953	12
Punting (Avg.)	Yale Lary, 1963	48.9
Punt Return (Avg.)	Jack Christiansen, 1952	21.5
Kickoff Return (Avg.)	Tom Watkins, 1965	34.4
Field Goals	Jason Hanson, 1993	34
Touchdowns (Tot.)	Barry Sanders, 1991	17
Points	Jason Hanson, 1995	132

INDIVIDUAL RECORDS—SINGLE GAME

Category	Name	Performance
Rushing (Yds.)	Barry Sanders, 11-13-94	237
Passing (Yds.)	Scott Mitchell, 11-23-95	410
Passing (TDs)	Gary Danielson, 12-9-78	5
Receiving (No.)	Herman Moore, 12-4-95	14
Receiving (Yds.)	Cloyce Box, 12-3-50	302
Interceptions	Don Doll, 10-23-49	*4
Field Goals	Garo Yepremian, 11-13-66	6
	Jason Hanson, 10-17-99	6
Touchdowns (Tot.)	Dutch Clark, 10-22-34	4
	Cloyce Box, 12-3-50	4
	Barry Sanders, 11-24-91	4
Points	Dutch Clark, 10-22-34	24
	Cloyce Box, 12-3-50	24
	Barry Sanders, 11-24-91	24

*NFL Record

COACHING HISTORY

Portsmouth Spartans 1930-33
(455-475-32)

1930	Hal (Tubby) Griffen	5-6-3
1931-36	George (Potsy) Clark	49-20-6
1937-38	Earl (Dutch) Clark	14-8-0
1939	Elmer (Gus) Henderson	6-5-0
1940	George (Potsy) Clark	5-5-1
1941-42	Bill Edwards*	4-9-1
1942	John Karcis	0-8-0
1943-47	Charles (Gus) Dorais	20-31-2
1948-50	Alvin (Bo) McMillin	12-24-0
1951-56	Raymond (Buddy) Parker	50-24-2
1957-64	George Wilson	55-45-6
1965-66	Harry Gilmer	10-16-2
1967-72	Joe Schmidt	43-35-7
1973	Don McCafferty	6-7-1
1974-76	Rick Forzano**	15-17-0
1976-77	Tommy Hudspeth	11-13-0
1978-84	Monte Clark	43-63-1
1985-88	Darryl Rogers***	18-40-0
1988-96	Wayne Fontes	67-71-0
1997-99	Bobby Ross	22-28-0

* Released after three games in 1942
** Resigned after four games in 1976
*** Released after 11 games in 1988

PONTIAC SILVERDOME

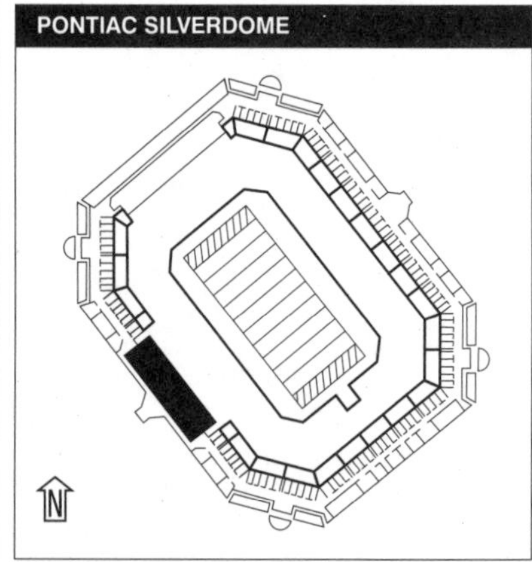

1999 TEAM RECORD

PRESEASON (1-3)

Date	Result		Opponent
8/13	L	31-35	at Atlanta
8/20	W	16-0	Cincinnati
8/28	L	10-31	at Miami
9/2	L	6-17	St. Louis

REGULAR SEASON (8-8)

Date	Result		Opponent	Att.
9/12	W	28-20	at Seattle	66,238
9/19	W	23-15	Green Bay	76,202
9/26	L	21-31	at Kansas City	78,384
10/10	L	10-20	San Diego	61,481
10/17	W	25-23	Minnesota	76,516
10/24	W	24-9	at Carolina	64,322
10/31	W	20-3	Tampa Bay	63,135
11/7	W	31-27	St. Louis	73,224
11/14	L	19-23	at Arizona	49,600
11/21	L	17-26	at Green Bay	59,869
11/25	W	21-17	Chicago	77,905
12/5	W	33-17	Washington	77,693
12/12	L	16-23	at Tampa Bay	65,536
12/19	L	10-28	at Chicago	66,944
12/25	L	7-17	Denver	73,158
1/2	L	17-24	at Minnesota	64,103

POSTSEASON (0-1)

Date	Result		Opponent	Att.
1/8	L	13-27	at Washington	79,411

SCORE BY PERIODS

Lions	61	132	47	82	0	— 322
Opponents	28	116	81	98	0	— 323

ATTENDANCE

Home 579,673 Away 518,106 Total 1,097,779
Single-game home record, 80,441 (12/20/81)
Single-season home record, 622,593 (1980)

1999 TEAM STATISTICS

	Lions	Opp.
Total First Downs	269	305
Rushing	67	87
Passing	179	185
Penalty	23	33
Third Down: Made/Att	81/222	84/213
Third Down Pct.	36.5	39.4
Fourth Down: Made/Att	6/17	4/13
Fourth Down Pct.	35.3	30.8
Total Net Yards	4,931	5,291
Avg. Per Game	308.2	330.7
Total Plays	978	1,017
Avg. Per Play	5.0	5.2
Net Yards Rushing	1,245	1,531
Avg. Per Game	77.8	95.7
Total Rushes	356	393
Net Yards Passing	3,686	3,760
Avg. Per Game	230.4	235.0
Sacked/Yards Lost	64/388	50/340
Gross Yards	4,074	4,100
Att./Completions	558/326	574/359
Completion Pct.	58.4	62.5
Had Intercepted	14	16
Punts/Average	86/42.3	82/42.0
Net Punting Avg.	86/34.8	82/35.8
Penalties/Yards	110/995	105/839
Fumbles/Ball Lost	21/8	32/16
Touchdowns	35	36
Rushing	8	12
Passing	22	21
Returns	5	3
Avg. Time of Possession	29:15	30:45

1999 INDIVIDUAL STATISTICS

Passing	Att.	Comp.	Yds.	Pct.	TD	Int.	Tkld.	Rate
Frerotte	288	175	2,117	60.8	9	7	28/202	83.6
Batch	270	151	1,957	55.9	13	7	36/186	84.1
Lions	558	326	4,074	58.4	22	14	64/388	83.9
Opponents	574	359	4,100	62.5	21	16	50/340	84.5

SCORING	TD R	TD P	TD Rt	PAT	FG	Saf	PTS
Hanson	0	0	0	28/29	26/32	0	106
Crowell	0	7	0	0/0	0/0	0	44
Morton	0	5	0	0/0	0/0	0	30
Irvin	4	0	0	0/0	0/0	0	24
Sloan	0	4	0	0/0	0/0	0	24
Batch	2	0	0	0/0	0/0	0	12
Fair	0	0	2	0/0	0/0	0	12
Hill	2	0	0	0/0	0/0	0	12
Moore	0	2	0	0/0	0/0	0	12
Stablein	0	1	0	0/0	0/0	0	8
Aldridge	0	0	1	0/0	0/0	0	6
Elliss	0	0	1	0/0	0/0	0	6
Howard	0	0	1	0/0	0/0	0	6
Rasby	0	1	0	0/0	0/0	0	6
Rivers	0	1	0	0/0	0/0	0	6
Schlesinger	0	1	0	0/0	0/0	0	6
Lions	8	22	5	28/29	26/32	1	322
Opponents	12	21	3	31/31	22/29	3	323

2-Pt. Conversions: Crowell, Stablein.
Team 2-6, Opponents 2-5.

RUSHING	Att.	Yds.	Avg.	LG	TD
Hill	144	542	3.8	45	2
Rivers	82	295	3.6	37	0
Irvin	36	133	3.7	51	4
Schlesinger	43	124	2.9	16	0
Batch	28	87	3.1	12t	2
Crowell	5	38	7.6	20	0
Frerotte	15	33	2.2	8	0
Olivo	1	1	1.0	1	0
Jett	2	-8	-4.0	0	0
Lions	356	1,245	3.5	51	8
Opponents	393	1,531	3.9	58t	12

RECEIVING	No.	Yds.	Avg.	LG	TD
Crowell	81	1,338	16.5	77t	7
Morton	80	1,129	14.1	48	5
Sloan	47	591	12.6	74t	4
Irvin	25	233	9.3	31	0
Rivers	22	173	7.9	31t	1
Schlesinger	21	151	7.2	25	1
Moore	16	197	12.3	26	2
Hill	13	77	5.9	15	0
Stablein	11	119	10.8	42	1
Olivo	4	24	6.0	12	0
Rasby	3	19	6.3	13	1
Chryplewicz	2	18	9.0	13	0
Uwaezuoke	1	5	5.0	5	0
Lions	326	4,074	12.5	77t	22
Opponents	359	4,100	11.4	75t	21

INTERCEPTIONS	No.	Yds.	Avg.	LG	TD
Rice	5	82	16.4	33	0
Fair	3	49	16.3	41t	1
Carrier	3	16	5.3	16	0
Bailey	2	39	19.5	31	0
Kowalkowski	1	29	29.0	29	0
Boyd	1	18	18.0	18	0
Kriewaldt	1	2	2.0	2	0
Lions	16	235	14.7	41t	1
Opponents	14	174	12.4	40t	1

PUNTING	No.	Yds.	Avg.	In 20	LG
Jett	86	3,637	42.3	27	62
Lions	86	3,637	42.3	27	62
Opponents	82	3,442	42.0	20	57

PUNT RETURNS	No.	FC	Yds.	Avg.	LG	TD
Uwaezuoke	18	9	150	8.3	20	0
Fair	11	4	97	8.8	36	0
Howard	6	3	115	19.2	68t	1
Irvin	2	0	15	7.5	15	0
Stablein	1	0	9	9.0	9	0
Lions	38	16	386	10.2	68t	1
Opponents	42	21	402	9.6	24	0

KICKOFF RETURNS	No.	Yds.	Avg.	LG	TD
Fair	34	752	22.1	91	0
Howard	15	298	19.9	35	0
Olivo	11	198	18.0	25	0
Talton	6	121	20.2	38	0
Irvin	3	21	7.0	21	0
Schlesinger	2	33	16.5	20	0
Morton	1	22	22.0	22	0
Lions	72	1,445	20.1	91	0
Opponents	60	1,242	20.7	95t	1

FIELD GOALS	1-19	20-29	30-39	40-49	50+
Hanson	0/0	8/8	4/4	10/12	4/8
Lions	0/0	8/8	4/4	10/12	4/8
Opponents	0/0	7/7	8/11	6/7	1/4

SACKS	No.
Porcher	15.0
Scroggins	8.5
Jones	7.0
Elliss	3.5
Aldridge	3.0
Bailey	2.0
Kirschke	2.0
Claiborne	1.5
Pringley	1.5
Kowalkowski	1.0
Owens	1.0
Pritchett	1.0
Rice	1.0
Stewart	1.0
Lions	50.0
Opponents	64.0

2000 DRAFT CHOICES

Round	Name	Pos.	College
1	Stockar McDougle	T	Oklahoma
2	Barrett Green	LB	West Virginia
3	Reuben Droughns	RB	Oregon
5	Todd Franz	DB	Tulsa
6	Quinton Reese	DE	Auburn
7	Alfonso Boone	DT	Mt. San Antonio J.C.

DETROIT LIONS

2000 VETERAN ROSTER

No.	Name	Pos.	Ht.	Wt.	Birthdate	NFL Exp.	College	Hometown	How Acq.	'99 Games/ Starts
24	Abrams, Kevin	CB	5-8	170	2/28/74	4	Syracuse	Tampa, Fla.	D2b-'97	1/0
55	Aldridge, Allen	LB	6-1	254	5/30/72	7	Houston	Missouri City, Tex.	UFA(Den)-'98	16/14
10	Batch, Charlie	QB	6-2	220	12/5/74	3	Eastern Michigan	Homestead, Pa.	D2b-'98	11/10
79	Beverly, Eric	C	6-3	294	3/28/74	3	Miami, Ohio	Bedford Heights, Ohio	FA-'97	16/2
65	Blaise, Kerlin	G	6-5	323	12/25/74	3	Miami	Orlando, Fla.	FA-'98	16/4
57	Boyd, Stephen	LB	6-0	242	8/22/72	6	Boston College	Valley Stream, N.Y.	D5a-'95	14/14
76	Brooks, Barrett	T	6-4	326	5/5/72	6	Kansas State	St. Louis, Mo.	UFA(Phil)-'99	16/12
44	Brown, Corwin	S	6-1	205	4/25/70	8	Michigan	Chicago, Ill.	FA-'99	13/1
39	Campbell, Lamar	CB	5-11	183	8/29/76	3	Wisconsin	Chester, Pa.	FA-'98	15/2
81	Chryplewicz, Pete	TE	6-5	261	4/27/74	4	Notre Dame	Sterling Heights, Mich.	D5a-'97	11/1
50	Claiborne, Chris	LB	6-3	255	7/26/78	2	Southern California	Riverside, Calif.	D1a-'99	15/13
77	Compton, Mike	C	6-6	298	9/18/70	8	West Virginia	Richland, Va.	D3b-'93	15/15
82	Crowell, Germane	WR	6-3	216	9/13/76	3	Virginia	Winston Salem, N.C.	D2a-'98	16/15
95	DeVries, Jared	DE	6-4	280	6/11/76	2	Iowa	Aplington, Iowa	D3-'99	2/0
94	Elliss, Luther	DT	6-5	305	3/22/73	6	Utah	Mancos, Colo.	D1-'95	15/14
23	Fair, Terry	CB	5-9	184	7/20/76	3	Tennessee	Phoenix, Ariz.	D1-'98	11/11
51	Fields, Scott	LB	6-2	220	4/22/73	2	Southern California	Ontario, Calif.	FA-'99	0*
71	Gibson, Aaron	T	6-4	380	9/27/77	2	Wisconsin	Indianapolis, Ind.	D1b-'99	0*
4	Hanson, Jason	K	5-11	182	6/17/70	9	Washington State	Spokane, Wash.	D2b-'92	16/0
64	Hartings, Jeff	G	6-3	295	9/7/72	5	Penn State	St. Henry, Ohio	D1b-'96	16/16
80	Howard, Desmond	WR	5-10	185	5/15/70	9	Michigan	Cleveland, Ohio	FA-'99	5/0
33	Irvin, Sedrick	RB	5-11	226	3/30/78	2	Michigan State	Miami, Fla.	D4-'99	14/0
19	Jett, John	P	6-0	197	11/11/68	8	East Carolina	Reedville, Va.	UFA(Dall)-'97	16/0
49	Johnson, Tony	TE	6-5	255	2/5/72	5	Alabama	Sardis, Miss.	FA-'00	0*
98	Jones, James	DT	6-2	295	2/6/69	10	Northern Iowa	Davenport, Iowa	UFA(Balt)-'99	16/16
99	Jordan, Richard	LB	6-1	256	12/1/74	4	Missouri Southern	Vian, Okla.	D7c-'97	9/0
67	Kirschke, Travis	DE	6-3	287	9/6/74	4	UCLA	Yorba Linda, Calif.	FA-'97	15/7
52	Kowalkowski, Scott	LB	6-2	220	8/23/68	10	Notre Dame	Orchard Lake, Mich.	FA-'94	16/3
58	Kriewaldt, Clint	LB	6-1	236	3/17/76	2	Wisconsin-Stevens Point	Shiocton, Wisc.	D6-'99	12/0
84	Moore, Herman	WR	6-4	224	10/20/69	10	Virginia	Danville, Va.	D1-'91	8/4
87	Morton, Johnnie	WR	6-0	190	10/7/71	7	Southern California	Torrance, Calif.	D1-'94	16/12
26	Olivo, Brock	RB	6-0	232	6/24/76	3	Missouri	Washington, Mo.	FA-'98	14/0
59	O'Neill, Kevin	LB	6-2	249	4/14/75	3	Bowling Green	Twinsburg, Ohio	FA-'98	4/0
91	Porcher, Robert	DE	6-3	282	7/30/69	9	South Carolina State	Wando, S.C.	D1-'92	15/14
92	Pringley, Mike	DE	6-4	277	5/22/76	2	North Carolina	Linden, N.J.	D7-'99	9/0
93	Pritchett, Kelvin	DT	6-3	319	10/24/69	10	Mississippi	Atlanta, Ga.	UFA(Jax)-'99	16/2
75	Ramirez, Tony	T	6-6	305	1/26/73	4	Northern Colorado	Lincoln, Neb.	D6-'97	12/3
89	Rasby, Walter	TE	6-3	251	9/7/72	7	Wake Forest	Washington, N.C.	UFA(Car)-'98	16/6
28	Rice, Ron	S	6-1	217	11/9/72	6	Eastern Michigan	Detroit, Mich.	FA-'95	16/16
72	Roberts, Ray	T	6-6	320	6/3/69	9	Virginia	Asheville, N.C.	UFA(Sea)-'96	14/14
74	Roque, Juan	T	6-8	332	2/6/74	4	Arizona State	Ontario, Calif.	D2a-'97	4/2
53	Russell, Matt	LB	6-2	256	7/5/73	4	Colorado	Belleville, Ill.	D4-'97	0*
16	Sauter, Cory	QB	6-4	215	11/21/74	2	Minnesota	Hutchinson, Minn.	FA-'99	0*
30	Schlesinger, Cory	RB	6-0	246	6/23/72	6	Nebraska	Duncan, Neb.	D6b-'95	16/11
45	Schulz, Kurt	S	6-1	208	12/12/68	9	Eastern Washington	Yakima, Wash.	UFA(Buff)-'00	16/16*
97	Scroggins, Tracy	DE	6-3	273	9/11/69	9	Tulsa	Checotah, Okla.	D2a-'92	14/11
62	Semple, Tony	G	6-5	303	12/20/70	7	Memphis	Lincoln, Ill.	D5-'94	12/12
86	Sloan, David	TE	6-6	260	6/8/72	6	New Mexico	Tollhouse, Calif.	D3-'95	16/15
83	Stablein, Brian	WR	6-1	194	4/14/70	7	Ohio State	Erie, Pa.	FA-'98	16/2
11	Stenstrom, Steve	QB	6-2	202	12/23/71	6	Stanford	El Toro, Calif.	FA-'00	6/3*
34	Stewart, James	RB	6-1	226	12/27/71	6	Tennessee	Morristown, Tenn.	UFA(Jax)-'00	14/7*
42	Stewart, Ryan	S	6-1	206	9/30/73	5	Georgia Tech	Moncks Corner, S.C.	FA-'97	2/0
29	Supernaw, Kywin	S	6-1	207	6/2/75	2	Indiana	Claremore, Okla.	FA-'98	2/0
25	Talton, Ty	S	5-11	201	5/10/76	2	Northern Iowa	Beloit, Wisc.	FA-'99	12/0
96	Taylor, Henry	DT	6-2	303	11/29/75	2	South Carolina	Barnwell, S.C.	FA-'98	8
18	Tomczak, Mike	QB	6-1	210	10/23/62	16	Ohio State	Calumet City, Ill.	UFA(Pitt)-'00	16/5*
32	Westbrook, Bryant	CB	6-0	198	12/19/74	4	Texas	Oceanside, Calif.	D1-'97	10/8

* Fields last active with Atlanta in '96; Gibson, Johnson (with New Orleans), and Russell missed '99 season because of injury; Sauter was inactive for 15 games; Schulz played 16 games with Buffalo; Stenstrom played 6 games with San Francisco; Stewart played 14 games with Jacksonville; Tomczak played 16 games with Pittsburgh.

Players lost to free agency (3): CB Robert Bailey (Balt; 16 games in '99), S Mark Carrier (Wash; 15), QB Gus Frerotte (Den; 9).

Also played with the Lions in '99—CB J.B. Brown (13 games), LB Andre Collins (7), C Greg Engel (1), CB Dwayne Harper, RB Greg Hill (14), DT Dan Owens (8), RB Ron Rivers (7), TE Ed Smith (3), WR Iheanyi Uwaezuoke (10).

COACHING STAFF

Head Coach,
Bobby Ross

Pro Career: Named the Lions' head coach January 13, 1997. In his first season with the Lions, Ross guided the club to victories in five of its final six games to earn an NFC wild-card berth. Detroit's 1999 playoff appearance marked the second time in Ross's first three years as Lions' head coach that he has led the club to the postseason. Joined the Lions following five seasons as the head coach of the San Diego Chargers. Led the Chargers to a 50-36 record, three playoff appearances in five years, including two AFC Western Division titles, the club's first AFC championship, and an appearance in Super Bowl XXIX. Began coaching career with Chiefs' special teams and defense in 1978-79 and offensive backs in 1980-81. No pro playing experience. Career record: 72-64.

Background: Played quarterback and defensive back for Virginia Military Institute (1956-58). Began coaching career at VMI in 1965. Moved on as an assistant at William & Mary (1967-1970), Rice (1971), and Maryland (1972). Head coach at The Citadel (1973-77). Compiled 39-19-1 record at Maryland (1982-86) as he led the Terrapins to three Atlantic Coast Conference titles and made four bowl game appearances in five seasons. Guided Georgia Tech (1987-1991) to first ACC title in school history. Under Ross, the Yellow Jackets won first national championship as country's only undefeated team (11-0-1) in 1990. Named consensus national coach of the year in 1990. Career collegiate record: 94-76-2.

Personal: Born December 23, 1935, Richmond, Va. Bobby and wife, Alice, live in West Bloomfield, Mich. and have five children—Chris, Kevin, Robbie, Mary, and Teresa.

ASSISTANT COACHES

Brian Baker, defensive line; born June 20, 1962, Baltimore, lives in Rochester, Mich. Linebacker Maryland 1980-83. No pro playing experience. College coach: Maryland 1984-85, Army 1986, Georgia Tech 1987-1995. Pro coach: San Diego Chargers 1996, joined Lions in 1997.

Don Clemons, defensive assistant; born February 15, 1954, Newark, N.J., lives in Rochester, Mich. Defensive end Muhlenberg College 1973-76. No pro playing experience. College coach: Kutztown State 1977-78, New Mexico 1979, Arizona State 1980-84. Pro coach: Joined Lions in 1985.

Sylvester Croom, offensive coordinator; born September 25, 1954, Tuscaloosa, Ala., lives in Rochester, Mich. Center Alabama 1971-74. Pro center New Orleans Saints 1975. College coach: Alabama 1976-1986. Pro coach: Tampa Bay Buccaneers 1987-1990, Indianapolis Colts 1991, San Diego Chargers 1992-96, joined Lions in 1997.

Frank Falks, running backs; born March 9, 1943, Tampa, lives in Rochester Hills, Mich. Linebacker Joplin (Mo.) J.C. 1963-64, Parsons College 1965-66. No pro playing experience. College coach: Parsons College 1967-69, Kansas State 1970-72, Arkansas 1973-77, Wyoming 1978-79, San Diego State 1980, Oklahoma State 1981-82, Southern California 1983-86, Arizona State 1987-1991, Ohio State 1992-93. Pro coach: San Diego Chargers 1994-96, joined Lions in 1997.

Robert Graf, asst. strength and conditioning; born January 25, 1967, Wichita Falls, Tex., lives in Auburn Hills, Mich. No college or pro playing experience. College coach: Texas A&M 1990-91, 1993-98. Pro coach: Joined Lions in 1999.

Bert Hill, strength and conditioning-asst. offensive line; born January 25, 1958, Montgomery, Ala., lives in Rochester Hills, Mich. Linebacker Marion (Ala.) Military Institute 1976-77, Wichita State 1978. No pro playing experience. College coach: Nicholls State 1981-82, Auburn 1983, Texas A&M 1984-88, Ohio State 1989. Pro coach: Joined Lions in 1990.

Stan Kwan, offense and special teams assistant; born November 2, 1967, Phoenix, lives in Rochester Hills, Mich. No college or pro playing experience. Pro coach: San Diego Chargers 1991-96, joined Lions in 1997.

John Misciagna, quality control-offense & administrative assistant; born December 11, 1954, Brooklyn, N.Y., lives in Auburn Hills, Mich. Guard Dickinson College 1973-76. No pro playing experience. College coach: Indiana (Pa.) University 1977, Columbia 1978-79, Maryland 1980-88, Georgia Tech 1989-1991. Pro coach: San Diego Chargers 1992-96, joined Lions in 1997.

Gary Moeller, asst. head coach-linebackers; born January 26, 1941, Lima, Ohio, lives in Ann Arbor, Mich. Center-linebacker Ohio State 1960-62. No pro playing experience. College coach: Miami (Ohio) 1967-68, Michigan 1969-1976, 1980-1994 (head coach 1990-94), Illinois 1977-79 (head coach). Pro coach: Cincinnati Bengals 1995-96, joined Lions in 1997.

Dennis Murphy, quality control-defense; born October 22, 1940, Endicott, N.Y., lives in Rochester, Mich. Tight end-defensive lineman Notre Dame 1959-1961. No pro playing experience. College coach: Notre Dame 1968-1974, Colgate 1975, Holy Cross 1976-77, Eastern Michigan 1978-1981, Maryland 1982-1991, Navy 1992-93. Pro coach: San Diego Chargers 1994-96, joined Lions in 1997.

Larry Peccatiello, defensive coordinator; born December 21, 1937, Newark, N.J., lives in Rochester, Mich. Receiver William & Mary 1955-58. No pro playing experience. College coach: William & Mary 1961-68, Navy 1969-1970, Rice 1971. Pro coach: Houston Oilers 1972-75, Seattle Seahawks 1976-1980, Washington Redskins 1981-1993, Cincinnati Bengals 1994-96, joined Lions in 1997.

Chuck Priefer, special teams; born July 26, 1944, Cleveland, lives in Rochester Hills, Mich. No college or pro playing experience. College coach: Miami (Ohio) 1977, North Carolina 1978-1983, Kent State 1986, Georgia Tech 1987-1991. Pro coach: Green Bay Packers 1984-85, San Diego Chargers 1992-96, joined Lions in 1997.

Golden Pat Ruel, offensive line, born December 5, 1950, Washington, D.C., lives in Auburn Hills, Mich. Guard Miami 1971-72. No pro playing experience. College coach: Miami 1973-76, Arkansas 1977-78, Washington State 1979-1981, Texas A&M 1982-84, Northern Illinois 1985-87, Kansas 1988-1996, Michigan State 1998-99. Pro coach: Joined Lions in 1999.

Richard Selcer, defensive backs; born August 22, 1937, Cincinnati, lives in Rochester, Mich. Running back Notre Dame 1955-58. No pro playing experience. College coach: Xavier 1962-64, 1970-71 (head coach), Cincinnati 1965-66, Brown 1967-69, Wisconsin 1972-74, Kansas State 1975-77, Southwestern Louisiana 1978-1980. Pro coach: Houston Oilers 1981-83, Cincinnati Bengals 1984-1991, Los Angeles/St. Louis Rams 1992-96, joined Lions in 1997.

Danny Smith, tight ends; born November 7, 1953, Pittsburgh, lives in Rochester Hills, Mich. Defensive back Edinboro State 1972-75. No pro playing experience. College coach: Edinboro State 1976, Clemson 1979, William & Mary 1980-83, The Citadel 1984-86, Georgia Tech 1987-1994. Pro coach: Philadelphia Eagles 1995-98, joined Lions in 1999.

Jerry Sullivan, wide receivers; born July 13, 1944, Miami, lives in Rochester Hills, Mich. Quarterback Florida State 1963-64. No pro playing experience. College coach: Kansas State 1971-72, Texas Tech 1973-75, South Carolina 1976-1982, Indiana 1983, Louisiana State 1984-1990, Ohio State 1991. Pro coach: San Diego Chargers 1992-96, joined Lions in 1997.

Jim Zorn, quarterbacks; born May 10, 1953, Whittier, Calif., lives in Bloomfield Hills, Mich. Quarterback Cal Poly-Pomona 1973-75. Pro quarterback Seattle Seahawks 1976-1984, Green Bay Packers 1985, Winnipeg Blue Bombers (CFL) 1986, Tampa Bay Buccaneers 1987. College coach: Boise State 1989-1991, Utah State 1992-94, Minnesota 1995-96. Pro coach: Seattle Seahawks 1997, joined Lions in 1998.

2000 FIRST-YEAR ROSTER

Name	Pos.	Ht.	Wt.	Birthdate	College	Hometown	How Acq.
Alexander, Tim (1)	WR	6-0	186	10/14/74	Oregon State	Sarasota, Fla.	FA
Bayes, Andrew	P	6-2	200	2/11/78	East Carolina	Hyattsville, Md.	FA
Boone, Alfonso	DT	6-3	305	1/11/76	Mt. San Antonio	Saginaw, Mich.	D7
Brominski, Steve	TE	6-4	264	10/24/76	Syracuse	Wilkes-Barre, Pa.	FA
Cameron, Delaunta (1)	LB	6-2	235	7/2/75	Georgia Tech	Arlington, Va.	FA
Cummings, Chris (1)	CB	5-8	185	1/5/74	Louisiana State	Dothan, Ala.	FA-'99
Dixon, Andre (1)	CB	6-1	200	12/4/75	Northeastern	Philadelphia, Pa.	FA-'99
Douglas, Henry (1)	WR	5-11	171	3/3/77	North Carolina A&T	Southern Pines, N.C.	FA
Droughns, Reuben	RB	5-11	207	8/21/78	Oregon	Anaheim, Calif.	D3
Foster, Larry	WR	5-10	196	11/7/76	Louisiana State	Harvey, La.	FA
Franz, Todd	CB	6-0	194	4/12/76	Tulsa	Weatherford, Okla.	D5
Garces, Pete	K	5-10	190	12/30/77	Idaho State	San Diego, Calif.	FA
Green, Barrett	LB	6-0	217	10/29/77	West Virginia	West Palm Beach, Fla.	D2
Hall, James	DE	6-2	271	2/4/77	Michigan	New Orleans, La.	FA
Hodge, Leroy	WR	6-1	215	2/5/77	Texas A&M	Rosenberg, Tex.	FA
Janus, Paul (1)	G	6-4	294	3/17/75	Northwestern	Edgerton, Wis.	FA-'99
Jensen, Casey	C	6-6	291	4/13/77	Michigan State	Eagen, Minn.	FA
Mankins, Jeremy	G	6-4	320	8/25/76	Boise State	Hughson, Calif.	FA
McDougle, Stockar	G	6-6	350	1/11/77	Oklahoma	Deerfield Beach, Fla.	D1
O'Brien, Nick	G	6-2	328	11/19/72	Texas A&M-Kingsville	Sickerville, N.J.	FA
O'Neill, Joe	LB	6-1	216	12/11/76	Bowling Green	Twinsburg, Ohio	FA
Powell, Sean	DT	6-1	292	1/23/74	New Mexico State	Torrance, Calif.	FA
Reece, Travis (1)	RB	6-3	251	4/3/75	Michigan State	Detroit, Mich.	FA-'98
Reese, Quinton	DE	6-4	252	8/26/77	Auburn	Birmingham, Ala.	D6
Rone, Andre' (1)	WR	5-10	180	4/14/76	Mississippi	Daytona Beach, Fla.	FA
Sanders, Charlie	RB	5-9	211	9/22/76	Emporia State	Rochester, Mich.	FA
Spicer, Paul (1)	DE	6-4	269	8/18/75	Saginaw Valley State	Indianapolis, Ind.	FA-'99
Vincent, Andy	T	6-4	306	6/11/78	Texas A&M	Sulphur, La.	FA
Wyrick, Jimmy	CB	5-9	179	12/31/76	Minnesota	DeSoto, Tex.	FA

The term NFL Rookie is defined as a player who is in his first season of professional football and has not been on the roster of another professional football team for any regular-season or postseason games. A Rookie is designated by an "R" on NFL rosters. Players who have been active in another professional football league or players who have NFL experience, including either preseason training camp or being on an Active List or Inactive List, or on Reserve/Injured or Reserve/Physically Unable to Perform for fewer than six regular-season games, are termed NFL First-Year Players. An NFL First-Year Player is designated by a "1" on NFL rosters. Thereafter, a player is credited with an additional year of experience for each season in which he accumulates six games on the Active List or Inactive List, or on Reserve/Injured or Reserve/Physically Unable to Perform.

NOTES

GREEN BAY PACKERS

National Football Conference
Central Division
Team Colors: Dark Green, Gold, and White
1265 Lombardi Avenue
Green Bay, Wisconsin 54304
Telephone: (920) 496-5700

CLUB OFFICIALS

President and CEO: Bob Harlan
Vice President: John Fabry
Secretary: Peter Platten
Treasurer: John Underwood
Exec. V.P. and General Manager: Ron Wolf
Senior Vice President of Administration: John Jones
Vice President of Personnel: Ken Herock
Director of Player Finance/Football Operations: Andrew Brandt
Exec. Assistant to the President: Phil Pionek
Exec. Director of Public Relations: Lee Remmel
Associate Director of Public Relations: Jeff Blumb
Assistant Director of Public Relations/Travel Coordinator: Aaron Popkey
Exec. Director of Player Programs and Community Affairs: Gill Byrd
Director of Family Programs: Sherry Schuldes
Director of Community Relations: Jeanne McKenna
Director of Marketing: Jeff Cieply
Ticket Director: Mark Wagner
Director of Administrative Affairs: Mark Schiefelbein
Director of Finance: Vicki Vannieuwenhoven
Director of Accounting: Duke Copp
Director of Computer Services: Wayne Wichlacz
Corporate Security Officer: Jerry Parins
Director of Pro Personnel: Reggie McKenzie
College Scouts: Lee Gissendaner, Brian Gutekunst, Shaun Herock, Alonzo Highsmith, Lenny McGill, Sam Seale, Red Cochran
Scouting Coordinator: Danny Mock
Strength and Conditioning Assistant: Mark Lovat
Director of Football Administration: Bruce Warwick
Video Director: Al Treml
Head Trainer: Pepper Burruss
Equipment Manager: Gordon (Red) Batty
Stadium Manager: Ted Eisenreich
Fields Supervisor: Allen Johnson
Stadium: Lambeau Field • **Capacity:** 60,890
1265 Lombardi Avenue
Green Bay, Wisconsin 54304
Playing Surface: Grass
Training Camp: St. Norbert College
De Pere, Wisconsin 54115

RECORD HOLDERS

INDIVIDUAL RECORDS—CAREER

Category	Name	Performance
Rushing (Yds.)	Jim Taylor, 1958-1966	8,207
Passing (Yds.)	Brett Favre, 1992-99	30,894
Passing (TDs)	Brett Favre, 1992-99	235
Receiving (No.)	Sterling Sharpe, 1988-1994	595
Receiving (Yds.)	James Lofton, 1978-1986	9,656
Interceptions	Bobby Dillon, 1952-59	52
Punting (Avg.)	Craig Hentrich, 1994-97	42.8
Punt Return (Avg.)	Desmond Howard, 1996, 1999	13.8
Kickoff Return (Avg.)	Travis Williams, 1967-1970	26.7
Field Goals	Chris Jacke, 1989-1996	173
Touchdowns (Tot.)	Don Hutson, 1935-1945	105
Points	Don Hutson, 1935-1945	823

INDIVIDUAL RECORDS—SINGLE SEASON

Category	Name	Performance
Rushing (Yds.)	Jim Taylor, 1962	1,474
Passing (Yds.)	Lynn Dickey, 1983	4,458
Passing (TDs)	Brett Favre, 1996	39
Receiving (No.)	Sterling Sharpe, 1993	112
Receiving (Yds.)	Robert Brooks, 1995	1,497
Interceptions	Irv Comp, 1943	10
Punting (Avg.)	Craig Hentrich, 1997	45.0
Punt Return (Avg.)	Billy Grimes, 1950	19.1
Kickoff Return (Avg.)	Travis Williams, 1967	*41.1
Field Goals	Chester Marcol, 1972	33
Touchdowns (Tot.)	Jim Taylor, 1962	19
Points	Paul Hornung, 1960	*176

INDIVIDUAL RECORDS—SINGLE GAME

Category	Name	Performance
Rushing (Yds.)	Dorsey Levens, 11-23-97	190
Passing (Yds.)	Lynn Dickey, 10-12-80	418
Passing (TDs)	Many times	5
	Last time by Brett Favre, 9-27-98	
Receiving (No.)	Don Hutson, 11-22-42	14
Receiving (Yds.)	Billy Howton, 10-21-56	257
Interceptions	Bobby Dillon, 11-26-53	*4
	Willie Buchanon, 9-24-78	*4
Field Goals	Chris Jacke, 11-11-90, 10-14-96	5
Touchdowns (Tot.)	Paul Hornung, 12-12-65	5
Points	Paul Hornung, 10-8-61	33

*NFL Record

2000 SCHEDULE

PRESEASON

Aug. 4	**New York Jets**	7:00
Aug. 13	at Denver	2:00
Aug. 21	at Miami	8:00
Aug. 26	**Cleveland**	4:00

REGULAR SEASON

Sept. 3	**New York Jets**	3:15
Sept. 10	at Buffalo	1:00
Sept. 17	**Philadelphia**	12:00
Sept. 24	at Arizona	1:05
Oct. 1	**Chicago**	3:15
Oct. 8	at Detroit	1:00
Oct. 15	**San Francisco**	3:15
Oct. 22	Open Date	
Oct. 29	at Miami	1:00
Nov. 6	**Minnesota** (Mon.)	8:00
Nov. 12	at Tampa Bay	4:15
Nov. 19	**Indianapolis**	12:00
Nov. 27	at Carolina (Mon.)	9:00
Dec. 3	at Chicago	7:35
Dec. 10	**Detroit**	12:00
Dec. 17	at Minnesota	12:00
Dec. 24	**Tampa Bay**	12:00

LAMBEAU FIELD

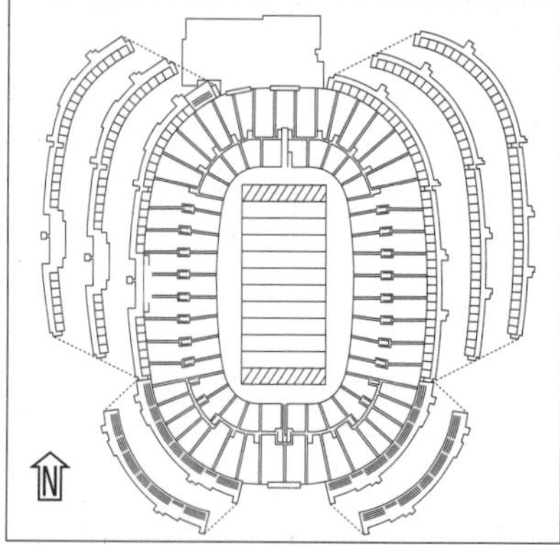

COACHING HISTORY

(581-463-36)

1921-49	Earl (Curly) Lambeau	212-106-21
1950-53	Gene Ronzani*	14-31-1
1953	Hugh Devore- Ray (Scooter) McLean**	0-2-0
1954-57	Lisle Blackbourn	17-31-0
1958	Ray (Scooter) McLean	1-10-1
1959-67	Vince Lombardi	98-30-4
1968-70	Phil Bengtson	20-21-1
1971-74	Dan Devine	25-28-4
1975-83	Bart Starr	53-77-3
1984-87	Forrest Gregg	25-37-1
1988-91	Lindy Infante	24-40-0
1992-98	Mike Holmgren	84-42-0
1999	Ray Rhodes	8-8-0

*Resigned after 10 games in 1953
**Co-coaches

1999 TEAM RECORD

PRESEASON (4-0)

Date	Result		Opponent
8/14	W	27-16	New York Jets
8/23	W	27-12	vs. Denver at Madison, Wisconsin
8/28	W	38-17	at New Orleans
9/2	W	25-17	Miami

REGULAR SEASON (8-8)

Date	Result		Opponent	Att.
9/12	W	28-24	Oakland	59,872
9/19	L	15-23	at Detroit	76,202
9/26	W	23-20	Minnesota	59,868
10/10	W	26-23	Tampa Bay	59,868
10/17	L	10-31	at Denver	73,352
10/24	W	31-3	at San Diego	68,274
11/1	L	7-27	Seattle	59,869
11/7	L	13-14	Chicago	59,867
11/14	L	13-27	at Dallas	64,634
11/21	W	26-17	Detroit	59,869
11/29	W	20-3	at San Francisco	68,304
12/5	W	35-19	at Chicago	66,944
12/12	L	31-33	Carolina	59,869
12/20	L	20-24	at Minnesota	64,203
12/26	L	10-29	at Tampa Bay	65,273
1/2	W	49-24	Arizona	59,818

SCORE BY PERIODS

Packers	44	123	73	117	0	—	357
Opponents	54	95	93	99	0	—	341

ATTENDANCE

Home 478,900 Away 545,599 Total 1,024,499
Single-game home record, 60,766 (9/1/97)
Single-season home record, 482,988 (1996)

1999 TEAM STATISTICS

	Packers	Opp.
Total First Downs	314	304
Rushing	87	103
Passing	196	177
Penalty	31	24
Third Down: Made/Att	77/209	87/223
Third Down Pct.	36.8	39.0
Fourth Down: Made/Att	2/9	8/20
Fourth Down Pct.	22.2	40.0
Total Net Yards	5,419	5,309
Avg. Per Game	338.7	331.8
Total Plays	1,027	1,040
Avg. Per Play	5.3	5.1
Net Yards Rushing	1,519	1,804
Avg. Per Game	94.9	112.8
Total Rushes	386	472
Net Yards Passing	3,900	3,505
Avg. Per Game	243.8	219.1
Sacked/Yards Lost	36/232	30/185
Gross Yards	4,132	3,690
Att./Completions	605/344	538/304
Completion Pct.	56.9	56.5
Had Intercepted	23	26
Punts/Average	80/39.1	69/42.8
Net Punting Avg.	80/34.0	69/36.8
Penalties/Yards	100/808	99/993
Fumbles/Ball Lost	28/13	36/15
Touchdowns	40	39
Rushing	13	16
Passing	23	20
Returns	4	3
Avg. Time of Possession	29:13	30:47

1999 INDIVIDUAL STATISTICS

Passing	Att.	Comp.	Yds.	Pct.	TD	Int.	Tkld.	Rate
Favre	595	341	4,091	57.3	22	23	35/223	74.7
Hasselbeck	10	3	41	30.0	1	0	1/9	77.5
Packers	605	344	4,132	56.9	23	23	36/232	74.8
Opponents	538	304	3,690	56.5	20	26	30/185	70.0

SCORING	TD R	TD P	TD Rt	PAT	FG	Saf	PTS
Longwell	0	0	0	38/38	25/30	0	113
Levens	9	1	0	0/0	0/0	0	60
Freeman	0	6	0	0/0	0/0	0	36
Bradford	0	5	0	0/0	0/0	0	32
Schroeder	0	5	0	0/0	0/0	0	30
Henderson	2	1	0	0/0	0/0	0	18
T. Davis	0	2	0	0/0	0/0	0	12
K. McKenzie	0	0	2	0/0	0/0	0	12
Parker	2	0	0	0/0	0/0	0	12
Thomason	0	2	0	0/0	0/0	0	12
Driver	0	1	0	0/0	0/0	0	6
Edwards	0	0	1	0/0	0/0	0	6
Mitchell	0	0	1	0/0	0/0	0	6
Packers	13	23	4	38/38	25/30	1	357
Opponents	16	20	3	35/35	24/31	0	341

2-Pt. Conversions: Bradford.
Team 1-2, Opponents 0-4.

RUSHING	Att.	Yds.	Avg.	LG	TD
Levens	279	1,034	3.7	36	9
Parker	36	184	5.1	26	2
Favre	28	142	5.1	20	0
Mitchell	29	117	4.0	15	0
Henderson	7	29	4.1	10	2
Hasselbeck	6	15	2.5	13	0
Freeman	1	-2	-2.0	-2	0
Packers	386	1,519	3.9	36	13
Opponents	472	1,804	3.8	51	16

RECEIVING	No.	Yds.	Avg.	LG	TD
Freeman	74	1,074	14.5	51	6
Schroeder	74	1,051	14.2	51	5
Levens	71	573	8.1	53	1
Bradford	37	637	17.2	74t	5
Henderson	30	203	6.8	22	1
T. Davis	20	204	10.2	33	2
Thomason	14	140	10.0	22	2
Mitchell	6	48	8.0	20	0
Chmura	5	55	11.0	16	0
Parker	4	15	3.8	7	0
Hall	3	33	11.0	13	0
Driver	3	31	10.3	12	1
Jordan	2	54	27.0	43	0
Crawford	1	14	14.0	14	0
Packers	344	4,132	12.0	74t	23
Opponents	304	3,690	12.1	88	20

INTERCEPTIONS	No.	Yds.	Avg.	LG	TD
M. McKenzie	6	4	0.7	4	0
Edwards	4	26	6.5	26t	1
T. Williams	4	12	3.0	12	0
Sharper	3	12	4.0	9	0
B. Williams	2	60	30.0	60	0
Vinson	2	21	10.5	21	0
Butler	2	0	0.0	0	0
Smith	1	2	2.0	2	0
Lyon	1	0	0.0	0	0
Nelson	1	0	0.0	0	0
Packers	26	137	5.3	60	1
Opponents	23	338	14.7	95t	2

PUNTING	No.	Yds.	Avg.	In 20	LG
Aguiar	75	2,954	39.4	20	64
Hanson	4	157	39.3	0	44
Longwell	1	19	19.0	1	19
Packers	80	3,130	39.1	21	64
Opponents	69	2,954	42.8	26	65

PUNT RETURNS	No.	FC	Yds.	Avg.	LG	TD
Howard	12	7	93	7.8	20	0
Edwards	10	4	90	9.0	45	0
Jordan	5	2	29	5.8	13	0
Mitchell	2	0	0	0.0	0	0
Packers	29	13	212	7.3	45	0
Opponents	39	24	333	8.5	41	0

KICKOFF RETURNS	No.	Yds.	Avg.	LG	TD
Mitchell	21	464	22.1	88t	1
Howard	19	364	19.2	31	0
Parker	15	268	17.9	40	0
Jordan	6	95	15.8	22	0
Henderson	2	23	11.5	16	0
R. McKenzie	1	13	13.0	13	0
Schroeder	1	10	10.0	10	0
Sharper	1	4	4.0	4	0
Packers	66	1,241	18.8	88t	1
Opponents	72	1,565	21.7	91	0

FIELD GOALS	1-19	20-29	30-39	40-49	50+
Longwell	0/0	8/9	8/9	8/10	1/2
Packers	0/0	8/9	8/9	8/10	1/2
Opponents	1/1	9/10	6/7	8/11	0/2

SACKS	No.
K. McKenzie	8.0
Holliday	6.0
Booker	3.5
S. Dotson	2.5
Lyon	2.0
B. Williams	2.0
Butler	1.0
Sharper	1.0
Vinson	1.0
Waddy	1.0
Hunt	0.5
Smith	0.5
Packers	30.0
Opponents	36.0

2000 DRAFT CHOICES

Round	Name	Pos.	College
1	Bubba Franks	TE	Miami
2	Chad Clifton	T	Tennessee
3	Steve Warren	DT	Nebraska
4	Na'il Diggs	LB	Ohio State
	Anthony Lucas	WR	Arkansas
	Gary Berry	DB	Ohio State
5	Kabeer Gbaja-Biamila	DE	San Diego State
	Joey Jamison	WR	Texas Southern
7	Mark Tauscher	T	Wisconsin
	Ron Moore	DT	Northwestern Oklahoma State
	Charles Lee	WR	Central Florida
	Eugene McCaslin	LB	Florida
	Rondell Mealey	RB	Louisiana State

GREEN BAY PACKERS

2000 VETERAN ROSTER

No.		Name	Pos.	Ht.	Wt.	Birthdate	NFL Exp.	College	Hometown	How Acq.	'99 Games/ Starts
70		Andruzzi, Joe	G	6-3	310	8/23/75	4	Southern Connecticut State	Staten Island, N.Y.	FA-'97	8/3
96	t-	Bowens, David	DE	6-2	255	7/3/77	2	Western Illinois	Orchard Lake, Mich.	T(Den)-'00	16/0*
85		Bradford, Corey	WR	6-1	205	12/8/75	3	Jackson State	Clinton, La.	D5-'98	16/2
2		Brooks, Aaron	QB	6-4	205	3/24/76	2	Virginia	Newport News, Va.	D4a-'99	0*
93	#	Brown, Gilbert	DT	6-2	345	2/22/71	8	Kansas	Detroit, Mich.	W(Minn)-'93	16/15
36		Butler, LeRoy	S	6-0	203	7/19/68	11	Florida State	Jacksonville, Fla.	D2-'90	16/16
61		Curry, Scott	T	6-5	300	12/25/75	2	Montana	Valier, Mont.	D6b-'99	5/1
60		Davis, Rob	LS	6-3	285	12/10/68	5	Shippenburg	Greenbelt, Md.	FA-'97	16/0
81		Davis, Tyrone	TE	6-4	255	6/30/72	5	Virginia	Halifax, Va.	FA-'97	16/13
72		Dotson, Earl	T	6-4	310	12/17/70	8	Texas A&I	Beaumont, Tex.	D3-'93	15/15
71		Dotson, Santana	DT	6-5	290	12/19/69	9	Baylor	Houston, Tex.	UFA(TB)-'96	12/12
80		Driver, Donald	WR	6-0	175	2/2/75	2	Alcorn State	Houston, Tex.	D7b-'99	6/1
24		Edwards, Antuan	CB-S	6-1	205	5/26/77	2	Clemson	Starkville, Miss.	D1-'99	16/1
4		Favre, Brett	QB	6-2	220	10/10/69	10	Southern Mississippi	Kiln, Miss.	T(Atl)-'92	16/16
58		Flanagan, Mike	C	6-5	295	11/10/73	5	UCLA	Sacramento, Calif.	D3a-'96	15/0
86		Freeman, Antonio	WR	6-1	198	5/27/72	6	Virginia Tech	Baltimore, Md.	D3d-'95	16/16
30	t-	Green, Ahman	RB	6-0	215	2/16/77	3	Nebraska	Omaha, Neb.	T(Sea)-'00	14/0*
88		Hall, Lamont	TE	6-4	260	11/16/74	2	Clemson	Clover, S.C.	FA-'99	14/0
55		Harris, Bernardo	LB	6-2	250	10/15/71	6	North Carolina	Chapel Hill, N.C.	FA-'95	16/15
11		Hasselbeck, Matt	QB	6-4	220	9/25/75	2	Boston College	Westwood, Mass.	FA-'99	16/0
75		Heimburger, Craig	G	6-2	318	2/3/77	2	Missouri	Belleville, Ill.	FA-'99	2/1
33		Henderson, William	RB	6-1	250	2/19/71	6	North Carolina	Chester, Va.	D3b-'95	16/13
90		Holliday, Vonnie	DE	6-5	300	12/11/75	3	North Carolina	Camden, S.C.	D1-'98	16/16
97		Hunt, Cletidus	DE	6-4	295	1/2/76	2	Kentucky State	Memphis, Tenn.	D3b-'99	11/1
12		Hutton, Tom	P	6-1	200	7/8/72	6	Tennessee	Memphis, Tenn.	UFA(Mia)-'00	14/0*
25		Levens, Dorsey	RB	6-1	228	5/21/70	7	Georgia Tech	Syracuse, N.Y.	D5b-'94	14/14
8		Longwell, Ryan	K	6-0	197	8/16/74	4	California	Bend, Ore.	W(SF)-'97	16/0
98		Lyon, Billy	DT	6-5	300	12/10/73	3	Marshall	Erlanger, Ky.	FA-'98	16/4
67		Maryland, Russell	DT	6-1	300	3/22/69	10	Miami	Chicago, Ill.	UFA(Oak)-'00	16/16*
56		Mays, Kivuusama	LB	6-3	248	1/7/75	3	North Carolina	Anniston, Ala.	W(Minn)-'99	3/1
27		McBride, Tod	CB-S	6-1	208	1/26/76	2	UCLA	Walnut, Calif.	W(Sea)-'99	15/0
43		McGarrahan, Scott	S	6-1	198	2/12/74	3	New Mexico	Arlington, Tex.	D6a-'98	13/0
34		McKenzie, Mike	CB	6-0	190	4/26/76	2	Memphis	Miami, Fla.	D3a-'99	16/16
63		McKenzie, Raleigh	G	6-2	290	2/8/63	16	Tennessee	Knoxville, Tenn.	UFA(SD)-'99	16/7
28		Mitchell, Basil	RB	5-10	200	9/7/75	2	Texas Christian	Mt. Pleasant, Tex.	FA-'99	16/2
53		Morton, Mike	LB	6-4	235	3/28/72	6	North Carolina	Kannapolis, N.C.	FA-'00	16/0*
57		Nelson, Jim	LB	6-1	238	4/16/75	2	Penn State	Pomfret, Md.	FA-'98	16/0
64		Newell, Mike	C	6-4	300	7/22/76	2	Colorado State	Littleton, Colo.	FA-'99	0*
22		Parker, De'Mond	RB	5-10	188	12/24/76	2	Oklahoma	Tulsa, Okla.	D5a-'99	11/1
62		Rivera, Marco	G	6-4	305	4/26/72	5	Penn State	Elmont, N.Y.	D6-'96	16/16
84		Schroeder, Bill	WR	6-3	205	1/9/71	5	Wisconsin-La Crosse	Sheboygan, Wis.	FA-'97	16/16
42		Sharper, Darren	S	6-2	210	11/3/75	4	William & Mary	Richmond, Va.	D2-'97	16/16
83	t-	Sinceno, Kaseem	TE	6-4	259	3/26/76	3	Syracuse	Liberty, N.Y.	T(Phil)-'00	0*
99		Smith, M. Jermaine	DT	6-3	298	2/3/72	3	Georgia	Augusta, Ga.	D4-'97	10/1
38		Snider, Matt	RB	6-2	243	1/26/76	2	Richmond	Wynnewood, Pa.	W(Car)-'99	8/1
91		Thierry, John	DE	6-4	260	9/4/71	7	Alcorn State	Plaisance, La.	UFA(Cle)-'00	16/10*
78		Verba, Ross	G-T	6-4	308	10/31/73	4	Iowa	West Des Moines, Iowa	D1-'97	11/10
54		Waddy, Jude	LB	6-2	220	9/12/75	3	William & Mary	Suitland, Md.	FA-'98	14/8
68		Wahle, Mike	T	6-6	306	3/29/77	3	Navy	Lake Arrowhead, Calif.	SD2-'98	16/13
51		Williams, Brian	LB	6-1	245	12/17/72	6	Southern California	Dallas, Tex.	D3c-'95	7/7
37		Williams, Tyrone	CB	5-11	195	5/31/73	5	Nebraska	Bradenton, Fla.	D3b-'96	16/16
52		Winters, Frank	C	6-3	305	1/23/64	14	Western Illinois	Union City, N.J.	PB(KC)-'92	16/16

* Bowens played 16 games with Denver in '99; Brooks was inactive for 16 games; Green played 14 games with Seattle; Hutton played 14 games with Miami; Maryland played 16 games with Oakland; Morton played 16 games with St. Louis; Newell was inactive for 7 games; Sinceno missed '99 season because of injury for Philadelphia; Thierry played 16 games with Cleveland.

Unrestricted free agent; subject to developments.

t- Packers traded for Bowens (Den), Green (Sea), and Sinceno (Phil).

Players lost through free agency (2)—DE Vaughn Booker (Cin, 14 games in '99), Keith McKenzie (Cle, 16).

Also played with Packers in '99—P Louie Aguiar (15 games), WR Jahine Arnold (1), S Rodney Artmore (5), DE Roy Barker (1), TE Mark Chmura (2), CB Keith Crawford (3), LB Anthony Davis (14), DT Antonio Dingle (6), P Chris Hanson (1), WR-KR Desmond Howard (8), WR Charles Jordan (4), LB George Koonce (15), TE Jeff Thomason (14), CB Fred Vinson (16).

COACHING STAFF

Head Coach,
Mike Sherman

Pro Career: Named the thirteenth head coach in Packers history January 18, 2000. Previously had served as Green Bay's tight ends coach for two seasons (1997-98) before following Mike Holmgren to the Seattle Seahawks in 1999 as offensive coordinator-tight ends coach. Oversaw vast improvement in the Seahawks' offense in his lone season with Seattle as it won the AFC West and made its first playoff appearance since 1988. Offensively, the Seahawks surged to twelfth in the NFL in total offense, up from twenty-third in 1998, and to eighth in the league in passing offense, up from twenty-fourth the previous year, while also ranking tenth in the NFL in points scored with 338. While a Green Bay assistant coach from 1997-98, he had played a major role in the continued success of Mark Chmura and the emergence of backup tight end Tyrone Davis, who caught 7 touchdown passes in 1998. The Packers participated in the playoffs both years and advanced to Super Bowl XXXII at the end of the 1997 season.

Background: After coaching for three seasons at the high school level, Sherman began a 16-year career in the collegiate ranks in 1981 at Pittsburgh, then went to Tulane in 1983. Subsequently spent four seasons at Holy Cross (1985-88), including the final year as offensive coordinator. Moved to Texas A&M in 1989 for the first of two highly successful stints with the Aggies. Tutored the school's offensive linemen from 1989-1993, including tackle Richmond Webb, who went on to become a seven-time Pro Bowl selection for Miami. Coached another Pro Bowl tackle, the Ravens' Jonathan Ogden, while spending the 1994 season at UCLA. Returned to Texas A&M in 1995 for two final seasons at the college level, and he was promoted to offensive coordinator following the '96 campaign but accepted an NFL assignment with the Packers only weeks later. Played offensive guard and tackle, as well as linebacker, for three seasons (1974, 1976-77) at Central Connecticut State University. Was a prep star at Algonquin Regional High School in Northboro, Mass.

Personal: Born December 19, 1954, in Norwood, Mass., Sherman holds a bachelor's degree in English from Central Connecticut State. He and his wife, Karen, have two daughters, Sarah and Emily, and two sons, Matthew and Benjamin, and live in Green Bay.

2000 FIRST-YEAR ROSTER

Name	Pos.	Ht.	Wt.	Birthdate	College	Hometown	How Acq.
Bell, Tyrone (1)	CB	6-2	210	10/20/74	North Alabama	West Point, Miss.	FA-'99
Berry, Gary	S	5-11	199	10/24/74	Ohio State	Worthington, Ohio	D4c
Bidwell, Josh (1)	P	6-3	225	3/13/76	Oregon	Winston, Ore.	D4b-'99
Brown, Bobby	WR	6-2	197	3/26/77	Notre Dame	Fort Lauderdale, Fla.	FA
Clifton, Chad	T	6-5	329	6/26/76	Tennessee	Martin, Tenn.	D2
Coutain, Kenny	WR	6-2	211	3/12/77	Memphis	Miami, Fla.	FA
Diggs, Na'il	LB	6-4	226	7/8/78	Ohio State	Los Angeles, Calif.	D4a
Franks, Bubba	TE	6-6	252	1/6/78	Miami	Big Spring, Tex.	D1
Gbaja-Biamila, Kabeer	DE	6-4	244	9/24/77	San Diego State	Los Angeles, Calif.	D5a
Goodman, Herbert	RB	5-11	204	8/31/77	Graceland	Miami, Fla.	FA
Goodson, Tyrone (1)	WR	6-2	195	2/24/74	Auburn	Brooksville, Fla.	FA-'99
Hart, Lawrence (1)	TE	6-4	260	9/19/76	Southern	Shreveport, La.	FA
Jamison, Joey	WR-KR	5-9	170	10/12/78	Texas Southern	Jacksonville, Fla.	D5b
Johnson, Damian	S	6-0	201	7/18/76	Alabama State	Vicksburg, Miss.	FA
Johnson, Kevin (1)	LB	6-0	225	12/27/73	Ohio State	Athens, Ga.	FA
Johnson, Steve (1)	CB	5-10	178	3/24/76	Tennessee	Powder Springs, Ga.	FA
Lee, Charles	WR	6-2	202	11/19/77	Central Florida	Homestead, Fla.	D7c
Lucas, Anthony	WR	6-3	192	11/20/76	Arkansas	Tallulah, La.	D4b
McCaslin, Eugene	LB	6-1	221	7/21/77	Florida	Tampa, Fla.	D7d
Mealey, Rondell	RB	6-0	206	2/24/77	Louisiana State	Destrehan, La.	D7e
Moore, Ron	DT	6-2	316	8/10/77	Northwestern Oklahoma St.	Sanford, Fla.	D7b
Newman, Adam	TE	6-5	246	12/8/77	Boston College	Westwood, Mass.	FA
Pittman, Bradley	CB	5-11	168	5/9/77	Southern	Lutcher, La.	FA
Purnell, David	K	5-10	185	5/11/77	Northwest Missouri State	Parkville, Mo.	FA
Sankey, Ben	QB	6-2	215	12/5/76	Wake Forest	Chicago, Ill.	FA
Tauscher, Mark	T	6-3	314	6/17/77	Wisconsin	Auburndale, Wis.	D7a
Terna, Scott (1)	P	5-11	210	12/5/77	Ohio State	Honolulu, Hawaii	FA
Warren, Steve	DT	6-1	307	1/22/78	Nebraska	Springfield, Mo.	D3
Williams, Travis	WR	6-3	203	5/22/78	Navy	Lexington, N.C.	FA

The term NFL Rookie is defined as a player who is in his first season of professional football and has not been on the roster of another professional football team for any regular-season or postseason games. A Rookie is designated by an "R" on NFL rosters. Players who have been active in another professional football league or players who have NFL experience, including either preseason training camp or being on an Active List or Inactive List, or on Reserve/Injured or Reserve/Physically Unable to Perform for fewer than six regular-season games, are termed NFL First-Year Players. An NFL First-Year Player is designated by a "1" on NFL rosters. Thereafter, a player is credited with an additional year of experience for each season in which he accumulates six games on the Active List or Inactive List, or on Reserve/Injured or Reserve/Physically Unable to Perform.

ASSISTANT COACHES

Larry Beightol, offensive line; born November 21, 1942, Pittsburgh, lives in Green Bay. Guard-linebacker Catawba College 1960-63. No pro playing experience. College coach: William & Mary 1968-1971, North Carolina State 1972-75, Auburn 1976, Arkansas 1977-78, 1980-82, Louisiana Tech 1979 (head coach), Missouri 1983-84. Pro coach: Atlanta Falcons 1985-86, Tampa Bay Buccaneers 1987-88, San Diego Chargers 1989, New York Jets 1990-94, Houston Oilers 1995, Miami Dolphins 1996-98, joined Packers in 1999.

Darrell Bevell, offensive assistant-quality control; born January 6, 1970, Yuma, Ariz., lives in De Pere, Wis. Quarterback Northern Arizona 1989, Wisconsin 1992-95. No pro playing experience. College coach: Westmar 1996, Iowa State 1997, Connecticut 1998-99. Pro coach: Joined Packers in 2000.

Kippy Brown, running backs; born March 6, 1955, Sweetwater, Tenn., lives in Green Bay. Quarterback Memphis State 1974-77. No pro playing experience. College coach: Memphis State 1978-1980, Louisville 1982, Tennessee 1983-89, 1993-94. Pro coach: New York Jets 1990-92, Tampa Bay Buccaneers 1995, Miami Dolphins 1996-99, joined Packers in 2000.

Billy Davis, defensive assistant-quality control; born November 5, 1965, Youngstown, Ohio, lives in Green Bay. Quarterback Cincinnati 1984-88. No pro playing experience. College coach: Michigan State 1990-91. Pro coach: Pittsburgh Steelers 1992-94, Carolina Panthers 1995-98, Cleveland Browns 1999, joined Packers in 2000.

Ed Donatell, defensive coordinator; born February 4, 1957, Akron, Ohio, lives in Green Bay. Defensive back Glenville State 1975-78. No pro playing experience. College coach: Kent State 1979-1980, Washington 1981-82, Pacific 1983-85, Idaho 1986-88, Cal State-Fullerton 1989. Pro coach: New York Jets 1990-94, Denver Broncos 1995-99, joined Packers in 2000.

Jethro Franklin, defensive line; born October 25, 1965, St. Lazaire, France, lives in De Pere, Wis. Defensive end San Jose (Calif.) C.C. 1984-85, Fresno State 1986-87. Pro defensive end Seattle Seahawks 1989. College coach: Fresno State 1991-98, UCLA 1999. Pro coach: Joined Packers in 2000.

Jeff Jagodzinski, tight ends; born October 12, 1963, Milwaukee, Wis., lives in Green Bay. Running back Wisconsin-Whitewater 1981-84. No pro playing experience. College coach: Wisconsin-Whitewater 1985, Northern Illinois 1986, Louisiana State 1987-88, East Carolina 1989-1996, Boston College 1997-98. Pro coach: Joined Packers in 1999.

Trent Miles, offensive assistant-quality control; born July 29, 1963, Terre Haute, Ind., lives in De Pere, Wis.Wide receiver Indiana State 1982-86. No pro playing experience. College coach: Indiana State 1987, New Mexico 1988-89, Oklahoma 1990, Northern Illinois 1991-94, Hawaii 1995-96, Fresno State 1997-99. Pro coach: Joined Packers in 2000.

Frank Novak, special teams; born May 18, 1938, Leominster, Mass., lives in De Pere, Wis. Quarterback Northern Michigan 1959-1961. No pro playing experience. College coach: Northern Michigan 1966-1972, East Carolina 1973, Virginia 1974-75, Western Illinois 1976-77, Holy Cross 1978-1983, Massachusetts 1986, Missouri 1988. Pro coach: Oklahoma Outlaws (USFL) 1984, Birmingham Stallions (USFL) 1985, Houston Oilers 1989-1994, Detroit Lions 1995-96, San Diego Chargers 1997-98, joined Packers in 2000.

Bo Pelini, linebackers; born December 13, 1967, Youngstown, Ohio, lives in Green Bay. Defensive back Ohio State 1986-1990. No pro playing experience. College coach: Iowa 1991-92. Pro coach: San Francisco 49ers 1994-96, New England Patriots 1997-99, joined Packers in 2000.

Tom Rossley, offensive coordinator; born August 9, 1946, Painesville, Ohio, lives in Green Bay. Wide receiver Cincinnati 1966-68. No pro playing experience. College coach: Arkansas 1972, Rice 1976, 1978-1981, Cincinnati 1977, Holy Cross 1986-87, Southern Methodist 1988-89, 1991-96 (head coach). Pro coach: Montreal Concorde (CFL) 1982-84, San Antonio Gunslingers (USFL) 1985, Denver Dynamite (Arena) 1987, Atlanta Falcons 1990, Chicago Bears 1997-98, Kansas City Chiefs 1999, joined Packers in 2000.

Barry Rubin, strength and conditioning; born June 25, 1957, Monroe, La., lives in Green Bay. Running back-punter Louisiana State 1976-77, tight end-punter Northwestern (La.) State 1978-1980. No pro playing experience. College coach: Northeast Louisiana 1981-83, 1987-1990, 1994, Louisiana State 1984-85. Pro coach: Joined Packers in 1995.

Ray Sherman, wide receivers; born November 27, 1951, Berkeley, Calif., lives in Green Bay. Wide receiver Lancey (Calif.) J.C. 1969-1970, Fresno State 1971-72. No pro playing experience. College coach: San Jose State 1974, California 1975, 1981, Michigan State 1976-77, Wake Forest 1978-1980, Purdue 1982-85, Georgia 1986-87. Pro coach: Houston Oilers 1988-89, Atlanta Falcons 1990, San Francisco 49ers 1991-93, New York Jets 1994, Minnesota Vikings 1995-97, 1999, Pittsburgh Steelers 1998, joined Packers in 2000.

Bob Slowik, defensive backs; born May 16, 1954, Pittsburgh, lives in Green Bay. Defensive back Delaware 1973-76. No pro playing experience. College coach: Delaware 1977-78, Florida 1979-1982, Drake 1983, Rutgers 1984-89, East Carolina 1990-91. Pro coach: Dallas Cowboys 1992, Chicago Bears 1993-98, Cleveland Browns 1999, joined Packers in 2000.

Lionel Washington, asst. defensive backs; born October 21, 1960, New Orleans, lives in Green Bay. Defensive back Tulane 1979-1982. Pro defensive back St. Louis Cardinals 1983-86, Los Angeles/Oakland Raiders 1987-1994, 1997, Denver Broncos 1995-96. Pro coach: Joined Packers in 1999.

MINNESOTA VIKINGS

National Football Conference
Central Division
Team Colors: Purple, Gold, and White
9520 Viking Drive
Eden Prairie, Minnesota 55344
Telephone: (612) 828-6500

CLUB OFFICIALS

Owners: Red & Charline McCombs
President: Gary Woods
Head Coach & VP of Football Operations: Dennis Green
Executive VP of Business Operations: Mike Kelly
Vice President of Player Personnel: Frank Gilliam
National Scout: Jerry Reichow
Director of Pro Personnel: Paul Wiggin
Player Personnel Coordinator: Scott Studwell
Director of Football Administration: Rob Brzezinski
Vice President of Sales and Marketing: Terri Huml
Vice President of Finance: Steve Poppen
Director of Research and Development: Mike Eayrs
Director of Public Relations: Bob Hagan
Director of Community Relations: Brad Madson
Director of Operations: Breck Spinner
Director of Ticket Sales: Phil Huebner
Equipment Manager: Dennis Ryan
Head Athletic Trainer: Chuck Barta
Video Director: Larry Kohout
Stadium: Hubert H. Humphrey Metrodome
•**Capacity:** 64,121
500 11th Avenue South
Minneapolis, Minnesota 55415
Playing Surface: AstroTurf
Training Camp: Minnesota State-Mankato
Mankato, Minnesota 56001

2000 SCHEDULE

PRESEASON

Aug. 5	**New Orleans**	7:00
Aug. 12	at San Diego	6:00
Aug. 18	**Arizona**	7:35
Aug. 24	at Indianapolis	7:00

REGULAR SEASON

Sept. 3	**Chicago**	12:00
Sept. 10	**Miami**	12:00
Sept. 17	at New England	4:15
Sept. 24	Open Date	
Oct. 1	at Detroit	1:00
Oct. 9	**Tampa Bay** (Mon.)	8:00
Oct. 15	at Chicago	7:35
Oct. 22	**Buffalo**	12:00
Oct. 29	at Tampa Bay	1:00
Nov. 6	at Green Bay (Mon.)	8:00
Nov. 12	**Arizona**	12:00
Nov. 19	**Carolina**	12:00
Nov. 23	at Dallas (Thu.)	3:05
Nov. 30	**Detroit** (Thu.)	7:35
Dec. 10	at St. Louis	12:00
Dec. 17	**Green Bay**	12:00
Dec. 24	at Indianapolis	4:15

RECORD HOLDERS

INDIVIDUAL RECORDS—CAREER

Category	Name	Performance
Rushing (Yds.)	Chuck Foreman, 1973-79	5,879
Passing (Yds.)	Fran Tarkenton, 1961-66, 1972-78	33,098
Passing (TDs)	Fran Tarkenton, 1961-66, 1972-78	239
Receiving (No.)	Cris Carter, 1990-99	835
Receiving (Yds.)	Cris Carter, 1990-99	10,238
Interceptions	Paul Krause, 1968-79	53
Punting (Avg.)	Harry Newsome, 1990-93	43.8
Punt Return (Avg.)	David Palmer, 1994-99	10.4
Kickoff Return (Avg.)	Charlie West, 1968-73	25.5
Field Goals	Fred Cox, 1963-77	282
Touchdowns (Tot.)	Cris Carter, 1990-99	95
Points	Fred Cox, 1963-77	1,365

INDIVIDUAL RECORDS—SINGLE SEASON

Category	Name	Performance
Rushing (Yds.)	Robert Smith, 1997	1,266
Passing (Yds.)	Warren Moon, 1994	4,264
Passing (TDs)	Randall Cunningham, 1998	34
Receiving (No.)	Cris Carter, 1994, 1995	122
Receiving (Yds.)	Randy Moss, 1999	1,413
Interceptions	Paul Krause, 1975	10
Punting (Avg.)	Bobby Walden, 1964	46.4
Punt Return (Avg.)	David Palmer, 1995	13.2
Kickoff Return (Avg.)	John Gilliam, 1972	26.3
Field Goals	Gary Anderson, 1998	35
Touchdowns (Tot.)	Chuck Foreman, 1975	22
Points	Gary Anderson, 1998	164

INDIVIDUAL RECORDS—SINGLE GAME

Category	Name	Performance
Rushing (Yds.)	Chuck Foreman, 10-24-76	200
Passing (Yds.)	Tommy Kramer, 11-2-86	490
Passing (TDs)	Joe Kapp, 9-28-69	*7
Receiving (No.)	Rickey Young, 12-16-79	15
Receiving (Yds.)	Sammy White, 11-7-76	210
Interceptions	Many Times	3
	Last time by Jack Del Rio, 12-5-93	
Field Goals	Rich Karlis, 11-5-89	*7
Touchdowns (Tot.)	Chuck Foreman, 12-20-75	4
	Ahmad Rashad, 9-2-79	4
Points	Chuck Foreman, 12-20-75	24
	Ahmad Rashad, 9-2-79	24

*NFL Record

VIKINGS COACHING HISTORY

(339-272-9)

Years	Coach	Record
1961-66	Norm Van Brocklin	29-51-4
1967-83	Bud Grant	161-99-5
1984	Les Steckel	3-13-0
1985	Bud Grant	7-9-0
1986-91	Jerry Burns	55-46-0
1992-99	Dennis Green	84-54-0

METRODOME

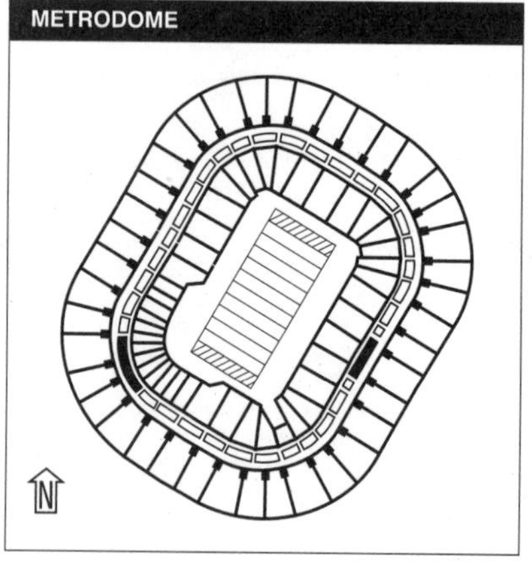

1999 TEAM RECORD

PRESEASON (2-2)

Date	Result		Opponent
8/13	L	21-36	New York Giants
8/21	W	24-17	at Cleveland
8/26	W	17-13	Philadelphia
9/3	L	17-38	at New York Jets

REGULAR SEASON (10-6)

Date	Result		Opponent	Att.
9/12	W	17-14	at Atlanta	69,555
9/19	L	17-22	Oakland	64,080
9/26	L	20-23	at Green Bay	59,868
10/3	W	21-14	Tampa Bay	64,106
10/10	L	22-24	Chicago	64,107
10/17	L	23-25	at Detroit	76,516
10/24	W	40-16	San Francisco	64,109
10/31	W	23-20	at Denver	75,021
11/8	W	27-17	Dallas	64,111
11/14	W	27-24	at Chicago (OT)	66,944
11/28	W	35-27	San Diego	64,232
12/6	L	17-24	at Tampa Bay	65,741
12/12	L	28-31	at Kansas City	78,932
12/20	W	24-20	Green Bay	64,203
12/26	W	34-17	at New York Giants	78,095
1/2	W	24-17	Detroit	64,103

(OT) Overtime

POSTSEASON (1-1)

Date	Result		Opponent	Att.
1/9	W	27-10	Dallas	64,056
1/16	L	37-49	at St. Louis	66,194

SCORE BY PERIODS

Vikings	59	166	64	107	3	—	399
Opponents	84	105	56	90	0	—	335

ATTENDANCE

Home 505,297 Away 568,161 Total 1,073,458
Single-game home record, 64,471 (11/22/98)
Single-season home record, 510,741 (1998)

1999 TEAM STATISTICS

	Vikings	Opp.
Total First Downs	324	320
Rushing	96	83
Passing	192	213
Penalty	36	24
Third Down: Made/Att.	89/204	89/227
Third Down Pct.	43.6	39.2
Fourth Down: Made/Att.	6/11	8/15
Fourth Down Pct.	54.5	53.3
Total Net Yards	5,793	5,597
Avg. Per Game	362.1	349.8
Total Plays	995	1,065
Avg. Per Play	5.8	5.3
Net Yards Rushing	1,804	1,617
Avg. Per Game	112.8	101.1
Total Rushes	422	413
Net Yards Passing	3,989	3,980
Avg. Per Game	249.3	248.8
Sacked/Yards Lost	43/329	46/272
Gross Yards	4,318	4,252
Att./Completions	530/316	606/373
Completion Pct.	59.6	61.6
Had Intercepted	21	12
Punts/Average	61/45.4	69/41.4
Net Punting Avg.	61/38.4	69/35.4
Penalties/Yards	114/955	108/880
Fumbles/Ball Lost	24/19	31/18
Touchdowns	49	35
Rushing	13	9
Passing	32	20
Returns	4	6
Avg. Time of Possession	29:21	30:39

1999 INDIVIDUAL STATISTICS

Passing	Att.	Comp.	Yds.	Pct.	TD	Int.	Tkld.	Rate
George	329	191	2,816	58.1	23	12	28/228	94.2
Cunningham	200	124	1,475	62.0	8	9	15/101	79.1
Moss	1	1	27	100.0	1	0	0/0	158.3
Vikings	530	316	4,318	59.6	32	21	43/329	89.3
Opponents	606	373	4,252	61.6	20	12	46/272	85.4

SCORING	TD R	TD P	TD Rt	PAT	FG	Saf	PTS
Anderson	0	0	0	46/46	19/30	0	103
Carter	0	13	0	0/0	0/0	0	78
Moss	0	11	1	0/0	0/0	0	72
Hoard	10	0	0	0/0	0/0	0	60
Hatchette	0	2	0	0/0	0/0	0	12
Reed	0	2	0	0/0	0/0	0	12
Smith	2	0	0	0/0	0/0	0	12
M. Williams	1	0	1	0/0	0/0	0	12
Crumpler	0	1	0	0/0	0/0	0	6
Glover	0	1	0	0/0	0/0	0	6
Jordan	0	1	0	0/0	0/0	0	6
Tate	0	0	1	0/0	0/0	0	6
Thomas	0	0	1	0/0	0/0	0	6
Walsh	0	1	0	0/0	0/0	0	6
Vikings	13	32	4	46/46	19/30	1	399
Opponents	9	20	6	32/32	29/42	1	335

2-Pt. Conversions: None.
Team 0-3, Opponents 2-3.

RUSHING	Att.	Yds.	Avg.	LG	TD
Smith	221	1,015	4.6	70t	2
Hoard	138	555	4.0	53	10
M. Williams	24	69	2.9	10	1
Cunningham	10	58	5.8	14	0
Moss	4	43	10.8	15	0
George	16	41	2.6	17	0
Palmer	3	12	4.0	7	0
Culpepper	3	6	2.0	9	0
Tate	1	4	4.0	4	0
Morrow	2	1	0.5	5	0
Vikings	422	1,804	4.3	70t	13
Opponents	413	1,617	3.9	63t	9

RECEIVING	No.	Yds.	Avg.	LG	TD
Carter	90	1,241	13.8	68	13
Moss	80	1,413	17.7	67t	11
Reed	44	643	14.6	50	2
Glover	28	327	11.7	31	1
Smith	24	166	6.9	34	0
Hoard	17	166	9.8	29	0
Hatchette	9	180	20.0	80t	2
Kleinsasser	6	13	2.2	11	0
Jordan	5	40	8.0	11	1
Palmer	4	25	6.3	13	0
Mills	3	30	10.0	14	0
Crumpler	2	35	17.5	31t	1
Walsh	2	24	12.0	18t	1
M. Williams	1	12	12.0	12	0
Tate	1	3	3.0	3	0
Vikings	316	4,318	13.7	80t	32
Opponents	373	4,252	11.4	80t	20

INTERCEPTIONS	No.	Yds.	Avg.	LG	TD
Griffith	3	0	0.0	0	0
Thomas	2	32	16.0	27t	1
Hitchcock	2	0	0.0	0	0
Tate	1	18	18.0	18	0
Wright	1	11	11.0	11	0
Bass	1	4	4.0	4	0
Randle	1	1	1.0	1	0
Miller	1	0	0.0	0	0
Vikings	12	66	5.5	27t	1
Opponents	21	302	14.4	68	3

PUNTING	No.	Yds.	Avg.	In 20	LG
Berger	61	2,769	45.4	18	75
Vikings	61	2,769	45.4	18	75
Opponents	69	2,855	41.4	22	63

PUNT RETURNS	No.	FC	Yds.	Avg.	LG	TD
Moss	17	4	162	9.5	64t	1
Palmer	12	5	93	7.8	18	0
Murphy	3	0	14	4.7	7	0
Tate	0	4	0	—	—	0
Vikings	32	13	269	8.4	64t	1
Opponents	28	8	246	8.8	25	0

KICKOFF RETURNS	No.	Yds.	Avg.	LG	TD
Palmer	27	621	23.0	51	0
Tate	25	627	25.1	76t	1
M. Williams	10	240	24.0	85t	1
Murphy	4	80	20.0	24	0
Morrow	1	20	20.0	20	0
Burrough	1	9	9.0	9	0
Jordan	1	0	0.0	0	0
Kleinsasser	1	0	0.0	0	0
Vikings	70	1,597	22.8	85t	2
Opponents	69	1,423	20.6	38	0

FIELD GOALS	1-19	20-29	30-39	40-49	50+
Anderson	0/0	6/8	9/11	4/9	0/2
Vikings	0/0	6/8	9/11	4/9	0/2
Opponents	1/1	9/9	10/16	9/15	0/1

SACKS	No.
Randle	10.0
Clemons	9.0
Doleman	8.0
T. Williams	5.0
Griffith	4.0
Rudd	3.0
Hitchcock	2.0
E. McDaniel	2.0
Ball	1.0
Burrough	1.0
Phillips	1.0
Vikings	46.0
Opponents	43.0

2000 DRAFT CHOICES

Round	Name	Pos.	College
1	Chris Hovan	DT	Boston College
2	Fred Robbins	DT	Wake Forest
	Michael Boireau	DE	Miami
3	Doug Chapman	RB	Marshall
4	Antonio Wilson	LB	Texas A&M-Commerce
	Tyronne Carter	DB	Minnesota
5	Troy Walters	WR	Stanford
7	Mike Malano	C	San Diego State
	Giles Cole	TE	Texas A&M-Kingsville
	Lewis Kelly	G	South Carolina State

MINNESOTA VIKINGS

2000 VETERAN ROSTER

No.	Name	Pos.	Ht.	Wt.	Birthdate	NFL Exp.	College	Hometown	How Acq.	'99 Games/ Starts
1	Anderson, Gary	K	5-11	170	7/16/59	19	Syracuse	Durban, South Africa	UFA(SF)-'98	16/0
96	Ball, Jerry	DT	6-1	330	12/15/64	14	Southern Methodist	Beaumont, Tex.	T(Cle)-'99	13/10
30	Banks, Antonio	CB	5-10	195	3/12/73	3	Virginia Tech	Newport News, Va.	FA-'99	6/1
32	Bass, Anthony	CB-S	6-1	200	3/27/75	3	Bethune Cookman	St. Alban, W. Va.	FA-'98	14/3
17	Berger, Mitch	P	6-4	221	6/24/72	5	Colorado	Vancouver, B.C., Canada	FA-'96	16/0
78	Birk, Matt	T	6-4	304	7/23/76	3	Harvard	St. Paul, Minn.	D6-'98	15/0
8	Bouman, Todd	QB	6-2	227	8/1/72	3	St. Cloud State	Ruthton, Minn.	FA-'97	0*
34	Bradford, Paul	CB	5-9	185	4/20/74	3	Portland State	East Palo Alto, Calif.	FA-'00	0*
6	Brister, Bubby	QB	6-3	205	8/15/62	14	Northeast Louisiana	Monroe, La.	FA-'00	2/0*
91	Burrough, John	DE	6-5	276	5/17/72	6	Wyoming	Pinedale, Wyo.	UFA(Atl)-'99	10/2
80	Carter, Cris	WR	6-3	220	11/25/65	14	Ohio State	Middletown, Ohio	W(Phil)-'90	16/16
87	Crumpler, Carlester	TE	6-6	253	9/5/71	7	East Carolina	Greenville, N.C.	UFA(Sea)-'99	11/1
11	Culpepper, Daunte	QB	6-4	250	1/28/77	2	Central Florida	Ocala, Fla.	D1a-'99	1/0
39	Davis, John	TE	6-4	260	5/14/73	5	Emporia State	Jasper, Tex.	FA-'00	16/0*
71	Dixon, David	G	6-5	346	1/5/69	7	Arizona State	Auckland, New Zealand	FA-'94	16/16
86	Fann, Chad	TE	6-3	250	6/7/70	7	Florida A&M	Jacksonville, Fla.	FA-'00	16/3*
23	Gray, Torrian	S	6-0	196	3/18/74	4	Virginia Tech	Lakeland, Fla.	D2-'97	0*
24	Griffith, Robert	S	5-11	198	11/30/70	7	San Diego State	San Diego, Calif.	FA-'94	16/16
53	Hall, Lemanski	LB	6-0	235	11/24/70	6	Alabama	Valley, Ala.	FA-'00	10/0*
89	Hatchette, Matthew	WR	6-2	201	5/1/74	4	Langston	Cleveland, Ohio	D7b-'97	13/0
67	Humphrey, Jay	T	6-6	313	6/20/76	2	Texas	Richardson, Tex.	D4b-'99	0*
55	Johnson, Olrick	LB	6-0	244	8/20/77	2	Florida A&M	Miami, Fla.	FA-'99	5/0
85	Jordan, Andrew	TE	6-6	272	6/21/72	6	Western Carolina	Charlotte, N.C.	FA-'99	11/1
46	Kidd, Carl	CB	6-1	205	6/14/73	3	Arkansas	Pine Bluff, Ark.	FA-'00	0*
40	Kleinsasser, Jim	RB	6-3	272	1/31/77	2	North Dakota	Carrington, N.D.	D2-'99	13/7
63	Lacina, Corbin	G	6-4	302	11/2/70	7	Augustana	St. Paul, Minn.	FA-'99	14/0
76	Liwienski, Chris	G-T	6-5	321	8/2/75	2	Indiana	Sterling Heights, Mich.	FA-'99	0*
36	Marshall, Anthony	S	6-1	212	9/16/70	5	Louisiana State	Mobile, Ala.	FA-'00	0*
58	McDaniel, Ed	LB	5-11	229	2/23/69	9	Clemson	Battesburgh, S.C.	D5-'92	16/16
33	Morrow, Harold	RB	5-11	224	2/24/73	5	Auburn	Maplesville, Ala.	W(Dall)-'96	16/0
84	Moss, Randy	WR	6-4	198	2/13/77	3	Marshall	Rand, W.Va.	D1-'98	16/16
22	Palmer, David	RB	5-8	172	11/19/72	7	Alabama	Birmingham, Ala.	D2a-'94	8/2
93	Randle, John	DT	6-1	287	12/12/67	11	Texas A&I	Hearne, Tex.	FA-'90	16/16
29	Rogers, Chris	CB	5-10	192	1/3/77	2	Howard	Largo, Md.	FA-'99	10/4
57	Rudd, Dwayne	LB	6-2	233	2/3/76	4	Alabama	Batesville, Miss.	D1-'97	16/16
59	Sauer, Craig	LB	6-1	235	12/13/72	5	Minnesota	Sartell, Minn.	FA-'00	16/3*
97	Sawyer, Talance	DE	6-2	272	6/14/76	2	Nevada-Las Vegas	Bastrop, La.	D6a-'99	2/0
90	Smith, Fernando	DE	6-6	287	8/2/71	7	Jackson State	Flint, Mich.	FA-'00	15/0*
26	Smith, Robert	RB	6-2	210	3/4/72	8	Ohio State	Euclid, Ohio	D1-'93	13/12
73	Steussie, Todd	T	6-6	308	12/1/70	7	California	Canoga Park, Calif.	D1b-'94	16/16
77	Stringer, Korey	T	6-4	339	5/8/74	6	Ohio State	Warren, Ohio	D1b-'95	16/16
28	Tate, Robert	CB	5-10	192	10/19/73	4	Cincinnati	Harrisburg, Pa.	D6-'97	16/1
27	Thibodeaux, Keith	CB	5-11	189	5/16/74	3	Northwestern State	Opelousas, La.	FA-'99	3/0
83	Thomas, Chris	WR	6-2	190	7/16/71	5	Cal Poly-San Luis Obispo	Ventura, Calif.	FA-'00	8/0*
42	Thomas, Orlando	S	6-1	211	10/21/72	6	Southwest Louisiana	Crowley, La.	D2a-'95	13/12
81	Walsh, Chris	WR	6-1	199	12/12/68	8	Stanford	Concord, Calif.	FA-'94	16/1
21	Williams, Moe	RB	6-1	205	7/26/74	5	Kentucky	Columbus, Ga.	D3-'96	14/0
94	Williams, Tony	DT	6-1	292	7/9/75	4	Memphis	Germantown, Tenn.	D5-'97	16/12
52	Wong, Kailee	LB	6-2	247	5/23/76	3	Stanford	Eugene, Ore.	D2-'98	13/8
20	Wright, Kenny	CB	6-1	196	9/14/77	2	Northwestern State, La.	Ruston, La.	D4a-'99	16/12

* Bouman was inactive for 16 games in '99; Bradford last active with San Diego in '97; Brister played 2 games with Denver; Davis played 16 games with Tampa Bay; Fann played 16 games with San Francisco; Gray missed '99 season because of injury; Hall played 10 games with Dallas; Humphrey inactive for 15 games; Kidd last active with Oakland in '96; Liwienski inactive for 4 games; Marshall last active with Philadelphia in '98; Sauer played 16 games with Atlanta; F. Smith played 15 games with Baltimore; C. Thomas played 2 games with Washington and 6 games with St. Louis.

Traded—Vikings traded DE Stalin Colinet (3 games in '99) to Cleveland.

Retired—Chris Doleman, 15-year defensive end, 14 games in '99.

Players lost to free agency (4): C Jeff Christy (TB; 16 games in '99), DE Duane Clemons (KC; 16), TE Andrew Glover (NO; 16), CB Jimmy Hitchcock (Car; 16).

Also played with the Vikings in '99—RB Obafemi Ayanbadejo (2 games), QB Randall Cunningham (6), CB Kevin Devine (2), QB Jeff George (12), DE Martin Harrison (4), RB Leroy Hoard (15), LB Rob Holmberg (16), LB Kivuusama Mays (11), G Randall McDaniel (16), CB Ramos McDonald (5), LB Corey Miller (5), RB John Henry Mills (15), C Mike Morris (16), WR Yo Murphy (1), DT Joe Phillips (16).

COACHING STAFF

Head Coach,
Dennis Green

Pro Career: Named the fifth head coach in Vikings history on January 10, 1992, Green is one of only seven people in the history of the league to lead his team to the playoffs in each of his first three seasons as an NFL head coach. Among active coaches, Green has guided his team longer than any other coach in the NFL and has led the Vikings to playoffs seven of his eight seasons at the helm, including three NFC Central titles. In 1998, Green led the Vikings to their best regular-season record (15-1) in franchise history and a trip to the NFC Championship game. Green also was named *Maxwell Club* and *Sports Illustrated* Coach of the Year (tie) following the 1998 season. In 1997, Green became the second winningest coach in franchise history. He also led Minnesota to its biggest come-from-behind playoff win, 23-22 over the Giants on December 27, 1997. In 1994, NFL Commissioner Paul Tagliabue appointed Green to the league's Competition Committee. He earned NFL coach of the year honors from the Washington Touchdown Club and NFC coach of the year honors from *United Press International* and *College and Pro Football Newsweekly.* Green's first pro coaching opportunity came as special teams coach for the 49ers in 1979. Green briefly played defensive back with British Columbia (CFL) in 1971. Career record: 84-54.

Background: A running back at Iowa from 1968-70, Green began his coaching career as a graduate assistant for Iowa in 1972. He coached running backs and receivers at Dayton in 1973, then running backs and receivers at Iowa from 1974-76. Green worked with running backs at Stanford in 1977-78. He returned to Stanford as offensive coordinator in 1980, then was head coach at Northwestern from 1981-85. Green was named Big Ten coach of the year in 1982. As head coach at Stanford from 1989-91, he led the Cardinal to the 1991 Aloha Bowl, its first bowl game since 1986.

Personal: Born February 17, 1949 in Harrisburg, Pa., Green earned his degree in recreation from Iowa. He and his wife, Marie, live in Minneapolis, with their daughter Vanessa and son Zachary. Green also has a daughter, Patti, and a son Jeremy.

2000 FIRST-YEAR ROSTER

Name	Pos.	Ht.	Wt.	Birthdate	College	Hometown	How Acq.
Abernathy, Chad (1)	T	6-5	302	7/2/76	Arkansas	Mountain View, Ark.	FA
Boireau, Michael	DE	6-4	274	7/24/78	Miami	North Miami Beach, Fla.	D2b
Carter, Tyrone	CB-S	5-8	190	3/31/76	Minnesota	Pompano Beach, Fla.	D4b
Cercone, Matt (1)	TE	6-5	255	11/30/75	Arizona State	Bakersfield, Calif.	FA
Chapman, Doug	RB	5-10	215	8/22/77	Marshall	Chesterfield, Va.	D3
Cockerham, Billy	QB	6-1	217	3/18/77	Minnesota	Clayton, Calif.	FA
Cole, Giles	TE	6-6	230	2/4/76	Texas A&M-Kingsville	Orange, Tex.	D7
Council, Keith (1)	DE	6-6	285	12/3/74	Hampton	Orlando, Fla.	FA-'99
Crosland, Andy	K	6-3	220	11/17/76	Miami	Dallas, Tex.	FA
Dalton, Antico (1)	LB	6-1	241	12/31/75	Hampton	Eden, N.C.	FA-'99
Daniel, Darryl (1)	WR	5-11	190	1/24/76	Syracuse	Lancaster, Pa.	FA-'99
Engelhardt, Tim	DT	6-2	279	5/12/78	New Mexico State	Alamagordo, N.M.	FA
Heffner-Liddaird, Brody	TE	6-4	234	6/12/77	Colorado	San Diego, Calif.	FA
Hovan, Chris	DT	6-2	305	5/12/78	Boston College	Rocky River, Ohio	D1
Jones, Carlos (1)	CB	5-11	190	8/31/73	Miami	New Orleans, La.	FA-'99
Kelly, Lewis	G-T	6-4	272	4/21/77	South Carolina State	Lithonia, Ga.	D7c
Lucas, Lenny	RB	6-3	232	3/24/77	Troy State	Macon, Ga.	FA
Malano, Mike	G-T	6-2	307	10/16/76	San Diego State	Scottsdale, Ariz.	D7a
McCullough, Carl (1)	RB	6-2	223	11/14/73	Wisconsin	St. Paul, Minn.	FA
Morgan, Don (1)	S	5-11	200	9/18/75	Nevada	Stockton, Calif.	FA-'99
Parker, Mike (1)	LB	6-1	230	7/12/75	Houston	Houston, Tex.	FA
Robbins, Fred	DT	6-4	312	3/25/77	Wake Forest	Pensacola, Fla.	D2a
Sawyer, Talance (1)	DE	6-2	272	6/14/76	Nevada-Las Vegas	Bastrop, La.	D6a-'99
Souder, James (1)	S	5-11	208	1/29/77	Bethune-Cookman	Newark, N.J.	FA-'00
Spann, Gregory	WR	6-2	205	4/16/73	Jackson State	Macon, Miss.	FA-'99
Walters, Troy	WR	5-7	171	12/15/76	Stanford	College Station, Tex.	D5b
Wilson, Antonio	LB	6-2	244	12/29/77	Texas A&M-Commerce	Dallas, Tex.	D4a
Wilson, Matt	WR	6-0	204	3/4/77	Bloomsburg State	Milton, Pa.	FA
Withrow, Corey (1)	C	6-2	282	4/5/75	Washington State	Spokane, Wash.	FA-'99
Young, Antwone	RB	6-2	270	1/28/77	San Diego State	Inglewood, Calif.	FA

The term NFL Rookie is defined as a player who is in his first season of professional football and has not been on the roster of another professional football team for any regular-season or postseason games. A Rookie is designated by an "R" on NFL rosters. Players who have been active in another professional football league or players who have NFL experience, including either preseason training camp or being on an Active List or Inactive List, or on Reserve/Injured or Reserve/Physically Unable to Perform for fewer than six regular-season games, are termed NFL First-Year Players. An NFL First-Year Player is designated by a "1" on NFL rosters. Thereafter, a player is credited with an additional year of experience for each season in which he accumulates six games on the Active List or Inactive List, or on Reserve/Injured or Reserve/Physically Unable to Perform.

ASSISTANT COACHES

Charlie Baggett, wide receivers; born January 21, 1953, Fayetteville, N.C., lives in Eden Prairie, Minn. Quarterback Michigan State 1972-75. No pro playing experience. College coach: Bowling Green 1977-1980, Minnesota 1981-82, Michigan State 1983-1992, 1995-98. Pro coach: Houston Oilers 1993-94, Green Bay Packers 1999, joined Vikings in 2000.

Dean Dalton, quality control; born July 27, 1963, Platteville, Wis., lives in Eden Prairie, Minn. Defensive back Air Force Academy 1981-82, Western Illinois 1983-84. College coach: Western Illinois 1984-85, Wisconsin 1986-87, Texas Southern 1988-89, Purdue 1990. Pro coach: Joined Vikings in 1999.

John Fontes, linebackers; born June 24, 1949, New Bedford, Mass., lives in Eden Prairie, Minn. Defensive back Iowa 1969-1970. No pro playing experience. College coach: Iowa 1971-72, Oregon State 1976-1980, Northwestern 1985, Miami 1986, Louisiana State 1987-89. Pro coach: Tampa Bay Storm (Arena League) 1991, Sacramento Surge (World League of American Football) 1992, Detroit Lions 1992-96, joined Vikings in 2000.

Carl Hargrave, running backs; born November 8, 1954, Frankfurt, Germany, lives in Eden Prairie, Minn. Defensive back Upper Iowa 1972-75. No pro playing experience. College coach: Upper Iowa 1977-1980, Northwestern 1981-85, Pittsburgh 1986, Houston 1987-1991, Iowa 1992-93. Pro coach: Joined Vikings in 1994.

Chuck Knox, Jr., defensive assistant; born February 19, 1965, Englewood, N.J., lives in Eden Prairie, Minn. Running back Arizona 1984-88. Pro coach: Los Angeles Rams 1993-94, Philadelphia Eagles 1995-98, Green Bay Packers 1999, joined Vikings in 2000.

Daryl Lawrence, asst. strength and conditioning; born October 20, 1965, Chicago Heights, Ill., lives in Shakopee, Minn. Attended Illinois State. No college or pro playing experience. College coach: Illinois State 1995-96, Army 1998-99. Pro coach: Minnesota Vikings 1997, rejoined Vikings in 2000.

Sherman Lewis, offensive coordinator; born June 29, 1942, Louisville, Ky., lives in Eden Prairie, Minn. Running back Michigan State 1960-63. Pro running back Toronto Argonauts (CFL) 1964-65, New York Jets 1966. College coach: Michigan State 1969-1982. Pro coach: San Francisco 49ers 1983-1991, Green Bay Packers 1992-99, joined Vikings in 2000.

Richard Solomon, defensive backs; born December 8, 1949, New Orleans, lives in Eden Prairie, Minn. Running back-defensive back Iowa 1970-73. No pro playing experience. College coach: Dubuque 1973-75, Southern Illinois 1976, Iowa 1977-78, Syracuse 1979, Illinois 1980-86. Pro coach: New York Giants 1987-1991 (scout), joined Vikings in 1992.

Emmitt Thomas, defensive coordinator; born June 3, 1943, Angleton, Texas, lives in Eden Prairie, Minn. Quarterback-receiver Bishop (Texas) College 1963-65. Pro defensive back Kansas City Chiefs 1966-1978. College coach: Central Missouri State 1979-1980. Pro coach: St. Louis Cardinals 1981-85, Washington Redskins 1986-1994, Philadelphia Eagles 1995-98, Green Bay Packers 1999, joined Vikings in 2000.

John Tice, tight ends; born June 22, 1960, Bayshore, N.Y., lives in Eden Prairie, Minn. Tight end Maryland 1978-1982. Pro tight end New Orleans Saints 1983-1992. Pro coach: Joined Vikings in 1999.

Mike Tice, offensive line; born February 2, 1959, Bayshore, N.Y., lives in Eden Prairie, Minn. Quarterback Maryland 1977-1980. Pro tight end Seattle Seahawks 1981-88, 1990-91, Washington Redskins 1989, Minnesota Vikings 1992-93, 1995. Pro coach: Joined Vikings in 1996.

Fred vonAppen, defensive line; born March 22, 1942, Eugene, Ore., lives in Eden Prairie, Minn. Lineman Linfield College 1961-63. No pro playing experience. College coach: Linfield College 1964-65, Arkansas 1969, 1981, UCLA 1970, Virginia Tech 1971, Oregon 1972-76, Stanford 1977-78, 1982, 1989, 1992-94, Pittsburgh 1990-91, Colorado 1995-96, Hawaii 1996-98 (head coach). Pro coach: Green Bay Packers 1979-1980, San Francisco 49ers 1983-88, joined Vikings in 2000.

Trent Walters, outside linebackers; born November 20, 1943, Knoxville, Tenn., lives in Eden Prairie, Minn. Defensive back Indiana 1963-65. Pro defensive back Edmonton Eskimos (CFL) 1966-67. College coach: Indiana 1968-1971, Louisville 1972, 1986-1990, Indiana 1973-1980, Washington 1981-83, Pittsburgh 1985, Texas A&M 1991-93. Pro coach: Cincinnati Bengals 1984, joined Vikings in 1994.

Steve Wetzel, strength and conditioning; born May 11, 1963, Washington, D.C., lives in Eden Prairie, Minn. Attended Slippery Rock. No college or pro playing experience. College coach: Maryland 1985-89, George Mason 1990. Pro coach: Washington Redskins 1990-91, joined Vikings in 1992.

Alex Wood, quarterbacks; born March 14, 1955, Massillion, Ohio, lives in Eden Prairie, Minn. Running back Iowa 1974-77. No pro playing experience. College coach: Iowa 1978, Kent 1979-1980, Southern Illinois 1981, Southern 1982-84, Wyoming 1985-86, Washington State 1987-88, Miami 1989-1992, Wake Forest 1993-94, James Madison (head coach) 1995-98. Pro coach: Joined Vikings in 1999.

Gary Zauner, special teams; born November 2, 1950, Milwaukee, Wis., lives in Eden Prairie, Minn. Kicker Wisconsin-LaCrosse 1968-1972. No pro playing experience. College coach: Brigham Young 1979-1980, San Diego State 1981-86, New Mexico 1987-88, Long Beach State 1990-91. Pro coach: Joined Vikings in 1994.

NEW ORLEANS SAINTS

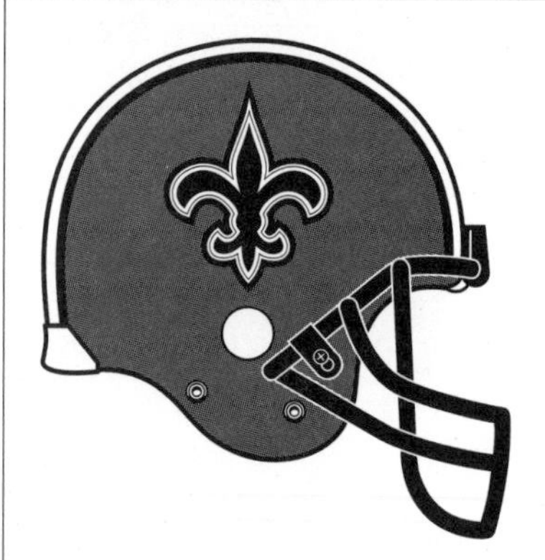

National Football Conference
Western Division
Team Colors: Old Gold, Black, and White
5800 Airline Drive
Metairie, Louisiana 70003
Telephone: (504) 733-0255

CLUB OFFICIALS

Owner: Tom Benson
General Manager of Football Operations: Randy Mueller
Director of Administration: Arnold D. Fielkow
Assistant General Manager of Football Operations: Charles Bailey
Director of Football Administration: Mickey Loomis
Director of Player Personnel: Rick Mueller
College Scouting Coordinator: Rick Thompson
Scouting Supervisor: Pat Mondock
Pro Scouts: Mike Baugh, Bill Quiner
Area Scouts: Matt Boockmeier, Cornell Gowdy, Tim Heffelfinger, Mark Sadowski, James Jefferson
Combine Scout: Andy Weidel
Player Personnel Assistant: Grant Neill
Equipment Manager: Dan Simmons
Head Athletic Trainer: Scottie Patton
Video Director: Joe Malota
Director of Player Development & Community Relations: Ricky Porter
Director of Media & Public Relations: Greg Bensel
Assistant Director of Media & Public Relations: Chris Pika
Football Operations Assistant: Omar Khan
Chief Financial Officer: Dennis Lauscha
Director of Marketing & Business Development: Wayne Hodes
Senior Director of Broadcasting & Special Sales Projects: Greg Suit
Director of Travel/Entertainment/Special Projects: Barra Birrcher
Director of Ticket Operations: James Nagaoka
Director of Ticket Sales: Mike Stanfield
Manager, Information Services: Jay Romig
Corporate Sales Manager/Director of Stadium Operations: Scott Sidwell
Facilities Manager: Terry Ashburn
Stadium: Louisiana Superdome
•**Capacity:** 65,044
1500 Poydras Street
New Orleans, Louisiana 70112
Playing Surface: AstroTurf
Training Camp: Nicholls State University
Thibodaux, LA 70310

2000 SCHEDULE

PRESEASON

July 29	at New York Jets	8:00
Aug. 5	at Minnesota	7:00
Aug. 12	vs. Indianapolis at West Lafayette, Indiana	7:00
Aug. 25	**Miami**	7:00

RECORD HOLDERS

INDIVIDUAL RECORDS—CAREER

Category	Name	Performance
Rushing (Yds.)	George Rogers, 1981-84	4,267
Passing (Yds.)	Archie Manning, 1971-1982	21,734
Passing (TDs)	Archie Manning, 1971-1982	115
Receiving (No.)	Eric Martin, 1985-1993	532
Receiving (Yds.)	Eric Martin, 1985-1993	7,854
Interceptions	Dave Waymer, 1980-89	37
Punting (Avg.)	Mark Royals, 1997-98	45.7
Punt Return (Avg.)	Mel Gray, 1986-88	13.4
Kickoff Return (Avg.)	Walter Roberts, 1967	26.3
Field Goals	Morten Andersen, 1982-1994	302
Touchdowns (Tot.)	Dalton Hilliard, 1986-1993	53
Points	Morten Andersen, 1982-1994	1,318

INDIVIDUAL RECORDS—SINGLE SEASON

Category	Name	Performance
Rushing (Yds.)	George Rogers, 1981	1,674
Passing (Yds.)	Jim Everett, 1995	3,970
Passing (TDs)	Jim Everett, 1995	26
Receiving (No.)	Eric Martin, 1988	85
Receiving (Yds.)	Eric Martin, 1989	1,090
Interceptions	Dave Whitsell, 1967	10
Punting (Avg.)	Mark Royals, 1997	45.9
Punt Return (Avg.)	Mel Gray, 1987	14.7
Kickoff Return (Avg.)	Don Shy, 1969	27.9
	Mel Gray, 1986	27.9
Field Goals	Morten Andersen, 1985	31
Touchdowns (Tot.)	Dalton Hilliard, 1989	18
Points	Morten Andersen, 1987	121

INDIVIDUAL RECORDS—SINGLE GAME

Category	Name	Performance
Rushing (Yds.)	George Rogers, 9-4-83	206
Passing (Yds.)	Archie Manning, 12-7-80	377
Passing (TDs)	Billy Kilmer, 11-2-69	6
Receiving (No.)	Tony Galbreath, 9-10-78	14
Receiving (Yds.)	Wes Chandler, 9-2-79	205
Interceptions	Tommy Myers, 9-3-78	3
	Dave Waymer, 10-6-85	3
	Reggie Sutton, 10-18-87	3
	Gene Atkins, 12-22-91	3
Field Goals	Many times	5
	Last time by Morten Andersen, 12-11-94	
Touchdowns (Tot.)	Many times	3
	Last time by Mario Bates, 12-4-94	
Points	Many times	18
	Last time by Mario Bates, 12-4-94	

REGULAR SEASON

Sept. 3	**Detroit**	12:00
Sept. 10	at San Diego	1:15
Sept. 17	at Seattle	1:15
Sept. 24	**Philadelphia**	12:00
Oct. 1	Open Date	
Oct. 8	at Chicago	12:00
Oct. 15	**Carolina**	12:00
Oct. 22	at Atlanta	1:00
Oct. 29	at Arizona	2:05
Nov. 5	**San Francisco**	12:00
Nov. 12	at Carolina	1:00
Nov. 19	**Oakland**	12:00
Nov. 26	at St. Louis	12:00
Dec. 3	**Denver**	12:00
Dec. 10	at San Francisco	1:15
Dec. 17	**Atlanta**	12:00
Dec. 24	**St. Louis**	12:00

LOUISIANA SUPERDOME

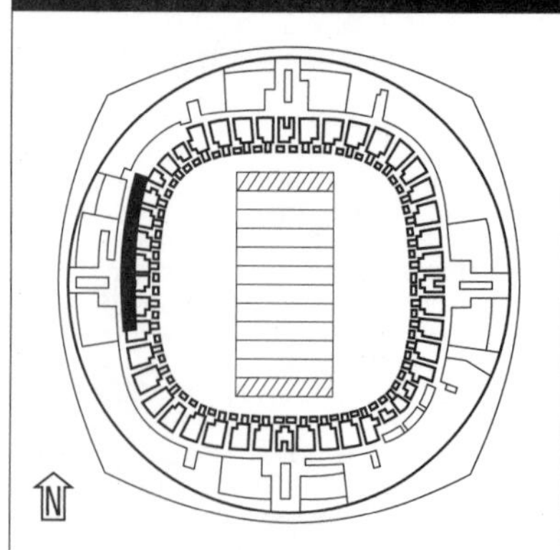

COACHING HISTORY

(192-305-5)

1967-70	Tom Fears*	13-34-2
1970-72	J.D. Roberts	7-25-3
1973-75	John North**	11-23-0
1975	Ernie Hefferle	1-7-0
1976-77	Hank Stram	7-21-0
1978-80	Dick Nolan***	15-29-0
1980	Dick Stanfel	1-3-0
1981-85	O.A. (Bum) Phillips****	27-42-0
1985	Wade Phillips	1-3-0
1986-96	Jim Mora#	93-78-0
1996	Rick Venturi	1-7-0
1997-99	Mike Ditka	15-33-0

*Released after seven games in 1970
**Released after six games in 1975
***Released after 12 games in 1980
****Resigned after 12 games in 1985
#Resigned after 8 games in 1996

1999 TEAM RECORD

PRESEASON (2-2)

Date	Result		Opponent
8/13	W	26-14	at Miami
8/21	L	7-37	Indianapolis
8/28	L	17-38	Green Bay
9/2	W	12-11	at Tennessee

REGULAR SEASON (3-13)

Date	Result		Opponent	Att.
9/12	W	19-10	Carolina	58,166
9/19	L	21-28	at San Francisco	67,685
10/3	L	10-14	at Chicago	66,944
10/10	L	17-20	Atlanta	57,289
10/17	L	21-24	Tennessee	51,875
10/24	L	3-31	at New York Giants	77,982
10/31	L	16-21	Cleveland	48,817
11/7	L	16-31	Tampa Bay	47,129
11/14	W	24-6	San Francisco	52,198
11/21	L	23-41	at Jacksonville	69,772
11/28	L	12-43	at St. Louis	65,864
12/5	L	12-35	at Atlanta	62,568
12/12	L	14-30	St. Louis	46,838
12/19	L	8-31	at Baltimore	67,597
12/24	W	31-24	Dallas	47,835
1/2	L	13-45	at Carolina	56,929

SCORE BY PERIODS

Saints	59	91	39	71	0	—	260
Opponents	79	124	104	127	0	—	434

ATTENDANCE

Home 380,671 Away 541,272 Total 921,943
Single-game home record, 70,940 (9/2/79)
Single-season home record, 548,728 (1992)

1999 TEAM STATISTICS

	Saints	Opp.
Total First Downs	288	297
Rushing	97	105
Passing	159	170
Penalty	32	22
Third Down: Made/Att	74/220	79/204
Third Down Pct.	33.6	38.7
Fourth Down: Made/Att.	8/22	8/11
Fourth Down Pct.	36.4	72.7
Total Net Yards	4,983	5,318
Avg. Per Game	311.4	332.4
Total Plays	1,055	966
Avg. Per Play	4.7	5.5
Net Yards Rushing	1,690	1,774
Avg. Per Game	105.6	110.9
Total Rushes	461	432
Net Yards Passing	3,293	3,544
Avg. Per Game	205.8	221.5
Sacked/Yards Lost	41/305	45/277
Gross Yards	3,598	3,821
Att./Completions	553/288	489/291
Completion Pct.	52.1	59.5
Had Intercepted	30	19
Punts/Average	83/39.5	77/41.3
Net Punting Avg.	83/34.9	77/36.2
Penalties/Yards	110/877	124/1,006
Fumbles/Ball Lost	26/9	22/15
Touchdowns	27	55
Rushing	9	15
Passing	16	34
Returns	2	6
Avg. Time of Possession	30:54	29:06

1999 INDIVIDUAL STATISTICS

Passing	Att.	Comp.	Yds.	Pct.	TD	Int.	Tkld.	Rate
Tolliver	268	139	1,916	51.9	7	16	19/152	58.9
Hobert	159	85	970	53.5	6	6	11/79	68.9
Delhomme	76	42	521	55.3	3	5	6/42	62.4
Wuerffel	48	22	191	45.8	0	3	5/32	30.8
L. Smith	1	0	0	0.0	0	0	0/0	39.6
Ri. Williams	1	0	0	0.0	0	0	0/0	39.6
Saints	553	288	3,598	52.1	16	30	41/305	59.6
Opponents	489	291	3,821	59.5	34	19	45/277	91.2

SCORING	TD R	TD P	TD Rt	PAT	FG	Saf	PTS
Brien	0	0	0	20/21	24/29	0	92
Poole	0	6	0	0/0	0/0	0	36
Kennison	0	4	0	0/0	0/0	0	26
Tolliver	3	0	0	0/0	0/0	0	18
Delhomme	2	0	0	0/0	0/0	0	12
Ri. Williams	2	0	0	0/0	0/0	0	12
Bech	0	1	0	0/0	0/0	0	8
Cleeland	0	1	0	0/0	0/0	0	8
Dawsey	0	1	0	0/0	0/0	0	6
Drakeford	0	0	1	0/0	0/0	0	6
Hastings	0	1	0	0/0	0/0	0	6
Hobert	1	0	0	0/0	0/0	0	6
Slutzker	0	1	0	0/0	0/0	0	6
L. Smith	0	1	0	0/0	0/0	0	6
Weary	0	0	1	0/0	0/0	0	6
Wuerffel	1	0	0	0/0	0/0	0	6
Saints	9	16	2	20/21	24/29	0	260
Opponents	15	34	6	54/54	16/23	0	434

2-Pt. Conversions: Bech, Cleeland, Kennison.
Team 3-6, Opponents 1-1.

RUSHING	Att.	Yds.	Avg.	LG	TD
Ri. Williams	253	884	3.5	25	2
L. Smith	60	205	3.4	24	0
Perry	48	180	3.8	22	0
Tolliver	26	142	5.5	33	3
Delhomme	11	72	6.5	27	2
Hobert	12	47	3.9	10	1
Craver	17	40	2.4	8	0
Davis	20	32	1.6	7	0
Wuerffel	2	29	14.5	29t	1
Kennison	3	20	6.7	15	0
Philyaw	4	16	4.0	18	0
Poole	1	14	14.0	14	0
Barnhardt	1	4	4.0	4	0
Hastings	1	4	4.0	4	0
Powell	1	1	1.0	1	0
Franklin	1	0	0.0	0	0
Saints	461	1,690	3.7	33	9
Opponents	432	1,774	4.1	40	15

RECEIVING	No.	Yds.	Avg.	LG	TD
Kennison	61	835	13.7	90t	4
Poole	42	796	19.0	67t	6
Hastings	40	564	14.1	42	1
Ri. Williams	28	172	6.1	29	0
Cleeland	26	325	12.5	31	1
L. Smith	20	151	7.6	26	1
Craver	19	154	8.1	29	0
Dawsey	16	196	12.3	57	1
Slutzker	11	164	14.9	42	1
Davis	7	53	7.6	20	0
Wilcox	6	61	10.2	19	0
Bech	4	65	16.3	23t	1
Perry	4	26	6.5	11	0
Philyaw	2	23	11.5	14	0
Franklin	2	13	6.5	8	0
Saints	288	3,598	12.5	90t	16
Opponents	291	3,821	13.1	62t	34

INTERCEPTIONS	No.	Yds.	Avg.	LG	TD
Ambrose	6	27	4.5	16	0
Clay	3	32	10.7	24	0
Kei. Mitchell	3	22	7.3	18	0
Weary	2	49	24.5	27	0
Fields	2	0	0.0	0	0
Kelly	1	6	6.0	6	0
Molden	1	2	2.0	2	0
Knight	1	0	0.0	0	0
Saints	19	138	7.3	27	0
Opponents	30	483	16.1	64t	4

PUNTING	No.	Yds.	Avg.	In 20	LG
Barnhardt	82	3,262	39.8	14	52
Brien	1	20	20.0	1	20
Saints	83	3,282	39.5	15	52
Opponents	77	3,183	41.3	24	60

PUNT RETURNS	No.	FC	Yds.	Avg.	LG	TD
Kennison	35	23	258	7.4	18	0
Saints	35	23	258	7.4	18	0
Opponents	43	25	283	6.6	74t	1

KICKOFF RETURNS	No.	Yds.	Avg.	LG	TD
Philyaw	53	1,165	22.0	55	0
Davis	20	424	21.2	35	0
Perry	2	6	3.0	16	0
Dawsey	1	20	20.0	20	0
Bech	1	12	12.0	12	0
Gammon	1	9	9.0	9	0
Craver	1	3	3.0	3	0
Saints	79	1,639	20.7	55	0
Opponents	60	1,473	24.6	95t	1

FIELD GOALS	1-19	20-29	30-39	40-49	50+
Brien	0/0	9/11	6/7	7/9	2/2
Saints	0/0	9/11	6/7	7/9	2/2
Opponents	1/1	2/2	7/8	4/8	2/4

SACKS	No.
Glover	8.5
Whitehead	7.0
B. Smith	6.0
Wilson	5.5
Martin	4.5
Fields	4.0
Kei. Mitchell	3.5
Tomich	3.0
Robbins	2.0
Hewitt	1.0
Saints	45.0
Opponents	41.0

2000 DRAFT CHOICE

Round	Name	Pos.	College
2	Darren Howard	DE	Kansas State
4	Terrelle Smith	RB	Arizona State
5	Tutan Reyes	T	Mississippi
	Austin Wheatley	TE	Iowa
	Chad Morton	RB	Southern California
6	Marc Bulger	QB	West Virginia
	Michael Hawthorne	DE	Purdue
	Sherrod Gideon	WR	Southern Mississippi
7	Kevin Houser	TE	Ohio State

NEW ORLEANS SAINTS

2000 VETERAN ROSTER

No.	Name	Pos.	Ht.	Wt.	Birthdate	NFL Exp.	College	Hometown	How Acq.	'99 Games/ Starts
69	Ackerman, Tom	C-G	6-3	296	9/6/72	5	Eastern Washington	Nooksack, Wash.	D5b-'96	16/8
18	Blake, Jeff	QB	6-0	210	12/4/70	9	East Carolina	Sanford, Fla.	UFA(Cin)-'00	14/12*
56	Bordano, Chris	LB	6-1	248	12/30/74	3	Southern Methodist	San Antonio, Tex.	D6-'98	15/12
10	Brien, Doug	K	6-0	180	11/25/70	7	California	Danville, Calif.	FA-'95	16/0
61	Burroughs, Justin	C	6-5	292	5/22/76	2	North Carolina State	Charlotte, N.C.	FA-'99	0*
51	Clarke, Phil	LB	6-0	241	1/19/77	2	Pittsburgh	Miami, Fla.	FA-'99	8/3
85	Cleeland, Cameron	TE	6-4	272	8/15/75	3	Washington	Sedro Woolley, Wash.	D2-'98	11/8
54	Clemons, Charlie	LB	6-2	250	7/4/72	4	Georgia	Griffin, Ga.	RFA(StL)-'00	16/0*
32	Craver, Aaron	RB	6-0	232	12/18/68	10	Fresno State	Compton, Calif.	UFA(SD)-'98	13/10
12	Delhomme, Jake	QB	6-2	205	1/10/75	2	Louisiana-Lafayette	Lafayette, La.	FA-'99	2/2
22	Drakeford, Tyronne	CB	5-11	185	6/21/71	7	Virginia Tech	Camden, S.C.	UFA(SF)-'98	10/5
55	Fields, Mark	LB	6-2	244	11/9/72	6	Washington State	Cerritos, Calif.	D1-'95	14/14
62	Fontenot, Jerry	C	6-3	300	11/21/66	12	Texas A&M	Lafayette, La.	UFA(Chi)-'97	16/16
82	Glover, Andrew	TE	6-6	252	8/12/67	10	Grambling State	Gonzales, La.	UFA(Minn)-'00	16/13*
97	Glover, La'Roi	DT	6-2	285	7/4/74	5	San Diego State	San Diego, Calif.	W(Oak)-'97	16/16
4	Gowin, Toby	P	5-10	167	3/30/75	4	North Texas	Jacksonville, Tex.	RFA(Dall)-'00	16/0*
79	Halapin, Mike	G	6-5	310	7/1/73	4	Pittsburgh	Vandergrift, Pa.	FA-'99	9/3
96	Hamiter, Uhuru	DT	6-4	280	3/14/73	3	Delaware State	Kingstree, S.C.	W(Phil)-'98	5/0
99	Hand, Norman	DT	6-3	310	9/4/72	6	Mississippi	Walterboro, S.C.	UFA(SD)-'00	14/14*
88	Hastings, Andre	WR	6-1	190	11/7/71	8	Georgia	Morrow, Ga.	UFA(Pitt)-'97	15/5
87	Horn, Joe	WR	6-1	206	1/16/72	5	Itawamba J.C., Miss.	New Haven, Conn.	UFA(KC)-'00	16/1
21	Israel, Steve	CB	5-11	197	3/16/69	9	Pittsburgh	Haddon Heights, N.J.	UFA(NE)'00	13/13
80	Jackson, Willie	WR	6-1	212	8/16/71	7	Florida	Gainesville, Fla.	FA-'00	16/2*
94	Johnson, Joe	DE	6-4	270	7/11/72	7	Louisville	St. Louis, Mo.	D1-'94	0*
27	Kelly, Rob	S	6-0	199	6/21/74	4	Ohio State	Newark, Ohio	D2a-'97	16/7
29	Knight, Sammy	S	6-0	205	9/10/75	4	Southern California	Riverside, Calif.	FA-'97	16/16
52	Merkerson, Ron	LB	6-2	247	8/30/75	2	Colorado	Las Vegas, Nev.	FA-'00	0*
59	Mitchell, Keith	LB	6-2	245	7/24/74	4	Texas A&M	Garland, Tex.	FA-'97	16/16
25	Molden, Alex	CB	5-10	190	8/4/73	5	Oregon	Colorado Springs, Colo.	D1-'96	13/0
65	Naeole, Chris	G	6-3	313	12/25/74	4	Colorado	Kaaawa, Hawaii	D1-'97	15/15
28	Oldham, Chris	DB	5-9	200	10/26/68	10	Oregon	Sacramento, Calif.	UFA(Pitt)-'00	15/0*
33	Perry, Wilmont	RB	6-1	235	2/24/75	3	Livingstone	Franklinton, N.C.	D5-'98	7/3
37	Philyaw, Dino	RB	5-10	205	10/30/70	4	Oregon	Dudley, N.C.	FA-'99	13/0
83	Poole, Keith	WR	6-0	193	6/18/74	4	Arizona State	Clovis, Calif.	D4b-'97	15/15
40	Powell, Marvin	RB	6-2	235	6/6/76	2	Southern California	Van Nuys, Calif.	FA-'99	9/0
70	Price, Marcus	T	6-6	321	3/3/72	3	Louisiana State	Port Arthur, Tex.	FA-'00	0*
86	Reed, Jake	WR	6-3	216	9/28/67	10	Grambling State	Covington, Ga.	UFA(Minn)-'00	16/8
77	Roaf, William	T	6-5	312	4/18/70	8	Louisiana Tech	Pine Bluff, Ark.	D1a-'93	16/16
17	Rodgers, Anthony	WR	6-3	190	12/11/73	2	Cal State-Northridge	Los Angeles, Calif.	FA-'00	0*
84	Slutzker, Scott	TE	6-4	240	12/20/72	5	Iowa	Hasbrouck Heights, N.J.	T(Ind)-'98	11/2
53	Spragan, Donnie	LB	6-4	240	7/12/76	2	Stanford	Union City, Calif.	FA-'99	0*
78	Terrell, Daryl	T	6-5	296	1/25/75	2	Southern Mississippi	Vossburg, Miss.	FA-'98	12/1
89	Thelwell, Ryan	WR	6-2	200	4/6/73	2	Minnesota	London, Ontario, Canada	FA-'00	0*
23	Thomas, Fred	CB	5-9	172	9/11/73	5	Tennessee-Martin	Bruce, Miss.	UFA(Sea)-'00	1/0*
11	Tolliver, Billy Joe	QB	6-1	217	2/7/66	11	Texas Tech	Boyd, Tex.	FA-'98	10/7
90	Tomich, Jared	DE	6-2	272	4/24/74	4	Nebraska	St. John, Ind.	D2b-'97	8/6
68	Turley, Kyle	T	6-5	300	9/24/75	3	San Diego State	Moreno Valley, Calif.	D1-'98	16/16
24	Weary, Fred	CB	5-10	181	4/12/74	3	Florida	Jacksonville, Fla.	D4a-'98	16/11
98	Whitehead, Willie	DE	6-3	285	1/26/73	2	Auburn	Tuskegee, Ala.	FA-'99	16/3
91	Williams, K.D.	LB	6-0	235	4/21/73	2	Henderson State	Tampa, Fla.	FA-'00	9/8
34	Williams, Ricky	RB	5-10	236	5/21/77	2	Texas	San Diego, Calif.	D1-'99	12/12
63	Williams, Wally	G-C	6-2	321	2/19/71	8	Florida A&M	Tallahassee, Fla.	UFA(Balt)-'99	6/6
16	Wilson, Robert	WR	5-11	176	6/23/74	2	Florida A&M	Monticello, Fla.	FA-'00	2/0
92	Wilson, Troy	DE	6-4	257	11/22/70	5	Pittsburg State, Kan.	Shawnee Heights, Kan.	W(SF)-'98	16/4

* Blake played 14 games with Cincinnati in '99; Burroughs and Spragan missed '99 season because of injury; Clemons played 16 games with St. Louis; Glover and Reed played 16 games with Minnesota; Hand played 14 games with San Diego; Jackson played 16 games with Cincinnati; Johnson missed '99 season because of injury; Merkerson was inactive for 2 games with New England; Oldham played 15 games with Pittsburgh; Price and Thelwell last active with San Diego in '98; Rodgers last active with San Diego in '97; Thomas played 1 game with Seattle; K.D. Williams played 9 games with Oakland; R. Wilson played 2 games with Seattle.

Traded—WR Eddie Kennison (16 games in '99) to Chicago.

Players lost through free agency (6): CB Ashley Ambrose (Atl; 16 games in '99), S JeRod Cherry (Oak; 16), C Kendall Gammon (KC; 16), LB Kevin Mitchell (Wash; 16), DT Austin Robbins (Oak; 14). DE Brady Smith (Atl; 16).

Also played with Saints in '99—LB Ink Aleaga (8 games), P Tommy Barnhardt (16), WR Brett Bech (8), CB Willie Clay (16), RB Troy Davis (16), WR Lawrence Dawsey (10), CB-S Chris Hewitt (12), QB Billy Joe Hobert (9), CB Earl Little (1), DT Wayne Martin (16), DE Darren Mickell (1), RB Lamar Smith (13), LB Vinson Smith (12).

COACHING STAFF

Head Coach,
Jim Haslett

Pro Career: Named the thirteenth head coach in Saints history on February 3, 2000. He joins the Saints following three seasons (1997-99) as defensive coordinator of the Pittsburgh Steelers, where they consistently ranked among the league's best defenses. He first held the position of defensive coordinator with the New Orleans Saints (1996), and they improved their defensive ranking from near the bottom of the league to among the league's best. He first joined the Saints as linebackers coach in 1995 after two seasons (1993-94) in the same capacity with the Los Angeles Raiders. From 1991-92, Haslett was defensive coordinator for the Sacramento Surge, who won a World League championship in 1992. Haslett was a second-round draft choice of the Buffalo Bills in 1979, when he was named all-rookie and captured *Associated Press* defensive rookie of the year honors. His playing career spanned nine seasons, including his first eight with the Bills. He concluded his playing career with the New York Jets in 1987. A year later, Haslett assumed his initial coaching post, handling the linebackers at the University of Buffalo. He was promoted to defensive coordinator (1989-1990).

Background: Haslett was a three-time All-America at defensive end at Indiana University of Pennsylvania (1975-78), graduating with a bachelor's degree in elementary education.

Personal: Born December 9, 1955 in Pittsburgh. Haslett and his wife Beth, have two daughters, Kelsey and Elizabeth, and a son, Chase.

2000 FIRST-YEAR ROSTER

Name	Pos.	Ht.	Wt.	Birthdate	College	Hometown	How Acq.
Brannon, Robert	DT	6-2	293	9/9/78	Iowa State	Rialto, Calif.	FA
Brooks, Jamal	LB	6-2	236	11/9/76	Hampton	Altadena, Calif.	FA
Brown, Cuncho (1)	TE	6-4	271	11/2/76	Penn State	Winston-Salem, N.C.	FA-'99
Bulger, Marc	QB	6-2	206	4/5/77	West Virginia	Pittsburgh, Pa.	D6a
Campbell, Amp	S	6-0	200	9/4/75	Michigan State	Sarasota, Fla.	FA
Cooper, D.J.	DE	6-3	283	4/19/76	Arkansas	Mesquite, Tex.	FA
Destefano, Pete	S	6-2	215	4/16/76	California	San Jose, Calif.	FA
Franklin, P.J. (1)	WR	5-10	180	9/28/77	Tulane	Amite, La.	FA-'99
Garnett, Winfield (1)	DT	6-6	305	7/24/76	Ohio State	Harvey, Ill.	FA
Garrett, Shannon (1)	CB	5-10	180	1/24/72	Mississippi College	Bay St. Louis, Miss.	FA
Gibson, Demond	DT	6-4	300	5/25/77	Pittsburgh	Pittsburgh, Pa.	FA
Gideon, Sherrod	WR	5-11	176	2/21/77	Southern Mississippi	Greenwood, Miss.	D6c
Harris, Corey (1)	CB	5-10	191	11/28/76	North Alabama	Warner-Robins, Ga.	FA-'99
Hawthorne, Michael	CB	6-3	196	1/26/75	Purdue	Sarasota, Fla.	D6b
Houser, Kevin	RB	6-2	250	8/23/77	Ohio State	Westlake, Ohio	D7
Howard, Darren	DE	6-3	281	11/19/76	Kansas State	St. Petersburg, Fla.	D2
Hunt, Robert (1)	G	6-3	307	7/22/75	Virginia	Newport News, Va.	FA-'99
Johnson, Eric (1)	S	6-3	218	6/28/72	Idaho State	Maben, Miss.	FA
Lafleur, Bill	P	5-11	200	2/25/76	Nebraska	Norfolk, Neb.	FA
McEndoo, Jason (1)	C	6-5	315	2/25/75	Washington State	Cosmopolis, Wash.	FA
Miles, Terrence	S	6-0	205	7/17/77	Kutztown, Pa.	Philadelphia, Pa.	FA
Morton, Chad	RB	5-8	186	4/4/77	Southern California	Torrance, Calif.	D5c
Newkirk, Robert (1)	DE	6-3	290	3/6/77	Michigan State	Belle Glade, Fla.	FA-'99
Posey, Carlos	CB	5-10	193	3/19/78	Missouri	Baton Rouge, La.	FA
Raynock, Chase	T	6-6	305	9/29/77	Montana	Billings, Mont.	FA
Reyes, Tutan	T	6-3	299	10/28/77	Mississippi	Queens, N.Y.	D5a
Schau, Tom (1)	C	6-5	290	12/30/75	Illinois	Bloomington, Ill.	FA-'99
Setzer, Bob (1)	DE	6-4	280	6/16/76	Boise State	Walnut Creek, Calif.	FA
Smith, Terrelle	RB	6-0	246	3/12/78	Arizona State	Mareno Valley, Calif.	D4
Stevens, L.C. (1)	WR	6-4	218	12/31/74	North Carolina	Clinton, N.C.	FA-'99
Thomas, Kevin (1)	DT	6-4	300	3/28/74	Delta State	Hammond, La.	FA
Tuipala, Joe (1)	LB	6-0	240	9/13/76	San Diego State	Ridgecrest, Calif.	FA-'99
Vaughn, Gerald (1)	S	6-3	195	4/8/70	Mississippi	Abbeville, Miss.	FA
Ward, Philip (1)	LB	6-3	230	11/11/74	UCLA	Compton, Calif.	FA
Warren, Brent (1)	G	6-5	338	2/10/75	Syracuse	Brockton, Mass.	FA
Wheatley, Austin	TE	6-3	254	11/16/77	Iowa	Milan, Ill.	D5b
Wieland, Matt (1)	K	6-0	190	1/29/75	Southwest Texas State	Yorktown, Tex.	FA

The term NFL Rookie is defined as a player who is in his first season of professional football and has not been on the roster of another professional football team for any regular-season or postseason games. A Rookie is designated by an "R" on NFL rosters. Players who have been active in another professional football league or players who have NFL experience, including either preseason training camp or being on an Active List or Inactive List, or on Reserve/Injured or Reserve/Physically Unable to Perform for fewer than six regular-season games, are termed NFL First-Year Players. An NFL First-Year Player is designated by a "1" on NFL rosters. Thereafter, a player is credited with an additional year of experience for each season in which he accumulates six games on the Active List or Inactive List, or on Reserve/Injured or Reserve/Physically Unable to Perform.

ASSISTANT COACHES

Hubbard Alexander, wide receivers; born February 14, 1939, Winston-Salem, N.C., lives in River Ridge, La. Center Tennessee State 1958-1961. No pro playing experience. College coach: Tennessee State 1962-63, Vanderbilt 1974-78, Miami 1979-1988. Pro coach: Dallas Cowboys 1989-1997, Minnesota Vikings 1998-99, joined Saints in 2000.

Dave Atkins, running backs; born May 18, 1949, Victoria, Texas, lives in River Ridge, La. Running back Texas-El Paso 1970-72. Pro running back San Francisco 49ers 1973, Honolulu Hawaiians (WFL) 1974, San Diego Chargers 1975. College coach: Texas El-Paso 1979-1980, San Diego State 1981-85. Pro coach: Philadelphia Eagles 1986-1992, New England Patriots 1993, Arizona Cardinals 1994-95, New Orleans Saints 1996, Minnesota Vikings 1997-99, rejoined Saints in 2000.

Joe Baker, secondary-special teams assistant; born June 29, 1969, Glen Ridge, N.J., lives in River Ridge, La. Wide receiver Princeton 1987-1990. No pro playing experience. College coach: East Stroudsburg 1991, Samford 1993, Wisconsin 1999. Pro coach: Birmingham Fire (WFL) 1992, Jacksonville Jaguars 1994-98, joined Saints in 2000.

John Bunting, linebackers; born July 15, 1950, Portland, Maine, lives in River Ridge, La. Linebacker North Carolina 1968-1971. Pro linebacker Philadelphia Eagles 1972-1982, Philadelphia Stars (USFL) 1983-84. College coach: Brown 1986, Rowan College 1987-1992 (head coach 1988-1992). Pro coach: Baltimore Stars (USFL) 1985, Kansas City Chiefs 1993-96, St. Louis Rams 1997-99, joined Saints in 2000.

Frank Cignetti, Jr., quarterbacks; born October 4, 1965, Pittsburgh, lives in Harahan, La. Defensive back Indiana (Pa.) 1984-87. No pro playing experience. College coach: Pittsburgh 1989, Indiana (Pa.) 1990-98. Pro coach: Kansas City Chiefs 1999, joined Saints in 2000.

Sam Clancy, defensive line; born May 29, 1958, Pittsburgh, lives in River Ridge, La. No college playing experience. Pro defensive lineman Seattle Seahawks 1982-83, Pittsburgh Maulers (USFL) 1984-85, Cleveland Browns 1985-88, Indianapolis Colts 1989-1993. Pro coach: Barcelona Dragons (NFLE) 1995-99, joined Saints in 2000.

Al Everest, special teams; born August 22, 1950, Santa Barbara, Calif., lives in River Ridge, La. Safety Southern Methodist 1970-71. No pro playing experience. College coach: Southern Methodist 1972, North Texas State 1973-74, Cameron (Okla.) 1974-75, U.S. International 1981-87. Pro coach: Arkansas Miners (PSFL) 1991-92, Birmingham Barracudas (CFL) 1995, Arizona Cardinals 1996-99, joined Saints in 2000.

Rock Gullickson, strength and conditioning; born April 11, 1955, Moorhead, Minn., lives in River Ridge, La. Guard Moorhead (Minn.) State 1973-76. College coach: Moorhead State 1978, Mayville (N.D.) State 1979-1980, South Dakota State 1981, Montana State 1982-89, Rutgers 1990-92, Texas 1993-97, Louisville 1998-99. Pro coach: Joined Saints in 2000.

Jack Henry, offensive line; born March 14, 1946, Wilmerding, Pa., lives in River Ridge, La. Linebacker Penn State 1964-65, guard Indiana (Pa.) 1967-68. No pro playing experience. College coach: West Virginia 1970, 1978-79, Edinboro 1973, Louisville 1974, Millersville 1975-76, Southern Illinois 1977, Appalachian State 1980, Wake Forest 1981-85, Indiana (Pa.) 1986-89, Pittsburgh 1993-95. Pro coach: Pittsburgh Steelers 1990-91, San Diego Chargers 1996, Detroit Lions 1997-99, joined Saints in 2000.

Evan Marcus, asst. strength and conditioning; born January 2, 1968, Cranford, N.J., lives in River Ridge, La. Tackle Ithaca College 1986-1990. No pro playing experience. College coach: Arizona State 1990-91, Rutgers 1993, Maryland 1994, Texas 1995-97, Louisville 1998-99. Pro coach: Joined Saints in 2000.

Mike McCarthy, offensive coordinator; born November 10, 1963, Pittsburgh, lives in Destrehan, La. Tight end Baker 1985-86. No pro playing experience. College coach: Fort Hays State 1987-88, Pittsburgh 1989-1992. Pro coach: Kansas City Chiefs 1993-98, Green Bay Packers 1999, joined Saints in 2000.

Winston Moss, defensive assistant; born December 24, 1965, Miami, lives in River Ridge, La. Linebacker Miami 1983-86. Pro linebacker Tampa Bay Buccaneers 1987-1990, Los Angeles Raiders 1991-94, Seattle Seahawks 1995-97. Pro coach: Seattle Seahawks 1998, joined Saints in 2000.

Bob Palcic, tight ends; born July 2, 1948, Gownada, N.Y., lives in River Ridge, La. Linebacker Dayton 1968-1970. No pro playing experience. College coach: Dayton 1974-75, Ball State 1976-77, Wisconsin 1978-1981, Arizona 1984-85, Ohio State 1986-1991, Southern California 1992, UCLA 1993. Pro coach: Atlanta Falcons 1994-96, Detroit Lions 1997-98, Cleveland Browns 1999, joined Saints in 2000.

Phil Pettey, offensive assistant; born April 17, 1961, Kenosha, Wis., lives in River Ridge, La. Guard Missouri 1984-86. Pro guard Washington Redskins 1987. College coach: LSU 1990, Pittsburgh 1991, Southern California 1999. Pro coach: Joined Saints in 2000.

Rick Venturi, asst. head coach–secondary; born February 23, 1946, Taylorville, Ill., lives in Destrehan, La. Quarterback-defensive back Northwestern 1965-67. No pro playing experience. College coach: Northwestern 1968-1972, 1978-1980 (head coach), Purdue 1973-76, Illinois 1977. Pro coach: Hamilton Tiger-Cats (CFL) 1981, Indianapolis Colts 1982-1993 (interim head coach for final 11 games of 1991), Cleveland Browns 1994-95, joined Saints in 1996 (interim head coach for final eight games of 1996).

Ron Zook, defensive coordinator; born April 28, 1954, Ashland, Ohio, lives in River Ridge, La. Defensive back Miami (Ohio) 1972-75. No pro playing experience. College coach: Murray State 1978-1980, Cincinnati 1981-82, Kansas 1983, Tennessee 1984-86, Virginia Tech 1987, Ohio State 1988-1990, Florida 1991-95. Pro coach: Pittsburgh Steelers 1996-98, Kansas City Chiefs 1999, joined Saints in 2000.

NEW YORK GIANTS

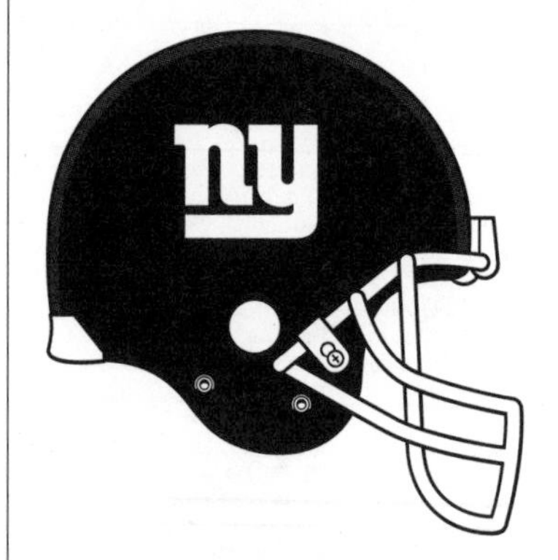

National Football Conference
Eastern Division
Team Colors: Blue, Red, and White
Giants Stadium
East Rutherford, New Jersey 07073
Telephone: (201) 935-8111

CLUB OFFICIALS

President/Co-CEO: Wellington T. Mara
Chairman/Co-CEO: Preston Robert Tisch
Executive Vice President/General Counsel: John K. Mara, Esq.
Treasurer: Jonathan Tisch
Vice President-General Manager: Ernie Accorsi
Vice President-Chief Financial Officer: John Pasquali
Vice President-Marketing: Rusty Hawley
Vice-President-Communications: Pat Hanlon
Assistant General Manager: Rick Donohue
Director of Player Personnel: Marv Sunderland
Director of Pro Personnel: David Gettleman
Assistant Director of Pro Personnel: Jerry Reese
Director of College Scouting: Jerry Shay
Director of Research and Development: Raymond J. Walsh, Jr.
Director of Player Development: Greg Gabriel
Pro Personnel Assistant: Geoff Mazza
Director of Promotion: Frank Mara
Ticket Manager: John Gorman
Director of Administration: Jim Phelan
Controller: Christine Procops
Director of Community Relations: Allison Stangeby
Director of Sales: Dan Lynch
Director of Corporate Sponsorship: Bill Smith
Director of Creative Services: Doug Murphy
Assistant Director of Community and Media Relations: Peter John-Baptiste
Assistant Director of Communications: Avis Roper
Head Athletic Trainer: Ronnie Barnes
Assistant Athletic Trainers: John Johnson, Steve Kennelly, Byron Hansen
Equipment Manager: Ed Wagner, Jr.
Stadium: Giants Stadium • **Capacity:** 79,469
East Rutherford, New Jersey 07073
Playing Surface: Natural Grass
Training Camp: University at Albany
1400 Washington Avenue
Albany, N.Y. 12222

2000 SCHEDULE

PRESEASON

Aug. 5	**Chicago**	8:00
Aug. 11	at Jacksonville	8:00
Aug. 18	at New York Jets	8:00
Aug. 25	**Baltimore**	8:00

REGULAR SEASON

Sept. 3	**Arizona**	1:00
Sept. 10	at Philadelphia	1:00
Sept. 17	at Chicago	3:15
Sept. 24	**Washington**	8:35
Oct. 1	at Tennessee	12:00
Oct. 8	at Atlanta	4:05
Oct. 15	**Dallas**	1:00
Oct. 22	Open Date	
Oct. 29	**Philadelphia**	4:05
Nov. 5	at Cleveland	1:00
Nov. 12	**St. Louis**	4:15
Nov. 19	**Detroit**	1:00
Nov. 26	at Arizona	6:35
Dec. 3	at Washington	1:00
Dec. 10	**Pittsburgh**	1:00
Dec. 17	at Dallas	7:35
Dec. 23	**Jacksonville** (Sat.)	12:30

RECORD HOLDERS

INDIVIDUAL RECORDS—CAREER

Category	Name	Performance
Rushing (Yds.)	Rodney Hampton, 1990-97	6,897
Passing (Yds.)	Phil Simms, 1979-1993	33,462
Passing (TDs)	Phil Simms, 1979-1993	199
Receiving (No.)	Joe Morrison, 1959-1972	395
Receiving (Yds.)	Frank Gifford, 1952-1960, 1962-64	5,434
Interceptions	Emlen Tunnell, 1948-1958	74
Punting (Avg.)	Don Chandler, 1956-1964	43.8
Punt Return (Avg.)	David Meggett, 1989-1994	11.0
Kickoff Return (Avg.)	Rocky Thompson, 1971-72	27.2
Field Goals	Pete Gogolak, 1966-1974	126
Touchdowns (Tot.)	Frank Gifford, 1952-1960, 1962-64	78
Points	Pete Gogolak, 1966-1974	646

INDIVIDUAL RECORDS—SINGLE SEASON

Category	Name	Performance
Rushing (Yds.)	Joe Morris, 1986	1,516
Passing (Yds.)	Phil Simms, 1984	4,044
Passing (TDs)	Y.A. Tittle, 1963	36
Receiving (No.)	Amani Toomer, 1999	79
Receiving (Yds.)	Homer Jones, 1967	1,209
Interceptions	Otto Schnellbacher, 1951	11
	Jim Patton, 1958	11
Punting (Avg.)	Don Chandler, 1959	46.6
Punt Return (Avg.)	Merle Hapes, 1942	15.5
Kickoff Return (Avg.)	John Salscheider, 1949	31.6
Field Goals	Ali Haji-Sheikh, 1983	35
Touchdowns (Tot.)	Joe Morris, 1985	21
Points	Ali Haji-Sheikh, 1983	127

INDIVIDUAL RECORDS—SINGLE GAME

Category	Name	Performance
Rushing (Yds.)	Gene Roberts, 11-12-50	218
Passing (Yds.)	Phil Simms, 10-13-85	513
Passing (TDs)	Y.A. Tittle, 10-28-62	*7
Receiving (No.)	Tiki Barber, 1-2-00	13
Receiving (Yds.)	Del Shofner, 10-28-62	269
Interceptions	Many times	3
	Last time by Terry Kinard, 9-27-87	
Field Goals	Joe Danelo, 10-18-81	6
Touchdowns (Tot.)	Ron Johnson, 10-2-72	4
	Earnest Gray, 9-7-80	4
	Rodney Hampton, 9-24-95	4
Points	Ron Johnson, 10-2-72	24
	Earnest Gray, 9-7-80	24
	Rodney Hampton, 9-24-95	24

*NFL Record

COACHING HISTORY

(552-465-33)

1925	Bob Folwell	8-4-0
1926	Joe Alexander	8-4-1
1927-28	Earl Potteiger	15-8-3
1929-30	LeRoy Andrews*	24-5-1
1930	Benny Friedman-Steve Owen	2-0-0
1931-53	Steve Owen	153-108-17
1954-60	Jim Lee Howell	55-29-4
1961-68	Allie Sherman	57-54-4
1969-73	Alex Webster	29-40-1
1974-76	Bill Arnsparger**	7-28-0
1976-78	John McVay	14-23-0
1979-82	Ray Perkins	24-35-0
1983-90	Bill Parcells	85-52-1
1991-92	Ray Handley	14-18-0
1993-96	Dan Reeves	32-34-0
1997-99	Jim Fassel	25-23-1

*Released after 15 games in 1930
**Released after seven games in 1976

GIANTS STADIUM

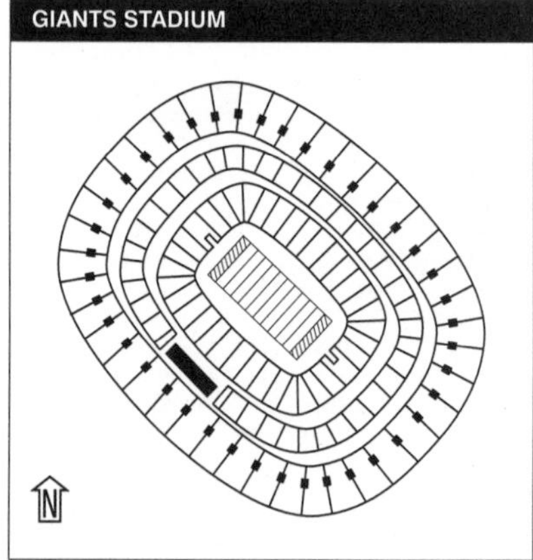

1999 TEAM RECORD

PRESEASON (2-2)

Date	Result		Opponent
8/13	W	36-21	at Minnesota
8/21	W	27-20	Jacksonville
8/28	L	10-16	New York Jets
9/3	L	24-28	at Baltimore

REGULAR SEASON (7-9)

Date	Result		Opponent	Att.
9/12	W	17-13	at Tampa Bay	65,026
9/19	L	21-50	Washington	77,622
9/26	L	14-16	at New England	59,169
10/3	W	16-15	Philadelphia	77,959
10/10	L	3-14	at Arizona	49,015
10/18	W	13-10	Dallas	78,204
10/24	W	31-3	New Orleans	77,982
10/31	W	23-17	at Philadelphia (OT)	66,481
11/14	L	19-27	Indianapolis	78,081
11/21	L	13-23	at Washington	78,641
11/28	L	24-34	Arizona	77,809
12/5	W	41-28	New York Jets	78,200
12/12	W	19-17	at Buffalo	72,527
12/19	L	10-31	at St. Louis	66,065
12/26	L	17-34	Minnesota	78,095
1/2	L	18-26	at Dallas	63,767

(OT) Overtime

SCORE BY PERIODS

Giants	54	82	36	121	6	—	299
Opponents	68	108	70	112	0	—	358

ATTENDANCE

Home 623,777 Away 515,876 Total 1,139,653
Single-game home record, 78,204 (10/18/99)
Single-season home record, 623,777 (1999)

1999 TEAM STATISTICS

	Giants	Opp.
Total First Downs	308	270
Rushing	87	81
Passing	197	170
Penalty	24	19
Third Down: Made/Att.	84/232	74/219
Third Down Pct.	36.2	33.8
Fourth Down: Made/Att.	12/19	5/17
Fourth Down Pct.	63.2	29.4
Total Net Yards	5,127	4,981
Avg. Per Game	320.4	311.3
Total Plays	1,075	990
Avg. Per Play	4.8	5.0
Net Yards Rushing	1,408	1,560
Avg. Per Game	88.0	97.5
Total Rushes	431	447
Net Yards Passing	3,719	3,421
Avg. Per Game	232.4	213.8
Sacked/Yards Lost	42/296	32/172
Gross Yards	4,015	3,593
Att./Completions	602/350	511/295
Completion Pct.	58.1	57.7
Had Intercepted	20	17
Punts/Average	89/41.0	78/43.9
Net Punting Avg.	89/35.1	78/35.7
Penalties/Yards	98/906	92/750
Fumbles/Ball Lost	29/12	23/7
Touchdowns	32	41
Rushing	11	13
Passing	17	20
Returns	4	8
Avg. Time of Possession	30:31	29:29

1999 INDIVIDUAL STATISTICS

Passing	Att.	Comp.	Yds.	Pct.	TD	Int.	Tkld.	Rate
K. Collins	331	190	2,318	57.4	8	11	16/112	73.3
Graham	271	160	1,697	59.0	9	9	26/184	74.6
Giants	602	350	4,015	58.1	17	20	42/296	73.9
Opponents	511	295	3,593	57.7	20	17	32/172	78.7

SCORING	TD R	TD P	TD Rt	PAT	FG	Saf	PTS
Blanchard	0	0	0	19/19	18/21	0	73
Toomer	0	6	0	0/0	0/0	0	36
Daluiso	0	0	0	9/9	7/9	0	30
Montgomery	3	0	0	0/0	0/0	0	20
Barber	0	2	1	0/0	0/0	0	18
Hilliard	0	3	0	0/0	0/0	0	18
Johnson	2	1	0	0/0	0/0	0	18
Mitchell	0	3	0	0/0	0/0	0	18
K. Collins	2	0	0	0/0	0/0	0	14
Way	2	0	0	0/0	0/0	0	12
Alford	0	1	0	0/0	0/0	0	6
Bennett	1	0	0	0/0	0/0	0	6
Graham	1	0	0	0/0	0/0	0	6
Jurevicius	0	1	0	0/0	0/0	0	6
Peter	0	0	1	0/0	0/0	0	6
Strahan	0	0	1	0/0	0/0	0	6
Weathers	0	0	1	0/0	0/0	0	6
Giants	11	17	4	28/28	25/30	0	299
Opponents	13	20	8	38/39	24/37	1	358

2-Pt. Conversions: K. Collins, Montgomery. Team 2-3, Opponents 0-2.

RUSHING	Att.	Yds.	Avg.	LG	TD
Montgomery	115	348	3.0	14	3
Barber	62	258	4.2	30	0
Brown	55	177	3.2	28	0
Johnson	61	143	2.3	17	2
Way	49	141	2.9	17	2
Graham	35	132	3.8	17	1
Bennett	29	126	4.3	40	1
K. Collins	19	36	1.9	11	2
Patten	1	27	27.0	27	0
Hilliard	3	16	5.3	24	0
Toomer	1	4	4.0	4	0
Comella	1	0	0.0	0	0
Giants	431	1,408	3.3	40	11
Opponents	447	1,560	3.5	72	13

RECEIVING	No.	Yds.	Avg.	LG	TD
Toomer	79	1,183	15.0	80t	6
Hilliard	72	996	13.8	46	3
Barber	66	609	9.2	56	2
Mitchell	58	520	9.0	25	3
Jurevicius	18	318	17.7	71	1
Johnson	12	86	7.2	28	1
Way	11	59	5.4	16	0
Patten	9	115	12.8	19	0
Cross	9	55	6.1	12	0
Comella	8	39	4.9	26	0
Bennett	4	27	6.8	16	0
Brown	2	2	1.0	1	0
Alford	1	7	7.0	7t	1
Graham	1	-1	-1.0	-1	0
Giants	350	4,015	11.5	80t	17
Opponents	295	3,593	12.2	90t	20

INTERCEPTIONS	No.	Yds.	Avg.	LG	TD
Ellsworth	6	80	13.3	26	0
Armstead	2	35	17.5	31	0
Garnes	2	7	3.5	4	0
Strahan	1	44	44.0	44t	1
Levingston	1	34	34.0	34	0
Sparks	1	28	28.0	28	0
Weathers	1	8	8.0	8t	1
Lincoln	1	0	0.0	0	0
Phillips	1	0	0.0	0	0
Sehorn	1	-4	-4.0	-4	0
Giants	17	232	13.6	44t	2
Opponents	20	322	16.1	70t	5

PUNTING	No.	Yds.	Avg.	In 20	LG
Maynard	89	3,651	41.0	31	63
Giants	89	3,651	41.0	31	63
Opponents	78	3,428	43.9	22	64

PUNT RETURNS	No.	FC	Yds.	Avg.	LG	TD
Barber	44	13	506	11.5	85t	1
Toomer	1	0	14	14.0	14	0
Giants	45	13	520	11.6	85t	1
Opponents	38	16	405	10.7	39t	1

KICKOFF RETURNS	No.	Yds.	Avg.	LG	TD
Patten	33	673	20.4	45	0
Levingston	22	532	24.2	35	0
Barber	12	266	22.2	41	0
Comella	2	31	15.5	17	0
Giants	69	1,502	21.8	45	0
Opponents	53	1,152	21.7	85t	1

FIELD GOALS	1-19	20-29	30-39	40-49	50+
Blanchard	0/0	7/7	2/4	9/10	0/0
Daluiso	0/0	4/4	3/3	0/2	0/0
Giants	0/0	11/11	5/7	9/12	0/0
Opponents	1/1	10/11	7/11	5/9	1/5

SACKS	No.
Armstead	9.0
Jones	7.5
Strahan	5.5
K. Hamilton	4.0
Widmer	3.0
Galyon	1.0
Garnes	1.0
Harris	1.0
Giants	32.0
Opponents	42.0

2000 DRAFT CHOICES

Round	Name	Pos.	College
1	Ron Dayne	RB	Wisconsin
2	Cornelius Griffin	DT	Alabama
3	Ron Dixon	WR	Lambuth
4	Brandon Short	LB	Penn State
5	Ralph Brown	DB	Nebraska
6	Dhani Jones	LB	Michigan
7	Jeremiah Parker	DE	California

NEW YORK GIANTS

2000 VETERAN ROSTER

No.	Name	Pos.	Ht.	Wt.	Birthdate	NFL Exp.	College	Hometown	How Acq.	'99 Games/ Starts
80	Alford, Brian	WR	6-1	190	6/7/75	3	Purdue	Oak Park, Mich.	D3-'98	2/0
98	Armstead, Jessie	LB	6-1	240	10/26/70	8	Miami	Dallas, Tex.	D8-'93	16/16
21	† Barber, Tiki	RB	5-10	200	4/7/75	4	Virginia	Roanoke, Va.	D2-'97	16/1
58	Barrow, Mike	LB	6-2	236	4/19/70	8	Miami	Homestead, Fla.	FA-'00	16/16*
44	Bennett, Sean	RB	6-1	230	11/9/75	2	Northwestern	Evansville, Ind.	D4-'99	9/2
76	Brown, Lomas	T	6-4	290	3/30/63	16	Florida	Miami, Fla.	UFA(Cle)-'00	10/10*
89	Campbell, Dan	TE	6-5	265	4/13/76	2	Texas A&M	Glen Rose, Tex.	D3-'99	12/1
18	† Cherry, Mike	QB	6-3	225	12/15/73	4	Murray State	Texarkana, Ark.	D6-'97	0*
57	Childress, O.J.	LB	6-1	245	12/6/75	2	Clemson	Hermitage, Tenn.	FA-'99	4/0
5	Collins, Kerry	QB	6-5	250	12/30/72	6	Penn State	Lebanon, Pa.	UFA(NO)-'99	10/7
34	Comella, Greg	RB	6-1	248	7/29/75	3	Stanford	Wellesley, Mass.	FA-'98	16/3
95	Cousins, Jomo	DE	6-5	285	9/4/74	2	Florida A&M	Seneca Valley, Calif.	FA-'00	0*
87	Cross, Howard	TE	6-5	285	8/8/67	12	Alabama	Huntsville, Ala.	D6-'89	16/15
3	Daluiso, Brad	PK	6-1	180	12/31/67	10	UCLA	San Diego, Calif.	FA-'93	6/0
69	† Engler, Derek	C	6-5	300	7/11/74	4	Wisconsin	St. Paul, Minn.	FA-'00	10/4
20	Garnes, Sam	S	6-3	225	7/12/74	4	Cincinnati	Bronx, N.Y.	D5-'97	16/16
17	Garrett, Jason	QB	6-2	200	3/28/66	8	Princeton	Chagrin, Ohio	UFA(Dall)-'00	5/2*
93	Hale, Ryan	DT	6-4	295	7/10/75	2	Arkansas	Rodgers, Ark.	D7a-'99	9/0
41	Hamilton, Conrad	CB	5-10	195	11/5/74	5	Eastern New Mexico	Alamogordo, N.M.	D7-'96	3/2
75	Hamilton, Keith	DT	6-6	295	5/25/71	9	Pittsburgh	Lynchburg, Va.	D4-'92	16/16
72	Hansen, Carl	DT	6-5	282	1/25/75	2	Stanford	Houston, Tex.	FA-'00	0*
88	Hilliard, Ike	WR	5-11	198	4/5/76	4	Florida	Patterson, La.	D1-'97	16/16
94	Jones, Cedric	DE	6-4	275	4/30/74	5	Oklahoma	Houston, Tex.	D1-'96	16/16
84	Jurevicius, Joe	WR	6-5	230	12/23/74	3	Penn State	Chardon, Ohio	D2-'98	16/1
24	Levingston, Bashir	CB	5-9	180	10/2/76	2	Eastern Washington	Seaside, Calif.	FA-'99	12/0
9	† Maynard, Brad	P	6-1	190	2/9/74	4	Ball State	Atlanta, Ind.	D3-'97	16/0
26	McDaniel, Emmanuel	CB	5-9	180	7/27/72	3	East Carolina	Griffin, Ga.	FA-'99	7/2
83	Mitchell, Pete	TE	6-2	248	10/9/71	6	Boston College	Royal Oak, Mich.	UFA(Jax)-'99	15/6
33	Montgomery, Joe	RB	5-10	230	6/8/76	2	Ohio State	Robbins, Ill.	D2-'99	7/5
51	Monty, Pete	LB	6-2	250	7/3/74	4	Wisconsin	Ft. Collins, Colo.	D4-'97	16/3
62	Parker, Glenn	G	6-5	311	4/22/66	11	Arizona	Huntington Beach, Calif.	FA-'00	12/11*
99	Peter, Christian	DT	6-3	300	10/5/72	4	Nebraska	Locust, N.J.	FA-'97	16/10
77	Petitgout, Luke	T	6-6	315	6/16/76	2	Notre Dame	Georgetown, Del.	D1-'99	15/8
91	Phillips, Ryan	LB	6-4	252	2/7/74	4	Idaho	Auburn, Wash.	D3-'97	16/16
78	Rosenthal, Mike	G	6-7	315	6/10/77	2	Notre Dame	Granger, Ind.	D5-'99	9/7
31	Sehorn, Jason	CB	6-2	215	4/15/71	7	Southern California	Mt. Shasta, Calif.	D2-'94	10/10
29	Settles, Tawambi	S	6-2	194	1/19/76	2	Duke	Chattanooga, Tenn.	FA-'00	0*
65	Stone, Ron	G	6-5	320	7/20/71	8	Boston College	Roxbury, Mass.	RFA(Dall)-'96	16/16
92	Strahan, Michael	DE	6-5	275	11/21/71	8	Texas Southern	Westbury, Tex.	D2-'93	16/16
23	Thomas, Dave	CB	6-3	218	8/25/68	8	Tennessee	Miami, Fla.	FA-'00	15/0*
81	Toomer, Amani	WR	6-3	205	9/8/74	5	Michigan	Berkeley, Calif.	D2-'96	16/16
35	Weathers, Andre	CB	6-0	190	8/6/76	2	Michigan	Flint, Mich.	D6b-'99	9/0
37	West, Lyle	S	6-0	215	12/20/76	2	San Jose State	Fremont, Calif.	D6a-'99	6/0
66	Whittle, Jason	G	6-4	305	3/7/75	2	Southwest Missouri State	Springfield, Mo.	FA-'98	16/1
96	Williams, George	DT	6-3	298	12/8/75	3	North Carolina State	Roseboro, N.C.	FA-'98	16/0
36	Williams, Shaun	S	6-2	215	10/10/76	3	UCLA	Encino, Calif.	D1-'98	11/0
52	Zeigler, Dusty	C	6-5	303	9/27/73	5	Notre Dame	Rincon, Ga.	UFA(Buff)-'00	15/15*

* Barrow played 16 games with Carolina in '99; Brown played 10 games with Cleveland; Cherry was inactive for 14 games; Cousins last active with Arizona in '98; Garrett played 5 games with Dallas; Hansen last active with N.Y. Jets in '98; Parker played 12 games with Kansas City; Settles last active with Jacksonville in '98; Thomas played 15 games with Jacksonville; Zeigler played 15 games with Buffalo.

† Restricted free agent; subject to developments.

Retired—Charles Way, 5-year running back, 11 games played in '99.

Players lost to free agency (6): K Cary Blanchard (Ariz; 10 games in '99), S Percy Ellsworth (Cle; 14), LB Scott Gaylon (Mia; 16), DT Bernard Holsey (Ind; 16), CB Jeremy Lincoln (Den; 15), T Roman Oben (Cle; 16).

Also played with Giants in '99—RB Gary Brown (3 games), LB Marcus Buckley (12), K Jose Cortez (1), T Scott Gragg (16), QB Kent Graham (9), DT Robert Harris (6), RB LeShon Johnson (16), T Toby Myles (8), WR David Patten (16), S Brandon Sanders (9), CB Phillippi Sparks (11), DB Tre Thomas (2), C Brian Williams (12), LB Corey Widmer (15).

COACHING STAFF

Head Coach,
Jim Fassel

Pro Career: Was named the fifteenth head coach in Giants history on January 15, 1997. Enters his fourth season as head coach of the Giants. In 1998, the Giants finished 8-8 by winning five of their last six games. In 1997, Fassel led his squad to a 10-5-1 record and a berth in the playoffs while capturing the NFC East title. He was named coach of the year by 11 media outlets as the Giants became the fifteenth team in NFL history to finish in first place in their division the season after finishing last. Fassel entered the NFL with the Giants in 1991 as quarterbacks coach, then as offensive coordinator in 1992. Fassel spent two campaigns as assistant head coach/offensive coordinator for the Denver Broncos (1993 and 1994), the 1995 season as quarterbacks coach for the Oakland Raiders, and was the offensive coordinator and quarterbacks coach for the Arizona Cardinals in 1996. Fassel has been credited with an ability to develop quarterbacks, including John Elway, Kent Graham, and Boomer Esiason. Career record: 25-23-1.

Background: Fassel began coaching in 1973 at his alma mater, Fullerton College, then was a player-coach for the Hawaii Hawaiians of the World Football League in 1974. He coached at Utah (1976), Weber State (1977-78), and Stanford (1979-1983). At Stanford, Fassel was credited with recruiting and coaching John Elway. Fassel entered the pro arena in 1984 as offensive coordinator for the New Orleans Breakers of the USFL, then returned to Utah as head coach (1985-89).

Personal: A native of Anaheim, California, Fassel led Fullerton College to the junior college national championship in 1967. He also played collegiately at Southern California with Seattle Seahawks head coach Mike Holmgren and at Long Beach State. He was drafted by the Chicago Bears in the seventh round of the 1972 NFL draft and played briefly with Chicago, the Houston Oilers, and San Diego Chargers. Born August 31, 1949 in Anaheim, Calif. Fassel and his wife, Kitty, have four children—John, Brian, Jana, and Mike.

ASSISTANT COACHES

Dave Brazil, defensive quality control; born March 25, 1936, Detroit, lives in East Rutherford, N.J. No college or pro playing experience. College coach: Holy Cross 1968, Tulsa 1969-1970, Eastern Michigan 1971-73, Boston College 1980, Kent State 1981-82. Pro coach: Detroit Wheels (WFL) 1974, Chicago Wind (WFL) 1975, Kansas City Chiefs 1984-88, Pittsburgh Steelers 1989-1991, joined Giants in 1992.

John Dunn, strength and conditioning; born July 22, 1956, Hillsdale, N.Y., lives in Wayne, N.J. Guard Penn State 1974-77. No pro playing experience. College coach: Penn State 1978. Pro coach: Washington Redskins 1984-86, Los Angeles Raiders 1987-89, San Diego Chargers 1990-96, joined Giants in 1997.

John Fox, defensive coordinator; born February 8, 1955, Virginia Beach, Va., lives in Wayne, N.J. Defensive back San Diego State 1975-77. No pro playing experience. College coach: U.S. International 1979, Boise State 1980, Long Beach State 1981, Utah 1982, Kansas 1983, 1985, Iowa State 1984, Pittsburgh 1986-88. Pro coach: Los Angeles Express (USFL) 1985, Pittsburgh Steelers 1989-1991, San Diego Chargers 1992-93, Los Angeles/Oakland Raiders 1994-95, St. Louis Rams 1996, joined Giants in 1997.

Mike Gillhamer, offensive assistant; born February 20, 1954, Oakland, lives in Somerset, N.J. Defensive back Humboldt State. No pro playing experience. College coach: College of the Sequoias 1979-1983, Weber State 1984, Utah 1985-89, San Jose State 1990-93, Nevada 1994-95, Rutgers 1996. Pro coach: Joined Giants in 1997.

Johnnie Lynn, defensive backs; born December 19, 1956, Los Angeles, lives in Wayne, N.J. Defensive back UCLA 1975-78. Pro defensive back New York Jets 1979-1986. College coach: Arizona 1988-1993. Pro coach: Tampa Bay Buccaneers 1994-95, San Francisco 49ers 1996, joined Giants in 1997.

Larry MacDuff, special teams; born June 22, 1948, Clinton, Iowa, lives in Mundham, N.J. Defensive end Fullerton C.C. 1966-67, Oklahoma 1968-69. No pro playing experience. College coach: Fullerton C.C. 1970, 1974-79, Stanford 1980-83, Hawaii 1984-86, Arizona 1987-1996. Pro coach: Joined Giants in 1997.

Denny Marcin, defensive line; born April 24, 1942, Cleveland, lives in Wayne, N.J. Defensive and offensive line Miami (Ohio) 1961-64. No pro playing experience. College coach: Miami (Ohio) 1974-77, North Carolina 1978-1987, Illinois 1988-1996. Pro coach: Joined Giants in 1997.

Jim McNally, offensive line; born December 13, 1943, Buffalo, lives in Cedar Grove, N.J. Guard Buffalo 1961-65. No pro playing experience. College coach: Buffalo 1966-1970, Marshall 1971-74, Boston College 1975-77, Wake Forest 1978-79. Pro coach: Cincinnati Bengals 1980-1994, Carolina Panthers 1995-98, joined Giants in 1999.

Tom Olivadotti, linebackers; born September 22, 1945, Long Beach, N.J., lives in Glennrock, N.J. Defensive back-wide receiver Upsala 1963-66. No pro playing experience. College coach: Princeton 1975-77, Boston College 1978-79, Miami 1980-83. Pro coach: Cleveland Browns 1985-86, Miami Dolphins 1987-1995, Minnesota Vikings 1996-99, joined Giants in 2000.

Sean Payton, offensive coordinator-quarterbacks; born December 29, 1963, San Mateo, Calif., lives in Wayne, N.J. Quarterback Eastern Illinois 1982-86. Pro quarterback Ottawa Rough Riders (CFL) 1987, Chicago Bears 1987. College coach: San Diego State 1988-89, 1992-93, Indiana State 1990-91, Miami (Ohio) 1994-95, Illinois 1996. Pro coach: Philadelphia Eagles 1997-98, joined Giants in 1999.

Mike Pope, tight ends; born March 15, 1942, Monroe, N.C., lives in Somerset, N.J. Quarterback Lenoir-Rhyne 1962-64. No pro playing experience. College coach: Florida State 1970-74, Texas Tech 1975-77, Mississippi 1978-1982. Pro coach: New York Giants 1983-1991, Cincinnati Bengals 1992-93, New England Patriots 1994-96, Washington Redskins 1997-99, joined Giants in 2000.

Jimmy Robinson, wide receivers; born January 3, 1953, Atlanta, lives in Wayne, N.J. Wide receiver Georgia Tech 1972-74. Pro wide receiver Atlanta Falcons 1975, New York Giants 1976-79, San Francisco 49ers 1980, Denver Broncos 1981. College coach: Georgia Tech 1986-89. Pro coach: Memphis Showboats (USFL) 1984-85, Atlanta Falcons 1990-93, Indianapolis Colts 1994-97, joined Giants in 1998.

Jim Skipper, asst. head coach-running backs; born January 23, 1949, Breaux Bridge, La., lives in Clifton, N.J. Defensive back Whittier College 1971-72. No pro playing experience. College coach: Cal Poly-Pomona 1974-76, San Jose State 1977-78, Pacific 1979, Oregon 1980-82. Pro coach: Philadelphia/Baltimore Stars (USFL) 1983-85, New Orleans Saints 1986-1995, Arizona Cardinals 1996, joined Giants in 1997.

Craig Stoddard, asst. strength and conditioning; born February 8, 1972, North Tarrytown, N.Y., lives in Hackensack, N.J. Linebacker Springfield College 1990-93. No pro playing experience. College coach: Penn State 1995-96. Pro coach: San Diego Chargers 1994, joined Giants in 1997.

2000 FIRST-YEAR ROSTER

Name	Pos.	Ht.	Wt.	Birthdate	College	Hometown	How Acq.
Aikins, Brian (1)	RB	6-1	253	10/18/75	Oklahoma State	Woodbridge, N.J.	FA
Bober, Chris	T	6-5	317	12/24/76	Nebraska-Omaha	Omaha, Neb.	FA
Brown, Ralph	CB	5-10	178	9/9/78	Nebraska	Hacienda Heights, Calif.	D5
Burke, Bill	QB	6-5	208	9/27/76	Michigan State	Warren, Ohio	FA
Dayne, Ron	RB	5-10	253	3/14/78	Wisconsin	Berlin, N.J.	D1
Dixon, Ron	WR	6-0	176	5/28/76	Lambuth	Wildwood, Fla.	D3
Elisara, Pita	T	6-4	300	11/16/76	Indiana	American Samoa	FA
Ellis, Lavell (1)	DE	6-4	267	9/5/76	Kent State	Warrensville Heights, Ohio	FA
Ferrara, Frank (1)	DE	6-3	273	12/25/75	Rhode Island	Brooklyn, N.Y.	FA-'99
Goff, Jim	T	6-4	295	12/7/77	Lafayette	Hawthorne, N.J.	FA
Golden, Jack	LB	6-1	225	1/28/77	Oklahoma State	Harvey, Ill.	FA
Griffin, Cornelius	DT	6-3	294	12/3/76	Alabama	Brundidge, Ala.	D2
Jones, Dhani	LB	6-1	235	2/22/78	Michigan	Potomac, Md.	D6
Keck, Tinker	S	6-1	200	8/10/76	Cincinnati	Goodland, Kan.	FA
Kiernan, Scott (1)	G	6-3	310	8/16/74	Syracuse	Cos Cob, Conn.	FA
Kuzora, John	T	6-5	308	9/30/75	Montclair State	Upper Saddle River, N.J.	FA
Lewis, Fred	CB	5-10	192	11/15/76	Louisiana Tech	Franklin, La.	FA
Lewis, Kevin	LB	6-1	227	10/6/78	Duke	Orlando, Fla.	FA
Mitchell, Cordell	RB	6-0	205	2/10/77	Penn State	Syracuse, N.Y.	FA
Nori, Mark (1)	G	6-4	306	1/1/74	Boston College	Philadelphia, Pa.	FA
Parker, Jeremiah	DE	6-5	275	11/15/77	California	Richmond, Calif.	D7
Pittman, Cedric	DE	6-4	257	6/8/77	Nevada-Reno	Colorado Springs, Colo.	FA
Prentiss, Kevin	WR	5-10	160	1/19/76	Mississippi State	Vicksburg, Miss.	FA
Rasheed, Duwad	RB	5-10	226	1/22/77	Duke	Birmingham, Ala.	FA
Schmitz, Brian	P-K	6-0	165	6/12/78	North Carolina	Park Ridge, Ill.	FA
Settles, Tawambi	S	6-2	194	1/19/76	Duke	Chattanooga, Tenn.	FA
Short, Brandon	LB	6-3	253	7/11/77	Penn State	McKeesport, Pa.	D4
Stephens, Reggie (1)	CB	5-9	200	2/21/75	Rutgers	Santa Cruz, Calif.	FA-'99
Strickland, Vernon (1)	LB	6-3	250	4/9/73	Georgia Tech	Newman, Ga.	FA
Talaeai, Faiva	DT	6-4	293	5/6/74	Oregon	San Francisco, Calif.	FA
Thomas, Mark (1)	TE	6-4	258	5/26/76	North Carolina State	Smithfield, N.C.	FA
Tucker, Anthony (1)	WR	6-0	190	2/27/76	Fresno State	Colorado Springs, Colo.	FA
Watkins, Jeremy	WR	5-11	166	1/27/76	Montana	Missoula, Mont.	FA
Young, Adam (1)	TE	6-4	260	4/15/77	Dartmouth	Concord, N.H.	FA
Ziemann, Chris	T	6-7	310	9/20/76	Michigan	Aurora, Ill.	FA

The term NFL Rookie is defined as a player who is in his first season of professional football and has not been on the roster of another professional football team for any regular-season or postseason games. A Rookie is designated by an "R" on NFL rosters. Players who have been active in another professional football league or players who have NFL experience, including either preseason training camp or being on an Active List or Inactive List, or on Reserve/Injured or Reserve/Physically Unable to Perform for fewer than six regular-season games, are termed NFL First-Year Players. An NFL First-Year Player is designated by a "1" on NFL rosters. Thereafter, a player is credited with an additional year of experience for each season in which he accumulates six games on the Active List or Inactive List, or on Reserve/Injured or Reserve/Physically Unable to Perform.

NOTES

PHILADELPHIA EAGLES

National Football Conference
Eastern Division
Team Colors: Midnight Green, Silver, Black, and White
Veterans Stadium
3501 South Broad Street
Philadelphia, Pennsylvania 19148
Telephone: (215) 463-2500

CLUB OFFICIALS

President/Chief Executive Officer: Jeffrey Lurie
Executive Vice President/Chief Operating Officer: Joe Banner
Director of Football Operations: Tom Modrak
Senior Vice President/Business Operations: Len Komoroski
Senior Vice President/Chief Financial Officer: Don Smolenski
Vice President, Corporate Sales: Dave Rowan
Executive Director of Eagles Youth Partnership: Sarah Helfman
Director of Pro Scouting: Mike McCartney
Director of College Scouting: John Goeller
Director of Administration: Vicki Chatley
Director of Public Relations: Ron Howard
Assistant Directors of Public Relations: Derek Boyko, Rich Burg
Director, Broadcasting/Exec. Producer Eagles Television Network: Rob Alberino
Director of Premium Services: Jason Gonella
Ticket Manager: Leo Carlin
Director of Merchandise: Steve Strawbridge
Director of Advertising and Promotions: Kim Babiak
Travel Coordinator: Tracey Bucher
Director of Security: Anthony (Butch) Buchanico
Director of Penthouse Operations: Christiana Noyalas
Head Athletic Trainer: Rick Burkholder
Asst. Athletic Trainer: Chris Peduzzi
Video Director: Mike Dougherty
Head Equipment Manager: John Hatfield
Stadium: Veterans Stadium • **Capacity:** 65,352
3501 South Broad Street
Philadelphia, Pennsylvania 19148
Playing Surface: AstroTurf-8
Training Camp: Lehigh University
Bethlehem, Pennsylvania 18015

2000 SCHEDULE

PRESEASON

July 30	at Cleveland	8:00
Aug. 5	at Baltimore	8:00
Aug. 18	**Tennessee**	7:30
Aug. 24	**Buffalo**	8:00

REGULAR SEASON

Sept. 3	at Dallas	3:05
Sept. 10	**New York Giants**	1:00
Sept. 17	at Green Bay	12:00
Sept. 24	at New Orleans	12:00
Oct. 1	**Atlanta**	8:35
Oct. 8	**Washington**	1:00
Oct. 15	at Arizona	1:15
Oct. 22	**Chicago**	1:00
Oct. 29	at New York Giants	4:05
Nov. 5	**Dallas**	1:00
Nov. 12	at Pittsburgh	1:00
Nov. 19	**Arizona**	1:00
Nov. 26	at Washington	1:00
Dec. 3	**Tennessee**	1:00
Dec. 10	at Cleveland	1:00
Dec. 17	Open Date	
Dec. 24	**Cincinnati**	1:00

RECORD HOLDERS

INDIVIDUAL RECORDS—CAREER

Category	Name	Performance
Rushing (Yds.)	Wilbert Montgomery, 1977-1984	6,538
Passing (Yds.)	Ron Jaworski, 1977-1986	26,963
Passing (TDs)	Ron Jaworski, 1977-1986	175
Receiving (No.)	Harold Carmichael, 1971-1983	589
Receiving (Yds.)	Harold Carmichael, 1971-1983	8,978
Interceptions	Bill Bradley, 1969-1976	34
	Eric Allen, 1988-1994	34
Punting (Avg.)	Joe Muha, 1946-1950	42.9
Punt Return (Avg.)	Steve Van Buren, 1944-1951	13.9
Kickoff Return (Avg.)	Steve Van Buren, 1944-1951	26.7
Field Goals	Paul McFadden, 1984-87	91
Touchdowns (Tot.)	Harold Carmichael, 1971-1983	79
Points	Bobby Walston, 1951-1962	881

INDIVIDUAL RECORDS—SINGLE SEASON

Category	Name	Performance
Rushing (Yds.)	Wilbert Montgomery, 1979	1,512
Passing (Yds.)	Randall Cunningham, 1988	3,808
Passing (TDs)	Sonny Jurgensen, 1961	32
Receiving (No.)	Irving Fryar, 1996	88
Receiving (Yds.)	Mike Quick, 1983	1,409
Interceptions	Bill Bradley, 1971	11
Punting (Avg.)	Joe Muha, 1948	47.2
Punt Return (Avg.)	Steve Van Buren, 1944	15.3
Kickoff Return (Avg.)	Al Nelson, 1972	29.1
Field Goals	Paul McFadden, 1984	30
Touchdowns (Tot.)	Steve Van Buren, 1945	18
Points	Paul McFadden, 1984	116

INDIVIDUAL RECORDS—SINGLE GAME

Category	Name	Performance
Rushing (Yds.)	Steve Van Buren, 11-27-49	205
Passing (Yds.)	Randall Cunningham, 9-17-89	447
Passing (TDs)	Adrian Burk, 10-17-54	*7
Receiving (No.)	Don Looney, 12-1-40	14
Receiving (Yds.)	Tommy McDonald, 12-10-60	237
Interceptions	Russ Craft, 9-24-50	*4
Field Goals	Tom Dempsey, 11-12-72	6
Touchdowns (Tot.)	Many times. Last time by Irving Fryar, 10-20-96	4
Points	Bobby Walston, 10-17-54	25

*NFL Record

VETERANS STADIUM

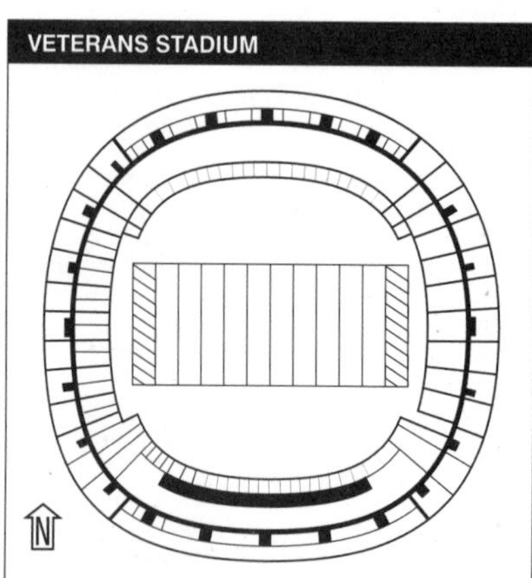

COACHING HISTORY

(405-490-25)

1933-35	Lud Wray	9-21-1
1936-40	Bert Bell	10-44-2
1941-50	Earle (Greasy) Neale*	66-44-5
1951	Alvin (Bo) McMillin**	2-0-0
1951	Wayne Millner	2-8-0
1952-55	Jim Trimble	25-20-3
1956-57	Hugh Devore	7-16-1
1958-60	Lawrence (Buck) Shaw	20-16-1
1961-63	Nick Skorich	15-24-3
1964-68	Joe Kuharich	28-41-1
1969-71	Jerry Williams***	7-22-2
1971-72	Ed Khayat	8-15-2
1973-75	Mike McCormack	16-25-1
1976-82	Dick Vermeil	57-51-0
1983-85	Marion Campbell****	17-29-1
1985	Fred Bruney	1-0-0
1986-90	Buddy Ryan	43-38-1
1991-94	Rich Kotite	37-29-0
1995-98	Ray Rhodes	30-36-1
1999	Andy Reid	5-11-0

*Co-coach with Walt Kiesling in Philadelphia-Pittsburgh merger in 1943
**Retired after two games in 1951
***Released after three games in 1971
****Released after 15 games in 1985

1999 TEAM RECORD

PRESEASON (1-3)

Date	Result		Opponent
8/12	L	7-10	Baltimore
8/20	L	9-10	at New York Jets
8/26	L	13-17	at Minnesota
9/2	W	30-17	Cleveland

REGULAR SEASON (5-11)

Date	Result		Opponent	Att.
9/12	L	24-25	Arizona	64,113
9/19	L	5-19	Tampa Bay	64,285
9/26	L	0-26	at Buffalo	70,872
10/3	L	15-16	at New York Giants	77,959
10/10	W	13-10	Dallas	66,669
10/17	W	20-16	at Chicago	66,944
10/24	L	13-16	at Miami	73,975
10/31	L	17-23	New York Giants (OT)	66,481
11/7	L	7-33	at Carolina	62,569
11/14	W	35-28	Washington	66,591
11/21	L	17-44	Indianapolis	65,521
11/28	L	17-20	at Washington (OT)	74,741
12/5	L	17-21	at Arizona	46,550
12/12	L	10-20	at Dallas	64,086
12/19	W	24-9	New England	65,475
1/2	W	38-31	St. Louis	60,700

(OT) Overtime

SCORE BY PERIODS

Eagles	71	77	38	86	0	—	272
Opponents	100	107	70	71	9	—	357

ATTENDANCE

Home 510,970 Away 547,546 Total 1,058,516
Single-game home record, 72,111 (11/1/81)
Single-season home record, 557,325 (1980)

1999 TEAM STATISTICS

	Eagles	Opp.
Total First Downs	218	328
Rushing	76	125
Passing	123	171
Penalty	19	32
Third Down: Made/Att	74/238	88/233
Third Down Pct.	31.1	37.8
Fourth Down: Made/Att	6/9	9/15
Fourth Down Pct.	66.7	60.0
Total Net Yards	3,830	54,62
Avg. Per Game	239.4	341.4
Total Plays	947	1,124
Avg. Per Play	4.0	4.9
Net Yards Rushing	1,746	2,001
Avg. Per Game	109.1	125.1
Total Rushes	424	519
Net Yards Passing	2,084	3,461
Avg. Per Game	130.3	216.3
Sacked/Yards Lost	49/321	37/272
Gross Yards	2,405	3,733
Att./Completions	474/235	568/322
Completion Pct.	49.6	56.7
Had Intercepted	18	28
Punts/Average	108/41.9	73/41.2
Net Punting Avg.	108/35.1	73/35.9
Penalties/Yards	102/905	89/719
Fumbles/Ball Lost	33/21	38/18
Touchdowns	29	36
Rushing	5	12
Passing	18	22
Returns	6	2
Avg. Time of Possession	27:03	32:57

1999 INDIVIDUAL STATISTICS

Passing	Att.	Comp.	Yds.	Pct.	TD	Int.	Tkld.	Rate
Pederson	227	119	1,276	52.4	7	9	20/109	62.9
McNabb	216	106	948	49.1	8	7	28/204	60.1
Detmer	29	10	181	34.5	3	2	0/0	62.6
Small	2	0	0	0.0	0	0	0/0	39.6
Staley	0	0	0	—	0	0	1/8	—
Eagles	474	235	2,405	49.6	18	18	49/321	61.4
Opponents	568	322	3,733	56.7	22	28	37/272	69.1

SCORING	TD R	TD P	TD Rt	PAT	FG	Saf	PTS
N. Johnson	0	0	0	25/25	18/25	0	79
Staley	4	2	0	0/0	0/0	0	36
Broughton	0	4	0	0/0	0/0	0	24
Small	0	4	0	0/0	0/0	0	24
Lewis	0	3	0	0/0	0/0	0	18
Jells	0	2	0	0/0	0/0	0	12
Akers	0	0	0	2/2	3/6	0	11
C. Johnson	0	1	0	0/0	0/0	1	8
Bieniemy	1	0	0	0/0	0/0	0	6
Brown	0	1	0	0/0	0/0	0	6
Dawkins	0	0	1	0/0	0/0	0	6
D. Douglas	0	1	0	0/0	0/0	0	6
A. Harris	0	0	1	0/0	0/0	0	6
Mamula	0	0	1	0/0	0/0	0	6
Rossum	0	0	1	0/0	0/0	0	6
Taylor	0	0	1	0/0	0/0	0	6
Whiting	0	0	1	0/0	0/0	0	6
McNabb	0	0	0	0/0	0/0	0	2
Weaver	0	0	0	0/0	0/0	0	2
Eagles	5	18	6	27/27	21/31	2	272
Opponents	12	22	2	33/33	36/45	0	357

2-Pt. Conversions: McNabb, Weaver.
Team 2-2, Opponents 0-2.

RUSHING	Att.	Yds.	Avg.	LG	TD
Staley	325	1,273	3.9	29	4
McNabb	47	313	6.7	27	0
Bieniemy	12	75	6.3	28	1
Pederson	20	33	1.7	19	0
Jam. Bostic	5	19	3.8	5	0
Watson	4	17	4.3	6	0
Turner	6	15	2.5	5	0
C. Martin	3	3	1.0	2	0
Detmer	2	-2	-1.0	-1	0
Eagles	424	1,746	4.1	29	5
Opponents	519	2,001	3.9	62t	12

RECEIVING	No.	Yds.	Avg.	LG	TD
Small	49	655	13.4	84t	4
Staley	41	294	7.2	19	2
C. Johnson	34	414	12.2	36	1
Broughton	26	295	11.3	33	4
Brown	18	188	10.4	27	1
Weaver	11	91	8.3	14	0
C. Martin	11	22	2.0	9	0
Jells	10	180	18.0	57t	2
Turner	9	46	5.1	14	0
D. Douglas	8	79	9.9	29t	1
Lewis	7	76	10.9	21	3
Jam. Bostic	5	8	1.6	7	0
Bieniemy	2	28	14.0	27	0
Finneran	2	21	10.5	11	0
T. Smith	1	14	14.0	14	0
McNabb	1	-6	-6.0	-6	0
Eagles	235	2,405	10.2	84t	18
Opponents	322	3,733	11.6	80t	22

INTERCEPTIONS	No.	Yds.	Avg.	LG	TD
Vincent	7	91	13.0	35	0
A. Harris	4	151	37.8	84	1
Dawkins	4	127	31.8	67t	1
Taylor	4	59	14.8	28	1
Trotter	2	30	15.0	30	0
Mamula	1	41	41.0	41t	1
Darling	1	33	33.0	33	0
Cook	1	29	29.0	29	0
Moore	1	28	28.0	28	0
Whiting	1	22	22.0	22t	1
Caldwell	1	12	12.0	12	0
Hauck	1	2	2.0	2	0
Eagles	28	625	22.3	84	5
Opponents	18	266	14.8	78t	2

PUNTING	No.	Yds.	Avg.	In 20	LG
Landeta	107	4,524	42.3	21	60
Eagles	108	4,524	41.9	21	60
Opponents	73	3,011	41.2	26	63

PUNT RETURNS	No.	FC	Yds.	Avg.	LG	TD
Rossum	28	17	250	8.9	39	0
C. Johnson	1	0	0	0.0	0	0
Brown	0	1	0	—	—	0
Eagles	29	18	250	8.6	39	0
Opponents	59	16	490	8.3	32	0

KICKOFF RETURNS	No.	Yds.	Avg.	LG	TD
Rossum	54	1,347	24.9	89t	1
Bieniemy	10	210	21.0	30	0
Whiting	3	49	16.3	21	0
Broughton	1	5	5.0	5	0
E. Smith	1	1	1.0	1	0
Reese	0	0	—	—	0
Eagles	69	1,612	23.4	89t	1
Opponents	57	1,305	22.9	48	0

FIELD GOALS	1-19	20-29	30-39	40-49	50+
N. Johnson	0/0	8/9	5/8	5/6	0/2
Akers	0/0	0/0	0/0	2/3	1/3
Eagles	0/0	8/9	5/8	7/9	1/5
Opponents	1/1	12/13	12/15	9/11	2/5

SACKS	No.
Mamula	8.5
Jefferson	4.0
Reese	3.0
T. Williams	3.0
W. Thomas	2.5
Trotter	2.5
H. Douglas	2.0
S. Martin	2.0
Dawkins	1.5
Caldwell	1.0
Cook	1.0
B. Johnson	1.0
H. Thomas	1.0
Vincent	1.0
Whiting	1.0
Eagles	37.0
Opponents	49.0

2000 DRAFT CHOICES

Round	Name	Pos.	College
1	Corey Simon	DT	Florida State
2	Todd Pinkston	WR	Southern Mississippi
	Bobby Williams	G	Arkansas
4	Gari Scott	WR	Michigan State
6	Thomas Hamner	RB	Minnesota
	John Frank	DE	Utah
	John Romero	C	California

PHILADELPHIA EAGLES

2000 VETERAN ROSTER

No.	Name	Pos.	Ht.	Wt.	Birthdate	NFL Exp.	College	Hometown	How Acq.	'99 Games/ Starts
2	Akers, David	K	5-10	180	12/9/74	2	Louisville	Lexington, Ky.	FA-'99	16/0
24	Autry, Darnell	RB	5-10	210	6/19/76	2	Northwestern	Tempe, Ariz.	FA-'98	0*
64	Barr, Robert	T	6-4	307	6/7/73	2	Rutgers	Wilkes-Barre, Pa.	FA-'99	0*
88	Bartrum, Mike	TE-LS	6-4	245	6/23/70	7	Marshall	Pomeroy, Ohio	FA-'00	16/0*
33	# Bieniemy, Eric	RB	5-7	205	8/15/69	10	Colorado	La Puente, Calif.	FA(Cin)-'99	16/0
55	Brandenburg, Dan	LB	6-2	255	2/16/73	4	Indiana State	Rensselaer, Ind.	FA(Buff)-'00	14/0*
6	Brice, Will	P	6-4	220	10/24/74	3	Virginia	Lancaster, S.C.	FA-'00	11/0*
84	Broughton, Luther	TE	6-2	248	11/30/74	4	Furman	Huger, S.C.	T(Car)-'99	16/3
85	Brown, Na	WR	6-0	187	2/22/77	2	North Carolina	Reidsville, N.C.	D4c-'99	12/5
74	Brzezinski, Doug	G	6-4	305	3/11/76	2	Boston College	Detroit, Mich.	D3-'99	16/16
56	Caldwell, Mike	LB	6-2	237	8/31/71	8	Middle Tennessee State	Oak Ridge, Tenn.	UFA(Ariz)-'98	14/2
68	Chung, Eugene	C-G	6-5	320	6/14/69	6	Virginia Tech	Vienna, Va.	FA-'00	0*
42	Cook, Rashard	S	5-11	197	4/18/77	2	Southern California	San Diego, Calif.	W(Chi)-'99	13/0
57	Darling, James	LB	6-0	250	12/29/74	4	Washington State	Kettle Falls, Wash.	D2-'97	15/10
93	Davis, Pernell	DT	6-2	320	5/19/76	2	Alabama-Birmingham	Birmingham, Ala.	D7b-'99	2/0
20	Dawkins, Brian	FS	5-11	200	10/13/73	5	Clemson	Jacksonville, Fla.	D2b-'96	16/16
10	Detmer, Koy	QB	6-1	195	7/5/73	4	Colorado	San Antonio, Tex.	D7a-'97	1/1
82	Douglas, Dameane	WR	6-0	195	3/15/76	2	California	Hanford, Calif.	W(Oak)-'99	14/0
53	Douglas, Hugh	LB-DE	6-2	280	8/23/71	6	Central State, Ohio	Mansfield, Ohio	T(NYJ)-'98	4/2
51	Emmons, Carlos	LB	6-5	250	9/3/73	5	Arkansas State	Greenwood, Miss.	UFA(Pitt)-'00	16/16*
52	Gardner, Barry	LB	6-0	248	12/13/76	2	Northwestern	Harvey, Ill.	D2-'99	16/5
96	Grasmanis, Paul	DT	6-2	298	8/2/74	5	Notre Dame	Jenison, Mich.	UFA(Den)-'00	5/0*
31	Harris, Al	CB	6-1	185	12/7/74	3	Texas A&M-Kingsville	Pompano Beach, Fla.	W(TB)-'98	16/6
45	# Hauck, Tim	S	5-10	187	12/20/66	11	Montana	Big Timber, Mont.	UFA(Ind)-'99	16/15
79	Jefferson, Greg	DE	6-3	280	8/31/71	6	Central Florida	Bartow, Fla.	D3a-'95	16/16
81	Johnson, Charles	WR	6-0	200	1/3/72	7	Colorado	San Bernardino, Calif.	UFA(Pitt)-'99	11/11
7	Landeta, Sean	P	6-0	215	1/6/62	16	Towson State	Towson, Md.	UFA(GB)-'99	16/0
89	Lewis, Chad	TE	6-6	252	10/5/71	4	Brigham Young	Orem, Utah	W(StL)-'99	6/4
59	Mamula, Mike	LB-DE	6-4	252	8/14/73	6	Boston College	Lackawanna, N.Y.	D1-95	16/13
38	Martin, Cecil	RB	6-0	235	7/8/75	2	Wisconsin	Evanston, Ill.	D6a-'99	12/5
71	Mayberry, Jermane	G-T	6-4	325	8/29/73	5	Texas A&M-Kingsville	Floresville, Tex.	D1-'96	13/5
5	McNabb, Donovan	QB	6-2	226	11/25/76	2	Syracuse	Mt. Carmel, Ill.	D1-'99	12/6
65	Miller, Bubba	C-G	6-1	305	1/24/73	5	Tennessee	Franklin, Tenn.	FA-'96	14/0
43	Moore, Damon	S	5-11	215	9/15/76	2	Ohio State	Fostoria, Ohio	D4b-'99	16/1
77	Palelei, Lonnie	G	6-3	310	10/15/70	7	Nevada-Las Vegas	Blue Springs, Mo.	UFA(NYG)-'99	16/12
14	Pederson, Doug	QB	6-3	216	1/31/68	8	Northeast Louisiana	Ferndale, Wash.	UFA(GB)-'99	16/9
36	Pritchett, Stanley	RB	6-1	240	12/22/73	5	South Carolina	Atlanta, Ga.	UFA(Mia)-'00	14/7*
58	Reese, Ike	LB	6-2	222	10/16/73	3	Michigan State	Cincinnati, Ohio	D5-'98	16/0
73	Ross, Oliver	T	6-4	310	9/27/74	3	Iowa State	Los Angeles, Calif.	FA-'99	0*
25	Rossum, Allen	CB-KR	5-8	178	10/22/75	3	Notre Dame	Dallas, Tex.	D3b-'98	16/0
69	Runyan, Jon	T	6-7	330	11/27/73	5	Michigan	Flint, Mich.	UFA(Tenn)-'00	16/16*
67	Schau, Ryan	G	6-6	300	12/30/75	2	Illinois	Bloomington, Ill.	FA-'99	1/0
80	Small, Torrance	WR	6-3	209	9/4/70	9	Alcorn State	Tampa, Fla.	UFA(Ind)-'99	15/15
19	Smith, Troy	WR	6-2	193	7/30/77	2	East Carolina	Greensville, N.C.	D6b-'99	1/0
22	Staley, Duce	RB	5-11	220	2/27/75	4	South Carolina	Columbia, S.C.	D3-'97	16/16
21	Taylor, Bobby	CB	6-3	216	12/28/73	6	Notre Dame	Longview, Tex.	D2a-'95	15/14
78	Thomas, Hollis	DT	6-0	306	1/10/74	5	Northern Illinois	St. Louis, Mo.	FA-'96	16/16
72	Thomas, Tra	T	6-7	349	11/20/74	3	Florida State	Deland, Fla.	D1-'98	16/15
83	Thomason, Jeff	TE	6-5	255	12/30/69	8	Oregon	Newport Beach, Calif.	T(GB)-'00	14/2*
54	Trotter, Jeremiah	LB	6-0	261	1/20/77	3	Stephen F. Austin	Hooks, Tex.	D3a-'98	16/16
86	Van Dyke, Alex	WR	6-0	205	7/24/74	5	Nevada	Sacramento, Calif.	FA-'99	2/0
23	Vincent, Troy	CB	6-1	200	6/8/71	9	Wisconsin	Trenton, N.J.	RFA(Mia)-'96	14/14
50	Wallace, Al	DE-LB	6-5	258	3/25/74	3	Maryland	Delray Beach, Fla.	UFA(Jax)-97	0*
35	Watson, Edwin	RB	6-0	225	9/29/76	3	Purdue	Pontiac, Mich.	UFA(Den)-'99	6/0
87	Weaver, Jed	TE	6-4	246	8/11/76	2	Oregon	Redmond, Ore.	D7a-'99	16/10
76	Welbourn, John	T-G	6-5	318	3/30/76	2	California	Palos Verdes, Calif.	D4a-'99	1/1
98	Whiting, Brandon	DT-DE	6-3	278	7/30/76	3	California	Long Beach, Calif.	D4a-'98	13/2
95	Williams, Tyrone	DE	6-4	292	10/22/72	3	Wyoming	Papillion, Neb.	FA-'99	4/0

* Autry last active with Philadelphia in '98; Barr last active with Seattle in '96; Bartrum played 16 games with New England in '99; Brandenburg played 14 games with Buffalo; Brice played 11 games with Cincinnati; Chung last active with Indianapolis in '97; Emmons played 16 games with Pittsburgh; Grasmanis played 5 games with Denver; Pritchett played 14 games with Miami; Ross was inactive for 15 games; Runyan played 16 games with Tennessee; Thomason played 14 games with Green Bay; Wallace missed '99 season because of injury.

Unrestricted free agent; subject to developments.

Players lost through free agency (2): G David Diaz-Infante (Den; 15), DT Steve Martin (KC; 16).

Also played with Eagles in '99—RB James Bostic (9 games), CB Jason Bostic (1), G-C Jeff Dellenbach (16), C Steve Everitt (16), WR Brian Finneran (3), DT Kelly Gregg (3), WR Dietrich Jells (14), DT Bill Johnson (6), K Norm Johnson (15), TE Ron Leshinski (1), TE Ed Smith (7), TE Justin Swift (1), LB William Thomas (14), RB Kevin Turner (8), DT Mark Wheeler (13), DT Ben Williams (3).

COACHING STAFF

Head Coach,
Andy Reid

Pro Career: Andy Reid became the twentieth head coach in franchise history on January 11, 1999. Reid joined the Eagles after spending the last seven seasons with the Green Bay Packers from 1992-98. With Green Bay, Reid helped the Packers reach the playoffs six consecutive times from 1993-98. During that span, Green Bay defeated the New England Patriots in Super Bowl XXXI and reached the NFL's title game again the following year. Reid played a significant role in helping put together Green Bay's renowned offensive attack. Indeed, Reid put his signature on nearly every part of the Packers' offense while coaching three different positions and assisting head coach Mike Holmgren and offensive coordinator Sherman Lewis with their game-planning duties. Prior to being the quarterbacks coach in 1997-98, Reid served as the Packers' tight ends and assistant offensive line coach. Career record: 5-11.

Background: Quality pass-blocking offensive lines, in both the Division I and II ranks, have been Reid's hallmark since launching his coaching career at San Francisco State in 1983. The school led the nation in passing offense and total offense for three consecutive years (1983-85) while he served as the school's offensive coordinator, offensive line coach, and strength coach. Reid moved to Northern Arizona as offensive line coach in 1986, to Texas-El Paso for two seasons (1987-88), and coached at Missouri from 1989-1991. Reid's coaching career began at his alma mater, Brigham Young, as a graduate assistant under LaVell Edwards in 1982. Reid first met Holmgren, who was a member of BYU's coaching staff, when Reid was an offensive tackle and guard on three Cougars Holiday Bowl teams. Reid went on to earn three varsity football letters, graduating with a bachelor's degree in physical education. He also received a master's degree in professional leadership in physical education and athletics.

Personal: Born in Los Angeles on March 19, 1958, Reid and his wife Tammy have five children—Garrett, Britt, Crosby, Drew Ann, and Spencer.

ASSISTANT COACHES

Tommy Brasher, defensive line; born Dec. 30, 1940, El Dorado, Ark., lives in Newtown Square, Pa. Linebacker Arkansas 1962-63. No pro playing experience. College coach: Arkansas 1970, Virginia Tech 1971, Northeast Louisiana 1974, 1976, Southern Methodist 1977-1981. Pro coach: Shreveport Steamer (WFL) 1975, New England Patriots 1982-84, Philadelphia Eagles 1985, Atlanta Falcons 1986-89, Tampa Bay Buccaneers 1990, Seattle Seahawks 1992-98, rejoined Eagles in 1999.

Juan Castillo, offensive line; born October 8, 1959, Port Isabel, Tex., lives in Mount Laurel, N.J. Linebacker Texas A&I (now Texas A&M-Kingsville) 1978-1980. Pro linebacker San Antonio Gunslingers (USFL) 1984-85. College coach: Texas A&M-Kingsville 1982-85, 1990-94. Pro coach: Joined Eagles in 1995.

Brad Childress, quarterbacks; born June 27, 1956, Aurora, Ill., lives in Cinnaminson, N.J. Eastern Illinois 1975-78. No pro playing experience. College coach: Illinois 1978-1984, Northern Arizona 1986-89, Utah 1990, Wisconsin 1991-98. Pro coach: Indianapolis Colts 1985, joined Eagles in 1999.

David Culley, wide receivers; born September 17, 1955, Sparta, Tenn., lives in Sewell, N.J. Quarterback Vanderbilt 1973-77. No pro playing experience. College coach: Austin Peay 1978, Vanderbilt 1979-1981, Middle Tennessee State 1982, Tennessee-Chattanooga 1983, Western Kentucky 1984, Southwestern Louisiana 1985-88, Texas-El Paso 1989-1990, Texas A&M 1991-93. Pro coach: Tampa Bay Buccaneers 1994-95, Pittsburgh Steelers 1996-1998, joined Eagles in 1999.

Rod Dowhower, offensive coordinator; born April 15, 1943, Ord, Neb., lives in Newtown Square, Pa. Quarterback San Diego State 1963-65. No pro playing experience. College coach: San Diego State 1966-1972, UCLA 1974-75, Boise State 1976, Stanford 1977-79 (head coach 1979), Vanderbilt 1995-96 (head coach). Pro coach: St. Louis Cardinals 1973, 1982-84, Denver Broncos 1980-1981, Indianapolis Colts 1985-86 (head coach), Atlanta Falcons 1987-89, Washington Redskins 1990-93, New York Giants 1997-98, joined Eagles in 1999.

Leslie Frazier, defensive backs; born April 3, 1959, Columbus, Miss., lives in Cherry Hill, N.J. Defensive back Alcorn State 1979-1980. Pro defensive back Chicago Bears 1981-86. College coach: Trinity (Ill.) College 1988-1996 (head coach), Illinois 1997-98. Pro coach: Joined Eagles in 1999.

John Harbaugh, special teams; born September 23, 1962, Perrysburg, Ohio, lives in Newtown Square, Pa. Defensive back Miami (Ohio) 1980-83. No pro playing experience. College coach: Western Michigan 1984-86, Pittsburgh 1987, Morehead State 1988, Cincinnati 1989-1996, Indiana 1997. Pro coach: Joined Eagles in 1998.

Jim Johnson, defensive coordinator; born May 26, 1941, Maywood, Ill., lives in Newtown Square, Pa. Quarterback Missouri 1959-1962. Pro tight end Buffalo Bills 1963-64. College coach: Missouri Southern 1967-68 (head coach), Drake 1969-1972, Indiana 1973-76, Notre Dame 1977-1980. Pro coach: Oklahoma Outlaws (USFL) 1984, Jacksonville Bulls (USFL) 1985, Phoenix Cardinals 1986-1993, Indianapolis Colts 1994-97, Seattle Seahawks 1998, joined Eagles in 1999.

Tom Melvin, offensive assistant-quality control; born October 1, 1961, Redwood City, Ca., lives in Cinnaminson, N.J. Offensive lineman San Francisco State 1982-83. No pro playing experience. College coach: San Francisco State 1984-85, Northern Arizona 1986-87, California-Santa Barbara 1988-1990, Occidental College 1991-98. Pro coach: Joined Eagles in 1999.

Ron Rivera, linebackers; born January 7, 1962, Fort Ord, Calif., lives in Cherry Hill, N.J. Linebacker California 1980-83. Pro linebacker Chicago Bears 1984-1992. Pro coach: Chicago Bears 1997-98, joined Eagles in 1999.

Pat Shurmur, tight ends-asst. offensive line; born April 14, 1965, Dearborn Heights, Mich., lives in Cinnaminson, N.J. Center Michigan State 1983-87. No pro playing experience. College coach: Michigan State 1988-1997, Stanford 1998. Pro coach: Joined Eagles in 1999.

Steve Spagnuolo, defensive asistant-quality control; born December 21, 1959, Witinsville, Mass., lives in Haddon Heights, N.J. Wide receiver Springfield College 1979-1981. No pro playing experience. College coach: Massachusetts 1982-83, Lafayette 1984-86, Connecticut 1987-1991, Maine 1993, Rutgers 1994-95, Bowling Green 1996-97. Pro coach: Barcelona Dragons (World League) 1992, Frankfurt Galaxy (NFL Europe) 1998, joined Eagles in 1999.

Ted Williams, running backs; born November 17, 1943, Lyons, Tex., lives in Sicklerville, N.J. No college or pro playing experience. College coach: UCLA 1980-89, Washington State 1991-93, Arizona 1994. Pro coach: Joined Eagles in 1995.

Mike Wolf, strength and conditioning; born May 15, 1965, Allentown, Pa., lives in Medford, N.J. Center Penn State 1983-87. No pro playing experience. College coach: Vanderbilt 1988-89, Lehigh 1990, Penn State 1991. Pro coach: Minnesota Vikings 1992-94, joined Eagles in 1995.

2000 FIRST-YEAR ROSTER

Name	Pos.	Ht.	Wt.	Birthdate	College	Hometown	How Acq.
Blackman, Jon (1)	T	6-6	290	10/8/75	Purdue	Yorkville, Ill.	FA
Bostic, Jason (1)	CB	5-9	181	6/30/76	Georgia Tech	Lauderhill, Fla.	FA-'99
Brown, Travis	QB	6-3	218	7/17/77	Northern Arizona	Phoenix, Ariz.	FA
Edwards, Eric (1)	CB	5-11	180	3/6/75	Oregon	Pasco, Wash.	FA
Francis, Tony	CB	6-1	206	7/26/77	Illinois	Glenwood, Ill.	FA
Frank, John	DE	6-4	280	7/1/74	Utah	Salt Lake City, Utah	D6b
Gregg, Kelly (1)	DT	6-0	285	11/1/76	Oklahoma	Edmond, Okla.	FA-'99
Hamner, Thomas	RB	6-0	197	12/25/76	Minnesota	Hamilton, Ohio	D6a
Johnson, Dwight	DT	6-4	285	1/30/77	Baylor	Waco, Tex.	FA
Marshall, Lemar (1)	S	6-2	208	12/17/76	Michigan State	Cincinnati, Ohio	FA-'99
Menendez, Rondel (1)	WR	5-9	178	5/18/75	Eastern Kentucky	Louisville, Ky.	W(Wash)
Nelson, Raki	WR	5-11	185	12/29/77	Notre Dame	Harrisburg, Pa.	FA
Pinkston, Todd	WR	6-2	170	4/23/77	Southern Mississippi	Forest, Miss.	D2a
Powlus, Ron (1)	QB	6-1	225	7/16/74	Notre Dame	Berwick, Pa.	FA
Reader, Jamie (1)	RB	5-11	238	5/4/74	Akron	Monessen, Pa.	FA-'99
Romero, John	C	6-3	326	10/3/76	California	Oakland, Calif.	D6c
Scott, Gari	WR	6-0	191	6/2/78	Michigan State	Riviera Beach, Fla.	D4
Simon, Corey	DT	6-2	293	3/2/77	Florida State	Pompano Beach, Fla.	D1
Southern, Anthony	RB	5-11	239	8/8/75	Virginia	Whiteville, N.C.	FA
Stockbauer, Marc	LB	6-3	235	9/25/77	Stanford	Baton Rouge, La.	FA
Tate, Mark (1)	CB	6-0	190	3/20/74	Penn State	Erie, Pa.	FA
Thurmon, Elijah	WR	6-3	206	8/2/78	Howard	Severn, Md.	FA
Williams, Bobby	G	6-3	320	9/25/76	Arkansas	Jefferson, Tex.	D2b
Wise, Ty	C	6-2	291	3/9/77	Miami	Pensacola, Fl.	FA

The term NFL Rookie is defined as a player who is in his first season of professional football and has not been on the roster of another professional football team for any regular-season or postseason games. A Rookie is designated by an "R" on NFL rosters. Players who have been active in another professional football league or players who have NFL experience, including either preseason training camp or being on an Active List or Inactive List, or on Reserve/Injured or Reserve/Physically Unable to Perform for fewer than six regular-season games, are termed NFL First-Year Players. An NFL First-Year Player is designated by a "1" on NFL rosters. Thereafter, a player is credited with an additional year of experience for each season in which he accumulates six games on the Active List or Inactive List, or on Reserve/Injured or Reserve/Physically Unable to Perform.

NOTES

ST. LOUIS RAMS

National Football Conference
Western Division
Team Colors: New Century Gold, Millennium Blue, and White
One Rams Way
St. Louis, Missouri 63045
Telephone: (314) 982-7267

CLUB OFFICIALS

Owner/Chairman: Georgia Frontiere
Owner/Vice Chairman: Stan Kroenke
President: John Shaw
President-Football Operations: Jay Zygmunt
Senior Vice President-Administration and General Counsel: Bob Wallace
Treasurer: Jeff Brewer
Vice President-Finance: Adrian Barr-Bracy
General Manager: Charley Armey
Vice President-Sales and Marketing: Phil Thomas
Director-College Scouting: Lawrence McCutchen
Director-Pro Scouting: Mike Ackerley
Vice President/Football Administration: Kevin Warren
Vice President-Ticket Operations: Michael T. Naughton
Director of Operations: John Oswald
Director of Public Relations: Rick Smith
Assistant Director of Public Relations: Duane Lewis
Head Trainer: Jim Anderson
Assistant Trainers: Dake Walden, Ron DuBuque
Equipment Manager: Todd Hewitt
Scouts: Dick Daniels, Ryan Grigson, Tom Marino Kevin McCabe, David Razzano, Harley Sewell
Stadium: Trans World Dome at America's Center
• **Capacity:** 66,000
701 Convention Plaza
St. Louis, Missouri 63101
Playing Surface: AstroTurf
Training Camp: Western Illinois University
Thompson Hall
Macomb, Illinois 61455

2000 SCHEDULE

PRESEASON

Aug. 5	**Oakland**	7:00
Aug. 14	at Tennessee	7:00
Aug. 19	**Buffalo**	7:00
Aug. 24	at Dallas	7:35

REGULAR SEASON

Sept. 4	**Denver** (Mon.)	8:00
Sept. 10	at Seattle	1:15
Sept. 17	**San Francisco**	12:00
Sept. 24	at Atlanta	1:00
Oct. 1	**San Diego**	12:00
Oct. 8	Open Date	
Oct. 15	**Atlanta**	12:00
Oct. 22	at Kansas City	12:00
Oct. 29	at San Francisco	1:05
Nov. 5	**Carolina**	7:35
Nov. 12	at New York Giants	4:15
Nov. 20	**Washington** (Mon.)	8:00
Nov. 26	**New Orleans**	12:00
Dec. 3	at Carolina	1:00
Dec. 10	**Minnesota**	12:00
Dec. 18	at Tampa Bay (Mon.)	9:00
Dec. 24	at New Orleans	12:00

RECORD HOLDERS

INDIVIDUAL RECORDS—CAREER

Category	Name	Performance
Rushing (Yds.)	Eric Dickerson, 1983-87	7,245
Passing (Yds.)	Jim Everett, 1986-1993	23,758
Passing (TDs)	Roman Gabriel, 1962-1972	154
Receiving (No.)	Henry Ellard, 1983-1993	593
Receiving (Yds.)	Henry Ellard, 1983-1993	9,761
Interceptions	Ed Meador, 1959-1970	46
Punting (Avg.)	Danny Villanueva, 1960-64	44.2
Punt Return (Avg.)	Henry Ellard, 1983-1992	11.3
Kickoff Return (Avg.)	Tom Wilson, 1956-1961	27.1
Field Goals	Mike Lansford, 1982-1990	158
Touchdowns (Tot.)	Eric Dickerson, 1983-87	58
Points	Mike Lansford, 1982-1990	789

INDIVIDUAL RECORDS—SINGLE SEASON

Category	Name	Performance
Rushing (Yds.)	Eric Dickerson, 1984	*2,105
Passing (Yds.)	Kurt Warner, 1999	4,353
Passing (TDs)	Kurt Warner, 1999	41
Receiving (No.)	Isaac Bruce, 1995	119
Receiving (Yds.)	Isaac Bruce, 1995	1,781
Interceptions	Dick (Night Train) Lane, 1952	*14
Punting (Avg.)	Danny Villanueva, 1962	45.5
Punt Return (Avg.)	Woodley Lewis, 1952	18.5
Kickoff Return (Avg.)	Verda (Vitamin T) Smith, 1950	33.7
Field Goals	David Ray, 1973	30
Touchdowns (Tot.)	Eric Dickerson, 1983	20
Points	David Ray, 1973	130

INDIVIDUAL RECORDS—SINGLE GAME

Category	Name	Performance
Rushing (Yds.)	Willie Ellison, 12-5-71	247
Passing (Yds.)	Norm Van Brocklin, 9-28-51	*554
Passing (TDs)	Many times.	5
	Last time by Kurt Warner, 10-10-99	
Receiving (No.)	Tom Fears, 12-3-50	*18
Receiving (Yds.)	Willie Anderson, 11-26-89	*336
Interceptions	Many times.	3
	Last time by Keith Lyle, 12-15-96	
Field Goals	Bob Waterfield, 12-9-51	5
Touchdowns (Tot.)	Bob Shaw, 12-11-49	4
	Elroy (Crazylegs) Hirsch, 9-28-51	4
	Harold Jackson, 10-14-73	4
	Az-Zahir Hakim, 10-3-99	4
	Isaac Bruce, 10-10-99	4
Points	Bob Shaw, 12-11-49	24
	Elroy (Crazylegs) Hirsch, 9-28-51	24
	Harold Jackson, 10-14-73	24
	Az-Zahir Hakim, 10-3-99	24
	Isaac Bruce, 10-10-99	24

*NFL Record

COACHING HISTORY

Cleveland 1937-1945, Los Angeles 1946-1994 (446-414-20)

1937-38	Hugo Bezdek*	1-13-0
1938	Art Lewis	4-4-0
1939-42	Earl (Dutch) Clark	16-26-2
1944	Aldo (Buff) Donelli	4-6-0
1945-46	Adam Walsh	16-5-1
1947	Bob Snyder	6-6-0
1948-49	Clark Shaughnessy	14-8-3
1950-52	Joe Stydahar**	19-9-0
1952-54	Hamp Pool	23-11-2
1955-59	Sid Gillman	28-32-1
1960-62	Bob Waterfield***	9-24-1
1962-65	Harland Svare	14-31-3
1966-70	George Allen	49-19-4
1971-72	Tommy Prothro	14-12-2
1973-77	Chuck Knox	57-20-1
1978-82	Ray Malavasi	43-36-0
1983-91	John Robinson	79-74-0
1992-94	Chuck Knox	15-33-0
1995-96	Rich Brooks	13-19-0
1997-99	Dick Vermeil	25-26-0

*Released after three games in 1938
**Resigned after one game in 1952
***Resigned after eight games in 1962

TRANS WORLD DOME

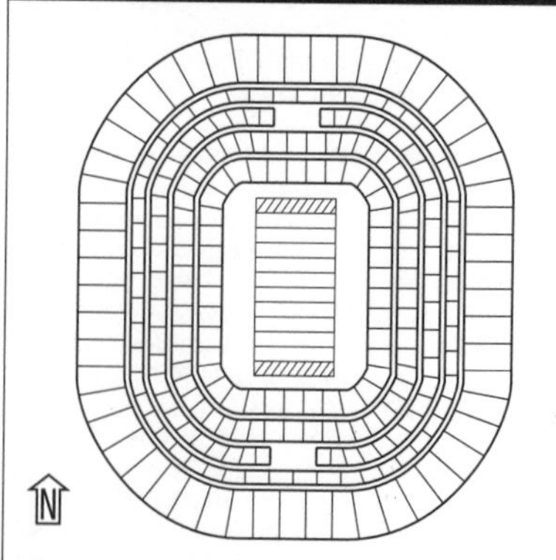

1999 TEAM RECORD

PRESEASON (2-2)

Date	Result		Opponent
8/7	L	17-18	Oakland
8/21	L	24-38	at Chicago
8/28	W	24-21	San Diego
9/2	W	17-6	at Detroit

REGULAR SEASON (13-3)

Date	Result		Opponent	Att.
9/12	W	27-10	Baltimore	62,100
9/26	W	35-7	Atlanta	63,253
10/3	W	38-10	at Cincinnati	45,481
10/10	W	42-20	San Francisco	65,872
10/17	W	41-13	at Atlanta	51,973
10/24	W	34-3	Cleveland	65,866
10/31	L	21-24	at Tennessee	66,415
11/7	L	27-31	at Detroit	73,224
11/14	W	35-10	Carolina	65,965
11/21	W	23-7	at San Francisco	68,193
11/28	W	43-12	New Orleans	65,864
12/5	W	34-21	at Carolina	62,285
12/12	W	30-14	at New Orleans	46,838
12/19	W	31-10	New York Giants	66,065
12/26	W	34-12	Chicago	65,941
1/2	L	31-38	at Philadelphia	60,700

POSTSEASON (3-0)

Date	Result		Opponent	Att.
1/16	W	49-37	Minnesota	66,194
1/23	W	11-6	Tampa Bay	66,496
1/30	W	23-16	vs. Tennessee, in Atlanta	72,625

SCORE BY PERIODS

Rams	123	170	106	127	0	—	526
Opponents	49	85	54	54	0	—	242

ATTENDANCE

Home 520,926 Away 475,109 Total 996,035
Single-game home record, 66,065 (12/19/99)
Single-season home record, 520,926 (1999)

1999 TEAM STATISTICS

	Rams	Opp.
Total First Downs	335	263
Rushing	102	53
Passing	207	189
Penalty	26	21
Third Down: Made/Att.	91/194	77/228
Third Down Pct.	46.9	33.8
Fourth Down: Made/Att.	5/8	12/25
Fourth Down Pct.	62.5	48.0
Total Net Yards	6,412	4,698
Avg. Per Game	400.8	293.6
Total Plays	994	991
Avg. Per Play	6.5	4.7
Net Yards Rushing	2,059	1,189
Avg. Per Game	128.7	74.3
Total Rushes	431	338
Net Yards Passing	4,353	3,509
Avg. Per Game	272.1	219.3
Sacked/Yards Lost	33/227	57/358
Gross Yards	4,580	3,867
Att./Completions	530/343	596/319
Completion Pct.	64.7	53.5
Had Intercepted	15	29
Punts/Average	60/41.1	86/42.7
Net Punting Avg.	60/34.8	86/36.5
Penalties/Yards	113/889	114/1,007
Fumbles/Ball Lost	30/16	21/7
Touchdowns	66	26
Rushing	13	4
Passing	42	19
Returns	11	3
Avg. Time of Possession	31:50	28:10

1999 INDIVIDUAL STATISTICS

Passing	Att.	Comp.	Yds.	Pct.	TD	Int.	Tkld.	Rate
Warner	499	325	4,353	65.1	41	13	29/201	109.2
Germaine	16	9	136	56.3	1	2	3/23	65.6
Justin	14	9	91	64.3	0	0	1/3	82.7
Faulk	1	0	0	0.0	0	0	0/0	39.6
Rams	530	343	4,580	64.7	42	15	33/227	106.6
Opponents	596	319	3,867	53.5	19	29	57/358	64.1

SCORING	TD R	TD P	TD Rt	PAT	FG	Saf	PTS
Wilkins	0	0	0	64/64	20/28	0	124
Bruce	0	12	0	0/0	0/0	0	74
Faulk	7	5	0	0/0	0/0	0	74
Hakim	0	8	1	0/0	0/0	0	54
Holt	0	6	0	0/0	0/0	0	36
R. Williams	0	6	0	0/0	0/0	0	36
Holcombe	4	1	0	0/0	0/0	0	30
M. Jones	0	0	3	0/0	0/0	0	18
Horne	0	0	2	0/0	0/0	0	12
Robinson	0	2	0	0/0	0/0	0	12
Wistrom	0	0	2	0/0	0/0	0	12
Bly	0	0	1	0/0	0/0	0	6
Bush	0	0	1	0/0	0/0	0	6
Hodgins	1	0	0	0/0	0/0	0	6
Lee	0	1	0	0/0	0/0	0	6
Lyght	0	0	1	0/0	0/0	0	6
Tucker	0	1	0	0/0	0/0	0	6
Warner	1	0	0	0/0	0/0	0	6
Fletcher	0	0	0	0/0	0/0	1	2
Rams	13	42	11	64/64	20/28	1	526
Opponents	4	19	3	22/23	20/26	0	242

2-Pt. Conversions: Bruce, Faulk.
Team 2-2, Opponents 2-3.

RUSHING	Att.	Yds.	Avg.	LG	TD
Faulk	253	1,381	5.5	58	7
Holcombe	78	294	3.8	34	4
Watson	47	179	3.8	21	0
Warner	23	92	4.0	22	1
Hakim	4	44	11.0	31	0
Bruce	5	32	6.4	11	0
Holt	3	25	8.3	14	0
Hodgins	7	10	1.4	3	1
Lee	3	3	1.0	4	0
Germaine	3	0	0.0	2	0
Justin	5	-1	-0.2	3	0
Rams	431	2,059	4.8	58	13
Opponents	338	1,189	3.5	40	4

RECEIVING	No.	Yds.	Avg.	LG	TD
Faulk	87	1,048	12.0	57t	5
Bruce	77	1,165	15.1	60	12
Holt	52	788	15.2	63t	6
Hakim	36	677	18.8	75t	8
Proehl	33	349	10.6	30	0
R. Williams	25	226	9.0	24	6
Holcombe	14	163	11.6	30	1
Robinson	6	76	12.7	30	2
Hodgins	6	35	5.8	10	0
Lee	3	22	7.3	15t	1
Lewis	1	12	12.0	12	0
Conwell	1	11	11.0	11	0
Thomas	1	6	6.0	6	0
Tucker	1	2	2.0	2t	1
Rams	343	4,580	13.4	75t	42
Opponents	319	3,867	12.1	71t	19

INTERCEPTIONS	No.	Yds.	Avg.	LG	TD
Lyght	6	112	18.7	57t	1
M. Jones	4	96	24.0	44t	2
McCleon	4	17	4.3	14	0
Bly	3	53	17.7	53t	1
Wistrom	2	131	65.5	91t	2
Allen	2	76	38.0	40	0
Bush	2	45	22.5	45t	1
Jenkins	2	16	8.0	14	0
Lyle	2	10	5.0	10	0
Coady	1	11	11.0	11	0
Clemons	1	0	0.0	0	0
Rams	29	567	19.6	91t	7
Opponents	15	266	17.7	60	2

PUNTING	No.	Yds.	Avg.	In 20	LG
Tuten	32	1,359	42.5	9	70
Horan	26	1,048	40.3	7	57
Wilkins	2	57	28.5	1	34
Rams	60	2,464	41.1	17	70
Opponents	86	3,674	42.7	26	65

PUNT RETURNS	No.	FC	Yds.	Avg.	LG	TD
Hakim	44	22	461	10.5	84t	1
Horne	5	0	22	4.4	9	0
Holt	3	2	15	5.0	11	0
Proehl	0	1	0	—	—	0
Rams	52	25	498	9.6	84t	1
Opponents	23	7	155	6.7	20	0

KICKOFF RETURNS	No.	Yds.	Avg.	LG	TD
Horne	30	892	29.7	101t	2
Carpenter	16	406	25.4	43	0
Hakim	2	35	17.5	20	0
Fletcher	2	13	6.5	13	0
Hodgins	2	4	2.0	4	0
McCollum	1	3	3.0	3	0
Bly	1	1	1.0	1	0
Proehl	0	0	—	—	0
Rams	54	1,354	25.1	101t	2
Opponents	85	2,115	24.9	69	0

FIELD GOALS	1-19	20-29	30-39	40-49	50+
Wilkins	1/1	5/5	6/7	7/11	1/4
Rams	1/1	5/5	6/7	7/11	1/4
Opponents	1/1	8/9	2/4	8/9	1/3

SACKS	No.
Carter	17.0
Farr	8.5
Wistrom	6.5
Zgonina	4.5
J. Williams	4.0
Clemons	3.0
Fletcher	3.0
Agnew	2.5
Lyght	2.5
McCleon	1.5
Jenkins	1.0
M. Jones	1.0
Lyle	1.0
Allen	0.5
Hobgood-Chittick	0.5
Rams	57.0
Opponents	33.0

2000 DRAFT CHOICES

Round	Name	Pos.	College
1	Trung Canidate	RB	Arizona
2	Jacoby Shepherd	DB	Oklahoma State
3	John St. Clair	C	Virginia
4	Kaulana Noa	T	Hawaii
5	Brian Young	DE	Texas-El Paso
6	Matt Bowen	DB	Iowa
7	Andrew Kline	G	San Diego State

ST. LOUIS RAMS

2000 VETERAN ROSTER

No.	Name	Pos.	Ht.	Wt.	Birthdate	NFL Exp.	College	Hometown	How Acq.	'99 Games/ Starts
99	Agnew, Ray	DT	6-3	285	12/9/67	11	North Carolina State	Winston Salem, N.C.	UFA(NYG)-'98	16/16
20	Allen, Taje	CB	5-10	185	11/6/73	4	Texas	Lubbock, Tex.	D5-'97	16/2
92	Barnes, Lionel	DE	6-4	264	4/19/76	2	Northeast Louisiana	Suffolk, England	D6-'99	3/0
32	Bly, Dre'	CB	5-9	185	5/22/77	2	North Carolina	Chesapeake, Va.	D2-'99	16/2
80	Bruce, Isaac	WR	6-0	188	11/10/72	7	Memphis	Fort Lauderdale, Fla.	D2a-'94	16/16
23	Bush, Devin	S	6-0	210	7/3/73	6	Florida State	Miami, Fla.	UFA(Atl)-'99	16/7
93	Carter, Kevin	DE	6-5	280	9/21/73	6	Florida	Tallahassee, Fla.	D1-'95	16/16
38	Coady, Rich	S	6-0	203	1/26/76	2	Texas A&M	Dallas, Tex.	D3-'99	16/0
54	Collins, Todd	LB	6-2	248	5/27/70	8	Carson-Newman	New Market, Tenn.	UFA(NE)-'99	16/13
84	Conwell, Ernie	TE	6-1	265	8/17/72	5	Washington	Kent, Wash.	D2b-'96	3/0
75	Farr, D'Marco	DT	6-1	280	6/9/71	7	Washington	Richmond, Calif.	FA-'94	16/16
28	Faulk, Marshall	RB	5-10	211	2/26/73	7	San Diego State	New Orleans, La.	T(Ind)-'99	16/16
59	Fletcher, London	LB	5-10	241	5/19/75	3	John Carroll	Cleveland, Ohio	FA-'98	16/16
9	Germaine, Joe	QB	6-0	203	8/11/75	2	Ohio State	Mesa, Ariz.	D4-'99	3/0
10	Green, Trent	QB	6-3	215	7/9/70	7	Indiana	St. Louis, Mo.	UFA(Wash)-'99	0/0*
81	Hakim, Az-Zahir	WR	5-10	178	6/3/77	3	San Diego State	Los Angeles, Calif.	D4a-'98	15/0
95	Hobgood-Chittick, Nate	DT	6-3	290	11/30/74	3	North Carolina	Allentown, Pa.	FA-'99	10/0
42	Hodgins, James	RB	5-11	230	4/30/77	2	San Jose State	San Jose, Calif.	FA-'99	15/0
25	Holcombe, Robert	RB	5-11	220	12/11/75	3	Illinois	Mesa, Ariz.	D2-'98	15/7
88	Holt, Torry	WR	6-0	190	6/5/76	2	North Carolina State	Greensboro, N.C.	D1-'99	16/15
82	Horne, Tony	WR	5-9	173	3/21/76	3	Clemson	Rockingham, N.C.	FA-'98	12/0
94	Hyder, Gaylon	DT	6-5	290	10/18/74	2	Texas Christian	Longview, Tex.	FA-'99	4/0
52	Jones, Mike	LB	6-1	240	4/15/69	10	Missouri	Kansas City, Mo.	UFA(Oak)-'97	16/16
57	Little, Leonard	LB	6-3	237	10/19/74	3	Tennessee	Asheville, N.C.	D3-'98	6/0
31	t- Loville, Derek	RB	5-10	210	7/4/68	10	Oregon	San Francisco, Calif.	T(Den)-'00	10/0*
41	T- Lyght, Todd	CB	6-0	190	2/9/69	10	Notre Dame	Flint, Mich.	D1-'91	16/16
35	Lyle, Keith	S	6-2	210	4/17/72	7	Virginia	Vienna, Va.	D3a-'94	9/9
21	McCleon, Dexter	CB	5-10	195	10/9/73	4	Clemson	Meridian, Miss.	D2-'97	15/15
67	McCollum, Andy	G	6-4	295	6/2/70	7	Toledo	Richfield, Ohio	UFA(NO)-'99	16/2
96	Moran, Sean	DT	6-3	275	6/5/73	5	Colorado State	Aurora, Colo.	UFA(Buff)-'00	16/0*
61	Nütten, Tom	G	6-5	300	6/8/71	4	Western Michigan	Magog, Quebec, Canada	FA-'98	14/14
76	Pace, Orlando	T	6-7	320	11/4/75	4	Ohio State	Sandusky, Ohio	D1-'97	16/16
91	Pelshak, Troy	LB	6-2	242	3/6/77	2	North Carolina A&T	Charlotte, N.C.	FA-'99	9/0
87	Proehl, Ricky	WR	6-0	190	3/7/68	11	Wake Forest	Hillsborough, N.J.	UFA(Chi)-'98	15/2
45	Robinson, Jeff	TE	6-4	275	2/20/70	8	Idaho	Spokane, Wash.	UFA(Den)-'97	16/9
73	Spikes, Cameron	G	6-2	310	11/6/76	2	Texas A&M	Bryan, Tex.	D5-'99	5/0
62	Timmerman, Adam	G	6-4	300	8/14/71	6	South Dakota State	Cherokee, Iowa	UFA(GB)-'99	16/16
50	Tucker, Ryan	C	6-5	305	6/12/75	4	Texas Christian	Midland, Tex.	D4-'97	16/0
11	Tuten, Rick	P	6-2	221	1/5/65	11	Florida State	Ocala, Fla.	UFA(Sea)-'98	8/0
13	Warner, Kurt	QB	6-2	220	6/22/71	3	Northern Iowa	Burlington, Iowa	FA-'98	16/16
33	Watson, Justin	RB	6-0	225	1/7/75	2	San Diego State	Pasadena, Calif.	FA-'99	8/0
14	Wilkins, Jeff	K	6-2	205	4/19/72	7	Youngstown State	Austintown, Ohio	RFA(SF)-'97	16/0
86	Williams, Roland	TE	6-5	269	4/27/75	3	Syracuse	Rochester, N.Y.	D4b-'98	16/15
98	Wistrom, Grant	DE	6-4	267	7/3/76	3	Nebraska	Webb City, Mo.	D1-'98	16/16
90	Zgonina, Jeff	DT	6-2	300	5/24/70	7	Purdue	Mundelein, Ill.	UFA(Ind)-'99	16/0

* Green missed '99 season because of injuries; Loville played 10 games with Denver in '99; Moran played 16 games with Buffalo.

t- Rams traded for Loville (Denver).

T- transition player; subject to developments.

Players lost through free agency (7): LB Charlie Clemons (NO; 16 games in '99), C Mike Gruttadauria (Ariz; 16), QB Paul Justin (Dall; 10), T Fred Miller (Tenn; 16); LB Mike Morton (GB; 16), WR Chris Thomas (Minn; 6 with StL, 2 with Wash), DE Jay Williams (Car; 16).

Traded—S Billy Jenkins (16 games in '99) to Denver.

Also played with Rams in '99—S Ron Carpenter (11 games), CB Clifton Crosby (1), RB Derrick Harris (1), P Mike Horan (8), RB Amp Lee (7), TE Chad Lewis (6), LB Lorenzo Styles (16).

COACHING STAFF

Head Coach,
Mike Martz

Pro Career: Named twenty-first head coach of the Rams on February 2, 2000. Is fifth head coach to take over a Super Bowl champion, the first since Barry Switzer was named coach of the Dallas Cowboys in 1994. Martz was the mastermind behind one of most explosive offenses in NFL history, as the 1999 Rams scored 526 points, third most in NFL annals. Supervised development of Kurt Warner, who set numerous club records on his way to MVP honors in both the regular season and the Super Bowl. Rejoined Rams last season after two seasons as quarterbacks coach of Washington Redskins, as he began NFL career with Rams in 1992 as offensive assistant. Coached tight ends, receivers, and quarterbacks through 1996 season.

Background: Played tight end at Fresno State 1972 after transferring from the University of California-Santa Barbara, which dropped football a season earlier. Began coaching career in 1973 at Bullard High School in Fresno, California, before moving to the collegiate ranks as an assistant at San Diego Mesa C.C. (1974, 1976-77), San Jose State (1975), and Santa Ana College (1978) before returning to his alma mater in 1979. Served as assistant at University of Pacific (1980-81) and Minnesota (1982) before moving to Arizona State, where he coached quarterbacks and receivers from 1983-87, and was offensive coordinator from 1987-1991.

Personal: Born May 13, 1951 in Sioux Falls, S.D. Graduated summa cum laude at Fresno State in 1973. Lives with wife Julie in Chesterfield, Mo., and has three sons and one daughter.

ASSISTANT COACHES

Steve Brown, secondary; born March 20, 1960, Sacramento, Calif., lives in Wildhorse, Mo. Defensive back Oregon 1978-1982. Pro cornerback Houston Oilers 1983-1990. Pro coach: Joined Rams in 1995.

Sam Clark, defensive assistant; born September 24, 1960, Hershey, Pa., lives in St. Louis. Attended Arizona. No college or pro playing experience. College coach: Princeton 1988, Northern Arizona 1989, Scottsdale C. C. (Ariz.) 1993-95, Bucknell 1996. Pro coach: Arizona Cardinals 1990-92, joined Rams in 1997.

Chris Clausen, strength and conditioning coordinator; born February 21, 1958, Evergreen Park, Ill., lives in St. Louis. Cornerback Indiana 1976-79. No pro playing experience. College coach: San Diego State 1987-88. Pro coach: San Diego Chargers 1989-1991, joined Rams in 1992.

Peter Giunta, asst. head coach-defensive coordinator; born August 11, 1956, Salem, Mass., lives in Chesterfield, Mo. Running back-defensive back Northeastern 1974-77. No pro playing experience. College coach: Penn State 1981-83, Brown 1984-87, Lehigh 1988-1990. Pro coach: Philadelphia Eagles 1991-94, New York Jets 1995-96, joined Rams in 1997.

Carl Hairston, defensive line; born December 15, 1952, Martinsville, Va., lives in Chesterfield, Mo. Defensive end Maryland-Eastern Shore 1972-75. Pro defensive end Philadelphia Eagles 1976-1983, Cleveland Browns 1984-89, Phoenix Cardinals 1990. Pro coach: Kansas City Chiefs 1995-96, joined Rams in 1997.

Mike Haluchak, linebackers; born November 28, 1949, Concord, Calif., lives in St. Louis. Linebacker Southern California 1967-1970. No pro playing experience. College coach: Southern California 1976-77, Cal State-Fullerton 1978, Pacific 1979-1980, California 1981, North Carolina State 1982. Pro coach: Oakland Invaders (USFL) 1983-85, San Diego Chargers 1986-1991, Cincinnati Bengals 1992-93, Washington Redskins 1994-96, New York Giants 1997-99, joined Rams in 2000.

Jim Hanifan, offensive line; born September 21, 1933, Compton, Calif., lives in St. Charles, Mo. Tight end California 1952-54. Pro tight end Toronto Argonauts (USFL) 1955. College coach: Yuba City J.C. (Calif.) 1959-1961, Glendale J.C. (Calif.) 1964-65, Utah 1966-69, California 1970-71, San Diego State 1972. Pro coach: St. Louis Cardinals 1973-78, 1980-85 (head coach), San Diego Chargers 1979, Atlanta Falcons 1987-89, Washington Redskins 1990-96, joined Rams in 1997.

Bobby Jackson, running backs; born February 16, 1940, Forsyth, Ga., lives in Chesterfield, Mo. Linebacker-running back Samford 1959-1962. No pro playing experience. College coach: Florida State 1965-69, Kansas State 1970-74, Louisville 1975-76, Tennessee 1977-1982. Pro coach: Atlanta Falcons 1983-86, San Diego Chargers 1987-1991, Phoenix Cardinals 1992-93, Washington Redskins 1994-99, joined Rams in 2000.

Dana LeDuc, strength and conditioning, born March 22, 1953, Tacoma, Wash., lives in St. Charles, Mo. No college or pro playing experience. College coach: Texas 1977-1992, Miami 1993-94. Pro coach: Seattle Seahawks 1995-98, joined Rams in 1999.

John Matsko, asst. head coach-offensive line; born February 2, 1951, Cleveland, lives in Lake St. Louis, Mo. Fullback Kent State 1970-73. No pro playing experience. College coach Kent State 1973, Miami (Ohio) 1974-75, 1977, North Carolina 1978-1984, Navy 1985, Arizona 1986, Southern California 1987-1991. Pro coach: Phoenix Cardinals 1992-93, New Orleans Saints 1994-96, New York Giants 1997-98, joined Rams in 1999.

Wilbert Montgomery, tight ends; born September 16, 1954, Greenville, Miss., lives in Chesterfield, Mo. Running back Abilene Christian 1973-76. Pro running back Philadelphia Eagles 1977-1984, Detroit Lions 1985-86. Pro coach: Joined Rams in 1997.

Larry Pasquale, special teams; born April 21, 1941, Brooklyn, N.Y., lives in St. Louis. Quarterback Bridgeport 1961-63. No pro playing experience. College coach: Slippery Rock State 1967, Boston University 1968, Navy 1969-1970, Massachusetts 1971-75, Idaho State 1976. Pro coach: Montreal Alouettes (CFL) 1977-78, Detroit Lions 1979, New York Jets 1980-89, San Diego Chargers 1990-91, Philadelphia Eagles 1992-94, Jacksonville Jaguars 1995-99, joined Rams in 2000.

John Ramsdell, quarterbacks; born August 16, 1954, Lafayette, Ind., lives in Chesterfield, Mo. Running back Springfield (Mass.) College 1972-75. No pro playing experience. College coach: San Francisco State 1976-77, Long Beach State 1978, Pacific 1979-1982, Oregon 1983-1994. Pro coach: Joined Rams in 1995.

Al Saunders, receivers, born February 1, 1947, London, England, lives in St. Louis. Defensive back San Jose State 1966-68. No pro playing experience. College coach: Southern California 1970-71, Missouri 1972, Utah State 1973-75, California 1976-1981, Tennessee 1982. Pro coach San Diego Chargers 1983-88 (head coach 1986-88), Kansas City Chiefs 1989-1998, joined Rams in 1999.

Howard Tippett, defensive assistant; born September 23, 1938, Tallassee, Ala., lives in Wildwood, Mo. Quarterback/free safety, East Tennessee State 1955-56. No pro playing experience: College coach: Tulane 1963-66, Houston 1967-69, West Virginia 1970-71, Wake Forest 1972, Mississippi State 1973, Washington State 1976, Oregon 1978-79, UCLA 1980, Illinois 1987. Pro coach: Jacksonville Express (WFL) 1974-75, Tampa Bay Buccaneers 1981-86, Green Bay Packers 1988-1991, Los Angeles Rams 1992-93, Detroit Lions 1994-96, rejoined Rams as scout in 1997.

Ken Zampese, offensive assistant; born July 19, 1967, Santa Maria, Calif., lives in O'Fallon, Mo. Wide receiver San Diego 1985-88. No pro playing experience. College coach: San Diego 1989, Southern California 1990-91, Northern Arizona 1992-95, Miami (Ohio) 1996-97. Pro coach: Philadelphia Eagles 1988, Green Bay 1999, joined Rams 2000.

2000 FIRST-YEAR ROSTER

Name	Pos.	Ht.	Wt.	Birthdate	College	Hometown	How Acq.
Anderson, Bennie	G	6-3	326	2/17/77	Tennessee State	St. Louis, Mo.	FA
Blevins, Darrius (1)	WR	6-2	216	4/2/76	Memphis	Morristown, Tenn.	FA
Bowen, Matt	S	6-1	202	11/12/76	Iowa	Glyn Elyn, Ill.	D6
Brown, Darwin	CB	5-11	175	7/6/77	Texas Tech	Tyler, Tex.	FA
Burley, Siaha	WR	5-11	175	7/16/77	Central Florida	Mesa, Ariz.	FA
Canidate, Trung	RB	5-11	192	3/3/77	Arizona	Phoenix, Ariz.	D1
Chatham, Matt (1)	LB	6-4	242	6/28/77	South Dakota	Sioux City, Iowa	FA
Crosby, Clifton (1)	CB	5-9	172	9/17/74	Maryland	Erie, Pa.	FA
Dodson, Damien	WR	5-7	167	6/21/78	Memphis	Memphis, Tenn.	FA
Fox, Derek	S	5-10	193	12/27/77	Penn State	Canton, Ohio	FA
Hall, Jeff (1)	K	6-0	185	7/30/76	Tennessee	Winchester, Tenn.	FA
Hass, Alex	TE	6-4	267	1/5/77	Minnesota	St. Peter, Minn.	FA
Jackson, Curtis	WR	5-10	190	9/22/73	Texas	Plano, Tex.	FA
Lewis, Derek (1)	TE	6-1	250	4/2/77	Texas	New Orleans, La.	FA
Jones, Bryan (1)	LB	6-3	210	12/21/75	Cal Poly-San Luis Obispo	Arroyo Grande, Calif.	FA
Kidd, James (1)	WR	5-8	165	3/4/74	Colorado	Sacramento, Calif.	FA
Kline, Andrew	G	6-2	303	10/5/76	San Diego State	Beverly Hills, Calif.	D7
Looker, Dane	WR	5-11	188	5/5/76	Washington	Puyallup, Wash.	FA
Marsau, Bill	T	6-5	294	4/16/77	Iowa State	Hudson, Iowa	FA
Mitchell, Barry	DT	6-3	254	3/18/74	Idaho	Aurora, Colo.	FA
McGuffey, Corte	QB	6-0	210	6/19/77	Northern Colorado	Riverson, Wyo.	FA
McNutt, Antoine	G	6-3	348	11/11/76	Tennessee State	Chicago, Ill.	FA
Miller, Keith	LB	6-1	238	7/9/76	California	San Diego, Calif.	FA
Mitchell, Lonny	WR	6-1	200	1/14/77	San Diego State	San Diego, Calif.	FA
Montgomery, Wendell	WR	6-2	209	5/12/77	Wyoming	Arvada, Colo.	FA
Noa, Kaulana	T	6-3	307	12/29/76	Hawaii	Honokaa, Hawaii	D4
O'Neal, Mike	P	6-0	190	10/19/75	Idaho	San Diego, Calif.	FA
Riti, Rob	C	6-1	293	12/2/76	Missouri	Hazelwood, Mo.	FA
Shepherd, Jacoby	CB	6-1	195	8/31/79	Oklahoma State	Luftin, Tex.	D2
Sherrod, Sam	DE	6-3	262	7/31/77	San Jose State	Pleasanton, Calif.	FA
St. Clair, John	C	6-4	293	7/15/77	Virginia	Roanoke, Va.	D3
Washington, Damon	RB	5-10	200	2/20/77	Colorado State	San Diego, Calif.	FA
Washington, T.J.	T	6-4	340	7/1/74	Virginia Tech	Melfa, Va.	FA
Young, Brian	DE	6-2	278	7/8/77	Texas El-Paso	El Paso, Tex.	D5

The term NFL Rookie is defined as a player who is in his first season of professional football and has not been on the roster of another professional football team for any regular-season or postseason games. A Rookie is designated by an "R" on NFL rosters. Players who have been active in another professional football league or players who have NFL experience, including either preseason training camp or being on an Active List or Inactive List, or on Reserve/Injured or Reserve/Physically Unable to Perform for fewer than six regular-season games, are termed NFL First-Year Players. An NFL First-Year Player is designated by a "1" on NFL rosters. Thereafter, a player is credited with an additional year of experience for each season in which he accumulates six games on the Active List or Inactive List, or on Reserve/Injured or Reserve/Physically Unable to Perform.

SAN FRANCISCO 49ERS

National Football Conference
Western Division
Team Colors: Forty Niners Gold and Cardinal
4949 Centennial Boulevard
Santa Clara, California 95054
Telephone: (408) 562-4949

CLUB OFFICIALS

Owner: Denise DeBartolo York
Vice President: Dr. John York
Vice President/General Manager: Bill Walsh
Vice President/CFO: Keith Lenhart
Vice President/Director of Football Administration: John McVay
Director of Player Personnel: Terry Donahue
Pro Personnel Director: Bill McPherson
Director of Communications and Marketing: Rodney Knox
Director of Public Relations: Kirk Reynolds
Ticket Manager: Lynn Carrozzi
Director of Stadium Operations: Murlan (Mo) Fowell
Video Director: Robert Yanagi
Trainer: Lindsy McLean
Equipment Manager: Kevin Lartigue
Stadium: 3Com Park • **Capacity:** 69,734
San Francisco, California 94124
Playing Surface: Grass
Training Camp: University of the Pacific
Stockton, California 95211

2000 SCHEDULE

PRESEASON

July 31	vs. New England at Canton, Ohio	8:00
Aug. 5	**San Diego**	6:00
Aug. 13	**Kansas City**	7:30
Aug. 19	at Seattle	8:00
Aug. 25	**Denver**	6:00

REGULAR SEASON

Sept. 3	at Atlanta	1:00
Sept. 10	**Carolina**	1:15
Sept. 17	at St. Louis	12:00
Sept. 24	at Dallas	12:00
Oct. 1	**Arizona**	1:15
Oct. 8	**Oakland**	1:15
Oct. 15	at Green Bay	3:15
Oct. 22	at Carolina	1:00
Oct. 29	**St. Louis**	1:05
Nov. 5	at New Orleans	12:00
Nov. 12	**Kansas City**	1:05
Nov. 19	**Atlanta**	1:15
Nov. 26	Open Date	
Dec. 3	at San Diego	1:05
Dec. 10	**New Orleans**	1:15
Dec. 17	**Chicago**	1:05
Dec. 23	at Denver (Sat.)	2:15

RECORD HOLDERS

INDIVIDUAL RECORDS—CAREER

Category	Name	Performance
Rushing (Yds.)	Joe Perry, 1950-1960, 1963	7,344
Passing (Yds.)	Joe Montana, 1979-1992	35,124
Passing (TDs)	Joe Montana, 1979-1992	244
Receiving (No.)	Jerry Rice, 1985-1999	*1,206
Receiving (Yds.)	Jerry Rice, 1985-1999	*18,442
Interceptions	Ronnie Lott, 1981-1990	51
Punting (Avg.)	Tommy Davis, 1959-1969	44.7
Punt Return (Avg.)	Dana McLemore, 1982-87	10.8
Kickoff Return (Avg.)	Abe Woodson, 1958-1964	29.4
Field Goals	Ray Wersching, 1977-1987	190
Touchdowns (Tot.)	Jerry Rice, 1985-1999	*180
Points	Jerry Rice, 1985-1999	1,088

INDIVIDUAL RECORDS—SINGLE SEASON

Category	Name	Performance
Rushing (Yds.)	Garrison Hearst, 1998	1,570
Passing (Yds.)	Steve Young, 1998	4,170
Passing (TDs)	Steve Young, 1998	36
Receiving (No.)	Jerry Rice, 1995	122
Receiving (Yds.)	Jerry Rice, 1995	*1,848
Interceptions	Dave Baker, 1960	10
	Ronnie Lott, 1986	10
Punting (Avg.)	Tommy Davis, 1965	45.8
Punt Return (Avg.)	Dana McLemore, 1982	22.3
Kickoff Return (Avg.)	Joe Arenas, 1953	34.4
Field Goals	Jeff Wilkins, 1996	30
Touchdowns (Tot.)	Jerry Rice, 1987	23
Points	Jerry Rice, 1987	138

INDIVIDUAL RECORDS—SINGLE GAME

Category	Name	Performance
Rushing (Yds.)	Garrison Hearst, 12-14-98	198
Passing (Yds.)	Joe Montana, 10-14-90	476
Passing (TDs)	Joe Montana, 10-14-90	6
Receiving (No.)	Jerry Rice, 11-20-94	16
Receiving (Yds.)	Jerry Rice, 12-18-95	289
Interceptions	Dave Baker, 12-4-60	*4
Field Goals	Ray Wersching, 10-16-83	6
	Jeff Wilkins, 9-29-96	6
Touchdowns (Tot.)	Jerry Rice, 10-14-90	5
Points	Jerry Rice, 10-14-90	30

*NFL Record

COACHING HISTORY

(421-319-13)

1950-54	Lawrence (Buck) Shaw	33-25-2
1955	Norman (Red) Strader	4-8-0
1956-58	Frankie Albert	19-17-1
1959-63	Howard (Red) Hickey*	27-27-1
1963-67	Jack Christiansen	26-38-3
1968-75	Dick Nolan	56-56-5
1976	Monte Clark	8-6-0
1977	Ken Meyer	5-9-0
1978	Pete McCulley**	1-8-0
1978	Fred O'Connor	1-6-0
1979-88	Bill Walsh	102-63-1
1989-96	George Seifert	108-35-0
1997-99	Steve Mariucci	31-21-0

*Resigned after three games in 1963
**Released after nine games in 1978

3COM PARK

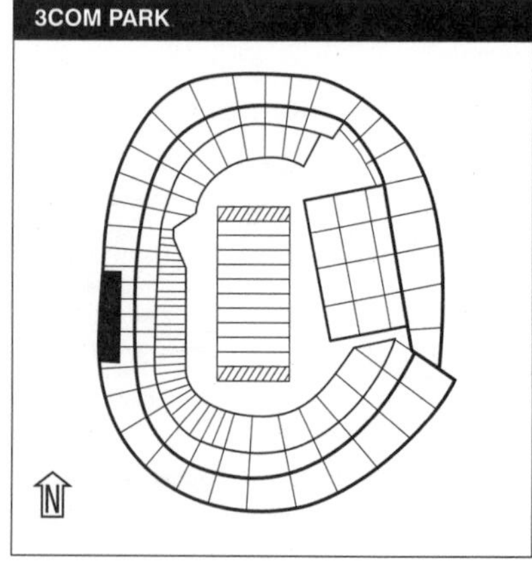

1999 TEAM RECORD

PRESEASON (3-1)

Date	Result		Opponent
8/12	W	31-24	San Diego
8/19	W	24-23	Seattle
8/30	W	16-8	at Oakland
9/3	L	3-34	at Denver

REGULAR SEASON (4-12)

Date	Result		Opponent	Att.
9/12	L	3-41	at Jacksonville	68,678
9/19	W	28-21	New Orleans	67,685
9/27	W	24-10	at Arizona	72,100
10/3	W	24-22	Tennessee	67,447
10/10	L	20-42	at St. Louis	65,872
10/17	L	29-31	Carolina	68,151
10/24	L	16-40	at Minnesota	64,109
11/7	L	6-27	Pittsburgh	68,657
11/14	L	6-24	at New Orleans	52,198
11/21	L	7-23	St. Louis	68,193
11/29	L	3-20	Green Bay	68,304
12/5	L	30-44	at Cincinnati	53,463
12/12	W	26-7	Atlanta	67,465
12/18	L	24-41	at Carolina	62,373
12/26	L	20-26	Washington (OT)	68,329
1/3	L	29-34	at Atlanta	57,980

(OT) Overtime

SCORE BY PERIODS

49ers	66	109	42	78	0	—	295
Opponents	92	143	130	82	6	—	453

ATTENDANCE

Home 544,228 Away 503,633 Total 1,047,861
Single-game home record, 69,014 (11/13/94)
Single-season home record, 544,228 (1999)

1999 TEAM STATISTICS

	49ers	Opp.
Total First Downs	300	315
Rushing	102	91
Passing	172	192
Penalty	26	32
Third Down: Made/Att	70/206	81/202
Third Down Pct.	34.0	40.1
Fourth Down: Made/Att	8/23	7/11
Fourth Down Pct.	34.8	63.6
Total Net Yards	5,380	5,687
Avg. Per Game	336.3	355.4
Total Plays	1,012	979
Avg. Per Play	5.3	5.8
Net Yards Rushing	2,095	1,619
Avg. Per Game	130.9	101.2
Total Rushes	418	426
Net Yards Passing	3,285	4,068
Avg. Per Game	205.3	254.3
Sacked/Yards Lost	34/241	32/227
Gross Yards	3,526	4,295
Att./Completions	560/324	521/317
Completion Pct.	57.9	60.8
Had Intercepted	19	13
Punts/Average	75/38.4	69/39.3
Net Punting Avg.	75/30.7	69/34.9
Penalties/Yards	120/1,045	96/760
Fumbles/Ball Lost	29/13	18/7
Touchdowns	33	53
Rushing	14	11
Passing	14	36
Returns	5	6
Avg. Time of Possession	30:17	29:43

1999 INDIVIDUAL STATISTICS

Passing	Att.	Comp.	Yds.	Pct.	TD	Int.	Tkld.	Rate
Garcia	375	225	2,544	60.0	11	11	15/104	77.9
Stenstrom	100	54	536	54.0	0	4	10/66	52.8
S. Young	84	45	446	53.6	3	4	8/63	60.9
Rice	1	0	0	0.0	0	0	0/0	39.6
Garner	0	0	0	—	0	0	1/8	—
49ers	560	324	3,526	57.9	14	19	34/241	70.7
Opponents	521	317	4,295	60.8	36	13	32/227	99.8

SCORING	TD R	TD P	TD Rt	PAT	FG	Saf	PTS
Richey	0	0	0	30/31	21/23	0	93
Garner	4	2	0	0/0	0/0	0	36
Rice	0	5	0	0/0	0/0	0	30
Beasley	4	0	0	0/0	0/0	0	24
Owens	0	4	0	0/0	0/0	0	24
Stokes	0	3	0	0/0	0/0	0	20
Garcia	2	0	0	0/0	0/0	0	12
Phillips	2	0	0	0/0	0/0	0	12
Walker	0	0	2	0/0	0/0	0	12
Bryant	0	0	1	0/0	0/0	0	6
Jervey	1	0	0	0/0	0/0	0	6
McMillian	0	0	1	0/0	0/0	0	6
Schulters	0	0	1	0/0	0/0	0	6
Vardell	1	0	0	0/0	0/0	0	6
B. Young	0	0	0	0/0	0/0	1	2
49ers	14	14	5	30/31	21/23	1	295
Opponents	11	36	6	50/50	27/32	1	453

2-Pt. Conversions: Stokes.
Team 1-2, Opponents 1-2.

RUSHING	Att.	Yds.	Avg.	LG	TD
Garner	241	1,229	5.1	53	4
Beasley	58	276	4.8	44t	4
Garcia	45	231	5.1	25	2
Phillips	30	144	4.8	68t	2
Jackson	15	75	5.0	11	0
S. Young	11	57	5.2	14	0
Jervey	6	49	8.2	33	1
Stenstrom	3	15	5.0	8	0
Rice	2	13	6.5	11	0
Vardell	6	6	1.0	5	1
Stanley	1	0	0.0	0	0
49ers	418	2,095	5.0	68t	14
Opponents	426	1,619	3.8	52	11

RECEIVING	No.	Yds.	Avg.	LG	TD
Rice	67	830	12.4	62	5
Owens	60	754	12.6	36	4
Garner	56	535	9.6	53	2
Stokes	34	429	12.6	47	3
Clark	34	347	10.2	24	0
Beasley	32	282	8.8	24	0
Phillips	15	152	10.1	47	0
Vardell	7	36	5.1	11	0
Harris	6	66	11.0	33	0
Cline	4	45	11.3	30	0
Jackson	3	6	2.0	4	0
Streets	2	25	12.5	14	0
Fann	2	8	4.0	6	0
Stenstrom	1	9	9.0	9	0
Jervey	1	2	2.0	2	0
49ers	324	3,526	10.9	62	14
Opponents	317	4,295	13.5	80t	36

INTERCEPTIONS	No.	Yds.	Avg.	LG	TD
Schulters	6	127	21.2	64t	1
T. McDonald	2	18	9.0	18	0
Walker	1	27	27.0	27t	1
McQuarters	1	25	25.0	25	0
Tubbs	1	8	8.0	8	0
R. McDonald	1	4	4.0	4	0
McMillian	1	0	0.0	0	0
49ers	13	209	16.1	64t	2
Opponents	19	286	15.1	93t	2

PUNTING	No.	Yds.	Avg.	In 20	LG
Stanley	69	2,737	39.7	20	70
Richey	4	146	36.5	1	45
49ers	75	2,883	38.4	21	70
Opponents	69	2,714	39.3	24	75

PUNT RETURNS	No.	FC	Yds.	Avg.	LG	TD
McQuarters	18	3	90	5.0	32	0
Harris	4	2	8	2.0	5	0
Preston	3	8	6	2.0	6	0
Givens	1	0	0	0.0	0	0
49ers	26	13	104	4.0	32	0
Opponents	33	11	399	12.1	70t	2

KICKOFF RETURNS	No.	Yds.	Avg.	LG	TD
McQuarters	26	568	21.8	37	0
Phillips	19	415	21.8	75	0
Preston	16	292	18.3	58	0
Jervey	8	191	23.9	48	0
Prioleau	3	73	24.3	32	0
Harris	2	26	13.0	15	0
Peterson	2	10	5.0	10	0
Lynch	1	4	4.0	4	0
49ers	77	1,579	20.5	75	0
Opponents	47	1,093	23.3	97t	1

FIELD GOALS	1-19	20-29	30-39	40-49	50+
Richey	1/1	7/7	7/8	5/6	1/1
49ers	1/1	7/7	7/8	5/6	1/1
Opponents	1/1	12/12	5/7	8/10	1/2

SACKS	No.
B. Young	11.0
Bryant	4.5
Haley	3.0
Woodall	2.5
T. McDonald	2.0
Posey	2.0
Tubbs	2.0
Buckner	1.0
Norton	1.0
Okeafor	1.0
Walker	1.0
Wilkins	1.0
49ers	32.0
Opponents	34.0

2000 DRAFT CHOICES

Round	Name	Pos.	College
1	Julian Peterson	LB	Michigan State
	Ahmed Plummer	DB	Ohio State
2	John Engelberger	DE	Virginia Tech
	Jason Webster	DB	Texas A&M
3	Giovanni Carmazzi	QB	Hofstra
	Jeff Ulbrich	LB	Hawaii
4	John Keith	DB	Furman
5	Paul Smith	RB	Texas-El Paso
	John Milem	DE	Lenoir-Rhyne
7	Tim Rattay	QB	Louisiana Tech
	Brian Jennings	TE	Arizona State

SAN FRANCISCO 49ERS

2000 VETERAN ROSTER

No.	Name	Pos.	Ht.	Wt.	Birthdate	NFL Exp.	College	Hometown	How Acq.	'99 Games/ Starts
40	Beasley, Fred	RB	6-1	235	9/18/74	2	Auburn	Montgomery, Ala.	D6-'98	13/11
82	Bell, Shonn	TE	6-5	257	10/25/74	2	Clinch Valley College	Stuarts Draft, Va.	FA-'99	2/0
31	† Bronson, Zack	S	6-1	195	1/28/74	4	McNeese State	Jasper, Tex.	FA-'97	15/2
65	Brown, Ray	G	6-5	318	12/12/62	15	Arkansas State	Marion, Ark.	UFA(Wash)-'96	16/16
90	Bryant, Junior	DT	6-4	278	1/16/71	6	Notre Dame	Omaha, Neb.	FA-'93	16/16
71	# Buckey, Jeff	T	6-4	295	8/7/74	5	Stanford	Bakersfield, Calif.	FA-'99	7/0
85	† Clark, Greg	TE	6-4	251	4/7/72	4	Stanford	Bountiful, Utah	D3-'97	12/11
67	Dalman, Chris	C	6-3	297	3/15/70	8	Stanford	Salinas, Calif.	D6-'93	15/15
63	Deese, Derrick	T	6-3	289	5/17/70	9	Southern California	Culver City, Calif.	FA-'92	16/16
79	Dercher, Dan	T	6-5	293	6/2/76	2	Kansas	Kansas City, Kan.	FA-'99	9/0
74	Fiore, Dave	T	6-4	290	8/10/74	5	Hofstra	Waldwick, N.J.	FA-'98	16/16
5	Garcia, Jeff	QB	6-1	195	2/24/70	2	San Jose State	Gilroy, Calif.	FA-'99	13/10
25	Garner, Charlie	RB	5-9	187	2/13/72	7	Tennessee	Fairfax, Va.	FA-'99	16/15
20	Hearst, Garrison	RB	5-11	215	1/4/71	8	Georgia	Lincolnton, Ga.	UFA(Cin)-'97	0*
66	Hopson, Tyrone	G	6-2	305	5/28/76	2	Eastern Kentucky	Hopkinsville, Ky.	D5-'99	1/0
22	Jackson, Terry	RB	6-1	218	1/10/76	2	Florida	Gainesville, Fla.	D5-'99	16/0
32	Jervey, Travis	RB	6-1	222	5/5/72	6	The Citadel	Columbia, S.C.	FA-'99	8/0
60	Lynch, Ben	C	6-4	295	11/18/72	2	California	Santa Rosa, Calif.	FA-'99	16/1
35	McDonald, Ramos	CB	5-11	194	4/30/76	3	New Mexico	Texarkana, Tex.	FA-'99	9/7
92	McGrew, Reggie	DT	6-1	301	12/16/76	2	Florida	Mayo, Fla.	D1-'99	0*
21	McQuarters, R.W.	CB	5-9	198	12/21/76	3	Oklahoma State	Tulsa, Okla.	D1-'98	11/4
24	Montgomery, Monty	CB	5-11	197	12/8/73	4	Houston	Dallas, Tex.	FA-'99	4/2
62	Newberry, Jeremy	G	6-5	315	3/23/76	3	California	Antioch, Calif.	D2-'98	16/16
51	Norton Jr., Ken	LB	6-2	254	9/29/66	13	UCLA	Los Angeles, Calif.	UFA(Dall)-'94	16/16
91	Okeafor, Chike	DE	6-4	248	3/27/76	2	Purdue	West Lafayette, Ind.	D3-'99	12/0
69	Ostrowski, Phil	G	6-4	291	9/23/75	3	Penn State	Wilkes-Barre, Pa.	D5-'98	15/0
81	Owens, Terrell	WR	6-3	217	12/7/73	5	Tennessee-Chattanooga	Alexander City, Ala.	D3-'96	14/14
26	Parker, Anthony	CB	6-1	200	12/4/75	2	Weber State	Denver, Colo.	D4-'99	0*
96	Posey, Jeff	DE	6-4	240	8/14/75	3	Southern Mississippi	Bassfield, Miss.	FA-'98	16/6
23	Prioleau, Pierson	CB	5-10	191	8/6/77	2	Virginia Tech	Charleston, S.C.	D4-'99	14/5
80	Rice, Jerry	WR	6-2	196	10/13/62	16	Mississippi Valley State	Crawford, Miss.	D1-'85	16/16
7	Richey, Wade	K	6-4	200	5/19/76	3	Louisiana State	Lafayette, La.	FA-'98	16/0
30	Schulters, Lance	S	6-2	195	5/27/75	3	Hofstra	Brooklyn, N.Y.	D4-'98	13/13
4	Stanley, Chad	P	6-3	205	1/29/76	2	Stephen F. Austin	Pittsburg, Tex.	FA-'99	16/0
83	Stokes, J.J.	WR	6-4	217	10/6/72	6	UCLA	San Diego, Calif.	D1-'95	16/4
55	Tubbs, Winfred	LB	6-4	254	9/24/70	7	Texas	Fairfield, Tex.	UFA(NO)-'98	16/15
56	Wesley, Joe	LB	6-1	229	11/10/76	2	Louisiana State	Jackson, Miss.	FA-'99	8/0
97	Young, Bryant	DT	6-3	291	1/27/72	7	Notre Dame	Chicago Heights, Ill.	D1-'94	16/16

* Hearst and Parker missed '99 season because of injury; McGrew was inactive for 4 games.

† Restricted free agents; subject to developments.

Unrestricted free agents; subject to developments.

Retired—Charles Haley, 14-year defensive end, 16 games in '99; Tommy Vardell, 8-year fullback, 6 games; Steve Young, 15-year quarterback, 3 games.

Also played with 49ers in '99—QB Pat Barnes (1 game), DT Shane Bonham (3), DT Brentson Buckner (16), TE Tony Cline (8), LB Chris Draft (7), TE Chad Fann (16), LB Reggie Givens (16), WR Mark Harris (16), DT Matt Keneley (7), LS Randy Kirk (3), S Tim McDonald (16), CB Mark McMillian (6), CB Craig Newsome (7), LB Anthony Peterson (12), RB Lawrence Phillips (8), KR Roell Preston (4), DT David Richie (1), CB Wasswa Serwanga (9), QB Steve Stenstrom (6), CB Darnell Walker (15), DE Marvin Washington (5), DE Gabe Wilkins (16), LB Lee Woodall (16), C-LS Joe Zelenka (13).

COACHING STAFF

Head Coach,
Steve Mariucci

Pro Career: Became the thirteenth head coach in 49ers history on January 16, 1997. One of thirteen head coaches since the NFL-AFL merger in 1970 to lead his team to a division title in his first season. He established an NFL mark for consecutive wins by a rookie head coach with an 11-game winning streak. He served as quarterbacks coach for the Green Bay Packers (1992-95). His first pro position was in 1985 when he was receivers coach for the USFL's Orlando Renegades. Later that fall, he had a brief stint with the Los Angeles Rams as quality control coach. Career record: 31-21.

Background: Three-time All-America quarterback at Northern Michigan. Began his coaching career at his alma mater (1978-79), and moved to Cal State-Fullerton (1980-82), and Louisville (1983-84). Joined the Southern California staff in 1986, then moved to California in 1987. In 1990-91, he served as the Bears' offensive coordinator. Became the head coach at California in 1996 and guided the squad to a 5-0 start and a berth in the Aloha Bowl.

Personal: Born November 4, 1955, in Iron Mountain, Mich. He and his wife, Gayle, have four children—Tyler, Adam, Stephen, and Brielle—and live in Saratoga, Calif.

ASSISTANT COACHES

Jerry Attaway, physical development; born January 3, 1946, Susanville, Calif., lives in San Jose, Calif. Defensive back Yuba, Calif. J.C. 1964-65, UC Davis 1967. No pro playing experience. College coach: UC Davis 1970-71, Idaho 1972-74, Utah State 1975-77, Southern California 1978-1982. Pro coach: Joined 49ers in 1983.

Mike Barnes, strength development; born March 13, 1966, Rochester, N.Y., lives in Pleasanton, Calif. No college or pro playing experience. College coach: Texas A&M 1990, California 1991-93. Pro coach: Joined 49ers in 1994.

Joe Barry, defensive quality control; born July 5, 1970, Boulder, Colo., lives in Santa Clara, Calif. Linebacker Southern California 1990-93. No pro playing experience. College coach: Southern California 1994-95, Northern Arizona 1996-98, Nevada-Las Vegas 1999. Pro coach: Joined 49ers in 2000.

Tom Batta, tight ends, born October 6, 1942, in Youngstown, Ohio, lives in Livermore, Calif. Offensive-defensive lineman Kent State 1961-63. No pro playing experience. College coach: Akron 1973, Colorado 1974-78, Kansas 1979-1982, North Carolina State 1983. Pro coach: Minnesota Vikings 1984-1993, Indianapolis Colts 1994-97, Pittsburgh Steelers 1998, joined 49ers in 1999.

Christopher Beake, defensive assistant; born September 10, 1972, Highlands Ranch, Colo., lives in Mountain View, Calif. Quarterback Air Force 1991-92. No pro playing experience. College coach: Air Force 1994-95. Pro coach: Joined 49ers in 1999.

Dwaine Board, defensive line; born November 29, 1956, Rocky Mount, Va., lives in Redwood City, Calif. Defensive lineman North Carolina A&T 1974-77. Pro defensive lineman San Francisco 49ers 1979-1987, New Orleans Saints 1988. Pro coach: Joined 49ers in 1991.

Bruce DeHaven, special teams; born September 6, 1948, Trousdale, Kan., lives in Livermore, Calif. Attended Southwestern (Kan.) College. No college or pro playing experience. College coach: Kansas 1979-1981, New Mexico State 1982. Pro coach: New Jersey Generals (USFL) 1983, Pittsburgh Maulers (USFL) 1984, Orlando Renegades (USFL) 1985, Buffalo Bills 1987-1999, joined 49ers in 2000.

Greg Knapp, quarterback; born March 5, 1963, Long Beach, Calif., lives in Los Gatos, Calif. Quarterback Cal State-Sacramento 1982-85. No pro playing experience. College coach: Cal State-Sacramento 1986-1994. Pro coach: Joined 49ers in 1995.

Brett Maxie, asst. secondary; born January 13, 1962, Dallas, lives in Santa Clara, Calif. Safety Texas Southern 1980-85. Pro safety New Orleans Saints 1985-1993, Atlanta Falcons 1994, Carolina Panthers 1995-96, San Francisco 49ers 1997. Pro coach: Carolina Panthers 1998, joined 49ers in 1999.

Jim Mora, defensive coordinator; born November 19, 1961, Los Angeles, lives in Los Gatos, Calif. Defensive back Washington 1980-83. No pro playing experience. College coach: Washington 1984. Pro coach: San Diego Chargers 1985-1991, New Orleans Saints 1992-96, joined 49ers in 1997.

Marty Mornhinweg, offensive coordinator; born March 29, 1962, Edmond, Okla., lives in Pleasanton, Calif. Quarterback Montana 1980-84. No pro playing experience. College coach: Montana 1985, Texas-El Paso 1986-87, Northern Arizona 1988, 1994, Southeast Missouri State 1989-1990, Missouri 1991-93. Pro coach: Green Bay Packers 1995-96, joined 49ers in 1997.

Pat Morris, offensive line; born April 7, 1954, Cleveland, lives in Mountain View, Calif. Offensive lineman Southern California 1972-75. No pro playing experience. College coach: Southern California 1976-77, 1983-86, Northern Arizona 1978, Minnesota 1979-1982, Michigan State 1987-1994, Stanford 1995-96. Pro coach: Joined 49ers in 1997.

Tom Rathman, running backs; born October 7, 1962, Grand Island, Neb., lives in Redwood City, Calif. Running back Nebraska 1983-85. Pro running back San Francisco 49ers 1986-1993, Los Angeles Raiders 1994. College coach: Menlo College 1996. Pro coach: Joined 49ers in 1997.

Richard Smith, linebackers; born October 17, 1955, Los Angeles, lives in Pleasanton, Calif. Offensive lineman Rio Hondo J.C. 1975-76, Fresno State 1977-78. No pro playing experience. College coach: Rio Hondo J.C. 1979-1980, Cal State-Fullerton 1981-83, California 1984-86, Arizona 1987. Pro coach: Houston Oilers 1988-1992, Denver Broncos 1993-96, joined 49ers in 1997.

George Stewart, wide receivers; born December 29, 1958, Little Rock, Ark., lives in Santa Clara, Calif. Guard Arkansas 1977-1980. No pro playing experience. College coach: Minnesota 1984-85, Notre Dame 1986-88. Pro coach: Pittsburgh Steelers 1989-1991, Tampa Bay Buccaneers 1992-95, joined 49ers in 1996.

Andy Sugarman, offensive assistant; born May 23, 1972, San Francisco, lives in Mountain View, Calif. No college or pro playing experience. College coach: California 1990-97. Pro coach: Joined 49ers in 1998.

2000 FIRST-YEAR ROSTER

Name	Pos.	Ht.	Wt.	Birthdate	College	Hometown	How Acq.
Allen, Mikki	S	5-11	193	11/15/77	Tennessee	Reno, Nev.	FA
Arrington, Jermaine	WR	5-9	176	7/3/77	Maryland	Pittsburg, Tex.	FA
Barzilauskas, Bo	DT	6-6	325	7/28/76	Valdosta State	Gilroy, Calif.	FA
Bell, Nate	DE	6-5	290	2/15/77	Southern	Greenwich, Conn.	FA
Benetka, Daniel	DT	6-4	310	11/17/74	Idaho	Los Angeles, Calif.	FA
Brumbaugh, James	DT	6-1	294	12/9/76	Auburn	Alexandria, La.	FA
Carmazzi, Giovanni	QB	6-3	224	4/14/77	Hofstra	New Orleans, La.	D3a
Carter, Dwight	WR	5-9	185	9/19/77	Hawaii	Adelphi, Md.	FA
Chew, Eric	WR	6-1	183	10/20/75	McNeese State	Bay City, Tex.	FA
Davenport, Joe Dean	TE	6-7	266	10/29/76	Arkansas	Tulsa, Okla.	FA
Dunlap, London	LB	6-3	232	2/10/77	Texas Christian	Dallas, Tex.	FA
Dupree, Terrence	TE	6-3	260	11/9/77	Duke	Fairfax, Va.	FA
Emanuel, Jim	LB	6-1	237	3/26/76	Hofstra	Denver, Colo.	FA
Engelberger, John	DE	6-4	260	10/18/76	Virginia Tech	El Paso, Tex.	D2a
Fields, Chafie	WR	6-1	200	2/4/77	Penn State	Ocean, N.J.	FA
Goodspeed, Dan	T	6-6	300	5/20/77	Kent State	Jasper, Tex.	FA
Grant, Lamar	CB	5-10	188	4/26/78	Duke	Columbia, S.C.	FA
Hall, Ricky	WR	6-2	207	1/17/76	Virginia Tech	Bradenton, Fla.	FA
Harris, Drae	CB	5-10	182	9/29/77	California	Crandall, Tex.	FA
Hart, Tracy	S	5-11	197	8/26/77	Southern Methodist	Texarkana, Tex.	FA
Heard, Ronnie	S	6-2	215	10/5/76	Mississippi	Houston, Tex.	FA
Hill, Marcus	S	6-3	217	6/1/76	Angelo State	Talent, Ore.	FA
Jennings, Brian	TE	6-5	238	10/14/76	Arizona State	Natchitoches, La.	D7b
Johnson, Tyronn	DT	6-1	295	10/18/78	Florida A&M	San Diego, Calif.	FA
Keith, John	S	6-1	207	2/4/77	Furman	Philadelphia, Pa.	D4
Killings, Cedric	DT	6-2	290	12/14/77	Carson-Newman	Overland Park, Kan.	FA
Ledford, Dwayne (1)	T	6-3	295	11/2/76	East Carolina	Memphis, Tenn.	FA-'99
Lewis, Jonas	RB	5-9	210	12/27/76	San Diego State	Hattiesburg, Miss.	FA
McMillan, Dyral	RB	5-9	217	1/11/77	South Florida	Springdale, Ark.	FA
Michel, Jake	LB	6-1	245	3/10/77	Northwestern State, La.	Colorado Springs, Colo.	FA
Milem, John	DE	6-7	290	6/9/75	Lenoir-Rhyne	San Jose, Calif.	D5b
Nicks, Ronnie	LB	6-1	244	12/18/77	Notre Dame	Jackson, Miss.	FA
Owen, Dustin	G-T	6-2	310	5/16/78	Hawaii	Santa Rosa, Calif.	FA
Parks, Tom	P	6-2	225	10/14/70	Mississippi State	Culver City, Calif.	FA
Payne, Greg	CB-S	5-10	190	12/3/77	Arizona	Los Osos, Calif.	FA
Pennington, Trey	TE	6-5	260	12/8/76	South Carolina	Marion, Ark.	FA
Peterson, Julian	LB	6-3	235	7/28/78	Michigan State	Hopkinsville, Ky.	D1a
Plummer, Ahmed	CB	5-11	191	3/26/76	Ohio State	Salinas, Calif.	D1b
Rattay, Tim	QB	6-1	215	3/15/77	Louisiana Tech	Miami, Fla.	D7a
Rice, Al	LB	6-1	218	11/6/77	Mississippi	Cleveland, Ohio	FA
Roques, Ryan	DB	5-11	190	8/5/77	UCLA	Morgantown, N.C.	FA
Scott, Danny	DE	6-3	263	3/19/76	Louisiana-Lafayette	New Orleans, La.	FA
Smith, Paul	RB	5-11	234	1/31/78	Texas-El Paso	Stanford, Calif.	D5a
Smith, Ricky	LB	6-3	250	12/1/75	Southwestern	Cola, S.C.	FA
Streets, Tai (1)	WR	6-1	193	4/20/77	Michigan	Matteson, Ill.	D6-'99
Swanson, Brennen	LB	6-2	238	10/18/76	Cal State-Northridge	Crawford, Miss.	FA
Swift, Justin (1)	TE	6-3	265	8/14/75	Kansas State	Alexander City, Ala.	FA-'99
Tenner, Jason (1)	T	6-5	275	8/17/77	Villanova	Stuarts Draft, Va.	FA-'99
Ulbrich, Jeff	LB	6-1	249	2/17/77	Hawaii	Mesa, Ariz.	D3b
Webster, Jason	CB	5-9	180	9/8/77	Texas A&M	Matteson, Ill.	D2b
White, Josh	RB	5-11	245	3/8/77	California	West Lafayette, Ind.	FA
Williams, Antonio	DT	6-7	300	1/19/76	South Carolina State	Concord, N.C.	FA
Williams, B.J.	S	6-1	197	8/11/76	Northwestern State, La.	Miami, Fla.	FA
Yates, Griff	RB	5-11	205	8/4/76	Southern Oregon	Heidelberg, Germany	FA

The term NFL Rookie is defined as a player who is in his first season of professional football and has not been on the roster of another professional football team for any regular-season or postseason games. A Rookie is designated by an "R" on NFL rosters. Players who have been active in another professional football league or players who have NFL experience, including either preseason training camp or being on an Active List or Inactive List, or on Reserve/Injured or Reserve/Physically Unable to Perform for fewer than six regular-season games, are termed NFL First-Year Players. An NFL First-Year Player is designated by a "1" on NFL rosters. Thereafter, a player is credited with an additional year of experience for each season in which he accumulates six games on the Active List or Inactive List, or on Reserve/Injured or Reserve/Physically Unable to Perform.

TAMPA BAY BUCCANEERS

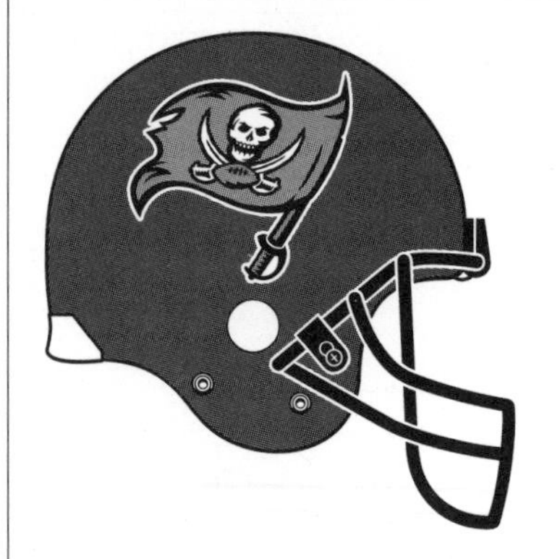

National Football Conference
Central Division
Team Colors: Buccaneer Red, Pewter, Black, and Orange
One Buccaneer Place
Tampa, Florida 33607
Telephone: (813) 870-2700

CLUB OFFICIALS

Owner/President: Malcolm Glazer
Executive Vice President: Bryan Glazer
Executive Vice President: Joel Glazer
Executive Vice President: Edward Glazer
General Manager: Rich McKay
Chief Financial Officer: Tom Alas
Director of Player Personnel: Jerry Angelo
Director of College Scouting: Tim Ruskell
Director of Football Administration: John Idzik
Executive Director of the Glazer Family Foundation: Veronica (Roni) Costello
Director of Communications: Reggie Roberts
Director of Marketing: George Woods
Director of Premium Seating: Jim Overton
Director of Community Relations: Stephanie Waller
Director of Player Programs: Kevin Winston
Director of Security: Andre Trescastro
College Scouts: Joe DiMarzo, Jr., Dennis Hickey, Ruston Webster, Mike Yowarsky
Coordinator of Pro Personnel: Mark Dominik
Pro Personnel Assistant: Leamon Boyd
Pro/College Scout: Lloyd Richards, Jr.
Director of Ticketing and Customer Relations: Mike Newquist
Director of Human Resources: Gene Magrini
Communications Coordinator: Carter Toole
Trainer: Todd Toriscelli
Assistant Trainer: Keith Abrams
Director of Rehabilitation: Jim Whalen
Equipment Manager: Darin Kerns
Assistant Equipment Manager: Mark Meschede
Video Director: Dave Levy
Assistant Video Director: Pat Brazil
Stadium: Raymond James Stadium
•Capacity: 66,321
Tampa, Florida 33607
Playing Surface: Grass
Training Camp: University of Tampa
Tampa, Florida 33606

2000 SCHEDULE

PRESEASON

Aug. 4	**Washington**	7:30
Aug. 10	at Miami	7:00
Aug. 20	at New England	4:00
Aug. 25	**Kansas City**	7:30

REGULAR SEASON

Sept. 3	at New England	1:00
Sept. 10	**Chicago**	1:00
Sept. 17	at Detroit	1:00
Sept. 24	**New York Jets**	4:15
Oct. 1	at Washington	4:15
Oct. 9	at Minnesota (Mon.)	8:00
Oct. 15	Open Date	
Oct. 19	**Detroit** (Thu.)	8:35
Oct. 29	**Minnesota**	1:00
Nov. 5	at Atlanta	1:00
Nov. 12	**Green Bay**	4:15
Nov. 19	at Chicago	12:00
Nov. 26	**Buffalo**	1:00
Dec. 3	**Dallas**	1:00
Dec. 10	at Miami	1:00
Dec. 18	**St. Louis** (Mon.)	9:00
Dec. 24	at Green Bay	12:00

RECORD HOLDERS

INDIVIDUAL RECORDS—CAREER

Category	Name	Performance
Rushing (Yds.)	James Wilder, 1981-89	5,957
Passing (Yds.)	Vinny Testaverde, 1987-1992	14,820
Passing (TDs)	Vinny Testaverde, 1987-1992	77
Receiving (No.)	James Wilder, 1981-89	430
Receiving (Yds.)	Mark Carrier, 1987-1992	5,018
Interceptions	Cedric Brown, 1976-1984	29
Punting (Avg.)	Tommy Barnhardt, 1996-98	42.6
Punt Return (Avg.)	Karl Williams, 1996-99	12.4
Kickoff Return (Avg.)	Reidel Anthony, 1997-99	23.3
Field Goals	Michael Husted, 1993-98	117
Touchdowns (Tot.)	James Wilder, 1981-89	46
Points	Michael Husted, 1993-98	502

INDIVIDUAL RECORDS—SINGLE SEASON

Category	Name	Performance
Rushing (Yds.)	James Wilder, 1984	1,544
Passing (Yds.)	Doug Williams, 1981	3,563
Passing (TDs)	Trent Dilfer, 1997, 1998	21
Receiving (No.)	Mark Carrier, 1989	86
Receiving (Yds.)	Mark Carrier, 1989	1,422
Interceptions	Cedric Brown, 1981	9
Punting (Avg.)	Mark Royals, 1999	43.1
Punt Return (Avg.)	Karl Williams, 1996	21.1
Kickoff Return (Avg.)	Karl Williams, 1996	27.4
Field Goals	Martin Gramatica, 1999	27
Touchdowns (Tot.)	James Wilder, 1984	13
Points	Martin Gramatica, 1999	106

INDIVIDUAL RECORDS—SINGLE GAME

Category	Name	Performance
Rushing (Yds.)	James Wilder, 11-6-83	219
Passing (Yds.)	Doug Williams, 11-16-80	486
Passing (TDs)	Steve DeBerg, 9-13-87	5
Receiving (No.)	James Wilder, 9-15-85	13
Receiving (Yds.)	Mark Carrier, 12-6-87	212
Interceptions	Many times. Last time by Damien Robinson, 12-26-99	2
Field Goals	Many times. Last time by Martin Gramatica, 11-21-99	4
Touchdowns (Tot.)	Jimmie Giles, 10-20-85	4
Points	Jimmie Giles, 10-20-85	24

COACHING HISTORY

(132-247-1)

1976-84	John McKay	45-91-1
1985-86	Leeman Bennett	4-28-0
1987-90	Ray Perkins*	19-41-0
1990-91	Richard Williamson	4-15-0
1992-95	Sam Wyche	23-41-0
1996-99	Tony Dungy	37-31-0

*Released after 13 games in 1990

RAYMOND JAMES STADIUM

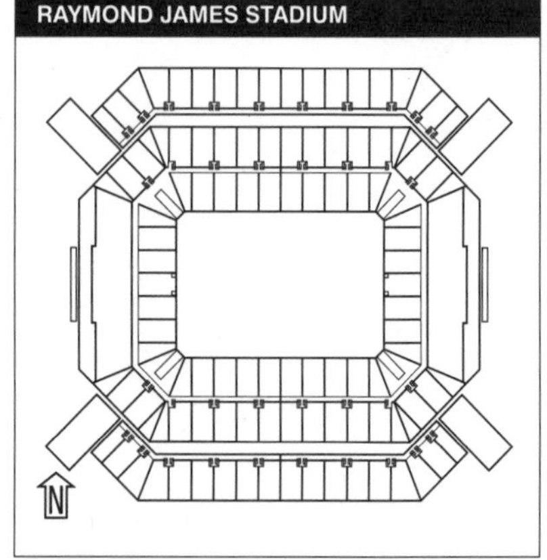

1999 TEAM RECORD

PRESEASON (4-0)

Date	Result		Opponent
8/14	W	30-3	Cleveland
8/21	W	17-7	at Kansas City
8/28	W	45-14	New England
9/3	W	16-13	at Washington

REGULAR SEASON (11-5)

Date	Result		Opponent	Att.
9/12	L	13-17	New York Giants	65,026
9/19	W	19-5	at Philadelphia	64,285
9/26	W	13-10	Denver	65,297
10/3	L	14-21	at Minnesota	64,106
10/10	L	23-26	at Green Bay	59,868
10/24	W	6-3	Chicago	65,283
10/31	L	3-20	at Detroit	63,135
11/7	W	31-16	at New Orleans	47,129
11/14	W	17-10	Kansas City	64,927
11/21	W	19-10	Atlanta	65,158
11/28	W	16-3	at Seattle	66,314
12/6	W	24-17	Minnesota	65,741
12/12	W	23-16	Detroit	65,536
12/19	L	0-45	at Oakland	46,395
12/26	W	29-10	Green Bay	65,273
1/2	W	20-6	at Chicago	66,944

POSTSEASON (1-1)

Date	Result		Opponent	Att.
1/15	W	14-13	Washington	65,835
1/23	L	6-11	at St. Louis	66,396

SCORE BY PERIODS

Buccaneers	34	106	42	88	0	—	270
Opponents	89	47	44	55	0	—	235

ATTENDANCE

Home 511,590 Away 472,982 Total 984,572
Single-game home record, 73,523 (12/7/97)
Single-season home record, 545,980 (1979)

1999 TEAM STATISTICS

	Buccaneers	Opp.
Total First Downs	245	228
Rushing	97	75
Passing	132	144
Penalty	16	9
Third Down: Made/Att	81/230	75/232
Third Down Pct.	35.2	32.3
Fourth Down: Made/Att	7/15	4/13
Fourth Down Pct.	46.7	30.8
Total Net Yards	4,254	4,280
Avg. Per Game	265.9	267.5
Total Plays	991	977
Avg. Per Play	4.3	4.4
Net Yards Rushing	1,776	1,407
Avg. Per Game	111.0	87.9
Total Rushes	502	361
Net Yards Passing	2,478	2,873
Avg. Per Game	154.9	179.6
Sacked/Yards Lost	42/303	43/291
Gross Yards	2,781	3,164
Att./Completions	447/268	573/302
Completion Pct.	60.0	52.7
Had Intercepted	16	21
Punts/Average	90/43.1	101/41.1
Net Punting Avg.	90/37.4	101/35.4
Penalties/Yards	75/583	88/727
Fumbles/Ball Lost	25/19	23/10
Touchdowns	27	23
Rushing	7	8
Passing	18	11
Returns	2	4
Avg. Time of Possession	32:11	27:49

1999 INDIVIDUAL STATISTICS

Passing	Att.	Comp.	Yds.	Pct.	TD	Int.	Tkld.	Rate
Dilfer	244	146	1,619	59.8	11	11	26/189	75.8
King	146	89	875	61.0	7	4	11/78	82.4
Zeier	55	32	270	58.2	0	1	5/36	63.4
Royals	2	1	17	50.0	0	0	0/0	79.2
Buccaneers	447	268	2,781	60.0	18	16	42/303	76.5
Opponents	573	302	3,164	52.7	11	21	43/291	60.1

SCORING	TD R	TD P	TD Rt	PAT	FG	Saf	PTS
Gramatica	0	0	0	25/25	27/32	0	106
Alstott	7	2	0	0/0	0/0	0	54
Moore	0	5	0	0/0	0/0	0	30
Green	0	3	0	0/0	0/0	0	18
Abraham	0	0	2	0/0	0/0	0	12
Dunn	0	2	0	0/0	0/0	0	12
Anthony	0	1	0	0/0	0/0	0	6
J. Davis	0	1	0	0/0	0/0	0	6
Emanuel	0	1	0	0/0	0/0	0	6
Hape	0	1	0	0/0	0/0	0	6
McDonald	0	1	0	0/0	0/0	0	6
McLeod	0	1	0	0/0	0/0	0	6
Culpepper	0	0	0	0/0	0/0	1	2
Buccaneers	7	18	2	25/25	27/32	1	270
Opponents	8	11	4	23/23	24/31	1	235

2-Pt. Conversions: None.
Team 0-2, Opponents 0-0.

RUSHING	Att.	Yds.	Avg.	LG	TD
Alstott	242	949	3.9	30	7
Dunn	195	616	3.2	33	0
Dilfer	35	144	4.1	28	0
King	18	38	2.1	8	0
Abdullah	5	12	2.4	10	0
Green	3	8	2.7	15	0
Zeier	3	7	2.3	8	0
Anthony	1	2	2.0	2	0
Buccaneers	502	1,776	3.5	33	7
Opponents	361	1,407	3.9	75t	8

RECEIVING	No.	Yds.	Avg.	LG	TD
Dunn	64	589	9.2	68	2
Green	56	791	14.1	62t	3
Anthony	30	296	9.9	30	1
Alstott	27	239	8.9	24	2
Moore	23	276	12.0	35t	5
Emanuel	22	238	10.8	39	1
Williams	21	176	8.4	14	0
McDonald	9	96	10.7	23	1
Hape	5	12	2.4	4	1
Murphy	4	28	7.0	9	0
Abdullah	2	11	5.5	8	0
J. Davis	2	7	3.5	6	1
McLeod	2	5	2.5	3t	1
Robinson	1	17	17.0	17	0
Buccaneers	268	2,781	10.4	68	18
Opponents	302	3,164	10.5	61t	11

INTERCEPTIONS	No.	Yds.	Avg.	LG	TD
Abraham	7	115	16.4	55t	2
Brooks	4	61	15.3	38	0
Barber	2	60	30.0	43	0
Robinson	2	36	18.0	36	0
Lynch	2	32	16.0	28	0
Nickerson	2	18	9.0	18	0
Kelly	1	26	26.0	26	0
Singleton	1	7	7.0	7	0
Buccaneers	21	355	16.9	55t	2
Opponents	16	144	9.0	37	1

PUNTING	No.	Yds.	Avg.	In 20	LG
Royals	90	3,882	43.1	23	66
Buccaneers	90	3,882	43.1	23	66
Opponents	101	4,150	41.1	27	61

PUNT RETURNS	No.	FC	Yds.	Avg.	LG	TD
Green	23	14	204	8.9	31	0
Williams	20	12	153	7.7	30	0
Buccaneers	43	26	357	8.3	31	0
Opponents	49	13	360	7.3	31	0

KICKOFF RETURNS	No.	Yds.	Avg.	LG	TD
Anthony	21	434	20.7	39	0
Murphy	14	307	21.9	55	0
Green	10	185	18.5	29	0
Dunn	8	156	19.5	34	0
Alstott	1	19	19.0	19	0
Williams	1	15	15.0	15	0
Moore	0	0	—	—	0
Buccaneers	55	1,116	20.3	55	0
Opponents	61	1,074	17.6	36	0

FIELD GOALS	1-19	20-29	30-39	40-49	50+
Gramatica	0/0	8/8	10/12	6/8	3/4
Buccaneers	0/0	8/8	10/12	6/8	3/4
Opponents	0/0	8/9	9/10	6/10	1/2

SACKS	No.
Sapp	12.5
Jones	7.0
Ahanotu	6.5
Culpepper	6.0
Abraham	2.0
Brooks	2.0
White	2.0
Barber	1.0
T. Jackson	1.0
McFarland	1.0
Lynch	0.5
Nickerson	0.5
Robinson	0.5
Singleton	0.5
Buccaneers	43.0
Opponents	42.0

2000 DRAFT CHOICES

Round	Name	Pos.	College
2	Cosey Coleman	G	Tennessee
3	Nate Webster	LB	Miami
5	James Whalen	TE	Kentucky
6	David Gibson	DB	Southern California
7	Joe Hamilton	QB	Georgia Tech

TAMPA BAY BUCCANEERS

2000 VETERAN ROSTER

No.	Name	Pos.	Ht.	Wt.	Birthdate	NFL Exp.	College	Hometown	How Acq.	'99 Games/ Starts
27	Abdullah, Rabih	RB	6-1	227	4/27/75	3	Lehigh	Roselle, NJ	FA-'98	15/1
21	Abraham, Donnie	CB	5-10	192	10/8/73	5	East Tennessee State	Orangeburg, S.C.	D3-'96	16/16
72	Ahanotu, Chidi	DE	6-2	285	10/11/70	8	California	Berkeley, Calif.	D6-'93	16/15
40	Alstott, Mike	RB	6-1	248	12/21/73	5	Purdue	Joliet, Ill.	D2-'96	16/16
85	Anthony, Reidel	WR	5-11	180	10/20/76	4	Florida	Glades Central, Fla.	D1b-'97	13/7
20	†- Barber, Ronde	CB	5-8	184	4/7/75	4	Virginia	Roanoke, Va.	D3b-'97	16/15
66	Blackman, Ken	G	6-6	320	11/8/72	5	Illinois	Abilene, Tex.	FA-'99	0/0
55	Brooks, Derrick	LB	6-0	235	4/18/73	6	Florida State	Pensacola, Fla.	D1b-'95	16/16
98	Cannida, James	DT	6-2	291	1/3/75	3	Nevada-Reno	Fremont, Calif.	D6a-'98	2/0
62	Christy, Jeff	C	6-2	285	2/3/69	8	Pittsburgh	Freeport, Pa.	UFA(Minn)-'00	16/16
77	Culpepper, Brad	DT	6-1	270	5/8/69	9	Florida	Tallahassee, Fla.	W (Minn)-'94	16/16
65	Dogins, Kevin	C-G	6-1	301	12/7/72	4	Texas A&M-Kingsville	Eagle Lake, Tex.	FA-'96	11/5
59	Duncan, Jamie	LB	6-0	242	7/20/75	3	Vanderbilt	Wilmington, Del.	D3-'98	16/0
28	Dunn, Warrick	RB	5-8	180	1/5/75	4	Florida State	Baton Rouge, La.	D1a-'97	15/15
37	Ellison, Jerry	RB	5-10	224	12/20/71	6	Tennessee-Chattanooga	Augusta, Ga.	FA-'00	12/0
50	Gooch, Jeff	RB	5-11	225	10/31/74	5	Austin Peay	Nashville, Tenn.	FA-'96	15/0
7	Martin Gramatica	K	5-8	170	11/27/75	2	Kansas State	LaBelle, Fla.	D3-'99	16/0
81	Green, Jacquez	WR	5-9	168	1/15/76	3	Florida	Fort Valley, Ga.	D2a-'98	16/10
82	Hape, Patrick	TE	6-4	262	6/6/74	4	Alabama	Kilen, Ala.	D5-'97	15/1
79	Hegamin, George	T	6-7	331	2/14/73	7	North Carolina State	Camden, N.J.	FA-'99	1/0
34	Jackson, Dexter	S	6-0	196	7/28/77	2	Florida State	Quincy, Fla.	D4-'99	12/0
97	Jackson, Tyoka	DE-DT	6-2	280	11/22/71	6	Penn State	Washington, D.C.	FA-'96	6/1
19	t- Johnson, Keyshawn	WR	6-4	212	7/22/72	5	Southern California	Los Angeles, Calif.	T(NYJ)-'00	16/16
78	Jones, Marcus	DE	6-6	278	8/15/73	5	North Carolina	Jacksonville, N.C.	D1b-'96	16/4
91	Jordan, Anthony	LB	6-3	240	12/19/74	3	Vanderbilt	Sewell, N.J.	FA-'00	0*
25	Kelly, Brian	CB	5-11	193	1/14/76	3	Southern California	Aurora, Colo.	D2b-'98	16/3
10	King, Shaun	QB	6-0	225	5/29/77	2	Tulane	St. Petersburg, Fla.	D2-'99	6/5
48	Kitts, Jim	RB	6-1	245	12/28/72	2	Ferrum	Chesapeake, Va.	FA-'00	0*
49	Lusk, Henry	TE	6-2	250	5/8/72	3	Utah	Monterey, Calif.	FA-'00	0*
47	Lynch, John	S	6-2	220	9/25/71	8	Stanford	Solana Beach, Calif.	D3-'93	16/16
64	McDaniel, Randall	G	6-3	287	12/19/64	12	Arizona State	Avondale, Ariz.	FA-'00	16/16
84	McDonald, Darnell	WR	6-3	199	5/26/76	2	Kansas State	Fairfax, N.J.	D7c-'99	9/0
92	McFarland, Anthony	DT	6-0	300	12/18/77	2	Louisiana State	Winnsboro, La.	D1-'99	14/0
95	McLaughlin, John	DE	6-4	247	11/13/75	2	California	Newhall, Calif.	D5-'99	12/0
43	McLeod, Kevin	RB	6-0	252	10/17/74	2	Auburn	Clarkston, Ga.	FA-'99	7/0
73	Middleton, Frank	G	6-3	334	10/25/74	4	Arizona	Beaumont, Tex.	D3a-'97	16/16
10	Milanovich, Scott	QB	6-3	220	1/25/73	4	Maryland	Butler, Pa.	FA-'00	0*
83	Moore, Dave	TE	6-2	258	11/11/69	8	Pittsburgh	Succasunna, N.J.	FA-'92	16/16
88	Murphy, Yo	WR	5-10	178	5/11/71	2	Idaho	Idaho Falls, Idaho	FA-'00	7/0
70	Odom, Jason	T	6-5	312	3/31/74	5	Florida	Bartow, Fla.	D4a-'96	3/3
57	Palmer, Mitch	C-LB	6-4	259	9/2/73	3	Colorado State	San Diego, Calif.	FA-'98	4/0
69	Pierson, Pete	T	6-5	315	2/4/71	6	Washington	Portland, Ore.	D5-'94	15/0
45	Purnell, Lovett	TE	6-3	245	4/7/72	5	West Virginia	Seadale, Del.	FA-'00	0*
53	Qurales, Shelton	LB	6-1	230	9/11/71	4	Vanderbilt	Whites Creek, Tenn.	FA-'97	16/14
24	Robinson, Damien	S	6-2	214	12/22/73	4	Iowa	Dallas, Tex.	FA-'97	16/16
3	Royals, Mark	P	6-5	215	6/22/65	12	Appalachian State	Mathews, Va.	FA-'99	16/0
99	Sapp, Warren	DT	6-2	303	12/19/72	6	Miami	Apopka, Fla.	D1a-'95	15/15
51	Singleton, Alshermond	LB	6-2	228	8/7/75	4	Temple	Irvington, N.J.	D4-'97	15/0
30	Smith, Shevin	S	5-11	204	6/17/75	3	Florida State	Miami, Fla.	D6b-'98	16/0
93	Stuckey, Sean	LB	6-0	230	10/22/75	2	Troy State	Daleville, Ala.	FA-'00	0*
90	Tatum, Kinnon	LB	6-0	222	7/19/75	3	Notre Dame	Fayetteville, N.C.	FA-'00	0*
68	Unutoa, Morris	C-LS	6-1	284	3/10/71	5	Brigham Young	Carson, Calif.	FA-'99	12/0
75	Washington, Todd	C-G	6-3	324	7/19/76	3	Virginia Tech	Melfa, Va.	D4-'98	6/0
94	White, Steve	DE	6-2	271	10/25/73	5	Tennessee	Memphis, Tenn.	FA-'96	13/13
86	Williams, Karl	WR	5-10	177	4/10/71	5	Texas A&M-Kingsville	Garland, Tex.	FA-'96	13/4
71	Wunsch, Jerry	T	6-6	339	1/21/74	4	Wisconsin	Wausau, Wis.	D2-'97	16/13
31	Young, Floyd	CB	6-0	179	11/23/75	4	Texas A&M-Kingsville	New Orleans, La.	FA-'97	6/0
15	Zeier, Eric	QB	6-1	214	9/6/72	6	Georgia	Marietta, Ga.	T(Balt)-'99	2/1

* Blackman was inactive for 6 games in '99; Christy played 16 games with Minnesota in '99; Ellison played 12 games with New England; Johnson played 16 games with N.Y. Jets; Jordan last active with Indianapolis in '98; Kitts last active with Green Bay in '99; Lusk last active with Washington in '98; McDaniel played 16 games with Minnesota; Milanovich was inactive for 5 games; Murphy played 7 games with Tampa Bay and 1 game with Minnesota; Purnell last active with Washington in 98; Stuckey last active with New England in '98; Tatum last active with Carolina in '98 .

†– Restricted free agent; subject to developments.

t – Buccaneers traded for Johnson (N.Y. Jets).

Players lost through free agency (2)—QB Trent Dilfer (Balt, 10 games in '99), LB Hardy Nickerson (Jax, 16).

Also played with Buccaneers in '99—LB Don Davis (14 games), TE John Davis (16), G Jorge Diaz (13), WR Bert Emanuel (11), T Paul Gruber (16), C Tony Mayberry (16), RB Fred McAfee (1), DE Regan Upshaw (1), S Eric Vance (6).

COACHING STAFF

Head Coach,
Tony Dungy

Pro Career: After 15 years as an NFL assistant coach, Dungy was named as the Buccaneers' sixth head coach on January 22, 1996, when he signed a six-year contract. Last season, Dungy's Buccaneers set a franchise record with 11 regular-season wins, captured their first NFC Central Division title in 18 years, and advanced to their first NFC Championship Game in 20 years. Tampa Bay also advanced to the playoffs in 1997 under Dungy, posting a 10-6 record and defeating the Detriot Lions in a wild-card game. Dungy's .544 winning percentage is the best in club history. Joined Tampa Bay after serving as Minnesota Vikings' defensive coordinator from 1992-95. Helped the Vikings' defense lead NFL with 95 interceptions during his four years in Minnesota. Prior to going to Vikings, spent 1989-1991 as defensive backs coach for Kansas City Chiefs. Also worked eight years as an assistant coach for the Pittsburgh Steelers under Chuck Noll as a defensive assistant (1981), defensive backs coach (1982-83), and as defensive coordinator (1984-88). At 25, was NFL's youngest assistant coach when hired by Steelers in 1981, then became league's youngest coordinator at age of 28. Began coaching career as defensive backs coach at University of Minnesota in 1980. As an NFL player, signed with Pittsburgh as a free agent in 1977 and played safety for Steelers for two seasons (1977-78). Had 9 interceptions (second in AFC with 6 in 1978) in 30 games for Pittsburgh and played in Super Bowl XIII victory over Dallas Cowboys. Had unusual distinction of making and throwing an interception in same 1977 game against Houston Oilers. Traded to San Francisco 49ers during 1979 training camp and played 15 games for 49ers. Was traded again prior to 1980 season to New York Giants in multi-player deal that sent current Minnesota Vikings defensive coordinator Ray Rhodes to 49ers. Career record: 37-31.

Background: Starred as quarterback at University of Minnesota from 1973-76. Finished career as school's all-time leader in attempts, completions, passing yards, and touchdown passes. Left Minnesota in fourth place in Big Ten history in total offense. Two-time team most valuable player, played in Hula Bowl, East-West Shrine Game, and Japan Bowl. Attended Parkside High School in Jackson, Michigan.

Personal: Born October 6, 1955, in Jackson, Michigan. Tony and his wife, Lauren, have three children including daughter Tiara (14), and sons James (12) and Eric (7). The family resides in Tampa.

ASSISTANT COACHES

Mark Asanovich, strength and conditioning; born May 20, 1959, Duluth, Minn., lives in Tampa. No college or pro playing experience. College coach: Ohio State 1985, Citadel 1986. Pro coach: Minnesota Vikings 1995, joined Buccaneers in 1996.

Wendell Avery, offensive assistant; born October 20, 1956, Corpus Christi, Tex., lives in Tampa. Quarterback Minnesota 1975-79. No pro playing experience. College coach: McCalister College (Minn.) 1982-83, Winona State 1990-91, Alabama A&M 1992-93, Savannah State 1994-96 (head coach, 1995-96), Fort Valley State 1998. Pro coach: Joined Buccaneers in 1999.

Clyde Christensen, quarterbacks; born January 28, 1958, Corvine, Calif., lives in Tampa. Quarterback Fresno (Calif.) J.C. 1975, North Carolina 1976-78. No pro playing experience. College coach: East Tennessee State 1980-82, Temple 1983-85, East Carolina 1986-88, Holy Cross 1989-90, South Carolina 1991, Maryland 1992-93, Clemson 1994-95. Pro coach: Joined Buccaneers in 1996.

Les Ebert, asst. strength and conditioning; born October 1, 1972, Brinard, Minn., lives in Tampa. Attended Minnesota-Duluth. No college or pro playing experience. Pro coach: Joined Buccaneers in 1999.

Herman Edwards, assistant head coach/defensive backs; born April 27, 1954, Monmouth, N.J., lives in Tampa. Defensive back California 1972, 1974, Monterey Peninsula (Calif.) J.C. 1973, San Diego State 1975-76. Pro defensive back Philadelphia Eagles 1977-85, Los Angeles Rams 1986, Atlanta Falcons 1986. College coach: San Jose State 1987-89. Pro coach: Kansas City Chiefs 1992-94 (scout 1990-91, 1995), joined Buccaneers in 1996.

Chris Foerster, offensive line; born October 12, 1961, Milwaukee, Wis., lives in Tampa. Center Colorado State 1979-82. No pro playing experience. College coach: Colorado State 1983-87, Stanford 1988-91, Minnesota 1992. Pro coach: Minnesota Vikings 1993-95, joined Buccaneers in 1996.

Monte Kiffin, defensive coordinator; born February 29, 1940, Lexington, Neb., lives in Tampa. Offensive/defensive tackle Nebraska 1959-63. Pro defensive end Winnipeg Blue Bombers (CFL) 1965. College coach: Nebraska 1966-76, Arkansas 1977-79, North Carolina State 1980-82 (head coach). Pro coach: Green Bay Packers 1983, Buffalo Bills 1984-85, Minnesota Vikings 1986-89, 1991-94, New York Jets 1990, New Orleans Saints 1995, joined Buccaneers in 1996.

Joe Marciano, special teams; born February 10, 1954, Scranton, Pa., lives in Tampa. Quarterback Temple 1972-75. No pro playing experience. College coach: East Stroudsburg 1977, Rhode Island 1978-79, Villanova 1980, Penn State 1981, Temple 1982. Pro coach: Philadelphia/Baltimore Stars (USFL) 1983-85, New Orleans Saints 1986-95, joined Buccaneers in 1996.

Rod Marinelli, defensive line; born July 13, 1949, Rosemead, Calif., lives in Tampa. Offensive/defensive tackle Utah 1968, offensive tackle California Lutheran 1970-72 (military service 1969-70). No pro playing experience. College coach: Utah State 1976-82, California 1983-91, Arizona State 1992-94, Southern California 1995. Pro coach: Joined Buccaneers in 1996.

Tony Nathan, running backs; born December 14, 1956, Birmingham, Ala., lives in Tampa. Running back Alabama 1975-78. Pro running back Miami Dolphins 1979-87. Pro coach: Miami Dolphins 1988-95, joined Buccaneers in 1996.

Kevin O'Dea, defensive assistant; born June 9, 1960, Williamsport, Va., lives in Tampa. Defensive back/wide receiver Lock Haven 1982-85. No pro playing experience. College coach: Lock Haven 1986, Cornell 1987, Virginia 1988-90, Penn State 1991-93. Pro coach: San Diego Chargers 1994-95, joined Buccaneers in 1996.

Lovie Smith, linebackers; born May 8, 1958, Gladewater, Tex., lives in Tampa. Linebacker Tulsa 1976-79. No pro playing experience. College coach: Tulsa 1983-86, Wisconsin 1987, Arizona State 1988-91, Kentucky 1992, Tennessee 1993-94, Ohio State 1995. Pro coach: Joined Buccaneers in 1996.

Les Steckel, offensive coordinator; born July 1, 1946, Whitehall, Pa., lives in Tampa. College coach: Colorado 1972-76, Navy 1977, Brown 1989, Colorado 1991-92. Pro coach: San Francisco 49ers 1978, Minnesota Vikings 1979-1984 (head coach, 1984), New England Patriots 1985-88, Denver Broncos 1993-94, Tennessee Titans/Oilers 1995-99, joined Buccaneers in 2000.

Ricky Thomas, tight ends; born March 29, 1965, London, England, lives in Tampa. Safety Alabama 1983-86. Pro safety Seattle Seahawks 1987. College coach: Kentucky 1996, Gardner-Webb 1996. Pro coach: Joined Buccaneers in 1997.

Charlie Williams, wide receivers; born January 31, 1958, Long Beach, Calif., lives in Tampa. Defensive back Long Beach City College 1977-78, Colorado State 1979-80. No pro playing experience. College coach: Colorado State 1981, Long Beach City College 1984-85, New Mexico State 1986-87, Texas Christian 1988-91, Minnesota 1992, Miami 1993-95. Pro coach: Joined Buccaneers in 1996.

2000 FIRST-YEAR ROSTER

Name	Pos.	Ht.	Wt.	Birthdate	College	Hometown	How Acq.
Blick, John	T	6-6	323	2/10/78	Penn State	Saylorsburg, Pa.	FA
Bradley, Carl	DT	6-2	228	2/22/78	Virginia Tech	Lynchburg, Va.	FA
Coleman, Cosey	G	6-4	322	10/27/78	Tennessee	Clarkston, Ga.	D2
Cooper, Ashley	S	6-0	207	1/11/78	Mississippi State	Fort Walton Beach, Fla.	FA
Curry, DeMarcus (1)	T	6-5	332	4/30/75	Auburn	Columbus, Ga.	FA-'99
Daniels, Chris	WR	6-3	219	3/30/77	Purdue	Clearwater, Fla.	FA
DeGroh, Eric (1)	C	6-4	318	4/16/77	West Virginia	Huron, Ohio	FA-'99
Freeman, Jason (1)	TE	6-3	249	11/14/76	Oklahoma	Muskogee, Okla.	FA
Gibson, David	S	6-1	210	11/5/77	Southern California	Santa Ana, Calif.	D6
Hamilton, Joe	QB	5-10	190	3/13/77	Georgia Tech	Alvin, S.C.	D7
Hogans, Tavarus	WR	5-10	191	8/16/78	Vanderbilt	DeFuniak Springs, Fla.	FA
Holman, Tarig	CB	6-0	195	10/14/76	Iowa	Randolf, N.J.	FA
Howard, Bobbie (1)	LB	5-10	226	6/14/77	Notre Dame	Ft. Lauderdale, Fla.	FA
Humphrey, Aaron	DE	6-3	260	9/22/77	Texas	Lubbock, Tex.	FA
Mallard, Deshone (1)	CB	5-10	188	1/22/76	Southern Mississppi	Jackson, Miss.	FA
McKenzie, Damonte	DT	6-2	280	3/25/76	Clemson	Lake City, S.C.	FA
Moreland, Earthwind	CB	5-11	185	6/13/77	Georgia Southern	Atlanta, Ga.	FA
O'Connor, Drew (1)	WR	6-3	224	2/2/76	Maine	Plainfield, N.J.	FA
Parrish, Terrance	CB	5-11	190	10/1/76	Southern Mississppi	Theodore, Ala.	FA
Sanford, Ketric	RB	5-8	204	7/6/78	Houston	Corsicana, Tex.	FA
Shay, John (1)	P	6-0	205	7/30/74	Temple	Philadelphia, Pa.	FA
Spencer, Jameion (1)	RB	6-1	245	1/21/77	Notre Dame	Monroe, La.	FA
Stecker, Aaron (1)	RB	5-10	205	11/13/75	Western Illinois	Green Bay, Wis.	FA
Tugbenyoh, Mawuko	DE	6-1	245	4/9/78	California	Concord, Calif.	FA
Webster, Nate	LB	5-11	225	11/29/79	Miami	Miami, Fla.	D3
Whalen, James	TE	6-2	228	12/11/77	Kentucky	Portland, Ore.	D5
Williams, Michael	WR	5-10	185	7/31/78	Arkansas	Bastrop, La.	FA
Yoder, Todd	TE	6-4	234	3/18/78	Vanderbilt	New Palestine, Ind.	FA

The term NFL Rookie is defined as a player who is in his first season of professional football and has not been on the roster of another professional football team for any regular-season or postseason games. A Rookie is designated by an "R" on NFL rosters. Players who have been active in another professional football league or players who have NFL experience, including either preseason training camp or being on an Active List or Inactive List, or on Reserve/Injured or Reserve/Physically Unable to Perform for fewer than six regular-season games, are termed NFL First-Year Players. An NFL First-Year Player is designated by a "1" on NFL rosters. Thereafter, a player is credited with an additional year of experience for each season in which he accumulates six games on the Active List or Inactive List, or on Reserve/Injured or Reserve/Physically Unable to Perform.

NOTES

WASHINGTON REDSKINS

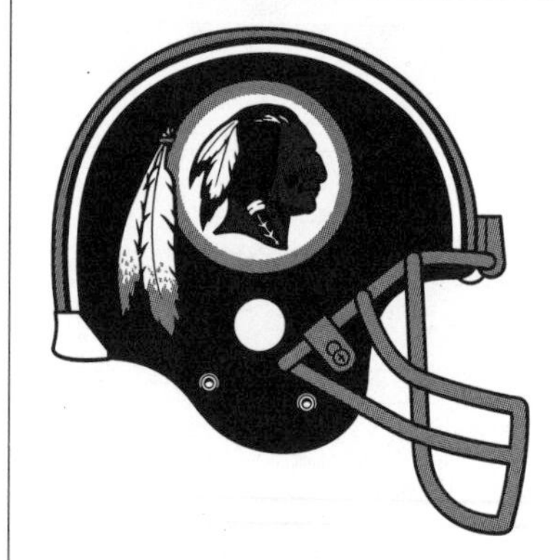

National Football Conference
Eastern Division
Team Colors: Burgundy and Gold
Redskin Park
P.O. Box 17247
Washington, D.C. 20041
Telephone: (703) 478-8900

CLUB OFFICIALS

Owner: Daniel M. Snyder
President/Director of Marketing: Steve Baldacci
Controller: Greg Dillon
Director of Player Personnel: Vinny Cerrato
Assistant General Manager: Bobby Mitchell
Contract Negotiator/Salary Cap: Joe Mendes
NFC Pro Coordinator: Mel Bratton
AFC Pro Coordinator: Charlie Brown
Director of College Scouting: Mike Faulkiner
College Scouts: Greg Henley, Stacy Harrison, Dan Shonka, Doug Kretz, Ron Nay, Hason Graham-BLESTO scout
Draft Room Coordinator: Mike Szabo
Director of Player Programs: John Jefferson
Dire ctor of Public Relations: Doug Green
Associate Director of Public Relations: Michelle Tessier
Publications Director: Casey Husband
Community Relations Manager: Marie Reynolds
Director, Washington Redskins Leadership Council: Alexander Hahn
Director of Administration: Barry Asimos
Video Director: Rob Porteus
Assistant Video Director: Mike Bracken
Ticket Manager: Jeff Ritter
Vice President–Stadium Operations: Michael Dillow
Head Trainer: Bubba Tyer
Assistant Trainers: Al Bellamy, Kevin Bastin
Equipment Manager: Jay Brunetti
Assistant Equipment Manager: Jeff Parsons
Stadium: FedEx Field
•**Capacity:** 80,116
Landover, Maryland 20785-4236
Playing Surface: Grass
Training Camp: Redskin Park
Ashburn, Virginia 20147

2000 SCHEDULE

PRESEASON

Aug. 4	at Tampa Bay	7:30
Aug. 11	**New England**	8:00
Aug. 19	at Cleveland	7:30
Aug. 25	**Pittsburgh**	8:00

REGULAR SEASON

Sept. 3	**Carolina**	1:00
Sept. 10	at Detroit	4:15
Sept. 18	**Dallas** (Mon.)	9:00
Sept. 24	at New York Giants	8:35
Oct. 1	**Tampa Bay**	4:15
Oct. 8	at Philadelphia	1:00
Oct. 15	**Baltimore**	1:00
Oct. 22	at Jacksonville	4:15
Oct. 30	**Tennessee** (Mon.)	9:00
Nov. 5	at Arizona	2:05
Nov. 12	Open Date	
Nov. 20	at St. Louis (Mon.)	8:00
Nov. 26	**Philadelphia**	1:00
Dec. 3	**New York Giants**	1:00
Dec. 10	at Dallas	3:15
Dec. 16	at Pittsburgh (Sat.)	12:30
Dec. 24	**Arizona**	1:00

RECORD HOLDERS

INDIVIDUAL RECORDS—CAREER

Category	Name	Performance
Rushing (Yds.)	John Riggins, 1976-79, 1981-85	7,472
Passing (Yds.)	Joe Theismann, 1974-1985	25,206
Passing (TDs)	Sammy Baugh, 1937-1952	187
Receiving (No.)	Art Monk, 1980-1993	888
Receiving (Yds.)	Art Monk, 1980-1993	12,028
Interceptions	Darrell Green, 1983-1999	50
Punting (Avg.)	Sammy Baugh, 1937-1952	*45.1
Punt Return (Avg.)	Johnny Williams, 1952-53	12.8
Kickoff Return (Avg.)	Bobby Mitchell, 1962-68	28.5
Field Goals	Mark Moseley, 1974-1986	263
Touchdowns (Tot.)	Charley Taylor, 1964-1977	90
Points	Mark Moseley, 1974-1986	1,206

INDIVIDUAL RECORDS—SINGLE SEASON

Category	Name	Performance
Rushing (Yds.)	Stephen Davis, 1999	1,405
Passing (Yds.)	Jay Schroeder, 1986	4,109
Passing (TDs)	Sonny Jurgensen, 1967	31
Receiving (No.)	Art Monk, 1984	106
Receiving (Yds.)	Bobby Mitchell, 1963	1,436
Interceptions	Dan Sandifer, 1948	13
Punting (Avg.)	Sammy Baugh, 1940	*51.4
Punt Return (Avg.)	Johnny Williams, 1952	15.3
Kickoff Return (Avg.)	Mike Nelms, 1981	29.7
Field Goals	Mark Moseley, 1983	33
Touchdowns (Tot.)	John Riggins, 1983	24
Points	Mark Moseley, 1983	161

INDIVIDUAL RECORDS—SINGLE GAME

Category	Name	Performance
Rushing (Yds.)	Gerald Riggs, 9-17-89	221
Passing (Yds.)	Sammy Baugh, 10-31-43	446
Passing (TDs)	Sammy Baugh, 10-31-43, 11-23-47	6
	Mark Rypien, 11-10-91	6
Receiving (No.)	Art Monk, 12-15-85	13
	Kelvin Bryant, 12-7-86	13
	Art Monk, 11-4-90	13
Receiving (Yds.)	Anthony Allen, 10-4-87	255
Interceptions	Sammy Baugh, 11-14-43	*4
	Dan Sandifer, 10-31-48	*4
Field Goals	Many times	5
	Last time by Chip Lohmiller, 10-25-92	
Touchdowns (Tot.)	Dick James, 12-17-61	4
	Larry Brown, 12-16-73	4
Points	Dick James, 12-17-61	24
	Larry Brown, 12-16-73	24

*NFL Record

COACHING HISTORY

Boston 1932-36
(493-431-27)

1932	Lud Wray	4-4-2
1933-34	William (Lone Star) Dietz	11-11-2
1935	Eddie Casey	2-8-1
1936-42	Ray Flaherty	56-23-3
1943	Arthur (Dutch) Bergman	7-4-1
1944-45	Dudley DeGroot	14-6-1
1946-48	Glen (Turk) Edwards	16-18-1
1949	John Whelchel*	3-3-1
1949-51	Herman Ball**	4-16-0
1951	Dick Todd	5-4-0
1952-53	Earl (Curly) Lambeau	10-13-1
1954-58	Joe Kuharich	26-32-2
1959-60	Mike Nixon	4-18-2
1961-65	Bill McPeak	21-46-3
1966-68	Otto Graham	17-22-3
1969	Vince Lombardi	7-5-2
1970	Bill Austin	6-8-0
1971-77	George Allen	69-35-1
1978-80	Jack Pardee	24-24-0
1981-92	Joe Gibbs	140-65-0
1993	Richie Petitbon	4-12-0
1994-99	Norv Turner	43-54-1

*Released after seven games in 1949
**Released after three games in 1951

FEDEX FIELD

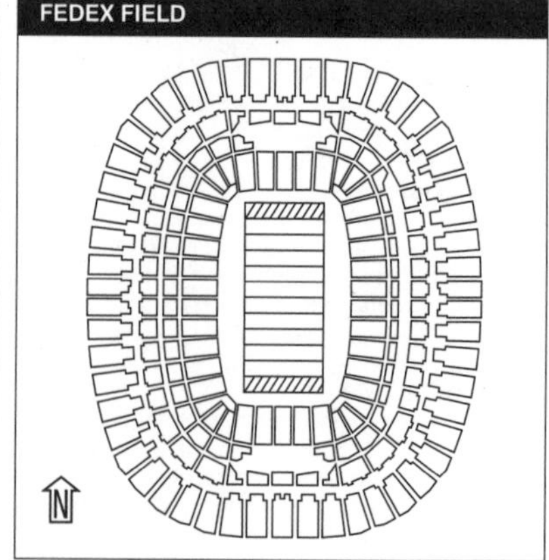

1999 TEAM RECORD

PRESEASON (3-1)

Date	Result		Opponent
8/13	W	20-14	at New England
8/20	W	20-19	Buffalo
8/28	W	27-14	at Pittsburgh
9/3	L	13-16	Tampa Bay

REGULAR SEASON (10-6)

Date	Result		Opponent	Att.
9/12	L	35-41	Dallas (OT)	79,237
9/19	W	50-21	at New York Giants	77,622
9/26	W	27-20	at New York Jets	78,161
10/3	W	38-36	Carolina	76,831
10/17	W	24-10	at Arizona	55,893
10/24	L	20-38	at Dallas	64,377
10/31	W	48-22	Chicago	77,621
11/7	L	17-34	Buffalo	78,721
11/14	L	28-35	at Philadelphia	66,591
11/21	W	23-13	New York Giants	78,641
11/28	W	20-17	Philadelphia (OT)	74,741
12/5	L	17-33	at Detroit	77,693
12/12	W	28-3	Arizona	75,851
12/19	L	21-24	at Indianapolis	57,013
12/26	W	26-20	at San Francisco (OT)	68,329
1/2	W	21-10	Miami	78,106

(OT) Overtime

POSTSEASON (1-1)

Date	Result		Opponent	Att.
1/8	W	27-13	Detroit	79,411
1/15	L	13-14	at Tampa Bay	65,835

SCORE BY PERIODS

Redskins	82	162	100	90	9	—	443
Opponents	78	89	63	141	6	—	377

ATTENDANCE

Home 628,535 Away 539,925 Total 1,168,460
Single-game home record, 78,925 (1/2/00)
Single-season home record, 628,535 (1999)

1999 TEAM STATISTICS

	Redskins	Opp.
Total First Downs	338	322
Rushing	121	107
Passing	183	193
Penalty	34	22
Third Down: Made/Att	77/203	91/232
Third Down Pct.	37.9	39.2
Fourth Down: Made/Att	9/18	11/21
Fourth Down Pct.	50.0	52.4
Total Net Yards	5,965	5,705
Avg. Per Game	372.8	356.6
Total Plays	1,031	1,068
Avg. Per Play	5.8	5.3
Net Yards Rushing	2,039	1,973
Avg. Per Game	127.4	123.3
Total Rushes	463	439
Net Yards Passing	3,926	3,732
Avg. Per Game	245.4	233.3
Sacked/Yards Lost	31/186	40/221
Gross Yards	4,112	3,953
Att./Completions	537/324	589/328
Completion Pct.	60.3	55.7
Had Intercepted	14	24
Punts/Average	71/41.2	74/42.7
Net Punting Avg.	71/34.2	74/37.1
Penalties/Yards	104/808	102/1,137
Fumbles/Ball Lost	31/11	22/13
Touchdowns	54	43
Rushing	23	16
Passing	26	23
Returns	5	4
Avg. Time of Possession	29:33	30:27

1999 INDIVIDUAL STATISTICS

Passing	Att.	Comp.	Yds.	Pct.	TD	Int.	Tkld.	Rate
B. Johnson	519	316	4,005	60.9	24	13	29/177	90.0
Peete	17	8	107	47.1	2	1	2/9	82.2
Conway	1	0	0	0.0	0	0	0/0	39.6
Redskins	537	324	4,112	60.3	26	14	31/186	89.5
Opponents	589	328	3,953	55.7	23	24	40/221	72.5

SCORING	TD R	TD P	TD Rt	PAT	FG	Saf	PTS
Conway	0	0	0	49/50	22/32	0	115
Davis	17	0	0	0/0	0/0	0	104
Westbrook	0	9	0	0/0	0/0	0	56
Connell	0	7	0	0/0	0/0	0	42
Alexander	0	3	0	0/0	0/0	0	18
Centers	0	3	0	0/0	0/0	0	18
Hicks	3	0	0	0/0	0/0	0	18
Fryar	0	2	0	0/0	0/0	0	12
B. Johnson	2	0	0	0/0	0/0	0	12
Sellers	0	2	0	0/0	0/0	0	12
Bailey	0	0	1	0/0	0/0	0	6
Barber	0	0	1	0/0	0/0	0	6
Coleman	0	0	1	0/0	0/0	0	6
Mitchell	1	0	0	0/0	0/0	0	6
Thrash	0	0	1	0/0	0/0	0	6
Wilkinson	0	0	1	0/0	0/0	0	6
Redskins	23	26	5	49/50	22/32	0	443
Opponents	16	23	4	38/38	25/30	0	377

2-Pt. Conversions: Davis, Westbrook.
Team 2-3, Opponents 3-4.

RUSHING	Att.	Yds.	Avg.	LG	TD
Davis	290	1,405	4.8	76t	17
Hicks	78	257	3.3	24	3
Mitchell	40	220	5.5	16	1
Centers	13	51	3.9	12	0
Thrash	1	37	37.0	37	0
Westbrook	7	35	5.0	12	0
B. Johnson	26	31	1.2	12	2
Connell	1	8	8.0	8	0
Peete	2	-1	-0.5	0	0
Weldon	5	-4	-0.8	0	0
Redskins	463	2,039	4.4	76t	23
Opponents	439	1,973	4.5	60t	16

RECEIVING	No.	Yds.	Avg.	LG	TD
Centers	69	544	7.9	33t	3
Westbrook	65	1,191	18.3	65t	9
Connell	62	1,132	18.3	62t	7
Mitchell	31	305	9.8	36	0
Alexander	29	324	11.2	27t	3
Fryar	26	254	9.8	30t	2
Davis	23	111	4.8	21	0
Hicks	8	72	9.0	25	0
Sellers	7	105	15.0	33t	2
Thrash	3	44	14.7	25	0
Jenkins	1	30	30.0	30	0
Redskins	324	4,112	12.7	65t	26
Opponents	328	3,953	12.1	76t	23

INTERCEPTIONS	No.	Yds.	Avg.	LG	TD
Stevens	6	61	10.2	25	0
Bailey	5	55	11.0	59t	1
Pounds	3	37	12.3	25	0
Green	3	33	11.0	25	0
Barber	2	70	35.0	70t	1
Shade	2	7	3.5	7	0
Wilkinson	1	88	88.0	88t	1
McMillian	1	24	24.0	24	0
Derek M. Smith	1	0	0.0	0	0
Redskins	24	375	15.6	88t	3
Opponents	14	129	9.2	29	0

PUNTING	No.	Yds.	Avg.	In 20	LG
M. Turk	62	2,564	41.4	16	57
Hansen	9	362	40.2	1	49
Redskins	71	2,926	41.2	17	57
Opponents	74	3,158	42.7	20	62

PUNT RETURNS	No.	FC	Yds.	Avg.	LG	TD
Mitchell	40	14	332	8.3	33	0
Pounds	1	0	0	0.0	0	0
Redskins	41	14	332	8.1	33	0
Opponents	27	11	279	10.3	70t	2

KICKOFF RETURNS	No.	Yds.	Avg.	LG	TD
Mitchell	43	893	20.8	45	0
Thrash	14	355	25.4	95t	1
Sellers	3	32	10.7	16	0
Bowie	1	0	0.0	0	0
Jenkins	1	10	10.0	10	0
Milstead	1	0	0.0	0	0
Redskins	63	1,290	20.5	95t	1
Opponents	77	1,772	23.0	89t	1

FIELD GOALS	1-19	20-29	30-39	40-49	50+
Conway	0/0	7/9	6/7	6/7	3/9
Redskins	0/0	7/9	6/7	6/7	3/9
Opponents	0/0	6/6	8/9	9/12	2/3

SACKS	No.
Wilkinson	8.0
Coleman	6.5
Lang	6.0
Kalu	3.5
Cook	3.0
Stubblefield	3.0
McMillian	1.5
Shade	1.5
Bailey	1.0
Barber	1.0
Boutte	1.0
Pounds	1.0
Derek M. Smith	1.0
Stevens	1.0
Francis	0.5
Jones	0.5
Redskins	40.0
Opponents	31.0

2000 DRAFT CHOICES

Round	Name	Pos.	College
1	LaVar Arrington	LB	Penn State
	Chris Samuels	T	Alabama
3	Lloyd Harrison	DB	North Carolina State
4	Michael Moore	G	Troy State
5	Quincy Sanders	DB	Nevada-Las Vegas
6	Todd Husak	QB	Stanford
7	Delbert Cowsette	DT	Maryland
	Ethan Howell	WR	Oklahoma State

WASHINGTON REDSKINS

2000 VETERAN ROSTER

No.	Name	Pos.	Ht.	Wt.	Birthdate	NFL Exp.	College	Hometown	How Acq.	'99 Games/ Starts
80	Alexander, Stephen	TE	6-4	246	11/7/75	3	Oklahoma	Chickasha, Okla.	D2-'98	15/15
24	Bailey, Champ	CB	6-1	184	6/22/78	2	Georgia	Folkston, Ga.	D1-'99	16/16
59	Barber, Shawn	LB	6-2	224	1/14/75	3	Richmond	Richmond, Va.	D4-'98	16/16
6	Barnhardt, Tommy	P	6-2	228	6/11/63	15	North Carolina	Matthews, N.C.	FA-'00	16/0*
79	Brown, Doug	DT	6-7	290	9/29/74	3	Simon Fraser	Coquittlam, B.C., Canada	FA-'98	10/0
26	Buckley, Curtis	CB	6-1	182	9/25/70	8	East Texas State	Oakdale, Calif.	FA-'99	7/0
27	Carrier, Mark	S	6-1	190	4/28/68	11	Southern California	Long Beach, Calif.	FA-'00	15/15*
37	Centers, Larry	RB	6-1	225	6/1/68	11	Stephen F. Austin	Tatum, Tex.	UFA(Ariz)-'99	16/12
99	Coleman, Marco	DE	6-3	267	12/18/69	9	Georgia Tech	Dayton, Ohio	UFA(SD)-'99	16/16
83	Connell, Albert	WR	6-1	179	5/13/74	4	Texas A&M	Brooklyn, N.Y.	D4-'97	15/14
5	Conway, Brett	K	6-2	192	3/8/75	4	Penn State	Liburn, Ga.	FA-'98	16/0
75	Cook, Anthony	DE	6-3	295	5/30/72	6	South Carolina State	Bennettsville, S.C.	UFA(Tenn) '99	16/7
48	Davis, Stephen	RB	6-1	234	3/1/74	5	Auburn	Spartanburg, S.C.	D4-'96	14/14
25	Denton, Tim	DB	5-11	182	2/2/73	3	Sam Houston	Galveston, Tex.	FA-'98	16/0
51	Fischer, Mark	C	6-3	293	7/29/74	3	Purdue	Cincinnati, Ohio	D5-'98	0*
86	Fryar, Irving	WR	6-1	198	9/28/62	17	Nebraska	Mount Holly, N.J.	FA-'99	16/1
3	George, Jeff	QB	6-4	215	12/8/67	10	Illinois	Indianapolis, Ind.	UFA(Minn)-'00	12/10*
58	Givens, Reggie	LB	6-0	234	10/3/71	3	Penn State	Emporia, Va.	FA-'00	16/0*
28	Green, Darrell	CB	5-8	184	2/15/60	18	Texas A&M	Houston, Tex.	D1-'83	16/16
64	Heck, Andy	T	6-6	298	1/1/67	12	Notre Dame	Fairfax, Va.	UFA(Phil)-'99	16/16
20	Hicks, Skip	RB	6-1	230	10/13/74	3	UCLA	Burkburnett, Tex.	D3-'98	10/2
76	Jansen, Jon	T	6-6	302	1/28/76	2	Michigan	Clawson, Mich.	D2-'99	16/16
88	Jenkins, James	TE	6-2	249	8/17/67	9	Rutgers	Staten Island, N.Y.	FA-'91	16/4
14	Johnson, Brad	QB	6-5	224	9/13/68	9	Florida State	Black Mountain, N.C.	T(Minn)-'99	16/16
77	Johnson, Tre´	G	6-2	326	8/30/71	7	Temple	Peekskill, N.Y.	D2-'94	16/16
54	Jones, Greg	LB	6-4	238	5/22/74	4	Colorado	Denver, Colo.	D2-'97	15/15
72	Kalu, Ndukwe	DE	6-3	246	8/3/75	4	Rice	San Antonio, Tex.	FA-'99	12/0
90	Lang, Kenard	DE	6-4	277	1/31/75	4	Miami	Orlando, Fla.	D1-'97	16/9
53	Mason, Eddie	LB	6-1	236	1/9/72	4	North Carolina	Siler City, N.C.	FA-'99	14/0
98	McCloud, Tyrus	LB	6-1	250	11/23/74	3	Louisville	Fort Lauderdale, Fla.	FA-'00	0*
55	Mitchell, Kevin	LB	6-1	254	1/1/71	7	Syracuse	Harrisburg, Pa.	FA-'00	16/1*
22	Murrell, Adrian	RB	5-11	210	10/16/70	8	West Virginia	Wahaiwa, Hawaii	FA-'00	16/12*
57	Peterson, Anthony	LB	6-0	232	1/23/72	7	Notre Dame	Monogahela, Pa.	UFA(SF)-'00	12/0*
52	Raymer, Cory	C	6-2	289	3/3/73	6	Wisconsin	Fond du Lac, Wis.	D2-'95	16/16
45	Sellers, Mike	RB	6-3	260	7/21/75	3	Walla Walla	Lacey, Wash.	FA-'98	16/2
29	Shade, Sam	S	6-1	201	6/14/73	6	Alabama	Birmingham, Ala.	UFA(Cin)-'99	16/16
63	Sims, Keith	G	6-3	318	6/17/67	10	Iowa State	Warren, N.J.	FA-'98	12/12
78	Smith, Bruce	DE	6-4	279	6/18/63	16	Virginia Tech	Norfolk, Va.	FA-'00	16/16*
50	Smith, Derek M	LB	6-2	239	1/18/75	4	Arizona State	American Folk, Utah	D3-'97	16/16
23	Stevens, Matt	S	6-0	206	6/15/73	5	Appalachian State	Chapel Hill, N.C.	FA-'98	15/1
94	Stubblefield, Dana	DT	6-2	315	11/14/70	8	Kansas	Cleves, Ohio	UFA(SF)-'98	16/16
71	Tanner, Barron	DT	6-3	310	9/14/73	4	Oklahoma	Athens, Tex.	T(Mia)-'99	0*
84	Thompson, Derrius	WR	6-2	215	7/5/77	2	Baylor	Cedar Hill, Tex.	FA-'99	1/0
87	Thrash, James	WR	6-1	200	4/28/75	4	Missouri Southern	Wewoka, Okla.	FA-'97	16/0
82	Westbrook, Michael	WR	6-3	220	7/7/72	6	Colorado	Detroit, Mich.	D1-'95	16/16
95	Wilkinson, Dan	DT	6-5	313	3/13/73	7	Ohio State	Dayton, Ohio	T(Cin)-'98	16/16
85	Zelenka, Joe	TE	6-3	280	3/9/76	2	Wake Forest	Cleveland, Ohio	T(SF)-'00	13/0*
34	Zellars, Ray	RB	5-11	233	3/25/73	5	Notre Dame	Pittsburgh, Pa.	FA-'00	0*

* Barnhardt played 16 with New Orleans in '99; Carrier played 15 games with Detroit; Fischer was inactive for 13 games; George played 12 games with Minnesota; Givens played 16 games with San Francisco; McCloud last active with Baltimore in '98; K. Mitchell played 16 games with New Orleans; Murrell played 16 games with Arizona; Peterson played 12 games with San Francisco; B. Smith played 16 games with Buffalo; Tanner was inactive for 16 games; Zelenka played 13 games with San Francisco; Zellars last active with New Orleans in '98.

Traded—P Matt Turk (14 games in '99) to Miami.

Players lost to free agency (3): G Brad Badger (14 games in '99), CB Darryl Pounds (Den; 16), G Kipp Vickers (Balt; 11).

Also played with Redskins in '99—DT Marc Boutte (6), RB Larry Bowie (2), T Jamie Brown (1), S Leomond Evans (15), LB James Francis (10), LB Kurt Gouveia (12), LB Malcolm Hamilton (4), P Brian Hansen (2), CB Mark McMillian (9), G Rod Milstead (6), RB-KR Brian Mitchell (16), DB Tito Paul (6), QB Rodney Peete (3), LB Twan Russell (9), S Matt Stevens (15), LB Fred Strickland (5), WR Chris Thomas (2), C Dan Tuck (16), QB Casey Weldon (2), DB Jamal Williams (3), DB Toby Wright (1).

COACHING STAFF

Head Coach,
Norv Turner

Pro Career: Enters his seventh season as head coach of the Washington Redskins after serving three years as the Dallas Cowboys' offensive coordinator. Last season, Turner guided the Redskins to their first NFC Eastern Division title since 1991. Turner guided the Cowboys' prolific offense during back-to-back Super Bowl championship seasons. He inherited a Cowboys' offense that finished twenty-eighth in total offense in 1990, and a year later improved to ninth. The Cowboys finished fourth in the league offensively in 1992-93. In three seasons under Turner, quarterback Troy Aikman compiled a 91.7 rating, and running back Emmitt Smith won three consecutive NFL rushing titles. Prior to joining the Cowboys, Turner coached six seasons (1985-1990) with the Los Angeles Rams where he oversaw the passing game. Quarterback Jim Everett enjoyed his best seasons under Turner, while Willie Anderson led the NFL in yards per catch in 1989 and 1990, and Henry Ellard was the league's leading receiver in 1988. Career record: 43-54-1.

Background: Turner played quarterback for three seasons at the University of Oregon (1972-74). He began his coaching career as a graduate assistant at Oregon in 1975. A year later, he moved to the University of Southern California, where he coached from 1976-1984.

Personal: Born May 17, 1952, in LeJeune, N.C. Turner and his wife, Nancy, live in Oakton, Va., and have three children—Scott, Stephanie, and Drew.

ASSISTANT COACHES

Jason Arapoff, asst. conditioning; born July 8, 1965, Weymouth, Mass., lives in Centreville, Va. Defensive back Springfield College 1985-88. No pro playing experience. Pro coach: Joined Redskins in 1992.

Rubin Carter, defensive line; born December 12, 1952, Ft. Lauderdale, Fla., lives in Laurel, Md. Defensive tackle Miami 1970-74. Pro defensive tackle Denver Broncos 1975-1986. College coach: Howard 1989-1993, San Jose State 1995-96, Maryland 1997-98. Pro coach: Denver Broncos 1987-88, joined Redskins in 1999.

Foge Fazio, linebackers; born February 28, 1939, Dawmont, W. Va., lives in Ashburn, Va. Linebacker-center Pittsburgh 1957-1960. No pro playing experience. College coach: Boston University 1967, Harvard 1968, Pittsburgh 1969-1972, 1977-1985 (head coach 1982-85), Cincinnati 1973-76, Notre Dame 1986-87. Pro coach: Atlanta Falcons 1988-89, New York Jets 1990-94, Minnesota Vikings 1995-99, joined Redskins in 2000.

Pat Flaherty, tight ends; born April 27, 1956, Hanover, Pa., lives in Ashburn, Va. Center East Stroudsburg 1976-79. No pro playing experience. College coach: East Stroudsburg 1980-81, Penn State 1982-83, Rutgers 1984-1991, East Carolina 1992, Wake Forest 1993-98, Iowa 1999. Pro coach: Joined Redskins in 2000.

Russ Grimm, offensive line; born May 2, 1959, Scottdale, Pa., lives in Fairfax, Va. Guard-center Pittsburgh 1977-1980. Pro guard Washington Redskins 1981-1991. Pro coach: Joined Redskins in 1992.

LeCharls McDaniel, special teams; born October 15, 1958, Fort Bragg, N.C., lives in Ashburn, Va. Cornerback Cal Poly-San Luis Obispo 1976-1980. Pro defensive back Washington Redskins 1981-82, New York Giants 1983. College coach: Hartnell College (Calif.) 1984-89, Cal Poly-San Luis Obispo 1992, San Diego State 1994-95. Pro coach: San Diego Chargers 1990-1991, Phoenix Cardinals 1993, joined Redskins in 1997.

Ron Meeks, defensive backs; born August 27, 1954, Jacksonville, lives in Reston, Va. Defensive back Arkansas State 1975-76. Pro defensive back Hamilton TIger-Cats (CFL) 1977-79, Ottawa Rough Riders (CFL) 1979, Toronto Argonauts (CFL) 1980-81. College coach: Arkansas State 1984-85, Miami 1986-87, New Mexico State 1988, Fresno State 1989-1990. Pro coach: Dallas Cowboys 1991, Cincinnati Bengals 1992-96, Atlanta Falcons 1997-99, joined Redskins in 2000.

Kirk Olivadotti, offensive assistant; born January 1, 1974, Wilmington, Del., lives in Ashburn, Va. Wide receiver Purdue 1992-96. No pro playing experience. College coach: Maine Maritime 1997, Indiana State 1998-99. Pro coach: Joined Redskins in 2000.

Rich Olson, quarterbacks; born July 7, 1948, Wilmington, Calif., lives in Herndon, Va. Quarterback-free safety Washington State 1968-69. No pro playing experience. College coach: Washington State 1970, Fresno State 1976, Southern California 1977, Southern Methodist 1978-1980, Arkansas 1981-83, Fresno State 1984-1991, Miami 1992-94. Pro coach: Seattle Seahawks 1995-98, joined Redskins in 1999.

Ray Rhodes, defensive coordinator; born October 20, 1950, Mexia, Tex., lives in Potomac Falls, Va. Running back-wide receiver Texas Christian 1969-1970, Tulsa 1972-73. Wide receiver-cornerback New York Giants 1974-79, San Francisco 49ers 1980. Pro coach: San Francisco 49ers 1981-1991, 1994, Green Bay Packers 1992-93, 1999 (head coach 1999), Philadelphia Eagles 1995-98 (head coach), joined Redskins in 2000.

Dan Riley, strength; born October 19, 1949, Syracuse, N.Y., lives in Ashburn, Va. Attended Keene State. No college or pro playing experience. College coach: Army 1973-76, Penn State 1977-1981. Pro coach: Joined Redskins in 1982.

Terry Robiskie, passing game coordinator; born November 12, 1954, New Orleans, lives in Clifton, Va. Running back Louisiana State 1973-76. Pro running back Oakland Raiders 1977-79, Miami Dolphins 1980-81. Pro coach: Los Angeles Raiders 1982-1993, joined Redskins in 1994.

Mike Trgovac, defensive line; born February 27, 1959, Youngstown, Ohio, lives in Ashburn, Va. Defensive lineman Michigan 1977-1980. No pro playing experience. College coach: Michgian 1984-85, Ball State 1986-88, Navy 1989, Colorado STate 1990-91, Notre Dame 1992-94. Pro coach: Philadelphia Eagles 1995-98, Green Bay Packers 1999, joined Redskins in 2000.

Jason Verduzco, defensive assistant; born born April 3, 1970, Clinton, N.Y., lives in Ashburn, Va. Quarterback Illinois 1989-1993. No pro playing experience. British Columbia Lions (CFL) 1993. College coach: Hamilton College 1994-96, Illinois 1997-99. Pro coach: Joined Redskins in 2000.

Kirby Wilson, running backs; born August 24, 1961, Los Angeles, lives in Franklin, Mass. Running back-wide receiver Pasadena C.C. (Calif.) 1978-79, Minnesota 1980-81. Pro cornerback Edmonton Eskimos (CFL) 1982, Oakland Invaders (USFL) 1984, Arizona Outlaws (USFL) 1985. College coach: Mt. San Antonio J.C. (Calif.) 1988-1992, Utah State 1993, Brigham Young 1994, Oklahoma State 1995, California 1996-97. Pro coach: New England Patriots 1998-99, joined Redskins in 2000.

2000 FIRST-YEAR ROSTER

Name	Pos.	Ht.	Wt.	Birthdate	College	Hometown	How Acq.
Arringotn, LaVar	LB	6-3	250	6/20/78	Penn State	Pittsburgh, Pa.	D1a
Bryant, Lamont	DE	6-3	260	10/11/76	Notre Dame	Georgetown, S.C.	FA
Cowsette, Delbert	DT	6-1	274	9/3/77	Maryland	Cleveland, Ohio	D7a
Deese, Jamie	WR	5-10	186	5/10/77	Wake Forest	Laurinburg, N.C.	FA
DeLoach, Jerry	DT	6-2	314	7/17/77	California	Elk Grove, Calif.	FA
Dukes, Chad (1)	RB	6-0	230	12/29/71	Pittsburgh	Albany, N.Y.	FA-'99
Elezovic, Peter	K	5-11	187	6/28/71	Michigan	Farmington Hills, Mich.	FA
Flemister, Zeron	TE	6-4	249	9/8/76	Iowa	Sioux City, Iowa	FA
Ham, Derrick (1)	DE	6-4	257	3/23/75	Miami	Merritt Island, Fla.	FA-'99
Harrison, Lloyd	CB	5-10	190	6/21/77	North Carolina State	Floral Park, N.Y.	D4
Howell, Ethan	WR	5-11	178	10/14/77	Oklahoma State	Monroe, La.	D7b
Husak, Todd	QB	6-3	216	7/6/78	Stanford	Long Beach, Calif.	D6
Johnson, Bryan	RB	6-10	234	1/18/78	Boise State	Pocatello, Idaho	FA
Kalich, Ryan	G	6-2	297	11/21/76	Florida	Houston, Tex.	FA
McIntosh, Ian	CB	5-9	176	2/15/78	Syracuse	Cheshire, Conn.	FA
Messina, Brad	G	6-5	297	2/11/77	Maryland	Bogota, N.J.	FA
Miller, Norman	RB	5-10	189	8/16/74	Texas A&M-Kingsville	Sacramento, Calif.	FA
Mitchell, Anthony	DE	6-5	245	10/26/76	Florida	Louisville, Miss.	FA
Moore, Michael	G	6-3	320	11/1/76	Troy State	Fayette, Ala.	D4
Murray, Leon	QB	6-2	207	1/10/77	Tennessee State	Shreveport, La.	FA
Nash, Tommy	WR	6-0	159	3/2/77	Wyoming	Tulsa, Okla.	FA
Osterhout, Jon	G	6-2	299	4/14/77	Cal State-Sacramento	Roseville, Calif.	FA
Percoats, Imani	WR	6-4	210	3/1/77	Oregon State	Merced, Calif.	FA
Pesak, Kevin	TE	6-2	222	4/18/75	Sam Houston	Alvin, Tex.	FA
Porter, Juan (1)	C	6-3	294	11/26/73	Ohio State	Cleveland, Ohio	FA-'99
Reed, Andre	LB	6-2	235	11/25/76	Jackson State	Jackson, Miss.	FA
Samuels, Chris	T	6-5	325	7/28/77	Alabama	Mobile, Ala.	D1b
Sanders, Quincy	S	6-1	204	4/8/77	Nevada-Las Vegas	Reno, Nev.	D5
Scanlon, Clay	S	6-2	198	6/24/76	Fort Hays State	Wakeeney, Kan.	FA
Silch, Ryan	T	6-4	315	1/31/77	Lindenwood	Plano, Tex.	FA
Smith, Chris	TE	6-4	257	4/28/78	Texas	Palestine, Tex.	FA
Smith, Derek G. (1)	T	6-6	309	4/13/76	Virginia Tech	Shenandoah Junction, W. Va.	D5-'99
Stevenson, Eric	DT	6-2	295	9/21/77	Oklahoma State	Crescent, Okla.	FA
Stiggers, Eric	WR	5-6	184	12/26/77	Colorado	Dallas, Tex.	FA
Symonette, Josh	S	5-10	180	5/8/78	Tennessee Tech	Miami, Fla.	FA
Terrell, David	CB	6-1	188	7/8/75	Texas-El Paso	Sweetwater, Tex.	FA
Walker, Jeff	P	5-10	218	2/14/77	Mississippi State	Grenada, Miss.	FA
Whitfield, Eric	CB	6-0	205	1/17/78	UCLA	Carson, Calif.	FA
Wilcox, Justin	CB	6-1	195	11/12/76	Oregon	Junction City, Ore.	FA
William, LaFann	CB	5-9	177	7/3/77	South Florida	Pahokee, Fla.	FA
Williams, Rodney	P	6-0	178	4/25/77	Georgia Tech	Decatur, Ga.	FA

The term NFL Rookie is defined as a player who is in his first season of professional football and has not been on the roster of another professional football team for any regular-season or postseason games. A Rookie is designated by an "R" on NFL rosters. Players who have been active in another professional football league or players who have NFL experience, including either preseason training camp or being on an Active List or Inactive List, or on Reserve/Injured or Reserve/Physically Unable to Perform for fewer than six regular-season games, are termed NFL First-Year Players. An NFL First-Year Player is designated by a "1" on NFL rosters. Thereafter, a player is credited with an additional year of experience for each season in which he accumulates six games on the Active List or Inactive List, or on Reserve/Injured or Reserve/Physically Unable to Perform.

1999 Season in Review

TRADES

1999 INTERCONFERENCE TRADES

Wide receiver **James McKnight** from Seattle to Dallas for the Cowboys' third-round selection in 2000. Seattle selected wide receiver **Darrell Jackson** (Florida) (6/25).

Tackle **Shar Pourdanesh** from Washington to Pittsburgh for the Steelers' seventh-round selection in 2000. Washington selected defensive tackle **Delbert Cowsette** (Maryland) (8/13).

Quarterback **Rick Mirer** from Green Bay to the New York Jets for the Jets' sixth-round selection in 2000. Green Bay traded the sixth-round selection acquired from New York to Seattle (8/21).

Defensive back **Tito Paul** from Denver to Washington for the Redskins' seventh-round selections in 2000 and 2001. Denver traded the seventh-round selection in 2000 acquired from Washington to Seattle (8/24).

Quarterback **Bobby Hoying** from Philadelphia to Oakland for the Raiders' sixth-round selection in 2000. Philadelphia selected defensive end **John Frank** (Utah) (8/24).

Quarterback **Paul Justin** from Oakland to St. Louis for the Rams' seventh-round selection in 2000. Oakland traded the seventh-round selection acquired from St. Louis to Indianapolis (8/30).

Wide receiver **Derrick Mayes** from Green Bay to Seattle for the Seahawks' seventh-round selection in 2000. Green Bay selected defensive tackle **Ron Moore** (Northwestern Oklahoma State) (8/31).

Tight end **Mitch Jacoby** from St. Louis to Kansas City for the Chiefs' sixth-round selection in 2000. St. Louis traded the sixth-round selection acquired from Kansas City to Denver (8/31).

Defensive tackle **Barron Tanner** from Miami to Washington for the Redskins' sixth-round selection in 2001 (9/4).

Quarterback **Jim Druckenmiller** from San Francisco to Miami for the Dolphins' seventh-round selection in 2000. San Francisco selected tight end **Brian Jennings** (Arizona State) (9/7).

Defensive back **Robert Williams** from Kansas City to San Francisco for the 49ers' seventh-round selection in 2000. Kansas City traded the seventh-round selection acquired from San Francisco to New Orleans (9/21).

Defensive tackle **Jerry Ball** from Cleveland to Minnesota for defensive end **Stalin Colinet** and the Vikings' seventh-round selection in 2000. Cleveland traded the seventh-round selection acquired from Minnesota to Miami (9/29).

Defensive end **Regan Upshaw** from Tampa Bay to Jacksonville for the Jaguars' sixth-round selection in 2001 (10/19).

1999 AFC TRADES

Running back **Sedrick Shaw** from New England to Cleveland for past consideration (4/22).

Tight end **John Burke** from San Diego to the New York Jets for the Jets' seventh-round selection in 2001 (8/10).

Defensive back **Cordell Taylor** from Jacksonville to Seattle for Seahawks' unannounced selection (9/5).

Wide receiver **Marcus Nash** from Denver to Miami for running back **John Avery** (9/21).

Running back **Karim Abdul-Jabbar** from Miami to Cleveland for the Browns' sixth-round selection in 2000. Miami selected defensive tackle **Earnest Grant** (Arkansas-Pine Bluff) (10/19).

1999 NFC TRADES

Quarterback **Rodney Peete** from Philadelphia to Washington for the Redskins' sixth-round selection in 2000. Philadelphia selected center **John Romero** (California) (4/28).

Linebacker **Mike Morton** from Green Bay to St. Louis for the Rams' seventh-round selection in 2001 (7/23).

Tackle **Jamie Wilson** from Carolina to Green Bay for Packers' unannounced selection (8/5).

Running back **Greg Hill** from St. Louis to Detroit for the Lions' seventh-round selection in 2000. The Rams selected guard **Andrew Kline** (San Diego State) and either Baltimore's fourth-round or fifth-round selection in 2000, whichever the Lions receive from the Ravens for Scott Mitchell (8/31).

Tackle **John Michels** from Green Bay to Philadelphia for defensive end **Jon Harris** (9/1).

Tight end **Luther Broughton** from Carolina to Philadelphia for the Eagles' seventh-round selection in 2001 (9/5).

Defensive back **Craig Newsome** from Green Bay to San Francisco for the 49ers' fifth-round selection in 2000. San Francisco reacquired the fifth-round selection from Green Bay (9/7).

2000 INTERCONFERENCE TRADES

Wide receiver **Joey Galloway** from Seattle to Dallas for the Cowboys' first-round selection in 2000 and first-round selection in 2001. Seattle selected running back **Shaun Alexander** (Alabama) (2/14).

New Orleans' seventh-round selection in 2000 to Kansas City for the Chiefs' seventh-round selection in 2000. New Orleans selected tight end **Kevin Houser** (Ohio State). Kansas City selected wide receiver **Desmond Kitchings** (Furman) (2/14).

Linebacker **Dave Bowens** from Denver to Green Bay for the Packers' seventh-round selection in 2001 (2/24).

Defensive back **Billy Jenkins** from St. Louis to Denver for the Broncos' fifth-round selection in 2000 and fifth-round selection in 2001. St. Louis selected defensive end **Brian Young** (Texas-El Paso) (3/7).

Punter **Matt Turk** from Washington to Miami for the Dolphins' seventh-round selection in 2001 (3/9).

Running back **Derek Loville** from Denver to St. Louis for the Rams' sixth-round selection in 2000. Denver selected running back **Mike Anderson** (Utah) (4/4).

Wide receiver **Keyshawn Johnson** from New York Jets to Tampa Bay for the Buccaneers' two first-round selections in 2000. New York selected linebacker **John Abraham** (South Carolina) and tight end **Anthony Becht** (West Virginia) (4/12).

New York Jets trade first-and second-round selections in 2000 to San Francisco for 49ers' first-round selection in 2000. San Francisco selected linebacker **Julian Peterson** (Michigan State) and defensive back **Jason Webster** (Texas A&M). New York selected defensive end **Shaun Ellis** (Tennessee) (4/15).

Defensive back **Fred Vinson** and sixth-round selection in 2000 from Green Bay to Seattle for the Seahawks' running back **Ahman Green** and their fifth-round selection in 2000. Green Bay selected wide receiver **Joey Jamison** (Texas Southern). Seattle selected defensive tackle **Tim Watson** (Rowan) (4/15).

Tennessee Titans trade their second-round selection in 2000 to Philadelphia for the Eagles' third- and fifth-round selection in 2000. Tennessee selected tight end **Erron Kinney** (Florida) and defensive back **Aric Morris** (Michigan State). Philadelphia selected guard **Bobby Williams** (Arkanas) (4/15).

San Francisco 49ers trade their fourth-and fifth-round selection in 2000 to Seattle for the Seahawks' third-round selection in 2000. San Francisco selected linebacker **Jeff Ulbrich** (Hawaii). Seattle selected linebacker **Isaiah Kacyvenski** (Harvard) and traded the third-round selection to Denver (4/15).

Philadelphia Eagles trade their fourth-round selection in 2000 to San Diego for the Chargers' third-round selection in 2001. San Diego selected wide receiver **Trevor Gaylor** (Miami, Ohio) (4/16).

New Orleans Saints trade their fifth-round selection in 2000 to Indianapolis for the Colts' fifth- and sixth-round selection in 2000. Indianapolis selected center **Matt Johnson** (Brigham Young). New Orleans selected tight end **Austin Wheatley** (Iowa) and defensive back **Michael Hawthorne** (Purdue) (4/16).

Cleveland Browns trade their three seventh-round selections in 2000 to Chicago for the Bears' two seventh-round selections in 2000. The Browns selected defensive end **Eric Chandler** (Jackson State) and defensive back **Rashidi Barnes** (Colorado). Chicago selected defensive end **James Cotton** (Ohio State) and defensive back **Mike Green** (Northwestern State, La.). Chicago traded a seventh-round selection acquired from Cleveland to Minnesota (4/16).

New England trades their seventh-round selection in 2000 to San Francisco for the 49ers' sixth-round selection in 2001. San Francisco selected quarterback **Tim Rattay** (Louisiana Tech) (4/16).

Chicago trades their seventh-round selection in 2000 to Miami for punter **Brent Bartholomew**. Miami selected defensive back **Jeff Harris** (Georgia) (4/16).

2000 AFC TRADES

Denver trades first-round selection in 2000 to Baltimore for the Ravens' first and second-round selections in 2000. Baltimore selected wide receiver **Travis Taylor** (Florida). Denver selected defensive back **Deltha O'Neal** (California) and defensive back **Kenoy Kennedy** (Arkansas) (4/13).

Seattle Seahawks trade their fifth-round selection in 2000 to Denver for the Broncos' sixth-and seventh-round selections in 2000. Denver selected wide receiver **Muneer Moore** (Richmond). Seattle selected wide receiver **James Williams** (Marshall) and traded the seventh-round selection acquired from Denver to Oakland for the Raiders' sixth-round selection in 2001 (4/16).

Oakland trades their sixth-round selection in 2001 to Seattle for the Seahawks' seventh-round selection in 2000. Oakland selected defensive back **Cliffton Black** (Southwest Texas State) (4/16).

Indianapolis Colts trade their sixth-round selection in 2001 to Oakland for the Raiders' seventh-round selection in 2000. Indianapolis selected defensive back **Rodregis Brooks** (Alabama-Birmingham) (4/16).

2000 NFC TRADES

Wide receiver **Eddie Kennison** from New Orleans to Chicago for the Bears' fifth-round selection in 2000. New Orleans traded the fifth-round selection acquired from Chicago to Indianapolis (2/22).

San Francisco 49ers trade their first-round selection in 2000 to Washington for the Redskins' two first-round selections and their fourth-and fifth-round selections in 2000. San Francisco selected defensive back **Ahmed Plummer** (Ohio State) and traded the fourth and fifth-round selections acquired from Washington to Seattle. Washington selected tackle **Chris Samuels** (Alabama) (2/28).

Tight end **Kaseem Sinceno** from Philadelphia to Green Bay for tight end **Jeff Thomason** (3/16).

Tampa Bay Buccaneers trade their second and fourth-round selections in 2000 to Carolina for the Panthers' second-round selection in 2000. Tampa Bay selected guard **Cosey Coleman** (Tennessee). Carolina selected defensive back **Deon Grant** (Tennessee) and defensive tackle **Alvin McKinley** (Mississippi State) (4/15).

San Francisco trades their fourth-round selection in 2000 to Green Bay for the Packers' fourth-and fifth-round selection in 2000. San Francisco selected defensive back **John Keith** (Furman) and running back **Paul Smith** (Texas-El Paso). Green Bay selected linebacker **Na'il Diggs** (Ohio State) (4/16).

Chicago trades their fourth-round selection in 2000 to St. Louis for the Rams' fourth-, fifth-, and seventh-round selections in 2000. St. Louis selected tackle **Kaulana Noa** (Hawaii). Chicago selected defensive back **Reggie Austin** (Wake Forest) and traded the fifth-round selection acquired from St. Louis to San Francisco for the 49ers' sixth- and seventh-round selections in 2000. Chicago traded the seventh-round selection acquired from St. Louis along with San Francisco's seventh-round selection to Cleveland for the Browns' two seventh-round selections and Minnesota's seventh-round selection in 2000 (4/16).

Chicago Bears trade their fifth-round selection in 2000 to San Francisco for the 49ers' sixth-and seventh-round selections in 2000. Chicago selected running back **Frank Murphy** (Kansas State) and traded the seventh-round selection acquired from San Francisco to Cleveland. San Francisco selected defensive end **John Milem** (Lenoir-Rhyne) (4/16).

PRESEASON FINAL STANDINGS

AMERICAN FOOTBALL CONFERENCE

Eastern Division

	W	L	T	Pct.	Pts.	OP
Buffalo	3	1	0	.750	89	47
Indianapolis	3	1	0	.750	94	61
N.Y. Jets	3	1	0	.750	80	63
Miami	2	2	0	.500	75	71
New England	1	3	0	.250	82	102

Central Division

	W	L	T	Pct.	Pts.	OP
Baltimore	4	0	0	1.000	85	61
Jacksonville	3	1	0	.750	113	49
Cleveland	2	3	0	.400	92	125
Pittsburgh	1	3	0	.250	71	86
Tennessee	1	3	0	.250	65	64
Cincinnati	0	4	0	.000	36	94

Western Division

	W	L	T	Pct.	Pts.	OP
Oakland	3	1	0	.750	79	43
Denver	3	2	0	.600	116	76
Kansas City	2	2	0	.500	69	95
Seattle	1	3	0	.250	102	86
San Diego	0	5	0	.000	99	122

NATIONAL FOOTBALL CONFERENCE

Eastern Division

	W	L	T	Pct.	Pts.	OP
Washington	3	1	0	.750	80	63
N.Y. Giants	2	2	0	.500	97	85
Arizona	1	3	0	.250	48	139
Philadelphia	1	3	0	.250	59	54
Dallas	1	4	0	.200	62	103

Central Division

	W	L	T	Pct.	Pts.	OP
Green Bay	4	0	0	1.000	117	62
Tampa Bay	4	0	0	1.000	108	37
Chicago	2	2	0	.500	94	95
Minnesota	2	2	0	.500	79	104
Detroit	1	3	0	.250	63	83

Western Division

	W	L	T	Pct.	Pts.	OP
San Francisco	3	1	0	.750	74	89
Atlanta	2	2	0	.500	72	83
Carolina	2	2	0	.500	77	96
New Orleans	2	2	0	.500	62	100
St. Louis	2	2	0	.500	82	83

AFC PRESEASON RECORDS—TEAM BY TEAM

Eastern Division

BUFFALO (3-1)

24	at Seattle	10
19	at Washington	20
30	at Cincinnati	3
16	Pittsburgh	14
89		47

INDIANAPOLIS (3-1)

6	at Chicago	9
20	Cincinnati	17
37	at New Orleans	7
31	Seattle	28
94		61

MIAMI (2-2)

14	New Orleans	26
13	at San Diego	10
31	Detroit	10
17	at Green Bay	25
75		71

NEW ENGLAND (1-3)

14	Washington	20
34	Dallas	14
14	at Tampa Bay	45
20	at Carolina	23
82		102

N.Y. JETS (3-1)

16	at Green Bay	27
10	Philadelphia	9
16	at N.Y. Giants	10
38	Minnesota	17
80		63

Central Division

BALTIMORE (4-0)

10	at Philadelphia	7
19	at Atlanta	6
28	Carolina	24
28	N.Y. Giants	24
85		61

CINCINNATI (0-4)

17	at Indianapolis	20
0	at Detroit	16
3	Buffalo	30
16	Atlanta	28
36		94

CLEVELAND (2-3)

20	vs. Dallas (OT) (b)	17
3	at Tampa Bay	30
17	Minnesota	24
35	Chicago	24
17	at Philadelphia	30
92		125

JACKSONVILLE (3-1)

35	Carolina	10
20	at N.Y. Giants	27
31	Kansas City	6
27	at Dallas	6
113		49

PITTSBURGH (1-3)

30	Chicago	23
13	at Carolina	20
14	Washington	27
14	at Buffalo	16
71		86

TENNESSEE (1-3)

20	at Kansas City	22
17	at Arizona	27
17	Atlanta	3
11	New Orleans	12
65		64

Western Division

DENVER (3-2)

20	San Diego (a)	17
38	Arizona	7
12	at Green Bay (c)	27
12	at Dallas	22
34	San Francisco	3
116		76

KANSAS CITY (2-2)

22	Tennessee	20
7	Tampa Bay	17
6	at Jacksonville	31
34	at San Diego	27
69		95

OAKLAND (3-1)

18	at St. Louis	17
10	Dallas	3
8	San Francisco	16
43	at Arizona	7
79		43

SAN DIEGO (0-5)

17	Denver (a)	20
24	at San Francisco	31
10	Miami	13
21	at St. Louis	24
27	Kansas City	34
99		122

SEATTLE (1-3)

10	Buffalo	24
23	at San Francisco	24
41	Arizona	7
28	at Indianapolis	31
102		86

NFC PRESEASON RECORDS—TEAM BY TEAM

Eastern Division

ARIZONA (1-3)

7	at Denver	38
27	Tennessee	17
7	at Seattle	41
7	Oakland	43
48		139

DALLAS (1-4)

17	Cleveland (OT) (b)	20
3	at Oakland	10
14	at New England	34
22	Denver	12
6	Jacksonville	27
62		103

N.Y. GIANTS (2-2)

36	at Minnesota	21
27	Jacksonville	20
10	N.Y. Jets	16
24	at Baltimore	28
97		85

PHILADELPHIA (1-3)

7	Baltimore	10
9	at N.Y. Jets	10
13	at Minnesota	17
30	Cleveland	17
59		54

WASHINGTON (3-1)

20	at New England	14
20	Buffalo	19
27	at Pittsburgh	14
13	Tampa Bay	16
80		63

Central Division

CHICAGO (2-2)

9	Indianapolis	6
23	at Pittsburgh	30
38	St. Louis	24
24	at Cleveland	35
94		95

DETROIT (1-3)

31	at Atlanta	35
16	Cincinnati	0
10	at Miami	31
6	St. Louis	17
63		83

GREEN BAY (4-0)

27	N.Y. Jets	16
27	Denver (c)	12
38	at New Orleans	17
25	Miami	17
117		62

MINNESOTA (2-2)

21	N.Y. Giants	36
24	at Cleveland	17
17	Philadelphia	13
17	at N.Y. Jets	38
79		104

TAMPA BAY (4-0)

30	Cleveland	3
17	at Kansas City	7
45	New England	14
16	at Washington	13
108		37

Western Division

ATLANTA (2-2)

35	Detroit	31
6	Baltimore	19
3	at Tennessee	17
28	at Cincinnati	16
72		83

CAROLINA (2-2)

10	at Jacksonville	35
20	Pittsburgh	13
24	at Baltimore	28
23	New England	20
77		96

NEW ORLEANS (2-2)

26	at Miami	14
7	Indianapolis	37
17	Green Bay	38
12	at Tennessee	11
62		100

ST. LOUIS (2-2)

17	Oakland	18
24	at Chicago	38
24	San Diego	21
17	at Detroit	6
82		83

SAN FRANCISCO (3-1)

31	San Diego	24
24	Seattle	23
16	at Oakland	8
3	at Denver	34
74		89

(OT) denotes overtime

(a) American Bowl at Sydney, Australia

(b) Pro Football Hall of Fame Game at Canton, Ohio

(c) at Madison, Wisconsin

1999 NFL STANDINGS/RESULTS

FINAL STANDINGS

AMERICAN FOOTBALL CONFERENCE

Eastern Division	W	L	T	Pct.	Pts.	OP
*Indianapolis	13	3	0	.813	423	333
#Buffalo	11	5	0	.688	320	229
#Miami	9	7	0	.563	326	336
New York Jets	8	8	0	.500	308	309
New England	8	8	0	.500	299	284
Central Division						
*Jacksonville	14	2	0	.875	396	217
#Tennessee	13	3	0	.813	392	324
Baltimore	8	8	0	.500	324	277
Pittsburgh	6	10	0	.375	317	320
Cincinnati	4	12	0	.250	283	460
Cleveland	2	14	0	.125	217	437
Western Division						
*Seattle	9	7	0	.563	338	298
Kansas City	9	7	0	.563	390	322
San Diego	8	8	0	.500	269	316
Oakland	8	8	0	.500	390	329
Denver	6	10	0	.375	314	318

NATIONAL FOOTBALL CONFERENCE

Eastern Division	W	L	T	Pct.	Pts.	OP
*Washington	10	6	0	.625	443	377
#Dallas	8	8	0	.500	352	276
New York Giants	7	9	0	.438	299	358
Arizona	6	10	0	.375	245	382
Philadelphia	5	11	0	.313	272	357
Central Division						
*Tampa Bay	11	5	0	.688	270	235
#Minnesota	10	6	0	.625	399	335
#Detroit	8	8	0	.500	322	323
Green Bay	8	8	0	.500	357	341
Chicago	6	10	0	.375	272	341
Western Division						
*St. Louis	13	3	0	.813	526	242
Carolina	8	8	0	.500	421	381
Atlanta	5	11	0	.313	285	380
San Francisco	4	12	0	.250	295	453
New Orleans	3	13	0	.188	260	434

*Division Champion; #Wild Card Team

Miami was third Wild Card ahead of Kansas City based on better record against common opponents (6-1 to Chiefs' 5-3). New York Jets finished ahead of New England based on better division record (4-4 to Patriots' 2-6). Seattle finished ahead of Kansas City based on head-to-head sweep (2-0). San Diego finished ahead of Oakland based on better division record (5-3 to Raiders' 3-5). Dallas was second Wild Card based on better record against common opponents (3-2 to Lions' 3-3) and better conference record than Carolina (7-5 to Panthers' 6-6). Detroit was third Wild Card based on better conference record than Green Bay (7-5 to Packers' 6-6) and better conference record than Carolina (7-5 to Panthers' 6-6).

WILD CARD PLAYOFFS

AFC

TENNESSEE 22, Buffalo 16
Miami 20, SEATTLE 17

NFC

WASHINGTON 27, Detroit 13
MINNESOTA 27, Dallas 10

DIVISIONAL PLAYOFFS

AFC

JACKSONVILLE 62, Miami 7
Tennessee 19, INDIANAPOLIS 16

NFC

TAMPA BAY 14, Washington 13
ST. LOUIS 49, Minnesota 37

CHAMPIONSHIP GAMES

AFC

Tennessee 33, JACKSONVILLE 14

NFC

ST. LOUIS 11, Tampa Bay 6

SUPER BOWL XXXIV

St. Louis (NFC) 23, Tennessee (AFC) 16
at Georgia Dome, Atlanta, Georgia

AFC-NFC PRO BOWL

NFC 51, AFC 31, at Aloha Stadium, Honolulu, Hawaii

Home teams in playoff games are indicated in CAPS.

AFC SEASON RECORDS—TEAM BY TEAM

BALTIMORE (8-8)

10	at St. Louis	27
20	PITTSBURGH	23
17	CLEVELAND	10
19	at Atlanta (OT)	13
11	at Tennessee	14
8	KANSAS CITY	35
10	BUFFALO	13
41	at Cleveland	9
3	at Jacksonville	6
34	at Cincinnati	31
23	JACKSONVILLE	30
41	TENNESSEE	14
31	at Pittsburgh	24
31	NEW ORLEANS	8
22	CINCINNATI	0
3	at New England	20
324		277

BUFFALO (11-5)

14	at Indianapolis	31
17	N.Y. JETS	3
26	PHILADELPHIA	0
23	at Miami	18
24	PITTSBURGH	21
14	OAKLAND	20
16	at Seattle	26
13	at Baltimore	10
34	at Washington	17
23	MIAMI	3
7	at N.Y. Jets	17
17	NEW ENGLAND	7
17	N.Y. GIANTS	19
31	at Arizona	21
13	at N. England (OT)	10
31	INDIANAPOLIS	6
320		229

CINCINNATI (4-12)

35	at Tennessee	36
7	SAN DIEGO	34
3	at Carolina	27
10	ST. LOUIS	38
18	at Cleveland	17
3	PITTSBURGH	17
10	at Indianapolis	31
10	JACKSONVILLE	41
20	at Seattle	37
14	TENNESSEE	24
31	BALTIMORE	34
27	at Pittsburgh	20
44	SAN FRANCISCO	30
44	CLEVELAND	28
0	at Baltimore	22
7	at Jacksonville	24
283		460

CLEVELAND (2-14)

0	PITTSBURGH	43
9	at Tennessee	26
10	at Baltimore	17
7	NEW ENGLAND	19
17	CINCINNATI	18
7	at Jacksonville	24
3	at St. Louis	34
21	at New Orleans	16
9	BALTIMORE	41
16	at Pittsburgh	15
17	CAROLINA	31
21	TENNESSEE	33
10	at San Diego	23
28	at Cincinnati	44
14	JACKSONVILLE	24
28	INDIANAPOLIS	29
217		437

DENVER (6-10)

21	MIAMI	38
10	at Kansas City	26
10	at Tampa Bay	13
13	N.Y. JETS	21
16	at Oakland	13
31	GREEN BAY	10
23	at New England	24
20	MINNESOTA	23
33	at San Diego	17
17	at Seattle	20
27	OAKLAND (OT)	21
10	KANSAS CITY	16
24	at Jacksonville	27
36	SEATTLE (OT)	30
17	at Detroit	7
6	SAN DIEGO	12
314		318

INDIANAPOLIS (13-3)

31	BUFFALO	14
28	at New England	31
27	at San Diego	19
31	MIAMI	34
16	at N.Y. Jets	13
31	CINCINNATI	10
34	DALLAS	24
25	KANSAS CITY	17
27	at N.Y. Giants	19
44	at Philadelphia	17
13	N.Y. JETS	6
37	at Miami	34
20	NEW ENGLAND	15
24	WASHINGTON	21
29	at Cleveland	28
6	at Buffalo	31
423		333

JACKSONVILLE (14-2)

41	SAN FRANCISCO	3
22	at Carolina	20
19	TENNESSEE	20
17	at Pittsburgh	3
16	at N.Y. Jets	6
24	CLEVELAND	7
41	at Cincinnati	10
30	at Atlanta	7
6	BALTIMORE	3
41	NEW ORLEANS	23
30	at Baltimore	23
20	PITTSBURGH	6
27	DENVER	24
24	at Cleveland	14
14	at Tennessee	41
24	CINCINNATI	7
396		217

KANSAS CITY (9-7)

17	at Chicago	20
26	DENVER	10
31	DETROIT	21
14	at San Diego	21
16	NEW ENGLAND	14
35	at Baltimore	8
34	SAN DIEGO	0
17	at Indianapolis	25
10	at Tampa Bay	17
19	SEATTLE	31
37	at Oakland	34
16	at Denver	10
31	MINNESOTA	28
35	PITTSBURGH	19
14	at Seattle	23
38	OAKLAND (OT)	41
390		322

MIAMI (9-7)

38	at Denver	21
19	ARIZONA	16
18	BUFFALO	23
34	at Indianapolis	31
31	at New England	30
16	PHILADELPHIA	13
16	at Oakland	9
17	TENNESSEE	0
3	at Buffalo	23
27	NEW ENGLAND	17
0	at Dallas	20
34	INDIANAPOLIS	37
20	at N.Y. Jets	28
12	SAN DIEGO	9
31	N.Y. JETS	38
10	at Washington	21
326		336

NEW ENGLAND (8-8)

30	at N.Y. Jets	28
31	INDIANAPOLIS	28
16	N.Y. GIANTS	14
19	at Cleveland	7
14	at Kansas City	16
30	MIAMI	31
24	DENVER	23
27	at Arizona	3
17	N.Y. JETS	24
17	at Miami	27
7	at Buffalo	17
13	DALLAS	6
15	at Indianapolis	20
9	at Philadelphia	24
10	BUFFALO (OT)	13
20	BALTIMORE	3
299		284

N.Y. JETS (8-8)

28	NEW ENGLAND	30
3	at Buffalo	17
20	WASHINGTON	27
21	at Denver	13
6	JACKSONVILLE	16
13	INDIANAPOLIS	16
23	at Oakland	24
12	ARIZONA	7
24	at New England	17
17	BUFFALO	7
6	at Indianapolis	13
28	at N.Y. Giants	41
28	MIAMI	20
22	at Dallas	21
38	at Miami	31
19	SEATTLE	9
308		309

OAKLAND (8-8)

24	at Green Bay	28
22	at Minnesota	17
24	CHICAGO	17
21	at Seattle	22
13	DENVER	16
20	at Buffalo	14
24	N.Y. JETS	23
9	MIAMI	16
28	SAN DIEGO	9
21	at Denver (OT)	27
34	KANSAS CITY	37
30	SEATTLE	21
14	at Tennessee	21
45	TAMPA BAY	0
20	at San Diego	23
41	at Kansas City (OT)	38
390		329

PITTSBURGH (6-10)

43	at Cleveland	0
23	at Baltimore	20
10	SEATTLE	29
3	JACKSONVILLE	17
21	at Buffalo	24
17	at Cincinnati	3
13	ATLANTA	9
27	at San Francisco	6
15	CLEVELAND	16
10	at Tennessee	16
20	CINCINNATI	27
6	at Jacksonville	20
24	BALTIMORE	31
19	at Kansas City	35
30	CAROLINA	20
36	TENNESSEE	47
317		320

SAN DIEGO (8-8)

34	at Cincinnati	7
19	INDIANAPOLIS	27
21	KANSAS CITY	14
20	at Detroit	10
13	SEATTLE	10
3	GREEN BAY	31
0	at Kansas City	34
17	DENVER	33
9	at Oakland	28
20	CHICAGO (OT)	23
27	at Minnesota	35
23	CLEVELAND	10
19	at Seattle	16
9	at Miami	12
23	OAKLAND	20
12	at Denver	6
269		316

SEATTLE (9-7)

20	DETROIT	28
14	at Chicago	13
29	at Pittsburgh	10
22	OAKLAND	21
10	at San Diego	13
26	BUFFALO	16
27	at Green Bay	7
37	CINCINNATI	20
20	DENVER	17
31	at Kansas City	19
3	TAMPA BAY	16
21	at Oakland	30
16	SAN DIEGO	19
30	at Denver (OT)	36
23	KANSAS CITY	14
9	at N.Y. Jets	19
338		298

TENNESSEE (13-3)

36	CINCINNATI	35
26	CLEVELAND	9
20	at Jacksonville	19
22	at San Francisco	24
14	BALTIMORE	11
24	at New Orleans	21
24	ST. LOUIS	21
0	at Miami	17
24	at Cincinnati	14
16	PITTSBURGH	10
33	at Cleveland	21
14	at Baltimore	41
21	OAKLAND	14
30	ATLANTA	17
41	JACKSONVILLE	14
47	at Pittsburgh	36
392		324

NFC SEASON RECORDS—TEAM BY TEAM

ARIZONA (6-10)

25	at Philadelphia	24
16	at Miami	19
10	SAN FRANCISCO	24
7	at Dallas	35
14	N.Y. GIANTS	3
10	WASHINGTON	24
3	NEW ENGLAND	27
7	at N.Y. Jets	12
23	DETROIT	19
13	DALLAS	9
34	at N.Y. Giants	24
21	PHILADELPHIA	17
3	at Washington	28
21	BUFFALO	31
14	at Atlanta	37
24	at Green Bay	49
245		382

ATLANTA (5-11)

14	MINNESOTA	17
7	at Dallas	24
7	at St. Louis	35
13	BALTIMORE (OT)	19
20	at New Orleans	17
13	ST. LOUIS	41
9	at Pittsburgh	13
27	CAROLINA	20
7	JACKSONVILLE	30
10	at Tampa Bay	19
28	at Carolina	34
35	NEW ORLEANS	12
7	at San Francisco	26
17	at Tennessee	30
37	ARIZONA	14
34	SAN FRANCISCO	29
285		380

CAROLINA (8-8)

10	at New Orleans	19
20	JACKSONVILLE	22
27	CINCINNATI	3
36	at Washington	38
31	at San Francisco	29
9	DETROIT	24
20	at Atlanta	27
33	PHILADELPHIA	7
10	at St. Louis	35
31	at Cleveland	17
34	ATLANTA	28
21	ST. LOUIS	34
33	at Green Bay	31
41	SAN FRANCISCO	24
20	at Pittsburgh	30
45	NEW ORLEANS	13
421		381

CHICAGO (6-10)

20	KANSAS CITY	17
13	SEATTLE	14
17	at Oakland	24
14	NEW ORLEANS	10
24	at Minnesota	22
16	PHILADELPHIA	20
3	at Tampa Bay	6
22	at Washington	48
14	at Green Bay	13
24	MINNESOTA (OT)	27
23	at San Diego (OT)	20
17	at Detroit	21
19	GREEN BAY	35
28	DETROIT	10
12	at St. Louis	34
6	TAMPA BAY	20
272		341

DALLAS (8-8)

41	at Washington (OT)	35
24	ATLANTA	7
35	ARIZONA	7
10	at Philadelphia	13
10	at N.Y. Giants	13
38	WASHINGTON	20
24	at Indianapolis	34
17	at Minnesota	27
27	GREEN BAY	13
9	at Arizona	13
20	MIAMI	0
6	at New England	13
20	PHILADELPHIA	10
21	N.Y. JETS	22
24	at New Orleans	31
26	N.Y. GIANTS	18
352		276

DETROIT (8-8)

28	at Seattle	20
23	GREEN BAY	15
21	at Kansas City	31
10	SAN DIEGO	20
25	MINNESOTA	23
24	at Carolina	9
20	TAMPA BAY	3
31	ST. LOUIS	27
19	at Arizona	23
17	at Green Bay	26
21	CHICAGO	17
33	WASHINGTON	17
16	at Tampa Bay	23
10	at Chicago	28
7	DENVER	17
17	at Minnesota	24
322		323

GREEN BAY (8-8)

28	OAKLAND	24
15	at Detroit	23
23	MINNESOTA	20
26	TAMPA BAY	23
10	at Denver	31
31	at San Diego	3
7	SEATTLE	27
13	CHICAGO	14
13	at Dallas	27
26	DETROIT	17
20	at San Francisco	3
35	at Chicago	19
31	CAROLINA	33
20	at Minnesota	24
10	at Tampa Bay	29
49	ARIZONA	24
357		341

MINNESOTA (10-6)

17	at Atlanta	14
17	OAKLAND	22
20	at Green Bay	23
21	TAMPA BAY	14
22	CHICAGO	24
23	at Detroit	25
40	SAN FRANCISCO	16
23	at Denver	20
27	DALLAS	17
27	at Chicago (OT)	24
35	SAN DIEGO	27
17	at Tampa Bay	24
28	at Kansas City	31
24	GREEN BAY	20
34	at N.Y. Giants	17
24	DETROIT	17
399		335

NEW ORLEANS (3-13)

19	CAROLINA	10
21	at San Francisco	28
10	at Chicago	14
17	ATLANTA	20
21	TENNESSEE	24
3	at N.Y. Giants	31
16	CLEVELAND	21
16	TAMPA BAY	31
24	SAN FRANCISCO	6
23	at Jacksonville	41
12	at St. Louis	43
12	at Atlanta	35
14	ST. LOUIS	30
8	at Baltimore	31
31	DALLAS	24
13	at Carolina	45
260		434

N.Y. GIANTS (7-9)

17	at Tampa Bay	13
21	WASHINGTON	50
14	at New England	16
16	PHILADELPHIA	15
3	at Arizona	14
13	DALLAS	10
31	NEW ORLEANS	3
23	at Philadelphia (OT)	17
19	INDIANAPOLIS	27
13	at Washington	23
24	ARIZONA	34
41	N.Y. JETS	28
19	at Buffalo	17
10	at St. Louis	31
17	MINNESOTA	34
18	at Dallas	26
299		358

PHILADELPHIA (5-11)

24	ARIZONA	25
5	TAMPA BAY	19
0	at Buffalo	26
15	at N.Y. Giants	16
13	DALLAS	10
20	at Chicago	16
13	at Miami	16
17	N.Y. GIANTS (OT)	23
7	at Carolina	33
35	WASHINGTON	28
17	INDIANAPOLIS	44
17	at Washington (OT)	20
17	at Arizona	21
10	at Dallas	20
24	NEW ENGLAND	9
38	ST. LOUIS	31
272		357

ST. LOUIS RAMS (13-3)

27	BALTIMORE	10
35	ATLANTA	7
38	at Cincinnati	10
42	SAN FRANCISCO	20
41	at Atlanta	13
34	CLEVELAND	3
21	at Tennessee	24
27	at Detroit	31
35	CAROLINA	10
23	at San Francisco	7
43	NEW ORLEANS	12
34	at Carolina	21
30	at New Orleans	14
31	N.Y. GIANTS	10
34	CHICAGO	12
31	at Philadelphia	38
526		242

SAN FRANCISCO (4-12)

3	at Jacksonville	41
28	NEW ORLEANS	21
24	at Arizona	10
24	TENNESSEE	22
20	at St. Louis	42
29	CAROLINA	31
16	at Minnesota	40
6	PITTSBURGH	27
6	at New Orleans	24
7	ST. LOUIS	23
3	GREEN BAY	20
30	at Cincinnati	44
26	ATLANTA	7
24	at Carolina	41
20	WASHINGTON (OT)	26
29	at Atlanta	34
295		453

TAMPA BAY (11-5)

13	N.Y. GIANTS	17
19	at Philadelphia	5
13	DENVER	10
14	at Minnesota	21
23	at Green Bay	26
6	CHICAGO	3
3	at Detroit	20
31	at New Orleans	16
17	KANSAS CITY	10
19	ATLANTA	10
16	at Seattle	3
24	MINNESOTA	17
23	DETROIT	16
0	at Oakland	45
29	GREEN BAY	10
20	at Chicago	6
270		235

WASHINGTON (10-6)

35	DALLAS (OT)	41
50	at N.Y. Giants	21
27	at N.Y. Jets	20
38	CAROLINA	36
24	at Arizona	10
20	at Dallas	38
48	CHICAGO	22
17	BUFFALO	34
28	at Philadelphia	35
23	N.Y. GIANTS	13
20	PHILADELPHIA (OT)	17
17	at Detroit	33
28	ARIZONA	3
21	at Indianapolis	24
26	at San Francisco (OT)	20
21	MIAMI	10
443		377

1999 WEEK BY WEEK

Attendance figures as they appear in the following, and in the club-by-club sections starting on page 28, are turnstile counts and not paid attendance. Paid attendance totals are on page 242.

FIRST WEEK SUMMARIES

American Football Conference

Eastern Division	**W**	**L**	**T**	**Pct.**	**Pts.**	**OP**
Indianapolis	1	0	0	1.000	31	14
Miami	1	0	0	1.000	38	21
New England	1	0	0	1.000	30	28
N.Y. Jets	0	1	0	.000	28	30
Buffalo	0	1	0	.000	14	31
Central Division						
Jacksonville	1	0	0	1.000	41	3
Pittsburgh	1	0	0	1.000	43	0
Tennessee	1	0	0	1.000	36	35
Baltimore	0	1	0	.000	13	20
Cincinnati	0	1	0	.000	14	23
Cleveland	0	1	0	.000	0	43
Western Division						
Denver	0	1	0	.000	21	38
Kansas City	0	1	0	.000	17	20
Oakland	0	1	0	.000	24	28
Seattle	0	1	0	.000	20	28
San Diego	0	0	0	.000	0	0

National Football Conference

Eastern Division	**W**	**L**	**T**	**Pct.**	**Pts.**	**OP**
Arizona	1	0	0	1.000	25	24
Dallas	1	0	0	1.000	41	35
N.Y. Giants	1	0	0	1.000	17	13
Philadelphia	0	1	0	.000	24	25
Washington	0	1	0	.000	35	41
Central Division						
Chicago	1	0	0	1.000	20	17
Detroit	1	0	0	1.000	28	20
Green Bay	1	0	0	1.000	28	24
Minnesota	1	0	0	1.000	17	14
Tampa Bay	0	1	0	.000	13	17
Western Division						
New Orleans	1	0	0	1.000	19	14
St. Louis	1	0	0	1.000	24	17
Atlanta	1	0	0	1.000	36	30
Carolina	0	1	0	.000	14	19
San Francisco	0	1	0	.000	17	24

SUNDAY, SEPTEMBER 12

ARIZONA 25, PHILADELPHIA 24—at Veterans Stadium, attendance 64,113. Chris Jacke's 31-yard field goal as time expired gave the Cardinals a comeback victory. Interception returns by Al Harris, to the Cardinals' 6-yard line, and Bryan Dawkins, to the Cardinals' 3, set up Eagles touchdowns just 2:03 apart late in the first quarter to give Philadelphia a 21-0 lead. The Cardinals responded with 2 Jacke field goal's, but Jake Plummer's third intercepted pass of the half, this time by James Darling, was returned 43 yards to the Cardinals' 8, setting up Norm Johnson's field goal as the half expired. Arizona put together scoring drives of 13 and 16 plays, with Jacke's 32-yard field goal cutting the deficit to 24-15 with 14:53 remaining. Plummer's 47-yard pass to Rob Moore was followed two plays later by the pair's 20-yard touchdown to cut the Eagles' lead to 24-22 with 4:03 left. On third-and-4 from the Eagles' 49 with 2:00 left, Kwamie Lassiter intercepted Doug Pederson's pass, which had deflected off the hands of Brian Finneran, and scampered 32 yards to the Eagles' 43. Plummer's 17-yard bootleg run set up Jacke's winning kick as time expired. It was Jacke's fourth game-winning field goal in five games as the Cardinals kicker. Plummer was 25 of 48 for 274 yards and 1 touchdown, with 3 interceptions. Pederson was 12 of 26 for 91 yards and 2 touchdowns, with 2 interceptions. Duce Staley carried 22 times for 103 yards.

Arizona	0	6	6	13	—	25
Philadelphia	21	3	0	0	—	24

Phil — Staley 24 run (Johnson kick)
Phil — Staley 3 pass from Pederson (Johnson kick)
Phil — Broughton 15 pass from Pederson (Johnson kick)
Ariz — FG Jacke 31
Ariz — FG Jacke 25
Phil — FG Johnson 25
Ariz — Bates 1 run (pass failed)
Ariz — FG Jacke 32
Ariz — Moore 20 pass from Plummer (Jacke kick)
Ariz — FG Jacke 31

ST. LOUIS 27, BALTIMORE 10—at Trans World Dome, attendance 62,100. With just 11 career NFL passes to his credit, Kurt Warner passed for 316 yards and 3 touchdowns to lead the Rams to victory. A 35-yard punt return by Az-zahir Hakim set up Jeff Wilkins' 36-yard field goal in the first quarter. Warner's performance varied in the first half, completing 2 of the Rams' last 4 possessions of the half with touchdown passes. However, the other 2 finished with interceptions, leading to Matt Stover's 25-yard field goal and the Ravens' lone points of the half. Scott Mitchell completed 5 of 7 passes on a late third-quarter drive, capped by a 28-yard touchdown pass to rookie Brandon Stokely to cut the deficit to 17-10. On the ensuing possession, Deron Jenkins's sack forced Warner to fumble early in the fourth quarter, and Fernando Smith recovered at the Rams' 30. However, the Ravens lost 6 yards on the next three plays, and Stover's 54-yard field-goal attempt sailed wide right. The Rams scored on their next two possessions, capped by rookie Torry Holt's 19-yard touchdown catch with 2:40 remaining, to finish the scoring. Warner was 28 of 44 for 316 yards and 3 touchdowns, with 2 interceptions. Mitchell was 17 of 40 for 188 yards and 1 touchdown, with 2 interceptions.

Baltimore	0	3	7	0	—	10
St. Louis	3	14	0	10	—	27

StL — FG Wilkins 36
StL — R. Williams 6 pass from Warner (Wilkins kick)
Balt — FG Stover 25
StL — Bruce 2 pass from Warner (Wilkins kick)
Balt — Stokley 28 pass from Mitchell (Stover kick)
StL — FG Wilkins 51
StL — Holt 19 pass from Warner (Wilkins kick)

INDIANAPOLIS 31, BUFFALO 14—at RCA Dome, attendance 56,238. Rookie Edgerrin James rushed for 112 yards and 1 touchdown, and Peyton Manning and Marvin Harrison connected for 2 touchdowns as the Colts defeated the Bills. James's 1-yard touchdown was set up by Manning's 50-yard pass to E.J. Green to the Bills' 1. The Bills drove inside the Colts' 25 three times in the first half, yet had just 2 field goals to show for their efforts. Jeff Burris's 28-yard interception return halted the other possession and led to Manning's first touchdown pass to Harrison. James's 40-yard run in the third quarter was followed two plays later by Harrison's second touchdown catch to give the Colts a 21-6 lead. The Bills responded with an 8-play touchdown drive, but Mike Vanderjagt's 35-yard field goal increased the lead to 10 points, and Tony Blevins's 74-yard interception return for a touchdown with 3:20 left iced the game. Manning was 21 of 33 for 284 yards and 2 touchdowns, with 2 interceptions. Harrison had 8 receptions for 121 yards, while Green had 5 catches for 124 yards. Along with James's 112 rushing yards, the Colts had 100-yard rushing and receiving days in the same game for the first time since October 27, 1985. Flutie was 22 of 42 for 300 yards and 1 touchdown, with 2 interceptions. Eric Moulds had 10 catches for 147 yards.

Buffalo	0	6	8	0	—	14
Indianapolis	7	7	7	10	—	31

Ind — James 1 run (Vanderjagt kick)
Buff — FG Christie 36
Ind — Harrison 5 pass from Manning (Vanderjagt kick)
Buff — FG Christie 29
Ind — Harrison 24 pass from Manning (Vanderjagt kick)
Buff — Reed 6 pass from Flutie (Linton run)
Ind — FG Vanderjagt 35
Ind — Blevins 74 interception return (Vanderjagt kick)

NEW ORLEANS 19, CAROLINA 10—at Superdome, attendance 58,166. Tyronne Drakeford returned a fumble on the season's opening kickoff for a touchdown, and the Saints' defense recorded 7 sacks to defeat the Panthers. The Saints recorded just 2 first downs in their first seven possessions, but the game was tied 10-10 at halftime. Austin Robbins recorded a defensive trifecta in the third quarter, as he sacked Steve Beuerlein, forced him to fumble, and recovered the ball at the Panthers' 20. Robbins's play led to Doug Brien's second field goal, and Billy Joe Hobert connected on a 67-yard touchdown pass to Keith Poole two minutes later. John Kasay missed a 53-yard field goal in the final minutes, allowing the Saints to run out the final 3:32. Hobert was 11 of 22 for 132 yards and 1 touchdown. Beuerlein was 16 of 32 for 207 yards and 1 touchdown, with 1 interception.

Carolina	0	10	0	0	—	10
New Orleans	7	3	9	0	—	19

NO — Drakeford 14 fumble return (Brien kick)
NO — FG Brien 46
Car — Walls 5 pass from Beuerlein (Kasay kick)
Car — FG Kasay 52
NO — FG Brien 21
NO — Poole 67 pass from Hobert (kick failed)

TENNESSEE 36, CINCINNATI 35—at Adelphia Coliseum, attendance 65,272. After losing a 19-point lead, Al Del Greco's 33-yard field goal with eight seconds left lifted the Titans to victory in their first game at Adelphia Coliseum. Steve McNair rushed for 1 touchdown and threw 2 scoring passes to Kevin Dyson as the Titans scored on four of their first five possessions, plus a blocked punt by Donald Mitchell for a safety, to take a 26-7 lead with 5:32 left in the first half. The Bengals scored twice in the half's final two minutes, the second set up by Greg Myers's 21-yard return of Yancey Thigpen's fumble, to cut the deficit to 26-21 at halftime. The Bengals' offense got hot in the second half and drove into Titans' territory on four of its first five possessions, leading to 1 touchdown and 2 field goals, to take a 35-26 lead with 7:56 remaining. McNair completed 12- and 20-yard passes to Dyson before finding Eddie George open for a 17-yard touchdown with 4:30 remaining. The Bengals failed to get a first down, and Thigpen's 21-yard punt return gave the Titans the ball at the Bengals' 49 with 2:24 left, setting up Del Greco's winning kick. Akili Smith's Hail Mary pass fell incomplete in the end zone as time expired. McNair was 21 of 32 for 341 yards and 3 touchdowns, with 1 interception. Dyson had 9 receptions for 162 yards. Jeff Blake was 18 of 31 for 182 yards and 2 touchdowns, with 2 interceptions.

Cincinnati	7	14	8	6	—	35
Tennessee	14	12	0	10	—	36

Tenn — McNair 1 run (Del Greco kick)
Cin — Dillon 1 run (Pelfrey kick)
Tenn — Dyson 13 pass from McNair (Del Greco kick)
Tenn — Safety, Mitchell blocked Brice punt out of end zone
Tenn — FG Del Greco 50
Cin — Carter 2 run (Jackson pass from Blake)
Cin — McGee 3 pass from Blake (run failed)
Cin — Jackson 17 pass from Blake (Milne pass from Blake)
Cin — FG Pelfrey 33
Cin — FG Pelfrey 38
Tenn — George 17 pass from McNair (Del Greco kick)
Tenn — FG Del Greco 33

DALLAS 41, WASHINGTON 35 (OT)—at Redskins Stadium, attendance 79,237. Troy Aikman's 76-yard touchdown pass to Raghib Ismail in overtime capped the Cowboys' 21-point comeback at Washington. Aikman completed touchdown passes to David LaFleur on each of the Cowboys' first two possessions of the game, but the Redskins drove into Cowboys' territory on each of its first nine possessions. Washington scored 4 touchdowns and added 2 field goals to score 32 unanswered points to take a 35-14 lead with 1:04 left in the third quarter. The lead would have been larger, but the Redskins lost 2 fumbles inside the Cowboys' 10. Trailing 35-21 with 4:30 left and faced with fourth-and-2, Emmitt Smith gained 3 yards to keep the drive alive. Aikman fired a 37-yard touchdown pass to Michael Irvin on the next play to cut the deficit to 35-28. The Cowboys forced a punt and drove 90 yards in 1:15, capped by Irvin's 12-yard scoring catch, to tie the game with 1:46 left. The Redskins reached the Cowboys' 23 with three seconds left and lined up for a field-goal attempt, but holder Matt Turk mishandled the snap and the game went to overtime. After a Redskins' punt, the Cowboys were faced with third-and-2. Aikman faked a handoff and found Ismail open deep down the middle for the game-winning 76-yard touchdown. Aikman was 28 of 49 for 362 yards, a career-high 5 touchdowns, and 3 interceptions. Ismail had 8 receptions for 149 yards. Irvin had 5 catches for 122 yards. Smith rushed 23 times for 109 yards. Brad Johnson was 20 of 33 for 382 yards and 2 touchdowns. Michael Westbrook had 5 catches for 159 yards, and Albert Connell had 4 for 137 yards. Stephen Davis rushed 24 times for 109 yards. The teams combined for 1,045 total yards.

Dallas	7	7	0	21	6	—	41
Washington	3	10	22	0	0	—	35

Dall — LaFleur 15 pass from Aikman (Cunningham kick)
Wash — FG Conway 25
Dall — LaFleur 14 pass from Aikman (Cunningham kick)
Wash — Westbrook 41 pass from Johnson (Conway kick)
Wash — FG Conway 42
Wash — Davis 3 run (Davis run)
Wash — Davis 7 run (Conway kick)
Wash — Connell 50 pass from Johnson (Conway kick)
Dall — E. Smith 1 run (Cunningham kick)
Dall — Irvin 37 pass from Aikman (Cunningham kick)
Dall — Irvin 12 pass from Aikman (Cunningham kick)
Dall — Ismail 76 pass from Aikman

DETROIT 28, SEATTLE 20—at Kingdome, attendance 66,238. Charlie Batch passed for 3 touchdowns, 2 to Germane Crowell, as the Lions spoiled Mike Holmgren's debut as the Seahawks' coach. Mark Carrier recovered Sean Dawkins's fumble four plays into the game, setting up Jason Hanson's 51-yard field goal. Following Todd Peterson's missed 32-yard field goal, Batch drove the Lions 77 yards, capped by a 16-yard touchdown pass to Crowell. Brock Olivo's recovery of Charlie Rogers's fumbled punt four minutes later led to Batch's second touchdown pass, and Deems Mays's punt snap less than a minute later sailed out of the end zone to give Detroit an 18-0 lead. On the first play following the safety, Willie Williams returned an interception 40 yards for a touchdown, but Batch and Crowell responded with a 41-yard touchdown connection on the ensuing drive. Jon Kitna fired 2 touchdown passes to Dawkins in the second half, the second cutting the deficit to 25-20 with 7:11 left. But the Lions drove five minutes for Hanson's 49-yard field goal, and Seattle failed to get a first down on its final possession. Batch was 16 of 26 for 216 yards and 3 touchdowns, with 1 interception. Crowell had 7 catches for 141 yards. Kitna was 20 of 30 for 202 yards and 2 touchdowns.

Detroit	3	22	0	3	—	28
Seattle	0	7	7	6	—	20

Det — FG Hanson 51
Det — Crowell 16 pass from Batch (Hanson kick)
Det — Sloan 5 pass from Batch (kick failed)
Det — Safety, punt snap went out of end zone
Sea — W. Williams 40 interception return (Peterson kick)
Det — Crowell 41 pass from Batch (Hanson kick)
Sea — Dawkins 26 pass from Kitna (Peterson kick)
Sea — Dawkins 3 pass from Kitna (pass failed)
Det — FG Hanson 49

CHICAGO 20, KANSAS CITY 17—at Soldier Field, attendance 58,381. Shane Matthews passed for 2 touchdowns in his first career start as the Bears scored on all four of their first-half possessions to defeat the Chiefs. With the Bears leading 7-3, Tony Parrish intercepted Elvis Grbac's pass and returned it 41 yards to set up the first of 2 Brian Gowins field goals, the second of which was successfully engineered by rookie Cade McNown, who played two series. Matthews drove the Bears on a 63-yard two-minute drive, capped by a 1-yard touchdown pass to John Allred to give the Bears a 20-3 halftime lead. Grbac's 86-yard touchdown pass to Derrick Alexander cut the deficit to 10 points, but after a fumble recovery, Pete Stoyanovich missed a 38-yard field-goal attempt late in the third quarter. Donnie Edwards returned Matthew's fourth-quarter fumble 79 yards for a touchdown, but the Chiefs failed to drive inside the Bears' 41 on their final three possessions. Matthews was 25 of 38 for 245 yards and 2 touchdowns, while McNown was 6 of 9 for 77 yards. Grbac was 20 of 42 for 283 yards and 1 touchdown, with 1 interception. Alexander had 6 receptions for 154 yards.

Kansas City	3	0	7	7	—	17
Chicago	7	13	0	0	—	20

KC — FG Stoyanovich 27
Chi — Enis 10 pass from Matthews (Gowins kick)
Chi — FG Gowins 21
Chi — FG Gowins 24
Chi — Allred 1 pass from Matthews (Gowins kick)
KC — Alexander 86 pass from Grbac (Stoyanovich kick)
KC — Edwards 79 fumble return (Stoyanovich kick)

MINNESOTA 17, ATLANTA 14—at Georgia Dome, attendance 69,555. In a rematch of the 1998 NFC Championship Game, the Vikings recovered 3 fumbles to defeat the Falcons. The Vikings scored their first 10 points off of fumbles by Richie Harris and Tim Dwight, and then drove 74 yards, capped by Leroy Hoard's 1-yard run, to take a 17-0 lead with 1:48 left in the first half. Chris Chandler and Chris Calloway connected four times on the ensuing five-play drive, including a 23-yard touchdown, to cut the deficit to 17-7 at halftime. Bob Christian's 1-yard run capped a 10-play drive early in the fourth quarter, and Gary Anderson missed a 30-yard field-goal attempt with 5:50 left. But Morten Andersen's 39-yard field-goal attempt sailed wide left with 3:38 to play. Randall Cunningham was 22 of 33 for 184 yards and 1 touchdown. Chandler was 17 of 30 for 258 yards and 1 touchdown.

Minnesota	0	17	0	0	—	17
Atlanta	0	7	0	7	—	14

Minn — Carter 2 pass from Cunningham (Anderson kick)
Minn — FG Anderson 36
Minn — Hoard 1 run (Anderson kick)
Atl — Calloway 23 pass from Chandler (Andersen kick)
Atl — Christian 1 run (Andersen kick)

NEW ENGLAND 30, N.Y. JETS 28—at Giants Stadium, attendance 78,227. Adam Vinatieri's 23-yard field goal with three seconds left lifted the Patriots past the Jets, which also lost Vinny Testaverde to a season-ending injury. Testaverde's 27-yard touchdown pass to Richie Anderson gave the Jets a 7-3 lead, but Lawyer Milloy's interception on the Jets' next drive led to Drew Bledsoe's 58-yard touchdown pass to Tony Simmons. On the ensuing possession, Testaverde, untouched, ruptured his Achilles tendon when he attempted to chase Curtis Martin's fumble. Tom Tupa's first pass, on the next play, was a 25-yard scoring strike to Keyshawn Johnson. Trailing 16-10 in the third quarter, Steve Israel sacked Tupa and forced him to fumble at the Jets' 11. Willie McGinest fell on the loose ball in the end zone to give the Patriots the lead. New England scored on its next two possessions to take a 27-16 lead. Tupa responded with a 5-play scoring drive, but his 2-point conversion pass to Johnson was stopped short of the end zone. Bryan Cox's 27-yard interception return with 9:34 remaining gave the Jets a 28-27 lead, but once again a completed 2-point conversion pass, this time from Rick Mirer to Eric Green, failed to reach the end zone. Chris Slade's interception at the Jets' 49 with 3:30 left set up Vinatieri's winning kick. Bledsoe was 21 of 30 for 340 yards and 1 touchdown, with 1 interception. Terry Glenn had 7 catches for 113 yards. Testaverde was 10 of 15 for 96 yards and 1 touchdown, with 1 interception. Tupa was 6 of 10 for 165 yards and 2 touchdowns, while Mirer was 4 of 11 for 28 yards, with 2 interceptions. Johnson had 8 receptions for 194 yards.

New England	3	7	17	3	—	30
N.Y. Jets	7	9	6	6	—	28

NE — FG Vinatieri 33
NYJ — Anderson 27 pass from Testaverde (Hall kick)
NE — Simmons 58 pass from Bledsoe (Vinatieri kick)
NYJ — K. Johnson 25 pass from Tupa (Hall kick)
NYJ — Safety, punt snap went out of end zone
NE — McGinest recovered fumble in end zone (Vinatieri kick)
NE — FG Vinatieri 21
NYJ — Baxter 7 pass from Tupa (pass failed)
NYJ — Cox 27 interception return (pass failed)
NE — FG Vinatieri 23

N.Y. GIANTS 17, TAMPA BAY 13—at Raymond James Stadium, attendance 65,026. Two defensive touchdowns were enough for the Giants to defeat the Buccaneers despite garnering just 4 first downs. Christian Peter's 38-yard return of Trent Dilfer's fumble gave the Giants an early lead. Late in the half, Dilfer's 39-yard pass to Bert Emanuel set up his 1-yard scoring toss to Dave Moore to give Tampa Bay a 10-7 halftime lead. Andre Weathers's 8-yard interception return for a touchdown late in the third quarter extended the Giants lead, but the Buccaneers responded with rookie Martin Gramatica's second field goal to trim the lead to 14-13. Percy Ellsworth's 5-yard interception return to the Buccaneers' 24 set up Brad Daluiso's 36-yard field goal with 12:10 remaining. Ellsworth intercepted Dilfer on Tampa Bay's next possession, and Phillippi Sparks intercepted Eric Zeier at the Buccaneers' 38 with 1:17 remaining to ice the game. Tampa Bay's defense permitted more than 20 yards on a possession just once in 15 drives as Tampa Bay outgained the Giants 254-107. Kent Graham was 12 of 23 for 91 yards. Dilfer was 15 of 31 for 174 yards and 1 touchdown, with 3 interceptions.

N.Y. Giants	7	0	7	3	—	17
Tampa Bay	0	10	3	0	—	13

NYG — Peter 38 fumble return (Daluiso kick)
TB — FG Gramatica 23
TB — Moore 1 pass from Dilfer (Gramatica kick)
NYG — Weathers 8 interception return (Daluiso kick)
TB — FG Gramatica 36
NYG — FG Daluiso 36

GREEN BAY 28, OAKLAND 24—at Lambeau Field, attendance 59,872. Brett Favre's 1-yard touchdown pass to Jeff Thomason with 11 seconds left capped an 82-yard drive in the final two minutes for the Packers. The Packers committed 3 first-half turnovers, one of which, an interception by Darrien Gordon, led to Randy Jordan's first touchdown run, gave Oakland a 10-7 halftime lead. Favre's 12-yard touchdown pass to Antonio Freeman concluded their first drive of the second half. But the Raiders scored on consecutive possessions, the first set up by K.D. Williams's 14-yard interception return to the Packers' 5, to take a 24-14 lead with 10:52 remaining. Favre, who reinjured a badly jammed thumb in the third quarter, completed 6 of 7 passes for 77 yards on the next drive, which culminated with Corey Bradford's 8-yard scoring reception, to cut the deficit to 24-21 with 7:20 to play. The Packers were forced to punt with 2:20 to play, but the Raiders failed to get a first down and punted with 1:51 remaining. Favre's 11-yard pass to Bill Schroeder on third-and-10 kept the drive going, and his 19-yard pass to Bradford at the Raiders' 1 set up the winning touchdown. Favre was 28 of 47 for 333 yards and 4 touchdowns, with 3 interceptions. Freeman had 7 catches for 111 yards. Rich Gannon was 16 of 31 for 227 yards, with 1 interception.

Oakland	3	7	7	7	—	24
Green Bay	7	0	7	14	—	28

GB — Schroeder 4 pass from Favre (Longwell kick)
Oak — FG Husted 41
Oak — Jordan 1 run (Husted kick)
GB — Freeman 12 pass from Favre (Longwell kick)
Oak — Wheatley 5 run (Husted kick)
GB — Bradford 8 pass from Favre (Longwell kick)
GB — Thomason 1 pass from Favre (Longwell kick)

JACKSONVILLE 41, SAN FRANCISCO 3—at ALLTEL Stadium, attendance 68,678. The Jaguars' defense forced 5 turnovers and recorded 4 sacks en route to scoring the game's final 41 points. In a game played in a steady downpour, the Jaguars took a 6-3 halftime lead. Mike Hollis's third field goal gave Jacksonville a 9-3 lead, and Jason Craft scooped up R.W. McQuarters's fumble on the ensuing kickoff and scampered 23 yards for a touchdown. Tony Brackens sacked Steve Young on fourth-and-1 to thwart the 49ers' next drive. The Jaguars then scored 17 points on their next three possessions, capped by James Stewart's 1-yard scoring run, to take a 34-3 lead with 9:13 remaining. Mark Brunell was 22 of 30 for 265 yards and 1 touchdown. Jimmy Smith had 6 catches for 139 yards. Steve Young was 9 of 26 for 96 yards, with 2 interceptions.

San Francisco	3	0	0	0	—	3
Jacksonville	3	3	18	17	—	41

SF — FG Richey 42
Jax — FG Hollis 41
Jax — FG Hollis 32
Jax — FG Hollis 50
Jax — Craft 23 fumble return (Brunell run)
Jax — D. Jones 4 pass from Brunell (Hollis kick)
Jax — FG Hollis 41
Jax — Stewart 1 run (Hollis kick)
Jax — Beasley 90 interception return (Hollis kick)

SUNDAY NIGHT, SEPTEMBER 12

PITTSBURGH 43, CLEVELAND 0—at Cleveland Browns Stadium, attendance 73,138. The Steelers scored more points (43) than yards allowed (40) as Cleveland lost its first game as an expansion team. In the Browns' first game since 1995, Ty Detmer completed a 13-yard pass to Leslie Shepherd on the Browns' first play, but Chris Oldham intercepted Detmer three plays later. Stewart's 1-yard scoring run five plays later was the first of eight consecutive scoring possessions for the Steelers. Four of the drives were more than 50 yards, and Richard Huntley scored 3 touchdowns. Mike Tomczak's 1-yard touchdown pass to Hines Ward gave Pittsburgh a 43-0 lead with 6:08 to play. The Steelers' defense, which recorded 3 sacks and forced 4 turnovers, did not permit a first down following the first quarter. Pittsburgh had more first downs (32-2), total yards (460-40), and time of possession (47:49-12:11). Stewart was 15 of 23 for 173 yards and 1 touchdown. Detmer was 6 of 13 for 52 yards, with 1 interception.

Pittsburgh	7	13	6	17	—	43
Cleveland	0	0	0	0	—	0

Pitt — Stewart 1 run (Brown kick)
Pitt — FG Brown 18
Pitt — Huntley 5 pass from Stewart (Brown kick)
Pitt — FG Brown 28
Pitt — Huntley 3 run (kick blocked)
Pitt — FG Brown 19
Pitt — Huntley 21 pass from Tomczak (Brown kick)
Pitt — Ward 1 pass from Tomczak (Brown kick)

MONDAY NIGHT, SEPTEMBER 13

MIAMI 38, DENVER 21—at Mile High Stadium, attendance 75,623. Dan Marino passed for 2 touchdowns as the Dolphins snapped the Broncos' 24-game home winning streak on the night John Elway's number was retired. Brian Griese's 61-yard touchdown pass to Ed McCaffrey capped the Broncos' first drive, and Denver was looking for more points but Jason Elam's 44-yard field-goal attempt early in the second quarter was blocked by Lorenzo Bromell. The Dolphins proceeded to score on their next four consecutive possessions, capped by rookie J.J. Johnson's 1-yard touchdown run to start the second half, to give Miami a 24-7 lead. After another Griese-to-McCaffrey touchdown, the Broncos forced a punt. But Zach Thomas sacked Griese at midfield on fourth-and-1 early in the fourth quarter, and Dan Marino engineered an 8-play drive, culminated by his 4-yard touchdown pass to O.J. McDuffie to give the Dolphins a 31-14 lead. Jason Taylor's 4-yard fumble return with 3:56 left ended any Denver comeback hopes. Marino was 15 of 23 for 215 yards and 2 touchdowns. Martin had 4 catches for 101 yards. Griese was 24 of 40 for 270 yards and 3 touchdowns, all to McCaffrey, who had 6 receptions for 105 yards.

Miami	0	17	7	14	—	38
Denver	7	0	7	7	—	21

Den — McCaffrey 61 pass from Griese (Elam kick)
Mia — Abdul-Jabbar 1 run (Mare kick)
Mia — Konrad 6 pass from Marino (Mare kick)
Mia — FG Mare 37
Mia — Johnson 1 run (Mare kick)
Den — McCaffrey 11 pass from Griese (Elam kick)
Mia — McDuffie 4 pass from Marino (Mare kick)
Mia — Taylor 4 fumble return (Mare kick)
Den — McCaffrey 4 pass from Griese (Elam kick)

SECOND WEEK SUMMARIES

AMERICAN FOOTBALL CONFERENCE

Eastern Division	W	L	T	Pct.	Pts.	OP
Miami	2	0	0	1.000	57	37
New England	2	0	0	1.000	61	56
Buffalo	1	1	0	.500	31	34
Indianapolis	1	1	0	.500	59	45
N.Y. Jets	0	2	0	.000	31	47
Central Division						
Jacksonville	2	0	0	1.000	63	23
Pittsburgh	2	0	0	1.000	66	20
Tennessee	2	0	0	1.000	62	44
Baltimore	0	2	0	.000	30	50
Cincinnati	0	2	0	.000	42	70
Cleveland	0	2	0	.000	9	69
Western Division						
San Diego	1	0	0	1.000	34	7
Kansas City	1	1	0	.500	43	30
Oakland	1	1	0	.500	46	45
Seattle	1	1	0	.500	34	41
Denver	0	2	0	.000	31	64

NATIONAL FOOTBALL CONFERENCE

Eastern Division	W	L	T	Pct.	Pts.	OP
Dallas	2	0	0	1.000	65	42
Arizona	1	1	0	.500	41	43
N.Y. Giants	1	1	0	.500	38	63
Washington	1	1	0	.500	85	62
Philadelphia	0	2	0	.000	29	44
Central Division						
Detroit	2	0	0	1.000	51	35
Chicago	1	1	0	.500	33	31
Green Bay	1	1	0	.500	43	47
Minnesota	1	1	0	.500	34	36
Tampa Bay	1	1	0	.500	32	22
Western Division						
St. Louis	1	0	0	1.000	27	10
New Orleans	1	1	0	.500	40	38
San Francisco	1	1	0	.500	31	62
Atlanta	0	2	0	.000	21	41
Carolina	0	2	0	.000	30	41

SUNDAY, SEPTEMBER 19

MIAMI 19, ARIZONA 16—at Pro Player Stadium, attendance 73,618. Olindo Mare's fourth field goal, which was set up by the Dolphins' fourth interception, lifted Miami to victory. The Dolphins led 6-0 in the second quarter before Chris Jacke's 36-yard field goal culminated a 14-play drive. Brock Marion fumbled the ensuing kickoff for Miami, and Joel Makovicka recovered to set up Jacke's second field goal. Rob Fredrickson then intercepted a Dan Marino pass on the next play from scrimmge and returned it 34 yards for a touchdown to give the Cardinals 13 points in a 1-minute, 34-second span. Marino worked the two-minute drill to perfection, capped by his 10-yard touchdown pass to Troy Drayton to tie the game at halftime. Andre Wadsworth's 23-yard interception return led to Jacke's third field goal, but Marion returned the ensuing kickoff 50 yards and Mare tied the game with a 48-yard field goal. Sam Madison's interception on the next play from scrimmage led to Mare's winning boot. Jacke missed a 32-yard field-goal attempt early in the fourth quarter, and Jake Plummer was intercepted twice in the final 10 minutes as Miami withheld the Cardinals' comeback efforts. Marino was 21 of 35 for 221 yards and 1 touchdown, with 2 interceptions. Plummer was 11 of 27 for 112 yards, with 4 interceptions.

Arizona	0	13	3	0	—	16
Miami	3	10	6	0	—	19

Mia — FG Mare 39
Mia — FG Mare 51
Ariz — FG Jacke 36
Ariz — FG Jacke 44
Ariz — Fredrickson 34 interception return (Jacke kick)
Mia — Drayton 10 pass from Marino (Mare kick)
Ariz — FG Jacke 38
Mia — FG Mare 48
Mia — FG Mare 44

TENNESSEE 26, CLEVELAND 9—at Adelphia Coliseum, attendance 65,904. Eddie George carried 31 times for 97 yards and 2 touchdowns as the Titans defeated the Browns. Eddie Robinson sacked rookie Tim Couch, making his first career start, for a safety late in the first quarter. George's 1-yard run capped the ensuing 12-play drive. The Browns, aided by a 15-yard facemask penalty, drove 10 yards to set up Phil Dawson's 41-yard field goal with 6:50 left in the half for the Browns' first points of the season. Tennessee answered with George's second 1-yard scoring run of the half to take a 16-3 lead. Another 12-play Titans' drive was capped by Al Del Greco's 35-yard field goal, but Cleveland scored its first touchdown on Couch's 39-yard bomb to Kevin Johnson with 2:51 left in the third quarter. Neil O'Donnell, starting for the injured Steve McNair, capped a 14-play drive with a 14-yard touchdown pass to Yancey Thigpen with 9:52 remaining. The Browns drove to the Titans' 11 in the final seconds, but Couch fumbled and Mike Jones recovered. The Titans had more first downs (24-12), total yards (412-173), and time of possession (41:20-18:40). O'Donnell was 31 of 40 for 310 yards and 1 touchdown. Couch was 12 of 24 for 134 yards, with 1 interception.

Cleveland	0	3	6	0	—	9
Tennessee	2	14	3	7	—	26

Tenn — Safety, E. Robinson sacked Couch in end zone
Tenn — George 1 run (Del Greco kick)
Cle — FG Dawson 41
Tenn — George 1 run (Del Greco kick)
Tenn — FG Del Greco 35
Cle — K. Johnson 39 pass from Couch (pass failed)
Tenn — Thigpen 14 pass from O'Donnell (Del Greco kick)

KANSAS CITY 26, DENVER 10—at Arrowhead Stadium, attendance 78,683. Kimble Anders rushed for 142 yards, Pete Stoyanovich kicked 4 field goals, and the Chiefs' defense forced 4 turnovers to give Gunther Cunningham his first victory. Stoyanovich kicked 2 field goals in the final three minutes of the first half to give the Chiefs a 6-3 halftime lead. Terrell Davis fumbled early in the second half, and Elvis Grbac completed a 49-yard pass to Derrick Alexander on the next play to set up Tony Richardson's 1-yard touchdown run. Brian Griese fumbled two plays later, and Derrick Thomas recovered at the Broncos' 27. Stoyanovich's 44-yard field goal four plays later gave the Chiefs a 16-3 lead. Trevor Pryce's interception at the Chiefs' 34 led to Davis's touchdown on the first play of the fourth quarter, but the Chiefs responded with a 66-yard drive, capped by Byron (Bam) Morris's 5-yard scoring run. Bubby Brister replaced Griese, but Eric Warfield's interception set up Stoyanovich's final field goal with 2:14 left. Anders injured his knee on the final drive and was placed on injured reserve. Grbac was 15 of 20 for 179 yards, with 1 interception. Alexander had 6 catches for 117 yards. Griese was 11 of 16 for 107 yards, with 1 interception, while Brister was 9 of 15 for 65 yards, with 1 interception.

Denver	0	3	0	7	—	10
Kansas City	0	6	10	10	—	26

Den — FG Elam 50
KC — FG Stoyanovich 19
KC — FG Stoyanovich 42
KC — Richardson 1 run (Stoyanovich kick)
KC — FG Stoyanovich 44
Den — Davis 1 run (Elam kick)
KC — Morris 5 run (Stoyanovich kick)
KC — FG Stoyanovich 27

DETROIT 23, GREEN BAY 15—at Pontiac Silverdome, attendance 76,202. Charlie Batch passed for 2 touchdowns and ran for another as the Lions defeated the Packers for the sixth time in the last seven games played between the two teams in Pontiac. Batch completed 45- and 74-yard touchdown passes early in the second quarter to stake the Lions to a 14-3 lead. Trailing 14-6 late in the third quarter, the Packers reached the Lions' 4. However, Brett Favre fumbled and Andre Collins recovered. However, Green Bay did get two points out of the series when, three plays later, Allen Aldridge's snap sailed over punter John Jett's head through the end zone for a safety. The Packers scored five plays after the ensuing free kick to take a 15-14 lead with 12:25 remaining. Terry Fair returned the ensuing kickoff 91 yards to set up Batch's 1-yard touchdown run, and Jason Hanson's field goal on the next possession gave Detroit a 23-15 lead with 2:46 left. The Packers reached the Lions' 27, but Favre's fourth-down pass fell incomplete. Batch was 9 of 16 for 219 yards and 2 touchdowns, with 2 interceptions. Johnnie Morton had 4 receptions for 118 yards. Favre was 20 of 41 for 288 yards, with 1 interception.

Green Bay	3	3	0	9	—	15
Detroit	0	14	0	9	—	23

GB — FG Longwell 45
Det — Morton 45 pass from Batch (Hanson kick)
Det — Sloan 74 pass from Batch (Hanson kick)
GB — FG Longwell 24
GB — Safety, snap out of end zone
GB — Levens 2 run (Longwell kick)
Det — Batch 1 run (pass failed)
Det — FG Hanson 48

NEW ENGLAND 31, INDIANAPOLIS 28—at Foxboro Stadium, attendance 59,640. Adam Vinatieri's 26-yard field goal with 35 seconds remaining capped the Patriots' 21-point comeback to defeat the Colts. The Colts scored on four of their last five possessions of the first half, three times on touchdown passes from Peyton Manning to Marvin Harrison. The Patriots didn't put together a sustained drive until their third possession of the second half, when Drew Bledsoe's 8-yard touchdown pass to Terry Allen with 4:35 left in the third quarter completed a 10-play, 81-yard drive. Ty Law forced and recovered Marcus Pollard's fumble at the Patriots' 42 early in the fourth quarter. Bledsoe completed a 3-yard touchdown pass to Ben Coates eight plays later to cut the lead to 28-21. On their next possession, Bledsoe's 10-yard touchdown pass to Coates capped a 10-play, 78-yard drive to tie the game with 3:03 remaining. Tedy Brushci forced Edgerrin James to fumble four plays later, and Brandon Mitchell recovered at the Colts' 37, which set up Vinatieri's winning kick. Bledsoe was 27 of 45 for 299 yards and 4 touchdowns. Terry Glenn had 7 catches for 122 yards. Manning was 18 of 30 for 223 yards and 3 touchdowns, with 2 interceptions. Harrison had 7 catches for 105 yards, and James rushed 32 times for 118 yards.

Indianapolis	14	14	0	0	—	28
New England	0	7	7	17	—	31

Ind — Harrison 42 pass from Manning (Vanderjagt kick)
Ind — Harrison 10 pass from Manning (Vanderjagt kick)
Ind — James 1 run (Vanderjagt kick)
NE — Jefferson 11 pass from Bledsoe (Vinatieri kick)
Ind — Harrison 8 pass from Manning (Vanderjagt kick)
NE — Allen 8 pass from Bledsoe (Vanderjagt kick)
NE — Coates 3 pass from Bledsoe (Vinatieri kick)
NE — Coates 10 pass from Bledsoe (Vinatieri kick)
NE — FG Vinatieri 26

JACKSONVILLE 22, CAROLINA 20—at Ericsson Stadium, attendance 64,261. James Stewart replaced an injured Fred Taylor and rushed for 124 yards and 2 second-half touchdowns to give the Jaguars a comeback victory. The Jaguars had drives of 69 and 70 yards in the first half, but settled for 2 Mike Hollis field goals. Carolina, meanwhile, put together a sustained 71-yard drive, which led to Steve Beuerlein's 10-yard touchdown pass to Wesley Walls, and a big play, Beuerlein's 60-yard touchdown pass to Muhsin Muhammad, to give the Panthers a 14-6 halftime lead. The Jaguars drove 79 yards in 15 plays to cut the lead to 14-12 on Stewart's 1-yard run. Fernando Bryant's interception at the Jaguars' 2 stifled a Carolina drive. However, the Jaguars drove the length of the field, only to have Kevin Greene recover Mark Brunell's fumble at the Panthers' 5 with 13:20 to play. Mike Hollis made a 31-yard field goal on the Jaguars' next possession to give Jacksonville a 15-14 lead, and Stewart scampered 44 yards with 1:48 remaining on the Jaguars' first play after stopping Carolina on downs to take a 22-14 lead. Beuerlein drove the Panthers 70 yards, capped by his 1-yard touchdown pass to Wesley Walls with 31 seconds left, but Lonnie Marts broke up Beuerlein's 2-point conversion pass intended for Walls.

Jacksonville	3	3	6	10	—	22
Carolina	0	14	0	6	—	20

Jax — FG Hollis 36
Jax — FG Hollis 40
Car — Walls 10 pass from Beuerlein (Kasay kick)
Car — Muhammad 60 pass from Beuerlein (Kasay kick)
Jax — Stewart 1 run (pass failed)
Jax — FG Hollis 31
Jax — Stewart 44 run (Hollis kick)
Car — Walls 1 pass from Beuerlein (pass failed)

SAN FRANCISCO 28, NEW ORLEANS 21—at 3Com Park, attendance 67,685. Lance Schulters's 64-yard interception return with 1:31 to play gave the 49ers a come-from-behind victory and improved coach Steve Mariucci's career home record to 17-0. The 49ers had an opportunity to take the lead just before halftime, but Ashley Ambrose's interception at the 49ers' 14 kept the game tied 14-14. The Saints drove 79 yards with the second half's opening possession, capped by Billy Joe Hobert's 12-yard scoring pass to Lawrence Dawsey. The 49ers reached the Saints' 3, but on fourth-and-goal from the 2-yard line Tommy Vardell was dropped for a 2-yard loss with 8:25 left. Steve Young engineered a 62-yard drive that culminated with his 4-yard touchdown pass to Terrell Owens with 2:03 remaining to tie the game. Two plays later, Schulters intercepted Hobert's pass over the middle and scampered down the left sideline for the go-ahead score. Ricky Williams was stopped near midfield, 7 yards shy of a first down, on a fourth-and-15 pass play to secure the 49ers' victory. Young was 23 of 35 for 258 yards and 2 touchdowns, with 1 interception. Hobert was 20 of 37 for 223 yards and 3 touchdowns, with 2 interceptions.

New Orleans	0	14	7	0	—	21
San Francisco	7	7	0	14	—	28

SF — Owens 5 pass from Young (Richey kick)
NO — Kennison 2 pass from Hobert (Brien kick)
NO — Poole 58 pass from Hobert (Brien kick)
SF — Vardell 1 run (Richey kick)
NO — Dawsey 12 pass from Hobert (Brien kick)
SF — Owens 4 pass from Young (Richey kick)
SF — Schulters 64 interception return (Richey kick)

OAKLAND 22, MINNESOTA 17—at Metrodome, attendance 64,080. Rich Gannon passed for 1 touchdown and ran for another as the ex-Vikings' quarterback guided the Raiders to victory. The Vikings drove into Raiders' territory on each of their first five possessions, but scored just 10 points because of 2 missed field goals and Randall Cunningham's fumble at the Raiders' 25. Oakland scored on five of their six drives during the second and third quarters, highlighted by Russell Maryland's interception that led to a field goal, and capped by Gannon's 5-yard run with 1:08 remaining in the quarter that gave the Raiders a 22-10 lead. The Vikings responded with an 80-yard scoring drive with Jake Reed's 28-yard touchdown catch still leaving 14:06 on the clock. But the Vikings were stopped on downs at the Raiders' 39 with 7:07 left, and Minnesota failed to get into Oakland territory on its final two possessions. Gannon was 21 of 33 for 248 yards and 1 touchdown. Cunningham was 23 of 39 for 364 yards and 2 touchdowns, with 2 interceptions. Jake Reed had 5 catches for 100 yards.

Oakland	0	6	16	0	—	22
Minnesota	7	3	0	7	—	17

Minn — Crumpler 31 pass from Cunningham (Anderson kick)
Oak — FG Husted 36
Minn — FG Anderson 37
Oak — FG Husted 37
Oak — Jett 9 pass from Gannon (Husted kick)
Oak — FG Husted 42
Oak — Gannon 5 run (pass failed)
Minn — Reed 28 pass from Cunningham (Anderson kick)

PITTSBURGH 23, BALTIMORE 20—at PSINet Stadium, attendance 68,956. Kris Brown's 36-yard field goal as time expired lifted the Steelers to victory against division rival Baltimore. Dewayne Washington's interception at the Ravens' 35 led to Kordell Stewart's 8-yard run less than five minutes into the game, and Richard Huntley's 17-yard scoring run with 1:46 remaining in the half gave the Steelers a 14-7 lead. Corey Harris's 63-yard kickoff return set up Matt Stover's 45-yard field goal just before halftime. Levon Kirkland's fumble recovery at the Ravens' 24 led to Brown's first field goal, and his second field goal, with 2:29 to play, increased Pittsburgh's lead to 23-20. Stoney Case, who had relieved Scott Mitchell in the third quarter, engineered a 6-play, 72-yard drive, capped by Qadry Ismail's 19-yard touchdown catch, to tie the game with 1:22 left. Will Blackwell returned the ensuing kickoff 37 yards to midfield, and Stewart completed 2 passes to set up Brown's winning kick. Stewart was 18 of 27 for 138 yards. Mitchell was 7 of 16 for 48 yards, with 2 interceptions, while Case was 7 of 15 for 130 yards and 1 touchdown. Errict Rhett rushed 22 times for 101 yards.

Pittsburgh	7	7	3	6	—	23
Baltimore	7	3	0	10	—	20

Pitt — Stewart 8 run (Brown kick)
Balt — Rhett 2 run (Stover kick)
Pitt — Huntley 17 run (Brown kick)
Balt — FG Stover 45
Pitt — FG Brown 32
Balt — FG Stover 28
Pitt — FG Brown 28
Balt — Ismail 19 pass from Case (Stover kick)
Pitt — FG Brown 36

SAN DIEGO 34, CINCINNATI 7—at Cinergy Field, attendance 47,660. After giving up a touchdown on the game's opening drive, the Chargers scored the game's last 34 points to defeat the Bengals. Fumble recoveries by Junior Seau and Scott Turner led to 10 of the Chargers' 13 points in the first quarter to take a 13-7 lead. Jim Harbaugh's 29-yard pass to Jeff Graham gave the Chargers a 20-7 lead with 2:08 left in the first half. The Bengals drove to their own 45, but Junior Seau sacked Jeff Blake and forced him to fumble. Gerald Dixon returned the fumble 27 yards for a 28-7 halftime lead. The Chargers' defense permitted just 8 total yards in the second half on 18 plays. Harbaugh was 15 of 26 for 164 yards and 2 touchdowns. Blake was 7 of 16 for 68 yards and 1 touchdown. Rookie Akili Smith made his debut after Seau's sack, and was 10 of 17 for 100 yards, with 1 interception.

San Diego	13	15	3	3	—	34
Cincinnati	7	0	0	0	—	7

Cin — McGee 12 pass from Blake (Pelfrey kick)
SD — FG Carney 27
SD — FG Carney 23
SD — Means 12 pass from Harbaugh (Carney kick)
SD — Graham 29 pass from Harbaugh (Carney kick)
SD — Dixon 27 fumble return (Ricks pass from Harbaugh)
SD — FG Carney 21
SD — FG Carney 42

SEATTLE 14, CHICAGO 13—at Soldier Field, attendance 66,944. Glenn Foley, who started in place of injured Jon Kitna, completed 2 fourth-quarter touchdown passes to give the Seahawks a come-from-behind victory in Chicago. The Seahawks got no closer than the Bears' 37 in the first half. The Bears, meanwhile, were deep into Seahawks' territory four times, but a missed field goal and a lost fumble by Curtis Enis at the Seahawks' 5 kept the score just 10-0 at halftime. Foley fumbled at the Bears' 7 early in the third quarter, and Brian Gowins's second field goal gave Chicago a 13-0 lead. Foley led the Seahawks on 80- and 85-yard touchdown drives, capped by his 49-yard touchdown pass to Fabien Bownes with 7:51 remaining, to give Seattle a 14-13 lead. The Bears regained possession at their own 25 with 2:44 left and successfully converted 2 fourth-down situations to reach the Seahawks' 30 with eight seconds left, but Gowins's 48-yard field-goal attempt sailed wide right. Foley was 18 of 30 for 283 yards and 2 touchdowns. Derrick Mayes had 7 catches for 137 yards. Shane Matthews was 22 of 42 for 212 yards.

Seattle	0	0	0	14	—	14
Chicago	0	10	3	0	—	13

Chi — Enis 2 run (Gowins kick)
Chi — FG Gowins 29
Chi — FG Gowins 43
Sea — Mayes 34 pass from Foley (Peterson kick)
Sea — Bownes 49 pass from Foley (Peterson kick)

TAMPA BAY 19, PHILADELPHIA 5—at Veterans Stadium, attendance 64,285. Trent Dilfer passed for 2 touchdowns, and the Buccaneers' defense permitted just 9 first downs and recorded 9 sacks as Tampa Bay defeated the Eagles. The Buccaneers scored on three of their first five possessions to take a 13-5 lead. The Eagles reached the Buccaneers' 9 just before halftime, but Norm Johnson missed a 26-yard field-goal attempt as the half expired. A 29-yard run by Warrick Dunn sparked the Buccaneers' first possession of the second half, setting up Dilfer's 17-yard touchdown pass to Mike Alstott. The Eagles managed just 1 first down on their final six possessions. Dilfer was 7 of 14 for 89 yards and 2 touchdowns, with 2 interceptions. Doug Pederson was 12 of 19 for 100 yards, with 1 interception, and rookie Donovan McNabb was 4 of 11 for 26 yards in his debut.

Tampa Bay	7	6	6	0	—	19
Philadelphia	5	0	0	0	—	5

TB — Emanuel 19 pass from Dilfer (Gramatica kick)
Phil — FG N. Johnson 39
Phil — Safety, snap went out of end zone
TB — FG Gramatica 51
TB — FG Gramatica 24
TB — Alstott 17 pass from Dilfer (run failed)

WASHINGTON 50, N.Y. GIANTS 21—at Giants Stadium, attendance 78,717. Stephen Davis rushed for 126 yards and 3 touchdowns as the Giants allowed their highest point total since 1966. Davis's touchdown runs capped 68-, 88-, and 54-yard drives on the Redskins' first three possessions to give Washington a 21-0 lead. Trailing 21-7, the Giants reached the Redskins' 25, but Shawn Barber intercepted Kent Graham's pass and returned it 70 yards for a touchdown. The Giants needed just two plays to score to cut the lead to 27-14 with 2:16 left in the half, but the Redskins drove 80 yards and scored on Brad Johnson's 1-yard touchdown pass to Stephen Alexander to give the Redskins a 33-14 halftime lead. Washington scored on three of its first four second-half possessions to take a 50-14 lead with 11:13 to play. Johnson was 20 of 28 for 231 yards and 3 touchdowns. Graham was 20 of 31 for 268 yards and 1 touchdown, with 1 interception. Ike Hilliard had 8 catches for 114 yards, while Amani Toomer had 5 receptions for 105 yards.

Washington	21	12	10	7	—	50
N.Y. Giants	0	14	0	7	—	21

Wash — Davis 1 run (Conway kick)
Wash — Davis 1 run (Conway kick)
Wash — Davis 19 run (Conway kick)
NYG — Way 7 run (Daluiso kick)
Wash — Barber 70 interception return (kick blocked)
NYG — L. Johnson 11 run (Daluiso kick)
Wash — Alexander 1 pass from Johnson (run failed)
Wash — FG Conway 48
Wash — Westbrook 15 pass from Johnson (Conway kick)
Wash — Alexander 27 pass from Johnson (Conway kick)
NYG — Hilliard 7 pass from Graham (Daluiso kick)

SUNDAY NIGHT, SEPTEMBER 19

BUFFALO 17, N.Y. JETS 3—at Ralph Wilson Stadium, attendance 68,839. Doug Flutie passed for 160 yards and ran for a touchdown as the Bills' defense permitted just 190 total yards to defeat the Jets. After Steve Christie's second missed field goal of the first half, the Jets drove to the Bills' 1, but Jerald Sowell was stopped on fourth-and-goal. The Bills' offense responded with a 12-play, 99-yard drive, capped by Antowain Smith's 1-yard touchdown run just 39 seconds before halftime. Flutie's 24-yard run on Buffalo's next possession gave the Bills a 14-0 lead. Rick Mirer completed 4 of 6 passes on the ensuing drive to set up John Hall's field goal, but the Jets failed to drive beyond their own 34-yard line in any of their remaining three possessions. The Bills outgained the Jets 224-74 on the ground, and owned a 36:24-23:36 edge in time of possession. Flutie was 15 of 25 for 160 yards. Smith carried 30 times for 113 yards. Mirer was 13 of 28 for 121 yards.

N.Y. Jets	0	0	3	0	—	3
Buffalo	0	7	7	3	—	17

Buff — A. Smith 1 run (Christie kick)
Buff — Flutie 24 run (Christie kick)
NYJ — FG Hall 31
Buff — FG Christie 35

MONDAY NIGHT, SEPTEMBER 20

DALLAS 24, ATLANTA 7—at Texas Stadium, attendance 63,663. Emmitt Smith rushed for 109 yards and 2 touchdowns and passed Tony Dorsett's career rushing total to become the NFL's fourth all-time leading rusher as the Cowboys defeated the Falcons. Trailing 3-0, the Falcons' Jamal Anderson suffered a season-ending knee injury midway through the first quarter. Dallas led 10-0 in the third quarter when Alonzo Spellman recovered Tony Graziani's fumble at the Falcons' 26, setting up Smith's second touchdown run. The Falcons gained some momentum in the fourth quarter when Ray Buchanan's end-zone interception stifled a Cowboys' drive and Danny Kanell replaced Graziani and completed a 45-yard touchdown pass to Tim Dwight to cut the lead to 17-7 with 4:00 left. The Falcons drove to the Cowboys' 4 on their next possession, but Greg Ellis intercepted Kanell's short pass and rumbled 87 yards with 46 seconds left. Troy Aikman was 10 of 22 for 109 yards, with 2 interceptions. Graziani, who started in place of injured Chris Chandler, was 7 of 16 for 90 yards, with 1 interception, and Kanell was 9 of 22 for 172 yards and 1 touchdown, with 2 interceptions. Without Anderson's presence, the Cowboys' recorded 5 sacks with constant blitzes.

Atlanta	0	0	0	7	—	7
Dallas	10	0	7	7	—	24

Dall — FG Cunningham 23
Dall — E. Smith 2 run (Cunningham kick)
Dall — E. Smith 7 run (Cunningham kick)
Atl — Dwight 45 pass from Kanell (Andersen kick)
Dall — Ellis 87 interception return (Cunningham kick)

THIRD WEEK SUMMARIES

AMERICAN FOOTBALL CONFERENCE

Eastern Division	W	L	T	Pct.	Pts.	OP
New England	3	0	0	1.000	77	70
Miami	2	0	0	1.000	57	37
Buffalo	2	1	0	.667	57	34
Indianapolis	2	1	0	.667	86	64
N.Y. Jets	0	3	0	.000	51	74
Central Division						
Tennessee	3	0	0	1.000	82	63
Jacksonville	2	1	0	.667	82	43
Pittsburgh	2	1	0	.667	76	49
Baltimore	1	2	0	.333	47	60
Cincinnati	0	3	0	.000	45	97
Cleveland	0	3	0	.000	19	86
Western Division						
Kansas City	2	1	0	.667	74	51
Oakland	2	1	0	.667	70	62
Seattle	2	1	0	.667	63	51
San Diego	1	1	0	.500	53	34
Denver	0	3	0	.000	41	77

NATIONAL FOOTBALL CONFERENCE

Eastern Division	W	L	T	Pct.	Pts.	OP
Dallas	2	0	0	1.000	65	42
Washington	2	1	0	.667	112	82
Arizona	1	2	0	.333	51	67
N.Y. Giants	1	2	0	.333	52	79
Philadelphia	0	3	0	.000	29	70
Central Division						
Detroit	2	1	0	.667	72	66
Green Bay	2	1	0	.667	66	67
Tampa Bay	2	1	0	.667	45	32
Chicago	1	2	0	.333	50	55
Minnesota	1	2	0	.333	54	59
Western Division						
St. Louis	2	0	0	1.000	62	17
San Francisco	2	1	0	.667	55	72
New Orleans	1	1	0	.500	40	38
Carolina	1	2	0	.333	57	44
Atlanta	0	3	0	.000	28	76

SUNDAY, SEPTEMBER 26

ST. LOUIS 35, ATLANTA 7—at Trans World Dome, attendance 63,253. Kurt Warner passed for 3 touchdowns and ran for another as the Rams won their first divisional game since 1997. The Rams scored on their first four possessions, on drives of 80, 78, 46, and 80 yards, to take a 28-0 lead with 6:35 remaining in the first half. The Falcons' lone drive inside the Rams' 40, on their first possession of the second half, led to their only touchdown to cut the lead to 28-7. Warner's 5-yard run on the ensuing drive finished the scoring. The Rams outgained the Falcons 442-233. Warner was 17 of 25 for 275 yards and 3 touchdowns. Marshall Faulk rushed 17 times for 105 yards. Chris Chandler was 5 of 9 for 28 yards, with 1 interception, before reaggravating his hamstring injury. Tony Graziani was 14 of 22 for 152 yards and 1 touchdown.

Atlanta	0	0	7	0	—	7
St. Louis	7	21	7	0	—	35

StL — Holcombe 1 run (Wilkins kick)
StL — Holt 38 pass from Warner (Wilkins kick)
StL — Bruce 46 pass from Warner (Wilkins kick)
StL — Faulk 17 pass from Warner (Wilkins kick)
Atl — Kozlowski 1 pass from Graziani (Andersen kick)
StL — Warner 5 run (Wilkins kick)

OAKLAND 24, CHICAGO 17—at Network Associates Coliseum, attendance 64,328. Tyrone Wheatley's 8-yard scoring run midway through the fourth quarter propelled the Raiders to victory despite committing 5 turnovers. The Raiders led 14-10 at halftime, but both teams missed numerous opportunities to increase their point total: the Bears drove inside the Raiders' 30 four times, but had a missed field goal and an interception thwart two drives; the Raiders drove inside the Bears' 40 four times, but lost two fumbles. Rosevelt Colvin's fumble recovery at the Raiders' 35 set up Shan Matthews's 16-yard touchdown pass to Curtis Enis in the third quarter to give the Bears a 17-14 lead. After Jeff Jaeger missed a 46-yard field-goal attempt moments later that would've extended the Bears' lead, Michael Husted tied the game with a 47-yard field goal with 13:13 left. Wheatley's scoring run on the Raiders' next drive gave Oakland a 24-17 lead, and the Bears failed to gain a first down in their final two possessions. Rich Gannon was 26 of 35 for 295 yards and 2 touchdowns, and rushed for a team-high 47 yards. Tim Brown had 9 catches for 121 yards. Matthews was 20 of 30 for 178 yards and 2 touchdowns, with 1 interception.

Chicago	7	3	7	0	—	17
Oakland	7	7	0	10	—	24

Oak — Brown 20 pass from Gannon (Husted kick)
Chi — Conway 11 pass from Matthews (Jaeger kick)
Chi — FG Jaeger 52
Oak — Dudley 13 pass from Gannon (Husted kick)
Chi — Enis 16 pass from Matthews (Jaeger kick)
Oak — FG Husted 47
Oak — Wheatley 8 run (Husted kick)

CAROLINA 27, CINCINNATI 3—at Ericsson Stadium, attendance 61,269. Tim Biakabutuka became just the third player since 1970 to have 2 touchdown runs of at least 60 yards in the same game, leading the Panthers to victory. Biakabutuka's 62-yard run, on the Panthers' first play from scrimmage, came after the first of three missed field goals by Doug Pelfrey. Damien Richardson's 27-yard interception return set up John Kasay's first field goal, and his second one as the half ended followed Pelfrey's second miss and gave the Panthers a 13-0 halftime lead. A fumble recovery by Artrell Hawkins at the Panthers' 26 led to Pelfrey's 39-yard field goal midway through the third quarter, cutting the deficit to 13-3. However, Biakabutuka's 67-yard jaunt, in which he swept left before cutting back to reverse field, came two plays later to destroy the Bengals' hopes. Steve Beuerlein was 17 of 23 for 204 yards and 1 touchdown. Muhsin Muhammad had 8 catches for 117 yards. Biakabutuka, who split time with Fred Lane, had 8 carries for 132 yards. Jeff Blake was 24 of 43 for 251 yards, with 1 interception. Corey Dillon carried 20 times for 113 yards.

Cincinnati	0	0	3	0	—	3
Carolina	10	3	7	7	—	27

Car — Biakabutuka 62 run (Kasay kick)
Car — FG Kasay 48
Car — FG Kasay 21
Cin — FG Pelfrey 39
Car — Biakabutuka 67 run (Kasay kick)
Car — Walls 4 pass from Beuerlein (Kasay kick)

BALTIMORE 17, CLEVELAND 10—at PSINet Stadium, attendance 68,803. Stoney Case, in his first start for the Ravens, scored on 2 short touchdown runs to give Baltimore a victory against the Browns. The Ravens led 3-0 when Tim Couch was sacked by Peter Boulware, fumbled, and Michael McCrary recovered at the Browns' 1. Case scored two plays later to give the Ravens a 10-0 halftime lead. After Rahim Abdullah's interception at the Ravens' 33 set up Phil Dawson's 49-yard field goal to cut the lead to 10-3, both teams used big plays, Case's 45-yard pass to Qadry Ismail and Couch's 61-yard pass to Terry Kirby, to set up touchdowns. Trailing 17-10 with 2:18 left, Chris McAlister intercepted Couch's long pass at the Ravens' 29 to secure coach Brian Billick's first victory. Case was 12 of 25 for 165 yards, with 3 interceptions. Errict Rhett carried 22 times for 113 yards. Couch was 13 of 32 for 123 yards and 1 touchdown, with 1 interception.

Cleveland	0	0	3	7	—	10
Baltimore	3	7	7	0	—	17

Balt — FG Stover 44
Balt — Case 1 run (Stover kick)
Cle — FG Dawson 49
Balt — Case 1 run (Stover kick)
Cle — K. Johnson 12 pass from Couch (Dawson kick)

TAMPA BAY 13, DENVER 10—at Raymond James Stadium, attendance 65,297. The Buccaneers' defense limited Denver to 8 first downs and 173 total yards. Mike Alstott's 28-yard touchdown run capped the Buccaneers' game-opening 78-yard drive. Chris Watson recovered Jacquez Green's muffed punt at the Buccaneers' 12 late in the first quarter, setting up Brian Griese's game-tying touchdown pass to Ed McCaffrey. The Buccaneers' responded with 2 second-quarter field goals, the second coming after Hardy Nickerson's 18-yard interception return to the Broncos' 33. Denver failed to penetrate Buccaneers' territory again until the fourth quarter, when Jason Elam kicked a 44-yard field goal to cut the lead to 13-10. The Broncos punted on fourth-and-7 from the Buccaneers' 35 with 5:51 left, and Denver failed to cross midfield in its final two possessions. Trent Dilfer was 15 of 18 for 135 yards. Alstott carried 25 times for 131 yards. Griese was 14 of 28 for 132 yards and 1 touchdown, with 1 interception.

Denver	7	0	0	3	—	10
Tampa Bay	7	6	0	0	—	13

TB — Alstott 28 run (Gramatica kick)
Den — McCaffrey 12 pass from Griese (Elam kick)
TB — FG Gramatica 38
TB — FG Gramatica 35
Den — FG Elam 44

KANSAS CITY 31, DETROIT 21—at Arrowhead Stadium, attendance 78,384. Elvis Grbac passed for 235 yards and 2 touchdowns to hand Detroit its first loss. Donnell Bennett's 44-yard run set up Rashaan Shehee's 6-yard scoring jaunt to break a 7-7 tie with 4:18 left in the half. The Chiefs then executed the 2-minute drill, which resulted in Pete Stoyanovich's 51-yard field goal just before halftime. Tamarick Vanover's 17-yard punt return and Grbac's third-down completion to Derrick Alexander set up Grbac's 25-yard touchdown pass to Joe Horn to give the Chiefs a 24-7 lead. The Lions immediately cut the deficit to 24-13 and got the ball back after a punt, but Cris Dishman intercepted Charlie Batch's tipped pass and returned the ball 25 yards to the Lions' 23 to set up Bennett's game-clinching 7-yard run with 10:38 left. Grbac was 20 of 29 for 235 yards and 2 touchdowns. Batch was 16 of 34 for 213 yards and 2 touchdowns, with 2 interceptions.

Detroit	0	7	6	8	—	21
Kansas City	7	10	7	7	—	31

KC — Gonzalez 15 pass from Grbac (Stoyanovich kick)
Det — Irvin 16 run (Hanson kick)
KC — Shehee 6 run (Stoyanovich kick)
KC — FG Stoyanovich 51
KC — Horn 25 pass from Grbac (Stoyanovich kick)
Det — Rasby 3 pass from Batch (pass failed)
KC — Bennett 7 run (Stoyanovich kick)
Det — Rivers 31 pass from Batch (Stablein pass from Batch)

INDIANAPOLIS 27, SAN DIEGO 19—at Qualcomm Stadium, attendance 56,942. Peyton Manning passed for 2 touchdowns and a club-record 404 yards as the Colts snapped a 10-game road losing streak. The Colts outgained the Chargers 279-129 in the first half, yet trailed at halftime 16-10 because of: Mike Vanderjagt making just 1 of 3 field-goal attempts; Brad Benta blocking Hunter Smith's punt and Darryll Lewis recovered it in the end zone for a touchdown; and late in the half, Larry Moore's Shotgun formation snap sailing past Manning out of the end zone for a safety. The Chargers led 19-13 entering the fourth quarter, but Manning engineered an 8-play, 83-yard drive, capped by his 12-yard scrambling scoring run with 11:41 left, and a 10-play, 69-yard drive that culminated with his 26-yard touchdown pass to Terrence Wilkins with 2:34 remaining. Tyrone Poole intercepted Jim Harbaugh-'s pass at the Colts' 7 as time expired to perserve the victory. Manning was 29 of 54 for 404 yards and 2 touchdowns, with 1 interception. Marvin Harrison had 13 catches for 196 yards. Harbaugh was 15 of 37 for 188 yards, with 1 interception.

Indianapolis	10	0	3	14	—	27
San Diego	0	16	3	0	—	19

Ind — FG Vanderjagt 35
Ind — Harrison 33 pass from Manning (Vanderjagt kick)
SD — Means 1 run (Carney kick)
SD — Lewis recovered blocked punt in end zone (Carney kick)
SD — Safety, ball snapped out of end zone
SD — FG Carney 50
Ind — FG Vanderjagt 42
Ind — Manning 12 run (Vanderjagt kick)
Ind — Wilkins 26 pass from Manning (Vanderjagt kick)

GREEN BAY 23, MINNESOTA 20—at Lambeau Field, attendance 59,868. Brett Favre's fourth-down 23-yard touchdown pass to Corey Bradford with 12 seconds left lifted the Packers past the Vikings. The Packers' offense struggled in the first half, but Antwan Edwards's 26-yard interception return helped forge a 10-10 halftime score. The clubs exchanged field goals to open the second half. Favre passed for 55 yards on a 68-yard drive to set up Ryan Longwell's 34-yard field goal with 4:25 remaining in the game. Randall Cunningham completed a 50-yard pass to Jake Reed two plays later and found Randy Moss open for a 10-yard touchdown with 1:56 left to give the Vikings a 20-16 lead. Favre completed 3 consecutive passes to reach the Vikings' 32 with 1:01 left, but this third-and-4 pass to Dorsey Levens netted just 3 yards. With the clock running, no timeouts, and needing 1 yard for a first down, Favre pumped right, whirled and found Bradford open in the end zone with 12 seconds left. Favre was 24 of 39 for 304 yards and 1 touchdown. Cunningham was 18 of 32 for 244 yards and 1 touchdown, with 2 interceptions. Reed had 6 catches for 108 yards.

Minnesota	7	3	3	7	—	20
Green Bay	0	10	3	10	—	23

Minn — Hoard 2 run (Anderson kick)
GB — FG Longwell 28
GB — Edwards 26 interception return (Longwell kick)
Minn — FG Anderson 34
Minn — FG Anderson 22
GB — FG Longwell 35
GB — FG Longwell 34
Minn — Moss 10 pass from Cunningham (Anderson kick)
GB — Bradford 23 pass from Favre (Longwell kick)

BUFFALO 26, PHILADELPHIA 0—at Ralph Wilson Stadium, attendance 70,872. The Bills' defense permitted just 11 first downs and 169 yards en route to recording its first shutout since 1992. The Bills drove into Eagles' territory during all seven of its first-half possessions, converting 4 field goals and 1 touchdown. The Eagles drove into Bills' territory just twice, and did not score because of Doug Pederson's lost fumble and Norm Johnson's missed 50-yard field-goal attempt. Philadelphia failed to run a play inside the Bills' 33 in the second half. Doug Flutie was 18 of 26 for 175 yards and 1 touchdown, with 1 interception. Pederson was 14 of 26 for 137 yards.

Philadelphia	0	0	0	0	—	0
Buffalo	9	10	7	0	—	26

Buff — FG Christie 24
Buff — FG Christie 29
Buff — FG Christie 19
Buff — Riemersma 15 pass from Flutie (Christie kick)
Buff — FG Christie 36
Buff — A. Smith 4 run (Christie kick)

SEATTLE 29, PITTSBURGH 10—at Three Rivers Stadium, attendance 57,881. The Seahawks scored 29 points without an offensive touchdown to defeat the Steelers. Merton Hanks intercepted Kordell Stewart's pass and returned it 23 yards for a touchdown 1:08 into the game to stake the Seahawks to a 7-0 lead. The Steelers were forced to punt on their next possession, and rookie Charlie Rogers scurried 94 yards for a touchdown to give Seattle a 14-0 lead 3:20 into the game and before the offense took a snap. Todd Peterson kicked 4 first-half field goals, the last set up by Jay Bellamy's interception, to give the Seahawks a 26-0 halftime lead. Mike Tomczak replaced Stewart but threw 2 interceptions inside the Seahawks' 25 to thwart Pittsburgh's comeback. Jon Kitna was 18 of 29 for 265 yards. Sean Dawkins had 5 catches for 105 yards. Stewart was 7 of 14 for 61 yards, with 3 interceptions. Tomczak was 14 of 27 for 159 yards and 1 touchdown, with 2 interceptions.

Seattle	17	9	0	3	—	29
Pittsburgh	0	0	0	10	—	10

Sea — Hanks 23 interception return (Peterson kick)
Sea — Rogers 94 punt return (Peterson kick)
Sea — FG Peterson 45
Sea — FG Peterson 51
Sea — FG Peterson 41
Sea — FG Peterson 26
Pitt — FG Brown 33
Sea — FG Peterson 38
Pitt — Edwards 16 pass from Tomczak (Brown kick)

TENNESSEE 20, JACKSONVILLE 19—at ALLTEL Stadium, attendance 61,502. Samari Rolle's interception in the end zone with 57 seconds left preserved the Titans' victory. The Jaguars led 3-0 late in the first half and could have extended the lead, but Anthony Dorsett intercepted Mark Brunell at the Titans' 23 and, just before halftime, holder Bryan Barker attempted to score on a fake field-goal attempt from the Titans' 15 but was stopped at the 2-yard line. Tennessee took advantage of James Stewart's fumble on the first play of the second half, which was recovered by Eddie Robinson at the Jaguars' 9 and set up Neil O'Donnell's 8-yard touchdown pass to Eddie George. The Jaguars reclaimed the lead late in the third quarter on Mark Brunell's touchdown pass and extended the advantage to 10 points 56 seconds later on Aaron Beasley's interception return. Al Del Greco kicked field goals to conclude the Titans' next two possessions, and Kenny Holmes's 19-yard interception return thwarted the Jaguars' ensuing drive. O'Donnell completed third-and-10 passes to George and Frank Wycheck to keep the drive alive, and Michael Roan's 12-yard touchdown catch with 3:26 left lifted Tennessee to a 20-17 lead. The Jaguars drove to the Titans' 3, but Rolle intercepted Brunell's pass that was underthrown to the back left corner of the end zone. Punter Craig Hentrich ran out of the end zone as time expired, accounting for the final margin. O'Donnell was 17 of 32 for 204 yards and 2 touchdowns, with 1 interception. Brunell was 22 of 42 for 232 yards and 1 touchdown, with 3 interceptions. Jimmy Smith had 10 catches for 129 yards.

Tennessee	0	0	7	13	—	20
Jacksonville	3	0	14	2	—	19

Jax — FG Hollis 42
Tenn — George 8 pass from O'Donnell (Del Greco kick)
Jax — Smith 11 pass from Brunell (Hollis kick)
Jax — Beasley 35 interception return (Hollis kick)
Tenn — FG Del Greco 44
Tenn — FG Del Greco 48
Tenn — Roan 12 pass from O'Donnell (Del Greco kick)
Jax — Safety, Hentrich ran out of end zone

WASHINGTON 27, N.Y. JETS 20—at Giants Stadium, attendance 78,161. Stephen Davis scored 3 touchdowns as the Redskins were victorious at Giants Stadium for the second consecutive weekend. Rick Mirer's 35-yard touchdown pass to Dedric Ward capped the Jets' 80-yard opening drive. The Redskins' potent offense was stifled until mounting consecutive drives of 76 and 74 yards, capped by Davis's 1-yard run just before halftime. Trailing 13-7, the Jets scored on consecutive possessions to take a 17-13 lead with 8:10 remaining. Two pass interference penalties on Ray Mickens aided the Redskins' ensuing 80-yard drive that gave them a 20-17 lead. Dan Wilkinson recovered Mirer's fumble at the Jets' 21 three plays later, setting up Davis's third run with 2:21 remaining. Kevin Williams's 81-yard kickoff return set up John Hall's 34-yard field goal with 1:45 left, and the Jets' failed to get the ball back. Brad Johnson was 17 of 28 for 241 yards. Mirer was 17 of 31 for 227 yards and 1 touchdown, with 1 interception.

Washington	0	10	3	14	—	27
N.Y. Jets	7	0	7	6	—	20

NYJ — Ward 35 pass from Mirer (Hall kick)
Wash — FG Conway 26
Wash — Davis 1 run (Conway kick)
Wash — FG Conway 50
NYJ — Martin 3 run (Hall kick)
NYJ — FG Hall 37
Wash — Davis 4 run (Conway kick)
Wash — Davis 7 run (Conway kick)
NYJ — FG Hall 34

SUNDAY NIGHT, SEPTEMBER 26

NEW ENGLAND 16, N.Y. GIANTS 14—at Foxboro Stadium, attendance 59,169. Kent Graham completed all 5 of his pass attempts on the Giants' opening drive, capped by his 6-yard touchdown pass to Leshon Johnson. The Patriots' defense kept the Giants' at bay until the fourth quarter, and the offense kicked field goals on their first 3 possessions of the second half to give New England a 16-7 lead with 3:12 left. The Giants drove 70 yards and cut the deficit to two points on Graham's 1-yard touchdown pass to Tiki Barber with 1:14 left. Ben Coates recovered the ensuing onside kick to preserve the Patriots' victory. Drew Bledsoe was 20 of 28 for 233 yards. Graham was 23 of 36 for 216 yards and 2 touchdowns.

N.Y. Giants	7	0	0	7	—	14
New England	0	7	6	3	—	16

NYG — L. Johnson 6 pass from Graham (Daluiso kick)
NE — Allen 1 run (Vinatieri kick)
NE — FG Vinatieri 38
NE — FG Vinatieri 19
NE — FG Vinatieri 41
NYG — Barber 1 pass from Graham (Daluiso kick)

MONDAY NIGHT, SEPTEMBER 27

SAN FRANCISCO 24, ARIZONA 10—at Sun Devil Stadium, attendance 72,100. Lawrence Phillips's 68-yard touchdown run in the final moments iced the 49ers' second consecutive victory. The victory was tempered, however, by the loss of Steve Young, who suffered a concussion when his head hit Dave Fiore's knee while he was being sacked by Aeneas Williams just before halftime. As the Cardinals' defense held the 49ers' without a first down in the third quarter, the offense scored 10 points to cut the deficit to 17-10. The Cardinals drove to the 49ers' 40 with 2:40 left, but, faced with fourth-and-11, decided to punt. After getting one first down, Phillips ran 68 yards over right tackle to extend the 49ers' lead to 24-10 with 1:42 remaining. Young was 13 of 23 for 92 yards and 1 touchdown, with 1 interception. Jeff Garcia was 5 of 6 for 30 yards. Phillips carried 9 times for 102 yards. Jake Plummer was 16 of 31 for 176 yards, with 2 interceptions.

San Francisco	14	3	0	7	—	24
Arizona	0	0	10	0	—	10

SF — Rice 13 pass from Young (Richey kick)
SF — Garner 11 run (Richey kick)
SF — FG Richey 33
Ariz — Bates 1 run (Jacke kick)
Ariz — FG Jacke 43
SF — Phillips 68 run (Richey kick)

FOURTH WEEK SUMMARIES

AMERICAN FOOTBALL CONFERENCE

Eastern Division	W	L	T	Pct.	Pts.	OP
New England	4	0	0	1.000	96	77
Buffalo	3	1	0	.750	80	52
Indianapolis	2	1	0	.667	86	64
Miami	2	1	0	.667	75	60
N.Y. Jets	1	3	0	.250	72	87
Central Division						
Jacksonville	3	1	0	.750	99	46
Tennessee	3	1	0	.750	104	87
Baltimore	2	2	0	.500	66	73
Pittsburgh	2	2	0	.500	79	66
Cincinnati	0	4	0	.000	55	135
Cleveland	0	4	0	.000	26	105
Western Division						
Seattle	3	1	0	.750	85	72
San Diego	2	1	0	.667	74	48
Kansas City	2	2	0	.500	88	72
Oakland	2	2	0	.500	91	84
Denver	0	4	0	.000	54	98

NATIONAL FOOTBALL CONFERENCE

Eastern Division	W	L	T	Pct.	Pts.	OP
Dallas	3	0	0	1.000	100	49
Washington	3	1	0	.750	150	118
N.Y. Giants	2	2	0	.500	68	94
Arizona	1	3	0	.250	58	102
Philadelphia	0	4	0	.000	44	86
Central Division						
Detroit	2	1	0	.667	72	66
Green Bay	2	1	0	.667	66	67
Chicago	2	2	0	.500	64	65
Minnesota	2	2	0	.500	75	73
Tampa Bay	2	2	0	.500	59	53
Western Division						
St. Louis	3	0	0	1.000	112	60
San Francisco	3	1	0	.750	62	44
New Orleans	1	2	0	.333	56	57
Carolina	1	3	0	.250	99	115
Atlanta	0	4	0	.000	58	75

SUNDAY, OCTOBER 3

DALLAS 35, ARIZONA 7—at Texas Stadium, attendance 64,169. Troy Aikman passed for 2 touchdowns and the Cowboys' defense forced 5 turnovers as Dallas exacted revenge for last season's wild-card defeat. George Teague's 32-yard interception return three plays into the game set the tone for the afternoon. The Cowboys' defense permitted just 3 first downs on Arizona's next seven possessions as Dallas took a 21-0 lead. Jake Plummer's 2-yard touchdown pass 11 seconds before halftime cut the deficit to 21-7, but Dallas emerged from the locker room with a 12-play, 73-yard drive, capped by Emmitt Smith's 1-yard touchdown run, to extend the lead back to 21 points. The Cardinals' last four possessions ended with turnovers, including a 98-yard fumble return by Greg Ellis early in the fourth quarter. Aikman was 15 of 21 for 192 yards and 2 touchdowns. Raghib Ismail had 4 receptions for 101 yards. Plummer was 16 of 33 for 111 yards and 1 touchdown, with 3 interceptions.

Arizona	0	7	0	0	—	7
Dallas	14	7	7	7	—	35

Dall — Teague 32 interception return (Cunningham kick)
Dall — Irvin 18 pass from Aikman (Cunningham kick)
Dall — Ismail 6 pass from Aikman (Cunningham kick)
Ariz — Makovicka 2 pass from Plummer (Jacke kick)
Dall — E. Smith 1 run (Cunningham kick)
Dall — Ellis 98 fumble return (Cunningham kick)

BALTIMORE 19, ATLANTA 13 (OT)—at Georgia Dome, attentendance 60,587. Stoney Case's 54-yard touchdown pass to Justin Armour 2:29 into overtime lifted the Ravens to victory. The Falcons led 6-3 at halftime and forged a 10-point advantage with 3:32 left in the third quarter on Danny Kanell's 30-yard touchdown pass to Jammi German. Case completed a 52-yard bomb to Patrick Johnson four plays later to cut the deficit to 13-10. Three plays later, Kim Herring recovered Byron Hanspard's fumble at the Falcons' 35 to set up Matt Stover's game-tying 26-yard field goal with 10:14 remaining. The Falcons reached the Ravens' 26 with 1:12 left, but a 10-yard holding penalty pushed Atlanta back, and Dan Reeves eschewed a 54-yard field-goal attempt with 1:01 left to punt. The Falcons won the overtime coin toss but went three and out. Three plays later, Case found Justin Armour open deep down the middle of the field for the winning touchdown. Case was 13 of 27 for 192 yards and 2 touchdowns. Errict Rhett had 27 carries for 136 yards. Kanell, who replaced an injured Tony Graziani in the second quarter, was 15 of 32 for 184 yards and 1 touchdown.

Baltimore	0	3	7	3	6	—	19
Atlanta	0	6	7	0	0	—	13

Balt — FG Stover 38
Atl — FG Andersen 41
Atl — FG Andersen 35
Atl — German 30 pass from Kanell (Andersen kick)
Balt — P. Johnson 52 pass from Case (Stover kick)
Balt — FG Stover 26
Balt — Armour 54 pass from Case

WASHINGTON 38, CAROLINA 36—at Redskins Stadium, attendance 76,831. Brett Conway's 31-yard field goal with six seconds remaining capped a wild game in which the Redskins overcame a 21-point deficit. The Panthers had touchdown drives of 72, 28, and 60 yards in the first quarter using 3, 3, and 2 plays, all capped by scoring runs by Tim Biakabutuka, to take a 21-0 lead. A field goal on their next possession gave Carolina a 24-7 lead with 10:12 left in the first half. The Redskins promptly scored 3 touchdowns in less than six minutes, the last of which was a 62-yard touchdown pass by Brad Johnson to Albert Connell, to take a 28-24 lead. The Panthers had a chance to retake the lead before halftime, but Darryl Pounds intercepted Steve Beuerlein's pass at the Redskins' 1 to quell the opportunity. Johnson and Connell connected early in the second half, and John Kasay missed a 52-yard field goal. The Redskins drove to the Panthers' 35, looking to extend their 11-point lead, but Michael Barrow sacked Johnson on fourth-and-5. Kasay kicked 43- and 45-yard field goals on the Panthers' next two possessions to cut the deficit to 35-30, and Beuerlein's 6-yard touchdown pass to Wesley Walls with 7:57 left gave Carolina a 36-35 lead. The Panthers recovered a fumbled punt return by Brian Mitchell at the Redskins' 31 with 4:19 remaining, but replay overruled the ruling. Johnson's 19-yard pass to Michael Westbrook to the Panthers' 12 set up Conway's winning kick. Johnson was 20 of 33 for 337 yards and 4 touchdowns. Westbrook had 8 catches for 140 yards, and Connell had 5 for 134 yards. Beuerlein was 23 of 47 for 334 yards and 1 touchdown, with 1 interception. Muhsin Muhammad had 8 catches for 151 yards. Biakabutuka had 12 carries for 142 yards.

Carolina	21	3	3	9	—	36
Washington	0	28	7	3	—	38

Car — Biakabutuka 60 run (Kasay kick)
Car — Biakabutuka 1 run (Kasay kick)
Car — Biakabutuka 45 run (Kasay kick)
Wash — Davis 1 run (Conway kick)
Car — FG Kasay 43
Wash — Westbrook 17 pass from Johnson (Conway kick)
Wash — Westbrook 11 pass from Johnson (Conway kick)
Wash — Connell 62 pass from Johnson (Conway kick)
Wash — Connell 32 pass from Johnson (Conway kick)
Car — FG Kasay 43
Car — FG Kasay 42
Car — Walls 6 pass from Beuerlein (pass failed)
Wash — FG Conway 31

JACKSONVILLE 17, PITTSBURGH 3—at Three Rivers Stadium, attendance 57,308. The Jaguars' defense forced 2 turnovers and recorded 4 sacks as the Jaguars won at Pittsburgh for the first time. The Jaguars led 7-0 just before halftime, but Travis Davis intercepted a pass at the Steelers' 43 to set up Kris Brown's 48-yard field goal as the half expired, cutting the deficit to 7-3. On Pittsburgh's first possession of the second half, Tony Brackens recovered Kordell Stewart's fumble at the Steelers' 45 to set up Mike Hollis's 27-yard field goal. The Jaguars twice stopped the Steelers on fourth-and-1, the second time when Pittsburgh attempted a flea-flicker from the Jaguars' 38 with 9:50 left. Hollis's second field goal nine plays later stretched Jacksonville's lead to 13-3 with 5:40 to play. Brackens forced Stewart to fumble the ball out of the end zone for a safety, and on Pittsburgh's next play from scrimmage, at its own 2-yard line, Joel Smeenge sacked Stewart for another safety with 54 seconds left. Mark Brunell was 10 of 25 for 85 yards and 1 touchdown, with 1 interception. Stewart was 15 of 32 for 126 yards, with 1 interception.

Jacksonville	0	7	3	7	—	17
Pittsburgh	0	3	0	0	—	3

Jax — McCardell 7 pass from Brunell (Hollis kick)
Pitt — FG Brown 48
Jax — FG Hollis 27
Jax — FG Hollis 41
Jax — Safety, Stewart fumbled ball out of end zone
Jax — Safety, Smeenge sacked Stewart in end zone

SAN DIEGO 21, KANSAS CITY 14—at Qualcomm Stadium, attendance 58,099. Erik Kramer passed for 2 touchdowns, and the Chargers' defense intercepted 4 passes to lead San Diego to victory. The Chiefs scored 2 first-quarter touchdowns, the first set up by Donnie Edwards's interception at the Chargers' 42 and the second set up by Tamarick Vanover's 28-yard punt return to the Chargers' 23. Michael Dumas's 24-yard interception return to the Chiefs' 10 led to Natrone Means's 4-yard scoring run midway through the second quarter, and Kramer's 18-yard touchdown pass to Kenny Bynum came two plays after punter Daniel Pope dropped a punt snap at the Chiefs' 18. Darryll Lewis's interception, plus a 15-yard personal foul penalty to the Chiefs' 22, set up Kramer's 11-yard scoring pass to Chris Penn early in the third quarter. The Chiefs reached the Chargers' 14 with 4:00 left, but a penalty and sack led to a fourth-down incomplete pass. On their last drive, Elvis Grbac completed an 18-yard pass to Tony Gonzalez to the Chargers' 14, but time expired before the Chiefs could snap the ball. Kramer, who had replaced an injured Jim Harbaugh, was 8 of 20 for 72 yards and 2 touchdowns, with 1 interception. Elvis Grbac was 19 of 40 for 200 yards and 2 touchdowns, with 4 interceptions.

Kansas City	14	0	0	0	—	14
San Diego	0	14	7	0	—	21

KC — Horn 31 pass from Grbac (Stoyanovich kick)
KC — Gonzalez 12 pass from Grbac (Stoyanovich kick)
SD — Means 4 run (Carney kick)
SD — Bynum 18 pass from Kramer (Carney kick)
SD — Penn 11 pass from Kramer (Carney kick)

NEW ENGLAND 19, CLEVELAND 7—at Cleveland Browns Stadium, attendance 72,368. Terry Glenn established career highs with 13 receptions for 214 yards as the Patriots defeated the Browns. Glenn's fumble at the Browns' 27 thwarted the Patriots' first drive. The Patriots drove inside the Browns' 10 two more times but were held to field goals, and Tim Couch's 64-yard touchdown pass to Kevin Johnson gave Cleveland a 7-6 halftime lead. Terry Allen's 3-yard run capped the second half's opening drive, and Drew Bledsoe found Glenn for a 54-yard touchdown on the first play of the fourth quarter. Cleveland failed to penetrate Patriots' territory in the final quarter. The Patriots had more first downs (23-12) and yards (434-235). Bledsoe was 28 of 42 for 389 yards and 1 touchdown. Couch was 12 of 27 for 195 yards and 1 touchdown.

New England	0	6	7	6	—	19
Cleveland	7	0	0	0	—	7

Cle — K. Johnson 64 pass from Couch (Dawson kick)
NE — FG Vinatieri 23
NE — FG Vinatieri 21
NE — Allen 3 run (Vinatieri kick)
NE — Glenn 54 pass from Bledsoe (pass failed)

CHICAGO 14, NEW ORLEANS 10—at Soldier Field, attendance 52,291. Shane Matthews passed for 2 touchdowns to Curtis Conway in the final two minutes to give Chicago a thrilling comeback victory. The Bears drove to the Saints' 12 in the first quarter, but Matthews fumbled and Wayne Martin recovered. Billy Joe Hobert's 2-yard scoring run late in the first half gave the Saints a 7-0 lead. The Bears threatened again in the third quarter, but Edgar Bennett fumbled at the Saints' 20, and Sammy Knight recovered. On the Bears' next possession, Ashley Ambrose intercepted Matthews at the Bears' 40 to set up Doug Brien's 30-yard field goal. Trailing 10-0, Jeff Jaeger missed a 32-yard field-goal attempt with 9:01 left, but Bryan Robinson stopped Lamar Smith for no gain on fourth-and-1 from the Bears' 21 with 4:35 left to keep Chicago in the game. Matthews completed 3 third-down passes, capped by a 22-yard touchdown pass to Conway with 1:48 left, to cut the deficit to 10-7. The Bears' defense forced a punt, and Chicago started from its own 33 with 1:08 left. Matthews completed 5 of 6 passes, with his last one a 6-yard pass to Conway with seven seconds left for the victory. Matthews was 25 of 39 for 224 yards and 2 touchdowns, with 2 interceptions. Conway had 8 catches for 103 yards. Hobert was 8 of 13 for 76 yards before leaving with an injury. Billy Joe Tolliver was 7 of 15 for 102 yards.

New Orleans	0	7	3	0	—	10
Chicago	0	0	0	14	—	14

NO — Hobert 2 run (Brien kick)
NO — FG Brien 30
Chi — Conway 22 pass from Matthews (Jaeger kick)
Chi — Conway 6 pass from Matthews (Jaeger kick)

N.Y. JETS 21, DENVER 13—at Mile High Stadium, attendance 74,181. In a rematch of the 1998 AFC Championship Game, Rick Mirer passed for 2 touchdowns, and the Jets intercepted 5 passes to defeat the Broncos in a game that saw Terrell Davis suffer a season-ending injury. The Broncos scored on their first two possessions to take a 10-7 lead. Late in the quarter, Victor Green intercepted Brian Griese's pass and returned it 15 yards to the Broncos' 18. As Green was tackled by Davis and Matt Lepsis, Davis's knee was injured. John Hall missed a 43-yard field-goal attempt moments later, and Jason Elam drilled a 51-yard field goal just before halftime to give Denver a 13-7 lead. The Jets got their offense going in the third quarter, driving inside the Broncos' 20 on four consecutive possessions: the Jets were stopped on downs at the Broncos' 18; Curtis Martin's 2- yard scoring run gave the Jets a 14-13 lead; Bill Romanowski intercepted Mirer at the Broncos' 1; and Dedric Ward caught a 16-yard touchdown pass with 5:57 remaining. Bubby Brister replaced Griese with 3:59 left, but was intercepted twice, the last by Marcus Coleman at midfield with 52 seconds left to preserve the Jets' victory. Mirer was 17 of 28 for 242 yards and 2 touchdowns, with 2 interceptions. Griese was 15 of 31 for 212 yards, with 3 interceptions.

N.Y. Jets	7	0	0	14	—	21
Denver	10	3	0	0	—	13

Den — FG Elam 26
NYJ — K. Johnson 26 pass from Mirer (Hall kick)
Den — Davis 1 run (Elam kick)
Den — FG Elam 51
NYJ — Martin 2 run (Hall kick)
NYJ — Ward 16 pass from Mirer (Hall kick)

N.Y. GIANTS 16, PHILADELPHIA 15—at Giants Stadium, attendance 73,274. Brad Daluiso kicked 3 field goals, and the Giants' defense recorded 5 sacks and forced 3 turnovers to defeat the Eagles. Kent Graham's 9-yard touchdown pass to Ike Hilliard capped a game-opening 57-yard drive for the Giants. The Eagles drove into Giants' territory, but Jason Sehorn intercepted Doug Pederson's pass at the Giants' 4. However, Sehorn attempted to lateral the ball before being tackled, and the ball went into the end zone where Phillippi Sparks fell on it for a safety. Bobby Taylor's 18-yard interception return at the end of the first quarter gave the Eagles a 9-7 lead. Daluiso's 35-yard field goal to end the half, and his 25-yard boot to conclude the opening drive of the second half gave the Giants a 4-point lead, only to have Norm Johnson kick 2 field goals, the second from 32 yards, to give Philadelphia a 15-13 lead with 12:37 remaining. Kerry Collins, who had replaced Graham a possession earlier, responded with a 67-yard drive, capped by Daluiso's third field goal with 7:43 to play. Gary Brown's 4-yard run on second-and-1 with 1:20 remaining clinched the victory. Graham was 15 of 29 for 171 yards and 1 touchdown, with 3 interceptions. Collins was 6 of 12 for 86 yards. Amani Toomer had 8 catches for 123 yards. Pederson was 6 of 15 for 75 yards, with 2 interceptions before being replaced by Donovan McNabb, who was 3 of 7 for 38 yards.

Philadelphia	9	0	3	3	—	15
N.Y. Giants	7	3	3	3	—	16

NYG — Hilliard 9 pass from Graham (Daluiso kick)
Phil — Safety, C. Johnson tackled Sparks in end zone
Phil — Taylor 18 interception return (N. Johnson kick)
NYG — FG Daluiso 35
NYG — FG Daluiso 25
Phil — FG N. Johnson 26
Phil — FG N. Johnson 32
NYG — FG Daluiso 23

ST. LOUIS 38, CINCINNATI 10—at Cinergy Field, attendance 45,481. Az-Zahir Hakim scored 4 touchdowns as the Rams remained undefeated. Doug Pelfrey's 26-yard field goal capped the Bengals' first drive, but the Rams put together drives of 76, 91, and 61 yards, twice capped by Kurt Warner to Hakim touchdown passes, to take a 21-3 lead. Hakim's 84-yard punt return, in which he weaved and hurdled players, two minutes into the second half, and his 18-yard touchdown catch late in the quarter, extended the Rams lead to 35-3. Akili Smith replaced an injured Jeff Blake in the third quarter and scored the Bengals' lone touchdown. Warner was 17 of 21 for 310 yards and 3 touchdowns. Isaac Bruce had 6 catches for 152 yards. Blake was 12 of 23 for 114 yards. Smith was 7 of 18 for 77 yards, with 1 interception.

St. Louis	7	14	14	3	—	38
Cincinnati	3	0	0	7	—	10

Cin — FG Pelfey 26
StL — Hakim 9 pass from Warner (Wilkins kick)
StL — Holcombe 1 run (Wilkins kick)
StL — Hakim 51 pass from Warner (Wilkins kick)
StL — Hakim 84 punt return from Warner (Wilkins kick)
StL — Hakim 18 pass from Warner (Wilkins kick)
StL — FG Wilkins 19
Cin — Smith 1 run (Pelfrey kick)

MINNESOTA 21, TAMPA BAY 14—at Metrodome, attendance 64,106. Randall Cunningham passed for 3 first-quarter touchdowns as the Vikings held off the Buccaneers. The Vikings drove 82, 39, and 86 yards on their first three possessions following Tampa Bay punts to take a 21-0 lead with 32 seconds left in the first quarter. The Buccaneers scored on their next possession, and Donnie Abraham intercepted a pass in the end zone just before halftime to keep Tampa Bay within 14 points. The Vikings once again had a chance to extend the lead, but John McLaughlin blocked Gary Anderson's 37-yard field-goal attempt with 10:08 remaining in the game. The blocked field goal spurred a 5-play, 72-yard drive, capped by Trent Dilfer's 26-yard touchdown pass to Reidel Anthony with 7:34 left. Tampa Bay got the ball back after a punt and drove to the Vikings' 21, but, on fourth-and-1, Dilfer's pass was intercepted by Corey Miller. Tampa Bay forced another punt, and the offense reached the Vikings' 18 with seven seconds left, but Dilfer's final 2 pass attempts fell incomplete in the end zone. Cunningham was 26 of 34 for 296 yards and 3 touchdowns, with 1 interception. Dilfer was 25 of 39 for 301 yards and 2 touchdowns, with 1 interception.

Tampa Bay	0	7	0	7	—	14
Minnesota	21	0	0	0	—	21

Minn — Moss 61 pass from Cunningham (Anderson kick)
Minn — Moss 27 pass from Cunningham (Anderson kick)
Minn — Glover 12 pass from Cunningham (Anderson kick)
TB — Moore 26 pass from Dilfer (Gramatica kick)
TB — Anthony 26 pass from Dilfer (Gramatica kick)

SAN FRANCISCO 24, TENNESSEE 22—at 3Com Park, attendance 67,447. The 49ers' defense stopped Eddie George on a 2-point conversion attempt with 1:48 remaining to give Jeff Garcia a victory in his first NFL start. George turned a screen pass into a 54-yard touchdown reception to give the Titans a 10-0 second-quarter lead. Garcia was 3-for-3 and scored from 1 yard on the ensuing drive, and his 21-yard touchdown pass to Charlie Garner two plays after R.J. McQuarters's 32-yard punt return gave the 49ers a 14-10 halftime lead. Consecutive fourth-quarter scoring drives gave the 49ers a 24-13 lead with 6:55 remaining. Al Del Greco kicked a 28-yard field goal with 3:38 left, and, following a punt, the Titans used the hook-and-ladder to convert a fourth-and-15 play that led to Neil O'Donnell's 32-yard touchdown pass to Yancey Thigpen with 1:48 left. However, the Titans attempted a pitch play on the 2-point conversion, and George was tackled at the 6-yard line. Tim McDonald recovered the ensuing onside kick to preserve the victory. Garcia was 21 of 33 for 243 yards and 2 touchdowns. O'Donnell was 20 of 40 for 355 yards and 2 touchdowns, with 1 interception. Thigpen had 6 catches for 143 yards.

Tennessee	3	7	3	9	—	22
San Francisco	0	14	0	10	—	24

Tenn — FG Del Greco 21
Tenn — George 54 pass from O'Donnell (Del Greco kick)
SF — Garcia 1 run (Richey kick)
SF — Garner 21 pass from Garcia (Richey kick)
Tenn — FG Del Greco 22
SF — FG Richey 39
SF — Owens 22 pass from Garcia (Richey kick)
Tenn — FG Del Greco 28
Tenn — Thigpen 32 pass from O'Donnell (run failed)

SUNDAY NIGHT, OCTOBER 3

SEATTLE 22, OAKLAND 21—at Kingdome, attendance 66,400. Todd Peterson kicked 3 field goals as Seattle moved into first place in the AFC West. The Raiders used drives of 77 and 87 yards to take a 14-3 lead. A 33-yard punt to midfield set up Jon Kitna's 29-yard touchdown pass to Derrick Mayes just before halftime to cut the deficit to 14-9. Eric Turner's 24-yard interception return to the Seahawks' 17 two plays into the second half set up Rich Gannon's 3-yard touchdown pass to Rickey Dudley. Kitna's 21-yard touchdown pass to Reggie Brown on the next drive cut the deficit to 21-16. Charlie Rogers's 68-yard punt return moments later led to Peterson's second field goal, and Darryl Williams's drive-stalling interception at the Seahawks' 18 set up Peterson's go-ahead field goal with 10:07 remaining. Michael Husted attempted a 61-yard field goal as time expired, but the kick landed in the end zone. Kitna was 15 of 30 for 213 yards and 2 touchdowns, with 1 interception. Gannon was 19 of 34 for 220 yards and 2 touchdowns, with 1 interception. Tyrone Wheatley carried 20 times for 100 yards.

Oakland	7	7	7	0	—	21
Seattle	3	6	10	3	—	22

Oak — Wheatley 7 run (Husted kick)
Sea — FG Peterson 28
Oak — Brown 6 pass from Gannon (Husted kick)
Sea — Mayes 29 pass from Kitna (pass failed)
Oak — Dudley 3 pass from Gannon (Husted kick)
Sea — Brown 21 pass from Kitna (Peterson kick)
Sea — FG Peterson 29
Sea — FG Peterson 45

MONDAY NIGHT, OCTOBER 4

BUFFALO 23, MIAMI 18—at Pro Player Stadium, attendance 74,724. The Bills' defense forced 3 turnovers, recorded 2 sacks, and scored a touchdown as Miami suffered its first loss. The Bills garnered 2 field goals in the first half but led 13-9 at halftime because of Gabe Northern's 59-yard fumble return late in the second quarter. The Bills' offense finally found the end zone, scoring on Doug Flutie's 6-yard pass to Eric Moulds with 10:02 left in the game to take a 20-12 lead. John Holecek's 35-yard interception return three plays later set up Steve Christie's third field goal to stretch the Bills' lead to 23-12 with 6:56 left. Dan Marino's 9-yard touchdown pass to O.J. McDuffie cut the deficit to 23-18 with 5:13 remaining, but Stanley Pritchett was stopped on the 2-point conversion attempt, and the Dolphins' failed to cross midfield on their final possession. Flutie was 12 of 25 for 186 yards and 1 touchdown. Marino was 22 of 42 for 251 yards and 1 touchdown, with 2 interceptions.

Buffalo	3	10	0	10	—	23
Miami	6	3	0	9	—	18

Buff — FG Christie 26
Mia — FG Mare 30
Mia — FG Mare 44
Buff — FG Christie 52
Buff — Northern 59 fumble return (Christie kick)
Mia — FG Mare 26
Mia — FG Mare 26
Buff — Moulds 6 pass from Flutie (Christie kick)
Buff — FG Christie 31
Mia — McDuffie 9 pass from Marino (run failed)

FIFTH WEEK SUMMARIES

AMERICAN FOOTBALL CONFERENCE

Eastern Division	W	L	T	Pct.	Pts.	OP
Buffalo	4	1	0	.800	104	73
New England	4	1	0	.800	110	93
Miami	3	1	0	.750	109	91
Indianapolis	2	2	0	.500	117	98
N.Y. Jets	1	4	0	.200	78	103
Central Division						
Jacksonville	4	1	0	.800	115	52
Tennessee	4	1	0	.800	118	98
Baltimore	2	3	0	.400	77	87
Pittsburgh	2	3	0	.400	100	90
Cincinnati	1	4	0	.200	73	152
Cleveland	0	5	0	.000	43	123
Western Division						
San Diego	3	1	0	.750	182	93
Seattle	3	1	0	.750	108	63
Kansas City	3	2	0	.600	104	86
Oakland	2	3	0	.400	104	100
Denver	1	4	0	.200	70	111

NATIONAL FOOTBALL CONFERENCE

Eastern Division	W	L	T	Pct.	Pts.	OP
Dallas	3	1	0	.750	110	62
Washington	3	1	0	.750	150	118
Arizona	2	3	0	.400	72	105
N.Y. Giants	2	3	0	.400	71	108
Philadelphia	1	4	0	.200	57	96
Central Division						
Green Bay	3	1	0	.750	92	90
Chicago	3	2	0	.600	88	87
Detroit	2	2	0	.500	82	86
Minnesota	2	3	0	.400	97	97
Tampa Bay	2	3	0	.400	82	79
Western Division						
St. Louis	4	0	0	1.000	142	47
San Francisco	3	1	0	.750	99	136
Carolina	1	3	0	.250	93	82
New Orleans	1	3	0	.250	67	72
Atlanta	1	4	0	.200	61	112

SUNDAY, OCTOBER 10

ATLANTA 20, NEW ORLEANS 17—at Louisiana Superdome, attendance 57,289. Morten Andersen kicked 2 fourth-quarter field goals as the defending NFC champions won their first game of the season. The Falcons drove 76 yards on their first possession but then fumbled on their next possession to set up a field goal. Billy Joe Hobert's club-record 90-yard touchdown pass to Eddie Kennison gave the Saints the lead, and a spectacular 23-yard diving touchdown catch by Brett Bech gave the Saints a 17-7 halftime lead. Tony Graziani's 62-yard pass to Jammi German set up Bob Christian's 1-yard run to open the second half. Ray Buchanan's interception at the Saints' 32 set up Andersen's tying field goal, and his go-ahead 44-yard boot came with 8:29 remaining. The Saints failed to drive inside the Falcons' 35 on their final two possessions. Graziani, who played for an injured Chris Chandler, was 11 of 20 for 162 yards and 1 touchdown. Hobert was 9 of 14 for 153 yards and 1 touchdown before being injured and replaced by Billy Joe Tolliver, who was 13 of 26 for 185 yards and 1 touchdown, with 2 interceptions.

Atlanta	7	0	7	6	—	20
New Orleans	0	17	0	0	—	17

Atl — Mathis 22 pass from Graziani (Andersen kick)
NO — FG Brien 42
NO — Kennison 90 pass from Hobert (Brien kick)
NO — Bech 23 pass from Tolliver (Brien kick)
Atl — Christian 1 run (Andersen kick)
Atl — FG Andersen 36
Atl — FG Andersen 44

TENNESSEE 14, BALTIMORE 11—at Adelphia Coliseum, attendance 65,487. The Titans won their tenth consecutive AFC Central game despite committing a club-record 15 penalties. Lorenzo Neal's 1-yard touchdown run capped the Titans' lone productive drive of the first half. The Ravens had an opportunity to take the lead late in the half, but Stoney Case fumbled and Henry Ford recovered at the Titans' 25 to preserve Tennessee's 7-6 lead. A 54-yard pass interference penalty led to Matt Stover's third field goal early in the second half, but the Titans responded with a 73-yard drive, capped by Neil O'Donnell's 27-yard touchdown pass to Yancey Thigpen, to take a 14-9 lead. Ray Lewis's tackle of Rodney Thomas for a safety late in the third quarter was as close as the Ravens could get, as their offense failed to penetrate the Titans' 40 in the final quarter. O'Donnell was 24 of 35 for 216 yards and 1 touchdown. Case was 15 of 37 for 207 yards.

Baltimore	3	3	5	0	—	11
Tennessee	7	0	7	0	—	14

Balt — FG Stover 44
Tenn — Neal 1 run (Del Greco kick)
Balt — FG Stover 46
Balt — FG Stover 50
Tenn — Thigpen 27 pass from O'Donnell (Del Greco kick)
Balt — Safety, Lewis tackled Thomas in end zone

CHICAGO 24, MINNESOTA 22—at Metrodome, attendance 64,107. Shane Matthews passed for 2 touchdowns, and the Bears' defense recorded 4 sacks and forced 5 turnovers to defeat the Vikings. The Vikings offense set up 4 Gary Anderson field goals in the first half, but 2 turnovers, a fumble by Jim Kleinsasser that Sean Harris fell on in the end zone and a pass interception by Terry Cousin, led to 14 points for the Bears. Chicago scored on its first 2 possessions of the second half to take a 24-15 lead with 12:21 remaining. Jeff Jaeger's third missed field goal, from 37 yards with 4:50 remaining, left the door open for Minnesota. Barry Minter's interception at the Bears' 18 with 3:08 left stymied the Vikings. Minnesota found the end zone, on Randall Cunningham's 18-yard pass to Chris Walsh, with two seconds left. Matthews was 19 of 28 for 184 yards and 2 touchdowns. Cunningham was 25 of 47 for 309 yards and 1 touchdown, with 3 interceptions. Randy Moss had 8 catches for 122 yards. Robert Smith rushed 12 times for 107 yards.

Chicago	7	7	7	3	—	24
Minnesota	3	9	3	7	—	22

Chi — Harris recovered fumble in end zone (Jaeger kick)
Minn — FG Anderson 26
Minn — FG Anderson 40
Minn — FG Anderson 23
Chi — Conway 30 pass from Matthews (Jaeger kick)
Minn — FG Anderson 26
Chi — Robinson 3 pass from Matthews (Jaeger kick)
Minn — FG Anderson 34
Chi — FG Jaeger 41
Minn — Walsh 18 pass from Cunningham (Anderson kick)

CINCINNATI 18, CLEVELAND 17—at Cleveland Browns Stadium, attendance 73,048. Akili Smith's 2-yard touchdown pass to Carl Pickens with five seconds remaining lifted the Bengals to victory in the battle of Ohio. Trailing 6-0, the Browns lined up for a 22-yard field-goal attempt in the second quarter. Holder Chris Gardocki pitched the ball to kicker Phil Dawson, who ran around left end for a touchdown. Tremain Mack fumbled the ensuing kickoff, recovered by Tarek Saleh, and Terry Kirby scored three plays later to give the Browns a 14-6 lead. Trailing 14-12 late in the third quarter, a poor punt snap by Cincinnati gave the Browns the ball at the Bengals' 19, setting up Dawson's field goal with 14:09 remaining. The Bengals gained possession at their own 20 with 2:04 remaining, and Smith deftly drove them downfield, including a fourth-and-4 9-yard pass to Darnay Scott, to set up his 2-yard pass to Pickens. In a game that for just the fourth time in NFL history featured two rookie first-round draft picks, Smith was 25 of 41 for 221 yards and 2 touchdowns, while Tim Couch was 15 of 27 for 164 yards, with 1 interception. Scott had 8 catches for 110 yards. Corey Dillon rushed 28 times for 168 yards.

Cincinnati	6	6	0	6	—	18
Cleveland	0	14	0	3	—	17

Cin — FG Pelfrey 27
Cin — FG Pelfrey 26
Cle — Dawson 4 run (Dawson kick)
Cle — Kirby 1 run (Dawson kick)
Cin — Pickens 5 pass from Smith (pass failed)
Cle — FG Dawson 33
Cin — Pickens 2 pass from Smith (run failed)

PHILADELPHIA 13, DALLAS 10—at Veterans Superdome, attendance 66,669. Doug Pederson's 28-yard touchdown pass to Charles Johnson with 1:07 left gave the Eagles their first victory. The Cowboys' defense limited the Eagles to just 25 yards and 1 first down in the first half. Dallas led 10-0 at halftime, but it easily could have been more: Emmitt Smith fumbled at the Eagles' 1, and William Thomas recovered; and Troy Vincent intercepted Troy Aikman's pass for a touchback. Leading 10-3, Richie Cunningham missed a 50-yard field-goal attempt with 9:00 left, setting up Norm Johnson's second consecutive field goal to cut the lead to 10-6 with 5:42 remaining. The Eagles' defense forced a punt, and six plays later Johnson caught Pederson's pass at the Cowboys' 10 and dove into the end zone for the Philadelphia touchdown. Bobby Taylor intercpeted Aikman moments later to preserve the victory. Michael Irvin was injured with 5:04 left in the first quarter. Pederson was 11 of 29 for 145 yards and 1 touchdown, with 1 interception. Duce Staley rushed 22 times for 110 yards. Aikman was 21 of 39 for 177 yards and 1 touchdown, with 2 interceptions. Smith rushed 30 times for 114 yards.

Dallas	3	7	0	0	—	10
Philadelphia	0	0	0	13	—	13

Dall — FG Cunningham 42
Dall — E. Smith 9 pass from Aikman (Cunningham kick)
Phil — FG N. Johnson 38
Phil — FG N. Johnson 31
Phil — C. Johnson 28 pass from Pederson (N. Johnson kick)

DENVER 16, OAKLAND 13—at Network Associates Coliseum, attendance 55,704. Jason Elam kicked 3 field goals, and the Broncos' defense recorded 6 sacks to give the defending Super Bowl champion their first victory. The Broncos led 3-0 in the second quarter but committed 2 turnovers in Raiders' territory. Oakland drove to the Broncos' 14, but Zack Crockett was stopped on fourth-and-1 with 3:56 left in the half. Spurred by the defense's momentum, the offense had consecutive scoring drives of 57 yards, capped by Brian Griese's 3-yard pass to Rod Smith with 16 seconds left in the half, to take a 13-0 lead. Oakland scored on its first three possessions of the second half, settling for a field goal on fourth-and-goal from the Broncos' 1 with 14:57 left, to tie the game 13-13. The Broncos responded with Elam's third field goal, and Tory James's interception at the Broncos' 23 with 57 seconds left clinched the victory. Griese was 17 of 29 for 234 yards and 1 touchdown, with 1 interception. Gannon was 25 of 36 for 248 yards and 1 touchdown, with 2 interceptions.

Denver	3	10	0	3	—	16
Oakland	0	0	10	3	—	13

Den — FG Elam 48
Den — FG Elam 47
Den — R. Smith 3 pass from Griese (Elam kick)
Oak — Walker 21 pass from Gannon (Husted kick)
Oak — FG Husted 47
Oak — FG Husted 19
Den — FG Elam 26

MIAMI 34, INDIANAPOLIS 31—at RCA Dome, attendance 56,810. Dan Marino's 2-yard touchdown pass to Oronde Gadsden with 27 seconds left capped a 25-point fourth quarter for the Dolphins. The Colts led 10-9 at halftime, but could have had more points except for Daryl Gardener's recovery of Edgerrin James's fumble at the Dolphins' 1 in the first quarter. The Colts scored on their first possession of the second half, and the defense stopped Cecil Collins's on four consecutive running plays inside the Colts' 4. On Miami's next possession, Marino did complete a 28-yard touchdown pass to Tony Martin with 12:08 to play, but Terrence Wilkins returned the ensuing kickoff 97 yards for a touchdown. Collins scooted 25 yards down the right sideline for a touchdown three minutes later to cut the deficit to 24-22, but Peyton Manning's 32-yard touchdown pass to Marcus Pollard four plays later increased Indianapolis' lead to 31-22 with 8:14 to play. Olindo Mare's fourth field goal with 3:20 left cut the deficit to six points, and Manning took a safety with 1:54 remaining. Faced with fourth-and-10 from midfield with 1:04 left, Marino threw a 48-yard bomb down the right sideline to Gadsden, and found Gadsden again two plays later for the winning touchdown. Marino was 25 of 38 for 393 yards and 2 touchdowns. Martin had 10 catches for 166 yards, and Gadsden had 4 for 123 yards. Manning was 17 of 24 for 274 yards and 3 touchdowns, with 1 interception.

Miami	3	6	0	25	—	34
Indianapolis	3	7	7	14	—	31

Ind — FG Vanderjagt 41
Mia — FG Mare 37
Mia — FG Mare 27
Ind — Harrison 33 pass from Manning (Vanderjagt kick)
Mia — FG Mare 21
Ind — Pollard 9 pass from Manning (Vanderjagt kick)
Mia — Martin 28 pass from Marino (pass failed)
Ind — Wilkins 97 kickoff return (Vanderjagt kick)
Mia — Collins 25 run (Mare kick)
Ind — Pollard 32 pass from Manning (Vanderjagt kick)
Mia — FG Mare 43
Mia — Safety, Manning ran out of end zone
Mia — Gadsden 2 pass from Marino (Mare kick)

KANSAS CITY 16, NEW ENGLAND 14—at Arrowhead Stadium, attendance 78,636. Adam Vinatieri's 32-yard field-goal attempt deflected off the right upright with four seconds left to enable the Chiefs to remain unbeaten at home. The Chiefs struggled in the first half, getting a field goal only after Chester McGlockton recovered Drew Bledsoe's fumble at the Patriots' 7. The Chiefs scored on their first three possessions of the second half to take a 16-7 lead with 4:42 left in the game. Bledsoe's 39-yard pass to Tony Simmons keyed an 8-play, 77-yard drive capped by Shawn Jefferson's touchdown catch with 2:43 left. The Patriots' defense forced a punt, and the Patriots started at their own 33 with 30 seconds left. Bledsoe's 27-yard pass to Shawn Jefferson at the Chiefs' 14 with nine seconds left set up Vinatieri's second miss of the half. Elvis Grbac was 18 of 26 for 198 yards, with 1 interception. Bledsoe was 23 of 45 for 334 yards and 2 touchdowns, with 2 interceptions. Tony Simmons had 7 catches for 107 yards.

New England	7	0	0	7	—	14
Kansas City	3	0	10	3	—	16

KC — FG Stoyanovich 22
NE — Glenn 49 pass from Bledsoe (Vinatieri kick)
KC — Bennett 1 run (Stoyanovich kick)
KC — FG Stoyanovich 41
KC — FG Stoyanovich 23
NE — Jefferson 8 pass from Bledsoe (Vinatieri kick)

ARIZONA 14, N.Y. GIANTS 3—at Sun Devil Stadium, attendance 49,015. Jake Plummer passed for a touchdown and threw for another. Kwamie Lassiter's recovery of Kerry Collins's fumble at the Giants' 30 set up Plummer's 1-yard scoring sneak. Later in the second quarter, Plummer parlayed a missed 42-yard field goal by Brad Daluiso into an 8-play, 68-yard drive, capped by David Boston's touchdown catch just 33 seconds before halftime. Daluiso's 31-yard field goal cut the deficit to 14-3, but the Cardinals' defense stopped the Giants on downs twice in the final five minutes, including once at the Cardinals' 10, to secure the victory. Plummer was 13 of 19 for 156 yards and 1 touchdown. Boston had 8 catches for 101 yards. Collins was 24 of 38 for 202 yards, with 1 interception.

N.Y. Giants	0	0	0	3	—	3
Arizona	0	14	0	0	—	14

Ariz — Plummer 1 run (Jacke kick)
Ariz — Boston 11 pass from Plummer (Jacke kick)
NYG — FG Daluiso 31

BUFFALO 24, PITTSBURGH 21—at Ralph Wilson Stadium, attendance 71,038. Doug Flutie passed for 261 yards and 3 touchdowns as the Bills remained undefeated at home. Antowain Smith fumbled on the Bills' first play from scrimmage, and Levon Kirkland recovered to set up Kordell Stewart's 12-yard touchdown pass to Hines Ward. The Bills responded by scoring on their next three drives, highlighted by Flutie's 49-yard scoring pass to Eric Moulds and capped by Steve Christie's 29-yard field goal with 4:31 left in the half. Stewart converted 2 third-down passes to set up Troy Edwards's 17-yard scoring grab just before halftime to trim the lead to 17-14. Sam Rogers's 24-yard interception return to the Steelers' 38, and Jonathan Linton's 3-yard run on fourth-and-1, led to Flutie's 8-yard touchdown pass to Jay Riemersma. Jerome Bettis's touchdown run with 2:44 left capped a 10-play drive, but the Steelers kicked deep, and Linton carried four consecutive times to garner first downs and secure the victory. Flutie was 21 of 32 for 261 yards and 3 touchdowns. Moulds had 6 catches for 122 yards. Stewart was 21 of 29 for 216 yards and 2 touchdowns, with 1 interception.

Pittsburgh	7	7	0	7	—	21
Buffalo	7	10	7	0	—	24

Pitt — Ward 12 pass from Stewart (Brown kick)
Buff — Gash 2 pass from Flutie (Christie kick)
Buff — Moulds 49 pass from Flutie (Christie kick)
Buff — FG Christie 29
Pitt — Edwards 17 pass from Stewart (Brown kick)
Buff — Riemersma 8 pass from Flutie (Christie kick)
Pitt — Bettis 1 run (Brown kick)

SAN DIEGO 20, DETROIT 10—at Pontiac Silverdome, attendance 61,481. The Chargers' defense recorded 6 sacks and forced 3 turnovers to defeat their former coach, Bobby Ross. The Lions had a chance to score early, but Lew Bush recovered Sedrick Irvin's fumble at the Chargers' 13. Charlie Batch's 41-yard touchdown pass to Germane Crowell put the Lions on the board, but the Chargers scored on their last two possessions of the half to tie the game 10-10. Tracy Simien's 4-yard interception return to the Lions' 13 set up John Carney's go-ahed field goal early in the third quarter. Carney missed a 47-yard field-goal attempt in the fourth quarter, but Cory Schlesinger fumbled three plays later, and Darryll Lewis scooped up the ball and scooted 42 yards into the end zone with 7:52 remaining. The Lions got no closer than the Chargers' 38 the remainder of the game. Erik Kramer was 20 of 34 for 208 yards, with 1 interception. Batch was 21 of 38 for 230 yards and 1 touchdown, with 1 interception.

San Diego	0	10	3	7	—	20
Detroit	7	3	0	0	—	10

Det — Crowell 41 pass from Batch (Hanson kick)
SD — FG Carney 33
Det — FG Hanson 23
SD — Stephens 3 run (Carney kick)
SD — FG Carney 24
SD — Lewis 42 fumble return (Carney kick)

ST. LOUIS 42, SAN FRANCISCO 20—at Trans World Dome, attendance 65,872. Isaac Bruce caught 4 of Kurt Warner's 5 touchdown passes as the Rams snapped a 17-game losing streak to the 49ers. Bruce capped each of the Rams' first three drives, covering 83, 64, and 45 yards, with touchdown receptions to give St. Louis a 21-3 lead with 1:12 left in the first quarter. The 49ers cut the deficit to 28-17 at halftime on Junior Bryant's recovery of Warner's fumble in the end zone just before intermission. Wade Richey's 43-yard field goal late in the third quarter pulled the 49ers to within eight points, but Tony Horne returned the ensuing kickoff 97 yards for a touchdown, and Warner and Bruce hooked up for the fourth time on the Rams' next drive to pull away. Warner was 20 of 23 for 323 yards and 5 touchdowns, with 1 interception. Bruce had 5 catches for 134 yards. Jeff Garcia was 22 of 36 for 233 yards, with 3 interceptions.

San Francisco	3	14	3	0	—	20
St. Louis	21	7	7	7	—	42

StL — Bruce 13 pass from Warner (Wilkins kick)
StL — Bruce 5 pass from Warner (Wilkins kick)
SF — FG Richey 42
StL — Bruce 45 pass from Warner (Wilkins kick)
SF — Phillips 2 run (Richey kick)
StL — Robinson 22 pass from Warner (Wilkins kick)

SF — Bryant fumble recovery in end zone (Richey kick)
SF — FG Richey 43
StL — Horne 97 kickoff return (Wilkins kick)
StL — Bruce 42 pass from Warner (Wilkins kick)

SUNDAY NIGHT, OCTOBER 10

GREEN BAY 26, TAMPA BAY 23—at Lambeau Field, attendance 59,868. Brett Favre's 21-yard touchdown pass to Antonio Freeman with 1:05 remaining gave the Packers a comeback victory. The Packers jumped to a quick 10-0 lead, the second score set up by Tyrone Williams's interception. Tampa Bay responded with four impressive drives, the first of which was stymied by Jermaine Smith's interception at the Packers' 8, but the next three produced 13 points and gave the Buccaneers a three-point lead. Ryan Longwell sandwiched field goals around halftime to give the Packers a 16-13 lead, but the Buccaneers responded with a 13-play, 7:24 drive, capped by Martin Gramatica's tying 36-yard field goal with 14:28 remaining. Longwell's 43-yard field goal with 5:57 left gave the Packers a 19-16 lead, and Keith McKenzie recovered Trent Dilfer's fumble at the Buccaneers' 19 three plays later. However, Longwell missed from 45 yards with 2:28 left, and Tampa Bay needed just four plays to march 65 yards, keyed by Dilfer's 27-yard scramble and capped by Mike Alstott's 22-yard scoring run with 1:45 left. Favre's 42-yard pass to Bill Schroeder set up his third-and-10 touchdown pass to Freeman between two defenders. Darren Sharper intercepted Dilfer's pass at the Packers' 33 to secure the victory. Favre was 22 of 40 for 390 yards and 2 touchdowns. Schroeder had 7 catches for 158 yards, while Freeman had 7 for 152. Dilfer was 16 of 26 for 110 yards and 1 touchdown, with 3 interceptions.

Tampa Bay	0	13	0	10	—	23
Green Bay	10	3	3	10	—	26

GB — Freeman 19 pass from Favre (Longwell kick)
GB — FG Longwell 42
TB — Dunn 16 pass from Dilfer (Gramatica kick)
TB — FG Gramatica 41
TB — FG Gramatica 36
GB — FG Longwell 49
GB — FG Longwell 38
TB — FG Gramatica 36
GB — FG Longwell 43
TB — Alstott 22 run (Gramatica kick)
GB — Freeman 21 pass from Favre (Longwell kick)

MONDAY NIGHT, OCTOBER 11

JACKSONVILLE 16, N.Y. JETS 6—at Giants Stadium, attendance 78,216. The Jaguars' defense limited the Jets to 230 yards while recording 4 sacks and forcing 2 turnovers to remain undefeated. The Jaguars methodically drove 61 yards in 13 plays on their opening possession, capped by James Stewart's 3-yard scoring run, to take a 7-0 lead. The Jaguars led 10-3 at halftime, and Mike Hollis's 44-yard field goal in the opening minutes of the second half stretched the lead to ten points. John Hall's 42-yard field goal with 8:53 remaining in the game got the Jets to within one score, but the Jets' went for a first down on fourth-and-6 from their own 6 with 2:37 left and Rick Mirer's pass fell incomplete. Hollis followed with a late field goal for the final margin. Mark Brunell was 21 of 35 for 215 yards. Mirer was 19 of 38 for 164 yards, with 2 interceptions.

Jacksonville	7	3	3	3	—	16
N.Y. Jets	0	3	0	3	—	6

Jax — Stewart 3 run (Hollis kick)
Jax — FG Hollis 32
NYJ — FG Hall 33
Jax — FG Hollis 44
NYJ — FG Hall 42
Jax — FG Hollis 21

SIXTH WEEK SUMMARIES

AMERICAN FOOTBALL CONFERENCE

Eastern Division	W	L	T	Pct.	Pts.	OP
Miami	4	1	0	.800	140	121
Buffalo	4	2	0	.600	118	93
New England	4	2	0	.600	140	124
Indianapolis	3	2	0	.400	133	111
N.Y. Jets	1	5	0	.167	91	119
Central Division						
Jacksonville	5	1	0	.833	139	59
Tennessee	5	1	0	.833	142	119
Pittsburgh	3	2	0	.600	117	93
Baltimore	2	3	0	.400	77	87
Cincinnati	1	5	0	.167	76	169
Cleveland	0	6	0	.000	50	147
Western Division						
San Diego	4	1	0	.800	107	68
Kansas City	3	2	0	.600	104	86
Seattle	3	2	0	.600	95	85
Oakland	3	3	0	.500	124	114
Denver	2	4	0	.333	101	121

NATIONAL FOOTBALL CONFERENCE

Eastern Division	W	L	T	Pct.	Pts.	OP
Washington	4	1	0	.800	174	128
Dallas	3	2	0	.600	120	75
N.Y. Giants	3	3	0	.500	84	118
Arizona	2	4	0	.333	82	129
Philadelphia	2	4	0	.333	77	112
Central Division						
Detroit	3	2	0	.600	107	109
Green Bay	3	2	0	.600	102	121
Chicago	3	3	0	.500	104	107
Tampa Bay	2	3	0	.400	82	79
Minnesota	2	4	0	.333	120	122
Western Division						
St. Louis	5	0	0	1.000	183	60
San Francisco	3	3	0	.500	128	167
Carolina	2	3	0	.400	124	111
New Orleans	1	4	0	.200	88	96
Atlanta	1	5	0	.167	74	153

SUNDAY, OCTOBER 17

CAROLINA 31, SAN FRANCISCO 29—at 3Com Park, attendance 68,151. Steve Beuerlein passed for a career-high 4 touchdowns as George Seifert won in his first game against his former team. The 49ers concluded each of their first three possessions with field goals to take a 9-3 lead. After Beuerlein's first touchdown pass, Darnell Walker returned an interception 27 yards for a touchdown to give the 49ers a 16-10 lead. However, Michael Bates returned the ensuing kickoff 72 yards to set up Muhsin Muhammad's 22-yard scoring grab, and Kevin Greene's fumble recovery at the 49ers' 25 just over a minute later led to Wesley Walls's 25-yard touchdown catch and the Panthers' 24-16 halftime lead. Donta Jones's recovery of Reggie Givens's fumbled punt was converted by Beuerlein two plays later, in the form of a 33-yard touchdown pass to Patrick Jeffers. After Mark McMillian's fumble return trimmed the deficit to 31-23, Jeff Garcia engineered a 63-yard scoring drive, capped by Jerry Rice's 11-yard catch with 1:28 left. But Garcia's two-point conversion pass fell incomplete, and the 49ers failed to cross midfield in their final possession. Beuerlein was 23 of 36 for 300 yards and 4 touchdowns, with 3 interceptions. Garcia was 22 of 45 for 236 yards and 1 touchdown.

Carolina	0	24	7	0	—	31
San Francisco	6	10	0	13	—	29

SF — FG Richey 38
SF — FG Richey 34
Car — FG Kasay 19
SF — FG Richey 40
Car — Jeffers 7 pass from Beuerlein (Kasay kick)
SF — Walker 27 interception return (Richey kick)
Car — Muhammad 22 pass from Beuerlein (Kasay kick)
Car — Walls 25 pass from Beuerlein (Kasay kick)
Car — Jeffers 33 pass from Beuerlein (Kasay kick)
SF — McMillan 41 fumble return (Richey kick)
SF — Rice 11 pass from Garcia (pass failed)

JACKSONVILLE 24, CLEVELAND 7—at ALLTEL Stadium, attendance 62,047. Reserve Jay Fiedler replaced an injured Mark Brunell and guided the Jaguars' to 3 second-half scoring drives as Jacksonville had to come-from-behind to defeat the Browns. The Browns' 12-play, 70-yard drive, which culminated with Tim Couch's 9-yard touchdown pass to Terry Kirby, vaulted the Browns to a 7-6 halftime lead. A rib injury early in the third quarter forced Brunell to the sideline, and it wasn't until Kevin Hardy recovered Terry Kirby's fumble at the Browns' 25 late in the third quarter that Kyle Brady caught a 7-yard touchdown pass from Fiedler. The Jaguars drove 70 and 42 yards on their next two possessions, with Mike Hollis's third field goal with 44 seconds left icing the victory. Brunell was 12 of 19 for 109 yards before being replaced by Fiedler, who was 12 of 14 for 113 yards and 1 touchdown. Couch was 18 of 23 for 161 yards and 1 touchdown.

Cleveland	0	7	0	0	—	7
Jacksonville	3	3	8	10	—	24

Jac — FG Hollis 20
Cle — Kirby 9 pass from Couch (Dawson kick)
Jac — FG Hollis 36
Jac — Brady 7 pass from Fiedler (Brady pass from Fiedler)
Jac — Stewart 2 run (Hollis kick)
Jac — FG Hollis 24

DENVER 31, GREEN BAY 10—at Mile High Stadium, attendance 73,352. Brian Griese passed for 2 touchdowns and ran for another as the Broncos' defense limited the Packers to just 5 first downs in a rematch of Super Bowl XXXII. Brian Williams's 60-yard interception return denied the Broncos a touchdown and set up Ryan Longwell's 50-yard field goal just before halftime to tie the game 3-3. Eric Brown's interception on the Packers' second play of the second half led to Griese's 10-yard touchdown pass to Ed McCaffrey. Brett Favre's 54-yard pass to Corey Bradford resulted in Dorsey Levens's game-tying touchdown midway through the quarter, but on the next play from scrimmage McCaffrey outleaped Tyrone Williams for a long pass, then carried and fought-off Darren Sharper the final 20 yards for a 78-yard touchdown. Ray Crockett intercepted Favre on the next play, leading to Olandis Gary's scoring run, and Griese's 88-yard pass to Bryon Chamberlain set up his own 2-yard run. Thanks to Gary's 37 carries for 124 yards, the Broncos controlled the ball for 45:14 and outgained the Packers 514-133. Griese was 19 of 31 for 363 yards and 2 touchdowns, with 1 interception, and McCaffrey had 5 receptions for 116 yards. Favre was 7 of 23 for 120 yards, with 3 interceptions.

Green Bay	0	3	7	0	—	10
Denver	3	0	21	7	—	31

Den — FG Elam 20
GB — FG Longwell 50
Den — McCaffrey 10 pass from Griese (Elam kick)
GB — Levens 1 run (Longwell kick)
Den — McCaffrey 78 pass from Griese (Elam kick)
Den — Gary 1 run (Elam kick)
Den — Griese 2 run (Elam kick)

INDIANAPOLIS 16, N.Y. JETS 13—at Giants Stadium, attendance 78,112. Ray Burris's goal-line interception set up Mike Vanderjagt's 27-yard field goal with 14 seconds left as the Colts had to come-from-behind to defeat the Jets. Spurred by starter Ray Lucas, the Jets dominated the first 16 minutes, driving deep into Colts' territory on their first four possessions, resulting in 1 missed and 2 made field goals and an 18-yard touchdown pass from Lucas to Richie Anderson. After a 6-play, 76-yard scoring drive in the second quarter, the Colts used two 12-play drives to set up Vanderjagt's first 2 field goals to tie the game with 12:06 remaining. After an exchange of punts, the Jets drove to the Colts' 3, only to have Burris step in front of Lucas's pass and return it 55 yards with 4:32 left and set up Vanderjagt's heroics. Peyton Manning was 21 of 35 for 210 yards and 1 touchdown, with 1 interception. Edgerrin James had 26 carries for 111 yards. Lucas was 16 of 30 for 137 yards and 1 touchdown, with 1 interception. Curtis Martin had 23 carries for 128 yards.

Indianapolis	0	7	3	6	—	16
N.Y. Jets	6	7	0	0	—	13

NYJ — FG Hall 45
NYJ — FG Hall 39
NYJ — R. Anderson 18 pass from Lucas (Hall kick)
Ind — Wilkins 22 pass from Manning (Vanderjagt kick)

Ind — FG Vanderjagt 31
Ind — FG Vanderjagt 18
Ind — FG Vanderjagt 27

MIAMI 31, NEW ENGLAND 30—at Foxboro Stadium, attendance 60,006. Damon Huard replaced an injured Dan Marino and guided the Dolphins to a comeback divisional victory on the road. Marino's second pass of the game was intercepted and returned 57 yards for a touchdown by Andy Katzenmoyer. After an exchange of punts, Huard replaced Marino and Ty Law intercepted Huard's first pass and scampered 27 yards for a touchdown. The Dolphins scored on their last five possessions of the half, with Huard's 69-yard touchdown pass to Tony Martin sandwiched between 4 Olindo Mare field goals, but the Patriots led 24-19 at intermission. Adam Vinatieri's third field goal, from 34 yards, gave the Patriots a 30-22 lead with 9:05 left. Following an exchange of punts, Huard's 13- and 14-yard scrambles set up Mare's club-record sixth field goal with 2:45 left. The Patriots went three-and-out, and Huard, starting from the Dolphins' 41, engineered a 14-play drive and converted 4 third-down situations, the last of which was his 5-yard touchdown pass to Stanley Pritchett with 23 seconds left to win the game. Huard, who was sacked 9 times but rushed 6 times for 54 yards, was 24 of 42 for 240 yards and 2 touchdowns, with 1 interception. Martin had 7 catches for 118 yards. Drew Bledsoe was 17 of 36 for 225 yards and 1 touchdown, with 1 interception.

Miami	3	16	0	12	—	31
New England	14	10	3	3	—	30

NE — Katzenmoyer 57 interception return (Vinatieri kick)
NE — Law 27 interception return (Vinatieri kick)
Mia — FG Mare 20
Mia — FG Mare 33
Mia — Martin 69 pass from Huard (Mare kick)
NE — FG Vinatieri 41
Mia — FG Mare 45
NE — Simmons 29 pass from Bledsoe (Vinatieri kick)
Mia — FG Mare 45
NE — FG Vinatieri 39
Mia — FG Mare 41
NE — FG Vinatieri 34
Mia — FG Mare 53
Mia — Pritchett 5 pass from Huard (pass failed)

DETROIT 25, MINNESOTA 23—at Pontiac Silverdome, attendance 76,516. Jason Hanson's 48-yard field goal with seven seconds left denied reserve Jeff George's comeback effort. Terry Fair intercepted Randall Cunningham's pass on the Vikings' fifth play and returned it 41 yards for a touchdown. Hanson added 4 field goals, 2 of which were set up by fumbles by Cunningham and Leroy Hoard, to take a 19-0 halftime lead. George replaced Cunningham to begin the second half and spearheaded a 20-point run, capped by Leroy Hoard's 2-yard run, to take a 20-19 lead with 13:30 remaining. Gus Frerotte, who had replaced an injured Charlie Batch at halftime, guided an 11-play, 54-yard drive that culminated with Hanson's fifth field goal with 7:06 left. The Vikings responded with an 11-play, 71-yard drive that resulted in Gary Anderson's 26-yard field goal with 1:40 remaining. With no time outs, Frerotte completed 5 passes and spiked the ball 4 times to get the Lions in position for Hanson's winning kick. Batch was 9 of 16 for 70 yards, and Frerotte was 15 of 24 for 140 yards. Cunningham was 10 of 15 for 78 yards, with 1 interception, and George was 10 of 12 for 214 yards and 2 touchdowns, with 1 interception.

Minnesota	0	0	14	9	—	23
Detroit	10	9	0	6	—	25

Det — Fair 41 interception return (Hanson kick)
Det — FG Hanson 21
Det — FG Hanson 49
Det — FG Hanson 29
Det — FG Hanson 30
Minn — Carter 17 pass from George (Anderson kick)
Minn — Moss 36 pass from George (Anderson kick)
Minn — Hoard 2 run (pass failed)
Det — FG Hanson 47
Minn — FG Anderson 26
Det — FG Hanson 48

OAKLAND 20, BUFFALO 14—at Ralph Wilson Stadium, attendance 71,113. Eric Turner's interception near the end zone as time expired gave the Raiders a hard-earned victory. Darrien Gordon intercepted Doug Flutie's pass on the game's first play, setting up Tyrone Wheatley's 3-yard run. Antowain Smith scampered 52 yards for a touchdown, but the Raiders responded with 5:47 and 7:07 drives that led to 2 Michael Husted field goals to take a 13-7 halftime lead. Wheatley's 11-yard touchdown run capped the opening drive of the second half and increased the lead to 20-7. Flutie's fourth-and-2 pass from the Raiders' 41 early in the fourth quarter went to Kevin Williams for 29 yards to set up Eric Moulds's touchdown catch. Husted missed a 32-yard field-goal attempt with 59 seconds left, and the Bills drove to the Raiders' 24 with two seconds left when Turner intercepted Flutie's pass near the goal line. The Raiders rushed 48 times for 195 yards and controlled the clock for 39:35. Rich Gannon was 15 of 22 for 155 yards. Flutie was 19 of 41 for 210 yards and 1 touchdown, with 3 interceptions.

Oakland	10	3	7	0	—	20
Buffalo	7	0	0	7	—	14

Oak — Wheatley 3 run (Husted kick)
Buff — A. Smith 52 run (Christie kick)
Oak — FG Husted 25
Oak — FG Husted 32
Oak — Wheatley 11 run (Husted kick)
Buff — Moulds 12 pass from Flutie (Christie kick)

PHILADELPHIA 20, CHICAGO 16—at Soldier Field, attendance 57,476. Doug Pederson passed for 2 touchdowns as the Eagles broke their 18-game road losing streak. Trailing 3-0, the Eagles scored 20 points in an 18-minute span on four consecutive possessions, the last of which was set up by Troy Vincent's 35-yard interception return to the Bears' 5, to give the Eagles a 20-6 lead. Chris Boniol missed a 32-yard field-goal attempt as the half expired, but Cade McNown's 80-yard touchdown pass to Marcus Robinson on the Bears' second play of the half trimmed the deficit to 20-13. Boniol's 44-yard field goal with 7:40 remaining cut the lead to 20-16, but the Bears got no closer than the Eagles' 31, where McNown's fourth-and-4 pass fell incomplete with 3:23 left. Pederson was 22 of 38 for 228 yards and 2 touchdowns. Duce Staley had 23 carries for 101 yards. McNown was 17 of 33 for 255 yards and 1 touchdown, with 2 interceptions.

Philadelphia	7	13	0	0	—	20
Chicago	3	3	7	3	—	16

Chi — FG Boniol 46
Phil — Jells 57 pass from Pederson (N. Johnson kick)
Phil — FG N. Johnson 28
Chi — FG Boniol 40
Phil — Broughton 3 pass from Pederson (N. Johnson kick)
Phil — FG N. Johnson 27
Chi — Robinson 80 pass from McNown (Boniol kick)
Chi — FG Boniol 44

PITTSBURGH 17, CINCINNATI 3—at Cinergy Field, attendance 59,669. Jerome Bettis rushed for 111 yards and 2 touchdowns as the Steelers improved to 3-1 against divisional opponents. Both of Bettis's scoring runs capped 49-yard drives and gave the Steelers a 14-3 halftime lead. The Bengals had chances to score more than just a field goal, but Doug Pelfrey missed a 41-yard attempt, and DeWayne Washington intercepted an Akili Smith pass in Steelers' territory. Bettis had runs of 17 and 14 yards in the fourth quarter to set up Kris Brown's 43-yard field goal, and Orpheus Roye stifled the Bengals' hopes with an interception at the Steelers' 4 with 3:51 remaining. Kordell Stewart was 17 of 29 for 134 yards. Smith was 19 of 38 for 207 yards, with 2 interceptions.

Pittsburgh	7	7	0	3	—	17
Cincinnati	3	0	0	0	—	3

Pitt — Bettis 1 run (Brown kick)
Cin — FG Pelfrey 37
Pitt — Bettis 5 run (Brown kick)
Pitt — FG Brown 43

ST. LOUIS 41, ATLANTA 13—at Georgia Dome, attendance 51,973. Marshall Faulk rushed for 181 yards and 1 touchdown, and the Rams scored on defense and special teams to remain undefeated. The Rams drove 76 and 60 yards on their first two possessions to take a 14-0 lead. After Chris Chandlers' 13-yard touchdown pass to Bob Christian cut the deficit to 14-7, Tony Horne returned the ensuing kickoff 101 yards for a touchdown. The Falcons' drove to the Rams' 9 late in the half, only to have Wistrom snare Chandler's pass and outrun everyone to the end zone. Leading 28-10 at halftime, Kevin Carter's fumble recovery and Billy Jenkins's interception led to Jeff Wilkins's field goals, and Faulk's 49-yard scamper set up Robert Holcombe's 1-yard plunge early in the fourth quarter. Kurt Warner was 13 of 20 for 111 yards and 1 touchdown. Chandler was 10 of 18 for 168 yards and 1 touchdown, with 1 interception. Tony Graziani also was 10 of 18, for 126 yards, with 1 interception.

St. Louis	14	14	6	7	—	41
Atlanta	0	10	0	3	—	13

StL — Bruce 4 pass from Warner (Wilkins kick)
StL — Faulk 6 run (Wilkins kick)
Atl — Christian 13 pass from Chandler (Andersen kick)
StL — Horne 101 kickoff return (Wilkins kick)
StL — Wistrom 91 interception return (Wilkins kick)
Atl — FG Andersen 20
StL — FG Wilkins 22
StL — FG Wilkins 49
StL — Holcombe 1 run (Wilkins kick)
Atl — FG Andersen 25

SAN DIEGO 13, SEATTLE 10—at Qualcomm Stadium, attendance 59,432. Despite committing 4 second-half turnovers, John Carney's 41-yard field goal as time expired kept the Chargers in first place. Seattle led 3-0 late in the first half, but Darryll Lewis's interception at the Seahawks' 34 led to Natrone Means's 5-yard touchdown run just before halftime. Brian Walker's 21-yard interception return in the third quarter set up Jon Kitna's 1-yard touchdown pass to Itula Mili to give Seattle a 10-7 lead. Erik Kramer was intercepted in the Chargers' next three possessions, but Seattle had to punt twice and Todd Peterson missed a 48-yard field-goal attempt. Kramer's 41-yard pass to Jeff Graham set up Carney's tying field goal with 2:54 left. San Diego forced a punt, and, starting from their own 32 with 1:34 left, Kramer completed 4 consecutive passes to set up Carney's heroics. Kramer was 27 of 44 for 296 yards, with 4 interceptions. Kitna was 17 of 29 for 151 yards and 1 touchdown, with 1 interception.

Seattle	0	3	7	0	—	10
San Diego	0	7	0	6	—	13

Sea — FG Peterson 40
SD — Means 5 run (Carney kick)
Sea — Mili 1 pass from Kitna (Peterson kick)
SD — FG Carney 28
SD — FG Carney 41

TENNESSEE 24, NEW ORLEANS 21—at Louisiana Superdome, attendance 51,875. Two fourth-quarter interceptions and a key play just before halftime keyed Tennessee's comeback victory. In the first half, Tennessee missed a 42-yard field-goal attempt, committed a fumble, and was intercepted in Saints' territory. Eric Molden's interception at the Titans' 19 set up Billy Joe Tolliver's 10-yard touchdown pass to Scott Slutzker to give the Saints a 10-0 lead. A pass interference penalty gave the Saints' the ball at the Titans' 1 with 12 seconds left in the half, but Barron Wortham stopped Ricky Williams for no gain and, with no timeouts left, the clock ran out. Neil O'Donnell passed for touchdowns to conclude two of Tennessee's first three possessions of the second half to take a 14-13 lead with 10:08 remaining. Jason Fisk's interception and 17-yard return to the Saints' 10 set up Al Del Greco's field goal with 2:58 left. Donald Mitchell intercepted Tolliver's pass on the next play from scrimmage and scampered 42 yards for a touchdown and a 24-13 Tennessee lead. Tolliver's 4-yard touchdown pass to Lamar Smith, and subsequent 2-point conversion, cut the deficit to three with 45 seconds left, but Derrick Mason recovered the onside kick to seal the victory. O'Donnell was 12 of 25 for 124 yards and 2 touchdowns, with 2 interceptions. Eddie George had 28 carries for 155 yards. Tolliver, who was making his first start for the injured Billy Joe Hobert, was 28 of 45 for 354 yards and 2 touchdowns, with 2 interceptions.

Tennessee	0	0	7	17	—	24
New Orleans	3	7	3	8	—	21

NO — FG Brien 24
NO — Slutzker 10 pass from Tolliver (Brien kick)

Tenn — Neal 4 pass from O'Donnell (Del Greco kick)
NO — FG Brien 42
Tenn — Dyson 11 pass from O'Donnell (Del Greco kick)
Tenn — FG Del Greco 19
Tenn — Mitchell 42 interception return (Del Greco kick)
NO — Smith 4 pass from Tolliver (Bech pass from Tolliver)

SUNDAY NIGHT, OCTOBER 17

WASHINGTON 24, ARIZONA 10—at Sun Devil Stadium, attendance 71,173. Twenty-one-year-old Champ Bailey became the youngest player in NFL history to intercept 3 passes in one game as the Redskins claimed sole possession of first place. Bailey returned his first interception 59 yards for a touchdown to snap a 3-3 tie and give the Redskins a 10-3 lead. His second pick came three plays later on a long pass. In the third quarter, the Redskins marched 90 yards in 12 plays, capped by Brad Johnson's 1-yard pass to Stephen Alexander, to give the Redskins a 17-3 lead. Dave Brown had replaced an injured Jake Plummer earlier in the quarter, but Bailey victimized him too, on the first play following Alexander's touchdown. Brown's 10-yard touchdown pass to Rob Moore trimmed the deficit to 17-10 with 6:59 remaining, but Skip Hicks scampered 14 yards for a touchdown with 2:03 left to finish the scoring. Johnson was 24 of 40 for 248 yards and 1 touchdown, with 2 interceptions. Albert Connell had 8 catches for 110 yards. Plummer was 12 of 23 for 99 yards, with 2 interceptions, before leaving with a broken finger. Brown was 8 of 20 for 117 yards and 1 touchdown, with 1 interception.

Washington	0	10	7	7	—	24
Arizona	3	0	0	7	—	10

Ariz — FG Jacke 44
Wash — FG Conway 36
Wash — Bailey 59 interception return (Conway kick)
Wash — Alexander 1 pass from B. Johnson (Conway kick)
Ariz — Moore 10 pass from Brown (Jacke kick)
Wash — Hicks 14 run (Conway kick)

MONDAY NIGHT, OCTOBER 18

N.Y. GIANTS 13, DALLAS 10—at Giants Stadium, attendance 78,204. Brad Daluiso's 21-yard field goal with one second remaining knocked the Cowboys out of a share for first place in the NFC East. The Cowboys drove inside the Giants' 30 three times in the first half, but Richie Cunningham missed a 48-yard field-goal attempt and, after Cunningham made a 38-yard field goal, Sam Garnes intercepted a Troy Aikman pass at the Giants' 7 to thwart a threat. On the ensuing drive, Graham completed 2 third-down passes to set up Daluiso's 27-yard field goal that tied the game 3-3 at halftime. Special teams hurt the Cowboys in the second half, as Cunningham missed a 41-yard attempt in the third quarter, and Tiki Barber scampered 85 yards with a punt return to give the Giants a 10-3 lead with 7:50 left. Aikman's 36-yard pass to Ernie Mills set up Emmitt Smith's tying 2-yard run with 1:57 left. Faced with second-and-10 from the Giants' 41, Graham dumped a short pass to Barber, who scurried 56 yards before being pulled down by Deion Sanders at the Cowboys' 3. Daluiso's field goal allowed one second left on the clock, and Sanders fielded the kickoff and lateraled to Kevin Mathis, who raced 60 yards and flipped the ball to Singor Mobley, who ran into the end zone. However, Sanders's lateral was ruled forward, which gave the Giants the victory. Graham was 15 of 21 for 183 yards. Aikman was 20 of 33 for 266 yards, with 1 interception.

Dallas	3	0	0	7	—	10
N.Y. Giants	0	3	0	10	—	13

Dall — FG Cunningham 38
NYG — FG Daluiso 27
NYG — Barber 85 punt return (Daluiso kick)
Dall — Smith 2 run (Cunningham kick)
NYG — FG Daluiso 21

SEVENTH WEEK SUMMARIES

AMERICAN FOOTBALL CONFERENCE

Eastern Division	W	L	T	Pct.	Pts.	OP
Miami	5	1	0	.833	156	134
New England	5	2	0	.714	164	147
Indianapolis	4	2	0	.667	164	121
Buffalo	4	3	0	.571	134	119
Indianapolis	1	6	0	.143	112	193
Central Division						
Jacksonville	5	1	0	.833	139	59
Tennessee	5	1	0	.833	142	119
Pittsburgh	4	3	0	.571	130	102
Baltimore	2	4	0	.333	85	122
Cincinnati	1	6	0	.143	86	200
Cleveland	0	7	0	.000	53	181
Western Division						
Kansas City	4	2	0	.667	139	94
San Diego	4	2	0	.667	110	99
Seattle	4	2	0	.667	121	101
Oakland	4	3	0	.571	148	137
Denver	2	5	0	.286	124	145

NATIONAL FOOTBALL CONFERENCE

Eastern Division	W	L	T	Pct.	Pts.	OP
Dallas	4	2	0	.667	158	95
Washington	4	2	0	.667	194	166
N.Y. Giants	4	3	0	.571	115	121
Arizona	2	4	0	.333	79	162
Philadelphia	2	5	0	.286	90	128
Central Division						
Detroit	4	2	0	.667	131	118
Green Bay	4	2	0	.667	133	124
Tampa Bay	3	3	0	.500	88	82
Chicago	3	4	0	.429	107	113
Minnesota	3	4	0	.429	160	138
Western Division						
St. Louis	6	0	0	1.000	217	63
San Francisco	3	4	0	.429	144	207
Carolina	2	4	0	.333	133	135
New Orleans	1	5	0	.167	91	127
Atlanta	1	6	0	.143	83	166

THURSDAY, OCTOBER 21

KANSAS CITY 35, BALTIMORE 8—at PSINet Stadium, attendance 68,771. James Hasty and Reggie Tongue each returned interceptions for touchdowns as the Chiefs downed the Ravens. Kansas City was held without a first down in six of their first seven possessions, but did manage a 9-play, 73-yard drive capped by Elvis Grbac's 11-yard touchdown pass to Tony Gonzalez early in the second quarter. The Ravens managed at least 1 first down in six of their eight first-half possessions, but Matt Stover missed a 37-yard field goal on their only scoring opportunity, and the Chiefs led 7-0 at halftime. Stoyanovich missed a field goal early in the third quarter, but Hasty intercepted Stoney Case's pass and returned it 56 yards for a touchdown. From the Chiefs' 43, Case's fourth-and-2 pass to Jermaine Lewis was incomplete, setting up Grbac's second touchdown pass to Gonzalez. Tongue intercepted Case moments later and scored, giving the Chiefs 21 points in less than 10 minutes, to increase their lead to 28-0. Grbac was 9 of 16 for 112 yards and 2 touchdowns. Case was 15 of 37 for 103 yards, with 3 interceptions.

Kansas City	0	7	7	21	—	35
Baltimore	0	0	0	8	—	8

KC — Gonzalez 11 pass from Grbac (Stoyanovich kick)
KC — Hasty 56 interception return (Stoyanovich kick)
KC — Gonzalez 22 pass from Grbac (Stoyanovich kick)
KC — Tongue 38 interception return (Stoyanovich kick)
Balt — Rhett 2 run (Evans run)
KC — Morris 1 run (Stoyanovich kick)

SUNDAY, OCTOBER 24

SEATTLE 26, BUFFALO 16—at Kingdome, attendance 66,301. Derrick Mayes caught 6 passes for 105 yards and 2 touchdowns as the Seahawks defeated the Bills. The Seahawks scored on their first three possessions to take a 13-0 lead. Two possessions later, Mayes caught a 27-yard third-down pass from Jon Kitna to keep alive a drive that culminated with the duo's 43-yard touchdown to increase the lead to 20-0. Doug Flutie passed for 2 second-half touchdowns to pull within 10 points. However, Michael Sinclair sacked Flutie and forced him to fumble the ball away near midfield with five minutes remaining, and Phillip Daniels sacked Flutie on fourth down with 1:54 left to clinch the victory. Kitna was 17 of 30 for 276 yards and 2 touchdowns. Flutie was 24 of 50 for 294 yards and 2 touchdowns, with 2 interceptions. Peerless Price had 5 receptions for 106 yards.

Buffalo	0	3	6	7	—	16
Seattle	13	10	0	3	—	26

Sea — Mayes 7 pass from Kitna (Peterson kick)
Sea — FG Peterson 40
Sea — FG Peterson 21
Sea — Mayes 43 pass from Kitna (Peterson kick)
Sea — FG Peterson 42
Buff — FG Christie 50
Buff — Price 18 pass from Flutie (bad snap)
Sea — FG Peterson 34
Buff — Riemersma 1 pass from Flutie (Christie kick)

TAMPA BAY 6, CHICAGO 3—at Raymond James Stadium, attendance 65,283. Martin Gramatica kicked 2 field goals, and Derrick Brooks intercepted 2 passes as the Buccaneers snapped a two-game losing streak. Gramatica made 2 field goals, but missed a 43-yard attempt, as Tampa Bay led a 6-0 in the third quarter. The Buccaneers' defense forced the Bears to punt their first seven possessions before Brooks intercepted Cade McNown at the Buccaneers' 36 to thwart the Bears' best drive. However, Gramatica missed another field goal, but Chris Boniol was errant from 44 yards early in the fourth quarter. Jim Miller's 50-yard pass to Bobby Engram set up Boniol's 28-yard boot with 2:24 left, and the Bears got the ball back at their own 29-yard line following a punt, but Brooks intercepeted Miller near midfield with 45 seconds left to preserve the victory. Trent Dilfer was 16 of 27 for 121 yards. McNown was 9 of 23 for 82 yards, with 1 interception. Miller was 10 of 22 for 117 yards, with 1 interception.

Chicago	0	0	0	3	—	3
Tampa Bay	3	3	0	0	—	6

TB — FG Gramatica 49
TB — FG Gramatica 34
Chi — FG Boniol 28

INDIANAPOLIS 31, CINCINNATI 10—at RCA Dome, attendance 55,996. Peyton Manning passed for 2 touchdowns, and Edgerrin James scored twice as the Colts surpassed last season's win total and gave coach Jim Mora his 100th career victory. The Colts scored on three consecutive second-quarter possessions to take a 24-0 first-half lead. The Bengals managed just 1 first down in their first seven possessions before Doug Pelfrey's 32-yard field goal just before halftime put the Bengals on the board. However, Manning's 10-yard touchdown pass to Ken Dilger capped an 11-play drive early in the fourth quarter and gave the Colts a 31-3 lead. Manning was 17 of 33 for 284 yards and 2 touchdowns, with 1 interception. Marvin Harrison had 8 receptions for 156 yards. Akili Smith was 12 of 24 for 122 yards.

Cincinnati	0	3	0	7	—	10
Indianapolis	7	17	0	7	—	31

Ind — Harrison 56 pass from Manning (Vanderjagt kick)
Ind — James 1 run (Vanderjagt kick)
Ind — James 2 run (Vanderjagt kick)
Ind — FG Vanderjagt 22
Cin — FG Pelfrey 32
Ind — Dilger 10 pass from Manning (Vanderjagt kick)
Cin — Scott 10 pass from Blake (Pelfrey kick)

ST. LOUIS 34, CLEVELAND 3—at Trans World Dome, attendance 65,866. Kurt Warner passed for 3 touchdowns as the NFL's lone unbeaten team defeated the Browns. The Rams took a 14-0 lead before the Browns ran a play, because of Charlie Clemons's recovery of Ronnie Powell's fumble on the kickoff return following Warner's first touchdown pass. The Browns did score on their first possession, but the Rams responded with an 8-play, 69-yard drive capped by Warner's second touchdown pass of the game to Roland Williams to take a 21-3 lead with 10:59 left in the half. The Browns drove to the Rams' 4, but Todd Lyght's interception thwarted the drive, and the Browns didn't drive inside the Rams' 30 the remainder of the game. Warner was 23 of 29 for 203 yards and 3 touchdowns. Marshall Faulk had 16 carries for 133 yards, including a 33-yard touchdown run early in the fourth quarter, and had a team-high 9 receptions for 67 yards. Tim Couch was 22 of 40 for 185 yards, with 2 interceptions.

Cleveland	3	0	0	0	—	3
St. Louis	14	7	3	10	—	34

StL — R. Williams 1 pass from Warner (Wilkins kick)
StL — Bruce 4 pass from Warner (Wilkins kick)
Cle — FG Dawson 47
StL — R. Williams 1 pass from Warner (Wilkins kick)
StL — FG Wilkins 28
StL — Faulk 33 run (Wilkins kick)
StL — FG Wilkins 36

NEW ENGLAND 24, DENVER 23—at Foxboro Stadium, attendance 60,011. Terry Allen rushed for 106 yards and 2 touchdowns as the Patriots fought off the Broncos. The Patriots jumped to a 10-0 lead before the Broncos had a first down. Denver responded with scoring drives of 67 and 88 yards, the second of which was keyed by Olandis Gary's 60-yard run, to tie the game 10-10. Drew Bledsoe's 67-yard pass to Terry Glenn set up Allen's 1-yard run just before halftime to give the Patriots a 17-10 lead. Leading 17-13 in the third quarter, Allen had 39- and 18-yard runs to set up his second touchdown and a 24-13 lead. Brian Griese's 7-yard scramble capped an 85-yard drive to cut the deficit to 24-20 in the opening minute of the fourth quarter. Jason Elam made a 30-yard field goal on the Broncos' next drive, and, after forcing a punt, the Broncos drove to the Patriots' 40, but Elam's 59-yard field-goal attempt fell short to give the Patriots there first victory against the Broncos in 19 years. Bledsoe was 13 of 22 for 214 yards. Griese was 25 of 38 for 316 yards and 1 touchdown. Ed McCaffrey had 5 receptions for 111 yards.

Denver	0	10	3	10	—	23
New England	10	7	7	0	—	24

NE — Faulk 15 run (Vinatieri kick)
NE — FG Vinatieri 28
Den — FG Elam 40
Den — R. Smith 28 pass from Griese (Elam kick)
NE — Allen 1 run (Vinatieri kick)
Den — FG Elam 28
NE — Allen 1 run (Vinatieri kick)
Den — Griese 7 run (Elam kick)
Den — FG Elam 30

DETROIT 24, CAROLINA 9—at Ericsson Stadium, attendance 64,322. Charlie Batch passed for 2 touchdowns as the Lions kept pace with the Packers atop the NFC Central standings. The Panthers had a chance to extend a 3-0 lead when Sean Gilbert intercepted a pass at the Lions' 14. However, Mark Carrier intercepted Steve Beuerlein's pass in the end zone three plays later, and the Lions' offense scored on their next two possessions to take a 10-3 lead. Field goals to end the half and begin the third quarter by John Kasay trimmed the Lions' lead to 10-9, but the Lions converted 2 third-down situations on an 8-play, 75-yard drive, capped by Batch's 22-yard scoring pass to David Sloan. Less than four minutes later, Batch's 4-yard touchdown pass to Brian Stablein gave the Lions a 24-9 lead late in the third quarter. The Panthers had a chance to get back into the game, but Ron Rice sacked Beuerlein and forced him to fumble. Tracy Scroggins recovered at the Lions' 20 to quell the threat with 11:16 remaining. The Panthers were stopped on downs at the Lions' 20 in the final minute to secure the victory. Batch was 16 of 27 for 210 yards and 2 touchdowns, with 1 interception. Beuerlein was 26 of 47 for 299 yards, with 1 interception.

Detroit	0	10	14	0	—	24
Carolina	3	3	3	0	—	9

Car — FG Kasay 21
Det — Irvin 1 run (Hanson kick)
Det — FG Hanson 29
Car — FG Kasay 30
Car — FG Kasay 23
Det — Sloan 22 pass from Batch (Hanson kick)
Det — Stablein 4 pass from Batch (Hanson kick)

GREEN BAY 31, SAN DIEGO 3—at Qualcomm Stadium, attendance 68,274. Brett Favre passed for 3 touchdowns as the Packers turned 6 interceptions into 24 points to knock the Chargers from atop the AFC West standings. In the first quarter, Mike McKenzie intercepted Erik Kramer's pass in the end zone for a touchback, which sparked an 80-yard drive by the Packers, capped by Favre's 7-yard touchdown pass to William Henderson. Fred Vinson intercepted Kramer at the Chargers' 28 two plays later, setting up Dorsey Levens's 6-yard scoring run. An interception by Jimmy Spencer at the Packers' 34 set up John Carney's field goal, and the Chargers had a chance to score in the final seconds of the half, but with six seconds left and no timeouts, Kramer scrambled for 3 yards to the Packers' 7 as time expired. A 44-yard pass interference penalty set up Favre's 6-yard touchdown pass to Bill Schroeder, and, after Tyrone Williams intercepted Kramer at the Packers' 1 to halt another long drive, the Packers marched 99 yards in 14 plays, culminated by Favre' 3-yard touchdown pass to Antonio Freeman for a 28-3 lead late in the third quarter. Favre was 12 of 22 for 173 yards and 3 touchdowns, with 1 interception. Kramer was 18 of 36 for 161 yards, with 3 interceptions, and Jim Harbaugh was 7 of 18 for 78 yards, with 3 interceptions in the fourth quarter.

Green Bay	7	7	14	3	—	31
San Diego	0	3	0	0	—	3

GB — Henderson 7 pass from Favre (Longwell kick)
GB — Levens 6 run (Longwell kick)
SD — FG Carney 28
GB — Schroeder 6 pass from Favre (Longwell kick)
GB — Freeman 3 pass from Favre (Longwell kick)
GB — FG Longwell 46

N.Y. GIANTS 31, NEW ORLEANS 3—at Giants Stadium, attendance 77,982. Kent Graham passed for 2 touchdowns and ran for another as the Giants defeated the Saints. Graham's 6-yard run capped a 12-play, 80-yard drive, but the Siants responded with Doug Brien's 25-yard field goal. The Giants then scored on three of their four second-quarter possessions, capped by Graham's 53-yard Hail Mary pass to Joe Jurevicius as the first half ended to give the Giants a 24-3 halftime edge. The Giants' defense intercepted 3 passes in the second half, twice in Giants' territory. The other was a 31-yard return by Jessie Armstead to the Saints' 12 that set up Joe Montgomery's touchdown run. Graham was 19 of 29 for 239 yards and 2 touchdowns, with 1 interception. Billy Joe Tolliver was 14 of 33 for 176 yards, with 3 interceptions. Ricky Williams rushed 24 times for 111 yards.

New Orleans	3	0	0	0	—	3
N.Y. Giants	7	17	7	0	—	31

NYG — Graham 6 run (Blanchard kick)
NO — FG Brien 25
NYG — FG Blanchard 41
NYG — Toomer 27 pass from Graham (Blanchard kick)
NYG — Jurevicius 53 pass from Graham (Blanchard kick)
NYG — Montgomery 12 run (Blanchard kick)

OAKLAND 24, N.Y. JETS 23—at Network Associates Coliseum, attendance 47,326. Rich Gannon's 5-yard touchdown pass to James Jett with 26 seconds remaining gave the Raiders a comeback victory against the Jets. With the score tied 3-3, Bryan Cox recovered Tyrone Wheatley's fumble at the Raiders' 9 to set up Rick Mirer's 9-yard scoring run. The Raiders proceeded to drive to the Jets' 4, but Gannon was sacked by Mo Lewis and fumbled. Omar Stoutmire recovered to stifle the drive and allow the Jets to maintain a 10-3 halftime lead. The Jets scored on their first two possessions of the second half, the second of which was set up by Victor Green's recovery of Wheatley's second fumble, to give the Jets a 20-3 lead. The Raiders drove 72 and 83 yards on their next two posessions to trim the deficit to 20-17 with 8:23 remaining, and the defense forced another punt. However, Aaron Glenn intercepted Gannon near midfield, and John Hall's 43-yard field goal with 1:55 left increased the Jets lead to 23-17. The Raiders then went 90 yards in 11 plays, highlighted by Gannon's 23-yard pass to Terry Mickens on third-and-10 and his 36-yard pass to Tim Brown to the Jets' 5, and capped by the Gannon's 5-yard pass to Jett with 26 seconds remaining. Marquis Walker intercepted Mirer near midfield to secure the victory. Mirer was 13 of 22 for 158 yards and 1 touchdown, with 2 interceptions. Gannon was 26 of 51 for 352 yards and 2 touchdowns, with 1 interception. Brown had 11 receptions for 190 yards. Mirer was 13 of 22 for 158 yards and 1 touchdown, with 2 interceptions. Curtis Martin had 26 carries for 123 yards.

N.Y. Jets	0	10	10	3	—	23
Oakland	3	0	7	14	—	24

Oak — FG Husted 25
NYJ — FG Hall 32
NYJ — Mirer 9 run (Hall kick)
NYJ — Green 2 pass from Mirer (Hall kick)
NYJ — FG Hall 37
Oak — Brown 45 pass from Gannon (Husted kick)
Oak — Crockett 3 run (Husted kick)
NYJ — FG Hall 43
Oak — Jett 5 pass from Gannon (Husted kick)

MIAMI 16, PHILADELPHIA 13—at Pro Player Stadium, attendance 73,975. Olindo Mare made 3 field goals, and Norm Johnson missed a 42-yard attempt in the final minute as the Dolphins remained in first place in the AFC East. Miami scored on its first two possessions, both of which featured successful third-down conversion runs by Damon Huard, to take a 10-0 lead, and Jason Taylor's fumble recovery at the Eagles' 27 set up Mare's second field goal and gave the Dolphins a 13-3 lead. Derrick Rodgers ended an Eagles' scoring opportunity just before halftime with an interception at the Dolphins' 20, but Philadelphia cut the lead to 13-10 late in the third quarter on Brian Dawkins's 67-yard interception return. The Dolphins responded with Mare's third field goal, but Johnson made a 44-yard attempt with 6:08 remaining. The Dolphins were attempting to run out the clock when William Thomas forced Cecil Collins to fumble, and Dawkins recovered the ball at the Eagles' 41 with 2:37 remaining. The Eagles reached the Dolphins' 24 with 59 seconds left, but Johnson's attempt was pushed wide right. The Dolphins' defense limited the Eagles to just 175 total yards. Huard was 15 of 21 for 142 yards, with 1 interception. Doug Pederson was 13 of 25 for 108 yards, with 1 interception.

Philadelphia	0	3	7	3	—	13
Miami	10	3	0	3	—	16

Mia — FG Mare 37
Mia — J. Johnson 18 run (Mare kick)
Phil — FG Akers 53
Mia — FG Mare 37
Phil — Dawkins 67 interception return (N. Johnson kick)
Mia — FG Mare 53
Phil — FG N. Johnson 44

MINNESOTA 40, SAN FRANCISCO 16—at Metrodome, attendance 64,109. Jeff George passed for 3 touchdowns in his first start of the season as the Vikings handed the 49ers their third consecutive defeat. The Vikings led 7-3 early in the second quarter when Darnell Walker recovered Leroy Hoard's fumble and raced 71 yards for a touchdown. The Vikings needed just 17 seconds to respond, as George hit Matthew Hatchette for an 80-yard touchdown. A missed field goal and interception in the end zone by Lance Schulters stifled the Vikings later in the quarter, but George's 7-yard touchdown pass to Andrew Jordan with 1:06 left in the half increased the lead to 21-13 and John Randle's interception at the 49ers' 15 with three seconds left set up Gary Anderson's 33-yard field goal as the half expired gave Minnesota a 24-13 lead. Wade Richey's field goal to open the third quarter cut the lead to 24-16, but the Vikings scored on their next two possessions to pull away. George was 15 of 28 for 250 yards and 3 touchdowns, with 1 interception. Hoard had 17 carries for 105 yards. Jeff Garcia was 14 of 31 for 188 yards, with 2 interceptions.

San Francisco	3	10	3	0	—	16
Minnesota	7	17	7	9	—	40

Minn — Hoard 1 run (Anderson kick)
SF — FG Richey 22
SF — Walker 71 fumble return (Richey kick)
Minn — Hatchette 80 pass from George (Anderson kick)
SF — FG Richey 31
Minn — Jordan 7 pass from George (Anderson kick)
Minn — FG Anderson 33
SF — FG Richey 26
Minn — M. Williams 9 run (Anderson kick)
Minn — Carter 2 pass from George (Anderson kick)
Minn — Safety, Fann penalized for holding in end zone

DALLAS 38, WASHINGTON 20—at Texas Stadium, attendance 64,377. Troy Aikman passed for 2 touchdowns and ran for another as the Cowboys joined the Redskins atop the NFC East. The Cowboys scored on their first three possessions, capped by Emmitt Smith's 1-yard run, to take a 17-0 lead with 8:59 remaining in the first half. Washington scored on its next two possessions to trim the lead to 17-10, and Brett Conway's field goal early in the second half cut the deficit to 17-13. Dallas drove 75 and 93 yards on its next two possessions to take a 31-20 lead with 10:50 left. Deion Sanders returned a punt 70 yards for a touchdown with 9:03 left to finish the scoring. Aikman was 20 of 32 for 244 yards and 2 touchdowns. Brad Johnson was 23 of 35 for 218 yards and 2 touchdowns.

Washington	0	10	10	0	—	20
Dallas	10	7	7	14	—	38

Dall — Ismail 13 pass from Aikman (Cunningham kick)
Dall — FG Cunningham 32
Dall — E. Smith 1 run (Cunningham kick)
Wash — Sellers 33 pass from B. Johnson (Conway kick)
Wash — FG Conway 36
Wash — FG Conway 24
Dall — LaFleur 4 pass from Aikman (Cunningham kick)
Wash — Connell 44 pass from B. Johnson (Conway kick)
Dall — Aikman 1 run (Cunningham kick)
Dall — Sanders 70 punt return (Cunningham kick)

MONDAY NIGHT, OCTOBER 25

PITTSBURGH 13, ATLANTA 9—at Three Rivers Stadium, attendance 58,141. The Steelers' defense kept the Falcons out of the end zone on five plays from inside the Steelers' 5-yard line in the final three minutes to improve to 8-0 at home under coach Bill Cowher on *Monday Night Football*. Chad Scott's 16-yard interception return to the Falcons' 11 set up Kordell Stewart's touchdown pass to Richard Huntley late in the first quarter. Rookie Kris Brown converted 2 second-quarter field goals to tie an NFL record with 11 consecutive made field goals to begin his career. The Steelers' 13-0 lead held up into the fourth quarter until Chandler engineered a 10-play, 56-yard drive, capped by a 5-yard touchdown pass to Terance Mathis, to cut the deficit to 13-7 with 6:42 remaining. Marty Carter recovered Jerome Bettis's fumble at the Steelers' 47 with 3:39 left, and Chandler's 40-yard pass to Mathis on the next play put the Falcons in scoring position. Ken Oxendine ran for 6 yards to the Steelers' 1, but Bob Christian lost 1 yard on 2 carries, and Oxendine was stopped at the 1-yard line on fourth down with 1:45 remaining. On fourth-and-2 from the Falcons' 9 with 1:24 left, punter Josh Miller stepped out of the end zone for a safety. Chandler completed a 27-yard pass over the middle to Tim Dwight to reach the Steelers' 5. With no timeouts, Chandler limped to the line and spiked the ball with two seconds left to set up one final play. However, his pass sailed behind Dwight in the end zone and the Steelers survived. Stewart was 13 of 21 for 127 yards and 1 touchdown. Chandler was 20 of 34 for 233 yards and 1 touchdown, with 1 interception. Mathis had 12 catches for 166 yards.

Atlanta	0	0	0	9	—	9
Pittsburgh	7	6	0	0	—	13

Pitt — Huntley 13 pass from Stewart (Brown kick)
Pitt — FG Brown 51
Pitt — FG Brown 25
Atl — Mathis 5 pass from Chandler (Andersen kick)
Atl — Safety, Miller stepped out of end zone

EIGHTH WEEK SUMMARIES

AMERICAN FOOTBALL CONFERENCE

Eastern Division	**W**	**L**	**T**	**Pct.**	**Pts.**	**OP**
Miami	6	1	0	.857	172	143
New England	6	2	0	.750	191	150
Indianapolis	5	2	0	.714	198	145
Buffalo	5	3	0	.625	147	129
N.Y. Jets	1	6	0	.143	114	143
Central Division						
Jacksonville	6	1	0	.857	180	69
Tennessee	6	1	0	.857	166	140
Pittsburgh	4	3	0	.571	130	102
Baltimore	2	5	0	.286	95	135
Cincinnati	1	7	0	.125	96	241
Cleveland	1	7	0	.125	74	197
Western Division						
Kansas City	5	2	0	.714	173	94
Seattle	5	2	0	.714	148	108
San Diego	4	3	0	.571	110	133
Oakland	4	4	0	.500	157	153
Denver	2	6	0	.250	144	168

NATIONAL FOOTBALL CONFERENCE

Eastern Division	**W**	**L**	**T**	**Pct.**	**Pts.**	**OP**
Washington	5	2	0	.714	242	188
N.Y. Giants	5	3	0	.625	138	138
Dallas	4	3	0	.571	182	129
Arizona	2	5	0	.286	85	156
Philadelphia	2	6	0	.250	107	151
Central Division						
Detroit	5	2	0	.714	151	121
Green Bay	4	3	0	.571	140	151
Minnesota	4	4	0	.500	183	158
Tampa Bay	3	4	0	.429	91	102
Chicago	3	5	0	.375	129	161
Western Division						
St. Louis	6	1	0	.857	238	87
San Francisco	3	4	0	.429	144	207
Carolina	2	5	0	.286	153	162
Atlanta	2	6	0	.250	110	186
New Orleans	1	6	0	.143	107	148

SUNDAY, OCTOBER 31

BUFFALO 13, BALTIMORE 10—at PSINet Stadium, attendance 68,673. Doug Flutie's 5-yard touchdown pass to Jonathan Linton with 1:35 remaining capped the Bills' comeback victory at Baltimore. Tony Banks, receiving his first start of the season, guided the Ravens on a 10-play, 50-yard scoring drive on their second possession, to take a 7-0 lead. Chris McAlister's interception at the Bills' 20 moments later led to Matt Stover's 37-yard field goal and a 10-0 lead. Pat Williams blocked Stover's 51-yard attempt with 2:03 left in the half, and the Bills converted the key special-teams play into a Steve Christie field goal to cut the deficit to 10-3 at halftime. Interceptions by Rod Woodson and Duane Starks in Ravens' territory stifled third-quarter drives by the Bills, but 2 turnovers by the Ravens in the fourth quarter led to their demise. First, Kurt Schulz's 26-yard interception return to the Ravens' 34 resulted in a 12-play, 13-yard drive, capped by Christie's 40-yard field goal that trimmed the score to 10-6 with 6:21 left. On the ensuing possession, Banks was scrambling for a first down when Gabe Northern forced him to fumble, and Sam Rogers recovered near midfield with 3:25 remaining. Flutie's 17-yard scramble on fourth-and-15 highlighted the game-clinching 9-play, 45-yard drive, culminated by Flutie's 5-yard touchdown pass to Linton. The Ravens failed to cross midfield with their final possession. Flutie was 18 of 40 for 155 yards and 1 touchdown, with 3 interceptions. Banks was 13 of 34 for 129 yards and 1 touchdown, with 1 interception.

Buffalo	0	3	0	10	—	13
Baltimore	10	0	0	0	—	10

Balt — Armour 7 pass from Banks (Stover kick)
Balt — FG Stover 37
Buff — FG Christie 25
Buff — FG Christie 40
Buff — Linton 5 pass from Flutie (Christie kick)

ATLANTA 27, CAROLINA 20—at Georgia Dome, attendance 52,594. Chris Chandler and Tim Dwight connected for 2 touchdowns, and the defense recorded 6 sacks and forced 5 turnovers as the Falcons won their first home game of the season. The Panthers led 3-0, but Atlanta scored on its next three possessions, the last of which was set up by Eugene Robinson's 7-yard interception return to the Panthers' 33, to take a 13-3 lead. Shane Dronett's 15-yard return of Steve Beuerlein's fumble to the Panthers' 5 in the third quarter set up Ken Oxendine's 1-yard run and gave Atlanta a 20-6 lead. Michael Bates quickly brought Carolina back into the game with a 100-yard kickoff return for a touchdown, but the Falcons responded with Dwight's second touchdown catch and the Panthers were stopped on downs at the Falcons' 41. Beuerlein fumbled the ball away at the Falcons' 29 on Carolina's next two possessions. Beuerlein's 54-yard pass to Donald Hayes set up his 1-yard sneak with 3:07 left, but Beuerlein was intercepted by Gerald McBurrows at the Panthers' 43 with 14 seconds left to secure the victory. Chandler was 14 of 21 for 201 yards and 2 touchdowns. Beuerlein was 21 of 35 for 256 yards, with 3 interceptions.

Carolina	3	3	7	7	—	20
Atlanta	7	6	7	7	—	27

Car — FG Kasay 31
Atl — Dwight 35 pass from Chandler (Andersen kick)
Atl — FG Andersen 39
Atl — FG Andersen 24
Car — FG Kasay 51
Atl — Oxendine 1 run (Andersen kick)
Car — Bates 100 kickoff return (Kasay kick)
Atl — Dwight 4 pass from Chandler (Andersen kick)
Car — Beuerlein 1 run (Kasay kick)

WASHINGTON 48, CHICAGO 22—at Redskins Stadium, attendance 77,621. Stephen Davis rushed for 145 yards and 2 touchdowns as the Redskins surpassed the Rams as the NFL's highest-scoring team. Davis raced 76 yards for a touchdown on the second play from scrimmage. Moments later, Dan Wilkinson intercepted Steve Matthews's pass and rumbled 88 yards for a touchdown. On Chicago's next possession, Matt Stevens dropped Curtis Enis for a 4-yard loss on fourth-and-1 at the Redskins' 22. The Redskins' offense responded by scoring on five of their next six possessions to take a 45-0 lead with 6:37 remaining in the third quarter. Cade McNown, who entered the game just before halftime, passed for 3 second-half touchdowns. Brad Johnson was 15 of 25 for 204 yards and 2 touchdowns. Matthews was 13 of 23 for 113 yards, with 1 interception, and McNown was 23 of 40 for 272 yards and 3 touchdowns, with 3 interceptions. Marcus Robinson had 9 receptions for 161 yards.

Chicago	0	0	14	8	—	22
Washington	14	17	14	3	—	48

Wash — Davis 76 run (Conway kick)
Wash — Wilkinson 88 interception return (Conway kick)
Wash — FG Conway 50
Wash — Johnson 1 run (Conway kick)
Wash — Westbrook 13 pass from Johnson (Conway kick)
Wash — Davis 2 run (Conway kick)
Wash — Centers 22 pass from Johnson (Conway kick)
Chi — Robinson 30 pass from McNown (Boniol kick)
Chi — Robinson 52 pass from McNown (Boniol kick)
Wash — FG Conway 51
Chi — Wetnight 3 pass from McNown (McNown run)

CLEVELAND 21, NEW ORLEANS 16—at Louisiana Superdome, attendance 48,817. The Browns won their first game since rejoining the NFL in dramatic fashion on Tim Couch's 56-yard Hail Mary touchdown pass to Kevin Johnson as time expired. A fumbled punt by David Dunn at the Browns' 15 led to the Saints' first touchdown, and Roy Barker's 14-yard interception return to the Saints' 22 set up Couch's touchdown pass to Marc Edwards to tie the game. Darius Holland's 14-yard return of Billy Joe Tolivers' fumble to the Saints' 22 set up Couch's 24-yard touchdown pass to Kevin Johnson midway through the third quarter to give the Browns a 14-10 lead. Doug Brien's 22-yard field goal cut the deficit to 14-13, but Ricky Williams's fumble at the Browns' 12 with 5:27 remaining thwarted a Saints opportunity. However, the Saints got the ball back, and Brien's 46-yard field goal with 21 seconds left gave New Orleans a 16-14 lead. Couch completed a 19-yard pass to Leslie Shepherd before launching his 56-yard touchdown pass to Johnson, who caught the ball after it had been tipped by two defenders. Couch was 11 of 19 for 193 yards and 3 touchdowns. Billy Joe Tolliver was

9 of 20 for 92 yards, with 1 interception. Williams rushed 40 times for a career-high 179 yards.

Cleveland	0	7	7	7	—	21
New Orleans	7	3	3	3	—	16

NO — Poole 5 pass from Hobert (Brien kick)
Cle — Edwards 27 pass from Couch (Dawson kick)
NO — FG Brien 49
Cle — K. Johnson 24 pass from Couch (Dawson kick)
NO — FG Brien 22
NO — FG Brien 46
Cle — K. Johnson 56 pass from Couch (Dawson kick)

INDIANAPOLIS 34, DALLAS 24—at RCA Dome, attendance 56,860. Edgerrin James tallied 205 total yards, and Mike Vanderjagt kicked 4 field goals as the Colts exploded for 28 second-half points to comeback and defeat the Cowboys. The Cowboys scored on their first three possessions, the second of which was set up by Darren Hambrick's blocked punt, to give the Cowboys a 17-3 lead. James's 37-yard run set up Vanderjagt's second field goal just before halftime to trim the deficit to 17-6. While the Cowboys failed to tally a first down on four of their first five possessions of the second half, the Colts scored on their first five possessions of the half. The Colts got a break when Terrence Wilkins fell on James's fumble in the end zone early in the third quarter to cut the Cowboys lead to 17-14. On the next play from scrimmage, Chad Bratzke sacked Aikman and forced him to fumble, with Bratzke recovering the ball at the Cowboys' 1 to set up James's touchdown. Aikman completed 4 of 4 passes on the next drive as Dallas retook the lead, but Peyton Manning's 40-yard touchdown pass to a wide- open Harrison on the first play of the fourth quarter gave the Colts the lead for good. Manning was 22 of 34 for 312 yards and 1 touchdown. James rushed 26 times for 113 yards. Aikman was 19 of 24 for 159 yards.

Dallas	10	7	7	0	—	24
Indianapolis	3	3	15	13	—	34

Dall — E. Smith 2 run (Cunningham kick)
Dall — FG Cunningham 24
Ind — FG Vanderjagt 43
Dall — Warren 4 run (Cunningham kick)
Ind — FG Vanderjagt 30
Ind — Wilkins recovered fumble in end zone (Harrison pass from Manning)
Ind — James 1 run (Vanderjagt kick)
Dall — E. Smith 4 run (Cunningham kick)
Ind — Harrison 40 pass from Manning (Vanderjagt kick)
Ind — FG Vanderjagt 33
Ind — FG Vanderjagt 27

JACKSONVILLE 41, CINCINNATI 10—at Cinergy Field, attendance 49,138. After a two-week layoff because of a pulled hamstring, Fred Taylor rushed for 128 yards and scored a touchdown as the Jaguars won their fourth consecutive game. The Jaguars scored on their first five possessions to take a 27-0 halftime lead. Taylor's 35-yard run highlighted the game's first drive, capped by his 1-yard plunge. Leading 14-0, Aaron Beasley's 38-yard interception return stifled the Bengals and led to Mike Hollis's field goal. On the Bengals ensuing possession, Donovin Darius's interception at the Jaguars' 2 stopped Cincinnati. The Jaguars proceeded to drive 98 yards, capped by Mark Brunell's 3-yard scoring pass to Jimmy Smith, to take a 24-0 lead, and Brunell's 38-yard pass to Tavian Banks on third-and-14 set up Hollis's 21-yard field goal just before halftime. Brunell, who didn't play in the fourth quarter, was 11 of 19 for 145 yards and 2 touchdowns. Akili Smith was 6 of 12 for 67 yards, with 2 interceptions, and reserve Jeff Blake was 13 of 23 for 155 yards and 1 touchdown.

Jacksonville	14	13	7	7	—	41
Cincinnati	0	0	3	7	—	10

Jax — Taylor 1 run (Hollis kick)
Jax — McCardell 23 pass from Brunell (Hollis kick)
Jax — FG Hollis 43
Jax — Smith 3 pass from Brunell (Hollis kick)
Jax — FG Hollis 21
Cin — FG Pelfrey 29
Jax — Stewart 1 run (Hollis kick)
Jax — Stewart 1 run (Hollis kick)
Cin — Jackson 15 pass from Blake (Pelfrey kick)

MIAMI 16, OAKLAND 9—at Network Associates Coliseum, attendance 49,138. Olindo Mare kicked 3 field goals, and the Dolphins' defense permitted just 187 yards as Miami won its fourth consecutive game. The score was 3-3 in the second quarter when Terrell Buckley's 15-yard interception return to the Dolphins' 49 led to Cecil Collins's 1-yard scoring run and a 10-3 Miami lead at halftime. The Dolphins led 13-9, but Mare missed a 46-yard attempt late in the third quarter, and Collins was stopped on fourth-and-1 from the Raiders' 12 with 6:59 left. However, the Raiders were forced to punt, and Mare made a 44-yard attempt to increase the lead to 16-9 with 3:21 remaining. The Raiders gained consecutive first downs to reach the Dolphins' 38, but Rich Gannon was sacked twice and the Raiders punted on fourth-and-24 with two minutes left. J.J. Johnson gained 4 yards on third-and-1 to seal the victory. Damon Huard, who was playing for the injured Dan Marino, was 16 of 32 for 221 yards. Gannon was 7 of 28 for 130 yards, with 1 interception. Tim Brown had 7 catches for 113 yards.

Miami	3	7	3	3	—	16
Oakland	3	0	6	0	—	9

Oak — FG Husted 49
Mia — FG Mare 21
Mia — Collins 1 run (Mare kick)
Oak — FG Husted 34
Mia — FG Mare 34
Oak — FG Husted 47
Mia — FG Mare 44

MINNESOTA 23, DENVER 20—at Mile High Stadium, attendance 75,021. Gary Anderson kicked a game-winning 23-yard field goal with one second left as the Vikings evened their record. The Broncos scored 3 times in the first nine minutes, with scoring drives of 70 and 66 yards sandwiched around Trevor Pryce's sack of Jeff George for a safety, to give the Broncos a 12-0 lead. Orlando Thomas's 27-yard interception return for a touchdown trimmed the deficit to 12-7, and after the Broncos were forced to punt, Leroy Hoard's 53-yard run on third-and-27 led to George's 37-yard touchdown pass to Cris Carter that gave the Vikings a 13-12 halftime lead. Jason Elam missed a 37-yard field-goal attempt in the third quarter that would have given the Broncos the lead, and the Vikings responded early in the fourth quarter by converting 2 third-down-and-long situations before George's second touchdown pass. Brian Griese completed 18- and 25-yard passes to Rod Smith to set up his 1-yard touchdown pass to Byron Chamberlain, and with the ensuing 2-point conversion run by Olandis Gary, to tie the game with 5:09 left. The Vikings responded with a 13-play, 73-yard drive in which George completed 5 of 7 passes, and the Vikings converted 2 third downs to set up Anderson's winning kick. George was 17 of 29 for 218 yards and 2 touchdowns. Carter had 8 receptions for 144 yards. Griese was 24 of 40 for 274 yards and 1 touchdown, with 1 interception. Smith had 7 receptions for 117 yards.

Minnesota	0	13	0	10	—	23
Denver	12	0	0	8	—	20

Den — Loville 36 run (Elam kick)
Den — Safety, Pryce sacked George in end zone
Den — FG Elam 19
Minn — Thomas 27 interception return (Anderson kick)
Minn — Carter 37 pass from George (pass failed)
Minn — Carter 16 pass from George (Anderson kick)
Den — Chamberlain 1 pass from Griese (Gary run)
Minn — FG Anderson 23

NEW ENGLAND 27, ARIZONA 3—at Sun Devil Stadium, attendance 55,830. Drew Bledsoe passed for 4 touchdowns, and the Patriots' defense permitted just 8 first downs to defeat the Cardinals. The first half was a battle of field position, and the Cardinals had to start all nine of their first-half possessions inside the Cardinals' 25 and never drove beyond the Patriots' 48. Meanwhile, the Patriots produced touchdown drives of just 53 and 61 yards, with a 64-yard touchdown pass from Bledsoe to Shawn Jefferson in between, en route to a 20-0 halftime lead. The Cardinals drove 60 yards for a field goal to begin the third quarter, but Bledsoe's 36-yard touchdown pass to Terry Glenn early in the fourth quarter put the game away. Bledsoe was 14 of 22 for 276 yards and 4 touchdowns. Jefferson had 3 receptions for 113 yards. Dave Brown, who played for an injured Jake Plummer, was 12 of 33 for 107 yards, with 2 interceptions.

New England	14	6	0	7	—	27
Arizona	0	0	3	0	—	3

NE — Warren 3 pass from Bledsoe (Vinatieri kick)
NE — Jefferson 64 pass from Bledsoe (Vinatieri kick)
NE — Jefferson 35 pass from Bledsoe (kick blocked)
Ariz — FG Jacke 24
NE — Glenn 36 pass from Bledose (Vinatieri kick)

N.Y. GIANTS 23, PHILADELPHIA 17 (OT)—at Veterans Stadium, attendance 66,481. Michael Strahan intercepted a pass and returned it 44 yards for a touchdown in overtime as the Giants won their third consecutive game with the help of two key plays by Christian Peter. With the score tied 3-3 in the second quarter, Cary Blanchard, in his first game with the Giants, missed a 35-yard field goal. The Eagles promptly scored on their next two possessions, capped by Doug Pederson's 84-yard touchdown pass to Torrance Small, to give the Eagles a 17-3 halftime lead. The Giants used a 16-play, 83-yard drive, which consumed nearly nine minutes, resulting in Leshon Johnson's 2-yard run, to cut the deficit to 17-10 with 13:07 remaining. The Eagles had a chance to extend their lead, but Peter blocked Norm Johnson's 33-yard field-goal attempt with 6:29 left. A 63-yard punt by Brad Maynard pinned the Eagles back to their own 3-yard line with 3:08 left, and, on third down, Keith Hamilton forced Duce Staley to fumble. Andre Weathers recovered at the Eagles' 5, and Kent Graham's 7-yard touchdown pass to Pete Mitchell two plays later tied the game with 2:00 left. Long-kicker David Akers's 59-yard field-goal attempt fell short, sending the game to overtime. The Eagles forced a punt, but on third-and-8 from the Giants' 45, Peter batted Pederson's pass in the air. Strahan snared the ball and lumbered 44 yards for his second career touchdown. Graham was 26 of 42 for 240 yards and 1 touchdown. Pederson was 18 of 28 for 256 yards and 1 touchdown, with 2 interceptions. Small had 4 receptions for 119 yards.

N.Y. Giants	3	0	0	14	6	—	23
Philadelphia	3	14	0	0	0	—	17

Phil — FG N. Johnson 28
NYG — FG Blanchard 28
Phil — Staley 21 run (N. Johnson kick)
Phil — Small 84 pass from Pederson (N. Johnson kick)
NYG — L. Johnson 2 run (Blanchard kick)
NYG — Mitchell 7 pass from Graham (Blanchard kick)
NYG — Strahan 44 interception return

TENNESSEE 24, ST. LOUIS 21—at Adelphia Coliseum, attendance 55,830. In a preview of Super Bowl XXXIV, Jeff Wilkins missed a 38-yard field-goal attempt with seven seconds remaining as the Titans improved to 6-1 for the first time since 1991. In his first game since back surgery six weeks earlier, Steve McNair passed for 2 touchdowns and ran for another in the first quarter to stake the Titans to a 21-0 lead. The Titans drove 80 yards with the game's first possession, and, after an exchange of punts, Joe Bowden sacked Kurt Warner and forced him to fumble. Barron Wortham's 8-yard return to the Rams' 15 set up McNair's second touchdown pass. Two plays later, Wortham recovered another Warner fumble, this time at the Rams' 26, and McNair went up the middle on a 10-yard scoring run two plays later to give Tennessee a 21-0 lead over the undefeated Rams, who had beaten their first six opponents by an average of 25.7 points. Warner's 57-yard touchdown pass to Marshall Faulk two plays into the second half started the Rams rally, and Warner's 3-yard scoring pass to Bruce on the next possession pulled the Rams within a touchdown. McNair's 34-yard pass to Yancey Thigpen on the ensuing possession led to Al Del Greco's 27-yard field goal and a 24-14 lead. Warner completed passes to 5 different players on an 11-play, 80-yard drive that resulted in his 15-yard touchdown pass to Amp Lee with 2:14 left. Lorenzo Styles recovered the ensuing onside kick, and Warner's 15-yard fourth-and-10 pass to Az-Zahir Hakim at the Titans' 29 set up Wilkins's game-tying attempt, which sailed wide right from 38 yards. McNair was 13 of 29 for 186 yards and 2 touchdowns. Warner was 29 of 46 for 328 yards and 3 touchdowns.

St. Louis	0	0	14	7	—	21
Tennessee	21	0	3	0	—	24

Tenn — Neal 1 pass from McNair (Del Greco kick)
Tenn — George 17 pass from McNair (Del Greco kick)
Tenn — McNair 10 run (Del Greco kick)
StL — Faulk 57 pass from Warner (Wilkins kick)
StL — Bruce 3 pass from Warner (Wilkins kick)
Tenn — FG Del Greco 27
StL — Lee 15 pass from Warner (Wilkins kick)

KANSAS CITY 34, SAN DIEGO 0—at Arrowhead Stadium, attendance 78,473. The Chiefs' defense tallied 5 sacks and forced 4 turnovers to record their first shutout since 1997. Cris Dishman's 7-yard interception return on the Chargers' third play set up Pete Stoyanovich's first field goal. Reggie Tongue's 7-yard fumble return three plays later gave the Chiefs a 10-0 lead 7:10 into the game. The Chiefs engineered 12- and 8-play drives in the second quarter to take a 20-0 lead, and Kansas City almost turned a near disaster into points at the end of the half when Michael Dumas blocked Darren Pope's punt as the half expired. The ball went directly to the Chiefs' Greg Manusky, who lumbered 84 yards before being pulled down by Chris Penn at the Chargers' 7 to end the half. The Chiefs scored twice in 29 seconds in the third quarter, the second of which was set up by Derrick Thomas's 20-yard interception return to the Chargers' 7, to take a 34-0 lead with 2:58 left in the third quarter. The Chiefs' defense stopped the Chargers' on third- and fourth-and-goal from the 1-yard line early in the fourth quarter, and on the next possession Jim Harbaugh's fourth-and-5 pass from the Chiefs' 15 fell incomplete. Elvis Grbac was 11 of 15 for 194 yards and 2 touchdowns. Derrick Alexander had 2 catches for 113 yards. Harbaugh was 18 of 34 for 174 yards, with 1 interception.

San Diego	0	0	0	0	—	0
Kansas City	10	10	14	0	—	34

KC — FG Stoyanovich 43
KC — Tongue 7 fumble return (Stoyanovich kick)
KC — FG Stoyanovich 39
KC — Horn 9 pass from Grbac (Stoyanovich kick)
KC — Alexander 81 pass from Grbac (Stoyanovich kick)
KC — Bennett 7 run (Stoyanovich kick)

SUNDAY NIGHT, OCTOBER 31

DETROIT 20, TAMPA BAY 3—at Pontiac Silverdome, attendance 63,135. Greg Hill rushed for 123 yards, and the Lions' defense forced 2 turnovers as Detroit won its third consecutive game and moved into first place in the NFC Central. Ron Rice blocked Martin Gramatica's 36-yard field-goal attempt late in the first quarter, and the Lions drove 44 yards to convert the block into three points. With the score tied 3-3, Tyree Talton downed John Jett's 47-yard punt at the Buccaneers' 1. Tampa Bay had to punt after three plays, and the Lions took over on the Buccaneers' 36. Hill's 27-yard run a few plays later set up Sedrick Irvin's 2-yard run and a 10-3 Lions lead. Chris Claiborne sacked Eric Zeier and forced him to fumble on the second play of the third quarter. Allen Aldridge recovered the fumble and went 21 yards for a touchdown. The Buccaneers reached the Lions' 1, but after a false start penalty, Mark Carrier forced Mike Alstott to fumble, and Claiborne recovered. Hill's 45-yard run set up Jason Hanson's 50-yard field goal to finish the scoring. Charlie Batch was 10 of 19 for 128 yards. Zeier, who was making his first start, was 29 of 44 for 256 yards. Warrick Dunn had 11 catches for 77 yards.

Tampa Bay	0	3	0	0	—	3
Detroit	0	10	7	3	—	20

Det — FG Hanson 47
TB — FG Gramatica 49
Det — Irvin 2 run (Hanson kick)
Det — Aldridge 21 fumble return (Hanson kick)
Det — FG Hanson 50

MONDAY NIGHT, NOVEMBER 1

SEATTLE 27, GREEN BAY 7—at Lambeau Field, attendance 59,869. Shawn Springs intercepted 2 passes and returned a blocked field goal for a touchdown as the Seahawks turned Packers' miscues into 21 points, allowing Mike Holmgren to defeat his former club. Springs stifled the Packers' first threat with an interception at the Seahawks' 8. On the Packers' next possession, Lamar King blocked Ryan Longwell's 50-yard field-goal attempt, which Springs recovered and returned 61 yards for a touchdown. Kerry Joseph's recovery of Dorsey Levens's fumble at the Packers' 37 set up Jon Kitna's 10-yard touchdown pass to Derrick Mayes to give Seattle a 14-7 lead. Willie Williams's interception at the Seahawks' 2 stopped the Packers just before halftime. The Seahawks drove 73 yards with the second half's opening drive to take a 21-7 lead. The Packers had a chance to cut into the deficit late in the third quarter, but Cortez Kennedy sacked Brett Favre and forced him to fumble at the Seahawks' 13. Michael Sinclair recovered, and the Seahawks intercepted Favre twice in a three-play stretch to set up fourth-quarter field goals. Kitna was 12 of 19 for 109 yards and 2 touchdowns. Ricky Watters had 31 carries for 125 yards. Favre was 14 of 35 for 180 yards and 1 touchdown, with 4 interceptions. Levens had 24 carries for 104 yards, and Corey Bradford had 3 receptions for 106 yards. The Seahawks' defense recorded 4 interceptions.

Seattle	7	7	7	6	—	27
Green Bay	0	7	0	0	—	7

Sea — Springs 61 blocked field goal return (Peterson kick)
GB — Bradford 74 pass from Favre (Longwell kick)
Sea — Mayes 10 pass from Kitna (Peterson kick)
Sea — Dawkins 2 pass from Kitna (Peterson kick)
Sea — FG Peterson 19
Sea — FG Peterson 29

NINTH WEEK SUMMARIES

AMERICAN FOOTBALL CONFERENCE

Eastern Division	W	L	T	Pct.	Pts.	OP
Miami	7	1	0	.875	189	143
Indianapolis	6	2	0	.750	223	162
New England	6	2	0	.750	191	150
Buffalo	6	3	0	.667	181	146
N.Y. Jets	2	6	0	.250	126	150
Central Division						
Jacksonville	7	1	0	.750	210	76
Tennessee	6	2	0	.750	166	157
Pittsburgh	5	3	0	.625	157	108
Baltimore	3	5	0	.375	136	144
Cincinnati	1	8	0	.111	116	278
Cleveland	1	8	0	.111	83	238
Western Division						
Seattle	6	2	0	.750	185	128
Kansas City	5	3	0	.625	190	119
Oakland	4	4	0	.500	157	153
San Diego	4	4	0	.500	127	166
Denver	3	5	0	.375	177	185

NATIONAL FOOTBALL CONFERENCE

Eastern Division	W	L	T	Pct.	Pts.	OP
N.Y. Giants	5	3	0	.625	138	138
Washington	5	3	0	.625	259	222
Dallas	4	4	0	.500	199	156
Arizona	2	6	0	.250	92	168
Philadelphia	2	7	0	.222	114	184
Central Division						
Detroit	6	2	0	.750	182	148
Minnesota	5	4	0	.556	210	175
Green Bay	4	4	0	.500	153	165
Tampa Bay	4	4	0	.500	122	118
Chicago	4	5	0	.444	143	174
Western Division						
St. Louis	6	2	0	.750	265	118
Carolina	3	5	0	.375	186	169
San Francisco	3	5	0	.375	150	234
Atlanta	2	7	0	.222	117	216
New Orleans	1	7	0	.125	123	179

SUNDAY, NOVEMBER 7

N.Y. JETS 12, ARIZONA 7—at Giants Stadium, attendance 77,857. Rick Mirer's 43-yard touchdown pass to Keyshawn Johnson in the fourth quarter allowed the Jets to snap their three-game losing streak. The Jets drove deep into Cardinals' territory three times in the first half, but were stopped on downs at the 5-yard line, and later in the half John Hall missed a 29-yard field goal. Dave Brown's 71-yard pass to Rob Moore immediately after the missed field goal set up Michael Pittman's 4-yard scoring run and gave the Cardinals a 7-3 halftime lead. The Jets were trailing 7-6 midway through the fourth quarter when the Cardinals' were forced to punt from their own 6-yard line. Dedric Ward returned the punt 6 yards to the Cardinals' 41. The Jets were faced with third-and-12 two plays later when Mirer found Johnson streaking deep down the middle. The Cardinals failed to gain a first down in their final two possessions. Mirer was 12 of 18 for 122 yards and 1 touchdown. Curtis Martin carried 38 times for 131 yards. Brown was 16 of 26 for 199 yards.

Arizona	0	7	0	0	—	7
N.Y. Jets	3	0	3	6	—	12

NYJ — FG Hall 44
Ariz — Pittman 4 run (Jacke kick)
NYJ — FG Hall 33
NYJ — K. Johnson 43 pass from Mirer (pass failed)

BALTIMORE 41, CLEVELAND 9—at Cleveland Browns Stadium, attendance 72,898. Errict Rhett rushed for 117 yards and 2 touchdowns, and Baltimore's defense permitted just 10 first downs and 150 yards as the Ravens defeated the Browns. The Ravens had touchdown drives of 73 and 80 yards in the first half en route to a 17-3 halftime lead, with the Browns' lone points set up by James Williams's recovery of Jermaine Lewis's fumbled punt at the Ravens' 17. The Browns reached the Ravens' 37 late in the third quarter, but Tim Couch's fourth-and-3 pass was incomplete. Rhett scampered 52 yards for a touchdown three plays later to extend Baltimore's lead to 24-3. Rod Woodson's 66-yard interception return of Ty Detmer's pass midway through the fourth quarter all but sealed the victory. Tony Banks was 14 of 25 for 129 yards and 1 touchdown. Couch was 9 of 21 for 57 yards, with 1 interception before being replaced in the fourth quarter by Detmer, who was 7 of 15 for 81 yards and 1 touchdown, with 1 interception.

Baltimore	7	10	7	17	—	41
Cleveland	3	0	0	6	—	9

Balt — Rhett 11 run (Stover kick)
Cle — FG Dawson 25
Balt — Ismail 28 pass from Banks (Stover kick)
Balt — FG Stover 28
Balt — Rhett 52 run (Stover kick)
Balt — FG Stover 44
Balt — Woodson 66 interception return (Stover kick)
Cle — Kirby 5 pass from Detmer (kick blocked)
Balt — Case 20 run (Stover kick)

BUFFALO 34, WASHINGTON 17—at Redskins Stadium, attendance 78,721. Doug Flutie passed for 2 touchdowns, and Antowain Smith rushed for 2 scores as the Bills held the ball for 41 minutes to defeat the Redskins. The Bills scored on five of their first six possessions, with each drive lasting at least 4:46, to take a 31-10 lead. The Redskins led 7-3 when Brett Conway missed a 55-yard field-goal attempt early in the second quarter. Flutie's 6-yard scoring pass to Bobby Collins gave the Bills a 10-7 lead, but the Redskins tied the game on Conway's field goal with 5:24 left in the half. Flutie ran 8 yards on fourth-and-5 to the Redskins' 15 to keep alive a late first-half drive that culminated with Smith's first touchdown 18 seconds before halftime. The Bills put together scoring drives of 75 and 69 yards in the third quarter to take a 31-10 lead, while permitting the Redskins to have the ball for just 2:28 of the third quarter. Flutie was 16 of 22 for 211 yards and 2 touchdowns. The Bills had 49 carries for 204 rushing yards and converted 9 of 15 third-down situations. Johnson was 19 of 37 for 232 yards and 1 touchdown, with 1 interception.

Buffalo	3	14	14	3	—	34
Washington	7	3	0	7	—	17

Wash — Davis 8 run (Conway kick)
Buff — FG Christie 23
Buff — Collins 6 pass from Flutie (Christie kick)
Wash — FG Conway 41
Buff — A. Smith 1 run (Christie kick)
Buff — A. Smith 10 run (Christie kick)
Buff — Moulds 14 pass from Flutie (Christie kick)
Wash — Connell 19 pass from Johnson (Conway kick)
Buff — FG Christie 21

CHICAGO 14, GREEN BAY 13—at Lambeau Field, attendance 59,867. In their first game since the death of club legend Walter Payton, the Bears' Bryan Robinson blocked Ryan Longwell's 28-yard field-goal attempt as time expired, snapping Chicago's 10-game losing streak against the Packers. Trailing 3-0, Glyn Milburn scampered 49 yards for a touchdown late in the first quarter. Chris Hudson's interception in the end zone stopped a second-quarter Packers' scoring threat, but Darren Sharper's interception at midfield set up Brett Favre's 7-yard touchdown pass to Tyrone Davis 30 seconds before halftime to give Green Bay a 10-7 lead. The Bears drove inside the Packers' 20 on their first three possessions of the second half, but scored just once. Keith McKenzie's fumble recovery at the Packers' 10 stopped one drive, and, leading 14-13 with 5:10 left, Chris Boniol missed a 34-yard field-goal attempt. A low snap contributed to Robinson's block as time expired. Jim Miller, who replaced Cade McNown in the first quarter, was 16 of 29 for 142 yards and 1 touchdown, with 3 interceptions. Favre was 27 of 41 for 267 yards and 1 touchdown, with 1 interception.

Chicago	7	0	7	0	—	14
Green Bay	3	7	0	3	—	13

GB — FG Longwell 37
Chi — Milburn 49 run (Boniol kick)
GB — Davis 7 pass from Favre (Longwell kick)
Chi — Engram 6 pass from Miller (Boniol kick)
GB — FG Longwell 26

SEATTLE 37, CINCINNATI 20—at Kingdome, attendance 66,303. Ricky Watters rushed for 133 yards and scored twice, and Jon Kitna passed for 3 touchdowns, as the Seahawks won for the sixth time in their last seven games. Cortez Kennedy's interception four plays into the game led to Watters's first touchdown, and his second touchdown capped a 7-play, 67-yard drive to give the Bengals a 14-3 lead with 6:36 remaining in the quarter. Leading 14-10, Kitna's 20-yard touchdown pass to Mike Pritchard capped a 7-play, 56-yard drive. After Deems May partially deflected a punt, the Seahawks needed just 30 yards, culminated by Kitna's third touchdown pass, to take a 28-10 lead. Trailing 31-13 late in the third quarter, Takeo Spikes's interception and return to the Seahawks' 33 gave the Bengals a scoring chance, but Jeff Blake's fourth-down pass to Willie Jackson was incomplete. Blake's 1-yard scoring run came with just 3:53 remaining, and Sean Dawkins recovered the ensuing onside kick to set up Todd Peterson's final field goal. Kitna was 14 of 24 for 202 yards and 3 touchdowns, with 2 interceptions. Blake was 18 of 35 for 287 yards and 1 touchdown, with 2 interceptions. Carl Pickens had 4 catches for 104 yards.

Cincinnati	10	0	3	7	—	20
Seattle	14	14	3	6	—	37

Sea — Watters 19 run (Peterson kick)
Cin — FG Pelfrey 50
Sea — Watters 8 pass from Kitna (Peterson kick)
Cin — Pickens 75 pass from Blake (Pelfrey kick)
Sea — Pritchard 20 pass from Kitna (Peterson kick)
Sea — Mayes 10 pass from Kitna (Peterson kick)
Sea — FG Peterson 29
Cin — FG Pelfrey 34
Sea — FG Peterson 45
Cin — Blake 1 run (Pelfrey kick)
Sea — FG Peterson 35

DENVER 33, SAN DIEGO 17—at Qualcomm Stadium, attendance 61,204. Olandis Gary rushed for 108 yards and 2 touchdowns, and Chris Miller played in his first game since 1995 as the Broncos handed the Chargers their third consecutive defeat. The Broncos led 3-0 when Bill Romanowski intercepted a Jim Harbaugh pass at the Chargers' 17 and returned it to the 1-yard line, where he fumbled and recovered the ball in the end zone for a touchdown. The Broncos led 13-3 at halftime, and Al Wilson's recovery of Chris Penn's fumble at the Chargers' 31 led to Gary's 23-yard scoring run midway through the third quarter. Harbaugh guided the Chargers to touchdown drives of 87 and 74 yards to trim the deficit to 23-17 with 9:17 remaining, and the defense forced the Broncos to punt. However, Penn fumbled again, and Detron Smith recovered at the Chargers' 38 to set up Jason Elam's 24-yard field goal with 4:18 left. Trevor Pryce sacked Harbaugh on fourth-and-13, giving the Broncos the ball at the Chargers' 9. Gary pierced the end zone three plays later to cap the scoring. Miller was 14 of 24 for 166 yards. Harbaugh was 25 of 39 for 235 yards and 2 touchdowns, with 2 interceptions.

Denver	3	10	7	13	—	33
San Diego	0	3	7	7	—	17

Den — FG Elam 44
Den — Romanowski recovered fumble in end zone
SD — FG Carney 46
Den — FG Elam 55
Den — Gary 23 run (Elam kick)
SD — F. Jones 7 pass from Harbaugh (Carney kick)
Den — FG Elam 41
SD — C. Jones 44 pass from Harbaugh (Carney kick)
Den — FG Elam 24
Den — Gary 5 run (Elam kick)

JACKSONVILLE 30, ATLANTA 7—at Georgia Dome, attendance 68,466. Mark Brunell passed for 3 touchdowns and the Jaguars' defense forced 4 turnovers to win their fifth consecutive game. Brunell's 44-yard touchdown pass to Jimmy Smith midway through the first quarter started the scoring, and Fred Taylor's 41-yard run set up his second touchdown pass. On the next play, Donovin Darius intercepted Chris Chandler's pass at the Jaguars' 44 and returned it 8 yards to set up Mike Hollis's 27-yard boot and give the Jaguars a 17-0 lead. Ray Buchanan blocked Hollis's field-goal attempt on the Jaguars' next possession, spearheading a 12-play, 81-yard scoring drive, with Tim Dwight's touchdown catch cutting the deficit to 17-7 at halftime. The Jaguars responded by scoring on their first two possessions of the second half to take a 27-7 lead. The Falcons failed to drive beyond the Jaguars' 45 in the second half. Brunell was 14 of 27 for 203 yards and 3 touchdowns. Chandler was 14 of 25 for 163 yards and 1 touchdown, with 2 interceptions.

Jacksonville	7	10	10	3	—	30
Atlanta	0	7	0	0	—	7

Jax — Smith 44 pass from Brunell (Hollis kick)
Jax — Jones 9 pass from Brunell (Hollis kick)
Jax — FG Hollis 27
Atl — Dwight 17 pass from Chandler (Andersen kick)
Jax — FG Hollis 24
Jax — McCardell 2 pass from Brunell (Hollis kick)
Jax — FG Hollis 34

INDIANAPOLIS 25, KANSAS CITY 17—at RCA Dome, attendance 56,689. Peyton Manning passed for a touchdown and ran for another, and Mike Vanderjagt converted 4 field goals as the Colts won their fourth consecutive game. The Colts drove the ball at will in the first half but led just 13-10 at halftime. Manning's fumble at the Chiefs' 5 stalled the Colts' first drive, and Chester McGlockton's interception at the Chiefs' 24 stopped the Colts just before halftime. The Chiefs marched 88 yards with the second half's opening kickoff to take a 17-13 lead on Elvis Grbac's touchdown pass to Kevin Lockett. Trailing 17-16, the Colts were forced to punt with 14:00 left, but Larry Parker fumbled and Tito Wooten recovered at the Colts' 46. Manning scrambled 7 yards for a touchdown six plays later to give the Colts a 22-17 lead with 10:49 remaining. Vanderjagt's fourth field goal gave the Colts a 25-17 lead with 1:14 left. The Chiefs got the ball on their own 30 and reached the Colts' 39 in the waning seconds, but with Elvis Grbac injured during the final drive, Warren Moon's Hail Mary pass was incomplete as time expired. Manning was 21 of 33 for 290 yards and 1 touchdown, with 1 interception. Edgerrin James had 20 carries for 109 yards. Grbac was 18 of 31 for 196 yards and 1 touchdown.

Kansas City	3	7	7	0	—	17
Indianapolis	3	10	3	9	—	25

Ind — FG Vanderjagt 47
KC — FG Stoyanovich 38
Ind — FG Vanderjagt 34
KC — Bennett 23 run (Stoyanovich kick)
Ind — James 30 pass from Manning (Vanderjagt kick)
KC — Lockett 18 pass from Grbac (Stoyanovich kick)
Ind — FG Vanderjagt 29
Ind — Manning 7 run (pass failed)
Ind — FG Vanderjagt 37

CAROLINA 33, PHILADELPHIA 7—at Ericsson Stadium, attendance 62,569. Steve Beuerlein passed for 3 touchdowns as the Panthers handed the Eagles their third consecutive defeat. The Panthers scored on six consecutive possessions from the second-thru-fourth quarters, and 4 of their 7 scoring drives were set up by turnovers. Beuerlein completed all 5 of his passes on an 80-yard drive that gave the Panthers a 10-0 lead. Barry Minter's fumble recovery at the Panthers' 40 led to Beuerlein's 12-yard touchdown pass to Muhsin Muhammad and a 17-0 lead with 3:04 left in the half. Kevin Greene's recovery of Donovan McNabb's fumble on the next play set up the first of 2 John Kasay field goals in the final 1:57 of the half to give the Panthers a 23-0 lead. The Eagles avoided the shutout on Ducee Staley's 14-yard run with 2:37 left. Beuerlein was 21 of 34 for 281 yards and 3 touchdowns. McNabb was 8 of 20 for 68 yards, with 1 interception. Staley rushed 17 times for 140 yards.

Philadelphia	0	0	0	7	—	7
Carolina	3	20	3	7	—	33

Car — FG Kasay 38
Car — Muhammad 4 pass from Beuerlein (Kasay kick)
Car — Muhammad 12 pass from Beuerlein (Kasay kick)
Car — FG Kasay 28
Car — FG Kasay 33
Car — FG Kasay 22
Car — Jeffers 22 pass from Beuerlein (Kasay kick)
Phil — Staley 14 run (N. Johnson kick)

PITTSBURGH 27, SAN FRANCISCO 6—at 3Com Park, attendance 68,657. Jerome Bettis rushed for 2 touchdowns as the Steelers won their third consecutive game and the 49ers dropped their fourth in a row. The Steelers scored on their first three possessions, in a span of less than eight minutes—the last of which was set up by Earl Holmes' fumble recovery at the 49ers' 19—to take a 17-3 lead early in the second quarter. Trailing 20-6 late in the third quarter, the 49ers' offense produced back-to-back drives, but Wade Richey missed a 49-yard field-goal attempt and Scott Shields's interception at the Steelers' 18 thwarted the second scoring chance. The 49ers were stopped on downs in their own territory three times in the final six minutes, with Bettis's 22-yard scoring run with 3:15 left for the final tally. Kordell Stewart was 15 of 26 for 139 yards and 1 touchdown. Jeff Garcia was 7 of 18 for 39 yards and was replaced in the fourth quarter by Steve Stenstrom, who was 5 of 15 for 54 yards, with 1 interception. Charlie Garner rushed 20 times for 166 yards.

Pittsburgh	14	3	3	7	—	27
San Francisco	3	3	0	0	—	6

Pitt — Bettis 1 run (Brown kick)
SF — FG Richey 19
Pitt — Ward 13 pass from Stewart (Brown kick)
Pitt — FG Brown 28
SF — FG Richey 20
Pitt — FG Brown 38
Pitt — Bettis 22 run (Brown kick)

DETROIT 31, ST. LOUIS 27—at Pontiac Silverdome, attendance 73,224. Gus Frerotte replaced an injured Charlie Batch and completed a 57-yard fourth-and-26 pass to Germane Crowell with one minute left to highlight Detroit's comeback victory against the Rams. The Rams led 12-10 at halftime on the strength of London Fletcher's safety from tackling Greg Hill in the end zone. In the third quarter, Terry Fair's 6-yard interception return to the Rams' 12 set up Cory Schlesinger's 3-yard touchdown pass from Frerotte, who replaced an injured Charlie Batch earlier in the quarter. A 33-yard pass from Frerotte to Crowell set up Jason Hanson's second field goal and gave the Lions a 21-12 lead. Kurt Warner's 75-yard touchdown pass to Az-Zahir Hakim cut the deficit to 21-19, but Frerotte's 31-yard pass to Sedrick Irvin set up Hanson's third field goal with 6:10 left. Warner promptly engineered an 8-play, 87-yard drive, capped by his 2-yard touchdown pass to tackle-eligible Ryan Tucker, to give the Rams a 27-24 lead with 2:42 left. Sacks by Kevin Carter and D'Marco Farr pushed the Lions into a fourth-and-26 situation from their own 21. However, Frerotte's deep pass down the left sideline was caught by Crowell, who was corralled at the Rams' 22. A pass interference penalty on Dexter McCleon three plays later gave the Lions a first down at the Rams' 12, and Frerotte found Johnnie Morton for the winning tally with 28 seconds left. Batch was 10 of 20 for 148 yards and 1 touchdown, while Frerotte was 12 of 16 for 209 yards and 2 touchdowns. Crowell had 8 receptions for 163 yards. Warner was 25 of 42 for 305 yards and 3 touchdowns, with 2 interceptions. Marshall Faulk had 10 receptions for 78 yards.

St. Louis	2	10	0	15	—	27
Detroit	0	10	11	10	—	31

StL — Safety, Fletcher tackles Hill in end zone
Det — Crowell 4 pass from Batch (Hanson kick)
StL — Robinson 6 pass from Warner (Wilkins kick)
Det — FG Hanson 29
StL — FG Wilkins 34
Det — Schlesinger 3 pass from Frerotte (Crowell pass from Frerotte)
Det — FG Hanson 43
StL — Hakim 75 pass from Warner (Wilkins kick)
Det — FG Hanson 44
StL — Tucker 2 pass from Warner (Bruce pass from Warner)
Det — Morton 12 pass from Frerotte (Hanson kick)

TAMPA BAY 31, NEW ORLEANS 16—at Louisiana Superdome, attendance 47,129. After a week's hiatus from the starting lineup, Trent Dilfer passed for 3 touchdowns as the Buccaneers handed the Saints their seventh consecutive defeat. Trailing 3-0, the Buccaneers drove 75, 54, and 42 yards to score on three consecutive possessions and take a 17-3 lead. Leading 17-6 in the third quarter, Derrick Brooks's 38-yard interception return to the Saints' 25 led to Dilfer's 10-yard touchdown pass to Darnell McDonald and a 24-6 advantage. It was 24-9 Tampa Bay with 2:06 left when Martin Gramatica missed a 51-yard field-goal attempt. The Saints needed just 1:18 to drive 59 yards, capped by Billy Joe Tolliver's 1-yard scoring pass to Keith Poole, to cut the deficit to 24-16. Dave Moore recovered the ensuing onside kick and, on fourth-and-2 with 21 seconds left, Mike Alstott barreled through the line and steamrolled 25 yards for the game-clinching touchdown. Dilfer, who was back in the lineup because Eric Zeier—the eighth week's starter—was injured, was 15 of 20 for 227 yards and 3 touchdowns. Alstott had 25 carries for 117 yards. Tolliver was 18 of 37 for 211 yards and 1 touchdown, with 2 interceptions.

Tampa Bay	7	10	7	7	—	31
New Orleans	3	3	0	10	—	16

NO — FG Brien 29
TB — Green 62 pass from Dilfer (Gramatica kick)
TB — FG Gramatica 45
TB — Davis 1 pass from Dilfer (Gramatica kick)
NO — FG Brien 39
TB — McDonald 10 pass from Dilfer (Gramatica kick)
NO — FG Brien 37
NO — Poole 1 pass from Tolliver (Brien kick)
TB — Alstott 25 run (Gramatica kick)

SUNDAY NIGHT, NOVEMBER 7

MIAMI 17, TENNESSEE 0—at Pro Player Stadium, attendance 74,109. Damon Huard passed for 2 touchdowns, and Sam Madison had 3 interceptions as the Dolphins extended their streak to 14 quarters without allowing an offensive touchdown. Al Del Greco's missed 32-yard field-goal attempt late in the first quarter propelled the Dolphins to a 12-play, 77-yard drive, with Huard completing 5 of 6 passes, to take a 7-0 lead. The Titans went for a first down on fourth-and-5 from the Dophins' 36 early in the second quarter, and Eddie George was stopped 2 yards short. Two plays later, Huard hit Tony Martin with a 43-yard touchdown pass. The Titans only drove inside the Dolphins' 40 once the rest of the game, and Steve McNair's fourth-and-goal pass from the Dolphins' 3 fell incomplete. Huard was 15 of 25 for 210 yards and 2 touchdowns. McNair was 22 of 42 for 205 yards, with 3 interceptions.

Tennessee	0	0	0	0	—	0
Miami	0	14	0	3	—	17

Mia — Pritchett 6 pass from Huard (Mare kick)
Mia — Martin 43 pass from Huard (Mare kick)
Mia — FG Mare 46

MONDAY NIGHT, NOVEMBER 8

MINNESOTA 27, DALLAS 17—at Metrodome, attendance 64,111. Jeff George passed for 3 touchdowns as the Vikings rebounded from a 17-0 deficit to defeat the Cowboys. The Cowboys dominated early, but Richie Cunningham missed 2 field goals before converting a 39-yard attempt. Midway through the second quarter, Emmitt Smith scampered 63 yards for a touchdown. However, he broke a bone in his hand as he stiff-armed Kenny Wright in the facemask on his way to the end zone. Charlie Williams recovered David Palmer's fumble on the ensuing kickoff, and on the first play, undaunted, Smith took the handoff and raced 24 yards for a touchdown, giving him 2 touchdowns in 18 seconds. Smith did leave the game after his second touchdown, and momentum shifted. Chris Doleman recovered Mark Stepnoski's bad Shotgun snap at the Cowboys' 21 just before halftime, setting up George's 4-yard touchdown pass to Randy Moss. Already without Smith, Troy Aikman was knocked from the game in the third-quarter with a concussion. The Cowboys garnered just 2 first downs in six second-half possessions. Meanwhile, the Vikings scored on four of their first five possessions, capped by 2 George touchdown passes, to take a 27-17 lead with 5:10 remaining. George was 17 of 30 for 218 yards and 3 touchdowns, with 1 interception. Cris Carter had 9 catches for 116 yards. Troy Aikman was 14 of 24 for 129 yards. Smith had 13 carries for 140 yards.

Dallas	0	17	0	0	—	17
Minnesota	0	7	6	14	—	27

Dall — FG Cunningham 39
Dall — E. Smith 63 run (Cunningham kick)
Dall — E. Smith 24 run (Cunningham kick)
Minn — Moss 4 pass from George (Anderson kick)
Minn — FG Anderson 31
Minn — FG Anderson 40
Minn — Carter 4 pass from George (Anderson kick)
Minn — Moss 47 pass from George (Anderson kick)

TENTH WEEK SUMMARIES

AMERICAN FOOTBALL CONFERENCE

Eastern Division	W	L	T	Pct.	Pts.	OP
Indianapolis	7	2	0	.778	250	181
Miami	7	2	0	.778	192	166
Buffalo	7	3	0	.700	204	149
New England	6	3	0	.667	208	174
N.Y. Jets	3	6	0	.333	150	167
Central Division						
Jacksonville	8	1	0	.889	216	79
Tennessee	7	2	0	.778	190	171
Pittsburgh	5	4	0	.556	172	124
Baltimore	3	6	0	.333	139	150
Cleveland	2	8	0	.200	99	253
Cincinnati	1	9	0	.100	130	302
Western Division						
Seattle	7	2	0	.778	205	145
Kansas City	5	4	0	.556	200	136
Oakland	5	4	0	.556	185	162
San Diego	4	5	0	.444	136	194
Denver	3	7	0	.300	194	205

NATIONAL FOOTBALL CONFERENCE

Eastern Division	W	L	T	Pct.	Pts.	OP
Dallas	5	4	0	.556	226	169
N.Y. Giants	5	4	0	.556	157	165
Washington	5	4	0	.556	287	257
Arizona	3	6	0	.333	115	187
Philadelphia	3	7	0	.300	149	212
Central Division						
Detroit	6	3	0	.667	201	171
Minnesota	6	4	0	.600	237	199
Tampa Bay	5	4	0	.556	139	128
Green Bay	4	5	0	.444	166	192
Chicago	4	6	0	.400	167	201
Western Division						
St. Louis	7	2	0	.778	300	128
Carolina	3	6	0	.333	196	204
San Francisco	3	6	0	.333	156	258
Atlanta	2	7	0	.222	117	216
New Orleans	2	7	0	.222	147	185

SUNDAY, NOVEMBER 14

JACKSONVILLE 6, BALTIMORE 3—at ALLTEL Stadium, attendance 67,391. Mike Hollis made 2 field goals as the Jaguars remained in first place despite making just 9 first downs. Dave Thomas blocked Kyle Richardson's punt early in the second quarter, and Corey Harris recovered at the Ravens' 14, setting up Hollis's first field goal. The Ravens responded by driving to the Jaguars' 27, but Aaron Pierce fumbled and Fernando Bryant recovered. Matt Stover's 23-yard field goal ended the half. The Jaguars put together a 15-play, 47-yard third-quarter drive to set up Hollis's go-ahead kick with 1:52 left in the third quarter. The Ravens threatened once in the fourth quarter, reaching the Jaguars' 34, but Gary Walker sacked Tony Banks on fourth-and-3 to preserve the victory. Mark Brunell was 20 of 29 for 118 yards. Banks was 10 of 21 for 73 yards, while Stoney Case was 7 of 12 for 103 yards.

Baltimore	0	3	0	0	—	3
Jacksonville	0	3	3	0	—	6

Jax — FG Hollis 28
Balt — FG Stover 23
Jax — FG Hollis 28

ST. LOUIS 35, CAROLINA 10—at Trans World Dome, attendance 65,965. Kurt Warner passed for 2 touchdowns as the Rams improved to 7-2 for the first time since 1988. The Panthers scored on their first possession, but the Rams used Warner's 53-yard pass to Marshall Faulk to set up his 22-yard touchdown pass to Isaac Bruce to tie the game. After Todd Lyght's interception return, the Rams' defense forced a punt and the offense marched 80 yards in 14 plays, capped by Warner's 19-yard touchdown pass to Roland Williams, to take a 21-7 lead. Mike Jones scooped up Wesley Walls's fumble and raced 35 yards for a touchdown early in the third quarter. The Panthers twice drove into Rams' territory in the second half, but were stopped on downs once and by Dre' Bly's interception at the Rams' 9. Warner was 19 of 29 for 283 yards and 2 touchdowns, with 1 interception. Steve Beuerlein was 24 of 39 for 286 yards and 1 touchdown, with 2 interceptions. Muhsin Muhammad had 9 receptions for 125 yards.

Carolina	7	3	0	0	—	10
St. Louis	14	7	7	7	—	35

Car — Walls 14 pass from Beuerlein (Kasay kick)
StL — Bruce 22 pass from Warner (Wilkins kick)
StL — Lyght 57 interception return (Wilkins kick)
StL — Williams 19 pass from Warner (Wilkins kick)
Car — FG Kasay 24
StL — Jones 37 fumble return (Wilkins kick)
StL — Faulk 18 run (Wilkins kick)

CLEVELAND 16, PITTSBURGH 15—at Three Rivers Stadium, attendance 58,213. Phil Dawson's 39-yard field goal as time expired allowed the Browns to snap the Steelers' three-game winning streak and exact revenge for the 43-0 loss to Pittsburgh in week one. Tim Couch's 35-yard touchdown pass to Kevin Johnson capped the game's first drive and gave the Browns a quick 7-0 lead. Trailing at halftime 7-3, Kordell Stewart's 8- and 21-yard runs led to Kris Brown's 32-yard field goal. Orpheus Roye recovered Couch's fumble at the Browns' 8 two plays later, setting up Richard Huntley's 5-yard touchdown run and giving the Steelers a 12-7 lead. Brown's third field goal increased the Steelers' lead to 15-7, and Pittsburgh had the ball with 6:30 left in the game when John Thierry intercepted Stewart at the Steelers' 23. Couch's 5-yard touchdown pass to Marc Edwards three plays later cut the deficit to 15-13, with Karim Abdul-Jabbar's 2-point conversion run attempt stopped short. The Browns forced a punt and got the ball on their own 20 with 1:51 left. Couch's 23-yard pass to Darrin Chiaverini, with a 15-yard roughing-the-passer penalty by Mike Vrabel tacked on, gave the Browns the ball at the Steelers' 37 with 1:43 left. A 7-yard pass to Terry Kirby and a couple of short runs by Abdul-Jabbar set the stage for Dawson's winning kick. Couch was 18 of 28 for 199 yards and 2 touchdowns, with 1 interception. Stewart was 15 of 32 for 137 yards, with 2 interceptions.

Cleveland	7	0	0	9	—	16
Pittsburgh	3	0	9	3	—	15

Cle — K. Johnson 35 pass from Couch (Dawson kick)
Pitt — FG Brown 41

Pitt — FG Brown 32
Pitt — Huntley 5 run (run failed)
Pitt — FG Brown 47
Cle — Edwards 5 pass from Couch (run failed)
Cle — FG Dawson 39

ARIZONA 23, DETROIT 19—at Sun Devil Stadium, attendance 49,600. Michael Pittman rushed for 153 yards and 1 touchdown as the Cardinals snapped a three-game losing streak. The Lions led 7-0 before the Cardinals rattled off 23 consecutive points. Dave Brown completed passes of 40, 46, and 33 yards to set up the Cardinals' first three scores and, after Jason Hanson missed a 57-yard field-goal attempt with 52 seconds left in the half, Brown completed a 16-yard pass to Frank Sanders on fourth-and-5 to the Lions' 31 to set up Chris Jacke's third field goal of the half and give Arizona a 16-7 halftime lead. Pittman's 58-yard touchdown run came on the Cardinals' first play of the second half and extended their lead to 23-7. The Lions answered immediately as Gus Frerotte's 77-yard touchdown pass to Germane Crowell on the next play cut the deficit to 23-13. Terry Fair's 35-yard fumble return for a score cut the deficit to 23-19 with 5:26 left, but the Lions went for 2 points and the pass play failed. The Lions reached the Cardinals' 10 in the waning moments, but Frerotte's final pass, intended for Crowell, was knocked down by Aeneas Williams at the goal line to preserve the victory. Brown was 16 of 30 for 209 yards. Frerotte, making his first start for the injured Charlie Batch, was 24 of 39 for a career-high 375 yards and 2 touchdowns. Crowell had 5 receptions for 142 yards, while Johnnie Morton had 4 catches for 110 yards.

Detroit	7	0	6	6	—	19
Arizona	3	13	7	0	—	23

Det — Sloan 7 pass from Frerotte (Hanson kick)
Ariz — FG Jacke 35
Ariz — Bates 3 run (Jacke kick)
Ariz — FG Jacke 35
Ariz — FG Jacke 49
Ariz — Pittman 58 run (Jacke kick)
Det — Crowell 77 pass from Frerotte (pass failed)
Det — Fair 35 fumble return (pass failed)

DALLAS 27, GREEN BAY 13—at Texas Stadium, attendance 64,634. Playing without injured stars Emmitt Smith and Troy Aikman, George Teague's 95-yard interception return for a touchdown in the final seconds secured the Cowboys eighth consecutive victory against the Packers in Dallas. The Cowboys led 7-0 when Vonnie Holliday recovered Chris Warren's fumble at the Cowboys' 24 to set up Ryan Longwell's 38-yard field goal with 1:07 left in the half. Jason Garrett's 32-yard pass to Eric Bjornson led to Richie Cunningham's 44-yard field goal as the half expired. Tyrone Williams recovered a Warren fumble at the Packers' 16 to thwart Dallas' first possession of the second half, but Garrett's 37-yard touchdown pass to Raghib Ismail gave Dallas a 17-3 lead and, following a blocked field goal by Flozell Adams, Cunningham's 47-yard boot gave the Cowboys a seemingly comfortable 20-3 lead with 10:40 remaining. The Packers drove 88 and 41 yards on their next two possessions to trim the deficit to 20-13 with 1:21 left. Darren Woodson could not hold onto the ensuing onside kick, and Fred Vinson recovered. The Packers reached the Cowboys' 25 with 21 seconds left, but Teague stepped in front of Favre's pass intended for Freeman and scampered untouched 95 yards for the game-clinching touchdown. Garrett was 13 of 23 for 199 yards and 2 touchdowns. Favre was 26 of 50 for 260 yards and 1 touchdown, with 2 interceptions. Freeman had 6 receptions for 110 yards.

Green Bay	0	3	0	10	—	13
Dallas	7	3	7	10	—	27

Dall — LaFleur 6 pass from Garrett (Cunningham kick)
GB — FG Longwell 38
Dall — FG Cunningham 44
Dall — Ismail 37 pass from Garrett (Cunningham kick)
Dall — FG Cunningham 47
GB — Freeman 28 pass from Favre (Longwell kick)
GB — FG Longwell 31
Dall — Teague 95 interception return (Cunningham kick)

INDIANAPOLIS 27, N.Y. GIANTS 19—at Giants Stadium, attendance 78,081. Marvin Harrison had 6 receptions for 109 yards and 2 touchdowns, as the Colts held off the Giants to win their fifth consecutive game. The Colts led 7-6 just before halftime and the Giants had a chance to take the lead, but Tito Wooten's interception at the Colts' 13 allowed Indianapolis to maintain their lead. The Giants had another chance to score at the start of the third quarter, but Thomas Randolph's interception in the end zone quelled the drive. The Colts responded with 17 points in a span of 6:22, capped by Terrence Wilkins's 39-yard punt return for a score to give the Colts a 24-6 lead with 2:44 left in the third quarter. Kent Graham passed for touchdowns on the Giants next two possessions, with a Mike Vanderjagt field goal in between, to trim the deficit to 27-19 with 6:50 left. A 32-yard punt return by Tiki Barber started the Giants' final possession. The Giants drove deep into Colts' territory, but Cornelius Bennett forced Pete Mitchell to fumble at the Colts' 15, and Wooten recovered with 1:21 left to preserve the victory. Manning was 20 of 35 for 237 yards and 2 touchdowns, with 1 interception. Edgerrin James carried 16 times for 108 yards. Graham was 27 of 50 for 253 yards and 2 touchdowns, with 2 interceptions.

Indianapolis	7	0	17	3	—	27
N.Y. Giants	0	6	0	13	—	19

Ind — Harrison 19 pass from Manning (Vanderjagt kick)
NYG — FG Blanchard 33
NYG — FG Blanchard 42
Ind — Harrison 57 pass from Manning (Vanderjagt kick)
Ind — FG Vanderjagt 40
Ind — Wilkins 39 punt return (Vanderjagt kick)
NYG — Toomer 33 pass from Graham (pass failed)
Ind — FG Vanderjagt 35
NYG — Mitchell 7 pass from Graham (Blanchard kick)

TAMPA BAY 17, KANSAS CITY 10—at Raymond James Stadium, attendance 64,927. Trent Dilfer passed for 2 touchdowns, and the Buccaneers' defense permitted just 11 first downs to offset the offense's 6 turnovers. The Chiefs tallied just 2 first downs in the first half, but trailed just 7-3 in the final minute of the half before Derrick Brooks recovered Donnell Bennett's fumble at the Chiefs' 13 to set up Martin Gramatica's 25-yard field goal. Each quarterback recorded a long touchdown pass in the second half, with Joe Horn's 50-yard catch cutting the deficit to 17-10 with 10:40 left. The Buccaneers lost 5 fumbles in the game, including 3 in Chiefs' territory in the second half, the last of which gave the Chiefs the ball at their own 21 with 2:47 left. Elvis Grbac's 18- and 22-yard passes to Tony Gonzalez allowed the Chiefs to reach the Buccaneers' 13 with 24 seconds left, but Hardy Nickerson intercepted Grbac at the goal line to preserve the victory. Dilfer was 17 of 27 for 270 yards and 2 touchdowns, with 1 interception. Jacquez Green had 7 catches for 164 yards. Grbac was 23 of 38 for 202 yards and 1 touchdown, with 1 interception.

Kansas City	3	0	0	7	—	10
Tampa Bay	0	10	7	0	—	17

KC — FG Stoyanovich 20
TB — Moore 35 pass from Dilfer (Gramatica kick)
TB — FG Gramatica 25
TB — Green 52 pass from Dilfer (Gramatica kick)
KC — Horn 50 pass from Grbac (Stoyanovich kick)

BUFFALO 23, MIAMI 3—at Ralph Wilson Stadium, attendance 72,810. The Bills scored on their first four possessions, and their defense limited the Dolphins to just 6 first downs and 101 total yards to snap Miami's five-game winning streak. Antoine Winfield intercepted Damon Huard's pass on the third play of the game to set up the first of Steve Christie's 3 first-quarter field goals. Jonathan Linton's 4-yard run capped an 11-play, 71-yard drive that gave the Bills a 16-0 lead before the Dolphins had registered a first down. Nate Jacquet's 25-yard punt return to the Bills' 34 set up Olindo Mare's field goal just before half, but Doug Flutie's 53-yard touchdown pass to Eric Moulds gave the Bills a 23-3 lead. The Dolphins garnered just 3 first downs in the second half. Flutie was 10 of 20 for 157 yards and 1 touchdown. Antowain Smith had 29 carries for 126 yards. Damon Huard was 9 of 25 for 65 yards, with 1 interception.

Miami	0	3	0	0	—	3
Buffalo	9	7	7	0	—	23

Buff — FG Christie 31
Buff — FG Christie 48
Buff — FG Christie 47
Buff — Linton 4 run (Christie kick)
Mia — FG Mare 30
Buff — Moulds 53 pass from Flutie (Christie kick)

MINNESOTA 27, CHICAGO 24 (OT)—at Soldier Field, attendance 61,481. Gary Anderson redeemed himself with a 38-yard field goal in overtime to cap a wild game that featured 915 offensive yards. Jim Miller, who made his first start of the season, completed touchdown passes of 77 yards to Marcus Robinson and 56 yards to Marty Booker in the first quarter to give the Bears a 14-7 lead. In the second quarter, Chris Doleman recovered Miller's fumble at the Bears' 7 to set up Jeff George's game-tying touchdown pass. The Bears led 17-14 and had a chance for more points just before halftime, but Jimmy Hitchcock intercepted Miller's pass at the Vikings' 10 to quell the drive. The Vikings drove to the Bears' 6 early in the third quarter, but George fumbled and Jim Flanigan recovered. On the Vikings' next possession, Anderson's 38-yard field goal tied the game. Randy Moss caught 4 passes on a 13-play, 96-yard fourth-quarter drive, capped by George's 1-yard touchdown pass to Cris Carter with 6:06 left to give the Vikings a 24-17 lead. After an exchange of punts, Miller completed 8 of 9 passes on an 87-yard drive, capped by Booker's second touchdown catch, the first 2 of his career, to tie the game with 49 seconds remaining. George then completed 44- and 42-yard passes to Moss, only to watch Anderson's 20-yard field-goal attempt sail wide left. Walt Harris intercepted George's pass at the Bears' 29 on the first play of overtime, but Boniol's 41-yard attempt three plays later was wide right. The Vikings drove 49 yards, aided by a 21-yard pass-interference penalty, to set up Anderson's game-winning boot. George was 25 of 44 for 374 yards and 3 touchdowns, with 1 interception. Moss had 12 receptions for 204 yards. Miller was 34 of 48 for 422 yards, the fourth-most in Bears' history, and 3 touchdowns, with 1 interception. Robinson had 7 receptions for 148 yards, and Booker had 7 for 134 yards.

Minnesota	7	7	3	7	3	—	27
Chicago	14	3	0	7	0	—	24

Chi — Robinson 77 pass from Miller (Boniol kick)
Minn — Carter 21 pass from George (Anderson kick)
Chi — Booker 56 pass from Miller (Boniol kick)
Minn — Carter 7 pass from George (Anderson kick)
Chi — FG Boniol 34
Minn — FG Anderson 38
Minn — Carter 1 pass from George (Anderson kick)
Chi — Booker 25 pass from Miller (Boniol kick)
Minn — FG Anderson 38

OAKLAND 28, SAN DIEGO 9—at Network Associates Coliseum, attendance 43,353. Rich Gannon passed for 4 touchdowns, and the Raiders' defense permitted just 225 yards to hand the Chargers their fourth consecutive defeat. Gannon's first touchdown pass was set up by Darrien Gordon's 21-yard punt return. On their next possession, the Raiders put together a 12-play, 97-yard drive to take a 14-0 lead. The Chargers were limited to 2 first downs in the first half, but when Michael Husted missed a 32-yard field-goal attempt as the half expired and John Carney began the second half with a 39-yard field goal, the Chargers trailed just 14-3. Gannon responded with a 10-play, 72-yard drive, highlighted by his 32-yard pass to James Jett, and capped by Gannon's second touchdown pass to Tyrone Wheatley. Gannon's 43-yard pass to Tim Brown led to his second touchdown pass to Rickey Dudley, with 5:58 remaining, to give the Raiders a 28-3 lead. Gannon was 18 of 24 for 254 yards and 4 touchdowns. Brown had 7 receptions for 117 yards. Jim Harbaugh was 18 of 32 for 204 yards and 1 touchdown.

San Diego	0	0	3	6	—	9
Oakland	14	0	7	7	—	28

Oak — Wheatley 26 pass from Gannon (Husted kick)
Oak — Dudley 2 pass from Gannon (Husted kick)
SD — FG Carney 39

Oak — Wheatley 7 pass from Gannon (Husted kick)
Oak — Dudley 12 pass from Gannon (Husted kick)
SD — F. Jones 11 pass from Harbaugh (pass failed)

NEW ORLEANS 24, SAN FRANCISCO 6—at Louisiana Superdome, attendance 52,198. Billy Joe Tolliver passed for 1 touchdown and ran for 2 scores as the Saints snapped a seven-game losing streak. Both teams played a ball-control offense in the first half. The Saints had drives of 77 and 89 yards to set up Tolliver touchdown runs, while the 49ers had two drives that exceeded eight minutes each, capped by Wade Richey field goals, giving the Saints a 14-6 halftime lead. The Saints' offense had scoring drives of 80 and 61 yards in the second half to take a 24-6 lead with 7:38 remaining. The 49ers mounted a late drive, but Willie Clay's end zone interception sealed just the second Saints' victory in their last 13 games with the 49ers. Tolliver was 12 of 15 for 242 yards and 1 touchdown. Steve Stenstrom, who made his first start of the season, was 18 of 32 for 157 yards, with 1 interception.

San Francisco	3	3	0	0	—	6
New Orleans	7	7	7	3	—	24

NO — Tolliver 2 run (Brien kick)
SF — FG Richey 52
NO — Tolliver 2 run (Brien kick)
SF — FG Richey 22
NO — Hastings 11 pass from Tolliver (Brien kick)
NO — FG Brien 28

TENNESSEE 24, CINCINNATI 14—at Cinergy Field, attendance 46,017. Eddie George rushed for 123 yards and 2 touchdowns as the Titans used turnovers to hand the Bengals their fifth consecutive defeat. George's 23-yard scamper capped the game's opening drive. Late in the first quarter, Josh Evans recovered Jeff Blake's fumble at the Bengals' 12, setting up Steve McNair's 1-yard sneak. Tremain Mack returned the second half's opening kickoff 99 yards for a touchdown, but two possession later the Bengals lost their second fumble of the game, with Blaine Bishop recovering Carl Pickens's fumble at the Bengals' 30. George scored two plays later, and when Craig Hentrich recovered Damon Griffin's fumble on the ensuing kickoff, Al Del Greco added a field goal. Blake fumbled at the Titans' 1 with 5:43 left to end a scoring chance. McNair was 12 of 25 for 103 yards. Blake was 18 of 32 for 236 yards and 1 touchdown, which came with 2:38 remaining.

Tennessee	14	0	10	0	—	24
Cincinnati	0	0	7	7	—	14

Tenn — George 23 run (Del Greco kick)
Tenn — McNair 1 run (Del Greco kick)
Cin — Mack 99 kickoff return (Pelfrey kick)
Tenn — George 14 run (Del Greco kick)
Tenn — FG Del Greco 26
Cin — Scott 24 pass from Blake (Pelfrey kick)

PHILADELPHIA 35, WASHINGTON 28—at Veterans Stadium, attendance 66,591. Eric Bieniemy's 11-yard run with 3:17 remaining snapped the Eagles' three-game losing streak. The Redskins scored 3 touchdowns in the first 17 minutes and had allowed just 57 yards, but led just 21-10 because of Allen Rossum's 89-yard kickoff return for a touchdown. Troy Vincent's 29-yard interception return to the Redskins' 11 with 1:15 left in the half set up Norm Johnson's 29-yard field goal to cut the deficit to 21-13. Hollis Thomas's recovery of Brad Johnson's fumble at the Redskins' 8 led to Johnson's third field goal, Duce Staley scampered 20 yards for a score two possessions later, and Mike Caldwell's 12-yard interception return to the Redskins' 29 set up Johnson's fourth successful kick to give the Eagles a 27-21 lead with 11:33 left. Johnson completed successive passes of 48 and 43 yards to Michael Westbrook to give the Redskins a 28-27 lead just 48 seconds later. The Eagles were forced to punt, but Al Harris's 17-yard interception return to midfield with 5:49 left led to Bieniemy's go-ahead touchdown with 3:17 remaining. The Redskins reached the Eagles' 28, but on fourth-and-4, Caldwell sacked Johnson as part of an all-out blitz to secure the victory. Donovan McNabb was 8 of 21 for 60 yards. Staley had 27 carries for 110 yards. The Redskins outgained the Eagles (424-266 yards), but committed 6 turnovers. Johnson was 18 of 33 for 313 yards and 2 touchdowns, with 3 interceptions. Davis had 25 carries for 122 yards. Westbrook had 4 receptions for 152 yards.

Washington	14	7	0	7	—	28
Philadelphia	10	3	11	11	—	35

Wash — Davis 2 run (Conway kick)
Phil — FG N. Johnson 49
Wash — Connell 54 pass from B. Johnson (Conway kick)
Phil — Rossum 89 kickoff return (N. Johnson kick)
Wash — Davis 1 run (Conway kick)
Phil — FG N. Johnson 29
Phil — FG N. Johnson 20
Phil — Staley 20 run (McNabb run)
Phil — FG N. Johnson 30
Wash — Westbrook 43 pass from B. Johnson (Conway kick)
Phil — Bieniemy 11 run (Weaver pass from McNabb)

SUNDAY NIGHT, NOVEMBER 14

SEATTLE 20, DENVER 17—at Kingdome, attendance 66,314. Jon Kitna passed for 2 touchdowns as the Seahawks improved to 7-2 for the first time since 1984. The Seahawks scored on their first two possessions to take a 10-0 lead, and Kerry Joseph's interception at the Seahawks' 1 just before halftime allowed Seattle to take a 10-0 lead into the locker room. Anthony Lynn recovered Ahman Green's fumble of the second half's opening kickoff, leading to Jason Elam's 25-yard field goal. On the next drive, Tory James intercepted Kitna at the Seahawks' 40, and Chris Miller's 23-yard touchdown pass to Ed McCaffrey seven plays later tied the game. Following a punt, Miller's 36-yard pass to Ed McCaffrey set up Howard Griffith's go-ahead touchdown catch. The Seahawks scored on their next two possessions, with Kitna completing 4 of 4 passes for 80 yards on the touchdown drive capped by Sean Dawkins's catch with 7:19 left to take a 20-17 lead. Miller completed a 42-yard pass to McCaffrey to the Seahawks' 38 with 10 seconds remaining, but the Broncos had no timeouts and Miller was unable to spike the ball before time expired. Kitna was 16 of 31 for 235 yards and 2 touchdowns, with 1 interception. Joey Galloway had 4 catches for 88 yards in his first game of the season. Miller was 20 of 30 for 239 yards and 2 touchdowns, with 1 interception.

Denver	0	0	17	0	—	17
Seattle	3	7	0	10	—	20

Sea — FG Peterson 35
Sea — Mayes 10 pass from Kitna (Peterson kick)
Den — FG Elam 35
Den — McCaffrey 23 pass from Miller (Elam kick)
Den — Griffith 1 pass from Miller (Elam kick)
Sea — FG Peterson 43
Sea — Dawkins 20 pass from Kitna (Peterson kick)

MONDAY NIGHT, NOVEMBER 15

N.Y. JETS 24, NEW ENGLAND 17—at Foxboro Stadium, attendance 59,077. Curtis Martin rushed for 149 yards and 2 touchdowns, and Ray Lucas, in just his second start, defeated his former team as the last-place Jets beat the Patriots. Lucas engineered two 58-yard drives to give the Jets a 14-3 lead late in the second quarter. Marcus Coleman's interception and 26-yard return to the Patriots' 36 with 48 seconds left in the half led to Lucas's 11-yard touchdown pass to Fred Baxter 28 seconds later to stake the Jets to a 21-3 halftime lead. A third-quarter interception at the Jets' 15 by Marvin Jones thwarted a Patriots' scoring opportunity and paved the way for a 19-play, 68-yard drive by the Jets that took 11:23, capped by John Hall's 26-yard field goal with 12:29 left, to give the Jets a 24-3 lead. Drew Bledsoe capped the Patriots' next two drives with touchdown passes, and Lawyer Milloy's interception and 17-yard return gave the Patriots the ball at the Jets' 27 with 5:58 remaining. However, 4 consecutive incompletions by Bledsoe gave the ball back to the Jets, and the Patriots never threatened again. Lucas was 18 of 31 for 153 yards and 2 touchdowns, with 2 interceptions. Bledsoe was 15 of 36 for 170 yards and 2 touchdowns, with 3 interceptions.

N.Y. Jets	0	21	0	3	—	24
New England	0	3	0	14	—	17

NYJ — K. Johnson 1 pass from Lucas (Hall kick)
NE — FG Vinatieri 22
NYJ — Martin 36 run (Hall kick)
NYJ — Baxter 11 pass from Lucas (Hall kick)
NYJ — FG Hall 26
NE — Faulk 13 pass from Bledsoe (Vinatieri kick)
NE — Brown 31 pass from Bledsoe (Vinatieri kick)

ELEVENTH WEEK SUMMARIES

AMERICAN FOOTBALL CONFERENCE						
Eastern Division	**W**	**L**	**T**	**Pct.**	**Pts.**	**OP**
Indianapolis	8	2	0	.800	294	198
Miami	8	2	0	.800	219	183
Buffalo	7	4	0	.636	211	166
New England	6	4	0	.600	225	201
N.Y. Jets	4	6	0	.400	167	174
Central Division						
Jacksonville	9	1	0	.900	257	102
Tennessee	8	2	0	.800	206	181
Pittsburgh	5	5	0	.500	182	140
Baltimore	4	6	0	.400	173	181
Cleveland	2	9	0	.182	116	284
Cincinnati	1	10	0	.091	161	336
Western Division						
Seattle	8	2	0	.800	236	164
Kansas City	5	5	0	.500	219	167
Oakland	5	5	0	.500	206	189
San Diego	4	6	0	.400	156	217
Denver	4	7	0	.364	221	226
NATIONAL FOOTBALL CONFERENCE						
Eastern Division	**W**	**L**	**T**	**Pct.**	**Pts.**	**OP**
Washington	6	4	0	.600	310	270
Dallas	5	5	0	.500	235	182
N.Y. Giants	5	5	0	.500	170	188
Arizona	4	6	0	.400	128	196
Philadelphia	3	8	0	.273	166	256
Central Division						
Detroit	6	4	0	.600	218	197
Minnesota	6	4	0	.600	237	199
Tampa Bay	6	4	0	.600	158	138
Green Bay	5	5	0	.500	192	209
Chicago	5	6	0	.455	190	221
Western Division						
St. Louis	8	2	0	.800	323	135
Carolina	4	6	0	.400	227	221
San Francisco	3	7	0	.300	163	281
Atlanta	2	8	0	.200	127	235
New Orleans	2	8	0	.200	170	226

SUNDAY, NOVEMBER 21

TAMPA BAY 19, ATLANTA 10—at Raymond James Stadium, attendance 65,158. Martin Gramatica kicked 4 field goals, and Donnie Abraham capped the day with a 47-yard interception return with 27 seconds left to give the Buccaneers a come-from-behind victory. The Falcons scored on their first two possessions to take a 10-0 lead, but the Buccaneers' defense limited Atlanta to just 3 first downs on its remaining nine possessions. Gramatica capped consecutive six-minute-plus drives with field goals to trim the deficit to 10-6 at halftime. The score was still 10-6 when Abraham intercepted Chris Chandler's pass at the Buccaneers' 34 with 9:15 left in the game. Mike Alstott's 8- and 13-yard runs set up Gramatica's 50-yard field goal with 6:32 left. The Buccaneers forced a punt, and Gramatica drilled a 53-yard attempt with 58 seconds left to give Tampa Bay its first lead of the game. The Falcons returned the kickoff to their own 33, but on third-and-7, Abraham intercepted Chandler again, and returned the ball 47 yards for the game-clinching points. Trent Dilfer was 15 of 31 for 142 yards, with 1 interception. Chandler was 14 of 25 for 109 yards, with 2 interceptions.

Atlanta	10	0	0	0	—	10
Tampa Bay	0	6	0	13	—	19

Atl — Dwight 8 run (Andersen kick)
Atl — FG Andersen 28
TB — FG Gramatica 24
TB — FG Gramatica 26
TB — FG Gramatica 50
TB — FG Gramatica 53
TB — Abraham 47 interception return (Gramatica kick)

BALTIMORE 34, CINCINNATI 31—at Cinergy Field, attendance 43,279. Matt Stover booted a 50-yard field goal as time expired to hand the Bengals their sixth consecutive defeat. Jeff Blake passed for 2 first-quarter touchdowns, the first of which was set up by Takeo Spikes's interception at the Ravens' 25, to give the Bengals a 14-0 lead. Tony Banks capped a 78-yard drive with a 3-yard touchdown pass to Greg Delong just before halftime to pull the Ravens within 14-10. The Ravens scored 3 touchdowns in a span of 3:40, jump-started by Banks's 73-yard pass to Billy Davis and capped by Duane Starks's 43-yard interception return for a score, to take a 31-14 lead with 4:38 remaining in the third quarter. Blake's 15-yard touchdown pass to Darnay Scott followed less than two minutes later, and Craig Yeast's 86-yard punt return with 9:09 left cut the deficit to 31-28. The Bengals forced a punt and got the ball on their own 20 with 5:28 left. The Bengals reached the Ravens' 1, but two running plays and an incomplete pass netted a 1-yard loss, and Doug Pelfrey kicked a 19-yard field goal with 1:50 remaining to tie the game at 31-31. The Ravens converted 2 third-down situations on their final drive to set up Stover's winning kick. Banks was 24 of 40 for 274 yards and 2 touchdowns, with 1 interception. Blake was 20 of 39 for 246 yards and 3 touchdowns, with 2 interceptions.

Baltimore	0	10	21	3	—	34
Cincinnati	14	0	7	10	—	31

Cin — Pickens 7 pass from Blake (Pelfrey kick)
Cin — Scott 23 pass from Blake (Pelfrey kick)
Balt — FG Stover 25
Balt — DeLong 3 pass from Banks (Stover kick)
Balt — Rhett 2 run (Stover kick)
Balt — Johnson 25 pass from Banks (Stover kick)
Balt — Starks 43 interception return (Stover kick)
Cin — Scott 15 pass from Blake (Pelfrey kick)
Cin — Yeast 86 punt return (Pelfrey kick)
Cin — FG Pelfrey 19
Balt — FG Stover 50

N.Y. JETS 17, BUFFALO 7—at Giants Stadium, attendance 79,285. Behind Ray Lucas, who began the season as a third-string quarterback, the Jets defeated an AFC East rival for the second time in six days. The Bills had ample opportunity to score in the first half. Steve Christie missed a 40-yard field-goal attempt, which allowed Lucas to engineer a 70-yard scoring drive, capped by his 9-yard run early in the second quarter. The next three possessions were disastrous for the Bills: Christie missed a 45-yard attempt; on third down from the Bills' 5, Ray Mickens stripped Doug Flutie and forced him to fumble in the end zone, which Eric Ogbogu recovered for a touchdown; and Victor Green intercepted Flutie at the Jets' 9 to stop a scoring drive. Flutie's 2-yard touchdown pass to Peerless Price trimmed the deficit to 17-7, but Ernie Logan tipped Flutie's pass and Jason Wiltz intercepted the ball at the Jets' 15 with 4:07 remaining. Lucas was 16 of 20 for 142 yards. Flutie was 22 of 40 for 220 yards and 1 touchdown, with 2 interceptions.

Buffalo	0	0	7	0	—	7
N.Y. Jets	0	14	3	0	—	17

NYJ — Lucas 9 run (Hall kick)
NYJ — Ogbogu recovered fumble in end zone (Hall kick)
NYJ — FG Hall 36
Buff — Price 2 run (Christie kick)

CAROLINA 31, CLEVELAND 17—at Cleveland Browns Stadium, attendance 72,818. Steve Beuerlein passed for 2 touchdowns, and William Floyd scored twice as the Panthers defeated the Browns. The score was tied 3-3 in the second quarter when Eric Metcalf's 31-yard kickoff return set up Floyd's first touchdown. Later in the half, Beuerlein's 8-yard touchdown pass to Wesley Walls capped a 13-play, 60-yard drive and gave Carolina a 17-3 halftime edge. The Panthers drove 77 and 54 yards with their first two possessions of the second half to take a 31-3 lead with 13:14 remaining. Beuerlein was 21 of 27 for 199 yards and 2 touchdowns. Tim Couch was 29 of 46 for 259 yards and 1 touchdown, with 2 interceptions.

Carolina	3	14	7	7	—	31
Cleveland	0	3	0	14	—	17

Car — FG Kasay 44
Cle — FG Dawson 23
Car — Floyd 1 run (Kasay kick)
Car — Walls 8 pass from Beuerlein (Kasay kick)
Car — Kinchen 1 pass from Beuerlein (Kasay kick)
Car — Floyd 1 run (Kasay kick)
Cle — Kirby 2 run (Dawson kick)
Cle — Chiaverini 12 pass from Couch (Dawson kick)

CHICAGO 23, SAN DIEGO 20 (OT)—at Qualcomm Stadium, attendance 56,055. Chris Boniol's 36-yard field goal in overtime handed the Chargers their fifth consecutive defeat. The first half concluded with Boniol missing a 33-yard field-goal attempt and the Chargers leading 10-3. Midway through the third quarter, Jim Miller's 25-yard third-down pass to Bobby Engram was followed one play later by his 38-yard touchdown pass to Marcus Robinson to tie the game. Miller's 30-yard pass to Robinson moments later set up Curtis Enis's 3-yard scoring run to give the Bears their first lead. Shane Burton blocked John Carney's 38-yard field-goal attempt in the fourth quarter, and Boniol culminated the following possession with a field goal to give the Bears a 20-10 lead with 5:22 left. Jim Harbaugh's 45-yard pass to Jeff Graham led to his 13-yard scoring pass to Tremayne Stephens, and, following a punt, the Chargers drove to the Bears' 10 only to have Graham drop a pass in the end zone with eight seconds left. Carney kicked a 28-yard field goal to send the game to overtime, where the Bears won the toss and used a 31-yard Miller-to-Robinson pass to set up Boniol's heroics. Miller was 25 of 38 for 357 yards and 1 touchdown. Robinson had 6 receptions for 163 yards, and Engram added 8 catches for 121 yards. Harbaugh was 29 of 46 for 273 yards and 2 touchdowns, with 1 interception.

Chicago	0	3	14	3	3	—	23
San Diego	7	3	0	10	0	—	20

SD — Davis 2 pass from Harbaugh (Carney kick)
Chi — FG Boniol 29
SD — FG Carney 28
Chi — Robinson 38 pass from Miller (Boniol kick)
Chi — Enis 3 run (Boniol kick)
Chi — FG Boniol 26
SD — Stephens 13 pass from Harbaugh (Carney kick)
SD — FG Carney 28
Chi — FG Boniol 36

ARIZONA 13, DALLAS 9—at Sun Devil Stadium, attendance 72,015. Dave Brown's touchdown pass to Rob Moore vaulted the Cardinals to just their second victory in their last 19 regular-season games against the Cowboys. The Cowboys drove into Cardinals' territory each of their first four possessions, but led just 7-3 at halftime after having to punt, get stopped on downs, and having missed a 48-yard field-goal attempt. The Cardinals grabbed their first lead on Dave Brown's 21-yard touchdown pass to Moore four plays into the second half, and Chris Jacke's 38-yard field goal with 11:30 remaining gave Arizona a 13-7 lead. The Cowboys reached the Cardinals' 10, but, facing second-and-2, Emmitt Smith gained 1 yard on three consecutive carries to hand the ball back to Arizona. Punter Scott Player ran out of the end zone for a safety with 1:49 remaining, and the Cowboys reached the Cardinals' 22 but Jason Garrett's fourth-and-3 pass to Raghib Ismail gained just 1 yard with 12 seconds left. Brown, playing for injured Jake Plummer, was 13 of 29 for 115 yards and 1 touchdown, with 2 interceptions. Garrett, playing for injured Troy Aikman, was 16 of 29 for 111 yards and 1 touchdown.

Dallas	7	0	0	2	—	9
Arizona	0	3	7	3	—	13

Dall — LaFleur 11 pass from Garrett (Cunningham kick)
Ariz — FG Jacke 24
Ariz — Moore 21 pass from Brown (Jacke kick)
Ariz — FG Jacke 38
Dall — Safety, Player ran out of end zone

GREEN BAY 26, DETROIT 17—at Lambeau Field, attendance 59,869. Ryan Longwell converted 4 field goals, and Brett Favre passed for 309 yards and 1 touchdown as the Packers knocked the Lions into a logjam atop the NFC Central. The Lions drove 84 yards to open the game and take a 7-0 lead. The Lions still led 7-0 early in the second quarter before the Packers scored on six of their next seven possessions, the last of which was set up by Fred Vinson's interception, to take a 26-17 lead with 12:52 remaining. Pass interference penalties deep in Lions' territory set up both Packers' touchdowns. The Lions reached the Packers' 6 in the final minute, but 4 consecutive Gus Frerotte incomplete passes quelled the rally. Favre was 26 of 40 for 309 yards and 1 touchdown. Dorsey Levens had 10 catches for 99 yards. Frerotte, starting for injured Charlie Batch, was 20 of 39 for 225 yards and 1 touchdown, with 2 interceptions. Germane Crowell had 8 receptions for 112 yards.

Detroit	7	10	0	0	—	17
Green Bay	0	12	11	3	—	26

Det — Irvin 2 run (Hanson kick)
GB — FG Longwell 23
GB — FG Longwell 33
Det — Crowell 14 pass from Frerotte (Hanson kick)
GB — Levens 1 run (pass failed)
Det — FG Hanson 46
GB — Bradford 17 pass from Favre (Bradford pass from Favre)
GB — FG Longwell 45
GB — FG Longwell 31

INDIANAPOLIS 44, PHILADELPHIA 17—at Veterans Stadium, attendance 65,521. Edgerrin James rushed for 152 yards and scored 3 touchdowns as the Colts won their sixth consecutive game. The Colts scored on their first five possessions, the last two set up by Donovan McNabb's fumbles at the Eagles' 7- and 10-yard lines respectively, to take a 27-0 lead with 11:27 left in the second quarter. The Colts led 30-3 at halftime. Peyton Manning's 80-yard touchdown pass to Terrence Wilkins on their first play of the second half extended the lead to 37-3. Cornelius Bennett recovered another McNabb fumble at the Eagles' 17 later in the quarter to set up Manning's touchdown pass to James for a 44-3 lead with 6:51 left in the quarter. Manning was 16 of 26 for 235 yards and 3 touchdowns. Wilkins had 4 receptions for 111 yards. McNabb was 19 of 36 for 165 yards and 1 touchdown, with 2 interceptions.

Indianapolis	17	13	14	0	—	44
Philadelphia	0	3	0	14	—	17

Ind — FG Vanderjagt 45
Ind — James 1 run (Vanderjagt kick)
Ind — James 62 run (Vanderjagt kick)
Ind — FG Vanderjagt 29
Ind — Harrison 5 pass from Manning (Vanderjagt kick)
Phil — FG Akers 48
Ind — FG Vanderjagt 34
Ind — Wilkins 80 pass from Manning (Vanderjagt kick)
Ind — James 17 pass from Manning (Vanderjagt kick)
Phil — Lewis 6 pass from McNabb (Akers kick)
Phil — Whiting 32 interception return (Akers kick)

MIAMI 27, NEW ENGLAND 17—at Pro Player Stadium, attendance 74,295. Damon Huard and Oronde Gadsden hooked up for 2 touchdowns, and the Dolphins intercepted 5 passes to defeat the Patriots. Chad Eaton recovered Damon Huard's fumble at the Dolphins' 7 to set up Terry Allen's touchdown run to begin the scoring. Drew Bledsoe's first intercepted pass was pilfered by Sam Madison, who returned it 13 yards to the Patriots' 9 to lead to Olindo Mare's field goal late in the first quarter. The game was tied 10-10 at halftime, but in the third quarter Huard engineered a 10-play, 80-yard drive, capped by a 3-yard touchdown pass to Gadsden. Terrell Buckley's 18-yard interception return to the Patriots' 10 set up J.J. Johnson's touchdown moments later to give Miami a 24-10 lead. Bledsoe's 68-yard touchdown pass to Shawn Jefferson two plays later trimmed the deficit to 24-17, but Jason Taylor's interception at the Patriots' 21 with 5:24 left led to Mare's 23-yard field goal to give Miami a 27-17 lead with 2:11 remaining. Jerry Wilson intercepted Bledsoe at the Dolphins' 21 with 1:05 left to preserve the victory. Bledsoe was 15 of 34 for 201 yards and 1 touchdown, with 5 interceptions. Huard was 18 of 30 for 131 yards and 2 touchdowns. Johnson had 31 carries for 106 yards.

New England	7	3	7	0	—	17
Miami	3	7	14	3	—	27

NE — Allen 6 run (Vinatieri kick)
Mia — FG Mare 19
NE — FG Vinatieri 27
Mia — Gadsden 4 pass from Huard (Mare kick)
Mia — Gadsden 3 pass from Huard (Mare kick)
Mia — Johnson 1 run (Mare kick)

NE — Jefferson 68 pass from Bledsoe (Vinatieri kick)
Mia — FG Mare 23

WASHINGTON 23, N.Y. GIANTS 13—at FedEx Field, attendance 78,641. Prior to the game, Redskins Stadium was officially renamed FedEx Field, but Stephen Davis felt at home regardless, rushing for 183 yards and 1 touchdown as the Redskins vaulted into first place in the NFC East. The Redskins led 10-3 and drove to the Giants' 1 late in the first half only to have Brad Johnson fumble and Keith Hamilton recover the ball. The Giants drove 71 yards in the final 1:40 of the half to set up Cary Blanchard's field goal and cut the deficit to 10-6. The Redskins led 13-6, but the Giants reached the Redskins' 49 at the beginning of the fourth quarter. On third down, Ndukwe Kalu sacked Kerry Collins and forced him to fumble. Marco Coleman caught the ball in midair and hustled 42 yards for a touchdown. The Giants responded with a 71-yard touchdown drive to trim the deficit to 20-13 with 10:26 left. After Brett Conway missed his third field-goal attempt of the game, the Giants drove to the Redskins' 27, but Collins fumbled the snap and Kenard Lang recovered with 4:05 left. Despite his tough day, Conway made a 37-yard field goal with 21 seconds left to clinch the victory. Johnson was 17 of 29 for 158 yards, with 1 interception. Collins was 13 of 21 for 221 yards, with 1 interception. Ike Hilliard had 4 receptions for 101 yards.

N.Y. Giants	0	6	0	7	—	13
Washington	7	3	3	10	—	23

Wash — Davis 1 run (Conway kick)
NYG — FG Blanchard 44
Wash — FG Conway 24
NYG — FG Blanchard 44
Wash — FG Conway 21
Wash — Coleman 42 fumble return (Conway kick)
NYG — Way 1 run (Blanchard kick)
Wash — FG Conway 37

TENNESSEE 16, PITTSBURGH 10—at Adelphia Coliseum, attendance 66,619. Steve McNair rushed for 2 touchdowns, and the Titans' defense recorded 5 sacks to win their twelfth consecutive game against an AFC Central opponent. McNair's short touchdown runs, the second of which came as he was hit in midair and flipped into the end zone, capped 74- and 82-yard drives to give Tennessee a 14-7 lead after the first quarter. The Titans' offense failed to drive deep into Steelers' territory the rest of the game, but Tennessee's defense forced Kordell Stewart to be flagged for intentional grounding in the end zone, a safety, to take a 16-7 third-quarter lead. Stewart engineered a 15-play, 68-yard drive to set up Kris Brown's 24-yard field goal with 6:55 left to pull within 16-10. The Steelers got the ball on their own 9 with 3:15 remaining, but Kenny Holmes intercepted Stewart at the Steelers' 18 with 1:53 remaining to preserve the victory. McNair was 14 of 26 for 149 yards, with 1 interception. Stewart was 18 of 30 for 177 yards and 1 touchdown, with 1 interception.

Pittsburgh	7	0	0	3	—	10
Tennessee	14	0	2	0	—	16

Tenn — McNair 2 run (Del Greco kick)
Pitt — Edwards 15 pass from Stewart (Brown kick)
Tenn — McNair 3 run (Del Greco kick)
Tenn — Safety, Stewart penalized for intentional grounding in end zone
Pitt — FG Brown 24

ST. LOUIS 23, SAN FRANCISCO 7—at 3Com Park, attendance 68,193. Marshall Faulk rushed for 126 yards, and the Rams' defense forced 5 turnovers to sweep the 49ers for the first time since 1980. The Rams had more than twice as many first downs in the first half (13-6), but led just 13-7 as the 49ers' defense forced the Rams to attempt 3 field goals, of which Jeff Wilkins converted 2 successfully. Mike Jones intercepted Steve Stenstrom's pass on the 49ers' third play of the second half and returned it 44 yards for a touchdown, and Wilkins added his third field goal later in the quarter to take a 23-7 lead. The Rams' defense forced 3 turnovers in the final 16 minutes to preserve the victory. Kurt Warner was 22 of 40 for 201 yards and 1 touchdown, with 1 interception. Stenstrom was 7 of 12 for 108 yards, with 1 interception. Jeff Garcia entered the game once the score was 23-7, and was 8 of 15 for 89 yards, with 2 interceptions. Terrell Owens had 6 catches for 120 yards.

St. Louis	3	10	10	0	—	23
San Francisco	0	7	0	0	—	7

StL — FG Wilkins 40
SF — Beasley 1 run (Richey kick)
StL — Bruce 5 pass from Warner (Wilkins kick)
StL — FG Wilkins 20
StL — Jones 44 interception return (Wilkins kick)
StL — FG Wilkins 49

SEATTLE 31, KANSAS CITY 19—at Arrowhead Stadium, attendance 78,714. Ricky Watters rushed for 107 yards and scored 3 touchdowns as the Seahawks won their fifth consecutive game. The Seahawks led 14-10 and were driving just before halftime when Jon Kitna fumbled and Marvcus Patton recovered the ball near midfield. Elvis Grbac converted 2 third-down situations to set up Pete Stoyanovich's 29-yard field goal just before halftime to trim the lead to 14-13. While the Seahawks' defense limited the Chiefs' to 2 first downs on their first five possessions of the second half, the offense increased the lead to 24-13, highlighted by Kitna's 45-yard touchdown pass to Sean Dawkins. Donnell Bennett's 4-yard touchdown run with 6:49 left in the fourth quarter cut the lead to 24-19, but Kevin Lockett failed to get into the end zone on the 2-point conversion attempt. Following an exchange of punts, Watters broke free for a 45-yard run to the Chiefs' 5 to set up his final touchdown with 2:43 left. Jon Kitna was 14 of 33 for 235 yards and 2 touchdowns, with 1 interception. Sean Dawkins had 5 receptions for 114 yards. Elvis Grbac was 30 of 49 for 322 yards, with 1 interception. Derrick Alexander had 8 catches for 101 yards.

Seattle	0	14	10	7	—	31
Kansas City	3	10	0	6	—	19

KC — FG Stoyanovich 29
Sea — Watters 2 run (Peterson kick)
KC — Bennett 1 run (Stoyanovich kick)
Sea — Watters 22 pass from Kitna (Peterson kick)
KC — FG Stoyanovich 29
Sea — FG Peterson 38
Sea — Dawkins 45 pass from Kitna (Peterson kick)
KC — Bennett 4 run (pass failed)
Sea — Watters 5 run (Peterson kick)

SUNDAY NIGHT, NOVEMBER 21

JACKSONVILLE 41, NEW ORLEANS 23—at ALLTEL Stadium, attendance 69,772. Mark Brunell passed for 351 yards and 2 touchdowns as the Jaguars won their seventh consecutive game. The Saints engineered touchdown drives of 80 and 79 yards, capped by Ricky Williams's first NFL touchdown, of 19 yards, to tie the game 14-14. The Jaguars drove to the Saints' 6, but Willie Clay's interception in the end zone thwarted the drive. The Saints took a brief 17-14 lead late in the half before Mike Hollis's 52-yard field goal as time expired tied the score. The Jaguars scored on their first two second-half possessions, as Brunell's 57-yard pass to Jimmy Smith set up the first touchdown and his 46-yard scoring pass to Smith moments later gave Jacksonville a 31-17 lead. Fernando Bryant's interception at the Saints' 29 led to James Stewart's second touchdown midway through the fourth quarter and gave the Jaguars a commanding 41-17 lead. Brunell was 19 of 30 for 351 yards and 2 touchdowns, with 1 interception. Smith had 9 receptions for 220 yards. Billy Joe Tolliver was 10 of 14 for 159 yards before being injured on Brant Boyer's sack and replaced by Billy Joe Hobert, who was 8 of 13 for 92 yards, with 1 interception.

New Orleans	7	10	0	6	—	23
Jacksonville	14	3	14	10	—	41

Jax — Barlow 74 punt return (Hollis kick)
NO — Tolliver 1 run (Brien kick)
Jax — Jones 8 pass from Brunell (Hollis kick)
NO — Williams 19 run (Brien kick)
NO — FG Brien 52
Jax — FG Hollis 45
Jax — Stewart 4 run (Hollis kick)
Jax — Smith 46 pass from Brunell (Hollis kick)
Jax — FG Hollis 32
Jax — Stewart 1 run (Hollis kick)
NO — Williams 1 run (pass failed)

MONDAY NIGHT, NOVEMBER 22

DENVER 27, OAKLAND 21 (OT)—at Mile High Stadium, attendance 70,012. Trevor Pryce forced Rich Gannon to fumble, and Olandis Gary scored the game-winning touchdown on the next play as the Broncos swept the season series from the Raiders. The Broncos scored on their first two possessions and led 15-0 with 6:37 left in the first half. Napoleon Kaufman's 47-yard kickoff return jump-started the Raiders, leading to Rich Gannon's 20-yard touchdown pass to Jon Ritchie. Charles Mincy recovered Gary's fumble at the Raiders' 20 just before halftime, keeping Oakland within eight points. Chris Watson fumbled the second half's kickoff, and Travian Smith recovered to set up Gannon's 12-yard touchdown pass to Rickey Dudley and game-tying 2-point conversion pass to James Jett. With the score tied 18-18, Darrien Gordon's 25-yard punt return to the Broncos' 35 set up Michael Husted's 44-yard field goal with 1:17 left. Brian Griese's fourth-down pass to Rod Smith kept the drive alive for Denver, and Jason Elam drilled a 53-yard field goal in the cold to tie the game with seven seconds remaining. The Raiders won the overtime coin toss, and Pryce sacked Gannon on third-and-4 and recovered the fumble. Gary broke through the left side of the line and raced into the end zone on the next play. Chris Miller was 12 of 27 for 122 yards before being replaced by Griese, who was 6 of 14 for 60 yards. Gannon was 17 of 34 for 222 yards and 2 touchdowns, with 1 interception.

Oakland	0	7	11	3	0	—	21
Denver	10	5	0	6	6	—	27

Den — Griffith 1 run (Elam kick)
Den — FG Elam 30
Den — Safety, D. Smith blocked punt out of end zone
Den — FG Elam 24
Oak — Ritchie 20 pass from Gannon (Husted kick)
Oak — Dudley 12 pass from Gannon (Jett pass from Gannon)
Oak — FG Husted 33
Den — FG Elam 38
Oak — FG Husted 44
Den — FG Elam 53
Den — Gary 24 run

TWELFTH WEEK SUMMARIES

AMERICAN FOOTBALL CONFERENCE

Eastern Division	**W**	**L**	**T**	**Pct.**	**Pts.**	**OP**
Indianapolis	9	2	0	.818	307	204
Miami	8	3	0	.727	219	203
Buffalo	8	4	0	.667	228	173
New England	6	5	0	.545	232	218
N.Y. Jets	4	7	0	.364	173	187
Central Division						
Jacksonville	10	1	0	.909	287	125
Tennessee	9	2	0	.818	239	202
Pittsburgh	5	6	0	.455	202	167
Baltimore	4	7	0	.364	196	211
Cincinnati	2	10	0	.167	188	356
Cleveland	2	10	0	.167	137	317
Western Division						
Seattle	8	3	0	.727	239	180
Kansas City	6	5	0	.545	256	201
Oakland	5	6	0	.455	240	226
Denver	4	7	0	.364	221	226
San Diego	4	7	0	.364	183	252

NATIONAL FOOTBALL CONFERENCE

Eastern Division	**W**	**L**	**T**	**Pct.**	**Pts.**	**OP**
Washington	7	4	0	.636	330	287
Dallas	6	5	0	.545	255	182
Arizona	5	6	0	.455	162	220
N.Y. Giants	5	6	0	.455	194	222
Philadelphia	3	9	0	.250	183	276
Central Division						
Detroit	7	4	0	.636	239	214
Minnesota	7	4	0	.636	272	226
Tampa Bay	7	4	0	.636	174	141
Green Bay	6	5	0	.545	212	212
Chicago	5	7	0	.417	207	242
Western Division						
St. Louis	9	2	0	.818	366	147
Carolina	5	6	0	.455	261	249
San Francisco	3	8	0	.273	166	301
Atlanta	2	9	0	.182	155	269
New Orleans	2	9	0	.182	182	269

THURSDAY, NOVEMBER 25

DETROIT 21, CHICAGO 17—at Pontiac Silverdome, attendance 77,905. Gus Frerotte passed for 2 first-half touchdowns, and the Lions held on to defeat the Bears. The Lions' defense limited the Bears to 1 first down in their first seven possessions, the last of which ended with Scott Kowalkowski's 29-yard interception return to the Bears' 1 to set up Frerotte's second touchdown pass and give the Lions a 21-0 lead with 1:45 left in the half. The Bears scored on their next two possessions to cut the deficit to 21-10, and Keith Burns's recovery of Iheanyi Uwaezuoke's fumbled punt near midfield led to Jim Miller's 23-yard touchdown pass to Marty Booker to make the score 21-17 with 14:53 remaining in the game. Frerotte completed 5 of 6 passes as the Lions were able to hold the ball for the final 6:09. Frerotte was 29 of 42 for 309 yards and 2 touchdowns. Miller was 25 of 37 for 204 yards and 2 touchdowns, with 1 interception.

Chicago	0	7	3	7	—	17
Detroit	7	14	0	0	—	21

Det — Crowell 45 pass from Frerotte (Hanson kick)
Det — Hill 29 run (Hanson kick)
Det — Morton 2 pass from Frerotte (Hanson kick)
Chi — Mayes 3 pass from Miller (Boniol kick)
Chi — FG Boniol 27
Chi — Booker 23 pass from Miller (Boniol kick)

DALLAS 20, MIAMI 0—at Texas Stadium, attendance 64,328. The Cowboys' defense intercepted 5 passes, including Dexter Coakley's 46-yard touchdown return to break a scoreless tie in the third quarter, as Dallas defeated Miami in the return of previously injured quarterbacks Troy Aikman and Dan Marino. The Dolphins drove inside the Cowboys' 35 three times in the first half, but Olindo Mare missed a 52-yard field-goal attempt, had a 47-yard attempt blocked by Flozell Adams, and Marino's fade pass in the corner of the end zone was intercepted by Deion Sanders. The Cowboys didn't penetrate the Dolphins' 35 until the fourth quarter, but Coakley's interception return midway through the third quarter had already given Dallas a 7-0 lead. Mare's third missed field goal late in the third quarter started a 44-yard drive capped by Richie Cunningham's 36-yard field goal with 11:47 left. Dallas recorded interceptions on the Dolphins' next three possessions, and turned the last two into points, highlighted by Aikman's 65-yard touchdown pass to Raghib Ismail. Aikman was 16 of 29 for 232 yards and 1 touchdown. Emmitt Smith had 31 carries for 103 yards. Ismail had 5 receptions for 125 yards. Marino was 14 of 35 for 176 yards, with 5 interceptions.

Miami	0	0	0	0	—	0
Dallas	0	0	7	13	—	20

Dall — Coakley 46 interception return (Cunningham kick)
Dall — FG Cunningham 36
Dall — Ismail 65 pass from Aikman (Cunningham kick)
Dall — FG Cunningham 23

SUNDAY, NOVEMBER 28

ARIZONA 34, N.Y. GIANTS 24—at Giants Stadium, attendance 77,809. Jake Plummer, who had missed a month with a broken finger, came off the bench in the second half to pass for 2 touchdowns as the Cardinals swept the Giants for the first time since 1979. The Giants scored on their last two possessions of the first half, capped by Cary Blanchard's 24-yard field goal with two seconds left, to take a 10-6 lead into the locker room. Rob Fredrickson's 23-yard interception return to the Giants' 16 set up Plummer's first scoring pass, and his 67-yard scoring drive late in the quarter culminated with his 9-yard touchdown pass to Johnny McWilliams to open the fourth quarter and give Arizona a 20-10 lead. Kerry Collins responded with an 88-yard touchdown drive, but Plummer answered with a 9-play, 60-yard drive, culminated by Mario Bates's 2-yard scoring plunge with 4:16 left. Eric Swann's 44-yard interception return for a touchdown with 1:57 remaining sealed the victory. Dave Brown was 11 of 17 for 126 yards before being replaced by Plummer, who was 12 of 18 for 125 yards and 2 touchdowns. Rob Moore had 7 receptions for 102 yards. Kerry Collins was 22 of 45 for 298 yards and 1 touchdown, with 3 interceptions.

Arizona	3	3	7	21	—	34
N.Y. Giants	0	10	0	14	—	24

Ariz — FG Jacke 39
NYG — Collins 1 run (Blanchard kick)
Ariz — FG Jacke 20
NYG — FG Blanchard 24
Ariz — Moore 2 pass from Plummer (Jacke kick)
Ariz — McWilliams 9 pass from Plummer (Jacke kick)
NYG — Bennett 1 run (Blanchard kick)
Ariz — Bates 2 run (Jacke kick)
Ariz — Swann 44 interception return (Jacke kick)
NYG — Barber 34 pass from Collins (Blanchard kick)

CINCINNATI 27, PITTSBURGH 20—at Three Rivers Stadium, attendance 50,907. Jeff Blake passed for 1 touchdown and ran for another as the Bengals built a 24-3 lead and held on to snap a six-game losing streak. The Bengals needed just 9 plays on their first two possessions, highlighted by Blake's 76- and 24-yard passes to Darnay Scott, and a 34-yard pass to Carl Pickens, to take a 14-0 lead 6:56 into the game. Rodney Heath's 58-yard interception return for a touchdown early in the second quarter ended Kordell Stewart's day and gave the Bengals a 21-3 lead. Takeo Spikes's recovery of Richard Huntley's fumble three plays later set up Doug Pelfrey's field goal and a 24-3 lead with 10:33 left in the first half. Mike Tomczak replaced Stewart and led the Steelers to successive scoring drives to make the halftime score 24-13. Tomczak needed just three plays in the second half to throw a 34-yard touchdown pass to Hines Ward to cut the deficit to 24-20. Pelfrey responded with a field goal, but the Bengals' defense stopped the Steelers on downs three times in the final 16 minutes, culminated by Tomczak's incomplete pass from the Bengals' 26 on fourth-and-6 with 49 seconds remaining. Blake was 15 of 28 for 241 yards and 1 touchdown, with 1 interception. Corey Dillon had 23 carries for 120 yards, and Scott had 4 receptions for 123 yards. Stewart was 5 of 11 for 36 yards, with 2 interceptions before being replaced by Tomczak, who was 19 of 35 for 264 yards and 2 touchdowns.

Cincinnati	14	10	3	0	—	27
Pittsburgh	3	10	7	0	—	20

Cin — Scott 76 pass from Blake (Pelfrey kick)
Cin — Blake 4 run (Pelfrey kick)
Pitt — FG Brown 35
Cin — Heath 58 interception return (Pelfrey kick)
Cin — FG Pelfrey 29
Pitt — FG Brown 33
Pitt — Shaw 15 pass from Tomczak (Brown kick)
Pitt — Ward 34 pass from Tomczak (Brown kick)
Cin — FG Pelfrey 29

JACKSONVILLE 30, BALTIMORE 23—at PSINet Stadium, attendance 68,428. Mark Brunell passed for 338 yards and 2 touchdowns as the Jaguars defeated the Ravens. The Ravens scored on their first two drives to take a 10-0 lead, and Matt Stover's 31-yard field goal just before halftime extended the lead to 13-7 at intermission. Interceptions in Ravens' territory by Ray Lewis and Rod Woodson stymied Jacksonville's two third-quarter drives, and Stover's third field goal in the final seconds of the third quarter extended the lead to 16-7. The Jaguars responded with a 61-yard scoring drive, capped by Brunell's 1-yard touchdown pass to Keenan McCardell. Tony Brackens intercepted Tony Banks's pass 16 seconds later and returned it for a touchdown to give the Jaguars a 22-16 lead. Banks's 46-yard pass to Jermaine Lewis set up his 3-yard touchdown pass to Chuck Evans to allow Baltimore to retake the lead, 23-22 with 6:26 remaining. Jacksonville drove 12 plays for 78 yards in the ensuing drive to take a 30-23 lead on James Stewart's 4-yard run with 1:39 left. Kevin Hardy sacked Banks three plays later and forced him to fumble. Brackens recovered the fumble with 1:06 left to preserve the victory. Brunell was 27 of 47 for 338 yards and 2 touchdowns, with 2 interceptions. Jimmy Smith had 10 receptions for 132 yards, and Keenan McCardell had 8 catches for 102 yards. Banks was 17 of 34 for 214 yards and 2 touchdowns, with 1 interception.

Jacksonville	0	7	0	23	—	30
Baltimore	10	3	3	7	—	23

Balt — Rhett 20 pass from Banks (Stover kick)
Balt — FG Stover 46
Jax — Smith 8 pass from Brunell (Hollis kick)
Balt — FG Stover 31
Balt — FG Stover 33
Jax — McCardell 1 pass from Brunell (Hollis kick)
Jax — Brackens 21 interception return (McCardell pass from Brunell)
Balt — Evans 3 pass from Banks (Stover kick)
Jax — Stewart 4 run (Smith pass from Brunell)

KANSAS CITY 37, OAKLAND 34—at Network Associates Coliseum, attendance 48,632. Chris Dishman scored 2 defensive touchdowns, and Pete Stoyanovich made a 44-yard field goal as time expired to lift the Chiefs to victory. With the score tied 13-13 in the third quarter, Dishman's 47-yard interception return for a touchdown gave Kansas City the lead. Oakland then scored 3 touchdowns in a span of 5:12 late in the third quarter. First, Napoleon Kaufman's 48-yard kickoff return led to Rich Gannon's 6-yard scoring run. Greg Biekert's 36-yard interception return to the Raiders' 3 three plays later set up Gannon's touchdown pass to Rickey Dudley, and then Charles Woodson's 15-yard interception return for a touchdown gave Oakland a 34-20 lead. However, Elvis Grbac's 73-yard touchdown pass to Tony Gonzalez three plays later cut into the deficit, and Dishman picked up Derrick Walker's fumble and raced 40 yards down the sideline for the tying touchdown with 6:24 left. Oakland drove to the Chiefs' 26, but Michael Husted missed a 44-yard field-goal attempt. The Chiefs responded by driving to the Raiders' 27, where Stoyanovich converted as time expired. Grbac was 18 of 27 for 226 yards and 1 touchdown, with 2 interceptions. Gannon was 19 of 29 for 232 yards and 2 touchdowns, with 2 interceptions.

Kansas City	0	10	10	17	—	37
Oakland	3	10	21	0	—	34

Oak — FG Husted 33
KC — Bennett 2 run (Stoyanovich kick)
Oak — FG Husted 30
KC — FG Stoyanovich 47
Oak — Dudley 16 pass from Gannon (Husted kick)
KC — FG Stoyanovich 37
KC — Dishman 47 interception return (Stoyanovich kick)
Oak — Gannon 6 run (Husted kick)
Oak — Dudley 3 pass from Gannon (Husted kick)
Oak — Woodson 15 interception return (Husted kick)
KC — Gonzalez 73 pass from Grbac (Stoyanovich kick)
KC — Dishman 40 fumble return (Stoyanovich kick)
KC — FG Stoyanovich 44

BUFFALO 17, NEW ENGLAND 7—at Ralph Wilson Stadium, attendance 72,111. Doug Flutie passed for 2 touchdowns as the Bills handed the Patriots their third consecutive defeat. The Bills scored on two of their four first-half possessions, highlighted by Flutie's 54-yard touchdown pass to Eric Moulds, to take a 10-0 lead into the locker room. Ken Irvin's interception at the Bills' 16 stopped the Patriots lone threat of the half. Flutie's 45-yard pass to Bobby Collins was immediatley followed by a 31-yard touchdown pass to Sam Gash. The Patriots responded by driving to the Bills' 6, but Kevin Faulk fumbled and Sam Rogers recovered to stymie the drive. Drew Bledsoe's 45-yard touchdown pass to Terry Glenn with 2:41 remaining averted the shutout. Flutie was 9 of 16 for 207 yards and 2 touchdowns. Bledsoe was 18 of 34 for 205 yards and 1 touchdown, with 1 interception.

New England	0	0	0	7	—	7
Buffalo	3	7	7	0	—	17

Buff — FG Christie 28
Buff — Moulds 54 pass from Flutie (Christie kick)
Buff — Gash 31 pass from Flutie (Christie kick)
NE — Glenn 45 pass from Bledsoe (Vinatieri kick)

ST. LOUIS 43, NEW ORLEANS 12—at Trans World Dome, attendance 65,864. Marshall Faulk rushed for 102 yards and 2 touchdowns as the Rams won their third consecutive game. Tony Horne's 64-yard kickoff return to begin the game set up Kurt Warner's 25-yard touchdown pass to Torry Holt three plays into the game. The Saints regrouped and put together first-half drives of 31, 50, 53, and 48 yards, which resulted in 4 Doug Brien field goals. The Rams were limited to 6 first downs in the first half, but Faulk's 1-yard scoring run, set up by a 35-yard pass interference penalty, allowed the Rams to take a 15-12 lead into the locker room. The Saints drove 68 yards to open the second half, but Brien's 24-yard field-goal attempt hit the left upright. The Rams needed just 7 plays to drive 80 yards, capped by Faulk's 6-yard run. St. Louis scored on all four of its second-half possessions, and the Saints never drove inside the Rams' 35 after the initial second-half opportunity. Warner was 15 of 27 for 213 yards and 2 touchdowns. Billy Joe Hobert was 23 of 41 for 254 yards, with 2 interceptions. Andre Hastings had 9 receptions for 113 yards.

New Orleans	3	9	0	0	—	12
St. Louis	7	8	7	21	—	43

StL — Holt 25 pass from Warner (Wilkins kick)
NO — FG Brien 51
NO — FG Brien 42
NO — FG Brien 45
StL — Faulk 1 run (Faulk run)
NO — FG Brien 35
StL — Faulk 6 run (Wilkins kick)
StL — Holcombe 3 run (Wilkins kick)
StL — Holt 20 pass from Warner (Wilkins kick)
StL — Hodgins 1 run (Wilkins kick)

INDIANAPOLIS 13, N.Y. JETS 6—at RCA Dome, attendance 56,689. Peyton Manning passed for 198 yards and 1 touchdown, and Wayne Chrebet could not hold onto Ray Lucas's game-tying pass in the end zone in the final moments as the Colts won their seventh consecutive game. The Jets drove 55 yards to set up John Hall's field goal to begin the game, and Edgerrin James's fumble on the Colts' first play from scrimmage was recovered at the Colts' 39 by Marvin Jones. Hall added his second field goal moments later, and the Jets had a quick 6-0 lead. The Colts responded with an 84-yard touchdown drive, and then Indianapolis drove to the Jets' 1 on their next possession, but Jason Wiltz intercepted Manning in the end zone. Mike Vanderjagt's 22-yard field goal just before halftime extended the Colts' lead to 10-6, but Manning was intercepted deep in Jets' territory again, this time at the Jets' 11 by Ray Mickens, to thwart a third-quarter scoring opportunity. Vanderjagt's 37-yard field goal increased the Colts' lead to 13-6 with 9:00 left. The Jets drove to the Colts' 17, but a holding penalty pushed them back and eventually set up a fourth-and-19 situation. Ray Lucas fired a strike into the end zone, but Chrebet was unable to hold onto the ball and the Colts ran out the clock. Manning was 23 of 31 for 198 yards and 1 touchdown, with 2 interceptions. Lucas was 12 of 22 for 102 yards.

N.Y. Jets	6	0	0	0	—	6
Indianapolis	7	3	0	3	—	13

NYJ — FG Hall 33
NYJ — FG Hall 30
Ind — Pollard 2 pass from Manning (Vanderjagt kick)
Ind — FG Vanderjagt 22
Ind — FG Vanderjagt 37

WASHINGTON 20, PHILADELPHIA 17 (OT)—at FedEx Field, attendance 74,741. Brett Conway redeemed himself for missing a 28-yard field-goal attempt as time expired in regulation by making a 27-yard field goal in overtime to allow the Redskins to stay in first place. The Redskins jumped out to a 10-0 lead before the Eagles drove 38 yards, keyed by Eric Bieniemy's fourth-and-9 run for 28 yards to the Redskins' 25, to set up Norm Johnson's field goal and trim the deficit to 10-3. Stephen Davis scored on a 1-yard run to culminate the opening drive of the second half and give the Redskins a 17-3 lead. Johnson missed a 47-yard field-goal attempt on the Eagles' first drive, but Donovan McNabb engineered two 91-yard scoring drives in the fourth quarter, both capped by Luther Broughton touchdown receptions, the second with 1:52 remaining, to tie the game. Brian Mitchell returned the ensuing kickoff 45 yards to set up Conway's game-winning attempt as time expired, but his 28-yard kick sailed wide right. The Redskins won the coin toss, and James Thrash returned the kickoff 48 yards to set up Conway's winning kick. Brad Johnson was 25 of 36 for 218 yards and 1 touchdown, with 1 interception. McNabb was 16 of 28 for 172 yards and 2 touchdowns.

Philadelphia	0	3	0	14	0	—	17
Washington	3	7	7	0	3	—	20

Wash — FG Conway 43
Wash — Sellers 6 pass from Johnson (Conway kick)
Phil — FG N. Johnson 34
Wash — Davis 1 run (Conway kick)
Phil — Broughton 3 pass from McNabb (N. Johnson kick)
Phil — Broughton 26 pass from McNabb (N. Johnson kick)
Wash — FG Conway 27

MINNESOTA 35, SAN DIEGO 27—at Metrodome, attendance 64,232. Jeff George passed for 363 yards and 4 touchdowns to offset Jim Harbaugh's 404 yards and 1 touchdown as the Vikings won their fifth consecutive game by outlasting the Chargers. The Chargers led 7-0, but George's 34-yard touchdown pass to Randy Moss on the first play of the second quarter tied the score. On the Vikings' next possession, George's 60-yard pass to Moss set up his 5-yard scoring pass to Jake Reed. Kailee Wong's fumble recovery at the Chargers' 31 led to Cris Carter's touchdown catch, and Tony Williams's fumble recovery at the Chargers' 27 two plays later led to Leroy Hoard's touchdown run to give Minnesota 28 points in just 11:20 and a 28-7 lead. The Chargers roared right back into the game, as Kenny Bynum took Harbaugh's short pass on the first play of the second half and raced 80 yards for a touchdown, and Michael Dumas returned an interception 68 yards to the Vikings' 7 to set up Tremayne Stephens's second touchdown. John Carney's field goal on the Chargers' next possession cut the deficit to 28-24, but George engineered a 7-play, 82-yard drive, capped by a 34-yard scoring pass to Carter. Trailing 35-27, with under five minutes remaining, the Chargers reached the Vikings' 17, but Robert Griffith intercepted Harbaugh's pass at the Vikings' 2 and Minnesota ran out the final 4:29. George was 28 of 43 for 363 yards and 4 touchdowns, with 2 interceptions. Robert Smith had 20 carries for 104 yards. Carter had 11 receptions for 136 yards, and Moss had 7 catches for 127. Harbaugh was 25 of 39 for 404 yards and 1 touchdown, with 1 interception. Jeff Graham had 6 catches for 141 yards.

San Diego	7	0	17	3	—	27
Minnesota	0	28	7	0	—	35

SD — Stephens 1 run (Carney kick)
Minn — Moss 34 pass from George (Anderson kick)
Minn — Reed 5 pass from George (Anderson kick)
Minn — Carter 4 pass from George (Anderson kick)
Minn — Hoard 4 run (Anderson kick)
SD — Bynum 80 pass from Harbaugh (Carney kick)
SD — Stephens 1 run (Carney kick)
SD — FG Carney 40
Minn — Carter 34 pass from George (Anderson kick)
SD — FG Carney 40

TAMPA BAY 16, SEATTLE 3—at Kingdome, attendance 66,314. The Buccaneers' defense forced 6 turnovers to take the pressure off third-string rookie Shaun King, who replaced an injured Trent Dilfer early in the third quarter, as the Buccaneers won their fourth consecutive game. With the score tied 3-3 in the second quarter, Hardy Nickerson intercepted a Jon Kitna pass and returned it 10 yards to the Seahawks' 25 to set up Martin Gramatica's 42-yard field goal and give the Buccaneers a 6-3 halftime lead. Dilfer suffered a broken right clavicle when sacked by Phillip Daniels early in the second half, but King was at the controls of a 67-yard drive that culminated with his 2-yard touchdown pass to Patrick Hape early in the fourth quarter to give Tampa Bay a 13-3 lead. Kitna fumbled three plays later, and Sapp recovered to set up Gramatica's third field goal. The Buccaneers' defense intercepted 2 passes in the final six minutes to seal the victory. Dilfer was 5 of 11 for 50 yards, and King was 3 of 7 for 32 yards and 1 touchdown. Kitna was 19 of 44 for 197 yards, with 5 interceptions.

Tampa Bay	0	6	0	10	—	16
Seattle	3	0	0	0	—	3

Sea — FG Peterson 25
TB — FG Gramatica 42
TB — FG Gramatica 40
TB — Hape 2 pass from King (Gramatica kick)
TB — FG Gramatica 37

TENNESSEE 33, CLEVELAND 21—at Cleveland Browns Stadium, attendance 72,008. Derrick Mason's punt return for a touchdown highlighted a 26-point outburst as the Titans won their thirteenth consecutive game against AFC Central opponents. The Browns scored 2 touchdowns in the span of 2:26, the first culminated a 15-play, 86-yard drive, and the second was capped by Tim Couch's 78-yard touchdown pass to Terry Kirby. The Titans responded with 2 Al Del Greco field goals to cut the deficit to 14-13 at halftime. Kevin Johnson fumbled a punt in the third quarter, and Greg Favors recovered at the Browns' 21 to set up Steve McNair's 1-yard scoring run. Later in the quarter, Mason returned a punt 65 yards for a touchdown to increase the Titans' lead to 26-14. Eddie George's 3-yard scoring run with 3:29 left iced the game. McNair was 18 of 36 for 179 yards. George had 26 carries for 113 yards. Couch was 19 of 35 for 261 yards and 2 touchdowns.

Tennessee	7	6	13	7	—	33
Cleveland	0	14	0	7	—	21

Tenn — George 14 run (Del Greco kick)
Cle — Couch 4 run (Dawson kick)
Cle — Kirby 78 pass from Couch (Dawson kick)
Tenn — FG Del Greco 27
Tenn — FG Del Greco 31
Tenn — McNair 1 run (Del Greco kick)
Tenn — Mason 65 punt return (run failed)
Tenn — George 5 run (Del Greco kick)
Cle — K. Johnson 6 pass from Couch (Dawson kick)

SUNDAY NIGHT, NOVEMBER 28

CAROLINA 34, ATLANTA 28—at Ericsson Stadium, attendance 55,507. Steve Beuerlein passed for 262 yards and 3 touchdowns as the Panthers withstood a late rally to defeat the Falcons. The Panthers scored on six of seven possessions spanning from late in the first quarter to early in the fourth quarter, with the lone non scoring possession ending with a missed 47-yard field goal. Chris Chandler's second touchdown pass of the first half gave the Falcons a 14-13 lead with 56 seconds left, but Beuerlein engineered a 7-play, 62-yard drive, culminated by a 1-yard touchdown pass to Patrick Jeffers with four seconds left to give Carolina a 20-14 halftime lead. Beuerlein's 11-yard touchdown pass to Wesley Walls with 12:47 remaining in the game gave the Panthers a secure-looking 34-14 lead. The Falcons roared back, as Chandler engineered scoring drives of 74 and 78 yards to cut the deficit to 34-28 on Terance Mathis's 18-yard touchdown catch with 3:12 remaining. Travis Hall recovered Beuerlein's fumble at the Panthers' 20 on the next play, but Kevin Greene forced Chandler to fumble two plays later and Esera Tuaolo recovered. The Panthers were forced to punt, and the Falcons, starting from their 31 with 1:06 left, could garner only one first down before Chandler's fourth-down pass sailed incomplete. Beuerlein was 18 of 27 for 262 yards and 3 touchdowns. Donald Hayes, who was a late replacement for injured Muhsin Muhammad, had 5 receptions for 133 yards. Chandler was 24 of 42 for 315 yards and 4 touchdowns. Tim Dwight had 5 catches for 102 yards.

Atlanta	0	14	0	14	—	28
Carolina	3	17	7	7	—	34

Car — FG Kasay 30
Car — FG Kasay 24
Atl — Oxendine 5 pass from Chandler (Andersen kick)
Car — Hayes 56 pass from Beuerlein (Kasay kick)
Atl — Christian 12 pass from Chandler (Andersen kick)
Car — Jeffers 1 pass from Beuerlein (Kasay kick)
Car — Biakabutuka 11 run (Kasay kick)
Car — Walls 11 pass from Beuerlein (Kasay kick)
Atl — Kozlowski 15 pass from Chandler (Andersen kick)
Atl — Mathis 18 pass from Chandler (Andersen kick)

MONDAY NIGHT, NOVEMBER 29

GREEN BAY 20, SAN FRANCISCO 3—at 3Com Park, attendance 68,304. Brett Favre passed for 246 yards and 2 touchdowns as the Packers handed the 49ers their seventh consecutive defeat. The 49ers drove deep into Packers territory twice early in the game, but LeRoy Butler's end-zone interception stifled one drive, and Wade Richey made a 35-yard field goal to culminate the other to give San Francisco a 3-0 lead. The Packers responded by driving inside the 49ers' 20 their last three possessions of the half, with Ryan Longwell hitting 1 of 2 field-goal attempts to give Green Bay a 10-3 halftime lead. The Packers added 10 points in the second half before the 49ers drove into Packers' territory, but a fumble by Fred Beasley with 9:12 left stymied one drive, and Steve Stenstrom's fourth-and-goal pass from the Packers' 1 fell incomplete with 2:10 remaining. Favre was 25 of 36 for 246 yards and 2 touchdowns. Stenstrom was 19 of 35 for 195 yards, with 1 interception.

Green Bay	0	10	7	3	—	20
San Francisco	0	3	0	0	—	3

SF — FG Richey 35
GB — Bradford 13 pass from Favre (Longwell kick)
GB — FG Longwell 23
GB — Davis 10 pass from Favre (Longwell kick)
GB — FG Longwell 22

THIRTEENTH WEEK SUMMARIES

AMERICAN FOOTBALL CONFERENCE

Eastern Division	W	L	T	Pct.	Pts.	OP
Indianapolis	10	2	0	.833	344	238
Buffalo	8	4	0	.667	228	173
Miami	8	4	0	.667	253	240
New England	7	5	0	.583	245	224
N.Y. Jets	4	8	0	.333	201	228
Central Division						
Jacksonville	11	1	0	.917	307	131
Tennessee	9	3	0	.750	253	243
Baltimore	5	7	0	.417	237	225
Pittsburgh	5	7	0	.417	208	187
Cincinnati	3	10	0	.231	232	386
Cleveland	2	11	0	.154	147	340
Western Division						
Seattle	8	4	0	.667	260	210
Kansas City	7	5	0	.583	272	211
Oakland	6	6	0	.500	270	247
San Diego	5	7	0	.417	206	262
Denver	4	8	0	.333	231	242

NATIONAL FOOTBALL CONFERENCE

Eastern Division	W	L	T	Pct.	Pts.	OP
Washington	7	5	0	.583	347	320
Arizona	6	6	0	.500	183	237
Dallas	6	6	0	.500	261	195
N.Y. Giants	6	6	0	.500	235	250
Philadelphia	3	10	0	.231	200	297
Central Division						
Detroit	8	4	0	.667	272	231
Tampa Bay	8	4	0	.667	198	158
Green Bay	7	5	0	.583	247	231
Minnesota	7	5	0	.583	289	250
Chicago	5	8	0	.385	226	277
Western Division						
St. Louis	10	2	0	.833	400	168
Carolina	5	7	0	.417	282	283
Atlanta	3	9	0	.250	190	281
San Francisco	3	9	0	.250	196	345
New Orleans	2	10	0	.167	194	304

THURSDAY, DECEMBER 2

JACKSONVILLE 20, PITTSBURGH 6—at ALLTEL Stadium, attendance 68,806. James Stewart rushed for 145 yards and 1 touchdown, and Mark Brunell added 308 yards and 1 touchdown through the air, as the Jaguars won their ninth consecutive game. Trailing 3-0, the Jaguars drove inside the Steelers' 20 three consecutive times in the second quarter but led just 6-3 at halftime after being held to 2 field goals and Carlos Emmons's recovery of Reggie Barlow's fumble at the Steelers' 9. Kris Brown's second field goal tied the game early in the third quarter, but the Jaguars needed just 8 plays to drive 86 yards, keyed by Stewart's 40-yard run, to set up Brunell's 27-yard touchdown pass to Jimmy Smith. Brunell's 49-yard pass to Keenan McCardell in the fourth quarter set up Stewart's scoring run, and Mike Tomczak's fourth-down incomplete pass from the Jaguars' 20 with 4:15 remaining preserved the Jaguars' victory. Brunell was 25 of 37 for 308 yards and 1 touchdown. Smith had 10 receptions for 124 yards. Tomczak was 19 of 39 for 194 yards.

Pittsburgh	3	0	3	0	—	6
Jacksonville	0	6	7	7	—	20

Pitt — FG Brown 40
Jax — FG Hollis 25
Jax — FG Hollis 32
Pitt — FG Brown 39
Jax — Smith 27 pass from Brunell (Hollis kick)
Jax — Stewart 1 run (Hollis kick)

SUNDAY, DECEMBER 5

SAN DIEGO 23, CLEVELAND 10—at Qualcomm Stadium, attendance 53,147. The Chargers' defense allowed just 202 yards and recorded 6 sacks en route to snapping their six-game losing streak. With the score tied 3-3 in the second quarter, Phil Dawson missed a 45-yard field-goal attempt. The Chargers responded with scoring drives of 63 and, following a 21-yard punt return by Robert Reed, 42 yards to take a 13-3 lead on Kenny Bynum's 1-yard scoring run. The Browns answered with a 9-play, 70-yard drive, capped by Tim Couch's 19-yard touchdown pass to Kevin Johnson six seconds before halftime, to trim the deficit to 13-10. The Chargers' defense buckled down in the second half, permitting just 1 first down in four possessions, while the offense began the half with a 15-play drive that concluded with a field goal and capped the day with Jermaine Fazande's 2-yard touchdown run with 6:28 to play. The Chargers added 3 first downs in the final five minutes to run out the clock. Jim Harbaugh was 16 of 23 for 161 yards. Couch was 18 of 29 for 184 yards and 1 touchdown, with 2 interceptions.

Cleveland	3	7	0	0	—	10
San Diego	3	10	3	7	—	23

Cle — FG Dawson 33
SD — FG Carney 44
SD — FG Carney 19
SD — Bynum 1 run (Carney kick)
Cle — K. Johnson 19 pass from Couch (Dawson kick)
SD — FG Carney 30
SD — Fazande 2 run (Carney kick)

GREEN BAY 35, CHICAGO 19—at Soldier Field, attendance 56,626. Battling fierce wind and rain, rookie De'-Mond Parker rushed for 113 yards and 2 touchdowns as the Packers won in Chicago for the sixth consecutive season. The Bears led 10-0, thanks to Barry Minter's 25-yard interception return, before the Packers scored 3 touchdowns in less than six minutes, the second of which was set up by a 27-yard punt and capped by Keith McKenzie's 45-yard return of punter Todd Sauerbrun's fumble. Shane Matthews's 56-yard pass to Bobby Engram led to Chris Boniol's field goal just before halftime to trim the deficit to 21-13. Antwan Edwards's fumbled punt return led to Curtis Enis's 1-yard scoring run, but Matthews's 2-point conversion pass attempt for Engram was incomplete. Leading 21-19, Parker culminated an 88-yard drive with a 12-yard scoring run with 9:02 remaining and, on the next possession, scampered 21 yards around right end for the final blow with 3:08 left. The Bears drove to the Packers' 16 in the final moments, but Santana Dotson stopped Enis on fourth-and-1 to ice the game. Favre was 17 of 24 for 155 yards and 1 touchdown, with 2 interceptions. Matthews was 20 of 37 for 223 yards, with 1 interception.

Green Bay	0	21	0	14	—	35
Chicago	7	6	6	0	—	19

Chi — Minter 25 interception return (Boniol kick)
Chi — FG Boniol 24
GB — Schroeder 6 pass from Favre (Longwell kick)
GB — Henderson 2 run (Longwell kick)
GB — K. McKenzie 45 fumble return (Longwell kick)
Chi — FG Boniol 23
Chi — Enis 1 run (pass failed)
GB — Parker 12 run (Longwell kick)
GB — Parker 21 run (Longwell kick)

INDIANAPOLIS 37, MIAMI 34—at Pro Player Stadium, attendance 74,096. Mike Vanderjagt made 2 field goals in the final five minutes, including a 53-yard boot as time expired, as the Colts won their eighth consecutive game by holding off the Dolphins. Edgerrin James's 41-yard touchdown run was followed 23 seconds later by Chad Cota's return of J.J. Johnson's fumble on the next play from scrimmage for a touchdown to take a 17-3 lead. The Colts led 24-10 at halftime, but Sam Madison's 21-yard interception return for a touchdown two plays into the second half cut the deficit to seven points. The Colts responded with Peyton Manning's 5-yard touchdown pass to Terrence Wilkins, but Dan Marino's 33-yard touchdown pass to Tony Martin cut the lead to 31-24, and Patrick Surtain's 28-yard interception return to the Dolphins' 49 four plays later led to Marino's 1-yard touchdown pass to Stanley Pritchett with 13:07 left to tie the game 31-31. Wilkins's 27-yard punt return set up Vanderjagt's 48-yard field goal with 4:24 left, but Marino completed 6 of 7 passes on the ensuing drive, capped by Olindo Mare's 32-yard field goal with 36 seconds left. Starting from the Colts' 32, Manning completed 16- and 18-yard passes on successive plays to Marvin Harrison to set up Vanderjagt's 53-yard field goal as time expired. Manning was 23 of 29 for 260 yards and 1 touchdown, with 2 interceptions. James had 23 carries for 130 yards, and Harrison had 8 catches for 125 yards. Marino was 24 of 38 for 313 yards and 3 touchdowns, with 1 interception. Martin had 6 catches for 109 yards, and Oronde Gadsden added 6 receptions for 103 yards.

Indianapolis	17	7	7	6	—	37
Miami	3	7	14	10	—	34

Ind — FG Vanderjagt 44
Mia — FG Mare 31
Ind — James 41 run (Vanderjagt kick)
Ind — Cota 25 fumble return (Vanderjagt kick)
Mia — Gadsden 24 pass from Marino (Mare kick)
Ind — James 1 run (Vanderjagt kick)
Mia — Madison 21 interception return (Mare kick)
Ind — Wilkins 5 pass from Manning (Vanderjagt kick)
Mia — Martin 33 pass from Marino (Mare kick)
Mia — Pritchett 1 pass from Marino (Mare kick)
Ind — FG Vanderjagt 48
Mia — FG Mare 32
Ind — FG Vanderjagt 53

KANSAS CITY 16, DENVER 10—at Mile High Stadium, attendance 73,855. Tamarick Vanover's 80-yard punt return for a touchdown with 4:53 remaining propelled the Chiefs to within one game of first place in the AFC West. Trailing 7-3, the Broncos, who did not garner a first down on four consecutive possessions following a game-opening field goal, rode the impetus of Chris Watson's 22-yard punt return to set up Olandis Gary's 3-yard scoring run and give Denver a 10-7 lead. Pete Stoyanovich's field goal just prior to halftime tied the game, and each team intercepted a pass deep in the other team's territory to stifle third-quarter scoring chances. Vanover fielded Tom Rouen's punt and tip-toed down the left sidelines for the 80-yard return. Holder Daniel Pope fumbled the snap on the extra point, keeping the score 16-10. After an exchange of punts, the Broncos reached their own 46 before Brian Griese threw 4 consecutive incompletions. Tony Richardson's 7-yard run on second-and-3 iced the game. Elvis Grbac was 20 of 34 for 183 yards and 1 touchdown, with 1 interception. Griese was 20 of 36 for 227 yards, with 1 interception. Rod Smith had 8 receptions for 106 yards.

Kansas City	0	10	0	6	—	16
Denver	3	7	0	0	—	10

Den — FG Elam 39
KC — Gonzalez 10 pass from Grbac (Stoyanovich kick)
Den — Gary 3 run (Elam kick)
KC — FG Stoyanovich 43
KC — Vanover 80 punt return (fumbled snap)

ATLANTA 35, NEW ORLEANS 12—at Georgia Dome, attendance 62,568. Chris Chandler passed for 2 touchdowns and ran for another, and Ray Buchanan intercepted 2 passes as the Falcons won their tenth consecutive game against the Saints. Trailing 3-0, the Falcons went on consecutive scoring drives of 36, 73, and 75 yards, capped by Chandler's 48-yard touchdown pass to Tim Dwight, to take a 21-6 halftime lead. Buchanan's first interception came three plays into the second half and led to Bob Christian's 1-yard run. Later in the quarter, Buchanan stepped in front of Danny Wuerffel's pass and scampered 52 yards for a touchdown and 35-6 lead. Chandler was 15 of 25 for 233 yards and 2 touchdowns, with 3 interceptions. Wuerffel, who replaced an injured Billy Joe Hobert in the second quarter, was 215 of 20 for 127 yards, with 2 interceptions.

New Orleans	3	3	0	6	—	12
Atlanta	7	14	14	0	—	35

NO — FG Brien 24
Atl — Mathis 8 pass from Chandler (Andersen kick)
Atl — Chandler 1 run (Andersen kick)
NO — FG Brien 34

Atl — Dwight 48 pass from Chandler (Andersen kick)
Atl — Christian 1 run (Andersen kick)
Atl — Buchanan 52 interception return (Andersen kick)
NO — Wuerffel 29 run (run failed)

N.Y. GIANTS 41, N.Y. JETS 28—at Giants Stadium, attendance 78,200. Kerry Collins passed for 341 yards to become the first Giants quarterback to exceed 300 passing yards since Phil Simms in November, 1993, en route to defeating the Jets. The Giants scored on their first three possessions, capped by Collins's 61-yard touchdown pass to Amani Toomer, to take a 17-0 lead just 9:32 into the game. Keyshawn Johnson's 13-yard touchdown catch in the second quarter got the Jets on the scoreboard, but the Giants answered with two more scoring drives, culminated by Cary Blanchard's 31-yard field goal just before halftime to give the Giants a 27-7 lead. Toomer's 9-yard touchdown catch capped a 16-play, 67-yard drive in the third quarter to extend the lead to 34-7. Trailing 34-14, Dorian Boose recovered Joe Montgomery's fumble at midfield with 4:50 left, setting up Ray Lucas's 10-yard touchdown pass to Wayne Chrebet with 4:14 left. Three plays later, faced with third-and-10, Collins's bomb to Toomer down the right sideline resulted in an 80-yard touchdown to ice the victory. Collins was 17 of 29 for 341 yards and 3 touchdowns. Rookie Joe Montgomery, making his first start, carried 38 times for 111 yards. Toomer had 6 catches for 181 yards, and Ike Hilliard added 6 receptions for 121 yards. Lucas was 31 of 48 for 284 yards and 4 touchdowns. Johnson had 10 receptions for 98 yards.

N.Y. Jets	0	7	0	21	—	28
N.Y. Giants	17	10	7	7	—	41

NYG — FG Blanchard 41
NYG — Montgomery 4 run (Blanchard kick)
NYG — Toomer 61 pass from Collins (Blanchard kick)
NYJ — K. Johnson 13 pass from Lucas (Hall kick)
NYG — Collins 1 run (Blanchard kick)
NYG — FG Blanchard 31
NYG — Toomer 9 pass from Collins (Blanchard kick)
NYJ — Green 10 pass from Lucas (Hall kick)
NYJ — Chrebet 10 pass from Lucas (Hall kick)
NYG — Toomer 80 pass from Collins (Blanchard kick)
NYJ — Chrebet 5 pass from Lucas (Hall kick)

ARIZONA 21, PHILADELPHIA 17—at Sun Devil Stadium, attendance 46,550. The Jake Plummer of 1998 revisited Sun Devil Stadium, as Plummer guided the Cardinals to 2 touchdowns in the final five minutes to win their fourth consecutive game and mark the eleventh time Plummer has led his team to a fourth-quarter comeback victory. Kwamie Lassiter's 78-yard interception return began the scoring, but Plummer was stopped on fourth-and-1 from the Cardinals' 31, leading to a short 4-play, 31-yard scoring drive for the Eagles to tie the game. Donovan McNabb's second touchdown pass of the quarter capped a 75-yard drive and gave the Eagles a 14-7 halftime lead. The Cardinals' offense failed to cross midfield in either the second or third quarters, and Norm Johnson's 29-yard field goal gave the Eagles a 17-7 lead. The Cardinals, beginning on their own 20 with 10:50 left in the game, drove 80 yards in 16 plays, capped by Plummer's 4-yard touchdown pass to David Boston with 4:31 remaining, to cut the deficit to 17-14. The Eagles failed to gain a first down and were forced to punt. On third-and-10 from the Eagles' 39 with 1:09 left, Plummer completed a 38-yard pass to Frank Sanders to set up Plummer's game-winning sneak with 57 seconds remaining. Plummer was 20 of 37 for 179 yards and 1 touchdown, with 1 interception. McNabb was 19 of 31 for 157 yards and 2 touchdowns, with 1 interception.

Philadelphia	0	14	3	0	—	17
Arizona	7	0	0	14	—	21

Ariz — Lassiter 78 interception return (Jacke kick)
Phil — Lewis 11 pass from McNabb (N. Johnson kick)
Phil — Douglas 29 pass from McNabb (N. Johnson kick)
Phil — FG N. Johnson 29
Ariz — Boston 4 pass from Plummer (Jacke kick)
Ariz — Plummer 1 run (Jacke kick)

ST. LOUIS 34, CAROLINA 21—at Ericsson Stadium, attendance 62,285. Kurt Warner passed for 351 yards and 3 touchdowns as the Rams fought off a late rally to defeat the Panthers. Az-Zahir Hakim caught 48- and 49-yard touchdown passes in the first half to help stake the Rams to a 21-0 lead. The lead could have been more, excpet for Mike Minter's interception in the end zone for a touchback. The Panthers drove 70 yards for a touchdown just before halftime, and then caught a break in the third quarter when Mike Jones intercepted Steve Beuerlein, only to fumble and allow Chris Terry to recover. Beuerlein found Donald Hayes open five plays later to trim the lead to 21-14. Jeff Wilkins's 44-yard field goal on the first play of the fourth quarter increased the Rams' lead to 24-14, but Beuerlein hit Patrick Jeffers with a 71-yard touchdown on the next play to pull within three. The Rams drove to the Panthers' 33 on their next possession, but Wilkins missed a 51-yard attempt to give the ball back to Carolina. However, three plays later Dre' Bly intercepted Beuerlein's pass and raced 53 yards for a touchdown with 9:48 remaining. The Panthers' offense failed to cross midfield the remainder of the game. Warner was 22 of 31 for 351 yards and 3 touchdowns, with 2 interceptions. Marshall Faulk had 22 carries for 118 yards. Hakim had 4 receptions for 122 yards, and Isaac Bruce added 6 for 111 yards. Beuerlein was 21 of 43 for 266 yards and 3 touchdowns, with 3 interceptions. Jeffers had 7 receptions for 107 yards.

St. Louis	14	7	0	13	—	34
Carolina	0	7	7	7	—	21

StL — R. Williams 14 pass from Warner (Wilkins kick)
StL — Hakim 48 pass from Warner (Wilkins kick)
StL — Hakim 49 pass from Warner (Wilkins kick)
Car — Walls 15 pass from Beuerlein (Kasay kick)
Car — Hayes 36 pass from Beuerlein (Kasay kick)
StL — FG Wilkins 44
Car — Jeffers 71 pass from Beuerlein (Kasay kick)
StL — Bly 53 interception return (Wilkins kick)
StL — FG Wilkins 29

CINCINNATI 44, SAN FRANCISCO 30—at Cinergy Field, attendance 53,463. Jeff Blake passed for 334 yards and 4 touchdowns, and Corey Dillon rushed for 133 yards and scored twice as the Bengals defeated the 49ers for the first time since 1974. The 49ers had the first opportunity to score, but Fred Beasley fumbled at the Bengals' 24 and John Copeland recovered. The Bengals drove 76 yards for a touchdown, beginning a stretch of five consecutive scoring possessions for Cincinnati. Leading 17-10, Blake hit Darnay Scott with a 58-yard touchdown pass with 2:09 left in the half and, after a 49ers punt, Doug Pelfrey added a 24-yard field goal as the half expired for a 27-10 lead. The 49ers scored touchdowns on their first three possessions of the second half, but in the midst of the offense's flurry, Mark Harris fumbled a punt at the 49ers' 21 to set up Pelfrey's 27-yard field goal, and Tremain Mack's 72-yard kickoff return led to Blake's third touchdown pass late in the third quarter. When J.J. Stokes hauled in Jeff Garcia's 11-yard touchdown pass with 14:11 remaining, the 49ers trailed 37-30. The Bengals drove 68 yards for their final touchdown, Blake's 13-yard pass to Carl Pickesn with 9:23 left, to take a 44-30 lead. The 49ers drove to the Bengals' 7, but Garcia's fourth-down pass was incomplete with 4:18 left. Blake was 20 of 31 for 334 yards and 4 touchdowns. Pickens had 7 catches for 107 yards. Garcia was 33 of 49 for a career-high 437 yards and 3 touchdowns, with 1 interception. Jerry Rice had 9 receptions for 157 yards, and Terrell Owens added 9 catches for 145 yards.

San Francisco	0	10	14	6	—	30
Cincinnati	10	17	10	7	—	44

Cin — Dillon 10 run (Pelfrey kick)
Cin — FG Pelfrey 29
SF — Garner 6 run (Richey kick)
Cin — Pickens 11 pass from Blake (Pelfrey kick)
SF — FG Richey 47
Cin — Scott 58 pass from Blake (Pelfrey kick)
Cin — FG Pelfrey 24
SF — Rice 7 pass from Garcia (Richey kick)
Cin — FG Pelfrey 27
SF — Rice 55 pass from Garcia (Richey kick)
Cin — Dillon 12 pass from Blake (Pelfrey kick)
SF — Stokes 11 pass from Garcia (kick failed)
Cin — Pickens 13 pass from Blake (Pelfrey kick)

OAKLAND 30, SEATTLE 21—at Network Associates Coliseum, attendance 44,716. Rich Gannon and Tim Brown combined for 2 touchdowns as the Raiders defeated the Seahawks. Gannon and Brown's 2 second-quarter touchdowns helped stake the Raiders to a 17-0 lead. The Seahawks responded with a 16-play, 73-yard touchdown drive just before halftime and a 67-yard touchdown drive to begin the second half to cut the deficit to 17-14. Unfazed, the Raiders drove 79 yards, keyed by Gannon completing 4 of 5 passes, to take a 24-14 lead on Zack Crockett's 1-yard plunge. Anthony Newman recovered Ricky Watters's fumble three plays later to set up Michael Husted's 41-yard field goal in the opening minute of the fourth quarter. Jon Kitna completed 4 of 5 passes on the ensuing drive, capped by a 3-yard scoring pass to Sean Dawkins to trim the deficit to 27-21 with 10:55 left. Husted missed a 51-yard field-goal attempt on the next drive, and the Seahawks reached the Raiders' 30. Newman intercepted a Kitna pass, and Napoleon Kaufman's 44-yard run set up Husted's game-clinching field goal with 1:53 remaining. Gannon was 22 of 39 for 245 yards and 2 touchdowns, with 2 interceptions. Gannon was 19 of 24 for 253 yards and 2 touchdowns, with 1 interception.

Seattle	0	7	7	7	—	21
Oakland	3	14	7	6	—	30

Oak — FG Husted 18
Oak — Brown 14 pass from Gannon (Husted kick)
Oak — Brown 5 pass from Gannon (Husted kick)
Sea — Watters 8 run (Peterson kick)
Sea — Galloway 31 pass from Kitna (Peterson kick)
Oak — Crockett 1 run (Husted kick)
Oak — FG Husted 41
Sea — Dawkins 3 pass from Kitna (Peterson kick)
Oak — FG Husted 23

BALTIMORE 41, TENNESSEE 14—at PSINet Stadium, attendance 67,854. Tony Banks passed for 4 touchdowns, and Rod Woodson tied an NFL record with his ninth career interception return for a touchdown as the Ravens snapped the Titans' 13-game AFC Central winning streak. The Ravens scored on three consecutive first-half possessions, one on a 76-yard touchdown pass to Patrick Johnson and another set up by Priest Holmes's 72-yard run, to claim a 17-11 lead before Al Del Greco trimmed the lead to three points with a 33-yard field goal just before halftime. The Ravens used a 28-yard punt return by Jermaine Lewis and a 40-yard defensive pass interference penalty to set up Justin Armour's 1-yard touchdown catch in the third quarter to give Baltimore a 24-14 lead. Trailing 27-14 with 7:04 left, Steve McNair's fourth-and-3 pass from near midfield fell incomplete. Banks's 39-yard touchdown pass to Lewis four plays later extended the lead to 34-14, and Woodson tied Ken Houston's record with 4:12 remaining when he stepped in front of McNair's pass and raced 47 yards down the right sideline for the game's final points. Banks was 18 of 31 for 332 yards and 4 touchdowns. Qadry Ismail had 5 catches for 113 yards, and Holmes had 9 carries for 100 yards. McNair was 28 of 48 for 288 yards, with 2 interceptions. Frank Wycheck had 10 receptions for 87 yards.

Tennessee	3	11	0	0	—	14
Baltimore	7	10	7	17	—	41

Tenn — FG Del Greco 39
Balt — Johnson 76 pass from Banks (Stover kick)
Balt — Lewis 6 pass from Banks (Stover kick)
Tenn — George 3 run (Harris run)
Balt — FG Stover 21
Tenn — FG Del Greco 33
Balt — Armour 1 pass from Banks (Stover kick)
Balt — FG Stover 27
Balt — Lewis 39 pass from Banks (Stover kick)
Balt — Woodson 47 interception return (Stover kick)

DETROIT 33, WASHINGTON 17—at Pontiac Silverdome, attendance 77,693. The Lions' defense forced 4 turnovers and recorded 5 sacks, and Desmond Howard returned a punt for a touchdown one day after being signed as a free agent, as the Lions snapped a 16-game regular-season losing streak to the Redskins that dated back to 1965. With the score tied 3-3, James Thrash returned a kickoff 95 yards for a touchdown, but the Lions needed just four plays to tie the game, on Gus Frerotte's 23-yard touchdown pass to Herman Moore, and took the lead two minutes later as Howard returned his first punt return for the Lions 68 yards for a touchdown. The Lions led 23-17 when Michael Westbrook fumbled and Chris Claiborne recovered at the Redskins' 37, setting up Jason Hanson's fourth field goal with 8:23 remaining. On the first play following the kickoff, James Jones knocked the ball from Brad Johnson's hands and Luther Elliss caught it in the air and ran into the end zone with the game's final points. Frerotte was 21 of 32 for 280 yards and 1 touchdown. Germane Crowell had 5 catches for 122 yards. Johnson was 26 of 43 for 249 yards and 1 touchdown, with 2 interceptions. Westbrook had 5 receptions for 108 yards.

Washington	3	7	7	0	—	17
Detroit	0	20	0	13	—	33

Wash — FG Conway 42
Det — FG Hanson 50
Wash — Thrash 95 kickoff return (Conway kick)
Det — Moore 23 pass from Frerotte (Hanson kick)
Det — Howard 68 punt return (Hanson kick)
Det — FG Hanson 45
Wash — Westbrook 39 pass from Johnson (Conway kick)
Det — FG Hanson 37
Det — FG Hanson 52
Det — Elliss 11 fumble return (Hanson kick)

SUNDAY NIGHT, DECEMBER 5

NEW ENGLAND 13, DALLAS 6—at Foxboro Stadium, attendance 66,532. The Patriots' defense permitted just 203 yards, and Terry Allen's 3-yard scoring run was the game's lone touchdown as the Patriots posted their first-ever victory against the Cowboys. The Cowboys gained just 3 first downs in the first half, but trailed just 6-3 at halftime thanks to Dexter Coakley's 18-yard interception return to the Patriots' 8 that set up a field goal. Richie Cunningham missed a game-tying 43-yard field-goal attempt late in the third quarter, and the Cowboys were stopped on fourth-and-2 from the Patriots' 35 with 12:04 left. Allen's 3-yard run capped the ensuing 65-yard drive, but Cunningham's 34-yard field goal gave the Cowboys a chance at 13-6 with 2:50 left. However, on third-and-6, Drew Bledsoe scrambled 6 yards for a game-clinching first down. Bledsoe was 14 of 25 for 176 yards, with 2 interceptions. Troy Aikman was 20 of 30 for 160 yards.

Dallas	3	0	0	3	—	6
New England	3	3	0	7	—	13

NE — FG Vinatieri 41
Dall — FG Cunningham 20
NE — FG Vinatieri 23
NE — Allen 3 run (Vinatieri kick)
Dall — FG Cunningham 34

MONDAY NIGHT, DECEMBER 6

TAMPA BAY 24, MINNESOTA 17—at Raymond James Stadium, attendance 65,741. The Buccaneers' defense forced 4 turnovers, to set up 14 points, and rookie Shaun King passed for 2 touchdowns in his first start as Tampa Bay won its fifth consecutive game. Donnie Abraham's 55-yard interception return for a touchdown 1:29 into the game gave the Buccaneers an early lead. Fumbles by King and Karl Williams, recovered at the Buccaneers' 22 and 10 respectively, set up 2 Vikings touchdowns late in the first half to give Minnesota a 14-10 halftime lead. King's 29-yard touchdown pass to Jacquez Green gave the Buccaneers the lead and, following Shelton Quarles's recovery of Yo Murphy's fumble on a punt return, King found Dave Moore for a touchdown with 11:46 remaining. The Vikings cut the deficit to 24-17 on Gary Anderson's field goal with 5:50 left, and got the ball back and reached the Buccaneers' 25 in the final minute. However, a false start and a Ronde Barber sack forced Jeff George to attempt a fourth-and-19 pass, which sailed incomplete with 16 seconds left. King was 11 of 19 of 93 yards and 2 touchdowns, with 1 interception. George was 26 of 45 for 271 yards and 1 touchdown, with 2 interceptions.

Minnesota	0	14	0	3	—	17
Tampa Bay	7	3	7	7	—	24

TB — Abraham 55 interception return (Gramatica kick)
TB — FG Gramatica 20
Minn — Hoard 1 run (Anderson kick)
Minn — Carter 1 pass from George (Anderson kick)
TB — Green 29 pass from King (Gramatica kick)
TB — Moore 1 pass from King (Gramatica kick)
Minn — FG Anderson 34

FOURTEENTH WEEK SUMMARIES

AMERICAN FOOTBALL CONFERENCE

Eastern Division	W	L	T	Pct.	Pts.	OP
Indianapolis	11	2	0	.846	364	253
Buffalo	8	5	0	.615	245	192
Miami	8	5	0	.615	273	268
New England	7	6	0	.538	260	244
N.Y. Jets	5	8	0	.385	229	248
Central Division						
Jacksonville	12	1	0	.923	334	155
Tennessee	10	3	0	.769	274	257
Baltimore	6	7	0	.462	268	249
Pittsburgh	5	8	0	.385	232	218
Cincinnati	4	10	0	.286	276	414
Cleveland	2	12	0	.143	175	384
Western Division						
Kansas City	8	5	0	.615	303	239
Seattle	8	5	0	.615	276	229
Oakland	6	7	0	.462	284	268
San Diego	6	7	0	.462	225	278
Denver	4	9	0	.308	255	269

NATIONAL FOOTBALL CONFERENCE

Eastern Division	W	L	T	Pct.	Pts.	OP
Washington	8	5	0	.615	375	323
Dallas	7	6	0	.538	281	205
N.Y. Giants	7	6	0	.538	254	267
Arizona	6	7	0	.462	186	265
Philadelphia	3	11	0	.214	210	317
Central Division						
Tampa Bay	9	4	0	.692	221	174
Detroit	8	5	0	.615	288	254
Green Bay	7	6	0	.538	278	264
Minnesota	7	6	0	.538	317	281
Chicago	5	8	0	.385	226	277
Western Division						
St. Louis	11	2	0	.846	430	182
Carolina	6	7	0	.462	315	314
San Francisco	4	9	0	.308	222	352
Atlanta	3	10	0	.231	197	307
New Orleans	2	11	0	.154	208	334

THURSDAY, DECEMBER 9

TENNESSEE 21, OAKLAND 14—at Adelphia Coliseum, attendance 66,357. Eddie George rushed for 199 yards and 2 fourth-quarter touchdowns as the Titans remained undefeated at home. The Raiders had three scoring opportunities in the first half, but Michael Husted missed 32- and 45-yard field-goal attempts and Samari Rolle recovered Rich Gannon's fumble at the Titans' 10 just before halftime to keep the game scoreless. The Titans scored touchdowns on their first three possessions of the second half, the last of which was set up by Steve Jackson's 2-yard interception return to the Raiders' 44, to take a 21-7 lead with 8:01 remaining. Gannon engineered an 86-yard drive, capped by his 2-yard touchdown pass to Rickey Dudley, to cut the deficit to 21-14 with 3:59 left. The Titans were forced to punt with 57 seconds left, but Darrien Gordon fumbled on the return and Donald Mitchell recovered at the Raiders' 20 to secure the victory. Steve McNair was 12 of 20 for 114 yards, with 1 interception. Gannon was 20 of 28 for 273 yards and 1 touchdown, with 1 interception.

Oakland	0	0	7	7	—	14
Tennessee	0	0	7	14	—	21

Tenn — McNair 1 run (Del Greco kick)
Oak — Crockett 1 run (Husted kick)
Tenn — George 8 run (Del Greco kick)
Tenn — George 19 run (Del Greco kick)
Oak — Dudley 2 pass from Gannon (Husted kick)

SUNDAY, DECEMBER 12

WASHINGTON 28, ARIZONA 3—at FedEx Field, attendance 31,124. Stephen Davis rushed 37 times for 189 yards and 1 touchdown, and the Redskins' defense permitted just 9 first downs to remain in first place in the NFC East. Davis's 50-yard scoring scamper just over four minutes into the game came two plays after he recovered Brad Johnson's fumble on third-and-2 and advanced it 6 yards for a first down. Trailing 14-3, Chris Jacke made a 36-yard field goal, but the Redskins were penalized for jumping off of another player, so the Cardinals took the points off the board. Two plays later, Champ Bailey intercepted Jake Plummer's pass in the end zone for a touchback. Later in the half, Adrian Murrell's fumble at the Redskins' 38 led to an 11-play, 62-yard drive, capped by Johnson's 25-yard pass to Michael Westbrook 11 seconds before halftime to give the Redskins a 21-3 lead. The Redskins' defense permitted just 2 second-half first downs. Johnson was 17 of 31 for 191 yards and 2 touchdowns, with 2 interceptions. Plummer was 15 of 32 for 147 yards, with 3 interceptions.

Arizona	3	0	0	0	—	3
Washington	7	14	0	7	—	28

Wash — Davis 50 run (Conway kick)
Ariz — FG Jacke 31
Wash — Fryar 7 pass from Johnson (Conway kick)
Wash — Westbrook 25 pass from Johnson (Conway kick)
Wash — Hicks 11 run (Conway kick)

SAN FRANCISCO 26, ATLANTA 7—at 3Com Park, attendance 67,465. Charlie Garner rushed for 107 yards and 1 touchdown, and Fred Beasley scored twice, as the 49ers' defense permitted just 7 first downs and 105 yards to snap their eight-game losing streak. Trailing 7-0, the Falcons drove 68 yards to the 49ers' 8, but Tim McDonald intercepted Chris Chandler's pass in the end zone for a touchback. The 49ers' offense responded with an 80-yard touchdown drive, and Bryant Young's sack for a safety three plays later staked San Francisco to a 16-0 lead. Winslow Oliver's 58-yard punt return for a touchdown trimmed the deficit to 19-7, but his fumble on a punt return at the Falcons' 17 late in the third quarter set up Beasley's second touchdown. Jeff Garcia was 16 of 24 for 160 yards. Chandler was 8 of 18 for 95 yards, with 1 interception.

Atlanta	0	0	7	0	—	7
San Francisco	7	12	0	7	—	26

SF — Garner 8 run (Richey kick)
SF — Beasley 2 run (Richey kick)
SF — Safety, Young sacked Chandler in end zone
SF — FG Richey 23
Atl — Oliver 58 punt return (Andersen kick)
SF — Beasley 1 run (Richey kick)

BALTIMORE 31, PITTSBURGH 24—at Three Rivers Stadium, attendance 46,715. Qadry Ismail caught 6 passes for a club-record 258 yards, including 3 touchdowns in excess of 50 yards. The game was tied 10-10 at halftime. Both of the Steelers' first-half scoring drives were set up by third-down receptions by Kordell Stewart, who had recently moved to wide receiver. The Ravens scored on all three of their third-quarter possessions, as Ismail burned man-for-man coverage for touchdown receptions of 54, 59, and 76 yards. Mike Tomczak's 11-yard touchdown pass to Stewart with 2:45 left in the game trimmed the deficit to 31-24, but Priest Holmes ran for 28 yards on third-and-7 in the final moments to seal the victory. Tony Banks was 8 of 26 for 268 yards and 3 touchdowns. Holmes had 18 carries for 130 yards. Tomczak was 22 of 41 for 249 yards and 2 touchdowns.

Baltimore	7	3	21	0	—	31
Pittsburgh	10	0	7	7	—	24

Pitt — Ward 21 pass from Bettis (Brown kick)
Balt — Holmes 64 run (Stover kick)
Pitt — FG Brown 31
Balt — FG Stover 19
Balt — Ismail 54 pass from Banks (Stover kick)
Pitt — Edwards 6 pass from Tomczak (Brown kick)
Balt — Ismail 59 pass from Banks (Stover kick)
Balt — Ismail 76 pass from Banks (Stover kick)
Pitt — Stewart 11 pass from Tomczak (Brown kick)

CAROLINA 33, GREEN BAY 31—at Lambeau Field, attendance 59,869. Steve Beuerlein's 5-yard scoring quarterback keeper as time expired gave the Panthers a stunning victory in Lambeau Field. In a wild game in which the team that won was the last team with the ball, there were no punts or turnovers in the second half. Brett Favre's 19-yard touchdown pass to Antonio Freeman just before halftime staked the Packers to a 14-10 lead at intermission.

Michael Bates returned the second half's opening kickoff 60 yards, and Beuerlein's 38-yard touchdown pass to Patrick Jeffers on the next play gave Carolina a 17-14 lead. An exchange of touchdowns and field goals, capped by John Kasay's 37-yard field goal with 7:38 remaining, gave the Panthers a 27-24 lead. The Packers responded with an 8-play drive to take a 31-27 lead with 4:00 left. Beuerlein's 18-yard pass to Wesley Walls on fourth-and-1 to the Packers' 8 was followed one play later by an apparent 8-yard touchdown pass to Walls. However, replay reversed the touchdown. The Panthers reached the 5-yard line for a fourth-and-goal with 45 seconds left, but the Packers permitted the Panthers to run the clock down to five seconds. Carolina called timeout, and Beuerlein took the snap, took two steps back, and then followed his blockers before diving into the end zone as time expired for the game's eighth and final lead change. Beuerlein was 29 of 43 for 373 yards and 3 touchdowns, with 1 interception. Jeffers had 8 receptions for 147 yards. Favre was 26 of 38 for 302 yards and 2 touchdowns, with 1 interception.

Carolina	3	7	14	9	—	33
Green Bay	7	7	7	10	—	31

Car — FG Kasay 20
GB — K. McKenzie 18 interception return (Longwell kick)
Car — Jeffers 35 pass from Beuerlein (Kasay kick)
GB — Freeman 19 pass from Favre (Longwell kick)
Car — Jeffers 38 pass from Beuerlein (Kasay kick)
GB — Driver 8 pass from Favre (Longwell kick)
Car — Kinchen 26 pass from Beuerlein (Kasay kick)
GB — FG Longwell 40
Car — FG Kasay 37
GB — Henderson 1 run (Longwell kick)
Car — Beuerlein 5 run (run failed)

CINCINNATI 44, CLEVELAND 28—at Cinergy Field, attendance 59,972. Corey Dillon rushed for 192 yards and 3 touchdowns as the Bengals won their third consecutive game. Craig Yeast's 81-yard punt return for a touchdown gave Cincinnati a 10-0 first-quarter lead, and Dillon's 50-yard run set up Clif Groce's 1-yard scoring plunge and gave the Bengals a 17-7 lead. The Browns had a chance to cut the deficit to three points, but Marc Edwards fumbled and Kimo von Oelhoffen recovered at the Bengals' 11. Dillon scored twice in the final three minutes of the half to give the Bengals a 30-15 halftime lead. Dillon carried 28 times for 192 yards and did not play most of the fourth quarter. Jeff Blake was 11 of 22 for 176 yards and 1 touchdown. Tim Couch was 16 of 28 for 239 yards and 2 touchdowns, with 2 interceptions. Kevin Johnson had 7 receptions for 135 yards.

Cleveland	7	8	6	7	—	28
Cincinnati	10	20	14	0	—	44

Cin — FG Pelfrey 28
Cin — Yeast 81 punt return (Pelfrey kick)
Cle — Abdul-Jabbar 8 pass from Couch (Dawson kick)
Cin — Groce 1 run (Pelfrey kick)
Cin — Dillon 2 run (bad snap)
Cle — Kirby 1 run (Couch run)
Cin — Dillon 2 run (Pelfrey kick)
Cin — Dillon 11 run (Pelfrey kick)
Cle — Smith 16 pass from Couch (pass failed)
Cin — Scott 52 pass from Blake (Pelfrey kick)
Cle — Chiaverini 19 pass from Detmer (Dawson kick)

TAMPA BAY 23, DETROIT 16—at Raymond James Stadium, attendance 65,536. Shaun King's 22-yard touchdown pass to Mike Alstott with 4:18 remaining propelled the Buccaneers past the Lions into first place in the NFC Central. The Lions scored on their first two possessions to take a 10-0 lead. Tampa Bay's lone offensive bright spot in the first half was a 68-yard pass to Warrick Dunn that set up King's 3-yard touchdown pass to Kevin McLeod just before halftime. Mark Carrier's interception at the Lions' 2 prevented a Tampa Bay touchdown, but Brad Culpepper sacked Frerotte for a safety on the next play to cut the deficit to 10-9. Two Jason Hanson field goals gave the Lions a 16-9 lead with 14:11 left, but King completed a 30-yard pass to Reidel Anthony on third-and-17 to jumpstart the offense, with Alstott plunging in from the 1-yard line with 9:26 left to tie the game. The Buccaneers' defense, which allowed a net zero yards in the fourth quarter, stepped up with a big play. John Lynch intercepted Frerotte's pass and returned the ball 28 yards to the Lions' 24 with 4:18 remaining, setting up King's winning pass to Alstott. King was 23 of 37 for 297 yards and 2 touchdowns, with 1 interception. Dunn had 6 receptions for 115 yards. Frerotte was 23 of 44 fro 241 yards, with 1 interception. Johnnie Morton had 7 catches for 107 yards.

Detroit	10	0	3	3	—	16
Tampa Bay	0	7	2	14	—	23

Det — FG Hanson 37
Det — Hill 10 run (Hanson kick)
TB — McLeod 3 pass from King (Gramatica kick)
TB — Safety, Culpepper sacked Frerotte in end zone
Det — FG Hanson 25
Det — FG Hanson 27
TB — Alstott 1 run (Gramatica kick)
TB — Alstott 22 pass from King (Gramatica kick)

N.Y. JETS 28, MIAMI 20—at Giants Stadium, attendance 78,246. Ray Lucas and Keyshawn Johnson connected for 2 fourth-quarter touchdowns that ignited a 22-point run as the Jets came from behind to hand the Dolphins their third consecutive defeat. Nate Jacquet's 35-yard punt return in the third quarter set up Stanley Pritchett's 1-yard run to give the Dolphins a 13-6 lead. Aaron Glenn's interception at the Dolphins' 39 in the final minute of the third quarter swung the game's momentum, leading to Lucas's 26-yard scoring pass to Johnson with 14:54 remaining to tie the game. The Dolphins failed to gain a first down on their next possession, and Curtis Martin's 9-yard run on fourth-and-1 set up Johnson's 24-yard scoring catch with 9:34 left. John Hall missed the extra point but redeemed himself with a 46-yard field goal with 2:51 left. Omar Stoutmire's 67-yard interception return with just over a minute later sealed the victory. Lucas was 22 of 38 for 230 yards and 2 touchdowns. Johnson had 11 receptions for 144 yards. Dan Marino was 18 of 39 for 192 yards, with 2 interceptions.

Miami	6	0	7	7	—	20
N.Y. Jets	0	6	0	22	—	28

Mia — FG Mare 24
Mia — FG Mare 33
NYJ — FG Hall 28
NYJ — FG Hall 31
Mia — Pritchett 1 run (Mare kick)
NYJ — K. Johnson 26 pass from Lucas (Hall kick)
NYJ — K. Johnson 24 pass from Lucas (kick failed)
NYJ — FG Hall 46
NYJ — Stoutmire 67 interception return (kick failed)
Mia — Gadsden 8 pass from Huard (Mare kick)

INDIANAPOLIS 20, NEW ENGLAND 15—at RCA Dome, attendance 56,975. Peyton Manning passed for 186 yards and 2 touchdowns, and Edgerrin James rushed for 101 yards and caught a touchdown pass, as the Colts won their ninth consecutive game. The Colts engineered touchdown drives of 72 and 60 yards in the first half and tacked on 2 Mike Vanderjaft field goals with their only possessions of the third quarter to take a 20-6 lead. Leading 20-9 early in the fourth quarter, Tyrone Poole stymied a Patriots scoring opportunity with an interception at the Colts' 24. The Patriots finally cracked the end zone on Drew Bledsoe's 10-yard touchdown pass to Shawn Jefferson with 3:07 remaining. The Patriots went for a 2-point conversion, and Bledsoe completed the pass to Ben Coates, but the tight end was stopped shy of the goal line. Jerry Ellison recovered the onside kick, but Manning fumbled the snap two plays later and Lawyer Milloy recovered at the Patriots' 33 with 2:11 left. Bledsoe passed for 2 first downs and reached the Colts' 22 before a third-down sack by Mike Peterson and Bledsoe's fourth-down incomplete pass ended the Patriots' comeback hopes. Manning was 15 of 27 for 186 yards and 2 touchdowns. Marvin Harrison had 6 receptions for 118 yards. Bledsoe was 31 of 44 for 379 yards and 1 touchdown, with 1 interception. Terry Glenn had 9 receptions for 148 yards.

New England	3	3	3	6	—	15
Indianapolis	7	7	6	0	—	20

Ind — Pollard 5 pass from Manning (Vanderjagt kick)
NE — FG Vinatieri 28
NE — FG Vinatieri 28
Ind — James 2 pass from Manning (Vanderjagt kick)
Ind — FG Vanderjagt 28
Ind — FG Vanderjagt 31
NE — FG Vinatieri 26
NE — Jefferson 10 pass from Bledsoe (pass failed)

N.Y. GIANTS 19, BUFFALO 17—at Ralph Wilson Stadium, attendance 72,527. Cary Blanchard's 48-yard field goal with 40 seconds left gave the Giants the victory and improved Jim Fassel's career road record to 9-0 in the month of December. The Giants led 6-3 late in the first half, but Doug Flutie's 23-yard touchdown pass to Thurman Thomas with 1:51 left in the half gave Buffalo the lead. Kerry Collins engineered a 67-yard drive in the half's final two minutes, capped by his 14-yard touchdown pass to Amani Toomer, to give the Giants a 13-10 halftime lead. After Steve Christie missed a 48-yard field goal, his second miss of the game, Blanchard drilled his third field goal, from 21 yards, to give the Giants a 16-10 lead. Marcellus Wiley's 52-yard interception return to the Giants' 22 set up Jonathan Linton's 2-yard scoring run with 9:34 remaining to give Buffalo a 17-16 lead. The Bills had a chance to run out the clock, but Keith Hamilton stuffed Linton at the line of scrimmage on fourth-and-1 from the Giants' 36 with 2:09 remaining. Collins's 15-yard third-and-15 pass to Tiki Barber was just enough for a first down at the Bills' 36, and Pete Mitchell's 5-yard catch on third down set up Blanchard's winning boot. Collins was 23 of 44 for 240 yards and 1 touchdown, with 1 interception. Flutie was 15 of 32 for 184 yards and 1 touchdown, with 1 interception.

N.Y. Giants	3	10	3	3	—	19
Buffalo	3	7	0	7	—	17

Buff — FG Christie 50
NYG — FG Blanchard 42
NYG — FG Blanchard 21
Buff — Thomas 23 pass from Flutie (Christie kick)
NYG — Toomer 14 pass from Collins (Blanchard kick)
NYG — FG Blanchard 21
Buff — Linton 2 run (Christie kick)
NYG — FG Blanchard 48

DALLAS 20, PHILADELPHIA 10—at Texas Stadium, attendance 64,086. Troy Aikman passed for 242 yards and 1 touchdown, and the Cowboys' defense forced 3 turnovers, as Dallas improved its home record to 6-0 despite losing Emmitt Smith and Greg Ellis to first-quarter injuries. The Eagles kicked an early field goal, but Darren Hambrick's interception at the Eagles' 22 quelled their only other first half threat, and Eddie Murray, coaxed out of retirement earlier in the week, booted 2 first-half field goals to give the Cowboys a 13-3 halftime lead. Dallas led 20-3 before Tyrone Williams recovered Chris Warren's fumble at the Eagles' 43 midway through the fourth quarter, which led to Doug Pederson's 25-yard touchdown pass to Na Brown. The Eagles failed to move the ball on their final possession, and the Cowboys ran out the clock. Aikman was 22 of 40 for 242 yards and 1 touchdown. Pederson, who replaced Donovan McNabb, was 8 of 12 for 108 yards and 1 touchdown. McNabb was 7 of 17 for 49 yards, with 1 interception.

Philadelphia	3	0	0	7	—	10
Dallas	7	6	7	0	—	20

Phil — FG N. Johnson 44
Dall — Warren 4 run (Murray kick)
Dall — FG Murray 30
Dall — FG Murray 34
Dall — LaFleur 8 pass from Aikman (Murray kick)
Phil — Brown 25 pass from Pederson (N. Johnson kick)

ST. LOUIS 30, NEW ORLEANS 14—at Louisiana Superdome, attendance 46,838. Marshall Faulk rushed for 154 yards and scored twice as the Rams won their fifth consecutive game. The Rams fell behind 14-7, thanks to Wayne Martin's fumble recovery and Billy Joe Tolliver's 2-yard touchdown pass to Cameron Cleeland, but the Rams scored on their next three possessions, the last two set up by Todd Lyght and Dexter McCleon interceptions, to take a 24-14 lead into the locker room. The Rams' powerful offense drove inside the Saints' 25 five times in the second half, but Jeff Wilkins made just 2 of 4 field-goal attempts and Fred Weary intercepted Kurt Warner. However, the Rams' defense permitted just 3 second-half first downs, and Taje Allen's interception deep in Rams' territory in the final moments sealed the victory. Warner was 21 of 31 for 346 yards and 2 touchdowns, with 1 interception. Torry Holt had 6 receptions for 113 yards, and Isaac Bruce added 4 for 102 yards. Tolliver was 12 of 28 for 188 yards and 1 touchdown, with 3 interceptions.

St. Louis	7	17	3	3	—	30
New Orleans	6	8	0	0	—	14

NO — FG Brien 29
StL — Holcombe 1 pass from Warner (Wilkins kick)
NO — FG Brien 26
NO — Cleeland 2 pass from Tolliver (Kennison pass from Tolliver)
StL — FG Wilkins 40
StL — Faulk 4 run (Wilkins kick)
StL — Faulk 30 pass from Warner (Wilkins kick)
StL — FG Wilkins 30
StL — FG Wilkins 38

SAN DIEGO 19, SEATTLE 16—at Kingdome, attendance 66,318. John Carney made all 4 of his field-goal attempts, while Todd Peterson missed 3 fourth-quarter field-goal attempts, the last with 1:10 remaining, as the Chargers held on to defeat the Seahawks. Jim Harbaugh started the game by completing all 4 of his pass attempts on the opening drive to set up Natrone Means's 1-yard touchdown run. Jimmy Spencer's interception at the Chargers' 12 moments later quelled a Seahawks' threat, and the teams exchanged field goals the remainder of the half. Seattle drove 67 yards to begin the second half, capped by Jon Kitna's 14-yard touchdown pass to Derrick Mayes, to give the Seahawks a 16-13 lead. Carney tied the game from 28 yards early in the fourth quarter. Peterson missed a 48-yard attempt, but on the next play Darryl Williams intercepted Harbaugh at the Chargers' 34. Peterson, however, missed the ensuing 52-yard attempt with 8:41 remaining. Later in the quarter, Jason Perry recovered Ricky Watters's fumble at the Seahawks' 27 to set up Carney's go-ahead 41-yard field goal with 3:19 remaining. The Seahawks marched 64 yards in nine plays to the Chargers' 20, but Peterson's 38-yard attempt hit the left upright with 1:10 left, and the Chargers ran the game's final play. Harbaugh was 20 of 35 for 229 yards, with 1 interception. Jeff Graham had 9 receptions for 114 yards. Kitna was 25 of 40 for 285 yards and 1 touchdown, with 1 interception.

San Diego	10	3	0	6	—	19
Seattle	3	6	7	0	—	16

SD — Means 1 run (Carney kick)
Sea — FG Peterson 28
SD — FG Carney 33
Sea — FG Peterson 40
SD — FG Carney 42
Sea — FG Peterson 33
Sea — Mayes 14 pass from Kitna (Peterson kick)
SD — FG Carney 28
SD — FG Carney 41

SUNDAY NIGHT, DECEMBER 12

KANSAS CITY 31, MINNESOTA 28—at Arrowhead Stadium, attendance 78,932. Pete Stoyanovich's 38-yard field goal with three second remaining lifted the Chiefs to their third consecutive victory. Kansas City scored on its first three possessions, the last two drives ending in Elvis Grbac touchdown passes to Tony Gonzalez. Robert Tate returned the ensuing kickoff 76 yards for a touchdown, and Jeff George's 8-yard touchdown pass to Matthew Hatchette just before halftime trimmed the deficit to 21-14. The Chiefs drove to the Vikings' 28 to begin the second half, but Duane Clemons recovered Grbac's fumbled snap, and George engineered a 14-play, 74-yard game-tying drive, capped by George's 12-yard scoring pass to Randy Moss. Randy Moss's muffed punt early in the fourth quarter gave the Chiefs excellent field position, but John Randle recovered Tony Richardson's fumble at the Vikings' 19 on the next play. Five plays later, Derrick Thomas chased down George for an 18-yard loss, forced him to fumble, and Eric Hicks scooped up the ball and rumbled 44 yards for the go-ahead touchdown with 8:01 remaining. Moss's second fumble of the quarter, on a pass at the Chiefs' 7 with 4:02 left, seemingly ruined the Vikings' comeback chances. Moss responded moments later with a 64-yard punt return for a touchdown to tie the game with 1:38 left. Grbac completed 4 consecutive passes in the final minute to set up Stoyanovich's winning kick. Grbac was 19 fo 29 for 215 yards and 2 touchdowns. George was 13 of 23 for 190 yards and 2 touchdowns. Robert Smith rushed 21 times for 118 yards.

Minnesota	0	14	7	7	—	28
Kansas City	14	7	0	10	—	31

KC — Bennett 2 run (Stoyanovich kick)
KC — Gonzalez 13 pass from Grbac (Stoyanovich kick)
KC — Gonzalez 9 pass from Grbac (Stoyanovich kick)
Minn — Tate 76 kickoff return (Anderson kick)
Minn — Hatchette 8 pass from George (Anderson kick)
Minn — Moss 12 pass from George (Anderson kick)
KC — Hicks 44 fumble return (Stoyanovich kick)
Minn — Moss 64 punt return (Anderson kick)
KC — FG Stoyanovich 38

MONDAY NIGHT, DECEMBER 13

JACKSONVILLE 27, DENVER 24—at ALLTEL Stadium, attendance 71,357. Mike Hollis's 23-yard field goal as time expired allowed Jacksonville to win its tenth consecutive game and escape with a victory against Denver. The Broncos drove 80 and 77 yards to score on their first two possessions and take a 14-0 lead. The Jaguars scored on their next three possessions, the last of which was set up by Aaron Beasley's interception at the Broncos' 33 and set up James Stewart's 1-yard run, to give Jacksonville a 3-point halftime lead. Brian Griese's 27-yard pass to Rod Smith on third-and-18 led to Jason Elam's tying 40-yard field goal late in the third quarter. The Jaguars' offense failed to gain a first down on seven consecutive possessions until Mark Brunell completed a 25-yard pass to Jimmy Smith. Fred Taylor broke free for a 38-yard touchdown run two plays later to give Jacksonville a 24-17 lead with 2:35 remaining. Five plays later, Griese found Byron Chamberlain wide open at the Jaguars' 35, and the tight end outran the coverage for a 57-yard game-tying touchdown with 1:43 left. Brunell's 21-yard pass to Damon Jones and a 25-yard pass interference penalty on the next play help set up Hollis's winning boot as time expired. Brunell was 11 of 25 for 115 yards. Griese was 21 of 33 for 275 yards and 2 touchdowns, with 2 interceptions.

Denver	7	7	3	7	—	24
Jacksonville	0	17	0	10	—	27

Den — Smith 22 pass from Griese (Elam kick)
Den — Gary 1 run (Elam kick)
Jax — Stewart 5 run (Hollis kick)
Jax — FG Hollis 49
Jax — Stewart 1 run (Hollis kick)
Den — FG Elam 40
Jax — Taylor 38 run (Hollis kick)
Den — Chamberlain 57 pass from Griese (Elam kick)
Jax — FG Hollis 23

FIFTEENTH WEEK SUMMARIES

AMERICAN FOOTBALL CONFERENCE

Eastern Division	W	L	T	Pct.	Pts.	OP
Indianapolis	12	2	0	.857	388	274
Buffalo	9	5	0	.643	276	213
Miami	9	5	0	.643	285	277
New England	7	7	0	.500	269	268
N.Y. Jets	6	8	0	.429	251	269
Central Division						
Jacksonville	13	1	0	.929	358	169
Tennessee	11	3	0	.786	304	274
Baltimore	7	7	0	.500	299	257
Pittsburgh	5	9	0	.357	251	253
Cincinnati	4	10	0	.286	276	414
Cleveland	2	13	0	.133	189	408
Western Division						
Kansas City	9	5	0	.643	338	258
Seattle	8	6	0	.571	306	265
Oakland	7	7	0	.500	329	268
San Diego	6	8	0	.429	234	290
Denver	5	9	0	.357	291	299

NATIONAL FOOTBALL CONFERENCE

Eastern Division	W	L	T	Pct.	Pts.	OP
Washington	8	6	0	.571	396	347
Dallas	7	7	0	.500	302	227
N.Y. Giants	7	7	0	.500	264	298
Arizona	6	8	0	.429	207	296
Philadelphia	4	11	0	.267	234	326
Central Division						
Tampa Bay	9	5	0	.643	221	219
Detroit	8	6	0	.571	298	282
Minnesota	8	6	0	.571	341	301
Green Bay	7	7	0	.500	298	288
Chicago	6	8	0	.429	254	287
Western Division						
St. Louis	12	2	0	.857	461	192
Carolina	7	7	0	.500	356	338
San Francisco	4	10	0	.286	246	393
Atlanta	3	11	0	.214	214	337
New Orleans	2	12	0	.143	216	365

SATURDAY, DECEMBER 18

KANSAS CITY 35, PITTSBURGH 19—at Arrowhead Stadium, attendance 78,697. Tony Gonzalez caught 2 touchdown passes, and the Chiefs' defense intercepted 4 passes as Kansas City handed the Steelers their sixth consecutive defeat. The Steelers scored on their first two possessions to take a 10-7 lead and attempted to extend the lead when Kris Brown's 49-yard field-goal attempt was blocked. In the second quarter, Donnie Edwards's 28-yard interception return for a touchdown gave the Chiefs a 14-10 lead, and Gonzalez's second touchdown capped a 76-yard march later in the half that gave Kansas City a 21-13 halftime lead. Derrick Alexander's 82-yard touchdown on a reverse, in which he received numerous good blocks, gave the Chiefs a 28-13 lead. The Chiefs' defense intercepted Mike Tomczak 3 times in the final quarter to preserve the victory. Elvis Grbac was 12 of 22 for 149 yards and 2 touchdowns. Tomczak was 23 of 46 for 278 yards and 2 touchdowns, with 4 interceptions.

Pittsburgh	10	3	0	6	—	19
Kansas City	7	14	7	7	—	35

Pitt — T. Edwards 12 pass from Tomczak (Brown kick)
KC — Gonzalez 15 pass from Grbac (Stoyanovich kick)
Pitt — FG Brown 42
KC — D. Edwards 28 interception return (Stoyanovich kick)
Pitt — FG Brown 47
KC — Alexander 82 run (Stoyanovich kick)
KC — Morris 10 run (Stoyanovich kick)
Pitt — Shaw 11 pass from Tomczak (pass failed)

CAROLINA 41, SAN FRANCISCO 24—at Ericsson Stadium, attendance 62,373. Steve Beuerlein passed for 368 yards and 4 touchdowns, 3 to Muhsin Muhammad, as the Panthers won their second consecutive game and stayed alive in the playoff chase. The Panthers scored on their first four possessions, the first two culminating with Beuerlein passes to Muhammad, to give Carolina a 24-10 lead with less than 18 minutes into the game. Fred Beasley's 44-yard run capped the opening drive of the second half and trimmed the deficit to 24-17, but Carolina needed just six plays to respond, as Beuerlein found Patrick Jeffers open for a 55-yard touchdown. Jeff Garcia's 17-yard touchdown pass to Charlie Garner on the opening play of the fourth quarter cut the deficit to 34-24, but the Panthers answered with a 12-play, 60-yard drive culminating with Beuerlein's third touchdown pass to Muhammad. The 49ers were stopped on downs inside the Panthers' 30 twice in the final four minutes. Beuerlein was 27 of 38 for 368 yards and 4 touchdowns. Jeffers had 8 receptions for 138 yards, and Muhammad had 11 for 126 yards. Garcia was 29 of 46 for 303 yards and 2 touchdowns, with 1 interception.

San Francisco	10	0	7	7	—	24
Carolina	17	7	10	7	—	41

Car — Muhammad 8 pass from Beuerlein (Cunningham kick)
SF — FG Richey 37
Car — Muhammad 14 pass from Beuerlein (Cunningham kick)
Car — FG Cunningham 21
SF — Rice 48 pass from Garcia (Richey kick)
Car — Floyd 2 run (Richey kick)
SF — Beasley 44 run (Richey kick)
Car — Jeffers 55 pass from Beuerlein (Cunningham kick)
Car — FG Cunningham 43
SF — Garner 17 pass from Garcia (Richey kick)
Car — Muhammad 7 pass from Beuerlein (Cunningham kick)

SUNDAY, DECEMBER 19

TENNESSEE 30, ATLANTA 17—at Adelphia Coliseum, attendance 66,196. The Titans' defense forced 6 turnovers as the franchise earned its first postseason berth since 1993 by defeating the Falcons. With the score tied 7-7 late in the first quarter, Steve McNair threw a lateral to tight end Frank Wycheck, who turned and completed a 61-yard touchdown pass to Isaac Byrd. Eddie Robinson's fumble recovery at the Titans' 48, the first of 4 second-quarter Falcons turnovers, led to Al Del Greco's 38-yard field goal and a 17-7 lead. Tennessee could not take advantage of the other 3 turnovers, however, and Danny Kanell's second touchdown pass of the game to Jammi German cut the deficit to 17-14. The Titans led just 20-17 when McNair ran 38 yards to the Falcons' 3 on fourth-and-1 to set up his 3-yard touchdown run. Henry Ford's fumble recovery later in the fourth quarter set up Del Greco's final field goal and secured the Titans' postseason berth. McNair was 15 of 29 for 216 yards and 1 touchdown. Chris Sanders had 5 receptions for 100 yards. Kanell was 18 of 29 for 237 yards and 2 touchdowns, with 2 interceptions.

Atlanta	7	7	3	0	—	17
Tennessee	14	6	0	10	—	30

Tenn — Sanders 48 pass from McNair (Del Greco kick)
Atl — German 16 pass from Kanell (Andersen kick)
Tenn — Byrd 61 pass from Wycheck (Del Greco kick)
Tenn — FG Del Greco 38
Atl — German 6 pass from Kanell (Andersen kick)
Tenn — FG Del Greco 27
Atl — FG Andersen 32
Tenn — McNair 3 run (Del Greco kick)
Tenn — FG Del Greco 43

CHICAGO 28, DETROIT 10—at Soldier Field, attendance 50,256. Cade McNown passed for 301 yards and 4 touchdowns, with Marcus Robinson contributing 11 receptions for 170 yards and 3 scores, as the Bears deprived the Lions from catching the Buccaneers. The Lions led 3-0 and were looking for more points early in the second quarter when Terry Cousins intercepted Gus Frerotte's pass at the Bears' 19. On the Lions' next possession, Chris Hudson intercepted Frerotte's pass and returned the ball 28 yards to the Lions' 47. McNown completed all 6 pass attempts on the ensuing drive, capped by his 4-yard touchdown pass to Bobby Engram. Jason Hanson missed a 50-yard field-goal attempt with 1:18 left in the half, and McNown and Robinson hooked up on a 1-yard pass seven seconds before halftime to give Chicago a 14-3 lead. Van Tuinei's fumble recovery at the Bears' 30 in the third quarter led to McNown's 36-yard scoring pass to Robinson. The pair completed the trifecta midway through the fourth quarter to take a 28-3 lead. McNown was 27 of 36 for 301 yards and 4 touchdowns, with 2 interceptions. McNown raised his passing total to 1,144 yards, and helped the Bears tie an NFL record with the 1993 Dolphins as the only teams with three quarterbacks with at least 1,000 passing yards. Engram had 10 receptions for 94 yards. Frerotte was 17 of 30 for 158 yards, with 3 interceptions. Johnnie Morton had 8 receptions for 100 yards.

Detroit	3	0	0	7	—	10
Chicago	0	14	7	7	—	28

Det — FG Hanson 24
Chi — Engram 4 pass from McNown (Boniol kick)
Chi — Robinson 1 pass from McNown (Boniol kick)
Chi — Robinson 36 pass from McNown (Boniol kick)
Chi — Robinson 42 pass from McNown (Boniol kick)
Det — Batch 12 run (Hanson kick)

JACKSONVILLE 24, CLEVELAND 14—at Cleveland Browns Stadium, attendance 72,038. Fred Taylor had 26 carries for 136 yards, including a game-breaking 41-yard touchdown run in the fourth quarter, as the Jaguars won their eleventh consecutive game. With the game scoreless early in the second quarter, Tim Couch fumbled and Lonnie Marts recovered at the Browns' 6 to set up Mark Brunell's 3-yard touchdown pass to Damon Jones. The Jaguars led 14-0 before a 31-yard pass interference penalty set up Terry Kirby's 1-yard run just before halftime. Couch left the game with a sprained left ankle, suffered when sacked by Tony Brackens, late in the first half, but the Browns refused to fold, and after Mike Hollis missed his second field goal of the game, Ty Detmer engineered a 62-yard drive capped by Darrin Chiaverini's 10-yard touchdown catch to trim the deficit to 17-14 late in the third quarter. The Browns' defense stopped Jacksonville three times from inside the Browns' 2-yard line early in the fourth quarter to get the ball back. However, Cleveland had to punt, and Taylor's 41-yard scoring scamper over left guard on the Jaguars' next play from scrimmage sealed the Browns' fate. Brunell was 21 of 33 for 267 yards and 1 touchdown, with 1 interception. Jimmy Smith had 8 receptions for 134 yards. Couch was 10 of 16 for 86 yards prior to the injury, while Detmer was 13 of 24 for 153 yards and 1 touchdown. Chiaverini had 10 receptions for 108 yards.

Jacksonville	0	14	3	7	—	24
Cleveland	0	7	7	0	—	14

Jax — D. Jones 3 pass from Brunell (Hollis kick)
Jax — Brunell 9 run (Hollis kick)
Cle — Kirby 1 run (Dawson kick)
Jax — FG Hollis 41
Cle — Chiaverini 10 pass from Detmer (Dawson kick)
Jax — Taylor 41 run (Hollis kick)

PHILADELPHIA 24, NEW ENGLAND 9—at Veterans Stadium, attendance 65,475. Koy Detmer passed for a career-high 3 touchdowns, and the Eagles' defense forced 7 turnovers and recorded 6 sacks as the Eagles improved to 5-0 all-time at home against the Patriots. Tony Simmons fumbled on the opening kickoff, and Mike Caldwell recovered at the Patriots' 24 to set up Norm Johnson's field goal. The Patriots' offense committed 2 turnovers deep in Eagles' territory, including a 30-yard interception return to midfield by Jeremiah Trotter. Detmer, making his first start of the season, connected on a 50-yard scoring pass to Torrance Small one play after Trotter's interception, and the Eagles led 10-0. The Patriots cut the deficit to 10-6 and were looking for more when Al Harris intercepted Drew Bledsoe's pass at the Eagles' 5 and returned it 75 yards before fumbling. Brian Dawkins recovered the ball and advanced it 9 yards to the Patriots' 11, where Detmer fired another touchdown pass to Small for a 17-6 halftime lead. Allen Rossum's 19-yard punt return in the third quarter set up Detmer's 44-yard touchdown pass to Dietrich Jells for a 24-9 lead. The Patriots drove inside the Eagles' 40 four times in the fourth quarter, but were stopped twice on downs and twice by interceptions. Detmer was 10 of 29 for 181 yards and 3 touchdowns, with 2 interceptions. Bledsoe was 23 of 49 for 331 yards, with 4 interceptions. Troy Brown had 5 receptions for 105 yards.

New England	0	6	3	0	—	9
Philadelphia	10	7	7	0	—	24

Phil — FG N. Johnson 43
Phil — Small 50 pass from Detmer (N. Johnson kick)
NE — FG Vinatieri 23
NE — FG Vinatieri 43
Phil — Small 11 pass from Detmer (N. Johnson kick)
NE — FG Vinatieri 46
Phil — Jells 44 pass from Detmer (N. Johnson kick)

BALTIMORE 31, NEW ORLEANS 8—at PSINet Stadium, attendance 67,597. Tony Banks passed for 298 yards and 3 touchdowns, and the Ravens' defense permitted just 8 first downs as the Ravens won their third consecutive game. Rod Woodson's 31-yard interception return late in the first quarter led to Matt Stover's 36-yard field goal. The Saints did not get inside the Ravens' 35 during the first half, and Banks engineered touchdown drives of 59 and 82 yards to stake Baltimore to a 17-0 lead. The Saints did not gain a first down on their first five possessions of the second half, and Banks's 47-yard touchdown pass to Qadry Ismail with 14:14 left in the game improved the Ravens' lead to 24-0. Billy Joe Tolliver's 57-yard pass to Lawrence Dawsey set up Keith Poole's 20-yard scoring grab, but Corey Harris's 24-yard interception return in the final moments dashed any comeback hopes for the Saints. Banks was 24 of 36 for 298 yards and 3 touchdowns, with 3 interceptions. Ismail had 7 receptions for 115 yards. Tolliver was 16 of 35 for 207 yards and 1 touchdown, with 3 interceptions, and Danny Wuerffel was 5 of 11 for 45 yards, with 1 interception.

New Orleans	0	0	0	8	—	8
Baltimore	3	14	0	14	—	31

Balt — FG Stover 36
Balt — Holmes 34 pass from Banks (Stover kick)
Balt — Armour 6 pass from Banks (Stover kick)
Balt — Ismail 47 pass from Banks (Stover kick)
NO — Poole 20 pass from Tolliver (Cleeland pass from Tolliver)
Balt — Harris 24 interception return (Stover kick)

ST. LOUIS 31, N.Y. GIANTS 10—at Trans World Dome, attendance 66,065. Kurt Warner passed for 319 yards and 2 touchdowns and the Rams' defense returned 2 interceptions for scores as the Rams clinched home-field advantage throughout the playoffs. The Rams led 10-0 at halftime, but Cary Blanchard's 23-yard field goal capped a 69-yard drive to begin the second half. The Giants forced a turnover in their own territory later in the quarter, but Devin Bush intercepted Kerry Collins's pass three plays later and returned it 45 yards for a touchdown. After Warner's second touchdown pass to Az-Zahir Hakim increased the lead to 24-3, Mike Jones returned an errant Collins pass 22 yards midway through the fourth quarter to take a commanding 31-3 lead. Warner was 18 of 32 for 319 yards and 2 touchdowns. Collins was 21 of 37 for 273 yards and 1 touchdown, with 2 interceptions. Amani Toomer had 9 receptions for 162 yards.

N.Y. Giants	0	0	3	7	—	10
St. Louis	3	7	7	14	—	31

StL — FG Wilkins 47
StL — Hakim 3 pass from Warner (Wilkins kick)
NYG — FG Blanchard 23
StL — Bush 45 interception return (Wilkins kick)
StL — Hakim 65 pass from Warner (Wilkins kick)
StL — M. Jones 22 interception return (Wilkins kick)
NYG — Hilliard 7 pass from Collins (Blanchard kick)

N.Y. JETS 22, DALLAS 21—at Texas Stadium, attendance 64,271. John Hall's 37-yard field goal with 1:35 to play allowed the Jets to hand the Cowboys their first home loss of the season. Trailing 6-0 early in the second quarter, Deion Sanders's 26-yard punt return set up Troy Aikman's 14-yard touchdown pass to Emmitt Smith to give the Cowboys a 7-6 lead. A 34-yard pass interference penalty on Kevin Smith led to Ray Lucas's 1-yard touchdown pass to Richie Anderson, but Aikman responded with a 53-yard pass to Chris Brazzell, which led to holder Eric Bjornson's 20-yard scoring run on a fake field goal to take a 14-13 lead. The Cowboys' momentum carried into the second half as Raghib Ismail scored on a 27-yard reverse, but Lucas took just six plays to answer, capped by Blake Spence's 2-yard touchdown catch. However, Lucas was stopped on the 2-point conversion attempt, and the Cowboys led 21-19. The Cowboys attempted to increase their lead early in the fourth quarter, but Victor Green's end-zone interception resulted in a touchback. Later in the quarter, Curtis Martin carried 9 times for 38 yards on an 11-play, 41-yard drive to set up Hall's go-ahead field goal with 1:35 left. The Cowboys failed to cross midfield in the final minute. Lucas was 20 of 34 for 229 yards and 2 touchdowns, with 1 interception. Martin had 26 carries for 113 yards, and Wayne Chrebet added 8 receptions for 108 yards. Aikman was 12 of 28 for 158 yards and 1 touchdown, with 2 interceptions. Emmitt Smith had 19 carries for 110 yards.

N.Y. Jets	6	7	6	3	—	22
Dallas	0	14	7	0	—	21

NYJ — FG Hall 47
NYJ — FG Hall 33
Dall — E. Smith 14 pass from Aikman (Murray kick)
NYJ — Anderson 1 pass from Lucas (Hall kick)
Dall — Bjornson 20 run (Murray kick)
Dall — Ismail 27 run (Murray kick)
NYJ — Spence 2 pass from Lucas (run failed)
NYJ — FG Hall 37

MIAMI 12, SAN DIEGO 9—at Pro Player Stadium, attendance 73,765. Olindo Mare made 4 field goals, and John Carney missed a 36-yard field-goal attempt with five seconds remaining, as the Dolphins snapped their three-game losing streak. The Dolphins had a 6-3 halftime lead as both teams converted field goals on their only drives into opponents' territories. Greg Jackson recovered Hunter Goodwin's fumble at the Dolphins' 34 late in the third quarter to set up Carney's tying field goal. Two possessions later Dan Marino fumbled, and Raylee Johnson recovered at the Dolphins' 4. But Daryl Gardener sacked Jim Harbaugh and the Chargers settled for Carney's go-ahead 31-yard field goal with 10:11 to play. A 15-yard penalty on the ensuing kickoff gave the Dolphins the ball in Chargers' territory and set up Mare's game-tying 30-yard field goal with 6:06 left. On the next play from scrimmage Rich Owens sacked Harbaugh and forced him to fumble. Brock Marion recovered at the Chargers' 20, and Mare gave the Dolphins the lead with a 31-yard field goal with 3:22 remaining. The Chargers strung together their longest drive of the game to reach the Dolphins' 18, but Carney's 36-yard field-goal attempt hit the left upright with five seconds remaining. Marino was 22 of 36 for 241 yards. Harbaugh was 20 of 40 for 178 yards.

San Diego	0	3	0	6	—	9
Miami	3	3	0	6	—	12

Mia — FG Mare 32
SD — FG Carney 23
Mia — FG Mare 21
SD — FG Carney 22
SD — FG Carney 31
Mia — FG Mare 30
Mia — FG Mare 31

DENVER 36, SEATTLE 30 (OT)—at Mile High Stadium, attendance 65,987. Glenn Cadrez scooped up Jon Kitna's fumble and rumbled 37 yards for a touchdown in overtime as the Broncos handed the Seahawks their fourth consecutive defeat. Behind the strength of Chris Watson's 81-yard punt return and Al Wilson's fumble recovery at the Seahawks' 43, the Broncos streaked to a 17-7 lead. Kerry Joseph's 61-yard kickoff return led to Ricky Watters's short touchdown run, but Jason Elam booted 2 third-quarter field goals to give Denver a 23-17 lead. Willie Williams's interception at the Broncos' 47 with 8:40 remaining led to Todd Peterson's 32-yard field goal with 3:41 left to trim the deficit to 23-20. Olandis Gary's 71-yard run set up Brian Griese's 9-yard touchdown pass to Dwayne Carswell to give Denver a seemingly commanding 30-20 lead with 1:47 remaining. Kitna completed all 3 of his pass attempts on the ensuing drive, with Derrick Mayes's 36-yard touchdown catch with 54 seconds left cutting the lead to 30-27. Joseph recovered the ensuing onside kick, and Peterson drilled a 45-yard field goal with 14 seconds left in regulation to tie the game. In overtime, Denver won the toss but failed to garner a first down. With all of the momentum, Kitna completed a 17-yard pass to Sean Dawkins for a first down, and reached the Broncos' 47. But on third-and-4, blitzing cornerback Ray Crockett blindsided Kitna, who fumbled and Cadrez scooped up the ball and ran untouched into the end zone for the winning touchdown. Griese was 20 of 39 for 180 yards and 2 touchdowns, with 2 interceptions. Gary had 22 carries for 183 yards. Kitna was 22 of 42 for 278 yards and 2 touchdowns. Watters had 16 carries for 115 yards.

Seattle	7	7	3	13	0	—	30
Denver	14	3	6	7	6	—	36

Den — Watson 81 punt return (Elam kick)
Sea — Pritchard 16 pass from Kitna (Peterson kick)
Den — Smith 14 pass from Griese (Elam kick)
Den — FG Elam 28
Sea — Watters 1 run (Peterson kick)
Den — FG Elam 46
Sea — FG Peterson 40
Den — FG Elam 33
Sea — FG Peterson 32
Den — Carswell 9 pass from Griese (Elam kick)
Sea — Mayes 36 pass from Kitna (Peterson kick)
Sea — FG Peterson 45
Den — Cadrez 37 fumble return

OAKLAND 45, TAMPA BAY 0—at Network Associates Coliseum, attendance 46,395. The Raiders' defense permitted just 137 yards, forced 3 turnovers, and recorded 4 sacks, and Tyrone Wheatley and Napoleon Kaufman each exceeded 100 yards, as the Raiders posted their first shutout in seven seasons. The Raiders scored on their first two possessions to lead 10-0, and Charles Woodson's 20-yard fumble return to the Buccaneers' 30 set up Wheatley's touchdown run on the next play, to take a 17-0 lead. Lance Johnstone's 13-yard return of Shaun King's fumble staked the Raiders to a 24-0 lead early in the third quarter, and Kaufman's 17-yard scoring scamper less than five minutes later gave Oakland a 31-0 lead. Tampa Bay had one scoring opportunity, but King's fourth-and-5 pass from the Raiders' 18 early in the fourth quarter fell incomplete. Kaufman's 75-yard touchdown run three plays later finished the scoring. Rich Gannon was 15 of 26 for 141 yards and 1 touchdown. Kaufman had 8 carries for 122 yards, and Wheatley rushed 19 times for 111 yards. King was 17 of 29 for 142 yards, with 1 interception.

Tampa Bay	0	0	0	0	—	0
Oakland	10	7	21	7	—	45

Oak — Brown 20 pass from Gannon (Nedney kick)
Oak — FG Nedney 26
Oak — Wheatley 30 run (Nedney kick)
Oak — Johnstone 13 fumble return (Nedney kick)
Oak — Kaufman 17 run (Nedney kick)
Oak — Wheatley 3 run (Nedney kick)
Oak — Kaufman 75 run (Nedney kick)

INDIANAPOLIS 24, WASHINGTON 21—at RCA Dome, attendance 57,013. Peyton Manning passed for 198 yards and 2 touchdowns, and Edgerrin James scored twice as the Colts clinched their first AFC East title since 1987. The Colts drove deep into Redskins' territory on all five of their first-half possessions, but managed just 10 points because of fumbles by Marvin Harrison and Peyton Manning, and Shawn Barber's interception in the end zone for a touchback. The Redskins strung together consecutive drives of 55, 58, and 66 yards to take a 13-10 halftime lead. Manning's 1-yard scoring pass to Ken Dilger on the opening play of the fourth quarter gave the Colts a 17-13 lead. The Redskins had an opportunity to cut the lead to one point, but Jason Belser blocked Brett Conway's 49-yard field-goal attempt. James scored six plays later to give the Colts a 24-13 lead with 5:57 left. After an exchange of punts, Brian Mitchell scored on a 6-yard run, and Brad Johnson completed a 2-point conversion pass to Michael Westbrook, to cut the deficit to 24-21 with 1:24 remaining. James Thrash recovered the ensuing onside kick, but the Redskins failed to garner a first down. Manning was 23 of 37 for 298 yards and 2 touchdowns, with 1 interception. Harrison had 9 receptions for 117 yards. Johnson was 16 of 30 for 237 yards and 1 touchdown.

Washington	3	10	0	8	—	21
Indianapolis	7	3	0	14	—	24

Ind — James 37 pass from Manning (Vanderjagt kick)
Wash — FG Conway 23
Wash — Connell 48 pass from Johnson (Conway kick)
Ind — FG Vanderjagt 43
Wash — FG Conway 32
Ind — Dilger 1 pass from Manning (Vanderjagt kick)
Ind — James 2 run (Vanderjagt kick)
Wash — Mitchell 6 run (Westbrook pass from Johnson)

SUNDAY NIGHT, DECEMBER 19

BUFFALO 31, ARIZONA 21—at Sun Devil Stadium, attendance 64,337. Doug Flutie passed for 239 yards and 2 touchdowns as the Bills won for the fifth time in seven games to remain in the AFC playoff chase. The Bills scored on two of their first three possessions, on 67- and 80-yard drives, to claim a 14-0 lead. Mario Bates's 2 second-quarter touchdowns, the second set up by Mac Cody's 26-yard punt return, tied the game just before halftime. Steve Christie's 33-yard field goal capped a 15-play, 60-yard drive that took 9:16 off the clock, and Flutie's 4-yard touchdown pass to Jay Riemersma with 3:01 remaining in the game culminated a 13-play, 78-yard drive that exhausted 7:33. Jake Plummer's 26-yard touchdown pass to Rob Moore with 1:49 left cut the deficit to 24-21, but Henry Jones fielded the ensuing onsides kick and scampered untouched 37 yards for a game-clinching touchdown. Flutie was 21 of 32 for 239 yards and 2 touchdowns, with 2 interceptions. Plummer was 11 of 29 for 119 yards and 1 touchdown, with 1 interception. The Bills controlled the ball for 39:30.

Buffalo	14	0	3	14	—	31
Arizona	0	14	0	7	—	21

Buff — Moulds 15 pass from Flutie (Christie kick)
Buff — Linton 6 run (Christie kick)
Ariz — Bates 1 run (Jacke kick)
Ariz — Bates 2 run (Jacke kick)
Buff — FG Christie 33
Buff — Riemersma 4 pass from Flutie (Christie kick)
Ariz — Moore 26 pass from Plummer (Jacke kick)
Buff — Jones 37 kickoff return (Christie kick)

MONDAY NIGHT, DECEMBER 20

MINNESOTA 24, GREEN BAY 20—at Metrodome, attendance 64,203. In a battle of 7-6 teams, Randy Moss caught 2 touchdown passes and Robert Griffith intercepted a pass in the end zone as time expired to propel the Vikings to victory. Dorsey Levens's 1-yard scoring run in the second quarter gave the Packers a 7-3 lead, and DeMond Parker recovered Robert Tate's fumbled kickoff return to set up Ryan Longwell's 26-yard field goal. Jeff George and Moss connected on a 57-yard touchdown three plays later, but Longwell added a second field goal just before halftime to give the Packers a 13-10 lead. Moss's second touchdown catch allowed the Vikings to retake the lead, but his fumbled punt moments later set up a Packers' field-goal attempt. The Packers faked the field goal, however, and holder Matt Hasselbeck completed a 9-yard touchdown pass to Jeff Thomason to give Green Bay a 20-17 lead with 12:31 left. Undaunted, the Vikings marched 64 yards in seven plays to retake the lead on a 1-yard plunge from Leroy Hoard with 8:58 remaining. The Packers reached the Vikings' 27, but Brett Favre's desperation pass was intercepted by Griffith in the end zone as time expired. George was 16 of 29 for 258 yards and 2 touchdowns. Moss had 5 receptions for 131 yards. Favre was 22 of 39 for 229 yards, with 2 interceptions.

Green Bay	0	13	0	7	—	20
Minnesota	0	10	7	7	—	24

Minn — FG Anderson 42
GB — Levens 1 run (Longwell kick)
GB — FG Longwell 26
Minn — Moss 57 pass from George (Anderson kick)
GB — FG Longwell 22
Minn — Moss 1 pass from George (Anderson kick)
GB — Thomason 9 pass from Hasselbeck (Longwell kick)
Minn — Hoard 1 run (Anderson kick)

SIXTEENTH WEEK SUMMARIES

AMERICAN FOOTBALL CONFERENCE

Eastern Division	W	L	T	Pct.	Pts.	OP
Indianapolis	13	2	0	.867	417	302
Buffalo	10	5	0	.667	289	223
Miami	9	6	0	.600	316	315
N.Y. Jets	7	8	0	.467	289	300
New England	7	8	0	.467	279	281
Central Division						
Jacksonville	13	2	0	.867	372	210
Tennessee	12	3	0	.800	345	288
Baltimore	8	7	0	.533	321	257
Pittsburgh	6	9	0	.400	281	273
Cincinnati	4	11	0	.267	276	436
Cleveland	2	14	0	.125	217	437
Western Division						
Seattle	9	6	0	.600	329	279
Kansas City	9	6	0	.600	352	281
Oakland	7	8	0	.467	349	291
San Diego	7	8	0	.467	257	310
Denver	6	9	0	.400	308	306

NATIONAL FOOTBALL CONFERENCE

Eastern Division	W	L	T	Pct.	Pts.	OP
Washington	9	6	0	.600	422	367
N.Y. Giants	7	8	0	.467	281	332
Dallas	7	8	0	.467	326	258
Arizona	6	9	0	.400	221	333
Philadelphia	4	11	0	.267	234	326
Central Division						
Tampa Bay	10	5	0	.667	250	229
Minnesota	9	6	0	.600	375	318
Detroit	8	7	0	.533	305	299
Green Bay	7	8	0	.467	308	317
Chicago	6	9	0	.400	266	321
Western Division						
St. Louis	13	2	0	.867	495	204
Carolina	7	8	0	.467	376	368
San Francisco	4	11	0	.267	266	419
Atlanta	4	11	0	.267	251	351
New Orleans	3	12	0	.200	247	389

FRIDAY, DECEMBER 24

NEW ORLEANS 31, DALLAS 24—at Louisiana Superdome, attendance 47,835. Jake Delhomme passed for 278 yards and 2 touchdowns in his first NFL start as the Saints dealt a serious blow to the Cowboys' playoff hopes. Fred Weary's 22-yard interception return to the Cowboys' 23 set up Delhomme's first-ever touchdown pass, 8 yards to Keith Poole, to give the Saints a 10-0 first-quarter lead. The Cowboys trailed 10-7 at halftime but took the opening kickoff of the second half and marched 61 yards, capped by Troy Aikman's 20-yard touchdown pass to Jason Tucker. Delhomme fumbled five plays later and Leon Lett recovered to set up Eddie Murray's field goal. The Saints answered two plays later as Delhomme's 51-yard touchdown pass to Eddie Kennison tied the game 17-17. Tucker's 50-yard kickoff return led to Aikman's 3-yard touchdown pass to David LaFleur, but Delhomme's 50-yard pass moments later set up the Louisiana native's 4-yard game-tying run. A 35-yard kickoff return by Tucker gave the Cowboys good field position, but Robert Newkirk forced Emmitt Smith to fumble, and Weary scooped up the ball and raced 58 yards for the go-ahead touchdown with 9:59 remaining. The Cowboys reached the Saints' 6 with 1:14 left, but Mark Fields intercepted Aikman's pass for a touchback to seal the victory. Delhomme was 16 of 27 for 278 yards and 2 touchdowns, with 1 interception. Aikman was 23 of 39 for 246 yards and 2 touchdowns, with 2 interceptions. Tucker became just the second player since 1995 to accumulate 300 combined net yards in a game (203 on returns, 128 on 7 receptions).

Dallas	0	7	17	0	—	24
New Orleans	10	0	7	14	—	31

NO — FG Brien 32
NO — Poole 8 pass from Delhomme (Brien kick)
Dall — Smith 1 run (Murray kick)
Dall — Tucker 20 pass from Aikman (Murray kick)
Dall — FG Murray 33
NO — Kennison 51 pass from Delhomme (Brien kick)
Dall — LaFleur 3 pass from Aikman (Murray kick)
NO — Delhomme 4 run (Brien kick)
NO — Weary 58 fumble return (Brien kick)

SATURDAY, DECEMBER 25

DENVER 17, DETROIT 7—at Pontiac Silverdome, attendance 73,158. Oldanis Gary rushed for a rookie club-record 185 yards, including 174 in the second half, as the Broncos handed the Lions their third consecutive defeat. The Broncos had the lone scoring opportunity of the first half, but Mark Carrier's interception in the end zone just before halftime kept the game scoreless. Gary's 45-yard touchdown run on the second play of the second half kick-started the Broncos' offense, which also produced scoring drives on its next two possessions to take a 17-0 lead. The Lions were stopped on downs at the Broncos' 27 with 10:10 remaining, and failed to score until 1:56 was left in the game. Brian Griese was 22 of 30 for 171 yards and 1 touchdown, with 1 interception. Charlie Batch was 21 of 40 for 267 yards with 1 touchdown. The Broncos' defense limited the Lions to just 12 carries for 32 yards, and recorded 5 sacks.

Denver	0	0	10	7	—	17
Detroit	0	0	0	7	—	7

Den — Gary 45 run (Elam kick)
Den — FG Elam 32
Den — Carswell 1 pass from Griese (Elam kick)
Det — Moore 13 pass from Batch (Hanson kick)

SUNDAY, DECEMBER 26

ATLANTA 37, ARIZONA 14—at Georgia Dome, attendance 47,074. Bob Christian rushed for 2 touchdowns as the Falcons eliminated the Cardinals from the playoff chase. The Falcons drove 69 yards with their first possession to take a 7-0 lead. However, the Cardinals responded with 86- and 74-yard scoring drives, both capped by Mario Bates 1-yard plunges, to take a 14-7 lead. The Falcons scored on their next two possessions, with Morten Andersen's 28-yard field goal with 42 seconds left in the half giving Atlanta a 17-14 lead. On second-and-7 from its own 23 with 35 seconds left in the half, Jake Plummer's pass was intercepted by Gerald McBurrows, who returned it 23 yards to the Cardinals' 28 to set up Andersen's second field goal. The Falcons came out of the locker room and engineered a 15-play, 80-yard drive that consumed 10:21, capped by Byron Hanspard's 1-yard run. The Cardinals were stopped on downs at the Falcons' 40, and Christian's 33-yard run with 10:06 remaining put the game out of reach. Chris Chandler was 14 of 23 for 230 yards and 1 touchdown. Hanspard had 26 carries for 102 yards. Plummer was 15 of 26 for 217 yards, with 2 interceptions. Frank Sanders had 3 receptions for 106 yards.

Arizona	0	14	0	0	—	14
Atlanta	7	13	7	10	—	37

Atl — Mathis 23 pass from Chandler (Andersen kick)
Ariz — Bates 1 run (Jacke kick)
Ariz — Bates 1 run (Jacke kick)
Atl — Christian 1 run (Andersen kick)
Atl — FG Andersen 28
Atl — FG Andersen 24
Atl — Hanspard 1 run (Andersen kick)
Atl — Christian 33 run (Andersen kick)
Atl — FG Andersen 41

BUFFALO 13, NEW ENGLAND 10 (OT)—at Foxboro Stadium, attendance 55,014. Steve Christie's 23-yard field goal in overtime capped a game with severe playoff implications and handed the Patriots their third consecutive defeat. The Bills' victory, along with Miami's loss to the Jets the next evening, gave Buffalo a playoff berth. In the first half both teams missed a scoring opportunity inside the opponents' 30 but also each made a field goal for a 3-3 halftime score. Chad Eaton returned Jonathan Linton's fumble 30 yards to the Bills' 14 early in the fourth quarter to set up Terry Allen's 14-yard scoring run on the next play. After an exchange of punts, Linton capped a 59-yard drive with a 1-yard plunge with 4:23 remaining. The Patriots reached the Bills' 15 in the final seconds of regulation, but Adam Vinatieri's 33-yard field-goal attempt sailed wide right. The Patriots won the overtime coin toss and drove to the Bills' 26, but Vinatieri's 44-yard attempt was short. After the Bills fumbled the ball away at the Patriots' 38, New England was forced to punt and Lee Johnson's boot went just 24 yards to give the Bills the ball at their own 42-yard line. Doug Flutie engineered a 10-play, 52-yard drive to set up Christie's winning boot 13:12 into overtime. Flutie was 22 of 35 for 212 yards. Drew Bledsoe was 10 of 21 for 101 yards. Allen had 27 carries for 126 yards.

Buffalo	3	0	0	7	3	—	13
New England	0	3	0	7	0	—	10

Buff — FG Christie 39
NE — FG Vinatieri 38
NE — Allen 14 run (Vinatieri kick)
Buff — Linton 1 run (Christie kick)
Buff — FG Christie 23

PITTSBURGH 30, CAROLINA 20—at Three Rivers Stadium, attendance 39,428. Jerome Bettis rushed for a season-high 137 yards and a steady snow hampered the Panthers' offense as the Steelers snapped their six-game losing streak. Trailing 3-0, the Panthers reached the Steelers' 1, but Levon Kirkland stripped Fred Lane, Travis Davis scooped up the ball in the end zone and raced 102 yards for a touchdown and 10-0 lead. It was the third-longest fumble return in NFL history. Lane answered less than two minutes later with a 41-yard touchdown run, but neither offense could be stopped the remainder of the half, as the Steelers' 80- and 73-yard scoring drives were countered by 2 long touchdown passes from Steve Beuerlein to Patrick Jeffers. The Steelers led 23-20 at halftime, but the snow fell at a more rapid pace in the second half and the Panthers failed to drive inside the Steelers' 35. Bettis's 8-yard scoring run with 2:26 left and Scott Shields' interception less than a minute later sealed the victory. Mike Tomczak was 13 of 23 for 94 yards and 1 touchdown, with 1 interception. Beuerlein was 18 of 35 for 263 yards and 2 touchdowns, with 1 interception. Jeffers had 5 receptions for 160 yards.

Carolina	7	13	0	0	—	20
Pittsburgh	10	13	0	7	—	30

Pitt — FG Brown 46
Pitt — Davis 102 fumble return (Brown kick)
Car — Lane 41 run (Cunningham kick)
Pitt — Huntley 25 run (fumbled snap)
Car — Jeffers 88 pass from Beuerlein (kick failed)
Pitt — Ward 9 pass from Tomczak (Brown kick)
Car — Jeffers 43 pass from Beuerlein (Cunningham kick)
Pitt — Bettis 8 run (Brown kick)

ST. LOUIS 34, CHICAGO 12—at Trans World Dome, attendance 65,941. Kurt Warner passed for 334 yards and 3 touchdowns as the Rams won their seventh consecutive game and eliminated the Bears from the playoff hunt. Jeff Wilkins missed a 48-yard field-goal attempt and Sean Harris intercepted Warner's pass in the end zone for a touchback as the Rams failed to score on their first two possessions. However, the Rams' quick-strike offense scored on its last three possessions of the first half, on drives of 82, 83, and 44 yards, drove 10 plays, 80 yards for a touchdown to open the second half, and Grant Wistrom's 40-yard interception return moments later gave the Rams a 31-0 lead. The Rams scored 31 points in a span of 15:28. Shane Matthews replaced an injured Cade McNown in the third quarter and had 2 late touchdown passes. Warner was 24 of 35 for 334 yards and 3 touchdowns, with 1 interception. Marshall Faulk had 12 receptions for 204 yards. McNown was 9 of 16 for 125 yards, with 1 interception before being replaced by Matthews, who was 23 of 39 for 266 yards and 2 touchdowns, with 1 interception. Bobby Engram had 13 receptions for 143 yards.

Chicago	0	0	6	6	—	12
St. Louis	0	17	14	3	—	34

StL — Faulk 48 pass from Warner (Wilkins kick)
StL — Williams 2 pass from Warner (Wilkins kick)
StL — FG Wilkins 38
StL — Bruce 4 pass from Warner (Wilkins kick)
StL — Wistrom 40 interception return (Wilkins kick)
Chi — Engram 8 pass from Matthews (kick failed)
Chi — Engram 4 pass from Matthews (pass failed)
StL — FG Wilkins 28

BALTIMORE 22, CINCINNATI 0—at PSINet Stadium, attendance 68,036. Matt Stover made 5 field goals and the Ravens' defense posted its first shutout in franchise history to win its fourth consecutive game. The Ravens scored on three consecutive first-half possessions, the third of which was set up by Tony Siragusa's fumble recovery near midfield, to take a 13-0 lead. The Bengals reached the Ravens' 13 later in the second quarter, but Duane Starks intercepted Blake's pass to stifle the threat. Rod Woodson's 44-yard interception return just before halftime led to Stover's third field goal and a 16-0 halftime lead. The Bengals reached the Ravens' 2 early in the fourth quarter, but, with a defensive automatic first-down penalty factored in, the Bengals ran six plays and could not score. The Bengals settled for a field-goal attempt, but Keith Washington blocked Doug Pelfrey's 20-yard attempt to preserve the shutout. Banks was 15 of 33 for 187 yards and 1 touchdown, with 1 interception. Jeff Blake was 20 of 37 for 187 yards, with 2 interceptions.

Cincinnati	0	0	0	0	—	0
Baltimore	7	9	0	6	—	22

Balt — Rhett 2 pass from Banks (Stover kick)
Balt — FG Stover 24
Balt — FG Stover 48
Balt — FG Stover 19
Balt — FG Stover 30
Balt — FG Stover 19

TAMPA BAY 29, GREEN BAY 10—at Raymond James Stadium, attendance 65,723. Damien Robinson had a career day and the Buccaneers converted 4 turnovers into 20 points to tie the club record for victories in a season. Derrick Brooks's recovery of Dorsey Levens's fumble at the Packers' 47 set up Martin Gramatica's first field goal. Gramatica's second field goal was set up by Mark Royals's 17-yard pass to Robinson on fourth-and-2 from the Packers' 40, and Robinson's interception at the Packers' 39 led to Gramatica's third field goal and a 9-0 lead. The Packers responded with two scoring drives, capped by Brett Favre's 20-yard touchdown pass to Levens just before halftime, to give the Packers a 10-9 lead. The Buccaneers regrouped, and Robinson's recovery of Bill Schroeder's fumble at the Packers' 23 led to Shaun King's 8-yard touchdown pass to Warrick Dunn. King completed passes three times on third down in an early fourth-quarter drive, capped by Mike Alstott's 5-yard scoring run to take a 22-10 lead with 11:30 remaining. Robinson capped his big day by intercepting Favre's pass midway through the fourth quarter and returning it 36 yards to the Packers' 28. Alstott rumbled 17 yards for a touchdown four plays later to seal the victory. King was 17 of 30 for 133 yards and 1 touchdown, with 1 interception. Favre was 25 of 48 for 234 yards and 1 touchdown, with 2 interceptions.

Green Bay	0	10	0	0	—	10
Tampa Bay	3	6	7	13	—	29

TB — FG Gramatica 49
TB — FG Gramatica 28
TB — FG Gramatica 33
GB — FG Longwell 46
GB — Levens 20 pass from Favre (Longwell kick)
TB — Dunn 8 pass from King (Gramatica kick)
TB — Alstott 5 run (pass failed)
TB — Alstott 17 run (Gramatica kick)

INDIANAPOLIS 29, CLEVELAND 28—at Cleveland Browns Stadium, attendance 72,618. Mike Vanderjagt's 21-yard field-goal attempt with four seconds remaining capped a fourth-quarter comeback and allowed the Colts to equal their club-record with eleven consecutive victories. Trailing 7-0, Peyton Manning completed a 30-yard pass to Marvin Harrison on fourth-and-8 to the Colts' 1 to set up Edgerrin James's 1-yard scoring run. Undaunted, the Browns answered with Ty Detmer's 28-yard pass to Darrin Chiaverini. Vanderjagt added 2 late field goals, the last set up by Terrence Wilkins's 39-yard punt return, to trim the deficit to 14-13 at halftime. Detmer, who was playing for injured Tim Couch, scored on an 8-yard run to cap the opening drive of the second half, but James's second 1-yard run of the game cut the deficit to 21-19. The Browns used a 21-yard run by Karim Abdul-Jabbar and 28-yard run by Marc Edwards to set up Kirby's second touchdown and give Cleveland a 28-19 lead after three quarters. James's third touchdown capped a 77-yard drive to trim the Browns' lead to 28-26, and, after forcing a punt, the Colts began at their own 43 with 4:12 left. Manning's 10-yard pass to James on third-and-4 to the Browns' 20 set up Vanderjagt's winning kick. Manning was 28 of 44 for 283 yards. James had 28 carries for 103 yards, and Harrison had 14 receptions for 138 yards. Detmer was 15 fo 26 for 173 yards and 1 touchdown.

Indianapolis	0	13	6	10	—	29
Cleveland	7	7	14	0	—	28

Cle — Kirby 1 run (Dawson kick)
Ind — James 1 run (Vanderjagt kick)
Cle — Chiaverini 28 pass from Detmer (Dawson kick)
Ind — FG Vanderjagt 41
Ind — FG Vanderjagt 19
Cle — Detmer 8 run (Dawson kick)
Ind — James 1 run (run failed)
Cle — Kirby 1 run (Dawson kick)
Ind — James 2 run (Vanderjagt kick)
Ind — FG Vanderjagt 21

TENNESSEE 41, JACKSONVILLE 14—at Adelphia Coliseum, attendance 66,641. Steve McNair passed for a career-high 5 touchdowns as the Titans defeated the Jaguars for the second time this season and finished 8-0 in their first season at Adelphia Coliseum. The Titans scored on four of their five first-half possessions, including touchdown drives of 78, 95, and 71 yards en route to a 24-7 halftime lead. Two more touchdown passes by McNair, the second of which followed Samari Rolle's 30-yard interception return to the Jaguars' 36, gave Tennessee a 38-7 lead with 3:24 remaining in the third quarter. The Jaguars' offense struggled without Mark Brunell, who left late in the first half with a sprained left knee. McNair was 23 of 33 for 291 yards and 5 touchdowns. George rushed 26 times for 102 yards. Mark Brunell was 4 of 11 for 95 yards, with 1 interception, while Jay Fiedler was 8 of 22 for 101 yards, with 2 interceptions. Jimmy Smith had 4 receptions for 104 yards.

Jacksonville	0	7	7	0	—	14
Tennessee	7	17	14	3	—	41

Tenn — Roan 4 pass from McNair (Del Greco kick)
Tenn — Harris 62 pass from McNair (Del Greco kick)
Tenn — FG Del Greco 30
Jax — Taylor 1 run (Hollis kick)
Tenn — Thigpen 2 pass from McNair (Del Greco kick)
Tenn — Byrd 65 pass from McNair (Del Greco kick)
Tenn — Dyson 13 pass from McNair (Del Greco kick)
Jax — Whitted 98 kickoff return (Hollis kick)
Tenn — FG Del Greco 20

SEATTLE 23, KANSAS CITY 14—at Kingdome, attendance 66,332. Jon Kitna passed for 216 yards and 2 touchdowns as the Seahawks snapped a four-game losing streak and, on the basis of their season sweep of the Cheifs, moved back into first place in the AFC West. Leading 3-0, Joey Galloway's 21-yard punt return set up Kitna's 20-yard scoring pass to Sean Dawkins. Darryl Williams's 4-yard interception return to the Chiefs' 48 in the second quarter led to Kitna's 9-yard touchdown pass to Derrick Mayes and a 17-0 lead. With the score 17-7, Shawn Springs's 27-yard interception return to the Chiefs' 6 led to Todd Peterson's 22-yard field goal and a 20-7 lead. Elvis Grbac responded three plays later with a 76-yard touchdown pass to Joe Horn, but the Seahawks answered with Peterson's 48-yard field goal to give Seattle a 23-14 lead late in the third quarter. The Chiefs failed to cross the Seahawks' 40 in their final six possessions as Seattle regained the advantage in the AFC West. Kitna was 18 of 30 for 216 yards and 2 touchdowns. Grbac was 22 of 42 for 254 yards and 2 touchdowns, with 3 interceptions.

Kansas City	0	7	7	0	—	14
Seattle	10	7	6	0	—	23

Sea — FG Peterson 31
Sea — Dawkins 20 pass from Kitna (Peterson kick)
Sea — Mayes 9 pass from Kitna (Peterson kick)
KC — Johnson 4 pass from Grbac (Stoyanovich kick)
Sea — FG Peterson 22
KC — Horn 76 pass from Grbac (Stoyanovich kick)
Sea — FG Peterson 48

MINNESOTA 34, N.Y. GIANTS 17—at Giants Stadium, attendance 78,095. Randy Moss's 27-yard touchdown pass to Cris Carter helped the Vikings, in conjunction with Carolina's loss, earn their seventh postseason appearance in the last eight seasons. The Vikings drove inside the Giants' 20 three times in the second quarter, scoring twice on short runs by Leroy Hoard and being turned away by Jeremy Lincoln's interception, as the Vikings took a 14-6 halftime lead. Antonio Bass's interception at the Giants' 27 late in the third quarter led to the Vikings' trickery, as Moss took a handoff on an end around and connected with Carter on the right side of the end zone for a 27-yard touchdown. Cary Blanchard's third field goal of the game, as the third quarter expired, cut the deficit to 21-9, but Moe Williams returned the ensuing kickoff 85 yards for a touchdown. Jeff George was 10 of 21 for 185 yards, with 2 interceptions. Robert Smith had 16 carries for 146 yards, including a 70-yard touchdown run. Carter had 5 receptions for 131 yards. Kerry Collins was 31 of 51 for 297 yards and 1 touchdown, with 1 interception.

Minnesota	0	14	7	13	—	34
N.Y. Giants	3	3	3	8	—	17

NYG — FG Blanchard 24
Minn — Hoard 3 run (Anderson kick)
NYG — FG Blanchard 43
Minn — Hoard 1 run (Anderson kick)
Minn — Carter 27 pass from Moss (Anderson kick)
NYG — FG Blanchard 42
Minn — Williams 85 kickoff return (Anderson kick)
NYG — Mitchell 1 pass from Collins (Collins run)
Minn — Smith 70 run (pass failed)

SAN DIEGO 23, OAKLAND 20—at Qualcomm Stadium, attendance 63,846. Jim Harbaugh passed for 325 yards and 2 touchdowns and John Carney added 3 field goals as the Chargers won for the third time in four games. The Raiders scored twice before the Chargers recorded a first down. San Diego's offense picked up steam in the second quarter, as Harbaugh's 18-yard touchdown pass to Fred McCrary tied the game with 1:53 left in the half, and Junior Seau's 16-yard interception return to the Raiders' 9 set up Carney's field goal as the half expired to give San Diego a 13-10 halftime lead. Oakland scored on its first two possessions of the second half, but Harbaugh's 49-yard pass to Jeff Graham on third-and-15 to the Raiders' 10 set up the combo's 10-yard touchdown to tie the game with 13:18 remaining. Following a Raiders punt, Carney made a 37-yard field goal with 8:09 remaining to give the Chargers a 23-20 lead. The Raiders drove to the Chargers' 27, but Joe Nedney's 44-yard field-goal attempt sailed wide left with 3:04 remaining, and Jermaine Fazande's 18-yard run on second-and-4 allowed the Chargers to run out the clock. Harbaugh was 23 of 36 for 325 yards and 2 touchdowns, with 1 interception. Graham had 3 receptions for 113 yards. Rich Gannon was 16 of 33 for 266 yards and 1 touchdown, with 1 interception. Tim Brown had 3 receptions for 109 yards.

Oakland	10	0	10	0	—	20
San Diego	0	13	0	10	—	23

Oak — FG Nedney 52
Oak — Crockett 1 run (Nedney kick)
SD — FG Carney 48
SD — McCrary 18 pass from Harbaugh (Carney kick)
SD — FG Carney 19
Oak — Dudley 7 pass from Gannon (Nedney kick)
Oak — FG Nedney 25
SD — Graham 10 pass from Harbaugh (Carney kick)
SD — FG Carney 37

SUNDAY NIGHT, DECEMBER 26

WASHINGTON 26, SAN FRANCISCO 20 (OT)—at 3Com Park, attendance 68,329. Brad Johnson's 33-yard touchdown pass to Larry Centers in overtime capped a 16-point run by the Redskins as Washington clinched its first NFC Eastern Division title since 1991. Wade Richey kicked 2 field goals in the final seven minutes of the first half to give the 49ers a 13-7. Charlie Garner's 40-yard run set up Jeff Garcia's 5-yard touchdown pass to J.J. Stokes late in the third quarter to give the 49ers a 20-10 lead. Matt Stevens's 10-yard interception return to the 49ers' 30 with 14:04 remaining sparked the Redskins' attack. The interception led to Brett Conway's 34-yard field goal, and Johnson's 1-yard run capped a 67-yard drive that tied the game with 3:28 remaining. The 49ers drove to the Redskins' 22, but Terry Jackson fumbled and Anthony Cook recovered with 1:33 remaining in regulation. In overtime, the Redskins won the toss and quickly drove downfield to set up Johnson's pass in the flat to Centers, who caught the ball at the 49ers' 31 and strolled into the end zone untouched. Johnson was 32 of 47 for 471 yards and 2 touchdowns, with 1 interception. Michael Westbrook had 7 receptions for 125 yards, and Albert Connell added 5 for 106 yards. Garcia was 17 of 29 for 168 yards and 1 touchdown, with 1 interception. Garner had 16 carries for 129 yards.

Washington	0	7	3	10	6 —	26
San Francisco	7	6	7	0	0 —	20

SF — Garner 4 run (Richey kick)
Wash — Westbrook 65 pass from Johnson (Conway kick)
SF — FG Richey 29
SF — FG Richey 25
Wash — FG Conway 47
SF — Stokes 5 pass from Garcia (Brien kick)
Wash — FG Conway 34
Wash — Johnson 1 run (Conway kick)
Wash — Centers 33 pass from Johnson

MONDAY NIGHT, DECEMBER 27

N.Y. JETS 38, MIAMI 31—at Pro Player Stadium, attendance 74,230. Ray Lucas passed for 190 yards and 3 touchdowns as the Jets won their third consecutive game in Dan Marino's final game in Miami. The Jets scored on their first two possessions to take a 10-7 lead, and Marcus Coleman intercepted a pass and returned it 98 yards for a touchdown to increase the Jets' lead to 17-7. The Dolphins responded with a 62-yard touchdown drive before halftime, and opened the second half with a 69-yard drive, capped by Marino's 32-yard touchdown pass to Tony Martin, to take a 21-17 lead. Roman Phifer's 4-yard interception return to the Dolphins' 1 set up Curtis Martin's 1-yard plunge, but Marino responded with a 7-for-8 effort on the ensuing drive to retake the lead, 28-24, on J.J. Johnson's 1-yard run with 13:32 remaining. The Jets could not be stopped, however, as Lucas connected with Wayne Chrebet for a 50-yard touchdown. And one play after Olindo Mare missed a 54-yard field-goal attempt, Lucas hit Dedric Ward with a 56-yard touchdown to take a 38-28 lead with 8:56 remaining. Mare made a 37-yard field goal with 2:20 remaining, but Coleman recovered the onside kick and the Jets ran out the clock. Lucas was 11 of 23 for 190 yards and 3 touchdowns. Marino was 29 of 52 for 322 yards and 3 touchdowns, with 3 interceptions. Martin had 6 catches for 102 yards.

N.Y. Jets	10	7	7	14 —	38
Miami	7	7	7	10 —	31

NYJ — K. Johnson 4 pass from Lucas (Hall kick)
Mia — Perry 1 pass from Marino (Mare kick)
NYJ — FG Hall 48
NYJ — Coleman 98 interception return (Hall kick)
Mia — Pritchett 3 pass from Marino (Mare kick)
Mia — Martin 32 pass from Marino (Mare kick)
NYJ — Martin 1 run (Hall kick)
Mia — Johnson 1 run (Mare kick)
NYJ — Chrebet 50 pass from Lucas (Hall kick)
NYJ — Ward 56 pass from Lucas (Hall kick)
Mia — FG Mare 37

SEVENTEENTH WEEK SUMMARIES

AMERICAN FOOTBALL CONFERENCE

Eastern Division	**W**	**L**	**T**	**Pct.**	**Pts.**	**OP**
Indianapolis	13	3	0	.813	423	333
Buffalo	11	5	0	.688	320	229
Miami	9	7	0	.563	326	336
N.Y. Jets	8	8	0	.500	308	309
New England	8	8	0	.500	299	284
Central Division						
Jacksonville	14	2	0	.875	396	217
Tennessee	13	3	0	.813	392	324
Baltimore	8	8	0	.500	324	277
Pittsburgh	6	10	0	.375	317	320
Cincinnati	4	12	0	.250	283	460
Cleveland	2	14	0	.125	217	437
Western Division						
Seattle	9	7	0	.563	338	298
Kansas City	9	7	0	.563	390	322
San Diego	8	8	0	.500	269	316
Oakland	8	8	0	.500	390	329
Denver	6	10	0	.375	314	318

NATIONAL FOOTBALL CONFERENCE

Eastern Division	**W**	**L**	**T**	**Pct.**	**Pts.**	**OP**
Washington	10	6	0	.625	443	377
Dallas	8	8	0	.500	352	276
N.Y. Giants	7	9	0	.438	299	358
Arizona	6	10	0	.375	245	382
Philadelphia	5	11	0	.313	272	357
Central Division						
Tampa Bay	11	5	0	.938	270	235
Minnesota	10	6	0	.625	399	335
Detroit	8	8	0	.500	322	323
Green Bay	8	8	0	.500	357	341
Chicago	6	10	0	.375	272	341
Western Division						
St. Louis	13	3	0	.813	526	242
Carolina	8	8	0	.500	421	381
Atlanta	5	11	0	.313	285	380
San Francisco	4	12	0	.250	295	453
New Orleans	3	13	0	.188	260	434

SUNDAY, JANUARY 2

GREEN BAY 49, ARIZONA 24—at Lambeau Field, attendance 59,818. Dorsey Levens rushed for 4 touchdowns, and the Packers held-off the Panthers in one tiebreaker, but the Cowboys' victory later in the day snapped the Packers' streak of postseason appearances at six games. The Packers entered the day 18 net points ahead of Carolina, and the Panthers at one point had a 31-0 lead, which forced the Packers to open up the offense in the second half. The Packers led just 7-3 midway through the second quarter before Mike McKenzie's interception near midfield led to Levens's first touchdown and gave the Packers a 14-3 halftime lead. Levens's second touchdown capped an 84-yard drive, but the Cardinals countered with a 77-yard scoring drive to cut the lead to 21-10. Needing to defeat Arizona by 18 more points than Carolina beat New Orleans, Basil Mitchell took the ensuing kickoff and raced 88 yards for a touchdown. After stopping Arizona on downs at the Cardinals' 47, Levens's 5-yard run gave Green Bay a 35-10 lead with 12:09 remaining. However, Mario Bates scored and the Packers were stopped on downs, thus leaving Green Bay with a 35-17 and Arizona with the ball with 7:22 left. Meanwhile, Carolina led 45-7 midway through the fourth quarter and had a momentary lead in the battle of net points. Needing to keep the Cardinals off the scoreboard, McKenzie intercepted Jake Plummer's pass at the Packers' 1 and sparked a 99-yard drive, capped by Brett Favre's 32-yard touchdown pass to Bill Schroeder, to give the Packers a 42-17 lead with 2:38 left. The Cardinals answered with a 62-yard scoring drive, capped by Plummer's 9-yard touchdown pass to Mac Cody with 1:31 left. The Cardinals then attempted an onsides kick, which Schroeder recovered, and, needing a touchdown, Levens scored four plays later to give Green Bay a 25-point victory. The Panthers gave up a touchdown after Levens's final touchdown and won by 32 points. Favre was 21 of 34 for 311 yards and 2 touchdowns, with 1 interceptions. Levens had 24 carries for 146 yards. Plummer was 35 of 57 for 396 yards and 2 touchdowns, with 3 interceptions. Rob Moore had 6 receptions for 120 yards. Frank Sanders had 13 receptions for 118 yards.

Arizona	0	3	7	14 —	24
Green Bay	7	7	14	21 —	49

GB — Schroeder 10 pass from Favre (Longwell kick)
Ariz — FG Jacke 23
GB — Levens 8 run (Longwell kick)
GB — Levens 1 run (Longwell kick)
Ariz — Sanders 6 pass from Plummer (Jacke kick)
GB — Mitchell 88 kickoff return (Longwell kick)
GB — Levens 5 run (Longwell kick)
Ariz — Bates 1 run (Jacke kick)
GB — Schroeder 32 pass from Favre (Longwell kick)
Ariz — Cody 9 pass from Plummer (Jacke kick)
GB — Levens 1 run (Longwell kick)

NEW ENGLAND 20, BALTIMORE 3—at Foxboro Stadium, attendance 50,263. Chad Eaton returned a fumble for a touchdown and the Patriots' defense forced 4 turnovers and recorded 7 sacks to snap the Ravens' four-game winning streak. The Ravens drove to the Patriots' 1 early in the second quarter, but were forced to settle for Matt Stover's 19-yard field goal. Troy Brown returned the ensuing kickoff 41 yards to set up Adam Vinatieri's 25-yard field goal. Brown's 52-yard punt return moments later set up Drew Bledsoe's 1-yard scoring pass to Mike Bartrum, and Vinatieri added a 51-yard field goal as the half expired for a 13-3 lead. Ted Johnson sacked Tony Banks in the third quarter and forced him to fumble. Eaton scooped up the ball and rumbled 23 yards for the game's final points. Banks was 18 of 26 for 163 yards, with 1 interception, and Stoney Case was 8 of 14 for 88 yards, with 1 interception. Patrick Johnson was 9 receptions for 114 yards. Bledsoe was 15 of 25 for 108 yards and 1 touchdown, with 1 interception.

Baltimore	0	3	0	0 —	3
New England	0	13	7	0 —	20

Balt — FG Stover 19
NE — FG Vinatieri 25
NE — Bartrum 1 pass from Bledsoe (Vinatieri kick)
NE — FG Vinatieri 51
NE — Eaton 23 fumble return (Vinatieri kick)

JACKSONVILLE 24, CINCINNATI 7—at ALLTEL Stadium, attendance 70,532. Fred Taylor scored 2 touchdowns and Jay Fiedler passed for 317 yards in place of injured Mark Brunell to allow the Jaguars to clinch AFC home-field advantage throughout the playoffs. The Bengals got the game's first break, when James Stewart fumbled going into the end zone and Clyde Simmons recovered for a touchback. Michael Basnight's 46-yard run on the ensuing possession led to Sedrick Shaw's 8-yard scoring run. The Jaguars responded scoring drives on three of their next four possessions, capped by Mike Hollis's 27-yard field goal just before halftime, to give Jacksonville a 17-7 lead. The Jaguars' defense did not allow the Bengals' to drive inside their own 35-yard line after the first quarter. Fiedler was 28 of 39 for 317 yards and 1 touchdown. Jimmy Smith had 14 receptions for 165 yards. Jeff Blake was 13 of 23 for 141 yards, with 2 interceptions.

Cincinnati	7	0	0	0 —	7
Jacksonville	7	10	0	7 —	24

Cin — Shaw 8 run (Pelfrey kick)
Jax — Taylor 13 run (Hollis kick)
Jax — McCardell 25 pass from Fiedler (Hollis kick)
Jax — FG Hollis 27
Jax — Taylor 1 run (Hollis kick)

MINNESOTA 24, DETROIT 17—at Metrodome, attendance 64,103. Randy Moss had 5 receptions for 155 yards, including a 67-yard touchdown, as the Vikings clinched a home game for the first weekend of the postseason. Duane Clemons recovered Charlie Batch's fumble at the Vikings' 35, and Jeff George completed a 53-yard pass to Moss to set up Robert Smith's 4-yard touchdown run less than six minutes into the game. The Lions used 14- and 12-play drives to tie the game 10-10, but the Vikings quick-strike attack responded as George fired a 67-yard touchdown to Moss. The Lions reached Vikings' territory on all six of their first half possessions, but had 2 turnovers, a punt, and a missed field goal. Leroy Hoard's 3-yard touchdown run with 4:56 remaining gave the Vikings a 24-10 lead. Gus Frerotte replaced Batch and completed a 36-yard touchdown to Johnnie Morton with 2:16 left, but Smith ran for 2 first downs to enable the Vikings to run out the clock. George was 14 of 24 for 275 yards and 1 touchdown, with 2 interceptions. Batch was 17 of 24 for 161 yards and 1 touchdown, and Frerotte was

14 of 22 for 180 yards and 1 touchdown, with 1 interception. Morton had 10 receptions for 128 yards.

Detroit	7	3	0	7	—	17
Minnesota	7	10	0	7	—	24

Minn — Smith 4 run (Anderson kick)
Det — Morton 6 pass from Batch (Hanson kick)
Minn — FG Anderson 44
Det — FG Hanson 39
Minn — Moss 67 pass from George (Anderson kick)
Minn — Hoard 3 run (Anderson kick)
Det — Morton 36 pass from Frerotte (Hanson kick)

BUFFALO 31, INDIANAPOLIS 6—at Ralph Wilson Stadium, attendance 61,959. Rob Johnson gave Doug Flutie a one-week break heading into the postseason and passed for 287 yards and 2 touchdowns to help the Bills snap the Colts' 11-game winning streak. Mike Vanderjagt had 2 first-half field goals for the Colts, but the Bills had drives of 83, 80, and 82 yards on their only three possessions of the half to take a 21-6 halftime lead. In the fourth quarter, a 6-yard punt return by Kevin Williams set up Johnson's second touchdown pass, and Steve Christie's 19-yard field goal with 3:37 remaining finished the scoring. The Bills' defense did not permit the Colts inside the Bills' 35 in five second-half possessions. Johnson was 24 of 32 for 287 yards and 2 touchdowns. Eric Moulds had 8 receptions for 110 yards. Peyton Manning was 18 of 29 for 163 yards.

Indianapolis	3	3	0	0	—	6
Buffalo	7	14	0	10	—	31

Ind — FG Vanderjagt 27
Buff — Smith 21 run (Christie kick)
Buff — Price 23 pass from Johnson (Christie kick)
Ind — FG Vanderjagt 24
Buff — Linton 3 run (Christie kick)
Buff — Collins 1 pass from Johnson (Christie kick)
Buff — FG Christie 19

WASHINGTON 21, MIAMI 10—at FedEx Field, attendance 78,106. Rodney Peete passed for 2 second-half touchdowns as the Redskins' defense forced 3 turnovers inside Redskins' territory to defeat the Dolphins, who had clinched a playoff berth earlier in the day when the Jets defeated the Seahawks. Darryl Pounds' fumble recovery at the Redskins' 34 and Mark McMillian's interception at the Redskins' 8 stalled the Dolphins' first two possessions. In the second quarter, a 41-yard pass interference penalty to the Dolphins' 8 set up Skip Hicks's touchdown run. Leading 7-3 at halftime, the Redskins needed just two plays to score on the second half's opening possessions. James Thrash went 37 yards on an end around and Peete, who had just replaced Brad Johnson, fired a 30-yard scoring strike to Irving Fryar. Peete's 4-yard touchdown pass to Larry Centers gave Washington a 21-3 lead, and Damon Huard, who had replaced Dan Marino, guided the Dolphins on an 80-yard drive in the final moments to finish the scoring. Johnson was 7 of 11 for 75 yards and Peete was 6 of 9 for 99 yards and 2 touchdowns. Marino was 11 of 24 for 118 yards, with 1 interception, and Huard, who entered the game to begin the second half, was 18 of 29 for 162 yards and 1 touchdown, with 1 interception.

Miami	0	3	0	7	—	10
Washington	0	7	7	7	—	21

Wash — Hicks 8 run (Conway kick)
Mia — FG Mare 39
Wash — Fryar 30 pass from Peete (Conway kick)
Wash — Centers 4 pass from Peete (Conway kick)
Mia — Gadsden 4 pass from Huard (Mare kick)

CAROLINA 45, NEW ORLEANS 13—at Ericsson Stadium, attendance 56,929. Steve Beuerlein passed for 322 yards and 5 touchdowns to defeat the Saints. However, the Panthers needed to outscore the Saints by 19 more points than the Packers would defeat the Cardinals, which did not happen and thus eliminated the Panthers from the postseason chase. It looked as if the Panthers may accomplish their feat, as Carolina struggled a bit on offense but allowed just 4 first-half first downs to the Saints and took a 17-0 halftime lead. With the Packers game going on simultaneously, Carolina put together scoring drives of 64 yards in 5 plays and 75 yards in 4 plays to take a 31-0 lead. Jake Delhomme's 27-yard scramble set up his 3-yard touchdown pass to Eddie Kennison with 13:00 remaining to trim the deficit to 31-7. However, Michael Bates returned the ensuing kickoff 95 yards for a touchdown, and when Beuerlein fired his fifth touchdown pass of the game, 32 yards to Patrick Jeffers, the Panthers had a 45-7 lead and momentary control of the net-point differential. But the Cardinals gave up a touchdown to the Packers in the final minute of their game to beat out the Panthers, and seconds later Delhomme scrambled into the end zone for a 9-yard touchdown with 18 seconds left. Beuerlein was 22 of 41 for 322 yards and 5 touchdowns. Jeffers had 7 receptions for 165 yards. Delhomme was 26 of 49 for 243 yard and 1 touchdown, with 4 interceptions. Keith Poole had 6 receptions for 104 yards.

New Orleans	0	0	0	13	—	13
Carolina	10	7	14	14	—	45

Car — FG Cunningham 27
Car — Muhammad 7 pass from Beuerlein (Cunningham kick)
Car — Walls 37 pass from Beuerlein (Cunningham kick)
Car — Walls 15 pass from Beuerlein (Cunningham kick)
Car — Jeffers 40 pass from Beuerlein (Cunningham kick)
NO — Kennison 3 pass from Delhomme (Brien kick)
Car — Bates 95 kickoff return (Cunningham kick)
Car — Jeffers 32 pass from Beuerlein (Cunningham kick)
NO — Delhomme 9 run (pass failed)

DALLAS 26, N.Y. GIANTS 18—at Texas Stadium, attendance 63,767. Troy Aikman passed for 288 yards and 2 touchdowns as the Cowboys clinched a wild-card berth. Jason Tucker's 79-yard kickoff return to begin the game sparked the Cowboys, who scored on their first four possessions to take a 16-0 lead. The Giants did not drive inside the Cowboys' 35 until the middle of the third quarter, and were forced to settle for Cary Blanchard's 29-yard field goal. The Cowboys responded quickly, as two plays later Aikman fired a quick slant to Tucker, who streaked into the end zone for a 90-yard touchdown and gave Dallas a 23-3 lead. The Giants' offense strung together two 80-yard scoring drives in the fourth quarter, including Kerry Collins's 7-yard touchdown pass to Brian Alford and Joe Montgomery's 2-point conversion run with 57 seconds left, but Dexter Coakley recovered the onsides kick to clinch the victory. Aikman was 23 of 32 for 288 yards and 2 touchdowns. Emmitt Smith had 22 carries for 122 yards, and Tucker had 4 receptions for 122 yards. Collins was 31 of 48 for 314 yards and 1 touchdown, with 1 interception. Tiki Barber had 13 receptions for 100 yards.

N.Y. Giants	0	0	3	15	—	18
Dallas	6	10	7	3	—	26

Dall — FG Murray 20
Dall — FG Murray 21
Dall — Ismail 4 pass from Aikman (Murray kick)
Dall — FG Murray 27
NYG — FG Blanchard 29
Dall — Tucker 90 pass from Aikman (Murray kick)
NYG — Montgomery 1 run (Blanchard kick)
Dall — FG Murray 40
NYG — Alford 7 pass from Collins (Montgomery run)

OAKLAND 41, KANSAS CITY 38 (OT)—at Arrowhead Stadium, attendance 79,026. Joe Nedney kicked a field goal in the final minute of regulation and then added the game-winner in overtime as the Raiders knocked the Chiefs out of postseason play. The Chiefs led 14-0 before they ran an offensive play, by virtue of Tamarick Vanover's punt return 1:57 into the game and James Hasty's 34-yard interception return for a touchdown on the next play. The Chiefs led 17-0 when Kenny Shedd returned Marquis Walker's blocked punt 20 yards for a touchdown. The Raiders drove 54, 52, and 60 yards to score on their last three possessions of the half, capped by Rich Gannon's 23-yard scoring pass to Tyrone Wheatley with 13 seconds remaining, to take a 28-24 halftime lead. The Chiefs drove 98 yards in 13 plays to retake the lead on Elvis Grbac's 15-yard touchdown pass to Joe Horn. The Raiders needed just two plays to respond as Gannon completed a 42-yard pass to Tim Brown and Wheatley scored on a 26-yard run. Both defense's stiffened, until Grbac's 39-yard touchdown pass to Kevin Lockett with 7:22 remaining gave Kansas City a 38-35 lead. Nedney's 38-yard field goal with 45 seconds left in regulation tied the game. The Raiders won the overtime toss, and Jon Baker's kickoff went out of bounds for the third time in the game, giving the Raiders the ball at their own 40. Gannon's 24-yard pass to Brown at the Chiefs' 16 set up Nedney's winning kick. Gannon was 25 of 47 for 324 yards and 3 touchdowns, with 2 interceptions. Brown had 6 receptions for 122 yards. Grbac was 20 of 39 for 243 yards and 3 touchdowns.

Oakland	7	21	7	3	3	—	41
Kansas City	17	7	7	7	0	—	38

KC — Vanover 84 punt return (Stoyanovich kick)
KC — Hasty 34 interception return (Stoyanovich kick)
KC — FG Stoyanovich 33
Oak — Shedd 20 blocked punt return (Nedney kick)
Oak — Crockett 12 pass from Gannon (Nedney kick)
Oak — Kaufman 22 pass from Gannon (Nedney kick)
KC — Gonzalez 7 pass from Grbac (Stoyanovich kick)
Oak — Wheatley 23 pass from Gannon (Nedney kick)
KC — Horn 15 pass from Grbac (Stoyanovich kick)
Oak — Wheatley 26 run (Nedney kick)
KC — Lockett 39 pass from Grbac (Stoyanovich kick)
Oak — FG Nedney 38
Oak — FG Nedney 33

PHILADELPHIA 38, ST. LOUIS 31—at Veterans Stadium, attendance 60,700. The Eagles' defense forced 7 turnovers and Al Harris and Mike Mamula each had interception returns for touchdowns as the Eagles snapped the Rams' seven-game winning streak. Marshall Faulk scored the first 2 Rams' touchdowns, and set the second one up with a 57-yard run, to give St. Louis a 14-3 lead. Dexter McCleon's interception at the Eagles' 33 led to Jeff Wilkins's 47-yard field goal to give the Rams a 17-10 lead, but Allen Rossum, who earlier in the half had a 69-yard kickoff return, added a 20-yard punt return to set up Donovan McNabb's 3-yard touchdown pass to Duce Staley just before halftime to tie the game at 17-17. Mamula intercepted Warner early in the second half and returned it 41 yards for a touchdown, but the Rams countered with Warner's 15-yard touchdown pass to Torry Holt. With both Faulk and Warner out of the game, the Rams reached the Eagles' 25 early in the fourth quarter, but Robert Holcombe fumbled and Barry Gardner recovered and returned the ball to the Eagles' 46. McNabb's 5-yard touchdown pass to Chad Lewis six plays later gave the Eagles a 31-24 lead. The Rams drove to the Eagles' 7, but Rashard Cook sacked Joe Germaine and forced him to fumble. Mamula recovered and, after an Eagles' punt, Cook intercepted a pass and returned it to the Rams' 26. Norm Johnson, however, missed a 39-yard field-goal attempt, and the Eagles clung to a 31-24 lead. Four plays later, Justin Watson fumbled and Tim Hauck recovered at the Eagles' 32. The Rams' defense forced a punt, but Harris intercepted Germaine's pass and returned it 17 yards for a touchdown and 38-24 lead with 1:16 left. Germaine fired a 63-yard scoring bomb to Holt on the next play, but Na' Brown recovered the ensuing onsides kick to clinch the victory. McNabb was 15 of 32 for 179 yards and 3 touchdowns, with 2 interceptions. Warner was 12 of 24 for 141 yards and 2 touchdowns, with 2 interceptions, and Germaine was 9 of 16 for 136 yards and 1 touchdown, with 2 interceptions. Holt had 5 receptions for 122 yards.

St. Louis	7	10	7	7	—	31
Philadelphia	3	14	7	14	—	38

StL — Faulk 8 pass from Warner (Wilkins kick)
Phil — FG Akers 46
StL — Faulk 1 run (Wilkins kick)
Phil — Small 63 pass from McNabb (N. Johnson kick)
StL — FG Wilkins 47
Phil — Staley 3 pass from McNabb (N. Johnson kick)
Phil — Mamula 41 interception return (N. Johnson kick)
StL — Holt 15 pass from Warner (Wilkins kick)

Phil — Lewis 5 pass from McNabb (N. Johnson kick)
Phil — Harris 17 interception return (N. Johnson kick)
StL — Holt 63 pass from Germaine (Wilkins kick)

SAN DIEGO 12, DENVER 6—at Mile High Stadium, attendance 69,278. Jermaine Fazande rushed for a career-high 183 yards to more than double his career output as the Chargers defeated the Broncos. Jim Harbaugh's 38-yard pass to Fred McCrary set up Fazande's 1-yard touchdown run early in the second quarter. Olandis Gary fumbled on the next play from scrimmage and Al Fotenot recovered, which led to John Carney's 25-yard field goal and a 9-0 lead. Fazande's 54-yard run on third-and-7 set up Carney's 28-yard field goal as the half expired. The Broncos, which had just 4 first downs in the first half, scored on two of their first three second-half possessions to trim the deficit to 12-6 with 13:57 remaining. Carney missed a 46-yard field-goal attempt with 9:27 left, and Fazande fumbled and Darrius Johnson recovered at the Broncos' 40 with 7:03 remaining. The Broncos reached the Chargers' 20, but Brian Griese's fourth-and-4 pass to Ed McCaffrey was incomplete with 2:23 left. With one final chance, Griese's Hail Mary pass from midfield fell incomplete. Harbaugh was 12 of 19 for 115 yards, with 2 interceptions. Fazande had 30 carries for 183 yards, and Jeff Graham had 6 receptions for 102 yards. Griese was 23 of 46 for 211 yards. Rod Smith had 9 catches for 106 yards.

San Diego	0	12	0	0	—	12
Denver	0	0	3	3	—	6

SD — Fazande 1 run (kick blocked)
SD — FG Carney 25
SD — FG Carney 28
Den — FG Elam 37
Den — FG Elam 50

N.Y. JETS 19, SEATTLE 9—at Giants Stadium, attendance 78,154. John Hall booted 4 field goals to give the Jets seven victories in their final nine games. Despite the loss, the Seahawks learned in the locker room moments after the game the Raiders had defeated the Chiefs, thus placing Seattle in the postseason for the first time since 1988. The Jets scored on their first three possessions en route to a 13-6 halftime lead. In the third quarter, Jon Kitna's 9-yard pass to Derrick Mayes on fourth-and-1 kept alive a drive that culminated with Todd Peterson's third field goal. Ray Lucas countered with a 23-yard pass to Wayne Chrebet and 34-yard pass to Curtis Martin to set up Hall's third field goal. The Seahawks failed to cross midfield the remainder of the game, and Hall's 35-yard field goal with 4:21 left finished the scoring. Lucas was 15 of 26 for 211 yards, with 2 interceptions. Martin had 34 carries for 158 yards. Kitna was 21 of 45 for 237 yards, with 2 interceptions.

Seattle	6	0	3	0	—	9
N.Y. Jets	3	10	3	3	—	19

Sea — FG Peterson 25
NYJ — FG Hall 23
Sea — FG Peterson 41
NYJ — Martin 1 run (Hall kick)
NYJ — FG Hall 30
Sea — FG Peterson 45
NYJ — FG Hall 31
NYJ — FG Hall 35

TAMPA BAY 20, CHICAGO 6—at Soldier Field, attendance 49,180. Shaun King passed for 178 yards and 1 touchdown as the Buccaneers won their first division title since 1981. The Buccaneers' defense allowed just 2 first downs in the first half, and Donnie Abraham's 13-yard interception return to the Bears' 29 set up Martin Gramatica's 25-yard field goal and Steve White's fumble recovery at the Bears' 14 led to Mike Alstott's 1-yard scoring run to give Tampa Bay a 10-0 halftime lead. Two Jaret Holmes field goal's cut the deficit to 13-6 early in the fourth quarter, but Warrick Dunn had a 33-yard run and the Buccaneers converted 2 third downs to set up King's 6-yard touchdown pass to Dave Moore with 7:33 remaining. The Bears were stopped on downs inside the Buccaneers' 30 twice in the final 3:48 to preserve the victory. King was 18 of 24 for 178 yards and 1 touchdown. Jacquez Green had 10 receptions for 113 yards. Cade McNown was 20 of 42 for 196 yards, with 1 interception.

Tampa Bay	0	10	3	7	—	20
Chicago	0	0	3	3	—	6

TB — FG Gramatica 25
TB — Alstott 1 run (Gramatica kick)
Chi — FG Holmes 39
TB — FG Gramatica 33
Chi — FG Holmes 31
TB — Moore 6 pass from King (Gramatica kick)

TENNESSEE 47, PITTSBURGH 36—at Three Rivers Stadium, attendance 63,565. The Titans' defense forced 4 turnovers, returned 2 fumbles for touchdowns, and recorded a safety as Tennessee set a franchise record for victories. With their postseason spot secure, Rodney Thomas scored on an 8-yard run to give the Titans a 14-7 lead midway through the second quarter. The Titans then exploded for 17 points in the last 1:11 of the first half: Joe Bowden's 29-yard interception return with 1:48 left in the half set up Neil O'Donnell's 26-yard touchdown pass to Frank Wycheck; Jevon Kearse sacked Mike Tomczak on the next play, forced him to fumble, and returned the fumble 6 yards for a touchdown with 1:01 left in the half; and Al Del Greco kicked a 42-yard field goal with nine seconds left after Josh Miller dropped the punt snap. O'Donnell's 24-yard touchdown pass to Michael Roan increased the Titans' lead to 40-15 with 2:56 left in the third quarter, but the Steelers countered with Richard Huntley's 37-yard run to set up Jerome Bettis's 1-yard plunge and, on the next play from scrimmage Joey Porter sacked O'Donnell, forced him to fumble, and returned it 46 yards for a touchdown to cut the lead to 40-29. Levon Kirkland intercepted an O'Donnell pass at the Titans' 28 two plays later, and the Steelers reached the Titans' 1, but on four successive plays Bettis gained minus-1, 1, 0, and 0 yards to turn the ball over on downs. The Steelers drove inside the Titans' 20 late in the fourth quarter, but Huntley fumbled and Denard Walker raced 83 yards for a touchdown with 3:59 left to ice the game. McNair was 9 of 11 for 107 yards and 1 touchdown, and O'Donnell was 6 of 12 for 109 yards and 2 touchdowns, with 1 interception. Tomczak was 21 of 39 for 309 yards and 2 touchdowns, with 1 interception. Bobby Shaw had 7 receptions for 131 yards.

Tennessee	7	24	9	7	—	47
Pittsburgh	7	0	22	7	—	36

Tenn — Wycheck 9 pass from McNair (Del Greco kick)
Pitt — Huntley 8 run (Brown kick)
Tenn — Thomas 11 run (Del Greco kick)
Tenn — Wycheck 26 pass from O'Donnell (Del Greco kick)
Tenn — Kearse 14 fumble return (Del Greco kick)
Tenn — FG Del Greco 42
Pitt — Ward 15 pass from Tomczak (Ward pass from Tomczak)
Tenn — Safety, Thornton sacked Tomczak in the end zone
Tenn — Roan 24 pass from O'Donnell (Del Greco kick)
Pitt — Bettis 1 run (Brown kick)
Pitt — Porter 46 fumble return (Brown kick)
Tenn — Walker 83 fumble return (Del Greco kick)
Pitt — Shaw 35 pass from Tomczak (Brown kick)

MONDAY NIGHT, JANUARY 3

ATLANTA 34, SAN FRANCISCO 29—at Georgia Dome, attendance 57,980. Chris Chandler passed for 306 yards and 3 touchdowns, and Tim Dwight scored 3 times, as the Falcons built a 31-7 lead and held on to defeat the 49ers. The game was tied 7-7 when Gerald McBurrows recovered Jeff Garcia's fumble at the Falcons' 46 with 1:53 left in the half. Morten Andersen made a 49-yard field goal with 1:08 left in the half, and Dwight returned a punt 70 yards for a touchdown with 12 seconds left to give the Falcons a 17-7 halftime lead. Chandler completed touchdown passes to Terance Mathis and Dwight to cap their first two possessions of the second half and give Atlanta a 31-7 lead with 3:49 left in the third quarter. Garcia engineered touchdown drives of 83, 80, and 95 yards on the 49ers' next three possessions to trim the deficit to 34-29 with 2:46 remaining. Garcia completed a 41-yard pass to Rice with 20 seconds left to get the 49ers close to midfield, but Garcia's Hail Mary pass as time expired fell incomplete. Chandler was 19 of 37 for 306 yards and 3 touchdowns. Dwight had 7 receptions for 162 yards. Garcia was 26 of 34 for 373 yards and 2 touchdowns. Rice had 6 catches for 143 yards, and Stokes added 5 receptions for 130 yards.

San Francisco	0	7	8	14	—	29
Atlanta	7	10	14	3	—	34

Atl — Dwight 5 pass from Chandler (Andersen kick)
SF — Owens 4 pass from Garcia (Richey kick)
Atl — FG Andersen 49
Atl — Dwight 70 punt return (Andersen kick)
Atl — Mathis 19 pass from Chandler (Andersen kick)
Atl — Dwight 60 pass from Chandler (Andersen kick)
SF — Jervey 1 run (Stokes pass from Garcia)
Atl — FG Andersen 38
SF — Garcia 5 run (Richey kick)
SF — Stokes 43 pass from Garcia (Richey kick)

EIGHTEENTH WEEK SUMMARIES

SATURDAY, JANUARY 8, 2000

AFC WILD CARD PLAYOFF GAME

TENNESSEE 22, BUFFALO 16—at Adelphia Coliseum, attendance 66,672. Kevin Dyson received a crossfield lateral from Frank Wycheck and raced 75 yards down the left sideline for a touchdown with three seconds remaining to lift the Titans past the Bills. The Titans' defense permitted just 3 first downs in the first half, and Jevon Kearse sacked Rob Johnson for a safety, as Tennessee took a 12-0 lead into the locker room. Antowain Smith's 44-yard run on the first play of the second half set up his 4-yard scoring jaunt, quickly cutting the deficit to 12-7. Johnson's 37-yard pass to Eric Moulds early in the fourth quarter led to Smith's go-ahead touchdown with 11:08 remaining, but Johnson's 2-point conversion pass attempt fell incomplete. A 16-yard punt return by Isaac Byrd with 6:15 remaining sparked the Titans, and five consecutive carries by Eddie George set up Al Del Greco's 36-yard field goal with 1:48 remaining to give Tennessee a 15-13 lead. With time winding down, Johnson, who lost a shoe on a 3-yard scramble, completed a 9-yard pass to Peerless Price with 20 seconds left to set up Steve Christie's go-ahead 41-yard field goal with 16 seconds remaining. Lorenzo Neal fielded Christie's ensuing kickoff at the Titans' 24, ran a yard and handed the ball to Wycheck, who began running to his right, stopped, and threw across field to a wide-open Dyson, who had a wall of blockers and streaked 75 yards untouched for the game's final points. McNair was 13 of 24 for 76 yards, with 1 interception. George had 29 carries for 106 yards. Johnson was 10 of 22 for 131 yards.

Buffalo	0	0	7	9	—	16
Tennessee	0	12	0	10	—	22

Tenn — Safety, Kearse sacked Johnson in end zone
Tenn — McNair 1 run (Del Greco kick)
Tenn — FG Del Greco 40
Buff — Smith 4 run (Christie kick)
Buff — Smith 1 run (pass failed)
Tenn — FG Del Greco 36
Buff — FG Christie 41
Tenn — Dyson 75 kickoff return lateral from Wycheck (Del Greco kick)

NFC WILD CARD PLAYOFF GAME

WASHINGTON 27, DETROIT 13—at FedEx Field, attendance 79,411. Stephen Davis rushed for 119 yards and 2 touchdowns as the Redskins scored on their first four, and five of their first six, possessions to defeat the Lions. The Lions forced the Redskins to punt on their first possession, but Clint Kriewaldt was flagged for running into punter Matt Turk, giving the Redskins a first down. A 41-yard pass interference penalty moments later set up Davis's first touchdown. Davis rumbled 58 yards to begin the Redskins' next possession, but injured his right knee on a 4-yard touchdown run to cap the drive. Champ Bailey's interception set up Conway's first field goal, and Davis returned to carry 5 times for 45 yards on the Redskins' fourth possession to lead to Conway's second field goal. Davis sat out the remainder of the game, but Washington put together one more scoring drive to take a 27-0 halftime lead. The Lions did not cross midfield until midway through the third quarter, and Lamar Campbell's blocked field-goal attempt led to Ron Rice's 94-yard return. Gus Frerotte's 5-yard touchdown pass to Ron Rivers came on the last play of the game. Brad Johnson was 15 of 31 for 174 yards and 1 touchdown, with 2 interceptions. Frerotte was 21 of 46 for 251 yards and 1 touchdown, with 2 interceptions. Washington had more rushing yards (223-45) and longer time of possession (38:28-21:32).

Detroit	0	0	0	13	—	13
Washington	14	13	0	0	—	27

Wash — Davis 1 run (Conway kick)
Wash — Davis 4 run (Conway kick)
Wash — FG Conway 33
Wash — FG Conway 23
Wash — Connell 30 pass from Johnson (Conway kick)
Det — Rice 94 blocked field goal return (pass failed)
Det — Rivers 5 pass from Frerotte (Hanson kick)

SUNDAY, JANUARY 9
NFC WILD CARD PLAYOFF GAME

MINNESOTA 27, DALLAS 10—at Metrodome, attendance 64,056. Robert Smith rushed for 140 yards and Jeff George passed for 3 touchdowns as the Vikings defeated the Cowboys. The Cowboys drove 73 and 79 yards on their first two possessions to claim a 10-3 lead. Anthony Bass recovered Robert Thomas's fumble at the Cowboys' 23 early in the second quarter, and four plays later Smith caught a screen pass from George and faked out George Teague at the 12-yard line before running into the end zone. George gave the Vikings their first lead with a 58-yard touchdown bomb to Randy Moss 28 seconds before halftime. The Vikings led 27-10 before the Cowboys put together two final drives, only to turn the ball over inside the Vikings' 20 on both occasions. George was 12 of 25 for 212 yards and 3 touchdowns. Moss had 5 receptions for 127 yards. Troy Aikman was 22 of 38 for 286 yards, with 1 interception. Raghib Ismail had 8 catches for 163 yards.

Dallas	10	0	0	0	—	10
Minnesota	3	14	3	7	—	27

Dall — FG Murray 18
Minn — FG Anderson 47
Dall — E. Smith 5 run (Murray kick)
Minn — R. Smith 26 pass from George (Anderson kick)
Minn — Moss 58 pass from George (Anderson kick)
Minn — FG Anderson 38
Minn — Carter 5 pass from George (Anderson kick)

AFC WILD CARD PLAYOFF GAME

MIAMI 20, SEATTLE 17—at Kingdome, attendance 66,170. J.J. Johnson rushed for 86 yards, and his 2-yard scoring run with 4:48 left vaulted the Dolphins past the Seahawks. The Seahawks led 10-3 at halftime, but Dan Marino completed 11- and 27-yard passes to O.J. McDuffie on the opening drive of the second half to set up his tying 1-yard touchdown pass to Oronde Gadsden. Charlie Rogers returned the ensuing kickoff 85 yards for a touchdown, but Olindo Mare's 50-yard field goal late in the quarter trimmed the deficit to 17-13. Faced with third-and-17 from his own 8-yard line with 8:26 remaining, Marino fired a 23-yard completion to Tony Martin. Marino completed a 20-yard pass to Martin and 24-yard pass to Gadsden to set up Johnson's go-ahead 2-yard run. Terrell Buckley's interception at the Seahawks' 42 clinched the victory. The Seahawks failed to cross midfield in the second half. Marino was 17 of 30 for 196 yards and 1 touchdown. Jon Kitna was 14 of 30 for 162 yards and 1 touchdown, with 2 interceptions. The Dolphins' defense recorded 6 sacks and limited the Seahawks to 171 total yards. This was the final game played in the Kingdome, the Seahawks only home since joining the NFL in 1976.

Miami	3	0	10	7	—	20
Seattle	7	3	7	0	—	17

Sea — Dawkins 9 pass from Kitna (Peterson kick)
Mia — FG Mare 32
Sea — FG Peterson 50
Mia — Gadsden 1 pass from Marino (Mare kick)
Sea — Rogers 85 kickoff return (Peterson kick)
Mia — FG Mare 50
Mia — Johnson 2 run (Mare kick)

NINETEENTH WEEK SUMMARIES
SATURDAY, JANUARY 15, 2000
AFC DIVISIONAL PLAYOFF GAME

JACKSONVILLE 62, MIAMI 7—at ALLTEL Stadium, attendance 75,173. The Jaguars scored 38 points in the first 17 minutes, 55 seconds en route to the highest point total in AFC postseason history. Mark Brunell's 8-yard touchdown pass to Jimmy Smith capped a game-opening 9-play, 73-yard drive. Aaron Beasley intercepted Dan Marino's pass on the Dolphins' first play, setting up Mike Hollis's 45-yard field goal with 6:19 remaining in the quarter. Two plays after a Dolphins' punt, Fred Taylor scampered 90 yards down the right sideline. On the next play from scrimmage, Tony Brackens stripped Marino, recovered the ball, and, after not being touched, was pushed into the end zone by teammates to give Jacksonville a 24-0 lead with 3:21 left in the quarter. Taylor dodged three tacklers en route to the end zone on a 39-yard screen pass on the first play of the second quarter. Corey Chamblin blocked the Dolphins' punt on the ensuing possession, and James Stewart scored three plays later to give the Jaguars a 38-0 lead before Miami had a first down. The Dolphins drove 80 yards just before halftime to get on the board, but Jacksonville, with reserve Jay Fiedler, scored on its first two possessions of the second half to take a 55-7 lead. Brunell was 5 of 9 for 105 yards and 2 touchdowns. Taylor carried 18 times for 135 yards. Marino was 11 of 25 for 95 yards and 1 touchdown, with 2 interceptions before being replaced in the third quarter by Damon Huard. The Jaguars had more first downs (21-10), total yards (520-131), registered 5 sacks, and forced 7 turnovers.

Miami	0	7	0	0	—	7
Jacksonville	24	17	14	7	—	62

Jax — Smith 8 pass from Brunell (Hollis kick)
Jax — FG Hollis 45
Jax — Taylor 90 run (Hollis kick)
Jax — Brackens 16 fumble return (Hollis kick)
Jax — Taylor 39 pass from Brunell (Hollis kick)
Jax — Stewart 25 run (Hollis kick)
Jax — FG Hollis 28
Mia — Gadsden 20 pass from Marino (Mare kick)
Jax — Smith 70 pass from Fiedler (Hollis kick)
Jax — Whitted 38 pass from Fiedler (Hollis kick)
Jax — Howard 5 run (Hollis kick)

NFC DIVISIONAL PLAYOFF GAME

TAMPA BAY 14, WASHINGTON 13—at Raymond James Stadium, attendance 65,835. Turnovers set up both of Tampa Bay's second half touchdowns, and an errant snap squashed the Redskins' field-goal attempt in the final minutes as the Buccaneers earned their first trip to the NFC Championship Game since 1979. The Redskins' defense forced 6 first-half punts, and Brett Conway's 28-yard field goal gave the Redskins a 3-0 halftime lead. Brian Mitchell returned the second half's opening kickoff 100 yards for a touchdown, and Darrell Green's interception in Buccaneers' territory set up Conway's second field goal to give Washington a 13-0 lead. John Lynch's interception at the Redskins' 27 sparked the Buccaneers' offense, which needed just 6 plays, capped by Mike Alstott's 2-yard run, to cut the deficit to 13-7 late in the third quarter. Warren Sapp recovered Brad Johnson's fumble at the Redskins' 32 early in the fourth quarter, and Alstott converted a fourth-and-1 to set up Shaun King's 1-yard touchdown pass to John Davis with 7:29 remaining. The Redskins reached the Buccaneers' 33 with 1:08 left, but Conway never got a chance to attempt the winning kick because of a poor snap by Dan Turk, which allowed Floyd Young to sack the holder, Johnson. King was 15 of 32 for 157 yards and 1 touchdown, with 1 interception. Johnson was 20 of 32 for 149 yards, with 1 interception. Both defenses were stifling, as Tampa Bay outgained Washington 186-157.

Washington	0	3	10	0	—	13
Tampa Bay	0	0	7	7	—	14

Wash — FG Conway 28
Wash — Mitchell 100 kickoff return (Conway kick)
Wash — FG Conway 48
TB — Alstott 2 run (Gramatica kick)
TB — Davis 1 pass from King (Gramatica kick)

SUNDAY, JANUARY 16
NFC DIVISIONAL PLAYOFF GAME

ST. LOUIS 49, MINNESOTA 37—at Trans World Dome, attendance 66,194. Kurt Warner passed for 391 yards and 5 touchdowns to put the Rams in the NFC Championship Game for the first time since 1989. Gary Anderson's 31-yard field goal capped the game's first drive, but on the Rams' first play, Warner found Isaac Bruce on a post pattern for a 77-yard touchdown. It took the Rams' four plays to score on their next possession, capped by Marshall Faulk's 41-yard scoring screen pass. The Vikings drove 96 yards to cut the deficit to 14-10, and Robert Griffith's fumble recovery near midfield set up Leroy Hoard's 4-yard scoring run to give the Vikings a 17-14 halftime lead. Trailing at halftime at home for the first time all season, Tony Horne promptly returned the second half's opening kickoff 95 yards for a touchdown. While the Vikings failed to gain a first down on their first four possessions (three punts and a fumble) of the second half, the Rams scored touchdowns on four of their first five possessions, capped by Warner's 2-yard touchdown pass to Roland Williams to give the Rams a 49-17 lead with 8:13 remaining. Jeff George engineered touchdown drives of 75, 63, and 85 yards in the final minutes. Warner was 27 of 33 for 391 yards and 5 touchdowns, with 1 interception, and completed passes to 10 different Rams. Bruce had 4 receptions for 133 yards. George was 29 of 50 for 423 yards and 4 touchdowns, with 1 interception. Randy Moss had 9 catches for 188 yards, and Cris Carter had 7 for 106 yards.

Minnesota	3	14	0	20	—	37
St. Louis	14	0	21	14	—	49

Minn — FG Anderson 31
StL — Bruce 77 pass from Warner (Wilkins kick)
StL — Faulk 41 pass from Warner (Wilkins kick)
Minn — Carter 22 pass from George (Anderson kick)
Minn — Hoard 4 run (Anderson kick)
StL — Horne 95 kickoff return (Wilkins kick)
StL — Faulk 1 run (Wilkins kick)
StL — Robinson 13 pass from Warner (Wilkins kick)
StL — Tucker 1 pass from Warner (Wilkins kick)
StL — Williams 2 pass from Warner (Wilkins kick)
Minn — Reed 4 pass from George (Hoard run)
Minn — Moss 44 pass from George (pass failed)
Minn — Moss 2 pass from George (pass failed)

AFC DIVISIONAL PLAYOFF GAME

TENNESSEE 19, INDIANAPOLIS 16—at RCA Dome, attendance 57,097. Eddie George rushed for 162 yards and scored the Titans' lone touchdown as the franchise formerly known as the Houston Oilers reached its first AFC Championship Game since 1979. The Colts led 9-6 at halftime, but George's 68-yard touchdown run on the third play of the second half gave the Titans a 13-9 lead. While the Colts had to punt to conclude their first four possessions of the second half, an Al Del Greco field goal gave Tennessee a 16-6 lead, and after an instant-replay reversal ruled that Terrence Wilkins stepped out of bounds on his own 34 during an 87-yard punt return, Del Greco added a second field goal to give the Titans a 19-9 lead with 4:19 left. The Colts were stopped on downs, but George fumbled three plays later, and Mark Thomas recovered with 3:11 left. Peyton Manning scrambled 15 yards for a touchdown to cut the deficit to 19-16 with 1:51 left, but Yancey Thigpen recovered the ensuing onside kick and the Colts had no timeouts to stop the clock. Steve McNair was 13 of 24 for 112 yards. Manning was 19 of 43 for 227 yards.

Tennessee	0	6	7	6	—	19
Indianapolis	3	6	0	7	—	16

Ind — FG Vanderjagt 40
Tenn — FG Del Greco 49
Ind — FG Vanderjagt 40
Tenn — FG Del Greco 37
Ind — FG Vanderjagt 34
Tenn — George 68 run (Del Greco kick)
Tenn — FG Del Greco 25
Tenn — FG Del Greco 43
Ind — Manning 15 run (Vanderjagt kick)

TWENTIETH WEEK SUMMARIES
SUNDAY, JANUARY 23, 2000
AFC CHAMPIONSHIP PLAYOFF GAME

TENNESSEE 33, JACKSONVILLE 14—at ALLTEL Stadium, attendance 75,206. Steve McNair rushed for 91 yards and 2 touchdowns and the Titans' defense forced 6 turnovers to earn the franchise's first-ever trip to the Super Bowl. The Jaguars marched 62 yards with their first possession and took a 7-0 lead on Mark Brunell's 7-yard touchdown pass to Kyle Brady. The Titans responded with a 44-yard kickoff return by Derrick Mason to set up McNair's tying touchdown pass to Yancey Thigpen. The Jaguars led 14-7 with 1:34 left in the first half when Reggie Barlow fumbled a punt at his own 19 and Steve Jackson recovered to set up Al Del Greco's 34-yard field goal. A roughing-the-passer and defensive-pass-interference penalties on the Titans' first drive of the second half set up McNair's 1-yard sneak to give the Titans a 17-10 lead. A fumble gave Tennessee excellent field position, but Frank Wycheck fumbled at the Jaguars' 1 and Lonnie Marts recovered. The Titans responded as Josh Evans sacked Brunell for a safety, and Derrick Mason returned the ensuinmg free kick 85 yards for a touchdown, to give Tennessee a 26-10 lead with 4:56 remaining in the third quarter. The Jaguars committed three turnovers in the fourth quarter, one of which led to a 51-yard scramble on third down by McNair to set up his second touchdown and finish the scoring. McNair was 14 of 23 for 112 yards and 1 touchdown, with 1 interception. Brunell was 19 of 38 for 226 yards and 1 touchdown, with 2 interceptions. Fred Taylor had 19 carries for 110 yards.

Tennessee	7	3	16	7	—	33
Jacksonville	7	7	0	0	—	14

Jax — Brady 7 pass from Brunell (Hollis kick)
Tenn — Thigpen 9 pass from McNair (Del Greco kick)
Jax — Stewart 33 run (Hollis kick)
Tenn — FG Del Greco 34
Tenn — McNair 1 run (Del Greco kick)
Tenn — Safety, Evans sacked Brunell in end zone
Tenn — Mason 80 kickoff return (Del Greco kick)
Tenn — McNair 1 run (Del Greco kick)

NFC CHAMPIONSHIP PLAYOFF GAME

ST. LOUIS 11, TAMPA BAY 6—at Trans World Dome, attendance 66,396. Kurt Warner's 30-yard touchdown pass to Ricky Proehl with 4:44 remaining lifted the Rams to their first Super Bowl in 20 seasons. On the game's first play, Steve White intercepted Warner's pass at the Rams' 20, but the Buccaneers had to settle for Martin Gramatica's field goal. The Rams immediatly responded with a field goal by Jeff Wilkins and took a 5-3 lead when Tony Mayberry's Shotgun snap from the Buccaneers' 20 on the first play of the second quarter sailed over Shaun King's head. King batted the ball out of the end zone for a safety, but Wilkins, who was battling patellar tendinitis in his non-kicking knee, missed a 44-yard attempt on the Rams' next possession. Todd Lyght's interception at the Rams' 33 just before the half allowed the Rams to maintain their 5-3 lead. King's 32-yard pass to Jacquez Green led to Gramatica's 23-yard field goal early in the third quarter, giving the Buccaneers a 6-5 lead. Warner was intercepted on the Rams' next two possessions, including once by Hardy Nickerson at the Buccaneers' 2, to maintain Tampa Bay's one-point lead. On third-and-11 from midfield with just over eight minutes remaining, Dre' Bly intercepted King's pass and returned it 9 yards to the Buccaneers' 44. Six plays later, on third-and-4 from the Buccaneers' 30, Warner read the blitz and lofted the ball down the left sideline to Proehl, who made a one-handed catch in the end zone despite Brian Kelly's step-for-step defense. The Buccaneers mounted one last attack, but King was sacked twice in the final two minutes, and his fourth-and-11 Hail Mary pass from the Rams' 35 was knocked down in the end zone. Warner was 26 of 43 for 258 yards and 1 touchdown, with 3 interceptions. Proehl, who had not caught a touchdown pass all season, finished with 6 receptions for 100 yards. King was 13 of 29 for 163 yards, with 2 interceptions.

Tampa Bay	3	0	3	0	—	6
St. Louis	3	2	0	6	—	11

TB — FG Gramatica 25
StL — FG Wilkins 24
StL — Safety, Mayberry's Shotgun snap went out of end zone
TB — FG Gramatica 23
StL — Proehl 30 pass from Warner (pass failed)

TWENTY-FIRST WEEK SUMMARY
SUNDAY, JANUARY 30, 2000
SUPER BOWL XXXIV

ST. LOUIS 23, TENNESSEE 16—at Georgia Dome, attendance 72,625. Mike Jones tackled Kevin Dyson at the 1-yard line as time expired, preserving the Rams' first-ever Super Bowl title. The Rams drove inside the Titans' 20 with each of their first six possessions, but compiled just 3 field goals and 1 touchdown to take a 16-0 lead. Holder Rick Tuten's bobbled snap averted a 35-yard field-goal attempt to conclude the Rams' first drive. The Titans responded with a 42-yard drive, their longest of the half, but Al Del Greco missed a 47-yard attempt. Jeff Wilkins added 3 field goals and missed a 34-yard attempt while the Titans did not threaten the rest of the half, giving the Rams a 9-0 lead at intermission despite outgaining the Titans in total yards (294-89). Tennessee drove 43 yards with the second half's opening kickoff, but Todd Lyght blocked Del Greco's 47-yard attempt to keep the Titans off the board. Kurt Warner's 31-yard pass to Isaac Bruce keyed the ensuing drive that was capped by Warner's 9-yard touchdown pass to Torry Holt with 7:20 left in the third quarter to give the Rams a 16-0 lead. The Titans responded with touchdown drives in excess of seven minutes on each of their next two possessions. Steve McNair's 23-yard scramble set up Eddie George's 1-yard run in the final minute of the third quarter. McNair's 2-point conversion pass to Frank Wycheck was incomplete, but the Titans' defense forced a punt and the offense drove 79 yards in 13 plays, highlighted by 21-yard passes from McNair to Isaac Byrd and Jackie Harris, and capped by George's 2-yard run to cut the deficit to 16-13 with 7:21 remaining. The Rams once again failed to get a first down, and following a punt, the Titans needed just 28 yards to set up Del Greco's game-tying 43-yard kick with 2:12 left. On the next play from scrimmage, Warner fired a deep pass down the right sideline to Bruce, who caught the ball at the Titans' 38, cut toward the inside, and outran the defense to the end zone to give the Rams a 23-16 lead with 1:54 left. The Titans drove downfield, and McNair avoided a sack and completed a 16-yard pass to Kevin Dyson to place Tennessee at the Rams' 10 with six seconds remaining. With no timeouts, McNair attempted a quick pass to a slanting Dyson, who caught the ball in stride at the Rams' 3. However, Jones reacted quickly and stepped up to tackle Dyson at the 1-yard line as time expired. Warner, who was named the game's most valuable player, was 24 of 45 for a Super Bowl-record 414 yards and 2 touchdowns. Bruce had 6 catches for 162 yards, and Holt had 7 for 109 yards. McNair was 22 of 36 for 214 yards. The Titans were the first team in Super Bowl history to comeback from a 16-point deficit.

St. Louis	3	6	7	7	—	23
Tennessee	0	0	6	10	—	16

StL — FG Wilkins 27
StL — FG Wilkins 29
StL — FG Wilkins 28
StL — Holt 9 pass from Warner (Wilkins kick)
Tenn — George 1 run (pass failed)
Tenn — George 2 run (Del Greco kick)
Tenn — FG Del Greco 43
StL — Bruce 73 pass from Warner (Wilkins kick)

TWENTY-SECOND WEEK SUMMARY
SUNDAY, FEBRUARY 6, 2000
2000 PRO BOWL GAME

AFC 23, NFC 10—at Aloha Stadium, attendance 50,075. Randy Moss earned player-of-the-game honors by setting records with 9 receptions for 212 yards as the NFC defeated the AFC in the highest-scoring Pro Bowl ever. Aeneas Williams intercepted Peyton Manning's pass and raced 62 yards down the left sideline to give the NFC an early 7-0 lead. Kurt Warner's 48-yard pass to Moss on the NFC's first possession set up Jason Hanson's first field goal. Mike Alstott and Jimmy Smith each scored twice in the first half, and Michael Bates's 66-yard kickoff return led to Hanson's Pro Bowl-record tying 51-yard field goal as the half expired to give the NFC a 27-21 lead. Alstott's third touchdown increased the NFC's lead to 37-21, and Derrick Brooks's interception of Mark Brunell and 20-yard return staked the NFC to a 44-24 lead with 11:12 left. The AFC responded with Manning's 52-yard touchdown pass to Smith with 6:30 remaining, but Steve Beuerlein found Moss with a 25-yard scoring pass with 1:05 left to finish the scoring. Warner led the three NFC quarterbacks by completing 8 of 11 passes for 123 yards. Alstott led all rushers with 13 carries for 67 yards. The NFC forced 6 turnovers. Manning was 17 of 23 for 270 yards and 2 touchdowns, with 2 interceptions. Smith had 8 receptions for 119 yards. The previous record, 64 points, was set in 1980.

AFC	7	14	0	10	—	31
NFC	10	17	10	14	—	51

NFC — A. Williams 62 interception return (Hanson kick)
NFC — FG Hanson 21
AFC — J. Smith 5 pass from Brunell (Mare kick)
NFC — Alstott 1 run (Hanson kick)
AFC — Gonzalez 10 pass from Gannon (Mare kick)
NFC — Alstott 3 run (Hanson kick)
AFC — J. Smith 21 pass from Manning (Mare kick)
NFC — FG Hanson 51
NFC — Alstott 1 run (Hanson kick)
NFC — FG Hanson 23
AFC — FG Mare 33
NFC — Brooks 20 interception return (Hanson kick)
AFC — J. Smith 52 pass from Manning (Mare kick)
NFC — Moss 25 pass from Beuerlein (Hanson kick)

1999 PRO FOOTBALL AWARDS

	NFL	AFC	NFC
ASSOCIATED PRESS			
Most Valuable Player	Kurt Warner		
Offensive Player of the Year	Marshall Faulk		
Defensive Player of the Year	Warren Sapp		
Offensive Rookie of the Year	Edgerrin James		
Defensive Rookie of the Year	Jevon Kearse		
Coach of the Year	Dick Vermeil		
Comeback Player of the Year	Bryant Young		
THE SPORTING NEWS			
Player of the Year	Kurt Warner		
Rookie of the Year	Edgerrin James		
Coach of the Year	Dick Vermeil		
FOOTBALL NEWS			
Player of the Year		Peyton Manning	Marshall Faulk
Coach of the Year	Dick Vermeil		
Offensive Rookie of the Year	Edgerrin James		
Defensive Rookie of the Year	Jevon Kearse		
PRO FOOTBALL WEEKLY/PFWA			
Executive of the Year	Bill Polian		
Most Valuable Player	Kurt Warner		
Defensive Most Valuable Player	Warren Sapp		
Defensive Rookie of the Year	Jevon Kearse		
Offensive Rookie of the Year	Edgerrin James		
Coach of the Year	Dick Vermeil		
Assistant Coach of the Year	Dom Capers		
Golden Toe	Craig Hentrich		
Comeback Player of the Year	Bryant Young		
FOOTBALL DIGEST			
Player of the Year	Kurt Warner		
Defensive Player of the Year	Warren Sapp		
Offensive Rookie of the Year	Edgerrin James		
Defensive Rookie of the Year	Jevon Kearse		
Coach of the Year	Dick Vermeil		
Comeback Player of the Year	Bryant Young		
Rookie Coach of the Year	Gunther Cunningham		
Offensive Coordinator of the Year	Mike Martz		
Defensive Coordinator of the Year	Dom Capers		
Executive of the Year	Bill Polian		
SPORTS ILLUSTRATED			
Player of the Year	Kurt Warner		
Coach of the Year	Dick Vermeil		
Rookie of the Year	Edgerrin James		
USA TODAY			
Coach of the Year		Jeff Fisher	Dick Vermeil
Offensive Rookie of the Year	Edgerrin James		
Defensive Rookie of the Year	Jevon Kearse		
Assistant Coach of the Year		Dom Capers	Mike Martz
COLLEGE AND PRO FOOTBALL NEWSWEEKLY			
Offensive Player of the Year	Marshall Faulk		
Defensive Player of the Year	Warren Sapp		
Offensive Rookie of the Year	Edgerrin James		
Defensive Rookie of the Year	Jevon Kearse		
Coach of the Year	Dick Vermeil		
Rookie Coach of the Year	(tie) Brian Billick Gunther Cunningham		
MAXWELL CLUB			
Player of the Year (Bert Bell Trophy)	Kurt Warner		
Coach of the Year (Earle "Greasy" Neale Trophy)	Dick Vermeil		
MILLER LITE PLAYER OF THE YEAR	Kurt Warner		
WALTER PAYTON NFL MAN OF THE YEAR	Cris Carter		
SUPER BOWL MOST VALUABLE PLAYER (Pete Rozelle Trophy)	Kurt Warner		
AFC-NFC PRO BOWL PLAYER OF THE GAME (Dan McGuire Award)	Randy Moss		

1999 PLAYERS OF THE WEEK/MONTH

1999 AFC PLAYERS OF THE WEEK

Week	Offense		Defense		Special Teams	
Week 1	QB	Dan Marino, Miami	DE	Willie McGinest, New England	K	Al Del Greco, Tennessee
Week 2	QB	Drew Bledsoe, New England	CB	Sam Madison, Miami	K	Kris Brown, Pittsburgh
Week 3	QB	Peyton Manning, Indianapolis	LB	Peter Boulware, Baltimore	KR	Charlie Rogers, Seattle
Week 4	WR	Terry Glenn, New England	LB	John Holecek, Buffalo	P	Bryan Barker, Jacksonville
Week 5	QB	Dan Marino, Miami	S	Rodney Harrison, San Diego	P	Bryan Barker, Jacksonville
Week 6	QB	Brian Griese, Denver	CB	Sam Madison, Miami	K	Olindo Mare, Miami
Week 7	WR	Tim Brown, Oakland	CB	James Hasty, Kansas City	K	Kris Brown, Pittsburgh
Week 8	RB	Edgerrin James, Indianapolis	CB	Shawn Springs, Seattle	PR	Nate Jacquet, Miami
Week 9	QB	Doug Flutie, Buffalo	CB	Sam Madison, Miami	K	Jason Elam, Denver
Week 10	QB	Rich Gannon, Oakland	CB	Marcus Coleman, New York Jets	P	Bryan Barker, Jacksonville
Week 11	RB	Edgerrin James, Indianapolis	LB	Glenn Cadrez, Denver	K	Matt Stover, Baltimore
Week 12	QB	Mark Brunell, Jacksonville	CB	Cris Dishman, Kansas City	KR	Derrick Mason, Tennessee
Week 13	QB	Jeff Blake, Cincinnati	DE	Michael McCrary, Baltimore	K	Mike Vanderjagt, Indianapolis
Week 14	WR	Qadry Ismail, Baltimore	LB	Eddie Robinson, Tennessee	K	John Carney, San Diego
Week 15	RB	Olandis Gary, Denver	LB	Donnie Edwards, Kansas City	K	Olindo Mare, Miami
Week 16	QB	Steve McNair, Tennessee	LB	Levon Kirkland, Pittsburgh	K	Matt Stover, Baltimore
Week 17	QB	Rob Johnson, Buffalo	LB	Ted Johnson, New England	K	John Hall, New York Jets

1999 AFC PLAYERS OF THE MONTH

Month	Offense		Defense		Special Teams	
September	WR	Marvin Harrison, Indianapolis	CB	Aaron Beasley, Jacksonville	K	Adam Vinatieri, New England
October	QB	Jon Kitna, Seattle	DE	Tony Brackens, Jacksonville	K	Olindo Mare, Miami
November	RB	Edgerrin James, Indianapolis	DE	Tony Brackens, Jacksonville	P	Tom Tupa, New York Jets
December	WR	Jimmy Smith, Jacksonville	DE	Jevon Kearse, Tennessee	P	Jeff Feagles, Seattle

1999 NFC PLAYERS OF THE WEEK

Week	Offense		Defense		Special Teams	
Week 1	QB	Troy Aikman, Dallas	DE	Robert Porcher, Detroit	K	Chris Jacke, Arizona
Week 2	QB	Brad Johnson, Washington	DT	Warren Sapp, Tampa Bay	KR	Terry Fair, Detroit
Week 3	QB	Kurt Warner, St. Louis	DE	Kenard Lang, Washington	LB	John McLaughlin, Tampa Bay
Week 4	QB	Brad Johnson, Washington	DT	John Randle, Minnesota	PR	Az-Zahir Hakim, St. Louis
Week 5	WR	Isaac Bruce, St. Louis	LB	Barry Minter, Chicago	K	Ryan Longwell, Green Bay
Week 6	RB	Marshall Faulk, St. Louis	CB	Champ Bailey, Washington	K	Jason Hanson, Detroit
		RB-PR Tiki Barber, New York Giants (PRIME TIME II AWARD)				
Week 7	QB	Jeff George, Minnesota	LB	Derrick Brooks, Tampa Bay	P	Toby Gowin, Dallas
Week 8	WR	Cris Carter, Minnesota	DE	Chuck Smith, Atlanta	DT	Christian Peter, New York Giants
Week 9	WR	Germane Crowell, Detroit	LB	Kevin Greene, Carolina	DE	Bryan Robinson, Chicago
Week 10	WR	Randy Moss, Minnesota	DE	Kevin Carter, St. Louis	KR	Allen Rossum, Philadelphia
Week 11	RB	Stephen Davis, Washington	CB	Donnie Abraham, Tampa Bay	K	Martin Gramatica, Tampa Bay
Week 12	WR	Cris Carter, Minnesota	LB	Dexter Coakley, Dallas	KR	Tony Horne, St. Louis
Week 13	QB	Kerry Collins, New York Giants	CB	Donnie Abraham, Tampa Bay	PR	Desmond Howard, Detroit
Week 14	QB	Steve Beuerlein, Carolina	DT	Bryant Young, San Francisco	K	Cary Blanchard, New York Giants
Week 15	WR	Marcus Robinson, Chicago	DE	Mike Mamula, Philadelphia	P	Mitch Berger, Minnesota
Week 16	RB	Marshall Faulk, St. Louis	CB	Fred Weary, New Orleans	KR	Moe Williams, Minnesota
Week 17	RB	Dorsey Levens, Green Bay	DT	John Randle, Minnesota	PR	Tim Dwight, Atlanta

1999 NFC PLAYERS OF THE MONTH

Month	Offense		Defense		Special Teams	
September	QB	Brett Favre, Green Bay	DT	Warren Sapp, Tampa Bay	P	Mitch Berger, Minnesota
October	QB	Kurt Warner, St. Louis	LB	Jessie Armstead, New York Giants	K	Jason Hanson, Detroit
November	WR	Cris Carter, Minnesota	DE	Kevin Carter, St. Louis	K	Martin Gramatica, Tampa Bay
December	WR	Patrick Jeffers, Carolina	DT	John Randle, Minnesota	KR	Jason Tucker, Dallas

1999 PLAYOFF PLAYERS OF THE WEEK

Round	Offense		Defense		Special Teams	
Wild Card	RB	Robert Smith, Minnesota	DE	Trace Armstrong, Miami	WR	Kevin Dyson & TE Frank Wycheck, Tennessee
Divisional	QB	Kurt Warner, St. Louis	DE	Steve White, Tampa Bay	K	Al Del Greco, Tennessee
Championship	QB	Steve McNair, Tennessee	CB	Dre' Bly, St. Louis	KR	Derrick Mason, Tennessee

1999 ROOKIES OF THE MONTH

Month	Offense (College)		Defense (College)
September	RB	Edgerrin James, Indianapolis (Miami)	DE Jevon Kearse, Tennessee (Florida)
October	QB	Tim Couch, Cleveland (Kentucky)	CB Champ Bailey, Washington (Georgia)
November	RB	Edgerrin James, Indianapolis (Miami)	DE Jevon Kearse, Tennessee (Florida)
December	QB	Shaun King, Tampa Bay (Tulane)	DE Jevon Kearse, Tennessee (Florida)

1999 PFW/PFWA ALL-PRO TEAM

Selected by Pro Football Weekly *and the Professional Football Writers of America*

Offense

Marvin Harrison, Indianapolis	Wide Receiver
Cris Carter, Minnesota	Wide Receiver
Tony Gonzalez, Kansas City	Tight End
Tony Boselli, Jacksonville	Tackle
Orlando Pace, St. Louis	Tackle
Larry Allen, Dallas	Guard
Bruce Matthews, Tennessee	Guard
Jeff Christy, Minnesota	Center
Kurt Warner, St. Louis	Quarterback
Marshall Faulk, St. Louis	Running Back
Edgerrin James, Indianapolis	Running Back

Defense

Jevon Kearse, Tennessee	End
Kevin Carter, St. Louis	End
Warren Sapp, Tampa Bay	Tackle
Darrell Russell, Oakland	Tackle
Derrick Brooks, Tampa Bay	Linebacker
Kevin Hardy, Jacksonville	Linebacker
Ray Lewis, Baltimore	Linebacker
Sam Madison, Miami	Cornerback
Charles Woodson, Oakland	Cornerback
John Lynch, Tampa Bay	Safety
Carnell Lake, Jacksonville	Safety

Specialists

Olindo Mare, Miami	Kicker
Mitch Berger, Minnesota	Punter
Tony Horne, St. Louis	Kick Returner
Charlie Rogers, Seattle	Punt Returner
Michael Bates, Carolina	Special Teams Player

1999 ASSOCIATED PRESS ALL-PRO TEAM

Selected by the Associated Press

Offense

Marvin Harrison, Indianapolis	Wide Receiver
Cris Carter, Minnesota	Wide Receiver
Tony Gonzalez, Kansas City	Tight End
Tony Boselli, Jacksonville	Tackle
Orlando Pace, St. Louis	Tackle
Larry Allen, Dallas	Guard
Bruce Matthews, Tennessee	Guard
Kevin Mawae, New York Jets	Center
Kurt Warner, St. Louis	Quarterback
Marshall Faulk, St. Louis	Running Back
Edgerrin James, Indianapolis	Running Back
Mike Alstott, Tampa Bay	Fullback

Defense

Jevon Kearse, Tennessee	End
Kevin Carter, St. Louis	End
Trevor Pryce, Denver	Tackle
Warren Sapp, Tampa Bay	Tackle
Derrick Brooks, Tampa Bay	Linebacker
Kevin Hardy, Jacksonville	Linebacker
Ray Lewis, Baltimore	Linebacker
Zach Thomas, Miami	Linebacker
Sam Madison, Miami	Cornerback
Charles Woodson, Oakland	Cornerback
John Lynch, Tampa Bay	Safety
Lawyer Milloy, New England	Safety

Specialists

Olindo Mare, Miami	Kicker
Glyn Milburn, Chicago	Kick Returner
Tom Tupa, New York Jets	Punter

1999 ALL-NFL TEAM

Selected by the Associated Press, Pro Football Weekly, *and the Professional Football Writers of America*

Offense

Marvin Harrison, Indianapolis (AP, PFW)	Wide Receiver
Cris Carter, Minnesota (AP, PFW)	Wide Receiver
Tony Gonzalez, Kansas City (AP, PFW)	Tight End
Tony Boselli, Jacksonville (AP, PFW)	Tackle
Orlando Pace, St. Louis (AP, PFW)	Tackle
Larry Allen, Dallas (AP, PFW)	Guard
Bruce Matthews, Tennessee (AP, PFW)	Guard
Jeff Christy, Minnesota (PFW)	Center
Kevin Mawae, New York Jets (AP)	Center
Kurt Warner, St. Louis (AP, PFW)	Quarterback
Marshall Faulk, St. Louis (AP, PFW)	Running Back
Edgerrin James, Indianapolis (AP, PFW)	Running Back
Mike Alstott, Tampa Bay (AP)	Fullback

Defense

Jevon Kearse, Tennessee (AP, PFW)	End
Kevin Carter, St. Louis (AP, PFW)	End
Warren Sapp, Tampa Bay (AP, PFW)	Tackle
Trevor Pryce, Denver (AP)	Tackle
Darrell Russell, Oakland (PFW)	Tackle
Derrick Brooks, Tampa Bay (AP, PFW)	Linebacker
Kevin Hardy, Jacksonville (AP, PFW)	Linebacker
Ray Lewis, Baltimore (AP, PFW)	Linebacker
Zach Thomas, Miami (AP)	Linebacker
Sam Madison, Miami (AP, PFW)	Cornerback
Charles Woodson, Oakland (AP, PFW)	Cornerback
John Lynch, Tampa Bay (AP, PFW)	Safety
Carnell Lake, Jacksonville (PFW)	Safety
Lawyer Milloy, New England (AP)	Safety

Specialists

Olindo Mare, Miami (AP, PFW)	Kicker
Mitch Berger, Minnesota (PFW)	Punter
Tom Tupa, New York Jets (AP)	Punter
Tony Horne, St. Louis (PFW)	Kick Returner
Glyn Milburn, Chicago (AP)	Kick Returner
Charlie Rogers, Seattle (PFW)	Punt Returner
Michael Bates, Carolina (PFW)	Special Teams Player

1999 ALL-PRO TEAMS

1999 FOOTBALL NEWS ALL-AFC TEAM

Selected by Football News

Offense

Jimmy Smith, Jacksonville	Wide Receiver
Marvin Harrison, Indianapolis	Wide Receiver
Tony Gonzalez, Kansas City	Tight End
Tony Boselli, Jacksonville	Tackle
Tarik Glenn, Indianapolis	Tackle
Bruce Matthews, Tennessee	Guard
Will Shields, Kansas City	Guard
Kevin Mawae, New York Jets	Center
Peyton Manning, Indianapolis	Quarterback
Curtis Martin, New York Jets	Running Back
Edgerrin James, Indianapolis	Running Back

Defense

Jevon Kearse, Tennessee	End
Tony Brackens, Jacksonville	End
Darrell Russell, Oakland	Tackle
Ted Washington, Buffalo	Tackle
Kevin Hardy, Jacksonville	Linebacker
Peter Boulware, Baltimore	Linebacker
Ray Lewis, Baltimore	Linebacker
Shawn Springs, Seattle	Cornerback
Sam Madison, Miami	Cornerback
Lawyer Milloy, New England	Safety
Carnell Lake, Jacksonville	Safety

Specialists

Charlie Rogers, Seattle	Punt Returner
Darren Bennett, San Diego	Punter
Tremain Mack, Cincinnati	Kick Returner
Mike Vanderjagt, Indianapolis	Kicker

1999 FOOTBALL NEWS ALL-NFC TEAM

Selected by Football News

Offense

Cris Carter, Minnesota	Wide Receiver
Isaac Bruce, St. Louis	Wide Receiver
Wesley Walls, Carolina	Tight End
Orlando Pace, St. Louis	Tackle
Erik Williams, Dallas	Tackle
Larry Allen, Dallas	Guard
Tre Johnson, Washington	Guard
Jeff Christy, Minnesota	Center
Kurt Warner, St. Louis	Quarterback
Stephen Davis, Washington	Running Back
Marshall Faulk, St. Louis	Running Back

Defense

Kevin Carter, St. Louis	End
Robert Porcher, Detroit	End
Warren Sapp, Tampa Bay	Tackle
Luther Elliss, Detroit	Tackle
Derrick Brooks, Tampa Bay	Linebacker
Jessie Armstead, New York Giants	Linebacker
Stephen Boyd, Detroit	Linebacker
Deion Sanders, Dallas	Cornerback
Todd Lyght, St. Louis	Cornerback
John Lynch, Tampa Bay	Safety
Brian Dawkins, Philadelphia	Safety

Specialists

Glyn Milburn, Chicago	Punt Returner
Mitch Berger, Minnesota	Punter
Tony Horne, St. Louis	Kick Returner
Jason Hanson, Detroit	Kicker

1999 PFW/PFWA ALL-ROOKIE TEAM

Selected by Pro Football Weekly *and the Professional Football Writers of America*

Offense

Kevin Johnson, Cleveland	Wide Receiver
Torry Holt, St. Louis	Wide Receiver
Jed Weaver, Philadelphia	Tight End
Jon Jansen, Washington	Tackle
Chris Terry, Carolina	Tackle
Randy Thomas, New York Jets	Guard
Doug Brzezinski, Philadelphia	Guard
Damien Woody, New England	Center
Tim Couch, Cleveland	Quarterback
Edgerrin James, Indianapolis	Running Back
Olandis Gary, Denver	Running Back

Defense

Jevon Kearse, Tennessee	End
Russell Davis, Chicago	End
Ebenezer Ekuban, Dallas	End
John Thorton, Tennessee	Tackle
Chris Claiborne, Detroit	Linebacker
Andy Katzenmoyer, New England	Linebacker
Mike Peterson, Indianapolis	Linebacker
Champ Bailey, Washington	Cornerback
Fernando Bryant, Jacksonville	Cornerback
Cory Hall, Cincinnati	Safety
Jason Perry, San Diego	Safety

Specialists

Martin Gramatica, Tampa Bay	Kicker
Hunter Smith, Indianapolis	Punter
Terrence Wilkins, Indianapolis	Kick Returner
Charlie Rogers, Seattle	Punt Returner
John McLaughlin, Tampa Bay	Special Teams Player

TEN BEST RUSHING PERFORMANCES, 1999

		Att.	Yards	TD
1.	Eddie George Tennessee vs. Oakland, Dec. 9	28	199	2
2.	Corey Dillon Cincinnati vs. Cleveland, Dec. 12	28	192	3
3.	Stephen Davis Washington vs. Arizona, Dec. 12	37	189	1
4.	Olandis Gary Denver vs. Detroit, Dec. 25	29	185	1
5.	Stephen Davis Washington vs. N.Y. Giants, Nov. 21	33	183	1
	Jermaine Fazande San Diego vs. Denver, Jan. 2	30	183	1
	Olandis Gary Denver vs. Seattle, Dec. 19	22	183	0
8.	Marshall Faulk St. Louis vs. Atlanta, Oct. 17	18	181	1
9.	Ricky Williams New Orleans vs. Cleveland, Oct. 31	40	179	0
10.	Corey Dillon Cincinnati vs. Cleveland, Oct. 10	28	168	0

100-YARD RUSHING PERFORMANCES, 1999

First Week

Edgerrin James, Indianapolis — 112 yards vs. Buffalo
Stephen Davis, Washington — 109 yards vs. Dallas
Emmitt Smith, Dallas — 109 yards vs. Washington
Duce Staley, Philadelphia — 103 yards vs. Arizona

Second Week

Dorsey Levens, Green Bay — 153 yards vs. Detroit
Kimble Anders, Kansas City — 142 yards vs. Denver
Stephen Davis, Washington — 126 yards vs. N.Y. Giants
James Stewart, Jacksonville — 124 yards vs. Carolina
Edgerrin James, Indianapolis — 118 yards vs. New England
Antowain Smith, Buffalo — 113 yards vs. N.Y. Jets
Emmitt Smith, Dallas — 109 yards vs. Atlanta
Errict Rhett, Baltimore — 101 yards vs. Pittsburgh

Third Week

Tshimanga Biakabutuka, Carolina — 132 yards vs. Cincinnati
Mike Alstott, Tampa Bay — 131 yards vs. Denver
Errict Rhett, Baltimore — 113 yards vs. Cleveland
Corey Dillon, Cincinnati — 113 yards vs. Carolina
Marshall Faulk, St. Louis — 105 yards vs. Atlanta
Lawrence Phillips, San Francisco — 102 yards vs. Arizona

Fourth Week

Tshimanga Biakabutuka, Carolina — 142 yards vs. Washington
Errict Rhett, Baltimore — 136 yards vs. Atlanta
Tyrone Wheatley, Oakland — 100 yards vs. Seattle

Fifth Week

Corey Dillon, Cincinnati — 168 yards vs. Cleveland
Emmitt Smith, Dallas — 114 yards vs. Philadelphia
Duce Staley, Philadelphia — 110 yards vs. Dallas
Robert Smith, Minnesota — 107 yards vs. Chicago

Sixth Week

Marshall Faulk, St. Louis — 181 yards vs. Atlanta
Eddie George, Tennessee — 155 yards vs. New Orleans
Curtis Martin, N.Y. Jets — 128 yards vs. Indianapolis
Olandis Gary, Denver — 124 yards vs. Green Bay
Edgerrin James, Indianapolis — 111 yards vs. N.Y. Jets
Jerome Bettis, Pittsburgh — 111 yards vs. Cincinnati
Duce Staley, Philadelphia — 101 yards vs. Chicago

Seventh Week

Marshall Faulk, St. Louis — 133 yards vs. Cleveland
Curtis Martin, N.Y. Jets — 123 yards vs. Oakland
Ricky Williams, New Orleans — 111 yards vs. N.Y. Giants
Terry Allen, New England — 106 yards vs. Denver
Leroy Hoard, Minnesota — 105 yards vs. San Francisco

Eighth Week

Ricky Williams, New Orleans — 179 yards vs. Cleveland
Stephen Davis, Washington — 143 yards vs. Chicago
Fred Taylor, Jacksonville — 128 yards vs. Cincinnati
Ricky Watters, Seattle — 125 yards vs. Green Bay
Greg Hill, Detroit — 123 yards vs. Tampa Bay
Edgerrin James, Indianapolis — 117 yards vs. Dallas
Dorsey Levens, Green Bay — 104 yards vs. Seattle

Ninth Week

Charlie Garner, San Francisco — 166 yards vs. Pittsburgh
Duce Staley, Philadelphia — 140 yards vs. Carolina
Emmitt Smith, Dallas — 140 yards vs. Minnesota
Ricky Watters, Seattle — 133 yards vs. Cincinnati
Curtis Martin, N.Y. Jets — 131 yards vs. Arizona
Fred Taylor, Jacksonville — 124 yards vs. Atlanta
Mike Alstott, Tampa Bay — 117 yards vs. New Orleans
Errict Rhett, Baltimore — 117 yards vs. Cleveland
Edgerrin James, Indianapolis — 109 yards vs. Kansas City
Olandis Gary, Denver — 108 yards vs. San Diego

Tenth Week

Curtis Martin, N.Y. Jets — 149 yards vs. New England
Michael Pittman, Arizona — 133 yards vs. Detroit
Antowain Smith, Buffalo — 126 yards vs. Miami
Eddie George, Tennessee — 123 yards vs. Cincinnati
Duce Staley, Philadelphia — 122 yards vs. Washington
Stephen Davis, Washington — 122 yards vs. Philadelphia
Edgerrin James, Indianapolis — 108 yards vs. N.Y. Giants

Eleventh Week

Stephen Davis, Washington — 183 yards vs. N.Y. Giants
Edgerrin James, Indianapolis — 152 yards vs. Philadelphia
Emmitt Smith, Dallas — 127 yards vs. Arizona
Marshall Faulk, St. Louis — 126 yards vs. San Francisco
Ricky Watters, Seattle — 107 yards vs. Kansas City
J.J. Johnson, Miami — 106 yards vs. New England

Twelfth Week

Corey Dillon, Cincinnati — 120 yards vs. Pittsburgh
Eddie George, Tennessee — 113 yards vs. Cleveland
Robert Smith, Minnesota — 104 yards vs. San Diego
Emmitt Smith, Dallas — 103 yards vs. Miami
Marshall Faulk, St. Louis — 102 yards vs. New Orleans

Thirteenth Week

James Stewart, Jacksonville — 145 yards vs. Pittsburgh
Corey Dillon, Cincinnati — 133 yards vs. San Francisco
Edgerrin James, Indianapolis — 130 yards vs. Miami
Marshall Faulk, St. Louis — 118 yards vs. Carolina
DeMond Parker, Green Bay — 113 yards vs. Chicago
Joe Montgomery, N.Y. Giants — 111 yards vs. N.Y. Jets
Priest Holmes, Baltimore — 100 yards vs. Tennessee

Fourteenth Week

Eddie George, Tennessee — 199 yards vs. Oakland
Corey Dillon, Cincinnati — 192 yards vs. Cleveland
Stephen Davis, Washington — 189 yards vs. Arizona
Marshall Faulk, St. Louis — 154 yards vs. New Orleans
Priest Holmes, Baltimore — 130 yards vs. Pittsburgh
Robert Smith, Minnesota — 118 yards vs. Kansas City
Charlie Garner, San Francisco — 107 yards vs. Atlanta
Edgerrin James, Indianapolis — 101 yards vs. New England

Fifteenth Week

Olandis Gary, Denver — 183 yards vs. Seattle
Fred Taylor, Jacksonville — 136 yards vs. Cleveland
Napoleon Kaufman, Oakland — 122 yards vs. Tampa Bay
Ricky Watters, Seattle — 115 yards vs. Denver
Curtis Martin, N.Y. Jets — 113 yards vs. Dallas
Tyrone Wheatley, Oakland — 111 yards vs. Tampa Bay
Emmitt Smith, Dallas — 110 yards vs. N.Y. Jets

1999 BEST PERFORMANCES

Sixteenth Week

Olandis Gary, Denver	185 yards vs. Detroit
Robert Smith, Minnesota	146 yards vs. N.Y. Giants
Jerome Bettis, Pittsburgh	137 yards vs. Carolina
Charlie Garner, San Francisco	129 yards vs. Washington
Terry Allen, New England	126 yards vs. Buffalo
Emmitt Smith, Dallas	110 yards vs. New Orleans
Edgerrin James, Indianapolis	103 yards vs. Cleveland
Eddie George, Tennessee	102 yards vs. Jacksonville
Byron Hanspard, Atlanta	102 yards vs. Arizona

Seventeenth Week

Jermaine Fazande, San Diego	183 yards vs. Denver
Curtis Martin, N.Y. Jets	158 yards vs. Seattle
Dorsey Levens, Green Bay	146 yards vs. Arizona
Emmitt Smith, Dallas	122 yards vs. N.Y. Giants

Times 100 or More (108)
James, 10; E. Smith, 9; Faulk, 7; Davis, Martin, 6; Dillon, George, Staley, 5; Gary, Rhett, R. Smith, Watters, 4; Garner, Levens, Taylor, 3; Allen, Alstott, Bettis, Biakabutuka, Holmes, A. Smith, Stewart, Wheatley, Williams, 2.

TEN BEST PASSING PERFORMANCES, 1999

		Att.	Comp.	Yards	TD
1.	Brad Johnson Washington vs. San Francisco, Dec. 26	47	32	471	2
2.	Jeff Garcia San Francisco vs. Cincinnati, Dec. 5	33	49	437	3
3.	Jim Miller Chicago vs. Minnesota, Nov. 14	48	34	422	3
4.	Jim Harbaugh San Diego vs. Minnesota, Nov. 28	39	25	404	1
	Peyton Manning Indianapolis vs. San Diego, Sept. 26	54	29	404	2
6.	Jake Plummer Arizona vs. Green Bay, Jan. 2	57	35	396	2
7.	Dan Marino Miami vs. Indianapolis, Oct. 10	38	25	393	2
8.	Brett Favre Green Bay vs. Tampa Bay, Oct. 10	40	22	390	2
9.	Drew Bledsoe New England vs. Cleveland, Oct. 3	42	28	389	1
10.	Brad Johnson Washington vs. Dallas, Sept. 12	33	20	382	2

300-YARD PASSING PERFORMANCES, 1999

First Week

Brad Johnson, Washington	382 yards vs. Dallas
Troy Aikman, Dallas	362 yards vs. Washington
Steve McNair, Tennessee	341 yards vs. Cincinnati
Drew Bledsoe, New England	340 yards vs. N.Y. Jets
Brett Favre, Green Bay	333 yards vs. Oakland
Kurt Warner, St. Louis	309 yards vs. Baltimore
Doug Flutie, Buffalo	300 yards vs. Indianapolis

Second Week

Randall Cunningham, Minnesota	364 yards vs. Oakland
Neil O'Donnell, Tennessee	310 yards vs. Cleveland

Third Week

Peyton Manning, Indianapolis	404 yards vs. San Diego
Brett Favre, Green Bay	304 yards vs. Minnesota

Fourth Week

Drew Bledsoe, New England	389 yards vs. Cleveland
Neil O'Donnell, Tennessee	355 yards vs. San Francisco
Brad Johnson, Washington	337 yards vs. Carolina
Steve Beuerlein, Carolina	334 yards vs. Washington
Kurt Warner, St. Louis	310 yards vs. Cincinnati
Trent Dilfer, Tampa Bay	301 yards vs. Minnesota

Fifth Week

Dan Marino, Miami	393 yards vs. Indianapolis
Brett Favre, Green Bay	390 yards vs. Tampa Bay
Drew Bledsoe, New England	334 yards vs. Kansas City
Kurt Warner, St. Louis	323 yards vs. San Francisco
Randall Cunningham, Minnesota	309 yards vs. Chicago

Sixth Week

Brian Griese, Denver	363 yards vs. Green Bay
Billy Joe Tolliver, New Orleans	354 yards vs. Tennessee
Steve Beuerlein, Carolina	300 yards vs. San Francisco

Seventh Week

Rich Gannon, Oakland	352 yards vs. N.Y. Jets
Brian Griese, Denver	316 yards vs. New England

Eighth Week

Kurt Warner, St. Louis	328 yards vs. Tennessee
Peyton Manning, Indianapolis	313 yards vs. Dallas

Ninth Week

Kurt Warner, St. Louis	305 yards vs. Detroit

Tenth Week

Jim Miller, Chicago	422 yards vs. Minnesota
Gus Frerotte, Detroit	375 yards vs. Arizona

Jeff George, Minnesota	374 yards vs. Chicago
Brad Johnson, Washington	313 yards vs. Philadelphia
Eleventh Week	
Jim Miller, Chicago	357 yards vs. San Diego
Mark Brunell, Jacksonville	351 yards vs. New Orleans
Elvis Grbac, Kansas City	320 yards vs. Seattle
Brett Favre, Green Bay	309 yards vs. Detroit
Twelfth Week	
Jim Harbaugh, San Diego	404 yards vs. Minnesota
Jeff George, Minnesota	363 yards vs. San Diego
Mark Brunell, Jacksonville	338 yards vs. Baltimore
Chris Chandler, Atlanta	315 yards vs. Carolina
Gus Frerotte, Detroit	309 yards vs. Chicago
Thirteenth Week	
Jeff Garcia, San Francisco	437 yards vs. Cincinnati
Kurt Warner, St. Louis	351 yards vs. Carolina
Kerry Collins, N.Y. Giants	341 yards vs. N.Y. Jets
Jeff Blake, Cincinnati	334 yards vs. San Francisco
Tony Banks, Baltimore	332 yards vs. Tennessee
Dan Marino, Miami	313 yards vs. Indianapolis
Mark Brunell, Jacksonville	308 yards vs. Pittsburgh
Fourteenth Week	
Drew Bledsoe, New England	379 yards vs. Indianapolis
Steve Beuerlein, Carolina	373 yards vs. Green Bay
Kurt Warner, St. Louis	346 yards vs. New Orleans
Brett Favre, Green Bay	302 yards vs. Carolina
Fifteenth Week	
Steve Beuerlein, Carolina	368 yards vs. San Francisco
Drew Bledsoe, New England	331 yards vs. Philadelphia
Kurt Warner, St. Louis	319 yards vs. N.Y. Giants
Jeff Garcia, San Francisco	303 yards vs. Carolina
Cade McNown, Chicago	301 yards vs. Detroit
Sixteenth Week	
Brad Johnson, Washington	471 yards vs. San Francisco
Kurt Warner, St. Louis	334 yards vs. Chicago
Jim Harbaugh, San Diego	325 yards vs. Oakland
Dan Marino, Miami	322 yards vs. N.Y. Jets
Seventeenth Week	
Jake Plummer, Arizona	396 yards vs. Green Bay
Jeff Garcia, San Francisco	373 yards vs. Atlanta
Rich Gannon, Oakland	324 yards vs. Kansas City
Steve Beuerlein, Carolina	322 yards vs. New Orleans
Jay Fiedler, Jacksonville	317 yards vs. Cincinnati
Kerry Collins, N.Y. Giants	314 yards vs. Dallas
Brett Favre, Green Bay	311 yards vs. Arizona
Mike Tomczak, Pittsburgh	309 yards vs. Tennessee
Chris Chandler, Atlanta	306 yards vs. San Francisco

Times 300 or more (72)
Warner, 9; Favre, 6; Beuerlein, Bledsoe, 5; Johnson, 4; Brunell, Garcia, Marino, 3; Chandler, Collins, Cunningham, Frerotte, Gannon, George, Griese, Harbaugh, Manning, Miller, O'Donnell, 2.

TEN BEST RECEIVING PERFORMANCES, 1999

		No.	Yards	TD
1.	Qadry Ismail, Baltimore vs. Pittsburgh, Dec. 12	6	258	3
2.	Jimmy Smith, Jacksonville vs. New Orleans, Nov. 21	9	220	1
3.	Terry Glenn, New England vs. Cleveland, Oct. 3	13	214	1
4.	Marshall Faulk, St. Louis vs. Chicago, Dec. 26	12	204	1
	Randy Moss, Minnesota vs. Chicago, Nov. 14	12	204	0
6.	Marvin Harrison, Indianapolis vs. San Diego, Sept. 26	13	196	1
7.	Keyshawn Johnson, N.Y. Jets vs. New England, Sept. 12	8	194	1
8.	Tim Brown, Oakland vs. N.Y. Jets, Oct. 24	11	190	1
9.	Amani Toomer, N.Y. Giants vs. N.Y. Jets, Dec. 5	6	181	3
10.	Marcus Robinson, Chicago vs. Detroit, Dec. 19	11	170	3

100-YARD RECEIVING PERFORMANCES, 1999

First Week	
Keyshawn Johnson, N.Y. Jets	194 yards vs. New England
Kevin Dyson, Tennessee	162 yards vs. Cincinnati
Michael Westbrook, Washington	159 yards vs. Dallas
Derrick Alexander, Kansas City	154 yards vs. Chicago
Raghib Ismail, Dallas	149 yards vs. Washington
Eric Moulds, Buffalo	147 yards vs. Indianapolis
Germane Crowell, Detroit	141 yards vs. Seattle
Jimmy Smith, Jacksonville	139 yards vs. San Francisco
Albert Connell, Washington	137 yards vs. Dallas
E.G. Green, Indianapolis	124 yards vs. Buffalo
Michael Irvin, Dallas	122 yards vs. Washington
Marvin Harrison, Indianapolis	121 yards vs. Buffalo
Terry Glenn, New England	113 yards vs. N.Y. Jets
Antonio Freeman, Green Bay	111 yards vs. Oakland
Ed McCaffrey, Denver	105 yards vs. Miami
Tony Martin, Miami	101 yards vs. Denver
Second Week	
Derrick Mayes, Seattle	137 yards vs. Chicago
Terry Glenn, New England	122 yards vs. Indianapolis
Johnnie Morton, Detroit	118 yards vs. Green Bay
Derrick Alexander, Kansas City	117 yards vs. Denver
Jimmy Smith, Jacksonville	115 yards vs. Carolina
Ike Hilliard, N.Y. Giants	114 yards vs. Washington
Marvin Harrison, Indianapolis	105 yards vs. New England
Amani Toomer, N.Y. Giants	105 yards vs. Washington
Muhsin Muhammad, Carolina	103 yards vs. Jacksonville
Jake Reed, Minnesota	100 yards vs. Oakland
Third Week	
Marvin Harrison, Indianapolis	196 yards vs. San Diego
Jimmy Smith, Jacksonville	129 yards vs. Tennessee
Tim Brown, Oakland	121 yards vs. Chicago
Muhsin Muhammad, Carolina	117 yards vs. Cincinnati
Jake Reed, Minnesota	108 yards vs. Green Bay
Sean Dawkins, Seattle	105 yards vs. Pittsburgh
Fourth Week	
Terry Glenn, New England	214 yards vs. Cleveland
Isaac Bruce, St. Louis	152 yards vs. Cincinnati
Muhsin Muhammad, Carolina	151 yards vs. Washington
Yancey Thigpen, Tennessee	143 yards vs. San Francisco
Michael Westbrook, Washington	140 yards vs. Carolina
Albert Connell, Washington	134 yards vs. Carolina

1999 BEST PERFORMANCES

Kevin Johnson, Cleveland	131 yards vs. New England
Amani Toomer, N.Y. Giants	123 yards vs. Philadelphia
Randy Moss, Minnesota	120 yards vs. Tampa Bay
Curtis Conway, Chicago	103 yards vs. New Orleans
Raghib Ismail, Dallas	101 yards vs. Arizona
Fifth Week	
Tony Martin, Miami	166 yards vs. Indianapolis
Bill Schroeder, Green Bay	158 yards vs. Tampa Bay
Antonio Freeman, Green Bay	152 yards vs. Tampa Bay
Eddie Kennison, New Orleans	138 yards vs. Atlanta
Isaac Bruce, St. Louis	134 yards vs. San Francisco
Oronde Gadsden, Miami	123 yards vs. Indianapolis
Randy Moss, Minnesota	122 yards vs. Chicago
Eric Moulds, Buffalo	122 yards vs. Pittsburgh
Darnay Scott, Cincinnati	110 yards vs. Cleveland
Tony Simmons, New England	107 yards vs. Kansas City
David Boston, Arizona	101 yards vs. N.Y. Giants
Sixth Week	
Marcus Robinson, Chicago	136 yards vs. Philadelphia
Randy Moss, Minnesota	125 yards vs. Detroit
Byron Chamberlain, Denver	123 yards vs. Green Bay
Tony Martin, Miami	118 yards vs. New England
Ed McCaffrey, Denver	116 yards vs. Green Bay
Albert Connell, Washington	110 yards vs. Arizona
Seventh Week	
Tim Brown, Oakland	190 yards vs. N.Y. Jets
Terance Mathis, Atlanta	166 yards vs. Pittsburgh
Marvin Harrison, Indianapolis	156 yards vs. Cincinnati
Ed McCaffrey, Denver	111 yards vs. New England
Peerless Price, Buffalo	106 yards vs. Seattle
Derrick Mayes, Seattle	105 yards vs. Buffalo
Eighth Week	
Marcus Robinson, Chicago	161 yards vs. Washington
Cris Carter, Minnesota	144 yards vs. Denver
Torrance Small, Philadelphia	119 yards vs. N.Y. Giants
Rod Smith, Denver	117 yards vs. Minnesota
Tim Brown, Oakland	113 yards vs. Miami
Shawn Jefferson, New England	113 yards vs. Arizona
Derrick Alexander, Kansas City	113 yards vs. San Diego
Corey Bradford, Green Bay	106 yards vs. Seattle
Ninth Week	
Germane Crowell, Detroit	163 yards vs. St. Louis
Cris Carter, Minnesota	116 yards vs. Dallas
Carl Pickens, Cincinnati	104 yards vs. Seattle
Tenth Week	
Randy Moss, Minnesota	204 yards vs. Chicago
Jacquez Green, Tampa Bay	164 yards vs. Kansas City
Michael Westbrook, Washington	152 yards vs. Philadelphia
Marcus Robinson, Chicago	148 yards vs. Minnesota
Germane Crowell, Detroit	142 yards vs. Arizona
Cris Carter, Minnesota	141 yards vs. Chicago
Marty Booker, Chicago	134 yards vs. Minnesota
Muhsin Muhammad, Carolina	125 yards vs. St. Louis
Ed McCaffrey, Denver	125 yards vs. Seattle
Tim Brown, Oakland	117 yards vs. San Diego
Antonio Freeman, Green Bay	110 yards vs. Dallas
Johnnie Morton, Detroit	110 yards vs. Arizona
Marvin Harrison, Indianapolis	109 yards vs. N.Y. Giants
Eleventh Week	
Jimmy Smith, Jacksonville	220 yards vs. New Orleans
Marcus Robinson, Chicago	163 yards vs. San Diego
Bobby Engram, Chicago	121 yards vs. San Diego
Terrell Owens, San Francisco	120 yards vs. St. Louis
Sean Dawkins, Seattle	114 yards vs. Kansas City
Germane Crowell, Detroit	112 yards vs. Green Bay
Terrence Wilkins, Indianapolis	111 yards vs. Philadelphia
Ike Hilliard, N.Y. Giants	101 yards vs. Washington
Derrick Alexander, Kansas City	101 yards vs. Seattle
Twelfth Week	
Jeff Graham, San Diego	141 yards vs. Minnesota
Cris Carter, Minnesota	136 yards vs. San Diego
Donald Hayes, Carolina	133 yards vs. Atlanta
Jimmy Smith, Jacksonville	132 yards vs. Baltimore
Randy Moss, Minnesota	127 yards vs. San Diego
Raghib Ismail, Dallas	125 yards vs. Miami
Darnay Scott, Cincinnati	123 yards vs. Pittsburgh
Andre Hastings, New Orleans	113 yards vs. St. Louis
Tim Dwight, Atlanta	102 yards vs. Carolina
Rob Moore, Arizona	102 yards vs. N.Y. Giants
Keenan McCardell, Jacksonville	102 yards vs. Baltimore
Thirteenth Week	
Amani Toomer, N.Y. Giants	181 yards vs. N.Y. Jets
Jerry Rice, San Francisco	157 yards vs. Cincinnati
Terrell Owens, San Francisco	145 yards vs. Cincinnati
Marvin Harrison, Indianapolis	125 yards vs. Miami
Jimmy Smith, Jacksonville	124 yards vs. Pittsburgh
Germane Crowell, Detroit	122 yards vs. Washington
Az-Zahir Hakim, St. Louis	122 yards vs. Carolina
Ike Hilliard, N.Y. Giants	121 yards vs. N.Y. Jets
Keenan McCardell, Jacksonville	113 yards vs. Pittsburgh
Qadry Ismail, Baltimore	113 yards vs. Tennessee
Isaac Bruce, St. Louis	111 yards vs. Carolina
Tony Martin, Miami	109 yards vs. Indianapolis
Michael Westbrook, Washington	108 yards vs. Detroit
Patrick Jeffers, Carolina	107 yards vs. St. Louis
Carl Pickens, Cincinnati	107 yards vs. San Francisco
Rod Smith, Denver	106 yards vs. Kansas City
Oronde Gadsden, Miami	103 yards vs. Indianapolis
Fourteenth Week	
Qadry Ismail, Baltimore	258 yards vs. Pittsburgh
Terry Glenn, New England	148 yards vs. Indianapolis
Patrick Jeffers, Carolina	147 yards vs. Green Bay
Keyshawn Johnson, N.Y. Jets	144 yards vs. Miami
Kevin Johnson, Cleveland	135 yards vs. Cincinnati
Marvin Harrison, Indianapolis	118 yards vs. New England
Warrick Dunn, Tampa Bay	115 yards vs. Detroit
Jeff Graham, San Diego	114 yards vs. Seattle
Torry Holt, St. Louis	113 yards vs. New Orleans
Johnnie Morton, Detroit	107 yards vs. Tampa Bay
Isaac Bruce, St. Louis	102 yards vs. New Orleans
Fifteenth Week	
Marcus Robinson, Chicago	170 yards vs. Detroit
Amani Toomer, N.Y. Giants	162 yards vs. St. Louis
Patrick Jeffers, Carolina	138 yards vs. San Francisco
Jimmy Smith, Jacksonville	134 yards vs. Cleveland
Randy Moss, Minnesota	131 yards vs. Green Bay
Muhsin Muhammad, Carolina	126 yards vs. San Francisco
Marvin Harrison, Indianapolis	117 yards vs. Washington
Qadry Ismail, Baltimore	115 yards vs. New Orleans
Darrin Chiaverini, Cleveland	108 yards vs. Jacksonville
Wayne Chrebet, N.Y. Jets	108 yards vs. Dallas
Tim Brown, New England	105 yards vs. Philadelphia
Johnnie Morton, Detroit	100 yards vs. Chicago
Chris Sanders, Tennessee	100 yards vs. Atlanta
Sixteenth Week	
Marshall Faulk, St. Louis	204 yards vs. Chicago
Patrick Jeffers, Carolina	160 yards vs. Pittsburgh
Bobby Engram, Chicago	143 yards vs. St. Louis
Marvin Harrison, Indianapolis	138 yards vs. Cleveland
Cris Carter, Minnesota	131 yards vs. N.Y. Giants
Jason Tucker, Dallas	128 yards vs. New Orleans
Michael Westbrook, Washington	125 yards vs. San Francisco
Jeff Graham, San Diego	113 yards vs. Oakland
Tim Brown, Oakland	109 yards vs. San Diego

Albert Connell, Washington	106 yards vs. San Francisco
Frank Sanders, Arizona	106 yards vs. Atlanta
Jimmy Smith, Jacksonville	104 yards vs. Tennessee
Tony Martin, Miami	102 yards vs. N.Y. Jets
Seventeenth Week	
Patrick Jeffers, Carolina	165 yards vs. New Orleans
Jimmy Smith, Jacksonville	165 yards vs. Cincinnati
Tim Dwight, Atlanta	162 yards vs. San Francisco
Randy Moss, Minnesota	155 yards vs. Detroit
Jerry Rice, San Francisco	143 yards vs. Atlanta
Bobby Shaw, Pittsburgh	131 yards vs. Tennessee
J.J. Stokes, San Francisco	130 yards vs. Atlanta
Johnnie Morton, Detroit	128 yards vs. Minnesota
Tim Brown, Oakland	122 yards vs. Kansas City
Torry Holt, St. Louis	122 yards vs. Philadelphia
Jason Tucker, Dallas	122 yards vs. N.Y. Giants
Germane Crowell, Detroit	120 yards vs. Minnesota
Rob Moore, Arizona	120 yards vs. Green Bay
Frank Sanders, Arizona	118 yards vs. Green Bay
Oronde Gadsden, Miami	114 yards vs. Washington
Patrick Johnson, Baltimore	114 yards vs. New England
Jacquez Green, Tampa Bay	113 yards vs. Chicago
Eric Moulds, Buffalo	110 yards vs. Indianapolis
Keenan McCardell, Jacksonville	108 yards vs. Cincinnati
Rod Smith, Denver	106 yards vs. San Diego
Keith Poole, New Orleans	104 yards vs. Carolina
Jeff Graham, San Diego	102 yards vs. Denver
Tiki Barber, N.Y. Giants	100 yards vs. Dallas

Times 100 or more (187)
Harrison, J. Smith, 9; Moss, 7; T. Brown, Crowell 6; Brown, Carter, Jeffers, Morton, Muhammad, Robinson, Westbrook, 5; Alexander, Bruce, Connell, Glenn, Graham, Martin, McCaffrey, Toomer, 4; Freeman, Gadsen, Hilliard, Q. Ismail, R. Ismail, McCardell, Moulds, R. Smith, 3; Dawkins, Dwight, Engram, Green, Hilliard, Holt, Kevin Johnson, Keyshawn Johnson, Mayes, Moore, Owens, Pickens, Reed, Rice, Sanders, Scott, Tucker, 2.

TOP QUARTERBACK SACK PERFORMANCES, 1999

(2.5 or More Sacks Per Game Needed to Qualify)

First Week	
Chad Bratzke, Indianapolis	3.0 vs. Buffalo
Robert Porcher, Detroit	3.0 vs. Seattle
Brady Smith, New Orleans	2.5 vs. Carolina
Second Week	
Chidi Ahanotu, Tampa Bay	3.0 vs. Philadelphia
Jevon Kearse, Tennessee	3.0 vs. Cleveland
Warren Sapp, Tampa Bay	3.0 vs. Philadelphia
Third Week	
Kenard Lang, Washington	3.0 vs. New York Jets
Trevor Pryce, Denver	3.0 vs. Tampa Bay
Clyde Simmons, Chicago	3.0 vs. Oakland
Fourth Week	
Tony Brackens, Jacksonville	2.5 vs. Pittsburgh
Fifth Week	
None	
Sixth Week	
None	
Seventh Week	
None	
Eighth Week	
Cortez Kennedy, Seattle	3.0 vs. Green Bay
Darrell Russell, Oakland	3.0 vs. Miami
Chuck Smith, Atlanta	3.0 vs. Carolina
Ninth Week	
D'Marco Farr, St. Louis	3.0 vs. Detroit
Kevin Carter, St. Louis	2.5 vs. Detroit
Henry Ford, Tennessee	2.5 vs. Miami
Tenth Week	
Kevin Carter, St. Louis	2.5 vs. Carolina
Eleventh Week	
Glenn Cadrez, Denver	3.0 vs. Oakland
Steve Foley, Cincinnati	3.0 vs. Baltimore
Twelfth Week	
Kevin Greene, Carolina	2.5 vs. Atlanta
Thirteenth Week	
Michael McCrary, Baltimore	3.5 vs. Tennessee
Lester Archambeau, Atlanta	3.0 vs. New Orleans
Raylee Johnson, San Diego	3.0 vs. Cleveland
John Thierry, Cleveland	3.0 vs. San Diego
Kevin Carter, St. Louis	2.5 vs. Carolina
Fourteenth Week	
Robert Porcher, Detroit	3.0 vs. Tampa Bay
Trevor Pryce, Denver	3.0 vs. Jacksonville
Fifteenth Week	
Chad Bratzke, Indianapolis	3.0 vs. Washington
La'Roi Glover, New Orleans	3.0 vs. Baltimore
Mike Mamula, Philadelphia	3.0 vs. New England
Sixteenth Week	
Lance Johnstone, Oakland	3.0 vs. San Diego
Michael McCrary, Baltimore	3.0 vs. Cincinnati
Seventeenth Week	
John Randle, Minnesota	3.0 vs. Detroit

1999 TEAM STATISTICS

AMERICAN FOOTBALL CONFERENCE OFFENSE

	Balt.	Buff.	Cin.	Cle.	Den.	Ind.	Jax	K.C.	Mia.	N.E.	NYJ	Oak.	Pitt.	S.D.	Sea.	Tenn.
First Downs	259	313	293	220	308	327	331	282	287	280	268	326	295	262	276	294
Rushing	87	117	111	64	107	89	116	108	81	72	111	110	111	69	65	109
Passing	148	173	161	134	168	200	194	164	188	184	139	196	159	171	179	167
Penalty	24	23	21	22	33	38	21	10	18	24	18	20	25	22	32	18
Rushes	431	519	442	313	465	419	514	521	445	425	486	488	495	410	408	459
Net Yds. Gained	1754	2040	2051	1150	1864	1660	2091	2082	1453	1426	1961	2084	1991	1246	1408	1811
Avg. Gain	4.1	3.9	4.6	3.7	4.0	4.0	4.1	4.0	3.3	3.4	4.0	4.3	4.0	3.0	3.5	3.9
Avg. Yds. per Game	109.6	127.5	128.2	71.9	116.5	103.8	130.7	130.1	90.8	89.1	122.6	130.3	124.4	77.9	88.0	113.2
Passes Attempted	546	513	548	492	554	546	535	502	589	540	476	520	535	583	525	527
Completed	270	290	300	271	319	338	320	295	329	305	272	306	301	332	288	304
% Completed	49.5	56.5	54.7	55.1	57.6	61.9	59.8	58.8	55.9	56.5	57.1	58.8	56.3	56.9	54.9	57.7
Total Yds. Gained	3360	3478	3504	2997	3646	4182	3716	3409	3736	3985	3001	3850	3118	3627	3629	3622
Times Sacked	56	27	49	60	34	14	36	26	37	56	37	49	37	46	38	25
Yds. Lost	336	185	278	385	227	116	221	170	251	349	210	241	235	284	232	137
Net Yds. Gained	3024	3293	3226	2612	3419	4066	3495	3239	3485	3636	2791	3609	2883	3343	3397	3485
Avg. Yds. per Game	189.0	205.8	201.6	163.3	213.7	254.1	218.4	202.4	217.8	227.3	174.4	225.6	180.2	208.9	212.3	217.8
Net Yds. per Pass Play	5.02	6.10	5.40	4.73	5.81	7.26	6.12	6.13	5.57	6.10	5.44	6.34	5.04	5.31	6.03	6.31
Yds. Gained per Comp.	12.44	11.99	11.68	11.06	11.43	12.37	11.61	11.56	11.36	13.07	11.03	12.58	10.36	10.92	12.60	11.91
Combined Net Yds. Gained	4778	5333	5277	3762	5283	5726	5586	5321	4938	5062	4752	5693	4874	4589	4805	5296
% Total Yds. Rushing	36.7	38.3	38.9	30.6	35.3	29.0	37.4	39.1	29.4	28.2	41.3	36.6	40.8	27.2	29.3	34.2
% Total Yds. Passing	63.3	61.7	61.1	69.4	64.7	71.0	62.6	60.9	70.6	71.8	58.7	63.4	59.2	72.8	70.7	65.8
Avg. Yds. per Game	298.6	333.3	329.8	235.1	330.2	357.9	349.1	332.6	308.6	316.4	297.0	355.8	304.6	286.8	300.3	331.0
Ball Control Plays	1033	1059	1039	865	1053	979	1085	1049	1071	1021	999	1057	1067	1039	971	1011
Avg. Yds. per Play	4.6	5.0	5.1	4.3	5.0	5.8	5.1	5.1	4.6	5.0	4.8	5.4	4.6	4.4	4.9	5.2
Avg. Time of Poss.	29:24	32:12	29:59	23:38	31:06	30:45	31:57	30:20	31:34	28:49	30:45	32:06	31:28	30:00	27:48	31:30
Third Down Efficiency	28.4	40.8	39.6	29.1	36.7	39.2	40.0	39.5	33.9	35.4	34.5	39.4	38.5	36.8	32.4	38.2
Had Intercepted	20	16	18	15	18	17	11	15	21	21	16	14	18	24	16	13
Yds. Opp Returned	220	288	305	153	231	189	149	166	567	299	148	239	304	196	210	227
Ret. by Opp. for TD	3	1	1	1	1	2	0	1	7	1	0	2	3	1	0	2
Punts	104	73	84	106	84	60	78	104	81	90	82	77	84	89	84	90
Yds. Punted	4355	2840	3219	4645	3908	2467	3260	4253	3322	3735	3693	3045	3795	3910	3425	3824
Avg. Yds. per Punt	41.9	38.9	38.3	43.8	46.5	41.1	41.8	40.9	41.0	41.5	45.0	39.5	45.2	43.9	40.8	42.5
Punt Returns	59	34	35	25	54	41	45	58	44	48	43	42	42	34	30	40
Yds. Returned	452	347	410	162	409	388	462	706	432	495	319	397	377	290	419	358
Avg. Yds. per Return	7.7	10.2	11.7	6.5	7.6	9.5	10.3	12.2	9.8	10.3	7.4	9.5	9.0	8.5	14.0	8.9
Returned for TD	0	0	2	0	1	1	1	2	0	0	0	0	0	0	1	1
Kickoff Returns	54	51	84	89	63	67	46	63	72	62	67	61	57	69	68	56
Yds. Returned	1098	1001	2020	1725	1398	1397	881	1182	1713	1498	1571	1140	1110	1312	1547	1042
Avg. Yds. per Return	20.3	19.6	24.0	19.4	22.2	20.9	19.2	18.8	23.8	24.2	23.4	18.7	19.5	19.0	22.8	18.6
Returned for TD	0	1	1	0	0	1	1	0	0	0	0	0	0	0	0	0
Fumbles	24	17	34	29	33	25	18	22	23	27	22	22	19	29	31	17
Lost	11	11	14	16	10	11	7	9	13	12	6	15	7	11	17	9
Out of Bounds	1	1	1	0	2	5	0	2	3	1	2	1	2	0	3	0
Own Rec. for TD	0	0	0	0	0	1	0	0	0	0	0	0	0	0	0	0
Opp. Rec. by	10	9	15	12	11	13	11	20	10	15	11	13	14	12	6	24
Opp. Rec. for TD	0	1	0	0	1	1	1	4	1	2	1	1	2	2	0	2
Penalties	125	97	126	92	114	81	90	126	111	95	87	98	119	104	98	114
Yds. Penalized	1010	789	1027	714	872	683	755	982	936	812	771	825	945	823	883	1069
Total Points Scored	324	320	283	217	314	423	396	390	326	299	308	390	317	269	338	392
Total TDs	34	35	33	28	32	46	42	47	30	32	33	45	35	25	34	46
TDs Rushing	9	12	11	9	13	15	20	14	8	9	7	18	14	10	5	19
TDs Passing	21	21	18	19	16	26	16	22	20	19	22	24	19	12	25	23
TDs on Ret. and Rec.	4	2	4	0	3	5	6	11	2	4	4	3	2	3	4	4
Extra Point Kicks	32	33	27	23	29	43	37	45	27	29	27	43	30	22	32	43
Extra Point Kicks Att.	32	33	27	24	29	43	37	45	27	30	29	43	31	23	32	43
2Pt Conversions	1	1	2	1	1	1	4	0	0	0	0	1	1	1	0	1
2Pt Conversions Att.	1	2	6	4	1	3	5	2	3	2	4	2	4	2	2	3
Safeties	1	0	0	0	2	0	3	0	1	0	1	0	0	1	0	4
Field Goals Made	28	25	18	8	29	34	31	21	39	26	27	25	25	31	34	21
Field Goals Attempted	33	34	27	12	36	38	38	28	46	33	33	38	29	36	40	25
% Successful	84.8	73.5	66.7	66.7	80.6	89.5	81.6	75.0	84.8	78.8	81.8	65.8	86.2	86.1	85.0	84.0

AMERICAN FOOTBALL CONFERENCE DEFENSE

	Balt.	Buff.	Cin.	Cle.	Den.	Ind.	Jax	K.C.	Mia.	N.E.	NYJ	Oak.	Pitt.	S.D.	Sea.	Tenn.
First Downs	260	244	316	368	267	304	248	281	252	281	299	266	260	279	313	300
Rushing	70	73	99	161	88	92	72	80	79	106	97	85	92	77	107	81
Passing	158	144	189	187	154	192	159	173	145	154	180	161	142	181	183	193
Penalty	32	27	28	20	25	20	17	28	28	21	22	20	26	21	23	26
Rushes	392	407	454	610	440	406	373	415	413	486	430	398	451	432	484	383
Net Yds. Gained	1231	1370	1699	2736	1737	1715	1444	1557	1476	1795	1703	1559	1958	1321	1934	1550
Avg. Gain	3.1	3.4	3.7	4.5	3.9	4.2	3.9	3.8	3.6	3.7	4.0	3.9	4.3	3.1	4.0	4.0
Avg. Yds. per Game	76.9	85.6	106.2	171.0	108.6	107.2	90.3	97.3	92.3	112.2	106.4	97.4	122.4	82.6	120.9	96.9
Passes Attempted	599	506	522	523	471	561	521	578	484	520	574	539	463	549	582	557
Completed	328	269	312	331	273	328	291	317	256	293	319	302	245	315	320	312
% Completed	54.8	53.2	59.8	63.3	58.0	58.5	55.9	54.8	52.9	56.3	55.6	56.0	52.9	57.4	55.0	56.0
Total Yds. Gained	3282	2889	4027	3457	3299	3775	3263	3768	3168	3281	3860	3630	3167	3847	3744	4000
Times Sacked	49	37	35	25	50	41	57	40	39	42	26	44	39	41	38	54
Yds. Lost	291	214	229	147	283	269	373	286	240	268	184	309	241	263	252	305
Net Yds. Gained	2991	2675	3798	3310	3016	3506	2890	3482	2928	3013	3676	3321	2926	3584	3492	3695
Avg. Yds. per Game	186.9	167.2	237.4	206.9	188.5	219.1	180.6	217.6	183.0	188.3	229.8	207.6	182.9	224.0	218.3	230.9
Net Yds. per Pass Play	4.62	4.93	6.82	6.04	5.79	5.82	5.00	5.63	5.60	5.36	6.13	5.70	5.83	6.07	5.63	6.05
Yds. Gained per Comp.	10.01	10.74	12.91	10.44	12.08	11.51	11.21	11.89	12.38	11.20	12.10	12.02	12.93	12.21	11.70	12.82
Combined Net Yds. Gained	4222	4045	5497	6046	4753	5221	4334	5039	4404	4808	5379	4880	4884	4905	5426	5245
% Total Yds. Rushing	29.2	33.9	30.9	45.3	36.5	32.8	33.3	30.9	33.5	37.3	31.7	31.9	40.1	26.9	35.6	29.6
% Total Yds. Passing	70.8	66.1	69.1	54.7	63.5	67.2	66.7	69.1	66.5	62.7	68.3	68.1	59.9	73.1	64.4	70.4
Avg. Yds. per Game	263.9	252.8	343.6	377.9	297.1	326.3	270.9	314.9	275.3	300.5	336.2	305.0	305.3	306.6	339.1	327.8
Ball Control Plays	1040	950	1011	1158	961	1008	951	1033	936	1048	1030	981	953	1022	1104	994
Avg. Yds. per Play	4.1	4.3	5.4	5.2	4.9	5.2	4.6	4.9	4.7	4.6	5.2	5.0	5.1	4.8	4.9	5.3
Avg. Time of Poss.	30:36	27:48	30:01	36:22	28:54	29:15	28:03	29:40	28:26	31:11	29:15	27:54	28:32	30:00	32:12	28:30
Third Down Efficiency	34.1	31.4	40.7	46.8	31.5	35.1	33.5	30.2	28.8	35.1	40.7	33.0	31.5	36.7	37.2	35.0
Intercepted By	21	12	12	8	15	10	19	25	18	16	24	20	14	15	30	16
Yds. Returned By	403	180	100	52	169	287	330	378	243	110	443	247	149	123	336	257
Returned for TD	4	0	1	0	1	1	3	5	1	2	3	1	0	0	2	1
Punts	115	93	71	66	92	83	96	98	85	95	78	82	92	85	81	80
Yds. Punted	4854	3875	3136	2702	4011	3437	3976	4260	3495	3914	3190	3542	3737	3439	3398	3435
Avg. Yds. per Punt	42.2	41.7	44.2	40.9	43.6	41.4	41.4	43.5	41.1	41.2	40.9	43.2	40.6	40.5	42.0	42.9
Punt Returns	43	23	45	68	43	29	37	46	42	36	47	38	39	41	36	45
Yds. Returned	468	226	498	762	600	469	259	406	424	345	427	479	392	343	370	335
Avg. Yds. per Return	10.9	9.8	11.1	11.2	14.0	16.2	7.0	8.8	10.1	9.6	9.1	12.6	10.1	8.4	10.3	7.4
Returned for TD	1	0	1	2	1	0	0	1	0	0	0	1	1	0	1	0
Kickoff Returns	70	68	57	42	70	83	64	78	58	64	63	77	67	67	81	76
Yds. Returned	1479	1504	1068	764	1457	1822	1474	1544	1282	1441	1589	1626	1209	1550	1500	1596
Avg. Yds. per Return	21.1	22.1	18.7	18.2	20.8	22.0	23.0	19.8	22.1	22.5	25.2	21.1	18.0	23.1	18.5	21.0
Returned for TD	0	0	0	0	0	0	0	1	1	0	0	0	0	0	0	2
Fumbles	25	14	27	25	29	22	31	31	19	29	24	26	29	30	17	39
Lost	10	9	15	12	11	13	11	20	10	15	11	13	14	12	6	24
Out of Bounds	2	1	1	3	0	0	4	0	1	0	4	1	1	4	1	1
Own Rec. for TD	0	0	0	0	0	0	0	0	0	0	0	0	0	0	0	0
Opp. Rec. by	11	11	14	16	10	11	7	9	13	12	6	15	7	11	17	9
Opp. Rec. for TD	1	1	1	0	1	0	0	0	2	0	1	1	2	1	1	1
Penalties	122	97	105	88	114	130	93	107	80	102	76	114	101	117	128	128
Yds. Penalized	1118	790	835	776	1016	1093	728	787	708	775	685	861	813	909	985	1010
Total Points Scored	277	229	460	437	318	333	217	322	336	284	309	329	320	316	298	324
Total TDs	31	23	53	49	35	36	24	38	35	30	33	36	36	34	30	39
TDs Rushing	6	9	22	29	15	12	6	10	6	6	16	10	10	8	9	8
TDs Passing	20	12	28	17	17	21	18	24	19	23	16	22	20	24	19	26
TDs on Ret. and Rec.	5	2	3	3	3	3	0	4	10	1	1	4	6	2	2	5
Extra Point Kicks	26	22	49	40	31	31	22	33	33	27	33	33	34	34	26	33
Extra Point Kicks Att.	27	22	50	41	32	31	22	33	35	27	33	33	35	34	27	33
2Pt Conversions	4	0	2	1	1	2	0	2	0	0	0	0	0	0	0	4
2Pt Conversions Att.	4	1	3	8	3	5	2	5	0	3	0	2	1	0	2	6
Safeties	0	0	1	1	0	2	0	0	0	1	0	1	5	0	1	2
Field Goals Made	19	23	29	33	25	26	17	19	31	25	26	26	20	26	30	15
Field Goals Attempted	25	31	32	39	29	29	18	25	40	30	31	32	26	38	38	22
% Successful	76.0	74.2	90.6	84.6	86.2	89.7	94.4	76.0	77.5	83.3	83.9	81.3	76.9	68.4	78.9	68.2

1999 TEAM STATISTICS

NATIONAL FOOTBALL CONFERENCE OFFENSE

	Ariz.	Atl.	Car.	Chi.	Dall.	Det.	G.B.	Minn.	N.O.	NYG	Phil.	St.L.	S.F.	T.B.	Wash.
First Downs	254	273	307	302	295	269	314	324	288	308	218	335	300	245	338
Rushing	77	68	78	82	129	67	87	96	97	87	76	102	102	97	121
Passing	150	179	208	203	139	179	196	192	159	197	123	207	172	132	183
Penalty	27	26	21	17	27	23	31	36	32	24	19	26	26	16	34
Rushes	396	373	356	396	493	356	386	422	461	431	424	431	418	502	463
Net Yds. Gained	1207	1196	1525	1387	2051	1245	1519	1804	1690	1408	1746	2059	2095	1776	2039
Avg. Gain	3.0	3.2	4.3	3.5	4.2	3.5	3.9	4.3	3.7	3.3	4.1	4.8	5.0	3.5	4.4
Avg. Yds. per Game	75.4	74.8	95.3	86.7	128.2	77.8	94.9	112.8	105.6	88.0	109.1	128.7	130.9	111.0	127.4
Passes Attempted	558	509	575	684	507	558	605	530	553	602	474	530	560	447	537
Completed	287	278	345	404	295	326	344	316	288	350	235	343	324	268	324
% Completed	51.4	54.6	60.0	59.1	58.2	58.4	56.9	59.6	52.1	58.1	49.6	64.7	57.9	60.0	60.3
Total Yds. Gained	3085	3691	4447	4352	3278	4074	4132	4318	3598	4015	2405	4580	3526	2781	4112
Times Sacked	45	49	51	38	24	64	36	43	41	42	49	33	34	42	31
Yds. Lost	282	345	286	216	151	388	232	329	305	296	321	227	241	303	186
Net Yds. Gained	2803	3346	4161	4136	3127	3686	3900	3989	3293	3719	2084	4353	3285	2478	3926
Avg. Yds. per Game	175.2	209.1	260.1	258.5	195.4	230.4	243.8	249.3	205.8	232.4	130.3	272.1	205.3	154.9	245.4
Net Yds. per Pass Play	4.65	6.00	6.65	5.73	5.89	5.93	6.08	6.96	5.54	5.77	3.98	7.73	5.53	5.07	6.91
Yds. Gained per Comp.	10.75	13.28	12.89	10.77	11.11	12.50	12.01	13.66	12.49	11.47	10.23	13.35	10.88	10.38	12.69
Combined Net Yds. Gained	4010	4542	5686	5523	5178	4931	5419	5793	4983	5127	3830	6412	5380	4254	5965
% Total Yds. Rushing	30.1	26.3	26.8	25.1	39.6	25.2	28.0	31.1	33.9	27.5	45.6	32.1	38.9	41.7	34.2
% Total Yds. Passing	69.9	73.7	73.2	74.9	60.4	74.8	72.0	68.9	66.1	72.5	54.4	67.9	61.1	58.3	65.8
Avg. Yds. per Game	250.6	283.9	355.4	345.2	323.6	308.2	338.7	362.1	311.4	320.4	239.4	400.8	336.3	265.9	372.8
Ball Control Plays	999	931	982	1118	1024	978	1027	995	1055	1075	947	994	1012	991	1031
Avg. Yds. per Play	4.0	4.9	5.8	4.9	5.1	5.0	5.3	5.8	4.7	4.8	4.0	6.5	5.3	4.3	5.8
Avg. Time of Poss.	27:10	28:44	29:23	29:24	31:51	29:15	29:13	29:21	30:54	30:31	27:03	31:50	30:17	32:11	29:33
Third Down Efficiency	32.6	34.7	38.3	36.8	35.2	36.5	36.8	43.6	33.6	36.2	31.1	46.9	34.0	35.2	37.9
Had Intercepted	30	19	15	22	13	14	23	21	30	20	18	15	19	16	14
Yds. Opp Returned	336	365	267	359	100	174	338	302	483	322	266	266	286	144	129
Ret. by Opp. for TD	2	3	3	2	0	1	2	3	4	5	2	2	2	1	0
Punts	94	80	65	85	81	86	80	61	83	89	108	60	75	90	71
Yds. Punted	3948	3163	2562	3478	3500	3637	3130	2769	3282	3651	4524	2464	2883	3882	2926
Avg. Yds. per Punt	42.0	39.5	39.4	40.9	43.2	42.3	39.1	45.4	39.5	41.0	41.9	41.1	38.4	43.1	41.2
Punt Returns	47	32	35	30	41	38	29	32	35	45	29	52	26	43	41
Yds. Returned	489	372	241	346	440	386	212	269	258	520	250	498	104	357	332
Avg. Yds. per Return	10.4	11.6	6.9	11.5	10.7	10.2	7.3	8.4	7.4	11.6	8.6	9.6	4.0	8.3	8.1
Returned for TD	0	2	0	0	1	1	0	1	0	1	0	1	0	0	0
Kickoff Returns	64	76	66	68	58	72	66	70	79	69	69	54	77	55	63
Yds. Returned	1403	1445	1475	1491	1372	1445	1241	1597	1639	1502	1612	1354	1579	1116	1290
Avg. Yds. per Return	21.9	19.0	22.3	21.9	23.7	20.1	18.8	22.8	20.7	21.8	23.4	25.1	20.5	20.3	20.5
Returned for TD	0	0	2	0	0	0	1	2	0	0	1	2	0	0	1
Fumbles	31	24	24	32	22	21	28	24	26	29	33	30	29	25	31
Lost	10	16	19	15	10	8	13	19	9	12	21	16	13	19	11
Out of Bounds	3	1	0	0	2	3	3	1	1	3	1	3	1	2	5
Own Rec. for TD	0	0	0	0	0	0	0	0	0	0	0	0	0	0	0
Opp. Rec. by	10	6	14	19	9	16	15	18	15	7	18	7	7	9	13
Opp. Rec. for TD	0	0	0	1	1	3	2	0	2	1	0	1	3	0	1
Penalties	70	110	106	117	136	110	100	114	110	98	102	113	120	75	104
Yds. Penalized	481	968	857	915	1196	995	808	955	877	906	905	889	1045	583	808
Total Points Scored	245	285	421	272	352	322	357	399	260	299	272	526	295	270	443
Total TDs	27	34	50	31	42	35	40	49	27	32	29	66	33	27	54
TDs Rushing	13	9	12	4	16	8	13	13	9	11	5	13	14	7	23
TDs Passing	11	22	36	25	20	22	23	32	16	17	18	42	14	18	26
TDs on Ret. and Rec.	3	3	2	2	6	5	4	4	2	4	6	11	5	2	5
Extra Point Kicks	26	34	46	27	41	28	38	46	20	28	27	64	30	25	49
Extra Point Kicks Att.	26	34	47	28	41	29	38	46	21	28	27	64	31	25	50
2Pt Conversions	0	0	0	1	0	2	1	0	3	2	2	2	1	0	2
2Pt Conversions Att.	1	0	3	3	0	6	2	3	6	3	2	2	2	2	3
Safeties	0	1	0	0	1	1	1	1	0	0	2	1	1	1	0
Field Goals Made	19	15	25	19	19	26	25	19	24	25	21	20	21	27	22
Field Goals Attempted	27	21	28	34	31	32	30	30	29	30	31	28	23	32	32
% Successful	70.4	71.4	89.3	55.9	61.3	81.3	83.3	63.3	82.8	83.3	67.7	71.4	91.3	84.4	68.8

NATIONAL FOOTBALL CONFERENCE DEFENSE

	Ariz.	Atl.	Car.	Chi.	Dall.	Det.	G.B.	Minn.	N.O.	NYG	Phil.	St.L.	S.F.	T.B.	Wash.
First Downs	301	293	331	310	266	305	304	320	297	270	328	263	315	228	322
Rushing	128	111	115	89	81	87	103	83	105	81	125	53	91	75	107
Passing	157	149	189	196	154	185	177	213	170	170	171	189	192	144	193
Penalty	16	33	27	25	31	33	24	24	22	19	32	21	32	9	22
Rushes	542	487	450	438	417	393	472	413	432	447	519	338	426	361	439
Net Yds. Gained	2265	2072	1898	1882	1442	1531	1804	1617	1774	1560	2001	1189	1619	1407	1973
Avg. Gain	4.2	4.3	4.2	4.3	3.5	3.9	3.8	3.9	4.1	3.5	3.9	3.5	3.8	3.9	4.5
Avg. Yds. per Game	141.6	129.5	118.6	117.6	90.1	95.7	112.8	101.1	110.9	97.5	125.1	74.3	101.2	87.9	123.3
Passes Attempted	493	468	557	583	545	574	538	606	489	511	568	596	521	573	589
Completed	294	274	327	354	297	359	304	373	291	295	322	319	317	302	328
% Completed	59.6	58.5	58.7	60.7	54.5	62.5	56.5	61.6	59.5	57.7	56.7	53.5	60.8	52.7	55.7
Total Yds. Gained	3386	3409	3840	4079	3615	4100	3690	4252	3821	3593	3733	3867	4295	3164	3953
Times Sacked	33	40	35	37	35	50	30	46	45	32	37	57	32	43	40
Yds. Lost	229	258	235	257	217	340	185	272	277	172	272	358	227	291	221
Net Yds. Gained	3157	3151	3605	3822	3398	3760	3505	3980	3544	3421	3461	3509	4068	2873	3732
Avg. Yds. per Game	197.3	196.9	225.3	238.9	212.4	235.0	219.1	248.8	221.5	213.8	216.3	219.3	254.3	179.6	233.3
Net Yds. per Pass Play	6.00	6.20	6.09	6.16	5.86	6.03	6.17	6.10	6.64	6.30	5.72	5.37	7.36	4.66	5.93
Yds. Gained per Comp.	11.52	12.44	11.74	11.52	12.17	11.42	12.14	11.40	13.13	12.18	11.59	12.12	13.55	10.48	12.05
Combined Net Yds. Gained	5422	5223	5503	5704	4840	5291	5309	5597	5318	4981	5462	4698	5687	4280	5705
% Total Yds. Rushing	41.8	39.7	34.5	33.0	29.8	28.9	34.0	28.9	33.4	31.3	36.6	25.3	28.5	32.9	34.6
% Total Yds. Passing	58.2	60.3	65.5	67.0	70.2	71.1	66.0	71.1	66.6	68.7	63.4	74.7	71.5	67.1	65.4
Avg. Yds. per Game	338.9	326.4	343.9	356.5	302.5	330.7	331.8	349.8	332.4	311.3	341.4	293.6	355.4	267.5	356.6
Ball Control Plays	1068	995	1042	1058	997	1017	1040	1065	966	990	1124	991	979	977	1068
Avg. Yds. per Play	5.1	5.2	5.3	5.4	4.9	5.2	5.1	5.3	5.5	5.0	4.9	4.7	5.8	4.4	5.3
Avg. Time of Poss.	32:51	31:16	30:37	30:36	28:09	30:45	30:47	30:39	29:06	29:29	32:57	28:10	29:43	27:49	30:27
Third Down Efficiency	40.5	39.1	41.6	40.6	32.1	39.4	39.0	39.2	38.7	33.8	37.8	33.8	40.1	32.3	39.2
Intercepted By	17	12	15	14	24	16	26	12	19	17	28	29	13	21	24
Yds. Returned By	276	166	169	229	442	235	137	66	138	232	625	567	209	355	375
Returned for TD	3	1	0	1	4	1	1	1	0	2	5	7	2	2	3
Punts	89	72	74	80	93	82	69	69	77	78	73	86	69	101	74
Yds. Punted	3775	2875	2924	3115	3836	3442	2954	2855	3183	3428	3011	3674	2714	4150	3158
Avg. Yds. per Punt	42.4	39.9	39.5	38.9	41.2	42.0	42.8	41.4	41.3	43.9	41.2	42.7	39.3	41.1	42.7
Punt Returns	53	26	32	36	43	42	39	28	43	38	59	23	33	49	27
Yds. Returned	340	119	158	266	459	402	333	246	283	405	490	155	399	360	279
Avg. Yds. per Return	6.4	4.6	4.9	7.4	10.7	9.6	8.5	8.8	6.6	10.7	8.3	6.7	12.1	7.3	10.3
Returned for TD	0	0	0	0	1	0	0	0	1	1	0	0	2	0	2
Kickoff Returns	59	55	76	57	62	60	72	69	60	53	57	85	47	61	77
Yds. Returned	1224	1221	1425	948	1259	1242	1565	1423	1473	1152	1305	2115	1093	1074	1772
Avg. Yds. per Return	20.7	22.2	18.8	16.6	20.3	20.7	21.7	20.6	24.6	21.7	22.9	24.9	23.3	17.6	23.0
Returned for TD	2	2	0	0	0	1	0	0	1	1	0	0	1	0	1
Fumbles	28	16	22	29	23	32	36	31	22	23	38	21	18	23	22
Lost	10	6	14	19	9	16	15	18	15	7	18	7	7	10	13
Out of Bounds	4	2	1	1	3	2	3	2	0	2	4	0	2	1	2
Own Rec. for TD	0	0	0	0	1	0	0	0	0	0	0	0	0	0	0
Opp. Rec. by	10	16	19	15	10	8	12	19	9	12	21	16	13	19	11
Opp. Rec. for TD	2	0	5	2	1	1	0	3	0	1	0	1	1	3	1
Penalties	112	126	109	89	107	105	99	108	124	92	89	114	96	88	102
Yds. Penalized	938	980	877	720	862	839	993	880	1006	750	719	1007	760	727	1137
Total Points Scored	382	380	381	341	276	323	341	335	434	358	357	242	453	235	377
Total TDs	48	43	47	38	28	36	39	35	55	41	36	26	53	23	43
TDs Rushing	17	18	13	11	6	12	16	9	15	13	12	4	11	8	16
TDs Passing	25	20	26	23	19	21	20	20	34	20	22	19	36	11	23
TDs on Ret. and Rec.	6	5	8	4	3	3	3	6	6	8	2	3	6	4	4
Extra Point Kicks	44	40	42	38	24	31	35	32	54	38	33	22	50	23	38
Extra Point Kicks Att.	45	40	43	38	24	31	35	32	54	39	33	23	50	23	38
2Pt Conversions	0	1	0	0	3	2	0	2	1	0	0	2	1	0	3
2Pt Conversions Att.	3	2	4	0	4	5	4	3	1	2	2	3	2	0	4
Safeties	1	1	0	0	0	3	0	1	0	1	0	0	1	1	0
Field Goals Made	16	26	19	25	26	22	24	29	16	24	36	20	27	24	25
Field Goals Attempted	24	35	25	36	33	29	31	42	23	37	45	26	32	31	30
% Successful	66.7	74.3	76.0	69.4	78.8	75.9	77.4	69.0	69.6	64.9	80.0	76.9	84.4	77.4	83.3

1999 TEAM STATISTICS

AFC, NFC, AND NFL SUMMARY

	AFC Offense Total	AFC Offense Average	AFC Defense Total	AFC Defense Average	NFC Offense Total	NFC Offense Average	NFC Defense Total	NFC Defense Average	NFL Total	NFL Average
First Downs	4621	288.8	4538	283.6	4370	291.3	4453	296.9	8991	290.0
Rushing	1527	95.4	1459	91.2	1366	91.1	1434	95.6	2893	93.3
Passing	2725	170.3	2695	168.4	2619	174.6	2649	176.6	5344	172.4
Penalty	369	23.1	384	24.0	385	25.7	370	24.7	754	24.3
Rushes	7240	452.5	6974	435.9	6308	420.5	6574	438.3	13548	437.0
Net Yds. Gained	28072	1754.5	26785	1674.1	24747	1649.8	26034	1735.6	52819	1703.8
Avg. Gain	—	3.9	—	3.8	—	3.9	—	4.0	—	3.9
Avg. Yds. per Game	—	109.7	—	104.6	—	103.1	—	108.5	—	106.5
Passes Attempted	8531	533.2	8549	534.3	8229	548.6	8211	547.4	16760	540.6
Completed	4840	302.5	4811	300.7	4727	315.1	4756	317.1	9567	308.6
% Completed	—	56.7	—	56.3	—	57.4	—	57.9	—	57.1
Total Yds. Gained	56860	3553.8	56457	3528.6	56394	3759.6	56797	3786.5	113254	3653.4
Times Sacked	627	39.2	657	41.1	622	41.5	592	39.5	1249	40.3
Yds. Lost	3857	241.1	4154	259.6	4108	273.9	3811	254.1	7965	256.9
Net Yds. Gained	53003	3312.7	52303	3268.9	52286	3485.7	52986	3532.4	105289	3396.4
Avg. Yds. per Game	—	207.0	—	204.3	—	217.9	—	220.8	—	212.3
Net Yds. per Pass Play	—	5.79	—	5.68	—	5.91	—	6.02	—	5.85
Yds. Gained per Comp.	—	11.75	—	11.73	—	11.93	—	11.94	—	11.84
Combined Net Yds. Gained	81075	5067.2	79088	4943.0	77033	5135.5	79020	5268.0	158108	5100.3
% Total Yds. Rushing	—	34.6	—	33.9	—	32.1	—	32.9	—	33.4
% Total Yds. Passing	—	65.4	—	66.1	—	67.9	—	67.1	—	66.6
Avg. Yds. per Game	—	316.7	—	308.9	—	321.0	—	329.3	—	318.8
Ball Control Plays	16398	1024.9	16180	1011.3	15159	1010.6	15377	1025.1	31557	1018.0
Avg. Yds. per Play	—	4.9	—	4.9	—	5.1	—	5.1	—	5.0
Third Down Efficiency	—	36.4	—	35.2	—	36.5	—	37.8	—	36.5
Interceptions	273	17.1	275	17.2	289	19.3	287	19.1	562	18.1
Yds. Returned	3891	243.2	3807	237.9	4137	275.8	4221	281.4	8028	259.0
Returned for TD	26	1.6	25	1.6	32	2.1	33	2.2	58	1.9
Punts	1370	85.6	1392	87.0	1208	80.5	1186	79.1	2578	83.2
Yds. Punted	57696	3606.0	58401	3650.1	49799	3319.9	49094	3272.9	107495	3467.6
Avg. Yds. per Punt	—	42.1	—	42.0	—	41.2	—	41.4	—	41.7
Punt Returns	674	42.1	658	41.1	555	37.0	571	38.1	1229	39.6
Yds. Returned	6423	401.4	6803	425.2	5074	338.3	4694	312.9	11497	370.9
Avg. Yds. per Return	—	9.5	—	10.3	—	9.1	—	8.2	—	9.4
Returned for TD	9	0.6	9	0.6	7	0.5	7	0.5	16	0.5
Kickoff Returns	1029	64.3	1085	67.8	1006	67.1	950	63.3	2035	65.6
Yds. Returned	21635	1352.2	22905	1431.6	21561	1437.4	20291	1352.7	43196	1393.4
Avg. Yds. per Return	—	21.0	—	21.1	—	21.4	—	21.4	—	21.2
Returned for TD	4	0.3	4	0.3	9	0.6	9	0.6	13	0.4
Fumbles	392	24.5	417	26.1	409	27.3	384	25.6	801	25.8
Lost	179	11.2	206	12.9	211	14.1	184	12.3	390	12.6
Out of Bounds	24	1.5	24	1.5	29	1.9	29	1.9	53	1.7
Own Rec. for TD	1	0.1	0	0.0	0	0.0	1	0.1	1	0.0
Opp. Rec.	206	12.9	179	11.2	183	12.2	210	14.0	389	12.5
Opp. Rec. for TD	19	1.2	13	0.8	15	1.0	21	1.4	34	1.1
Penalties	1677	104.8	1702	106.4	1585	105.7	1560	104.0	3262	105.2
Yds. Penalized	13896	868.5	13889	868.1	13188	879.2	13195	879.7	27084	873.7
Total Points Scored	5306	331.6	5109	319.3	5018	334.5	5215	347.7	10324	333.0
Total TDs	577	36.1	562	35.1	576	38.4	591	39.4	1153	37.2
TDs Rushing	193	12.1	182	11.4	170	11.3	181	12.1	363	11.7
TDs Passing	323	20.2	326	20.4	342	22.8	339	22.6	665	21.5
TDs on Ret. and Rec.	61	3.8	54	3.4	64	4.3	71	4.7	125	4.0
Extra Point Kicks	522	32.6	507	31.7	529	35.3	544	36.3	1051	33.9
Extra Point Kicks Att.	528	33.0	515	32.2	535	35.7	548	36.5	1063	34.3
2Pt Conversions	15	0.9	16	1.0	16	1.1	15	1.0	31	1.0
2Pt Conversions Att.	46	2.9	45	2.8	38	2.5	39	2.6	84	2.7
Safeties	13	0.8	14	0.9	10	0.7	9	0.6	23	0.7
Field Goals Made	422	26.4	390	24.4	327	21.8	359	23.9	749	24.2
Field Goals Attempted	526	32.9	485	30.3	438	29.2	479	31.9	964	31.1
% Successful	—	80.2	—	80.4	—	74.7	—	74.9	—	77.7

CLUB LEADERS

	Offense	Defense
First Downs	Wash. 338	T.B. 228
Rushing	Dall. 129	St.L. 53
Passing	Car. 208	Pitt. 142
Penalty	Ind. 38	T.B. 9
Rushes	K.C. 521	St.L. 338
Net Yds. Gained	S.F. 2095	St.L. 1189
Avg. Gain	S.F. 5.0	S.D. 3.1
Passes Attempted	Chi. 684	Pitt. 463
Completed	Chi. 404	Pitt. 245
% Completed	St.L. 64.7	T.B. 52.7
Total Yds. Gained	St.L. 4580	Buff. 2889
Times Sacked	Ind. 14	Jax. & St.L. 57
Yds. Lost	Ind. 116	Jax. 373
Net Yds. Gained	St.L. 4353	Buff. 2675
Net Yds. per Pass Play	St.L. 7.7	Balt. 4.6
Yds. Gained per Comp.	Minn. 13.7	Balt. 10.0
Combined Net Yds. Gained	St.L. 6412	Buff. 4045
% Total Yds. Rushing	Phil. 45.6	St.L. 25.3
% Total Yds. Passing	Chi. 74.9	Cle. 54.7
Ball Control Plays	Chi. 1118	Mia. 936
Avg. Yds. per Play	St.L. 6.5	Balt. 4.1
Avg. Time of Poss.	Buff. 32:12	—
Third Down Efficiency	St.L. 46.9	Mia. 28.8
Interceptions	—	Sea. 30
Yds. Returned	—	Phil. 625
Returned for TD	—	St.L. 7
Punts	Phil. 108	—
Yds. Punted	Cle. 4645	—
Avg. Yds. per Punt	Den. 46.5	—
Punt Returns	Balt. 59	Buff. & St.L. 23
Yds. Returned	K.C. 706	Atl. 119
Avg. Yds. per Return	Sea. 14.0	Atl. 4.6
Returned for TD	Three tied 2	—
Kickoff Returns	Cle. 89	Cle. 42
Yds. Returned	Cin. 2020	Cle. 764
Avg. Yds. per Return	St.L. 25.1	Chi. 16.6
Returned for TD	Three tied 2	—
Total Points Scored	St.L. 526	Jax. 217
Total TDs	St.L. 66	Buff. & T.B. 23
TDs Rushing	Wash. 23	St.L. 4
TDs Passing	St.L. 42	T.B. 11
TDs on Ret. and Rec.	KC & St.L. 11	Jax. 0
Extra Points	St.L. 64	Three tied 22
2-Point Conversions	Jax. 4	—
Safeties	Tenn. 4	—
Field Goals Made	Mia. 39	Tenn. 15
Field Goals Attempted	Mia. 46	Jax. 18
% Successful	S.F. 91.3	N.Y.G. 64.9

NFL CLUB RANKINGS BY YARDS

	Offense			Defense		
	Total	Rush	Pass	Total	Rush	Pass
Arizona	29	29	27	22	30	10
Atlanta	27	30	17	16	29	9
Baltimore	24	16	25	2	2	6
Buffalo	11	8	19T	*1	4	*1
Carolina	6	20	2	26	24	23
Chicago	8	26	3	29	23	29
Cincinnati	15	6T	23	25	16	28
Cleveland	31	31	29	31	31	11
Dallas	16	6T	24	9	6	13
Denver	14	12	15	7	19	8
Detroit	21	28	9	18	9	27
Green Bay	9	21	7	19	22	18
Indianapolis	4	19	4	15	18	19
Jacksonville	7	2	12	4	7	3
Kansas City	12	4	22	14	11	16
Miami	20	22	13T	5	8	5
Minnesota	3	14	5	27	14	30
New England	18	23	10	8	21	7
New Orleans	19	18	19T	20	20	21
N.Y. Giants	17	24T	8	13	13	14
N.Y. Jets	25	11	28	21	17	24
Oakland	5	3	11	10	12	12
Philadelphia	30	17	31	24	28	15
Pittsburgh	22	10	26	11	26	4
St. Louis	*1	5	*1	6	*1	20
San Diego	26	27	18	12	3	22
San Francisco	10	*1	21	28	15	31
Seattle	23	24T	16	23	25	17
Tampa Bay	28	15	30	3	5	2
Tennessee	13	13	13T	17	10	25
Washington	2	9	6	30	27	26

T = Tied for position
* = League Leader

AFC TAKEAWAYS/GIVEAWAYS

	Takeaways			Giveaways			Net
	Int	Fum	Total	Int	Fum	Total	Diff.
Kansas City	25	20	45	15	9	24	+21
Tennessee	16	24	40	13	9	22	+18
N.Y. Jets	24	11	35	16	6	22	+13
Jacksonville	19	11	30	11	7	18	+12
Oakland	20	13	33	14	15	29	+4
Pittsburgh	14	14	28	18	7	25	+3
Seattle	30	6	36	16	17	33	+3
Baltimore	21	10	31	20	11	31	0
Denver	15	11	26	18	10	28	-2
New England	16	15	31	21	12	33	-2
Cincinnati	12	15	27	18	14	32	-5
Indianapolis	10	13	23	17	11	28	-5
Buffalo	12	9	21	16	11	27	-6
Miami	18	10	28	21	13	34	-6
San Diego	15	12	27	24	11	35	-8
Cleveland	8	12	20	15	16	31	-11

NFC TAKEAWAYS/GIVEAWAYS

	Takeaways			Giveaways			Net
	Int	Fum	Total	Int	Fum	Total	Diff.
Washington	24	13	37	14	11	25	+12
Dallas	24	9	33	13	10	23	+10
Detroit	16	16	32	14	8	22	+10
Philadelphia	28	18	46	18	21	39	+7
Green Bay	26	15	41	23	13	36	+5
St. Louis	29	7	36	15	16	31	+5
Chicago	14	19	33	22	15	37	-4
Tampa Bay	21	10	31	16	19	35	-4
Carolina	15	14	29	15	19	34	-5
New Orleans	19	15	34	30	9	39	-5
N.Y. Giants	17	7	24	20	12	32	-8
Minnesota	12	18	30	21	19	40	-10
San Francisco	13	7	20	19	13	32	-12
Arizona	17	10	27	30	10	40	-13
Atlanta	12	6	18	19	16	35	-17

1999 INDIVIDUAL STATISTICS—SCORING

SCORING

Points
- **AFC:** 145—Mike Vanderjagt, Indianapolis
- **NFC:** 124—Jeff Wilkins, St. Louis

Touchdowns
- **AFC:** 17—Edgerrin James, Indianapolis
- **NFC:** 17—Stephen Davis, Washington

Extra Points
- **NFC:** 64—Jeff Wilkins, St. Louis
- **AFC:** 45—Pete Stoyanovich, Kansas City

Field Goals
- **AFC:** 39—Olindo Mare, Miami
- **NFC:** 27—Martin Gramatica, Tampa Bay

Field Goal Attempts
- **AFC:** 46—Olindo Mare, Miami
- **NFC:** 32—Brett Conway, Washington
  Martin Gramatica, Tampa Bay
  Jason Hanson, Detroit

Longest Field Goal
- **AFC:** 55—Jason Elam, Denver at San Diego, November 7
- **NFC:** 53—David Akers, Philadelphia at Miami, October 24
  Martin Gramatica, Tampa Bay vs. Atlanta, November 21

Most Points, Game
- **NFC:** 24—Az-Zahir Hakim, St. Louis at Cincinnati, October 3 (4 TD)
  Isaac Bruce, St. Louis vs. San Francisco, October 10 (4 TD)
  Dorsey Levens, Green Bay vs. Ariz.ona, January 2 (4 TD)
- **AFC:** 19—Olindo Mare, Miami at New England, October 17 (6 FG, 1 XP)

Team Leaders, Points

AFC: BALTIMORE, 116, Matt Stover; BUFFALO, 108, Steve Christie; CINCINNATI, 81, Doug Pelfrey; CLEVELAND, 54, Terry Kirby; DENVER, 116, Jason Elam; INDIANAPOLIS, 145, Mike Vanderjagt; JACKSONVILLE, 130, Mike Hollis; KANSAS CITY, 108, Pete Stoyanovich; MIAMI, 144, Olindo Mare; NEW ENGLAND, 107, Adam Vinatieri; N.Y. JETS, 108, John Hall; OAKLAND, 90, Michael Husted; PITTSBURGH, 105, Kris Brown; SAN DIEGO, 115, John Carney; SEATTLE, 134, Todd Peterson; TENNESSEE, 106, Al Del Greco.

NFC: ARIZONA, 83, Chris Jacke; ATLANTA, 79, Morten Andersen; CAROLINA, 99, John Kasay; CHICAGO, 54, Marcus Robinson; DALLAS, 78, Emmitt Smith; DETROIT, 106, Jason Hanson; GREEN BAY, 113, Ryan Longwell; MINNESOTA, 103, Gary Anderson; NEW ORLEANS, 92, Doug Brien; N.Y. GIANTS, 73, Cary Blanchard; PHILADELPHIA, 79, Norm Johnson; ST. LOUIS, 124, Jeff Wilkins; SAN FRANCISCO, 93, Wade Richey; TAMPA BAY, 106, Martin Gramatica; WASHINGTON, 115, Brett Conway.

Team Champion
- **NFC:** 526—St. Louis
- **AFC:** 423—Indianapolis

AFC SCORING—TEAM

	TD	TDR	TDP	TDM	Extra Pt. Made	Kicks Att.	2-Point Made	Tries Att.	FG	FGA	SAF	PTS
Indianapolis	46	15	26	5	43	43	1	3	34	38	0	423
Jacksonville	42	20	16	6	37	37	4	5	31	38	3	396
Tennessee	46	19	23	4	43	43	1	3	21	25	4	392
Kansas City	47	14	22	11	45	45	0	2	21	28	0	390
Oakland	45	18	24	3	43	43	1	2	25	38	0	390
Seattle	34	5	25	4	32	32	0	2	34	40	0	338
Miami	30	8	20	2	27	27	0	3	39	46	1	326
Baltimore	34	9	21	4	32	32	1	1	28	33	1	324
Buffalo	35	12	21	2	33	33	1	2	25	34	0	320
Pittsburgh	35	14	19	2	30	31	1	4	25	29	0	317
Denver	32	13	16	3	29	29	1	1	29	36	2	314
N.Y. Jets	33	7	22	4	27	29	0	4	27	33	1	308
New England	32	9	19	4	29	30	0	2	26	33	0	299
Cincinnati	33	11	18	4	27	27	2	6	18	27	0	283
San Diego	25	10	12	3	22	23	1	2	31	36	1	269
Cleveland	28	9	19	0	23	24	1	4	8	12	0	217
AFC Total	577	193	323	61	522	528	15	46	422	526	13	5306
AFC Average	36.1	12.1	20.2	3.8	32.6	33.0	0.9	2.9	26.4	32.9	0.8	331.6

NFC SCORING—TEAM

	TD	TDR	TDP	TDM	Extra Pt. Made	Kicks Att.	2-Point Made	Tries Att.	FG	FGA	SAF	PTS
St. Louis	66	13	42	11	64	64	2	2	20	28	1	526
Washington	54	23	26	5	49	50	2	3	22	32	0	443
Carolina	50	12	36	2	46	47	0	3	25	28	0	421
Minnesota	49	13	32	4	46	46	0	3	19	30	1	399
Green Bay	40	13	23	4	38	38	1	2	25	30	1	357
Dallas	42	16	20	6	41	41	0	0	19	31	1	352
Detroit	35	8	22	5	28	29	2	6	26	32	1	322
N.Y. Giants	32	11	17	4	28	28	2	3	25	30	0	299
San Francisco	33	14	14	5	30	31	1	2	21	23	1	295
Atlanta	34	9	22	3	34	34	0	0	15	21	1	285
Chicago	31	4	25	2	27	28	1	3	19	34	0	272
Philadelphia	29	5	18	6	27	27	2	2	21	31	2	272
Tampa Bay	27	7	18	2	25	25	0	2	27	32	1	270
New Orleans	27	9	16	2	20	21	3	6	24	29	0	260
Arizona	27	13	11	3	26	26	0	1	19	27	0	245
NFC Total	576	170	342	64	529	535	16	38	327	438	10	5018
NFC Average	38.4	11.3	22.8	4.3	35.3	35.7	1.1	2.5	21.8	29.2	0.7	334.5
League Total	1153	363	665	125	1051	1063	31	84	749	964	23	10324
League Average	37.2	11.7	21.5	4.0	33.9	34.3	1.0	2.7	24.2	31.1	0.7	333.0

NFL TOP TEN SCORERS—NONKICKERS

	TD	TDR	TDP	TDM	2-PT	PTS
Davis, Stephen, Wash.	17	17	0	0	1	104
James, Edgerrin, Ind.	17	13	4	0	0	102
Carter, Cris, Minn.	13	0	13	0	0	78
George, Eddie, Tenn.	13	9	4	0	0	78
Smith, Emmitt, Dall.	13	11	2	0	0	78
Stewart, James, Jax.	13	13	0	0	0	78
Bruce, Isaac, St.L.	12	0	12	0	1	74
Faulk, Marshall, St.L.	12	7	5	0	1	74
Harrison, Marvin, Ind.	12	0	12	0	1	74
Jeffers, Patrick, Car.	12	0	12	0	0	72
Moss, Randy, Minn.	12	0	11	1	0	72
Walls, Wesley, Car.	12	0	12	0	0	72

NFL TOP TEN SCORERS—KICKERS

	XP	XPA	FG	FGA	PTS
Vanderjagt, Mike, Ind.	43	43	34	38	145
Mare, Olindo, Mia.	27	27	39	46	144
Peterson, Todd, Sea.	32	32	34	40	134
Hollis, Mike, Jax.	37	37	31	38	130
Wilkins, Jeff, St.L.	64	64	20	28	124
Elam, Jason, Den.	29	29	29	36	116
Stover, Matt, Balt.	32	32	28	33	116
Carney, John, S.D.	22	23	31	36	115
Conway, Brett, Wash.	49	50	22	32	115
Longwell, Ryan, G.B.	38	38	25	30	113

AFC SCORERS—INDIVIDUAL

Kickers

	XP	XPA	FG	FGA	PTS
Vanderjagt, Mike, Ind.	43	43	34	38	145
Mare, Olindo, Mia.	27	27	39	46	144
Peterson, Todd, Sea.	32	32	34	40	134
Hollis, Mike, Jax.	37	37	31	38	130
Elam, Jason, Den.	29	29	29	36	116
Stover, Matt, Balt.	32	32	28	33	116
Carney, John, S.D.	22	23	31	36	115
Christie, Steve, Buff.	33	33	25	34	108
Hall, John, NYJ	27	29	27	33	108
Stoyanovich, Pete, K.C.	45	45	21	28	108
Vinatieri, Adam, N.E.	29	30	26	33	107
Del Greco, Al, Tenn.	43	43	21	25	106
Brown, Kris, Pitt.	30	31	25	29	105
Husted, Michael, Oak.	30	30	20	31	90
Pelfrey, Doug, Cin.	27	27	18	27	81
Dawson, Phil, Cle.	23	24	8	12	#53
Nedney, Joe, Oak.	13	13	5	7	28

 # Also scored one touchdown.

Nonkickers

	TD	TDR	TDP	TDM	2-PT	PTS
James, Edgerrin, Ind.	17	13	4	0	0	102
George, Eddie, Tenn.	13	9	4	0	0	78
Stewart, James, Jax.	13	13	0	0	0	78
Harrison, Marvin, Ind.	12	0	12	0	1	74
Gonzalez, Tony, K.C.	11	0	11	0	0	66
Wheatley, Tyrone, Oak.	11	8	3	0	0	66
Mayes, Derrick, Sea.	10	0	10	0	0	60
Allen, Terry, N.E.	9	8	1	0	0	54
Dudley, Rickey, Oak.	9	0	9	0	0	54
Kirby, Terry, Cle.	9	6	3	0	0	54
Bennett, Donnell, K.C.	8	8	0	0	0	48
Huntley, Richard, Pitt.	8	5	3	0	0	48
Johnson, Kevin, Cle.	8	0	8	0	0	48
Johnson, Keyshawn, NYJ	8	0	8	0	0	48
McNair, Steve, Tenn.	8	8	0	0	0	48
Gary, Olandis, Den.	7	7	0	0	1	44
Ward, Hines, Pitt.	7	0	7	0	1	44
Bettis, Jerome, Pitt.	7	7	0	0	0	42
Dawkins, Sean, Sea.	7	0	7	0	0	42
McCaffrey, Ed, Den.	7	0	7	0	0	42
Moulds, Eric, Buff.	7	0	7	0	0	42
Rhett, Errict, Balt.	7	5	2	0	0	42
Scott, Darnay, Cin.	7	0	7	0	0	42
Watters, Ricky, Sea.	7	5	2	0	0	42
Wilkins, Terrence, Ind.	7	0	4	3	0	42
Linton, Jonathan, Buff.	6	5	1	0	1	38
Smith, Jimmy, Jax.	6	0	6	0	1	38
Brown, Tim, Oak.	6	0	6	0	0	36
Dillon, Corey, Cin.	6	5	1	0	0	36
Gadsden, Oronde, Mia.	6	0	6	0	0	36
Horn, Joe, K.C.	6	0	6	0	0	36
Ismail, Qadry, Balt.	6	0	6	0	0	36
Jefferson, Shawn, N.E.	6	0	6	0	0	36
Pickens, Carl, Cin.	6	0	6	0	0	36
Smith, Antowain, Buff.	6	6	0	0	0	36
Taylor, Fred, Jax.	6	6	0	0	0	36
McCardell, Keenan, Jax.	5	0	5	0	1	32
Crockett, Zack, Oak.	5	4	1	0	0	30
Edwards, Troy, Pitt.	5	0	5	0	0	30
Martin, Curtis, NYJ	5	5	0	0	0	30
Martin, Tony, Mia.	5	0	5	0	0	30
Means, Natrone, S.D.	5	4	1	0	0	30
Pritchett, Stanley, Mia.	5	1	4	0	0	30
Armour, Justin, Balt.	4	0	4	0	0	24
Chiaverini, Darrin, Cle.	4	0	4	0	0	24
Dyson, Kevin, Tenn.	4	0	4	0	0	24
Glenn, Terry, N.E.	4	0	4	0	0	24
Johnson, J.J., Mia.	4	4	0	0	0	24
Jones, Damon, Jax.	4	0	4	0	0	24
Pollard, Marcus, Ind.	4	0	4	0	0	24
Riemersma, Jay, Buff.	4	0	4	0	0	24
Smith, Rod, Den.	4	0	4	0	0	24
Stephens, Tremayne, S.D.	4	3	1	0	0	24
Thigpen, Yancey, Tenn.	4	0	4	0	0	24
Alexander, Derrick S., K.C.	3	1	2	0	0	18
Anderson, Richie, NYJ	3	0	3	0	0	18
Bynum, Kenny, S.D.	3	1	2	0	0	18
Case, Stoney, Balt.	3	3	0	0	0	18
Chrebet, Wayne, NYJ	3	0	3	0	0	18
Johnson, Pat, Balt.	3	0	3	0	0	18
Kaufman, Napoleon, Oak.	3	2	1	0	0	18
Morris, Bam, K.C.	3	3	0	0	0	18
Neal, Lorenzo, Tenn.	3	1	2	0	0	18
Price, Peerless, Buff.	3	0	3	0	0	18
Roan, Michael, Tenn.	3	0	3	0	0	18
Shaw, Bobby, Pitt.	3	0	3	0	0	18
Stewart, Kordell, Pitt.	3	2	1	0	0	18
Ward, Dedric, NYJ	3	0	3	0	0	18
Jackson, Willie, Cin.	2	0	2	0	1	14
Jett, James, Oak.	2	0	2	0	1	14
Abdul-Jabbar, Karim, Mia.-Cle.	2	1	1	0	0	12
Baxter, Fred, NYJ	2	0	2	0	0	12
Beasley, Aaron, Jax.	2	0	0	2	0	12
Blake, Jeff, Cin.	2	2	0	0	0	12
Byrd, Isaac, Tenn.	2	0	2	0	0	12
Carswell, Dwayne, Den.	2	0	2	0	0	12
Chamberlain, Byron, Den.	2	0	2	0	0	12
Coates, Ben, N.E.	2	0	2	0	0	12
Collins, Bobby, Buff.	2	0	2	0	0	12
Collins, Cecil, Mia.	2	2	0	0	0	12
Davis, Terrell, Den.	2	2	0	0	0	12
Dilger, Ken, Ind.	2	0	2	0	0	12
Dishman, Cris, K.C.	2	0	0	2	0	12
Edwards, Donnie, K.C.	2	0	0	2	0	12
Edwards, Marc, Cle.	2	0	2	0	0	12
Faulk, Kevin, N.E.	2	1	1	0	0	12
Fazande, Jermaine, S.D.	2	2	0	0	0	12
Gannon, Rich, Oak.	2	2	0	0	0	12
Gash, Sam, Buff.	2	0	2	0	0	12
Graham, Jeff, S.D.	2	0	2	0	0	12
Green, Eric, NYJ	2	0	2	0	0	12
Griese, Brian, Den.	2	2	0	0	0	12
Griffith, Howard, Den.	2	1	1	0	0	12
Hasty, James, K.C.	2	0	0	2	0	12
Holmes, Priest, Balt.	2	1	1	0	0	12
Jones, Freddie, S.D.	2	0	2	0	0	12
Jordan, Randy, Oak.	2	2	0	0	0	12
Lewis, Darryll, S.D.	2	0	0	2	0	12
Lewis, Jermaine, Balt.	2	0	2	0	0	12
Lockett, Kevin, K.C.	2	0	2	0	0	12
Manning, Peyton, Ind.	2	2	0	0	0	12
McDuffie, O.J., Mia.	2	0	2	0	0	12
McGee, Tony, Cin.	2	0	2	0	0	12
Pritchard, Mike, Sea.	2	0	2	0	0	12
Simmons, Tony, N.E.	2	0	2	0	0	12
Tongue, Reggie, K.C.	2	0	0	2	0	12
Vanover, Tamarick, K.C.	2	0	0	2	0	12
Woodson, Rod, Balt.	2	0	0	2	0	12
Wycheck, Frank, Tenn.	2	0	2	0	0	12
Yeast, Craig, Cin.	2	0	0	2	0	12
Brady, Kyle, Jax.	1	0	1	0	1	8
Brunell, Mark, Jax.	1	1	0	0	1	8
Couch, Tim, Cle.	1	1	0	0	1	8

1999 INDIVIDUAL STATISTICS—SCORING

	TD	TDR	TDP	TDM	2-PT	PTS
Evans, Chuck, Balt.	1	0	1	0	1	8
Harris, Jackie, Tenn.	1	0	1	0	1	8
Madison, Sam, Mia.	1	0	0	1	0	*8
Barlow, Reggie, Jax.	1	0	0	1	0	6
Bartrum, Mike, N.E.	1	0	1	0	0	6
Blevins, Tony, Ind.	1	0	0	1	0	6
Bownes, Fabien, Sea.	1	0	1	0	0	6
Brackens, Tony, Jax.	1	0	0	1	0	6
Brown, Reggie, Sea.	1	0	1	0	0	6
Brown, Troy, N.E.	1	0	1	0	0	6
Cadrez, Glenn, Den.	1	0	0	1	0	6
Carter, Ki-Jana, Cin.	1	1	0	0	0	6
Coleman, Marcus, NYJ	1	0	0	1	0	6
Cota, Chad, Ind.	1	0	0	1	0	6
Cox, Bryan, NYJ	1	0	0	1	0	6
Craft, Jason, Jax.	1	0	0	1	0	6
Davis, Reggie, S.D.	1	0	1	0	0	6
Davis, Travis, Pitt.	1	0	0	1	0	6
DeLong, Greg, Balt.	1	0	1	0	0	6
Detmer, Ty, Cle.	1	1	0	0	0	6
Dixon, Gerald, S.D.	1	0	0	1	0	6
Drayton, Troy, Mia.	1	0	1	0	0	6
Eaton, Chad, N.E.	1	0	0	1	0	6
Flutie, Doug, Buff.	1	1	0	0	0	6
Galloway, Joey, Sea.	1	0	1	0	0	6
Groce, Clif, Cin.	1	1	0	0	0	6
Hanks, Merton, Sea.	1	0	0	1	0	6
Harris, Corey, Balt.	1	0	0	1	0	6
Heath, Rodney, Cin.	1	0	0	1	0	6
Hicks, Eric, K.C.	1	0	0	1	0	6
Johnson, Lonnie, K.C.	1	0	1	0	0	6
Johnstone, Lance, Oak.	1	0	0	1	0	6
Jones, Charlie, S.D.	1	0	1	0	0	6
Jones, Henry, Buff.	1	0	0	1	0	6
Katzenmoyer, Andy, N.E.	1	0	0	1	0	6
Kearse, Jevon, Tenn.	1	0	0	1	0	6
Konrad, Rob, Mia.	1	0	1	0	0	6
Law, Ty, N.E.	1	0	0	1	0	6
Loville, Derek, Den.	1	1	0	0	0	6
Lucas, Ray, NYJ	1	1	0	0	0	6
Mack, Tremain, Cin.	1	0	0	1	0	6
Mason, Derrick, Tenn.	1	0	0	1	0	6
McCrary, Fred, S.D.	1	0	1	0	0	6
McGinest, Willie, N.E.	1	0	0	1	0	6
Mili, Itula, Sea.	1	0	1	0	0	6
Mirer, Rick, NYJ	1	1	0	0	0	6
Mitchell, Donald, Tenn.	1	0	0	1	0	6
Northern, Gabe, Buff.	1	0	0	1	0	6
Ogbogu, Eric, NYJ	1	0	0	1	0	6
Penn, Chris, S.D.	1	0	1	0	0	6
Perry, Ed, Mia.	1	0	1	0	0	6
Porter, Joey, Pitt.	1	0	0	1	0	6
Reed, Andre, Buff.	1	0	1	0	0	6
Richardson, Tony, K.C.	1	1	0	0	0	6
Ritchie, Jon, Oak.	1	0	1	0	0	6
Rogers, Charlie, Sea.	1	0	0	1	0	6
Romanowski, Bill, Den.	1	0	0	1	0	6
Sanders, Chris, Tenn.	1	0	1	0	0	6
Shaw, Sedrick, Cin.	1	1	0	0	0	6
Shedd, Kenny, Oak.	1	0	0	1	0	6
Shehee, Rashaan, K.C.	1	1	0	0	0	6
Smith, Irv, Cle.	1	0	1	0	0	6
Smith, Akili, Cin.	1	1	0	0	0	6
Spence, Blake, NYJ	1	0	1	0	0	6
Springs, Shawn, Sea.	1	0	0	1	0	6
Starks, Duane, Balt.	1	0	0	1	0	6
Stokley, Brandon, Balt.	1	0	1	0	0	6
Stoutmire, Omar, NYJ	1	0	0	1	0	6
Taylor, Jason, Mia.	1	0	0	1	0	6
Thomas, Rodney, Tenn.	1	1	0	0	0	6
Thomas, Thurman, Buff.	1	0	1	0	0	6
Walker, Denard, Tenn.	1	0	0	1	0	6
Walker, Derrick, Oak.	1	0	1	0	0	6
Warren, Lamont, N.E.	1	0	1	0	0	6
Watson, Chris, Den.	1	0	0	1	0	6
Whitted, Alvis, Jax.	1	0	0	1	0	6
Williams, Willie, Sea.	1	0	0	1	0	6
Woodson, Charles, Oak.	1	0	0	1	0	6
Lewis, Ray, Balt.	0	0	0	0	0	*2
Milne, Brian, Cin.	0	0	0	0	1	2
Pryce, Trevor, Den.	0	0	0	0	0	*2
Ricks, Mikhael, S.D.	0	0	0	0	1	2

	XP	XPA	FG	FGA		PTS
Smeenge, Joel, Jax.	0	0	0	0	0	*2
Thornton, John, Tenn.	0	0	0	0	0	*2

** Safety*

Team safeties credited to Denver, Jacksonville (2), N.Y. Jets, San Diego, Tennessee (3).

NFC SCORERS—INDIVIDUAL

Kickers

	XP	XPA	FG	FGA	PTS
Wilkins, Jeff, St.L.	64	64	20	28	124
Conway, Brett, Wash.	49	50	22	32	115
Longwell, Ryan, G.B.	38	38	25	30	113
Gramatica, Martin, T.B.	25	25	27	32	106
Hanson, Jason, Det.	28	29	26	32	106
Anderson, Gary, Minn.	46	46	19	30	103
Kasay, John, Car.	33	33	22	25	99
Richey, Wade, S.F.	30	31	21	23	93
Brien, Doug, N.O.	20	21	24	29	92
Cunningham, Richie, Dall.-Car.	44	45	15	25	89
Jacke, Chris, Ariz.	26	26	19	27	83
Andersen, Morten, Atl.	34	34	15	21	79
Johnson, Norm, Phil.	25	25	18	25	79
Blanchard, Cary, NYG	19	19	18	21	73
Boniol, Chris, Chi.	17	18	11	18	50
Murray, Eddie, Dall.	10	10	7	9	31
Daluiso, Brad, NYG	9	9	7	9	30
Gowins, Brian, Chi.	3	3	4	6	15
Jaeger, Jeff, Chi.	7	7	2	8	13
Akers, David, Phil.	2	2	3	6	11
Holmes, Jaret, Chi.	0	0	2	2	6

Nonkickers

	TD	TDR	TDP	TDM	2-PT	PTS
Davis, Stephen, Wash.	17	17	0	0	1	104
Carter, Cris, Minn.	13	0	13	0	0	78
Smith, Emmitt, Dall.	13	11	2	0	0	78
Bruce, Isaac, St.L.	12	0	12	0	1	74
Faulk, Marshall, St.L.	12	7	5	0	1	74
Jeffers, Patrick, Car.	12	0	12	0	0	72
Moss, Randy, Minn.	12	0	11	1	0	72
Walls, Wesley, Car.	12	0	12	0	0	72
Hoard, Leroy, Minn.	10	10	0	0	0	60
Levens, Dorsey, G.B.	10	9	1	0	0	60
Westbrook, Michael, Wash.	9	0	9	0	1	56
Alstott, Mike, T.B.	9	7	2	0	0	54
Bates, Mario, Ariz.	9	9	0	0	0	54
Dwight, Tim, Atl.	9	1	7	1	0	54
Hakim, Az-Zahir, St.L.	9	0	8	1	0	54
Robinson, Marcus, Chi.	9	0	9	0	0	54
Muhammad, Muhsin, Car.	8	0	8	0	0	48
Crowell, Germane, Det.	7	0	7	0	1	44
Christian, Bob, Atl.	7	5	2	0	0	42
Connell, Albert, Wash.	7	0	7	0	0	42
Ismail, Raghib, Dall.	7	1	6	0	0	42
LaFleur, David, Dall.	7	0	7	0	0	42
Biakabutuka, Tim, Car.	6	6	0	0	0	36
Freeman, Antonio, G.B.	6	0	6	0	0	36
Garner, Charlie, S.F.	6	4	2	0	0	36
Holt, Torry, St.L.	6	0	6	0	0	36
Mathis, Terance, Atl.	6	0	6	0	0	36
Poole, Keith, N.O.	6	0	6	0	0	36
Staley, Duce, Phil.	6	4	2	0	0	36
Toomer, Amani, NYG	6	0	6	0	0	36
Williams, Roland, St.L.	6	0	6	0	0	36
Bradford, Corey, G.B.	5	0	5	0	1	32
Enis, Curtis, Chi.	5	3	2	0	0	30
Holcombe, Robert, St.L.	5	4	1	0	0	30
Moore, Dave, T.B.	5	0	5	0	0	30
Moore, Rob, Ariz.	5	0	5	0	0	30
Morton, Johnnie, Det.	5	0	5	0	0	30
Rice, Jerry, S.F.	5	0	5	0	0	30
Schroeder, Bill, G.B.	5	0	5	0	0	30
Kennison, Eddie, N.O.	4	0	4	0	1	26
Beasley, Fred, S.F.	4	4	0	0	0	24
Broughton, Luther, Phil.	4	0	4	0	0	24
Conway, Curtis, Chi.	4	0	4	0	0	24
Engram, Bobby, Chi.	4	0	4	0	0	24
Irvin, Sedrick, Det.	4	4	0	0	0	24
Owens, Terrell, S.F.	4	0	4	0	0	24
Sloan, David, Det.	4	0	4	0	0	24

1999 INDIVIDUAL STATISTICS—SCORING

	TD	TDR	TDP	TDM	2-PT	PTS
Small, Torrance, Phil.	4	0	4	0	0	24
Montgomery, Joe, NYG	3	3	0	0	1	20
Stokes, J.J., S.F.	3	0	3	0	1	20
Alexander, Stephen, Wash.	3	0	3	0	0	18
Barber, Tiki, NYG	3	0	2	1	0	18
Booker, Marty, Chi.	3	0	3	0	0	18
Centers, Larry, Wash.	3	0	3	0	0	18
Floyd, William, Car.	3	3	0	0	0	18
German, Jammi, Atl.	3	0	3	0	0	18
Green, Jacquez, T.B.	3	0	3	0	0	18
Henderson, William, G.B.	3	2	1	0	0	18
Hicks, Skip, Wash.	3	3	0	0	0	18
Hilliard, Ike, NYG	3	0	3	0	0	18
Irvin, Michael, Dall.	3	0	3	0	0	18
Johnson, LeShon, NYG	3	2	1	0	0	18
Jones, Mike A., St.L.	3	0	0	3	0	18
Lewis, Chad, Phil.	3	0	3	0	0	18
Mitchell, Pete, NYG	3	0	3	0	0	18
Tolliver, Billy Joe, N.O.	3	3	0	0	0	18
Collins, Kerry, NYG	2	2	0	0	1	14
Abraham, Donnie, T.B.	2	0	0	2	0	12
Batch, Charlie, Det.	2	2	0	0	0	12
Bates, Michael, Car.	2	0	0	2	0	12
Beuerlein, Steve, Car.	2	2	0	0	0	12
Boston, David, Ariz.	2	0	2	0	0	12
Davis, Tyrone, G.B.	2	0	2	0	0	12
Delhomme, Jake, N.O.	2	2	0	0	0	12
Dunn, Warrick, T.B.	2	0	2	0	0	12
Ellis, Greg, Dall.	2	0	0	2	0	12
Fair, Terry, Det.	2	0	0	2	0	12
Fryar, Irving, Wash.	2	0	2	0	0	12
Garcia, Jeff, S.F.	2	2	0	0	0	12
Hatchette, Matt, Minn.	2	0	2	0	0	12
Hayes, Donald, Car.	2	0	2	0	0	12
Hill, Greg, Det.	2	2	0	0	0	12
Horne, Tony, St.L.	2	0	0	2	0	12
Jells, Dietrich, Phil.	2	0	2	0	0	12
Johnson, Brad, Wash.	2	2	0	0	0	12
Kinchen, Brian, Car.	2	0	2	0	0	12
Kozlowski, Brian, Atl.	2	0	2	0	0	12
McKenzie, Keith, G.B.	2	0	0	2	0	12
Moore, Herman, Det.	2	0	2	0	0	12
Oxendine, Ken, Atl.	2	1	1	0	0	12
Parker, De'Mond, G.B.	2	2	0	0	0	12
Phillips, Lawrence, S.F.	2	2	0	0	0	12
Pittman, Michael, Ariz.	2	2	0	0	0	12
Plummer, Jake, Ariz.	2	2	0	0	0	12
Reed, Jake, Minn.	2	0	2	0	0	12
Robinson, Jeff, St.L.	2	0	2	0	0	12
Sellers, Mike, Wash.	2	0	2	0	0	12
Smith, Robert, Minn.	2	2	0	0	0	12
Teague, George, Dall.	2	0	0	2	0	12
Thomason, Jeff, G.B.	2	0	2	0	0	12
Tucker, Jason, Dall.	2	0	2	0	0	12
Walker, Darnell, S.F.	2	0	0	2	0	12
Warren, Chris, Dall.	2	2	0	0	0	12
Way, Charles, NYG	2	2	0	0	0	12
Williams, Ricky, N.O.	2	2	0	0	0	12
Williams, Moe, Minn.	2	1	0	1	0	12
Wistrom, Grant, St.L.	2	0	0	2	0	12
Bech, Brett, N.O.	1	0	1	0	1	8
Cleeland, Cameron, N.O.	1	0	1	0	1	8
Johnson, Charles, Phil.	1	0	1	0	0	*8
Stablein, Brian, Det.	1	0	1	0	1	8
Aikman, Troy, Dall.	1	1	0	0	0	6
Aldridge, Allen, Det.	1	0	0	1	0	6
Alford, Brian, NYG	1	0	1	0	0	6
Allred, John, Chi.	1	0	1	0	0	6
Anthony, Reidel, T.B.	1	0	1	0	0	6
Bailey, Champ, Wash.	1	0	0	1	0	6
Barber, Shawn, Wash.	1	0	0	1	0	6
Bennett, Sean, NYG	1	1	0	0	0	6
Bieniemy, Eric, Phil.	1	1	0	0	0	6
Bjornson, Eric, Dall.	1	1	0	0	0	6
Bly, Dre', St.L.	1	0	0	1	0	6
Brown, Na, Phil.	1	0	1	0	0	6
Bryant, Junior, S.F.	1	0	0	1	0	6
Buchanan, Ray, Atl.	1	0	0	1	0	6
Bush, Devin, St.L.	1	0	0	1	0	6
Calloway, Chris, Atl.	1	0	1	0	0	6
Chandler, Chris, Atl.	1	1	0	0	0	6
Coakley, Dexter, Dall.	1	0	0	1	0	6
Cody, Mac, Ariz.	1	0	1	0	0	6
Coleman, Marco, Wash.	1	0	0	1	0	6
Crumpler, Carlester, Minn.	1	0	1	0	0	6
Davis, John, T.B.	1	0	1	0	0	6
Dawkins, Brian, Phil.	1	0	0	1	0	6
Dawsey, Lawrence, N.O.	1	0	1	0	0	6
Douglas, Dameane, Phil.	1	0	1	0	0	6
Drakeford, Tyronne, N.O.	1	0	0	1	0	6
Driver, Donald, G.B.	1	0	1	0	0	6
Edwards, Antuan, G.B.	1	0	0	1	0	6
Elliss, Luther, Det.	1	0	0	1	0	6
Emanuel, Bert, T.B.	1	0	1	0	0	6
Fredrickson, Rob, Ariz.	1	0	0	1	0	6
Glover, Andrew, Minn.	1	0	1	0	0	6
Graham, Kent, NYG	1	1	0	0	0	6
Hanspard, Byron, Atl.	1	1	0	0	0	6
Hape, Patrick, T.B.	1	0	1	0	0	6
Harris, Al, Phil.	1	0	0	1	0	6
Harris, Sean, Chi.	1	0	0	1	0	6
Hastings, Andre, N.O.	1	0	1	0	0	6
Hobert, Billy Joe, N.O.	1	1	0	0	0	6
Hodgins, James, St.L.	1	1	0	0	0	6
Howard, Desmond, Det.	1	0	0	1	0	6
Jervey, Travis, S.F.	1	1	0	0	0	6
Jordan, Andrew, Minn.	1	0	1	0	0	6
Jurevicius, Joe, NYG	1	0	1	0	0	6
Lane, Fred, Car.	1	1	0	0	0	6
Lassiter, Kwamie, Ariz.	1	0	0	1	0	6
Lee, Amp, St.L.	1	0	1	0	0	6
Lyght, Todd, St.L.	1	0	0	1	0	6
Makovicka, Joel, Ariz.	1	0	1	0	0	6
Mamula, Mike, Phil.	1	0	0	1	0	6
Mayes, Alonzo, Chi.	1	0	1	0	0	6
McDonald, Darnell, T.B.	1	0	1	0	0	6
McLeod, Kevin, T.B.	1	0	1	0	0	6
McMillian, Mark, S.F.	1	0	0	1	0	6
McWilliams, Johnny, Ariz.	1	0	1	0	0	6
Milburn, Glyn, Chi.	1	1	0	0	0	6
Minter, Barry, Chi.	1	0	0	1	0	6
Mitchell, Basil, G.B.	1	0	0	1	0	6
Mitchell, Brian, Wash.	1	1	0	0	0	6
Oliver, Winslow, Atl.	1	0	0	1	0	6
Peter, Christian, NYG	1	0	0	1	0	6
Rasby, Walter, Det.	1	0	1	0	0	6
Rivers, Ron, Det.	1	0	1	0	0	6
Rossum, Allen, Phil.	1	0	0	1	0	6
Sanders, Deion, Dall.	1	0	0	1	0	6
Sanders, Frank, Ariz.	1	0	1	0	0	6
Schlesinger, Cory, Det.	1	0	1	0	0	6
Schulters, Lance, S.F.	1	0	0	1	0	6
Slutzker, Scott, N.O.	1	0	1	0	0	6
Smith, Lamar, N.O.	1	0	1	0	0	6
Strahan, Michael, NYG	1	0	0	1	0	6
Swann, Eric, Ariz.	1	0	0	1	0	6
Tate, Robert, Minn.	1	0	0	1	0	6
Taylor, Bobby, Phil.	1	0	0	1	0	6
Thomas, Orlando, Minn.	1	0	0	1	0	6
Thrash, James, Wash.	1	0	0	1	0	6
Tucker, Ryan, St.L.	1	0	1	0	0	6
Vardell, Tommy, S.F.	1	1	0	0	0	6
Walsh, Chris, Minn.	1	0	1	0	0	6
Warner, Kurt, St.L.	1	1	0	0	0	6
Weary, Fred, N.O.	1	0	0	1	0	6
Weathers, Andre, NYG	1	0	0	1	0	6
Wetnight, Ryan, Chi.	1	0	1	0	0	6
Whiting, Brandon, Phil.	1	0	0	1	0	6
Wilkinson, Dan, Wash.	1	0	0	1	0	6
Wuerffel, Danny, N.O.	1	1	0	0	0	6
Culpepper, Brad, T.B.	0	0	0	0	0	*2
Fletcher, London, St.L.	0	0	0	0	0	*2
Hambrick, Darren, Dall.	0	0	0	0	0	*2
McNabb, Donovan, Phil.	0	0	0	0	1	2
McNown, Cade, Chi.	0	0	0	0	1	2
Weaver, Jed, Phil.	0	0	0	0	1	2
Young, Bryant, S.F.	0	0	0	0	0	*2

** Safety*
Team safeties credited to Atlanta, Detroit, Green Bay, Minnesota, Philadelphia.

1999 INDIVIDUAL STATISTICS—FIELD GOALS

FIELD GOALS

Field Goal Percentage
- **NFC:** .913—Wade Richey, San Francisco
- **AFC:** .895—Mike Vanderjagt, Indianapolis

Field Goals
- **AFC:** 39—Olindo Mare, Miami
- **NFC:** 27—Martin Gramatica, Tampa Bay

Field Goal Attempts
- **AFC:** 46—Olindo Mare, Miami
- **NFC:** 32—Brett Conway, Washington
  Martin Gramatica, Tampa Bay
  Jason Hanson, Detroit

AFC FIELD GOALS—TEAM

	FG	FGA	Pct.	Long
Indianapolis	34	38	.895	53
Pittsburgh	25	29	.862	51
San Diego	31	36	.861	50
Seattle	34	40	.850	51
Baltimore	28	33	.848	50
Miami	39	46	.848	54
Tennessee	21	25	.840	50
N.Y. Jets	27	33	.818	48
Jacksonville	31	38	.816	50
Denver	29	36	.806	55
New England	26	33	.788	51
Kansas City	21	28	.750	51
Buffalo	25	34	.735	52
Cincinnati	18	27	.667	50
Cleveland	8	12	.667	49
Oakland	25	38	.658	52
AFC Total	422	526	—	55
AFC Average	26.4	32.9	.802	—

Longest Field Goal
- **AFC:** 55—Jason Elam, Denver at San Diego, November 7
- **NFC:** 53—David Akers, Philadelphia at Miami, October 24
  Martin Gramatica, Tampa Bay vs. Atlanta, November 21

Average Yards Made
- **NFC:** 39.2—Jason Hanson, Detroit
- **AFC:** 36.8—Jason Elam, Denver

NFC FIELD GOALS—TEAM

	FG	FGA	Pct.	Long
San Francisco	21	23	.913	52
Carolina	25	28	.893	52
Tampa Bay	27	32	.844	53
Green Bay	25	30	.833	50
N.Y. Giants	25	30	.833	48
New Orleans	24	29	.828	52
Detroit	26	32	.813	52
Atlanta	15	21	.714	49
St. Louis	20	28	.714	51
Ariz.ona	19	27	.704	49
Washington	22	32	.688	51
Philadelphia	21	31	.677	53
Minnesota	19	30	.633	44
Dallas	19	31	.613	47
Chicago	19	34	.559	52
NFC Total	327	438	—	53
NFC Average	21.8	29.2	.747	—
League Total	749	964	—	55
League Average	24.2	31.1	.777	—

AFC FIELD GOALS—INDIVIDUAL

	1-19 Yards	20-29 Yards	30-39 Yards	40-49 Yards	50 or Longer	Totals	Avg. Yds. Att.	Avg. Yds. Made	Avg. Yds. Miss	Long
Vanderjagt, Mike, Ind.	2-2	10-10	11-13	10-11	1-2	34-38	34.9	33.9	43.3	53
	1.000	1.000	.846	.909	.500	.895				
Brown, Kris, Pitt.	2-2	5-5	9-10	8-11	1-1	25-29	36.3	35.4	42.5	51
	1.000	1.000	.900	.727	1.000	.862				
Carney, John, S.D.	2-2	13-13	6-8	9-12	1-1	31-36	33.8	32.5	41.8	50
	1.000	1.000	.750	.750	1.000	.861				
Peterson, Todd, Sea.	1-1	10-10	8-11	14-16	1-2	34-40	36.4	35.5	41.3	51
	1.000	1.000	.727	.875	.500	.850				
Stover, Matt, Balt.	4-4	9-9	6-8	7-7	2-5	28-33	35.1	33.0	46.8	50
	1.000	1.000	.750	1.000	.400	.848				
Mare, Olindo, Mia.	1-1	9-9	17-17	9-14	3-5	39-46	36.9	35.0	47.3	54
	1.000	1.000	1.000	.643	.600	.848				
Del Greco, Al, Tenn.	1-1	8-8	7-9	4-6	1-1	21-25	33.6	32.5	39.0	50
	1.000	1.000	.778	.667	1.000	.840				
Hall, John, NYJ	0-0	3-4	17-17	7-12	0-0	27-33	37.0	35.7	42.7	48
	—	.750	1.000	.583	—	.818				
Hollis, Mike, Jax.	0-0	12-13	8-9	10-15	1-1	31-38	35.1	33.5	42.4	50
	—	.923	.889	.667	1.000	.816				
Elam, Jason, Den.	1-1	8-8	7-8	8-11	5-8	29-36	39.2	36.8	49.0	55
	1.000	1.000	.875	.727	.625	.806				
Vinatieri, Adam, N.E.	1-1	14-14	5-7	5-9	1-2	26-33	33.5	31.0	42.7	51
	1.000	1.000	.714	.556	.500	.788				
Stoyanovich, Pete, K.C.	1-1	7-7	5-6	7-13	1-1	21-28	37.2	35.0	43.6	51
	1.000	1.000	.833	.538	1.000	.750				
Christie, Steve, Buff.	2-2	10-10	7-10	3-9	3-3	25-34	35.4	32.9	42.3	52
	1.000	1.000	.700	.333	1.000	.735				
Pelfrey, Doug, Cin.	1-1	9-11	7-12	0-2	1-1	18-27	32.2	31.4	33.8	50
	1.000	.818	.583	.000	1.000	.667				
Husted, Michael, Oak.	2-2	3-3	7-11	8-12	0-3	20-31	38.2	35.2	43.8	49
	1.000	1.000	.636	.667	.000	.645				
(Nonqualifiers)										
Dawson, Phil, Cle.	0-0	2-2	3-5	3-5	0-0	8-12	38.1	36.3	41.8	49
	—	1.000	.600	.600	—	.667				
Nedney, Joe, Oak.	0-0	2-2	2-2	0-1	1-2	5-7	38.6	34.8	48.0	52
	—	1.000	1.000	.000	.500	.714				
AFC Totals	21-21	134-138	132-163	112-166	23-38	422-526	35.8	34.1	42.8	55
	1.000	.971	.810	.675	.605	.802				

Leader based on percentage, minimum 16 field-goal attempts

NFC FIELD GOALS—INDIVIDUAL

	1-19 Yards	20-29 Yards	30-39 Yards	40-49 Yards	50 or Longer	Totals	Avg. Yds. Att.	Avg. Yds. Made	Avg. Yds. Miss	Long
Richey, Wade, S.F.	1-1	7-7	7-8	5-6	1-1	21-23	34.2	33.3	44.0	52
	1.000	1.000	.875	.833	1.000	.913				
Kasay, John, Car.	1-1	8-8	6-6	5-6	2-4	22-25	35.0	32.9	50.7	52
	1.000	1.000	1.000	.833	.500	.880				
Blanchard, Cary, NYG	0-0	7-7	2-4	9-10	0-0	18-21	35.0	34.5	38.3	48
	—	1.000	.500	.900	—	.857				
Gramatica, Martin, T.B.	0-0	8-8	10-12	6-8	3-4	27-32	37.2	36.0	43.4	53
	—	1.000	.833	.750	.750	.844				
Longwell, Ryan, G.B.	0-0	8-9	8-9	8-10	1-2	25-30	35.8	35.1	39.4	50
	—	.889	.889	.800	.500	.833				
Brien, Doug, N.O.	0-0	9-11	6-7	7-9	2-2	24-29	35.8	35.4	37.4	52
	—	.818	.857	.778	1.000	.828				
Hanson, Jason, Det.	0-0	8-8	4-4	10-12	4-8	26-32	41.6	39.2	52.2	52
	—	1.000	1.000	.833	.500	.813				
Johnson, Norm, Phil.	0-0	8-9	5-8	5-6	0-2	18-25	35.1	33.7	38.9	49
	—	.889	.625	.833	.000	.720				
Andersen, Morten, Atl.	1-1	5-5	5-8	4-6	0-1	15-21	36.0	33.5	42.2	49
	1.000	1.000	.625	.667	.000	.714				
Wilkins, Jeff, St.L.	1-1	5-5	6-7	7-11	1-4	20-28	38.9	36.3	45.6	51
	1.000	1.000	.857	.636	.250	.714				
Jacke, Chris, Ariz.	0-0	5-5	10-12	4-7	0-3	19-27	37.1	33.8	44.9	49
	—	1.000	.833	.571	.000	.704				
Conway, Brett, Wash.	0-0	7-9	6-7	6-7	3-9	22-32	38.8	35.9	45.3	51
	—	.778	.857	.857	.333	.688				
Anderson, Gary, Minn.	0-0	6-8	9-11	4-9	0-2	19-30	35.7	32.9	40.4	44
	—	.750	.818	.444	.000	.633				
Boniol, Chris, Chi.	0-0	6-6	2-6	3-5	0-1	11-18	34.4	32.2	37.9	46
	—	1.000	.333	.600	.000	.611				
Cunningham, Richie, Dall.-Car.	0-0	6-8	5-6	4-10	0-1	15-25	35.8	32.9	40.2	47
	—	.750	.833	.400	.000	.600				
(Nonqualifiers)										
Daluiso, Brad, NYG	0-0	4-4	3-3	0-2	0-0	7-9	31.2	28.3	41.5	36
	—	1.000	1.000	.000	—	.778				
Murray, Eddie, Dall.	0-0	3-3	3-4	1-2	0-0	7-9	31.9	29.3	41.0	40
	—	1.000	.750	.500	—	.778				
Jaeger, Jeff, Chi.	0-0	0-0	0-2	1-5	1-1	2-8	44.1	46.5	43.3	52
	—	—	.000	.200	1.000	.250				
Akers, David, Phil.	0-0	0-0	0-0	2-3	1-3	3-6	50.7	49.0	52.3	53
	—	—	—	.667	.333	.500				
Gowins, Brian, Chi.	0-0	3-3	0-0	1-2	0-1	4-6	35.8	29.3	49.0	43
	—	1.000	—	.500	.000	.667				
Holmes, Jaret, Chi.	0-0	0-0	2-2	0-0	0-0	2-2	35.0	35.0	—	39
	—	—	1.000	—	—	1.000				
NFC Totals	4-4	113-123	99-126	92-136	19-49	327-438	36.7	34.7	42.9	53
	1.000	.919	.786	.676	.388	.747				
League Totals	25-25	247-261	231-289	204-302	42-87	749-964	36.2	34.3	42.9	55
	1.000	.946	.799	.675	.483	.777				

Leader based on percentage, minimum 16 field-goal attempts

RUSHING

Yards
- **AFC:** 1553—Edgerrin James, Indianapolis
- **NFC:** 1405—Stephen Davis, Washington

Yards, Game
- **AFC:** 199—Eddie George, Tennessee vs. Oakland, December 9 (28 attempts, 2 TD)
- **NFC:** 189—Stephen Davis, Washington vs. Ariz.ona, December 12 (37 attempts, TD)

Longest
- **AFC:** 82—Derrick S. Alexander, Kansas City vs. Pittsburgh, December 18 - TD
- **NFC:** 76—Stephen Davis, Washington vs. Ariz.ona, December 12 - TD

Attempts
- **AFC:** 369—Edgerrin James, Indianapolis
- **NFC:** 329—Emmitt Smith, Dallas

Attempts, Game
- **NFC:** 40—Ricky Williams, New Orleans vs. Cleveland, October 31 (179 yards, 0 TD)
- **AFC:** 38—Curtis Martin, N.Y. Jets vs. Ariz.ona, November 7 (131 yards, 0 TD)

Yards Per Attempt
- **NFC:** 5.5—Marshall Faulk, St. Louis
- **AFC:** 5.2—Napoleon Kaufman, Oakland

Touchdowns
- **NFC:** 17—Stephen Davis, Washington
- **AFC:** 13—Edgerrin James, Indianapolis; James Stewart, Jacksonville

Team Leaders, Yards
- **AFC:** BALTIMORE: 852, Errict Rhett; BUFFALO: 695, Jonathan Linton; CINCINNATI: 1200, Corey Dillon; CLEVELAND: 452, Terry Kirby; DENVER: 1159, Olandis Gary; INDIANAPOLIS: 1553, Edgerrin James; JACKSONVILLE: 931, James Stewart; KANSAS CITY: 627, Donnell Bennett; MIAMI: 558, J.J. Johnson; NEW ENGLAND: 896, Terry Allen; N.Y. JETS: 1464, Curtis Martin; OAKLAND: 936, Tyrone Wheatley; PITTSBURGH: 1091, Jerome Bettis; SAN DIEGO: 365, Jermaine Fazande; SEATTLE: 1210, Ricky Watters; TENNESSEE: 1304, Eddie George
- **NFC:** ARIZONA: 553, Adrian Murrell; ATLANTA: 452, Ken Oxendine; CAROLINA: 718, Tim Biakabutuka; CHICAGO: 916, Curtis Enis; DALLAS: 1397, Emmitt Smith; DETROIT: 542, Greg Hill; GREEN BAY: 1034, Dorsey Levens; MINNESOTA: 1015, Robert Smith; NEW ORLEANS: 884, Ricky Williams; N.Y. GIANTS: 348, Joe Montgomery; PHILADELPHIA: 1273, Duce Staley; ST. LOUIS: 1381, Marshall Faulk; SAN FRANCISCO: 1229, Charlie Garner; TAMPA BAY: 949, Mike Alstott; WASHINGTON: 1405, Stephen Davis

Team Champion
- **NFC:** 2095—San Francisco
- **AFC:** 2091—Jacksonville

1999 INDIVIDUAL STATISTICS—RUSHING

AFC RUSHING—TEAM

	Att.	Yards	Avg.	Long	TD
Jacksonville	514	2091	4.1	52	20
Oakland	488	2084	4.3	75t	18
Kansas City	521	2082	4.0	82t	14
Cincinnati	442	2051	4.6	50	11
Buffalo	519	2040	3.9	52t	12
Pittsburgh	495	1991	4.0	52	14
N.Y. Jets	486	1961	4.0	50	7
Denver	465	1864	4.0	71	13
Tennessee	459	1811	3.9	40	19
Baltimore	431	1754	4.1	72	9
Indianapolis	419	1660	4.0	72	15
Miami	445	1453	3.3	34	8
New England	425	1426	3.4	43	9
Seattle	408	1408	3.5	45	5
San Diego	410	1246	3.0	54	10
Cleveland	313	1150	3.7	40	9
AFC Total	7240	28072	3.9	82t	193
AFC Average	452.5	1754.5	3.9	—	12.1

NFC RUSHING—TEAM

	Att.	Yards	Avg.	Long	TD
San Francisco	418	2095	5.0	68t	14
St. Louis	431	2059	4.8	58	13
Dallas	493	2051	4.2	63t	16
Washington	463	2039	4.4	76t	23
Minnesota	422	1804	4.3	70t	13
Tampa Bay	502	1776	3.5	33	7
Philadelphia	424	1746	4.1	29	5
New Orleans	461	1690	3.7	33	9
Carolina	356	1525	4.3	67t	12
Green Bay	386	1519	3.9	36	13
N.Y. Giants	431	1408	3.3	40	11
Chicago	396	1387	3.5	49t	4
Detroit	356	1245	3.5	51	8
Arizona	396	1207	3.0	58t	13
Atlanta	373	1196	3.2	33t	9
NFC Total	6308	24747	3.9	76t	170
NFC Average	420.5	1649.8	3.9	—	11.3
League Total	13548	52819	—	82t	363
League Average	437.0	1703.8	3.9	—	11.7

NFL TOP TEN RUSHERS

	Att.	Yards	Avg.	Long	TD
James, Edgerrin, Ind.	369	1553	4.2	72	13
Martin, Curtis, NYJ	367	1464	4.0	50	5
Davis, Stephen, Wash.	290	1405	4.8	76t	17
Smith, Emmitt, Dall.	329	1397	4.2	63t	11
Faulk, Marshall, St.L.	253	1381	5.5	58	7
George, Eddie, Tenn.	320	1304	4.1	40	9
Staley, Duce, Phil.	325	1273	3.9	29	4
Garner, Charlie, S.F.	241	1229	5.1	53	4
Watters, Ricky, Sea.	325	1210	3.7	45	5
Dillon, Corey, Cin.	263	1200	4.6	50	5

AFC RUSHERS—INDIVIDUAL

	Att.	Yards	Avg.	Long	TD
James, Edgerrin, Ind.	369	1553	4.2	72	13
Martin, Curtis, NYJ	367	1464	4.0	50	5
George, Eddie, Tenn.	320	1304	4.1	40	9
Watters, Ricky, Sea.	325	1210	3.7	45	5
Dillon, Corey, Cin.	263	1200	4.6	50	5
Gary, Olandis, Den.	276	1159	4.2	71	7
Bettis, Jerome, Pitt.	299	1091	3.6	35	7
Wheatley, Tyrone, Oak.	242	936	3.9	30t	8
Stewart, James, Jax.	249	931	3.7	44t	13
Allen, Terry, N.E.	254	896	3.5	39	8
Rhett, Errict, Balt.	236	852	3.6	52t	5
Taylor, Fred, Jax.	159	732	4.6	52	6
Kaufman, Napoleon, Oak.	138	714	5.2	75t	2
Linton, Jonathan, Buff.	205	695	3.4	18	5
Bennett, Donnell, K.C.	161	627	3.9	44	8
Smith, Antowain, Buff.	165	614	3.7	52t	6
Huntley, Richard, Pitt.	93	567	6.1	52	5
Johnson, J.J., Mia.	164	558	3.4	34	4
Holmes, Priest, Balt.	89	506	5.7	72	1
Flutie, Doug, Buff.	88	476	5.4	24t	1
Kirby, Terry, Cle.	130	452	3.5	28	6
Abdul-Jabbar, Karim, Mia.-Cle.	143	445	3.1	21	1
Collins, Cecil, Mia.	131	414	3.2	25t	2
Morris, Byron (Bam), K.C.	120	414	3.5	24	3
Richardson, Tony, K.C.	84	387	4.6	26	1
Fazande, Jermaine, S.D.	91	365	4.0	54	2
McNair, Steve, Tenn.	72	337	4.7	38	8
Blake, Jeff, Cin.	63	332	5.3	16	2
Basnight, Michael, Cin.	62	308	5.0	46	0
Gannon, Rich, Oak.	46	298	6.5	39	2
Bynum, Kenny, S.D.	92	287	3.1	25	1
Means, Natrone, S.D.	112	277	2.5	15	4
Couch, Tim, Cle.	40	267	6.7	40	1
Stewart, Kordell, Pitt.	56	258	4.6	21	2
Shehee, Rashaan, K.C.	65	238	3.7	18	1
Faulk, Kevin, N.E.	67	227	3.4	43	1
Davis, Terrell, Den.	67	211	3.1	26	2
Brunell, Mark, Jax.	47	208	4.4	15	1
Loville, Derek, Den.	40	203	5.1	36t	1
Anders, Kimble, K.C.	32	181	5.7	46	0
Thomas, Rodney, Tenn.	43	164	3.8	22	1
Pritchett, Stanley, Mia.	47	158	3.4	25	1
Thomas, Thurman, Buff.	36	152	4.2	31	0
Lucas, Ray, NYJ	41	144	3.5	21	1
Case, Stoney, Balt.	36	141	3.9	28	3
Griese, Brian, Den.	46	138	3.0	23	2
Evans, Chuck, Balt.	38	134	3.5	12	0
Parmalee, Bernie, NYJ	27	133	4.9	18	0
Cloud, Mike, K.C.	35	128	3.7	14	0
Fletcher, Terrell, S.D.	48	126	2.6	16	0
Harbaugh, Jim, S.D.	34	126	3.7	16	0
Huard, Damon, Mia.	28	124	4.4	25	0
Green, Ahman, Sea.	26	120	4.6	21	0
Warren, Lamont, N.E.	35	120	3.4	18	0
Smith, Akili, Cin.	19	114	6.0	24	1
Bledsoe, Drew, N.E.	42	101	2.4	25	0
Denson, Autry, Mia.	28	98	3.5	20	0
Banks, Tony, Balt.	24	93	3.9	12	0
Crockett, Zack, Oak.	45	91	2.0	7	4
Mirer, Rick, NYJ	21	89	4.2	12	1
Anderson, Richie, NYJ	16	84	5.3	16	0
Alexander, Derrick S., K.C.	2	82	41.0	82t	1
Banks, Tavian, Jax.	23	82	3.6	21	0
Manning, Peyton, Ind.	35	73	2.1	13	2
Griffith, Howard, Den.	17	66	3.9	13	1
Johnson, Rob, Buff.	8	61	7.6	25	0
Stephens, Tremayne, S.D.	24	61	2.5	9	3
Kitna, Jon, Sea.	35	56	1.6	10	0
Howard, Chris, Jax.	13	55	4.2	22	0
Zereoue, Amos, Pitt.	18	48	2.7	8	0
Mack, Stacey, Jax.	7	40	5.7	19	0
Miller, Chris, Den.	8	40	5.0	13	0
Brown, Reggie, Sea.	14	38	2.7	9	0
Detmer, Ty, Cle.	6	38	6.3	11	1
Gordon, Lennox, Buff.	11	38	3.5	13	0
Edwards, Marc, Cle.	6	35	5.8	28	0
Jordan, Randy, Oak.	9	32	3.6	12	2
Milne, Brian, Cin.	3	30	10.0	26	0
Williams, Nick, Cin.	10	30	3.0	8	0
Elias, Keith, Ind.	13	28	2.2	8	0
Stone, Dwight, NYJ	2	27	13.5	36	0
Carter, Tony, N.E.	6	26	4.3	9	0
Fiedler, Jay, Jax.	13	26	2.0	15	0
Shaw, Harold, N.E.	9	23	2.6	12	0
Groce, Clif, Cin.	8	22	2.8	8	1
Shaw, Sedrick, Cle.-Cin.	7	22	3.1	10	1
Avery, John, Den.	5	21	4.2	11	0
Tomczak, Mike, Pitt.	16	19	1.2	17	0
Witman, Jon, Pitt.	6	18	3.0	7	0
Brister, Bubby, Den.	2	17	8.5	17	0
Konrad, Rob, Mia.	9	16	1.8	5	0
Carter, Ki-Jana, Cin.	6	15	2.5	8	1
Horn, Joe, K.C.	2	15	7.5	9	0
Jones, George, Cle.	8	15	1.9	9	0
Johnson, Lee, N.E.	2	13	6.5	13	0
Williams, Kevin R., Buff.	1	13	13.0	13	0
Floyd, Chris, N.E.	6	12	2.0	6	0
Johnson, Pat, Balt.	1	12	12.0	12	0
Ritchie, Jon, Oak.	5	12	2.4	5	0
Lewis, Jermaine, Balt.	5	11	2.2	4	0
Ricks, Mikhael, S.D.	2	11	5.5	7	0

	Att.	Yards	Avg.	Long	TD
Ellison, Jerry, N.E.	2	10	5.0	8	0
Grbac, Elvis, K.C.	19	10	0.5	8	0
Whitted, Alvis, Jax.	1	9	9.0	9	0
Tupa, Tom, NYJ	2	8	4.0	4	0
Smith, Detron, Den.	1	7	7.0	7	0
Barker, Bryan, Jax.	1	6	6.0	6	0
Johnson, Keyshawn, NYJ	5	6	1.2	12	0
Shepherd, Leslie, Cle.	1	5	5.0	5	0
Sowell, Jerald, NYJ	3	5	1.7	3	0
Brown, Tim, Oak.	1	4	4.0	4	0
Dawson, Phil, Cle.	1	4	4.0	4t	1
Fuamatu-Ma'afala, Chris, Pitt.	1	4	4.0	4	0
Harrison, Marvin, Ind.	1	4	4.0	4	0
Ismail, Qadry, Balt.	1	4	4.0	4	0
Jacquet, Nate, Mia.	1	4	4.0	4	0
Dyson, Kevin, Tenn.	1	3	3.0	3	0
Johnson, Leon, NYJ	1	2	2.0	2	0
Lynn, Anthony, Den.	2	2	1.0	1	0
Salaam, Rashaan, Cle.	1	2	2.0	2	0
Shelton, Daimon, Jax.	1	2	2.0	2	0
Wilkins, Terrence, Ind.	1	2	2.0	2	0
Hentrich, Craig, Tenn.	2	1	0.5	1	0
Kramer, Erik, S.D.	5	1	0.2	3	0
Mitchell, Scott, Balt.	1	1	1.0	1	0
Moulds, Eric, Buff.	1	1	1.0	1	0
Neal, Lorenzo, Tenn.	2	1	0.5	1t	1
O'Donnell, Neil, Tenn.	19	1	0.1	4	0
Bennett, Darren, S.D.	1	0	0.0	0	0
Feagles, Jeff, Sea.	2	0	0.0	0	0
Mohr, Chris, Buff.	1	0	0.0	0	0
Pope, Daniel, K.C.	1	0	0.0	0	0
Rouen, Tom, Den.	1	0	0.0	0	0
Strong, Mack, Sea.	1	0	0.0	0	0
Foley, Glenn, Sea.	3	-1	-0.3	0	0
Galloway, Joey, Sea.	1	-1	-1.0	-1	0
Van Pelt, Alex, Buff.	1	-1	-1.0	-1	0
Ward, Dedric, NYJ	1	-1	-1.0	-1	0
Friesz, John, N.E.	2	-2	-1.0	-1	0
Hicks, Robert, Buff.	1	-2	-2.0	-2	0
Ward, Hines, Pitt.	2	-2	-1.0	3	0
Zolak, Scott, Mia.	2	-2	-1.0	-1	0
Gonzalez, Pete, Pitt.	2	-3	-1.5	-1	0
Hoying, Bobby, Oak.	2	-3	-1.5	-1	0
Covington, Scott, Cin.	2	-4	-2.0	-2	0
Johnson, Kevin, Cle.	1	-6	-6.0	-6	0
Marino, Dan, Mia.	6	-6	-1.0	0	0
Martin, Tony, Mia.	1	-6	-6.0	-6	0
Price, Peerless, Buff.	1	-7	-7.0	-7	0
Jones, Charlie, S.D.	1	-8	-8.0	-8	0
Miller, Josh, Pitt.	2	-9	-4.5	0	0
Bownes, Fabien, Sea.	1	-14	-14.0	-14	0
Powell, Ronnie, Cle.	1	-14	-14.0	-14	0
Yeast, Craig, Cin.	2	-16	-8.0	-3	0

t = Touchdown
Leader based on most yards gained

NFC RUSHERS—INDIVIDUAL

	Att.	Yards	Avg.	Long	TD
Davis, Stephen, Wash.	290	1405	4.8	76t	17
Smith, Emmitt, Dall.	329	1397	4.2	63t	11
Faulk, Marshall, St.L.	253	1381	5.5	58	7
Staley, Duce, Phil.	325	1273	3.9	29	4
Garner, Charlie, S.F.	241	1229	5.1	53	4
Levens, Dorsey, G.B.	279	1034	3.7	36	9
Smith, Robert, Minn.	221	1015	4.6	70t	2
Alstott, Mike, T.B.	242	949	3.9	30	7
Enis, Curtis, Chi.	287	916	3.2	19	3
Williams, Ricky, N.O.	253	884	3.5	25	2
Biakabutuka, Tim, Car.	138	718	5.2	67t	6
Dunn, Warrick, T.B.	195	616	3.2	33	0
Hoard, Leroy, Minn.	138	555	4.0	53	10
Murrell, Adrian, Ariz.	193	553	2.9	22	0
Hill, Greg, Det.	144	542	3.8	45	2
Lane, Fred, Car.	115	475	4.1	41t	1
Oxendine, Ken, Atl.	141	452	3.2	20	1
Warren, Chris, Dall.	99	403	4.1	25	2
Hanspard, Byron, Atl.	136	383	2.8	15	1
Montgomery, Joe, NYG	115	348	3.0	14	3
McNabb, Donovan, Phil.	47	313	6.7	27	0
Rivers, Ron, Det.	82	295	3.6	37	0
Holcombe, Robert, St.L.	78	294	3.8	34	4
Pittman, Michael, Ariz.	64	289	4.5	58t	2
Beasley, Fred, S.F.	58	276	4.8	44t	4
Barber, Tiki, NYG	62	258	4.2	30	0
Hicks, Skip, Wash.	78	257	3.3	24	3
Garcia, Jeff, S.F.	45	231	5.1	25	2
Mitchell, Brian, Wash.	40	220	5.5	16	1
Smith, Lamar, N.O.	60	205	3.4	24	0
Bates, Mario, Ariz.	72	202	2.8	16	9
Parker, De'Mond, G.B.	36	184	5.1	26	2
Perry, Wilmont, N.O.	48	180	3.8	22	0
Watson, Justin, St.L.	47	179	3.8	21	0
Brown, Gary, NYG	55	177	3.2	28	0
Christian, Bob, Atl.	38	174	4.6	33t	5
McNown, Cade, Chi.	32	160	5.0	18	0
Dilfer, Trent, T.B.	35	144	4.1	28	0
Phillips, Lawrence, S.F.	30	144	4.8	68t	2
Johnson, LeShon, NYG	61	143	2.3	17	2
Favre, Brett, G.B.	28	142	5.1	20	0
Tolliver, Billy Joe, N.O.	26	142	5.5	33	3
Way, Charles, NYG	49	141	2.9	17	2
Irvin, Sedrick, Det.	36	133	3.7	51	4
Graham, Kent, NYG	35	132	3.8	17	1
Bennett, Sean, NYG	29	126	4.3	40	1
Beuerlein, Steve, Car.	27	124	4.6	16	2
Schlesinger, Cory, Det.	43	124	2.9	16	0
Plummer, Jake, Ariz.	39	121	3.1	17	2
Allen, James, Chi.	32	119	3.7	13	0
Mitchell, Basil, G.B.	29	117	4.0	15	0
Ismail, Raghib, Dall.	13	110	8.5	27t	1
Milburn, Glyn, Chi.	16	102	6.4	49t	1
Warner, Kurt, St.L.	23	92	4.0	22	1
Batch, Charlie, Det.	28	87	3.1	12t	2
Floyd, William, Car.	35	78	2.2	16	3
Bieniemy, Eric, Phil.	12	75	6.3	28	1
Jackson, Terry, S.F.	15	75	5.0	11	0
Delhomme, Jake, N.O.	11	72	6.5	27	2
Johnson, Anthony, Car.	25	72	2.9	23	0
Williams, Moe, Minn.	24	69	2.9	10	1
Anderson, Jamal, Atl.	19	59	3.1	20	0
Cunningham, Randall, Minn.	10	58	5.8	14	0
Chancey, Robert, Dall.	14	57	4.1	11	0
Chandler, Chris, Atl.	16	57	3.6	14	1
Young, Steve, S.F.	11	57	5.2	14	0
Centers, Larry, Wash.	13	51	3.9	12	0
Brown, Dave, Ariz.	13	49	3.8	10	0
Jervey, Travis, S.F.	6	49	8.2	33	1
Hobert, Billy Joe, N.O.	12	47	3.9	10	1
Hakim, Az-Zahir, St.L.	4	44	11.0	31	0
Moss, Randy, Minn.	4	43	10.8	15	0
George, Jeff, Minn.	16	41	2.6	17	0
Craver, Aaron, N.O.	17	40	2.4	8	0
Crowell, Germane, Det.	5	38	7.6	20	0
King, Shaun, T.B.	18	38	2.1	8	0
Thrash, James, Wash.	1	37	37.0	37	0
Collins, Kerry, NYG	19	36	1.9	11	2
Thomas, Robert, Dall.	8	35	4.4	10	0
Westbrook, Michael, Wash.	7	35	5.0	12	0
Frerotte, Gus, Det.	15	33	2.2	8	0
Pederson, Doug, Phil.	20	33	1.7	19	0
Bruce, Isaac, St.L.	5	32	6.4	11	0
Davis, Troy, N.O.	20	32	1.6	7	0
Oliver, Winslow, Atl.	8	32	4.0	10	0
Johnson, Brad, Wash.	26	31	1.2	12	2
Matthews, Shane, Chi.	14	31	2.2	14	0
Henderson, William, G.B.	7	29	4.1	10	2
Wuerffel, Danny, N.O.	2	29	14.5	29t	1
Bennett, Edgar, Chi.	6	28	4.7	15	0
Dwight, Tim, Atl.	5	28	5.6	9	1
Patten, David, NYG	1	27	27.0	27	0
Holt, Torry, St.L.	3	25	8.3	14	0
Bjornson, Eric, Dall.	1	20	20.0	20t	1
Kennison, Eddie, N.O.	3	20	6.7	15	0
Metcalf, Eric, Car.	2	20	10.0	17	0
Bostic, James, Phil.	5	19	3.8	5	0
Watson, Edwin, Phil.	4	17	4.3	6	0
Hilliard, Ike, NYG	3	16	5.3	24	0
Jeffers, Patrick, Car.	2	16	8.0	23	0
Philyaw, Dino, N.O.	4	16	4.0	18	0
Hasselbeck, Matt, G.B.	6	15	2.5	13	0
Stenstrom, Steve, S.F.	3	15	5.0	8	0
Turner, Kevin, Phil.	6	15	2.5	5	0
Poole, Keith, N.O.	1	14	14.0	14	0

1999 INDIVIDUAL STATISTICS—RUSHING/PASSING

	Att.	Yards	Avg.	Long	TD
Rice, Jerry, S.F.	2	13	6.5	11	0
Abdullah, Rabih, T.B.	5	12	2.4	10	0
Bates, Michael, Car.	3	12	4.0	12	0
Garrett, Jason, Dall.	6	12	2.0	9	0
Palmer, David, Minn.	3	12	4.0	7	0
Engram, Bobby, Chi.	2	11	5.5	9	0
Graziani, Tony, Atl.	9	11	1.2	10	0
Aikman, Troy, Dall.	21	10	0.5	7	1
Hodgins, James, St.L.	7	10	1.4	3	1
Miller, Jim, Chi.	3	9	3.0	9	0
Booker, Marty, Chi.	1	8	8.0	8	0
Connell, Albert, Wash.	1	8	8.0	8	0
Green, Jacquez, T.B.	3	8	2.7	15	0
Tucker, Jason, Dall.	1	8	8.0	8	0
Brooks, Macey, Chi.	1	7	7.0	7	0
Hetherington, Chris, Car.	2	7	3.5	5	0
Makovicka, Joel, Ariz.	8	7	0.9	7	0
Zeier, Eric, T.B.	3	7	2.3	8	0
Culpepper, Daunte, Minn.	3	6	2.0	9	0
Vardell, Tommy, S.F.	6	6	1.0	5	1
Barnhardt, Tommy, N.O.	1	4	4.0	4	0
Carruth, Rae, Car.	1	4	4.0	4	0
Hastings, Andre, N.O.	1	4	4.0	4	0
Tate, Robert, Minn.	1	4	4.0	4	0
Tillman, Pat, Ariz.	1	4	4.0	4	0
Toomer, Amani, NYG	1	4	4.0	4	0
Lee, Amp, St.L.	3	3	1.0	4	0
Martin, Cecil, Phil.	3	3	1.0	2	0
Anthony, Reidel, T.B.	1	2	2.0	2	0
Lewis, Jeff, Car.	4	1	0.3	4	0
Morrow, Harold, Minn.	2	1	0.5	5	0
Olivo, Brock, Det.	1	1	1.0	1	0
Powell, Marvin, N.O.	1	1	1.0	1	0
Boston, David, Ariz.	5	0	0.0	7	0
Comella, Greg, NYG	1	0	0.0	0	0
Franklin, P.J., N.O.	1	0	0.0	0	0
Germaine, Joe, St.L.	3	0	0.0	2	0
Mathis, Terance, Atl.	1	0	0.0	0	0
Stanley, Chad, S.F.	1	0	0.0	0	0
Justin, Paul, St.L.	5	-1	-0.2	3	0
Mills, Ernie, Dall.	1	-1	-1.0	-1	0
Peete, Rodney, Wash.	2	-1	-0.5	0	0
Bono, Steve, Car.	2	-2	-1.0	-1	0
Conway, Curtis, Chi.	1	-2	-2.0	-2	0
Detmer, Koy, Phil.	2	-2	-1.0	-1	0
Freeman, Antonio, G.B.	1	-2	-2.0	-2	0
Sauerbrun, Todd, Chi.	1	-2	-2.0	-2	0
Weldon, Casey, Wash.	5	-4	-0.8	0	0
Jett, John, Det.	2	-8	-4.0	0	0
Player, Scott, Ariz.	1	-18	-18.0	-18	0

t = Touchdown
Leader based on most yards gained

PASSING

Highest Rating
NFC: 109.2—Kurt Warner, St. Louis
AFC: 90.7—Peyton Manning, Indianapolis

Completion Percentage
NFC: 65.1—Kurt Warner, St. Louis
AFC: 62.1—Peyton Manning, Indianapolis

Attempts
NFC: 595—Brett Favre, Green Bay
AFC: 539—Drew Bledsoe, New England

Completions
NFC: 343—Steve Beuerlein, Carolina
AFC: 331—Peyton Manning, Indianapolis

Yards
NFC: 4436—Steve Beuerlein, Carolina
AFC: 4135—Peyton Manning, Indianapolis

Yards, Game
NFC: 471—Brad Johnson, Washington at San Francisco, December 26 (32-47, 2 TD) (OT)
AFC: 404—Peyton Manning, Indianapolis at San Diego, September 26 (29-54, 2 TD)
404—Jim Harbaugh, San Diego at Minnesota, November 28 (25-39, 1 TD)

Longest
NFC: 90—Billy Joe Hobert (to Eddie Kennison), New Orleans vs. Atlanta, October 10 - TD
90—Troy Aikman (to Jason Tucker), Dallas vs. N.Y. Giants, January 2 - TD
AFC: 88—Brian Griese (to Byron Chamberlain), Denver vs. Green Bay, October 17

Yards Per Attempt
NFC: 8.72—Kurt Warner, St. Louis
AFC: 7.76—Peyton Manning, Indianapolis

Touchdown Passes
NFC: 41—Kurt Warner, St. Louis
AFC: 26—Peyton Manning, Indianapolis

Touchdown Passes, Game
AFC: 5—Steve McNair, Tennessee vs. Jacksonville, December 26 (23-33, 291 yards)
NFC: 5—Troy Aikman, Dallas at Washington, September 12 (28-49, 362 yards) (OT)
Kurt Warner, St. Louis vs. San Francisco, October 10 (20-23, 323 yards)
Steve Beuerlein, Carolina vs. New Orleans, January 2 (22-41, 322 yards)

Lowest Interception Percentage
AFC: 2.0—Mark Brunell, Jacksonville
NFC: 2.2—Shane Matthews, Chicago

Team Champion (Most Net Yards)
NFC: 4353—St. Louis
AFC: 4066—Indianapolis

AFC PASSING—TEAM

	Att.	Comp.	Pct. Comp.	Gross Yards	Sacked	Yds. Lost	Net Yards	Yds./ Att.	Yds./ Comp.	TD	Pct. TD	Long	Int.	Pct. Int.
Indianapolis	546	338	61.9	4182	14	116	4066	7.66	12.37	26	4.76	80t	17	3.1
New England	540	305	56.5	3985	56	349	3636	7.38	13.07	19	3.52	68t	21	3.9
Oakland	520	306	58.8	3850	49	241	3609	7.40	12.58	24	4.62	50	14	2.7
Miami	589	329	55.9	3736	37	251	3485	6.34	11.36	20	3.40	69t	21	3.6
Jacksonville	535	320	59.8	3716	36	221	3495	6.95	11.61	16	2.99	62	11	2.1
Denver	554	319	57.6	3646	34	227	3419	6.58	11.43	16	2.89	88	18	3.2
Seattle	525	288	54.9	3629	38	232	3397	6.91	12.60	25	4.76	51	16	3.0
San Diego	583	332	56.9	3627	46	284	3343	6.22	10.92	12	2.06	80t	24	4.1
Tennessee	527	304	57.7	3622	25	137	3485	6.87	11.91	23	4.36	65t	13	2.5
Cincinnati	548	300	54.7	3504	49	278	3226	6.39	11.68	18	3.28	76t	18	3.3
Buffalo	513	290	56.5	3478	27	185	3293	6.78	11.99	21	4.09	54t	16	3.1
Kansas City	502	295	58.8	3409	26	170	3239	6.79	11.56	22	4.38	86t	15	3.0
Baltimore	546	270	49.5	3360	56	336	3024	6.15	12.44	21	3.85	76t	20	3.7
Pittsburgh	535	301	56.3	3118	37	235	2883	5.83	10.36	19	3.55	49	18	3.4
N.Y. Jets	476	272	57.1	3001	37	210	2791	6.30	11.03	22	4.62	65	16	3.4
Cleveland	492	271	55.1	2997	60	385	2612	6.09	11.06	19	3.86	78t	15	3.0
AFC Total	8531	4840	—	56860	627	3857	53003	—	—	323	—	88	273	—
AFC Average	533.2	302.5	56.7	3553.8	39.2	241.1	3312.7	6.67	11.75	20.2	3.8	—	17.1	3.2

NFC PASSING—TEAM

	Att.	Comp.	Pct. Comp.	Gross Yards	Sacked	Yds. Lost	Net Yards	Yds./ Att.	Yds./ Comp.	TD	Pct. TD	Long	Int.	Pct. Int.
St. Louis	530	343	64.7	4580	33	227	4353	8.64	13.35	42	7.92	75t	15	2.8
Carolina	575	345	60.0	4447	51	286	4161	7.73	12.89	36	6.26	88t	15	2.6
Chicago	684	404	59.1	4352	38	216	4136	6.36	10.77	25	3.65	80t	22	3.2
Minnesota	530	316	59.6	4318	43	329	3989	8.15	13.66	32	6.04	80t	21	4.0
Green Bay	605	344	56.9	4132	36	232	3900	6.83	12.01	23	3.80	74t	23	3.8
Washington	537	324	60.3	4112	31	186	3926	7.66	12.69	26	4.84	65t	14	2.6
Detroit	558	326	58.4	4074	64	388	3686	7.30	12.50	22	3.94	77t	14	2.5
N.Y. Giants	602	350	58.1	4015	42	296	3719	6.67	11.47	17	2.82	80t	20	3.3
Atlanta	509	278	54.6	3691	49	345	3346	7.25	13.28	22	4.32	62	19	3.7
New Orleans	553	288	52.1	3598	41	305	3293	6.51	12.49	16	2.89	90t	30	5.4
San Francisco	560	324	57.9	3526	34	241	3285	6.30	10.88	14	2.50	62	19	3.4
Dallas	507	295	58.2	3278	24	151	3127	6.47	11.11	20	3.94	90t	13	2.6
Arizona	558	287	51.4	3085	45	282	2803	5.53	10.75	11	1.97	71	30	5.4
Tampa Bay	447	268	60.0	2781	42	303	2478	6.22	10.38	18	4.03	68	16	3.6
Philadelphia	474	235	49.6	2405	49	321	2084	5.07	10.23	18	3.80	84t	18	3.8
NFC Total	8229	4727	—	56394	622	4108	52286	—	—	342	—	90t	289	—
NFC Average	548.6	315.1	57.4	3759.6	41.5	273.9	3485.7	6.85	11.93	22.8	4.2	—	19.3	3.5
League Total	16760	9567	—	113254	1249	7965	105289	—	—	665	—	90t	562	—
League Average	540.6	308.6	57.1	3653.4	40.3	256.9	3396.4	6.76	11.84	21.5	4.0	—	18.1	3.4

Leader based on net yards

NFL TOP TEN PASSERS

	Att.	Comp.	Pct. Comp.	Yds.	Avg. Gain	TD	Pct. TD	Long	Int.	Pct. Int.	Sack	Yds. Lost	Rating Points
Warner, Kurt, St.L.	499	325	65.1	4353	8.72	41	8.2	75t	13	2.6	29	201	109.2
Beuerlein, Steve, Car.	571	343	60.1	4436	7.77	36	6.3	88t	15	2.6	50	280	94.6
George, Jeff, Minn.	329	191	58.1	2816	8.56	23	7.0	80t	12	3.6	28	228	94.2
Manning, Peyton, Ind.	533	331	62.1	4135	7.76	26	4.9	80t	15	2.8	14	116	90.7
Johnson, Brad, Wash.	519	316	60.9	4005	7.72	24	4.6	65t	13	2.5	29	177	90.0
Gannon, Rich, Oak.	515	304	59.0	3840	7.46	24	4.7	50	14	2.7	49	241	86.5
Lucas, Ray, NYJ	272	161	59.2	1678	6.17	14	5.1	56t	6	2.2	11	69	85.1
Batch, Charlie, Det.	270	151	55.9	1957	7.25	13	4.8	74t	7	2.6	36	186	84.1
Frerotte, Gus, Det.	288	175	60.8	2117	7.35	9	3.1	77t	7	2.4	28	202	83.6
Chandler, Chris, Atl.	307	174	56.7	2339	7.62	16	5.2	60t	11	3.6	32	230	83.5

AFC PASSING—INDIVIDUAL

	Att.	Comp.	Pct. Comp.	Yds.	Avg. Gain	TD	Pct. TD	Long	Int.	Pct. Int.	Sack	Yds. Lost	Rating Points
Manning, Peyton, Ind.	533	331	62.1	4135	7.76	26	4.9	80t	15	2.8	14	116	90.7
Gannon, Rich, Oak.	515	304	59.0	3840	7.46	24	4.7	50	14	2.7	49	241	86.5
Lucas, Ray, NYJ	272	161	59.2	1678	6.17	14	5.1	56t	6	2.2	11	69	85.1
Brunell, Mark, Jax.	441	259	58.7	3060	6.94	14	3.2	62	9	2.0	29	174	82.0
Grbac, Elvis, K.C.	499	294	58.9	3389	6.79	22	4.4	86t	15	3.0	26	170	81.7
Banks, Tony, Balt.	320	169	52.8	2136	6.68	17	5.3	76t	8	2.5	33	190	81.2
McNair, Steve, Tenn.	331	187	56.5	2179	6.58	12	3.6	65t	8	2.4	16	74	78.6
Kitna, Jon, Sea.	495	270	54.5	3346	6.76	23	4.6	51	16	3.2	32	198	77.7
Blake, Jeff, Cin.	389	215	55.3	2670	6.86	16	4.1	76t	12	3.1	30	168	77.6
Tomczak, Mike, Pitt.	258	139	53.9	1625	6.30	12	4.7	49	8	3.1	15	104	75.8
Griese, Brian, Den.	452	261	57.7	3032	6.71	14	3.1	88	14	3.1	27	176	75.6
Bledsoe, Drew, N.E.	539	305	56.6	3985	7.39	19	3.5	68t	21	3.9	55	342	75.6
Flutie, Doug, Buff.	478	264	55.2	3171	6.63	19	4.0	54t	16	3.3	26	176	75.1
Couch, Tim, Cle.	399	223	55.9	2447	6.13	15	3.8	78t	13	3.3	56	359	73.2
Harbaugh, Jim, S.D.	434	249	57.4	2761	6.36	10	2.3	80t	14	3.2	37	208	70.6
Marino, Dan, Mia.	369	204	55.3	2448	6.63	12	3.3	62	17	4.6	9	66	67.4
Stewart, Kordell, Pitt.	275	160	58.2	1464	5.32	6	2.2	42	10	3.6	22	131	64.9
Nonqualifiers													
Tupa, Tom, NYJ	11	6	54.5	165	15.00	2	18.2	65	0	0.0	3	30	139.2
Johnson, Rob, Buff.	34	25	73.5	298	8.76	2	5.9	42	0	0.0	1	9	119.5
Foley, Glenn, Sea.	30	18	60.0	283	9.43	2	6.7	49t	0	0.0	6	34	113.6
O'Donnell, Neil, Tenn.	195	116	59.5	1382	7.09	10	5.1	54t	5	2.6	9	63	87.6
Fiedler, Jay, Jax.	94	61	64.9	656	6.98	2	2.1	25t	2	2.1	7	47	83.5
Huard, Damon, Mia.	216	125	57.9	1288	5.96	8	3.7	69t	4	1.9	28	185	79.8
Miller, Chris, Den.	81	46	56.8	527	6.51	2	2.5	42	1	1.2	7	51	79.6
Testaverde, Vinny, NYJ	15	10	66.7	96	6.40	1	6.7	27t	1	6.7	0	0	78.8
Detmer, Ty, Cle.	91	47	51.6	548	6.02	4	4.4	35	2	2.2	4	26	75.7
Mirer, Rick, NYJ	176	95	54.0	1062	6.03	5	2.8	50	9	5.1	22	102	60.4
Smith, Akili, Cin.	153	80	52.3	805	5.26	2	1.3	39	6	3.9	19	110	55.6
Case, Stoney, Balt.	170	77	45.3	988	5.81	3	1.8	54t	8	4.7	17	116	50.3
Kramer, Erik, S.D.	141	78	55.3	788	5.59	2	1.4	41	10	7.1	7	62	46.6
Mitchell, Scott, Balt.	56	24	42.9	236	4.21	1	1.8	28t	4	7.1	6	30	31.5
Brister, Bubby, Den.	20	12	60.0	87	4.35	0	0.0	11	3	15.0	0	0	30.6
Walsh, Steve, Ind.	13	7	53.8	47	3.62	0	0.0	11	2	15.4	0	0	22.4
Fewer than 10 attempts													
Bettis, Jerome, Pitt.	1	1	100.0	21	21.00	1	100.0	21t	0	0.0	0	0	158.3
Brown, Troy, N.E.	1	0	0.0	0	0.00	0	0.0	0	0	0.0	0	0	39.6

1999 INDIVIDUAL STATISTICS—PASSING

Covington, Scott, Cin.	5	4	80.0	23	4.60	0	0.0	8	0	0.0	0	0	85.8
Gonzalez, Pete, Pitt.	1	1	100.0	8	8.00	0	0.0	8	0	0.0	0	0	100.0
Hoying, Bobby, Oak.	5	2	40.0	10	2.00	0	0.0	7	0	0.0	0	0	47.9
Johnson, Kevin, Cle.	1	0	0.0	0	0.00	0	0.0	0	0	0.0	0	0	39.6
Johnson, Keyshawn, NYJ	1	0	0.0	0	0.00	0	0.0	0	0	0.0	1	9	39.6
Kirby, Terry, Cle.	1	1	100.0	2	2.00	0	0.0	2	0	0.0	0	0	79.2
Moon, Warren, K.C.	3	1	33.3	20	6.67	0	0.0	20	0	0.0	0	0	57.6
Moreno, Moses, S.D.	7	5	71.4	78	11.14	0	0.0	45	0	0.0	1	3	108.0
Pickens, Carl, Cin.	1	1	100.0	6	6.00	0	0.0	6	0	0.0	0	0	91.7
Reed, Robert, S.D.	0	0	—	0	—	0	—	—	0	—	1	11	—
Ricks, Mikhael, S.D.	1	0	0.0	0	0.00	0	0.0	0	0	0.0	0	0	39.6
Smith, Rod, Den.	1	0	0.0	0	0.00	0	0.0	0	0	0.0	0	0	39.6
Sowell, Jerald, NYJ	1	0	0.0	0	0.00	0	0.0	0	0	0.0	0	0	39.6
Van Pelt, Alex, Buff.	1	1	100.0	9	9.00	0	0.0	9	0	0.0	0	0	104.2
Warren, Lamont, N.E.	0	0	—	0	—	0	—	—	0	—	1	7	—
Wycheck, Frank, Tenn.	1	1	100.0	61	61.00	1	100.0	61t	0	0.0	0	0	158.3
Zolak, Scott, Mia.	4	0	0.0	0	0.00	0	0.0	0	0	0.0	0	0	39.6

t = Touchdown
Leader based on rating points, minimum 224 attempts

NFC PASSING—INDIVIDUAL

	Att.	Comp.	Pct. Comp.	Yds.	Avg. Gain	TD	Pct. TD	Long	Int.	Pct. Int.	Sack	Yds. Lost	Rating Points
Warner, Kurt, St.L.	499	325	65.1	4353	8.72	41	8.2	75t	13	2.6	29	201	109.2
Beuerlein, Steve, Car.	571	343	60.1	4436	7.77	36	6.3	88t	15	2.6	50	280	94.6
George, Jeff, Minn.	329	191	58.1	2816	8.56	23	7.0	80t	12	3.6	28	228	94.2
Johnson, Brad, Wash.	519	316	60.9	4005	7.72	24	4.6	65t	13	2.5	29	177	90.0
Batch, Charlie, Det.	270	151	55.9	1957	7.25	13	4.8	74t	7	2.6	36	186	84.1
Frerotte, Gus, Det.	288	175	60.8	2117	7.35	9	3.1	77t	7	2.4	28	202	83.6
Chandler, Chris, Atl.	307	174	56.7	2339	7.62	16	5.2	60t	11	3.6	32	230	83.5
Aikman, Troy, Dall.	442	263	59.5	2964	6.71	17	3.8	90t	12	2.7	19	130	81.1
Matthews, Shane, Chi.	275	167	60.7	1645	5.98	10	3.6	56	6	2.2	13	79	80.6
Garcia, Jeff, S.F.	375	225	60.0	2544	6.78	11	2.9	62	11	2.9	15	104	77.9
Dilfer, Trent, T.B.	244	146	59.8	1619	6.64	11	4.5	62t	11	4.5	26	189	75.8
Favre, Brett, G.B.	595	341	57.3	4091	6.88	22	3.7	74t	23	3.9	35	223	74.7
Graham, Kent, NYG	271	160	59.0	1697	6.26	9	3.3	56	9	3.3	26	184	74.6
Collins, Kerry, NYG	331	190	57.4	2318	7.00	8	2.4	80t	11	3.3	16	112	73.3
McNown, Cade, Chi.	235	127	54.0	1465	6.23	8	3.4	80t	10	4.3	18	94	66.7
Pederson, Doug, Phil.	227	119	52.4	1276	5.62	7	3.1	84t	9	4.0	20	109	62.9
Tolliver, Billy Joe, N.O.	268	139	51.9	1916	7.15	7	2.6	57	16	6.0	19	152	58.9
Plummer, Jake, Ariz.	381	201	52.8	2111	5.54	9	2.4	63	24	6.3	27	152	50.8
Nonqualifiers													
Miller, Jim, Chi.	174	110	63.2	1242	7.14	7	4.0	77t	6	3.4	7	43	83.5
Justin, Paul, St.L.	14	9	64.3	91	6.50	0	0.0	27	0	0.0	1	3	82.7
King, Shaun, T.B.	146	89	61.0	875	5.99	7	4.8	68	4	2.7	11	78	82.4
Peete, Rodney, Wash.	17	8	47.1	107	6.29	2	11.8	30t	1	5.9	2	9	82.2
Cunningham, Randall, Minn.	200	124	62.0	1475	7.38	8	4.0	61t	9	4.5	15	101	79.1
Hasselbeck, Matt, G.B.	10	3	30.0	41	4.10	1	10.0	19	0	0.0	1	9	77.5
Garrett, Jason, Dall.	64	32	50.0	314	4.91	3	4.7	37t	1	1.6	5	21	73.3
Kanell, Danny, Atl.	84	42	50.0	593	7.06	4	4.8	52	4	4.8	5	37	69.2
Hobert, Billy Joe, N.O.	159	85	53.5	970	6.10	6	3.8	90t	6	3.8	11	79	68.9
Germaine, Joe, St.L.	16	9	56.3	136	8.50	1	6.3	63t	2	12.5	3	23	65.6
Graziani, Tony, Atl.	118	62	52.5	759	6.43	2	1.7	62	4	3.4	12	78	64.2
Zeier, Eric, T.B.	55	32	58.2	270	4.91	0	0.0	38	1	1.8	5	36	63.4
Detmer, Koy, Phil.	29	10	34.5	181	6.24	3	10.3	50t	2	6.9	0	0	62.6
Delhomme, Jake, N.O.	76	42	55.3	521	6.86	3	3.9	51t	5	6.6	6	42	62.4
Young, Steve, S.F.	84	45	53.6	446	5.31	3	3.6	53	4	4.8	8	63	60.9
McNabb, Donovan, Phil.	216	106	49.1	948	4.39	8	3.7	63t	7	3.2	28	204	60.1
Brown, Dave, Ariz.	169	84	49.7	944	5.59	2	1.2	71	6	3.6	18	130	55.9
Stenstrom, Steve, S.F.	100	54	54.0	536	5.36	0	0.0	32	4	4.0	10	66	52.8
Wuerffel, Danny, N.O.	48	22	45.8	191	3.98	0	0.0	22	3	6.3	5	32	30.8
Fewer than 10 attempts													
Bono, Steve, Car.	1	0	0.0	0	0.00	0	0.0	0	0	0.0	0	0	39.6
Conway, Brett, Wash.	1	0	0.0	0	0.00	0	0.0	0	0	0.0	0	0	39.6
Faulk, Marshall, St.L.	1	0	0.0	0	0.00	0	0.0	0	0	0.0	0	0	39.6
Garner, Charlie, S.F.	0	0	—	0	—	0	—	—	0	—	1	8	—
Greisen, Chris, Ariz.	6	1	16.7	4	0.67	0	0.0	4	0	0.0	0	0	39.6
Lewis, Jeff, Car.	3	2	66.7	11	3.67	0	0.0	12	0	0.0	1	6	72.9
Moss, Randy, Minn.	1	1	100.0	27	27.00	1	100.0	27t	0	0.0	0	0	158.3
Pittman, Michael, Ariz.	1	1	100.0	26	26.00	0	0.0	26	0	0.0	0	0	118.8
Rice, Jerry, S.F.	1	0	0.0	0	0.00	0	0.0	0	0	0.0	0	0	39.6
Royals, Mark, T.B.	2	1	50.0	17	8.50	0	0.0	17	0	0.0	0	0	79.2
Sanders, Deion, Dall.	1	0	0.0	0	0.00	0	0.0	0	0	0.0	0	0	39.6
Sanders, Frank, Ariz.	1	0	0.0	0	0.00	0	0.0	0	0	0.0	0	0	39.6
Small, Torrance, Phil.	2	0	0.0	0	0.00	0	0.0	0	0	0.0	0	0	39.6
Smith, Lamar, N.O.	1	0	0.0	0	0.00	0	0.0	0	0	0.0	0	0	39.6
Staley, Duce, Phil.	0	0	—	0	—	0	—	—	0	—	1	8	—
Williams, Ricky, N.O.	1	0	0.0	0	0.00	0	0.0	0	0	0.0	0	0	39.6

t = Touchdown
Leader based on rating points, minimum 224 attempts

PASS RECEIVING

Receptions

AFC: 116—Jimmy Smith, Jacksonville
NFC: 96—Muhsin Muhammad, Carolina

Receptions, Game

AFC: 14—Marvin Harrison, Indianapolis at Cleveland, December 26 (138 yards, 0 TD)
14—Jimmy Smith, Jacksonville vs. Cincinnati, January 2 (165 yards, 0 TD)
NFC: 13—Bobby Engram, Chicago at St. Louis, December 26 (143 yards, 2 TD)
13—Frank Sanders, Ariz.ona at Green Bay, January 2 (118 yards, 1 TD)
13—Tiki Barber, N.Y. Giants at Dallas, January 2 (100 yards, 0 TD)

Yards

AFC: 1663—Marvin Harrison, Indianapolis
NFC: 1413—Randy Moss, Minnesota

Yards, Game

AFC: 258—Qadry Ismail, Baltimore at Pittsburgh, December 12 (6 receptions, 3 TD)
NFC: 204—Marshall Faulk, St. Louis vs. Chicago, December 26 (12 receptions, 1 TD)
204—Randy Moss, Minnesota at Chicago, November 14 (12 receptions, 1 TD) (OT)

Longest

NFC: 90—Eddie Kennison (from Billy Joe Hobert), New Orleans vs. Atlanta, October 10 - TD
90—Jason Tucker (from Troy Aikman), Dallas vs. N.Y. Giants, January 2 - TD
AFC: 88—Byron Chamberlain (from Brian Griese), Denver vs. Green Bay, October 17

Yards Per Reception

NFC: 20.9—Tim Dwight, Atlanta
AFC: 17.5—Shawn Jefferson, New England

Touchdowns

NFC: 13—Cris Carter, Minnesota
AFC: 12—Marvin Harrison, Indianapolis

Team Leaders, Receptions

AFC: BALTIMORE 68, Qadry Ismail; BUFFALO 65, Eric Moulds; CINCINNATI 68, Darnay Scott; CLEVELAND 66, Kevin Johnson; DENVER 79, Rod Smith; INDIANAPOLIS 115, Marvin Harrison; JACKSONVILLE 116, Jimmy Smith; KANSAS CITY 76, Tony Gonzalez; MIAMI 67, Tony Martin; NEW ENGLAND 69, Terry Glenn; N.Y. JETS 89, Keyshawn Johnson; OAKLAND 90, Tim Brown; PITTSBURGH 61, Troy Edwards, Hines Ward; SAN DIEGO 57, Jeff Graham; SEATTLE 62, Derrick Mayes; TENNESSEE 69, Frank Wycheck

NFC: ARIZONA 79, Frank Sanders; ATLANTA 81, Terance Mathis; CAROLINA 96, Muhsin Muhammad; CHICAGO 88, Bobby Engram; DALLAS 80, Raghib Ismail; DETROIT 81, Germane Crowell; GREEN BAY 74, Antonio Freeman, Bill Schroeder; MINNESOTA 90, Cris Carter; NEW ORLEANS 61, Eddie Kennison; N.Y. GIANTS 79, Amani Toomer; PHILADELPHIA 49, Torrance Small; ST. LOUIS 87, Marshall Faulk; SAN FRANCISCO 67, Jerry Rice; TAMPA BAY 64, Warrick Dunn; WASHINGTON 69, Larry Centers

NFL TOP TEN PASS RECEIVERS

	No.	Yards	Avg.	Long	TD
Smith, Jimmy, Jax.	116	1636	14.1	62	6
Harrison, Marvin, Ind.	115	1663	14.5	57t	12
Muhammad, Muhsin, Car.	96	1253	13.1	60t	8
Brown, Tim, Oak.	90	1344	14.9	47	6
Carter, Cris, Minn.	90	1241	13.8	68	13
Johnson, Keyshawn, NYJ	89	1170	13.1	65	8
Engram, Bobby, Chi.	88	947	10.8	56	4
Faulk, Marshall, St.L.	87	1048	12.0	57t	5
Robinson, Marcus, Chi.	84	1400	16.7	80t	9
Crowell, Germane, Det.	81	1338	16.5	77t	7
Mathis, Terance, Atl.	81	1016	12.5	52	6

NFL TOP TEN PASS RECEIVERS BY YARDS

	Yards	No.	Avg.	Long	TD
Harrison, Marvin, Ind.	1663	115	14.5	57t	12
Smith, Jimmy, Jax.	1636	116	14.1	62	6
Moss, Randy, Minn.	1413	80	17.7	67t	11
Robinson, Marcus, Chi.	1400	84	16.7	80t	9
Brown, Tim, Oak.	1344	90	14.9	47	6
Crowell, Germane, Det.	1338	81	16.5	77t	7
Muhammad, Muhsin, Car.	1253	96	13.1	60t	8
Carter, Cris, Minn.	1241	90	13.8	68	13
Westbrook, Michael, Wash.	1191	65	18.3	65t	9
Toomer, Amani, NYG	1183	79	15.0	80t	6

AFC RECEIVERS—INDIVIDUAL

	No.	Yards	Avg.	Long	TD
Smith, Jimmy, Jax.	116	1636	14.1	62	6
Harrison, Marvin, Ind.	115	1663	14.5	57t	12
Brown, Tim, Oak.	90	1344	14.9	47	6
Johnson, Keyshawn, NYJ	89	1170	13.1	65	8
Smith, Rod, Den.	79	1020	12.9	71	4
McCardell, Keenan, Jax.	78	891	11.4	49	5
Gonzalez, Tony, K.C.	76	849	11.2	73t	11
McCaffrey, Ed, Den.	71	1018	14.3	78t	7
Glenn, Terry, N.E.	69	1147	16.6	67	4
Wycheck, Frank, Tenn.	69	641	9.3	35	2
Ismail, Qadry, Balt.	68	1105	16.3	76t	6
Scott, Darnay, Cin.	68	1022	15.0	76t	7
Martin, Tony, Mia.	67	1037	15.5	69t	5
Johnson, Kevin, Cle.	66	986	14.9	64t	8
Moulds, Eric, Buff.	65	994	15.3	54t	7
Mayes, Derrick, Sea.	62	829	13.4	43t	10
James, Edgerrin, Ind.	62	586	9.5	54	4
Edwards, Troy, Pitt.	61	714	11.7	41	5
Ward, Hines, Pitt.	61	638	10.5	42	7
Dawkins, Sean, Sea.	58	992	17.1	45t	7
Kirby, Terry, Cle.	58	528	9.1	78t	3
Graham, Jeff, S.D.	57	968	17.0	54	2
Pickens, Carl, Cin.	57	737	12.9	75t	6
Jones, Freddie, S.D.	56	670	12.0	36	2
Alexander, Derrick S., K.C.	54	832	15.4	86t	2
Dyson, Kevin, Tenn.	54	658	12.2	47t	4
Reed, Andre, Buff.	52	536	10.3	30	1
Gadsden, Oronde, Mia.	48	803	16.7	62	6
Chrebet, Wayne, NYJ	48	631	13.1	50t	3
George, Eddie, Tenn.	47	458	9.7	54t	4
Ritchie, Jon, Oak.	45	408	9.1	20t	1
Fletcher, Terrell, S.D.	45	360	8.0	25	0
Martin, Curtis, NYJ	45	259	5.8	34	0
Chiaverini, Darrin, Cle.	44	487	11.1	28t	4
McDuffie, O.J., Mia.	43	516	12.0	34	2
Pritchett, Stanley, Mia.	43	312	7.3	30	4
Wilkins, Terrence, Ind.	42	565	13.5	80t	4
Jefferson, Shawn, N.E.	40	698	17.5	68t	6
Dilger, Ken, Ind.	40	479	12.0	30	2
Ricks, Mikhael, S.D.	40	429	10.7	50	0
Watters, Ricky, Sea.	40	387	9.7	25	2
Dudley, Rickey, Oak.	39	555	14.2	35	9
Jett, James, Oak.	39	552	14.2	43	2
Thigpen, Yancey, Tenn.	38	648	17.1	35	4
Armour, Justin, Balt.	37	538	14.5	54t	4
Riemersma, Jay, Buff.	37	496	13.4	38	4
McCrary, Fred, S.D.	37	201	5.4	38	1
Brown, Troy, N.E.	36	471	13.1	37	1
Horn, Joe, K.C.	35	586	16.7	76t	6
Fauria, Christian, Sea.	35	376	10.7	25	0
Lockett, Kevin, K.C.	34	426	12.5	39t	2
Pollard, Marcus, Ind.	34	374	11.0	33	4
Konrad, Rob, Mia.	34	251	7.4	25	1
Brown, Reggie, Sea.	34	228	6.7	26	1
Chamberlain, Byron, Den.	32	488	15.3	88	2
Coates, Ben, N.E.	32	370	11.6	27	2
Brady, Kyle, Jax.	32	346	10.8	30	1
Drayton, Troy, Mia.	32	299	9.3	26	1
Evans, Chuck, Balt.	32	235	7.3	27	1
Price, Peerless, Buff.	31	393	12.7	45	3
Williams, Kevin R., Buff.	31	381	12.3	35	0
Jackson, Willie, Cin.	31	369	11.9	29	2
Dillon, Corey, Cin.	31	290	9.4	23	1
Hawkins, Courtney, Pitt.	30	285	9.5	23	0
Johnson, Pat, Balt.	29	526	18.1	76t	3
Anderson, Richie, NYJ	29	302	10.4	29	3
Warren, Lamont, N.E.	29	262	9.0	21	1
Linton, Jonathan, Buff.	29	228	7.9	28	1
Shaw, Bobby, Pitt.	28	387	13.8	49	3
Huntley, Richard, Pitt.	27	253	9.4	25	3
Edwards, Marc, Cle.	27	212	7.9	27t	2
Pritchard, Mike, Sea.	26	375	14.4	51	2
McGee, Tony, Cin.	26	344	13.2	35	2
Harris, Jackie, Tenn.	26	297	11.4	62t	1
Griffith, Howard, Den.	26	192	7.4	20	1
Lewis, Jermaine, Balt.	25	281	11.2	46	2
Groce, Clif, Cin.	25	154	6.2	14	0
Smith, Irv, Cle.	24	222	9.3	22	1
Carswell, Dwayne, Den.	24	201	8.4	20	2
Rhett, Errict, Balt.	24	169	7.0	20t	2
Richardson, Tony, K.C.	24	141	5.9	29	0

1999 INDIVIDUAL STATISTICS—PASS RECEIVING

	No.	Yards	Avg.	Long	TD
Shepherd, Leslie, Cle.	23	274	11.9	36	0
Sharpe, Shannon, Den.	23	224	9.7	24	0
Galloway, Joey, Sea.	22	335	15.2	48	1
Ward, Dedric, NYJ	22	325	14.8	56t	3
Green, E.G., Ind.	21	287	13.7	50	0
Rison, Andre, K.C.	21	218	10.4	20	0
Wheatley, Tyrone, Oak.	21	196	9.3	28	3
Gary, Olandis, Den.	21	159	7.6	21	0
Bettis, Jerome, Pitt.	21	110	5.2	17	0
Stewart, James, Jax.	21	108	5.1	19	0
Sanders, Chris, Tenn.	20	336	16.8	48t	1
Mickens, Terry, Oak.	20	261	13.1	30	0
Blackwell, Will, Pitt.	20	186	9.3	26	0
Gash, Sam, Buff.	20	163	8.2	31t	2
Carter, Tony, N.E.	20	108	5.4	20	0
Simmons, Tony, N.E.	19	276	14.5	58t	2
Jones, Damon, Jax.	19	221	11.6	31	4
Brisby, Vincent, N.E.	18	266	14.8	40	0
Green, Yatil, Mia.	18	234	13.0	27	0
Kaufman, Napoleon, Oak.	18	181	10.1	50	1
Bruener, Mark, Pitt.	18	176	9.8	29	0
Shehee, Rashaan, K.C.	18	136	7.6	17	0
Stephens, Tremayne, S.D.	18	133	7.4	22	1
Penn, Chris, S.D.	17	257	15.1	43	1
Abdul-Jabbar, Karim, Mia.-Cle.	17	84	4.9	21	1
Bynum, Kenny, S.D.	16	209	13.1	80t	2
Barlow, Reggie, Jax.	16	202	12.6	31	0
Basnight, Michael, Cin.	16	172	10.8	47	0
Parmalee, Bernie, NYJ	15	113	7.5	23	0
Johnson, J.J., Mia.	15	100	6.7	17	0
Byrd, Isaac, Tenn.	14	261	18.6	65t	2
Pathon, Jerome, Ind.	14	163	11.6	38	0
Battaglia, Marco, Cin.	14	153	10.9	30	0
Banks, Tavian, Jax.	14	137	9.8	38	0
Allen, Terry, N.E.	14	125	8.9	38	1
Holmes, Priest, Balt.	13	104	8.0	34t	1
DeLong, Greg, Balt.	13	52	4.0	9	1
Davis, Reggie, S.D.	12	137	11.4	46	1
Griffin, Damon, Cin.	12	112	9.3	20	0
Witman, Jon, Pitt.	12	106	8.8	38	0
Faulk, Kevin, N.E.	12	98	8.2	19	1
Shelton, Daimon, Jax.	12	87	7.3	13	0
Pierce, Aaron, Balt.	11	102	9.3	26	0
Loville, Derek, Den.	11	50	4.5	15	0
Johnson, Lonnie, K.C.	10	98	9.8	19	1
Williams, Nick, Cin.	10	96	9.6	19	0
Jones, Charlie, S.D.	10	90	9.0	44t	1
Taylor, Fred, Jax.	10	83	8.3	41	0
Bennett, Donnell, K.C.	10	41	4.1	12	0
Campbell, Mark, Cle.	9	131	14.6	21	0
Collins, Bobby, Buff.	9	124	13.8	45	2
Stewart, Kordell, Pitt.	9	113	12.6	28	1
Cooper, Andre, Den.	9	98	10.9	21	0
Roan, Michael, Tenn.	9	93	10.3	24t	3
Thomas, Rodney, Tenn.	9	72	8.0	26	0
Means, Natrone, S.D.	9	51	5.7	12t	1
Brigham, Jeremy, Oak.	8	108	13.5	29	0
Mason, Derrick, Tenn.	8	89	11.1	31	0
Jordan, Randy, Oak.	8	82	10.3	30	0
Lyons, Mitch, Pitt.	8	81	10.1	25	0
Baxter, Fred, NYJ	8	66	8.3	24	2
Crockett, Zack, Oak.	8	56	7.0	12t	1
Goodwin, Hunter, Mia.	8	55	6.9	14	0
Walker, Derrick, Oak.	7	71	10.1	21t	1
Rutledge, Rod, N.E.	7	66	9.4	13	0
Green, Eric, NYJ	7	37	5.3	10t	2
Morris, Byron (Bam), K.C.	7	37	5.3	9	0
Neal, Lorenzo, Tenn.	7	27	3.9	8	2
Davis, Billy, Balt.	6	121	20.2	73	0
Early, Quinn, NYJ	6	83	13.8	24	0
Loud, Kamil, Buff.	6	66	11.0	20	0
Collins, Cecil, Mia.	6	32	5.3	12	0
Miller, Billy, Den.	5	59	11.8	26	0
Mili, Itula, Sea.	5	28	5.6	8	1
Bownes, Fabien, Sea.	4	68	17.0	49t	1
Collins, Ryan, Balt.	4	62	15.5	28	0
Ellison, Jerry, N.E.	4	50	12.5	23	0
Shields, Paul, Ind.	4	37	9.3	21	0
Jackson, Sheldon, Buff.	4	34	8.5	16	0
Denson, Autry, Mia.	4	28	7.0	10	0
Ofodile, A.J., Balt.	4	25	6.3	9	0
Avery, John, Den.	4	24	6.0	11	0
Smith, Detron, Den.	4	23	5.8	11	0
Pupunu, Alfred, S.D.	4	17	4.3	11	0
Elias, Keith, Ind.	4	16	4.0	7	0
Kent, Joey, Tenn.	3	42	14.0	25	0
McGriff, Travis, Den.	3	37	12.3	15	0
Thomas, Thurman, Buff.	3	37	12.3	23t	1
Davis, Terrell, Den.	3	26	8.7	10	0
Cloud, Mike, K.C.	3	25	8.3	12	0
Carter, Ki-Jana, Cin.	3	24	8.0	11	0
Doering, Chris, Den.	3	22	7.3	9	0
Yeast, Craig, Cin.	3	20	6.7	8	0
Spence, Blake, NYJ	3	15	5.0	9	1
Perry, Ed, Mia.	3	8	2.7	5	1
Shaw, Sedrick, Cle.-Cin.	3	4	1.3	7	0
Davis, Zola, Cle.	2	38	19.0	25	0
Smith, Antowain, Buff.	2	32	16.0	23	0
Shaw, Harold, N.E.	2	31	15.5	29	0
Cushing, Matt, Pitt.	2	29	14.5	22	0
Johnson, Malcolm, Pitt.	2	23	11.5	18	0
McKenzie, Kevin, Mia.	2	18	9.0	13	0
Zereoue, Amos, Pitt.	2	17	8.5	14	0
Floyd, Chris, N.E.	2	16	8.0	11	0
Anders, Kimble, K.C.	2	14	7.0	9	0
Purnell, Lovett, Balt.	2	10	5.0	5	0
Seau, Junior, S.D.	2	8	4.0	6	0
Powell, Ronnie, Cle.	1	45	45.0	45	0
Stokley, Brandon, Balt.	1	28	28.0	28t	1
Williams, Jermaine, Oak.	1	20	20.0	20	0
Woodson, Charles, Oak.	1	19	19.0	19	0
Jacquet, Nate, Mia.	1	18	18.0	18	0
Howard, Chris, Jax.	1	8	8.0	8	0
Jones, Isaac, Ind.	1	8	8.0	8	0
Jacoby, Mitch, K.C.	1	6	6.0	6	0
Smith, Akili, Cin.	1	6	6.0	6	0
Clark, Desmond, Den.	1	5	5.0	5	0
Hundon, James, Cin.	1	5	5.0	5	0
Strong, Mack, Sea.	1	5	5.0	5	0
Bush, Steve, Cin.	1	4	4.0	4	0
Dunn, David, Cle.	1	4	4.0	4	0
Greene, Scott, Ind.	1	4	4.0	4	0
Bobo, Orlando, Cle.	1	3	3.0	3	0
Ayanbadejo, Obafemi, Balt.	1	2	2.0	2	0
Bartrum, Mike, N.E.	1	1	1.0	1t	1
Reed, Robert, S.D.	1	1	1.0	1	0
Huard, Damon, Mia.	1	0	0.0	0	0
Gannon, Rich, Oak.	1	-3	-3.0	-3	0
Wiegert, Zach, Jax.	1	-3	-3.0	-3	0
Hicks, Robert, Buff.	1	-6	-6.0	-6	0

t = Touchdown
Leader based on receptions

NFC RECEIVERS—INDIVIDUAL

	No.	Yards	Avg.	Long	TD
Muhammad, Muhsin, Car.	96	1253	13.1	60t	8
Carter, Cris, Minn.	90	1241	13.8	68	13
Engram, Bobby, Chi.	88	947	10.8	56	4
Faulk, Marshall, St.L.	87	1048	12.0	57t	5
Robinson, Marcus, Chi.	84	1400	16.7	80t	9
Crowell, Germane, Det.	81	1338	16.5	77t	7
Mathis, Terance, Atl.	81	1016	12.5	52	6
Moss, Randy, Minn.	80	1413	17.7	67t	11
Morton, Johnnie, Det.	80	1129	14.1	48	5
Ismail, Raghib, Dall.	80	1097	13.7	76t	6
Toomer, Amani, NYG	79	1183	15.0	80t	6
Sanders, Frank, Ariz.	79	954	12.1	63	1
Bruce, Isaac, St.L.	77	1165	15.1	60	12
Freeman, Antonio, G.B.	74	1074	14.5	51	6
Schroeder, Bill, G.B.	74	1051	14.2	51	5
Hilliard, Ike, NYG	72	996	13.8	46	3
Levens, Dorsey, G.B.	71	573	8.1	53	1
Centers, Larry, Wash.	69	544	7.9	33t	3
Rice, Jerry, S.F.	67	830	12.4	62	5
Barber, Tiki, NYG	66	609	9.2	56	2
Westbrook, Michael, Wash.	65	1191	18.3	65t	9
Dunn, Warrick, T.B.	64	589	9.2	68	2
Jeffers, Patrick, Car.	63	1082	17.2	88t	12
Walls, Wesley, Car.	63	822	13.0	37t	12
Connell, Albert, Wash.	62	1132	18.3	62t	7
Kennison, Eddie, N.O.	61	835	13.7	90t	4
Owens, Terrell, S.F.	60	754	12.6	36	4

1999 INDIVIDUAL STATISTICS—PASS RECEIVING

	No.	Yards	Avg.	Long	TD
Mitchell, Pete, NYG	58	520	9.0	25	3
Green, Jacquez, T.B.	56	791	14.1	62t	3
Garner, Charlie, S.F.	56	535	9.6	53	2
Holt, Torry, St.L.	52	788	15.2	63t	6
Small, Torrance, Phil.	49	655	13.4	84t	4
Murrell, Adrian, Ariz.	49	335	6.8	23	0
Sloan, David, Det.	47	591	12.6	74t	4
Enis, Curtis, Chi.	45	340	7.6	28	2
Reed, Jake, Minn.	44	643	14.6	50	2
Conway, Curtis, Chi.	44	426	9.7	30t	4
Poole, Keith, N.O.	42	796	19.0	67t	6
Staley, Duce, Phil.	41	294	7.2	19	2
Hastings, Andre, N.O.	40	564	14.1	42	1
Boston, David, Ariz.	40	473	11.8	43	2
Christian, Bob, Atl.	40	354	8.9	36	2
Wetnight, Ryan, Chi.	38	277	7.3	22	1
Bradford, Corey, G.B.	37	637	17.2	74t	5
Moore, Rob, Ariz.	37	621	16.8	71	5
Hakim, Az-Zahir, St.L.	36	677	18.8	75t	8
LaFleur, David, Dall.	35	322	9.2	25	7
Stokes, J.J., S.F.	34	429	12.6	47	3
Johnson, Charles, Phil.	34	414	12.2	36	1
Clark, Greg, S.F.	34	347	10.2	24	0
Warren, Chris, Dall.	34	224	6.6	24	0
Proehl, Ricky, St.L.	33	349	10.6	30	0
Dwight, Tim, Atl.	32	669	20.9	60t	7
Beasley, Fred, S.F.	32	282	8.8	24	0
Mitchell, Brian, Wash.	31	305	9.8	36	0
Mills, Ernie, Dall.	30	325	10.8	36	0
Anthony, Reidel, T.B.	30	296	9.9	30	1
Hardy, Terry, Ariz.	30	222	7.4	23	0
Henderson, William, G.B.	30	203	6.8	22	1
Alexander, Stephen, Wash.	29	324	11.2	27t	3
Glover, Andrew, Minn.	28	327	11.7	31	1
Williams, Ricky, N.O.	28	172	6.1	29	0
Alstott, Mike, T.B.	27	239	8.9	24	2
Smith, Emmitt, Dall.	27	119	4.4	14t	2
Cleeland, Cameron, N.O.	26	325	12.5	31	1
Broughton, Luther, Phil.	26	295	11.3	33	4
Fryar, Irving, Wash.	26	254	9.8	30t	2
Irvin, Sedrick, Det.	25	233	9.3	31	0
Williams, Roland, St.L.	25	226	9.0	24	6
Smith, Robert, Minn.	24	166	6.9	34	0
Tucker, Jason, Dall.	23	439	19.1	90t	2
Moore, Dave, T.B.	23	276	12.0	35t	5
Biakabutuka, Tim, Car.	23	189	8.2	32	0
Lane, Fred, Car.	23	163	7.1	23	0
Davis, Stephen, Wash.	23	111	4.8	21	0
Calloway, Chris, Atl.	22	314	14.3	33	1
Emanuel, Bert, T.B.	22	238	10.8	39	1
Rivers, Ron, Det.	22	173	7.9	31t	1
Floyd, William, Car.	21	179	8.5	25	0
Williams, Karl, T.B.	21	176	8.4	14	0
Schlesinger, Cory, Det.	21	151	7.2	25	1
Davis, Tyrone, G.B.	20	204	10.2	33	2
Milburn, Glyn, Chi.	20	151	7.6	22	0
Smith, Lamar, N.O.	20	151	7.6	26	1
Booker, Marty, Chi.	19	219	11.5	57t	3
Craver, Aaron, N.O.	19	154	8.1	29	0
Jurevicius, Joe, NYG	18	318	17.7	71	1
Brown, Na, Phil.	18	188	10.4	27	1
Oxendine, Ken, Atl.	17	172	10.1	32	1
Hoard, Leroy, Minn.	17	166	9.8	29	0
Moore, Herman, Det.	16	197	12.3	26	2
Dawsey, Lawrence, N.O.	16	196	12.3	57	1
Pittman, Michael, Ariz.	16	196	12.3	46	0
Santiago, O.J., Atl.	15	174	11.6	46	0
Phillips, Lawrence, S.F.	15	152	10.1	47	0
Carruth, Rae, Car.	14	200	14.3	43	0
Holcombe, Robert, St.L.	14	163	11.6	30	1
Brooks, Macey, Chi.	14	160	11.4	30	0
Thomason, Jeff, G.B.	14	140	10.0	22	2
Bennett, Edgar, Chi.	14	116	8.3	34	0
Johnson, Anthony, Car.	13	103	7.9	22	0
Allred, John, Chi.	13	102	7.8	26	1
Hill, Greg, Det.	13	77	5.9	15	0
German, Jammi, Atl.	12	219	18.3	62	3
Ogden, Jeff, Dall.	12	144	12.0	25	0
Johnson, LeShon, NYG	12	86	7.2	28	1
Hayes, Donald, Car.	11	270	24.5	56t	2
Slutzker, Scott, N.O.	11	164	14.9	42	1
Metcalf, Eric, Car.	11	133	12.1	33	0

	No.	Yards	Avg.	Long	TD
Kozlowski, Brian, Atl.	11	122	11.1	26	2
Stablein, Brian, Det.	11	119	10.8	42	1
Weaver, Jed, Phil.	11	91	8.3	14	0
McWilliams, Johnny, Ariz.	11	71	6.5	11	1
Way, Charles, NYG	11	59	5.4	16	0
Martin, Cecil, Phil.	11	22	2.0	9	0
Jells, Dietrich, Phil.	10	180	18.0	57t	2
Irvin, Michael, Dall.	10	167	16.7	37t	3
Harris, Ronnie, Atl.	10	164	16.4	24	0
Bjornson, Eric, Dall.	10	131	13.1	32	0
Still, Bryan, S.D.-Atl.	10	110	11.0	28	0
Hanspard, Byron, Atl.	10	93	9.3	34	0
Makovicka, Joel, Ariz.	10	70	7.0	15	1
Thomas, Robert, Dall.	10	64	6.4	13	0
Hatchette, Matt, Minn.	9	180	20.0	80t	2
Patten, David, NYG	9	115	12.8	19	0
McDonald, Darnell, T.B.	9	96	10.7	23	1
Allen, James, Chi.	9	91	10.1	17	0
Cross, Howard, NYG	9	55	6.1	12	0
Turner, Kevin, Phil.	9	46	5.1	14	0
Kelly, Reggie, Atl.	8	146	18.3	50	0
Lewis, Chad, St.L.-Phil.	8	88	11.0	21	3
Mayes, Alonzo, Chi.	8	82	10.3	24	1
Douglas, Dameane, Phil.	8	79	9.9	29t	1
Oliver, Winslow, Atl.	8	74	9.3	14	0
Hicks, Skip, Wash.	8	72	9.0	25	0
Comella, Greg, NYG	8	39	4.9	26	0
Baker, Eugene, Atl.	7	118	16.9	36	0
Sellers, Mike, Wash.	7	105	15.0	33t	2
McGarity, Wane, Dall.	7	70	10.0	18	0
Davis, Troy, N.O.	7	53	7.6	20	0
Vardell, Tommy, S.F.	7	36	5.1	11	0
Robinson, Jeff, St.L.	6	76	12.7	30	2
Harris, Mark, S.F.	6	66	11.0	33	0
Wilcox, Josh, N.O.	6	61	10.2	19	0
Cody, Mac, Ariz.	6	60	10.0	16	1
Mitchell, Basil, G.B.	6	48	8.0	20	0
Hodgins, James, St.L.	6	35	5.8	10	0
Hallock, Ty, Chi.	6	22	3.7	7	0
Kleinsasser, Jimmy, Minn.	6	13	2.2	11	0
Brazzell, Chris, Dall.	5	114	22.8	53	0
Chmura, Mark, G.B.	5	55	11.0	16	0
Kinchen, Brian, Car.	5	45	9.0	26t	2
Jordan, Andrew, Minn.	5	40	8.0	11	1
Bates, Mario, Ariz.	5	34	6.8	18	0
Lucky, Mike, Dall.	5	25	5.0	8	0
Hape, Patrick, T.B.	5	12	2.4	4	1
Bostic, James, Phil.	5	8	1.6	7	0
Bech, Brett, N.O.	4	65	16.3	23t	1
Cline, Tony, S.F.	4	45	11.3	30	0
Murphy, Yo, T.B.	4	28	7.0	9	0
Bennett, Sean, NYG	4	27	6.8	16	0
Perry, Wilmont, N.O.	4	26	6.5	11	0
Palmer, David, Minn.	4	25	6.3	13	0
Olivo, Brock, Det.	4	24	6.0	12	0
Sanders, Deion, Dall.	4	24	6.0	9	0
Parker, De'Mond, G.B.	4	15	3.8	7	0
Jordan, Charles, Sea.-G.B.	3	60	20.0	43	0
McCullough, Andy, Ariz.	3	45	15.0	31	0
Thrash, James, Wash.	3	44	14.7	25	0
Hall, Lamont, G.B.	3	33	11.0	13	0
Driver, Donald, G.B.	3	31	10.3	12	1
Mills, John Henry, Minn.	3	30	10.0	14	0
Lee, Amp, St.L.	3	22	7.3	15t	1
Rasby, Walter, Det.	3	19	6.3	13	1
Jackson, Terry, S.F.	3	6	2.0	4	0
Crumpler, Carlester, Minn.	2	35	17.5	31t	1
Anderson, Jamal, Atl.	2	34	17.0	32	0
Bieniemy, Eric, Phil.	2	28	14.0	27	0
Streets, Tai, S.F.	2	25	12.5	14	0
Walsh, Chris, Minn.	2	24	12.0	18t	1
Philyaw, Dino, N.O.	2	23	11.5	14	0
Finneran, Brian, Phil.	2	21	10.5	11	0
Bates, D'Wayne, Chi.	2	19	9.5	11	0
Chryplewicz, Pete, Det.	2	18	9.0	13	0
Franklin, P.J., N.O.	2	13	6.5	8	0
Abdullah, Rabih, T.B.	2	11	5.5	8	0
Lester, Tim, Dall.	2	9	4.5	6	0
Fann, Chad, S.F.	2	8	4.0	6	0
Davis, John, T.B.	2	7	3.5	6	1
McLeod, Kevin, T.B.	2	5	2.5	3t	1
Brown, Gary, NYG	2	2	1.0	1	0

1999 INDIVIDUAL STATISTICS—PASS RECEIVING/INTERCEPTIONS

	No.	Yards	Avg.	Long	TD
Jenkins, James, Wash.	1	30	30.0	30	0
Robinson, Damien, T.B.	1	17	17.0	17	0
Crawford, Keith, G.B.	1	14	14.0	14	0
Smith, Troy, Phil.	1	14	14.0	14	0
Williams, Moe, Minn.	1	12	12.0	12	0
Conwell, Ernie, St.L.	1	11	11.0	11	0
Stenstrom, Steve, S.F.	1	9	9.0	9	0
Monroe, Rodrick, Atl.	1	8	8.0	8	0
Alford, Brian, NYG	1	7	7.0	7t	1
Mangum, Kris, Car.	1	6	6.0	6	0
Thomas, Chris, St.L.	1	6	6.0	6	0
Uwaezuoke, Iheanyi, Det.	1	5	5.0	5	0
Johnston, Daryl, Dall.	1	4	4.0	4	0
McKinley, Dennis, Ariz.	1	4	4.0	4	0
Tate, Robert, Minn.	1	3	3.0	3	0
Bates, Michael, Car.	1	2	2.0	2	0
Jervey, Travis, S.F.	1	2	2.0	2	0
Tucker, Ryan, St.L.	1	2	2.0	2t	1
Graham, Kent, NYG	1	-1	-1.0	-1	0
McNabb, Donovan, Phil.	1	-6	-6.0	-6	0

t = Touchdown
Leader based on receptions

INTERCEPTIONS

Interceptions
AFC: 7—James Hasty, Kansas City
Sam Madison, Miami
Rod Woodson, Baltimore
NFC: 7—Donnie Abraham, Tampa Bay
Troy Vincent, Philadelphia

Interceptions, Game
NFC: 3—Champ Bailey, Washington at Arizona, October 17
AFC: 3—Sam Madison, Miami vs. Tennessee, November 7
Samari Rolle, Tennessee vs. Jacksonville, December 26

Yards
AFC: 200—Aaron Beasley, Jacksonville
NFC: 151—Al Harris, Philadelphia

Longest
AFC: 98—Marcus Colelman, N.Y. Jets at Miami, December 27 - TD
NFC: 95—George Teague, Dallas vs. Green Bay, November 14 - TD

Touchdowns
AFC: 2—Aaron Beasley, Jacksonville
James Hasty, Kansas City
Rod Woodson, Baltimore
NFC: 2—Donnie Abraham, Tampa Bay
Mike A. Jones, St. Louis
George Teague, Dallas
Grant Wistrom, St. Louis

Team Leaders, Interceptions
AFC: BALTIMORE, 7, Rod Woodson; BUFFALO, 3, Kurt Schulz; CINCINNATI, 3, Rodney Heath; CLEVELAND, 2, Marquez Pope; DENVER, 5, Tory James; INDIANAPOLIS, 3, Tyrone Poole; JACKSONVILLE, 6, Aaron Beasley; KANSAS CITY, 7, James Hasty; MIAMI, 7, Sam Madison; NEW ENGLAND, 4, Lawyer Milloy; N.Y. JETS, 6, Marcus Coleman; OAKLAND, 3, Eric Allen, Darrien Gordon; Eric Turner; PITTSBURGH, 4, Scott Shields, Dewayne Washington; SAN DIEGO, 4, Darryll Lewis, Jimmy Spencer; SEATTLE, 5, Shawn Springs, Willie Williams; TENNESSEE, 4, Samari Rolle
NFC: ARIZONA, 2, Rob Fredrickson, Tom Knight, Kwamie Lassiter, Pat Tillman, Aeneas Williams; ATLANTA, 4, Ray Buchanan; CAROLINA, 5, Eric Davis; CHICAGO, 3, Chris Hudson; DALLAS, 4, Dexter Coakley; DETROIT, 5, Ron Rice; GREEN BAY, 6, Mike McKenzie; MINNESOTA, 3, Robert Griffith; NEW ORLEANS, 6, Ashley Ambrose; N.Y. GIANTS, 6, Percy Ellsworth; PHILADELPHIA, 7, Troy Vincent; ST. LOUIS, 6, Todd Lyght; SAN FRANCISCO, 6, Lance Schulters; TAMPA BAY, 7, Donnie Abraham; WASHINGTON, 6, Matt Stevens

Team Champion
AFC: 30—Seattle
NFC: 29—St. Louis

AFC INTERCEPTIONS—TEAM

	No.	Yards	Avg.	Long	TD
Seattle	30	336	11.2	42	2
Kansas City	25	378	15.1	56t	5
N.Y. Jets	24	443	18.5	98t	3
Baltimore	21	403	19.2	66t	4
Oakland	20	247	12.4	36	1
Jacksonville	19	330	17.4	93t	3
Miami	18	243	13.5	42	1
New England	16	110	6.9	57t	2
Tennessee	16	257	16.1	43	1
Denver	15	169	11.3	45	1
San Diego	15	123	8.2	68	0
Pittsburgh	14	149	10.6	25	0
Buffalo	12	180	15.0	52	0
Cincinnati	12	100	8.3	58t	1
Indianapolis	10	287	28.7	74t	1
Cleveland	8	52	6.5	14	0
AFC Total	275	3807	13.8	98t	25
AFC Average	17.2	237.9	13.8	—	1.6

NFC INTERCEPTIONS—TEAM

	No.	Yards	Avg.	Long	TD
St. Louis	29	567	19.6	91t	7
Philadelphia	28	625	22.3	84	5
Green Bay	26	137	5.3	60	1
Dallas	24	442	18.4	95t	4
Washington	24	375	15.6	88t	3
Tampa Bay	21	355	16.9	55t	2
New Orleans	19	138	7.3	27	0
Arizona	17	276	16.2	78t	3
N.Y. Giants	17	232	13.6	44t	2
Detroit	16	235	14.7	41t	1
Carolina	15	169	11.3	44	0
Chicago	14	229	16.4	41	1
San Francisco	13	209	16.1	64t	2
Atlanta	12	166	13.8	52t	1
Minnesota	12	66	5.5	27t	1
NFC Total	287	4221	14.7	95t	33
NFC Average	19.1	281.4	14.7	—	2.2
League Total	562	8028	—	98t	58
League Average	18.1	259.0	14.3	—	1.9

NFL TOP TEN INTERCEPTORS

	No.	Yards	Avg.	Long	TD
Abraham, Donnie, T.B.	7	115	16.4	55t	2
Hasty, James, K.C.	7	98	14.0	56t	2
Madison, Sam, Mia.	7	164	23.4	42	1
Vincent, Troy, Phil.	7	91	13.0	35	0
Woodson, Rod, Balt.	7	195	27.9	66t	2
Ambrose, Ashley, N.O.	6	27	4.5	16	0
Beasley, Aaron, Jax.	6	200	33.3	93t	2
Coleman, Marcus, NYJ	6	165	27.5	98t	1
Ellsworth, Percy, NYG	6	80	13.3	26	0
Lyght, Todd, St.L.	6	112	18.7	57t	1
McKenzie, Mike, G.B.	6	4	0.7	4	0
Schulters, Lance, S.F.	6	127	21.2	64t	1
Stevens, Matt, Wash.	6	61	10.2	25	0

AFC INTERCEPTIONS—INDIVIDUAL

	No.	Yards	Avg.	Long	TD
Woodson, Rod, Balt.	7	195	27.9	66t	2
Madison, Sam, Mia.	7	164	23.4	42	1
Hasty, James, K.C.	7	98	14.0	56t	2
Beasley, Aaron, Jax.	6	200	33.3	93t	2
Coleman, Marcus, NYJ	6	165	27.5	98t	1
Dishman, Cris, K.C.	5	95	19.0	47t	1
Green, Victor, NYJ	5	92	18.4	32	0
Springs, Shawn, Sea.	5	77	15.4	42	0
James, Tory, Den.	5	59	11.8	45	0
Starks, Duane, Balt.	5	59	11.8	43t	1
Edwards, Donnie, K.C.	5	50	10.0	28t	1
Williams, Willie, Sea.	5	43	8.6	40t	1
McAlister, Chris, Balt.	5	28	5.6	21	0
Shields, Scott, Pitt.	4	75	18.8	25	0
Rolle, Samari, Tenn.	4	65	16.3	30	0
Williams, Darryl, Sea.	4	41	10.3	21	0
Darius, Donovin, Jax.	4	37	9.3	29	0
Milloy, Lawyer, N.E.	4	17	4.3	17	0
Lewis, Darryll, S.D.	4	9	2.3	5	0
Bellamy, Jay, Sea.	4	4	1.0	7	0
Spencer, Jimmy, S.D.	4	1	0.3	1	0
Washington, Dewayne, Pitt.	4	1	0.3	1	0
Lewis, Ray, Balt.	3	97	32.3	60	0
Poole, Tyrone, Ind.	3	85	28.3	38	0
Joseph, Kerry, Sea.	3	82	27.3	40	0
Heath, Rodney, Cin.	3	72	24.0	58t	1
Gordon, Darrien, Oak.	3	44	14.7	28	0

1999 INDIVIDUAL STATISTICS—INTERCEPTIONS

	No.	Yards	Avg.	Long	TD
Turner, Eric, Oak.	3	43	14.3	24	0
Romanowski, Bill, Den.	3	35	11.7	18t	1
Allen, Eric, Oak.	3	33	11.0	31	0
Canty, Chris, Sea.	3	26	8.7	19	0
Schulz, Kurt, Buff.	3	26	8.7	26	0
Glenn, Aaron, NYJ	3	20	6.7	12	0
Carter, Chris, N.E.	3	13	4.3	8	0
Sidney, Dainon, Tenn.	3	12	4.0	7	0
Buckley, Terrell, Mia.	3	3	1.0	18	0
Serwanga, Kato, N.E.	3	2	0.7	2	0
Warfield, Eric, K.C.	3	0	0.0	0	0
Blevins, Tony, Ind.	2	115	57.5	74t	1
Stoutmire, Omar, NYJ	2	97	48.5	67t	1
Dumas, Mike, S.D.	2	92	46.0	68	0
Burris, Jeff, Ind.	2	83	41.5	55	0
Biekert, Greg, Oak.	2	57	28.5	36	0
Carter, Dale, Den.	2	48	24.0	34	0
Carter, Tom, Chi.-Cin.	2	36	18.0	36	0
Thomas, Dave, Jax.	2	36	18.0	36	0
Hanks, Merton, Sea.	2	30	15.0	23t	1
Marion, Brock, Mia.	2	30	15.0	28	0
Surtain, Patrick, Mia.	2	28	14.0	28	0
Mincy, Charles, Oak.	2	23	11.5	21	0
Law, Ty, N.E.	2	20	10.0	27t	1
Phifer, Roman, NYJ	2	20	10.0	16	0
Holmes, Kenny, Tenn.	2	17	8.5	19	0
Brackens, Tony, Jax.	2	16	8.0	16t	1
Copeland, John, Cin.	2	16	8.0	12	0
Newman, Anthony, Oak.	2	16	8.0	16	0
Pope, Marquez, Cle.	2	15	7.5	13	0
Crockett, Ray, Den.	2	14	7.0	10	0
Winfield, Antoine, Buff.	2	13	6.5	10	0
Kennedy, Cortez, Sea.	2	12	6.0	7	0
Spikes, Takeo, Cin.	2	7	3.5	7	0
Wiltz, Jason, NYJ	2	5	2.5	5	0
Mickens, Ray, NYJ	2	2	1.0	2	0
Dimry, Charles, S.D.	2	1	0.5	1	0
Bryant, Fernando, Jax.	2	0	0.0	0	0
Tongue, Reggie, K.C.	1	80	80.0	46t	1
Katzenmoyer, Andy, N.E.	1	57	57.0	57t	1
Wiley, Marcellus, Buff.	1	52	52.0	52	0
Dorsett, Anthony, Tenn.	1	43	43.0	43	0
Mitchell, Donald, Tenn.	1	42	42.0	42t	1
Holecek, John, Buff.	1	35	35.0	35	0
McGlockton, Chester, K.C.	1	30	30.0	30	0
Bowden, Joe, Tenn.	1	29	29.0	29	0
Smith, Thomas, Buff.	1	29	29.0	29	0
Cox, Bryan, NYJ	1	27	27.0	27t	1
Walker, Denard, Tenn.	1	27	27.0	27	0
McElmurry, Blaine, Jax.	1	26	26.0	26	0
Harris, Corey, Balt.	1	24	24.0	24t	1
Rogers, Sam, Buff.	1	24	24.0	24	0
Kirkland, Levon, Pitt.	1	23	23.0	23	0
Emmons, Carlos, Pitt.	1	22	22.0	22	0
Walker, Brian, Sea.	1	21	21.0	21	0
Thomas, Derrick, K.C.	1	20	20.0	20	0
Fisk, Jason, Tenn.	1	17	17.0	17	0
Scott, Chad, Pitt.	1	16	16.0	16	0
Seau, Junior, S.D.	1	16	16.0	16	0
Jones, Marvin, NYJ	1	15	15.0	15	0
Woodson, Charles, Oak.	1	15	15.0	15t	1
Barker, Roy, Cle.	1	14	14.0	14	0
Williams, K.D., Oak.	1	14	14.0	14	0
Brown, Eric, Den.	1	13	13.0	13	0
Wilson, Jerry, Mia.	1	13	13.0	13	0
McCutcheon, Daylon, Cle.	1	12	12.0	12	0
Marts, Lonnie, Jax.	1	10	10.0	10	0
Oldham, Chris, Pitt.	1	9	9.0	9	0
Thierry, John, Cle.	1	8	8.0	8	0
Bell, Myron, Cin.	1	5	5.0	5	0
Boyer, Brant, Jax.	1	5	5.0	5	0
Rodgers, Derrick, Mia.	1	5	5.0	5	0
Woods, Jerome, K.C.	1	5	5.0	5	0
Simien, Tracy, S.D.	1	4	4.0	4	0
Wooten, Tito, Ind.	1	4	4.0	4	0
Jones, Lenoy, Cle.	1	3	3.0	3	0
Robertson, Marcus, Tenn.	1	3	3.0	3	0
Jackson, Steve, Tenn.	1	2	2.0	2	0
Maryland, Russell, Oak.	1	2	2.0	2	0
Roye, Orpheus, Pitt.	1	2	2.0	2	0
Bruschi, Tedy, N.E.	1	1	1.0	1	0
Davis, Travis, Pitt.	1	1	1.0	1	0
Irvin, Ken, Buff.	1	1	1.0	1	0
Abdullah, Rahim, Cle.	1	0	0.0	0	0
Blackmon, Roosevelt, Cin.	1	0	0.0	0	0
Coghill, George, Den.	1	0	0.0	0	0
Greer, Donovan, Buff.	1	0	0.0	0	0
Hall, Cory, Cin.	1	0	0.0	0	0
Harrison, Rodney, S.D.	1	0	0.0	0	0
Israel, Steve, N.E.	1	0	0.0	0	0
Johnstone, Lance, Oak.	1	0	0.0	0	0
Little, Earl, Cle.	1	0	0.0	0	0
Martin, Emanuel, Buff.	1	0	0.0	0	0
Myers, Greg, Cin.	1	0	0.0	0	0
Patton, Marvcus, K.C.	1	0	0.0	0	0
Pryce, Trevor, Den.	1	0	0.0	0	0
Randolph, Thomas, Ind.	1	0	0.0	0	0
Slade, Chris, N.E.	1	0	0.0	0	0
Smith, Darrin, Sea.	1	0	0.0	0	0
Taylor, Jason, Mia.	1	0	0.0	0	0
Thomas, Ratcliff, Ind.	1	0	0.0	0	0
Thomas, Zach, Mia.	1	0	0.0	0	0
Walker, Marquis, Oak.	1	0	0.0	0	0

t = Touchdown
Leader based on interceptions

NFC INTERCEPTIONS—INDIVIDUAL

	No.	Yards	Avg.	Long	TD
Abraham, Donnie, T.B.	7	115	16.4	55t	2
Vincent, Troy, Phil.	7	91	13.0	35	0
Schulters, Lance, S.F.	6	127	21.2	64t	1
Lyght, Todd, St.L.	6	112	18.7	57t	1
Ellsworth, Percy, NYG	6	80	13.3	26	0
Stevens, Matt, Wash.	6	61	10.2	25	0
Ambrose, Ashley, N.O.	6	27	4.5	16	0
McKenzie, Mike, G.B.	6	4	0.7	4	0
Rice, Ron, Det.	5	82	16.4	33	0
Bailey, Champ, Wash.	5	55	11.0	59t	1
Davis, Eric, Car.	5	49	9.8	16	0
Harris, Al, Phil.	4	151	37.8	84	1
Dawkins, Brian, Phil.	4	127	31.8	67t	1
Coakley, Dexter, Dall.	4	119	29.8	46t	1
Jones, Mike A., St.L.	4	96	24.0	44t	2
Buchanan, Ray, Atl.	4	81	20.3	52t	1
Brooks, Derrick, T.B.	4	61	15.3	38	0
Taylor, Bobby, Phil.	4	59	14.8	28	1
Edwards, Antuan, G.B.	4	26	6.5	26t	1
McCleon, Dexter, St.L.	4	17	4.3	14	0
Williams, Tyrone, G.B.	4	12	3.0	12	0
Teague, George, Dall.	3	127	42.3	95t	2
Minter, Mike, Car.	3	69	23.0	44	0
Bly, Dre', St.L.	3	53	17.7	53t	1
Fair, Terry, Det.	3	49	16.3	41t	1
Pounds, Darryl, Wash.	3	37	12.3	25	0
Green, Darrell, Wash.	3	33	11.0	25	0
Clay, Willie, N.O.	3	32	10.7	24	0
Hudson, Chris, Chi.	3	28	9.3	28	0
Reese, Izell, Dall.	3	28	9.3	24	0
Mitchell, Keith, N.O.	3	22	7.3	18	0
Carrier, Mark, Det.	3	16	5.3	16	0
Sharper, Darren, G.B.	3	12	4.0	9	0
Robinson, Eugene, Atl.	3	7	2.3	7	0
Sanders, Deion, Dall.	3	2	0.7	2	0
Griffith, Robert, Minn.	3	0	0.0	0	0
Hawthorne, Duane, Dall.	3	-2	-0.7	0	0
Wistrom, Grant, St.L.	2	131	65.5	91t	2
Lassiter, Kwamie, Ariz.	2	110	55.0	78t	1
Allen, Taje, St.L.	2	76	38.0	40	0
Barber, Shawn, Wash.	2	70	35.0	70t	1
Minter, Barry, Chi.	2	66	33.0	34t	1
McBurrows, Gerald, Atl.	2	64	32.0	41	0
Barber, Ronde, T.B.	2	60	30.0	43	0
Williams, Brian, G.B.	2	60	30.0	60	0
Fredrickson, Rob, Ariz.	2	57	28.5	34t	1
Weary, Fred, N.O.	2	49	24.5	27	0
Bush, Devin, St.L.	2	45	22.5	45t	1
Hambrick, Darren, Dall.	2	44	22.0	25	0
Bailey, Robert, Det.	2	39	19.5	31	0
Robinson, Damien, T.B.	2	36	18.0	36	0
Armstead, Jessie, NYG	2	35	17.5	31	0
Lynch, John, T.B.	2	32	16.0	28	0
Thomas, Orlando, Minn.	2	32	16.0	27t	1
Trotter, Jeremiah, Phil.	2	30	15.0	30	0

1999 INDIVIDUAL STATISTICS—PUNTING

	No.	Yards	Avg.	Long	TD
McMillian, Mark, S.F.-Wash.	2	24	12.0	24	0
Vinson, Fred, G.B.	2	21	10.5	21	0
Alexander, Brent, Car.	2	18	9.0	18	0
McDonald, Tim, S.F.	2	18	9.0	18	0
Nickerson, Hardy, T.B.	2	18	9.0	18	0
Jenkins, Billy, St.L.	2	16	8.0	14	0
Knight, Tom, Ariz.	2	16	8.0	16	0
Booker, Michael, Atl.	2	10	5.0	10	0
Lyle, Keith, St.L.	2	10	5.0	10	0
Garnes, Sam, NYG	2	7	3.5	4	0
Shade, Sam, Wash.	2	7	3.5	7	0
Tillman, Pat, Ariz.	2	7	3.5	6	0
Williams, Aeneas, Ariz.	2	5	2.5	8	0
Woodson, Darren, Dall.	2	5	2.5	5	0
Cousin, Terry, Chi.	2	1	0.5	1	0
Evans, Doug, Car.	2	1	0.5	1	0
Butler, LeRoy, G.B.	2	0	0.0	0	0
Fields, Mark, N.O.	2	0	0.0	0	0
Hitchcock, Jimmy, Minn.	2	0	0.0	0	0
Wilkinson, Dan, Wash.	1	88	88.0	88t	1
Ellis, Greg, Dall.	1	87	87.0	87t	1
Strahan, Michael, NYG	1	44	44.0	44t	1
Swann, Eric, Ariz.	1	42	42.0	42t	1
Mamula, Mike, Phil.	1	41	41.0	41t	1
Parrish, Tony, Chi.	1	41	41.0	41	0
Burton, Shane, Chi.	1	37	37.0	37	0
Levingston, Bashir, NYG	1	34	34.0	34	0
Darling, James, Phil.	1	33	33.0	33	0
Cook, Rashard, Phil.	1	29	29.0	29	0
Kowalkowski, Scott, Det.	1	29	29.0	29	0
Moore, Damon, Phil.	1	28	28.0	28	0
Sparks, Phillippi, NYG	1	28	28.0	28	0
Richardson, Damien, Car.	1	27	27.0	27	0
Walker, Darnell, S.F.	1	27	27.0	27t	1
Kelly, Brian, T.B.	1	26	26.0	26	0
McQuarters, R.W., S.F.	1	25	25.0	25	0
Wadsworth, Andre, Ariz.	1	23	23.0	23	0
Whiting, Brandon, Phil.	1	22	22.0	22t	1
Boyd, Stephen, Det.	1	18	18.0	18	0
Tate, Robert, Minn.	1	18	18.0	18	0
Smith, Kevin, Dall.	1	16	16.0	16	0
Burns, Keith, Chi.	1	15	15.0	15	0
Bennett, Tommy, Ariz.	1	13	13.0	13	0
Caldwell, Mike, Phil.	1	12	12.0	12	0
Coady, Rich, St.L.	1	11	11.0	11	0
Wright, Kenny, Minn.	1	11	11.0	11	0
Godfrey, Randall, Dall.	1	10	10.0	10	0
Tubbs, Winfred, S.F.	1	8	8.0	8	0
Weathers, Andre, NYG	1	8	8.0	8t	1
Singleton, Alshermond, T.B.	1	7	7.0	7	0
Flanigan, Jim, Chi.	1	6	6.0	6	0
Kelly, Rob, N.O.	1	6	6.0	6	0
Nguyen, Dat, Dall.	1	6	6.0	6	0
Bass, Anthony, Minn.	1	4	4.0	4	0
Carter, Marty, Atl.	1	4	4.0	4	0
Gilbert, Sean, Car.	1	4	4.0	4	0
McDonald, Ramos, S.F.	1	4	4.0	4	0
Hauck, Tim, Phil.	1	2	2.0	2	0
Kriewaldt, Clint, Det.	1	2	2.0	2	0
McCleskey, J.J., Ariz.	1	2	2.0	2	0
Molden, Alex, N.O.	1	2	2.0	2	0
Smith, Jermaine, G.B.	1	2	2.0	2	0
Chavous, Corey, Ariz.	1	1	1.0	1	0
Randle, John, Minn.	1	1	1.0	1	0
Wells, Dean, Car.	1	1	1.0	1	0
Clemons, Charlie, St.L.	1	0	0.0	0	0
Drake, Jerry, Ariz.	1	0	0.0	0	0
Harris, Sean, Chi.	1	0	0.0	0	0
Knight, Sammy, N.O.	1	0	0.0	0	0
Lincoln, Jeremy, NYG	1	0	0.0	0	0
Lyon, Billy, G.B.	1	0	0.0	0	0
McKinnon, Ronald, Ariz.	1	0	0.0	0	0
Miller, Corey, Minn.	1	0	0.0	0	0
Nelson, Jim, G.B.	1	0	0.0	0	0
Phillips, Ryan, NYG	1	0	0.0	0	0
Smith, Derek M., Wash.	1	0	0.0	0	0
Harris, Walt, Chi.	1	-1	-1.0	-1	0
Sehorn, Jason, NYG	1	-4	-4.0	-4	0

t = Touchdown
Leader based on interceptions

PUNTING

Average Yards Per Punt
AFC: 46.5—Tom Rouen, Denver
NFC: 45.4—Mitch Berger, Minnesota

Net Average Yards Per Punt
AFC: 38.7—Darren Bennett, San Diego
NFC: 38.4—Mitch Berger, Minnesota

Longest
AFC: 83—Bryan Barker, Jacksonville at N.Y. Jets, October 11
NFC: 75—Mitch Berger, Minnesota vs. San Francisco, October 24

Punts
NFC: 107—Sean Landeta, Philadelphia
AFC: 106—Chris Gardocki, Cleveland

Punts, Game
NFC: 12—Brad Maynard, N.Y. Giants at Tampa Bay, September 12 (526 yards)
AFC: 10—Chris Gardocki, Cleveland at Baltimore, September 26 (447 yards)
Lee Johnson, New England at Ariz.ona, October 31 (376 yards)

Team Champion
AFC: 46.5—Denver
NFC: 45.4—Minnesota

AFC PUNTING—TEAM

	Total Punts	Yards	Long	Avg.	TB	Blk.	Opp. Ret.	Ret. Yds.	In 20	Net. Avg.
Denver	84	3908	65	46.5	16	0	43	600	19	35.6
Pittsburgh	84	3795	75	45.2	10	0	39	392	27	38.1
N.Y. Jets	82	3693	69	45.0	7	0	47	427	26	38.1
San Diego	89	3910	60	43.9	6	0	41	343	32	38.7
Cleveland	106	4645	61	43.8	11	0	68	762	20	34.6
Tennessee	90	3824	78	42.5	3	0	45	335	35	38.1
Baltimore	104	4355	63	41.9	10	1	43	468	39	35.5
Jacksonville	78	3260	83	41.8	6	0	37	259	32	36.9
New England	90	3735	58	41.5	14	0	36	345	23	34.6
Indianapolis	60	2467	61	41.1	8	2	29	469	16	30.6
Miami	81	3322	63	41.0	4	0	42	424	23	34.8
Kansas City	104	4253	64	40.9	10	2	46	406	21	35.1
Seattle	84	3425	59	40.8	5	0	36	370	34	35.2
Oakland	77	3045	56	39.5	4	1	38	479	25	32.3
Buffalo	73	2840	60	38.9	7	0	23	226	20	33.9
Cincinnati	84	3219	72	38.3	5	2	45	498	13	31.2
AFC Total	1370	57696	83	—	126	8	658	6803	405	—
AFC Average	85.6	3606.0	—	42.1	7.9	0.5	41.1	425.2	25.3	35.3

NFC PUNTING—TEAM

	Total Punts	Yards	Long	Avg.	TB	Blk.	Opp. Ret.	Ret. Yds.	In 20	Net. Avg.
Minnesota	61	2769	75	45.4	9	0	28	246	18	38.4
Dallas	81	3500	64	43.2	10	0	43	459	24	35.1
Tampa Bay	90	3882	66	43.1	8	0	49	360	23	37.4
Detroit	86	3637	62	42.3	12	0	42	402	27	34.8
Ariz.ona	94	3948	60	42.0	8	0	53	340	18	36.7
Philadelphia	108	4524	60	41.9	12	1	59	490	21	35.1
Washington	71	2926	57	41.2	11	0	27	279	17	34.2
St. Louis	60	2464	70	41.1	11	0	23	155	17	34.8
N.Y. Giants	89	3651	63	41.0	6	0	38	405	31	35.1
Chicago	85	3478	65	40.9	10	0	36	266	20	35.4
New Orleans	83	3282	52	39.5	5	0	43	283	15	34.9
Atlanta	80	3163	55	39.5	4	0	26	119	27	37.1
Carolina	65	2562	56	39.4	1	0	32	158	18	36.7
Green Bay	80	3130	64	39.1	4	0	39	333	21	34.0
San Francisco	75	2883	70	38.4	9	2	33	399	21	30.7
NFC Total	1208	49799	75	—	120	3	571	4694	318	—
NFC Average	80.5	3319.9	—	41.2	8.0	0.2	38.1	312.9	21.2	35.4
League Total	2578	107495	83	—	246	11	1229	11497	723	—
League Average	83.2	3467.6	—	41.7	7.9	0.4	39.6	370.9	23.3	35.3

NFL TOP TEN PUNTERS

	No.	Yards	Long	Avg.	Total Punts	TB	Blk.	Opp. Ret.	Ret. Yds.	In 20	Net. Avg.
Rouen, Tom, Den.	84	3908	65	46.5	84	16	0	43	600	19	35.6
Berger, Mitch, Minn.	61	2769	75	45.4	61	9	0	28	246	18	38.4
Miller, Josh, Pitt.	84	3795	75	45.2	84	10	0	39	392	27	38.1
Tupa, Tom, NYJ	81	3659	69	45.2	81	7	0	47	427	25	38.2
Bennett, Darren, S.D.	89	3910	60	43.9	89	6	0	41	343	32	38.7
Gardocki, Chris, Cle.	106	4645	61	43.8	106	11	0	68	762	20	34.6
Gowin, Toby, Dall.	81	3500	64	43.2	81	10	0	43	459	24	35.1
Royals, Mark, T.B.	90	3882	66	43.1	90	8	0	49	360	23	37.4
Smith, Hunter, Ind.	58	2467	61	42.5	60	8	2	29	469	16	30.6
Hentrich, Craig, Tenn.	90	3824	78	42.5	90	3	0	45	335	35	38.1

AFC PUNTERS—INDIVIDUAL

	No.	Yards	Long	Avg.	Total Punts	TB	Blk.	Opp. Ret.	Ret. Yds.	In 20	Net. Avg.
Rouen, Tom, Den.	84	3908	65	46.5	84	16	0	43	600	19	35.6
Miller, Josh, Pitt.	84	3795	75	45.2	84	10	0	39	392	27	38.1
Tupa, Tom, NYJ	81	3659	69	45.2	81	7	0	47	427	25	38.2
Bennett, Darren, S.D.	89	3910	60	43.9	89	6	0	41	343	32	38.7
Gardocki, Chris, Cle.	106	4645	61	43.8	106	11	0	68	762	20	34.6
Smith, Hunter, Ind.	58	2467	61	42.5	60	8	2	29	469	16	30.6
Hentrich, Craig, Tenn.	90	3824	78	42.5	90	3	0	45	335	35	38.1
Richardson, Kyle, Balt.	103	4355	63	42.3	104	10	1	43	468	39	35.5
Barker, Bryan, Jax.	78	3260	83	41.8	78	6	0	37	259	32	36.9
Pope, Daniel, K.C.	101	4218	64	41.8	103	10	2	46	406	20	35.1
Johnson, Lee, N.E.	90	3735	58	41.5	90	14	0	36	345	23	34.6
Brice, Will, Cin.	60	2475	72	41.3	62	4	2	36	406	12	32.1
Hutton, Tom, Mia.	73	2978	63	40.8	73	3	0	37	358	22	35.1
Feagles, Jeff, Sea.	84	3425	59	40.8	84	5	0	36	370	34	35.2
Araguz, Leo, Oak.	76	3045	56	40.1	77	4	1	38	479	25	32.3
Mohr, Chris, Buff.	73	2840	60	38.9	73	7	0	23	226	20	33.9
Nonqualifiers											
Costello, Brad, Cin.	22	744	44	33.8	22	1	0	9	92	1	28.7
Bartholomew, Brent, Mia.	7	308	51	44.0	7	1	0	4	60	1	32.6
Mare, Olindo, Mia.	1	36	36	36.0	1	0	0	1	6	0	30.0
Stoyanovich, Pete, K.C.	1	35	35	35.0	1	0	0	0	0	1	35.0
Hall, John, NYJ	1	34	34	34.0	1	0	0	0	0	1	34.0

Leader based on average, minimum 40 punts

NFC PUNTERS—INDIVIDUAL

	No.	Yards	Long	Avg.	Total Punts	TB	Blk.	Opp. Ret.	Ret. Yds.	In 20	Net. Avg.
Berger, Mitch, Minn.	61	2769	75	45.4	61	9	0	28	246	18	38.4
Gowin, Toby, Dall.	81	3500	64	43.2	81	10	0	43	459	24	35.1
Royals, Mark, T.B.	90	3882	66	43.1	90	8	0	49	360	23	37.4
Jett, John, Det.	86	3637	62	42.3	86	12	0	42	402	27	34.8
Landeta, Sean, Phil.	107	4524	60	42.3	108	12	1	59	490	21	35.1
Player, Scott, Ariz.	94	3948	60	42.0	94	8	0	53	340	18	36.7
Turk, Matt, Wash.	62	2564	57	41.4	62	10	0	22	159	16	35.6
Maynard, Brad, NYG	89	3651	63	41.0	89	6	0	38	405	31	35.1
Sauerbrun, Todd, Chi.	85	3478	65	40.9	85	10	0	36	266	20	35.4
Barnhardt, Tommy, N.O.	82	3262	52	39.8	82	5	0	43	283	14	35.1
Stanley, Chad, S.F.	69	2737	70	39.7	71	9	2	31	374	20	30.7
Stryzinski, Dan, Atl.	80	3163	55	39.5	80	4	0	26	119	27	37.1
Walter, Ken, Car.	65	2562	56	39.4	65	1	0	32	158	18	36.7
Aguiar, Louie, G.B.	75	2954	64	39.4	75	4	0	37	330	20	33.9
Nonqualifiers											
Tuten, Rick, St.L.	32	1359	70	42.5	32	7	0	11	101	9	34.9
Horan, Mike, St.L.	26	1048	57	40.3	26	4	0	11	51	7	35.3
Hansen, Brian, Wash.	9	362	49	40.2	9	1	0	5	120	1	24.7
Hanson, Chris, G.B.	4	157	44	39.3	4	0	0	2	3	0	38.5
Richey, Wade, S.F.	4	146	45	36.5	4	0	0	2	25	1	30.3
Wilkins, Jeff, St.L.	2	57	34	28.5	2	0	0	1	3	1	27.0
Brien, Doug, N.O.	1	20	20	20.0	1	0	0	0	0	1	20.0
Longwell, Ryan, G.B.	1	19	19	19.0	1	0	0	0	0	1	19.0

Leader based on average, minimum 40 punts

PUNT RETURNS

Yards Per Return
AFC: 14.5—Charlie Rogers, Seattle
NFC: 11.7—Mac Cody, Arizona

Yards
AFC: 627—Tamarick Vanover, Kansas City
NFC: 506—Tiki Barber, N.Y. Giants

Yards, Game
NFC: 147—Az-Zahir Hakim, St. Louis at Cincinnati, October 3 (5 returns, 1 TD)
AFC: 139—Tamarick Vanover, Kansas City at Denver, December 5 (7 returns, 1 TD)

Longest
NFC: 85—Tiki Barber, N.Y. Giants vs. Dallas, October 18 - TD
AFC: 94—Charlie Rogers, Seattle at Pittsburgh, September 26 - TD

Returns
AFC: 57—Jermaine Lewis, Baltimore
NFC: 44—Tiki Barber, N.Y. Giants
Az-Zahir Hakim, St. Louis

Returns, Game
AFC: 7—Tamarick Vanover, Kansas City vs. Detroit, September 26 (104 yards, 0 TD)
Jermaine Lewis, Baltimore at Cleveland, November 7 (49 yards, 0 TD)
Tamarick Vanover, Kansas City at Denver, December 5 (139 yards, 1 TD)
Jermaine Lewis, Baltimore vs. New Orleans, December 19 (34 yards, 0 TD)
NFC: 7—Az-Zahir Hakim, St. Louis at Tennessee, October 31 (68 yards, 0 TD)

Fair Catches
NFC: 23—Eddie Kennison, New Orleans
AFC: 19—Chris Penn, San Diego

Touchdowns
AFC: 2—Tamarick Vanover, Kansas City
Craig Yeast, Cincinnati
NFC: 1—by many

Team Champion
AFC: 14.0—Seattle
NFC: 11.6—Atlanta

AFC PUNT RETURNS—TEAM

	No.	FC	Yards	Avg.	Long	TD
Seattle	30	24	419	14.0	94t	1
Kansas City	58	19	706	12.2	84t	2
Cincinnati	35	10	410	11.7	86t	2
New England	48	17	495	10.3	52	0
Jacksonville	45	21	462	10.3	74t	1
Buffalo	34	17	347	10.2	27	0
Miami	44	13	432	9.8	45	0
Indianapolis	41	18	388	9.5	39t	1
Oakland	42	14	397	9.5	78	0
Pittsburgh	42	14	377	9.0	48	0
Tennessee	40	17	358	8.9	65t	1
San Diego	34	25	290	8.5	33	0
Baltimore	59	20	452	7.7	33	0
Denver	54	10	409	7.6	81t	1
N.Y. Jets	43	14	319	7.4	23	0
Cleveland	25	13	162	6.5	15	0
AFC Total	674	266	6423	9.5	94t	9
AFC Average	42.1	16.6	401.4	9.5	—	0.6

NFC PUNT RETURNS—TEAM

	No.	FC	Yards	Avg.	Long	TD
Atlanta	32	17	372	11.6	70t	2
N.Y. Giants	45	13	520	11.6	85t	1
Chicago	30	19	346	11.5	54	0
Dallas	41	9	440	10.7	76	1
Arizona	47	13	489	10.4	43	0
Detroit	38	16	386	10.2	68t	1
St. Louis	52	25	498	9.6	84t	1
Philadelphia	29	18	250	8.6	39	0
Minnesota	32	13	269	8.4	64t	1
Tampa Bay	43	26	357	8.3	31	0
Washington	41	14	332	8.1	33	0
New Orleans	35	23	258	7.4	18	0
Green Bay	29	13	212	7.3	45	0
Carolina	35	18	241	6.9	30	0
San Francisco	26	13	104	4.0	32	0
NFC Total	555	250	5074	9.1	85t	7
NFC Average	37.0	16.7	338.3	9.1	—	0.5
League Total	1229	516	11497	—	94t	16
League Average	39.6	16.6	370.9	9.4	—	0.5

NFL TOP TEN PUNT RETURNERS

	No.	FC	Yards	Avg.	Long	TD
Rogers, Charlie, Sea.	22	18	318	14.5	94t	1
Jacquet, Nate, Mia.	28	0	351	12.5	45	0
Vanover, Tamarick, K.C.	51	18	627	12.3	84t	2
Cody, Mac, Ariz.	32	12	373	11.7	31	0
Milburn, Glyn, Chi.	30	19	346	11.5	54	0
Barber, Tiki, NYG	44	13	506	11.5	85t	1
Sanders, Deion, Dall.	30	1	344	11.5	76	1
Dwight, Tim, Atl.	20	12	220	11.0	70t	1
Barlow, Reggie, Jax.	38	17	414	10.9	74t	1
Brown, Troy, N.E.	38	13	405	10.7	52	0

AFC—INDIVIDUAL PUNT RETURNERS

	No.	FC	Yards	Avg.	Long	TD
Rogers, Charlie, Sea.	22	18	318	14.5	94t	1
Jacquet, Nate, Mia.	28	0	351	12.5	45	0
Vanover, Tamarick, K.C.	51	18	627	12.3	84t	2
Barlow, Reggie, Jax.	38	17	414	10.9	74t	1
Brown, Troy, N.E.	38	13	405	10.7	52	0
Williams, Kevin R., Buff.	33	17	331	10.0	27	0
Wilkins, Terrence, Ind.	41	17	388	9.5	39t	1
Gordon, Darrien, Oak.	42	14	397	9.5	78	0
Edwards, Troy, Pitt.	25	4	234	9.4	48	0
Mason, Derrick, Tenn.	26	15	225	8.7	65t	1
Griffin, Damon, Cin.	23	3	195	8.5	34	0
Lewis, Jermaine, Balt.	57	18	452	7.9	33	0
Watson, Chris, Den.	44	8	334	7.6	81t	1
Ward, Dedric, NYJ	38	12	288	7.6	23	0
Penn, Chris, S.D.	21	19	148	7.0	18	0
Nonqualifiers						
Johnson, Kevin, Cle.	19	10	128	6.7	15	0
Hawkins, Courtney, Pitt.	11	6	49	4.5	14	0
Yeast, Craig, Cin.	10	6	209	20.9	86t	2
Faulk, Kevin, N.E.	10	4	90	9.0	20	0
Jones, Charlie, S.D.	9	6	93	10.3	33	0
Buckley, Terrell, Mia.	8	5	13	1.6	8	0
McDuffie, O.J., Mia.	7	8	62	8.9	21	0
McGriff, Travis, Den.	7	1	50	7.1	20	0
McCardell, Keenan, Jax.	6	4	41	6.8	19	0
Parker, Larry, K.C.	5	1	51	10.2	35	0
Shaw, Bobby, Pitt.	4	3	53	13.3	17	0
Dunn, David, Cle.	4	1	25	6.3	13	0
Sawyer, Corey, NYJ	4	1	25	6.3	11	0
Galloway, Joey, Sea.	3	1	54	18.0	21	0
Reed, Robert, S.D.	3	0	49	16.3	21	0
Coghill, George, Den.	3	1	25	8.3	10	0
Gibson, Damon, Cle.	2	2	9	4.5	8	0
Byrd, Isaac, Tenn.	2	0	8	4.0	8	0
Jackson, Willie, Cin.	2	1	6	3.0	8	0
Woodson, Rod, Balt.	2	2	0	0.0	7	0
Blackwell, Will, Pitt.	1	1	39	39.0	39	0
Rolle, Samari, Tenn.	1	0	23	23.0	23	0
Thigpen, Yancey, Tenn.	1	0	21	21.0	21	0
George, Spencer, Tenn.	1	0	18	18.0	18	0
Horn, Joe, K.C.	1	0	18	18.0	18	0
Price, Peerless, Buff.	1	0	16	16.0	16	0
Lockett, Kevin, K.C.	1	0	10	10.0	10	0

1999 INDIVIDUAL STATISTICS—PUNT RETURNS/KICKOFF RETURNS

	No.	FC	Yards	Avg.	Long	TD
Logan, Mike, Jax.	1	0	7	7.0	7	0
Johnson, Leon, NYJ	1	1	6	6.0	6	0
Sidney, Dainon, Tenn.	1	0	4	4.0	4	0
Ward, Hines, Pitt.	1	0	2	2.0	2	0
Turner, Scott, S.D.	1	0	0	0.0	0	0
Joseph, Kerry, Sea.	0	2	0	—	—	0
Pathon, Jerome, Ind.	0	1	0	—	—	0

t = Touchdown
Leader based on average return, minimum 20 returns

NFC—INDIVIDUAL PUNT RETURNERS

	No.	FC	Yards	Avg.	Long	TD
Cody, Mac, Ariz.	32	12	373	11.7	31	0
Milburn, Glyn, Chi.	30	19	346	11.5	54	0
Barber, Tiki, NYG	44	13	506	11.5	85t	1
Sanders, Deion, Dall.	30	1	344	11.5	76	1
Dwight, Tim, Atl.	20	12	220	11.0	70t	1
Hakim, Az-Zahir, St.L.	44	22	461	10.5	84t	1
Rossum, Allen, Phil.	28	17	250	8.9	39	0
Green, Jacquez, T.B.	23	14	204	8.9	31	0
Mitchell, Brian, Wash.	40	14	332	8.3	33	0
Williams, Karl, T.B.	20	12	153	7.7	30	0
Kennison, Eddie, N.O.	35	23	258	7.4	18	0
Metcalf, Eric, Car.	34	18	238	7.0	30	0
Nonqualifiers						
Howard, Desmond, G.B.-Det.	18	10	208	11.6	68t	1
Uwaezuoke, Iheanyi, Det.	18	9	150	8.3	20	0
McQuarters, R.W., S.F.	18	3	90	5.0	32	0
Moss, Randy, Minn.	17	4	162	9.5	64t	1
Oliver, Winslow, Atl.	12	5	152	12.7	58t	1
Palmer, David, Minn.	12	5	93	7.8	18	0
Preston, Roell, Tenn.-Mia.-S.F.	12	10	71	5.9	12	0
Fair, Terry, Det.	11	4	97	8.8	36	0
Edwards, Antuan, G.B.	10	4	90	9.0	45	0
Jordan, Charles, Sea.-G.B.	10	5	76	7.6	15	0
Boston, David, Ariz.	7	0	62	8.9	43	0
Horne, Tony, St.L.	5	0	22	4.4	9	0
Tucker, Jason, Dall.	4	2	52	13.0	41	0
Ogden, Jeff, Dall.	4	2	28	7.0	10	0
Pittman, Michael, Ariz.	4	0	16	4.0	7	0
Harris, Mark, S.F.	4	2	8	2.0	5	0
Knight, Tom, Ariz.	3	1	38	12.7	27	0
McGarity, Wane, Dall.	3	4	16	5.3	9	0
Holt, Torry, St.L.	3	2	15	5.0	11	0
Murphy, Yo, Minn.	3	0	14	4.7	7	0
Irvin, Sedrick, Det.	2	0	15	7.5	15	0
Mitchell, Basil, G.B.	2	0	0	0.0	0	0
Toomer, Amani, NYG	1	0	14	14.0	14	0
Stablein, Brian, Det.	1	0	9	9.0	9	0
Johnson, Anthony, Car.	1	0	3	3.0	3	0
Givens, Reggie, S.F.	1	0	0	0.0	0	0
Johnson, Charles, Phil.	1	0	0	0.0	0	0
McCleskey, J.J., Ariz.	1	0	0	0.0	0	0
Pounds, Darryl, Wash.	1	0	0	0.0	0	0
Brown, Na, Phil.	0	1	0	—	—	0
Proehl, Ricky, St.L.	0	1	0	—	—	0
Tate, Robert, Minn.	0	4	0	—	—	0

t = Touchdown
Leader based on average return, minimum 20 returns

KICKOFF RETURNS

Yards Per Return
NFC: 29.7—Tony Horne, St. Louis
AFC: 27.1—Tremain Mack, Cincinnati

Yards
AFC: 1524—Brock Marion, Miami
NFC: 1426—Glyn Milburn, Chicago

Yards, Game
NFC: 222—Allen Rossum, Philadelphia vs. Washington, November 14 (5 returns, 1 TD)
AFC: 190—Charlie Rogers, Seattle at N.Y. Jets, January 2 (7 returns, 0 TD)

Longest
NFC: 101—Tony Horne, St. Louis at Atlanta, October 17 - TD
AFC: 99—Tremain Mack, Cleveland vs. Tennessee, November 14 - TD

Returns
AFC: 63—Brock Marion, Miami
NFC: 61—Glyn Milburn, Chicago

Returns, Game
NFC: 8—Allen Rossum, Philadelphia vs. Indianapolis, November 21 (192 yards, 0 TD)
AFC: 7—Tremain Mack, Cincinnati at Seattle, November 7 (132 yards, 0 TD)
Napoleon Kaufman, Oakland vs. Kansas City, November 28 (141 yards, 0 TD)
Brock Marion, Miami at N.Y. Jets, December 12 (143 yards, 0 TD)
Charlie Rogers, Seattle at N.Y. Jets, January 2 (190 yards, 0 TD)

Touchdowns
NFC: 2—Michael Bates, Carolina
Tony Horne, St. Louis
AFC: 1—Henry Jones, Buffalo
Tremain Mack, Cincinnati
Alvis Whitted, Jacksonville
Terrence Wilkins, Indianapolis

Team Champion
NFC: 25.1 St. Louis
AFC: 24.2 New England

AFC KICKOFF RETURNS—TEAM

	No.	Yards	Avg.	Long	TD
New England	62	1498	24.2	95	0
Cincinnati	84	2020	24.0	99t	1
Miami	72	1713	23.8	93	0
N.Y. Jets	67	1571	23.4	81	0
Seattle	68	1547	22.8	61	0
Denver	63	1398	22.2	71	0
Indianapolis	67	1397	20.9	97t	1
Baltimore	54	1098	20.3	66	0
Buffalo	51	1001	19.6	62	1
Pittsburgh	57	1110	19.5	44	0
Cleveland	89	1725	19.4	43	0
Jacksonville	46	881	19.2	98t	1
San Diego	69	1312	19.0	37	0
Kansas City	63	1182	18.8	29	0
Oakland	61	1140	18.7	48	0
Tennessee	56	1042	18.6	41	0
AFC Total	1029	21635	21.0	99t	4
AFC Average	64.3	1352.2	21.0	—	0.3

NFC KICKOFF RETURNS—TEAM

	No.	Yards	Avg.	Long	TD
St. Louis	54	1354	25.1	101t	2
Dallas	58	1372	23.7	79	0
Philadelphia	69	1612	23.4	89t	1
Minnesota	70	1597	22.8	85t	2
Carolina	66	1475	22.3	100t	2
Chicago	68	1491	21.9	93	0
Arizona	64	1403	21.9	68	0
N.Y. Giants	69	1502	21.8	45	0
New Orleans	79	1639	20.7	55	0
San Francisco	77	1579	20.5	75	0
Washington	63	1290	20.5	95t	1
Tampa Bay	55	1116	20.3	55	0
Detroit	72	1445	20.1	91	0
Atlanta	76	1445	19.0	40	0
Green Bay	66	1241	18.8	88t	1
NFC Total	1006	21561	21.4	101t	9
NFC Average	67.1	1437.4	21.4	—	0.6
League Total	2035	43196	—	101t	13
League Average	65.6	1393.4	21.2	—	0.4

NFL TOP TEN KICKOFF RETURNERS

	No.	Yards	Avg.	Long	TD
Horne, Tony, St.L.	30	892	29.7	101t	2
Tucker, Jason, Dall.	22	613	27.9	79	0
Mack, Tremain, Cin.	51	1382	27.1	99t	1
Tate, Robert, Minn.	25	627	25.1	76t	1
Rossum, Allen, Phil.	54	1347	24.9	89t	1
Bates, Michael, Car.	52	1287	24.8	100t	2
Stone, Dwight, NYJ	28	689	24.6	50	0
Marion, Brock, Mia.	62	1524	24.6	93	0
Levingston, Bashir, NYG	22	532	24.2	35	0
Faulk, Kevin, N.E.	39	943	24.2	95	0

1999 INDIVIDUAL STATISTICS—KICKOFF RETURNS

AFC KICKOFF RETURNERS—INDIVIDUAL

	No.	Yards	Avg.	Long	TD
Mack, Tremain, Cin.	51	1382	27.1	99t	1
Stone, Dwight, NYJ	28	689	24.6	50	0
Marion, Brock, Mia.	62	1524	24.6	93	0
Faulk, Kevin, N.E.	39	943	24.2	95	0
Watson, Chris, Den.	48	1138	23.7	71	0
Green, Ahman, Sea.	36	818	22.7	54	0
Powell, Ronnie, Cle.	44	986	22.4	43	0
Glenn, Aaron, NYJ	27	601	22.3	46	0
Wilkins, Terrence, Ind.	51	1134	22.2	97t	1
Harris, Corey, Balt.	38	843	22.2	66	0
Bynum, Kenny, S.D.	37	781	21.1	37	0
Vanover, Tamarick, K.C.	44	886	20.1	29	0
Williams, Kevin R., Buff.	42	840	20.0	62	0
Kaufman, Napoleon, Oak.	42	831	19.8	48	0
Mason, Derrick, Tenn.	41	805	19.6	41	0
Nonqualifiers					
Barlow, Reggie, Jax.	19	396	20.8	56	0
Rogers, Charlie, Sea.	18	465	25.8	49	0
Stephens, Tremayne, S.D.	18	335	18.6	28	0
Huntley, Richard, Pitt.	15	336	22.4	41	0
Griffin, Damon, Cin.	15	296	19.7	42	0
Blackwell, Will, Pitt.	14	282	20.1	37	0
Edwards, Troy, Pitt.	13	234	18.0	44	0
Kirby, Terry, Cle.	11	230	20.9	28	0
Jordan, Randy, Oak.	10	207	20.7	28	0
Avery, John, Mia.-Den.	9	192	21.3	33	0
Dunn, David, Cle.	9	180	20.0	27	0
Horn, Joe, K.C.	9	165	18.3	28	0
Brown, Troy, N.E.	8	271	33.9	54	0
Whitted, Alvis, Jax.	8	187	23.4	98t	1
Lewis, Jermaine, Balt.	8	158	19.8	25	0
Hill, Madre, Cle.	8	137	17.1	27	0
Williams, Nick, Cin.	8	109	13.6	24	0
Zereoue, Amos, Pitt.	7	169	24.1	35	0
Fletcher, Terrell, S.D.	7	112	16.0	22	0
Jackson, Willie, Cin.	6	179	29.8	46	0
Williams, Kevin L., NYJ	6	166	27.7	81	0
Joseph, Kerry, Sea.	6	132	22.0	61	0
Simmons, Tony, N.E.	6	132	22.0	29	0
Pathon, Jerome, Ind.	6	123	20.5	31	0
Mack, Stacey, Jax.	6	112	18.7	32	0
Branch, Calvin, Oak.	6	96	16.0	20	0
Jones, Tebucky, N.E.	5	113	22.6	28	0
Elias, Keith, Ind.	5	82	16.4	21	0
Banks, Tavian, Jax.	5	78	15.6	20	0
Reed, Robert, S.D.	5	72	14.4	21	0
Saleh, Tarek, Cle.	5	43	8.6	14	0
Farmer, Robert, NYJ	4	84	21.0	30	0
Miller, Billy, Den.	4	79	19.8	30	0
George, Spencer, Tenn.	4	63	15.8	22	0
Ismail, Qadry, Balt.	4	55	13.8	19	0
Jackson, Lenzie, Jax.	3	58	19.3	23	0
Bennett, Donnell, K.C.	3	51	17.0	24	0
Wilson, Jerry, Mia.	3	50	16.7	23	0
Yeast, Craig, Cin.	3	50	16.7	22	0
Lyons, Mitch, Pitt.	3	42	14.0	17	0
Campbell, Mark, Cle.	3	28	9.3	10	0
Smith, Irv, Cle.	3	15	5.0	10	0
Muhammad, Steve, Ind.	2	41	20.5	22	0
Porter, Daryl, Buff.	2	41	20.5	24	0
Bownes, Fabien, Sea.	2	40	20.0	33	0
Chiaverini, Darrin, Cle.	2	35	17.5	22	0
Little, Earl, Cle.	2	34	17.0	20	0
Johnson, Leon, NYJ	2	31	15.5	17	0
Cloud, Mike, K.C.	2	28	14.0	18	0
Johnson, J.J., Mia.	2	26	13.0	19	0
Loud, Kamil, Buff.	2	26	13.0	15	0
Warren, Lamont, N.E.	2	25	12.5	16	0
Kent, Joey, Tenn.	2	24	12.0	13	0
Loville, Derek, Den.	2	22	11.0	12	0
McCardell, Keenan, Jax.	2f	19	9.5	10	0
Byrd, Isaac, Tenn.	2	16	8.0	9	0
Fauria, Christian, Sea.	2	15	7.5	8	0
Neal, Lorenzo, Tenn.	2	15	7.5	14	0
Cline, Tony, Pitt.	2	8	4.0	8	0
Manusky, Greg, K.C.	2	6	3.0	6	0
Jones, Henry, Buff.	1	37	37.0	37t	1
Price, Peerless, Buff.	1	27	27.0	27	0
Jacquet, Nate, Mia.	1	26	26.0	26	0
Johnson, Kevin, Cle.	1	25	25.0	25	0
Logan, Mike, Jax.	1	25	25.0	25	0
Parker, Larry, K.C.	1	24	24.0	24	0
Ward, Hines, Pitt.	1	24	24.0	24	0
McDuffie, O.J., Mia.	1	17	17.0	17	0
Springs, Shawn, Sea.	1	15	15.0	15	0
Thomas, Zach, Mia.	1	15	15.0	15	0
Greene, Scott, Ind.	1	14	14.0	14	0
Ellison, Jerry, N.E.	1	13	13.0	13	0
Gash, Sam, Buff.	1	13	13.0	13	0
Jones, George, Cle.	1	12	12.0	12	0
McAlister, Chris, Balt.	1	12	12.0	12	0
Smith, Detron, Den.	1	12	12.0	11	0
Washington, Keith, Balt.	1	12	12.0	12	0
DeLong, Greg, Balt.	1f	11	11.0	11	0
Gordon, Lennox, Buff.	1	11	11.0	11	0
Johnson, Lonnie, K.C.	1	11	11.0	11	0
Parten, Ty, K.C.	1	11	11.0	11	0
Smith, Rod, Den.	1	10	10.0	10	0
Fuamatu-Ma'afala, Chris, Pitt.	1	9	9.0	9	0
Still, Bryan, S.D.	1	8	8.0	8	0
Pierce, Aaron, Balt.	1	7	7.0	7	0
Chamblin, Corey, Jax.	1	6	6.0	6	0
Collins, Bobby, Buff.	1	6	6.0	6	0
Treu, Adam, Oak.	1	6	6.0	6	0
Vrabel, Mike, Pitt.	1	6	6.0	6	0
Dillon, Corey, Cin.	1	4	4.0	4	0
McCrary, Fred, S.D.	1	4	4.0	4	0
Shields, Paul, Ind.	1	3	3.0	3	0
Sullivan, Chris, N.E.	1	1	1.0	1	0
Ashmore, Darryl, Oak.	1	0	0.0	0	0
Austin, Billy, Ind.	1	0	0.0	0	0
Mincy, Charles, Oak.	1	0	0.0	0	0
Shelton, Daimon, Jax.	1	0	0.0	0	0
Jones, Damon, Jax.	0f	0	—	—	0

t = Touchdown
f = Fair Catch
Leader based on average return, minimum 20 returns

NFC KICKOFF RETURNERS—INDIVIDUAL

	No.	Yards	Avg.	Long	TD
Horne, Tony, St.L.	30f	892	29.7	101t	2
Tucker, Jason, Dall.	22	613	27.9	79	0
Tate, Robert, Minn.	25	627	25.1	76t	1
Rossum, Allen, Phil.	54	1347	24.9	89t	1
Bates, Michael, Car.	52	1287	24.8	100t	2
Levingston, Bashir, NYG	22	532	24.2	35	0
Bates, Mario, Ariz.	52	1231	23.7	68	0
Milburn, Glyn, Chi.	61	1426	23.4	93	0
Palmer, David, Minn.	27	621	23.0	51	0
Fair, Terry, Det.	34	752	22.1	91	0
Mitchell, Basil, G.B.	21	464	22.1	88t	1
Philyaw, Dino, N.O.	53	1165	22.0	55	0
McQuarters, R.W., S.F.	26	568	21.8	37	0
Dwight, Tim, Atl.	44	944	21.5	40	0
Davis, Troy, N.O.	20	424	21.2	35	0
Mitchell, Brian, Wash.	43	893	20.8	45	0
Anthony, Reidel, T.B.	21	434	20.7	39	0
Patten, David, NYG	33	673	20.4	45	0
Preston, Roell, Tenn.-S.F.	21	411	19.6	58	0
Howard, Desmond, G.B.-Det.	34	662	19.5	35	0
Oliver, Winslow, Atl.	24	441	18.4	28	0
Nonqualifiers					
Phillips, Lawrence, S.F.	19	415	21.8	75	0
Mathis, Kevin, Dall.	18	408	22.7	37	0
Murphy, Yo, T.B.-Minn.	18	387	21.5	55	0
Carpenter, Ron, St.L.	16	406	25.4	43	0
Parker, De'Mond, G.B.	15	268	17.9	40	0
Thrash, James, Wash.	14	355	25.4	95t	1
Barber, Tiki, NYG	12	266	22.2	41	0
Ogden, Jeff, Dall.	12	252	21.0	29	0
Olivo, Brock, Det.	11	198	18.0	25	0
Williams, Moe, Minn.	10	240	24.0	85t	1
Bieniemy, Eric, Phil.	10	210	21.0	30	0
Green, Jacquez, T.B.	10	185	18.5	29	0
Jordan, Charles, Sea.-G.B.	9	157	17.4	24	0
Jervey, Travis, S.F.	8	191	23.9	48	0
Dunn, Warrick, T.B.	8	156	19.5	34	0
Talton, Tyree, Det.	6	121	20.2	38	0
Sanders, Deion, Dall.	4	87	21.8	31	0
Cody, Mac, Ariz.	4	76	19.0	29	0
Metcalf, Eric, Car.	4	56	14.0	31	0
Prioleau, Pierson, S.F.	3	73	24.3	32	0

1999 INDIVIDUAL STATISTICS—KICKOFF RETURNS/FUMBLES

	No.	Yards	Avg.	Long	TD
Lane, Fred, Car.	3	58	19.3	22	0
Bennett, Edgar, Chi.	3	53	17.7	20	0
Whiting, Brandon, Phil.	3	49	16.3	21	0
Williams, Elijah, Atl.	3	37	12.3	18	0
Tillman, Pat, Ariz.	3	33	11.0	18	0
Sellers, Mike, Wash.	3	32	10.7	16	0
Kinchen, Brian, Car.	3	29	9.7	15	0
Irvin, Sedrick, Det.	3	21	7.0	21	0
Hakim, Az-Zahir, St.L.	2	35	17.5	20	0
Schlesinger, Cory, Det.	2	33	16.5	20	0
Comella, Greg, NYG	2	31	15.5	17	0
Pittman, Michael, Ariz.	2	31	15.5	22	0
Harris, Mark, S.F.	2	26	13.0	15	0
Henderson, William, G.B.	2	23	11.5	16	0
Mangum, Kris, Car.	2	20	10.0	13	0
Kozlowski, Brian, Atl.	2	19	9.5	10	0
Fletcher, London, St.L.	2	13	6.5	13	0
Hallock, Ty, Chi.	2	10	5.0	7	0
Peterson, Tony, S.F.	2	10	5.0	10	0
Perry, Wilmont, N.O.	2	6	3.0	16	0
Hodgins, James, St.L.	2	4	2.0	4	0
Morton, Johnnie, Det.	1	22	22.0	22	0
Dawsey, Lawrence, N.O.	1	20	20.0	20	0
Morrow, Harold, Minn.	1	20	20.0	20	0
Alstott, Mike, T.B.	1	19	19.0	19	0
Hetherington, Chris, Car.	1	16	16.0	16	0
Williams, Karl, T.B.	1	15	15.0	15	0
Lassiter, Kwamie, Ariz.	1	13	13.0	13	0
McKenzie, Raleigh, G.B.	1	13	13.0	13	0
Bech, Brett, N.O.	1	12	12.0	12	0
Jenkins, James, Wash.	1	10	10.0	10	0
Makovicka, Joel, Ariz.	1	10	10.0	10	0
Schroeder, Bill, G.B.	1	10	10.0	10	0
Burrough, John, Minn.	1	9	9.0	9	0
Dishman, Chris, Ariz.	1	9	9.0	9	0
Gammon, Kendall, N.O.	1	9	9.0	9	0
Johnson, Anthony, Car.	1	9	9.0	9	0
Noble, Brandon, Dall.	1	9	9.0	9	0
Broughton, Luther, Phil.	1	5	5.0	5	0
Harris, Ronnie, Atl.	1	5	5.0	5	0
Lynch, Ben, S.F.	1	4	4.0	4	0
Sharper, Darren, G.B.	1	4	4.0	4	0
Coakley, Dexter, Dall.	1	3	3.0	3	0
Craver, Aaron, N.O.	1	3	3.0	3	0
McCollum, Andy, St.L.	1	3	3.0	3	0
Wiegmann, Casey, Chi.	1	2	2.0	2	0
Bly, Dre', St.L.	1f	1	1.0	1	0
German, Jammi, Atl.	1	1	1.0	1	0
Smith, Ed, Phil.	1	1	1.0	1	0
Bowie, Larry, Wash.	1	0	0.0	0	0
Jordan, Andrew, Minn.	1	0	0.0	0	0
Kleinsasser, Jimmy, Minn.	1	0	0.0	0	0
Milstead, Rod, Wash.	1	0	0.0	0	0
Tuinei, Van, Chi.	1	0	0.0	0	0
Marshall, Whit, Atl.	1	-2	-2.0	-2	0

t = Touchdown
f = Fair Catch
Leader based on average return, minimum 20 returns

FUMBLES

Most Fumbles
AFC: 16—Brian Griese, Denver
NFC: 12—Steve Beuerlein, Carolina
Brad Johnson, Washington

Most Fumbles, Game
AFC: 4—Jim Harbaugh, San Diego vs. Oakland, December 26
NFC: 4—Kurt Warner, St. Louis at Tennessee, October 31

Own Fumbles Recovered
AFC: 9—Brian Griese, Denver
NFC: 5—Tiki Barber, N.Y. Giants
Jake Plummer, Arizona

Most Own Fumbles Recovered, Game
AFC: 3—Mark Brunell, Jacksonville vs. Denver, December 13
NFC: 2—many times

Opponents' Fumbles Recovered
AFC: 4—Ryan McNeil, Cleveland
Takeo Spikes, Cincinnati
NFC: 4—Duane Clemons, Minnesota
Keith McKenzie, Green Bay

Most Opponents' Fumbles Recovered, Game
AFC: 2—Phil Hansen, Buffalo vs. Philadelphia, September 26
Fernando Smith, Baltimore at Atlanta, October 3
Ryan McNeil, Cleveland vs. New England, October 3
Barron Wortham, Tennessee vs. St. Louis, October 31
Reggie Tongue, Kansas City at Tampa Bay, November 14
NFC: 1—many times

Yards
AFC: 120—Travis Davis, Pittsburgh
NFC: 98—Greg Ellis, Dallas

Longest
AFC: 102—Travis Davis, Pittsburgh vs. Carolina, December 26 - TD
NFC: 98—Greg Ellis, Dallas vs. Ariz.ona, October 3 - TD

AFC FUMBLES—TEAM

	Fum.	Own Rec.	Fum. OB	TD	Opp. Rec.	TD	Fum. Yards	Tot. Rec.
Buffalo	17	5	1	0	9	1	75	14
Tennessee	17	8	0	0	24	2	96	32
Jacksonville	18	11	0	0	11	1	43	22
Pittsburgh	19	10	2	0	14	2	146	24
Kansas City	22	11	2	0	20	4	178	31
N.Y. Jets	22	14	2	0	11	1	-20	25
Oakland	22	6	1	0	13	1	107	19
Miami	23	7	3	0	10	1	33	17
Baltimore	24	12	1	0	10	0	-25	22
Indianapolis	25	9	5	1	13	1	0	22
New England	27	14	1	0	15	2	16	29
Cleveland	29	13	0	0	12	0	3	25
San Diego	29	18	0	0	12	2	6	30
Seattle	31	11	3	0	6	0	-14	17
Denver	33	21	2	0	11	1	1	32
Cincinnati	34	19	1	0	15	0	-14	34
AFC Total	392	189	24	1	206	19	631	395
AFC Average	24.5	11.8	1.5	0.1	12.9	1.2	39.4	24.7

NFC FUMBLES—TEAM

	Fum.	Own Rec.	Fum. OB	TD	Opp. Rec.	TD	Fum. Yards	Tot. Rec.
Detroit	21	10	3	0	16	3	100	26
Dallas	22	10	2	0	9	1	60	19
Atlanta	24	7	1	0	6	0	11	13
Carolina	24	5	0	0	14	0	37	19
Minnesota	24	4	1	0	18	0	8	22
Tampa Bay	25	4	2	0	9	0	-15	13
New Orleans	26	16	1	0	15	2	79	31
Green Bay	28	13	3	0	15	2	68	28
N.Y. Giants	29	14	3	0	7	1	26	21
San Francisco	29	15	1	0	7	3	95	22
St. Louis	30	11	3	0	7	1	100	18
Arizona	31	18	3	0	10	0	-4	28
Washington	31	15	5	0	13	1	43	28
Chicago	32	17	0	0	19	1	2	36
Philadelphia	33	11	1	0	18	0	32	29
NFC Total	409	170	29	0	183	15	642	353
NFC Average	27.3	11.3	1.9	0.0	12.2	1.0	42.8	23.5
League Total	801	359	53	1	389	34	1273	748
League Average	25.8	11.6	1.7	0.0	12.5	1.1	41.1	24.1

Fum OB = Fumbled out of bounds, includes fumbled through the end zone.

AFC TOUCHDOWNS ON FUMBLE RECOVERIES

1—Cadrez, Glenn, Den.; 1—Cota, Chad, Ind.; 1—Craft, Jason, Jax.; 1—Davis, Travis, Pitt.; 1—Dishman, Cris, K.C.; 1—Dixon, Gerald, S.D.; 1—Eaton, Chad, N.E.; 1—Edwards, Donnie, K.C.; 1—Hicks, Eric, K.C.; 1—Johnstone, Lance, Oak.; 1—Kearse, Jevon, Tenn.; 1—Lewis, Darryll, S.D.; 1—McGinest, Willie, N.E.; 1—Northern, Gabe, Buff.; 1—Ogbogu, Eric, NYJ; 1—Porter, Joey, Pitt.; 1—Taylor, Jason, Mia.; 1—Tongue, Reggie, K.C.; 1—Walker, Denard, Tenn.; 1—Wilkins, Terrence, Ind.

NFC TOUCHDOWNS ON FUMBLE RECOVERIES

2—McKenzie, Keith, G.B.; 1—Aldridge, Allen, Det.; 1—Bryant, Junior, S.F.; 1—Coleman, Marco, Wash.; 1—Drakeford, Tyronne, N.O.; 1—Ellis, Greg, Dall.; 1—Elliss, Luther, Det.; 1—Fair, Terry, Det.; 1—Harris, Sean, Chi.; 1—Jones, Mike A., St.L.; 1—McMillian, Mark, S.F.-Wash.; 1—Peter, Christian, NYG; 1—Walker, Darnell, S.F.; 1—Weary, Fred, N.O.

1999 INDIVIDUAL STATISTICS—FUMBLES

AFC FUMBLES—INDIVIDUAL

	Fum.	Own Rec.	Opp. Rec.	Yards	Tot. Rec.
Abdul-Jabbar, Karim, Cle.	0	1	0	0	1
Adams, Sam, Sea.	0	0	1	0	1
Albright, Ethan, Buff.	1	0	0	-8	0
Allen, Eric, Oak.	0	0	1	0	1
Allen, Terry, N.E.	8	1	0	0	1
Anders, Kimble, K.C.	1	0	0	0	0
Anderson, Willie, Cin.	0	1	0	0	1
Armstrong, Bruce, N.E.	0	1	0	0	1
Austin, Billy, Ind.	0	1	0	0	1
Banks, Tony, Balt.	11	2	0	0	2
Barber, Mike, Ind.	0	1	0	0	1
Barlow, Reggie, Jax.	4	1	0	0	1
Barndt, Tom, K.C.	0	0	1	0	1
Bartrum, Mike, N.E.	1	0	0	-7	0
Basnight, Michael, Cin.	1	1	0	0	1
Baxter, Fred, NYJ	0	1	0	0	1
Bellamy, Jay, Sea.	0	1	0	0	1
Bennett, Cornelius, Ind.	0	0	2	0	2
Bennett, Donnell, K.C.	1	0	0	0	0
Bettis, Jerome, Pitt.	2	3	0	1	3
Binn, David, S.D.	1	0	0	-36	0
Bishop, Blaine, Tenn.	0	0	2	0	2
Blackwell, Will, Pitt.	1	0	0	0	0
Blake, Jeff, Cin.	12	7	0	-28	7
Bledsoe, Drew, N.E.	8	6	0	-13	6
Blevins, Tony, Ind.	0	0	2	2	2
Bloedorn, Greg, Sea.	1	0	0	-6	0
Boose, Dorian, NYJ	0	0	1	0	1
Boselli, Tony, Jax.	0	3	0	0	3
Bowden, Joe, Tenn.	0	0	3	11	3
Bowens, David, Den.	0	1	0	0	1
Brackens, Tony, Jax.	0	0	2	6	2
Braham, Rich, Cin.	0	1	0	0	1
Bratzke, Chad, Ind.	1	0	1	3	1
Brice, Will, Cin.	0	1	0	0	1
Brown, Chad, Sea.	0	0	1	0	1
Brown, Eric, Den.	2	1	0	0	1
Brown, Reggie, Sea.	1	0	0	0	0
Brown, Troy, N.E.	1	1	1	0	2
Bruener, Mark, Pitt.	0	2	0	4	2
Brunell, Mark, Jax.	6	3	0	-2	3
Bruschi, Tedy, N.E.	0	0	1	0	1
Bryant, Fernando, Jax.	0	0	3	27	3
Buckley, Terrell, Mia.	1	0	0	0	0
Bush, Lewis, S.D.	0	0	1	0	1
Bynum, Kenny, S.D.	3	3	0	0	3
Byrd, Isaac, Tenn.	1	0	0	0	0
Cadrez, Glenn, Den.	0	1	3	74	4
Campbell, Mark, Cle.	0	2	0	0	2
Carney, John, S.D.	0	1	0	0	1
Carter, Tony, N.E.	0	1	0	0	1
Carter, Chris, N.E.	0	1	1	0	2
Case, Stoney, Balt.	2	2	0	-3	2
Chester, Larry, Ind.	0	0	1	0	1
Chiaverini, Darrin, Cle.	0	1	0	0	1
Christie, Steve, Buff.	0	1	0	0	1
Coleman, Marcus, NYJ	0	0	1	0	1
Collins, Cecil, Mia.	2	1	0	0	1
Cota, Chad, Ind.	0	0	1	25	1
Couch, Tim, Cle.	14	4	0	-11	4
Cowart, Sam, Buff.	0	0	1	0	1
Cox, Bryan, NYJ	0	0	1	0	1
Craft, Jason, Jax.	0	0	1	23	1
Crockett, Ray, Den.	0	0	1	0	1
Davis, Reggie, S.D.	0	0	1	0	1
Davis, Terrell, Den.	1	1	0	0	1
Davis, Travis, Pitt.	0	0	1	102	1
Davis, Billy, Balt.	0	0	1	0	1
Dawkins, Sean, Sea.	1	0	0	0	0
Dilger, Ken, Ind.	1	1	0	0	1
Dillon, Corey, Cin.	3	1	0	0	1
Dishman, Cris, K.C.	0	1	2	40	3
Dixon, Gerald, S.D.	0	0	1	27	1
Dunn, David, Cle.	3	1	0	0	1
Eaton, Chad, N.E.	0	0	3	53	3
Edwards, Donnie, K.C.	0	0	2	79	2
Edwards, Marc, Cle.	1	0	0	0	0
Edwards, Troy, Pitt.	4	2	1	0	3
Emmons, Carlos, Pitt.	0	0	3	2	3
Evans, Chuck, Balt.	0	1	0	0	1

	Fum.	Own Rec.	Opp. Rec.	Yards	Tot. Rec.
Evans, Josh, Tenn.	0	0	2	0	2
Farmer, Robert, NYJ	1	1	0	0	1
Faulk, Kevin, N.E.	3	0	0	-9	0
Fauria, Christian, Sea.	1	0	0	0	0
Favors, Greg, Tenn.	0	0	1	0	1
Fazande, Jermaine, S.D.	2	0	0	0	0
Fiedler, Jay, Jax.	1	0	0	0	0
Fletcher, Terrell, S.D.	1	1	0	0	1
Flutie, Doug, Buff.	6	1	0	-5	1
Foley, Glenn, Sea.	1	0	0	0	0
Foley, Steve, Cin.	0	0	2	0	2
Fontenot, Albert, S.D.	0	0	1	0	1
Ford, Henry, Tenn.	0	0	2	0	2
Fortin, Roman, S.D.	0	2	0	0	2
Fuller, Corey, Cle.	0	0	2	0	2
Gannon, Rich, Oak.	8	1	0	-5	1
Gardener, Daryl, Mia.	0	0	1	33	1
Gary, Olandis, Den.	2	1	0	0	1
Gash, Sam, Buff.	0	1	0	0	1
George, Eddie, Tenn.	5	1	0	0	1
Gibson, Oliver, Cin.	0	0	1	0	1
Glenn, Aaron, NYJ	0	0	1	0	1
Glenn, Terry, N.E.	2	1	0	0	1
Goff, Mike, Cin.	0	1	0	0	1
Gogan, Kevin, Mia.	0	1	0	0	1
Gonzalez, Tony, K.C.	2	1	0	0	1
Goodwin, Hunter, Mia.	1	0	0	0	0
Gordon, Darrien, Oak.	3	1	1	40	2
Gray, Chris, Sea.	0	1	0	0	1
Grbac, Elvis, K.C.	7	1	0	0	1
Green, Ahman, Sea.	2	1	0	0	1
Green, Victor, NYJ	0	0	2	9	2
Griese, Brian, Den.	16	9	0	-46	9
Griffin, Damon, Cin.	5	2	0	0	2
Griffith, Howard, Den.	0	1	0	0	1
Grunhard, Tim, K.C.	0	1	0	0	1
Hall, Cory, Cin.	0	0	1	0	1
Hansen, Phil, Buff.	0	0	2	24	2
Harbaugh, Jim, S.D.	12	4	0	-20	4
Hardy, Kevin, Jax.	0	0	1	0	1
Harrison, Marvin, Ind.	2	1	0	0	1
Harrison, Nolan, Pitt.	0	0	1	0	1
Hawkins, Artrell, Cin.	0	0	1	0	1
Heath, Rodney, Cin.	0	0	2	-4	2
Hentrich, Craig, Tenn.	0	1	1	0	2
Herring, Kim, Balt.	0	0	2	0	2
Hicks, Eric, K.C.	0	0	2	44	2
Hill, Ray, Mia.	0	1	0	1	1
Holland, Darius, Cle.	0	0	1	14	1
Hollier, Dwight, Mia.	0	1	0	0	1
Holmes, Earl, Pitt.	0	0	1	0	1
Holmes, Priest, Balt.	0	1	0	0	1
Horn, Joe, K.C.	0	1	0	0	1
Huard, Damon, Mia.	3	1	0	-5	1
Huntley, Richard, Pitt.	3	0	0	0	0
Ismail, Qadry, Balt.	2	0	0	0	0
Israel, Steve, N.E.	0	0	2	0	2
Izzo, Larry, Mia.	0	0	1	0	1
Jackson, Brad, Balt.	0	0	1	0	1
Jackson, Grady, Oak.	0	0	1	0	1
Jackson, Greg, S.D.	0	0	1	0	1
Jackson, Steve, Tenn.	0	1	1	0	2
Jackson, Willie, Cin.	1	1	0	0	1
Jacquet, Nate, Mia.	1	0	0	0	0
James, Edgerrin, Ind.	8	2	0	0	2
Jefferson, Shawn, N.E.	0	1	0	0	1
Jenkins, Kerry, NYJ	0	1	0	0	1
Johnson, Darrius, Den.	0	1	1	0	2
Johnson, Ellis, Ind.	0	0	1	0	1
Johnson, J.J., Mia.	2	1	0	0	1
Johnson, Kevin, Cle.	1	1	0	0	1
Johnson, Pat, Balt.	1	1	0	12	1
Johnson, Raylee, S.D.	0	0	1	0	1
Johnson, Leon, NYJ	1	0	0	0	0
Johnstone, Lance, Oak.	0	0	1	13	1
Jones, Charlie, S.D.	1	1	0	0	1
Jones, Lenoy, Cle.	1	0	0	0	0
Jones, Marvin, NYJ	0	0	1	0	1
Jones, Mike D., Tenn.	0	0	1	0	1
Jones, Walter, Sea.	0	1	0	0	1
Jordan, Randy, Oak.	2	0	0	0	0

1999 INDIVIDUAL STATISTICS—FUMBLES

	Fum.	Own Rec.	Opp. Rec.	Yards	Tot. Rec.
Joseph, Kerry, Sea.	0	0	1	0	1
Kaufman, Napoleon, Oak.	3	2	0	0	2
Kearse, Jevon, Tenn.	0	0	1	14	1
Killens, Terry, Tenn.	0	0	1	0	1
Kirby, Terry, Cle.	4	2	0	0	2
Kirkland, Levon, Pitt.	0	0	2	0	2
Kitna, Jon, Sea.	14	6	0	-9	6
Konrad, Rob, Mia.	3	1	0	0	1
Kramer, Erik, S.D.	3	1	0	-7	1
Law, Ty, N.E.	1	0	1	0	1
Leeuwenburg, Jay, Cin.	1	0	0	0	0
Lewis, Darryll, S.D.	0	0	2	42	2
Lewis, Jermaine, Balt.	1	0	1	0	1
Lewis, Mo, NYJ	0	0	1	0	1
Lewis, Ray, Balt.	1	0	0	0	0
Linton, Jonathan, Buff.	4	1	0	0	1
Little, Earl, N.O.-Cle.	1	0	0	0	0
Long, Kevin, Tenn.	1	0	0	-10	0
Loville, Derek, Den.	1	0	0	-12	0
Lucas, Ray, NYJ	8	4	0	-28	4
Lynn, Anthony, Den.	0	0	1	0	1
Machado, J.P., NYJ	0	1	0	0	1
Mack, Tremain, Cin.	3	1	0	0	1
Manning, Peyton, Ind.	6	2	0	-5	2
Manusky, Greg, K.C.	0	0	1	0	1
Marino, Dan, Mia.	5	0	0	0	0
Marion, Brock, Mia.	2	0	1	0	1
Martin, Curtis, NYJ	2	2	0	0	2
Marts, Lonnie, Jax.	0	0	2	3	2
Maryland, Russell, Oak.	0	0	1	0	1
May, Deems, Sea.	1	0	0	-12	0
Mayes, Derrick, Sea.	1	0	0	0	0
McCardell, Keenan, Jax.	1	1	0	0	1
McCrary, Michael, Balt.	0	0	1	0	1
McDuffie, O.J., Mia.	2	0	0	0	0
McGinest, Willie, N.E.	0	0	2	2	2
McGlockton, Chester, K.C.	1	0	1	-2	1
McGriff, Travis, Den.	1	1	0	0	1
McKenzie, Kevin, Mia.	1	0	0	0	0
McNair, Steve, Tenn.	3	1	0	0	1
McNeil, Ryan, Cle.	0	0	4	0	4
Mickens, Terry, Oak.	1	0	0	0	0
Mili, Itula, Sea.	1	0	0	0	0
Miller, Chris, Den.	2	0	0	-6	0
Miller, Josh, Pitt.	1	0	0	-11	0
Milloy, Lawyer, N.E.	0	0	2	0	2
Mincy, Charles, Oak.	0	0	1	0	1
Mirer, Rick, NYJ	3	2	0	-1	2
Mitchell, Brandon, N.E.	0	0	1	0	1
Mitchell, Donald, Tenn.	0	0	1	0	1
Mitchell, Jeff, Balt.	2	0	0	-36	0
Mitchell, Scott, Balt.	1	0	0	0	0
Moore, Larry, Ind.	2	0	0	-25	0
Morris, Byron (Bam), K.C.	3	1	0	0	1
Moulds, Eric, Buff.	1	0	0	0	0
Myers, Greg, Cin.	0	0	1	21	1
Newman, Anthony, Oak.	0	0	1	0	1
Northern, Gabe, Buff.	0	0	1	59	1
O'Donnell, Neil, Tenn.	5	3	0	-14	3
Ogbogu, Eric, NYJ	0	0	2	0	2
Ogden, Jonathan, Balt.	0	2	0	2	2
Oldham, Chris, Pitt.	0	0	1	0	1
Olson, Benji, Tenn.	0	1	0	0	1
Ostroski, Jerry, Buff.	1	0	0	-2	0
Owens, Rich, Mia.	0	0	1	0	1
Parker, Larry, K.C.	1	0	0	0	0
Parker, Vaughn, S.D.	0	1	0	0	1
Patton, Marvcus, K.C.	0	0	3	0	3
Penn, Chris, S.D.	3	1	0	0	1
Perry, Jason, S.D.	0	0	1	0	1
Peterson, Mike, Ind.	0	0	1	0	1
Pickens, Carl, Cin.	1	0	0	0	0
Pierce, Aaron, Balt.	1	0	0	0	0
Pollard, Marcus, Ind.	2	0	0	0	0
Pope, Daniel, K.C.	1	1	0	-11	1
Porter, Joey, Pitt.	0	0	2	50	2
Powell, Ronnie, Cle.	3	0	0	0	0
Pryce, Trevor, Den.	0	0	1	0	1
Randolph, Thomas, Ind.	0	0	1	0	1
Reed, Andre, Buff.	0	1	0	0	1
Reed, Robert, S.D.	1	0	0	0	0

	Fum.	Own Rec.	Opp. Rec.	Yards	Tot. Rec.
Rehberg, Scott, Cle.	0	1	0	0	1
Richardson, Tony, K.C.	1	0	0	0	0
Robbins, Barret, Oak.	0	1	0	0	1
Robinson, Eddie, Tenn.	0	0	3	1	3
Rodgers, Derrick, Mia.	0	0	2	0	2
Rogers, Charlie, Sea.	3	0	0	0	0
Rogers, Sam, Buff.	0	0	2	7	2
Rolle, Samari, Tenn.	1	0	1	3	1
Romanowski, Bill, Den.	1	1	0	0	1
Rouen, Tom, Den.	0	1	0	0	1
Roye, Orpheus, Pitt.	0	0	1	0	1
Russell, Darrell, Oak.	0	0	1	0	1
Rutledge, Rod, N.E.	1	0	0	0	0
Saleh, Tarek, Cle.	0	0	1	0	1
Schulz, Kurt, Buff.	0	0	1	0	1
Seau, Junior, S.D.	0	0	1	0	1
Serwanga, Kato, N.E.	0	0	1	0	1
Shaw, Sedrick, Cle.	1	0	0	0	0
Shehee, Rashaan, K.C.	1	0	0	0	0
Shelton, Daimon, Jax.	0	0	1	0	1
Shields, Will, K.C.	0	1	0	0	1
Simien, Tracy, S.D.	0	0	1	0	1
Simmons, Brian, Cin.	0	0	1	0	1
Simmons, Jason, Pitt.	0	1	0	0	1
Simmons, Tony, N.E.	1	0	0	0	0
Sinclair, Michael, Sea.	0	0	1	13	1
Siragusa, Tony, Balt.	0	0	1	0	1
Smith, Antowain, Buff.	4	0	0	0	0
Smith, Bruce, Buff.	0	0	1	0	1
Smith, Detron, Den.	0	0	1	0	1
Smith, Fernando, Balt.	0	0	3	0	3
Smith, Jimmy, Jax.	1	0	0	0	0
Smith, Akili, Cin.	4	1	0	-3	1
Smith, Rod, Den.	1	0	0	0	0
Smith, Thomas, Buff.	0	0	1	0	1
Smith, Travian, Oak.	0	0	1	1	1
Spears, Marcus, K.C.	0	1	0	0	1
Spikes, Takeo, Cin.	0	0	4	0	4
Springs, Shawn, Sea.	0	0	1	0	1
Steed, Joel, Pitt.	0	0	1	4	1
Stephens, Tremayne, S.D.	2	3	0	0	3
Stewart, James, Jax.	4	1	0	0	1
Stewart, Kordell, Pitt.	4	1	0	0	1
Stewart, Rayna, Jax.	0	1	0	0	1
Stone, Dwight, NYJ	3	2	0	0	2
Stoutmire, Omar, NYJ	0	0	1	0	1
Szott, David, K.C.	0	1	0	0	1
Taylor, Jason, Mia.	0	0	2	4	2
Teague, Trey, Den.	1	0	0	-9	0
Thigpen, Yancey, Tenn.	1	0	0	0	0
Thomas, Derrick, K.C.	0	0	1	0	1
Thomas, Mark, Ind.	0	0	1	0	1
Thompson, Mike, Cle.	0	0	2	0	2
Tomczak, Mike, Pitt.	3	0	0	-6	0
Tongue, Reggie, K.C.	0	0	3	9	3
Treu, Adam, Oak.	1	0	0	0	0
Tupa, Tom, NYJ	1	0	0	0	0
Turner, Eric, Oak.	0	0	2	34	2
Turner, Scott, S.D.	0	0	1	0	1
Vanover, Tamarick, K.C.	3	1	0	0	1
von Oelhoffen, Kimo, Cin.	0	0	1	0	1
Vrabel, Mike, Pitt.	0	1	0	0	1
Wade, John, Jax.	1	0	0	-14	0
Walker, Brian, Sea.	0	1	0	0	1
Walker, Denard, Tenn.	0	0	1	83	1
Walker, Derrick, Oak.	1	0	0	0	0
Ward, Dedric, NYJ	2	0	0	0	0
Ward, Hines, Pitt.	1	0	0	0	0
Washington, Keith, Balt.	1	1	0	0	1
Watson, Chris, Den.	5	2	1	0	3
Watters, Ricky, Sea.	4	0	0	0	0
Wheatley, Tyrone, Oak.	3	1	0	0	1
Wiegert, Zach, Jax.	0	1	0	0	1
Wilkins, Terrence, Ind.	3	1	0	0	1
Williams, Dan, K.C.	0	0	2	0	2
Williams, Darryl, Sea.	0	0	1	0	1
Williams, James E., Cle.	0	0	2	0	2
Williams, Nick, Cin.	1	0	0	0	0
Williams, K.D., Oak.	0	0	1	0	1
Williams, Kevin L., NYJ	1	0	0	0	0
Williams, Robert, K.C.	0	0	1	0	1

1999 INDIVIDUAL STATISTICS—FUMBLES

	Fum.	Own Rec.	Opp. Rec.	Yards	Tot. Rec.
Wilson, Al, Den.	0	0	2	0	2
Wooden, Shawn, Mia.	0	0	2	0	2
Woods, Jerome, K.C.	0	0	1	19	1
Woodson, Charles, Oak.	0	0	1	24	1
Woodson, Rod, Balt.	1	2	0	0	2
Woody, Damien, N.E.	1	1	0	-10	1
Wooten, Tito, Ind.	0	0	2	0	2
Wortham, Barron, Tenn.	0	0	3	8	3
Wright, Lawrence, Cin.	0	0	1	0	1
Wynn, Renaldo, Jax.	0	0	1	0	1
Yeast, Craig, Cin.	2	1	0	0	1

Yards includes aborted plays, own recoveries, and opponents' recoveries.

NFC FUMBLES—INDIVIDUAL

	Fum.	Own Rec.	Opp. Rec.	Yards	Tot. Rec.
Adams, Flozell, Dall.	0	1	0	0	1
Aikman, Troy, Dall.	8	2	0	-12	2
Aldridge, Allen, Det.	1	0	1	8	1
Alstott, Mike, T.B.	6	0	0	0	0
Ambrose, Ashley, N.O.	0	0	2	29	2
Anthony, Reidel, T.B.	1	0	0	0	0
Banks, Antonio, Minn.	0	0	1	0	1
Barber, Tiki, NYG	5	5	0	0	5
Barnhardt, Tommy, N.O.	1	1	0	0	1
Barrow, Micheal, Car.	0	0	1	0	1
Batch, Charlie, Det.	4	0	0	0	0
Bates, Mario, Ariz.	2	0	1	0	1
Bates, Michael, Car.	1	0	0	0	0
Beasley, Fred, S.F.	2	2	0	0	2
Bennett, Edgar, Chi.	1	0	0	0	0
Bennett, Tommy, Ariz.	0	0	1	0	1
Berger, Mitch, Minn.	0	0	1	0	1
Beuerlein, Steve, Car.	12	0	0	-4	0
Biakabutuka, Tim, Car.	3	0	0	0	0
Bostic, James, Phil.	2	0	0	0	0
Boston, David, Ariz.	2	1	0	0	1
Bowie, Larry, Wash.	1	1	0	0	1
Bradford, Corey, G.B.	1	0	0	0	0
Brooks, Macey, Chi.	0	0	1	0	1
Brooks, Derrick, T.B.	0	0	2	4	2
Broughton, Luther, Phil.	0	1	0	0	1
Brown, Dave, Ariz.	4	1	0	0	1
Brown, Doug, Wash.	0	0	1	0	1
Brown, Gary, NYG	1	0	0	0	0
Brown, Ray, S.F.	0	2	0	0	2
Bryant, Junior, S.F.	0	0	1	0	1
Burns, Keith, Chi.	0	0	1	0	1
Bush, Devin, St.L.	0	1	1	31	2
Butler, LeRoy, G.B.	0	0	1	0	1
Caldwell, Mike, Phil.	0	0	1	0	1
Carrier, Mark, Det.	0	0	1	6	1
Carter, Kevin, St.L.	0	0	2	0	2
Carter, Marty, Atl.	0	0	1	0	1
Carter, Tom, Chi.	0	0	1	21	1
Centers, Larry, Wash.	2	1	0	0	1
Chandler, Chris, Atl.	7	4	0	-14	4
Christian, Bob, Atl.	1	0	0	0	0
Claiborne, Chris, Det.	0	0	3	27	3
Clark, Greg, S.F.	1	0	0	0	0
Cleeland, Cameron, N.O.	1	0	0	0	0
Clemons, Charlie, St.L.	0	0	1	0	1
Clemons, Duane, Minn.	0	0	4	0	4
Cody, Mac, Ariz.	2	1	0	0	1
Coleman, Marco, Wash.	0	0	1	42	1
Collins, Andre, Det.	0	0	1	0	1
Collins, Kerry, NYG	11	2	0	-27	2
Colvin, Rosevelt, Chi.	0	0	1	0	1
Compton, Mike, Det.	0	2	0	8	2
Connell, Albert, Wash.	1	1	0	0	1
Conway, Brett, Wash.	0	1	0	0	1
Conway, Curtis, Chi.	2	0	0	0	0
Cook, Anthony, Wash.	0	0	1	0	1
Cousin, Terry, Chi.	0	0	1	0	1
Craver, Aaron, N.O.	1	1	0	0	1
Crowell, Germane, Det.	1	1	0	0	1
Culpepper, Daunte, Minn.	1	1	0	-2	1
Cunningham, Randall, Minn.	2	0	0	-1	0
Davis, Eric, Car.	1	0	1	0	1
Davis, Stephen, Wash.	4	2	0	0	2
Davis, Troy, N.O.	1	0	0	0	0
Dawkins, Brian, Phil.	0	1	1	0	2
Deese, Derrick, S.F.	0	4	0	0	4
Delhomme, Jake, N.O.	1	0	0	0	0
Diaz, Jorge, T.B.	0	1	0	0	1
Dilfer, Trent, T.B.	6	0	0	-4	0
Doleman, Chris, Minn.	0	0	2	7	2
Drake, Jerry, Ariz.	0	0	1	0	1
Drakeford, Tyronne, N.O.	0	0	1	20	1
Dronett, Shane, Atl.	0	0	1	15	1
Dunn, Warrick, T.B.	3	1	0	0	1
Dwight, Tim, Atl.	2	0	0	0	0
Edwards, Antuan, G.B.	1	0	0	0	0
Ellis, Greg, Dall.	0	0	1	98	1
Elliss, Luther, Det.	0	0	2	11	2
Ellsworth, Percy, NYG	0	0	1	15	1
Engram, Bobby, Chi.	2	1	1	0	2
Enis, Curtis, Chi.	4	2	0	0	2
Evans, Leomont, Wash.	0	0	1	0	1
Everitt, Steve, Phil.	0	1	0	0	1
Fair, Terry, Det.	2	0	1	35	1
Fann, Chad, S.F.	1	1	0	0	1
Faulk, Marshall, St.L.	2	0	0	0	0
Favre, Brett, G.B.	9	1	0	-2	1
Fields, Mark, N.O.	0	0	1	0	1
Flanigan, Jim, Chi.	0	0	1	0	1
Floyd, William, Car.	1	1	0	0	1
Fontenot, Jerry, N.O.	0	1	0	0	1
Fredrickson, Rob, Ariz.	0	0	1	0	1
Freeman, Antonio, G.B.	1	1	0	0	1
Frerotte, Gus, Det.	3	1	0	0	1
Garcia, Frank, Car.	0	2	0	0	2
Garcia, Jeff, S.F.	5	1	0	-1	1
Gardner, Barry, Phil.	0	0	1	20	1
Garner, Charlie, S.F.	4	0	0	0	0
George, Jeff, Minn.	8	2	0	0	2
Germaine, Joe, St.L.	1	0	0	0	0
Givens, Reggie, S.F.	1	0	0	0	0
Glover, La'Roi, N.O.	0	0	1	2	1
Gragg, Scott, NYG	0	1	0	0	1
Graham, Aaron, Ariz.	1	1	0	0	1
Graham, Kent, NYG	4	2	0	0	2
Gramatica, Martin, T.B.	0	0	1	0	1
Graziani, Tony, Atl.	4	2	0	-8	2
Green, Darrell, Wash.	0	0	1	4	1
Green, Jacquez, T.B.	1	0	0	0	0
Greene, Kevin, Car.	0	0	3	8	3
Hakim, Az-Zahir, St.L.	6	3	0	0	3
Hall, Travis, Atl.	0	0	1	0	1
Hallock, Ty, Chi.	0	0	1	0	1
Hamilton, Keith, NYG	0	0	2	0	2
Hanspard, Byron, Atl.	1	0	0	0	0
Hardy, Terry, Ariz.	1	0	0	0	0
Harris, Al, Phil.	1	0	0	0	0
Harris, Bernardo, G.B.	0	1	0	0	1
Harris, Mark, S.F.	1	0	0	0	0
Harris, Ronnie, Atl.	1	0	0	0	0
Harris, Sean, Chi.	0	0	2	0	2
Harris, Walt, Chi.	0	0	1	0	1
Hartings, Jeff, Det.	0	2	0	1	2
Hasselbeck, Matt, G.B.	1	1	0	-16	1
Hauck, Tim, Phil.	0	0	1	0	1
Henderson, William, G.B.	1	0	0	0	0
Hetherington, Chris, Car.	0	0	1	0	1
Hicks, Skip, Wash.	1	0	0	0	0
Hill, Greg, Det.	1	0	0	0	0
Hoard, Leroy, Minn.	4	0	0	0	0
Hobert, Billy Joe, N.O.	2	1	0	-8	1
Holcombe, Robert, St.L.	4	0	0	0	0
Holdman, Warrick, Chi.	0	0	1	33	1
Holliday, Vonnie, G.B.	0	0	1	0	1
Holmes, Lester, Ariz.	0	1	0	0	1
Holsey, Bernard, NYG	0	1	0	1	1
Holt, Torry, St.L.	4	1	0	0	1
Hunt, Cletidus, G.B.	0	0	1	0	1
Irvin, Sedrick, Det.	2	0	0	0	0
Ismail, Raghib, Dall.	1	0	0	0	0
Jackson, Terry, S.F.	1	0	0	0	0
Jeffers, Patrick, Car.	0	1	0	3	1
Jefferson, Greg, Phil.	0	0	2	4	2
Jett, John, Det.	1	0	0	0	0

	Fum.	Own Rec.	Opp. Rec.	Yards	Tot. Rec.
Johnson, Anthony, Car.	1	0	0	0	0
Johnson, Charles, Phil.	2	1	0	0	1
Johnson, Tre', Wash.	0	3	0	0	3
Johnson, Brad, Wash.	12	2	0	-8	2
Johnson, LeShon, NYG	2	0	0	0	0
Johnston, Daryl, Dall.	0	1	0	0	1
Jones, James, Det.	0	0	1	0	1
Jones, Donta, Car.	0	0	1	0	1
Jones, Mike A., St.L.	1	0	2	42	2
Jordan, Charles, G.B.	1	1	0	0	1
Joyce, Matt, Ariz.	0	1	0	0	1
Jurevicius, Joe, NYG	1	0	0	0	0
Kelly, Jeff, Atl.	0	0	1	0	1
Kelly, Rob, N.O.	0	0	1	0	1
Kennison, Eddie, N.O.	6	4	0	0	4
Kinchen, Brian, Car.	0	0	1	0	1
King, Shaun, T.B.	4	1	0	0	1
Kirschke, Travis, Det.	0	0	1	0	1
Kleinsasser, Jimmy, Minn.	2	0	0	0	0
Knight, Sammy, N.O.	0	0	1	0	1
Kozlowski, Brian, Atl.	1	0	0	0	0
Kreutz, Olin, Chi.	1	2	0	-17	2
LaFleur, David, Dall.	0	1	0	0	1
Landeta, Sean, Phil.	1	1	0	0	1
Lane, Fred, Car.	1	0	0	0	0
Lang, Kenard, Wash.	0	0	1	0	1
Lassiter, Kwamie, Ariz.	0	0	2	0	2
Lee, Amp, St.L.	0	1	0	0	1
Lett, Leon, Dall.	0	0	2	0	2
Levens, Dorsey, G.B.	5	0	0	0	0
Levingston, Bashir, NYG	1	0	0	0	0
Makovicka, Joel, Ariz.	1	1	0	0	1
Mamula, Mike, Phil.	0	0	2	0	2
Martin, Wayne, N.O.	0	0	2	0	2
Martin, Steve, Phil.	0	0	1	0	1
Mathis, Kevin, Dall.	1	1	0	0	1
Matthews, Shane, Chi.	7	2	0	-14	2
Mayberry, Tony, T.B.	1	0	0	-15	0
McBride, Tod, G.B.	0	0	2	0	2
McBurrows, Gerald, Atl.	0	0	1	0	1
McDaniel, Ed, Minn.	0	0	2	0	2
McDonald, Tim, S.F.	0	0	1	0	1
McGarrahan, Scott, G.B.	0	1	0	0	1
McIver, Everett, Dall.	0	1	0	0	1
McKenzie, Keith, G.B.	0	0	4	63	4
McKinley, Dennis, Ariz.	0	1	1	0	2
McKinnon, Ronald, Ariz.	0	0	1	0	1
McMillian, Mark, S.F.-Wash.	1	0	1	41	1
McNabb, Donovan, Phil.	8	0	0	-3	0
McNown, Cade, Chi.	6	2	0	-2	2
McQuarters, R.W., S.F.	1	0	0	0	0
McWilliams, Johnny, Ariz.	1	1	0	0	1
Metcalf, Eric, Car.	2	0	0	0	0
Milburn, Glyn, Chi.	4	2	0	0	2
Miller, Jim, Chi.	4	3	0	-19	3
Minter, Barry, Chi.	0	0	1	0	1
Minter, Mike, Car.	0	0	2	30	2
Mitchell, Basil, G.B.	2	1	1	0	2
Mitchell, Brian, Wash.	2	1	1	5	2
Mitchell, Keith, N.O.	0	0	1	0	1
Mitchell, Pete, NYG	1	0	0	0	0
Montgomery, Joe, NYG	2	0	0	0	0
Moore, Damon, Phil.	0	0	1	0	1
Morrow, Harold, Minn.	0	0	1	0	1
Moss, Randy, Minn.	3	0	0	0	0
Muhammad, Muhsin, Car.	1	0	0	0	0
Murphy, Yo, T.B.-Minn.	1	0	0	0	0
Murrell, Adrian, Ariz.	4	0	0	0	0
Nelson, Jim, G.B.	0	0	1	0	1
Noble, Brandon, Dall.	0	0	1	0	1
Nutten, Tom, St.L.	0	1	0	0	1
Oben, Roman, NYG	0	2	0	0	2
Oliver, Winslow, Atl.	2	0	0	0	0
Olivo, Brock, Det.	0	0	1	0	1
Owens, Terrell, S.F.	1	0	0	0	0
Oxendine, Ken, Atl.	5	0	0	0	0
Palmer, David, Minn.	1	0	0	0	0
Parker, De'Mond, G.B.	1	1	1	0	2
Pederson, Doug, Phil.	7	0	0	0	0
Perry, Todd, Chi.	0	1	0	0	1
Perry, Wilmont, N.O.	0	1	0	0	1
Peter, Christian, NYG	0	0	1	38	1
Peterson, Tony, S.F.	1	0	0	0	0
Phillips, Lawrence, S.F.	2	2	0	0	2
Philyaw, Dino, N.O.	1	1	0	0	1
Pittman, Kavika, Dall.	0	0	2	0	2
Pittman, Michael, Ariz.	3	1	0	0	1
Plummer, Jake, Ariz.	7	5	0	-4	5
Pounds, Darryl, Wash.	1	0	1	2	1
Preston, Roell, S.F.	1	1	0	0	1
Quarles, Shelton, T.B.	0	0	1	0	1
Ramirez, Tony, Det.	0	1	0	0	1
Randle, John, Minn.	0	0	3	0	3
Raymer, Cory, Wash.	0	1	0	0	1
Rice, Ron, Det.	0	0	1	0	1
Rice, Simeon, Ariz.	0	0	1	0	1
Rivera, Marco, G.B.	0	1	0	0	1
Roaf, Willie, N.O.	0	1	0	0	1
Robbins, Austin, N.O.	0	0	1	0	1
Roberts, Ray, Det.	0	1	0	0	1
Robinson, Damien, T.B.	0	0	2	0	2
Rossum, Allen, Phil.	6	2	0	0	2
Rudd, Dwayne, Minn.	0	0	1	0	1
Samuel, Khari, Chi.	0	0	1	0	1
Sanders, Deion, Dall.	1	0	0	0	0
Sanders, Frank, Ariz.	2	1	0	0	1
Sapp, Warren, T.B.	0	0	2	0	2
Sauerbrun, Todd, Chi.	1	0	0	0	0
Schlesinger, Cory, Det.	4	1	0	0	1
Schroeder, Bill, G.B.	3	0	0	0	0
Scroggins, Tracy, Det.	0	0	2	4	2
Scurlock, Mike, Car.	0	0	1	0	1
Sehorn, Jason, NYG	1	0	0	-1	0
Sellers, Mike, Wash.	1	0	0	0	0
Shade, Sam, Wash.	0	0	1	0	1
Sharper, Darren, G.B.	0	0	1	9	1
Simmons, Clyde, Chi.	0	0	1	0	1
Slutzker, Scott, N.O.	1	0	0	0	0
Smith, Brady, N.O.	0	0	2	0	2
Smith, Chuck, Atl.	0	0	1	18	1
Smith, Derek M., Wash.	0	0	1	0	1
Smith, Emmitt, Dall.	5	1	0	0	1
Smith, Frankie, Chi.	0	0	1	0	1
Smith, Lamar, N.O.	1	0	0	0	0
Smith, Jermaine, G.B.	1	0	0	0	0
Smith, Robert, Minn.	1	0	0	0	0
Sparks, Phillippi, NYG	0	1	0	0	1
Spellman, Alonzo, Dall.	0	0	1	0	1
Stablein, Brian, Det.	1	1	0	0	1
Staley, Duce, Phil.	5	2	0	0	2
Stanley, Chad, S.F.	0	1	0	0	1
Stenstrom, Steve, S.F.	3	0	0	-1	0
Stepnoski, Mark, Dall.	1	1	0	-26	1
Steussie, Todd, Minn.	0	1	0	0	1
Stevens, Matt, Wash.	0	0	1	0	1
Stokes, J.J., S.F.	1	1	0	0	1
Strahan, Michael, NYG	0	0	2	0	2
Stubblefield, Dana, Wash.	0	0	1	0	1
Styles, Lorenzo, St.L.	0	1	0	0	1
Swift, Michael, Car.	0	0	1	0	1
Tate, Robert, Minn.	1	0	0	0	0
Taylor, Bobby, Phil.	0	0	3	0	3
Teague, George, Dall.	0	0	1	0	1
Terry, Chris, Car.	0	1	1	0	2
Thomas, Hollis, Phil.	0	0	1	2	1
Thomas, Orlando, Minn.	0	0	1	0	1
Thomas, William, Phil.	0	0	1	9	1
Thomas, Tra, Phil.	0	1	0	0	1
Tillman, Pat, Ariz.	1	1	0	0	1
Timmerman, Adam, St.L.	0	1	0	0	1
Tobeck, Robbie, Atl.	0	1	0	0	1
Tolliver, Billy Joe, N.O.	4	2	0	-24	2
Trotter, Jeremiah, Phil.	0	0	1	0	1
Tuaolo, Esera, Car.	0	0	1	0	1
Tubbs, Winfred, S.F.	0	0	1	0	1
Tucker, Jason, Dall.	1	1	0	0	1
Tuinei, Van, Chi.	0	0	2	0	2
Turk, Matt, Wash.	1	0	0	0	0
Turner, Kevin, Phil.	1	1	0	0	1
Uwaezuoke, Iheanyi, Det.	1	0	0	0	0
Verba, Ross, G.B.	0	1	0	2	1
Villarrial, Chris, Chi.	0	2	0	0	2

1999 INDIVIDUAL STATISTICS—FUMBLES/SACKS

	Fum.	Own Rec.	Opp. Rec.	Yards	Tot. Rec.
Wahle, Mike, G.B.	0	1	0	0	1
Walker, Darnell, S.F.	0	0	2	71	2
Walls, Wesley, Car.	1	0	0	0	0
Warner, Kurt, St.L.	9	0	0	-4	0
Warren, Chris, Dall.	4	0	0	0	0
Watson, Justin, St.L.	2	0	0	0	0
Weary, Fred, N.O.	0	2	2	60	4
Weathers, Andre, NYG	0	0	1	0	1
Weldon, Casey, Wash.	1	1	0	-2	1
Wells, Mike, Chi.	0	0	1	0	1
Westbrook, Bryant, Det.	0	0	1	0	1
Westbrook, Michael, Wash.	3	1	0	0	1
Wheeler, Mark, Phil.	0	0	1	0	1
White, Steve, T.B.	0	0	1	0	1
Wilkinson, Dan, Wash.	0	0	1	0	1
Williams, Aeneas, Ariz.	0	1	1	0	2
Williams, Brian, G.B.	0	1	0	0	1
Williams, Charlie, Dall.	0	0	1	0	1
Williams, Ricky, N.O.	6	1	0	0	1
Williams, Karl, T.B.	2	1	0	0	1
Williams, Roland, St.L.	0	2	0	0	2
Williams, Tony, Minn.	0	0	1	0	1
Williams, Tyrone, Phil.	0	0	1	0	1
Williams, Tyrone, G.B.	1	0	2	12	2
Winters, Frank, G.B.	0	1	0	0	1
Wistrom, Grant, St.L.	1	0	1	31	1
Wong, Kailee, Minn.	0	0	1	4	1
Young, Steve, S.F.	2	0	0	0	0
Zeier, Eric, T.B.	1	0	0	0	0
Zelenka, Joe, S.F.	1	0	1	-15	1

Yards includes aborted plays, own recoveries, and opponents' recoveries.

SACKS

Most Sacks
NFC: 17.0—Kevin Carter, St. Louis
AFC: 14.5—Jevon Kearse, Tennessee

Most Sacks, Game
AFC: 3.5—Michael McCrary, Baltimore vs. Tennessee, December 5
NFC: 3.0—many times

Team Champion
AFC: 57—Jacksonville
NFC: 57—St. Louis

Team Leaders, Sacks

AFC—BALTIMORE: 11.5, Michael McCrary; BUFFALO: 7.0, Bruce Smith; CINCINNATI: 6.0, Michael Bankston; CLEVELAND: 7.0, John Thierry; DENVER: 13.0, Trevor Pryce; INDIANAPOLIS: 12.0, Chad Bratzke; JACKSONVILLE: 12.0, Tony Brackens; KANSAS CITY: 7.0, Derrick Thomas; MIAMI: 8.5, Rich Owens; NEW ENGLAND: 9.0, Willie McGinest; N.Y. JETS: 5.5, Mo Lewis; OAKLAND: 10.0, Lance Johnstone; PITTSBURGH: 8.5, Jason Gildon; SAN DIEGO: 10.5, Raylee Johnson; SEATTLE: 9.0, Phillip Daniels; TENNESSEE: 14.5, Jevon Kearse

NFC—ARIZONA: 16.5, Simeon Rice; ATLANTA: 10.0, Chuck Smith; CAROLINA: 12.0, Kevin Greene; CHICAGO: 7.0, Clyde Simmons; DALLAS: 7.5, Greg Ellis; DETROIT: 15.0, Robert Porcher; GREEN BAY: 8.0, Keith McKenzie; MINNESOTA: 10.0, John Randle; NEW ORLEANS: 8.5, La'Roi Glover; N.Y. GIANTS: 9.0, Jessie Armstead; PHILADELPHIA: 8.5, Mike Mamula; ST. LOUIS: 17.0, Kevin Carter; SAN FRANCISCO: 11.0, Bryant Young; TAMPA BAY: 12.5, Warren Sapp; WASHINGTON: 8.0, Dan Wilkinson

AFC SACKS—TEAM

	Sacks	Yards
Jacksonville	57	373
Tennessee	54	305
Denver	50	283
Baltimore	49	291
Oakland	44	309
New England	42	268
Indianapolis	41	269
San Diego	41	263
Kansas City	40	286
Miami	39	240
Pittsburgh	39	241
Seattle	38	252
Buffalo	37	214
Cincinnati	35	229
N.Y. Jets	26	184
Cleveland	25	147
AFC Total	657	4154
AFC Average	41.1	259.6

NFC SACKS—TEAM

	Sacks	Yards
St. Louis	57	358
Detroit	50	340
Minnesota	46	272
New Orleans	45	277
Tampa Bay	43	291
Atlanta	40	258
Washington	40	221
Chicago	37	257
Philadelphia	37	272
Carolina	35	235
Dallas	35	217
Arizona	33	229
N.Y. Giants	32	172
San Francisco	32	227
Green Bay	30	185
NFC Total	592	3811
NFC Average	39.5	254.1
League Total	1249	7965
League Average	40.3	256.9

SACKS—TOP TEN LEADERS

Carter, Kevin, St.L.	17.0
Rice, Simeon, Ariz.	16.5
Porcher, Robert, Det.	15.0
Kearse, Jevon, Tenn.	14.5
Pryce, Trevor, Den.	13.0
Sapp, Warren, T.B.	12.5
Brackens, Tony, Jax.	12.0
Bratzke, Chad, Ind.	12.0
Greene, Kevin, Car.	12.0
McCrary, Michael, Balt.	11.5

AFC SACKS—INDIVIDUAL

Kearse, Jevon, Tenn.	14.5
Pryce, Trevor, Den.	13.0
Brackens, Tony, Jax.	12.0
Bratzke, Chad, Ind.	12.0
McCrary, Michael, Balt.	11.5
Hardy, Kevin, Jax.	10.5
Johnson, Raylee, S.D.	10.5
Boulware, Peter, Balt.	10.0
Johnstone, Lance, Oak.	10.0
Walker, Gary, Jax.	10.0
Russell, Darrell, Oak.	9.5
Daniels, Phillip, Sea.	9.0
McGinest, Willie, N.E.	9.0
Gildon, Jason, Pitt.	8.5
Owens, Rich, Mia.	8.5
Armstrong, Trace, Mia.	7.5
Johnson, Ellis, Ind.	7.5
Cadrez, Glenn, Den.	7.0
Smith, Bruce, Buff.	7.0
Tanuvasa, Maa, Den.	7.0
Thierry, John, Cle.	7.0
Thomas, Derrick, K.C.	7.0
Burnett, Rob, Balt.	6.5
Kennedy, Cortez, Sea.	6.5
Patton, Marvcus, K.C.	6.5
Smith, Neil, Den.	6.5
Bankston, Michael, Cin.	6.0
Emmons, Carlos, Pitt.	6.0
Hansen, Phil, Buff.	6.0
Robinson, Eddie, Tenn.	6.0
Sinclair, Michael, Sea.	6.0
Brown, Chad, Sea.	5.5
Ford, Henry, Tenn.	5.5
Lewis, Mo, NYJ	5.5
O'Neal, Leslie, K.C.	5.5
Parrella, John, S.D.	5.5
Bennett, Cornelius, Ind.	5.0
Bromell, Lorenzo, Mia.	5.0
Flowers, Lethon, Pitt.	5.0
Fontenot, Albert, S.D.	5.0
Gardener, Daryl, Mia.	5.0
Smeenge, Joel, Jax.	5.0
Wiley, Marcellus, Buff.	5.0
Williams, Dan, K.C.	5.0
Bryant, Tony, Oak.	4.5
Gibson, Oliver, Cin.	4.5
Miller, Jamir, Cle.	4.5
Phifer, Roman, NYJ	4.5
Roye, Orpheus, Pitt.	4.5
Slade, Chris, N.E.	4.5
Thornton, John, Tenn.	4.5
Boyer, Brant, Jax.	4.0
Copeland, John, Cin.	4.0
Dixon, Gerald, S.D.	4.0
Fisk, Jason, Tenn.	4.0
Hand, Norman, S.D.	4.0
Hicks, Eric, K.C.	4.0
Holmes, Kenny, Tenn.	4.0
Jackson, Grady, Oak.	4.0
Sharper, Jamie, Balt.	4.0
von Oelhoffen, Kimo, Cin.	4.0
Williams, Alfred, Den.	4.0
Bowden, Joe, Tenn.	3.5
Evans, Josh, Tenn.	3.5
Foley, Steve, Cin.	3.5
Katzenmoyer, Andy, N.E.	3.5
Lake, Carnell, Jax.	3.5
Lewis, Ray, Balt.	3.5
Northern, Gabe, Buff.	3.5
Seau, Junior, S.D.	3.5
Siragusa, Tony, Balt.	3.5
Barton, Eric, Oak.	3.0
Eaton, Chad, N.E.	3.0

Edwards, Donnie, K.C.	3.0
Logan, Ernie, NYJ	3.0
Mitchell, Brandon, N.E.	3.0
Oldham, Chris, Pitt.	3.0
Peterson, Mike, Ind.	3.0
Rogers, Sam, Buff.	3.0
Rolle, Samari, Tenn.	3.0
Simmons, Brian, Cin.	3.0
Smith, Larry, Jax.	3.0
Spikes, Takeo, Cin.	3.0
Steed, Joel, Pitt.	3.0
Thomas, Henry, N.E.	3.0
Thomas, Mark, Ind.	3.0
Whigham, Larry, N.E.	3.0
Wilson, Reinard, Cin.	3.0
Wilson, Jerry, Mia.	3.0
Alexander, Derrick L., Cle.	2.5
Barndt, Tom, K.C.	2.5
Bishop, Blaine, Tenn.	2.5
Harris, James, Oak.	2.5
Hasselbach, Harald, Den.	2.5
Price, Shawn, Buff.	2.5
Taylor, Jason, Mia.	2.5
Washington, Ted, Buff.	2.5
Williams, Pat, Buff.	2.5
Barker, Roy, Cle.	2.0
Bell, Myron, Cin.	2.0
Biekert, Greg, Oak.	2.0
Bruschi, Tedy, N.E.	2.0
Burris, Jeff, Ind.	2.0
Collons, Ferric, N.E.	2.0
Crockett, Ray, Den.	2.0
Dumas, Mike, S.D.	2.0
Farrior, James, NYJ	2.0
Hanks, Merton, Sea.	2.0
Harvey, Richard, Oak.	2.0
Holland, Darius, Cle.	2.0
Johnson, Ted, N.E.	2.0
King, Lamar, Sea.	2.0
Kirkland, Levon, Pitt.	2.0
LaBounty, Matt, Sea.	2.0
Marts, Lonnie, Jax.	2.0
McCormack, Hurvin, Cle.	2.0
Mickens, Ray, NYJ	2.0
Milloy, Lawyer, N.E.	2.0
Mohring, Mike, S.D.	2.0
Parker, Riddick, Sea.	2.0
Pleasant, Anthony, NYJ	2.0
Porter, Joey, Pitt.	2.0
Smith, Fernando, Balt.	2.0
Surtain, Patrick, Mia.	2.0
Tongue, Reggie, K.C.	2.0
Vrabel, Mike, Pitt.	2.0
Wayne, Nate, Den.	2.0
Webster, Larry, Balt.	2.0
Beasley, Aaron, Jax.	1.5
Bowens, Tim, Mia.	1.5
Brown, Eric, Den.	1.5
King, Shawn, Ind.	1.5
Maryland, Russell, Oak.	1.5
McGlockton, Chester, K.C.	1.5
Payne, Seth, Jax.	1.5
Perry, Marlo, Buff.	1.5
Traylor, Keith, Den.	1.5
Wynn, Renaldo, Jax.	1.5
Adams, Sam, Sea.	1.0
Belser, Jason, Ind.	1.0
Berry, Bert, Ind.	1.0
Blevins, Tony, Ind.	1.0
Bowens, David, Den.	1.0
Braxton, Tyrone, Den.	1.0
Brown, Cornell, Balt.	1.0
Brown, Lance, Pitt.	1.0
Buckley, Terrell, Mia.	1.0
Bush, Lewis, S.D.	1.0
Carter, Chris, N.E.	1.0
Chester, Larry, Ind.	1.0
Cowart, Sam, Buff.	1.0
Cummings, Joe, Buff.	1.0
Curtis, Canute, Cin.	1.0
Dalton, Lional, Balt.	1.0
Ferguson, Jason, NYJ	1.0
Gordon, Darrien, Oak.	1.0
Gordon, Dwayne, NYJ	1.0
Harris, Corey, Balt.	1.0
Harrison, Rodney, S.D.	1.0
Hasty, James, K.C.	1.0
Henry, Kevin, Pitt.	1.0
Holecek, John, Buff.	1.0
Israel, Steve, N.E.	1.0
Jackson, Calvin, Mia.	1.0
Jenkins, DeRon, Balt.	1.0
Jones, Marvin, NYJ	1.0
Jones, Mike D., Tenn.	1.0
Lyle, Rick, NYJ	1.0
Marion, Brock, Mia.	1.0
McCutcheon, Daylon, Cle.	1.0
McNeil, Ryan, Cle.	1.0
Miller, Arnold, Cle.	1.0
Ogbogu, Eric, NYJ	1.0
Osborne, Chuck, Oak.	1.0
Paup, Bryce, Jax.	1.0
Poole, Tyrone, Ind.	1.0
Rainer, Wali, Cle.	1.0
Ransom, Derrick, K.C.	1.0
Roberson, James, Jax.	1.0
Ross, Adrian, Cin.	1.0
Royal, Andre, Ind.	1.0
Serwanga, Kato, N.E.	1.0
Shields, Scott, Pitt.	1.0
Simien, Tracy, S.D.	1.0
Smith, Darrin, Sea.	1.0
Stoutmire, Omar, Cle.	1.0
Sullivan, Chris, N.E.	1.0
Sword, Sam, Oak.	1.0
Thomas, Zach, Mia.	1.0
Trapp, James, Balt.	1.0
Walker, Marquis, Oak.	1.0
Washington, Keith, Balt.	1.0
Whittington, Bernard, Ind.	1.0
Williams, Jamal, S.D.	1.0
Williams, K.D., Oak.	1.0
Wilson, Al, Den.	1.0
Wiltz, Jason, NYJ	1.0
Curry, Eric, Jax.	0.5
Frederick, Mike, Tenn.	0.5
Harden, Cedric, S.D.	0.5
Jackson, Steve, Tenn.	0.5
Law, Ty, N.E.	0.5
Moran, Sean, Buff.	0.5
Robertson, Marcus, Tenn.	0.5
Spires, Greg, N.E.	0.5
Wortham, Barron, Tenn.	0.5

NFC SACKS—INDIVIDUAL

Carter, Kevin, St.L.	17.0
Rice, Simeon, Ariz.	16.5
Porcher, Robert, Det.	15.0
Sapp, Warren, T.B.	12.5
Greene, Kevin, Car.	12.0
Young, Bryant, S.F.	11.0
Randle, John, Minn.	10.0
Smith, Chuck, Atl.	10.0
Armstead, Jessie, NYG	9.0
Clemons, Duane, Minn.	9.0
Farr, D'Marco, St.L.	8.5
Glover, La'Roi, N.O.	8.5
Mamula, Mike, Phil.	8.5
Scroggins, Tracy, Det.	8.5
Doleman, Chris, Minn.	8.0
McKenzie, Keith, G.B.	8.0
Wilkinson, Dan, Wash.	8.0
Ellis, Greg, Dall.	7.5
Jones, Cedric, NYG	7.5
Jones, James, Det.	7.0
Jones, Marcus, T.B.	7.0
Simmons, Clyde, Chi.	7.0
Whitehead, Willie, N.O.	7.0
Ahanotu, Chidi, T.B.	6.5
Coleman, Marco, Wash.	6.5
Dronett, Shane, Atl.	6.5
Wistrom, Grant, St.L.	6.5
Culpepper, Brad, T.B.	6.0
Flanigan, Jim, Chi.	6.0
Holliday, Vonnie, G.B.	6.0
Lang, Kenard, Wash.	6.0
Smith, Brady, N.O.	6.0
Archambeau, Lester, Atl.	5.5
Strahan, Michael, NYG	5.5
Wilson, Troy, N.O.	5.5
Hennings, Chad, Dall.	5.0
Robinson, Bryan, Chi.	5.0
Spellman, Alonzo, Dall.	5.0
Williams, Tony, Minn.	5.0
Bryant, Junior, S.F.	4.5
Hall, Travis, Atl.	4.5
Martin, Wayne, N.O.	4.5
Peter, Jason, Car.	4.5
Zgonina, Jeff, St.L.	4.5
Barrow, Micheal, Car.	4.0
Fields, Mark, N.O.	4.0
Griffith, Robert, Minn.	4.0
Hamilton, Keith, NYG	4.0
Jefferson, Greg, Phil.	4.0
Swann, Eric, Ariz.	4.0
Williams, Jay, St.L.	4.0
Booker, Vaughn, G.B.	3.5
Elliss, Luther, Det.	3.5
Kalu, Ndukwe, Wash.	3.5
Mitchell, Keith, N.O.	3.5
Tuggle, Jessie, Atl.	3.5
Aldridge, Allen, Det.	3.0
Burton, Shane, Chi.	3.0
Clemons, Charlie, St.L.	3.0
Cook, Anthony, Wash.	3.0
Fletcher, London, St.L.	3.0
Haley, Charles, S.F.	3.0
Minter, Barry, Chi.	3.0
Noble, Brandon, Dall.	3.0
Pittman, Kavika, Dall.	3.0
Reese, Ike, Phil.	3.0
Rucker, Mike, Car.	3.0
Rudd, Dwayne, Minn.	3.0
Stubblefield, Dana, Wash.	3.0
Tomich, Jared, N.O.	3.0
Widmer, Corey, NYG	3.0
Williams, Tyrone, Phil.	3.0
Agnew, Ray, St.L.	2.5
Burke, Tom, Ariz.	2.5
Dotson, Santana, G.B.	2.5
Ekuban, Ebenezer, Dall.	2.5
Gilbert, Sean, Car.	2.5
Hambrick, Darren, Dall.	2.5
Jones, Ernest, Car.	2.5
Kerney, Patrick, Atl.	2.5
Lyght, Todd, St.L.	2.5
Thomas, William, Phil.	2.5
Trotter, Jeremiah, Phil.	2.5
Tuinei, Van, Chi.	2.5
Woodall, Lee, S.F.	2.5
Abraham, Donnie, T.B.	2.0
Bailey, Robert, Det.	2.0
Ball, Jerry, Cle.-Minn.	2.0
Brooking, Keith, Atl.	2.0
Brooks, Derrick, T.B.	2.0
Colvin, Rosevelt, Chi.	2.0
Davis, Russell, Chi.	2.0
Douglas, Hugh, Phil.	2.0
Edwards, Antonio, Car.	2.0
Fredrickson, Rob, Ariz.	2.0
Hitchcock, Jimmy, Minn.	2.0
Holdman, Warrick, Chi.	2.0
Kirschke, Travis, Det.	2.0
Lyon, Billy, G.B.	2.0
Martin, Steve, Phil.	2.0
McDaniel, Ed, Minn.	2.0
McDonald, Tim, S.F.	2.0
Posey, Jeff, S.F.	2.0
Robbins, Austin, N.O.	2.0
Tubbs, Winfred, S.F.	2.0
Wadsworth, Andre, Ariz.	2.0
White, Steve, T.B.	2.0
Williams, Brian, G.B.	2.0
Claiborne, Chris, Det.	1.5
Crockett, Henri, Atl.	1.5
Dawkins, Brian, Phil.	1.5
Lett, Leon, Dall.	1.5
McCleon, Dexter, St.L.	1.5
McMillian, Mark, S.F.-Wash.	1.5
Pringley, Mike, Det.	1.5
Shade, Sam, Wash.	1.5
Bailey, Champ, Wash.	1.0
Barber, Ronde, T.B.	1.0
Barber, Shawn, Wash.	1.0
Boutte, Marc, Wash.	1.0
Buchanan, Ray, Atl.	1.0
Buckner, Brentson, S.F.	1.0
Burrough, John, Minn.	1.0
Butler, LeRoy, G.B.	1.0
Caldwell, Mike, Phil.	1.0
Coakley, Dexter, Dall.	1.0
Cook, Rashard, Phil.	1.0
Drake, Jerry, Ariz.	1.0
Galyon, Scott, NYG	1.0
Garnes, Sam, NYG	1.0
Godfrey, Randall, Dall.	1.0
Harris, Robert, NYG	1.0
Harris, Walt, Chi.	1.0
Hewitt, Chris, N.O.	1.0
Hudson, Chris, Chi.	1.0
Jackson, Tyoka, T.B.	1.0
Jenkins, Billy, St.L.	1.0
Johnson, Bill, Phil.	1.0
Jones, Mike A., St.L.	1.0
Kowalkowski, Scott, Det.	1.0
Lyle, Keith, St.L.	1.0
McBurrows, Gerald, Atl.	1.0
McFarland, Anthony, T.B.	1.0
McKinnon, Ronald, Ariz.	1.0
Minter, Mike, Car.	1.0
Nguyen, Dat, Dall.	1.0
Norton, Ken, S.F.	1.0
Okeafor, Chike, S.F.	1.0
Ottis, Brad, Ariz.	1.0
Owens, Dan, Det.	1.0
Phillips, Joe, Minn.	1.0
Pounds, Darryl, Wash.	1.0
Pritchett, Kelvin, Det.	1.0
Rice, Ron, Det.	1.0
Richardson, Damien, Car.	1.0
Sapp, Patrick, Ariz.	1.0
Sauer, Craig, Atl.	1.0
Sharper, Darren, G.B.	1.0
Smith, Derek M., Wash.	1.0
Smith, Frankie, Chi.	1.0
Stevens, Matt, Wash.	1.0
Stewart, Ryan, Det.	1.0
Swinger, Rashod, Ariz.	1.0
Thomas, Hollis, Phil.	1.0
Tuaolo, Esera, Car.	1.0
Vincent, Troy, Phil.	1.0
Vinson, Fred, G.B.	1.0
Waddy, Jude, G.B.	1.0
Walker, Darnell, S.F.	1.0
Walz, Zack, Ariz.	1.0
Wells, Mike, Chi.	1.0
Whiting, Brandon, Phil.	1.0
Wilkins, Gabe, S.F.	1.0
Woodson, Darren, Dall.	1.0
Zellner, Peppi, Dall.	1.0
Allen, Taje, St.L.	0.5
Francis, James, Wash.	0.5
Hobgood-Chittick, Nate, St.L.	0.5
Hunt, Cletidus, G.B.	0.5
Jones, Greg, Wash.	0.5
Lynch, John, T.B.	0.5
McDonald, Ricardo, Chi.	0.5
Nickerson, Hardy, T.B.	0.5
Robinson, Damien, T.B.	0.5
Singleton, Alshermond, T.B.	0.5
Smith, Jermaine, G.B.	0.5
Wells, Dean, Car.	0.5

1999 ATTENDANCE

1999 NFL PAID ATTENDANCE BREAKDOWN

	Games	Attendance	Average
NFL Preseason Total	64	3,762,331	58,786
NFL Regular-Season Total	248	16,206,640	65,349
NFL Postseason Total	12	793,759	66,147
NFL All Games	324	20,762,730	64,083

1.1-MILLION CLUB

During the 1999 season, seven teams drew more than 1.1 million paid attendance home and away during the regular season. The Washington Redskins drew an NFL leading 1,168,460 fans in 1999.

Team	Total Paid Home Attendance	Total Paid Visiting Attendance	Total Paid Attendance
Washington	628,535	539,925	1,168,460
New York Jets	624,847	519,699	1,144,546
New York Giants	623,777	515,876	1,139,653
Kansas City	629,569	504,921	1,134,490
Miami	592,161	538,805	1,130,966
Denver	593,811	534,542	1,128,353
Buffalo	562,499	540,413	1,102,912

For complete year-by-year attendance records, see page 385.

Inside the Numbers

RECORDS FOR NFL TEAMS FOR MOST POINTS IN A GAME (REGULAR SEASON ONLY)

Note: *When the record has been achieved more than once, only the most recent game is shown; summaries are listed in alphabetical order by conference. Bold face indicates team holding record.*

BALTIMORE RAVENS
December 5, 1999, at Baltimore

Tennessee .... 3 11 0 0 — 14
Baltimore .... 7 10 7 17 — 41

TD: Balt—Jermaine Lewis 2, Justin Armour, Pat Johnson, Rod Woodson; Tenn—Eddie George. TD Passes: Balt—Tony Banks 4. FG: Balt—Matt Stover 2; Tenn—Al Del Greco 2.

BUFFALO BILLS
September 18, 1966, at Buffalo

Miami .... 3 7 0 14 — 24
Buffalo .... 21 27 3 7 — 58

TD: Buff—Bobby Burnett 2, Butch Byrd 2, Jack Spikes 2, Bobby Crockett, Jack Kemp; Mia—Dave Kocourek, Bo Roberson, John Roderick. TD Passes: Buff—Jack Kemp, Daryle Lamonica; Mia—George Wilson 3. FG: Buff—Booth Lusteg; Mia—Gene Mingo.

CINCINNATI BENGALS
December 17, 1989, at Cincinnati

Houston .... 0 0 0 7 — 7
Cincinnati .... 21 10 21 9 — 61

TD: Cin—Eddie Brown 2, Eric Ball, James Brooks, Ira Hillary, Rodney Holman, Tim McGee, Craig Taylor; Hou—Lorenzo White. TD Passes: Cin—Boomer Esiason 4, Erik Wilhelm. FG: Cin—Jim Breech 2.

CLEVELAND BROWNS
November 7, 1954, at Cleveland

Washington .... 0 3 0 0 — 3
Cleveland .... 13 14 21 14 — 62

TD: Clev—Darrell Brewster 2, Mo Bassett, Ken Gorgal, Otto Graham, Dub Jones, Dante Lavelli, Curley Morrison. TD Passes: Clev—George Ratterman 3, Otto Graham. FG: Clev—Lou Groza 2; Wash—Vic Janowicz.

DENVER BRONCOS
October 6, 1963, at Denver

San Diego .... 13 7 0 14 — 34
Denver .... 3 14 9 24 — 50

TD: Den—Lionel Taylor 2, Goose Gonsoulin, Gene Prebola, Donnie Stone; SD—Keith Lincoln 2, Lance Alworth, Paul Lowe, Jacque MacKinnon. TD Passes: Den—John McCormick 3; SD—Tobin Rote 3, John Hadl 2. FG: Den—Gene Mingo 5.

INDIANAPOLIS COLTS
December 12, 1976, at Baltimore

Buffalo .... 3 3 7 7 — 20
Baltimore Colts .... 7 13 28 10 — 58

TD: Balt—Roger Carr, Raymond Chester, Glenn Doughty, Roosevelt Leaks, Derrel Luce, Lydell Mitchell, Howard Stevens; Buff—Bob Chandler, O.J. Simpson. TD Passes: Balt—Bert Jones 3; Buff—Gary Marangi. FG: Balt—Toni Linhart 3; Buff—George Jakowenko 2.

JACKSONVILLE JAGUARS
November 1, 1998, at Baltimore

Jacksonville .... 14 28 0 3 — 45
Baltimore .... 7 6 0 6 — 19

TD: Jac—Fred Taylor 2, Donovin Darius, Daimon Shelton, Jimmy Smith, Alvis Whitted; Balt—Pat Johnson, Jermaine Lewis, Floyd Turner. TD Passes: Jac—Mark Brunell 2; Balt—Jim Harbaugh 3. FG: Jac—Mike Hollis.

KANSAS CITY CHIEFS
September 7, 1963, at Denver

Kansas City .... 14 14 21 10 — 59
Denver .... 0 7 0 0 — 7

TD: KC—Chris Burford 2, Frank Jackson 2, Dave Grayson, Abner Haynes, Sherrill Headrick, Curtis McClinton; Den—Lionel Taylor. TD Passes: KC—Len Dawson 4, Curtis McClinton; Den—Mickey Slaughter. FG: KC—Tommy Brooker.

MIAMI DOLPHINS
November 24, 1977, at St. Louis

Miami .... 14 14 20 7 — 55
St. Louis Cardinals .... 7 0 0 7 — 14

TD: Mia—Nat Moore 3, Gary Davis, Duriel Harris, Leroy Harris, Benny Malone, Andre Tillman; StL—Ike Harris, Terry Metcalf. TD Passes: Mia—Bob Griese 6; StL—Jim Hart.

NEW ENGLAND PATRIOTS
September 9, 1979, at New England

New York Jets .... 3 0 0 0 — 3
New England .... 14 21 7 14 — 56

TD: NE—Harold Jackson 3, Stanley Morgan 2, Allan Clark, Andy Johnson, Don Westbrook. TD Passes: NE—Steve Grogan 5, Tom Owen. FG: NYJ—Pat Leahy.

NEW YORK JETS
November 17, 1985, at New York

Tampa Bay .... 14 7 7 0 — 28
New York Jets .... 17 24 14 7 — 62

TD: NYJ—Mickey Shuler 3, Johnny Hector 2, Tony Paige, Al Toon, Wesley Walker; TB—James Wilder 2, Kevin House, Calvin Magee. TD Passes: NYJ—Ken O'Brien 5; TB—Steve DeBerg 2. FG: NYJ—Pat Leahy 2.

OAKLAND RAIDERS
December 22, 1963, at Oakland

Houston .... 14 21 14 0 — 49
Oakland .... 7 28 7 10 — 52

TD: Oak—Art Powell 4, Clem Daniels, Claude Gibson, Ken Herock; Hou—Willard Dewveall 2, Dave Smith 2, Charley Hennigan, Bob McLeod, Charley Tolar. TD Passes: Oak—Tom Flores 6; Hou—George Blanda 5. FG: Oak—Mike Mercer.

PITTSBURGH STEELERS
November 30, 1952, at Pittsburgh

New York Giants .... 0 0 7 0 — 7
Pittsburgh .... 14 14 7 28 — 63

TD: Pitt—Lynn Chandnois 2, Dick Hensley 2, Jack Butler, George Hays, Ray Mathews, Ed Modzelewski, Elbie Nickel; NYG—Bill Stribling. TD Passes: Pitt—Jim Finks 4, Gary Kerkorian; NYG—Tom Landry.

SAN DIEGO CHARGERS
December 22, 1963, at San Diego

Denver .... 7 10 3 0 — 20
San Diego .... 10 16 10 22 — 58

TD: SD—Paul Lowe 2, Chuck Allen, Bobby Jackson, Dave Kocourek, Keith Lincoln, Jacque MacKinnon; Den—Billy Joe, Donnie Stone. TD Passes: SD—John Hadl, Tobin Rote; Den—Don Breaux. FG: SD—George Blair 3; Den—Gene Mingo 2.

SEATTLE SEAHAWKS
October 30, 1977, at Seattle

Buffalo .... 3 0 7 7 — 17
Seattle .... 14 28 7 7 — 56

TD: Sea—Steve Largent 2, Duke Fergerson, Al Hunter, David Sims, Sherman Smith, Don Testerman, Jim Zorn; Buff—Joe Ferguson, John Kimbrough. TD Passes: Sea—Jim Zorn 4; Buff—Joe Ferguson. FG: Buff—Carson Long.

TENNESSEE TITANS
December 9, 1990, at Houston

Cleveland .... 0 7 7 0 — 14
Houston Oilers .... 14 31 7 6 — 58

TD: Hou—Lorenzo White 4, Ernest Givins, Leonard Harris, Tony Jones, Terry Kinard; Clev—Eric Metcalf 2. TD Passes: Hou—Warren Moon 2, Cody Carlson; Clev—Bernie Kosar. FG: Hou—Teddy Garcia.

ARIZONA CARDINALS
November 13, 1949, at New York

Chicago Cardinals .... 7 31 14 13 — 65
New York Bulldogs .... 7 0 6 7 — 20

TD: Chi—Red Cochran 2, Pat Harder 2, Bill Dewell, Mel Kutner, Bob Ravensburg, Vic Schwall, Charlie Trippi; NY—Joe Golding, Frank Muehlheuser, Johnny Rauch. TD Passes: Chi—Paul Christman 3, Jim Hardy 3; NY—Bobby Layne. FG: Chi—Pat Harder.

ATLANTA FALCONS
September 16, 1973, at New Orleans

Atlanta .... 0 24 21 17 — 62
New Orleans .... 0 0 7 0 — 7

TD: Atl—Ken Burrow 2, Eddie Ray 2, Wes Chesson, Tom Hayes, Art Malone, Joe Profit; NO—Bill Butler. TD Passes: Atl—Dick Shiner 3, Bob Lee; NO—Archie Manning. FG: Atl—Nick Mike-Mayer 2.

CAROLINA PANTHERS
January 2, 2000, at Carolina

New Orleans .... 0 0 0 13 — 13
Carolina .... 10 7 14 14 — 45

TD: Car—Patrick Jeffers 2, Wesley Walls 2, Michael Bates, Muhsin Muhammad; NO—Jake Delhomme, Eddie Kennison. TD Passes: Car—Steve Beuerlein 5; NO—Jake Delhomme. FG: Car—Richie Cunningham.

CHICAGO BEARS
December 7, 1980, at Chicago

Green Bay .... 0 7 0 0 — 7
Chicago .... 0 28 13 20 — 61

TD: Chi—Walter Payton 3, Brian Baschnagel, Robin Earl, Roland Harper, Willie McClendon, Len Walterscheid, Rickey Watts; GB—James Lofton. TD Passes: Chi—Vince Evans 3; GB—Lynn Dickey.

DALLAS COWBOYS
October 12, 1980, at Dallas

San Francisco .... 0 7 0 7 — 14
Dallas .... 14 24 14 7 — 59

TD: Dall—Drew Pearson 3, Ron Springs 2, Tony Dorsett, Billy Joe DuPree, Robert Newhouse; SF—Dwight Clark 2. TD Passes: Dall—Danny White 4; SF—Steve DeBerg 2. FG: Dall—Rafael Septien.

DETROIT LIONS
November 27, 1997, at Detroit

Chicago .... 14 6 0 0 — 20
Detroit .... 3 14 17 21 — 55

TD: Det—Herman Moore, Johnnie Morton, Ron Rivers, Barry Sanders 3, Tracy Scroggins; Chi—Raymont Harris, Ricky Proehl. TD Passes: Det—Scott Mitchell 2; Chi—Erik Kramer. FG: Det—Jason Hanson 2; Chi—Jeff Jaeger 2.

GREEN BAY PACKERS
October 7, 1945, at Milwaukee

Detroit .... 0 7 7 7 — 21
Green Bay .... 0 41 9 7 — 57

TD: GB—Don Hutson 4, Charley Brock, Irv Comp, Ted Fritsch, Clyde Goodnight; Det—Chuck Fenenbock, John Greene, Bob Westfall. TD Passes: GB—Tex McKay 4, Lou Brock, Irv Comp; Det—Dave Ryan.

MINNESOTA VIKINGS
October 18, 1970, at Minnesota

Dallas .... 3 3 0 7 — 13
Minnesota .... 14 20 17 3 — 54

TD: Minn—Clint Jones 2, Ed Sharockman 2, John Beasley, Dave Osborn; Dall—Calvin Hill. TD Pass: Minn—Gary Cuozzo. FG: Minn—Fred Cox 4; Dall—Mike Clark 2.

NEW ORLEANS SAINTS
November 21, 1976, at Seattle

New Orleans .... 3 17 28 3 — 51
Seattle .... 6 0 7 14 — 27

TD: NO—Bobby Douglass 2, Tony Galbreath, Chuck Muncie, Tom Myers, Elex Price; Sea—Sherman Smith 2, Steve Largent, Jim Zorn. TD Pass: Sea—Bill Munson. FG: NO—Rich Szaro 3.

NEW YORK GIANTS
November 26, 1972, at New York

Philadelphia .... 3 7 0 0 — 10
New York Giants .... 14 24 10 14 — 62

TD: NYG—Don Herrmann 2, Ron Johnson 2, Bob Tucker 2, Randy Johnson; Phil—Harold Jackson. TD Passes: NYG—Norm Snead 3, Randy Johnson 2; Phil—John Reaves. FG: NYG—Pete Gogolak 2; Phil—Tom Dempsey.

PHILADELPHIA EAGLES
November 6, 1934, at Philadelphia

Cincinnati Reds .... 0 0 0 0 — 0
Philadelphia .... 26 6 12 20 — 64

TD: Phil—Joe Carter 3, Swede Hanson 3, Marvin Ellstrom, Roger Kirkman, Ed Matesic, Ed Storm. TD Passes: Phil—Ed Matesic 2, Albert Weiner 2, Marvin Elstrom.

ST. LOUIS RAMS
October 22, 1950, at Los Angeles

Baltimore .... 13 0 7 7 — 27
Los Angeles Rams .... 21 14 14 21 — 70

TD: LA—Bob Boyd 2, Vitamin T. Smith 2, Tom Fears,

Elroy (Crazylegs) Hirsch, Dick Hoerner, Ralph Pasquariello, Dan Towler, Bob Waterfield; Balt—Chet Mutryn 2, Adrian Burk, Billy Stone. TD Passes: LA—Norm Van Brocklin 2, Bob Waterfield 2, Glenn Davis; Balt—Adrian Burk 3.

SAN FRANCISCO 49ERS
October 18, 1992, at San Francisco

Atlanta	7	3	0	7	— 17
San Francisco	21	21	14	0	— 56

TD: SF—Jerry Rice 3, Ricky Watters 3, Brent Jones, Tom Rathman; Atl—Michael Haynes, Jason Phillips. TD Passes: SF—Steve Young 3; Atl—Chris Miller, Wade Wilson. FG: Atl—Norm Johnson.

TAMPA BAY BUCCANEERS
September 13, 1987, at Tampa Bay

Atlanta	0	3	0	7	— 10
Tampa Bay	14	13	7	14	— 48

TD: TB—Gerald Carter 2, Cliff Austin, Steve Bartalo, Mark Carrier, Phil Freeman, Calvin Magee; Atl—Stacey Bailey. TD Passes: TB—Steve DeBerg 5; Atl—Scott Campbell. FG: Atl—Mick Luckhurst.

WASHINGTON REDSKINS
November 27, 1966, at Washington

New York Giants	0	14	14	13	— 41
Washington	13	21	14	24	— 72

TD: Wash—A.D. Whitfield 3, Brig Owens 2, Charley Taylor 2, Rickie Harris, Joe Don Looney, Bobby Mitchell; NYG—Allen Jacobs, Homer Jones, Dan Lewis, Joe Morrison, Aaron Thomas, Gary Wood. TD Passes: Wash—Sonny Jurgensen 3; NYG—Gary Wood 2, Tom Kennedy. FG: Wash—Charlie Gogolak.

TEAMS THAT FINISHED IN FIRST PLACE IN THEIR DIVISION THE SEASON AFTER FINISHING IN LAST PLACE

Season	Team	Record	Previous Season
1967	Houston	9-4-1	*3-11-0
1968	Minnesota	8-6-0	3- 8-3
1970	Cincinnati	8-6-0	4- 9-1
1970	San Francisco	10-3-1	4- 8-2
1972	Green Bay	10-4-0	4- 8-2
1975	Baltimore	10-4-0	2-12-0
1979	Tampa Bay	10-6-0	5-11-0
1981	Cincinnati	12-4-0	6-10-0
1987	Indianapolis	9-6-0	3-13-0
1988	Cincinnati	12-4-0	4-11-0
1990	Cincinnati	9-7-0	8- 8-0
1991	Denver	12-4-0	5-11-0
1992	San Diego	11-5-0	4-12-0
1993	Detroit	10-6-0	5-11-0
1997	N.Y. Giants	10-5-1	6-10-0
1999	Indianapolis	13-3-0	3-13-0
1999	St. Louis	13-3-0	*4-12-0

**tied for last place*

RECORDS OF NFL TEAMS, 1990-1999

AFC	W	L	T	Pct.	Division Titles	Playoff Berths	Postseason Record	Super Bowl Record
Buffalo	103	57	0	.644	4	8	10-8	0-4
Kansas City	102	58	0	.638	3	7	3-7	0-0
Jacksonville	49	31	0	.613	2	4	4-4	0-0
Miami	95	65	0	.594	2	7	5-7	0-0
Denver	94	66	0	.588	3	5	8-3	2-0
Pittsburgh	93	67	0	.581	5	6	5-6	0-1
Tennessee	88	72	0	.550	2	5	4-5	0-1
Oakland	82	78	0	.513	1	3	2-3	0-0
San Diego	74	86	0	.463	2	3	3-3	0-1
Seattle	70	90	0	.438	1	1	0-1	0-0
New England	68	92	0	.425	2	4	3-4	0-1
Indianapolis	66	94	0	.413	1	3	2-3	0-0
N.Y. Jets	65	95	0	.406	1	2	1-2	0-0
Baltimore	24	39	1	.383	0	0	0-0	0-0
Cleveland	41	71	0	.366	0	1	1-1	0-0
Cincinnati	52	108	0	.325	1	1	1-1	0-0

Oakland totals include L.A. Raiders, 1990-94
Tennessee totals include Houston, 1990-96

NFC	W	L	T	Pct.	Division Titles	Playoff Berths	Postseason Record	Super Bowl Record
San Francisco	113	47	0	.706	6	8	9-7	1-0
Dallas	101	59	0	.631	6	8	12-5	3-0
Minnesota	95	65	0	.594	3	7	3-7	0-0
Green Bay	93	67	0	.581	3	6	9-5	1-1
N.Y. Giants	83	76	1	.522	2	3	4-2	1-0
Philadelphia	80	79	1	.503	0	4	2-4	0-0
Washington	79	80	1	.497	2	4	6-3	1-0
Detroit	79	81	0	.494	2	6	1-6	0-0
Carolina	38	42	0	.475	1	1	1-1	0-0
Chicago	73	87	0	.456	1	3	2-3	0-0
Atlanta	72	88	0	.450	1	3	3-3	0-1
New Orleans	71	89	0	.444	1	3	0-3	0-0
Tampa Bay	67	93	0	.419	1	2	2-2	0-0
Arizona	58	102	0	.363	0	1	1-1	0-0
St. Louis	58	102	0	.363	1	1	3-0	1-0

Arizona totals include Phoenix, 1990-93
St. Louis totals include L.A. Rams, 1990-94

HOME RECORDS, 1990-1999

AFC	W-L-T	Pct.	NFC	W-L-T	Pct.
Kansas City	63-17-0	.788	San Francisco	64-16-0	.800
Buffalo	60-20-0	.750	Dallas	60-20-0	.750
Denver	60-20-0	.750	Green Bay	59-21-0	.738
Jacksonville	30-10-0	.750	Minnesota	53-27-0	.663
Pittsburgh	58-22-0	.725	Detroit	52-28-0	.650
Miami	55-25-0	.688	Philadelphia	50-30-0	.625
Tennessee	49-31-0	.613	Atlanta	49-31-0	.613
Oakland	44-36-0	.550	Washington	47-32-1	.594
Seattle	42-38-0	.525	N.Y. Giants	47-33-0	.588
San Diego	41-39-0	.513	Tampa Bay	45-35-0	.563
New England	39-41-0	.488	Carolina	22-18-0	.550
Baltimore	15-16-1	.484	Chicago	44-36-0	.550
Indianapolis	37-43-0	.463	New Orleans	40-40-0	.500
N.Y. Jets	35-45-0	.438	Arizona	37-43-0	.463
Cincinnati	34-46-0	.425	St. Louis	34-46-0	.425
Cleveland	22-34-0	.393			

Arizona totals include Phoenix, 1990-93
Oakland totals include L.A. Raiders, 1990-94
St. Louis totals include L.A. Rams, 1990-94
Tennessee totals include Houston, 1990-96

ROAD RECORDS, 1990-1999

AFC	W-L-T	Pct.	NFC	W-L-T	Pct.
Buffalo	43-37-0	.538	San Francisco	49-31-0	.613
Miami	40-40-0	.500	Minnesota	42-38-0	.525
Kansas City	39-41-0	.488	Dallas	41-39-0	.513
Tennessee	39-41-0	.488	N.Y. Giants	36-43-1	.456
Jacksonville	19-21-0	.475	Green Bay	34-46-0	.425
Oakland	38-42-0	.475	Carolina	16-24-0	.400
Pittsburgh	35-45-0	.438	Washington	32-48-0	.400
Denver	34-46-0	.425	New Orleans	31-49-0	.388
San Diego	33-47-0	.413	Philadelphia	30-49-1	.381
N.Y. Jets	30-50-0	.375	Chicago	29-51-0	.363
Indianapolis	29-51-0	.363	Detroit	27-53-0	.338
New England	29-51-0	.363	St. Louis	24-56-0	.300
Seattle	28-52-0	.350	Atlanta	23-57-0	.288
Cleveland	19-37-0	.339	Tampa Bay	22-58-0	.275
Baltimore	9-23-0	.281	Arizona	21-59-0	.263
Cincinnati	18-62-0	.225			

Arizona totals include Phoenix, 1990-93
Oakland totals include L.A. Raiders, 1990-94
St. Louis totals include L.A. Rams, 1990-94
Tennessee totals include Houston, 1990-96

RECORDS BY MONTHS, 1990-1999

AFC	Sept. W-L-T	Oct. W-L-T	Nov. W-L-T	Dec. W-L-T	Total W-L-T	Pct.
Buffalo	26-11	25-13	29-15	23-18	103- 57-0	.644
Kansas City	30-11	21-15	26-16	25-16	102- 58-0	.638
Jacksonville	11- 9	11- 9	14- 6	13- 7	49- 31-0	.613
Miami	26- 9	26-14	24-19	19-23	95- 65-0	.594
Denver	26-15	22-14	27-14	19-23	94- 66-0	.588
Pittsburgh	22-17	24-13	27-16	20-21	93- 67-0	.581
Tennessee	19-20	22-15	22-20	25-17	88- 72-0	.550
Oakland	20-21	24-13	17-23	21-21	82- 78-0	.513
San Diego	19-21	17-21	18-23	20-21	74- 86-0	.463
Seattle	17-23	17-20	19-22	17-25	70- 90-0	.438
New England	17-20	13-27	18-23	20-22	68- 92-0	.425
Indianapolis	12-25	17-22	15-27	22-20	66- 94-0	.413
N.Y. Jets	13-27	15-23	23-18	14-27	65- 95-0	.406
Baltimore	8-8	3-11	5-12-1	8- 8	24- 39-1	.383
Cleveland	13-14	13-14	7-21	8-22	41- 71-0	.366
Cincinnati	10-28	6-33	16-26	20-21	52-108-0	.325

Oakland totals include L.A. Raiders, 1990-94
Tennessee totals include Houston, 1990-96
September totals include August
December totals include January

NFC	Sept. W-L-T	Oct. W-L-T	Nov. W-L-T	Dec. W-L-T	Total W-L-T	Pct.
San Francisco	28-11	27-10	29-13	29-13	113- 47-0	.706
Dallas	23-14	27-12	28-17	23-16	101- 59-0	.631
Minnesota	25-16	20-16	25-16	25-17	95- 65-0	.594

INSIDE THE NUMBERS

	Sept. W-L-T	Oct. W-L-T	Nov. W-L-T	Dec. W-L-T	Total W-L-T	Pct.
Green Bay	24-17	18-15	26-17	25-18	93- 67-0	.581
N.Y. Giants	21-18	21-17	18-23-1	23-18	83- 76-1	.522
Philadelphia	17-21	22-16	20-22-1	21-20	80- 79-1	.503
Washington	22-17	17-20	16-26-1	24-17	79- 80-1	.497
Detroit	21-21	18-16	20-24	20-20	79- 81-0	.494
Carolina	6-12	8-12	12-10	12- 8	38- 42-0	.475
Chicago	17-24	22-14	19-24	15-25	73- 87-0	.456
Atlanta	11-28	17-21	24-17	20-22	72- 88-0	.450
New Orleans	18-21	16-22	19-22	18-24	71- 89-0	.444
Tampa Bay	17-24	12-24	18-24	20-21	67- 93-0	.419
Arizona	12-27	12-26	18-25	16-24	58-102-0	.363
St. Louis	19-20	11-26	12-30	16-26	58-102-0	.363

Arizona totals include Phoenix, 1990-93
St. Louis totals include L.A. Rams, 1990-94
September totals include August
December totals include January

TAKEAWAYS/GIVEAWAYS, 1990-1999

	Takeaways			Giveaways			
AFC	Int.	Fum.	Total	Int.	Fum.	Total	Net.Diff.
Kansas City	184	181	365	122	115	237	128
Pittsburgh	201	149	350	163	132	295	55
N.Y. Jets	184	146	330	170	130	300	30
Jacksonville	72	68	140	67	49	116	24
Miami	176	120	296	159	135	294	2
Buffalo	179	133	312	183	132	315	-3
Denver	161	125	286	156	135	291	-5
Seattle	188	144	332	191	148	339	-7
Tennessee	176	150	326	170	163	333	-7
San Diego	191	112	303	202	116	318	-15
Cincinnati	154	123	277	165	133	298	-21
Baltimore	70	34	104	71	56	127	-23
New England	172	139	311	196	141	337	-26
Cleveland	97	88	185	124	101	225	-40
Oakland	148	121	269	170	139	309	-40
Indianapolis	128	124	252	176	124	300	-48

Oakland totals include L.A. Raiders, 1990-94
Tennessee totals include Houston, 1990-96

	Takeaways			Giveaways			
NFC	Int.	Fum.	Total	Int.	Fum.	Total	Net.Diff.
N.Y. Giants	184	117	301	131	108	239	62
San Francisco	193	122	315	142	129	271	44
Minnesota	199	138	337	177	119	296	41
Dallas	159	120	279	128	112	240	39
Washington	195	120	315	179	98	277	38
Philadelphia	199	144	343	169	155	324	19
Detroit	166	127	293	168	116	284	9
Green Bay	184	126	310	183	135	318	-8
Chicago	166	139	305	170	144	314	-9
Carolina	88	71	159	93	81	174	-15
New Orleans	167	155	322	206	147	353	-31
Atlanta	155	138	293	192	135	327	-34
Tampa Bay	151	136	287	200	135	335	-48
St. Louis	184	112	296	188	158	346	-50
Arizona	163	145	308	223	146	369	-61

Arizona totals include Phoenix, 1990-93
St. Louis totals include L.A. Rams, 1990-94

BEST TAKEAWAY/GIVEAWAY DIFFERENTIAL, SEASON

+43 Washington, 1983
+26 Kansas City, 1990
+25 N.Y. Giants, 1997

HIGH AND LOW SINGLE-GAME YARDAGE TOTALS, 1990-1999

Most Total Yards, Game
676 Washington vs. Detroit, Nov. 4, 1990 (OT)
615 Arizona vs. Washington, Nov. 10, 1996 (OT)
598 San Francisco vs. Buffalo, Sept. 13, 1992
590 San Francisco vs. Atlanta, Oct. 18, 1992
583 Houston vs. Dallas, Nov. 10, 1991 (OT)

Fewest Total Yards, Game
40 Cleveland vs. Pittsburgh, Sept. 12, 1999
62 Seattle vs. Dallas, Oct. 11, 1992
82 Denver vs. Philadelphia, Sept. 20, 1992
87 Seattle vs. Philadelphia, Dec. 13, 1992 (OT)
89 Philadelphia vs. Washington, Sept. 30, 1991
Seattle vs. Kansas City, Dec. 24, 1995

Most Yards Rushing, Game
328 San Francisco vs. Detroit, Dec. 14, 1998
315 Buffalo vs. Atlanta, Nov. 22, 1992
310 Kansas City vs. Detroit, Oct. 14, 1990
304 Philadelphia vs. New England, Nov. 4, 1990
302 N.Y. Jets vs. Indianapolis, Sept. 20, 1998

Fewest Yards Rushing, Game
4 Indianapolis vs. Detroit, Sept. 22, 1991
Buffalo vs. Tennessee, Nov. 23, 1997
8 Oakland vs. Kansas City, Dec. 3, 1995
Dallas vs. New Orleans, Dec. 6, 1998
9 Cleveland vs. Pittsburgh, Sept. 12, 1999

Most Yards Passing, Game
507 Arizona vs. Washington, Nov. 10, 1996 (OT)
505 Houston vs. Kansas City, Dec. 16, 1990
483 Cincinnati vs. L.A. Rams, Oct. 7, 1990 (OT)
482 Washington vs. Detroit, Nov. 4, 1990 (OT)
475 San Francisco vs. L.A. Rams, Nov. 28, 1993

Fewest Yards Passing, Game
-19 San Diego vs. Kansas City, Sept. 20, 1998
12 Carolina vs. Buffalo, Sept. 10, 1995
Philadelphia vs. Seattle, Sept. 6, 1998
13 Seattle vs. Oakland, Dec. 22, 1996
15 New England vs. Atlanta, Nov. 29, 1992

NFL INDIVIDUAL LEADERS, 1990-1999

Points		Touchdowns		Field Goals	
1,130	Gary Anderson	147	Emmitt Smith	253	Gary Anderson
1,100	Pete Stoyanovich	110	Jerry Rice	248	Pete Stoyanovich
1,080	Morten Andersen	95	Cris Carter	246	Steve Christie
1,065	Steve Christie	95	Barry Sanders	245	Morten Andersen
1,028	Norm Johnson	81	Ricky Watters	243	John Carney

Rushes		Rushing Yards		Rushing TDs	
3,243	Emmitt Smith	13,963	Emmitt Smith	136	Emmitt Smith
2,782	Barry Sanders	13,799	Barry Sanders	85	Barry Sanders
2,344	Thurman Thomas	9,813	Thurman Thomas	70	Ricky Watters
2,272	Ricky Watters	9,083	Ricky Watters	68	Terry Allen
2,106	Jerome Bettis	8,463	Jerome Bettis	60	Marcus Allen

Pass Attempts		Completions		Passing Yards	
4,708	Dan Marino	2,793	Dan Marino	33,508	Dan Marino
4,352	Brett Favre	2,659	Brett Favre	30,894	Brett Favre
4,348	Warren Moon	2,634	Warren Moon	30,817	Warren Moon
4,180	John Elway	2,587	Troy Aikman	30,280	John Elway
4,160	Troy Aikman	2,458	John Elway	29,561	Troy Aikman

TD Passes		Receptions		Reception Yards	
235	Brett Favre	860	Jerry Rice	12,078	Jerry Rice
200	Dan Marino	835	Cris Carter	10,872	Michael Irvin
200	Steve Young	726	Tim Brown	10,238	Cris Carter
189	Warren Moon	692	Michael Irvin	10,211	Tim Brown
180	John Elway	650	Andre Rison	9,368	Rob Moore

Receiving TDs		Interceptions		Sacks	
103	Jerry Rice	46	Rod Woodson	116.5	Derrick Thomas
95	Cris Carter	42	Eugene Robinson	113.5	Kevin Greene
74	Andre Rison	41	Aeneas Williams	113.5	Bruce Smith
70	Tim Brown	39	Deion Sanders	111.5	Reggie White
63	Carl Pickens	38	Cris Dishman	107.0	Chris Doleman

NFL GAMES IN WHICH A TEAM HAS SCORED 60 OR MORE POINTS

(Home team in capitals)

Regular Season
WASHINGTON 72, New York Giants 41 ....November 27, 1966
LOS ANGELES RAMS 70, Baltimore 27 ....October 22, 1950
Chicago Cardinals 65, NEW YORK BULLDOGS 20 ....November 13, 1949
LOS ANGELES RAMS 65, Detroit 24 ....October 29, 1950
PHILADELPHIA 64, Cincinnati 0 ....November 6, 1934
CHICAGO CARDINALS 63, New York Giants 35 ....October 17, 1948
AKRON 62, Oorang 0 ....October 29, 1922
PITTSBURGH 62, New York Giants 7 ....November 30, 1952
CLEVELAND 62, New York Giants 14 ....December 6, 1953
CLEVELAND 62, Washington 3 ....November 7, 1954
NEW YORK GIANTS 62, Philadelphia 10 ....November 26, 1972
Atlanta 62, NEW ORLEANS 7 ....September 16, 1973
NEW YORK JETS 62, Tampa Bay 28 ....November 17, 1985
CHICAGO 61, San Francisco 20 ....December 12, 1965
Cincinnati 61, HOUSTON 17 ....December 17, 1972
CHICAGO 61, Green Bay 7 ....December 7, 1980
CINCINNATI 61, Houston 7 ....December 17, 1989
ROCK ISLAND 60, Evansville 0 ....October 15, 1922
CHICAGO CARDINALS 60, Rochester 0 ....October 7, 1923

Postseason
Chicago Bears 73, WASHINGTON 0 ....December 8, 1940
JACKSONVILLE 62, Miami 7 ....January 15, 2000

YOUNGEST AND OLDEST PLAYERS IN NFL IN 1999

10 Youngest Players	Birthdate	Games	Starts	Position
David Boston, Arizona	8/19/78	16	8	WR
Edgerrin James, Indianapolis	8/1/78	16	16	RB
Chris Claiborne, Detroit	7/26/78	15	13	LB
Champ Bailey, Washington	6/22/78	16	16	CB
Lennox Gordon, Buffalo	4/9/78	8	0	RB
Sedrick Irvin, Detroit	3/30/78	14	0	RB
Anthony McFarland, Tampa Bay	12/18/77	14	0	DT
Andy Katzenmoyer, New England	12/2/77	16	11	LB
Damien Woody, New England	11/3/77	16	16	C
Keion Carpenter, Buffalo	10/31/77	10	0	DB

10 Oldest Players	Birthdate	Games	Starts	Position
Eddie Murray, Dallas	8/29/56	4	0	K
Warren Moon, Kansas City	11/18/56	1	0	QB
Mike Horan, St. Louis	2/1/59	8	0	P
Gary Anderson, Minnesota	7/16/59	16	0	K
Darrell Green, Washington	2/15/60	16	16	CB
Norm Johnson, Philadelphia	5/31/60	15	0	K
Morten Andersen, Atlanta	8/19/60	16	0	K
Brian Hansen, Washington	10/26/60	2	0	P
Trey Junkin, Arizona	1/23/61	16	0	TE
Mike Morris, Minnesota	2/22/61	16	0	C

YOUNGEST AND OLDEST REGULAR STARTERS BY POSITION IN 1999

Minimum: 8 Games Started

	Youngest		Oldest	
QB	7/31/77	Tim Couch, Cle.	9/15/61	Dan Marino, Mia.
RB	8/1/78	Edgerrin James, Ind.	4/16/67	Chuck Evans, Balt.
WR	8/19/78	David Boston, Ariz.	10/13/62	Jerry Rice, S.F.
TE	8/11/76	Jed Weaver, Phil.	2/26/66	Wesley Walls, Car.
C	11/3/77	Damien Woody, N.E.	1/23/64	Frank Winters, G.B.
G	12/7/76	Alan Faneca, Pitt.	8/8/61	Bruce Matthews, Tenn.
T	3/29/77	Mike Wahle, G.B.	3/30/63	Lomas Brown, Cle.
DE	9/3/76	Jevon Kearse, Tenn.	10/16/61	Chris Doleman, Minn.
DT	5/27/76	Darrell Russell, Oak.	12/15/64	Jerry Ball, Cle.-Minn.
LB	7/26/78	Chris Claiborne, Det.	7/31/62	Kevin Greene, Car.
CB	6/22/78	Champ Bailey, Wash.	2/15/60	Darrell Green, Wash.
S	12/5/76	Cory Hall, Cin.	5/28/63	Eugene Robinson, Atl.

EMMITT SMITH'S CAREER RUSHING VS. EACH OPPONENT

Opponent	Games	Rushes	Yards	Yards Per Rush	Yards Per Game	TD
Arizona	20	425	1,822	4.3	91.1	24
Atlanta	7	143	695	4.9	99.3	9
Buffalo	1	15	25	1.7	25.0	1
Carolina	2	23	115	5.0	57.5	1
Chicago	4	67	322	4.8	80.5	1
Cincinnati	3	56	222	4.0	74.0	1
Cleveland	2	58	224	3.9	112.0	1
Denver	3	72	269	3.7	89.7	3
Detroit	3	64	276	4.3	92.0	4
Green Bay	6	139	567	4.1	94.5	6
Indianapolis	3	73	298	4.1	99.3	4
Jacksonville	1	24	75	3.1	75.0	1
Kansas City	3	56	193	3.4	64.3	2
Miami	3	69	228	3.3	76.0	0
Minnesota	4	70	438	6.3	109.5	8
New England	2	46	160	3.5	80.0	0
New Orleans	5	104	387	3.7	77.4	3
N.Y. Giants	19	376	1,689	4.5	88.9	15
N.Y. Jets	3	54	256	4.7	85.3	0
Oakland	3	79	321	4.1	107.0	7
Philadelphia	20	450	2,083	4.6	104.2	12
Pittsburgh	3	89	349	3.9	116.3	2
St. Louis	2	40	134	3.4	67.0	1
San Diego	2	24	70	2.9	35.0	2
San Francisco	6	110	422	3.8	70.3	4
Seattle	2	39	152	3.9	76.0	2
Tampa Bay	2	39	169	4.3	84.5	1
Tennessee	3	49	161	3.3	53.7	1
Washington	18	390	1,841	4.7	102.3	20
Totals	155	3,243	13,963	4.3	90.1	136

Arizona totals include eight games vs. Phoenix
Oakland totals include one game vs. L.A. Raiders
St. Louis totals include two games vs. L.A. Rams
Tennessee totals include two games vs. Houston

BARRY SANDERS'S CAREER RUSHING VS. EACH OPPONENT

Opponent	Games	Rushes	Yards	Yards Per Rush	Yards Per Game	TD
Arizona	4	83	415	5.0	103.8	2
Atlanta	8	169	681	4.0	85.1	5
Baltimore	1	19	41	2.2	41.0	0
Buffalo	3	70	260	3.7	86.7	2
Chicago	19	368	1,846	5.0	97.2	12
Cincinnati	3	73	450	6.2	150.0	5
Cleveland	3	76	389	5.1	129.7	4
Dallas	3	79	357	4.5	119.0	0
Denver	1	23	147	6.4	147.0	1
Green Bay	19	384	2,059	5.4	108.4	7
Indianapolis	2	54	395	7.3	197.5	4
Jacksonville	2	40	178	4.5	89.0	2
Kansas City	2	36	167	4.6	83.5	2
Miami	3	74	332	4.5	110.7	1
Minnesota	19	363	1,858	5.1	97.8	11
New England	2	50	279	5.6	139.5	2
New Orleans	5	75	307	4.1	61.4	2
N.Y. Giants	5	89	424	4.8	84.8	2
N.Y. Jets	3	66	425	6.4	141.7	3
Oakland	2	34	212	6.2	106.0	2
Philadelphia	2	36	189	5.3	94.5	2
Pittsburgh	4	67	236	3.5	59.0	1
St. Louis	2	52	148	2.8	74.0	1
San Diego	1	16	51	3.2	51.0	2
San Francisco	6	107	452	4.2	75.3	2
Seattle	3	47	258	5.5	86.0	2
Tampa Bay	19	392	2,195	5.6	115.5	14
Tennessee	3	60	199	3.3	66.3	4
Washington	4	60	319	5.3	79.8	2
Totals	153	3,062	15,269	5.0	99.8	99

Arizona totals include two games vs. Phoenix
Oakland totals include one game vs. L.A. Raiders
St. Louis totals include two games vs. L.A. Rams
Tennessee totals include three games vs. Houston

RICKY WATTERS'S CAREER RUSHING VS. EACH OPPONENT

Opponent	Games	Rushes	Yards	Yards Per Rush	Yards Per Game	TD
Arizona	9	195	723	3.7	80.3	6
Atlanta	7	120	584	4.9	83.4	7
Baltimore	1	11	37	3.4	37.0	0
Buffalo	3	57	209	3.7	69.7	0
Carolina	1	21	33	1.6	33.0	1
Chicago	2	35	112	3.2	56.0	0
Cincinnati	3	64	309	4.8	103.0	5
Cleveland	1	13	83	6.4	83.0	0
Dallas	9	177	733	4.1	81.4	4
Denver	6	94	330	3.5	55.0	5
Detroit	4	59	231	3.9	57.8	2
Green Bay	3	64	244	3.8	81.3	1
Indianapolis	2	39	211	5.4	105.5	1
Jacksonville	1	15	44	2.9	44.0	0
Kansas City	5	102	393	3.9	78.6	4
Miami	1	25	173	6.9	173.0	1
Minnesota	3	29	82	2.8	27.3	1
New England	1	19	104	5.5	104.0	1
New Orleans	7	147	675	4.6	96.4	0
N.Y. Giants	7	149	640	4.3	91.4	5
N.Y. Jets	4	61	244	4.0	61.0	2
Oakland	6	116	373	3.2	62.2	3
Philadelphia	4	39	163	4.2	40.8	1
Pittsburgh	4	80	239	3.0	59.8	0
St. Louis	7	134	524	3.9	74.9	5
San Diego	6	116	359	3.1	59.8	3
San Francisco	1	14	42	3.0	42.0	0
Seattle	1	21	69	3.3	69.0	2
Tampa Bay	5	74	305	4.1	61.0	3
Tennessee	1	14	63	4.5	63.0	0
Washington	8	168	752	4.5	94.0	7
Totals	123	2,272	9,083	4.0	73.8	70

Arizona totals include two games vs. Phoenix
Oakland totals include one game vs. L.A. Raiders
St. Louis totals include six games vs. L.A. Rams

INSIDE THE NUMBERS

THURMAN THOMAS'S CAREER RUSHING VS. EACH OPPONENT

Opponent	Games	Rushes	Yards	Yards Per Rush	Yards Per Game	TD
Arizona	2	39	165	4.2	82.5	0
Atlanta	3	51	264	5.2	88.0	1
Carolina	2	29	110	3.8	55.0	2
Chicago	3	37	151	4.1	50.3	1
Cincinnati	5	74	334	4.5	66.8	1
Cleveland	2	40	144	3.6	72.0	2
Dallas	2	47	126	2.7	63.0	1
Denver	6	93	390	4.2	65.0	3
Detroit	2	30	131	4.4	65.5	0
Green Bay	4	85	330	3.9	82.5	2
Indianapolis	22	304	1,230	4.0	55.9	7
Jacksonville	2	15	60	4.0	30.0	0
Kansas City	5	76	213	2.8	42.6	1
Miami	20	364	1,620	4.5	81.0	8
Minnesota	3	48	199	4.1	66.3	1
New England	23	415	1,888	4.5	82.1	10
New Orleans	2	40	155	3.9	77.5	2
N.Y. Giants	4	87	294	3.4	73.5	2
N.Y. Jets	22	349	1,590	4.6	72.3	7
Oakland	6	84	376	4.5	62.7	3
Philadelphia	3	53	174	3.3	58.0	1
Pittsburgh	6	118	510	4.3	85.0	1
St. Louis	4	77	369	4.8	92.3	4
San Francisco	4	43	174	4.0	43.5	1
Seattle	4	68	216	3.2	54.0	0
Tampa Bay	2	24	55	2.3	27.5	0
Tennessee	7	103	434	4.2	62.0	2
Washington	3	56	236	4.2	78.7	2
Totals	173	2,849	11,938	4.2	69.8	65

Arizona totals include one game vs. Phoenix
Oakland totals include five games vs. L.A. Raiders
St. Louis totals include two games vs. L.A. Rams
Tennessee totals include six games vs. Houston

DAN MARINO'S CAREER PASSING VS. EACH OPPONENT

Opponent	Games	Att.	Cmp.	Pct.	Yards	Avg. Gain	TD	Int.	Sacked
Arizona	4	119	77	64.7	1,033	8.68	8	2	3/21
Atlanta	4	166	96	57.8	1,216	7.33	5	8	3/15
Baltimore	1	27	19	70.4	189	7.00	0	0	0/0
Buffalo	30	1,001	614	61.3	7,553	7.55	50	35	42/351
Carolina	1	21	14	66.7	140	6.67	0	1	1/9
Chicago	5	156	81	51.9	1,129	7.24	8	5	12/78
Cincinnati	6	219	143	65.3	1,680	7.67	11	2	6/47
Cleveland	6	205	126	61.5	1,661	8.10	11	5	4/33
Dallas	5	178	93	52.2	1,211	6.80	7	9	5/43
Denver	3	104	63	60.6	960	9.23	9	1	3/25
Detroit	4	152	89	58.6	1,016	6.68	4	3	4/28
Green Bay	6	218	133	61.0	1,568	7.19	12	7	6/37
Indianapolis	33	1,030	624	60.6	7,537	7.32	54	17	29/186
Jacksonville	1	49	30	61.2	323	6.59	2	1	2/16
Kansas City	7	243	142	58.4	1,687	6.94	12	4	4/35
Minnesota	2	91	49	53.8	695	7.64	5	6	1/5
New England	30	1,027	608	59.2	7,382	7.19	42	46	28/207
New Orleans	4	145	87	60.0	905	6.24	8	3	6/42
N.Y. Giants	2	60	30	50.0	324	5.40	1	4	4/25
N.Y. Jets	30	1,125	656	58.3	8,651	7.69	72	36	42/262
Oakland	10	347	196	56.5	2,356	6.79	18	11	11/90
Philadelphia	3	127	72	56.7	987	7.77	6	2	5/45
Pittsburgh	10	306	193	63.1	2,195	7.17	13	10	10/68
St. Louis	5	182	112	61.5	1,309	7.19	13	6	4/24
San Diego	6	238	150	63.0	1,775	7.46	11	3	8/52
San Francisco	4	144	84	58.3	942	6.54	5	5	8/56
Seattle	2	68	40	58.8	504	7.41	3	4	3/25
Tampa Bay	4	154	98	63.6	1,110	7.21	9	1	1/10
Tennessee	9	291	161	55.3	2,025	6.96	11	11	13/88
Washington	5	165	87	52.7	1,298	7.87	10	4	2/7
Totals	242	8,358	4.967	59.4	61,361	7.34	420	252	270/1,930

Arizona totals include one game vs. St. Louis, one game vs. Phoenix
Indianapolis totals include two games vs. Baltimore Colts
Oakland totals include seven games vs. L.A. Raiders
St. Louis totals include three games vs. L.A. Rams
Tennessee totals include eight games vs. Houston

BRETT FAVRE'S CAREER PASSING VS. EACH OPPONENT

Opponent	Games	Att.	Cmp.	Pct.	Yards	Avg. Gain	TD	Int.	Sacked
Arizona	1	34	21	61.8	311	9.15	2	1	2/12
Atlanta	2	87	62	71.3	597	6.86	3	2	4/26
Baltimore	1	41	22	53.7	260	6.34	2	2	1/8
Buffalo	2	58	34	58.6	370	6.38	5	1	1/9
Carolina	3	117	76	65.0	902	7.71	6	2	9/68
Chicago	16	494	315	63.8	3,686	7.46	32	17	29/178
Cincinnati	3	117	76	65.0	902	7.71	6	2	9/68
Cleveland	2	61	43	70.5	433	7.10	3	0	4/22
Dallas	6	240	138	57.5	1,383	5.76	11	4	12/91
Denver	3	93	47	50.5	635	6.83	5	8	2/12
Detroit	16	569	355	62.4	4,295	7.55	27	22	28/185
Indianapolis	1	25	18	72.0	363	14.52	3	2	3/29
Jacksonville	1	30	20	66.7	202	6.73	2	1	2/9
Kansas City	2	83	47	56.6	527	6.35	3	4	8/50
Miami	2	88	55	62.5	615	6.99	4	1	5/20
Minnesota	15	468	282	60.3	3,094	6.61	21	18	36/229
New England	2	81	48	59.3	533	6.58	4	2	5/42
New Orleans	2	62	39	62.9	458	7.39	5	0	8/39
N.Y. Giants	3	102	62	60.8	687	6.74	4	3	6/37
N.Y. Jets	1	28	20	71.4	183	6.54	2	0	1/11
Oakland	2	75	42	56.0	523	6.97	5	3	5/24
Philadelphia	6	207	115	55.6	1,527	7.38	10	9	11/61
Pittsburgh	3	90	59	65.6	745	8.28	4	1	7/44
St. Louis	7	219	130	59.4	1,471	6.72	10	10	15/124
San Diego	3	78	47	60.3	550	7.05	6	3	5/56
San Francisco	3	124	67	54.0	910	7.34	6	5	5/29
Seattle	2	69	34	49.3	389	5.64	5	4	5/28
Tampa Bay	16	555	357	64.3	3,891	7.01	31	8	35/176
Tennessee	2	52	33	63.5	408	7.85	4	1	5/11
Washington	1	5	0	0.0	0	0.00	0	2	1/11
Totals	129	4,352	2,659	61.1	30,894	7.10	235	141	267/1,686

Oakland totals include one game vs. L.A. Raiders
St. Louis totals include four games vs. L.A. Rams
Tennessee totals include one game vs. Houston

WARREN MOON'S CAREER PASSING VS. EACH OPPONENT

Opponent	Games	Att.	Cmp.	Pct.	Yards	Avg. Gain	TD	Int.	Sacked
Arizona	5	174	98	56.3	1,296	7.45	11	4	12/101
Atlanta	5	194	111	57.2	1,429	7.37	11	6	12/55
Baltimore	1	19	12	63.2	140	7.37	1	1	3/23
Buffalo	8	206	117	56.8	1,528	7.42	7	9	12/94
Carolina	1	34	19	55.9	209	6.15	2	1	4/17
Chicago	8	281	168	59.8	2,019	7.19	9	8	19/141
Cincinnati	20	649	383	59.0	4,902	7.55	37	22	37/310
Cleveland	19	590	336	56.9	4,315	7.31	25	22	42/314
Dallas	5	177	104	58.8	1,259	7.11	6	5	21/148
Denver	6	198	113	57.1	1,409	7.12	9	3	14/93
Detroit	7	223	142	63.7	1,824	8.18	9	8	12/95
Green Bay	6	222	126	56.8	1,291	5.82	8	10	14/133
Indianapolis	9	296	185	62.5	2,446	8.26	14	8	15/97
Kansas City	12	352	217	61.6	2,614	7.43	13	11	36/251
Miami	6	148	102	68.9	1,236	8.35	8	6	11/112
Minnesota	3	95	58	61.1	592	6.23	2	2	14/106
New England	4	136	76	55.9	946	6.96	6	4	5/41
New Orleans	7	248	144	58.1	1,746	7.04	11	6	16/107
N.Y. Giants	4	142	84	59.2	1,008	7.10	4	4	8/56
N.Y. Jets	5	192	125	65.1	1,500	7.81	8	7	10/86
Oakland	7	254	142	55.9	1,908	7.51	13	11	21/165
Philadelphia	2	67	37	55.2	466	6.96	3	0	4/36
Pittsburgh	21	648	364	56.2	4,604	7.10	25	30	46/334
St. Louis	5	193	109	56.5	1,424	7.38	4	9	11/81
San Diego	8	280	149	53.2	1,910	6.82	11	9	13/87
San Francisco	6	192	109	56.8	1,359	7.08	14	8	16/98
Seattle	4	145	87	60.0	970	6.69	5	6	6/44
Tampa Bay	6	216	132	61.1	1,498	6.94	7	7	9/63
Tennessee	2	83	55	66.3	549	6.61	2	2	3/30
Washington	4	135	69	51.1	720	5.33	5	3	7/51
Totals	206	6,789	3,973	58.5	49,117	7.23	290	232	453/3,369

Arizona totals include one game vs. St. Louis, one game vs. Phoenix
Oakland totals include four games vs. L.A. Raiders
St. Louis totals include four games vs. L.A. Rams
Tennessee totals include one game vs. Houston

TROY AIKMAN'S CAREER PASSING VS. EACH OPPONENT

Opponent	Games	Att.	Cmp.	Pct.	Yards	Avg. Gain	TD	Int.	Sacked
Arizona	19	493	315	63.9	4,106	8.33	21	13	20/131
Atlanta	5	115	77	67.0	1,052	9.15	8	5	5/30
Buffalo	2	78	44	56.4	461	5.91	0	5	2/11
Carolina	1	26	14	53.8	180	6.92	1	0	4/42
Chicago	3	84	43	51.2	414	4.93	2	2	6/41
Cincinnati	3	108	62	57.4	833	7.71	5	5	2/23
Cleveland	2	73	45	61.6	462	6.33	3	2	4/20
Denver	3	78	48	61.5	515	6.60	6	1	2/9
Detroit	3	106	70	66.0	765	7.22	3	3	4/30
Green Bay	6	182	127	69.8	1,381	7.59	4	4	7/44
Indianapolis	3	79	57	72.2	588	7.44	2	0	6/41
Jacksonville	1	32	21	65.6	262	8.19	2	0	2/24
Kansas City	3	93	60	64.5	583	6.27	5	3	4/29
Miami	4	146	102	69.9	1,037	7.10	6	2	2/13
Minnesota	4	148	91	61.5	1,038	7.01	3	0	4/23
New England	2	58	36	62.1	329	5.67	0	2	6/45
New Orleans	5	155	92	59.4	970	6.26	3	6	6/64
N.Y. Giants	21	542	360	66.4	3,953	7.29	18	12	24/145
N.Y. Jets	3	95	58	61.1	659	6.94	3	7	7/46
Oakland	2	49	35	71.4	461	9.41	1	0	6/31
Philadelphia	20	532	281	52.8	3,027	5.69	15	18	49/320
Pittsburgh	2	62	40	64.5	540	8.71	5	1	0/0
St. Louis	3	103	58	56.3	754	7.32	7	2	4/25
San Diego	2	59	34	57.6	415	7.03	1	1	6/39
San Francisco	6	179	103	57.5	1,155	6.45	3	8	14/97
Seattle	2	65	43	66.2	469	7.22	2	3	2/7
Tampa Bay	2	53	30	56.6	332	6.26	2	2	5/38
Tennessee	3	106	65	61.3	844	7.96	4	4	8/38
Washington	19	554	331	59.7	3,725	6.72	23	16	35/251
Totals	154	4,453	2,742	61.6	31,310	7.03	158	127	246/1,657

Arizona totals include eight games vs. Phoenix
Oakland totals include one game vs. L.A. Raiders
St. Louis totals include three games vs. L.A. Rams
Tennessee totals include two games vs. Houston

STEVE YOUNG'S CAREER PASSING VS. EACH OPPONENT

Opponent	Games	Att.	Cmp.	Pct.	Yards	Avg. Gain	TD	Int.	Sacked
Arizona	6	154	82	53.2	977	6.34	6	3	11/81
Atlanta	19	519	342	65.9	4,784	9.22	37	15	31/184
Buffalo	5	162	100	61.7	1,380	8.52	7	5	17/105
Carolina	6	203	134	66.0	1,582	7.79	10	5	15/53
Chicago	6	136	75	55.1	993	7.30	8	3	9/52
Cincinnati	2	55	32	58.2	453	8.24	2	5	5/29
Cleveland	3	34	19	55.9	274	8.06	0	3	1/8
Dallas	6	108	71	65.7	887	8.21	6	2	11/53
Denver	3	66	42	63.6	626	9.48	4	3	3/19
Detroit	10	236	161	68.2	1,846	7.82	14	4	16/116
Green Bay	6	148	83	56.1	854	5.77	3	7	33/231
Indianapolis	3	116	75	64.7	811	6.99	4	3	13/53
Jacksonville	1	26	9	34.6	96	3.69	0	2	2/18
Kansas City	4	81	54	66.7	617	7.62	2	4	13/78
Miami	1	27	19	70.4	220	8.15	2	1	0/0
Minnesota	10	268	174	64.9	2,218	8.28	14	9	30/139
New England	4	104	77	74.0	973	9.36	10	4	12/63
New Orleans	20	482	320	66.4	3,669	7.61	29	6	58/340
N.Y. Giants	6	120	72	60.0	759	6.33	5	1	8/50
N.Y. Jets	3	89	54	60.7	708	7.96	6	1	3/17
Oakland	2	67	37	55.2	525	7.84	4	3	4/20
Philadelphia	5	115	73	63.5	805	7.00	5	3	9/59
Pittsburgh	3	72	48	66.7	493	6.85	6	3	4/21
St. Louis	17	417	279	66.9	3,568	8.56	28	7	28/146
San Diego	4	101	73	72.3	911	9.02	7	1	9/50
Seattle	2	18	11	61.1	136	7.56	1	0	0/0
Tampa Bay	5	95	66	69.5	883	9.29	8	0	5/28
Tennessee	3	30	16	53.3	187	6.23	0	2	2/10
Washington	4	100	69	69.0	889	8.89	4	2	7/33
Totals	169	4,149	2,667	64.3	33,124	7.98	232	107	358/2,055

Arizona totals include two games vs. St. Louis, three games vs. Phoenix
Oakland totals include two games vs. L.A. Raiders
St. Louis totals include 12 games vs. L.A. Rams
Tennessee totals include three games vs. Houston

JERRY RICE'S CAREER RECEIVING VS. EACH OPPONENT

Opponent	Games	Rec.	Yards	Yds./Rec.	Yds./Game	TD
Arizona	6	28	493	17.6	82.2	6
Atlanta	27	166	2,641	15.9	97.8	25
Baltimore	1	6	58	9.7	58.0	1
Buffalo	4	14	158	11.3	39.5	1
Carolina	8	52	726	14.0	90.8	3
Chicago	5	24	424	17.7	84.8	7
Cincinnati	5	32	508	15.9	101.6	4
Cleveland	3	19	275	14.5	91.7	4
Dallas	7	43	671	15.6	95.9	4
Denver	4	19	306	16.1	76.5	2
Detroit	9	42	559	13.3	62.1	2
Green Bay	7	41	639	15.6	91.3	7
Indianapolis	4	22	414	78.8	103.5	5
Jacksonville	1	2	17	8.5	17.0	0
Kansas City	3	13	178	13.7	59.3	2
Miami	3	18	304	16.9	101.3	5
Minnesota	10	55	919	16.7	91.9	10
New England	5	24	409	17.0	81.8	6
New Orleans	28	138	1,935	14.0	69.1	14
N.Y. Giants	8	37	550	14.9	68.8	5
N.Y. Jets	4	21	351	16.7	87.8	3
Oakland	4	18	362	20.1	90.5	2
Philadelphia	6	31	490	15.8	81.7	5
Pittsburgh	5	29	280	9.7	56.0	4
St. Louis	28	149	2,312	15.5	82.6	20
San Diego	3	27	465	17.2	155.0	4
Seattle	3	14	272	19.4	90.7	4
Tampa Bay	8	47	710	15.1	88.8	10
Tennessee	5	34	330	9.7	66.0	2
Washington	8	41	686	16.7	85.8	2
Totals	222	1,206	18,442	15.3	83.8	169

Arizona totals include one game vs. St. Louis, four games vs. Phoenix
Oakland totals include four games vs. L.A. Raiders
St. Louis totals include 20 games vs. L.A. Rams
Tennessee totals include four games vs. Houston

ANDRE REED'S CAREER RECEIVING VS. EACH OPPONENT

Opponent	Games	Rec.	Yards	Yds./Rec.	Yds./Game	TD
Arizona	3	3	42	14.0	14.0	0
Atlanta	2	9	170	18.9	85.0	1
Baltimore	1	7	76	10.9	76.0	0
Carolina	2	2	17	8.5	8.5	0
Chicago	4	16	185	11.6	46.3	0
Cincinnati	7	24	344	14.3	49.1	2
Cleveland	5	25	347	13.9	69.4	2
Dallas	2	6	46	7.7	23.0	0
Denver	7	34	478	14.1	68.3	3
Detroit	3	15	184	12.3	61.3	2
Green Bay	3	21	249	11.9	83.0	3
Indianapolis	28	128	1,718	13.4	61.4	16
Jacksonville	2	6	57	9.5	28.5	0
Kansas City	7	36	557	15.5	79.6	5
Miami	28	122	1,731	14.2	61.8	10
Minnesota	4	18	247	13.7	61.8	0
New England	26	101	1,610	15.9	61.9	8
New Orleans	3	8	74	9.3	24.7	0
N.Y. Giants	4	15	273	18.2	68.3	2
N.Y. Jets	29	110	1,408	12.8	48.6	12
Oakland	7	35	499	14.3	71.3	1
Philadelphia	5	20	224	11.2	44.8	3
Pittsburgh	9	39	457	11.7	50.8	3
St. Louis	3	14	170	12.1	56.7	2
San Diego	3	16	232	14.5	77.3	2
San Francisco	2	20	259	13.0	129.5	0
Seattle	4	10	154	15.4	38.5	1
Tampa Bay	3	8	119	14.9	39.7	0
Tennessee	10	49	756	15.4	75.6	6
Washington	5	24	412	17.2	82.4	2
Totals	221	941	13,095	13.9	62.4	86

Arizona totals include one game vs. St. Louis, one game vs. Phoenix
Oakland totals include five games vs. L.A. Raiders
St. Louis totals include two games vs. L.A. Rams
Tennessee totals include nine games vs. Houston

INSIDE THE NUMBERS

HERMAN MOORE'S CAREER RECEIVING VS. EACH OPPONENT

Opponent	Games	Rec.	Yards	Yds./Rec.	Yds./Game	TD
Arizona	4	16	238	14.9	59.5	1
Atlanta	6	32	629	19.7	104.8	7
Baltimore	1	10	120	12.0	120.0	0
Buffalo	3	17	310	18.2	103.3	1
Chicago	18	81	1,071	13.2	59.5	5
Cincinnati	2	12	172	14.3	86.0	0
Cleveland	2	11	177	16.1	88.5	0
Dallas	3	12	156	13.0	52.0	1
Denver	1	4	62	15.5	62.0	1
Green Bay	16	72	970	13.5	60.6	10
Indianapolis	2	2	16	8.0	8.0	0
Jacksonville	2	12	175	14.6	87.5	1
Kansas City	1	7	84	12.0	84.0	0
Miami	3	11	133	12.1	44.3	1
Minnesota	17	79	1,162	14.7	68.4	7
New England	2	10	141	14.1	70.5	0
New Orleans	2	15	153	10.2	76.5	1
N.Y. Giants	3	20	243	12.2	81.0	2
N.Y. Jets	2	10	109	10.9	54.5	0
Oakland	1	10	109	10.9	109.0	2
Philadelphia	2	9	111	12.3	55.5	0
Pittsburgh	3	23	350	15.2	116.7	2
St. Louis	1	6	120	20.0	120.0	0
San Diego	1	3	39	13.0	39.0	0
San Francisco	7	34	441	13.0	63.0	5
Seattle	3	14	153	10.9	51.0	3
Tampa Bay	13	66	842	12.8	64.8	4
Tennessee	2	9	193	21.4	96.5	3
Washington	4	19	185	9.7	46.3	2
Totals	127	626	8,664	13.8	74.1	59

Arizona totals include two games vs. Phoenix
St. Louis totals include one game vs. L.A. Rams
Tennessee totals include two games vs. Houston

CRIS CARTER'S CAREER RECEIVING VS. EACH OPPONENT

Opponent	Games	Rec.	Yards	Yds./Rec.	Yds./Game	TD
Arizona	12	53	774	14.6	64.5	11
Atlanta	4	20	324	16.2	81.0	6
Baltimore	1	11	85	7.7	85.0	1
Buffalo	3	18	242	13.4	80.7	2
Carolina	2	9	108	12.0	54.0	3
Chicago	21	121	1,367	11.3	65.1	8
Cincinnati	4	25	310	12.4	77.5	3
Cleveland	3	12	166	13.8	55.3	0
Dallas	8	38	503	13.2	62.9	7
Denver	6	28	403	14.4	67.2	5
Detroit	20	89	995	11.2	49.8	8
Green Bay	19	89	1,062	11.9	55.9	8
Indianapolis	1	5	89	17.8	89.0	3
Jacksonville	1	4	27	6.8	27.0	1
Kansas City	4	15	199	13.3	49.8	3
Miami	2	7	81	11.6	40.5	3
Minnesota	2	5	30	6.0	15.0	1
New England	4	24	276	11.5	69.0	1
New Orleans	7	37	433	11.7	61.9	4
N.Y. Giants	10	24	460	19.2	46.0	3
N.Y. Jets	3	18	219	12.2	73.0	2
Oakland	5	26	327	12.6	65.4	1
Philadelphia	2	11	209	19.0	104.5	3
Pittsburgh	2	9	140	15.6	70.0	2
St. Louis	4	12	165	13.8	41.3	1
San Diego	3	20	258	12.9	86.0	2
San Francisco	8	38	367	9.7	45.9	6
Seattle	3	12	217	18.1	72.3	1
Tampa Bay	21	95	1,141	12.0	54.3	9
Tennessee	4	23	289	12.6	72.3	4
Washington	8	26	422	16.2	52.8	2
Totals	197	924	11,688	12.6	64.9	114

Arizona totals include two games vs. St. Louis, six games vs. Phoenix
Oakland totals include three games vs. L.A. Raiders
St. Louis totals include three games vs. L.A. Rams
Tennessee totals include three games vs. Houston

TIM BROWN'S CAREER RECEIVING VS. EACH OPPONENT

Opponent	Games	Rec.	Yards	Yds./Rec.	Yds./Game	TD
Arizona	1	2	13	6.5	13.0	0
Atlanta	4	18	298	16.6	74.5	2
Baltimore	2	9	99	11.0	49.5	2
Buffalo	7	24	536	22.3	76.6	5
Carolina	1	10	163	16.3	163.0	0
Chicago	4	17	192	11.3	48.0	2
Cincinnati	7	24	434	18.1	62.0	6
Cleveland	2	2	29	14.5	14.5	0
Dallas	3	18	224	12.4	74.7	1
Denver	22	95	1,288	13.6	58.5	8
Detroit	2	6	48	8.0	24.0	1
Green Bay	3	13	161	12.4	53.7	0
Indianapolis	2	9	116	12.9	58.0	0
Jacksonville	2	19	224	11.8	112.0	1
Kansas City	21	100	1,423	14.2	67.8	5
Miami	8	43	563	13.1	70.4	5
Minnesota	4	16	175	10.9	43.8	1
New England	1	2	46	23.0	46.0	0
New Orleans	4	16	199	12.4	49.8	2
N.Y. Giants	3	11	254	23.1	84.7	2
N.Y. Jets	5	39	620	15.9	124.0	4
Philadelphia	2	9	115	12.8	57.5	1
Pittsburgh	3	9	82	9.1	27.3	0
St. Louis	4	11	203	18.5	50.8	1
San Diego	23	96	1,297	13.5	56.4	7
San Francisco	3	10	112	11.2	37.3	1
Seattle	22	89	1,381	15.5	62.8	10
Tampa Bay	3	13	180	13.8	60.0	1
Tennessee	5	21	293	14.0	58.6	5
Washington	3	19	176	9.3	58.7	2
Totals	176	770	10,944	14.2	65.9	75

St. Louis totals include three games vs. L.A. Rams
Tennessee totals include three games vs. Houston

MICHAEL IRVIN'S CAREER RECEIVING VS. EACH OPPONENT

Opponent	Games	Rec.	Yards	Yds./Rec.	Yds./Game	TD
Arizona	21	83	1,507	18.2	71.8	9
Atlanta	9	43	673	15.7	74.8	3
Buffalo	1	8	115	14.4	115.0	0
Carolina	2	8	213	26.6	106.5	1
Chicago	3	16	213	13.3	71.0	1
Cincinnati	4	24	431	18.0	107.8	1
Cleveland	3	18	248	13.8	82.7	1
Denver	3	18	237	13.2	79.0	2
Detroit	3	16	304	19.0	101.3	1
Green Bay	7	38	633	16.7	90.4	4
Indianapolis	1	7	112	16.0	112.0	0
Jacksonville	1	3	57	19.0	57.0	0
Kansas City	3	18	214	11.9	71.3	1
Miami	2	15	217	14.5	108.5	1
Minnesota	4	28	411	14.7	102.8	2
New England	1	6	76	12.7	76.0	0
New Orleans	6	22	342	15.5	57.0	0
N.Y. Giants	18	75	1,107	14.8	61.5	4
N.Y. Jets	2	10	184	18.4	92.0	2
Oakland	3	16	252	15.8	84.0	1
Philadelphia	20	64	1,047	16.4	52.4	5
Pittsburgh	4	26	522	20.1	130.5	4
St. Louis	2	10	239	23.9	119.5	2
San Diego	1	7	103	14.7	103.0	0
San Francisco	7	43	508	11.8	72.6	3
Seattle	2	14	211	15.1	105.5	0
Tampa Bay	2	2	42	21.0	21.0	1
Tennessee	4	16	259	16.2	64.8	3
Washington	20	96	1,427	14.9	71.4	13
Totals	159	750	11,904	15.9	74.9	65

Arizona totals include 10 games vs. Phoenix
Oakland totals include one game vs. L.A. Raiders
St. Louis totals include two games vs. L.A. Rams
Tennessee totals include three games vs. Houston

MORTEN ANDERSEN'S CAREER KICKING VS. EACH OPPONENT

Opponent	Games	FG	FGA	FG%	Long FG	XP	XPA	Pts.
Arizona	12	21	21	100.0	52	32	33	95
Atlanta	25	40	51	78.4	49	56	58	176
Baltimore	1	2	3	66.7	41	1	1	7
Buffalo	4	7	11	63.6	50	7	7	28
Carolina	10	18	20	90.0	51	21	21	75
Chicago	6	5	8	62.5	60	14	14	29
Cincinnati	5	5	8	62.5	49	17	17	32
Cleveland	4	7	8	87.5	53	7	7	28
Dallas	11	18	25	72.0	54	18	18	72
Denver	4	4	8	50.0	55	14	15	26
Detroit	9	10	16	62.5	50	18	18	48
Green Bay	6	10	11	90.9	52	15	15	45
Indianapolis	3	3	5	60.0	46	11	11	20
Jacksonville	2	1	2	50.0	46	3	3	6
Kansas City	4	4	5	80.0	50	7	7	19
Miami	5	5	7	71.4	35	15	15	30
Minnesota	10	15	19	78.9	47	17	17	62
New England	6	10	12	83.3	54	16	16	46
New Orleans	10	20	25	80.0	55	26	26	86
N.Y. Giants	8	15	17	88.2	45	15	15	60
N.Y. Jets	6	10	11	90.9	53	12	12	42
Oakland	5	7	9	77.8	51	11	11	32
Philadelphia	10	18	22	81.8	56	19	19	73
Pittsburgh	5	7	9	77.8	50	9	9	30
St. Louis	33	51	59	86.4	51	80	82	233
San Diego	4	3	7	42.9	35	9	9	18
San Francisco	35	53	65	81.5	59	56	58	215
Seattle	4	6	7	85.7	47	8	8	26
Tampa Bay	15	24	32	75.0	50	33	33	105
Tennessee	6	9	13	69.2	47	13	13	40
Washington	7	8	14	57.1	45	11	11	35
Totals	276	416	531	78.3	60	592	600	1,840

Arizona totals include five games vs. St. Louis, four games vs. Phoenix
Oakland totals include four games vs. L.A. Raiders
St. Louis totals include 23 games vs. L.A. Rams
Tennessee totals include five games vs. Houston

GARY ANDERSON'S CAREER KICKING VS. EACH OPPONENT

Opponent	Games	FG	FGA	FG%	Long FG	XP	XPA	Pts.
Arizona	7	13	18	72.2	44	18	18	57
Atlanta	7	8	10	80.0	39	26	26	50
Baltimore	1	6	6	100.0	46	2	2	20
Buffalo	9	14	17	82.4	49	19	19	61
Carolina	3	6	7	85.7	48	9	9	27
Chicago	8	13	17	76.5	50	17	17	56
Cincinnati	26	39	48	81.3	52	60	60	177
Cleveland	26	35	52	67.3	49	47	47	152
Dallas	12	20	26	76.9	48	24	24	84
Denver	11	19	23	82.6	42	24	24	81
Detroit	9	15	22	68.2	44	21	21	66
Green Bay	8	12	16	75.0	42	17	18	53
Indianapolis	7	10	12	83.3	53	21	21	51
Jacksonville	1	3	3	100.0	53	5	5	14
Kansas City	10	23	29	79.3	49	24	24	93
Miami	9	14	19	73.7	48	23	23	65
Minnesota	5	3	7	42.9	44	10	10	19
New England	7	10	10	100.0	49	17	17	47
New Orleans	8	20	22	90.9	51	18	18	78
N.Y. Giants	8	10	12	83.3	46	18	18	48
N.Y. Jets	8	13	19	68.4	45	24	24	63
Oakland	5	5	12	41.7	37	8	8	23
Philadelphia	4	5	7	71.4	52	9	9	24
St. Louis	7	9	11	81.8	46	19	19	46
San Diego	14	25	27	92.6	55	41	42	116
San Francisco	5	8	11	72.7	50	12	12	36
Seattle	10	13	15	86.7	43	10	10	49
Tampa Bay	8	9	12	75.0	44	18	18	45
Tennessee	26	47	52	90.4	54	50	52	191
Washington	8	12	13	92.3	49	20	21	56
Totals	277	439	555	79.1	55	631	636	1,948

Arizona totals include one game vs. St. Louis, one game vs. Phoenix
Indianapolis totals include one game vs. Baltimore
Oakland totals include three games vs. L.A. Raiders
Tennessee totals include 25 games vs. Houston
St. Louis totals include three games vs. L.A. Rams

INSIDE THE NUMBERS

STARTING RECORDS OF ACTIVE NFL QUARTERBACKS

Minimum: 10 starts

	W - L - T	Pct.
Kurt Warner	13 - 3	.813
Steve Bono	28 - 14	.667
Doug Flutie	26 - 13	.667
Steve Young	94 - 49	.657
Brett Favre	82 - 43	.656
Mark Brunell	44 - 24	.647
Brad Johnson	25 - 14	.641
Randall Cunningham	79 - 50 - 1	.612
Elvis Grbac	25 - 16	.610
Steve McNair	29 - 20	.592
Troy Aikman	90 - 64	.584
Mike Tomczak	42 - 31	.575
Jon Kitna	12 - 9	.571
Drew Bledsoe	58 - 47	.552
Neil O'Donnell	53 - 44	.546
Kordell Stewart	23 - 20	.535
Rich Gannon	39 - 35	.527
Steve Walsh	20 - 18	.526
Wade Wilson	36 - 33	.522
Rodney Peete	37 - 35	.514
Warren Moon	102 - 100	.505
Charlie Batch	11 - 11	.500
Trent Dilfer	38 - 38	.500
Danny Kanell	10 - 10 - 1	.500
Peyton Manning	16 - 16	.500
Bubby Brister	37 - 38	.493
Jim Harbaugh	66 - 69	.489
Ty Detmer	10 - 11	.476
Chris Chandler	52 - 58	.473
Steve Beuerlein	38 - 43	.469
Kerry Collins	26 - 30	.464
Erik Kramer	31 - 36	.463
Kent Graham	15 - 18	.455
Scott Mitchell	30 - 36	.455
Dave Brown	26 - 32	.448
Trent Green	6 - 8	.429
Jake Plummer	15 - 21	.417
Vinny Testaverde	60 - 85 - 1	.414
Gus Frerotte	21 - 30 - 1	.413
Todd Collins	7 - 10	.412
Craig Erickson	14 - 21	.400
Jeff George	45 - 72	.385
Jeff Blake	25 - 41	.379
Tony Banks	20 - 33	.377
Chris Miller	34 - 58	.370
Rick Mirer	22 - 38	.367
John Friesz	13 - 25	.342
Eric Zeier	4 - 8	.333
Billy Joe Tolliver	15 - 32	.319
Brian Griese	4 - 9	.308
Paul Justin	3 - 7	.300
Bobby Hoying	3 - 9 - 1	.269
Billy Joe Hobert	4 - 13	.235
Jeff Garcia	2 - 8	.200
Tim Couch	2 - 12	.143
Steve Stenstrom	1 - 9	.100

ALL-TIME RANKINGS OF PLAYERS IN FOUR CATEGORIES THAT DETERMINE NFL PASSER RATING

Minimum: 1,500 Attempts

COMPLETION PERCENTAGE	Pct.	Att.	Comp.
Steve Young	64.28	4,149	2,667
Joe Montana	63.24	5,391	3,409
Troy Aikman	61.58	4,453	2,742
Brett Favre	61.10	4,352	2,659
Jim Kelly	60.14	4,779	2,874
Mark Brunell	60.05	2,160	1,297
Ken Stabler	59.85	3,793	2,270
Danny White	59.69	2,950	1,761
Dan Marino	59.43	8,358	4,967
Ken Anderson	59.31	4,475	2,654

AVERAGE YARDS PER PASS	Avg.	Att.	Yards
Otto Graham	8.63	1,565	13,499
Sid Luckman	8.42	1,744	14,686
Norm Van Brocklin	8.16	2,895	23,611
Steve Young	7.98	4,149	33,124
Ed Brown	7.85	1,987	15,600
Bart Starr	7.85	3,149	24,718
Johnny Unitas	7.76	5,186	40,239
Earl Morrall	7.74	2,689	20,809
Dan Fouts	7.68	5,604	43,040
Len Dawson	7.67	3,741	28,711

TOUCHDOWN PERCENTAGE	Pct.	Att.	TD
Sid Luckman	7.86	1,744	137
Frank Ryan	6.99	2,133	149
Len Dawson	6.39	3,741	239
Daryle Lamonica	6.31	2,601	164
Sammy Baugh	6.24	2,995	187
Charley Conerly	6.11	2,833	173
Bob Waterfield	6.00	1,617	97
Earl Morrall	5.99	2,689	161
Sonny Jurgensen	5.98	4,262	255
Norm Van Brocklin	5.98	2,895	173

INTERCEPTION PERCENTAGE	Pct.	Att.	Int.
Neil O'Donnell	2.03	3,057	62
Mark Brunell	2.41	2,160	52
Steve Bono	2.47	1,701	42
Joe Montana	2.58	5,391	139
Steve Young	2.58	4,149	107
Bernie Kosar	2.59	3,365	87
Ken O'Brien	2.72	3,602	98
Jeff George	2.79	3,731	104
Jeff Blake	2.83	2,230	63
Troy Aikman	2.85	4,453	127

HIGHEST NFL POSTSEASON PASSER RATINGS (MINIMUM: 150 ATTEMPTS)

	Games	Att.	Comp.	Pct.	Yds.	Avg. Gain	TD	Int.	Rating
Bart Starr	10	213	130	61.0	1,753	8.23	15	3	104.8
Joe Montana	23	734	460	62.7	5,772	7.86	45	21	95.6
Ken Anderson	6	166	110	66.3	1,321	7.96	9	6	93.5
Joe Theismann	10	211	128	60.7	1,782	8.45	11	7	91.4
Brett Favre	14	449	270	60.1	3,390	7.55	25	12	91.1
Troy Aikman	16	502	320	63.7	3,849	7.67	23	17	88.3
Steve Young	22	471	292	62.0	3,326	7.06	20	13	85.8
Warren Moon	10	403	259	64.3	2,870	7.12	17	14	84.9
Ken Stabler	13	351	203	57.8	2,641	7.52	19	13	84.2
Bernie Kosar	10	270	152	56.3	1,953	7.23	16	10	83.5

HIGHEST NFL POSTSEASON PASSER RATINGS, ACTIVE PLAYERS (MINIMUM: 150 ATTEMPTS)

	Games	Att.	Comp.	Pct.	Yds.	Avg. Gain	TD	Int.	Rating
Brett Favre	14	449	270	60.1	3,390	7.55	25	12	91.1
Troy Aikman	16	502	320	63.7	3,849	7.67	23	17	88.3
Steve Young	22	471	292	62.0	3,326	7.06	20	13	85.8
Warren Moon	10	403	259	64.3	2,870	7.12	17	14	84.9
Wade Wilson	7	185	99	53.5	1,322	7.15	7	6	75.6
Neil O'Donnell	7	273	158	57.9	1,690	6.19	9	8	74.9
Randall Cunningham	12	365	192	52.6	2,426	6.65	12	9	74.3
Jim Harbaugh	5	163	83	50.9	906	5.56	6	5	67.2
Mark Brunell	9	255	127	49.8	1,550	6.08	10	10	65.6
Drew Bledsoe	3	231	119	51.5	1,233	5.34	5	12	52.8

RETIRED UNIFORM NUMBERS IN NFL

AFC

Baltimore: None
Buffalo: None
Cincinnati: Bob Johnson 54
Cleveland: Otto Graham 14
Jim Brown 32
Ernie Davis 45
Don Fleming 46
Lou Groza 76
Denver: John Elway 7
Frank Tripucka 18
Floyd Little 44
Indianapolis: Johnny Unitas 19
Buddy Young 22
Lenny Moore 24
Art Donovan 70
Jim Parker 77
Raymond Berry 82
Gino Marchetti 89
Jacksonville None
Kansas City: Jan Stenerud 3
Len Dawson 16
Abner Haynes 28
Stone Johnson 33
Mack Lee Hill 36
Willie Lanier 63
Bobby Bell 78
Buck Buchanan 86
Miami: Bob Griese 12
New England: Gino Cappelletti 20
Mike Haynes 40
Steve Nelson 57
John Hannah 73
Jim Hunt 79
Bob Dee 89
New York Jets: Joe Namath 12
Don Maynard 13
Oakland: None
Pittsburgh: Ernie Stautner 70
San Diego: Dan Fouts 14
Seattle: "Fans/the twelfth man" 12
Steve Largent 80
Tennessee: Earl Campbell 34
Jim Norton 43
Mike Munchak 63
Elvin Bethea 65

NFC

Arizona: Larry Wilson 8
Stan Mauldin 77
J.V. Cain 88
Marshall Goldberg 99
Atlanta: Steve Bartowski 10
William Andrews 31
Jeff Van Note 57
Tommy Nobis 60
Carolina None
Chicago: Bronko Nagurski 3
George McAfee 5
George Halas 7
Willie Galimore 28
Walter Payton 34
Gale Sayers 40
Brian Piccolo 41
Sid Luckman 42
Dick Butkus 51
Bill Hewitt 56
Bill George 61
Bulldog Turner 66
Red Grange 77
Dallas: None
Detroit: Dutch Clark 7
Bobby Layne 22
Doak Walker 37
Joe Schmidt 56
Chuck Hughes 85
Charlie Sanders 88
Green Bay: Tony Canadeo 3
Don Hutson 14
Bart Starr 15
Ray Nitschke 66
Minnesota: Fran Tarkenton 10
Paul Krause 22
Jim Marshall 70
Alan Page 88
New Orleans: Jim Taylor 31
Doug Atkins 81
New York Giants: Ray Flaherty 1
Tuffy Leemans 4
Mel Hein 7
Phil Simms 11
Y.A. Tittle 14
Al Blozis 32
Joe Morrison 40
Charlie Conerly 42
Ken Strong 50
Lawrence Taylor 56
Philadelphia: Steve Van Buren 15
Tom Brookshier 40
Pete Retzlaff 44
Chuck Bednarik 60
Al Wistert 70
Jerome Brown 99
St. Louis: Bob Waterfield 7
Merlin Olsen 74
Jackie Slater 78
San Francisco: John Brodie 12
Joe Montana 16
Joe Perry 34
Jimmy Johnson 37
Hugh McElhenny 39
Charlie Krueger 70
Leo Nomellini 73
Dwight Clark 87
Tampa Bay: Lee Roy Selmon 63
Washington: Sammy Baugh 33

INSIDE THE NUMBERS

NFL INDIVIDUAL LEADERS OVER RECENT SEASONS

Points

Last 2 Seasons		Last 3 Seasons		Last 4 Seasons	
267	Gary Anderson	392	Gary Anderson	507	Gary Anderson
249	Mike Vanderjagt	372	Mike Hollis	489	Mike Hollis
248	Steve Christie	367	Jason Elam	486	Al Del Greco
243	Jason Elam	361	Ryan Longwell	476	Jason Elam
243	Olindo Mare	360	Olindo Mare	469	Adam Vinatieri

Touchdowns

Last 2 Seasons		Last 3 Seasons		Last 4 Seasons	
29	Randy Moss	40	Terrell Davis	55	Terrell Davis
28	Emmitt Smith	38	Cris Carter	48	Cris Carter
25	Cris Carter	32	Antonio Freeman	47	Emmitt Smith
25	Terrell Davis	32	Emmitt Smith	41	Antonio Freeman
23	Fred Taylor	30	Marshall Faulk	37	Two tied

Field Goals

Last 2 Seasons		Last 3 Seasons		Last 4 Seasons	
61	Olindo Mare	89	Olindo Mare	116	Al Del Greco
61	Mike Vanderjagt	84	Al Del Greco	113	Mike hollis
58	Steve Christie	83	Gary Anderson	109	Adam Vinatieri
57	Three tied	83	Mike Hollis	108	Gary Anderson
		82	Two tied	106	Steve Christie

Rushes

Last 2 Seasons		Last 3 Seasons		Last 4 Seasons	
736	Curtis Martin	1,025	Eddie George	1,360	Eddie George
668	Eddie George	1,010	Curtis Martin	1,326	Curtis Martin
648	Emmitt Smith	990	Jerome Bettis	1,310	Jerome Bettis
644	Ricky Watters	929	Ricky Watters	1,282	Ricky Watters
615	Jerome Bettis	909	Emmitt Smith	1,236	Emmitt Smith

Rushing Yards

Last 2 Seasons		Last 3 Seasons		Last 4 Seasons	
2,751	Curtis Martin	3,997	Eddie George	5,507	Terrell Davis
2,729	Emmitt Smith	3,969	Terrell Davis	5,372	Jerome Bettis
2,700	Marshall Faulk	3,941	Jerome Bettis	5,365	Eddie George
2,598	Eddie George	3,911	Curtis Martin	5,097	Barry Sanders
2,449	Ricky Watters	3,803	Emmitt Smith	5,063	Curtis Martin

Rushing TDs

Last 2 Seasons		Last 3 Seasons		Last 4 Seasons	
24	Emmitt Smith	38	Terrell Davis	51	Terrell Davis
23	Terrell Davis	28	Emmitt Smith	40	Emmitt Smith
20	Fred Taylor	23	Leroy Hoard	35	Terry Allen
19	Leroy Hoard	23	James Stewart	34	Ricky Watters
17	Stephen Davis	22	Three tied	33	Karim Abdul-Jabbar

Passes

Last 2 Seasons		Last 3 Seasons		Last 4 Seasons	
1,146	Brett Favre	1,659	Brett Favre	2,202	Brett Favre
1,108	Peyton Manning	1,542	Drew Bledsoe	2,165	Drew Bledsoe
1,020	Drew Bledsoe	1,454	Dan Marino	1,827	Dan Marino
928	Jake Plummer	1,275	Troy Aikman	1,787	Mark Brunell
914	Steve Beuerlein	1,238	Steve McNair	1,740	Troy Aikman

Completions

Last 2 Seasons		Last 3 Seasons		Last 4 Seasons	
688	Brett Favre	992	Brett Favre	1,317	Brett Favre
657	Peyton Manning	882	Drew Bledsoe	1,255	Drew Bledsoe
568	Drew Bledsoe	833	Dan Marino	1,084	Mark Brunell
559	Steve Beuerlein	742	Troy Aikman	1,054	Dan Marino
525	Jake Plummer	731	Mark Brunell	1,038	Troy Aikman

Passing Yards

Last 2 Seasons		Last 3 Seasons		Last 4 Seasons	
8,303	Brett Favre	12,170	Brett Favre	16,069	Brett Favre
7,874	Peyton Manning	11,324	Drew Bledsoe	15,410	Drew Bledsoe
7,618	Drew Bledsoe	9,725	Dan Marino	13,309	Mark Brunell
7,049	Steve Beuerlein	8,942	Mark Brunell	12,520	Dan Marino
6,145	Rich Gannon	8,577	Troy Aikman	11,703	Troy Aikman

Touchdown Passes

Last 2 Seasons		Last 3 Seasons		Last 4 Seasons	
53	Steve Beuerlein	88	Brett Favre	127	Brett Favre
53	Brett Favre	67	Drew Bledsoe	94	Drew Bledsoe
52	Peyton Manning	61	Chris Chandler	81	Vinny Testaverde
42	Randall Cunningham	59	Steve Beuerlein	77	Chris Chandler
41	Two tied	58	Steve Young	75	John Elway

Receptions

Last 2 Seasons		Last 3 Seasons		Last 4 Seasons	
194	Jimmy Smith	276	Jimmy Smith	365	Tim Brown
174	Marvin Harrison	275	Tim Brown	359	Jimmy Smith
173	Marshall Faulk	257	Cris Carter	353	Cris Carter
172	Keyshawn Johnson	247	Marvin Harrison	312	Keenan McCardell
171	Tim Brown	243	Frank Sanders	312	Frank Sanders

Reception Yards

Last 2 Seasons		Last 3 Seasons		Last 4 Seasons	
2,818	Jimmy Smith	4,142	Jimmy Smith	5,386	Jimmy Smith
2,726	Randy Moss	3,764	Tim Brown	4,868	Tim Brown
2,498	Antonio Freeman	3,741	Antonio Freeman	4,674	Antonio Freeman
2,439	Marvin Harrison	3,422	Rod Smith	4,484	Cris Carter
2,362	Eric Moulds	3,321	Cris Carter	4,293	Tony Martin

Receiving Touchdowns

Last 2 Seasons		Last 3 Seasons		Last 4 Seasons	
28	Randy Moss	38	Cris Carter	48	Cris Carter
25	Cris Carter	32	Antonio Freeman	41	Antonio Freeman
20	Antonio Freeman	28	Randy Moss	33	Marvin Harrison
19	Marvin Harrison	26	Terrell Owens	33	Wesley Walls
18	Two tied	25	Two tied	32	Ed McCaffrey

Interceptions

Last 2 Seasons		Last 3 Seasons		Last 4 Seasons	
15	Sam Madison	16	Ray Buchanan	22	Keith Lyle
13	Rod Woodson	16	Sam Madison	22	Rod Woodson
12	Shawn Springs	16	Rod Woodson	21	Terrell Buckley
11	Five tied	15	Four tied	20	Eric Davis
				20	Darryl Williams

Sacks

Last 2 Seasons		Last 3 Seasons		Last 4 Seasons	
29.0	Kevin Carter	39.0	Robert Porcher	52.0	Kevin Greene
27.0	Kevin Greene	37.5	Kevin Greene	49.0	Robert Porcher
26.5	Robert Porcher	36.5	Kevin Carter	48.5	Michael McCrary
26.5	Simeon Rice	36.0	John Randle	47.5	John Randle
26.0	Michael McCrary	35.0	Two tied	47.5	Michael Sinclair

NFL TEAM LEADERS OVER RECENT SEASONS

Highest Won-Lost Percentage

Last 2 Seasons		Last 3 Seasons		Last 4 Seasons	
.781	Jacksonville	.750	Jacksonville	.703	Denver
.781	Minnesota	.708	Minnesota	.703	Green Bay
.656	Buffalo	.667	Denver	.703	Jacksonville
.656	Tennessee	.667	Green Bay	.672	Minnesota
.625	Two tied	.604	Five tied	.641	San Francisco

Most Points

Last 2 Seasons		Last 3 Seasons		Last 4 Seasons	
955	Minnesota	1,309	Minnesota	1,678	Denver
815	Denver	1,287	Denver	1,643	Green Bay
811	St. Louis	1,187	Green Bay	1,607	Minnesota
788	Jacksonville	1,182	Jacksonville	1,547	San Francisco
774	San Francisco	1,149	San Francisco	1,507	Jacksonville

Most Total Yards

Last 2 Seasons		Last 3 Seasons		Last 4 Seasons	
12,180	San Francisco	17,411	Minnesota	23,038	Denver
12,057	Minnesota	17,292	San Francisco	22,798	San Francisco
11,375	Denver	17,247	Denver	22,615	Minnesota
11,055	Green Bay	16,669	Green Bay	22,204	Green Bay
10,975	Washington	16,224	Jacksonville	21,984	Jacksonville

Most Rushing Yards

Last 2 Seasons		Last 3 Seasons		Last 4 Seasons	
4,639	San Francisco	6,710	Denver	9,072	Denver
4,332	Denver	6,608	San Francisco	8,803	Pittsburgh
4,201	Buffalo	6,504	Pittsburgh	8,455	San Francisco
4,193	Jacksonville	6,195	Tennessee	8,145	Tennessee
4,065	Dallas	5,983	Buffalo	7,884	Buffalo

Most Passing Yards

Last 2 Seasons		Last 3 Seasons		Last 4 Seasons	
8,317	Minnesota	11,715	Green Bay	15,412	Green Bay
8,010	Green Bay	11,630	Minnesota	15,288	Minnesota
7,696	Indianapolis	10,846	New England	14,747	New England
7,541	San Francisco	10,838	Indianapolis	14,421	Jacksonville
7,483	Carolina	10,684	San Francisco	14,343	San Francisco

***Fewest Turnovers**

Last 2 Seasons		Last 3 Seasons		Last 4 Seasons	
38	Dallas	58	Jacksonville	88	Jacksonville
38	Jacksonville	61	Dallas	90	Dallas
41	Tennessee	67	Tennessee	97	Tennessee
46	N.Y. Jets	68	N.Y. Jets	100	Kansas City
47	Two tied	69	Denver	101	Four tied

***Fewest Points Allowed**

Last 2 Seasons		Last 3 Seasons		Last 4 Seasons	
530	Tampa Bay	793	Tampa Bay	1,086	Tampa Bay
551	Dallas	862	N.Y. Jets	1,115	Dallas
555	Jacksonville	865	Dallas	1,152	Green Bay
562	Buffalo	873	Jacksonville	1,187	Pittsburgh
575	N.Y. Jets	902	New England	1,189	Denver

Last 2 Seasons		Last 3 Seasons		Last 4 Seasons	
***Fewest Total Yards Allowed**					
8,625	Tampa Bay	13,253	Tampa Bay	18,067	Tampa Bay
8,736	Buffalo	13,589	Buffalo	18,326	Buffalo
8,839	Miami	14,203	Miami	18,799	Green Bay
9,113	San Diego	14,279	San Diego	18,829	Denver
9,430	Oakland	14,359	Denver	18,902	Dallas
***Fewest Rushing Yards Allowed**					
2,461	San Diego	4,159	San Diego	5,914	San Diego
2,863	Buffalo	4,595	San Francisco	6,092	San Francisco
2,936	Baltimore	4,607	Tampa Bay	6,118	Tennessee
2,987	Miami	4,626	Baltimore	6,158	Denver
2,990	Tampa Bay	4,655	Buffalo	6,324	Buffalo
***Fewest Passing Yards Allowed**					
5,635	Tampa Bay	8,646	Tampa Bay	11,571	Tampa Bay
5,852	Miami	8,934	Buffalo	12,002	Buffalo
5,873	Buffalo	9,104	Philadelphia	12,083	Philadelphia
6,181	Philadelphia	9,403	Miami	12,261	Green Bay
6,197	Oakland	9,465	Dallas	12,271	Dallas
Most Opponents' Turnovers					
78	Kansas City	112	Kansas City	139	Kansas City
78	Seattle	107	Seattle	139	Seattle
68	Oakland	98	St. Louis	137	St. Louis
66	Arizona	97	New Orleans	135	Green Bay
66	New Orleans	96	Green Bay	131	Pittsburgh

**Cleveland excluded from all lists.*

RECORDS OF TEAMS ON OPENING DAY, 1933-1999

AFC	W	L	T	Pct.	Longest W Strk.	Longest L Strk.	Current Streak
Jacksonville	4	1	0	.800	4	1	W-4
Denver	25	14	1	.641	4	4	L-1
Miami	19	14	1	.576	8	5	W-8
Kansas City	23	17	0	.575	7	4	L-1
San Diego	23	17	0	.575	6	6	W-2
Cleveland	26	21	0	.553	5	5	L-2
Oakland	21	19	0	.525	5	5	L-4
Tennessee	21	19	0	.525	4	3	W-3
Pittsburgh	32	29	4	.525	4	3	W-2
Indianapolis	24	23	1	.511	8	8	W-1
New England	19	21	0	.475	6	3	W-1
Cincinnati	15	17	0	.469	4	4	L-2
Buffalo	16	24	0	.400	6	5	L-3
N.Y. Jets	16	24	0	.400	3	5	L-2
Baltimore	1	3	0	.250	1	3	L-3
Seattle	6	18	0	.250	3	8	L-1

NFC	W	L	T	Pct.	Longest W Strk.	Longest L Strk.	Current Streak
Dallas	30	9	1	.769	17	3	W-3
N.Y. Giants	38	25	4	.603	4	3	W-3
Chicago	39	27	1	.591	9	6	W-1
Minnesota	22	16	1	.579	4	3	W-4
St. Louis	34	28	0	.548	5	6	W-1
Green Bay	35	29	3	.547	5	6	W-4
Detroit	34	31	2	.523	7	4	W-1
San Francisco	25	24	1	.510	5	3	L-1
Atlanta	17	17	0	.500	5	3	L-1
Washington	31	32	4	.492	6	5	L-2
Arizona	27	38	1	.415	6	7	W-1
Philadelphia	26	39	1	.400	5	9	L-3
Tampa Bay	9	15	0	.375	3	5	L-2
New Orleans	9	24	0	.273	2	6	W-2
Carolina	1	4	0	.200	1	3	L-3

Kansas City totals include Dallas Texans, 1960-62.
Oakland totals include L.A. Raiders, 1982-94.
San Diego totals include L.A. Chargers, 1960.
Indianapolis totals include Baltimore, 1953-83.
Tennessee totals include Houston, 1960-96.
New England totals include Boston, 1960-70.
St. Louis totals include Cleveland, 1937-42 and 1944-45, and L.A. Rams, 1946-94.
Detroit totals include Portsmouth, 1933.
Arizona totals include Chi. Cardinals, 1933-59, St. Louis, 1960-87, and Phoenix, 1988-93.
NOTE: All tied games occurred prior to 1972, when calculation of ties in percentages as half-win, half-loss was begun.

OLDEST INDIVIDUAL SINGLE-SEASON OR SINGLE-GAME RECORDS IN NFL RECORD & FACT BOOK

Regular-Season Records That Have Not Been Surpassed or Tied

Most Points, Game—40, Ernie Nevers, Chi. Cardinals vs. Chi. Bears, Nov. 28, 1929 (6-td, 4-pat)

Most Touchdowns Rushing, Game—6, Ernie Nevers, Chi. Cardinals vs. Chi. Bears, Nov. 28, 1929

Highest Punting Average, Season (Qualifiers)—51.40, Sammy Baugh, Washington, 1940 (35-1,799)

Highest Punting Average, Game (minimum: 4 punts)—61.75, Bob Cifers, Detroit vs. Chi. Bears, Nov. 24, 1946 (4-247)

Highest Average Gain, Pass Receptions, Season (minimum: 24 receptions)—32.58, Don Currivan, Boston, 1947 (24-782)

Highest Average Gain, Passing, Game (minimum: 20 passes)—18.58, Sammy Baugh, Washington vs. Boston, Oct. 31, 1948 (24-446)

Most Touchdowns, Fumble Recoveries, Game—2, Fred (Dippy) Evans, Chi. Bears vs. Washington, Nov. 28, 1948

Most Yards Gained, Intercepted Passes, Rookie, Season—301, Don Doll, Detroit, 1949

Most Passes Had Intercepted, Game—8, Jim Hardy, Chi. Cardinals vs. Philadelphia, Sept. 24, 1950

Highest Average Gain, Rushing, Game (minimum: 10 attempts)—17.09, Marion Motley, Cleveland vs. Pittsburgh, Oct. 29, 1950 (11-188)

Highest Kickoff Return Average, Game (minimum: 3 returns)—73.50, Wally Triplett, Detroit vs. Los Angeles, Oct. 29, 1950 (4-294)

Most Pass Receptions, Game—18, Tom Fears, Los Angeles vs. Green Bay, Dec. 3, 1950

Highest Punt Return Average, Season (Qualifiers)—23.00, Herb Rich, Baltimore, 1950 (12-276)

Highest Punt Return Average, Rookie, Season (Qualifiers)—23.00, Herb Rich, Baltimore, 1950 (12-276)

Most Yards Passing, Game—554, Norm Van Brocklin, Los Angeles vs. N.Y. Yanks, Sept. 28, 1951

Most Touchdowns, Punt Returns, Rookie, Season—4, Jack Christiansen, Detroit, 1951

Most Interceptions By, Season—14, Dick (Night Train) Lane, Los Angeles, 1952

Most Interceptions By, Rookie, Season—14, Dick (Night Train) Lane, Los Angeles, 1952

Highest Average Gain, Passing, Season (Qualifiers)—11.17, Tommy O'Connell, Cleveland, 1957 (110-1,229)

Most Points, Season—176, Paul Hornung, Green Bay, 1960 (15-td, 41-pat,15-fg)

Most Yards Gained, Pass Receptions, Rookie, Season—1,473, Bill Groman, Houston, 1960

INSIDE THE NUMBERS

LONGEST WINNING STREAKS SINCE 1970

Regular-Season Games

16	Miami, 1971-73	(1 in 1971, 14 in 1972, 1 in 1973)
16	Miami, 1983-84	(5 in 1983, 11 in 1984)
15	San Francisco, 1989-90	(5 in 1989, 10 in 1990)
14	Oakland, 1976-77	(10 in 1976, 4 in 1977)
14	Denver, 1997-98	(1 in 1997, 13 in 1998)
13	Minnesota, 1974-75	(3 in 1974, 10 in 1975)
13	Chicago, 1984-85	(1 in 1984, 12 in 1985)
13	N.Y. Giants, 1989-90	(3 in 1989, 10 in 1990)
12	Washington, 1990-91	(1 in 1990, 11 in 1991)
11	Pittsburgh, 1975	
11	Baltimore, 1975-76	(9 in 1975, 2 in 1976)
11	Chicago, 1986-87	(7 in 1986, 4 in 1987)
11	Houston, 1993	
11	San Francisco, 1997	
11	Jacksonville, 1999	
11	Indianapolis, 1999	
10	Miami, 1973	
10	Pittsburgh, 1976-77	(9 in 1976, 1 in 1977)
10	Denver, 1984	
10	San Francisco, 1994	

NFL PLAYOFF APPEARANCES BY SEASONS

Team offs	Number of Seasons in Play
Dallas	26
N.Y. Giants	24
Cleveland	23
St. Louis	23
Minnesota	22
Chicago	21
San Francisco	20
Washington	20
Green Bay	19
Miami	19
Pittsburgh	19
Oakland	18
Buffalo	17
Tennessee	16
Detroit	14
Indianapolis	14
Philadelphia	14
Denver	13
Kansas City	13
San Diego	12
New England	10
N.Y. Jets	8
Cincinnati	7
Arizona	6
Atlanta	6
Seattle	5
Tampa Bay	5
Jacksonville	4
New Orleans	4
Carolina	1

TEAMS IN SUPER BOWL CONTENTION, 1978-1999

	With 3 Weeks to Play	With 2 Weeks to Play	With 1 Week to Play
1999	23	20	16
1998	22	19	14
1997	22	18	14
1996	23	21	13
1995	*27	21	*18
1994	25	*22	15
1993	20	18	16
1992	20	16	14
1991	20	18	13
1990	23	20	15
1989	21	18	17
1988	21	18	15
1987	19	19	15
1986	19	17	14
1985	21	18	13
1984	18	14	13
1983	24	19	15
1982	20	17	16
1981	21	20	16
1980	20	14	12
1979	19	15	13
1978	20	17	12

*NFL Record

GAMES DECIDED BY 7 POINTS OR LESS AND 3 POINTS OR LESS (1970-1998)

	Games Decided by 7 Points or Less	Games Decided by 3 Points or Less
1970	59 of 182 (32.4%)	34 of 182 (18.7%)
1971	76 of 182 (41.8%)	35 of 182 (19.2%)
1972	71 of 182 (39.0%)	38 of 182 (20.9%)
1973	60 of 182 (32.9%)	28 of 182 (15.4%)
1974	91 of 182 (50.0%)	37 of 182 (20.3%)
1975	62 of 182 (34.1%)	35 of 182 (19.2%)
1976	73 of 196 (37.2%)	38 of 196 (19.4%)
1977	85 of 196 (43.4%)	36 of 196 (18.4%)
1978	108 of 224 (48.2%)	49 of 224 (21.9%)
1979	104 of 224 (46.4%)	51 of 224 (22.8%)
1980	108 of 224 (48.2%)	58 of 224 (25.9%)
1981	91 of 224 (40.6%)	60 of 224 (26.8%)
1982	61 of 126 (48.4%)	33 of 126 (26.2%)
1983	106 of 224 (47.3%)	54 of 224 (24.1%)
1984	95 of 224 (42.4%)	58 of 224 (25.9%)
1985	87 of 224 (38.8%)	38 of 224 (17.0%)
1986	106 of 224 (47.3%)	48 of 224 (21.4%)
1987	99 of 210 (47.1%)	40 of 210 (19.0%)
1988	113 of 224 (50.4%)	62 of 224 (27.7%)
1989	107 of 224 (47.8%)	55 of 224 (24.6%)
1990	97 of 224 (43.3%)	54 of 224 (24.1%)
1991	112 of 224 (50.0%)	57 of 224 (25.4%)
1992	88 of 224 (39.3%)	48 of 224 (21.4%)
1993	*105 of 224 (46.9%)	53 of 224 (23.7%)
1994	115 of 224 (51.3%)	60 of 224 (26.8%)
1995	115 of 240 (47.9%)	61 of 240 (25.4%)
1996	109 of 240 (45.4%)	47 of 240 (19.6%)
1997	111 of 240 (46.3%)	67 of 240 (27.9%)
1998	113 of 240 (47.1%)	50 of 240 (20.8%)
1999	115 of 248 (46.4%)	**64 of 248 (25.8%)

*Week record: Dec. 11-13, 1993 (Week 15), 12 of 14 games (86%) decided by 7 points or less.
**Week record: Oct. 10-11, 1999 (Week 5), 10 of 14 games (71%) decided by 3 points or less.

1999 RECORDS OF TEAMS IN CLOSE GAMES

AFC	Overall Record	Decided by 8 Pts. or Less	Decided By 3 Pts. or Less
Baltimore	8-8	4-5	1-4
Buffalo	11-5	4-2	3-1
Cincinnati	4-12	2-2	1-2
Cleveland	2-14	2-3	1-2
Denver	6-10	3-8	1-5
Indianapolis	13-3	9-2	4-2
Jacksonville	14-2	4-1	3-1
Kansas City	9-7	4-5	3-2
Miami	9-7	6-4	5-1
New England	8-8	5-5	4-3
N.Y. Jets	8-8	6-5	1-3
Oakland	8-8	5-8	2-4
Pittsburgh	6-10	2-5	1-2
San Diego	8-8	5-4	3-2
Seattle	9-7	3-4	3-2
Tennessee	13-3	7-1	5-1

NFC	Overall Record	Decided by 8 Pts. or Less	Decided By 3 Pts. or Less
Arizona	6-10	4-2	1-1
Atlanta	5-11	3-4	1-1
Carolina	8-8	3-3	2-2
Chicago	6-10	5-6	4-3
Dallas	8-8	2-6	0-3
Detroit	8-8	5-3	1-0
Green Bay	8-8	3-4	2-2
Minnesota	10-6	7-6	3-4
New Orleans	3-13	1-5	0-2
N.Y. Giants	7-9	5-3	3-1
Philadelphia	5-11	4-6	1-4
St. Louis	13-3	0-3	0-1
San Francisco	4-12	2-3	1-1
Tampa Bay	11-5	5-3	2-1
Washington	10-6	4-3	2-1

SUPER BOWL CHAMPIONS THAT DID NOT MAKE PLAYOFFS THE FOLLOWING YEAR

Denver—Super Bowl XXXIII champions did not make playoffs in the 1999 season.
N.Y. Giants—Super Bowl XXV champions did not make playoffs in the 1991 season.
Washington—Super Bowl XXII champions did not make playoffs in the 1988 season.
N.Y. Giants—Super Bowl XXI champions did not make playoffs in the 1987 season.
San Francisco—Super Bowl XVI champions did not make playoffs in the 1982 season.
Oakland—Super Bowl XV champions did not make playoffs in the 1981 season.
Pittsburgh—Super Bowl XIV champions did not make playoffs in the 1980 season.
Kansas City—Super Bowl IV champions did not make playoffs in the 1970 season.
Green Bay—Super Bowl II champions did not make playoffs in the 1968 season.

NON-DIVISION WINNERS THAT PLAYED IN SUPER BOWL

1999	Tennessee Titans (Lost to St. Louis 23-16)	Super Bowl XXXIV
1997	Denver Broncos (Defeated Green Bay, 31-24)	Super Bowl XXXII
1992	Buffalo Bills (Lost to Dallas, 52-17)	Super Bowl XXVII
1985	New England Patriots (Lost to Chicago, 46-10)	Super Bowl XX
1980	Oakland Raiders (Defeated Philadelphia, 27-10)	Super Bowl XV
1975	Dallas Cowboys (Lost to Pittsburgh, 21-17)	Super Bowl X
1969	Kansas City Chiefs (Defeated Minnesota, 23-7)	Super Bowl IV

TEAMS AT OR UNDER .500 IN POSTSEASON PLAY

1999	Dallas Cowboys	8-8
1999	Detroit Lions	8-8
1991	New York Jets	8-8
1990	New Orleans Saints	8-8
1985	Cleveland Browns	8-8
1982	Cleveland Browns	4-5
1982	Detroit Lions	4-5
1969	Houston Oilers	6-6-2

COLDEST NFL GAMES ON RECORD

-13 degrees (-48 degree wind chill)—December 31, 1967, Lambeau Field, Green Bay, Wisconsin, NFL Championship (Green Bay 21, Dallas 17)
-9 degrees (-59 degree wind chill)—January 10, 1982, Riverfront Stadium, Cincinnati, Ohio, AFC Championship (Cincinnati 27, San Diego 7)
0 degrees (-32 degree wind chill)—January 15, 1994, Rich Stadium, Orchard Park, New York, AFC Divisional Playoff (Buffalo 29, Los Angeles Raiders 23)
1 degree (wind chill not recorded)—January 4, 1981, Cleveland Stadium, Cleveland, Ohio, AFC Divisional Playoff (Oakland 14, Cleveland 12)

1999 NFL SCORE BY QUARTERS

AFC Offense	1	2	3	4	OT	PTS
Indianapolis	112	114	88	109	0	423
Jacksonville	61	109	103	123	0	396
Tennessee	113	97	85	97	0	392
Kansas City	84	105	93	108	0	390
Oakland	80	89	151	67	3	390
Seattle	86	104	70	78	0	338
Miami	50	106	58	112	0	326
Baltimore	64	84	85	85	6	324
Buffalo	68	98	73	78	3	320
Pittsburgh	102	72	60	83	0	317
Denver	79	58	77	88	12	314
N.Y. Jets	55	101	48	104	0	308
New England	61	84	67	87	0	299
Cincinnati	91	70	58	64	0	283
San Diego	40	112	46	71	0	269
Cleveland	37	77	43	60	0	217

NFC Offense	1	2	3	4	OT	PTS
St. Louis	123	170	106	127	0	526
Washington	82	162	100	90	9	443
Carolina	90	155	89	87	0	421
Minnesota	59	166	64	107	3	399
Green Bay	44	123	73	117	0	357
Dallas	87	92	80	87	6	352
Detroit	61	132	47	82	0	322
N.Y. Giants	54	82	36	121	6	299
San Francisco	66	109	42	78	0	295
Atlanta	52	94	73	66	0	285
Chicago	52	69	84	64	3	272
Philadelphia	71	77	38	86	0	272
Tampa Bay	34	106	42	88	0	270
New Orleans	59	91	39	71	0	260
Arizona	19	97	50	79	0	245

AFC Defense	1	2	3	4	OT	PTS
Jacksonville	44	81	40	52	0	217
Buffalo	66	80	23	60	0	229
Baltimore	47	71	51	108	0	277
New England	70	101	56	54	3	284
Seattle	53	109	59	71	6	298
N.Y. Jets	66	81	78	84	0	309
San Diego	91	80	93	49	3	316
Denver	34	115	62	107	0	318
Pittsburgh	100	102	59	59	0	320
Kansas City	50	133	74	62	3	322
Tennessee	44	93	103	84	0	324
Oakland	64	81	71	107	6	329
Indianapolis	51	109	63	110	0	333
Miami	73	83	75	105	0	336
Cleveland	75	146	99	117	0	437
Cincinnati	124	166	92	78	0	460

NFC Defense	1	2	3	4	OT	PTS
Tampa Bay	89	47	44	55	0	235
St. Louis	49	85	54	54	0	242
Dallas	28	56	76	116	0	276
Detroit	28	116	81	98	0	323
Minnesota	84	105	56	90	0	335
Chicago	64	135	47	92	3	341
Green Bay	54	95	93	99	0	341
Philadelphia	100	107	70	71	9	357
N.Y. Giants	68	108	70	112	0	358
Washington	78	89	63	141	6	377
Atlanta	75	156	59	84	6	380
Carolina	78	111	67	125	0	381
Arizona	118	97	56	111	0	382
New Orleans	79	124	104	127	0	434
San Francisco	92	143	130	82	6	453
NFL Totals	2,136	3,205	2,168	2,764	51	10,324

TEAM LEADERS

Offense	Most Scored	Fewest Scored
1st Quarter	123 St. Louis	19 Arizona
2nd Quarter	170 St. Louis	58 Denver
3rd Quarter	151 Oakland	36 N.Y. Giants
4th Quarter	127 St. Louis	60 Cleveland

Defense	Most Allowed	Fewest Allowed
1st Quarter	124 Cincinnati	28 Dallas Detroit
2nd Quarter	166 Cincinnati	47 Tampa Bay
3rd Quarter	130 San Francisco	23 Buffalo
4th Quarter	141 Washington	49 San Diego

LARGEST TRADES IN NFL HISTORY

(Based on number of players or draft choices involved)

18—October 13, 1989—RB Herschel Walker from the Dallas Cowboys to Minnesota. Dallas also traded its third-round choice in 1990, its tenth-round choice in 1990, and its third-round choice in 1991 to Minnesota. Minnesota traded LB Jesse Solomon, LB David Howard, CB Issiac Holt, and DE Alex Stewart along with its first-round choice in 1990, its second-round choice in 1990, its sixth-round choice in 1990, its first-round choice in 1991, its second-round choice in 1991, its first-round choice in 1992, its second-round choice in 1992, and its third-round choice in 1992 to Dallas. Minnesota traded RB Darrin Nelson to Dallas, which traded Nelson to San Diego for the Chargers' fifth-round choice in 1990, which Dallas then sent to Minnesota.

15—March 26, 1953—T Mike McCormack, DT Don Colo, LB Tom Catlin, DB John Petitbon, and G Herschell Forester from Baltimore to Cleveland for DB Don Shula, DB Bert Rechichar, DB Carl Taseff, LB Ed Sharkey, E Gern Nagler, QB Harry Agganis, T Dick Batten, T Stu Sheets, G Art Spinney, and G Elmer Willhoite.

15—January 28, 1971—LB Marlin McKeever, first- and third-round choices in 1971, and third-, fourth-, fifth-, sixth-, and seventh-round choices in 1972 from Washington to the Los Angeles Rams for LB Maxie Baughan, LB Jack Pardee, LB Myron Pottios, RB Jeff Jordan, G John Wilbur, DT Diron Talbert, and a fifth-round choice in 1971.

12—June 13, 1952—Selection rights to Les Richter from the Dallas Texans to the Los Angeles Rams for RB Dick Hoerner, DB Tom Keane, DB George Sims, C Joe Reid, HB Billy Baggett, T Jack Halliday, FB Dick McKissack, LB Vic Vasicek, E Richard Wilkins, C Aubrey Phillips, and RB Dave Anderson.

10—March 23, 1959—HB Ollie Matson from the Chicago Cardinals to the Los Angeles Rams for T Frank Fuller, DE Glenn Holtzman, T Ken Panfil, DT Art Hauser, E John Tracey, FB Larry Hickman, HB Don Brown, the Rams second-round choice in 1960, and a player to be delivered during the 1959 training camp.

10—October 31, 1987—RB Eric Dickerson from the Los Angeles Rams to Indianapolis. The rights to LB Cornelius Bennett from Indianapolis to Buffalo. Indianapolis running back Owen Gill and the Colts' first- and second-round choices in 1988 and second-round choice in 1989, plus Bills running back Greg Bell and Buffalo's first-round choice in 1988 and first- and second-round choices in 1989 to the Rams.

OTHER SIGNIFICANT TRADES

March 21, 1967—QB Fran Tarkenton from Minnesota to the New York Giants for the Giants' first- and second-round selections in 1967, first-round selection in 1968, and second-round selection in 1969.

January 27, 1972—QB Fran Tarkenton from the New York Giants to Minnesota for QB Norm Snead, WR Bob Grim, RB Vince Clements, and the Vikings' first-round selection in 1972 and second-round selection in 1973.

June 8, 1973—QB Roman Gabriel from Los Angeles to Philadelphia for WR Harold Jackson, RB Tony Baker, the Eagles' first-round selection in 1974, and the Eagles' first- and third-round selections in 1975.

October 22, 1974—QB John Hadl from Los Angeles to Green Bay for the Packers' first- and third-round selections in 1975, Baltimore's second-round selection in 1975, and the Packers' first- and second-round selections in 1976.

April 5, 1976—QB Jim Plunkett from New England to San Francisco for the 49ers' first-round selection in 1976, Houston's first-round selection in 1976, the 49ers' first- and second-round selections in 1977, and QB Tom Owen.

April 17, 1999—Washington's first-round selection in 1999 (fifth overall) to New Orleans for the Saints first-round selection in 1999 (12th overall); third-round, fourth-round, fifth-round, sixth-round, and seventh-round selections in 1999; and first-round and third-round selections in 2000. The Saints drafted Texas RB Ricky Williams.

INSIDE THE NUMBERS

GREATEST COMEBACKS IN NFL HISTORY

(Most Points Overcome To Win Game)

REGULAR SEASON GAMES

FROM 28 POINTS BEHIND TO WIN:
December 7, 1980, at San Francisco

New Orleans	14	21	0	0	0	— 35
San Francisco	0	7	14	14	3	— 38

NO — Harris 33 pass from Manning (Ricardo kick)
NO — Childs 21 pass from Manning (Ricardo kick)
NO — Holmes 1 run (Ricardo kick)
SF — Solomon 57 punt return (Wersching kick)
NO — Holmes 1 run (Ricardo kick)
NO — Harris 41 pass from Manning (Ricardo kick)
SF — Montana 1 run (Wersching kick)
SF — Clark 71 pass from Montana (Wersching kick)
SF — Solomon 14 pass from Montana (Wersching kick)
SF — Elliott 7 run (Wersching kick)
SF — FG Wersching 36

	N.O.	S.F.
First Downs	27	24
Total Yards	519	430
Yards Rushing	143	176
Yards Passing	376	254
Turnovers	3	0

FROM 26 POINTS BEHIND TO WIN:
September 21, 1997, at Buffalo

Indianapolis	14	12	0	9	— 35
Buffalo	0	10	6	21	— 37

Ind — Bailey 10 pass from Harbaugh (Blanchard kick)
Ind — Faulk 10 run (Blanchard kick)
Ind — FG Blanchard 39
Ind — FG Blanchard 36
Ind — FG Blanchard 49
Ind — FG Blanchard 22
Buff — Johnson 16 pass from Collins (Christie kick)
Buff — FG Christie 27
Buff — A. Smith 15 run (2-pt attempt failed)
Ind — FG Blanchard 25
Buff — Early 4 pass from Collins (Christie kick)
Buff — A. Smith 1 run (Christie kick)
Buff — A. Smith 54 run (Christie kick)
Ind — Harrison 2 pass from Justin (2-pt attempt failed)

	Ind.	Buff.
First Downs	17	25
Total Yards	322	393
Yards Rushing	124	163
Yards Passing	198	230
Turnovers	1	5

FROM 25 POINTS BEHIND TO WIN:
November 8, 1987, at St. Louis

Tampa Bay	7	7	14	0	— 28
St. Louis	0	3	0	28	— 31

TB — Carrier 5 pass from DeBerg (Igwebuike kick)
TB — Carter 3 pass from DeBerg (Igwebuike kick)
StL — FG Gallery 31
TB — Smith 34 pass from DeBerg (Igwebuike kick)
TB — Smith 3 run (Igwebuike kick)
StL — Awalt 4 pass from Lomax (Gallery kick)
StL — Noga 23 fumble recovery (Gallery kick)
StL — J. Smith 11 pass from Lomax (Gallery kick)
StL — J. Smith 17 pass from Lomax (Gallery kick)

	T.B.	St.L.
First Downs	26	26
Total Yards	377	415
Yards Rushing	83	137
Yards Passing	294	278
Turnovers	1	2

FROM 24 POINTS BEHIND TO WIN:
October 27, 1946, at Washington

Philadelphia	0	0	14	14	— 28
Washington	10	14	0	0	— 24

Wash — Rosato 2 run (Poillon kick)
Wash — FG Poillon 28
Wash — Rosato 4 run (Poillon kick)
Wash — Lapka recovered fumble in end zone (Poillon kick)
Phil — Steele 1 run (Lio kick)
Phil — Pritchard 45 pass from Thompson (Lio kick)
Phil — Steinke 7 pass from Thompson (Lio kick)
Phil — Ferrante 30 pass from Thompson (Lio kick)

	Phil.	Wash.
First Downs	14	8
Total Yards	262	127
Yards Rushing	34	66
Yards Passing	228	61
Turnovers	6	3

FROM 24 POINTS BEHIND TO WIN:
October 20, 1957, at Detroit

Baltimore	7	14	6	0	— 27
Detroit	0	3	7	21	— 31

Balt — Mutscheller 15 pass from Unitas (Rechichar kick)
Det — FG Martin 47
Balt — Moore 72 pass from Unitas (Rechichar kick)
Balt — Mutscheller 52 pass from Unitas (Rechichar kick)
Balt — Moore 4 pass from Unitas (kick failed)
Det — Junker 14 pass from Rote (Layne kick)
Det — Cassady 26 pass from Layne (Layne kick)
Det — Johnson 1 run (Layne kick)
Det — Cassady 29 pass from Layne (Layne kick)

	Balt.	Det.
First Downs	15	20
Total Yards	322	369
Yards Rushing	117	178
Yards Passing	205	191
Turnovers	6	4

FROM 24 POINTS BEHIND TO WIN:
October 25, 1959, at Minneapolis

Philadelphia	0	0	21	7	— 28
Chicago Cardinals	7	10	7	0	— 24

Cardinals — Crow 10 pass from Roach (Conrad kick)
Cardinals — J. Hill 77 blocked field goal return (Conrad kick)
Cardinals — FG Conrad 15
Cardinals — Lane 37 interception return (Conrad kick)
Phil — Barnes 1 run (Walston kick)
Phil — McDonald 29 pass from Van Brocklin (Walston kick)
Phil — Barnes 2 run (Walston kick)
Phil — McDonald 22 pass from Van Brocklin (Walston kick)

	Phil.	Cardinals
First Downs	22	14
Total Yards	399	313
Yards Rushing	168	163
Yards Passing	231	150
Turnovers	2	6

FROM 24 POINTS BEHIND TO WIN:
October 23, 1960, at Denver

Boston	10	7	7	0	— 24
Denver	0	0	14	17	— 31

Bos — FG Cappelletti 12
Bos — Colclough 10 pass from Songin (Cappelletti kick)
Bos — Wells 6 pass from Songin (Cappelletti kick)
Bos — Miller 47 pass from Songin (Cappelletti kick)
Den — Carmichael 21 pass from Tripucka (Mingo kick)
Den — Jessup 19 pass from Tripucka (Mingo kick)
Den — Carmichael 35 lateral from Taylor, pass from Tripucka (Mingo kick)
Den — Taylor 8 pass from Tripucka (Mingo kick)
Den — FG Mingo 9

	Bos.	Den.
First Downs	19	16
Total Yards	434	326
Yards Rushing	211	65
Yards Passing	223	261
Turnovers	7	4

FROM 24 POINTS BEHIND TO WIN:
December 15, 1974, at Miami

New England	21	3	0	3	— 27
Miami	0	17	7	10	— 34

NE — Hannah recovered fumble in end zone (J. Smith kick)
NE — Sanders 23 interception return (J. Smith kick)
NE — Herron 4 pass from Plunkett (J. Smith kick)
NE — FG J. Smith 46
Mia — Nottingham 1 run (Yepremian kick)
Mia — Baker 37 pass from Morrall (Yepremian kick)
Mia — FG Yepremian 28
Mia — Baker 46 pass from Morrall (Yepremian kick)
NE — FG J. Smith 34
Mia — Nottingham 2 run (Yepremian kick)
Mia — FG Yepremian 40

	N.E.	Mia.
First Downs	18	18
Total Yards	333	333
Yards Rushing	114	61
Yards Passing	219	272
Turnovers	3	4

FROM 24 POINTS BEHIND TO WIN:
December 4, 1977, at Minnesota

San Francisco	0	10	14	3	— 27
Minnesota	0	0	7	21	— 28

SF — Delvin Williams 2 run (Wersching kick)
SF — FG Wersching 31
SF — Dave Williams 80 kickoff return (Wersching kick)
SF — Delvin Williams 5 run (Wersching kick)
Minn— McClanahan 15 pass from Lee (Cox kick)
Minn— Rashad 8 pass from Kramer (Cox kick)
Minn— Tucker 9 pass from Kramer (Cox kick)
SF — FG Wersching 31
Minn— S. White 69 pass from Kramer (Cox kick)

	S.F.	Minn.
First Downs	19	18
Total Yards	243	309
Yards Rushing	196	52
Yards Passing	47	257
Turnovers	2	5

FROM 24 POINTS BEHIND TO WIN:
September 23, 1979, at Denver

Seattle	10	10	14	0	— 34
Denver	0	10	21	6	— 37

Sea — FG Herrera 28
Sea — Doornink 5 run (Herrera kick)
Den — FG Turner 27
Sea — Doornink 5 run (Herrera kick)
Den — Armstrong 2 run (Turner kick)
Sea — FG Herrera 22
Sea — McCullum 13 pass from Zorn (Herrera kick)
Sea — Smith 1 run (Herrera kick)
Den — Studdard 2 pass from Morton (Turner kick)
Den — Moses 11 pass from Morton (Turner kick)
Den — Upchurch 35 pass from Morton (Turner kick)
Den — Lytle 1 run (kick failed)

	Sea.	Den.
First Downs	22	23
Total Yards	350	344
Yards Rushing	153	90
Yards Passing	197	254
Turnovers	4	3

FROM 24 POINTS BEHIND TO WIN:
September 23, 1979, at Cincinnati

Houston	0	10	17	0	3	—30
Cincinnati	14	10	0	3	0	—27

Cin — Johnson 1 run (Bahr kick)
Cin — Alexander 2 run (Bahr kick)
Cin — Johnson 1 run (Bahr kick)
Cin — FG Bahr 52
Hou — Burrough 35 pass from Pastorini (Fritsch kick)
Hou — FG Fritsch 33
Hou — Campbell 8 run (Fritsch kick)
Hou — Caster 22 pass from Pastorini (Fritsch kick)
Hou — FG Fritsch 47
Cin — FG Bahr 55
Hou — FG Fritsch 29

	Hou.	Cin.
First Downs	19	21
Total Yards	361	265
Yards Rushing	177	165
Yards Passing	184	100
Turnovers	3	2

FROM 24 POINTS BEHIND TO WIN:
November 22, 1982, at Los Angeles

San Diego	10	14	0	0	— 24
L.A. Raiders	0	7	14	7	— 28

SD — FG Benirschke 19
SD — Scales 29 pass from Fouts (Benirschke kick)
SD — Muncie 2 run (Benirschke kick)
SD — Muncie 1 run (Benirschke kick)
Raiders — Christensen 1 pass from Plunkett (Bahr kick)
Raiders — Allen 3 run (Bahr kick)
Raiders — Allen 6 run (Bahr kick)
Raiders — Hawkins 1 run (Bahr kick)

	S.D.	Raiders
First Downs	26	23
Total Yards	411	326
Yards Rushing	72	181
Yards Passing	339	145
Turnovers	4	2

FROM 24 POINTS BEHIND TO WIN:
September 26, 1988, at Denver

L.A. Raiders	0	0	14	13	3	— 30
Denver	7	17	0	3	0	— 27

Den — Dorsett 1 run (Karlis kick)
Den — Dorsett 1 run (Karlis kick)
Den — Sewell 7 pass from Elway (Karlis kick)
Den — FG Karlis 39
Raiders — Smith 40 pass from Schroeder (Bahr kick)
Raiders — Smith 42 pass from Schroeder (Bahr kick)
Raiders — FG Bahr 28
Raiders — Allen 4 run (Bahr kick)
Den — FG Karlis 25
Raiders — FG Bahr 44
Raiders — FG Bahr 35

	Raiders	Den.
First Downs	20	23
Total Yards	363	398
Yards Rushing	128	189
Yards Passing	235	209
Turnovers	1	5

FROM 24 POINTS BEHIND TO WIN:
December 6, 1992, at Tampa

L.A. Rams	0	3	21	7	— 31
Tampa Bay	6	21	0	0	— 27

TB — FG Murray 34
TB — FG Murray 47
TB — Armstrong 81 pass from Testaverde (Murray kick)
TB — Jones 26 fumble recovery (Murray kick)
Rams — FG Zendejas 18
TB — Carrier 10 pass from Testaverde (Murray kick)
Rams — Anderson 40 pass from Everett (Zendejas kick)
Rams — Chadwick 27 pass from Everett (Zendejas kick)
Rams — Lang 1 run (Zendejas kick)
Rams — Carter 8 pass from Everett (Zendejas kick)

	Rams	T.B.
First Downs	21	16
Total Yards	405	313
Yards Rushing	63	150
Yards Passing	342	163
Turnovers	3	3

POSTSEASON GAMES

FROM 32 POINTS BEHIND TO WIN:
AFC First-Round Playoff Game
January 3, 1993, at Buffalo

Houston	7	21	7	3	0	— 38
Buffalo	3	0	28	7	3	— 41

Hou — Jeffires 3 pass from Moon (Del Greco kick)
Buff — FG Christie 36
Hou — Slaughter 7 pass from Moon (Del Greco kick)
Hou — Duncan 26 pass from Moon (Del Greco kick)
Hou — Jeffires 27 pass from Moon (Del Greco kick)
Hou — McDowell 58 interception return (Del Greco kick)
Buff — Davis 1 run (Christie kick)
Buff — Beebe 38 pass from Reich (Christie kick)
Buff — Reed 26 pass from Reich (Christie kick)
Buff — Reed 18 pass from Reich (Christie kick)
Buff — Reed 17 pass from Reich (Christie kick)
Hou — FG Del Greco 26
Buff — FG Christie 32

	Hou.	Buff.
First Downs	27	19
Total Yards	429	366
Yards Rushing	82	98
Yards Passing	347	268
Turnovers	2	1

FROM 20 POINTS BEHIND TO WIN:
Western Conference Playoff Game
December 22, 1957, at San Francisco

Detroit	0	7	14	10	— 31
San Francisco	14	10	3	0	— 27

SF — Owens 34 pass from Tittle (Soltau kick)
SF — McElhenny 47 pass from Tittle (Soltau kick)
Det — Junker 4 pass from Rote (Martin kick)
SF — Wilson 12 pass from Tittle (Soltau kick)
SF — FG Soltau 25
SF — FG Soltau 10
Det — Tracy 2 run (Martin kick)
Det — Tracy 58 run (Martin kick)
Det — Gedman 3 run (Martin kick)
Det — FG Martin 14

	Det.	S.F.
First Downs	22	20
Total Yards	324	351
Yards Rushing	129	127
Yards Passing	195	224
Turnovers	5	4

FROM 18 POINTS BEHIND TO WIN:
NFC Divisional Playoff Game
December 23, 1972, at San Francisco

Dallas	3	10	0	17	— 30
San Francisco	7	14	7	0	— 28

SF — Washington 97 kickoff return (Gossett kick)
Dall — FG Fritsch 37
SF — Schreiber 1 run (Gossett kick)
SF — Schreiber 1 run (Gossett kick)
Dall — FG Fritsch 45
Dall — Alworth 28 pass from Morton (Fritsch kick)
SF — Schreiber 1 run (Gossett kick)
Dall — FG Fritsch 27
Dall — Parks 20 pass from Staubach (Fritsch kick)
Dall — Sellers 10 pass from Staubach (Fritsch kick)

	Dall.	S.F.
First Downs	22	13
Total Yards	402	255
Yards Rushing	165	105
Yards Passing	237	150
Turnovers	5	3

FROM 18 POINTS BEHIND TO WIN:
AFC Divisional Playoff Game
January 4, 1986, at Miami

Cleveland	7	7	7	0	— 21
Miami	3	0	14	7	— 24

Mia — FG Reveiz 51
Clev — Newsome 16 pass from Kosar (Bahr kick)
Clev — Byner 21 run (Bahr kick)
Clev — Byner 66 run (Bahr kick)
Mia — Moore 6 pass from Marino (Reveiz kick)
Mia — Davenport 31 run (Reveiz kick)
Mia — Davenport 1 run (Reveiz kick)

	Clev.	Mia.
First Downs	17	20
Total Yards	313	330
Yards Rushing	251	92
Yards Passing	62	238
Turnovers	1	1

RECORDS OF NFL TEAMS SINCE 1970 AFL-NFL MERGER

AFC	W - L - T	Pct.	Division Titles	Playoff Berths	Post-season Record	Super Bowl Record
Miami	293-161-2	.645	11	19	19-17	2-3
Jacksonville**	49- 31-0	.613	2	4	4-4	0-0
Oakland	271-179-6	.602	9	15	18-12	3-0
Pittsburgh	269-186-1	.591	14	18	21-14	4-1
Denver	262-188-6	.581	9	13	16-11	2-4
Kansas City	228-221-7	.508	4	9	3-9	0-0
Buffalo	223-231-2	.491	7	13	12-13	0-4
Cleveland+	196-209-3	.484	6	10	4-10	0-0
Seattle*	173-199-0	.465	2	5	3-5	0-0
New England	212-244-0	.465	4	9	6-9	0-2
Tennessee	210-244-2	.463	2	11	10-11	0-1
Cincinnati	207-249-0	.454	5	7	5-7	0-2
San Diego	204-247-5	.453	5	7	6-7	0-1
Indianapolis	193-261-2	.425	6	9	6-8	1-0
N.Y. Jets	191-263-2	.421	1	6	4-6	0-0
Baltimore***	24- 39-1	.383	0	0	0-0	0-0

NFC	W - L - T	Pct.	Division Titles	Playoff Berths	Post-season Record	Super Bowl Record
Dallas	285-171-0	.625	15	22	31-17	5-3
San Francisco	277-176-3	.611	16	19	24-14	5-0
Minnesota	271-183-2	.596	13	20	14-20	0-3
Washington	267-187-2	.588	6	14	19-11	3-2
St. Louis	242-210-4	.535	9	15	13-14	1-1
Chicago	225-230-1	.495	6	10	7-9	1-0
Green Bay	215-233-8	.480	4	8	10-7	1-1
Carolina**	38- 42-0	.475	1	1	1-1	0-0
N.Y. Giants	214-239-3	.473	4	8	10-6	2-0
Philadelphia	212-237-7	.472	2	10	5-10	0-1
Detroit	206-246-4	.456	3	9	1-9	0-0
Arizona	189-261-6	.421	2	4	1-4	0-0
Atlanta	189-263-4	.418	2	6	4-6	0-1
New Orleans	180-272-4	.398	1	4	0-4	0-0
Tampa Bay*	129-242-1	.348	3	5	3-5	0-0

*Entered NFL in 1976.
**Entered NFL in 1995.
***Entered NFL in 1996.
+ Did not play 1996-98.
Oakland totals include L.A. Raiders, 1982-94.
Tennessee totals include Houston, 1970-96.
Indianapolis totals include Baltimore, 1970-83.
St. Louis totals include L.A. Rams, 1970-94.
Arizona totals include St. Louis, 1970-87, and Phoenix, 1988-93.
Tie games before 1972 are not calculated in won-lost percentage.
In 1982, because of players' strike, the divisional format was abandoned; L.A. Raiders and Washington won regular-season conference titles, not included in "Division Titles" totals listed above. Sixteen teams were awarded playoff berths, included in totals listed above.

INSIDE THE NUMBERS

ALL-TIME REGULAR-SEASON RECORDS OF CURRENT NFL TEAMS

AFC

BALTIMORE RAVENS

	All Games			Home Games			Road Games		
Season	W	L	T	W	L	T	W	L	T
1996	4	12		4	4		0	8	
1997	6	9	1	3	4	1	3	5	
1998	6	10		4	4		2	6	
1999	8	8		4	4		4	4	
	24	39	1	15	16	1	9	23	

BUFFALO BILLS

	All Games			Home Games			Road Games		
Season	W	L	T	W	L	T	W	L	T
1960	5	8	1	3	4		2	4	1
1961	6	8		2	5		4	3	
1962	7	6	1	3	3	1	4	3	
1963	7	6	1	4	2	1	3	4	
1964	12	2		6	1		6	1	
1965	10	3	1	5	2		5	1	1
1966	9	4	1	4	2	1	5	2	
1967	4	10		2	5		2	5	
1968	1	12	1	1	6		0	6	1
1969	4	10		4	3		0	7	
1970	3	10	1	1	6		2	4	1
1971	1	13		1	6		0	7	
1972	4	9	1	2	4	1	2	5	
1973	9	5		5	2		4	3	
1974	9	5		5	2		4	3	
1975	8	6		3	4		5	2	
1976	2	12		1	6		1	6	
1977	3	11		1	6		2	5	
1978	5	11		4	4		1	7	
1979	7	9		3	5		4	4	
1980	11	5		6	2		5	3	
1981	10	6		7	1		3	5	
1982	4	5		4	1		0	4	
1983	8	8		3	5		5	3	
1984	2	14		2	6		0	8	
1985	2	14		2	6		0	8	
1986	4	12		3	5		1	7	
1987	7	8		4	4		3	4	
1988	12	4		8	0		4	4	
1989	9	7		6	2		3	5	
1990	13	3		8	0		5	3	
1991	13	3		7	1		6	2	
1992	11	5		6	2		5	3	
1993	12	4		6	2		6	2	
1994	7	9		4	4		3	5	
1995	10	6		6	2		4	4	
1996	10	6		7	1		3	5	
1997	6	10		4	4		2	6	
1998	10	6		6	2		4	4	
1999	11	5		6	2		5	3	
	288	300	8	165	130	4	123	170	4

CINCINNATI BENGALS

	All Games			Home Games			Road Games		
Season	W	L	T	W	L	T	W	L	T
1968	3	11		2	5		1	6	
1969	4	9	1	4	3		0	6	1
1970	8	6		5	2		3	4	
1971	4	10		3	4		1	6	
1972	8	6		4	3		4	3	
1973	10	4		7	0		3	4	
1974	7	7		4	3		3	4	
1975	11	3		6	1		5	2	
1976	10	4		6	1		4	3	
1977	8	6		5	2		3	4	
1978	4	12		3	5		1	7	
1979	4	12		4	4		0	8	
1980	6	10		3	5		3	5	
1981	12	4		6	2		6	2	
1982	7	2		4	0		3	2	
1983	7	9		4	4		3	5	
1984	8	8		5	3		3	5	
1985	7	9		5	3		2	6	
1986	10	6		6	2		4	4	
1987	4	11		1	7		3	4	
1988	12	4		8	0		4	4	
1989	8	8		5	3		3	5	
1990	9	7		5	3		4	4	
1991	3	13		3	5		0	8	
1992	5	11		3	5		2	6	
1993	3	13		3	5		0	8	
1994	3	13		2	6		1	7	
1995	7	9		3	5		4	4	
1996	8	8		6	2		2	6	
1997	7	9		6	2		1	7	
1998	3	13		1	7		2	6	
1999	4	12		2	6		2	6	
	214	269	1	134	108		80	161	1

CLEVELAND BROWNS*

	All Games			Home Games			Road Games		
Season	W	L	T	W	L	T	W	L	T
1950	10	2		5	1		5	1	
1951	11	1		6	0		5	1	
1952	8	4		4	2		4	2	
1953	11	1		6	0		5	1	
1954	9	3		5	1		4	2	
1955	9	2	1	5	1		4	1	1
1956	5	7		1	5		4	2	
1957	9	2	1	6	0		3	2	1
1958	9	3		4	2		5	1	
1959	7	5		3	3		4	2	
1960	8	3	1	4	2		4	1	1
1961	8	5	1	4	3		4	2	1
1962	7	6	1	4	2	1	3	4	
1963	10	4		5	2		5	2	
1964	10	3	1	5	1	1	5	2	
1965	11	3		5	2		6	1	
1966	9	5		5	2		4	3	
1967	9	5		6	1		3	4	
1968	10	4		5	2		5	2	
1969	10	3	1	5	1	1	5	2	
1970	7	7		4	3		3	4	
1971	9	5		4	3		5	2	
1972	10	4		4	3		6	1	
1973	7	5	2	5	1	1	2	4	1
1974	4	10		3	4		1	6	
1975	3	11		3	4		0	7	
1976	9	5		6	1		3	4	
1977	6	8		2	5		4	3	
1978	8	8		5	3		3	5	
1979	9	7		5	3		4	4	
1980	11	5		6	2		5	3	
1981	5	11		3	5		2	6	
1982	4	5		2	2		2	3	
1983	9	7		6	2		3	5	
1984	5	11		2	6		3	5	
1985	8	8		5	3		3	5	
1986	12	4		6	2		6	2	
1987	10	5		5	2		5	3	
1988	10	6		6	2		4	4	
1989	9	6	1	5	2	1	4	4	
1990	3	13		2	6		1	7	
1991	6	10		3	5		3	5	
1992	7	9		4	4		3	5	
1993	7	9		4	4		3	5	
1994	11	5		6	2		5	3	
1995	5	11		3	5		2	6	
1999	2	14		0	8		2	6	
	376	280	10	202	125	5	174	155	5

Did not play from 1996-98.

DENVER BRONCOS

	All Games			Home Games			Road Games		
Season	W	L	T	W	L	T	W	L	T
1960	4	9	1	2	4	1	2	5	
1961	3	11		2	5		1	6	
1962	7	7		3	4		4	3	
1963	2	11	1	2	5		0	6	1
1964	2	11	1	2	4	1	0	7	
1965	4	10		2	5		2	5	
1966	4	10		3	4		1	6	
1967	3	11		1	6		2	5	
1968	5	9		3	4		2	5	
1969	5	8	1	4	2	1	1	6	
1970	5	8	1	3	3	1	2	5	
1971	4	9	1	2	4	1	2	5	
1972	5	9		3	4		2	5	
1973	7	5	2	3	3	1	4	2	1
1974	7	6	1	3	3	1	4	3	
1975	6	8		5	2		1	6	
1976	9	5		6	1		3	4	
1977	12	2		6	1		6	1	
1978	10	6		6	2		4	4	
1979	10	6		6	2		4	4	
1980	8	8		4	4		4	4	
1981	10	6		8	0		2	6	
1982	2	7		1	4		1	3	
1983	9	7		6	2		3	5	
1984	13	3		7	1		6	2	
1985	11	5		6	2		5	3	
1986	11	5		7	1		4	4	
1987	10	4	1	7	1		3	3	1
1988	8	8		6	2		2	6	
1989	11	5		6	2		5	3	
1990	5	11		4	4		1	7	
1991	12	4		7	1		5	3	
1992	8	8		7	1		1	7	
1993	9	7		5	3		4	4	
1994	7	9		4	4		3	5	
1995	8	8		6	2		2	6	
1996	13	3		8	0		5	3	
1997	12	4		8	0		4	4	
1998	14	2		8	0		6	2	
1999	6	10		3	5		3	5	
	301	285	10	185	107	7	116	178	3

INDIANAPOLIS COLTS*

	All Games			Home Games			Road Games		
Season	W	L	T	W	L	T	W	L	T
1953	3	9		2	4		1	5	
1954	3	9		2	4		1	5	
1955	5	6	1	4	1	1	1	5	
1956	5	7		4	2		1	5	
1957	7	5		4	2		3	3	
1958	9	3		6	0		3	3	
1959	9	3		4	2		5	1	
1960	6	6		4	2		2	4	
1961	8	6		5	2		3	4	
1962	7	7		3	4		4	3	
1963	8	6		4	3		4	3	
1964	12	2		7	1		5	1	
1965	10	3	1	5	2		5	1	1
1966	9	5		5	2		4	3	
1967	11	1	2	6	0	1	5	1	1
1968	13	1		6	1		7	0	
1969	8	5	1	4	2	1	4	3	
1970	11	2	1	5	1	1	6	1	
1971	10	4		5	2		5	2	
1972	5	9		2	5		3	4	
1973	4	10		3	4		1	6	
1974	2	12		0	7		2	5	
1975	10	4		5	2		5	2	
1976	11	3		6	1		5	2	
1977	10	4		6	1		4	3	
1978	5	11		2	6		3	5	
1979	5	11		3	5		2	6	
1980	7	9		2	6		5	3	
1981	2	14		1	7		1	7	
1982	0	8	1	0	3	1	0	5	
1983	7	9		3	5		4	4	
1984	4	12		2	6		2	6	
1985	5	11		4	4		1	7	
1986	3	13		1	7		2	6	
1987	9	6		4	4		5	2	
1988	9	7		6	2		3	5	
1989	8	8		6	2		2	6	
1990	7	9		3	5		4	4	
1991	1	15		0	8		1	7	
1992	9	7		4	4		5	3	
1993	4	12		2	6		2	6	
1994	8	8		5	3		3	5	
1995	9	7		5	3		4	4	
1996	9	7		6	2		3	5	
1997	3	13		2	6		1	7	
1998	3	13		3	5		0	8	
1999	13	3		7	1		6	2	
	326	345	7	178	157	5	148	188	2

includes Baltimore Colts (1953-83).

JACKSONVILLE JAGUARS

	All Games			Home Games			Road Games		
Season	W	L	T	W	L	T	W	L	T
1995	4	12		2	6		2	6	
1996	9	7		7	1		2	6	
1997	11	5		7	1		4	4	
1998	11	5		7	1		4	4	
1999	14	2		7	1		7	1	
	49	31		30	10		19	21	

KANSAS CITY CHIEFS*

	All Games			Home Games			Road Games		
Season	W	L	T	W	L	T	W	L	T
1960	8	6		5	2		3	4	
1961	6	8		4	3		2	5	
1962	11	3		6	1		5	2	
1963	5	7	2	4	3		1	4	2
1964	7	7		4	3		3	4	
1965	7	5	2	5	2		2	3	2
1966	11	2	1	4	2	1	7	0	
1967	9	5		4	3		5	2	
1968	12	2		6	1		6	1	
1969	11	3		6	1		5	2	
1970	7	5	2	4	1	2	3	4	
1971	10	3	1	7	0		3	3	1
1972	8	6		3	4		5	2	
1973	7	5	2	5	1	1	2	4	1
1974	5	9		1	6		4	3	
1975	5	9		3	4		2	5	
1976	5	9		1	6		4	3	
1977	2	12		1	6		1	6	
1978	4	12		3	5		1	7	
1979	7	9		3	5		4	4	
1980	8	8		3	5		5	3	
1981	9	7		5	3		4	4	
1982	3	6		2	2		1	4	
1983	6	10		5	3		1	7	
1984	8	8		5	3		3	5	
1985	6	10		5	3		1	7	
1986	10	6		6	2		4	4	
1987	4	11		3	4		1	7	
1988	4	11	1	4	4		0	7	1
1989	8	7	1	5	3		3	4	1
1990	11	5		6	2		5	3	
1991	10	6		6	2		4	4	
1992	10	6		7	1		3	5	
1993	11	5		7	1		4	4	
1994	9	7		5	3		4	4	
1995	13	3		8	0		5	3	
1996	9	7		5	3		4	4	
1997	13	3		8	0		5	3	
1998	7	9		5	3		2	6	
1999	9	7		6	2		3	5	
	315	269	12	185	108	4	130	161	8

**includes Dallas Texans (1960-62).*

MIAMI DOLPHINS

	All Games			Home Games			Road Games		
Season	W	L	T	W	L	T	W	L	T
1966	3	11		2	5		1	6	
1967	4	10		4	3		0	7	
1968	5	8	1	1	5	1	4	3	
1969	3	10	1	2	4	1	1	6	
1970	10	4		6	1		4	3	
1971	10	3	1	6	1		4	2	1
1972	14	0		7	0		7	0	
1973	12	2		7	0		5	2	
1974	11	3		7	0		4	3	
1975	10	4		5	2		5	2	
1976	6	8		3	4		3	4	
1977	10	4		6	1		4	3	
1978	11	5		7	1		4	4	
1979	10	6		6	2		4	4	
1980	8	8		5	3		3	5	
1981	11	4	1	6	1	1	5	3	
1982	7	2		4	0		3	2	
1983	12	4		7	1		5	3	
1984	14	2		7	1		7	1	
1985	12	4		8	0		4	4	
1986	8	8		4	4		4	4	
1987	8	7		4	3		4	4	
1988	6	10		4	4		2	6	
1989	8	8		4	4		4	4	
Season	W	L	T	W	L	T	W	L	T
1990	12	4		7	1		5	3	
1991	8	8		5	3		3	5	
1992	11	5		6	2		5	3	
1993	9	7		4	4		5	3	
1994	10	6		6	2		4	4	
1995	9	7		5	3		4	4	
1996	8	8		4	4		4	4	
1997	9	7		6	2		3	5	
1998	10	6		7	1		3	5	
1999	9	7		5	3		4	4	
	308	200	4	177	75	3	131	125	1

NEW ENGLAND PATRIOTS*

	All Games			Home Games			Road Games		
Season	W	L	T	W	L	T	W	L	T
1960	5	9		3	4		2	5	
1961	9	4	1	4	2	1	5	2	
1962	9	4	1	6	1		3	3	1
1963	7	6	1	5	1	1	2	5	
1964	10	3	1	4	2	1	6	1	
1965	4	8	2	1	4	2	3	4	
1966	8	4	2	4	2	1	4	2	1
1967	3	10	1	2	4		1	6	1
1968	4	10		2	5		2	5	
1969	4	10		2	5		2	5	
1970	2	12		1	6		1	6	
1971	6	8		5	2		1	6	
1972	3	11		2	5		1	6	
1973	5	9		3	4		2	5	
1974	7	7		3	4		4	3	
1975	3	11		2	5		1	6	
1976	11	3		6	1		5	2	
1977	9	5		6	1		3	4	
1978	11	5		5	3		6	2	
1979	9	7		6	2		3	5	
1980	10	6		6	2		4	4	
1981	2	14		2	6		0	8	
1982	5	4		3	1		2	3	
1983	8	8		5	3		3	5	
1984	9	7		5	3		4	4	
1985	11	5		7	1		4	4	
1986	11	5		4	4		7	1	
1987	8	7		5	3		3	4	
1988	9	7		7	1		2	6	
1989	5	11		3	5		2	6	
1990	1	15		0	8		1	7	
1991	6	10		4	4		2	6	
1992	2	14		1	7		1	7	
1993	5	11		3	5		2	6	
1994	10	6		5	3		5	3	
1995	6	10		3	5		3	5	
1996	11	5		6	2		5	3	
1997	10	6		6	2		4	4	
1998	9	7		6	2		3	5	
1999	8	8		5	3		3	5	
	275	312	9	158	133	6	117	179	3

**includes Boston Patriots (1960-70).*

NEW YORK JETS*

	All Games			Home Games			Road Games		
Season	W	L	T	W	L	T	W	L	T
1960	7	7		3	4		4	3	
1961	7	7		5	2		2	5	
1962	5	9		2	5		3	4	
1963	5	8	1	4	2	1	1	6	
1964	5	8	1	5	1	1	0	7	
1965	5	8	1	3	3	1	2	5	
1966	6	6	2	4	3		2	3	2
1967	8	5	1	4	2	1	4	3	
1968	11	3		6	1		5	2	
1969	10	4		5	2		5	2	
1970	4	10		2	5		2	5	
1971	6	8		4	3		2	5	
1972	7	7		4	3		3	4	
1973	4	10		2	4		2	6	
1974	7	7		3	4		4	3	
1975	3	11		1	6		2	5	
1976	3	11		2	5		1	6	
1977	3	11		1	6		2	5	
1978	8	8		4	4		4	4	
1979	8	8		6	2		2	6	
Season	W	L	T	W	L	T	W	L	T
1980	4	12		2	6		2	6	
1981	10	5	1	6	2		4	3	1
1982	6	3		3	1		3	2	
1983	7	9		2	6		5	3	
1984	7	9		3	5		4	4	
1985	11	5		7	1		4	4	
1986	10	6		5	3		5	3	
1987	6	9		4	4		2	5	
1988	8	7	1	5	2	1	3	5	
1989	4	12		1	7		3	5	
1990	6	10		3	5		3	5	
1991	8	8		4	4		4	4	
1992	4	12		3	5		1	7	
1993	8	8		3	5		5	3	
1994	6	10		4	4		2	6	
1995	3	13		2	6		1	7	
1996	1	15		0	8		1	7	
1997	9	7		5	3		4	4	
1998	12	4		7	1		5	3	
1999	8	8		4	4		4	4	
	260	328	8	143	149	5	117	179	3

**includes New York Titans (1960-62).*

OAKLAND RAIDERS*

	All Games			Home Games			Road Games		
Season	W	L	T	W	L	T	W	L	T
1960	6	8		3	4		3	4	
1961	2	12		1	6		1	6	
1962	1	13		1	6		0	7	
1963	10	4		6	1		4	3	
1964	5	7	2	5	2		0	5	2
1965	8	5	1	5	2		3	3	1
1966	8	5	1	3	3	1	5	2	
1967	13	1		7	0		6	1	
1968	12	2		6	1		6	1	
1969	12	1	1	7	0		5	1	1
1970	8	4	2	6	1		2	3	2
1971	8	4	2	5	1	1	3	3	1
1972	10	3	1	5	1	1	5	2	
1973	9	4	1	5	2		4	2	1
1974	12	2		6	1		6	1	
1975	11	3		6	1		5	2	
1976	13	1		7	0		6	1	
1977	11	3		6	1		5	2	
1978	9	7		4	4		5	3	
1979	9	7		6	2		3	5	
1980	11	5		6	2		5	3	
1981	7	9		4	4		3	5	
1982	8	1		4	0		4	1	
1983	12	4		6	2		6	2	
1984	11	5		6	2		5	3	
1985	12	4		7	1		5	3	
1986	8	8		3	5		5	3	
1987	5	10		3	5		2	5	
1988	7	9		3	5		4	4	
1989	8	8		7	1		1	7	
1990	12	4		6	2		6	2	
1991	9	7		5	3		4	4	
1992	7	9		5	3		2	6	
1993	10	6		5	3		5	3	
1994	9	7		4	4		5	3	
1995	8	8		4	4		4	4	
1996	7	9		4	4		3	5	
1997	4	12		2	6		2	6	
1998	8	8		4	4		4	4	
1999	8	8		5	3		3	5	
	348	237	11	193	102	3	155	135	8

**includes Los Angeles Raiders (1982-94).*

PITTSBURGH STEELERS*

	All Games			Home Games			Road Games		
Season	W	L	T	W	L	T	W	L	T
1933	3	6	2	2	3		1	3	2
1934	2	10		1	5		1	5	
1935	4	8		2	5		2	3	
1936	6	6		4	1		2	5	
1937	4	7		2	4		2	3	
1938	2	9		0	5		2	4	
1939	1	9	1	1	4		0	5	1
1940	2	7	2	1	2	2	1	5	
1941	1	9	1	1	4		0	5	1

INSIDE THE NUMBERS

Season	All Games W	L	T	Home Games W	L	T	Road Games W	L	T
1942	7	4		3	2		4	2	
1945	2	8		1	4		1	4	
1946	5	5	1	4	1		1	4	1
1947	8	4		5	1		3	3	
1948	4	8		4	2		0	6	
1949	6	5	1	3	2	1	3	3	
1950	6	6		2	4		4	2	
1951	4	7	1	1	4	1	3	3	
1952	5	7		2	4		3	3	
1953	6	6		3	3		3	3	
1954	5	7		4	2		1	5	
1955	4	8		3	2		1	6	
1956	5	7		3	3		2	4	
1957	6	6		4	2		2	4	
1958	7	4	1	5	1		2	3	1
1959	6	5	1	3	2	1	3	3	
1960	5	6	1	4	2		1	4	1
1961	6	8		4	3		2	5	
1962	9	5		4	3		5	2	
1963	7	4	3	5	0	2	2	4	1
1964	5	9		2	5		3	4	
1965	2	12		1	6		1	6	
1966	5	8	1	3	3	1	2	5	
1967	4	9	1	1	6		3	3	1
1968	2	11	1	1	6		1	5	1
1969	1	13		1	6		0	7	
1970	5	9		4	3		1	6	
1971	6	8		5	2		1	6	
1972	11	3		7	0		4	3	
1973	10	4		7	1		3	3	
1974	10	3	1	5	2		5	1	1
1975	12	2		6	1		6	1	
1976	10	4		6	1		4	3	
1977	9	5		6	1		3	4	
1978	14	2		7	1		7	1	
1979	12	4		8	0		4	4	
1980	9	7		6	2		3	5	
1981	8	8		5	3		3	5	
1982	6	3		4	0		2	3	
1983	10	6		4	4		6	2	
1984	9	7		6	2		3	5	
1985	7	9		5	3		2	6	
1986	6	10		4	4		2	6	
1987	8	7		4	3		4	4	
1988	5	11		4	4		1	7	
1989	9	7		4	4		5	3	
1990	9	7		6	2		3	5	
1991	7	9		5	3		2	6	
1992	11	5		7	1		4	4	
1993	9	7		6	2		3	5	
1994	12	4		7	1		5	3	
1995	11	5		6	2		5	3	
1996	10	6		7	1		3	5	
1997	11	5		7	1		4	4	
1998	7	9		5	3		2	6	
1999	6	10		2	6		4	4	
	426	439	19	255	175	8	171	264	11

**includes Pittsburgh Pirates (1933-40).*

SAN DIEGO CHARGERS*

Season	All Games W	L	T	Home Games W	L	T	Road Games W	L	T
1960	10	4		5	2		5	2	
1961	12	2		6	1		6	1	
1962	4	10		3	4		1	6	
1963	11	3		6	1		5	2	
1964	8	5	1	4	3		4	2	1
1965	9	2	3	4	1	2	5	1	1
1966	7	6	1	5	2		2	4	1
1967	8	5	1	5	2	1	3	3	
1968	9	5		4	3		5	2	
1969	8	6		5	2		3	4	
1970	5	6	3	2	3	2	3	3	1
1971	6	8		6	1		0	7	
1972	4	9	1	2	5		2	4	1
1973	2	11	1	2	5		0	6	1
1974	5	9		3	4		2	5	
1975	2	12		1	6		1	6	
1976	6	8		3	4		3	4	
1977	7	7		3	4		4	3	
1978	9	7		5	3		4	4	
1979	12	4		7	1		5	3	
1980	11	5		6	2		5	3	
1981	10	6		5	3		5	3	
1982	6	3		3	1		3	2	
1983	6	10		4	4		2	6	
1984	7	9		4	4		3	5	
1985	8	8		6	2		2	6	
1986	4	12		2	6		2	6	
1987	8	7		4	3		4	4	
1988	6	10		3	5		3	5	
1989	6	10		4	4		2	6	
1990	6	10		3	5		3	5	
1991	4	12		3	5		1	7	
1992	11	5		6	2		5	3	
1993	8	8		4	4		4	4	
1994	11	5		5	3		6	2	
1995	9	7		5	3		4	4	
1996	8	8		5	3		3	5	
1997	4	12		2	6		2	6	
1998	5	11		4	4		1	7	
1999	8	8		4	4		4	4	
	290	295	11	163	130	5	127	165	6

**includes Los Angeles Chargers (1960).*

SEATTLE SEAHAWKS

Season	All Games W	L	T	Home Games W	L	T	Road Games W	L	T
1976	2	12		1	6		1	6	
1977	5	9		3	4		2	5	
1978	9	7		5	3		4	4	
1979	9	7		5	3		4	4	
1980	4	12		0	8		4	4	
1981	6	10		5	3		1	7	
1982	4	5		3	2		1	3	
1983	9	7		5	3		4	4	
1984	12	4		7	1		5	3	
1985	8	8		5	3		3	5	
1986	10	6		7	1		3	5	
1987	9	6		6	2		3	4	
1988	9	7		5	3		4	4	
1989	7	9		3	5		4	4	
1990	9	7		5	3		4	4	
1991	7	9		5	3		2	6	
1992	2	14		1	7		1	7	
1993	6	10		4	4		2	6	
1994	6	10		3	5		3	5	
1995	8	8		5	3		3	5	
1996	7	9		4	4		3	5	
1997	8	8		4	4		4	4	
1998	8	8		6	2		2	6	
1999	9	7		5	3		4	4	
	173	199		102	85		71	114	

TENNESSEE TITANS*

Season	All Games W	L	T	Home Games W	L	T	Road Games W	L	T
1960	10	4		6	1		4	3	
1961	10	3	1	6	1		4	2	1
1962	11	3		6	1		5	2	
1963	6	8		4	3		2	5	
1964	4	10		3	4		1	6	
1965	4	10		3	4		1	6	
1966	3	11		3	4		0	7	
1967	9	4	1	5	2		4	2	1
1968	7	7		3	4		4	3	
1969	6	6	2	4	2	1	2	4	1
1970	3	10	1	1	6		2	4	1
1971	4	9	1	3	3	1	1	6	
1972	1	13		1	6		0	7	
1973	1	13		0	7		1	6	
1974	7	7		3	4		4	3	
1975	10	4		5	2		5	2	
1976	5	9		3	4		2	5	
1977	8	6		5	2		3	4	
1978	10	6		5	3		5	3	
1979	11	5		6	2		5	3	
1980	11	5		6	2		5	3	
1981	7	9		5	3		2	6	
1982	1	8		1	4		0	4	
1983	2	14		2	6		0	8	
1984	3	13		2	6		1	7	
1985	5	11		4	4		1	7	
1986	5	11		4	4		1	7	
1987	9	6		5	2		4	4	
1988	10	6		7	1		3	5	
1989	9	7		6	2		3	5	
1990	9	7		6	2		3	5	
1991	11	5		7	1		4	4	
1992	10	6		5	3		5	3	
1993	12	4		7	1		5	3	
1994	2	14		2	6		0	8	
1995	7	9		3	5		4	4	
1996	8	8		2	6		6	2	
1997	8	8		6	2		2	6	
1998	8	8		3	5		5	3	
1999	13	3		8	0		5	3	
	280	310	6	166	130	2	114	180	4

**includes Houston Oilers (1960-96) and Tennessee Oilers (1997-98).*

NFC

ARIZONA CARDINALS*

Season	All Games W	L	T	Home Games W	L	T	Road Games W	L	T
1920	6	2	2	5	1	1	1	1	1
1921	3	3	2	3	3	1	0	0	1
1922	8	3		8	3		0	0	
1923	8	4		8	3		0	1	
1924	5	4	1	5	3	1	0	1	
1925	11	2	1	11	2		0	0	1
1926	5	6	1	3	3		2	3	1
1927	3	7	1	2	3	1	1	4	
1928	1	5		1	1		0	4	
1929	6	6	1	3	2		3	4	1
1930	5	6	2	3	2		2	4	2
1931	5	4		3	0		2	4	
1932	2	6	2	1	2	1	1	4	1
1933	1	9	1	0	4	1	1	5	
1934	5	6		2	2		3	4	
1935	6	4	2	2	2		4	2	2
1936	3	8	1	3	1	1	0	7	
1937	5	5	1	1	3		4	2	1
1938	2	9		1	4		1	5	
1939	1	10		0	4		1	6	
1940	2	7	2	2	1	1	0	6	1
1941	3	7	1	0	3	1	3	4	
1942	3	8		2	2		1	6	
1943	0	10		0	3		0	7	
1945	1	9		0	3		1	6	
1946	6	5		2	2		4	3	
1947	9	3		5	0		4	3	
1948	11	1		5	1		6	0	
1949	6	5	1	2	3	1	4	2	
1950	5	7		3	3		2	4	
1951	3	9		1	5		2	4	
1952	4	8		2	4		2	4	
1953	1	10	1	0	5	1	1	5	
1954	2	10		2	4		0	6	
1955	4	7	1	3	2	1	1	5	
1956	7	5		4	2		3	3	
1957	3	9		0	6		3	3	
1958	2	9	1	1	4	1	1	5	
1959	2	10		2	4		0	6	
1960	6	5	1	3	2	1	3	3	
1961	7	7		3	4		4	3	
1962	4	9	1	2	4	1	2	5	
1963	9	5		3	4		6	1	
1964	9	3	2	4	1	1	5	2	1
1965	5	9		2	5		3	4	
1966	8	5	1	5	1	1	3	4	
1967	6	7	1	3	3	1	3	4	
1968	9	4	1	4	2	1	5	2	
1969	4	9	1	3	4		1	5	1
1970	8	5	1	6	1		2	4	1
1971	4	9	1	1	5	1	3	4	
1972	4	9	1	2	5		2	4	1
1973	4	9	1	2	4	1	2	5	
1974	10	4		5	2		5	2	
1975	11	3		6	1		5	2	
1976	10	4		6	1		4	3	
1977	7	7		4	3		3	4	
1978	6	10		3	5		3	5	

Season	All Games W	L	T	Home Games W	L	T	Road Games W	L	T
1979	5	11		3	5		2	6	
1980	5	11		2	6		3	5	
1981	7	9		5	3		2	6	
1982	5	4		1	3		4	1	
1983	8	7	1	4	3	1	4	4	
1984	9	7		5	3		4	4	
1985	5	11		4	4		1	7	
1986	4	11	1	3	5		1	6	1
1987	7	8		4	3		3	5	
1988	7	9		4	4		3	5	
1989	5	11		2	6		3	5	
1990	5	11		3	5		2	6	
1991	4	12		2	6		2	6	
1992	4	12		3	5		1	7	
1993	7	9		4	4		3	5	
1994	8	8		5	3		3	5	
1995	4	12		3	5		1	7	
1996	7	9		5	3		2	6	
1997	4	12		3	5		1	7	
1998	9	7		5	3		4	4	
1999	6	10		4	4		2	6	
	421	572	39	242	250	22	179	322	17

**includes Chicago Cardinals (1920-59), St. Louis Cardinals (1960-87), and Phoenix Cardinals (1988-93).*

ATLANTA FALCONS

Season	All Games W	L	T	Home Games W	L	T	Road Games W	L	T
1966	3	11		1	6		2	5	
1967	1	12	1	1	5	1	0	7	
1968	2	12		1	6		1	6	
1969	6	8		4	3		2	5	
1970	4	8	2	3	4		1	4	2
1971	7	6	1	4	3		3	3	1
1972	7	7		4	3		3	4	
1973	9	5		4	3		5	2	
1974	3	11		2	5		1	6	
1975	4	10		3	4		1	6	
1976	4	10		3	4		1	6	
1977	7	7		4	3		3	4	
1978	9	7		7	1		2	6	
1979	6	10		3	5		3	5	
1980	12	4		6	2		6	2	
1981	7	9		4	4		3	5	
1982	5	4		2	3		3	1	
1983	7	9		4	4		3	5	
1984	4	12		2	6		2	6	
1985	4	12		3	5		1	7	
1986	7	8	1	2	5	1	5	3	
1987	3	12		2	6		1	6	
1988	5	11		2	6		3	5	
1989	3	13		3	5		0	8	
1990	5	11		5	3		0	8	
1991	10	6		6	2		4	4	
1992	6	10		5	3		1	7	
1993	6	10		4	4		2	6	
1994	7	9		5	3		2	6	
1995	9	7		7	1		2	6	
1996	3	13		2	6		1	7	
1997	7	9		3	5		4	4	
1998	14	2		8	0		6	2	
1999	5	11		4	4		1	7	
	201	306	5	123	132	2	78	174	3

CAROLINA PANTHERS

Season	W	L	T	W	L	T	W	L	T
1995	7	9		5	3		2	6	
1996	12	4		8	0		4	4	
1997	7	9		2	6		5	3	
1998	4	12		2	6		2	6	
1999	8	8		5	3		3	5	
	38	42		22	18		16	24	

CHICAGO BEARS*

Season	All Games W	L	T	Home Games W	L	T	Road Games W	L	T
1920	10	1	2	6	0	1	4	1	1
1921	9	1	1	9	1	1	0	0	
1922	9	3		7	1		2	2	
1923	9	2	1	7	1	1	2	1	

Season	All Games W	L	T	Home Games W	L	T	Road Games W	L	T
1924	6	1	4	5	0	3	1	1	1
1925	9	5	3	7	1	1	2	4	2
1926	12	1	3	10	0	2	2	1	1
1927	9	3	2	7	1	1	2	2	1
1928	7	5	1	6	3		1	2	1
1929	4	9	2	1	5	2	3	4	
1930	9	4	1	5	2	1	4	2	
1931	8	5		6	3		2	2	
1932	7	1	6	6	1	1	1	0	5
1933	10	2	1	6	0		4	2	1
1934	13	0		5	0		8	0	
1935	6	4	2	1	2	2	5	2	
1936	9	3		3	1		6	2	
1937	9	1	1	4	1		5	0	1
1938	6	5		2	3		4	2	
1939	8	3		4	1		4	2	
1940	8	3		5	0		3	3	
1941	10	1		5	1		5	0	
1942	11	0		6	0		5	0	
1943	8	1	1	5	0		3	1	1
1944	6	3	1	4	0	1	2	3	
1945	3	7		2	3		1	4	
1946	8	2	1	4	1	1	4	1	
1947	8	4		4	2		4	2	
1948	10	2		5	1		5	1	
1949	9	3		5	1		4	2	
1950	9	3		6	0		3	3	
1951	7	5		3	3		4	2	
1952	5	7		3	3		2	4	
1953	3	8	1	1	4	1	2	4	
1954	8	4		4	2		4	2	
1955	8	4		5	1		3	3	
1956	9	2	1	6	0		3	2	1
1957	5	7		2	4		3	3	
1958	8	4		5	1		3	3	
1959	8	4		4	2		4	2	
1960	5	6	1	4	2		1	4	1
1961	8	6		5	2		3	4	
1962	9	5		4	3		5	2	
1963	11	1	2	6	0	1	5	1	1
1964	5	9		2	5		3	4	
1965	9	5		5	2		4	3	
1966	5	7	2	4	1	2	1	6	
1967	7	6	1	3	3	1	4	3	
1968	7	7		2	5		5	2	
1969	1	13		1	6		0	7	
1970	6	8		3	4		3	4	
1971	6	8		4	3		2	5	
1972	4	9	1	1	5	1	3	4	
1973	3	11		1	6		2	5	
1974	4	10		4	3		0	7	
1975	4	10		3	4		1	6	
1976	7	7		4	3		3	4	
1977	9	5		5	2		4	3	
1978	7	9		4	4		3	5	
1979	10	6		6	2		4	4	
1980	7	9		5	3		2	6	
1981	6	10		4	4		2	6	
1982	3	6		2	2		1	4	
1983	8	8		5	3		3	5	
1984	10	6		6	2		4	4	
1985	15	1		8	0		7	1	
1986	14	2		7	1		7	1	
1987	11	4		6	2		5	2	
1988	12	4		7	1		5	3	
1989	6	10		4	4		2	6	
1990	11	5		7	1		4	4	
1991	11	5		6	2		5	3	
1992	5	11		4	4		1	7	
1993	7	9		3	5		4	4	
1994	9	7		5	3		4	4	
1995	9	7		5	3		4	4	
1996	7	9		6	2		1	7	
1997	4	12		2	6		2	6	
1998	4	12		3	5		1	7	
1999	6	10		3	5		3	5	
	612	428	42	360	179	24	252	249	18

**includes Decatur Staleys (1920) and Chicago Staleys (1921).*

DALLAS COWBOYS

Season	All Games W	L	T	Home Games W	L	T	Road Games W	L	T
1960	0	11	1	0	6		0	5	1
1961	4	9	1	2	4	1	2	5	
1962	5	8	1	2	4	1	3	4	
1963	4	10		3	4		1	6	
1964	5	8	1	2	4	1	3	4	
1965	7	7		5	2		2	5	
1966	10	3	1	6	1		4	2	1
1967	9	5		5	2		4	3	
1968	12	2		5	2		7	0	
1969	11	2	1	6	0	1	5	2	
1970	10	4		6	1		4	3	
1971	11	3		6	1		5	2	
1972	10	4		5	2		5	2	
1973	10	4		6	1		4	3	
1974	8	6		5	2		3	4	
1975	10	4		5	2		5	2	
1976	11	3		6	1		5	2	
1977	12	2		6	1		6	1	
1978	12	4		7	1		5	3	
1979	11	5		6	2		5	3	
1980	12	4		8	0		4	4	
1981	12	4		8	0		4	4	
1982	6	3		3	2		3	1	
1983	12	4		6	2		6	2	
1984	9	7		5	3		4	4	
1985	10	6		7	1		3	5	
1986	7	9		3	5		4	4	
1987	7	8		3	4		4	4	
1988	3	13		1	7		2	6	
1989	1	15		0	8		1	7	
1990	7	9		5	3		2	6	
1991	11	5		6	2		5	3	
1992	13	3		7	1		6	2	
1993	12	4		6	2		6	2	
1994	12	4		6	2		6	2	
1995	12	4		6	2		6	2	
1996	10	6		6	2		4	4	
1997	6	10		5	3		1	7	
1998	10	6		6	2		4	4	
1999	8	8		7	1		1	7	
	352	236	6	198	95	4	154	141	2

DETROIT LIONS*

Season	All Games W	L	T	Home Games W	L	T	Road Games W	L	T
1930	5	6	3	5	1	2	0	5	1
1931	11	3		8	0		3	3	
1932	6	2	4	3	0	2	3	2	2
1933	6	5		4	1		2	4	
1934	10	3		6	2		4	1	
1935	7	3	2	5	0	1	2	3	1
1936	8	4		5	1		3	3	
1937	7	4		4	2		3	2	
1938	7	4		4	3		3	1	
1939	6	5		4	2		2	3	
1940	5	5	1	3	3		2	2	1
1941	4	6	1	3	2		1	4	1
1942	0	11		0	7		0	4	
1943	3	6	1	2	2	1	1	4	
1944	6	3	1	4	2		2	1	1
1945	7	3		4	1		3	2	
1946	1	10		1	5		0	5	
1947	3	9		2	4		1	5	
1948	2	10		2	4		0	6	
1949	4	8		2	4		2	4	
1950	6	6		4	2		2	4	
1951	7	4	1	3	3	1	4	1	
1952	9	3		6	1		3	2	
1953	10	2		5	1		5	1	
1954	9	2	1	5	0	1	4	2	
1955	3	9		3	4		0	5	
1956	9	3		5	1		4	2	
1957	8	4		5	1		3	3	
1958	4	7	1	2	4		2	3	1
1959	3	8	1	2	4		1	4	1
1960	7	5		5	1		2	4	
1961	8	5	1	2	5		6	0	1
1962	11	3		7	0		4	3	
1963	5	8	1	3	3	1	2	5	
1964	7	5	2	3	3	1	4	2	1

	All Games			Home Games			Road Games		
Season	W	L	T	W	L	T	W	L	T
1965	6	7	1	2	4	1	4	3	
1966	4	9	1	3	4		1	5	1
1967	5	7	2	3	4		2	3	2
1968	4	8	2	1	4	2	3	4	
1969	9	4	1	5	2		4	2	1
1970	10	4		6	1		4	3	
1971	7	6	1	3	4		4	2	1
1972	8	5	1	5	2		3	3	1
1973	6	7	1	4	3		2	4	1
1974	7	7		5	2		2	5	
1975	7	7		4	3		3	4	
1976	6	8		5	2		1	6	
1977	6	8		5	2		1	6	
1978	7	9		5	3		2	6	
1979	2	14		2	6		0	8	
1980	9	7		6	2		3	5	
1981	8	8		7	1		1	7	
1982	4	5		2	3		2	2	
1983	9	7		6	2		3	5	
1984	4	11	1	2	5	1	2	6	
1985	7	9		6	2		1	7	
1986	5	11		1	7		4	4	
1987	4	11		1	6		3	5	
1988	4	12		2	6		2	6	
1989	7	9		4	4		3	5	
1990	6	10		3	5		3	5	
1991	12	4		8	0		4	4	
1992	5	11		3	5		2	6	
1993	10	6		5	3		5	3	
1994	9	7		6	2		3	5	
1995	10	6		7	1		3	5	
1996	5	11		4	4		1	7	
1997	9	7		6	2		3	5	
1998	5	11		4	4		1	7	
1999	8	8		6	2		2	6	
	448	465	32	278	191	14	170	274	18

includes Portsmouth Spartans (1930-33).

GREEN BAY PACKERS

	All Games			Home Games			Road Games		
Season	W	L	T	W	L	T	W	L	T
1921	3	2	1	2	1		1	1	1
1922	4	3	3	4	1	1	0	2	2
1923	7	2	1	4	2	1	3	0	
1924	7	4		5	0		2	4	
1925	8	5		6	0		2	5	
1926	7	3	3	4	1	2	3	2	1
1927	7	2	1	6	1		1	1	1
1928	6	4	3	2	2	2	4	2	1
1929	12	0	1	5	0		7	0	1
1930	10	3	1	6	0		4	3	1
1931	12	2		8	0		4	2	
1932	10	3	1	5	0	1	5	3	
1933	5	7	1	3	2	1	2	5	
1934	7	6		4	2		3	4	
1935	8	4		5	2		3	2	
1936	10	1	1	5	1		5	0	1
1937	7	4		3	2		4	2	
1938	8	3		4	2		4	1	
1939	9	2		4	1		5	1	
1940	6	4	1	4	2		2	2	1
1941	10	1		4	1		6	0	
1942	8	2	1	4	1		4	1	1
1943	7	2	1	2	1	1	5	1	
1944	8	2		5	0		3	2	
1945	6	4		4	1		2	3	
1946	6	5		2	3		4	2	
1947	6	5	1	4	2		2	3	1
1948	3	9		2	4		1	5	
1949	2	10		1	5		1	5	
1950	3	9		3	3		0	6	
1951	3	9		2	4		1	5	
1952	6	6		3	3		3	3	
1953	2	9	1	1	5		1	4	1
1954	4	8		2	4		2	4	
1955	6	6		5	1		1	5	
1956	4	8		2	4		2	4	
1957	3	9		1	5		2	4	
1958	1	10	1	1	4	1	0	6	
1959	7	5		4	2		3	3	
1960	8	4		4	2		4	2	

	All Games			Home Games			Road Games		
Season	W	L	T	W	L	T	W	L	T
1961	11	3		6	1		5	2	
1962	13	1		7	0		6	1	
1963	11	2	1	6	1		5	1	1
1964	8	5	1	4	3		4	2	1
1965	10	3	1	6	1		4	2	1
1966	12	2		6	1		6	1	
1967	9	4	1	4	2	1	5	2	
1968	6	7	1	2	5		4	2	1
1969	8	6		5	2		3	4	
1970	6	8		4	3		2	5	
1971	4	8	2	3	3	1	1	5	1
1972	10	4		4	3		6	1	
1973	5	7	2	3	2	2	2	5	
1974	6	8		4	3		2	5	
1975	4	10		3	4		1	6	
1976	5	9		4	3		1	6	
1977	4	10		2	5		2	5	
1978	8	7	1	5	2	1	3	5	
1979	5	11		4	4		1	7	
1980	5	10	1	4	4		1	6	1
1981	8	8		4	4		4	4	
1982	5	3	1	3	1		2	2	1
1983	8	8		5	3		3	5	
1984	8	8		5	3		3	5	
1985	8	8		5	3		3	5	
1986	4	12		1	7		3	5	
1987	5	9	1	2	5	1	3	4	
1988	4	12		2	6		2	6	
1989	10	6		6	2		4	4	
1990	6	10		3	5		3	5	
1991	4	12		2	6		2	6	
1992	9	7		6	2		3	5	
1993	9	7		6	2		3	5	
1994	9	7		7	1		2	6	
1995	11	5		7	1		4	4	
1996	13	3		8	0		5	3	
1997	13	3		8	0		5	3	
1998	11	5		7	1		4	4	
1999	8	8		5	3		3	5	
	559	453	36	323	184	16	236	269	20

MINNESOTA VIKINGS

	All Games			Home Games			Road Games		
Season	W	L	T	W	L	T	W	L	T
1961	3	11		3	4		0	7	
1962	2	11	1	1	5	1	1	6	
1963	5	8	1	3	4		2	4	1
1964	8	5	1	4	3		4	2	1
1965	7	7		2	5		5	2	
1966	4	9	1	2	5		2	4	1
1967	3	8	3	1	4	2	2	4	1
1968	8	6		4	3		4	3	
1969	12	2		7	0		5	2	
1970	12	2		7	0		5	2	
1971	11	3		5	2		6	1	
1972	7	7		3	4		4	3	
1973	12	2		7	0		5	2	
1974	10	4		4	3		6	1	
1975	12	2		7	0		5	2	
1976	11	2	1	6	0	1	5	2	
1977	9	5		5	2		4	3	
1978	8	7	1	5	3		3	4	1
1979	7	9		5	3		2	6	
1980	9	7		5	3		4	4	
1981	7	9		5	3		2	6	
1982	5	4		4	1		1	3	
1983	8	8		3	5		5	3	
1984	3	13		2	6		1	7	
1985	7	9		4	4		3	5	
1986	9	7		5	3		4	4	
1987	8	7		5	3		3	4	
1988	11	5		7	1		4	4	
1989	10	6		8	0		2	6	
1990	6	10		4	4		2	6	
1991	8	8		4	4		4	4	
1992	11	5		5	3		6	2	
1993	9	7		4	4		5	3	
1994	10	6		6	2		4	4	
1995	8	8		6	2		2	6	
1996	9	7		5	3		4	4	
1997	9	7		5	3		4	4	

	All Games			Home Games			Road Games		
Season	W	L	T	W	L	T	W	L	T
1998	15	1		8	0		7	1	
1999	10	6		6	2		4	4	
	323	250	9	182	106	4	141	144	5

NEW ORLEANS SAINTS

	All Games			Home Games			Road Games		
Season	W	L	T	W	L	T	W	L	T
1967	3	11		2	5		1	6	
1968	4	9	1	3	4		1	5	1
1969	5	9		3	4		2	5	
1970	2	11	1	2	5		0	6	1
1971	4	8	2	2	4	1	2	4	1
1972	2	11	1	2	5		0	6	1
1973	5	9		5	2		0	7	
1974	5	9		4	3		1	6	
1975	2	12		2	5		0	7	
1976	4	10		2	5		2	5	
1977	3	11		2	5		1	6	
1978	7	9		3	5		4	4	
1979	8	8		3	5		5	3	
1980	1	15		0	8		1	7	
1981	4	12		2	6		2	6	
1982	4	5		2	3		2	2	
1983	8	8		5	3		3	5	
1984	7	9		3	5		4	4	
1985	5	11		3	5		2	6	
1986	7	9		4	4		3	5	
1987	12	3		6	1		6	2	
1988	10	6		5	3		5	3	
1989	9	7		5	3		4	4	
1990	8	8		5	3		3	5	
1991	11	5		6	2		5	3	
1992	12	4		6	2		6	2	
1993	8	8		4	4		4	4	
1994	7	9		3	5		4	4	
1995	7	9		4	4		3	5	
1996	3	13		2	6		1	7	
1997	6	10		3	5		3	5	
1998	6	10		4	4		2	6	
1999	3	13		3	5		0	8	
	192	301	5	110	138	1	82	163	4

NEW YORK GIANTS

	All Games			Home Games			Road Games		
Season	W	L	T	W	L	T	W	L	T
1925	8	4		7	2		1	2	
1926	8	4	1	5	2	1	3	2	
1927	11	1	1	7	1		4	0	1
1928	4	7	2	1	2	2	3	5	
1929	13	1	1	7	1		6	0	1
1930	13	4		6	2		7	2	
1931	7	6	1	4	2	1	3	4	
1932	4	6	2	3	2	1	1	4	1
1933	11	3		7	0		4	3	
1934	8	5		5	1		3	4	
1935	9	3		4	2		5	1	
1936	5	6	1	3	3	1	2	3	
1937	6	3	2	4	2	1	2	1	1
1938	8	2	1	6	1		2	1	1
1939	9	1	1	6	0		3	1	1
1940	6	4	1	4	3		2	1	1
1941	8	3		5	2		3	1	
1942	5	5	1	3	2	1	2	3	
1943	6	3	1	4	2		2	1	1
1944	8	1	1	5	1		3	0	1
1945	3	6	1	2	4		1	2	1
1946	7	3	1	5	1	1	2	2	
1947	2	8	2	2	3	1	0	5	1
1948	4	8		2	4		2	4	
1949	6	6		2	4		4	2	
1950	10	2		5	1		5	1	
1951	9	2	1	5	1		4	1	1
1952	7	5		2	4		5	1	
1953	3	9		2	4		1	5	
1954	7	5		4	2		3	3	
1955	6	5	1	4	1	1	2	4	
1956	8	3	1	4	1	1	4	2	
1957	7	5		3	3		4	2	
1958	9	3		5	1		4	2	
1959	10	2		5	1		5	1	
1960	6	4	2	1	3	2	5	1	

	All Games			Home Games			Road Games		
Season	W	L	T	W	L	T	W	L	T
1961	10	3	1	4	2	1	6	1	
1962	12	2		6	1		6	1	
1963	11	3		5	2		6	1	
1964	2	10	2	2	5		0	5	2
1965	7	7		3	4		4	3	
1966	1	12	1	1	6		0	6	1
1967	7	7		5	2		2	5	
1968	7	7		3	4		4	3	
1969	6	8		5	2		1	6	
1970	9	5		5	2		4	3	
1971	4	10		1	6		3	4	
1972	8	6		4	3		4	3	
1973	2	11	1	2	4	1	0	7	
1974	2	12		0	7		2	5	
1975	5	9		2	5		3	4	
1976	3	11		3	4		0	7	
1977	5	9		3	4		2	5	
1978	6	10		5	3		1	7	
1979	6	10		4	4		2	6	
1980	4	12		2	6		2	6	
1981	9	7		4	4		5	3	
1982	4	5		2	3		2	2	
1983	3	12	1	1	7		2	5	1
1984	9	7		6	2		3	5	
1985	10	6		6	2		4	4	
1986	14	2		8	0		6	2	
1987	6	9		5	3		1	6	
1988	10	6		5	3		5	3	
1989	12	4		7	1		5	3	
1990	13	3		7	1		6	2	
1991	8	8		5	3		3	5	
1992	6	10		4	4		2	6	
1993	11	5		6	2		5	3	
1994	9	7		4	4		5	3	
1995	5	11		3	5		2	6	
1996	6	10		3	5		3	5	
1997	10	5	1	6	2		4	3	1
1998	8	8		5	3		3	5	
1999	7	9		4	4		3	5	
	538	446	33	305	205	16	233	241	17

PHILADELPHIA EAGLES

	All Games			Home Games			Road Games		
Season	W	L	T	W	L	T	W	L	T
1933	3	5	1	2	3	1	1	2	
1934	4	7		2	4		2	3	
1935	2	9		0	5		2	4	
1936	1	11		1	6		0	5	
1937	2	8	1	0	5	1	2	3	
1938	5	6		2	3		3	3	
1939	1	9	1	1	3	1	0	6	
1940	1	10		1	4		0	6	
1941	2	8	1	1	4	1	1	4	
1942	2	9		0	5		2	4	
1944	7	1	2	3	1	2	4	0	
1945	7	3		6	0		1	3	
1946	6	5		3	2		3	3	
1947	8	4		6	1		2	3	
1948	9	2	1	6	0		3	2	1
1949	11	1		6	0		5	1	
1950	6	6		2	4		4	2	
1951	4	8		1	5		3	3	
1952	7	5		4	2		3	3	
1953	7	4	1	5	0	1	2	4	
1954	7	4	1	5	1		2	3	1
1955	4	7	1	4	2		0	5	1
1956	3	8	1	2	3	1	1	5	
1957	4	8		3	3		1	5	
1958	2	9	1	2	4		0	5	1
1959	7	5		5	1		2	4	
1960	10	2		5	1		5	1	
1961	10	4		5	2		5	2	
1962	3	10	1	2	5		1	5	1
1963	2	10	2	1	5	1	1	5	1
1964	6	8		3	4		3	4	
1965	5	9		2	5		3	4	
1966	9	5		5	2		4	3	
1967	6	7	1	5	2		1	5	1
1968	2	12		1	6		1	6	
1969	4	9	1	2	5		2	4	1
1970	3	10	1	3	3	1	0	7	
1971	6	7	1	3	4		3	3	1
1972	2	11	1	0	6	1	2	5	
1973	5	8	1	4	3		1	5	1
1974	7	7		5	2		2	5	
1975	4	10		2	5		2	5	
1976	4	10		2	5		2	5	
1977	5	9		4	3		1	6	
1978	9	7		5	3		4	4	
1979	11	5		5	3		6	2	
1980	12	4		7	1		5	3	
1981	10	6		6	2		4	4	
1982	3	6		1	4		2	2	
1983	5	11		1	7		4	4	
1984	6	9	1	5	3		1	6	1
1985	7	9		4	4		3	5	
1986	5	10	1	2	5	1	3	5	
1987	7	8		4	4		3	4	
1988	10	6		5	3		5	3	
1989	11	5		6	2		5	3	
1990	10	6		6	2		4	4	
1991	10	6		4	4		6	2	
1992	11	5		8	0		3	5	
1993	8	8		3	5		5	3	
1994	7	9		5	3		2	6	
1995	10	6		6	2		4	4	
1996	10	6		5	3		5	3	
1997	6	9	1	6	2		0	7	1
1998	3	13		3	5		0	8	
1999	5	11		4	4		1	7	
	391	475	24	228	210	12	163	265	12

ST. LOUIS RAMS*

	All Games			Home Games			Road Games		
Season	W	L	T	W	L	T	W	L	T
1937	1	10		0	5		1	5	
1938	4	7		2	2		2	5	
1939	5	5	1	3	2	1	2	3	
1940	4	6	1	3	1	1	1	5	
1941	2	9		1	4		1	5	
1942	5	6		3	2		2	4	
1944	4	6		1	2		3	4	
1945	9	1		4	0		5	1	
1946	6	4	1	3	2		3	2	1
1947	6	6		3	3		3	3	
1948	6	5	1	3	2	1	3	3	
1949	8	2	2	5	1		3	1	2
1950	9	3		5	1		4	2	
1951	8	4		5	2		3	2	
1952	9	3		5	1		4	2	
1953	8	3	1	5	1		3	2	1
1954	6	5	1	3	2	1	3	3	
1955	8	3	1	5	1		3	2	1
1956	4	8		4	2		0	6	
1957	6	6		5	1		1	5	
1958	8	4		4	2		4	2	
1959	2	10		0	6		2	4	
1960	4	7	1	2	3	1	2	4	
1961	4	10		4	3		0	7	
1962	1	12	1	0	7		1	5	1
1963	5	9		3	4		2	5	
1964	5	7	2	3	2	2	2	5	
1965	4	10		3	4		1	6	
1966	8	6		5	2		3	4	
1967	11	1	2	5	1	1	6	0	1
1968	10	3	1	5	2		5	1	1
1969	11	3		5	2		6	1	
1970	9	4	1	3	3	1	6	1	
1971	8	5	1	4	2	1	4	3	
1972	6	7	1	4	3		2	4	1
1973	12	2		7	0		5	2	
1974	10	4		6	1		4	3	
1975	12	2		6	1		6	1	
1976	10	3	1	5	2		5	1	1
1977	10	4		7	0		3	4	
1978	12	4		6	2		6	2	
1979	9	7		4	4		5	3	
1980	11	5		6	2		5	3	
1981	6	10		4	4		2	6	
1982	2	7		1	4		1	3	
1983	9	7		5	3		4	4	
1984	10	6		5	3		5	3	
1985	11	5		6	2		5	3	
1986	10	6		6	2		4	4	
1987	6	9		3	4		3	5	
1988	10	6		4	4		6	2	
1989	11	5		6	2		5	3	
1990	5	11		2	6		3	5	
1991	3	13		2	6		1	7	
1992	6	10		4	4		2	6	
1993	5	11		3	5		2	6	
1994	4	12		3	5		1	7	
1995	7	9		4	4		3	5	
1996	6	10		4	4		2	6	
1997	5	11		2	6		3	5	
1998	4	12		2	6		2	6	
1999	13	3		8	0		5	3	
	433	394	20	239	169	10	194	225	10

includes Cleveland Rams (1937-42, 1944-45) and Los Angeles Rams (1946-94).

SAN FRANCISCO 49ERS

	All Games			Home Games			Road Games		
Season	W	L	T	W	L	T	W	L	T
1950	3	9		3	3		0	6	
1951	7	4	1	5	1		2	3	1
1952	7	5		3	3		4	2	
1953	9	3		5	1		4	2	
1954	7	4	1	4	2		3	2	1
1955	4	8		2	4		2	4	
1956	5	6	1	3	3		2	3	1
1957	8	4		5	1		3	3	
1958	6	6		4	2		2	4	
1959	7	5		4	2		3	3	
1960	7	5		3	3		4	2	
1961	7	6	1	5	1	1	2	5	
1962	6	8		1	6		5	2	
1963	2	12		2	5		0	7	
1964	4	10		3	4		1	6	
1965	7	6	1	4	2	1	3	4	
1966	6	6	2	4	2	1	2	4	1
1967	7	7		3	4		4	3	
1968	7	6	1	3	3	1	4	3	
1969	4	8	2	3	3	1	1	5	1
1970	10	3	1	5	1	1	5	2	
1971	9	5		4	3		5	2	
1972	8	5	1	4	2	1	4	3	
1973	5	9		3	4		2	5	
1974	6	8		3	4		3	4	
1975	5	9		2	5		3	4	
1976	8	6		4	3		4	3	
1977	5	9		3	4		2	5	
1978	2	14		2	6		0	8	
1979	2	14		2	6		0	8	
1980	6	10		4	4		2	6	
1981	13	3		7	1		6	2	
1982	3	6		0	5		3	1	
1983	10	6		4	4		6	2	
1984	15	1		7	1		8	0	
1985	10	6		5	3		5	3	
1986	10	5	1	6	2		4	3	1
1987	13	2		6	1		7	1	
1988	10	6		4	4		6	2	
1989	14	2		6	2		8	0	
1990	14	2		6	2		8	0	
1991	10	6		7	1		3	5	
1992	14	2		7	1		7	1	
1993	10	6		6	2		4	4	
1994	13	3		7	1		6	2	
1995	11	5		6	2		5	3	
1996	12	4		6	2		6	2	
1997	13	3		8	0		5	3	
1998	12	4		8	0		4	4	
1999	4	12		3	5		1	7	
	397	304	13	214	136	7	183	168	6

TAMPA BAY BUCCANEERS

	All Games			Home Games			Road Games		
Season	W	L	T	W	L	T	W	L	T
1976	0	14		0	7		0	7	
1977	2	12		1	6		1	6	
1978	5	11		3	5		2	6	
1979	10	6		5	3		5	3	
1980	5	10	1	2	5	1	3	5	
1981	9	7		6	2		3	5	
1982	5	4		4	1		1	3	
1983	2	14		1	7		1	7	

Season	All Games W	L	T	Home Games W	L	T	Road Games W	L	T
1984	6	10		6	2		0	8	
1985	2	14		2	6		0	8	
1986	2	14		1	7		1	7	
1987	4	11		2	5		2	6	
1988	5	11		3	5		2	6	
1989	5	11		2	6		3	5	
1990	6	10		4	4		2	6	
1991	3	13		3	5		0	8	
1992	5	11		3	5		2	6	
1993	5	11		3	5		2	6	
1994	6	10		4	4		2	6	
1995	7	9		5	3		2	6	
1996	6	10		5	3		1	7	
1997	10	6		5	3		5	3	
1998	8	8		6	2		2	6	
1999	11	5		7	1		4	4	
	129	242	1	83	102	1	46	140	

WASHINGTON REDSKINS*

Season	All Games W	L	T	Home Games W	L	T	Road Games W	L	T
1932	4	4	2	2	3	1	2	1	1
1933	5	5	2	4	2		1	3	2
1934	6	6		4	3		2	3	
1935	2	8	1	2	5		0	3	1
1936	7	5		4	3		3	2	
1937	8	3		4	2		4	1	
1938	6	3	2	3	1	1	3	2	1
1939	8	2	1	5	0	1	3	2	
1940	9	2		6	0		3	2	
1941	6	5		4	2		2	3	
1942	10	1		5	1		5	0	
1943	6	3	1	4	2		2	1	1
1944	6	3	1	4	2		2	1	1
1945	8	2		6	0		2	2	
1946	5	5	1	3	2	1	2	3	
1947	4	8		4	2		0	6	
1948	7	5		4	2		3	3	
1949	4	7	1	3	3		1	4	1
1950	3	9		1	5		2	4	
1951	5	7		2	4		3	3	
1952	4	8		1	5		3	3	
1953	6	5	1	3	3		3	2	1
1954	3	9		3	3		0	6	
1955	8	4		3	3		5	1	
1956	6	6		4	2		2	4	
1957	5	6	1	2	3	1	3	3	
1958	4	7	1	3	2	1	1	5	
1959	3	9		2	4		1	5	
1960	1	9	2	1	4	1	0	5	1
1961	1	12	1	1	6		0	6	1
1962	5	7	2	3	4		2	3	2
1963	3	11		1	6		2	5	
1964	6	8		4	3		2	5	
1965	6	8		3	4		3	4	
1966	7	7		4	3		3	4	
1967	5	6	3	2	4	1	3	2	2
1968	5	9		3	4		2	5	
1969	7	5	2	4	2	1	3	3	1
1970	6	8		4	3		2	5	
1971	9	4	1	4	2	1	5	2	
1972	11	3		6	1		5	2	
1973	10	4		7	0		3	4	
1974	10	4		6	1		4	3	
1975	8	6		5	2		3	4	
1976	10	4		5	2		5	2	
1977	9	5		5	2		4	3	
1978	8	8		5	3		3	5	
1979	10	6		6	2		4	4	
1980	6	10		4	4		2	6	
1981	8	8		5	3		3	5	
1982	8	1		3	1		5	0	
1983	14	2		7	1		7	1	
1984	11	5		7	1		4	4	
1985	10	6		5	3		5	3	
1986	12	4		7	1		5	3	
1987	11	4		6	1		5	3	
1988	7	9		4	4		3	5	
1989	10	6		4	4		6	2	
1990	10	6		7	1		3	5	
1991	14	2		7	1		7	1	
1992	9	7		6	2		3	5	
1993	4	12		3	5		1	7	
1994	3	13		0	8		3	5	
1995	6	10		4	4		2	6	
1996	9	7		5	3		4	4	
1997	8	7	1	5	2	1	3	5	
1998	6	10		4	4		2	6	
1999	10	6		6	2		4	4	
	471	416	27	273	182	11	198	234	16

includes Boston Braves (1932) and Boston Redskins (1933-36).

History

PRO FOOTBALL HALL OF FAME

The Professional Football Hall of Fame is located in Canton, Ohio, site of the organizational meeting on September 17, 1920, from which the National Football League evolved. The NFL recognized Canton as the Hall of Fame site on April 27, 1961. Canton area individuals, foundations, and companies donated almost $400,000 in cash and services to provide funds for the construction of the original two-building complex, which was dedicated on September 7, 1963. Since that time, the Hall added three buildings with major expansion projects in 1971, 1978, and 1995. The Hall's largest-ever expansion, a $9.2 million project, was completed in early fall 1995. With the new fifth building, the Hall's size is now 82,307-square feet, more than four times its original size.

The expanded Hall represents the sport of pro football in many ways—through (1) GameDay Stadium, a dynamic two-part turntable theater featuring NFL action in Cinemascope for the first time, (2) a standard theater showing NFL films hourly, (3) six large exhibition areas where the history of pro football is detailed in memento, picture, and story form, (4) an extensive library and research center, and (5) a new and enlarged museum store.

In recent years, the Pro Football Hall of Fame has become an extremely popular tourist attraction. At the end of 1999, a total of 6,704,310 fans had visited the Hall of Fame.

New members of the Pro Football Hall of Fame are elected annually by a 36-member National Board of Selectors, made up of media representatives from every league city, five at-large representatives, and a representative of the Pro Football Writers of America. Between four and seven new members are elected each year. An affirmative vote of approximately 80 percent is needed for election.

Any fan may nominate any eligible player or contributor simply by writing to the Pro Football Hall of Fame. Players must be retired five years to be eligible, while a coach need only to be retired with no time limit specified. Contributors (administrators, owners, *et al.*) may be elected while they are still active.

The charter class of 17 enshrinees was elected in 1963 and the honor roll now stands at 204 with the election of a five-man class in 2000. That class consists of Howie Long, Ronnie Lott, Joe Montana, Dan Rooney, and Dave Wilcox.

ROSTER OF MEMBERS

HERB ADDERLEY
Defensive back. 6-1, 200. Born in Philadelphia, Pennsylvania, June 8, 1939. Michigan State. Inducted in 1980. 1961-69 Green Bay Packers, 1970-72 Dallas Cowboys. **Highlights:** 48 interceptions, 7 touchdowns. Played in four Super Bowls, five Pro Bowls.

LANCE ALWORTH
Wide receiver. 6-0, 184. Born in Houston, Texas, August 3, 1940. Arkansas. Inducted in 1978. 1962-70 San Diego Chargers, 1971-72 Dallas Cowboys. **Highlights:** 542 receptions for 10,266 yards, 85 touchdowns. All-AFL seven times, seven All-Star games.

DOUG ATKINS
Defensive end. 6-8, 275. Born in Humboldt, Tennessee, May 8, 1930. Tennessee. Inducted in 1982. 1953-54 Cleveland Browns, 1955-66 Chicago Bears, 1967-69 New Orleans Saints. **Highlights:** Eight Pro Bowls, All-NFL four times. Played for 17 years, 205 games.

MORRIS (RED) BADGRO
End. 6-0, 190. Born in Orilla, Washington, December 1, 1902. Died July 13, 1998. Southern California. Inducted in 1981. 1927 New York Yankees, 1930-35 New York Giants, 1936 Brooklyn Dodgers. **Highlights:** All-NFL three times. Scored first touchdown in NFL Championship Game series.

LEM BARNEY
Cornerback. 6-0, 190. Born in Gulfport, Mississippi, September 8, 1945. Jackson State. Inducted in 1992. 1967-77 Detroit Lions. **Highlights:** 56 interceptions for 1,077 yards, 11 touchdowns (7 defensive, 4 special teams). Seven Pro Bowls, All-NFL/NFC four times.

CLIFF BATTLES
Halfback. 6-1, 201. Born in Akron, Ohio, May 1, 1910. Died April 28, 1981. West Virginia Wesleyan. Inducted in 1968. 1932 Boston Braves, 1933-36 Boston Redskins, 1937 Washington Redskins. **Highlights:** NFL rushing champion 1932, 1937. First to gain more than 200 yards in a game, 1933.

SAMMY BAUGH
Quarterback. 6-2, 180. Born in Temple, Texas, March 17, 1914. Texas Christian. Inducted in 1963. 1937-52 Washington Redskins. **Highlights:** Charter enshrinee. Six-time NFL passing leader. NFL passing, punting, interception champ, 1943.

CHUCK BEDNARIK
Center-linebacker. 6-3, 230. Born in Bethlehem, Pennsylvania, May 1, 1925. Pennsylvania. Inducted in 1967. 1949-62 Philadelphia Eagles. **Highlights:** Eight Pro Bowls. Missed three games in 14 years. Named NFL all-time center, 1969.

BERT BELL
Team owner. Commissioner. Born in Philadelphia, Pennsylvania, February 25, 1895. Died October 11, 1959. Pennsylvania. Inducted in 1963. 1933-40 Philadelphia Eagles, 1941-42 Pittsburgh Steelers, 1943 Phil-Pitt, 1944 Card-Pitt, 1945-46 Pittsburgh Steelers. Commissioner, 1946-59. **Highlights:** Charter enshrinee. Built NFL image as commissioner, 1946-1959. Set up long-term television policies.

BOBBY BELL
Linebacker. 6-4, 225. Born in Shelby, North Carolina, June 17, 1940. Minnesota. Inducted in 1983. 1963-74 Kansas City Chiefs. **Highlights:** 26 interceptions. All-AFL/AFC eight times. Nine career touchdowns, 1 on onside kick return.

RAYMOND BERRY
End. 6-2, 187. Born in Corpus Christi, Texas, February 27, 1933. Southern Methodist. Inducted in 1973. 1955-67 Baltimore Colts. **Highlights:** 631 receptions for 9,275 yards, 68 touchdowns. Set NFL title game mark with 12 catches for 178 yards, 1958.

CHARLES W. BIDWILL, SR.
Team owner. Born in Chicago, Illinois, September 16, 1895. Died April 19, 1947. Loyola of Chicago. Inducted in 1967. 1933-43 Chicago Cardinals, 1944 Card-Pitt, 1945-47 Chicago Cardinals. **Highlights:** Guiding light for NFL during depression years. Built famous "Dream Backfield."

FRED BILETNIKOFF
Wide receiver. 6-1, 190. Born in Erie, Pennsylvania, February 23, 1943. Florida State. Inducted in 1988. 1965-78 Oakland Raiders. **Highlights:** 589 receptions for 8,974 yards, 76 touchdowns. 40 catches 10 straight years. MVP, Super Bowl XI.

GEORGE BLANDA
Quarterback-kicker. 6-2, 215. Born in Youngwood, Pennsylvania, September 17, 1927. Kentucky. Inducted in 1981. 1949-58 Chicago Bears, 1950 Baltimore Colts, 1960-66 Houston Oilers, 1967-75 Oakland Raiders. **Highlights:** Record 2,002 career points. 26-season, 340-game career longest in NFL history.

MEL BLOUNT
Cornerback. 6-3, 205. Born in Vidalia, Georgia, April 10, 1948. Southern University. Inducted in 1989. 1970-83 Pittsburgh Steelers. **Highlights:** 57 interceptions for 736 yards. NFL defensive MVP, 1975. Played in five Pro Bowls.

TERRY BRADSHAW
Quarterback. 6-3, 210. Born in Shreveport, Louisiana, September 2, 1948. Louisiana Tech. Inducted in 1989. 1970-83 Pittsburgh Steelers. **Highlights:** 27,989 yards passing, 212 touchdowns. MVP in Super Bowls XIII, XIV.

JIM BROWN
Fullback. 6-2, 228. Born in St. Simons, Georgia, February 17, 1936. Syracuse. Inducted in 1971. 1957-65 Cleveland Browns. **Highlights:** 12,312 yards rushing, 756 points. Led NFL rushers eight years. Nine consecutive Pro Bowls.

PAUL BROWN
Coach. Born in Norwalk, Ohio, September 7, 1908. Died August 5, 1991. Miami (Ohio). Inducted in 1967. 1946-49 Cleveland Browns (AAFC), 1950-62 Cleveland Browns. **Highlights:** Built Cleveland dynasty with 167-53-8 record, four AAFC titles, three NFL crowns. Returned to coaching with Cincinnati Bengals after induction, 1968-1975.

ROOSEVELT BROWN
Tackle. 6-3, 255. Born in Charlottesville, Virginia, October 20, 1932. Morgan State. Inducted in 1975. 1953-65 New York Giants. **Highlights:** All-NFL eight consecutive years, nine Pro Bowls. NFL's lineman of year, 1956.

WILLIE BROWN
Cornerback. 6-1, 210. Born in Yazoo City, Mississippi, December 2, 1940. Grambling. Inducted in 1984. 1963-66 Denver Broncos, 1967-78 Oakland Raiders. **Highlights:** 54 interceptions for 472 yards. Scored on 75-yard interception in Super Bowl XI.

BUCK BUCHANAN
Defensive tackle. 6-7, 274. Born in Gainesville, Alabama, September 10, 1940. Died July 16, 1992. Grambling. Inducted in 1990. 1963-75 Kansas City Chiefs. **Highlights:** Led Chiefs defensive efforts in Super Bowl I, IV. Did not miss a game in 13 years.

DICK BUTKUS
Linebacker. 6-3, 245. Born in Chicago, Illinois, December 9, 1942. Illinois. Inducted in 1979. 1965-73 Chicago Bears. **Highlights:** All-NFL six years, eight consecutive Pro Bowls. 25 fumble recoveries.

EARL CAMPBELL
Running back. 5-11, 233. Born in Tyler, Texas, March 29, 1955. Texas. Inducted in 1991. 1978-84 Houston Oilers, 1984-85 New Orleans Saints. **Highlights:** 9,407 yards rushing, 74 touchdowns. 1,934 yards rushing in 1980, including four games with at least 200 yards.

TONY CANADEO
Halfback. 5-11, 195. Born in Chicago, Illinois, May 5, 1919. Gonzaga. Inducted in 1974. 1941-44, 1946-52 Green Bay Packers. **Highlights:** Two-way player. Third player to rush for 1,000 yards in single season, 1949.

JOE CARR
NFL president. Born in Columbus, Ohio, October 22, 1880. Died May 20, 1939. Did not attend college. Inducted in 1963. President, 1921-39 National Football League. **Highlights:** Charter enshrinee. NFL co-organizer, 1920. Introduced standard player's contract.

GUY CHAMBERLIN
End. Coach. 6-2, 210. Born in Blue Springs, Nebraska, January 16, 1894. Died April 4, 1967. Nebraska. Inducted in 1965. 1919 Canton Bulldogs, 1920 Decatur Staleys, 1921 Chicago Staleys, player-coach 1922-23 Canton Bulldogs, 1924 Cleveland Bulldogs, 1925-26 Frankford Yellow Jackets, 1927-28 Chicago Cardinals. **Highlights:** Player-coach of four NFL championship teams. Six-year coaching record 58-16-7.

JACK CHRISTIANSEN
Safety. 6-1, 185. Born in Sublette, Kansas, December 20, 1928. Died June 29, 1986. Colorado State. Inducted in 1970. 1951-58 Detroit Lions. **Highlights:** 46 interceptions. NFL interception leader, 1953, 1957. Eight punt returns for touchdowns.

EARL (DUTCH) CLARK
Quarterback. 6-0, 185. Born in Fowler, Colorado, October 11, 1906. Died August 5, 1978. Colorado College. Inducted in 1963. 1931-32 Portsmouth Spartans, 1934-38 Detroit Lions. **Highlights:** Charter enshrinee. NFL scoring champion three years. Led Lions to 1935 NFL title.

GEORGE CONNOR
Tackle-linebacker. 6-3, 240. Born in Chicago, Illinois, January 21, 1925. Holy Cross, Notre Dame. Inducted in 1975. 1948-55 Chicago Bears. **Highlights:** All-NFL at three positions—T, DT, LB. All-NFL five years. Played in first four Pro Bowls.

JIMMY CONZELMAN
Quarterback. Coach. Team owner. 6-0, 180. Born in St. Louis, Missouri, March 6, 1898. Died July 31, 1970. Washington of St. Louis. Inducted in 1964. 1920 Decatur Staleys, 1921-22 Rock Island Independents, 1923-24 Milwaukee Badgers; owner-coach 1925-26 Detroit Panthers; player-coach 1927-29, coach 1930 Providence Steam Roller; coach 1940-42, 1946-48 Chicago Cardinals. **Highlights:** Player-coach of four NFL teams in 1920's. Coached Cardinals to 1947 NFL crown.

LOU CREEKMUR
Tackle-guard. 6-4, 255. Born in Hopelawn, New Jersey. January 22, 1927. William & Mary. Inducted in 1996. 1950-59 Detroit Lions. **Highlights:** All-NFL six times, twice at guard and four times at tackle. Selected to eight Pro Bowls and played on three NFL championship teams.

LARRY CSONKA
Running back. 6-3, 235. Born in Stow, Ohio, December 25, 1946. Syracuse. Inducted in 1987. 1968-74, 1979 Miami Dolphins, 1976-78 New York Giants. **Highlights:** 8,081 yards rushing, 68 touchdowns. MVP Super Bowl VIII. Only 21 fumbles in 1,891 carries and 106 receptions.

AL DAVIS
Team, League Administrator. Born in Brockton, Massachusetts, July 4, 1929. Wittenberg, Syracuse. Inducted in 1992. 1963-81, 1995-present Oakland Raiders, 1982-94 Los Angeles Raiders, 1966 American Football League. **Highlights:** Only person to serve in pros as personnel assistant, scout, assistant coach, head coach, general manager, commissioner, team owner/CEO.

WILLIE DAVIS
Defensive end. 6-3, 245. Born in Lisbon, Louisiana, July 24, 1934. Grambling. Inducted in 1981. 1958-59 Cleveland Browns, 1960-69 Green Bay Packers. **Highlights:** All-NFL five seasons, five Pro Bowls. Did not miss game in 12-year career.

LEN DAWSON
Quarterback. 6-0, 190. Born in Alliance, Ohio, June 20, 1935. Purdue. Inducted in 1987. 1957-59 Pittsburgh Steelers, 1960-61 Cleveland Browns, 1962 Dallas Texans, 1963-75 Kansas City Chiefs. **Highlights:** 28,711 yards passing, 239 touchdowns. Four AFL passing crowns. MVP, Super Bowl IV.

ERIC DICKERSON
Running back. 6-3, 220. Born in Sealy, Texas, September 2, 1960. Southern Methodist. Inducted in 1999. 1983-87 Los Angeles Rams, 1987-91 Indianapolis Colts, 1992 Los Angeles Raiders, 1993 Atlanta Falcons. **Highlights:** Rushed for 13,259 career yards, including an NFL record 2,105 yards in 1984. All-Pro five times, six Pro Bowls.

DAN DIERDORF
Tackle. 6-3, 290. Born in Canton, Ohio, June 29, 1949. Michigan. Inducted in 1996. 1971-83 St. Louis Cardinals. **Highlights:** All-Pro five times, played in six Pro Bowls, named NFL's best blocker three times.

MIKE DITKA
Tight end. 6-3, 225. Born in Carnegie, Pennsylvania, October 18, 1939. Pittsburgh. Inducted in 1988. 1961-66 Chicago Bears, 1967-68 Philadelphia Eagles, 1969-72 Dallas Cowboys. **Highlights:** 427 receptions for 5,812 yards, 43 touchdowns. First tight end selected to Hall of Fame. Five consecutive Pro Bowls.

ART DONOVAN
Defensive tackle. 6-3, 265. Born in Bronx, New York, June 5, 1925. Boston College. Inducted in 1968. 1950 Baltimore Colts, 1951 New York Yanks, 1952 Dallas Texans, 1953-61 Baltimore Colts. **Highlights:** Five Pro Bowls. Vital part of Baltimore's climb to powerhouse status in 1950s.

TONY DORSETT
Running back. 5-11, 184. Born in Rochester, Pennsylvania, April 7, 1954. Pittsburgh. Inducted in 1994. 1977-87 Dallas Cowboys, 1988 Denver Broncos. **Highlights:** 12,739 yards rushing, 398 receptions, 91 touchdowns. Ran record 99 yards for touchdown vs. Minnesota, January, 1983.

JOHN (PADDY) DRISCOLL
Quarterback. 5-11, 160. Born in Evanston, Illinois, January 11, 1896. Died June 29, 1968. Northwestern. Inducted in 1965. 1919 Hammond Pros, 1920 Decatur Staleys, 1920-25 Chicago Cardinals, 1926-29 Chicago Bears. **Highlights:** All-NFL seven times. Dropkicked record 4 field goals in one game, 1925.

BILL DUDLEY
Halfback. 5-10, 176. Born in Bluefield, Virginia, December 24, 1921. Virginia. Inducted in 1966. 1942, 1945-46 Pittsburgh Steelers, 1947-49 Detroit Lions, 1950-51, 1953 Washington Redskins. **Highlights:** Won NFL rushing, interception, punt return titles, 1946. All-NFL 1942, 1946, and 1947.

ALBERT GLEN (TURK) EDWARDS
Tackle. 6-2, 260. Born in Mold, Washington, September 28, 1907. Died January 12, 1973. Washington State. Inducted in 1969. 1932 Boston Braves, 1933-36 Boston Redskins, 1937-40 Washington Redskins. **Highlights:** All-NFL 1932-34, 1936, 1937. Steamrolling blocker, smothering tackler.

WEEB EWBANK
Coach. Born in Richmond, Indiana, May 6, 1907. Died November 17, 1998. Miami (Ohio). Inducted in 1978. 1954-62 Baltimore Colts, 1963-73 New York Jets. **Highlights:** Only coach to win championships in both NFL, AFL. Led both Colts (1958) and Jets (1968) to championships.

TOM FEARS
End. 6-2, 215. Born in Los Angeles, California, December 3, 1923. Died January 4, 2000. Santa Clara, UCLA. Inducted in 1970. 1948-56 Los Angeles Rams. **Highlights:** 400 receptions for 5,397 yards, 38 touchdowns. Led NFL receivers first three seasons. Record 18 receptions in single game.

JIM FINKS
Administrator. Born in St. Louis, Missouri, August 31, 1927. Died May 8, 1994. Tulsa. Inducted 1995. 1964-73 Minnesota Vikings, 1974-82 Chicago Bears, 1986-93 New Orleans Saints. **Highlights:** Developed Vikings, Bears, Saints—all teams with losing records—into winners.

RAY FLAHERTY
Coach. Born in Spokane, Washington, September 1, 1903. Died July 19, 1994. Gonzaga. Inducted in 1976. 1936 Boston Redskins, 1937-42 Washington Redskins, 1946-48 New York Yankees (AAFC), 1949 Chicago Hornets (AAFC). **Highlights:** 82-41-5 coaching record. Introduced screen pass in 1937 title game and platoon system.

LEN FORD
Defensive end. 6-5, 260. Born in Washington, D.C., February 18, 1926. Died March 14, 1972. Morgan State, Michigan. Inducted in 1976. 1948-49 Los Angeles Dons (AAFC), 1950-57 Cleveland Browns, 1958 Green Bay Packers. **Highlights:** All-NFL five times, four Pro Bowls. Recovered 20 opponents' fumbles.

DAN FORTMANN
Guard. 6-0, 210. Born in Pearl River, New York, April 11, 1916. Died May 24, 1995. Colgate. Inducted in 1965. 1936-43 Chicago Bears. **Highlights:** At 20, became youngest starter in NFL. All-NFL six consecutive years.

DAN FOUTS
Quarterback. 6-3, 210. Born in San Francisco, California, June 10, 1951. Oregon. Inducted in 1993. 1973-1987 San Diego Chargers. **Highlights:** 43,040 passing yards, 254 touchdowns. Six Pro Bowls, NFL MVP, 1982.

FRANK GATSKI
Center. 6-3, 240. Born in Farmington, West Virginia, March 18, 1922. Marshall, Auburn. Inducted in 1985. 1946-49 Cleveland Browns (AAFC), 1950-56 Cleveland Browns, 1957 Detroit Lions. **Highlights:** Never missed game in high school, college, or pro football. Played 11 championship games, winning eight.

BILL GEORGE
Linebacker. 6-2, 230. Born in Waynesburg, Pennsylvania, October 27, 1930. Died September 30, 1982. Wake Forest. Inducted in 1974. 1952-65 Chicago Bears, 1966 Los Angeles Rams. **Highlights:** All-NFL eight years, eight consecutive Pro Bowls. 14 years of service, longest of any Bears player.

JOE GIBBS
Coach. Born in Mocksville, North Carolina, November 25, 1940. Cerritos (Calif.) J.C., San Diego State. Inducted in 1996. 1981-92 Washington Redskins. **Highlights:** 124-60-0 record in regular season, 16-5 in postseason, including four Super Bowl appearances—winning three. Won 10 or more games eight times.

FRANK GIFFORD
Halfback. 6-1, 195. Born in Santa Monica, California, August 16, 1930. Southern California. Inducted in 1977. 1952-60, 1962-64 New York Giants. **Highlights:** Starred on both offense and defense. Seven Pro Bowls, 1956 NFL player of the year.

SID GILLMAN
Coach. Born in Minneapolis, Minnesota, October 26, 1911. Ohio State. Inducted in 1983. 1955-59 Los Angeles Rams, 1960 Los Angeles Chargers, 1961-69, 1971 San Diego Chargers, 1973-74 Houston Oilers. **Highlights:** 123-104-7 coaching record. First to win division titles in both NFL, AFL.

PRO FOOTBALL HALL OF FAME

OTTO GRAHAM
Quarterback. 6-1, 195. Born in Waukegan, Illinois, December 6, 1921. Northwestern. Inducted in 1965. 1946-49 Cleveland Browns (AAFC), 1950-55 Cleveland Browns. **Highlights:** 23,584 passing yards, 174 touchdowns. Guided Browns to 10 division or league crowns in 10 years.

HAROLD (RED) GRANGE
Halfback. 6-0, 185. Born in Forksville, Pennsylvania, June 13, 1903. Died January 28, 1991. Illinois. Inducted in 1963. 1925 Chicago Bears, 1926 New York Yankees (AFL), 1927 New York Yankees, 1929-34 Chicago Bears. **Highlights:** Nicknamed "Galloping Ghost." Name produced first huge pro football crowds.

BUD GRANT
Coach. Born in Superior, Wisconsin, May 20, 1927. Minnesota. Inducted in 1994. 1967-83, 1985 Minnesota Vikings. **Highlights:** 168-108-5 coaching record. Led Vikings to 11 division championships, four Super Bowls.

JOE GREENE
Defensive tackle. 6-4, 260. Born in Temple, Texas, September 24, 1946. North Texas State. Inducted in 1987. 1969-81 Pittsburgh Steelers. **Highlights:** NFL defensive player of the year, 1972, 1974. Four-time Super Bowl champion, 10 Pro Bowls.

FORREST GREGG
Tackle. 6-4, 250. Born in Birthright, Texas, October 18, 1933. Southern Methodist. Inducted in 1977. 1956, 1958-70 Green Bay Packers, 1971 Dallas Cowboys. **Highlights:** Played 188 consecutive games. Nine Pro Bowls. Played on six NFL championship teams, three Super Bowl winners.

BOB GRIESE
Quarterback. 6-1, 190. Born in Evansville, Indiana, February 3, 1945. Purdue. Inducted in 1990. 1967-80 Miami Dolphins. **Highlights:** 25,092 passing yards, 192 touchdowns. Led Miami to three AFC titles, Super Bowl VII, VIII wins.

LOU GROZA
Tackle-kicker. 6-3, 250. Born in Martins Ferry, Ohio, January 25, 1924. Ohio State. Inducted in 1974. 1946-49 Cleveland Browns (AAFC), 1950-59, 1961-67 Cleveland Browns. **Highlights:** 1,608 points in 21 years. Nine Pro Bowls, All-NFL six years. NFL player of the year, 1954.

JOE GUYON
Halfback. 6-1, 180. Born on White Earth Indian Reservation, Minnesota, November 26, 1892. Died November 27, 1971. Carlisle, Georgia Tech. Inducted in 1966. 1919-20 Canton Bulldogs, 1921 Cleveland Indians, 1922-23 Oorang Indians, 1924 Rock Island Independents, 1924-25 Kansas City Cowboys, 1927 New York Giants. **Highlights:** Touchdown pass gave Giants victory over Bears to win 1927 championship.

GEORGE HALAS
End. Coach. Team owner. Born in Chicago, Illinois, February 2, 1895. Died October 31, 1983. Illinois. Inducted in 1963. Player-coach 1920 Decatur Staleys, 1921 Chicago Staleys, 1922-29 Chicago Bears; coach 1933-42, 1946-55, 1958-67 Chicago Bears. **Highlights:** Charter enshrinee. 324 coaching wins. Only person associated with NFL throughout first 50 years. Coached Bears 40 seasons, won six NFL titles.

JACK HAM
Linebacker. 6-1, 225. Born in Johnstown, Pennsylvania, December 23, 1948. Penn State. Inducted in 1988. 1971-82 Pittsburgh Steelers. **Highlights:** Won four Super Bowls, 21 opponents' fumbles recovered, 32 interceptions. Eight consecutive Pro Bowls.

JOHN HANNAH
Guard. 6-3, 265. Born in Canton, Georgia, April 4, 1951. Alabama. Inducted in 1991. 1973-85 New England Patriots. **Highlights:** Renowned as premier guard of era. All-Pro 10 years, nine Pro Bowls.

FRANCO HARRIS
Running back. 6-2, 225. Born in Fort Dix, New Jersey, March 7, 1950. Penn State. Inducted in 1990. 1972-83 Pittsburgh Steelers, 1984 Seattle Seahawks. **Highlights:** 12,120 rushing yards, 100 total touchdowns. 1,556 rushing yards in 19 postseason games. MVP in Super Bowl IX.

MIKE HAYNES
Cornerback. 6-2, 195. Born in Denison, Texas, July 1, 1953. Arizona State. Inducted in 1997. 1976-82 New England Patriots, 1983-89 Los Angeles Raiders. **Highlights:** Defensive rookie of the year. Selected to nine Pro Bowls and intercepted 46 passes, plus one pick in Super Bowl XVIII.

ED HEALEY
Tackle. 6-3, 220. Born in Indian Orchard, Massachusetts, December 28, 1894. Died December 9, 1978. Dartmouth. Inducted in 1964. 1920-22 Rock Island Independents, 1922-27 Chicago Bears. **Highlights:** Two-way star. Perennial all-pro with Bears.

MEL HEIN
Center. 6-2, 225. Born in Redding, California, August 22, 1909. Died January 31, 1992. Washington State. Inducted in 1963. 1931-45 New York Giants. **Highlights:** Charter enshrinee. 60-minute regular for 15 years. All-NFL eight consecutive years.

TED HENDRICKS
Linebacker. 6-7, 235. Born in Guatemala City, Guatemala, November 1, 1947. Miami. Inducted in 1990. 1969-73 Baltimore Colts, 1974 Green Bay Packers, 1975-81 Oakland Raiders, 1982-83 Los Angeles Raiders. **Highlights:** 25 blocked field goals, extra points, and punts, 26 interceptions. Played in 215 consecutive games.

WILBUR (PETE) HENRY
Tackle. 6-0, 250. Born in Mansfield, Ohio, October 31, 1897. Died February 7, 1952. Washington & Jefferson. Inducted in 1963. 1920-23, 1925-26 Canton Bulldogs, 1927 New York Giants, 1927-28 Pottsville Maroons. **Highlights:** Largest player of his time at 250 pounds. Bulwark of Canton's championship lines.

ARNIE HERBER
Quarterback. 6-0, 200. Born in Green Bay, Wisconsin, April 2, 1910. Died October 14, 1969. Wisconsin, Regis College. Inducted in 1966. 1930-40 Green Bay Packers, 1944-45 New York Giants. **Highlights:** NFL passing leader 1932, 1934, 1936. Came out of retirement to lead 1944 Giants to NFL Eastern crown.

BILL HEWITT
End. 5-11, 191. Born in Bay City, Michigan, October 8, 1909. Died January 14, 1947. Michigan. Inducted in 1971. 1932-36 Chicago Bears, 1937-39 Philadelphia Eagles, 1943 Phil-Pitt. **Highlights:** First to be named all-NFL with two teams—1933, 1934, 1936 Bears; 1937 Eagles.

CLARKE HINKLE
Fullback. 5-11, 201. Born in Toronto, Ohio, April 10, 1909. Died November 9, 1988. Bucknell. Inducted in 1964. 1932-41 Green Bay Packers. **Highlights:** 3,860 yards rushing, 379 points. Fullback on offense, linebacker on defense.

ELROY (CRAZYLEGS) HIRSCH
Halfback-end. 6-2, 190. Born in Wausau, Wisconsin, June 17, 1923. Wisconsin, Michigan. Inducted in 1968. 1946-48 Chicago Rockets (AAFC), 1949-57 Los Angeles Rams. **Highlights:** 387 receptions for 7,029 yards, 60 touchdowns. Key part of Rams' revolutionary "three end" offense, 1949.

PAUL HORNUNG
Halfback. 6-2, 220. Born in Louisville, Kentucky, December 23, 1935. Notre Dame. Inducted in 1986. 1957-62, 1964-66 Green Bay Packers. **Highlights:** 760 points. Led NFL scorers three years, including record 176 points, 1960. Record 19 points scored in 1961 NFL title game.

KEN HOUSTON
Safety. 6-3, 198. Born in Lufkin, Texas, November 12, 1944. Prairie View A&M. Inducted in 1986. 1967-72 Houston Oilers, 1973-80 Washington Redskins. **Highlights:** 49 interceptions, 898 yards, 9 touchdowns. NFL's premier strong safety of 1970s. 12 Pro Bowls.

ROBERT (CAL) HUBBARD
Tackle. 6-5, 250. Born in Keytesville, Missouri, October 31, 1900. Died October 17, 1977. Centenary, Geneva. Inducted in 1963. 1927-28 New York Giants, 1929-33, 1935 Green Bay Packers, 1936 New York Giants, 1936 Pittsburgh Pirates. **Highlights:** Charter enshrinee. Most feared lineman of his time. All-NFL six years, 1927-29, 1931-33.

SAM HUFF
Linebacker. 6-1, 230. Born in Morgantown, West Virginia, October 4, 1934. West Virginia. Inducted in 1982. 1956-63 New York Giants, 1964-67, 1969 Washington Redskins. **Highlights:** 30 interceptions. Played in six NFL title games, five Pro Bowls. Redskins player-coach, 1969.

LAMAR HUNT
Team owner. Born in El Dorado, Arkansas, August 2, 1932. Southern Methodist. Inducted in 1972. 1960-62 Dallas Texans, 1963-present Kansas City Chiefs. **Highlights:** Driving force behind organization of AFL. Spearheaded merger negotiations with NFL, 1966.

DON HUTSON
End. 6-1, 180. Born in Pine Bluff, Arkansas, January 31, 1913. Died June 26, 1997. Alabama. Inducted in 1963. 1935-45 Green Bay Packers. **Highlights:** 488 receptions for 7,991 yards, 99 touchdowns. NFL receiving champion eight years. NFL MVP, 1941, 1942.

JIMMY JOHNSON
Cornerback. 6-2, 187. Born in Dallas, Texas, March 31, 1938. UCLA. Inducted in 1994. 1961-76 San Francisco 49ers. **Highlights:** 47 interceptions for 615 yards. Five Pro Bowls. Opposing passers avoided throwing in his area.

JOHN HENRY JOHNSON
Fullback. 6-2, 225. Born in Waterproof, Louisiana, November 24, 1929. St. Mary's, Arizona State. Inducted in 1987. 1954-56 San Francisco 49ers, 1957-59 Detroit Lions, 1960-65 Pittsburgh Steelers, 1966 Houston Oilers. **Highlights:** 6,803 yards rushing, 55 total touchdowns. Member of San Francisco's "Fabulous Foursome" backfield.

CHARLIE JOINER
Wide receiver. 5-11, 180. Born in Many, Louisiana, October 14, 1947. Grambling. Inducted in 1996. 1969-72 Houston Oilers, 1972-75 Cincinnati Bengals, 1976-86 San Diego Chargers. **Highlights:** 750 receptions for 12,146 yards and 65 touchdowns. Played 18 seasons, 239 games, most ever for wide receiver.

DAVID (DEACON) JONES
Defensive end. 6-5, 260. Born in Eatonville, Florida, December 9, 1938. South Carolina State, Mississippi Vocational. Inducted in 1980. 1961-71 Los Angeles Rams, 1972-73 San Diego Chargers, 1974 Washington Redskins. **Highlights:** Specialized in quarterback 'sacks,' a term he invented. Unanimous all-league five consecutive years.

STAN JONES
Guard-defensive tackle. 6-1, 250. Born in Altoona, Pennsylvania, November 24, 1931. Maryland. Inducted in 1991. 1954-65 Chicago Bears, 1966 Washington Redskins. **Highlights:** Seven consecutive Pro Bowls. First to rely on weightlifting for football preparation.

HENRY JORDAN
Defensive tackle, 6-3, 240. Born in Emporia, Virginia, January 26, 1935. Died February 21, 1977. Virginia. Inducted in 1995. 1957-58 Cleveland Browns, 1959-69 Green Bay Packers. **Highlights:** Fixture at DT during Packers' dynasty. Played in four Pro Bowls, seven NFL title games, Super Bowls I, II.

SONNY JURGENSEN
Quarterback. 6-0, 203. Born in Wilmington, North Carolina, August 23, 1934. Duke. Inducted in 1983. 1957-63 Philadelphia Eagles, 1964-74 Washington Redskins. **Highlights:** 32,224 yards passing, 255 touchdowns, 82.63 passer rating. Surpassed 3,000 yards passing in five seasons.

LEROY KELLY
Running back. 6-0, 205. Born in Philadelphia, Pennsylvania, May 20, 1942. Morgan State. Inducted in 1994. 1964-73 Cleveland Browns. **Highlights:** 7,274 yards rushing, 90 total touchdowns, 1,000-yard rusher first three years as starter. Punt return champion, 1965.

WALT KIESLING
Guard. Coach. 6-2, 245. Born in St. Paul, Minnesota, March 27, 1903. Died March 2, 1962. St. Thomas (Minnesota). Inducted in 1966. 1926-27 Duluth Eskimos, 1928 Pottsville Maroons, 1929-33 Chicago Cardinals, 1934 Chicago Bears, 1935-36 Green Bay Packers, 1937-38 Pittsburgh Pirates; coach, 1939 Pittsburgh Pirates, 1940-42 Pittsburgh Steelers; co-coach, 1943 Phil-Pitt, 1944 Card-Pitt; coach, 1954-56 Pittsburgh Steelers. **Highlights:** 34-year career as pro player, assistant coach, head coach. Led Steelers to first winning season, 1942.

FRANK (BRUISER) KINARD
Tackle. 6-1, 210. Born in Pelahatchie, Mississippi, October 23, 1914. Died September 7, 1985. Mississippi. Inducted in 1971. 1938-43 Brooklyn Dodgers, 1944 Brooklyn Tigers, 1946-47 New York Yankees (AAFC). **Highlights:** First man to earn both All-NFL, All-AAFC honors. Out because of injury only once.

PAUL KRAUSE
Safety. 6-3, 200. Born in Flint, Michigan, February 19, 1942. Iowa. Inducted in 1998. 1964-67 Washington Redskins, 1968-79 Minnesota Vikings. **Highlights:** NFL all-time leader with 81 interceptions. Played in eight Pro Bowls. Starting safety in four Super Bowls.

EARL (CURLY) LAMBEAU
Coach. Born in Green Bay, Wisconsin, April 9, 1898. Died June 1, 1965. Notre Dame. Inducted in 1963. 1919-49 Green Bay Packers, 1950-51 Chicago Cardinals, 1952-53 Washington Redskins. **Highlights:** 229-134-22 coaching record with six NFL championships. Founded pre-NFL Packers, 1919.

JACK LAMBERT
Linebacker. 6-4, 220. Born in Mantua, Ohio, July 8, 1952. Kent State. Inducted in 1990. 1974-84 Pittsburgh Steelers. **Highlights:** Leader of 'Steel Curtain.' NFL defensive player of year in 1976, nine Pro Bowls.

TOM LANDRY
Coach. Born in Mission, Texas, September 11, 1924. Texas. Inducted in 1990. 1960-88 Dallas Cowboys. **Highlights:** 270-178-6 coaching record. 20 consecutive winning seasons. Innovator on offense and defense.

DICK (NIGHT TRAIN) LANE
Cornerback. 6-2, 210. Born in Austin, Texas, April 16, 1928. Scottsbluff Junior College. Inducted in 1974. 1952-53 Los Angeles Rams, 1954-59 Chicago Cardinals, 1960-65 Detroit Lions. **Highlights:** 68 interceptions for 1,207 yards, 5 touchdowns. Record 14 interceptions as rookie. Seven Pro Bowls.

JIM LANGER
Center. 6-2, 255. Born in Little Falls, Minnesota, May 16, 1948. South Dakota State. Inducted in 1987. 1970-79 Miami Dolphins, 1980-81 Minnesota Vikings. **Highlights:** Played every offensive down in Dolphins' perfect 1972 season. Six Pro Bowls.

WILLIE LANIER
Linebacker. 6-1, 245. Born in Clover, Virginia, August 21, 1945. Morgan State. Inducted in 1986. 1967-77 Kansas City Chiefs. **Highlights:** 27 interceptions. Defensive star in Super Bowl IV upset. Nicknamed 'Contact' for ferocious tackling.

STEVE LARGENT
Wide receiver. 5-11, 191. Born in Tulsa, Oklahoma, September 28, 1954, Tulsa. Inducted in 1995. 1976-89 Seattle Seahawks. **Highlights:** 819 receptions for 13,089 yards, 100 touchdowns. Receptions in 177 consecutive games.

YALE LARY
Defensive back-punter. 5-11, 189. Born in Fort Worth, Texas, November 24, 1930. Texas A&M. Inducted in 1979. 1952-53, 1956-64 Detroit Lions. **Highlights:** 50 interceptions. Three NFL punting crowns, three touchdowns on punt returns. Nine Pro Bowls.

DANTE LAVELLI
End. 6-0, 199. Born in Hudson, Ohio, February 23, 1923. Ohio State. Inducted in 1975. 1946-49 Cleveland Browns (AAFC), 1950-56 Cleveland Browns. **Highlights:** 386 receptions for 6,488 yards, 62 touchdowns. 24 catches in six NFL title games.

BOBBY LAYNE
Quarterback. 6-2, 190. Born in Santa Ana, Texas, December 19, 1926. Died December 1, 1986. Texas. Inducted in 1967. 1948 Chicago Bears, 1949 New York Bulldogs, 1950-58 Detroit Lions, 1958-62 Pittsburgh Steelers. **Highlights:** 26,768 yards passing, 196 touchdowns, 2,451 yards rushing. Late touchdown pass won 1953 NFL title game.

ALPHONSE (TUFFY) LEEMANS
Fullback. 6-0, 200. Born in Superior, Wisconsin, November 12, 1912. Died January 19, 1979. Oregon, George Washington. Inducted in 1978. 1936-43 New York Giants. **Highlights:** 3,132 yards rushing, 2,324 yards passing, 422 yards receiving. Led NFL rushers as rookie, 1936.

BOB LILLY
Defensive tackle. 6-5, 260. Born in Olney, Texas, July 26, 1939. Texas Christian. Inducted in 1980. 1961-74 Dallas Cowboys. **Highlights:** Eleven Pro Bowls. Played 196 consecutive games. Foundation of great Dallas defensive units.

LARRY LITTLE
Guard. 6-1, 265. Born in Groveland, Georgia, November 2, 1945. Bethune-Cookman. Inducted in 1993. 1967-68 San Diego Chargers, 1969-80 Miami Dolphins. **Highlights:** Five Pro Bowls, started in three Super Bowls. Epitome of powerful Dolphins rushing game of 1970s.

VINCE LOMBARDI
Coach. Born in Brooklyn, New York, June 11, 1913. Died September 3, 1970. Fordham. Inducted in 1971. 1959-67 Green Bay Packers, 1969 Washington Redskins. **Highlights:** 105-35-6 coaching record in 10 years, including five NFL titles and victories in Super Bowls I and II.

HOWIE LONG
Defensive end. 6-5, 268. Born in Somerville, Massachusetts, January 6, 1960. Villanova. Inducted in 2000. 1981-1993 Oakland/Los Angeles Raiders. **Highlights:** All-Pro 1983, 1984, 1985. Named All-AFC four times, 1983-1986. Eight Pro Bowls.

RONNIE LOTT
Cornerback-safety. 6-0, 203. Born in Albuquerque, New Mexico, May 8, 1959. Southern California. Inducted in 2000. 1981-90 San Francisco 49ers, 1991-92 Los Angeles Raiders, 1993-94 New York Jets. **Highlights:** Ten Pro Bowls, 63 career interceptions, and was named to the NFL's 75th Anniversary Team.

SID LUCKMAN
Quarterback. 6-0, 195. Born in Brooklyn, New York, November 21, 1916. Died July 5, 1998. Columbia. Inducted in 1965. 1939-50 Chicago Bears. **Highlights:** 137 touchdown passes. All-NFL five times. League MVP in 1943.

WILLIAM ROY (LINK) LYMAN
Tackle. 6-2, 252. Born in Table Rock, Nebraska, November 30, 1898. Died December 16, 1972. Nebraska. Inducted in 1964. 1922-23, 1925 Canton Bulldogs, 1924 Cleveland Bulldogs, 1925 Frankford Yellow Jackets, 1926-28, 1930-31, 1933-34 Chicago Bears. **Highlights:** Played for four NFL champions. In 16 seasons of college and pro football, played on one losing team.

TOM MACK
Guard. 6-3, 250. Born in Cleveland, Ohio, November 1, 1943. Michigan. Inducted in 1999. 1966-78 Los Angeles Rams. **Highlights:** Never missed a game in entire 184-game career. Elected to 11 Pro Bowls.

JOHN MACKEY
Tight end. 6-2, 224. Born in New York, New York, September 24, 1941. Syracuse. Inducted in 1992. 1963-71 Baltimore Colts, 1972 San Diego Chargers. **Highlights:** 331 receptions for 5,236 yards, 38 touchdowns. Second tight end to enter Hall of Fame.

TIM MARA
Team owner. Born in New York, New York, July 29, 1887. Died February 17, 1959. Did not attend college. Inducted in 1963. 1925-59 New York Giants. **Highlights:** Charter enshrinee. Founder of New York Giants. Built team into powerhouse winning four NFL titles, 10 division titles.

WELLINGTON MARA
Team owner. Born in New York, New York, August 14, 1916. Fordham. Inducted in 1997. 1937-present New York Giants. **Highlights:** Lifetime contributor to NFL and New York Giants. Worked as Giants' ballboy, secretary, vice-president, president and co-CEO. NFC president 1984-present.

GINO MARCHETTI
Defensive end. 6-4, 245. Born in Smithers, West Virginia, January 2, 1927. San Francisco. Inducted in 1972. 1952 Dallas Texans, 1953-64, 1966 Baltimore Colts. **Highlights:** Named top defensive end of NFL's first 50 years. 10 consecutive Pro Bowls. All-NFL seven times.

GEORGE PRESTON MARSHALL
Team owner. Born in Grafton, West Virginia, October 11, 1897. Died August 9, 1969. Randolph-Macon. Inducted in 1963. 1932 Boston Braves, 1933-36 Boston Redskins, 1937-69 Washington Redskins. **Highlights:** Charter enshrinee. Sponsored progressive rules changes. Organized first team band, pioneered halftime shows.

OLLIE MATSON
Halfback. 6-2, 220. Born in Trinity, Texas, May 1, 1930. San Francisco. Inducted in 1972. 1952, 1954-58 Chicago Cardinals, 1959-62 Los Angeles Rams, 1963 Detroit Lions, 1964-66 Philadelphia Eagles. **Highlights:** Nine touchdowns on kickoff, punt returns. Traded for nine players in 1959.

PRO FOOTBALL HALL OF FAME

DON MAYNARD
Wide receiver. 6-1, 185. Born in Crosbyton, Texas, January 25, 1935. Texas Western. Inducted in 1987. 1958 New York Giants, 1960-62 New York Titans, 1963-72 New York Jets, 1973 St. Louis Cardinals. **Highlights:** 633 receptions for 11,834 yards, 88 touchdowns. At least 50 catches and 1,000 yards in five different seasons.

GEORGE McAFEE
Halfback. 6-0, 177. Born in Corbin, Kentucky, March 13, 1918. Duke. Inducted in 1966. 1940-41, 1945-50 Chicago Bears. **Highlights:** Two-way star. 25 interceptions, 234 points. Career punt-return average of 12.78 yards per return.

MIKE McCORMACK
Tackle. 6-4, 250. Born in Chicago, Illinois, June 21, 1930. Kansas. Inducted in 1984. 1951 New York Yanks, 1954-62 Cleveland Browns. **Highlights:** Excelled as offensive right tackle for eight years. Six Pro Bowls.

TOMMY McDONALD
Wide receiver. 5-9, 175. Born in Roy, New Mexico, July 26, 1934. Oklahoma. Inducted in 1998. 1957-63 Philadelphia Eagles, 1964 Dallas Cowboys, 1965-66 Los Angeles Rams, 1967 Atlanta Falcons, 1968 Cleveland Browns. **Highlights:** Recorded 495 receptions for 8,410 yards, 84 touchdowns.

HUGH McELHENNY
Halfback. 6-1, 198. Born in Los Angeles, California, December 31, 1928. Washington. Inducted in 1970. 1952-60 San Francisco 49ers, 1961-62 Minnesota Vikings, 1963 New York Giants, 1964 Detroit Lions. **Highlights:** 5,281 rushing yards, 360 points. Totaled 11,369 yards rushing, receiving, and returning kicks.

JOHNNY (BLOOD) McNALLY
Halfback. 6-0, 185. Born in New Richmond, Wisconsin, November 27, 1903. Died November 28, 1985. Notre Dame, St. John's (Minnesota). Inducted in 1963. 1925-26 Milwaukee Badgers, 1926-27 Duluth Eskimos, 1928 Pottsville Maroons, 1929-33, 1935-36 Green Bay Packers, 1934 Pittsburgh Pirates; player-coach, 1937-38 Pittsburgh Pirates. **Highlights:** 49 touchdowns, 296 points in 14 seasons with five teams.

MIKE MICHALSKE
Guard. 6-0, 209. Born in Cleveland, Ohio, April 24, 1903. Died October 26, 1983. Penn State. Inducted in 1964. 1926 New York Yankees (AFL), 1927-28 New York Yankees, 1929-35, 1937 Green Bay Packers. **Highlights:** Anchored Packers' championship lines, 1929-1931. First guard enshrined in Canton.

WAYNE MILLNER
End. 6-0, 191. Born in Roxbury, Massachusetts, January 31, 1913. Died November 19, 1976. Notre Dame. Inducted in 1968. 1936 Boston Redskins, 1937-41, 1945 Washington Redskins. **Highlights:** Redskins' all-time leader with 124 catches when retired. 55- and 78-yard touchdown receptions in 1937 NFL Championship Game.

BOBBY MITCHELL
Running back-wide receiver. 6-0, 195. Born in Hot Springs, Arkansas, June 6, 1935. Illinois. Inducted in 1983. 1958-61 Cleveland Browns, 1962-68 Washington Redskins. **Highlights:** 91 touchdowns, including 8 on kickoff and punt returns. 14,078 combined yards.

RON MIX
Tackle. 6-4, 255. Born in Los Angeles, California, March 10, 1938. Southern California. Inducted in 1979. 1960 Los Angeles Chargers, 1961-69 San Diego Chargers, 1971 Oakland Raiders. **Highlights:** All-AFL nine times. Only two holding penalties in 10 years with the Chargers.

JOE MONTANA
Quarterback. 6-2, 200. Born in New Eagle, Pennsylvania, June, 11, 1956. Notre Dame. Inducted in 2000. 1979-92 San Francisco 49ers, 1993-94 Kansas City Chiefs. **Highlights:** MVP in Super Bowl's XVI, XIX, and XXIV. Eight Pro Bowls and ALL-NFL three times.

LENNY MOORE
Flanker-running back. 6-1, 198. Born in Reading, Pennsylvania, November 25, 1933. Penn State. Inducted in 1975. 1956-67 Baltimore Colts. **Highlights:** From 1963-65, scored touchdowns in record 18 consecutive games. 113 career touchdowns, 12,451 combined net yards.

MARION MOTLEY
Fullback. 6-1, 238. Born in Leesburg, Georgia, June 5, 1920. South Carolina State, Nevada. Inducted in 1968. 1946-49 Cleveland Browns (AAFC), 1950-53 Cleveland Browns, 1955 Pittsburgh Steelers. **Highlights:** AAFC's all-time rushing champion. Led league in rushing in first NFL season.

ANTHONY MUÑOZ
Tackle. 6-6, 278. Born in Ontario, California, August 19, 1958. Southern California. Inducted in 1998. 1980-92 Cincinnati Bengals. **Highlights:** All-Pro choice 11 consecutive years, 1981-91. Selected to 11 straight Pro Bowls.

GEORGE MUSSO
Guard-tackle. 6-2, 270. Born in Collinsville, Illinois. April 8, 1910. Millikin. Inducted in 1982. 1933-44 Chicago Bears. **Highlights:** First player to achieve All-NFL status at two positions—tackle in 1935 and guard in 1937.

BRONKO NAGURSKI
Fullback. 6-2, 225. Born in Rainy River, Ontario, Canada, November 3, 1908. Died January 7, 1990. Minnesota. Inducted in 1963. 1930-37, 1943 Chicago Bears. **Highlights:** Charter enshrinee. 2,778 rushing yards in nine seasons. All-NFL three times.

JOE NAMATH
Quarterback. 6-2, 200. Born in Beaver Falls, Pennsylvania, May 31, 1943. Alabama. Inducted in 1985. 1965-76 New York Jets, 1977 Los Angeles Rams. **Highlights:** First quarterback to pass for more than 4,000 yards in season, 1967. Guaranteed, delivered victory over Colts in Super Bowl III.

EARLE (GREASY) NEALE
Coach. Born in Parkersburg, West Virginia, November 5, 1891. Died November 2, 1973. West Virginia Wesleyan. Inducted in 1969. 1941-42, 1944-50 Philadelphia Eagles; co-coach, 1943 Phil-Pitt. **Highlights:** Turned Eagles into winners with three consecutive division crowns, NFL championships in 1948 and 1949.

ERNIE NEVERS
Fullback. 6-1, 205. Born in Willow River, Minnesota, June 11, 1903. Died May 3, 1976. Stanford. Inducted in 1963. 1926-27 Duluth Eskimos, 1929-31 Chicago Cardinals. **Highlights:** Charter enshrinee. Holds NFL's longest-standing record, 40 points in one game in 1929.

OZZIE NEWSOME
Tight end. 6-2, 232. Born in Muscle Shoals, Alabama, March 16, 1956. Alabama. Inducted in 1999. 1978-90 Cleveland Browns. **Highlights:** Leading tight end receiver in NFL history with 662 receptions for 7,980 yards.

RAY NITSCHKE
Linebacker. 6-3, 235. Born in Elmwood Park, Illinois, December 29, 1936. Died March 8, 1998. Illinois. Inducted in 1978. 1958-72 Green Bay Packers. **Highlights:** MVP of 1962 title game. Named NFL's all-time linebacker in 1969.

CHUCK NOLL
Coach. Born in Cleveland, Ohio, January 5, 1932. Dayton. Inducted in 1993. 1969-91 Pittsburgh Steelers. **Highlights:** Coached for 23 years. Only coach to win four Super Bowl titles (IX, X, XIII, XIV).

LEO NOMELLINI
Defensive tackle. 6-3, 264. Born in Lucca, Italy, June 19, 1924. Minnesota. Inducted in 1969. 1950-63 San Francisco 49ers. **Highlights:** Played every 49ers game for 14 seasons. 10 Pro Bowls.

MERLIN OLSEN
Defensive tackle. 6-5, 270. Born in Logan, Utah, September 15, 1940. Utah State. Inducted in 1982. 1962-76 Los Angeles Rams. **Highlights:** Member of the Fearsome Foursome. Named to 14 consecutive Pro Bowls, Rams' all-time team.

JIM OTTO
Center. 6-2, 255. Born in Wausau, Wisconsin, January 5, 1938. Miami. Inducted in 1980. 1960-74 Oakland Raiders. **Highlights:** Named AFL's all-time center. Played in 210 games, 12 AFL All-Star Games or Pro Bowls, six AFL/AFC title games.

STEVE OWEN
Tackle. Coach. 6-2, 235. Born in Cleo Springs, Oklahoma, April 21, 1898. Died May 17, 1964. Phillips. Inducted in 1966. 1924-25 Kansas City Cowboys, 1925 Cleveland Bulldogs, 1926-31, 1933 New York Giants; coach, 1931-53 New York Giants. **Highlights:** Both player and coach. Coached Giants to record of 153-108-17, eight divisional titles, two NFL championships.

ALAN PAGE
Defensive tackle. 6-4, 225. Born in Canton, Ohio, August 7, 1945. Notre Dame. Inducted in 1988. 1967-78 Minnesota Vikings, 1978-81 Chicago Bears. **Highlights:** Dominating defensive tackle played in 218 consecutive games, four Super Bowls. Won league MVP honors in 1971.

CLARENCE (ACE) PARKER
Quarterback. 5-11, 168. Born in Portsmouth, Virginia, May 17, 1912. Duke. Inducted in 1972. 1937-41 Brooklyn Dodgers, 1945 Boston Yanks, 1946 New York Yankees (AAFC). **Highlights:** Two-way threat. Two-time All-NFL performer, league MVP in 1940.

JIM PARKER
Guard-tackle. 6-3, 273. Born in Macon, Georgia, April 3, 1934. Ohio State. Inducted in 1973. 1957-67 Baltimore Colts. **Highlights:** First full-time offensive lineman elected to Hall of Fame. All-NFL eight consecutive years, eight Pro Bowls.

WALTER PAYTON
Running back. 5-10, 202. Born in Columbia, Mississippi, July 25, 1954. Died November 1, 1999. Jackson State. Inducted in 1993. 1975-87 Chicago Bears. **Highlights:** NFL's all-time leading rusher with 16,726 yards. Holds single-game rushing record of 275 yards.

JOE PERRY
Fullback. 6-0, 200. Born in Stevens, Arkansas, January 22, 1927. Compton Junior College. Inducted in 1969. 1948-49 San Francisco 49ers (AAFC), 1950-60, 1963 San Francisco 49ers, 1961-62 Baltimore Colts. **Highlights:** First player in NFL history to gain 1,000 yards two consecutive seasons. 12,505 combined yards.

PETE PIHOS
End. 6-1, 210. Born in Orlando, Florida, October 22, 1923. Indiana. Inducted in 1970. 1947-55 Philadelphia Eagles. **Highlights:** Three-time NFL receiving champion. Caught winning touchdown in 1949 NFL Championship Game.

HUGH (SHORTY) RAY
Supervisor of officials 1938-52. Born in Highland Park, Illinois, September 21, 1884. Died September 16, 1956. Illinois. Inducted in 1966. **Highlights:** Supervisor of Officials, 1938-1952. Streamlined rules to improve game tempo, player safety.

DAN REEVES
Team owner. Born in New York, New York, June 30, 1912. Died April 15, 1971. Georgetown. Inducted in 1967. 1941-45 Cleveland Rams, 1946-71 Los Angeles Rams. **Highlights:** Moved Rams to Los Angeles in 1946 and opened up West Coast to pro football. First postwar owner to sign African-American player.

MEL RENFRO
Cornerback-safety. 6-0, 192. Born in Houston, Texas, December 30, 1941. Oregon. Inducted in 1996. 1964-77 Dallas Cowboys. **Highlights:** 52 interceptions for 626 yards and 3 touchdowns. Also added 842 yards on punt returns, 2,246 yards on kickoff returns. Elected to Pro Bowl first 10 seasons.

JOHN RIGGINS
Running back. 6-2, 240. Born in Seneca, Kansas, August 4, 1949. Kansas. Inducted in 1992. 1971-75 New York Jets, 1976-79, 1981-85 Washington Redskins. **Highlights:** 11,352 rushing yards, 116 total touchdowns. MVP of Super Bowl XVII with 166 rushing yards including game-winning 43-yard touchdown.

JIM RINGO
Center. 6-2, 230. Born in Orange, New Jersey, November 21, 1931. Syracuse. Inducted in 1981. 1953-63 Green Bay Packers, 1964-67 Philadelphia Eagles. **Highlights:** Ten-time Pro Bowl selection, six-time All-NFL selection. Started in then-record 182 consecutive games.

ANDY ROBUSTELLI
Defensive end. 6-0, 230. Born in Stamford, Connecticut, December 6, 1925. Arnold College. Inducted in 1971. 1951-55 Los Angeles Rams, 1956-64 New York Giants. **Highlights:** Anchored defense in eight championship games. Named NFL's top player in 1962.

ART ROONEY
Team owner. Born in Coulterville, Pennsylvania, January 27, 1901. Died August 25, 1988. Georgetown, Duquesne. Inducted in 1964. 1933-39 Pittsburgh Pirates, 1940-42, 1945-88 Pittsburgh Steelers, 1943 Phil-Pitt, 1944 Card-Pitt. **Highlights:** Founded Pittsburgh Pirates in 1933 and renamed them Steelers in 1940. Team won four Super Bowls in 1970s.

DAN ROONEY
Team owner. Born in Pittsburgh, Pennsylvania, July, 20, 1932. Inducted in 2000. 1955-present Pittsburgh Steelers. **Highlights:** Has been on the board of directors for the NFL Trust Fund, NFL Films, and Scheduling Committee. Played a key role in the labor agreement reached in 1993 between the NFL owners and players.

PETE ROZELLE
Commissioner. Born in South Gate, California, March 1, 1926. Died December 6, 1996. Compton Junior College, San Francisco. Inducted in 1985. Commissioner, 1960-89. **Highlights:** Negotiated first league-wide television contract in 1962. Generally recognized as premiere commissioner in all of sports. Credited with making NFL the nation's most popular sport.

BOB ST. CLAIR
Tackle. 6-9, 265. Born in San Francisco, California, February 18, 1931. San Francisco, Tulsa. Inducted in 1990. 1953-63 San Francisco 49ers. **Highlights:** Exceptional offensive lineman. Also played goal-line defense and had 10 blocked field goals, 1956.

GALE SAYERS
Running back. 6-0, 200. Born in Wichita, Kansas, May 30, 1943. Kansas. Inducted in 1977. 1965-71 Chicago Bears. **Highlights:** Broke into league by scoring rookie-record 22 touchdowns. Led league in rushing in 1966, 1969. MVP of three Pro Bowls.

JOE SCHMIDT
Linebacker. 6-0, 222. Born in Pittsburgh, Pennsylvania, January 18, 1932. Pittsburgh. Inducted in 1973. 1953-65 Detroit Lions. **Highlights:** 24 interceptions. Lions' team captain for nine years. Mastered middle linebacker position that evolved in 1950s.

TEX SCHRAMM
Team president-general manager. Born in San Gabriel, California, June 2, 1920. Texas. Inducted in 1991. 1947-56 Los Angeles Rams. 1960-89 Dallas Cowboys. **Highlights:** Played prominent role in AFL-NFL merger. Chairman of Competition Committee from 1966-1988.

LEE ROY SELMON
Defensive end. 6-3, 250. Born in Eufaula, Oklahoma, October 20, 1954. Oklahoma. Inducted in 1995. 1976-84 Tampa Bay Buccaneers. **Highlights:** 78½ sacks, 380 quarterback pressures, forced 28 fumbles. Six consecutive Pro Bowl selections.

BILLY SHAW
Guard. 6-2, 258. Born in Natchez, Mississippi, December 15, 1938. Georgia Tech. Inducted in 1999. 1961-69 Buffalo Bills. **Highlights:** First player who played entire career in AFL to be elected to Hall of Fame. Named to AFL's all-time team.

ART SHELL
Tackle. 6-5, 285. Born in Charleston, South Carolina, November 26, 1946. Maryland State-Eastern Shore. Inducted in 1989. 1968-81 Oakland Raiders, 1982 Los Angeles Raiders. **Highlights:** Cornerstone of Raiders' offensive line in 1970s. 207 regular-season games, 24 postseason games, eight Pro Bowls.

DON SHULA
Coach. Born in Painesville, Ohio, January 4, 1930. John Carroll. Inducted in 1997. 1963-69 Baltimore Colts, 1970-1995 Miami Dolphins. **Highlights:** Won more games (347) than any coach in NFL history. Won two Super Bowl titles, including Super Bowl VII when Dolphins recorded NFL's only perfect season (17-0).

O.J. SIMPSON
Running back. 6-1, 212. Born in San Francisco, California, July 9, 1947. City College (San Francisco), Southern California. Inducted in 1985. 1969-77 Buffalo Bills, 1978-79 San Francisco 49ers. **Highlights:** In 1973, became first player to rush for 2,000 yards in season. Finished career with four rushing titles, 11,236 yards.

MIKE SINGLETARY
Linebacker. 6-0, 230. Born in Houston, Texas, October 9, 1958. Baylor. Inducted in 1998. 1981-92 Chicago Bears. **Highlights:** All-Pro choice eight times and All-NFC nine consecutive seasons. Selected to 10 Pro Bowls.

JACKIE SMITH
Tight end. 6-4, 232. Born in Columbia, Mississippi, February 23, 1940. Northwestern State (Louisiana). Inducted in 1994. 1963-77 St. Louis Cardinals, 1978 Dallas Cowboys. **Highlights:** 480 receptions for 7,918 yards, 40 touchdowns. Third tight end to be elected to Hall of Fame.

BART STARR
Quarterback. 6-1, 200. Born in Montgomery, Alabama, January 9, 1934. Alabama. Inducted in 1977. 1956-71 Green Bay Packers. **Highlights:** Quarterbacked Packers to six division titles, five NFL titles, and first two Super Bowls in which he was MVP.

ROGER STAUBACH
Quarterback. 6-3, 202. Born in Cincinnati, Ohio, February 5, 1942. New Mexico Military Institute, Navy. Inducted in 1985. 1969-79 Dallas Cowboys. **Highlights:** Led Cowboys to four NFC titles and victories in Super Bowls VI, XII. When retired, 83.4 career passer rating was best of all time.

ERNIE STAUTNER
Defensive tackle. 6-2, 235. Born in Prinzing-by-Cham, Bavaria, April 20, 1925. Boston College. Inducted in 1969. 1950-63 Pittsburgh Steelers. **Highlights:** Played in nine Pro Bowls and won the best lineman award in 1957. Recorded 3 safeties.

JAN STENERUD
Kicker. 6-2, 190. Born in Fetsund, Norway, November 26, 1942. Montana State. Inducted in 1991. 1967-79 Kansas City Chiefs, 1980-83 Green Bay Packers, 1984-85 Minnesota Vikings. **Highlights:** 1,699 points on 580 extra points, 373 field goals. First pure placekicker to enter Hall of Fame.

DWIGHT STEPHENSON
Center. 6-2, 255. Born in Murfreesboro, North Carolina, November 20, 1957. Alabama. Inducted in 1998. 1980-87 Miami Dolphins. **Highlights:** Recognized as premier center of his time. All-Pro, All-AFC five straight years. Selected to five Pro Bowls.

KEN STRONG
Halfback. 5-11, 210. Born in West Haven, Connecticut, August 6, 1906. Died October 5, 1979. New York University. Inducted in 1967. 1929-32 Staten Island Stapletons, 1933-35, 1939, 1944-47 New York Giants, 1936-37 New York Yanks (AFL). **Highlights:** Scored 17 points to lead Giants to victory in 1934 'Sneakers' game, led NFL with 64 points, 1933.

JOE STYDAHAR
Tackle. 6-4, 230. Born in Kaylor, Pennsylvania, March 17, 1912. Died March 23, 1977. West Virginia. Inducted in 1967. 1936-42, 1945-46 Chicago Bears. **Highlights:** One of stalwarts of Bears' 'Monsters of the Midway.' Played on five divisional, three NFL championship teams.

FRAN TARKENTON
Quarterback. 6-0, 185. Born in Richmond, Virginia, February 3, 1940. Georgia. Inducted in 1986. 1961-66, 1972-78 Minnesota Vikings, 1967-71 New York Giants. **Highlights:** At retirement, held NFL records for attempts (6,467), completions (3,686), yards (47,003), and touchdowns (342). Four touchdowns passes in first NFL game.

CHARLEY TAYLOR
Running back-wide receiver. 6-3, 210. Born in Grand Prairie, Texas, September 28, 1941. Arizona State. Inducted in 1984. 1964-75, 1977 Washington Redskins. **Highlights:** Won rookie of year honors as running back. Switched to wide receiver and won receiving titles in 1966, 1967.

JIM TAYLOR
Fullback. 6-0, 216. Born in Baton Rouge, Louisiana, September 20, 1935. Louisiana State. Inducted in 1976. 1958-66 Green Bay Packers, 1967 New Orleans Saints. **Highlights:** 8,597 rushing yards, 558 points. In 1962, led league in rushing and scoring with 19 touchdowns.

LAWRENCE TAYLOR
Linebacker. 6-3, 237. Born in Williamsburg, Virginia, February 4, 1959. North Carolina. Inducted in 1999. 1981-93 New York Giants. **Highlights:** Redefined the position of outside linebacker. All-Pro nine times, 10 Pro Bowls. NFL MVP in 1986.

PRO FOOTBALL HALL OF FAME

JIM THORPE
Halfback. 6-1, 190. Born in Prague, Oklahoma, May 28, 1888. Died March 28, 1953. Carlisle. Inducted in 1963. 1915-17, 1919-20, 1926 Canton Bulldogs, 1921 Cleveland Indians, 1922-23 Oorang Indians, 1924 Rock Island Independents, 1925 New York Giants, 1928 Chicago Cardinals. **Highlights:** Charter enshrinee. First president of American Professional Football Association, 1920. Played for 12 seasons.

Y.A. TITTLE
Quarterback. 6-0, 200. Born in Marshall, Texas, October 24, 1926. Louisiana State. Inducted in 1971. 1948-49 Baltimore Colts (AAFC), 1950 Baltimore Colts, 1951-60 San Francisco 49ers, 1961-64 New York Giants. **Highlights:** 33,070 yards, 242 touchdowns. 33 touchdown passes in 1962 and 36 in 1963. Two-time league MVP.

GEORGE TRAFTON
Center. 6-2, 235. Born in Chicago, Illinois, December 6, 1896. Died September 5, 1971. Notre Dame. Inducted in 1964. 1920 Decatur Staleys, 1921 Chicago Staleys, 1922-32 Chicago Bears. **Highlights:** First center to snap with one hand. Named top NFL center of 1920s.

CHARLEY TRIPPI
Halfback-quarterback. 6-0, 185. Born in Pittston, Pennsylvania, December 14, 1922. Georgia. Inducted in 1968. 1947-55 Chicago Cardinals. **Highlights:** One of football's most versatile performers. Played halfback five years, quarterback for two, defense for two.

EMLEN TUNNELL
Safety. 6-1, 200. Born in Bryn Mawr, Pennsylvania, March 29, 1925. Died July 22, 1975. Toledo, Iowa. Inducted in 1967. 1948-58 New York Giants, 1959-61 Green Bay Packers. **Highlights:** 79 interceptions. Gained more yards on kickoff, punt, and interception returns (924) in 1952 than that season's NFL rushing leader.

CLYDE (BULLDOG) TURNER
Center. 6-2, 235. Born in Plains, Texas, March 10, 1919. Died October 30, 1998. Hardin-Simmons. Inducted in 1966. 1940-52 Chicago Bears. **Highlights:** Anchored defense for four NFL championship teams, including 4 interceptions in five title games.

JOHNNY UNITAS
Quarterback. 6-1, 195. Born in Pittsburgh, Pennsylvania, May 7, 1933. Louisville. Inducted in 1979. 1956-72 Baltimore Colts, 1973 San Diego Chargers. **Highlights:** 40,239 passing yards, 290 touchdowns. Led Colts to two NFL championships. Passed for at least one touchdown in 47 consecutive games.

GENE UPSHAW
Guard. 6-5, 255. Born in Robstown, Texas, August 15, 1945. Texas A & I. Inducted in 1987. 1967-81 Oakland Raiders. **Highlights:** Premier guard of his era played in 10 AFL/AFC Championship Games, three Super Bowls, seven Pro Bowls.

NORM VAN BROCKLIN
Quarterback. 6-1, 190. Born in Eagle Butte, South Dakota, March 15, 1926. Died May 2, 1983. Oregon. Inducted in 1971. 1949-57 Los Angeles Rams, 1958-60 Philadelphia Eagles. **Highlights:** NFL-record 554 yards passing in 1951 season opener. Guided Eagles to NFL crown as league MVP in 1960.

STEVE VAN BUREN
Halfback. 6-1, 200. Born in La Ceiba, Honduras, December 28, 1920. Louisiana State. Inducted in 1965. 1944-51 Philadelphia Eagles. **Highlights:** Four-time rushing champion. Won 1944 punt-return title and was 1945 kickoff-return champion.

DOAK WALKER
Halfback. 5-11, 173. Born in Dallas, Texas, January 1, 1927. Died September 27, 1998. Southern Methodist. Inducted in 1986. 1950-55 Detroit Lions. **Highlights:** 534 points. Won two NFL scoring titles. Had winning 67-yard scoring run in 1952 title game.

BILL WALSH
Coach. Born in Los Angeles, California, November 30, 1931. San Jose State. Inducted in 1993. 1979-88 San Francisco 49ers. **Highlights:** 102-63-1 coaching record. Guided 49ers to three Super Bowl titles (XVI, XIX, XXIII) in 10 years.

PAUL WARFIELD
Wide receiver. 6-0, 188. Born in Warren, Ohio, November 28, 1942. Ohio State. Inducted in 1983. 1964-69, 1976-77 Cleveland Browns, 1970-74 Miami Dolphins. **Highlights:** 8,565 yards receiving, 85 touchdowns. Eight-time Pro Bowl player. Key to both Cleveland and Miami offenses.

BOB WATERFIELD
Quarterback. 6-2, 200. Born in Elmira, New York, July 26, 1920. Died March 25, 1983. UCLA. Inducted in 1965. 1945 Cleveland Rams, 1946-52 Los Angeles Rams. **Highlights:** NFL MVP as rookie in 1945 and led Rams to NFL title. Grabbed 20 interceptions in limited defensive duties.

MIKE WEBSTER
Center. 6-2, 260. Born in Tomahawk, Wisconsin, March 18, 1952. Wisconsin. Inducted in 1997. 1974-88 Pittsburgh Steelers, 1989-90 Kansas City Chiefs. **Highlights:** Played in 245 games, nine Pro Bowls, and won four Super Bowls during 17-year career.

ARNIE WEINMEISTER
Defensive tackle. 6-4, 235. Born in Rhein, Saskatchewan, Canada, March 23, 1923. Washington. Inducted in 1984. 1948-49 New York Yankees (AAFC), 1950-53 New York Giants. **Highlights:** Dominant defensive tackle of his time. Four-time All-NFL selection, four Pro Bowls.

RANDY WHITE
Defensive tackle. 6-4, 265. Born in Pittsburgh, Pennsylvania, January 15, 1953. Maryland. Inducted in 1994. 1975-88 Dallas Cowboys. **Highlights:** Missed only one game in 14 seasons. Co-MVP of Super Bowl XII. Nine-time Pro Bowl selection.

DAVE WILCOX
Linebacker. 6-3, 241. Born in Ontario, Oregon, September, 29, 1942. Boise State, Oregon. Inducted in 2000. 1964-74 San Francisco 49ers. **Highlights:** Seven Pro Bowls, All-NFL five times. Missed only one game because of injury.

BILL WILLIS
Guard. 6-2, 215. Born in Columbus, Ohio, October 5, 1921. Ohio State. Inducted in 1977. 1946-49 Cleveland Browns (AAFC), 1950-53 Cleveland Browns. **Highlights:** Two-way player who excelled on defense. Four-time All-NFL player, played in three Pro Bowls.

LARRY WILSON
Safety. 6-0, 190. Born in Rigby, Idaho, March 24, 1938. Utah. Inducted in 1978. 1960-72 St. Louis Cardinals. **Highlights:** 52 interceptions. Had interception in seven consecutive games in 1966. Made "safety blitz" famous.

KELLEN WINSLOW
Tight end. 6-5, 250. Born in St. Louis, Missouri, November 5, 1957. Missouri. Inducted in 1995. 1979-87 San Diego Chargers **Highlights:** 541 receptions for 6,741 yards, 45 touchdowns. 13 catches, blocked field goal in 1981 playoff win over Miami.

ALEX WOJCIECHOWICZ
Center. 6-0, 235. Born in South River, New Jersey, August 12, 1915. Died July 13, 1992. Fordham. Inducted in 1968. 1938-46 Detroit Lions, 1946-50 Philadelphia Eagles. **Highlights:** One of league's first iron men. Played both ways for eight years with Lions.

WILLIE WOOD
Safety. 5-10, 190. Born in Washington, D.C., December 23, 1936. Southern California. Inducted in 1989. 1960-71 Green Bay Packers. **Highlights:** 48 interceptions. Competed in six NFL Championship Games and Super Bowls I and II.

ENSHRINEES BY YEAR OF INDUCTION

**Deceased*
(Date of enshrinement in parentheses)

1963 CHARTER CLASS
(September 7, 1963)
Sammy Baugh
Bert Bell*
Joe Carr*
Earl (Dutch) Clark*
Harold (Red) Grange*
George Halas*
Mel Hein*
Wilbur (Pete) Henry*
Robert (Cal) Hubbard*
Don Hutson*
Earl (Curly) Lambeau*
Tim Mara*
George Preston Marshall*
John (Blood) McNally*
Bronko Nagurski*
Ernie Nevers*
Jim Thorpe*

CLASS OF 1964
(September 6, 1964)
Jimmy Conzelman*
Ed Healey*
Clarke Hinkle*
William Roy (Link) Lyman*
Mike Michalske*
Art Rooney*
George Trafton*

CLASS OF 1965
(September 12, 1965)
Guy Chamberlin*
John (Paddy) Driscoll*
Dan Fortmann*
Otto Graham
Sid Luckman*
Steve Van Buren
Bob Waterfield*

CLASS OF 1966
(September 17, 1966)
Bill Dudley
Joe Guyon*
Arnie Herber*
Walt Kiesling*
George McAfee
Steve Owen*
Hugh (Shorty) Ray*
Clyde (Bulldog) Turner*

CLASS OF 1967
(August 5, 1967)
Chuck Bednarik
Charles W. Bidwill, Sr.*
Paul Brown*
Bobby Layne*
Dan Reeves*
Ken Strong*
Joe Stydahar*
Emlen Tunnell*

CLASS OF 1968
(August 3, 1968)
Cliff Battles*
Art Donovan
Elroy (Crazylegs) Hirsch
Wayne Millner*
Marion Motley
Charley Trippi
Alex Wojciechowicz*

CLASS OF 1969
(September 13, 1969)
Albert Glen (Turk) Edwards*
Earle (Greasy) Neale*
Leo Nomellini
Joe Perry
Ernie Stautner

CLASS OF 1970
(August 8, 1970)
Jack Christiansen*
Tom Fears
Hugh McElhenny
Pete Pihos

CLASS OF 1971
(July 31, 1971)
Jim Brown
Bill Hewitt*
Frank (Bruiser) Kinard*
Vince Lombardi*
Andy Robustelli
Y. A. Tittle
Norm Van Brocklin*

CLASS OF 1972
(July 29, 1972)
Lamar Hunt
Gino Marchetti
Ollie Matson
Clarence (Ace) Parker

CLASS OF 1973
(July 28, 1973)
Raymond Berry
Jim Parker
Joe Schmidt

CLASS OF 1974
(July 27, 1974)
Tony Canadeo
Bill George*
Lou Groza
Dick (Night Train) Lane

CLASS OF 1975
(August 2, 1975)
Roosevelt Brown
George Connor
Dante Lavelli
Lenny Moore

CLASS OF 1976
(July 24, 1976)
Ray Flaherty*
Len Ford*
Jim Taylor

CLASS OF 1977
(July 30, 1977)
Frank Gifford
Forrest Gregg
Gale Sayers
Bart Starr
Bill Willis

CLASS OF 1978
(July 29, 1978)
Lance Alworth
Weeb Ewbank*
Alphonse (Tuffy) Leemans*
Ray Nitschke*
Larry Wilson

CLASS OF 1979
(July 28, 1979)
Dick Butkus
Yale Lary
Ron Mix
Johnny Unitas

CLASS OF 1980
(August 2, 1980)
Herb Adderley
David (Deacon) Jones
Bob Lilly
Jim Otto

CLASS OF 1981
(August 1, 1981)
Morris (Red) Badgro*
George Blanda
Willie Davis
Jim Ringo

CLASS OF 1982
(August 7, 1982)
Doug Atkins
Sam Huff
George Musso
Merlin Olsen

CLASS OF 1983
(July 30, 1983)
Bobby Bell
Sid Gillman
Sonny Jurgensen
Bobby Mitchell
Paul Warfield

CLASS OF 1984
(July 28, 1984)
Willie Brown
Mike McCormack
Charley Taylor
Arnie Weinmeister

CLASS OF 1985
(August 3, 1985)
Frank Gatski
Joe Namath
Pete Rozelle*
O. J. Simpson
Roger Staubach

CLASS OF 1986
(August 2, 1986)
Paul Hornung
Ken Houston
Willie Lanier
Fran Tarkenton
Doak Walker*

CLASS OF 1987
(August 8, 1987)
Larry Csonka
Len Dawson
Joe Greene
John Henry Johnson
Jim Langer
Don Maynard
Gene Upshaw

CLASS OF 1988
(July 30, 1988)
Fred Biletnikoff
Mike Ditka
Jack Ham
Alan Page

CLASS OF 1989
(August 5, 1989)
Mel Blount
Terry Bradshaw
Art Shell
Willie Wood

CLASS OF 1990
(August 4, 1990)
Buck Buchanan*
Bob Griese
Franco Harris
Ted Hendricks
Jack Lambert
Tom Landry
Bob St. Clair

CLASS OF 1991
(July 27, 1991)
Earl Campbell
John Hannah
Stan Jones
Tex Schramm
Jan Stenerud

CLASS OF 1992
(August 1, 1992)
Lem Barney
Al Davis
John Mackey
John Riggins

CLASS OF 1993
(July 31, 1993)
Dan Fouts
Larry Little
Chuck Noll
Walter Payton
Bill Walsh

CLASS OF 1994
(July 30, 1994)
Tony Dorsett
Bud Grant
Jimmy Johnson
Leroy Kelly
Jackie Smith
Randy White

CLASS OF 1995
(July 29, 1995)
Jim Finks*
Henry Jordan*
Steve Largent
Lee Roy Selmon
Kellen Winslow

CLASS OF 1996
(July 27, 1996)
Lou Creekmur
Dan Dierdorf
Joe Gibbs
Charlie Joiner
Mel Renfro

CLASS OF 1997
(July 26, 1997)
Mike Haynes
Wellington Mara
Don Shula
Mike Webster

CLASS OF 1998
(August 1, 1998)
Paul Krause
Tommy McDonald
Anthony Muñoz
Mike Singletary
Dwight Stephenson

CLASS OF 1999
(August 7, 1999)
Eric Dickerson
Tom Mack
Ozzie Newsome
Billy Shaw
Lawrence Taylor

CLASS OF 2000
(July 29, 2000)
Howie Long
Ronnie Lott
Joe Montana
Dan Rooney
Dave Wilcox

CHRONOLOGY OF PROFESSIONAL FOOTBALL

1869
Rutgers and Princeton played a college soccer football game, the first ever, November 6. The game used modified London Football Association rules. During the next seven years, rugby gained favor with the major eastern schools over soccer, and modern football began to develop from rugby.

1876
At the Massasoit convention, the first rules for American football were written. Walter Camp, who would become known as the father of American football, first became involved with the game.

1892
In an era in which football was a major attraction of local athletic clubs, an intense competition between two Pittsburgh-area clubs, the Allegheny Athletic Association (AAA) and the Pittsburgh Athletic Club (PAC), led to the making of the first professional football player. Former Yale All-America guard William (Pudge) Heffelfinger was paid $500 by the AAA to play in a game against the PAC, becoming the first person to be paid to play football, November 12. The AAA won the game 4-0 when Heffelfinger picked up a PAC fumble and ran 35 yards for a touchdown.

1893
The Pittsburgh Athletic Club signed one of its players, probably halfback Grant Dibert, to the first known pro football contract, which covered all of the PAC's games for the year.

1895
John Brallier became the first football player to openly turn pro, accepting $10 and expenses to play for the Latrobe YMCA against the Jeannette Athletic Club.

1896
The Allegheny Athletic Association team fielded the first completely professional team for its abbreviated two-game season.

1897
The Latrobe Athletic Association football team went entirely professional, becoming the first team to play a full season with only professionals.

1898
A touchdown was changed from four points to five.

1899
Chris O'Brien formed a neighborhood team, which played under the name the Morgan Athletic Club, on the south side of Chicago. The team later became known as the Normals, then the Racine (for a street in Chicago) Cardinals, the Chicago Cardinals, the St. Louis Cardinals, the Phoenix Cardinals, and, in 1994, the Arizona Cardinals. The team remains the oldest continuing operation in pro football.

1900
William C. Temple took over the team payments for the Duquesne Country and Athletic Club, becoming the first known individual club owner.

1902
Baseball's Philadelphia Athletics, managed by Connie Mack, and the Philadelphia Phillies formed professional football teams, joining the Pittsburgh Stars in the first attempt at a pro football league, named the National Football League. The Athletics won the first night football game ever played, 39-0 over Kanaweola AC at Elmira, New York, November 21.

All three teams claimed the pro championship for the year, but the league president, Dave Berry, named the Stars the champions. Pitcher Rube Waddell was with the Athletics, and pitcher Christy Mathewson a fullback for Pittsburgh.

The first World Series of pro football, actually a five-team tournament, was played among a team made up of players from both the Athletics and the Phillies, but simply named New York; the New York Knickerbockers; the Syracuse AC; the Warlow AC; and the Orange (New Jersey) AC at New York's original Madison Square Garden. New York and Syracuse played the first indoor football game before 3,000, December 28. Syracuse, with Glen (Pop) Warner at guard, won 6-0 and went on to win the tournament.

1903
The Franklin (Pa.) Athletic Club won the second and last World Series of pro football over the Oreos AC of Asbury Park, New Jersey; the Watertown Red and Blacks; and the Orange AC.

Pro football was popularized in Ohio when the Massillon Tigers, a strong amateur team, hired four Pittsburgh pros to play in the season-ending game against Akron. At the same time, pro football declined in the Pittsburgh area, and the emphasis on the pro game moved west from Pennsylvania to Ohio.

1904
A field goal was changed from five points to four.

Ohio had at least seven pro teams, with Massillon winning the Ohio Independent Championship, that is, the pro title. Talk surfaced about forming a state-wide league to end spiraling salaries brought about by constant bidding for players and to write universal rules for the game. The feeble attempt to start the league failed.

Halfback Charles Follis signed a contract with the Shelby (Ohio) AC, making him the first known black pro football player.

1905
The Canton AC, later to become known as the Bulldogs, became a professional team. Massillon again won the Ohio League championship.

1906
The forward pass was legalized. The first authenticated pass completion in a pro game came on October 27, when George (Peggy) Parratt of Massillon threw a completion to Dan (Bullet) Riley in a victory over a combined Benwood-Moundsville team.

Arch-rivals Canton and Massillon, the two best pro teams in America, played twice, with Canton winning the first game but Massillon winning the second and the Ohio League championship. A betting scandal and the financial disaster wrought upon the two clubs by paying huge salaries caused a temporary decline in interest in pro football in the two cities and, somewhat, throughout Ohio.

1909
A field goal dropped from four points to three.

1912
A touchdown was increased from five points to six.

Jack Cusack revived a strong pro team in Canton.

1913
Jim Thorpe, a former football and track star at the Carlisle Indian School (Pa.) and a double gold medal winner at the 1912 Olympics in Stockholm, played for the Pine Village Pros in Indiana.

1915
Massillon again fielded a major team, reviving the old rivalry with Canton. Cusack signed Thorpe to play for Canton for $250 a game.

1916
With Thorpe and former Carlisle teammate Pete Calac starring, Canton went 9-0-1, won the Ohio League championship, and was acclaimed the pro football champion.

1917
Despite an upset by Massillon, Canton again won the Ohio League championship.

1919
Canton again won the Ohio League championship, despite the team having been turned over from Cusack to Ralph Hay. Thorpe and Calac were joined in the backfield by Joe Guyon.

Earl (Curly) Lambeau and George Calhoun organized the Green Bay Packers. Lambeau's employer at the Indian Packing Company provided $500 for equipment and allowed the team to use the company field for practices. The Packers went 10-1.

1920
Pro football was in a state of confusion due to three major problems: dramatically rising salaries; players continually jumping from one team to another following the highest offer; and the use of college players still enrolled in school. A league in which all the members would follow the same rules seemed the answer. An organizational meeting, at which the Akron Pros, Canton Bulldogs, Cleveland Indians, and Dayton Triangles were represented, was held at the Jordan and Hupmobile auto showroom in Canton, Ohio, August 20. This meeting resulted in the formation of the American Professional Football Conference.

A second organizational meeting was held in Canton, September 17. The teams were from four states—Akron, Canton, Cleveland, and Dayton from Ohio; the Hammond Pros and Muncie Flyers from Indiana; the Rochester Jeffersons from New York; and the Rock Island Independents, Decatur Staleys, and Racine Cardinals from Illinois. The name of the league was changed to the American Professional Football Association. Hoping to capitalize on his fame, the members elected Thorpe president; Stanley Cofall of Cleveland was elected vice president. A membership fee of $100 per team was charged to give an appearance of respectability, but no team ever paid it. Scheduling was left up to the teams, and there were wide variations, both in the overall number of games played and in the number played against APFA member teams.

Four other teams—the Buffalo All-Americans, Chicago Tigers, Columbus Panhandles, and Detroit Heralds—joined the league sometime during the year. On September 26, the first game featuring an APFA team was played at Rock Island's Douglas Park. A crowd of 800 watched the Independents defeat the St. Paul Ideals 48-0. A week later, October 3, the first game matching two APFA teams was held. At Triangle Park, Dayton defeated Columbus 14-0, with Lou Partlow of Dayton scoring the first touchdown in a game between Association teams. The same day, Rock Island defeated Muncie 45-0.

By the beginning of December, most of the teams in the APFA had abandoned their hopes for a championship, and some of them, including the Chicago Tigers and the Detroit Heralds, had finished their seasons, disbanded, and had their franchises canceled by the Association. Four teams—Akron, Buffalo, Canton, and Decatur—still had championship aspirations, but a series of late-season games among them left Akron as the only undefeated team in the Association. At one of these games, Akron sold tackle Bob Nash to Buffalo for $300 and five percent of the gate receipts—the first APFA player deal.

1921
At the league meeting in Akron, April 30, the championship of the 1920 season was awarded to the Akron Pros. The APFA was reorganized, with Joe Carr of the Columbus Panhandles named president and Carl Storck of Dayton secretary-treasurer. Carr moved the Association's headquarters to Columbus, drafted a league constitution and by-laws, gave teams territorial rights, restricted player movements, developed membership criteria for the franchises, and issued standings for the first time, so that the APFA would have a clear champion.

The Association's membership increased to 22 teams, including the Green Bay Packers, who were awarded to John Clair of the Acme Packing Company.

Thorpe moved from Canton to the Cleveland Indians, but he was hurt early in the season and played very little.

A.E. Staley turned the Decatur Staleys over to player-coach George Halas, who moved the team to Cubs Park in Chicago. Staley paid Halas

$5,000 to keep the name Staleys for one more year. Halas made halfback Ed (Dutch) Sternaman his partner.

Player-coach Fritz Pollard of the Akron Pros became the first black head coach.

The Staleys claimed the APFA championship with a 9-1-1 record, as did Buffalo at 9-1-2. Carr ruled in favor of the Staleys, giving Halas his first championship.

1922
After admitting the use of players who had college eligibility remaining during the 1921 season, Clair and the Green Bay management withdrew from the APFA, January 28. Curly Lambeau promised to obey league rules and then used $50 of his own money to buy back the franchise. Bad weather and low attendance plagued the Packers, and Lambeau went broke, but local merchants arranged a $2,500 loan for the club. A public nonprofit corporation was set up to operate the team, with Lambeau as head coach and manager.

The American Professional Football Association changed its name to the National Football League, June 24. The Chicago Staleys became the Chicago Bears.

The NFL fielded 18 teams, including the new Oorang Indians of Marion, Ohio, an all-Indian team featuring Thorpe, Joe Guyon, and Pete Calac, and sponsored by the Oorang dog kennels.

Canton, led by player-coach Guy Chamberlin and tackles Link Lyman and Wilbur (Pete) Henry, emerged as the league's first true powerhouse, going 10-0-2.

1923
For the first time, all of the franchises considered to be part of the NFL fielded teams. Thorpe played his second and final season for the Oorang Indians. Against the Bears, Thorpe fumbled, and Halas picked up the ball and returned it 98 yards for a touchdown, a record that would last until 1972.

Canton had its second consecutive undefeated season, going 11-0-1 for the NFL title.

1924
The league had 18 franchises, including new ones in Kansas City, Kenosha, and Frankford, a section of Philadelphia. League champion Canton, successful on the field but not at the box office, was purchased by the owner of the Cleveland franchise, who kept the Canton franchise inactive, while using the best players for his Cleveland team, which he renamed the Bulldogs. Cleveland won the title with a 7-1-1 record.

1925
Five new franchises were admitted to the NFL—the New York Giants, who were awarded to Tim Mara and Billy Gibson for $500; the Detroit Panthers, featuring Jimmy Conzelman as owner, coach, and tailback; the Providence Steam Roller; a new Canton Bulldogs team; and the Pottsville Maroons, who had been perhaps the most successful independent pro team. The NFL established its first player limit, at 16 players.

Late in the season, the NFL made its greatest coup in gaining national recognition. Shortly after the University of Illinois season ended in November, All-America halfback Harold (Red) Grange signed a contract to play with the Chicago Bears. On Thanksgiving Day, a crowd of 36,000—the largest in pro football history—watched Grange and the Bears play the Chicago Cardinals to a scoreless tie at Wrigley Field. At the beginning of December, the Bears left on a barnstorming tour that saw them play eight games in 12 days, in St. Louis, Philadelphia, New York City, Washington, Boston, Pittsburgh, Detroit, and Chicago. A crowd of 73,000 watched the game against the Giants at the Polo Grounds, helping assure the future of the troubled NFL franchise in New York. The Bears then played nine more games in the South and West, including a game in Los Angeles, in which 75,000 fans watched them defeat the Los Angeles Tigers in the Los Angeles Memorial Coliseum.

Pottsville and the Chicago Cardinals were the top contenders for the league title, with Pottsville winning a late-season meeting 21-7. Pottsville scheduled a game against a team of former Notre Dame players for Shibe Park in Philadelphia. Frankford lodged a protest not only because the game was in Frankford's protected territory, but because it was being played the same day as a Yellow Jackets home game. Carr gave three different notices forbidding Pottsville to play the game, but Pottsville played anyway, December 12. That day, Carr fined the club, suspended it from all rights and privileges (including the right to play for the NFL championship), and returned its franchise to the league. The Cardinals, who ended the season with the best record in the league, were named the 1925 champions.

1926
Grange's manager, C.C. Pyle, told the Bears that Grange wouldn't play for them unless he was paid a five-figure salary and given one-third ownership of the team. The Bears refused. Pyle leased Yankee Stadium in New York City, then petitioned for an NFL franchise. After he was refused, he started the first American Football League. It lasted one season and included Grange's New York Yankees and eight other teams. The AFL champion Philadelphia Quakers played a December game against the New York Giants, seventh in the NFL, and the Giants won 31-0. At the end of the season, the AFL folded.

Halas pushed through a rule that prohibited any team from signing a player whose college class had not graduated.

The NFL grew to 22 teams, including the Duluth Eskimos, who signed All-America fullback Ernie Nevers of Stanford, giving the league a gate attraction to rival Grange. The 15-member Eskimos, dubbed the Iron Men of the North, played 29 exhibition and league games, 28 on the road, and Nevers played in all but 29 minutes of them.

Frankford edged the Bears for the championship, despite Halas having obtained John (Paddy) Driscoll from the Cardinals. On December 4, the Yellow Jackets scored in the final two minutes to defeat the Bears 7-6 and move ahead of them in the standings.

1927
At a special meeting in Cleveland, April 23, Carr decided to secure the NFL's future by eliminating the financially weaker teams and consolidating the quality players onto a limited number of more successful teams. The new-look NFL dropped to 12 teams, and the center of gravity of the league left the Midwest, where the NFL had started, and began to emerge in the large cities of the East. One of the new teams was Grange's New York Yankees, but Grange suffered a knee injury and the Yankees finished in the middle of the pack. The NFL championship was won by the cross-town rival New York Giants, who posted 10 shutouts in 13 games.

1928
Grange and Nevers both retired from pro football, and Duluth disbanded, as the NFL was reduced to only 10 teams. The Providence Steam Roller of Jimmy Conzelman and Pearce Johnson won the championship, playing in the Cycledrome, a 10,000-seat oval that had been built for bicycle races.

1929
Chris O'Brien sold the Chicago Cardinals to David Jones, July 27.

The NFL added a fourth official, the field judge, July 28.

Grange and Nevers returned to the NFL. Nevers scored six rushing touchdowns and four extra points as the Cardinals beat Grange's Bears 40-6, November 28. The 40 points set a record that remains the NFL's oldest.

Providence became the first NFL team to host a game at night under floodlights, against the Cardinals, November 3.

The Packers added back Johnny Blood (McNally), tackle Cal Hubbard, and guard Mike Michalske, and won their first NFL championship, edging the Giants, who featured quarterback Benny Friedman.

1930
Dayton, the last of the NFL's original franchises, was purchased by William B. Dwyer and John C. Depler, moved to Brooklyn, and renamed the Dodgers. The Portsmouth, Ohio, Spartans entered the league.

The Packers edged the Giants for the title, but the most improved team was the Bears. Halas retired as a player and replaced himself as coach of the Bears with Ralph Jones, who refined the T-formation by introducing wide ends and a halfback in motion. Jones also introduced rookie All-America fullback-tackle Bronko Nagurski.

The Giants defeated a team of former Notre Dame players coached by Knute Rockne 22-0 before 55,000 at the Polo Grounds, December 14. The proceeds went to the New York Unemployment Fund to help those suffering because of the Great Depression, and the easy victory helped give the NFL credibility with the press and the public.

1931
The NFL decreased to 10 teams, and halfway through the season the Frankford franchise folded. Carr fined the Bears, Packers, and Portsmouth $1,000 each for using players whose college classes had not graduated.

The Packers won an unprecedented third consecutive title, beating out the Spartans, who were led by rookie backs Earl (Dutch) Clark and Glenn Presnell.

1932
George Preston Marshall, Vincent Bendix, Jay O'Brien, and M. Dorland Doyle were awarded a franchise for Boston, July 9. Despite the presence of two rookies—halfback Cliff Battles and tackle Glen (Turk) Edwards—the new team, named the Braves, lost money and Marshall was left as the sole owner at the end of the year.

NFL membership dropped to eight teams, the lowest in history. Official statistics were kept for the first time. The Bears and the Spartans finished the season in the first-ever tie for first place. After the season finale, the league office arranged for an additional regular-season game to determine the league champion. The game was moved indoors to Chicago Stadium because of bitter cold and heavy snow. The arena allowed only an 80-yard field that came right to the walls. The goal posts were moved from the end lines to the goal lines and, for safety, inbounds lines or hashmarks where the ball would be put in play were drawn 10 yards from the walls that butted against the sidelines. The Bears won 9-0, December 18, scoring the winning touchdown on a two-yard pass from Nagurski to Grange. The Spartans claimed Nagurski's pass was thrown from less than five yards behind the line of scrimmage, violating the existing passing rule, but the play stood.

1933
The NFL, which long had followed the rules of college football, made a number of significant changes from the college game for the first time and began to develop rules serving its needs and the style of play it preferred. The innovations from the 1932 championship game—inbounds line or hashmarks and goal posts on the goal lines—were adopted. Also the forward pass was legalized from anywhere behind the line of scrimmage, February 25.

Marshall and Halas pushed through a proposal that divided the NFL into two divisions, with the winners to meet in an annual championship game, July 8.

Three new franchises joined the league—the Pittsburgh Pirates of Art Rooney, the Philadelphia Eagles of Bert Bell and Lud Wray, and the Cincinnati Reds. The Staten Island Stapletons suspended operations for a year, but never returned to the league.

Halas bought out Sternaman, became sole owner of the Bears, and reinstated himself as head coach. Marshall changed the name of the Boston Braves to the Redskins. David Jones sold the Chicago Cardinals to Charles W. Bidwill.

In the first NFL Championship Game scheduled before the season, the Western Division champion Bears defeated the Eastern Division champion Giants 23-21 at Wrigley Field, December 17.

1934
G.A. (Dick) Richards purchased the Portsmouth Spartans, moved them to Detroit, and renamed them the Lions.

Professional football gained new prestige when the Bears were matched against the best college football players in the first Chicago College All-Star Game, August 31. The game ended in a scoreless tie before 79,432 at Soldier Field.

The Cincinnati Reds lost their first eight games, then were suspended from the league for defaulting on payments. The St. Louis Gunners, an independent team, joined the NFL by buying the Cincinnati franchise and went 1-2 the last three weeks.

Rookie Beattie Feathers of the Bears became the NFL's first 1,000-yard rusher, gaining 1,004 on 101 carries. The Thanksgiving Day game between the Bears and the Lions became the first NFL game broadcast nationally, with Graham McNamee the announcer for NBC radio.

In the championship game, on an extremely cold and icy day at the Polo Grounds, the Giants trailed the Bears 13-3 in the third quarter before changing to basketball shoes for better footing. The Giants won 30-13 in what has come to be known as the Sneakers Game, December 9.

The player waiver rule was adopted, December 10.

1935
The NFL adopted Bert Bell's proposal to hold an annual draft of college players, to begin in 1936, with teams selecting in an inverse order of finish, May 19. The inbounds line or hashmarks were moved nearer the center of the field, 15 yards from the sidelines.

All-America end Don Hutson of Alabama joined Green Bay. The Lions defeated the Giants 26-7 in the NFL Championship Game, December 15.

1936
There were no franchise transactions for the first year since the formation of the NFL. It also was the first year in which all member teams played the same number of games.

The Eagles made University of Chicago halfback and Heisman Trophy winner Jay Berwanger the first player ever selected in the NFL draft, February 8. The Eagles traded his rights to the Bears, but Berwanger never played pro football. The first player selected to actually sign was the number-two pick, Riley Smith of Alabama, who was selected by Boston.

A rival league was formed, and it became the second to call itself the American Football League. The Boston Shamrocks were its champions.

Because of poor attendance, Marshall, the owner of the host team, moved the Championship Game from Boston to the Polo Grounds in New York. Green Bay defeated the Redskins 21-6, December 13.

1937
Homer Marshman was granted a Cleveland franchise, named the Rams, February 12. Marshall moved the Redskins to Washington, D.C., February 13. The Redskins signed TCU All-America tailback Sammy Baugh, who led them to a 28-21 victory over the Bears in the NFL Championship Game, December 12.

The Los Angeles Bulldogs had an 8-0 record to win the AFL title, but then the 2-year-old league folded.

1938
At the suggestion of Halas, Hugh (Shorty) Ray became a technical advisor on rules and officiating to the NFL. A new rule called for a 15-yard penalty for roughing the passer.

Rookie Byron (Whizzer) White of the Pittsburgh Pirates led the NFL in rushing. The Giants defeated the Packers 23-17 for the NFL title, December 11.

Marshall, *Los Angeles Times* sports editor Bill Henry, and promoter Tom Gallery established the Pro Bowl game between the NFL champion and a team of pro all-stars.

1939
The New York Giants defeated the Pro All-Stars 13-10 in the first Pro Bowl, at Wrigley Field, Los Angeles, January 15.

Carr, NFL president since 1921, died in Columbus, May 20. Carl Storck was named acting president, May 25.

An NFL game was televised for the first time when NBC broadcast the Brooklyn Dodgers-Philadelphia Eagles game from Ebbets Field to the approximately 1,000 sets then in New York.

Green Bay defeated New York 27-0 in the NFL Championship Game, December 10 at Milwaukee. NFL attendance exceeded 1 million in a season for the first time, reaching 1,071,200.

1940
A six-team rival league, the third to call itself the American Football League, was formed, and the Columbus Bullies won its championship.

Halas's Bears, with additional coaching by Clark Shaughnessy of Stanford, defeated the Redskins 73-0 in the NFL Championship Game, December 8. The game, which was the most decisive victory in NFL history, popularized the Bears' T-formation with a man-in-motion. It was the first championship carried on network radio, broadcast by Red Barber to 120 stations of the Mutual Broadcasting System, which paid $2,500 for the rights.

Art Rooney sold the Pittsburgh franchise to Alexis Thompson, December 9, then bought part interest in the Philadelphia Eagles.

1941
Elmer Layden was named the first Commissioner of the NFL, March 1; Storck, the acting president, resigned, April 5. NFL headquarters were moved to Chicago.

Bell and Rooney traded the Eagles to Thompson for the Pirates, then re-named their new team the Steelers. Homer Marshman sold the Rams to Daniel F. Reeves and Fred Levy, Jr.

The league by-laws were revised to provide for playoffs in case there were ties in division races, and sudden-death overtimes in case a playoff game was tied after four quarters. An official *NFL Record Manual* was published for the first time.

Columbus again won the championship of the AFL, but the two-year-old league then folded.

The Bears and the Packers finished in a tie for the Western Division championship, setting up the first divisional playoff game in league history. The Bears won 33-14, then defeated the Giants 37-9 for the NFL championship, December 21.

1942
Players departing for service in World War II depleted the rosters of NFL teams. Halas left the Bears in midseason to join the Navy, and Luke Johnsos and Heartley (Hunk) Anderson served as co-coaches as the Bears went 11-0 in the regular season. The Redskins defeated the Bears 14-6 in the NFL Championship Game, December 13.

1943
The Cleveland Rams, with co-owners Reeves and Levy in the service, were granted permission to suspend operations for one season, April 6. Levy transferred his stock in the team to Reeves, April 16.

The NFL adopted free substitution, April 7. The league also made the wearing of helmets mandatory and approved a 10-game schedule for all teams.

Philadelphia and Pittsburgh were granted permission to merge for one season, June 19. The team, known as Phil-Pitt (and called the Steagles by fans), divided home games between the two cities, and Earle (Greasy) Neale of Philadelphia and Walt Kiesling of Pittsburgh served as co-coaches. The merger automatically dissolved the last day of the season, December 5.

Ted Collins was granted a franchise for Boston, to become active in 1944.

Sammy Baugh led the league in passing, punting, and interceptions. He led the Redskins to a tie with the Giants for the Eastern Division title, and then to a 28-0 victory in a divisional playoff game. The Bears beat the Redskins 41-21 in the NFL Championship Game, December 26.

1944
Collins, who had wanted a franchise in Yankee Stadium in New York, named his new team in Boston the Yanks. Cleveland resumed operations. The Brooklyn Dodgers changed their name to the Tigers.

Coaching from the bench was legalized, April 20.

The Cardinals and the Steelers were granted permission to merge for one year under the name Card-Pitt, April 21. Phil Handler of the Cardinals and Walt Kiesling of the Steelers served as co-coaches. The merger automatically dissolved the last day of the season, December 3.

In the NFL Championship Game, Green Bay defeated the New York Giants 14-7, December 17.

1945
The inbounds lines or hashmarks were moved from 15 yards away from the sidelines to nearer the center of the field—20 yards from the sidelines.

Brooklyn and Boston merged into a team that played home games in both cities and was known simply as The Yanks. The team was coached by former Boston head coach Herb Kopf. In December, the Brooklyn franchise withdrew from the NFL to join the new All-America Football Conference; all the players on its active and reserve lists were assigned to The Yanks, who once again became the Boston Yanks.

Halas rejoined the Bears late in the season after service with the U.S. Navy. Although Halas took over much of the coaching duties, Anderson and Johnsos remained the coaches of record throughout the season.

Steve Van Buren of Philadelphia led the NFL in rushing, kickoff returns, and scoring.

After the Japanese surrendered ending World War II, a count showed that the NFL service roster, limited to men who had played in league games, totaled 638, 21 of whom had died in action.

Rookie quarterback Bob Waterfield led Cleveland to a 15-14 victory over Washington in the NFL Championship Game, December 16.

1946
The contract of Commissioner Layden was not renewed, and Bert Bell, the co-owner of the Steelers, replaced him, January 11. Bell moved the league headquarters from Chicago to the Philadelphia suburb of Bala-Cynwyd.

Free substitution was withdrawn and substitutions were limited to no more than three men at a time. Forward passes were made automatically incomplete upon striking the goal posts, January 11.

The NFL took on a truly national appearance for the first time when Reeves was granted permission by the league to move his NFL champion Rams to Los Angeles.

Halfback Kenny Washington (March 21) and end Woody Strode (May 7) signed with the Los Angeles Rams to become the first African-Americans to play in the NFL in the modern era. Guard Bill Willis (August 6) and running back Marion Motley (August 9) joined the AAFC with the Cleveland Browns.

The rival All-America Football Conference began play with eight teams. The Cleveland Browns, coached by Paul Brown, won the AAFC's first championship, defeating the New York Yankees 14-9.

Bill Dudley of the Steelers led the NFL in rushing, interceptions, and punt returns, and won the league's most valuable player award.

Backs Frank Filchock and Merle Hapes of the Giants were questioned about an attempt by a New York man to fix the championship game with the Bears. Bell suspended Hapes but allowed Filchock to play; he played well, but Chicago won 24-14, December 15.

1947
The NFL added a fifth official, the back judge.

A bonus choice was made for the first time in the NFL draft. One team each year would select the special choice before the first round began. The Chicago Bears won a lottery and the rights to the first choice and drafted back Bob Fenimore of Oklahoma A&M.

The Cleveland Browns again won the AAFC title, defeating the New York Yankees 14-3.

Charles Bidwill, Sr., owner of the Cardinals, died April 19, but his wife and sons retained ownership of the team. On December 28, the Cardinals won the NFL Championship Game 28-21 over the Philadelphia Eagles, who had beaten Pittsburgh 21-0 in a playoff.

1948
Plastic helmets were prohibited. A flexible artificial tee was permitted at the kickoff. Officials other than the referee were equipped with whistles, not horns, January 14.

Fred Mandel sold the Detroit Lions to a syndicate headed by D. Lyle Fife, January 15.

Halfback Fred Gehrke of the Los Angeles Rams painted horns on the Rams' helmets, the first modern helmet emblems in pro football.

The Cleveland Browns won their third straight championship in the AAFC, going 14-0 and then defeating the Buffalo Bills 49-7.

In a blizzard, the Eagles defeated the Cardinals 7-0 in the NFL Championship Game, December 19.

1949
Alexis Thompson sold the champion Eagles to a syndicate headed by James P. Clark, January 15. The Boston Yanks became the New York Bulldogs, sharing the Polo Grounds with the Giants.

Free substitution was adopted for one year, January 20.

The NFL had two 1,000-yard rushers in the same season for the first time—Steve Van Buren of Philadelphia and Tony Canadeo of Green Bay.

The AAFC played its season with a one-division, seven-team format. On December 9, Bell announced a merger agreement in which three AAFC franchises—Cleveland, San Francisco, and Baltimore—would join the NFL in 1950. The Browns won their fourth consecutive AAFC title, defeating the 49ers 21-7, December 11.

In a heavy rain, the Eagles defeated the Rams 14-0 in the NFL Championship Game, December 18.

1950
Unlimited free substitution was restored, opening the way for the era of two platoons and specialization in pro football, January 20.

Curly Lambeau, founder of the franchise and Green Bay's head coach since 1921, resigned under fire, February 1.

The name National Football League was restored after about three months as the National-American Football League. The American and National conferences were created to replace the Eastern and Western divisions, March 3.

The New York Bulldogs became the Yanks and divided the players of the former AAFC Yankees with the Giants. A special allocation draft was held in which the 13 teams drafted the remaining AAFC players, with special consideration for Baltimore, which received 15 choices compared to 10 for other teams.

The Los Angeles Rams became the first NFL team to have all of its games—both home and away—televised. The Washington Redskins followed the Rams in arranging to televise their games; other teams made deals to put selected games on television.

In the first game of the season, former AAFC champion Cleveland defeated NFL champion Philadelphia 35-10. For the first time, deadlocks occurred in both conferences and playoffs were necessary. The Browns defeated the Giants in the American and the Rams defeated the Bears in the National. Cleveland defeated Los Angeles 30-28 in the NFL Championship Game, December 24.

1951
The Pro Bowl game, dormant since 1942, was revived under a new format matching the all-stars of each conference at the Los Angeles Memorial Coliseum. The American Conference defeated the National Conference 28-27, January 14.

Abraham Watner returned the Baltimore franchise and its player contracts back to the NFL for $50,000. Baltimore's former players were made available for drafting at the same time as college players, January 18.

A rule was passed that no tackle, guard, or center would be eligible to catch a forward pass, January 18.

The Rams reversed their television policy and televised only road games.

The NFL Championship Game was televised coast-to-coast for the first time, December 23. The DuMont Network paid $75,000 for the rights to the game, in which the Rams defeated the Browns 24-17.

1952
Ted Collins sold the New York Yanks' franchise back to the NFL, January 19. A new franchise was awarded to a group in Dallas after it purchased the assets of the Yanks, January 24. The new Texans went 1-11, with the owners turning the franchise back to the league in midseason. For the last five games of the season, the commissioner's office operated the Texans as a road team, using Hershey, Pennsylvania, as a home base. At the end of the season the franchise was canceled, the last time an NFL team failed.

The Pittsburgh Steelers abandoned the Single-Wing for the T-formation, the last pro team to do so.

The Detroit Lions won their first NFL championship in 17 years, defeating the Browns 17-7 in the title game, December 28.

1953
A Baltimore group headed by Carroll Rosenbloom was granted a franchise and was awarded the holdings of the defunct Dallas organization, January 23. The team, named the Colts, put together the largest trade in league history, acquiring 10 players from Cleveland in exchange for five.

The names of the American and National conferences were changed to the Eastern and Western conferences, January 24.

Jim Thorpe died, March 28.

Mickey McBride, founder of the Cleveland Browns, sold the franchise to a syndicate headed by Dave R. Jones, June 10.

The NFL policy of blacking out home games was upheld by Judge Allan K. Grim of the U.S. District Court in Philadelphia, November 12.

The Lions again defeated the Browns in the NFL Championship Game, winning 17-16, December 27.

1954
The Canadian Football League began a series of raids on NFL teams, signing quarterback Eddie LeBaron and defensive end Gene Brito of Washington and defensive tackle Arnie Weinmeister of the Giants, among others.

Fullback Joe Perry of the 49ers became the first player in league history to gain 1,000 yards rushing in consecutive seasons.

Cleveland defeated Detroit 56-10 in the NFL Championship Game, December 26.

1955
The sudden-death overtime rule was used for the first time in a preseason game between the Rams and Giants at Portland, Oregon, August 28. The Rams won 23-17 three minutes into overtime.

A rule change declared the ball dead immediately if the ball carrier touched the ground with any part of his body except his hands or feet while in the grasp of an opponent.

The Baltimore Colts made an 80-cent phone call to Johnny Unitas and signed him as a free agent. Another quarterback, Otto Graham, played his last game as the Browns defeated the Rams 38-14 in the NFL Championship Game, December 26. Graham had quarterbacked the Browns to 10 championship-game appearances in 10 years.

NBC replaced DuMont as the network for the title game, paying a rights fee of $100,000.

1956
The NFL Players Association was founded.

Grabbing an opponent's facemask (other than the ball carrier) was made illegal. Using radio receivers to communicate with players on the field was prohibited. A natural leather ball with white end stripes replaced the white ball with black stripes for night games.

The Giants moved from the Polo Grounds to Yankee Stadium.

Halas retired as coach of the Bears, and was replaced by Paddy Driscoll.

CBS became the first network to broadcast some NFL regular-season games to selected television markets across the nation.

The Giants routed the Bears 47-7 in the NFL Championship Game, December 30.

1957
Pete Rozelle was named general manager of the Rams. Anthony J. Morabito, founder and co-owner of the 49ers, died of a heart attack during a game against the Bears at Kezar Stadium, October 28. An NFL-record crowd of 102,368 saw the 49ers-Rams game at the Los Angeles Memorial Coliseum, November 10.

The Lions came from 20 points down to post a 31-27 playoff victory over the 49ers, December 22. Detroit defeated Cleveland 59-14 in the NFL Championship Game, December 29.

1958
The bonus selection in the draft was eliminated, January 29. The last selection was quarterback King Hill of Rice by the Chicago Cardinals.

Halas reinstated himself as coach of the Bears.

Jim Brown of Cleveland gained an NFL-record 1,527 yards rushing. In a divisional playoff game, the Giants held Brown to eight yards and defeated Cleveland 10-0.

Baltimore, coached by Weeb Ewbank, defeated the Giants 23-17 in the first sudden-death overtime in an NFL Championship Game, December 28. The game ended when Colts fullback Alan Ameche scored on a one-yard touchdown run after 8:15 of overtime.

1959
Vince Lombardi was named head coach of the Green Bay Packers, January 28. Tim Mara, the co-founder of the Giants, died, February 17.

Lamar Hunt of Dallas announced his intentions to form a second pro football league. The first meeting was held in Chicago, August 14, and consisted of Hunt representing Dallas; Bob Howsam, Denver; K.S. (Bud) Adams, Houston; Barron Hilton, Los Angeles; Max Winter and Bill Boyer, Minneapolis; and Harry Wismer, New York City. They made plans to begin play in 1960.

The new league was named the American Football League, August 22. Buffalo, owned by Ralph Wilson, became the seventh franchise, October 28. Boston, owned by William H. Sullivan, became the eighth team, November 22. The first AFL draft, lasting 33 rounds, was held, November 22. Joe Foss was named AFL Commissioner, November 30. An additional draft of 20 rounds was held by the AFL, December 2.

NFL Commissioner Bert Bell died of a heart attack suffered at Franklin

Field, Philadelphia, during the last two minutes of a game between the Eagles and the Steelers, October 11. Treasurer Austin Gunsel was named president in the office of the commissioner, October 14.

The Colts again defeated the Giants in the NFL Championship Game, 31-16, December 27.

1960

Pete Rozelle was elected NFL Commissioner as a compromise choice on the twenty-third ballot, January 26. Rozelle moved the league offices to New York City.

Hunt was elected AFL president for 1960, January 26. Minneapolis withdrew from the AFL, January 27, and the same ownership was given an NFL franchise for Minnesota (to start in 1961), January 28. Dallas received an NFL franchise for 1960, January 28. Oakland received an AFL franchise, January 30.

The AFL adopted the two-point option on points after touchdown, January 28. A no-tampering verbal pact, relative to players' contracts, was agreed to between the NFL and AFL, February 9.

The NFL owners voted to allow the transfer of the Chicago Cardinals to St. Louis, March 13.

The AFL signed a five-year television contract with ABC, June 9.

The Boston Patriots defeated the Buffalo Bills 28-7 before 16,000 at Buffalo in the first AFL preseason game, July 30. The Denver Broncos defeated the Patriots 13-10 before 21,597 at Boston in the first AFL regular-season game, September 9.

Philadelphia defeated Green Bay 17-13 in the NFL Championship Game, December 26.

1961

The Houston Oilers defeated the Los Angeles Chargers 24-16 before 32,183 in the first AFL Championship Game, January 1.

Detroit defeated Cleveland 17-16 in the first Playoff Bowl, or Bert Bell Benefit Bowl, between second-place teams in each conference in Miami, January 7.

End Willard Dewveall of the Bears played out his option and joined the Oilers, becoming the first player to move deliberately from one league to the other, January 14.

Ed McGah, Wayne Valley, and Robert Osborne bought out their partners in the ownership of the Raiders, January 17. The Chargers were transferred to San Diego, February 10. Dave R. Jones sold the Browns to a group headed by Arthur B. Modell, March 22. The Howsam brothers sold the Broncos to a group headed by Calvin Kunz and Gerry Phipps, May 26.

NBC was awarded a two-year contract for radio and television rights to the NFL Championship Game for $615,000 annually, $300,000 of which was to go directly into the NFL Player Benefit Plan, April 5.

Canton, Ohio, where the league that became the NFL was formed in 1920, was chosen as the site of the Pro Football Hall of Fame, April 27. Dick McCann, a former Redskins executive, was named executive director.

A bill legalizing single-network television contracts by professional sports leagues was introduced in Congress by Representative Emanuel Celler. It passed the House and Senate and was signed into law by President John F. Kennedy, September 30.

Houston defeated San Diego 10-3 for the AFL championship, December 24. Green Bay won its first NFL championship since 1944, defeating the New York Giants 37-0, December 31.

1962

The Western Division defeated the Eastern Division 47-27 in the first AFL All-Star Game, played before 20,973 in San Diego, January 7.

Both leagues prohibited grabbing any player's facemask. The AFL voted to make the scoreboard clock the official timer of the game.

The NFL entered into a single-network agreement with CBS for telecasting all regular-season games for $4.65 million annually, January 10.

Judge Roszel Thompson of the U.S. District Court in Baltimore ruled against the AFL in its antitrust suit against the NFL, May 21. The AFL had charged the NFL with monopoly and conspiracy in areas of expansion, television, and player signings. The case lasted two and a half years, the trial two months.

McGah and Valley acquired controlling interest in the Raiders, May 24. The AFL assumed financial responsibility for the New York Titans, November 8. With Commissioner Rozelle as referee, Daniel F. Reeves regained the ownership of the Rams, outbidding his partners in sealed-envelope bidding for the team, November 27.

The Dallas Texans defeated the Oilers 20-17 for the AFL championship at Houston after 17 minutes, 54 seconds of overtime on a 25-yard field goal by Tommy Brooker, December 23. The game lasted a record 77 minutes, 54 seconds.

Judge Edward Weinfeld of the U.S. District Court in New York City upheld the legality of the NFL's television blackout within a 75-mile radius of home games and denied an injunction that would have forced the championship game between the Giants and the Packers to be televised in the New York City area, December 28. The Packers beat the Giants 16-7 for the NFL title, December 30.

1963

The Dallas Texans transferred to Kansas City, becoming the Chiefs, February 8. The New York Titans were sold to a five-man syndicate headed by David (Sonny) Werblin, March 28. Weeb Ewbank became the Titans' new head coach and the team's name was changed to the Jets, April 15. They began play in Shea Stadium.

NFL Properties, Inc., was founded to serve as the licensing arm of the NFL.

Rozelle indefinitely suspended Green Bay halfback Paul Hornung and Detroit defensive tackle Alex Karras for placing bets on their own teams and on other NFL games; he also fined five other Detroit players $2,000 each for betting on one game in which they did not participate, and the Detroit Lions Football Company $2,000 on each of two counts for failure to report information promptly and for lack of sideline supervision.

Paul Brown, head coach of the Browns since their inception, was fired and replaced by Blanton Collier. Don Shula replaced Weeb Ewbank as head coach of the Colts.

The AFL allowed the Jets and Raiders to select players from other franchises in hopes of giving the league more competitive balance, May 11.

NBC was awarded exclusive network broadcasting rights for the 1963 AFL Championship Game for $926,000, May 23.

The Pro Football Hall of Fame was dedicated at Canton, Ohio, September 7.

The U.S. Fourth Circuit Court of Appeals reaffirmed the lower court's finding for the NFL in the $10-million suit brought by the AFL, ending three and a half years of litigation, November 21.

Jim Brown of Cleveland rushed for an NFL single-season record 1,863 yards.

Boston defeated Buffalo 26-8 in the first divisional playoff game in AFL history, December 28.

The Bears defeated the Giants 14-10 in the NFL Championship Game, a record sixth and last title for Halas in his thirty-sixth season as the Bears' coach, December 29.

1964

The Chargers defeated the Patriots 51-10 in the AFL Championship Game, January 5.

William Clay Ford, the Lions' president since 1961, purchased the team, January 10. A group representing the late James P. Clark sold the Eagles to a group headed by Jerry Wolman, January 21. Carroll Rosenbloom, the majority owner of the Colts since 1953, acquired complete ownership of the team, January 23.

The AFL signed a five-year, $36-million television contract with NBC to begin with the 1965 season, January 29.

Commissioner Rozelle negotiated an agreement on behalf of the NFL clubs to purchase Ed Sabol's Blair Motion Pictures, which was renamed NFL Films, March 5.

Hornung and Karras were reinstated by Rozelle, March 16.

CBS submitted the winning bid of $14.1 million per year for the NFL regular-season television rights for 1964 and 1965, January 24. CBS acquired the rights to the championship games for 1964 and 1965 for $1.8 million per game, April 17.

Pete Gogolak of Cornell signed a contract with Buffalo, becoming the first soccer-style kicker in pro football.

Buffalo defeated San Diego 20-7 in the AFL Championship Game, December 26. Cleveland defeated Baltimore 27-0 in the NFL Championship Game, December 27.

1965

The NFL teams pledged not to sign college seniors until completion of all their games, including bowl games, and empowered the Commissioner to discipline the clubs up to as much as the loss of an entire draft list for a violation of the pledge, February 15.

The NFL added a sixth official, the line judge, February 19. The color of the officials' penalty flags was changed from white to bright gold, April 5.

Atlanta was awarded an NFL franchise for 1966, with Rankin Smith, Sr., as owner, June 30. Miami was awarded an AFL franchise for 1966, with Joe Robbie and Danny Thomas as owners, August 16.

Field Judge Burl Toler became the first black official in NFL history, September 19.

According to a Harris survey, sports fans chose professional football (41 percent) as their favorite sport, overtaking baseball (38 percent) for the first time, October.

Green Bay defeated Baltimore 13-10 in sudden-death overtime in a Western Conference playoff game. Don Chandler kicked a 25-yard field goal for the Packers after 13 minutes, 39 seconds of overtime, December 26. The Packers then defeated the Browns 23-12 in the NFL Championship Game, January 2.

In the AFL Championship Game, the Bills again defeated the Chargers, 23-0, December 26.

CBS acquired the rights to the NFL regular-season games in 1966 and 1967, with an option for 1968, for $18.8 million per year, December 29.

1966

The AFL-NFL war reached its peak, as the leagues spent a combined $7 million to sign their 1966 draft choices. The NFL signed 75 percent of its 232 draftees, the AFL 46 percent of its 181. Of the 111 common draft choices, 79 signed with the NFL, 28 with the AFL, and 4 went unsigned.

Buddy Young became the first African-American to work in the league office when Commissioner Rozelle named him director of player relations, February 1.

The rights to the 1966 and 1967 NFL Championship Games were sold to CBS for $2 million per game, February 14.

Foss resigned as AFL Commissioner, April 7. Al Davis, the head coach and general manager of the Raiders, was named to replace him, April 8.

Goal posts offset from the goal line, painted bright yellow, and with uprights 20 feet above the cross-bar were made standard in the NFL, May 16.

A series of secret meetings regarding a possible AFL-NFL merger were held in the spring between Hunt of Kansas City and Tex Schramm of Dallas. Rozelle announced the merger, June 8. Under the agreement, the two leagues would combine to form an expanded league with 24 teams, to be increased to 26 in 1968 and to 28 by 1970 or soon thereafter. All existing franchises would be retained, and no franchises would be transferred outside their metropolitan areas. While maintaining separate schedules through 1969, the leagues agreed to play an annual AFL-NFL World Championship Game beginning in January, 1967, and to hold a combined draft, also beginning in 1967. Preseason games would be held between teams of each league starting in 1967. Official regular-season play would start in 1970 when the two leagues would officially merge to form one league with two conferences. Rozelle was named Commissioner of the expanded league setup.

Davis rejoined the Raiders, and Milt Woodard was named president of the AFL, July 25.

The St. Louis Cardinals moved into newly constructed Busch Memorial Stadium.

Barron Hilton sold the Chargers to a group headed by Eugene Klein and Sam Schulman, August 25.

Congress approved the AFL-NFL merger, passing legislation exempting the agreement itself from antitrust action, October 21.

New Orleans was awarded an NFL franchise to begin play in 1967, November 1. John Mecom, Jr., of Houston was designated majority stockholder and president of the franchise, December 15.

The NFL was realigned for the 1967-69 seasons into the Capitol and Century Divisions in the Eastern Conference and the Central and Coastal Divisions in the Western Conference, December 2. New Orleans and the New York Giants agreed to switch divisions in 1968 and return to the 1967 alignment in 1969.

The rights to the Super Bowl for four years were sold to CBS and NBC for $9.5 million, December 13.

1967

Green Bay earned the right to represent the NFL in the first AFL-NFL World Championship Game by defeating Dallas 34-27, January 1. The same day, Kansas City defeated Buffalo 31-7 to represent the AFL. The Packers defeated the Chiefs 35-10 before 61,946 fans at the Los Angeles Memorial Coliseum in the first game between AFL and NFL teams, January 15. The winning players' share for the Packers was $15,000 each, and the losing players' share for the Chiefs was $7,500 each. The game was televised by both CBS and NBC.

The "sling-shot" goal post and a six-foot-wide border around the field were made standard in the NFL, February 22.

Baltimore made Bubba Smith, a Michigan State defensive lineman, the first choice in the first combined AFL-NFL draft, March 14.

The AFL awarded a franchise to begin play in 1968 to Cincinnati, May 24. A group with Paul Brown as part owner, general manager, and head coach, was awarded the Cincinnati franchise, September 27.

Arthur B. Modell, the president of the Cleveland Browns, was elected president of the NFL, May 28.

Defensive back Emlen Tunnell of the New York Giants became the first black player to enter the Pro Football Hall of Fame, August 5.

An AFL team defeated an NFL team for the first time, when Denver beat Detroit 13-7 in a preseason game, August 5.

Green Bay defeated Dallas 21-17 for the NFL championship on a last-minute 1-yard quarterback sneak by Bart Starr in 13-below-zero temperature at Green Bay, December 31. The same day, Oakland defeated Houston 40-7 for the AFL championship.

1968

Green Bay defeated Oakland 33-14 in Super Bowl II at Miami, January 14. The game had the first $3-million gate in pro football history.

Vince Lombardi resigned as head coach of the Packers, but remained as general manager, January 28.

Werblin sold his shares in the Jets to his partners Don Lillis, Leon Hess, Townsend Martin, and Phil Iselin, May 21. Lillis assumed the presidency of the club, but then died July 23. Iselin was appointed president, August 6.

Halas retired for the fourth and last time as head coach of the Bears, May 27.

The Oilers left Rice Stadium for the Astrodome and became the first NFL team to play its home games in a domed stadium.

The movie *Heidi* became a footnote in sports history when NBC didn't show the last :50 of the Jets-Raiders game in order to permit the children's special to begin on time. The Raiders scored two touchdowns in the last 42 seconds to win 43-32, November 17.

Ewbank became the first coach to win titles in both the NFL and AFL when his Jets defeated the Raiders 27-23 for the AFL championship, December 29. The same day, Baltimore defeated Cleveland 34-0.

1969

The AFL established a playoff format for the 1969 season, with the winner in one division playing the runner-up in the other, January 11.

An AFL team won the Super Bowl for the first time, as the Jets defeated the Colts 16-7 at Miami, January 12 in Super Bowl III. The title Super Bowl was recognized by the NFL for the first time.

Vince Lombardi became part owner, executive vice-president, and head coach of the Washington Redskins, February 7.

Wolman sold the Eagles to Leonard Tose, May 1.

Baltimore, Cleveland, and Pittsburgh agreed to join the AFL teams to form the 13-team American Football Conference of the NFL in 1970, May 17. The NFL also agreed on a playoff format that would include one "wild-card" team per conference—the second-place team with the best record.

Monday Night Football was signed for 1970. ABC acquired the rights to televise 13 NFL regular-season Monday night games in 1970, 1971, and 1972.

George Preston Marshall, president emeritus of the Redskins, died at 72, August 9.

The NFL marked its fiftieth year by the wearing of a special patch by each of the 16 teams.

1970

Kansas City defeated Minnesota 23-7 in Super Bowl IV at New Orleans, January 11. The gross receipts of approximately $3.8 million were the largest ever for a one-day sports event.

Four-year television contracts, under which CBS would televise all NFC games and NBC all AFC games (except Monday night games) and the two would divide televising the Super Bowl and AFC-NFC Pro Bowl games, were announced, January 26.

Art Modell resigned as president of the NFL, March 12. Milt Woodard resigned as president of the AFL, March 13. Lamar Hunt was elected president of the AFC and George Halas was elected president of the NFC, March 19.

The merged 26-team league adopted rules changes putting names on the backs of players' jerseys, making a point after touchdown worth only one point, and making the scoreboard clock the official timing device of the game, March 18.

The Players Negotiating Committee and the NFL Players Association announced a four-year agreement guaranteeing approximately $4,535,000 annually to player pension and insurance benefits, August 3. The owners also agreed to contribute $250,000 annually to improve or implement items such as disability payments, widows' benefits, maternity benefits, and dental benefits. The agreement also provided for increased preseason game and per diem payments, averaging approximately $2.6 million annually.

The Pittsburgh Steelers moved into Three Rivers Stadium. The Cincinnati Bengals moved to Riverfront Stadium.

Lombardi died of cancer at 57, September 3.

The Super Bowl trophy was renamed the Vince Lombardi trophy, September 10.

Tom Dempsey of New Orleans kicked a game-winning NFL-record 63-yard field goal against Detroit, November 8.

1971

Baltimore defeated Dallas 16-13 on Jim O'Brien's 32-yard field goal with five seconds to go in Super Bowl V at Miami, January 17. The NBC telecast was viewed in an estimated 23,980,000 homes, the largest audience ever for a one-day sports event.

The NFC defeated the AFC 27-6 in the first AFC-NFC Pro Bowl at Los Angeles, January 24.

The Boston Patriots changed their name to the New England Patriots, March 25. Their new stadium, Schaefer Stadium, was dedicated in a 20-14 preseason victory over the Giants.

The Philadelphia Eagles left Franklin Field and played their games at the new Veterans Stadium.

The San Francisco 49ers left Kezar Stadium and moved their games to Candlestick Park.

Daniel F. Reeves, the president and general manager of the Rams, died at 58, April 15.

The Dallas Cowboys moved from the Cotton Bowl into their new home, Texas Stadium, October 24.

Miami defeated Kansas City 27-24 in sudden-death overtime in an AFC Divisional Playoff Game, December 25. Garo Yepremian kicked a 37-yard field goal for the Dolphins after 22 minutes, 40 seconds of overtime, as the game lasted 82 minutes, 40 seconds overall, making it the longest game in history.

1972

Dallas defeated Miami 24-3 in Super Bowl VI at New Orleans, January 16. The CBS telecast was viewed in an estimated 27,450,000 homes, the top-rated one-day telecast ever.

The inbounds lines or hashmarks were moved nearer the center of the field, 23 yards, 1 foot, 9 inches from the sidelines, March 23. The method of determining won-lost percentage in standings changed. Tie games, previously not counted in the standings, were made equal to a half-game won and a half-game lost, May 24.

Robert Irsay purchased the Los Angeles Rams and transferred ownership of the club to Carroll Rosenbloom in exchange for the Baltimore Colts, July 13.

William V. Bidwill purchased the stock of his brother Charles (Stormy) Bidwill to become the sole owner of the St. Louis Cardinals, September 2.

The National District Attorneys Association endorsed the position of professional leagues in opposing proposed legalization of gambling on professional team sports, September 28.

Franco Harris's "Immaculate Reception" gave the Steelers their first postseason win ever, 13-7 over the Raiders, December 23.

1973

Rozelle announced that all Super Bowl VII tickets were sold and that the game would be telecast in Los Angeles, the site of the game, on an experimental basis, January 3.

Miami defeated Washington 14-7 in Super Bowl VII at Los Angeles, completing a 17-0 season, the first perfect-record regular-season and post-season mark in NFL history, January 14. The NBC telecast was viewed by approximately 75 million people.

The AFC defeated the NFC 33-28 in the Pro Bowl in Dallas, the first time since 1942 that the game was played outside Los Angeles, January 21.

A jersey numbering system was adopted, April 5: 1-19 for quarterbacks and specialists, 20-49 for running backs and defensive backs, 50-59 for centers and linebackers, 60-79 for defensive linemen and interior offensive linemen other than centers, and 80-89 for wide receivers and tight ends. Players who had been in the NFL in 1972 could continue to use old numbers.

NFL Charities, a nonprofit organization, was created to derive an income from monies generated from NFL Properties' licensing of NFL trademarks and team names, June 26. NFL Charities was set up to support education and charitable activities and to supply economic support to persons formerly associated with professional football who were no longer able to support themselves.

Congress adopted experimental legislation (for three years) requiring any NFL game that had been declared a sellout 72 hours prior to kickoff to be made available for local televising, September 14. The legislation provided for an annual review to be made by the Federal Communications Commission.

The Buffalo Bills moved their home games from War Memorial Stadium to Rich Stadium in nearby Orchard Park. The Giants tied the Eagles 23-23 in the final game in Yankee Stadium, September 23. The Giants played the rest of their home games at the Yale Bowl in New Haven, Connecticut.

A rival league, the World Football League, was formed and was reported in operation, October 2. It had plans to start play in 1974.

O.J. Simpson of Buffalo became the first player to rush for more than 2,000 yards in a season, gaining 2,003.

1974

Miami defeated Minnesota 24-7 in Super Bowl VIII at Houston, the second consecutive Super Bowl championship for the Dolphins, January 13. The CBS telecast was viewed by approximately 75 million people.

Rozelle was given a 10-year contract effective January 1, 1973, February 27.

Tampa Bay was awarded a franchise to begin operation in 1976, April 24.

Sweeping rules changes were adopted to add action and tempo to games: one sudden-death overtime period was added for preseason and regular-season games; the goal posts were moved from the goal line to the end lines; kickoffs were moved from the 40- to the 35-yard line; after missed field goals from beyond the 20, the ball was to be returned to the line of scrimmage; restrictions were placed on members of the punting team to open up return possibilities; roll-blocking and cutting of wide receivers was eliminated; the extent of downfield contact a defender could have with an eligible receiver was restricted; the penalties for offensive holding, illegal use of the hands, and tripping were reduced from 15 to 10 yards; wide receivers blocking back toward the ball within three yards of the line of scrimmage were prevented from blocking below the waist, April 25.

Seattle was awarded an NFL franchise to begin play in 1976, June 4. Lloyd W. Nordstrom, president of the Seattle Seahawks, and Hugh Culverhouse, president of the Tampa Bay Buccaneers, signed franchise agreements, December 5.

The Birmingham Americans defeated the Florida Blazers 22-21 in the WFL World Bowl, winning the league championship, December 5.

1975

Pittsburgh defeated Minnesota 16-6 in Super Bowl IX at New Orleans, the Steelers' first championship since entering the NFL in 1933. The NBC telecast was viewed by approximately 78 million people.

The Memphis Southmen of the WFL signed Larry Csonka, Jim Kiick, and Paul Warfield of Miami, March 31.

The divisional winners with the highest won-loss percentage were made the home team for the divisional playoffs, and the surviving winners with the highest percentage made home teams for the championship games, June 26.

Referees were equipped with wireless microphones for all preseason, regular-season, and playoff games.

The Lions moved to the new Pontiac Silverdome. The Giants played their home games in Shea Stadium. The Saints moved into the Louisiana Superdome.

The World Football League folded, October 22.

1976

Pittsburgh defeated Dallas 21-17 in Super Bowl X in Miami. The Steelers joined Green Bay and Miami as the only teams to win two Super Bowls; the Cowboys became the first wild-card team to play in the Super Bowl. The CBS telecast was viewed by an estimated 80 million people, the largest television audience in history.

Lloyd Nordstrom, the president of the Seahawks, died at 66, January 20. His brother Elmer succeeded him as majority representative of the team.

The owners awarded Super Bowl XII, to be played on January 15, 1978, to New Orleans. They also adopted the use of two 30-second clocks for all games, visible to both players and fans to note the official time between the ready-for-play signal and snap of the ball, March 16.

A veteran player allocation was held to stock the Seattle and Tampa Bay franchises with 39 players each, March 30-31. In the college draft, Seattle and Tampa Bay each received eight extra choices, April 8-9.

The Giants moved into new Giants Stadium in East Rutherford, New Jersey.

The Steelers defeated the College All-Stars in a storm-shortened Chicago College All-Star Game, the last of the series, July 23. St. Louis defeated San Diego 20-10 in a preseason game before 38,000 in Korakuen Stadium, Tokyo, in the first NFL game outside of North America, August 16.

1977

Oakland defeated Minnesota 32-14 in Super Bowl XI at Pasadena, January 9. The paid attendance was a pro record 103,438. The NBC telecast was viewed by 81.9 million people, the largest ever to view a sports event. The victory was the fifth consecutive for the AFC in the Super Bowl.

The NFL Players Association and the NFL Management Council ratified a collective bargaining agreement extending until 1982, covering five football seasons while continuing the pension plan—including years 1974, 1975, and 1976—with contributions totaling more than $55 million. The total cost of the agreement was estimated at $107 million. The agreement called for a college draft at least through 1986; contained a no-strike, no-suit clause; established a 43-man active player limit; reduced pension vesting to four years; provided for increases in minimum salaries and preseason and postseason pay; improved insurance, medical, and dental benefits; modified previous practices in player movement and control; and reaffirmed the NFL Commissioner's disciplinary authority. Additionally, the agreement called for the NFL member clubs to make payments totaling $16 million the next 10 years to settle various legal disputes, February 25.

The San Francisco 49ers were sold to Edward J. DeBartolo, Jr., March 28.

A 16-game regular season, 4-game preseason was adopted to begin in 1978, March 29. A second wild-card team was adopted for the playoffs beginning in 1978, with the wild-card teams to play each other and the winners advancing to a round of eight postseason series.

The Seahawks were permanently aligned in the AFC Western Division and the Buccaneers in the NFC Central Division, March 31.

The owners awarded Super Bowl XIII, to be played on January 21, 1979, to Miami, to be played in the Orange Bowl; Super Bowl XIV, to be played January 20, 1980, was awarded to Pasadena, to be played in the Rose Bowl, June 14.

Rules changes were adopted to open up the passing game and to cut down on injuries. Defenders were permitted to make contact with eligible receivers only once; the head slap was outlawed; offensive linemen were prohibited from thrusting their hands to an opponent's neck, face, or head; and wide receivers were prohibited from clipping, even in the legal clipping zone.

Rozelle negotiated contracts with the three television networks to televise all NFL regular-season and postseason games, plus selected preseason games, for four years beginning with the 1978 season. ABC was awarded yearly rights to 16 Monday night games, four prime-time games, the AFC-NFC Pro Bowl, and the Hall of Fame games. CBS received the rights to all NFC regular-season and postseason games (except those in the ABC package) and to Super Bowls XIV and XVI. NBC received the rights to all AFC regular-season and postseason games (except those in the ABC package) and to Super Bowls XIII and XV. Industry sources considered it the largest single television package ever negotiated, October 12.

Chicago's Walter Payton set a single-game rushing record with 275 yards (40 carries) against Minnesota, November 20.

1978

Dallas defeated Denver 27-10 in Super Bowl XII, held indoors for the first time, at the Louisiana Superdome in New Orleans, January 15. The CBS telecast was viewed by more than 102 million people, meaning the game was watched by more viewers than any other show of any kind in the history of television. Dallas's victory was the first for the NFC in six years.

According to a Louis Harris Sports Survey, 70 percent of the nation's sports fans said they followed football, compared to 54 percent who followed baseball. Football increased its lead as the country's favorite, 26 percent to 16 percent for baseball, January 19.

A seventh official, the side judge, was added to the officiating crew, March 14.

The NFL continued a trend toward opening up the game. Rules changes permitted a defender to maintain contact with a receiver within five yards of the line of scrimmage, but restricted contact beyond that point. The pass-blocking rule was interpreted to permit the extending of arms and open hands, March 17.

A study on the use of instant replay as an officiating aid was made during seven nationally televised preseason games.

The NFL played for the first time in Mexico City, with the Saints defeating the Eagles 14-7 in a preseason game, August 5.

Bolstered by the expansion of the regular-season schedule from 14 to 16 weeks, NFL paid attendance exceeded 12 million (12,771,800) for the first time. The per-game average of 57,017 was the third-highest in league history and the most since 1973.

1979

Pittsburgh defeated Dallas 35-31 in Super Bowl XIII at Miami to become the first team ever to win three Super Bowls, January 21. The NBC telecast was viewed in 35,090,000 homes, by an estimated 96.6 million fans.

The owners awarded three future Super Bowl sites: Super Bowl XV to the Louisiana Superdome in New Orleans, to be played on January 25, 1981; Super Bowl XVI to the Pontiac Silverdome in Pontiac, Michigan, to be played on January 24, 1982; and Super Bowl XVII to Pasadena's Rose Bowl, to be played on January 30, 1983, March 13.

NFL rules changes emphasized additional player safety. The changes prohibited players on the receiving team from blocking below the waist during kickoffs, punts, and field-goal attempts; prohibited the wearing of torn or altered equipment and exposed pads that could be hazardous; extended the zone in which there could be no crackback blocks; and instructed officials to quickly whistle a play dead when a quarterback was clearly in the grasp of a tackler, March 16.

Rosenbloom, the president of the Rams, drowned at 72, April 2. His widow, Georgia, assumed control of the club.

1980

Pittsburgh defeated the Los Angeles Rams 31-19 in Super Bowl XIV at Pasadena to become the first team to win four Super Bowls, January 20. The game was viewed in a record 35,330,000 homes.

The AFC-NFC Pro Bowl, won 37-27 by the NFC, was played before 48,060 fans at Aloha Stadium in Honolulu, Hawaii. It was the first time in the 30-year history of the Pro Bowl that the game was played in a non-NFL city.

Rules changes placed greater restrictions on contact in the area of the head, neck, and face. Under the heading of "personal foul," players were prohibited from directly striking, swinging, or clubbing on the head, neck, or face. Starting in 1980, a penalty could be called for such contact whether or not the initial contact was made below the neck area.

CBS, with a record bid of $12 million, won the national radio rights to 26 NFL regular-season games, including Monday Night Football, and all 10 postseason games for the 1980-83 seasons.

The Los Angeles Rams moved their home games to Anaheim Stadium in nearby Orange County, California.

The Oakland Raiders joined the Los Angeles Coliseum Commission's antitrust suit against the NFL. The suit contended the league violated antitrust laws in declining to approve a proposed move by the Raiders from Oakland to Los Angeles.

NFL regular-season attendance of nearly 13.4 million set a record for the third year in a row. The average paid attendance for the 224-game 1980 regular season was 59,787, the highest in the league's 61-year history. NFL games in 1980 were played before 92.4 percent of total stadium capacity.

Television ratings in 1980 were the second-best in NFL history, trailing only the combined ratings of the 1976 season. All three networks posted gains, and NBC's 15.0 rating was its best ever. CBS and ABC had their best ratings since 1977, with 15.3 and 20.8 ratings, respectively. CBS Radio reported a record audience of 7 million for Monday night and special games.

1981
Oakland defeated Philadelphia 27-10 in Super Bowl XV at the Louisiana Superdome in New Orleans, to become the first wild-card team to win a Super Bowl, January 25.

Edgar F. Kaiser, Jr., purchased the Denver Broncos from Gerald and Allan Phipps, February 26.

The owners adopted a disaster plan for re-stocking a team should the club be involved in a fatal accident, March 20.

The owners awarded Super Bowl XVIII to Tampa, to be played in Tampa Stadium on January 22, 1984, June 3.

A CBS-New York Times poll showed that 48 percent of sports fans preferred football to 31 percent for baseball.

The NFL teams hosted 167 representatives from 44 predominantly black colleges during training camps for a total of 289 days. The program was adopted for renewal during each training camp period.

NFL regular-season attendance—13.6 million for an average of 60,745—set a record for the fourth year in a row. It also was the first time the per-game average exceeded 60,000. NFL games in 1981 were played before 93.8 percent of total stadium capacity.

ABC and CBS set all-time rating highs. ABC finished with a 21.7 rating and CBS with a 17.5 rating. NBC was down slightly to 13.9.

1982
San Francisco defeated Cincinnati 26-21 in Super Bowl XVI at the Pontiac Silverdome, in the first Super Bowl held in the North, January 24. The CBS telecast achieved the highest rating of any televised sports event ever, 49.1 with a 73.0 share. The game was viewed by a record 110.2 million fans. CBS Radio reported a record 14 million listeners for the game.

The NFL signed a five-year contract with the three television networks (ABC, CBS, and NBC) to televise all NFL regular-season and postseason games starting with the 1982 season.

The owners awarded the 1983, 1984, and 1985 AFC-NFC Pro Bowls to Honolulu's Aloha Stadium.

A jury ruled against the NFL in the antitrust trial brought by the Los Angeles Coliseum Commission and the Oakland Raiders, May 7. The verdict cleared the way for the Raiders to move to Los Angeles, where they defeated Green Bay 24-3 in their first preseason game, August 29.

The 1982 season was reduced from a 16-game schedule to nine as the result of a 57-day players' strike. The strike was called by the NFLPA at midnight on Monday, September 20, following the Green Bay at New York Giants game. Play resumed November 21-22 following ratification of the Collective Bargaining Agreement by NFL owners, November 17 in New York.

Under the Collective Bargaining Agreement, which was to run through the 1986 season, the NFL draft was extended through 1992 and the veteran free-agent system was left basically unchanged. A minimum salary schedule for years of experience was established; training camp and postseason pay were increased; players' medical, insurance, and retirement benefits were increased; and a severance-pay system was introduced to aid in career transition, a first in professional sports.

Despite the players' strike, the average paid attendance in 1982 was 58,472, the fifth-highest in league history.

The owners awarded the sites of two Super Bowls, December 14: Super Bowl XIX, to be played on January 20, 1985, to Stanford University Stadium in Stanford, California, with San Francisco as host team; and Super Bowl XX, to be played on January 26, 1986, to the Louisiana Superdome in New Orleans.

1983
Because of the shortened season, the NFL adopted a format of 16 teams competing in a Super Bowl Tournament for the 1982 playoffs. The NFC's number-one seed, Washington, defeated the AFC's number-two seed, Miami, 27-17 in Super Bowl XVII at the Rose Bowl in Pasadena, January 30.

Super Bowl XVII was the second-highest rated live television program of all time, giving the NFL a sweep of the top 10 live programs in television history. The game was viewed in more than 40 million homes, the largest ever for a live telecast.

George Halas, the owner of the Bears and the last surviving member of the NFL's second organizational meeting, died at 88, October 31.

1984
The Los Angeles Raiders defeated Washington 38-9 in Super Bowl XVIII at Tampa Stadium, January 22. The game achieved a 46.4 rating and 71.0 share.

An 11-man group headed by H.R. (Bum) Bright purchased the Dallas Cowboys from Clint Murchison, Jr., March 20. Club president Tex Schramm was designated as managing general partner.

Wellington Mara was named president of the NFC, March 20.

Patrick Bowlen purchased a majority interest in the Denver Broncos from Edgar Kaiser, Jr., March 21.

The Colts relocated to Indianapolis, March 28. Their new home became the Hoosier Dome.

The owners awarded two Super Bowl sites at their May 23-25 meetings: Super Bowl XXI, to be played on January 25, 1987, to the Rose Bowl in Pasadena; and Super Bowl XXII, to be played on January 31, 1988, to San Diego Jack Murphy Stadium.

The New York Jets moved their home games to Giants Stadium in East Rutherford, New Jersey.

Alex G. Spanos purchased a majority interest in the San Diego Chargers from Eugene V. Klein, August 28.

Houston defeated Pittsburgh 23-20 to mark the one-hundredth overtime game in regular-season play since overtime was adopted in 1974, December 2.

On the field, many all-time records were set: Dan Marino of Miami passed for 5,084 yards and 48 touchdowns; Eric Dickerson of the Los Angeles Rams rushed for 2,105 yards; Art Monk of Washington caught 106 passes; and Walter Payton of Chicago broke Jim Brown's career rushing mark, finishing the season with 13,309 yards.

According to a CBS Sports/*New York Times* survey, 53 percent of the nation's sports fans said they most enjoyed watching football, compared to 18 percent for baseball, December 2-4.

NFL paid attendance exceeded 13 million for the fifth consecutive complete regular season when 13,398,112, an average of 59,813, attended games. The figure was the second-highest in league history. Teams averaged 42.4 points per game, the second-highest total since the 1970 merger.

1985
San Francisco defeated Miami 38-16 in Super Bowl XIX at Stanford Stadium in Stanford, California, January 20. The game was viewed on television by more people than any other live event in history. President Ronald Reagan, who took his second oath of office before tossing the coin for the game, was one of 115,936,000 viewers. The game drew a 46.4 rating and a 63.0 share. In addition, 6 million people watched the Super Bowl in the United Kingdom and a similar number in Italy. Super Bowl XIX had a direct economic impact of $113.5 million on the San Francisco Bay area.

NBC Radio and the NFL entered into a two-year agreement granting NBC the radio rights to a 37-game package in each of the 1985-86 seasons, March 6. The package included 27 regular-season games and 10 postseason games.

The owners awarded two Super Bowl sites at their annual meeting, March 10-15: Super Bowl XXIII, to be played on January 22, 1989, to the proposed Dolphins Stadium in Miami; and Super Bowl XXIV, to be played on January 28, 1990, to the Louisiana Superdome in New Orleans.

Norman Braman, in partnership with Edward Leibowitz, bought the Philadelphia Eagles from Leonard Tose, April 29.

Bruce Smith, a Virginia Tech defensive lineman selected by Buffalo, was the first player chosen in the fiftieth NFL draft, April 30.

A group headed by Tom Benson, Jr., was approved to purchase the New Orleans Saints from John W. Mecom, Jr., June 3.

The NFL owners adopted a resolution calling for a series of overseas preseason games, beginning in 1986, with one game to be played in England/Europe and/or one game in Japan each year. The game would be a fifth preseason game for the clubs involved and all arrangements and selection of the clubs would be under the control of the Commissioner, May 23.

The league-wide conversion to videotape from movie film for coaching study was approved.

Commissioner Rozelle was authorized to extend the commitment to Honolulu's Aloha Stadium for the AFC-NFC Pro Bowl for 1988, 1989, and 1990, October 15.

The NFL set a single-weekend paid attendance record when 902,657 tickets were sold for the weekend of October 27-28.

A Louis Harris poll in December revealed that pro football remained the sport most followed by Americans. Fifty-nine percent of those surveyed followed pro football, compared with 54 percent who followed baseball.

The Chicago-Miami Monday game had the highest rating, 29.6, and share, 46.0, of any prime-time game in NFL history, December 2. The game was viewed in more than 25 million homes.

The NFL showed a ratings increase on all three networks for the season, gaining 4 percent on NBC, 10 on CBS, and 16 on ABC.

1986
Chicago defeated New England 46-10 in Super Bowl XX at the Louisiana Superdome, January 26. The Patriots had earned the right to play the Bears by becoming the first wild-card team to win three consecutive games on the road. The NBC telecast replaced the final episode of *M*A*S*H* as the most-viewed television program in history, with an audience of 127 million viewers, according to A.C. Nielsen figures. In addition to drawing a 48.3 rating

and a 70 percent share in the United States, Super Bowl XX was televised to 59 foreign countries and beamed via satellite to the QE II. An estimated 300 million Chinese viewed a tape delay of the game in March. NBC Radio figures indicated an audience of 10 million for the game.

Super Bowl XX injected more than $100 million into the New Orleans-area economy, and fans spent $250 per day and a record $17.69 per person on game day.

The owners adopted limited use of instant replay as an officiating aid, prohibited players from wearing or otherwise displaying equipment, apparel, or other items that carry commercial names, names of organizations, or personal messages of any type, March 11.

After an 11-week trial, a jury in U.S. District Court in New York awarded the United States Football League one dollar in its $1.7 billion antitrust suit against the NFL. The jury rejected all of the USFL's television-related claims, which were the self-proclaimed heart of the USFL's case, July 29.

Chicago defeated Dallas 17-6 at Wembley Stadium in London in the first American Bowl. The game drew a sellout crowd of 82,699 and the NBC national telecast in this country produced a 12.4 rating and 36 percent share, making it the second-highest-rated daytime preseason game and highest daytime preseason television audience ever with 10.65-million viewers, August 3.

Monday Night Football became the longest-running prime-time series in the history of the ABC network.

Instant replay was used to reverse two plays in 31 preseason games. During the regular season, 374 plays were closely reviewed by replay officials, leading to 38 reversals in 224 games. Eighteen plays were closely reviewed by instant replay in 10 postseason games with three reversals.

1987

The New York Giants defeated Denver 39-20 in Super Bowl XXI and captured their first NFL title since 1956. The game, played in Pasadena's Rose Bowl, drew a sellout crowd of 101,063. According to A.C. Nielsen figures, the CBS broadcast of the game was viewed in the U.S. on television by 122.64-million people, making the telecast the second most-watched television show of all-time behind Super Bowl XX. The game was watched live or on tape in 55 foreign countries and NBC Radio's broadcast of the game was heard by a record 10.1 million people.

The NFL set an all-time paid attendance mark of 17,304,463 for all games, including preseason, regular-season, and postseason. Average regular-season game attendance (60,663) exceeded the 60,000 figure for only the second time in league history.

New three-year TV contracts with ABC, CBS, and NBC were announced for 1987-89 at the NFL annual meeting in Maui, Hawaii, March 15. Commissioner Rozelle and Broadcast Committee Chairman Art Modell also announced a three-year contract with ESPN to televise 13 prime-time games each season. The ESPN contract was the first with a cable network. However, NFL games on ESPN also were scheduled for regular television in the city of the visiting team and in the home city if the game was sold out 72 hours in advance.

Owners also voted to continue in effect for one year the instant replay system used during the 1986 season.

A special payment program was adopted to benefit nearly 1,000 former NFL players who participated in the League before the current Bert Bell NFL Pension Plan was created and made retroactive to the 1959 season. Players covered by the new program spent at least five years in the League and played all or part of their career prior to 1959. Each vested player would receive $60 per month for each year of service in the League for life.

Possible sites for Super Bowl XXV were reduced to five locations by the NFL Super Bowl XXV Site Selection Committee: Anaheim Stadium, Los Angeles Memorial Coliseum, Joe Robbie Stadium, San Diego Jack Murphy Stadium, and Tampa Stadium.

NFL and CBS Radio jointly announced agreement granting CBS the radio rights to a 40-game package in each of the next three NFL seasons, 1987-89, April 7.

NFL owners awarded Super Bowl XXV, to be played on January 27, 1991, to Tampa Stadium, May 20.

Over 400 former NFL players from the pre-1959 era received first payments from NFL owners, July 1.

The NFL's debut on ESPN produced the two highest-rated and most-watched sports programs in basic cable history. The Chicago at Miami game on August 16 drew an 8.9 rating in 3.81 million homes. Those records fell two weeks later when the Los Angeles Raiders at Dallas game achieved a 10.2 cable rating in 4.36 million homes.

Fifty-eight preseason games drew a record paid attendance of 3,116,870.

The 1987 season was reduced from a 16-game season to 15 as the result of a 24-day players' strike. The strike was called by the NFLPA on Tuesday, September 22, following the New England at New York Jets game. Games scheduled for the third weekend were canceled but the games of weeks four, five, and six were played with replacement teams. Striking players returned for the seventh week of the season, October 25.

In a three-team deal involving 10 players and/or draft choices, the Los Angeles Rams traded running back Eric Dickerson to the Indianapolis Colts for six draft choices and two players. Buffalo obtained the rights to linebacker Cornelius Bennett from Indianapolis, sending Greg Bell and three draft choices to the Rams. The Colts added Owen Gill and three draft choices of their own to complete the deal with the Rams, October 31.

The Chicago at Minnesota game became the highest-rated and most-watched sports program in basic cable history when it drew a 14.4 cable rating in 6.5 million homes, December 6.

Instant replay was used to reverse eight plays in 52 preseason games. During the strike-shortened 210-game regular season, 490 plays were closely reviewed by replay officials, leading to 57 reversals. Eighteen plays were closely reviewed by instant replay in 10 postseason games, with three reversals.

1988

Washington defeated Denver 42-10 in Super Bowl XXII to earn its second victory this decade in the NFL Championship Game. The game, played for the first time in San Diego Jack Murphy Stadium, drew a sellout crowd of 73,302. According to A.C. Nielsen figures, the ABC broadcast of the game was viewed in the U.S. on television by 115,000,000 people. The game was seen live or on tape in 60 foreign countries, including the People's Republic of China, and CBS's radio broadcast of the game was heard by 13.7 million people.

A total of 811 players shared in the postseason pool of $16.9 million, the most ever distributed in a single season.

In a unanimous 3-0 decision, the 2nd Circuit Court of Appeals in New York upheld the verdict of the jury that in July, 1986, had awarded the United States Football League one dollar in its $1.7 billion antitrust suit against the NFL. In a 91-page opinion, Judge Ralph K. Winter said the USFL sought through court decree the success it failed to gain among football fans, March 10.

By a 23-5 margin, owners voted to continue the instant replay system for the third consecutive season with the Instant Replay Official to be assigned to a regular seven-man, on-the-field crew. At the NFL annual meeting in Phoenix, Arizona, a 45-second clock was also approved to replace the 30-second clock. For a normal sequence of plays, the interval between plays was changed to 45 seconds from the time the ball is signaled dead until it is snapped on the succeeding play.

NFL owners approved the transfer of the Cardinals' franchise from St. Louis to Phoenix; approved two supplemental drafts each year—one prior to training camp and one prior to the regular season; and voted to initiate an annual series of games in Japan/Asia as early as the 1989 preseason, March 14-18.

The NFL Annual Selection Meeting returned to a separate two-day format and for the first time originated on a Sunday. ESPN drew a 3.6 rating during their seven-hour coverage of the draft, which was viewed in 1.6 million homes, April 24-25.

Art Rooney, founder and owner of the Steelers, died at 87, August 25.

Johnny Grier became the first African-American referee in NFL history, September 4.

Paid and average attendance of 934,271 and 66,734 at 14 games on October 16-17 set single weekend records.

Commissioner Rozelle announced that two teams would play a preseason game as part of the American Bowl series on August 6, 1989, in the Korakuen Tokyo Dome in Japan, December 16.

NFL regular-season paid attendance of 13,535,335 and the average of 60,427 was the third highest all-time. Buffalo set an NFL team single-season, in-house attendance mark of 622,793.

1989

San Francisco defeated Cincinnati 20-16 in Super Bowl XXIII. The game, played for the first time at Joe Robbie Stadium in Miami, was attended by a sellout crowd of 75,129. NBC's telecast of the game was watched by an estimated 110,780,000 viewers, according to A.C. Nielsen, making it the sixth most-watched program in television history. The game was seen live or on tape in 60 foreign countries, including an estimated 300 million in China. The CBS Radio broadcast of the game was heard by 11.2 million people.

Commissioner Rozelle announced his retirement, pending the naming of a successor, March 22 at the NFL annual meeting in Palm Desert, California.

Following the announcement, AFC president Lamar Hunt and NFC president Wellington Mara announced the formation of a six-man search committee composed of Art Modell, Robert Parins, Dan Rooney, and Ralph Wilson. Hunt and Mara served as co-chairmen.

By a 24-4 margin, owners voted to continue the instant replay system for the fourth straight season. A strengthened policy regarding anabolic steroids and masking agents was announced by Commissioner Rozelle. NFL clubs called for strong disciplinary measures in cases of feigned injuries and adopted a joint proposal by the Long-Range Planning and Finance committees regarding player personnel rules, March 19-23.

Two hundred twenty-nine unconditional free agents signed with new teams under management's Plan B system, April 1.

Jerry Jones purchased a majority interest in the Dallas Cowboys from H.R. (Bum) Bright, April 18.

Tex Schramm was named president of the new World League of American Football to work with a six-man committee of Dan Rooney, chairman; Norman Braman, Lamar Hunt, Victor Kiam, Mike Lynn, and Bill Walsh, April 18.

NFL and CBS Radio jointly announced agreement extending CBS's radio rights to an annual 40-game package through the 1994 season, April 18.

NFL owners awarded Super Bowl XXVI, to be played on January 26, 1992, to Minneapolis, May 24.

As of opening day, September 10, of the 229 Plan B free agents, 111 were active and 23 others were on teams' reserve lists. Ninety-two others were waived and three retired.

Art Shell was named head coach of the Los Angeles Raiders making him the NFL's first black head coach since Fritz Pollard coached the Akron Pros in 1921, October 3.

The site of the New England Patriots at San Francisco 49ers game scheduled for Candlestick Park on October 22 was switched to Stanford Stadium in the aftermath of the Bay Area Earthquake of October 17. The change was announced on October 19.

Paul Tagliabue became the seventh chief executive of the NFL on October 26 when he was chosen to succeed Commissioner Pete Rozelle on the sixth ballot of a three-day meeting in Cleveland, Ohio.

In all, 12 ballots were required to select Tagliabue. Two were conducted at a meeting in Chicago on July 6, and four at a meeting in Dallas on October 10-11. On the twelfth ballot, with Seattle absent, Tagliabue received more than the 19 affirmative votes required for election from among the 27 clubs present.

The transfer from Commissioner Rozelle to Commissioner Tagliabue took place at 12:01 A.M. on Sunday, November 5.

NFL Charities donated $1 million through United Way to benefit Bay Area earthquake victims, November 6.

NFL paid attendance of 17,399,538 was the highest total in league history. This included a total of 13,625,662 for an average of 60,829—both NFL records—for the 224-game regular season.

1990

San Francisco defeated Denver 55-10 in Super Bowl XXIV at the Louisiana Superdome, January 28. San Francisco joined Pittsburgh as the NFL's only teams to win four Super Bowls.

The NFL announced revisions in its 1990 draft eligibility rules. College juniors became eligible but must renounce their collegiate football eligibility before applying for the NFL Draft, February 16.

Commissioner Tagliabue announced NFL teams will play their 16-game schedule over 17 weeks in 1990 and 1991 and 16 games over 18 weeks in 1992 and 1993, February 27.

The NFL revised its playoff format to include two additional wild-card teams (one per conference).

Commissioner Tagliabue and Broadcast Committee Chairman Art Modell announced a four-year contract with Turner Broadcasting to televise nine Sunday-night games.

New four-year TV agreements were ratified for 1990-93 for ABC, CBS, NBC, ESPN, and TNT at the NFL annual meeting in Orlando, Florida, March 12. The contracts totaled $3.6 billion, the largest in TV history.

The NFL announced plans to expand its American Bowl series of preseason games. In addition to games in London and Tokyo, American Bowl games were scheduled for Berlin, Germany, and Montreal, Canada, in 1990.

For the fifth straight year, NFL owners voted to continue a limited system of Instant Replay. Beginning in 1990, the replay official will have a two-minute time limit to make a decision. The vote was 21-7, March 12.

Commissioner Tagliabue announced the formation of a Committee on Expansion and Realignment, March 13. He also named a Player Advisory Council, comprised of 12 former NFL players, March 14.

One-hundred eighty-four Plan B unconditional free agents signed with new teams, April 2.

Commissioner Tagliabue appointed Dr. John Lombardo as the League's Drug Advisor for Anabolic Steroids, April 25 and named Dr. Lawrence Brown as the League's Advisor for Drugs of Abuse, May 17.

NFL owners awarded Super Bowl XXVIII, to be played in 1994, to the proposed Georgia Dome, May 23.

Commissioner Tagliabue named NFL referee Jerry Seeman as NFL Director of Officiating, replacing Art McNally, who announced his retirement after 31 years on the field and at the league office, July 12.

NFL International Week was celebrated with four preseason games in seven days in Tokyo, London, Berlin, and Montreal. More than 200,000 fans on three continents attended the four games, August 4-11.

Commissioner Tagliabue announced the NFL Teacher of the Month program in which the League furnishes grants and scholarships in recognition of teachers who provided a positive influence upon NFL players in elementary and secondary schools, September 20.

For the first time since 1957, every NFL club won at least one of its first four games, October 1.

The Super Bowl Most Valuable Player trophy was renamed the Pete Rozelle trophy, October 8.

NFL total paid attendance of 17,665,671 was the highest total in League history. The regular-season total paid attendance of 13,959,896 and average of 62,321 for 224 games were the highest ever, surpassing the previous records set in the 1989 season.

1991

The New York Giants defeated Buffalo 20-19 in Super Bowl XXV to capture their second title in five years. The game was played before a sellout crowd of 73,813 at Tampa Stadium and became the first Super Bowl decided by one point, January 26. The ABC broadcast of the game was seen by more than 112-million people in the United States and was seen live or taped in 60 other countries.

NFL playoff games earned the top television rating spot of the week for each week of the month-long playoffs, January 29.

A total of 693 players shared in the postseason pool of $14.9 million.

New York businessman Robert Tisch purchased a 50 percent interest in the New York Giants from Mrs. Helen Mara Nugent and her children, Tim Mara and Maura Mara Concannon, February 2.

Commissioner Tagliabue named Neil Austrian to the newly created position of President of the NFL to be chief operating officer for League-wide business and financial operations, February 27.

NFL clubs voted to continue a limited system of Instant Replay for the sixth consecutive year. The vote was 21-7, March 19.

The NFL launched the World League of American Football, the first sports league to operate on a weekly basis on two separate continents, March 23.

NFL Charities presented a $250,000 donation to the United Service Organization. The donation was the second largest single grant ever by NFL Charities, April 5.

Commissioner Tagliabue named Harold Henderson as Executive Vice President for Labor Relations and Chairman of the NFL Management Council Executive Committee, April 8.

Russell Maryland, a University of Miami defensive lineman, was selected by Dallas, becoming the first player chosen in the 1991 NFL draft, April 21.

NFL clubs approved a recommendation by the Expansion and Realignment Committee to add two teams for the 1994 season, resulting in six divisions of five teams each, May 22.

NFL clubs awarded Super Bowl XXIX, to be played on January 29, 1995, to Miami, May 23.

"NFL International Week" featured six 1990 playoff teams playing nationally televised games in London, Berlin, and Tokyo on July 28 and August 3-4. The games drew more than 150,000 fans.

Paul Brown, founder of the Cleveland Browns and Cincinnati Bengals, died at age 82, August 5.

NFL clubs approved a resolution establishing an international division, reporting to the President of the NFL. A three-year financial plan for the World League was approved by NFL clubs at a meeting in Dallas, October 23.

1992

The NFL agreed to provide a minimum of $2.5 million in financial support to the NFL Alumni Association and assistance to NFL Alumni-related programs. The agreement included contributions from NFL Charities to the Pre-59ers and Dire Need Programs for former players, January 25.

The Washington Redskins defeated the Buffalo Bills 37-24 in Super Bowl XXVI to capture their third world championship in 10 years, January 26. The game was played before a sellout crowd of 63,130 at the Hubert H. Humphrey Metrodome in Minneapolis and attracted the second largest television audience in Super Bowl history. The CBS broadcast was seen by more than 123 million people nationally, second only to the 127 million who viewed Super Bowl XX.

For the third consecutive season, NFL total paid attendance reached a record level. Total paid attendance was 17,752,139 for the 296 preseason, regular-season, and postseason games, February 3.

The use in officiating of a limited system of Instant Replay for a seventh consecutive year was not approved. The vote was 17-11 in favor of approval (21 votes were required), March 18.

Steve Emtman, a University of Washington defensive lineman, was selected by Indianapolis, becoming the first player chosen in the 1992 NFL draft, April 26.

St. Louis businessman James Orthwein purchased controlling interest in the New England Patriots from Victor Kiam, May 11.

In a Harris Poll taken during the NFL offseason, professional football again was declared the nation's most popular sport. Professional football finished atop similar surveys conducted by Harris in 1985 and 1989, May 23.

NFL clubs accepted the report of the Expansion Committee at a league meeting in Pasadena. The report names five cities as finalists for the two expansion teams—Baltimore, Charlotte, Jacksonville, Memphis, and St. Louis, May 19.

At a league meeting in Dallas, NFL clubs approved a proposal by the World League Board of Directors to restructure the World League and place future emphasis on its international success, September 17.

1993

The NFL and lawyers for the players announced a settlement of various lawsuits and an agreement on the terms of a seven-year deal that included a new player system to be in place through the 1999 season, January 6.

Commissioner Tagliabue announced the establishment of the "NFL World Partnership Program" to develop amateur football internationally through a series of clinics conducted by former NFL players and coaches, January 14.

As part of Super Bowl XXVII, the NFL announced the creation of the first NFL Youth Education Town, a facility located in south central Los Angeles for inner city youth. January 25.

The Dallas Cowboys defeated the Buffalo Bills 52-17 in Super Bowl XXVII to capture their first NFL title since 1978. The game was played before a crowd of 98,374 at the Rose Bowl in Pasadena, California. The NBC broadcast of the game was the most watched program in television history and was seen by 133,400,000 people in the United States. The game also was seen live or taped in 101 other countries. The rating for the game was 45.1, the tenth highest for any televised sports event, January 31.

A total of 695 players shared in the postseason pool of $14.9 million, February 15.

For the fourth consecutive season, the NFL total paid attendance reached a record level. Total paid attendance was 17,784,354 for the 296 preseason, regular-season, and postseason games, March 4.

NFL clubs awarded Super Bowl XXX to the city of Phoenix, to be played on January 28, 1996, at Sun Devil Stadium, March 23.

Drew Bledsoe, a quarterback from Washington State, was selected by New England, becoming the first player chosen in the 1993 NFL draft, April 25.

The NFL and the NFL Players Association officially signed a 7-year Collective Bargaining Agreement in Washington, D.C., which guarantees more than $1 billion in pension, health, and post-career benefits for current and retired players—the most extensive benefits plan in pro sports. It was the NFL's first CBA since the 1982 agreement expired in 1987, June 29.

Ron Bernard was named president

of NFL Enterprises, a newly formed division of the NFL responsible for NFL Films, home video, and special domestic and international television programming, August 19.

NFL announced plans to allow fans, for the first time ever, to join players and coaches in selecting the annual AFC and NFC Pro Bowl teams, October 12.

NFL clubs unanimously awarded the league's twenty-ninth franchise to the Carolina Panthers at a meeting in Chicago. NFL clubs also awarded Super Bowl XXXI to New Orleans and Super Bowl XXXII to San Diego, October 26.

At the same meeting in Chicago, NFL clubs approved a plan to form a European league with joint venture partners, October 27.

Don Shula became the winningest coach in NFL history when Miami beat Philadelphia to give Shula his 325th victory, one more than George Halas, November 14.

NFL clubs awarded the league's thirtieth franchise to the Jacksonville Jaguars at a meeting in Chicago, November 30.

The NFL announced new 4-year television agreements with ABC, ESPN, TNT, and NFL newcomer FOX, which took over the NFC package from CBS, December 18.

The NFL completed its new TV agreements by announcing that NBC would retain the rights to the AFC package, December 20.

1994

The NFL announced that a regular-season paid attendance record was set in 1993. Attendance averaged 62,354, topping the previous record of 62,321 set in 1990, January 6.

The Dallas Cowboys defeated the Buffalo Bills 30-13 in Super Bowl XXVIII to become the fifth team to win back-to-back Super Bowl titles. The game was viewed by the largest U.S. audience in television history—134.8 million people. The game's 45.5 rating was the highest for a Super Bowl since 1987 and the tenth highest-rated Super Bowl ever, January 30.

NFL clubs unanimously approved the transfer of the New England Patriots from James Orthwein to Robert Kraft at a meeting in Orlando, February 22.

In an effort to increase offensive production, NFL clubs at the league's annual meeting in Orlando adopted a package of changes, including modifications in line play, chucking rules, and the roughing-the-passer rule, plus the adoption of the two-point conversion and moving the spot of the kickoff back to the 30-yard line, March 22.

NFL clubs approved the transfer of the majority interest in the Miami Dolphins from the Robbie family to H. Wayne Huizenga, March 23.

The NFL and FOX announced the formation of a joint venture to create a six-team World League to begin play in Europe in April, 1995, March 23.

The NFL announced a total paid attendance record for the fifth consecutive year, with 17,951,831 in paid attendance for all 1993 games, March 23.

Dan Wilkinson, a defensive tackle from Ohio State, was selected by Cincinnati as the first overall selection in the draft, April 24.

The Carolina Panthers earned the right to select first in the 1995 NFL draft by winning a coin toss with the Jacksonville Jaguars. The Jaguars received the second selection in the 1995 draft, April 24.

NFL clubs approved the transfer of the Philadelphia Eagles from Norman Braman to Jeffrey Lurie, May 6.

The NFL launched "NFL Sunday Ticket," a new season subscription service for satellite television dish owners, June 1.

Sara Levinson, president/business director of MTV, was named president of NFL Properties, July 12.

An all-time NFL record crowd of 112,376 attended the American Bowl game between Dallas and Houston in Mexico City. It concluded the biggest American Bowl series in NFL history with four games attracting a record 256,666 fans, August 15.

The NFL 75th Anniversary All-Time Team was announced at a press conference at Radio City Music Hall, August 30.

The NFL reached agreement on a new seven-year contract with its game officials, September 22.

The NFL Management Council and the NFL Players Association announced an agreement on the formulation and implementation of the most comprehensive drug and alcohol policy in sports, October 28.

At an NFL meeting in Chicago, Commissioner Tagliabue slotted the two new expansion teams into the AFC Central (Jacksonville Jaguars) and NFC West (Carolina Panthers) for the 1995 season only. He also appointed a special committee on realignment to make recommendations on the 1996 season and beyond, November 2.

The NFL set a regular-season paid attendance record for the second consecutive year, topping 14 million for the first time (14,034,977), December 27.

1995

The San Francisco 49ers became the first team to win five Super Bowls when they defeated the San Diego Chargers 49-26 in Super Bowl XXIX at Joe Robbie Stadium in Miami, January 29.

Carolina and Jacksonville stocked their expansion rosters with a total of 66 players from other NFL teams in a veteran player allocation draft in New York, February 16.

CBS Radio and the NFL agreed to a new four-year contract for an annual 53-game package of games, continuing a relationship that spanned 15 of the past 17 years, February 22.

NFL total paid attendance for all 1994 season games reached a record level for the sixth consecutive year, exceeding 18 million for the first time (18,010,264), March 9.

NFL clubs approved the transfer of the Tampa Bay Buccaneers from the estate of the late Hugh Culverhouse to South Florida businessman Malcolm Glazer, March 13.

A total of $20.3 million, the largest NFL postseason pool ever, was divided among 729 players who participated in the 1994 playoffs, March 13.

A series of safety-related rules changes were adopted at a league meeting in Phoenix, primarily related to the use of the helmet against defenseless players, March 14.

After a two-year hiatus, the World League of American Football returned to action with six teams in Europe, April 8.

The NFL became the first major sports league to establish a site on the Internet system of on-line computer communication, April 10.

The transfer of the Rams from Los Angeles to St. Louis was approved by a vote of the NFL clubs at a meeting in Dallas, April 12.

ABC's *NFL Monday Night Football* finished the 1994-95 television season as the fifth highest-rated show out of 146 with a 17.8 average rating, the highest finish in the 25-year history of the series, April 18.

Ki-Jana Carter, a running back from Penn State, was selected by the Cincinnati Bengals as the first overall selection in the draft, April 22.

In an ABC News Poll taken during the NFL offseason, America's sports fans chose football as their favorite spectator sport by more than a 2-to-1 margin over basketball and baseball (35%-16%-12%), April 26.

The Frankfurt Galaxy defeated the Amsterdam Admirals 26-22 to win the 1995 World Bowl before a crowd of 23,847 in Amsterdam's Olympic Stadium, June 23.

Former NFL quarterback and Rhein Fire general manager Oliver Luck was named President of the World League, July 13.

The transfer of the Raiders from Los Angeles to Oakland was approved by a vote of the NFL clubs at a meeting in Chicago, July 22.

Jacksonville Municipal Stadium opened before a sold-out crowd of more than 70,000 for the first preseason game in Jaguars history, August 18.

NFL Charities and 50 NFL players donated $1 million to the United Negro College Fund in honor of the fiftieth anniversity of the UNCF and the integration of the modern NFL, September 15.

The Pro Football Hall Of Fame in Canton, Ohio, completed an $8.9 million expansion including a $4 million contribution by the NFL clubs, October 14.

The Trans World Dome opened in St. Louis before a sold-out crowd of 65,598 as the Rams defeated the Carolina Panthers 28-17, November 12.

NFL paid attendance totaled 963,521 for 15 games in Week 12, the highest weekend total in the league's 76-year history, November 19-20.

On the field, many significant records and milestones were achieved: Miami's Dan Marino surpassed Pro Football Hall of Famer Fran Tarkenton in four major passing categories—attempts, completions, yards, and touchdowns—to become the NFL's all-time career leader. San Francisco's Jerry Rice became the all-time reception and receiving-yardage leader with career totals of 942 catches and 15,123 yards. Dallas' Emmitt Smith scored 25 touchdowns, breaking the season record of 24 set by Washington's John Riggins in 1983.

1996

The Dallas Cowboys won their third Super Bowl title in four years when they defeated the Pittsburgh Steelers 27-17 in Super Bowl XXX at Sun Devil Stadium in Tempe, Arizona. The game was viewed by the largest audience in U.S. television history—138.5 million people, January 28.

An agreement between the NFL and the city of Cleveland regarding the Cleveland Browns' relocation was approved by a vote of the NFL clubs, February 9. According to the agreement, the city of Cleveland retained the Browns' heritage and records, including the name, logo, colors, history, playing records, trophies, and memorabilia, and committed to building a new 72,000-seat stadium for a reactivated Browns' franchise to begin play there no later than 1999. Art Modell received approval to move his franchise to Baltimore and rename it.

NFL total paid attendance for all 1995 games reached a record level for the seventh consecutive year, exceeding 19 million for the first time (19,202,757), March 7.

A total of $21.5 million, the largest NFL postseason pool ever, was divided among 717 players who participated in the 1995 playoffs, March 11.

Keyshawn Johnson, a wide receiver from Southern California, was selected by the New York Jets as the first overall selection in the draft, April 20.

The transfer of the Oilers from Houston to Nashville for the 1998 season was approved by a vote of the NFL clubs at a meeting in Atlanta, April 30.

The Scottish Claymores defeated the Frankfurt Galaxy 32-27 to win the 1996 World Bowl in front of 38,982 at Murrayfield Stadium in Edinburgh, Scotland, June 23.

The NFL returned to Baltimore when the new Baltimore Ravens defeated the Philadelphia Eagles 17-9 in a preseason game before a crowd of 63,804 at Memorial Stadium, August 3.

Ericsson Stadium opened in Charlotte, North Carolina before a crowd of 65,350 as the Carolina Panthers defeated the Chicago Bears 30-12 in a preseason game, August 3.

Points scored totaled 762 and NFL paid attendance totaled 964,079 for 15 games in Week 11, the highest weekend totals in either category in the league's 77-year history, November 10-11.

Former NFL Commissioner Pete Rozelle died at his home in Rancho Santa Fe, California. Rozelle, regarded as the premiere commissioner in sports history, led the NFL for 29 years, from 1960-1989, December 6.

1997

Indianapolis Colts owner Robert Irsay died from complications related to a stroke he suffered in 1995. Irsay acquired the club in 1972 when he traded his Los Angeles Rams to Carrol Rosenbloom for the Colts. He later moved the Colts from Baltimore to Indianapolis in 1984, January 14.

The Green Bay Packers won their first NFL title in 29 years by defeating the New England Patriots 35-21 in Super Bowl XXXI at the Louisiana Superdome in New Orleans. The game was viewed by the fourth-largest audience in U.S. television history—128 million people, January 26.

A total of $24.3 million, the largest NFL postseason pool ever, was divided among 730 players who participated in the 1996 playoffs, March 11.

The rules governing cross-ownership were modified, permitting NFL club owners to also own teams in other sports in their home market or markets without NFL teams. The vote was 24-5 (one abstention) in favor of approval, March 11.

Washington Redskins owner Jack Kent Cooke died at his home in Washington, D.C. Cooke became majority owner in 1974 and the Redskins won three Super Bowls under his leadership, April 6.

Orlando Pace, an offensive tackle from Ohio State, was selected by the St. Louis Rams as the first overall selection in the draft, April 19.

The Barcelona Dragons defeated the Rhein Fire 38-24 to win the 1997 World Bowl in front of 31,100 fans at Estadi Olimpic de Montjuic in Barcelona, Spain, June 22.

NFL clubs approved the transfer of the Seattle Seahawks from Ken Behring to Paul Allen, August 19.

Jack Kent Cooke Stadium opened in Raljon, Maryland before a crowd of 78,270 as the Washington Redskins defeated the Arizona Cardinals 19-13, September 14.

The 10,000th regular-season game in NFL history was played when the Seattle Seahawks defeated the Tennessee Oilers 16-13 at the Kingdome in Seattle, October 5.

Atlanta Falcons owner Rankin Smith died of heart failure three days prior to his seventy-third birthday. Smith was the founder of the Falcons and was instrumental in bringing Super Bowls XXVIII and XXXIV to Atlanta, October 26.

NFL paid attendance totaled 999,778 for 15 games in Week 12, the highest weekend total in league history, November 16-17.

Regular-season paid attendance in 1997 rose to 14,967,314 for an average of 62,364 per game. That total was the second-highest all-time, behind the 15,043,562 of 1995, December 23.

1998

The NFL reached agreement on record eight-year television contracts with four networks. ABC (*Monday Night Football*) and FOX (NFC) retained their previous rights, CBS took over the AFC package from NBC, and ESPN won the right to broadcast the entire Sunday night cable package, January 13.

The World League was renamed the NFL Europe League, January 22.

The Denver Broncos won their first Super Bowl by defeating the defending champion Green Bay Packers 31-24 in Super Bowl XXXII at Qualcomm Stadium in San Diego. The game tied Super Bowl XXVII for the third-largest audience in U.S. television history with 133.4 million viewers, January 25.

The NFL clubs approved a six-year extension of the Collective Bargaining Agreement through 2003. The extended CBA also created a $100 million fund for youth football, March 22.

The NFL clubs unanimously approved an expansion team for Cleveland to fulfill the commitment to return the Browns to the field in 1999, March 23.

NFL paid attendance of 19,049,886 for all games played during the 1997 season was the second highest in league history. In 1995, 19,202,757 fans paid to attend games, March 23.

A total of $25.1 million, the largest NFL postseason pool ever, was divided among 737 players who participated in the 1997 playoffs, March 24.

Peyton Manning, a quarterback from Tennessee, was selected by the Indianapolis Colts as the first overall selection in the draft, April 18.

The Rhein Fire defeated the Frankfurt Galaxy 34-10 to win the 1998 World Bowl in front of 47,846 fans in Frankfurt's Waldstadion—the biggest crowd to witness a World Bowl since 1991, June 14.

NFL clubs approved the transfer of the Minnesota Vikings from a 10-man ownership group to Red McCombs, July 28.

The NFL Stadium at Camden Yards opened in Baltimore, Maryland before a crowd of 65,938 as the Baltimore Ravens defeated the Chicago Bears 19-14 in a preseason game, August 8.

Raymond James Stadium opened in Tampa, Florida before a crowd of 62,410 as the Tampa Bay Buccaneers defeated the Chicago Bears 27-15, September 20.

NFL paid attendance totaled 997,835 for 15 games in Week 1, the highest opening weekend total in league history and the second-highest total ever. In 1997, paid attendance totaled 999,778 for 15 games in Week 12, September 6-7.

A Harris Poll says 55 percent of adults follow professional football, up 4 percent from 1997 and 6 percent from 1992, October 15.

Tennessee Oilers owner Bud Adams announced the team will change its name to the Tennessee Titans following the 1998 season. The NFL announced that the name Oilers will be retired–a first in league history, November 14.

1999

The Denver Broncos won their second consecutive Super Bowl title by defeating the NFC champion Atlanta Falcons 34-19 in Super Bowl XXXIII at Pro Player Stadium in Miami. The game was viewed by 127.5 million viewers, the sixth most-watched program in U.S. television history, January 31.

Jim Pyne, a center allocated by the Detroit Lions, was the first selection of the Cleveland Browns in the 1999 NFL Expansion Draft. The Browns eventually selected 37 players, February 9.

CBS Radio/Westwood One agreed to a 3-year extension of their exclusive national radio rights to NFL games, March 11.

NFL paid attendance of 19,741,493 for all games played during the 1998 season was the highest in league history, topping the 19,202,757 fans who paid to attend games in 1995. The 1998 regular-season total paid attendance of 15,364,873 for an average of 64,020 were also records, March 15.

By a vote of 28-3, the owners adopted an instant replay system as an officiating aid for the 1999 season, March 17.

Tim Couch, a quarterback from Kentucky, was selected by the Cleveland Browns as the first overall selection in the draft, April 17.

New York Jets owner Leon Hess died from complications of a blood disease. Hess had been involved in the ownership of the Jets since 1963 and was sole owner of the club since 1984, May 9.

A group led by Washington area businessman Daniel Snyder is approved by NFL clubs as the new owner of the Washington Redskins at a league meeting in Atlanta, May 25.

The Frankfurt Galaxy became the first team in NFL Europe League history to win a second World Bowl by defeating the Barcelona Dragons 38-24 at Rheinstadion, in Düsseldorf, Germany, June 27.

The Cleveland Browns returned to the field for the first time since 1995 and defeated the Dallas Cowboys 20-17 in overtime in the annual Hall of Fame Game at Canton, Ohio, August 9.

Cleveland Browns Stadium opened in Cleveland, Ohio before a crowd of 71,398 as the Minnesota Vikings defeated the Browns in a preseason game, 24-17, August 21.

Adelphia Coliseum opened in Nashville, Tennessee before a crowd of 65,729 with the Tennessee Titans defeating the Atlanta Falcons 17-3 in a preseason game, August 26.

Houston, Texas and owner Robert McNair were awarded the NFL's thirty-second franchise in a vote of the NFL clubs at a league meeting in Atlanta. The team will begin play in 2002. The NFL clubs also voted to realign into eight divisions of four teams each for the 2002 season, October 6.

Walter Payton, the NFL's all-time leading rusher, died of liver cancer at the age of 45. Payton played for the Chicago Bears from 1975-1987 and rushed for an NFL-record 16,726 yards. He played in a club-record 186 consecutive games from 1975-1987 and was voted to nine Pro Bowls. He was selected to the Pro Football Hall of Fame in 1993, November 1.

Former NFL Commissioner Pete Rozelle, who guided a still-developing league to its position today as America's most popular sport, was named by *The Sporting News* as the most powerful person in sports in the 20th Century, December 15.

2000

Johnson & Johnson heir Robert Wood Johnson IV was approved by NFL clubs as the new owner of the New York Jets at a league meeting, January 18.

The St. Louis Rams won their first Super Bowl by defeating the AFC champion Tennessee Titans 23-16 in Super Bowl XXXIV at the Georgia Dome in Atlanta. The game was viewed by 132.5 million viewers, the fifth most-watched program in U.S. television history, January 30.

For the first time in league history, paid attendance topped 16 million for the regular season and more than 65,000 per game, an increase of 1,300 per game over 1998. Paid attendance for all NFL games increased in 1999 for the third year in a row and was the highest ever in the 80-year history of the league. It marked the first time in league history that the 20-million paid attendance mark was reached for all games in a season, March 27.

Courtney Brown, a defensive end from Penn State, was selected by the Cleveland Browns as the first overall selection in the draft, April 15.

NFL COMMISSIONERS AND PRESIDENTS*

1920 .... Jim Thorpe, President
1921-39 .... Joe Carr, President
1939-41 .... Carl Storck, President
1941-46 .... Elmer Layden, Commissioner
1946-59 .... Bert Bell, Commissioner
1960-89 .... Pete Rozelle, Commissioner
1989-present .... Paul Tagliabue, Commissioner

**NFL treasurer Austin Gunsel served as president in the office of the commissioner following the death of Bert Bell (Oct. 11, 1959) until the election of Pete Rozelle (Jan. 26, 1960).*

PAST STANDINGS

1999

AMERICAN CONFERENCE

Eastern Division

	W	L	T	Pct.	Pts.	OP
Indianapolis	13	3	0	.813	423	333
Buffalo*	11	5	0	.688	320	229
Miami*	9	7	0	.563	326	336
N.Y. Jets	8	8	0	.500	308	309
New England	8	8	0	.500	299	284

Central Division

	W	L	T	Pct.	Pts.	OP
Jacksonville	14	2	0	.875	396	217
Tennessee*	13	3	0	.813	392	324
Baltimore	8	8	0	.500	324	277
Pittsburgh	6	10	0	.375	317	320
Cincinnati	4	12	0	.250	283	460
Cleveland	2	14	0	.125	217	437

Western Division

	W	L	T	Pct.	Pts.	OP
Seattle	9	7	0	.563	338	298
Kansas City	9	7	0	.563	390	322
San Diego	8	8	0	.500	269	316
Oakland	8	8	0	.500	390	329
Denver	6	10	0	.375	314	318

NATIONAL CONFERENCE

Eastern Division

	W	L	T	Pct.	Pts.	OP
Washington	10	6	0	.625	443	377
Dallas*	8	8	0	.500	352	276
N.Y. Giants	7	9	0	.438	299	358
Arizona	6	10	0	.375	245	382
Philadelphia	5	11	0	.313	272	357

Central Division

	W	L	T	Pct.	Pts.	OP
Tampa Bay	11	5	0	.688	270	235
Minnesota*	10	6	0	.625	399	335
Detroit*	8	8	0	.500	322	323
Green Bay	8	8	0	.500	357	341
Chicago	6	10	0	.375	272	341

Western Division

	W	L	T	Pct.	Pts.	OP
St. Louis	13	3	0	.813	526	242
Carolina	8	8	0	.500	421	381
Atlanta	5	11	0	.313	285	380
San Francisco	4	12	0	.250	295	453
New Orleans	3	13	0	.188	260	434

**Wild-Card qualifier for playoffs*

Miami was third Wild Card ahead of Kansas City based on better record against common opponents (6-1 to Chiefs' 5-3). New York Jets finished ahead of New England based on better division record (4-4 to Patriots' 2-6). Seattle finished ahead of Kansas City based on head-to-head sweep (2-0). San Diego finished ahead of Oakland based on better division record (5-3 to Raiders' 3-5). Dallas was second Wild Card based on better record against common opponents (3-2 to Lions' 3-3) and better conference record than Carolina (7-5 to Panthers' 6-6). Detroit was third Wild Card based on better conference record than Green Bay (7-5 to Packers' 6-6) and better conference record than Carolina (7-5 to Panthers' 6-6).

Wild-Card playoffs: TENNESSEE 22, Buffalo 16; Miami 20, SEATTLE 17
Divisional playoffs: JACKSONVILLE 62, Miami 7; Tennessee 19, INDIANAPOLIS 16
AFC Championship: Tennessee 33, JACKSONVILLE 14
Wild-Card playoffs: WASHINGTON 27, Detroit 13; MINNESOTA 27, Dallas 10
Divisional playoffs: TAMPA BAY 14, Washington 13; ST. LOUIS 49, Minnesota 37
NFC Championship: ST. LOUIS 11, Tampa Bay 6
Super Bowl XXXIV: St. Louis (NFC) 23, Tennessee (AFC) 16
at Georgia Dome, Atlanta, Georgia

In Past Standings section, home teams in playoff games are indicated by capital letters.

1998

AMERICAN CONFERENCE

Eastern Division

	W	L	T	Pct.	Pts.	OP
N.Y. Jets	12	4	0	.750	416	266
Miami*	10	6	0	.625	321	265
Buffalo*	10	6	0	.625	400	333
New England*	9	7	0	.563	337	329
Indianapolis	3	13	0	.188	310	444

Central Division

	W	L	T	Pct.	Pts.	OP
Jacksonville	11	5	0	.688	392	338
Tennessee	8	8	0	.500	330	320
Pittsburgh	7	9	0	.438	263	303
Baltimore	6	10	0	.375	269	335
Cincinnati	3	13	0	.188	268	452

Western Division

	W	L	T	Pct.	Pts.	OP
Denver	14	2	0	.875	501	309
Oakland	8	8	0	.500	288	356
Seattle	8	8	0	.500	372	310
Kansas City	7	9	0	.438	327	363
San Diego	5	11	0	.313	241	342

NATIONAL CONFERENCE

Eastern Division

	W	L	T	Pct.	Pts.	OP
Dallas	10	6	0	.625	381	275
Arizona*	9	7	0	.563	325	378
N.Y. Giants	8	8	0	.500	287	309
Washington	6	10	0	.375	319	421
Philadelphia	3	13	0	.188	161	344

Central Division

	W	L	T	Pct.	Pts.	OP
Minnesota	15	1	0	.938	556	296
Green Bay*	11	5	0	.688	408	319
Tampa Bay	8	8	0	.500	314	295
Detroit	5	11	0	.313	306	378
Chicago	4	12	0	.250	276	368

Western Division

	W	L	T	Pct.	Pts.	OP
Atlanta	14	2	0	.875	442	289
San Francisco*	12	4	0	.750	479	328
New Orleans	6	10	0	.375	305	359
Carolina	4	12	0	.250	336	413
St. Louis	4	12	0	.250	285	378

**Wild-Card qualifier for playoffs*

Miami finished ahead of Buffalo based on better net division points (6 to Bills' 0). Oakland finished ahead of Seattle based on head-to-head sweep (2-0). Carolina finished ahead of St. Louis based on head-to-head sweep (2-0).

Wild-Card playoffs: MIAMI 24, Buffalo 17; JACKSONVILLE 25, New England 10
Divisional playoffs: DENVER 38, Miami 3; N.Y. JETS 34, Jacksonville 24
AFC Championship: DENVER 23, N.Y. Jets 10
Wild-Card playoffs: Arizona 20, DALLAS 7; SAN FRANCISCO 30, Green Bay 27
Divisional playoffs: ATLANTA 20, San Francisco 18; MINNESOTA 41, Arizona 21
NFC Championship: Atlanta 30, MINNESOTA 27 (OT)
Super Bowl XXXIII: Denver (AFC) 34, Atlanta (NFC) 19,
at Pro Player Stadium, Miami, Florida

1997

AMERICAN CONFERENCE

Eastern Division

	W	L	T	Pct.	Pts.	OP
New England	10	6	0	.625	369	289
Miami*	9	7	0	.563	339	327
N.Y. Jets	9	7	0	.563	348	287
Buffalo	6	10	0	.375	255	367
Indianapolis	3	13	0	.188	313	401

Central Division

	W	L	T	Pct.	Pts.	OP
Pittsburgh	11	5	0	.688	372	307
Jacksonville*	11	5	0	.688	394	318
Tennessee	8	8	0	.500	333	310
Cincinnati	7	9	0	.438	355	405
Baltimore	6	9	1	.406	326	345

Western Division

	W	L	T	Pct.	Pts.	OP
Kansas City	13	3	0	.813	375	232
Denver*	12	4	0	.750	472	287
Seattle	8	8	0	.500	365	362
Oakland	4	12	0	.250	324	419
San Diego	4	12	0	.250	266	425

NATIONAL CONFERENCE

Eastern Division

	W	L	T	Pct.	Pts.	OP
N.Y. Giants	10	5	1	.656	307	265
Washington	8	7	1	.531	327	289
Philadelphia	6	9	1	.406	317	372
Dallas	6	10	0	.375	304	314
Arizona	4	12	0	.250	283	379

Central Division

	W	L	T	Pct.	Pts.	OP
Green Bay	13	3	0	.813	422	282
Tampa Bay*	10	6	0	.625	299	263
Detroit*	9	7	0	.563	379	306
Minnesota*	9	7	0	.563	354	359
Chicago	4	12	0	.250	263	421

Western Division

	W	L	T	Pct.	Pts.	OP
San Francisco	13	3	0	.813	375	265
Carolina	7	9	0	.438	265	314
Atlanta	7	9	0	.438	320	361
New Orleans	6	10	0	.375	237	327
St. Louis	5	11	0	.313	299	359

**Wild-Card qualifier for playoffs*

Miami finished ahead of New York Jets based on head-to-head sweep (2-0). Pittsburgh finished ahead of Jacksonville based on better net division points (78 to Jaguars' 23). Oakland finished ahead of San Diego based on better division record (2-6 to Chargers' 1-7). Detroit finished ahead of Minnesota based on head-to-head sweep (2-0). Carolina finished ahead of Atlanta based on head-to-head sweep (2-0).

Wild-Card playoffs: DENVER 42, Jacksonville 17; NEW ENGLAND 17, Miami 3
Divisional playoffs: PITTSBURGH 7, New England 6; Denver 14, KANSAS CITY 10
AFC championship: Denver 24, PITTSBURGH 21
Wild-Card playoffs: Minnesota 23, N.Y. GIANTS 22; TAMPA BAY 20, Detroit 10
Divisional playoffs: SAN FRANCISCO 38, Minnesota 22; GREEN BAY 21, Tampa Bay 7
NFC championship: Green Bay 23, SAN FRANCISCO 10
Super Bowl XXXII: Denver (AFC) 31, Green Bay (NFC) 24, at Qualcomm Stadium,
San Diego, California

1996

AMERICAN CONFERENCE

Eastern Division

	W	L	T	Pct.	Pts.	OP
New England	11	5	0	.688	418	313
Buffalo*	10	6	0	.625	319	266
Indianapolis*	9	7	0	.563	317	334
Miami	8	8	0	.500	339	325
N.Y. Jets	1	15	0	.063	279	454

Central Division

	W	L	T	Pct.	Pts.	OP
Pittsburgh	10	6	0	.625	344	257
Jacksonville*	9	7	0	.563	325	335
Cincinnati	8	8	0	.500	372	369
Houston	8	8	0	.500	345	319
Baltimore	4	12	0	.250	371	441

Western Division

	W	L	T	Pct.	Pts.	OP
Denver	13	3	0	.813	391	275
Kansas City	9	7	0	.563	297	300
San Diego	8	8	0	.500	310	376
Oakland	7	9	0	.438	340	293
Seattle	7	9	0	.438	317	376

NATIONAL CONFERENCE

Eastern Division

	W	L	T	Pct.	Pts.	OP
Dallas	10	6	0	.625	286	250
Philadelphia*	10	6	0	.625	363	341
Washington	9	7	0	.563	364	312
Arizona	7	9	0	.438	300	397
N.Y. Giants	6	10	0	.375	242	297

Central Division

	W	L	T	Pct.	Pts.	OP
Green Bay	13	3	0	.813	456	210
Minnesota*	9	7	0	.563	298	315
Chicago	7	9	0	.438	283	305
Tampa Bay	6	10	0	.375	221	293
Detroit	5	11	0	.313	302	368

Western Division

	W	L	T	Pct.	Pts.	OP
Carolina	12	4	0	.750	367	218
San Francisco*	12	4	0	.750	398	257
St. Louis	6	10	0	.375	303	409
Atlanta	3	13	0	.188	309	461
New Orleans	3	13	0	.188	229	339

**Wild-Card qualifier for playoffs*

Jacksonville was second Wild Card ahead of Indianapolis and Kansas City based on better conference record (7-5 to Colts' 6-6 and Chiefs' 5-7). Indianapolis was third Wild Card based on head-to-head victory over Kansas City (1-0). Cincinnati finished ahead of Houston based on better net division points (19 to Oilers' 11). Oakland finished ahead of Seattle based on better division record (3-5 to Seahawks' 2-6). Dallas finished ahead of Philadelphia based on better record against common opponents (8-5 to Eagles' 7-6). Minnesota was third Wild Card based on better conference record than Washington (8-4 to Redskins' 6-6). Carolina finished ahead of San Francisco based on head-to-head sweep (2-0). Atlanta finished ahead of New Orleans based on head-to-head sweep (2-0).

Wild-Card playoffs: Jacksonville 30, BUFFALO 27; PITTSBURGH 42, Indianapolis 14
Divisional playoffs: Jacksonville 30, DENVER 27; NEW ENGLAND 28, Pittsburgh 3
AFC championship: NEW ENGLAND 20, Jacksonville 6
Wild-Card playoffs: DALLAS 40, Minnesota 15; SAN FRANCISCO 14, Philadelphia 0
Divisional playoffs: GREEN BAY 35, San Francisco 14; CAROLINA 26, Dallas 17
NFC championship: GREEN BAY 30, Carolina 13
Super Bowl XXXI: Green Bay (NFC) 35, New England (AFC) 21, at Louisiana
Superdome, New Orleans, Louisiana

1995

AMERICAN CONFERENCE

Eastern Division

	W	L	T	Pct.	Pts.	OP
Buffalo	10	6	0	.625	350	335
Indianapolis*	9	7	0	.563	331	316
Miami*	9	7	0	.563	398	332
New England	6	10	0	.375	294	377
N.Y. Jets	3	13	0	.188	233	384

Central Division

	W	L	T	Pct.	Pts.	OP
Pittsburgh	11	5	0	.688	407	327
Cincinnati	7	9	0	.438	349	374
Houston	7	9	0	.438	348	324
Cleveland	5	11	0	.313	289	356
Jacksonville	4	12	0	.250	275	404

Western Division

	W	L	T	Pct.	Pts.	OP
Kansas City	13	3	0	.813	358	241
San Diego*	9	7	0	.563	321	323
Seattle	8	8	0	.500	363	366
Denver	8	8	0	.500	388	345
Oakland	8	8	0	.500	348	332

NATIONAL CONFERENCE

Eastern Division

	W	L	T	Pct.	Pts.	OP
Dallas	12	4	0	.750	435	291
Philadelphia*	10	6	0	.625	318	338
Washington	6	10	0	.375	326	359
N.Y. Giants	5	11	0	.313	290	340
Arizona	4	12	0	.250	275	422

Central Division

	W	L	T	Pct.	Pts.	OP
Green Bay	11	5	0	.688	404	314
Detroit*	10	6	0	.625	436	336
Chicago	9	7	0	.563	392	360
Minnesota	8	8	0	.500	412	385
Tampa Bay	7	9	0	.438	238	335

Western Division

	W	L	T	Pct.	Pts.	OP
San Francisco	11	5	0	.688	457	258
Atlanta*	9	7	0	.563	362	349
St. Louis	7	9	0	.438	309	418
Carolina	7	9	0	.438	289	325
New Orleans	7	9	0	.438	319	348

**Wild-Card qualifier for playoffs*

Indianapolis finished ahead of Miami based on head-to-head sweep (2-0). San Diego was first Wild Card based on head-to-head victory over Indianapolis (1-0). Cincinnati finished ahead of Houston based on better division record (4-4 to Oilers' 3-5). Seattle finished ahead of Denver and Oakland based on best head-to-head record (3-1 to Broncos' 2-2 and Raiders' 1-3). Denver finished ahead of Oakland based on head-to-head sweep (2-0). Philadelphia was first Wild Card ahead of Detroit based on better conference record (9-3 to Lions' 7-5). Atlanta was third Wild Card ahead of Chicago based on better record against common opponents (4-2 to Bears' 3-3). St. Louis finished ahead of Carolina and New Orleans based on best head-to-head record (3-1 to Panthers' 1-3 and Saints' 2-2). Carolina finished ahead of New Orleans based on better conference record (4-8 to 3-9).

Wild-Card playoffs: BUFFALO 37, Miami 22; Indianapolis 35, SAN DIEGO 20
Divisional playoffs: PITTSBURGH 40, Buffalo 21; Indianapolis 10, KANSAS CITY 7
AFC championship: PITTSBURGH 20, Indianapolis 16
Wild-Card playoffs: PHILADELPHIA 58, Detroit 37; GREEN BAY 37, Atlanta 20
Divisional playoffs: Green Bay 27, SAN FRANCISCO 17; DALLAS 30, Philadelphia 11
NFC championship: DALLAS 38, Green Bay 27
Super Bowl XXX: Dallas (NFC) 27, Pittsburgh (AFC)17, at Sun Devil Stadium, Tempe, Arizona

1994

AMERICAN CONFERENCE

Eastern Division

	W	L	T	Pct.	Pts.	OP
Miami	10	6	0	.625	389	327
New England*	10	6	0	.625	351	312
Indianapolis	8	8	0	.500	307	320
Buffalo	7	9	0	.438	340	356
N.Y. Jets	6	10	0	.375	264	320

Central Division

	W	L	T	Pct.	Pts.	OP
Pittsburgh	12	4	0	.750	316	234
Cleveland*	11	5	0	.688	340	204
Cincinnati	3	13	0	.188	276	406
Houston	2	14	0	.125	226	352

Western Division

	W	L	T	Pct.	Pts.	OP
San Diego	11	5	0	.688	381	306
Kansas City*	9	7	0	.563	319	298
L.A. Raiders	9	7	0	.563	303	327
Denver	7	9	0	.438	347	396
Seattle	6	10	0	.375	287	323

NATIONAL CONFERENCE

Eastern Division

	W	L	T	Pct.	Pts.	OP
Dallas	12	4	0	.750	414	248
N.Y. Giants	9	7	0	.563	279	305
Arizona	8	8	0	.500	235	267
Philadelphia	7	9	0	.438	308	308
Washington	3	13	0	.188	320	412

Central Division

	W	L	T	Pct.	Pts.	OP
Minnesota	10	6	0	.625	356	314
Green Bay*	9	7	0	.563	382	287
Detroit*	9	7	0	.563	357	342
Chicago*	9	7	0	.563	271	307
Tampa Bay	6	10	0	.375	251	351

Western Division

	W	L	T	Pct.	Pts.	OP
San Francisco	13	3	0	.813	505	296
New Orleans	7	9	0	.438	348	407
Atlanta	7	9	0	.438	317	385
L.A. Rams	4	12	0	.250	286	365

**Wild-Card qualifier for playoffs*

Miami finished ahead of New England based on a head-to-head sweep (2-0). Kansas City finished ahead of L.A. Raiders based on a head-to-head sweep (2-0). Green Bay was first Wild Card based on best head-to-head record (3-1) vs. Detroit (2-2) and Chicago (1-3) and better conference record (8-4) than N.Y. Giants (6-6). Detroit was second Wild Card based on better division record (4-4) than Chicago (3-5) and head-to-head sweep of N.Y. Giants (1-0). Chicago was third Wild Card based on better record against common opponents (4-4) than N.Y. Giants (3-5). New Orleans finished ahead of Atlanta based on a head-to-head sweep (2-0).

Wild-Card playoffs: MIAMI 27, Kansas City 17; CLEVELAND 20, New England 13
Divisional playoffs: PITTSBURGH 29, Cleveland 9; SAN DIEGO 22, Miami 21
AFC championship: San Diego 17, PITTSBURGH 13
Wild-Card playoffs: GREEN BAY 16, Detroit 12; Chicago 35, MINNESOTA 18
Divisional playoffs: SAN FRANCISCO 44, Chicago 15; DALLAS 35, Green Bay 9
NFC championship: SAN FRANCISCO 38, Dallas 28
Super Bowl XXIX: San Francisco (NFC) 49, San Diego (AFC) 26, at Joe Robbie Stadium, Miami, Florida

1993

AMERICAN CONFERENCE

Eastern Division

	W	L	T	Pct.	Pts.	OP
Buffalo	12	4	0	.750	329	242
Miami	9	7	0	.563	349	351
N.Y. Jets	8	8	0	.500	270	247
New England	5	11	0	.313	238	286
Indianapolis	4	12	0	.250	189	378

Central Division

	W	L	T	Pct.	Pts.	OP
Houston	12	4	0	.750	368	238
Pittsburgh*	9	7	0	.563	308	281
Cleveland	7	9	0	.438	304	307
Cincinnati	3	13	0	.188	187	319

Western Division

	W	L	T	Pct.	Pts.	OP
Kansas City	11	5	0	.688	328	291
L.A. Raiders*	10	6	0	.625	306	326
Denver*	9	7	0	.563	373	284
San Diego	8	8	0	.500	322	290
Seattle	6	10	0	.375	280	314

NATIONAL CONFERENCE

Eastern Division

	W	L	T	Pct.	Pts.	OP
Dallas	12	4	0	.750	376	229
N.Y. Giants*	11	5	0	.688	288	205
Philadelphia	8	8	0	.500	293	315
Phoenix	7	9	0	.438	326	269
Washington	4	12	0	.250	230	345

Central Division

	W	L	T	Pct.	Pts.	OP
Detroit	10	6	0	.625	298	292
Minnesota*	9	7	0	.563	277	290
Green Bay*	9	7	0	.563	340	282
Chicago	7	9	0	.438	234	230
Tampa Bay	5	11	0	.313	237	376

Western Division

	W	L	T	Pct.	Pts.	OP
San Francisco	10	6	0	.625	473	295
New Orleans	8	8	0	.500	317	343
Atlanta	6	10	0	.375	316	385
L.A. Rams	5	11	0	.313	221	367

**Wild-Card qualifier for playoffs*

Minnesota finished ahead of Green Bay based on a head-to-head sweep (2-0).

Wild-Card playoffs: KANSAS CITY 27, Pittsburgh 24 (OT); L.A. RAIDERS 42, Denver 24
Divisional playoffs: BUFFALO 29, L.A. Raiders 23; Kansas City 28, HOUSTON 20
AFC championship: BUFFALO 30, Kansas City 13
Wild-Card playoffs: Green Bay 28, DETROIT 24; N.Y. GIANTS 17, Minnesota 10
Divisional playoffs: SAN FRANCISCO 44, N.Y. Giants 3; DALLAS 27, Green Bay 17
NFC championship: DALLAS 38, San Francisco 21
Super Bowl XXVIII: Dallas (NFC) 30, Buffalo (AFC) 13, at Georgia Dome, Atlanta, Georgia

1992

AMERICAN CONFERENCE

Eastern Division

	W	L	T	Pct.	Pts.	OP
Miami	11	5	0	.688	340	281
Buffalo*	11	5	0	.688	381	283
Indianapolis	9	7	0	.563	216	302
N.Y. Jets	4	12	0	.250	220	315
New England	2	14	0	.125	205	363

Central Division

	W	L	T	Pct.	Pts.	OP
Pittsburgh	11	5	0	.688	299	225
Houston*	10	6	0	.625	352	258
Cleveland	7	9	0	.438	272	275
Cincinnati	5	11	0	.313	274	364

Western Division

	W	L	T	Pct.	Pts.	OP
San Diego	11	5	0	.688	335	241
Kansas City*	10	6	0	.625	348	282
Denver	8	8	0	.500	262	329
L.A. Raiders	7	9	0	.438	249	281
Seattle	2	14	0	.125	140	312

NATIONAL CONFERENCE

Eastern Division

	W	L	T	Pct.	Pts.	OP
Dallas	13	3	0	.813	409	243
Philadelphia*	11	5	0	.688	354	245
Washington*	9	7	0	.563	300	255
N.Y. Giants	6	10	0	.375	306	367
Phoenix	4	12	0	.250	243	332

Central Division

	W	L	T	Pct.	Pts.	OP
Minnesota	11	5	0	.688	374	249
Green Bay	9	7	0	.563	276	296
Tampa Bay	5	11	0	.313	267	365
Chicago	5	11	0	.313	295	361
Detroit	5	11	0	.313	273	332

Western Division

	W	L	T	Pct.	Pts.	OP
San Francisco	14	2	0	.875	431	236
New Orleans*	12	4	0	.750	330	202
Atlanta	6	10	0	.375	327	414
L.A. Rams	6	10	0	.375	313	383

**Wild-Card qualifier for playoffs*

Miami finished ahead of Buffalo based on better conference record (9-3 to 7-5). Tampa Bay finished ahead of Chicago and Detroit based on better conference record (5-9 to Bears' 4-8 and Lions' 3-9). Atlanta finished ahead of L.A. Rams based on better record against common opponents (5-7 to 4-8).

Wild-Card playoffs: SAN DIEGO 17, Kansas City 0; BUFFALO 41, Houston 38 (OT)
Divisional playoffs: Buffalo 24, PITTSBURGH 3; MIAMI 31, San Diego 0
AFC championship: Buffalo 29, MIAMI 10
Wild-Card playoffs: Washington 24, MINNESOTA 7; Philadelphia 36, NEW ORLEANS 20
Divisional playoffs: SAN FRANCISCO 20, Washington 13; DALLAS 34, Philadelphia 10
NFC championship: Dallas 30, SAN FRANCISCO 20
Super Bowl XXVII: Dallas (NFC) 52, Buffalo (AFC) 17, at Rose Bowl, Pasadena, California

PAST STANDINGS

1991

AMERICAN CONFERENCE

Eastern Division

	W	L	T	Pct.	Pts.	OP
Buffalo	13	3	0	.813	458	318
N.Y. Jets*	8	8	0	.500	314	293
Miami	8	8	0	.500	343	349
New England	6	10	0	.375	211	305
Indianapolis	1	15	0	.063	143	381

Central Division

	W	L	T	Pct.	Pts.	OP
Houston	11	5	0	.688	386	251
Pittsburgh	7	9	0	.438	292	344
Cleveland	6	10	0	.375	293	298
Cincinnati	3	13	0	.188	263	435

Western Division

	W	L	T	Pct.	Pts.	OP
Denver	12	4	0	.750	304	235
Kansas City*	10	6	0	.625	322	252
L.A. Raiders*	9	7	0	.563	298	297
Seattle	7	9	0	.438	276	261
San Diego	4	12	0	.250	274	342

NATIONAL CONFERENCE

Eastern Division

	W	L	T	Pct.	Pts.	OP
Washington	14	2	0	.875	485	224
Dallas*	11	5	0	.688	342	310
Philadelphia	10	6	0	.625	285	244
N.Y. Giants	8	8	0	.500	281	297
Phoenix	4	12	0	.250	196	344

Central Division

	W	L	T	Pct.	Pts.	OP
Detroit	12	4	0	.750	339	295
Chicago*	11	5	0	.688	299	269
Minnesota	8	8	0	.500	301	306
Green Bay	4	12	0	.250	273	313
Tampa Bay	3	13	0	.188	199	365

Western Division

	W	L	T	Pct.	Pts.	OP
New Orleans	11	5	0	.688	341	211
Atlanta*	10	6	0	.625	361	338
San Francisco	10	6	0	.625	393	239
L.A. Rams	3	13	0	.188	234	390

**Wild-Card qualifiers for playoffs*

New York Jets finished ahead of Miami based on head-to-head sweep (2-0). Atlanta finished ahead of San Francisco based on head-to-head sweep (2-0).

Wild-Card playoffs: KANSAS CITY 10, L.A. Raiders 6;
HOUSTON 17, N.Y. Jets 10

Divisional playoffs: DENVER 26, Houston 24; BUFFALO 37, Kansas City 14

AFC championship: BUFFALO 10, Denver 7

Wild-Card playoffs: Atlanta 27, NEW ORLEANS 20; Dallas 17, CHICAGO 13

Divisional playoffs: WASHINGTON 24, Atlanta 7; DETROIT 38, Dallas 6

NFC championship: WASHINGTON 41, Detroit 10

Super Bowl XXVI: Washington (NFC) 37, Buffalo (AFC) 24, at Hubert H. Humphrey Metrodome, Minneapolis, Minnesota

1990

AMERICAN CONFERENCE

Eastern Division

	W	L	T	Pct.	Pts.	OP
Buffalo	13	3	0	.813	428	263
Miami*	12	4	0	.750	336	242
Indianapolis	7	9	0	.438	281	353
N.Y. Jets	6	10	0	.375	295	345
New England	1	15	0	.063	181	446

Central Division

	W	L	T	Pct.	Pts.	OP
Cincinnati	9	7	0	.563	360	352
Houston*	9	7	0	.563	405	307
Pittsburgh	9	7	0	.563	292	240
Cleveland	3	13	0	.188	228	462

Western Division

	W	L	T	Pct.	Pts.	OP
L.A. Raiders	12	4	0	.750	337	268
Kansas City*	11	5	0	.688	369	257
Seattle	9	7	0	.563	306	286
San Diego	6	10	0	.375	315	281
Denver	5	11	0	.313	331	374

NATIONAL CONFERENCE

Eastern Division

	W	L	T	Pct.	Pts.	OP
N.Y. Giants	13	3	0	.813	335	211
Philadelphia*	10	6	0	.625	396	299
Washington*	10	6	0	.625	381	301
Dallas	7	9	0	.438	244	308
Phoenix	5	11	0	.313	268	396

Central Division

	W	L	T	Pct.	Pts.	OP
Chicago	11	5	0	.688	348	280
Tampa Bay	6	10	0	.375	264	367
Detroit	6	10	0	.375	373	413
Green Bay	6	10	0	.375	271	347
Minnesota	6	10	0	.375	351	326

Western Division

	W	L	T	Pct.	Pts.	OP
San Francisco	14	2	0	.875	353	239
New Orleans*	8	8	0	.500	274	275
L.A. Rams	5	11	0	.313	345	412
Atlanta	5	11	0	.313	348	365

**Wild-Card qualifiers for playoffs*

Cincinnati won AFC Central title based on best head-to-head record (3-1) against Houston (2-2) and Pittsburgh (1-3). Houston was Wild Card based on better conference record (8-4) than Seattle (7-5) and Pittsburgh (6-6). Philadelphia finished second in the NFC East based on better division record (5-3) than Washington (4-4). Tampa Bay was second in NFC Central based on 5-1 record vs. Detroit, Green Bay, and Minnesota. Detroit finished third based on best net division points (minus 8) against Green Bay (minus 40) in fourth. Minnesota was fifth based on 4-8 conference record. The Los Angeles Rams finished third in NFC West based on net points in division (plus 1) vs. Atlanta (minus 31).

Wild-Card playoffs: MIAMI 17, Kansas City 16; CINCINNATI 41, Houston 14

Divisional playoffs: BUFFALO 44, Miami 34; L.A. RAIDERS 20, Cincinnati 10

AFC championship: BUFFALO 51, L.A. Raiders 3

Wild-Card playoffs: Washington 20, PHILADELPHIA 6; CHICAGO 16, New Orleans 6

Divisional playoffs: SAN FRANCISCO 28, Washington 10; N.Y. GIANTS 31, Chicago 3

NFC championship: N.Y. Giants 15, SAN FRANCISCO 13

Super Bowl XXV: N.Y. Giants (NFC) 20, Buffalo (AFC) 19, at Tampa Stadium, Tampa, Florida

1989

AMERICAN CONFERENCE

Eastern Division

	W	L	T	Pct.	Pts.	OP
Buffalo	9	7	0	.563	409	317
Indianapolis	8	8	0	.500	298	301
Miami	8	8	0	.500	331	379
New England	5	11	0	.313	297	391
N.Y. Jets	4	12	0	.250	253	411

Central Division

	W	L	T	Pct.	Pts.	OP
Cleveland	9	6	1	.594	334	254
Houston*	9	7	0	.563	365	412
Pittsburgh*	9	7	0	.563	265	326
Cincinnati	8	8	0	.500	404	285

Western Division

	W	L	T	Pct.	Pts.	OP
Denver	11	5	0	.688	362	226
Kansas City	8	7	1	.531	318	286
L.A. Raiders	8	8	0	.500	315	297
Seattle	7	9	0	.438	241	327
San Diego	6	10	0	.375	266	290

NATIONAL CONFERENCE

Eastern Division

	W	L	T	Pct.	Pts.	OP
N.Y. Giants	12	4	0	.750	348	252
Philadelphia*	11	5	0	.688	342	274
Washington	10	6	0	.625	386	308
Phoenix	5	11	0	.313	258	377
Dallas	1	15	0	.063	204	393

Central Division

	W	L	T	Pct.	Pts.	OP
Minnesota	10	6	0	.625	351	275
Green Bay	10	6	0	.625	362	356
Detroit	7	9	0	.438	312	364
Chicago	6	10	0	.375	358	377
Tampa Bay	5	11	0	.313	320	419

Western Division

	W	L	T	Pct.	Pts.	OP
San Francisco	14	2	0	.875	442	253
L.A. Rams*	11	5	0	.688	426	344
New Orleans	9	7	0	.563	386	301
Atlanta	3	13	0	.188	279	437

**Wild-Card qualifiers for playoffs*

Indianapolis finished ahead of Miami in AFC East because of better conference record (7-5 vs. 6-8). Houston finished ahead of Pittsburgh in AFC Central because of head-to-head sweep (2-0). Minnesota finished ahead of Green Bay in NFC Central because of better division record (6-2 vs. 5-3).

Wild-Card playoff: Pittsburgh 26, HOUSTON 23 (OT)

Divisional playoffs: CLEVELAND 34, Buffalo 30; DENVER 24, Pittsburgh 23

AFC championship: DENVER 37, Cleveland 21

Wild-Card playoff: L.A. Rams 21, PHILADELPHIA 7

Divisional playoffs: L.A. Rams 19, N.Y. GIANTS 13 (OT);
SAN FRANCISCO 41, Minnesota 13

NFC championship: SAN FRANCISCO 30, L.A. Rams 3

Super Bowl XXIV: San Francisco (NFC) 55, Denver (AFC) 10, at Louisiana Superdome, New Orleans, Louisiana

1988

AMERICAN CONFERENCE

Eastern Division

	W	L	T	Pct.	Pts.	OP
Buffalo	12	4	0	.750	329	237
Indianapolis	9	7	0	.563	354	315
New England	9	7	0	.563	250	284
N.Y. Jets	8	7	1	.531	372	354
Miami	6	10	0	.375	319	380

Central Division

	W	L	T	Pct.	Pts.	OP
Cincinnati	12	4	0	.750	448	329
Cleveland*	10	6	0	.625	304	288
Houston*	10	6	0	.625	424	365
Pittsburgh	5	11	0	.313	336	421

Western Division

	W	L	T	Pct.	Pts.	OP
Seattle	9	7	0	.563	339	329
Denver	8	8	0	.500	327	352
L.A. Raiders	7	9	0	.438	325	369
San Diego	6	10	0	.375	231	332
Kansas City	4	11	1	.281	254	320

NATIONAL CONFERENCE

Eastern Division

	W	L	T	Pct.	Pts.	OP
Philadelphia	10	6	0	.625	379	319
N.Y. Giants	10	6	0	.625	359	304
Washington	7	9	0	.438	345	387
Phoenix	7	9	0	.438	344	398
Dallas	3	13	0	.188	265	381

Central Division

	W	L	T	Pct.	Pts.	OP
Chicago	12	4	0	.750	312	215
Minnesota*	11	5	0	.688	406	233
Tampa Bay	5	11	0	.313	261	350
Detroit	4	12	0	.250	220	313
Green Bay	4	12	0	.250	240	315

Western Division

	W	L	T	Pct.	Pts.	OP
San Francisco	10	6	0	.625	369	294
L.A. Rams*	10	6	0	.625	407	293
New Orleans	10	6	0	.625	312	283
Atlanta	5	11	0	.313	244	315

**Wild-Card qualifiers for playoffs*

Indianapolis finished second in AFC East on basis of better record against common opponents (7-5) over New England (6-6). Cleveland gained first AFC Wild-Card position based on better division record (4-2) over Houston (3-3). Philadelphia finished first in NFC East on basis of head-to-head sweep over New York Giants. Washington finished third in NFC East on basis of better division record (4-4) over Phoenix (3-5). Detroit finished fourth in NFC Central on basis of head-to-head sweep over Green Bay. San Francisco finished first in NFC West based on better head-to-head record (3-1) over Los Angeles Rams (2-2) and New Orleans (1-3). Los Angeles Rams finished second in NFC West on basis of better division record (4-2) over New Orleans (3-3) and earned Wild-Card position based on better conference record (8-4) over New York Giants (9-5) and New Orleans (6-6).

Wild-Card playoff: Houston 24, CLEVELAND 23

Divisional playoffs: CINCINNATI 21, Seattle 13; BUFFALO 17, Houston 10

AFC championship: CINCINNATI 21, Buffalo 10

Wild-Card playoff: MINNESOTA 28, Los Angeles Rams 17

Divisional playoffs: CHICAGO 20, Philadelphia 12;
SAN FRANCISCO 34, Minnesota 9

NFC championship: San Francisco 28, CHICAGO 3

Super Bowl XXIII: San Francisco (NFC) 20, Cincinnati (AFC) 16, at Joe Robbie Stadium, Miami, Florida

1987

AMERICAN CONFERENCE

Eastern Division

	W	L	T	Pct.	Pts.	OP
Indianapolis	9	6	0	.600	300	238
New England	8	7	0	.533	320	293
Miami	8	7	0	.533	362	335
Buffalo	7	8	0	.467	270	305
N.Y. Jets	6	9	0	.400	334	360

Central Division

	W	L	T	Pct.	Pts.	OP
Cleveland	10	5	0	.667	390	239
Houston*	9	6	0	.600	345	349
Pittsburgh	8	7	0	.533	285	299
Cincinnati	4	11	0	.267	285	370

Western Division

	W	L	T	Pct.	Pts.	OP
Denver	10	4	1	.700	379	288
Seattle*	9	6	0	.600	371	314
San Diego	8	7	0	.533	253	317
L.A. Raiders	5	10	0	.333	301	289
Kansas City	4	11	0	.267	273	388

NATIONAL CONFERENCE

Eastern Division

	W	L	T	Pct.	Pts.	OP
Washington	11	4	0	.733	379	285
Dallas	7	8	0	.467	340	348
St. Louis	7	8	0	.467	362	368
Philadelphia	7	8	0	.467	337	380
N.Y. Giants	6	9	0	.400	280	312

Central Division

	W	L	T	Pct.	Pts.	OP
Chicago	11	4	0	.733	356	282
Minnesota*	8	7	0	.533	336	335
Green Bay	5	9	1	.367	255	300
Tampa Bay	4	11	0	.267	286	360
Detroit	4	11	0	.267	269	384

Western Division

	W	L	T	Pct.	Pts.	OP
San Francisco	13	2	0	.867	459	253
New Orleans*	12	3	0	.800	422	283
L.A. Rams	6	9	0	.400	317	361
Atlanta	3	12	0	.200	205	436

**Wild-Card qualifiers for playoffs*

Houston gained first AFC Wild-Card position on better conference record (7-4) over Seattle (5-6).

Wild-Card playoff: HOUSTON 23, Seattle 20 (OT)

Divisional playoffs: CLEVELAND 38, Indianapolis 21; DENVER 34, Houston 10

AFC championship: DENVER 38, Cleveland 33

Wild-Card playoff: Minnesota 44, NEW ORLEANS 10

Divisional playoffs: Minnesota 36, SAN FRANCISCO 24; Washington 21, CHICAGO 17

NFC championship: WASHINGTON 17, Minnesota 10

Super Bowl XXII: Washington (NFC) 42, Denver (AFC) 10, at San Diego Jack Murphy Stadium, San Diego, California

Note: 1987 regular season was reduced from 16 to 15 games for each team due to players' strike.

1986

AMERICAN CONFERENCE

Eastern Division

	W	L	T	Pct.	Pts.	OP
New England	11	5	0	.688	412	307
N.Y. Jets*	10	6	0	.625	364	386
Miami	8	8	0	.500	430	405
Buffalo	4	12	0	.250	287	348
Indianapolis	3	13	0	.188	229	400

Central Division

	W	L	T	Pct.	Pts.	OP
Cleveland	12	4	0	.750	391	310
Cincinnati	10	6	0	.625	409	394
Pittsburgh	6	10	0	.375	307	336
Houston	5	11	0	.313	274	329

Western Division

	W	L	T	Pct.	Pts.	OP
Denver	11	5	0	.688	378	327
Kansas City*	10	6	0	.625	358	326
Seattle	10	6	0	.625	366	293
L.A. Raiders	8	8	0	.500	323	346
San Diego	4	12	0	.250	335	396

NATIONAL CONFERENCE

Eastern Division

	W	L	T	Pct.	Pts.	OP
N.Y. Giants	14	2	0	.875	371	236
Washington*	12	4	0	.750	368	296
Dallas	7	9	0	.438	346	337
Philadelphia	5	10	1	.344	256	312
St. Louis	4	11	1	.281	218	351

Central Division

	W	L	T	Pct.	Pts.	OP
Chicago	14	2	0	.875	352	187
Minnesota	9	7	0	.563	398	273
Detroit	5	11	0	.313	277	326
Green Bay	4	12	0	.250	254	418
Tampa Bay	2	14	0	.125	239	473

Western Division

	W	L	T	Pct.	Pts.	OP
San Francisco	10	5	1	.656	374	247
L.A. Rams*	10	6	0	.625	309	267
Atlanta	7	8	1	.469	280	280
New Orleans	7	9	0	.438	288	287

**Wild-Card qualifiers for playoffs*

New York Jets gained first AFC Wild-Card position on better conference record (8-4) over Kansas City (9-5), Seattle (7-5), and Cincinnati (7-5). Kansas City gained second Wild Card based on better conference record (9-5) over Seattle (7-5) and Cincinnati (7-5).

Wild-Card playoff: NEW YORK JETS 35, Kansas City 15

Divisional playoffs: CLEVELAND 23, New York Jets 20 (OT); DENVER 22, New England 17

AFC championship: Denver 23, CLEVELAND 20 (OT)

Wild-Card playoff: WASHINGTON 19, Los Angeles Rams 7

Divisional playoffs: Washington 27, CHICAGO 13 NEW YORK GIANTS 49, San Francisco 3

NFC championship: NEW YORK GIANTS 17, Washington 0

Super Bowl XXI: New York Giants (NFC) 39, Denver (AFC) 20, at Rose Bowl, Pasadena, California

1985

AMERICAN CONFERENCE

Eastern Division

	W	L	T	Pct.	Pts.	OP
Miami	12	4	0	.750	428	320
N.Y. Jets*	11	5	0	.688	393	264
New England*	11	5	0	.688	362	290
Indianapolis	5	11	0	.313	320	386
Buffalo	2	14	0	.125	200	381

Central Division

	W	L	T	Pct.	Pts.	OP
Cleveland	8	8	0	.500	287	294
Cincinnati	7	9	0	.438	441	437
Pittsburgh	7	9	0	.438	379	355
Houston	5	11	0	.313	284	412

Western Division

	W	L	T	Pct.	Pts.	OP
L.A. Raiders	12	4	0	.750	354	308
Denver	11	5	0	.688	380	329
Seattle	8	8	0	.500	349	303
San Diego	8	8	0	.500	467	435
Kansas City	6	10	0	.375	317	360

NATIONAL CONFERENCE

Eastern Division

	W	L	T	Pct.	Pts.	OP
Dallas	10	6	0	.625	357	333
N.Y. Giants*	10	6	0	.625	399	283
Washington	10	6	0	.625	297	312
Philadelphia	7	9	0	.438	286	310
St. Louis	5	11	0	.313	278	414

Central Division

	W	L	T	Pct.	Pts.	OP
Chicago	15	1	0	.938	456	198
Green Bay	8	8	0	.500	337	355
Minnesota	7	9	0	.438	346	359
Detroit	7	9	0	.438	307	366
Tampa Bay	2	14	0	.125	294	448

Western Division

	W	L	T	Pct.	Pts.	OP
L.A. Rams	11	5	0	.688	340	277
San Francisco*	10	6	0	.625	411	263
New Orleans	5	11	0	.313	294	401
Atlanta	4	12	0	.250	282	452

**Wild-Card qualifiers for playoffs*

New York Jets gained first AFC Wild-Card position on better conference record (9-3) over New England (8-4) and Denver (8-4). New England gained second AFC Wild-Card position based on better record against common opponents (4-2) than Denver (3-3). Dallas won NFC Eastern Division title based on better record (4-0) against New York Giants (1-3) and Washington (1-3). New York Giants gained first NFC Wild-Card position based on better conference record (8-4) over San Francisco (7-5) and Washington (6-6). San Francisco gained second NFC Wild-Card position based on head-to-head victory over Washington.

Wild-Card playoff: New England 26, NEW YORK JETS 14

Divisional playoffs: MIAMI 24, Cleveland 21; New England 27, LOS ANGELES RAIDERS 20

AFC championship: New England 31, MIAMI 14

Wild-Card playoff: NEW YORK GIANTS 17, San Francisco 3

Divisional playoffs: LOS ANGELES RAMS 20, Dallas 0; CHICAGO 21, New York Giants 0

NFC championship: CHICAGO 24, Los Angeles Rams 0

Super Bowl XX: Chicago (NFC) 46, New England (AFC) 10, at Louisiana Superdome, New Orleans, Louisiana

1984

AMERICAN CONFERENCE

Eastern Division

	W	L	T	Pct.	Pts.	OP
Miami	14	2	0	.875	513	298
New England	9	7	0	.563	362	352
N.Y. Jets	7	9	0	.438	332	364
Indianapolis	4	12	0	.250	239	414
Buffalo	2	14	0	.125	250	454

Central Division

	W	L	T	Pct.	Pts.	OP
Pittsburgh	9	7	0	.563	387	310
Cincinnati	8	8	0	.500	339	339
Cleveland	5	11	0	.313	250	297
Houston	3	13	0	.188	240	437

Western Division

	W	L	T	Pct.	Pts.	OP
Denver	13	3	0	.813	353	241
Seattle*	12	4	0	.750	418	282
L.A. Raiders*	11	5	0	.688	368	278
Kansas City	8	8	0	.500	314	324
San Diego	7	9	0	.438	394	413

NATIONAL CONFERENCE

Eastern Division

	W	L	T	Pct.	Pts.	OP
Washington	11	5	0	.688	426	310
N.Y. Giants*	9	7	0	.563	299	301
St. Louis	9	7	0	.563	423	345
Dallas	9	7	0	.563	308	308
Philadelphia	6	9	1	.406	278	320

Central Division

	W	L	T	Pct.	Pts.	OP
Chicago	10	6	0	.625	325	248
Green Bay	8	8	0	.500	390	309
Tampa Bay	6	10	0	.375	335	380
Detroit	4	11	1	.281	283	408
Minnesota	3	13	0	.188	276	484

Western Division

	W	L	T	Pct.	Pts.	OP
San Francisco	15	1	0	.938	475	227
L.A. Rams*	10	6	0	.625	346	316
New Orleans	7	9	0	.438	298	361
Atlanta	4	12	0	.250	281	382

**Wild-Card qualifiers for playoffs*

New York Giants won Wild-Card berth based on best head-to-head record (3-1) against St. Louis (2-2) and Dallas (1-3). St. Louis finished ahead of Dallas based on better division record (5-3 to 3-5).

Wild-Card playoff: SEATTLE 13, Los Angeles Raiders 7

Divisional playoffs: MIAMI 31, Seattle 10; Pittsburgh 24, DENVER 17

AFC championship: MIAMI 45, Pittsburgh 28

Wild-Card playoff: New York Giants 16, LOS ANGELES RAMS 13

Divisional playoffs: SAN FRANCISCO 21, New York Giants 10; Chicago 23, WASHINGTON 19

NFC championship: SAN FRANCISCO 23, Chicago 0

Super Bowl XIX: San Francisco (NFC) 38, Miami (AFC) 16, at Stanford Stadium, Stanford, California

PAST STANDINGS

1983

AMERICAN CONFERENCE

Eastern Division

	W	L	T	Pct.	Pts.	OP
Miami	12	4	0	.750	389	250
New England	8	8	0	.500	274	289
Buffalo	8	8	0	.500	283	351
Baltimore	7	9	0	.438	264	354
N.Y. Jets	7	9	0	.438	313	331

Central Division

	W	L	T	Pct.	Pts.	OP
Pittsburgh	10	6	0	.625	355	303
Cleveland	9	7	0	.563	356	342
Cincinnati	7	9	0	.438	346	302
Houston	2	14	0	.125	288	460

Western Division

	W	L	T	Pct.	Pts.	OP
L.A. Raiders	12	4	0	.750	442	338
Seattle*	9	7	0	.563	403	397
Denver*	9	7	0	.563	302	327
San Diego	6	10	0	.375	358	462
Kansas City	6	10	0	.375	386	367

NATIONAL CONFERENCE

Eastern Division

	W	L	T	Pct.	Pts.	OP
Washington	14	2	0	.875	541	332
Dallas*	12	4	0	.750	479	360
St. Louis	8	7	1	.531	374	428
Philadelphia	5	11	0	.313	233	322
N.Y. Giants	3	12	1	.219	267	347

Central Division

	W	L	T	Pct.	Pts.	OP
Detroit	9	7	0	.563	347	286
Green Bay	8	8	0	.500	429	439
Chicago	8	8	0	.500	311	301
Minnesota	8	8	0	.500	316	348
Tampa Bay	2	14	0	.125	241	380

Western Division

	W	L	T	Pct.	Pts.	OP
San Francisco	10	6	0	.625	432	293
L.A. Rams*	9	7	0	.563	361	344
New Orleans	8	8	0	.500	319	337
Atlanta	7	9	0	.438	370	389

**Wild-Card qualifiers for playoffs*

Seattle and Denver gained Wild-Card berths over Cleveland because of their victories over the Browns.

Wild-Card playoff: SEATTLE 31, Denver 7
Divisional playoffs: Seattle 27, MIAMI 20; LOS ANGELES RAIDERS 38, Pittsburgh 10
AFC championship: LOS ANGELES RAIDERS 30, Seattle 14
Wild-Card playoff: Los Angeles Rams 24, DALLAS 17
Divisional playoffs: SAN FRANCISCO 24, Detroit 23; WASHINGTON 51, L.A. Rams 7
NFC championship: WASHINGTON 24, San Francisco 21
Super Bowl XVIII: Los Angeles Raiders (AFC) 38, Washington (NFC) 9, at Tampa Stadium, Tampa, Florida

1982

AMERICAN CONFERENCE

	W	L	T	Pct.	Pts.	OP
L.A. Raiders	8	1	0	.889	260	200
Miami	7	2	0	.778	198	131
Cincinnati	7	2	0	.778	232	177
Pittsburgh	6	3	0	.667	204	146
San Diego	6	3	0	.667	288	221
N.Y. Jets	6	3	0	.667	245	166
New England	5	4	0	.556	143	157
Cleveland	4	5	0	.444	140	182
Buffalo	4	5	0	.444	150	154
Seattle	4	5	0	.444	127	147
Kansas City	3	6	0	.333	176	184
Denver	2	7	0	.222	148	226
Houston	1	8	0	.111	136	245
Baltimore	0	8	1	.056	113	236

NATIONAL CONFERENCE

	W	L	T	Pct.	Pts.	OP
Washington	8	1	0	.889	190	128
Dallas	6	3	0	.667	226	145
Green Bay	5	3	1	.611	226	169
Minnesota	5	4	0	.556	187	198
Atlanta	5	4	0	.556	183	199
St. Louis	5	4	0	.556	135	170
Tampa Bay	5	4	0	.556	158	178
Detroit	4	5	0	.444	181	176
New Orleans	4	5	0	.444	129	160
N.Y. Giants	4	5	0	.444	164	160
San Francisco	3	6	0	.333	209	206
Chicago	3	6	0	.333	141	174
Philadelphia	3	6	0	.333	191	195
L.A. Rams	2	7	0	.222	200	250

As the result of a 57-day players' strike, the 1982 NFL regular season schedule was reduced from 16 weeks to 9. At the conclusion of the regular season, the NFL conducted a 16-team postseason Super Bowl Tournament. Eight teams from each conference were seeded 1-8 based on their records during the season.

Miami finished ahead of Cincinnati based on better conference record (6-1 to 6-2). Pittsburgh won common games tie-breaker with San Diego (3-1 to 2-1) after New York Jets were eliminated from three-way tie based on conference record (Pittsburgh and San Diego 5-3 vs. Jets 2-3). Cleveland finished ahead of Buffalo and Seattle based on better conference record (4-3 to 3-3 to 3-5). Minnesota (4-1), Atlanta (4-3), St. Louis (5-4), Tampa Bay (3-3) seeds were determined by best won-lost record in conference games. Detroit finished ahead of New Orleans and the New York Giants based on better conference record (4-4 to 3-5 to 3-5).

First round playoff: MIAMI 28, New England 13
LOS ANGELES RAIDERS 27, Cleveland 10
New York Jets 44, CINCINNATI 17
San Diego 31, PITTSBURGH 28
Second round playoff: New York Jets 17, LOS ANGELES RAIDERS 14
MIAMI 34, San Diego 13
AFC championship: MIAMI 14, New York Jets 0
First round playoff: WASHINGTON 31, Detroit 7
GREEN BAY 41, St. Louis 16
MINNESOTA 30, Atlanta 24
DALLAS 30, Tampa Bay 17
Second round playoff: WASHINGTON 21, Minnesota 7
DALLAS 37, Green Bay 26
NFC championship: WASHINGTON 31, Dallas 17
Super Bowl XVII: Washington (NFC) 27, Miami (AFC) 17, at Rose Bowl, Pasadena, California

1981

AMERICAN CONFERENCE

Eastern Division

	W	L	T	Pct.	Pts.	OP
Miami	11	4	1	.719	345	275
N.Y. Jets*	10	5	1	.656	355	287
Buffalo*	10	6	0	.625	311	276
Baltimore	2	14	0	.125	259	533
New England	2	14	0	.125	322	370

Central Division

	W	L	T	Pct.	Pts.	OP
Cincinnati	12	4	0	.750	421	304
Pittsburgh	8	8	0	.500	356	297
Houston	7	9	0	.438	281	355
Cleveland	5	11	0	.313	276	375

Western Division

	W	L	T	Pct.	Pts.	OP
San Diego	10	6	0	.625	478	390
Denver	10	6	0	.625	321	289
Kansas City	9	7	0	.563	343	290
Oakland	7	9	0	.438	273	343
Seattle	6	10	0	.375	322	388

NATIONAL CONFERENCE

Eastern Division

	W	L	T	Pct.	Pts.	OP
Dallas	12	4	0	.750	367	277
Philadelphia*	10	6	0	.625	368	221
N.Y. Giants*	9	7	0	.563	295	257
Washington	8	8	0	.500	347	349
St. Louis	7	9	0	.438	315	408

Central Division

	W	L	T	Pct.	Pts.	OP
Tampa Bay	9	7	0	.563	315	268
Detroit	8	8	0	.500	397	322
Green Bay	8	8	0	.500	324	361
Minnesota	7	9	0	.438	325	369
Chicago	6	10	0	.375	253	324

Western Division

	W	L	T	Pct.	Pts.	OP
San Francisco	13	3	0	.813	357	250
Atlanta	7	9	0	.438	426	355
Los Angeles	6	10	0	.375	303	351
New Orleans	4	12	0	.250	207	378

**Wild-Card qualifiers for playoffs*

San Diego finished ahead of Denver based on better division record (6-2 to 5-3). Buffalo won a Wild-Card playoff berth over Denver as the result of a 9-7 victory in head-to-head competition.

Wild-Card playoff: Buffalo 31, NEW YORK JETS 27
Divisional playoffs: San Diego 41, MIAMI 38 (OT); CINCINNATI 28, Buffalo 21
AFC championship: CINCINNATI 27, San Diego 7
Wild-Card playoff: New York Giants 27, PHILADELPHIA 21
Divisional playoffs: DALLAS 38, Tampa Bay 0; SAN FRANCISCO 38, New York Giants 24
NFC championship: SAN FRANCISCO 28, Dallas 27
Super Bowl XVI: San Francisco (NFC) 26, Cincinnati (AFC) 21, at Silverdome, Pontiac, Michigan

1980

AMERICAN CONFERENCE

Eastern Division

	W	L	T	Pct.	Pts.	OP
Buffalo	11	5	0	.688	320	260
New England	10	6	0	.625	441	325
Miami	8	8	0	.500	266	305
Baltimore	7	9	0	.438	355	387
N.Y. Jets	4	12	0	.250	302	395

Central Division

	W	L	T	Pct.	Pts.	OP
Cleveland	11	5	0	.688	357	310
Houston*	11	5	0	.688	295	251
Pittsburgh	9	7	0	.563	352	313
Cincinnati	6	10	0	.375	244	312

Western Division

	W	L	T	Pct.	Pts.	OP
San Diego	11	5	0	.688	418	327
Oakland*	11	5	0	.688	364	306
Kansas City	8	8	0	.500	319	336
Denver	8	8	0	.500	310	323
Seattle	4	12	0	.250	291	408

NATIONAL CONFERENCE

Eastern Division

	W	L	T	Pct.	Pts.	OP
Philadelphia	12	4	0	.750	384	222
Dallas*	12	4	0	.750	454	311
Washington	6	10	0	.375	261	293
St. Louis	5	11	0	.313	299	350
N.Y. Giants	4	12	0	.250	249	425

Central Division

	W	L	T	Pct.	Pts.	OP
Minnesota	9	7	0	.563	317	308
Detroit	9	7	0	.563	334	272
Chicago	7	9	0	.438	304	264
Tampa Bay	5	10	1	.344	271	341
Green Bay	5	10	1	.344	231	371

Western Division

	W	L	T	Pct.	Pts.	OP
Atlanta	12	4	0	.750	405	272
Los Angeles*	11	5	0	.688	424	289
San Francisco	6	10	0	.375	320	415
New Orleans	1	15	0	.063	291	487

**Wild-Card qualifiers for playoffs*

Philadelphia won division title over Dallas on the basis of best net points in division games (plus 84 net points to plus 50). Minnesota won division title because of a better conference record than Detroit (8-4 to 9-5). Cleveland won division title because of a better conference record than Houston (8-4 to 7-5). San Diego won division title over Oakland on the basis of best net points in division games (plus 60 net points to plus 37).

Wild-Card playoff: OAKLAND 27, Houston 7
Divisional playoffs: SAN DIEGO 20, Buffalo 14; Oakland 14, CLEVELAND 12
AFC championship: Oakland 34, SAN DIEGO 27
Wild-Card playoff: DALLAS 34, Los Angeles 13
Divisional playoffs: PHILADELPHIA 31, Minnesota 16; Dallas 30, ATLANTA 27
NFC championship: PHILADELPHIA 20, Dallas 7
Super Bowl XV: Oakland (AFC) 27, Philadelphia (NFC) 10, at Louisiana Superdome, New Orleans, Louisiana

1979

AMERICAN CONFERENCE

Eastern Division

	W	L	T	Pct.	Pts.	OP
Miami	10	6	0	.625	341	257
New England	9	7	0	.563	411	326
N.Y. Jets	8	8	0	.500	337	383
Buffalo	7	9	0	.438	268	279
Baltimore	5	11	0	.313	271	351

Central Division

	W	L	T	Pct.	Pts.	OP
Pittsburgh	12	4	0	.750	416	262
Houston*	11	5	0	.688	362	331
Cleveland	9	7	0	.563	359	352
Cincinnati	4	12	0	.250	337	421

Western Division

	W	L	T	Pct.	Pts.	OP
San Diego	12	4	0	.750	411	246
Denver*	10	6	0	.625	289	262
Seattle	9	7	0	.563	378	372
Oakland	9	7	0	.563	365	337
Kansas City	7	9	0	.438	238	262

NATIONAL CONFERENCE

Eastern Division

	W	L	T	Pct.	Pts.	OP
Dallas	11	5	0	.688	371	313
Philadelphia*	11	5	0	.688	339	282
Washington	10	6	0	.625	348	295
N.Y. Giants	6	10	0	.375	237	323
St. Louis	5	11	0	.313	307	358

Central Division

	W	L	T	Pct.	Pts.	OP
Tampa Bay	10	6	0	.625	273	237
Chicago*	10	6	0	.625	306	249
Minnesota	7	9	0	.438	259	337
Green Bay	5	11	0	.313	246	316
Detroit	2	14	0	.125	219	365

Western Division

	W	L	T	Pct.	Pts.	OP
Los Angeles	9	7	0	.563	323	309
New Orleans	8	8	0	.500	370	360
Atlanta	6	10	0	.375	300	388
San Francisco	2	14	0	.125	308	416

**Wild-Card qualifiers for playoffs*

Dallas won division title because of a better conference record than Philadelphia (10-2 to 9-3). Tampa Bay won division title because of a better division record than Chicago (6-2 to 5-3). Chicago won a Wild-Card berth over Washington on the basis of best net points in all games (plus 57 net points to plus 53).

Wild-Card playoff: HOUSTON 13, Denver 7

Divisional playoffs: Houston 17, SAN DIEGO 14; PITTSBURGH 34, Miami 14

AFC championship: PITTSBURGH 27, Houston 13

Wild-Card playoff: PHILADELPHIA 27, Chicago 17

Divisional playoffs: TAMPA BAY 24, Philadelphia 17; Los Angeles 21, DALLAS 19

NFC championship: Los Angeles 9, TAMPA BAY 0

Super Bowl XIV: Pittsburgh (AFC) 31, Los Angeles (NFC) 19, at Rose Bowl, Pasadena, California

1978

AMERICAN CONFERENCE

Eastern Division

	W	L	T	Pct.	Pts.	OP
New England	11	5	0	.688	358	286
Miami*	11	5	0	.688	372	254
N.Y. Jets	8	8	0	.500	359	364
Buffalo	5	11	0	.313	302	354
Baltimore	5	11	0	.313	239	421

Central Division

	W	L	T	Pct.	Pts.	OP
Pittsburgh	14	2	0	.875	356	195
Houston*	10	6	0	.625	283	298
Cleveland	8	8	0	.500	334	356
Cincinnati	4	12	0	.250	252	284

Western Division

	W	L	T	Pct.	Pts.	OP
Denver	10	6	0	.625	282	198
Oakland	9	7	0	.563	311	283
Seattle	9	7	0	.563	345	358
San Diego	9	7	0	.563	355	309
Kansas City	4	12	0	.250	243	327

NATIONAL CONFERENCE

Eastern Division

	W	L	T	Pct.	Pts.	OP
Dallas	12	4	0	.750	384	208
Philadelphia*	9	7	0	.563	270	250
Washington	8	8	0	.500	273	283
St. Louis	6	10	0	.375	248	296
N.Y. Giants	6	10	0	.375	264	298

Central Division

	W	L	T	Pct.	Pts.	OP
Minnesota	8	7	1	.531	294	306
Green Bay	8	7	1	.531	249	269
Detroit	7	9	0	.438	290	300
Chicago	7	9	0	.438	253	274
Tampa Bay	5	11	0	.313	241	259

Western Division

	W	L	T	Pct.	Pts.	OP
Los Angeles	12	4	0	.750	316	245
Atlanta*	9	7	0	.563	240	290
New Orleans	7	9	0	.438	281	298
San Francisco	2	14	0	.125	219	350

**Wild-Card qualifiers for playoffs*

New England won division title on the basis of a better division record than Miami (6-2 to 5-3). Minnesota won division title because of a better head-to-head record against Green Bay (1-0-1).

Wild-Card playoff: Houston 17, MIAMI 9

Divisional playoffs: Houston 31, NEW ENGLAND 14; PITTSBURGH 33, Denver 10

AFC championship: PITTSBURGH 34, Houston 5

Wild-Card playoff: ATLANTA 14, Philadelphia 13

Divisional playoffs: DALLAS 27, Atlanta 20; LOS ANGELES 34, Minnesota 10

NFC championship: Dallas 28, LOS ANGELES 0

Super Bowl XIII: Pittsburgh (AFC) 35, Dallas (NFC) 31, at Orange Bowl, Miami, Florida

1977

AMERICAN CONFERENCE

Eastern Division

	W	L	T	Pct.	Pts.	OP
Baltimore	10	4	0	.714	295	221
Miami	10	4	0	.714	313	197
New England	9	5	0	.643	278	217
N.Y. Jets	3	11	0	.214	191	300
Buffalo	3	11	0	.214	160	313

Central Division

	W	L	T	Pct.	Pts.	OP
Pittsburgh	9	5	0	.643	283	243
Houston	8	6	0	.571	299	230
Cincinnati	8	6	0	.571	238	235
Cleveland	6	8	0	.429	269	267

Western Division

	W	L	T	Pct.	Pts.	OP
Denver	12	2	0	.857	274	148
Oakland*	11	3	0	.786	351	230
San Diego	7	7	0	.500	222	205
Seattle	5	9	0	.357	282	373
Kansas City	2	12	0	.143	225	349

NATIONAL CONFERENCE

Eastern Division

	W	L	T	Pct.	Pts.	OP
Dallas	12	2	0	.857	345	212
Washington	9	5	0	.643	196	189
St. Louis	7	7	0	.500	272	287
Philadelphia	5	9	0	.357	220	207
N.Y. Giants	5	9	0	.357	181	265

Central Division

	W	L	T	Pct.	Pts.	OP
Minnesota	9	5	0	.643	231	227
Chicago*	9	5	0	.643	255	253
Detroit	6	8	0	.429	183	252
Green Bay	4	10	0	.286	134	219
Tampa Bay	2	12	0	.143	103	223

Western Division

	W	L	T	Pct.	Pts.	OP
Los Angeles	10	4	0	.714	302	146
Atlanta	7	7	0	.500	179	129
San Francisco	5	9	0	.357	220	260
New Orleans	3	11	0	.214	232	336

**Wild-Card qualifier for playoffs*

Baltimore won division title on the basis of a better conference record than Miami (9-3 to 8-4). Chicago won a Wild-Card berth over Washington on the basis of best net points in conference games (plus 48 net points to plus 4).

Divisional playoffs: DENVER 34, Pittsburgh 21; Oakland 37, BALTIMORE 31 (OT)

AFC championship: DENVER 20, Oakland 17

Divisional playoffs: DALLAS 37, Chicago 7; Minnesota 14, LOS ANGELES 7

NFC championship: DALLAS 23, Minnesota 6

Super Bowl XII: Dallas (NFC) 27, Denver (AFC) 10, at Louisiana Superdome, New Orleans, Louisiana

1976

AMERICAN CONFERENCE

Eastern Division

	W	L	T	Pct.	Pts.	OP
Baltimore	11	3	0	.786	417	246
New England*	11	3	0	.786	376	236
Miami	6	8	0	.429	263	264
N.Y. Jets	3	11	0	.214	169	383
Buffalo	2	12	0	.143	245	363

Central Division

	W	L	T	Pct.	Pts.	OP
Pittsburgh	10	4	0	.714	342	138
Cincinnati	10	4	0	.714	335	210
Cleveland	9	5	0	.643	267	287
Houston	5	9	0	.357	222	273

Western Division

	W	L	T	Pct.	Pts.	OP
Oakland	13	1	0	.929	350	237
Denver	9	5	0	.643	315	206
San Diego	6	8	0	.429	248	285
Kansas City	5	9	0	.357	290	376
Tampa Bay	0	14	0	.000	125	412

NATIONAL CONFERENCE

Eastern Division

	W	L	T	Pct.	Pts.	OP
Dallas	11	3	0	.786	296	194
Washington*	10	4	0	.714	291	217
St. Louis	10	4	0	.714	309	267
Philadelphia	4	10	0	.286	165	286
N.Y. Giants	3	11	0	.214	170	250

Central Division

	W	L	T	Pct.	Pts.	OP
Minnesota	11	2	1	.821	305	176
Chicago	7	7	0	.500	253	216
Detroit	6	8	0	.429	262	220
Green Bay	5	9	0	.357	218	299

Western Division

	W	L	T	Pct.	Pts.	OP
Los Angeles	10	3	1	.750	351	190
San Francisco	8	6	0	.571	270	190
Atlanta	4	10	0	.286	172	312
New Orleans	4	10	0	.286	253	346
Seattle	2	12	0	.143	229	429

**Wild-Card qualifier for playoffs*

Baltimore won division title on the basis of a better division record than New England (7-1 to 6-2). Pittsburgh won division title because of a two-game sweep over Cincinnati. Washington won Wild-Card berth over St. Louis because of a two-game sweep over Cardinals.

Divisional playoffs: OAKLAND 24, New England 21; Pittsburgh 40, BALTIMORE 14

AFC championship: OAKLAND 24, Pittsburgh 7

Divisional playoffs: MINNESOTA 35, Washington 20; Los Angeles 14, DALLAS 12

NFC championship: MINNESOTA 24, Los Angeles 13

Super Bowl XI: Oakland (AFC) 32, Minnesota (NFC) 14, at Rose Bowl, Pasadena, California

PAST STANDINGS

1975

AMERICAN CONFERENCE

Eastern Division

	W	L	T	Pct.	Pts.	OP
Baltimore	10	4	0	.714	395	269
Miami	10	4	0	.714	357	222
Buffalo	8	6	0	.571	420	355
New England	3	11	0	.214	258	358
N.Y. Jets	3	11	0	.214	258	433

Central Division

	W	L	T	Pct.	Pts.	OP
Pittsburgh	12	2	0	.857	373	162
Cincinnati*	11	3	0	.786	340	246
Houston	10	4	0	.714	293	226
Cleveland	3	11	0	.214	218	372

Western Division

	W	L	T	Pct.	Pts.	OP
Oakland	11	3	0	.786	375	255
Denver	6	8	0	.429	254	307
Kansas City	5	9	0	.357	282	341
San Diego	2	12	0	.143	189	345

NATIONAL CONFERENCE

Eastern Division

	W	L	T	Pct.	Pts.	OP
St. Louis	11	3	0	.786	356	276
Dallas*	10	4	0	.714	350	268
Washington	8	6	0	.571	325	276
N.Y. Giants	5	9	0	.357	216	306
Philadelphia	4	10	0	.286	225	302

Central Division

	W	L	T	Pct.	Pts.	OP
Minnesota	12	2	0	.857	377	180
Detroit	7	7	0	.500	245	262
Chicago	4	10	0	.286	191	379
Green Bay	4	10	0	.286	226	285

Western Division

	W	L	T	Pct.	Pts.	OP
Los Angeles	12	2	0	.857	312	135
San Francisco	5	9	0	.357	255	286
Atlanta	4	10	0	.286	240	289
New Orleans	2	12	0	.143	165	360

**Wild-Card qualifier for playoffs*

Baltimore won division title on the basis of a two-game sweep over Miami.

Divisional playoffs: PITTSBURGH 28, Baltimore 10; OAKLAND 31, Cincinnati 28

AFC championship: PITTSBURGH 16, Oakland 10

Divisional playoffs: LOS ANGELES 35, St. Louis 23; Dallas 17, MINNESOTA 14

NFC championship: Dallas 37, LOS ANGELES 7

Super Bowl X: Pittsburgh (AFC) 21, Dallas (NFC) 17, at Orange Bowl, Miami, Florida

1974

AMERICAN CONFERENCE

Eastern Division

	W	L	T	Pct.	Pts.	OP
Miami	11	3	0	.786	327	216
Buffalo*	9	5	0	.643	264	244
New England	7	7	0	.500	348	289
N.Y. Jets	7	7	0	.500	279	300
Baltimore	2	12	0	.143	190	329

Central Division

	W	L	T	Pct.	Pts.	OP
Pittsburgh	10	3	1	.750	305	189
Cincinnati	7	7	0	.500	283	259
Houston	7	7	0	.500	236	282
Cleveland	4	10	0	.286	251	344

Western Division

	W	L	T	Pct.	Pts.	OP
Oakland	12	2	0	.857	355	228
Denver	7	6	1	.536	302	294
Kansas City	5	9	0	.357	233	293
San Diego	5	9	0	.357	212	285

NATIONAL CONFERENCE

Eastern Division

	W	L	T	Pct.	Pts.	OP
St. Louis	10	4	0	.714	285	218
Washington*	10	4	0	.714	320	196
Dallas	8	6	0	.571	297	235
Philadelphia	7	7	0	.500	242	217
N.Y. Giants	2	12	0	.143	195	299

Central Division

	W	L	T	Pct.	Pts.	OP
Minnesota	10	4	0	.714	310	195
Detroit	7	7	0	.500	256	270
Green Bay	6	8	0	.429	210	206
Chicago	4	10	0	.286	152	279

Western Division

	W	L	T	Pct.	Pts.	OP
Los Angeles	10	4	0	.714	263	181
San Francisco	6	8	0	.429	226	236
New Orleans	5	9	0	.357	166	263
Atlanta	3	11	0	.214	111	271

**Wild-Card qualifier for playoffs*

St. Louis won division title because of a two-game sweep over Washington.

Divisional playoffs: OAKLAND 28, Miami 26; PITTSBURGH 32, Buffalo 14

AFC championship: Pittsburgh 24, OAKLAND 13

Divisional playoffs: MINNESOTA 30, St. Louis 14; LOS ANGELES 19, Washington 10

NFC championship: MINNESOTA 14, Los Angeles 10

Super Bowl IX: Pittsburgh (AFC) 16, Minnesota (NFC) 6, at Tulane Stadium, New Orleans, Louisiana

1973

AMERICAN CONFERENCE

Eastern Division

	W	L	T	Pct.	Pts.	OP
Miami	12	2	0	.857	343	150
Buffalo	9	5	0	.643	259	230
New England	5	9	0	.357	258	300
Baltimore	4	10	0	.286	226	341
N.Y. Jets	4	10	0	.286	240	306

Central Division

	W	L	T	Pct.	Pts.	OP
Cincinnati	10	4	0	.714	286	231
Pittsburgh*	10	4	0	.714	347	210
Cleveland	7	5	2	.571	234	255
Houston	1	13	0	.071	199	447

Western Division

	W	L	T	Pct.	Pts.	OP
Oakland	9	4	1	.679	292	175
Denver	7	5	2	.571	354	296
Kansas City	7	5	2	.571	231	192
San Diego	2	11	1	.179	188	386

NATIONAL CONFERENCE

Eastern Division

	W	L	T	Pct.	Pts.	OP
Dallas	10	4	0	.714	382	203
Washington*	10	4	0	.714	325	198
Philadelphia	5	8	1	.393	310	393
St. Louis	4	9	1	.321	286	365
N.Y. Giants	2	11	1	.179	226	362

Central Division

	W	L	T	Pct.	Pts.	OP
Minnesota	12	2	0	.857	296	168
Detroit	6	7	1	.464	271	247
Green Bay	5	7	2	.429	202	259
Chicago	3	11	0	.214	195	334

Western Division

	W	L	T	Pct.	Pts.	OP
Los Angeles	12	2	0	.857	388	178
Atlanta	9	5	0	.643	318	224
New Orleans	5	9	0	.357	163	312
San Francisco	5	9	0	.357	262	319

**Wild-Card qualifier for playoffs*

Cincinnati won division title on the basis of a better conference record than Pittsburgh (8-3 to 7-4). Dallas won division title on the basis of a better point differential in head-to-head games against Washington (net 13 points).

Divisional playoffs: OAKLAND 33, Pittsburgh 14; MIAMI 34, Cincinnati 16

AFC championship: MIAMI 27, Oakland 10

Divisional playoffs: MINNESOTA 27, Washington 20; DALLAS 27, Los Angeles 16

NFC championship: Minnesota 27, DALLAS 10

Super Bowl VIII: Miami (AFC) 24, Minnesota (NFC) 7, at Rice Stadium, Houston, Texas

1972

AMERICAN CONFERENCE

Eastern Division

	W	L	T	Pct.	Pts.	OP
Miami	14	0	0	1.000	385	171
N.Y. Jets	7	7	0	.500	367	324
Baltimore	5	9	0	.357	235	252
Buffalo	4	9	1	.321	257	377
New England	3	11	0	.214	192	446

Central Division

	W	L	T	Pct.	Pts.	OP
Pittsburgh	11	3	0	.786	343	175
Cleveland*	10	4	0	.714	268	249
Cincinnati	8	6	0	.571	299	229
Houston	1	13	0	.071	164	380

Western Division

	W	L	T	Pct.	Pts.	OP
Oakland	10	3	1	.750	365	248
Kansas City	8	6	0	.571	287	254
Denver	5	9	0	.357	325	350
San Diego	4	9	1	.321	264	344

NATIONAL CONFERENCE

Eastern Division

	W	L	T	Pct.	Pts.	OP
Washington	11	3	0	.786	336	218
Dallas*	10	4	0	.714	319	240
N.Y. Giants	8	6	0	.571	331	247
St. Louis	4	9	1	.321	193	303
Philadelphia	2	11	1	.179	145	352

Central Division

	W	L	T	Pct.	Pts.	OP
Green Bay	10	4	0	.714	304	226
Detroit	8	5	1	.607	339	290
Minnesota	7	7	0	.500	301	252
Chicago	4	9	1	.321	225	275

Western Division

	W	L	T	Pct.	Pts.	OP
San Francisco	8	5	1	.607	353	249
Atlanta	7	7	0	.500	269	274
Los Angeles	6	7	1	.464	291	286
New Orleans	2	11	1	.179	215	361

**Wild-Card qualifier for playoffs*

Divisional playoffs: PITTSBURGH 13, Oakland 7; MIAMI 20, Cleveland 14

AFC championship: Miami 21, PITTSBURGH 17

Divisional playoffs: Dallas 30, SAN FRANCISCO 28; WASHINGTON 16, Green Bay 3

NFC championship: WASHINGTON 26, Dallas 3

Super Bowl VII: Miami (AFC) 14, Washington (NFC) 7, at Memorial Coliseum, Los Angeles, California

1971

AMERICAN CONFERENCE

Eastern Division

	W	L	T	Pct.	Pts.	OP
Miami	10	3	1	.769	315	174
Baltimore*	10	4	0	.714	313	140
New England	6	8	0	.429	238	325
N.Y. Jets	6	8	0	.429	212	299
Buffalo	1	13	0	.071	184	394

Central Division

	W	L	T	Pct.	Pts.	OP
Cleveland	9	5	0	.643	285	273
Pittsburgh	6	8	0	.429	246	292
Houston	4	9	1	.308	251	330
Cincinnati	4	10	0	.286	284	265

Western Division

	W	L	T	Pct.	Pts.	OP
Kansas City	10	3	1	.769	302	208
Oakland	8	4	2	.667	344	278
San Diego	6	8	0	.429	311	341
Denver	4	9	1	.308	203	275

NATIONAL CONFERENCE

Eastern Division

	W	L	T	Pct.	Pts.	OP
Dallas	11	3	0	.786	406	222
Washington*	9	4	1	.692	276	190
Philadelphia	6	7	1	.462	221	302
St. Louis	4	9	1	.308	231	279
N.Y. Giants	4	10	0	.286	228	362

Central Division

	W	L	T	Pct.	Pts.	OP
Minnesota	11	3	0	.786	245	139
Detroit	7	6	1	.538	341	286
Chicago	6	8	0	.429	185	276
Green Bay	4	8	2	.333	274	298

Western Division

	W	L	T	Pct.	Pts.	OP
San Francisco	9	5	0	.643	300	216
Los Angeles	8	5	1	.615	313	260
Atlanta	7	6	1	.538	274	277
New Orleans	4	8	2	.333	266	347

**Wild-Card qualifier for playoffs*

Divisional playoffs: Miami 27, KANSAS CITY 24 (OT); Baltimore 20, CLEVELAND 3

AFC championship: MIAMI 21, Baltimore 0

Divisional playoffs: Dallas 20, MINNESOTA 12; SAN FRANCISCO 24, Washington 20

NFC championship: DALLAS 14, San Francisco 3

Super Bowl VI: Dallas (NFC) 24, Miami (AFC) 3, at Tulane Stadium, New Orleans, Louisiana

1970

AMERICAN CONFERENCE

Eastern Division

	W	L	T	Pct.	Pts.	OP
Baltimore	11	2	1	.846	321	234
Miami*	10	4	0	.714	297	228
N.Y. Jets	4	10	0	.286	255	286
Buffalo	3	10	1	.231	204	337
Boston Patriots	2	12	0	.143	149	361

Central Division

	W	L	T	Pct.	Pts.	OP
Cincinnati	8	6	0	.571	312	255
Cleveland	7	7	0	.500	286	265
Pittsburgh	5	9	0	.357	210	272
Houston	3	10	1	.231	217	352

Western Division

	W	L	T	Pct.	Pts.	OP
Oakland	8	4	2	.667	300	293
Kansas City	7	5	2	.583	272	244
San Diego	5	6	3	.455	282	278
Denver	5	8	1	.385	253	264

NATIONAL CONFERENCE

Eastern Division

	W	L	T	Pct.	Pts.	OP
Dallas	10	4	0	.714	299	221
N.Y. Giants	9	5	0	.643	301	270
St. Louis	8	5	1	.615	325	228
Washington	6	8	0	.429	297	314
Philadelphia	3	10	1	.231	241	332

Central Division

	W	L	T	Pct.	Pts.	OP
Minnesota	12	2	0	.857	335	143
Detroit*	10	4	0	.714	347	202
Chicago	6	8	0	.429	256	261
Green Bay	6	8	0	.429	196	293

Western Division

	W	L	T	Pct.	Pts.	OP
San Francisco	10	3	1	.769	352	267
Los Angeles	9	4	1	.692	325	202
Atlanta	4	8	2	.333	206	261
New Orleans	2	11	1	.154	172	347

**Wild-Card qualifier for playoffs*

Divisional playoffs: BALTIMORE 17, Cincinnati 0; OAKLAND 21, Miami 14

AFC championship: BALTIMORE 27, Oakland 17

Divisional playoffs: DALLAS 5, Detroit 0; San Francisco 17, MINNESOTA 14

NFC championship: Dallas 17, SAN FRANCISCO 10

Super Bowl V: Baltimore (AFC) 16, Dallas (NFC) 13, at Orange Bowl, Miami, Florida

1969 NFL

EASTERN CONFERENCE

Capitol Division

	W	L	T	Pct.	Pts.	OP
Dallas	11	2	1	.846	369	223
Washington	7	5	2	.583	307	319
New Orleans	5	9	0	.357	311	393
Philadelphia	4	9	1	.308	279	377

Century Division

	W	L	T	Pct.	Pts.	OP
Cleveland	10	3	1	.769	351	300
N.Y. Giants	6	8	0	.429	264	298
St. Louis	4	9	1	.308	314	389
Pittsburgh	1	13	0	.071	218	404

WESTERN CONFERENCE

Coastal Division

	W	L	T	Pct.	Pts.	OP
Los Angeles	11	3	0	.786	320	243
Baltimore	8	5	1	.615	279	268
Atlanta	6	8	0	.429	276	268
San Francisco	4	8	2	.333	277	319

Central Division

	W	L	T	Pct.	Pts.	OP
Minnesota	12	2	0	.857	379	133
Detroit	9	4	1	.692	259	188
Green Bay	8	6	0	.571	269	221
Chicago	1	13	0	.071	210	339

Conference championships: Cleveland 38, DALLAS 14; MINNESOTA 23, Los Angeles 20

NFL championship: MINNESOTA 27, Cleveland 7

Super Bowl IV: Kansas City (AFL) 23, Minnesota (NFL) 7, at Tulane Stadium, New Orleans, Louisiana

1969 AFL

EASTERN DIVISION

	W	L	T	Pct.	Pts.	OP
N.Y. Jets	10	4	0	.714	353	269
Houston	6	6	2	.500	278	279
Boston Patriots	4	10	0	.286	266	316
Buffalo	4	10	0	.286	230	359
Miami	3	10	1	.231	233	332

WESTERN DIVISION

	W	L	T	Pct.	Pts.	OP
Oakland	12	1	1	.923	377	242
Kansas City	11	3	0	.786	359	177
San Diego	8	6	0	.571	288	276
Denver	5	8	1	.385	297	344
Cincinnati	4	9	1	.308	280	367

Divisional playoffs: Kansas City 13, N.Y. JETS 6; OAKLAND 56, Houston 7

AFL championship: Kansas City 17, OAKLAND 7

1968 NFL

EASTERN CONFERENCE

Capitol Division

	W	L	T	Pct.	Pts.	OP
Dallas	12	2	0	.857	431	186
N.Y. Giants	7	7	0	.500	294	325
Washington	5	9	0	.357	249	358
Philadelphia	2	12	0	.143	202	351

Century Division

	W	L	T	Pct.	Pts.	OP
Cleveland	10	4	0	.714	394	273
St. Louis	9	4	1	.692	325	289
New Orleans	4	9	1	.308	246	327
Pittsburgh	2	11	1	.154	244	397

WESTERN CONFERENCE

Coastal Division

	W	L	T	Pct.	Pts.	OP
Baltimore	13	1	0	.929	402	144
Los Angeles	10	3	1	.769	312	200
San Francisco	7	6	1	.538	303	310
Atlanta	2	12	0	.143	170	389

Central Division

	W	L	T	Pct.	Pts.	OP
Minnesota	8	6	0	.571	282	242
Chicago	7	7	0	.500	250	333
Green Bay	6	7	1	.462	281	227
Detroit	4	8	2	.333	207	241

Conference championships: CLEVELAND 31, Dallas 20; BALTIMORE 24, Minnesota 14

NFL championship: Baltimore 34, CLEVELAND 0

Super Bowl III: N.Y. Jets (AFL) 16, Baltimore (NFL) 7, at Orange Bowl, Miami, Florida

1968 AFL

EASTERN DIVISION

	W	L	T	Pct.	Pts.	OP
N.Y. Jets	11	3	0	.786	419	280
Houston	7	7	0	.500	303	248
Miami	5	8	1	.385	276	355
Boston Patriots	4	10	0	.286	229	406
Buffalo	1	12	1	.077	199	367

WESTERN DIVISION

	W	L	T	Pct.	Pts.	OP
Oakland	12	2	0	.857	453	233
Kansas City	12	2	0	.857	371	170
San Diego	9	5	0	.643	382	310
Denver	5	9	0	.357	255	404
Cincinnati	3	11	0	.214	215	329

Western Division playoff: OAKLAND 41, Kansas City 6

AFL championship: N.Y. JETS 27, Oakland 23

1967 NFL

EASTERN CONFERENCE

Capitol Division

	W	L	T	Pct.	Pts.	OP
Dallas	9	5	0	.643	342	268
Philadelphia	6	7	1	.462	351	409
Washington	5	6	3	.455	347	353
New Orleans	3	11	0	.214	233	379

Century Division

	W	L	T	Pct.	Pts.	OP
Cleveland	9	5	0	.643	334	297
N.Y. Giants	7	7	0	.500	369	379
St. Louis	6	7	1	.462	333	356
Pittsburgh	4	9	1	.308	281	320

WESTERN CONFERENCE

Coastal Division

	W	L	T	Pct.	Pts.	OP
Los Angeles	11	1	2	.917	398	196
Baltimore	11	1	2	.917	394	198
San Francisco	7	7	0	.500	273	337
Atlanta	1	12	1	.077	175	422

Central Division

	W	L	T	Pct.	Pts.	OP
Green Bay	9	4	1	.692	332	209
Chicago	7	6	1	.538	239	218
Detroit	5	7	2	.417	260	259
Minnesota	3	8	3	.273	233	294

Los Angeles won division title on the basis of advantage in points (58-34) in two games vs. Baltimore.

Conference championships: DALLAS 52, Cleveland 14; GREEN BAY 28, Los Angeles 7

NFL championship: GREEN BAY 21, Dallas 17

Super Bowl II: Green Bay (NFL) 33, Oakland (AFL) 14, at Orange Bowl, Miami, Florida

1967 AFL

EASTERN DIVISION

	W	L	T	Pct.	Pts.	OP
Houston	9	4	1	.692	258	199
N.Y. Jets	8	5	1	.615	371	329
Buffalo	4	10	0	.286	237	285
Miami	4	10	0	.286	219	407
Boston Patriots	3	10	1	.231	280	389

WESTERN DIVISION

	W	L	T	Pct.	Pts.	OP
Oakland	13	1	0	.929	468	233
Kansas City	9	5	0	.643	408	254
San Diego	8	5	1	.615	360	352
Denver	3	11	0	.214	256	409

AFL championship: OAKLAND 40, Houston 7

PAST STANDINGS

1966 NFL

EASTERN CONFERENCE	W	L	T	Pct.	Pts.	OP
Dallas	10	3	1	.769	445	239
Cleveland	9	5	0	.643	403	259
Philadelphia	9	5	0	.643	326	340
St. Louis	8	5	1	.615	264	265
Washington	7	7	0	.500	351	355
Pittsburgh	5	8	1	.385	316	347
Atlanta	3	11	0	.214	204	437
N.Y. Giants	1	12	1	.077	263	501

WESTERN CONFERENCE	W	L	T	Pct.	Pts.	OP
Green Bay	12	2	0	.857	335	163
Baltimore	9	5	0	.643	314	226
Los Angeles	8	6	0	.571	289	212
San Francisco	6	6	2	.500	320	325
Chicago	5	7	2	.417	234	272
Detroit	4	9	1	.308	206	317
Minnesota	4	9	1	.308	292	304

NFL championship: Green Bay 34, DALLAS 27
Super Bowl I: Green Bay (NFL) 35, Kansas City (AFL) 10, at Memorial Coliseum, Los Angeles, California

1966 AFL

EASTERN DIVISION	W	L	T	Pct.	Pts.	OP
Buffalo	9	4	1	.692	358	255
Boston Patriots	8	4	2	.677	315	283
N.Y. Jets	6	6	2	.500	322	312
Houston	3	11	0	.214	335	396
Miami	3	11	0	.214	213	362

WESTERN DIVISION	W	L	T	Pct.	Pts.	OP
Kansas City	11	2	1	.846	448	276
Oakland	8	5	1	.615	315	288
San Diego	7	6	1	.538	335	284
Denver	4	10	0	.286	196	381

AFL championship: Kansas City 31, BUFFALO 7

1965 NFL

EASTERN CONFERENCE	W	L	T	Pct.	Pts.	OP
Cleveland	11	3	0	.786	363	325
Dallas	7	7	0	.500	325	280
N.Y. Giants	7	7	0	.500	270	338
Washington	6	8	0	.429	257	301
Philadelphia	5	9	0	.357	363	359
St. Louis	5	9	0	.357	296	309
Pittsburgh	2	12	0	.143	202	397

WESTERN CONFERENCE	W	L	T	Pct.	Pts.	OP
Green Bay	10	3	1	.769	316	224
Baltimore	10	3	1	.769	389	284
Chicago	9	5	0	.643	409	275
San Francisco	7	6	1	.538	421	402
Minnesota	7	7	0	.500	383	403
Detroit	6	7	1	.462	257	295
Los Angeles	4	10	0	.286	269	328

Western Conference playoff: GREEN BAY 13, Baltimore 10 (OT)
NFL championship: GREEN BAY 23, Cleveland 12

1965 AFL

EASTERN DIVISION	W	L	T	Pct.	Pts.	OP
Buffalo	10	3	1	.769	313	226
N.Y. Jets	5	8	1	.385	285	303
Boston Patriots	4	8	2	.333	244	302
Houston	4	10	0	.286	298	429

WESTERN DIVISION	W	L	T	Pct.	Pts.	OP
San Diego	9	2	3	.818	340	227
Oakland	8	5	1	.615	298	239
Kansas City	7	5	2	.583	322	285
Denver	4	10	0	.286	303	392

AFL championship: Buffalo 23, SAN DIEGO 0

1964 NFL

EASTERN CONFERENCE	W	L	T	Pct.	Pts.	OP
Cleveland	10	3	1	.769	415	293
St. Louis	9	3	2	.750	357	331
Philadelphia	6	8	0	.429	312	313
Washington	6	8	0	.429	307	305
Dallas	5	8	1	.385	250	289
Pittsburgh	5	9	0	.357	253	315
N.Y. Giants	2	10	2	.167	241	399

WESTERN CONFERENCE	W	L	T	Pct.	Pts.	OP
Baltimore	12	2	0	.857	428	225
Green Bay	8	5	1	.615	342	245
Minnesota	8	5	1	.615	355	296
Detroit	7	5	2	.583	280	260
Los Angeles	5	7	2	.417	283	339
Chicago	5	9	0	.357	260	379
San Francisco	4	10	0	.286	236	330

NFL championship: CLEVELAND 27, Baltimore 0

1964 AFL

EASTERN DIVISION	W	L	T	Pct.	Pts.	OP
Buffalo	12	2	0	.857	400	242
Boston Patriots	10	3	1	.769	365	297
N.Y. Jets	5	8	1	.385	278	315
Houston	4	10	0	.286	310	355

WESTERN DIVISION	W	L	T	Pct.	Pts.	OP
San Diego	8	5	1	.615	341	300
Kansas City	7	7	0	.500	366	306
Oakland	5	7	2	.417	303	350
Denver	2	11	1	.154	240	438

AFL championship: BUFFALO 20, San Diego 7

1963 NFL

EASTERN CONFERENCE	W	L	T	Pct.	Pts.	OP
N.Y. Giants	11	3	0	.786	448	280
Cleveland	10	4	0	.714	343	262
St. Louis	9	5	0	.643	341	283
Pittsburgh	7	4	3	.636	321	295
Dallas	4	10	0	.286	305	378
Washington	3	11	0	.214	279	398
Philadelphia	2	10	2	.167	242	381

WESTERN CONFERENCE	W	L	T	Pct.	Pts.	OP
Chicago	11	1	2	.917	301	144
Green Bay	11	2	1	.846	369	206
Baltimore	8	6	0	.571	316	285
Detroit	5	8	1	.385	326	265
Minnesota	5	8	1	.385	309	390
Los Angeles	5	9	0	.357	210	350
San Francisco	2	12	0	.143	198	391

NFL championship: CHICAGO 14, N.Y. Giants 10

1963 AFL

EASTERN DIVISION	W	L	T	Pct.	Pts.	OP
Boston Patriots	7	6	1	.538	327	257
Buffalo	7	6	1	.538	304	291
Houston	6	8	0	.429	302	372
N.Y. Jets	5	8	1	.385	249	399

WESTERN DIVISION	W	L	T	Pct.	Pts.	OP
San Diego	11	3	0	.786	399	255
Oakland	10	4	0	.714	363	282
Kansas City	5	7	2	.417	347	263
Denver	2	11	1	.154	301	473

Eastern Division playoff: Boston 26, BUFFALO 8
AFL championship: SAN DIEGO 51, Boston 10

1962 NFL

EASTERN CONFERENCE	W	L	T	Pct.	Pts.	OP
N.Y. Giants	12	2	0	.857	398	283
Pittsburgh	9	5	0	.643	312	363
Cleveland	7	6	1	.538	291	257
Washington	5	7	2	.417	305	376
Dallas Cowboys	5	8	1	.385	398	402
St. Louis	4	9	1	.308	287	361
Philadelphia	3	10	1	.231	282	356

WESTERN CONFERENCE	W	L	T	Pct.	Pts.	OP
Green Bay	13	1	0	.929	415	148
Detroit	11	3	0	.786	315	177
Chicago	9	5	0	.643	321	287
Baltimore	7	7	0	.500	293	288
San Francisco	6	8	0	.429	282	331
Minnesota	2	11	1	.154	254	410
Los Angeles	1	12	1	.077	220	334

NFL championship: Green Bay 16, N.Y. GIANTS 7

1962 AFL

EASTERN DIVISION	W	L	T	Pct.	Pts.	OP
Houston	11	3	0	.786	387	270
Boston Patriots	9	4	1	.692	346	295
Buffalo	7	6	1	.538	309	272
N.Y. Titans	5	9	0	.357	278	423

WESTERN DIVISION	W	L	T	Pct.	Pts.	OP
Dallas Texans	11	3	0	.786	389	233
Denver	7	7	0	.500	353	334
San Diego	4	10	0	.286	314	392
Oakland	1	13	0	.071	213	370

AFL championship: Dallas Texans 20, HOUSTON 17 (OT)

1961 NFL

EASTERN CONFERENCE	W	L	T	Pct.	Pts.	OP
N.Y. Giants	10	3	1	.769	368	220
Philadelphia	10	4	0	.714	361	297
Cleveland	8	5	1	.615	319	270
St. Louis	7	7	0	.500	279	267
Pittsburgh	6	8	0	.429	295	287
Dallas Cowboys	4	9	1	.308	236	380
Washington	1	12	1	.077	174	392

WESTERN CONFERENCE	W	L	T	Pct.	Pts.	OP
Green Bay	11	3	0	.786	391	223
Detroit	8	5	1	.615	270	258
Baltimore	8	6	0	.571	302	307
Chicago	8	6	0	.571	326	302
San Francisco	7	6	1	.538	346	272
Los Angeles	4	10	0	.286	263	333
Minnesota	3	11	0	.214	285	407

NFL championship: GREEN BAY 37, N.Y. Giants 0

1961 AFL

EASTERN DIVISION	W	L	T	Pct.	Pts.	OP
Houston	10	3	1	.769	513	242
Boston Patriots	9	4	1	.692	413	313
N.Y. Titans	7	7	0	.500	301	390
Buffalo	6	8	0	.429	294	342

WESTERN DIVISION	W	L	T	Pct.	Pts.	OP
San Diego	12	2	0	.857	396	219
Dallas Texans	6	8	0	.429	334	343
Denver	3	11	0	.214	251	432
Oakland	2	12	0	.143	237	458

AFL championship: Houston 10, SAN DIEGO 3

1960 NFL

EASTERN CONFERENCE	W	L	T	Pct.	Pts.	OP
Philadelphia	10	2	0	.833	321	246
Cleveland	8	3	1	.727	362	217
N.Y. Giants	6	4	2	.600	271	261
St. Louis	6	5	1	.545	288	230
Pittsburgh	5	6	1	.455	240	275
Washington	1	9	2	.100	178	309

WESTERN CONFERENCE	W	L	T	Pct.	Pts.	OP
Green Bay	8	4	0	.667	332	209
Detroit	7	5	0	.583	239	212
San Francisco	7	5	0	.583	208	205
Baltimore	6	6	0	.500	288	234
Chicago	5	6	1	.455	194	299
L.A. Rams	4	7	1	.364	265	297
Dallas Cowboys	0	11	1	.000	177	369

NFL championship: PHILADELPHIA 17, Green Bay 13

1960 AFL

EASTERN CONFERENCE	W	L	T	Pct.	Pts.	OP
Houston	10	4	0	.714	379	285
N.Y. Titans	7	7	0	.500	382	399
Buffalo	5	8	1	.385	296	303
Boston	5	9	0	.357	286	349

WESTERN CONFERENCE	W	L	T	Pct.	Pts.	OP
L.A. Chargers	10	4	0	.714	373	336
Dallas Texans	8	6	0	.571	362	253
Oakland	6	8	0	.429	319	388
Denver	4	9	1	.308	309	393

AFL championship: HOUSTON 24, L.A. Chargers 16

1959

EASTERN CONFERENCE

	W	L	T	Pct.	Pts.	OP
N.Y. Giants	10	2	0	.833	284	170
Cleveland	7	5	0	.583	270	214
Philadelphia	7	5	0	.583	268	278
Pittsburgh	6	5	1	.545	257	216
Washington	3	9	0	.250	185	350
Chi. Cardinals	2	10	0	.167	234	324

WESTERN CONFERENCE

	W	L	T	Pct.	Pts.	OP
Baltimore	9	3	0	.750	374	251
Chi. Bears	8	4	0	.667	252	196
Green Bay	7	5	0	.583	248	246
San Francisco	7	5	0	.583	255	237
Detroit	3	8	1	.273	203	275
Los Angeles	2	10	0	.167	242	315

NFL championship: BALTIMORE 31, N.Y. Giants 16

1958

EASTERN CONFERENCE

	W	L	T	Pct.	Pts.	OP
N.Y. Giants	9	3	0	.750	246	183
Cleveland	9	3	0	.750	302	217
Pittsburgh	7	4	1	.636	261	230
Washington	4	7	1	.364	214	268
Chi. Cardinals	2	9	1	.182	261	356
Philadelphia	2	9	1	.182	235	306

WESTERN CONFERENCE

	W	L	T	Pct.	Pts.	OP
Baltimore	9	3	0	.750	381	203
Chi. Bears	8	4	0	.667	298	230
Los Angeles	8	4	0	.667	344	278
San Francisco	6	6	0	.500	257	324
Detroit	4	7	1	.364	261	276
Green Bay	1	10	1	.091	193	382

Eastern Conference playoff: N.Y. GIANTS 10, Cleveland 0
NFL championship: Baltimore 23, N.Y. GIANTS 17 (OT)

1957

EASTERN CONFERENCE

	W	L	T	Pct.	Pts.	OP
Cleveland	9	2	1	.818	269	172
N.Y. Giants	7	5	0	.583	254	211
Pittsburgh	6	6	0	.500	161	178
Washington	5	6	1	.455	251	230
Philadelphia	4	8	0	.333	173	230
Chi. Cardinals	3	9	0	.250	200	299

WESTERN CONFERENCE

	W	L	T	Pct.	Pts.	OP
Detroit	8	4	0	.667	251	231
San Francisco	8	4	0	.667	260	264
Baltimore	7	5	0	.583	303	235
Los Angeles	6	6	0	.500	307	278
Chi. Bears	5	7	0	.417	203	211
Green Bay	3	9	0	.250	218	311

Western Conference playoff: Detroit 31, SAN FRANCISCO 27
NFL championship: DETROIT 59, Cleveland 14

1956

EASTERN CONFERENCE

	W	L	T	Pct.	Pts.	OP
N.Y. Giants	8	3	1	.727	264	197
Chi. Cardinals	7	5	0	.583	240	182
Washington	6	6	0	.500	183	225
Cleveland	5	7	0	.417	167	177
Pittsburgh	5	7	0	.417	217	250
Philadelphia	3	8	1	.273	143	215

WESTERN CONFERENCE

	W	L	T	Pct.	Pts.	OP
Chi. Bears	9	2	1	.818	363	246
Detroit	9	3	0	.750	300	188
San Francisco	5	6	1	.455	233	284
Baltimore	5	7	0	.417	270	322
Green Bay	4	8	0	.333	264	342
Los Angeles	4	8	0	.333	291	307

NFL championship: N.Y. GIANTS 47, Chi. Bears 7

1955

EASTERN CONFERENCE

	W	L	T	Pct.	Pts.	OP
Cleveland	9	2	1	.818	349	218
Washington	8	4	0	.667	246	222
N.Y. Giants	6	5	1	.545	267	223
Chi. Cardinals	4	7	1	.364	224	252
Philadelphia	4	7	1	.364	248	231
Pittsburgh	4	8	0	.333	195	285

WESTERN CONFERENCE

	W	L	T	Pct.	Pts.	OP
Los Angeles	8	3	1	.727	260	231
Chi. Bears	8	4	0	.667	294	251
Green Bay	6	6	0	.500	258	276
Baltimore	5	6	1	.455	214	239
San Francisco	4	8	0	.333	216	298
Detroit	3	9	0	.250	230	275

NFL championship: Cleveland 38, LOS ANGELES 14

1954

EASTERN CONFERENCE

	W	L	T	Pct.	Pts.	OP
Cleveland	9	3	0	.750	336	162
Philadelphia	7	4	1	.636	284	230
N.Y. Giants	7	5	0	.583	293	184
Pittsburgh	5	7	0	.417	219	263
Washington	3	9	0	.250	207	432
Chi. Cardinals	2	10	0	.167	183	347

WESTERN CONFERENCE

	W	L	T	Pct.	Pts.	OP
Detroit	9	2	1	.818	337	189
Chi. Bears	8	4	0	.667	301	279
San Francisco	7	4	1	.636	313	251
Los Angeles	6	5	1	.545	314	285
Green Bay	4	8	0	.333	234	251
Baltimore	3	9	0	.250	131	279

NFL championship: CLEVELAND 56, Detroit 10

1953

EASTERN CONFERENCE

	W	L	T	Pct.	Pts.	OP
Cleveland	11	1	0	.917	348	162
Philadelphia	7	4	1	.636	352	215
Washington	6	5	1	.545	208	215
Pittsburgh	6	6	0	.500	211	263
N.Y. Giants	3	9	0	.250	179	277
Chi. Cardinals	1	10	1	.091	190	337

WESTERN CONFERENCE

	W	L	T	Pct.	Pts.	OP
Detroit	10	2	0	.833	271	205
San Francisco	9	3	0	.750	372	237
Los Angeles	8	3	1	.727	366	236
Chi. Bears	3	8	1	.273	218	262
Baltimore	3	9	0	.250	182	350
Green Bay	2	9	1	.182	200	338

NFL championship: DETROIT 17, Cleveland 16

1952

AMERICAN CONFERENCE

	W	L	T	Pct.	Pts.	OP
Cleveland	8	4	0	.667	310	213
N.Y. Giants	7	5	0	.583	234	231
Philadelphia	7	5	0	.583	252	271
Pittsburgh	5	7	0	.417	300	273
Chi. Cardinals	4	8	0	.333	172	221
Washington	4	8	0	.333	240	287

NATIONAL CONFERENCE

	W	L	T	Pct.	Pts.	OP
Detroit	9	3	0	.750	344	192
Los Angeles	9	3	0	.750	349	234
San Francisco	7	5	0	.583	285	221
Green Bay	6	6	0	.500	295	312
Chi. Bears	5	7	0	.417	245	326
Dallas Texans	1	11	0	.083	182	427

National Conference playoff: DETROIT 31, Los Angeles 21
NFL championship: Detroit 17, CLEVELAND 7

1951

AMERICAN CONFERENCE

	W	L	T	Pct.	Pts.	OP
Cleveland	11	1	0	.917	331	152
N.Y. Giants	9	2	1	.818	254	161
Washington	5	7	0	.417	183	296
Pittsburgh	4	7	1	.364	183	235
Philadelphia	4	8	0	.333	234	264
Chi. Cardinals	3	9	0	.250	210	287

NATIONAL CONFERENCE

	W	L	T	Pct.	Pts.	OP
Los Angeles	8	4	0	.667	392	261
Detroit	7	4	1	.636	336	259
San Francisco	7	4	1	.636	255	205
Chi. Bears	7	5	0	.583	286	282
Green Bay	3	9	0	.250	254	375
N.Y. Yanks	1	9	2	.100	241	382

NFL championship: LOS ANGELES 24, Cleveland 17

1950

AMERICAN CONFERENCE

	W	L	T	Pct.	Pts.	OP
Cleveland	10	2	0	.833	310	144
N.Y. Giants	10	2	0	.833	268	150
Philadelphia	6	6	0	.500	254	141
Pittsburgh	6	6	0	.500	180	195
Chi. Cardinals	5	7	0	.417	233	287
Washington	3	9	0	.250	232	326

NATIONAL CONFERENCE

	W	L	T	Pct.	Pts.	OP
Los Angeles	9	3	0	.750	466	309
Chi. Bears	9	3	0	.750	279	207
N.Y. Yanks	7	5	0	.583	366	367
Detroit	6	6	0	.500	321	285
Green Bay	3	9	0	.250	244	406
San Francisco	3	9	0	.250	213	300
Baltimore	1	11	0	.083	213	462

American Conference playoff: CLEVELAND 8, N.Y. Giants 3
National Conference playoff: LOS ANGELES 24, Chi. Bears 14
NFL championship: CLEVELAND 30, Los Angeles 28

1949

EASTERN DIVISION

	W	L	T	Pct.	Pts.	OP
Philadelphia	11	1	0	.917	364	134
Pittsburgh	6	5	1	.545	224	214
N.Y. Giants	6	6	0	.500	287	298
Washington	4	7	1	.364	268	339
N.Y. Bulldogs	1	10	1	.091	153	368

WESTERN DIVISION

	W	L	T	Pct.	Pts.	OP
Los Angeles	8	2	2	.800	360	239
Chi. Bears	9	3	0	.750	332	218
Chi. Cardinals	6	5	1	.545	360	301
Detroit	4	8	0	.333	237	259
Green Bay	2	10	0	.167	114	329

NFL championship: Philadelphia 14, LOS ANGELES 0

1948

EASTERN DIVISION

	W	L	T	Pct.	Pts.	OP
Philadelphia	9	2	1	.818	376	156
Washington	7	5	0	.583	291	287
N.Y. Giants	4	8	0	.333	297	388
Pittsburgh	4	8	0	.333	200	243
Boston	3	9	0	.250	174	372

WESTERN DIVISION

	W	L	T	Pct.	Pts.	OP
Chi. Cardinals	11	1	0	.917	395	226
Chi. Bears	10	2	0	.833	375	151
Los Angeles	6	5	1	.545	327	269
Green Bay	3	9	0	.250	154	290
Detroit	2	10	0	.167	200	407

NFL championship: PHILADELPHIA 7, Chi. Cardinals 0

1947

EASTERN DIVISION

	W	L	T	Pct.	Pts.	OP
Philadelphia	8	4	0	.667	308	242
Pittsburgh	8	4	0	.667	240	259
Boston	4	7	1	.364	168	256
Washington	4	8	0	.333	295	367
N.Y. Giants	2	8	2	.200	190	309

WESTERN DIVISION

	W	L	T	Pct.	Pts.	OP
Chi. Cardinals	9	3	0	.750	306	231
Chi. Bears	8	4	0	.667	363	241
Green Bay	6	5	1	.545	274	210
Los Angeles	6	6	0	.500	259	214
Detroit	3	9	0	.250	231	305

Eastern Division playoff: Philadelphia 21, PITTSBURGH 0
NFL championship: CHI. CARDINALS 28, Philadelphia 21

1946

EASTERN DIVISION

	W	L	T	Pct.	Pts.	OP
N.Y. Giants	7	3	1	.700	236	162
Philadelphia	6	5	0	.545	231	220
Washington	5	5	1	.500	171	191
Pittsburgh	5	5	1	.500	136	117
Boston	2	8	1	.200	189	273

WESTERN DIVISION

	W	L	T	Pct.	Pts.	OP
Chi. Bears	8	2	1	.800	289	193
Los Angeles	6	4	1	.600	277	257
Green Bay	6	5	0	.545	148	158
Chi. Cardinals	6	5	0	.545	260	198
Detroit	1	10	0	.091	142	310

NFL championship: Chi. Bears 24, N.Y. GIANTS 14

PAST STANDINGS

1945

EASTERN DIVISION

	W	L	T	Pct.	Pts.	OP
Washington	8	2	0	.800	209	121
Philadelphia	7	3	0	.700	272	133
N.Y. Giants	3	6	1	.333	179	198
Boston	3	6	1	.333	123	211
Pittsburgh	2	8	0	.200	79	220

WESTERN DIVISION

	W	L	T	Pct.	Pts.	OP
Cleveland	9	1	0	.900	244	136
Detroit	7	3	0	.700	195	194
Green Bay	6	4	0	.600	258	173
Chi. Bears	3	7	0	.300	192	235
Chi. Cardinals	1	9	0	.100	98	228

NFL championship: CLEVELAND 15, Washington 14

1944

EASTERN DIVISION

	W	L	T	Pct.	Pts.	OP
N.Y. Giants	8	1	1	.889	206	75
Philadelphia	7	1	2	.875	267	131
Washington	6	3	1	.667	169	180
Boston	2	8	0	.200	82	233
Brooklyn	0	10	0	.000	69	166

WESTERN DIVISION

	W	L	T	Pct.	Pts.	OP
Green Bay	8	2	0	.800	238	141
Chi. Bears	6	3	1	.667	258	172
Detroit	6	3	1	.667	216	151
Cleveland	4	6	0	.400	188	224
Card-Pitt	0	10	0	.000	108	328

NFL championship: Green Bay 14, N.Y. GIANTS 7

1943

EASTERN DIVISION

	W	L	T	Pct.	Pts.	OP
Washington	6	3	1	.667	229	137
N.Y. Giants	6	3	1	.667	197	170
Phil-Pitt	5	4	1	.556	225	230
Brooklyn	2	8	0	.200	65	234

WESTERN DIVISION

	W	L	T	Pct.	Pts.	OP
Chi. Bears	8	1	1	.889	303	157
Green Bay	7	2	1	.778	264	172
Detroit	3	6	1	.333	178	218
Chi. Cardinals	0	10	0	.000	95	238

Eastern Division playoff: Washington 28, N.Y. GIANTS 0
NFL championship: CHI. BEARS 41, Washington 21

1942

EASTERN DIVISION

	W	L	T	Pct.	Pts.	OP
Washington	10	1	0	.909	227	102
Pittsburgh	7	4	0	.636	167	119
N.Y. Giants	5	5	1	.500	155	139
Brooklyn	3	8	0	.273	100	168
Philadelphia	2	9	0	.182	134	239

WESTERN DIVISION

	W	L	T	Pct.	Pts.	OP
Chi. Bears	11	0	0	1.000	376	84
Green Bay	8	2	1	.800	300	215
Cleveland	5	6	0	.455	150	207
Chi. Cardinals	3	8	0	.273	98	209
Detroit	0	11	0	.000	38	263

NFL championship: WASHINGTON 14, Chi. Bears 6

1941

EASTERN DIVISION

	W	L	T	Pct.	Pts.	OP
N.Y. Giants	8	3	0	.727	238	114
Brooklyn	7	4	0	.636	158	127
Washington	6	5	0	.545	176	174
Philadelphia	2	8	1	.200	119	218
Pittsburgh	1	9	1	.100	103	276

WESTERN DIVISION

	W	L	T	Pct.	Pts.	OP
Chi. Bears	10	1	0	.909	396	147
Green Bay	10	1	0	.909	258	120
Detroit	4	6	1	.400	121	195
Chi. Cardinals	3	7	1	.300	127	197
Cleveland	2	9	0	.182	116	244

Western Division playoff: CHI. BEARS 33, Green Bay 14
NFL championship: CHI. BEARS 37, N.Y. Giants 9

1940

EASTERN DIVISION

	W	L	T	Pct.	Pts.	OP
Washington	9	2	0	.818	245	142
Brooklyn	8	3	0	.727	186	120
N.Y. Giants	6	4	1	.600	131	133
Pittsburgh	2	7	2	.222	60	178
Philadelphia	1	10	0	.091	111	211

WESTERN DIVISION

	W	L	T	Pct.	Pts.	OP
Chi. Bears	8	3	0	.727	238	152
Green Bay	6	4	1	.600	238	155
Detroit	5	5	1	.500	138	153
Cleveland	4	6	1	.400	171	191
Chi. Cardinals	2	7	2	.222	139	222

NFL championship: Chi. Bears 73, WASHINGTON 0

1939

EASTERN DIVISION

	W	L	T	Pct.	Pts.	OP
N.Y. Giants	9	1	1	.900	168	85
Washington	8	2	1	.800	242	94
Brooklyn	4	6	1	.400	108	219
Philadelphia	1	9	1	.100	105	200
Pittsburgh	1	9	1	.100	114	216

WESTERN DIVISION

	W	L	T	Pct.	Pts.	OP
Green Bay	9	2	0	.818	233	153
Chi. Bears	8	3	0	.727	298	157
Detroit	6	5	0	.545	145	150
Cleveland	5	5	1	.500	195	164
Chi. Cardinals	1	10	0	.091	84	254

NFL championship: GREEN BAY 27, N.Y. Giants 0

1938

EASTERN DIVISION

	W	L	T	Pct.	Pts.	OP
N.Y. Giants	8	2	1	.800	194	79
Washington	6	3	2	.667	148	154
Brooklyn	4	4	3	.500	131	161
Philadelphia	5	6	0	.455	154	164
Pittsburgh	2	9	0	.182	79	169

WESTERN DIVISION

	W	L	T	Pct.	Pts.	OP
Green Bay	8	3	0	.727	223	118
Detroit	7	4	0	.636	119	108
Chi. Bears	6	5	0	.545	194	148
Cleveland	4	7	0	.364	131	215
Chi. Cardinals	2	9	0	.182	111	168

NFL championship: N.Y. GIANTS 23, Green Bay 17

1937

EASTERN DIVISION

	W	L	T	Pct.	Pts.	OP
Washington	8	3	0	.727	195	120
N.Y. Giants	6	3	2	.667	128	109
Pittsburgh	4	7	0	.364	122	145
Brooklyn	3	7	1	.300	82	174
Philadelphia	2	8	1	.200	86	177

WESTERN DIVISION

	W	L	T	Pct.	Pts.	OP
Chi. Bears	9	1	1	.900	201	100
Green Bay	7	4	0	.636	220	122
Detroit	7	4	0	.636	180	105
Chi. Cardinals	5	5	1	.500	135	165
Cleveland	1	10	0	.091	75	207

NFL championship: Washington 28, CHI. BEARS 21

1936

EASTERN DIVISION

	W	L	T	Pct.	Pts.	OP
Boston	7	5	0	.583	149	110
Pittsburgh	6	6	0	.500	98	187
N.Y. Giants	5	6	1	.455	115	163
Brooklyn	3	8	1	.273	92	161
Philadelphia	1	11	0	.083	51	206

WESTERN DIVISION

	W	L	T	Pct.	Pts.	OP
Green Bay	10	1	1	.909	248	118
Chi. Bears	9	3	0	.750	222	94
Detroit	8	4	0	.667	235	102
Chi. Cardinals	3	8	1	.273	74	143

NFL championship: Green Bay 21, Boston 6, at Polo Grounds, N.Y.

1935

EASTERN DIVISION

	W	L	T	Pct.	Pts.	OP
N.Y. Giants	9	3	0	.750	180	96
Brooklyn	5	6	1	.455	90	141
Pittsburgh	4	8	0	.333	100	209
Boston	2	8	1	.200	65	123
Philadelphia	2	9	0	.182	60	179

WESTERN DIVISION

	W	L	T	Pct.	Pts.	OP
Detroit	7	3	2	.700	191	111
Green Bay	8	4	0	.667	181	96
Chi. Bears	6	4	2	.600	192	106
Chi. Cardinals	6	4	2	.600	99	97

NFL championship: DETROIT 26, N.Y. Giants 7
One game between Boston and Philadelphia was canceled.

1934

EASTERN DIVISION

	W	L	T	Pct.	Pts.	OP
N.Y. Giants	8	5	0	.615	147	107
Boston	6	6	0	.500	107	94
Brooklyn	4	7	0	.364	61	153
Philadelphia	4	7	0	.364	127	85
Pittsburgh	2	10	0	.167	51	206

WESTERN DIVISION

	W	L	T	Pct.	Pts.	OP
Chi. Bears	13	0	0	1.000	286	86
Detroit	10	3	0	.769	238	59
Green Bay	7	6	0	.538	156	112
Chi. Cardinals	5	6	0	.455	80	84
St. Louis	1	2	0	.333	27	61
Cincinnati	0	8	0	.000	10	243

NFL championship: N.Y. GIANTS 30, Chi. Bears 13

1933

EASTERN DIVISION

	W	L	T	Pct.	Pts.	OP
N.Y. Giants	11	3	0	.786	244	101
Brooklyn	5	4	1	.556	93	54
Boston	5	5	2	.500	103	97
Philadelphia	3	5	1	.375	77	158
Pittsburgh	3	6	2	.333	67	208

WESTERN DIVISION

	W	L	T	Pct.	Pts.	OP
Chi. Bears	10	2	1	.833	133	82
Portsmouth	6	5	0	.545	128	87
Green Bay	5	7	1	.417	170	107
Cincinnati	3	6	1	.333	38	110
Chi. Cardinals	1	9	1	.100	52	101

NFL championship: CHI. BEARS 23, N.Y. Giants 21

1932

	W	L	T	Pct.
Chicago Bears	7	1	6	.875
Green Bay Packers	10	3	1	.769
Portsmouth Spartans	6	2	4	.750
Boston Braves	4	4	2	.500
New York Giants	4	6	2	.400
Brooklyn Dodgers	3	9	0	.250
Chicago Cardinals	2	6	2	.250
Staten Island Stapletons	2	7	3	.222

Chicago Bears and Portsmouth finished regularly scheduled games tied for first place. Bears won playoff game, which counted in standings, 9-0.

1931

	W	L	T	Pct.
Green Bay Packers	12	2	0	.857
Portsmouth Spartans	11	3	0	.786
Chicago Bears	8	5	0	.615
Chicago Cardinals	5	4	0	.556
New York Giants	7	6	1	.538
Providence Steam Roller	4	4	3	.500
Staten Island Stapletons	4	6	1	.400
Cleveland Indians	2	8	0	.200
Brooklyn Dodgers	2	12	0	.143
Frankford Yellow Jackets	1	6	1	.143

1930

	W	L	T	Pct.
Green Bay Packers	10	3	1	.769
New York Giants	13	4	0	.765
Chicago Bears	9	4	1	.692
Brooklyn Dodgers	7	4	1	.636
Providence Steam Roller	6	4	1	.600
Staten Island Stapletons	5	5	2	.500
Chicago Cardinals	5	6	2	.455
Portsmouth Spartans	5	6	3	.455
Frankford Yellow Jackets	4	13	1	.222
Minneapolis Red Jackets	1	7	1	.125
Newark Tornadoes	1	10	1	.091

1929

	W	L	T	Pct.
Green Bay Packers	12	0	1	1.000
New York Giants	13	1	1	.929
Frankford Yellow Jackets	10	4	5	.714
Chicago Cardinals	6	6	1	.500
Boston Bulldogs	4	4	0	.500
Staten Island Stapletons	3	4	3	.429
Providence Steam Roller	4	6	2	.400
Orange Tornadoes	3	5	4	.375
Chicago Bears	4	9	2	.308
Buffalo Bisons	1	7	1	.125
Minneapolis Red Jackets	1	9	0	.100
Dayton Triangles	0	6	0	.000

1928

	W	L	T	Pct.
Providence Steam Roller	8	1	2	.889
Frankford Yellow Jackets	11	3	2	.786
Detroit Wolverines	7	2	1	.778
Green Bay Packers	6	4	3	.600
Chicago Bears	7	5	1	.583
New York Giants	4	7	2	.364
New York Yankees	4	8	1	.333
Pottsville Maroons	2	8	0	.200
Chicago Cardinals	1	5	0	.167
Dayton Triangles	0	7	0	.000

1927

	W	L	T	Pct.
New York Giants	11	1	1	.917
Green Bay Packers	7	2	1	.778
Chicago Bears	9	3	2	.750
Cleveland Bulldogs	8	4	1	.667
Providence Steam Roller	8	5	1	.615
New York Yankees	7	8	1	.467
Frankford Yellow Jackets	6	9	3	.400
Pottsville Maroons	5	8	0	.385
Chicago Cardinals	3	7	1	.300
Dayton Triangles	1	6	1	.143
Duluth Eskimos	1	8	0	.111
Buffalo Bisons	0	5	0	.000

1926

	W	L	T	Pct.
Frankford Yellow Jackets	14	1	2	.933
Chicago Bears	12	1	3	.923
Pottsville Maroons	10	2	2	.833
Kansas City Cowboys	8	3	0	.727
Green Bay Packers	7	3	3	.700
Los Angeles Buccaneers	6	3	1	.667
New York Giants	8	4	1	.667
Duluth Eskimos	6	5	3	.545
Buffalo Rangers	4	4	2	.500
Chicago Cardinals	5	6	1	.455
Providence Steam Roller	5	7	1	.417
Detroit Panthers	4	6	2	.400
Hartford Blues	3	7	0	.300
Brooklyn Lions	3	8	0	.273
Milwaukee Badgers	2	7	0	.222
Akron Pros	1	4	3	.200
Dayton Triangles	1	4	1	.200
Racine Tornadoes	1	4	0	.200
Columbus Tigers	1	6	0	.143
Canton Bulldogs	1	9	3	.100
Hammond Pros	0	4	0	.000
Louisville Colonels	0	4	0	.000

1925

	W	L	T	Pct.
Chicago Cardinals	11	2	1	.846
Pottsville Maroons	10	2	0	.833
Detroit Panthers	8	2	2	.800
New York Giants	8	4	0	.667
Akron Indians	4	2	2	.667
Frankford Yellow Jackets	13	7	0	.650
Chicago Bears	9	5	3	.643
Rock Island Independents	5	3	3	.625
Green Bay Packers	8	5	0	.615
Providence Steam Roller	6	5	1	.545
Canton Bulldogs	4	4	0	.500
Cleveland Bulldogs	5	8	1	.385
Kansas City Cowboys	2	5	1	.286
Hammond Pros	1	4	0	.200
Buffalo Bisons	1	6	2	.143
Duluth Kelleys	0	3	0	.000
Rochester Jeffersons	0	6	1	.000
Milwaukee Badgers	0	6	0	.000
Dayton Triangles	0	7	1	.000
Columbus Tigers	0	9	0	.000

1924

	W	L	T	Pct.
Cleveland Bulldogs	7	1	1	.875
Chicago Bears	6	1	4	.857
Frankford Yellow Jackets	11	2	1	.846
Duluth Kelleys	5	1	0	.833
Rock Island Independents	5	2	2	.714
Green Bay Packers	7	4	0	.636
Racine Legion	4	3	3	.571
Chicago Cardinals	5	4	1	.556
Buffalo Bisons	6	5	0	.545
Columbus Tigers	4	4	0	.500
Hammond Pros	2	2	1	.500
Milwaukee Badgers	5	8	0	.385
Akron Indians	2	6	0	.250
Dayton Triangles	2	6	0	.250
Kansas City Blues	2	7	0	.222
Kenosha Maroons	0	4	1	.000
Minneapolis Marines	0	6	0	.000
Rochester Jeffersons	0	7	0	.000

1923

	W	L	T	Pct.
Canton Bulldogs	11	0	1	1.000
Chicago Bears	9	2	1	.818
Green Bay Packers	7	2	1	.778
Milwaukee Badgers	7	2	3	.778
Cleveland Indians	3	1	3	.750
Chicago Cardinals	8	4	0	.667
Duluth Kelleys	4	3	0	.571
Buffalo All-Americans	5	4	3	.556
Columbus Tigers	5	4	1	.556
Racine Legion	4	4	2	.500
Toledo Maroons	3	3	2	.500
Rock Island Independents	2	3	3	.400
Minneapolis Marines	2	5	2	.286
St. Louis All-Stars	1	4	2	.200
Hammond Pros	1	5	1	.167
Dayton Triangles	1	6	1	.143
Akron Indians	1	6	0	.143
Oorang Indians	1	10	0	.091
Louisville Brecks	0	3	0	.000
Rochester Jeffersons	0	4	0	.000

1922

	W	L	T	Pct.
Canton Bulldogs	10	0	2	1.000
Chicago Bears	9	3	0	.750
Chicago Cardinals	8	3	0	.727
Toledo Maroons	5	2	2	.714
Rock Island Independents	4	2	1	.667
Racine Legion	6	4	1	.600
Dayton Triangles	4	3	1	.571
Green Bay Packers	4	3	3	.571
Buffalo All-Americans	5	4	1	.556
Akron Pros	3	5	2	.375
Milwaukee Badgers	2	4	3	.333
Oorang Indians	3	6	0	.333
Minneapolis Marines	1	3	0	.250
Louisville Brecks	1	3	0	.250
Evansville Crimson Giants	0	3	0	.000
Rochester Jeffersons	0	4	1	.000
Hammond Pros	0	5	1	.000
Columbus Panhandles	0	8	0	.000

1921

	W	L	T	Pct.
Chicago Staleys	9	1	1	.900
Buffalo All-Americans	9	1	2	.900
Akron Pros	8	3	1	.727
Canton Bulldogs	5	2	3	.714
Rock Island Independents	4	2	1	.667
Evansville Crimson Giants	3	2	0	.600
Green Bay Packers	3	2	1	.600
Dayton Triangles	4	4	1	.500
Chicago Cardinals	3	3	2	.500
Rochester Jeffersons	2	3	0	.400
Cleveland Indians	3	5	0	.375
Washington Senators	1	2	0	.333
Cincinnati Celts	1	3	0	.250
Hammond Pros	1	3	1	.250
Minneapolis Marines	1	3	0	.250
Detroit Heralds	1	5	1	.167
Columbus Panhandles	1	8	0	.111
Tonawanda Kardex	0	1	0	.000
Muncie Flyers	0	2	0	.000
Louisville Brecks	0	2	0	.000
New York Giants	0	2	0	.000

1920*

	W	L	T	Pct.
Akron Pros	8	0	3	1.000
Decatur Staleys	10	1	2	.909
Buffalo All-Americans	9	1	1	.900
Chicago Cardinals	6	2	2	.750
Rock Island Independents	6	2	2	.750
Dayton Triangles	5	2	2	.714
Rochester Jeffersons	6	3	2	.667
Canton Bulldogs	7	4	2	.636
Detroit Heralds	2	3	3	.400
Cleveland Tigers	2	4	2	.333
Chicago Tigers	2	5	1	.286
Hammond Pros	2	5	0	.286
Columbus Panhandles	2	6	2	.250
Muncie Flyers	0	1	0	.000

**No official standings were maintained for the 1920 season, and the championship was awarded to the Akron Pros in a League meeting on April 30, 1921. Clubs played schedules that included games against nonleague opponents.*

ALL-TIME TEAM VS. TEAM RESULTS

RS=REGULAR SEASON
PS=POSTSEASON
***ARIZONA vs. ATLANTA**
RS: Cardinals lead series, 13-7
1966—Falcons, 16-10 (A)
1968—Cardinals, 17-12 (StL)
1971—Cardinals, 26-9 (A)
1973—Cardinals, 32-10 (A)
1975—Cardinals, 23-20 (StL)
1978—Cardinals, 42-21 (StL)
1980—Falcons, 33-27 (StL) OT
1981—Falcons, 41-20 (A)
1982—Cardinals, 23-20 (A)
1986—Falcons, 33-13 (A)
1987—Cardinals, 34-21 (A)
1989—Cardinals, 34-20 (P)
1990—Cardinals, 24-13 (A)
1991—Cardinals, 16-10 (P)
1992—Falcons, 20-17 (A)
1993—Cardinals, 27-10 (A)
1994—Falcons, 10-6 (Atl)
1995—Cardinals, 40-37 (Ariz) OT
1997—Cardinals, 29-26 (Ariz)
1999—Falcons, 37-14 (Atl)
(RS Pts.—Cardinals 474, Falcons 419)
**Franchise known as Phoenix prior to 1994 and in St. Louis prior to 1988*
***ARIZONA vs. BALTIMORE**
RS: Cardinals lead series, 1-0
1997—Cardinals, 16-13 (B)
(RS Pts.—Cardinals 16, Ravens 13)
***ARIZONA vs. BUFFALO**
RS: Bills lead series, 4-3
1971—Cardinals, 28-23 (B)
1975—Bills, 32-14 (StL)
1981—Cardinals, 24-0 (StL)
1984—Cardinals, 37-7 (StL)
1986—Bills, 17-10 (B)
1990—Bills, 45-14 (B)
1999—Bills, 31-21 (A)
(RS Pts.—Bills 155, Cardinals 148)
**Franchise known as Phoenix prior to 1994 and in St. Louis prior to 1988*
ARIZONA vs. CAROLINA
RS: Panthers lead series, 1-0
1995—Panthers, 27-7 (C)
(RS Pts.—Panthers 27, Cardinals 7)
***ARIZONA vs. **CHICAGO**
RS: Bears lead series, 52-26-6
(NP denotes Normal Park;
Wr denotes Wrigley Field;
Co denotes Comiskey Park;
So denotes Soldier Field;
all Chicago)
1920—Cardinals, 7-6 (NP)
Staleys, 10-0 (Wr)
1921—Tie, 0-0 (Wr)
1922—Cardinals, 6-0 (Co)
Cardinals, 9-0 (Co)
1923—Bears, 3-0 (Wr)
1924—Bears, 6-0 (Wr)
Bears, 21-0 (Co)
1925—Cardinals, 9-0 (Co)
Tie, 0-0 (Wr)
1926—Bears, 16-0 (Wr)
Bears, 10-0 (So)
Tie, 0-0 (Wr)
1927—Bears, 9-0 (NP)
Cardinals, 3-0 (Wr)
1928—Bears, 15-0 (NP)
Bears, 34-0 (Wr)
1929—Tie, 0-0 (Wr)
Cardinals, 40-6 (Co)
1930—Bears, 32-6 (Co)
Bears, 6-0 (Wr)
1931—Bears, 26-13 (Wr)
Bears, 18-7 (Wr)
1932—Tie, 0-0 (Wr)
Bears, 34-0 (Wr)
1933—Bears, 12-9 (Wr)
Bears, 22-6 (Wr)
1934—Bears, 20-0 (Wr)
Bears, 17-6 (Wr)
1935—Tie, 7-7 (Wr)
Bears, 13-0 (Wr)
1936—Bears, 7-3 (Wr)
Cardinals, 14-7 (Wr)
1937—Bears, 16-7 (Wr)
Bears, 42-28 (Wr)
1938—Bears, 16-13 (So)
Bears, 34-28 (Wr)
1939—Bears, 44-7 (Wr)
Bears, 48-7 (Co)
1940—Cardinals, 21-7 (Co)
Bears, 31-23 (Wr)
1941—Bears, 53-7 (Wr)
Bears, 34-24 (Co)
1942—Bears, 41-14 (Wr)
Bears, 21-7 (Co)
1943—Bears, 20-0 (Wr)
Bears, 35-24 (Co)
1945—Cardinals, 16-7 (Wr)
Bears, 28-20 (Co)
1946—Bears, 34-17 (Co)
Cardinals, 35-28 (Wr)
1947—Cardinals, 31-7 (Co)
Cardinals, 30-21 (Wr)
1948—Bears, 28-17 (Co)
Cardinals, 24-21 (Wr)
1949—Bears, 17-7 (Co)
Bears, 52-21 (Wr)
1950—Bears, 27-6 (Wr)
Cardinals, 20-10 (Co)
1951—Cardinals, 28-14 (Co)
Cardinals, 24-14 (Wr)
1952—Cardinals, 21-10 (Co)
Bears, 10-7 (Wr)
1953—Cardinals, 24-17 (Wr)
1954—Bears, 29-7 (Co)
1955—Cardinals, 53-14 (Co)
1956—Bears, 10-3 (Wr)
1957—Bears, 14-6 (Co)
1958—Bears, 30-14 (Wr)
1959—Bears, 31-7 (So)
1965—Bears, 34-13 (Wr)
1966—Cardinals, 24-17 (StL)
1967—Bears, 30-3 (Wr)
1969—Cardinals, 20-17 (StL)
1972—Bears, 27-10 (StL)
1975—Cardinals, 34-20 (So)
1977—Cardinals, 16-13 (StL)
1978—Bears, 17-10 (So)
1979—Bears, 42-6 (So)
1982—Cardinals, 10-7 (So)
1984—Cardinals, 38-21 (StL)
1990—Bears, 31-21 (P)
1994—Bears, 19-16 (A) OT
1998—Cardinals, 20-7 (A)
(RS Pts.—Bears 1,574, Cardinals 1,034)
**Franchise known as Phoenix prior to 1994, in St. Louis prior to 1988, and in Chicago prior to 1960*
***Franchise in Decatur prior to 1921 and known as Staleys prior to 1922*
***ARIZONA vs. CINCINNATI**
RS: Bengals lead series, 4-2
1973—Bengals, 42-24 (C)
1979—Bengals, 34-28 (C)
1985—Cardinals, 41-27 (StL)
1988—Bengals, 21-14 (C)
1994—Cardinals, 28-7 (A)
1997—Bengals, 24-21 (C)
(RS Pts.—Cardinals 156, Bengals 155)
**Franchise known as Phoenix prior to 1994 and in St. Louis prior to 1988*
***ARIZONA vs. CLEVELAND**
RS: Browns lead series, 32-10-3
1950—Browns, 34-24 (Cle)
Browns, 10-7 (Chi)
1951—Browns, 34-17 (Chi)
Browns, 49-28 (Cle)
1952—Browns, 28-13 (Cle)
Browns, 10-0 (Chi)
1953—Browns, 27-7 (Chi)
Browns, 27-16 (Cle)
1954—Browns, 31-7 (Cle)
Browns, 35-3 (Chi)
1955—Browns, 26-20 (Chi)
Browns, 35-24 (Cle)
1956—Cardinals, 9-7 (Chi)
Cardinals, 24-7 (Cle)
1957—Browns, 17-7 (Chi)
Browns, 31-0 (Cle)
1958—Browns, 35-28 (Cle)
Browns, 38-24 (Chi)
1959—Browns, 34-7 (Chi)
Browns, 17-7 (Cle)
1960—Browns, 28-27 (Cle)
Tie, 17-17 (StL)
1961—Browns, 20-17 (Cle)
Browns, 21-10 (StL)
1962—Browns, 34-7 (StL)
Browns, 38-14 (Cle)
1963—Cardinals, 20-14 (Cle)
Browns, 24-10 (StL)
1964—Tie, 33-33 (Cle)
Cardinals, 28-19 (StL)
1965—Cardinals, 49-13 (Cle)
Browns, 27-24 (StL)
1966—Cardinals, 34-28 (Cle)
Browns, 38-10 (StL)
1967—Browns, 20-16 (Cle)
Browns, 20-16 (StL)
1968—Cardinals, 27-21 (Cle)
Cardinals, 27-16 (StL)
1969—Tie, 21-21 (Cle)
Browns, 27-21 (StL)
1974—Cardinals, 29-7 (StL)
1979—Browns, 38-20 (StL)
1985—Cardinals, 27-24 (Cle) OT
1988—Browns, 29-21 (P)
1994—Browns, 32-0 (Cle)
(RS Pts.—Browns 1,141, Cardinals 797)
**Franchise known as Phoenix prior to 1994, in St. Louis prior to 1988, and in Chicago prior to 1960*
***ARIZONA vs. DALLAS**
RS: Cowboys lead series, 50-24-1
PS: Cardinals lead series, 1-0
1960—Cardinals, 12-10 (StL)
1961—Cardinals, 31-17 (D)
Cardinals, 31-13 (StL)
1962—Cardinals, 28-24 (D)
Cardinals, 52-20 (StL)
1963—Cardinals, 34-7 (D)
Cowboys, 28-24 (StL)
1964—Cardinals, 16-6 (D)
Cowboys, 31-13 (StL)
1965—Cardinals, 20-13 (StL)
Cowboys, 27-13 (D)
1966—Tie, 10-10 (StL)
Cowboys, 31-17 (D)
1967—Cowboys, 46-21 (D)
1968—Cowboys, 27-10 (StL)
1969—Cowboys, 24-3 (D)
1970—Cardinals, 20-7 (StL)
Cardinals, 38-0 (D)
1971—Cowboys, 16-13 (StL)
Cowboys, 31-12 (D)
1972—Cowboys, 33-24 (D)
Cowboys, 27-6 (StL)
1973—Cowboys, 45-10 (D)
Cowboys, 30-3 (StL)
1974—Cardinals, 31-28 (StL)
Cowboys, 17-14 (D)
1975—Cowboys, 37-31 (D) OT
Cardinals, 31-17 (StL)
1976—Cardinals, 21-17 (StL)
Cowboys, 19-14 (D)
1977—Cowboys, 30-24 (StL)
Cardinals, 24-17 (D)
1978—Cowboys, 21-12 (D)
Cowboys, 24-21 (StL) OT
1979—Cowboys, 22-21 (StL)
Cowboys, 22-13 (D)
1980—Cowboys, 27-24 (StL)
Cowboys, 31-21 (D)
1981—Cowboys, 30-17 (D)
Cardinals, 20-17 (StL)
1982—Cowboys, 24-7 (StL)
1983—Cowboys, 34-17 (StL)
Cowboys, 35-17 (D)
1984—Cardinals, 31-20 (D)
Cowboys, 24-17 (StL)
1985—Cardinals, 21-10 (StL)
Cowboys, 35-17 (D)
1986—Cowboys, 31-7 (StL)
Cowboys, 37-6 (D)
1987—Cardinals, 24-13 (StL)
Cowboys, 21-16 (D)
1988—Cowboys, 17-14 (P)
Cardinals, 16-10 (D)
1989—Cardinals, 19-10 (D)
Cardinals, 24-20 (P)
1990—Cardinals, 20-3 (P)
Cowboys, 41-10 (D)
1991—Cowboys, 17-9 (P)
Cowboys, 27-7 (D)
1992—Cowboys, 31-20 (D)
Cowboys, 16-10 (P)
1993—Cowboys, 17-10 (P)
Cowboys, 20-15 (D)
1994—Cowboys, 38-3 (D)
Cowboys, 28-21 (A)
1995—Cowboys, 34-20 (D)
Cowboys, 37-13 (A)
1996—Cowboys, 17-3 (D)
Cowboys, 10-6 (A)
1997—Cardinals, 25-22 (A) OT
Cowboys, 24-6 (D)
1998—Cowboys, 38-10 (D)
Cowboys, 35-28 (A)
**Cardinals, 20-7 (D)
1999—Cowboys, 35-7 (D)
Cardinals, 13-9 (A)
(RS Pts.—Cowboys 1,739, Cardinals 1,309)
(PS Pts.—Cardinals 20, Cowboys 7)
**Franchise known as Phoenix prior to 1994 and in St. Louis prior to 1988*
***NFC First-Round Playoff*
***ARIZONA vs. DENVER**
RS: Broncos lead series, 4-0-1
1973—Tie, 17-17 (StL)
1977—Broncos, 7-0 (D)
1989—Broncos, 37-0 (P)
1991—Broncos, 24-19 (D)
1995—Broncos, 38-6 (D)
(RS Pts.—Broncos 123, Cardinals 42)
**Franchise known as Phoenix prior to 1994 and in St. Louis prior to 1988*
***ARIZONA vs. **DETROIT**
RS: Lions lead series, 27-19-5
1930—Tie, 0-0 (Port)
Cardinals, 23-0 (C)
1931—Cardinals, 20-19 (C)
1932—Tie, 7-7 (Port)
1933—Spartans, 7-6 (Port)
1934—Lions, 6-0 (D)
Lions, 17-13 (C)
1935—Tie, 10-10 (D)
Lions, 7-6 (C)
1936—Lions, 39-0 (D)
Lions, 14-7 (C)
1937—Lions, 16-7 (C)
Lions, 16-7 (D)
1938—Lions, 10-0 (D)
Lions, 7-3 (C)
1939—Lions, 21-3 (D)
Lions, 17-3 (C)
1940—Tie, 0-0 (Buffalo)
Lions, 43-14 (C)
1941—Tie, 14-14 (C)
Lions, 21-3 (D)
1942—Cardinals, 13-0 (C)
Cardinals, 7-0 (D)
1943—Lions, 35-17 (D)
Lions, 7-0 (Buffalo)
1945—Lions, 10-0 (Milwaukee)
Lions, 26-0 (D)
1946—Cardinals, 34-14 (C)
Cardinals, 36-14 (D)
1947—Cardinals, 45-21 (C)

Cardinals, 17-7 (D)
1948—Cardinals, 56-20 (C)
Cardinals, 28-14 (D)
1949—Lions, 24-7 (C)
Cardinals, 42-19 (D)
1959—Lions, 45-21 (D)
1961—Lions, 45-14 (StL)
1967—Cardinals, 38-28 (StL)
1969—Lions, 20-0 (D)
1970—Lions, 16-3 (D)
1973—Lions, 20-16 (StL)
1975—Cardinals, 24-13 (D)
1978—Cardinals, 21-14 (StL)
1980—Lions, 20-7 (D)
Cardinals, 24-23 (StL)
1989—Cardinals, 16-13 (D)
1993—Lions, 26-20 (D)
Lions, 21-14 (Phx)
1995—Cardinals, 20-17 (D)
1998—Cardinals, 17-15 (D)
1999—Cardinals, 23-19 (A)
(RS Pts.—Lions 857, Cardinals 736)
**Franchise known as Phoenix prior to 1994, in St. Louis prior to 1988, and in Chicago prior to 1960*
***Franchise in Portsmouth prior to 1934 and known as the Spartans*

***ARIZONA vs. GREEN BAY**
RS: Packers lead series, 40-21-4
PS: Packers lead series, 1-0
1921—Tie, 3-3 (C)
1922—Cardinals, 16-3 (C)
1924—Cardinals, 3-0 (C)
1925—Cardinals, 9-6 (C)
1926—Cardinals, 13-7 (GB)
Packers, 3-0 (C)
1927—Packers, 13-0 (GB)
Tie, 6-6 (C)
1928—Packers, 20-0 (GB)
1929—Packers, 9-2 (GB)
Packers, 7-6 (C)
Packers, 12-0 (C)
1930—Packers, 14-0 (GB)
Cardinals, 13-6 (C)
1931—Packers, 26-7 (GB)
Cardinals, 21-13 (C)
1932—Packers, 15-7 (GB)
Packers, 19-9 (C)
1933—Packers, 14-6 (C)
1934—Packers, 15-0 (GB)
Cardinals, 9-0 (Mil)
Cardinals, 6-0 (C)
1935—Cardinals, 7-6 (GB)
Cardinals, 3-0 (Mil)
Cardinals, 9-7 (C)
1936—Packers, 10-7 (GB)
Packers, 24-0 (Mil)
Tie, 0-0 (C)
1937—Cardinals, 14-7 (GB)
Packers, 34-13 (Mil)
1938—Packers, 28-7 (Mil)
Packers, 24-22 (Buffalo)
1939—Packers, 14-10 (GB)
Packers, 27-20 (Mil)
1940—Packers, 31-6 (Mil)
Packers, 28-7 (C)
1941—Packers, 14-13 (Mil)
Packers, 17-9 (GB)
1942—Packers, 17-13 (C)
Packers, 55-24 (GB)
1943—Packers, 28-7 (C)
Packers, 35-14 (Mil)
1945—Packers, 33-14 (GB)
1946—Packers, 19-7 (C)
Cardinals, 24-6 (GB)
1947—Cardinals, 14-10 (GB)
Cardinals, 21-20 (C)
1948—Cardinals, 17-7 (Mil)
Cardinals, 42-7 (C)
1949—Cardinals, 39-17 (Mil)
Cardinals, 41-21 (C)
1955—Packers, 31-14 (GB)
1956—Packers, 24-21 (C)
1962—Packers, 17-0 (Mil)
1963—Packers, 30-7 (StL)
1967—Packers, 31-23 (StL)
1969—Packers, 45-28 (GB)
1971—Tie, 16-16 (StL)
1973—Packers, 25-21 (GB)
1976—Cardinals, 29-0 (StL)
1982—**Packers, 41-16 (GB)
1984—Packers, 24-23 (GB)
1985—Cardinals, 43-28 (StL)
1988—Packers, 26-17 (P)
1990—Packers, 24-21 (P)
1999—Packers, 49-24 (GB)
(RS Pts.—Packers 1,127, Cardinals 847)
(PS Pts.—Packers 41, Cardinals 16)
**Franchise known as Phoenix prior to 1994, in St. Louis prior to 1988, and in Chicago prior to 1960*
***NFC First-Round Playoff*

***ARIZONA vs. **INDIANAPOLIS**
RS: Series tied, 6-6
1961—Colts, 16-0 (B)
1964—Colts, 47-27 (B)
1968—Colts, 27-0 (B)
1972—Cardinals, 10-3 (B)
1976—Cardinals, 24-17 (StL)
1978—Colts, 30-17 (StL)
1980—Cardinals, 17-10 (B)
1981—Cardinals, 35-24 (B)
1984—Cardinals, 34-33 (I)
1990—Cardinals, 20-17 (P)
1992—Colts, 16-13 (I)
1996—Colts, 20-13 (I)
(RS Pts.—Colts 260, Cardinals 210)
**Franchise known as Phoenix prior to 1994 and in St. Louis prior to 1988*
***Franchise in Baltimore prior to 1984*

***ARIZONA vs. KANSAS CITY**
RS: Chiefs lead series, 5-1-1
1970—Tie, 6-6 (KC)
1974—Chiefs, 17-13 (StL)
1980—Chiefs, 21-13 (StL)
1983—Chiefs, 38-14 (KC)
1986—Cardinals, 23-14 (StL)
1995—Chiefs, 24-3 (A)
1998—Chiefs, 34-24 (KC)
(RS Pts.—Chiefs 154, Cardinals 96)
**Franchise known as Phoenix prior to 1994 and in St. Louis prior to 1988*

***ARIZONA vs. MIAMI**
RS: Dolphins lead series, 8-0
1972—Dolphins, 31-10 (M)
1977—Dolphins, 55-14 (StL)
1978—Dolphins, 24-10 (M)
1981—Dolphins, 20-7 (StL)
1984—Dolphins, 36-28 (StL)
1990—Dolphins, 23-3 (M)
1996—Dolphins, 38-10 (A)
1999—Dolphins, 19-16 (M)
(RS Pts.—Dolphins 246, Cardinals 98)
**Franchise known as Phoenix prior to 1994 and in St. Louis prior to 1988*

***ARIZONA vs. MINNESOTA**
RS: Cardinals lead series, 8-7
PS: Vikings lead series, 2-0
1963—Cardinals, 56-14 (M)
1967—Cardinals, 34-24 (M)
1969—Vikings, 27-10 (StL)
1972—Cardinals, 19-17 (M)
1974—Vikings, 28-24 (StL)
**Vikings, 30-14 (M)
1977—Cardinals, 27-7 (M)
1979—Cardinals, 37-7 (StL)
1981—Cardinals, 30-17 (StL)
1983—Cardinals, 41-31 (StL)
1991—Vikings, 34-7 (M)
Vikings, 28-0 (P)
1994—Cardinals, 17-7 (A)
1995—Vikings, 30-24 (A) OT
1996—Vikings, 41-17 (M)
1997—Vikings, 20-19 (A)
1998—**Vikings, 41-21 (M)
(RS Pts.—Cardinals 362, Vikings 332)
(PS Pts.—Vikings 71, Cardinals 35)
**Franchise known as Phoenix prior to 1994 and in St. Louis prior to 1988*
***NFC Divisional Playoff*

***ARIZONA vs. **NEW ENGLAND**
RS: Cardinals lead series, 6-4
1970—Cardinals, 31-0 (StL)
1975—Cardinals, 24-17 (StL)
1978—Patriots, 16-6 (StL)
1981—Cardinals, 27-20 (NE)
1984—Cardinals, 33-10 (NE)
1990—Cardinals, 34-14 (P)
1991—Cardinals, 24-10 (P)
1993—Patriots, 23-21 (P)
1996—Patriots, 31-0 (NE)
1999—Patriots, 27-3 (A)
(RS Pts.—Cardinals 203, Patriots 168)
**Franchise known as Phoenix prior to 1994 and in St. Louis prior to 1988*
***Franchise in Boston prior to 1971*

***ARIZONA vs. NEW ORLEANS**
RS: Cardinals lead series, 12-10
1967—Cardinals, 31-20 (StL)
1968—Cardinals, 21-20 (NO)
Cardinals, 31-17 (StL)
1969—Saints, 51-42 (StL)
1970—Cardinals, 24-17 (StL)
1974—Saints, 14-0 (NO)
1977—Cardinals, 49-31 (StL)
1980—Cardinals, 40-7 (NO)
1981—Cardinals, 30-3 (StL)
1982—Cardinals, 21-7 (NO)
1983—Saints, 28-17 (NO)
1984—Saints, 34-24 (NO)
1985—Cardinals, 28-16 (StL)
1986—Saints, 16-7 (StL)
1987—Cardinals, 24-19 (StL)
1990—Saints, 28-7 (NO)
1991—Saints, 27-3 (P)
1992—Saints, 30-21 (P)
1993—Saints, 20-17 (P)
1996—Cardinals, 28-14 (NO)
1997—Saints, 27-10 (NO)
1998—Cardinals, 19-17 (A)
(RS Pts.—Cardinals 494, Saints 463)
**Franchise known as Phoenix prior to 1994 and in St. Louis prior to 1988*

***ARIZONA vs. N.Y. GIANTS**
RS: Giants lead series, 73-39-2
1926—Giants, 20-0 (NY)
1927—Giants, 28-7 (NY)
1929—Giants, 24-21 (NY)
1930—Giants, 25-12 (NY)
Giants, 13-7 (C)
1935—Cardinals, 14-13 (NY)
1936—Giants, 14-6 (NY)
1938—Giants, 6-0 (NY)
1939—Giants, 17-7 (NY)
1941—Cardinals, 10-7 (NY)
1942—Giants, 21-7 (NY)
1943—Giants, 24-13 (NY)
1946—Giants, 28-24 (NY)
1947—Giants, 35-31 (NY)
1948—Cardinals, 63-35 (NY)
1949—Giants, 41-38 (C)
1950—Cardinals, 17-3 (C)
Giants, 51-21 (NY)
1951—Giants, 28-17 (NY)
Giants, 10-0 (C)
1952—Cardinals, 24-23 (NY)
Giants, 28-6 (C)
1953—Giants, 21-7 (NY)
Giants, 23-20 (C)
1954—Giants, 41-10 (C)
Giants, 31-17 (NY)
1955—Cardinals, 28-17 (C)
Giants, 10-0 (NY)
1956—Cardinals, 35-27 (C)
Giants, 23-10 (NY)
1957—Giants, 27-14 (NY)
Giants, 28-21 (C)
1958—Giants, 37-7 (Buffalo)
Cardinals, 23-6 (NY)
1959—Giants, 9-3 (NY)
Giants, 30-20 (Minn)
1960—Giants, 35-14 (StL)
Cardinals, 20-13 (NY)
1961—Cardinals, 21-10 (NY)
Giants, 24-9 (StL)
1962—Giants, 31-14 (StL)
Giants, 31-28 (NY)
1963—Giants, 38-21 (StL)
Cardinals, 24-17 (NY)
1964—Giants, 34-17 (NY)
Tie, 10-10 (StL)
1965—Giants, 14-10 (NY)
Giants, 28-15 (StL)
1966—Cardinals, 24-19 (StL)
Cardinals, 20-17 (NY)
1967—Giants, 37-20 (StL)
Giants, 37-14 (NY)
1968—Cardinals, 28-21 (NY)
1969—Cardinals, 42-17 (StL)
Giants, 49-6 (NY)
1970—Giants, 35-17 (NY)
Giants, 34-17 (StL)
1971—Giants, 21-20 (StL)
Cardinals, 24-7 (NY)
1972—Giants, 27-21 (NY)
Giants, 13-7 (StL)
1973—Cardinals, 35-27 (StL)
Giants, 24-13 (New Haven)
1974—Cardinals, 23-21 (New Haven)
Cardinals, 26-14 (StL)
1975—Cardinals, 26-14 (StL)
Cardinals, 20-13 (NY)
1976—Cardinals, 27-21 (StL)
Cardinals, 17-14 (NY)
1977—Cardinals, 28-0 (StL)
Giants, 27-7 (NY)
1978—Cardinals, 20-10 (StL)
Giants, 17-0 (NY)
1979—Cardinals, 27-14 (NY)
Cardinals, 29-20 (StL)
1980—Giants, 41-35 (StL)
Cardinals, 23-7 (NY)
1981—Giants, 34-14 (NY)
Giants, 20-10 (StL)
1982—Cardinals, 24-21 (StL)
1983—Tie, 20-20 (StL) OT
Cardinals, 10-6 (NY)
1984—Giants, 16-10 (NY)
Cardinals, 31-21 (StL)
1985—Giants, 27-17 (NY)
Giants, 34-3 (StL)
1986—Giants, 13-6 (StL)
Giants, 27-7 (NY)
1987—Giants, 30-7 (NY)
Cardinals, 27-24 (StL)
1988—Cardinals, 24-17 (P)
Giants, 44-7 (NY)
1989—Giants, 35-7 (NY)
Giants, 20-13 (P)
1990—Giants, 20-19 (NY)
Giants, 24-21 (P)
1991—Giants, 20-9 (NY)
Giants, 21-14 (P)
1992—Giants, 31-21 (NY)
Cardinals, 19-0 (P)
1993—Giants, 19-17 (NY)
Cardinals, 17-6 (P)
1994—Giants, 20-17 (A)
Cardinals, 10-9 (NY)
1995—Giants, 27-21 (NY) OT
Giants, 10-6 (A)
1996—Giants, 16-8 (NY)
Cardinals, 31-23 (A)
1997—Giants, 27-13 (A)
Giants, 19-10 (NY)
1998—Giants, 34-7 (NY)
Giants, 23-19 (A)
1999—Cardinals, 14-3 (A)
Cardinals, 34-24 (NY)
(RS Pts.—Giants 2,512, Cardinals 1,943)
**Franchise known as Phoenix prior to 1994, in St. Louis prior to 1988,*

ALL-TIME TEAM VS. TEAM RESULTS

and in Chicago prior to 1960
***ARIZONA vs. N.Y. JETS**
RS: Jets lead series, 3-2
1971—Cardinals, 17-10 (StL)
1975—Cardinals, 37-6 (NY)
1978—Jets, 23-10 (NY)
1996—Jets, 31-21 (A)
1999—Jets, 12-7 (NY)
(RS Pts.—Cardinals 92, Jets 82)
**Franchise known as Phoenix prior to 1994 and in St. Louis prior to 1988*
***ARIZONA vs. **OAKLAND**
RS: Raiders lead series, 3-1
1973—Raiders, 17-10 (StL)
1983—Cardinals, 34-24 (LA)
1989—Raiders, 16-14 (LA)
1998—Raiders, 23-20 (A)
(RS Pts.—Raiders 80, Cardinals 78)
**Franchise known as Phoenix prior to 1994 and in St. Louis prior to 1988*
***Franchise in Los Angeles from 1982-1994*
***ARIZONA vs. PHILADELPHIA**
RS: Cardinals lead series, 51-48-5
PS: Series tied, 1-1
1935—Cardinals, 12-3 (C)
1936—Cardinals, 13-0 (C)
1937—Tie, 6-6 (P)
1938—Eagles, 7-0 (Erie, Pa.)
1941—Eagles, 21-14 (P)
1945—Eagles, 21-6 (P)
1947—Cardinals, 45-21 (P)
**Cardinals, 28-21 (C)
1948—Cardinals, 21-14 (C)
**Eagles, 7-0 (P)
1949—Eagles, 28-3 (P)
1950—Eagles, 45-7 (C)
Cardinals, 14-10 (P)
1951—Eagles, 17-14 (C)
1952—Eagles, 10-7 (P)
Cardinals, 28-22 (C)
1953—Eagles, 56-17 (C)
Eagles, 38-0 (P)
1954—Eagles, 35-16 (C)
Eagles, 30-14 (P)
1955—Tie, 24-24 (C)
Eagles, 27-3 (P)
1956—Cardinals, 20-6 (P)
Cardinals, 28-17 (C)
1957—Eagles, 38-21 (C)
Cardinals, 31-27 (P)
1958—Tie, 21-21 (C)
Eagles, 49-21 (P)
1959—Eagles, 28-24 (Minn)
Eagles, 27-17 (P)
1960—Eagles, 31-27 (P)
Eagles, 20-6 (StL)
1961—Cardinals, 30-27 (P)
Eagles, 20-7 (StL)
1962—Cardinals, 27-21 (P)
Cardinals, 45-35 (StL)
1963—Cardinals, 28-24 (P)
Cardinals, 38-14 (StL)
1964—Cardinals, 38-13 (P)
Cardinals, 36-34 (StL)
1965—Eagles, 34-27 (P)
Eagles, 28-24 (StL)
1966—Cardinals, 16-13 (StL)
Cardinals, 41-10 (P)
1967—Cardinals, 48-14 (StL)
1968—Cardinals, 45-17 (P)
1969—Eagles, 34-30 (StL)
1970—Cardinals, 35-20 (P)
Cardinals, 23-14 (StL)
1971—Eagles, 37-20 (StL)
Eagles, 19-7 (P)
1972—Tie, 6-6 (P)
Cardinals, 24-23 (StL)
1973—Cardinals, 34-23 (P)
Eagles, 27-24 (StL)
1974—Cardinals, 7-3 (StL)
Cardinals, 13-3 (P)
1975—Cardinals, 31-20 (StL)
Cardinals, 24-23 (P)
1976—Cardinals, 33-14 (StL)
Cardinals, 17-14 (P)
1977—Cardinals, 21-17 (P)
Cardinals, 21-16 (StL)
1978—Cardinals, 16-10 (P)
Eagles, 14-10 (StL)
1979—Eagles, 24-20 (StL)
Eagles, 16-13 (P)
1980—Cardinals, 24-14 (StL)
Eagles, 17-3 (P)
1981—Eagles, 52-10 (StL)
Eagles, 38-0 (P)
1982—Cardinals, 23-20 (P)
1983—Cardinals, 14-11 (P)
Cardinals, 31-7 (StL)
1984—Cardinals, 34-14 (P)
Cardinals, 17-16 (StL)
1985—Eagles, 30-7 (P)
Eagles, 24-14 (StL)
1986—Cardinals, 13-10 (StL)
Tie, 10-10 (P) OT
1987—Eagles, 28-23 (StL)
Cardinals, 31-19 (P)
1988—Eagles, 31-21 (P)
Eagles, 23-17 (Phx)
1989—Eagles, 17-5 (Phx)
Eagles, 31-14 (P)
1990—Cardinals, 23-21 (P)
Eagles, 23-21 (Phx)
1991—Cardinals, 26-10 (P)
Eagles, 34-14 (Phx)
1992—Eagles, 31-14 (Phx)
Eagles, 7-3 (P)
1993—Eagles, 23-17 (P)
Cardinals, 16-3 (Phx)
1994—Eagles, 17-7 (P)
Cardinals, 12-6 (A)
1995—Eagles, 31-19 (A)
Eagles, 21-20 (P)
1996—Cardinals, 36-30 (A)
Eagles, 29-19 (P)
1997—Eagles, 13-10 (P) OT
Cardinals, 31-21 (A)
1998—Cardinals, 17-3 (A)
Cardinals, 20-17 (P) OT
1999—Cardinals, 25-24 (P)
Cardinals, 21-17 (A)
(RS Pts.—Eagles 2,173, Cardinals 2,041)
(PS Pts.—Eagles 28, Cardinals 28)
**Franchise known as Phoenix prior to 1994, in St. Louis prior to 1988, and in Chicago prior to 1960*
***NFL Championship*
***ARIZONA vs. **PITTSBURGH**
RS: Steelers lead series, 30-22-3
1933—Pirates, 14-13 (C)
1935—Pirates, 17-13 (P)
1936—Cardinals, 14-6 (C)
1937—Cardinals, 13-7 (P)
1939—Cardinals, 10-0 (P)
1940—Tie, 7-7 (P)
1942—Steelers, 19-3 (P)
1945—Steelers, 23-0 (P)
1946—Steelers, 14-7 (P)
1948—Cardinals, 24-7 (P)
1950—Steelers, 28-17 (C)
Steelers, 28-7 (P)
1951—Steelers, 28-14 (C)
1952—Steelers, 34-28 (C)
Steelers, 17-14 (P)
1953—Steelers, 31-28 (P)
Steelers, 21-17 (C)
1954—Cardinals, 17-14 (C)
Steelers, 20-17 (P)
1955—Steelers, 14-7 (P)
Cardinals, 27-13 (C)
1956—Steelers, 14-7 (P)
Cardinals, 38-27 (C)
1957—Steelers, 29-20 (P)
Steelers, 27-2 (C)
1958—Steelers, 27-20 (C)
Steelers, 38-21 (P)
1959—Cardinals, 45-24 (C)
Steelers, 35-20 (P)
1960—Steelers, 27-14 (P)
Cardinals, 38-7 (StL)
1961—Steelers, 30-27 (P)
Cardinals, 20-0 (StL)
1962—Steelers, 26-17 (StL)
Steelers, 19-7 (P)
1963—Steelers, 23-10 (P)
Cardinals, 24-23 (StL)
1964—Cardinals, 34-30 (StL)
Cardinals, 21-20 (P)
1965—Cardinals, 20-7 (P)
Cardinals, 21-17 (StL)
1966—Steelers, 30-9 (P)
Cardinals, 6-3 (StL)
1967—Cardinals, 28-14 (P)
Tie, 14-14 (StL)
1968—Tie, 28-28 (StL)
Cardinals, 20-10 (P)
1969—Cardinals, 27-14 (P)
Cardinals, 47-10 (StL)
1972—Steelers, 25-19 (StL)
1979—Steelers, 24-21 (StL)
1985—Steelers, 23-10 (P)
1988—Cardinals, 31-14 (Phx)
1994—Cardinals, 20-17 (A) OT
1997—Steelers, 26-20 (A) OT
(RS Pts.—Steelers 1,064, Cardinals 1,023)
**Franchise known as Phoenix prior to 1994, in St. Louis prior to 1988, and in Chicago prior to 1960*
***Steelers known as Pirates prior to 1941*
***ARIZONA vs. **ST. LOUIS**
RS: Rams lead series, 23-21-2
PS: Rams lead series, 1-0
1937—Cardinals, 6-0 (Clev)
Cardinals, 13-7 (Chi)
1938—Cardinals, 7-6 (Clev)
Cardinals, 31-17 (Chi)
1939—Rams, 24-0 (Chi)
Rams, 14-0 (Clev)
1940—Rams, 26-14 (Clev)
Cardinals, 17-7 (Chi)
1941—Rams, 10-6 (Clev)
Cardinals, 7-0 (Chi)
1942—Cardinals, 7-0 (Buffalo)
Rams, 7-3 (Clev)
1945—Rams, 21-0 (Clev)
Rams, 35-21 (Chi)
1946—Cardinals, 34-10 (Chi)
Rams, 17-14 (LA)
1947—Rams, 27-7 (LA)
Cardinals, 17-10 (Chi)
1948—Cardinals, 27-22 (LA)
Cardinals, 27-24 (Chi)
1949—Tie, 28-28 (Chi)
Cardinals, 31-27 (LA)
1951—Rams, 45-21 (LA)
1953—Tie, 24-24 (Chi)
1954—Rams, 28-17 (LA)
1958—Rams, 20-14 (Chi)
1960—Cardinals, 43-21 (LA)
1965—Rams, 27-3 (StL)
1968—Rams, 24-13 (StL)
1970—Rams, 34-13 (LA)
1972—Cardinals, 24-14 (StL)
1975—***Rams, 35-23 (LA)
1976—Cardinals, 30-28 (LA)
1979—Rams, 21-0 (LA)
1980—Rams, 21-13 (StL)
1984—Rams, 16-13 (StL)
1985—Rams, 46-14 (LA)
1986—Rams, 16-10 (StL)
1987—Rams, 27-24 (StL)
1988—Cardinals, 41-27 (LA)
1989—Rams, 37-14 (LA)
1991—Cardinals, 24-14 (LA)
1992—Cardinals, 20-14 (LA)
1993—Cardinals, 38-10 (P)
1994—Rams, 14-12 (LA)
1996—Cardinals, 31-28 (A) OT
1998—Cardinals, 20-17 (StL)
(RS Pts.—Rams 912, Cardinals 793)
(PS Pts.—Rams 35, Cardinals 23)
**Franchise known as Phoenix prior to 1994, in St. Louis prior to 1988, and in Chicago prior to 1960*
***Franchise in Los Angeles prior to 1995 and in Cleveland prior to 1946*
****NFC Divisional Playoff*
***ARIZONA vs. SAN DIEGO**
RS: Chargers lead series, 6-2
1971—Chargers, 20-17 (SD)
1976—Chargers, 43-24 (SD)
1983—Cardinals, 44-14 (StL)
1987—Chargers, 28-24 (SD)
1989—Chargers, 24-13 (P)
1992—Chargers, 27-21 (P)
1995—Chargers, 28-25 (SD)
1998—Cardinals, 16-13 (A)
(RS Pts.—Chargers 197, Cardinals 184)
**Franchise known as Phoenix prior to 1994, in St. Louis prior to 1988,*
***ARIZONA vs. SAN FRANCISCO**
RS: 49ers lead series, 11-9
1951—Cardinals, 27-21 (SF)
1957—Cardinals, 20-10 (SF)
1962—49ers, 24-17 (StL)
1964—Cardinals, 23-13 (SF)
1968—49ers, 35-17 (SF)
1971—49ers, 26-14 (StL)
1974—Cardinals, 34-9 (SF)
1976—Cardinals, 23-20 (StL) OT
1978—Cardinals, 16-10 (SF)
1979—Cardinals, 13-10 (StL)
1980—49ers, 24-21 (SF) OT
1982—49ers, 31-20 (StL)
1983—49ers, 42-27 (StL)
1986—49ers, 43-17 (SF)
1987—49ers, 34-28 (SF)
1988—Cardinals, 24-23 (P)
1991—49ers, 14-10 (SF)
1992—Cardinals, 24-14 (P)
1993—49ers, 28-14 (SF)
1999—49ers, 24-10 (A)
(RS Pts.—49ers 455, Cardinals 399)
**Franchise known as Phoenix prior to 1994, in St. Louis prior to 1988, and in Chicago prior to 1960*
***ARIZONA vs. SEATTLE**
RS: Cardinals lead series, 5-1
1976—Cardinals, 30-24 (S)
1983—Cardinals, 33-28 (StL)
1989—Cardinals, 34-24 (S)
1993—Cardinals, 30-27 (S) OT
1995—Cardinals, 20-14 (A) OT
1998—Seahawks, 33-14 (S)
(RS Pts.—Cardinals 161, Seahawks 150)
**Franchise known as Phoenix prior to 1994 and in St. Louis prior to 1988*
***ARIZONA vs. TAMPA BAY**
RS: Series tied, 7-7
1977—Buccaneers, 17-7 (TB)
1981—Buccaneers, 20-10 (TB)
1983—Cardinals, 34-27 (TB)
1985—Buccaneers, 16-0 (TB)
1986—Cardinals, 30-19 (TB)
Cardinals, 21-17 (StL)
1987—Cardinals, 31-28 (StL)
Cardinals, 31-14 (TB)
1988—Cardinals, 30-24 (TB)
1989—Buccaneers, 14-13 (P)
1992—Buccaneers, 23-7 (TB)
Buccaneers, 7-3 (P)
1996—Cardinals, 13-9 (A)
1997—Buccaneers, 19-18 (TB)
(RS Pts.—Buccaneers 254, Cardinals 248)
**Franchise known as Phoenix prior to 1994 and in St. Louis prior to 1988*
***ARIZONA vs. **TENNESSEE**
RS: Cardinals lead series, 4-3
1970—Cardinals, 44-0 (StL)
1974—Cardinals, 31-27 (H)
1979—Cardinals, 24-17 (H)
1985—Oilers, 20-10 (StL)

1988—Oilers, 38-20 (H)
1994—Cardinals, 30-12 (H)
1997—Oilers, 41-14 (T)
(RS Pts.—Cardinals 173, Titans 155)
Franchise known as Phoenix prior to 1994 and in St. Louis prior to 1988
**Franchise in Houston prior to 1997; known as Oilers prior to 1999*

***ARIZONA vs. **WASHINGTON**
RS: Redskins lead series, 66-43-2
1932—Cardinals, 9-0 (B)
Braves, 8-6 (C)
1933—Redskins, 10-0 (C)
Tie, 0-0 (B)
1934—Redskins, 9-0 (B)
1935—Cardinals, 6-0 (B)
1936—Redskins, 13-10 (B)
1937—Cardinals, 21-14 (W)
1939—Redskins, 28-7 (W)
1940—Redskins, 28-21 (W)
1942—Redskins, 28-0 (W)
1943—Redskins, 13-7 (W)
1945—Redskins, 24-21 (W)
1947—Redskins, 45-21 (W)
1949—Cardinals, 38-7 (C)
1950—Cardinals, 38-28 (W)
1951—Redskins, 7-3 (C)
Redskins, 20-17 (W)
1952—Redskins, 23-7 (C)
Cardinals, 17-6 (W)
1953—Redskins, 24-13 (C)
Redskins, 28-17 (W)
1954—Cardinals, 38-16 (C)
Redskins, 37-20 (W)
1955—Cardinals, 24-10 (W)
Redskins, 31-0 (C)
1956—Cardinals, 31-3 (W)
Redskins, 17-14 (C)
1957—Redskins, 37-14 (C)
Cardinals, 44-14 (W)
1958—Cardinals, 37-10 (C)
Redskins, 45-31 (W)
1959—Cardinals, 49-21 (C)
Redskins, 23-14 (W)
1960—Cardinals, 44-7 (StL)
Cardinals, 26-14 (W)
1961—Cardinals, 24-0 (W)
Cardinals, 38-24 (StL)
1962—Redskins, 24-14 (W)
Tie, 17-17 (StL)
1963—Cardinals, 21-7 (W)
Cardinals, 24-20 (StL)
1964—Cardinals, 23-17 (W)
Cardinals, 38-24 (StL)
1965—Cardinals, 37-16 (W)
Redskins, 24-20 (StL)
1966—Cardinals, 23-7 (StL)
Redskins, 26-20 (W)
1967—Cardinals, 27-21 (W)
1968—Cardinals, 41-14 (StL)
1969—Redskins, 33-17 (W)
1970—Cardinals, 27-17 (StL)
Redskins, 28-27 (W)
1971—Redskins, 24-17 (StL)
Redskins, 20-0 (W)
1972—Redskins, 24-10 (W)
Redskins, 33-3 (StL)
1973—Cardinals, 34-27 (StL)
Redskins, 31-13 (W)
1974—Cardinals, 17-10 (W)
Cardinals, 23-20 (StL)
1975—Redskins, 27-17 (W)
Cardinals, 20-17 (StL) OT
1976—Redskins, 20-10 (W)
Redskins, 16-10 (StL)
1977—Redskins, 24-14 (W)
Redskins, 26-20 (StL)
1978—Redskins, 28-10 (StL)
Cardinals, 27-17 (W)
1979—Redskins, 17-7 (StL)
Redskins, 30-28 (W)
1980—Redskins, 23-0 (W)
Redskins, 31-7 (StL)
1981—Cardinals, 40-30 (StL)
Redskins, 42-21 (W)
1982—Redskins, 12-7 (StL)
Redskins, 28-0 (W)
1983—Redskins, 38-14 (StL)
Redskins, 45-7 (W)
1984—Cardinals, 26-24 (StL)
Redskins, 29-27 (W)
1985—Redskins, 27-10 (W)
Redskins, 27-16 (StL)
1986—Redskins, 28-21 (W)
Redskins, 20-17 (StL)
1987—Redskins, 28-21 (W)
Redskins, 34-17 (StL)
1988—Cardinals, 30-21 (P)
Redskins, 33-17 (W)
1989—Redskins, 30-28 (W)
Redskins, 29-10 (P)
1990—Redskins, 31-0 (W)
Redskins, 38-10 (P)
1991—Redskins, 34-0 (W)
Redskins, 20-14 (P)
1992—Cardinals, 27-24 (P)
Redskins, 41-3 (W)
1993—Cardinals, 17-10 (W)
Cardinals, 36-6 (P)
1994—Cardinals, 19-16 (W) OT
Cardinals, 17-15 (A)
1995—Redskins, 27-7 (W)
Cardinals, 24-20 (A)
1996—Cardinals, 37-34 (W) OT
Cardinals, 27-26 (A)
1997—Redskins, 19-13 (W) OT
Redskins, 38-28 (A)
1998—Cardinals, 29-27 (A)
Cardinals, 45-42 (W)
1999—Redskins, 24-10 (A)
Redskins, 28-3 (W)
(RS Pts.—Redskins 2,477, Cardinals 2,085)
Franchise known as Phoenix prior to 1994, in St. Louis prior to 1988, and in Chicago prior to 1960
**Franchise in Boston prior to 1937 and known as Braves prior to 1933*

ATLANTA vs. ARIZONA
RS: Cardinals lead series, 13-7;
See Arizona vs. Atlanta

ATLANTA vs. BALTIMORE
RS: Ravens lead series, 1-0
1999—Ravens, 19-13 (A) OT
(RS Pts.—Ravens 19, Falcons 13)

ATLANTA vs. BUFFALO
RS: Bills lead series, 4-3
1973—Bills, 17-6 (A)
1977—Bills, 3-0 (B)
1980—Falcons, 30-14 (B)
1983—Falcons, 31-14 (A)
1989—Falcons, 30-28 (A)
1992—Bills, 41-14 (B)
1995—Bills, 23-17 (B)
(RS Pts.—Bills 140, Falcons 128)

ATLANTA vs. CAROLINA
RS: Series tied, 5-5
1995—Falcons, 23-20 (A) OT
Panthers, 21-17 (C)
1996—Panthers, 29-6 (C)
Falcons, 20-17 (A)
1997—Panthers, 9-6 (A)
Panthers, 21-12 (C)
1998—Falcons, 19-14 (C)
Falcons, 51-23 (A)
1999—Falcons, 27-20 (A)
Panthers, 34-28 (C)
(RS Pts.—Falcons 209, Panthers 208)

ATLANTA vs. CHICAGO
RS: Falcons lead series, 10-9
1966—Bears, 23-6 (C)
1967—Bears, 23-14 (A)
1968—Falcons, 16-13 (C)
1969—Falcons, 48-31 (A)
1970—Bears, 23-14 (A)
1972—Falcons, 37-21 (C)
1973—Falcons, 46-6 (A)
1974—Falcons, 13-10 (A)
1976—Falcons, 10-0 (C)
1977—Falcons, 16-10 (C)
1978—Bears, 13-7 (C)
1980—Falcons, 28-17 (A)
1983—Falcons, 20-17 (C)
1985—Bears, 36-0 (C)
1986—Bears, 13-10 (A)
1990—Bears, 30-24 (C)
1992—Bears, 41-31 (C)
1993—Bears, 6-0 (C)
1998—Falcons, 20-13 (A)
(RS Pts.—Falcons 360, Bears 346)

ATLANTA vs. CINCINNATI
RS: Bengals lead series, 7-2
1971—Falcons, 9-6 (C)
1975—Bengals, 21-14 (A)
1978—Bengals, 37-7 (C)
1981—Bengals, 30-28 (A)
1984—Bengals, 35-14 (C)
1987—Bengals, 16-10 (A)
1990—Falcons, 38-17 (A)
1993—Bengals, 21-17 (C)
1996—Bengals, 41-31 (C)
(RS Pts.—Bengals 224, Falcons 168)

ATLANTA vs. CLEVELAND
RS: Browns lead series, 8-2
1966—Browns, 49-17 (A)
1968—Browns, 30-7 (C)
1971—Falcons, 31-14 (C)
1976—Browns, 20-17 (A)
1978—Browns, 24-16 (A)
1981—Browns, 28-17 (C)
1984—Browns, 23-7 (A)
1987—Browns, 38-3 (C)
1990—Browns, 13-10 (C)
1993—Falcons, 17-14 (A)
(RS Pts.—Browns 253, Falcons 142)

ATLANTA vs. DALLAS
RS: Cowboys lead series, 12-6
PS: Cowboys lead series, 2-0
1966—Cowboys, 47-14 (A)
1967—Cowboys, 37-7 (D)
1969—Cowboys, 24-17 (A)
1970—Cowboys, 13-0 (D)
1974—Cowboys, 24-0 (A)
1976—Falcons, 17-10 (A)
1978—*Cowboys, 27-20 (D)
1980—*Cowboys, 30-27 (A)
1985—Cowboys, 24-10 (D)
1986—Falcons, 37-35 (D)
1987—Falcons, 21-10 (D)
1988—Cowboys, 26-20 (D)
1989—Falcons 27-21 (A)
1990—Falcons, 26-7 (A)
1991—Cowboys, 31-27 (D)
1992—Cowboys, 41-17 (A)
1993—Falcons, 27-14 (A)
1995—Cowboys, 28-13 (A)
1996—Cowboys, 32-28 (D)
1999—Cowboys, 24-7 (D)
(RS Pts.—Cowboys 448, Falcons 315)
(PS Pts.—Cowboys 57, Falcons 47)
NFC Divisional Playoff

ATLANTA vs. DENVER
RS: Broncos lead series, 6-3
PS: Broncos lead series, 1-0
1970—Broncos, 24-10 (D)
1972—Falcons, 23-20 (A)
1975—Falcons, 35-21 (A)
1979—Broncos, 20-17 (A) OT
1982—Falcons, 34-27 (D)
1985—Broncos, 44-28 (A)
1988—Broncos, 30-14 (D)
1994—Broncos, 32-28 (D)
1997—Broncos, 29-21 (A)
1998—*Broncos, 34-19 (Miami)
(RS Pts.—Broncos 247, Falcons 210)
(PS Pts.—Broncos 34, Falcons 19)
*Super Bowl XXXIII

ATLANTA vs. DETROIT
RS: Lions lead series, 20-7
1966—Lions, 28-10 (D)
1967—Lions, 24-3 (D)
1968—Lions, 24-7 (A)
1969—Lions, 27-21 (D)
1971—Lions, 41-38 (D)
1972—Lions, 26-23 (A)
1973—Lions, 31-6 (D)
1975—Lions, 17-14 (A)
1976—Lions, 24-10 (D)
1977—Falcons, 17-6 (A)
1978—Falcons, 14-0 (A)
1979—Lions, 24-23 (D)
1980—Falcons, 43-28 (A)
1983—Falcons, 30-14 (D)
1984—Lions, 27-24 (A) OT
1985—Lions, 28-27 (A)
1986—Falcons, 20-6 (D)
1987—Lions, 30-13 (A)
1988—Lions, 31-17 (D)
1989—Lions, 31-24 (A)
1990—Lions, 21-14 (D)
1993—Lions, 30-13 (D)
1994—Lions, 31-28 (D) OT
1995—Falcons, 34-22 (A)
1996—Lions, 28-24 (D)
1997—Lions, 28-17 (D)
1998—Falcons, 24-17 (D)
(RS Pts.—Lions 644, Falcons 538)

ATLANTA vs. GREEN BAY
RS: Packers lead series, 10-9
PS: Packers lead series, 1-0
1966—Packers, 56-3 (Mil)
1967—Packers, 23-0 (Mil)
1968—Packers, 38-7 (A)
1969—Packers, 28-10 (GB)
1970—Packers, 27-24 (GB)
1971—Falcons, 28-21 (A)
1972—Falcons, 10-9 (Mil)
1974—Falcons, 10-3 (A)
1975—Packers, 22-13 (GB)
1976—Packers, 24-20 (A)
1979—Falcons, 25-7 (A)
1981—Falcons, 31-17 (GB)
1982—Packers, 38-7 (A)
1983—Falcons, 47-41 (A) OT
1988—Falcons, 20-0 (A)
1989—Packers, 23-21 (Mil)
1991—Falcons, 35-31 (A)
1992—Falcons, 24-10 (A)
1994—Packers, 21-17 (Mil)
1995—*Packers, 37-20 (GB)
(RS Pts.—Packers 439, Falcons 352)
(PS Pts.—Packers 37, Falcons 20)
NFC First-Round Playoff

ATLANTA vs. *INDIANAPOLIS
RS: Colts lead series, 10-1
1966—Colts, 19-7 (A)
1967—Colts, 38-31 (B)
Colts, 49-7 (A)
1968—Colts, 28-20 (A)
Colts, 44-0 (B)
1969—Colts, 21-14 (A)
Colts, 13-6 (B)
1974—Colts, 17-7 (A)
1986—Colts, 28-23 (A)
1989—Colts, 13-9 (I)
1998—Falcons, 28-21 (A)
(RS Pts.—Colts 291, Falcons 152)
Franchise in Baltimore prior to 1984

ATLANTA vs. JACKSONVILLE
RS: Jaguars lead series, 2-0
1996—Jaguars, 19-17 (J)
1999—Jaguars, 30-7 (A)
(RS Pts.—Jaguars 49, Falcons 24)

ATLANTA vs. KANSAS CITY
RS: Chiefs lead series, 4-0
1972—Chiefs, 17-14 (A)
1985—Chiefs, 38-10 (KC)
1991—Chiefs, 14-3 (KC)
1994—Chiefs, 30-10 (A)
(RS Pts.—Chiefs 99, Falcons 37)

ATLANTA vs. MIAMI
RS: Dolphins lead series, 6-2

ALL-TIME TEAM VS. TEAM RESULTS

1970—Dolphins, 20-7 (A)
1974—Dolphins, 42-7 (M)
1980—Dolphins, 20-17 (A)
1983—Dolphins, 31-24 (M)
1986—Falcons, 20-14 (M)
1992—Dolphins, 21-17 (M)
1995—Dolphins, 21-20 (M)
1998—Falcons, 38-16 (A)
(RS Pts.—Dolphins 185, Falcons 150)

ATLANTA vs. MINNESOTA
RS: Vikings lead series, 13-6
PS: Series tied, 1-1
1966—Falcons, 20-13 (M)
1967—Falcons, 21-20 (A)
1968—Vikings, 47-7 (M)
1969—Falcons, 10-3 (A)
1970—Vikings, 37-7 (A)
1971—Vikings, 24-7 (M)
1973—Falcons, 20-14 (A)
1974—Vikings, 23-10 (M)
1975—Vikings, 38-0 (M)
1977—Vikings, 14-7 (A)
1980—Vikings, 24-23 (M)
1981—Falcons, 31-30 (A)
1982—*Vikings, 30-24 (M)
1984—Vikings, 27-20 (M)
1985—Falcons, 14-13 (A)
1987—Vikings, 24-13 (M)
1989—Vikings, 43-17 (M)
1991—Vikings, 20-19 (A)
1996—Vikings, 23-17 (A)
1998—**Falcons, 30-27 (M) OT
1999—Vikings, 17-14 (A)
(RS Pts.—Vikings 454, Falcons 277)
(PS Pts.—Vikings 57, Falcons 54)
NFC First-Round Playoff
***NFC Championship*

ATLANTA vs. NEW ENGLAND
RS: Falcons lead series, 6-3
1972—Patriots, 21-20 (NE)
1977—Patriots, 16-10 (A)
1980—Falcons, 37-21 (NE)
1983—Falcons, 24-13 (A)
1986—Patriots, 25-17 (NE)
1989—Falcons, 16-15 (A)
1992—Falcons, 34-0 (A)
1995—Falcons, 30-17 (A)
1998—Falcons, 41-10 (NE)
(RS Pts.—Falcons 229, Patriots 138)

ATLANTA vs. NEW ORLEANS
RS: Falcons lead series, 37-24
PS: Falcons lead series, 1-0
1967—Saints, 27-24 (NO)
1969—Falcons, 45-17 (A)
1970—Falcons, 14-3 (NO)
Falcons, 32-14 (A)
1971—Falcons, 28-6 (A)
Falcons, 24-20 (NO)
1972—Falcons, 21-14 (NO)
Falcons, 36-20 (A)
1973—Falcons, 62-7 (NO)
Falcons, 14-10 (A)
1974—Saints, 14-13 (NO)
Saints, 13-3 (A)
1975—Falcons, 14-7 (A)
Saints, 23-7 (NO)
1976—Saints, 30-0 (NO)
Falcons, 23-20 (A)
1977—Saints, 21-20 (NO)
Falcons, 35-7 (A)
1978—Falcons, 20-17 (NO)
Falcons, 20-17 (A)
1979—Falcons, 40-34 (NO) OT
Saints, 37-6 (A)
1980—Falcons, 41-14 (NO)
Falcons, 31-13 (A)
1981—Falcons, 27-0 (A)
Falcons, 41-10 (NO)
1982—Falcons, 35-0 (A)
Saints, 35-6 (NO)
1983—Saints, 19-17 (A)
Saints, 27-10 (NO)
1984—Falcons, 36-28 (NO)
Saints, 17-13 (A)
1985—Falcons, 31-24 (A)
Falcons, 16-10 (NO)
1986—Falcons, 31-10 (NO)
Saints, 14-9 (A)
1987—Saints, 38-0 (A)
1988—Saints, 29-21 (A)
Saints, 10-9 (NO)
1989—Saints, 20-13 (NO)
Saints, 26-17 (A)
1990—Falcons, 28-27 (A)
Saints, 10-7 (NO)
1991—Saints, 27-6 (A)
Falcons, 23-20 (NO) OT
*Falcons, 27-20 (NO)
1992—Saints, 10-7 (A)
Saints, 22-14 (NO)
1993—Saints, 34-31 (A)
Falcons, 26-15 (NO)
1994—Saints, 33-32 (NO)
Saints, 29-20 (A)
1995—Falcons, 27-24 (NO) OT
Falcons, 19-14 (A)
1996—Falcons, 17-15 (A)
Falcons, 31-15 (NO)
1997—Falcons, 23-17 (NO)
Falcons, 20-3 (A)
1998—Falcons, 31-23 (A)
Falcons, 27-17 (NO)
1999—Falcons, 20-17 (NO)
Falcons, 35-12 (A)
(RS Pts.—Falcons 1,349, Saints 1,106)
(PS Pts.—Falcons 27, Saints 20)
NFC First-Round Playoff

ATLANTA vs. N.Y. GIANTS
RS: Falcons lead series, 7-6
1966—Falcons, 27-16 (NY)
1968—Falcons, 24-21 (A)
1971—Giants, 21-17 (A)
1974—Falcons, 14-7 (New Haven)
1977—Falcons, 17-3 (A)
1978—Falcons, 23-20 (A)
1979—Giants, 24-3 (NY)
1981—Giants, 27-24 (A) OT
1982—Falcons, 16-14 (NY)
1983—Giants, 16-13 (A) OT
1984—Giants, 19-7 (A)
1988—Giants, 23-16 (A)
1998—Falcons, 34-20 (NY)
(RS Pts.—Falcons 235, Giants 231)

ATLANTA vs. N.Y. JETS
RS: Series tied, 4-4
1973—Falcons, 28-20 (NY)
1980—Jets, 14-7 (A)
1983—Falcons, 27-21 (NY)
1986—Jets, 28-14 (A)
1989—Jets, 27-7 (NY)
1992—Falcons, 20-17 (A)
1995—Falcons, 13-3 (A)
1998—Jets, 28-3 (NY)
(RS Pts.—Jets 158, Falcons 119)

ATLANTA vs. *OAKLAND
RS: Raiders lead series, 6-3
1971—Falcons, 24-13 (A)
1975—Raiders, 37-34 (O) OT
1979—Raiders, 50-19 (O)
1982—Raiders, 38-14 (A)
1985—Raiders, 34-24 (A)
1988—Falcons, 12-6 (LA)
1991—Falcons, 21-17 (A)
1994—Raiders, 30-17 (LA)
1997—Raiders, 36-31 (A)
(RS Pts.—Raiders 261, Falcons 196)
Franchise in Los Angeles from 1982-1994

ATLANTA vs. PHILADELPHIA
RS: Series tied, 9-9-1
PS: Falcons lead series, 1-0
1966—Eagles, 23-10 (P)
1967—Eagles, 38-7 (A)
1969—Falcons, 27-3 (P)
1970—Tie, 13-13 (P)
1973—Falcons, 44-27 (P)
1976—Eagles, 14-13 (A)
1978—*Falcons, 14-13 (A)
1979—Falcons, 14-10 (P)
1980—Falcons, 20-17 (P)
1981—Eagles, 16-13 (P)
1983—Eagles, 28-24 (A)
1984—Falcons, 26-10 (A)
1985—Eagles, 23-17 (P) OT
1986—Eagles, 16-0 (A)
1988—Falcons, 27-24 (P)
1990—Eagles, 24-23 (A)
1994—Falcons, 28-21 (A)
1996—Eagles, 33-18 (A)
1997—Falcons, 20-17 (A)
1998—Falcons, 17-12 (A)
(RS Pts.—Eagles 369, Falcons 361)
(PS Pts.—Falcons 14, Eagles 13)
NFC First-Round Playoff

ATLANTA vs. PITTSBURGH
RS: Steelers lead series, 11-1
1966—Steelers, 57-33 (A)
1968—Steelers, 41-21 (A)
1970—Falcons, 27-16 (A)
1974—Steelers, 24-17 (P)
1978—Steelers, 31-7 (P)
1981—Steelers, 34-20 (A)
1984—Steelers, 35-10 (P)
1987—Steelers, 28-12 (A)
1990—Steelers, 21-9 (P)
1993—Steelers, 45-17 (A)
1996—Steelers, 20-17 (A)
1999—Steelers, 13-9 (P)
(RS Pts.—Steelers 365, Falcons 199)

ATLANTA vs. *ST. LOUIS
RS: Rams lead series, 41-23-2
1966—Rams, 19-14 (A)
1967—Rams, 31-3 (A)
Rams, 20-3 (LA)
1968—Rams, 27-14 (LA)
Rams, 17-10 (A)
1969—Rams, 17-7 (LA)
Rams, 38-6 (A)
1970—Tie, 10-10 (LA)
Rams, 17-7 (A)
1971—Tie, 20-20 (LA)
Rams, 24-16 (A)
1972—Falcons, 31-3 (A)
Rams, 20-7 (LA)
1973—Rams, 31-0 (LA)
Falcons, 15-13 (A)
1974—Rams, 21-0 (LA)
Rams, 30-7 (A)
1975—Rams, 22-7 (LA)
Rams, 16-7 (A)
1976—Rams, 30-14 (A)
Rams, 59-0 (LA)
1977—Falcons, 17-6 (A)
Rams, 23-7 (LA)
1978—Rams, 10-0 (LA)
Falcons, 15-7 (A)
1979—Rams, 20-14 (LA)
Rams, 34-13 (A)
1980—Falcons, 13-10 (A)
Rams, 20-17 (LA) OT
1981—Rams, 37-35 (A)
Rams, 21-16 (LA)
1982—Falcons, 34-17 (A)
1983—Rams, 27-21 (LA)
Rams, 36-13 (A)
1984—Falcons, 30-28 (LA)
Rams, 24-10 (A)
1985—Rams, 17-6 (LA)
Falcons, 30-14 (A)
1986—Falcons, 26-14 (A)
Rams, 14-7 (LA)
1987—Falcons, 24-20 (A)
Rams, 33-0 (LA)
1988—Rams, 33-0 (A)
Rams, 22-7 (LA)
1989—Rams, 31-21 (A)
Rams, 26-14 (LA)
1990—Rams, 44-24 (LA)
Falcons, 20-13 (A)
1991—Falcons, 31-14 (A)
Falcons, 31-14 (LA)
1992—Falcons, 30-28 (A)
Rams, 38-27 (LA)
1993—Falcons, 30-24 (A)
Falcons, 13-0 (LA)
1994—Falcons, 31-13 (A)
Falcons, 8-5 (LA)
1995—Rams, 21-19 (StL)
Falcons, 31-6 (A)
1996—Rams, 59-16 (StL)
Rams, 34-27 (A)
1997—Falcons, 34-31 (A)
Falcons, 27-21 (StL)
1998—Falcons, 37-15 (A)
Falcons, 21-10 (StL)
1999—Rams, 35-7 (StL)
Rams, 41-13 (A)
(RS Pts.—Rams 1,495, Falcons 1,065)
Franchise in Los Angeles prior to 1995

ATLANTA vs. SAN DIEGO
RS: Falcons lead series, 5-1
1973—Falcons, 41-0 (SD)
1979—Falcons, 28-26 (SD)
1988—Chargers, 10-7 (A)
1991—Falcons, 13-10 (SD)
1994—Falcons, 10-9 (A)
1997—Falcons, 14-3 (SD)
(RS Pts.—Falcons 113, Chargers 58)

ATLANTA vs. SAN FRANCISCO
RS: 49ers lead series, 41-24-1
PS: Falcons lead series, 1-0
1966—49ers, 44-7 (A)
1967—49ers, 38-7 (SF)
49ers, 34-28 (A)
1968—49ers, 28-13 (SF)
49ers, 14-12 (A)
1969—Falcons, 24-12 (A)
Falcons, 21-7 (SF)
1970—Falcons, 21-20 (A)
49ers, 24-20 (SF)
1971—Falcons, 20-17 (A)
49ers, 24-3 (SF)
1972—49ers, 49-14 (A)
49ers, 20-0 (SF)
1973—49ers, 13-9 (A)
Falcons, 17-3 (SF)
1974—49ers, 16-10 (A)
49ers, 27-0 (SF)
1975—Falcons, 17-3 (SF)
Falcons, 31-9 (A)
1976—49ers, 15-0 (SF)
Falcons, 21-16 (A)
1977—Falcons, 7-0 (SF)
49ers, 10-3 (A)
1978—Falcons, 20-17 (SF)
Falcons, 21-10 (A)
1979—49ers, 20-15 (SF)
Falcons, 31-21 (A)
1980—Falcons, 20-17 (SF)
Falcons, 35-10 (A)
1981—Falcons, 34-17 (A)
49ers, 17-14 (SF)
1982—Falcons, 17-7 (SF)
1983—49ers, 24-20 (SF)
Falcons, 28-24 (A)
1984—49ers, 14-5 (SF)
49ers, 35-17 (A)
1985—49ers, 35-16 (SF)
49ers, 38-17 (A)
1986—Tie, 10-10 (A) OT
49ers, 20-0 (SF)
1987—49ers, 25-17 (A)
49ers, 35-7 (SF)
1988—Falcons, 34-17 (SF)
49ers, 13-3 (A)
1989—49ers, 45-3 (SF)
49ers, 23-10 (A)
1990—49ers, 19-13 (SF)
49ers, 45-35 (A)
1991—Falcons, 39-34 (SF)
Falcons, 17-14 (A)
1992—49ers, 56-17 (SF)

49ers, 41-3 (A)
1993—49ers, 37-30 (SF)
Falcons, 27-24 (A)
1994—49ers, 42-3 (A)
49ers, 50-14 (SF)
1995—49ers, 41-10 (SF)
Falcons, 28-27 (A)
1996—49ers, 39-17 (SF)
49ers, 34-10 (A)
1997—49ers, 34-7 (SF)
49ers, 35-28 (A)
1998—49ers, 31-20 (SF)
Falcons, 31-19 (A)
*Falcons, 20-18 (A)
1999—49ers, 26-7 (SF)
Falcons, 34-29 (A)
(RS Pts.—49ers 1,614, Falcons 1,089)
(PS Pts.—Falcons 20, 49ers 18)
NFC Divisional Playoff
ATLANTA vs. SEATTLE
RS: Seahawks lead series, 4-2
1976—Seahawks, 30-13 (S)
1979—Seahawks, 31-28 (A)
1985—Seahawks, 30-26 (S)
1988—Seahawks, 31-20 (A)
1991—Falcons, 26-13 (A)
1997—Falcons, 24-17 (S)
(RS Pts.—Seahawks 152, Falcons 137)
ATLANTA vs. TAMPA BAY
RS: Series tied, 8-8
1977—Falcons, 17-0 (TB)
1978—Buccaneers, 14-9 (TB)
1979—Falcons, 17-14 (A)
1981—Buccaneers, 24-23 (TB)
1984—Buccaneers, 23-6 (TB)
1986—Falcons, 23-20 (TB) OT
1987—Buccaneers, 48-10 (TB)
1988—Falcons, 17-10 (A)
1990—Buccaneers, 23-17 (TB)
1991—Falcons, 43-7 (A)
1992—Falcons, 35-7 (TB)
1993—Buccaneers, 31-24 (A)
1994—Falcons, 34-13 (A)
1995—Falcons, 24-21 (TB)
1997—Buccaneers, 31-10 (A)
1999—Buccaneers, 19-10 (TB)
(RS Pts.—Falcons 319, Buccaneers 305)
ATLANTA vs. *TENNESSEE
RS: Series tied, 5-5
1972—Falcons, 20-10 (A)
1976—Oilers, 20-14 (H)
1978—Falcons, 20-14 (A)
1981—Falcons, 31-27 (H)
1984—Falcons, 42-10 (A)
1987—Oilers, 37-33 (H)
1990—Falcons, 47-27 (A)
1993—Oilers, 33-17 (H)
1996—Oilers, 23-13 (A)
1999—Titans, 30-17 (T)
(RS Pts.—Falcons 254, Titans 231)
**Franchise in Houston prior to 1997; known as Oilers prior to 1999*
ATLANTA vs. WASHINGTON
RS: Redskins lead series, 13-4-1
PS: Redskins lead series, 1-0
1966—Redskins, 33-20 (W)
1967—Tie, 20-20 (A)
1969—Redskins, 27-20 (W)
1972—Redskins, 24-13 (W)
1975—Redskins, 30-27 (A)
1977—Redskins, 10-6 (W)
1978—Falcons, 20-17 (A)
1979—Redskins, 16-7 (A)
1980—Falcons, 10-6 (A)
1983—Redskins, 37-21 (W)
1984—Redskins, 27-14 (W)
1985—Redskins, 44-10 (A)
1987—Falcons, 21-20 (A)
1989—Redskins, 31-30 (A)
1991—Redskins, 56-17 (W)
*Redskins, 24-7 (W)
1992—Redskins, 24-17 (W)
1993—Redskins, 30-17 (W)
1994—Falcons, 27-20 (W)
(RS Pts.—Redskins 472, Falcons 317)
(PS Pts.—Redskins 24, Falcons 7)
NFC Divisional Playoff

BALTIMORE vs. ARIZONA
RS: Cardinals lead series, 1-0;
See Arizona vs. Baltimore
BALTIMORE vs. ATLANTA
RS: Ravens lead series, 1-0;
See Atlanta vs. Baltimore
BALTIMORE vs. BUFFALO
RS: Bills lead series, 1-0
1999—Bills, 13-10 (Balt)
(RS Pts.—Bills 13, Ravens 10)
BALTIMORE vs. CAROLINA
RS: Panthers lead series, 1-0
1996—Panthers, 27-16 (C)
(RS Pts.—Panthers 27, Ravens 16)
BALTIMORE vs. CHICAGO
RS: Bears lead series, 1-0
1998—Bears, 24-3 (C)
(RS Pts.—Bears 24, Ravens 3)
BALTIMORE vs. CINCINNATI
RS: Ravens lead series, 5-3
1996—Bengals, 24-21 (B)
Bengals, 21-14 (C)
1997—Ravens, 23-10 (B)
Bengals, 16-14 (C)
1998—Ravens, 31-24 (B)
Ravens, 20-13 (C)
1999—Ravens, 34-31 (C)
Ravens, 22-0 (B)
(RS Pts.—Ravens 179, Bengals 139)
BALTIMORE vs. CLEVELAND
RS: Ravens lead series, 2-0
1999—Ravens, 17-10 (B)
Ravens, 41-9 (C)
(RS Pts.—Ravens 58, Browns 19)
BALTIMORE vs. DENVER
RS: Broncos lead series, 1-0
1996—Broncos, 45-34 (D)
(RS Pts.—Broncos 45, Ravens 34)
BALTIMORE vs. DETROIT
RS: Ravens lead series, 1-0
1998—Ravens, 19-10 (B)
(RS Pts.—Ravens 19, Lions 10)
BALTIMORE vs. GREEN BAY
RS: Packers lead series, 1-0
1998—Packers, 28-10 (GB)
(RS Pts.—Packers 28, Ravens 10)
BALTIMORE vs. INDIANAPOLIS
RS: Series tied, 1-1
1996—Colts, 26-21 (I)
1998—Ravens, 38-31 (B)
(RS Pts.—Ravens 59, Colts 57)
BALTIMORE vs. JACKSONVILLE
RS: Jaguars lead series, 8-0
1996—Jaguars, 30-27 (J)
Jaguars, 28-25 (B) OT
1997—Jaguars, 28-27 (B)
Jaguars, 29-27 (J)
1998—Jaguars, 24-10 (J)
Jaguars, 45-19 (B)
1999—Jaguars, 6-3 (J)
Jaguars, 30-23 (B)
(RS Pts.—Jaguars 220, Ravens 161)
BALTIMORE vs. KANSAS CITY
RS: Chiefs lead series, 1-0
1999—Chiefs, 35-8 (B)
(RS Pts.—Chiefs 35, Ravens 8)
BALTIMORE vs. MIAMI
RS: Dolphins lead series, 1-0
1997—Dolphins, 24-13 (B)
(RS Pts.—Dolphins 24, Ravens 13)
BALTIMORE vs. MINNESOTA
RS: Vikings lead series, 1-0
1998—Vikings, 38-28 (B)
(RS Pts.—Vikings 38, Ravens 28)
BALTIMORE vs. NEW ENGLAND
RS: Patriots lead series, 2-0
1996—Patriots, 46-38 (B)
1999—Patriots, 20-3 (NE)
(RS Pts.—Patriots 66, Ravens 41)
BALTIMORE vs. NEW ORLEANS
RS: Ravens lead series, 2-0
1996—Ravens, 17-10 (B)
1999—Ravens, 31-8 (B)
(RS Pts.—Ravens 48, Saints 18)
BALTIMORE vs. N.Y. GIANTS
RS: Ravens lead series, 1-0
1997—Ravens, 24-23 (NY)
(RS Pts.—Ravens 24, Giants 23)
BALTIMORE vs. N.Y. JETS
RS: Series tied, 1-1
1997—Jets, 19-16 (NY) OT
1998—Ravens, 24-10 (NY)
(RS Pts.—Ravens 40, Jets 29)
BALTIMORE vs. OAKLAND
RS: Ravens lead series, 2-0
1996—Ravens, 19-14 (B)
1998—Ravens, 13-10 (B)
(RS Pts.—Ravens 32, Raiders 24)
BALTIMORE vs. PHILADELPHIA
RS: Series tied, 0-0-1
1997—Tie, 10-10 (B) OT
(RS Pts.—Ravens 10, Eagles 10)
BALTIMORE vs. PITTSBURGH
RS: Steelers lead series, 6-2
1996—Steelers, 31-17 (P)
Ravens, 31-17 (B)
1997—Steelers, 42-34 (B)
Steelers, 37-0 (P)
1998—Steelers, 20-13 (B)
Steelers, 16-6 (P)
1999—Steelers, 23-20 (B)
Ravens, 31-24 (P)
(RS Pts.—Steelers 210, Ravens 152)
BALTIMORE vs. ST. LOUIS
RS: Series tied, 1-1
1996—Ravens, 37-31 (B) OT
1999—Rams, 27-10 (StL)
(RS Pts.—Rams 58, Ravens 47)
BALTIMORE vs. SAN DIEGO
RS: Chargers lead series, 2-0
1997—Chargers, 21-17 (SD)
1998—Chargers, 14-13 (SD)
(RS Pts.—Chargers 35, Ravens 30)
BALTIMORE vs. SAN FRANCISCO
RS: 49ers lead series, 1-0
1996—49ers, 38-20 (SF)
(RS Pts.—49ers 38, Ravens 20)
BALTIMORE vs. SEATTLE
RS: Ravens lead series, 1-0
1997—Ravens, 31-24 (B)
(RS Pts.—Ravens 31, Seahawks 24)
BALTIMORE vs. *TENNESSEE
RS: Titans lead series, 5-3
1996—Oilers, 29-13 (H)
Oilers, 24-21 (B)
1997—Ravens, 36-10 (T)
Ravens, 21-19 (B)
1998—Oilers, 12-8 (B)
Oilers, 16-14 (T)
1999—Titans, 14-11 (T)
Ravens, 41-14 (B)
(RS Pts.—Ravens 165, Titans 138)
**Franchise in Houston prior to 1997; known as Oilers prior to 1999*
BALTIMORE vs. WASHINGTON
RS: Ravens lead series, 1-0
1997—Ravens, 20-17 (W)
(RS Pts.—Ravens 20, Redskins 17)

BUFFALO vs. ARIZONA
RS: Bills lead series, 4-3;
See Arizona vs. Buffalo
BUFFALO vs. ATLANTA
RS: Bills lead series, 4-3;
See Atlanta vs. Buffalo
BUFFALO vs. BALTIMORE
RS: Bills lead series, 1-0;
See Baltimore vs. Buffalo
BUFFALO vs. CAROLINA
RS: Bills lead series, 2-0
1995—Bills, 31-9 (B)
1998—Bills, 30-14 (C)
(RS Pts.—Bills 61, Panthers 23)
BUFFALO vs. CHICAGO
RS: Bears lead series, 5-2
1970—Bears, 31-13 (C)
1974—Bills, 16-6 (B)
1979—Bears, 7-0 (B)
1988—Bears, 24-3 (C)
1991—Bills, 35-20 (B)
1994—Bears, 20-13 (C)
1997—Bears, 20-3 (C)
(RS Pts.—Bears 128, Bills 83)
BUFFALO vs. CINCINNATI
RS: Series tied, 9-9
PS: Bengals lead series, 2-0
1968—Bengals, 34-23 (C)
1969—Bills, 16-13 (B)
1970—Bengals, 43-14 (B)
1973—Bengals, 16-13 (B)
1975—Bengals, 33-24 (C)
1978—Bills, 5-0 (B)
1979—Bills, 51-24 (B)
1980—Bills, 14-0 (C)
1981—Bengals, 27-24 (C) OT
*Bengals, 28-21 (C)
1983—Bills, 10-6 (C)
1984—Bengals, 52-21 (C)
1985—Bengals, 23-17 (B)
1986—Bengals, 36-33 (C) OT
1988—Bengals, 35-21 (C)
**Bengals, 21-10 (C)
1989—Bills, 24-7 (B)
1991—Bills, 35-16 (B)
1996—Bills, 31-17 (B)
1998—Bills, 33-20 (C)
(RS Pts.—Bills 409, Bengals 402)
(PS Pts.—Bengals 49, Bills 31)
AFC Divisional Playoff
***AFC Championship*
BUFFALO vs. CLEVELAND
RS: Browns lead series, 7-4
PS: Browns lead series, 1-0
1972—Browns, 27-10 (C)
1974—Bills, 15-10 (C)
1977—Browns, 27-16 (B)
1978—Browns, 41-20 (C)
1981—Bills, 22-13 (B)
1984—Browns, 13-10 (B)
1985—Browns, 17-7 (C)
1986—Browns, 21-17 (B)
1987—Browns, 27-21 (C)
1989—*Browns, 34-30 (C)
1990—Bills, 42-0 (C)
1995—Bills, 22-19 (C)
(RS Pts.—Browns 215, Bills 202)
(PS Pts.—Browns 34, Bills 30)
AFC Divisional Playoff
BUFFALO vs. DALLAS
RS: Series tied, 3-3
PS: Cowboys lead series, 2-0
1971—Cowboys, 49-37 (B)
1976—Cowboys, 17-10 (D)
1981—Cowboys, 27-14 (D)
1984—Bills, 14-3 (B)
1992—*Cowboys, 52-17 (Pasadena)
1993—Bills, 13-10 (D)
**Cowboys, 30-13 (Atlanta)
1996—Bills, 10-7 (B)
(RS Pts.—Cowboys 113, Bills 98)
(PS Pts.—Cowboys 82, Bills 30)
Super Bowl XXVII
***Super Bowl XXVIII*
BUFFALO vs. DENVER
RS: Bills lead series, 17-12-1
PS: Bills lead series, 1-0
1960—Broncos, 27-21 (B)
Tie, 38-38 (D)
1961—Broncos, 22-10 (B)
Bills, 23-10 (D)
1962—Broncos, 23-20 (B)
Bills, 45-38 (D)
1963—Bills, 30-28 (D)
Bills, 27-17 (B)

ALL-TIME TEAM VS. TEAM RESULTS

1964—Bills, 30-13 (B)
Bills, 30-19 (D)
1965—Bills, 30-15 (D)
Bills, 31-13 (B)
1966—Bills, 38-21 (B)
1967—Bills, 17-16 (D)
Broncos, 21-20 (B)
1968—Broncos, 34-32 (D)
1969—Bills, 41-28 (B)
1970—Broncos, 25-10 (B)
1975—Bills, 38-14 (B)
1977—Broncos, 26-6 (D)
1979—Broncos, 19-16 (B)
1981—Bills, 9-7 (B)
1984—Broncos, 37-7 (B)
1987—Bills, 21-14 (B)
1989—Broncos, 28-14 (B)
1990—Bills, 29-28 (B)
1991—*Bills, 10-7 (B)
1992—Bills, 27-17 (B)
1994—Bills, 27-20 (B)
1995—Broncos, 22-7 (D)
1997—Broncos, 23-20 (B) OT
(RS Pts.—Bills 714, Broncos 663)
(PS Pts.—Bills 10, Broncos 7)
*AFC Championship

BUFFALO vs. DETROIT
RS: Lions lead series, 3-2-1
1972—Tie, 21-21 (B)
1976—Lions, 27-14 (D)
1979—Bills, 20-17 (D)
1991—Lions, 17-14 (B) OT
1994—Lions, 35-21 (D)
1997—Bills, 22-13 (B)
(RS Pts.—Lions 130, Bills 112)

BUFFALO vs. GREEN BAY
RS: Bills lead series, 5-2
1974—Bills, 27-7 (GB)
1979—Bills, 19-12 (B)
1982—Packers, 33-21 (Mil)
1988—Bills, 28-0 (B)
1991—Bills, 34-24 (Mil)
1994—Bills 29-20 (B)
1997—Packers, 31-21 (GB)
(RS Pts.—Bills 179, Packers 127)

BUFFALO vs. *INDIANAPOLIS
RS: Bills lead series, 34-24-1
1970—Tie, 17-17 (Balt)
Colts, 20-14 (Buff)
1971—Colts, 43-0 (Buff)
Colts, 24-0 (Balt)
1972—Colts, 17-0 (Buff)
Colts, 35-7 (Balt)
1973—Bills, 31-13 (Buff)
Bills, 24-17 (Balt)
1974—Bills, 27-14 (Balt)
Bills, 6-0 (Buff)
1975—Bills, 38-31 (Balt)
Colts, 42-35 (Buff)
1976—Colts, 31-13 (Buff)
Colts, 58-20 (Balt)
1977—Colts, 17-14 (Balt)
Colts, 31-13 (Buff)
1978—Bills, 24-17 (Buff)
Bills, 21-14 (Balt)
1979—Bills, 31-13 (Balt)
Colts, 14-13 (Buff)
1980—Colts, 17-12 (Buff)
Colts, 28-24 (Balt)
1981—Bills, 35-3 (Balt)
Bills, 23-17 (Buff)
1982—Bills, 20-0 (Buff)
1983—Bills, 28-23 (Buff)
Bills, 30-7 (Balt)
1984—Colts, 31-17 (I)
Bills, 21-15 (Buff)
1985—Colts, 49-17 (I)
Bills, 21-9 (Buff)
1986—Bills, 24-13 (Buff)
Colts, 24-14 (I)
1987—Colts, 47-6 (Buff)
Bills, 27-3 (I)
1988—Bills, 34-23 (Buff)
Colts, 17-14 (I)
1989—Colts, 37-14 (I)
Bills, 30-7 (Buff)
1990—Bills, 26-10 (Buff)
Bills, 31-7 (I)
1991—Bills, 42-6 (Buff)
Bills, 35-7 (I)
1992—Bills, 38-0 (Buff)
Colts, 16-13 (I) OT
1993—Bills, 23-9 (Buff)
Bills, 30-10 (I)
1994—Colts, 27-17 (Buff)
Colts, 10-9 (I)
1995—Bills, 20-14 (Buff)
Bills, 16-10 (I)
1996—Bills, 16-13 (Buff) OT
Colts, 13-10 (I) OT
1997—Bills, 37-35 (B)
Bills, 9-6 (I)
1998—Bills, 31-24 (I)
Bills, 34-11 (B)
1999—Colts, 31-14 (I)
Bills, 31-6 (B)
(RS Pts.—Bills 1,241, Colts 1,103)
Franchise in Baltimore prior to 1984

BUFFALO vs. JACKSONVILLE
RS: Series tied, 1-1
PS: Jaguars lead series, 1-0
1996—*Jaguars, 30-27 (B)
1997—Jaguars, 20-14 (B)
1998—Bills, 17-16 (B)
(RS Pts.—Jaguars 36, Bills 31)
(PS Pts.—Jaguars 30, Bills 27)
AFC First-Round Playoff

BUFFALO vs. *KANSAS CITY
RS: Bills lead series, 17-14-1
PS: Bills lead series, 2-1
1960—Texans, 45-28 (B)
Texans, 24-7 (D)
1961—Bills, 27-24 (B)
Bills, 30-20 (D)
1962—Texans, 41-21 (D)
Bills, 23-14 (B)
1963—Tie, 27-27 (B)
Bills, 35-26 (KC)
1964—Bills, 34-17 (B)
Bills, 35-22 (KC)
1965—Bills, 23-7 (KC)
Bills, 34-25 (B)
1966—Chiefs, 42-20 (B)
Bills, 29-14 (KC)
**Chiefs, 31-7 (B)
1967—Chiefs, 23-13 (KC)
1968—Chiefs, 18-7 (B)
1969—Chiefs, 29-7 (B)
Chiefs, 22-19 (KC)
1971—Chiefs, 22-9 (KC)
1973—Bills, 23-14 (B)
1976—Bills, 50-17 (B)
1978—Bills, 28-13 (B)
Chiefs, 14-10 (KC)
1982—Bills, 14-9 (B)
1983—Bills, 14-9 (KC)
1986—Chiefs, 20-17 (B)
Bills, 17-14 (KC)
1991—Chiefs, 33-6 (KC)
***Bills, 37-14 (B)
1993—Chiefs, 23-7 (KC)
****Bills, 30-13 (B)
1994—Bills, 44-10 (B)
1996—Bills, 20-9 (B)
1997—Chiefs, 22-16 (KC)
(RS Pts.—Bills 694, Chiefs 669)
(PS Pts.—Bills 74, Chiefs 58)
Franchise in Dallas prior to 1963 and known as Texans
***AFL Championship*
****AFC Divisional Playoff*
*****AFC Championship*

BUFFALO vs. MIAMI
RS: Dolphins lead series, 42-25-1
PS: Bills lead series, 3-1
1966—Bills, 58-24 (B)
Bills, 29-0 (M)
1967—Bills, 35-13 (B)
Dolphins, 17-14 (M)
1968—Tie, 14-14 (M)
Dolphins, 21-17 (B)
1969—Dolphins, 24-6 (M)
Bills, 28-3 (B)
1970—Dolphins, 33-14 (B)
Dolphins, 45-7 (M)
1971—Dolphins, 29-14 (B)
Dolphins, 34-0 (M)
1972—Dolphins, 24-23 (M)
Dolphins, 30-16 (B)
1973—Dolphins, 27-6 (M)
Dolphins, 17-0 (B)
1974—Dolphins, 24-16 (B)
Dolphins, 35-28 (M)
1975—Dolphins, 35-30 (B)
Dolphins, 31-21 (M)
1976—Dolphins, 30-21 (B)
Dolphins, 45-27 (M)
1977—Dolphins, 13-0 (B)
Dolphins, 31-14 (M)
1978—Dolphins, 31-24 (M)
Dolphins, 25-24 (B)
1979—Dolphins, 9-7 (B)
Dolphins, 17-7 (M)
1980—Bills, 17-7 (B)
Dolphins, 17-14 (M)
1981—Bills, 31-21 (B)
Dolphins, 16-6 (M)
1982—Dolphins, 9-7 (B)
Dolphins, 27-10 (M)
1983—Dolphins, 12-0 (B)
Bills, 38-35 (M) OT
1984—Dolphins, 21-17 (B)
Dolphins, 38-7 (M)
1985—Dolphins, 23-14 (B)
Dolphins, 28-0 (M)
1986—Dolphins, 27-14 (M)
Dolphins, 34-24 (B)
1987—Bills, 34-31 (M) OT
Bills, 27-0 (B)
1988—Bills, 9-6 (B)
Bills, 31-6 (M)
1989—Bills, 27-24 (M)
Bills, 31-17 (B)
1990—Dolphins, 30-7 (M)
Bills, 24-14 (B)
*Bills, 44-34 (B)
1991—Bills, 35-31 (B)
Bills, 41-27 (M)
1992—Dolphins, 37-10 (B)
Bills, 26-20 (M)
**Bills, 29-10 (M)
1993—Dolphins, 22-13 (B)
Bills, 47-34 (M)
1994—Bills, 21-11 (B)
Bills, 42-31 (M)
1995—Dolphins, 23-6 (M)
Bills, 23-20 (B)
***Bills, 37-22 (B)
1996—Dolphins, 21-7 (B)
Dolphins, 16-14 (M)
1997—Bills, 9-6 (B)
Dolphins, 30-13 (M)
1998—Dolphins, 13-7 (M)
Bills, 30-24 (B)
***Dolphins, 24-17 (M)
1999—Bills, 23-18 (M)
Bills, 23-3 (B)
(RS Pts.—Dolphins 1,511, Bills 1,279)
(PS Pts.—Bills 127, Dolphins 90)
AFC Divisional Playoff
***AFC Championship*
****AFC First-Round Playoff*

BUFFALO vs. MINNESOTA
RS: Vikings lead series, 6-2
1971—Vikings, 19-0 (M)
1975—Vikings, 35-13 (B)
1979—Vikings, 10-3 (M)
1982—Bills, 23-22 (B)
1985—Vikings, 27-20 (B)
1988—Bills, 13-10 (B)
1994—Vikings, 21-17 (B)
1997—Vikings, 34-13 (B)
(RS Pts.—Vikings 178, Bills 102)

BUFFALO vs. *NEW ENGLAND
RS: Patriots lead series, 40-38-1
PS: Patriots lead series, 1-0
1960—Bills, 13-0 (Bos)
Bills, 38-14 (Buff)
1961—Patriots, 23-21 (Buff)
Patriots, 52-21 (Bos)
1962—Tie, 28-28 (Buff)
Patriots, 21-10 (Bos)
1963—Bills, 28-21 (Buff)
Patriots, 17-7 (Bos)
**Patriots, 26-8 (Buff)
1964—Patriots, 36-28 (Buff)
Bills, 24-14 (Bos)
1965—Bills, 24-7 (Buff)
Bills, 23-7 (Bos)
1966—Patriots, 20-10 (Buff)
Patriots, 14-3 (Bos)
1967—Patriots, 23-0 (Buff)
Bills, 44-16 (Bos)
1968—Patriots, 16-7 (Buff)
Patriots, 23-6 (Bos)
1969—Bills, 23-16 (Buff)
Patriots, 35-21 (Bos)
1970—Bills, 45-10 (Bos)
Patriots, 14-10 (Buff)
1971—Patriots, 38-33 (NE)
Bills, 27-20 (Buff)
1972—Bills, 38-14 (Buff)
Bills, 27-24 (NE)
1973—Bills, 31-13 (NE)
Bills, 37-13 (Buff)
1974—Bills, 30-28 (Buff)
Bills, 29-28 (NE)
1975—Bills, 45-31 (Buff)
Bills, 34-14 (NE)
1976—Patriots, 26-22 (Buff)
Patriots, 20-10 (NE)
1977—Bills, 24-14 (NE)
Patriots, 20-7 (Buff)
1978—Patriots, 14-10 (Buff)
Patriots, 26-24 (NE)
1979—Patriots, 26-6 (Buff)
Bills, 16-13 (NE) OT
1980—Bills, 31-13 (Buff)
Patriots, 24-2 (NE)
1981—Bills, 20-17 (Buff)
Bills, 19-10 (NE)
1982—Patriots, 30-19 (NE)
1983—Patriots, 31-0 (Buff)
Patriots, 21-7 (NE)
1984—Patriots, 21-17 (Buff)
Patriots, 38-10 (NE)
1985—Patriots, 17-14 (Buff)
Patriots, 14-3 (NE)
1986—Patriots, 23-3 (Buff)
Patriots, 22-19 (NE)
1987—Patriots, 14-7 (NE)
Patriots, 13-7 (Buff)
1988—Bills, 16-14 (NE)
Bills, 23-20 (Buff)
1989—Bills, 31-10 (Buff)
Patriots, 33-24 (NE)
1990—Bills, 27-10 (NE)
Bills, 14-0 (Buff)
1991—Bills, 22-17 (Buff)
Patriots, 16-13 (NE)
1992—Bills, 41-7 (NE)
Bills, 16-7 (Buff)
1993—Bills, 38-14 (Buff)
Bills, 13-10 (NE) OT
1994—Bills, 38-35 (NE)
Patriots, 41-17 (Buff)
1995—Patriots, 27-14 (NE)
Patriots, 35-25 (Buff)
1996—Bills, 17-10 (Buff)
Patriots, 28-25 (NE)
1997—Patriots, 33-6 (NE)
Patriots, 31-10 (B)

1998—Bills, 13-10 (B)
Patriots, 25-21 (NE)
1998—Bills, 17-7 (B)
Bills, 13-10 (NE) OT
(RS Pts.—Patriots 1,567, Bills 1,556)
(PS Pts.—Patriots 26, Bills 8)
**Franchise in Boston prior to 1971*
***Division Playoff*

BUFFALO vs. NEW ORLEANS
RS: Bills lead series, 4-2
1973—Saints, 13-0 (NO)
1980—Bills, 35-26 (NO)
1983—Bills, 27-21 (B)
1989—Saints, 22-19 (B)
1992—Bills, 20-16 (NO)
1998—Bills, 45-33 (NO)
(RS Pts.—Bills 146, Saints 131)

BUFFALO vs. N.Y. GIANTS
RS: Bills lead series, 5-3
PS: Giants lead series, 1-0
1970—Giants, 20-6 (NY)
1975—Giants, 17-14 (B)
1978—Bills, 41-17 (B)
1987—Bills, 6-3 (B) OT
1990—Bills, 17-13 (NY)
*Giants, 20-19 (Tampa)
1993—Bills, 17-14 (B)
1996—Bills, 23-20 (NY) OT
1999—Giants, 19-17 (B)
(RS Pts.—Bills 141, Giants 123)
(PS Pts.—Giants 20, Bills 19)
**Super Bowl XXV*

BUFFALO vs. *N.Y. JETS
RS: Bills lead series, 44-34
PS: Bills lead series, 1-0
1960—Titans, 27-3 (NY)
Titans, 17-13 (B)
1961—Bills, 41-31 (B)
Titans, 21-14 (NY)
1962—Titans, 17-6 (B)
Bills, 20-3 (NY)
1963—Bills, 45-14 (B)
Bills, 19-10 (NY)
1964—Bills, 34-24 (B)
Bills, 20-7 (NY)
1965—Bills, 33-21 (B)
Jets, 14-12 (NY)
1966—Bills, 33-23 (NY)
Bills, 14-3 (B)
1967—Bills, 20-17 (B)
Jets, 20-10 (NY)
1968—Bills, 37-35 (B)
Jets, 25-21 (NY)
1969—Jets, 33-19 (B)
Jets, 16-6 (NY)
1970—Bills, 34-31 (B)
Bills, 10-6 (NY)
1971—Jets, 28-17 (NY)
Jets, 20-7 (B)
1972—Jets, 41-24 (B)
Jets, 41-3 (NY)
1973—Bills, 9-7 (B)
Bills, 34-14 (NY)
1974—Bills, 16-12 (B)
Jets, 20-10 (NY)
1975—Bills, 42-14 (B)
Bills, 24-23 (NY)
1976—Jets, 17-14 (NY)
Jets, 19-14 (B)
1977—Jets, 24-19 (B)
Bills, 14-10 (NY)
1978—Jets, 21-20 (B)
Jets, 45-14 (NY)
1979—Bills, 46-31 (B)
Bills, 14-12 (NY)
1980—Bills, 20-10 (B)
Bills, 31-24 (NY)
1981—Bills, 31-0 (B)
Jets, 33-14 (NY)
**Bills, 31-27 (NY)
1983—Jets, 34-10 (B)
Bills, 24-17 (NY)
1984—Jets, 28-26 (B)
Jets, 21-17 (NY)
1985—Jets, 42-3 (NY)
Jets, 27-7 (B)
1986—Jets, 28-24 (B)
Jets, 14-13 (NY)
1987—Jets, 31-28 (B)
Bills, 17-14 (NY)
1988—Bills, 37-14 (NY)
Bills, 9-6 (B) OT
1989—Bills, 34-3 (B)
Bills, 37-0 (NY)
1990—Bills, 30-7 (NY)
Bills, 30-27 (B)
1991—Bills, 23-20 (NY)
Bills, 24-13 (B)
1992—Bills, 24-20 (NY)
Jets, 24-17 (B)
1993—Bills, 19-10 (NY)
Bills, 16-14 (B)
1994—Jets, 23-3 (B)
Jets, 22-17 (NY)
1995—Bills, 29-10 (B)
Bills, 28-26 (NY)
1996—Bills, 25-22 (NY)
Bills, 35-10 (B)
1997—Bills, 28-22 (NY)
Bills, 20-10 (B)
1998—Jets, 34-12 (NY)
Jets, 17-10 (B)
1999—Bills, 17-3 (B)
Jets, 17-7 (NY)
(RS Pts.—Bills 1,601, Jets 1,511)
(PS Pts.—Bills 31, Jets 27)
**Jets known as Titans prior to 1963*
***AFC First-Round Playoff*

BUFFALO vs. *OAKLAND
RS: Raiders lead series, 16-15
PS: Bills lead series, 2-0
1960—Bills, 38-9 (B)
Raiders, 20-7 (O)
1961—Raiders, 31-22 (B)
Bills, 26-21 (O)
1962—Bills, 14-6 (B)
Bills, 10-6 (O)
1963—Raiders, 35-17 (O)
Bills, 12-0 (B)
1964—Bills, 23-20 (B)
Raiders, 16-13 (O)
1965—Bills, 17-12 (B)
Bills, 17-14 (O)
1966—Bills, 31-10 (O)
1967—Raiders, 24-20 (B)
Raiders, 28-21 (O)
1968—Raiders, 48-6 (B)
Raiders, 13-10 (O)
1969—Raiders, 50-21 (O)
1972—Raiders, 28-16 (O)
1974—Bills, 21-20 (B)
1977—Raiders, 34-13 (O)
1980—Bills, 24-7 (B)
1983—Raiders, 27-24 (B)
1987—Raiders, 34-21 (LA)
1988—Bills, 37-21 (B)
1990—Bills, 38-24 (B)
**Bills, 51-3 (B)
1991—Bills, 30-27 (LA) OT
1992—Raiders, 20-3 (LA)
1993—Raiders, 25-24 (B)
***Bills, 29-23 (B)
1998—Bills, 44-21 (B)
1999—Raiders, 20-14 (B)
(RS Pts.—Raiders 671, Bills 634)
(PS Pts.—Bills 80, Raiders 26)
**Franchise in Los Angeles from 1982-1994*
***AFC Championship*
****AFC Divisional Playoff*

BUFFALO vs. PHILADELPHIA
RS: Bills lead series, 5-4
1973—Bills, 27-26 (B)
1981—Eagles, 20-14 (B)
1984—Eagles, 27-17 (B)
1985—Eagles, 21-17 (P)
1987—Eagles, 17-7 (P)
1990—Bills, 30-23 (B)
1993—Bills, 10-7 (P)
1996—Bills, 24-17 (P)
1999—Bills, 26-0 (B)
(RS Pts.—Bills 172, Eagles 158)

BUFFALO vs. PITTSBURGH
RS: Series tied, 8-8
PS: Steelers lead series, 2-1
1970—Steelers, 23-10 (P)
1972—Steelers, 38-21 (B)
1974—*Steelers, 32-14 (P)
1975—Bills, 30-21 (P)
1978—Steelers, 28-17 (B)
1979—Steelers, 28-0 (P)
1980—Bills, 28-13 (B)
1982—Bills, 13-0 (B)
1985—Steelers, 30-24 (P)
1986—Bills, 16-12 (B)
1988—Bills, 36-28 (B)
1991—Bills, 52-34 (B)
1992—Bills, 28-20 (B)
*Bills, 24-3 (P)
1993—Steelers, 23-0 (P)
1994—Steelers, 23-10 (P)
1995—*Steelers, 40-21 (P)
1996—Steelers, 24-6 (P)
1999—Bills, 24-21 (B)
(RS Pts.—Steelers 366, Bills 315)
(PS Pts.—Steelers 75, Bills 59)
**AFC Divisional Playoff*

BUFFALO vs. *ST. LOUIS
RS: Series tied, 4-4
1970—Rams, 19-0 (B)
1974—Rams, 19-14 (LA)
1980—Bills, 10-7 (B) OT
1983—Rams, 41-17 (LA)
1989—Bills, 23-20 (B)
1992—Bills, 40-7 (B)
1995—Bills, 45-27 (StL)
1998—Rams, 34-33 (B)
(RS Pts.—Bills 182, Rams 174)
**Franchise in Los Angeles prior to 1995*

BUFFALO vs. *SAN DIEGO
RS: Chargers lead series, 17-7-2
PS: Bills lead series, 2-1
1960—Chargers, 24-10 (B)
Bills, 32-3 (LA)
1961—Chargers, 19-11 (B)
Chargers, 28-10 (SD)
1962—Bills, 35-10 (B)
Bills, 40-20 (SD)
1963—Chargers, 14-10 (SD)
Chargers, 23-13 (B)
1964—Bills, 30-3 (B)
Bills, 27-24 (SD)
**Bills, 20-7 (B)
1965—Chargers, 34-3 (B)
Tie, 20-20 (SD)
**Bills, 23-0 (SD)
1966—Chargers, 27-7 (SD)
Tie, 17-17 (B)
1967—Chargers, 37-17 (B)
1968—Chargers, 21-6 (B)
1969—Chargers, 45-6 (SD)
1971—Chargers, 20-3 (SD)
1973—Chargers, 34-7 (SD)
1976—Chargers, 34-13 (B)
1979—Chargers, 27-19 (SD)
1980—Bills, 26-24 (SD)
***Chargers, 20-14 (SD)
1981—Bills, 28-27 (SD)
1985—Chargers, 14-9 (B)
Chargers, 40-7 (SD)
1998—Chargers, 16-14 (SD)
(RS Pts.—Chargers 605, Bills 420)
(PS Pts.—Bills 57, Chargers 27)
**Franchise in Los Angeles prior to 1961*
***AFL Championship*
****AFC Divisional Playoff*

BUFFALO vs. SAN FRANCISCO
RS: Bills lead series, 4-3
1972—Bills, 27-20 (B)
1980—Bills, 18-13 (SF)
1983—49ers, 23-10 (B)
1989—49ers, 21-10 (SF)
1992—Bills, 34-31 (SF)
1995—49ers, 27-17 (SF)
1998—Bills, 26-21 (B)
(RS Pts.—49ers 156, Bills 142)

BUFFALO vs. SEATTLE
RS: Seahawks lead series, 5-2
1977—Seahawks, 56-17 (S)
1984—Seahawks, 31-28 (S)
1988—Bills, 13-3 (S)
1989—Seahawks, 17-16 (S)
1995—Bills, 27-21 (B)
1996—Seahawks, 26-18 (S)
1999—Seahawks, 26-16 (S)
(RS Pts.—Seahawks 180, Bills 135)

BUFFALO vs. TAMPA BAY
RS: Buccaneers lead series, 4-2
1976—Bills, 14-9 (TB)
1978—Buccaneers, 31-10 (TB)
1982—Buccaneers, 24-23 (TB)
1986—Buccaneers, 34-28 (TB)
1988—Buccaneers, 10-5 (TB)
1991—Bills, 17-10 (TB)
(RS Pts.—Buccaneers 118, Bills 97)

BUFFALO vs. *TENNESSEE
RS: Titans lead series, 22-13
PS: Bills lead series, 2-1
1960—Bills, 25-24 (B)
Oilers, 31-23 (H)
1961—Bills, 22-12 (H)
Oilers, 28-16 (B)
1962—Oilers, 28-23 (B)
Oilers, 17-14 (H)
1963—Oilers, 31-20 (B)
Oilers, 28-14 (H)
1964—Bills, 48-17 (H)
Bills, 24-10 (B)
1965—Oilers, 19-17 (B)
Bills, 29-18 (H)
1966—Bills, 27-20 (B)
Bills, 42-20 (H)
1967—Oilers, 20-3 (B)
Oilers, 10-3 (H)
1968—Oilers, 30-7 (B)
Oilers, 35-6 (H)
1969—Oilers, 17-3 (B)
Oilers, 28-14 (H)
1971—Oilers, 20-14 (B)
1974—Oilers, 21-9 (B)
1976—Oilers, 13-3 (B)
1978—Oilers, 17-10 (H)
1983—Bills, 30-13 (B)
1985—Bills, 20-0 (B)
1986—Oilers, 16-7 (H)
1987—Bills, 34-30 (B)
1988—**Bills, 17-10 (B)
1989—Bills, 47-41 (H) OT
1990—Oilers, 27-24 (H)
1992—Oilers, 27-3 (H)
***Bills, 41-38 (B) OT
1993—Bills, 35-7 (B)
1994—Bills, 15-7 (H)
1995—Oilers, 28-17 (B)
1997—Oilers, 31-14 (T)
1999—***Titans, 22-16 (T)
(RS Pts.—Titans 741, Bills 662)
(PS Pts.—Bills 74, Titans 70)
**Franchise in Houston prior to 1997; known as Oilers prior to 1999*
***AFC Divisional Playoff*
****AFC First-Round Playoff*

BUFFALO vs. WASHINGTON
RS: Bills lead series, 5-4
PS: Redskins lead series, 1-0
1972—Bills, 24-17 (W)
1977—Redskins, 10-0 (B)
1981—Bills, 21-14 (B)
1984—Redskins, 41-14 (W)
1987—Redskins, 27-7 (B)
1990—Redskins, 29-14 (W)
1991—*Redskins, 37-24 (Minneapolis)

ALL-TIME TEAM VS. TEAM RESULTS

1993—Bills, 24-10 (B)
1996—Bills, 38-13 (B)
1999—Bills, 34-17 (W)
(RS Pts.—Redskins 178, Bills 176)
(PS Pts.—Redskins 37, Bills 24)
Super Bowl XXVI

CAROLINA vs. ARIZONA
RS: Panthers lead series, 1-0;
See Arizona vs. Carolina
CAROLINA vs. ATLANTA
RS: Series tied, 5-5;
See Atlanta vs. Carolina
CAROLINA vs. BALTIMORE
RS: Panthers lead series, 1-0
See Baltimore vs. Carolina
CAROLINA vs. BUFFALO
RS: Bills lead series, 2-0;
See Buffalo vs. Carolina
CAROLINA vs. CHICAGO
RS: Bears lead series, 1-0
1995—Bears, 31-27 (Chi)
(RS Pts.—Bears 31, Panthers 27)
CAROLINA vs. CINCINNATI
RS: Panthers lead series, 1-0
1999—Panthers, 27-3 (Car)
(RS Pts.—Panthers 27, Bengals 3)
CAROLINA vs. CLEVELAND
RS: Panthers lead series, 1-0
1999—Panthers, 31-17 (Cle)
(RS Pts.—Panthers 31, Browns 17)
CAROLINA vs. DALLAS
RS: Series tied, 1-1
PS: Panthers lead series, 1-0
1996—*Panthers, 26-17 (C)
1997—Panthers, 23-13 (D)
1998—Cowboys, 27-20 (D)
(RS Pts.—Panthers 43, Cowboys 40)
(PS Pts.—Panthers 26, Cowboys 17)
NFC Divisional Playoff
CAROLINA vs. DENVER
RS: Broncos lead series, 1-0
1997—Broncos, 34-0 (D)
(RS Pts.—Broncos 34, Panthers 0)
CAROLINA vs. DETROIT
RS: Lions lead series, 1-0
1999—Lions, 24-9 (C)
(RS Pts.—Lions 24, Panthers 9)
CAROLINA vs. GREEN BAY
RS: Packers lead series, 2-1
PS: Packers lead series, 1-0
1996—*Packers, 30-13 (GB)
1997—Packers, 31-10 (C)
1998—Packers, 37-30 (C)
1999—Panthers, 33-31 (GB)
(RS Pts.—Packers 99, Panthers 73)
(PS Pts.—Packers 30, Panthers 13)
NFC Championship
CAROLINA vs. INDIANAPOLIS
RS: Panthers lead series, 2-0
1995—Panthers, 13-10 (C)
1998—Panthers, 27-19 (I)
(RS Pts.—Panthers 40, Colts 29)
CAROLINA vs. JACKSONVILLE
RS: Jaguars lead series, 2-0
1996—Jaguars, 24-14 (J)
1999—Jaguars, 22-20 (C)
(RS Pts.—Jaguars 46, Panthers 34)
CAROLINA vs. KANSAS CITY
RS: Chiefs lead series, 1-0
1997—Chiefs, 35-14 (C)
(RS Pts.—Chiefs 35, Panthers 14)
CAROLINA vs. MIAMI
RS: Dolphins lead series, 1-0
1998—Dolphins, 13-9 (C)
(RS Pts.—Dolphins 13, Panthers 9)
CAROLINA vs. MINNESOTA
RS: Vikings lead series, 2-0
1996—Vikings, 14-12 (M)
1997—Vikings, 21-14 (M)
(RS Pts.—Vikings 35, Panthers 26)
CAROLINA vs. NEW ENGLAND
RS: Panthers lead series, 1-0
1995—Panthers, 20-17 (NE) OT
(RS Pts.—Panthers 20, Patriots 17)
CAROLINA vs. NEW ORLEANS
RS: Panthers lead series, 6-4
1995—Panthers, 20-3 (C)
Saints, 34-26 (NO)
1996—Panthers, 22-20 (NO)
Panthers, 19-7 (C)
1997—Panthers, 13-0 (NO)
Saints, 16-13 (C)
1998—Saints, 19-14 (NO)
Panthers, 31-17 (C)
1999—Saints, 19-10 (NO)
Panthers, 45-13 (C)
(RS Pts.—Panthers 213, Saints 148)
CAROLINA vs. N.Y. GIANTS
RS: Panthers lead series, 1-0
1995—Panthers, 27-17 (C)
(RS Pts.—Panthers 27, Giants 17)
CAROLINA vs. N.Y. JETS
RS: Series tied, 1-1
1995—Panthers, 26-15 (C)
1998—Jets, 48-21 (NY)
(RS Pts.—Jets 63, Panthers 47)
CAROLINA vs. OAKLAND
RS: Panthers lead series, 1-0
1997—Panthers, 38-14 (C)
(RS Pts.—Panthers 38, Raiders 14)
CAROLINA vs. PHILADELPHIA
RS: Series tied, 1-1
1996—Eagles, 20-9 (P)
1999—Panthers, 33-7 (C)
(RS Pts.—Panthers 42, Eagles 27)
CAROLINA vs. PITTSBURGH
RS: Series tied, 1-1
1996—Panthers, 18-14 (C)
1999—Steelers, 30-20 (P)
(RS Pts.—Steelers 44, Panthers 38)
CAROLINA vs. ST. LOUIS
RS: Series tied, 5-5
1995—Rams, 31-10 (C)
Rams, 28-17 (StL)
1996—Panthers, 45-13 (C)
Panthers, 20-10 (StL)
1997—Panthers, 16-10 (StL)
Rams, 30-18 (C)
1998—Panthers, 24-20 (StL)
Panthers, 20-13 (C)
1999—Rams, 35-10 (StL)
Rams, 34-21 (C)
(RS Pts.—Rams 224, Panthers 201)
CAROLINA vs. SAN DIEGO
RS: Panthers lead series, 1-0
1997—Panthers, 26-7 (SD)
(RS Pts.—Panthers 26, Chargers 7)
CAROLINA vs. SAN FRANCISCO
RS: Series tied, 5-5
1995—Panthers, 13-7 (SF)
49ers, 31-10 (C)
1996—Panthers, 23-7 (C)
Panthers, 30-24 (SF)
1997—49ers, 34-21 (C)
49ers, 27-19 (SF)
1998—49ers, 25-23 (SF)
49ers, 31-28 (C) OT
1999—Panthers, 31-29 (SF)
Panthers, 41-24 (C)
(RS Pts.—49ers 239, Panthers 239)
CAROLINA vs. TAMPA BAY
RS: Buccaneers lead series, 2-1
1995—Buccaneers, 20-13 (C)
1996—Panthers, 24-0 (C)
1998—Buccaneers, 16-13 (TB)
(RS Pts.—Panthers 50, Buccaneers 36)
CAROLINA vs. *TENNESSEE
RS: Panthers lead series, 1-0
1996—Panthers, 31-6 (H)
(RS Pts.—Panthers 31, Titans 6)
**Franchise in Houston prior to 1997; known as Oilers prior to 1999*
CAROLINA vs. WASHINGTON
RS: Redskins lead series, 4-0
1995—Redskins, 20-17 (W)
1997—Redskins, 24-10 (C)
1998—Redskins, 28-25 (C)
1999—Redskins, 38-36 (W)
(RS Pts.—Redskins 110, Panthers 88)

CHICAGO vs. ARIZONA
RS: Bears lead series, 52-26-6;
See Arizona vs. Chicago
CHICAGO vs. ATLANTA
RS: Falcons lead series, 10-9;
See Atlanta vs. Chicago
CHICAGO vs. BALTIMORE
RS: Bears lead series, 1-0;
See Baltimore vs. Chicago
CHICAGO vs. BUFFALO
RS: Bears lead series, 5-2;
See Buffalo vs. Chicago
CHICAGO vs. CAROLINA
RS: Bears lead series, 1-0;
See Carolina vs. Chicago
CHICAGO vs. CINCINNATI
RS: Bengals lead series, 4-2
1972—Bengals, 13-3 (Chi)
1980—Bengals, 17-14 (Chi) OT
1986—Bears, 44-7 (Cin)
1989—Bears, 17-14 (Chi)
1992—Bengals, 31-28 (Chi) OT
1995—Bengals, 16-10 (Cin)
(RS Pts.—Bears 116, Bengals 98)
CHICAGO vs. CLEVELAND
RS: Browns lead series, 8-3
1951—Browns, 42-21 (Cle)
1954—Browns, 39-10 (Chi)
1960—Browns, 42-0 (Cle)
1961—Bears, 17-14 (Chi)
1967—Browns, 24-0 (Cle)
1969—Browns, 28-24 (Chi)
1972—Bears, 17-0 (Cle)
1980—Browns, 27-21 (Cle)
1986—Bears, 41-31 (Chi)
1989—Browns, 27-7 (Cle)
1992—Browns, 27-14 (Cle)
(RS Pts.—Browns 301, Bears 172)
CHICAGO vs. DALLAS
RS: Cowboys lead series, 9-8
PS: Cowboys lead series, 2-0
1960—Bears, 17-7 (C)
1962—Bears, 34-33 (D)
1964—Cowboys, 24-10 (C)
1968—Cowboys, 34-3 (C)
1971—Bears, 23-19 (C)
1973—Cowboys, 20-17 (C)
1976—Cowboys, 31-21 (D)
1977—*Cowboys, 37-7 (D)
1979—Cowboys, 24-20 (D)
1981—Cowboys, 10-9 (D)
1984—Cowboys, 23-14 (C)
1985—Bears, 44-0 (D)
1986—Bears, 24-10 (D)
1988—Bears, 17-7 (C)
1991—**Cowboys, 17-13 (C)
1992—Cowboys, 27-14 (D)
1996—Bears, 22-6 (C)
1997—Cowboys, 27-3 (D)
1998—Bears, 13-12 (C)
(RS Pts.—Cowboys 314, Bears 305)
(PS Pts.—Cowboys 54, Bears 20)
**NFC Divisional Playoff*
***NFC First-Round Playoff*
CHICAGO vs. DENVER
RS: Broncos lead series, 6-5
1971—Broncos, 6-3 (D)
1973—Bears, 33-14 (D)
1976—Broncos, 28-14 (C)
1978—Broncos, 16-7 (D)
1981—Bears, 35-24 (C)
1983—Bears, 31-14 (C)
1984—Bears, 27-0 (C)
1987—Broncos, 31-29 (D)
1990—Bears, 16-13 (D) OT
1993—Broncos, 13-3 (C)
1996—Broncos, 17-12 (D)
(RS Pts.—Bears 210, Broncos 176)

CHICAGO vs. *DETROIT
RS: Bears lead series, 78-57-5
1930—Spartans, 7-6 (P)
Bears, 14-6 (C)
1931—Bears, 9-6 (C)
Spartans, 3-0 (P)
1932—Tie, 13-13 (C)
Tie, 7-7 (P)
Bears, 9-0 (C)
1933—Bears, 17-14 (C)
Bears, 17-7 (P)
1934—Bears, 19-16 (D)
Bears, 10-7 (C)
1935—Tie, 20-20 (C)
Lions, 14-2 (D)
1936—Bears, 12-10 (C)
Lions, 13-7 (D)
1937—Bears, 28-20 (C)
Bears, 13-0 (D)
1938—Lions, 13-7 (C)
Lions, 14-7 (D)
1939—Lions, 10-0 (C)
Bears, 23-13 (D)
1940—Bears, 7-0 (C)
Lions, 17-14 (D)
1941—Bears, 49-0 (C)
Bears, 24-7 (D)
1942—Bears, 16-0 (C)
Bears, 42-0 (D)
1943—Bears, 27-21 (D)
Bears, 35-14 (C)
1944—Tie, 21-21 (C)
Lions, 41-21 (D)
1945—Lions, 16-10 (D)
Lions, 35-28 (C)
1946—Bears, 42-6 (C)
Bears, 45-24 (D)
1947—Bears, 33-24 (C)
Bears, 34-14 (D)
1948—Bears, 28-0 (C)
Bears, 42-14 (D)
1949—Bears, 27-24 (C)
Bears, 28-7 (D)
1950—Bears, 35-21 (D)
Bears, 6-3 (C)
1951—Bears, 28-23 (D)
Lions, 41-28 (C)
1952—Bears, 24-23 (C)
Lions, 45-21 (D)
1953—Lions, 20-16 (C)
Lions, 13-7 (D)
1954—Lions, 48-23 (D)
Bears, 28-24 (C)
1955—Bears, 24-14 (D)
Bears, 21-20 (C)
1956—Lions, 42-10 (D)
Bears, 38-21 (C)
1957—Bears, 27-7 (D)
Lions, 21-13 (C)
1958—Bears, 20-7 (D)
Bears, 21-16 (C)
1959—Bears, 24-14 (D)
Bears, 25-14 (C)
1960—Bears, 28-7 (C)
Lions, 36-0 (D)
1961—Bears, 31-17 (D)
Lions, 16-15 (C)
1962—Lions, 11-3 (D)
Bears, 3-0 (C)
1963—Bears, 37-21 (D)
Bears, 24-14 (C)
1964—Lions, 10-0 (C)
Bears, 27-24 (D)
1965—Bears, 38-10 (C)
Bears, 17-10 (D)
1966—Lions, 14-3 (D)
Tie, 10-10 (C)
1967—Bears, 14-3 (C)
Bears, 27-13 (D)
1968—Lions, 42-0 (D)
Lions, 28-10 (C)
1969—Lions, 13-7 (D)
Lions, 20-3 (C)

1970—Lions, 28-14 (D)
Lions, 16-10 (C)
1971—Bears, 28-23 (D)
Lions, 28-3 (C)
1972—Lions, 38-24 (C)
Lions, 14-0 (D)
1973—Lions, 30-7 (C)
Lions, 40-7 (D)
1974—Bears, 17-9 (C)
Lions, 34-17 (D)
1975—Lions, 27-7 (D)
Bears, 25-21 (C)
1976—Bears, 10-3 (C)
Lions, 14-10 (D)
1977—Bears, 30-20 (C)
Bears, 31-14 (D)
1978—Bears, 19-0 (D)
Lions, 21-17 (C)
1979—Bears, 35-7 (C)
Lions, 20-0 (D)
1980—Bears, 24-7 (C)
Bears, 23-17 (D) OT
1981—Lions, 48-17 (D)
Lions, 23-7 (C)
1982—Lions, 17-10 (D)
Bears, 20-17 (C)
1983—Lions, 31-17 (D)
Lions, 38-17 (C)
1984—Bears, 16-14 (C)
Bears, 30-13 (D)
1985—Bears, 24-3 (C)
Bears, 37-17 (D)
1986—Bears, 13-7 (C)
Bears, 16-13 (D)
1987—Bears, 30-10 (C)
1988—Bears, 24-7 (D)
Bears, 13-12 (C)
1989—Bears, 47-27 (D)
Lions, 27-17 (C)
1990—Bears, 23-17 (C) OT
Lions, 38-21 (D)
1991—Bears, 20-10 (C)
Lions, 16-6 (D)
1992—Bears, 27-24 (C)
Lions, 16-3 (D)
1993—Bears, 10-6 (D)
Lions, 20-14 (C)
1994—Lions, 21-16 (D)
Bears, 20-10 (C)
1995—Lions, 24-17 (C)
Lions, 27-7 (D)
1996—Lions, 35-16 (D)
Bears, 31-14 (C)
1997—Lions, 32-7 (C)
Lions, 55-20 (D)
1998—Bears, 31-27 (C)
Lions, 26-3 (D)
1999—Lions, 21-17 (D)
Bears, 28-10 (C)
(RS Pts.—Bears 2,599, Lions 2,458)
Franchise in Portsmouth prior to 1934 and known as the Spartans

***CHICAGO vs. GREEN BAY**
RS: Bears lead series, 82-70-6
PS: Bears lead series, 1-0
1921—Staleys, 20-0 (C)
1923—Bears, 3-0 (GB)
1924—Bears, 3-0 (C)
1925—Packers, 14-10 (GB)
Bears, 21-0 (C)
1926—Tie, 6-6 (GB)
Bears, 19-13 (C)
Tie, 3-3 (C)
1927—Bears, 7-6 (GB)
Bears, 14-6 (C)
1928—Tie, 12-12 (GB)
Packers, 16-6 (C)
Packers, 6-0 (C)
1929—Packers, 23-0 (GB)
Packers, 14-0 (C)
Packers, 25-0 (C)
1930—Packers, 7-0 (GB)
Packers, 13-12 (C)
Bears, 21-0 (C)
1931—Packers, 7-0 (GB)
Packers, 6-2 (C)
Bears, 7-6 (C)
1932—Tie, 0-0 (GB)
Packers, 2-0 (C)
Bears, 9-0 (C)
1933—Bears, 14-7 (GB)
Bears, 10-7 (C)
Bears, 7-6 (C)
1934—Bears, 24-10 (GB)
Bears, 27-14 (C)
1935—Packers, 7-0 (GB)
Packers, 17-14 (C)
1936—Bears, 30-3 (GB)
Packers, 21-10 (C)
1937—Bears, 14-2 (GB)
Packers, 24-14 (C)
1938—Bears, 2-0 (GB)
Packers, 24-17 (C)
1939—Packers, 21-16 (GB)
Bears, 30-27 (C)
1940—Bears, 41-10 (GB)
Bears, 14-7 (C)
1941—Bears, 25-17 (GB)
Packers, 16-14 (C)
**Bears, 33-14 (C)
1942—Bears, 44-28 (GB)
Bears, 38-7 (C)
1943—Tie, 21-21 (GB)
Bears, 21-7 (C)
1944—Packers, 42-28 (GB)
Bears, 21-0 (C)
1945—Packers, 31-21 (GB)
Bears, 28-24 (C)
1946—Bears, 30-7 (GB)
Bears, 10-7 (C)
1947—Packers, 29-20 (GB)
Bears, 20-17 (C)
1948—Bears, 45-7 (GB)
Bears, 7-6 (C)
1949—Bears, 17-0 (GB)
Bears, 24-3 (C)
1950—Packers, 31-21 (GB)
Bears, 28-14 (C)
1951—Bears, 31-20 (GB)
Bears, 24-13 (C)
1952—Bears, 24-14 (GB)
Packers, 41-28 (C)
1953—Bears, 17-13 (GB)
Tie, 21-21 (C)
1954—Bears, 10-3 (GB)
Bears, 28-23 (C)
1955—Packers, 24-3 (GB)
Bears, 52-31 (C)
1956—Bears, 37-21 (GB)
Bears, 38-14 (C)
1957—Packers, 21-17 (GB)
Bears, 21-14 (C)
1958—Bears, 34-20 (GB)
Bears, 24-10 (C)
1959—Packers, 9-6 (GB)
Bears, 28-17 (C)
1960—Bears, 17-14 (GB)
Packers, 41-13 (C)
1961—Packers, 24-0 (GB)
Packers, 31-28 (C)
1962—Packers, 49-0 (GB)
Packers, 38-7 (C)
1963—Bears, 10-3 (GB)
Bears, 26-7 (C)
1964—Packers, 23-12 (GB)
Packers, 17-3 (C)
1965—Packers, 23-14 (GB)
Bears, 31-10 (C)
1966—Packers, 17-0 (C)
Packers, 13-6 (GB)
1967—Packers, 13-10 (GB)
Packers, 17-13 (C)
1968—Bears, 13-10 (GB)
Packers, 28-27 (C)
1969—Packers, 17-0 (GB)
Packers, 21-3 (C)
1970—Packers, 20-19 (GB)
Bears, 35-17 (C)
1971—Packers, 17-14 (C)
Packers, 31-10 (GB)
1972—Packers, 20-17 (GB)
Packers, 23-17 (C)
1973—Bears, 31-17 (GB)
Packers, 21-0 (C)
1974—Bears, 10-9 (C)
Packers, 20-3 (Mil)
1975—Bears, 27-14 (C)
Packers, 28-7 (GB)
1976—Bears, 24-13 (C)
Bears, 16-10 (GB)
1977—Bears, 26-0 (GB)
Bears, 21-10 (C)
1978—Packers, 24-14 (GB)
Bears, 14-0 (C)
1979—Bears, 6-3 (C)
Bears, 15-14 (GB)
1980—Packers, 12-6 (GB) OT
Bears, 61-7 (C)
1981—Packers, 16-9 (C)
Packers, 21-17 (GB)
1983—Packers, 31-28 (GB)
Bears, 23-21 (C)
1984—Bears, 9-7 (GB)
Packers, 20-14 (C)
1985—Bears, 23-7 (C)
Bears, 16-10 (GB)
1986—Bears, 25-12 (GB)
Bears, 12-10 (C)
1987—Bears, 26-24 (GB)
Bears, 23-10 (C)
1988—Bears, 24-6 (GB)
Bears, 16-0 (C)
1989—Packers, 14-13 (GB)
Packers, 40-28 (C)
1990—Bears, 31-13 (GB)
Bears, 27-13 (C)
1991—Bears, 10-0 (GB)
Bears, 27-13 (C)
1992—Bears, 30-10 (GB)
Packers, 17-3 (C)
1993—Packers, 17-3 (GB)
Bears, 30-17 (C)
1994—Packers, 33-6 (C)
Packers, 40-3 (GB)
1995—Packers, 27-24 (C)
Packers, 35-28 (GB)
1996—Packers, 37-6 (C)
Packers, 28-17 (GB)
1997—Packers, 38-24 (GB)
Packers, 24-23 (C)
1998—Packers, 26-20 (GB)
Packers, 16-13 (C)
1999—Bears, 14-13 (GB)
Packers, 35-19 (C)
(RS Pts.—Bears 2,675, Packers 2,482)
(PS Pts.—Bears 33, Packers 14)
**Bears known as Staleys prior to 1922*
***Division Playoff*

CHICAGO vs. *INDIANAPOLIS
RS: Colts lead series, 21-16
1953—Colts, 13-9 (B)
Colts, 16-14 (C)
1954—Bears, 28-9 (C)
Bears, 28-13 (B)
1955—Colts, 23-17 (B)
Bears, 38-10 (C)
1956—Colts, 28-21 (B)
Bears, 58-27 (C)
1957—Colts, 21-10 (B)
Colts, 29-14 (C)
1958—Colts, 51-38 (B)
Colts, 17-0 (C)
1959—Bears, 26-21 (B)
Colts, 21-7 (C)
1960—Colts, 42-7 (B)
Colts, 24-20 (C)
1961—Bears, 24-10 (C)
Bears, 21-20 (B)
1962—Bears, 35-15 (C)
Bears, 57-0 (B)
1963—Bears, 10-3 (C)
Bears, 17-7 (B)
1964—Colts, 52-0 (B)
Colts, 40-24 (C)
1965—Colts, 26-21 (C)
Bears, 13-0 (B)
1966—Bears, 27-17 (C)
Colts, 21-16 (B)
1967—Colts, 24-3 (C)
1968—Colts, 28-7 (B)
1969—Colts, 24-21 (C)
1970—Colts, 21-20 (B)
1975—Colts, 35-7 (C)
1983—Colts, 22-19 (B) OT
1985—Bears, 17-10 (C)
1988—Bears, 17-13 (I)
1991—Bears, 31-17 (I)
(RS Pts.—Colts 770, Bears 742)
**Franchise in Baltimore prior to 1984*

CHICAGO vs. JACKSONVILLE
RS: Series tied, 1-1
1995—Bears, 30-27 (J)
1998—Jaguars, 24-23 (C)
(RS Pts.—Bears 53, Jaguars 51)

CHICAGO vs. KANSAS CITY
RS: Bears lead series, 5-3
1973—Chiefs, 19-7 (KC)
1977—Bears, 28-27 (C)
1981—Bears, 16-13 (KC) OT
1987—Bears, 31-28 (C)
1990—Chiefs, 21-10 (C)
1993—Bears, 19-17 (KC)
1996—Chiefs, 14-10 (KC)
1999—Bears, 20-17 (C)
(RS Pts.—Chiefs 156, Bears 141)

CHICAGO vs. MIAMI
RS: Dolphins lead series, 5-3
1971—Dolphins, 34-3 (M)
1975—Dolphins, 46-13 (C)
1979—Dolphins, 31-16 (M)
1985—Dolphins, 38-24 (M)
1988—Bears, 34-7 (C)
1991—Dolphins, 16-13 (C) OT
1994—Bears, 17-14 (M)
1997—Bears, 36-33 (M) OT
(RS Pts.—Dolphins 219, Bears 156)

CHICAGO vs. MINNESOTA
RS: Vikings lead series, 42-33-2
PS: Bears lead series, 1-0
1961—Vikings, 37-13 (M)
Bears, 52-35 (C)
1962—Bears, 13-0 (M)
Bears, 31-30 (C)
1963—Bears, 28-7 (M)
Tie, 17-17 (C)
1964—Bears, 34-28 (M)
Vikings, 41-14 (C)
1965—Bears, 45-37 (M)
Vikings, 24-17 (C)
1966—Bears, 13-10 (M)
Bears, 41-28 (C)
1967—Bears, 17-7 (M)
Tie, 10-10 (C)
1968—Bears, 27-17 (M)
Bears, 26-24 (C)
1969—Vikings, 31-0 (C)
Vikings, 31-14 (M)
1970—Vikings, 24-0 (C)
Vikings, 16-13 (M)
1971—Bears, 20-17 (M)
Vikings, 27-10 (C)
1972—Bears, 13-10 (C)
Vikings, 23-10 (M)
1973—Vikings, 22-13 (C)
Vikings, 31-13 (M)
1974—Vikings, 11-7 (M)
Vikings, 17-0 (C)
1975—Vikings, 28-3 (M)
Vikings, 13-9 (C)
1976—Vikings, 20-19 (M)
Bears, 14-13 (C)
1977—Vikings, 22-16 (M) OT

ALL-TIME TEAM VS. TEAM RESULTS

Bears, 10-7 (C)
1978—Vikings, 24-20 (C)
Vikings, 17-14 (M)
1979—Bears, 26-7 (C)
Vikings, 30-27 (M)
1980—Vikings, 34-14 (C)
Vikings, 13-7 (M)
1981—Vikings, 24-21 (M)
Bears, 10-9 (C)
1982—Vikings, 35-7 (M)
1983—Vikings, 23-14 (C)
Bears, 19-13 (M)
1984—Bears, 16-7 (C)
Bears, 34-3 (M)
1985—Bears, 33-24 (M)
Bears, 27-9 (C)
1986—Bears, 23-0 (C)
Vikings, 23-7 (M)
1987—Bears, 27-7 (C)
Bears, 30-24 (M)
1988—Vikings, 31-7 (C)
Vikings, 28-27 (M)
1989—Bears, 38-7 (C)
Vikings, 27-16 (M)
1990—Bears, 19-16 (C)
Vikings, 41-13 (M)
1991—Bears, 10-6 (C)
Bears, 34-17 (M)
1992—Vikings, 21-20 (M)
Vikings, 38-10 (C)
1993—Vikings, 10-7 (M)
Vikings, 19-12 (C)
1994—Vikings, 42-14 (C)
Vikings, 33-27 (M) OT
*Bears, 35-18 (M)
1995—Bears, 31-14 (C)
Bears, 14-6 (M)
1996—Vikings, 20-14 (C)
Bears, 15-13 (M)
1997—Vikings, 27-24 (C)
Vikings, 29-22 (M)
1998—Vikings, 31-28 (C)
Vikings, 48-22 (M)
1999—Bears, 24-22 (M)
Vikings, 27-24 (C) OT
RS Pts.—Vikings 1,614, Bears 1,430)
(PS Pts.—Bears 35, Vikings 18)
NFC First-Round Playoff

CHICAGO vs. NEW ENGLAND
RS: Patriots lead series, 5-2
PS: Bears lead series, 1-0
1973—Patriots, 13-10 (C)
1979—Patriots, 27-7 (C)
1982—Bears, 26-13 (C)
1985—Bears, 20-7 (C)
*Bears, 46-10 (New Orleans)
1988—Patriots, 30-7 (NE)
1994—Patriots, 13-3 (C)
1997—Patriots, 31-3 (NE)
(RS Pts.—Patriots 134, Bears 76)
(PS Pts.—Bears 46, Patriots 10)
Super Bowl XX

CHICAGO vs. NEW ORLEANS
RS: Bears lead series, 10-8
PS: Bears lead series, 1-0
1968—Bears, 23-17 (NO)
1970—Bears, 24-3 (NO)
1971—Bears, 35-14 (C)
1973—Saints, 21-16 (NO)
1974—Bears, 24-10 (C)
1975—Bears, 42-17 (NO)
1977—Saints, 42-24 (C)
1980—Bears, 22-3 (C)
1982—Saints, 10-0 (C)
1983—Saints, 34-31 (NO) OT
1984—Bears, 20-7 (C)
1987—Saints, 19-17 (C)
1990—*Bears, 16-6 (C)
1991—Bears, 20-17 (NO)
1992—Saints, 28-6 (NO)
1994—Bears, 17-7 (C)
1996—Saints, 27-24 (NO)
1997—Saints, 20-17 (C)
1999—Bears, 14-10 (C)
(RS Pts.—Bears 376, Saints 306)
(PS Pts.—Bears 16, Saints 6)
NFC First-Round Playoff

CHICAGO vs. N.Y. GIANTS
RS: Bears lead series, 25-16-2
PS: Bears lead series, 5-3
1925—Bears, 19-7 (NY)
Giants, 9-0 (C)
1926—Bears, 7-0 (C)
1927—Giants, 13-7 (NY)
1928—Bears, 13-0 (C)
1929—Giants, 26-14 (C)
Giants, 34-0 (NY)
Giants, 14-9 (C)
1930—Giants, 12-0 (C)
Bears, 12-0 (NY)
1931—Bears, 6-0 (C)
Bears, 12-6 (NY)
Giants, 25-6 (C)
1932—Bears, 28-8 (NY)
Bears, 6-0 (C)
1933—Bears, 14-10 (C)
Giants, 3-0 (NY)
*Bears, 23-21 (C)
1934—Bears, 27-7 (C)
Bears, 10-9 (NY)
*Giants, 30-13 (NY)
1935—Bears, 20-3 (NY)
Giants, 3-0 (C)
1936—Bears, 25-7 (NY)
1937—Tie, 3-3 (NY)
1939—Giants, 16-13 (NY)
1940—Bears, 37-21 (NY)
1941—*Bears, 37-9 (C)
1942—Bears, 26-7 (NY)
1943—Bears, 56-7 (NY)
1946—Giants, 14-0 (NY)
*Bears, 24-14 (NY)
1948—Bears, 35-14 (C)
1949—Giants, 35-28 (NY)
1956—Tie, 17-17 (NY)
*Giants, 47-7 (NY)
1962—Giants, 26-24 (C)
1963—*Bears, 14-10 (C)
1965—Bears, 35-14 (NY)
1967—Bears, 34-7 (C)
1969—Giants, 28-24 (NY)
1970—Bears, 24-16 (NY)
1974—Bears, 16-13 (C)
1977—Bears, 12-9 (NY) OT
1985—**Bears, 21-0 (C)
1987—Bears, 34-19 (C)
1990—**Giants, 31-3 (NY)
1991—Bears, 20-17 (C)
1992—Giants, 27-14 (C)
1993—Giants, 26-20 (C)
1995—Bears, 27-24 (NY)
(RS Pts.—Bears 734, Giants 556)
(PS Pts.—Giants 162, Bears 142)
NFL Championship
**NFC Divisional Playoff*

CHICAGO vs. N.Y. JETS
RS: Bears lead series, 4-2
1974—Jets, 23-21 (C)
1979—Bears, 23-13 (C)
1985—Bears, 19-6 (NY)
1991—Bears, 19-13 (C) OT
1994—Bears, 19-7 (NY)
1997—Jets, 23-15 (C)
(RS Pts.—Bears 116, Jets 85)

CHICAGO vs. *OAKLAND
RS: Raiders lead series, 6-4
1972—Raiders, 28-21 (O)
1976—Raiders, 28-27 (C)
1978—Raiders, 25-19 (C) OT
1981—Bears, 23-6 (O)
1984—Bears, 17-6 (C)
1987—Bears, 6-3 (LA)
1990—Raiders, 24-10 (LA)
1993—Raiders, 16-14 (C)
1996—Bears, 19-17 (C)
1999—Raiders, 24-17 (O)
(RS Pts.—Raiders 177, Bears 173)
Franchise in Los Angeles from 1982-1994

CHICAGO vs. PHILADELPHIA
RS: Bears lead series, 24-5-1
PS: Series tied, 1-1
1933—Tie, 3-3 (P)
1935—Bears, 39-0 (P)
1936—Bears, 17-0 (P)
Bears, 28-7 (P)
1938—Bears, 28-6 (P)
1939—Bears, 27-14 (C)
1941—Bears, 49-14 (P)
1942—Bears, 45-14 (C)
1944—Bears, 28-7 (P)
1946—Bears, 21-14 (C)
1947—Bears, 40-7 (C)
1948—Eagles, 12-7 (P)
1949—Bears, 38-21 (C)
1955—Bears, 17-10 (C)
1961—Eagles, 16-14 (P)
1963—Bears, 16-7 (C)
1968—Bears, 29-16 (P)
1970—Bears, 20-16 (C)
1972—Bears, 21-12 (P)
1975—Bears, 15-13 (C)
1979—*Eagles, 27-17 (P)
1980—Eagles, 17-14 (P)
1983—Bears, 7-6 (P)
Bears, 17-14 (C)
1986—Bears, 13-10 (C) OT
1987—Bears, 35-3 (P)
1988—**Bears, 20-12 (C)
1989—Bears, 27-13 (C)
1993—Bears, 17-6 (P)
1994—Eagles, 30-22 (P)
1995—Bears, 20-14 (C)
1999—Eagles, 20-16 (C)
(RS Pts.—Bears 690, Eagles 342)
(PS Pts.—Eagles 39, Bears 37)
NFC First-Round Playoff
**NFC Divisional Playoff*

CHICAGO vs. *PITTSBURGH
RS: Bears lead series, 16-6-1
1934—Bears, 28-0 (P)
1935—Bears, 23-7 (P)
1936—Bears, 27-9 (P)
Bears, 26-6 (C)
1937—Bears, 7-0 (P)
1939—Bears, 32-0 (P)
1941—Bears, 34-7 (C)
1945—Bears, 28-7 (C)
1947—Bears, 49-7 (C)
1949—Bears, 30-21 (C)
1958—Steelers, 24-10 (P)
1959—Bears, 27-21 (C)
1963—Tie, 17-17 (P)
1967—Steelers, 41-13 (P)
1969—Bears, 38-7 (C)
1971—Bears, 17-15 (C)
1975—Steelers, 34-3 (P)
1980—Steelers, 38-3 (P)
1986—Bears, 13-10 (C) OT
1989—Bears, 20-0 (P)
1992—Bears, 30-6 (C)
1995—Steelers, 37-34 (C) OT
1998—Steelers, 17-12 (P)
(RS Pts.—Bears 521, Steelers 331)
Steelers known as Pirates prior to 1941

CHICAGO vs. *ST. LOUIS
RS: Bears lead series, 47-32-3
PS: Series tied, 1-1
1937—Bears, 20-2 (Clev)
Bears, 15-7 (C)
1938—Rams, 14-7 (C)
Rams, 23-21 (Clev)
1939—Bears, 30-21 (Clev)
Bears, 35-21 (C)
1940—Bears, 21-14 (Clev)
Bears, 47-25 (C)
1941—Bears, 48-21 (Clev)
Bears, 31-13 (C)
1942—Bears, 21-7 (Clev)
Bears, 47-0 (C)
1944—Rams, 19-7 (Clev)
Bears, 28-21 (C)
1945—Rams, 17-0 (Clev)
Rams, 41-21 (C)
1946—Tie, 28-28 (C)
Bears, 27-21 (LA)
1947—Bears, 41-21 (LA)
Rams, 17-14 (C)
1948—Bears, 42-21 (C)
Bears, 21-6 (LA)
1949—Rams, 31-16 (C)
Rams, 27-24 (LA)
1950—Bears, 24-20 (LA)
Bears, 24-14 (C)
**Rams, 24-14 (LA)
1951—Rams, 42-17 (C)
1952—Rams, 31-7 (LA)
Rams, 40-24 (C)
1953—Rams, 38-24 (LA)
Bears, 24-21 (C)
1954—Rams, 42-38 (LA)
Bears, 24-13 (C)
1955—Bears, 31-20 (LA)
Bears, 24-3 (C)
1956—Bears, 35-24 (LA)
Bears, 30-21 (C)
1957—Bears, 34-26 (C)
Bears, 16-10 (LA)
1958—Bears, 31-10 (C)
Rams, 41-35 (LA)
1959—Rams, 28-21 (C)
Bears, 26-21 (LA)
1960—Bears, 34-27 (C)
Tie, 24-24 (LA)
1961—Bears, 21-17 (LA)
Bears, 28-24 (C)
1962—Bears, 27-23 (LA)
Bears, 30-14 (C)
1963—Bears, 52-14 (LA)
Bears, 6-0 (C)
1964—Bears, 38-17 (C)
Bears, 34-24 (LA)
1965—Rams, 30-28 (LA)
Bears, 31-6 (C)
1966—Rams, 31-17 (LA)
Bears, 17-10 (C)
1967—Rams, 28-17 (C)
1968—Bears, 17-16 (LA)
1969—Rams, 9-7 (C)
1971—Rams, 17-3 (LA)
1972—Tie, 13-13 (C)
1973—Rams, 26-0 (C)
1975—Rams, 38-10 (LA)
1976—Rams, 20-12 (LA)
1977—Bears, 24-23 (C)
1979—Bears, 27-23 (C)
1981—Rams, 24-7 (C)
1982—Bears, 34-26 (LA)
1983—Rams, 21-14 (LA)
1984—Rams, 29-13 (LA)
1985—***Bears, 24-0 (C)
1986—Rams, 20-17 (C)
1988—Rams, 23-3 (LA)
1989—Bears, 20-10 (C)
1990—Bears, 38-9 (C)
1993—Rams, 20-6 (LA)
1994—Bears, 27-13 (C)
1995—Rams, 34-28 (StL)
1996—Bears, 35-9 (C)
1997—Bears, 13-10 (StL)
1998—Rams, 20-12 (C)
1999—Rams, 34-12 (StL)
(RS Pts.—Bears 1,897, Rams 1,679)
(PS Pts.—Bears 38, Rams 24)
Franchise in Los Angeles prior to 1995 and in Cleveland prior to 1946
**Conference Playoff*
***NFC Championship*

CHICAGO vs. SAN DIEGO
RS: Series tied, 4-4
1970—Chargers, 20-7 (C)
1974—Chargers, 28-21 (SD)

1978—Chargers, 40-7 (SD)
1981—Bears, 20-17 (C) OT
1984—Chargers, 20-7 (SD)
1993—Bears, 16-13 (SD)
1996—Bears, 27-14 (C)
1999—Bears, 23-20 (SD) OT
(RS Pts.—Chargers 172, Bears 128)

CHICAGO vs. SAN FRANCISCO
RS: Series tied, 25-25-1
PS: 49ers lead series, 3-0
1950—Bears, 32-20 (SF)
Bears, 17-0 (C)
1951—Bears, 13-7 (C)
1952—49ers, 40-16 (C)
Bears, 20-17 (SF)
1953—49ers, 35-28 (C)
49ers, 24-14 (SF)
1954—49ers, 31-24 (C)
Bears, 31-27 (SF)
1955—49ers, 20-19 (C)
Bears, 34-23 (SF)
1956—Bears, 31-7 (C)
Bears, 38-21 (SF)
1957—49ers, 21-17 (C)
49ers, 21-17 (SF)
1958—Bears, 28-6 (C)
Bears, 27-14 (SF)
1959—49ers, 20-17 (SF)
Bears, 14-3 (C)
1960—Bears, 27-10 (C)
49ers, 25-7 (SF)
1961—Bears, 31-0 (C)
49ers, 41-31 (SF)
1962—Bears, 30-14 (SF)
49ers, 34-27 (C)
1963—49ers, 20-14 (SF)
Bears, 27-7 (C)
1964—49ers, 31-21 (SF)
Bears, 23-21 (C)
1965—49ers, 52-24 (SF)
Bears, 61-20 (C)
1966—Tie, 30-30 (C)
49ers, 41-14 (SF)
1967—Bears, 28-14 (SF)
1968—Bears, 27-19 (C)
1969—49ers, 42-21 (SF)
1970—49ers, 37-16 (C)
1971—49ers, 13-0 (SF)
1972—49ers, 34-21 (C)
1974—49ers, 34-0 (C)
1975—49ers, 31-3 (SF)
1976—Bears, 19-12 (SF)
1978—Bears, 16-13 (SF)
1979—Bears, 28-27 (SF)
1981—49ers, 28-17 (SF)
1983—Bears, 13-3 (C)
1984—*49ers, 23-0 (SF)
1985—Bears, 26-10 (SF)
1987—49ers, 41-0 (SF)
1988—Bears, 10-9 (C)
*49ers, 28-3 (C)
1989—49ers, 26-0 (SF)
1991—49ers, 52-14 (SF)
1994—**49ers, 44-15 (SF)
(RS Pts.—49ers 1,148, Bears 1,063)
(PS Pts.—49ers 95, Bears 18)
NFC Championship
***NFC Divisional Playoff*

CHICAGO vs. SEATTLE
RS: Seahawks lead series, 5-2
1976—Bears, 34-7 (S)
1978—Seahawks, 31-29 (C)
1982—Seahawks, 20-14 (S)
1984—Seahawks, 38-9 (S)
1987—Seahawks, 34-21 (C)
1990—Bears, 17-0 (C)
1999—Seahawks, 14-13 (C)
(RS Pts.—Seahawks 144, Bears 137)

CHICAGO vs. TAMPA BAY
RS: Bears lead series, 30-14
1977—Bears, 10-0 (TB)
1978—Buccaneers, 33-19 (TB)
Bears, 14-3 (C)
1979—Buccaneers, 17-13 (C)
Bears, 14-0 (TB)
1980—Bears, 23-0 (C)
Bears, 14-13 (TB)
1981—Bears, 28-17 (C)
Buccaneers, 20-10 (TB)
1982—Buccaneers, 26-23 (TB) OT
1983—Bears, 17-10 (C)
Bears, 27-0 (TB)
1984—Bears, 34-14 (C)
Bears, 44-9 (TB)
1985—Bears, 38-28 (C)
Bears, 27-19 (TB)
1986—Bears, 23-3 (TB)
Bears, 48-14 (C)
1987—Bears, 20-3 (C)
Bears, 27-26 (TB)
1988—Bears, 28-10 (C)
Bears, 27-15 (TB)
1989—Buccaneers, 42-35 (TB)
Buccaneers, 32-31 (C)
1990—Bears, 26-6 (TB)
Bears, 27-14 (C)
1991—Bears, 21-20 (TB)
Bears, 27-0 (C)
1992—Bears, 31-14 (C)
Buccaneers, 20-17 (TB)
1993—Bears, 47-17 (C)
Buccaneers, 13-10 (TB)
1994—Bears, 21-9 (C)
Bears, 20-6 (TB)
1995—Bears, 25-6 (TB)
Bears, 31-10 (C)
1996—Bears, 13-10 (C)
Buccaneers, 34-19 (TB)
1997—Bears, 13-7 (C)
Buccaneers, 31-15 (TB)
1998—Buccaneers, 27-15 (TB)
Buccaneers, 31-17 (C)
1999—Buccaneers, 6-3 (TB)
Buccaneers, 20-6 (C)
(RS Pts.—Bears 998, Buccaneers 655)

CHICAGO vs. *TENNESSEE
RS: Series tied, 4-4
1973—Bears, 35-14 (C)
1977—Oilers, 47-0 (H)
1980—Oilers, 10-6 (C)
1986—Bears, 20-7 (H)
1989—Oilers, 33-28 (C)
1992—Oilers, 24-7 (H)
1995—Bears, 35-32 (C)
1998—Bears, 23-20 (T)
(RS Pts.—Titans 187, Bears 154)
**Franchise in Houston prior to 1997; known as Oilers prior to 1999*

CHICAGO vs. *WASHINGTON
RS: Bears lead series, 18-15-1
PS: Redskins lead series, 4-3
1932—Tie, 7-7 (B)
1933—Bears, 7-0 (C)
Redskins, 10-0 (B)
1934—Bears, 21-0 (B)
1935—Bears, 30-14 (B)
1936—Bears, 26-0 (B)
1937—**Redskins, 28-21 (C)
1938—Bears, 31-7 (C)
1940—Redskins, 7-3 (W)
**Bears, 73-0 (W)
1941—Bears, 35-21 (C)
1942—**Redskins, 14-6 (W)
1943—Redskins, 21-7 (W)
**Bears, 41-21 (C)
1945—Redskins, 28-21 (W)
1946—Bears, 24-20 (C)
1947—Bears, 56-20 (W)
1948—Bears, 48-13 (C)
1949—Bears, 31-21 (W)
1951—Bears, 27-0 (W)
1953—Bears, 27-24 (W)
1957—Redskins, 14-3 (C)
1964—Redskins, 27-20 (W)
1968—Redskins, 38-28 (C)
1971—Bears, 16-15 (C)
1974—Redskins, 42-0 (W)
1976—Bears, 33-7 (C)
1978—Bears, 14-10 (W)
1980—Bears, 35-21 (C)
1981—Redskins, 24-7 (C)
1984—***Bears, 23-19 (W)
1985—Bears, 45-10 (C)
1986—***Redskins, 27-13 (C)
1987—***Redskins, 21-17 (C)
1988—Bears, 34-14 (W)
1989—Redskins, 38-14 (W)
1990—Redskins, 10-9 (W)
1991—Redskins, 20-7 (C)
1996—Redskins, 10-3 (W)
1997—Redskins, 31-8 (C)
1999—Redskins, 48-22 (W)
(RS Pts.—Bears 699, Redskins 592)
(PS Pts.—Bears 194, Redskins 130)
**Franchise in Boston prior to 1937 and known as Braves prior to 1933*
***NFL Championship*
****NFC Divisional Playoff*

CINCINNATI vs. ARIZONA
RS: Bengals lead series, 4-2;
See Arizona vs. Cincinnati

CINCINNATI vs. ATLANTA
RS: Bengals lead series, 7-2;
See Atlanta vs. Cincinnati

CINCINNATI vs. BALTIMORE
RS: Ravens lead series, 5-3;
See Baltimore vs. Cincinnati

CINCINNATI vs. BUFFALO
RS: Series tied, 9-9
PS: Bengals lead series, 2-0;
See Buffalo vs. Cincinnati

CINCINNATI vs. CAROLINA
RS: Panthers lead series, 1-0;
See Carolina vs. Cincinnati

CINCINNATI vs. CHICAGO
RS: Bengals lead series, 4-2;
See Chicago vs. Cincinnati

CINCINNATI vs. CLEVELAND
RS: Browns lead series, 27-26
1970—Browns, 30-27 (Cle)
Bengals, 14-10 (Cin)
1971—Browns, 27-24 (Cin)
Browns, 31-27 (Cle)
1972—Browns, 27-6 (Cle)
Browns, 27-24 (Cin)
1973—Browns, 17-10 (Cle)
Bengals, 34-17 (Cin)
1974—Bengals, 33-7 (Cin)
Bengals, 34-24 (Cle)
1975—Bengals, 24-17 (Cin)
Browns, 35-23 (Cle)
1976—Bengals, 45-24 (Cle)
Bengals, 21-6 (Cin)
1977—Browns, 13-3 (Cin)
Bengals, 10-7 (Cle)
1978—Browns, 13-10 (Cle) OT
Bengals, 48-16 (Cin)
1979—Browns, 28-27 (Cle)
Bengals, 16-12 (Cin)
1980—Browns, 31-7 (Cle)
Browns, 27-24 (Cin)
1981—Browns, 20-17 (Cin)
Bengals, 41-21 (Cle)
1982—Bengals, 23-10 (Cin)
1983—Browns, 17-7 (Cle)
Bengals, 28-21 (Cin)
1984—Bengals, 12-9 (Cin)
Bengals, 20-17 (Cle) OT
1985—Bengals, 27-10 (Cin)
Browns, 24-6 (Cle)
1986—Bengals, 30-13 (Cle)
Browns, 34-3 (Cin)
1987—Browns, 34-0 (Cin)
Browns, 38-24 (Cle)
1988—Bengals, 24-17 (Cin)
Browns, 23-16 (Cle)
1989—Bengals, 21-14 (Cin)
Bengals, 21-0 (Cle)
1990—Bengals, 34-13 (Cle)
Bengals, 21-14 (Cin)
1991—Browns, 14-13 (Cle)
Bengals, 23-21 (Cin)
1992—Bengals, 30-10 (Cin)
Browns, 37-21 (Cle)
1993—Browns, 27-14 (Cle)
Browns, 28-17 (Cin)
1994—Browns, 28-20 (Cin)
Browns, 37-13 (Cle)
1995—Browns, 29-26 (Cin) OT
Browns, 26-10 (Cle)
1999—Bengals, 18-17 (Cle)
Bengals, 44-28 (Cin)
(RS Pts.—Bengals 1,115, Browns 1,097)

CINCINNATI vs. DALLAS
RS: Cowboys lead series, 4-3
1973—Cowboys, 38-10 (D)
1979—Cowboys, 38-13 (D)
1985—Bengals, 50-24 (C)
1988—Bengals, 38-24 (D)
1991—Cowboys, 35-23 (D)
1994—Cowboys, 23-20 (C)
1997—Bengals, 31-24 (C)
(RS Pts.—Cowboys 206, Bengals 185)

CINCINNATI vs. DENVER
RS: Broncos lead series, 14-6
1968—Bengals, 24-10 (C)
Broncos, 10-7 (D)
1969—Broncos, 30-23 (C)
Broncos, 27-16 (D)
1971—Bengals, 24-10 (D)
1972—Bengals, 21-10 (C)
1973—Broncos, 28-10 (D)
1975—Bengals, 17-16 (D)
1976—Bengals, 17-7 (C)
1977—Broncos, 24-13 (C)
1979—Broncos, 10-0 (D)
1981—Bengals, 38-21 (C)
1983—Broncos, 24-17 (D)
1984—Broncos, 20-17 (D)
1986—Broncos, 34-28 (D)
1991—Broncos, 45-14 (D)
1994—Broncos, 15-13 (D)
1996—Broncos, 14-10 (C)
1997—Broncos, 38-20 (D)
1998—Broncos, 33-26 (C)
(RS Pts.—Broncos 426, Bengals 355)

CINCINNATI vs. DETROIT
RS: Bengals lead series, 4-3
1970—Lions, 38-3 (D)
1974—Lions, 23-19 (C)
1983—Bengals, 17-9 (C)
1986—Bengals, 24-17 (D)
1989—Bengals, 42-7 (C)
1992—Lions, 19-13 (C)
1998—Bengals, 34-28 (D) OT
(RS Pts.—Bengals 152, Lions 141)

CINCINNATI vs. GREEN BAY
RS: Packers lead series, 5-4
1971—Packers, 20-17 (GB)
1976—Bengals, 28-7 (C)
1977—Bengals, 17-7 (Mil)
1980—Packers, 14-9 (GB)
1983—Bengals, 34-14 (C)
1986—Bengals, 34-28 (Mil)
1992—Packers, 24-23 (GB)
1995—Packers, 24-10 (GB)
1998—Packers, 13-6 (C)
(RS Pts.—Bengals 178, Packers 151)

CINCINNATI vs. *INDIANAPOLIS
RS: Colts lead series, 11-8
PS: Colts lead series, 1-0
1970—**Colts, 17-0 (B)
1972—Colts, 20-19 (C)
1974—Bengals, 24-14 (B)
1976—Colts, 28-27 (B)
1979—Colts, 38-28 (B)
1980—Bengals, 34-33 (C)
1981—Bengals, 41-19 (B)
1982—Bengals, 20-17 (B)
1983—Colts, 34-31 (C)
1987—Bengals, 23-21 (I)

ALL-TIME TEAM VS. TEAM RESULTS

1989—Colts, 23-12 (C)
1990—Colts, 34-20 (C)
1992—Colts, 21-17 (C)
1993—Colts, 9-6 (C)
1994—Colts, 17-13 (C)
1995—Bengals, 24-21 (I) OT
1996—Bengals, 31-24 (C)
1997—Bengals, 28-13 (I)
1998—Colts, 39-26 (I)
1999—Colts, 31-10 (I)
(RS Pts.—Colts 456, Bengals 434)
(PS Pts.—Colts 17, Bengals 0)
Franchise in Baltimore prior to 1984
**AFC Divisional Playoff*

CINCINNATI vs. JACKSONVILLE
RS: Jaguars lead series, 6-4
1995—Bengals, 24-17 (C)
Bengals, 17-13 (J)
1996—Bengals, 28-21 (C)
Jaguars, 30-27 (J)
1997—Jaguars, 21-13 (J)
Bengals, 31-26 (C)
1998—Jaguars, 24-11 (J)
Jaguars, 34-17 (C)
1999—Jaguars, 41-10 (C)
Jaguars, 24-7 (J)
(RS Pts.—Jaguars 251, Bengals 185)

CINCINNATI vs. KANSAS CITY
RS: Chiefs lead series, 11-9
1968—Chiefs, 13-3 (KC)
Chiefs, 16-9 (C)
1969—Bengals, 24-19 (C)
Chiefs, 42-22 (KC)
1970—Chiefs, 27-19 (C)
1972—Bengals, 23-16 (KC)
1973—Bengals, 14-6 (C)
1974—Bengals, 33-6 (C)
1976—Bengals, 27-24 (KC)
1977—Bengals, 27-7 (KC)
1978—Chiefs, 24-23 (C)
1979—Chiefs, 10-7 (C)
1980—Bengals, 20-6 (KC)
1983—Chiefs, 20-15 (KC)
1984—Chiefs, 27-22 (C)
1986—Chiefs, 24-14 (KC)
1987—Bengals, 30-27 (C) OT
1988—Chiefs, 31-28 (KC)
1989—Bengals, 21-17 (KC)
1993—Chiefs, 17-15 (KC)
(RS Pts.—Bengals 396, Chiefs 379)

CINCINNATI vs. MIAMI
RS: Dolphins lead series, 11-3
PS: Dolphins lead series, 1-0
1968—Dolphins, 24-22 (C)
Bengals, 38-21 (M)
1969—Bengals, 27-21 (C)
1971—Dolphins, 23-13 (C)
1973—*Dolphins, 34-16 (M)
1974—Dolphins, 24-3 (M)
1977—Bengals, 23-17 (C)
1978—Dolphins, 21-0 (M)
1980—Dolphins, 17-16 (M)
1983—Dolphins, 38-14 (M)
1987—Dolphins, 20-14 (C)
1989—Dolphins, 20-13 (C)
1991—Dolphins, 37-13 (M)
1994—Dolphins, 23-7 (C)
1995—Dolphins, 26-23 (C)
(RS Pts.—Dolphins 332, Bengals 226)
(PS Pts.—Dolphins 34, Bengals 16)
AFC Divisional Playoff

CINCINNATI vs. MINNESOTA
RS: Vikings lead series, 5-4
1973—Bengals, 27-0 (C)
1977—Vikings, 42-10 (M)
1980—Bengals, 14-0 (C)
1983—Vikings, 20-14 (M)
1986—Bengals, 24-20 (C)
1989—Vikings, 29-21 (M)
1992—Vikings, 42-7 (C)
1995—Bengals, 27-24 (C)
1998—Vikings, 24-3 (M)
(RS Pts.—Vikings 201, Bengals 147)

CINCINNATI vs. *NEW ENGLAND
RS: Patriots lead series, 9-7
1968—Patriots, 33-14 (B)
1969—Patriots, 25-14 (C)
1970—Bengals, 45-7 (C)
1972—Bengals, 31-7 (NE)
1975—Bengals, 27-10 (C)
1978—Patriots, 10-3 (C)
1979—Patriots, 20-14 (C)
1984—Patriots, 20-14 (NE)
1985—Patriots, 34-23 (NE)
1986—Bengals, 31-7 (NE)
1988—Patriots, 27-21 (NE)
1990—Bengals, 41-7 (C)
1991—Bengals, 29-7 (C)
1992—Bengals, 20-10 (C)
1993—Patriots, 7-2 (NE)
1994—Patriots, 31-28 (C)
(RS Pts.—Bengals 357, Patriots 262)
Franchise in Boston prior to 1971

CINCINNATI vs. NEW ORLEANS
RS: Saints lead series, 5-4
1970—Bengals, 26-6 (C)
1975—Bengals, 21-0 (NO)
1978—Saints, 20-18 (C)
1981—Saints, 17-7 (NO)
1984—Bengals, 24-21 (NO)
1987—Saints, 41-24 (C)
1990—Saints, 21-7 (C)
1993—Saints, 20-13 (NO)
1996—Bengals, 30-15 (C))
(RS Pts.—Bengals 170, Saints 161)

CINCINNATI vs. N.Y. GIANTS
RS: Bengals lead series, 4-2
1972—Bengals, 13-10 (C)
1977—Bengals, 30-13 (C)
1985—Bengals, 35-30 (C)
1991—Bengals, 27-24 (C)
1994—Giants, 27-20 (NY)
1997—Giants, 29-27 (NY)
(RS Pts.—Bengals 152, Giants 133)

CINCINNATI vs. N.Y. JETS
RS: Jets lead series, 10-6
PS: Jets lead series, 1-0
1968—Jets, 27-14 (NY)
1969—Jets, 21-7 (C)
Jets, 40-7 (NY)
1971—Jets, 35-21 (NY)
1973—Bengals, 20-14 (C)
1976—Bengals, 42-3 (NY)
1981—Bengals, 31-30 (NY)
1982—*Jets, 44-17 (C)
1984—Jets, 43-23 (NY)
1985—Jets, 29-20 (C)
1986—Bengals, 52-21 (C)
1987—Jets, 27-20 (NY)
1988—Bengals, 36-19 (C)
1990—Bengals, 25-20 (C)
1992—Jets, 17-14 (NY)
1993—Jets, 17-12 (NY)
1997—Jets, 31-14 (C)
(RS Pts.—Jets 394, Bengals 358)
(PS Pts.—Jets 44, Bengals 17)
AFC First-Round Playoff

CINCINNATI vs. *OAKLAND
RS: Raiders lead series, 16-7
PS: Raiders lead series, 2-0
1968—Raiders, 31-10 (O)
Raiders, 34-0 (C)
1969—Bengals, 31-17 (C)
Raiders, 37-17 (O)
1970—Bengals, 31-21 (C)
1971—Raiders, 31-27 (O)
1972—Raiders, 20-14 (C)
1974—Raiders, 30-27 (O)
1975—Bengals, 14-10 (C)
**Raiders, 31-28 (O)
1976—Raiders, 35-20 (O)
1978—Raiders, 34-21 (C)
1980—Raiders, 28-17 (O)
1982—Bengals, 31-17 (C)
1983—Raiders, 20-10 (C)
1985—Raiders, 13-6 (LA)
1988—Bengals, 45-21 (LA)
1989—Raiders, 28-7 (LA)
1990—Raiders, 24-7 (LA)
**Raiders, 20-10 (LA)
1991—Raiders, 38-14 (C)
1992—Bengals, 24-21 (C) OT
1993—Bengals, 16-10 (C)
1995—Raiders, 20-17 (C)
1998—Raiders, 27-10 (O)
(RS Pts.—Raiders 567, Bengals 416)
(PS Pts.—Raiders 51, Bengals 38)
Franchise in Los Angeles from 1982-1994
**AFC Divisional Playoff*

CINCINNATI vs. PHILADELPHIA
RS: Bengals lead series, 6-2
1971—Bengals, 37-14 (C)
1975—Bengals, 31-0 (P)
1979—Bengals, 37-13 (C)
1982—Bengals, 18-14 (P)
1988—Bengals, 28-24 (P)
1991—Eagles, 17-10 (P)
1994—Bengals, 33-30 (C)
1997—Eagles, 44-42 (P)
(RS Pts.—Bengals 236, Eagles 156)

CINCINNATI vs. PITTSBURGH
RS: Steelers lead series, 33-26
1970—Steelers, 21-10 (P)
Bengals, 34-7 (C)
1971—Steelers, 21-10 (P)
Steelers, 21-13 (C)
1972—Bengals, 15-10 (C)
Steelers, 40-17 (P)
1973—Bengals, 19-7 (C)
Steelers, 20-13 (P)
1974—Bengals, 17-10 (C)
Steelers, 27-3 (P)
1975—Steelers, 30-24 (C)
Steelers, 35-14 (P)
1976—Steelers, 23-6 (P)
Steelers, 7-3 (C)
1977—Steelers, 20-14 (P)
Bengals, 17-10 (C)
1978—Steelers, 28-3 (C)
Steelers, 7-6 (P)
1979—Bengals, 34-10 (C)
Steelers, 37-17 (P)
1980—Bengals, 30-28 (C)
Bengals, 17-16 (P)
1981—Bengals, 34-7 (C)
Bengals, 17-10 (P)
1982—Steelers, 26-20 (P) OT
1983—Steelers, 24-14 (C)
Bengals, 23-10 (P)
1984—Steelers, 38-17 (P)
Bengals, 22-20 (C)
1985—Bengals, 37-24 (P)
Bengals, 26-21 (C)
1986—Bengals, 24-22 (C)
Steelers, 30-9 (P)
1987—Steelers, 23-20 (P)
Steelers, 30-16 (C)
1988—Bengals, 17-12 (P)
Bengals, 42-7 (C)
1989—Bengals, 41-10 (C)
Bengals, 26-16 (P)
1990—Bengals, 27-3 (C)
Bengals, 16-12 (P)
1991—Steelers, 33-27 (C) OT
Steelers, 17-10 (P)
1992—Steelers, 20-0 (P)
Steelers, 21-9 (C)
1993—Steelers, 34-7 (P)
Steelers, 24-16 (C)
1994—Steelers, 14-10 (P)
Steelers, 38-15 (C)
1995—Bengals, 27-9 (P)
Steelers, 49-31 (C)
1996—Steelers, 20-10 (P)
Bengals, 34-24 (C)
1997—Steelers, 26-10 (C)
Steelers, 20-3 (P)
1998—Bengals, 25-20 (C)
Bengals, 25-24 (P)
1999—Steelers, 17-3 (C)
Bengals, 27-20 (P)
(RS Pts.—Steelers 1,210, Bengals 1,073)

CINCINNATI vs. *ST. LOUIS
RS: Bengals lead series, 5-4
1972—Rams, 15-12 (LA)
1976—Bengals, 20-12 (C)
1978—Bengals, 20-19 (LA)
1981—Bengals, 24-10 (C)
1984—Rams, 24-14 (C)
1990—Bengals, 34-31 (LA) OT
1993—Bengals, 15-3 (C)
1996—Rams, 26-16 (StL)
1999—Rams, 38-10 (C)
(RS Pts.—Rams 178, Bengals 165)
Franchise in Los Angeles prior to 1995

CINCINNATI vs. SAN DIEGO
RS: Chargers lead series, 15-9
PS: Bengals lead series, 1-0
1968—Chargers, 29-13 (SD)
Chargers, 31-10 (C)
1969—Bengals, 34-20 (C)
Chargers, 21-14 (SD)
1970—Bengals, 17-14 (SD)
1971—Bengals, 31-0 (C)
1973—Bengals, 20-13 (SD)
1974—Chargers, 20-17 (C)
1975—Bengals, 47-17 (C)
1977—Chargers, 24-3 (SD)
1978—Chargers, 22-13 (SD)
1979—Chargers, 26-24 (C)
1980—Chargers, 31-14 (C)
1981—Bengals, 40-17 (SD)
*Bengals, 27-7 (C)
1982—Chargers, 50-34 (SD)
1985—Chargers, 44-41 (C)
1987—Chargers, 10-9 (C)
1988—Bengals, 27-10 (C)
1990—Bengals, 21-16 (SD)
1992—Chargers, 27-10 (SD)
1994—Chargers, 27-10 (SD)
1996—Chargers, 27-14 (SD)
1997—Bengals, 38-31 (C)
1999—Chargers, 34-7 (C)
(RS Pts.—Chargers 561, Bengals 508)
(PS Pts.—Bengals 27, Chargers 7)
AFC Championship

CINCINNATI vs. SAN FRANCISCO
RS: 49ers lead series, 7-2
PS: 49ers lead series, 2-0
1974—Bengals, 21-3 (SF)
1978—49ers, 28-12 (SF)
1981—49ers, 21-3 (C)
*49ers, 26-21 (Detroit)
1984—49ers, 23-17 (SF)
1987—49ers, 27-26 (C)
1988—**49ers, 20-16 (Miami)
1990—49ers, 20-17 (C) OT
1993—49ers, 21-8 (SF)
1996—49ers, 28-21 (SF)
1999—Bengals, 44-30 (C)
(RS Pts.—49ers 201, Bengals 169)
(PS Pts.—49ers 46, Bengals 37)
Super Bowl XVI
**Super Bowl XXIII*

CINCINNATI vs. SEATTLE
RS: Seahawks lead series, 8-7
PS: Bengals lead series, 1-0
1977—Bengals, 42-20 (C)
1981—Bengals, 27-21 (C)
1982—Bengals, 24-10 (C)
1984—Seahawks, 26-6 (C)
1985—Seahawks, 28-24 (C)
1986—Bengals, 34-7 (C)
1987—Bengals, 17-10 (S)
1988—*Bengals, 21-13 (C)
1989—Seahawks, 24-17 (C)
1990—Seahawks, 31-16 (S)
1991—Seahawks, 13-7 (C)
1992—Bengals, 21-3 (S)
1993—Seahawks, 19-10 (C)
1994—Bengals, 20-17 (S) OT

1995—Seahawks, 24-21 (S)
1999—Seahawks, 37-20 (S)
(RS Pts.—Bengals 306, Seahawks 290)
(PS Pts.—Bengals 21, Seahawks 13)
*AFC Divisional Playoff

CINCINNATI vs. TAMPA BAY
RS: Series tied, 3-3
1976—Bengals, 21-0 (C)
1980—Buccaneers, 17-12 (C)
1983—Bengals, 23-17 (TB)
1989—Bengals, 56-23 (C)
1995—Buccaneers, 19-16 (TB)
1998—Buccaneers, 35-0 (C)
(RS Pts.—Bengals 128, Buccaneers 111)

CINCINNATI vs. *TENNESSEE
RS: Titans lead series, 33-28-1
PS: Bengals lead series, 1-0
1968—Oilers, 27-17 (C)
1969—Tie, 31-31 (H)
1970—Oilers, 20-13 (C)
Bengals, 30-20 (H)
1971—Oilers, 10-6 (H)
Bengals, 28-13 (C)
1972—Bengals, 30-7 (C)
Bengals, 61-17 (H)
1973—Bengals, 24-10 (C)
Bengals, 27-24 (H)
1974—Oilers, 34-21 (C)
Oilers, 20-3 (H)
1975—Bengals, 21-19 (H)
Bengals, 23-19 (C)
1976—Bengals, 27-7 (H)
Bengals, 31-27 (C)
1977—Bengals, 13-10 (C) OT
Oilers, 21-16 (H)
1978—Bengals, 28-13 (C)
Oilers, 17-10 (H)
1979—Oilers, 30-27 (C) OT
Oilers, 42-21 (H)
1980—Oilers, 13-10 (C)
Oilers, 23-3 (H)
1981—Oilers, 17-10 (H)
Bengals, 34-21 (C)
1982—Bengals, 27-6 (C)
Bengals, 35-27 (H)
1983—Bengals, 55-14 (H)
Bengals, 38-10 (C)
1984—Bengals, 13-3 (C)
Bengals, 31-13 (H)
1985—Oilers, 44-27 (H)
Bengals, 45-27 (C)
1986—Bengals, 31-28 (C)
Oilers, 32-28 (H)
1987—Oilers, 31-29 (C)
Oilers, 21-17 (H)
1988—Bengals, 44-21 (C)
Oilers, 41-6 (H)
1989—Oilers, 26-24 (H)
Bengals, 61-7 (C)
1990—Oilers, 48-17 (H)
Bengals, 40-20 (C)
**Bengals, 41-14 (C)
1991—Oilers, 30-7 (C)
Oilers, 35-3 (H)
1992—Oilers, 38-24 (C)
Oilers, 26-10 (H)
1993—Oilers, 28-12 (H)
Oilers, 38-3 (C)
1994—Oilers, 20-13 (H)
Bengals, 34-31 (C)
1995—Oilers, 38-28 (C)
Bengals, 32-25 (H)
1996—Oilers, 30-27 (C) OT
Bengals, 21-13 (H)
1997—Oilers, 30-7 (T)
Bengals, 41-14 (C)
1998—Oilers, 23-14 (C)
Oilers, 44-14 (T)
1999—Titans, 36-35 (T)
Titans, 24-14 (C)
(RS Pts.—Bengals 1,472, Titans 1,454)
(PS Pts.—Bengals 41, Titans 14)
*Franchise in Houston prior to 1997; known as Oilers prior to 1999
**AFC First-Round Playoff

CINCINNATI vs. WASHINGTON
RS: Redskins lead series, 4-2
1970—Redskins, 20-0 (W)
1974—Bengals, 28-17 (C)
1979—Redskins, 28-14 (W)
1985—Redskins, 27-24 (W)
1988—Bengals, 20-17 (C) OT
1991—Redskins, 34-27 (C)
(RS Pts.—Redskins 143, Bengals 113)

CLEVELAND vs. ARIZONA
RS: Browns lead series, 32-10-3;
See Arizona vs. Cleveland

CLEVELAND vs. ATLANTA
RS: Browns lead series, 8-2;
See Atlanta vs. Cleveland

CLEVELAND vs. BALTIMORE
RS: Ravens lead series, 2-0;
See Baltimore vs. Cleveland

CLEVELAND vs. BUFFALO
RS: Browns lead series, 7-4
PS: Browns lead series, 1-0;
See Buffalo vs. Cleveland

CLEVELAND vs. ATLANTA
RS: Browns lead series, 8-2;
See Atlanta vs. Cleveland

CLEVELAND vs. CAROLINA
RS: Panthers lead series, 1-0;
See Carolina vs. Cleveland

CLEVELAND vs. CINCINNATI
RS: Browns lead series, 27-26;
See Cincinnati vs. Cleveland

CLEVELAND vs. DALLAS
RS: Browns lead series, 15-9
PS: Browns lead series, 2-1
1960—Browns, 48-7 (D)
1961—Browns, 25-7 (C)
Browns, 38-17 (D)
1962—Browns, 19-10 (C)
Cowboys, 45-21 (D)
1963—Browns, 41-24 (D)
Browns, 27-17 (C)
1964—Browns, 27-6 (C)
Browns, 20-16 (D)
1965—Browns, 23-17 (C)
Browns, 24-17 (D)
1966—Browns, 30-21 (C)
Cowboys, 26-14 (D)
1967—Cowboys, 21-14 (C)
*Cowboys, 52-14 (D)
1968—Cowboys, 28-7 (C)
*Browns, 31-20 (C)
1969—Browns, 42-10 (C)
*Browns, 38-14 (D)
1970—Cowboys, 6-2 (C)
1974—Cowboys, 41-17 (D)
1979—Browns, 26-7 (C)
1982—Cowboys, 31-14 (D)
1985—Cowboys, 20-7 (D)
1988—Browns, 24-21 (C)
1991—Cowboys, 26-14 (C)
1994—Browns, 19-14 (D)
(RS Pts.—Browns 543, Cowboys 455)
(PS Pts.—Cowboys 86, Browns 83)
*Conference Championship

CLEVELAND vs. DENVER
RS: Broncos lead series, 13-5
PS: Broncos lead series, 3-0
1970—Browns, 27-13 (D)
1971—Broncos, 27-0 (C)
1972—Browns, 27-20 (D)
1974—Browns, 23-21 (C)
1975—Broncos, 16-15 (D)
1976—Broncos, 44-13 (D)
1978—Broncos, 19-7 (C)
1980—Broncos, 19-16 (C)
1981—Broncos, 23-20 (D) OT
1983—Broncos, 27-6 (D)
1984—Broncos, 24-14 (C)
1986—*Broncos, 23-20 (C) OT
1987—*Broncos, 38-33 (D)
1988—Broncos, 30-7 (D)
1989—Browns, 16-13 (C)
*Broncos, 37-21 (D)
1990—Browns, 30-29 (D)
1991—Broncos, 17-7 (C)
1992—Broncos, 12-0 (C)
1993—Broncos, 29-14 (C)
1994—Broncos, 26-14 (D)
(RS Pts.—Broncos 409, Browns 256)
(PS Pts.—Broncos 98, Browns 74)
*AFC Championship

CLEVELAND vs. DETROIT
RS: Lions lead series, 12-3
PS: Lions lead series, 3-1
1952—Lions, 17-6 (D)
*Lions, 17-7 (C)
1953—*Lions, 17-16 (D)
1954—Lions, 14-10 (C)
*Browns, 56-10 (C)
1957—Lions, 20-7 (D)
*Lions, 59-14 (D)
1958—Lions, 30-10 (C)
1963—Lions, 38-10 (D)
1964—Browns, 37-21 (C)
1967—Lions, 31-14 (D)
1969—Lions, 28-21 (C)
1970—Lions, 41-24 (C)
1975—Lions, 21-10 (D)
1983—Browns, 31-26 (D)
1986—Browns, 24-21 (C)
1989—Lions, 13-10 (D)
1992—Lions, 24-14 (D)
1995—Lions, 38-20 (D)
(RS Pts.—Lions 383, Browns 248)
(PS Pts.—Lions 103, Browns 93)
*NFL Championship

CLEVELAND vs. GREEN BAY
RS: Packers lead series, 8-6
PS: Packers lead series, 1-0
1953—Browns, 27-0 (Mil)
1955—Browns, 41-10 (C)
1956—Browns, 24-7 (Mil)
1961—Packers, 49-17 (C)
1964—Packers, 28-21 (Mil)
1965—*Packers, 23-12 (GB)
1966—Packers, 21-20 (C)
1967—Packers, 55-7 (Mil)
1969—Browns, 20-7 (C)
1972—Packers, 26-10 (C)
1980—Browns, 26-21 (C)
1983—Packers, 35-21 (Mil)
1986—Packers, 17-14 (C)
1992—Browns, 17-6 (C)
1995—Packers, 31-20 (C)
(RS Pts.—Packers 313, Browns 285)
(PS Pts.—Packers 23, Browns 12)
*NFL Championship

CLEVELAND vs. *INDIANAPOLIS
RS: Browns lead series, 13-8
PS: Series tied, 2-2
1956—Colts, 21-7 (C)
1959—Browns, 38-31 (B)
1962—Colts, 36-14 (C)
1964—**Browns, 27-0 (C)
1968—Browns, 30-20 (B)
**Colts, 34-0 (C)
1971—Browns, 14-13 (B)
***Colts, 20-3 (C)
1973—Browns, 24-14 (C)
1975—Colts, 21-7 (B)
1978—Browns, 45-24 (B)
1979—Browns, 13-10 (C)
1980—Browns, 28-27 (B)
1981—Browns, 42-28 (C)
1983—Browns, 41-23 (C)
1986—Browns, 24-9 (I)
1987—Colts, 9-7 (C)
***Browns, 38-21 (C)
1988—Browns, 23-17 (C)
1989—Colts, 23-17 (I) OT
1991—Browns, 31-0 (I)
1992—Colts, 14-3 (I)
1993—Colts, 23-10 (I)
1994—Browns, 21-14 (I)
1999—Colts, 29-28 (C)
(RS Pts.—Browns 467, Colts 406)
(PS Pts.—Colts 75, Browns 68)
*Franchise in Baltimore prior to 1984
**NFL Championship
***AFC Divisional Playoff

CLEVELAND vs. JACKSONVILLE
RS: Jaguars lead series, 4-0
1995—Jaguars, 23-15 (C)
Jaguars, 24-21 (J)
1999—Jaguars, 24-7 (J)
Jaguars, 24-14 (C)
(RS Pts.—Jaguars 95, Browns 57)

CLEVELAND vs. KANSAS CITY
RS: Browns lead series, 8-7-2
1971—Chiefs, 13-7 (KC)
1972—Chiefs, 31-7 (C)
1973—Tie, 20-20 (KC)
1975—Browns, 40-14 (C)
1976—Chiefs, 39-14 (KC)
1977—Browns, 44-7 (C)
1978—Chiefs, 17-3 (KC)
1979—Browns, 27-24 (KC)
1980—Browns, 20-13 (C)
1984—Chiefs, 10-6 (KC)
1986—Browns, 20-7 (C)
1988—Browns, 6-3 (KC)
1989—Tie, 10-10 (C) OT
1990—Chiefs, 34-0 (KC)
1991—Browns, 20-15 (C)
1994—Chiefs, 20-13 (KC)
1995—Browns, 35-17 (C)
(RS Pts.—Chiefs 294, Browns 292)

CLEVELAND vs. MIAMI
RS: Dolphins lead series, 6-4
PS: Dolphins lead series, 2-0
1970—Browns, 28-0 (M)
1972—*Dolphins, 20-14 (M)
1973—Dolphins, 17-9 (C)
1976—Browns, 17-13 (C)
1979—Browns, 30-24 (C) OT
1985—*Dolphins, 24-21 (M)
1986—Browns, 26-16 (C)
1988—Dolphins, 38-31 (M)
1989—Dolphins, 13-10 (M) OT
1990—Dolphins, 30-13 (C)
1992—Dolphins, 27-23 (C)
1993—Dolphins, 24-14 (C)
(RS Pts.—Dolphins 202, Browns 201)
(PS Pts.—Dolphins 44, Browns 35)
*AFC Divisional Playoff

CLEVELAND vs. MINNESOTA
RS: Vikings lead series, 8-3
PS: Vikings lead series, 1-0
1965—Vikings, 27-17 (C)
1967—Browns, 14-10 (C)
1969—Vikings, 51-3 (M)
*Vikings, 27-7 (M)
1973—Vikings, 26-3 (M)
1975—Vikings, 42-10 (C)
1980—Vikings, 28-23 (M)
1983—Vikings, 27-21 (C)
1986—Browns, 23-20 (M)
1989—Browns, 23-17 (C) OT
1992—Vikings, 17-13 (M)
1995—Vikings, 27-11 (M)
(RS Pts.—Vikings 292, Browns 161)
(PS Pts.—Vikings 27, Browns 7)
*NFL Championship

CLEVELAND vs. NEW ENGLAND
RS: Browns lead series, 10-5
PS: Browns lead series, 1-0
1971—Browns, 27-7 (C)
1974—Browns, 21-14 (NE)
1977—Browns, 30-27 (C) OT
1980—Patriots, 34-17 (NE)
1982—Browns, 10-7 (C)
1983—Browns, 30-0 (NE)
1984—Patriots, 17-16 (C)
1985—Browns, 24-20 (C)
1987—Browns, 20-10 (NE)
1991—Browns, 20-0 (NE)

ALL-TIME TEAM VS. TEAM RESULTS

1992—Browns, 19-17 (NE)
1993—Patriots, 20-17 (C)
1994—Browns, 13-6 (C)
*Browns, 20-13 (C)
1995—Patriots, 17-14 (NE)
1999—Patriots, 19-7 (C)
(RS Pts.—Browns 285, Patriots 215)
(PS Pts.—Browns 20, Patriots 13)
*AFC First-Round Playoff

CLEVELAND vs. NEW ORLEANS
RS: Browns lead series, 10-3
1967—Browns, 42-7 (NO)
1968—Browns, 24-10 (NO)
Browns, 35-17 (C)
1969—Browns, 27-17 (NO)
1971—Browns, 21-17 (NO)
1975—Browns, 17-16 (C)
1978—Browns, 24-16 (NO)
1981—Browns, 20-17 (C)
1984—Saints, 16-14 (C)
1987—Saints, 28-21 (NO)
1990—Saints, 25-20 (NO)
1993—Browns, 17-13 (C)
1999—Browns, 21-16 (NO)
(RS Pts.—Browns 303, Saints 215)

CLEVELAND vs. N.Y. GIANTS
RS: Browns lead series, 25-17-2
PS: Series tied, 1-1
1950—Giants, 6-0 (C)
Giants, 17-13 (NY)
*Browns, 8-3 (C)
1951—Browns, 14-13 (C)
Browns, 10-0 (NY)
1952—Giants, 17-9 (C)
Giants, 37-34 (NY)
1953—Browns, 7-0 (NY)
Browns, 62-14 (C)
1954—Browns, 24-14 (C)
Browns, 16-7 (NY)
1955—Browns, 24-14 (C)
Tie, 35-35 (NY)
1956—Giants, 21-9 (C)
Browns, 24-7 (NY)
1957—Browns, 6-3 (C)
Browns, 34-28 (NY)
1958—Giants, 21-17 (C)
Giants, 13-10 (NY)
*Giants, 10-0 (NY)
1959—Giants, 10-6 (C)
Giants, 48-7 (NY)
1960—Giants, 17-13 (C)
Browns, 48-34 (NY)
1961—Giants, 37-21 (C)
Tie, 7-7 (NY)
1962—Browns, 17-7 (C)
Giants, 17-13 (NY)
1963—Browns, 35-24 (NY)
Giants, 33-6 (C)
1964—Browns, 42-20 (C)
Browns, 52-20 (NY)
1965—Browns, 38-14 (NY)
Browns, 34-21 (C)
1966—Browns, 28-7 (NY)
Browns, 49-40 (C)
1967—Giants, 38-34 (NY)
Browns, 24-14 (C)
1968—Browns, 45-10 (C)
1969—Browns, 28-17 (C)
Giants, 27-14 (NY)
1973—Browns, 12-10 (C)
1977—Browns, 21-7 (NY)
1985—Browns, 35-33 (NY)
1991—Giants, 13-10 (NY)
1994—Giants, 16-13 (C)
(RS Pts.—Browns 1,000, Giants 808)
(PS Pts.—Giants 13, Browns 8)
*Conference Playoff

CLEVELAND vs. N.Y. JETS
RS: Browns lead series, 9-6
PS: Browns lead series, 1-0
1970—Browns, 31-21 (C)
1972—Browns, 26-10 (NY)
1976—Browns, 38-17 (C)
1978—Browns, 37-34 (C) OT
1979—Browns, 25-22 (NY) OT
1980—Browns, 17-14 (C)
1981—Jets, 14-13 (C)
1983—Browns, 10-7 (C)
1984—Jets, 24-20 (C)
1985—Jets, 37-10 (NY)
1986—*Browns, 23-20 (C) OT
1988—Jets, 23-3 (C)
1989—Browns, 38-24 (C)
1990—Jets, 24-21 (NY)
1991—Jets, 17-14 (C)
1994—Browns, 27-7 (C)
(RS Pts.—Browns 330, Jets 295)
(PS Pts.—Browns 23, Jets 20)
*AFC Divisional Playoff

CLEVELAND vs. *OAKLAND
RS: Raiders lead series, 8-4
PS: Raiders lead series, 2-0
1970—Raiders, 23-20 (O)
1971—Raiders, 34-20 (C)
1973—Browns, 7-3 (O)
1974—Raiders, 40-24 (C)
1975—Raiders, 38-17 (O)
1977—Raiders, 26-10 (C)
1979—Raiders, 19-14 (O)
1980—**Raiders, 14-12 (C)
1982—***Raiders, 27-10 (LA)
1985—Raiders, 21-20 (C)
1986—Raiders, 27-14 (LA)
1987—Browns, 24-17 (LA)
1992—Browns, 28-16 (LA)
1993—Browns, 19-16 (LA)
(RS Pts.—Raiders 280, Browns 217)
(PS Pts.—Raiders 41, Browns 22)
*Franchise in Los Angeles from 1982-1994
**AFC Divisional Playoff
***AFC First-Round Playoff

CLEVELAND vs. PHILADELPHIA
RS: Browns lead series, 31-12-1
1950—Browns, 35-10 (P)
Browns, 13-7 (C)
1951—Browns, 20-17 (C)
Browns, 24-9 (P)
1952—Browns, 49-7 (P)
Eagles, 28-20 (C)
1953—Browns, 37-13 (C)
Eagles, 42-27 (P)
1954—Eagles, 28-10 (P)
Browns, 6-0 (C)
1955—Browns, 21-17 (C)
Eagles, 33-17 (P)
1956—Browns, 16-0 (P)
Browns, 17-14 (C)
1957—Browns, 24-7 (C)
Eagles, 17-7 (P)
1958—Browns, 28-14 (C)
Browns, 21-14 (P)
1959—Browns, 28-7 (C)
Browns, 28-21 (P)
1960—Browns, 41-24 (P)
Eagles, 31-29 (C)
1961—Eagles, 27-20 (P)
Browns, 45-24 (C)
1962—Eagles, 35-7 (P)
Tie, 14-14 (C)
1963—Browns, 37-7 (C)
Browns, 23-17 (P)
1964—Browns, 28-20 (P)
Browns, 38-24 (C)
1965—Browns, 35-17 (P)
Browns, 38-34 (C)
1966—Browns, 27-7 (C)
Eagles, 33-21 (P)
1967—Eagles, 28-24 (P)
1968—Browns, 47-13 (C)
1969—Browns, 27-20 (P)
1972—Browns, 27-17 (P)
1976—Browns, 24-3 (C)
1979—Browns, 24-19 (P)
1982—Eagles, 24-21 (C)
1988—Browns, 19-3 (C)
1991—Eagles, 32-30 (C)
1994—Browns, 26-7 (P)
(RS Pts.—Browns 1,120, Eagles 785)

CLEVELAND vs. PITTSBURGH
RS: Browns lead series, 53-41
PS: Steelers lead series, 1-0
1950—Browns, 30-17 (P)
Browns, 45-7 (C)
1951—Browns, 17-0 (C)
Browns, 28-0 (P)
1952—Browns, 21-20 (P)
Browns, 29-28 (C)
1953—Browns, 34-16 (C)
Browns, 20-16 (P)
1954—Steelers, 55-27 (P)
Browns, 42-7 (C)
1955—Browns, 41-14 (C)
Browns, 30-7 (P)
1956—Browns, 14-10 (P)
Steelers, 24-16 (C)
1957—Browns, 23-12 (P)
Browns, 24-0 (C)
1958—Browns, 45-12 (P)
Browns, 27-10 (C)
1959—Steelers, 17-7 (P)
Steelers, 21-20 (C)
1960—Browns, 28-20 (C)
Steelers, 14-10 (P)
1961—Browns, 30-28 (P)
Steelers, 17-13 (C)
1962—Browns, 41-14 (P)
Browns, 35-14 (C)
1963—Browns, 35-23 (C)
Steelers, 9-7 (P)
1964—Steelers, 23-7 (C)
Browns, 30-17 (P)
1965—Browns, 24-19 (C)
Browns, 42-21 (P)
1966—Browns, 41-10 (C)
Steelers, 16-6 (P)
1967—Browns, 21-10 (C)
Browns, 34-14 (P)
1968—Browns, 31-24 (C)
Browns, 45-24 (P)
1969—Browns, 42-31 (C)
Browns, 24-3 (P)
1970—Browns, 15-7 (C)
Steelers, 28-9 (P)
1971—Browns, 27-17 (C)
Steelers, 26-9 (P)
1972—Browns, 26-24 (C)
Steelers, 30-0 (P)
1973—Steelers, 33-6 (P)
Browns, 21-16 (C)
1974—Steelers, 20-16 (P)
Steelers, 26-16 (C)
1975—Steelers, 42-6 (C)
Steelers, 31-17 (P)
1976—Steelers, 31-14 (P)
Browns, 18-16 (C)
1977—Steelers, 28-14 (C)
Steelers, 35-31 (P)
1978—Steelers, 15-9 (P) OT
Steelers, 34-14 (C)
1979—Steelers, 51-35 (C)
Steelers, 33-30 (P) OT
1980—Browns, 27-26 (C)
Steelers, 16-13 (P)
1981—Steelers, 13-7 (P)
Steelers, 32-10 (C)
1982—Browns, 10-9 (C)
Steelers, 37-21 (P)
1983—Steelers, 44-17 (P)
Browns, 30-17 (C)
1984—Browns, 20-10 (C)
Steelers, 23-20 (P)
1985—Browns, 17-7 (C)
Steelers, 10-9 (P)
1986—Browns, 27-24 (P)
Browns, 37-31 (C) OT
1987—Browns, 34-10 (C)
Browns, 19-13 (P)
1988—Browns, 23-9 (P)
Browns, 27-7 (C)
1989—Browns, 51-0 (P)
Steelers, 17-7 (C)
1990—Browns, 13-3 (C)
Steelers, 35-0 (P)
1991—Browns, 17-14 (C)
Steelers, 17-10 (P)
1992—Browns, 17-9 (C)
Steelers, 23-13 (P)
1993—Browns, 28-23 (C)
Steelers, 16-9 (P)
1994—Steelers, 17-10 (C)
Steelers, 17-7 (P)
*Steelers, 29-9 (P)
1995—Steelers, 20-3 (P)
Steelers, 20-17 (C)
1999—Steelers, 43-0 (C)
Browns, 16-15 (P)
(RS Pts.—Browns 2,005, Steelers 1,814)
(PS Pts.—Steelers 29, Browns 9)
*AFC Divisional Playoff

CLEVELAND vs. *ST. LOUIS
RS: Series tied, 8-8
PS: Browns lead series, 2-1
1950—**Browns, 30-28 (C)
1951—Browns, 38-23 (LA)
**Rams, 24-17 (LA)
1952—Browns, 37-7 (C)
1955—**Browns, 38-14 (LA)
1957—Browns, 45-31 (C)
1958—Browns, 30-27 (LA)
1963—Browns, 20-6 (C)
1965—Rams, 42-7 (LA)
1968—Rams, 24-6 (C)
1973—Rams, 30-17 (LA)
1977—Rams, 9-0 (C)
1978—Browns, 30-19 (C)
1981—Rams, 27-16 (LA)
1984—Rams, 20-17 (LA)
1987—Browns, 30-17 (C)
1990—Rams, 38-23 (C)
1993—Browns, 42-14 (LA)
1999—Rams, 34-3 (StL)
(RS Pts.—Rams 368, Browns 361)
(PS Pts.—Browns 85, Rams 66)
*Franchise in Los Angeles prior to 1995
**NFL Championship

CLEVELAND vs. SAN DIEGO
RS: Chargers lead series, 10-6-1
1970—Chargers, 27-10 (C)
1972—Browns, 21-17 (SD)
1973—Tie, 16-16 (C)
1974—Chargers, 36-35 (SD)
1976—Browns, 21-17 (C)
1977—Chargers, 37-14 (SD)
1981—Chargers, 44-14 (C)
1982—Chargers, 30-13 (C)
1983—Browns, 30-24 (SD) OT
1985—Browns, 21-7 (SD)
1986—Browns, 47-17 (C)
1987—Chargers, 27-24 (SD) OT
1990—Chargers, 24-14 (C)
1991—Browns, 30-24 (SD) OT
1992—Chargers, 14-13 (C)
1995—Chargers, 31-13 (SD)
1999—Chargers, 23-10 (SD)
(RS Pts.—Chargers 415, Browns 346)

CLEVELAND vs. SAN FRANCISCO
RS: Browns lead series, 9-6
1950—Browns, 34-14 (C)
1951—49ers, 24-10 (SF)
1953—Browns, 23-21 (C)
1955—Browns, 38-3 (SF)
1959—49ers, 21-20 (C)
1962—Browns, 13-10 (SF)
1968—Browns, 33-21 (SF)
1970—49ers, 34-31 (SF)
1974—Browns, 7-0 (C)
1978—Browns, 24-7 (C)
1981—Browns, 15-12 (SF)
1984—49ers, 41-7 (C)
1987—49ers, 38-24 (SF)
1990—49ers, 20-17 (SF)

1993—Browns, 23-13 (C)
(RS Pts.—Browns 319, 49ers 279)

CLEVELAND vs. SEATTLE
RS: Seahawks lead series, 9-4
1977—Seahawks, 20-19 (S)
1978—Seahawks, 47-24 (S)
1979—Seahawks, 29-24 (C)
1980—Browns, 27-3 (S)
1981—Seahawks, 42-21 (S)
1982—Browns, 21-7 (S)
1983—Seahawks, 24-9 (C)
1984—Seahawks, 33-0 (S)
1985—Seahawks, 31-13 (S)
1988—Seahawks, 16-10 (C)
1989—Browns, 17-7 (S)
1993—Seahawks, 22-5 (S)
1994—Browns, 35-9 (C)
(RS Pts.—Seahawks 290, Browns 225)

CLEVELAND vs. TAMPA BAY
RS: Browns lead series, 5-0
1976—Browns, 24-7 (TB)
1980—Browns, 34-27 (TB)
1983—Browns, 20-0 (C)
1989—Browns, 42-31 (TB)
1995—Browns, 22-6 (C)
(RS Pts.—Browns 142, Buccaneers 71)

CLEVELAND vs. *TENNESSEE
RS: Browns lead series, 30-23
PS: Titans lead series, 1-0
1970—Browns, 28-14 (C)
Browns, 21-10 (H)
1971—Browns, 31-0 (C)
Browns, 37-24 (H)
1972—Browns, 23-17 (H)
Browns, 20-0 (C)
1973—Browns, 42-13 (C)
Browns, 23-13 (H)
1974—Browns, 20-7 (C)
Oilers, 28-24 (H)
1975—Oilers, 40-10 (C)
Oilers, 21-10 (H)
1976—Browns, 21-7 (H)
Browns, 13-10 (C)
1977—Browns, 24-23 (H)
Oilers, 19-15 (C)
1978—Oilers, 16-13 (C)
Oilers, 14-10 (H)
1979—Oilers, 31-10 (H)
Browns, 14-7 (C)
1980—Oilers, 16-7 (C)
Browns, 17-14 (H)
1981—Oilers, 9-3 (C)
Oilers, 17-13 (H)
1982—Browns, 20-14 (H)
1983—Browns, 25-19 (C) OT
Oilers, 34-27 (H)
1984—Browns, 27-10 (C)
Browns, 27-20 (H)
1985—Browns, 21-6 (H)
Browns, 28-21 (C)
1986—Browns, 23-20 (H)
Browns, 13-10 (C) OT
1987—Oilers, 15-10 (C)
Browns, 40-7 (H)
1988—Oilers, 24-17 (H)
Browns, 28-23 (C)
**Oilers, 24-23 (C)
1989—Browns, 28-17 (C)
Browns, 24-20 (H)
1990—Oilers, 35-23 (C)
Oilers, 58-14 (H)
1991—Oilers, 28-24 (H)
Oilers, 17-14 (C)
1992—Browns, 24-14 (H)
Oilers, 17-14 (C)
1993—Oilers, 27-20 (C)
Oilers, 19-17 (H)
1994—Browns, 11-8 (H)
Browns, 34-10 (C)
1995—Browns, 14-7 (H)
Oilers, 37-10 (C)
1999—Titans, 26-9 (T)
Titans, 33-21 (C)
(RS Pts.—Browns 1,056, Titans 966)
(PS Pts.—Titans 24, Browns 23)
Franchise in Houston prior to 1997; known as Oilers prior to 1999
***AFC First-Round Playoff*

CLEVELAND vs. WASHINGTON
RS: Browns lead series, 32-9-1
1950—Browns, 20-14 (C)
Browns, 45-21 (W)
1951—Browns, 45-0 (C)
1952—Browns, 19-15 (C)
Browns, 48-24 (W)
1953—Browns, 30-14 (W)
Browns, 27-3 (C)
1954—Browns, 62-3 (C)
Browns, 34-14 (W)
1955—Redskins, 27-17 (C)
Browns, 24-14 (W)
1956—Redskins, 20-9 (W)
Redskins, 20-17 (C)
1957—Browns, 21-17 (C)
Tie, 30-30 (W)
1958—Browns, 20-10 (W)
Browns, 21-14 (C)
1959—Browns, 34-7 (C)
Browns, 31-17 (W)
1960—Browns, 31-10 (W)
Browns, 27-16 (C)
1961—Browns, 31-7 (C)
Browns, 17-6 (W)
1962—Redskins, 17-16 (C)
Redskins, 17-9 (W)
1963—Browns, 37-14 (C)
Browns, 27-20 (W)
1964—Browns, 27-13 (W)
Browns, 34-24 (C)
1965—Browns, 17-7 (W)
Browns, 24-16 (C)
1966—Browns, 38-14 (W)
Browns, 14-3 (C)
1967—Browns, 42-37 (C)
1968—Browns, 24-21 (W)
1969—Browns, 27-23 (C)
1971—Browns, 20-13 (W)
1975—Redskins, 23-7 (C)
1979—Redskins, 13-9 (C)
1985—Redskins, 14-7 (C)
1988—Browns, 17-13 (W)
1991—Redskins, 42-17 (W)
(RS Pts.—Browns 1,073, Redskins 667)

DALLAS vs. ARIZONA
RS: Cowboys lead series, 50-24-1
PS: Cardinals lead series, 1-0;
See Arizona vs. Dallas

DALLAS vs. ATLANTA
RS: Cowboys lead series, 12-6
PS: Cowboys lead series, 2-0;
See Atlanta vs. Dallas

DALLAS vs. BUFFALO
RS: Series tied, 3-3
PS: Cowboys lead series, 2-0;
See Buffalo vs. Dallas

DALLAS vs. CAROLINA
RS: Series tied, 1-1
PS: Panthers lead series, 1-0;
See Carolina vs. Dallas

DALLAS vs. CHICAGO
RS: Cowboys lead series, 9-8
PS: Cowboys lead series, 2-0;
See Chicago vs. Dallas

DALLAS vs. CINCINNATI
RS: Cowboys lead series, 4-3;
See Cincinnati vs. Dallas

DALLAS vs. CLEVELAND
RS: Browns lead series, 15-9
PS: Browns lead series, 2-1;
See Cleveland vs. Dallas

DALLAS vs. DENVER
RS: Cowboys lead series, 4-3
PS: Cowboys lead series, 1-0
1973—Cowboys, 22-10 (Den)
1977—Cowboys, 14-6 (Dal)
*Cowboys, 27-10 (New Orleans)
1980—Broncos, 41-20 (Den)
1986—Broncos, 29-14 (Den)
1992—Cowboys, 31-27 (Den)
1995—Cowboys, 31-21 (Dal)
1998—Broncos, 42-23 (Den)
(RS Pts.—Broncos 176, Cowboys 155)
(PS Pts.—Cowboys 27, Broncos 10)
**Super Bowl XII*

DALLAS vs. DETROIT
RS: Cowboys lead series, 7-6
PS: Series tied, 1-1
1960—Lions, 23-14 (Det)
1963—Cowboys, 17-14 (Dal)
1968—Cowboys, 59-13 (Dal)
1970—*Cowboys, 5-0 (Dal)
1972—Cowboys, 28-24 (Dal)
1975—Cowboys, 36-10 (Det)
1977—Cowboys, 37-0 (Dal)
1981—Lions, 27-24 (Det)
1985—Lions, 26-21 (Det)
1986—Cowboys, 31-7 (Det)
1987—Lions, 27-17 (Det)
1991—Lions, 34-10 (Det)
*Lions, 38-6 (Det)
1992—Cowboys, 37-3 (Det)
1994—Lions, 20-17 (Dal) OT
(RS Pts.—Cowboys 348, Lions 228)
(PS Pts.—Lions 38, Cowboys 11)
**NFC Divisional Playoff*

DALLAS vs. GREEN BAY
RS: Cowboys lead series, 10-9
PS: Cowboys lead series, 4-2
1960—Packers, 41-7 (GB)
1964—Packers, 45-21 (D)
1965—Packers, 13-3 (Mil)
1966—*Packers, 34-27 (D)
1967—*Packers, 21-17 (GB)
1968—Packers, 28-17 (D)
1970—Cowboys, 16-3 (D)
1972—Packers, 16-13 (Mil)
1975—Packers, 19-17 (D)
1978—Cowboys, 42-14 (Mil)
1980—Cowboys, 28-7 (Mil)
1982—**Cowboys, 37-26 (D)
1984—Cowboys, 20-6 (D)
1989—Packers, 31-13 (GB)
Packers, 20-10 (D)
1991—Cowboys, 20-17 (Mil)
1993—Cowboys, 36-14 (D)
***Cowboys, 27-17 (D)
1994—Cowboys, 42-31 (D)
***Cowboys, 35-9 (D)
1995—Cowboys, 34-24 (D)
****Cowboys, 38-27 (D)
1996—Cowboys, 21-6 (D)
1997—Packers, 45-17 (GB)
1999—Cowboys, 27-13 (D)
(RS Pts.—Cowboys 404, Packers 393)
(PS Pts.—Cowboys 181, Packers 134)
**NFL Championship*
***NFC Second-Round Playoff*
****NFC Divisional Playoff*
*****NFC Championship*

DALLAS vs. *INDIANAPOLIS
RS: Cowboys lead series, 7-4
PS: Colts lead series, 1-0
1960—Colts, 45-7 (D)
1967—Colts, 23-17 (B)
1969—Cowboys, 27-10 (D)
1970—**Colts, 16-13 (Miami)
1972—Cowboys, 21-0 (B)
1976—Cowboys, 30-27 (D)
1978—Cowboys, 38-0 (D)
1981—Cowboys, 37-13 (B)
1984—Cowboys, 22-3 (D)
1993—Cowboys, 27-3 (I)
1996—Colts, 25-24 (D)
1999—Colts, 34-24 (I)
(RS Pts.—Cowboys 274, Colts 183)
(PS Pts.—Colts 16, Cowboys 13)
**Franchise in Baltimore prior to 1984*
***Super Bowl V*

DALLAS VS. JACKSONVILLE
RS: Cowboys lead series, 1-0
1997—Cowboys, 26-22 (D)
(RS Pts.—Cowboys 26, Jaguars 22)

DALLAS vs. KANSAS CITY
RS: Cowboys lead series, 4-3
1970—Cowboys, 27-16 (KC)
1975—Chiefs, 34-31 (D)
1983—Cowboys, 41-21 (D)
1989—Chiefs, 36-28 (KC)
1992—Cowboys, 17-10 (D)
1995—Cowboys, 24-12 (D)
1998—Chiefs, 20-17 (KC)
(RS Pts.—Cowboys 185, Chiefs 149)

DALLAS vs. MIAMI
RS: Dolphins lead series, 6-3
PS: Cowboys lead series, 1-0
1971—*Cowboys, 24-3 (New Orleans)
1973—Dolphins, 14-7 (D)
1978—Dolphins, 23-16 (M)
1981—Cowboys, 28-27 (D)
1984—Dolphins, 28-21 (M)
1987—Dolphins, 20-14 (D)
1989—Dolphins, 17-14 (D)
1993—Dolphins, 16-14 (D)
1996—Cowboys, 29-10 (M)
1999—Cowboys, 20-0 (D)
(RS Pts.—Cowboys 163, Dolphins 155)
(PS Pts.—Cowboys 24, Dolphins 3)
**Super Bowl VI*

DALLAS vs. MINNESOTA
RS: Cowboys lead series, 9-8
PS: Cowboys lead series, 4-2
1961—Cowboys, 21-7 (D)
Cowboys, 28-0 (M)
1966—Cowboys, 28-17 (D)
1968—Cowboys, 20-7 (M)
1970—Vikings, 54-13 (M)
1971—*Cowboys, 20-12 (M)
1973—**Vikings, 27-10 (D)
1974—Vikings, 23-21 (D)
1975—*Cowboys, 17-14 (M)
1977—Cowboys, 16-10 (M) OT
**Cowboys, 23-6 (D)
1978—Vikings, 21-10 (D)
1979—Cowboys, 36-20 (M)
1982—Vikings, 31-27 (M)
1983—Cowboys, 37-24 (M)
1987—Vikings, 44-38 (D) OT
1988—Vikings, 43-3 (D)
1993—Cowboys, 37-20 (M)
1995—Cowboys, 23-17 (M) OT
1996—***Cowboys, 40-15 (D)
1998—Vikings, 46-36 (D)
1999—Vikings, 27-17 (M)
***Vikings, 27-10 (M)
(RS Pts.—Cowboys 411, Vikings 411)
(PS Pts.—Cowboys 120, Vikings 101)
**NFC Divisional Playoff*
***NFC Championship*
****NFC First-Round Playoff*

DALLAS vs. NEW ENGLAND
RS: Cowboys lead series, 7-1
1971—Cowboys, 44-21 (D)
1975—Cowboys, 34-31 (NE)
1978—Cowboys, 17-10 (D)
1981—Cowboys, 35-21 (NE)
1984—Cowboys, 20-17 (D)
1987—Cowboys, 23-17 (NE) OT
1996—Cowboys, 12-6 (D)
1999—Patriots, 13-6 (NE)
(RS Pts.—Cowboys 191, Patriots 136)

DALLAS vs. NEW ORLEANS
RS: Cowboys lead series, 14-5
1967—Cowboys, 14-10 (D)
Cowboys, 27-10 (NO)
1968—Cowboys, 17-3 (NO)
1969—Cowboys, 21-17 (NO)
Cowboys, 33-17 (D)
1971—Saints, 24-14 (NO)
1973—Cowboys, 40-3 (D)
1976—Cowboys, 24-6 (NO)
1978—Cowboys, 27-7 (D)

ALL-TIME TEAM VS. TEAM RESULTS

1982—Cowboys, 21-7 (D)
1983—Cowboys, 21-20 (D)
1984—Cowboys, 30-27 (D) OT
1988—Saints, 20-17 (NO)
1989—Saints, 28-0 (NO)
1990—Cowboys, 17-13 (D)
1991—Cowboys, 23-14 (D)
1994—Cowboys, 24-16 (NO)
1998—Saints, 22-3 (NO)
1999—Saints, 31-24 (NO)
(RS Pts.—Cowboys 397, Saints 295)

DALLAS vs. N.Y. GIANTS
RS: Cowboys lead series, 47-26-2
1960—Tie, 31-31 (NY)
1961—Giants, 31-10 (D)
Cowboys, 17-16 (NY)
1962—Giants, 41-10 (D)
Giants, 41-31 (NY)
1963—Giants, 37-21 (NY)
Giants, 34-27 (D)
1964—Tie, 13-13 (D)
Cowboys, 31-21 (NY)
1965—Cowboys, 31-2 (D)
Cowboys, 38-20 (NY)
1966—Cowboys, 52-7 (D)
Cowboys, 17-7 (NY)
1967—Cowboys, 38-24 (D)
1968—Giants, 27-21 (D)
Cowboys, 28-10 (NY)
1969—Cowboys, 25-3 (D)
1970—Cowboys, 28-10 (D)
Giants, 23-20 (NY)
1971—Cowboys, 20-13 (D)
Cowboys, 42-14 (NY)
1972—Cowboys, 23-14 (NY)
Giants, 23-3 (D)
1973—Cowboys, 45-28 (D)
Cowboys, 23-10 (New Haven)
1974—Giants, 14-6 (D)
Cowboys, 21-7 (New Haven)
1975—Cowboys, 13-7 (NY)
Cowboys, 14-3 (D)
1976—Cowboys, 24-14 (NY)
Cowboys, 9-3 (D)
1977—Cowboys, 41-21 (D)
Cowboys, 24-10 (NY)
1978—Cowboys, 34-24 (NY)
Cowboys, 24-3 (D)
1979—Cowboys, 16-14 (NY)
Cowboys, 28-7 (D)
1980—Cowboys, 24-3 (D)
Giants, 38-35 (NY)
1981—Cowboys, 18-10 (D)
Giants, 13-10 (NY) OT
1983—Cowboys, 28-13 (D)
Cowboys, 38-20 (NY)
1984—Giants, 28-7 (NY)
Giants, 19-7 (D)
1985—Cowboys, 30-29 (NY)
Cowboys, 28-21 (D)
1986—Cowboys, 31-28 (D)
Giants, 17-14 (NY)
1987—Cowboys, 16-14 (NY)
Cowboys, 33-24 (D)
1988—Giants, 12-10 (D)
Giants, 29-21 (NY)
1989—Giants, 30-13 (D)
Giants, 15-0 (NY)
1990—Giants, 28-7 (D)
Giants, 31-17 (NY)
1991—Cowboys, 21-16 (D)
Giants, 22-9 (NY)
1992—Cowboys, 34-28 (NY)
Cowboys, 30-3 (D)
1993—Cowboys, 31-9 (D)
Cowboys, 16-13 (NY) OT
1994—Cowboys, 38-10 (D)
Giants, 15-10 (NY)
1995—Cowboys, 35-0 (NY)
Cowboys, 21-20 (D)
1996—Cowboys, 27-0 (D)
Giants, 20-6 (NY)
1997—Giants, 20-17 (NY)
Giants, 20-7 (D)
1998—Cowboys, 31-7 (NY)
Cowboys, 16-6 (D)
1999—Giants, 13-10 (NY)
Cowboys, 26-18 (D)
(RS Pts.—Cowboys 1,671, Giants 1,289)

DALLAS vs. N.Y. JETS
RS: Cowboys lead series, 5-2
1971—Cowboys, 52-10 (D)
1975—Cowboys, 31-21 (NY)
1978—Cowboys, 30-7 (NY)
1987—Cowboys, 38-24 (NY)
1990—Jets, 24-9 (NY)
1993—Cowboys, 28-7 (NY)
1999—Jets, 22-21 (D)
(RS Pts.—Cowboys 209, Jets 115)

DALLAS vs. *OAKLAND
RS: Raiders lead series, 4-3
1974—Raiders, 27-23 (O)
1980—Cowboys, 19-13 (O)
1983—Raiders, 40-38 (D)
1986—Raiders, 17-13 (D)
1992—Cowboys, 28-13 (LA)
1995—Cowboys, 34-21 (O)
1998—Raiders, 13-12 (D)
(RS Pts.—Cowboys 167, Raiders 144)
**Franchise in Los Angeles from 1982-1994*

DALLAS vs. PHILADELPHIA
RS: Cowboys lead series, 48-30
PS: Cowboys lead series, 2-1
1960—Eagles, 27-25 (D)
1961—Eagles, 43-7 (D)
Eagles, 35-13 (P)
1962—Cowboys, 41-19 (D)
Eagles, 28-14 (P)
1963—Eagles, 24-21 (P)
Cowboys, 27-20 (D)
1964—Eagles, 17-14 (D)
Eagles, 24-14 (P)
1965—Eagles, 35-24 (D)
Cowboys, 21-19 (P)
1966—Cowboys, 56-7 (D)
Eagles, 24-23 (P)
1967—Eagles, 21-14 (P)
Cowboys, 38-17 (D)
1968—Cowboys, 45-13 (P)
Cowboys, 34-14 (D)
1969—Cowboys, 38-7 (P)
Cowboys, 49-14 (D)
1970—Cowboys, 17-7 (P)
Cowboys, 21-17 (D)
1971—Cowboys, 42-7 (P)
Cowboys, 20-7 (D)
1972—Cowboys, 28-6 (D)
Cowboys, 28-7 (P)
1973—Eagles, 30-16 (P)
Cowboys, 31-10 (D)
1974—Eagles, 13-10 (P)
Cowboys, 31-24 (D)
1975—Cowboys, 20-17 (P)
Cowboys, 27-17 (D)
1976—Cowboys, 27-7 (D)
Cowboys, 26-7 (P)
1977—Cowboys, 16-10 (P)
Cowboys, 24-14 (D)
1978—Cowboys, 14-7 (D)
Cowboys, 31-13 (P)
1979—Eagles, 31-21 (D)
Cowboys, 24-17 (P)
1980—Eagles, 17-10 (P)
Cowboys, 35-27 (D)
*Eagles, 20-7 (P)
1981—Cowboys, 17-14 (P)
Cowboys, 21-10 (D)
1982—Eagles, 24-20 (D)
1983—Cowboys, 37-7 (D)
Cowboys, 27-20 (P)
1984—Cowboys, 23-17 (D)
Cowboys, 26-10 (P)
1985—Eagles, 16-14 (P)
Cowboys, 34-17 (D)
1986—Cowboys, 17-14 (P)
Eagles, 23-21 (D)
1987—Cowboys, 41-22 (D)
Eagles, 37-20 (P)
1988—Eagles, 24-23 (P)
Eagles, 23-7 (D)
1989—Eagles, 27-0 (D)
Eagles, 20-10 (P)
1990—Eagles, 21-20 (D)
Eagles, 17-3 (P)
1991—Eagles, 24-0 (D)
Cowboys, 25-13 (P)
1992—Eagles, 31-7 (P)
Cowboys, 20-10 (D)
**Cowboys, 34-10 (D)
1993—Cowboys, 23-10 (P)
Cowboys, 23-17 (D)
1994—Cowboys, 24-13 (D)
Cowboys, 31-19 (P)
1995—Cowboys, 34-12 (D)
Eagles, 20-17 (P)
**Cowboys, 30-11 (D)
1996—Cowboys, 23-19 (P)
Eagles, 31-21 (D)
1997—Cowboys, 21-20 (D)
Eagles, 13-12 (P)
1998—Cowboys, 34-0 (P)
Cowboys, 13-9 (D)
1999—Eagles, 13-10 (P)
Cowboys, 20-10 (D)
(RS Pts.—Cowboys 1,776, Eagles 1,367)
(PS Pts.—Cowboys 71, Eagles 41)
**NFC Championship*
***NFC Divisional Playoff*

DALLAS vs. PITTSBURGH
RS: Cowboys lead series, 14-11
PS: Steelers lead series, 2-1
1960—Steelers, 35-28 (D)
1961—Cowboys, 27-24 (D)
Steelers, 37-7 (P)
1962—Steelers, 30-28 (D)
Cowboys, 42-27 (P)
1963—Steelers, 27-21 (P)
Steelers, 24-19 (D)
1964—Steelers, 23-17 (P)
Cowboys, 17-14 (D)
1965—Steelers, 22-13 (P)
Cowboys, 24-17 (D)
1966—Cowboys, 52-21 (D)
Cowboys, 20-7 (P)
1967—Cowboys, 24-21 (P)
1968—Cowboys, 28-7 (D)
1969—Cowboys, 10-7 (P)
1972—Cowboys, 17-13 (D)
1975—*Steelers, 21-17 (Miami)
1977—Steelers, 28-13 (P)
1978—**Steelers, 35-31 (Miami)
1979—Steelers, 14-3 (P)
1982—Steelers, 36-28 (D)
1985—Cowboys, 27-13 (D)
1988—Steelers, 24-21 (P)
1991—Cowboys, 20-10 (D)
1994—Cowboys, 26-9 (P)
1995—***Cowboys, 27-17 (Tempe)
1997—Cowboys, 37-7 (P)
(RS Pts.—Cowboys 569, Steelers 497)
(PS Pts.—Cowboys 75, Steelers 73)
**Super Bowl X*
***Super Bowl XIII*
****Super Bowl XXX*

DALLAS vs. *ST. LOUIS
RS: Rams lead series, 9-8
PS: Series tied, 4-4
1960—Rams, 38-13 (D)
1962—Cowboys, 27-17 (LA)
1967—Rams, 35-13 (D)
1969—Rams, 24-23 (LA)
1971—Cowboys, 28-21 (D)
1973—Rams, 37-31 (LA)
**Cowboys, 27-16 (D)
1975—Cowboys, 18-7 (D)
***Cowboys, 37-7 (LA)
1976—**Rams, 14-12 (D)
1978—Rams, 27-14 (LA)
***Cowboys, 28-0 (LA)
1979—Cowboys, 30-6 (D)
**Rams, 21-19 (D)
1980—Rams, 38-14 (LA)
****Cowboys, 34-13 (D)
1981—Cowboys, 29-17 (D)
1983—****Rams, 24-17 (D)
1984—Cowboys, 20-13 (LA)
1985—**Rams, 20-0 (LA)
1986—Rams, 29-10 (LA)
1987—Cowboys, 29-21 (LA)
1989—Rams, 35-31 (D)
1990—Cowboys, 24-21 (LA)
1992—Rams, 27-23 (D)
(RS Pts.—Rams 413, Cowboys 377)
(PS Pts.—Cowboys 174, Rams 115)
**Franchise in Los Angeles prior to 1995*
***NFC Divisional Playoff*
****NFC Championship*
*****NFC First-Round Playoff*

DALLAS vs. SAN DIEGO
RS: Cowboys lead series, 5-1
1972—Cowboys, 34-28 (SD)
1980—Cowboys, 42-31 (D)
1983—Chargers, 24-23 (SD)
1986—Cowboys, 24-21 (SD)
1990—Cowboys, 17-14 (D)
1995—Cowboys, 23-9 (SD)
(RS Pts.—Cowboys 163, Chargers 127)

DALLAS vs. SAN FRANCISCO
RS: 49ers lead series, 12-7-1
PS: Cowboys lead series, 5-2
1960—49ers, 26-14 (D)
1963—49ers, 31-24 (SF)
1965—Cowboys, 39-31 (D)
1967—49ers, 24-16 (SF)
1969—Tie, 24-24 (D)
1970—*Cowboys, 17-10 (SF)
1971—*Cowboys, 14-3 (D)
1972—49ers, 31-10 (D)
**Cowboys, 30-28 (SF)
1974—Cowboys, 20-14 (D)
1977—Cowboys, 42-35 (SF)
1979—Cowboys, 21-13 (SF)
1980—Cowboys, 59-14 (D)
1981—49ers, 45-14 (SF)
*49ers, 28-27 (SF)
1983—49ers, 42-17 (SF)
1985—49ers, 31-16 (SF)
1989—49ers, 31-14 (D)
1990—49ers, 24-6 (D)
1992—*Cowboys, 30-20 (SF)
1993—Cowboys, 26-17 (D)
*Cowboys, 38-21 (D)
1994—49ers, 21-14 (SF)
*49ers, 38-28 (SF)
1995—49ers, 38-20 (D)
1996—Cowboys, 20-17 (SF) OT
1997—49ers, 17-10 (SF)
(RS Pts.—49ers 526, Cowboys 426)
(PS Pts.—Cowboys 184, 49ers 148)
**NFC Championship*
***NFC Divisional Playoff*

DALLAS vs. SEATTLE
RS: Cowboys lead series, 5-1
1976—Cowboys, 28-13 (S)
1980—Cowboys, 51-7 (D)
1983—Cowboys, 35-10 (S)
1986—Seahawks, 31-14 (D)
1992—Cowboys, 27-0 (D)
1998—Cowboys, 30-22 (D)
(RS Pts.—Cowboys 185, Seahawks 83)

DALLAS vs. TAMPA BAY
RS: Cowboys lead series, 6-0
PS: Cowboys lead series, 2-0
1977—Cowboys, 23-7 (D)
1980—Cowboys, 28-17 (D)
1981—*Cowboys, 38-0 (D)
1982—Cowboys, 14-9 (D)
**Cowboys, 30-17 (D)
1983—Cowboys, 27-24 (D) OT
1990—Cowboys, 14-10 (D)

Cowboys, 17-13 (TB)
(RS Pts.—Cowboys 123, Buccaneers 80)
(PS Pts.—Cowboys 68, Buccaneers 17)
NFC Divisional Playoff
***NFC First-Round Playoff*

DALLAS vs. *TENNESSEE
RS: Cowboys lead series, 5-4
1970—Cowboys, 52-10 (D)
1974—Cowboys, 10-0 (H)
1979—Oilers, 30-24 (D)
1982—Cowboys, 37-7 (H)
1985—Cowboys, 17-10 (H)
1988—Oilers, 25-17 (D)
1991—Oilers, 26-23 (H) OT
1994—Cowboys, 20-17 (D)
1997—Oilers, 27-14 (D)
(RS Pts.—Cowboys 214, Titans 152)
Franchise in Houston prior to 1997; known as Oilers prior to 1999

DALLAS vs. WASHINGTON
RS: Cowboys lead series, 45-31-2
PS: Redskins lead series, 2-0
1960—Redskins, 26-14 (W)
1961—Tie, 28-28 (D)
Redskins, 34-24 (W)
1962—Tie, 35-35 (D)
Cowboys, 38-10 (W)
1963—Redskins, 21-17 (W)
Cowboys, 35-20 (D)
1964—Cowboys, 24-18 (D)
Redskins, 28-16 (W)
1965—Cowboys, 27-7 (D)
Redskins, 34-31 (W)
1966—Cowboys, 31-30 (W)
Redskins, 34-31 (D)
1967—Cowboys, 17-14 (W)
Redskins, 27-20 (D)
1968—Cowboys, 44-24 (W)
Cowboys, 29-20 (D)
1969—Cowboys, 41-28 (W)
Cowboys, 20-10 (D)
1970—Cowboys, 45-21 (W)
Cowboys, 34-0 (D)
1971—Redskins, 20-16 (D)
Cowboys, 13-0 (W)
1972—Redskins, 24-20 (W)
Cowboys, 34-24 (D)
*Redskins, 26-3 (W)
1973—Redskins, 14-7 (W)
Cowboys, 27-7 (D)
1974—Redskins, 28-21 (W)
Cowboys, 24-23 (D)
1975—Redskins, 30-24 (W) OT
Cowboys, 31-10 (D)
1976—Cowboys, 20-7 (W)
Redskins, 27-14 (D)
1977—Cowboys, 34-16 (D)
Cowboys, 14-7 (W)
1978—Redskins, 9-5 (W)
Cowboys, 37-10 (D)
1979—Redskins, 34-20 (W)
Cowboys, 35-34 (D)
1980—Cowboys, 17-3 (W)
Cowboys, 14-10 (D)
1981—Cowboys, 26-10 (W)
Cowboys, 24-10 (D)
1982—Cowboys, 24-10 (W)
*Redskins, 31-17 (W)
1983—Cowboys, 31-30 (W)
Redskins, 31-10 (D)
1984—Redskins, 34-14 (W)
Redskins, 30-28 (D)
1985—Cowboys, 44-14 (D)
Cowboys, 13-7 (W)
1986—Cowboys, 30-6 (D)
Redskins, 41-14 (W)
1987—Redskins, 13-7 (D)
Redskins, 24-20 (W)
1988—Redskins, 35-17 (D)
Cowboys, 24-17 (W)
1989—Redskins, 30-7 (D)
Cowboys, 13-3 (W)
1990—Redskins, 19-15 (W)
Cowboys, 27-17 (D)
1991—Redskins, 33-31 (D)
Cowboys, 24-21 (W)
1992—Cowboys, 23-10 (D)
Redskins, 20-17 (W)
1993—Redskins, 35-16 (W)
Cowboys, 38-3 (D)
1994—Cowboys, 34-7 (W)
Cowboys, 31-7 (D)
1995—Redskins, 27-23 (W)
Redskins, 24-17 (D)
1996—Cowboys, 21-10 (D)
Redskins, 37-10 (W)
1997—Redskins, 21-16 (W)
Cowboys, 17-14 (D)
1998—Cowboys, 31-10 (W)
Cowboys, 23-7 (D)
1999—Cowboys, 41-35 (W) OT
Cowboys, 38-20 (D)
(RS Pts.—Cowboys 1,867, Redskins 1,528)
(PS Pts.—Redskins 57, Cowboys 20)
NFC Championship

DENVER vs. ARIZONA
RS: Broncos lead series, 4-0-1;
See Arizona vs. Denver

DENVER vs. ATLANTA
RS: Broncos lead series, 6-3
PS: Broncos lead series, 1-0;
See Atlanta vs. Denver

DENVER vs. BALTIMORE
RS: Broncos lead series, 1-0;
See Baltimore vs. Denver

DENVER vs. BUFFALO
RS: Bills lead series, 17-12-1
PS: Bills lead series, 1-0;
See Buffalo vs. Denver

DENVER vs. CAROLINA
RS: Broncos lead series, 1-0;
See Carolina vs. Denver

DENVER vs. CHICAGO
RS: Broncos lead series, 6-5;
See Chicago vs. Denver

DENVER vs. CINCINNATI
Broncos lead series, 14-6;
See Cincinnati vs. Denver

DENVER vs. CLEVELAND
RS: Broncos lead series, 13-5
PS: Broncos lead series, 3-0;
See Cleveland vs. Denver

DENVER vs. DALLAS
RS: Cowboys lead series, 4-3
PS: Cowboys lead series, 1-0;
See Dallas vs. Denver

DENVER vs. DETROIT
RS: Broncos lead series, 5-3
1971—Lions, 24-20 (Den)
1974—Broncos, 31-27 (Det)
1978—Lions, 17-14 (Det)
1981—Broncos, 27-21 (Den)
1984—Broncos, 28-7 (Det)
1987—Broncos, 34-0 (Den)
1990—Lions, 40-27 (Det)
1999—Broncos, 17-7 (Det)
(RS Pts.—Broncos 198, Lions 143)

DENVER vs. GREEN BAY
RS: Broncos lead series, 5-3-1
PS: Broncos lead series, 1-0
1971—Packers, 34-13 (Mil)
1975—Broncos, 23-13 (D)
1978—Broncos, 16-3 (D)
1984—Broncos, 17-14 (D)
1987—Tie, 17-17 (Mil) OT
1990—Broncos, 22-13 (D)
1993—Packers, 30-27 (GB)
1996—Packers, 41-6 (GB)
1997—*Broncos, 31-24 (San Diego)
1999—Broncos, 31-10 (D)
(RS Pts.—Packers 175, Broncos 172)
(PS Pts.—Broncos 31, Packers 24)
Super Bowl XXXII

DENVER vs. *INDIANAPOLIS
RS: Broncos lead series, 9-2
1974—Broncos, 17-6 (B)
1977—Broncos, 27-13 (D)
1978—Colts, 7-6 (B)
1981—Broncos, 28-10 (D)
1983—Broncos, 17-10 (B)
Broncos, 21-19 (D)
1985—Broncos, 15-10 (I)
1988—Colts, 55-23 (I)
1989—Broncos, 14-3 (D)
1990—Broncos, 27-17 (I)
1993—Broncos, 35-13 (D)
(RS Pts.—Broncos 230, Colts 163)
Franchise in Baltimore prior to 1984

DENVER vs. JACKSONVILLE
RS: Broncos lead series, 2-1
PS: Series tied, 1-1
1995—Broncos, 31-23 (D)
1996—*Jaguars, 30-27 (D)
1997—**Broncos, 42-17 (D)
1998—Broncos, 37-24 (D)
1999—Jaguars, 27-24 (J)
(RS Pts.—Broncos 92, Jaguars 74)
(PS Pts.—Broncos 69, Jaguars 47)
AFC Divisional Playoff
***AFC First-Round Playoff*

DENVER vs. *KANSAS CITY
RS: Chiefs lead series, 45-34
PS: Broncos lead series, 1-0
1960—Texans, 17-14 (D)
Texans, 34-7 (Dal)
1961—Texans, 19-12 (D)
Texans, 49-21 (Dal)
1962—Texans, 24-3 (D)
Texans, 17-10 (Dal)
1963—Chiefs, 59-7 (D)
Chiefs, 52-21 (KC)
1964—Broncos, 33-27 (D)
Chiefs, 49-39 (KC)
1965—Chiefs, 31-23 (D)
Chiefs, 45-35 (KC)
1966—Chiefs, 37-10 (KC)
Chiefs, 56-10 (D)
1967—Chiefs, 52-9 (KC)
Chiefs, 38-24 (D)
1968—Chiefs, 34-2 (KC)
Chiefs, 30-7 (D)
1969—Chiefs, 26-13 (D)
Chiefs, 31-17 (KC)
1970—Broncos, 26-13 (D)
Chiefs, 16-0 (KC)
1971—Chiefs, 16-3 (D)
Chiefs, 28-10 (KC)
1972—Chiefs, 45-24 (D)
Chiefs, 24-21 (KC)
1973—Chiefs, 16-14 (KC)
Broncos, 14-10 (D)
1974—Broncos, 17-14 (KC)
Chiefs, 42-34 (D)
1975—Broncos, 37-33 (D)
Chiefs, 26-13 (KC)
1976—Broncos, 35-26 (KC)
Broncos, 17-16 (D)
1977—Broncos, 23-7 (D)
Broncos, 14-7 (KC)
1978—Broncos, 23-17 (KC) OT
Broncos, 24-3 (D)
1979—Broncos, 24-10 (KC)
Broncos, 20-3 (D)
1980—Chiefs, 23-17 (D)
Chiefs, 31-14 (KC)
1981—Chiefs, 28-14 (KC)
Broncos, 16-13 (D)
1982—Chiefs, 37-16 (D)
1983—Broncos, 27-24 (D)
Chiefs, 48-17 (KC)
1984—Broncos, 21-0 (D)
Chiefs, 16-13 (KC)
1985—Broncos, 30-10 (KC)
Broncos, 14-13 (D)
1986—Broncos, 38-17 (D)
Chiefs, 37-10 (KC)
1987—Broncos, 26-17 (KC)
Broncos, 20-17 (D)
1988—Chiefs, 20-13 (KC)
Broncos, 17-11 (D)
1989—Broncos, 34-20 (D)
Broncos, 16-13 (KC)
1990—Broncos, 24-23 (D)
Chiefs, 31-20 (KC)
1991—Broncos, 19-16 (D)
Broncos, 24-20 (KC)
1992—Broncos, 20-19 (D)
Chiefs, 42-20 (KC)
1993—Chiefs, 15-7 (KC)
Broncos, 27-21 (D)
1994—Chiefs, 31-28 (D)
Broncos, 20-17 (KC) OT
1995—Chiefs, 21-7 (D)
Chiefs, 20-17 (KC)
1996—Chiefs, 17-14 (KC)
Broncos, 34-7 (D)
1997—Broncos, 19-3 (D)
Chiefs, 24-22 (KC)
**Broncos, 14-10 (KC)
1998—Broncos, 30-7 (KC)
Broncos, 35-31 (D)
1999—Chiefs, 26-10 (KC)
Chiefs, 16-10 (D)
(RS Pts.—Chiefs 1,901, Broncos 1,490)
(PS Pts.—Broncos 14, Chiefs 10)
Franchise in Dallas prior to 1963 and known as Texans
***AFC Divisional Playoff*

DENVER vs. MIAMI
RS: Dolphins lead series, 7-2-1
PS: Broncos lead series, 1-0
1966—Dolphins, 24-7 (M)
Broncos, 17-7 (D)
1967—Dolphins, 35-21 (M)
1968—Broncos, 21-14 (D)
1969—Dolphins, 27-24 (M)
1971—Tie, 10-10 (D)
1975—Dolphins, 14-13 (M)
1985—Dolphins, 30-26 (D)
1998—Dolphins, 31-21 (M)
*Broncos, 38-3 (D)
1999—Dolphins, 38-21 (D)
(RS Pts.—Dolphins 230, Broncos 181)
(PS Pts.—Broncos 38, Dolphins 3)
AFC Divisonal Playoff

DENVER vs. MINNESOTA
RS: Vikings lead series, 6-4
1972—Vikings, 23-20 (D)
1978—Vikings, 12-9 (M) OT
1981—Broncos, 19-17 (D)
1984—Broncos, 42-21 (D)
1987—Vikings, 34-27 (M)
1990—Vikings, 27-22 (M)
1991—Broncos, 13-6 (M)
1993—Vikings, 26-23 (D)
1996—Broncos, 21-17 (M)
1999—Vikings, 23-20 (D)
(RS Pts.—Broncos 216, Vikings 206)

DENVER vs. *NEW ENGLAND
RS: Broncos lead series, 20-13
PS: Broncos lead series, 1-0
1960—Broncos, 13-10 (B)
Broncos, 31-24 (D)
1961—Patriots, 45-17 (B)
Patriots, 28-24 (D)
1962—Patriots, 41-16 (B)
Patriots, 33-29 (D)
1963—Broncos, 14-10 (D)
Patriots, 40-21 (B)
1964—Patriots, 39-10 (D)
Patriots, 12-7 (B)
1965—Broncos, 27-10 (B)
Patriots, 28-20 (D)
1966—Patriots, 24-10 (D)
Broncos, 17-10 (B)
1967—Broncos, 26-21 (D)
1968—Patriots, 20-17 (D)
Broncos, 35-14 (B)
1969—Broncos, 35-7 (D)
1972—Broncos, 45-21 (D)
1976—Patriots, 38-14 (NE)

ALL-TIME TEAM VS. TEAM RESULTS

1979—Broncos, 45-10 (D)
1980—Patriots, 23-14 (NE)
1984—Broncos, 26-19 (D)
1986—Broncos, 27-20 (D)
**Broncos, 22-17 (D)
1987—Broncos, 31-20 (D)
1988—Broncos, 21-10 (D)
1991—Broncos, 9-6 (NE)
Broncos, 20-3 (D)
1995—Broncos, 37-3 (NE)
1996—Broncos, 34-8 (NE)
1997—Broncos, 34-13 (D)
1998—Broncos, 27-21 (D)
1999—Patriots, 24-23 (NE)
(RS Pts.—Broncos 776, Patriots 655)
(PS Pts.—Broncos 22, Patriots 17)
**Franchise in Boston prior to 1971*
***AFC Divisional Playoff*

DENVER vs. NEW ORLEANS
RS: Broncos lead series, 4-2
1970—Broncos, 31-6 (NO)
1974—Broncos, 33-17 (D)
1979—Broncos, 10-3 (D)
1985—Broncos, 34-23 (D)
1988—Saints, 42-0 (NO)
1994—Saints, 30-28 (D)
(RS Pts.—Broncos 136, Saints 121)

DENVER vs. N.Y. GIANTS
RS: Giants lead series, 4-3
PS: Giants lead series, 1-0
1972—Giants, 29-17 (NY)
1976—Broncos, 14-13 (D)
1980—Broncos, 14-9 (NY)
1986—Giants, 19-16 (NY)
*Giants, 39-20 (Pasadena)
1989—Giants, 14-7 (D)
1992—Broncos, 27-13 (D)
1998—Giants, 20-16 (NY)
(RS Pts.—Giants 117, Broncos 111)
(PS Pts.—Giants 39, Broncos 20)
**Super Bowl XXI*

DENVER vs. *N.Y. JETS
RS: Series tied, 13-13-1
PS: Broncos lead series, 1-0
1960—Titans, 28-24 (NY)
Titans, 30-27 (D)
1961—Titans, 35-28 (NY)
Broncos, 27-10 (D)
1962—Broncos, 32-10 (NY)
Titans, 46-45 (D)
1963—Tie, 35-35 (NY)
Jets, 14-9 (D)
1964—Jets, 30-6 (NY)
Broncos, 20-16 (D)
1965—Broncos, 16-13 (D)
Jets, 45-10 (NY)
1966—Jets, 16-7 (D)
1967—Jets, 38-24 (D)
Broncos, 33-24 (NY)
1968—Broncos, 21-13 (NY)
1969—Broncos, 21-19 (D)
1973—Broncos, 40-28 (NY)
1976—Broncos, 46-3 (D)
1978—Jets, 31-28 (D)
1980—Broncos, 31-24 (D)
1986—Jets, 22-10 (NY)
1992—Broncos, 27-16 (D)
1993—Broncos, 26-20 (NY)
1994—Jets, 25-22 (NY) OT
1996—Broncos, 31-6 (D)
1998—**Broncos, 23-10 (D)
1999—Jets, 21-13 (D)
(RS Pts.—Broncos 659, Jets 618)
(PS Pts.—Broncos 23, Jets 10)
**Jets known as Titans prior to 1963*
***AFC Championship*

DENVER vs. *OAKLAND
RS: Raiders lead series, 49-28-2
PS: Series tied, 1-1
1960—Broncos, 31-14 (D)
Raiders, 48-10 (O)
1961—Raiders, 33-19 (O)
Broncos, 27-24 (D)
1962—Broncos, 44-7 (D)
Broncos, 23-6 (O)
1963—Raiders, 26-10 (D)
Raiders, 35-31 (O)
1964—Raiders, 40-7 (O)
Tie, 20-20 (D)
1965—Raiders, 28-20 (D)
Raiders, 24-13 (O)
1966—Raiders, 17-3 (D)
Raiders, 28-10 (O)
1967—Raiders, 51-0 (O)
Raiders, 21-17 (D)
1968—Raiders, 43-7 (D)
Raiders, 33-27 (O)
1969—Raiders, 24-14 (D)
Raiders, 41-10 (O)
1970—Raiders, 35-23 (O)
Raiders, 24-19 (D)
1971—Raiders, 27-16 (D)
Raiders, 21-13 (O)
1972—Broncos, 30-23 (O)
Raiders, 37-20 (D)
1973—Tie, 23-23 (D)
Raiders, 21-17 (O)
1974—Raiders, 28-17 (D)
Broncos, 20-17 (O)
1975—Raiders, 42-17 (D)
Raiders, 17-10 (O)
1976—Raiders, 17-10 (D)
Raiders, 19-6 (O)
1977—Broncos, 30-7 (O)
Raiders, 24-14 (D)
**Broncos, 20-17 (D)
1978—Broncos, 14-6 (D)
Broncos, 21-6 (O)
1979—Raiders, 27-3 (O)
Raiders, 14-10 (D)
1980—Raiders, 9-3 (O)
Raiders, 24-21 (D)
1981—Broncos, 9-7 (D)
Broncos, 17-0 (O)
1982—Raiders, 27-10 (LA)
1983—Raiders, 22-7 (D)
Raiders, 22-20 (LA)
1984—Broncos, 16-13 (D)
Broncos, 22-19 (LA) OT
1985—Raiders, 31-28 (LA) OT
Raiders, 17-14 (D) OT
1986—Broncos, 38-36 (D)
Broncos, 21-10 (LA)
1987—Broncos, 30-14 (D)
Broncos, 23-17 (LA)
1988—Raiders, 30-27 (D) OT
Raiders, 21-20 (LA)
1989—Broncos, 31-21 (D)
Raiders, 16-13 (LA) OT
1990—Raiders, 14-9 (LA)
Raiders, 23-20 (D)
1991—Raiders, 16-13 (LA)
Raiders, 17-16 (D)
1992—Broncos, 17-13 (D)
Raiders, 24-0 (LA)
1993—Raiders, 23-20 (D)
Raiders, 33-30 (LA) OT
***Raiders, 42-24 (LA)
1994—Raiders, 48-16 (D)
Raiders, 23-13 (LA)
1995—Broncos, 27-0 (D)
Broncos, 31-28 (O)
1996—Broncos, 22-21 (O)
Broncos, 24-19 (D)
1997—Raiders, 28-25 (O)
Broncos, 31-3 (D)
1998—Broncos, 34-17 (O)
Broncos, 40-14 (D)
1999—Broncos, 16-13 (O)
Broncos, 27-21 (D) OT
(RS Pts.—Raiders 1,752, Broncos 1,477)
(PS Pts.—Raiders 59, Broncos 44)
**Franchise in Los Angeles from 1982-1994*
***AFC Championship*
****AFC First-Round Playoff*

DENVER vs. PHILADELPHIA
RS: Eagles lead series, 6-3
1971—Eagles, 17-16 (P)
1975—Broncos, 25-10 (D)
1980—Eagles, 27-6 (P)
1983—Eagles, 13-10 (D)
1986—Broncos, 33-7 (P)
1989—Eagles, 28-24 (D)
1992—Eagles, 30-0 (P)
1995—Eagles, 31-13 (P)
1998—Broncos, 41-16 (D)
(RS Pts.—Eagles 179, Broncos 168)

DENVER vs. PITTSBURGH
RS: Broncos lead series, 10-6-1
PS: Broncos lead series, 3-2
1970—Broncos, 16-13 (D)
1971—Broncos, 22-10 (P)
1973—Broncos, 23-13 (P)
1974—Tie, 35-35 (D) OT
1975—Steelers, 20-9 (P)
1977—Broncos, 21-7 (D)
*Broncos, 34-21 (D)
1978—Steelers, 21-17 (D)
*Steelers, 33-10 (P)
1979—Steelers, 42-7 (P)
1983—Broncos, 14-10 (P)
1984—*Steelers, 24-17 (D)
1985—Broncos, 31-23 (P)
1986—Broncos, 21-10 (P)
1988—Steelers, 39-21 (P)
1989—Broncos, 34-7 (D)
*Broncos, 24-23 (D)
1990—Steelers, 34-17 (D)
1991—Broncos, 20-13 (D)
1993—Broncos, 37-13 (D)
1997—Steelers, 35-24 (P)
**Broncos, 24-21 (P)
(RS Pts.—Broncos 369, Steelers 345)
(PS Pts.—Steelers 122, Broncos 109)
**AFC Divisional Playoff*
***AFC Championship*

DENVER vs. *ST. LOUIS
RS: Series tied, 4-4
1972—Broncos, 16-10 (LA)
1974—Rams, 17-10 (D)
1979—Rams, 13-9 (D)
1982—Broncos, 27-24 (LA)
1985—Rams, 20-16 (LA)
1988—Broncos, 35-24 (D)
1994—Rams, 27-21 (LA)
1997—Broncos, 35-14 (D)
(RS Pts.—Broncos 169, Rams 149)
**Franchise in Los Angeles prior to 1995*

DENVER vs. *SAN DIEGO
RS: Broncos lead series, 43-36-1
1960—Chargers, 23-19 (D)
Chargers, 41-33 (LA)
1961—Chargers, 37-0 (SD)
Chargers, 19-16 (D)
1962—Broncos, 30-21 (D)
Broncos, 23-20 (SD)
1963—Broncos, 50-34 (D)
Chargers, 58-20 (SD)
1964—Chargers, 42-14 (SD)
Chargers, 31-20 (D)
1965—Chargers, 34-31 (SD)
Chargers, 33-21 (D)
1966—Chargers, 24-17 (SD)
Broncos, 20-17 (D)
1967—Chargers, 38-21 (D)
Chargers, 24-20 (SD)
1968—Chargers, 55-24 (SD)
Chargers, 47-23 (D)
1969—Broncos, 13-0 (D)
Chargers, 45-24 (SD)
1970—Chargers, 24-21 (SD)
Tie, 17-17 (D)
1971—Broncos, 20-16 (D)
Chargers, 45-17 (SD)
1972—Chargers, 37-14 (SD)
Broncos, 38-13 (D)
1973—Broncos, 30-19 (D)
Broncos, 42-28 (SD)
1974—Broncos, 27-7 (D)
Chargers, 17-0 (SD)
1975—Broncos, 27-17 (SD)
Broncos, 13-10 (D) OT
1976—Broncos, 26-0 (D)
Broncos, 17-0 (SD)
1977—Broncos, 17-14 (SD)
Broncos, 17-9 (D)
1978—Broncos, 27-14 (D)
Chargers, 23-0 (SD)
1979—Broncos, 7-0 (D)
Chargers, 17-7 (SD)
1980—Chargers, 30-13 (D)
Broncos, 20-13 (SD)
1981—Broncos, 42-24 (D)
Chargers, 34-17 (SD)
1982—Chargers, 23-3 (D)
Chargers, 30-20 (SD)
1983—Broncos, 14-6 (D)
Chargers, 31-7 (SD)
1984—Broncos, 16-13 (SD)
Broncos, 16-13 (D)
1985—Chargers, 30-10 (SD)
Broncos, 30-24 (D) OT
1986—Broncos, 31-14 (SD)
Chargers, 9-3 (D)
1987—Broncos, 31-17 (SD)
Broncos, 24-0 (D)
1988—Broncos, 34-3 (D)
Broncos, 12-0 (SD)
1989—Broncos, 16-10 (D)
Chargers, 19-16 (SD)
1990—Chargers, 19-7 (SD)
Broncos, 20-10 (D)
1991—Broncos, 27-19 (D)
Broncos, 17-14 (SD)
1992—Broncos, 21-13 (D)
Chargers, 24-21 (SD)
1993—Broncos, 34-17 (D)
Chargers, 13-10 (SD)
1994—Chargers, 37-34 (D)
Broncos, 20-15 (SD)
1995—Chargers, 17-6 (SD)
Broncos, 30-27 (D)
1996—Broncos, 28-17 (D)
Chargers, 16-10 (SD)
1997—Broncos, 38-28 (SD)
Broncos, 38-3 (D)
1998—Broncos, 27-10 (D)
Broncos, 31-16 (SD)
1999—Broncos, 33-17 (SD)
Chargers, 12-6 (D)
(RS Pts.—Chargers 1,659, Broncos 1,656)
**Franchise in Los Angeles prior to 1961*

DENVER vs. SAN FRANCISCO
RS: Series tied, 4-4
PS: 49ers lead series, 1-0
1970—49ers, 19-14 (SF)
1973—49ers, 36-34 (D)
1979—Broncos, 38-28 (SF)
1982—Broncos, 24-21 (D)
1985—Broncos, 17-16 (D)
1988—Broncos, 16-13 (SF) OT
1989—*49ers, 55-10 (New Orleans)
1994—49ers, 42-19 (SF)
1997—49ers, 34-17 (SF)
(RS Pts.—49ers 209, Broncos 179)
(PS Pts.—49ers 55, Broncos 10)
**Super Bowl XXIV*

DENVER vs. SEATTLE
RS: Broncos lead series, 29-16
PS: Seahawks lead series, 1-0
1977—Broncos, 24-13 (S)
1978—Broncos, 28-7 (D)
Broncos, 20-17 (S) OT
1979—Broncos, 37-34 (D)
Seahawks, 28-23 (S)
1980—Broncos, 36-20 (D)
Broncos, 25-17 (S)
1981—Seahawks, 13-10 (S)
Broncos, 23-13 (D)
1982—Seahawks, 17-10 (D)
Seahawks, 13-11 (S)

1983—Seahawks, 27-19 (S)
Broncos, 38-27 (D)
*Seahawks, 31-7 (S)
1984—Seahawks, 27-24 (D)
Broncos, 31-14 (S)
1985—Broncos, 13-10 (D) OT
Broncos, 27-24 (S)
1986—Broncos, 20-13 (D)
Seahawks, 41-16 (S)
1987—Broncos, 40-17 (D)
Seahawks, 28-21 (S)
1988—Seahawks, 21-14 (D)
Seahawks, 42-14 (S)
1989—Broncos, 24-21 (S) OT
Broncos, 41-14 (D)
1990—Broncos, 34-31 (D) OT
Seahawks, 17-12 (S)
1991—Broncos, 16-10 (D)
Seahawks, 13-10 (S)
1992—Seahawks, 16-13 (S) OT
Broncos, 10-6 (D)
1993—Broncos, 28-17 (D)
Broncos, 17-9 (S)
1994—Broncos, 16-9 (S)
Broncos, 17-10 (D)
1995—Seahawks, 27-10 (S)
Seahawks, 31-27 (D)
1996—Broncos, 30-20 (S)
Broncos, 34-7 (D)
1997—Broncos, 35-14 (S)
Broncos, 30-27 (D)
1998—Broncos, 21-16 (S)
Broncos, 28-21 (D)
1999—Seahawks, 20-17 (S)
Broncos, 36-30 (D) OT
(RS Pts.—Broncos 1,030, Seahawks 869)
(PS Pts.—Seahawks 31, Broncos 7)
AFC First-Round Playoff

DENVER vs. TAMPA BAY
RS: Broncos lead series, 3-2
1976—Broncos, 48-13 (D)
1981—Broncos, 24-7 (TB)
1993—Buccaneers, 17-10 (D)
1996—Broncos, 27-23 (D)
1999—Buccaneers, 13-10 (TB)
(RS Pts.—Broncos 119, Buccaneers 73)

DENVER vs. *TENNESSEE
RS: Titans lead series, 20-11-1
PS: Broncos lead series, 2-1
1960—Oilers, 45-25 (D)
Oilers, 20-10 (H)
1961—Oilers, 55-14 (D)
Oilers, 45-14 (H)
1962—Broncos, 20-10 (D)
Oilers, 34-17 (H)
1963—Oilers, 20-14 (H)
Oilers, 33-24 (D)
1964—Oilers, 38-17 (D)
Oilers, 34-15 (H)
1965—Broncos, 28-17 (D)
Broncos, 31-21 (H)
1966—Oilers, 45-7 (H)
Broncos, 40-38 (D)
1967—Oilers, 10-6 (H)
Oilers, 20-18 (D)
1968—Oilers, 38-17 (H)
1969—Oilers, 24-21 (H)
Tie, 20-20 (D)
1970—Oilers, 31-21 (H)
1972—Broncos, 30-17 (D)
1973—Broncos, 48-20 (H)
1974—Broncos, 37-14 (D)
1976—Oilers, 17-3 (H)
1977—Broncos, 24-14 (H)
1979—**Oilers, 13-7 (H)
1980—Oilers, 20-16 (D)
1983—Broncos, 26-14 (H)
1985—Broncos, 31-20 (D)
1987—Oilers, 40-10 (D)
***Broncos, 34-10 (D)
1991—Oilers, 42-14 (H)
***Broncos, 26-24 (D)
1992—Broncos, 27-21 (D)
1995—Oilers, 42-33 (H)
(RS Pts.—Titans 879, Broncos 678)
(PS Pts.—Broncos 67, Titans 47)
Franchise in Houston prior to 1997; known as the Oilers prior to 1999
***AFC First-Round Playoff*
****AFC Divisional Playoff*

DENVER vs. WASHINGTON
RS: Broncos lead series, 5-3
PS: Redskins lead series, 1-0
1970—Redskins, 19-3 (D)
1974—Redskins, 30-3 (W)
1980—Broncos, 20-17 (D)
1986—Broncos, 31-30 (D)
1987—*Redskins, 42-10 (San Diego)
1989—Broncos, 14-10 (W)
1992—Redskins, 34-3 (W)
1995—Broncos, 38-31 (D)
1998—Broncos, 38-16 (W)
(RS Pts.—Redskins 187, Broncos 150)
(PS Pts.—Redskins 42, Broncos 10)
Super Bowl XXII

DETROIT vs. ARIZONA
RS: Lions lead series, 27-19-5;
See Arizona vs. Detroit

DETROIT vs. ATLANTA
RS: Lions lead series, 20-7;
See Atlanta vs. Detroit

DETROIT vs. BALTIMORE
RS: Ravens lead series, 1-0;
See Baltimore vs. Detroit

DETROIT vs. BUFFALO
RS: Lions lead series, 3-2-1;
See Buffalo vs. Detroit

DETROIT vs. CAROLINA
RS: Lions lead series, 1-0;
See Carolina vs. Detroit

DETROIT vs. CHICAGO
RS: Bears lead series, 78-57-5;
See Chicago vs. Detroit

DETROIT vs. CINCINNATI
RS: Bengals lead series, 4-3;
See Cincinnati vs. Detroit

DETROIT vs. CLEVELAND
RS: Lions lead series, 12-3
PS: Lions lead series, 3-1;
See Cleveland vs. Detroit

DETROIT vs. DALLAS
RS: Cowboys lead series, 7-6
PS: Series tied, 1-1;
See Dallas vs. Detroit

DETROIT vs. DENVER
RS: Broncos lead series, 5-3;
See Denver vs. Detroit

***DETROIT vs. GREEN BAY**
RS: Packers lead series, 71-61-7
PS: Packers lead series, 2-0
1930—Packers, 47-13 (GB)
Tie, 6-6 (P)
1932—Packers, 15-10 (GB)
Spartans, 19-0 (P)
1933—Packers, 17-0 (GB)
Spartans, 7-0 (P)
1934—Lions, 3-0 (GB)
Packers, 3-0 (D)
1935—Packers, 13-9 (Mil)
Packers, 31-7 (GB)
Lions, 20-10 (D)
1936—Packers, 20-18 (GB)
Packers, 26-17 (D)
1937—Packers, 26-6 (GB)
Packers, 14-13 (D)
1938—Lions, 17-7 (GB)
Packers, 28-7 (D)
1939—Packers, 26-7 (GB)
Packers, 12-7 (D)
1940—Lions, 23-14 (GB)
Packers, 50-7 (D)
1941—Packers, 23-0 (GB)
Packers, 24-7 (D)
1942—Packers, 38-7 (Mil)
Packers, 28-7 (D)
1943—Packers, 35-14 (GB)
Packers, 27-6 (D)
1944—Packers, 27-6 (Mil)
Packers, 14-0 (D)
1945—Packers, 57-21 (Mil)
Lions, 14-3 (D)
1946—Packers, 10-7 (Mil)
Packers, 9-0 (D)
1947—Packers, 34-17 (GB)
Packers, 35-14 (D)
1948—Packers, 33-21 (GB)
Lions, 24-20 (D)
1949—Packers, 16-14 (Mil)
Lions, 21-7 (D)
1950—Lions, 45-7 (GB)
Lions, 24-21 (D)
1951—Lions, 24-17 (GB)
Lions, 52-35 (D)
1952—Lions, 52-17 (GB)
Lions, 48-24 (D)
1953—Lions, 14-7 (GB)
Lions, 34-15 (D)
1954—Lions, 21-17 (GB)
Lions, 28-24 (D)
1955—Packers, 20-17 (GB)
Lions, 24-10 (D)
1956—Lions, 20-16 (GB)
Packers, 24-20 (D)
1957—Lions, 24-14 (GB)
Lions, 18-6 (D)
1958—Tie, 13-13 (GB)
Lions, 24-14 (D)
1959—Packers, 28-10 (GB)
Packers, 24-17 (D)
1960—Packers, 28-9 (GB)
Lions, 23-10 (D)
1961—Lions, 17-13 (Mil)
Packers, 17-9 (D)
1962—Packers, 9-7 (GB)
Lions, 26-14 (D)
1963—Packers, 31-10 (Mil)
Tie, 13-13 (D)
1964—Packers, 14-10 (D)
Packers, 30-7 (GB)
1965—Packers, 31-21 (D)
Lions, 12-7 (GB)
1966—Packers, 23-14 (GB)
Packers, 31-7 (D)
1967—Tie, 17-17 (GB)
Packers, 27-17 (D)
1968—Lions, 23-17 (GB)
Tie, 14-14 (D)
1969—Packers, 28-17 (D)
Lions, 16-10 (GB)
1970—Lions, 40-0 (GB)
Lions, 20-0 (D)
1971—Lions, 31-28 (D)
Tie, 14-14 (Mil)
1972—Packers, 24-23 (D)
Packers, 33-7 (GB)
1973—Tie, 13-13 (GB)
Lions, 34-0 (D)
1974—Packers, 21-19 (Mil)
Lions, 19-17 (D)
1975—Lions, 30-16 (Mil)
Lions, 13-10 (D)
1976—Packers, 24-14 (GB)
Lions, 27-6 (D)
1977—Lions, 10-6 (D)
Packers, 10-9 (GB)
1978—Packers, 13-7 (D)
Packers, 35-14 (Mil)
1979—Packers, 24-16 (Mil)
Packers, 18-13 (D)
1980—Lions, 29-7 (Mil)
Lions, 24-3 (D)
1981—Lions, 31-27 (D)
Packers, 31-17 (GB)
1982—Lions, 30-10 (GB)
Lions, 27-24 (D)
1983—Lions, 38-14 (D)
Lions, 23-20 (Mil) OT
1984—Packers, 41-9 (GB)
Lions, 31-28 (D)
1985—Packers, 43-10 (GB)
Packers, 26-23 (D)
1986—Lions, 21-14 (GB)
Packers, 44-40 (D)
1987—Lions, 19-16 (GB) OT
Packers, 34-33 (D)
1988—Lions, 19-9 (Mil)
Lions, 30-14 (D)
1989—Packers, 23-20 (Mil) OT
Lions, 31-22 (D)
1990—Packers, 24-21 (D)
Lions, 24-17 (GB)
1991—Lions, 23-14 (D)
Lions, 21-17 (GB)
1992—Packers, 27-13 (D)
Packers, 38-10 (Mil)
1993—Packers, 26-17 (Mil)
Lions, 30-20 (D)
**Packers, 28-24 (D)
1994—Packers, 38-30 (Mil)
Lions, 34-31 (D)
**Packers, 16-12 (GB)
1995—Packers, 30-21 (GB)
Lions, 24-16 (D)
1996—Packers, 28-18 (GB)
Packers, 31-3 (D)
1997—Lions, 26-15 (D)
Packers, 20-10 (GB)
1998—Packers, 38-19 (GB)
Lions, 27-20 (D)
1999—Lions, 23-15 (D)
Packers, 26-17 (GB)
(RS: Pts.—Packers 2,795, Lions 2,523)
(PS Pts.—Packers 44, Lions 36)
Franchise in Portsmouth prior to 1934 and known as the Spartans
***NFC First-Round Playoff*

DETROIT vs. *INDIANAPOLIS
RS: Lions lead series, 18-17-2
1953—Lions, 27-17 (B)
Lions, 17-7 (D)
1954—Lions, 35-0 (D)
Lions, 27-3 (B)
1955—Colts, 28-13 (B)
Lions, 24-14 (D)
1956—Lions, 31-14 (B)
Lions, 27-3 (D)
1957—Colts, 34-14 (B)
Lions, 31-27 (D)
1958—Colts, 28-15 (B)
Colts, 40-14 (D)
1959—Colts, 21-9 (B)
Colts, 31-24 (D)
1960—Lions, 30-17 (D)
Lions, 20-15 (B)
1961—Lions, 16-15 (B)
Colts, 17-14 (D)
1962—Lions, 29-20 (B)
Lions, 21-14 (D)
1963—Colts, 25-21 (D)
Colts, 24-21 (B)
1964—Colts, 34-0 (D)
Lions, 31-14 (B)
1965—Colts, 31-7 (B)
Tie, 24-24 (D)
1966—Colts, 45-14 (B)
Lions, 20-14 (D)
1967—Colts, 41-7 (B)
1968—Colts, 27-10 (D)
1969—Tie, 17-17 (B)
1973—Colts, 29-27 (D)
1977—Lions, 13-10 (B)
1980—Colts, 10-9 (D)
1985—Colts, 14-6 (I)
1991—Lions, 33-24 (I)
1997—Lions, 32-10 (D)
(RS Pts.—Colts 758, Lions 730)
Franchise in Baltimore prior to 1984

DETROIT vs. JACKSONVILLE
RS: Series tied, 1-1
1995—Lions, 44-0 (D)
1998—Jaguars, 37-22 (J)

ALL-TIME TEAM VS. TEAM RESULTS

(RS Pts.—Lions 66, Jaguars 37)

DETROIT vs. KANSAS CITY
RS: Chiefs lead series, 6-3
1971—Lions, 32-21 (D)
1975—Chiefs, 24-21 (KC) OT
1980—Chiefs, 20-17 (KC)
1981—Lions, 27-10 (D)
1987—Chiefs, 27-20 (D)
1988—Lions, 7-6 (KC)
1990—Chiefs, 43-24 (KC)
1996—Chiefs, 28-24 (D)
1999—Chiefs, 31-21 (KC)
(RS Pts.—Chiefs 210, Lions 193)

DETROIT vs. MIAMI
RS: Dolphins lead series, 4-2
1973—Dolphins, 34-7 (M)
1979—Dolphins, 28-10 (D)
1985—Lions, 31-21 (D)
1991—Lions, 17-13 (D)
1994—Dolphins, 27-20 (M)
1997—Dolphins, 33-30 (M)
(RS Pts.—Dolphins 156, Lions 115)

DETROIT vs. MINNESOTA
RS: Vikings lead series, 47-28-2
1961—Lions, 37-10 (M)
Lions, 13-7 (D)
1962—Lions, 17-6 (M)
Lions, 37-23 (D)
1963—Lions, 28-10 (D)
Vikings, 34-31 (M)
1964—Lions, 24-20 (M)
Tie, 23-23 (D)
1965—Lions, 31-29 (M)
Vikings, 29-7 (D)
1966—Lions, 32-31 (M)
Vikings, 28-16 (D)
1967—Tie, 10-10 (M)
Lions, 14-3 (D)
1968—Vikings, 24-10 (M)
Vikings, 13-6 (D)
1969—Vikings, 24-10 (M)
Vikings, 27-0 (D)
1970—Vikings, 30-17 (D)
Vikings, 24-20 (M)
1971—Vikings, 16-13 (D)
Vikings, 29-10 (M)
1972—Vikings, 34-10 (D)
Vikings, 16-14 (M)
1973—Vikings, 23-9 (D)
Vikings, 28-7 (M)
1974—Vikings, 7-6 (D)
Lions, 20-16 (M)
1975—Vikings, 25-19 (M)
Lions, 17-10 (D)
1976—Vikings, 10-9 (D)
Vikings, 31-23 (M)
1977—Vikings, 14-7 (M)
Vikings, 30-21 (D)
1978—Vikings, 17-7 (M)
Lions, 45-14 (D)
1979—Vikings, 13-10 (D)
Vikings, 14-7 (M)
1980—Lions, 27-7 (D)
Vikings, 34-0 (M)
1981—Vikings, 26-24 (M)
Lions, 45-7 (D)
1982—Vikings, 34-31 (D)
1983—Vikings, 20-17 (M)
Lions, 13-2 (D)
1984—Vikings, 29-28 (D)
Lions, 16-14 (M)
1985—Vikings, 16-13 (M)
Lions, 41-21 (D)
1986—Lions, 13-10 (M)
Vikings, 24-10 (D)
1987—Vikings, 34-19 (M)
Vikings, 17-14 (D)
1988—Vikings, 44-17 (M)
Vikings, 23-0 (D)
1989—Vikings, 24-17 (M)
Vikings, 20-7 (D)
1990—Lions, 34-27 (M)
Vikings, 17-7 (D)
1991—Lions, 24-20 (D)
Lions, 34-14 (M)
1992—Lions, 31-17 (D)
Vikings, 31-14 (M)
1993—Lions, 30-27 (M)
Vikings, 13-0 (D)
1994—Vikings, 10-3 (M)
Lions, 41-19 (D)
1995—Vikings, 20-10 (M)
Lions, 44-38 (D)
1996—Vikings, 17-13 (M)
Vikings, 24-22 (D)
1997—Lions, 38-15 (D)
Lions, 14-13 (M)
1998—Vikings, 29-6 (M)
Vikings, 34-13 (D)
1999—Lions, 25-23 (D)
Vikings, 24-17 (M)
(RS Pts.—Vikings 1,590, Lions 1,409)

DETROIT vs. NEW ENGLAND
RS: Series tied, 3-3
1971—Lions, 34-7 (NE)
1976—Lions, 30-10 (D)
1979—Patriots, 24-17 (NE)
1985—Patriots, 23-6 (NE)
1993—Lions, 19-16 (NE) OT
1994—Patriots, 23-17 (D)
(RS Pts.—Lions 123, Patriots 103)

DETROIT vs. NEW ORLEANS
RS: Saints lead series, 8-6-1
1968—Tie, 20-20 (D)
1970—Saints, 19-17 (NO)
1972—Lions, 27-14 (D)
1973—Saints, 20-13 (NO)
1974—Lions, 19-14 (D)
1976—Saints, 17-16 (NO)
1977—Lions, 23-19 (D)
1979—Saints, 17-7 (NO)
1980—Lions, 24-13 (D)
1988—Saints, 22-14 (D)
1989—Lions, 21-14 (D)
1990—Lions, 27-10 (NO)
1992—Saints, 13-7 (D)
1993—Saints, 14-3 (NO)
1997—Saints, 35-17 (NO)
(RS Pts.—Saints 261, Lions 255)

***DETROIT vs. N.Y. GIANTS**
RS: Lions lead series, 18-17-1
PS: Lions lead series, 1-0
1930—Giants, 19-6 (P)
1931—Spartans, 14-6 (P)
Giants, 14-0 (NY)
1932—Spartans, 7-0 (P)
Spartans, 6-0 (NY)
1933—Spartans, 17-7 (P)
Giants, 13-10 (NY)
1934—Lions, 9-0 (D)
1935—**Lions, 26-7 (D)
1936—Giants, 14-7 (NY)
Lions, 38-0 (D)
1937—Lions, 17-0 (NY)
1939—Lions, 18-14 (D)
1941—Giants, 20-13 (NY)
1943—Tie, 0-0 (D)
1945—Giants, 35-14 (NY)
1947—Lions, 35-7 (D)
1949—Lions, 45-21 (NY)
1953—Lions, 27-16 (NY)
1955—Giants, 24-19 (D)
1958—Giants, 19-17 (D)
1962—Giants, 17-14 (NY)
1964—Lions, 26-3 (D)
1967—Lions, 30-7 (NY)
1969—Lions, 24-0 (D)
1972—Lions, 30-16 (D)
1974—Lions, 20-19 (D)
1976—Giants, 24-10 (NY)
1982—Giants, 13-6 (D)
1983—Lions, 15-9 (D)
1988—Giants, 30-10 (NY)
Giants, 13-10 (D) OT
1989—Giants, 24-14 (NY)
1990—Giants, 20-0 (NY)
1994—Lions, 28-25 (NY) OT
1996—Giants, 35-7 (D)
1997—Giants, 26-20 (D) OT
(RS Pts.—Lions 583, Giants 510)
(PS Pts.—Lions 26, Giants 7)
**Franchise in Portsmouth prior to 1934 and known as the Spartans*
***NFL Championship*

DETROIT vs. N.Y. JETS
RS: Lions lead series, 5-3
1972—Lions, 37-20 (D)
1979—Jets, 31-10 (NY)
1982—Jets, 28-13 (D)
1985—Lions, 31-20 (D)
1988—Jets, 17-10 (D)
1991—Lions, 34-20 (D)
1994—Lions, 18-7 (NY)
1997—Lions, 13-10 (D)
(RS Pts.—Lions 166, Jets 153)

DETROIT vs. *OAKLAND
RS: Raiders lead series, 6-2
1970—Lions, 28-14 (D)
1974—Raiders, 35-13 (O)
1978—Raiders, 29-17 (O)
1981—Lions, 16-0 (D)
1984—Raiders, 24-3 (D)
1987—Raiders, 27-7 (LA)
1990—Raiders, 38-31 (D)
1996—Raiders, 37-21 (O)
(RS Pts.—Raiders 204, Lions 136)
**Franchise in Los Angeles from 1982-1994*

***DETROIT vs. PHILADELPHIA**
RS: Lions lead series, 12-11-2
PS: Eagles lead series, 1-0
1933—Spartans, 25-0 (P)
1934—Lions, 10-0 (P)
1935—Lions, 35-0 (D)
1936—Lions, 23-0 (P)
1938—Eagles, 21-7 (D)
1940—Lions, 21-0 (P)
1941—Lions, 21-17 (D)
1945—Lions, 28-24 (D)
1948—Eagles, 45-21 (P)
1949—Eagles, 22-14 (D)
1951—Lions, 28-10 (P)
1954—Tie, 13-13 (D)
1957—Lions, 27-16 (P)
1960—Eagles, 28-10 (P)
1961—Eagles, 27-24 (D)
1965—Lions, 35-28 (P)
1968—Eagles, 12-0 (D)
1971—Eagles, 23-20 (D)
1974—Eagles, 28-17 (P)
1977—Lions, 17-13 (D)
1979—Eagles, 44-7 (P)
1984—Tie, 23-23 (D) OT
1986—Lions, 13-11 (P)
1995—**Eagles, 58-37 (P)
1996—Eagles, 24-17 (P)
1998—Eagles, 10-9 (P)
(RS Pts.—Lions 465, Eagles 439)
(PS Pts.—Eagles 58, Lions 37)
**Franchise in Portsmouth prior to 1934 and known as the Spartans*
***NFC First-Round Playoff*

DETROIT vs. *PITTSBURGH
RS: Lions lead series, 14-12-1
1934—Lions, 40-7 (D)
1936—Lions, 28-3 (D)
1937—Lions, 7-3 (D)
1938—Lions, 16-7 (D)
1940—Pirates, 10-7 (D)
1942—Steelers, 35-7 (D)
1946—Lions, 17-7 (D)
1947—Steelers, 17-10 (P)
1948—Lions, 17-14 (D)
1949—Steelers, 14-7 (P)
1950—Lions, 10-7 (D)
1952—Lions, 31-6 (P)
1953—Lions, 38-21 (D)
1955—Lions, 31-28 (P)
1956—Lions, 45-7 (D)
1959—Tie, 10-10 (P)
1962—Lions, 45-7 (D)
1966—Steelers, 17-3 (P)
1967—Steelers, 24-14 (D)
1969—Steelers, 16-13 (P)
1973—Steelers, 24-10 (P)
1983—Lions, 45-3 (D)
1986—Steelers, 27-17 (P)
1989—Steelers, 23-3 (D)
1992—Steelers, 17-14 (P)
1995—Steelers, 23-20 (P)
1998—Lions, 19-16 (D) OT
(RS Pts.—Lions 524, Steelers 393)
**Steelers known as Pirates prior to 1941*

DETROIT vs. *ST. LOUIS
RS: Rams lead series, 39-36-1
PS: Lions lead series, 1-0
1937—Lions, 28-0 (C)
Lions, 27-7 (D)
1938—Rams, 21-17 (C)
Lions, 6-0 (D)
1939—Lions, 15-7 (D)
Rams, 14-3 (C)
1940—Lions, 6-0 (D)
Rams, 24-0 (C)
1941—Lions, 17-7 (D)
Lions, 14-0 (C)
1942—Rams, 14-0 (D)
Rams, 27-7 (C)
1944—Rams, 20-17 (D)
Lions, 26-14 (C)
1945—Rams, 28-21 (D)
1946—Rams, 35-14 (LA)
Rams, 41-20 (D)
1947—Rams, 27-13 (D)
Rams, 28-17 (LA)
1948—Rams, 44-7 (LA)
Rams, 34-27 (D)
1949—Rams, 27-24 (LA)
Rams, 21-10 (D)
1950—Rams, 30-28 (D)
Rams, 65-24 (LA)
1951—Rams, 27-21 (D)
Lions, 24-22 (LA)
1952—Lions, 17-14 (LA)
Lions, 24-16 (D)
**Lions, 31-21 (D)
1953—Rams, 31-19 (D)
Rams, 37-24 (LA)
1954—Lions, 21-3 (D)
Lions, 27-24 (LA)
1955—Rams, 17-10 (D)
Rams, 24-13 (LA)
1956—Lions, 24-21 (D)
Lions, 16-7 (LA)
1957—Lions, 10-7 (D)
Rams, 35-17 (LA)
1958—Rams, 42-28 (D)
Lions, 41-24 (LA)
1959—Lions, 17-7 (LA)
Lions, 23-17 (D)
1960—Rams, 48-35 (LA)
Lions, 12-10 (D)
1961—Lions, 14-13 (D)
Lions, 28-10 (LA)
1962—Lions, 13-10 (D)
Lions, 12-3 (LA)
1963—Lions, 23-2 (LA)
Rams, 28-21 (D)
1964—Tie, 17-17 (LA)
Lions, 37-17 (D)
1965—Lions, 20-0 (D)
Lions, 31-7 (LA)
1966—Rams, 14-7 (D)
Rams, 23-3 (LA)
1967—Rams, 31-7 (D)
1968—Rams, 10-7 (LA)
1969—Lions, 28-0 (D)
1970—Lions, 28-23 (LA)
1971—Rams, 21-13 (D)
1972—Lions, 34-17 (LA)
1974—Rams, 16-13 (LA)
1975—Rams, 20-0 (D)

1976—Rams, 20-17 (D)
1980—Lions, 41-20 (LA)
1981—Rams, 20-13 (LA)
1982—Lions, 19-14 (LA)
1983—Rams, 21-10 (LA)
1986—Rams, 14-10 (LA)
1987—Rams, 37-16 (D)
1988—Rams, 17-10 (LA)
1991—Lions, 21-10 (D)
1993—Lions, 16-13 (LA)
1999—Lions, 31-27 (D)
(RS Pts.—Rams 1,463, Lions 1,371)
(PS Pts.—Lions 31, Rams 21)
Franchise in Los Angeles prior to 1995 and in Cleveland prior to 1946
***Conference Playoff*

DETROIT vs. SAN DIEGO
RS: Chargers lead series, 4-3
1972—Lions, 34-20 (D)
1977—Lions, 20-0 (D)
1978—Lions, 31-14 (D)
1981—Chargers, 28-23 (SD)
1984—Chargers, 27-24 (SD)
1996—Chargers, 27-21 (SD)
1999—Chargers, 20-10 (D)
(RS Pts.—Lions 163, Chargers 136)

DETROIT vs. SAN FRANCISCO
RS: 49ers lead series, 29-26-1
PS: Series tied, 1-1
1950—Lions, 24-7 (D)
49ers, 28-27 (SF)
1951—49ers, 20-10 (D)
49ers, 21-17 (SF)
1952—49ers, 17-3 (SF)
49ers, 28-0 (D)
1953—Lions, 24-21 (D)
Lions, 14-10 (SF)
1954—49ers, 37-31 (SF)
Lions, 48-7 (D)
1955—49ers, 27-24 (D)
49ers, 38-21 (SF)
1956—Lions, 20-17 (D)
Lions, 17-13 (SF)
1957—49ers, 35-31 (SF)
Lions, 31-10 (D)
*Lions, 31-27 (SF)
1958—49ers, 24-21 (SF)
Lions, 35-21 (D)
1959—49ers, 34-13 (D)
49ers, 33-7 (SF)
1960—49ers, 14-10 (D)
Lions, 24-0 (SF)
1961—49ers, 49-0 (D)
Tie, 20-20 (SF)
1962—Lions, 45-24 (D)
Lions, 38-24 (SF)
1963—Lions, 26-3 (D)
Lions, 45-7 (SF)
1964—Lions, 26-17 (SF)
Lions, 24-7 (D)
1965—49ers, 27-21 (D)
49ers, 17-14 (SF)
1966—49ers, 27-24 (SF)
49ers, 41-14 (D)
1967—Lions, 45-3 (SF)
1968—49ers, 14-7 (D)
1969—Lions, 26-14 (SF)
1970—Lions, 28-7 (D)
1971—49ers, 31-27 (SF)
1973—Lions, 30-20 (D)
1974—Lions, 17-13 (D)
1975—Lions, 28-17 (SF)
1977—49ers, 28-7 (SF)
1978—Lions, 33-14 (D)
1980—Lions, 17-13 (D)
1981—Lions, 24-17 (D)
1983—**49ers, 24-23 (SF)
1984—49ers, 30-27 (D)
1985—Lions, 23-21 (D)
1988—49ers, 20-13 (SF)
1991—49ers, 35-3 (SF)
1992—49ers, 24-6 (SF)
1993—49ers, 55-17 (D)
1994—49ers, 27-21 (D)
1995—Lions, 27-24 (D)
1996—49ers, 24-14 (SF)
1998—49ers, 35-13 (SF)
(RS Pts.—49ers 1,211, Lions 1,202)
(PS Pts.—Lions 54, 49ers 51)
**Conference Playoff*
***NFC Divisional Playoff*

DETROIT vs. SEATTLE
RS: Series tied, 4-4
1976—Lions, 41-14 (S)
1978—Seahawks, 28-16 (S)
1984—Seahawks, 38-17 (S)
1987—Seahawks, 37-14 (D)
1990—Seahawks, 30-10 (S)
1993—Lions, 30-10 (D)
1996—Lions, 17-16 (D)
1999—Lions, 28-20 (S)
(RS Pts.—Seahawks 193, Lions 173)

DETROIT vs. TAMPA BAY
RS: Lions lead series, 25-19
PS: Buccaneers lead series, 1-0
1977—Lions, 16-7 (D)
1978—Lions, 15-7 (TB)
Lions, 34-23 (D)
1979—Buccaneers, 31-16 (TB)
Buccaneers, 16-14 (D)
1980—Lions, 24-10 (TB)
Lions, 27-14 (D)
1981—Buccaneers, 28-10 (TB)
Buccaneers, 20-17 (D)
1982—Buccaneers, 23-21 (TB)
1983—Lions, 11-0 (TB)
Lions, 23-20 (D)
1984—Buccaneers, 21-17 (TB)
Lions, 13-7 (D) OT
1985—Lions, 30-9 (D)
Buccaneers, 19-16 (TB) OT
1986—Buccaneers, 24-20 (D)
Lions, 38-17 (TB)
1987—Buccaneers, 31-27 (D)
Lions, 20-10 (TB)
1988—Buccaneers, 23-20 (D)
Buccaneers, 21-10 (TB)
1989—Lions, 17-16 (TB)
Lions, 33-7 (D)
1990—Buccaneers, 38-21 (D)
Buccaneers, 23-20 (TB)
1991—Lions, 31-3 (D)
Buccaneers, 30-21 (TB)
1992—Buccaneers, 27-23 (D)
Lions, 38-7 (TB)
1993—Buccaneers, 27-10 (TB)
Lions, 23-0 (D)
1994—Buccaneers, 24-14 (TB)
Lions, 14-9 (D)
1995—Lions, 27-24 (D)
Lions, 37-10 (TB)
1996—Lions, 21-6 (D)
Lions, 27-0 (TB)
1997—Buccaneers, 24-17 (D)
Lions, 27-9 (TB)
*Buccaneers, 20-10 (TB)
1998—Lions, 27-6 (D)
Lions, 28-25 (TB)
1999—Lions, 20-3 (D)
Buccaneers, 23-16 (TB)
(RS Pts—Lions 951, Buccaneers 722)
(PS Pts.—Buccaneers 20, Lions 10)
**NFC First-Round Playoff*

DETROIT vs. *TENNESSEE
RS: Titans lead series, 4-3
1971—Lions, 31-7 (H)
1975—Oilers, 24-8 (H)
1983—Oilers, 27-17 (H)
1986—Lions, 24-13 (D)
1989—Oilers, 35-31 (H)
1992—Oilers, 24-21 (D)
1995—Lions, 24-17 (H)
(RS Pts.—Lions 156, Titans 147)
**Franchise in Houston prior to 1997; known as Oilers prior to 1999*

***DETROIT vs. **WASHINGTON**
RS: Redskins lead series, 24-9
PS: Redskins lead series, 3-0
1932—Spartans, 10-0 (P)
1933—Spartans, 13-0 (B)
1934—Lions, 24-0 (D)
1935—Lions, 17-7 (B)
Lions, 14-0 (D)
1938—Redskins, 7-5 (D)
1939—Redskins, 31-7 (W)
1940—Redskins, 20-14 (D)
1942—Redskins, 15-3 (D)
1943—Redskins, 42-20 (W)
1946—Redskins, 17-16 (W)
1947—Lions, 38-21 (D)
1948—Redskins, 46-21 (W)
1951—Lions, 35-17 (D)
1956—Redskins, 18-17 (W)
1965—Lions, 14-10 (D)
1968—Redskins, 14-3 (W)
1970—Redskins, 31-10 (W)
1973—Redskins, 20-0 (D)
1976—Redskins, 20-7 (W)
1978—Redskins, 21-19 (D)
1979—Redskins, 27-24 (D)
1981—Redskins, 33-31 (W)
1982—***Redskins, 31-7 (W)
1983—Redskins, 38-17 (W)
1984—Redskins, 28-14 (W)
1985—Redskins, 24-3 (W)
1987—Redskins, 20-13 (W)
1990—Redskins, 41-38 (D) OT
1991—Redskins, 45-0 (W)
****Redskins, 41-10 (W)
1992—Redskins, 13-10 (W)
1995—Redskins, 36-30 (W) OT
1997—Redskins, 30-7 (W)
1999—Lions, 33-17 (D)
***Redskins, 27-13 (W)
(RS Pts.—Redskins 709, Lions 527)
(PS Pts.—Redskins 99, Lions 30)
**Franchise in Portsmouth prior to 1934 and known as the Spartans.*
***Franchise in Boston prior to 1937*
****NFC First-Round Playoff*
*****NFC Championship*

GREEN BAY vs. ARIZONA
RS: Packers lead series, 40-21-4
PS: Packers lead series, 1-0;
See Arizona vs. Green Bay

GREEN BAY vs. ATLANTA
RS: Packers lead series, 10-9
PS: Packers lead series, 1-0;
See Atlanta vs. Green Bay

GREEN BAY vs. BALTIMORE
RS: Packers lead series, 1-0;
See Baltimore vs. Green Bay

GREEN BAY vs. BUFFALO
RS: Bills lead series, 5-2
See Buffalo vs. Green Bay

GREEN BAY vs. CAROLINA
RS: Packers lead series, 2-1
PS: Packers lead series, 1-0;
See Carolina vs. Green Bay

GREEN BAY vs. CHICAGO
RS: Bears lead series, 82-70-6
PS: Bears lead series, 1-0;
See Chicago vs. Green Bay

GREEN BAY vs. CINCINNATI
RS: Packers lead series, 5-4;
See Cincinnati vs. Green Bay

GREEN BAY vs. CLEVELAND
RS: Packers lead series, 8-6
PS: Packers lead series, 1-0;
See Cleveland vs. Green Bay

GREEN BAY vs. DALLAS
RS: Cowboys lead series, 10-9
PS: Cowboys lead series, 4-2;
See Dallas vs. Green Bay

GREEN BAY vs. DENVER
RS: Broncos lead series, 5-3-1
PS: Broncos lead series, 1-0;
See Denver vs. Green Bay

GREEN BAY vs. DETROIT
RS: Packers lead series, 71-61-7
PS: Packers lead series, 2-0;
See Detroit vs. Green Bay

GREEN BAY vs. *INDIANAPOLIS
RS: Colts lead series, 19-18-1
PS: Packers lead series, 1-0
1953—Packers, 37-14 (GB)
Packers, 35-24 (B)
1954—Packers, 7-6 (B)
Packers, 24-13 (Mil)
1955—Colts, 24-20 (Mil)
Colts, 14-10 (B)
1956—Packers, 38-33 (Mil)
Colts, 28-21 (B)
1957—Colts, 45-17 (Mil)
Packers, 24-21 (B)
1958—Colts, 24-17 (Mil)
Colts, 56-0 (B)
1959—Colts, 38-21 (B)
Colts, 28-24 (Mil)
1960—Packers, 35-21 (GB)
Colts, 38-24 (B)
1961—Packers, 45-7 (GB)
Colts, 45-21 (B)
1962—Packers, 17-6 (B)
Packers, 17-13 (GB)
1963—Packers, 31-20 (GB)
Packers, 34-20 (B)
1964—Colts, 21-20 (GB)
Colts, 24-21 (B)
1965—Packers, 20-17 (Mil)
Packers, 42-27 (B)
**Packers, 13-10 (GB) OT
1966—Packers, 24-3 (Mil)
Packers, 14-10 (B)
1967—Colts, 13-10 (B)
1968—Colts, 16-3 (GB)
1969—Colts, 14-6 (B)
1970—Colts, 13-10 (Mil)
1974—Packers, 20-13 (B)
1982—Tie, 20-20 (B) OT
1985—Colts, 37-10 (I)
1988—Colts, 20-13 (GB)
1991—Packers, 14-10 (Mil)
1997—Colts, 41-38 (I)
(RS Pts.—Colts 837, Packers 804)
(PS Pts.—Packers 13, Colts 10)
**Franchise in Baltimore prior to 1984*
***Conference Playoff*

GREEN BAY vs. JACKSONVILLE
RS: Packers lead series, 1-0
1995—Packers, 24-14 (J)
(RS Pts.—Packers 24, Jaguars 14)

GREEN BAY vs. KANSAS CITY
RS: Chiefs lead series, 5-1-1
PS: Packers lead series, 1-0
1966—*Packers, 35-10 (Los Angeles)
1973—Tie, 10-10 (Mil)
1977—Chiefs, 20-10 (KC)
1987—Packers, 23-3 (KC)
1989—Chiefs, 21-3 (GB)
1990—Chiefs, 17-3 (GB)
1993—Chiefs, 23-16 (KC)
1996—Chiefs, 27-20 (KC)
(RS Pts.—Chiefs 121, Packers 85)
(PS Pts.—Packers 35, Chiefs 10)
**Super Bowl I*

GREEN BAY vs. MIAMI
RS: Dolphins lead series, 8-1
1971—Dolphins, 27-6 (Mia)
1975—Dolphins, 31-7 (GB)
1979—Dolphins, 27-7 (Mia)
1985—Dolphins, 34-24 (GB)
1988—Dolphins, 24-17 (Mia)
1989—Dolphins, 23-20 (Mia)
1991—Dolphins, 16-13 (Mia)
1994—Dolphins, 24-14 (Mil)
1997—Packers, 23-18 (GB)
(RS Pts.—Dolphins 224, Packers 131)

GREEN BAY vs. MINNESOTA
RS: Vikings lead series, 39-37-1

ALL-TIME TEAM VS. TEAM RESULTS

1961—Packers, 33-7 (Minn)
Packers, 28-10 (Mil)
1962—Packers, 34-7 (GB)
Packers, 48-21 (Minn)
1963—Packers, 37-28 (Minn)
Packers, 28-7 (GB)
1964—Vikings, 24-23 (GB)
Packers, 42-13 (Minn)
1965—Packers, 38-13 (Minn)
Packers, 24-19 (GB)
1966—Vikings, 20-17 (GB)
Packers, 28-16 (Minn)
1967—Vikings, 10-7 (Mil)
Packers, 30-27 (Minn)
1968—Vikings, 26-13 (Mil)
Vikings, 14-10 (Minn)
1969—Vikings, 19-7 (Minn)
Vikings, 9-7 (Mil)
1970—Packers, 13-10 (Mil)
Vikings, 10-3 (Minn)
1971—Vikings, 24-13 (GB)
Vikings, 3-0 (Minn)
1972—Vikings, 27-13 (GB)
Packers, 23-7 (Minn)
1973—Vikings, 11-3 (Minn)
Vikings, 31-7 (GB)
1974—Vikings, 32-17 (GB)
Packers, 19-7 (Minn)
1975—Vikings, 28-17 (GB)
Vikings, 24-3 (Minn)
1976—Vikings, 17-10 (Mil)
Vikings, 20-9 (Minn)
1977—Vikings, 19-7 (Minn)
Vikings, 13-6 (GB)
1978—Vikings, 21-7 (Minn)
Tie, 10-10 (GB) OT
1979—Vikings, 27-21 (Minn) OT
Packers, 19-7 (Mil)
1980—Packers, 16-3 (GB)
Packers, 25-13 (Minn)
1981—Vikings, 30-13 (Mil)
Packers, 35-23 (Minn)
1982—Packers, 26-7 (Mil)
1983—Vikings, 20-17 (GB) OT
Packers, 29-21 (Minn)
1984—Packers, 45-17 (Mil)
Packers, 38-14 (Minn)
1985—Packers, 20-17 (Mil)
Packers, 27-17 (Minn)
1986—Vikings, 42-7 (Minn)
Vikings, 32-6 (GB)
1987—Packers, 23-16 (Minn)
Packers, 16-10 (Mil)
1988—Packers, 34-14 (Minn)
Packers, 18-6 (GB)
1989—Vikings, 26-14 (Minn)
Packers, 20-19 (Mil)
1990—Packers, 24-10 (Mil)
Vikings, 23-7 (Minn)
1991—Vikings, 35-21 (GB)
Packers, 27-7 (Minn)
1992—Vikings, 23-20 (GB) OT
Vikings, 27-7 (Minn)
1993—Vikings, 15-13 (Minn)
Vikings, 21-17 (Mil)
1994—Packers, 16-10 (GB)
Vikings, 13-10 (M) OT
1995—Packers, 38-21 (GB)
Vikings, 27-24 (M)
1996—Vikings, 30-21 (M)
Packers, 38-10 (GB)
1997—Packers, 38-32 (GB)
Packers, 27-11 (M)
1998—Vikings, 37-24 (GB)
Vikings, 28-14 (M)
1999—Packers, 23-20 (GB)
Vikings, 24-20 (M)
(RS Pts.—Packers 1,532, Vikings 1,409)

GREEN BAY vs. NEW ENGLAND
RS: Series tied, 3-3
PS: Packers lead series, 1-0
1973—Patriots, 33-24 (NE)
1979—Packers, 27-14 (GB)
1985—Patriots, 26-20 (NE)
1988—Packers, 45-3 (Mil)
1994—Patriots, 17-16 (NE)
1996—*Packers, 35-21 (New Orleans)
1997—Packers, 28-10 (NE)
(RS Pts.—Packers 160, Patriots 103)
(PS Pts.—Packers 35, Patriots 21)
Super Bowl XXXI

GREEN BAY vs. NEW ORLEANS
RS: Packers lead series, 13-4
1968—Packers, 29-7 (Mil)
1971—Saints, 29-21 (Mil)
1972—Packers, 30-20 (NO)
1973—Packers, 30-10 (Mil)
1975—Saints, 20-19 (NO)
1976—Packers, 32-27 (Mil)
1977—Packers, 24-20 (NO)
1978—Packers, 28-17 (Mil)
1979—Packers, 28-19 (Mil)
1981—Packers, 35-7 (NO)
1984—Packers, 23-13 (NO)
1985—Packers, 38-14 (Mil)
1986—Saints, 24-10 (NO)
1987—Saints, 33-24 (NO)
1989—Packers, 35-34 (GB)
1993—Packers, 19-17 (NO)
1995—Packers, 34-23 (NO)
(RS Pts.—Packers 459, Saints 334)

GREEN BAY vs. N.Y. GIANTS
RS: Packers lead series, 23-20-2
PS: Packers lead series, 4-1
1928—Giants, 6-0 (GB)
Packers, 7-0 (NY)
1929—Packers, 20-6 (NY)
1930—Packers, 14-7 (GB)
Giants, 13-6 (NY)
1931—Packers, 27-7 (GB)
Packers, 14-10 (NY)
1932—Packers, 13-0 (GB)
Giants, 6-0 (NY)
1933—Giants, 10-7 (Mil)
Giants, 17-6 (NY)
1934—Packers, 20-6 (Mil)
Giants, 17-3 (NY)
1935—Packers, 16-7 (GB)
1936—Packers, 26-14 (NY)
1937—Giants, 10-0 (NY)
1938—Giants, 15-3 (NY)
*Giants, 23-17 (NY)
1939—*Packers, 27-0 (Mil)
1940—Giants, 7-3 (NY)
1942—Tie, 21-21 (NY)
1943—Packers, 35-21 (NY)
1944—Giants, 24-0 (NY)
*Packers, 14-7 (NY)
1945—Packers, 23-14 (NY)
1947—Tie, 24-24 (NY)
1948—Giants, 49-3 (Mil)
1949—Giants, 30-10 (GB)
1952—Packers, 17-3 (NY)
1957—Giants, 31-17 (GB)
1959—Giants, 20-3 (NY)
1961—Packers, 20-17 (Mil)
*Packers, 37-0 (GB)
1962—*Packers, 16-7 (NY)
1967—Packers, 48-21 (NY)
1969—Packers, 20-10 (Mil)
1971—Giants, 42-40 (GB)
1973—Packers, 16-14 (New Haven)
1975—Packers, 40-14 (Mil)
1980—Giants, 27-21 (NY)
1981—Packers, 27-14 (NY)
Packers, 26-24 (Mil)
1982—Packers, 27-19 (NY)
1983—Giants, 27-3 (NY)
1985—Packers, 23-20 (GB)
1986—Giants, 55-24 (NY)
1987—Giants, 20-10 (NY)
1992—Giants, 27-7 (NY)
1995—Packers, 14-6 (GB)
1998—Packers, 37-3 (NY)
(RS Pts.—Giants 755, Packers 741)
(PS Pts.—Packers 111, Giants 37)
NFL Championship

GREEN BAY vs. N.Y. JETS
RS: Jets lead series, 5-2
1973—Packers, 23-7 (Mil)
1979—Jets, 27-22 (GB)
1981—Jets, 28-3 (NY)
1982—Jets, 15-13 (NY)
1985—Jets, 24-3 (Mil)
1991—Jets, 19-16 (NY) OT
1994—Packers, 17-10 (GB)
(RS Pts.—Jets 130, Packers 97)

GREEN BAY vs. *OAKLAND
RS: Raiders lead series, 5-3
PS: Packers lead series, 1-0
1967—**Packers, 33-14 (Miami)
1972—Raiders, 20-14 (GB)
1976—Raiders, 18-14 (O)
1978—Raiders, 28-3 (GB)
1984—Raiders, 28-7 (LA)
1987—Raiders, 20-0 (GB)
1990—Packers, 29-16 (LA)
1993—Packers, 28-0 (GB)
1999—Packers, 28-24 (GB)
(RS Pts.—Raiders 154, Packers 123)
(PS Pts.—Packers 33, Raiders 14)
Franchise in Los Angeles from 1982-1994
***Super Bowl II*

GREEN BAY vs. PHILADELPHIA
RS: Packers lead series, 21-9
PS: Eagles lead series, 1-0
1933—Packers, 35-9 (GB)
Packers, 10-0 (P)
1934—Packers, 19-6 (GB)
1935—Packers, 13-6 (P)
1937—Packers, 37-7 (Mil)
1939—Packers, 23-16 (P)
1940—Packers, 27-20 (GB)
1942—Packers, 7-0 (P)
1946—Packers, 19-7 (P)
1947—Eagles, 28-14 (P)
1951—Packers, 37-24 (GB)
1952—Packers, 12-10 (Mil)
1954—Packers, 37-14 (P)
1958—Packers, 38-35 (GB)
1960—*Eagles, 17-13 (P)
1962—Packers, 49-0 (P)
1968—Packers, 30-13 (GB)
1970—Packers, 30-17 (Mil)
1974—Eagles, 36-14 (P)
1976—Packers, 28-13 (GB)
1978—Eagles, 10-3 (P)
1979—Eagles, 21-10 (GB)
1987—Packers, 16-10 (GB) OT
1990—Eagles, 31-0 (P)
1991—Eagles, 20-3 (GB)
1992—Packers, 27-24 (Mil)
1993—Eagles, 20-17 (GB)
1994—Eagles, 13-7 (P)
1996—Packers, 39-13 (GB)
1997—Eagles, 10-9 (P)
1998—Packers, 24-16 (GB)
(RS Pts.—Packers 634, Eagles 449)
(PS Pts.—Eagles 17, Packers 13)
NFL Championship

GREEN BAY vs. *PITTSBURGH
RS: Packers lead series, 18-12
1933—Packers, 47-0 (GB)
1935—Packers, 27-0 (GB)
Packers, 34-14 (P)
1936—Packers, 42-10 (Mil)
1938—Packers, 20-0 (GB)
1940—Packers, 24-3 (Mil)
1941—Packers, 54-7 (P)
1942—Packers, 24-21 (Mil)
1946—Packers, 17-7 (GB)
1947—Steelers, 18-17 (Mil)
1948—Steelers, 38-7 (P)
1949—Steelers, 30-7 (Mil)
1951—Packers, 35-33 (Mil)
Steelers, 28-7 (P)
1953—Steelers, 31-14 (P)
1954—Steelers, 21-20 (GB)
1957—Packers, 27-10 (P)
1960—Packers, 19-13 (P)
1963—Packers, 33-14 (Mil)
1965—Packers, 41-9 (P)
1967—Steelers, 24-17 (GB)
1969—Packers, 38-34 (P)
1970—Packers, 20-12 (P)
1975—Steelers, 16-13 (Mil)
1980—Steelers, 22-20 (P)
1983—Steelers, 25-21 (GB)
1986—Steelers, 27-3 (P)
1992—Packers, 17-3 (GB)
1995—Packers, 24-19 (GB)
1998—Steelers, 27-20 (P)
(RS Pts.—Packers 709, Steelers 516)
Steelers known as Pirates prior to 1941

GREEN BAY vs. *ST. LOUIS
RS: Rams lead series, 43-39-2
PS: Packers lead series, 1-0
1937—Packers, 35-10 (C)
Packers, 35-7 (GB)
1938—Packers, 26-17 (GB)
Packers, 28-7 (C)
1939—Rams, 27-24 (GB)
Packers, 7-6 (C)
1940—Packers, 31-14 (GB)
Tie, 13-13 (C)
1941—Packers, 24-7 (Mil)
Packers, 17-14 (C)
1942—Packers, 45-28 (GB)
Packers, 30-12 (C)
1944—Packers, 30-21 (GB)
Packers, 42-7 (C)
1945—Rams, 27-14 (GB)
Rams, 20-7 (C)
1946—Rams, 21-17 (Mil)
Rams, 38-17 (LA)
1947—Packers, 17-14 (Mil)
Packers, 30-10 (LA)
1948—Packers, 16-0 (GB)
Rams, 24-10 (LA)
1949—Rams, 48-7 (GB)
Rams, 35-7 (LA)
1950—Rams, 45-14 (Mil)
Rams, 51-14 (LA)
1951—Rams, 28-0 (Mil)
Rams, 42-14 (LA)
1952—Rams, 30-28 (Mil)
Rams, 45-27 (LA)
1953—Rams, 38-20 (Mil)
Rams, 33-17 (LA)
1954—Packers, 35-17 (Mil)
Rams, 35-27 (LA)
1955—Packers, 30-28 (Mil)
Rams, 31-17 (LA)
1956—Packers, 42-17 (Mil)
Rams, 49-21 (LA)
1957—Rams, 31-27 (Mil)
Rams, 42-17 (LA)
1958—Rams, 20-7 (GB)
Rams, 34-20 (LA)
1959—Rams, 45-6 (Mil)
Packers, 38-20 (LA)
1960—Rams, 33-31 (Mil)
Packers, 35-21 (LA)
1961—Packers, 35-17 (GB)
Packers, 24-17 (LA)
1962—Packers, 41-10 (Mil)
Packers, 20-17 (LA)
1963—Packers, 42-10 (GB)
Packers, 31-14 (LA)
1964—Rams, 27-17 (Mil)
Tie, 24-24 (LA)
1965—Packers, 6-3 (Mil)
Rams, 21-10 (LA)
1966—Packers, 24-13 (GB)
Packers, 27-23 (LA)
1967—Rams, 27-24 (LA)
**Packers, 28-7 (Mil)
1968—Rams, 16-14 (Mil)
1969—Rams, 34-21 (LA)
1970—Rams, 31-21 (GB)
1971—Rams, 30-13 (LA)

1973—Rams, 24-7 (LA)
1974—Packers, 17-6 (Mil)
1975—Rams, 22-5 (LA)
1977—Rams, 24-6 (Mil)
1978—Rams, 31-14 (LA)
1980—Rams, 51-21 (LA)
1981—Rams, 35-23 (LA)
1982—Packers, 35-23 (Mil)
1983—Packers, 27-24 (Mil)
1984—Packers, 31-6 (Mil)
1985—Rams, 34-17 (LA)
1988—Rams, 34-7 (GB)
1989—Rams, 41-38 (LA)
1990—Packers, 36-24 (GB)
1991—Rams, 23-21 (LA)
1992—Packers, 28-13 (GB)
1993—Packers, 36-6 (Mil)
1994—Packers, 24-17 (GB)
1995—Rams, 17-14 (GB)
1996—Packers, 24-9 (StL)
1997—Packers, 17-7 (GB)
(RS Pts.—Rams 1,967, Packers 1,858)
(PS Pts.—Packers 28, Rams 7)
Franchise in Los Angeles prior to 1995 and in Cleveland prior to 1946
***Conference Championship*

GREEN BAY vs. SAN DIEGO
RS: Packers lead series, 6-1
1970—Packers, 22-20 (SD)
1974—Packers, 34-0 (GB)
1978—Packers, 24-3 (SD)
1984—Chargers, 34-28 (GB)
1993—Packers, 20-13 (SD)
1996—Packers, 42-10 (GB)
1999—Packers, 31-3 (SD)
(RS Pts.—Packers 201, Chargers 83)

GREEN BAY vs. SAN FRANCISCO
RS: 49ers lead series, 25-24-1
PS: Packers lead series, 3-1
1950—Packers, 25-21 (GB)
49ers, 30-14 (SF)
1951—49ers, 31-19 (SF)
1952—49ers, 24-14 (SF)
1953—49ers, 37-7 (Mil)
49ers, 48-14 (SF)
1954—49ers, 23-17 (Mil)
49ers, 35-0 (SF)
1955—Packers, 27-21 (Mil)
Packers, 28-7 (SF)
1956—49ers, 17-16 (GB)
49ers, 38-20 (SF)
1957—49ers, 24-14 (Mil)
49ers, 27-20 (SF)
1958—49ers, 33-12 (Mil)
49ers, 48-21 (SF)
1959—Packers, 21-20 (GB)
Packers, 36-14 (SF)
1960—Packers, 41-14 (Mil)
Packers, 13-0 (SF)
1961—Packers, 30-10 (GB)
49ers, 22-21 (SF)
1962—Packers, 31-13 (Mil)
Packers, 31-21 (SF)
1963—Packers, 28-10 (Mil)
Packers, 21-17 (SF)
1964—Packers, 24-14 (Mil)
49ers, 24-14 (SF)
1965—Packers, 27-10 (GB)
Tie, 24-24 (SF)
1966—49ers, 21-20 (SF)
Packers, 20-7 (Mil)
1967—Packers, 13-0 (GB)
1968—49ers, 27-20 (SF)
1969—Packers, 14-7 (Mil)
1970—49ers, 26-10 (SF)
1972—Packers, 34-24 (Mil)
1973—49ers, 20-6 (SF)
1974—49ers, 7-6 (SF)
1976—49ers, 26-14 (GB)
1977—Packers, 16-14 (Mil)
1980—Packers, 23-16 (Mil)
1981—49ers, 13-3 (Mil)
1986—49ers, 31-17 (Mil)
1987—49ers, 23-12 (GB)
1989—Packers, 21-17 (SF)
1990—49ers, 24-20 (GB)
1995—*Packers, 27-17 (SF)
1996—Packers, 23-20 (GB) OT
*Packers, 35-14 (GB)
1997—**Packers, 23-10 (SF)
1998—Packers, 36-22 (GB)
***49ers, 30-27 (SF)
1999—Packers, 20-3 (SF)
(RS Pts.—49ers 1,025, Packers 978)
(PS Pts.—Packers 112, 49ers 71)
**NFC Divisional Playoff*
***NFC Championship*
****NFC First-Round Playoff*

GREEN BAY vs. SEATTLE
RS: Series tied, 4-4
1976—Packers, 27-20 (Mil)
1978—Packers, 45-28 (Mil)
1981—Packers, 34-24 (GB)
1984—Seahawks, 30-24 (Mil)
1987—Seahawks, 24-13 (S)
1990—Seahawks, 20-14 (Mil)
1996—Packers, 31-10 (S)
1999—Seahawks, 27-7 (GB)
(RS Pts.—Packers 195, Seahawks 183)

GREEN BAY vs. TAMPA BAY
RS: Packers lead series, 26-15-1
PS: Packers lead series, 1-0
1977—Packers, 13-0 (TB)
1978—Packers, 9-7 (GB)
Packers, 17-7 (TB)
1979—Buccaneers, 21-10 (GB)
Buccaneers, 21-3 (TB)
1980—Tie, 14-14 (TB) OT
Buccaneers, 20-17 (Mil)
1981—Buccaneers, 21-10 (GB)
Buccaneers, 37-3 (TB)
1983—Packers, 55-14 (GB)
Packers, 12-9 (TB) OT
1984—Buccaneers, 30-27 (TB) OT
Packers, 27-14 (GB)
1985—Packers, 21-0 (GB)
Packers, 20-17 (TB)
1986—Packers, 31-7 (Mil)
Packers, 21-7 (TB)
1987—Buccaneers, 23-17 (Mil)
1988—Buccaneers, 13-10 (GB)
Buccaneers, 27-24 (TB)
1989—Buccaneers, 23-21 (GB)
Packers, 17-16 (TB)
1990—Buccaneers, 26-14 (TB)
Packers, 20-10 (Mil)
1991—Packers, 15-13 (GB)
Packers, 27-0 (TB)
1992—Buccaneers, 31-3 (TB)
Packers, 19-14 (Mil)
1993—Packers, 37-14 (TB)
Packers, 13-10 (GB)
1994—Packers, 30-3 (GB)
Packers, 34-19 (TB)
1995—Packers, 35-13 (GB)
Buccaneers, 13-10 (TB) OT
1996—Packers, 34-3 (TB)
Packers, 13-7 (GB)
1997—Packers, 21-16 (GB)
Packers, 17-6 (TB)
*Packers, 21-7 (GB)
1998—Packers, 23-15 (GB)
Buccaneers, 24-22 (TB)
1999—Packers, 26-23 (GB)
Buccaneers, 29-10 (TB)
(RS Pts.—Packers 822, Buccaneers 637)
(PS Pts.—Packers 21, Buccaneers 7)
**NFC Divisional Playoff*

GREEN BAY vs. *TENNESSEE
RS: Packers lead series, 4-3
1972—Packers, 23-10 (H)
1977—Oilers, 16-10 (GB)
1980—Oilers, 22-3 (GB)
1983—Packers, 41-38 (H) OT
1986—Oilers, 31-3 (GB)
1992—Packers, 16-14 (H)
1998—Packers, 30-22 (GB)
(RS Pts.—Titans 153, Packers 126)
**Franchise in Houston prior to 1997; known as Oilers prior to 1999*

GREEN BAY vs. *WASHINGTON
RS: Packers lead series, 13-12-1
PS: Series tied, 1-1
1932—Packers, 21-0 (B)
1933—Tie, 7-7 (GB)
Redskins, 20-7 (B)
1934—Packers, 10-0 (B)
1936—Packers, 31-2 (GB)
Packers, 7-3 (B)
**Packers, 21-6 (New York)
1937—Redskins, 14-6 (W)
1939—Packers, 24-14 (Mil)
1941—Packers, 22-17 (W)
1943—Redskins, 33-7 (Mil)
1946—Packers, 20-7 (W)
1947—Packers, 27-10 (Mil)
1948—Redskins, 23-7 (Mil)
1949—Redskins, 30-0 (W)
1950—Packers, 35-21 (Mil)
1952—Packers, 35-20 (Mil)
1958—Redskins, 37-21 (W)
1959—Packers, 21-0 (GB)
1968—Packers, 27-7 (W)
1972—Redskins, 21-16 (W)
***Redskins, 16-3 (W)
1974—Redskins, 17-6 (GB)
1977—Redskins, 10-9 (W)
1979—Redskins, 38-21 (W)
1983—Packers, 48-47 (GB)
1986—Redskins, 16-7 (GB)
1988—Redskins, 20-17 (Mil)
(RS Pts.—Packers 459, Redskins 434)
(PS Pts.—Packers 24, Redskins 22)
**Franchise in Boston prior to 1937 and known as Braves prior to 1933*
***NFL Championship*
****NFC Divisional Playoff*

INDIANAPOLIS vs. ARIZONA
RS: Series tied, 6-6;
See Arizona vs. Indianapolis

INDIANAPOLIS vs. ATLANTA
RS: Colts lead series, 10-1;
See Atlanta vs. Indianapolis

INDIANAPOLIS vs. BALTIMORE
RS: Series tied, 1-1;
See Baltimore vs. Indianapolis

INDIANAPOLIS vs. BUFFALO
RS: Bills lead series, 34-24-1;
See Buffalo vs. Indianapolis

INDIANAPOLIS vs. CAROLINA
RS: Panthers lead series, 2-0;
See Carolina vs. Indianapolis

INDIANAPOLIS vs. CHICAGO
RS: Colts lead series, 21-16;
See Chicago vs. Indianapolis

INDIANAPOLIS vs. CINCINNATI
RS: Colts lead series, 11-8
PS: Colts lead series, 1-0;
See Cincinnati vs. Indianapolis

INDIANAPOLIS vs. CLEVELAND
RS: Browns lead series, 13-8
PS: Series tied, 2-2;
See Cleveland vs. Indianapolis

INDIANAPOLIS vs. DALLAS
RS: Cowboys lead series, 7-4
PS: Colts lead series, 1-0;
See Dallas vs. Indianapolis

INDIANAPOLIS vs. DENVER
RS: Broncos lead series, 9-2;
See Denver vs. Indianapolis

INDIANAPOLIS vs. DETROIT
RS: Lions lead series, 18-17-2;
See Detroit vs. Indianapolis

INDIANAPOLIS vs. GREEN BAY
RS: Colts lead series, 19-18-1
PS: Packers lead series, 1-0;
See Green Bay vs. Indianapolis

INDIANAPOLIS vs. JACKSONVILLE
RS: Colts lead series, 1-0
1995—Colts, 41-31 (J)
(RS Pts.—Colts 41, Jaguars 31)

***INDIANAPOLIS vs. KANSAS CITY**
RS: Series tied, 6-6
PS: Colts lead series, 1-0
1970—Chiefs, 44-24 (B)
1972—Chiefs, 24-10 (KC)
1975—Colts, 28-14 (B)
1977—Colts, 17-6 (KC)
1979—Chiefs, 14-0 (KC)
Chiefs, 10-7 (B)
1980—Colts, 31-24 (KC)
Chiefs, 38-28 (B)
1985—Chiefs, 20-7 (KC)
1990—Colts, 23-19 (I)
1995—**Colts, 10-7 (KC)
1996—Colts, 24-19 (KC)
1999—Colts, 25-17 (I)
(RS Pts.—Chiefs 249, Colts 224)
(PS Pts.—Colts 10, Chiefs 7)
**Franchise in Baltimore prior to 1984*
***AFC Divisional Playoff*

***INDIANAPOLIS vs. MIAMI**
RS: Dolphins lead series, 40-20
PS: Dolphins lead series, 1-0
1970—Colts, 35-0 (B)
Dolphins, 34-17 (M)
1971—Dolphins, 17-14 (M)
Colts, 14-3 (B)
**Dolphins, 21-0 (M)
1972—Dolphins, 23-0 (B)
Dolphins, 16-0 (M)
1973—Dolphins, 44-0 (M)
Colts, 16-3 (B)
1974—Dolphins, 17-7 (M)
Dolphins, 17-16 (B)
1975—Colts, 33-17 (M)
Colts, 10-7 (B) OT
1976—Colts, 28-14 (B)
Colts, 17-16 (M)
1977—Colts, 45-28 (B)
Dolphins, 17-6 (M)
1978—Dolphins, 42-0 (B)
Dolphins, 26-8 (M)
1979—Dolphins, 19-0 (M)
Dolphins, 28-24 (B)
1980—Colts, 30-17 (M)
Dolphins, 24-14 (B)
1981—Dolphins, 31-28 (B)
Dolphins, 27-10 (M)
1982—Dolphins, 24-20 (M)
Dolphins, 34-7 (B)
1983—Dolphins, 21-7 (B)
Dolphins, 37-0 (M)
1984—Dolphins, 44-7 (M)
Dolphins, 35-17 (I)
1985—Dolphins, 30-13 (M)
Dolphins, 34-20 (I)
1986—Dolphins, 30-10 (M)
Dolphins, 17-13 (I)
1987—Dolphins, 23-10 (I)
Colts, 40-21 (M)
1988—Colts, 15-13 (I)
Colts, 31-28 (M)
1989—Dolphins, 19-13 (M)
Colts, 42-13 (I)
1990—Dolphins, 27-7 (I)
Dolphins, 23-17 (M)
1991—Dolphins, 17-6 (M)
Dolphins, 10-6 (I)
1992—Colts, 31-20 (M)
Dolphins, 28-0 (I)
1993—Dolphins, 24-20 (I)
Dolphins, 41-27 (M)
1994—Dolphins, 22-21 (M)
Colts, 10-6 (I)
1995—Colts, 27-24 (M) OT
Colts, 36-28 (I)
1996—Colts, 10-6 (I)
Dolphins, 37-13 (M)
1997—Dolphins, 16-10 (M)

Colts, 41-0 (I)
1998—Dolphins, 24-15 (I)
Dolphins, 27-14 (M)
1999—Dolphins, 34-31 (I)
Colts, 37-34 (M)
(RS Pts.—Dolphins 1,358, Colts 1,016)
(PS Pts.—Dolphins 21, Colts 0)
Franchise in Baltimore prior to 1984
***AFC Championship*

***INDIANAPOLIS vs. MINNESOTA**
RS: Colts lead series, 11-7-1
PS: Colts lead series, 1-0
1961—Colts, 34-33 (B)
Vikings, 28-20 (M)
1962—Colts, 34-7 (M)
Colts, 42-17 (B)
1963—Colts, 37-34 (M)
Colts, 41-10 (B)
1964—Vikings, 34-24 (M)
Colts, 17-14 (B)
1965—Colts, 35-16 (B)
Colts, 41-21 (M)
1966—Colts, 38-23 (M)
Colts, 20-17 (B)
1967—Tie, 20-20 (M)
1968—Colts, 21-9 (B)
**Colts, 24-14 (B)
1969—Vikings, 52-14 (M)
1971—Vikings, 10-3 (M)
1982—Vikings, 13-10 (M)
1988—Vikings, 12-3 (M)
1997—Vikings, 39-28 (M)
(RS Pts.—Colts 482, Vikings 409)
(PS Pts.—Colts 24, Vikings 14)
Franchise in Baltimore prior to 1984
***Conference Championship*

***INDIANAPOLIS vs. **NEW ENGLAND**
RS: Patriots lead series, 36-23
1970—Colts, 14-6 (Bos)
Colts, 27-3 (Balt)
1971—Colts, 23-3 (NE)
Patriots, 21-17 (Balt)
1972—Colts, 24-17 (NE)
Colts, 31-0 (Balt)
1973—Patriots, 24-16 (NE)
Colts, 18-13 (Balt)
1974—Patriots, 42-3 (NE)
Patriots, 27-17 (Balt)
1975—Patriots, 21-10 (NE)
Colts, 34-21 (Balt)
1976—Colts, 27-13 (NE)
Patriots, 21-14 (Balt)
1977—Patriots, 17-3 (NE)
Colts, 30-24 (Balt)
1978—Colts, 34-27 (NE)
Patriots, 35-14 (Balt)
1979—Colts, 31-26 (Balt)
Patriots, 50-21 (NE)
1980—Patriots, 37-21 (Balt)
Patriots, 47-21 (NE)
1981—Colts, 29-28 (NE)
Colts, 23-21 (Balt)
1982—Patriots, 24-13 (Balt)
1983—Colts, 29-23 (NE) OT
Colts, 12-7 (Balt)
1984—Patriots, 50-17 (I)
Patriots, 16-10 (NE)
1985—Patriots, 34-15 (NE)
Patriots, 38-31 (I)
1986—Patriots, 33-3 (NE)
Patriots, 30-21 (I)
1987—Colts, 30-16 (I)
Patriots, 24-0 (NE)
1988—Patriots, 21-17 (NE)
Colts, 24-21 (I)
1989—Patriots, 23-20 (I) OT
Patriots, 22-16 (NE)
1990—Patriots, 16-14 (I)
Colts, 13-10 (NE)
1991—Patriots, 16-7 (I)
Patriots, 23-17 (NE) OT
1992—Patriots, 37-34 (I) OT
Colts, 6-0 (NE)
1993—Colts, 9-6 (I)
Patriots, 38-0 (NE)
1994—Patriots, 12-10 (I)
Patriots, 28-13 (NE)
1995—Colts, 24-10 (NE)
Colts, 10-7 (I)
1996—Patriots, 27-9 (I)
Patriots, 27-13 (NE)
1997—Patriots, 31-6 (I)
Patriots, 20-17 (NE)
1998—Patriots, 29-6 (NE)
Patriots, 21-16 (I)
1999—Patriots, 31-28 (NE)
Colts, 20-15 (I)
(RS Pts.—Patriots 1,330, Colts 1,032)
Franchise in Baltimore prior to 1984
***Franchise in Boston prior to 1971*

***INDIANAPOLIS vs. NEW ORLEANS**
RS: Saints lead series, 4-3
1967—Colts, 30-10 (B)
1969—Colts, 30-10 (NO)
1973—Colts, 14-10 (B)
1986—Saints, 17-14 (I)
1989—Saints, 41-6 (NO)
1995—Saints, 17-14 (NO)
1998—Saints, 19-13 (I) OT
(RS Pts.—Colts 124, Saints 121)
Franchise in Baltimore prior to 1984

***INDIANAPOLIS vs. N.Y. GIANTS**
RS: Colts lead series, 6-5
PS: Colts lead series, 2-0
1954—Colts, 20-14 (B)
1955—Giants, 17-7 (NY)
1958—Giants, 24-21 (NY)
**Colts, 23-17 (NY) OT
1959—**Colts, 31-16 (B)
1963—Giants, 37-28 (B)
1968—Colts, 26-0 (NY)
1971—Colts, 31-7 (NY)
1975—Colts, 21-0 (NY)
1979—Colts, 31-7 (NY)
1990—Giants, 24-7 (I)
1993—Giants, 20-6 (NY)
1999—Colts, 27-19 (NY)
(RS Pts.—Colts 225, Giants 169)
(PS Pts.—Colts 54, Giants 33)
Franchise in Baltimore prior to 1984
***NFL Championship*

***INDIANAPOLIS vs. N.Y. JETS**
RS: Colts lead series, 36-23
PS: Jets lead series, 1-0
1968—**Jets 16-7 (Miami)
1970—Colts, 29-22 (NY)
Colts, 35-20 (B)
1971—Colts, 22-0 (B)
Colts, 14-13 (NY)
1972—Jets, 44-34 (B)
Jets, 24-20 (NY)
1973—Jets, 34-10 (B)
Jets, 20-17 (NY)
1974—Colts, 35-20 (NY)
Jets, 45-38 (B)
1975—Colts, 45-28 (NY)
Colts, 52-19 (B)
1976—Colts, 20-0 (NY)
Colts, 33-16 (B)
1977—Colts, 20-12 (NY)
Colts, 33-12 (B)
1978—Jets, 33-10 (B)
Jets, 24-16 (NY)
1979—Colts, 10-8 (B)
Jets, 30-17 (NY)
1980—Colts, 17-14 (NY)
Colts, 35-21 (B)
1981—Jets, 41-14 (B)
Jets, 25-0 (NY)
1982—Jets, 37-0 (NY)
1983—Colts, 17-14 (NY)
Jets, 10-6 (B)
1984—Jets, 23-14 (I)
Colts, 9-5 (NY)
1985—Jets, 25-20 (NY)
Jets, 35-17 (I)
1986—Jets, 26-7 (I)
Jets, 31-16 (NY)
1987—Colts, 6-0 (I)
Colts, 19-14 (NY)
1988—Colts, 38-14 (I)
Jets, 34-16 (NY)
1989—Colts, 17-10 (NY)
Colts, 27-10 (I)
1990—Colts, 17-14 (I)
Colts, 29-21 (NY)
1991—Jets, 17-6 (I)
Colts, 28-27 (NY)
1992—Colts, 6-3 (I) OT
Colts, 10-6 (NY)
1993—Jets, 31-17 (I)
Colts, 9-6 (NY)
1994—Jets, 16-6 (NY)
Colts, 28-25 (I)
1995—Colts, 27-24 (NY) OT
Colts, 17-10 (I)
1996—Colts, 21-7 (NY)
Colts, 34-29 (I)
1997—Jets, 16-12 (I)
Colts, 22-14 (NY)
1998—Jets, 44-6 (NY)
Colts, 24-23 (I)
1999—Colts, 16-13 (NY)
Colts, 13-6 (I)
(RS Pts.—Jets 1,165, Colts 1,153)
(PS Pts.—Jets 16, Colts 7)
Franchise in Baltimore prior to 1984
***Super Bowl III*

***INDIANAPOLIS vs **OAKLAND**
RS: Raiders lead series, 5-2
PS: Series tied, 1-1
1970—***Colts, 27-17 (B)
1971—Colts, 37-14 (O)
1973—Raiders, 34-21 (B)
1975—Raiders, 31-20 (B)
1977—****Raiders, 37-31 (B) OT
1984—Raiders, 21-7 (LA)
1986—Colts, 30-24 (LA)
1991—Raiders, 16-0 (LA)
1995—Raiders, 30-17 (O)
(RS Pts.—Raiders 170, Colts 132)
(PS Pts.—Colts 58, Raiders 54)
Franchise in Baltimore prior to 1984
***Franchise in Los Angeles from 1982-1994*
****AFC Championship*
*****AFC Divisional Playoff*

***INDIANAPOLIS vs. PHILADELPHIA**
RS: Colts lead series, 8-6
1953—Eagles, 45-14 (P)
1965—Colts, 34-24 (B)
1967—Colts, 38-6 (P)
1969—Colts, 24-20 (B)
1970—Colts, 29-10 (B)
1974—Eagles, 30-10 (P)
1978—Eagles, 17-14 (B)
1981—Eagles, 38-13 (P)
1983—Colts, 22-21 (P)
1984—Eagles, 16-7 (P)
1990—Colts, 24-23 (P)
1993—Eagles, 20-10 (I)
1996—Colts, 37-10 (I)
1999—Colts, 44-17 (P)
(RS Pts.—Colts 320, Eagles 297)
Franchise in Baltimore prior to 1984

***INDIANAPOLIS vs. PITTSBURGH**
RS: Steelers lead series, 12-4
PS: Steelers lead series, 4-0
1957—Steelers, 19-13 (B)
1968—Colts, 41-7 (P)
1971—Colts, 34-21 (B)
1974—Steelers, 30-0 (P)
1975—**Steelers, 28-10 (P)
1976—**Steelers, 40-14 (B)
1977—Colts, 31-21 (B)
1978—Steelers, 35-13 (P)
1979—Steelers, 17-13 (P)
1980—Steelers, 20-17 (B)
1983—Steelers, 24-13 (B)
1984—Colts, 17-16 (I)
1985—Steelers, 45-3 (P)
1987—Steelers, 21-7 (P)
1991—Steelers, 21-3 (I)
1992—Steelers, 30-14 (P)
1994—Steelers, 31-21 (P)
1995—***Steelers, 20-16 (P)
1996—****Steelers, 42-14 (P)
1997—Steelers, 24-22 (P)
(RS Pts.—Steelers 382, Colts 262)
(PS Pts.—Steelers 130, Colts 54)
Franchise in Baltimore prior to 1984
***AFC Divisional Playoff*
****AFC Championship*
*****AFC First-Round Playoff*

***INDIANAPOLIS vs. **ST. LOUIS**
RS: Colts lead series, 21-16-2
1953—Rams, 21-13 (B)
Rams, 45-2 (LA)
1954—Rams, 48-0 (B)
Colts, 22-21 (LA)
1955—Tie, 17-17 (B)
Rams, 20-14 (LA)
1956—Colts, 56-21 (B)
Rams, 31-7 (LA)
1957—Colts, 31-14 (B)
Rams, 37-21 (LA)
1958—Colts, 34-7 (B)
Rams, 30-28 (LA)
1959—Colts, 35-21 (B)
Colts, 45-26 (LA)
1960—Colts, 31-17 (B)
Rams, 10-3 (LA)
1961—Colts, 27-24 (B)
Rams, 34-17 (LA)
1962—Colts, 30-27 (B)
Colts, 14-2 (LA)
1963—Rams, 17-16 (LA)
Colts, 19-16 (B)
1964—Colts, 35-20 (B)
Colts, 24-7 (LA)
1965—Colts, 35-20 (B)
Colts, 20-17 (LA)
1966—Colts, 17-3 (LA)
Rams, 23-7 (B)
1967—Tie, 24-24 (B)
Rams, 34-10 (LA)
1968—Colts, 27-10 (B)
Colts, 28-24 (LA)
1969—Rams, 27-20 (B)
Colts, 13-7 (LA)
1971—Colts, 24-17 (B)
1975—Rams, 24-13 (LA)
1986—Rams, 24-7 (I)
1989—Rams, 31-17 (LA)
1995—Colts, 21-18 (I)
(RS Pts.—Rams 836, Colts 824)
Franchise in Baltimore prior to 1984
***Franchise in Los Angeles prior to 1995*

***INDIANAPOLIS vs. SAN DIEGO**
RS: Chargers lead series, 12-7
PS: Colts lead series, 1-0
1970—Colts, 16-14 (SD)
1972—Chargers, 23-20 (B)
1976—Colts, 37-21 (SD)
1981—Chargers, 43-14 (B)
1982—Chargers, 44-26 (SD)
1984—Chargers, 38-10 (I)
1986—Chargers, 17-3 (I)
1987—Chargers, 16-13 (I)
Colts, 20-7 (SD)
1988—Colts, 16-0 (SD)
1989—Colts, 10-6 (I)
1992—Chargers, 34-14 (I)
Chargers, 26-0 (SD)
1993—Chargers, 31-0 (I)
1995—Chargers, 27-24 (I)
**Colts, 35-20 (SD)
1996—Chargers, 26-19 (I)
1997—Chargers, 35-19 (SD)
1998—Colts, 17-12 (I)
1999—Colts, 27-19 (SD)
(RS Pts.—Chargers 439, Colts 305)

(PS Pts.—Colts 35, Chargers 20)
Franchise in Baltimore prior to 1984
***AFC First-Round Playoff*

***INDIANAPOLIS vs. SAN FRANCISCO**
RS: Colts lead series, 22-17
1953—49ers, 38-21 (B)
49ers, 45-14 (SF)
1954—Colts, 17-13 (B)
49ers, 10-7 (SF)
1955—Colts, 26-14 (B)
49ers, 35-24 (SF)
1956—49ers, 20-17 (B)
49ers, 30-17 (SF)
1957—Colts, 27-21 (B)
49ers, 17-13 (SF)
1958—Colts, 35-27 (B)
49ers, 21-12 (SF)
1959—Colts, 45-14 (B)
Colts, 34-14 (SF)
1960—49ers, 30-22 (B)
49ers, 34-10 (SF)
1961—Colts, 20-17 (B)
Colts, 27-24 (SF)
1962—49ers, 21-13 (B)
Colts, 22-3 (SF)
1963—Colts, 20-14 (SF)
Colts, 20-3 (B)
1964—Colts, 37-7 (B)
Colts, 14-3 (SF)
1965—Colts, 27-24 (B)
Colts, 34-28 (SF)
1966—Colts, 36-14 (B)
Colts, 30-14 (SF)
1967—Colts, 41-7 (B)
Colts, 26-9 (SF)
1968—Colts, 27-10 (B)
Colts, 42-14 (SF)
1969—49ers, 24-21 (B)
49ers, 20-17 (SF)
1972—49ers, 24-21 (SF)
1986—49ers, 35-14 (SF)
1989—49ers, 30-24 (I)
1995—Colts, 18-17 (I)
1998—49ers, 34-31 (SF)
(RS Pts.—Colts 923, 49ers 779)
**Franchise in Baltimore prior to 1984*

***INDIANAPOLIS vs. SEATTLE**
RS: Colts lead series, 4-3
1977—Colts, 29-14 (S)
1978—Colts, 17-14 (S)
1991—Seahawks, 31-3 (S)
1994—Colts, 17-15 (I)
Colts, 31-19 (S)
1997—Seahawks, 31-3 (I)
1998—Seahawks, 27-23 (S)
(RS Pts.—Seahawks 151, Colts 123)
**Franchise in Baltimore prior to 1984*

***INDIANAPOLIS vs. TAMPA BAY**
RS: Colts lead series, 5-4
1976—Colts, 42-17 (B)
1979—Buccaneers, 29-26 (B) OT
1985—Colts, 31-23 (TB)
1987—Colts, 24-6 (I)
1988—Colts, 35-31 (I)
1991—Buccaneers, 17-3 (TB)
1992—Colts, 24-14 (TB)
1994—Buccaneers, 24-10 (TB)
1997—Buccaneers, 31-28 (I)
(RS Pts.—Colts 223, Buccaneers 192)
**Franchise in Baltimore prior to 1984*

***INDIANAPOLIS vs. **TENNESSEE**
RS: Series tied, 7-7
PS: Titans lead series, 1-0
1970—Colts, 24-20 (H)
1973—Oilers, 31-27 (B)
1976—Colts, 38-14 (B)
1979—Oilers, 28-16 (B)
1980—Oilers, 21-16 (H)
1983—Colts, 20-10 (B)
1984—Colts, 35-21 (H)
1985—Colts, 34-16 (I)
1986—Oilers, 31-17 (H)
1987—Colts, 51-27 (I)
1988—Oilers, 17-14 (I) OT
1990—Oilers, 24-10 (H)
1992—Oilers, 20-10 (I)
1994—Colts, 45-21 (I)
1999—***Titans, 19-16 (I)
(RS Pts.—Colts 357, Titans 301)
(PS Pts.—Titans 19, Colts 16)
**Franchise in Baltimore prior to 1984*
***Franchise in Houston prior to 1997; known as Oilers prior to 1999*
****AFC Divisional Playoff*

***INDIANAPOLIS vs. WASHINGTON**
RS: Colts lead series, 17-9
1953—Colts, 27-17 (B)
1954—Redskins, 24-21 (W)
1955—Redskins, 14-13 (B)
1956—Colts, 19-17 (B)
1957—Colts, 21-17 (W)
1958—Colts, 35-10 (B)
1959—Redskins, 27-24 (W)
1960—Colts, 20-0 (B)
1961—Colts, 27-6 (W)
1962—Colts, 34-21 (B)
1963—Colts, 36-20 (W)
1964—Colts, 45-17 (B)
1965—Colts, 38-7 (W)
1966—Colts, 37-10 (B)
1967—Colts, 17-13 (W)
1969—Colts, 41-17 (B)
1973—Redskins, 22-14 (W)
1977—Colts, 10-3 (B)
1978—Colts, 21-17 (B)
1981—Redskins, 38-14 (W)
1984—Redskins, 35-7 (I)
1990—Colts, 35-28 (I)
1993—Redskins, 30-24 (W)
1994—Redskins, 41-27 (I)
1996—Redskins, 31-16 (W)
1999—Colts, 24-21 (I)
(RS Pts.—Colts 647, Redskins 503)
**Franchise in Baltimore prior to 1984*

JACKSONVILLE vs. ATLANTA
RS: Jaguars lead series, 2-0;
See Atlanta vs. Jacksonville

JACKSONVILLE vs. BALTIMORE
RS: Jaguars lead series, 8-0;
See Baltimore vs. Jacksonville

JACKSONVILLE vs. BUFFALO
RS: Series tied, 1-1
PS: Jaguars lead series, 1-0;
See Buffalo vs. Jacksonville

JACKSONVILLE vs. CAROLINA
RS: Jaguars lead series, 2-0;
See Carolina vs. Jacksonville

JACKSONVILLE vs. CHICAGO
RS: Series tied, 1-1;
See Chicago vs. Jacksonville

JACKSONVILLE vs. CINCINNATI
RS: Jaguars lead series, 6-4;
See Cincinnati vs. Jacksonville

JACKSONVILLE vs. CLEVELAND
RS: Jaguars lead series, 4-0;
See Cleveland vs. Jacksonville

JACKSONVILLE vs. DALLAS
RS: Cowboys lead series, 1-0;
See Dallas vs. Jacksonville

JACKSONVILLE vs. DENVER
RS: Broncos lead series, 2-1
PS: Series tied, 1-1;
See Denver vs. Jacksonville

JACKSONVILLE vs. DETROIT
RS: Series tied, 1-1;
See Detroit vs. Jacksonville

JACKSONVILLE vs. GREEN BAY
RS: Packers lead series, 1-0;
See Green Bay vs. Jacksonville

JACKSONVILLE vs. INDIANAPOLIS
RS: Colts lead series, 1-0;
See Indianapolis vs. Jacksonville

JACKSONVILLE vs. KANSAS CITY
RS: Jaguars lead series, 2-0
1997—Jaguars, 24-10 (J)
1998—Jaguars, 21-16 (J)
(RS Pts.—Jaguars 45, Chiefs 26)

JACKSONVILLE vs. MIAMI
RS: Jaguars lead series, 1-0
PS: Jaguars lead series, 1-0
1998—Jaguars, 28-21 (J)
1999—*Jaguars, 62-7 (J)
(RS Pts.—Jaguars 28, Dolphins 21)
(PS Pts.—Jaguars 62, Dolphins 7)
**AFC Divisional Playoff*

JACKSONVILLE vs. MINNESOTA
RS: Vikings lead series, 1-0
1998—Vikings, 50-10 (M)
(RS Pts.—Vikings 50, Jaguars 10)

JACKSONVILLE vs. NEW ENGLAND
RS: Patriots lead series, 2-0
PS: Series tied, 1-1
1996—Patriots, 28-25 (NE) OT
*Patriots, 20-6 (NE)
1997—Patriots, 26-20 (J)
1998—**Jaguars, 25-10 (J)
(RS Pts.—Patriots 54, Jaguars 45)
(PS Pts.—Jaguars 31, Patriots 30)
**AFC Championship*
***AFC First-Round Playoff*

JACKSONVILLE vs. NEW ORLEANS
RS: Series tied, 1-1
1996—Saints, 17-13 (NO)
1999—Jaguars, 41-23 (J)
(RS Pts.—Jaguars 54, Saints 40)

JACKSONVILLE vs. N.Y. GIANTS
RS: Jaguars lead series, 1-0
1997—Jaguars, 40-13 (J)
(RS Pts.—Jaguars 40, Giants 13)

JACKSONVILLE vs. N.Y. JETS
RS: Jaguars lead series, 2-1
PS: Jets lead series, 1-0
1995—Jets, 27-10 (NY)
1996—Jaguars, 21-17 (J)
1998—*Jets, 34-24 (NY)
1999—Jaguars, 16-6 (NY)
(RS Pts.—Jets 50, Jaguars 47)
(PS Pts.—Jets 34, Jaguars 24
**AFC Divisional Playoff*

JACKSONVILLE vs. OAKLAND
RS: Series tied, 1-1
1996—Raiders, 17-3 (O)
1997—Jaguars, 20-9 (O)
(RS Pts.—Raiders 26, Jaguars 23)

JACKSONVILLE vs. PHILADELPHIA
RS: Jaguars lead series, 1-0
1997—Jaguars, 38-21 (J)
(RS Pts.—Jaguars 38, Eagles 21)

JACKSONVILLE vs. PITTSBURGH
RS: Jaguars lead series, 6-4
1995—Jaguars, 20-16 (J)
Steelers, 24-7 (P)
1996—Jaguars, 24-9 (J)
Steelers, 28-3 (P)
1997—Jaguars, 30-21 (J)
Steelers, 23-17 (P) OT
1998—Steelers, 30-15 (P)
Jaguars, 21-3 (J)
1999—Jaguars, 17-3 (P)
Jaguars, 20-6 (J)
(RS Pts.—Jaguars 174, Steelers 163)

JACKSONVILLE vs. ST. LOUIS
RS: Rams lead series, 1-0
1996—Rams, 17-14 (StL)
(RS Pts.—Rams 17, Jaguars 14)

JACKSONVILLE vs. SAN FRANCISCO
RS: Jaguars lead series, 1-0
1999—Jaguars, 41-3 (J)
(RS Pts.—Jaguars 41, 49ers 3)

JACKSONVILLE vs. SEATTLE
RS: Series tied, 1-1
1995—Seahawks, 47-30 (J)
1996—Jaguars, 20-13 (J)
(RS Pts.—Seahawks 60, Jaguars 50)

JACKSONVILLE vs. TAMPA BAY
RS: Series tied, 1-1
1995—Buccaneers, 17-16 (TB)
1998—Jaguars, 29-24 (J)
(RS Pts.—Jaguars 45, Buccaneers 41)

JACKSONVILLE vs. *TENNESSEE
RS: Series tied, 5-5
PS: Titans lead, 1-0
1995—Oilers, 10-3 (J)
Jaguars, 17-16 (H)
1996—Oilers, 34-27 (J)
Jaguars, 23-17 (H)
1997—Jaguars, 30-24 (T)
Jaguars, 17-9 (J)
1998—Jaguars, 27-22 (T)
Oilers, 16-13 (J)
1999—Titans, 20-19 (J)
Titans, 41-14 (T)
**Titans, 33-14 (J)
(RS Pts.—Titans 209, Jaguars 190)
(PS Pts.—Titans 33, Jaguars 14)
**Franchise in Houston prior to 1997; known as Oilers prior to 1999*
***AFC Championship*

JACKSONVILLE vs. WASHINGTON
RS: Redskins lead series, 1-0
1997—Redskins, 24-12 (W)
(RS Pts.—Redskins 24, Jaguars 12)

KANSAS CITY vs. ARIZONA
RS: Chiefs lead series, 5-1-1;
See Arizona vs. Kansas City

KANSAS CITY vs. ATLANTA
RS: Chiefs lead series, 4-0;
See Atlanta vs. Kansas City

KANSAS CITY vs. BALTIMORE
RS: Chiefs lead series, 1-0;
See Baltimore vs. Kansas City

KANSAS CITY vs. BUFFALO
RS: Bills lead series, 17-14-1
PS: Bills lead series, 2-1;
See Buffalo vs. Kansas City

KANSAS CITY vs. CARLOINA
RS: Chiefs lead series, 1-0;
See Carolina vs. Kansas City

KANSAS CITY vs. CHICAGO
RS: Bears lead series, 5-3;
See Chicago vs. Kansas City

KANSAS CITY vs. CINCINNATI
RS: Chiefs lead series, 11-9;
See Cincinnati vs. Kansas City

KANSAS CITY vs. CLEVELAND
RS: Browns lead series, 8-7-2;
See Cleveland vs. Kansas City

KANSAS CITY vs. DALLAS
RS: Cowboys lead series, 4-3;
See Dallas vs. Kansas City

KANSAS CITY vs. DENVER
RS: Chiefs lead series, 45-34
PS: Broncos lead series, 1-0;
See Denver vs. Kansas City

KANSAS CITY vs. DETROIT
RS: Chiefs lead series, 6-3;
See Detroit vs. Kansas City

KANSAS CITY vs. GREEN BAY
RS: Chiefs lead series, 5-1-1
PS: Packers lead series, 1-0;
See Green Bay vs. Kansas City

KANSAS CITY vs. INDIANAPOLIS
RS: Series tied, 6-6
PS: Colts lead series, 1-0;
See Indianapolis vs. Kansas City

KANSAS CITY vs. JACKSONVILLE
RS: Jaguars lead series, 2-0;
See Jacksonville vs. Kansas City

KANSAS CITY vs. MIAMI
RS: Series tied, 10-10
PS: Dolphins lead series, 3-0
1966—Chiefs, 34-16 (KC)
Chiefs, 19-18 (M)
1967—Chiefs, 24-0 (M)
Chiefs, 41-0 (KC)
1968—Chiefs, 48-3 (M)
1969—Chiefs, 17-10 (KC)
1971—*Dolphins, 27-24 (KC) OT
1972—Dolphins, 20-10 (KC)
1974—Dolphins, 9-3 (M)

ALL-TIME TEAM VS. TEAM RESULTS

1976—Chiefs, 20-17 (M) OT
1981—Dolphins, 17-7 (KC)
1983—Dolphins, 14-6 (M)
1985—Dolphins, 31-0 (M)
1987—Dolphins, 42-0 (M)
1989—Chiefs, 26-21 (KC)
Chiefs, 27-24 (M)
1990—**Dolphins, 17-16 (M)
1991—Chiefs, 42-7 (KC)
1993—Dolphins, 30-10 (M)
1994—Dolphins, 45-28 (M)
**Dolphins, 27-17 (M)
1995—Dolphins, 13-6 (M)
1997—Dolphins, 17-14 (M)
(RS Pts.—Chiefs 382, Dolphins 354)
(PS Pts.—Dolphins 71, Chiefs 57)
AFC Divisional Playoff
***AFC First-Round Playoff*

KANSAS CITY vs. MINNESOTA
RS: Chiefs lead series, 4-3
PS: Chiefs lead series, 1-0
1969—*Chiefs, 23-7 (New Orleans)
1970—Vikings, 27-10 (M)
1974—Vikings, 35-15 (KC)
1981—Chiefs, 10-6 (M)
1990—Chiefs, 24-21 (KC)
1993—Vikings, 30-10 (M)
1996—Chiefs, 21-6 (M)
1999—Chiefs, 31-28 (KC)
(RS Pts.—Vikings 153, Chiefs 121)
(PS Pts.—Chiefs 23, Vikings 7)
Super Bowl IV

***KANSAS CITY vs. **NEW ENGLAND**
RS: Chiefs lead series, 15-8-3
1960—Patriots, 42-14 (B)
Texans, 34-0 (D)
1961—Patriots, 18-17 (D)
Patriots, 28-21 (B)
1962—Texans, 42-28 (D)
Texans, 27-7 (B)
1963—Tie, 24-24 (B)
Chiefs, 35-3 (KC)
1964—Patriots, 24-7 (B)
Patriots, 31-24 (KC)
1965—Chiefs, 27-17 (KC)
Tie, 10-10 (B)
1966—Chiefs, 43-24 (B)
Tie, 27-27 (KC)
1967—Chiefs, 33-10 (B)
1968—Chiefs, 31-17 (KC)
1969—Chiefs, 31-0 (B)
1970—Chiefs, 23-10 (KC)
1973—Chiefs, 10-7 (NE)
1977—Patriots, 21-17 (NE)
1981—Patriots, 33-17 (NE)
1990—Chiefs, 37-7 (NE)
1992—Chiefs, 27-20 (KC)
1995—Chiefs, 31-26 (KC)
1998—Patriots, 40-10 (NE)
1999—Chiefs, 16-14 (KC)
(RS Pts.—Chiefs 635, Patriots 488)
Franchise located in Dallas prior to 1963 and known as Texans
***Franchise in Boston prior to 1971*

KANSAS CITY vs. NEW ORLEANS
RS: Chiefs lead series, 4-3
1972—Chiefs, 20-17 (NO)
1976—Saints, 27-17 (KC)
1982—Saints, 27-17 (NO)
1985—Chiefs, 47-27 (NO)
1991—Saints, 17-10 (KC)
1994—Chiefs, 30-17 (NO)
1997—Chiefs, 25-13 (KC)
(RS Pts.—Chiefs 166, Saints 145)

KANSAS CITY vs. N.Y. GIANTS
RS: Giants lead series, 7-2
1974—Giants, 33-27 (KC)
1978—Giants, 26-10 (NY)
1979—Giants, 21-17 (KC)
1983—Chiefs, 38-17 (KC)
1984—Giants, 28-27 (NY)
1988—Giants, 28-12 (NY)
1992—Giants, 35-21 (NY)
1995—Chiefs, 20-17 (KC) OT
1998—Giants, 28-7 (NY)
(RS Pts.—Giants 233, Chiefs 179)

***KANSAS CITY vs. **N.Y. JETS**
RS: Chiefs lead series, 14-13-1
PS: Series tied, 1-1
1960—Titans, 37-35 (D)
Titans, 41-35 (NY)
1961—Titans, 28-7 (NY)
Texans, 35-24 (D)
1962—Texans, 20-17 (D)
Texans, 52-31 (NY)
1963—Jets, 17-0 (NY)
Chiefs, 48-0 (KC)
1964—Jets, 27-14 (NY)
Chiefs, 24-7 (KC)
1965—Chiefs, 14-10 (NY)
Jets, 13-10 (KC)
1966—Chiefs, 32-24 (NY)
1967—Chiefs, 42-18 (KC)
Chiefs, 21-7 (NY)
1968—Jets, 20-19 (KC)
1969—Chiefs, 34-16 (NY)
***Chiefs, 13-6 (NY)
1971—Jets, 13-10 (NY)
1974—Chiefs, 24-16 (KC)
1975—Jets, 30-24 (KC)
1982—Chiefs, 37-13 (KC)
1984—Jets, 17-16 (KC)
Jets, 28-7 (NY)
1986—****Jets, 35-15 (NY)
1987—Jets, 16-9 (KC)
1988—Tie, 17-17 (NY)
Chiefs, 38-34 (KC)
1992—Chiefs, 23-7 (NY)
1998—Jets, 20-17 (KC)
(RS Pts.—Chiefs 664, Jets 548)
(PS Pts.—Jets 41, Chiefs 28)
Franchise in Dallas prior to 1963 and known as Texans
***Jets known as Titans prior to 1963*
****Inter-Divisional Playoff*
*****AFC First-Round Playoff*

***KANSAS CITY vs. **OAKLAND**
RS: Chiefs lead series, 40-37-2
PS: Chiefs lead series, 2-1
1960—Texans, 34-16 (O)
Raiders, 20-19 (D)
1961—Texans, 42-35 (O)
Texans, 43-11 (D)
1962—Texans, 26-16 (O)
Texans, 35-7 (D)
1963—Raiders, 10-7 (O)
Raiders, 22-7 (KC)
1964—Chiefs, 21-9 (O)
Chiefs, 42-7 (KC)
1965—Raiders, 37-10 (O)
Chiefs, 14-7 (KC)
1966—Chiefs, 32-10 (O)
Raiders, 34-13 (KC)
1967—Raiders, 23-21 (O)
Raiders, 44-22 (KC)
1968—Chiefs, 24-10 (KC)
Raiders, 38-21 (O)
***Raiders, 41-6 (O)
1969—Raiders, 27-24 (KC)
Raiders, 10-6 (O)
****Chiefs, 17-7 (O)
1970—Tie, 17-17 (KC)
Raiders, 20-6 (O)
1971—Tie, 20-20 (O)
Chiefs, 16-14 (KC)
1972—Chiefs, 27-14 (KC)
Raiders, 26-3 (O)
1973—Chiefs, 16-3 (KC)
Raiders, 37-7 (O)
1974—Raiders, 27-7 (O)
Raiders, 7-6 (KC)
1975—Chiefs, 42-10 (KC)
Raiders, 28-20 (O)
1976—Raiders, 24-21 (KC)
Raiders, 21-10 (O)
1977—Raiders, 37-28 (KC)
Raiders, 21-20 (O)
1978—Raiders, 28-6 (O)
Raiders, 20-10 (KC)
1979—Chiefs, 35-7 (KC)
Chiefs, 24-21 (O)
1980—Raiders, 27-14 (KC)
Chiefs, 31-17 (O)
1981—Chiefs, 27-0 (KC)
Chiefs, 28-17 (O)
1982—Raiders, 21-16 (KC)
1983—Raiders, 21-20 (LA)
Raiders, 28-20 (KC)
1984—Raiders, 22-20 (KC)
Raiders, 17-7 (LA)
1985—Chiefs, 36-20 (KC)
Raiders, 19-10 (LA)
1986—Raiders, 24-17 (KC)
Chiefs, 20-17 (LA)
1987—Raiders, 35-17 (LA)
Chiefs, 16-10 (KC)
1988—Raiders, 27-17 (KC)
Raiders, 17-10 (LA)
1989—Chiefs, 24-19 (KC)
Raiders, 20-14 (LA)
1990—Chiefs, 9-7 (KC)
Chiefs, 27-24 (LA)
1991—Chiefs, 24-21 (KC)
Chiefs, 27-21 (LA)
*****Chiefs, 10-6 (KC)
1992—Chiefs, 27-7 (KC)
Raiders, 28-7 (LA)
1993—Chiefs, 24-9 (KC)
Chiefs, 31-20 (LA)
1994—Chiefs, 13-3 (KC)
Chiefs, 19-9 (LA)
1995—Chiefs, 23-17 (KC) OT
Chiefs, 29-23 (O)
1996—Chiefs, 19-3 (KC)
Raiders, 26-7 (O)
1997—Chiefs, 28-27 (O)
Chiefs, 30-0 (KC)
1998—Chiefs, 28-8 (KC)
Chiefs, 31-24 (O)
1999—Chiefs, 37-34 (O)
Raiders, 41-38 (KC) OT
(RS Pts.—Chiefs 1,646, Raiders 1,525)
(PS Pts.—Raiders 54, Chiefs 33)
Franchise in Dallas prior to 1963 and known as Texans
***Franchise in Los Angeles from 1982-1994*
****Division Playoff*
*****AFL Championship*
******AFC First-Round Playoff*

KANSAS CITY vs. PHILADELPHIA
RS: Chiefs lead series, 2-1
1972—Eagles, 21-20 (KC)
1992—Chiefs, 24-17 (KC)
1998—Chiefs, 24-21 (P)
(RS Pts.—Chiefs 68, Eagles 59)

KANSAS CITY vs. PITTSBURGH
RS: Steelers lead series, 15-7
PS: Chiefs lead series, 1-0
1970—Chiefs, 31-14 (P)
1971—Chiefs, 38-16 (KC)
1972—Steelers, 16-7 (P)
1974—Steelers, 34-24 (KC)
1975—Steelers, 28-3 (P)
1976—Steelers, 45-0 (KC)
1978—Steelers, 27-24 (P)
1979—Steelers, 30-3 (KC)
1980—Steelers, 21-16 (P)
1981—Chiefs, 37-33 (P)
1982—Steelers, 35-14 (P)
1984—Chiefs, 37-27 (P)
1985—Steelers, 36-28 (KC)
1986—Chiefs, 24-19 (P)
1987—Steelers, 17-16 (KC)
1988—Steelers, 16-10 (P)
1989—Steelers, 23-17 (P)
1992—Steelers, 27-3 (KC)
1993—*Chiefs, 27-24 (KC) OT
1996—Steelers, 17-7 (KC)
1997—Chiefs, 13-10 (KC)
1998—Steelers, 20-13 (KC)
1999—Chiefs, 35-19 (KC)
(RS Pts.—Steelers 530, Chiefs 400)
(PS Pts.—Chiefs 27, Steelers 24)
AFC First-Round Playoff

KANSAS CITY vs. *ST. LOUIS
RS: Rams lead series, 4-2
1973—Rams, 23-13 (KC)
1982—Rams, 20-14 (LA)
1985—Rams, 16-0 (KC)
1991—Chiefs, 27-20 (LA)
1994—Rams, 16-0 (KC)
1997—Chiefs, 28-20 (StL)
(RS Pts.—Rams 115, Chiefs 82)
Franchise in Los Angeles prior to 1995

***KANSAS CITY vs. **SAN DIEGO**
RS: Chiefs lead series, 41-37-1
PS: Chargers lead series, 1-0
1960—Chargers, 21-20 (LA)
Texans, 17-0 (D)
1961—Chargers, 26-10 (D)
Chargers, 24-14 (SD)
1962—Chargers, 32-28 (SD)
Texans, 26-17 (D)
1963—Chargers, 24-10 (SD)
Chargers, 38-17 (KC)
1964—Chargers, 28-14 (KC)
Chiefs, 49-6 (SD)
1965—Tie, 10-10 (SD)
Chiefs, 31-7 (KC)
1966—Chiefs, 24-14 (KC)
Chiefs, 27-17 (SD)
1967—Chargers, 45-31 (SD)
Chargers, 17-16 (KC)
1968—Chiefs, 27-20 (KC)
Chiefs, 40-3 (SD)
1969—Chiefs, 27-9 (SD)
Chiefs, 27-3 (KC)
1970—Chiefs, 26-14 (KC)
Chargers, 31-13 (SD)
1971—Chargers, 21-14 (SD)
Chiefs, 31-10 (KC)
1972—Chiefs, 26-14 (SD)
Chargers, 27-17 (KC)
1973—Chiefs, 19-0 (SD)
Chiefs, 33-6 (KC)
1974—Chiefs, 24-14 (SD)
Chargers, 14-7 (KC)
1975—Chiefs, 12-10 (SD)
Chargers, 28-20 (KC)
1976—Chargers, 30-16 (KC)
Chiefs, 23-20 (SD)
1977—Chargers, 23-7 (KC)
Chiefs, 21-16 (SD)
1978—Chargers, 29-23 (SD) OT
Chiefs, 23-0 (KC)
1979—Chargers, 20-14 (KC)
Chargers, 28-7 (SD)
1980—Chargers, 24-7 (KC)
Chargers, 20-7 (SD)
1981—Chargers, 42-31 (KC)
Chargers, 22-20 (SD)
1982—Chiefs, 19-12 (KC)
1983—Chargers, 17-14 (KC)
Chargers, 41-38 (SD)
1984—Chiefs, 31-13 (KC)
Chiefs, 42-21 (SD)
1985—Chargers, 31-20 (SD)
Chiefs, 38-34 (KC)
1986—Chiefs, 42-41 (KC)
Chiefs, 24-23 (SD)
1987—Chiefs, 20-13 (KC)
Chargers, 42-21 (SD)
1988—Chargers, 24-23 (KC)
Chargers, 24-13 (SD)
1989—Chargers, 21-6 (SD)
Chargers, 20-13 (KC)
1990—Chiefs, 27-10 (KC)
Chiefs, 24-21 (SD)
1991—Chiefs, 14-13 (SD)
Chiefs, 20-17 (KC) OT
1992—Chiefs, 24-10 (SD)

Chiefs, 16-14 (KC)
***Chargers, 17-0 (SD)
1993—Chiefs, 17-14 (SD)
Chiefs, 28-24 (KC)
1994—Chargers, 20-6 (SD)
Chargers, 14-13 (KC)
1995—Chiefs, 29-23 (KC) OT
Chiefs, 22-7 (SD)
1996—Chargers, 22-19 (SD)
Chargers, 28-14 (KC)
1997—Chiefs, 31-3 (KC)
Chiefs, 29-7 (SD)
1998—Chiefs, 23-7 (KC)
Chargers, 38-37 (SD)
1999—Chargers, 21-14 (SD)
Chiefs, 34-0 (KC)
(RS Pts.—Chiefs 1,711, Chargers 1,514)
(PS Pts.—Chargers 17, Chiefs 0)
Franchise in Dallas prior to 1963 and known as Texans
**Franchise in Los Angeles prior to 1961*
***AFC First-Round Playoff*

KANSAS CITY vs. SAN FRANCISCO
RS: 49ers lead series, 4-3
1971—Chiefs, 26-17 (SF)
1975—49ers, 20-3 (KC)
1982—49ers, 26-13 (KC)
1985—49ers, 31-3 (SF)
1991—49ers, 28-14 (SF)
1994—Chiefs, 24-17 (KC)
1997—Chiefs, 44-9 (KC)
(PS Pts.—49ers 148, Chiefs 127)

KANSAS CITY vs. SEATTLE
RS: Chiefs lead series, 27-16
1977—Seahawks, 34-31 (KC)
1978—Seahawks, 13-10 (KC)
Seahawks, 23-19 (S)
1979—Chiefs, 24-6 (S)
Chiefs, 37-21 (KC)
1980—Seahawks, 17-16 (KC)
Chiefs, 31-30 (S)
1981—Chiefs, 20-14 (S)
Chiefs, 40-13 (KC)
1983—Chiefs, 17-13 (KC)
Seahawks, 51-48 (S) OT
1984—Seahawks, 45-0 (S)
Chiefs, 34-7 (KC)
1985—Chiefs, 28-7 (KC)
Seahawks, 24-6 (S)
1986—Seahawks, 23-17 (S)
Chiefs, 27-7 (KC)
1987—Seahawks, 43-14 (S)
Chiefs, 41-20 (KC)
1988—Seahawks, 31-10 (S)
Chiefs, 27-24 (KC)
1989—Chiefs, 20-16 (S)
Chiefs, 20-10 (KC)
1990—Seahawks, 19-7 (S)
Seahawks, 17-16 (KC)
1991—Chiefs, 20-13 (KC)
Chiefs, 19-6 (S)
1992—Chiefs, 26-7 (KC)
Chiefs, 24-14 (S)
1993—Chiefs, 31-16 (S)
Chiefs, 34-24 (KC)
1994—Chiefs, 38-23 (KC)
Seahawks, 10-9 (S)
1995—Chiefs, 34-10 (S)
Chiefs, 26-3 (KC)
1996—Chiefs, 35-17 (S)
Chiefs, 34-16 (KC)
1997—Chiefs, 20-17 (KC) OT
Chiefs, 19-14 (S)
1998—Chiefs, 17-6 (KC)
Seahawks, 24-12 (S)
1999—Seahawks, 31-19 (KC)
Seahawks, 23-14 (S)
(RS Pts.—Chiefs 991, Seahawks 802)

KANSAS CITY vs. TAMPA BAY
RS: Chiefs lead series, 5-3
1976—Chiefs, 28-19 (TB)
1978—Buccaneers, 30-13 (KC)
1979—Buccaneers, 3-0 (TB)
1981—Chiefs, 19-10 (KC)
1984—Chiefs, 24-20 (KC)
1986—Chiefs, 27-20 (KC)
1993—Chiefs, 27-3 (TB)
1999—Buccaneers, 17-10 (TB)
(RS Pts.—Chiefs 148, Buccaneers 122)

***KANSAS CITY vs. **TENNESSEE**
RS: Chiefs lead series, 24-17
PS: Chiefs lead series, 2-0
1960—Oilers, 20-10 (H)
Texans, 24-0 (D)
1961—Texans, 26-21 (D)
Oilers, 38-7 (H)
1962—Texans, 31-7 (H)
Oilers, 14-6 (D)
***Texans, 20-17 (H) OT
1963—Chiefs, 28-7 (KC)
Oilers, 28-7 (H)
1964—Chiefs, 28-7 (KC)
Chiefs, 28-19 (H)
1965—Chiefs, 52-21 (KC)
Oilers, 38-36 (H)
1966—Chiefs, 48-23 (KC)
1967—Chiefs, 25-20 (H)
Oilers, 24-19 (KC)
1968—Chiefs, 26-21 (H)
Chiefs, 24-10 (KC)
1969—Chiefs, 24-0 (KC)
1970—Chiefs, 24-9 (KC)
1971—Chiefs, 20-16 (H)
1973—Chiefs, 38-14 (KC)
1974—Chiefs, 17-7 (H)
1975—Oilers, 17-13 (KC)
1977—Oilers, 34-20 (H)
1978—Oilers, 20-17 (KC)
1979—Oilers, 20-6 (H)
1980—Chiefs, 21-20 (KC)
1981—Chiefs, 23-10 (KC)
1983—Chiefs, 13-10 (H) OT
1984—Oilers, 17-16 (KC)
1985—Oilers, 23-20 (H)
1986—Chiefs, 27-13 (KC)
1988—Oilers, 7-6 (H)
1989—Chiefs, 34-0 (KC)
1990—Oilers, 27-10 (KC)
1991—Oilers, 17-7 (H)
1992—Oilers, 23-20 (H) OT
1993—Oilers, 30-0 (H)
****Chiefs, 28-20 (H)
1994—Chiefs, 31-9 (KC)
1995—Chiefs, 20-13 (KC)
1996—Chiefs, 20-19 (H)
(RS Pts.—Chiefs 872, Titans 693)
(PS Pts.—Chiefs 48, Titans 37)
Franchise in Dallas prior to 1963 and known as Texans
**Franchise in Houston prior to 1997; known as Oilers prior to 1999*
***AFL Championship*
****AFC Divisional Playoff*

KANSAS CITY vs. WASHINGTON
RS: Chiefs lead series, 4-1
1971—Chiefs, 27-20 (KC)
1976—Chiefs, 33-30 (W)
1983—Redskins, 27-12 (W)
1992—Chiefs, 35-16 (KC)
1995—Chiefs, 24-3 (KC)
(RS Pts.—Chiefs 131, Redskins 96)

MIAMI vs. ARIZONA
RS: Dolphins lead series, 8-0;
See Arizona vs. Miami

MIAMI vs. ATLANTA
RS: Dolphins lead series, 6-2;
See Atlanta vs. Miami

MIAMI vs. BALTIMORE
RS: Dolphins lead series, 1-0;
See Baltimore vs. Miami

MIAMI vs. BUFFALO
RS: Dolphins lead series, 42-25-1
PS: Bills lead series, 3-1;
See Buffalo vs. Miami

MIAMI vs. CAROLINA
RS: Dolphins lead series, 1-0;
See Carolina vs. Miami

MIAMI vs. CHICAGO
RS: Dolphins lead series, 6-3;
See Chicago vs. Miami

MIAMI vs. CINCINNATI
RS: Dolphins lead series, 11-3
PS: Dolphins lead series, 1-0;
See Cincinnati vs. Miami

MIAMI vs. CLEVELAND
RS: Dolphins lead series, 6-4
PS: Dolphins lead series, 2-0;
See Cleveland vs. Miami

MIAMI vs. DALLAS
RS: Dolphins lead series, 6-3
PS: Cowboys lead series, 1-0;
See Dallas vs. Miami

MIAMI vs. DENVER
RS: Dolphins lead series, 7-2-1
PS: Broncos lead series, 1-0;
See Denver vs. Miami

MIAMI vs. DETROIT
RS: Dolphins lead series, 4-2;
See Detroit vs. Miami

MIAMI vs. GREEN BAY
RS: Dolphins lead series, 8-1;
See Green Bay vs. Miami

MIAMI vs. INDIANAPOLIS
RS: Dolphins lead series, 40-20
PS: Dolphins lead series, 1-0;
See Indianapolis vs. Miami

MIAMI vs. JACKSONVILLE
RS: Jaguars lead series, 1-0
PS: Jaguars lead series, 1-0;
See Jacksonville vs. Miami

MIAMI vs. KANSAS CITY
RS: Series tied, 10-10
PS: Dolphins lead series, 3-0;
See Kansas City vs. Miami

MIAMI vs. MINNESOTA
RS: Dolphins lead series, 4-2
PS: Dolphins lead series, 1-0
1972—Dolphins, 16-14 (Minn)
1973—*Dolphins, 24-7 (Houston)
1976—Vikings, 29-7 (Mia)
1979—Dolphins, 27-12 (Minn)
1982—Dolphins, 22-14 (Mia)
1988—Dolphins, 24-7 (Mia)
1994—Vikings, 38-35 (M)
(RS Pts.—Dolphins 131, Vikings 114)
(PS Pts.—Dolphins 24, Vikings 7)
Super Bowl VIII

MIAMI vs. *NEW ENGLAND
RS: Dolphins lead series, 40-26
PS: Patriots lead series, 2-1
1966—Patriots, 20-14 (M)
1967—Patriots, 41-10 (B)
Dolphins, 41-32 (M)
1968—Dolphins, 34-10 (B)
Dolphins, 38-7 (M)
1969—Dolphins, 17-16 (B)
Patriots, 38-23 (Tampa)
1970—Patriots, 27-14 (B)
Dolphins, 37-20 (M)
1971—Dolphins, 41-3 (M)
Patriots, 34-13 (NE)
1972—Dolphins, 52-0 (M)
Dolphins, 37-21 (NE)
1973—Dolphins, 44-23 (M)
Dolphins, 30-14 (NE)
1974—Patriots, 34-24 (NE)
Dolphins, 34-27 (M)
1975—Dolphins, 22-14 (NE)
Dolphins, 20-7 (M)
1976—Patriots, 30-14 (NE)
Dolphins, 10-3 (M)
1977—Dolphins, 17-5 (M)
Patriots, 14-10 (NE)
1978—Patriots, 33-24 (NE)
Dolphins, 23-3 (M)
1979—Patriots, 28-13 (NE)
Dolphins, 39-24 (M)
1980—Patriots, 34-0 (NE)
Dolphins, 16-13 (M) OT
1981—Dolphins, 30-27 (NE) OT
Dolphins, 24-14 (M)
1982—Patriots, 3-0 (NE)
**Dolphins, 28-13 (M)
1983—Dolphins, 34-24 (M)
Patriots, 17-6 (NE)
1984—Dolphins, 28-7 (M)
Dolphins, 44-24 (NE)
1985—Patriots, 17-13 (NE)
Dolphins, 30-27 (M)
***Patriots, 31-14 (M)
1986—Patriots, 34-7 (NE)
Patriots, 34-27 (M)
1987—Patriots, 28-21 (NE)
Patriots, 24-10 (M)
1988—Patriots, 21-10 (NE)
Patriots, 6-3 (M)
1989—Dolphins, 24-10 (NE)
Dolphins, 31-10 (M)
1990—Dolphins, 27-24 (NE)
Dolphins, 17-10 (M)
1991—Dolphins, 20-10 (NE)
Dolphins, 30-20 (M)
1992—Dolphins, 38-17 (M)
Dolphins, 16-13 (NE) OT
1993—Dolphins, 17-13 (M)
Patriots, 33-27 (NE) OT
1994—Dolphins, 39-35 (M)
Dolphins, 23-3 (NE)
1995—Dolphins, 20-3 (NE)
Patriots, 34-17 (M)
1996—Dolphins, 24-10 (M)
Patriots, 42-23 (NE)
1997—Patriots, 27-24 (NE)
Patriots, 14-12 (M)
**Patriots, 17-3 (NE)
1998—Dolphins, 12-9 (M) OT
Patriots, 26-23 (NE)
1999—Dolphins, 31-30 (NE)
Dolphins, 27-17 (M)
(RS Pts.—Dolphins 1,520, Patriots 1,292)
(PS Pts.—Patriots 61, Dolphins 45)
Franchise in Boston prior to 1971
**AFC First-Round Playoff*
***AFC Championship*

MIAMI vs. NEW ORLEANS
RS: Dolphins lead series, 5-3
1970—Dolphins, 21-10 (M)
1974—Dolphins, 21-0 (NO)
1980—Dolphins, 21-16 (M)
1983—Saints, 17-7 (NO)
1986—Dolphins, 31-27 (NO)
1992—Saints, 24-13 (NO)
1995—Saints, 33-30 (NO)
1998—Dolphins, 30-10 (M)
(RS Pts.—Dolphins 174, Saints 137)

MIAMI vs. N.Y. GIANTS
RS: Giants lead series, 3-1
1972—Dolphins, 23-13 (NY)
1990—Giants, 20-3 (NY)
1993—Giants, 19-14 (M)
1996—Giants, 17-7 (M)
(RS Pts.—Giants 69, Dolphins 47)

MIAMI vs. N.Y. JETS
RS: Dolphins lead series, 34-33-1
PS: Dolphins lead series, 1-0
1966—Jets, 19-14 (M)
Jets, 30-13 (NY)
1967—Jets, 29-7 (NY)
Jets, 33-14 (M)
1968—Jets, 35-17 (NY)
Jets, 31-7 (M)
1969—Jets, 34-31 (NY)
Jets, 27-9 (M)
1970—Dolphins, 20-6 (NY)
Dolphins, 16-10 (M)
1971—Jets, 14-10 (M)
Dolphins, 30-14 (NY)
1972—Dolphins, 27-17 (NY)
Dolphins, 28-24 (M)
1973—Dolphins, 31-3 (M)
Dolphins, 24-14 (NY)

1974—Dolphins, 21-17 (M)
Jets, 17-14 (NY)
1975—Dolphins, 43-0 (NY)
Dolphins, 27-7 (M)
1976—Dolphins, 16-0 (M)
Dolphins, 27-7 (NY)
1977—Dolphins, 21-17 (M)
Dolphins, 14-10 (NY)
1978—Jets, 33-20 (NY)
Jets, 24-13 (M)
1979—Jets, 33-27 (NY)
Jets, 27-24 (M)
1980—Jets, 17-14 (NY)
Jets, 24-17 (M)
1981—Tie, 28-28 (M) OT
Jets, 16-15 (NY)
1982—Dolphins, 45-28 (NY)
Dolphins, 20-19 (M)
*Dolphins, 14-0 (M)
1983—Dolphins, 32-14 (NY)
Dolphins, 34-14 (M)
1984—Dolphins, 31-17 (NY)
Dolphins, 28-17 (M)
1985—Jets, 23-7 (NY)
Dolphins, 21-17 (M)
1986—Jets, 51-45 (NY) OT
Dolphins, 45-3 (M)
1987—Jets, 37-31 (NY) OT
Dolphins, 37-28 (M)
1988—Jets, 44-30 (M)
Jets, 38-34 (NY)
1989—Jets, 40-33 (M)
Dolphins, 31-23 (NY)
1990—Dolphins, 20-16 (M)
Dolphins, 17-3 (NY)
1991—Jets, 41-23 (NY)
Jets, 23-20 (M) OT
1992—Jets, 26-14 (NY)
Dolphins, 19-17 (M)
1993—Jets, 24-14 (M)
Jets, 27-10 (NY)
1994—Dolphins, 28-14 (M)
Dolphins, 28-24 (NY)
1995—Dolphins, 52-14 (M)
Jets, 17-16 (NY)
1996—Dolphins, 36-27 (M)
Dolphins, 31-28 (NY)
1997—Dolphins, 31-20 (NY)
Dolphins, 24-17 (M)
1998—Jets, 20-9 (NY)
Jets, 21-16 (M)
1999—Jets, 28-20 (NY)
Jets, 38-31 (M)
(RS Pts.—Dolphins 1,602, Jets 1,475)
(PS Pts.—Dolphins 14, Jets 0)
AFC Championship

MIAMI vs. *OAKLAND
RS: Raiders lead series, 15-8-1
PS: Raiders lead series, 2-1
1966—Raiders, 23-14 (M)
Raiders, 21-10 (O)
1967—Raiders, 31-17 (O)
1968—Raiders, 47-21 (M)
1969—Raiders, 20-17 (O)
Tie, 20-20 (M)
1970—Dolphins, 20-13 (M)
**Raiders, 21-14 (O)
1973—Raiders, 12-7 (O)
***Dolphins, 27-10 (M)
1974—**Raiders, 28-26 (O)
1975—Raiders, 31-21 (M)
1978—Dolphins, 23-6 (M)
1979—Raiders, 13-3 (O)
1980—Raiders, 16-10 (O)
1981—Raiders, 33-17 (M)
1983—Raiders, 27-14 (LA)
1984—Raiders, 45-34 (M)
1986—Raiders, 30-28 (M)
1988—Dolphins, 24-14 (LA)
1990—Raiders, 13-10 (M)
1992—Dolphins, 20-7 (M)
1994—Dolphins, 20-17 (M) OT
1996—Raiders, 17-7 (O)
1997—Dolphins, 34-16 (O)
1998—Dolphins, 27-17 (O)
1999—Dolphins, 16-9 (O)
(RS Pts.—Raiders 498, Dolphins 434)
(PS Pts.—Dolphins 67, Raiders 59)
**Franchise in Los Angeles from 1982-1994*
***AFC Divisional Playoff*
****AFC Championship*

MIAMI vs. PHILADELPHIA
RS: Dolphins lead series, 7-3
1970—Eagles, 24-17 (P)
1975—Dolphins, 24-16 (M)
1978—Eagles, 17-3 (P)
1981—Dolphins, 13-10 (M)
1984—Dolphins, 24-23 (M)
1987—Dolphins, 28-10 (P)
1990—Dolphins, 23-20 (M) OT
1993—Dolphins, 19-14 (P)
1996—Eagles, 35-28 (P)
1999—Dolphins, 16-13 (M)
(RS Pts.—Dolphins 195, Eagles 182)

MIAMI vs. PITTSBURGH
RS: Dolphins lead series, 9-7
PS: Dolphins lead series, 2-1
1971—Dolphins, 24-21 (M)
1972—*Dolphins, 21-17 (P)
1973—Dolphins, 30-26 (M)
1976—Steelers, 14-3 (P)
1979—**Steelers, 34-14 (P)
1980—Steelers, 23-10 (P)
1981—Dolphins, 30-10 (M)
1984—Dolphins, 31-7 (P)
*Dolphins, 45-28 (M)
1985—Dolphins, 24-20 (M)
1987—Dolphins, 35-24 (M)
1988—Steelers, 40-24 (P)
1989—Steelers, 34-14 (M)
1990—Dolphins, 28-6 (P)
1993—Steelers, 21-20 (M)
1994—Steelers, 16-13 (P) OT
1995—Dolphins, 23-10 (M)
1996—Steelers, 24-17 (M)
1998—Dolphins, 21-0 (M)
(RS Pts.—Dolphins 347, Steelers 296)
(PS Pts.—Dolphins 80, Steelers 79)
**AFC Championship*
***AFC Divisional Playoff*

MIAMI vs. *ST. LOUIS
RS: Dolphins lead series, 7-1
1971—Dolphins, 20-14 (LA)
1976—Rams, 31-28 (M)
1980—Dolphins, 35-14 (LA)
1983—Dolphins, 30-14 (M)
1986—Dolphins, 37-31 (LA) OT
1992—Dolphins, 26-10 (M)
1995—Dolphins, 41-22 (StL)
1998—Dolphins, 14-0 (M)
(RS Pts.—Dolphins 231, Rams 136)
**Franchise in Los Angeles prior to 1995*

MIAMI vs. SAN DIEGO
RS: Chargers lead series, 10-7
PS: Series tied, 2-2
1966—Chargers, 44-10 (SD)
1967—Chargers, 24-0 (SD)
Dolphins, 41-24 (M)
1968—Chargers, 34-28 (SD)
1969—Chargers, 21-14 (M)
1972—Dolphins, 24-10 (M)
1974—Dolphins, 28-21 (SD)
1977—Chargers, 14-13 (M)
1978—Dolphins, 28-21 (SD)
1980—Chargers, 27-24 (M) OT
1981—*Chargers, 41-38 (M) OT
1982—**Dolphins, 34-13 (M)
1984—Chargers, 34-28 (SD) OT
1986—Chargers, 50-28 (SD)
1988—Dolphins, 31-28 (M)
1991—Chargers, 38-30 (SD)
1992—*Dolphins, 31-0 (M)
1993—Chargers, 45-20 (SD)
1994—*Chargers, 22-21 (SD)
1995—Dolphins, 24-14 (SD)
1999—Dolphins, 12-9 (M)
(RS Pts.—Chargers 458, Dolphins 383)
(PS Pts.—Dolphins 124, Chargers 76)
**AFC Divisional Playoff*
***AFC Second-Round Playoff*

MIAMI vs. SAN FRANCISCO
RS: Dolphins lead series, 4-3
PS: 49ers lead series, 1-0
1973—Dolphins, 21-13 (M)
1977—Dolphins, 19-15 (SF)
1980—Dolphins, 17-13 (M)
1983—Dolphins, 20-17 (SF)
1984—*49ers, 38-16 (Stanford)
1986—49ers, 31-16 (M)
1992—49ers, 27-3 (SF)
1995—49ers, 44-20 (M)
(RS Pts.—49ers 160, Dolphins 116)
(PS Pts.—49ers 38, Dolphins 16)
**Super Bowl XIX*

MIAMI vs. SEATTLE
RS: Dolphins lead series, 4-2
PS: Dolphins lead series, 2-1
1977—Dolphins, 31-13 (M)
1979—Dolphins, 19-10 (M)
1983—*Seahawks, 27-20 (M)
1984—*Dolphins, 31-10 (M)
1987—Seahawks, 24-20 (S)
1990—Dolphins, 24-17 (M)
1992—Dolphins, 19-17 (S)
1996—Seahawks, 22-15 (M)
1999—**Dolphins, 20-17 (S)
(RS Pts.—Dolphins 128, Seahawks 103)
(PS Pts.—Dolphins 71, Seahawks 54)
**AFC Divisional Playoff*
***AFC First-Round Playoff*

MIAMI vs. TAMPA BAY
RS: Dolphins lead series, 4-2
1976—Dolphins, 23-20 (TB)
1982—Buccaneers, 23-17 (TB)
1985—Dolphins, 41-38 (M)
1988—Dolphins, 17-14 (TB)
1991—Dolphins, 33-14 (M)
1997—Buccaneers, 31-21 (TB)
(RS Pts.—Dolphins 152, Buccaneers 140)

MIAMI vs. *TENNESSEE
RS: Dolphins lead series, 14-11
PS: Titans lead series, 1-0
1966—Dolphins, 20-13 (H)
Dolphins, 29-28 (M)
1967—Oilers, 17-14 (H)
Oilers, 41-10 (M)
1968—Oilers, 24-10 (M)
Dolphins, 24-7 (H)
1969—Oilers, 22-10 (H)
Oilers, 32-7 (M)
1970—Dolphins, 20-10 (H)
1972—Dolphins, 34-13 (M)
1975—Oilers, 20-19 (H)
1977—Dolphins, 27-7 (M)
1978—Oilers, 35-30 (H)
**Oilers, 17-9 (M)
1979—Oilers, 9-6 (M)
1981—Dolphins, 16-10 (H)
1983—Dolphins, 24-17 (H)
1984—Dolphins, 28-10 (M)
1985—Oilers, 26-23 (H)
1986—Dolphins, 28-7 (M)
1989—Oilers, 39-7 (H)
1991—Oilers, 17-13 (M)
1992—Dolphins, 19-16 (M)
1996—Dolphins, 23-20 (H)
1997—Dolphins, 16-13 (M) OT
1999—Dolphins, 17-0 (M)
(RS Pts.—Dolphins 474, Titans 453)
(PS Pts.—Titans 17, Dolphins 9)
**Franchise in Houston prior to 1997; known as Oilers prior to 1999*
***AFC First-Round Playoff*

MIAMI vs. WASHINGTON
RS: Dolphins lead series, 5-3
PS: Series tied, 1-1
1972—*Dolphins, 14-7 (Los Angeles)
1974—Redskins, 20-17 (W)
1978—Dolphins, 16-0 (W)
1981—Dolphins, 13-10 (M)
1982—**Redskins, 27-17 (Pasadena)
1984—Dolphins, 35-17 (W)
1987—Dolphins, 23-21 (M)
1990—Redskins, 42-20 (W)
1993—Dolphins, 17-10 (M)
1999—Redskins, 21-10 (W)
(RS Pts.—Dolphins 151, Redskins 141)
(PS Pts.—Redskins 34, Dolphins 31)
**Super Bowl VII*
***Super Bowl XVII*

MINNESOTA vs. ARIZONA
RS: Cardinals lead series, 8-7
PS: Vikings lead series, 2-0;
See Arizona vs. Minnesota

MINNESOTA vs. ATLANTA
RS: Vikings lead series, 13-6
PS: Series tied, 1-1;
See Atlanta vs. Minnesota

MINNESOTA vs. BALTIMORE
RS: Vikings lead series, 1-0;
See Baltimore vs. Minnesota

MINNESOTA vs. BUFFALO
RS: Vikings lead series, 6-2;
See Buffalo vs. Minnesota

MINNESOTA vs. CAROLINA
RS: Vikings lead series, 2-0;
See Carolina vs. Minnesota

MINNESOTA vs. CHICAGO
RS: Vikings lead series, 42-33-2
PS: Bears lead series, 1-0;
See Chicago vs. Minnesota

MINNESOTA vs. CINCINNATI
RS: Vikings lead series, 5-4;
See Cincinnati vs. Minnesota

MINNESOTA vs. CLEVELAND
RS: Vikings lead series, 8-3
PS: Vikings lead series, 1-0;
See Cleveland vs. Minnesota

MINNESOTA vs. DALLAS
RS: Cowboys lead series, 9-8
PS: Cowboys lead series, 4-2;
See Dallas vs. Minnesota

MINNESOTA vs. DENVER
RS: Vikings lead series, 6-4;
See Denver vs. Minnesota

MINNESOTA vs. DETROIT
RS: Vikings lead series, 47-28-2;
See Detroit vs. Minnesota

MINNESOTA vs. GREEN BAY
RS: Vikings lead series, 39-37-1;
See Green Bay vs. Minnesota

MINNESOTA vs. INDIANAPOLIS
RS: Colts lead series, 11-7-1
PS: Colts lead series, 1-0;
See Indianapolis vs. Minnesota

MINNESOTA vs. JACKSONVILLE
RS: Vikings lead series, 1-0;
See Jacksonville vs. Minnesota

MINNESOTA vs. KANSAS CITY
RS: Chiefs lead series, 4-3
PS: Chiefs lead series, 1-0;
See Kansas City vs. Minnesota

MINNESOTA vs. MIAMI
RS: Dolphins lead series, 4-2
PS: Dolphins lead series, 1-0;
See Miami vs. Minnesota

MINNESOTA vs. *NEW ENGLAND
RS: Patriots lead series, 4-3
1970—Vikings, 35-14 (B)
1974—Patriots, 17-14 (M)
1979—Patriots, 27-23 (NE)
1988—Vikings, 36-6 (M)
1991—Patriots, 26-23 (NE) OT
1994—Patriots, 26-20 (NE) OT
1997—Vikings, 23-18 (M)
(RS Pts.—Vikings 174, Patriots 134)
**Franchise in Boston prior to 1971*

MINNESOTA vs. NEW ORLEANS
RS: Vikings lead series, 14-6
PS: Vikings lead series, 1-0

1968—Saints, 20-17 (NO)
1970—Vikings, 26-0 (M)
1971—Vikings, 23-10 (NO)
1972—Vikings, 37-6 (M)
1974—Vikings, 29-9 (M)
1975—Vikings, 20-7 (NO)
1976—Vikings, 40-9 (NO)
1978—Saints, 31-24 (NO)
1980—Vikings, 23-20 (NO)
1981—Vikings, 20-10 (M)
1983—Saints, 17-16 (NO)
1985—Saints, 30-23 (M)
1986—Vikings, 33-17 (M)
1987—*Vikings, 44-10 (NO)
1988—Vikings, 45-3 (M)
1990—Vikings, 32-3 (M)
1991—Saints, 26-0 (NO)
1993—Saints, 17-14 (M)
1994—Vikings, 21-20 (M)
1995—Vikings, 43-24 (M)
1998—Vikings, 31-24 (M)
(RS Pts.—Vikings 517, Saints 303)
(PS Pts.—Vikings 44, Saints 10)
NFC First-Round Playoff

MINNESOTA vs. N.Y. GIANTS
RS: Vikings lead series, 8-5
PS: Series tied, 1-1
1964—Vikings, 30-21 (NY)
1965—Vikings, 40-14 (M)
1967—Vikings, 27-24 (M)
1969—Giants, 24-23 (NY)
1971—Vikings, 17-10 (NY)
1973—Vikings, 31-7 (New Haven)
1976—Vikings, 24-7 (M)
1986—Giants, 22-20 (M)
1989—Giants, 24-14 (NY)
1990—Giants, 23-15 (NY)
1993—*Giants, 17-10 (NY)
1994—Vikings, 27-10 (NY)
1996—Giants, 15-10 (NY)
1997—*Vikings, 23-22 (NY)
1999—Vikings, 34-17 (NY)
(RS Pts.—Vikings 312, Giants 218)
(PS Pts.—Giants 39, Vikings 33)
NFC First-Round Playoff

MINNESOTA vs. N.Y. JETS
RS: Jets lead series, 5-1
1970—Jets, 20-10 (NY)
1975—Vikings, 29-21 (M)
1979—Jets, 14-7 (NY)
1982—Jets, 42-14 (M)
1994—Jets, 31-21 (M)
1997—Jets, 23-21 (NY)
(RS Pts.—Jets 151, Vikings 102)

MINNESOTA vs. *OAKLAND
RS: Raiders lead series, 7-3
PS: Raiders lead series, 1-0
1973—Vikings, 24-16 (M)
1976—**Raiders, 32-14 (Pasadena)
1977—Raiders, 35-13 (O)
1978—Raiders, 27-20 (O)
1981—Raiders, 36-10 (M)
1984—Raiders, 23-20 (LA)
1987—Vikings, 31-20 (M)
1990—Raiders, 28-24 (M)
1993—Raiders, 24-7 (LA)
1996—Vikings, 16-13 (O) OT
1999—Raiders, 22-17 (M)
(RS Pts.—Raiders 244, Vikings 182)
(PS Pts.—Raiders 32, Vikings 14)
Franchise in Los Angeles from 1982-1994
**Super Bowl XI*

MINNESOTA vs. PHILADELPHIA
RS: Vikings lead series, 11-6
PS: Eagles lead series, 1-0
1962—Vikings, 31-21 (M)
1963—Vikings, 34-13 (P)
1968—Vikings, 24-17 (P)
1971—Vikings, 13-0 (P)
1973—Vikings, 28-21 (M)
1976—Vikings, 31-12 (P)
1978—Vikings, 28-27 (M)
1980—Eagles, 42-7 (M)
*Eagles, 31-16 (P)
1981—Vikings, 35-23 (M)
1984—Eagles, 19-17 (P)
1985—Vikings, 28-23 (P)
Eagles, 37-35 (M)
1988—Vikings, 23-21 (M)
1989—Eagles, 10-9 (P)
1990—Eagles, 32-24 (P)
1992—Eagles, 28-17 (P)
1997—Vikings, 28-19 (M)
(RS Pts.—Vikings 412, Eagles 365)
(PS Pts.—Eagles 31, Vikings 16)
NFC Divisional Playoff

MINNESOTA vs. PITTSBURGH
RS: Vikings lead series, 8-4
PS: Steelers lead series, 1-0
1962—Steelers, 39-31 (P)
1964—Vikings, 30-10 (M)
1967—Vikings, 41-27 (P)
1969—Vikings, 52-14 (M)
1972—Steelers, 23-10 (P)
1974—*Steelers, 16-6 (New Orleans)
1976—Vikings, 17-6 (M)
1980—Steelers, 23-17 (M)
1983—Vikings, 17-14 (P)
1986—Vikings, 31-7 (M)
1989—Steelers, 27-14 (P)
1992—Vikings, 6-3 (P)
1995—Vikings, 44-24 (P)
(RS Pts.—Vikings 310, Steelers 217)
(PS Pts.—Steelers 16, Vikings 6)
Super Bowl IX

MINNESOTA vs. *ST. LOUIS
RS: Vikings lead series, 16-11-2
PS: Vikings lead series, 5-2
1961—Rams, 31-17 (LA)
Vikings, 42-21 (M)
1962—Vikings, 38-14 (LA)
Tie, 24-24 (M)
1963—Rams, 27-24 (LA)
Vikings, 21-13 (M)
1964—Rams, 22-13 (LA)
Vikings, 34-13 (M)
1965—Vikings, 38-35 (LA)
Vikings, 24-13 (M)
1966—Vikings, 35-7 (M)
Rams, 21-6 (LA)
1967—Rams, 39-3 (LA)
1968—Rams, 31-3 (M)
1969—Vikings, 20-13 (LA)
**Vikings, 23-20 (M)
1970—Vikings, 13-3 (M)
1972—Vikings, 45-41 (LA)
1973—Vikings, 10-9 (M)
1974—Rams, 20-17 (LA)
***Vikings, 14-10 (M)
1976—Tie, 10-10 (M) OT
***Vikings, 24-13 (M)
1977—Rams, 35-3 (LA)
****Vikings, 14-7 (LA)
1978—Rams, 34-17 (M)
****Rams, 34-10 (LA)
1979—Rams, 27-21 (LA) OT
1985—Rams, 13-10 (LA)
1987—Vikings, 21-16 (LA)
1988—*****Vikings, 28-17 (M)
1989—Vikings, 23-21 (M) OT
1991—Vikings, 20-14 (M)
1992—Vikings, 31-17 (LA)
1998—Vikings, 38-31 (StL)
1999—****Rams, 49-37 (StL)
(RS Pts.—Vikings 621, Rams 615)
(PS Pts.—Rams 150, Vikings 150)
Franchise in Los Angeles prior to 1995
**Conference Championship*
***NFC Championship*
****NFC Divisional Playoff*
*****NFC First-Round Playoff*

MINNESOTA vs. SAN DIEGO
RS: Series tied, 4-4
1971—Chargers, 30-14 (SD)
1975—Vikings, 28-13 (M)
1978—Chargers, 13-7 (M)
1981—Vikings, 33-31 (SD)
1984—Chargers, 42-13 (M)
1985—Vikings, 21-17 (M)
1993—Chargers, 30-17 (M)
1999—Vikings, 35-27 (M)
(RS Pts.—Chargers 203, Vikings 168)

MINNESOTA vs. SAN FRANCISCO
RS: Series tied, 17-17-1
PS: 49ers lead series, 4-1
1961—49ers, 38-24 (M)
49ers, 38-28 (SF)
1962—49ers, 21-7 (SF)
49ers, 35-12 (M)
1963—Vikings, 24-20 (SF)
Vikings, 45-14 (M)
1964—Vikings, 27-22 (SF)
Vikings, 24-7 (M)
1965—Vikings, 42-41 (SF)
49ers, 45-24 (M)
1966—Tie, 20-20 (SF)
Vikings, 28-3 (SF)
1967—49ers, 27-21 (M)
1968—Vikings, 30-20 (SF)
1969—Vikings, 10-7 (M)
1970—*49ers, 17-14 (M)
1971—49ers, 13-9 (M)
1972—49ers, 20-17 (SF)
1973—Vikings, 17-13 (SF)
1975—Vikings, 27-17 (M)
1976—49ers, 20-16 (SF)
1977—Vikings, 28-27 (M)
1979—Vikings, 28-22 (M)
1983—49ers, 48-17 (M)
1984—49ers, 51-7 (SF)
1985—Vikings, 28-21 (M)
1986—Vikings, 27-24 (SF) OT
1987—*Vikings, 36-24 (SF)
1988—49ers, 24-21 (SF)
*49ers, 34-9 (SF)
1989—*49ers, 41-13 (SF)
1990—49ers, 20-17 (M)
1991—Vikings, 17-14 (M)
1992—49ers, 20-17 (M)
1993—49ers, 38-19 (SF)
1994—Vikings, 21-14 (M)
1995—49ers, 37-30 (SF)
1997—49ers, 28-17 (SF)
*49ers, 38-22 (SF)
1999—Vikings, 40-16 (M)
(RS Pts.—49ers 845, Vikings 786)
(PS Pts.—49ers 154, Vikings 94)
NFC Divisional Playoff

MINNESOTA vs. SEATTLE
RS: Seahawks lead series, 4-2
1976—Vikings, 27-21 (M)
1978—Seahawks, 29-28 (S)
1984—Seahawks, 20-12 (M)
1987—Seahawks, 28-17 (S)
1990—Vikings, 24-21 (S)
1996—Seahawks, 42-23 (S)
(RS Pts.—Seahawks 161, Vikings 131)

MINNESOTA vs. TAMPA BAY
RS: Vikings lead series, 29-15
1977—Vikings, 9-3 (TB)
1978—Buccaneers, 16-10 (M)
Vikings, 24-7 (TB)
1979—Buccaneers, 12-10 (M)
Vikings, 23-22 (TB)
1980—Vikings, 38-30 (M)
Vikings, 21-10 (TB)
1981—Buccaneers, 21-13 (TB)
Vikings, 25-10 (M)
1982—Vikings, 17-10 (M)
1983—Vikings, 19-16 (TB) OT
Buccaneers, 17-12 (M)
1984—Buccaneers, 35-31 (TB)
Vikings, 27-24 (M)
1985—Vikings, 31-16 (TB)
Vikings, 26-7 (M)
1986—Vikings, 23-10 (TB)
Vikings, 45-13 (M)
1987—Buccaneers, 20-10 (TB)
Vikings, 23-17 (M)
1988—Vikings, 14-13 (M)
Vikings, 49-20 (TB)
1989—Vikings, 17-3 (M)
Vikings, 24-10 (TB)
1990—Buccaneers, 23-20 (M) OT
Buccaneers, 26-13 (TB)
1991—Vikings, 28-13 (M)
Vikings, 26-24 (TB)
1992—Vikings, 26-20 (M)
Vikings, 35-7 (TB)
1993—Vikings, 15-0 (M)
Buccaneers, 23-10 (TB)
1994—Vikings, 36-13 (TB)
Buccaneers, 20-17 (M) OT
1995—Buccaneers, 20-17 (TB) OT
Vikings, 31-17 (M)
1996—Buccaneers, 24-13 (TB)
Vikings, 21-10 (M)
1997—Buccaneers, 28-14 (M)
Vikings, 10-6 (TB)
1998—Vikings, 31-7 (M)
Buccaneers, 27-24 (TB)
1999—Vikings, 21-14 (M)
Buccaneers, 24-17 (TB)
(RS Pts.—Vikings 966, Buccaneers 708)

MINNESOTA vs. *TENNESSEE
RS: Vikings lead series, 5-3
1974—Vikings, 51-10 (M)
1980—Oilers, 20-16 (H)
1983—Vikings, 34-14 (M)
1986—Oilers, 23-10 (H)
1989—Vikings, 38-7 (M)
1992—Oilers, 17-13 (M)
1995—Vikings, 23-17 (M) OT
1998—Vikings, 26-16 (T)
(RS Pts.—Vikings 211, Titans 124)
Franchise in Houston prior to 1997; known as Oilers prior to 1999

MINNESOTA vs. WASHINGTON
RS: Redskins lead series, 6-5
PS: Redskins lead series, 3-2
1968—Vikings, 27-14 (M)
1970—Vikings, 19-10 (W)
1972—Redskins, 24-21 (M)
1973—*Vikings, 27-20 (M)
1975—Redskins, 31-30 (W)
1976—*Vikings, 35-20 (M)
1980—Vikings, 39-14 (W)
1982—**Redskins, 21-7 (W)
1984—Redskins, 31-17 (M)
1986—Redskins, 44-38 (W) OT
1987—Redskins, 27-24 (M) OT
***Redskins, 17-10 (W)
1992—Redskins, 15-13 (M)
****Redskins, 24-7 (M)
1993—Vikings, 14-9 (W)
1998—Vikings, 41-7 (M)
(RS Pts.—Vikings 283, Redskins 226)
(PS Pts.—Redskins 102, Vikings 86)
NFC Divisional Playoff
**NFC Second-Round Playoff*
***NFC Championship*
****NFC First-Round Playoff*

NEW ENGLAND vs. ARIZONA
RS: Cardinals lead series, 6-4;
See Arizona vs. New England

NEW ENGLAND vs. ATLANTA
RS: Falcons lead series, 6-3;
See Atlanta vs. New England

NEW ENGLAND vs. BALTIMORE
RS: Patriots lead series, 2-0;
See Baltimore vs. New England

NEW ENGLAND vs. BUFFALO
RS: Patriots lead series, 40-38-1
PS: Patriots lead series, 1-0;
See Buffalo vs. New England

NEW ENGLAND vs. CAROLINA
RS: Panthers lead series, 1-0;
See Carolina vs. New England

ALL-TIME TEAM VS. TEAM RESULTS

NEW ENGLAND vs. CHICAGO
RS: Patriots lead series, 5-2
PS: Bears lead series, 1-0;
See Chicago vs. New England
NEW ENGLAND vs. CINCINNATI
RS: Patriots lead series, 9-7;
See Cincinnati vs. New England
NEW ENGLAND vs. CLEVELAND
RS: Browns lead series, 10-5
PS: Browns lead series, 1-0;
See Cleveland vs. New England
NEW ENGLAND vs. DALLAS
RS: Cowboys lead series, 7-1;
See Dallas vs. New England
NEW ENGLAND vs. DENVER
RS: Broncos lead series, 20-13
PS: Broncos lead series, 1-0;
See Denver vs. New England
NEW ENGLAND vs. DETROIT
RS: Series tied, 3-3;
See Detroit vs. New England
NEW ENGLAND vs. GREEN BAY
RS: Series tied, 3-3
PS: Packers lead series, 1-0;
See Green Bay vs. New England
NEW ENGLAND vs. INDIANAPOLIS
RS: Patriots lead series, 36-23;
See Indianapolis vs. New England
NEW ENGLAND vs. JACKSONVILLE
RS: Patriots lead series, 2-0
PS: Series tied, 1-1;
See Jacksonville vs. New England
NEW ENGLAND vs. KANSAS CITY
RS: Chiefs lead series, 15-8-3;
See Kansas City vs. New England
NEW ENGLAND vs. MIAMI
RS: Dolphins lead series, 40-26
PS: Patriots lead series, 2-1;
See Miami vs. New England
NEW ENGLAND vs. MINNESOTA
RS: Patriots lead series, 4-3;
See Minnesota vs. New England
NEW ENGLAND vs. NEW ORLEANS
RS: Patriots lead series, 6-3
1972—Patriots, 17-10 (NO)
1976—Patriots, 27-6 (NE)
1980—Patriots, 38-27 (NO)
1983—Patriots, 7-0 (NE)
1986—Patriots, 21-20 (NO)
1989—Saints, 28-24 (NE)
1992—Saints, 31-14 (NE)
1995—Saints, 31-17 (NE)
1998—Patriots, 30-27 (NO)
(RS Pts.—Patriots 195, Saints 180)
***NEW ENGLAND vs. N.Y. GIANTS**
RS: Series tied, 3-3
1970—Giants, 16-0 (B)
1974—Patriots, 28-20 (New Haven)
1987—Giants, 17-10 (NY)
1990—Giants, 13-10 (NE)
1996—Patriots, 23-22 (NY)
1999—Patriots, 16-14 (NE)
(RS Pts.—Giants 102, Patriots 87)
**Franchise in Boston prior to 1971*
***NEW ENGLAND vs. **N.Y. JETS**
RS: Jets lead series, 43-35-1
PS: Patriots lead series, 1-0
1960—Patriots, 28-24 (NY)
Patriots, 38-21 (B)
1961—Titans, 21-20 (B)
Titans, 37-30 (NY)
1962—Patriots, 43-14 (NY)
Patriots, 24-17 (B)
1963—Patriots, 38-14 (B)
Jets, 31-24 (NY)
1964—Patriots, 26-10 (B)
Jets, 35-14 (NY)
1965—Jets, 30-20 (B)
Patriots, 27-23 (NY)
1966—Tie, 24-24 (B)
Jets, 38-28 (NY)
1967—Jets, 30-23 (NY)
Jets, 29-24 (B)
1968—Jets, 47-31 (Birmingham)
Jets, 48-14 (NY)
1969—Jets, 23-14 (B)
Jets, 23-17 (NY)
1970—Jets, 31-21 (B)
Jets, 17-3 (NY)
1971—Patriots, 20-0 (NE)
Jets, 13-6 (NY)
1972—Jets, 41-13 (NE)
Jets, 34-10 (NY)
1973—Jets, 9-7 (NE)
Jets, 33-13 (NY)
1974—Patriots, 24-0 (NY)
Jets, 21-16 (NE)
1975—Jets, 36-7 (NY)
Jets, 30-28 (NE)
1976—Patriots, 41-7 (NE)
Patriots, 38-24 (NY)
1977—Jets, 30-27 (NY)
Patriots, 24-13 (NE)
1978—Patriots, 55-21 (NE)
Patriots, 19-17 (NY)
1979—Patriots, 56-3 (NE)
Jets, 27-26 (NY)
1980—Patriots, 21-11 (NY)
Patriots, 34-21 (NE)
1981—Jets, 28-24 (NY)
Jets, 17-6 (NE)
1982—Jets, 31-7 (NE)
1983—Patriots, 23-13 (NE)
Jets, 26-3 (NY)
1984—Patriots, 28-21 (NY)
Patriots, 30-20 (NE)
1985—Patriots, 20-13 (NE)
Jets, 16-13 (NY) OT
***Patriots, 26-14 (NY)
1986—Patriots, 20-6 (NY)
Jets, 31-24 (NE)
1987—Jets, 43-24 (NY)
Patriots, 42-20 (NE)
1988—Patriots, 28-3 (NE)
Patriots, 14-13 (NY)
1989—Patriots, 27-24 (NY)
Jets, 27-26 (NE)
1990—Jets, 37-13 (NE)
Jets, 42-7 (NY)
1991—Jets, 28-21 (NE)
Patriots, 6-3 (NY)
1992—Jets, 30-21 (NY)
Patriots, 24-3 (NE)
1993—Jets, 45-7 (NY)
Jets, 6-0 (NE)
1994—Jets, 24-17 (NY)
Patriots, 24-13 (NE)
1995—Patriots, 20-7 (NY)
Patriots, 31-28 (NE)
1996—Patriots, 31-27 (NY)
Patriots, 34-10 (NE)
1997—Patriots, 27-24 (NE) OT
Jets, 24-19 (NY)
1998—Jets, 24-14 (NE)
Jets, 31-10 (NY)
1999—Patriots, 30-28 (NY)
Jets, 24-17 (NE)
(RS Pts.—Jets 1,788, Patriots 1,748)
(PS Pts.—Patriots 26, Jets 14)
**Franchise in Boston prior to 1971*
***Jets known as Titans prior to 1963*
****AFC First-Round Playoff*
***NEW ENGLAND vs. **OAKLAND**
RS: Raiders lead series, 13-12-1
PS: Series tied, 1-1
1960—Raiders, 27-14 (O)
Patriots, 34-28 (B)
1961—Patriots, 20-17 (B)
Patriots, 35-21 (O)
1962—Patriots, 26-16 (B)
Raiders, 20-0 (O)
1963—Patriots, 20-14 (O)
Patriots, 20-14 (B)
1964—Patriots, 17-14 (O)
Tie, 43-43 (B)
1965—Raiders, 24-10 (B)
Raiders, 30-21 (O)
1966—Patriots, 24-21 (B)
1967—Raiders, 35-7 (O)
Raiders, 48-14 (B)
1968—Raiders, 41-10 (O)
1969—Raiders, 38-23 (B)
1971—Patriots, 20-6 (NE)
1974—Raiders, 41-26 (O)
1976—Patriots, 48-17 (NE)
***Raiders, 24-21 (O)
1978—Patriots, 21-14 (O)
1981—Raiders, 27-17 (O)
1985—Raiders, 35-20 (NE)
***Patriots, 27-20 (LA)
1987—Patriots, 26-23 (NE)
1989—Raiders, 24-21 (LA)
1994—Raiders, 21-17 (NE)
(RS Pts.—Raiders 659, Patriots 554)
(PS Pts.—Patriots 48, Raiders 44)
**Franchise in Boston prior to 1971*
***Franchise in Los Angeles from 1982-1994*
****AFC Divisional Playoff*
NEW ENGLAND vs. PHILADELPHIA
RS: Eagles lead series, 6-2
1973—Eagles, 24-23 (P)
1977—Patriots, 14-6 (NE)
1978—Patriots, 24-14 (NE)
1981—Eagles, 13-3 (P)
1984—Eagles, 27-17 (P)
1987—Eagles, 34-31 (NE) OT
1990—Eagles, 48-20 (P)
1999—Eagles, 24-9 (P)
(RS Pts.—Eagles 190, Patriots 141)
NEW ENGLAND vs. PITTSBURGH
RS: Steelers lead series, 11-4
PS: Series tied, 1-1
1972—Steelers, 33-3 (P)
1974—Steelers, 21-17 (NE)
1976—Patriots, 30-27 (P)
1979—Steelers, 16-13 (NE) OT
1981—Steelers, 27-21 (P) OT
1982—Steelers, 37-14 (P)
1983—Patriots, 28-23 (P)
1986—Patriots, 34-0 (P)
1989—Steelers, 28-10 (P)
1990—Steelers, 24-3 (P)
1991—Steelers, 20-6 (P)
1993—Steelers, 17-14 (P)
1995—Steelers, 41-27 (P)
1996—*Patriots, 28-3 (NE)
1997—Steelers, 24-21 (NE) OT
*Steelers, 7-6 (P)
1998—Patriots, 23-9 (P)
(RS Pts.—Steelers 347, Patriots 264)
(PS Pts.—Patriots 34, Steelers 10)
**AFC Divisional Playoff*
NEW ENGLAND vs. *ST. LOUIS
RS: Rams lead series, 4-3
1974—Patriots, 20-14 (NE)
1980—Rams, 17-14 (NE)
1983—Patriots, 21-7 (LA)
1986—Patriots, 30-28 (LA)
1989—Rams, 24-20 (NE)
1992—Rams, 14-0 (LA)
1998—Rams, 32-18 (StL)
(RS Pts.—Rams 136, Patriots 123)
**Franchise in Los Angeles prior to 1995*
***NEW ENGLAND vs. **SAN DIEGO**
RS: Patriots lead series, 16-11-2
PS: Chargers lead series, 1-0
1960—Patriots, 35-0 (LA)
Chargers, 45-16 (B)
1961—Chargers, 38-27 (B)
Patriots, 41-0 (SD)
1962—Patriots, 24-20 (B)
Patriots, 20-14 (SD)
1963—Chargers, 17-13 (SD)
Chargers, 7-6 (B)
***Chargers, 51-10 (SD)
1964—Patriots, 33-28 (SD)
Chargers, 26-17 (B)
1965—Tie, 10-10 (B)
Patriots, 22-6 (SD)
1966—Chargers, 24-0 (SD)
Patriots, 35-17 (B)
1967—Chargers, 28-14 (SD)
Tie, 31-31 (SD)
1968—Chargers, 27-17 (B)
1969—Chargers, 13-10 (B)
Chargers, 28-18 (SD)
1970—Chargers, 16-14 (B)
1973—Patriots, 30-14 (NE)
1975—Patriots, 33-19 (SD)
1977—Patriots, 24-20 (SD)
1978—Patriots, 28-23 (NE)
1979—Patriots, 27-21 (NE)
1983—Patriots, 37-21 (NE)
1994—Patriots, 23-17 (NE)
1996—Patriots, 45-7 (SD)
1997—Patriots, 41-7 (NE)
(RS Pts.—Patriots 691, Chargers 544)
(PS Pts.—Chargers 51, Patriots 10)
**Franchise in Boston prior to 1971*
***Franchise in Los Angeles prior to 1961*
****AFL Championship*
NEW ENGLAND vs. SAN FRANCISCO
RS: 49ers lead series, 7-2
1971—49ers, 27-10 (SF)
1975—Patriots, 24-16 (NE)
1980—49ers, 21-17 (SF)
1983—49ers, 33-13 (NE)
1986—49ers, 29-24 (NE)
1989—49ers, 37-20 (SF)
1992—49ers, 24-12 (NE)
1995—49ers, 28-3 (SF)
1998—Patriots, 24-21 (NE)
(RS Pts.—49ers 236, Patriots 147)
NEW ENGLAND vs. SEATTLE
RS: Seahawks lead series, 7-6
1977—Patriots, 31-0 (NE)
1980—Patriots, 37-31 (S)
1982—Patriots, 16-0 (S)
1983—Seahawks, 24-6 (S)
1984—Patriots, 38-23 (NE)
1985—Patriots, 20-13 (S)
1986—Seahawks, 38-31 (NE)
1988—Patriots, 13-7 (NE)
1989—Seahawks, 24-3 (NE)
1990—Seahawks, 33-20 (NE)
1992—Seahawks, 10-6 (NE)
1993—Seahawks, 17-14 (NE)
Seahawks, 10-9 (S)
(RS Pts.—Patriots 244, Seahawks 230)
NEW ENGLAND vs. TAMPA BAY
RS: Patriots lead series, 3-1
1976—Patriots, 31-14 (TB)
1985—Patriots, 32-14 (TB)
1988—Patriots, 10-7 (NE) OT
1997—Buccaneers, 27-7 (TB)
(RS Pts.—Patriots 80, Buccaneers 62)
***NEW ENGLAND vs. **TENNESSEE**
RS: Patriots lead series, 18-14-1
PS: Titans lead series, 1-0
1960—Oilers, 24-10 (B)
Oilers, 37-21 (H)
1961—Tie, 31-31 (B)
Oilers, 27-15 (H)
1962—Patriots, 34-21 (B)
Oilers, 21-17 (H)
1963—Patriots, 45-3 (B)
Patriots, 46-28 (H)
1964—Patriots, 25-24 (B)
Patriots, 34-17 (H)
1965—Oilers, 31-10 (H)
Patriots, 42-14 (B)
1966—Patriots, 27-21 (B)
Patriots, 38-14 (H)
1967—Patriots, 18-7 (B)
Oilers, 27-6 (H)
1968—Oilers, 16-0 (B)
Oilers, 45-17 (H)
1969—Patriots, 24-0 (B)
Oilers, 27-23 (H)
1971—Patriots, 28-20 (NE)
1973—Patriots, 32-0 (H)

1975—Oilers, 7-0 (NE)
1978—Oilers, 26-23 (NE)
***Oilers, 31-14 (NE)
1980—Oilers, 38-34 (H)
1981—Patriots, 38-10 (NE)
1982—Patriots, 29-21 (NE)
1987—Patriots, 21-7 (H)
1988—Oilers, 31-6 (H)
1989—Patriots, 23-13 (NE)
1991—Patriots, 24-20 (NE)
1993—Oilers, 28-14 (NE)
1998—Patriots, 27-16 (NE)
(RS Pts.—Patriots 782, Titans 672)
(PS Pts.—Titans 31, Patriots 14)
Franchise in Boston prior to 1971
**Franchise in Houston prior to 1997; known as Oilers prior to 1999*
****AFC Divisional Playoff*

NEW ENGLAND vs. WASHINGTON
RS: Redskins lead series, 5-1
1972—Patriots, 24-23 (NE)
1978—Redskins, 16-14 (NE)
1981—Redskins, 24-22 (W)
1984—Redskins, 26-10 (NE)
1990—Redskins, 25-10 (NE)
1996—Redskins, 27-22 (NE)
(RS Pts.—Redskins 141, Patriots 102)

NEW ORLEANS vs. ARIZONA
RS: Cardinals lead series, 12-10;
See Arizona vs. New Orleans

NEW ORLEANS vs. ATLANTA
RS: Falcons lead series, 37-24
PS: Falcons lead series, 1-0;
See Atlanta vs. New Orleans

NEW ORLEANS vs. BALTIMORE
RS: Ravens lead series, 2-0;
See Baltimore vs. New Orleans

NEW ORLEANS vs. BUFFALO
RS: Bills lead series, 4-2;
See Buffalo vs. New Orleans

NEW ORLEANS vs. CAROLINA
RS: Panthers lead series, 6-4;
See Carolina vs. New Orleans

NEW ORLEANS vs. CHICAGO
RS: Bears lead series, 10-8
PS: Bears lead series, 1-0;
See Chicago vs. New Orleans

NEW ORLEANS vs. CINCINNATI
RS: Saints lead series, 5-4;
See Cincinnati vs. New Orleans

NEW ORLEANS vs. CLEVELAND
RS: Browns lead series, 10-3;
See Cleveland vs. New Orleans

NEW ORLEANS vs. DALLAS
RS: Cowboys lead series, 14-5;
See Dallas vs. New Orleans

NEW ORLEANS vs. DENVER
RS: Broncos lead series, 4-2;
See Denver vs. New Orleans

NEW ORLEANS vs. DETROIT
RS: Saints lead series, 8-6-1;
See Detroit vs. New Orleans

NEW ORLEANS vs. GREEN BAY
RS: Packers lead series, 13-4;
See Green Bay vs. New Orleans

NEW ORLEANS vs. INDIANAPOLIS
RS: Saints lead series, 4-3;
See Indianapolis vs. New Orleans

NEW ORLEANS vs. JACKSONVILLE
RS: Series tied, 1-1;
See Jacksonville vs. New Orleans

NEW ORLEANS vs. KANSAS CITY
RS: Chiefs lead series, 4-3;
See Kansas City vs. New Orleans

NEW ORLEANS vs. MIAMI
RS: Dolphins lead series, 5-3;
See Miami vs. New Orleans

NEW ORLEANS vs. MINNESOTA
RS: Vikings lead series, 14-6
PS: Vikings lead series, 1-0;
See Minnesota vs. New Orleans

NEW ORLEANS vs. NEW ENGLAND
RS: Patriots lead series, 6-3;
See New England vs. New Orleans

NEW ORLEANS vs. N.Y. GIANTS
RS: Giants lead series, 12-8
1967—Giants, 27-21 (NY)
1968—Giants, 38-21 (NY)
1969—Saints, 25-24 (NY)
1970—Saints, 14-10 (NO)
1972—Giants, 45-21 (NY)
1975—Giants, 28-14 (NY)
1978—Saints, 28-17 (NO)
1979—Saints, 24-14 (NO)
1981—Giants, 20-7 (NY)
1984—Saints, 10-3 (NY)
1985—Giants, 21-13 (NO)
1986—Giants, 20-17 (NY)
1987—Saints, 23-14 (NO)
1988—Giants, 13-12 (NO)
1993—Giants, 24-14 (NO)
1994—Saints, 27-22 (NO)
1995—Giants, 45-29 (NY)
1996—Saints 17-3 (NY)
1997—Giants, 14-9 (NY)
1999—Giants, 31-3 (NY)
(RS Pts.—Giants 433, Saints 349)

NEW ORLEANS vs. N.Y. JETS
RS: Series tied, 4-4
1972—Jets, 18-17 (NY)
1977—Jets, 16-13 (NO)
1980—Saints, 21-20 (NY)
1983—Jets, 31-28 (NO)
1986—Jets, 28-23 (NY)
1989—Saints, 29-14 (NO)
1992—Saints, 20-0 (NY)
1995—Saints, 12-0 (NY)
(RS Pts.—Saints 163, Jets 127)

NEW ORLEANS vs. *OAKLAND
RS: Raiders lead series, 4-3-1
1971—Tie, 21-21 (NO)
1975—Raiders, 48-10 (O)
1979—Raiders, 42-35 (NO)
1985—Raiders, 23-13 (LA)
1988—Saints, 20-6 (NO)
1991—Saints, 27-0 (NO)
1994—Raiders, 24-19 (LA)
1997—Saints, 13-10 (O)
(RS Pts.—Raiders 174, Saints 158)
Franchise in Los Angeles from 1982-1994

NEW ORLEANS vs. PHILADELPHIA
RS: Eagles lead series, 12-8
PS: Eagles lead series, 1-0
1967—Saints, 31-24 (NO)
Eagles, 48-21 (P)
1968—Eagles, 29-17 (P)
1969—Eagles, 13-10 (P)
Saints, 26-17 (NO)
1972—Saints, 21-3 (NO)
1974—Saints, 14-10 (NO)
1977—Eagles, 28-7 (P)
1978—Eagles, 24-17 (NO)
1979—Eagles, 26-14 (NO)
1980—Eagles, 34-21 (NO)
1981—Eagles, 31-14 (NO)
1983—Saints, 20-17 (P) OT
1985—Saints, 23-21 (NO)
1987—Eagles, 27-17 (P)
1989—Saints, 30-20 (NO)
1991—Saints, 13-6 (P)
1992—Eagles, 15-13 (P)
*Eagles, 36-20 (NO)
1993—Eagles, 37-26 (P)
1995—Eagles, 15-10 (NO)
(RS Pts.—Eagles 445, Saints 365)
(PS Pts.—Eagles 36, Saints 20)
**NFC First-Round Playoff*

NEW ORLEANS vs. PITTSBURGH
RS: Steelers lead series, 6-5
1967—Steelers, 14-10 (NO)
1968—Saints, 16-12 (P)
Saints, 24-14 (NO)
1969—Saints, 27-24 (NO)
1974—Steelers, 28-7 (NO)
1978—Steelers, 20-14 (P)
1981—Steelers, 20-6 (NO)
1984—Saints, 27-24 (NO)
1987—Saints, 20-16 (P)
1990—Steelers, 9-6 (NO)
1993—Steelers, 37-14 (P)
(RS Pts.—Steelers 218, Saints 171)

NEW ORLEANS vs. *ST. LOUIS
RS: Rams lead series, 34-26
1967—Rams, 27-13 (NO)
1969—Rams, 36-17 (LA)
1970—Rams, 30-17 (NO)
Rams, 34-16 (LA)
1971—Saints, 24-20 (NO)
Rams, 45-28 (LA)
1972—Rams, 34-14 (LA)
Saints, 19-16 (NO)
1973—Rams, 29-7 (LA)
Rams, 24-13 (NO)
1974—Rams, 24-0 (LA)
Saints, 20-7 (NO)
1975—Rams, 38-14 (LA)
Rams, 14-7 (NO)
1976—Rams, 16-10 (NO)
Rams, 33-14 (LA)
1977—Rams, 14-7 (LA)
Saints, 27-26 (NO)
1978—Rams, 26-20 (NO)
Saints, 10-3 (LA)
1979—Rams, 35-17 (NO)
Saints, 29-14 (LA)
1980—Rams, 45-31 (LA)
Rams, 27-7 (NO)
1981—Saints, 23-17 (NO)
Saints, 21-13 (LA)
1983—Rams, 30-27 (LA)
Rams, 26-24 (NO)
1984—Rams, 28-10 (NO)
Rams, 34-21 (LA)
1985—Rams, 28-10 (LA)
Saints, 29-3 (NO)
1986—Saints, 6-0 (NO)
Rams, 26-13 (LA)
1987—Saints, 37-10 (NO)
Saints, 31-14 (LA)
1988—Rams, 12-10 (NO)
Saints, 14-10 (LA)
1989—Saints, 40-21 (LA)
Rams, 20-17 (NO) OT
1990—Saints, 24-20 (LA)
Saints, 20-17 (NO)
1991—Saints, 24-7 (NO)
Saints, 24-17 (LA)
1992—Saints, 13-10 (NO)
Saints, 37-14 (LA)
1993—Saints, 37-6 (LA)
Rams, 23-20 (NO)
1994—Saints, 37-34 (NO)
Saints, 31-15 (LA)
1995—Rams, 17-13 (StL)
Saints, 19-10 (NO)
1996—Rams, 26-10 (NO)
Rams, 14-13 (StL)
1997—Rams, 38-24 (StL)
Rams, 34-27 (NO)
1998—Saints, 24-17 (StL)
Saints, 24-3 (NO)
1999—Rams, 43-12 (StL)
Rams, 30-14 (NO)
(RS Pts.—Rams 1,304, Saints 1,161)
Franchise in Los Angeles prior to 1995

NEW ORLEANS vs. SAN DIEGO
RS: Chargers lead series, 6-1
1973—Chargers, 17-14 (SD)
1977—Chargers, 14-0 (NO)
1979—Chargers, 35-0 (NO)
1988—Saints, 23-17 (SD)
1991—Chargers, 24-21 (SD)
1994—Chargers, 36-22 (NO)
1997—Chargers, 20-6 (NO)
(RS Pts.—Chargers 163, Saints 86)

NEW ORLEANS vs. SAN FRANCISCO
RS: 49ers lead series, 43-16-2
1967—49ers, 27-13 (SF)
1969—Saints, 43-38 (NO)
1970—Tie, 20-20 (SF)
49ers, 38-27 (NO)
1971—49ers, 38-20 (NO)
Saints, 26-20 (SF)
1972—49ers, 37-2 (NO)
Tie, 20-20 (SF)
1973—49ers, 40-0 (SF)
Saints, 16-10 (NO)
1974—49ers, 17-13 (NO)
49ers, 35-21 (SF)
1975—49ers, 35-21 (SF)
49ers, 16-6 (NO)
1976—49ers, 33-3 (SF)
49ers, 27-7 (NO)
1977—49ers, 10-7 (NO) OT
49ers, 20-17 (SF)
1978—Saints, 14-7 (SF)
Saints, 24-13 (NO)
1979—Saints, 30-21 (SF)
Saints, 31-20 (NO)
1980—49ers, 26-23 (NO)
49ers, 38-35 (SF) OT
1981—49ers, 21-14 (SF)
49ers, 21-17 (NO)
1982—Saints, 23-20 (SF)
1983—49ers, 32-13 (NO)
49ers, 27-0 (SF)
1984—49ers, 30-20 (SF)
49ers, 35-3 (NO)
1985—Saints, 20-17 (SF)
49ers, 31-19 (NO)
1986—49ers, 26-17 (SF)
Saints, 23-10 (NO)
1987—49ers, 24-22 (NO)
Saints, 26-24 (SF)
1988—49ers, 34-33 (NO)
49ers, 30-17 (SF)
1989—49ers, 24-20 (NO)
49ers, 31-13 (SF)
1990—49ers, 13-12 (NO)
Saints, 13-10 (SF)
1991—Saints, 10-3 (NO)
49ers, 38-24 (SF)
1992—49ers, 16-10 (NO)
49ers, 21-20 (SF)
1993—Saints, 16-13 (NO)
49ers, 42-7 (SF)
1994—49ers, 24-13 (SF)
49ers, 35-14 (NO)
1995—49ers, 24-22 (NO)
Saints, 11-7 (SF)
1996—49ers, 27-11 (SF)
49ers, 24-17 (NO)
1997—49ers, 33-7 (SF)
49ers, 23-0 (NO)
1998—49ers, 31-0 (NO)
49ers, 31-20 (SF)
1999—49ers, 28-21 (SF)
Saints, 24-6 (NO)
(RS Pts.—49ers 1,492, Saints 1,011)

NEW ORLEANS vs. SEATTLE
RS: Saints lead series, 4-2
1976—Saints, 51-27 (S)
1979—Seahawks, 38-24 (S)
1985—Seahawks, 27-3 (NO)
1988—Saints, 20-19 (S)
1991—Saints, 27-24 (NO)
1997—Saints, 20-17 (NO) OT
(RS Pts.—Seahawks 152, Saints 145)

NEW ORLEANS vs. TAMPA BAY
RS: Saints lead series, 13-6
1977—Buccaneers, 33-14 (NO)
1978—Saints, 17-10 (TB)
1979—Saints, 42-14 (TB)
1981—Buccaneers, 31-14 (NO)
1982—Buccaneers, 13-10 (NO)
1983—Saints, 24-21 (TB)
1984—Saints, 17-13 (NO)
1985—Saints, 20-13 (NO)

ALL-TIME TEAM VS. TEAM RESULTS

1986—Saints, 38-7 (NO)
1987—Saints, 44-34 (NO)
1988—Saints, 13-9 (NO)
1989—Buccaneers, 20-10 (TB)
1990—Saints, 35-7 (NO)
1991—Saints, 23-7 (NO)
1992—Saints, 23-21 (NO)
1994—Saints, 9-7 (TB)
1996—Buccaneers, 13-7 (TB)
1998—Saints, 9-3 (NO)
1999—Buccaneers, 31-16 (NO)
(RS Pts.—Saints 385, Buccaneers 307)

NEW ORLEANS vs. *TENNESSEE
RS: Titans lead series, 5-4-1
1971—Tie, 13-13 (H)
1976—Oilers, 31-26 (NO)
1978—Oilers, 17-12 (NO)
1981—Saints, 27-24 (H)
1984—Saints, 27-10 (H)
1987—Saints, 24-10 (NO)
1990—Oilers, 23-10 (H)
1993—Saints, 33-21 (NO)
1996—Oilers, 31-14 (NO)
1999—Titans, 24-21 (NO)
(RS Pts.—Saints 207, Titans 204)
**Franchise in Houston prior to 1997; known as Oilers prior to 1999*

NEW ORLEANS vs. WASHINGTON
RS: Redskins lead series, 12-5
1967—Redskins, 30-10 (NO)
Saints, 30-14 (W)
1968—Saints, 37-17 (NO)
1969—Redskins, 26-20 (NO)
Redskins, 17-14 (W)
1971—Redskins, 24-14 (W)
1973—Saints, 19-3 (NO)
1975—Redskins, 41-3 (W)
1979—Saints, 14-10 (W)
1980—Redskins, 22-14 (W)
1982—Redskins, 27-10 (NO)
1986—Redskins, 14-6 (NO)
1988—Redskins, 27-24 (W)
1989—Redskins, 16-14 (NO)
1990—Redskins, 31-17 (W)
1992—Saints, 20-3 (NO)
1994—Redskins, 38-24 (NO)
(RS Pts.—Redskins 360, Saints 290)

N.Y. GIANTS vs. ARIZONA
RS: Giants lead series, 73-39-2;
See Arizona vs. N.Y. Giants

N.Y. GIANTS vs. ATLANTA
RS: Falcons lead series, 7-6;
See Atlanta vs. N.Y. Giants

N.Y. GIANTS vs. BALTIMORE
RS: Ravens lead series, 1-0;
See Baltimore vs. N.Y. Giants

N.Y. GIANTS vs. BUFFALO
RS: Bills lead series, 5-3
PS: Giants lead series, 1-0;
See Buffalo vs. N.Y. Giants

N.Y. GIANTS vs. CAROLINA
RS: Panthers lead series, 1-0;
See Carolina vs. N.Y. Giants

N.Y. GIANTS vs. CHICAGO
RS: Bears lead series, 25-16-2
PS: Bears lead series, 5-3;
See Chicago vs. N.Y. Giants

N.Y. GIANTS vs. CINCINNATI
RS: Bengals lead series, 4-2;
See Cincinnati vs. N.Y. Giants

N.Y. GIANTS vs. CLEVELAND
RS: Browns lead series, 25-17-2
PS: Series tied, 1-1;
See Cleveland vs. N.Y. Giants

N.Y. GIANTS vs. DALLAS
RS: Cowboys lead series, 47-26-2;
See Dallas vs. N.Y. Giants

N.Y. GIANTS vs. DENVER
RS: Giants lead series, 4-3
PS: Giants lead series, 1-0;
See Denver vs. N.Y. Giants

N.Y. GIANTS vs. DETROIT
RS: Lions lead series, 18-17-1
PS: Lions lead series, 1-0;
See Detroit vs. N.Y. Giants

N.Y. GIANTS vs. GREEN BAY
RS: Packers lead series, 23-20-2
PS: Packers lead series, 4-1;
See Green Bay vs. N.Y. Giants

N.Y. GIANTS vs. INDIANAPOLIS
RS: Colts lead series, 6-5
PS: Colts lead series, 2-0;
See Indianapolis vs. N.Y. Giants

N.Y. GIANTS vs. JACKSONVILLE
RS: Jaguars lead series, 1-0;
See Jacksonville vs. N.Y. Giants

N.Y. GIANTS vs. KANSAS CITY
RS: Giants lead series, 7-2;
See Kansas City vs. N.Y. Giants

N.Y. GIANTS vs. MIAMI
RS: Giants lead series, 3-1;
See Miami vs. N.Y. Giants

N.Y. GIANTS vs. MINNESOTA
RS: Vikings lead series, 8-5
PS: Series tied, 1-1;
See Minnesota vs. N.Y. Giants

N.Y. GIANTS vs. NEW ENGLAND
RS: Series tied, 3-3;
See New England vs. N.Y. Giants

N.Y. GIANTS vs. NEW ORLEANS
RS: Giants lead series, 12-8;
See New Orleans vs. N.Y. Giants

N.Y. GIANTS vs. N.Y. JETS
RS: Giants lead series, 5-4
1970—Giants, 22-10 (NYJ)
1974—Jets, 26-20 (New Haven) OT
1981—Jets, 26-7 (NYG)
1984—Giants, 20-10 (NYJ)
1987—Giants, 20-7 (NYG)
1988—Jets, 27-21 (NYJ)
1993—Jets, 10-6 (NYG)
1996—Giants, 13-6 (NYJ)
1999—Giants, 41-28 (NYG)
(RS Pts.—Giants 170, Jets 150)

N.Y. GIANTS vs. *OAKLAND
RS: Raiders lead series, 6-2
1973—Raiders, 42-0 (O)
1980—Raiders, 33-17 (NY)
1983—Raiders, 27-12 (LA)
1986—Giants, 14-9 (LA)
1989—Giants, 34-17 (NY)
1992—Raiders, 13-10 (LA)
1995—Raiders, 17-13 (NY)
1998—Raiders, 20-17 (O)
(RS Pts.—Raiders 178, Giants 117)
**Franchise in Los Angeles from 1982-1994*

N.Y. GIANTS vs. PHILADELPHIA
RS: Giants lead series, 70-58-2
PS: Giants lead series, 1-0
1933—Giants, 56-0 (NY)
Giants, 20-14 (P)
1934—Giants, 17-0 (NY)
Eagles, 6-0 (P)
1935—Giants, 10-0 (NY)
Giants, 21-14 (P)
1936—Eagles, 10-7 (P)
Giants, 21-17 (NY)
1937—Giants, 16-7 (P)
Giants, 21-0 (NY)
1938—Eagles, 14-10 (P)
Giants, 17-7 (NY)
1939—Giants, 13-3 (P)
Giants, 27-10 (NY)
1940—Giants, 20-14 (P)
Giants, 17-7 (NY)
1941—Giants, 24-0 (P)
Giants, 16-0 (NY)
1942—Giants, 35-17 (NY)
Giants, 14-0 (P)
1944—Eagles, 24-17 (NY)
Tie, 21-21 (P)
1945—Eagles, 38-17 (P)
Giants, 28-21 (NY)
1946—Eagles, 24-14 (P)
Giants, 45-17 (NY)
1947—Eagles, 23-0 (P)
Eagles, 41-24 (NY)
1948—Eagles, 45-0 (P)
Eagles, 35-14 (NY)
1949—Eagles, 24-3 (NY)
Eagles, 17-3 (P)
1950—Giants, 7-3 (NY)
Giants, 9-7 (P)
1951—Giants, 26-24 (NY)
Giants, 23-7 (P)
1952—Giants, 31-7 (P)
Eagles, 14-10 (NY)
1953—Eagles, 30-7 (P)
Giants, 37-28 (NY)
1954—Giants, 27-14 (NY)
Eagles, 29-14 (P)
1955—Eagles, 27-17 (P)
Giants, 31-7 (NY)
1956—Giants, 20-3 (NY)
Giants, 21-7 (P)
1957—Giants, 24-20 (P)
Giants, 13-0 (NY)
1958—Eagles, 27-24 (P)
Giants, 24-10 (NY)
1959—Eagles, 49-21 (P)
Giants, 24-7 (NY)
1960—Eagles, 17-10 (NY)
Eagles, 31-23 (P)
1961—Giants, 38-21 (NY)
Giants, 28-24 (P)
1962—Giants, 29-13 (P)
Giants, 19-14 (NY)
1963—Giants, 37-14 (P)
Giants, 42-14 (NY)
1964—Eagles, 38-7 (P)
Eagles, 23-17 (NY)
1965—Giants, 16-14 (P)
Giants, 35-27 (NY)
1966—Eagles, 35-17 (P)
Eagles, 31-3 (NY)
1967—Giants, 44-7 (NY)
1968—Giants, 34-25 (P)
Giants, 7-6 (NY)
1969—Eagles, 23-20 (NY)
1970—Giants, 30-23 (NY)
Eagles, 23-20 (P)
1971—Eagles, 23-7 (P)
Eagles, 41-28 (NY)
1972—Giants, 27-12 (P)
Giants, 62-10 (NY)
1973—Tie, 23-23 (NY)
Eagles, 20-16 (P)
1974—Eagles, 35-7 (P)
Eagles, 20-7 (New Haven)
1975—Giants, 23-14 (P)
Eagles, 13-10 (NY)
1976—Eagles, 20-7 (P)
Eagles, 10-0 (NY)
1977—Eagles, 28-10 (NY)
Eagles, 17-14 (P)
1978—Eagles, 19-17 (NY)
Eagles, 20-3 (P)
1979—Eagles, 23-17 (P)
Eagles, 17-13 (NY)
1980—Eagles, 35-3 (P)
Eagles, 31-16 (NY)
1981—Eagles, 24-10 (NY)
Giants, 20-10 (P)
*Giants, 27-21 (P)
1982—Giants, 23-7 (NY)
Giants, 26-24 (P)
1983—Eagles, 17-13 (NY)
Giants, 23-0 (P)
1984—Giants, 28-27 (NY)
Eagles, 24-10 (P)
1985—Giants, 21-0 (NY)
Giants, 16-10 (P) OT
1986—Giants, 35-3 (NY)
Giants, 17-14 (P)
1987—Giants, 20-17 (P)
Giants, 23-20 (NY) OT
1988—Eagles, 24-13 (P)
Eagles, 23-17 (NY) OT
1989—Eagles, 21-19 (P)
Eagles, 24-17 (NY)
1990—Giants, 27-20 (NY)
Eagles, 31-13 (P)
1991—Eagles, 30-7 (P)
Eagles, 19-14 (NY)
1992—Eagles, 47-34 (NY)
Eagles, 20-10 (P)
1993—Giants, 21-10 (NY)
Giants, 7-3 (P)
1994—Giants, 28-23 (NY)
Giants, 16-13 (P)
1995—Eagles, 17-14 (NY)
Eagles, 28-19 (P)
1996—Eagles, 19-10 (NY)
Eagles, 24-0 (P)
1997—Giants, 31-17 (NY)
Giants, 31-21 (P)
1998—Giants, 20-0 (NY)
Giants, 20-10 (P)
1999—Giants, 16-15 (NY)
Giants, 23-17 (P) OT
(RS Pts.—Giants 2,476, Eagles 2,317)
(PS Pts.—Giants 27, Eagles 21)
**NFC First-Round Playoff*

N.Y. GIANTS vs. *PITTSBURGH
RS: Giants lead series, 42-27-3
1933—Giants, 23-2 (P)
Giants, 27-3 (NY)
1934—Giants, 14-12 (P)
Giants, 17-7 (NY)
1935—Giants, 42-7 (P)
Giants, 13-0 (NY)
1936—Pirates, 10-7 (P)
1937—Giants, 10-7 (P)
Giants, 17-0 (NY)
1938—Giants, 27-14 (P)
Pirates, 13-10 (NY)
1939—Giants, 14-7 (P)
Giants, 23-7 (NY)
1940—Tie, 10-10 (P)
Giants, 12-0 (NY)
1941—Giants, 37-10 (P)
Giants, 28-7 (NY)
1942—Steelers, 13-10 (P)
Steelers, 17-9 (NY)
1945—Giants, 34-6 (P)
Steelers, 21-7 (NY)
1946—Giants, 17-14 (P)
Giants, 7-0 (NY)
1947—Steelers, 38-21 (NY)
Steelers, 24-7 (P)
1948—Giants, 34-27 (NY)
Steelers, 38-28 (P)
1949—Steelers, 28-7 (P)
Steelers, 21-17 (NY)
1950—Giants, 18-7 (P)
Steelers, 17-6 (NY)
1951—Tie, 13-13 (P)
Giants, 14-0 (NY)
1952—Steelers, 63-7 (P)
1953—Steelers, 24-14 (P)
Steelers, 14-10 (NY)
1954—Giants, 30-6 (P)
Giants, 24-3 (NY)
1955—Steelers, 30-23 (P)
Steelers, 19-17 (NY)
1956—Giants, 38-10 (NY)
Giants, 17-14 (P)
1957—Giants, 35-0 (NY)
Steelers, 21-10 (P)
1958—Giants, 17-6 (NY)
Steelers, 31-10 (P)
1959—Giants, 21-16 (P)
Steelers, 14-9 (NY)
1960—Giants, 19-17 (P)
Giants, 27-24 (NY)
1961—Giants, 17-14 (P)
Giants, 42-21 (NY)
1962—Giants, 31-27 (P)
Steelers, 20-17 (NY)

1963—Steelers, 31-0 (P)
Giants, 33-17 (NY)
1964—Steelers, 27-24 (P)
Steelers, 44-17 (NY)
1965—Giants, 23-13 (P)
Giants, 35-10 (NY)
1966—Tie, 34-34 (P)
Steelers, 47-28 (NY)
1967—Giants, 27-24 (P)
Giants, 28-20 (NY)
1968—Giants, 34-20 (P)
1969—Giants, 10-7 (NY)
Giants, 21-17 (P)
1971—Steelers, 17-13 (P)
1976—Steelers, 27-0 (NY)
1985—Giants, 28-10 (NY)
1991—Giants, 23-20 (P)
1994—Steelers, 10-6 (NY)
(RS Pts.—Giants 1,399, Steelers 1,189)
Steelers known as Pirates prior to 1941

N.Y. GIANTS vs. *ST. LOUIS
RS: Rams lead series, 23-9
PS: Series tied, 1-1
1938—Giants, 28-0 (NY)
1940—Rams, 13-0 (NY)
1941—Giants, 49-14 (NY)
1945—Rams, 21-17 (NY)
1946—Rams, 31-21 (NY)
1947—Rams, 34-10 (LA)
1948—Rams, 52-37 (NY)
1953—Rams, 21-7 (LA)
1954—Rams, 17-16 (NY)
1959—Giants, 23-21 (LA)
1961—Giants, 24-14 (NY)
1966—Rams, 55-14 (LA)
1968—Rams, 24-21 (LA)
1970—Rams, 31-3 (NY)
1973—Rams, 40-6 (LA)
1976—Rams, 24-10 (LA)
1978—Rams, 20-17 (NY)
1979—Giants, 20-14 (LA)
1980—Rams, 28-7 (NY)
1981—Giants, 10-7 (NY)
1983—Rams, 16-6 (NY)
1984—Rams, 33-12 (LA)
**Giants, 16-13 (LA)
1985—Giants, 24-19 (NY)
1988—Rams, 45-31 (NY)
1989—Rams, 31-10 (LA)
***Rams, 19-13 (NY) OT
1990—Giants, 31-7 (LA)
1991—Rams, 19-13 (NY)
1992—Rams, 38-17 (LA)
1993—Giants, 20-10 (NY)
1994—Rams, 17-10 (LA)
1997—Rams, 13-3 (StL)
1999—Rams, 31-10 (StL)
(RS Pts.—Rams 760, Giants 527)
(PS Pts.—Rams 32, Giants 29)
Franchise in Los Angeles prior to 1995 and in Cleveland prior to 1946
***NFC First-Round Playoff*
****NFC Divisional Playoff*

N.Y. GIANTS vs. SAN DIEGO
RS: Giants lead series, 5-3
1971—Giants, 35-17 (NY)
1975—Giants, 35-24 (NY)
1980—Chargers, 44-7 (SD)
1983—Chargers, 41-34 (NY)
1986—Giants, 20-7 (NY)
1989—Giants, 20-13 (SD)
1995—Chargers, 27-17 (NY)
1998—Giants, 34-16 (SD)
(RS Pts.—Giants 202, Chargers 189)

N.Y. GIANTS vs. SAN FRANCISCO
RS: 49ers lead series, 12-11
PS: Series tied, 3-3
1952—Giants, 23-14 (NY)
1956—Giants, 38-21 (SF)
1957—49ers, 27-17 (NY)
1960—Giants, 21-19 (SF)
1963—Giants, 48-14 (NY)
1968—49ers, 26-10 (NY)
1972—Giants, 23-17 (SF)
1975—Giants, 26-23 (SF)
1977—Giants, 20-17 (NY)
1978—Giants, 27-10 (NY)
1979—Giants, 32-16 (NY)
1980—49ers, 12-0 (SF)
1981—49ers, 17-10 (SF)
*49ers, 38-24 (SF)
1984—49ers, 31-10 (NY)
*49ers, 21-10 (SF)
1985—**Giants, 17-3 (NY)
1986—Giants, 21-17 (SF)
*Giants, 49-3 (NY)
1987—49ers, 41-21 (NY)
1988—49ers, 20-17 (NY)
1989—49ers, 34-24 (SF)
1990—49ers, 7-3 (SF)
***Giants, 15-13 (SF)
1991—Giants, 16-14 (NY)
1992—49ers, 31-14 (NY)
1993—*49ers, 44-3 (SF)
1995—49ers, 20-6 (SF)
1998—49ers, 31-7 (SF)
(RS Pts.—49ers 479, Giants 434)
(PS Pts.—49ers 122, Giants 118)
**NFC Divisional Playoff*
***NFC First-Round Playoff*
****NFC Championship*

N.Y. GIANTS vs. SEATTLE
RS: Giants lead series, 5-3
1976—Giants, 28-16 (NY)
1980—Giants, 27-21 (S)
1981—Giants, 32-0 (S)
1983—Seahawks, 17-12 (NY)
1986—Seahawks, 17-12 (S)
1989—Giants, 15-3 (NY)
1992—Giants, 23-10 (NY)
1995—Seahawks, 30-28 (S)
(RS Pts.—Giants 177, Seahawks 114)

N.Y. GIANTS vs. TAMPA BAY
RS: Giants lead series, 9-5
1977—Giants, 10-0 (TB)
1978—Giants, 19-13 (TB)
Giants, 17-14 (NY)
1979—Giants, 17-14 (NY)
Buccaneers, 31-3 (TB)
1980—Buccaneers, 30-13 (TB)
1984—Giants, 17-14 (NY)
Buccaneers, 20-17 (TB)
1985—Giants, 22-20 (NY)
1991—Giants, 21-14 (TB)
1993—Giants, 23-7 (NY)
1997—Buccaneers, 20-8 (NY)
1998—Buccaneers, 20-3 (TB)
1999—Giants, 17-13 (TB)
(RS Pts.—Buccaneers 230, Giants 207)

N.Y. GIANTS vs. *TENNESSEE
RS: Giants lead series, 5-1
1973—Giants, 34-14 (NY)
1982—Giants, 17-14 (NY)
1985—Giants, 35-14 (H)
1991—Giants, 24-20 (NY)
1994—Giants, 13-10 (H)
1997—Oilers, 10-6 (T)
(RS Pts.—Giants 129, Titans 82)
Franchise in Houston prior to 1997; known as Oilers prior to 1999

N.Y. GIANTS vs. *WASHINGTON
RS: Giants lead series, 75-55-4
PS: Series tied, 1-1
1932—Braves, 14-6 (B)
Tie, 0-0 (NY)
1933—Redskins, 21-20 (B)
Giants, 7-0 (NY)
1934—Giants, 16-13 (B)
Giants, 3-0 (NY)
1935—Giants, 20-12 (B)
Giants, 17-6 (NY)
1936—Giants, 7-0 (B)
Redskins, 14-0 (NY)
1937—Redskins, 13-3 (W)
Redskins, 49-14 (NY)
1938—Giants, 10-7 (W)
Giants, 36-0 (NY)
1939—Tie, 0-0 (W)
Giants, 9-7 (NY)
1940—Redskins, 21-7 (W)
Giants, 21-7 (NY)
1941—Giants, 17-10 (W)
Giants, 20-13 (NY)
1942—Giants, 14-7 (W)
Redskins, 14-7 (NY)
1943—Giants, 14-10 (NY)
Giants, 31-7 (W)
**Redskins, 28-0 (NY)
1944—Giants, 16-13 (NY)
Giants, 31-0 (W)
1945—Redskins, 24-14 (NY)
Redskins, 17-0 (W)
1946—Redskins, 24-14 (W)
Giants, 31-0 (NY)
1947—Redskins, 28-20 (W)
Giants, 35-10 (NY)
1948—Redskins, 41-10 (W)
Redskins, 28-21 (NY)
1949—Giants, 45-35 (W)
Giants, 23-7 (NY)
1950—Giants, 21-17 (W)
Giants, 24-21 (NY)
1951—Giants, 35-14 (W)
Giants, 28-14 (NY)
1952—Giants, 14-10 (W)
Redskins, 27-17 (NY)
1953—Redskins, 13-9 (W)
Redskins, 24-21 (NY)
1954—Giants, 51-21 (W)
Giants, 24-7 (NY)
1955—Giants, 35-7 (NY)
Giants, 27-20 (W)
1956—Redskins, 33-7 (W)
Giants, 28-14 (NY)
1957—Giants, 24-20 (W)
Redskins, 31-14 (NY)
1958—Giants, 21-14 (W)
Giants, 30-0 (NY)
1959—Giants, 45-14 (NY)
Giants, 24-10 (W)
1960—Tie, 24-24 (NY)
Giants, 17-3 (W)
1961—Giants, 24-21 (W)
Giants, 53-0 (NY)
1962—Giants, 49-34 (NY)
Giants, 42-24 (W)
1963—Giants, 24-14 (W)
Giants, 44-14 (NY)
1964—Giants, 13-10 (NY)
Redskins, 36-21 (W)
1965—Redskins, 23-7 (NY)
Giants, 27-10 (W)
1966—Giants, 13-10 (NY)
Redskins, 72-41 (W)
1967—Redskins, 38-34 (W)
1968—Giants, 48-21 (NY)
Giants, 13-10 (W)
1969—Redskins, 20-14 (W)
1970—Giants, 35-33 (NY)
Giants, 27-24 (W)
1971—Redskins, 30-3 (NY)
Redskins, 23-7 (W)
1972—Redskins, 23-16 (NY)
Redskins, 27-13 (W)
1973—Redskins, 21-3 (New Haven)
Redskins, 27-24 (W)
1974—Redskins, 13-10 (New Haven)
Redskins, 24-3 (W)
1975—Redskins, 49-13 (W)
Redskins, 21-13 (NY)
1976—Redskins, 19-17 (W)
Giants, 12-9 (NY)
1977—Giants, 20-17 (NY)
Giants, 17-6 (W)
1978—Giants, 17-6 (NY)
Redskins, 16-13 (W) OT
1979—Redskins, 27-0 (W)
Giants, 14-6 (NY)
1980—Redskins, 23-21 (NY)
Redskins, 16-13 (W)
1981—Giants, 17-7 (W)
Redskins, 30-27 (NY) OT
1982—Redskins, 27-17 (NY)
Redskins, 15-14 (W)
1983—Redskins, 33-17 (NY)
Redskins, 31-22 (W)
1984—Redskins, 30-14 (W)
Giants, 37-13 (NY)
1985—Giants, 17-3 (NY)
Redskins, 23-21 (W)
1986—Giants, 27-20 (NY)
Giants, 24-14 (W)
***Giants, 17-0 (NY)
1987—Redskins, 38-12 (NY)
Redskins, 23-19 (W)
1988—Giants, 27-20 (NY)
Giants, 24-23 (W)
1989—Giants, 27-24 (W)
Giants, 20-17 (NY)
1990—Giants, 24-20 (W)
Giants, 21-10 (NY)
1991—Redskins, 17-13 (NY)
Redskins, 34-17 (W)
1992—Giants, 24-7 (W)
Redskins, 28-10 (NY)
1993—Giants, 41-7 (W)
Giants, 20-6 (NY)
1994—Giants, 31-23 (NY)
Giants, 21-19 (W)
1995—Giants, 24-15 (W)
Giants, 20-13 (NY)
1996—Redskins, 31-10 (NY)
Redskins, 31-21 (W)
1997—Tie, 7-7 (W) OT
Giants, 30-10 (NY)
1998—Giants, 31-24 (NY)
Redskins, 21-14 (W)
1999—Redskins, 50-21 (NY)
Redskins, 23-13 (W)
(RS Pts.—Giants 2,673, Redskins 2,434)
(PS Pts.—Redskins 28, Giants 17)
Franchise in Boston prior to 1937 and known as Braves prior to 1933
***Division Playoff*
****NFC Championship*

N.Y. JETS vs. ARIZONA
RS: Jets lead series, 3-2;
See Arizona vs. N.Y. Jets

N.Y. JETS vs. ATLANTA
RS: Series tied, 4-4;
See Atlanta vs. N.Y. Jets

N.Y. JETS vs BALTIMORE
RS: Series tied, 1-1;
See Baltimore vs. N.Y. Jets

N.Y. JETS vs. BUFFALO
RS: Bills lead series, 44-34
PS: Bills lead series, 1-0;
See Buffalo vs. N.Y. Jets

N.Y. JETS vs. CAROLINA
RS: Series tied, 1-1;
See Carolina vs. N.Y. Jets

N.Y. JETS vs. CHICAGO
RS: Bears lead series, 4-2;
See Chicago vs. N.Y. Jets

N.Y. JETS vs. CINCINNATI
RS: Jets lead series, 10-6
PS: Jets lead series, 1-0;
See Cincinnati vs. N.Y. Jets

N.Y. JETS vs. CLEVELAND
RS: Browns lead series, 9-6
PS: Browns lead series, 1-0;
See Cleveland vs. N.Y. Jets

N.Y. JETS vs. DALLAS
RS: Cowboys lead series, 5-2;
See Dallas vs. N.Y. Jets

N.Y. JETS vs. DENVER
RS: Series tied, 13-13-1
PS: Broncos lead series, 1-0;
See Denver vs. N.Y. Jets

ALL-TIME TEAM VS. TEAM RESULTS

N.Y. JETS vs. DETROIT
RS: Lions lead series, 5-3;
See Detroit vs. N.Y. Jets
N.Y. JETS vs. GREEN BAY
RS: Jets lead series, 5-2;
See Green Bay vs. N.Y. Jets
N.Y. JETS vs. INDIANAPOLIS
RS: Colts lead series, 36-23
PS: Jets lead series, 1-0;
See Indianapolis vs. N.Y. Jets
N.Y. JETS vs. JACKSONVILLE
RS: Jaguars lead series, 2-1
PS: Jets lead series, 1-0;
See Jacksonville vs. N.Y. Jets
N.Y. JETS vs. KANSAS CITY
RS: Chiefs lead series, 14-13-1
PS: Series tied, 1-1;
See Kansas City vs. N.Y. Jets
N.Y. JETS vs. MIAMI
RS: Dolphins lead series, 34-33-1
PS: Dolphins lead series, 1-0;
See Miami vs. N.Y. Jets
N.Y. JETS vs. MINNESOTA
RS: Jets lead series, 5-1;
See Minnesota vs. N.Y. Jets
N.Y. JETS vs. NEW ENGLAND
RS: Jets lead series, 43-35-1
PS: Patriots lead series, 1-0;
See New England vs. N.Y. Jets
N.Y. JETS vs. NEW ORLEANS
RS: Series tied, 4-4;
See New Orleans vs. N.Y. Jets
N.Y. JETS vs. N.Y. GIANTS
RS: Giants lead series, 5-4;
See N.Y. Giants vs. N.Y. Jets
***N.Y. JETS vs. **OAKLAND**
RS: Raiders lead series, 17-10-2
PS: Jets lead series, 2-0
1960—Raiders, 28-27 (NY)
Titans, 31-28 (O)
1961—Titans, 14-6 (O)
Titans, 23-12 (NY)
1962—Titans, 28-17 (O)
Titans, 31-21 (NY)
1963—Jets, 10-7 (NY)
Raiders, 49-26 (O)
1964—Jets, 35-13 (NY)
Raiders, 35-26 (O)
1965—Tie, 24-24 (NY)
Raiders, 24-14 (O)
1966—Raiders, 24-21 (NY)
Tie, 28-28 (O)
1967—Jets, 27-14 (NY)
Raiders, 38-29 (O)
1968—Raiders, 43-32 (O)
***Jets, 27-23 (NY)
1969—Raiders, 27-14 (NY)
1970—Raiders, 14-13 (NY)
1972—Raiders, 24-16 (O)
1977—Raiders, 28-27 (NY)
1979—Jets, 28-19 (NY)
1982—****Jets, 17-14 (LA)
1985—Raiders, 31-0 (LA)
1989—Raiders, 14-7 (NY)
1993—Raiders, 24-20 (LA)
1995—Raiders, 47-10 (NY)
1996—Raiders, 34-13 (NY)
1997—Jets 23-22 (NY)
1999—Raiders, 24-23 (O)
(RS Pts.—Raiders 719, Jets 620)
(PS Pts.—Jets 44, Raiders 37)
Jets known as Titans prior to 1963
***Franchise in Los Angeles from 1982-1994*
****AFL Championship*
*****AFC Second-Round Playoff*
N.Y. JETS vs. PHILADELPHIA
RS: Eagles lead series, 6-0
1973—Eagles, 24-23 (P)
1977—Eagles, 27-0 (P)
1978—Eagles, 17-9 (P)
1987—Eagles, 38-27 (NY)
1993—Eagles, 35-30 (NY)
1996—Eagles, 21-20 (NY)
(RS Pts.—Eagles 162, Jets 109)
N.Y. JETS vs. PITTSBURGH
RS: Steelers lead series, 12-1
1970—Steelers, 21-17 (P)
1973—Steelers, 26-14 (P)
1975—Steelers, 20-7 (NY)
1977—Steelers, 23-20 (NY)
1978—Steelers, 28-17 (NY)
1981—Steelers, 38-10 (P)
1983—Steelers, 34-7 (NY)
1984—Steelers, 23-17 (NY)
1986—Steelers, 45-24 (NY)
1988—Jets, 24-20 (NY)
1989—Steelers, 13-0 (NY)
1990—Steelers, 24-7 (NY)
1992—Steelers, 27-10 (P)
(RS Pts.—Steelers 342, Jets 174)
N.Y. JETS vs. *ST. LOUIS
RS: Rams lead series, 7-2
1970—Jets, 31-20 (LA)
1974—Rams, 20-13 (NY)
1980—Rams, 38-13 (LA)
1983—Jets, 27-24 (NY) OT
1986—Rams, 17-3 (NY)
1989—Rams, 38-14 (LA)
1992—Rams, 18-10 (LA)
1995—Rams, 23-20 (NY)
1998—Rams, 30-10 (StL)
(RS Pts.—Rams 228, Jets 141)
**Franchise in Los Angeles prior to 1995*
***N.Y. JETS vs. **SAN DIEGO**
RS: Chargers lead series, 17-9-1
1960—Chargers, 21-7 (NY)
Chargers, 50-43 (LA)
1961—Chargers, 25-10 (NY)
Chargers, 48-13 (SD)
1962—Chargers, 40-14 (SD)
Titans, 23-3 (NY)
1963—Chargers, 24-20 (SD)
Chargers, 53-7 (NY)
1964—Tie, 17-17 (NY)
Chargers, 38-3 (SD)
1965—Chargers, 34-9 (NY)
Chargers, 38-7 (SD)
1966—Jets, 17-16 (NY)
Chargers, 42-27 (SD)
1967—Jets, 42-31 (SD)
1968—Jets, 23-20 (NY)
Jets, 37-15 (SD)
1969—Chargers, 34-27 (SD)
1971—Chargers, 49-21 (SD)
1974—Jets, 27-14 (NY)
1975—Chargers, 24-16 (SD)
1983—Jets, 41-29 (SD)
1989—Jets, 20-17 (SD)
1990—Chargers, 39-3 (NY)
Chargers, 38-17 (SD)
1991—Jets, 24-3 (NY)
1994—Chargers, 21-6 (NY)
(RS Pts.—Chargers 783, Jets 521)
**Jets known as Titans prior to 1963*
***Franchise in Los Angeles prior to 1961*
N.Y. JETS vs. SAN FRANCISCO
RS: 49ers lead series, 7-1
1971—49ers, 24-21 (NY)
1976—49ers, 17-6 (SF)
1980—49ers, 37-27 (NY)
1983—Jets, 27-13 (SF)
1986—49ers, 24-10 (SF)
1989—49ers, 23-10 (NY)
1992—49ers, 31-14 (NY)
1998—49ers, 36-30 (SF) OT
(RS Pts.—49ers 205, Jets 145)
N.Y. JETS vs. SEATTLE
RS: Seahawks lead series, 8-7
1977—Seahawks, 17-0 (NY)
1978—Seahawks, 24-17 (NY)
1979—Seahawks, 30-7 (S)
1980—Seahawks, 27-17 (NY)
1981—Seahawks, 19-3 (NY)
Seahawks, 27-23 (S)
1983—Seahawks, 17-10 (NY)
1985—Jets, 17-14 (NY)
1986—Jets, 38-7 (S)
1987—Jets, 30-14 (NY)
1991—Seahawks, 20-13 (S)
1995—Jets, 16-10 (S)
1997—Jets, 41-3 (S)
1998—Jets, 32-31 (NY)
1999—Jets, 19-9 (NY)
(RS Pts.—Jets 283, Seahawks 269)
N.Y. JETS vs. TAMPA BAY
RS: Jets lead series, 6-1
1976—Jets, 34-0 (NY)
1982—Jets, 32-17 (NY)
1984—Buccaneers, 41-21 (TB)
1985—Jets, 62-28 (NY)
1990—Jets, 16-14 (TB)
1991—Jets, 16-13 (NY)
1997—Jets, 31-0 (NY)
(RS Pts.—Jets 212, Buccaneers 113)
***N.Y. JETS vs. **TENNESSEE**
RS: Titans lead series, 20-13-1
PS: Titans lead series, 1-0
1960—Oilers, 27-21 (H)
Oilers, 42-28 (NY)
1961—Oilers, 49-13 (H)
Oilers, 48-21 (NY)
1962—Oilers, 56-17 (H)
Oilers, 44-10 (NY)
1963—Jets, 24-17 (NY)
Oilers, 31-27 (H)
1964—Jets, 24-21 (NY)
Oilers, 33-17 (H)
1965—Oilers, 27-21 (H)
Jets, 41-14 (NY)
1966—Jets, 52-13 (NY)
Oilers, 24-0 (H)
1967—Tie, 28-28 (NY)
1968—Jets, 20-14 (H)
Jets, 26-7 (NY)
1969—Jets, 26-17 (NY)
Jets, 34-26 (H)
1972—Oilers, 26-20 (H)
1974—Oilers, 27-22 (NY)
1977—Oilers, 20-0 (H)
1979—Oilers, 27-24 (H) OT
1980—Jets, 31-28 (NY) OT
1981—Jets, 33-17 (NY)
1984—Oilers, 31-20 (H)
1988—Jets, 45-3 (NY)
1990—Jets, 17-12 (H)
1991—Oilers, 23-20 (NY)
***Oilers, 17-10 (H)
1993—Oilers, 24-0 (H)
1994—Oilers, 24-10 (H)
1995—Oilers, 23-6 (H)
1996—Oilers, 35-10 (NY)
1998—Jets, 24-3 (T)
(RS Pts.—Titans 861, Jets 732)
(PS Pts.—Titans 17, Jets 10)
**Jets known as Titans prior to 1963*
***Franchise in Houston prior to 1997; known as Oilers prior to 1999*
****AFC First-Round Playoff*
N.Y. JETS vs. WASHINGTON
RS: Redskins lead series, 6-1
1972—Redskins, 35-17 (NY)
1976—Redskins, 37-16 (NY)
1978—Redskins, 23-3 (W)
1987—Redskins, 17-16 (W)
1993—Jets, 3-0 (W)
1996—Redskins, 31-16 (W)
1999—Redskins, 27-20 (NY)
(RS Pts.—Redskins 170, Jets 91)

OAKLAND vs. ARIZONA
RS: Raiders lead series, 3-1;
See Arizona vs. Oakland
OAKLAND vs. ATLANTA
RS: Raiders lead series, 6-3;
See Atlanta vs. Oakland
OAKLAND vs. BALTIMORE
RS: Ravens lead series, 2-0;
See Baltimore vs. Oakland
OAKLAND vs. BUFFALO
RS: Raiders lead series, 16-15
PS: Bills lead series, 2-0;
See Buffalo vs. Oakland
OAKLAND vs CAROLINA
RS: Panthers lead series, 1-0;
See Carolina vs Oakland
OAKLAND vs. CHICAGO
RS: Raiders lead series, 6-4;
See Chicago vs. Oakland
OAKLAND vs. CINCINNATI
RS: Raiders lead series, 16-7
PS: Raiders lead series, 2-0;
See Cincinnati vs. Oakland
OAKLAND vs. CLEVELAND
RS: Raiders lead series, 8-4
PS: Raiders lead series, 2-0;
See Cleveland vs. Oakland
OAKLAND vs. DALLAS
RS: Raiders lead series, 4-3;
See Dallas vs. Oakland
OAKLAND vs. DENVER
RS: Raiders lead series, 49-28-2
PS: Series tied, 1-1;
See Denver vs. Oakland
OAKLAND vs. DETROIT
RS: Raiders lead series, 6-2;
See Detroit vs. Oakland
OAKLAND vs. GREEN BAY
RS: Raiders lead series, 5-3
PS: Packers lead series, 1-0;
See Green Bay vs. Oakland
OAKLAND vs. INDIANAPOLIS
RS: Raiders lead series, 5-2
PS: Series tied, 1-1;
See Indianapolis vs. Oakland
OAKLAND vs. JACKSONVILLE
RS: Series tied, 1-1;
See Jacksonville vs. Oakland
OAKLAND vs. KANSAS CITY
RS: Chiefs lead series, 40-37-2
PS: Chiefs lead series, 2-1;
See Kansas City vs. Oakland
OAKLAND vs. MIAMI
RS: Raiders lead series, 15-8-1
PS: Raiders lead series, 2-1;
See Miami vs. Oakland
OAKLAND vs. MINNESOTA
RS: Raiders lead series, 7-3
PS: Raiders lead series, 1-0;
See Minnesota vs. Oakland
OAKLAND vs. NEW ENGLAND
RS: Raiders lead series, 13-12-1
PS: Series tied, 1-1;
See New England vs. Oakland
OAKLAND vs. NEW ORLEANS
RS: Raiders lead series, 4-3-1;
See New Orleans vs. Oakland
OAKLAND vs. N.Y. GIANTS
RS: Raiders lead series, 6-2;
See N.Y. Giants vs. Oakland
OAKLAND vs. N.Y. JETS
RS: Raiders lead series, 17-10-2
PS: Jets lead series, 2-0;
See N.Y. Jets vs. Oakland
***OAKLAND vs. PHILADELPHIA**
RS: Eagles lead series, 4-3
PS: Raiders lead series, 1-0
1971—Raiders, 34-10 (O)
1976—Raiders, 26-7 (P)
1980—Eagles, 10-7 (P)
**Raiders, 27-10 (New Orleans)
1986—Eagles, 33-27 (LA) OT
1989—Eagles, 10-7 (P)
1992—Eagles, 31-10 (P)
1995—Raiders, 48-17 (O)
(RS Pts.—Raiders 159, Eagles 118)
(PS Pts.—Raiders 27, Eagles 10)
**Franchise in Los Angeles from 1982-1994*
***Super Bowl XV*

***OAKLAND vs. PITTSBURGH**
RS: Raiders lead series, 7-5
PS: Series tied, 3-3
1970—Raiders, 31-14 (O)
1972—Steelers, 34-28 (P)
**Steelers, 13-7 (P)
1973—Steelers, 17-9 (O)
**Raiders, 33-14 (O)
1974—Raiders, 17-0 (P)
***Steelers, 24-13 (O)
1975—***Steelers, 16-10 (P)
1976—Raiders, 31-28 (O)
***Raiders, 24-7 (O)
1977—Raiders, 16-7 (P)
1980—Raiders, 45-34 (P)
1981—Raiders, 30-27 (O)
1983—**Raiders, 38-10 (LA)
1984—Steelers, 13-7 (LA)
1990—Raiders, 20-3 (LA)
1994—Steelers, 21-3 (LA)
1995—Steelers, 29-10 (O)
(RS Pts.—Raiders 247, Steelers 227)
(PS Pts.—Raiders 125, Steelers 84)
**Franchise in Los Angeles from 1982-1994*
***AFC Divisional Playoff*
****AFC Championship*

***OAKLAND vs. **ST. LOUIS**
RS: Raiders lead series, 7-2
1972—Raiders, 45-17 (O)
1977—Rams, 20-14 (LA)
1979—Raiders, 24-17 (LA)
1982—Raiders, 37-31 (LA Raiders)
1985—Raiders, 16-6 (LA Rams)
1988—Rams, 22-17 (LA Raiders)
1991—Raiders, 20-17 (LA Raiders)
1994—Raiders, 20-17 (LA Rams)
1997—Raiders, 35-17 (O)
(RS Pts.—Raiders 228, Rams 164)
**Franchise in Los Angeles from 1982-1994*
***Franchise in Los Angeles prior to 1995*

***OAKLAND vs. **SAN DIEGO**
RS: Raiders lead series, 48-30-2
PS: Raiders lead series, 1-0
1960—Chargers, 52-28 (LA)
Chargers, 41-17 (O)
1961—Chargers, 44-0 (SD)
Chargers, 41-10 (O)
1962—Chargers, 42-33 (O)
Chargers, 31-21 (SD)
1963—Raiders, 34-33 (SD)
Raiders, 41-27 (O)
1964—Chargers, 31-17 (SD)
Raiders, 21-20 (O)
1965—Chargers, 17-6 (O)
Chargers, 24-14 (SD)
1966—Chargers, 29-20 (O)
Raiders, 41-19 (SD)
1967—Raiders, 51-10 (O)
Raiders, 41-21 (SD)
1968—Chargers, 23-14 (O)
Raiders, 34-27 (SD)
1969—Raiders, 24-12 (SD)
Raiders, 21-16 (O)
1970—Tie, 27-27 (SD)
Raiders, 20-17 (O)
1971—Raiders, 34-0 (SD)
Raiders, 34-33 (O)
1972—Tie, 17-17 (O)
Raiders, 21-19 (SD)
1973—Raiders, 27-17 (SD)
Raiders, 31-3 (O)
1974—Raiders, 14-10 (SD)
Raiders, 17-10 (O)
1975—Raiders, 6-0 (SD)
Raiders, 25-0 (O)
1976—Raiders, 27-17 (SD)
Raiders, 24-0 (O)
1977—Raiders, 24-0 (O)
Chargers, 12-7 (SD)
1978—Raiders, 21-20 (SD)
Chargers, 27-23 (O)
1979—Chargers, 30-10 (SD)
Raiders, 45-22 (O)
1980—Chargers, 30-24 (SD) OT
Raiders, 38-24 (O)
***Raiders, 34-27 (SD)
1981—Chargers, 55-21 (O)
Chargers, 23-10 (SD)
1982—Raiders, 28-24 (LA)
Raiders, 41-34 (SD)
1983—Raiders, 42-10 (SD)
Raiders, 30-14 (LA)
1984—Raiders, 33-30 (LA)
Raiders, 44-37 (SD)
1985—Raiders, 34-21 (LA)
Chargers, 40-34 (SD) OT
1986—Raiders, 17-13 (LA)
Raiders, 37-31 (SD) OT
1987—Chargers, 23-17 (LA)
Chargers, 16-14 (SD)
1988—Raiders, 24-13 (LA)
Raiders, 13-3 (SD)
1989—Raiders, 40-14 (LA)
Chargers, 14-12 (SD)
1990—Raiders, 24-9 (SD)
Raiders, 17-12 (LA)
1991—Chargers, 21-13 (LA)
Raiders, 9-7 (SD)
1992—Chargers, 27-3 (SD)
Chargers, 36-14 (LA)
1993—Chargers, 30-23 (LA)
Raiders, 12-7 (SD)
1994—Chargers, 26-24 (LA)
Raiders, 24-17 (SD)
1995—Raiders, 17-7 (O)
Chargers, 12-6 (SD)
1996—Chargers, 40-34 (O)
Raiders, 23-14 (SD)
1997—Chargers, 25-10 (O)
Raiders, 38-13 (SD)
1998—Raiders, 7-6 (O)
Raiders, 17-10 (SD)
1999—Raiders, 28-9 (O)
Chargers, 23-20 (SD)
(RS Pts.—Raiders 1,858, Chargers 1,661)
(PS Pts.—Raiders 34, Chargers 27)
**Franchise in Los Angeles from 1982-1994*
***Franchise in Los Angeles prior to 1961*
****AFC Championship*

***OAKLAND vs. SAN FRANCISCO**
RS: Raiders lead series, 5-3
1970—49ers, 38-7 (O)
1974—Raiders, 35-24 (SF)
1979—Raiders, 23-10 (O)
1982—Raiders, 23-17 (SF)
1985—49ers, 34-10 (LA)
1988—Raiders, 9-3 (SF)
1991—Raiders, 12-6 (LA)
1994—49ers, 44-14 (SF)
(RS Pts.—49ers 176, Raiders 133)
**Franchise in Los Angeles from 1982-1994*

***OAKLAND vs. SEATTLE**
RS: Raiders lead series, 24-20
PS: Series tied, 1-1
1977—Raiders, 44-7 (O)
1978—Seahawks, 27-7 (S)
Seahawks, 17-16 (O)
1979—Seahawks, 27-10 (S)
Seahawks, 29-24 (O)
1980—Raiders, 33-14 (O)
Raiders, 19-17 (S)
1981—Raiders, 20-10 (O)
Raiders, 32-31 (S)
1982—Raiders, 28-23 (LA)
1983—Seahawks, 38-36 (S)
Seahawks, 34-21 (LA)
**Raiders, 30-14 (LA)
1984—Raiders, 28-14 (LA)
Seahawks, 17-14 (S)
***Seahawks, 13-7 (S)
1985—Seahawks, 33-3 (S)
Raiders, 13-3 (LA)
1986—Raiders, 14-10 (LA)
Seahawks, 37-0 (S)
1987—Seahawks, 35-13 (LA)
Raiders, 37-14 (S)
1988—Seahawks, 35-27 (S)
Seahawks, 43-37 (LA)
1989—Seahawks, 24-20 (LA)
Seahawks, 23-17 (S)
1990—Raiders, 17-13 (S)
Raiders, 24-17 (LA)
1991—Raiders, 23-20 (S) OT
Raiders, 31-7 (LA)
1992—Raiders, 19-0 (S)
Raiders, 20-3 (LA)
1993—Raiders, 17-13 (S)
Raiders, 27-23 (LA)
1994—Seahawks, 38-9 (LA)
Raiders, 17-16 (S)
1995—Raiders, 34-14 (O)
Seahawks, 44-10 (S)
1996—Raiders, 27-21 (S)
Seahawks, 28-21 (O)
1997—Seahawks, 45-34 (S)
Seahawks, 22-21 (O)
1998—Raiders, 31-18 (S)
Raiders, 20-17 (O)
1999—Seahawks, 22-21 (S)
Raiders, 30-21 (O)
(RS Pts.—Raiders 966, Seahawks 964)
(PS Pts.—Raiders 37, Seahawks 27)
**Franchise in Los Angeles from 1982-1994*
***AFC Championship*
****AFC First-Round Playoff*

***OAKLAND vs. TAMPA BAY**
RS: Raiders lead series, 4-1
1976—Raiders, 49-16 (O)
1981—Raiders, 18-16 (O)
1993—Raiders, 27-20 (LA)
1996—Buccaneers, 20-17 (TB) OT
1999—Raiders, 45-0 (O)
(RS Pts.—Raiders 156, Buccaneers 72)
**Franchise in Los Angeles from 1982-1994*

***OAKLAND vs. **TENNESSEE**
RS: Raiders lead series, 20-15
PS: Raiders lead series, 3-0
1960—Oilers, 37-22 (O)
Raiders, 14-13 (H)
1961—Oilers, 55-0 (H)
Oilers, 47-16 (O)
1962—Oilers, 28-20 (O)
Oilers, 32-17 (H)
1963—Raiders, 24-13 (H)
Raiders, 52-49 (O)
1964—Oilers, 42-28 (H)
Raiders, 20-10 (O)
1965—Raiders, 21-17 (O)
Raiders, 33-21 (H)
1966—Oilers, 31-0 (H)
Raiders, 38-23 (O)
1967—Raiders, 19-7 (H)
***Raiders, 40-7 (O)
1968—Raiders, 24-15 (H)
1969—Raiders, 21-17 (O)
****Raiders, 56-7 (O)
1971—Raiders, 41-21 (O)
1972—Raiders, 34-0 (H)
1973—Raiders, 17-6 (H)
1975—Oilers, 27-26 (O)
1976—Raiders, 14-13 (H)
1977—Raiders, 34-29 (O)
1978—Raiders, 21-17 (O)
1979—Oilers, 31-17 (H)
1980—*****Raiders, 27-7 (O)
1981—Oilers, 17-16 (H)
1983—Raiders, 20-6 (LA)
1984—Raiders, 24-14 (H)
1986—Raiders, 28-17 (H)
1988—Oilers, 38-35 (H)
1989—Oilers, 23-7 (H)
1991—Oilers, 47-17 (H)
1994—Raiders, 17-14 (LA)
1997—Oilers, 24-21 (T) OT
1999—Titans, 21-14 (T)
(RS Pts.—Titans 822, Raiders 772)
(PS Pts.—Raiders 123, Titans 21)
**Franchise in Los Angeles from 1982-1994*
***Franchise in Houston prior to 1997; known as Oilers prior to 1999*
****AFL Championship*
*****Inter-Divisional Playoff*
******AFC First-Round Playoff*

***OAKLAND vs. WASHINGTON**
RS: Raiders lead series, 6-3
PS: Raiders lead series, 1-0
1970—Raiders, 34-20 (O)
1975—Raiders, 26-23 (W) OT
1980—Raiders, 24-21 (O)
1983—Redskins, 37-35 (W)
**Raiders, 38-9 (Tampa)
1986—Redskins, 10-6 (W)
1989—Raiders, 37-24 (LA)
1992—Raiders, 21-20 (W)
1995—Raiders, 20-8 (W)
1998—Redskins, 29-19 (O)
(RS Pts.—Raiders 222, Redskins 192)
(PS Pts.—Raiders 38, Redskins 9)
**Franchise in Los Angeles from 1982-1994*
***Super Bowl XVIII*

PHILADELPHIA vs. ARIZONA
RS: Cardinals lead series, 51-48-5
PS: Series tied, 1-1;
See Arizona vs. Philadelphia
PHILADELPHIA vs. ATLANTA
RS: Series tied, 9-9-1
PS: Falcons lead series, 1-0;
See Atlanta vs. Philadelphia
PHILADELPHIA vs. BALTIMORE
RS: Series tied, 0-0-1;
See Baltimore vs. Philadelphia
PHILADELPHIA vs. BUFFALO
RS: Bills lead series, 5-4;
See Buffalo vs. Philadelphia
PHILADELPHIA vs. CAROLINA
RS: Series tied, 1-1;
See Carolina vs. Philadelphia
PHILADELPHIA vs. CHICAGO
RS: Bears lead series, 24-5-1
PS: Series tied, 1-1;
See Chicago vs. Philadelphia
PHILADELPHIA vs. CINCINNATI
RS: Bengals lead series, 6-2;
See Cincinnati vs. Philadelphia
PHILADELPHIA vs. CLEVELAND
RS: Browns lead series, 31-12-1;
See Cleveland vs. Philadelphia
PHILADELPHIA vs. DALLAS
RS: Cowboys lead series, 48-30
PS: Cowboys lead series, 2-1;
See Dallas vs. Philadelphia
PHILADELPHIA vs. DENVER
RS: Eagles lead series, 6-3;
See Denver vs. Philadelphia
PHILADELPHIA vs. DETROIT
RS: Lions lead series, 12-11-2
PS: Eagles lead series, 1-0;
See Detroit vs. Philadelphia
PHILADELPHIA vs. GREEN BAY
RS: Packers lead series, 21-9
PS: Eagles lead series, 1-0;
See Green Bay vs. Philadelphia
PHILADELPHIA vs. INDIANAPOLIS
RS: Colts lead series, 8-6;
See Indianapolis vs. Philadelphia
PHILADELPHIA vs. JACKSONVILLE
RS: Jaguars lead series, 1-0;
See Jacksonville vs. Philadelphia
PHILADELPHIA vs. KANSAS CITY
RS: Chiefs lead series, 2-1;
See Kansas City vs. Philadelphia

ALL-TIME TEAM VS. TEAM RESULTS

PHILADELPHIA vs. MIAMI
RS: Dolphins lead series, 7-3;
See Miami vs. Philadelphia
PHILADELPHIA vs. MINNESOTA
RS: Vikings lead series, 11-6
PS: Eagles lead series, 1-0;
See Minnesota vs. Philadelphia
PHILADELPHIA vs. NEW ENGLAND
RS: Eagles lead series, 6-2;
See New England vs. Philadelphia
PHILADELPHIA vs. NEW ORLEANS
RS: Eagles lead series, 12-8
PS; Eagles lead series, 1-0;
See New Orleans vs. Philadelphia
PHILADELPHIA vs. N.Y. GIANTS
RS: Giants lead series, 70-58-2
PS: Giants lead series, 1-0;
See N.Y. Giants vs. Philadelphia
PHILADELPHIA vs. N.Y. JETS
RS: Eagles lead series, 6-0;
See N.Y. Jets vs. Philadelphia
PHILADELPHIA vs. OAKLAND
RS: Eagles lead series, 4-3
PS: Raiders lead series, 1-0;
See Oakland vs. Philadelphia
PHILADELPHIA vs. *PITTSBURGH
RS: Eagles lead series, 44-26-3
PS: Eagles lead series, 1-0
1933—Eagles, 25-6 (Phila)
1934—Eagles, 17-0 (Pitt)
Pirates, 9-7 (Phila)
1935—Pirates, 17-7 (Phila)
Eagles, 17-6 (Pitt)
1936—Pirates, 17-0 (Pitt)
Pirates, 6-0 (Johnstown, Pa.)
1937—Pirates, 27-14 (Pitt)
Pirates, 16-7 (Pitt)
1938—Eagles, 27-7 (Buffalo)
Eagles, 14-7 (Charleston, W. Va.)
1939—Eagles, 17-14 (Phila)
Pirates, 24-12 (Pitt)
1940—Pirates, 7-3 (Pitt)
Eagles, 7-0 (Phila)
1941—Eagles, 10-7 (Pitt)
Tie, 7-7 (Phila)
1942—Eagles, 24-14 (Pitt)
Steelers, 14-0 (Phila)
1945—Eagles, 45-3 (Pitt)
Eagles, 30-6 (Phila)
1946—Steelers, 10-7 (Pitt)
Eagles, 10-7 (Phila)
1947—Steelers, 35-24 (Pitt)
Eagles, 21-0 (Phila)
**Eagles, 21-0 (Pitt)
1948—Eagles, 34-7 (Pitt)
Eagles, 17-0 (Phila)
1949—Eagles, 38-7 (Pitt)
Eagles, 34-17 (Phila)
1950—Eagles, 17-10 (Pitt)
Steelers, 9-7 (Phila)
1951—Eagles, 34-13 (Pitt)
Steelers, 17-13 (Phila)
1952—Eagles, 31-25 (Pitt)
Eagles, 26-21 (Phila)
1953—Eagles, 23-17 (Phila)
Eagles, 35-7 (Pitt)
1954—Eagles, 24-22 (Phila)
Steelers, 17-7 (Pitt)
1955—Steelers, 13-7 (Pitt)
Eagles, 24-0 (Phila)
1956—Eagles, 35-21 (Pitt)
Eagles, 14-7 (Phila)
1957—Steelers, 6-0 (Pitt)
Eagles, 7-6 (Phila)
1958—Steelers, 24-3 (Pitt)
Steelers, 31-24 (Phila)
1959—Eagles, 28-24 (Phila)
Steelers, 31-0 (Pitt)
1960—Eagles, 34-7 (Phila)
Steelers, 27-21 (Pitt)
1961—Eagles, 21-16 (Phila)
Eagles, 35-24 (Pitt)
1962—Steelers, 13-7 (Pitt)
Steelers, 26-17 (Phila)
1963—Tie, 21-21 (Phila)
Tie, 20-20 (Pitt)
1964—Eagles, 21-7 (Phila)
Eagles, 34-10 (Pitt)
1965—Steelers, 20-14 (Phila)
Eagles, 47-13 (Pitt)
1966—Eagles, 31-14 (Pitt)
Eagles, 27-23 (Phila)
1967—Eagles, 34-24 (Phila)
1968—Steelers, 6-3 (Pitt)
1969—Eagles, 41-27 (Phila)
1970—Eagles, 30-20 (Phila)
1974—Steelers, 27-0 (Pitt)
1979—Eagles, 17-14 (Phila)
1988—Eagles, 27-26 (Pitt)
1991—Eagles, 23-14 (Phila)
1994—Steelers, 14-3 (Pitt)
1997—Eagles, 23-20 (Phila)
(RS Pts.—Eagles 1,385, Steelers 1,041)
(PS Pts.—Eagles 21, Steelers 0)
**Steelers known as Pirates prior to 1941*
***Division Playoff*
PHILADELPHIA vs. *ST. LOUIS
RS: Rams lead series, 15-14-1
PS: Series tied, 1-1
1937—Rams, 21-3 (P)
1939—Rams, 35-13 (Colorado Springs)
1940—Rams, 21-13 (C)
1942—Rams, 24-14 (Akron)
1944—Eagles, 26-13 (P)
1945—Eagles, 28-14 (P)
1946—Eagles, 25-14 (LA)
1947—Eagles, 14-7 (P)
1948—Tie, 28-28 (LA)
1949—Eagles, 38-14 (P)
**Eagles, 14-0 (LA)
1950—Eagles, 56-20 (P)
1955—Rams, 23-21 (P)
1956—Rams, 27-7 (LA)
1957—Rams, 17-13 (LA)
1959—Eagles, 23-20 (P)
1964—Rams, 20-10 (LA)
1967—Rams, 33-17 (LA)
1969—Rams, 23-17 (P)
1972—Rams, 34-3 (P)
1975—Rams, 42-3 (P)
1977—Rams, 20-0 (LA)
1978—Rams, 16-14 (P)
1983—Eagles, 13-9 (P)
1985—Rams, 17-6 (P)
1986—Eagles, 34-20 (P)
1988—Eagles, 30-24 (P)
1989—***Rams, 21-7 (P)
1990—Eagles, 27-21 (LA)
1995—Eagles, 20-9 (P)
1998—Eagles, 17-14 (P)
1999—Eagles, 38-31 (P)
(RS Pts.—Rams 631, Eagles 571)
(PS Pts.—Rams 21, Eagles 21)
**Franchise in Los Angeles prior to 1995 and in Cleveland prior to 1946*
***NFL Championship*
****NFC First-Round Playoff*
PHILADELPHIA vs. SAN DIEGO
RS: Chargers lead series, 5-2
1974—Eagles, 13-7 (SD)
1980—Chargers, 22-21 (SD)
1985—Chargers, 20-14 (SD)
1986—Eagles, 23-7 (P)
1989—Chargers, 20-17 (SD)
1995—Chargers, 27-21 (P)
1998—Chargers, 13-10 (SD)
(RS Pts.—Eagles 119, Chargers 116)
PHILADELPHIA vs. SAN FRANCISCO
RS: 49ers lead series, 14-6-1
PS: 49ers lead series, 1-0
1951—Eagles, 21-14 (P)
1953—49ers, 31-21 (SF)
1956—Tie, 10-10 (P)
1958—49ers, 30-24 (P)
1959—49ers, 24-14 (SF)
1964—49ers, 28-24 (P)
1966—Eagles, 35-34 (SF)
1967—49ers, 28-27 (P)
1969—49ers, 14-13 (SF)
1971—49ers, 31-3 (P)
1973—49ers, 38-28 (SF)
1975—Eagles, 27-17 (P)
1983—Eagles, 22-17 (SF)
1984—49ers, 21-9 (P)
1985—49ers, 24-13 (SF)
1989—49ers, 38-28 (P)
1991—49ers, 23-7 (P)
1992—49ers, 20-14 (SF)
1993—Eagles, 37-34 (SF) OT
1994—Eagles, 40-8 (SF)
1996—*49ers, 14-0 (SF)
1997—49ers, 24-12 (P)
(RS Pts.—49ers 508, Eagles 429)
(PS Pts.—49ers 14, Eagles 0)
**NFC First-Round Playoff*
PHILADELPHIA vs. SEATTLE
RS: Eagles lead series, 4-3
1976—Eagles, 27-10 (P)
1980—Eagles, 27-20 (S)
1986—Seahawks, 24-20 (S)
1989—Eagles, 31-7 (P)
1992—Eagles, 20-17 (S) OT
1995—Seahawks, 26-14 (S)
1998—Seahawks, 38-0 (P)
(RS Pts.—Seahawks 142, Eagles 139)
PHILADELPHIA vs. TAMPA BAY
RS: Series tied, 3-3
PS: Buccaneers lead series, 1-0
1977—Eagles, 13-3 (P)
1979—*Buccaneers, 24-17 (TB)
1981—Eagles, 20-10 (P)
1988—Eagles, 41-14 (TB)
1991—Buccaneers, 14-13 (TB)
1995—Buccaneers, 21-6 (P)
1999—Buccaneers, 19-5 (P)
(RS Pts.—Eagles 98, Buccaneers 81)
(PS Pts.—Buccaneers 24, Eagles 17)
**NFC Divisional Playoff*
PHILADELPHIA vs. *TENNESSEE
RS: Eagles lead series, 6-0
1972—Eagles, 18-17 (H)
1979—Eagles, 26-20 (H)
1982—Eagles, 35-14 (P)
1988—Eagles, 32-23 (P)
1991—Eagles, 13-6 (H)
1994—Eagles, 21-6 (P)
(RS Pts.—Eagles 145, Titans 86)
**Franchise in Houston prior to 1997; known as Oilers prior to 1999*
PHILADELPHIA vs. *WASHINGTON
RS: Redskins lead series, 70-54-5
PS: Redskins lead series, 1-0
1934—Redskins, 6-0 (B)
Redskins, 14-7 (P)
1935—Eagles, 7-6 (B)
1936—Redskins, 26-3 (P)
Redskins, 17-7 (B)
1937—Eagles, 14-0 (W)
Redskins, 10-7 (P)
1938—Redskins, 26-23 (P)
Redskins, 20-14 (W)
1939—Redskins, 7-0 (P)
Redskins, 7-6 (W)
1940—Redskins, 34-17 (P)
Redskins, 13-6 (W)
1941—Redskins, 21-17 (P)
Redskins, 20-14 (W)
1942—Redskins, 14-10 (P)
Redskins, 30-27 (W)
1944—Tie, 31-31 (P)
Eagles, 37-7 (W)
1945—Redskins, 24-14 (W)
Eagles, 16-0 (P)
1946—Eagles, 28-24 (W)
Redskins, 27-10 (P)
1947—Eagles, 45-42 (P)
Eagles, 38-14 (W)
1948—Eagles, 45-0 (W)
Eagles, 42-21 (P)
1949—Eagles, 49-14 (P)
Eagles, 44-21 (W)
1950—Eagles, 35-3 (P)
Eagles, 33-0 (W)
1951—Redskins, 27-23 (P)
Eagles, 35-21 (W)
1952—Eagles, 38-20 (P)
Redskins, 27-21 (W)
1953—Tie, 21-21 (P)
Redskins, 10-0 (W)
1954—Eagles, 49-21 (W)
Eagles, 41-33 (P)
1955—Redskins, 31-30 (P)
Redskins, 34-21 (W)
1956—Eagles, 13-9 (P)
Redskins, 19-17 (W)
1957—Eagles, 21-12 (P)
Redskins, 42-7 (W)
1958—Redskins, 24-14 (P)
Redskins, 20-0 (W)
1959—Eagles, 30-23 (P)
Eagles, 34-14 (W)
1960—Eagles, 19-13 (P)
Eagles, 38-28 (W)
1961—Eagles, 14-7 (P)
Eagles, 27-24 (W)
1962—Redskins, 27-21 (P)
Eagles, 37-14 (W)
1963—Eagles, 37-24 (W)
Redskins, 13-10 (P)
1964—Redskins, 35-20 (W)
Redskins, 21-10 (P)
1965—Redskins, 23-21 (W)
Eagles, 21-14 (P)
1966—Redskins, 27-13 (P)
Eagles, 37-28 (W)
1967—Eagles, 35-24 (P)
Tie, 35-35 (W)
1968—Redskins, 17-14 (W)
Redskins, 16-10 (P)
1969—Tie, 28-28 (W)
Redskins, 34-29 (P)
1970—Redskins, 33-21 (P)
Redskins, 24-6 (W)
1971—Tie, 7-7 (W)
Redskins, 20-13 (P)
1972—Redskins, 14-0 (W)
Redskins, 23-7 (P)
1973—Redskins, 28-7 (P)
Redskins, 38-20 (W)
1974—Redskins, 27-20 (P)
Redskins, 26-7 (W)
1975—Eagles, 26-10 (P)
Eagles, 26-3 (W)
1976—Redskins, 20-17 (P) OT
Redskins, 24-0 (W)
1977—Redskins, 23-17 (W)
Redskins, 17-14 (P)
1978—Redskins, 35-30 (W)
Eagles, 17-10 (P)
1979—Eagles, 28-17 (P)
Redskins, 17-7 (W)
1980—Eagles, 24-14 (P)
Eagles, 24-0 (W)
1981—Eagles, 36-13 (P)
Redskins, 15-13 (W)
1982—Redskins, 37-34 (P) OT
Redskins, 13-9 (W)
1983—Redskins, 23-13 (P)
Redskins, 28-24 (W)
1984—Redskins, 20-0 (W)
Eagles, 16-10 (P)
1985—Eagles, 19-6 (W)
Redskins, 17-12 (P)
1986—Redskins, 41-14 (W)
Redskins, 21-14 (P)
1987—Redskins, 34-24 (W)
Eagles, 31-27 (P)
1988—Redskins, 17-10 (W)
Redskins, 20-19 (P)
1989—Eagles, 42-37 (W)
Redskins, 10-3 (P)
1990—Redskins, 13-7 (W)

Eagles, 28-14 (P)
**Redskins, 20-6 (P)
1991—Redskins, 23-0 (W)
Eagles, 24-22 (P)
1992—Redskins, 16-12 (W)
Eagles, 17-13 (P)
1993—Eagles, 34-31 (P)
Eagles, 17-14 (W)
1994—Eagles, 21-17 (P)
Eagles, 31-29 (W)
1995—Eagles, 37-34 (P) (OT)
Eagles, 14-7 (W)
1996—Eagles, 17-14 (W)
Redskins, 26-21 (P)
1997—Eagles, 24-10 (P)
Redskins, 35-32 (W)
1998—Eagles, 17-12 (P)
Redskins, 28-3 (W)
1999—Eagles, 35-28 (P)
Redskins, 20-17 (W) OT
(RS Pts.—Eagles 2,616, Redskins 2,584)
(PS Pts.—Redskins 20, Eagles 6)
Franchise in Boston prior to 1937
***NFC First-Round Playoff*

PITTSBURGH vs. ARIZONA
RS: Steelers lead series, 30-22-3;
See Arizona vs. Pittsburgh
PITTSBURGH vs. ATLANTA
RS: Steelers lead series, 11-1;
See Atlanta vs. Pittsburgh
PITTSBURGH vs. BALTIMORE
RS: Steelers lead series, 6-2;
See Baltimore vs. Pittsburgh
PITTSBURGH vs. BUFFALO
RS: Series tied, 8-8
PS: Steelers lead series, 2-1;
See Buffalo vs. Pittsburgh
PITTSBURGH vs. CAROLINA
RS: Series tied, 1-1;
See Carolina vs. Pittsburgh
PITTSBURGH vs. CHICAGO
RS: Bears lead series, 16-6-1;
See Chicago vs. Pittsburgh
PITTSBURGH vs. CINCINNATI
RS: Steelers lead series, 33-26;
See Cincinnati vs. Pittsburgh
PITTSBURGH vs. CLEVELAND
RS: Browns lead series, 53-41
PS: Steelers lead series, 1-0;
See Cleveland vs. Pittsburgh
PITTSBURGH vs. DALLAS
RS: Cowboys lead series, 14-11
PS: Steelers lead series, 2-1;
See Dallas vs. Pittsburgh
PITTSBURGH vs. DENVER
RS: Broncos lead series, 10-6-1
PS: Broncos lead series, 3-2;
See Denver vs. Pittsburgh
PITTSBURGH vs. DETROIT
RS: Lions lead series, 14-12-1;
See Detroit vs. Pittsburgh
PITTSBURGH vs. GREEN BAY
RS: Packers lead series, 18-12;
See Green Bay vs. Pittsburgh
PITTSBURGH vs. INDIANAPOLIS
RS: Steelers lead series, 12-4
PS: Steelers lead series, 4-0;
See Indianapolis vs. Pittsburgh
PITTSBURGH vs. JACKSONVILLE
RS: Jaguars lead series, 6-4;
See Jacksonville vs. Pittsburgh
PITTSBURGH vs. KANSAS CITY
RS: Steelers lead series, 15-7
PS: Chiefs lead series, 1-0;
See Kansas City vs. Pittsburgh
PITTSBURGH vs. MIAMI
RS: Dolphins lead series, 9-7
PS: Dolphins lead series, 2-1;
See Miami vs. Pittsburgh
PITTSBURGH vs. MINNESOTA
RS: Vikings lead series, 8-4
PS: Steelers lead series, 1-0;
See Minnesota vs. Pittsburgh
PITTSBURGH vs. NEW ENGLAND
RS: Steelers lead series, 11-4
PS: Series tied, 1-1;
See New England vs. Pittsburgh
PITTSBURGH vs. NEW ORLEANS
RS: Steelers lead series, 6-5;
See New Orleans vs. Pittsburgh
PITTSBURGH vs. N.Y. GIANTS
RS: Giants lead series, 42-27-3;
See N.Y. Giants vs. Pittsburgh
PITTSBURGH vs. N.Y. JETS
RS: Steelers lead series, 12-1;
See N.Y. Jets vs. Pittsburgh
PITTSBURGH vs. OAKLAND
RS: Raiders lead series, 7-5
PS: Series tied, 3-3;
See Oakland vs. Pittsburgh
PITTSBURGH vs. PHILADELPHIA
RS: Eagles lead series, 44-26-3
PS: Eagles lead series, 1-0;
See Philadelphia vs. Pittsburgh
***PITTSBURGH vs. **ST. LOUIS**
RS: Rams lead series, 14-5-2
PS: Steelers lead series, 1-0
1938—Rams, 13-7 (New Orleans)
1939—Tie, 14-14 (C)
1941—Rams, 17-14 (Akron)
1947—Rams, 48-7 (P)
1948—Rams, 31-14 (LA)
1949—Tie, 7-7 (P)
1952—Rams, 28-14 (LA)
1955—Rams, 27-26 (LA)
1956—Steelers, 30-13 (P)
1961—Rams, 24-14 (LA)
1964—Rams, 26-14 (P)
1968—Rams, 45-10 (LA)
1971—Rams, 23-14 (P)
1975—Rams, 10-3 (LA)
1978—Rams, 10-7 (LA)
1979—***Steelers, 31-19 (Pasadena)
1981—Steelers, 24-0 (P)
1984—Steelers, 24-14 (P)
1987—Rams, 31-21 (LA)
1990—Steelers, 41-10 (P)
1993—Rams, 27-0 (LA)
1996—Steelers, 42-6 (P)
(RS Pts.—Rams 424, Steelers 347)
(PS Pts.—Steelers 31, Rams 19)
Steelers known as Pirates prior to 1941
***Franchise in Los Angeles prior to 1995 and in Cleveland prior to 1946*
****Super Bowl XIV*
PITTSBURGH vs. SAN DIEGO
RS: Steelers lead series, 16-5
PS: Chargers lead series, 2-0
1971—Steelers, 21-17 (P)
1972—Steelers, 24-2 (SD)
1973—Steelers, 38-21 (P)
1975—Steelers, 37-0 (SD)
1976—Steelers, 23-0 (P)
1977—Steelers, 10-9 (SD)
1979—Chargers, 35-7 (SD)
1980—Chargers, 26-17 (SD)
1982—*Chargers, 31-28 (P)
1983—Steelers, 26-3 (P)
1984—Steelers, 52-24 (P)
1985—Chargers, 54-44 (SD)
1987—Steelers, 20-16 (SD)
1988—Chargers, 20-14 (SD)
1989—Steelers, 20-17 (P)
1990—Steelers, 36-14 (P)
1991—Steelers, 26-20 (P)
1992—Steelers, 23-6 (SD)
1993—Steelers,.16-3 (P)
1994—Chargers, 37-34 (SD)
**Chargers, 17-13 (P)
1995—Steelers, 31-16 (P)
1996—Steelers, 16-3 (P)
(RS Pts.—Steelers 535, Chargers 343)
(PS Pts.—Chargers 48, Steelers 41)
AFC First-Round Playoff
***AFC Championship*

PITTSBURGH vs. SAN FRANCISCO
RS: 49ers lead series, 9-8
1951—49ers, 28-24 (P)
1952—Steelers, 24-7 (SF)
1954—49ers, 31-3 (SF)
1958—49ers, 23-20 (SF)
1961—Steelers, 20-10 (P)
1965—49ers, 27-17 (SF)
1968—49ers, 45-28 (P)
1973—Steelers, 37-14 (SF)
1977—Steelers, 27-0 (P)
1978—Steelers, 24-7 (SF)
1981—49ers, 17-14 (P)
1984—Steelers, 20-17 (SF)
1987—Steelers, 30-17 (P)
1990—49ers, 27-7 (SF)
1993—49ers, 24-13 (P)
1996—49ers, 25-15 (P)
1999—Steelers, 27-6 (SF)
(RS Pts.—Steelers 350, 49ers 325)
PITTSBURGH vs. SEATTLE
RS: Seahawks lead series, 7-6
1977—Steelers, 30-20 (P)
1978—Steelers, 21-10 (P)
1981—Seahawks, 24-21 (S)
1982—Seahawks, 16-0 (S)
1983—Steelers, 27-21 (S)
1986—Seahawks, 30-0 (S)
1987—Steelers, 13-9 (P)
1991—Seahawks, 27-7 (P)
1992—Steelers, 20-14 (P)
1993—Seahawks, 16-6 (S)
1994—Seahawks, 30-13 (S)
1998—Steelers, 13-10 (P)
1999—Seahawks, 29-10 (P)
(RS Pts.—Seahawks 256, Steelers 181)
PITTSBURGH vs. TAMPA BAY
RS: Steelers lead series, 4-1
1976—Steelers, 42-0 (P)
1980—Steelers, 24-21 (TB)
1983—Steelers, 17-12 (P)
1989—Steelers, 31-22 (TB)
1998—Buccaneers, 16-3 (TB)
(RS Pts.—Steelers 117, Buccaneers 71)
PITTSBURGH vs. *TENNESSEE
RS: Steelers lead series, 35-24
PS: Steelers lead series, 3-0
1970—Oilers, 19-7 (P)
Steelers, 7-3 (H)
1971—Steelers, 23-16 (P)
Oilers, 29-3 (H)
1972—Steelers, 24-7 (P)
Steelers, 9-3 (H)
1973—Steelers, 36-7 (H)
Steelers, 33-7 (P)
1974—Steelers, 13-7 (H)
Oilers, 13-10 (P)
1975—Steelers, 24-17 (P)
Steelers, 32-9 (H)
1976—Steelers, 32-16 (P)
Steelers, 21-0 (H)
1977—Oilers, 27-10 (H)
Steelers, 27-10 (P)
1978—Oilers, 24-17 (P)
Steelers, 13-3 (H)
**Steelers, 34-5 (P)
1979—Steelers, 38-7 (P)
Oilers, 20-17 (H)
**Steelers, 27-13 (P)
1980—Steelers, 31-17 (P)
Oilers, 6-0 (H)
1981—Steelers, 26-13 (P)
Oilers, 21-20 (H)
1982—Steelers, 24-10 (H)
1983—Steelers, 40-28 (H)
Steelers, 17-10 (P)
1984—Steelers, 35-7 (P)
Oilers, 23-20 (H) OT
1985—Steelers, 20-0 (P)
Steelers, 30-7 (H)
1986—Steelers, 22-16 (H) OT
Steelers, 21-10 (P)
1987—Oilers, 23-3 (P)
Oilers, 24-16 (H)
1988—Oilers, 34-14 (P)
Steelers, 37-34 (H)
1989—Oilers, 27-0 (H)
Oilers, 23-16 (P)
***Steelers, 26-23 (H) OT
1990—Steelers, 20-9 (P)
Oilers, 34-14 (H)
1991—Steelers, 26-14 (P)
Oilers, 31-6 (H)
1992—Steelers, 29-24 (H)
Steelers, 21-20 (P)
1993—Oilers, 23-3 (H)
Oilers, 26-17 (P)
1994—Steelers, 30-14 (P)
Steelers, 12-9 (H) OT
1995—Steelers, 34-17 (H)
Steelers, 21-7 (P)
1996—Steelers, 30-16 (P)
Oilers, 23-13 (H)
1997—Steelers, 37-24 (P)
Oilers, 16-6 (T)
1998—Oilers, 41-31 (P)
Oilers, 23-14 (T)
1999—Titans, 16-10 (T)
Titans, 47-36 (P)
(RS Pts.—Steelers 1,198, Titans 1,011)
(PS Pts.—Steelers 87, Titans 41)
Franchise in Houston prior to 1997; known as Oilers prior to 1999
***AFC Championship*
****AFC First-Round Playoff*
***PITTSBURGH vs. **WASHINGTON**
RS: Redskins lead series, 42-28-3
1933—Redskins, 21-6 (P)
Pirates, 16-14 (B)
1934—Redskins, 7-0 (P)
Redskins, 39-0 (B)
1935—Pirates, 6-0 (P)
Redskins, 13-3 (B)
1936—Pirates, 10-0 (P)
Redskins, 30-0 (B)
1937—Redskins, 34-20 (W)
Pirates, 21-13 (P)
1938—Redskins, 7-0 (P)
Redskins, 15-0 (W)
1939—Redskins, 44-14 (W)
Redskins, 21-14 (P)
1940—Redskins, 40-10 (P)
Redskins, 37-10 (W)
1941—Redskins, 24-20 (P)
Redskins, 23-3 (W)
1942—Redskins, 28-14 (W)
Redskins, 14-0 (P)
1945—Redskins, 14-0 (P)
Redskins, 24-0 (W)
1946—Tie, 14-14 (W)
Steelers, 14-7 (P)
1947—Redskins, 27-26 (W)
Steelers, 21-14 (P)
1948—Redskins, 17-14 (W)
Steelers, 10-7 (P)
1949—Redskins, 27-14 (P)
Redskins, 27-14 (W)
1950—Steelers, 26-7 (W)
Redskins, 24-7 (P)
1951—Redskins, 22-7 (P)
Steelers, 20-10 (W)
1952—Redskins, 28-24 (P)
Steelers, 24-23 (W)
1953—Redskins, 17-9 (P)
Steelers, 14-13 (W)
1954—Steelers, 37-7 (P)
Redskins, 17-14 (W)
1955—Redskins, 23-14 (P)
Redskins, 28-17 (W)
1956—Steelers, 30-13 (P)
Steelers, 23-0 (W)
1957—Steelers, 28-7 (P)
Redskins, 10-3 (W)
1958—Steelers, 24-16 (P)
Tie, 14-14 (W)
1959—Redskins, 23-17 (P)

ALL-TIME TEAM VS. TEAM RESULTS

Steelers, 27-6 (W)
1960—Tie, 27-27 (W)
Steelers, 22-10 (P)
1961—Steelers, 20-0 (P)
Steelers, 30-14 (W)
1962—Steelers, 23-21 (P)
Steelers, 27-24 (W)
1963—Steelers, 38-27 (P)
Steelers, 34-28 (W)
1964—Redskins, 30-0 (P)
Steelers, 14-7 (W)
1965—Redskins, 31-3 (P)
Redskins, 35-14 (W)
1966—Redskins, 33-27 (P)
Redskins, 24-10 (W)
1967—Redskins, 15-10 (P)
1968—Redskins, 16-13 (W)
1969—Redskins, 14-7 (P)
1973—Steelers, 21-16 (P)
1979—Steelers, 38-7 (P)
1985—Redskins, 30-23 (P)
1988—Redskins, 30-29 (W)
1991—Redskins, 41-14 (P)
1997—Steelers, 14-13 (P)
(RS Pts.—Redskins 1,403, Steelers 1,131)
Steelers known as Pirates prior to 1941
***Franchise in Boston prior to 1937*

ST. LOUIS vs. ARIZONA
RS: Rams lead series, 23-21-2
PS: Rams lead series, 1-0;
See Arizona vs. St. Louis
ST. LOUIS vs. ATLANTA
RS: Rams lead series, 41-23-2;
See Atlanta vs. St. Louis
ST. LOUIS vs. BALTIMORE
RS: Series tied, 1-1;
See Baltimore vs. St. Louis
ST. LOUIS vs. BUFFALO
RS: Series tied, 4-4;
See Buffalo vs. St. Louis
ST. LOUIS vs. CAROLINA
RS: Series tied, 5-5;
See Carolina vs. St. Louis
ST. LOUIS vs. CHICAGO
RS: Bears lead series, 47-32-3
PS: Series tied, 1-1;
See Chicago vs. St. Louis
ST. LOUIS vs. CINCINNATI
RS: Bengals lead series, 5-4;
See Cincinnati vs. St. Louis
ST. LOUIS vs. CLEVELAND
RS: Series tied, 8-8
PS: Browns lead series, 2-1;
See Cleveland vs. St. Louis
ST. LOUIS vs. DALLAS
RS: Rams lead series, 9-8
PS: Series tied, 4-4;
See Dallas vs. St. Louis
ST. LOUIS vs. DENVER
RS: Series tied, 4-4;
See Denver vs. St. Louis
ST. LOUIS vs. DETROIT
RS: Rams lead series, 39-36-1
PS: Lions lead series, 1-0;
See Detroit vs. St. Louis
ST. LOUIS vs. GREEN BAY
RS: Rams lead series, 43-39-2
PS: Packers lead series, 1-0;
See Green Bay vs. St. Louis
ST. LOUIS vs. INDIANAPOLIS
RS: Colts lead series, 21-16-2;
See Indianapolis vs. St. Louis
ST. LOUIS vs. JACKSONVILLE
RS: Rams lead series, 1-0;
See Jacksonville vs. St. Louis
ST. LOUIS vs. KANSAS CITY
RS: Rams lead series, 4-2;
See Kansas City vs. St. Louis
ST. LOUIS vs. MIAMI
RS: Dolphins lead series, 7-1;
See Miami vs. St. Louis
ST. LOUIS vs. MINNESOTA
RS: Vikings lead series, 16-11-2
PS: Vikings lead series, 5-2;
See Minnesota vs. St. Louis
ST. LOUIS vs. NEW ENGLAND
RS: Rams lead series, 4-3;
See New England vs. St. Louis
ST. LOUIS vs. NEW ORLEANS
RS: Rams lead series, 34-26;
See New Orleans vs. St. Louis
ST. LOUIS vs. N.Y. GIANTS
RS: Rams lead series, 23-9
PS: Series tied, 1-1;
See N.Y. Giants vs. St. Louis
ST. LOUIS vs. N.Y. JETS
RS: Rams lead series, 7-2;
See N.Y. Jets vs. St. Louis
ST. LOUIS vs. OAKLAND
RS: Raiders lead series, 7-2;
See Oakland vs. St. Louis
ST. LOUIS vs. PHILADELPHIA
RS: Rams lead series, 15-14-1
PS: Series tied, 1-1;
See Philadelphia vs. St. Louis
ST. LOUIS vs. PITTSBURGH
RS: Rams lead series, 14-5-2
PS: Steelers lead series, 1-0;
See Pittsburgh vs. St. Louis
***ST. LOUIS vs. SAN DIEGO**
RS: Series tied, 3-3
1970—Rams, 37-10 (LA)
1975—Rams, 13-10 (SD) OT
1979—Chargers, 40-16 (LA)
1988—Chargers, 38-24 (LA)
1991—Rams, 30-24 (LA)
1994—Chargers, 31-17 (SD)
(RS Pts.—Chargers 153, Rams 137)
**Franchise in Los Angeles prior to 1995*
***ST. LOUIS vs. SAN FRANCISCO**
RS: Rams lead series, 50-48-2
PS: 49ers lead series, 1-0
1950—Rams, 35-14 (SF)
Rams, 28-21 (LA)
1951—49ers, 44-17 (SF)
Rams, 23-16 (LA)
1952—Rams, 35-9 (LA)
Rams, 34-21 (SF)
1953—49ers, 31-30 (SF)
49ers, 31-27 (LA)
1954—Tie, 24-24 (LA)
Rams, 42-34 (SF)
1955—Rams, 23-14 (SF)
Rams, 27-14 (LA)
1956—49ers, 33-30 (SF)
Rams, 30-6 (LA)
1957—49ers, 23-20 (SF)
Rams, 37-24 (LA)
1958—Rams, 33-3 (SF)
Rams, 56-7 (LA)
1959—49ers, 34-0 (SF)
49ers, 24-16 (LA)
1960—49ers, 13-9 (SF)
49ers, 23-7 (LA)
1961—49ers, 35-0 (SF)
Rams, 17-7 (LA)
1962—Rams, 28-14 (SF)
49ers, 24-17 (LA)
1963—Rams, 28-21 (LA)
Rams, 21-17 (SF)
1964—Rams, 42-14 (LA)
49ers, 28-7 (SF)
1965—49ers, 45-21 (LA)
49ers, 30-27 (SF)
1966—Rams, 34-3 (LA)
49ers, 21-13 (SF)
1967—49ers, 27-24 (LA)
Rams, 17-7 (SF)
1968—Rams, 24-10 (LA)
Tie, 20-20 (SF)
1969—Rams, 27-21 (SF)
Rams, 41-30 (LA)
1970—49ers, 20-6 (LA)
Rams, 30-13 (SF)
1971—Rams, 20-13 (SF)
Rams, 17-6 (LA)
1972—Rams, 31-7 (LA)
Rams, 26-16 (SF)
1973—Rams, 40-20 (SF)
Rams, 31-13 (LA)
1974—Rams, 37-14 (LA)
Rams, 15-13 (SF)
1975—Rams, 23-14 (SF)
49ers, 24-23 (LA)
1976—49ers, 16-0 (LA)
Rams, 23-3 (SF)
1977—Rams, 34-14 (LA)
Rams, 23-10 (SF)
1978—Rams, 27-10 (LA)
Rams, 31-28 (SF)
1979—Rams, 27-24 (LA)
Rams, 26-20 (SF)
1980—Rams, 48-26 (LA)
Rams, 31-17 (SF)
1981—49ers, 20-17 (SF)
49ers, 33-31 (LA)
1982—49ers, 30-24 (LA)
Rams, 21-20 (SF)
1983—Rams, 10-7 (SF)
49ers, 45-35 (LA)
1984—49ers, 33-0 (LA)
49ers, 19-16 (SF)
1985—49ers, 28-14 (LA)
Rams, 27-20 (SF)
1986—Rams, 16-13 (LA)
49ers, 24-14 (SF)
1987—49ers, 31-10 (LA)
49ers, 48-0 (SF)
1988—49ers, 24-21 (LA)
Rams, 38-16 (SF)
1989—Rams, 13-12 (SF)
49ers, 30-27 (LA)
**49ers, 30-3 (SF)
1990—Rams, 28-17 (SF)
49ers, 26-10 (LA)
1991—49ers, 27-10 (SF)
49ers, 33-10 (LA)
1992—49ers, 27-24 (SF)
49ers, 27-10 (LA)
1993—49ers, 40-17 (SF)
49ers, 35-10 (LA)
1994—49ers, 34-19 (LA)
49ers, 31-27 (SF)
1995—49ers, 44-10 (StL)
49ers, 41-13 (SF)
1996—49ers, 34-0 (SF)
49ers, 28-11 (StL)
1997—49ers, 15-12 (StL)
49ers, 30-10 (SF)
1998—49ers, 28-10 (StL)
49ers, 38-19 (SF)
1999—Rams, 42-20 (StL)
Rams, 23-7 (SF)
(RS Pts.—49ers 2,213, Rams 2,209)
(PS Pts.—49ers 30, Rams 3)
**Franchise in Los Angeles prior to 1995*
***NFC Championship*
***ST. LOUIS vs. SEATTLE**
RS: Rams lead series, 4-2
1976—Rams, 45-6 (LA)
1979—Rams, 24-0 (S)
1985—Rams, 35-24 (S)
1988—Rams, 31-10 (LA)
1991—Seahawks, 23-9 (S)
1997—Seahawks, 17-9 (StL)
(RS Pts.—Rams 153, Seahawks 80)
**Franchise in Los Angeles prior to 1995*
***ST. LOUIS vs. TAMPA BAY**
RS: Rams lead series, 8-3
PS: Rams lead series, 2-0
1977—Rams, 31-0 (LA)
1978—Rams, 26-23 (LA)
1979—Buccaneers, 21-6 (TB)
**Rams, 9-0 (TB)
1980—Buccaneers, 10-9 (TB)
1984—Rams, 34-33 (TB)
1985—Rams, 31-27 (TB)
1986—Rams, 26-20 (LA) OT
1987—Rams, 35-3 (LA)
1990—Rams, 35-14 (TB)
1992—Rams, 31-27 (TB)
1994—Buccaneers, 24-14 (TB)
1999—**Rams, 11-6 (StL)
(RS Pts.—Rams 278, Buccaneers 202)
(PS Pts.—Rams 20, Buccaneers 6)
**Franchise in Los Angeles prior to 1995*
***NFC Championship*
***ST. LOUIS vs. **TENNESSEE**
RS: Rams lead series, 5-3
PS: Rams lead series, 1-0
1973—Rams, 31-26 (H)
1978—Rams, 10-6 (H)
1981—Oilers, 27-20 (LA)
1984—Rams, 27-16 (LA)
1987—Oilers, 20-16 (H)
1990—Rams, 17-13 (LA)
1993—Rams, 28-13 (H)
1999—Titans, 24-21 (T)
***Rams, 23-16 (Atlanta)
(RS Pts.—Rams 170, Titans 145)
(PS Pts.—Rams 23, Titans 16)
**Franchise in Los Angeles prior to 1995*
***Franchise in Houston prior to 1997; known as Oilers prior to 1999*
****Super Bowl XXXIV*
***ST. LOUIS vs. WASHINGTON**
RS: Redskins lead series, 17-6-1
PS: Series tied, 2-2
1937—Redskins, 16-7 (C)
1938—Redskins, 37-13 (W)
1941—Redskins, 17-13 (W)
1942—Redskins, 33-14 (W)
1944—Redskins, 14-10 (W)
1945—**Rams, 15-14 (C)
1948—Rams, 41-13 (W)
1949—Rams, 53-27 (LA)
1951—Redskins, 31-21 (W)
1962—Redskins, 20-14 (W)
1963—Redskins, 37-14 (LA)
1967—Tie, 28-28 (LA)
1969—Rams, 24-13 (W)
1971—Redskins, 38-24 (LA)
1974—Redskins, 23-17 (LA)
***Rams, 19-10 (LA)
1977—Redskins, 17-14 (W)
1981—Redskins, 30-7 (LA)
1983—Redskins, 42-20 (LA)
***Redskins, 51-7 (W)
1986—****Redskins, 19-7 (W)
1987—Rams, 30-26 (W)
1991—Redskins, 27-6 (LA)
1993—Rams, 10-6 (LA)
1994—Redskins, 24-21 (LA)
1995—Redskins, 35-23 (StL)
1996—Redskins, 17-10 (StL)
1997—Rams, 23-20 (W)
(RS Pts.—Redskins 591, Rams 457)
(PS Pts.—Redskins 94, Rams 48)
**Franchise in Los Angeles prior to 1995 and in Cleveland prior to 1946*
***NFL Championship*
****NFC Divisional Playoff*
*****NFC First-Round Playoff*

SAN DIEGO vs. ARIZONA
RS: Chargers lead series, 6-2;
See Arizona vs. San Diego
SAN DIEGO vs. ATLANTA
RS: Falcons lead series, 5-1;
See Atlanta vs. San Diego
SAN DIEGO vs BALTIMORE
RS: Chargers lead series, 2-0;
See Baltimore vs. San Diego
SAN DIEGO vs. BUFFALO
RS: Chargers lead series, 17-7-2
PS: Bills lead series, 2-1;
See Buffalo vs. San Diego
SAN DIEGO vs. CAROLINA
RS: Panthers lead series, 1-0;
See Carolina vs. San Diego

SAN DIEGO vs. CHICAGO
RS: Series tied, 4-4;
See Chicago vs. San Diego
SAN DIEGO vs. CINCINNATI
RS: Chargers lead series, 15-9
PS: Bengals lead series, 1-0;
See Cincinnati vs. San Diego
SAN DIEGO vs. CLEVELAND
RS: Chargers lead series, 10-6-1;
See Cleveland vs. San Diego
SAN DIEGO vs. DALLAS
RS: Cowboys lead series, 5-1;
See Dallas vs. San Diego
SAN DIEGO vs. DENVER
RS: Broncos lead series, 43-36-1;
See Denver vs. San Diego
SAN DIEGO vs. DETROIT
RS: Chargers lead series, 4-3;
See Detroit vs. San Diego
SAN DIEGO vs. GREEN BAY
RS: Packers lead series, 6-1;
See Green Bay vs. San Diego
SAN DIEGO vs. INDIANAPOLIS
RS: Chargers lead series, 12-7
PS: Colts lead series, 1-0;
See Indianapolis vs. San Diego
SAN DIEGO vs. KANSAS CITY
RS: Chiefs lead series, 41-37-1
PS: Chargers lead series, 1-0;
See Kansas City vs. San Diego
SAN DIEGO vs. MIAMI
RS: Chargers lead series, 10-7
PS: Series tied, 2-2;
See Miami vs. San Diego
SAN DIEGO vs. MINNESOTA
RS: Series tied, 4-4;
See Minnesota vs. San Diego
SAN DIEGO vs. NEW ENGLAND
RS: Patriots lead series, 16-11-2
PS: Chargers lead series, 1-0;
See New England vs. San Diego
SAN DIEGO vs. NEW ORLEANS
RS: Chargers lead series, 6-1;
See New Orleans vs. San Diego
SAN DIEGO vs. N.Y. GIANTS
RS: Giants lead series, 5-3;
See N.Y. Giants vs. San Diego
SAN DIEGO vs. N.Y. JETS
RS: Chargers lead series, 17-9-1;
See N.Y. Jets vs. San Diego
SAN DIEGO vs. OAKLAND
RS: Raiders lead series, 48-30-2
PS: Raiders lead series, 1-0;
See Oakland vs. San Diego
SAN DIEGO vs. PHILADELPHIA
RS: Chargers lead series, 5-2;
See Philadelphia vs. San Diego
SAN DIEGO vs. PITTSBURGH
RS: Steelers lead series, 16-5
PS: Chargers lead series, 2-0;
See Pittsburgh vs. San Diego
SAN DIEGO vs. ST. LOUIS
RS: Series tied, 3-3
See St. Louis vs. San Diego
SAN DIEGO vs. SAN FRANCISCO
RS: 49ers lead series, 5-3
PS: 49ers lead series, 1-0
1972—49ers, 34-3 (SF)
1976—Chargers, 13-7 (SD) OT
1979—Chargers, 31-9 (SD)
1982—Chargers, 41-37 (SF)
1988—49ers, 48-10 (SD)
1991—49ers, 34-14 (SF)
1994—49ers, 38-15 (SD)
*49ers, 49-26 (Miami)
1997—49ers, 17-10 (SF)
(RS Pts.—49ers 224, Chargers 137)
(PS Pts.—49ers 49, Chargers 26)
**Super Bowl XXIX*
SAN DIEGO vs. SEATTLE
RS: Chargers lead series, 22-20
1977—Chargers, 30-28 (S)
1978—Chargers, 24-20 (S)
Chargers, 37-10 (SD)
1979—Chargers, 33-16 (S)
Chargers, 20-10 (SD)
1980—Chargers, 34-13 (S)
Chargers, 21-14 (SD)
1981—Chargers, 24-10 (SD)
Seahawks, 44-23 (S)
1983—Seahawks, 34-31 (S)
Chargers, 28-21 (SD)
1984—Seahawks, 31-17 (S)
Seahawks, 24-0 (SD)
1985—Seahawks, 49-35 (SD)
Seahawks, 26-21 (S)
1986—Seahawks, 33-7 (S)
Seahawks, 34-24 (SD)
1987—Seahawks, 34-3 (S)
1988—Chargers, 17-6 (SD)
Seahawks, 17-14 (S)
1989—Seahawks, 17-16 (SD)
Seahawks, 10-7 (S)
1990—Chargers, 31-14 (S)
Seahawks, 13-10 (SD) OT
1991—Seahawks, 20-9 (S)
Chargers, 17-14 (SD)
1992—Chargers, 17-6 (SD)
Chargers, 31-14 (S)
1993—Chargers, 18-12 (SD)
Seahawks, 31-14 (S)
1994—Chargers, 24-10 (S)
Chargers, 35-15 (SD)
1995—Chargers, 14-10 (SD)
Chargers, 35-25 (S)
1996—Chargers, 29-7 (SD)
Seahawks, 32-13 (S)
1997—Seahawks, 26-22 (S)
Seahawks, 37-31 (SD)
1998—Seahawks, 27-20 (SD)
Seahawks, 38-17 (S)
1999—Chargers, 13-10 (SD)
Chargers, 19-16 (S)
(RS Pts.—Chargers 885, Seahawks 878)
SAN DIEGO vs. TAMPA BAY
RS: Chargers lead series, 6-1
1976—Chargers, 23-0 (TB)
1981—Chargers, 24-23 (TB)
1987—Chargers, 17-13 (TB)
1990—Chargers, 41-10 (SD)
1992—Chargers, 29-14 (SD)
1993—Chargers, 32-17 (TB)
1996—Buccaneers, 25-17 (SD)
(RS Pts.—Chargers 183, Buccaneers 102)
***SAN DIEGO vs. **TENNESSEE**
RS: Chargers lead series, 19-13-1
PS: Titans lead series, 3-0
1960—Oilers, 38-28 (H)
Chargers, 24-21 (LA)
***Oilers, 24-16 (H)
1961—Chargers, 34-24 (SD)
Oilers, 33-13 (H)
***Oilers, 10-3 (SD)
1962—Oilers, 42-17 (SD)
Oilers, 33-27 (H)
1963—Chargers, 27-0 (SD)
Chargers 20-14 (H)
1964—Chargers, 27-21 (SD)
Chargers, 20-17 (H)
1965—Chargers, 31-14 (SD)
Chargers, 37-26 (H)
1966—Chargers, 28-22 (H)
1967—Chargers, 13-3 (SD)
Oilers, 24-17 (H)
1968—Chargers, 30-14 (SD)
1969—Chargers, 21-17 (H)
1970—Tie, 31-31 (SD)
1971—Oilers, 49-33 (H)
1972—Chargers, 34-20 (SD)
1974—Oilers, 21-14 (H)
1975—Oilers, 33-17 (H)
1976—Chargers, 30-27 (SD)
1978—Chargers, 45-24 (H)
1979—****Oilers, 17-14 (SD)
1984—Chargers, 31-14 (SD)
1985—Oilers, 37-35 (H)
1986—Chargers, 27-0 (SD)
1987—Oilers, 33-18 (H)
1989—Oilers, 34-27 (SD)
1990—Oilers, 17-7 (SD)
1992—Oilers, 27-0 (H)
1993—Chargers, 18-17 (SD)
1998—Chargers, 13-7 (T)
(RS Pts.—Chargers 794, Titans 754)
(PS Pts.—Titans 51, Chargers 33)
**Franchise in Los Angeles prior to 1961*
***Franchise in Houston prior to 1997; known as Oilers prior to 1999*
****AFL Championship*
*****AFC Divisional Playoff*
SAN DIEGO vs. WASHINGTON
RS: Redskins lead series, 6-0
1973—Redskins, 38-0 (W)
1980—Redskins, 40-17 (W)
1983—Redskins, 27-24 (SD)
1986—Redskins, 30-27 (SD)
1989—Redskins, 26-21 (W)
1998—Redskins, 24-20 (W)
(RS Pts.—Redskins 185, Chargers 109)

SAN FRANCISCO vs. ARIZONA
RS: 49ers lead series, 11-9;
See Arizona vs. San Francisco
SAN FRANCISCO vs. ATLANTA
RS: 49ers lead series, 41-24-1
PS: Falcons lead series, 1-0;
See Atlanta vs. San Francisco
SAN FRANCISCO vs. BALTIMORE
RS: 49ers lead series, 1-0;
See Baltimore vs. San Francisco
SAN FRANCISCO vs. BUFFALO
RS: Bills lead series, 4-3;
See Buffalo vs. San Francisco
SAN FRANCISCO vs. CAROLINA
RS: Series tied, 5-5;
See Carolina vs. San Francisco
SAN FRANCISCO vs. CHICAGO
RS: Series tied, 25-25-1
PS: 49ers lead series, 3-0;
See Chicago vs. San Francisco
SAN FRANCISCO vs. CINCINNATI
RS: 49ers lead series, 7-2
PS: 49ers lead series, 2-0;
See Cincinnati vs. San Francisco
SAN FRANCISCO vs. CLEVELAND
RS: Browns lead series, 9-6;
See Cleveland vs. San Francisco
SAN FRANCISCO vs. DALLAS
RS: 49ers lead series, 12-7-1
PS: Cowboys lead series, 5-2;
See Dallas vs. San Francisco
SAN FRANCISCO vs. DENVER
RS: Series tied, 4-4
PS: 49ers lead series, 1-0;
See Denver vs. San Francisco
SAN FRANCISCO vs. DETROIT
RS: 49ers lead series, 29-26-1
PS: Series tied, 1-1;
See Detroit vs. San Francisco
SAN FRANCISCO vs. GREEN BAY
RS: 49ers lead series, 25-24-1
PS: Packers lead series, 3-1;
See Green Bay vs. San Francisco
SAN FRANCISCO vs. INDIANAPOLIS
RS: Colts lead series, 22-17;
See Indianapolis vs. San Francisco
SAN FRANCISCO vs. JACKSONVILLE
RS: Jaguars lead series, 1-0;
See Jacksonville vs. San Francisco
SAN FRANCISCO vs. KANSAS CITY
RS: 49ers lead series, 4-3;
See Kansas City vs. San Francisco
SAN FRANCISCO vs. MIAMI
RS: Dolphins lead series, 4-3
PS: 49ers lead series, 1-0;
See Miami vs. San Francisco
SAN FRANCISCO vs. MINNESOTA
RS: Series tied, 17-17-1
PS: 49ers lead series, 4-1;
See Minnesota vs. San Francisco
SAN FRANCISCO vs. NEW ENGLAND
RS: 49ers lead series, 7-2;
See New England vs. San Francisco
SAN FRANCISCO vs. NEW ORLEANS
RS: 49ers lead series, 43-16-2;
See New Orleans vs. San Francisco
SAN FRANCISCO vs. N.Y. GIANTS
RS: 49ers lead series, 12-11
PS: Series tied, 3-3;
See N.Y. Giants vs. San Francisco
SAN FRANCISCO vs. N.Y. JETS
RS: 49ers lead series, 7-1;
See N.Y. Jets vs. San Francisco
SAN FRANCISCO vs. OAKLAND
RS: Raiders lead series, 5-3;
See Oakland vs. San Francisco
SAN FRANCISCO vs. PHILADELPHIA
RS: 49ers lead series, 14-6-1
PS: 49ers lead series, 1-0;
See Philadelphia vs. San Francisco
SAN FRANCISCO vs. PITTSBURGH
RS: 49ers lead series, 9-8;
See Pittsburgh vs. San Francisco
SAN FRANCISCO vs. ST. LOUIS
RS: Rams lead series, 50-48-2
PS: 49ers lead series, 1-0;
See St. Louis vs. San Francisco
SAN FRANCISCO vs. SAN DIEGO
RS: 49ers lead series, 5-3
PS: 49ers lead series, 1-0;
See San Diego vs. San Francisco
SAN FRANCISCO vs. SEATTLE
RS: 49ers lead series, 4-2
1976—49ers, 37-21 (S)
1979—Seahawks, 35-24 (SF)
1985—49ers, 19-6 (SF)
1988—49ers, 38-7 (S)
1991—49ers, 24-22 (S)
1997—Seahawks, 38-9 (S)
(RS Pts.—49ers 151, Seahawks 129)
SAN FRANCISCO vs. TAMPA BAY
RS: 49ers lead series, 12-2
1977—49ers, 20-10 (SF)
1978—49ers, 6-3 (SF)
1979—49ers, 23-7 (SF)
1980—Buccaneers, 24-23 (SF)
1983—49ers, 35-21 (SF)
1984—49ers, 24-17 (SF)
1986—49ers, 31-7 (TB)
1987—49ers, 24-10 (TB)
1989—49ers, 20-16 (TB)
1990—49ers, 31-7 (SF)
1992—49ers, 21-14 (SF)
1993—49ers, 45-21 (TB)
1994—49ers, 41-16 (SF)
1997—Buccaneers, 13-6 (TB)
(RS Pts.—49ers 350, Buccaneers 186)
SAN FRANCISCO vs. *TENNESSEE
RS: 49ers lead series, 7-3
1970—49ers, 30-20 (H)
1975—Oilers, 27-13 (SF)
1978—Oilers, 20-19 (H)
1981—49ers, 28-6 (SF)
1984—49ers, 34-21 (H)
1987—49ers, 27-20 (SF)
1990—49ers, 24-21 (H)
1993—Oilers, 10-7 (SF)
1996—49ers, 10-9 (H)
1999—49ers, 24-22 (SF)
(RS Pts.—49ers 216, Titans 176)
**Franchise in Houston prior to 1997; known as Oilers prior to 1999*
SAN FRANCISCO vs. WASHINGTON
RS: 49ers lead series, 12-7-1
PS: 49ers lead series, 3-1
1952—49ers, 23-17 (W)
1954—49ers, 41-7 (SF)
1955—Redskins, 7-0 (W)
1961—49ers, 35-3 (SF)
1967—Redskins, 31-28 (W)
1969—Tie, 17-17 (SF)
1970—49ers, 26-17 (SF)

ALL-TIME TEAM VS. TEAM RESULTS

1971—*49ers, 24-20 (SF)
1973—Redskins, 33-9 (W)
1976—Redskins, 24-21 (SF)
1978—Redskins, 38-20 (W)
1981—49ers, 30-17 (W)
1983—**Redskins, 24-21 (W)
1984—49ers, 37-31 (SF)
1985—49ers, 35-8 (W)
1986—Redskins, 14-6 (W)
1988—49ers, 37-21 (SF)
1990—49ers, 26-13 (SF)
*49ers, 28-10 (SF)
1992—*49ers, 20-13 (SF)
1994—49ers, 37-22 (W)
1996—49ers, 19-16 (W) OT
1998—49ers, 45-10 (W)
1999—Redskins, 26-20 (SF) OT
(RS Pts.—49ers 512, Redskins 372)
(PS Pts.—49ers 93, Redskins 67)
NFC Divisional Playoff
***NFC Championship*

SEATTLE vs. ARIZONA
RS: Cardinals lead series, 5-1;
See Arizona vs. Seattle
SEATTLE vs. ATLANTA
RS: Seahawks lead series, 4-2;
See Atlanta vs. Seattle
SEATTLE vs. BALTIMORE
RS: Ravens lead series, 1-0;
See Baltimore vs. Seattle
SEATTLE vs. BUFFALO
RS: Seahawks lead series, 5-2;
See Buffalo vs. Seattle
SEATTLE vs. CHICAGO
RS: Seahawks lead series, 5-2;
See Chicago vs. Seattle
SEATTLE vs. CINCINNATI
RS: Seahawks lead series, 8-7
PS: Bengals lead series, 1-0;
See Cincinnati vs. Seattle
SEATTLE vs. CLEVELAND
RS: Seahawks lead series, 9-4;
See Cleveland vs. Seattle
SEATTLE vs. DALLAS
RS: Cowboys lead series, 5-1;
See Dallas vs. Seattle
SEATTLE vs. DENVER
RS: Broncos lead series, 29-16
PS: Seahawks lead series, 1-0;
See Denver vs. Seattle
SEATTLE vs. DETROIT
RS: Series tied, 4-4;
See Detroit vs. Seattle
SEATTLE vs. GREEN BAY
RS: Series tied, 4-4;
See Green Bay vs. Seattle
SEATTLE vs. INDIANAPOLIS
RS: Colts lead series, 4-3;
See Indianapolis vs. Seattle
SEATTLE vs. JACKSONVILLE
RS: Series tied, 1-1;
See Jacksonville vs. Seattle
SEATTLE vs. KANSAS CITY
RS: Chiefs lead series, 27-16;
See Kansas City vs. Seattle
SEATTLE vs. MIAMI
RS: Dolphins lead series, 4-2
PS: Dolphins lead series, 2-1;
See Miami vs. Seattle
SEATTLE vs. MINNESOTA
RS: Seahawks lead series, 4-2;
See Minnesota vs. Seattle
SEATTLE vs. NEW ENGLAND
RS: Seahawks lead series, 7-6;
See New England vs. Seattle
SEATTLE vs. NEW ORLEANS
RS: Saints lead series, 4-2;
See New Orleans vs. Seattle
SEATTLE vs. N.Y. GIANTS
RS: Giants lead series, 5-3;
See N.Y. Giants vs. Seattle
SEATTLE vs. N.Y. JETS
RS: Seahawks lead series, 8-7;
See N.Y. Jets vs. Seattle
SEATTLE vs. OAKLAND
RS: Raiders lead series, 24-20
PS: Series tied, 1-1;
See Oakland vs. Seattle
SEATTLE vs. PHILADELPHIA
RS: Eagles lead series, 4-3;
See Philadelphia vs. Seattle
SEATTLE vs. PITTSBURGH
RS: Seahawks lead series, 7-6;
See Pittsburgh vs. Seattle
SEATTLE vs. ST. LOUIS
RS: Rams lead series, 4-2;
See St. Louis vs. Seattle
SEATTLE vs. SAN DIEGO
RS: Chargers lead series, 22-20;
See San Diego vs. Seattle
SEATTLE vs. SAN FRANCISCO
RS: 49ers lead series, 4-2;
See San Francisco vs. Seattle
SEATTLE vs. TAMPA BAY
RS: Seahawks lead series, 4-1
1976—Seahawks, 13-10 (TB)
1977—Seahawks, 30-23 (S)
1994—Seahawks, 22-21 (S)
1996—Seahawks, 17-13 (TB)
1999—Buccaneers, 16-3 (S)
(RS Pts.—Seahawks 85, Buccaneers 83)
SEATTLE vs. *TENNESSEE
RS: Seahawks lead series, 8-4
PS: Titans lead series, 1-0
1977—Oilers, 22-10 (S)
1979—Seahawks, 34-14 (S)
1980—Seahawks, 26-7 (H)
1981—Oilers, 35-17 (H)
1982—Oilers, 23-21 (H)
1987—**Oilers, 23-20 (H) OT
1988—Seahawks, 27-24 (S)
1990—Seahawks, 13-10 (S) OT
1993—Oilers, 24-14 (H)
1994—Seahawks, 16-14 (H)
1996—Seahawks, 23-16 (S)
1997—Seahawks, 16-13 (S)
1998—Seahawks, 20-18 (S)
(RS Pts.—Seahawks 237, Titans 220)
(PS Pts.—Titans 23, Seahawks 20)
**Franchise in Houston prior to 1997; known as Oilers prior to 1999*
***AFC First-Round Playoff*
SEATTLE vs. WASHINGTON
RS: Redskins lead series, 5-4
1976—Redskins, 31-7 (W)
1980—Seahawks, 14-0 (W)
1983—Redskins, 27-17 (S)
1986—Redskins, 19-14 (W)
1989—Redskins, 29-0 (S)
1992—Redskins, 16-3 (S)
1994—Seahawks, 28-7 (W)
1995—Seahawks, 27-20 (W)
1998—Seahawks, 24-14 (S)
(RS Pts.—Redskins 163, Seahawks 134)

TAMPA BAY vs. ARIZONA
RS: Series tied, 7-7;
See Arizona vs. Tampa Bay
TAMPA BAY vs. ATLANTA
RS: Series tied, 8-8;
See Atlanta vs. Tampa Bay
TAMPA BAY vs. BUFFALO
RS: Buccaneers lead series, 4-2;
See Buffalo vs. Tampa Bay
TAMPA BAY vs. CAROLINA
RS: Buccaneers lead series, 2-1;
See Carolina vs. Tampa Bay
TAMPA BAY vs. CHICAGO
RS: Bears lead series, 30-14;
See Chicago vs. Tampa Bay
TAMPA BAY vs. CINCINNATI
RS: Series tied, 3-3;
See Cincinnati vs. Tampa Bay
TAMPA BAY vs. CLEVELAND
RS: Browns lead series, 5-0;
See Cleveland vs. Tampa Bay
TAMPA BAY vs. DALLAS
RS: Cowboys lead series, 6-0
PS: Cowboys lead series, 2-0;
See Dallas vs. Tampa Bay
TAMPA BAY vs. DENVER
RS: Broncos lead series, 3-2;
See Denver vs. Tampa Bay
TAMPA BAY vs. DETROIT
RS: Lions lead series, 25-19
PS: Buccaneers lead series, 1-0;
See Detroit vs. Tampa Bay
TAMPA BAY vs. GREEN BAY
RS: Packers lead series, 26-15-1
PS: Packers lead series, 1-1;
See Green Bay vs. Tampa Bay
TAMPA BAY vs. INDIANAPOLIS
RS: Colts lead series, 5-4;
See Indianapolis vs. Tampa Bay
TAMPA BAY vs. JACKSONVILLE
RS: Series tied, 1-1;
See Jacksonville vs. Tampa Bay
TAMPA BAY vs. KANSAS CITY
RS: Chiefs lead series, 5-3;
See Kansas City vs. Tampa Bay
TAMPA BAY vs. MIAMI
RS: Dolphins lead series, 4-2;
See Miami vs. Tampa Bay
TAMPA BAY vs. MINNESOTA
RS: Vikings lead series, 29-15;
See Minnesota vs. Tampa Bay
TAMPA BAY vs. NEW ENGLAND
RS: Patriots lead series, 3-1;
See New England vs. Tampa Bay
TAMPA BAY vs. NEW ORLEANS
RS: Saints lead series, 13-6;
See New Orleans vs. Tampa Bay
TAMPA BAY vs. N.Y. GIANTS
RS: Giants lead series, 9-5;
See N.Y. Giants vs. Tampa Bay
TAMPA BAY vs. N.Y. JETS
RS: Jets lead series, 6-1;
See N.Y. Jets vs. Tampa Bay
TAMPA BAY vs. OAKLAND
RS: Raiders lead series, 4-1;
See Oakland vs. Tampa Bay
TAMPA BAY vs. PHILADELPHIA
RS: Series tied, 3-3
PS: Buccaneers lead series, 1-0;
See Philadelphia vs. Tampa Bay
TAMPA BAY vs. PITTSBURGH
RS: Steelers lead series, 4-1;
See Pittsburgh vs. Tampa Bay
TAMPA BAY vs. ST. LOUIS
RS: Rams lead series, 8-3
PS: Rams lead series, 2-0;
See St. Louis vs. Tampa Bay
TAMPA BAY vs. SAN DIEGO
RS: Chargers lead series, 6-1;
See San Diego vs. Tampa Bay
TAMPA BAY vs. SAN FRANCISCO
RS: 49ers lead series, 12-2;
See San Francisco vs. Tampa Bay
TAMPA BAY vs. SEATTLE
RS: Seahawks lead series, 4-1;
See Seattle vs. Tampa Bay
TAMPA BAY vs. *TENNESSEE
RS: Titans lead series, 5-1
1976—Oilers, 20-0 (H)
1980—Oilers, 20-14 (H)
1983—Buccaneers, 33-24 (TB)
1989—Oilers, 20-17 (H)
1995—Oilers, 19-7 (H)
1998—Oilers, 31-22 (TB)
(RS Pts.—Titans 134, Buccaneers 93)
**Franchise in Houston prior to 1997; known as Oilers prior to 1999*
TAMPA BAY vs. WASHINGTON
RS: Redskins lead series, 5-4
PS: Buccaneers lead series, 1-0;
1977—Redskins, 10-0 (TB)
1982—Redskins, 21-13 (TB)
1989—Redskins, 32-28 (W)
1993—Redskins, 23-17 (TB)
1994—Buccaneers, 26-21 (TB)
Buccaneers, 17-14 (W)
1995—Buccaneers, 14-6 (TB)
1996—Buccaneers, 24-10 (TB)
1998—Redskins, 20-16 (W)
1999—*Buccaneers, 14-13 (TB)
(RS Pts.—Redskins 157, Buccaneers 155)
(PS Pts.—Buccaneers 14, Redskins 13)
NFC Divisional Playoff

TENNESSEE VS. ARIZONA
RS: Cardinals lead series, 4-3;
See Arizona vs. Tennessee
TENNESSEE vs. ATLANTA
RS: Falcons lead series, 5-5;
See Atlanta vs. Tennessee
TENNESSEE vs. BALTIMORE
RS: Titans lead series, 5-3;
See Baltimore vs. Tennessee
TENNESSEE vs. BUFFALO
RS: Titans lead series, 22-13
PS: Bills lead series, 2-1;
See Buffalo vs. Tennessee
TENNESSEE vs. CAROLINA
RS: Panthers lead series, 1-0;
See Carolina vs. Tennessee
TENNESSEE vs. CHICAGO
RS: Series tied, 4-4;
See Chicago vs. Tennessee
TENNESSEE vs. CINCINNATI
RS: Titans lead series, 33-28-1
PS: Bengals lead series, 1-0;
See Cincinnati vs. Tennessee
TENNESSEE vs. CLEVELAND
RS: Browns lead series, 30-23
PS: Titans lead series, 1-0;
See Cleveland vs. Tennessee
TENNESSEE vs. DALLAS
RS: Cowboys lead series, 5-4
See Dallas vs. Tennessee
TENNESSEE vs. DENVER
RS: Titans lead series, 20-11-1
PS: Broncos lead series, 2-1;
See Denver vs. Tennessee
TENNESSEE vs. DETROIT
RS: Titans lead series, 4-3;
See Detroit vs. Tennessee
TENNESSEE vs. GREEN BAY
RS: Packers lead series, 4-3;
See Green Bay vs. Tennessee
TENNESSEE vs. INDIANAPOLIS
RS: Series tied, 7-7
PS: Titans lead series, 1-0;
See Indianapolis vs. Tennessee
TENNESSEE vs. JACKSONVILLE
RS: Series tied, 5-5
PS: Titans lead series, 1-0;
See Jacksonville vs. Tennessee
TENNESSEE vs. KANSAS CITY
RS: Chiefs lead series, 24-17
PS: Chiefs lead series, 2-0;
See Kansas City vs. Tennessee
TENNESSEE vs. MIAMI
RS: Dolphins lead series, 14-11
PS: Titans lead series, 1-0;
See Miami vs. Tennessee
TENNESSEE vs. MINNESOTA
RS: Vikings lead series, 5-3;
See Minnesota vs. Tennessee
TENNESSEE vs. NEW ENGLAND
RS: Patriots lead series, 18-14-1
PS: Titans lead series, 1-0;
See New England vs. Tennessee
TENNESSEE vs. NEW ORLEANS
RS: Titans lead series, 5-4-1;
See New Orleans vs. Tennessee
TENNESSEE vs. N.Y. GIANTS
RS: Giants lead series, 5-1;
See N.Y. Giants vs. Tennessee

TENNESSEE vs. N.Y. JETS
RS: Titans lead series, 20-13-1
PS: Titans lead series, 1-0;
See N.Y. Jets vs. Tennessee
TENNESSEE vs. OAKLAND
RS: Raiders lead series, 20-15
PS: Raiders lead series, 3-0;
See Oakland vs. Tennessee
TENNESSEE vs. PHILADELPHIA
RS: Eagles lead series, 6-0;
See Philadelphia vs. Tennessee
TENNESSEE vs. PITTSBURGH
RS: Steelers lead series, 35-24
PS: Steelers lead series, 3-0;
See Pittsburgh vs. Tennessee
TENNESSEE vs. ST. LOUIS
RS: Rams lead series, 5-3
PS: Rams lead series, 1-0;
See St. Louis vs. Tennessee
TENNESSEE vs. SAN DIEGO
RS: Chargers lead series, 19-13-1
PS: Titans lead series, 3-0;
See San Diego vs. Tennessee
TENNESSEE vs. SAN FRANCISCO
RS: 49ers lead series, 7-3;
See San Francisco vs. Tennessee
TENNESSEE vs. SEATTLE
RS: Seahawks lead series, 8-4
PS: Titans lead series, 1-0;
See Seattle vs. Tennessee
TENNESSEE vs. TAMPA BAY
RS: Titans lead series, 5-1;
See Tampa Bay vs. Tennessee
***TENNESSEE vs. WASHINGTON**
RS: Titans lead series, 4-3
1971—Redskins, 22-13 (W)
1975—Oilers, 13-10 (H)
1979—Oilers, 29-27 (W)
1985—Redskins, 16-13 (W)
1988—Oilers, 41-17 (H)
1991—Redskins, 16-13 (W) OT
1997—Oilers, 28-14 (T)
(RS—Titans 150, Redskins 122)
**Franchise in Houston prior to 1997; known as Oilers prior to 1999*

WASHINGTON vs. ARIZONA
RS: Redskins lead series, 66-43-2;
See Arizona vs. Washington
WASHINGTON vs. ATLANTA
RS: Redskins lead series, 13-4-1
PS: Redskins lead series, 1-0;
See Atlanta vs. Washington
WASHINGTON vs BALTIMORE
RS: Ravens lead series, 1-0;
See Baltimore vs. Washington
WASHINGTON vs. BUFFALO
RS: Bills lead series, 5-4
PS: Redskins lead series, 1-0;
See Buffalo vs. Washington
WASHINGTON vs. CAROLINA
RS: Redskins lead series, 4-0;
See Carolina vs. Washington
WASHINGTON vs. CHICAGO
RS: Bears lead series, 18-15-1
PS: Redskins lead series, 4-3;
See Chicago vs. Washington
WASHINGTON vs. CINCINNATI
RS: Redskins lead series, 4-2;
See Cincinnati vs. Washington
WASHINGTON vs. CLEVELAND
RS: Browns lead series, 32-9-1;
See Cleveland vs. Washington
WASHINGTON vs. DALLAS
RS: Cowboys lead series, 45-31-2
PS: Redskins lead series, 2-0;
See Dallas vs. Washington
WASHINGTON vs. DENVER
RS: Broncos lead series, 5-3
PS: Redskins lead series, 1-0;
See Denver vs. Washington
WASHINGTON vs. DETROIT
RS: Redskins lead series, 24-9
PS: Redskins lead series, 3-0;
See Detroit vs. Washington
WASHINGTON vs. GREEN BAY
RS: Packers lead series, 13-12-1
PS: Series tied, 1-1;
See Green Bay vs. Washington
WASHINGTON vs. INDIANAPOLIS
RS: Colts lead series, 17-9;
See Indianapolis vs. Washington
WASHINGTON vs. JACKSONVILLE
RS: Redskins lead series, 1-0;
See Jacksonville vs. Washington
WASHINGTON vs. KANSAS CITY
RS: Chiefs lead series, 4-1;
See Kansas City vs. Washington
WASHINGTON vs. MIAMI
RS: Dolphins lead series, 5-3
PS: Series tied, 1-1;
See Miami vs. Washington
WASHINGTON vs. MINNESOTA
RS: Redskins lead series, 6-5
PS: Redskins lead series, 3-2;
See Minnesota vs. Washington
WASHINGTON vs. NEW ENGLAND
RS: Redskins lead series, 5-1;
See New England vs. Washington
WASHINGTON vs. NEW ORLEANS
RS: Redskins lead series, 12-5;
See New Orleans vs. Washington
WASHINGTON vs. N.Y. GIANTS
RS: Giants lead series, 75-55-4
PS: Series tied, 1-1;
See N.Y. Giants vs. Washington
WASHINGTON vs. N.Y. JETS
RS: Redskins lead series, 6-1;
See N.Y. Jets vs. Washington
WASHINGTON vs. OAKLAND
RS: Raiders lead series, 6-3
PS: Raiders lead series, 1-0;
See Oakland vs. Washington
WASHINGTON vs. PHILADELPHIA
RS: Redskins lead series, 70-54-5
PS: Redskins lead series, 1-0;
See Philadelphia vs. Washington
WASHINGTON vs. PITTSBURGH
RS: Redskins lead series, 42-28-3;
See Pittsburgh vs. Washington
WASHINGTON vs. ST. LOUIS
RS: Redskins lead series, 17-6-1
PS: Series tied, 2-2;
See St. Louis vs. Washington
WASHINGTON vs. SAN DIEGO
RS: Redskins lead series, 6-0;
See San Diego vs. Washington
WASHINGTON vs. SAN FRANCISCO
RS: 49ers lead series, 12-7-1
PS: 49ers lead series, 3-1;
See San Francisco vs. Washington
WASHINGTON vs. SEATTLE
RS: Redskins lead series, 5-4;
See Seattle vs. Washington
WASHINGTON vs. TAMPA BAY
RS: Redskins lead series, 5-4
PS: Buccaneers lead series, 1-0;
See Tampa Bay vs. Washington
WASHINGTON vs. TENNESSEE
RS: Titans lead series, 4-3;
See Tennessee vs. Washington

SUPER BOWL SUMMARIES

RESULTS

Super Bowl	Date	Winner (Share)	Loser (Share)	Score	Site	Attendance
XXXIV	1-30-00	St. Louis ($58,000)	Tennessee ($33,000)	23-16	Atlanta	72,625
XXXIII	1-31-99	Denver ($53,000)	Atlanta ($32,500)	34-19	Miami	74,803
XXXII	1-25-98	Denver ($48,000)	Green Bay ($29,000)	31-24	San Diego	68,912
XXXI	1-26-97	Green Bay ($48,000)	New England ($29,000)	35-21	New Orleans	72,301
XXX	1-28-96	Dallas ($42,000)	Pittsburgh ($27,000)	27-17	Tempe	76,347
XXIX	1-29-95	San Francisco ($42,000)	San Diego ($26,000)	49-26	Miami	74,107
XXVIII	1-30-94	Dallas ($38,000)	Buffalo ($23,500)	30-13	Atlanta	72,817
XXVII	1-31-93	Dallas ($36,000)	Buffalo ($18,000)	52-17	Pasadena	98,374
XXVI	1-26-92	Washington ($36,000)	Buffalo ($18,000)	37-24	Minneapolis	63,130
XXV	1-27-91	N.Y. Giants ($36,000)	Buffalo ($18,000)	20-19	Tampa	73,813
XXIV	1-28-90	San Francisco ($36,000)	Denver ($18,000)	55-10	New Orleans	72,919
XXIII	1-22-89	San Francisco ($36,000)	Cincinnati ($18,000)	20-16	Miami	75,129
XXII	1-31-88	Washington ($36,000)	Denver ($18,000)	42-10	San Diego	73,302
XXI	1-25-87	N.Y. Giants ($36,000)	Denver ($18,000)	39-20	Pasadena	101,063
XX	1-26-86	Chicago ($36,000)	New England ($18,000)	46-10	New Orleans	73,818
XIX	1-20-85	San Francisco ($36,000)	Miami ($18,000)	38-16	Stanford	84,059
XVIII	1-22-84	L.A. Raiders ($36,000)	Washington ($18,000)	38-9	Tampa	72,920
XVII	1-30-83	Washington ($36,000)	Miami ($18,000)	27-17	Pasadena	103,667
XVI	1-24-82	San Francisco ($18,000)	Cincinnati ($9,000)	26-21	Pontiac	81,270
XV	1-25-81	Oakland ($18,000)	Philadelphia ($9,000)	27-10	New Orleans	76,135
XIV	1-20-80	Pittsburgh ($18,000)	Los Angeles ($9,000)	31-19	Pasadena	103,985
XIII	1-21-79	Pittsburgh ($18,000)	Dallas ($9,000)	35-31	Miami	79,484
XII	1-15-78	Dallas ($18,000)	Denver ($9,000)	27-10	New Orleans	75,583
XI	1-9-77	Oakland ($15,000)	Minnesota ($7,500)	32-14	Pasadena	103,438
X	1-18-76	Pittsburgh ($15,000)	Dallas ($7,500)	21-17	Miami	80,187
IX	1-12-75	Pittsburgh ($15,000)	Minnesota ($7,500)	16-6	New Orleans	80,997
VIII	1-13-74	Miami ($15,000)	Minnesota ($7,500)	24-7	Houston	71,882
VII	1-14-73	Miami ($15,000)	Washington ($7,500)	14-7	Los Angeles	90,182
VI	1-16-72	Dallas ($15,000)	Miami ($7,500)	24-3	New Orleans	81,023
V	1-17-71	Baltimore ($15,000)	Dallas ($7,500)	16-13	Miami	79,204
IV	1-11-70	Kansas City ($15,000)	Minnesota ($7,500)	23-7	New Orleans	80,562
III	1-12-69	N.Y. Jets ($15,000)	Baltimore ($7,500)	16-7	Miami	75,389
II	1-14-68	Green Bay ($15,000)	Oakland ($7,500)	33-14	Miami	75,546
I	1-15-67	Green Bay ($15,000)	Kansas City ($7,500)	35-10	Los Angeles	61,946

SUPER BOWL COMPOSITE STANDINGS

	W	L	Pct.	Pts.	OP
San Francisco 49ers	5	0	1.000	188	89
New York Giants	2	0	1.000	59	39
Chicago Bears	1	0	1.000	46	10
New York Jets	1	0	1.000	16	7
Pittsburgh Steelers	4	1	.800	120	100
Green Bay Packers	3	1	.750	127	76
Oakland/L.A. Raiders	3	1	.750	111	66
Dallas Cowboys	5	3	.625	221	132
Washington Redskins	3	2	.600	122	103
Baltimore Colts	1	1	.500	23	29
Kansas City Chiefs	1	1	.500	33	42
St. Louis/L.A. Rams	1	1	.500	42	47
Miami Dolphins	2	3	.400	74	103
Denver Broncos	2	4	.333	115	206
Atlanta Falcons	0	1	.000	19	34
Philadelphia Eagles	0	1	.000	10	27
San Diego Chargers	0	1	.000	26	49
Tennessee Titans	0	1	.000	16	23
Cincinnati Bengals	0	2	.000	37	46
New England Patriots	0	2	.000	31	81
Buffalo Bills	0	4	.000	73	139
Minnesota Vikings	0	4	.000	34	95

SUPER BOWL MOST VALUABLE PLAYERS*

Super Bowl I — QB Bart Starr, Green Bay
Super Bowl II — QB Bart Starr, Green Bay
Super Bowl III — QB Joe Namath, N.Y. Jets
Super Bowl IV — QB Len Dawson, Kansas City
Super Bowl V — LB Chuck Howley, Dallas
Super Bowl VI — QB Roger Staubach, Dallas
Super Bowl VII — S Jake Scott, Miami
Super Bowl VIII — RB Larry Csonka, Miami
Super Bowl IX — RB Franco Harris, Pittsburgh
Super Bowl X — WR Lynn Swann, Pittsburgh
Super Bowl XI — WR Fred Biletnikoff, Oakland
Super Bowl XII — DT Randy White and DE Harvey Martin, Dallas
Super Bowl XIII — QB Terry Bradshaw, Pittsburgh
Super Bowl XIV — QB Terry Bradshaw, Pittsburgh
Super Bowl XV — QB Jim Plunkett, Oakland
Super Bowl XVI — QB Joe Montana, San Francisco
Super Bowl XVII — RB John Riggins, Washington
Super Bowl XVIII — RB Marcus Allen, L.A. Raiders
Super Bowl XIX — QB Joe Montana, San Francisco
Super Bowl XX — DE Richard Dent, Chicago
Super Bowl XXI — QB Phil Simms, N.Y. Giants
Super Bowl XXII — QB Doug Williams, Washington
Super Bowl XXIII — WR Jerry Rice, San Francisco
Super Bowl XXIV — QB Joe Montana, San Francisco
Super Bowl XXV — RB Ottis Anderson, N.Y. Giants
Super Bowl XXVI — QB Mark Rypien, Washington
Super Bowl XXVII — QB Troy Aikman, Dallas
Super Bowl XXVIII — RB Emmitt Smith, Dallas
Super Bowl XXIX — QB Steve Young, San Francisco
Super Bowl XXX — CB Larry Brown, Dallas
Super Bowl XXXI — KR-PR Desmond Howard, Green Bay
Super Bowl XXXII — RB Terrell Davis, Denver
Super Bowl XXXIII — QB John Elway, Denver
Super Bowl XXXIV — QB Kurt Warner, St. Louis

* Award named Pete Rozelle Trophy since Super Bowl XXV.

SUPER BOWL XXXIV

Georgia Dome, Atlanta, Georgia
January 30, 2000, Attendance: 72,625

ST. LOUIS 23, TENNESSEE 16—Mike Jones tackled Kevin Dyson at the 1-yard line as time expired, preserving the Rams' first-ever Super Bowl title. The Rams drove inside the Titans' 20 with each of their first six possessions, but compiled just 3 field goals and 1 touchdown to take a 16-0 lead. Holder Rick Tuten's bobbled snap averted a 35-yard field-goal attempt to conclude the Rams' first drive. The Titans responded with a 42-yard drive, their longest of the half, but Al Del Greco missed a 47-yard attempt. Jeff Wilkins added 3 field goals and missed a 34-yard attempt while the Titans did not threaten the rest of the half, giving the Rams a 9-0 lead at intermission despite outgaining the Titans in total yards (294-89). Tennessee drove 43 yards with the second half's opening kickoff, but Todd Lyght blocked Del Greco's 47-yard attempt to keep the Titans off the board. Kurt Warner's 31-yard pass to Isaac Bruce keyed the ensuing drive that was capped by Warner's 9-yard touchdown pass to Torry Holt with 7:20 left in the third quarter to give the Rams a 16-0 lead. The Titans responded with touchdown drives in excess of seven minutes on each of their next two possessions. Steve McNair's 23-yard scramble set up Eddie George's 1-yard run in the final minute of the third quarter. McNair's 2-point conversion pass to Frank Wycheck was incomplete, but the Titans' defense forced a punt and the offense drove 79 yards in 13 plays, highlighted by 21-yard passes from McNair to Isaac Byrd and Jackie Harris, and capped by George's 2-yard run to cut the deficit to 16-13 with 7:21 remaining. The Rams once again failed to get a first down, and following a punt, the Titans needed just 28 yards to set up Del Greco's game-tying 43-yard kick with 2:12 left. On the next play from scrimmage, Warner fired a deep pass down the right sideline to Bruce, who caught the ball at the Titans' 38, cut toward the inside, and outran the defense to the end zone to give the Rams a 23-16 lead with 1:54 left. The Titans drove downfield, and McNair avoided a sack and completed a 16-yard pass to Kevin Dyson to place Tennessee at the Rams' 10 with six seconds remaining. With no timeouts, McNair attempted a quick pass to a slanting Dyson, who caught the ball in stride at the Rams' 3. However, Jones reacted quickly and stepped up to tackle Dyson at the 1-yard line as time expired. Warner, who was named the game's most valuable player, was 24 of 45 for a Super Bowl-record 414 yards and 2 touchdowns. Bruce had 6 catches for 162 yards, and Holt had 7 for 109 yards. McNair was 22 of 36 for 214 yards. The Titans were the first team in Super Bowl history to comeback from a 16-point deficit.

St. Louis (23)	Offense	Tennessee (16)
Torry Holt	WR	Kevin Dyson
Orlando Pace	LT	Brad Hopkins
Tom Nutten	LG	Bruce Matthews
Mark Gruttadauria	C	Kevin Long
Adam Timmerman	RG	Benji Olson
Fred Miller	RT	Jon Runyan
Roland Williams	TE	Fred Wycheck

Isaac Bruce	WR	Isaac Byrd
Kurt Warner	QB	Steve McNair
Robert Holcombe	RB	Eddie George
Marshall Faulk	FB	Jackie Harris
	Defense	
Kevin Carter	LE	Jevon Kearse
Ray Agnew	LT	Josh Evans
D'Marco Farr	RT	Jason Fisk
Grant Wistrom	RE	Kenny Holmes
Mike Jones	LLB	Eddie Robinson
London Fletcher	MLB	Barron Wortham
Todd Collins	RLB	Joe Bowden
Todd Lyght	LCB	Denard Walker
Dexter McCleon	RCB	Samari Rolle
Billy Jenkins	SS	Blaine Bishop
Keith Lyle	FS	Anthony Dorsett

SUBSTITUTIONS

ST. LOUIS—Offense: K—Jeff Wilkins. P—Mike Horan. RB—James Hodgins, Amp Lee. WR—Az-Zahir Hakim, Tony Horne, Ricky Proehl. TE—Ernie Conwell, Jeff Robinson. G—Andy McCollum. C—Ryan Tucker. Defense: DE—Jay Williams. DT—Nate Hobgood-Chittick, Jeff Zgonina. LB—Charlie Clemons, Leonard Little, Mike Morton, Lorenzo Styles. CB—Dre' Bly. S—Devin Bush, Rich Coady. DNP—Taje Allen, Paul Justin. Inactive: QB—Joe Germaine. RB—Justin Watson. WR—Chris Thomas. T—Matt Willig. G—Cameron Spikes. DE—Lionel Barnes. LB—Troy Pelshak. S—Ron Carpenter.

TENNESSEE—Offense: K—Al Del Greco. P—Craig Hentrich. RB—Robert Thomas. FB—Lorenzo Neal. WR—Chris Sanders, Derrick Mason, Joey Kent. TE—Larry Brown. G—Jason Layman. Defense: DT—Joe Salave'a, John Thornton. DE-DT—Henry Ford, Mike Jones. LB—Doug Colman, Greg Favors, Terry Killens. CB—Donald Mitchell, George McCullough, Dainon Sidney. S—Steve Jackson, Perry Phenix. DNP—Jason Matthews, Neil O'Donnell. Inactive: QB—Kevin Daft. RB—Spencer George. WR—Yancey Thigpen. G—Zach Piller. C—Craig Page. DE—Mike Frederick. LB—Phil Glover. S—Marcus Robertson.

OFFICIALS

Referee—Bob McElwee. Umpire—Ron Botchan. Line Judge—Byron Boston. Side Judge—Tom Fincken. Head Linesman—Earnie Frantz. Back Judge—Bill Leavy. Field Judge—Al Jury. Replay Official—Mark Burns.

SCORING

St. Louis (NFC)	3	6	7	7	—	23
Tennessee (AFC)	0	0	6	10	—	16

StL — FG Wilkins 27
StL — FG Wilkins 29
StL — FG Wilkins 28
StL — Holt 9 pass from Warner (Wilkins kick)
Tenn — George 1 run (pass failed)
Tenn — George 2 run (Del Greco kick)
Tenn — FG Del Greco 43
StL — Bruce 73 pass from Warner (Wilkins kick)

TEAM STATISTICS	STL.	TENN.
Total First Downs	23	27
Rushing	1	12
Passing	18	13
Penalty	4	2
Total Net Yardage	436	367
Total Offensive Plays	59	73
Average Gain Per Offensive Play	7.4	5.0
Rushes	13	36
Yards Gained Rushing (Net)	29	159
Average Yards per Rush	2.2	4.4
Passes Attempted	45	36
Passes Completed	24	22
Had Intercepted	0	0
Tackled Attempting to Pass	1	1
Yards Lost Attempting to Pass	7	6
Yards Gained Passing (Net)	407	208
Punts	2	3
Average Distance	38.5	43.0
Punt Returns	2	1
Punt Return Yardage	8	(-1)
Kickoff Returns	4	5
Kickoff Return Yardage	55	122
Interception Return Yardage	0	0
Total Return Yardage	63	121
Fumbles	2	0
Fumbles Lost	0	0
Own Fumbles Recovered	2	0
Opponent Fumbles Recovered	0	0
Penalties	8	7
Yards Penalized	60	45
Field Goals	3	1
Field Goals Attempted	4	3
Third-Down Efficiency	5/12	6/13
Fourth-Down Efficiency	0/1	1/1
Time of Possession	23:34	36:26

INDIVIDUAL STATISTICS

RUSHING: StL: Faulk 10-17, Holcombe 1-11, Warner 1-1, Horan 1-0. TENN: E. George 28-95, McNair 8-64.

PASSING: StL: Warner 24-45-414-0. TENN: Chandler 19-35-219-1.

RECEIVING: StL: Holt 7-109, Bruce 6-162, Faulk 5-90, Hakim 1-17, Conwell 1-16, Proehl 1-11, R. Williams 1-9, Holcombe 1-1, Miller 1-(-1). TENN: Harris 7-64, Wycheck 5-35, Dyson 4-41, E. George 2-35, Byrd 2-21, Mason 2-18.

KICKOFF RETURNS: StL: Horne 4-55, Morton 0-0. TENN: Mason 5-122.

PUNT RETURNS: StL: Hakim 2-8. TENN: Mason 1-(-1).

PUNTING: StL: Horan 2-77-47-0. TENN: Hentrich 3-129-49-0.

SACKS: StL: Carter. TENN: Fisk.

SUPER BOWL XXXIII

Pro Player Stadium, Miami, Florida
January 31, 1999, Attendance: 74,803

DENVER 34, ATLANTA 19—John Elway, in his last game, passed for 336 yards and ran for a touchdown to earn most valuable player honors as the Broncos became the first AFC team to win consecutive Super Bowls since the Steelers won XIII and XIV. A 25-yard pass interference penalty on Ray Crockett assisted the Falcons' nine-play, 48-yard game-opening drive that was capped by Morten Andersen's 32-yard field goal. Elway's 41-yard pass to Rod Smith kept alive Denver's ensuing drive and led to Howard Griffith's 1-yard touchdown run. Ronnie Bradford's interception and return to the Broncos' 35 late in the first quarter gave Atlanta excellent field position. However, Jamal Anderson was stopped for no gain on third-and-1 and thrown for a 2-yard loss on fourth down. Denver capitalized on its defensive effort with Jason Elam's 26-yard field goal. The Falcons responded by driving to the Broncos' 8, but Andersen's 26-yard field-goal attempt sailed wide right and on the next play, Elway fired an 80-yard touchdown pass to Smith to turn a possible 10-6 game into a 17-3 Broncos lead. Andersen's 28-yard field goal and 2 misses by Elam on the Broncos' first two second-half possessions gave Atlanta an opportunity to climb back into the game. However, Darrien Gordon dashed the Falcons' hopes with interceptions on consecutive possessions inside the Broncos' 20 to stop drives and set up Broncos touchdowns. Gordon returned the first interception, on a tipped pass, 58 yards to the Falcons' 24 to set up Griffith's second touchdown five plays later, and picked the second pass off at the Broncos' 2 and returned it 50 yards. Terrell Davis turned a short pass into a 39-yard gain, and Elway scored two plays later to give Denver a 31-6 lead. Tim Dwight returned the ensuing kickoff for a touchdown, and, after a field goal by Elam, the Falcons' offense scored with 2:04 remaining on Chandler's 3-yard pass to Tony Martin. Byron Chamberlain recovered the ensuing onside kick, but Tyrone Braxton recovered Anderson's fumble at the Falcons' 33 with 1:30 remaining to ice the game. The Falcons drove inside the Broncos' 30 seven times, but tallied just 1 touchdown and 2 field goals, throwing 2 interceptions, missing 1 field goal, and turning the ball over 1 time on downs during the other possessions. Elway was 18 of 29 for 336 yards and 1 touchdown, with 1 interception. Davis had 25 carries for 102 yards. Smith had 5 receptions for 152 yards. Chandler was 19 of 35 for 219 yards and 1 touchdown, with 3 interceptions.

Denver (AFC)	7	10	0	17	—	34
Atlanta (NFC)	3	3	0	13	—	19

Atl — FG Andersen 32 (5:25)
Den — Griffith 1 run (Elam kick) (11:05)
Den — FG Elam 26 (5:43)
Den — R. Smith 80 pass from Elway (Elam kick) (10:06)
Atl — FG Andersen 28 (12:35)
Den — Griffith 1 run (Elam kick) (:04)
Den — Elway 3 run (Elam kick) (3:40)
Atl — Dwight 94 kickoff return (Andersen kick) (3:59)
Den — FG Elam 37 (7:52)
Atl — Mathis 3 pass from Chandler (pass failed) (12:56)

SUPER BOWL XXXII

Qualcomm Stadium, San Diego, California
January 25, 1998, Attendance: 68,912

DENVER 31, GREEN BAY 24—Terrell Davis rushed for 157 yards and a Super Bowl-record 3 touchdowns to lead the Broncos to their first NFL championship and break the NFC's streak of Super Bowl victories at 13. The defending Super Bowl champion Packers took the opening kickoff and marched 76 yards in just over four minutes, scoring the first points on Brett Favre's 22-yard touchdown pass to Antonio Freeman. The Broncos responded with a 10-play, 58-yard drive capped by Davis's 1-yard run to tie the game. Tyrone Braxton intercepted Favre two plays later, and John Elway scored on a third-and-goal play to begin the second quarter. Steve Atwater forced Favre to fumble three plays later, and Neil Smith recovered at the Packers' 33. Jason Elam converted a 51-yard field goal, the second longest in Super Bowl history, to give the Broncos a 17-7 lead with 12:21 left in the half. After an exchange of punts, the Packers produced a 17-play, 95-yard drive that consumed 7:26 and finished with Favre's 6-yard touchdown pass to Mark Chmura on third-and-5 with 12 seconds left in the half. Tyrone Williams forced and recovered Davis's fumble at the Broncos' 26 on the first play from scrimmage in the second half. However, the Broncos' defense kept the Packers out of the end zone as Ryan Longwell's 27-yard field goal tied the game with 11:59 left in the third quarter. After another exchange of punts, Elway's 36-yard pass to Ed McCaffrey keyed a 13-play, 92-yard drive capped by Davis's 1-yard touchdown run with 34 seconds left in the third quarter. Tim McKyer recovered Freeman's fumble at the Packers' 22 on the ensuing kickoff return, giving the Broncos a golden opportunity, but Eugene Robinson intercepted Elway's pass in the end zone on the next play. Sparked by Robinson's play, the Packers took just four plays, three on passes to Freeman, to score the tying touchdown with 13:32 remaining. Each defense stiffened, forcing two punts, but the Broncos got great field position following Craig Hentrich's 39-yard punt to the Packers' 49 with 3:27 left and the score tied 24-24. Davis rushed for 2 yards on the first play, but Darrius Holland's 15-yard facemask penalty moved the ball to the Packers' 32. Elway threw a 23-yard pass to Howard Griffith two plays later, and after a holding penalty, Davis rushed 17 yards to the Packers' 1 with 1:47 left. After a timeout, Davis waltzed into the end zone to give Denver a 31-24 lead with 1:45 remaining. Freeman returned the kickoff 22 yards to the Broncos' 30, and Favre completed 22- and 13-yard screen passes to Dorsey Levens to reach the Broncos' 35 with 1:04 left. But after a 4-yard pass to Levens and incompletions to Freeman and Brooks, John Mobley knocked away Favre's pass to Chmura with 32 seconds left to give the Broncos the Vince Lombardi Trophy. Elway was 12 of 22 for 123 yards, with 1 interception. Favre was 25 of 42 for 256 yards and 1 touchdown, with 1 interception. Freeman had 9 receptions for 126 yards. Davis was named the game's most valuable player.

Green Bay (NFC)	7	7	3	7	—	24
Denver (AFC)	7	10	7	7	—	31

GB — Freeman 22 pass from Favre (Longwell kick) (4:02)
Den — Davis 1 run (Elam kick) (9:21)
Den — Elway 1 run (Elam kick) (:05)
Den — FG Elam 51 (2:39)
GB — Chmura 6 pass from Favre (Longwell kick) (14:48)
GB — FG Longwell 27 (3:01)
Den — Davis 1 run (Elam kick) (14:26)
GB — Freeman 13 pass from Favre (Longwell kick) (1:28)
Den — Davis 1 run (Elam kick) (13:15)

SUPER BOWL XXXI

Louisiana Superdome, New Orleans, Louisiana
January 26, 1997, Attendance: 72,301

GREEN BAY 35, NEW ENGLAND 21— Desmond Howard returned a kickoff 99 yards for a touchdown and Brett Favre passed for 2 touchdowns and ran for a score as the Packers won their first Super Bowl in twenty-nine years. Howard, en route to garnering the MVP trophy, equaled a Super Bowl record with 244 total return yards. It was Favre's arm that struck first, as he hit Andre Rison for a 54-yard touchdown pass on the Packers' second play from scrimmage to take a 7-0 lead. Two plays later Doug Evans made a diving interception of Drew Bledsoe's pass at the 28-yard line, setting up Chris Jacke's field goal and giving the Packers a 10-0 lead just 6:18 into the Super Bowl. The Patriots answered with touchdowns on their next two possessions. Craig Newsome's pass interference penalty set up the first touchdown and a 44-yard completion from Bledsoe to Terry Glenn preceeding Ben Coates's touchdown gave New England its first and only lead. The 24 combined first quarter points were the most in Super Bowl history. Green Bay struck again 56 seconds into the second quarter as Favre hit Antonio Freeman with a Super Bowl-record 81-yard touchdown bomb. Jacke booted his second field goal on Green Bay's next possession. After a Mike Prior interception, Favre orchestrated a 74-yard, nearly 6-minute drive that concluded with a diving Favre touching the ball against the pylon to give Green Bay a 27-14 halftime lead. Curtis Martin brought the Patriots to within a score by running in from 18 yards out with 3:27 left in the third quarter. But Howard broke the Patriots' spirit by returning the ensuing kickoff a Super Bowl-record 99 yards. Favre found Mark Chmura for the 2-point conversion to finish the scoring. Bledsoe was intercepted twice in the fourth quarter as the Patriots never crossed midfield in 4 fourth-quarter possessions. Reggie White set a Super Bowl record with 3 sacks. Favre completed 14 of 27 passes for 246 yards, with no interceptions. Bledsoe completed 11 more passes than Favre, but for just 7 more yards, and threw 4 interceptions.

New England (AFC)	14	0	7	0	—	21
Green Bay (NFC)	10	17	8	0	—	35

GB — Rison 54 pass from Favre (Jacke kick) (3:32)
GB — FG Jacke 37 (6:18)
NE — Byars 1 pass from Bledsoe (Vinatieri kick) (8:25)
NE — Coates 4 pass from Bledsoe (Vinatieri kick) (12:27)
GB — Freeman 81 pass from Favre (Jacke kick) (0:56)
GB — FG Jacke 31 (6:45)
GB — Favre 2 run (Jacke kick) (13:49)
NE — Martin 18 run (Vinatieri kick) (11:33)
GB — Howard 99 kickoff return (Chmura pass from Favre) (11:50)

SUPER BOWL XXX

Sun Devil Stadium, Tempe, Arizona
January 28, 1996, Attendance: 76,347

DALLAS 27, PITTSBURGH 17—Cornerback Larry Brown's 2 interceptions led to 14 second-half points and helped lift the Cowboys to their third Super Bowl victory in the last four seasons and their record-tying fifth title overall. Brown's interceptions foiled the comeback efforts of the Steelers, and earned him the Pete Rozelle Trophy as the game's most valuable player. Dallas scored on each of its first three possessions, taking a 13-0 lead on Troy Aikman's 3-yard touchdown pass to Jay Novacek and a pair of field goals by Chris Boniol. Neil O'Donnell's 6-yard touchdown pass to Yancey Thigpen 13 seconds before halftime pulled Pittsburgh within 6 points, and the Steelers had the ball near midfield midway through the third quarter. But O'Donnell's third-down pass was intercepted by Brown at the Cowboys' 38-yard line, and his 44-yard return carried to Pittsburgh's 18. After Aikman's 17-yard completion to Michael Irvin, Emmitt Smith ran 1 yard for the touchdown that put Dallas ahead again by 13 points. The Steelers rallied, though, behind Norm Johnson's 46-yard field goal, a successful surprise onside kick, and Byron (Bam) Morris's 1-yard touchdown run with 6:36 to play in the game. And when they forced a punt and took possession at their own 32-yard line trailing only 20-17 with 4:15 remaining, it appeared they might have a chance to break the NFC's recent domination in the Super Bowl. But on second down, Brown struck again, intercepting O'Donnell's pass at the 39 and returning it 33 yards to the 6. Two plays later, Smith barreled over from 4 yards out for the clinching touchdown with 3:43 to go. Pittsburgh limited the Cowboys' powerful running game to only 56 yards and enjoyed a whopping 201-61 advantage in total yards in the second half, but could not overcome the 3 interceptions (another came on the game's final play) thrown by O'Donnell, the NFL's career leader for fewest interceptions per pass attempt. In all, O'Donnell completed 28 of 49 passes for 239 yards. Morris rushed for a game-high 73 yards on 19 carries. For Dallas, Aikman completed 15 of 23 pass attempts for 209 yards. The Cowboys' victory was the twelfth in a row for NFC teams over AFC teams in the Super Bowl.

Dallas (NFC)	10	3	7	7	—	27
Pittsburgh (AFC)	0	7	0	10	—	17

Dall — FG Boniol 42 (2:55)
Dall — Novacek 3 pass from Aikman (Boniol kick) (9:37)
Dall — FG Boniol 35 (8:57)
Pitt — Thigpen 6 pass from O'Donnell (N. Johnson kick) (14:47)
Dall — E. Smith 1 run (Boniol kick) (8:18)
Pitt — FG N. Johnson 46 (3:40)
Pitt — Morris 1 run (N. Johnson kick) (8:24)
Dall — E. Smith 4 run (Boniol kick) (11:17)

SUPER BOWL XXIX

Joe Robbie Stadium, Miami, Florida
January 29, 1995, Attendance: 74,107

SAN FRANCISCO 49, SAN DIEGO 26—Steve Young passed for a record 6 touchdowns, and the 49ers became the first team to win five Super Bowls when they routed the Chargers. Young, the game's most valuable player, directed an explosive offense that generated 7 touchdowns, 28 first downs, and 455 total yards. He completed 24 of 36 passes for 325 yards, and broke the record of 5 touchdown passes set by fromer 49ers quarterback Joe Montana in Super Bowl XXIV. San Francisco wasted little time scoring, taking the lead for good on Young's 44-yard touchdown pass to Jerry Rice only three plays and 1:24 into the game. The next time they had the ball, the 49ers marched 79 yards in four plays, taking a 14-0 lead when Young teamed with running back Ricky Watters on a 51-yard touchdown pass with 10:05 still to play in the opening period. San Diego then put together its most impressive possession of the game, a 13-play, 78-yard drive that consumed more than 7 minutes and was capped by Natrone Means's 1-yard touchdown run, to cut its deficit to 14-7 late in the quarter. But San Francisco countered with a 70-yard drive of its own, and Young's 5-yard touchdown pass to fullback William Floyd made it 21-7. Young's fourth touchdown pass of the half, 8 yards to Watters 4:44 before halftime, increased the advantage to 28-7, and the Chargers could get no closer than 18 points after that. Watters, who ran 9 yards for a touchdown in the third quarter, equaled the Super Bowl record with 3 touchdowns. Rice also scored 3 touchdowns (the second time in his career he'd done that in a Super Bowl) while catching 10 passes for 149 yards. He established career records for receptions, yards, and touchdowns in a Super Bowl. Young, who scrambled 21 yards and 15 yards to set up touchdowns in the first half, was the game's leading rusher with 49 yards on 5 carries. San Diego's Means, who rushed for 1,350 yards during the regular season, was limited to 33 yards on 13 attempts. Chargers quarterback Stan Humphries completed 24 of 49 passes for 275 yards. Rookie Andre Coleman became only the third player in Super Bowl history to return a kickoff for a touchdown, going 98 yards in the third quarter. The 75 points scored by the two teams established another record, breaking the previous mark of 69 set in Dallas's 52-17 victory over Buffalo in XXVII. The 49ers' victory was the eleventh straight for NFC teams over AFC teams in the Super Bowl.

San Diego (AFC)	7	3	8	8	—	26
San Francisco (NFC)	14	14	14	7	—	49

SF — Rice 44 pass from S. Young (Brien kick) (1:24)
SF — Watters 51 pass from S. Young (Brien kick) (4:55)
SD — Means 1 run (Carney kick) (12:16)
SF — Floyd 5 pass from S. Young (Brien kick) (1:58)
SF — Watters 8 pass from S. Young (Brien kick) (10:16)
SD — FG Carney 31 (13:16)
SF — Watters 9 run (Brien kick) (5:25)
SF — Rice 15 pass from S. Young (Brien kick) (11:42)
SD — Coleman 98 kickoff return (Seay pass from Humphries) (11:59)
SF — Rice 7 pass from S. Young (Brien kick) (1:11)
SD — Martin 30 pass from Humphries (Pupunu pass from Humphries) (12:35)

SUPER BOWL XXVIII

Georgia Dome, Atlanta, Georgia
January 30, 1994, Attendance: 72,817

DALLAS 30, BUFFALO 13—Emmitt Smith rushed for 132 yards and 2 second-half touchdowns to power the Cowboys to their second consecutive NFL title. By winning, Dallas joined San Francisco and Pittsburgh as the only franchises with four Super Bowl victories. The Bills, meanwhile, extended a dubious string by losing in the Super Bowl for the fourth consecutive year. To win, the Cowboys had to rally from a 13-6 halftime deficit. Buffalo had forged its lead on Thurman Thomas's 4-yard touchdown run and a pair of field goals by Steve Christie, including a 54-yard kick, the longest in Super Bowl history. But just 55 seconds into the second half, Thomas was stripped of the ball by Dallas defensive tackle Leon Lett. Safety James Washington recovered and weaved his way 46 yards for a touchdown to tie the game at 13-13. After forcing the Bills to punt, the Cowboys began their next possession on their 36-yard line and Smith, the game's most valuable player, took over. He carried 7 times for 61 yards on the ensuing 8-play, 64-yard drive, capping the march with a 15-yard touchdown run to give Dallas the lead for good with 8:42 remaining in the third quarter. Early in the fourth quarter, Washington intercepted Jim Kelly's pass and returned it 12 yards to Buffalo's 34. A penalty moved the ball back to the 39, but Smith carried twice for 10 yards and caught a screen pass for 9, and quarterback Troy Aikman completed a 16-yard pass to Alvin Harper to give the Cowboys a first-and-goal at the 6. Smith took it from there, cracking the end zone on fourth-and-goal from the 1 to put Dallas ahead 27-13 with 9:50 remaining. Eddie Murray's third field goal, from 20 yards with 2:50 left, ended any doubt about the game's outcome. Smith had 30 carries in all, with 19 of his attempts and 92 yards coming after intermission. Washington, normally a reserve who played most of the game because the Cowboys used five defensive backs to combat the Bills' No-Huddle offense, had 11 tackles and forced another fumble by Thomas in the first quarter. Aikman completed 19 of 27 passes for 207 yards. Buffalo's Kelly completed a Super Bowl-record 31 passes in 50 attempts for 260 yards. Dallas, the first team in NFL history to begin the regular season 0-2 and go on to win the Super Bowl, also became the fifth to win back-to-back titles, following Green Bay, Miami, Pittsburgh (the Steelers did it twice), and San Francisco. Buffalo became the third team, along with Minnesota and Denver, to lose four Super Bowls. The Cowboys' victory was the tenth in succession for the NFC over the AFC.

Dallas (NFC)	6	0	14	10	— 30
Buffalo (AFC)	3	10	0	0	— 13

Dall — FG Murray 41 (2:19)
Buff — FG Christie 54 (4:41)
Dall — FG Murray 24 (11:05)
Buff — Thomas 4 run (Christie kick) (2:34)
Buff — FG Christie 28 (15:00)
Dall — Washington 46 fumble return (Murray kick) (0:55)
Dall — E. Smith 15 run (Murray kick) (6:18)
Dall — E. Smith 1 run (Murray kick) (5:10)
Dall — FG Murray 20 (12:10)

SUPER BOWL XXVII

Rose Bowl, Pasadena, California
January 31, 1993, Attendance: 98,374

DALLAS 52, BUFFALO 17—Troy Aikman passed for 4 touchdowns, Emmitt Smith rushed for 108 yards, and the Cowboys converted 9 turnovers into 35 points while coasting to the victory. Dallas's win was its third in its record sixth Super Bowl appearance; the Bills became the first team to drop three in succession. Buffalo led 7-0 until the first 2 of its record number of turnovers helped the Cowboys take the lead for good late in the opening quarter. First, Dallas safety James Washington intercepted Jim Kelly's pass and returned it 13 yards to the Bills' 47, setting up Aikman's 23-yard touchdown pass to tight end Jay Novacek with 1:36 remaining in the period. On the next play from scrimmage, Kelly was sacked by Charles Haley and fumbled at the Bills' 2-yard line where the Cowboys' Jimmie Jones picked up the loose ball and ran 2 yards for a touchdown. Dallas, which recovered 5 fumbles and intercepted 4 passes, struck just as quickly late in the first half, when Aikman tossed 19- and 18-yard touchdown passes to Michael Irvin 18 seconds apart to give the Cowboys a 28-10 lead at intermission. The second score was set up when Bills running back Thurman Thomas lost a fumble at his 19-yard line. Buffalo scored for the last time when backup quarterback Frank Reich, playing because Kelly was injured while attempting to pass midway through the second quarter, threw a 40-yard touchdown pass to Don Beebe on the final play of the third period to trim the deficit to 31-17. But Dallas put the game out of reach by scoring three times in a span of 2:33 of the fourth quarter. Aikman, the game's most valuable player, completed 22 of 30 passes for 273 yards. The victory was the ninth in succession for the NFC over the AFC.

Buffalo (AFC)	7	3	7	0	— 17
Dallas (NFC)	14	14	3	21	— 52

Buff — Thomas 2 run (Christie kick) (5:00)
Dall — Novacek 23 pass from Aikman (Elliott kick) (13:24)
Dall — J. Jones 2 fumble recovery return (Elliott kick) (13:39)
Buff — FG Christie 21 (11:36)
Dall — Irvin 19 pass from Aikman (Elliott kick) (13:06)
Dall — Irvin 18 pass from Aikman (Elliott kick) (13:24)
Dall — FG Elliott 20 (6:39)
Buff — Beebe 40 pass from Reich (Christie kick) (15:00)
Dall — Harper 45 pass from Aikman (Elliott kick) (4:56)
Dall — E. Smith 10 run (Elliott kick) (6:48)
Dall — Norton 9 fumble recovery return (Elliott kick) (7:29)

SUPER BOWL XXVI

Metrodome, Minneapolis, Minnesota
January 26, 1992, Attendance: 63,130

WASHINGTON 37, BUFFALO 24—Mark Rypien passed for 292 yards and 2 touchdowns as the Redskins overwhelmed the Bills to win their third Super Bowl in the past 10 years. Rypien, the game's most valuable player, completed 18 of 33 passes, including a 10-yard scoring strike to Earnest Byner and a 30-yard touchdown to Gary Clark. The latter came late in the third quarter after Buffalo had trimmed a 24-0 deficit to 24-10, and effectively put the game out of reach. Washington went on to lead by as much as 37-10 before the Bills made it close wih a pair of touchdowns in the final six minutes. Though the Redskins struggled early, converting their first three drives inside the Bills' 20-yard line into only 3 points, they built a 17-0 halftime lead. And they made it 24-0 just 16 seconds into the second half, after Kurt Gouveia intercepted Buffalo quarterback Jim Kelly's pass on the first play of the third quarter and returned it 23 yards to the Bills' 2. One play later, Gerald Riggs scored his second touchdown of the game to make it 24-0. Kelly, forced to bring Buffalo from behind, completed 28 of a Super Bowl-record 58 passes for 275 yards and 2 touchdowns, but was intercepted 4 times. Bills running back Thurman Thomas, who had an AFC-high 1,407 yards rushing and an NFL-best 2,038 total yards from scrimmage during the regular season, ran for only 13 yards on 10 carries and was limited to 27 yards on 4 receptions. Clark had 7 catches for 114 yards and Art Monk added 7 for 113 for the Redskins, who amassed 417 yards of total offense while limiting the explosive Bills to 283. Washington's Joe Gibbs became only the third head coach to win three Super Bowls.

Washington (NFC)	0	17	14	6	— 37
Buffalo (AFC)	0	0	10	14	— 24

Wash — FG Lohmiller 34 (1:58)
Wash — Byner 10 pass from Rypien (Lohmiller kick) (5:06)
Wash — Riggs 1 run (Lohmiller kick) (7:43)
Wash — Riggs 2 run (Lohmiller kick) (0:16)
Buff — FG Norwood 21 (3:01)
Buff — Thomas 1 run (Norwood kick) (9:02)
Wash — Clark 30 pass from Rypien (Lohmiller kick) (13:36)
Wash — FG Lohmiller 25 (0:06)
Wash — FG Lohmiller 39 (3:24)
Buff — Metzelaars 2 pass from Kelly (Norwood kick) (9:01)
Buff — Beebe 4 pass from Kelly (Norwood kick) (11:05)

SUPER BOWL XXV

Tampa Stadium, Tampa, Florida
January 27, 1991, Attendance: 73,813

NEW YORK GIANTS 20, BUFFALO 19—The NFC champion New York Giants won their second Super Bowl in five years with a 20-19 victory over AFC titlist Buffalo. New York, employing its ball-control offense, had possession for 40 minutes, 33 seconds, a Super Bowl record. The Bills, who scored 95 points in their previous two playoff games leading to Super Bowl XXV, had the ball for less than eight minutes in the second half and just 19:27 for the game. Fourteen of New York's 73 plays came on its initial drive of the third quarter, which covered 75 yards and consumed a Super Bowl-record 9:29 before running back Ottis Anderson ran 1 yard for a touchdown. Giants quarterback Jeff Hostetler kept the long drive going by converting three third-down plays—an 11-yard pass to running back David Meggett on third-and-eight, a 14-yard toss to wide receiver Mark Ingram on third-and-13, and a 9-yard pass to Howard Cross on third-and-four—to give New York a 17-12 lead in the third quarter. Buffalo jumped to a 12-3 lead midway through the second quarter before Hostetler completed a 14-yard scoring strike to wide receiver Stephen Baker to close the score to 12-10 at halftime. Buffalo's Thurman Thomas ran 31 yards for a touchdown on the opening play of the fourth quarter to help Buffalo recapture the lead 19-17. Matt Bahr's 21-yard field goal gave the Giants a 20-19 lead, but Buffalo's Scott Norwood had a chance to win the game with seconds remaining before his 47-yard field-goal attempt sailed wide right. Hostetler completed 20 of 32 passes for 222 yards and 1 touchdown. Anderson rushed 21 times for 102 yards and 1 touchdown to capture most-valuable-player honors. Thomas totaled 190 scrimmage yards, rushing 15 times for 135 yards and catching 5 passes for 55 yards.

Buffalo (AFC)	3	9	0	7	— 19
N.Y. Giants (NFC)	3	7	7	3	— 20

NYG — FG Bahr 28 (7:46)
Buff — FG Norwood 23 (9:09)
Buff — D. Smith 1 run (Norwood kick) (2:30)
Buff — Safety, B. Smith tackled Hostetler in end zone (6:33)
NYG — Baker 14 pass from Hostetler (Bahr kick) (14:35)
NYG — Anderson 1 run (Bahr kick) (9:29)
Buff — Thomas 31 run (Norwood kick) (0:08)
NYG — FG Bahr 21 (7:40)

SUPER BOWL XXIV

Louisiana Superdome, New Orleans, Louisiana
January 28, 1990, Attendance: 72,919

SAN FRANCISCO 55, DENVER 10—NFC titlist San Francisco won its fourth Super Bowl championship with a 55-10 victory over AFC champion Denver. The 49ers, who also won Super Bowls XVI, XIX, and XXIII, tied the Pittsburgh Steelers for most Super Bowl victories. The Steelers captured Super Bowls IX, X, XIII, and XIV. San Francisco's 55 points broke the previous Super Bowl scoring mark of 46 points by Chicago in Super Bowl XX. San Francisco scored touchdowns on four of its six first-half possessions to hold a 27-3 lead at halftime. Interceptions by Michael Walter and Chet Brooks ended the Broncos' first two possessions of the second half. San Francisco quarterback Joe Montana was named the Super Bowl most valuable player for a record third time. Montana completed 22 of 29 passes for 297 yards and a Super Bowl-record 5 touchdowns. Jerry Rice, Super Bowl XXIII most valuable player, caught 7 passes for 148 yards and 3 touchdowns. The 49ers' domination included first downs (28 to 12), net yards (461 to 167), and time of possession (39:31 to 20:29).

San Francisco (NFC)	13	14	14	14	— 55
Denver (AFC)	3	0	7	0	— 10

SF — Rice 20 pass from Montana (Cofer kick) (4:54)
Den — FG Treadwell 42 (8:13)
SF — Jones 7 pass from Montana (kick failed) (14:57)
SF — Rathman 1 run (Cofer kick) (7:45)
SF — Rice 38 pass from Montana (Cofer kick) (14:26)
SF — Rice 28 pass from Montana (Cofer kick) (2:12)
SF — Taylor 35 pass from Montana (Cofer kick) (5:16)
Den — Elway 3 run (Treadwell kick) (8:07)
SF — Rathman 3 run (Cofer kick) (0:03)
SF — Craig 1 run (Cofer kick) (1:13)

SUPER BOWL XXIII

Joe Robbie Stadium, Miami, Florida
January 22, 1989, Attendance: 75,129

SAN FRANCISCO 20, CINCINNATI 16—NFC champion San Francisco captured its third Super Bowl of the 1980s by defeating AFC champion Cincinnati 20-16. The 49ers, who also won Super Bowls XVI and XIX, became the first NFC team to win three Super Bowls. Pittsburgh, with four Super Bowl titles (IX, X, XIII, and XIV), and the Oakland/Los Angeles Raiders, with three (XI, XV, and XVIII), lead AFC franchises. Even though San Francisco held an advantage in total net yards (453 to 229), the 49ers found themselves trailing the Bengals late in the game. With the score 13-13, Cincinnati took a 16-13 lead on Jim Breech's 40-yard field goal with 3:20 remaining. It was Breech's third field goal of the day, following earlier successes from 34 and 43 yards.

The 49ers started their winning drive at their 8-yard line. Over the next 11 plays, San Francisco covered 92 yards with the decisive score coming on a 10-yard pass from quarterback Joe Montana to wide receiver John Taylor with 34 seconds remaining. At halftime, the score was 3-3, the first time in Super Bowl history the game was tied at intermission. After the teams traded third-period field goals, the Bengals jumped ahead 13-6 on Stanford Jennings's 93-yard kickoff return for a touchdown with 34 seconds remaining in the quarter. The 49ers didn't waste any time coming back as they covered 85 yards in four plays, concluding with Montana's 14-yard scoring pass to Jerry Rice 57 seconds into the final stanza. Rice was named the game's most valuable player after compiling 11 catches for a Super Bowl-record 215 yards. Montana completed 23 of 36 passes for a Super Bowl-record 357 yards and 2 touchdowns.

Cincinnati (AFC)	0	3	10	3	—	16
San Francisco (NFC)	3	0	3	14	—	20

SF — FG Cofer 41 (11:46)
Cin — FG Breech 34 (13:45)
Cin — FG Breech 43 (9:21)
SF — FG Cofer 32 (14:10)
Cin — Jennings 93 kickoff return (Breech kick) (14:26)
SF — Rice 14 pass from Montana (Cofer kick) (0:57)
Cin — FG Breech 40 (11:40)
SF — Taylor 10 pass from Montana (Cofer kick) (14:26)

SUPER BOWL XXII

San Diego Jack Murphy Stadium, San Diego, California
January 31, 1988, Attendance: 73,302

WASHINGTON 42, DENVER 10—NFC champion Washington won Super Bowl XXII and its second NFL championship of the 1980s with a 42-10 decision over AFC champion Denver. The Redskins, who also won Super Bowl XVII, enjoyed a record-setting second quarter en route to the victory. The Broncos broke in front 10-0 when quarterback John Elway threw a 56-yard touchdown pass to wide receiver Ricky Nattiel on the Broncos' first play from scrimmage. Following a Washington punt, Denver's Rich Karlis kicked a 24-yard field goal to cap a seven-play, 61-yard scoring drive. The Redskins then erupted for 35 points on five straight possessions in the second period and coasted thereafter. The 35 points established an NFL postseason mark for most points in a period. Redskins quarterback Doug Williams led the second-period explosion by passing for a Super Bowl record-tying 4 touchdowns, including 80- and 50-yard passes to wide receiver Ricky Sanders, a 27-yard toss to wide receiver Gary Clark, and an 8-yard pass to tight end Clint Didier. Washington scored 5 touchdowns in 18 plays with total time of possession of only 5:47. Overall, Williams completed 18 of 29 passes for 340 yards and was named the game's most valuable player. His pass-yardage total eclipsed the Super Bowl record of 331 yards by Joe Montana of San Francisco in Super Bowl XIX. Sanders ended with 193 yards on 8 catches, breaking the previous Super Bowl yardage record of 161 yards by Lynn Swann of Pittsburgh in Game X. Rookie running back Timmy Smith was the game's leading rusher with 22 carries for a Super Bowl-record 204 yards, breaking the previous mark of 191 yards by Marcus Allen of the Raiders in Game XVIII. Smith also scored twice on runs of 58 and 4 yards. Washington's 6 touchdowns and 602 total yards gained also set Super Bowl records. Redskins cornerback Barry Wilburn had 2 of the team's 3 interceptions, and strong safety Alvin Walton had 2 of Washington's 5 sacks.

Washington (NFC)	0	35	0	7	—	42
Denver (AFC)	10	0	0	0	—	10

Den — Nattiel 56 pass from Elway (Karlis kick) (1:57)
Den — FG Karlis 24 (5:51)
Wash — Sanders 80 pass from Williams (Haji-Sheikh kick) (0:53)
Wash — Clark 27 pass from Williams (Haji-Sheikh kick) (4:45)
Wash — Smith 58 run (Haji-Sheikh kick) (8:33)
Wash — Sanders 50 pass from Williams (Haji-Sheikh kick) (11:18)
Wash — Didier 8 pass from Williams (Haji-Sheikh kick) (13:56)
Wash — Smith 4 run (Haji-Sheikh kick) (1:51)

SUPER BOWL XXI

Rose Bowl, Pasadena, California
January 25, 1987, Attendance: 101,063

NEW YORK GIANTS 39, DENVER 20—The NFC champion New York Giants captured their first NFL title since 1956 when they downed the AFC champion Denver Broncos 39-20 in Super Bowl XXI. The victory marked the NFC's fifth NFL title in the past six seasons. The Broncos, behind the passing of quarterback John Elway, who was 13 of 20 for 187 yards in the first half, held a 10-9 lead at intermission, the narrowest half-time margin in Super Bowl history. Denver's Rich Karlis opened the scoring with a Super Bowl record-tying 48-yard field goal. New York drove 78 yards in nine plays on the next series to take a 7-3 lead on quarterback Phil Simms's 6-yard touchdown pass to tight end Zeke Mowatt. The Broncos came right back with a 58-yard scoring drive on six plays capped by Elway's 4-yard touchdown run. The only scoring in the second period was the sack of Elway in the end zone by defensive end George Martin for a New York safety. The Giants produced a key defensive stand early in the second quarter when the Broncos had a first down at the New York 1-yard line, but failed to score on three running plays and Karlis's 23-yard missed field-goal attempt. The Giants took command of the game in the third period en route to a 30-point second half, the most ever scored in one half of Super Bowl play. New York took the lead for good on tight end Mark Bavaro's 13-yard touchdown catch 4:52 into the third period. The nine-play, 63-yard scoring drive included the successful conversion of a fourth-and-1 play on the New York 46-yard line. Denver was limited to only 2 net yards on 10 offensive plays in the third period. Simms set Super Bowl records for most consecutive completions (10) and highest completion percentage (88 percent on 22 completions in 25 attempts). He also passed for 268 yards and 3 touchdowns and was named the game's most valuable player. New York running back Joe Morris was the game's leading rusher with 20 carries for 67 yards. Denver wide receiver Vance Johnson led all receivers with 5 catches for 121 yards.

Denver (AFC)	10	0	0	10	—	20
N.Y. Giants (NFC)	7	2	17	13	—	39

Den — FG Karlis 48 (4:09)
NYG — Mowatt 6 pass from Simms (Allegre kick) (9:33)
Den — Elway 4 run (Karlis kick) (12:54)
NYG — Safety, Martin tackled Elway in end zone (12:14)
NYG — Bavaro 13 pass from Simms (Allegre kick) (4:52)
NYG — FG Allegre 21 (11:06)
NYG — Morris 1 run (Allegre kick) (14:36)
NYG — McConkey 6 pass from Simms (Allegre kick) (4:04)
Den — FG Karlis 28 (8:59)
NYG — Anderson 2 run (kick failed) (10:42)
Den — V. Johnson 47 pass from Elway (Karlis kick) (12:54)

SUPER BOWL XX

Louisiana Superdome, New Orleans, Louisiana
January 26, 1986, Attendance: 73,818

CHICAGO 46, NEW ENGLAND 10—The NFC champion Chicago Bears, seeking their first NFL title since 1963, scored a Super Bowl-record 46 points in downing AFC champion New England 46-10 in Super Bowl XX. The previous record for most points in a Super Bowl was 38, shared by San Francisco in XIX and the Los Angeles Raiders in XVIII. The Bears' league-leading defense tied the Super Bowl record for sacks (7) and limited the Patriots to a record-low 7 rushing yards. New England took the quickest lead in Super Bowl history when Tony Franklin kicked a 36-yard field goal with 1:19 elapsed in the first period. The score came about because of Larry McGrew's fumble recovery at the Chicago 19-yard line. However, the Bears rebounded for a 23-3 first-half lead, while building a yardage advantage of 236 total yards to New England's minus 19. Running back Matt Suhey rushed 8 times for 37 yards, including an 11-yard touchdown run, and caught 1 pass for 24 yards in the first half. After the Patriot's first drive of the second half ended with a punt to the Bears' 4-yard line, Chicago marched 96 yards in nine plays with quarterback Jim McMahon's 1-yard scoring run capping the drive. McMahon became the first quarterback in Super Bowl history to rush for a pair of touchdowns. The Bears completed their scoring via a 28-yard interception return by reserve cornerback Reggie Phillips, a 1-yard run by defensive tackle/fullback William Perry, and a safety when defensive end Henry Waechter tackled Patriots quarterback Steve Grogan in the end zone. Bears defensive end Richard Dent became the fourth defender to be named the game's most valuable player after contributing 1½ sacks. The Bears' victory margin of 36 points was the largest in Super Bowl history, bettering the previous mark of 29 by the Los Angeles Raiders when they topped Washington 38-9 in Game XVIII. McMahon completed 12 of 20 passes for 256 yards before leaving the game in the fourth period with a wrist injury. The NFL's all-time leading rusher, Bears running back Walter Payton, carried 22 times for 61 yards. Wide receiver Willie Gault caught 4 passes for 129 yards, the fourth-most receiving yards in a Super Bowl. Chicago coach Mike Ditka became the second man (Tom Flores of Raiders was the other) to win a Super Bowl ring as a player and as a coach.

Chicago (NFC)	13	10	21	2	—	46
New England (AFC)	3	0	0	7	—	10

NE — FG Franklin 36 (1:19)
Chi — FG Butler 28 (5:40)
Chi — FG Butler 24 (13:34)
Chi — Suhey 11 run (Butler kick) (14:37)
Chi — McMahon 2 run (Butler kick) (7:36)
Chi — FG Butler 24 (15:00)
Chi — McMahon 1 run (Butler kick) (7:38)
Chi — Phillips 28 interception return (Butler kick) (8:44)
Chi — Perry 1 run (Butler kick) (11:38)
NE — Fryar 8 pass from Grogan (Franklin kick) (1:46)
Chi — Safety, Waechter tackled Grogan in end zone (9:24)

SUPER BOWL XIX

Stanford Stadium, Stanford, California
January 20, 1985, Attendance: 84,059

SAN FRANCISCO 38, MIAMI 16—The San Francisco 49ers captured their second Super Bowl title with a dominating offense and a defense that tamed Miami's explosive passing attack. The Dolphins held a 10-7 lead at the end of the first period, which represented the most points scored by two teams in an opening quarter of a Super Bowl. However, the 49ers used excellent field position in the second period to build a 28-16 halftime lead. Running back Roger Craig set a Super Bowl record by scoring 3 touchdowns on pass receptions of 8 and 16 yards and a run of 2 yards. San Francisco's Joe Montana was voted the game's most valuable player. He joined Green Bay's Bart Starr and Pittsburgh's Terry Bradshaw as the only two-time Super Bowl most valuable players. Montana completed 24 of 35 passes for a Super Bowl-record 331 yards and 3 touchdowns, and rushed 5 times for 59 yards, including a 6-yard touchdown. Craig had 58 yards on 15 carries and caught 7 passes for 77 yards. Wendell Tyler rushed 13 times for 65 yards and had 4 catches for 70 yards. Dwight Clark had 6 receptions for 77 yards, while Russ Francis had 5 for 60. San Francisco's 537 total net yards bettered the previous Super Bowl record of 429 yards by Oakland in Super Bowl XI. The 49ers also held a time of possession advantage over the Dolphins of 37:11 to 22:49.

Miami (AFC)	10	6	0	0 —	16
San Francisco (NFC)	7	21	10	0 —	38

Mia — FG von Schamann 37 (7:36)
SF — Monroe 33 pass from Montana (Wersching kick) (11:48)
Mia — D. Johnson 2 pass from Marino (von Schamann kick) (14:15)
SF — Craig 8 pass from Montana (Wersching kick) (3:26)
SF — Montana 6 run (Wersching kick) (8:02)
SF — Craig 2 run (Wersching kick) (12:55)
Mia — FG von Schamann 31 (14:48)
Mia — FG von Schamann 30 (15:00)
SF — FG Wersching 27 (4:48)
SF — Craig 16 pass from Montana (Wersching kick) (8:42)

SUPER BOWL XVIII

Tampa Stadium, Tampa, Florida
January 22, 1984, Attendance: 72,920

LOS ANGELES RAIDERS 38, WASHINGTON 9—The Los Angeles Raiders dominated the Washington Redskins from the beginning in Super Bowl XVIII and achieved the most lopsided victory in Super Bowl history, surpassing Green Bay's 35-10 win over Kansas City in Super Bowl I. The Raiders took a 7-0 lead 4:52 into the game when Derrick Jensen blocked Jeff Hayes's punt and recovered it in the end zone for a touchdown. With 9:14 remaining in the first half, Raiders quarterback Jim Plunkett fired a 12-yard touchdown pass to wide receiver Cliff Branch to complete a three-play, 65-yard drive. Washington cut the Raiders' lead to 14-3 on a 24-yard field goal by Mark Moseley. With seven seconds left in the first half, Raiders linebacker Jack Squirek intercepted Joe Theismann's pass at the Redskins' 5-yard line and ran it in for a touchdown to give Los Angeles a 21-3 halftime lead. In the third period, running back Marcus Allen, who rushed for a Super Bowl-record 191 yards on 20 carries, increased the Raiders' lead to 35-9 on touchdown runs of 5 and 74 yards, the latter erasing the Super Bowl record of 58 yards set by Baltimore's Tom Matte in Game III. Allen was named the game's most valuable player. The victory over Washington raised Raiders coach Tom Flores' playoff record to 8-1, including a 27-10 win against Philadelphia in Super Bowl XV. The 38 points scored by the Raiders were the highest total by a Super Bowl team. The previous high was 35 points by Green Bay in Game I.

Washington (NFC)	0	3	6	0 —	9
L.A. Raiders (AFC)	7	14	14	3 —	38

Raiders — Jensen recovered blocked punt in end zone (Bahr kick) (4:52)
Raiders — Branch 12 pass from Plunkett (Bahr kick) (5:46)
Wash — FG Moseley 24 (11:55)
Raiders — Squirek 5 interception return (Bahr kick) (14:53)
Wash — Riggins 1 run (kick blocked) (4:08)
Raiders — Allen 5 run (Bahr kick) (7:54)
Raiders — Allen 74 run (Bahr kick) (15:00)
Raiders — FG Bahr 21 (12:36)

SUPER BOWL XVII

Rose Bowl, Pasadena, California
January 30, 1983, Attendance: 103,667

WASHINGTON 27, MIAMI 17—Fullback John Riggins ran for a Super Bowl-record 166 yards on 38 carries to spark Washington to a 27-17 victory over AFC champion Miami. It was Riggins's fourth straight 100-yard rushing game during the playoffs, also a record. The win marked Washington's first NFL title since 1942, and was only the second time in Super Bowl history NFL/NFC teams scored consecutive victories (Green Bay did it in Super Bowls I and II and San Francisco won Super Bowl XVI). The Redskins, under second-year head coach Joe Gibbs, used a balanced offense that accounted for 400 total yards (a Super Bowl-record 276 yards rushing and 124 passing), second in Super Bowl history to 429 yards by Oakland in Super Bowl XI. The Dolphins built a 17-10 halftime lead on a 76-yard touchdown pass from quarterback David Woodley to wide receiver Jimmy Cefalo 6:49 into the first period, a 20-yard field goal by Uwe von Schamann with 6:00 left in the half, and a Super Bowl-record 98-yard kickoff return by Fulton Walker with 1:38 remaining. Washington had tied the score at 10-10 with 1:51 left on a 4-yard touchdown pass from Joe Theismann to wide receiver Alvin Garrett. Mark Moseley started the Redskins' scoring with a 31-yard field goal late in the first period, and added a 20-yard kick midway through the third period to cut the Dolphins' lead to 17-13. Riggins, who was voted the game's most valuable player, gave Washington its first lead of the game with 10:01 left when he ran 43 yards off left tackle for a touchdown in a fourth-and-1 situation. Wide receiver Charlie Brown caught a 6-yard scoring pass from Theismann with 1:55 left to complete the scoring. The Dolphins managed only 176 yards (142 in first half). Theismann completed 15 of 23 passes for 143 yards, with 2 touchdowns and 2 interceptions. For Miami, Woodley was 4 of 14 for 97 yards, with 1 touchdown, and 1 interception. Don Strock was 0 for 3 in relief.

Miami (AFC)	7	10	0	0 —	17
Washington (NFC)	0	10	3	14 —	27

Mia — Cefalo 76 pass from Woodley (von Schamann kick) (6:49)
Wash — FG Moseley 31 (0:21)
Mia — FG von Schamann 20 (9:00)
Wash — Garrett 4 pass from Theismann (Moseley kick) (13:09)
Mia — Walker 98 kickoff return (von Schamann kick) (13:22)
Wash — FG Moseley 20 (6:51)
Wash — Riggins 43 run (Moseley kick) (4:59)
Wash — Brown 6 pass from Theismann (Moseley kick) (13:05)

SUPER BOWL XVI

Pontiac Silverdome, Pontiac, Michigan
January 24, 1982, Attendance: 81,270

SAN FRANCISCO 26, CINCINNATI 21—Ray Wersching's Super Bowl record-tying 4 field goals and Joe Montana's controlled passing helped lift the San Francisco 49ers to their first NFL championship with a 26-21 victory over Cincinnati. The 49ers built a game-record 20-0 halftime lead via Montana's 1-yard touchdown run, which capped an 11-play, 68-yard drive; fullback Earl Cooper's 11-yard scoring pass from Montana, which climaxed a Super Bowl record 92-yard drive on 12 plays; and Wersching's 22- and 26-yard field goals. The Bengals rebounded in the second half, closing the gap to 20-14 on quarterback Ken Anderson's 5-yard run and Dan Ross's 4-yard reception from Anderson, who established Super Bowl passing records for completions (25) and completion percentage (73.5 percent on 25 of 34). Wersching added early fourth-period field goals of 40 and 23 yards to increase the 49ers' lead to 26-14. The Bengals managed to score on an Anderson-to-Ross 3-yard pass with only 16 seconds remaining. Ross set a Super Bowl record with 11 receptions for 104 yards. Montana, the game's most valuable player, completed 14 of 22 passes for 157 yards. Cincinnati compiled 356 yards to San Francisco's 275, which marked the first time in Super Bowl history that the team that gained the most yards from scrimmage lost the game.

San Francisco (NFC)	7	13	0	6 —	26
Cincinnati (AFC)	0	0	7	14 —	21

SF — Montana 1 run (Wersching kick) (9:08)
SF — Cooper 11 pass from Montana (Wersching kick) (8:07)
SF — FG Wersching 22 (14:45)
SF — FG Wersching 26 (14:58)
Cin — Anderson 5 run (Breech kick) (3:35)
Cin — Ross 4 pass from Anderson (Breech kick) (4:54)
SF — FG Wersching 40 (9:35)
SF — FG Wersching 23 (13:03)
Cin — Ross 3 pass from Anderson (Breech kick) (14:44)

SUPER BOWL XV

Louisiana Superdome, New Orleans, Louisiana
January 25, 1981, Attendance: 76,135

OAKLAND 27, PHILADELPHIA 10—Jim Plunkett passed for 3 touchdowns, including an 80-yard strike to Kenny King, as the Raiders became the first wild-card team to win the Super Bowl. Plunkett's touchdown bomb to King—the longest play in Super Bowl history—gave Oakland a decisive 14-0 lead with nine seconds left in the first period. Linebacker Rod Martin had set up Oakland's first touchdown, a 2-yard reception by Cliff Branch, with a 17-yard interception return to the Eagles' 30-yard line. The Eagles never recovered from that early deficit, managing only Tony Franklin's field goal (30 yards) and an 8-yard touchdown pass from Ron Jaworski to Keith Krepfle. Plunkett, who became a starter in the sixth game of the season, completed 13 of 21 for 261 yards and was named the game's most valuable player. Oakland won 9 of 11 games with Plunkett starting, but that was good enough only for second place in the AFC West, although they tied division winner San Diego with an 11-5 record. The Raiders, who had previously won Super Bowl XI over Minnesota, had to win three playoff games to get to the championship game. Oakland defeated Houston 27-7 at home followed by road victories over Cleveland (14-12) and San Diego (34-27). Oakland's Mark van Eeghen was the game's leading rusher with 75 yards on 18 carries. Philadelphia's Wilbert Montgomery led all receivers with 6 receptions for 91 yards. Branch had 5 for 67 and Harold Carmichael of Philadelphia 5 for 83. Martin finished the game with 3 interceptions, a Super Bowl record.

Oakland (AFC)	14	0	10	3 —	27
Philadelphia (NFC)	0	3	0	7 —	10

Oak — Branch 2 pass from Plunkett (Bahr kick) (6:04)
Oak — King 80 pass from Plunkett (Bahr kick) (14:51)
Phil — FG Franklin 30 (4:32)
Oak — Branch 29 pass from Plunkett (Bahr kick) (2:36)
Oak — FG Bahr 46 (10:25)
Phil — Krepfle 8 pass from Jaworski (Franklin kick) (1:01)
Oak — FG Bahr 35 (6:31)

SUPER BOWL XIV

Rose Bowl, Pasadena, California
January 20, 1980, Attendance: 103,985

PITTSBURGH 31, LOS ANGELES 19—Terry Bradshaw completed 14 of 21 passes for 309 yards and set two passing records as the Steelers became the first team to win four Super Bowls. Despite 3 interceptions by the Rams, Bradshaw kept his poise and brought the Steelers from behind twice in the second half. Trailing 13-10 at halftime, Pittsburgh went ahead 17-13 when Bradshaw hit Lynn Swann with a 47-yard touchdown pass after 2:48 of the third quarter. On the Rams' next possession Vince Ferragamo, who completed 15 of 25 passes for 212 yards, responded with a 50-yard pass to Billy Waddy that moved Los Angeles from its 26 to the Steelers' 24. On the following play, Lawrence McCutcheon connected with Ron Smith on a halfback option pass that gave the Rams a 19-17 lead. On Pittsburgh's initial possession of the final period, Bradshaw lofted a 73-yard scoring pass to John Stallworth to put the Steelers in front to stay 24-19. Franco Harris scored on a 1-yard run later in the quarter to seal the verdict. A 45-yard pass from Bradshaw to Stallworth was the key play in the drive to Harris's score. Bradshaw, the game's most valuable player for the second straight year, set career Super Bowl records for most touchdown passes (9) and most passing yards (932). Larry Anderson gave the Steelers excellent field position throughout the game with 5 kickoff returns for a record 162 yards.

Los Angeles (NFC)	7	6	6	0 —	19
Pittsburgh (AFC)	3	7	7	14 —	31

Pitt — FG Bahr 41 (7:29)
LA — Bryant 1 run (Corral kick) (12:16)

Pitt — Harris 1 run (Bahr kick) (2:08)
LA — FG Corral 31 (7:39)
LA — FG Corral 45 (14:46)
Pitt — Swann 47 pass from Bradshaw (Bahr kick) (2:48)
LA — Smith 24 pass from McCutcheon (kick failed) (4:45)
Pitt — Stallworth 73 pass from Bradshaw (Bahr kick) (2:56)
Pitt — Harris 1 run (Bahr kick) (13:11)

SUPER BOWL XIII

Orange Bowl, Miami, Florida
January 21, 1979, Attendance: 79,484

PITTSBURGH 35, DALLAS 31—Terry Bradshaw passed for a record 4 touchdowns to lead the Steelers to victory. The Steelers became the first team to win three Super Bowls, mostly because of Bradshaw's accurate arm. Bradshaw, voted the game's most valuable player, completed 17 of 30 passes for 318 yards, a personal high. Four of those passes went for touchdowns—2 to John Stallworth and the third, with 26 seconds remaining in the second period, to Rocky Bleier for a 21-14 halftime lead. The Cowboys scored twice before intermission on Roger Staubach's 39-yard pass to Tony Hill and a 37-yard fumble return by linebacker Mike Hegman, who stole the ball from Bradshaw. The Steelers broke open the contest with 2 touchdowns in a span of 19 seconds midway through the final period. Franco Harris rambled 22 yards up the middle to give the Steelers a 28-17 lead with 7:10 left. Pittsburgh got the ball right back when Randy White fumbled the kickoff and Dennis Winston recovered for the Steelers. On first down, Bradshaw fired his fourth touchdown pass, an 18-yard pass to Lynn Swann to boost the Steelers' lead to 35-17 with 6:51 to play. The Cowboys refused to let the Steelers run away with the contest. Staubach connected with Billy Joe DuPree on a 7-yard scoring pass with 2:23 left. Then the Cowboys recovered an onside kick and Staubach took them in for another score, passing 4 yards to Butch Johnson with 22 seconds remaining. Bleier recovered another onside kick with 17 seconds left to seal the victory for the Steelers.

Pittsburgh (AFC)	7	14	0	14	—	35
Dallas (NFC)	7	7	3	14	—	31

Pitt — Stallworth 28 pass from Bradshaw (Gerela kick) (5:13)
Dall — Hill 39 pass from Staubach (Septien kick) (15:00)
Dall — Hegman 37 fumble recovery return (Septien kick) (2:52)
Pitt — Stallworth 75 pass from Bradshaw (Gerela kick) (4:35)
Pitt — Bleier 7 pass from Bradshaw (Gerela kick) (14:34)
Dall — FG Septien 27 (12:24)
Pitt — Harris 22 run (Gerela kick) (7:50)
Pitt — Swann 18 pass from Bradshaw (Gerela kick) (8:09)
Dall — DuPree 7 pass from Staubach (Septien kick) (12:37)
Dall — B. Johnson 4 pass from Staubach (Septien kick) (14:38)

SUPER BOWL XII

Louisiana Superdome, New Orleans, Louisiana
January 15, 1978, Attendance: 75,583

DALLAS 27, DENVER 10—The Cowboys evened their Super Bowl record at 2-2 by defeating Denver before a sellout crowd of 75,583, plus 102,010,000 television viewers, the largest audience ever to watch a sporting event. Dallas converted 2 interceptions into 10 points and Efren Herrera added a 35-yard field goal for a 13-0 halftime advantage. In the third period Craig Morton engineered a drive to the Cowboys' 30 and Jim Turner's 47-yard field goal made the score 13-3. After an exchange of punts, Butch Johnson made a spectacular diving catch in the end zone to complete a 45-yard pass from Roger Staubach and put the Cowboys ahead 20-3. Following Rick Upchurch's 67-yard kickoff return, Norris Weese guided the Broncos to a touchdown to cut the Dallas lead to 20-10. Dallas clinched the victory when running back Robert Newhouse tossed a 29-yard touchdown pass to Golden Richards with 7:04 remaining in the game. It was the first pass thrown by Newhouse since 1975. Harvey Martin and Randy White, who were named co-most valuable players, led the Cowboys' defense, which recovered 4 fumbles and intercepted 4 passes.

Dallas (NFC)	10	3	7	7	—	27
Denver (AFC)	0	0	10	0	—	10

Dall — Dorsett 3 run (Herrera kick) (10:31)
Dall — FG Herrera 35 (13:29)
Dall — FG Herrera 43 (3:44)
Den — FG Turner 47 (2:28)
Dall — Johnson 45 pass from Staubach (Herrera kick) (8:01)
Den — Lytle 1 run (Turner kick) (9:21)
Dall — Richards 29 pass from Newhouse (Herrera kick) (7:56)

SUPER BOWL XI

Rose Bowl, Pasadena, California
January 9, 1977, Attendance: 103,438

OAKLAND 32, MINNESOTA 14—The Raiders won their first NFL championship before a record Super Bowl crowd plus 81 million television viewers, the largest audience ever to watch a sporting event. The Raiders gained a record-breaking 429 yards, including running back Clarence Davis's 137 rushing yards. Wide receiver Fred Biletnikoff made 4 key receptions, which earned him the game's most valuable player trophy. Oakland scored on three successive possessions in the second quarter to build a 16-0 halftime lead. Errol Mann's 24-yard field goal opened the scoring, then the AFC champions put together drives of 64 and 35 yards, scoring on a 1-yard pass from Ken Stabler to Dave Casper and a 1-yard run by Pete Banaszak. The Raiders increased their lead to 19-0 on a 40-yard field goal in the third quarter, but Minnesota responded with a 12-play, 58-yard drive late in the period, with Fran Tarkenton passing 8 yards to wide receiver Sammy White to cut the deficit to 19-7. Two fourth-quarter interceptions clinched the title for the Raiders. One set up Banaszak's second touchdown run, the other resulted in cornerback Willie Brown's Super Bowl-record 75-yard interception return.

Oakland (AFC)	0	16	3	13	—	32
Minnesota (NFC)	0	0	7	7	—	14

Oak — FG Mann 24 (0:48)
Oak — Casper 1 pass from Stabler (Mann kick) (7:50)
Oak — Banaszak 1 run (kick failed) (11:27)
Oak — FG Mann 40 (9:44)
Minn — S. White 8 pass from Tarkenton (Cox kick) (14:13)
Oak — Banaszak 2 run (Mann kick) (7:21)
Oak — Brown 75 interception return (kick failed) (9:17)
Minn — Voigt 13 pass from Lee (Cox kick) (14:35)

SUPER BOWL X

Orange Bowl, Miami, Florida
January 18, 1976, Attendance: 80,187

PITTSBURGH 21, DALLAS 17—The Steelers won the Super Bowl for the second year in a row on Terry Bradshaw's 64-yard touchdown pass to Lynn Swann and an aggressive defense that snuffed out a late rally by the Cowboys with an end-zone interception on the final play of the game. In the fourth quarter, Pittsburgh ran on fourth down and gave up the ball on the Cowboys' 39 with 1:22 to play. Roger Staubach ran and passed for 2 first downs but his last desperation pass was picked off by Glen Edwards. Dallas's scoring was the result of 2 touchdown passes by Staubach, one to Drew Pearson for 29 yards and the other to Percy Howard for 34 yards. Toni Fritsch had a 36-yard field goal. The Steelers scored on 2 touchdown passes by Bradshaw, 1 to Randy Grossman for 7 yards and the long bomb to Swann. Roy Gerela had 36- and 18-yard field goals. Reggie Harrison blocked a punt through the end zone for a safety. Swann set a Super Bowl record by gaining 161 yards on his 4 receptions.

Dallas (NFC)	7	3	0	7	—	17
Pittsburgh (AFC)	7	0	0	14	—	21

Dall — D. Pearson 29 pass from Staubach (Fritsch kick) (4:36)
Pitt — Grossman 7 pass from Bradshaw (Gerela kick) (9:03)
Dall — FG Fritsch 36 (0:15)
Pitt — Safety, Harrison blocked Hoopes's punt through end zone (3:32)
Pitt — FG Gerela 36 (6:19)
Pitt — FG Gerela 18 (8:23)
Pitt — Swann 64 pass from Bradshaw (kick failed) (11:58)
Dall — P. Howard 34 pass from Staubach (Fritsch kick) (13:12)

SUPER BOWL IX

Tulane Stadium, New Orleans, Louisiana
January 12, 1975, Attendance: 80,997

PITTSBURGH 16, MINNESOTA 6—AFC champion Pittsburgh, in its initial Super Bowl appearance, and NFC champion Minnesota, making a third bid for its first Super Bowl title, struggled through a first half in which the only score was produced by the Steelers' defense when Dwight White downed Vikings' quarterback Fran Tarkenton in the end zone for a safety 7:49 into the second period. The Steelers forced another break and took advantage on the second-half kickoff when Minnesota's Bill Brown fumbled and Marv Kellum recovered for Pittsburgh on the Vikings' 30. After Rocky Bleier failed to gain on first down, Franco Harris carried 3 consecutive times for 24 yards, a loss of 3, and a 9-yard touchdown and a 9-0 lead. Though its offense was completely stymied by Pittsburgh's defense, Minnesota managed to move into a threatening position after 4:27 of the final period when Matt Blair blocked Bobby Walden's punt and Terry Brown recovered the ball in the end zone for a touchdown. Fred Cox's kick failed and the Steelers led 9-6. Pittsburgh wasted no time putting the victory away. The Steelers took the ensuing kickoff and marched 66 yards in 11 plays, climaxed by Terry Bradshaw's 4-yard scoring pass to Larry Brown with 3:31 left. Pittsburgh's defense permitted Minnesota only 119 yards total offense, including a Super Bowl low of 17 rushing yards. The Steelers, meanwhile, gained 333 yards, including Harris's record 158 yards on 34 carries.

Pittsburgh (AFC)	0	2	7	7	—	16
Minnesota (NFC)	0	0	0	6	—	6

Pitt — Safety, White downed Tarkenton in end zone (7:49)
Pitt — Harris 9 run (Gerela kick) (1:35)
Minn — T. Brown recovered blocked punt in end zone (kick failed) (4:27)
Pitt — L. Brown 4 pass from Bradshaw (Gerela kick) (11:29)

SUPER BOWL VIII

Rice Stadium, Houston, Texas
January 13, 1974, Attendance: 71,882

MIAMI 24, MINNESOTA 7—The defending NFL champion Dolphins, representing the AFC for the third straight year, scored the first two times they had possession on marches of 62 and 56 yards while the Miami defense limited the Vikings to only seven plays in the first period. Larry Csonka climaxed the initial 10-play drive with a 5-yard touchdown bolt through right guard after 5:27 had elapsed. Four plays later, Miami began another 10-play scoring drive, which ended with Jim Kiick bursting 1 yard through the middle for another touchdown after 13:38 of the period. Garo Yepremian added a 28-yard field goal midway in the second period for a 17-0 Miami lead. Minnesota then drove from its 20 to a second-and-2 situation on the Miami 7 yard line with 1:18 left in the half. But on two plays, Miami limited Oscar Reed to 1 yard. On fourth-and-1 from the 6, Reed went over right tackle, but Dolphins middle linebacker Nick Buoniconti jarred the ball loose and Jake Scott recovered for Miami to halt the Minnesota threat. The Vikings were unable to muster enough offense in the second half to threaten the Dolphins. Csonka rushed 33 times for a Super Bowl-record 145 yards. Bob Griese of Miami completed 6 of 7 passes for 73 yards.

Minnesota (NFC)	0	0	0	7	— 7
Miami (AFC)	14	3	7	0	— 24

Mia — Csonka 5 run (Yepremian kick) (9:33)
Mia — Kiick 1 run (Yepremian kick) (13:38)
Mia — FG Yepremian 28 (8:58)
Mia — Csonka 2 run (Yepremian kick) (6:16)
Minn — Tarkenton 4 run (Cox kick) (1:35)

SUPER BOWL VII

Memorial Coliseum, Los Angeles, California
January 14, 1973, Attendance: 90,182

MIAMI 14, WASHINGTON 7—The Dolphins played virtually perfect football in the first half as their defense permitted the Redskins to cross midfield only once and their offense turned good field position into 2 touchdowns. On its third possession, Miami opened its first scoring drive from the Dolphins' 37 yard line. An 18-yard pass from Bob Griese to Paul Warfield preceded by three plays Griese's 28-yard touchdown pass to Howard Twilley. After Washington moved from its 17 to the Miami 48 with two minutes remaining in the first half, Dolphins linebacker Nick Buoniconti intercepted Billy Kilmer's pass at the Miami 41 and returned it to the Washington 27. Jim Kiick ran for 3 yards, Larry Csonka for 3, Griese passed to Jim Mandich for 19, and Kiick gained 1 to the 1-yard line. With 18 seconds left until intermission, Kiick scored from the 1. Washington's only touchdown came with 2:07 left in the game and resulted from a misplayed field-goal attempt and fumble by Garo Yepremian, with the Redskins' Mike Bass picking the ball out of the air and running 49 yards for the score. Dolphins safety Jake Scott, who had 2 interceptions, including 1 in the end zone to kill a Redskins' drive, was voted the game's most valuable player.

Miami (AFC)	7	7	0	0	— 14
Washington (NFC)	0	0	0	7	— 7

Mia — Twilley 28 pass from Griese (Yepremian kick) (14:59)
Mia — Kiick 1 run (Yepremian kick) (14:42)
Wash — Bass 49 fumble recovery return (Knight kick) (12:53)

SUPER BOWL VI

Tulane Stadium, New Orleans, Louisiana
January 16, 1972, Attendance: 81,023

DALLAS 24, MIAMI 3—The Cowboys rushed for a record 252 yards and their defense limited the Dolphins to a low of 185 yards while not permitting a touchdown for the first time in Super Bowl history. Dallas converted Chuck Howley's recovery of Larry Csonka's first fumble of the season into a 3-0 advantage and led at halftime 10-3. After Dallas received the second-half kickoff, Duane Thomas led a 71-yard march in eight plays for a 17-3 margin. Howley intercepted Bob Griese's pass at the 50 and returned it to the Miami 9 early in the fourth period, and three plays later Roger Staubach passed 7 yards to Mike Ditka for the final touchdown. Thomas rushed for 95 yards and Walt Garrison gained 74. Staubach, voted the game's most valuable player, completed 12 of 19 passes for 119 yards and 2 touchdowns.

Dallas (NFC)	3	7	7	7	— 24
Miami (AFC)	0	3	0	0	— 3

Dall — FG Clark 9 (13:37)
Dall — Alworth 7 pass from Staubach (Clark kick) (13:45)
Mia — FG Yepremian 31 (14:56)
Dall — D. Thomas 3 run (Clark kick) (5:17)
Dall — Ditka 7 pass from Staubach (Clark kick) (3:18)

SUPER BOWL V

Orange Bowl, Miami, Florida
January 17, 1971, Attendance: 79,204

BALTIMORE 16, DALLAS 13—A 32-yard field goal by rookie kicker Jim O'Brien brought the Baltimore Colts a victory over the Dallas Cowboys in the final five seconds of Super Bowl V. The game between the champions of the AFC and NFC was played on artificial turf for the first time. Dallas led 13-6 at the half but interceptions by Rick Volk and Mike Curtis set up a Baltimore touchdown and O'Brien's decisive kick in the fourth period. Earl Morrall relieved an injured Johnny Unitas late in the first half, although Unitas completed the Colts' only scoring pass. It caromed off receiver Eddie Hinton's fingertips, off Dallas defensive back Mel Renfro, and finally settled into the grasp of John Mackey, who went 45 yards to score on a 75-yard play.

Baltimore (AFC)	0	6	0	10	— 16
Dallas (NFC)	3	10	0	0	— 13

Dall — FG Clark 14 (9:28)
Dall — FG Clark 30 (0:08)
Balt — Mackey 75 pass from Unitas (kick blocked) (0:05)
Dall — Thomas 7 pass from Morton (Clark kick) (7:07)
Balt — Nowatzke 2 run (O'Brien kick) (7:25)
Balt — FG O'Brien 32 (14:55)

SUPER BOWL IV

Tulane Stadium, New Orleans, Louisiana
January 11, 1970, Attendance: 80,562

KANSAS CITY 23, MINNESOTA 7—The AFL squared the Super Bowl at two games apiece with the NFL, building a 16-0 halftime lead behind Len Dawson's superb quarterbacking and a powerful defense. Dawson, the fourth consecutive quarterback to be chosen the Super Bowl's top player, called an almost flawless game, completing 12 of 17 passes and hitting Otis Taylor on a 46-yard play for the final Chiefs touchdown. The Kansas City defense limited Minnesota's strong rushing game to 67 yards and had 3 interceptions and 2 fumble recoveries. The crowd of 80,562 set a Super Bowl record, as did the gross receipts of $3,817,872.69.

Minnesota (NFL)	0	0	7	0	— 7
Kansas City (AFL)	3	13	7	0	— 23

KC — FG Stenerud 48 (8:08)
KC — FG Stenerud 32 (1:40)
KC — FG Stenerud 25 (7:08)
KC — Garrett 5 run (Stenerud kick) (9:26)
Minn — Osborn 4 run (Cox kick) (10:28)
KC — Taylor 46 pass from Dawson (Stenerud kick) (13:38)

SUPER BOWL III

Orange Bowl, Miami, Florida
January 12, 1969, Attendance: 75,389

NEW YORK JETS 16, BALTIMORE 7—Jets quarterback Joe Namath "guaranteed" victory on the Thursday before the game, then went out and led the AFL to its first Super Bowl victory over a Baltimore team that had lost only once in 16 games all season. Namath, chosen the outstanding player, completed 17 of 28 passes for 206 yards and directed a steady attack that dominated the NFL champions after the Jets' defense had intercepted Colts quarterback Earl Morrall 3 times in the first half. The Jets had 337 total yards, including 121 rushing yards by Matt Snell. Johnny Unitas, who had missed most of the season with a sore elbow, came off the bench and led Baltimore to its only touchdown late in the fourth quarter after New York led 16-0.

New York Jets (AFL)	0	7	6	3	— 16
Baltimore (NFL)	0	0	0	7	— 7

NYJ — Snell 4 run (Turner kick) (5:57)
NYJ — FG Turner 32 (4:52)
NYJ — FG Turner 30 (11:02)
NYJ — FG Turner 9 (1:34)
Balt — Hill 1 run (Michaels kick) (11:41)

SUPER BOWL II

Orange Bowl, Miami, Florida
January 14, 1968, Attendance: 75,546

GREEN BAY 33, OAKLAND 14—Green Bay, after winning its third consecutive NFL championship, won the Super Bowl title for the second straight year, defeating the AFL champion Raiders in a game that drew the first $3-million gate in football history. Bart Starr again was chosen the game's most valuable player as he completed 13 of 24 passes for 202 yards and 1 touchdown and directed a Packers' attack that was in control all the way after building a 16-7 halftime lead. Don Chandler kicked 4 field goals and all-pro cornerback Herb Adderley capped the Green Bay scoring with a 60-yard interception return. The game marked the last for Vince Lombardi as Packers coach, ending nine years at Green Bay in which he won six Western Conference championships, five NFL championships, and two Super Bowls.

Green Bay (NFL)	3	13	10	7	— 33
Oakland (AFL)	0	7	0	7	— 14

GB — FG Chandler 39 (5:07)
GB — FG Chandler 20 (3:08)
GB — Dowler 62 pass from Starr (Chandler kick) (4:10)
Oak — Miller 23 pass from Lamonica (Blanda kick) (8:45)
GB — FG Chandler 43 (14:59)
GB — Anderson 2 run (Chandler kick) (9:06)
GB — FG Chandler 31 (14:58)
GB — Adderley 60 interception return (Chandler kick) (3:57)
Oak — Miller 23 pass from Lamonica (Blanda kick) (5:47)

SUPER BOWL I

Memorial Coliseum, Los Angeles, California
January 15, 1967, Attendance: 61,946

GREEN BAY 35, KANSAS CITY 10—The Green Bay Packers opened the Super Bowl series by defeating the AFL champion Chiefs behind the passing of Bart Starr, the receiving of Max McGee, and a key interception by all-pro safety Willie Wood. Green Bay broke open the game with 3 second-half touchdowns, the first of which was set up by Wood's 50-yard return of an interception. McGee, filling in for ailing Boyd Dowler after having caught only 4 passes all season, caught 7 from Starr for 138 yards and 2 touchdowns. Elijah Pitts ran for 2 other scores. The Chiefs' 10 points came in the second quarter, the only touchdown on a 7-yard pass from Len Dawson to Curtis McClinton. Starr completed 16 of 23 passes for 250 yards and 2 touchdowns and was chosen the most valuable player. The Packers collected $15,000 per man and the Chiefs $7,500—the largest single-game shares in the history of team sports.

Kansas City (AFL)	0	10	0	0	— 10
Green Bay (NFL)	7	7	14	7	— 35

GB — McGee 37 pass from Starr (Chandler kick) (8:56)
KC — McClinton 7 pass from Dawson (Mercer kick) (4:20)
GB — Taylor 14 run (Chandler kick) (10:23)
KC — FG Mercer 31 (14:06)
GB — Pitts 5 run (Chandler kick) (2:27)
GB — McGee 13 pass from Starr (Chandler kick) (14:09)
GB — Pitts 1 run (Chandler kick) (8:25)

AFC CHAMPIONSHIP GAME RESULTS

Includes AFL Championship Games (1960-69)

Season	Date	Winner (Share)	Loser (Share)	Score	Site	Attendance
1999	Jan. 23	Tennessee ($33,000)	Jacksonville ($33,000)	33-14	Jacksonville	75,206
1998	Jan. 17	Denver ($32,500)	N.Y. Jets ($32,500)	23-10	Denver	75,482
1997	Jan. 11	Denver ($30,000)	Pittsburgh ($30,000)	24-21	Pittsburgh	61,382
1996	Jan. 12	New England ($29,000)	Jacksonville ($29,000)	20-6	New England	60,190
1995	Jan. 14	Pittsburgh ($27,000)	Indianapolis ($27,000)	20-16	Pittsburgh	61,062
1994	Jan. 15	San Diego ($26,000)	Pittsburgh ($26,000)	17-13	Pittsburgh	61,545
1993	Jan. 23	Buffalo ($23,500)	Kansas City ($23,500)	30-13	Buffalo	76,642
1992	Jan. 17	Buffalo ($18,000)	Miami ($18,000)	29-10	Miami	72,703
1991	Jan. 12	Buffalo ($18,000)	Denver ($18,000)	10-7	Buffalo	80,272
1990	Jan. 20	Buffalo ($18,000)	L.A. Raiders ($18,000)	51-3	Buffalo	80,325
1989	Jan. 14	Denver ($18,000)	Cleveland ($18,000)	37-21	Denver	76,046
1988	Jan. 8	Cincinnati ($18,000)	Buffalo ($18,000)	21-10	Cincinnati	59,747
1987	Jan. 17	Denver ($18,000)	Cleveland ($18,000)	38-33	Denver	76,197
1986	Jan. 11	Denver ($18,000)	Cleveland ($18,000)	23-20*	Cleveland	79,973
1985	Jan. 12	New England ($18,000)	Miami ($18,000)	31-14	Miami	75,662
1984	Jan. 6	Miami ($18,000)	Pittsburgh ($18,000)	45-28	Miami	76,029
1983	Jan. 8	L.A. Raiders ($18,000)	Seattle ($18,000)	30-14	Los Angeles	91,445
1982	Jan. 23	Miami ($18,000)	N.Y. Jets ($18,000)	14-0	Miami	67,396
1981	Jan. 10	Cincinnati ($9,000)	San Diego ($9,000)	27-7	Cincinnati	46,302
1980	Jan. 11	Oakland ($9,000)	San Diego ($9,000)	34-27	San Diego	52,675
1979	Jan. 6	Pittsburgh ($9,000)	Houston ($9,000)	27-13	Pittsburgh	50,475
1978	Jan. 7	Pittsburgh ($9,000)	Houston ($9,000)	34-5	Pittsburgh	50,725
1977	Jan. 1	Denver ($9,000)	Oakland ($9,000)	20-17	Denver	75,044
1976	Dec. 26	Oakland ($8,500)	Pittsburgh ($5,500)	24-7	Oakland	53,821
1975	Jan. 4	Pittsburgh ($8,500)	Oakland ($5,500)	16-10	Pittsburgh	50,609
1974	Dec. 29	Pittsburgh ($8,500)	Oakland ($5,500)	24-13	Oakland	53,800
1973	Dec. 30	Miami ($8,500)	Oakland ($5,500)	27-10	Miami	79,325
1972	Dec. 31	Miami ($8,500)	Pittsburgh ($5,500)	21-17	Pittsburgh	50,845
1971	Jan. 2	Miami ($8,500)	Baltimore ($5,500)	21-0	Miami	76,622
1970	Jan. 3	Baltimore ($8,500)	Oakland ($5,500)	27-17	Baltimore	54,799
1969	Jan. 4	Kansas City ($7,755)	Oakland ($6,252)	17-7	Oakland	53,564
1968	Dec. 29	N.Y. Jets ($7,007)	Oakland ($5,349)	27-23	New York	62,627
1967	Dec. 31	Oakland ($6,321)	Houston ($4,996)	40-7	Oakland	53,330
1966	Jan. 1	Kansas City ($5,309)	Buffalo ($3,799)	31-7	Buffalo	42,080
1965	Dec. 26	Buffalo ($5,189)	San Diego ($3,447)	23-0	San Diego	30,361
1964	Dec. 26	Buffalo ($2,668)	San Diego ($1,738)	20-7	Buffalo	40,242
1963	Jan. 5	San Diego ($2,498)	Boston ($1,596)	51-10	San Diego	30,127
1962	Dec. 23	Dallas ($2,206)	Houston ($1,471)	20-17*	Houston	37,981
1961	Dec. 24	Houston ($1,792)	San Diego ($1,111)	10-3	San Diego	29,556
1960	Jan. 1	Houston ($1,025)	L.A. Chargers ($718)	24-16	Houston	32,183

**Sudden death overtime*

AFC CHAMPIONSHIP GAME COMPOSITE STANDINGS

	W	L	Pct.	Pts.	OP
Cincinnati Bengals	2	0	1.000	48	17
Denver Broncos	6	1	.857	172	132
Buffalo Bills	6	2	.750	180	92
Kansas City Chiefs*	3	1	.750	81	61
Miami Dolphins	5	2	.714	152	115
New England Patriots**	2	1	.667	61	71
Pittsburgh Steelers	5	5	.500	207	188
Tennessee Titans##	3	4	.429	109	154
Indianapolis Colts#	1	2	.333	43	58
New York Jets	1	2	.333	37	60
Oakland/L.A. Raiders	4	8	.333	228	264
San Diego Chargers***	2	6	.250	128	161
Seattle Seahawks	0	1	.000	14	30
Jacksonville Jaguars	0	2	.000	20	53
Cleveland Browns	0	3	.000	74	98

**One game played when franchise was in Dallas (Texans). (Won 20-17)*

***One game played when franchise was in Boston. (Lost 51-10)*

****One game played when franchise was in Los Angeles. (Lost 24-16)*

#Two games played when franchise was in Baltimore. (Won 27-17, lost 21-0)

##Six games played when franchise was in Houston and known as Oilers. (Won 2, lost 4)

1999 AFC CHAMPIONSHIP GAME

ALLTEL Stadium, Jacksonville, Florida

January 23, 2000, Attendance: 75,206

TENNESSEE 33, JACKSONVILLE 14—Steve McNair rushed for 91 yards and 2 touchdowns and the Titans' defense forced 6 turnovers to earn the franchise's first-ever trip to the Super Bowl. The Jaguars marched 62 yards with their first possession and took a 7-0 lead on Mark Brunell's 7-yard touchdown pass to Kyle Brady. The Titans responded with a 44-yard kickoff return by Derrick Mason to set up McNair's tying touchdown pass to Yancey Thigpen. The Jaguars led 14-7 with 1:34 left in the first half when Reggie Barlow fumbled a punt at his own 19 and Steve Jackson recovered to set up Al Del Greco's 34-yard field goal. A roughing-the-passer and defensive-pass-interference penalties on the Titans' first drive of the second half set up McNair's 1-yard sneak to give the Titans a 17-10 lead. A fumble gave Tennessee excellent field position, but Frank Wycheck fumbled at the Jaguars' 1 and Lonnie Marts recovered. The Titans responded as Josh Evans sacked Brunell for a safety, and Derrick Mason returned the ensuinmg free kick 85 yards for a touchdown, to give Tennessee a 26-10 lead with 4:56 remaining in the third quarter. The Jaguars committed three turnovers in the fourth quarter, one of which led to a 51-yard scramble on third down by McNair to set up his second touchdown and finish the scoring. McNair was 14 of 23 for 112 yards and 1 touchdown, with 1 interception. Brunell was 19 of 38 for 226 yards and 1 touchdown, with 2 interceptions. Fred Taylor had 19 carries for 110 yards.

Tennessee (33)	Offense	Jacksonville (14)
Kevin Dyson	WR	Jimmy Smith
Brad Hopkins	LT	Ben Coleman
Bruce Matthews	LG	Rich Tylski
Kevin Long	C	John Wade
Benji Olson	RG	Zach Wiegert
Jon Runyan	RT	Leon Searcy
Frank Wycheck	TE	Kyle Brady
Yancey Thigpen	WR	Keenan McCardell
Steve McNair	QB	Mark Brunell
Eddie George	RB	Fred Taylor
Jackie Harris	TE	Damon Jones
	Defense	
Jevon Kearse	LE	Renaldo Wynn
Josh Evans	LT	Gary Walker
Jason Fisk	RT	Seth Payne
Kenny Holmes	RE	Tony Brackens
Eddie Robinson	LLB-SLB	Bryce Paup
Barron Wortham	MLB	Lonnie Marts
Joe Bowden	RLB-WLB	Kevin Hardy
Denard Walker	LCB	Fernando Bryant
Samari Rolle	RCB	Aaron Beasley
Blaine Bishop	SS	Donovin Darius
Marcus Robertson	FS	Carnell Lake

SUBSTITUTIONS

Tennessee—Offense: G—Jason Layman. WR—Isaac Byrd, Derrick Mason, Roell Preston, Chris Sanders. RB—Lorenzo Neal, Rodney Thomas. P—Craig Hentrich. K—Al Del Greco. Defense: DT-DE—Henry Ford, Mike Jones. DT—Joe Salave'a, John Thornton. DE—Eric Ogbogu. LB—Doug Colman, Greg Favors, Terry Killens. DB—Anthony Dorsett, Steve Jackson, Donald Mitchell, Perry Phenix, Dainon Sidney. DNP—Jason Mathews, Neil O'Donnell.

Jacksonville—Offense: C—Quentin Neujahr. T/G—Steve Ingram. TE—Rich Griffith. WR—Reggie Barlow, Alvis Whitted. RB—Chris Howard, Daimon Shelton, James Stewart. P—Bryan Barker. K—Mike Hollis, Steve Lindsey. Defense: DT—Emarlos Leroy, Larry Smith. DE—Joel Smeenge, Regan Upshaw. LB—Brant Boyer, Corey Terry. DB—Corey Chamblin, Jason Craft, Blaine McElmurry, Rayna Stewart, Dave Thomas. DNP—Jay Fiedler.

OFFICIALS

Referee—Bernie Kukar. Umpire—Jim Quirk. Line Judge—Ron Baynes. Side Judge—Rick Patterson. Head Linesman—John Schleyer. Back Judge—Scott Green. Field Judge—Bill Lovett.

SCORING

Tennessee	7	3	16	7	— 33
Jacksonville	7	7	0	0	— 14

Jax — Brady 7 pass from Brunell (Hollis kick)
Tenn — Thigpen 9 pass from McNair (Del Greco kick)
Jax — Stewart 33 run (Hollis kick)
Tenn — FG Del Greco 34
Tenn — McNair 1 run (Del Greco kick)
Tenn — Safety, Evans sacked Brunell in end zone
Tenn — Mason 80 kickoff return (Del Greco kick)
Tenn — McNair 1 run (Del Greco kick)

TEAM STATISTICS	Tenn	Jax
Total First Downs	17	20
Rushing	8	5
Passing	7	13
Penalty	2	2
Total Net Yardage	289	360
Total Offensive Plays	58	64
Average Gain Per Offensive Play	5.0	5.6
Rushes	34	23
Yards Gained Rushing (Net)	177	144
Average Yards per Rush	5.2	6.3
Passes Attempted	23	38
Passes Completed	14	19
Had Intercepted	1	2
Tackled Attempting to Pass	1	3
Yards Lost Attempting to Pass	0	10
Yards Gained Passing (Net)	112	216
Punts	5	3
Average Distance	39.8	45.3
Punt Returns	2	3
Punt Return Yardage	14	2
Kickoff Returns	4	6
Kickoff Return Yardage	174	80
Interception Return Yardage	0	1
Total Return Yardage	188	83
Fumbles	5	5
Fumbles Lost	3	4
Own Fumbles Recovered	2	1
Opponent Fumbles Recovered	4	3
Penalties	5	9
Yards Penalized	39	100
Field Goals	1	0
Field Goals Attempted	1	0
Third-Down Efficiency	3/10	3/10
Fourth-Down Efficiency	0/0	0/2
Time of Possession	31:36	28:24

INDIVIDUAL STATISTICS

RUSHING: TENN: McNair 9-91, George 25-86. JAX: Taylor 19-100, Stewart 3-35, Brunell 1-(-1).

PASSING: TENN: McNair 23-14-112-1. JAX: Brunell 38-19-226-2.

RECEIVING: TENN: Harris 3-33, George 3-19, Byrd 2-19, Thigpen 2-16, Wycheck 2-12, Dyson 1-12, Neal 1-1. JAX: McCardell 6-67, Smith 5-92, Brady 5-44, Taylor 2-16, Jones 1-7.

KICKOFF RETURNS: TENN: Mason 4-174. JAX: Barlow 3-58, Whitted 3-22.

PUNT RETURNS: TENN: Mason 2-14. JAX: Barlow 3-2.

PUNTING: TENN: Hentrich 5-199-39.8. JAX: Barker 3-136-45.3.

INTERCEPTIONS: TENN: Mitchell 1-0, Robertson 1-0. JAX: Bryant 1-1.

SACKS: TENN: Bishop 1, Holmes 1, Evans 0.5, Fisk 0.5. JAX: Brackens 1.

NFC CHAMPIONSHIP GAME RESULTS

Includes NFL Championship Games (1933-69)

Season	Date	Winner (Share)	Loser (Share)	Score	Site	Attendance
1999	Jan. 23	St. Louis ($33,000)	Tampa Bay ($33,000)	11-6	St. Louis	66,396
1998	Jan. 17	Atlanta ($32,500)	Minnesota ($32,500)	30-27*	Minnesota	64,060
1997	Jan. 11	Green Bay ($30,000)	San Francisco ($30,000)	23-10	San Francisco	68,987
1996	Jan. 12	Green Bay ($29,000)	Carolina ($29,000)	30-13	Green Bay	60,216
1995	Jan. 14	Dallas ($27,000)	Green Bay ($27,000)	38-27	Dallas	65,135
1994	Jan. 15	San Francisco ($26,000)	Dallas ($26,000)	38-28	San Francisco	69,125
1993	Jan. 23	Dallas ($23,500)	San Francisco ($23,500)	38-21	Dallas	64,902
1992	Jan. 17	Dallas ($18,000)	San Francisco ($18,000)	30-20	San Francisco	64,920
1991	Jan. 12	Washington ($18,000)	Detroit ($18,000)	41-10	Washington	55,585
1990	Jan. 20	N.Y. Giants ($18,000)	San Francisco ($18,000)	15-13	San Francisco	65,750
1989	Jan. 14	San Francisco ($18,000)	L.A. Rams ($18,000)	30-3	San Francisco	65,634
1988	Jan. 8	San Francisco ($18,000)	Chicago ($18,000)	28-3	Chicago	66,946
1987	Jan. 17	Washington ($18,000)	Minnesota ($18,000)	17-10	Washington	55,212
1986	Jan. 11	New York Giants ($18,000)	Washington ($18,000)	17-0	East Rutherford	76,891
1985	Jan. 12	Chicago ($18,000)	L.A. Rams ($18,000)	24-0	Chicago	66,030
1984	Jan. 6	San Francisco ($18,000)	Chicago ($18,000)	23-0	San Francisco	61,336
1983	Jan. 8	Washington ($18,000)	San Francisco ($18,000)	24-21	Washington	55,363
1982	Jan. 22	Washington ($18,000)	Dallas ($18,000)	31-17	Washington	55,045
1981	Jan. 10	San Francisco ($9,000)	Dallas ($9,000)	28-27	San Francisco	60,525
1980	Jan. 11	Philadelphia ($9,000)	Dallas ($9,000)	20-7	Philadelphia	71,522
1979	Jan. 6	Los Angeles ($9,000)	Tampa Bay ($9,000)	9-0	Tampa Bay	72,033
1978	Jan. 7	Dallas ($9,000)	Los Angeles ($9,000)	28-0	Los Angeles	71,086
1977	Jan. 1	Dallas ($9,000)	Minnesota ($9,000)	23-6	Dallas	64,293
1976	Dec. 26	Minnesota ($8,500)	Los Angeles ($5,500)	24-13	Minnesota	48,379
1975	Jan. 4	Dallas ($8,500)	Los Angeles ($5,500)	37-7	Los Angeles	88,919
1974	Dec. 29	Minnesota ($8,500)	Los Angeles ($5,500)	14-10	Minnesota	48,444
1973	Dec. 30	Minnesota ($8,500)	Dallas ($5,500)	27-10	Dallas	64,422
1972	Dec. 31	Washington ($8,500)	Dallas ($5,500)	26-3	Washington	53,129
1971	Jan. 2	Dallas ($8,500)	San Francisco ($5,500)	14-3	Dallas	63,409
1970	Jan. 3	Dallas ($8,500)	San Francisco ($5,500)	17-10	San Francisco	59,364
1969	Jan. 4	Minnesota ($7,930)	Cleveland ($5,118)	27-7	Minnesota	46,503
1968	Dec. 29	Baltimore ($9,306)	Cleveland ($5,963)	34-0	Cleveland	78,410
1967	Dec. 31	Green Bay ($7,950)	Dallas ($5,299)	21-17	Green Bay	50,861
1966	Jan. 1	Green Bay ($9,813)	Dallas ($6,527)	34-27	Dallas	74,152
1965	Jan. 2	Green Bay ($7,819)	Cleveland ($5,288)	23-12	Green Bay	50,777
1964	Dec. 27	Cleveland ($8,052)	Baltimore ($5,571)	27-0	Cleveland	79,544
1963	Dec. 29	Chicago ($5,899)	New York ($4,218)	14-10	Chicago	45,801
1962	Dec. 30	Green Bay ($5,888)	New York ($4,166)	16-7	New York	64,892
1961	Dec. 31	Green Bay ($5,195)	New York ($3,339)	37-0	Green Bay	39,029
1960	Dec. 26	Philadelphia ($5,116)	Green Bay ($3,105)	17-13	Philadelphia	67,325
1959	Dec. 27	Baltimore ($4,674)	New York ($3,083)	31-16	Baltimore	57,545
1958	Dec. 28	Baltimore ($4,718)	New York ($3,111)	23-17*	New York	64,185
1957	Dec. 29	Detroit ($4,295)	Cleveland ($2,750)	59-14	Detroit	55,263
1956	Dec. 30	New York ($3,779)	Chi. Bears ($2,485)	47-7	New York	56,836
1955	Dec. 26	Cleveland ($3,508)	Los Angeles ($2,316)	38-14	Los Angeles	85,693
1954	Dec. 26	Cleveland ($2,478)	Detroit ($1,585)	56-10	Cleveland	43,827
1953	Dec. 27	Detroit ($2,424)	Cleveland ($1,654)	17-16	Detroit	54,577
1952	Dec. 28	Detroit ($2,274)	Cleveland ($1,712)	17-7	Cleveland	50,934
1951	Dec. 23	Los Angeles ($2,108)	Cleveland ($1,483)	24-17	Los Angeles	57,522
1950	Dec. 24	Cleveland ($1,113)	Los Angeles ($686)	30-28	Cleveland	29,751
1949	Dec. 18	Philadelphia ($1,094)	Los Angeles ($739)	14-0	Los Angeles	27,980
1948	Dec. 19	Philadelphia ($1,540)	Chi. Cardinals ($874)	7-0	Philadelphia	36,309
1947	Dec. 28	Chi. Cardinals ($1,132)	Philadelphia ($754)	28-21	Chicago	30,759
1946	Dec. 15	Chi. Bears ($1,975)	New York ($1,295)	24-14	New York	58,346
1945	Dec. 16	Cleveland ($1,469)	Washington ($902)	15-14	Cleveland	32,178

Season	Date	Winner (Share)	Loser (Share)	Score	Site	Attendance
1944	Dec. 17	Green Bay ($1,449)	New York ($814)	14-7	New York	46,016
1943	Dec. 26	Chi. Bears ($1,146)	Washington ($765)	41-21	Chicago	34,320
1942	Dec. 13	Washington ($965)	Chi. Bears ($637)	14-6	Washington	36,006
1941	Dec. 21	Chi. Bears ($430)	New York ($288)	37-9	Chicago	13,341
1940	Dec. 8	Chi. Bears ($873)	Washington ($606)	73-0	Washington	36,034
1939	Dec. 10	Green Bay ($703.97)	New York ($455.57)	27-0	Milwaukee	32,279
1938	Dec. 11	New York ($504.45)	Green Bay ($368.81)	23-17	New York	48,120
1937	Dec. 12	Washington ($225.90)	Chi. Bears ($127.78)	28-21	Chicago	15,870
1936	Dec. 13	Green Bay ($250)	Boston ($180)	21-6	New York	29,545
1935	Dec. 15	Detroit ($313.35)	New York ($200.20)	26-7	Detroit	15,000
1934	Dec. 9	New York ($621)	Chi. Bears ($414.02)	30-13	New York	35,059
1933	Dec. 17	Chi. Bears ($210.34)	New York ($140.22)	23-21	Chicago	26,000

**Sudden death overtime*

NFC CHAMPIONSHIP GAME COMPOSITE STANDINGS

	W	L	Pct.	Pts.	OP
Atlanta Falcons	1	0	1.000	30	27
Philadelphia Eagles	4	1	.800	79	48
Green Bay Packers	10	3	.769	303	177
Baltimore Colts	3	1	.750	88	60
Detroit Lions	4	2	.667	139	141
Washington Redskins*	7	5	.583	222	255
Minnesota Vikings	4	3	.571	135	110
Chicago Bears	7	6	.538	286	245
Dallas Cowboys	8	8	.500	361	319
Arizona Cardinals**	1	1	.500	28	28
San Francisco 49ers	5	7	.417	245	222
Cleveland Browns	4	7	.364	224	253
New York Giants	5	11	.313	240	322
St. Louis Rams***	4	9	.308	134	276
Carolina Panthers	0	1	.000	13	30
Tampa Bay Buccaneers	0	2	.000	6	20

**One game played when franchise was in Boston. (Lost 21-6)*

***Both games played when franchise was in Chicago. (Won 28-21, lost 7-0)*

****One game played when franchise was in Cleveland (Won 15-14), and 11 games when franchise was in Los Angeles (Won 2, lost 9, scored 108 points, allowed 256 points).*

1999 NFC CHAMPIONSHIP GAME

Trans World Dome, St. Louis, Missouri
January 23, 2000, Attendance: 66,396

ST. LOUIS 11, TAMPA BAY 6—Kurt Warner's 30-yard touchdown pass to Ricky Proehl with 4:44 remaining lifted the Rams to their first Super Bowl in 20 seasons. On the game's first play, Steve White intercepted Warner's pass at the Rams' 20, but the Buccaneers had to settle for Martin Gramatica's field goal. The Rams immediatly responded with a field goal by Jeff Wilkins and took a 5-3 lead when Tony Mayberry's Shotgun snap from the Buccaneers' 20 on the first play of the second quarter sailed over Shaun King's head. King batted the ball out of the end zone for a safety, but Wilkins, who was battling patellar tendinitis in his non-kicking knee, missed a 44-yard attempt on the Rams' next possession. Todd Lyght's interception at the Rams' 33 just before the half allowed the Rams to maintain their 5-3 lead. King's 32-yard pass to Jacquez Green led to Gramatica's 23-yard field goal early in the third quarter, giving the Buccaneers a 6-5 lead. Warner was intercepted on the Rams' next two possessions, including once by Hardy Nickerson at the Buccaneers' 2, to maintain Tampa Bay's one-point lead. On third-and-11 from midfield with just over eight minutes remaining, Dre' Bly intercepted King's pass and returned it 9 yards to the Buccaneers' 44. Six plays later, on third-and-4 from the Buccaneers' 30, Warner read the blitz and lofted the ball down the left sideline to Proehl, who made a one-handed catch in the end zone despite Brian Kelly's step-for-step defense. The Buccaneers mounted one last attack, but King was sacked twice in the final two minutes, and his fourth-and-11 Hail Mary pass from the Rams' 35 was knocked down in the end zone. Warner was 26 of 43 for 258 yards and 1 touchdown, with 3 interceptions. Proehl, who had not caught a touchdown pass all season, finished with 6 receptions for 100 yards. King was 13 of 29 for 163 yards, with 2 interceptions.

Tampa Bay (6)	Offense	St. Louis (11)
Karl Williams	WR	Torry Holt
Pete Pierson	LT	Orlando Pace
Jorge Diaz	LG	Tom Nutten
Tony Mayberry	C	Mark Gruttadauria
Frank Middleton	RG	Amda Timmerman
Jerry Wunsch	RT	Fred Miller
Dave Moore	TE	Roland Williams
Patrick Hape	WR	Isaac Bruce
Shaun King	QB	Kurt Warner
Mike Alstott	FB	Robert Holcombe
Warrick Dunn	RB	Marshall Faulk
	Defense	
Chidi Ahanotu	LE	Kevin Carter
Brad Culpepper	LT	Ray Agnew
Warren Sapp	RT	D'Marco Farr
Steve White	RE	Grant Wistrom
Shelton Quarles	SLB-LLB	Mike Jones
Hardy Nickerson	MLB	London Fletcher
Derrick Brooks	WLB-RLB	Todd Collins
Donnie Abraham	LCB	Todd Lyght
Ronde Barber	RCB	Dexter McCleon
John Lynch	SS	Billy Jenkins
Damien Robinson	FS	Devin Bush

SUBSTITUTIONS

Tampa Bay—Offense: C-G—Kevin Dogins, Todd Washington. C-LS—Morris Unutoa. G-T—George Hegamin. TE—John Davis. WR—Bert Emanuel, Jacquez Green, Darnell McDonald. RB—Fred McAfee, Kevin McLeod. P—Mark Royals. K—Martin Gramatica. Defense: DT—Anthony McFarland. DE—Marcus Jones, John McLaughlin. LB—Don Davis, Jamie Duncan, Jeff Gooch. DB—Dexter Jackson, Brian Kelly, Shevin Smith, Floyd Young. DNP—Eric Zeier.

St. Louis—Offense: C—Ryan Tucker. G—Andy McCollum. TE—Ernie Conwell, Jeff Robinson. WR—Az-Zahir Hakim, Tony Horne, Ricky Proehl. RB—James Hodgins, Amp Lee. P—Mike Horan. K—Jeff Wilkins. Defense: DT—Nate Hobgood-Chittick, Jeff Zgonina. DE—Jay Williams. LB—Charlie Clemons, Leonard Little, Mike Morton, Lorenzo Styles. DB—Taje Allen, Dre' Bly, Rich Coady, Keith Lyle. DNP—Paul Justin.

OFFICIALS

Referee—Bill Carollo. Umpire—Ed Coukart. Line Judge—Walt Anderson. Side Judge—Neely Dunn. Head Linesman—Mark Baltz. Back Judge—Ron Spitler. Field Judge—Tim Millis.

SCORING

Tampa Bay	3	0	3	0	— 6
St. Louis	3	2	0	6	— 11

TB — FG Gramatica 25
StL — FG Wilkins 24
StL — Safety, Mayberry's Shotgun snap went out of end zone
TB — FG Gramatica 23
StL — Proehl 30 pass from Warner (pass failed)

TEAM STATISTICS	TB	StL
Total First Downs	12	17
Rushing	4	3
Passing	7	14
Penalty	1	0
Total Net Yardage	203	309
Total Offensive Plays	57	64
Average Gain Per Offensive Play	3.6	4.8
Rushes	23	21
Yards Gained Rushing (Net)	77	51
Average Yards per Rush	3.3	2.4
Passes Attempted	29	43
Passes Completed	13	26
Had Intercepted	2	3
Tackled Attempting to Pass	5	0
Yards Lost Attempting to Pass	37	0
Yards Gained Passing (Net)	126	258
Punts	5	4
Average Distance	40.4	43.8
Punt Returns	4	3
Punt Return Yardage	45	25
Kickoff Returns	3	2
Kickoff Return Yardage	60	38
Interception Return Yardage	21	28
Total Return Yardage	126	91
Fumbles	3	2
Fumbles Lost	0	0
Own Fumbles Recovered	3	2
Opponent Fumbles Recovered	0	0
Penalties	3	7
Yards Penalized	15	48
Field Goals	2	1
Field Goals Attempted	2	2
Third-Down Efficiency	5/14	7/15
Fourth-Down Efficiency	0/1	0/0
Time of Possession	26:59	33:01

INDIVIDUAL STATISTICS

RUSHING: TB: Alstott 12-39, Dunn 9-35, King 2-3. StL: Faulk 17-44, Hakim 1-6, Holcombe 1-2, Warner 2-(-1).

PASSING: TB: King 29-13-163-2. StL: Warner 26-43-258-3.

RECEIVING: TB: Green 4-59, Dunn 4-37, Williams 2-28, Emanuel 1-22, Alstott 1-9, Moore 1-8. StL: Holt 7-68, Proehl 6-100, Bruce 3-22, Faulk 3-5, Hakim 2-27, Holcombe 2-5, Williams 1-22, Robinson 1-11, Conwell 1-(-2).

KICKOFF RETURNS: TB: Dunn 3-60. StL: Horne 2-38

PUNT RETURNS: TB: Williams 4-45. StL: Hakim 3-25.

PUNTING: TB: Royals 5-202-40.4. StL: Horan 4-175-43.8.

SACKS: StL: Carter 1, Clemons 1, Farr 1, Wistrom 1, Zgonina 1.

AFC DIVISIONAL PLAYOFFS RESULTS

Includes Second-Round Playoff Games (1982), AFC Inter-Divisional Games (1969), and special playoff games to break ties for AFL Division Championships (1963, 1968)

Season	Date	Winner (Share)	Loser (Share)	Score	Site	Attendance
1999	Jan. 16	Tennessee ($16,000)	Indianapolis ($16,000)	19-16	Indianapolis	57,097
	Jan. 15	Jacksonville ($16,000)	Miami ($16,000)	62-7	Jacksonville	75,173
1998	Jan. 10	N.Y. Jets ($15,000)	Jacksonville ($15,000)	34-24	East Rutherford	78,817
	Jan. 9	Denver ($15,000)	Miami ($15,000)	38-3	Denver	75,729
1997	Jan. 4	Denver ($15,000)	Kansas City ($15,000)	14-10	Kansas City	76,965
	Jan. 3	Pittsburgh ($15,000)	New England ($15,000)	7-6	Pittsburgh	61,228
1996	Jan. 5	New England ($14,000)	Pittsburgh ($14,000)	28-3	New England	60,188
	Jan. 4	Jacksonville ($14,000)	Denver ($14,000)	30-27	Denver	75,678
1995	Jan. 7	Indianapolis ($13,000)	Kansas City ($13,000)	10-7	Kansas City	77,594
	Jan. 6	Pittsburgh ($13,000)	Buffalo ($13,000)	40-21	Pittsburgh	59,072
1994	Jan. 8	San Diego ($12,000)	Miami ($12,000)	22-21	San Diego	63,381
	Jan. 7	Pittsburgh ($12,000)	Cleveland ($12,000)	29-9	Pittsburgh	58,185
1993	Jan. 16	Kansas City ($12,000)	Houston ($12,000)	28-20	Houston	64,011
	Jan. 15	Buffalo ($12,000)	L.A. Raiders ($12,000)	29-23	Buffalo	61,923
1992	Jan. 10	Miami ($10,000)	San Diego ($10,000)	31-0	Miami	71,224
	Jan. 9	Buffalo ($10,000)	Pittsburgh ($10,000)	24-3	Pittsburgh	60,407
1991	Jan. 5	Buffalo ($10,000)	Kansas City ($10,000)	37-14	Buffalo	80,182
	Jan. 4	Denver ($10,000)	Houston ($10,000)	26-24	Denver	75,301
1990	Jan. 13	L.A. Raiders ($10,000)	Cincinnati ($10,000)	20-10	Los Angeles	92,045
	Jan. 12	Buffalo ($10,000)	Miami ($10,000)	44-34	Buffalo	77,087
1989	Jan. 7	Denver ($10,000)	Pittsburgh ($10,000)	24-23	Denver	75,477
	Jan. 6	Cleveland ($10,000)	Buffalo ($10,000)	34-30	Cleveland	78,921
1988	Jan. 1	Buffalo ($10,000)	Houston ($10,000)	17-10	Buffalo	79,532
	Dec. 31	Cincinnati ($10,000)	Seattle ($10,000)	21-13	Cincinnati	58,560
1987	Jan. 10	Denver ($10,000)	Houston ($10,000)	34-10	Denver	75,440
	Jan. 9	Cleveland ($10,000)	Indianapolis ($10,000)	38-21	Cleveland	79,372
1986	Jan. 4	Denver ($10,000)	New England ($10,000)	22-17	Denver	75,262
	Jan. 3	Cleveland ($10,000)	N.Y. Jets ($10,000)	23-20*	Cleveland	79,720
1985	Jan. 5	New England ($10,000)	L.A. Raiders ($10,000)	27-20	Los Angeles	87,163
	Jan. 4	Miami ($10,000)	Cleveland ($10,000)	24-21	Miami	74,667
1984	Dec. 30	Pittsburgh ($10,000)	Denver ($10,000)	24-17	Denver	74,981
	Dec. 29	Miami ($10,000)	Seattle ($10,000)	31-10	Miami	73,469
1983	Jan. 1	L.A. Raiders ($10,000)	Pittsburgh ($10,000)	38-10	Los Angeles	90,380
	Dec. 31	Seattle ($10,000)	Miami ($10,000)	27-20	Miami	74,136
1982	Jan. 16	Miami ($10,000)	San Diego ($10,000)	34-13	Miami	71,383
	Jan. 15	N.Y. Jets ($10,000)	L.A. Raiders ($10,000)	17-14	Los Angeles	90,038
1981	Jan. 3	Cincinnati ($5,000)	Buffalo ($5,000)	28-21	Cincinnati	55,420
	Jan. 2	San Diego ($5,000)	Miami ($5,000)	41-38*	Miami	73,735
1980	Jan. 4	Oakland ($5,000)	Cleveland ($5,000)	14-12	Cleveland	78,245
	Jan. 3	San Diego ($5,000)	Buffalo ($5,000)	20-14	San Diego	52,253
1979	Dec. 30	Pittsburgh ($5,000)	Miami ($5,000)	34-14	Pittsburgh	50,214
	Dec. 29	Houston ($5,000)	San Diego ($5,000)	17-14	San Diego	51,192
1978	Dec. 31	Houston ($5,000)	New England ($5,000)	31-14	New England	60,735
	Dec. 30	Pittsburgh ($5,000)	Denver ($5,000)	33-10	Pittsburgh	50,230
1977	Dec. 24	Oakland ($5,000)	Baltimore ($5,000)	37-31*	Baltimore	59,925
	Dec. 24	Denver ($5,000)	Pittsburgh ($5,000)	34-21	Denver	75,059
1976	Dec. 19	Pittsburgh [$]	Baltimore [$]	40-14	Baltimore	59,296
	Dec. 18	Oakland [$]	New England [$]	24-21	Oakland	53,050
1975	Dec. 28	Oakland [$]	Cincinnati [$]	31-28	Oakland	53,030
	Dec. 27	Pittsburgh [$]	Baltimore [$]	28-10	Pittsburgh	49,557
1974	Dec. 22	Pittsburgh [$]	Buffalo [$]	32-14	Pittsburgh	49,841
	Dec. 21	Oakland [$]	Miami [$]	28-26	Oakland	53,023
1973	Dec. 23	Miami [$]	Cincinnati [$]	34-16	Miami	78,928
	Dec. 22	Oakland [$]	Pittsburgh [$]	33-14	Oakland	52,646
1972	Dec. 24	Miami [$]	Cleveland [$]	20-14	Miami	78,916
	Dec. 23	Pittsburgh [$]	Oakland [$]	13-7	Pittsburgh	50,327
1971	Dec. 26	Baltimore [$]	Cleveland [$]	20-3	Cleveland	70,734
	Dec. 25	Miami [$]	Kansas City [$]	27-24*	Kansas City	50,374
1970	Dec. 27	Oakland [$]	Miami [$]	21-14	Oakland	52,594
	Dec. 26	Baltimore [$]	Cincinnati [$]	17-0	Baltimore	49,694
1969	Dec. 21	Oakland [$]	Houston [$]	56-7	Oakland	53,539
	Dec. 20	Kansas City [$]	N.Y. Jets [$]	13-6	New York	62,977
1968	Dec. 22	Oakland [$]	Kansas City [$]	41-6	Oakland	53,605
1963	Dec. 28	Boston [$]	Buffalo [$]	26-8	Buffalo	33,044

**Sudden death overtime.*

$ Players received 1/14 of annual salary for playoff appearances.

1999 AFC DIVISIONAL PLAYOFF GAMES

RCA Dome, Indianapolis, Indiana
January 16, 2000, Attendance: 57,097

TENNESSEE 19, INDIANAPOLIS 16—Eddie George rushed for 162 yards and scored the Titans' lone touchdown as the franchise formerly known as the Houston Oilers reached its first AFC Championship Game since 1979. The Colts led 9-6 at halftime, but George's 68-yard touchdown run on the third play of the second half gave the Titans a 13-9 lead. While the Colts had to punt to conclude their first four possessions of the second half, an Al Del Greco field goal gave Tennessee a 16-6 lead, and after an instant-replay reversal ruled that Terrence Wilkins stepped out of bounds on his own 34 during an 87-yard punt return, Del Greco added a second field goal to give the Titans a 19-9 lead with 4:19 left. The Colts were stopped on downs, but George fumbled three plays later, and Mark Thomas recovered with 3:11 left. Peyton Manning scrambled 15 yards for a touchdown to cut the deficit to 19-16 with 1:51 left, but Yancey Thigpen recovered the ensuing onside kick and the Colts had no timeouts to stop the clock. Steve McNair was 13 of 24 for 112 yards. Manning was 19 of 43 for 227 yards.

Tennessee	0	6	7	6	—	19
Indianapolis	3	6	0	7	—	16

Ind — FG Vanderjagt 40
Tenn — FG Del Greco 49
Ind — FG Vanderjagt 40
Tenn — FG Del Greco 37
Ind — FG Vanderjagt 34

PLAYOFF GAMES SUMMARIES

Tenn — George 68 run (Del Greco kick)
Tenn — FG Del Greco 25
Tenn — FG Del Greco 43
Ind — Manning 15 run (Vanderjagt kick)

ALLTEL Stadium, Jacksonville, Florida
January 10, 2000, Attendance: 75,173
JACKSONVILLE 62, MIAMI 7—The Jaguars scored 38 points in the first 17 minutes, 55 seconds en route to the highest point total in AFC postseason history. Mark Brunell's 8-yard touchdown pass to Jimmy Smith capped a game-opening 9-play, 73-yard drive. Aaron Beasley intercepted Dan Marino's pass on the Dolphins' first play, setting up Mike Hollis's 45-yard field goal with 6:19 remaining in the quarter. Two plays after a Dolphins' punt, Fred Taylor scampered 90 yards down the right sideline. On the next play from scrimmage, Tony Brackens stripped Marino, recovered the ball, and, after not being touched, was pushed into the end zone by teammates to give Jacksonville a 24-0 lead with 3:21 left in the quarter. Taylor dodged three tacklers en route to the end zone on a 39-yard screen pass on the first play of the second quarter. Corey Chamblin blocked the Dolphins' punt on the ensuing possession, and James Stewart scored three plays later to give the Jaguars a 38-0 lead before Miami had a first down. The Dolphins drove 80 yards just before halftime to get on the board, but Jacksonville, with reserve Jay Fiedler, scored on its first two possessions of the second half to take a 55-7 lead. Brunell was 5 of 9 for 105 yards and 2 touchdowns. Taylor carried 18 times for 135 yards. Marino was 11 of 25 for 95 yards and 1 touchdown, with 2 interceptions before being replaced in the third quarter by Damon Huard. The Jaguars had more first downs (21-10), total yards (520-131), registered 5 sacks, and forced 7 turnovers.

Miami	0	7	0	0 —	7
Jacksonville	24	17	14	7 —	62

Jax — Smith 8 pass from Brunell (Hollis kick)
Jax — FG Hollis 45
Jax — Taylor 90 run (Hollis kick)
Jax — Brackens 16 fumble return (Hollis kick)
Jax — Taylor 39 pass from Brunell (Hollis kick)
Jax — Stewart 25 run (Hollis kick)
Jax — FG Hollis 28
Mia — Gadsden 20 pass from Marino (Mare kick)
Jax — Smith 70 pass from Fiedler (Hollis kick)
Jax — Whitted 38 pass from Fiedler (Hollis kick)
Jax — Howard 5 run (Hollis kick)

NFC DIVISIONAL PLAYOFFS RESULTS

Includes Second-Round Playoff Games (1982), NFL Conference Championship Games (1967-69), and special playoff games to break ties for NFL Division or Conference Championships (1941, 1943, 1947, 1950, 1952, 1957, 1958, 1965)

Season	Date	Winner (Share)	Loser (Share)	Score	Site	Attendance
1999	Jan. 16	St. Louis ($16,000)	Minnesota ($16,000)	49-37	St. Louis	66,194
	Jan. 15	Tampa Bay ($16,000)	Washington ($16,000)	14-13	Tampa Bay	65,835
1998	Jan. 10	Minnesota ($15,000)	Arizona ($15,000)	41-21	Minnesota	63,760
	Jan. 9	Atlanta ($15,000)	San Francisco ($15,000)	20-18	Atlanta	70,262
1997	Jan. 4	Green Bay ($15,000)	Tampa Bay ($15,000)	21-7	Green Bay	60,327
	Jan. 3	San Francisco ($15,000)	Minnesota ($15,000)	38-22	San Francisco	65,018
1996	Jan. 5	Carolina ($14,000)	Dallas ($14,000)	26-17	Carolina	72,808
	Jan. 4	Green Bay ($14,000)	San Francisco ($14,000)	35-14	Green Bay	60,787
1995	Jan. 7	Dallas ($13,000)	Philadelphia ($13,000)	30-11	Dallas	64,371
	Jan. 6	Green Bay ($13,000)	San Francisco ($13,000)	27-17	San Francisco	69,311
1994	Jan. 8	Dallas ($12,000)	Green Bay ($12,000)	35-9	Dallas	64,745
	Jan. 7	San Francisco ($12,000)	Chicago ($12,000)	44-15	San Francisco	64,644
1993	Jan. 16	Dallas ($12,000)	Green Bay ($12,000)	27-17	Dallas	64,790
	Jan. 15	San Francisco ($12,000)	N.Y. Giants ($12,000)	44-3	San Francisco	67,143
1992	Jan. 10	Dallas ($10,000)	Philadelphia ($10,000)	34-10	Dallas	63,721
	Jan. 9	San Francisco ($10,000)	Washington ($10,000)	20-13	San Francisco	64,991
1991	Jan. 5	Detroit ($10,000)	Dallas ($10,000)	38-6	Detroit	78,290
	Jan. 4	Washington ($10,000)	Atlanta ($10,000)	24-7	Washington	55,181
1990	Jan. 13	N.Y. Giants ($10,000)	Chicago ($10,000)	31-3	East Rutherford	77,025
	Jan. 12	San Francisco ($10,000)	Washington ($10,000)	28-10	San Francisco	65,292
1989	Jan. 7	L.A. Rams ($10,000)	N.Y. Giants ($10,000)	19-13*	East Rutherford	76,526
	Jan. 6	San Francisco ($10,000)	Minnesota ($10,000)	41-13	San Francisco	64,918
1988	Jan. 1	San Francisco ($10,000)	Minnesota ($10,000)	34-9	San Francisco	61,848
	Dec. 31	Chicago ($10,000)	Philadelphia ($10,000)	20-12	Chicago	65,534
1987	Jan. 10	Washington ($10,000)	Chicago ($10,000)	21-17	Chicago	65,268
	Jan. 9	Minnesota ($10,000)	San Francisco ($10,000)	36-24	San Francisco	63,008
1986	Jan. 4	N.Y. Giants ($10,000)	San Francisco ($10,000)	49-3	East Rutherford	75,691
	Jan. 3	Washington ($10,000)	Chicago ($10,000)	27-13	Chicago	65,524
1985	Jan. 5	Chicago ($10,000)	N.Y. Giants ($10,000)	21-0	Chicago	65,670
	Jan. 4	L.A. Rams ($10,000)	Dallas ($10,000)	20-0	Anaheim	66,581
1984	Dec. 30	Chicago ($10,000)	Washington ($10,000)	23-19	Washington	55,431
	Dec. 29	San Francisco ($10,000)	N.Y. Giants ($10,000)	21-10	San Francisco	60,303
1983	Jan. 1	Washington ($10,000)	L.A. Rams ($10,000)	51-7	Washington	54,440
	Dec. 31	San Francisco ($10,000)	Detroit ($10,000)	24-23	San Francisco	59,979
1982	Jan. 16	Dallas ($10,000)	Green Bay ($10,000)	37-26	Dallas	63,972
	Jan. 15	Washington ($10,000)	Minnesota ($10,000)	21-7	Washington	54,593
1981	Jan. 3	San Francisco ($5,000)	N.Y. Giants ($5,000)	38-24	San Francisco	58,360
	Jan. 2	Dallas ($5,000)	Tampa Bay ($5,000)	38-0	Dallas	64,848
1980	Jan. 4	Dallas ($5,000)	Atlanta ($5,000)	30-27	Atlanta	59,793
	Jan. 3	Philadelphia ($5,000)	Minnesota ($5,000)	31-16	Philadelphia	70,178
1979	Dec. 30	Los Angeles ($5,000)	Dallas ($5,000)	21-19	Dallas	64,792
	Dec. 29	Tampa Bay ($5,000)	Philadelphia ($5,000)	24-17	Tampa Bay	71,402
1978	Dec. 31	Los Angeles ($5,000)	Minnesota ($5,000)	34-10	Los Angeles	70,436
	Dec. 30	Dallas ($5,000)	Atlanta ($5,000)	27-20	Dallas	63,406
1977	Dec. 26	Dallas ($5,000)	Chicago ($5,000)	37-7	Dallas	63,260
	Dec. 26	Minnesota ($5,000)	Los Angeles ($5,000)	14-7	Los Angeles	70,203
1976	Dec. 19	Los Angeles [$]	Dallas [$]	14-12	Dallas	63,283
	Dec. 18	Minnesota [$]	Washington [$]	35-20	Minnesota	47,466
1975	Dec. 28	Dallas [$]	Minnesota [$]	17-14	Minnesota	48,050
	Dec. 27	Los Angeles [$]	St. Louis [$]	35-23	Los Angeles	73,459
1974	Dec. 22	Los Angeles [$]	Washington [$]	19-10	Los Angeles	77,925
	Dec. 21	Minnesota [$]	St. Louis [$]	30-14	Minnesota	48,150
1973	Dec. 23	Dallas [$]	Los Angeles [$]	27-16	Dallas	63,272
	Dec. 22	Minnesota [$]	Washington [$]	27-20	Minnesota	48,040
1972	Dec. 24	Washington [$]	Green Bay [$]	16-3	Washington	52,321
	Dec. 23	Dallas [$]	San Francisco [$]	30-28	San Francisco	59,746
1971	Dec. 26	San Francisco [$]	Washington [$]	24-20	San Francisco	45,327
	Dec. 25	Dallas [$]	Minnesota [$]	20-12	Minnesota	47,307
1970	Dec. 27	San Francisco [$]	Minnesota [$]	17-14	Minnesota	45,103
	Dec. 26	Dallas [$]	Detroit [$]	5-0	Dallas	69,613

1969	Dec. 28	Cleveland [$]	Dallas [$]	38-14	Dallas	69,321
	Dec. 27	Minnesota [$]	Los Angeles [$]	23-20	Minnesota	47,900
1968	Dec. 22	Baltimore [$]	Minnesota [$]	24-14	Baltimore	60,238
	Dec. 21	Cleveland [$]	Dallas [$]	31-20	Cleveland	81,497
1967	Dec. 24	Dallas [$]	Cleveland [$]	52-14	Dallas	70,786
	Dec. 23	Green Bay [$]	Los Angeles [$]	28-7	Milwaukee	49,861
1965	Dec. 26	Green Bay [$]	Baltimore [$]	13-10*	Green Bay	50,484
1958	Dec. 21	N.Y. Giants (#)	Cleveland (#)	10-0	New York	61,274
1957	Dec. 22	Detroit (#)	San Francisco (#)	31-27	San Francisco	60,118
1952	Dec. 21	Detroit (#)	Los Angeles (#)	31-21	Detroit	47,645
1950	Dec. 17	Los Angeles (#)	Chicago Bears (#)	24-14	Los Angeles	83,501
	Dec. 17	Cleveland (#)	N.Y. Giants (#)	8-3	Cleveland	33,054
1947	Dec. 21	Philadelphia (#)	Pittsburgh (#)	21-0	Pittsburgh	35,729
1943	Dec. 19	Washington (¢)	N.Y. Giants (¢)	28-0	New York	42,800
1941	Dec. 14	Chicago Bears (¢)	Green Bay (¢)	33-14	Chicago	43,425

** Sudden death overtime*
[$] Players received 1/14 of annual salary for playoff appearances.
 # Players received 1/12 of annual salary for playoff appearances.
¢ Players received 1/10 of annual salary for playoff appearances.

1999 NFC DIVISIONAL PLAYOFF GAMES

Trans World Dome, St. Louis, Missouri
January 16, 2000, Attendance: 66,194

ST. LOUIS 49, MINNESOTA 37—Kurt Warner passed for 391 yards and 5 touchdowns to put the Rams in the NFC Championship Game for the first time since 1989. Gary Anderson's 31-yard field goal capped the game's first drive, but on the Rams' first play, Warner found Isaac Bruce on a post pattern for a 77-yard touchdown. It took the Rams' four plays to score on their next possession, capped by Marshall Faulk's 41-yard scoring screen pass. The Vikings drove 96 yards to cut the deficit to 14-10, and Robert Griffith's fumble recovery near midfield set up Leroy Hoard's 4-yard scoring run to give the Vikings a 17-14 halftime lead. Trailing at halftime at home for the first time all season, Tony Horne promptly returned the second half's opening kickoff 95 yards for a touchdown. While the Vikings failed to gain a first down on their first four possessions (three punts and a fumble) of the second half, the Rams scored touchdowns on four of their first five possessions, capped by Warner's 2-yard touchdown pass to Roland Williams to give the Rams a 49-17 lead with 8:13 remaining. Jeff George engineered touchdown drives of 75, 63, and 85 yards in the final minutes. Warner was 27 of 33 for 391 yards and 5 touchdowns, with 1 interception, and completed passes to 10 different Rams. Bruce had 4 receptions for 133 yards. George was 29 of 50 for 423 yards and 4 touchdowns, with 1 interception. Randy Moss had 9 catches for 188 yards, and Cris Carter had 7 for 106 yards.

Minnesota	3	14	0	20	—	37
St. Louis	14	0	21	14	—	49

Minn — FG Anderson 31
StL — Bruce 77 pass from Warner (Wilkins kick)
StL — Faulk 41 pass from Warner (Wilkins kick)
Minn — Carter 22 pass from George (Anderson kick)
Minn — Hoard 4 run (Anderson kick)
StL — Horne 95 kickoff return (Wilkins kick)
StL — Faulk 1 run (Wilkins kick)
StL — Robinson 13 pass from Warner (Wilkins kick)
StL — Tucker 1 pass from Warner (Wilkins kick)
StL — Williams 2 pass from Warner (Wilkins kick)
Minn — Reed 4 pass from George (Hoard run)
Minn — Moss 44 pass from George (pass failed)
Minn — Moss 2 pass from George (pass failed)

Raymond James Stadium, Tampa, Florida
January 15, 2000, Attendance: 65,835

TAMPA BAY 14, WASHINGTON 13—Turnovers set up both of Tampa Bay's second half touchdowns, and an errant snap squashed the Redskins' field-goal attempt in the final minutes as the Buccaneers earned their first trip to the NFC Championship Game since 1979. The Redskins' defense forced 6 first-half punts, and Brett Conway's 28-yard field goal gave the Redskins a 3-0 halftime lead. Brian Mitchell returned the second half's opening kickoff 100 yards for a touchdown, and Darrell Green's interception in Buccaneers' territory set up Conway's second field goal to give Washington a 13-0 lead. John Lynch's interception at the Redskins' 27 sparked the Buccaneers' offense, which needed just 6 plays, capped by Mike Alstott's 2-yard run, to cut the deficit to 13-7 late in the third quarter. Warren Sapp recovered Brad Johnson's fumble at the Redskins' 32 early in the fourth quarter, and Alstott converted a fourth-and-1 to set up Shaun King's 1-yard touchdown pass to John Davis with 7:29 remaining. The Redskins reached the Buccaneers' 33 with 1:08 left, but Conway never got a chance to attempt the winning kick because of a poor snap by Dan Turk, which allowed Floyd Young to sack the holder, Johnson. King was 15 of 32 for 157 yards and 1 touchdown, with 1 interception. Johnson was 20 of 32 for 149 yards, with 1 interception. Both defenses were stifling, as Tampa Bay outgained Washington 186-157.

Washington	0	3	10	0	—	13
Tampa Bay	0	0	7	7	—	14

Wash — FG Conway 28
Wash — Mitchell 100 kickoff return (Conway kick)
Wash — FG Conway 48
TB — Alstott 2 run (Gramatica kick)
TB — Davis 1 pass from King (Gramatica kick)

AFC WILD CARD PLAYOFF GAMES RESULTS

Season	Date	Winner (Share)	Loser (Share)	Score	Site	Attendance
1999	Jan. 9	Miami ($10,000)	Seattle ($16,000)	20-17	Seattle	66,170
	Jan. 8	Tennessee ($10,000)	Buffalo ($10,000)	22-16	Nashville	66,672
1998	Jan. 3	Jacksonville ($15,000)	New England ($10,000)	25-10	Jacksonville	71,139
	Jan. 2	Miami ($10,000)	Buffalo ($10,000)	24-17	Miami	72,698
1997	Dec. 28	New England ($15,000)	Miami ($10,000)	17-3	New England	60,041
	Dec. 27	Denver ($10,000)	Jacksonville ($10,000)	42-17	Denver	74,481
1996	Dec. 29	Pittsburgh ($14,000)	Indianapolis ($10,000)	42-14	Pittsburgh	58,078
	Dec. 28	Jacksonville ($10,000)	Buffalo ($10,000)	30-27	Buffalo	70,213
1995	Dec. 31	Indianapolis ($7,500)	San Diego ($7,500)	35-20	San Diego	61,182
	Dec. 30	Buffalo ($13,000)	Miami ($7,500)	37-22	Buffalo	73,103
1994	Jan. 1	Cleveland ($7,500)	New England ($7,500)	20-13	Cleveland	77,452
	Dec. 31	Miami ($12,000)	Kansas City ($7,500)	27-17	Miami	67,487
1993	Jan. 9	L.A. Raiders ($7,500)	Denver ($7,500)	42-24	Los Angeles	65,314
	Jan. 8	Kansas City ($12,000)	Pittsburgh ($7,500)	27-24*	Kansas City	74,515
1992	Jan. 3	Buffalo ($6,000)	Houston ($6,000)	41-38*	Buffalo	75,141
	Jan. 2	San Diego ($10,000)	Kansas City ($6,000)	17-0	San Diego	58,278
1991	Dec. 29	Houston ($10,000)	N.Y. Jets ($6,000)	17-10	Houston	61,485
	Dec. 28	Kansas City ($6,000)	L.A. Raiders ($6,000)	10-6	Kansas City	75,827
1990	Jan. 6	Cincinnati ($10,000)	Houston ($6,000)	41-14	Cincinnati	60,012
	Jan. 5	Miami ($6,000)	Kansas City ($6,000)	17-16	Miami	67,276
1989	Dec. 31	Pittsburgh ($6,000)	Houston ($6,000)	26-23*	Houston	59,406
1988	Dec. 26	Houston ($6,000)	Cleveland ($6,000)	24-23	Cleveland	75,896
1987	Jan. 3	Houston ($6,000)	Seattle ($6,000)	23-20*	Houston	50,519
1986	Dec. 28	N.Y. Jets ($6,000)	Kansas City ($6,000)	35-15	East Rutherford	75,210
1985	Dec. 28	New England ($6,000)	N.Y. Jets ($6,000)	26-14	East Rutherford	75,945
1984	Dec. 22	Seattle ($6,000)	L.A. Raiders ($6,000)	13-7	Seattle	62,049
1983	Dec. 24	Seattle ($6,000)	Denver ($6,000)	31-7	Seattle	64,275
1982	Jan. 9	N.Y. Jets ($6,000)	Cincinnati ($6,000)	44-17	Cincinnati	57,560
	Jan. 9	San Diego ($6,000)	Pittsburgh ($6,000)	31-28	Pittsburgh	53,546
	Jan. 8	L.A. Raiders ($6,000)	Cleveland ($6,000)	27-10	Los Angeles	56,555

PLAYOFF GAMES SUMMARIES

Season	Date	Winner (Share)	Loser (Share)	Score	Site	Attendance
	Jan. 8	Miami ($6,000)	New England ($6,000)	28-13	Miami	68,842
1981	Dec. 27	Buffalo ($3,000)	N.Y. Jets ($3,000)	31-27	New York	57,050
1980	Dec. 28	Oakland ($3,000)	Houston ($3,000)	27-7	Oakland	53,333
1979	Dec. 23	Houston ($3,000)	Denver ($3,000)	13-7	Houston	48,776
1978	Dec. 24	Houston ($3,000)	Miami ($3,000)	17-9	Miami	72,445

**Sudden death overtime*

1999 AFC WILD CARD PLAYOFF GAMES

Kingdome, Seattle, Washington
January 9, 2000, Attendance: 66,170

MIAMI 20, SEATTLE 17—J.J. Johnson rushed for 86 yards, and his 2-yard scoring run with 4:48 left vaulted the Dolphins past the Seahawks. The Seahawks led 10-3 at halftime, but Dan Marino completed 11- and 27-yard passes to O.J. McDuffie on the opening drive of the second half to set up his tying 1-yard touchdown pass to Oronde Gadsden. Charlie Rogers returned the ensuing kickoff 85 yards for a touchdown, but Olindo Mare's 50-yard field goal late in the quarter trimmed the deficit to 17-13. Faced with third-and-17 from his own 8-yard line with 8:26 remaining, Marino fired a 23-yard completion to Tony Martin. Marino completed a 20-yard pass to Martin and 24-yard pass to Gadsden to set up Johnson's go-ahead 2-yard run. Terrell Buckley's interception at the Seahawks' 42 clinched the victory. The Seahawks failed to cross midfield in the second half. Marino was 17 of 30 for 196 yards and 1 touchdown. Jon Kitna was 14 of 30 for 162 yards and 1 touchdown, with 2 interceptions. The Dolphins' defense recorded 6 sacks and limited the Seahawks to 171 total yards. This was the final game played in the Kingdome, the Seahawks only home since joining the NFL in 1976.

Miami	3	0	10	7	—	20
Seattle	7	3	7	0	—	17

Sea — Dawkins 9 pass from Kitna (Peterson kick)
Mia — FG Mare 32
Sea — FG Peterson 50
Mia — Gadsden 1 pass from Marino (Mare kick)
Sea — Rogers 85 kickoff return (Peterson kick)
Mia — FG Mare 50
Mia — Johnson 2 run (Mare kick)

Adelphia Coliseum, Nashville, Tennessee
January 8, 2000, Attendance: 66,672

TENNESSEE 22, BUFFALO 16—Kevin Dyson received a crossfield lateral from Frank Wycheck and raced 75 yards down the left sideline for a touchdown with three seconds remaining to lift the Titans past the Bills. The Titans' defense permitted just 3 first downs in the first half, and Jevon Kearse sacked Rob Johnson for a safety, as Tennessee took a 12-0 lead into the locker room. Antowain Smith's 44-yard run on the first play of the second half set up his 4-yard scoring jaunt, quickly cutting the deficit to 12-7. Johnson's 37-yard pass to Eric Moulds early in the fourth quarter led to Smith's go-ahead touchdown with 11:08 remaining, but Johnson's 2-point conversion pass attempt fell incomplete. A 16-yard punt return by Isaac Byrd with 6:15 remaining sparked the Titans, and five consecutive carries by Eddie George set up Al Del Greco's 36-yard field goal with 1:48 remaining to give Tennessee a 15-13 lead. With time winding down, Johnson, who lost a shoe on a 3-yard scramble, completed a 9-yard pass to Peerless Price with 20 seconds left to set up Steve Christie's go-ahead 41-yard field goal with 16 seconds remaining. Lorenzo Neal fielded Christie's ensuing kickoff at the Titans' 24, ran a yard and handed the ball to Wycheck, who began running to his right, stopped, and threw across field to a wide-open Dyson, who had a wall of blockers and streaked 75 yards untouched for the game's final points. McNair was 13 of 24 for 76 yards, with 1 interception. George had 29 carries for 106 yards. Johnson was 10 of 22 for 131 yards.

Buffalo	0	0	7	9	—	16
Tennessee	0	12	0	10	—	22

Tenn — Safety, Kearse sacked Johnson in end zone
Tenn — McNair 1 run (Del Greco kick)
Tenn — FG Del Greco 40
Buff — Smith 4 run (Christie kick)
Buff — Smith 1 run (pass failed)
Tenn — FG Del Greco 36
Buff — FG Christie 41
Tenn — Dyson 75 kickoff return lateral from Wycheck (Del Greco kick)

NFC WILD CARD PLAYOFF GAMES RESULTS

Season	Date	Winner (Share)	Loser (Share)	Score	Site	Attendance
1999	Jan. 9	Minnesota ($10,000)	Dallas ($10,000)	27-10	Minneapolis	64,056
	Jan. 8	Washington ($16,000)	Detroit ($10,000)	27-13	Washington	79,411
1998	Jan. 3	San Francisco ($10,000)	Green Bay ($10,000)	30-27	San Francisco	66,506
	Jan. 2	Arizona ($10,000)	Dallas ($15,000)	20-7	Dallas	62,969
1997	Dec. 28	Tampa Bay ($10,000)	Detroit ($10,000)	20-10	Tampa Bay	73,361
	Dec. 27	Minnesota ($10,000)	N.Y. Giants ($15,000)	23-22	East Rutherford	77,497
1996	Dec. 29	San Francisco ($10,000)	Philadelphia ($10,000)	14-0	San Francisco	56,460
	Dec. 28	Dallas ($14,000)	Minnesota ($10,000)	40-15	Dallas	64,682
1995	Dec. 31	Green Bay ($13,000)	Atlanta ($7,500)	37-20	Green Bay	60,453
	Dec. 30	Philadelphia ($7,500)	Detroit ($7,500)	58-37	Philadelphia	66,099
1994	Jan. 1	Chicago ($7,500)	Minnesota ($12,000)	35-18	Minnesota	60,347
	Dec. 31	Green Bay ($7,500)	Detroit ($7,500)	16-12	Green Bay	58,125
1993	Jan. 9	N.Y. Giants ($7,500)	Minnesota ($7,500)	17-10	East Rutherford	75,089
	Jan. 8	Green Bay ($7,500)	Detroit ($12,000)	28-24	Detroit	68,479
1992	Jan. 3	Philadelphia ($6,000)	New Orleans ($6,000)	36-20	New Orleans	68,893
	Jan. 2	Washington ($6,000)	Minnesota ($10,000)	24-7	Minnesota	57,353
1991	Dec. 29	Dallas ($6,000)	Chicago ($6,000)	17-13	Chicago	62,594
	Dec. 28	Atlanta ($6,000)	New Orleans ($10,000)	27-20	New Orleans	68,794
1990	Jan. 6	Chicago ($10,000)	New Orleans ($6,000)	16-6	Chicago	60,767
	Jan. 5	Washington ($6,000)	Philadelphia ($6,000)	20-6	Philadelphia	65,287
1989	Dec. 31	L.A. Rams ($6,000)	Philadelphia ($6,000)	21-7	Philadelphia	65,479
1988	Dec. 26	Minnesota ($6,000)	L.A. Rams ($6,000)	28-17	Minnesota	61,204
1987	Jan. 3	Minnesota ($6,000)	New Orleans ($6,000)	44-10	New Orleans	68,546
1986	Dec. 28	Washington ($6,000)	L.A. Rams ($6,000)	19-7	Washington	54,567
1985	Dec. 29	N.Y. Giants ($6,000)	San Francisco ($6,000)	17-3	East Rutherford	75,131
1984	Dec. 23	N.Y. Giants ($6,000)	L.A. Rams ($6,000)	16-13	Anaheim	67,037
1983	Dec. 26	L.A. Rams ($6,000)	Dallas ($6,000)	24-17	Dallas	62,118
1982	Jan. 9	Dallas ($6,000)	Tampa Bay ($6,000)	30-17	Dallas	65,042
	Jan. 9	Minnesota ($6,000)	Atlanta ($6,000)	30-24	Minnesota	60,560
	Jan. 8	Green Bay ($6,000)	St. Louis ($6,000)	41-16	Green Bay	54,282
	Jan. 8	Washington ($6,000)	Detroit ($6,000)	31-7	Washington	55,045
1981	Dec. 27	N.Y. Giants ($3,000)	Philadelphia ($3,000)	27-21	Philadelphia	71,611
1980	Dec. 28	Dallas ($3,000)	Los Angeles ($3,000)	34-13	Dallas	63,052
1979	Dec. 23	Philadelphia ($3,000)	Chicago ($3,000)	27-17	Philadelphia	69,397
1978	Dec. 24	Atlanta ($3,000)	Philadelphia ($3,000)	14-13	Atlanta	59,403

1999 NFC WILD CARD PLAYOFF GAMES

Metrodome, Minneapolis, Minnesota
January 9, 2000, Attendance: 64,056

MINNESOTA 27, DALLAS 10—Robert Smith rushed for 140 yards and Jeff George passed for 3 touchdowns as the Vikings defeated the Cowboys. The Cowboys drove 73 and 79 yards on their first two possessions to claim a 10-3 lead. Anthony Bass recovered Robert Thomas's fumble at the Cowboys' 23 early in the second quarter, and four plays later Smith caught a screen pass from George and faked out George Teague at the 12-yard line before running into the end zone. George gave the Vikings their first lead with a 58-yard touchdown bomb to Randy Moss 28 seconds before halftime. The Vikings led 27-10 before the Cowboys put together two final drives, only to turn the ball over inside the Vikings' 20 on both occasions. George was 12 of 25 for 212 yards and 3 touchdowns. Moss had 5 receptions for 127 yards. Troy Aikman was 22 of 38 for 286 yards, with 1 interception. Raghib Ismail had 8 catches for 163 yards.

Dallas	10	0	0	0	— 10
Minnesota	3	14	3	7	— 27

Dall — FG Murray 18
Minn — FG Anderson 47
Dall — E. Smith 5 run (Murray kick)
Minn — R. Smith 26 pass from George (Anderson kick)
Minn — Moss 58 pass from George (Anderson kick)
Minn — FG Anderson 38
Minn — Carter 5 pass from George (Anderson kick)

FedEx Field, Landover, Maryland
January 8, 2000, Attendance: 79,411

WASHINGTON 27, DETROIT 13—Stephen Davis rushed for 119 yards and 2 touchdowns as the Redskins scored on their first four, and five of their first six, possessions to defeat the Lions. The Lions forced the Redskins to punt on their first possession, but Clint Kriewaldt was flagged for running into punter Matt Turk, giving the Redskins a first down. A 41-yard pass interference penalty moments later set up Davis's first touchdown. Davis rumbled 58 yards to begin the Redskins' next possession, but injured his right knee on a 4-yard touchdown run to cap the drive. Champ Bailey's interception set up Conway's first field goal, and Davis returned to carry 5 times for 45 yards on the Redskins' fourth possession to lead to Conway's second field goal. Davis sat out the remainder of the game, but Washington put together one more scoring drive to take a 27-0 halftime lead. The Lions did not cross midfield until midway through the third quarter, and Lamar Campbell's blocked field-goal attempt led to Ron Rice's 94-yard return. Gus Frerotte's 5-yard touchdown pass to Ron Rivers came on the last play of the game. Brad Johnson was 15 of 31 for 174 yards and 1 touchdown, with 2 interceptions. Frerotte was 21 of 46 for 251 yards and 1 touchdown, with 2 interceptions. Washington had more rushing yards (223-45) and longer time of possession (38:28-21:32).

Detroit	0	0	0	13	— 13
Washington	14	13	0	0	— 27

Wash — Davis 1 run (Conway kick)
Wash — Davis 4 run (Conway kick)
Wash — FG Conway 33
Wash — FG Conway 23
Wash — Connell 30 pass from Johnson (Conway kick)
Det — Rice 94 blocked field goal return (pass failed)
Det — Rivers 5 pass from Frerotte (Hanson kick)

AFC-NFC PRO BOWL SUMMARIES

AFC-NFC PRO BOWL AT A GLANCE RESULTS (1971-2000)

NFC leads series, 16-14

Year	Date	Winner (Share)	Loser (Share)	Score	Site	Attendance
2000	Feb. 6	NFC ($25,000)	AFC ($12,500)	51-31	Honolulu	50,112
1999	Feb. 7	AFC ($25,000)	NFC ($12,500)	23-10	Honolulu	50,075
1998	Feb. 1	AFC ($25,000)	NFC ($12,500)	29-24	Honolulu	49,995
1997	Feb. 2	AFC ($20,000)	NFC ($10,000)	26-23 (OT)	Honolulu	50,031
1996	Feb. 4	NFC ($20,000)	AFC ($10,000)	20-13	Honolulu	50,034
1995	Feb. 5	AFC ($20,000)	NFC ($10,000)	41-13	Honolulu	49,121
1994	Feb. 6	NFC ($20,000)	AFC ($10,000)	17-3	Honolulu	50,026
1993	Feb. 7	AFC ($10,000)	NFC ($5,000)	23-20 (OT)	Honolulu	50,007
1992	Feb. 2	NFC ($10,000)	AFC ($5,000)	21-15	Honolulu	50,209
1991	Feb. 3	AFC ($10,000)	NFC ($5,000)	23-21	Honolulu	50,345
1990	Feb. 4	NFC ($10,000)	AFC ($5,000)	27-21	Honolulu	50,445
1989	Jan. 29	NFC ($10,000)	AFC ($5,000)	34-3	Honolulu	50,113
1988	Feb. 7	AFC ($10,000)	NFC ($5,000)	15-6	Honolulu	50,113
1987	Feb. 1	AFC ($10,000)	NFC ($5,000)	10-6	Honolulu	50,101
1986	Feb. 2	NFC ($10,000)	AFC ($5,000)	28-24	Honolulu	50,101
1985	Jan. 27	AFC ($10,000)	NFC ($5,000)	22-14	Honolulu	50,385
1984	Jan. 29	NFC ($10,000)	AFC ($5,000)	45-3	Honolulu	50,445
1983	Feb. 6	NFC ($10,000)	AFC ($5,000)	20-19	Honolulu	49,883
1982	Jan. 31	AFC ($5,000)	NFC ($2,500)	16-13	Honolulu	50,402
1981	Feb. 1	NFC ($5,000)	AFC ($2,500)	21-7	Honolulu	50,360
1980	Jan. 27	NFC ($5,000)	AFC ($2,500)	37-27	Honolulu	49,800
1979	Jan. 29	NFC ($5,000)	AFC ($2,500)	13-7	Los Angeles	46,281
1978	Jan. 23	NFC ($5,000)	AFC ($2,500)	14-13	Tampa	51,337
1977	Jan. 17	AFC ($2,000)	NFC ($1,500)	24-14	Seattle	64,752
1976	Jan. 26	NFC ($2,000)	AFC ($1,500)	23-20	New Orleans	30,546
1975	Jan. 20	NFC ($2,000)	AFC ($1,500)	17-10	Miami	26,484
1974	Jan. 20	AFC ($2,000)	NFC ($1,500)	15-13	Kansas City	66,918
1973	Jan. 21	AFC ($2,000)	NFC ($1,500)	33-28	Dallas	37,091
1972	Jan. 23	AFC ($2,000)	NFC ($1,500)	26-13	Los Angeles	53,647
1971	Jan. 24	NFC ($2,000)	AFC ($1,500)	27-6	Los Angeles	48,222

2000 AFC-NFC PRO BOWL

Aloha Stadium, Honolulu, Hawaii
February 6, 2000, Attendance: 50,112

NFC 51, AFC 31—Randy Moss earned player-of-the-game honors by setting records with 9 receptions for 212 yards as the NFC defeated the AFC in the highest-scoring Pro Bowl ever. Aeneas Williams intercepted Peyton Manning's pass and raced 62 yards down the left sideline to give the NFC an early 7-0 lead. Kurt Warner's 48-yard pass to Moss on the NFC's first possession set up Jason Hanson's first field goal. Mike Alstott and Jimmy Smith each scored twice in the first half, and Michael Bates's 66-yard kickoff return led to Hanson's Pro Bowl-record tying 51-yard field goal as the half expired to give the NFC a 27-21 lead. Alstott's third touchdown increased the NFC's lead to 37-21, and Derrick Brooks's interception of Mark Brunell and 20-yard return staked the NFC to a 44-24 lead with 11:12 left. The AFC responded with Manning's 52-yard touchdown pass to Smith with 6:30 remaining, but Steve Beuerlein found Moss with a 25-yard scoring pass with 1:05 left to finish the scoring. Warner led the three NFC quarterbacks by completing 8 of 11 passes for 123 yards. Alstott led all rushers with 13 carries for 67 yards. The NFC forced 6 turnovers. Manning was 17 of 23 for 270 yards and 2 touchdowns, with 2 interceptions. Smith had 8 receptions for 119 yards. The previous record, 64 points, was set in 1980.

AFC (31)	Offense	NFC (51)
Marvin Harrison (Indianapolis)	WR	Isaac Bruce (St. Louis)
Jonathan Ogden (Baltimore)	LT	Orlando Pace (St. Louis)
Bruce Matthews (Tennessee)	LG	Randall McDaniel (Minnesota)
Kevin Mawae (N.Y. Jets)	C	Jeff Christy (Minnesota)
Ruben Brown (Buffalo)	RG	Tre Johnson (Washington)
Leon Searcy (Jacksonville)	RT	William Roaf (New Orleans)
Tony Gonzalez (Kansas City)	TE	Wesley Walls (Carolina)
Jimmy Smith (Jacksonville)	WR	Cris Carter (Minnesota)
Peyton Manning (Indianapolis)	QB	Kurt Warner (St. Louis)
Sam Gash (Buffalo)	RB	Mike Alstott (Tampa Bay)
Edgerrin James (Indianapolis)	RB	Marshall Faulk (St. Louis)
	Defense	
Tony Brackens (Jacksonville)	LE	Kevin Carter (St. Louis)
Darrell Russell (Oakland)	IL	Luther Elliss (Detroit)
Trevor Pryce (Denver)	IL	Warren Sapp (Tampa Bay)
Jevon Kearse (Tennessee)	RE	Michael Strahan (N.Y. Giants)
Kevin Hardy (Jacksonville)	LOLB	Derrick Brooks (Tampa Bay)
Zach Thomas (Miami)	ILB	Hardy Nickerson (Tampa Bay)
Peter Boulware (Baltimore)	ROLB	Jessie Armstead (N.Y. Giants)
Sam Madison (Miami)	LCB	Todd Lyght (St. Louis)
Charles Woodson (Oakland)	RCB	Aeneas Williams (Arizona)
Lawyer Milloy (New England)	SS	John Lynch (Tampa Bay)
Carnell Lake (Jacksonville)	FS	Lance Schulters (San Francisco)

SUBSTITUTIONS

AFC—Offense: G—Will Shields (Kansas City). T—Walter Jones (Seattle). C—Tim Grunhard (Kansas City). TE—Frank Wycheck (Tennessee). WR—Terry Glenn (New England), Keyshawn Johnson (N.Y. Jets). RB—Corey Dillon (Cincinnati), Eddie George (Tennessee), Detron Smith (Denver). QB—Mark Brunell (Jacksonville), Rich Gannon (Oakland). P—Tom Tupa (N.Y. Jets). K—Olindo Mare (Miami). Defense: IL—Cortez Kennedy (Seattle). DE—Michael McCrary (Baltimore). LB—Chad Brown (Seattle), Mo Lewis (N.Y. Jets), Junior Seau (San Diego). DB—James Hasty (Kansas City), Tremain Mack (Cincinnati), Rod Woodson (Baltimore).

NFC—Offense: G—Adam Timmerman (St. Louis). T—Erik Williams (Dallas). C—Tony Mayberry (Tampa Bay). TE—David Sloan (Detroit). WR—Michael Bates (Carolina), Randy Moss (Minnesota), Muhsin Muhammad (Carolina). RB—Stephen Davis (Washington), Glyn Milburn (Chicago), Emmitt Smith (Dallas). QB—Steve Beuerlein (Carolina), Brad Johnson (Washington). P—Mitch Berger (Minnesota). K—Jason Hanson (Detroit). Defense: IL—D'Marco Farr (St. Louis). DE—Robert Porcher (Detroit), Simeon Rice (Arizona). LB—Stephen Boyd (Detroit), Dexter Coakley (Dallas). DB—Brian Dawkins (Philadelphia), Troy Vincent (Philadelphia).

HEAD COACHES

AFC—Tom Coughlin (Jacksonville)
NFC—Tony Dungy (Tampa Bay)

OFFICIALS

Referee—Tom White. Umpire—Jeff Rice. Side Judge—Gary Lane. Linesman—Sid Semon. Back Judge—Jack Vaughan. Field Judge—Tom Sifferman. Line Judge—Dave Anderson.

AFC	7	14	0	10	—	31
NFC	10	17	10	14	—	51

NFC — A. Williams 62 interception return (Hanson kick)
NFC — FG Hanson 21
AFC — J. Smith 5 pass from Brunell (Mare kick)
NFC — Alstott 1 run (Hanson kick)
AFC — Gonzalez 10 pass from Gannon (Mare kick)
NFC — Alstott 3 run (Hanson kick)
AFC — J. Smith 21 pass from Manning (Mare kick)
NFC — FG Hanson 51
NFC — Alstott 1 run (Hanson kick)
NFC — FG Hanson 23
AFC — FG Mare 33
NFC — Brooks 20 interception return (Hanson kick)
AFC — J. Smith 52 pass from Manning (Mare kick)
NFC — Moss 25 pass from Beuerlein (Hanson kick)

TEAM STATISTICS	NFC	AFC
Total First Downs	19	21
Rushing	7	1
Passing	12	18

Penalty	0	2
Total Net Yardage	370	397
Total Offensive Plays	70	69
Average Gain Per Offensive Play	5.3	5.8
Rushes	37	20
Yards Gained Rushing (Net)	110	48
Average Yards per Rush	3.0	2.4
Passes Attempted	31	49
Passes Completed	18	27
Had Intercepted	0	5
Tackled Attempting to Pass	2	0
Yards Lost Attempting to Pass	(-12)	0
Yards Gained Passing (Net)	260	349
Punts	6	5
Average Distance	44.2	47.0
Punt Returns	4	4
Punt Return Yardage	99	56
Kickoff Returns	6	5
Kickoff Return Yardage	232	153
Interception Return Yardage	86	0
Total Return Yardage	417	209
Fumbles	4	2
Fumbles Lost	1	1
Own Fumbles Recovered	3	1
Opponent Fumbles Recovered	1	1
Penalties	8	6
Yards Penalized	41	45
Field Goals	3	1
Field Goals Attempted	3	1
Third-Down Efficiency	8/16	4/12
Fourth-Down Efficiency	1/1	0/1
Time of Possession	33:49	26:11

INDIVIDUAL STATISTICS

RUSHING: NFC: Alstott 13-67-3, Faulk 13-39-0, E. Smith 7-10-0, Davis 1-1-0, B. Johnson 1-(-3)-0, Beuerlein 2-(-4)-0. AFC: George 9-42-0, James 9-14-0, Dillon 1-(-3)-0, Manning 1-(-5)-0.

PASSING: NFC: Warner 11-8-123-0-0, Beuerlein 7-4-85-1-0, B. Johnson 13-6-64-0-0. AFC: Manning 23-17-270-2-2, Brunell 14-6-44-1-2, Gannon 11-4-35-1-1.

RECEIVING: NFC: Moss 9-212-1, Carter 5-27-0, Muhammad 2-24-0, Faulk 1-5-0, E. Smith 1-4-0. AFC: J. Smith 8-119-3, K. Johnson 5-35-0, Gonzalez 4-55-0, Harrison 4-35-0, Glenn 3-69-0, Wycheck 1-16-0, James 1-11-0, Dillon 1-9-0.

KICKOFF RETURNS: NFC: Bates 4-168, Milburn 2-64. AFC: Mack 2-65, Dillon 2-57, Glenn 1-31.

PUNT RETURNS: NFC: Milburn 2-53, Moss 2-46. AFC: Woodson 4-30, Mack 1-26.

PUNTING: NFC: Berger 6-265-44.2. AFC: Tupa 5-235-47.0.

INTERCEPTIONS: NFC: Dawkins 2-4, Williams 1-62, Brooks 1-20, Coakley 1-0.

SACKS: AFC: McCrary, R. Woodson.

1999 AFC-NFC PRO BOWL

Aloha Stadium, Honolulu, Hawaii
February 7, 1999, Attendance: 50,075

AFC 23, NFC 10—John Elway, appearing in uniform on a football field for the final time, drove the AFC to its initial touchdown and then watched a strong defensive effort as the AFC won the Pro Bowl for the third consecutive season. Elway capped a game-opening 61-yard drive with a touchdown pass to Sam Gash. The AFC led 10-3 late in the first half when Deion Sanders intercepted a Vinny Testaverde pass at the NFC's 10 and raced downfield, only to be caught by Ed McCaffrey at the AFC 3-yard line as the half expired. The NFC drove into AFC territory early in the second half, but Ty Law thwarted the NFC's spirits with a 67-yard interception return for a touchdown to give the AFC a 17-3 lead with 9:42 left in the third quarter. The NFC reached the end zone three minutes later as Emmitt Smith scored, but the AFC responded with a field goal on its ensuing possession. Jason Elam's third field goal with 1:02 remaining finished the scoring. Elway played just one drive and was 4 of 5 for 55 yards and 1 touchdown. Keyshawn Johnson had 7 catches for 87 yards and shared player-of-the-game honors with Law. Chandler completed 9 of 25 passes for 133 yards en route to leading the NFC to its only touchdown. Randy Moss had 7 catches for 108 yards.

NFC	3	0	7	0	—	10
AFC	7	3	10	3	—	23

AFC — Gash 3 pass from Elway (Elam kick)
NFC — FG Anderson 23
AFC — FG Elam 23
AFC — Law 67 interception return (Elam kick)
NFC — E. Smith 3 run (Anderson kick)
AFC — FG Elam 46
AFC — FG Elam 26

1998 AFC-NFC PRO BOWL

Aloha Stadium, Honolulu, Hawaii
February 1, 1998, Attendance: 49,995

AFC 29, NFC 24—Warren Moon guided the AFC to points on all three of his drives, including the winning touchdown from 1 yard with 1:49 left as the AFC scored the game's final 15 points to beat the NFC. Steve Young threw a 22-yard touchdown pass to Herman Moore to cap the game's opening drive and give the NFC a 7-0 lead. Late in the first quarter, Mark Brunell threw a 17-yard touchdown pass to Andre Rison to tie the game. Both touchdown passes came on third-and-8 plays. The NFC responded with a 7-play, 71-yard drive capped by Young's 36-yard touchdown pass to Rob Moore. Trent Dilfer guided the NFC to its third touchdown, keyed by a 21-yard pass to Irving Fryar and 23-yard pass to Mike Alstott, and capped by Dorsey Levens's 12-yard touchdown run with 1:36 left in the half to give the NFC a 21-7 lead. The NFC had a chance to pad its lead on its first possession of the second half, but Jason Hanson missed a 44-yard field goal. The AFC bounced back with a 10-play, 65-yard drive that culminated with Drew Bledsoe's 14-yard touchdown pass to Jimmy Smith late in the third quarter. After Hanson's 35-yard field goal gave the NFC a 24-14 lead with 13:42 left, Moon entered the game and drove the AFC into field-goal range, where Mike Hollis drilled a 48-yard attempt with 8:51 left. Attempting to grind out the clock, Warrick Dunn fumbled, and Darryl Williams recovered at the AFC's 49 with 3:03 remaining. After a holding penalty moved the AFC back 10 yards, Moon fired a 57-yard pass to Tim Brown to set up Eddie George's 4-yard run with 2:31 left. The AFC went for the lead instead of a tie, but Moon's pass to Rison fell incomplete. However, the AFC got the ball back when Chris Chandler fumbled the snap on the NFC's first play, and Michael Sinclair recovered at the NFC's 16 with 2:19 left. Three runs by George set up Moon's winning sneak with 1:49 remaining. Moon's 2-point conversion pass to Brown was incomplete, keeping the AFC's lead at 29-24. The NFC was unable to move beyond its own 31-yard line in the final moments, and the AFC prevailed. Tim Brown had 5 receptions for 129 yards. Moon, who was 4 of 8 for 89 yards, earned player of the game honors.

AFC	7	0	7	15	—	29
NFC	7	14	0	3	—	24

NFC —H. Moore 22 pass from Young (Hanson kick)
AFC —Rison 17 pass from Brunell (Hollis kick)
NFC —R. Moore 36 pass from Young (Hanson kick)
NFC —Levens 12 run (Hanson kick)
AFC —J. Smith 14 pass from Bledsoe (Hollis kick)
NFC —FG Hanson 35
AFC —FG Hollis 48
AFC —George 4 run (pass failed)
AFC —Moon 1 run (pass failed)

1997 AFC-NFC PRO BOWL

Aloha Stadium, Honolulu, Hawaii
February 2, 1997, Attendance: 50,031

AFC 26, NFC 23 (OT)—Cary Blanchard's 37-yard field goal 8:16 into overtime gave the AFC a 26-23 victory. The field goal was an ironic ending to a game that saw Blanchard and NFC kicker John Kasay, who each broke the previous single-season record of 35 field goals, combine to miss 5 of 8 field-goal attempts. The NFC scored on its first two possessions, with Vikings guard Randall McDaniel, who lined up as a fullback, scoring his first professional touchdown to give the NFC a 9-0 lead. However, the follies of the kicking unit began as holder Matt Turk muffed the snap on the extra point attempt. Blanchard booted a 28-yard field goal with 27 seconds left in the half to cut the NFC's lead to 9-3. In the third quarter, Barry Sanders scored from 6 yards out, but Kerry Collins was sacked on the 2-point attempt. A 41-yard pass from Drew Bledsoe to Tony Martin led to Curtis Martin's 3-yard run, and after Ashley Ambrose ran an interception back 54 yards for a touchdown 11 seconds into the fourth quarter, the AFC found itself with a 16-15 lead. The NFC drove for more than six minutes, only to have Kasay miss a 40-yard field goal attempt. After an AFC punt, Cris Carter caught a 47-yard touchdown bomb from Gus Frerotte to put the NFC ahead 23-16. After each team punted, the AFC got the ball on its own 20-yard line with 55 seconds left. Mark Brunell hit Tim Brown with an 80-yard bomb down the right sideline to tie the game with 44 seconds left. Wesley Walls caught a 33-yard pass to give the NFC a chance to win in regulation, but Kasay missed a 39-yard attempt and the game went to overtime. The AFC won the overtime toss, but Blanchard missed a 41-yard field goal attempt. The NFC had to punt after three plays, and Brunell hit Ben Coates with a 43-yard pass on the AFC's first play. After three running plays failed to gain a first down, Blanchard trotted onto the field and made the game-winning kick. The teams combined for a Pro Bowl record 962 total yards. Brunell, who completed 12 of 22 pass attempts for 236 yards, was selected as the player of the game.

AFC	0	3	7	13	3	— 26
NFC	9	0	6	8	0	— 23

NFC — FG Kasay 20
NFC — R. McDaniel 5 pass from Favre (muffed snap)
AFC — FG Blanchard 28
NFC — Sanders 6 run (pass failed)
AFC — Martin 3 run (Blanchard kick)
AFC — Ambrose 54 interception return (pass failed)
NFC — Carter 53 pass from Frerotte (Walls pass from Frerotte)
AFC — T. Brown 80 pass from Brunell (Blanchard kick)
AFC — FG Blanchard 37

1996 AFC-NFC PRO BOWL

Aloha Stadium, Honolulu, Hawaii
February 4, 1996, Attendance: 50,034

NFC 20, AFC 13—Jerry Rice had 6 receptions for 82 yards and 1 touchdown to earn player of the game honors in the NFC's victory. The 49ers' wide receiver, who was named to the Pro Bowl for the tenth consecutive year, caught a 1-yard touchdown pass from Packers quarterback Brett Favre 1:41 into the second quarter to cap an 80-yard drive and give the NFC the lead for good at 10-7. The AFC had taken a 7-0 lead 2:26 into the game when Bengals quarterback Jeff Blake connected with Steelers wide receiver Yancey Thigpen on a Pro Bowl-record 93-yard touchdown pass. The NFC increased its advantage to 20-7 at halftime on Redskins linebacker Ken Harvey's 36-yard interception return for a touchdown and Falcons kicker Morten Andersen's 24-yard field goal. The AFC trimmed its deficit to 20-13 when Colts quarterback Jim Harbaugh teamed with Patriots running back Curtis Martin on a 17-yard touchdown pass in the final minute of the third quarter, but its bid to win or tie was rebuffed twice in the final minutes of the fourth quarter. First, 49ers safety Tim McDonald intercepted Harbaugh's pass in the end zone with 1:50 remaining. Then, after the AFC forced a punt and got the ball back near midfield, Harbaugh drove his team to the NFC's 9-yard line in the closing seconds. But he spiked the ball once to stop the clock and threw 3 consecutive incompletions as time ran out. The AFC outgained the NFC 390 total yards to 287, but its quarterbacks suffered 4 interceptions, including 3 off Harbaugh, the NFL's leading passer during the regular season. The NFC raised its edge to 15-11 in Pro Bowl games since the AFL-NFL merger in 1970.

NFC	3	17	0	0	—	20
AFC	7	0	6	0	—	13

AFC — Thigpen 93 pass from Blake (Elam kick)
NFC — FG Andersen 36
NFC — Rice 1 pass from Favre (Andersen kick)
NFC — Harvey 36 interception return (Andersen kick)
NFC — FG Andersen 24
AFC — Martin 17 pass from Harbaugh (kick failed)

AFC-NFC PRO BOWL SUMMARIES

1995 AFC-NFC PRO BOWL

Aloha Stadium, Honolulu, Hawaii
February 5, 1995, Attendance: 49,121

AFC 41, NFC 13—Colts rookie Marshall Faulk rushed for a Pro Bowl-record 180 yards to key the AFC's rout of the NFC. Faulk, who earned the Dan McGuire Trophy as the player of the game, averaged nearly 14 yards on his 13 carries and shattered the previous rushing mark of 112 yards set by O.J. Simpson in the 1973 game. Faulk's 49-yard touchdown run from punt formation in the fourth quarter was the longest in Pro Bowl history. The Seahawks' Chris Warren added 127 yards on 14 carries as the AFC amassed records for rushing yards (400) and total yards (552). Steelers tight end Eric Green caught 2 touchdown passes for the victors. The NFC managed only 196 total yards, a large chunk coming when 49ers quarterback Steve Young and Vikings wide receiver Cris Carter teamed on a 51-yard touchdown pass in the first quarter. That gave the NFC a 10-0 advantage, but the AFC rallied in the second quarter and took the lead for good when the Browns' Leroy Hoard scored on a 4-yard touchdown run 2:07 before halftime.

AFC	0	17	3	21	—	41
NFC	10	0	3	0	—	13

NFC — FG Reveiz 28
NFC — Carter 51 pass from Young (Reveiz kick)
AFC — Green 22 pass from Elway (Carney kick)
AFC — FG Carney 22
AFC — Hoard 4 run (Carney kick)
NFC — FG Reveiz 49
AFC — FG Carney 23
AFC — Warren 11 run (Carney kick)
AFC — Green 16 pass from Hostetler (Carney kick)
AFC — Faulk 49 run (Carney kick)

1994 AFC-NFC PRO BOWL

Aloha Stadium, Honolulu, Hawaii
February 6, 1994, Attendance: 50,026

NFC 17, AFC 3—The NFC converted a blocked punt and a fumble recovery into touchdowns just 2:20 apart in the second half of its victory over the AFC. With the score tied 3-3 late in the third quarter, Saints linebacker Renaldo Turnbull deflected a punt by the Oilers' Greg Montgomery, and the NFC took possession at the AFC's 48-yard line. A 32-yard pass from Bobby Hebert to Falcons teammate Andre Rison positioned Rams running back Jerome Bettis for a 4-yard touchdown run with 1:27 left in the third quarter. Moments later, Rams defensive tackle Sean Gilbert recovered a fumble by Oilers quarterback Warren Moon at the AFC's 19. Hebert then teamed with the Vikings' Cris Carter on a 15-yard touchdown pass 53 seconds into the fourth period. The NFC kept the AFC out of the end zone by maintaining possession for more than 38 minutes and forcing 6 turnovers. Rison earned the Dan McGuire Trophy as the player of the game by catching 6 passes for 86 yards. The victory was the fourth in the last six years for the NFC, which leads the series 14-10.

NFC	3	0	7	7	—	17
AFC	0	3	0	0	—	3

NFC — FG Johnson 35
AFC — FG Anderson 25
NFC — Bettis 4 run (Johnson kick)
NFC — Carter 15 pass from Hebert (Johnson kick)

1993 AFC-NFC PRO BOWL

Aloha Stadium, Honolulu, Hawaii
February 7, 1993, Attendance: 50,007

AFC 23, NFC 20—Nick Lowery's 33-yard field goal 4:09 into overtime gave the American Conference all-stars an unlikely 23-20 victory over the National Conference. Despite being overwhelmed by the NFC in first downs (30-9), and total yards (471-114), the AFC won because it forced 6 turnovers, blocked a pair of field goals (1 of which was returned for a touchdown), and returned an interception for a score. Special-teams star Steve Tasker of the Bills earned the Dan McGuire Trophy as the player of the game for making 4 tackles, forcing a fumble, and blocking a field goal. The block came with eight minutes left in regulation and the game tied at 13-13. The Raiders' Terry McDaniel picked up the loose ball and ran 28 yards for a touchdown and a 20-13 AFC lead. The NFC rallied behind 49ers quarterback Steve Young, whose fourth-down, 23-yard touchdown pass to Giants running back Rodney Hampton tied the game at 20-20 with 10 seconds left in regulation. Young completed 18 of 32 passes for 196 yards but was intercepted 3 times and lost a fumble when sacked in overtime. Raiders defensive end Howie Long fell on that fumble at the NFC 28-yard line, and five plays later, Lowery converted the winning field goal.

AFC	0	10	3	7	3 —	23
NFC	3	10	0	7	0 —	20

NFC — FG Andersen 27
AFC — Seau 31 interception return (Lowery kick)
NFC — FG Andersen 37
NFC — Irvin 9 pass from Aikman (Andersen kick)
AFC — FG Lowery 42
AFC — FG Lowery 29
AFC — McDaniel 28 blocked field goal return (Lowery kick)
NFC — Hampton 23 pass from Young (Andersen kick)
AFC — FG Lowery 33

1992 AFC-NFC PRO BOWL

Aloha Stadium, Honolulu, Hawaii
February 2, 1992, Attendance: 50,209

NFC 21, AFC 15—Atlanta's Chris Miller threw an 11-yard touchdown pass to San Francisco's Jerry Rice with 4:04 remaining in the game to lift the NFC over the AFC. It was the NFC's thirteenth win in the 22-game series. The AFC had taken a 15-14 lead when the Raiders' Jeff Jaeger kicked a 27-yard field goal 1:49 into the fourth quarter. But the NFC, aided by a key roughing-the-passer penalty on a third-down incompletion from the AFC 24-yard line, drove 85 yards to the winning score. The Cowboys' Michael Irvin, playing in his first Pro Bowl, caught 8 passes for 125 yards, including a 13-yard touchdown in the first quarter, and was named the player of the game. Rice had 7 catches for 77 yards. Mark Rypien of Washington, the Super Bowl most valuable player one week earlier, completed 11 of 18 passes for 165 yards and 2 touchdowns for the NFC, including a 35-yard pass to Redskins teammate Gary Clark just 26 seconds before halftime. Miller completed 7 of his 10 attempts for 85 yards.

NFC	7	7	0	7	—	21
AFC	7	5	0	3	—	15

AFC — Clayton 4 pass from Kelly (Jaeger kick)
NFC — Irvin 13 pass from Rypien (Lohmiller kick)
AFC — Safety, Townsend tackled Byner in end zone
AFC — FG Jaeger 48
NFC — Clark 35 pass from Rypien (Lohmiller kick)
AFC — FG Jaeger 27
NFC — Rice 11 pass from Miller (Lohmiller kick)

1991 AFC-NFC PRO BOWL

Aloha Stadium, Honolulu, Hawaii
February 3, 1991, Attendance: 50,345

AFC 23, NFC 21—Buffalo's Jim Kelly and Houston's Ernest Givins combined for a 13-yard scoring pass late in the fourth quarter to rally the AFC over the NFC. Phoenix rookie Johnny Johnson scored on runs of 1 and 9 yards to put the NFC ahead 14-3 in the third quarter. Buffalo's Andre Reed, who led all receivers with 4 catches for 80 yards, caught a 20-yard scoring reception from Kelly early in the fourth quarter to move the AFC to within 1 point. Barry Sanders ran 22 yards for a touchdown to increase the NFC's lead to 21-13. Miami's Jeff Cross blocked a 46-yard field-goal attempt by New Orleans's Morten Andersen with seven seconds remaining to preserve the win. Buffalo's Bruce Smith recorded 3 sacks and also had a blocked field goal. Kelly, who completed 13 of 19 passes for 210 yards and 2 touchdowns, was presented the Dan McGuire Award as player of the game. The AFC's victory narrowed the NFC's Pro Bowl series lead to 12-9.

AFC	3	0	3	17	—	23
NFC	0	7	7	7	—	21

AFC — FG Lowery 26
NFC — J. Johnson 1 run (Andersen kick)
AFC — FG Lowery 43
NFC — J. Johnson 9 run (Andersen kick)
AFC — Reed 20 pass from Kelly (Lowery kick)
NFC — Sanders 22 run (Andersen kick)
AFC — FG Lowery 34
AFC — Givins 13 pass from Kelly (Lowery kick)

1990 AFC-NFC PRO BOWL

Aloha Stadium, Honolulu, Hawaii
February 4, 1990, Attendance: 50,445

NFC 27, AFC 21—The NFC captured its second straight Pro Bowl as the defense accounted for a pair of touchdowns and forced 5 turnovers before the eleventh consecutive sellout crowd at Aloha Stadium. The AFC held a 7-6 halftime edge on a 1-yard scoring run by Christian Okoye of the Chiefs. The NFC then rallied with 21 unanswered points in the third quarter. David Meggett of the Giants began the comeback with an 11-yard touchdown reception from Philadelphia's Randall Cunningham. The Rams' Jerry Gray followed with a 51-yard interception return for a score and the Vikings' Keith Millard added an 8-yard fumble return for a touchdown four minutes later to give the NFC a commanding 27-7 lead. Seattle's Dave Krieg rallied the AFC with a 5-yard touchdown pass to Miami's Ferrell Edmunds. Cleveland's Mike Johnson then returned an interception 22 yards for a score to pull the AFC to within 27-21. Gray, who was credited with 7 tackles, was given the Dan McGuire Award as player of the game. Krieg led all quarterbacks by completing 15 of 23 for 148 yards and 1 touchdown. Buffalo's Thurman Thomas topped all receivers with 5 catches for 47 yards, while Indianapolis's Eric Dickerson led all rushers with 46 yards on 15 carries. The win gave the NFC a 12-8 advantage in Pro Bowl games since 1971.

NFC	3	3	21	0	—	27
AFC	0	7	0	14	—	21

NFC — FG Murray 23
NFC — FG Murray 41
AFC — Okoye 1 run (Treadwell kick)
NFC — Meggett 11 pass from Cunningham (Murray kick)
NFC — Gray 51 interception return (Murray kick)
NFC — Millard 8 fumble recovery return (Murray kick)
AFC — Edmunds 5 pass from Krieg (Treadwell kick)
AFC — M. Johnson 22 interception return (Treadwell kick)

1989 AFC-NFC PRO BOWL

Aloha Stadium, Honolulu, Hawaii
January 29, 1989, Attendance: 50,113

NFC 34, AFC 3—The NFC scored 34 unanswered points to snap a two-game losing streak to the AFC before the tenth straight sellout crowd in Honolulu's Aloha Stadium. Bills kicker Scott Norwood provided the AFC's only points on a 38-yard field goal 6:23 into the game. Touchdown runs by Dallas's Herschel Walker (4 yards) and Atlanta's John Settle (1) brought the NFC a 14-3 halftime lead. Walker added a 7-yard scoring run, the Saints' Morten Andersen kicked field goals of 27 and 51 yards, and Los Angeles Rams' wide receiver Henry Ellard caught an 8-yard scoring pass from Minnesota quarterback Wade Wilson in the second half to complete the scoring. Chicago running back Neal Anderson and Philadelphia quarterback Randall Cunningham, who were both appearing in their first Pro Bowl, also played major roles in the NFC's victory. Anderson rushed 13 times for 85 yards and had 2 receptions for 17. Cunningham, who was voted the game's outstanding player, completed 10 of 14 passes for 63 yards and rushed for 49 yards. The NFC, which had 5 takeaways, outgained the AFC 355 yards to 167 and held a time-of-possession advantage of 35:18 to 24:42. Houston quarterback Warren Moon completed 13 of 20 passes for 134 yards for the AFC. The win gave the NFC an 11-8 advantage in Pro

Bowl games.

AFC	3	0	0	0	—	3
NFC	7	7	10	10	—	34

AFC — FG Norwood 38
NFC — Walker 4 run (Andersen kick)
NFC — Settle 1 run (Andersen kick)
NFC — FG Andersen 27
NFC — Walker 7 run (Andersen kick)
NFC — FG Andersen 51
NFC — Ellard 8 pass from Wilson (Andersen kick)

1988 AFC-NFC PRO BOWL

Aloha Stadium, Honolulu, Hawaii
February 7, 1988, Attendance: 50,113

AFC 15, NFC 6—Led by a tenacious pass rush, the AFC defeated the NFC for the second consecutive year before the ninth straight sellout crowd in Honolulu's Aloha Stadium. Buffalo quarterback Jim Kelly scored the game's lone touchdown on a 1-yard run for a 7-6 halftime lead. Colts kicker Dean Biasucci added field goals from 37 and 30 yards to complete the AFC's scoring. Saints kicker Morten Andersen had 25- and 36-yard field goals to account for the NFC's points. AFC defenders held the NFC to 213 yards and recorded 8 sacks. Bills defensive end Bruce Smith, who had 2 sacks among his 5 tackles, was voted the game's outstanding player. Oilers running back Mike Rozier led all rushers with 49 yards on 9 carries. Jets wide receiver Al Toon had 5 receptions for 75 yards. The AFC generated 341 yards total offense and held a time-of-possession advantage of 34:14 to 25:46. By winning, the AFC cut the NFC's lead in the Pro Bowl series to 10-8.

NFC	0	6	0	0	—	6
AFC	0	7	6	2	—	15

NFC — FG Andersen 25
AFC — Kelly 1 run (Biasucci kick)
NFC — FG Andersen 36
AFC — FG Biasucci 37
AFC — FG Biasucci 30
AFC — Safety, Montana forced out of end zone

1987 AFC-NFC PRO BOWL

Aloha Stadium, Honolulu, Hawaii
February 1, 1987, Attendance: 50,101

AFC 10, NFC 6—The AFC defeated the NFC in the lowest-scoring game in AFC-NFC Pro Bowl history. The AFC took a 10-0 halftime lead on Broncos quarterback John Elway's 10-yard touchdown pass to Raiders tight end Todd Christensen and Patriots kicker Tony Franklin's 26-yard field goal. The AFC defense made the lead stand by forcing the NFC to settle for a pair of field goals from 38 and 19 yards by Saints kicker Morten Andersen after the NFC had first downs at the AFC 31-, 7-, 16-, 15-, 5-, and 7-yard lines. Both AFC scores were set up by fumble recoveries by Seahawks linebacker Fredd Young and Dolphins linebacker John Offerdahl, respectively. Eagles defensive end Reggie White, who tied a Pro Bowl record with 4 sacks among his 7 solo tackles, was voted the game's outstanding player. The AFC victory cut the NFC's lead in the Pro Bowl series to 10-7.

AFC	7	3	0	0	—	10
NFC	0	0	3	3	—	6

AFC — Christensen 10 pass from Elway (Franklin kick)
AFC — FG Franklin 26
NFC — FG Andersen 38
NFC — FG Andersen 19

1986 AFC-NFC PRO BOWL

Aloha Stadium, Honolulu, Hawaii
February 2, 1986, Attendance: 50,101

NFC 28, AFC 24—New York Giants quarterback Phil Simms brought the NFC back from a 24-7 halftime deficit to defeat the AFC. Simms, who completed 15 of 27 passes for 212 yards and 3 touchdowns, was named the most valuable player of the game. The AFC had taken its first-half lead behind a 2-yard run by Los Angeles Raiders running back Marcus Allen, who also threw a 51-yard scoring pass to San Diego wide receiver Wes Chandler, an 11-yard touchdown catch by Pittsburgh wide receiver Louis Lipps, and a 34-yard field goal by Steelers kicker Gary Anderson. Minnesota's Joey Browner accounted for the NFC's only score before halftime with a 48-yard interception return. After intermission, the NFC blanked the AFC while scoring 3 touchdowns via a 15-yard catch by Washington wide receiver Art Monk, a 2-yard reception by Dallas tight end Doug Cosbie, and a 15-yard catch by Tampa Bay tight end Jimmie Giles with 2:47 remaining in the game. The victory gave the NFC a 10-6 Pro Bowl record against the AFC.

NFC	0	7	7	14	—	28
AFC	7	17	0	0	—	24

AFC — Allen 2 run (Anderson kick)
NFC — Browner 48 interception return (Andersen kick)
AFC — Chandler 51 pass from Allen (Anderson kick)
AFC — FG Anderson 34
AFC — Lipps 11 pass from O'Brien (Anderson kick)
NFC — Monk 15 pass from Simms (Andersen kick)
NFC — Cosbie 2 pass from Simms (Andersen kick)
NFC — Giles 15 pass from Simms (Andersen kick)

1985 AFC-NFC PRO BOWL

Aloha Stadium, Honolulu, Hawaii
January 27, 1985, Attendance: 50,385

AFC 22, NFC 14—Defensive end Art Still of the Kansas City Chiefs recovered a fumble and returned it 83 yards for a touchdown to clinch the AFC's victory over the NFC. Still's touchdown came in the fourth period with the AFC trailing 14-12 and was one of several outstanding defensive plays in a Pro Bowl dominated by two record-breaking defenses. The teams combined for a Pro Bowl-record 17 sacks, including 4 by New York Jets defensive end Mark Gastineau, who was named the game's outstanding player. The AFC's first score came on a safety when Gastineau tackled running back Eric Dickerson of the Los Angeles Rams in the end zone. The AFC's second score, a 6-yard pass from Miami's Dan Marino to Los Angeles Raiders running back Marcus Allen, was set up by a partial block of a punt by Seahawks linebacker Fredd Young. The NFC leads the series 9-6.

AFC	0	9	0	13	—	22
NFC	0	0	7	7	—	14

AFC — Safety, Gastineau tackled Dickerson in end zone
AFC — Allen 6 pass from Marino (Johnson kick)
NFC — Lofton 13 pass from Montana (Stenerud kick)
NFC — Payton 1 run (Stenerud kick)
AFC — FG Johnson 33
AFC — Still 83 fumble recovery return (Johnson kick)
AFC — FG Johnson 22

1984 AFC-NFC PRO BOWL

Aloha Stadium, Honolulu, Hawaii
January 29, 1984, Attendance: 50,445

NFC 45, AFC 3—The NFC won its sixth Pro Bowl in the last seven seasons by routing the AFC. The NFC was led by the passing of most valuable player Joe Theismann of Washington, who completed 21 of 27 passes for 242 yards and 3 touchdowns. Theismann set Pro Bowl records for completions and touchdown passes. The NFC established Pro Bowl marks for most points scored and fewest points allowed. Running back William Andrews of Atlanta had 6 carries for 43 yards and caught 4 passes for 49 yards, including scoring receptions of 16 and 2 yards. Los Angeles Rams rookie Eric Dickerson gained 46 yards on 11 carries, including a 14-yard touchdown run, and had 45 yards on 5 catches. Rams safety Nolan Cromwell had a 44-yard interception return for a touchdown early in the third period to give the NFC a commanding 24-3 lead. Green Bay wide receiver James Lofton caught an 8-yard touchdown pass, while tight end teammate Paul Coffman had a 6-yard scoring catch.

NFC	3	14	14	14	—	45
AFC	0	3	0	0	—	3

NFC — FG Haji-Sheikh 23
NFC — Andrews 16 pass from Theismann (Haji-Sheikh kick)
NFC — Andrews 2 pass from Montana (Haji-Sheikh kick)
AFC — FG Anderson 43
NFC — Cromwell 44 interception return (Haji-Sheikh kick)
NFC — Lofton 8 pass from Theismann (Haji-Sheikh kick)
NFC — Coffman 6 pass from Theismann (Haji-Sheikh kick)
NFC — Dickerson 14 run (Haji-Sheikh kick)

1983 AFC-NFC PRO BOWL

Aloha Stadium, Honolulu, Hawaii
February 6, 1983, Attendance: 49,883

NFC 20, AFC 19—Dallas's Danny White threw an 11-yard touchdown pass to the Packers' John Jefferson with 35 seconds remaining to rally the NFC over the AFC. White, who completed 14 of 26 passes for 162 yards, kept the winning 65-yard drive alive with a 14-yard completion to Jefferson on a fourth-and-7 play at the AFC 25. The AFC was ahead 12-10 at halftime and increased the lead to 19-10 in the third period, when Marcus Allen scored on a 1-yard run. San Diego's Dan Fouts, who attempted 30 passes, set Pro Bowl records for most completions (17) and yards (274). Pittsburgh's John Stallworth was the AFC's leading receiver with 7 catches for 67 yards. William Andrews topped the NFC with 5 receptions for 48 yards. Fouts and Jefferson were co-winners of the player of the game award.

AFC	9	3	7	0	—	19
NFC	0	10	0	10	—	20

AFC — Walker 34 pass from Fouts (Benirschke kick)
AFC — Safety, Still tackled Theismann in end zone
NFC — Andrews 3 run (Moseley kick)
NFC — FG Moseley 35
AFC — FG Benirschke 29
AFC — Allen 1 run (Benirschke kick)
NFC — FG Moseley 41
NFC — Jefferson 11 pass from D. White (Moseley kick)

1982 AFC-NFC PRO BOWL

Aloha Stadium, Honolulu, Hawaii
January 31, 1982, Attendance: 50,402

AFC 16, NFC 13—Nick Lowery of Kansas City kicked a 23-yard field goal with three seconds remaining to give the AFC a last-second victory over the NFC. Lowery's kick climaxed a 69-yard drive directed by quarterback Dan Fouts. The NFC gained a 13-13 tie with 2:43 to go when Dallas's Tony Dorsett ran 4 yards for a touchdown. In the drive to the winning field goal, Fouts completed 3 passes, including a 23-yard toss to San Diego teammate Kellen Winslow that put the ball on the NFC's 5-yard line. Two plays later, Lowery kicked the field goal. Winslow, who caught 6 passes for 86 yards, was named co-player of the game along with Tampa Bay defensive end Lee Roy Selmon.

NFC	0	6	0	7	—	13
AFC	0	0	13	3	—	16

NFC — Giles 4 pass from Montana (kick blocked)
AFC — Muncie 2 run (kick failed)
AFC — Campbell 1 run (Lowery kick)
NFC — Dorsett 4 run (Septien kick)
AFC — FG Lowery 23

1981 AFC-NFC PRO BOWL

Aloha Stadium, Honolulu, Hawaii
February 1, 1981, Attendance: 50,360

NFC 21, AFC 7—Eddie Murray kicked 4 field goals and Steve Bartkowski fired a 55-yard scoring pass to Alfred Jenkins to lead the NFC to its fourth straight victory over the AFC and a 7-4 edge in the series. Murray was named the game's most valuable player and missed tying Garo Yepremian's Pro Bowl record of 5 field goals when a 37-yard attempt hit the crossbar with 22 seconds remaining. The AFC's only score came on a 9-yard pass from Brian Sipe to Stanley Morgan in the second period. Bartkowski completed 9 of 21 passes for 173 yards, while Sipe connected on 10 of 15 for 142 yards. Ottis Anderson led all rushers with 70 yards on 10 carries. Earl Campbell, the NFL's leading rusher in 1980, was limited to 24 yards on 8 attempts.

AFC	0	7	0	0	—	7
NFC	3	6	0	12	—	21

NFC — FG Murray 31
AFC — Morgan 9 pass from Sipe (J. Smith kick)
NFC — FG Murray 31
NFC — FG Murray 34
NFC — Jenkins 55 pass from Bartkowski (Murray kick)
NFC — FG Murray 36
NFC — Safety, Shell called for holding in end zone

1980 AFC-NFC PRO BOWL

Aloha Stadium, Honolulu, Hawaii
January 27, 1980, Attendance: 49,800

NFC 37, AFC 27—Running back Chuck Muncie of New Orleans ran for 2 touchdowns and threw a 25-yard option pass for another score to give the NFC its third consecutive victory over the AFC. Muncie, who was selected the game's most valuable player, snapped a 3-3 tie on a 1-yard touchdown run at 1:41 of the second quarter, then scored on an 11-yard run in the fourth quarter for the NFC's final touchdown. Two scoring records were set in the game— 37 points by the NFC, eclipsing the 33 by the AFC in 1973, and the 64 points by both teams, surpassing the 61 scored in 1973.

NFC	3	20	7	7	—	37
AFC	3	7	10	7	—	27

NFC — FG Moseley 37
AFC — FG Fritsch 19
NFC — Muncie 1 run (Moseley kick)
AFC — Pruitt 1 pass from Bradshaw (Fritsch kick)
NFC — D. Hill 13 pass from Manning (kick failed)
NFC — T. Hill 25 pass from Muncie (Moseley kick)
NFC — Henry 86 punt return (Moseley kick)
AFC — Campbell 2 run (Fritsch kick)
AFC — FG Fritsch 29
NFC — Muncie 11 run (Moseley kick)
AFC — Campbell 1 run (Fritsch kick)

1979 AFC-NFC PRO BOWL

Memorial Coliseum, Los Angeles, California
January 29, 1979, Attendance: 46,281

NFC 13, AFC 7—Roger Staubach completed 9 of 15 passes for 125 yards, including the winning touchdown on a 19-yard strike to Dallas Cowboys teammate Tony Hill in the third period. The winning drive began at the AFC's 45-yard line after a shanked punt. Staubach hit Ahmad Rashad with passes of 15 and 17 yards to set up Hill's decisive catch. The victory gave the NFC a 5-4 advantage in Pro Bowl games. Rashad, who accounted for 89 yards on 5 receptions, was named the player of the game. The AFC led 7-6 at halftime on Bob Griese's 8-yard scoring toss to Steve Largent late in the second quarter. Largent finished the game with 5 receptions for 75 yards. The NFC scored first as Archie Manning marched his team 70 yards in 11 plays, capped by Wilbert Montgomery's 2-yard touchdown run. The AFC's Earl Campbell was the game's leading rusher with 66 yards on 12 carries.

AFC	0	7	0	0	—	7
NFC	0	6	7	0	—	13

NFC — Montgomery 2 run (kick failed)
AFC — Largent 8 pass from Griese (Yepremian kick)
NFC — T. Hill 19 pass from Staubach (Corral kick)

1978 AFC-NFC PRO BOWL

Tampa Stadium, Tampa, Florida
January 23, 1978, Attendance: 51,337

NFC 14, AFC 13—Walter Payton, the NFL's leading rusher in 1977, sparked a second-half comeback to give the NFC the win and tie the series between the two conferences at four victories each. Payton, who was the game's most valuable player, gained 77 yards on 13 carries and scored the tying touchdown on a 1-yard burst with 7:37 left in the game. Efren Herrera kicked the winning extra point. The AFC dominated the first half of the game, taking a 13-0 lead on field goals of 21 and 39 yards by Toni Linhart and a 10-yard touchdown pass from Ken Stabler to Oakland teammate Cliff Branch. On the NFC's first possession of the second half, Pat Haden put together the first touchdown drive after Eddie Brown returned Ray Guy's punt to the AFC 46-yard line. Haden connected on all 4 of his passes on that drive, finally hitting Terry Metcalf with a 4-yard scoring toss. The NFC continued to rally and, with Jim Hart at quarterback, moved 63 yards in 12 plays for the go-ahead score. During the winning drive, Hart completed 5 of 6 passes for 38 yards and Payton picked up 20 more on the ground.

AFC	3	10	0	0	—	13
NFC	0	0	7	7	—	14

AFC — FG Linhart 21
AFC — Branch 10 pass from Stabler (Linhart kick)
AFC — FG Linhart 39
NFC — Metcalf 4 pass from Haden (Herrera kick)
NFC — Payton 1 run (Herrera kick)

1977 AFC-NFC PRO BOWL

Kingdome, Seattle, Washington
January 17, 1977, Attendance: 64,752

AFC 24, NFC 14—O.J. Simpson's 3-yard touchdown burst at 7:03 of the first quarter gave the AFC a lead it would not surrender, breaking a two-game NFC win streak and giving the American Conference stars a 4-3 series lead. The AFC took a 17-7 lead midway through the second period on the first of 2 Ken Anderson touchdown passes, a 12-yard toss to Charlie Joiner. But the NFC mounted a 73-yard drive capped by Lawrence McCutcheon's 1-yard touchdown plunge to pull within 17-14 at the half. Following a scoreless third quarter, player of the game Mel Blount thwarted a possible NFC score when he intercepted Jim Hart's pass in the end zone. Less than three minutes later, Blount again picked off a Hart pass. That set up Anderson's 27-yard touchdown strike to the Raiders' Cliff Branch for the final score.

NFC	0	14	0	0	—	14
AFC	10	7	0	7	—	24

AFC — Simpson 3 run (Linhart kick)
AFC — FG Linhart 31
NFC — Thomas 15 run (Bakken kick)
AFC — Joiner 12 pass from Anderson (Linhart kick)
NFC — McCutcheon 1 run (Bakken kick)
AFC — Branch 27 pass from Anderson (Linhart kick)

1976 AFC-NFC PRO BOWL

Superdome, New Orleans, Louisiana
January 26, 1976, Attendance: 30,546

NFC 23, AFC 20—Mike Boryla, a late substitute who did not enter the game until 5:39 remained, lifted the National Football Conference to the victory over the American Football Conference with 2 touchdown passes in the final minutes. It was the second straight NFC win, squaring the series at 3-3. Until Boryla started firing the ball the AFC was in control, leading 13-0 at the half. Boryla entered the game after Billy Johnson had raced 90 yards with a punt to make the score 20-9 in favor of the AFC. He floated a 14-yard touchdown pass to Terry Metcalf and later fired an 8-yard scoring pass to Mel Gray for the winner.

AFC	0	13	0	7	—	20
NFC	0	0	9	14	—	23

AFC — FG Stenerud 20
AFC — FG Stenerud 35
AFC — Burrough 64 pass from Pastorini (Stenerud kick)
NFC — FG Bakken 42
NFC — Foreman 4 pass from Hart (kick blocked)
AFC — Johnson 90 punt return (Stenerud kick)
NFC — Metcalf 14 pass from Boryla (Bakken kick)
NFC — Gray 8 pass from Boryla (Bakken kick)

1975 AFC-NFC PRO BOWL

Orange Bowl, Miami, Florida
January 20, 1975, Attendance: 26,484

NFC 17, AFC 10—Los Angeles quarterback James Harris, who took over the NFC offense after Jim Hart of St. Louis suffered a laceration above his right eye in the second period, threw 2 touchdown passes early in the fourth period to pace the NFC to its second victory in the five-game Pro Bowl series. The NFC win snapped a three-game AFC victory string. Harris, who was named the player of the game, connected with St. Louis's Mel Gray for an 8-yard touchdown 2:03 into the final period. One minute and 24 seconds later, following a fumble recovery by Washington's Ken Houston, Harris tossed another 8-yard scoring pass to Washington's Charley Taylor for the decisive points.

NFC	0	3	0	14	—	17
AFC	0	0	10	0	—	10

NFC — FG Marcol 33
AFC — Warfield 32 pass from Griese (Gerela kick)
AFC — FG Gerela 33
NFC — Gray 8 pass from J. Harris (Marcol kick)
NFC — Taylor 8 pass from J. Harris (Marcol kick)

1974 AFC-NFC PRO BOWL

Arrowhead Stadium, Kansas City, Missouri
January 20, 1974, Attendance: 66,918

AFC 15, NFC 13—Miami's Garo Yepremian's fifth field goal—a 42-yard kick with 21 seconds remaining—gave the AFC its third straight victory since the NFC won the inaugural game following the 1970 season. The field goal by Yepremian, who was voted the game's outstanding player, offset a 21-yard field goal by Atlanta's Nick Mike-Mayer that had given the NFC a 13-12 advantage with 1:41 remaining. The only touchdown in the game was scored by the NFC on a 14-yard pass from Philadelphia's Roman Gabriel to Lawrence McCutcheon of the Los Angeles Rams.

NFC	0	10	0	3	—	13
AFC	3	3	3	6	—	15

AFC — FG Yepremian 16
NFC — FG Mike-Mayer 27
NFC — McCutcheon 14 pass from Gabriel (Mike-Mayer kick)
AFC — FG Yepremian 37
AFC — FG Yepremian 27
AFC — FG Yepremian 41
NFC — FG Mike-Mayer 21
AFC — FG Yepremian 42

1973 AFC-NFC PRO BOWL

Texas Stadium, Irving, Texas
January 21, 1973, Attendance: 37,091

AFC 33, NFC 28—Paced by the rushing and receiving of player of the game O.J. Simpson, the AFC erased a 14-0 first period deficit and built a commanding 33-14 lead midway through the fourth period before the NFC managed 2 touchdowns in the final minute of play. Simpson rushed for 112 yards and caught 3 passes for 58 more to gain unanimous recognition in the balloting for player of the game. John Brockington scored 3 touchdowns for the NFC.

AFC	0	10	10	13	—	33
NFC	14	0	0	14	—	28

NFC — Brockington 1 run (Marcol kick)
NFC — Brockington 3 pass from Kilmer (Marcol kick)
AFC — Simpson 7 run (Gerela kick)
AFC — FG Gerela 18
AFC — FG Gerela 22
AFC — Hubbard 11 run (Gerela kick)
AFC — O. Taylor 5 pass from Lamonica (kick failed)
AFC — Bell 12 interception return (Gerela kick)
NFC — Brockington 1 run (Marcol kick)
NFC — Kwalick 12 pass from Snead (Marcol kick)

1972 AFC-NFC PRO BOWL

Memorial Coliseum, Los Angeles, California
January 23, 1972, Attendance: 53,647

AFC 26, NFC 13—Kansas City's Jan Stenerud kicked 4 field goals to lead the AFC from a 6-0 deficit to victory. The AFC defense picked off 3 passes. Stenerud was selected as the outstanding offensive player and his Kansas City teammate, linebacker Willie Lanier, was the game's outstanding defensive player.

AFC	0	3	13	10	—	26
NFC	0	6	0	7	—	13

NFC — Grim 50 pass from Landry (kick failed)
AFC — FG Stenerud 25
AFC — FG Stenerud 23
AFC — FG Stenerud 48
AFC — Morin 5 pass from Dawson (Stenerud kick)
AFC — FG Stenerud 42
NFC — V. Washington 2 run (Knight kick)
AFC — F. Little 6 run (Stenerud kick)

1971 AFC-NFC PRO BOWL

Memorial Coliseum, Los Angeles, California
January 24, 1971, Attendance: 48,222

NFC 27, AFC 6—Mel Renfro of Dallas broke open the first meeting between the American Football Conference and National Football Conference all-star teams as he returned a pair of punts 82 and 56 yards for touchdowns in the final period to clinch the NFC victory over the AFC. Renfro was voted the game's outstanding back and linebacker Fred Carr of Green Bay the outstanding lineman.

AFC	0	3	3	0	—	6
NFC	0	3	10	14	—	27

AFC — FG Stenerud 37
NFC — FG Cox 13
NFC — Osborn 23 pass from Brodie (Cox kick)
NFC — FG Cox 35
AFC — FG Stenerud 16
NFC — Renfro 82 punt return (Cox kick)
NFC — Renfro 56 punt return (Cox kick)

PRO BOWL ALL-TIME RESULTS

PRO BOWL ALL-TIME RESULTS

Date	Result	Site (attendance)	Honored players
Jan. 15, 1939	New York Giants 13, Pro All-Stars 10	Wrigley Field, Los Angeles (20,000)	
Jan. 14, 1940	Green Bay 16, NFL All-Stars 7	Gilmore Stadium, Los Angeles (18,000)	
Dec. 29, 1940	Chicago Bears 28, NFL All-Stars 14	Gilmore Stadium, Los Angeles (21,624)	
Jan. 4, 1942	Chicago Bears 35, NFL All-Stars 24	Polo Grounds, New York (17,725)	
Dec. 27, 1942	NFL All-Stars 17, Washington 14	Shibe Park, Philadelphia (18,671)	
Jan. 14, 1951	American Conf. 28, National Conf. 27	Los Angeles Memorial Coliseum (53,676)	Otto Graham, Cleveland, player of the game
Jan. 12, 1952	National Conf. 30, American Conf. 13	Los Angeles Memorial Coliseum (19,400)	Dan Towler, Los Angeles, player of the game
Jan. 10, 1953	National Conf. 27, American Conf. 7	Los Angeles Memorial Coliseum (34,208)	Don Doll, Detroit, player of the game
Jan. 17, 1954	East 20, West 9	Los Angeles Memorial Coliseum (44,214)	Chuck Bednarik, Philadelphia, player of the game
Jan. 16, 1955	West 26, East 19	Los Angeles Memorial Coliseum (43,972)	Billy Wilson, San Francisco, player of the game
Jan. 15, 1956	East 31, West 30	Los Angeles Memorial Coliseum (37,867)	Ollie Matson, Chi. Cardinals, player of the game
Jan. 13, 1957	West 19, East 10	Los Angeles Memorial Coliseum (44,177)	Bert Rechichar, Baltimore, outstanding back Ernie Stautner, Pittsburgh, outstanding lineman
Jan. 12, 1958	West 26, East 7	Los Angeles Memorial Coliseum (66,634)	Hugh McElhenny, San Francisco, outstanding back Gene Brito, Washington, outstanding lineman
Jan. 11, 1959	East 28, West 21	Los Angeles Memorial Coliseum (72,250)	Frank Gifford, N.Y. Giants, outstanding back Doug Atkins, Chi. Bears, outstanding lineman
Jan. 17, 1960	West 38, East 21	Los Angeles Memorial Coliseum (56,876)	Johnny Unitas, Baltimore, outstanding back Gene (Big Daddy) Lipscomb, Baltimore, outstanding lineman
Jan. 15, 1961	West 35, East 31	Los Angeles Memorial Coliseum (62,971)	Johnny Unitas, Baltimore, outstanding back Sam Huff, N.Y. Giants, outstanding lineman
Jan. 7, 1962	AFL West 47, East 27	Balboa Stadium, San Diego (20,973)	Cotton Davidson, Dallas Texans, player of the game
Jan. 14, 1962	NFL West 31, East 30	Los Angeles Memorial Coliseum (57,409)	Jim Brown, Cleveland, outstanding back Henry Jordan, Green Bay, outstanding lineman
Jan. 13, 1963	AFL West 21, East 14	Balboa Stadium, San Diego (27,641)	Curtis McClinton, Dallas Texans, outstanding offensive player Earl Faison, San Diego, outstanding defensive player
Jan. 13, 1963	NFL East 30, West 20	Los Angeles Memorial Coliseum (61,374)	Jim Brown, Cleveland, outstanding back Gene (Big Daddy) Lipscomb, Pittsburgh, outstanding lineman
Jan. 12, 1964	NFL West 31, East 17	Los Angeles Memorial Coliseum (67,242)	Johnny Unitas, Baltimore, player of the game Gino Marchetti, Baltimore, outstanding lineman
Jan. 19, 1964	AFL West 27, East 24	Balboa Stadium, San Diego (20,016)	Keith Lincoln, San Diego, outstanding offensive player Archie Matsos, Oakland, outstanding defensive player
Jan. 10, 1965	NFL West 34, East 14	Los Angeles Memorial Coliseum (60,598)	Fran Tarkenton, Minnesota, outstanding back Terry Barr, Detroit, outstanding lineman
Jan. 16, 1965	AFL West 38, East 14	Jeppesen Stadium, Houston (15,446)	Keith Lincoln, San Diego, outstanding offensive player Willie Brown, Denver, outstanding defensive player
Jan. 15, 1966	AFL All-Stars 30, Buffalo 19	Rice Stadium, Houston (35,572)	Joe Namath, N.Y. Jets, most valuable player, offense Frank Buncom, San Diego, most valuable player, defense
Jan. 15, 1966	NFL East 36, West 7	Los Angeles Memorial Coliseum (60,124)	Jim Brown, Cleveland, outstanding back Dale Meinert, St. Louis, outstanding lineman
Jan. 21, 1967	AFL East 30, West 23	Oakland-Alameda County Coliseum (18,876)	Babe Parilli, Boston, outstanding offensive player Verlon Biggs, N.Y. Jets, outstanding defensive player
Jan. 22, 1967	NFL East 20, West 10	Los Angeles Memorial Coliseum (15,062)	Gale Sayers, Chicago, outstanding back Floyd Peters, Philadelphia, outstanding lineman
Jan. 21, 1968	AFL East 25, West 24	Gator Bowl, Jacksonville, Fla. (40,103)	Joe Namath and Don Maynard, N.Y. Jets, out. off. players Leslie (Speedy) Duncan, San Diego, out. def. player
Jan. 21, 1968	NFL West 38, East 20	Los Angeles Memorial Coliseum (53,289)	Gale Sayers, Chicago, outstanding back Dave Robinson, Green Bay, outstanding lineman
Jan. 19, 1969	AFL West 38, East 25	Gator Bowl, Jacksonville, Fla. (41,058)	Len Dawson, Kansas City, outstanding offensive player George Webster, Houston, outstanding defensive player
Jan. 19, 1969	NFL West 10, East 7	Los Angeles Memorial Coliseum (32,050)	Roman Gabriel, Los Angeles, outstanding back Merlin Olsen, Los Angeles, outstanding lineman
Jan. 17, 1970	AFL West 26, East 3	Astrodome, Houston (30,170)	John Hadl, San Diego, player of the game
Jan. 18, 1970	NFL West 16, East 13	Los Angeles Memorial Coliseum (57,786)	Gale Sayers, Chicago, outstanding back George Andrie, Dallas, outstanding lineman
Jan. 24, 1971	NFC 27, AFC 6	Los Angeles Memorial Coliseum (48,222)	Mel Renfro, Dallas, outstanding back Fred Carr, Green Bay, outstanding lineman
Jan. 23, 1972	AFC 26, NFC 13	Los Angeles Memorial Coliseum (53,647)	Jan Stenerud, Kansas City, outstanding offensive player Willie Lanier, Kansas City, outstanding defensive player
Jan. 21, 1973	AFC 33, NFC 28	Texas Stadium, Irving (37,091)	O.J. Simpson, Buffalo, player of the game
Jan. 20, 1974	AFC 15, NFC 13	Arrowhead Stadium, Kansas City (66,918)	Garo Yepremian, Miami, player of the game
Jan. 20, 1975	NFC 17, AFC 10	Orange Bowl, Miami (26,484)	James Harris, Los Angeles, player of the game
Jan. 26, 1976	NFC 23, AFC 20	Louisiana Superdome, New Orleans (30,546)	Billy Johnson, Houston, player of the game
Jan. 17, 1977	AFC 24, NFC 14	Kingdome, Seattle (64,752)	Mel Blount, Pittsburgh, player of the game
Jan. 23, 1978	NFC 14, AFC 13	Tampa Stadium (51,337)	Walter Payton, Chicago, player of the game
Jan. 29, 1979	NFC 13, AFC 7	Los Angeles Memorial Coliseum (46,281)	Ahmad Rashad, Minnesota, player of the game
Jan. 27, 1980	NFC 37, AFC 27	Aloha Stadium, Honolulu (49,800)	Chuck Muncie, New Orleans, player of the game
Feb. 1, 1981	NFC 21, AFC 7	Aloha Stadium, Honolulu (50,360)	Eddie Murray, Detroit, player of the game
Jan. 31, 1982	AFC 16, NFC 13	Aloha Stadium, Honolulu (50,402)	Kellen Winslow, San Diego, and Lee Roy Selmon, Tampa Bay, players of the game
Feb. 6, 1983	NFC 20, AFC 19	Aloha Stadium, Honolulu (49,883)	Dan Fouts, San Diego, and John Jefferson, Green Bay, players of the game
Jan. 29, 1984	NFC 45, AFC 3	Aloha Stadium, Honolulu (50,445)	Joe Theismann, Washington, player of the game
Jan. 27, 1985	AFC 22, NFC 14	Aloha Stadium, Honolulu (50,385)	Mark Gastineau, N.Y. Jets, player of the game
Feb. 2, 1986	NFC 28, AFC 24	Aloha Stadium, Honolulu (50,101)	Phil Simms, N.Y. Giants, player of the game
Feb. 1, 1987	AFC 10, NFC 6	Aloha Stadium, Honolulu (50,101)	Reggie White, Philadelphia, player of the game
Feb. 7, 1988	AFC 15, NFC 6	Aloha Stadium, Honolulu (50,113)	Bruce Smith, Buffalo, player of the game
Jan. 29, 1989	NFC 34, AFC 3	Aloha Stadium, Honolulu (50,113)	Randall Cunningham, Philadelphia, player of the game
Feb. 4, 1990	NFC 27, AFC 21	Aloha Stadium, Honolulu (50,445)	Jerry Gray, L.A. Rams, player of the game
Feb. 3, 1991	AFC 23, NFC 21	Aloha Stadium, Honolulu (50,345)	Jim Kelly, Buffalo, player of the game
Feb. 2, 1992	NFC 21, AFC 15	Aloha Stadium, Honolulu (50,209)	Michael Irvin, Dallas, player of the game
Feb. 7, 1993	AFC 23, NFC 20 (OT)	Aloha Stadium, Honolulu (50,007)	Steve Tasker, Buffalo, player of the game
Feb. 6, 1994	NFC 17, AFC 3	Aloha Stadium, Honolulu (50,026)	Andre Rison, Atlanta, player of the game
Feb. 5, 1995	AFC 41, NFC 13	Aloha Stadium, Honolulu (49,121)	Marshall Faulk, Indianapolis, player of the game
Feb. 4, 1996	NFC 20, AFC 13	Aloha Stadium, Honolulu (50,034)	Jerry Rice, San Francisco, player of the game
Feb. 2, 1997	AFC 26, NFC 23 (OT)	Aloha Stadium, Honolulu (50,031)	Mark Brunell, Jacksonville, player of the game
Feb. 1, 1998	AFC 29, NFC 24	Aloha Stadium, Honolulu (49,995)	Warren Moon, Seattle, player of the game
Feb. 7, 1999	AFC 23, NFC 10	Aloha Stadium, Honolulu (50,075)	Keyshawn Johnson, N.Y. Jets and Ty Law, New England, co-players of the game
Feb. 6, 2000	NFC 51, AFC 31	Aloha Stadium, Honolulu (50,112)	Randy Moss, Minnesota, player of the game

PRO FOOTBALL HALL OF FAME GAME

1962 New York Giants 21, St. Louis Cardinals 21
1963 Pittsburgh Steelers 16, Cleveland Browns 7
1964 Baltimore Colts 48, Pittsburgh Steelers 17
1965 Washington Redskins 20, Detroit Lions 3
1966 No game
1967 Philadelphia Eagles 28, Cleveland Browns 13
1968 Chicago Bears 30, Dallas Cowboys 24
1969 Green Bay Packers 38, Atlanta Falcons 24
1970 New Orleans Saints 14, Minnesota Vikings 13
1971 Los Angeles Rams (NFC) 17, Houston Oilers (AFC) 6
1972 Kansas City Chiefs (AFC) 23, New York Giants (NFC) 17
1973 San Francisco 49ers (NFC) 20, New England Patriots (AFC) 7
1974 St. Louis Cardinals (NFC) 21, Buffalo Bills (AFC) 13
1975 Washington Redskins (NFC) 17, Cincinnati Bengals (AFC) 9
1976 Denver Broncos (AFC) 10, Detroit Lions (NFC) 7
1977 Chicago Bears (NFC) 20, New York Jets (AFC) 6
1978 Philadelphia Eagles (NFC) 17, Miami Dolphins (AFC) 3
1979 Oakland Raiders (AFC) 20, Dallas Cowboys (NFC) 13
1980* San Diego Chargers (AFC) 0, Green Bay Packers (NFC) 0
1981 Cleveland Browns (AFC) 24, Atlanta Falcons (NFC) 10
1982 Minnesota Vikings (NFC) 30, Baltimore Colts (AFC) 14
1983 Pittsburgh Steelers (AFC) 27, New Orleans Saints (NFC) 14
1984 Seattle Seahawks (AFC) 38, Tampa Bay Buccaneers (NFC) 0
1985 New York Giants (NFC) 21, Houston Oilers (AFC) 20
1986 New England Patriots (AFC) 21, St. Louis Cardinals (NFC) 16
1987 San Francisco 49ers (NFC) 20, Kansas City Chiefs (AFC) 7
1988 Cincinnati Bengals (AFC) 14, Los Angeles Rams (NFC) 7
1989 Washington Redskins (NFC) 31, Buffalo Bills (AFC) 6
1990 Chicago Bears (NFC) 13, Cleveland Browns (AFC) 0
1991 Detroit Lions (NFC) 14, Denver Broncos (AFC) 3
1992 New York Jets (AFC) 41, Philadelphia Eagles (NFC) 14
1993 Los Angeles Raiders (AFC) 19, Green Bay Packers (NFC) 3
1994 Atlanta Falcons (NFC) 21, San Diego Chargers (AFC) 17
1995 Carolina Panthers (NFC) 20, Jacksonville Jaguars (AFC) 14
1996 Indianapolis Colts (AFC) 10, New Orleans Saints (NFC) 3
1997 Minnesota Vikings (NFC) 28, Seattle Seahawks (AFC) 26
1998 Tampa Bay Buccaneers (NFC) 30, Pittsburgh Steelers (AFC) 6
1999 Cleveland Browns (AFC) 20, Dallas Cowboys (NFC) 17 (OT)

**Game called with 5:29 remaining because of severe thunder and lightning.*

NFL INTERNATIONAL GAMES

Date	Site	Teams
Aug. 12, 1950	Ottawa, Canada	N.Y. Giants 27, Ottawa Rough Riders 6
Aug. 11, 1951	Ottawa, Canada	N.Y. Giants 41, Ottawa Rough Riders 18
Aug. 5, 1959	Toronto, Canada	Chi. Cardinals 55, Tor. Argonauts 26
Aug. 3, 1960	Toronto, Canada	Pittsburgh 43, Toronto Argonauts 16
Aug. 15, 1960	Toronto, Canada	Chicago 16, N.Y. Giants 7
Aug. 2, 1961	Toronto, Canada	St. Louis 36, Toronto Argonauts 7
Aug. 5, 1961	Montreal, Canada	Chicago 34, Montreal Allouettes 16
Aug. 8, 1961	Hamilton, Canada	Hamilton Tiger-Cats 38, Buffalo 21
Sept. 11, 1969	Montreal, Canada	Pittsburgh 17, N.Y. Giants 13
Aug. 25, 1969	Montreal, Canada	Detroit 22, Boston 9
Aug. 16, 1976	Tokyo, Japan	St. Louis 20, San Diego 10
Aug. 5, 1978	Mexico City, Mexico	New Orleans 14, Philadelphia 7
Aug. 6, 1983	London, England	Minnesota 28, St. Louis 10
*Aug. 3, 1986	London, England	Chicago 17, Dallas 6
*Aug. 9, 1987	London, England	L.A. Rams 28, Denver 27
*July 31, 1988	London, England	Miami 27, San Francisco 21
Aug. 14, 1988	Goteborg, Sweden	Minnesota 28, Chicago 21
Aug. 18, 1988	Montreal, Canada	N.Y. Jets 11, Cleveland 7
*Aug. 5, 1989	Tokyo, Japan	L.A. Rams 16, San Francisco 13 (OT)
*Aug. 6, 1989	London, England	Philadelphia 17, Cleveland 13
*Aug. 4, 1990	Tokyo, Japan	Denver 10, Seattle 7
*Aug. 5, 1990	London, England	New Orleans 17, L.A. Raiders 10
*Aug. 9, 1990	Montreal, Canada	Pittsburgh 30, New England 14
*Aug. 11, 1990	Berlin, Germany	L.A. Rams 19, Kansas City 3
*July 28, 1991	London, England	Buffalo 17, Philadelphia 13
*Aug. 3, 1991	Berlin, Germany	San Francisco 21, Chicago 7
*Aug. 3, 1991	Tokyo, Japan	Miami 19, L.A. Raiders 17
*Aug. 1, 1992	Tokyo, Japan	Houston 34, Dallas 23
*Aug. 15, 1992	Berlin, Germany	Miami 31, Denver 27
*Aug. 16, 1992	London, England	San Francisco 17, Washington 15
*July 31, 1993	Tokyo, Japan	New Orleans 28, Philadelphia 16
*Aug. 1, 1993	Barcelona, Spain	San Francisco 21, Pittsburgh 14
*Aug. 7, 1993	Berlin, Germany	Minnesota 20, Buffalo 6
*Aug. 8, 1993	London, England	Dallas 13, Detroit 13 (OT)
Aug. 14, 1993	Toronto, Canada	Cleveland 12, New England 9
*July 31, 1994	Barcelona, Spain	L.A. Raiders 25, Denver 22
*Aug. 6, 1994	Tokyo, Japan	Minnesota 17, Kansas City 9
*Aug. 13, 1994	Berlin, Germany	N.Y. Giants 28, San Diego 20
*Aug. 15, 1994	Mexico City, Mexico	Houston 6, Dallas 0
*Aug. 5, 1995	Tokyo, Japan	Denver 24, San Francisco 10
*Aug. 12, 1995	Toronto, Canada	Buffalo 9, Dallas 7
*July 27, 1996	Tokyo, Japan	San Diego 20, Pittsburgh 10
*Aug. 5, 1996	Monterrey, Mexico	Kansas City 32, Dallas 6
*July 27, 1997	Dublin, Ireland	Pittsburgh 30, Chicago 17
*Aug. 4, 1997	Mexico City, Mexico	Miami 38, Denver 19
*Aug. 16, 1997	Toronto, Canada	Green Bay 35, Buffalo 3
*Aug. 1, 1998	Tokyo, Japan	Green Bay 27, Kansas City 24 (OT)
*Aug. 15, 1998	Vancouver, Canada	San Francisco 24, Seattle 21
*Aug. 17, 1998	Mexico City, Mexico	New England 21, Dallas 3
*Aug. 7, 1999	Sydney, Australia	Denver 20, San Diego 17

**American Bowl Game*

CHICAGO ALL-STAR GAME

Pro teams won 31, lost 9, and tied 2. The game was discontinued after 1976.

Year	Date	Winner	Loser	Attendance
1976*	July 23	Pittsburgh 24	All-Stars 0	52,895
1975	Aug. 1	Pittsburgh 21	All-Stars 14	54,103
1974		No game was played		
1973	July 27	Miami 14	All-Stars 3	54,103
1972	July 28	Dallas 20	All-Stars 7	54,162
1971	July 30	Baltimore 24	All-Stars 17	52,289
1970	July 31	Kansas City 24	All-Stars 3	69,940
1969	Aug. 1	N.Y. Jets 26	All-Stars 24	74,208
1968	Aug. 2	Green Bay 34	All-Stars 17	69,917
1967	Aug. 4	Green Bay 27	All-Stars 0	70,934
1966	Aug. 5	Green Bay 38	All-Stars 0	72,000
1965	Aug. 6	Cleveland 24	All-Stars 16	68,000
1964	Aug. 7	Chicago 28	All-Stars 17	65,000
1963	Aug. 2	All-Stars 20	Green Bay 17	65,000
1962	Aug. 3	Green Bay 42	All-Stars 20	65,000
1961	Aug. 4	Philadelphia 28	All-Stars 14	66,000
1960	Aug. 12	Baltimore 32	All-Stars 7	70,000
1959	Aug. 14	Baltimore 29	All-Stars 0	70,000
1958	Aug. 15	All-Stars 35	Detroit 19	70,000
1957	Aug. 9	N.Y. Giants 22	All-Stars 12	75,000
1956	Aug. 10	Cleveland 26	All-Stars 0	75,000
1955	Aug. 12	All-Stars 30	Cleveland 27	75,000
1954	Aug. 13	Detroit 31	All-Stars 6	93,470
1953	Aug. 14	Detroit 24	All-Stars 10	93,818
1952	Aug. 15	Los Angeles 10	All-Stars 7	88,316
1951	Aug. 17	Cleveland 33	All-Stars 0	92,180
1950	Aug. 11	All-Stars 17	Philadelphia 7	88,885
1949	Aug. 12	Philadelphia 38	All-Stars 0	93,780
1948	Aug. 20	Chi. Cardinals 28	All-Stars 0	101,220
1947	Aug. 22	All-Stars 16	Chi. Bears 0	105,840
1946	Aug. 23	All-Stars 16	Los Angeles 0	97,380
1945	Aug. 30	Green Bay 19	All-Stars 7	92,753
1944	Aug. 30	Chi. Bears 24	All-Stars 21	48,769
1943	Aug. 25	All-Stars 27	Washington 7	48,471
1942	Aug. 28	Chi. Bears 21	All-Stars 0	101,100
1941	Aug. 28	Chi. Bears 37	All-Stars 13	98,203
1940	Aug. 29	Green Bay 45	All-Stars 28	84,567
1939	Aug. 30	N.Y. Giants 9	All-Stars 0	81,456
1938	Aug. 31	All-Stars 28	Washington 16	74,250
1937	Sept. 1	All-Stars 6	Green Bay 0	84,560
1936	Sept. 3	Detroit 7	All-Stars 7 (tie)	76,000
1935	Aug. 29	Chi. Bears 5	All-Stars 0	77,450
1934	Aug. 31	Chi. Bears 0	All-Stars 0 (tie)	79,432

**Game shortened because of thunderstorms.*

NFL PLAYOFF BOWL

Consolation game that matched conference runners-up.
Western Conference won 8, Eastern Conference won 2.
All games played at Miami's Orange Bowl.

1970 Los Angeles Rams 31, Dallas Cowboys 0
1969 Dallas Cowboys 17, Minnesota Vikings 13
1968 Los Angeles Rams 30, Cleveland Browns 6
1967 Baltimore Colts 20, Philadelphia Eagles 14
1966 Baltimore Colts 35, Dallas Cowboys 3
1965 St. Louis Cardinals 24, Green Bay Packers 17
1964 Green Bay Packers 40, Cleveland Browns 23
1963 Detroit Lions 17, Pittsburgh Steelers 10
1962 Detroit Lions 28, Philadelphia Eagles 10
1961 Detroit Lions 17, Cleveland Browns 16

INTERCONFERENCE GAMES

AFC VS. NFC (REGULAR SEASON), 1970-1999

	Mia	Oak	KC	Pitt	Den	Cin	Sea	Cle	Buff	SD	Balt	Jax	Tenn	NYJ	NE	Ind	TB	TOTALS
1970	2-1	1-2	0-2-1	0-3	2-2	1-2		0-3	0-3	1-2			0-3	2-1	0-3	3-0		12-27-1
1971	3-0	1-1-1	2-1	1-2	1-3	1-2		2-1	0-3	2-1			0-2-1	0-3	0-3	2-1		15-23-2
1972	3-0	3-0	2-1	2-1	1-3	2-1		1-2	2-0-1	0-3			0-3	1-2	3-0	0-3		20-19-1
1973	3-0	2-1	1-1-1	3-0	0-3-1	2-1		1-2	2-1	1-2			0-3	0-3	2-1	2-1		19-19-2
1974	2-1	3-0	1-2	3-0	2-2	2-1		1-2	2-1	1-2			0-3	2-1	3-0	1-2		23-17
1975	3-0	3-0	2-1	2-1	2-1	3-0		1-3	1-2	0-3			3-0	0-3	1-2	2-1		23-17
1976	0-2	3-0	1-1	1-1	2-0	2-0		2-0	0-2	2-0			2-0	0-2	1-1	0-2	0-1	16-12
1977	2-0	1-1	1-1	2-0	1-1	2-1	1-0	1-1	1-1	1-1			2-0	1-1	2-0	1-1		19-9
1978	3-1	4-0	0-2	3-1	2-2	2-2	3-1	4-0	1-1	2-2			2-2	1-3	2-2	2-2		31-21
1979	4-0	4-0	0-2	3-1	3-1	2-2	3-1	3-1	2-2	3-1			2-2	3-1	3-1	1-1		36-16
1980	4-0	2-2	2-0	4-0	3-1	2-2	1-3	3-1	3-1	2-2			4-0	1-3	1-3	1-1		33-19
1981	3-1	2-2	2-2	3-1	3-1	2-2	0-2	3-1	1-3	2-2			1-3	2-0	0-4	0-4		24-28
1982	1-1	3-0	0-3	1-0	2-1	1-0	1-0	0-2	1-2	1-0			0-3	4-0	0-1	0-1-1		15-14-1
1983	3-1	2-2	2-2	2-2	0-2	3-1	1-3	2-2	1-3	2-2			1-3	3-1	2-2	2-0		26-26
1984	4-0	3-1	1-1	3-1	3-1	2-2	4-0	1-3	1-3	4-0			0-4	0-2	0-4	0-4		26-26
1985	3-1	3-1	2-2	1-3	3-1	2-2	2-2	1-3	0-2	1-1			1-3	2-2	3-1	3-1		27-25
1986	2-2	1-3	1-1	2-2	3-1	3-1	3-1	2-2	1-1	0-4			2-2	2-2	3-1	1-3		26-26
1987	3-0	2-2	1-2	2-2	2-1-1	1-2	4-0	2-2	1-2	2-0			2-2	0-4	0-3	1-0		23-22-1
1988	3-1	1-3	0-2	1-3	3-1	4-0	1-3	4-0	2-2	2-2			3-1	2-0	2-2	2-2		30-22
1989	2-0	2-2	2-0	3-1	2-2	2-2	0-4	3-1	1-3	2-2			3-1	1-3	0-4	1-3		24-28
1990	2-2	3-1	4-0	3-1	1-3	1-3	2-2	1-3	3-1	1-1			1-3	2-0	0-4	2-2		26-26
1991	3-1	2-2	2-2	0-4	2-0	1-3	1-3	0-4	3-1	1-3			1-3	2-2	1-1	0-4		19-33
1992	2-2	2-2	2-2	1-3	1-3	1-3	0-4	2-2	4-0	2-0			3-1	0-4	0-4	2-0		22-30
1993	3-1	3-1	2-2	2-2	1-3	2-2	0-2	3-1	4-0	2-2			2-2	2-2	1-1	0-4		27-25
1994	2-2	3-1	3-1	2-2	1-3	1-3	2-0	3-1	1-3	2-2			0-4	1-3	4-0	0-2		25-27
1995	2-2	3-1	3-1	2-2	2-2	2-2	3-1	1-3	3-1	3-1		0-4	1-3	0-4	0-4	2-2		27-33
1996	1-3	1-3	4-0	2-2	3-1	2-2	2-2		4-0	1-3	2-2	2-2	2-2	1-3	2-2	3-1		32-28
1997	1-3	2-2	4-0	2-2	3-1	2-2	2-2		1-3	1-3	2-1-1	2-2	4-0	3-1	1-3	1-3		31-28-1
1998	3-1	3-1	3-1	2-2	3-1	1-3	3-1		3-1	1-3	1-3	3-1	1-3	2-2	2-2	0-4		31-29
1999	2-2	3-1	2-2	3-0	2-2	1-2	2-2	1-2	3-1	1-3	2-1	4-0	3-1	2-2	3-1	4-0		38-22
Total	74-31	71-38-1	52-40-2	61-45	59-49-2	55-51	41-39	48-48	52-49-1	46-53	7-7-1	11-9	46-62-1	42-60	42-60	39-55-1	0-1	746-697-9

NFC VS. AFC (REGULAR SEASON), 1970-1999

	Dall	SF	Car	Wash	Phil	Minn	StL	NYG	Chi	Det	GB	NO	Ariz	Atl	TB	Sea	TOTALS
1970	3-0	4-0		2-1	2-1	2-1	2-1	3-0	1-2	3-0	2-1	0-3	2-0-1	1-2			27-12-1
1971	3-0	2-1		1-2	1-2	2-1	1-2	1-2	1-2	4-0	2-1	0-1-2	2-1	3-0			23-15-2
1972	3-0	2-1		1-2	2-1	1-2	1-2	1-2	1-2	2-0-1	2-1	0-3	1-2	2-2			19-20-1
1973	2-1	1-2		2-1	2-1	2-1	3-0	1-2	2-2	0-3	1-1-1	1-2	0-2-1	2-1			19-19-2
1974	2-1	0-3		2-1	2-1	2-1	3-1	1-2	0-3	1-2	2-1	0-3	2-1	0-3			17-23
1975	2-1	1-2		1-2	0-3	4-0	3-0	2-1	0-3	1-2	0-3	0-3	2-1	1-2			17-23
1976	2-0	1-1		1-1	0-2	2-0	1-1	0-2	0-2	2-0	0-2	1-2	1-1	0-2		1-0	12-16
1977	1-1	0-2		1-1	1-1	1-1	2-0	0-2	1-1	2-0	0-3	0-2	0-2	0-2	0-1		9-19
1978	3-1	1-3		2-2	3-1	1-3	2-2	1-1	0-4	2-2	2-2	1-3	0-4	1-3	2-0		21-31
1979	1-3	0-4		2-2	2-2	1-3	2-2	1-1	2-2	0-4	1-3	0-4	1-3	1-3	2-0		16-36
1980	3-1	2-2		1-3	3-1	1-3	2-2	1-3	0-4	0-2	1-3	1-3	1-1	2-2	1-3		19-33
1981	4-0	3-1		2-2	3-1	1-3	1-3	1-1	4-0	2-2	1-1	2-2	3-1	1-3	0-4		28-24
1982	2-1	1-3			2-1	1-3	1-2	1-0	1-1	0-1	1-1-1	1-0		1-1	2-1		14-15-1
1983	2-2	2-2		4-0	1-1	4-0	1-3	0-4	1-1	1-3	2-2	1-3	3-1	3-1	1-3		26-26
1984	2-2	3-1		3-1	3-1	0-4	3-1	2-0	2-2	0-4	0-4	3-1	3-1	1-3	1-1		26-26
1985	3-1	3-1		4-0	1-1	2-0	3-1	2-2	3-1	2-2	0-4	0-4	2-2	0-4	0-4		25-27
1986	1-3	4-0		3-1	2-2	1-3	2-2	3-1	4-0	1-3	1-3	1-3	1-1	1-3	1-1		26-26
1987	2-1	3-1		2-1	3-1	2-1	1-2	2-1	2-2	0-4	1-2-1	4-0	0-1	0-4	0-2		22-23-1
1988	0-4	2-2		1-3	2-2	2-2	2-2	1-1	3-1	1-1	1-3	4-0	1-3	1-3	1-3		22-30
1989	0-2	4-0		2-2	3-1	2-2	3-1	4-0	2-2	1-3	0-2	4-0	1-3	2-2	0-4		28-24
1990	1-1	4-0		3-1	1-3	2-2	2-2	3-1	2-2	1-3	1-3	2-2	2-2	2-2	0-2		26-26
1991	3-1	3-1		4-0	4-0	0-2	1-3	3-1	2-2	4-0	1-3	3-1	1-1	3-1	1-3		33-19
1992	4-0	3-1		2-2	3-1	3-1	2-2	2-2	1-3	2-2	3-1	3-1	0-2	2-2	0-2		30-22
1993	2-2	2-2		1-3	2-2	2-2	2-2	2-2	2-2	2-0	3-1	2-2	1-1	1-3	1-3		25-27
1994	3-1	3-1		1-1	1-3	2-2	2-2	3-1	3-1	2-2	1-3	1-3	3-1	1-3	1-1		27-25
1995	4-0	3-1	3-1	0-4	1-3	3-1	1-3	0-4	2-2	3-1	4-0	4-0	1-3	2-2	2-2		33-27
1996	2-2	4-0	3-1	3-1	2-2	1-3	2-2	2-2	2-2	1-3	3-1	1-3	0-4	0-4	2-2		28-32
1997	2-2	2-2	2-2	1-3	2-1-1	3-1	0-4	1-3	2-2	2-2	3-1	2-2	1-3	2-2	3-1		28-31-1
1998	1-3	2-2	1-3	2-2	0-4	4-0	3-1	3-1	2-2	1-3	3-1	1-3	1-3	3-1	2-2		29-31
1999	1-3	1-3	2-2	2-2	1-3	2-2	3-1	2-2	2-2	1-3	2-2	0-4	0-4	0-4	3-1		22-38
Total	64-40	66-45	11-9	56-47	55-49-1	56-50	57-52	49-47	50-57	44-57-1	44-59-1	43-63-2	36-55-2	39-70	26-46	1-0	697-746-9

INTERCONFERENCE GAMES

1999 INTERCONFERENCE GAMES

(Home Team in capital letters)

AFC 38, NFC 22

AFC Victories

JACKSONVILLE 41, San Francisco 3
MIAMI 19, Arizona 16
Jacksonville 22, CAROLINA 20
Oakland 22, MINNESOTA 17
Seattle 14, CHICAGO 13
OAKLAND 24, Chicago 17
KANSAS CITY 31, Detroit 21
BUFFALO 26, Philadelphia 0
NEW ENGLAND 16, New York Giants 14
Baltimore 19, ATLANTA 13 (OT)
San Diego 20, DETROIT 10
DENVER 31, Green Bay 10
Tennessee 24, NEW ORLEANS 21
MIAMI 16, Philadelphia 13
PITTSBURGH 13, Atlanta 9
Cleveland 21, NEW ORLEANS 16
INDIANAPOLIS 34, Dallas 24
New England 27, ARIZONA 3
TENNESSEE 24, St. Louis 21
Seattle 27, GREEN BAY 7
NEW YORK JETS 12, Arizona 7
Buffalo 34, WASHINGTON 17
Jacksonville 30, ATLANTA 7
Pittsburgh 27, SAN FRANCISCO 6
Indianapolis 27, NEW YORK GIANTS 19
Indianapolis 44, PHILADELPHIA 17
JACKSONVILLE 41, New Orleans 23
CINCINNATI 44, San Francisco 30
NEW ENGLAND 13, Dallas 6
KANSAS CITY 31, Minnesota 28
TENNESSEE 30, Atlanta 17
BALTIMORE 31, New Orleans 8
New York Jets 22, DALLAS 21
OAKLAND 45, Tampa Bay 0
INDIANAPOLIS 24, Washington 21
Buffalo 31, ARIZONA 21
Denver 17, DETROIT 7
PITTSBURGH 30, Carolina 20

NFC Victories

CHICAGO 20, Kansas City 17
GREEN BAY 28, Oakland 24
Detroit 28, SEATTLE 20
CAROLINA 27, Cincinnati 3
TAMPA BAY 13, Denver 10
Washington 27, NEW YORK JETS 20
St. Louis 38, CINCINNATI 10
SAN FRANCISCO 24, Tennessee 22
ST. LOUIS 34, Cleveland 3
Green Bay 31, SAN DIEGO 3
Minnesota 23, DENVER 20
TAMPA BAY 17, Kansas City 10
Carolina 31, CLEVELAND 17
Chicago 23, SAN DIEGO 20 (OT)
DALLAS 20, Miami 0
MINNESOTA 35, San Diego 27
Tampa Bay 16, SEATTLE 3
NEW YORK GIANTS 41, New York Jets 28
New York Giants 19, BUFFALO 17
PHILADELPHIA 24, New England 9
WASHINGTON 21, Miami 10
ST. LOUIS 27, Baltimore 10

REGULAR SEASON INTERCONFERENCE RECORDS, 1970-1999

AMERICAN FOOTBALL CONFERENCE

Eastern Division	W	L	T	Pct.
Miami	74	31	0	.705
Buffalo	52	49	1	.510
New England	42	60	0	.412
New York Jets	42	60	0	.412
Indianapolis	39	55	1	.411
Central Division				
Pittsburgh	61	45	0	.575
Jacksonville	11	9	0	.550
Cincinnati	55	51	0	.519
Cleveland	48	48	0	.500
Baltimore	7	7	1	.467
Tennessee	46	62	1	.422
Western Division				
Oakland	71	38	1	.645
Kansas City	52	40	2	.553
Denver	59	49	2	.536
Seattle*	41	39	0	.513
San Diego	46	53	0	.465

NATIONAL FOOTBALL CONFERENCE

Eastern Division	W	L	T	Pct.
Dallas	64	40	0	.615
Washington	56	47	0	.544
Philadelphia	55	49	1	.524
New York Giants	49	47	0	.510
Arizona	36	55	2	.387
Central Division				
Minnesota	56	50	0	.528
Chicago	50	57	0	.467
Detroit	44	57	1	.431
Green Bay	44	59	3	.415
Tampa Bay*	26	47	0	.356
Western Division				
San Francisco	66	45	0	.595
St. Louis	57	52	0	.559
Carolina	11	9	0	.550
New Orleans	43	63	2	.398
Atlanta	39	70	0	.358

**Records include one game played between Seattle and Tampa Bay, won by the Seahwaks 13-10, in their inaugural season (1976) when Seattle competed in the NFC and Tampa Bay in the AFC.*

INTERCONFERENCE VICTORIES, 1970-1999

REGULAR SEASON

	AFC	NFC	Tie
1970	12	27	1
1971	15	23	2
1972	20	19	1
1973	19	19	2
1974	23	17	0
1975	23	17	0
1976	16	12	0
1977	19	9	0
1978	31	21	0
1979	36	16	0
1980	33	19	0
1981	24	28	0
1982	15	14	1
1983	26	26	0
1984	26	26	0
1985	27	25	0
1986	26	26	0
1987	23	22	1
1988	30	22	0
1989	24	28	0
1990	26	26	0
1991	19	33	0
1992	22	30	0
1993	27	25	0
1994	25	27	0
1995	27	33	0
1996	32	28	0
1997	31	28	1
1998	31	29	0
1999	38	22	0
Total	746	697	9

PRESEASON

	AFC	NFC	Tie
1970	21	28	1
1971	28	28	3
1972	27	25	4
1973	23	35	2
1974	35	25	0
1975	30	26	1
1976	30	31	0
1977	38	25	0
1978	20	19	0
1979	25	18	0
1980	22	20	1
1981	18	19	0
1982	25	16	0
1983	15	24	0
1984	16	19	0
1985	10	22	1
1986	22	17	0
1987	22	22	0
1988	23	16	1
1989	16	27	0
1990	15	29	0
1991	19	27	0
1992	30	22	0
1993	17	22	0
1994	22	16	0
1995	19	26	0
1996	27	19	0
1997	26	17	0
1998	34	16	0
1999	22	25	0
Total	697	681	14

RECORDS AFTER BYE WEEKS, 1990-99

AFC

Team	Record	Team	Record
Baltimore	1-3	Miami	8-3
Buffalo	9-7	New England	4-7
Cincinnati	3-8	N.Y. Jets	5-6
Cleveland	2-5	Oakland	6-5
Denver	8-3	Pittsburgh	6-5
Indianapolis	4-7	San Diego	5-6
Jacksonville	4-1	Seattle	3-8
Kansas City	8-3	Tennessee	6-5

RECORDS AFTER BYE WEEKS, 1990-99

NFC

Team	Record	Team	Record
Arizona	5-6	New Orleans	5-6
Atlanta	7-4	N.Y. Giants	2-9
Carolina	2-3	Philadelphia	7-4
Chicago	8-3	St. Louis	5-6
Dallas	9-2	San Francisco	5-6
Detroit	5-6	Tampa Bay	4-7
Green Bay	5-6	Washington	5-6
Minnesota	9-2		

MONDAY NIGHT FOOTBALL, 1970-1999

(Home Team in capitals, games listed in chronological order.)

1999
Miami 38, DENVER 21
DALLAS 24, Atlanta 7
San Francisco 24, ARIZONA 10
Buffalo 23, MIAMI 18
Jacksonville 16, NEW YORK JETS 6
NEW YORK GIANTS 13, Dallas 10
PITTSBURGH 13, Atlanta 9
Seattle 27, GREEN BAY 7
MINNESOTA 27, Dallas 17
New York Jets 24, NEW ENGLAND 17
DENVER 27, Oakland 21 (OT)
Green Bay 20, SAN FRANCISCO 3
TAMPA BAY 24, Minnesota 17
JACKSONVILLE 27, Denver 24
MINNESOTA 24, Green Bay 20
New York Jets 38, MIAMI 31
ATLANTA 34, San Francisco 29

1998
DENVER 27, New England 21
San Francisco 45, WASHINGTON 10
Dallas 31, NEW YORK GIANTS 7
DETROIT 27, Tampa Bay 6
Minnesota 37, GREEN BAY 24
JACKSONVILLE 28, Miami 21
New York Jets 24, NEW ENGLAND 14
Pittsburgh 20, KANSAS CITY 13
Dallas 34, PHILADELPHIA 0
PITTSBURGH 27, Green Bay 20
Denver 30, KANSAS CITY 7
NEW ENGLAND 26, Miami 23
SAN FRANCISCO 35, New York Giants 7
TAMPA BAY 24, Green Bay 22
SAN FRANCISCO 35, Detroit 13
MIAMI 31, Denver 21
JACKSONVILLE 21, Pittsburgh 3

1997
GREEN BAY 38, Chicago 24
Kansas City 28, OAKLAND 27
DALLAS 21, Philadelphia 20
JACKSONVILLE 30, Pittsburgh 21
San Francisco 34, CAROLINA 21
DENVER 34, New England 13
WASHINGTON 21, Dallas 16
Buffalo 9, INDIANAPOLIS 6
Green Bay 28, NEW ENGLAND 10
Chicago 36, MIAMI 33 (OT)
KANSAS CITY 13, Pittsburgh 10
San Francisco 24, PHILADELPHIA 12
MIAMI 30, Buffalo 13
DENVER 31, Oakland 3
Green Bay 27, MINNESOTA 11
Carolina 23, DALLAS 13
SAN FRANCISCO 34, Denver 17
New England 14, MIAMI 12

1996
CHICAGO 22, Dallas 6
GREEN BAY 39, Philadelphia 13
PITTSBURGH 24, Buffalo 6
INDIANAPOLIS 10, Miami 6
Dallas 23, PHILADELPHIA 19
Pittsburgh 17, KANSAS CITY 7
GREEN BAY 23, San Francisco 20 (OT)
Oakland 23, SAN DIEGO 14
Chicago 15, MINNESOTA 13
Denver 22, OAKLAND 21
SAN DIEGO 27, Detroit 21
DALLAS 21, Green Bay 6
Pittsburgh 24, MIAMI 17
San Francisco 34, ATLANTA 10
OAKLAND 26, Kansas City 7
MIAMI 16, Buffalo 14
SAN FRANCISCO 24, Detroit 14

1995
Dallas 35, NEW YORK GIANTS 0
Green Bay 27, CHICAGO 24
MIAMI 23, Pittsburgh 10
DETROIT 27, San Francisco 24
Buffalo 22, CLEVELAND 19
KANSAS CITY 29, San Diego 23 (OT)
DENVER 27, Oakland 0
NEW ENGLAND 27, Buffalo 14
Chicago 14, MINNESOTA 6
DALLAS 34, Philadelphia 12
PITTSBURGH 20, Cleveland 3
San Francisco 44, MIAMI 20
SAN DIEGO 12, Oakland 6
DETROIT 27, Chicago 7
MIAMI 13, Kansas City 6
SAN FRANCISCO 37, Minnesota 30
Dallas 37, ARIZONA 13

1994
SAN FRANCISCO 44, Los Angeles Raiders 14
PHILADELPHIA 30, Chicago 22
Detroit 20, DALLAS 17 (OT)
BUFFALO 27, Denver 20
PITTSBURGH 30, Houston 14
Minnesota 27, NEW YORK GIANTS 10
Kansas City 31, DENVER 28
PHILADELPHIA 21, Houston 6
Green Bay 33, CHICAGO 6
DALLAS 38, New York Giants 10
PITTSBURGH 23, Buffalo 10
New York Giants 13, HOUSTON 10
San Francisco 35, NEW ORLEANS 14
Los Angeles Raiders 24, SAN DIEGO 17
MIAMI 45, Kansas City 28
Dallas 24, NEW ORLEANS 16
MINNESOTA 21, San Francisco 14

1993
WASHINGTON 35, Dallas 16
CLEVELAND 23, San Francisco 13
KANSAS CITY 15, Denver 7
Pittsburgh 45, ATLANTA 17
MIAMI 17, Washington 10
BUFFALO 35, Houston 7
Los Angeles Raiders 23, DENVER 20
Minnesota 19, CHICAGO 12
BUFFALO 24, Washington 10
KANSAS CITY 23, Green Bay 16
PITTSBURGH 23, Buffalo 0
SAN FRANCISCO 42, New Orleans 7
San Diego 31, INDIANAPOLIS 0
DALLAS 23, Philadelphia 17
Pittsburgh 21, MIAMI 20
New York Giants 24, NEW ORLEANS 14
SAN DIEGO 45, Miami 20
Philadelphia 37, SAN FRANCISCO 34 (OT)

1992
DALLAS 23, Washington 10
Miami 27, CLEVELAND 23
New York Giants 27, CHICAGO 14
KANSAS CITY 27, Los Angeles Raiders 7
PHILADELPHIA 31, Dallas 7
WASHINGTON 34, Denver 3
PITTSBURGH 20, Cincinnati 0
Buffalo 24, NEW YORK JETS 20
Minnesota 38, CHICAGO 10
San Francisco 41, ATLANTA 3
Buffalo 26, MIAMI 20
NEW ORLEANS 20, Washington 3
SEATTLE 16, Denver 13 (OT)
HOUSTON 24, Chicago 7
MIAMI 20, Los Angeles Raiders 7
Dallas 41, ATLANTA 17
SAN FRANCISCO 24, Detroit 6

1991
NEW YORK GIANTS 16, San Francisco 14
Washington 33, DALLAS 31
HOUSTON 17, Kansas City 7
CHICAGO 19, New York Jets 13 (OT)
WASHINGTON 23, Philadelphia 0
KANSAS CITY 33, Buffalo 6
New York Giants 23, PITTSBURGH 20
BUFFALO 35, Cincinnati 16
KANSAS CITY 24, Los Angeles Raiders 21
PHILADELPHIA 30, New York Giants 7
Chicago 34, MINNESOTA 17
Buffalo 41, MIAMI 27
San Francisco 33, LOS ANGELES RAMS 10
Philadelphia 13, HOUSTON 6
MIAMI 37, Cincinnati 13
NEW ORLEANS 27, Los Angeles Raiders 0
SAN FRANCISCO 52, Chicago 14

1990
San Francisco 13, NEW ORLEANS 12
DENVER 24, Kansas City 23
Buffalo 30, NEW YORK JETS 7
SEATTLE 31, Cincinnati 16
Cleveland 30, DENVER 29
PHILADELPHIA 32, Minnesota 24
Cincinnati 34, CLEVELAND 13
PITTSBURGH 41, Los Angeles Rams 10
New York Giants 24, INDIANAPOLIS 7
PHILADELPHIA 28, Washington 14
Los Angeles Raiders 13, MIAMI 10
HOUSTON 27, Buffalo 24
SAN FRANCISCO 7, New York Giants 3
Los Angeles Raiders 38, DETROIT 31
San Francisco 26, LOS ANGELES RAMS 10
NEW ORLEANS 20, Los Angeles Rams 17

1989
New York Giants 27, WASHINGTON 24
Denver 28, BUFFALO 14
CINCINNATI 21, Cleveland 14
CHICAGO 27, Philadelphia 13
Los Angeles Raiders 14, NEW YORK JETS 7
BUFFALO 23, Los Angeles Rams 20
CLEVELAND 27, Chicago 7
NEW YORK GIANTS 24, Minnesota 14
SAN FRANCISCO 31, New Orleans 13
HOUSTON 26, Cincinnati 24
Denver 14, WASHINGTON 10
SAN FRANCISCO 34, New York Giants 24
SEATTLE 17, Buffalo 16
San Francisco 30, LOS ANGELES RAMS 27
NEW ORLEANS 30, Philadelphia 20
MINNESOTA 29, Cincinnati 21

1988
NEW YORK GIANTS 27, Washington 20
Dallas 17, PHOENIX 14
CLEVELAND 23, Indianapolis 17
Los Angeles Raiders 30, DENVER 27 (OT)
NEW ORLEANS 20, Dallas 17
PHILADELPHIA 24, New York Giants 13
Buffalo 37, NEW YORK JETS 14
CHICAGO 10, San Francisco 9
INDIANAPOLIS 55, Denver 23
HOUSTON 24, Cleveland 17
Buffalo 31, MIAMI 6
SAN FRANCISCO 37, Washington 21
SEATTLE 35, Los Angeles Raiders 27
LOS ANGELES RAMS 23, Chicago 3
MIAMI 38, Cleveland 31
MINNESOTA 28, Chicago 27

MONDAY NIGHT FOOTBALL

1987
CHICAGO 34, New York Giants 19
NEW YORK JETS 43, New England 24
San Francisco 41, NEW YORK GIANTS 21
DENVER 30, Los Angeles Raiders 14
Washington 13, DALLAS 7
CLEVELAND 30, Los Angeles Rams 17
MINNESOTA 34, Denver 27
DALLAS 33, New York Giants 24
NEW YORK JETS 30, Seattle 14
DENVER 31, Chicago 29
Los Angeles Rams 30, WASHINGTON 26
Los Angeles Raiders 37, SEATTLE 14
MIAMI 37, New York Jets 28
SAN FRANCISCO 41, Chicago 0
Dallas 29, LOS ANGELES RAMS 21
New England 24, MIAMI 10

1986
DALLAS 31, New York Giants 28
Denver 21, PITTSBURGH 10
Chicago 25, GREEN BAY 12
Dallas 31, ST. LOUIS 7
SEATTLE 33, San Diego 7
CINCINNATI 24, Pittsburgh 22
NEW YORK JETS 22, Denver 10
NEW YORK GIANTS 27, Washington 20
Los Angeles Rams 20, CHICAGO 17
CLEVELAND 26, Miami 16
WASHINGTON 14, San Francisco 6
MIAMI 45, New York Jets 3
New York Giants 21, SAN FRANCISCO 17
SEATTLE 37, Los Angeles Raiders 0
Chicago 16, DETROIT 13
New England 34, MIAMI 27

1985
DALLAS 44, Washington 14
CLEVELAND 17, Pittsburgh 7
Los Angeles Rams 35, SEATTLE 24
Cincinnati 37, PITTSBURGH 24
WASHINGTON 27, St. Louis 10
NEW YORK JETS 23, Miami 7
CHICAGO 23, Green Bay 7
LOS ANGELES RAIDERS 34, San Diego 21
ST. LOUIS 21, Dallas 10
DENVER 17, San Francisco 16
WASHINGTON 23, New York Giants 21
SAN FRANCISCO 19, Seattle 6
MIAMI 38, Chicago 24
Los Angeles Rams 27, SAN FRANCISCO 20
MIAMI 30, New England 27
L.A. Raiders 16, L.A. RAMS 6

1984
Dallas 20, LOS ANGELES RAMS 13
SAN FRANCISCO 37, Washington 31
Miami 21, BUFFALO 17
LOS ANGELES RAIDERS 33, San Diego 30
PITTSBURGH 38, Cincinnati 17
San Francisco 31, NEW YORK GIANTS 10
DENVER 17, Green Bay 14
Los Angeles Rams 24, ATLANTA 10
Seattle 24, SAN DIEGO 0
WASHINGTON 27, Atlanta 14
SEATTLE 17, Los Angeles Raiders 14
NEW ORLEANS 27, Pittsburgh 24
MIAMI 28, New York Jets 17
SAN DIEGO 20, Chicago 7
Los Angeles Raiders 24, DETROIT 3
MIAMI 28, Dallas 21

1983
Dallas 31, WASHINGTON 30
San Diego 17, KANSAS CITY 14
LOS ANGELES RAIDERS 27, Miami 14
NEW YORK GIANTS 27, Green Bay 3
New York Jets 34, BUFFALO 10
Pittsburgh 24, CINCINNATI 14
GREEN BAY 48, Washington 47
ST. LOUIS 20, New York Giants 20 (OT)
Washington 27, SAN DIEGO 24
DETROIT 15, New York Giants 9
Los Angeles Rams 36, ATLANTA 13
New York Jets 31, NEW ORLEANS 28
MIAMI 38, Cincinnati 14
DETROIT 13, Minnesota 2
Green Bay 12, TAMPA BAY 9 (OT)
SAN FRANCISCO 42, Dallas 17

1982
Pittsburgh 36, DALLAS 28
Green Bay 27, NEW YORK GIANTS 19
LOS ANGELES RAIDERS 28, San Diego 24
TAMPA BAY 23, Miami 17
New York Jets 28, DETROIT 13
Dallas 37, HOUSTON 7
SAN DIEGO 50, Cincinnati 34
MIAMI 27, Buffalo 10
MINNESOTA 31, Dallas 27

1981
San Diego 44, CLEVELAND 14
Oakland 36, MINNESOTA 10
Dallas 35, NEW ENGLAND 21
Los Angeles 24, CHICAGO 7
PHILADELPHIA 16, Atlanta 13
BUFFALO 31, Miami 21
DETROIT 48, Chicago 17
PITTSBURGH 26, Houston 13
DENVER 19, Minnesota 17
DALLAS 27, Buffalo 14
SEATTLE 44, San Diego 23
ATLANTA 31, Minnesota 30
MIAMI 13, Philadelphia 10
OAKLAND 30, Pittsburgh 27
LOS ANGELES 21, Atlanta 16
SAN DIEGO 23, Oakland 10

1980
Dallas 17, WASHINGTON 3
Houston 16, CLEVELAND 7
PHILADELPHIA 35, New York Giants 3
NEW ENGLAND 23, Denver 14
CHICAGO 23, Tampa Bay 0
DENVER 20, Washington 17
Oakland 45, PITTSBURGH 34
NEW YORK JETS 17, Miami 14
CLEVELAND 27, Chicago 21
HOUSTON 38, New England 34
Oakland 19, SEATTLE 17
Los Angeles 27, NEW ORLEANS 7
OAKLAND 9, Denver 3
MIAMI 16, New England 13 (OT)
LOS ANGELES 38, Dallas 14
SAN DIEGO 26, Pittsburgh 17

1979
Pittsburgh 16, NEW ENGLAND 13 (OT)
Atlanta 14, PHILADELPHIA 10
WASHINGTON 27, New York Giants 0
CLEVELAND 26, Dallas 7
GREEN BAY 27, New England 14
OAKLAND 13, Miami 3
NEW YORK JETS 14, Minnesota 7
PITTSBURGH 42, Denver 7
Seattle 31, ATLANTA 28
Houston 9, MIAMI 6
Philadelphia 31, DALLAS 21
LOS ANGELES 20, Atlanta 14
SEATTLE 30, New York Jets 7
Oakland 42, NEW ORLEANS 35
HOUSTON 20, Pittsburgh 17
SAN DIEGO 17, Denver 7

1978
DALLAS 38, Baltimore 0
MINNESOTA 12, Denver 9 (OT)
Baltimore 34, NEW ENGLAND 27
Minnesota 24, CHICAGO 20
WASHINGTON 9, Dallas 5
MIAMI 21, Cincinnati 0
DENVER 16, Chicago 7
Houston 24, PITTSBURGH 17
ATLANTA 15, Los Angeles 7
BALTIMORE 21, Washington 17
Oakland 34, CINCINNATI 21
HOUSTON 35, Miami 30
Pittsburgh 24, SAN FRANCISCO 7
SAN DIEGO 40, Chicago 7
Cincinnati 20, LOS ANGELES 19
MIAMI 23, New England 3

1977
PITTSBURGH 27, San Francisco 0
CLEVELAND 30, New England 27 (OT)
Oakland 37, KANSAS CITY 28
CHICAGO 24, Los Angeles 23
PITTSBURGH 20, Cincinnati 14
LOS ANGELES 35, Minnesota 3
ST. LOUIS 28, New York Giants 0
BALTIMORE 10, Washington 3
St. Louis 24, DALLAS 17
WASHINGTON 10, Green Bay 9
OAKLAND 34, Buffalo 13
MIAMI 17, Baltimore 6
Dallas 42, SAN FRANCISCO 35

1976
Miami 30, BUFFALO 21
Oakland 24, KANSAS CITY 21
Washington 20, PHILADELPHIA 17 (OT)
MINNESOTA 17, Pittsburgh 6
San Francisco 16, LOS ANGELES 0
NEW ENGLAND 41, New York Jets 7
WASHINGTON 20, St. Louis 10
BALTIMORE 38, Houston 14
CINCINNATI 20, Los Angeles 12
DALLAS 17, Buffalo 10
Baltimore 17, MIAMI 16
SAN FRANCISCO 20, Minnesota 16
OAKLAND 35, Cincinnati 20

1975
Oakland 31, MIAMI 21
DENVER 23, Green Bay 13
Dallas 36, DETROIT 10
WASHINGTON 27, St. Louis 17
New York Giants 17, BUFFALO 14
Minnesota 13, CHICAGO 9
Los Angeles 42, PHILADELPHIA 3
Kansas City 34, DALLAS 31
CINCINNATI 33, Buffalo 24
Pittsburgh 32, HOUSTON 9
MIAMI 20, New England 7
OAKLAND 17, Denver 10
SAN DIEGO 24, New York Jets 16

1974
BUFFALO 21, Oakland 20
PHILADELPHIA 13, Dallas 10
WASHINGTON 30, Denver 3
MIAMI 21, New York Jets 17
DETROIT 17, San Francisco 13
CHICAGO 10, Green Bay 9
PITTSBURGH 24, Atlanta 17
Los Angeles 15, SAN FRANCISCO 13
Minnesota 28, ST. LOUIS 24
Kansas City 42, DENVER 34
Pittsburgh 28, NEW ORLEANS 7
MIAMI 24, Cincinnati 3
Washington 23, LOS ANGELES 17

1973
GREEN BAY 23, New York Jets 7
DALLAS 40, New Orleans 3
DETROIT 31, Atlanta 6
WASHINGTON 14, Dallas 7
Miami 17, CLEVELAND 9
DENVER 23, Oakland 23
BUFFALO 23, Kansas City 14
PITTSBURGH 21, Washington 16
KANSAS CITY 19, Chicago 7
ATLANTA 20, Minnesota 14
SAN FRANCISCO 20, Green Bay 6
MIAMI 30, Pittsburgh 26
LOS ANGELES 40, New York Giants 6

1972
Washington 24, MINNESOTA 21
Kansas City 20, NEW ORLEANS 17
New York Giants 27, PHILADELPHIA 12
Oakland 34, HOUSTON 0
Green Bay 24, DETROIT 23
CHICAGO 13, Minnesota 10
DALLAS 28, Detroit 24
Baltimore 24, NEW ENGLAND 17
Cleveland 21, SAN DIEGO 17
WASHINGTON 24, Atlanta 13
MIAMI 31, St. Louis 10
Los Angeles 26, SAN FRANCISCO 16
OAKLAND 24, New York Jets 16

1971
Minnesota 16, DETROIT 13
ST. LOUIS 17, New York Jets 10
Oakland 34, CLEVELAND 20
DALLAS 20, New York Giants 13
KANSAS CITY 38, Pittsburgh 16
MINNESOTA 10, Baltimore 3
GREEN BAY 14, Detroit 14
BALTIMORE 24, Los Angeles 17
SAN DIEGO 20, St. Louis 17
ATLANTA 28, Green Bay 21
MIAMI 34, Chicago 3
Kansas City 26, SAN FRANCISCO 17
Washington 38, LOS ANGELES 24

1970
CLEVELAND 31, New York Jets 21
Kansas City 44, BALTIMORE 24
DETROIT 28, Chicago 14
Green Bay 22, SAN DIEGO 20
OAKLAND 34, Washington 20
MINNESOTA 13, Los Angeles 3
PITTSBURGH 21, Cincinnati 10
Baltimore 13, GREEN BAY 10
St. Louis 38, DALLAS 0
PHILADELPHIA 23, New York Giants 20
Miami 20, ATLANTA 7
Cleveland 21, HOUSTON 10
Detroit 28, LOS ANGELES 23

MONDAY NIGHT FOOTBALL

MONDAY NIGHT WON-LOST RECORDS, 1970-1999

AMERICAN FOOTBALL CONFERENCE

	Balt.	Buff.	Cin.	Cle.	Den.	Ind.	Jax.	K.C.	Mia.	N.E.	N.Y.J.	Oak.	Pitt.	S.D.	Sea.	Tenn.
Total	0-0	17-19	7-16	13-11	19-23-1	10-8	5-0	16-12	35-28	7-17	12-17	33-17-1	28-18	14-12	12-5	11-11
1999		1-0			1-2		2-0		1-2	0-1	2-1	0-1	1-0		1-0	
1998					2-1		2-0	0-2	1-2	1-2	1-0		2-1			
1997		1-1			2-1	0-1	1-0	2-0	1-2	1-2		0-2	0-2			
1996		0-2			1-0	1-0		0-2	1-2			2-1	3-0	1-1		
1995		1-1		0-2	1-0			1-1	2-1	1-0		0-2	1-1	1-1		
1994		1-1			0-2			1-1	1-0			1-1	2-0	0-1		0-3
1993		2-1		1-0	0-2	0-1		2-0	1-2			1-0	3-0	2-0		0-1
1992		2-0	0-1	0-1	0-2			1-0	2-1		0-1	0-2	1-0		1-0	1-0
1991		2-1	0-2					2-1	1-1		0-1	0-2	0-1			1-1
1990		1-1	1-1	1-1	1-1	0-1		0-1	0-1		0-1	2-0	1-0		1-0	1-0
1989		1-2	1-2	1-1	2-0						0-1	1-0			1-0	1-0
1988		2-0		1-2	0-2	1-1			1-1		0-1	1-1			1-0	1-0
1987				1-0	2-1				1-1	1-1	2-1	1-1			0-2	
1986			1-0	1-0	1-1				1-2	1-0	1-1	0-1	0-2	0-1	2-0	
1985			1-0	1-0	1-0				2-1	0-1	1-0	2-0	0-2	0-1	0-2	
1984		0-1	0-1		1-0				3-0		0-1	2-1	1-1	1-2	2-0	
1983		0-1	0-2					0-1	1-1		2-0	1-0	1-0	1-1		
1982		0-1	0-1		0-1				1-1		1-0	1-0	1-0	1-1		0-1
1981		1-1		0-1	1-0				1-1	0-1		2-1	1-1	2-1	1-0	0-1
1980				1-1	1-2				1-1	1-2	1-0	3-0	0-2	1-0	0-1	2-0
1979				1-0	0-2				0-2	0-2	1-1	2-0	2-1	1-0	2-0	2-0
1978			1-2		1-1	2-1			2-1	0-2		1-0	1-1	1-0		2-0
1977		0-1	0-1	1-0		1-1		0-1	1-0	0-1		2-0	2-0			
1976		0-2	1-1			2-0		0-1	1-1	1-0	0-1	2-0	0-1			0-1
1975		0-2	1-0		1-1			1-0	1-1	0-1	0-1	2-0	1-0	1-0		0-1
1974		1-0	0-1		0-2			1-0	2-0		0-1	0-1	2-0			
1973		1-0		0-1	0-0-1			1-1	2-0		0-1	0-0-1	1-1			
1972				1-0		1-0		1-0	1-0	0-1	0-1	2-0		0-1		0-1
1971				0-1		1-1		2-0	1-0		0-1	1-0	0-1	1-0		
1970			0-1	2-0		1-1		1-0	1-0		0-1	1-0	1-0	0-1		0-1

NATIONAL FOOTBALL CONFERENCE

	Ariz.	Atl.	Car.	Chi.	Dall.	Det.	G.B.	Minn.	N.O.	N.Y.G.	Phil.	St. L.	S.F.	T.B.	Wash.
Total	5-10-1	6-17	1-1	16-28	33-25	11-12-1	15-17-1	19-18	6-12	15-22-1	14-16	17-20	34-20	3-3	23-22
1999	0-1	1-2			1-2		1-2	2-1		1-0			1-2	1-0	
1998					2-0	1-1	0-3	1-0		0-2	0-1		3-0	1-1	0-1
1997			1-1	1-1	1-2		3-0	0-1			0-2		3-0		1-0
1996		0-1		2-0	2-1	0-2	2-1	0-1			0-2		2-1		
1995	0-1			1-2	3-0	2-0	1-0	0-2		0-1	0-1		2-1		
1994				0-2	2-1	1-0	1-0	2-0	0-2	1-2	2-0		2-1		
1993		0-1		0-1	1-1		0-1	1-0	0-2	1-0	1-1		1-2		1-2
1992		0-2		0-3	2-1	0-1		1-0	1-0	1-0	1-0		2-0		1-2
1991				2-1	0-1			0-1	1-0	2-1	2-1	0-1	2-1		2-0
1990						0-1		0-1	1-1	1-1	2-0	0-3	3-0		0-1
1989				1-1				1-1	1-1	2-1	0-2	0-2	3-0		0-2
1988	0-1			1-2	1-1			1-0	1-0	1-0	1-1	1-0	1-1		0-2
1987				1-2	2-1			1-0		0-3		1-2	2-0		1-1
1986	0-1			2-1	2-0	0-1	0-1			2-1		1-0	0-2		1-1
1985	1-1			1-1	1-1		0-1			0-1		2-1	1-2		2-1
1984		0-2		0-1	1-1	0-1	0-1		1-0	0-1		1-1	2-0		1-1
1983	0-0-1	0-1			1-1	2-0	2-1	0-1	0-1	1-1-1		1-0	1-0	0-1	1-2
1982					1-2	0-1	1-0	1-0		0-1				1-0	
1981		1-2		0-2	2-0	1-0		0-3			1-1	2-0			
1980				1-1	1-1				0-1	0-1	1-0	2-0		0-1	0-2
1979		1-2			0-2		1-0	0-1	0-1	0-1	1-1	1-0			1-0
1978		1-0		0-3	1-1			2-0				0-2	0-1		1-1
1977	2-0			1-0	1-1		0-1	0-1		0-1		1-1	0-2		1-1
1976	0-1				1-0			1-1			0-1	0-2	2-0		2-0
1975	0-1			0-1	1-1	0-1	0-1	1-0		1-0	0-1	1-0			1-0
1974	0-1	0-1		1-0	0-1	1-0	0-1	1-0	0-1		1-0	1-1	0-2		2-0
1973		1-1		0-1	1-1	1-0	1-1	0-1	0-1	0-1		1-0	1-0		1-1
1972	0-1	0-1		1-0	1-0	0-2	1-0	0-2	0-1	1-0	0-1	1-0	0-1		2-0
1971	1-1	1-0		0-1	1-0	0-1-1	0-1-1	2-0		0-1		0-2	0-1		1-0
1970	1-0	0-1		0-1	0-1	2-0	1-1	1-0		0-1	1-0	0-2			0-1

Compiled by Elias Sports Bureau
*Set or tied NFL all-time record.

MONDAY NIGHT RECORDS

SCORING
TOUCHDOWNS
Most Touchdowns, Game
4 Ron Johnson, N.Y. Giants at Philadelphia, Oct. 2, 1972
4 Earl Campbell, Houston vs. Miami, Nov. 20, 1978
4 Marcus Allen, L.A. Raiders vs. San Diego, Sept. 24, 1984
4 Eric Dickerson, Indianapolis vs. Denver, Oct. 31, 1988
4 Emmitt Smith, Dallas at N.Y. Giants, Sept. 4. 1995
FIELD GOALS
Most Field Goals, Game
7 Chris Boniol, Dallas vs. Green Bay, Nov. 18, 1996*
5 Tim Mazzetti, Atlanta vs. Los Angeles, Oct. 30, 1978
5 Roger Ruzek, Dallas at L.A. Rams, Dec. 21, 1987
5 Rich Karlis, Minnesota vs. Cincinnati, Dec. 25, 1989
5 Nick Lowery, Kansas City vs. Denver, Sept. 20, 1993
5 Chris Jacke, Green Bay vs. San Francisco, Oct. 14, 1996 (OT)
5 Richie Cunningham, Dallas vs. Philadelphia, Sept. 15, 1997

RUSHING
YARDS GAINED
Most Yards Rushing, Game
221 Bo Jackson, L.A. Raiders at Seattle, Nov. 30, 1987
214 Thurman Thomas, Buffalo at N.Y. Jets, Sept. 24, 1990
199 Earl Campbell, Houston vs. Miami, Nov. 20, 1978
Longest Run From Scrimage, Game
99 Tony Dorsett, Dallas at Minnesota, Jan. 3, 1983 (TD)*
91 Bo Jackson, L.A. Raiders at Seattle, Nov. 30, 1987 (TD)
83 James Lofton, Green Bay at N.Y. Giants, Sept. 20, 1982 (TD)
TOUCHDOWNS
Most Rushing Touchdowns, Game
4 Earl Campbell, Houston vs. Miami, Nov. 20, 1978
4 Eric Dickerson, Indianapolis vs. Denver, Oct. 31, 1988
4 Emmitt Smith, Dallas at N.Y. Giants, Sept. 4, 1995

PASSING
YARDS GAINED
Most Yards Passing, Game
458 Joe Montana, San Francisco at L.A. Rams, Dec. 11, 1989
447 Ken Anderson, Cincinnati vs. Buffalo, Nov. 17, 1975
445 Charley Johnson, Denver vs. Kansas City, Nov. 18, 1974
Longest Pass Play
99 Brett Favre to Robert Brooks, Green Bay at Chicago, Sept. 11, 1995 (TD)*
97 Bernie Kosar to Webster Slaughter, Cleveland vs. Chicago, Oct. 23, 1989 (TD)
95 Joe Montana to John Taylor, San Francisco at L.A. Rams, Dec. 11, 1989 (TD)
TOUCHDOWNS
Most Touchdown Passes, Game
5 Dave Krieg, Seattle vs. L.A. Raiders, Nov. 28, 1988
5 Jim Kelly, Buffalo vs. Cincinnati, Oct. 21, 1991

PASS RECEIVING
RECEPTIONS
Most Pass Receptions, Game
14 Herman Moore, Detroit vs. Chicago, Dec. 4, 1995
14 Jerry Rice, San Francisco vs. Minnesota, Dec. 18, 1995
13 Andre Reed, Buffalo vs. Denver, Sept. 18, 1989
YARDS GAINED
Most Yards on Pass Receptions, Game
289 Jerry Rice, San Francisco vs. Minnesota, Dec. 18, 1995
286 John Taylor, San Francisco at L.A. Rams, Dec. 11, 1989
260 Wes Chandler, San Diego vs. Cincinnati, Dec. 20, 1982
TOUCHDOWNS
Most Touchdown Pass Receptions, Game
3 Ron Johnson, N.Y. Giants at Philadelphia, Oct. 2, 1972
3 Wesley Walker, N.Y. Jets at Detroit, Dec. 6, 1982
3 Steve Largent, Seattle at San Diego, Oct. 29, 1984
3 Mark Clayton, Miami vs. Dallas, Dec. 17, 1984
3 Jerry Rice, San Francisco vs. Chicago, Dec. 14, 1987
3 Jerry Rice, San Francisco vs. Minnesota, Dec. 18, 1995
3 Lamar Thomas, Miami vs. Denver, Dec. 21, 1998
3 Ed McCaffrey, Denver vs. Miami, Sept. 13, 1999

INTERCEPTIONS BY
Most Interceptions, Game
4 Dick Anderson, Miami vs. Pittsburgh, Dec. 3, 1973*
3 Johnny Robinson, Kansas City at Baltimore, Sept. 28, 1970
3 Charlie Babb, Miami vs. Oakland, Sept. 22, 1975
3 Charles Phillips, Oakland vs. Denver, Dec. 8, 1975
3 Mark Murphy, Washington at San Diego, Oct. 31, 1983
3 Ken Easley, Seattle at San Diego, Oct. 29, 1984
3 Dwayne Harper, San Diego vs. Oakland, Nov. 27, 1995
Longest Interception Return
102 Eddie Anderson, L.A. Raiders at Miami, Dec. 14, 1992 (TD)
98 Marcus Coleman, N.Y. Jets vs. Miami, Dec. 27, 1999 (TD)
94 Nolan Cromwell, L.A. Rams vs. Atlanta, Dec. 14, 1981
94 Walker Lee Ashley, Minnesota vs. Chicago, Dec. 19, 1988 (TD)

PUNTING
Longest Punt
83 Bryan Barker, Jacksonville vs. N.Y. Jets, Oct. 11, 1999
74 Craig Colquitt, Pittsburgh vs. Oakland, Dec. 7, 1981
73 Tom Tupa, New England at Denver, Oct. 6, 1997

PUNT RETURNS
Longest Punt Return
95 John Taylor, San Francisco vs. Washington, Nov. 21, 1988 (TD)
94 Dennis McKinnon, Chicago vs. N.Y. Giants, Sept. 14, 1987 (TD)
91 JoJo Townsell, N.Y. Jets vs. Seattle, Nov. 9, 1987 (TD)

KICKOFF RETURNS
Longest Kickoff Return
105 Terry Fair, Detroit vs. Tampa Bay, Sept. 28, 1998 (TD)
102 Harold Hart, Oakland at Miami, Sept. 22, 1975 (TD)
101 Roell Preston, Green Bay vs. Minnesota, Oct. 5, 1998 (TD)

FUMBLES
Longest Fumble Return
99 Don Griffin, San Francisco vs. Chicago, Dec. 23, 1991 (TD)
96 Joe Lavender, Philadelphia vs. Dallas, Sept. 23, 1974 (TD)
88 Keith McKenzie, Pittsburgh vs. Green Bay, Nov. 9, 1998 (TD)

THANKSGIVING DAY RECORDS

SCORING
Most Touchdowns, Game
6 Ernie Nevers, Chi. Cardinals vs. Chi. Bears, Nov. 28, 1929*
4 Sterling Sharpe, Green Bay at Dallas, Nov. 24, 1994
3 By many players

RUSHING
Most Yards Rushing, Game
273 O.J. Simpson, Buffalo at Detroit, Nov. 25, 1976
198 Bob Hoernschemeyer, Detroit vs. N.Y. Yankees, Nov. 23, 1950
195 Earl Campbell, Houston at Dallas, Nov. 22, 1979

PASSING
Most Yards Passing, Game
455 Troy Aikman, Dallas vs. Minnesota, Nov. 26, 1998
410 Scott Mitchell, Detroit vs. Minnesota, Nov. 23, 1995
384 Warren Moon, Minnesota at Detroit, Nov. 23, 1995

PASS RECEIVING
RECEPTIONS
Most Pass Receptions, Game
12 Brett Perriman, Detroit vs. Minnesota, Nov. 23, 1995
11 Daryl Johnston, Dallas vs. Miami, Nov. 25, 1993
Michael Irvin, Dallas vs Kansas City, Nov. 23 1995
YARDS GAINED
Most Yards on Pass Receptions, Game
303 Jim Benton, Cleveland at Detroit, Nov. 22, 1945
185 Lance Alworth, San Diego vs. Buffalo, Nov. 26, 1964
184 Anthony Carter, Minnesota at Dallas, Nov. 26, 1987 (OT)

THURSDAY-SUNDAY NIGHT FOOTBALL, 1974-1999

(Home Team in capitals, games listed in chronological order.)

1999
Pittsburgh 43, CLEVELAND 0 (Sun.)
BUFFALO 17, N.Y. Jets 3 (Sun.)
NEW ENGLAND 16, N.Y. Giants 14 (Sun.)
SEATTLE 22, Oakland 21 (Sun.)
GREEN BAY 26, Tampa Bay 23 (Sun.)
Washington 24, ARIZONA 10 (Sun.)
Kansas City 35, BALTIMORE 8 (Thurs.)
DETROIT 20, Tampa Bay 3 (Sun.)
MIAMI 17, Tennessee 0 (Sun.)
SEATTLE 20, Denver 17 (Sun.)
JACKSONVILLE 41, New Orleans 23 (Sun.)
CAROLINA 34, Atlanta 28 (Sun.)
JACKSONVILLE 20, Pittsburgh 6 (Thurs.)
NEW ENGLAND 13, Dallas 6 (Sun.)
TENNESSEE 21, Oakland 14 (Thurs.)
KANSAS CITY 31, Minnesota 28 (Sun.)
Buffalo 31, ARIZONA 21 (Sun.)
Washington 26, SAN FRANCISCO 20 (OT) (Sun.)

1998
KANSAS CITY 28, Oakland 8 (Sun.)
NEW ENGLAND 29, Indianapolis 6 (Sun.)
ARIZONA 17, Philadelphia 3 (Sun.)
BALTIMORE 31, Cincinnati 24 (Sun.)
KANSAS CITY 17, Seattle 6 (Sun.)
Atlanta 34, NEW YORK GIANTS 20 (Sun.)
DETROIT 27, Green Bay 20 (Thurs.)
Buffalo 30, CAROLINA 14 (Sun.)
Oakland 31, SEATTLE 18 (Sun.)
Tennessee 31, TAMPA BAY 22 (Sun.)
DETROIT 26, Chicago 3 (Sun.)
SAN FRANCISCO 31, New Orleans 20 (Sun.)
Denver 31, SAN DIEGO 16 (Sun.)
PHILADELPHIA 17, St. Louis 14 (Thurs.)
MINNESOTA 48, Chicago 22 (Sun.)
New York Jets 21, MIAMI 16 (Sun.)
MINNESOTA 50, Jacksonville 10 (Sun.)
Dallas 23, WASHINGTON 7 (Sun.)

1997
Washington 24, CAROLINA 10 (Sun.)
ARIZONA 25, Dallas 22 (OT) (Sun.)
NEW ENGLAND 27, New York Jets 24 (OT) (Sun.)
TAMPA BAY 31, Miami 21 (Sun.)
MINNESOTA 28, Philadelphia 19 (Sun.)
New Orleans 20, CHICAGO 17 (Sun.)
PITTSBURGH 24, Indianapolis 22 (Sun.)
KANSAS CITY 31, San Diego 3 (Thurs.)
CAROLINA 21, Atlanta 12 (Sun.)
GREEN BAY 20, Detroit 10 (Sun.)
PITTSBURGH 37, Baltimore 0 (Sun.)
Oakland 38, SAN DIEGO 13 (Sun.)
WASHINGTON 7, New York Giants 7 (OT) (Sun.)
Denver 38, SAN DIEGO 28 (Sun.)
CINCINNATI 41, Tennessee 14 (Thurs.)
MIAMI 33, Detroit 30 (Sun.)
Chicago 13, ST. LOUIS 10 (Sun.)
SEATTLE 38, San Francisco 9 (Sun.)

1996
Buffalo 23, NEW YORK GIANTS 20 (OT) (Sun.)
Miami 38, ARIZONA 10 (Sun.)
DENVER 27, Tampa Bay 23 (Sun.)
Philadelphia 33, ATLANTA 18 (Sun.)
WASHINGTON 31, New York Jets 16 (Sun.)
Houston 30, CINCINNATI 27 (OT) (Sun.)
INDIANAPOLIS 26, Baltimore 21 (Sun.)
KANSAS CITY 34, Seattle 16 (Thurs.)
NEW ENGLAND 28, Buffalo 25 (Sun.)
San Francisco 24, NEW ORLEANS 17 (Sun.)
CAROLINA 27, New York Giants 17 (Sun.)
Minnesota 16, OAKLAND 13 (OT) (Sun.)
Green Bay 24, ST. LOUIS 9 (Sun.)
New England 45, SAN DIEGO 7 (Sun.)
INDIANAPOLIS 37, Philadelphia 10 (Thurs.)
Minnesota 24, DETROIT 22 (Sun.)
JACKSONVILLE 20, Seattle 13 (Sun.)
SAN DIEGO 16, Denver 10 (Sun.)

1995
DENVER 22, Buffalo 7 (Sun.)
Philadelphia 31, ARIZONA 19 (Sun.)
Dallas 23, MINNESOTA 17 (OT) (Sun.)
Green Bay 24, JACKSONVILLE 14 (Sun.)
Oakland 47, NEW YORK JETS 10 (Sun.)
Denver 37, NEW ENGLAND 3 (Sun.)
ST. LOUIS 21, Atlanta 19 (Thurs.)
Cincinnati 27, PITTSBURGH 9 (Thurs.)
New York Giants 24, WASHINGTON 15 (Sun.)
Miami 24, SAN DIEGO 14 (Sun.)
PHILADELPHIA 31, Denver 13 (Sun.)
KANSAS CITY 20, Houston 13 (Sun.)
NEW ORLEANS 34, Carolina 26 (Sun.)
New York Giants 10, ARIZONA 6 (Thurs.)
SAN FRANCISCO 27, Buffalo 17 (Sun.)
TAMPA BAY 13, Green Bay 10 (OT) (Sun.)
SEATTLE 44, Oakland 10 (Sun.)
INDIANAPOLIS 10, New England 7 (Sat.)

1994
San Diego 17, DENVER 34 (Sun.)
New York Giants 20, ARIZONA 17 (Sun.)
Kansas City 30, ATLANTA 10 (Sun.)
Chicago 19, NEW YORK JETS 7 (Sun.)
Miami 23, CINCINNATI 7 (Sun.)
PHILADELPHIA 21, Washington 17 (Sun.)
Cleveland 11, HOUSTON 8 (Thurs.)
MINNESOTA 13, Green Bay 10 (OT) (Thurs.)
ARIZONA 20, Pittsburgh 17 (OT) (Sun.)
KANSAS CITY 13, Los Angeles Raiders 3 (Sun.)
DETROIT 14, Tampa Bay 9 (Sun.)
SAN FRANCISCO 31, Los Angeles Rams 27 (Sun.)
New England 12, INDIANAPOLIS 10 (Sun.)
MINNESOTA 33, Chicago 27 (OT) (Thurs.)
Buffalo 42, MIAMI 31 (Sun.)
New Orleans 29, ATLANTA 20 (Sun.)
Los Angeles Raiders 17, SEATTLE 16 (Sun.)
MIAMI 27, Detroit 20 (Sun.)

1993
NEW ORLEANS 33, Houston 21 (Sun.)
Los Angeles Raiders 17, SEATTLE 13 (Sun.)
Dallas 17, PHOENIX 10 (Sun.)
NEW YORK JETS 45, New England 7 (Sun.)
BUFFALO 17, New York Giants 14 (Sun.)
GREEN BAY 30, Denver 27 (Sun.)
ATLANTA 30, Los Angeles Rams 24 (Thurs.)
MIAMI 41, Indianapolis 27 (Sun.)
Detroit 30, MINNESOTA 27 (Sun.)
WASHINGTON 30, Indianapolis 24 (Sun.)
Chicago 16, SAN DIEGO 13 (Sun.)
TAMPA BAY 23, Minnesota 10 (Sun.)
HOUSTON 23, Pittsburgh 3 (Sun.)
SAN FRANCISCO 21, Cincinnati 8 (Sun.)
Green Bay 20, SAN DIEGO 13 (Sun.)
Philadelphia 20, INDIANAPOLIS 10 (Sun.)
MINNESOTA 30, Kansas City 10 (Sun.)
HOUSTON 24, New York Jets 0 (Sun.)

1992
DENVER 17, Los Angeles Raiders 13 (Sun.)
Philadelphia 31, PHOENIX 14 (Sun.)
BUFFALO 38, Indianapolis 0 (Sun.)
San Francisco 16, NEW ORLEANS 10 (Sun.)
NEW YORK JETS 30, New England 21 (Sun.)
NEW ORLEANS 13, Los Angeles Rams 10 (Sun.)
MINNESOTA 31, Detroit 14 (Thurs.)
Pittsburgh 27, KANSAS CITY 3 (Sun.)
New York Giants 24, WASHINGTON 7 (Sun.)
Cincinnati 31, CHICAGO 28 (OT) (Sun.)
DENVER 27, New York Giants 13 (Sun.)
Kansas City 24, SEATTLE 14 (Sun.)
SAN DIEGO 27, Los Angeles Raiders 3 (Sun.)
NEW ORLEANS 22, Atlanta 14 (Thurs.)
Los Angeles Rams 31, TAMPA BAY 27 (Sun.)
Green Bay 16, HOUSTON 14 (Sun.)
MIAMI 19, New York Jets 17 (Sun.)
HOUSTON 27, Buffalo 3 (Sun.)

1991
WASHINGTON 45, Detroit 0 (Sun.)
Houston 30, CINCINNATI 7 (Sun.)
NEW ORLEANS 24, Los Angeles Rams 7 (Sun.)
Dallas 17, PHOENIX 9 (Sun.)
Denver 13, MINNESOTA 6 (Sun.)
Pittsburgh 21, INDIANAPOLIS 3 (Sun.)
Los Angeles Raiders 23, SEATTLE 20 (Sun.)
Chicago 10, GREEN BAY 0 (Thurs.)
Washington 17, NEW YORK GIANTS 13 (Sun.)
DENVER 20, Pittsburgh 13 (Sun.)
MIAMI 30, New England 20 (Sun.)
HOUSTON 28, Cleveland 24 (Sun.)
Atlanta 23, NEW ORLEANS 20 (OT) (Sun.)
Los Angeles Raiders 9, SAN DIEGO 7 (Sun.)
Minnesota 26, TAMPA BAY 24 (Sun.)
Buffalo 35, INDIANAPOLIS 7 (Sun.)
SEATTLE 23, Los Angeles Rams 9 (Sun.)

1990
NEW YORK GIANTS 27, Philadelphia 20 (Sun.)
PITTSBURGH 20, Houston 9 (Sun.)
TAMPA BAY 23, Detroit 20 (Sun.)
Washington 38, PHOENIX 10 (Sun.)
BUFFALO 38, Los Angeles Raiders 24 (Sun.)
CHICAGO 38, Los Angeles Rams 9 (Sun.)
MIAMI 17, New England 10 (Thurs.)
ATLANTA 38, Cincinnati 17 (Sun.)
MINNESOTA 27, Denver 22 (Sun.)
San Francisco 24, DALLAS 6 (Sun.)
CINCINNATI 27, Pittsburgh 3 (Sun.)
Seattle 13, SAN DIEGO 10 (Sun.)
MINNESOTA 23, Green Bay 7 (Sun.)
MIAMI 23, Philadelphia 20 (Sun.)
DETROIT 38, Chicago 21 (Sun.)
INDIANAPOLIS 35, Washington 28 (Sat.)
SEATTLE 17, Denver 12 (Sun.)
HOUSTON 34, Pittsburgh 14 (Sun.)

1989
Dallas 13, WASHINGTON 3 (Sun.)
SAN DIEGO 14, Los Angeles Raiders 12 (Sun.)
INDIANAPOLIS 27, New York Jets 10 (Sun.)
Los Angeles Rams 20, NEW ORLEANS 17 (Sun.)
MINNESOTA 27, Chicago 16 (Sun.)
MIAMI 31, New England 10 (Sun.)
SEATTLE 23, Los Angeles Raiders 17 (Sun.)
Cleveland 24, HOUSTON 20 (Sat.)

1988
HOUSTON 41, Washington 17 (Sun.)
Los Angeles Raiders 13, SAN DIEGO 3 (Sun.)
Minnesota 43, DALLAS 3 (Sun.)
New England 6, MIAMI 3 (Sun.)
New York Giants 13, NEW ORLEANS 12 (Sun.)
Pittsburgh 37, HOUSTON 34 (Sun.)
SEATTLE 42, Denver 14 (Sun.)
Los Angeles Rams 38, SAN FRANCISCO 16 (Sun.)

1987
NEW YORK GIANTS 17, New England 10 (Sun.)
SAN DIEGO 16, Los Angeles Raiders 14 (Sun.)
Miami 20, DALLAS 14 (Sun.)
SAN FRANCISCO 38, Cleveland 24 (Sun.)
Chicago 30, MINNESOTA 24 (Sun.)
SEATTLE 28, Denver 21 (Sun.)
MIAMI 23, Washington 21 (Sun.)
SAN FRANCISCO 48, Los Angeles Rams 0 (Sun.)

1986
New England 20, NEW YORK JETS 6 (Thurs.)
Cincinnati 30, CLEVELAND 13 (Thurs.)
Los Angeles Raiders 37, SAN DIEGO 31 (OT) (Thurs.)
LOS ANGELES RAMS 29, Dallas 10 (Sun.)
SAN FRANCISCO 24, Los Angeles Rams 14 (Fri.)

1985
KANSAS CITY 36, Los Angeles Raiders 20 (Thurs.)
Chicago 33, MINNESOTA 24 (Thurs.)
Dallas 30, NEW YORK GIANTS 29 (Sun.)
SAN DIEGO 54, Pittsburgh 44 (Sun.)
Denver 27, SEATTLE 24 (Fri.)

1984
Pittsburgh 23, NEW YORK JETS 17 (Thurs.)
Denver 24, CLEVELAND 14 (Sun.)
DALLAS 30, New Orleans 27 (Sun.)
Washington 31, MINNESOTA 17 (Thurs.)
SAN FRANCISCO 19, Los Angeles Rams 16 (Fri.)

1983
San Francisco 48, MINNESOTA 17 (Thurs.)
CLEVELAND 17, Cincinnati 7 (Thurs.)
Los Angeles Raiders 40, DALLAS 38 (Sun.)
Los Angeles Raiders 42, SAN DIEGO 10 (Thurs.)
MIAMI 34, New York Jets 14 (Fri.)

1982
BUFFALO 23, Minnesota 22 (Thurs.)
SAN FRANCISCO 30, Los Angeles Rams 24 (Thurs.)
ATLANTA 17, San Francisco 7 (Sun.)

1981
MIAMI 30, Pittsburgh 10 (Thurs.)
Philadelphia 20, BUFFALO 14 (Thurs.)
DALLAS 29, Los Angeles 17 (Sun.)
HOUSTON 17, Cleveland 13 (Thurs.)

1980
TAMPA BAY 10, Los Angeles 9 (Thurs.)
DALLAS 42, San Diego 31 (Sun.)
San Diego 27, MIAMI 24 (OT) (Thurs.)
HOUSTON 6, Pittsburgh 0 (Thurs.)

1979
Los Angeles 13, DENVER 9 (Thurs.)
DALLAS 30, Los Angeles 6 (Sun.)
OAKLAND 45, San Diego 22 (Thurs.)
MIAMI 39, New England 24 (Thurs.)

1978
New England 21, OAKLAND 14 (Sun.)
Minnesota 21, DALLAS 10 (Thurs.)
LOS ANGELES 10, Pittsburgh 7 (Sun.)
Denver 21, OAKLAND 6 (Sun.)

1977
Minnesota 30, DETROIT 21 (Sat.)

1976
Los Angeles 20, DETROIT 17 (Sat.)

1975
LOS ANGELES 10, Pittsburgh 3 (Sat.)

1974
OAKLAND 27, Dallas 23 (Sat.)

OVERTIME GAMES

HISTORY OF OVERTIME GAMES

PRESEASON

Aug. 28, 1955	Los Angeles 23, New York Giants 17, at Portland, Oregon
Aug. 24, 1962	Denver 27, Dallas Texans 24, at Fort Worth, Texas
Aug. 10, 1974	San Diego 20, New York Jets 14, at San Diego
Aug. 17, 1974	Pittsburgh 33, Philadelphia 30, at Philadelphia
Aug. 17, 1974	Dallas 19, Houston 13, at Dallas
Aug. 17, 1974	Cincinnati 13, Atlanta 7, at Atlanta
Sept. 6, 1974	Buffalo 23, New York Giants 17, at Buffalo
Aug. 9, 1975	Baltimore 23, Denver 20, at Denver
Aug. 30, 1975	New England 20, Green Bay 17, at Milwaukee
Sept. 13, 1975	Minnesota 14, San Diego 14, at San Diego
Aug. 1, 1976	New England 13, New York Giants 7, at New England
Aug. 2, 1976	Kansas City 9, Houston 3, at Kansas City
Aug. 20, 1976	New Orleans 26, Baltimore 20, at Baltimore
Sept. 4, 1976	Dallas 26, Houston 20, at Dallas
Aug. 13, 1977	Seattle 23, Dallas 17, at Seattle
Aug. 28, 1977	New England 13, Pittsburgh 10, at New England
Aug. 28, 1977	New York Giants 24, Buffalo 21, at East Rutherford, N.J.
Aug. 2, 1979	Seattle 12, Minnesota 9, at Minnesota
Aug. 4, 1979	Los Angeles 20, Oakland 14, at Los Angeles
Aug. 24, 1979	Denver 20, New England 17, at Denver
Aug. 23, 1980	Tampa Bay 20, Cincinnati 14, at Tampa Bay
Aug. 5, 1981	San Francisco 27, Seattle 24, at Seattle
Aug. 29, 1981	New Orleans 20, Detroit 17, at New Orleans
Aug. 28, 1982	Miami 17, Kansas City 17, at Kansas City
Sept. 3, 1982	Miami 16, New York Giants 13, at Miami
Aug. 6, 1983	L.A. Raiders 26, San Francisco 23, at Los Angeles
Aug. 6, 1983	Atlanta 13, Washington 10, at Atlanta
Aug. 13, 1983	St. Louis 27, Chicago 24, at St. Louis
Aug. 18, 1983	New York Jets 20, Cincinnati 17, at Cincinnati
Aug. 27, 1983	Chicago 20, Kansas City 17, at Chicago
Aug. 11, 1984	Pittsburgh 20, Philadelphia 17, at Pittsburgh
Aug. 9, 1985	Buffalo 10, Detroit 10, at Pontiac, Mich.
Aug. 10, 1985	Minnesota 16, Miami 13, at Miami
Aug. 17, 1985	Dallas 27, San Diego 24, at San Diego
Aug. 24, 1985	N.Y. Giants 34, N.Y. Jets 31, at East Rutherford, N.J.
Aug. 15, 1986	Washington 27, Pittsburgh 24, at Washington
Aug. 15, 1986	Detroit 30, Seattle 27, at Detroit
Aug. 23, 1986	Los Angeles Rams 20, San Diego 17, at Anaheim
Aug. 30, 1986	Minnesota 23, Indianapolis 20, at Indianapolis
Aug. 23, 1987	Philadelphia 19, New England 13, at New England
Sept. 5, 1987	Cleveland 30, Green Bay 24, at Milwaukee
Sept. 6, 1987	Kansas City 13, St. Louis 10, at Memphis, Tenn.
Aug. 11, 1988	Seattle 16, Detroit 13, at Detroit
Aug. 19, 1988	Miami 16, Denver 13, at Miami
Aug. 19, 1988	Green Bay 21, Kansas City 21, at Milwaukee
Aug. 20, 1988	Houston 20, Los Angeles Rams 17, at Anaheim
Aug. 21, 1988	Minnesota 19, Phoenix 16, at Phoenix
Aug. 5, 1989	Los Angeles Rams 16, San Francisco 13, at Tokyo, Japan
Aug. 26, 1989	Denver 24, Dallas 21, at Denver
Sept. 1, 1989	N.Y. Jets 15, Kansas City 13, at Kansas City
Aug. 24, 1990	Cincinnati 13, New England 10, at New England
Aug. 16, 1991	Cleveland 24, Washington 21, at Washington
Aug. 17, 1991	Cincinnati 27, Minnesota 24, at Cincinnati
Aug. 23, 1991	Dallas 20, Atlanta 17, at Dallas
Aug. 24, 1991	Cincinnati 19, Green Bay 16, at Green Bay
Aug. 22, 1992	Los Angeles Rams 16, Green Bay 13, at Anaheim
Aug. 8, 1993	Dallas 13, Detroit 13, at London, England
Aug. 12, 1995	Washington 16, Houston 13, at Knoxville, Tenn.
Aug. 19, 1995	Indianapolis 20, Green Bay 17, at Green Bay
Aug. 3, 1996	Minnesota 23, San Diego 20, at Minnesota
Aug. 10, 1996	San Francisco 16, San Diego 13, at San Francisco
Aug. 1, 1998	Green Bay 27, Kansas City 24, at Tokyo, Japan
Aug. 7, 1998	Detroit 13, Arizona 10, at Pontiac, Mich.
Aug. 22, 1998	Minnesota 25, Carolina 22, at Charlotte, N.C.
Aug. 9, 1999	Cleveland 20, Dallas 17, at Canton, Ohio

REGULAR SEASON

Sept. 22, 1974—Pittsburgh 35, Denver 35, at Denver; Steelers win toss. Gilliam's pass intercepted and returned by Rowser to Denver's 42. Turner misses 41-yard field goal. Walden punts and Greer returns to Broncos' 39. Van Heusen punts and Edwards returns to Steelers' 16. Game ends with Steelers on own 26.

Nov. 10, 1974—New York Jets 26, New York Giants 20, at New Haven, Conn.; Giants win toss. Gogolak misses 42-yard field goal. Namath passes to Boozer for five yards and touchdown at 6:53.

Sept. 28, 1975—Dallas 37, St. Louis 31, at Dallas; Cardinals win toss. Hart's pass intercepted and returned by Jordan to Cardinals' 37. Staubach passes to DuPree for three yards and touchdown at 7:53.

Oct. 12, 1975—Los Angeles 13, San Diego 10, at San Diego; Chargers win toss. Partee punts to Rams' 14. Dempsey kicks 22-yard field goal at 9:27.

Nov. 2, 1975—Washington 30, Dallas 24, at Washington; Cowboys win toss. Staubach's pass intercepted and returned by Houston to Cowboys' 35. Kilmer runs one yard for touchdown at 6:34.

Nov. 16, 1975—St. Louis 20, Washington 17, at St. Louis; Cardinals win toss. Bakken kicks 37-yard field goal at 7:00.

Nov. 23, 1975—Kansas City 24, Detroit 21, at Kansas City; Lions win toss. Chiefs take over on downs at own 38. Stenerud kicks 26-yard field goal at 6:44.

Nov. 23, 1975—Oakland 26, Washington 23, at Washington; Redskins win toss. Bragg punts to Raiders' 42. Blanda kicks 27-yard field goal at 7:13.

Nov. 30, 1975—Denver 13, San Diego 10, at Denver; Broncos win toss. Turner kicks 25-yard field goal at 4:13.

Nov. 30, 1975—Oakland 37, Atlanta 34, at Oakland; Falcons win toss. James punts to Raiders' 16. Guy punts and Herron returns to Falcons' 41. Nick Mike-Mayer misses 45-yard field goal. Guy punts into Falcons' end zone. James punts to Raiders' 39. Blanda kicks 36-yard field goal at 15:00.

Dec. 14, 1975—Baltimore 10, Miami 7, at Baltimore; Dolphins win toss. Seiple punts to Colts' 4. Linhart kicks 31-yard field goal at 12:44.

Sept. 19, 1976—Minnesota 10, Los Angeles 10, at Minnesota; Vikings win toss. Tarkenton's pass intercepted by Monte Jackson and returned to Minnesota 16. Allen blocks Dempsey's 30-yard field goal attempt, ball rolls into end zone for touchback. Clabo punts and Scribner returns to Rams' 20. Rusty Jackson punts to Vikings' 35. Tarkenton's pass intercepted by Kay at Rams' 1, no return. Game ends with Rams on own 3.

***Sept. 27, 1976—Washington 20, Philadelphia 17,** at Philadelphia; Eagles win toss. Jones punts and E. Brown loses one yard on return to Redskins' 40. Bragg punts 51 yards into end zone for touchback. Jones punts and E. Brown returns to Redskins' 42. Bragg punts and Marshall returns to Eagles' 41. Boryla's pass intercepted by Dusek at Redskins' 37, no return. Bragg punts and Bradley returns. Philadelphia holding penalty moves ball back to Eagles' 8. Boryla pass intercepted by E. Brown and returned to Eagles' 22. Moseley kicks 29-yard field goal at 12:49.

Oct. 17, 1976—Kansas City 20, Miami 17, at Miami; Chiefs win toss. Wilson punts into end zone for touchback. Bulaich fumbles into Kansas City end zone, Collier recovers for touchback. Stenerud kicks 34-yard field goal at 14:48.

Oct. 31, 1976—St. Louis 23, San Francisco 20, at St. Louis; Cardinals win toss. Joyce punts and Leonard fumbles on return, Jones recovers at 49ers' 43. Bakken kicks 21-yard field goal at 6:42.

Dec. 5, 1976—San Diego 13, San Francisco 7, at San Diego; Chargers win toss. Morris runs 13 yards for touchdown at 5:12.

Sept. 18, 1977—Dallas 16, Minnesota 10, at Minnesota; Vikings win toss. Dallas starts on Vikings' 47 after a punt early in the overtime period. Staubach scores seven plays later on a four-yard run at 6:14.

***Sept. 26, 1977—Cleveland 30, New England 27,** at Cleveland; Browns win toss. Sipe throws a 22-yard pass to Logan at Patriots' 19. Cockroft kicks 35-yard field goal at 4:45.

Oct. 16, 1977—Minnesota 22, Chicago 16, at Minnesota; Bears win toss. Parsons punts 53 yards to Vikings' 18. Minnesota drives to Bears' 11. On a first-and-10, Vikings fake a field goal and holder Krause hits Voigt with a touchdown pass at 6:45.

Oct. 30, 1977—Cincinnati 13, Houston 10, at Cincinnati; Bengals win toss. Bahr kicks a 22-yard field goal at 5:51.

Nov. 13, 1977—San Francisco 10, New Orleans 7, at New Orleans; Saints win toss. Saints fail to move ball and Blanchard punts to 49ers' 41. Wersching kicks a 33-yard field goal at 6:33.

Dec. 18, 1977—Chicago 12, New York Giants 9, at East Rutherford, N.J.; Giants win toss. The ball changes hands eight times before Thomas kicks a 28-yard field goal at 14:51.

Sept. 10, 1978—Cleveland 13, Cincinnati 10, at Cleveland; Browns win toss. Collins returns kickoff 41 yards to Browns' 47. Cockroft kicks 27-yard field goal at 4:30.

***Sept. 11, 1978—Minnesota 12, Denver 9,** at Minnesota; Vikings win toss. Danmeier kicks 44-yard field goal at 2:56.

Sept. 24, 1978—Pittsburgh 15, Cleveland 9, at Pittsburgh; Steelers win toss. Cunningham scores on a 37-yard "gadget" pass from Bradshaw at 3:43. Steelers start winning drive on their 21.

Sept. 24, 1978—Denver 23, Kansas City 17, at Kansas City; Broncos win toss. Dilts punts to Kansas City. Chiefs advance to Broncos' 40 where Reed fails to make first down on fourth-and-one situation. Broncos march downfield. Preston scores two-yard touchdown at 10:28.

Oct. 1, 1978—Oakland 25, Chicago 19, at Chicago; Bears win toss. Both teams punt on first possession. On Chicago's second offensive series, Colzie intercepts Avellini's pass and returns it to Bears' 3. Three plays later, Whittington runs two yards for a touchdown at 5:19.

Oct. 15, 1978—Dallas 24, St. Louis 21, at St. Louis; Cowboys win toss. Dallas drives from its 23 into field goal range. Septien kicks 27-yard field goal at 3:28.

Oct. 29, 1978—Denver 20, Seattle 17, at Seattle; Broncos win toss. Ball changes hands four times before Turner kicks 18-yard field goal at 12:59.

Nov. 12, 1978—San Diego 29, Kansas City 23, at San Diego; Chiefs win toss. Fouts hits Jefferson for decisive 14-yard touchdown pass on the last play (15:00) of overtime period.

Nov. 12, 1978—Washington 16, New York Giants 13, at Washington; Redskins win toss. Moseley kicks winning 45-yard field goal at 8:32 after missing first down field goal attempt of 35 yards at 4:50.

Nov. 26, 1978—Green Bay 10, Minnesota 10, at Green Bay; Packers win toss.

Both teams have possession of the ball four times.

Dec. 9, 1978—Cleveland 37, New York Jets 34, at Cleveland; Browns win toss. Cockroft kicks 22-yard field goal at 3:07.

Sept. 2, 1979—Atlanta 40, New Orleans 34, at New Orleans; Falcons win toss. Bartkowski's pass intercepted by Myers and returned to Falcons' 46. Erxleben punts to Falcons' 4. James punts to Chandler on Saints' 43. Erxleben punts and Ryckman returns to Falcons' 28. James punts and Chandler returns to Saints' 36. Erxleben retrieves punt snap on Saints' 1 and attempts pass. Mayberry intercepts and returns six yards for touchdown at 8:22.

Sept. 2, 1979—Cleveland 25, New York Jets 22, at New York; Jets win toss. Leahy's 43-yard field goal attempt goes wide right at 4:41. Evans's punt blocked by Dykes is recovered by Newton. Ramsey punts into end zone for touchback. Evans punts and Harper returns to Jets' 24. Robinson's pass intercepted by Davis and returned 33 yards to Jets' 31. Cockroft kicks 27-yard field goal at 14:45.

***Sept. 3, 1979—Pittsburgh 16, New England 13,** at Foxboro; Patriots win toss. Hare punts to Swann at Steelers' 31. Bahr kicks 41-yard field goal at 5:10.

Sept. 9, 1979—Tampa Bay 29, Baltimore 26, at Baltimore; Colts win toss. Landry fumbles, recovered by Kollar at Colts' 14. O'Donoghue kicks 31-yard, first-down field goal at 1:41.

Sept. 16, 1979—Denver 20, Atlanta 17, at Atlanta; Broncos win toss. Broncos march 65 yards to Falcons' 7. Turner kicks 24-yard field goal at 6:15.

Sept. 23, 1979—Houston 30, Cincinnati 27, at Cincinnati; Oilers win toss. Parsley punts and Lusby returns to Bengals' 33. Bahr's 32-yard field goal attempt is wide right at 8:05. Parsley's punt downed on Bengals' 5. McInally punts and Ellender returns to Bengals' 42. Fritsch's third down, 29-yard field goal attempt hits left upright and bounces through at 14:28.

Sept. 23, 1979—Minnesota 27, Green Bay 21, at Minnesota; Vikings win toss. Kramer throws 50-yard touchdown pass to Rashad at 3:18.

Oct. 28, 1979—Houston 27, New York Jets 24, at Houston; Oilers win toss. Oilers march 58 yards to Jets' 18. Fritsch kicks 35-yard field goal at 5:10.

Nov. 18, 1979—Cleveland 30, Miami 24, at Cleveland; Browns win toss. Sipe passes 39 yards to Rucker for touchdown at 1:59.

Nov. 25, 1979—Pittsburgh 33, Cleveland 30, at Pittsburgh; Browns win toss. Sipe's pass intercepted by Blount on Steelers' 4. Bradshaw pass intercepted by Bolton on Browns' 12. Evans punts and Bell returns to Steelers' 17. Bahr kicks 37-yard field goal at 14:51.

Nov. 25, 1979—Buffalo 16, New England 13, at Foxboro; Patriots win toss. Hare's punt downed on Bills' 38. Jackson punts and Morgan returns to Patriots' 20. Grogan's pass intercepted by Haslett and returned to Bills' 42. Ferguson's 51-yard pass to Butler sets up N. Mike-Mayer's 29-yard field goal at 9:15.

Dec. 2, 1979—Los Angeles 27, Minnesota 21, at Los Angeles; Rams win toss. Clark punts and Miller returns to Vikings' 25. Kramer's pass intercepted by Brown and returned to Rams' 40. Cromwell, holding for 22-yard field goal attempt, runs around left end untouched for winning score at 6:53.

Sept. 7, 1980—Green Bay 12, Chicago 6, at Green Bay; Bears win toss. Parsons punts and Nixon returns 16 yards. Five plays later, Marcol returns own blocked field goal attempt 24 yards for touchdown at 6:00.

Sept. 14, 1980—San Diego 30, Oakland 24, at San Diego; Raiders win toss. Pastorini's first-down pass intercepted by Edwards. Millen intercepts Fouts' first-down pass and returns to San Diego 46. Bahr's 50-yard field goal attempt partially blocked by Williams and recovered on Chargers' 32. Eight plays later, Fouts throws 24-yard touchdown pass to Jefferson at 8:09.

Sept. 14, 1980—San Francisco 24, St. Louis 21, at San Francisco; Cardinals win toss. Swider punts and Robinson returns to 49ers' 32. San Francisco drives 52 yards to St. Louis 16, where Wersching kicks 33-yard field goal at 4:12.

Oct. 12, 1980—Green Bay 14, Tampa Bay 14, at Tampa Bay; Packers win toss. Teams trade punts twice. Lee returns second Tampa Bay punt to Green Bay 42. Dickey completes three passes to Buccaneers' 18, where Birney's 36-yard field goal attempt is wide right as time expires.

Nov. 9, 1980—Atlanta 33, St. Louis 27, at St. Louis; Falcons win toss. Strong runs 21 yards for touchdown at 4:20.

#Nov. 20, 1980—San Diego 27, Miami 24, at Miami; Chargers win toss. Partridge punts into end zone, Dolphins take over on their own 20. Woodley's pass for Nathan intercepted by Lowe and returned 28 yards to Dolphins' 12. Benirschke kicks 28-yard field goal at 7:14.

Nov. 23, 1980—New York Jets 31, Houston 28, at New York; Jets win toss. Leahy kicks 38-yard field goal at 3:58.

Nov. 27, 1980—Chicago 23, Detroit 17, at Detroit; Bears win toss. Williams returns kickoff 95 yards for touchdown at 0:21.

Dec. 7, 1980—Buffalo 10, Los Angeles 7, at Buffalo; Rams win toss. Corral punts and Hooks returns to Bills' 34. Ferguson's 30-yard pass to Lewis sets up N. Mike-Mayer's 30-yard field goal at 5:14.

Dec. 7, 1980—San Francisco 38, New Orleans 35, at San Francisco; Saints win toss. Erxleben's punt downed by Hardy on 49ers' 27. Wersching kicks 36-yard field goal at 7:40.

***Dec. 8, 1980—Miami 16, New England 13,** at Miami; Dolphins win toss. Von Schamann kicks 23-yard field goal at 3:20.

Dec. 14, 1980—Cincinnati 17, Chicago 14, at Chicago; Bengals win toss. Breech kicks 28-yard field goal at 4:23.

Dec. 21, 1980—Los Angeles 20, Atlanta 17, at Los Angeles; Rams win toss. Corral's punt downed at Rams' 37. James punts into end zone for touchback. Corral's punt downed on Falcons' 17. Bartkowski fumbles when hit by Harris, recovered by Delaney. Corral kicks 23-yard field goal on first play of possession at 7:00.

Sept. 27, 1981—Cincinnati 27, Buffalo 24, at Cincinnati; Bills win toss. Cater punts into end zone for touchback. Bengals drive to the Bills' 10 where Breech kicks 28-yard field goal at 9:33.

Sept. 27, 1981—Pittsburgh 27, New England 21, at Pittsburgh; Patriots win toss. Hubach punts and Smith returns five yards to midfield. Four plays later Bradshaw throws 24-yard touchdown pass to Swann at 3:19.

Oct. 4, 1981—Miami 28, New York Jets 28, at Miami; Jets win toss. Teams trade punts twice. Leahy's 48-yard field goal attempt is wide right as time expires.

Oct. 25, 1981—New York Giants 27, Atlanta 24, at Atlanta; Giants win toss. Jennings' punt goes out of bounds at New York 47. Bright returns Atlanta punt to Giants' 14. Woerner fair catches punt at own 28. Andrews fumbles on first play, recovered by Van Pelt. Danelo kicks 40-yard field goal four plays later at 9:20.

Oct. 25, 1981—Chicago 20, San Diego 17, at Chicago; Bears win toss. Teams trade punts. Bears' second punt returned by Brooks to Chargers' 33. Fouts pass intercepted by Fencik and returned 32 yards to San Diego 27. Roveto kicks 27-yard field goal seven plays later at 9:30.

Nov. 8, 1981—Chicago 16, Kansas City 13, at Kansas City; Bears win toss. Teams trade punts. Kansas City takes over on downs on its own 38. Fuller's fumble recovered by Harris on Chicago 36. Roveto's 37-yard field goal wide, but Chiefs penalized for leverage. Roveto's 22-yard field goal attempt three plays later is good at 13:07.

Nov. 8, 1981—Denver 23, Cleveland 20, at Denver; Browns win toss. D. Smith recovers Hill's fumble at Denver 48. Morton's 33-yard pass to Upchurch and 6-yard run by Preston set up Steinfort's 30-yard field goal at 4:10.

Nov. 8, 1981—Miami 30, New England 27, at New England; Dolphins win toss. Orosz punts and Morgan returns six yards to New England 26. Grogan's pass intercepted by Brudzinski who returns 19 yards to Patriots' 26. Von Schamann kicks 30-yard field goal on first down at 7:09.

Nov. 15, 1981—Washington 30, New York Giants 27, at New York; Giants win toss. Nelms returns Giants' punt 26 yards to New York 47. Five plays later Moseley kicks 48-yard field goal at 3:44.

Dec. 20, 1981—New York Giants 13, Dallas 10, at New York; Cowboys win toss and kick off. Jennings punts to Dallas 40. Taylor recovers Dorsett's fumble on second down. Danelo's 33-yard field goal attempt hits right upright and bounces back. White's pass for Pearson intercepted by Hunt and returned seven yards to Dallas 24. Four plays later Danelo kicks 35-yard field goal at 6:19.

Sept. 12, 1982—Washington 37, Philadelphia 34, at Philadelphia; Redskins win toss. Theismann completes five passes for 63 yards to set up Moseley's 26-yard field goal at 4:47.

Sept. 19, 1982—Pittsburgh 26, Cincinnati 20, at Pittsburgh; Bengals win toss. Anderson's pass intended for Kreider intercepted by Woodruff and returned 30 yards to Cincinnati 2. Bradshaw completes two-yard touchdown pass to Stallworth on first down at 1:08.

Dec. 19, 1982—Baltimore 20, Green Bay 20, at Baltimore; Packers win toss. K. Anderson intercepts Dickey's first-down pass and returns to Packers' 42. Miller's 44-yard field goal attempt blocked by G. Lewis. Teams trade punts before Stenerud's 47-yard field goal attempt is wide right. Teams trade punts again before time expires in Colts possession.

Jan. 2, 1983—Tampa Bay 26, Chicago 23, at Tampa; Bears win toss. Parsons punts to T. Bell at Buccaneers' 40. Capece kicks 33-yard field goal at 3:14.

Sept. 4, 1983—Baltimore 29, New England 23, at New England; Patriots win toss. Cooks runs 52 yards with fumble recovery three plays into overtime at 0:30.

Sept. 4, 1983—Green Bay 41, Houston 38, at Houston; Packers win toss. Stenerud kicks 42-yard field goal at 5:55.

Sept. 11, 1983—New York Giants 16, Atlanta 13, at Atlanta; Giants win toss. Dennis returns kickoff 54 yards to Atlanta 41. Haji-Sheikh kicks 30-yard field goal at 3:38.

Sept. 18, 1983—New Orleans 34, Chicago 31, at New Orleans; Bears win toss. Parsons punts and Groth returns five yards to New Orleans 34. Stabler pass intercepted by Schmidt at Chicago 47. Parsons punt downed by Gentry at New Orleans 2. Stabler gains 36 yards in four passes; Wilson 38 on six carries. Andersen kicks 41-yard field goal at 10:57.

Sept. 18, 1983—Minnesota 19, Tampa Bay 16, at Tampa; Vikings win toss. Coleman punts and Bell returns eight yards to Tampa Bay 47. Capece's 33-yard field goal attempt sails wide at 7:26. Dils and Young combine for 48-yard gain to Tampa Bay 27. Ricardo kicks 42-yard field goal at 9:27.

Sept. 25, 1983—Baltimore 22, Chicago 19, at Baltimore; Colts win toss. Allegre kicks 33-yard field goal nine plays later at 4:51.

Sept. 25, 1983—Cleveland 30, San Diego 24, at San Diego; Browns win toss. Walker returns kickoff 33 yards to Cleveland 37. Sipe completes 48-yard touchdown pass to Holt four plays later at 1:53.

Sept. 25, 1983—New York Jets 27, Los Angeles Rams 24, at New York; Jets win toss. Ramsey punts to Irvin who returns to 25 but penalty puts Rams on own 13. Holmes 30-yard interception return sets up Leahy's 26-yard field goal at 3:22.

Oct. 9, 1983—Buffalo 38, Miami 35, at Miami; Dolphins win toss. Von Schamann's 52-yard field goal attempt goes wide at 12:36. Cater punts to Clayton who loses 11 to own 13. Von Schamann's 43-yard field goal attempt sails wide at 5:15. Danelo kicks 36-yard field goal nine plays later at 13:58.

Oct. 9, 1983—Dallas 27, Tampa Bay 24, at Dallas; Cowboys win toss. Septien's 51-yard field goal attempt goes wide but Buccaneers penalized for roughing kicker. Septien kicks 42-yard field goal at 4:38.

Oct. 23, 1983—Kansas City 13, Houston 10, at Houston; Chiefs win toss. Lowery kicks 41-yard field goal 13 plays later at 7:41.

Oct. 23, 1983—Minnesota 20, Green Bay 17, at Green Bay; Packers win toss. Scribner's punt downed on Vikings' 42. Ricardo kicks 32-yard field goal eight plays later at 5:05.

***Oct. 24, 1983—New York Giants 20, St. Louis 20,** at St. Louis; Cardinals win toss. Teams trade punts before O'Donoghue's 44-yard field goal attempt is wide left. Jennings' punt returned by Bird to St. Louis 21. Lomax pass intercepted by Haynes who loses six yards to New York 33. Jennings' punt downed on St. Louis 17. O'Donoghue's 19-yard field goal attempt is wide right. Rutledge's pass intercepted by L. Washington who returns 25 yards to New York 25. O'Donoghue's 42-yard field goal attempt is wide right. Rutledge's pass intercepted by W. Smith at St. Louis 33 to end game.

Oct. 30, 1983—Cleveland 25, Houston 19, at Cleveland; Oilers win toss. Teams trade punts. Nielsen's pass intercepted by Whitwell who returns to Houston 20. Green runs 20 yards for touchdown on first down at 6:34.

Nov. 20, 1983—Detroit 23, Green Bay 20, at Milwaukee; Packers win toss. Scribner punts and Jenkins returns 14 yards to Green Bay 45. Murray's 33-yard field goal attempt is wide left at 9:32. Whitehurst's pass intercepted by Watkins and returned to Green Bay 27. Murray kicks 37-yard field goal four plays later at 8:30.

Nov. 27, 1983—Atlanta 47, Green Bay 41, at Atlanta; Packers win toss. K. Johnson returns interception 31 yards for touchdown at 2:13.

Nov. 27, 1983—Seattle 51, Kansas City 48, at Seattle; Seahawks win toss. Dixon's 47-yard kickoff return sets up N. Johnson's 42-yard field goal at 1:36.

Dec. 11, 1983—New Orleans 20, Philadelphia 17, at Philadelphia; Eagles win toss. Runager punts to Groth who fair catches on New Orleans 32. Stabler completes two passes for 36 yards to Goodlow to set up Andersen's 50-yard field goal at 5:30.

***Dec. 12, 1983—Green Bay 12, Tampa Bay 9,** at Tampa; Packers win toss. Stenerud kicks 23-yard field goal 11 plays later at 4:07.

Sept. 9, 1984—Detroit 27, Atlanta 24, at Atlanta; Lions win toss. Murray kicks 48-yard field goal nine plays later at 5:06.

Sept. 30, 1984—Tampa Bay 30, Green Bay 27, at Tampa; Packers win toss. Scribner punts 44 yards to Tampa Bay 2. Epps returns Garcia's punt three yards to Green Bay 27. Scribner's punt downed on Buccaneers' 33. Ariri kicks 46-yard field goal 11 plays later at 10:32.

Oct. 14, 1984—Detroit 13, Tampa Bay 7, at Detroit; Buccaneers win toss. Tampa Bay drives to Lions' 39 before Wilder fumbles. Five plays later Danielson hits Thompson with 37-yard touchdown pass at 4:34.

Oct. 21, 1984—Dallas 30, New Orleans 27, at Dallas; Cowboys win toss. Septien kicks 41-yard field goal eight plays later at 3:42.

Oct. 28, 1984—Denver 22, Los Angeles Raiders 19, at Los Angeles; Raiders win toss. Hawkins fumble recovered by Foley at Denver 7. Teams trade punts. Karlis's 42-yard field goal attempt is wide left. Teams trade punts. Wilson pass intercepted by R. Jackson at Los Angeles 45, returned 23 yards to Los Angeles 22. Karlis kicks 35-yard field goal two plays later at 15:00.

Nov. 4, 1984—Philadelphia 23, Detroit 23, at Detroit; Lions win toss. Lions drive to Eagles' 3 in eight plays. Murray's 21-yard field goal attempt hits right upright and bounces back. Jaworski's pass intercepted by Watkins at Detroit 5. Teams trade punts. Cooper returns Black's punt five yards to Eagles' 14. Time expires four plays later with Eagles on own 21.

Nov. 18, 1984—San Diego 34, Miami 28, at San Diego; Chargers win toss. McGee scores eight plays later on a 25-yard run at 3:17.

Dec. 2, 1984—Cincinnati 20, Cleveland 17, at Cleveland; Browns win toss. Simmons returns Cox's punt 30 yards to Cleveland 35. Breech kicks 35-yard field goal seven plays later at 4:34.

Dec. 2, 1984—Houston 23, Pittsburgh 20, at Houston; Oilers win toss. Cooper kicks 30-yard field goal 16 plays later at 5:53.

Sept. 8, 1985—St. Louis 27, Cleveland 24, at Cleveland; Cardinals win toss. O'Donoghue kicks 35-yard field goal nine plays later at 5:27.

Sept. 29, 1985—New York Giants 16, Philadelphia 10, at Philadelphia; Eagles win toss. Jaworski's pass tipped by Quick and intercepted by Patterson who returns 29 yards for touchdown at 0:55.

Oct. 20, 1985—Denver 13, Seattle 10, at Denver; Seahawks win toss. Teams trade punts twice. Krieg's pass intercepted by Hunter and returned to Seahawks' 15. Karlis kicks 24-yard field goal four plays later at 9:19.

Nov. 10, 1985—Philadelphia 23, Atlanta 17, at Philadelphia; Falcons win toss. Donnelly's 62-yard punt goes out of bounds at Eagles' 1. Jaworski completes 99-yard touchdown pass to Quick two plays later at 1:49.

Nov. 10, 1985—San Diego 40, Los Angeles Raiders 34, at San Diego; Chargers win toss. James scores on 17-yard run seven plays later at 3:44.

Nov. 17, 1985—Denver 30, San Diego 24, at Denver; Chargers win toss. Thomas' 40-yard field goal attempt blocked by Smith and returned 60 yards by Wright for touchdown at 4:45.

Nov. 24, 1985—New York Jets 16, New England 13, at New York; Jets win toss. Teams trade punts twice. Patriots' second punt returned 46 yards by Sohn to Patriots' 15. Leahy kicks 32-yard field goal one play later at 10:05.

Nov. 24, 1985—Tampa Bay 19, Detroit 16, at Tampa; Lions win toss. Teams trade punts. Lions' punt downed on Buccaneers' 38. Igwebuike kicks 24-yard field goal 11 plays later at 12:31.

Nov. 24, 1985—Los Angeles Raiders 31, Denver 28, at Los Angeles; Raiders win toss. Bahr kicks 32-yard field goal six plays later at 2:42.

Dec. 8, 1985—Los Angeles Raiders 17, Denver 14, at Denver; Broncos win toss. Teams trade punts twice. Elway's fumble recovered by Townsend at Broncos' 8. Bahr kicks 26-yard field goal one play later at 4:55.

Sept. 14, 1986—Chicago 13, Philadelphia 10, at Chicago; Eagles win toss. Crawford's fumble of kickoff recovered by Jackson at Eagles' 35. Butler kicks 23-yard field goal 10 plays later at 5:56.

Sept. 14, 1986—Cincinnati 36, Buffalo 33, at Cincinnati; Bills win toss. Zander intercepts Kelly's first-down pass and returns it to Bills' 17. Breech kicks 20-yard field goal two plays later at 0:56.

Sept. 21, 1986—New York Jets 51, Miami 45, at New York; Jets win toss. O'Brien completes 43-yard touchdown pass to Walker five plays later at 2:35.

Sept. 28, 1986—Pittsburgh 22, Houston 16, at Houston; Oilers win toss. Johnson's punt returned 41 yards by Woods to Oilers' 15. Abercrombie scores on three-yard run three plays later at 2:35.

Sept. 28, 1986—Atlanta 23, Tampa Bay 20, at Tampa; Falcons win toss. Teams trade punts. Luckhurst kicks 34-yard field goal 10 plays later at 12:35.

Oct. 5, 1986—Los Angeles Rams 26, Tampa Bay 20, at Anaheim; Rams win toss. Dickerson scores four plays later on 42-yard run at 2:16.

Oct. 12, 1986—Minnesota 27, San Francisco 24, at San Francisco; Vikings win toss. C. Nelson kicks 28-yard field goal nine plays later at 4:27.

Oct. 19, 1986—San Francisco 10, Atlanta 10, at Atlanta; Falcons win toss. Teams trade punts twice. Donnelly punts to 49ers' 27. The following play Wilson recovers Rice's fumble at 49ers' 46 as time expires.

Nov. 2, 1986—Washington 44, Minnesota 38, at Washington; Redskins win toss. Schroeder completes 38-yard touchdown pass to Clark four plays later at 1:46.

Nov. 20, 1986—Los Angeles Raiders 37, San Diego 31, at San Diego; Raiders win toss. Teams trade punts. Allen scores five plays later on 28-yard run at 8:33.

Nov. 23, 1986—Cleveland 37, Pittsburgh 31, at Cleveland; Browns win toss. Teams trade punts. Six plays later Kosar hits Slaughter with 36-yard touchdown pass at 6:37.

Nov. 30, 1986—Chicago 13, Pittsburgh 10, at Chicago; Bears win toss and kick off. Newsome's punt returned by Barnes to Chicago 49. Butler kicks 42-yard field goal five plays later at 3:55.

Nov. 30, 1986—Philadelphia 33, Los Angeles Raiders 27, at Los Angeles; Eagles win toss. Teams trade punts. Long recovers Cunningham's fumble at Philadelphia 42. Waters returns Allen's fumble 81 yards to Los Angeles 4. Cunningham scores on one-yard run two plays later at 6:53.

Nov. 30, 1986—Cleveland 13, Houston 10, at Cleveland; Oilers win toss and kick off. Gossett punts to Houston 39. Luck's pass intercepted by Minnifield at Cleveland 21. Gossett punts to Houston 34. Luck's pass intercepted by Minnifield at Cleveland 43 who returns 20 yards to Houston 37. Moseley kicks 29-yard field goal nine plays later at 14:44.

Dec. 7, 1986—St. Louis 10, Philadelphia 10, at Philadelphia; Cardinals win toss. White blocks Schubert's 40-yard field goal attempt. Teams trade punts. McFadden's 43-yard field goal attempt is wide left. Schubert's 37-yard field goal attempt is wide right. Cavanaugh's pass intercepted by Carter and returned to Eagles' 48 to end game.

Dec. 14, 1986—Miami 37, Los Angeles Rams 31, at Anaheim; Dolphins win toss. Marino completes 20-yard touchdown pass to Duper six plays later at 3:04.

Sept. 20, 1987—Denver 17, Green Bay 17, at Milwaukee; Packers win toss. Del Greco's 47-yard field goal attempt is short. Teams trade punts. Elway intercepted by Noble who returns 10 yards to Green Bay 34. Davis fumbles on next play and Smith recovers. Two plays later, Karlis's 40-yard field goal attempt is wide left. Time expires two plays later with Packers on own 23.

Oct. 11, 1987—Detroit 19, Green Bay 16, at Green Bay; Lions win toss. Prindle's 42-yard field goal attempt is wide left. Packers punt downed on Detroit 17. Prindle kicks 31-yard field goal 16 plays later at 12:26.

Oct. 18, 1987—New York Jets 37, Miami 31, at New York; Jets win toss. Teams trade punts. Ryan intercepted by Hooper at Jets' 47 who returns 11 yards. Mackey intercepted by Haslett at Jets' 37 who returns 9 yards. Jets punt. Mackey intercepted by Radachowsky who returns 45 yards to Miami 24. Ryan completes eight-yard touchdown pass to Hunter five plays later at 14:26.

Oct. 18, 1987—Green Bay 16, Philadelphia 10, at Green Bay; Packers win toss. Hargrove scores on seven-yard run 10 plays later at 5:04.

Oct. 18, 1987—Buffalo 6, New York Giants 3, at Buffalo; Bills win toss. Schlopy's 28-yard field goal attempt is wide left. Teams trade punts. Rutledge intercepted by Clark who returns 23 yards to Buffalo 40. Schlopy kicks 27-yard field goal nine plays later at 14:41.

Oct. 25, 1987—Buffalo 34, Miami 31, at Miami; Bills win toss. Norwood kicks 27-yard field goal seven plays later at 4:12.

Nov. 1, 1987—San Diego 27, Cleveland 24, at San Diego; Browns win toss. Kosar intercepted by Glenn who returns 20 yards to Browns' 25. Abbott kicks 33-yard field goal three plays later at 2:16.

Nov. 15, 1987—Dallas 23, New England 17, at New England; Cowboys win toss. Walker scores on 60-yard run four plays later at 1:50.

Nov. 26, 1987—Minnesota 44, Dallas 38, at Dallas; Vikings win toss. Coleman's punt downed by Hilton at Cowboys' 37. White intercepted by Studwell who returns 12 yards to Vikings' 37. D. Nelson scores on 24-yard run seven plays later at 7:51.

Nov. 29, 1987—Philadelphia 34, New England 31, at New England; Patriots win toss. Ramsey intercepted by Joyner who returns 29 yards to Eagles' 32. Fryar fair catches Teltschik's punt at Patriots' 13. Franklin's 46-yard field goal attempt is short. McFadden's 39-yard field goal attempt is wide left. Tatupu fumbles on next play and Cobb recovers. McFadden kicks 38-yard field goal four plays later at 12:16.

Dec. 6, 1987—New York Giants 23, Philadelphia 20, at New York; Giants win toss and kick off. Teams trade punts twice. Teltschik's punt is returned 16 yards by McConkey to Eagles' 33. Three plays later, Allegre's 50-yard field goal attempt is blocked by Joyner and returned 25 yards by Hoage to Eagles' 30. McConkey returns Teltschik's punt four yards to Giants' 44. Allegre kicks 28-yard field goal four plays later at 10:42.

Dec. 6, 1987—Cincinnati 30, Kansas City 27, at Cincinnati; Bengals win toss. Teams trade punts. Breech kicks 32-yard field goal 16 plays later at 9:44.

Dec. 26, 1987—Washington 27, Minnesota 24, at Minnesota; Redskins win toss. Haji-Sheikh kicks 26-yard field goal six plays later at 2:09.

Sept. 4, 1988—Houston 17, Indianapolis 14, at Indianapolis; Colts win toss. Dickerson fumble recovered by Lyles who returns six yards to Colts' 42. Zendejas kicks 35-yard field goal six plays later at 3:51.

***Sept. 26, 1988—Los Angeles Raiders 30, Denver 27,** at Denver; Broncos win toss. Teams trade punts twice. Elway intercepted by Lee who returns 20 yards to Broncos' 31. Bahr kicks 35-yard field goal four plays later at 12:35.

Oct. 2, 1988—New York Jets 17, Kansas City 17, at New York; Chiefs win toss. Chiefs punt goes into end zone for touchback. Leahy's 44-yard field goal attempt is wide right. Chiefs punt is returned by Townsell to Jets' 26. Burruss recovers McNeil's fumble at Chiefs' 11. DeBerg intercepted by Humphery at Jets' 49. Three plays later, time expires.

Oct. 9, 1988—Denver 16, San Francisco 13, at San Francisco; Broncos win toss and kick off. Young intercepted by Haynes at Broncos' 32. Denver punt downed at 49ers' 5. Young intercepted by Wilson who returns seven yards to 49ers' 5. Karlis kicks 22-yard field goal two plays later at 8:11.

Oct. 30, 1988—New York Giants 13, Detroit 10, at Detroit; Lions win toss. James's fumble recovered by Taylor at Lions' 22. Three plays later, McFadden kicks 33-yard field goal at 1:13.

Nov. 20, 1988—Buffalo 9, New York Jets 6, at Buffalo; Jets win toss. Vick's fumble recovered by Bennett at Bills' 32. Norwood kicks 30-yard field goal five plays later at 3:47.

Nov. 20, 1988—Philadelphia 23, New York Giants 17, at New York; Eagles win toss. Philadelphia's punt goes into end zone for touchback. Hostetler intercepted by Hoage who returns 11 yards to Giants' 41. Six plays later, Zendejas's 30-yard field-goal attempt is blocked and ball is recovered behind line of scrimmage by Eagles' Simmons, who runs 15 yards for touchdown at 3:09.

Dec. 11, 1988—New England 10, Tampa Bay 7, at New England; Buccaneers win toss and kick off. Staurovsky kicks 27-yard field goal six plays later at 3:08.

Dec. 17, 1988—Cincinnati 20, Washington 17, at Cincinnati; Bengals win toss. Cincinnati's punt returned by Oliphant to Redskins' 16. Grant recovers Williams's fumble at Redskins' 17. Breech kicks 20-yard field goal three plays later at 7:01.

Sept. 24, 1989—Buffalo 47, Houston 41, at Houston; Oilers win toss. Johnson returns Brady's kickoff 17 yards to Oilers' 19. Oilers drive to Buffalo 25, Zendejas's 37-yard field goal blocked, but Bills offsides and Zendejas's second attempt is wide left. Bills' ball and Kelly completes series of passes, including 28-yard game-winner to Andre Reed, at 8:42.

Oct. 8, 1989—Miami 13, Cleveland 10, at Miami; Browns win toss. Metcalf returns Stoyanovich's kickoff 20 yards to Browns' 28. Browns drive ball 46 yards in eight plays; Bahr wide left on 44-yard field goal attempt. Dolphins ball. Browns called for pass interference on Marino pass to Banks at Cleveland 47. Two plays later, Banks's 20-yard reception at Browns' 23 sets up winning 35-yard field goal by Stoyanovich at 6:23.

Oct. 22, 1989—Denver 24, Seattle 21, at Seattle; Seahawks win toss. Treadwell's 56-yard kickoff returned 18 yards by Jefferson to Seahawks' 27. Seahawks drive to Broncos' 22 in 10 plays, but Johnson's 40-yard field goal attempt wide left. Smith intercepts a Krieg pass and returns it 28 yards to Seahawks' 10. Treadwell kicks winning 27-yard field goal at 7:46.

Oct. 29, 1989—New England 23, Indianapolis 20, at Indianapolis; Patriots win toss. Biasucci kickoff returned 13 yards to Patriots' 23 by Martin. Holding penalty brings ball back to Patriots' 13. After six plays, Feagles punt returned 11 yards by Verdin to Colts' 28. Six plays later, Colts punt to Martin at Patriots' 12. Grogan completes three straight passes to Patriots' 44. Five consecutive runs put New England on Colts' 33. Davis kicks a 51-yard winning field goal for Patriots at 9:46.

Oct. 29, 1989—Green Bay 23, Detroit 20, at Milwaukee; Lions win toss. Sanders touchback on Jacke kickoff. On first play, Murphy intercepts Lions' Peete and returns it three yards to Lions' 26. Fullwood gains five yards on three plays to set up Jacke's 38-yard field goal at 2:14.

Nov. 5, 1989—Minnesota 23, Los Angeles Rams 21, at Minneapolis; Rams win toss. Karlis's kick returned 18 yards by Delpino to Rams' 19. Drive stops at Rams' 28. Merriweather blocks Hatcher's punt at 12. Ball rolls out of end zone for safety.

Nov. 19, 1989—Cleveland 10, Kansas City 10, at Cleveland; Browns win toss. Browns punt three times; Chiefs twice; before Kansas City's Lowery misses 47-yard field goal with 17 seconds remaining in overtime. Kosar's pass intercepted as time expired.

Nov. 26, 1989—Los Angeles Rams 20, New Orleans 17, at New Orleans; Saints win toss. Lansford's kickoff returned 27 yards to Saints' 30. After four plays, Barnhardt punts to Rams' 15. Saints penalized 35 yards for interference to Rams' 43. Three plays later, Everett hits Anderson with 14-yard pass to Saints' 40, then 26-yarder to put Rams in field goal position. Lansford kicks 31-yard field goal at 6:38.

Dec. 3, 1989—Los Angeles Raiders 16, Denver 13, at Los Angeles; Broncos win toss. Bell returns Jaeger kickoff 14 yards to Broncos' 18. Broncos' penalized for illegal block to Broncos' 9. Elway completes three passes for two first downs. On third and eight Elway sacked for 10-yard loss. Horan punts, Adams calls for fair catch at Raiders' 29. Dyal's 26-yard reception moves Raiders to Denver 43. Raiders move ball 34 yards in three plays to set up Jaeger's 26-yard field goal at 7:02.

Dec. 10, 1989—Indianapolis 23, Cleveland 17, at Indianapolis; Browns win toss. Teams trade punts. McNeil returns Colts' punt 42 yards to 42. Seven plays later, Bahr misses 35-yard field goal attempt. Three plays later, Stark punts and McNeil returns ball to 50-yard line. Two plays later, Prior intercepts Kosar's pass at Colts' 42 and returns it 58 yards for touchdown at 10:54.

Dec. 17, 1989—Cleveland 23, Minnesota 17, at Cleveland; Browns win toss. Browns punt to Vikings' 18. Six plays later, Vikings punt to Browns' 22. Nine plays later, Bahr lines up to attempt 31-yard field goal. Holder Pagel takes snap and passes 14 yards to Waiters for touchdown at 9:30.

Sept. 23, 1990—Denver 34, Seattle 31, at Denver; Seahawks win toss. Loville returns kickoff 19 yards to Seahawks' 27. Seahawks drive to Broncos' 26, where Johnson misses 44-yard field goal wide right. Broncos take over and Elway completes series of passes to set up Treadwell's 25-yard field goal at 9:14.

Sept. 30, 1990—Tampa Bay 23, Minnesota 20, at Minnesota; Vikings win toss. Vikings drive to Buccaneers' 31; Igwebuike's 48-yard field goal attempt wide left. Buccaneers drive to Vikings' 43 and punt. Gannon's pass is intercepted at Vikings' 26 by Wayne Haddix. Buccaneers drive to Vikings' 19 to set up Christie's 36-yard field goal at 9:11.

Oct. 7, 1990—Cincinnati 34, Los Angeles Rams 31, at Anaheim; Rams win toss. Berry returns kickoff to Rams' 21. After 3 plays, English punts and Green downs ball at Bengals' 25. After 3 plays, Johnson punts and Sutton downs ball at Rams' 29-yard line. After 3 plays, English punts and Price signals fair catch at Bengals' 47. Esiason completes series of passes to 26-yard line to set up Breech's 44-yard field goal at 11:56.

Nov. 4, 1990—Washington 41, Detroit 38, at Detroit; Redskins win toss. Howard downs kickoff on Redskins' 15. After 3 plays, Mojsiejenko punts to Redskins' 45. After 3 plays, Arnold punts to Redskins' 10. Rutledge completes series of passes to set up Lohmiller's 34-yard field goal at 9:10.

Nov. 18, 1990—Chicago 16, Denver 13, at Denver; Broncos win toss. Ezor returns kickoff to Broncos' 12. Both teams have ball twice and have to punt after each possession. Broncos punt after third possession of overtime and Bailey returns 20 yards to Broncos' 34. Harbaugh completes 10-yard pass to Thornton to set up Butler's 44-yard field goal at 13:14.

Nov. 25, 1990—Seattle 13, San Diego 10, at San Diego; Chargers win toss. Lewis returns kickoff to Chargers' 22. After 2 plays, Cox fumbles and ball is recovered by Porter at Chargers' 23. After two plays, Johnson kicks 40-yard field goal at 3:01.

Dec. 2, 1990—Chicago 23, Detroit 17, at Chicago; Lions win toss. Gray returns kickoff to Lions' 35. After 10 plays, Murray misses 35-yard field goal. Bears take possession at Chicago 20. Harbaugh completes 50-yard game-winning pass to Anderson at 10:57.

Dec. 2, 1990—Seattle 13, Houston 10, at Seattle; Seahawks win toss. Warren returns kickoff to Seahawks' 13. After 5 plays, Donnelly punts to Oilers' 23-yard line. Ford's fumble recovered by Wyman. Seahawks take possession at Oilers' 27. After 2 plays, Johnson kicks 42-yard field goal at 4:25.

Dec. 9, 1990—Miami 23, Philadelphia 20, at Miami; Eagles win toss. After 11 plays, Feagles punts to Dolphins' 26. After 6 plays, Roby punts to Eagles' 14 and Harris returns to 25. After 3 plays, Feagles punts to Dolphins' 43. Marino completes series of passes to Eagles' 22. Stoyanovich kicks 39-yard field goal at 12:32.

Dec. 9, 1990—San Francisco 20, Cincinnati 17, at Cincinnati; 49ers win toss. Carter returns kickoff to 49ers' 19. After 10 plays, Cofer kicks 23-yard field goal at 6:12.

Sept. 23, 1991—Chicago 19, New York Jets 13, at Chicago; Jets win toss. Mathis returns kickoff seven yards to New York's 12. Jets drive to New York 26; Bailey returns punt to Chicago 39. Bears drive to Jets' 44-yard line and punt into the end zone. Jets drive to Bears' 11 where Leahy's 28-yard field goal attempt is wide left. Bears drive from 20 to Jets' 1 where Harbaugh runs for touchdown at 14:42.

Oct. 13, 1991—Los Angeles Raiders 23, Seattle 20, at Seattle. Seahawks win toss. Seahawks begin on 20. After 5 plays, Tuten punts and Brown signals fair catch at Raiders' 24. After 3 plays, Gossett punts and Land downs ball at Seattle 9. After 1 play, Lott intercepts at Seahawks' 19 to set up Jaeger's game-winning 37-yard field goal at 6:37.

Oct. 20, 1991—Cleveland 30, San Diego 24, at San Diego; Chargers win toss. After kickoff, Chargers drive to Browns' 45 and punt to Browns' 6 where Hendrickson downs ball. Browns drive to 38 and punt; Taylor fair catches on Chargers' 14. After 3 plays, Brandon intercepts at Chargers' 30 and scores at 5:58.

Oct. 20, 1991—New England 26, Minnesota 23, at New England; Patriots win toss. Martin returns kickoff 18 yards to New England 22. Patriots drive to Minnesota 19. Staurovsky's 36-yard field goal attempt is wide left. Minnesota drives to the 50 where Newsome punts into end zone. On first play, McMillian intercepts at the 40 for Minnesota. After 2 plays, Marion causes Jordan fumble and Pool recovers at New England 20. New England drives to Minnesota 24 where Staurovsky kicks 42-yard field goal as time expires.

Nov. 3, 1991—New York Jets 19, Green Bay 16, at New York; Packers win toss. Thompson returns kickoff 30 yards to Packers' 39. Green Bay drives to New York 24 where Jacke's 42-yard field goal attempt is wide right. Jets drive to 50. Aguiar's punt is fumbled by Sikahema and recovered by New York at Packers' 23. After 2 plays, Leahy kicks 37-yard field goal at 9:40.

Nov. 3, 1991—Washington 16, Houston 13, at Washington; Redskins win toss. Mitchell returns kickoff 9 yards to Washington 14. After 4 plays, Goodburn punts and Givins returns to Houston 31. After 1 play, Moon's pass is intercepted by Green at Oilers' 35. After 3 plays, Lohmiller kicks 41-yard field goal at 4:01.

Nov. 10, 1991—Houston 26, Dallas 23, at Houston; Oilers win toss. Pinkett returns kickoff 20 yards to Houston 24. After 6 plays, Montgomery punts and Martin returns to Dallas 24. Cowboys drive to Oilers' 24 where Smith fumbles and McDowell recovers at Oilers' 15. Houston drives to Dallas 5 where Del Greco kicks 23-yard field goal at 14:31.

Nov. 10, 1991—Pittsburgh 33, Cincinnati 27, at Cincinnati; Pittsburgh wins toss. Woodson downs kickoff for touchback. After 3 plays, Stryzinski punts and Barber returns 7 yards to Cincinnati 38. Bengals drive to Pittsburgh 37 where Woods fumbles and Lloyd returns recovery to Cincinnati 44. After 2 plays, O'Donnell passes to Green for 26-yard touchdown at 6:32.

Nov. 24, 1991—Atlanta 23, New Orleans 20, at New Orleans; Atlanta wins toss. Falcons begin at 20. After 3 plays, Fulhage punts and Fenerty signals fair catch at New Orleans 43. After 3 plays, Barnhardt punts and Thompson downs ball at Atlanta 23. After 3 plays, Fulhage punts and Fenerty fair catches at New Orleans 25. Saints drive to Atlanta 38 where Andersen misses 55-yard field-goal attempt. After 1 play, Rozier fumbles and Martin recovers on 50. Saints drive to Atlanta 38 where Barnhardt punts to Falcons' 2. Atlanta drives to New Orleans 33 where Johnson kicks 50-yard field goal at 13:03.

Nov. 24, 1991—Miami 16, Chicago 13, at Chicago; Miami wins toss. Butler kicks to Miami 20 where Paige returns kickoff 15 yards to 35. Miami drives to Chicago 9 where Stoyanovich kicks 27-yard field goal at 4:11.

Dec. 8, 1991—Buffalo 30, Los Angeles Raiders 27, at Los Angeles; Raiders win toss. Daluiso kicks into end zone for touchback. On third play, Kelso intercepts for Buffalo and returns ball to Bills' 36. Bills drive to Los Angeles 24 where Norwood kicks 42-yard field goal at 2:34.

Dec. 8, 1991—Kansas City 20, San Diego 17, at Kansas City; Chiefs win toss. Carney kicks to Kansas City 10 where Stradford returns 23 yards to 33. After 3 plays, Barker punts to San Diego 4. Chargers drive to 40 where Kidd punts 60 yards into end zone for touchback. Kansas City drives to San Diego 39 where Barker punts 38 yards to 1. After 3 plays, Kidd punts 41 yards to San Diego 42 where Stradford returns 12 yards to 30. Chiefs drive to San Diego 1 where Lowery kicks 18-yard field goal at 11:26.

Dec. 8, 1991—New England 23, Indianapolis 17, at New England; Indianapolis wins toss. Baumann kicks off to Indianapolis 2 where Martin returns 23 yards to 25. After 3 downs, Stark punts to New England 17 where Henderson returns 8 yards to 25. New England drives to 50 where McCarthy punts and Prior signals fair catch at Indianapolis 15. After 3 plays, Stark punts to New England 40 where Henderson returns 7 yards to 47. After 2 plays, Millen passes to Timpson for 45-yard touchdown at 8:55.

Dec. 22, 1991—Detroit 17, Buffalo 14, at Buffalo; Detroit wins toss. Daluiso kicks off to Detroit 20 where Dozier returns 15 yards to Lions 35. Lions drive to Bills' 3 where Murray kicks 21-yard field goal at 4:23.

Dec. 22, 1991—New York Jets 23, Miami 20, at Miami; Jets win toss. Aguiar kicks to Miami's 30 where Logan returns 3 yards to the 33. After 4 downs, Stoyanovich punts to Jets' 15 where Baty returns 8 yards to 23. Jets drive to Miami 12 where Allegre kicks 30-yard field goal at 6:33.

Sept. 6, 1992—Minnesota 23, Green Bay 20, at Green Bay. Vikings win toss. Nelson returns kickoff 14 yards to the Minnesota 23. After 5 plays, Newsome punts 49 yards to Green Bay 21 where Brooks returns 12 yards to the 33. After 2 plays, Glenn intercepts pass at the Vikings' 48. On first play, Allen fumbles and Billups recovers at Green Bay 35. After 3 plays, McJulien punts 33 yards to Vikings' 35. Vikings drive to Minnesota 48; Newsome punts 52 yards for touchback. After 3 plays, McJulien punts and Parker returns 10 yards to Green Bay 48. Vikings drive to Packers' 9 where Reveiz kicks 26-yard field goal at 10:20.

Sept. 13, 1992—Cincinnati 24, Los Angeles Raiders 21, at Cincinnati. Raiders win toss. Land returns kickoff 13 yards but fumbles at Los Angeles's 20; ball recovered by Bengals' Bennett at Raiders' 21. After 1 play, Breech kicks 34-yard field goal at 1:01.

Sept. 20, 1992—Houston 23, Kansas City 20, at Houston. Chiefs win toss. Carter returns kickoff 25 yards to Kansas City 28. On third play of drive, Birden fumbles at Kansas City 34; ball recovered by Houston's D. Smith at Chiefs' 23. After one play, Del Greco kicks 39-yard field goal at 1:55.

Oct. 11, 1992—Indianapolis 6, New York Jets 3, at Indianapolis. Colts win toss. Verdin returns kickoff 33 yards to Colts' 36. Colts drive to Jets' 30 where Biasucci kicks 47-yard field goal at 3:01.

Nov. 8, 1992—Cincinnati 31, Chicago 28, at Chicago. Bears win toss. Lewis returns kickoff 22 yards to Chicago's 29. Bears drive to Chicago's 46 where Gardocki punts; fair catch by Wright at the Cincinnati 17. Bengals drive to Bears' 18 where Breech kicks 36-yard field goal at 8:39.

Nov. 15, 1992—New England 37, Indianapolis 34, at Indianapolis. Colts win toss. Verdin returns kickoff 10 yards to Colts' 20; holding penalty brings ball back to Colts' 10. After two plays, Henderson intercepts pass at Colts' 38 and returns it 9 yards to the 29. In three plays, Patriots drive to 1 where Baumann kicks 18-yard field goal at 3:25.

Nov. 29, 1992—Indianapolis 16, Buffalo 13, at Indianapolis. Colts win toss. Verdin returns kickoff 24 yards to Colts' 22. Colts drive to Buffalo 22 where Biasucci kicks 40-yard field goal at 3:51.

***Nov. 30, 1992—Seattle 16, Denver 13,** at Seattle. Seahawks win toss. Daluiso kicks through end zone for touchback. After three plays, Tuten punts 53 yards to Denver 18 where Marshall returns for no gain. After three plays, Rodriguez punts 29 yards to Seattle 45 where Warren signals fair catch. Seahawks drive to Denver 15 where Kasay's 33-yard field goal attempt misses. Broncos take over at Denver 20. After three plays, Rodriguez punts 43 yards to Seattle 38 where Warren signals for fair catch. After four plays, Tuten punts 39 yards to Denver 4 where Daniels downs punt. After three plays, Rodriguez punts 46 yards to Denver 48 where Warren returns 10 yards to the 38. Seahawks drive to Denver 14 where Kasay kicks 32-yard field goal at 11:10.

Dec. 13, 1992—Philadelphia 20, Seattle 17, at Seattle. Eagles win toss. Sydner returns kick 12 yards to Eagles' 16; illegal block penalty brings ball back to 8. Eagles drive to Philadelphia 45 where Feagles punts for a touchback. After 6 plays, Tuten punts 45 yards to Philadelphia 22 where Sydner returns 7 yards to 29. After 6 plays, Feagles punts 44 yards to Seattle 26 where Warren returns 5 yards to 31. After 5 plays, Tuten punts 32 yards to Philadelphia 20 where Sydner signals for fair catch. Eagles drive to Seattle 27 where Ruzek kicks 44-yard field goal with no time remaining.

Dec. 27, 1992—Miami 16, New England 13, at New England. Patriots win toss. Lockwood returns kickoff 15 yards to Patriots' 21. After three plays, McCarthy punts 39 yards to Miami 33 where Miller returns 2 yards to the 35. Miami drives to New England 18 where Stoyanovich kicks 35-yard field goal at 8:17.

Sept. 12, 1993—Detroit 19, New England 16, at New England. Patriots win toss. Patriots begin at 20. After 3 plays, Saxon punts 42 yards to Detroit 29 where Gray returns 12 yards to the 41. After 3 plays, Arnold punts 41 yards to New England 12 where Brown returns 16 yards to the 28. Patriots drive to Detroit 44 where Saxon punts into the end zone for a touchback. Detroit drives to New England 20 where Hanson kicks 38-yard field goal at 11:04.

Nov. 7, 1993—Buffalo 13, New England 10, at New England. Patriots win toss. T. Brown returns kickoff 27 yards to Patriots 30. Patriots drive to Buffalo 48 where Bills take over on downs. Bills drive to New England 25 where Metzelaars fumbles, and C. Brown recovers. After 3 plays, Saxon punts 46 yards to Buffalo 24 where Copeland returns 11 yards to the 35. Bills drive to New England 14 where Christie kicks 32-yard field goal at 9:22.

Dec. 19, 1993—Phoenix 30, Seattle 27, at Seattle. Cardinals win toss. Bailey returns kickoff 14 yards to Cardinals 20. Cardinals drive to Seattle 23 where Davis kicks 41-yard field goal at 6:45.

Jan. 2, 1994—Dallas 16, New York Giants 13, at New York. Giants win toss. Meggett returns kickoff 19 yards to Giants 19. After 6 plays, Horan punts 45 yards to Cowboys 25 where Widmer downs punt. Cowboys drive to Giants' 23 where Murray kicks 41-yard field goal at 10:44.

Jan. 2, 1994—New England 33, Miami 27, at New England. Dolphins win toss. McDuffie returns kickoff 21 yards to Miami 27. After 3 plays, Hatcher punts 43 yards to New England 29 where Harris returns 6 yards to the 35. After 2 plays, Brown intercepts pass from Bledsoe and returns 3 yards to Miami 49. After 3 plays, Hatcher punts 37 yards to New England 14 where Harris returns 18 yards to the 32. After 2 plays, Bledsoe passes 36 yards to Timpson for touchdown at 4:44.

Jan. 2, 1994—Los Angeles Raiders 33, Denver 30, at Los Angeles. Broncos win toss. Delpino returns kickoff 12 yards to Denver 25. Broncos drive to Los Angeles 22 where Elam's 40-yard field goal attempt is wide left. Raiders drive to Denver 29 where Jaeger kicks 47-yard field goal at 7:10.

***Jan. 3, 1994—Philadelphia 37, San Francisco 34,** at San Francisco. 49ers win toss. Walker returns kickoff, 19 yards to San Francisco 27. 49ers drive to Philadelphia 14 where Cofer misses 32-yard field goal. Eagles start at their 20-yard line, and, after 3 plays, Feagles punts 48 yards to San Francisco 36 where Carter fumbles and 49ers recover. After 7 plays, Wilmsmeyer punts 57 yards to Philadelphia 6 where Sikahema returns 16 yards to the 22. Eagles drive to San Francisco 10 where Ruzek kicks 28-yard field goal with no time remaining.

Sept. 4, 1994—Detroit 31, Atlanta 28, at Detroit. Falcons win toss. Falcons start at their own 16 after holding penalty on kickoff. After 3 plays, Alexander punts 41 yards to Detroit 39 where Clay returns 12 yards to Atlanta 49. Detroit drives to Atlanta 20 where Hanson kicks 37-yard field goal with 9:46 remaining.

Sept. 11, 1994—New York Jets 25, Denver 22, at New York. Jets win toss. Murrell returns kickoff 24 yards to New York 33. Jets drive to Denver 22 where Lowery kicks 39-yard field goal with 11:03 remaining.

***Sept. 19, 1994—Detroit 20, Dallas 17,** at Dallas. Lions win toss. Gray returns kickoff 24 yards to Detroit 32. Lions drive to Dallas 34 where Hanson's 51-yard field-goal attempt is blocked by Lett. Cowboys take possession at Dallas 42. Cowboys drive to Detroit 37 where Kennard fumbles and Swilling recovers. Lions take possession at Detroit 45. After 6 plays, Montgomery punts 31 yards to Dallas 16. Cowboys drive to Dallas 49 where Aikman fumbles and Thomas recovers at Dallas 43. Lions drive to Dallas 26 where Hanson kicks 44-yard field goal with 27 seconds remaining.

Oct. 16, 1994—Arizona 19, Washington 16, at Washington. Redskins win toss. Mitchell returns kickoff 27 yards to Washington 41. Redskins drive to Arizona 34 where Lohmiller's 51-yard field-goal attempt is blocked by Joyner and recovered by Williams who returns it to the Washington 37. After 5 plays, Peterson's 45-yard field-goal attempt is wide right. Redskins take possession at the Washington 36. After 3 plays, Roby punts 36 yards to the Arizona 37 where Robinson returns 3 yards to the 40. After 3 plays, Feagles punts 51 yards for a touchback. After 1 play, Shuler's pass is intercepted by Hoage who returns it to the Washington 12. Peterson kicks 29-yard field goal with 5:00 remaining.

Oct. 16, 1994—Miami 20, Los Angeles Raiders 17, at Miami. Dolphins win toss. McDuffie returns kickoff 19 yards to Miami 23. Dolphins drive to Los Angeles 12 where Stoyanovich kicks 29-yard field goal with 9:14 remaining.

#Oct. 20, 1994—Minnesota 13, Green Bay 10, at Minnesota. Vikings win toss. Ismail returns kickoff 22 yards to Minnesota 29. Vikings drive to Green Bay 9 where Fuad Reveiz kicks 27-yard field goal with 10:34 remaining.

Oct. 30, 1994—Detroit 28, New York Giants 25, at New York. Giants win toss. Lewis returns kickoff 16 yards to New York 27. After 3 plays, Horan punts 42 yards to Detroit 24 where Gray calls for fair catch. Detroit drives to New York 6 where Hanson kicks 24-yard field goal with 8:17 remaining.

Oct. 30, 1994—Arizona 20, Pittsburgh 17, at Arizona. Steelers win toss. Johnson returns kickoff 24 yards to Pittsburgh 30 where he fumbles and Arizona's Merritt recovers at Pittsburgh 32. After 3 plays, Davis kicks 51-yard field goal with 13:20 remaining.

Nov. 6, 1994—Cincinnati 20, Seattle 17, at Seattle. Seahawks win toss. Warren returns kickoff 32 yards to Seattle 33. After 3 plays, Tuten punts 37 yards to Cincinnati 28 where Sawyer calls for fair catch. After 3 plays, Johnson punts 64 yards to Seattle 2 where Truitt downs ball. Seahawks drive to Seattle 38 where Tuten punts 50 yards to Cincinnati 12 and Sawyer returns 5 yards to 17. Blake passes to Scott for 76 yards to Seattle 7. Pelfrey kicks 26-yard field goal with 6:46 remaining.

Nov. 6, 1994—Pittsburgh 12, Houston 9, at Houston. Steelers win toss. Stone returns kickoff 15 yards to Pittsburgh 28. After 3 plays, Royals punts 53 yards to Houston 13 where Givins downs ball. After 3 plays, Camarillo punts 57 yards to Pittsburgh 31 where Woodson returns 20 yards to Houston 49. After 3 plays, Royals punts 43 yards to Houston 15 where Coleman returns 3 yards to 18. After 5 plays, Camarillo punts 57 yards to Pittsburgh 12 where Hastings returns 12 yards to 24. Steelers drive to Houston 41 where Royals punts 29 yards to Houston 12, and Coleman calls for fair catch. Brown fumbles on first play and Jones recovers at Houston 22. After 1 play, Anderson kicks 40-yard field goal with 3:36 remaining.

Nov. 13, 1994—New England 26, Minnesota 20, at New England. Patriots win toss. Thompson returns kickoff 27 yards to New England 33. Patriots drive to Minnesota 14 where Bledsoe passes 14 yards to Turner for touchdown with 10:50 remaining.

Nov. 20, 1994—Pittsburgh 16, Miami 13, at Pittsburgh. Steelers win toss. Stone returns kickoff 15 yards to Pittsburgh 16. Steelers drive to Miami 39 where they lose possession on downs. Dolphins drive to Pittsburgh 47 where Arnold punts 35 yards to Pittsburgh 12 and Oliver downs ball. Steelers drive to Miami 21 where Anderson kicks 39-yard field goal with 4:41 remaining.

Nov. 27, 1994—Chicago 19, Arizona 16, at Arizona. Cardinals win toss. Levy returns kickoff 31 yards to Arizona 45. After 5 plays, Feagles punts 38 yards to the end zone for a touchback. Bears drive to Arizona 10 where Butler kicks 27-yard field goal with 6:49 remaining.

Nov. 27, 1994—Tampa Bay 20, Minnesota 17, at Minnesota. Buccaneers win toss. Harris returns kickoff 12 yards to Tampa Bay 38. After 6 plays, Stryzinski punts 40 yards to Minnesota 4 where Guliford muffs punt and Buccaneers' Brady recovers. Husted kicks 22-yard field goal with 12:52 remaining.

#Dec. 1, 1994—Minnesota 33, Chicago 27, at Minnesota. Bears win toss. Lewis returns kickoff 23 yards to Chicago 33. Bears drive to Minnesota 22 where Butler's 40-yard field goal attempt is wide left. After 1 play, Moon passes 65 yards to Carter for touchdown with 9:14 remaining.

Dec. 4, 1994—Denver 20, Kansas City 17, at Kansas City. Broncos win toss. Milburn returns kickoff 24 yards to Denver 29. After 3 plays, Millen fumbles and Phillips recovers at Denver 35. After 4 plays, Allen fumbles and Smith recovers at Denver 27. After 6 plays, Rouen punts 45 yards to Kansas City 25 where Hughes calls for fair catch. After 3 plays, Aguiar punts 33 yards to Denver 42 where Chiefs down ball. Broncos drive to Kansas City 17 where Elam kicks 34-yard field goal with 2:48 remaining.

Sept. 3, 1995—Cincinnati 24, Indianapolis 21, at Indianapolis. Bengals win toss. Dunn returns kickoff 15 yards to Bengals' 17. Cincinnati drives to Indianapolis 29 where Pelfrey kicks 47-yard field goal with 12:24 remaining.

Sept. 3, 1995—Atlanta 23, Carolina 20, at Atlanta. Panthers win toss. Baldwin downs kickoff for touchback. Panthers drive to Carolina 42 where Reich fumbles and ball is recovered by Archambeau at Carolina 31. Falcons drive to Panthers' 16 where Andersen kicks 35-yard field goal with 8:43 remaining.

Sept. 10, 1995—Indianapolis 27, New York Jets 24, at New York. Jets win toss. Carter downs kickoff for touchback. Jets punt downed at Colts' 37. Colts drive to Jets' 35 where Cofer kicks 52-yard field goal with 10:33 remaining.

Sept. 10, 1995—Kansas City 20, New York Giants 17, at Kansas City. Chiefs win toss. Vanover returns kickoff 30 yards to Chiefs' 28. Aguiar punts to Giants' 3. Horan punts to Chiefs' 49. Chiefs drive to Giants' 6 where Elliott kicks 23-yard field goal with 7:11 left.

Sept. 17, 1995—Dallas 23, Minnesota 17, at Minnesota. Cowboys win toss. K. Williams returns kickoff 23 yards to Cowboys' 27. E. Smith scores on 31-yard run with 12:34 left.

Sept. 17, 1995—Kansas City 23, Oakland 17, at Kansas City. Chiefs win toss. Vanover returns kickoff 28 yards to Chiefs' 41. M. Allen fumbles, ball recovered by Robbins at Raiders' 38. Hasty intercepts pass at Chiefs' 36 and returns it 64 yards for touchdown with 10:33 left.

Sept. 17, 1995—Atlanta 27, New Orleans 24, at Atlanta. Saints win toss. Hughes returns kickoff 21 yards to Saints' 17. Metcalf returns Wilmsmeyer's punt 18 yards to Saints' 39. Stryzinski punts, fair catch by Hughes at Saints' 14. Wilmsmeyer punt downed at Falcons' 6. Falcons drive to Saints' 3 where Andersen kicks 21-yard field goal with 7:02 left.

Oct. 8, 1995—Indianapolis 27, Miami 24, at Miami. Colts win toss. Warren returns kickoff 25 yards to Colts' 33. Colts drive to Dolphins' 10 where Blanchard kicks 27-yard field goal with 10:02 left.

Oct. 8, 1995—New York Giants 27, Arizona 21, at New York. Cardinals win toss. Terry returns kickoff 20 yards to Cardinals' 23. Hamilton recovers Krieg's fumble at Cardinals' 36. Lynch recovers Brown's fumble at Cardinals' 38. Armstead intercepts pass at Giants' 42 and returns it 58 yards for touchdown with 10:55 left.

Oct. 8, 1995—Minnesota 23, Houston 17, at Minnesota. Vikings win toss. Palmer returns kickoff 10 yards to Vikings' 15. Saxon's punt downed at Oilers' 8. Washington intercepts pass at Vikings' 47 and returns it 25 yards to Oilers' 28. R. Smith scores on 20-yard run with 7:50 left.

Oct. 8, 1995—Philadelphia 37, Washington 34, at Philadelphia. Redskins win toss. Redskins take possession at their 20 after touchback. Turk punt out of bounds at Eagles' 9. Eagles drive to Redskins' 18 where Anderson kicks 35-yard field goal with 4:54 left.

*** Oct. 9, 1995—Kansas City 29, San Diego 23,** at Kansas City. Chargers win toss. Coleman returns kickoff 24 yards to Chargers' 28. Vanover makes fair catch of Bennett's punt at Chiefs' 15. Coleman makes fair catch of Aguiar's punt at Chargers' 43. Vanover returns Bennett's punt 86 yards for a touchdown with 7:33 left.

Oct. 15, 1995—Tampa Bay 20, Minnesota 17, at Tampa Bay. Buccaneers win toss. Edmonds returns kickoff 19 yards to Buccaneers' 22. A. Lee returns Roby's punt to Vikings' 48. Vikings drive to Tampa Bays' 35 where Reveiz's 53-yard field-goal attempt is wide right. Buccaneers take over at own 43 and drive to Vikings' 33 where Husted kicks 51-yard field goal with 8:37 left.

Oct. 22, 1995—Washington 36, Detroit 30, at Washington. Redskins win toss. B. Mitchell returns kickoff 16 yards to Redskins' 27. Turk's punt downed at Lions' 4. D. Green intercepts S. Mitchell's pass and returns it 7 yards for touchdown with 11:19 left.

Oct. 29, 1995—Carolina 20, New England 17, at New England. Panthers win toss. Baldwin returns kickoff 22 yards to Panthers' 25. Meggett makes fair catch of Barnhardt's punt at Patriots' 9. Guliford returns O'Neill's punt 9 yards to Patriots' 32. Panthers drive to Patriots' 12 where Kasay kicks 29-yard field goal with 7:52 left.

Oct. 29, 1995—Cleveland 29, Cincinnati 26, at Cincinnati. Browns win toss. Hunter returns kickoff 31 yards to Browns' 31. Bieniemy returns Tupa's punt 9 yards to Bengals' 37. McCardell makes fair catch of Johnson's punt at Browns' 12. Bieniemy returns Tupa's punt 0 yards to Bengals' 38. Hall intercepts Blake's pass and returns it 5 yards to Bengals' 45. Browns drive to Bengals' 11 where Stover kicks 28-yard field goal with 8:30 left.

Oct. 29, 1995—Arizona 20, Seattle 14, at Arizona. Cardinals win toss. Dowdell returns kickoff 16 yards to Cardinals' 25. Cardinals drive to Seahawks' 10 where G. Davis' 27-yard field goal attempt is blocked. L. Lynch intercepts Friesz's pass at Cardinals' 28 and returns it 72 yards for a touchdown with 3:44 left.

Nov. 5, 1995—Pittsburgh 37, Chicago 34, at Chicago. Bears win toss. Timpson returns kickoff 23 yards to Bears' 33. Hastings returns Sauerbrun's punt 2 yards to Steelers' 31. Steelers drive to Bears' 6 where N. Johnson kicks 24-yard field goal with 6:41 left.

Nov. 12, 1995—Minnesota 30, Arizona 24, at Arizona. Vikings win toss. A. Lee returns kickoff 20 yards to Vikings' 25. Moon throws 50-yard touchdown pass to Ismail with 12:44 left.

Nov. 26, 1995—Arizona 40, Atlanta 37, at Arizona. Falcons win toss. J. Anderson returns kickoff 20 yards to Falcons' 20. Stryzinski fumbles punt snap. Recovered by England at Falcons' 10 where G. Davis kicks 28-yard field goal with 13:17 left.

Dec. 10, 1995—Tampa Bay 13, Green Bay 10, at Tampa Bay. Buccaneers win toss. Edmonds returns kickoff 24 yards to Buccaneers' 23. Tampa Bay drives to Packers' 29 where Husted kicks 47-yard field goal with 11:14 remaining.

Sept. 1, 1996—Buffalo 23, New York Giants 20, at New York. Bills win toss. Daluiso kick is a touchback. Bills drive to Buffalo 46. Toomer returns Mohr's punt to Giants' 16. Dave Brown's fumble recovered by Spielman at Giants' 33. Bills drive to Giants' 16 where Christie kicks 34-yard field goal with 5:52 remaining.

Sept. 22, 1996—New England 28, Jacksonville 25, at New England. Patriots win toss. T. Brown returns kickoff 18 yards to Patriots' 29. Patriots drive to Jaguars' 22 where Vinatieri kicks 40-yard field goal with 12:24 remaining.

Sept. 29, 1996—Arizona 31, St. Louis 28, at Arizona. Cardinals win toss. Lohmiller kick is a touchback. Cardinals drive to Rams' 7 where G. Davis kicks 24-yard field goal with 13:06 remaining.

Oct. 6, 1996—Buffalo 16, Indianapolis 13, at Buffalo. Colts win toss. Christie kick is a touchback. Colts drive to Indianapolis 32. Burris returns Gardocki's punt to Bills' 35. Bills drive to Colts' 48. Mohr punts out of bounds at Colts' 14. Colts drive to Indianapolis 9. Burris returns Gardocki's punt to Colts' 48. Bills drive to Colts' 22 where Christie kicks 39-yard field goal with 5:38 remaining.

Oct. 6, 1996—Houston 30, Cincinnati 27, at Cincinnati. Bengals win toss. Dunn returns kickoff 23 yards to Bengals' 34. Bengals drive to Cincinnati 36. Floyd returns L. Johnson's punt to Oilers' 18. Oilers drive to Bengals' 31 where Del Greco kicks 49-yard field goal with 7:53 remaining.

*** Oct. 14, 1996—Green Bay 23, San Francisco 20,** at Green Bay. 49ers win toss. D. Carter returns kickoff 23 yards to 49ers' 22. 49ers' drive to San Francisco 25. Howard makes fair catch of Thompson's punt at Packers' 44. Packers drive to 49ers' 35 where Jacke kicks 53-yard field goal with 11:19 remaining.

Oct. 27, 1996—Baltimore 37, St. Louis 31, at Baltimore. Rams win toss. J. Thomas returns kickoff 17 yard to Rams' 17. Rams drive to Ravens' 15. F. Miller fumble in field goal formation recovered by S. Moore at Ravens' 17. Ravens drive to Baltimore 49 and turn ball over on downs. Rams drive to Ravens' 40 and turn ball over on downs. Testaverde throws 22-yard scoring pass to M. Jackson with 10 seconds remaining.

Nov. 10, 1996—Dallas 20, San Francisco 17, at San Francisco. Cowboys win toss. H. Walker returns kickoff 10 yards to Cowboys' 23. Cowboys drive to 49ers' 11 where Boniol kicks 29-yard field goal with 8:43 remaining.

Nov. 10, 1996—Arizona 37, Washington 34, at Washington. Arizona wins toss. Blanton's kickoff is a touchback. Cardinals drive to Redskins' 15 where Butler misses 32-yard field goal. Redskins drive to Cardinals' 43 where Turk punts for touchback. L. Johnson fumble returned by Morrison to Cardinals' 27. Redskins drive to Cardinals' 31 where Blanton misses 48-yard field goal. Cardinals drive to Redskins' 15 where Butler kicks 32-yard field goal with 33 seconds remaining.

Nov. 10, 1996—Tampa Bay 20, Oakland 17, at Tampa Bay. Tampa Bay wins toss. M. Marshall returns kickoff 15 yards to Bucs' 17. Bucs drive to Tampa Bay 36. T. Brown returns Barnhardt's punt four yards to Raiders' 22. Raiders drive to Oakland 25. M. Marshall returns Gossett's punt nine yards to Bucs' 39. Bucs drive to Raiders' 4 where Husted kicks 23-yard field goal with 3:04 remaining.

Nov. 17, 1996—Minnesota 16, Oakland 13, at Oakland. Oakland wins toss. Kaufman returns kickoff 32 yards to Raiders' 27. Raiders drive to Oakland 46 where Gossett punts to Vikings' 17. Vikings drive to Raiders' 12 where Sisson kicks 31-yard field goal with 3:07 remaining.

Nov. 24, 1996—Jacksonville 28, Baltimore 25, at Baltimore. Jacksonville wins toss. Jordon returns kickoff 16 yards to Jaguars' 30. Jaguars drive to Jacksonville 37. Barker's punt is downed at Ravens' 6. Ravens drive to Jaguars' 37 where Pritchett recovers Byner's fumble. Jaguars drive to Ravens' 15 where Hollis kicks 34-yard field goal with 5:54 remaining.

Nov. 24, 1996—San Francisco 19, Washington 16, at Washington. San Francisco wins toss. D. Carter returns kickoff 20 yards to 49ers' 32. 49ers drive to Redskins' 20 where Wilkins kicks 38-yard field goal with 11:36 remaining.

Dec. 1, 1996—Indianapolis 13, Buffalo 10, at Indianapolis. Buffalo wins toss. Moulds returns kickoff 26 yards to Bills' 25. Bills drive to Buffalo 49. Stock returns Mohr's punt one yard to Colts' 16. Colts drive to Bills' 32 where Blanchard kicks 49-yard field goal with 4:14 remaining.

Aug. 31, 1997—Tennessee 24, Oakland 21, at Tennessee. Oilers win toss. Gray returns kickoff 32 yards to Tennessee 33. Oilers drive to Tennessee 38. Roby's punt is downed at the Oakland 33. Raiders drive to Oakland 32. Gray returns Araguz punt to Tennessee 35. Oilers drive to Oakland 15 where Del Greco kicks 33-yard field goal with 8:03 remaining.

Sept. 7, 1997—Miami 16, Tennessee 13, at Miami. Dolphins win toss. Spikes returns kickoff 48 yards to Tennessee 45. Dolphins drive to Tennessee 11 where Mare kicks 29-yard field goal with 12:45 remaining.

Sept. 7, 1997— Arizona 25, Dallas 22, at Arizona. Cowboys win toss. Walker returns kickoff 21 yards to Dallas 25. Cowboys drive to Arizona 43. Gowin punts 43 yards for a touchback. Cardinals drive to Dallas 44. Graham fumbles. Cowboys drive to Arizona 42. Williams fumbles. Cardinals drive to Dallas 3 where Butler kicks 20-yard field goal with 6:30 remaining.

Sept. 14, 1997—Washington 19, Arizona 13, at Washington. Cardinals win toss. K. Williams returns kickoff 27 yards to Arizona 34. Cardinals drive to Arizona 40. McElroy fumbles. Redskins drive to Arizona 40. Westbrook catches 40-yard touchdown pass from Frerotte with 13:24 remaining.

Sept. 14, 1997—New England 27, New York Jets 24, at New England. Patriots win toss. Hall's kickoff is a touchback. Patriots drive to New England 15. Bledsoe pass intercepted by O. Smith. Jets drive to New York 46. Hansen punts 47 yards. Meggett returns to New England 21. Patriots drive to New York 17 where Vinatieri kicks 34-yard field goal with 6:57 remaining.

Sept. 28, 1997—Kansas City 20, Seattle 17, at Kansas City. Seahawks win toss. Broussard returns kickoff 12 yards to Seattle 14. Seahawks drive to Seattle 17. Vanover returns Tuten punt 8 yards to Kansas City 26. Chiefs drive to Seattle 44. Aguiar punt downed at Seattle 11. Seahawks drive to Seattle 26. Moon pass intercepted by Woods and returned 13 yards to 50. Chiefs drive to Seattle 23 where Stoyanovich kicks 41-yard field goal with 1:56 remaining.

Oct. 19, 1997—Philadelphia 13, Arizona 10, at Philadelphia. Cardinals win toss. K. Williams returns kickoff 28 yards to Arizona 42. Cardinals drive to Philadelphia 48. Feagles punts 48 yards for touchback. Eagles drive to Arizona 7 where Boniol kicks 24-yard field goal with 10:58 remaining.

Oct. 19, 1997—New York Giants 26, Detroit 20, at Detroit. Giants win toss. Pegram returns kickoff 16 yards to New York 18. Giants drive to New York 32. Calloway catches 68-yard touchdown pass from Kanell with 13:20 remaining.

Oct. 26, 1997—Denver 23, Buffalo 20, at Buffalo. Denver wins toss and elects to kickoff. Holmes returns kickoff 20 yards to Buffalo 25. Bills drive to Buffalo 23. Mohr punt downed at Denver 40. Broncos drive to Buffalo 48. Rouen punt downed at Buffalo 1. Bills drive to Buffalo 20. Gordon returns Mohr punt to Denver 42. Broncos drive to Buffalo 15 where Elam kicks 33-yard field goal with 1:56 remaining.

Oct. 26, 1997—Pittsburgh 23, Jacksonville 17, at Pittsburgh. Pittsburgh wins toss. Coleman returns kickoff 23 yards to Pittsburgh 23. Steelers drive to Jacksonville 17. Bettis catches 17-yard touchdown pass from Stewart with 11:13 remaining.

Oct. 27, 1997—Chicago 36, Miami 33, at Miami. Miami wins toss. McPhail returns kickoff 23 yards to Miami 27. Dolphins drive to Miami 36. Kidd punts out of bounds at Chicago 10. Bears drive to the Chicago 39. Sauerbrun punt out of bounds at Miami 27. Reeves recovers Marino fumble at Miami 17. Bears drive to Miami 17 where Jaeger kicks 35-yard field goal with 5:35 remaining.

Nov. 2, 1997—New York Jets 19, Baltimore 16, at New York. New York wins toss. Stover's kickoff is a touchback. Jets drive to Baltimore 20 where Hall kicks 37-yard field goal with 10:02 remaining.

Nov. 16, 1997—Philadelphia 10, Baltimore 10, at Baltimore. Philadelphia wins toss. Stover's kickoff is a touchback. Eagles drive to Philadelphia 19. Hutton punts 36 yards to Baltimore 45. Ravens drive to Baltimore 36 where Eagles take over on downs. Eagles drive to Baltimore 33 where Ravens take over on downs. Ravens drive to Baltimore 37. Montgomery punts 55 yards, and Solomon returns to Philadelphia 22. Eagles drive to Philadelphia 16. Hutton punts 41 yards, and Roe returns to Baltimore 46. Ravens drive to Philadelphia 35 where Stover's 53-yard field-goal attempt is no good. Eagles drive to Baltimore 22 where Boniol's 40-yard field-goal is no good as time expires.

Nov. 16, 1997—New Orleans 20, Seattle 17, at New Orleans. Seattle wins toss. Brien's kickoff is a touchback. Seahawks start at Seattle 20 where Moon's pass intercepted by Tubbs who returns 15 yards to Seattle 20. Saints Brien kicks 38-yard field goal with 14:43 remaining.

Nov. 23, 1997—New York Giants 7, Washington 7, at Washington. Washington wins toss. Davis returns kickoff 28 yards to Washington 39. Redskins drive to Washington 36 where Hostetler's pass intercepted by Sehorn who returns minus-2 yards before lateralling to Wooten who returns 5 yards to New York 41. Giants drive to New York 26 where Maynard punts 37 yards to Washington 37. Redskins drive to New York 39 where Hostetler fumble is recovered by Harris at New York 40. Giants drive to New York 43 where Maynard punts 57 yards for a touchback. Washington drives to New York 41. Giants take over on downs at New York 40. Giants drive to Washington 36 where Daluiso's 54-yard field-goal attempt is no good. Redskins drive to Washington 45 where Hostetler's pass intercepted by Sparks at New York 49. Giants drive to Washington 36 where Maynard punts 36 yards for a touchback. Redskins drive to New York 36 where Blanton's 54-yard field-goal attempt is no good. Giants drive to New York 45 where Kanell's pass intercepted by Patton who laterals to Pounds who returns 11 yards to Washington 24 as time expires.

Nov. 30, 1997—Pittsburgh 26, Arizona 20, at Arizona. Arizona wins toss. K. Williams returns kickoff 11 yards to Arizona 23. Cardinals drive to Arizona 18 where Feagles punts 43 yards. Hawkins returns punt 9 yards to Pittsburgh 48. Steelers drive to Arizona 10 where Bettis scores on a 10-yard touchdown run with 9:26 remaining.

Dec. 13, 1997—Pittsburgh 24, New England 21, at New England. Pittsburgh wins toss. Coleman returns kickoff 19 yards to Pittsburgh 26. Steelers drive to New England 13 where Johnson kicks a 31-yard field goal with 10:17 remaining.

Sept. 6, 1998—San Francisco 36, New York Jets 30, at San Francisco. Jets win toss. Richey's kickoff is a touchback. Jets drive to New York 11. Gallery punts 48 yards. McQuarters returns to New York 43. 49ers drive to New York 44. Howard punts 23 yards to New York 21. Johnson calls fair catch. Jets drive to New York 47. Gallery's 49-yard punt downed at San Francisco 4. Hearst runs for a 96-yard touchdown with 10:52 remaining.

Sept. 13, 1998—Cincinnati 34, Detroit 28, at Detroit. Lions win toss. Johnson's kickoff is a touchback. Lions drive to Detroit 47 where Mitchell's pass is intercepted by Sawyer and returned for a 58-yard touchdown with 12:54 remaining.

Sept. 27, 1998—New Orleans 19, Indianapolis 13, at Indianapolis. Saints win toss. Gardocki's kickoff is returned by Ismail to New Orleans 28. Saints drive to New Orleans 30. Royals punts 64 yards. Poole returns to Indianapolis 12. Colts drive to Indianapolis 20. Gardocki punts 58 yards. Hastings returns to New Orleans 29. Saints drive to New Orleans 32. Royals punts 59 yards. Punt downed at Indianapolis 9. Colts drive to Indianapolis 44 where Manning's pass is intercepted by Drakeford and returned to Indianapolis 36. Saints drive to Indianapolis 33. Wuerffel throws 33-yard touchdown pass to Cleeland with 8:50 remaining.

Oct. 25, 1998—Miami 12, New England 9, at Miami. Dolphins win toss. Vinatieri's kickoff is returned by Avery to Miami 15. Dolphins drive to New England 26 where Mare kicks 43-yard field goal with 10:24 remaining.

Nov. 26, 1998—Detroit 19, Pittsburgh 16, at Detroit. Lions win toss. Johnson's kickoff is returned by Fair to Detroit 35. Lions drive to Pittsburgh 24 where Hanson kicks 42-yard field goal with 12:08 remaining.

Dec. 6, 1998—San Francisco 31, Carolina 28, at Carolina. Panthers win toss. Richey's kickoff is returned by Floyd to Carolina 36. Panthers drive to Carolina 38 where Beuerlein's fumble is recovered by Doleman at Carolina 30. 49ers drive to Carolina 5 where Richey kicks 23-yard field goal with 10:44 remaining.

Dec. 13, 1998—Arizona 20, Philadelphia 17, at Philadelphia. Cardinals win toss. Boniol's kickoff is returned by Metcalf to Arizona 28. Cardinals drive to Philadelphia 15 where Jacke kicks 32-yard field goal with 10:30 remaining.

Sept. 12, 1999—Dallas 41, Washington 35, at Washington. Redskins win toss. T. Gowin's kickoff is returned by B. Mitchell to Washington 24. Redskins drive to Washington 47. M. Turk punts 48 yards. Punt downed at Dallas 5. Cowboys drive to Dallas 24. Aikman passes 76-yard touchdown to R. Ismail with 10:51 remaining.

Oct. 3, 1999—Baltimore 19, Atlanta 13, at Atlanta. Falcons win toss. M. Stover's kickoff is returned by W. Oliver to Atlanta 18. Falcons drive to Atlanta 23. D. Stryzinski punts 41 yards, out of bounds at Baltimore 36. Baltimore drives to Baltimore 46. S. Case passes 54-yard touchdown to J. Armour with 12:31 remaining.

Oct. 31, 1999—New York Giants 23, Philadelphia 17, at Philadelphia. Giants win toss. D. Akers' kickoff is returned by B. Levingston to New York 27. New York drives to Giants 31. B Maynard punts 43 yards to Philadelphia 26. A. Rossum returns to Eagles 28. D. Pederson drives to New York 45. D. Pederson's pass is intercepted by M.Strahan at Philadelphia 44. Giants' Peter batted ball up in the air as D. Pederson backpedaled. M.Strahan for 44 yards and touchdown with 10:36 remaining.

Nov. 14, 1999—Minnesota 27, Chicago 24, at Chicago. Vikings win toss. C. Boniol kicks to Minnesota 2, M. Williams touchback. Minnesota starts from own 20. J. George's pass is intercepted by W. Harris at Minnesota 29 for -1 yard. Chicago starts at Minnesota 29 and moves to Minnesota 23. C. Boniol's 41-yard field goal is no good. Minnesota starts from own 31 and drives to Chicago 20. G. Anderson kicks 38-yard field goal with 5:58 remaining.

Nov. 21, 1999—Chicago 23, San Diego 20, at San Diego. Bears win toss. Chicago starts from own 22. J. Miller completes four consecutive passes and Bears drive to San Diego 22. C. Enis rushes twice to San Diego 19. C. Boniol kicks 36-yard field goal with 10:02 remaining.

* **Nov. 22, 1999—Denver 27, Oakland 21, at Denver.** Broncos win toss. Denver starts from own 33 and drives to Broncos' 35. T. Rouen punts 46 yards to Oakland 19. Oakland starts at own 19 and drives to Raiders' 25. R. Gannon fumbles and Broncos' T. Pryce recovers at Oakland 25. Denver running back O. Gary scores on 24-yard run with 12:20 remaining.

Nov. 28, 1999—Washington 20, Philadelphia 17, at Washington. Redskins win toss. D. Akers' kickoff is returned by J. Thrash for 48 yards to Philadelphia 46. B. Johnson completes 20-yard pass to A. Connell to Philadelphia 26. B. Johnson completes 9-yard pass to B. Mitchell to Philadelphia 9. B. Mitchell runs for seven yards to Philadelphia 2. On third-down, Washington attempts field goal from Philadelphia 2. B. Johnson fumbles and recovers at Philadelphia 9. B. Conway kicks 27-yard field goal with 10:26 remaining.

Dec. 19, 1999—Denver 36, Seattle 30, at Denver. Broncos win toss. T. Peterson kicks to Denver 8. C. Watson returns kick to Denver 27 for 19 yards. Broncos do not convert a first down. T. Rouen punts 46 yards, out of bounds at Seattle 25. J. Kitna passes to S. Dawkins for 17 yards at Seattle 47. R. Watters runs for 6 yards to Denver 47. J. Kitna sacked for 11-yard loss by R. Crockett. J. Kitna fumbles, forced by R. Crockett, recovered by G. Cadrez at Seattle 37. G. Cadrez for 37 yards and touchdown with 12:26 remaining.

Dec. 26, 1999—Washington 26, San Francisco 20, at San Francisco. Redskins win toss. W. Richey kicks to Washington 9, J. Thrash returns 13 yards to Washington 22. B. Johnson passes to S. Hicks for 25 yards to Washington 47. L. Centers runs for 12 yards to San Francisco 33. B. Johnson passes to L. Centers for 33 yards and touchdown with 13:00 remaining.

Dec. 26, 1999—Buffalo 13, New England 10, at New England. Patriots win toss. New England's A. Vinatieri misses 44-yard field goal from Buffalo 26. Buffalo takes over at Bills 34. D. Flutie passes to E. Moulds to New England 21 for 17 yards. E. Moulds fumbles, recovered by T. Bruschi at Patriots 21. New England drives to own 34. L. Johnson punts from New England 34 to Buffalo 42. D. Flutie passes to P. Price for 7 yards to New England 44. D. Flutie passes to E. Moulds for 11 yards to New England 27. T. Thomas runs for 9 yards to New England 6. S. Christie kicks 23-yard field goal with 1:48 remaining.

Jan. 2, 2000—Oakland 41, Kansas City 38, at Kansas City. Raiders win toss. J. Baker kicks 69 yards from Kansas City 30 to Oakland 1 and out of bounds. Oakland starts at Raiders 40. R. Gannon passes to R. Dudley for 21 yards to Kansas City 40. R. Gannon passes to T. Brown at Kansas City 16 for 24 yards. Z. Crockett runs to Kansas City 15 for 1 yard. J. Nedney kicks 33-yard field goal with 11:47 remaining.

**indicates Monday night game*
#indicates Thursday night game

POSTSEASON

Dec. 28, 1958—Baltimore 23, New York Giants 17, at New York in NFL Championship Game. Giants win toss. Maynard returns kickoff to Giants' 20. Chandler punts and Taseff returns one yard to Colts' 20. Colts win at 8:15 on a 1-yard run by Ameche.

Dec. 23, 1962—Dallas Texans 20, Houston Oilers 17, at Houston in AFL Championship Game. Texans win toss and kick off. Jancik returns kickoff to Oilers' 33. Norton punts and Jackson makes fair catch on Texans' 22. Wilson punts and Jancik makes fair catch on Oilers' 45. Robinson intercepts Blanda's pass and returns 13 yards to Oilers' 47. Wilson's punt rolls dead at Oilers' 12. Hull intercepts Blanda's pass and returns 23 yards to midfield. Texans win at 17:54 on a 25-yard field goal by Brooker.

Dec. 26, 1965—Green Bay 13, Baltimore 10, at Green Bay in NFL Divisional Playoff Game. Packers win toss. Moore returns kickoff to Packers' 22. Chandler punts and Haymond returns nine yards to Colts' 41. Gilburg punts and Wood makes fair catch at Packers' 21. Chandler punts and Haymond returns one yard to Colts' 41. Michaels misses 47-yard field goal. Packers win at 13:39 on 25-yard field goal by Chandler.

Dec. 25, 1971—Miami 27, Kansas City 24, at Kansas City in AFC Divisional Playoff Game. Chiefs win toss. Podolak, after a lateral from Buchanan, returns kickoff to Chiefs' 46. Stenerud's 42-yard field goal is blocked. Seiple punts and Podolak makes fair catch at Chiefs' 17. Wilson punts and Scott returns 18 yards to Dolphins' 39. Yepremian misses 62-yard field goal. Scott intercepts Dawson's pass and returns 13 yards to Dolphins' 46. Seiple punts and Podolak loses one yard to Chiefs' 15. Wilson punts and Scott makes fair catch on Dolphins' 30. Dolphins win at 22:40 on a 37-yard field goal by Yepremian.

Dec. 24, 1977—Oakland 37, Baltimore 31, at Baltimore in AFC Divisional Playoff Game. Colts win toss. Raiders start on own 42 following a punt late in the first overtime. Oakland works way into field-goal range on Stabler's 19-yard pass to Branch at Colts' 26. Four plays later, on the second play of the second overtime, Stabler hits Casper with a 10-yard touchdown pass at 15:43.

Jan. 2, 1982—San Diego 41, Miami 38, at Miami in AFC Divisional Playoff Game. Chargers win toss. San Diego drives from its 13 to Miami 8. On second-and-goal, Benirschke misses 27-yard field goal attempt wide left at 9:15. Miami has the ball twice and San Diego twice more before the Dolphins get their third possession. Miami drives from the San Diego 46 to Chargers' 17 and on fourth-and-two, von Schamann's 34-yard field goal attempt is blocked by San Diego's Winslow after 11:27. Fouts then completes four of five passes, including a 39-yarder to Joiner that puts the ball on Dolphins' 10. On first down, Benirschke kicks a 29-yard field goal at 13:52. San Diego's winning drive covered 74 yards in six plays.

Jan. 3, 1987—Cleveland 23, New York Jets 20, at Cleveland in AFC Divisional Playoff Game. Jets win toss. Jets' punt downed at Browns' 26. Moseley's 23-yard field goal attempt is wide right. Teams trade punts. Jets' second punt downed at Browns' 31. First overtime period expires eight plays later with Browns in possession at Jets' 42. Moseley kicks 27-yard field goal four plays into second overtime at 17:02.

Jan. 11, 1987—Denver 23, Cleveland 20, at Cleveland in AFC Championship Game. Browns win toss. Broncos hold Browns on four downs. Browns' punt returned four yards to Denver's 25. Elway completes 22- and 28-yard passes to set up Karlis's 33-yard field goal nine plays into drive at 5:38.

Jan. 3, 1988—Houston 23, Seattle 20, at Houston in AFC Wild Card Game. Seahawks win toss. Rodriguez punts to K. Johnson who returns one yard to Houston 15. Zendejas kicks 32-yard field goal 12 plays later at 8:05.

Dec. 31, 1989—Pittsburgh 26, Houston 23, at Houston in AFC Wild Card Playoff Game. Steelers win toss. Steelers punt to Oilers. Oilers' fumble recovered by Woodson and returned three yards. Four plays and 13 yards later, Anderson kicks a 50-yard field goal at 3:26.

Jan. 7, 1990—Los Angeles Rams 19, New York Giants 13, at New York in NFC Divisional Game. Rams win toss. Everett completes two passes to move ball to Giants' 48. White called for pass interference; ball spotted on Giants' 25. Everett hits Anderson with a 30-yard touchdown pass at 1:06.

Jan. 3, 1993—Buffalo 41, Houston 38, at Buffalo in AFC Wild Card Game. Houston wins toss. Oilers begin at 20. After 2 plays, Moon's pass is intercepted by Odomes who returns ball 2 yards to Houston 35. After 2 plays, Christie kicks 32-yard field goal at 3:06.

Jan. 8, 1994—Kansas City 27, Pittsburgh 24, at Kansas City in AFC Wild Card Game. Kansas City wins toss. Hughes returns kickoff 20 yards to Kansas City 25. After 3 plays, Barker punts 48 yards to Pittsburgh 18 where Woodson returns 8 yards to the 26. After 6 plays, Royals punts 30 yards to Kansas City 20. Kansas City drives to Pittsburgh 14 where Lowery kicks 32-yard field goal at 11:03.

Jan. 17, 1999—Atlanta 30, Minnesota 27, at Minnesota in NFC Championship Game. Minnesota wins toss. Palmer returns kickoff 30 yards to Minnesota 29. After four plays, Berger punts 51 yards to Atlanta 7 where Dwight returns 8 yards to Atlanta 15. Falcons drive to Atlanta 36. Stryzinski punts 37 yards to Vikings' 27. Palmer calls fair catch. Vikings drive to Minnesota 39. Berger punts 52 yards to Atlanta 9. Downed by Vikings. Atlanta drives to Minnesota 21 where Andersen kicks 38-yard field goal at 11:52.

NFL POSTSEASON OVERTIME GAMES

(BY LENGTH OF GAME)

Dec. 25, 1971	Miami 27, KANSAS CITY 24	82:40
Dec. 23, 1962	Dallas Texans 20, HOUSTON 17	77:54
Jan. 3, 1987	CLEVELAND 23, New York Jets 20	77:02
Dec. 24, 1977	Oakland 37, BALTIMORE 31	75:43
Jan. 2, 1982	San Diego 41, MIAMI 38	73:52
Dec. 26, 1965	GREEN BAY 13, Baltimore 10	73:39
Jan. 17, 1999	Atlanta 30, MINNESOTA 27	71:52
Jan. 8, 1994	KANSAS CITY 27, Pittsburgh 24	71:03
Dec. 28, 1958	Baltimore 23, N.Y. GIANTS 17	68:15
Jan. 3, 1988	HOUSTON 23, Seattle 20	68:05
Jan. 11, 1987	Denver 23, CLEVELAND 20	65:38
Dec. 31, 1989	Pittsburgh 26, HOUSTON 23	63:26
Jan. 3, 1993	BUFFALO 41, Houston 38	63:06
Jan. 7, 1990	Los Angeles Rams 19, N.Y. GIANTS 13	61:06

Home team in CAPS

There have been 14 overtime postseason games dating back to 1958. In 13 cases, both teams had at least one possession. Last time: 1/17/99, Atlanta 30, MINNESOTA 27.

OVERTIME GAMES

OVERTIME WON-LOST RECORDS, 1974-1999
(REGULAR SEASON)

AFC	W	L	T	Pct.
Baltimore	2	2	1	.500
Buffalo	12	6	0	.667
Cincinnati	13	7	0	.650
Cleveland	12	8	1	.595
Denver	15	9	2	.615
Indianapolis	9	8	1	.528
Jacksonville	1	2	0	.333
Kansas City	8	8	2	.500
Miami	10	14	1	.420
New England	9	17	0	.346
New York Jets	10	9	2	.524
Oakland	11	12	0	.478
Pittsburgh	13	5	1	.711
San Diego	7	11	0	.389
Seattle	4	12	0	.250
Tennessee	8	13	0	.380

NFC	W	L	T	Pct.
Arizona	12	10	2	.542
Atlanta	7	10	1	.417
Carolina	1	2	0	.333
Chicago	12	12	0	.500
Dallas	10	6	0	.625
Detroit	10	10	1	.500
Green Bay	6	10	4	.400
Minnesota	14	12	2	.536
New Orleans	4	7	0	.364
New York Giants	9	10	2	.476
Philadelphia	8	11	3	.432
St. Louis	6	7	1	.464
San Francisco	7	8	1	.469
Tampa Bay	9	7	1	.559
Washington	13	8	1	.614

OVERTIME GAMES BY YEAR
(REGULAR SEASON)

1999-11	1992-10	1985-10	1978-11
1998-7	1991-15	1984-9	1977-6
1997-17	1990-10	1983-19	1976-5
1996-14	1989-11	1982-4	1975-9
1995-21	1988-9	1981-10	1974-2
1994-16	1987-13	1980-13	
1993-7	1986-16	1979-12	

OVERTIME GAME SUMMARY—1974-1999
There have been 287 overtime games in regular-season play since the rule was adopted in 1974 (11 in 1999 season). Breakdown follows:

211(7) times both teams had at least one possession (74%)
144(8) times the team which won the toss won the game (50%)
128(3) times the team which lost the toss won the game (45%)
15(0) games ended tied (5%). Last time: Nov. 23, 1997, N.Y. Giants 7, at Washington 7.
76(4) times the team which won the toss drove for winning score (55 FG, 21 TD) (26%)
7(0) times the team which won the toss elected to kick off (4 wins) (2%)
195(5) games were decided by a field goal (68%)
76(6) games were decided by a touchdown (25%)
1(0) games were decided by a safety (.3%)

Note: The number in parentheses represents the 1999 season total in each category.

MOST OVERTIME GAMES, SEASON
5 Green Bay Packers, 1983
4 Denver Broncos, 1985
Cleveland Browns, 1989
Minnesota Vikings, 1994
Arizona Cardinals, 1995
Minnesota Vikings, 1995
Arizona Cardinals, 1997
3 By many teams, last time: Washington Redskins, 1999

LONGEST CONSECUTIVE GAME STREAKS WITHOUT OVERTIME (Current)
57 Green Bay Packers (last OT game, 10/14/96 vs. San Francisco)
(Record: 110, St. Louis/Phoenix Cardinals, 12/7/86-12/19/93)

SHORTEST OVERTIME GAMES
0:17 New Orleans 20, Seattle 17; 11/16/97
0:21 Chicago 23, Detroit 17; 11/27/80—only kickoff return for TD
0:30 Baltimore 29, New England 23; 9/4/83

LONGEST OVERTIME GAMES
(ALL POSTSEASON GAMES)
22:40 Miami 27, Kansas City 24; 12/25/71
17:54 Dallas Texans 20, Houston 17; 12/23/62
17:02 Cleveland 23, New York Jets 20; 1/3/87

OVERTIME SCORING SUMMARY
195 were decided by a field goal
33 were decided by a touchdown pass
22 were decided by a touchdown run
11 were decided by interceptions (Atlanta 40, New Orleans 34, 9/2/79; Atlanta 47, Green Bay 41, 11/27/83; New York Giants 16, Philadelphia 10, 9/29/85; Indianapolis 23, Cleveland 17, 12/10/89; Cleveland 30, San Diego 24, 10/20/91; Kansas City 23, Oakland 17, 9/17/95; New York Giants 27, Arizona 21, 10/8/95; Washington 36, Detroit 30, 10/22/95; Arizona 20, Seattle 14, 10/29/95; Cincinnati 34, Detroit 28, 9/13/98; New York Giants 23, Washington 17, 10/31/99)
2 were decided on a fake field goal/touchdown pass (Minnesota 22, Chicago 16, 10/16/77; Cleveland 23, Minnesota 17, 12/17/89)
2 were decided by a fumble recovery (Baltimore 29, New England 23, 9/4/83; Denver 36, Seattle 30, 12/19/99)
1 was decided by a kickoff return (Chicago 23, Detroit 17, 11/27/80)
1 was decided by a punt return (Kansas City 29, San Diego 23, 10/9/95)
1 was decided on a fake field goal/touchdown run (Los Angeles Rams 27, Minnesota 21, 12/2/79)
1 was decided on a blocked field goal (Denver 30, San Diego 24, 11/17/85)
1 was decided on a blocked field goal/recovery by kicker (Green Bay 12, Chicago 6, 9/7/80)
1 was decided on a blocked field goal/recovery by kicking team (Philadelphia 23, New York Giants 17, 11/20/88)
1 was decided by a safety (Minnesota 23, Los Angeles Rams 21, 11/5/89)
15 ended tied

OVERTIME RECORDS
Longest Touchdown Pass
99 Yards — Ron Jaworski to Mike Quick, Philadelphia 23, Atlanta 17 (11/10/85)
76 Yards — Troy Aikman to Raghib Ismail, Dallas 41, Washington 35 (9/12/99)
68 Yards — Danny Kanell to Chris Calloway, New York Giants 26, Detroit 20 (10/20/97)

Longest Touchdown Run
96 Yards — Garrison Hearst, San Francisco 36, N.Y. Jets 30 (9/6/98)
60 Yards — Herschel Walker, Dallas 23, New England 17 (11/15/87)
42 Yards — Eric Dickerson, Los Angeles Rams 26, Tampa Bay 20 (10/5/86)

Longest Field Goal
53 Yards — Chris Jacke, Green Bay 23, San Francisco 20 (10/4/96)
52 Yards — Mike Cofer, Indianapolis 27, N.Y. Jets 24 (9/10/95)
51 Yards — Greg Davis, New England 23, Indianapolis 20 (10/29/89)
Greg Davis, Arizona 20, Pittsburgh 17 (10/30/94)
Michael Husted, Tampa Bay 20, Minnesota 17 (10/15/95)

Longest Touchdown Plays
99 Yards — (Pass) Ron Jaworski to Mike Quick, Philadelphia 23, Atlanta 17 (11/10/85)
96 Yards — (Run) Garrison Hearst, San Francisco 36, N.Y. Jets 30 (9/6/98)
95 Yards — (Kickoff return) Dave Williams, Chicago 23, Detroit 17 (11/27/80)
86 Yards — (Punt return) Tamarick Vanover, Kansas City 29, San Diego 23 (10/9/95)
76 Yards — (Pass) Troy Aikman to Raghib Ismail, Dallas 41, Washington 35 (9/12/99)

NFL PAID ATTENDANCE

For detailed 1999 attendance, see page 242.

Year	Regular Season	Average	Postseason	Total
1999	#16,206,640 (248 games)	#65,349	793,759 (12)	#17,000,399
1998	15,364,873 (240 games)	64,020	822,885 (12)	16,187,758
1997	14,967,314 (240 games)	62,364	801,879 (12)	15,769,193
1996	14,612,417 (240 games)	60,885	769,310 (12)	15,381,727
1995	15,043,562 (240 games)	62,682	790,906 (12)	15,834,468
1994	14,030,435 (224 games)	62,636	779,738 (12)	14,810,173
1993	13,966,843 (224 games)	62,352	814,607 (12)	14,781,450
1992	13,828,887 (224 games)	61,736	815,910 (12)	14,644,797
1991	13,841,459 (224 games)	61,792	813,247 (12)	14,654,706
1990	13,959,896 (224 games)	62,321	847,543 (12)	14,807,439
1989	13,625,662 (224 games)	60,829	685,771 (10)	14,311,433
1988	13,539,848 (224 games)	60,446	658,317 (10)	14,198,165
1987	*11,406,166 (210 games)	54,315	656,977 (10)	12,063,143
1986	13,588,551 (224 games)	60,663	734,002 (10)	14,322,553
1985	13,345,047 (224 games)	59,567	710,768 (10)	14,055,815
1984	13,398,112 (224 games)	59,813	665,194 (10)	14,063,306
1983	13,277,222 (224 games)	59,273	675,513 (10)	13,952,735
1982	**7,367,438 (126 games)	58,472	1,033,153 (16)	8,400,591
1981	13,606,990 (224 games)	60,745	637,763 (10)	14,244,753
1980	13,392,230 (224 games)	59,787	624,430 (10)	14,016,660
1979	13,182,039 (224 games)	58,848	630,326 (10)	13,812,365
1978	12,771,800 (224 games)	57,017	624,388 (10)	13,396,188
1977	11,018,632 (196 games)	56,218	534,925 (8)	11,553,557
1976	11,070,543 (196 games)	56,482	492,884 (8)	11,563,427
1975	10,213,193 (182 games)	56,116	475,919 (8)	10,689,112
1974	10,236,322 (182 games)	56,244	438,664 (8)	10,674,986
1973	10,730,933 (182 games)	58,961	525,433 (8)	11,256,366
1972	10,445,827 (182 games)	57,395	483,345 (8)	10,929,172
1971	10,076,035 (182 games)	55,363	483,891 (8)	10,559,926
1970	9,533,333 (182 games)	52,381	458,493 (8)	9,991,826
1969	6,096,127 (112 games) NFL	54,430	162,279 (3)	6,258,406
	2,843,373 (70 games) AFL	40,620	167,088 (3)	3,010,461
1968	5,882,313 (112 games) NFL	52,521	215,902 (3)	6,098,215
	2,635,004 (70 games) AFL	37,643	114,438 (2)	2,749,442
1967	5,938,924 (112 games) NFL	53,026	166,208 (3)	6,105,132
	2,295,697 (63 games) AFL	36,439	53,330 (1)	2,349,027
1966	5,337,044 (105 games) NFL	50,829	74,152 (1)	5,411,196
	2,160,369 (63 games) AFL	34,291	42,080 (1)	2,202,449
1965	4,634,021 (98 games) NFL	47,286	100,304 (2)	4,734,325
	1,782,384 (56 games) AFL	31,828	30,361 (1)	1,812,745
1964	4,563,049 (98 games) NFL	46,562	79,544 (1)	4,642,593
	1,447,875 (56 games) AFL	25,855	40,242 (1)	1,488,117
1963	4,163,643 (98 games) NFL	42,486	45,801 (1)	4,209,444
	1,208,697 (56 games) AFL	21,584	63,171 (2)	1,271,868
1962	4,003,421 (98 games) NFL	40,851	64,892 (1)	4,068,313
	1,147,302 (56 games) AFL	20,487	37,981 (1)	1,185,283
1961	3,986,159 (98 games) NFL	40,675	39,029 (1)	4,025,188
	1,002,657 (56 games) AFL	17,904	29,556 (1)	1,032,213
1960	3,128,296 (78 games) NFL	40,106	67,325 (1)	3,195,621
	926,156 (56 games) AFL	16,538	32,183 (1)	958,339
1959	3,140,000 (72 games)	43,617	57,545 (1)	3,197,545
1958	3,006,124 (72 games)	41,752	123,659 (2)	3,129,783
1957	2,836,318 (72 games)	39,393	119,579 (2)	2,955,897
1956	2,551,263 (72 games)	35,434	56,836 (1)	2,608,099
1955	2,521,836 (72 games)	35,026	85,693 (1)	2,607,529
1954	2,190,571 (72 games)	30,425	43,827 (1)	2,234,398
1953	2,164,585 (72 games)	30,064	54,577 (1)	2,219,162
1952	2,052,126 (72 games)	28,502	97,507 (2)	2,149,633
1951	1,913,019 (72 games)	26,570	57,522 (1)	1,970,541
1950	1,977,753 (78 games)	25,356	136,647 (3)	2,114,400
1949	1,391,735 (60 games)	23,196	27,980 (1)	1,419,715
1948	1,525,243 (60 games)	25,421	36,309 (1)	1,561,552
1947	1,837,437 (60 games)	30,624	66,268 (2)	1,903,705
1946	1,732,135 (55 games)	31,493	58,346 (1)	1,790,481
1945	1,270,401 (50 games)	25,408	32,178 (1)	1,302,579
1944	1,019,649 (50 games)	20,393	46,016 (1)	1,065,665
1943	969,128 (40 games)	24,228	71,315 (2)	1,040,443
1942	887,920 (55 games)	16,144	36,006 (1)	923,926
1941	1,108,615 (55 games)	20,157	55,870 (2)	1,164,485
1940	1,063,025 (55 games)	19,328	36,034 (1)	1,099,059
1939	1,071,200 (55 games)	19,476	32,279 (1)	1,103,479
1938	937,197 (55 games)	17,040	48,120 (1)	985,317
1937	963,039 (55 games)	17,510	15,878 (1)	978,917
1936	816,007 (54 games)	15,111	29,545 (1)	845,552
1935	638,178 (53 games)	12,041	15,000 (1)	653,178
1934	492,684 (60 games)	8,211	35,059 (1)	527,743

 # Record

**Players' 24-day strike reduced 224-game schedule to 210 games.*

***Players' 57-day strike reduced 224-game schedule to 126 games.*

NFL'S TOP 10 PAID ATTENDANCE WEEKENDS

Weekend	Games	Attendance
November 21-22, 1999	15	1,027,861
September 19-20, 1999	15	1,010,820
November 23-24, 1997	15	999,778
September 6-7, 1998	15	997,835
November 25, 28-29, 1999	15	995,802
December 13-14, 1998	15	992,659
September 13-14, 1999	15	987,779
December 20-21, 1998	15	987,518
November 8-9, 1998	15	984,630
December 18-20, 1999	15	984,274

NFL'S 10 HIGHEST SCORING WEEKENDS

Point Total	Date	Weekend
762	November 10-11, 1996	11th
761	October 16-17, 1983	7th
740	November 29-30, 1998	13th
739	November 23, 26-27, 1995	13th
736	October 25-26, 1987	7th
734	November 19-20, 1995	12th
732	November 9-10, 1980	10th
725	November 24, 27-28, 1983	13th
719	November 27, 30-December 1, 1997	14th
714	September 17-18, 1989	2nd

TOP 10 TELEVISED SPORTS EVENTS OF ALL-TIME

(Based on A.C. Nielsen Figures)

Program	Date	Network	Share	Rating
Super Bowl XVI	1/24/82	CBS	73%	49.1
Super Bowl XVII	1/30/83	NBC	69%	48.6
Winter Olympics	2/23/94	CBS	64%	48.5
Super Bowl XX	1/26/86	NBC	70%	48.3
Super Bowl XII	1/15/78	CBS	67%	47.2
Super Bowl XIII	1/21/79	NBC	74%	47.1
Super Bowl XVIII	1/22/84	CBS	71%	46.4
Super Bowl XIX	1/20/85	ABC	63%	46.4
Super Bowl XIV	1/20/80	CBS	67%	46.3
Super Bowl XXX	1/28/96	NBC	68%	46.0

TEN MOST WATCHED TV PROGRAMS & ESTIMATED TOTAL NUMBER OF VIEWERS

(Based on A.C. Nielsen Figures)

Program	Date	Network	*Total Viewers
Super Bowl XXX	Jan. 28, 1996	NBC	138,488,000
Super Bowl XXVIII	Jan. 30, 1994	NBC	134,800,000
Super Bowl XXXII	Jan. 25, 1998	NBC	133,400,000
Super Bowl XXVII	Jan. 31, 1993	NBC	133,400,000
Super Bowl XXXIV	Jan. 30, 2000	ABC	132,500,000
Super Bowl XXXI	Jan. 26, 1997	FOX	128,900,000
Super Bowl XXXIII	Jan. 31, 1999	FOX	127,500,000
Super Bowl XX	Jan. 26, 1986	NBC	127,000,000
Winter Olympics	Feb. 23, 1994	CBS	126,686,000
Super Bowl XXIX	Jan. 29, 1995	ABC	125,216,000

**Watched some portion of the broadcast*

NFL'S TOP 10 TEAM SINGLE-SEASON HOME PAID ATTENDANCE TOTALS

Year	Club	Games	Attendance
1980	Detroit Lions	8	634,204
1988	Buffalo Bills	8	631,818
1991	Buffalo Bills	8	631,786
1992	Buffalo Bills	8	630,978
1997	Kansas City Chiefs	8	629,763
1999	Kansas City Chiefs	8	629,569
1998	Kansas City Chiefs	8	629,209
1999	Washington Redskins	8	628,535
1996	Kansas City Chiefs	8	628,460
1994	Kansas City Chiefs	8	626,612

NFL'S TOP FIVE PAID ATTENDANCE TOTALS FOR ALL GAMES

Year	Preseason	Regular Season	Postseason	All Games
1999	3,762,331	16,206,640	793,759	20,762,730
1998	3,553,735	15,364,873	822,885	19,741,493
1995	3,368,289	15,043,562	790,906	19,202,757
1997	3,280,693	14,967,314	801,879	19,049,886
1996	3,267,254	14,612,417	769,310	18,648,981
1994	3,200,091	14,030,435	779,738	18,010,264

TEN HIGHEST-RATED ABC NFL MONDAY NIGHT FOOTBALL GAMES OF ALL-TIME

(Based on A.C. Nielsen Figures)

Game	Date	Share	Rating
Chicago at Miami	12/2/85	46%	29.6
N.Y. Giants at San Francisco	12/3/90	42%	26.9
Dallas at Washington	10/2/78	43%	26.8
Pittsburgh at San Diego	12/22/80	40%	25.3
Philadelphia at Miami	11/30/81	40%	25.3
Pittsburgh at Houston	12/10/79	40%	25.1
Dallas at Miami	12/17/84	40%	25.1
Pittsburgh at Dallas	9/13/82	42%	24.9
Cincinnati at Oakland	12/6/76	40%	24.7
Dallas at Washington	10/8/73	40%	24.6
Minnesota at Atlanta	11/19/73	40%	24.6

NFL'S 10 BIGGEST SINGLE-GAME ATTENDANCE TOTALS

Date	Site	Game	Teams	Attendance
August 15, 1994	Azteca Stadium	American Bowl (Mexico City)	Cowboys vs. Oilers	112,376
August 17, 1998	Azteca Stadium	American Bowl (Mexico City)	Cowboys vs. Patriots	106,424
August 22, 1947	Soldier Field	College All-Star	Bears vs. All-Stars	105,840
August 4, 1997	Estadio Guillermo Canedo	American Bowl (Mexico City)	Broncos vs. Dolphins	104,629
January 20, 1980	Rose Bowl	Super Bowl XIV	Steelers vs. Rams	103,985
January 30, 1983	Rose Bowl	Super Bowl XVII	Redskins vs. Dolphins	103,667
January 9, 1977	Rose Bowl	Super Bowl XI	Raiders vs. Vikings	103,438
November 10, 1957	L.A. Coliseum	Regular Season	49ers at Rams	102,368
January 25, 1987	Rose Bowl	Super Bowl XXI	Giants vs. Broncos	101,643
August 20, 1948	Soldier Field	College All-Star	Cardinals vs. All-Stars	101,220

NUMBER-ONE DRAFT CHOICES

Season	Date	Team	Player	Position	College
2000	April 15-16	Cleveland	Courtney Brown	DE	Penn State
1999	April 17-18	Cleveland	Tim Couch	QB	Kentucky
1998	April 18-19	Indianapolis	Peyton Manning	QB	Tennessee
1997	April 19-20	St. Louis	Orlando Pace	T	Ohio State
1996	April 20-21	New York Jets	Keyshawn Johnson	WR	Southern California
1995	April 22-23	Cincinnati	Ki-Jana Carter	RB	Penn State
1994	April 24-25	Cincinnati	Dan Wilkinson	DT	Ohio State
1993	April 25-26	New England	Drew Bledsoe	QB	Washington State
1992	April 26-27	Indianapolis	Steve Emtman	DT	Washington
1991	April 21-22	Dallas	Russell Maryland	DT	Miami
1990	April 22-23	Indianapolis	Jeff George	QB	Illinois
1989	April 23-24	Dallas	Troy Aikman	QB	UCLA
1988	April 24-25	Atlanta	Aundray Bruce	LB	Auburn
1987	April 28-29	Tampa Bay	Vinny Testaverde	QB	Miami
1986	April 29-30	Tampa Bay	Bo Jackson	RB	Auburn
1985	April 30-May 1	Buffalo	Bruce Smith	DE	Virginia Tech
1984	May 1-2	New England	Irving Fryar	WR	Nebraska
1983	April 26-27	Baltimore	John Elway	QB	Stanford
1982	April 27-28	New England	Kenneth Sims	DT	Texas
1981	April 28-29	New Orleans	George Rogers	RB	South Carolina
1980	April 29-30	Detroit	Billy Sims	RB	Oklahoma
1979	May 3-4	Buffalo	Tom Cousineau	LB	Ohio State
1978	May 2-3	Houston	Earl Campbell	RB	Texas
1977	May 3-4	Tampa Bay	Ricky Bell	RB	Southern California
1976	April 8-9	Tampa Bay	Lee Roy Selmon	DE	Oklahoma
1975	January 28-29	Atlanta	Steve Bartkowski	QB	California
1974	January 29-30	Dallas	Ed Jones	DE	Tennessee State
1973	January 30-31	Houston	John Matuszak	DE	Tampa
1972	February 1-2	Buffalo	Walt Patulski	DE	Notre Dame
1971	January 28-29	New England	Jim Plunkett	QB	Stanford
1970	January 27-28	Pittsburgh	Terry Bradshaw	QB	Louisiana Tech
1969	January 28-29	Buffalo (AFL)	O.J. Simpson	RB	Southern California
1968	January 30-31	Minnesota	Ron Yary	T	Southern California
1967	March 14	Baltimore	Bubba Smith	DT	Michigan State
1966	November 27, 1965	Atlanta	Tommy Nobis	LB	Texas
	November 28, 1965	Miami (AFL)	Jim Grabowski	RB	Illinois
1965	November 28, 1964	New York Giants	Tucker Frederickson	RB	Auburn
	November 28, 1964	Houston (AFL)	Lawrence Elkins	E	Baylor
1964	December 2, 1963	San Francisco	Dave Parks	E	Texas Tech
	November 30, 1963	Boston (AFL)	Jack Concannon	QB	Boston College
1963	December 3, 1962	Los Angeles	Terry Baker	QB	Oregon State
	December 1, 1962	Kansas City (AFL)	Buck Buchanan	DT	Grambling
1962	December 4, 1961	Washington	Ernie Davis	RB	Syracuse
	December 2, 1961	Oakland (AFL)	Roman Gabriel	QB	North Carolina State
1961	December 27-28, 1960	Minnesota	Tommy Mason	RB	Tulane
	November 23, 1960	Buffalo (AFL)	Ken Rice	G	Auburn
1960	Secret Draft	Los Angeles	Billy Cannon	RB	Louisiana State
	November 22, December 2, 1959	(AFL had no formal first pick)			
1959	December 2, 1958	Green Bay	Randy Duncan	QB	Iowa
1958	December 2, 1957	Chicago Cardinals	King Hill	QB	Rice
1957	November 27, 1956	Green Bay	Paul Hornung	HB	Notre Dame
1956	November 29, 1955	Pittsburgh	Gary Glick	DB	Colorado A&M
1955	January 27-28	Baltimore	George Shaw	QB	Oregon
1954	January 28	Cleveland	Bobby Garrett	QB	Stanford
1953	January 22	San Francisco	Harry Babcock	E	Georgia
1952	January 17	Los Angeles	Bill Wade	QB	Vanderbilt
1951	January 18-19	New York Giants	Kyle Rote	HB	Southern Methodist
1950	January 21-22	Detroit	Leon Hart	E	Notre Dame
1949	December 21, 1948	Philadelphia	Chuck Bednarik	C	Pennsylvania
1948	December 19, 1947	Washington	Harry Gilmer	QB	Alabama
1947	December 16, 1946	Chicago Bears	Bob Fenimore	HB	Oklahoma A&M
1946	January 14	Boston	Frank Dancewicz	QB	Notre Dame
1945	April 6	Chicago Cardinals	Charley Trippi	HB	Georgia
1944	April 19	Boston	Angelo Bertelli	QB	Notre Dame
1943	April 8	Detroit	Frank Sinkwich	HB	Georgia
1942	December 22, 1941	Pittsburgh	Bill Dudley	HB	Virginia
1941	December 10, 1940	Chicago Bears	Tom Harmon	HB	Michigan
1940	December 9, 1939	Chicago Cardinals	George Cafego	HB	Tennessee
1939	December 8, 1938	Chicago Cardinals	Ki Aldrich	C	Texas Christian
1938	December 12, 1937	Cleveland	Corbett Davis	FB	Indiana
1937	December 12, 1936	Philadelphia	Sam Francis	FB	Nebraska
1936	February 8	Philadelphia	Jay Berwanger	HB	Chicago

Note: From 1947 through 1958, the first selection in the draft was a Bonus pick, awarded to the winner of a random draw. That club, in turn, forfeited its last-round draft choice. The winner of the Bonus choice was eliminated from future draws. The system was abolished after 1958, by which time all clubs had received a Bonus choice.

FIRST-ROUND SELECTIONS

FIRST-ROUND SELECTIONS

If club had no first-round selection, first player drafted is listed with round in parentheses.

ARIZONA CARDINALS

Year	Player, College, Position
1936	Jim Lawrence, Texas Christian, B
1937	Ray Buivid, Marquette, B
1938	Jack Robbins, Arkansas, B
1939	Charles (Ki) Aldrich, Texas Christian, C
1940	George Cafego, Tennessee, B
1941	John Kimbrough, Texas A&M, B
1942	Steve Lach, Duke, B
1943	Glenn Dobbs, Tulsa, B
1944	Pat Harder, Wisconsin, B
1945	Charley Trippi, Georgia, B
1946	Dub Jones, Louisiana State, B
1947	DeWitt (Tex) Coulter, Army, T
1948	Jim Spavital, Oklahoma A&M, B
1949	Bill Fischer, Notre Dame, G
1950	Jack Jennings, Ohio State, T (2)
1951	Jerry Groom, Notre Dame, C
1952	Ollie Matson, San Francisco, B
1953	Johnny Olszewski, California, B
1954	Lamar McHan, Arkansas, B
1955	Max Boydston, Oklahoma, E
1956	Joe Childress, Auburn, B
1957	Jerry Tubbs, Oklahoma, C
1958	King Hill, Rice, B
	John David Crow, Texas A&M, B
1959	Bill Stacy, Mississippi State, B
1960	George Izo, Notre Dame, QB
1961	Ken Rice, Auburn, T
1962	Fate Echols, Northwestern, DT
	Irv Goode, Kentucky, C
1963	Jerry Stovall, Louisiana State, S
	Don Brumm, Purdue, DE
1964	Ken Kortas, Louisville, DT
1965	Joe Namath, Alabama, QB
1966	Carl McAdams, Oklahoma, LB
1967	Dave Williams, Washington, WR
1968	MacArthur Lane, Utah State, RB
1969	Roger Wehrli, Missouri, DB
1970	Larry Stegent, Texas A&M, RB
1971	Norm Thompson, Utah, CB
1972	Bobby Moore, Oregon, RB-WR
1973	Dave Butz, Purdue, DT
1974	J.V. Cain, Colorado, TE
1975	Tim Gray, Texas A&M, DB
1976	Mike Dawson, Arizona, DT
1977	Steve Pisarkiewicz, Missouri, QB
1978	Steve Little, Arkansas, K
	Ken Greene, Washington State, DB
1979	Ottis Anderson, Miami, RB
1980	Curtis Greer, Michigan, DE
1981	E.J. Junior, Alabama, LB
1982	Luis Sharpe, UCLA, T
1983	Leonard Smith, McNeese State, DB
1984	Clyde Duncan, Tennessee, WR
1985	Freddie Joe Nunn, Mississippi, LB
1986	Anthony Bell, Michigan State, LB
1987	Kelly Stouffer, Colorado State, QB
1988	Ken Harvey, California, LB
1989	Eric Hill, Louisiana State, LB
	Joe Wolf, Boston College, G
1990	Anthony Thompson, Indiana, RB (2)
1991	Eric Swann, No College, DE
1992	Tony Sacca, Penn State, QB (2)
1993	Garrison Hearst, Georgia, RB
	Ernest Dye, South Carolina, T
1994	Jamir Miller, UCLA, LB
1995	Frank Sanders, Auburn, WR (2)
1996	Simeon Rice, Illinois, DE
1997	Tom Knight, Iowa, DB
1998	Andre Wadsworth, Florida State, DE
1999	David Boston, Ohio State, WR
	L.J. Shelton, Eastern Michigan, T
2000	Thomas Jones, Virginia, RB

ATLANTA FALCONS

Year	Player, College, Position
1966	Tommy Nobis, Texas, LB
	Randy Johnson, Texas A&I, QB
1967	Leo Carroll, San Diego State, DE (2)
1968	Claude Humphrey, Tennessee State, DE
1969	George Kunz, Notre Dame, T
1970	John Small, Citadel, LB
1971	Joe Profit, Northeast Louisiana, RB
1972	Clarence Ellis, Notre Dame, DB
1973	Greg Marx, Notre Dame, DT (2)
1974	Gerald Tinker, Kent State, WR (2)
1975	Steve Bartkowski, California, QB
1976	Bubba Bean, Texas A&M, RB
1977	Warren Bryant, Kentucky, T
	Wilson Faumuina, San Jose State, DT
1978	Mike Kenn, Michigan, T
1979	Don Smith, Miami, DE
1980	Junior Miller, Nebraska, TE
1981	Bobby Butler, Florida State, DB
1982	Gerald Riggs, Arizona State, RB
1983	Mike Pitts, Alabama, DE
1984	Rick Bryan, Oklahoma, DT
1985	Bill Fralic, Pittsburgh, T
1986	Tony Casillas, Oklahoma, NT
	Tim Green, Syracuse, LB
1987	Chris Miller, Oregon, QB
1988	Aundray Bruce, Auburn, LB
1989	Deion Sanders, Florida State, DB
	Shawn Collins, Northern Arizona, WR
1990	Steve Broussard, Washington State, RB
1991	Bruce Pickens, Nebraska, DB
	Mike Pritchard, Colorado, WR
1992	Bob Whitfield, Stanford, T
	Tony Smith, Southern Mississippi, RB
1993	Lincoln Kennedy, Washington, T
1994	Bert Emanuel, Rice, WR (2)
1995	Devin Bush, Florida State, DB
1996	Shannon Brown, Alabama, DT (3)
1997	Michael Booker, Nebraska, DB
1998	Keith Brooking, Georgia Tech, LB
1999	Patrick Kerney, Virginia, DE
2000	Travis Claridge, Southern California, T (2)

BALTIMORE RAVENS

Year	Player, College, Position
1996	Jonathan Ogden, UCLA, T
	Ray Lewis, Miami, LB
1997	Peter Boulware, Florida State, DE
1998	Duane Starks, Miami, DB
1999	Chris McAlister, Arizona, DB
2000	Jamal Lewis, Tennessee, RB
	Travis Taylor, Florida, WR

BUFFALO BILLS

Year	Player, College, Position
1960	Richie Lucas, Penn State, QB
1961	Ken Rice, Auburn, T
1962	Ernie Davis, Syracuse, RB
1963	Dave Behrman, Michigan State, C
1964	Carl Eller, Minnesota, DE
1965	Jim Davidson, Ohio State, T
1966	Mike Dennis, Mississippi, RB
1967	John Pitts, Arizona State, S
1968	Haven Moses, San Diego State, WR
1969	O.J. Simpson, Southern California, RB
1970	Al Cowlings, Southern California, DE
1971	J.D. Hill, Arizona State, WR
1972	Walt Patulski, Notre Dame, DE
1973	Paul Seymour, Michigan, TE
	Joe DeLamielleure, Michigan State, G
1974	Reuben Gant, Oklahoma State, TE
1975	Tom Ruud, Nebraska, LB
1976	Mario Clark, Oregon, DB
1977	Phil Dokes, Oklahoma State, DT
1978	Terry Miller, Oklahoma State, RB
1979	Tom Cousineau, Ohio State, LB
	Jerry Butler, Clemson, WR
1980	Jim Ritcher, North Carolina State, C
1981	Booker Moore, Penn State, RB
1982	Perry Tuttle, Clemson, WR
1983	Tony Hunter, Notre Dame, TE
	Jim Kelly, Miami, QB
1984	Greg Bell, Notre Dame, RB
1985	Bruce Smith, Virginia Tech, DE
	Derrick Burroughs, Memphis State, DB
1986	Ronnie Harmon, Iowa, RB
	Will Wolford, Vanderbilt, T
1987	Shane Conlan, Penn State, LB
1988	Thurman Thomas, Oklahoma State, RB (2)
1989	Don Beebe, Chadron, Neb., WR (3)
1990	James Williams, Fresno State, DB
1991	Henry Jones, Illinois, DB
1992	John Fina, Arizona, T
1993	Thomas Smith, North Carolina, DB
1994	Jeff Burris, Notre Dame, DB
1995	Ruben Brown, Pittsburgh, G
1996	Eric Moulds, Mississippi State, WR
1997	Antowain Smith, Houston, RB
1998	Sam Cowart, Florida State, LB (2)
1999	Antoine Winfield, Ohio State, DB
2000	Erik Flowers, Arizona State, DE

CAROLINA PANTHERS

Year	Player, College, Position
1995	Kerry Collins, Penn State, QB
	Tyrone Poole, Ft. Valley State, DB
	Blake Brockermeyer, Texas, T
1996	Tim Biakabutuka, Michigan, RB
1997	Rae Carruth, Colorado, WR
1998	Jason Peter, Nebraska, DT
1999	Chris Terry, Georgia, T (2)
2000	Rashard Anderson, Jackson State, DB

CHICAGO BEARS

Year	Player, College, Position
1936	Joe Stydahar, West Virginia, T
1937	Les McDonald, Nebraska, E
1938	Joe Gray, Oregon State, B
1939	Sid Luckman, Columbia, QB
	Bill Osmanski, Holy Cross, B
1940	Clyde (Bulldog) Turner, Hardin-Simmons, C
1941	Tom Harmon, Michigan, B
	Norm Standlee, Stanford, B
	Don Scott, Ohio State, B
1942	Frankie Albert, Stanford, B
1943	Bob Steber, Missouri, B
1944	Ray Evans, Kansas, B
1945	Don Lund, Michigan, B
1946	Johnny Lujack, Notre Dame, QB
1947	Bob Fenimore, Oklahoma State, B
	Don Kindt, Wisconsin, B
1948	Bobby Layne, Texas, QB
	Max Bumgardner, Texas, E
1949	Dick Harris, Texas, C
1950	Chuck Hunsinger, Florida, B
	Fred Morrison, Ohio State, B
1951	Bob Williams, Notre Dame, B
	Billy Stone, Bradley, B
	Gene Schroeder, Virginia, E
1952	Jim Dooley, Miami, B
1953	Billy Anderson, Compton (Calif.) J.C., B
1954	Stan Wallace, Illinois, B
1955	Ron Drzewiecki, Marquette, B
1956	Menan (Tex) Schriewer, Texas, E
1957	Earl Leggett, Louisiana State, T
1958	Chuck Howley, West Virginia, G
1959	Don Clark, Ohio State, B
1960	Roger Davis, Syracuse, G
1961	Mike Ditka, Pittsburgh, E
1962	Ronnie Bull, Baylor, RB
1963	Dave Behrman, Michigan State, C
1964	Dick Evey, Tennessee, DT
1965	Dick Butkus, Illinois, LB
	Gale Sayers, Kansas, RB
	Steve DeLong, Tennessee, T
1966	George Rice, Louisiana State, DT
1967	Loyd Phillips, Arkansas, DE
1968	Mike Hull, Southern California, RB
1969	Rufus Mayes, Ohio State, T
1970	George Farmer, UCLA, WR (3)
1971	Joe Moore, Missouri, RB
1972	Lionel Antoine, Southern Illinois, T
	Craig Clemons, Iowa, DB
1973	Wally Chambers, Eastern Kentucky, DE
1974	Waymond Bryant, Tennessee State, LB
	Dave Gallagher, Michigan, DT
1975	Walter Payton, Jackson State, RB
1976	Dennis Lick, Wisconsin, T
1977	Ted Albrecht, California, T

1978 Brad Shearer, Texas, DT (3)
1979 Dan Hampton, Arkansas, DT
Al Harris, Arizona State, DE
1980 Otis Wilson, Louisville, LB
1981 Keith Van Horne, Southern California, T
1982 Jim McMahon, Brigham Young, QB
1983 Jim Covert, Pittsburgh, T
Willie Gault, Tennessee, WR
1984 Wilber Marshall, Florida, LB
1985 William Perry, Clemson, DT
1986 Neal Anderson, Florida, RB
1987 Jim Harbaugh, Michigan, QB
1988 Brad Muster, Stanford, RB
Wendell Davis, Louisiana State, WR
1989 Donnell Woolford, Clemson, DB
Trace Armstrong, Florida, DE
1990 Mark Carrier, Southern California, DB
1991 Stan Thomas, Texas, T
1992 Alonzo Spellman, Ohio State, DE
1993 Curtis Conway, Southern California, WR
1994 John Thierry, Alcorn State, DE
1995 Rashaan Salaam, Colorado, RB
1996 Walt Harris, Mississippi State, DB
1997 John Allred, Southern California, TE (2)
1998 Curtis Enis, Penn State, RB
1999 Cade McNown, UCLA, QB
2000 Brian Urlacher, New Mexico, LB

CINCINNATI BENGALS

Year Player, College, Position
1968 Bob Johnson, Tennessee, C
1969 Greg Cook, Cincinnati, QB
1970 Mike Reid, Penn State, DT
1971 Vernon Holland, Tennessee State, T
1972 Sherman White, California, DE
1973 Isaac Curtis, San Diego State, WR
1974 Bill Kollar, Montana State, DT
1975 Glenn Cameron, Florida, LB
1976 Billy Brooks, Oklahoma, WR
Archie Griffin, Ohio State, RB
1977 Eddie Edwards, Miami, DT
Wilson Whitley, Houston, DT
Mike Cobb, Michigan State, TE
1978 Ross Browner, Notre Dame, DT
Blair Bush, Washington, C
1979 Jack Thompson, Washington State, QB
Charles Alexander, Louisiana State, RB
1980 Anthony Muñoz, Southern California, T
1981 David Verser, Kansas, WR
1982 Glen Collins, Mississippi State, DE
1983 Dave Rimington, Nebraska, C
1984 Ricky Hunley, Arizona, LB
Pete Koch, Maryland, DE
Brian Blados, North Carolina, T
1985 Eddie Brown, Miami, WR
Emanuel King, Alabama, LB
1986 Joe Kelly, Washington, LB
Tim McGee, Tennessee, WR
1987 Jason Buck, Brigham Young, DE
1988 Rickey Dixon, Oklahoma, DB
1989 Eric Ball, UCLA, RB (2)
1990 James Francis, Baylor, LB
1991 Alfred Williams, Colorado, LB
1992 David Klingler, Houston, QB
Darryl Williams, Miami, DB
1993 John Copeland, Alabama, DE
1994 Dan Wilkinson, Ohio State, DT
1995 Ki-Jana Carter, Penn State, RB
1996 Willie Anderson, Auburn, T
1997 Reinard Wilson, Florida State, LB
1998 Takeo Spikes, Auburn, LB
Brian Simmons, North Carolina, LB
1999 Akili Smith, Oregon, QB
2000 Peter Warrick, Florida State, WR

CLEVELAND BROWNS

Year Player, College, Position
1950 Ken Carpenter, Oregon State, B
1951 Ken Konz, Louisiana State, B
1952 Bert Rechichar, Tennessee, DB
Harry Agganis, Boston U., QB
1953 Doug Atkins, Tennessee, DE
1954 Bobby Garrett, Stanford, QB
John Bauer, Illinois, G
1955 Kurt Burris, Oklahoma, C
1956 Preston Carpenter, Arkansas, B
1957 Jim Brown, Syracuse, RB
1958 Jim Shofner, Texas Christian, DB
1959 Rich Kreitling, Illinois, DE
1960 Jim Houston, Ohio State, DE
1961 Bobby Crespino, Mississippi, TE
1962 Gary Collins, Maryland, WR
Leroy Jackson, Western Illinois, RB
1963 Tom Hutchinson, Kentucky, WR
1964 Paul Warfield, Ohio State, WR
1965 James Garcia, Purdue, T (2)
1966 Milt Morin, Massachusetts, TE
1967 Bob Matheson, Duke, LB
1968 Marvin Upshaw, Trinity, Tex., DT-DE
1969 Ron Johnson, Michigan, RB
1970 Mike Phipps, Purdue, QB
Bob McKay, Texas, T
1971 Clarence Scott, Kansas State, CB
1972 Thom Darden, Michigan, DB
1973 Steve Holden, Arizona State, WR
Pete Adams, Southern California, T
1974 Billy Corbett, Johnson C. Smith, T (2)
1975 Mack Mitchell, Houston, DE
1976 Mike Pruitt, Purdue, RB
1977 Robert Jackson, Texas A&M, LB
1978 Clay Matthews, Southern California, LB
Ozzie Newsome, Alabama, TE
1979 Willis Adams, Houston, WR
1980 Charles White, Southern California, RB
1981 Hanford Dixon, Southern Mississippi, DB
1982 Chip Banks, Southern California, LB
1983 Ron Brown, Arizona State, WR (2)
1984 Don Rogers, UCLA, DB
1985 Greg Allen, Florida State, RB (2)
1986 Webster Slaughter, San Diego State, WR (2)
1987 Mike Junkin, Duke, LB
1988 Clifford Charlton, Florida, LB
1989 Eric Metcalf, Texas, RB
1990 Leroy Hoard, Michigan, RB (2)
1991 Eric Turner, UCLA, DB
1992 Tommy Vardell, Stanford, RB
1993 Steve Everitt, Michigan, C
1994 Antonio Langham, Alabama, DB
Derrick Alexander, Michigan, WR
1995 Craig Powell, Ohio State, LB
1999 Tim Couch, Kentucky, QB
2000 Courtney Brown, Penn State, DE

DALLAS COWBOYS

Year Player, College, Position
1960 None
1961 Bob Lilly, Texas Christian, DT
1962 Sonny Gibbs, Texas Christian, QB (2)
1963 Lee Roy Jordan, Alabama, LB
1964 Scott Appleton, Texas, DT
1965 Craig Morton, California, QB
1966 John Niland, Iowa, G
1967 Phil Clark, Northwestern, DB (3)
1968 Dennis Homan, Alabama, WR
1969 Calvin Hill, Yale, RB
1970 Duane Thomas, West Texas State, RB
1971 Tody Smith, Southern California, DE
1972 Bill Thomas, Boston College, RB
1973 Billy Joe DuPree, Michigan State, TE
1974 Ed (Too Tall) Jones, Tennessee State, DE
Charley Young, North Carolina State, RB
1975 Randy White, Maryland, LB
Thomas Henderson, Langston, LB
1976 Aaron Kyle, Wyoming, DB
1977 Tony Dorsett, Pittsburgh, RB
1978 Larry Bethea, Michigan State, DE
1979 Robert Shaw, Tennessee, C
1980 Bill Roe, Colorado, LB (3)
1981 Howard Richards, Missouri, T
1982 Rod Hill, Kentucky State, DB
1983 Jim Jeffcoat, Arizona State, DE
1984 Billy Cannon, Jr., Texas A&M, LB
1985 Kevin Brooks, Michigan, DE
1986 Mike Sherrard, UCLA, WR
1987 Danny Noonan, Nebraska, DT
1988 Michael Irvin, Miami, WR
1989 Troy Aikman, UCLA, QB
1990 Emmitt Smith, Florida, RB
1991 Russell Maryland, Miami, DT
Alvin Harper, Tennessee, WR
Kelvin Pritchett, Mississippi, DT
1992 Kevin Smith, Texas A&M, DB
Robert Jones, East Carolina, LB
1993 Kevin Williams, Miami, WR (2)
1994 Shante Carver, Arizona State, DE
1995 Sherman Williams, Alabama, RB (2)
1996 Kavika Pittman, McNeese State, DE (2)
1997 David LaFleur, Louisiana State, TE
1998 Greg Ellis, North Carolina, DE
1999 Ebenezer Ekuban, North Carolina, DE
2000 Dwayne Goodrich, Tennessee, DB (2)

DENVER BRONCOS

Year Player, College, Position
1960 Roger LeClerc, Trinity, Conn., C
1961 Bob Gaiters, New Mexico State, RB
1962 Merlin Olsen, Utah State, DT
1963 Kermit Alexander, UCLA, CB
1964 Bob Brown, Nebraska, T
1965 Dick Butkus, Illinois, LB (2)
1966 Jerry Shay, Purdue, DT
1967 Floyd Little, Syracuse, RB
1968 Curley Culp, Arizona State, DE (2)
1969 Grady Cavness, Texas-El Paso, DB (2)
1970 Bob Anderson, Colorado, RB
1971 Marv Montgomery, Southern California, T
1972 Riley Odoms, Houston, TE
1973 Otis Armstrong, Purdue, RB
1974 Randy Gradishar, Ohio State, LB
1975 Louis Wright, San Jose State, DB
1976 Tom Glassic, Virginia, G
1977 Steve Schindler, Boston College, G
1978 Don Latimer, Miami, DT
1979 Kelvin Clark, Nebraska, T
1980 Rulon Jones, Utah State, DE (2)
1981 Dennis Smith, Southern California, DB
1982 Gerald Willhite, San Jose State, RB
1983 Chris Hinton, Northwestern, G
1984 Andre Townsend, Mississippi, DE (2)
1985 Steve Sewell, Oklahoma, RB
1986 Jim Juriga, Illinois, T (4)
1987 Ricky Nattiel, Florida, WR
1988 Ted Gregory, Syracuse, NT
1989 Steve Atwater, Arkansas, DB
1990 Alton Montgomery, Houston, DB (2)
1991 Mike Croel, Nebraska, LB
1992 Tommy Maddox, UCLA, QB
1993 Dan Williams, Toledo, DE
1994 Allen Aldridge, Houston, LB (2)
1995 Jamie Brown, Florida A&M, T (4)
1996 John Mobley, Kutztown, LB
1997 Trevor Pryce, Clemson, DT
1998 Marcus Nash, Tennessee, WR
1999 Al Wilson, Tennessee, LB
2000 Deltha O'Neal, California, DB

DETROIT LIONS

Year Player, College, Position
1936 Sid Wagner, Michigan State, G
1937 Lloyd Cardwell, Nebraska, B
1938 Alex Wojciechowicz, Fordham, C
1939 John Pingel, Michigan State, B
1940 Doyle Nave, Southern California, B
1941 Jim Thomason, Texas A&M, B
1942 Bob Westfall, Michigan, B
1943 Frank Sinkwich, Georgia, B
1944 Otto Graham, Northwestern, B
1945 Frank Szymanski, Notre Dame, C
1946 Bill Dellastatious, Missouri, B
1947 Glenn Davis, Army, B
1948 Y.A. Tittle, Louisiana State, B
1949 John Rauch, Georgia, B
1950 Leon Hart, Notre Dame, E
Joe Watson, Rice, C
1951 Dick Stanfel, San Francisco, G (2)
1952 Yale Lary, Texas A&M, B (3)
1953 Harley Sewell, Texas, G
1954 Dick Chapman, Rice, T
1955 Dave Middleton, Auburn, B

FIRST-ROUND SELECTIONS

1956 Hopalong Cassady, Ohio State, B
1957 Bill Glass, Baylor, G
1958 Alex Karras, Iowa, T
1959 Nick Pietrosante, Notre Dame, B
1960 John Robinson, Louisiana State, S
1961 Danny LaRose, Missouri, T (2)
1962 John Hadl, Kansas, QB
1963 Daryl Sanders, Ohio State, T
1964 Pete Beathard, Southern California, QB
1965 Tom Nowatzke, Indiana, RB
1966 Nick Eddy, Notre Dame, RB (2)
1967 Mel Farr, UCLA, RB
1968 Greg Landry, Massachusetts, QB
Earl McCullouch, Southern California, WR
1969 Altie Taylor, Utah State, RB (2)
1970 Steve Owens, Oklahoma, RB
1971 Bob Bell, Cincinnati, DT
1972 Herb Orvis, Colorado, DE
1973 Ernie Price, Texas A&I, DE
1974 Ed O'Neil, Penn State, LB
1975 Lynn Boden, South Dakota State, G
1976 James Hunter, Grambling, DB
Lawrence Gaines, Wyoming, RB
1977 Walt Williams, New Mexico State, DB (2)
1978 Luther Bradley, Notre Dame, DB
1979 Keith Dorney, Penn State, T
1980 Billy Sims, Oklahoma, RB
1981 Mark Nichols, San Jose State, WR
1982 Jimmy Williams, Nebraska, LB
1983 James Jones, Florida, RB
1984 David Lewis, California, TE
1985 Lomas Brown, Florida, T
1986 Chuck Long, Iowa, QB
1987 Reggie Rogers, Washington, DE
1988 Bennie Blades, Miami, DB
1989 Barry Sanders, Oklahoma State, RB
1990 Andre Ware, Houston, QB
1991 Herman Moore, Virginia, WR
1992 Robert Porcher, South Carolina State, DE
1993 Ryan McNeil, Miami, DB (2)
1994 Johnnie Morton, Southern California, WR
1995 Luther Elliss, Utah, DT
1996 Reggie Brown, Texas A&M, LB
Jeff Hartings, Penn State, G
1997 Bryant Westbrook, Texas, DB
1998 Terry Fair, Tennessee, DB
1999 Chris Claiborne, Southern California, LB
Aaron Gibson, Wisconsin, T
2000 Stockar McDougle, Oklahoma, T

GREEN BAY PACKERS

Year Player, College, Position

1936 Russ Letlow, San Francisco, G
1937 Eddie Jankowski, Wisconsin, B
1938 Cecil Isbell, Purdue, B
1939 Larry Buhler, Minnesota, B
1940 Harold Van Every, Minnesota, B
1941 George Paskvan, Wisconsin, B
1942 Urban Odson, Minnesota, T
1943 Dick Wildung, Minnesota, T
1944 Merv Pregulman, Michigan, G
1945 Walt Schlinkman, Texas Tech, B
1946 Johnny (Strike) Strzykalski, Marquette, B
1947 Ernie Case, UCLA, B
1948 Earl (Jug) Girard, Wisconsin, B
1949 Stan Heath, Nevada, B
1950 Clayton Tonnemaker, Minnesota, C
1951 Bob Gain, Kentucky, T
1952 Babe Parilli, Kentucky, QB
1953 Al Carmichael, Southern California, B
1954 Art Hunter, Notre Dame, T
Veryl Switzer, Kansas State, B
1955 Tom Bettis, Purdue, G
1956 Jack Losch, Miami, B
1957 Paul Hornung, Notre Dame, B
Ron Kramer, Michigan, E
1958 Dan Currie, Michigan State, C
1959 Randy Duncan, Iowa, B
1960 Tom Moore, Vanderbilt, RB
1961 Herb Adderley, Michigan State, CB
1962 Earl Gros, Louisiana State, RB
1963 Dave Robinson, Penn State, LB
1964 Lloyd Voss, Nebraska, DT
1965 Donny Anderson, Texas Tech, RB
Lawrence Elkins, Baylor, E
1966 Jim Grabowski, Illinois, RB
Gale Gillingham, Minnesota, T
1967 Bob Hyland, Boston College, C
Don Horn, San Diego State, QB
1968 Fred Carr, Texas-El Paso, LB
Bill Lueck, Arizona, G
1969 Rich Moore, Villanova, DT
1970 Mike McCoy, Notre Dame, DT
Rich McGeorge, Elon, TE
1971 John Brockington, Ohio State, RB
1972 Willie Buchanon, San Diego State, DB
Jerry Tagge, Nebraska, QB
1973 Barry Smith, Florida State, WR
1974 Barty Smith, Richmond, RB
1975 Bill Bain, Southern California, G (2)
1976 Mark Koncar, Colorado, T
1977 Mike Butler, Kansas, DE
Ezra Johnson, Morris Brown, DE
1978 James Lofton, Stanford, WR
John Anderson, Michigan, LB
1979 Eddie Lee Ivery, Georgia Tech, RB
1980 Bruce Clark, Penn State, DE
George Cumby, Oklahoma, LB
1981 Rich Campbell, California, QB
1982 Ron Hallstrom, Iowa, G
1983 Tim Lewis, Pittsburgh, DB
1984 Alphonso Carreker, Florida State, DE
1985 Ken Ruettgers, Southern California, T
1986 Kenneth Davis, Texas Christian, RB (2)
1987 Brent Fullwood, Auburn, RB
1988 Sterling Sharpe, South Carolina, WR
1989 Tony Mandarich, Michigan State, T
1990 Tony Bennett, Mississippi, LB
Darrell Thompson, Minnesota, RB
1991 Vinnie Clark, Ohio State, DB
1992 Terrell Buckley, Florida State, DB
1993 Wayne Simmons, Clemson, LB
George Teague, Alabama, DB
1994 Aaron Taylor, Notre Dame, T
1995 Craig Newsome, Arizona State, DB
1996 John Michels, Southern California, T
1997 Ross Verba, Iowa, T
1998 Vonnie Holliday, North Carolina, DT
1999 Antuan Edwards, Clemson, DB
2000 Bubba Franks, Miami, TE

INDIANAPOLIS COLTS

Year Player, College, Position

1953 Billy Vessels, Oklahoma, B
1954 Cotton Davidson, Baylor, B
1955 George Shaw, Oregon, B
Alan Ameche, Wisconsin, FB
1956 Lenny Moore, Penn State, B
1957 Jim Parker, Ohio State, G
1958 Lenny Lyles, Louisville, B
1959 Jackie Burkett, Auburn, C
1960 Ron Mix, Southern California, T
1961 Tom Matte, Ohio State, RB
1962 Wendell Harris, Louisiana State, S
1963 Bob Vogel, Ohio State, T
1964 Marv Woodson, Indiana, CB
1965 Mike Curtis, Duke, LB
1966 Sam Ball, Kentucky, T
1967 Bubba Smith, Michigan State, DT
Jim Detwiler, Michigan, RB
1968 John Williams, Minnesota, G
1969 Eddie Hinton, Oklahoma, WR
1970 Norman Bulaich, Texas Christian, RB
1971 Don McCauley, North Carolina, RB
Leonard Dunlap, North Texas State, DB
1972 Tom Drougas, Oregon, T
1973 Bert Jones, Louisiana State, QB
Joe Ehrmann, Syracuse, DT
1974 John Dutton, Nebraska, DE
Roger Carr, Louisiana Tech, WR
1975 Ken Huff, North Carolina, G
1976 Ken Novak, Purdue, DT
1977 Randy Burke, Kentucky, WR
1978 Reese McCall, Auburn, TE
1979 Barry Krauss, Alabama, LB
1980 Curtis Dickey, Texas A&M, RB
Derrick Hatchett, Texas, DB
1981 Randy McMillan, Pittsburgh, RB
Donnell Thompson, North Carolina, DT
1982 Johnie Cooks, Mississippi State, LB
Art Schlichter, Ohio State, QB
1983 John Elway, Stanford, QB
1984 Leonard Coleman, Vanderbilt, DB
Ron Solt, Maryland, G
1985 Duane Bickett, Southern California, LB
1986 Jon Hand, Alabama, DE
1987 Cornelius Bennett, Alabama, LB
1988 Chris Chandler, Washington, QB (3)
1989 Andre Rison, Michigan State, WR
1990 Jeff George, Illinois, QB
1991 Shane Curry, Miami, DE (2)
1992 Steve Emtman, Washington, DT
Quentin Coryatt, Texas A&M, LB
1993 Sean Dawkins, California, WR
1994 Marshall Faulk, San Diego State, RB
Trev Alberts, Nebraska, LB
1995 Ellis Johnson, Florida, DT
1996 Marvin Harrison, Syracuse, WR
1997 Tarik Glenn, California, T
1998 Peyton Manning, Tennessee, QB
1999 Edgerrin James, Miami, RB
2000 Rob Morris, Brigham Young, LB

JACKSONVILLE JAGUARS

Year Player, College, Position

1995 Tony Boselli, Southern California, T
James Stewart, Tennessee, RB
1996 Kevin Hardy, Illinois, LB
1997 Renaldo Wynn, Notre Dame, DT
1998 Fred Taylor, Florida, RB
Donovin Darius, Syracuse, DB
1999 Fernando Bryant, Alabama, DB
2000 R. Jay Soward, Southern California, WR

KANSAS CITY CHIEFS

Year Player, College, Position

1960 Don Meredith, Southern Methodist, QB
1961 E.J. Holub, Texas Tech, C
1962 Ronnie Bull, Baylor, RB
1963 Buck Buchanan, Grambling, DT
Ed Budde, Michigan State, G
1964 Pete Beathard, Southern California, QB
1965 Gale Sayers, Kansas, RB
1966 Aaron Brown, Minnesota, DE
1967 Gene Trosch, Miami, DE-DT
1968 Mo Moorman, Texas A&M, G
George Daney, Texas-El Paso, G
1969 Jim Marsalis, Tennessee State, CB
1970 Sid Smith, Southern California, T
1971 Elmo Wright, Houston, WR
1972 Jeff Kinney, Nebraska, RB
1973 Gary Butler, Rice, TE (2)
1974 Woody Green, Arizona State, RB
1975 Elmore Stephens, Kentucky, TE (2)
1976 Rod Walters, Iowa, G
1977 Gary Green, Baylor, DB
1978 Art Still, Kentucky, DE
1979 Mike Bell, Colorado State, DE
Steve Fuller, Clemson, QB
1980 Brad Budde, Southern California, G
1981 Willie Scott, South Carolina, TE
1982 Anthony Hancock, Tennessee, WR
1983 Todd Blackledge, Penn State, QB
1984 Bill Maas, Pittsburgh, DT
John Alt, Iowa, T
1985 Ethan Horton, North Carolina, RB
1986 Brian Jozwiak, West Virginia, T
1987 Paul Palmer, Temple, RB
1988 Neil Smith, Nebraska, DE
1989 Derrick Thomas, Alabama, LB
1990 Percy Snow, Michigan State, LB
1991 Harvey Williams, Louisiana State, RB
1992 Dale Carter, Tennessee, DB
1993 Will Shields, Nebraska, G (3)
1994 Greg Hill, Texas A&M, RB
1995 Trezelle Jenkins, Michigan, T
1996 Jerome Woods, Memphis, DB
1997 Tony Gonzalez, California, TE
1998 Victor Riley, Auburn, T

1999 John Tait, Brigham Young, T
2000 Sylvester Morris, Jackson State, WR

MIAMI DOLPHINS

Year	Player, College, Position
1966	Jim Grabowski, Illinois, RB
	Rick Norton, Kentucky, QB
1967	Bob Griese, Purdue, QB
1968	Larry Csonka, Syracuse, RB
	Doug Crusan, Indiana, T
1969	Bill Stanfill, Georgia, DE
1970	Jim Mandich, Michigan, TE (2)
1971	Otto Stowe, Iowa State, WR (2)
1972	Mike Kadish, Notre Dame, DT
1973	Chuck Bradley, Oregon, C (2)
1974	Donald Reese, Jackson State, DE
1975	Darryl Carlton, Tampa, T
1976	Larry Gordon, Arizona State, LB
	Kim Bokamper, San Jose State, LB
1977	A.J. Duhe, Louisiana State, DT
1978	Guy Benjamin, Stanford, QB (2)
1979	Jon Giesler, Michigan, T
1980	Don McNeal, Alabama, DB
1981	David Overstreet, Oklahoma, RB
1982	Roy Foster, Southern California, G
1983	Dan Marino, Pittsburgh, QB
1984	Jackie Shipp, Oklahoma, LB
1985	Lorenzo Hampton, Florida, RB
1986	John Offerdahl, Western Michigan, LB (2)
1987	John Bosa, Boston College, DE
1988	Eric Kumerow, Ohio State, DE
1989	Sammie Smith, Florida State, RB
	Louis Oliver, Florida, DB
1990	Richmond Webb, Texas A&M, T
1991	Randal Hill, Miami, WR
1992	Troy Vincent, Wisconsin, DB
	Marco Coleman, Georgia Tech, LB
1993	O.J. McDuffie, Penn State, WR
1994	Tim Bowens, Mississippi, DT
1995	Billy Milner, Houston, T
1996	Daryl Gardener, Baylor, DT
1997	Yatil Green, Miami, WR
1998	John Avery, Mississippi, RB
1999	James Johnson, Mississippi State, RB (2)
2000	Todd Wade, Mississippi, T (2)

MINNESOTA VIKINGS

Year	Player, College, Position
1961	Tommy Mason, Tulane, RB
1962	Bill Miller, Miami, WR (3)
1963	Jim Dunaway, Mississippi, T
1964	Carl Eller, Minnesota, DE
1965	Jack Snow, Notre Dame, WR
1966	Jerry Shay, Purdue, DT
1967	Clint Jones, Michigan State, RB
	Gene Washington, Michigan State, WR
	Alan Page, Notre Dame, DT
1968	Ron Yary, Southern California, T
1969	Ed White, California, G (2)
1970	John Ward, Oklahoma State, DT
1971	Leo Hayden, Ohio State, RB
1972	Jeff Siemon, Stanford, LB
1973	Chuck Foreman, Miami, RB
1974	Fred McNeill, UCLA, LB
	Steve Riley, Southern California, T
1975	Mark Mullaney, Colorado State, DE
1976	James White, Oklahoma State, DT
1977	Tommy Kramer, Rice, QB
1978	Randy Holloway, Pittsburgh, DE
1979	Ted Brown, North Carolina State, RB
1980	Doug Martin, Washington, DT
1981	Mardye McDole, Mississippi State, WR (2)
1982	Darrin Nelson, Stanford, RB
1983	Joey Browner, Southern California, DB
1984	Keith Millard, Washington State, DE
1985	Chris Doleman, Pittsburgh, LB
1986	Gerald Robinson, Auburn, DE
1987	D.J. Dozier, Penn State, RB
1988	Randall McDaniel, Arizona State, G
1989	David Braxton, Wake Forest, LB (2)
1990	Mike Jones, Texas A&M, TE (3)
1991	Carlos Jenkins, Michigan State, LB (3)
1992	Robert Harris, Southern University, DE (2)
1993	Robert Smith, Ohio State, RB
1994	DeWayne Washington, N. Carolina St., DB
	Todd Steussie, California, T
1995	Derrick Alexander, Florida State, DE
	Korey Stringer, Ohio State, T
1996	Duane Clemons, California, DE
1997	Dwayne Rudd, Alabama, LB
1998	Randy Moss, Marshall, WR
1999	Daunte Culpepper, Central Florida, QB
	Dimitrius Underwood, Michigan State, DE
2000	Chris Hovan, Boston College, DT

NEW ENGLAND PATRIOTS

Year	Player, College, Position
1960	Ron Burton, Northwestern, RB
1961	Tommy Mason, Tulane, RB
1962	Gary Collins, Maryland, WR
1963	Art Graham, Boston College, WR
1964	Jack Concannon, Boston College, QB
1965	Jerry Rush, Michigan State, DE
1966	Karl Singer, Purdue, T
1967	John Charles, Purdue, S
1968	Dennis Byrd, North Carolina State, DE
1969	Ron Sellers, Florida State, WR
1970	Phil Olsen, Utah State, DE
1971	Jim Plunkett, Stanford, QB
1972	Tom Reynolds, San Diego State, WR (2)
1973	John Hannah, Alabama, G
	Sam Cunningham, So. California, RB
	Darryl Stingley, Purdue, WR
1974	Steve Corbett, Boston College, G (2)
1975	Russ Francis, Oregon, TE
1976	Mike Haynes, Arizona State, DB
	Pete Brock, Colorado, C
	Tim Fox, Ohio State, DB
1977	Raymond Clayborn, Texas, DB
	Stanley Morgan, Tennessee, WR
1978	Bob Cryder, Alabama, G
1979	Rick Sanford, South Carolina, DB
1980	Roland James, Tennessee, DB
	Vagas Ferguson, Notre Dame, RB
1981	Brian Holloway, Stanford, T
1982	Kenneth Sims, Texas, DT
	Lester Williams, Miami, DT
1983	Tony Eason, Illinois, QB
1984	Irving Fryar, Nebraska, WR
1985	Trevor Matich, Brigham Young, C
1986	Reggie Dupard, Southern Methodist, RB
1987	Bruce Armstrong, Louisville, T
1988	John Stephens, Northwestern St., La., RB
1989	Hart Lee Dykes, Oklahoma State, WR
1990	Chris Singleton, Arizona, LB
	Ray Agnew, North Carolina State, DE
1991	Pat Harlow, Southern California, T
	Leonard Russell, Arizona State, RB
1992	Eugene Chung, Virginia Tech, T
1993	Drew Bledsoe, Washington State, QB
1994	Willie McGinest, Southern California, DE
1995	Ty Law, Michigan, DB
1996	Terry Glenn, Ohio State, WR
1997	Chris Canty, Kansas State, DB
1998	Robert Edwards, Georgia, RB
	Tebucky Jones, Syracuse, DB
1999	Damien Woody, Boston College, C
	Andy Katzenmoyer, Ohio State, LB
2000	Adrian Klemm, Hawaii, T (2)

NEW ORLEANS SAINTS

Year	Player, College, Position
1967	Les Kelley, Alabama, RB
1968	Kevin Hardy, Notre Dame, DE
1969	John Shinners, Xavier, G
1970	Ken Burrough, Texas Southern, WR
1971	Archie Manning, Mississippi, QB
1972	Royce Smith, Georgia, G
1973	Derland Moore, Oklahoma, DE (2)
1974	Rick Middleton, Ohio State, LB
1975	Larry Burton, Purdue, WR
	Kurt Schumacher, Ohio State, T
1976	Chuck Muncie, California, RB
1977	Joe Campbell, Maryland, DE
1978	Wes Chandler, Florida, WR
1979	Russell Erxleben, Texas, P-K
1980	Stan Brock, Colorado, T
1981	George Rogers, South Carolina, RB
1982	Lindsay Scott, Georgia, WR
1983	Steve Korte, Arkansas, G (2)
1984	James Geathers, Wichita State, DE
1985	Alvin Toles, Tennessee, LB
1986	Jim Dombrowski, Virginia, T
1987	Shawn Knight, Brigham Young, DT
1988	Craig Heyward, Pittsburgh, RB
1989	Wayne Martin, Arkansas, DE
1990	Renaldo Turnbull, West Virginia, DE
1991	Wesley Carroll, Miami, WR (2)
1992	Vaughn Dunbar, Indiana, RB
1993	Willie Roaf, Louisiana Tech, T
	Irv Smith, Notre Dame, TE
1994	Joe Johnson, Louisville, DE
1995	Mark Fields, Washington State, LB
1996	Alex Molden, Oregon, DB
1997	Chris Naeole, Colorado, G
1998	Kyle Turley, San Diego State, T
1999	Ricky Williams, Texas, RB
2000	Darren Howard, Kansas State, DE (2)

NEW YORK GIANTS

Year	Player, College, Position
1936	Art Lewis, Ohio U., T
1937	Ed Widseth, Minnesota, T
1938	George Karamatic, Gonzaga, B
1939	Walt Neilson, Arizona, B
1940	Grenville Lansdell, Southern California, B
1941	George Franck, Minnesota, B
1942	Merle Hapes, Mississippi, B
1943	Steve Filipowicz, Fordham, B
1944	Billy Hillenbrand, Indiana, B
1945	Elmer Barbour, Wake Forest, B
1946	George Connor, Notre Dame, T
1947	Vic Schwall, Northwestern, B
1948	Tony Minisi, Pennsylvania, B
1949	Paul Page, Southern Methodist, B
1950	Travis Tidwell, Auburn, B
1951	Kyle Rote, Southern Methodist, B
	Jim Spavital, Oklahoma A&M, B
1952	Frank Gifford, Southern California, B
1953	Bobby Marlow, Alabama, B
1954	Ken Buck, Pacific, C (2)
1955	Joe Heap, Notre Dame, B
1956	Henry Moore, Arkansas, B (2)
1957	Sam DeLuca, South Carolina, T (2)
1958	Phil King, Vanderbilt, B
1959	Lee Grosscup, Utah, B
1960	Lou Cordileone, Clemson, G
1961	Bruce Tarbox, Syracuse, G (2)
1962	Jerry Hillebrand, Colorado, LB
1963	Frank Lasky, Florida, T (2)
1964	Joe Don Looney, Oklahoma, RB
1965	Tucker Frederickson, Auburn, RB
1966	Francis Peay, Missouri, T
1967	Louis Thompson, Alabama, DT (4)
1968	Dick Buzin, Penn State, T (2)
1969	Fred Dryer, San Diego State, DE
1970	Jim Files, Oklahoma, LB
1971	Rocky Thompson, West Texas State, WR
1972	Eldridge Small, Texas A&I, DB
	Larry Jacobson, Nebraska, DE
1973	Brad Van Pelt, Michigan State, LB (2)
1974	John Hicks, Ohio State, G
1975	Al Simpson, Colorado State, T (2)
1976	Troy Archer, Colorado, DE
1977	Gary Jeter, Southern California, DT
1978	Gordon King, Stanford, T
1979	Phil Simms, Morehead State, QB
1980	Mark Haynes, Colorado, DB
1981	Lawrence Taylor, North Carolina, LB
1982	Butch Woolfolk, Michigan, RB
1983	Terry Kinard, Clemson, DB
1984	Carl Banks, Michigan State, LB
	William Roberts, Ohio State, T
1985	George Adams, Kentucky, RB
1986	Eric Dorsey, Notre Dame, DE
1987	Mark Ingram, Michigan State, WR
1988	Eric Moore, Indiana, T
1989	Brian Williams, Minnesota, C-G
1990	Rodney Hampton, Georgia, RB

FIRST-ROUND SELECTIONS

1991 Jarrod Bunch, Michigan, RB
1992 Derek Brown, Notre Dame, TE
1993 Michael Strahan, Texas Southern, DE (2)
1994 Thomas Lewis, Indiana, WR
1995 Tyrone Wheatley, Michigan, RB
1996 Cedric Jones, Oklahoma, DE
1997 Ike Hilliard, Florida, WR
1998 Shaun Williams, UCLA, DB
1999 Luke Petitgout, Notre Dame, T
2000 Ron Dayne, Wisconsin, RB

NEW YORK JETS

Year	Player, College, Position
1960	George Izo, Notre Dame, QB
1961	Tom Brown, Minnesota, G
1962	Sandy Stephens, Minnesota, QB
1963	Jerry Stovall, Louisiana State, S
1964	Matt Snell, Ohio State, RB
1965	Joe Namath, Alabama, QB
	Tom Nowatzke, Indiana, RB
1966	Bill Yearby, Michigan, DT
1967	Paul Seiler, Notre Dame, T
1968	Lee White, Weber State, RB
1969	Dave Foley, Ohio State, T
1970	Steve Tannen, Florida, CB
1971	John Riggins, Kansas, RB
1972	Jerome Barkum, Jackson State, WR
	Mike Taylor, Michigan, LB
1973	Burgess Owens, Miami, DB
1974	Carl Barzilauskas, Indiana, DT
1975	Anthony Davis, Southern California, RB (2)
1976	Richard Todd, Alabama, QB
1977	Marvin Powell, Southern California, T
1978	Chris Ward, Ohio State, T
1979	Marty Lyons, Alabama, DE
1980	Johnny (Lam) Jones, Texas, WR
1981	Freeman McNeil, UCLA, RB
1982	Bob Crable, Notre Dame, LB
1983	Ken O'Brien, Cal-Davis, QB
1984	Russell Carter, Southern Methodist, DB
	Ron Faurot, Arkansas, DE
1985	Al Toon, Wisconsin, WR
1986	Mike Haight, Iowa, T
1987	Roger Vick, Texas A&M, RB
1988	Dave Cadigan, Southern California, T
1989	Jeff Lageman, Virginia, LB
1990	Blair Thomas, Penn State, RB
1991	Browning Nagle, Louisville, QB (2)
1992	Johnny Mitchell, Nebraska, TE
1993	Marvin Jones, Florida State, LB
1994	Aaron Glenn, Texas A&M, DB
1995	Kyle Brady, Penn State, TE
	Hugh Douglas, Central State, Ohio, DE
1996	Keyshawn Johnson, Southern California, WR
1997	James Farrior, Virginia, LB
1998	Dorian Boose, Washington State, DE (2)
1999	Randy Thomas, Mississippi State, G (2)
2000	Shaun Ellis, Tennessee, DE
	John Abraham, South Carolina, LB
	Chad Pennington, Marshall, QB
	Anthony Becht, West Virginia, TE

OAKLAND RAIDERS

Year	Player, College, Position
1960	Dale Hackbart, Wisconsin, CB
1961	Joe Rutgens, Illinois, DT
1962	Roman Gabriel, North Carolina State, QB
1963	George Wilson, Alabama, RB (6)
1964	Tony Lorick, Arizona State, RB
1965	Harry Schuh, Memphis State, T
1966	Rodger Bird, Kentucky, S
1967	Gene Upshaw, Texas A&I, G
1968	Eldridge Dickey, Tennessee State, QB
1969	Art Thoms, Syracuse, DT
1970	Raymond Chester, Morgan State, TE
1971	Jack Tatum, Ohio State, S
1972	Mike Siani, Villanova, WR
1973	Ray Guy, Southern Mississippi, P
1974	Henry Lawrence, Florida A&M, T
1975	Neal Colzie, Ohio State, DB
1976	Charles Philyaw, Texas Southern, DT (2)
1977	Mike Davis, Colorado, DB (2)
1978	Dave Browning, Washington, DE (2)
1979	Willie Jones, Florida State, DE (2)
1980	Marc Wilson, Brigham Young, QB
1981	Ted Watts, Texas Tech, DB
	Curt Marsh, Washington, T
1982	Marcus Allen, Southern California, RB
1983	Don Mosebar, Southern California, T
1984	Sean Jones, Northeastern, DE (2)
1985	Jessie Hester, Florida State, WR
1986	Bob Buczkowski, Pittsburgh, DE
1987	John Clay, Missouri, T
1988	Tim Brown, Notre Dame, WR
	Terry McDaniel, Tennessee, DB
	Scott Davis, Illinois, DE
1989	Jeff Francis, Tennessee, QB (6)
1990	Anthony Smith, Arizona, DE
1991	Todd Marinovich, Southern California, QB
1992	Chester McGlockton, Clemson, DE
1993	Patrick Bates, Texas A&M, DB
1994	Rob Fredrickson, Michigan State, LB
1995	Napoleon Kaufman, Washington, RB
1996	Rickey Dudley, Ohio State, TE
1997	Darrell Russell, Southern California, DT
1998	Charles Woodson, Michigan, DB
	Mo Collins, Florida, T
1999	Matt Stinchcomb, Georgia, T
2000	Sebastian Janikowski, Florida State, K

PHILADELPHIA EAGLES

Year	Player, College, Position
1936	Jay Berwanger, Chicago, B
1937	Sam Francis, Nebraska, B
1938	Jim McDonald, Ohio State, B
1939	Davey O'Brien, Texas Christian, B
1940	George McAfee, Duke, B
1941	Art Jones, Richmond, B (2)
1942	Pete Kmetovic, Stanford, B
1943	Joe Muha, Virginia Military, B
1944	Steve Van Buren, Louisiana State, B
1945	John Yonaker, Notre Dame, E
1946	Leo Riggs, Southern California, B
1947	Neill Armstrong, Oklahoma A&M, E
1948	Clyde (Smackover) Scott, Arkansas, B
1949	Chuck Bednarik, Pennsylvania, C
	Frank Tripucka, Notre Dame, B
1950	Harry (Bud) Grant, Minnesota, E
1951	Ebert Van Buren, Louisiana State, B
	Chet Mutryn, Xavier, B
1952	Johnny Bright, Drake, B
1953	Al Conway, Army, B (2)
1954	Neil Worden, Notre Dame, B
1955	Dick Bielski, Maryland, B
1956	Bob Pellegrini, Maryland, C
1957	Clarence Peaks, Michigan State, B
1958	Walt Kowalczyk, Michigan State, B
1959	J.D. Smith, Rice, T (2)
1960	Ron Burton, Northwestern, RB
1961	Art Baker, Syracuse, RB
1962	Pete Case, Georgia, G (2)
1963	Ed Budde, Michigan State, G
1964	Bob Brown, Nebraska, T
1965	Ray Rissmiller, Georgia, T (2)
1966	Randy Beisler, Indiana, DE
1967	Harry Jones, Arkansas, RB
1968	Tim Rossovich, Southern California, DE
1969	Leroy Keyes, Purdue, RB
1970	Steve Zabel, Oklahoma, TE
1971	Richard Harris, Grambling, DE
1972	John Reaves, Florida, QB
1973	Jerry Sisemore, Texas, T
	Charle Young, Southern California, TE
1974	Mitch Sutton, Kansas, DT (3)
1975	Bill Capraun, Miami, T (7)
1976	Mike Smith, Florida, DE (4)
1977	Skip Sharp, Kansas, DB (5)
1978	Reggie Wilkes, Georgia Tech, LB (3)
1979	Jerry Robinson, UCLA, LB
1980	Roynell Young, Alcorn State, DB
1981	Leonard Mitchell, Houston, DE
1982	Mike Quick, North Carolina State, WR
1983	Michael Haddix, Mississippi State, RB
1984	Kenny Jackson, Penn State, WR
1985	Kevin Allen, Indiana, T
1986	Keith Byars, Ohio State, RB
1987	Jerome Brown, Miami, DT
1988	Keith Jackson, Oklahoma, TE
1989	Jessie Small, Eastern Kentucky, LB (2)
1990	Ben Smith, Georgia, DB
1991	Antone Davis, Tennessee, T
1992	Siran Stacy, Alabama, RB (2)
1993	Lester Holmes, Jackson State, T
	Leonard Renfro, Colorado, DT
1994	Bernard Williams, Georgia, T
1995	Mike Mamula, Boston College, DE
1996	Jermane Mayberry, Texas A&M-Kingsville, T
1997	Jon Harris, Virginia, DE
1998	Tra Thomas, Florida State, T
1999	Donovan McNabb, Syracuse, QB
2000	Corey Simon, Florida State, DT

PITTSBURGH STEELERS

Year	Player, College, Position
1936	Bill Shakespeare, Notre Dame, B
1937	Mike Basrak, Duquesne, C
1938	Byron (Whizzer) White, Colorado, B
1939	Bill Patterson, Baylor, B (3)
1940	Kay Eakin, Arkansas, B
1941	Chet Gladchuk, Boston College, C (2)
1942	Bill Dudley, Virginia, B
1943	Bill Daley, Minnesota, B
1944	Johnny Podesto, St. Mary's, Calif., B
1945	Paul Duhart, Florida, B
1946	Felix (Doc) Blanchard, Army, B
1947	Hub Bechtol, Texas, E
1948	Dan Edwards, Georgia, E
1949	Bobby Gage, Clemson, B
1950	Lynn Chandnois, Michigan State, B
1951	Butch Avinger, Alabama, B
1952	Ed Modzelewski, Maryland, B
1953	Ted Marchibroda, St. Bonaventure, B
1954	Johnny Lattner, Notre Dame, B
1955	Frank Varrichione, Notre Dame, T
1956	Gary Glick, Colorado A&M, B
	Art Davis, Mississippi State, B
1957	Len Dawson, Purdue, B
1958	Larry Krutko, West Virginia, B (2)
1959	Tom Barnett, Purdue, B (8)
1960	Jack Spikes, Texas Christian, RB
1961	Myron Pottios, Notre Dame, LB (2)
1962	Bob Ferguson, Ohio State, RB
1963	Frank Atkinson, Stanford, T (8)
1964	Paul Martha, Pittsburgh, S
1965	Roy Jefferson, Utah, WR (2)
1966	Dick Leftridge, West Virginia, RB
1967	Don Shy, San Diego State, RB (2)
1968	Mike Taylor, Southern California, T
1969	Joe Greene, North Texas State, DT
1970	Terry Bradshaw, Louisiana Tech, QB
1971	Frank Lewis, Grambling, WR
1972	Franco Harris, Penn State, RB
1973	J.T. Thomas, Florida State, DB
1974	Lynn Swann, Southern California, WR
1975	Dave Brown, Michigan, DB
1976	Bennie Cunningham, Clemson, TE
1977	Robin Cole, New Mexico, LB
1978	Ron Johnson, Eastern Michigan, DB
1979	Greg Hawthorne, Baylor, RB
1980	Mark Malone, Arizona State, QB
1981	Keith Gary, Oklahoma, DE
1982	Walter Abercrombie, Baylor, RB
1983	Gabriel Rivera, Texas Tech, DT
1984	Louis Lipps, Southern Mississippi, WR
1985	Darryl Sims, Wisconsin, DE
1986	John Rienstra, Temple, G
1987	Rod Woodson, Purdue, DB
1988	Aaron Jones, Eastern Kentucky, DE
1989	Tim Worley, Georgia, RB
	Tom Ricketts, Pittsburgh, T
1990	Eric Green, Liberty, TE
1991	Huey Richardson, Florida, DE
1992	Leon Searcy, Miami, T
1993	Deon Figures, Colorado, DB
1994	Charles Johnson, Colorado, WR
1995	Mark Bruener, Washington, TE
1996	Jamain Stephens, North Carolina A&T, T
1997	Chad Scott, Maryland, DB
1998	Alan Faneca, Louisiana State, G

1999 Troy Edwards, Lousiana Tech, WR
2000 Plaxico Burress, Michigan State, WR

ST. LOUIS RAMS

Year Player, College, Position
1937 Johnny Drake, Purdue, B
1938 Corbett Davis, Indiana, B
1939 Parker Hall, Mississippi, B
1940 Ollie Cordill, Rice, B
1941 Rudy Mucha, Washington, C
1942 Jack Wilson, Baylor, B
1943 Mike Holovak, Boston College, B
1944 Tony Butkovich, Illinois, B
1945 Elroy (Crazylegs) Hirsch, Wisconsin, B
1946 Emil Sitko, Notre Dame, B
1947 Herman Wedemeyer, St. Mary's, Calif., B
1948 Tom Keane, West Virginia, B (2)
1949 Bobby Thomason, Virginia Military, B
1950 Ralph Pasquariello, Villanova, B
Stan West, Oklahoma, G
1951 Bud McFadin, Texas, G
1952 Bill Wade, Vanderbilt, QB
Bob Carey, Michigan State, E
1953 Donn Moomaw, UCLA, C
Ed Barker, Washington State, E
1954 Ed Beatty, Cincinnati, C
1955 Larry Morris, Georgia Tech, C
1956 Joe Marconi, West Virginia, B
Charles Horton, Vanderbilt, B
1957 Jon Arnett, Southern California, B
Del Shofner, Baylor, E
1958 Lou Michaels, Kentucky, T
Jim Phillips, Auburn, E
1959 Dick Bass, Pacific, B
Paul Dickson, Baylor, T
1960 Billy Cannon, Louisiana State, RB
1961 Marlin McKeever, Southern California, E-LB
1962 Roman Gabriel, North Carolina State, QB
Merlin Olsen, Utah State, DT
1963 Terry Baker, Oregon State, QB
Rufus Guthrie, Georgia Tech, G
1964 Bill Munson, Utah State, QB
1965 Clancy Williams, Washington State, CB
1966 Tom Mack, Michigan, G
1967 Willie Ellison, Texas Southern, RB (2)
1968 Gary Beban, UCLA, QB (2)
1969 Larry Smith, Florida, RB
Jim Seymour, Notre Dame, WR
Bob Klein, Southern California, TE
1970 Jack Reynolds, Tennessee, LB
1971 Isiah Robertson, Southern, LB
Jack Youngblood, Florida, DE
1972 Jim Bertelsen, Texas, RB (2)
1973 Cullen Bryant, Colorado, DB (2)
1974 John Cappelletti, Penn State, RB
1975 Mike Fanning, Notre Dame, DT
Dennis Harrah, Miami, T
Doug France, Ohio State, T
1976 Kevin McLain, Colorado State, LB
1977 Bob Brudzinski, Ohio State, LB
1978 Elvis Peacock, Oklahoma, RB
1979 George Andrews, Nebraska, LB
Kent Hill, Georgia Tech, T
1980 Johnnie Johnson, Texas, DB
1981 Mel Owens, Michigan, LB
1982 Barry Redden, Richmond, RB
1983 Eric Dickerson, Southern Methodist, RB
1984 Hal Stephens, East Carolina, DE (5)
1985 Jerry Gray, Texas, DB
1986 Mike Schad, Queen's University, Canada, T
1987 Donald Evans, Winston-Salem, DE (2)
1988 Gaston Green, UCLA, RB
Aaron Cox, Arizona State, WR
1989 Bill Hawkins, Miami, DE
Cleveland Gary, Miami, RB
1990 Bern Brostek, Washington, C
1991 Todd Lyght, Notre Dame, DB
1992 Sean Gilbert, Pittsburgh, DE
1993 Jerome Bettis, Notre Dame, RB
1994 Wayne Gandy, Auburn, T
1995 Kevin Carter, Florida, DE
1996 Lawrence Phillips, Nebraska, RB
Eddie Kennison, Louisiana State, WR
1997 Orlando Pace, Ohio State, T
1998 Grant Wistrom, Nebraska, DE
1999 Torry Holt, North Carolina State, WR
2000 Trung Canidate, Arizona, RB

SAN DIEGO CHARGERS

Year Player, College, Position
1960 Monty Stickles, Notre Dame, E
1961 Earl Faison, Indiana, DE
1962 Bob Ferguson, Ohio State, RB
1963 Walt Sweeney, Syracuse, G
1964 Ted Davis, Georgia Tech, LB
1965 Steve DeLong, Tennessee, DE
1966 Don Davis, Cal State-Los Angeles, DT
1967 Ron Billingsley, Wyoming, DE
1968 Russ Washington, Missouri, DT
Jimmy Hill, Texas A&I, DB
1969 Marty Domres, Columbia, QB
Bob Babich, Miami, Ohio, LB
1970 Walker Gillette, Richmond, WR
1971 Leon Burns, Long Beach State, RB
1972 Pete Lazetich, Stanford, DE (2)
1973 Johnny Rodgers, Nebraska, WR
1974 Bo Matthews, Colorado, RB
Don Goode, Kansas, LB
1975 Gary Johnson, Grambling, DT
Mike Williams, Louisiana State, DB
1976 Joe Washington, Oklahoma, RB
1977 Bob Rush, Memphis State, C
1978 John Jefferson, Arizona State, WR
1979 Kellen Winslow, Missouri, TE
1980 Ed Luther, San Jose State, QB (4)
1981 James Brooks, Auburn, RB
1982 Hollis Hall, Clemson, DB (7)
1983 Billy Ray Smith, Arkansas, LB
Gary Anderson, Arkansas, WR
Gill Byrd, San Jose State, DB
1984 Mossy Cade, Texas, DB
1985 Jim Lachey, Ohio State, G
1986 Leslie O'Neal, Oklahoma State, DE
James FitzPatrick, Southern California, T
1987 Rod Bernstine, Texas A&M, TE
1988 Anthony Miller, Tennessee, WR
1989 Burt Grossman, Pittsburgh, DE
1990 Junior Seau, Southern California, LB
1991 Stanley Richard, Texas, DB
1992 Chris Mims, Tennessee, DE
1993 Darrien Gordon, Stanford, DB
1994 Isaac Davis, Arkansas, G (2)
1995 Terrance Shaw, Stephen F. Austin, DB (2)
1996 Bryan Still, Virginia Tech, WR (2)
1997 Freddie Jones, North Carolina, TE (2)
1998 Ryan Leaf, Washington State, QB
1999 Jermaine Fazande, Oklahoma, RB (2)
2000 Rogers Beckett, Marshall, DB (2)

SAN FRANCISCO 49ERS

Year Player, College, Position
1950 Leo Nomellini, Minnesota, T
1951 Y.A. Tittle, Louisiana State, B
1952 Hugh McElhenny, Washington, B
1953 Harry Babcock, Georgia, E
Tom Stolhandske, Texas, E
1954 Bernie Faloney, Maryland, B
1955 Dickie Moegle, Rice, B
1956 Earl Morrall, Michigan State, B
1957 John Brodie, Stanford, B
1958 Jim Pace, Michigan, B
Charlie Krueger, Texas A&M, T
1959 Dave Baker, Oklahoma, B
Dan James, Ohio State, C
1960 Monty Stickles, Notre Dame, E
1961 Jimmy Johnson, UCLA, CB
Bernie Casey, Bowling Green, WR
Bill Kilmer, UCLA, QB
1962 Lance Alworth, Arkansas, WR
1963 Kermit Alexander, UCLA, CB
1964 Dave Parks, Texas Tech, WR
1965 Ken Willard, North Carolina, RB
George Donnelly, Illinois, DB
1966 Stan Hindman, Mississippi, DE
1967 Steve Spurrier, Florida, QB
Cas Banaszek, Northwestern, T
1968 Forrest Blue, Auburn, C
1969 Ted Kwalick, Penn State, TE
Gene Washington, Stanford, WR
1970 Cedrick Hardman, North Texas State, DE
Bruce Taylor, Boston U., DB
1971 Tim Anderson, Ohio State, DB
1972 Terry Beasley, Auburn, WR
1973 Mike Holmes, Texas Southern, DB
1974 Wilbur Jackson, Alabama, RB
Bill Sandifer, UCLA, DT
1975 Jimmy Webb, Mississippi State, DT
1976 Randy Cross, UCLA, C (2)
1977 Elmo Boyd, Eastern Kentucky, WR (3)
1978 Ken MacAfee, Notre Dame, TE
Dan Bunz, Cal State-Long Beach, LB
1979 James Owens, UCLA, WR (2)
1980 Earl Cooper, Rice, RB
Jim Stuckey, Clemson, DT
1981 Ronnie Lott, Southern California, DB
1982 Bubba Paris, Michigan, T (2)
1983 Roger Craig, Nebraska, RB (2)
1984 Todd Shell, Brigham Young, LB
1985 Jerry Rice, Mississippi Valley State, WR
1986 Larry Roberts, Alabama, DE (2)
1987 Harris Barton, North Carolina, T
Terrence Flagler, Clemson, RB
1988 Danny Stubbs, Miami, DE (2)
1989 Keith DeLong, Tennessee, LB
1990 Dexter Carter, Florida State, RB
1991 Ted Washington, Louisville, DT
1992 Dana Hall, Washington, DB
1993 Dana Stubblefield, Kansas, DT
Todd Kelly, Tennessee, DE
1994 Bryant Young, Notre Dame, DT
William Floyd, Florida State, RB
1995 J.J. Stokes, UCLA, WR
1996 Israel Ifeanyi, Southern California, DE (2)
1997 Jim Druckenmiller, Virginia Tech, QB
1998 R.W. McQuarters, Oklahoma State, DB
1999 Reggie McGrew, Florida, DT
2000 Julian Peterson, Michigan State, LB
Ahmed Plummer, Ohio State, DB

SEATTLE SEAHAWKS

Year Player, College, Position
1976 Steve Niehaus, Notre Dame, DT
1977 Steve August, Tulsa, G
1978 Keith Simpson, Memphis State, DB
1979 Manu Tuiasosopo, UCLA, DT
1980 Jacob Green, Texas A&M, DE
1981 Ken Easley, UCLA, DB
1982 Jeff Bryant, Clemson, DE
1983 Curt Warner, Penn State, RB
1984 Terry Taylor, Southern Illinois, DB
1985 Owen Gill, Iowa, RB (2)
1986 John L. Williams, Florida, RB
1987 Tony Woods, Pittsburgh, LB
1988 Brian Blades, Miami, WR (2)
1989 Andy Heck, Notre Dame, T
1990 Cortez Kennedy, Miami, DT
1991 Dan McGwire, San Diego State, QB
1992 Ray Roberts, Virginia, T
1993 Rick Mirer, Notre Dame, QB
1994 Sam Adams, Texas A&M, DT
1995 Joey Galloway, Ohio State, WR
1996 Pete Kendall, Boston College, T
1997 Shawn Springs, Ohio State, DB
Walter Jones, Florida State, T
1998 Anthony Simmons, Clemson, LB
1999 Lamar King, Saginaw Valley State, DE
2000 Shaun Alexander, Alabama, RB
Chris McIntosh, Wisconsin, T

TAMPA BAY BUCCANEERS

Year Player, College, Position
1976 Lee Roy Selmon, Oklahoma, DT
1977 Ricky Bell, Southern California, RB
1978 Doug Williams, Grambling, QB
1979 Greg Roberts, Oklahoma, G (2)
1980 Ray Snell, Wisconsin, G
1981 Hugh Green, Pittsburgh, LB
1982 Sean Farrell, Penn State, G
1983 Randy Grimes, Baylor, C (2)

FIRST-ROUND SELECTIONS

Year	Player, College, Position
1984	Keith Browner, Southern California, LB (2)
1985	Ron Holmes, Washington, DE
1986	Bo Jackson, Auburn, RB
	Roderick Jones, Southern Methodist, DB
1987	Vinny Testaverde, Miami, QB
1988	Paul Gruber, Wisconsin, T
1989	Broderick Thomas, Nebraska, LB
1990	Keith McCants, Alabama, LB
1991	Charles McRae, Tennessee, T
1992	Courtney Hawkins, Michigan State, WR (2)
1993	Eric Curry, Alabama, DE
1994	Trent Dilfer, Fresno State, QB
1995	Warren Sapp, Miami, DT
	Derrick Brooks, Florida State, LB
1996	Regan Upshaw, California, DE
	Marcus Jones, North Carolina, DT
1997	Warrick Dunn, Florida State, RB
	Reidel Anthony, Florida, WR
1998	Jacquez Green, Florida, WR (2)
1999	Anthony McFarland, Louisiana State, DT
2000	Cosey Coleman, Tennessee, G (2)

TENNESSEE TITANS

Year	Player, College, Position
1960	Billy Cannon, Louisiana State, RB
1961	Mike Ditka, Pittsburgh, E
1962	Ray Jacobs, Howard Payne, DT
1963	Danny Brabham, Arkansas, LB
1964	Scott Appleton, Texas, DT
1965	Lawrence Elkins, Baylor, WR
1966	Tommy Nobis, Texas, LB
1967	George Webster, Michigan State, LB
	Tom Regner, Notre Dame, G
1968	Mac Haik, Mississippi, WR (2)
1969	Ron Pritchard, Arizona State, LB
1970	Doug Wilkerson, N. Carolina Central, G
1971	Dan Pastorini, Santa Clara, QB
1972	Greg Sampson, Stanford, DE
1973	John Matuszak, Tampa, DE
	George Amundson, Iowa State, RB
1974	Steve Manstedt, Nebraska, LB (4)
1975	Robert Brazile, Jackson State, LB
	Don Hardeman, Texas A&I, RB
1976	Mike Barber, Louisiana Tech, TE (2)
1977	Morris Towns, Missouri, T
1978	Earl Campbell, Texas, RB
1979	Mike Stensrud, Iowa State, DE (2)
1980	Angelo Fields, Michigan State, T (2)
1981	Michael Holston, Morgan State, WR (3)
1982	Mike Munchak, Penn State, G
1983	Bruce Matthews, Southern California, T
1984	Dean Steinkuhler, Nebraska, T
1985	Ray Childress, Texas A&M, DE
	Richard Johnson, Wisconsin, DB
1986	Jim Everett, Purdue, QB
1987	Alonzo Highsmith, Miami, RB
	Haywood Jeffires, North Carolina St., WR
1988	Lorenzo White, Michigan State, RB
1989	David Williams, Florida, T
1990	Lamar Lathon, Houston, LB
1991	Mike Dumas, Indiana, DB (2)
1992	Eddie Robinson, Alabama State, LB (2)
1993	Brad Hopkins, Illinois, T
1994	Henry Ford, Arkansas, DE
1995	Steve McNair, Alcorn State, QB
1996	Eddie George, Ohio State, RB
1997	Kenny Holmes, Miami, DE
1998	Kevin Dyson, Utah, WR
1999	Jevon Kearse, Florida, DE
2000	Keith Bulluck, Syracuse, LB

WASHINGTON REDSKINS

Year	Player, College, Position
1936	Riley Smith, Alabama, B
1937	Sammy Baugh, Texas Christian, B
1938	Andy Farkas, Detroit, B
1939	I.B. Hale, Texas Christian, T
1940	Ed Boell, New York U., B
1941	Forest Evashevski, Michigan, B
1942	Orban (Spec) Sanders, Texas, B
1943	Jack Jenkins, Missouri, B
1944	Mike Micka, Colgate, B
1945	Jim Hardy, Southern California, B
1946	Cal Rossi, UCLA, B*
1947	Cal Rossi, UCLA, B
1948	Harry Gilmer, Alabama, B
	Lowell Tew, Alabama, B
1949	Rob Goode, Texas A&M, B
1950	George Thomas, Oklahoma, B
1951	Leon Heath, Oklahoma, B
1952	Larry Isbell, Baylor, B
1953	Jack Scarbath, Maryland, B
1954	Steve Meilinger, Kentucky, E
1955	Ralph Guglielmi, Notre Dame, B
1956	Ed Vereb, Maryland, B
1957	Don Bosseler, Miami, B
1958	Mike Sommer, George Washington, B (2)
1959	Don Allard, Boston College, B
1960	Richie Lucas, Penn State, QB
1961	Norman Snead, Wake Forest, QB
	Joe Rutgens, Illinois, DT
1962	Ernie Davis, Syracuse, RB
1963	Pat Richter, Wisconsin, TE
1964	Charley Taylor, Arizona State, RB-WR
1965	Bob Breitenstein, Tulsa, T (2)
1966	Charlie Gogolak, Princeton, K
1967	Ray McDonald, Idaho, RB
1968	Jim Smith, Oregon, DB
1969	Eugene Epps, Texas-El Paso, DB (2)
1970	Bill Bundige, Colorado, DT (2)
1971	Cotton Speyrer, Texas, WR (2)
1972	Moses Denson, Maryland State, RB (8)
1973	Charles Cantrell, Lamar, G (5)
1974	Jon Keyworth, Colorado, TE (6)
1975	Mike Thomas, Nevada-Las Vegas, RB (6)
1976	Mike Hughes, Baylor, G (5)
1977	Duncan McColl, Stanford, DE (4)
1978	Tony Green, Florida, RB (6)
1979	Don Warren, San Diego State, TE (4)
1980	Art Monk, Syracuse, WR
1981	Mark May, Pittsburgh, T
1982	Vernon Dean, San Diego State, DB (2)
1983	Darrell Green, Texas A&I, DB
1984	Bob Slater, Oklahoma, DT (2)
1985	Tory Nixon, San Diego State, DB (2)
1986	Markus Koch, Boise State, DE (2)
1987	Brian Davis, Nebraska, DB (2)
1988	Chip Lohmiller, Minnesota, K (2)
1989	Tracy Rocker, Auburn, DT (3)
1990	Andre Collins, Penn State, LB (2)
1991	Bobby Wilson, Michigan State, DT
1992	Desmond Howard, Michigan, WR
1993	Tom Carter, Notre Dame, DB
1994	Heath Shuler, Tennessee, QB
1995	Michael Westbrook, Colorado, WR
1996	Andre Johnson, Penn State, T
1997	Kenard Lang, Miami, DE
1998	Stephen Alexander, Oklahoma, TE (2)
1999	Champ Bailey, Georgia, DB
2000	LaVar Arrington, Penn State, LB
	Chris Samuels, Alabama, T

**Choice lost because of ineligibility*

ASSOCIATED PRESS NFL MOST VALUABLE PLAYERS

NFL MOST VALUABLE PLAYERS NAMED BY *ASSOCIATED PRESS* IN BALLOTING BY A NATIONWIDE PANEL OF MEDIA:

YEAR	PLAYER	POS.	TEAM	ACCOMPLISHMENTS
1957	Jim Brown	RB	Cleveland Browns	Rushed for league-leading 942 yards and added 9 TDs as a rookie.
1958	Gino Marchetti	DE	Baltimore Colts	Leader of defense that permitted league-low 1,291 rushing yards and division-low 203 points.
1959	Charley Conerly	QB	New York Giants	Passed for 14 TDs vs. 4 interceptions. Led offense to division-leading 284 points.
1960	Norm Van Brocklin	QB	Philadelphia Eagles	Guided Eagles to first division title since 1949. Passed for 2,471 yards and 24 TDs.
	Joe Schmidt	LB	Detroit Lions	Team went 7-2 after 0-3 start when he returned from injury. Scored 2 defensive TDs.
1961	Paul Hornung	RB	Green Bay Packers	Led league in scoring for second straight season with 146 points (10 TD, 15 FG, 41 PAT).
1962	Jim Taylor	RB	Green Bay Packers	League rushing champion with 1,474 yards. Scored then all-time record 19 touchdowns.
1963	Y.A. Tittle	QB	New York Giants	Set then all-time season record with 36 TD passes. Guided league's top offense (5,024 yards).
1964	Johnny Unitas	QB	Baltimore Colts	Guided Colts to NFL's best record (12-2) and league's top offensive attack (4,779 yards).
1965	Jim Brown	RB	Cleveland Browns	Leader of NFL's top rushing attack. Led league with 1,544 yards, added 21 total TDs.
1966	Bart Starr	QB	Green Bay Packers	Passed for 14 touchdowns vs. 3 interceptions. Led Packers to league-best 12-2 record.
1967	Johnny Unitas	QB	Baltimore Colts	Passed for 3,428 yards and 20 touchdowns. Led Colts to 11-1-2 record.
1968	Earl Morrall	QB	Baltimore Colts	Guided Colts to NFL-best 13-1 record. Led league with 26 touchdown passes.
1969	Roman Gabriel	QB	Los Angeles Rams	Led NFL with 24 touchdown passes. Guided Rams to 11-3 record.
1970	John Brodie	QB	San Francisco 49ers	Took 49ers to first-ever division title. Threw NFL-best 24 TD passes.
1971	Alan Page	DT	Minnesota Vikings	Led defense that allowed NFL-low 139 points. Vikings won fourth straight NFC Central title.
1972	Larry Brown	RB	Washington Redskins	Led conference with 1,216 rushing yards. Redskins had NFC-best 11-3 record.
1973	O.J. Simpson	RB	Buffalo Bills	Rushed for then all-time record 2,003 yards, including three 200-yard performances.
1974	Ken Stabler	QB	Oakland Raiders	Led league with 26 touchdown passes vs. 12 interceptions. Raiders had NFL-best 12-2 record.
1975	Fran Tarkenton	QB	Minnesota Vikings	Tied for league-best 12-2 record. Led NFC with 91.7 passer rating.
1976	Bert Jones	QB	Baltimore Colts	Threw 24 touchdowns vs. 9 interceptions for 102.5 passer rating.
1977	Walter Payton	RB	Chicago Bears	Rushed for league-leading 1,852 yards and 16 total touchdowns.
1978	Terry Bradshaw	QB	Pittsburgh Steelers	Led Steelers to league-leading 14-2 mark. Set team record with 28 TD passes.
1979	Earl Campbell	RB	Houston Oilers	Led league with 1,697 rushing yards and 19 touchdowns.
1980	Brian Sipe	QB	Cleveland Browns	NFL-best 91.4 passer rating. Set Browns' records with 30 TD passes and 4,132 yards.
1981	Ken Anderson	QB	Cincinnati Bengals	Led Bengals to first division title since 1973. NFL-high 98.5 passer rating.
1982	Mark Moseley	K	Washington Redskins	Converted 20 of 21 FGs. Set then consecutive field-goal record at 23 (including last three in '81).
1983	Joe Theismann	QB	Washington Redskins	Leader of offense that scored NFL record 541 points. Redskins had NFL-best 14-2 record.
1984	Dan Marino	QB	Miami Dolphins	Set NFL records with 5,084 yards and 48 TD passes. Led Dolphins to AFC-best 14-2 mark.
1985	Marcus Allen	RB	Los Angeles Raiders	Rushed for league-leading 1,759 yards. Tied for AFC lead with 11 rushing touchdowns.
1986	Lawrence Taylor	LB	New York Giants	Recorded league-high 20.5 sacks, and led Giants' second-ranked defense (297.3).
1987	John Elway	QB	Denver Broncos	In 12 games, passed for 19 TDs and 3,198 yards, including four 300-yard games.
1988	Boomer Esiason	QB	Cincinnati Bengals	Led NFL with 97.4 passer rating. Tied for AFC lead with 28 TD passes.
1989	Joe Montana	QB	San Francisco 49ers	Set then NFL record with 112.4 passer rating, including 70.2 completion percentage.
1990	Joe Montana	QB	San Francisco 49ers	Led 49ers to league-best 14-2 record. Completed NFC-high 61.7 percent of passes.
1991	Thurman Thomas	RB	Buffalo Bills	Recorded league-high 2,038 yards from scrimmage (1,407 rushing, 631 receiving).
1992	Steve Young	QB	San Francisco 49ers	NFL's top passer with 107.0 rating. Led 49ers to league-best 14-2 record.
1993	Emmitt Smith	RB	Dallas Cowboys	Led league in rushing (1,486 yards) for third straight year despite missing first two games.
1994	Steve Young	QB	San Francisco 49ers	Compiled NFL all-time best 112.8 passer rating. Completed more than 70 percent of his passes.
1995	Brett Favre	QB	Green Bay Packers	Led league with 38 touchdown passes and NFC with 99.5 passer rating.
1996	Brett Favre	QB	Green Bay Packers	Led Packers to top conference record (13-3). Threw NFL-best 39 TD passes.
1997	Brett Favre	QB	Green Bay Packers	Led league with 35 touchdown passes. Led NFC with 3,867 passing yards
	Barry Sanders	RB	Detroit Lions	Rushed for all-time second-best 2,053 yards, including record 14 straight 100-yard games.
1998	Terrell Davis	RB	Denver Broncos	Rushed for 2,008 yards and scored league-best 23 total touchdowns.
1999	Kurt Warner	QB	St. Louis Rams	Became the second QB in history to throw for 40 touchdowns in a season (41).

Total *Associated Press* NFL MVPs: 45
Two-time Winners: Jim Brown, Brett Favre (3), Joe Montana, Johnny Unitas, Steve Young

ASSOCIATED PRESS NFL MVP BY POSITION

Quarterback:	27	**Defensive End:**	1
Running Back:	13	**Defensive Tackle:**	1
Linebacker:	2	**Kicker:**	1

ASSOCIATED PRESS MVPs WHO WON SUPER BOWL/NFL CHAMPIONSHIP IN SAME SEASON: 14

1958	Gino Marchetti	Baltimore Colts
1960	Norm Van Brocklin	Philadelphia Eagles
1961	Paul Hornung	Green Bay Packers
1962	Jim Taylor	Green Bay Packers
1966	Bart Starr	Green Bay Packers
1968	Earl Morrall	Baltimore Colts
1978	Terry Bradshaw	Pittsburgh Steelers
1982	Mark Moseley	Washington Redskins
1986	Lawrence Taylor	New York Giants
1989	Joe Montana	San Francisco 49ers
1993	Emmitt Smith	Dallas Cowboys
1994	Steve Young	San Francisco 49ers
1996	Brett Favre	Green Bay Packers
1998	Terrell Davis	Denver Broncos
1999	Kurt Warner	St. Louis Rams

ASSOCIATED PRESS MVPs BY TEAM

6	Green Bay Packers
5	Baltimore Colts San Francisco 49ers
3	Cleveland Browns New York Giants Washington Redskins
2	Buffalo Bills Cincinnati Bengals Denver Broncos Detroit Lions Minnesota Vikings Oakland/Los Angeles Raiders St. Louis/Los Angeles Rams
1	Chicago Bears Dallas Cowboys Houston Oilers Miami Dolphins Philadelphia Eagles Pittsburgh Steelers

MILLER LITE PLAYERS OF THE YEAR

YEAR	PLAYER	POS.	TEAM
1989	Joe Montana	QB	San Francisco 49ers
1990	Joe Montana	QB	San Francisco 49ers
1991	Thurman Thomas	RB	Buffalo Bills
1992	Steve Young	QB	San Francisco 49ers
1993	Emmitt Smith	RB	Dallas Cowboys
1994	Steve Young	QB	San Francisco 49ers
1995	Brett Favre	QB	Green Bay Packers
1996	Brett Favre	QB	Green Bay Packers
1997	Barry Sanders	RB	Detroit Lions
1998	Randall Cunningham	QB	Minnesota Vikings
1999	Kurt Warner	QB	St. Louis Rams

ALL-TIME NFL TEAMS

75TH ANNIVERSARY ALL-TIME TEAM

Chosen by a selection committee of media and league personnel in 1994.

Position	Name	Team(s)	Ht.	Wt.	College
OFFENSE					
QB	Sammy Baugh	Washington Redskins (1937-52)	6-2	180	Texas Christian
QB	Otto Graham	Cleveland Browns (1946-55)	6-1	195	Northwestern
QB	Joe Montana	San Francisco 49ers (1979-92), Kansas City Chiefs (1993-94)	6-2	195	Notre Dame
QB	Johnny Unitas	Baltimore Colts (1956-72), San Diego Chargers (1973)	6-1	195	Louisville
RB	Jim Brown	Cleveland Browns (1957-65)	6-2	232	Syracuse
RB	Marion Motley	Cleveland Browns (1946-53), Pittsburgh Steelers (1955)	6-1	238	Nevada-Reno
RB	Bronko Nagurski	Chicago Bears (1930-37, 1943)	6-2	225	Minnesota
RB	Walter Payton	Chicago Bears (1975-87)	5-10	202	Jackson State
RB	Gale Sayers	Chicago Bears (1965-71)	6-0	200	Kansas
RB	O.J. Simpson	Buffalo Bills (1969-77), San Francisco 49ers (1978-79)	6-1	212	Southern California
RB	Steve Van Buren	Philadelphia Eagles (1944-51)	6-1	200	Louisiana State
WR	Lance Alworth	San Diego Chargers (1962-70), Dallas Cowboys (1971-72)	6-0	184	Arkansas
WR	Raymond Berry	Baltimore Colts (1955-67)	6-2	187	Southern Methodist
WR	Don Hutson	Green Bay Packers (1935-45)	6-1	180	Alabama
WR	Jerry Rice	San Francisco 49ers (1985-present)	6-2	200	Miss. Valley State
TE	Mike Ditka	Chicago Bears (1961-66), Philadelphia Eagles (1967-68), Dallas Cowboys (1969-72)	6-3	225	Pittsburgh
TE	Kellen Winslow	San Diego Chargers (1979-87)	6-5	250	Missouri
T	Roosevelt Brown	New York Giants (1953-65)	6-3	255	Morgan State
T	Forrest Gregg	Green Bay Packers (1956, 1958-70)	6-4	250	Southern Methodist
T	Anthony Muñoz	Cincinnati Bengals (1980-92)	6-6	285	Southern California
G	John Hannah	New England Patriots (1973-85)	6-3	265	Alabama
G	Jim Parker	Baltimore Colts (1957-67)	6-3	273	Ohio State
G	Gene Upshaw	Oakland Raiders (1967-81)	6-5	255	Texas A&I
C	Mel Hein	New York Giants (1931-45)	6-2	225	Washington State
C	Mike Webster	Pittsburgh Steelers (1974-88), Kansas City Chiefs (1989-90)	6-2	250	Wisconsin
DEFENSE					
DE	David (Deacon) Jones	Los Angeles Rams (1961-71), San Diego Chargers (1972-73), Washington Redskins (1974)	6-5	250	Miss. Vocational
DE	Gino Marchetti	Dallas Texans (1952), Baltimore Colts (1953-64,1966)	6-4	245	San Francisco
DE	Reggie White	Philadelphia Eagles (1985-95), Green Bay Packers (1993-present)	6-5	290	Tennessee
DT	Joe Greene	Pittsburgh Steelers (1969-81)	6-4	260	North Texas State
DT	Bob Lilly	Dallas Cowboys (1961-74)	6-5	260	Texas Christian
DT	Merlin Olsen	Los Angeles Rams (1962-76)	6-5	270	Utah State
LB	Dick Butkus	Chicago Bears (1965-73)	6-3	245	Illinois
LB	Jack Ham	Pittsburgh Steelers (1971-82)	6-1	225	Penn State
LB	Ted Hendricks	Baltimore Colts (1969-73), Green Bay Packers (1974), Oakland/L.A. Raiders (1975-83)	6-7	235	Miami
LB	Jack Lambert	Pittsburgh Steelers (1974-84)	6-4	220	Kent State
LB	Willie Lanier	Kansas City Chiefs (1967-77)	6-1	245	Morgan State
LB	Ray Nitschke	Green Bay Packers (1958-72)	6-3	235	Illinois
LB	Lawrence Taylor	New York Giants (1981-93)	6-3	243	North Carolina
CB	Mel Blount	Pittsburgh Steelers (1970-83)	6-3	205	Southern
CB	Mike Haynes	New England Patriots (1976-82), Los Angeles Raiders (1983-89)	6-2	190	Arizona State
CB	Dick (Night Train) Lane	Los Angeles Rams (1952-53), Chicago Cardinals (1954-59), Detroit Lions (1960-65)	6-2	210	Scottsbluff JC
CB	Rod Woodson	Pittsburgh Steelers (1987-96), San Francisco 49ers (1997)	6-0	200	Purdue
S	Ken Houston	Houston Oilers (1967-72), Washington Redskins (1973-80)	6-3	198	Prairie View A&M
S	Ronnie Lott	San Francisco 49ers (1981-90), Los Angeles Raiders (1991-92), New York Jets (1993-94)	6-0	200	Southern California
S	Larry Wilson	St. Louis Cardinals (1960-72)	6-0	190	Utah
SPECIAL TEAMS					
P	Ray Guy	Oakland/L.A. Raiders (1973-86)	6-3	190	Southern Miss.
K	Jan Stenerud	Kansas City Chiefs (1967-79), Green Bay Packers (1980-83), Minnesota Vikings (1984-85)	6-2	190	Montana State
PR	Billy (White Shoes) Johnson	Houston Oilers (1974-80), Atlanta Falcons (1982-87), Washington Redskins (1988)	5-9	170	Widener
KR	Gale Sayers	Chicago Bears (1965-71)	6-0	200	Kansas

75TH ANNIVERSARY ALL-TWO-WAY TEAM

Positions	
Quarterback, Defensive Halfback, Punter	Sammy Baugh
Center, Linebacker	Chuck Bednarik
Quarterback, Defensive Halfback, Punter	Earl (Dutch) Clark
Tackle, Defensive Tackle	George Connor
Guard, Defensive Tackle	Danny Fortmann
Center, Defensive Tackle	Mel Hein
Tackle, Defensive Tackle, Punter	Wilbur (Pete) Henry
Back, Defensive Halfback	Bill Hewitt
Fullback, Linebacker, Kicker	Clarke Hinkle
Tackle, Defensive Tackle	Cal Hubbard
End, Defensive Halfback	Don Hutson
Back, Defensive Back	George McAfee
Fullback, Linebacker	Marion Motley
Guard-Tackle, Defensive Tackle	George Musso
Fullback, Linebacker	Bronko Nagurski
Halfback, Defensive Halfback	Ernie Nevers
End, Defensive Back	Pete Pihos
Tackle, Defensive Tackle	Joe Stydahar
Running Back, Defensive Back	Steve Van Buren

50TH ANNIVERSARY TEAM

Chosen by the Hall of Fame Selection Committee in 1969.

Offense	
Split End	Don Hutson
Tight End	John Mackey
Tackle	Cal Hubbard
Guard	Jerry Kramer
Center	Chuck Bednarik
Flanker	Elroy Hirsch
Quarterback	Johnny Unitas
Halfback	Jim Thorpe
Halfback	Gale Sayers
Fullback	Jim Brown
Kicker	Lou Groza

Defense	
End	Gino Marchetti
Tackle	Leo Nomellini
Linebacker	Ray Nitschke
Cornerback	Dick (Night Train) Lane
Safety	Emlen Tunnell

SUPER BOWL SILVER ANNIVERSARY TEAM

Chosen by the fans in 1990 prior to Super Bowl XXV.

Head Coach — Vince Lombardi

Offense	
Quarterback	Joe Montana
Running Back	Franco Harris
Running Back	Larry Csonka
Wide Receiver	Lynn Swann
Wide Receiver	Jerry Rice
Tight End	Dave Casper
Tackle	Art Shell
Tackle	Forrest Gregg
Guard	Gene Upshaw
Guard	Jerry Kramer
Center	Mike Webster

Defense	
Defensive End	L.C. Greenwood
Defensive End	Ed (Too Tall) Jones
Defensive Tackle	Joe Greene
Defensive Tackle	Randy White
Inside Linebacker	Jack Lambert
Inside Linebacker	Mike Singletary
Outside Linebacker	Jack Ham
Outside Linebacker	Ted Hendricks
Cornerback	Ronnie Lott
Cornerback	Mel Blount
Safety	Donnie Shell
Safety	Willie Wood

Special Teams	
Punter	Ray Guy
Kicker	Jan Stenerud
Kick Returner	John Taylor

ALL-TIME NFL TEAMS

All-Decade teams chosen by the Hall of Fame Selection Committee Members.

1920's ALL-DECADE TEAM

End	Guy Chamberlin
End	Lavern Dilweg
End	George Halas
Tackle	Ed Healey
Tackle	Wilbur (Pete) Henry
Tackle	Cal Hubbard
Tackle	Steve Owen
Guard	Hunk Anderson
Guard	Walt Kiesling
Guard	Mike Michalske
Center	George Trafton
Quarterback	Jimmy Conzelman
Quarterback	John (Paddy) Driscoll
Halfback	Harold (Red) Grange
Halfback	Joe Guyon
Halfback	Earl (Curly) Lambeau
Halfback	Jim Thorpe
Fullback	Ernie Nevers

1930's ALL-DECADE TEAM

End	Bill Hewitt
End	Don Hutson
End	Wayne Millner
End	Gaynell Tinsley
Tackle	George Christensen
Tackle	Frank Cope
Tackle	Glen (Turk) Edwards
Tackle	Bill Lee
Tackle	Joe Stydahar
Guard	Grover (Ox) Emerson
Guard	Dan Fortmann
Guard	Charles (Buckets) Goldenberg
Guard	Russ Letlow
Center	Mel Hein
Center	George Svendsen
Quarterback	Earl (Dutch) Clark
Quarterback	Arnie Herber
Quarterback	Cecil Isbell
Halfback	Cliff Battles
Halfback	Johnny (Blood) McNally
Halfback	Beattie Feathers
Halfback	Alphonse (Tuffy) Leemans
Halfback	Ken Strong
Fullback	Clarke Hinkle
Fullback	Bronko Nagurski

1940's ALL-DECADE TEAM

End	Jim Benton
End	Jack Ferrante
End	Ken Kavanaugh
End	Dante Lavelli
End	Pete Pihos
End	Mac Speedie
End	Ed Sprinkle
Tackle	Al Blozis
Tackle	George Connor
Tackle	Frank (Bucko) Kilroy
Tackle	Buford (Baby) Ray
Tackle	Vic Sears
Tackle	Al Wistert
Guard	Bruno Banducci
Guard	Bill Edwards
Guard	Garrard (Buster) Ramsey
Guard	Bill Willis
Guard	Len Younce
Center	Charley Brock
Center	Clyde (Bulldog) Turner
Center	Alex Wojciechowicz
Quarterback	Sammy Baugh
Quarterback	Sid Luckman
Quarterback	Bob Waterfield
Halfback	Tony Canadeo
Halfback	Bill Dudley
Halfback	George McAfee
Halfback	Charley Trippi
Halfback	Steve Van Buren
Halfback	Byron (Whizzer) White
Fullback	Pat Harder
Fullback	Marion Motley
Fullback	Bill Osmanski

1950's ALL-DECADE TEAM

Offense

End	Raymond Berry
End	Tom Fears
End	Bobby Walston
Halfback-End	Elroy (Crazylegs) Hirsch
Tackle	Roosevelt Brown
Tackle	Bob St. Clair
Guard	Dick Barwegan
Guard	Jim Parker
Guard	Dick Stanfel
Center	Chuck Bednarik
Quarterback	Otto Graham
Quarterback	Bobby Layne
Quarterback	Norm Van Brocklin
Halfback	Frank Gifford
Halfback	Ollie Matson
Halfback	Hugh McElhenny
Halfback	Lenny Moore
Fullback	Alan Ameche
Fullback	Joe Perry
Kicker	Lou Groza

Defense

End	Len Ford
End	Gino Marchetti
Tackle	Art Donovan
Tackle	Leo Nomellini
Tackle	Ernie Stautner
Linebacker	Joe Fortunato
Linebacker	Bill George
Linebacker	Sam Huff
Linebacker	Joe Schmidt
Halfback	Jack Butler
Halfback	Dick (Night Train) Lane
Safety	Jack Christiansen
Safety	Yale Lary
Safety	Emlen Tunnell

1960's ALL-DECADE TEAM

Offense

Split End	Del Shofner
Split End	Charley Taylor
Flanker	Gary Collins
Flanker	Boyd Dowler
Tight End	John Mackey
Tackle	Bob Brown
Tackle	Forrest Gregg
Tackle	Ralph Neely
Guard	Gene Hickerson
Guard	Jerry Kramer
Guard	Howard Mudd
Center	Jim Ringo
Quarterback	Sonny Jurgensen
Quarterback	Bart Starr
Quarterback	Johnny Unitas
Halfback	John David Crow
Halfback	Paul Hornung
Halfback	Leroy Kelly
Halfback	Gale Sayers
Fullback	Jim Brown
Fullback	Jim Taylor
Kicker	Jim Bakken

Defense

End	Doug Atkins
End	Willie Davis
End	David (Deacon) Jones
Tackle	Alex Karras
Tackle	Bob Lilly
Tackle	Merlin Olsen
Linebacker	Dick Butkus
Linebacker	Larry Morris
Linebacker	Ray Nitschke
Linebacker	Tommy Nobis
Linebacker	Dave Robinson
Cornerback	Herb Adderley
Cornerback	Lem Barney
Cornerback	Bobby Boyd
Safety	Eddie Meador
Safety	Larry Wilson
Safety	Willie Wood
Punter	Don Chandler

1970's ALL-DECADE TEAM

Offense

Wide Receiver	Harold Carmichael
Wide Receiver	Drew Pearson
Wide Receiver	Lynn Swann
Wide Receiver	Paul Warfield
Tight End	Dave Casper
Tight End	Charlie Sanders
Tackle	Dan Dierdorf
Tackle	Art Shell
Tackle	Rayfield Wright
Tackle	Ron Yary
Guard	Joe DeLamielleure
Guard	John Hannah
Guard	Larry Little
Guard	Gene Upshaw
Center	Jim Langer
Center	Mike Webster
Quarterback	Terry Bradshaw
Quarterback	Ken Stabler
Quarterback	Roger Staubach
Running Back	Earl Campbell
Running Back	Franco Harris
Running Back	Walter Payton
Running Back	O.J. Simpson
Kicker	Garo Yepremian

Defense

End	Carl Eller
End	L.C. Greenwood
End	Harvey Martin
End	Jack Youngblood
Tackle	Joe Greene
Tackle	Bob Lilly
Tackle	Merlin Olsen
Tackle	Alan Page
Linebacker	Bobby Bell
Linebacker	Robert Brazile
Linebacker	Dick Butkus
Linebacker	Jack Ham
Linebacker	Ted Hendricks
Linebacker	Jack Lambert
Cornerback	Willie Brown
Cornerback	Jimmy Johnson
Cornerback	Roger Wehrli
Cornerback	Louis Wright
Safety	Dick Anderson
Safety	Cliff Harris
Safety	Ken Houston
Safety	Larry Wilson
Punter	Ray Guy

1980's ALL-DECADE TEAM

Offense

Wide Receiver	Jerry Rice
Wide Receiver	Steve Largent
Wide Receiver	James Lofton
Wide Receiver	Art Monk
Tight End	Kellen Winslow
Tight End	Ozzie Newsome
Tackle	Anthony Munoz
Tackle	Jim Covert
Tackle	Gary Zimmerman
Tackle	Joe Jacoby
Guard	John Hannah
Guard	Russ Grimm
Guard	Bill Fralic
Guard	Mike Munchak
Center	Dwight Stephenson
Center	Mike Webster
Quarterback	Joe Montana
Quarterback	Dan Fouts
Running Back	Walter Payton
Running Back	Eric Dickerson
Running Back	Roger Craig
Running Back	John Riggins

Defense

End	Reggie White
End	Howie Long
End	Lee Roy Selmon
End	Bruce Smith
Tackle	Randy White
Tackle	Dan Hampton
Tackle	Keith Millard
Tackle	Dave Butz
Linebacker	Mike Singletary
Linebacker	Lawrence Taylor
Linebacker	Ted Hendricks
Linebacker	Jack Lambert
Linebacker	Andre Tippett
Linebacker	John Anderson
Linebacker	Carl Banks
Cornerback	Mike Haynes
Cornerback	Mel Blount
Cornerback	Frank Minnifield
Cornerback	Lester Hayes
Safety	Ronnie Lott
Safety	Kenny Easley
Safety	Deron Cherry
Safety	Joey Browner
Safety	Nolan Cromwell

Specialists

Punter	Sean Landeta
Punter	Reggie Roby
Kicker	Morten Andersen
Kicker	Gary Anderson
Kicker	Eddie Murray
Punt Returner	Billy (White Shoes) Johnson
Punt Returner	John Taylor
Kick Returner	Mike Nelms
Kick Returner	Rick Upchurch
Coach	Bill Walsh
Coach	Chuck Noll

ALL-TIME NFL TEAMS

ALL-TIME AFL TEAM

Chosen by 1969 AFL Hall of Fame Selection Committee members.

Offense

Flanker	Lance Alworth
End	Don Maynard
Tight End	Fred Arbanas
Tackle	Ron Mix
Tackle	Jim Tyrer
Guard	Ed Budde
Guard	Billy Shaw
Center	Jim Otto
Quarterback	Joe Namath
Running Back	Clem Daniels
Running Back	Paul Lowe

Defense

End	Jerry Mays
End	Gerry Philbin
Tackle	Houston Antwine
Tackle	Tom Sestak
Linebacker	Bobby Bell
Linebacker	George Webster
Linebacker	Nick Buoniconti
Cornerback	Willie Brown
Cornerback	Dave Grayson
Safety	Johnny Robinson
Safety	George Saimes

Special Teams

Kicker	George Blanda
Punter	Jerrel Wilson

ALL-TIME NFL TEAM

Chosen by members of the Hall of Fame Selection Committee in 2000 for the book NFL's Greatest.

Offense

Wide Receiver	Don Hutson
Wide Receiver	Jerry Rice
Tight End	John Mackey
Tackle	Roosevelt Brown
Tackle	Anthony Muñoz
Guard	John Hannah
Guard	Jim Parker
Center	Mike Webster
Quarterback	Johnny Unitas
Running Back	Jim Brown
Running Back	Walter Payton

Defense

End	Deacon Jones
End	Reggie White
Tackle	Joe Greene
Tackle	Bob Lilly
Middle Linebacker	Dick Butkus
Outside Linebacker	Jack Ham
Outside Linebacker	Lawrence Taylor
Cornerback	Mel Blount
Cornerback	Dick (Night Train) Lane
Safety	Ronnie Lott
Safety	Larry Wilson

Special Teams

Kicker	Jan Stenerud
Punter	Ray Guy
Kick Returner	Gale Sayers
Punt Returner	Deion Sanders
Special Teams	Steve Tasker

AFL-NFL 1960-1984 ALL-STAR TEAM

Chosen by the Hall of Fame Selection Committee in 1985.

Offense

Quarterback	Johnny Unitas
Running Back	Jim Brown
Running Back	O.J. Simpson
Wide Receiver	Lance Alworth
Wide Receiver	Raymond Berry
Tight End	Kellen Winslow
Tight End	Forrest Gregg
Tight End	Ron Mix
Guard	Jim Parker
Guard	John Hannah
Center	Jim Otto

Defense

End	Gino Marchetti
End	Willie Davis
Tackle	Bob Lilly
Tackle	Merlin Olsen
Linebacker	Dick Butkus
Linebacker	Jack Lambert
Linebacker	Ray Nitschke
Cornerback	Willie Brown
Cornerback	Dick (Night Train) Lane
Safety	Larry Wilson
Safety	Yale Lary

Special Teams

Punter	Ray Guy
Kicker	Jan Stenerud
Kick Returner	Gale Sayers
Kick Returner	Rick Upchurch
Coach	Don Shula
Coach	Vince Lombardi

Records

ALL-TIME RECORDS

Compiled by Elias Sports Bureau

The following records reflect all available official information on the National Football League from its formation in 1920 to date. Also included are all applicable records from the American Football League, 1960-69.

Individuals eligible for Rookie records are players who were in their first season of professional football and had not been on the roster of another professional football team, including teams in other leagues, for any regular-season or postseason games in a previous season. Eligible players, therefore, include those who were under contract to a National Football League club for a previous season but were terminated prior to their club's first regular-season game and not re-signed, or who were placed on Reserve/Injured (or another category of the Reserve List) prior to their club's first regular-season game and were not activated during the rest of the regular season or postseason.

INDIVIDUAL RECORDS

SERVICE

Most Seasons

26 George Blanda, Chi. Bears, 1949, 1950-58; Baltimore, 1950; Houston, 1960-66; Oakland, 1967-75
21 Earl Morrall, San Francisco, 1956; Pittsburgh, 1957-58; Detroit, 1958-64; N.Y. Giants, 1965-67; Baltimore, 1968-71; Miami, 1972-76
20 Jim Marshall, Cleveland, 1960; Minnesota, 1961-79
Jackie Slater, L.A. Rams, 1976-94; St. Louis, 1995

Most Seasons, One Club

20 Jackie Slater, L.A. Rams, 1976-94; St. Louis, 1995
19 Jim Marshall, Minnesota, 1961-79
18 Jim Hart, St. Louis, 1966-83
Jeff Van Note, Atlanta, 1969-86
Pat Leahy, N.Y. Jets, 1974-91

Most Games Played, Career

340 George Blanda, Chi. Bears, 1949, 1950-58; Baltimore, 1950; Houston, 1960-66; Oakland, 1967-75
282 Jim Marshall, Cleveland, 1960; Minnesota, 1961-79
278 Clay Matthews, Cleveland, 1978-93; Atlanta, 1994-96

Most Consecutive Games Played, Career

282 Jim Marshall, Cleveland, 1960; Minnesota, 1961-79
240 Mick Tingelhoff, Minnesota, 1962-78
234 Jim Bakken, St. Louis, 1962-78

SCORING

Most Seasons Leading League

5 Don Hutson, Green Bay, 1940-44
Gino Cappelletti, Boston, 1961, 1963-66
3 Earl (Dutch) Clark, Portsmouth, 1932; Detroit, 1935-36
Pat Harder, Chi. Cardinals, 1947-49
Paul Hornung, Green Bay, 1959-61
2 Jack Manders, Chi. Bears, 1934, 1937
Gordy Soltau, San Francisco, 1952-53
Doak Walker, Detroit, 1950, 1955
Gene Mingo, Denver, 1960, 1962
Jim Turner, N.Y. Jets, 1968-69
Fred Cox, Minnesota, 1969-70
Chester Marcol, Green Bay, 1972, 1974
John Smith, New England, 1979-80

Most Consecutive Seasons Leading League

5 Don Hutson, Green Bay, 1940-44
4 Gino Cappelletti, Boston, 1963-66
3 Pat Harder, Chi. Cardinals, 1947-49
Paul Hornung, Green Bay, 1959-61

POINTS

Most Points, Career

2,002 George Blanda, Chi. Bears, 1949, 1950-58; Baltimore, 1950; Houston, 1960-66; Oakland, 1967-75 (9-td, 943-pat, 335-fg)
1,948 Gary Anderson, Pittsburgh, 1982-94; Philadelphia, 1995-96; San Francisco, 1997; Minnesota, 1998-99
1,840 Morten Andersen, New Orleans, 1982-94; Atlanta, 1995-99

Most Points, Season

176 Paul Hornung, Green Bay, 1960 (15-td, 41-pat, 15-fg)
164 Gary Anderson, Minnesota, 1998 (59-pat, 35-fg)
161 Mark Moseley, Washington, 1983 (62-pat, 33-fg)

Most Points, No Touchdowns, Season

164 Gary Anderson, Minnesota, 1998 (59-pat, 35-fg)
161 Mark Moseley, Washington, 1983 (62-pat, 33-fg)
149 Chip Lohmiller, Washington, 1991 (56-pat, 31-fg)

Most Seasons, 100 or More Points

12 Morten Andersen, New Orleans, 1985-89, 1991-94; Atlanta, 1995, 1997-98
Gary Anderson, Pittsburgh, 1983-85, 1988, 1991-94; Philadelphia, 1996; San Francisco, 1997; Minnesota, 1998-99
11 Nick Lowery, Kansas City, 1981, 1983-86, 1988-93
9 Norm Johnson, Seattle, 1983-84, 1986, 1988, 1990; Atlanta, 1993; Pittsburgh, 1995-97
Pete Stoyanovich, Miami, 1990-95; Kansas City, 1997-99

Most Points, Rookie, Season

144 Kevin Butler, Chicago, 1985 (51-pat, 31-fg)
132 Gale Sayers, Chicago, 1965 (22-td)
128 Doak Walker, Detroit, 1950 (11-td, 38-pat, 8-fg)
Chester Marcol, Green Bay, 1972 (29-pat, 33-fg)

Most Points, Game

40 Ernie Nevers, Chi. Cardinals vs. Chi. Bears, Nov. 28, 1929 (6-td, 4-pat)
36 Dub Jones, Cleveland vs. Chi. Bears, Nov. 25, 1951 (6-td)
Gale Sayers, Chicago vs. San Francisco, Dec. 12, 1965 (6-td)
33 Paul Hornung, Green Bay vs. Baltimore, Oct. 8, 1961 (4-td, 6-pat, 1-fg)

Most Consecutive Games Scoring

254 Morten Andersen, New Orleans, 1982-94; Atlanta, 1995-99 (current)
186 Jim Breech, Oakland, 1979; Cincinnati, 1980-92
155 Ray Wersching, San Francisco, 1977-87

TOUCHDOWNS

Most Seasons Leading League

8 Don Hutson, Green Bay, 1935-38, 1941-44
3 Jim Brown, Cleveland, 1958-59, 1963
Lance Alworth, San Diego, 1964-66
Emmitt Smith, Dallas, 1992, 1994-95
2 By many players

Most Consecutive Seasons Leading League

4 Don Hutson, Green Bay, 1935-38, 1941-44
3 Lance Alworth, San Diego, 1964-66
2 By many players

Most Touchdowns, Career

180 Jerry Rice, San Francisco, 1985-99 (10-r, 169-p, 1-ret)
147 Emmitt Smith, Dallas, 1990-99 (136-r, 11-p)
145 Marcus Allen, L.A. Raiders, 1982-92; Kansas City, 1993-97 (123-r, 21-p, 1-ret)

Most Touchdowns, Season

25 Emmitt Smith, Dallas, 1995 (25-r)
24 John Riggins, Washington, 1983 (24-r)
23 O.J. Simpson, Buffalo, 1975 (16-r, 7-p)
Jerry Rice, San Francisco, 1987 (1-r, 22-p)
Terrell Davis, Denver, 1998 (21-r, 2-p)

Most Touchdowns, Rookie, Season

22 Gale Sayers, Chicago, 1965 (14-r, 6-p, 2-ret)
20 Eric Dickerson, L.A. Rams, 1983 (18-r, 2-p)
17 Randy Moss, Minnesota, 1998 (17-p)
Fred Taylor, Jacksonville, 1998 (14-r, 3-p)
Edgerrin James, Indianapolis, 1999 (13-r, 4-p)

Most Touchdowns, Game

6 Ernie Nevers, Chi. Cardinals vs. Chi. Bears, Nov. 28, 1929 (6-r)
Dub Jones, Cleveland vs. Chi. Bears, Nov. 25, 1951 (4-r, 2-p)
Gale Sayers, Chicago vs. San Francisco, Dec. 12, 1965 (4-r, 1-p, 1-ret)
5 Bob Shaw, Chi. Cardinals vs. Baltimore, Oct. 2, 1950 (5-p)
Jim Brown, Cleveland vs. Baltimore, Nov. 1, 1959 (5-r)
Abner Haynes, Dall. Texans vs. Oakland, Nov. 26, 1961 (4-r, 1-p)
Billy Cannon, Houston vs. N.Y. Titans, Dec. 10, 1961 (3-r, 2-p)
Cookie Gilchrist, Buffalo vs. N.Y. Jets, Dec. 8, 1963 (5-r)
Paul Hornung, Green Bay vs. Baltimore, Dec. 12, 1965 (3-r, 2-p)
Kellen Winslow, San Diego vs. Oakland, Nov. 22, 1981 (5-p)
Jerry Rice, San Francisco vs. Atlanta, Oct. 14, 1990 (5-p)
James Stewart, Jacksonville vs. Philadelphia, Oct. 12, 1997 (5-r)
4 By many players. Last time: Dorsey Levens, Green Bay vs. Arizona, Jan. 2, 2000 (4-r)

Most Consecutive Games Scoring Touchdowns

18 Lenny Moore, Baltimore, 1963-65
14 O.J. Simpson, Buffalo, 1975
13 John Riggins, Washington, 1982-83
George Rogers, Washington, 1985-86
Jerry Rice, San Francisco, 1986-87

POINTS AFTER TOUCHDOWN

Most Seasons Leading League

8 George Blanda, Chi. Bears, 1956; Houston, 1961-62; Oakland, 1967-69, 1972, 1974
4 Bob Waterfield, Cleveland, 1945; Los Angeles, 1946, 1950, 1952
3 Earl (Dutch) Clark, Portsmouth, 1932; Detroit, 1935-36
Jack Manders, Chi. Bears, 1933-35
Don Hutson, Green Bay, 1941-42, 1945

Most (Kicking) Points After Touchdown Attempted, Career

959 George Blanda, Chi. Bears, 1949, 1950-58; Baltimore, 1950; Houston, 1960-66; Oakland, 1967-75
657 Lou Groza, Cleveland, 1950-59, 1961-67
645 Norm Johnson, Seattle, 1982-90; Atlanta, 1991-94; Pittsburgh, 1995-98; Philadelphia, 1999

Most (Kicking) Points After Touchdown Attempted, Season
70 Uwe von Schamann, Miami, 1984
65 George Blanda, Houston, 1961
64 Jeff Wilkins, St. Louis, 1999

Most (Kicking) Points After Touchdown Attempted, Game
10 Charlie Gogolak, Washington vs. N.Y. Giants, Nov. 27, 1966
9 Pat Harder, Chi. Cardinals vs. N.Y. Giants, Oct. 17, 1948; vs. N.Y. Bulldogs, Nov. 13, 1949
Bob Waterfield, Los Angeles vs. Baltimore, Oct. 22, 1950
Bob Thomas, Chicago vs. Green Bay, Dec. 7, 1980
8 By many players

Most (One-Point) Points After Touchdown, Career
943 George Blanda, Chi. Bears, 1949, 1950-58; Baltimore, 1950; Houston, 1960-66; Oakland, 1967-75
641 Lou Groza, Cleveland, 1950-59, 1961-67
638 Norm Johnson, Seattle, 1982-90; Atlanta, 1991-94; Pittsburgh, 1995-98; Philadelphia, 1999

Most (One-Point) Points After Touchdown, Season
66 Uwe von Schamann, Miami, 1984
64 George Blanda, Houston, 1961
Jeff Wilkins, St. Louis, 1999
62 Mark Moseley, Washington, 1983

Most (One-Point) Points After Touchdown, Game
9 Pat Harder, Chi. Cardinals vs. N.Y. Giants, Oct. 17, 1948
Bob Waterfield, Los Angeles vs. Baltimore, Oct. 22, 1950
Charlie Gogolak, Washington vs. N.Y. Giants, Nov. 27, 1966
8 By many players

Most Consecutive (Kicking) Points After Touchdown
301 Norm Johnson, Atlanta, 1991-94; Pittsburgh, 1995-98; Philadelphia, 1999 (current)
264 Jason Elam, Denver, 1993-99 (current)
250 Eddie Murray, Detroit, 1988-91; Kansas City, 1992; Tampa Bay, 1992; Dallas, 1993; Philadelphia, 1994; Washington, 1995; Minnesota, 1997

Highest (Kicking) Points After Touchdown Percentage, Career (200 points after touchdown)
99.65 Jason Elam, Denver, 1993-99 (289-288)
99.43 Tommy Davis, San Francisco, 1959-69 (350-348)
99.21 Gary Anderson, Pittsburgh, 1982-94; Philadelphia, 1995-96; San Francisco, 1997; Minnesota, 1998-99 (636-631)

Most (Kicking) Points After Touchdown, No Misses, Season
64 Jeff Wilkins, St. Louis, 1999
59 Gary Anderson, Minnesota, 1998
58 Jason Elam, Denver, 1998

Most (Kicking) Points After Touchdown, No Misses, Game
9 Pat Harder, Chi. Cardinals vs. N.Y. Giants, Oct. 17, 1948
Bob Waterfield, Los Angeles vs. Baltimore, Oct. 22, 1950
8 By many players

Most Two-Point Conversions, Career
Two-point conversion records include AFL (1960-69) and NFL (since 1994).
6 Terance Mathis, Atlanta, 1994-99
5 Cris Carter, Minnesota, 1994-99
Rob Moore, N.Y. Jets, 1994; Arizona, 1995-99
4 Gino Cappelletti, Boston, 1960-69
Jerry Rice, San Francisco, 1994-99
Lamar Smith, Seattle, 1994-97; New Orleans, 1998-99
Floyd Turner, Indianapolis, 1994-95; Baltimore, 1996, 1998
Marvin Harrison, Indianapolis, 1996-99
Willie Jackson, Jacksonville, 1995-97; Cincinnati, 1998-99
Keenan McCardell, Cleveland, 1994-95; Jacksonville, 1996-99

Most Two-Point Conversions, Season
3 Gino Cappelletti, Boston, 1960
Richie Lucas, Buffalo, 1961
Ronnie Harmon, San Diego, 1994
Haywood Jeffires, Houston, 1994
Tom Tupa, Cleveland, 1994
Terance Mathis, Atlanta, 1995
Lamar Smith, Seattle, 1996
Cris Carter, Minnesota, 1997
Terrell Davis, Denver, 1997
2 By many players

Most Two-Point Conversions, Game
2 Brett Perriman, Detroit vs. Green Bay, Nov. 6, 1994
Michael Jackson, Baltimore vs. New England, Oct. 6, 1996
Terrell Davis, Denver vs. Atlanta, Sept. 28, 1997
Charles Johnson, Pittsburgh vs. Tennessee, Nov. 1, 1998

FIELD GOALS

Most Seasons Leading League
5 Lou Groza, Cleveland, 1950, 1952-54, 1957
4 Jack Manders, Chi. Bears, 1933-34, 1936-37
Ward Cuff, N.Y. Giants, 1938-39, 1943; Green Bay, 1947
Mark Moseley, Washington, 1976-77, 1979, 1982
3 Bob Waterfield, Los Angeles, 1947, 1949, 1951
Gino Cappelletti, Boston, 1961, 1963-64
Fred Cox, Minnesota, 1965, 1969-70
Jan Stenerud, Kansas City, 1967, 1970, 1975

Most Consecutive Seasons Leading League
3 Lou Groza, Cleveland, 1952-54
2 Jack Manders, Chi. Bears, 1933-34
Armand Niccolai, Pittsburgh, 1935-36
Jack Manders, Chi. Bears, 1936-37
Ward Cuff, N.Y. Giants, 1938-39
Clark Hinkle, Green Bay, 1940-41
Cliff Patton, Philadelphia, 1948-49
Gino Cappelletti, Boston, 1963-64
Jim Turner, N.Y. Jets, 1968-69
Fred Cox, Minnesota, 1969-70
Mark Moseley, Washington, 1976-77
Chip Lohmiller, Washington, 1991-92
Pete Stoyanovich, Miami, 1991-92

Most Field Goals Attempted, Career
637 George Blanda, Chi. Bears, 1949, 1950-58; Baltimore, 1950; Houston, 1960-66; Oakland, 1967-75
558 Jan Stenerud, Kansas City, 1967-79; Green Bay, 1980-83; Minnesota, 1984-85
555 Gary Anderson, Pittsburgh, 1982-94; Philadelphia, 1995-96; San Francisco, 1997; Minnesota, 1998-99

Most Field Goals Attempted, Season
49 Bruce Gossett, Los Angeles, 1966
Curt Knight, Washington, 1971
48 Chester Marcol, Green Bay, 1972
47 Jim Turner, N.Y. Jets, 1969
David Ray, Los Angeles, 1973
Mark Moseley, Washington, 1983

Most Field Goals Attempted, Game
9 Jim Bakken, St. Louis vs. Pittsburgh, Sept. 24, 1967
8 Lou Michaels, Pittsburgh vs. St. Louis, Dec. 2, 1962
Garo Yepremian, Detroit vs. Minnesota, Nov. 13, 1966
Jim Turner, N.Y. Jets vs. Buffalo, Nov. 3, 1968
7 By many players

Most Field Goals, Career
439 Gary Anderson, Pittsburgh, 1982-94; Philadelphia, 1995-96; San Francisco, 1997; Minnesota, 1998-99
416 Morten Andersen, New Orleans, 1982-94; Atlanta, 1995-99
383 Nick Lowery, New England, 1978; Kansas City, 1980-93; N.Y. Jets, 1994-96

Most Field Goals, Season
39 Olindo Mare, Miami, 1999
37 John Kasay, Carolina, 1996
36 Cary Blanchard, Indianapolis, 1996
Al Del Greco, Tennessee, 1998

Most Field Goals, Rookie, Season
35 Ali Haji-Sheikh, N.Y. Giants, 1983
34 Richie Cunningham, Dallas, 1997
33 Chester Marcol, Green Bay, 1972

Most Field Goals, Game
7 Jim Bakken, St. Louis vs. Pittsburgh, Sept. 24, 1967
Rich Karlis, Minnesota vs. L.A. Rams, Nov. 5, 1989 (OT)
Chris Boniol, Dallas vs. Green Bay, Nov. 18, 1996
6 Gino Cappelletti, Boston vs. Denver, Oct. 4, 1964
Garo Yepremian, Detroit vs. Minnesota, Nov. 13, 1966
Jim Turner, N.Y. Jets vs. Buffalo, Nov. 3, 1968
Tom Dempsey, Philadelphia vs. Houston, Nov. 12, 1972
Bobby Howfield, N.Y. Jets vs. New Orleans, Dec. 3, 1972
Jim Bakken, St. Louis vs. Atlanta, Dec. 9, 1973
Joe Danelo, N.Y. Giants vs. Seattle, Oct. 18, 1981
Ray Wersching, San Francisco vs. New Orleans, Oct. 16, 1983
Gary Anderson, Pittsburgh vs. Denver, Oct. 23, 1988
John Carney, San Diego vs. Seattle, Sept. 5, 1993
John Carney, San Diego vs. Houston, Sept. 19, 1993
Doug Pelfrey, Cincinnati vs. Seattle, Nov. 6, 1994 (OT)
Norm Johnson, Atlanta vs. New Orleans, Nov. 13, 1994
Jeff Wilkins, San Francisco vs. Atlanta, Sept. 29, 1996
Steve Christie, Buffalo vs. N.Y. Jets, Oct. 20, 1996
Greg Davis, San Diego vs. Oakland, Oct. 5, 1997
Gary Anderson, Minnesota vs. Baltimore, Dec. 13, 1998
Olindo Mare, Miami vs. New England, Oct. 17, 1999
Jason Hanson, Detroit vs. Minnesota, Oct. 17, 1999
5 By many players

Most Field Goals, One Quarter
4 Garo Yepremian, Detroit vs. Minnesota, Nov. 13, 1966 (second quarter)
Curt Knight, Washington vs. N.Y. Giants, Nov. 15, 1970 (second quarter)
Roger Ruzek, Dallas vs. N.Y. Giants, Nov. 2, 1987 (fourth quarter)
Cary Blanchard, Indianapolis vs. Buffalo, Sept. 21 1997 (second quarter)
3 By many players

ALL-TIME RECORDS

Most Consecutive Games Scoring Field Goals
31 Fred Cox, Minnesota, 1968-70
28 Jim Turner, N.Y. Jets, 1970; Denver, 1971-72
Chip Lohmiller, Washington, 1988-90
23 Morten Andersen, New Orleans, 1986-88

Most Consecutive Field Goals
40 Gary Anderson, San Francisco, 1997; Minnesota, 1998 (current)
31 Fuad Reveiz, Minnesota, 1994-95
29 John Carney, San Diego, 1992-93

Longest Field Goal
63 Tom Dempsey, New Orleans vs. Detroit, Nov. 8, 1970
Jason Elam, Denver vs. Jacksonville, Oct. 25, 1998
60 Steve Cox, Cleveland vs. Cincinnati, Oct. 21, 1984
Morten Andersen, New Orleans vs. Chicago, Oct. 27, 1991
59 Tony Franklin, Philadelphia vs. Dallas, Nov. 12, 1979
Pete Stoyanovich, Miami vs. N.Y. Jets, Nov. 12, 1989
Steve Christie, Buffalo vs. Miami, Sept. 26, 1993
Morten Andersen, Atlanta vs. San Francisco, Dec. 24, 1995

Highest Field Goal Percentage, Career (100 field goals)
81.67 John Carney, Tampa Bay, 1988-89; L.A. Rams, 1990; San Diego, 1990-99 (300-245)
81.60 Mike Hollis, Jacksonville, 1995-99 (163-133)
81.01 Todd Peterson, Arizona, 1994; Seattle, 1995-99 (158-128)

Highest Field Goal Percentage, Season (Qualifiers)
100.00 Tony Zendejas, L.A. Rams, 1991 (17-17)
Gary Anderson, Minnesota, 1998 (35-35)
96.43 Chris Boniol, Dallas, 1995 (28-27)
96.30 Norm Johnson, Atlanta, 1993 (27-26)
Pete Stoyanovich, Kansas City, 1997 (27-26)

Most Field Goals, No Misses, Game
7 Rich Karlis, Minnesota vs. L.A. Rams, Nov. 5, 1989 (OT)
Chris Boniol, Dallas vs. Green Bay, Nov. 18, 1996
6 Gino Cappelletti, Boston vs. Denver, Oct. 4, 1964
Joe Danelo, N.Y. Giants vs. Seattle, Oct. 18, 1981
Ray Wersching, San Francisco vs. New Orleans, Oct. 16, 1983
Gary Anderson, Pittsburgh vs. Denver, Oct. 23, 1988
John Carney, San Diego vs. Seattle, Sept. 5, 1993
John Carney, San Diego vs. Houston, Sept. 19, 1993
Doug Pelfrey, Cincinnati vs. Seattle, Nov. 6, 1994 (OT)
Norm Johnson, Atlanta vs. New Orleans, Nov. 13, 1994
Jeff Wilkins, San Francisco vs. Atlanta, Sept. 29, 1996
Greg Davis, San Diego vs. Oakland, Oct. 5, 1997
Gary Anderson, Minnesota vs. Baltimore, Dec. 13, 1998
Olindo Mare, Miami vs. New England, Oct. 17, 1999
5 By many players

Most Field Goals, 50 or More Yards, Career
35 Morten Andersen, New Orleans, 1982-94; Atlanta, 1995-99
22 Nick Lowery, New England, 1978; Kansas City, 1980-93; N.Y. Jets, 1994-96
Jason Elam, Denver, 1993-99
21 Eddie Murray, Detroit, 1980-91; Kansas City, 1992; Tampa Bay, 1992; Dallas, 1993, 1999; Philadelphia, 1994; Washington, 1995; Minnesota, 1997

Most Field Goals, 50 or More Yards, Season
8 Morten Andersen, Atlanta, 1995
6 Dean Biasucci, Indianapolis, 1988
Chris Jacke, Green Bay, 1993
Tony Zendejas, L.A. Rams, 1993
Mike Vanderjagt, Indianapolis, 1998
5 Fred Steinfort, Denver, 1980
Norm Johnson, Seattle, 1986
Kevin Butler, Chicago, 1993
Jason Elam, Denver, 1995
Cary Blanchard, Indianapolis, 1996
Jason Elam, Denver, 1999

Most Field Goals, 50 or More Yards, Game
3 Morten Andersen, Atlanta vs. New Orleans, Dec. 10, 1995
2 By many players. Last time:
Jason Hanson, Detroit vs. Washington, Dec. 5, 1999

SAFETIES

Most Safeties, Career
4 Ted Hendricks, Baltimore, 1969-73; Green Bay, 1974; Oakland, 1975-81; L.A. Raiders, 1982-83
Doug English, Detroit, 1975-79, 1981-85
3 Bill McPeak, Pittsburgh, 1949-57
Charlie Krueger, San Francisco, 1959-73
Ernie Stautner, Pittsburgh, 1950-63
Jim Katcavage, N.Y. Giants, 1956-68
Roger Brown, Detroit, 1960-66; Los Angeles, 1967-69
Bruce Maher, Detroit, 1960-67; N.Y. Giants, 1968-69
Ron McDole, St. Louis, 1961; Houston, 1962; Buffalo, 1963-70; Washington, 1971-78
Alan Page, Minnesota, 1967-78; Chicago, 1979-81
Lyle Alzado, Denver, 1971-78; Cleveland, 1979-81; L.A. Raiders, 1982-85
Rulon Jones, Denver, 1980-88
Steve McMichael, New England, 1980; Chicago, 1981-93; Green Bay, 1994
Kevin Greene, L.A. Rams, 1985-92; Pittsburgh, 1993-95; Carolina, 1996, 1998-99; San Francisco, 1997
Burt Grossman, San Diego, 1989-93; Philadelphia, 1994
Eric Swann, Phoenix, 1991-93; Arizona, 1994-99
Dan Saleaumua, Detroit, 1987-88; Kansas City, 1989-96; Seattle, 1997-98
Derrick Thomas, Kansas City, 1989-99
Bryant Young, San Francisco, 1994-99
2 By many players

Most Safeties, Season
2 Tom Nash, Green Bay, 1932
Roger Brown, Detroit, 1962
Ron McDole, Buffalo, 1964
Alan Page, Minnesota, 1971
Fred Dryer, Los Angeles, 1973
Benny Barnes, Dallas, 1973
James Young, Houston, 1977
Doug English, Detroit, 1983
Don Blackmon, New England, 1985
Tim Harris, Green Bay, 1988
Brian Jordan, Atlanta, 1991
Burt Grossman, San Diego, 1992
Rod Stephens, Seattle, 1993
Bryant Young, San Francisco, 1996

Most Safeties, Game
2 Fred Dryer, Los Angeles vs. Green Bay, Oct. 21, 1973

RUSHING

Most Seasons Leading League
8 Jim Brown, Cleveland, 1957-61, 1963-65
4 Steve Van Buren, Philadelphia, 1945, 1947-49
O.J. Simpson, Buffalo, 1972-73, 1975-76
Eric Dickerson, L.A. Rams, 1983-84, 1986; Indianapolis, 1988
Emmitt Smith, Dallas, 1991-93, 1995
Barry Sanders, Detroit, 1990, 1994, 1996-97
3 Earl Campbell, Houston, 1978-80

Most Consecutive Seasons Leading League
5 Jim Brown, Cleveland, 1957-61
3 Steve Van Buren, Philadelphia, 1947-49
Jim Brown, Cleveland, 1963-65
Earl Campbell, Houston, 1978-80
Emmitt Smith, Dallas, 1991-93
2 Bill Paschal, N.Y. Giants, 1943-44
Joe Perry, San Francisco, 1953-54
Jim Nance, Boston, 1966-67
Leroy Kelly, Cleveland, 1967-68
O.J. Simpson, Buffalo, 1972-73; 1975-76
Eric Dickerson, L.A. Rams, 1983-84
Barry Sanders, Detroit, 1996-97

ATTEMPTS

Most Seasons Leading League
6 Jim Brown, Cleveland, 1958-59, 1961, 1963-65
4 Steve Van Buren, Philadelphia, 1947-50
Walter Payton, Chicago, 1976-79
3 Cookie Gilchrist, Buffalo, 1963-64; Denver, 1965
Jim Nance, Boston, 1966-67, 1969
O.J. Simpson, Buffalo, 1973-75
Eric Dickerson, L.A. Rams, 1983, 1986; Indianapolis, 1988
Emmitt Smith, Dallas, 1991, 1994-95

Most Consecutive Seasons Leading League
4 Steve Van Buren, Philadelphia, 1947-50
Walter Payton, Chicago, 1976-79
3 Jim Brown, Cleveland, 1963-65
Cookie Gilchrist, Buffalo, 1963-64; Denver, 1965
O.J. Simpson, Buffalo, 1973-75
2 By many players

Most Attempts, Career
3,838 Walter Payton, Chicago, 1975-87
3,243 Emmitt Smith, Dallas, 1990-99
3,062 Barry Sanders, Detroit, 1989-98

Most Attempts, Season
410 Jamal Anderson, Atlanta, 1998
407 James Wilder, Tampa Bay, 1984
404 Eric Dickerson, L.A. Rams, 1986

Most Attempts, Rookie, Season
390 Eric Dickerson, L.A. Rams, 1983
378 George Rogers, New Orleans, 1981
369 Edgerrin James, Indianapolis, 1999

Most Attempts, Game
45 Jamie Morris, Washington vs. Cincinnati, Dec. 17, 1988 (OT)
43 Butch Woolfolk, N.Y. Giants vs. Philadelphia, Nov. 20, 1983
James Wilder, Tampa Bay vs. Green Bay, Sept. 30, 1984 (OT)
42 James Wilder, Tampa Bay vs. Pittsburgh, Oct. 30, 1983
Terrell Davis, Denver vs. Buffalo, Oct. 26, 1997 (OT)

YARDS GAINED

Most Yards Gained, Career
16,726 Walter Payton, Chicago, 1975-87
15,269 Barry Sanders, Detroit, 1989-98
13,963 Emmitt Smith, Dallas, 1990-99

Most Seasons, 1,000 or More Yards Rushing
10 Walter Payton, Chicago, 1976-81, 1983-86
Barry Sanders, Detroit, 1989-98
9 Emmitt Smith, Dallas, 1991-99
8 Franco Harris, Pittsburgh, 1972, 1974-79, 1983
Tony Dorsett, Dallas, 1977-81, 1983-85
Thurman Thomas, Buffalo, 1989-96

Most Consecutive Seasons, 1,000 or More Yards Rushing
10 Barry Sanders, Detroit, 1989-98 (current)
9 Emmitt Smith, Dallas, 1991-99 (current)
8 Thurman Thomas, Buffalo, 1989-96

Most Yards Gained, Season
2,105 Eric Dickerson, L.A. Rams, 1984
2,053 Barry Sanders, Detroit, 1997
2,008 Terrell Davis, Denver, 1998

Most Yards Gained, Rookie, Season
1,808 Eric Dickerson, L.A. Rams, 1983
1,674 George Rogers, New Orleans, 1981
1,605 Ottis Anderson, St. Louis, 1979

Most Yards Gained, Game
275 Walter Payton, Chicago vs. Minnesota, Nov. 20, 1977
273 O.J. Simpson, Buffalo vs. Detroit, Nov. 25, 1976
250 O.J. Simpson, Buffalo vs. New England, Sept. 16, 1973

Most Games, 200 or More Yards Rushing, Career
6 O.J. Simpson, Buffalo, 1969-77; San Francisco, 1978-79
4 Jim Brown, Cleveland, 1957-65
Earl Campbell, Houston, 1978-84; New Orleans, 1984-85
Barry Sanders, Detroit, 1989-98
3 Eric Dickerson, L.A. Rams, 1983-87; Indianapolis, 1987-91; L.A. Raiders, 1992; Atlanta, 1993
Greg Bell, Buffalo, 1984-87; L.A. Rams, 1987-89; L.A. Raiders, 1990
Terrell Davis, Denver, 1995-98

Most Games, 200 or More Yards Rushing, Season
4 Earl Campbell, Houston, 1980
3 O.J. Simpson, Buffalo, 1973
2 Jim Brown, Cleveland, 1963
O.J. Simpson, Buffalo, 1976
Walter Payton, Chicago, 1977
Eric Dickerson, L.A. Rams, 1984
Greg Bell, L.A. Rams, 1989
Terrell Davis, Denver, 1997
Barry Sanders, Detroit, 1997

Most Consecutive Games, 200 or More Yards Rushing
2 O.J. Simpson, Buffalo, 1973, 1976
Earl Campbell, Houston, 1980

Most Games, 100 or More Yards Rushing, Career
77 Walter Payton, Chicago, 1975-87
76 Barry Sanders, Detroit, 1989-98
64 Eric Dickerson, L.A. Rams, 1983-87; Indianapolis, 1987-91; L.A. Raiders, 1992; Atlanta, 1993
Emmitt Smith, Dallas, 1990-99

Most Games, 100 or More Yards Rushing, Season
14 Barry Sanders, Detroit, 1997
12 Eric Dickerson, L.A. Rams, 1984
Barry Foster, Pittsburgh, 1992
Jamal Anderson, Atlanta, 1998
11 O.J. Simpson, Buffalo, 1973
Earl Campbell, Houston, 1979
Marcus Allen, L.A. Raiders, 1985
Eric Dickerson, L.A. Rams, 1986
Emmitt Smith, Dallas, 1995
Terrell Davis, Denver, 1998

Most Consecutive Games, 100 or More Yards Rushing
14 Barry Sanders, Detroit, 1997
11 Marcus Allen, L.A. Raiders, 1985-86
9 Walter Payton, Chicago, 1985

Longest Run From Scrimmage
99 Tony Dorsett, Dallas vs. Minnesota, Jan. 3, 1983 (TD)
97 Andy Uram, Green Bay vs. Chi. Cardinals, Oct. 8, 1939 (TD)
Bob Gage, Pittsburgh vs. Chi. Bears, Dec. 4, 1949 (TD)
96 Jim Spavital, Baltimore vs. Green Bay, Nov. 5, 1950 (TD)
Bob Hoernschemeyer, Detroit vs. N.Y. Yanks, Nov. 23, 1950 (TD)
Garrison Hearst, San Francisco vs. N.Y. Jets, Sept. 6, 1998 (TD)

AVERAGE GAIN

Highest Average Gain, Career (750 attempts)
5.22 Jim Brown, Cleveland, 1957-65 (2,359-12,312)
5.14 Eugene (Mercury) Morris, Miami, 1969-75; San Diego, 1976 (804-4,133)
5.00 Gale Sayers, Chicago, 1965-71 (991-4,956)

Highest Average Gain, Season (Qualifiers)
8.44 Beattie Feathers, Chi. Bears, 1934 (119-1,004)
7.98 Randall Cunningham, Philadelphia 1990 (118-942)
6.87 Bobby Douglass, Chicago, 1972 (141-968)

Highest Average Gain, Game (10 attempts)
17.09 Marion Motley, Cleveland vs. Pittsburgh, Oct. 29, 1950 (11-188)
16.70 Bill Grimes, Green Bay vs. N.Y. Yanks, Oct. 8, 1950 (10-167)
16.57 Bobby Mitchell, Cleveland vs. Washington, Nov. 15, 1959 (14-232)

TOUCHDOWNS

Most Seasons Leading League
5 Jim Brown, Cleveland, 1957-59, 1963, 1965
4 Steve Van Buren, Philadelphia, 1945, 1947-49
3 Abner Haynes, Dall. Texans, 1960-62
Cookie Gilchrist, Buffalo, 1962-64
Paul Lowe, L.A. Chargers, 1960; San Diego, 1961, 1965
Leroy Kelly, Cleveland, 1966-68
Emmitt Smith, Dallas, 1992, 1994-95

Most Consecutive Seasons Leading League
3 Steve Van Buren, Philadelphia, 1947-49
Jim Brown, Cleveland, 1957-59
Abner Haynes, Dall. Texans, 1960-62
Cookie Gilchrist, Buffalo, 1962-64
Leroy Kelly, Cleveland, 1966-68

Most Touchdowns, Career
136 Emmitt Smith, Dallas, 1990-99
123 Marcus Allen, L.A. Raiders, 1982-92; Kansas City, 1993-97
110 Walter Payton, Chicago, 1975-87

Most Touchdowns, Season
25 Emmitt Smith, Dallas, 1995
24 John Riggins, Washington, 1983
21 Joe Morris, N.Y. Giants, 1985
Emmitt Smith, Dallas, 1994
Terry Allen, Washington, 1996
Terrell Davis, Denver, 1998

Most Touchdowns, Rookie, Season
18 Eric Dickerson, L.A. Rams, 1983
15 Ickey Woods, Cincinnati, 1988
14 Gale Sayers, Chicago, 1965
Barry Sanders, Detroit, 1989
Curtis Martin, New England, 1995
Fred Taylor, Jacksonville, 1998

Most Touchdowns, Game
6 Ernie Nevers, Chi. Cardinals vs. Chi. Bears, Nov. 28, 1929
5 Jim Brown, Cleveland vs. Baltimore, Nov. 1, 1959
Cookie Gilchrist, Buffalo vs. N.Y. Jets, Dec. 8, 1963
James Stewart, Jacksonville vs. Philadelphia, Oct. 12, 1997
4 By many players

Most Consecutive Games Rushing for Touchdowns
13 John Riggins, Washington, 1982-83
George Rogers, Washington, 1985-86
11 Lenny Moore, Baltimore, 1963-64
Emmitt Smith, Dallas, 1994-95
Emmitt Smith, Dallas, 1995
10 Greg Bell, L.A. Rams, 1988-89
Terry Allen, Washington, 1995-96

PASSING

Most Seasons Leading League
6 Sammy Baugh, Washington, 1937, 1940, 1943, 1945, 1947, 1949
Steve Young San Francisco, 1991-94, 1996-97
4 Len Dawson, Dall. Texans; 1962; Kansas City, 1964, 1966, 1968
Roger Staubach, Dallas, 1971, 1973, 1978-79
Ken Anderson, Cincinnati, 1974-75, 1981-82
3 Arnie Herber, Green Bay, 1932, 1934, 1936
Norm Van Brocklin, Los Angeles, 1950, 1952, 1954
Bart Starr, Green Bay, 1962, 1964, 1966

ALL-TIME RECORDS

Most Consecutive Seasons Leading League
4 Steve Young, San Francisco, 1991-94
2 Cecil Isbell, Green Bay, 1941-42
Milt Plum, Cleveland, 1960-61
Ken Anderson, Cincinnati, 1974-75, 1981-82
Roger Staubach, Dallas, 1978-79
Steve Young, San Francisco, 1996-97

PASSER RATING

Highest Passer Rating, Career (1,500 attempts)
96.8 Steve Young, Tampa Bay, 1985-86; San Francisco, 1987-99
92.3 Joe Montana, San Francisco, 1979-90, 1992; Kansas City, 1993-94
87.1 Brett Favre, Atlanta, 1991; Green Bay, 1992-99

Highest Passer Rating, Season (Qualifiers)
112.8 Steve Young, San Francisco, 1994
112.4 Joe Montana, San Francisco, 1989
110.4 Milt Plum, Cleveland, 1960

Highest Passer Rating, Rookie, Season (Qualifiers)
96.0 Dan Marino, Miami, 1983
88.2 Greg Cook, Cincinnati, 1969
84.0 Charlie Conerly, N.Y. Giants, 1948

ATTEMPTS

Most Seasons Leading League
5 Dan Marino, Miami, 1984, 1986, 1988, 1992, 1997
4 Sammy Baugh, Washington, 1937, 1943, 1947-48
Johnny Unitas, Baltimore, 1957, 1959-61
George Blanda, Chi. Bears, 1953; Houston, 1963-65
3 Arnie Herber, Green Bay, 1932, 1934, 1936
Sonny Jurgensen, Washington, 1966-67, 1969
Drew Bledsoe, New England, 1994-96

Most Consecutive Seasons Leading League
3 Johnny Unitas, Baltimore, 1959-61
George Blanda, Houston, 1963-65
Drew Bledsoe, New England, 1994-96
2 By many players

Most Passes Attempted, Career
8,358 Dan Marino, Miami, 1983-99
7,250 John Elway, Denver, 1983-98
6,789 Warren Moon, Houston, 1984-93; Minnesota, 1994-96; Seattle, 1997-98; Kansas City, 1999

Most Passes Attempted, Season
691 Drew Bledsoe, New England, 1994
655 Warren Moon, Houston, 1991
636 Drew Bledsoe, New England, 1995

Most Passes Attempted, Rookie, Season
575 Peyton Manning, Indianapolis, 1998
486 Rick Mirer, Seattle, 1993
439 Jim Zorn, Seattle, 1976

Most Passes Attempted, Game
70 Drew Bledsoe, New England vs. Minnesota, Nov. 13, 1994 (OT)
68 George Blanda, Houston vs. Buffalo, Nov. 1, 1964
66 Chris Miller, Atlanta vs. Detroit, Dec. 24, 1989

COMPLETIONS

Most Seasons Leading League
6 Dan Marino, Miami, 1984-86, 1988, 1992, 1997
5 Sammy Baugh, Washington, 1937, 1943, 1945, 1947-48
4 George Blanda, Chi. Bears, 1953; Houston, 1963-65
Sonny Jurgensen, Philadelphia, 1961; Washington, 1966-67, 1969

Most Consecutive Seasons Leading League
3 George Blanda, Houston, 1963-65
Dan Marino, Miami, 1984-86
2 By many players

Most Passes Completed, Career
4,967 Dan Marino, Miami, 1983-99
4,123 John Elway, Denver, 1983-98
3,973 Warren Moon, Houston, 1984-93; Minnesota, 1994-96; Seattle, 1997-98; Kansas City, 1999

Most Passes Completed, Season
404 Warren Moon, Houston, 1991
400 Drew Bledsoe, New England, 1994
385 Dan Marino, Miami, 1994

Most Passes Completed, Rookie, Season
326 Peyton Manning, Indianapolis, 1998
274 Rick Mirer, Seattle, 1993
223 Tim Couch, Cleveland, 1999

Most Passes Completed, Game
45 Drew Bledsoe, New England vs. Minnesota, Nov. 13, 1994 (OT)
42 Richard Todd, N.Y. Jets vs. San Francisco, Sept. 21, 1980
Vinny Testaverde, N.Y. Jets vs. Seattle, Dec. 6, 1998
41 Warren Moon, Houston vs. Dallas, Nov. 10, 1991 (OT)

Most Consecutive Passes Completed
22 Joe Montana, San Francisco vs. Cleveland (5), Nov. 29, 1987; vs. Green Bay (17), Dec. 6, 1987
20 Ken Anderson, Cincinnati vs. Houston, Jan. 2, 1983
Hugh Millen, Denver vs. L.A. Raiders (7), Dec. 11, 1994; vs. San Francisco (13), Dec. 17, 1994
Steve Young, San Francisco vs. Washington, Nov. 24, 1996
18 Steve DeBerg, Denver vs. L.A. Rams (17), Dec. 12, 1982; vs. Kansas City (1), Dec. 19, 1982
Lynn Dickey, Green Bay vs. Houston, Sept. 4, 1983
Joe Montana, San Francisco vs. L.A. Rams (13), Oct. 28, 1984; vs. Cincinnati (5), Nov. 4, 1984
Don Majkowski, Green Bay vs. New Orleans, Sept. 18, 1989
Boomer Esiason, N.Y. Jets vs. Miami (5), Sept. 12, 1993; vs. New England (13), Sept. 26, 1993

COMPLETION PERCENTAGE

Most Seasons Leading League
8 Len Dawson, Dall. Texans, 1962; Kansas City, 1964-69, 1975
7 Sammy Baugh, Washington, 1940, 1942-43, 1945, 1947-49
5 Joe Montana, San Francisco, 1980-81, 1985, 1987, 1989
Steve Young, San Francisco, 1992, 1994-97

Most Consecutive Seasons Leading League
6 Len Dawson, Kansas City, 1964-69
4 Steve Young, San Francisco, 1994-97
3 Sammy Baugh, Washington, 1947-49
Otto Graham, Cleveland, 1953-55
Milt Plum, Cleveland, 1959-61

Highest Completion Percentage, Career (1,500 attempts)
64.28 Steve Young, Tampa Bay, 1985-86; San Francisco, 1987-99 (4,149-2,667)
63.24 Joe Montana, San Francisco, 1979-90, 1992; Kansas City, 1993-94 (5,391-3,409)
61.58 Troy Aikman, Dallas, 1989-99 (4,453-2,742)

Highest Completion Percentage, Season (Qualifiers)
70.55 Ken Anderson, Cincinnati, 1982 (309-218)
70.33 Sammy Baugh, Washington, 1945 (182-128)
70.28 Steve Young, San Francisco, 1994 (461-324)

Highest Completion Percentage, Rookie, Season (Qualifiers)
58.45 Dan Marino, Miami, 1983 (296-173)
57.14 Jim McMahon, Chicago, 1982 (210-120)
57.10 Charlie Batch, Detroit, 1998 (303-173)

Highest Completion Percentage, Game (20 attempts)
91.30 Vinny Testaverde, Cleveland vs. L.A. Rams, Dec. 26, 1993 (23-21)
90.91 Ken Anderson, Cincinnati vs. Pittsburgh, Nov. 10, 1974 (22-20)
90.48 Lynn Dickey, Green Bay vs. New Orleans, Dec. 13, 1981 (21-19)

YARDS GAINED

Most Seasons Leading League
5 Sonny Jurgensen, Philadelphia, 1961-62; Washington, 1966-67, 1969
Dan Marino, Miami, 1984-86, 1988, 1992
4 Sammy Baugh, Washington, 1937, 1940, 1947-48
Johnny Unitas, Baltimore, 1957, 1959-60, 1963
Dan Fouts, San Diego, 1979-82
3 Arnie Herber, Green Bay, 1932, 1934, 1936
Sid Luckman, Chi. Bears, 1943, 1945-46
John Brodie, San Francisco, 1965, 1968, 1970
John Hadl, San Diego, 1965, 1968, 1971
Joe Namath, N.Y. Jets, 1966-67, 1972

Most Consecutive Seasons Leading League
4 Dan Fouts, San Diego, 1979-82
3 Dan Marino, Miami, 1984-86
2 By many players

Most Yards Gained, Career
61,361 Dan Marino, Miami, 1983-99
51,475 John Elway, Denver, 1983-98
49,117 Warren Moon, Houston, 1984-93; Minnesota, 1994-96; Seattle, 1997-98; Kansas City, 1999

Most Seasons, 3,000 or More Yards Passing
13 Dan Marino, Miami, 1984-92, 1994-95, 1997-98
12 John Elway, Denver, 1985-91, 1993-97
9 Warren Moon, Houston, 1984, 1986, 1989-91, 1993; Minnesota, 1994-95; Seattle, 1997

Most Yards Gained, Season
5,084 Dan Marino, Miami, 1984
4,802 Dan Fouts, San Diego, 1981
4,746 Dan Marino, Miami, 1986

Most Yards Gained, Rookie, Season
3,739 Peyton Manning, Indianapolis, 1998
2,833 Rick Mirer, Seattle, 1993
2,717 Kerry Collins, Carolina, 1995

Most Yards Gained, Game
554 Norm Van Brocklin, Los Angeles vs. N.Y. Yanks, Sept. 28, 1951
527 Warren Moon, Houston vs. Kansas City, Dec. 16, 1990
522 Boomer Esiason, Arizona vs. Washington, Nov. 10, 1996

Most Games, 400 or More Yards Passing, Career
13 Dan Marino, Miami, 1983-99
7 Joe Montana, San Francisco, 1979-90, 1992; Kansas City, 1993-94
Warren Moon, Houston, 1984-93; Minnesota, 1994-96; Seattle, 1997-98; Kansas City, 1999
6 Dan Fouts, San Diego, 1973-87

Most Games, 400 or More Yards Passing, Season
4 Dan Marino, Miami, 1984
3 Dan Marino, Miami, 1986
2 By many players

Most Consecutive Games, 400 or More Yards Passing
2 Dan Fouts, San Diego, 1982
Dan Marino, Miami, 1984
Phil Simms, N.Y. Giants, 1985

Most Games, 300 or More Yards Passing, Career
63 Dan Marino, Miami, 1983-99
51 Dan Fouts, San Diego, 1973-87
49 Warren Moon, Houston, 1984-93; Minnesota, 1994-96; Seattle, 1997-98; Kansas City, 1999

Most Games, 300 or More Yards Passing, Season
9 Dan Marino, Miami, 1984
Warren Moon, Houston, 1990
Kurt Warner, St. Louis, 1999
8 Dan Fouts, San Diego, 1980
7 Dan Fouts, San Diego, 1981
Bill Kenney, Kansas City, 1983
Neil Lomax, St. Louis, 1984
Dan Fouts, San Diego, 1985
Brett Favre, Green Bay, 1995
Steve Young, San Francisco, 1998

Most Consecutive Games, 300 or More Yards Passing
6 Steve Young, San Francisco, 1998
5 Joe Montana, San Francisco, 1982
4 Dan Fouts, San Diego, 1979
Dan Fouts, San Diego, 1980-81
Bill Kenney, Kansas City, 1983
Joe Montana, San Francisco, 1985-86
Joe Montana, San Francisco, 1990
Warren Moon, Houston, 1990
Drew Bledsoe, New England, 1993-94
Kurt Warner, St. Louis, 1999

Longest Pass Completion (All TDs except as noted)
99 Frank Filchock (to Farkas), Washington vs. Pittsburgh, Oct. 15, 1939
George Izo (to Mitchell), Washington vs. Cleveland, Sept. 15, 1963
Karl Sweetan (to Studstill), Detroit vs. Baltimore, Oct. 16, 1966
Sonny Jurgensen (to Allen), Washington vs. Chicago, Sept. 15, 1968
Jim Plunkett (to Branch), L.A. Raiders vs. Washington, Oct. 2, 1983
Ron Jaworski (to Quick), Philadelphia vs. Atlanta, Nov. 10, 1985
Stan Humphries (to Martin), San Diego vs. Seattle, Sept. 18, 1994
Brett Favre (to Brooks), Green Bay vs. Chicago, Sept. 11, 1995
98 Doug Russell (to Tinsley), Chi. Cardinals vs. Cleveland, Nov. 27, 1938
Ogden Compton (to Lane), Chi. Cardinals vs. Green Bay, Nov. 13, 1955
Bill Wade (to Farrington), Chicago Bears vs. Detroit, Oct. 8, 1961
Jacky Lee (to Dewveall), Houston vs. San Diego, Nov. 25, 1962
Earl Morrall (to Jones), N.Y. Giants vs. Pittsburgh, Sept. 11, 1966
Jim Hart (to Moore), St. Louis vs. Los Angeles, Dec. 10, 1972 (no TD)
Bobby Hebert (to Haynes), Atlanta vs. New Orleans, Sept. 12, 1993
Charlie Batch (to Morton), Detroit vs. Chicago, Oct. 4, 1998
97 Pat Coffee (to Tinsley), Chi. Cardinals vs. Chi. Bears, Dec. 5, 1937
Bobby Layne (to Box), Detroit vs. Green Bay, Nov. 26, 1953
George Shaw (to Tarr), Denver vs. Boston, Sept. 21, 1962
Bernie Kosar (to Slaughter), Cleveland vs. Chicago, Oct. 23, 1989
Steve Young (to Taylor), San Francisco vs. Atlanta, Nov. 3, 1991

AVERAGE GAIN

Most Seasons Leading League
7 Sid Luckman, Chi. Bears, 1939-43, 1946-47
5 Steve Young, San Francisco, 1991-94, 1997
3 Arnie Herber, Green Bay, 1932, 1934, 1936
Norm Van Brocklin, Los Angeles, 1950, 1952, 1954
Len Dawson, Dall. Texans, 1962; Kansas City, 1966, 1968
Bart Starr, Green Bay, 1966-68

Most Consecutive Seasons Leading League
5 Sid Luckman, Chi. Bears, 1939-43
4 Steve Young, San Francisco, 1991-94
3 Bart Starr, Green Bay, 1966-68

Highest Average Gain, Career (1,500 attempts)
8.63 Otto Graham, Cleveland, 1950-55 (1,565-13,499)
8.42 Sid Luckman, Chi. Bears, 1939-50 (1,744-14,686)
8.16 Norm Van Brocklin, Los Angeles, 1949-57; Philadelphia, 1958-60 (2,895-23,611)

Highest Average Gain, Season (Qualifiers)
11.17 Tommy O'Connell, Cleveland, 1957 (110-1,229)
10.86 Sid Luckman, Chi. Bears, 1943 (202-2,194)
10.55 Otto Graham, Cleveland, 1953 (258-2,722)

Highest Average Gain, Rookie, Season (Qualifiers)
9.411 Greg Cook, Cincinnati, 1969 (197-1,854)
9.409 Bob Waterfield, Cleveland, 1945 (171-1,609)
8.36 Zeke Bratkowski, Chi. Bears, 1954 (130-1,087)

Highest Average Gain, Game (20 attempts)
18.58 Sammy Baugh, Washington vs. Boston, Oct. 31, 1948 (24-446)
18.50 Johnny Unitas, Baltimore vs. Atlanta, Nov. 12, 1967 (20-370)
17.71 Joe Namath, N.Y. Jets vs. Baltimore, Sept. 24, 1972 (28-496)

TOUCHDOWNS

Most Seasons Leading League
4 Johnny Unitas, Baltimore, 1957-60
Len Dawson, Dall. Texans, 1962; Kansas City, 1963, 1965-66
Steve Young, San Francisco, 1992-94, 1998
3 Arnie Herber, Green Bay, 1932, 1934, 1936
Sid Luckman, Chi. Bears, 1943, 1945-46
Y.A. Tittle, San Francisco, 1955; N.Y. Giants, 1962-63
Dan Marino, Miami, 1984-86
Brett Favre, Green Bay, 1995-97
2 By many players

Most Consecutive Seasons Leading League
4 Johnny Unitas, Baltimore, 1957-60
3 Dan Marino, Miami, 1984-86
Steve Young, San Francisco, 1992-94
Brett Favre, Green Bay, 1995-97
2 By many players

Most Touchdown Passes, Career
420 Dan Marino, Miami, 1983-99
342 Fran Tarkenton, Minnesota, 1961-66, 1972-78; N.Y. Giants, 1967-71
300 John Elway, Denver, 1983-98

Most Touchdown Passes, Season
48 Dan Marino, Miami, 1984
44 Dan Marino, Miami, 1986
41 Kurt Warner, St. Louis, 1999

Most Touchdown Passes, Rookie, Season
26 Peyton Manning, Indianapolis, 1998
22 Charlie Conerly, N.Y. Giants, 1948
20 Dan Marino, Miami, 1983

Most Touchdown Passes, Game
7 Sid Luckman, Chi. Bears vs. N.Y. Giants, Nov. 14, 1943
Adrian Burk, Philadelphia vs. Washington, Oct. 17, 1954
George Blanda, Houston vs. N.Y. Titans, Nov. 19, 1961
Y.A. Tittle, N.Y. Giants vs. Washington, Oct. 28, 1962
Joe Kapp, Minnesota vs. Baltimore, Sept. 28, 1969
6 By many players. Last time:
Mark Rypien, Washington vs. Atlanta, Nov. 10, 1991

Most Games, Four or More Touchdown Passes, Career
21 Dan Marino, Miami, 1983-99
17 Johnny Unitas, Baltimore, 1956-72; San Diego, 1973
14 Brett Favre, Atlanta, 1991; Green Bay, 1992-99

Most Games, Four or More Touchdown Passes, Season
6 Dan Marino, Miami, 1984
5 Dan Marino, Miami, 1986
Brett Favre, Green Bay, 1996
4 George Blanda, Houston, 1961
Vince Ferragamo, Los Angeles, 1980
Steve Young, San Francisco, 1994
Randall Cunningham, Minnesota, 1998

Most Consecutive Games, Four or More Touchdown Passes
4 Dan Marino, Miami, 1984
2 By many players

Most Consecutive Games, Touchdown Passes
47 Johnny Unitas, Baltimore, 1956-60
30 Dan Marino, Miami, 1985-87
28 Dave Krieg, Seattle, 1983-85

HAD INTERCEPTED

Most Consecutive Passes Attempted, None Intercepted
308 Bernie Kosar, Cleveland, 1990-91
294 Bart Starr, Green Bay, 1964-65
279 Jeff George, Indianapolis, 1993; Atlanta, 1994

Most Passes Had Intercepted, Career
277 George Blanda, Chi. Bears, 1949, 1950-58; Baltimore, 1950; Houston, 1960-66; Oakland, 1967-75
268 John Hadl, San Diego, 1962-72; Los Angeles, 1973-74; Green Bay, 1974-75; Houston, 1976-77
266 Fran Tarkenton, Minnesota, 1961-66, 1972-78;

N.Y. Giants, 1967-71

Most Passes Had Intercepted, Season

42 George Blanda, Houston, 1962
35 Vinny Testaverde, Tampa Bay, 1988
34 Frank Tripucka, Denver, 1960

Most Passes Had Intercepted, Game

8 Jim Hardy, Chi. Cardinals vs. Philadelphia, Sept. 24, 1950
7 Parker Hall, Cleveland vs. Green Bay, Nov. 8, 1942
Frank Sinkwich, Detroit vs. Green Bay, Oct. 24, 1943
Bob Waterfield, Los Angeles vs. Green Bay, Oct. 17, 1948
Zeke Bratkowski, Chicago vs. Baltimore, Oct. 2, 1960
Tommy Wade, Pittsburgh vs. Philadelphia, Dec. 12, 1965
Ken Stabler, Oakland vs. Denver, Oct. 16, 1977
Steve DeBerg, Tampa Bay vs. San Francisco, Sept. 7, 1986
6 By many players

Most Attempts, No Interceptions, Game

70 Drew Bledsoe, New England vs. Minnesota, Nov. 13, 1994 (OT)
63 Rich Gannon, Minnesota vs. New England, Oct. 20, 1991 (OT)
60 Davey O'Brien, Philadelphia vs. Washington, Dec. 1, 1940

LOWEST PERCENTAGE, PASSES HAD INTERCEPTED

Most Seasons Leading League, Lowest Percentage, Passes Had Intercepted

5 Sammy Baugh, Washington, 1940, 1942, 1944-45, 1947
3 Charlie Conerly, N.Y. Giants, 1950, 1956, 1959
Bart Starr, Green Bay, 1962, 1964, 1966
Roger Staubach, Dallas, 1971, 1977, 1979
Ken Anderson, Cincinnati, 1972, 1981-82
Ken O'Brien, N.Y. Jets, 1985, 1987-88
2 By many players

Lowest Percentage, Passes Had Intercepted, Career (1,500 attempts)

2.03 Neil O'Donnell, Pittsburgh, 1991-95; N.Y. Jets, 1996-97; Cincinnati, 1998; Tennessee, 1999 (3,057-62)
2.41 Mark Brunell, Green Bay, 1994; Jacksonville, 1995-99 (2,160-52)
2.47 Steve Bono, Minnesota, 1985-86; Pittsburgh, 1987-88; San Francisco, 1989, 1991-93; Kansas City, 1994-96; Green Bay, 1997; St. Louis, 1998; Carolina, 1999 (1,701-42)

Lowest Percentage, Passes Had Intercepted, Season (Qualifiers)

0.66 Joe Ferguson, Buffalo, 1976 (151-1)
0.90 Steve DeBerg, Kansas City, 1990 (444-4)
1.16 Steve Bartkowski, Atlanta, 1983 (432-5)

Lowest Percentage, Passes Had Intercepted, Rookie, Season (Qualifiers)

1.98 Charlie Batch, Detroit, 1998 (303-6)
2.03 Dan Marino, Miami, 1983 (296-6)
2.10 Gary Wood, N.Y. Giants, 1964 (143-3)

TIMES SACKED

Times Sacked has been compiled since 1963.

Most Times Sacked, Career

516 John Elway, Denver, 1983-98
494 Dave Krieg, Seattle, 1980-91; Kansas City, 1992-93; Detroit, 1994; Arizona, 1995; Chicago, 1996; Tennessee, 1997-98
483 Fran Tarkenton, Minnesota, 1963-66, 1972-78; N.Y. Giants, 1967-71

Most Times Sacked, Season

72 Randall Cunningham, Philadelphia, 1986
62 Ken O'Brien, N.Y. Jets, 1985
61 Neil Lomax, St. Louis, 1985

Most Times Sacked, Game

12 Bert Jones, Baltimore vs. St. Louis, Oct. 26, 1980
Warren Moon, Houston vs. Dallas, Sept. 29, 1985
11 Charley Johnson, St. Louis vs. N.Y. Giants, Nov. 1, 1964
Bart Starr, Green Bay vs. Detroit, Nov. 7, 1965
Jack Kemp, Buffalo vs. Oakland, Oct. 15, 1967
Bob Berry, Atlanta vs. St. Louis, Nov. 24, 1968
Greg Landry, Detroit vs. Dallas, Oct. 6, 1975
Ron Jaworski, Philadelphia vs. St. Louis, Dec. 18, 1983
Paul McDonald, Cleveland vs. Kansas City, Sept. 30, 1984
Archie Manning, Minnesota vs. Chicago, Oct. 28, 1984
Steve Pelluer, Dallas vs. San Diego, Nov. 16, 1986
Randall Cunningham, Philadelphia vs. L.A. Raiders, Nov. 30, 1986 (OT)
David Norrie, N.Y. Jets vs. Dallas, Oct. 4, 1987
Troy Aikman, Dallas vs. Philadelphia, Sept. 15, 1991
Bernie Kosar, Cleveland vs. Indianapolis, Sept. 6, 1992
10 By many players

PASS RECEIVING

Most Seasons Leading League

8 Don Hutson, Green Bay, 1936-37, 1939, 1941-45
5 Lionel Taylor, Denver, 1960-63, 1965
3 Tom Fears, Los Angeles, 1948-50
Pete Pihos, Philadelphia, 1953-55
Billy Wilson, San Francisco, 1954, 1956-57
Raymond Berry, Baltimore, 1958-60
Lance Alworth, San Diego, 1966, 1968-69
Sterling Sharpe, Green Bay, 1989, 1992-93

Most Consecutive Seasons Leading League

5 Don Hutson, Green Bay, 1941-45
4 Lionel Taylor, Denver, 1960-63
3 Tom Fears, Los Angeles, 1948-50
Pete Pihos, Philadelphia, 1953-55
Raymond Berry, Baltimore, 1958-60

Most Pass Receptions, Career

1,206 Jerry Rice, San Francisco, 1985-99
941 Andre Reed, Buffalo, 1985-99
940 Art Monk, Washington, 1980-93; N.Y. Jets, 1994; Philadelphia, 1995

Most Seasons, 50 or More Pass Receptions

13 Jerry Rice, San Francisco, 1986-96, 1998-99
Andre Reed, Buffalo, 1986-94, 1996-99
10 Steve Largent, Seattle, 1976, 1978-81, 1983-87
Gary Clark, Washington, 1985-92; Phoenix, 1993; Arizona, 1994
Henry Ellard, L.A. Rams, 1985, 1987-91, 1993; Washington, 1994-96
9 Art Monk, Washington, 1980-81, 1984-86, 1988-91
James Lofton, Green Bay, 1979-81, 1983-86; Buffalo, 1991-92
Cris Carter, Minnesota, 1991-99

Most Pass Receptions, Season

123 Herman Moore, Detroit, 1995
122 Cris Carter, Minnesota, 1994
Cris Carter, Minnesota, 1995
Jerry Rice, San Francisco, 1995
119 Isaac Bruce, St. Louis, 1995

Most Pass Receptions, Rookie, Season

90 Terry Glenn, New England, 1996
83 Earl Cooper, San Francisco, 1980
81 Keith Jackson, Philadelphia, 1988

Most Pass Receptions, Game

18 Tom Fears, Los Angeles vs. Green Bay, Dec. 3, 1950
17 Clark Gaines, N.Y. Jets vs. San Francisco, Sept. 21, 1980
16 Sonny Randle, St. Louis vs. N.Y. Giants, Nov. 4, 1962
Jerry Rice, San Francisco vs. L.A. Rams, Nov. 20, 1994
Keenan McCardell, Jacksonville vs. St. Louis, Oct. 20, 1996

Most Consecutive Games, Pass Receptions

209 Jerry Rice, San Francisco, 1985-99 (current)
183 Art Monk, Washington, 1980-93; N.Y. Jets, 1994; Philadelphia, 1995
177 Steve Largent, Seattle, 1977-89

YARDS GAINED

Most Seasons Leading League

7 Don Hutson, Green Bay, 1936, 1938-39, 1941-44
6 Jerry Rice, San Francisco, 1986, 1989-90, 1993-95
3 Raymond Berry, Baltimore, 1957, 1959-60
Lance Alworth, San Diego, 1965-66, 1968

Most Consecutive Seasons Leading League

4 Don Hutson, Green Bay, 1941-44
3 Jerry Rice, San Francisco, 1993-95
2 By many players

Most Yards Gained, Career

18,442 Jerry Rice, San Francisco, 1985-99
14,004 James Lofton, Green Bay, 1978-86; L.A. Raiders, 1987-88; Buffalo, 1989-92; L.A. Rams, 1993; Philadelphia, 1993
13,777 Henry Ellard, L.A. Rams, 1983-1993; Washington, 1994-97; New England-Washington, 1998

Most Seasons, 1,000 or More Yards, Pass Receiving

12 Jerry Rice, San Francisco, 1986-96, 1998
8 Steve Largent, Seattle, 1978-81, 1983-86
7 Lance Alworth, San Diego, 1963-69
Henry Ellard, L.A. Rams, 1988-91; Washington 1994-96
Michael Irvin, Dallas, 1991-95, 1997-98
Tim Brown, L.A. Raiders, 1993-94; Oakland, 1995-99
Cris Carter, Minnesota, 1993-99

Most Yards Gained, Season

1,848 Jerry Rice, San Francisco, 1995
1,781 Isaac Bruce, St. Louis, 1995
1,746 Charley Hennigan, Houston, 1961

Most Yards Gained, Rookie, Season

1,473 Bill Groman, Houston, 1960
1,313 Randy Moss, Minnesota, 1998
1,231 Bill Howton, Green Bay, 1952

Most Yards Gained, Game

336 Willie Anderson, L.A. Rams vs. New Orleans, Nov. 26, 1989 (OT)
309 Stephone Paige, Kansas City vs. San Diego, Dec. 22, 1985
303 Jim Benton, Cleveland vs. Detroit, Nov. 22, 1945

Most Games, 200 or More Yards Pass Receiving, Career

5 Lance Alworth, San Diego, 1962-70; Dallas, 1971-72
4 Don Hutson, Green Bay, 1935-45
Charley Hennigan, Houston, 1960-66
Jerry Rice, San Francisco, 1985-99
3 Don Maynard, N.Y. Giants, 1958; N.Y. Jets, 1960-72; St. Louis, 1973

Wes Chandler, New Orleans, 1978-81; San Diego, 1981-87; San Francisco, 1988
Isaac Bruce, L.A. Rams, 1994; St. Louis, 1995-99

Most Games, 200 or More Yards Pass Receiving, Season
3 Charley Hennigan, Houston, 1961
2 Don Hutson, Green Bay, 1942
Gene Roberts, N.Y. Giants, 1949
Lance Alworth, San Diego, 1963
Don Maynard, N.Y. Jets, 1968

Most Games, 100 or More Yards Pass Receiving, Career
66 Jerry Rice, San Francisco, 1985-99
50 Don Maynard, N.Y. Giants, 1958; N.Y. Jets, 1960-72; St. Louis, 1973
47 Michael Irvin, Dallas, 1988-99

Most Games, 100 or More Yards Pass Receiving, Season
11 Michael Irvin, Dallas, 1995
10 Charley Hennigan, Houston, 1961
Herman Moore, Detroit, 1995
9 Elroy (Crazylegs) Hirsch, Los Angeles, 1951
Bill Groman, Houston, 1960
Lance Alworth, San Diego, 1965
Don Maynard, N.Y. Jets, 1967
Stanley Morgan, New England, 1986
Mark Carrier, Tampa Bay, 1989
Robert Brooks, Green Bay, 1995
Isaac Bruce, St. Louis, 1995
Jerry Rice, San Francisco, 1995
Marvin Harrison, Indianapolis, 1999
Jimmy Smith, Jacksonville, 1999

Most Consecutive Games, 100 or More Yards Pass Receiving
7 Charley Hennigan, Houston, 1961
Michael Irvin, Dallas, 1995
6 Raymond Berry, Baltimore, 1960
Bill Groman, Houston, 1961
Pat Studstill, Detroit, 1966
Isaac Bruce, St. Louis, 1995
5 Elroy (Crazylegs) Hirsch, Los Angeles, 1951
Bob Boyd, Los Angeles, 1954
Terry Barr, Detroit, 1963
Lance Alworth, San Diego, 1966
Don Maynard, N.Y. Jets, 1968-69
Harold Jackson, Philadelphia, 1971-72
Patrick Jeffers, Carolina, 1999 (current)

Longest Pass Reception (All TDs except as noted)
99 Andy Farkas (from Filchock), Washington vs. Pittsburgh, Oct. 15, 1939
Bobby Mitchell (from Izo), Washington vs. Cleveland, Sept. 15, 1963
Pat Studstill (from Sweetan), Detroit vs. Baltimore, Oct. 16, 1966
Gerry Allen (from Jurgensen), Washington vs. Chicago, Sept. 15, 1968
Cliff Branch (from Plunkett), L.A. Raiders vs. Washington, Oct. 2, 1983
Mike Quick (from Jaworski), Philadelphia vs. Atlanta, Nov. 10, 1985
Tony Martin (from Humphries), San Diego vs. Seattle, Sept. 18, 1994
Robert Brooks (from Favre), Green Bay vs. Chicago, Sept. 11, 1995
98 Gaynell Tinsley (from Russell), Chi. Cardinals vs. Cleveland, Nov. 17, 1938
Dick (Night Train) Lane (from Compton), Chi. Cardinals vs. Green Bay, Nov. 13, 1955
John Farrington (from Wade), Chicago vs. Detroit, Oct. 8, 1961
Willard Dewveall (from Lee), Houston vs. San Diego, Nov. 25, 1962
Homer Jones (from Morrall), N.Y. Giants vs. Pittsburgh, Sept. 11, 1966
Bobby Moore (from Hart), St. Louis vs. Los Angeles, Dec. 10, 1972 (no TD)
Michael Haynes (from Hebert), Atlanta vs. New Orleans, Sept. 12, 1993
Johnnie Morton (from Batch), Detroit vs. Chicago, Oct. 4, 1998
97 Gaynell Tinsley (from Coffee), Chi. Cardinals vs. Chi. Bears, Dec. 5, 1937
Cloyce Box (from Layne), Detroit vs. Green Bay, Nov. 26, 1953
Jerry Tarr (from Shaw), Denver vs. Boston, Sept. 21, 1962
Webster Slaughter (from Kosar), Cleveland vs. Chicago, Oct. 23, 1989
John Taylor (from Young), San Francisco vs. Atlanta, Nov. 3, 1991

AVERAGE GAIN

Highest Average Gain, Career (200 receptions)
22.26 Homer Jones, N.Y. Giants, 1964-69; Cleveland, 1970 (224-4,986)
20.83 Buddy Dial, Pittsburgh, 1959-63; Dallas, 1964-66 (261-5,436)
20.24 Harlon Hill, Chi. Bears, 1954-61; Pittsburgh, 1962; Detroit, 1962 (233-4,717)

Highest Average Gain, Season (24 receptions)
32.58 Don Currivan, Boston, 1947 (24-782)
31.44 Bucky Pope, Los Angeles, 1964 (25-786)
28.60 Bobby Duckworth, San Diego, 1984 (25-715)

Highest Average Gain, Game (3 receptions)
60.67 Bill Groman, Houston vs. Denver, Nov. 20, 1960 (3-182)
Homer Jones, N.Y. Giants vs. Washington, Dec. 12, 1965 (3-182)
60.33 Don Currivan, Boston vs. Washington, Nov. 30, 1947 (3-181)
59.67 Bobby Duckworth, San Diego vs. Chicago, Dec. 3, 1984 (3-179)

TOUCHDOWNS

Most Seasons Leading League
9 Don Hutson, Green Bay, 1935-38, 1940-44
6 Jerry Rice, San Francisco, 1986-87, 1989-91, 1993
3 Lance Alworth, San Diego, 1964-66
Cris Carter, Minnesota, 1995, 1997, 1999

Most Consecutive Seasons Leading League
5 Don Hutson, Green Bay, 1940-44
4 Don Hutson, Green Bay, 1935-38
3 Lance Alworth, San Diego, 1964-66
Jerry Rice, San Francisco, 1989-91

Most Touchdowns, Career
169 Jerry Rice, San Francisco, 1985-99
114 Cris Carter, Philadelphia, 1987-89; Minnesota, 1990-99
100 Steve Largent, Seattle, 1976-89

Most Touchdowns, Season
22 Jerry Rice, San Francisco, 1987
18 Mark Clayton, Miami, 1984
Sterling Sharpe, Green Bay, 1994
17 Don Hutson, Green Bay, 1942
Elroy (Crazylegs) Hirsch, Los Angeles, 1951
Bill Groman, Houston, 1961
Jerry Rice, San Francisco, 1989
Cris Carter, Minnesota, 1995
Carl Pickens, Cincinnati, 1995
Randy Moss, Minnesota, 1998

Most Touchdowns, Rookie, Season
17 Randy Moss, Minnesota, 1998
13 Bill Howton, Green Bay, 1952
John Jefferson, San Diego, 1978
12 Harlon Hill, Chi. Bears, 1954
Bill Groman, Houston, 1960
Mike Ditka, Chicago, 1961
Bob Hayes, Dallas, 1965

Most Touchdowns, Game
5 Bob Shaw, Chi. Cardinals vs. Baltimore, Oct. 2, 1950
Kellen Winslow, San Diego vs. Oakland, Nov. 22, 1981
Jerry Rice, San Francisco vs. Atlanta, Oct. 14, 1990
4 By many players. Last time:
Isaac Bruce, St. Louis vs. San Francisco, Oct. 10, 1999

Most Consecutive Games, Touchdowns
13 Jerry Rice, San Francisco, 1986-87
11 Elroy (Crazylegs) Hirsch, Los Angeles, 1950-51
Buddy Dial, Pittsburgh, 1959-60
10 Carl Pickens, Cincinnati, 1994-95

INTERCEPTIONS BY

Most Seasons Leading League
3 Everson Walls, Dallas, 1981-82, 1985
2 Dick (Night Train) Lane, Los Angeles, 1952; Chi. Cardinals, 1954
Jack Christiansen, Detroit, 1953, 1957
Milt Davis, Baltimore, 1957, 1959
Dick Lynch, N.Y. Giants, 1961, 1963
Johnny Robinson, Kansas City, 1966, 1970
Bill Bradley, Philadelphia, 1971-72
Emmitt Thomas, Kansas City, 1969, 1974
Ronnie Lott, San Francisco, 1986; L.A. Raiders, 1991

Most Interceptions By, Career
81 Paul Krause, Washington, 1964-67; Minnesota, 1968-79
79 Emlen Tunnell, N.Y. Giants, 1948-58; Green Bay, 1959-61
68 Dick (Night Train) Lane, Los Angeles, 1952-53; Chi. Cardinals, 1954-59; Detroit, 1960-65

Most Interceptions By, Season
14 Dick (Night Train) Lane, Los Angeles, 1952
13 Dan Sandifer, Washington, 1948
Orban (Spec) Sanders, N.Y. Yanks, 1950
Lester Hayes, Oakland, 1980
12 By nine players

Most Interceptions By, Rookie, Season
14 Dick (Night Train) Lane, Los Angeles, 1952
13 Dan Sandifer, Washington, 1948
12 Woodley Lewis, Los Angeles, 1950
Paul Krause, Washington, 1964

Most Interceptions By, Game
4 Sammy Baugh, Washington vs. Detroit, Nov. 14, 1943
Dan Sandifer, Washington vs. Boston, Oct. 31, 1948
Don Doll, Detroit vs. Chi. Cardinals, Oct. 23, 1949
Bob Nussbaumer, Chi. Cardinals vs. N.Y. Bulldogs, Nov. 13, 1949
Russ Craft, Philadelphia vs. Chi. Cardinals, Sept. 24, 1950
Bobby Dillon, Green Bay vs. Detroit, Nov. 26, 1953

Jack Butler, Pittsburgh vs. Washington, Dec. 13, 1953
Austin (Goose) Gonsoulin, Denver vs. Buffalo, Sept. 18, 1960
Jerry Norton, St. Louis vs. Washington, Nov. 20, 1960; vs. Pittsburgh, Nov. 26, 1961
Dave Baker, San Francisco vs. L.A. Rams, Dec. 4, 1960
Bobby Ply, Dall. Texans vs. San Diego, Dec. 16, 1962
Bobby Hunt, Kansas City vs. Houston, Oct. 4, 1964
Willie Brown, Denver vs. N.Y. Jets, Nov. 15, 1964
Dick Anderson, Miami vs. Pittsburgh, Dec. 3, 1973
Willie Buchanon, Green Bay vs. San Diego, Sept. 24, 1978
Deron Cherry, Kansas City vs. Seattle, Sept. 29, 1985
Kwamie Lassiter, Arizona vs. San Diego, Dec. 27, 1998

Most Consecutive Games, Passes Intercepted By

8 Tom Morrow, Oakland, 1962-63
7 Tom Landry, N.Y. Giants, 1950-51
Paul Krause, Washington, 1964
Larry Wilson, St. Louis, 1966
Ben Davis, Cleveland, 1968
6 By many players. Last time:
Barry Wilburn, Washington, 1987

YARDS GAINED

Most Seasons Leading League

2 Dick (Night Train) Lane, Los Angeles, 1952; Chi. Cardinals, 1954
Herb Adderley, Green Bay, 1965, 1969
Dick Anderson, Miami, 1968, 1970

Most Yards Gained, Career

1,282 Emlen Tunnell, N.Y. Giants, 1948-58; Green Bay, 1959-61
1,207 Dick (Night Train) Lane, Los Angeles, 1952-53; Chi. Cardinals, 1954-59; Detroit, 1960-65
1,185 Paul Krause, Washington, 1964-67; Minnesota, 1968-79

Most Yards Gained, Season

349 Charlie McNeil, San Diego, 1961
303 Deion Sanders, San Francisco, 1994
301 Don Doll, Detroit, 1949

Most Yards Gained, Rookie, Season

301 Don Doll, Detroit, 1949
298 Dick (Night Train) Lane, Los Angeles, 1952
275 Woodley Lewis, Los Angeles, 1950

Most Yards Gained, Game

177 Charlie McNeil, San Diego vs. Houston, Sept. 24, 1961
170 Louis Oliver, Miami vs. Buffalo, Oct. 4, 1992
167 Dick Jauron, Detroit vs. Chicago, Nov. 18, 1973

Longest Return (All TDs)

103 Vencie Glenn, San Diego vs. Denver, Nov. 29, 1987
Louis Oliver, Miami vs. Buffalo, Oct. 4, 1992
102 Bob Smith, Detroit vs. Chi. Bears, Nov. 24, 1949
Erich Barnes, N.Y. Giants vs. Dall. Cowboys, Oct. 15, 1961
Gary Barbaro, Kansas City vs. Seattle, Dec. 11, 1977
Louis Breeden, Cincinnati vs. San Diego, Nov. 8, 1981
Eddie Anderson, L.A. Raiders vs. Miami, Dec. 14, 1992
Donald Frank, San Diego vs. L.A. Raiders, Oct. 31, 1993
101 Richie Petitbon, Chicago vs Los Angeles, Dec. 9, 1962
Henry Carr, N.Y. Giants vs. Los Angeles, Nov. 13, 1966
Tony Greene, Buffalo vs. Kansas City, Oct. 3, 1976
Tom Pridemore, Atlanta vs. San Francisco, Sept. 20, 1981

TOUCHDOWNS

Most Touchdowns, Career

9 Ken Houston, Houston, 1967-72; Washington, 1973-80
Rod Woodson, Pittsburgh, 1987-96; San Francisco, 1997; Baltimore, 1998-99
8 Deion Sanders, Atlanta, 1989-93; San Francisco, 1994; Dallas, 1995-99
7 Herb Adderley, Green Bay, 1961-69; Dallas, 1970-72
Erich Barnes, Chi. Bears, 1958-60; N.Y. Giants, 1961-64; Cleveland, 1965-70
Lem Barney, Detroit, 1967-77

Most Touchdowns, Season

4 Ken Houston, Houston, 1971
Jim Kearney, Kansas City, 1972
Eric Allen, Philadelphia, 1993
3 Dick Harris, San Diego, 1961
Dick Lynch, N.Y. Giants, 1963
Herb Adderley, Green Bay, 1965
Lem Barney, Detroit, 1967
Miller Farr, Houston, 1967
Monte Jackson, Los Angeles, 1976
Rod Perry, Los Angeles, 1978
Ronnie Lott, San Francisco, 1981
Lloyd Burruss, Kansas City, 1986
Wayne Haddix, Tampa Bay, 1990
Robert Massey, Phoenix, 1992
Ray Buchanan, Indianapolis, 1994
Deion Sanders, San Francisco, 1994
Mark McMillian, Kansas City, 1997
Otis Smith, N.Y. Jets, 1997
Jimmy Hitchcock, Minnesota, 1998
2 By many players

Most Touchdowns, Rookie, Season

3 Lem Barney, Detroit, 1967
Ronnie Lott, San Francisco, 1981
2 By many players

Most Touchdowns, Game

2 Bill Blackburn, Chi. Cardinals vs. Boston, Oct. 24, 1948
Dan Sandifer, Washington vs. Boston, Oct. 31, 1948
Bob Franklin, Cleveland vs. Chicago, Dec. 11, 1960
Bill Stacy, St. Louis vs. Dall. Cowboys, Nov. 5, 1961
Jerry Norton, St. Louis vs. Pittsburgh, Nov. 26, 1961
Miller Farr, Houston vs. Buffalo, Dec. 7, 1968
Ken Houston, Houston vs. San Diego, Dec. 19, 1971
Jim Kearney, Kansas City vs. Denver, Oct. 1, 1972
Lemar Parrish, Cincinnati vs. Houston, Dec. 17, 1972
Dick Anderson, Miami vs. Pittsburgh, Dec. 3, 1973
Prentice McCray, New England vs. N.Y. Jets, Nov. 21, 1976
Kenny Johnson, Atlanta vs. Green Bay, Nov. 27, 1983 (OT)
Mike Kozlowski, Miami vs. N.Y. Jets, Dec. 16, 1983
Dave Brown, Seattle vs. Kansas City, Nov. 4, 1984
Lloyd Burruss, Kansas City vs. San Diego, Oct. 19, 1986
Henry Jones, Buffalo vs. Indianapolis, Sept. 20, 1992
Robert Massey, Phoenix vs. Washington, Oct. 4, 1992
Eric Allen, Philadelphia vs. New Orleans, Dec. 26, 1993
Ken Norton, San Francisco vs. St. Louis, Oct. 22, 1995
Otis Smith, N.Y. Jets vs. Tampa Bay, Dec. 14, 1997
Dewayne Washington, Pittsburgh vs. Jacksonville, Nov. 22, 1998

PUNTING

Most Seasons Leading League

4 Sammy Baugh, Washington, 1940-43
Jerrel Wilson, Kansas City, 1965, 1968, 1972-73
3 Yale Lary, Detroit, 1959, 1961, 1963
Jim Fraser, Denver, 1962-64
Ray Guy, Oakland, 1974-75, 1977
Rohn Stark, Baltimore, 1983; Indianapolis, 1985-86
2 By many players

Most Consecutive Seasons Leading League

4 Sammy Baugh, Washington, 1940-43
3 Jim Fraser, Denver, 1962-64
2 By many players

PUNTS

Most Punts, Career

1,154 Dave Jennings, N.Y. Giants, 1974-84; N.Y. Jets, 1985-87
1,141 Rohn Stark, Baltimore, 1982-83; Indianapolis, 1984-94; Pittsburgh, 1995; Carolina, 1996; Seattle, 1997
1,083 John James, Atlanta, 1972-81; Detroit, 1982, Houston, 1982-84

Most Punts, Season

114 Bob Parsons, Chicago, 1981
111 Brad Maynard, N.Y. Giants, 1997
109 John James, Atlanta, 1978

Most Punts, Rookie, Season

111 Brad Maynard, N.Y. Giants, 1997
108 John Teltschik, Philadelphia, 1986
101 Daniel Pope, Kansas City, 1999

Most Punts, Game

16 Leo Araguz, Oakland vs. San Diego, Oct. 11, 1998
15 John Teltschik, Philadelphia vs. N.Y. Giants, Dec. 6, 1987 (OT)
14 Dick Nesbitt, Chi. Cardinals vs. Chi. Bears, Nov. 30, 1933
Keith Molesworth, Chi. Bears vs. Green Bay, Dec. 10, 1933
Sammy Baugh, Washington vs. Philadelphia, Nov. 5, 1939
Carl Kinscherf, N.Y. Giants vs. Detroit, Nov. 7, 1943
George Taliaferro, N.Y. Yanks vs. Los Angeles, Sept. 28, 1951

Longest Punt

98 Steve O'Neal, N.Y. Jets vs. Denver, Sept. 21, 1969
94 Joe Lintzenich, Chi. Bears vs. N.Y. Giants, Nov. 16, 1931
93 Shawn McCarthy, New England vs. Buffalo, Nov. 3, 1991

AVERAGE YARDAGE

Highest Average, Punting, Career (250 punts)

45.10 Sammy Baugh, Washington, 1937-52 (338-15,245)
44.68 Tommy Davis, San Francisco, 1959-69 (511-22,833)
44.55 Darren Bennett, San Diego, 1995-99 (432-19,244)

Highest Average, Punting, Season (Qualifiers)

51.40 Sammy Baugh, Washington, 1940 (35-1,799)
48.94 Yale Lary, Detroit, 1963 (35-1,713)
48.73 Sammy Baugh, Washington, 1941 (30-1,462)

Highest Average, Punting, Rookie, Season (Qualifiers)
45.92 Frank Sinkwich, Detroit, 1943 (12-551)
45.66 Tommy Davis, San Francisco, 1959 (59-2,694)
45.57 David Lee, Baltimore, 1966 (49-2,233)

Highest Average, Punting, Game (4 punts)
61.75 Bob Cifers, Detroit vs. Chi. Bears, Nov. 24, 1946 (4-247)
61.60 Roy McKay, Green Bay vs. Chi. Cardinals, Oct. 28, 1945 (5-308)
59.50 Darren Bennett, San Diego vs. Pittsburgh, Oct. 1, 1995 (4-238)

PUNTS HAD BLOCKED

Most Consecutive Punts, None Blocked
623 Dave Jennings, N.Y. Giants, 1976-83
619 Ray Guy, Oakland, 1979-81; L.A. Raiders, 1982-86
618 Chris Gardocki, Chicago, 1992-94; Indianapolis, 1995-98; Cleveland, 1999

Most Punts Had Blocked, Career
14 Herman Weaver, Detroit, 1970-76; Seattle, 1977-80
Harry Newsome, Pittsburgh, 1985-89; Minnesota, 1990-93
12 Jerrel Wilson, Kansas City, 1963-77; New England, 1978
Tom Blanchard, N.Y. Giants, 1971-73; New Orleans, 1974-78; Tampa Bay, 1979-81
11 David Lee, Baltimore, 1966-78

Most Punts Had Blocked, Season
6 Harry Newsome, Pittsburgh, 1988
4 Bryan Wagner, Cleveland, 1990
3 By many players

PUNT RETURNS

Most Seasons Leading League
3 Les (Speedy) Duncan, San Diego, 1965-66; Washington, 1971
Rick Upchurch, Denver, 1976, 1978, 1982
2 Dick Christy, N.Y. Titans, 1961-62
Claude Gibson, Oakland, 1963-64
Billy (White Shoes) Johnson, Houston, 1975, 1977
Mel Gray, New Orleans, 1987; Detroit, 1991

PUNT RETURNS

Most Punt Returns, Career
349 David Meggett, N.Y. Giants, 1989-94; New England, 1995-97; N.Y. Jets, 1998
317 Brian Mitchell, Washington, 1990-99
315 Eric Metcalf, Cleveland, 1989-94; Atlanta, 1995-96; San Diego, 1997; Arizona, 1998; Carolina, 1999

Most Punt Returns, Season
70 Danny Reece, Tampa Bay, 1979
62 Fulton Walker, Miami-L.A. Raiders, 1985
58 J.T. Smith, Kansas City, 1979
Greg Pruitt, L.A. Raiders, 1983
Leo Lewis, Minnesota, 1988
Desmond Howard, Green Bay, 1996

Most Punt Returns, Rookie, Season
57 Lew Barnes, Chicago, 1986
54 James Jones, Dallas, 1980
53 Louis Lipps, Pittsburgh, 1984

Most Punt Returns, Game
11 Eddie Brown, Washington vs. Tampa Bay, Oct. 9, 1977
10 Theo Bell, Pittsburgh vs. Buffalo, Dec. 16, 1979
Mike Nelms, Washington vs. New Orleans, Dec. 26, 1982
Ronnie Harris, New England vs. Pittsburgh, Dec. 5, 1993
9 Rodger Bird, Oakland vs. Denver, Sept. 10, 1967
Ralph McGill, San Francisco vs. Atlanta, Oct. 29, 1972
Ed Podolak, Kansas City vs. San Diego, Nov. 10, 1974
Anthony Leonard, San Francisco vs. New Orleans, Oct. 17, 1976
Butch Johnson, Dallas vs. Buffalo, Nov. 15, 1976
Larry Marshall, Philadelphia vs. Tampa Bay, Sept. 18, 1977
Nesby Glasgow, Baltimore vs. Kansas City, Sept. 2, 1979
Mike Nelms, Washington vs. St. Louis, Dec. 21, 1980
Leon Bright, N.Y. Giants vs. Philadelphia, Dec. 11, 1982
Pete Shaw, N.Y. Giants vs. Philadelphia, Nov. 20, 1983
Cleotha Montgomery, L.A. Raiders vs. Detroit, Dec. 10, 1984
Phil McConkey, N.Y. Giants vs. Philadelphia, Dec. 6, 1987 (OT)
Andre Hastings, Pittsburgh vs. Cleveland, Nov. 13, 1995

FAIR CATCHES

Most Fair Catches, Career
151 Brian Mitchell, Washington, 1990-99
121 Mel Gray, New Orleans, 1986-88; Detroit, 1989-94; Houston, 1995-96; Tennessee, 1997; Philadelphia, 1997
114 David Meggett, N.Y. Giants, 1989-94; New England, 1995-97; N.Y. Jets, 1998

Most Fair Catches, Season
27 Leo Lewis, Minnesota, 1989
26 Eric Guliford, New Orleans, 1997
Glyn Milburn, Detroit, 1997
25 Mark Konecny, Philadelphia, 1988
Phil McConkey, N.Y. Giants, 1988
Chris Warren, Seattle, 1992
Eddie Kennison, St. Louis, 1998

Most Fair Catches, Game
7 Lem Barney, Detroit vs. Chicago, Nov. 21, 1976
Bobby Morse, Philadelphia vs. Buffalo, Dec. 27, 1987
6 Jake Scott, Miami vs. Buffalo, Dec. 20, 1970
Greg Pruitt, L.A. Raiders vs. Seattle, Oct. 7, 1984
Phil McConkey, San Diego vs. Kansas City, Dec. 17, 1989
Gerald McNeil, Houston vs. Pittsburgh, Sept. 16, 1990
Bobby Engram, Chicago vs. Minnesota, Sept. 15, 1996
Eddie Kennison, New Orleans vs. Baltimore, Dec. 19, 1999
5 By many players

YARDS GAINED

Most Seasons Leading League
3 Alvin Haymond, Baltimore, 1965-66; Los Angeles, 1969
2 Bill Dudley, Pittsburgh, 1942, 1946
Emlen Tunnell, N.Y. Giants, 1951-52
Dick Christy, N.Y. Titans, 1961-62
Claude Gibson, Oakland, 1963-64
Rodger Bird, Oakland, 1966-67
J.T. Smith, Kansas City, 1979-80
Vai Sikahema, St. Louis, 1986-87
David Meggett, N.Y. Giants, 1989-90
Tamarick Vanover, Kansas City, 1995, 1999

Most Yards Gained, Career
3,708 David Meggett, N.Y. Giants, 1989-94; New England, 1995-97; N.Y. Jets, 1998
3,476 Brian Mitchell, Washington, 1990-99
3,317 Billy (White Shoes) Johnson, Houston, 1974-80; Atlanta, 1982-87; Washington, 1988

Most Yards Gained, Season
875 Desmond Howard, Green Bay, 1996
692 Fulton Walker, Miami-L.A. Raiders, 1985
666 Greg Pruitt, L.A. Raiders, 1983

Most Yards Gained, Rookie, Season
656 Louis Lipps, Pittsburgh, 1984
655 Neal Colzie, Oakland, 1975
619 Leon Johnson, N.Y. Jets, 1997

Most Yards Gained, Game
207 LeRoy Irvin, Los Angeles vs. Atlanta, Oct. 11, 1981
205 George Atkinson, Oakland vs. Buffalo, Sept. 15, 1968
184 Tom Watkins, Detroit vs. San Francisco, Oct. 6, 1963
Jermaine Lewis, Baltimore vs. Seattle, Dec. 7, 1997

Longest Punt Return (All TDs)
103 Robert Bailey, L.A. Rams vs. New Orleans, Oct. 23, 1994
98 Gil LeFebvre, Cincinnati vs. Brooklyn, Dec. 3, 1933
Charlie West, Minnesota vs. Washington, Nov. 3, 1968
Dennis Morgan, Dallas vs. St. Louis, Oct. 13, 1974
Terance Mathis, N.Y. Jets vs. Dallas, Nov. 4, 1990
97 Greg Pruitt, L.A. Raiders vs. Washington, Oct. 2, 1983

AVERAGE YARDAGE

Highest Average, Career (75 returns)
12.78 George McAfee, Chi. Bears, 1940-41, 1945-50 (112-1,431)
12.75 Jack Christiansen, Detroit, 1951-58 (85-1,084)
12.55 Claude Gibson, San Diego, 1961-62; Oakland, 1963-65 (110-1,381)

Highest Average, Season (Qualifiers)
23.00 Herb Rich, Baltimore, 1950 (12-276)
21.47 Jack Christiansen, Detroit, 1952 (15-322)
21.28 Dick Christy, N.Y. Titans, 1961 (18-383)

Highest Average, Rookie, Season (Qualifiers)
23.00 Herb Rich, Baltimore, 1950 (12-276)
20.88 Jerry Davis, Chi. Cardinals, 1948 (16-334)
20.73 Frank Sinkwich, Detroit, 1943 (11-228)

Highest Average, Game (3 returns)
47.67 Chuck Latourette, St. Louis vs. New Orleans, Sept. 29, 1968 (3-143)
47.33 Johnny Roland, St. Louis vs. Philadelphia, Oct. 2, 1966 (3-142)
45.67 Dick Christy, N.Y. Titans vs. Denver, Sept. 24, 1961 (3-137)

TOUCHDOWNS

Most Touchdowns, Career
9 Eric Metcalf, Cleveland, 1989-94; Atlanta, 1995-96; San Diego, 1997; Arizona, 1998; Carolina, 1999
8 Jack Christiansen, Detroit, 1951-58
Rick Upchurch, Denver, 1975-83

7 David Meggett, N.Y. Giants, 1989-94; New England, 1995-97; N.Y. Jets, 1998
Brian Mitchell, Washington, 1990-99
Desmond Howard, Washington, 1992-94; Jacksonville, 1995; Green Bay, 1996, 1999; Oakland, 1997-98; Detroit, 1999

Most Touchdowns, Season
4 Jack Christiansen, Detroit, 1951
Rick Upchurch, Denver, 1976
3 Emlen Tunnell, N.Y. Giants, 1951
Billy (White Shoes) Johnson, Houston, 1975
LeRoy Irvin, Los Angeles, 1981
Desmond Howard, Green Bay, 1996
Darrien Gordon, Denver, 1997
Eric Metcalf, San Diego, 1997
2 By many players

Most Touchdowns, Rookie, Season
4 Jack Christiansen, Detroit, 1951
2 By many players

Most Touchdowns, Game
2 Jack Christiansen, Detroit vs. Los Angeles, Oct. 14, 1951; vs. Green Bay, Nov. 22, 1951
Dick Christy, N.Y. Titans vs. Denver, Sept. 24, 1961
Rick Upchurch, Denver vs. Cleveland, Sept. 26, 1976
LeRoy Irvin, Los Angeles vs. Atlanta, Oct. 11, 1981
Vai Sikahema, St. Louis vs. Tampa Bay, Dec. 21, 1986
Todd Kinchen, L.A. Rams vs. Atlanta, Dec. 27, 1992
Eric Metcalf, Cleveland vs. Pittsburgh, Oct. 24, 1993; San Diego vs. Cincinnati, Nov. 2, 1997
Darrien Gordon, Denver vs. Carolina, Nov. 9, 1997
Jermaine Lewis, Baltimore vs. Seattle, Dec. 7, 1997

KICKOFF RETURNS

Most Seasons Leading League
3 Abe Woodson, San Francisco, 1959, 1962-63
2 Lynn Chandnois, Pittsburgh, 1951-52
Bobby Jancik, Houston, 1962-63
Travis Williams, Green Bay, 1967; Los Angeles, 1971
Mel Gray, Detroit, 1991, 1994
Michael Bates, Carolina, 1996-97

KICKOFF RETURNS

Most Kickoff Returns, Career
421 Mel Gray, New Orleans, 1986-88; Detroit, 1989-94; Houston, 1995-96; Tennessee, 1997; Philadelphia, 1997
Brian Mitchell, Washington, 1990-99
338 Glyn Milburn, Denver, 1993-95; Detroit, 1996-97; Chicago, 1998-99
292 Kevin Williams, Dallas, 1993-96; Arizona, 1997; Buffalo, 1998-99

Most Kickoff Returns, Season
70 Tyrone Hughes, New Orleans, 1996
66 Tyrone Hughes, New Orleans, 1995
64 Glyn Milburn, Detroit, 1996

Most Kickoff Returns, Rookie, Season
56 Tony Horne, St. Louis, 1998
55 Stump Mitchell, St. Louis, 1981
54 Leeland McElroy, Arizona, 1996

Most Kickoff Returns, Game
10 Desmond Howard, Oakland vs. Seattle, Oct. 26, 1997
9 Noland Smith, Kansas City vs. Oakland, Nov. 23, 1967
Dino Hall, Cleveland vs. Pittsburgh, Oct. 7, 1979
Paul Palmer, Kansas City vs. Seattle, Sept. 20, 1987
Eric Metcalf, Atlanta vs. San Francisco, Sept. 29, 1996; vs. St. Louis, Nov. 10, 1996
Michael Bates, Carolina vs. Atlanta, Oct. 4, 1998
8 By many players

YARDS GAINED

Most Seasons Leading League
3 Bruce Harper, N.Y. Jets, 1977-79
Tyrone Hughes, New Orleans, 1994-96
2 Marshall Goldberg, Chi. Cardinals, 1941-42
Woodley Lewis, Los Angeles, 1953-54
Al Carmichael, Green Bay, 1956-57
Timmy Brown, Philadelphia, 1961, 1963
Bobby Jancik, Houston, 1963, 1966
Ron Smith, Atlanta, 1966-67

Most Yards Gained, Career
10,250 Mel Gray, New Orleans, 1986-88; Detroit, 1989-94; Houston, 1995-96; Tennessee, 1997; Philadelphia, 1997
9,586 Brian Mitchell, Washington, 1990-99
8,168 Glyn Milburn, Denver, 1993-95; Detroit, 1996-97; Chicago, 1998-99

Most Yards Gained, Season
1,791 Tyrone Hughes, New Orleans, 1996
1,627 Glyn Milburn, Detroit, 1996
1,617 Tyrone Hughes, New Orleans, 1995

Most Yards Gained, Rookie, Season
1,428 Terry Fair, Detroit, 1998
1,345 Buster Rhymes, Minnesota, 1985
1,306 Tony Horne, St. Louis, 1998

Most Yards Gained, Game
304 Tyrone Hughes, New Orleans vs. L.A. Rams, Oct. 23, 1994
294 Wally Triplett, Detroit vs. Los Angeles, Oct. 29, 1950
256 Roell Preston, Green Bay vs. Minnesota, Oct. 5, 1998

Longest Kickoff Return (All TDs)
106 Al Carmichael, Green Bay vs. Chi. Bears, Oct. 7, 1956
Noland Smith, Kansas City vs. Denver, Dec. 17, 1967
Roy Green, St. Louis vs. Dallas, Oct. 21, 1979
105 Frank Seno, Chi. Cardinals vs. N.Y. Giants, Oct. 20, 1946
Ollie Matson, Chi. Cardinals vs. Washington, Oct. 14, 1956
Abe Woodson, San Francisco vs. Los Angeles, Nov. 8, 1959
Timmy Brown, Philadelphia vs. Cleveland, Sept. 17, 1961
Jon Arnett, Los Angeles vs. Detroit, Oct. 29, 1961
Eugene (Mercury) Morris, Miami vs. Cincinnati, Sept. 14, 1969
Travis Williams, Los Angeles vs. New Orleans, Dec. 5, 1971
Terry Fair, Detroit vs. Tampa Bay, Sept. 28, 1998
104 By many players

AVERAGE YARDAGE

Highest Average, Career (75 returns)
30.56 Gale Sayers, Chicago, 1965-71 (91-2,781)
29.57 Lynn Chandnois, Pittsburgh, 1950-56 (92-2,720)
28.69 Abe Woodson, San Francisco, 1958-64; St. Louis, 1965-66 (193-5,538)

Highest Average, Season (Qualifiers)
41.06 Travis Williams, Green Bay, 1967 (18-739)
37.69 Gale Sayers, Chicago, 1967 (16-603)
35.50 Ollie Matson, Chi. Cardinals, 1958 (14-497)

Highest Average, Rookie, Season (Qualifiers)
41.06 Travis Williams, Green Bay, 1967 (18-739)
33.08 Tom Moore, Green Bay, 1960 (12-397)
32.88 Duriel Harris, Miami, 1976 (17-559)

Highest Average, Game (3 returns)
73.50 Wally Triplett, Detroit vs. Los Angeles, Oct. 29, 1950 (4-294)
67.33 Lenny Lyles, San Francisco vs. Baltimore, Dec. 18, 1960 (3-202)
65.33 Ken Hall, Houston vs. N.Y. Titans, Oct. 23, 1960 (3-196)

TOUCHDOWNS

Most Touchdowns, Career
6 Ollie Matson, Chi. Cardinals, 1952, 1954-58; L.A. Rams, 1959-62; Detroit, 1963; Philadelphia, 1964
Gale Sayers, Chicago, 1965-71
Travis Williams, Green Bay, 1967-70; Los Angeles, 1971
Mel Gray, New Orleans, 1986-88; Detroit, 1989-94; Houston, 1995-96; Tennessee, 1997; Philadelphia, 1997
5 Bobby Mitchell, Cleveland, 1958-61; Washington, 1962-68
Abe Woodson, San Francisco, 1958-64; St. Louis, 1965-66
Timmy Brown, Green Bay, 1959; Philadelphia, 1960-67; Baltimore, 1968
4 Cecil Turner, Chicago, 1968-73
Ron Brown, L.A. Rams, 1984-89, 1991; L.A. Raiders, 1990
Jon Vaughn, New England, 1991-92; Seattle, 1993-94; Kansas City, 1994
Andre Coleman, San Diego, 1994-96; Seattle, 1997; Pittsburgh, 1997-98
Tamarick Vanover, Kansas City, 1995-99
Michael Bates, Seattle, 1993-94; Cleveland, 1995; Carolina, 1996-99

Most Touchdowns, Season
4 Travis Williams, Green Bay, 1967
Cecil Turner, Chicago, 1970
3 Verda (Vitamin T) Smith, Los Angeles, 1950
Abe Woodson, San Francisco, 1963
Gale Sayers, Chicago, 1967
Raymond Clayborn, New England, 1977
Ron Brown, L.A. Rams, 1985
Mel Gray, Detroit, 1994
2 By many players

Most Touchdowns, Rookie, Season
4 Travis Williams, Green Bay, 1967
3 Raymond Clayborn, New England, 1977
2 By many players

Most Touchdowns, Game
2 Timmy Brown, Philadelphia vs. Dallas, Nov. 6, 1966
Travis Williams, Green Bay vs. Cleveland, Nov. 12, 1967
Ron Brown, L.A. Rams vs. Green Bay, Nov. 24, 1985
Tyrone Hughes, New Orleans vs. L.A. Rams, Oct. 23, 1994

COMBINED KICK RETURNS

Most Combined Kick Returns, Career

738 Brian Mitchell, Washington, 1990-99 (p-317; k-421)
673 Mel Gray, New Orleans, 1986-88; Detroit, 1989-94; Houston, 1995-96; Tennessee, 1997; Philadelphia, 1997 (p-252, k-421)
601 David Meggett, N.Y. Giants, 1989-94; New England, 1995-97; N.Y. Jets, 1998 (p-349; k-252)

Most Combined Kick Returns, Season

103 Brian Mitchell, Washington, 1998 (p-44; k-59)
102 Glyn Milburn, Detroit, 1997 (p-47, k-55)
101 Roell Preston, Green Bay, 1998 (p-44; k-57)

Most Combined Kick Returns, Game

13 Stump Mitchell, St. Louis vs. Atlanta, Oct. 18, 1981 (p-6, k-7)
Ronnie Harris, New England vs. Pittsburgh, Dec. 5, 1993 (p-10, k-3)
12 Mel Renfro, Dallas vs. Green Bay, Nov. 29, 1964 (p-4, k-8)
Larry Jones, Washington vs. Dallas, Dec. 13, 1975 (p-6, k-6)
Eddie Brown, Washington vs. Tampa Bay, Oct. 9, 1977 (p-11, k-1)
Nesby Glasgow, Baltimore vs. Denver, Sept. 2, 1979 (p-9, k-3)
11 By many players

YARDS GAINED

Most Yards Returned, Career

13,062 Brian Mitchell, Washington, 1990-99 (p-3,476; k-9,586)
13,003 Mel Gray, New Orleans, 1986-88; Detroit, 1989-94; Houston, 1995-96; Tennessee, 1997; Philadelphia, 1997 (p-2,753; k-10,250)
10,680 Glyn Milburn, Denver, 1993-95; Detroit, 1996-97; Chicago, 1998-99 (p-2,512; k-8,168)

Most Yards Returned, Season

1,943 Tyrone Hughes, New Orleans, 1996 (p-152, k-1,791)
1,930 Brian Mitchell, Washington, 1994 (p-452, k-1,478)
1,920 Kevin Williams, Arizona, 1997 (p-462, k-1,458)

Most Yards Returned, Game

347 Tyrone Hughes, New Orleans vs. L.A. Rams, Oct. 23, 1994 (p-43, k-304)
294 Wally Triplett, Detroit vs. Los Angeles, Oct. 29, 1950 (k-294)
Woodley Lewis, Los Angeles vs. Detroit, Oct. 18, 1953 (p-120, k-174)
289 Eddie Payton, Detroit vs. Minnesota, Dec. 17, 1977 (p-105, k-184)

TOUCHDOWNS

Most Touchdowns, Career

11 Eric Metcalf, Cleveland, 1989-94; Atlanta, 1995-96; San Diego, 1997; Arizona, 1998; Carolina, 1999 (p-9; k-2)
9 Ollie Matson, Chi. Cardinals, 1952, 1954-58; Los Angeles, 1959-62; Detroit, 1963; Philadelphia, 1964-66 (p-3, k-6)
Mel Gray, New Orleans, 1986-88; Detroit, 1989-94; Houston, 1995-96; Tennessee, 1997; Philadelphia, 1997 (p-3, k-6)
Brian Mitchell, Washington, 1990-99 (p-7; k-2)
Deion Sanders, Atlanta, 1989-93; San Francisco, 1994; Dallas, 1995-99 (p-6; k-3)
8 Jack Christiansen, Detroit, 1951-58 (p-8)
Bobby Mitchell, Cleveland, 1958-61; Washington, 1962-68 (p-3, k-5)
Gale Sayers, Chicago, 1965-71 (p-2, k-6)
Rick Upchurch, Denver, 1975-83 (p-8)
Billy (White Shoes) Johnson, Houston, 1974-80; Atlanta, 1982-87; Washington, 1988 (p-6, k-2)
David Meggett, N.Y. Giants, 1989-94; New England, 1995-97; N.Y. Jets, 1998 (p-7; k-1)
Tamarick Vanover, Kansas City, 1995-99 (p-4; k-4)

Most Touchdowns, Season

4 Jack Christiansen, Detroit, 1951 (p-4)
Emlen Tunnell, N.Y. Giants, 1951 (p-3, k-1)
Gale Sayers, Chicago, 1967 (p-1, k-3)
Travis Williams, Green Bay, 1967 (k-4)
Cecil Turner, Chicago, 1970 (k-4)
Billy Johnson, Houston, 1975 (p-3, k-1)
Rick Upchurch, Denver, 1976 (p-4)
3 Verda (Vitamin T) Smith, Los Angeles, 1950 (k-3)
Abe Woodson, San Francisco, 1963 (k-3)
Raymond Clayborn, New England, 1977 (k-3)
Billy Johnson, Houston, 1977 (p-2, k-1)
LeRoy Irvin, Los Angeles, 1981 (p-3)
Ron Brown, L.A. Rams, 1985 (k-3)
Tyrone Hughes, New Orleans, 1993 (p-2, k-1)
Mel Gray, Detroit, 1994 (k-3)
Andre Coleman, San Diego, 1995 (p-2; k-1)
Tamarick Vanover, Kansas City, 1995 (p-1, k-2)
Desmond Howard, Green Bay, 1996 (p-3)
Darrien Gordon, Denver, 1997 (p-3)
Eric Metcalf, San Diego, 1997 (p-3)
Glyn Milburn, Chicago, 1998 (p-2; k-1)
Roell Preston, Green Bay, 1998 (p-2; k-1)
2 By many players

Most Touchdowns, Game

2 Jack Christiansen, Detroit vs. Los Angeles, Oct. 14, 1951 (p-2); vs. Green Bay, Nov. 22, 1951 (p-2)
Jim Patton, N.Y. Giants vs. Washington, Oct. 30, 1955 (p-1, k-1)
Bobby Mitchell, Cleveland vs. Philadelphia, Nov. 23, 1958 (p-1, k-1)
Dick Christy, N.Y. Titans vs. Denver, Sept. 24, 1961 (p-2)
Al Frazier, Denver vs. Boston, Dec. 3, 1961 (p-1, k-1)
Timmy Brown, Philadelphia vs. Dallas, Nov. 6, 1966 (k-2)
Travis Williams, Green Bay vs. Cleveland, Nov. 12, 1967 (k-2); vs. Pittsburgh, Nov. 2, 1969 (p-1, k-1)
Gale Sayers, Chicago vs. San Francisco, Dec. 3, 1967 (p-1, k-1)
Rick Upchurch, Denver vs. Cleveland, Sept. 26, 1976 (p-2)
Eddie Payton, Detroit vs. Minnesota, Dec. 17, 1977 (p-1, k-1)
LeRoy Irvin, Los Angeles vs. Atlanta, Oct. 11, 1981 (p-2)
Ron Brown, L.A. Rams vs. Green Bay, Nov. 24, 1985 (k-2)
Vai Sikahema, St. Louis vs. Tampa Bay, Dec. 21, 1986 (p-2)
Todd Kinchen, L.A. Rams vs. Atlanta, Dec. 27, 1992 (p-2)
Eric Metcalf, Cleveland vs. Pittsburgh, Oct. 24, 1993 (p-2); San Diego vs. Cincinnati, Nov. 2, 1997 (p-2)
Tyrone Hughes, New Orleans vs. L.A. Rams, Oct. 23, 1994 (k-2)
Darrien Gordon, Denver vs. Carolina, Nov. 9, 1997 (p-2)
Jermaine Lewis, Baltimore vs. Seattle, Dec. 7, 1997 (p-2)

FUMBLES

Most Fumbles, Career

160 Warren Moon, Houston, 1984-93; Minnesota, 1994-96; Seattle, 1997-98; Kansas City, 1999
153 Dave Krieg, Seattle, 1980-91; Kansas City, 1992-93; Detroit, 1994; Arizona, 1995; Chicago, 1996; Tennessee, 1997-98
137 John Elway, Denver, 1983-98

Most Fumbles, Season

21 Tony Banks, St. Louis, 1996
18 Dave Krieg, Seattle, 1989
Warren Moon, Houston, 1990
17 Dan Pastorini, Houston, 1973
Warren Moon, Houston, 1984
Randall Cunningham, Philadelphia, 1989

Most Fumbles, Game

7 Len Dawson, Kansas City vs. San Diego, Nov. 15, 1964
6 Sam Etcheverry, St. Louis vs. N.Y. Giants, Sept, 17, 1961
Dave Krieg, Seattle vs. Kansas City, Nov. 5, 1989
Brett Favre, Green Bay vs. Tampa Bay, Dec. 7, 1998
5 Paul Christman, Chi. Cardinals vs. Green Bay, Nov. 10, 1946
Charlie Conerly, N.Y. Giants vs. San Francisco, Dec. 1, 1957
Jack Kemp, Buffalo vs. Houston, Oct. 29, 1967
Roman Gabriel, Philadelphia vs. Oakland, Nov. 21, 1976
Randall Cunningham, Philadelphia vs. L.A. Raiders, Nov. 30, 1986 (OT)
Willie Totten, Buffalo vs. Indianapolis, Oct. 4, 1987
Dave Walter, Cincinnati vs. Seattle, Oct. 11, 1987
Dave Krieg, Seattle vs. San Diego, Nov. 25, 1990 (OT)
Andre Ware, Detroit vs. Green Bay, Dec. 6, 1992
Steve Beuerlein, Carolina vs. San Francisco, Nov. 8, 1998

FUMBLES RECOVERED

Most Fumbles Recovered, Career, Own and Opponents'

55 Warren Moon, Houston, 1984-93, Minnesota, 1994-96; Seattle, 1997-98; Kansas City, 1999 (55 own)
47 Dave Krieg, Seattle, 1980-91; Kansas City, 1992-93; Detroit, 1994; Arizona, 1995; Chicago, 1996; Tennessee, 1997-98 (47 own)
45 Boomer Esiason, Cincinnati, 1984-92, 1997; N.Y. Jets, 1993-95; Arizona, 1996 (45 own)

Most Fumbles Recovered, Season, Own and Opponents'

9 Don Hultz, Minnesota, 1963 (9 opp)
Dave Krieg, Seattle, 1989 (9 own)
Brian Griese, Denver, 1999 (9 own)
8 Paul Christman, Chi. Cardinals, 1945 (8 own)
Joe Schmidt, Detroit, 1955 (8 opp)
Bill Butler, Minnesota, 1963 (8 own)
Kermit Alexander, San Francisco, 1965 (4 own, 4 opp)
Jack Lambert, Pittsburgh, 1976 (1 own, 7 opp)
Danny White, Dallas, 1981 (8 own)
Dan Marino, Miami, 1988 (7 own, 1 opp)
Tony Banks, St. Louis, 1998 (8 own)
7 By many players

Most Fumbles Recovered, Game, Own and Opponents'

4 Otto Graham, Cleveland vs. N.Y. Giants, Oct. 25, 1953 (4 own)
Sam Etcheverry, St. Louis vs. N.Y. Giants, Sept. 17, 1961 (4 own)
Roman Gabriel, Los Angeles vs. San Francisco, Oct. 12, 1969 (4 own)
Joe Ferguson, Buffalo vs. Miami, Sept. 18, 1977 (4 own)
Randall Cunningham, Philadelphia vs. L.A. Raiders, Nov. 30, 1986 (OT) (4 own)
3 By many players

OWN FUMBLES RECOVERED

Most Own Fumbles Recovered, Career

55 Warren Moon, Houston, 1984-93; Minnesota, 1994-96; Seattle, 1997-98; Kansas City, 1999 (55 own)
47 Dave Krieg, Seattle, 1980-91; Kansas City, 1992-93; Detroit, 1994; Arizona, 1995; Chicago, 1996; Tennessee, 1997-98 (47 own)
45 Boomer Esiason, Cincinnati, 1984-92, 1997; N.Y. Jets, 1993-95; Arizona, 1996 (45 own)

Most Own Fumbles Recovered, Season

9 Dave Krieg, Seattle, 1989
Brian Griese, Denver, 1999
8 Paul Christman, Chi. Cardinals, 1945
Bill Butler, Minnesota, 1963
Danny White, Dallas, 1981
Tony Banks, St. Louis, 1998
7 By many players

Most Own Fumbles Recovered, Game

4 Otto Graham, Cleveland vs. N.Y. Giants, Oct. 25, 1953
Sam Etcheverry, St. Louis vs. N.Y. Giants, Sept. 17, 1961
Roman Gabriel, Los Angeles vs. San Francisco, Oct. 12, 1969
Joe Ferguson, Buffalo vs. Miami, Sept. 18, 1977
Randall Cunningham, Philadelphia vs. L.A. Raiders, Nov. 30, 1986 (OT)
3 By many players

OPPONENTS' FUMBLES RECOVERED

Most Opponents' Fumbles Recovered, Career

29 Jim Marshall, Cleveland, 1960; Minnesota, 1961-79
28 Rickey Jackson, New Orleans, 1981-93; San Francisco, 1994-95
26 Kevin Greene, L.A. Rams, 1985-92; Pittsburgh, 1993-95; Carolina, 1996, 1998-99; San Francisco, 1997

Most Opponents' Fumbles Recovered, Season

9 Don Hultz, Minnesota, 1963
8 Joe Schmidt, Detroit, 1955
7 Alan Page, Minnesota, 1970
Jack Lambert, Pittsburgh, 1976
Ray Childress, Houston, 1988
Rickey Jackson, New Orleans, 1990

Most Opponents' Fumbles Recovered, Game

3 Corwin Clatt, Chi. Cardinals vs. Detroit, Nov. 6, 1949
Vic Sears, Philadelphia vs. Green Bay, Nov. 2, 1952
Ed Beatty, San Francisco vs. Los Angeles, Oct. 7, 1956
Ron Carroll, Houston vs. Cincinnati, Oct. 27, 1974
Maurice Spencer, New Orleans vs. Atlanta, Oct. 10, 1976
Steve Nelson, New England vs. Philadelphia, Oct. 8, 1978
Charles Jackson, Kansas City vs. Pittsburgh, Sept. 6, 1981
Willie Buchanon, San Diego vs. Denver, Sept. 27, 1981
Joey Browner, Minnesota vs. San Francisco, Sept. 8, 1985
Ray Childress, Houston vs. Washington, Oct. 30, 1988
John Thierry, Chicago vs. Houston, Oct. 22, 1995
Stephen Boyd, Detroit vs. Chicago, Oct. 4, 1998
Darryl Williams, Seattle vs. Kansas City, Oct. 4, 1998
2 By many players

YARDS RETURNING FUMBLES

Longest Fumble Run (All TDs)

104 Jack Tatum, Oakland vs. Green Bay, Sept. 24, 1972
102 Travis Davis, Pittsburgh vs. Carolina, Dec. 26, 1999
100 Chris Martin, Kansas City vs. Miami, Oct. 13, 1991

TOUCHDOWNS

Most Touchdowns, Career (Total)

5 Jessie Tuggle, Atlanta, 1987-99
4 Bill Thompson, Denver, 1969-81
Derrick Thomas, Kansas City, 1989-99
3 By many players

Most Touchdowns, Season (Total)

2 Harold McPhail, Boston, 1934
Harry Ebding, Detroit, 1937
John Morelli, Boston, 1944
Frank Maznicki, Boston, 1947
Fred (Dippy) Evans, Chi. Bears, 1948
Ralph Heywood, Boston, 1948
Art Tait, N.Y. Yanks, 1951
John Dwyer, Los Angeles, 1952
Leo Sugar, Chi. Cardinals, 1957
Doug Cline, Houston, 1961
Jim Bradshaw, Pittsburgh, 1964
Royce Berry, Cincinnati, 1970
Ahmad Rashad, Buffalo, 1974
Tim Gray, Kansas City, 1977
Charles Phillips, Oakland, 1978
Kenny Johnson, Atlanta, 1981
George Martin, N.Y. Giants, 1981
Del Rodgers, Green Bay, 1982
Mike Douglass, Green Bay, 1983
Shelton Robinson, Seattle, 1983
Erik McMillan, N.Y. Jets, 1989
Les Miller, San Diego, 1990
Seth Joyner, Philadelphia, 1991
Robert Goff, New Orleans, 1992
Willie Clay, Detroit, 1993
Tyrone Hughes, New Orleans, 1994
Chad Brown, Seattle, 1997
Marcus Robertson, Tennessee, 1997
Dwayne Rudd, Minnesota, 1998
Keith McKenzie, Green Bay, 1999

Most Touchdowns, Career (Own recovered)

2 Ken Kavanaugh, Chi. Bears, 1940-41, 1945-50
Mike Ditka, Chicago, 1961-66; Philadelphia, 1967-68; Dallas, 1969-72
Gail Cogdill, Detroit, 1960-68; Baltimore, 1968; Atlanta, 1969-70
Ahmad Rashad, St. Louis, 1972-73; Buffalo, 1974; Minnesota, 1976-82
Jim Mitchell, Atlanta, 1969-79
Drew Pearson, Dallas, 1973-83
Del Rodgers, Green Bay, 1982, 1984; San Francisco, 1987-88

Most Touchdowns, Season (Own recovered)

2 Ahmad Rashad, Buffalo, 1974
Del Rodgers, Green Bay, 1982
1 By many players

Most Touchdowns, Career (Opponents' recovered)

5 Jessie Tuggle, Atlanta, 1987-99
4 Derrick Thomas, Kansas City, 1989-99
3 By many players

Most Touchdowns, Season (Opponents' recovered)

2 Harold McPhail, Boston, 1934
Harry Ebding, Detroit, 1937
John Morelli, Boston, 1944
Frank Maznicki, Boston, 1947
Fred (Dippy) Evans, Chi. Bears, 1948
Ralph Heywood, Boston, 1948
Art Tait, N.Y. Yanks, 1951
John Dwyer, Los Angeles, 1952
Leo Sugar, Chi. Cardinals, 1957
Doug Cline, Houston, 1961
Jim Bradshaw, Pittsburgh, 1964
Royce Berry, Cincinnati, 1970
Tim Gray, Kansas City, 1977
Charles Phillips, Oakland, 1978
Kenny Johnson, Atlanta, 1981
George Martin, N.Y. Giants, 1981
Mike Douglass, Green Bay, 1983
Shelton Robinson, Seattle, 1983
Erik McMillan, N.Y. Jets, 1989
Les Miller, San Diego, 1990
Seth Joyner, Philadelphia, 1991
Robert Goff, New Orleans, 1992
Willie Clay, Detroit, 1993
Tyrone Hughes, New Orleans, 1994
Chad Brown, Seattle, 1997
Marcus Robertson, Tennessee, 1997
Dwayne Rudd, Minnesota, 1998
Keith McKenzie, Green Bay, 1999

Most Touchdowns, Game (Opponents' recovered)

2 Fred (Dippy) Evans, Chi. Bears vs. Washington, Nov. 28, 1948

COMBINED NET YARDS GAINED

Rushing, receiving, interception returns, punt returns, kickoff returns, and fumble returns

Most Seasons Leading League

5 Jim Brown, Cleveland, 1958-61, 1964
4 Brian Mitchell, Washington, 1994-96, 1998
3 Cliff Battles, Boston, 1932-33; Washington, 1937
Gale Sayers, Chicago, 1965-67
Eric Dickerson, L.A. Rams, 1983-84, 1986
Thurman Thomas, Buffalo, 1989, 1991-92

Most Consecutive Seasons Leading League

4 Jim Brown, Cleveland, 1958-61
3 Gale Sayers, Chicago, 1965-67
Brian Mitchell, Washington, 1994-96
2 Cliff Battles, Boston, 1932-33
Charley Trippi, Chi. Cardinals, 1948-49
Timmy Brown, Philadelphia, 1962-63
Floyd Little, Denver, 1967-68
James Brooks, San Diego, 1981-82
Eric Dickerson, L.A. Rams, 1983-84
Thurman Thomas, Buffalo, 1991-92

ATTEMPTS

Most Attempts, Career

4,368 Walter Payton, Chicago, 1975-87
3,694 Emmitt Smith, Dallas, 1990-99
3,624 Marcus Allen, L.A. Raiders, 1982-92; Kansas City, 1993-97

Most Attempts, Season

496 James Wilder, Tampa Bay, 1984
449 Marcus Allen, L.A. Raiders, 1985
442 Eric Dickerson, L.A. Rams, 1983

Most Attempts, Rookie, Season

442 Eric Dickerson, L.A. Rams, 1983
433 Edgerrin James, Indianapolis, 1999
401 Curtis Martin, New England, 1995

Most Attempts, Game

48 James Wilder, Tampa Bay vs. Pittsburgh, Oct. 30, 1983
47 James Wilder, Tampa Bay vs. Green Bay, Sept. 30, 1984 (OT)
Terrell Davis, Denver vs. Buffalo, Oct. 26, 1997 (OT)
46 Gerald Riggs, Atlanta vs. L.A. Rams, Nov. 17, 1985

YARDS GAINED

Most Yards Gained, Career

21,803 Walter Payton, Chicago, 1975-87
19,075 Jerry Rice, San Francisco, 1985-99
18,308 Barry Sanders, Detroit, 1989-98

Most Yards Gained, Season

2,535 Lionel James, San Diego, 1985
2,477 Brian Mitchell, Washington, 1994
2,462 Terry Metcalf, St. Louis, 1975

Most Yards Gained, Rookie, Season

2,317 Tim Brown, L.A. Raiders, 1988
2,272 Gale Sayers, Chicago, 1965
2,212 Eric Dickerson, L.A. Rams, 1983

Most Yards Gained, Game

404 Glyn Milburn, Denver vs. Seattle, Dec. 10, 1995
373 Billy Cannon, Houston vs. N.Y. Titans, Dec. 10, 1961
347 Tyrone Hughes, New Orleans vs. L.A. Rams, Oct. 23, 1994

SACKS

Sacks have been compiled since 1982.

Most Seasons Leading League

2 Mark Gastineau, N.Y. Jets, 1983-84
Reggie White, Philadelphia, 1987-88
Kevin Greene, Pittsburgh, 1994; Carolina, 1996

Most Sacks, Career

192.5 Reggie White, Philadelphia, 1985-92; Green Bay, 1993-98
171.0 Bruce Smith, Buffalo, 1985-99
160.0 Kevin Greene, L.A. Rams, 1985-92; Pittsburgh, 1993-95; Carolina, 1996, 1998-99; San Francisco, 1997

Most Sacks, Season

22 Mark Gastineau, N.Y. Jets, 1984
21 Reggie White, Philadelphia, 1987
Chris Doleman, Minnesota, 1989
20.5 Lawrence Taylor, N.Y. Giants, 1986

Most Sacks, Rookie, Season

14.5 Jevon Kearse, Tennessee, 1999
12.5 Leslie O'Neal, San Diego, 1986
Simeon Rice, Arizona, 1996
12 Charles Haley, San Francisco, 1986

Most Sacks, Game

7 Derrick Thomas, Kansas City vs. Seattle, Nov. 11, 1990
6 Fred Dean, San Francisco vs. New Orleans, Nov. 13, 1983
Derrick Thomas, Kansas City vs. Oakland, Sept. 6, 1998
5.5 William Gay, Detroit vs. Tampa Bay, Sept. 4, 1983

Most Seasons, 10 or More Sacks

12 Reggie White, Philadelphia, 1985-92; Green Bay, 1993, 1995, 1997-98
Bruce Smith, Buffalo, 1986-90, 1992-98
10 Kevin Greene, L.A. Rams, 1988-90, 1992; Pittsburgh, 1993-94; Carolina, 1996, 1998-99; San Francisco, 1997
8 Richard Dent, Chicago, 1984-88, 1990-91, 1993
Leslie O'Neal, San Diego, 1986, 1989-90, 1992-95; St. Louis, 1997
Chris Doleman, Minnesota, 1987, 1989-90, 1992-93; San Francisco, 1996-98
John Randle, Minnesota, 1992-99

Most Consecutive Seasons, 10 or More Sacks

9 Reggie White, Philadelphia, 1985-92; Green Bay, 1993
8 John Randle, Minnesota, 1992-99 (current)
7 Lawrence Taylor, N.Y. Giants, 1984-1990
Bruce Smith, Buffalo, 1992-98

MISCELLANEOUS

Longest Return of Missed Field Goal (All TDs)

104 Aaron Glenn, N.Y. Jets vs. Indianapolis, Nov. 15, 1998
101 Al Nelson, Philadelphia vs. Dallas, Sept. 26, 1971
100 Al Nelson, Philadelphia vs. Cleveland, Dec. 11, 1966
Ken Ellis, Green Bay vs. N.Y. Giants, Sept. 19, 1971

TEAM RECORDS

CHAMPIONSHIPS

Most Seasons League Champion

12 Green Bay, 1929-31, 1936, 1939, 1944, 1961-62, 1965-67, 1996
9 Chi. Bears, 1921, 1932-33, 1940-41, 1943, 1946, 1963, 1985
6 N.Y. Giants, 1927, 1934, 1938, 1956, 1986, 1990

Most Consecutive Seasons League Champion

3 Green Bay, 1929-31
Green Bay, 1965-67
2 Canton, 1922-23
Chi. Bears, 1932-33
Chi. Bears, 1940-41
Philadelphia, 1948-49
Detroit, 1952-53
Cleveland, 1954-55
Baltimore, 1958-59
Houston, 1960-61
Green Bay, 1961-62
Buffalo, 1964-65
Miami, 1972-73
Pittsburgh, 1974-75
Pittsburgh, 1978-79
San Francisco, 1988-89
Dallas, 1992-93
Denver, 1997-98

Most Times Finishing First, Regular Season

19 N.Y. Giants, 1927, 1933-35, 1938-39, 1941, 1944, 1946, 1956, 1958-59, 1961-63, 1986, 1989-90, 1997
Dallas, 1966-71, 1973, 1976-79, 1981, 1985, 1992-96, 1998
18 Clev. Browns, 1950-55, 1957, 1964-65, 1967-69, 1971, 1980, 1985-87, 1989
Chi. Bears, 1921, 1932-34, 1937, 1940-43, 1946, 1956, 1963, 1984-88, 1990
17 Green Bay, 1929-31, 1936, 1938-39, 1944, 1960-62, 1965-67, 1972, 1995-97

Most Consecutive Times Finishing First, Regular Season

7 Los Angeles, 1973-79
6 Cleveland, 1950-55
Dallas, 1966-71
Minnesota, 1973-78
Pittsburgh, 1974-79
5 Oakland, 1972-76
Chicago, 1984-88
San Francisco, 1986-90
Dallas, 1992-96

GAMES WON

Most Consecutive Games Won

17 Chi. Bears, 1933-34
16 Chi. Bears, 1941-42
Miami, 1971-73
Miami, 1983-84
15 L.A. Chargers/San Diego, 1960-61
San Francisco, 1989-90

Most Consecutive Games Without Defeat

25 Canton, 1921-23 (won 22, tied 3)
24 Chi. Bears, 1941-43 (won 23, tied 1)
23 Green Bay, 1928-30 (won 21, tied 2)

Most Games Won, Season

15 San Francisco, 1984
Chicago, 1985
Minnesota, 1998
14 Frankford, 1926
Miami, 1972
Pittsburgh, 1978
Washington, 1983
Miami, 1984
Chicago, 1986
N.Y. Giants, 1986
San Francisco, 1989
San Francisco, 1990
Washington, 1991
San Francisco, 1992
Atlanta, 1998

Denver, 1998
Jacksonville, 1999
13 By many teams

Most Consecutive Games Won, Season
14 Miami, 1972
13 Chi. Bears, 1934
Denver, 1998
12 Minnesota, 1969
Chicago, 1985

Most Consecutive Games Won, Start of Season
14 Miami, 1972, entire season
13 Chi. Bears, 1934, entire season
Denver, 1998
12 Chicago, 1985

Most Consecutive Games Won, End of Season
14 Miami, 1972, entire season
13 Chi. Bears, 1934, entire season
11 Chi. Bears, 1942, entire season
Cleveland, 1951
Houston, 1993

Most Consecutive Games Without Defeat, Season
14 Miami, 1972 (won 14)
13 Chi. Bears, 1926 (won 11, tied 2)
Green Bay, 1929 (won 12, tied 1)
Chi. Bears, 1934 (won 13)
Baltimore, 1967 (won 11, tied 2)
Denver, 1998 (won 13)
12 Canton, 1922 (won 10, tied 2)
Canton, 1923 (won 11, tied 1)
Minnesota, 1969 (won 12)
Chicago, 1985 (won 12)

Most Consecutive Games Without Defeat, Start of Season
14 Miami, 1972 (won 14), entire season
13 Chi. Bears, 1926 (won 11, tied 2)
Green Bay, 1929 (won 12, tied 1), entire season
Chi. Bears, 1934 (won 13), entire season
Baltimore, 1967 (won 11, tied 2)
Denver, 1998 (won 13)
12 Canton, 1922 (won 10, tied 2), entire season
Canton, 1923 (won 11, tied 1), entire season
Chicago, 1985 (won 12)

Most Consecutive Games Without Defeat, End of Season
14 Miami, 1972 (won 14), entire season
13 Green Bay, 1929 (won 12, tied 1), entire season
Chi. Bears, 1934 (won 13), entire season
12 Canton, 1922 (won 10, tied 2), entire season
Canton, 1923 (won 11, tied 1), entire season

Most Consecutive Home Games Won
27 Miami, 1971-74
25 Green Bay, 1995-98
24 Denver, 1996-98

Most Consecutive Home Games Without Defeat
30 Green Bay, 1928-33 (won 27, tied 3)
27 Miami, 1971-74 (won 27)
25 Chi. Bears, 1923-25 (won 19, tied 6)
Green Bay, 1995-98 (won 25)

Most Consecutive Road Games Won
18 San Francisco, 1988-90
11 L.A. Chargers/San Diego, 1960-61
San Francisco, 1987-88
10 Chi. Bears, 1941-42
Dallas, 1968-69
New Orleans, 1987-88

Most Consecutive Road Games Without Defeat
18 San Francisco, 1988-90 (won 18)
13 Chi. Bears, 1941-43 (won 12, tied 1)
12 Green Bay, 1928-30 (won 10, tied 2)

Most Shutout Games Won or Tied, Season
10 Pottsville, 1926 (won 9, tied 1)
N.Y. Giants, 1927 (won 9, tied 1)
9 Akron, 1921 (won 8, tied 1)
Canton, 1922 (won 7, tied 2)
Frankford, 1926 (won 9)
Frankford, 1929 (won 6, tied 3)
8 By many teams

Most Consecutive Shutout Games Won or Tied
13 Akron, 1920-21 (won 10, tied 3)
7 Pottsville, 1926 (won 6, tied 1)
Detroit, 1934 (won 7)
6 Buffalo, 1920-21 (won 5, tied 1)
Frankford, 1926 (won 6)
Detroit, 1926 (won 4, tied 2)
N.Y. Giants, 1926-27 (won 5, tied 1)

GAMES LOST

Most Consecutive Games Lost
26 Tampa Bay, 1976-77
19 Chi. Cardinals, 1942-43, 1945
Oakland, 1961-62
18 Houston, 1972-73

Most Consecutive Games Without Victory
26 Tampa Bay, 1976-77 (lost 26)
23 Rochester, 1922-25 (lost 21, tied 2)
Washington, 1960-61 (lost 20, tied 3)
19 Dayton, 1927-29 (lost 18, tied 1)
Chi. Cardinals, 1942-43, 1945 (lost 19)
Oakland, 1961-62 (lost 19)

Most Games Lost, Season
15 New Orleans, 1980
Dallas, 1989
New England, 1990
Indianapolis, 1991
N.Y. Jets, 1996
14 By many teams

Most Consecutive Games Lost, Season
14 Tampa Bay, 1976
New Orleans, 1980
Baltimore, 1981
New England, 1990
13 Oakland, 1962
Pittsburgh, 1969
Indianapolis, 1986
12 Tampa Bay, 1977

Most Consecutive Games Lost, Start of Season
14 Tampa Bay, 1976, entire season
New Orleans, 1980
13 Oakland, 1962
Indianapolis, 1986
12 Tampa Bay, 1977

Most Consecutive Games Lost, End of Season
14 Tampa Bay, 1976, entire season
New England, 1990
13 Pittsburgh, 1969
11 Philadelphia, 1936
Detroit, 1942, entire season
Houston, 1972

Most Consecutive Games Without Victory, Season
14 Tampa Bay, 1976 (lost 14), entire season
New Orleans, 1980 (lost 14)
Baltimore, 1981 (lost 14)
New England, 1990 (lost 14)
13 Washington, 1961 (lost 12, tied 1)
Oakland, 1962 (lost 13)
Pittsburgh, 1969 (lost 13)
Indianapolis, 1986 (lost 13)
12 Dall. Cowboys, 1960 (lost 11, tied 1), entire season
Tampa Bay, 1977 (lost 12)

Most Consecutive Games Without Victory, Start of Season
14 Tampa Bay, 1976 (lost 14), entire season
New Orleans, 1980 (lost 14)
13 Washington, 1961 (lost 12, tied 1)
Oakland, 1962 (lost 13)
Indianapolis, 1986 (lost 13)
12 Dall. Cowboys, 1960 (lost 11, tied 1), entire season
Tampa Bay, 1977 (lost 12)

Most Consecutive Games Without Victory, End of Season
14 Tampa Bay, 1976, (lost 14), entire season
New England, 1990 (lost 14)
13 Pittsburgh, 1969 (lost 13)
12 Dall. Cowboys, 1960 (lost 11, tied 1), entire season

Most Consecutive Home Games Lost
14 Dallas, 1988-89
13 Houston, 1972-73
Tampa Bay, 1976-77
N.Y. Jets, 1995-97
11 Oakland, 1961-62
Los Angeles, 1961-63
Cincinnati, 1998-99

Most Consecutive Home Games Without Victory
14 Dallas, 1988-89 (lost 14)
13 Houston, 1972-73 (lost 13)
Tampa Bay, 1976-77 (lost 13)
N.Y. Jets, 1995-97 (lost 13)
12 Philadelphia, 1936-38 (lost 11, tied 1)

Most Consecutive Road Games Lost
23 Houston, 1981-84
22 Buffalo, 1983-86

19 Tampa Bay, 1983-85
Atlanta, 1988-91

Most Consecutive Road Games Without Victory
23 Houston, 1981-84 (lost 23)
22 Buffalo, 1983-86 (lost 22)
19 Tampa Bay, 1983-85 (lost 19)
Atlanta, 1988-91 (lost 19)

Most Shutout Games Lost or Tied, Season
8 Frankford, 1927 (lost 6, tied 2)
Brooklyn, 1931 (lost 8)
7 Dayton, 1925 (lost 6, tied 1)
Orange, 1929 (lost 4, tied 3)
Frankford, 1931 (lost 6, tied 1)
6 By many teams

Most Consecutive Shutout Games Lost or Tied
8 Rochester, 1922-24 (lost 8)
7 Hammond, 1922-23 (lost 6, tied 1)
6 Providence, 1926-27 (lost 5, tied 1)
Brooklyn, 1942-43 (lost 6)

TIE GAMES

Most Tie Games, Season
6 Chi. Bears, 1932
5 Frankford, 1929
4 Chi. Bears, 1924
Orange, 1929
Portsmouth, 1932

Most Consecutive Tie Games
3 Chi. Bears, 1932
2 By many teams

SCORING

Most Seasons Leading League
10 Chi. Bears, 1932, 1934-35, 1939, 1941-43, 1946-47, 1956
9 San Francisco, 1953, 1965, 1970, 1987, 1989, 1992-95
7 Green Bay, 1931, 1936-38, 1961-62, 1996
L.A./St. Louis Rams, 1950-52, 1957, 1967, 1973, 1999

Most Consecutive Seasons Leading League
4 San Francisco, 1992-1995
3 Green Bay, 1936-38
Chi. Bears, 1941-43
Los Angeles, 1950-52
Oakland, 1967-69
2 By many teams

POINTS

Most Points, Season
556 Minnesota, 1998
541 Washington, 1983
526 St. Louis, 1999

Fewest Points, Season (Since 1932)
37 Cincinnati/St. Louis, 1934
38 Cincinnati, 1933
Detroit, 1942
51 Pittsburgh, 1934
Philadelphia, 1936

Most Points, Game
72 Washington vs. N.Y. Giants, Nov. 27, 1966
70 Los Angeles vs. Baltimore, Oct. 22, 1950
65 Chi. Cardinals vs. N.Y. Bulldogs, Nov. 13, 1949
Los Angeles vs. Detroit, Oct. 29, 1950

Most Points, Both Teams, Game
113 Washington (72) vs. N.Y. Giants (41), Nov. 27, 1966
101 Oakland (52) vs. Houston (49), Dec. 22, 1963
99 Seattle (51) vs. Kansas City (48), Nov. 27, 1983 (OT)

Fewest Points, Both Teams, Game
0 In many games. Last time: N.Y. Giants vs. Detroit, Nov. 7, 1943

Most Points, Shutout Victory, Game
64 Philadelphia vs. Cincinnati, Nov. 6, 1934
62 Akron vs. Oorang, Oct. 29, 1922
60 Rock Island vs. Evansville, Oct. 15, 1922
Chi. Cardinals vs. Rochester, Oct. 7, 1923

Fewest Points, Shutout Victory, Game
2 Green Bay vs. Chi. Bears, Oct. 16, 1932
Chi. Bears vs. Green Bay, Sept. 18, 1938

Most Points Overcome to Win Game
28 San Francisco vs. New Orleans, Dec. 7, 1980 (OT) (trailed 7-35, won 38-35)
26 Buffalo vs. Indianapolis, Sept., 21, 1997 (trailed 26-0, won 37-35)
25 St. Louis vs. Tampa Bay, Nov. 8, 1987 (trailed 3-28, won 31-28)

Most Points Overcome to Tie Game
31 Denver vs. Buffalo, Nov. 27, 1960 (trailed 7-38, tied 38-38)
28 Los Angeles vs. Philadelphia, Oct. 3, 1948 (trailed 0-28, tied 28-28)

Most Points, Each Half
1st: 49 Green Bay vs. Tampa Bay, Oct. 2, 1983
48 Buffalo vs. Miami, Sept. 18, 1966
45 Green Bay vs. Cleveland, Nov. 12, 1967
Indianapolis vs. Denver, Oct. 31, 1988
Houston vs. Cleveland, Dec. 9, 1990
2nd: 49 Chi. Bears vs. Philadelphia, Nov. 30, 1941
48 Chi. Cardinals vs. Baltimore, Oct. 2, 1950
N.Y. Giants vs. Baltimore, Nov. 19, 1950
45 Cincinnati vs. Houston, Dec. 17, 1972

Most Points, Both Teams, Each Half
1st: 70 Houston (35) vs. Oakland (35), Dec. 22, 1963
62 N.Y. Jets (41) vs. Tampa Bay (21), Nov. 17, 1985
59 St. Louis (31) vs. Philadelphia (28), Dec. 16, 1962
2nd: 65 Washington (38) vs. N.Y. Giants (27), Nov. 27, 1966
62 L.A. Raiders (31) vs. San Diego (31), Jan. 2, 1983
58 New England (37) vs. Baltimore (21), Nov. 23, 1980
N.Y. Jets (37) vs. New England (21), Sept. 21, 1987

Most Points, One Quarter
41 Green Bay vs. Detroit, Oct. 7, 1945 (second quarter)
Los Angeles vs. Detroit, Oct. 29, 1950 (third quarter)
37 Los Angeles vs. Green Bay, Sept. 21, 1980 (second quarter)
35 Chi. Cardinals vs. Boston, Oct. 24, 1948 (third quarter)
Green Bay vs. Cleveland, Nov. 12, 1967 (first quarter)
Green Bay vs. Tampa Bay, Oct. 2, 1983 (second quarter)

Most Points, Both Teams, One Quarter
49 Oakland (28) vs. Houston (21), Dec. 22, 1963 (second quarter)
48 Green Bay (41) vs. Detroit (7), Oct. 7, 1945 (second quarter)
Los Angeles (41) vs. Detroit (7), Oct. 29, 1950 (third quarter)
47 St. Louis (27) vs. Philadelphia (20), Dec. 13, 1964 (second quarter)

Most Points, Each Quarter
1st: 35 Green Bay vs. Cleveland, Nov. 12, 1967
31 Buffalo vs. Kansas City, Sept. 13, 1964
28 By eight teams
2nd: 41 Green Bay vs. Detroit, Oct. 7, 1945
37 Los Angeles vs. Green Bay, Sept. 21, 1980
35 Green Bay vs. Tampa Bay, Oct. 2, 1983
3rd: 41 Los Angeles vs. Detroit, Oct. 29, 1950
35 Chi. Cardinals vs. Boston, Oct. 24, 1948
28 By 10 teams
4th: 31 Oakland vs. Denver, Dec. 17, 1960
Oakland vs. San Diego, Dec. 8, 1963
Atlanta vs. Green Bay, Sept. 13, 1981
28 By many teams

Most Points, Both Teams, Each Quarter
1st: 42 Green Bay (35) vs. Cleveland (7), Nov. 12, 1967
35 Dall. Texans (21) vs. N.Y. Titans (14), Nov. 11, 1962
Dallas (28) vs. Philadelphia (7), Oct. 19, 1969
Kansas City (21) vs. Seattle (14), Dec. 11, 1977
Detroit (21) vs. L.A. Raiders (14), Dec. 10, 1990
Dallas (21) vs. Atlanta (14), Dec. 22, 1991
34 Los Angeles (21) vs. Baltimore (13), Oct. 22, 1950
Oakland (21) vs. Atlanta (13), Nov. 30, 1975
2nd: 49 Oakland (28) vs. Houston (21), Dec. 22, 1963
48 Green Bay (41) vs. Detroit (7), Oct. 7, 1945
47 St. Louis (27) vs. Philadelphia (20), Dec. 13, 1964
3rd: 48 Los Angeles (41) vs. Detroit (7), Oct. 29, 1950
42 Washington (28) vs. Philadelphia (14), Oct. 1, 1955
41 Green Bay (21) vs. N.Y. Yanks (20), Oct. 8, 1950
4th: 42 Chi. Cardinals (28) vs. Philadelphia (14), Dec. 7, 1947
Green Bay (28) vs. Chi. Bears (14), Nov. 6, 1955
N.Y. Jets (28) vs. Boston (14), Oct. 27, 1968
Pittsburgh (21) vs. Cleveland (21), Oct. 18, 1969
41 Baltimore (27) vs. New England (14), Sept. 18, 1978
New England (27) vs. Baltimore (14), Nov. 23, 1980
40 Chicago (21) vs. Tampa Bay (19), Nov. 19, 1989

Most Consecutive Games Scoring
354 San Francisco, 1977-99 (current)
274 Cleveland, 1950-71
218 Dallas, 1970-85

TOUCHDOWNS

Most Seasons Leading League, Touchdowns
13 Chi. Bears, 1932, 1934-35, 1939, 1941-44, 1946-48, 1956, 1965
7 Dallas, 1966, 1968, 1971, 1973, 1977-78, 1980
San Francisco, 1953, 1970, 1987, 1992-95
6 Oakland, 1967-69, 1972, 1974, 1977
San Diego, 1963, 1965, 1979, 1981-82, 1985
Green Bay, 1932, 1937-38, 1961-62, 1996

Most Consecutive Seasons Leading League, Touchdowns
4 Chi. Bears, 1941-44
Los Angeles, 1949-52
San Francisco, 1992-95

3 Chi. Bears, 1946-48
Baltimore, 1957-59
Oakland, 1967-69
2 By many teams

Most Touchdowns, Season
70 Miami, 1984
66 Houston, 1961
San Francisco, 1994
St. Louis, 1999
64 Los Angeles, 1950
Minnesota, 1998

Fewest Touchdowns, Season (Since 1932)
3 Cincinnati, 1933
4 Cincinnati/St. Louis, 1934
5 Detroit, 1942

Most Touchdowns, Game
10 Philadelphia vs. Cincinnati, Nov. 6, 1934
Los Angeles vs. Baltimore, Oct. 22, 1950
Washington vs. N.Y. Giants, Nov. 27, 1966
9 Chi. Cardinals vs. Rochester, Oct. 7, 1923
Chi. Cardinals vs. N.Y. Giants, Oct. 17, 1948
Chi. Cardinals vs. N.Y. Bulldogs, Nov. 13, 1949
Los Angeles vs. Detroit, Oct. 29, 1950
Pittsburgh vs. N.Y. Giants, Nov. 30, 1952
Chicago vs. San Francisco, Dec. 12, 1965
Chicago vs. Green Bay, Dec. 7, 1980
8 By many teams

Most Touchdowns, Both Teams, Game
16 Washington (10) vs. N.Y. Giants (6), Nov. 27, 1966
14 Chi. Cardinals (9) vs. N.Y. Giants (5), Oct. 17, 1948
Los Angeles (10) vs. Baltimore (4), Oct. 22, 1950
Houston (7) vs. Oakland (7), Dec. 22, 1963
13 New Orleans (7) vs. St. Louis (6), Nov. 2, 1969
Kansas City (7) vs. Seattle (6), Nov. 27, 1983 (OT)
San Diego (8) vs. Pittsburgh (5), Dec. 8, 1985
N.Y. Jets (7) vs. Miami (6), Sept. 21, 1986 (OT)

Most Consecutive Games Scoring Touchdowns
166 Cleveland, 1957-69
97 Oakland, 1966-73
96 Kansas City, 1963-70

POINTS AFTER TOUCHDOWN

Most (One-Point) Points After Touchdown, Season
66 Miami, 1984
65 Houston, 1961
64 St. Louis, 1999

Fewest (One-Point) Points After Touchdown, Season
2 Chi. Cardinals, 1933
3 Cincinnati, 1933
Pittsburgh, 1934
4 Cincinnati/St. Louis, 1934

Most (One-Point) Points After Touchdown, Game
10 Los Angeles vs. Baltimore, Oct. 22, 1950
9 Chi. Cardinals vs. N.Y. Giants, Oct. 17, 1948
Pittsburgh vs. N.Y. Giants, Nov. 30, 1952
Washington vs. N.Y. Giants, Nov. 27, 1966
8 By many teams

Most (One-Point) Points After Touchdown, Both Teams, Game
14 Chi. Cardinals (9) vs. N.Y. Giants (5), Oct. 17, 1948
Houston (7) vs. Oakland (7), Dec. 22, 1963
Washington (9) vs. N.Y. Giants (5), Nov. 27, 1966
13 Los Angeles (10) vs. Baltimore (3), Oct. 22, 1950
12 In many games

Most Two-Point Conversions, Season
6 Miami, 1994
Minnesota, 1997
5 Arizona, 1995
Baltimore, 1996
Jacksonville, 1996
Chicago, 1997
San Francisco, 1998
4 By many teams

Most Two-Point Conversions, Game
3 Baltimore vs. New England, Oct. 6, 1996
Pittsburgh vs. Tennessee, Nov. 1, 1998
2 Denver vs. Oakland, Oct. 1, 1961
Oakland vs. San Diego, Sept. 30, 1962
Kansas City vs. Houston, Oct. 24, 1965
Houston vs. N.Y. Jets, Dec. 6, 1969
Seattle vs. Kansas City, Oct. 23, 1994
Tampa Bay vs. San Francisco, Oct. 23, 1994
Detroit vs. Green Bay, Nov. 6, 1994
Washington vs. San Francisco, Nov. 6, 1994
Carolina vs. New Orleans, Nov. 26, 1995
Miami vs. Indianapolis, Nov. 26, 1995
New England vs. Baltimore, Oct. 6, 1996
Minnesota vs. Seattle, Nov. 10, 1996
Denver vs. Atlanta, Sept. 28, 1997
Kansas City vs. St. Louis, Oct. 26, 1997
Indianapolis vs. Green Bay, Nov. 16, 1997
Carolina vs. St. Louis, Dec. 20, 1997
Cincinnati vs. Tennessee, Sept. 12, 1999
Philadelphia vs. Washington, Nov. 14, 1999
Jacksonville vs. Baltimore, Nov. 28, 1999

Most Two-Point Conversions, Both Teams, Game
5 Baltimore (3) vs. New England (2), Oct. 6, 1996
3 Seattle (2) vs. Kansas City (1), Oct. 23, 1994
Minnesota (2) vs. Seattle (1), Nov. 10, 1996
Pittsburgh (3) vs. Tennessee (0), Nov. 1, 1998
2 In many games

FIELD GOALS

Most Seasons Leading League, Field Goals
11 Green Bay, 1935-36, 1940-43, 1946-47, 1955, 1972, 1974
8 Washington, 1945, 1956, 1971, 1976-77, 1979, 1982, 1992
7 N.Y. Giants, 1933, 1937, 1939, 1941, 1944, 1959, 1983

Most Consecutive Seasons Leading League, Field Goals
4 Green Bay, 1940-43
3 Cleveland, 1952-54
2 By many teams

Most Field Goals Attempted, Season
49 Los Angeles, 1966
Washington, 1971
48 Green Bay, 1972
47 N.Y. Jets, 1969
Los Angeles, 1973
Washington, 1983

Fewest Field Goals Attempted, Season (Since 1938)
0 Chi. Bears, 1944
2 Cleveland, 1939
Card-Pitt, 1944
Boston, 1946
Chi. Bears, 1947
3 Chi. Bears, 1945
Cleveland, 1945

Most Field Goals Attempted, Game
9 St. Louis vs. Pittsburgh, Sept. 24, 1967
8 Pittsburgh vs. St. Louis, Dec. 2, 1962
Detroit vs. Minnesota, Nov. 13, 1966
N.Y. Jets vs. Buffalo, Nov. 3, 1968
7 By many teams

Most Field Goals Attempted, Both Teams, Game
11 St. Louis (6) vs. Pittsburgh (5), Nov. 13, 1966
Washington (6) vs. Chicago (5), Nov. 14, 1971
Green Bay (6) vs. Detroit (5), Sept. 29, 1974
Washington (6) vs. N.Y. Giants (5), Nov. 14, 1976
10 In many games

Most Field Goals, Season
39 Miami, 1999
37 Carolina, 1996
36 Indianapolis, 1996
Tennessee, 1998

Fewest Field Goals, Season (Since 1932)
0 Boston, 1932, 1935
Chi. Cardinals, 1932, 1945
Green Bay, 1932, 1944
N.Y. Giants, 1932
Brooklyn, 1944
Card-Pitt, 1944
Chi. Bears, 1944, 1947
Boston, 1946
Baltimore, 1950
Dallas, 1952

Most Field Goals, Game
7 St. Louis vs. Pittsburgh, Sept. 24, 1967
Minnesota vs. L.A. Rams, Nov. 5, 1989 (OT)
Dallas vs. Green Bay, Nov. 18, 1996
6 Boston vs. Denver, Oct. 4, 1964
Detroit vs. Minnesota, Nov. 13, 1966
N.Y. Jets vs. Buffalo, Nov. 3, 1968
Philadelphia vs. Houston, Nov. 12, 1972
N.Y. Jets vs. New Orleans, Dec. 3, 1972
St. Louis vs. Atlanta, Dec. 9, 1973
N.Y. Giants vs. Seattle, Oct. 18, 1981
San Francisco vs. New Orleans, Oct. 16, 1983
Pittsburgh vs. Denver, Oct. 23, 1988

San Diego vs. Seattle, Sept. 5, 1993
San Diego vs. Houston, Sept. 19, 1993
Cincinnati vs. Seattle, Nov. 6, 1994
Atlanta vs. New Orleans, Nov. 13, 1994
San Francisco vs. Atlanta, Sept. 29, 1996
Buffalo vs. N.Y. Jets, Oct. 20, 1996
San Diego vs. Oakland, Oct. 5, 1997
Minnesota vs. Baltimore, Dec. 13, 1998
Detroit vs. Minnesota, Oct. 17, 1999
Miami vs. New England, Oct. 17, 1999
5 By many teams

Most Field Goals, Both Teams, Game
9 San Diego (5) vs. Kansas City (4), Sept. 29, 1996
Miami (6) vs. New England (3), Oct. 17, 1999
8 Cleveland (4) vs. St. Louis (4), Sept. 20, 1964
Chicago (5) vs. Philadelphia (3), Oct. 20, 1968
Washington (5) vs. Chicago (3), Nov. 14, 1971
Kansas City (5) vs. Buffalo (3), Dec. 19, 1971
Detroit (4) vs. Green Bay (4), Sept. 29, 1974
Cleveland (5) vs. Denver (3), Oct. 19, 1975
New England (4) vs. San Diego (4), Nov. 9, 1975
San Francisco (6) vs. New Orleans (2), Oct. 16, 1983
Seattle (5) vs. L.A. Raiders (3), Dec. 18, 1988
Atlanta (6) vs. New Orleans (2), Nov. 13, 1994
Indianapolis (4) vs. San Diego (4), Nov. 3, 1996
7 In many games

Most Consecutive Games Scoring Field Goals
31 Minnesota, 1968-70
28 Washington, 1988-90
23 Minnesota, 1997-99

SAFETIES

Most Safeties, Season
4 Cleveland, 1927
Detroit, 1962
Seattle, 1993
San Francisco, 1996
Tennessee, 1999
3 By many teams

Most Safeties, Game
3 L.A. Rams vs. N.Y. Giants, Sept. 30, 1984
2 N.Y. Giants vs. Pottsville, Oct. 30, 1927
Chi. Bears vs. Pottsville, Nov. 13, 1927
Detroit vs. Brooklyn, Dec. 1, 1935
N.Y. Giants vs. Pittsburgh, Sept. 17, 1950
N.Y. Giants vs. Washington, Nov. 5, 1961
Chicago vs. Pittsburgh, Nov. 9, 1969
Dallas vs. Philadelphia, Nov. 19, 1972
Los Angeles vs. Green Bay, Oct. 21, 1973
Oakland vs. San Diego, Oct. 26, 1975
Denver vs. Seattle, Jan. 2, 1983
New Orleans vs. Cleveland, Sept. 13, 1987
Buffalo vs. Denver, Nov. 8, 1987
San Francisco vs. St. Louis, Sept. 8, 1996
Jacksonville vs. Pittsburgh, Oct. 3, 1999

Most Safeties, Both Teams, Game
3 L.A. Rams (3) vs. N.Y. Giants (0), Sept. 30, 1984
2 Chi. Cardinals (1) vs. Frankford (1), Nov. 19, 1927
Chi. Cardinals (1) vs. Cincinnati (1), Nov. 12, 1933
Chi. Bears (1) vs. San Francisco (1), Oct. 19, 1952
Cincinnati (1) vs. Los Angeles (1), Oct. 22, 1972
Chi. Bears (1) vs. San Francisco (1), Sept. 19, 1976
Baltimore (1) vs. Miami (1), Oct. 29, 1978
Atlanta (1) vs. Detroit (1), Oct. 5, 1980
Houston (1) vs. Philadelphia (1), Oct. 2, 1988
Cleveland (1) vs. Seattle (1), Nov. 14, 1993
Arizona (1) vs. Houston (1), Dec. 4, 1994
(Also see previous record)

FIRST DOWNS

Most Seasons Leading League
9 Chi. Bears, 1935, 1939, 1941, 1943, 1945, 1947-49, 1955
7 San Diego, 1965, 1969, 1980-83, 1985
6 L.A. Rams, 1946, 1950-51, 1954, 1957, 1973
San Francisco, 1965, 1987, 1989, 1993-94, 1998

Most Consecutive Seasons Leading League
4 San Diego, 1980-83
3 Chi. Bears, 1947-49
2 By many teams

Most First Downs, Season
387 Miami, 1984
381 San Francisco, 1998
380 San Diego, 1985

Fewest First Downs, Season
51 Cincinnati, 1933
64 Pittsburgh, 1935
67 Philadelphia, 1937

Most First Downs, Game
39 N.Y. Jets vs. Miami, Nov. 27, 1988
Washington vs. Detroit, Nov. 4, 1990 (OT)
38 Los Angeles vs. N.Y. Giants, Nov. 13, 1966
37 Green Bay vs. Philadelphia, Nov. 11, 1962

Fewest First Downs, Game
0 N.Y. Giants vs. Green Bay, Oct. 1, 1933
Pittsburgh vs. Boston, Oct. 29, 1933
Philadelphia vs. Detroit, Sept. 20, 1935
N.Y. Giants vs. Washington, Sept. 27, 1942
Denver vs. Houston, Sept. 3, 1966

Most First Downs, Both Teams, Game
62 San Diego (32) vs. Seattle (30), Sept. 15, 1985
59 Miami (31) vs. Buffalo (28), Oct. 9, 1983 (OT)
Seattle (33) vs. Kansas City (26), Nov. 27, 1983 (OT)
N.Y. Jets (32) vs. Miami (27), Sept. 21, 1986 (OT)
N.Y. Jets (39) vs. Miami (20), Nov. 27, 1988
58 Los Angeles (30) vs. Chi. Bears (28), Oct. 24, 1954
Denver (34) vs. Kansas City (24), Nov. 18, 1974
Atlanta (35) vs. New Orleans (23), Sept. 2, 1979 (OT)
Pittsburgh (36) vs. Cleveland (22), Nov. 25, 1979 (OT)
San Diego (34) vs. Miami (24), Nov. 18, 1984 (OT)
Cincinnati (32) vs. San Diego (26), Sept. 22, 1985

Fewest First Downs, Both Teams, Game
7 Chi. Cardinals (2) vs. Detroit (5), Sept. 15, 1940
9 Pittsburgh (1) vs. Boston (8), Oct. 27, 1935
Boston (4) vs. Brooklyn (5), Nov. 24, 1935
N.Y. Giants (3) vs. Detroit (6), Nov. 7, 1943
Pittsburgh (4) vs. Chi. Cardinals (5), Nov. 11, 1945
N.Y. Bulldogs (1) vs. Philadelphia (8), Sept. 22, 1949
10 N.Y. Giants (4) vs. Washington (6), Dec. 11, 1960

Most First Downs, Rushing, Season
181 New England, 1978
177 Los Angeles, 1973
176 Chicago, 1985

Fewest First Downs, Rushing, Season
36 Cleveland, 1942
Boston, 1944
39 Brooklyn, 1943
40 Philadelphia, 1940
Detroit, 1945

Most First Downs, Rushing, Game
25 Philadelphia vs. Washington, Dec. 2, 1951
23 St. Louis vs. New Orleans, Oct. 5, 1980
21 Cleveland vs. Philadelphia, Dec. 13, 1959
Green Bay vs. Philadelphia, Nov. 11, 1962
Los Angeles vs. New Orleans, Nov. 25, 1973
Pittsburgh vs. Kansas City, Nov. 7, 1976
New England vs. Denver, Nov. 28, 1976
Oakland vs. Green Bay, Sept. 17, 1978
Buffalo vs. Washington, Nov. 3, 1996
San Francisco vs. Detroit, Dec. 14, 1998

Fewest First Downs, Rushing, Game
0 By many teams. Last time: Detroit vs. Minnesota, Jan. 2, 2000

Most First Downs, Rushing, Both Teams, Game
36 Philadelphia (25) vs. Washington (11), Dec. 2, 1951
31 Detroit (18) vs. Washington (13), Sept. 30, 1951
30 Los Angeles (17) vs. Minnesota (13), Nov. 5, 1961
New Orleans (17) vs. Green Bay (13), Sept. 9, 1979
New Orleans (16) vs. San Francisco (14), Nov. 11, 1979
New England (16) vs. Kansas City (14), Oct. 4, 1981

Fewest First Downs, Rushing, Both Teams, Game
2 Houston (0) vs. Denver (2), Dec. 2, 1962
N.Y. Jets, (1) vs. St. Louis (1), Dec. 3, 1995
Miami (1) vs. San Diego (1), Dec. 19, 1999
New Orleans (0) vs. Baltimore (2), Dec. 19, 1999
3 Philadelphia (1) vs. Pittsburgh (2), Oct. 27, 1957
Boston (1) vs. Buffalo (2), Nov. 15, 1964
Los Angeles (0) vs. San Francisco (3), Dec. 6, 1964
Pittsburgh (1) vs. St. Louis (2), Nov. 13, 1966
Seattle (1) vs. New Orleans (2), Sept. 1, 1991
New Orleans (0) vs. N.Y. Jets (3), Dec. 24, 1995
Philadelphia (1) vs. Carolina (2), Oct. 27, 1996
San Diego (1) vs. New Orleans (2), Sept. 7, 1997
New Orleans (1) vs. Tampa Bay (2), Oct, 25, 1998
New England (1) vs. Miami (2), Oct. 25, 1998 (OT)
Miami (1) vs. New England (2), Nov. 23, 1998
4 In many games

Most First Downs, Passing, Season
259 San Diego, 1985
251 Houston, 1990
250 Miami, 1986
Fewest First Downs, Passing, Season
18 Pittsburgh, 1941
23 Brooklyn, 1942
N.Y. Giants, 1944
24 N.Y. Giants, 1943
Most First Downs, Passing, Game
29 N.Y. Giants vs. Cincinnati, Oct. 13, 1985
27 San Diego vs. Seattle, Sept. 15, 1985
26 Miami vs. Cleveland, Dec. 12, 1988
Fewest First Downs, Passing, Game
0 By many teams. Last time:
San Diego vs. Kansas City, Sept. 20, 1998
Most First Downs, Passing, Both Teams, Game
43 San Diego (23) vs. Cincinnati (20), Dec. 20, 1982
Miami (24) vs. N.Y. Jets (19), Sept. 21, 1986 (OT)
42 San Francisco (22) vs. San Diego (20), Dec. 11, 1982
41 San Diego (27) vs. Seattle (14), Sept. 15, 1985
Miami (26) vs. Cleveland (15), Dec. 12, 1988
Fewest First Downs, Passing, Both Teams, Game
0 Brooklyn vs. Pittsburgh, Nov. 29, 1942
1 Green Bay (0) vs. Cleveland (1), Sept. 21, 1941
Pittsburgh (0) vs. Brooklyn (1), Oct. 11, 1942
N.Y. Giants (0) vs. Detroit (1), Nov. 7, 1943
Pittsburgh (0) vs. Chi. Cardinals (1), Nov. 11, 1945
N.Y. Bulldogs (0) vs. Philadelphia (1), Sept. 22, 1949
Chicago (0) vs. Buffalo (1), Oct. 7, 1979
2 In many games
Most First Downs, Penalty, Season
43 Denver, 1994
42 Chicago, 1987
41 Denver, 1986
Fewest First Downs, Penalty, Season
2 Brooklyn, 1940
4 Chi. Cardinals, 1940
N.Y. Giants, 1942, 1944
Washington, 1944
Cleveland, 1952
Kansas City, 1969
5 Brooklyn, 1939
Chi. Bears, 1939
Detroit, 1953
Los Angeles, 1953
Houston, 1982
Most First Downs, Penalty, Game
11 Denver vs. Houston, Oct. 6, 1985
9 Chi. Bears vs. Cleveland, Nov. 25, 1951
Baltimore vs. Pittsburgh, Oct. 30, 1977
N.Y. Jets vs. Houston, Sept. 18, 1988
8 Philadelphia vs. Detroit, Dec. 2, 1979
Cincinnati vs. N.Y. Jets, Oct. 6, 1985
Buffalo vs. Houston, Sept. 20, 1987
Houston vs. Atlanta, Sept. 9, 1990
Kansas City vs. L.A. Raiders, Oct. 3, 1993
San Francisco vs. New Orleans, Oct. 11, 1998
Most First Downs, Penalty, Both Teams, Game
12 Buffalo (7) vs. San Francisco (5), Oct. 4, 1998
11 Chi. Bears (9) vs. Cleveland (2), Nov. 25, 1951
Cincinnati (8) vs. N.Y. Jets (3), Oct. 6, 1985
Denver (11) vs. Houston (0), Oct. 6, 1985
Detroit (6) vs. Dallas (5), Nov. 8, 1987
N.Y. Jets (9) vs. Houston (2), Sept. 18, 1988
Kansas City (8) vs. L.A. Raiders (3), Oct. 3, 1993
Detroit (6) vs. San Diego (5), Nov. 11, 1996
10 In many games

NET YARDS GAINED RUSHING AND PASSING

Most Seasons Leading League
12 Chi. Bears, 1932, 1934-35, 1939, 1941-44, 1947, 1949, 1955-56
7 San Diego, 1963, 1965, 1980-83, 1985
L.A./St. Louis Rams, 1946, 1950-51, 1954, 1957, 1973, 1999
6 Baltimore, 1958-60, 1964, 1967, 1976
Dall. Cowboys, 1966, 1968-69, 1971, 1974, 1977
San Francisco, 1965, 1987, 1989, 1992-93, 1998
Most Consecutive Seasons Leading League
4 Chi. Bears, 1941-44
San Diego, 1980-83
3 Baltimore, 1958-60
Houston, 1960-62
Oakland, 1968-70
2 By many teams
Most Yards Gained, Season
6,936 Miami, 1984
6,800 San Francisco, 1998
6,744 San Diego, 1981
Fewest Yards Gained, Season
1,150 Cincinnati, 1933
1,443 Chi. Cardinals, 1934
1,486 Chi. Cardinals, 1933
Most Yards Gained, Game
735 Los Angeles vs. N.Y. Yanks, Sept. 28, 1951
683 Pittsburgh vs. Chi. Cardinals, Dec. 13, 1958
682 Chi. Bears vs. N.Y. Giants, Nov. 14, 1943
Fewest Yards Gained, Game
–7 Seattle vs. Los Angeles, Nov. 4, 1979
–5 Denver vs. Oakland, Sept. 10, 1967
14 Chi. Cardinals vs. Detroit, Sept. 15, 1940
Most Yards Gained, Both Teams, Game
1,133 Los Angeles (636) vs. N.Y. Yanks (497), Nov. 19, 1950
1,102 San Diego (661) vs. Cincinnati (441), Dec. 20, 1982
1,087 St. Louis (589) vs. Philadelphia (498), Dec. 16, 1962
Fewest Yards Gained, Both Teams, Game
30 Chi. Cardinals (14) vs. Detroit (16), Sept. 15, 1940
136 Chi. Cardinals (50) vs. Green Bay (86), Nov. 18, 1934
154 N.Y. Giants (51) vs. Washington (103), Dec. 11, 1960
Most Consecutive Games, 400 or More Yards Gained
11 San Diego, 1982-83
6 Houston, 1961-62
San Diego, 1981
San Francisco, 1987
5 Chi. Bears, 1947
Philadelphia, 1953
Chi. Bears, 1955
Oakland, 1968
New England, 1981
Cincinnati, 1986
San Francisco, 1994
San Francisco, 1998
St. Louis, 1999 (current)
Most Consecutive Games, 300 or More Yards Gained
29 Los Angeles, 1949-51
26 Miami, 1983-85
25 Miami, 1993-95

RUSHING

Most Seasons Leading League
16 Chi. Bears, 1932, 1934-35, 1939-42, 1951, 1955-56, 1968, 1977, 1983-86
7 Buffalo, 1962, 1964, 1973, 1975, 1982, 1991-92
6 Cleveland, 1958-59, 1963, 1965-67
San Francisco, 1952-54, 1987, 1998-99
Most Consecutive Seasons Leading League
4 Chi. Bears, 1939-42
Chi. Bears, 1983-86
3 Detroit, 1936-38
San Francisco, 1952-54
Cleveland, 1965-67
2 By many teams

ATTEMPTS

Most Rushing Attempts, Season
681 Oakland, 1977
674 Chicago, 1984
671 New England, 1978
Fewest Rushing Attempts, Season
211 Philadelphia, 1982
219 San Francisco, 1982
225 Houston, 1982
Most Rushing Attempts, Game
72 Chi. Bears vs. Brooklyn, Oct. 20, 1935
70 Chi. Cardinals vs. Green Bay, Dec. 5, 1948
69 Chi. Cardinals vs. Green Bay, Dec. 6, 1936
Kansas City vs. Cincinnati, Sept. 3, 1978
Fewest Rushing Attempts, Game
6 Chi. Cardinals vs. Boston, Oct. 29, 1933
7 Oakland vs. Buffalo, Oct. 15, 1963
Houston vs. N.Y. Giants, Dec. 8, 1985
Seattle vs. L.A. Raiders, Nov. 17, 1991
Green Bay vs. Miami, Sept. 11, 1994
8 Denver vs. Oakland, Dec. 17, 1960

Buffalo vs. St. Louis, Sept. 9, 1984
Detroit vs. San Francisco, Oct. 20, 1991
Atlanta vs. Detroit, Sept. 5, 1993

Most Rushing Attempts, Both Teams, Game
108 Chi. Cardinals (70) vs. Green Bay (38), Dec. 5, 1948
105 Oakland (62) vs. Atlanta (43), Nov. 30, 1975 (OT)
104 Chi. Bears (64) vs. Pittsburgh (40), Oct. 18, 1936

Fewest Rushing Attempts, Both Teams, Game
34 Atlanta (12) vs. Houston (22), Dec. 5, 1993
Atlanta (15) vs. San Francisco (19), Dec. 24, 1995
35 Seattle (15) vs. New Orleans (20), Sept. 1, 1991
36 Houston (15) vs. N.Y. Jets (21), Oct. 13, 1991
St. Louis (16) vs. Detroit (20), Nov. 7, 1999
Detroit (15) vs. Washington (21), Dec. 5, 1999
Tennessee (14) vs. Baltimore (22), Dec. 5, 1999

YARDS GAINED

Most Yards Gained Rushing, Season
3,165 New England, 1978
3,088 Buffalo, 1973
2,986 Kansas City, 1978

Fewest Yards Gained Rushing, Season
298 Philadelphia, 1940
467 Detroit, 1946
471 Boston, 1944

Most Yards Gained Rushing, Game
426 Detroit vs. Pittsburgh, Nov. 4, 1934
423 N.Y. Giants vs. Baltimore, Nov. 19, 1950
420 Boston vs. N.Y. Giants, Oct. 8, 1933

Fewest Yards Gained Rushing, Game
–53 Detroit vs. Chi. Cardinals, Oct. 17, 1943
–36 Philadelphia vs. Chi. Bears, Nov. 19, 1939
–33 Phil-Pitt vs. Brooklyn, Oct. 2, 1943

Most Yards Gained Rushing, Both Teams, Game
595 Los Angeles (371) vs. N.Y. Yanks (224), Nov. 18, 1951
574 Chi. Bears (396) vs. Pittsburgh (178), Oct. 10, 1934
558 Boston (420) vs. N.Y. Giants (138), Oct. 8, 1933

Fewest Yards Gained Rushing, Both Teams, Game
–15 Detroit (–53) vs. Chi. Cardinals (38), Oct. 17, 1943
4 Detroit (–10) vs. Chi. Cardinals (14), Sept. 15, 1940
62 L.A. Rams (15) vs. San Francisco (47), Dec. 6, 1964

AVERAGE GAIN

Highest Average Gain, Rushing, Season
5.74 Cleveland, 1963
5.65 San Francisco, 1954
5.56 San Diego, 1963

Lowest Average Gain, Rushing, Season
0.94 Philadelphia, 1940
1.45 Boston, 1944
1.55 Pittsburgh, 1935

TOUCHDOWNS

Most Touchdowns, Rushing, Season
36 Green Bay, 1962
33 Pittsburgh, 1976
30 Chi. Bears, 1941
New England, 1978
Washington, 1983

Fewest Touchdowns, Rushing, Season
1 Brooklyn, 1934
2 Chi. Cardinals, 1933
Cincinnati, 1933
Pittsburgh, 1934
Philadelphia, 1935
Philadelphia, 1936
Philadelphia, 1937
Philadelphia, 1938
Pittsburgh, 1940
Philadelphia, 1972
N.Y. Jets, 1995
3 By many teams

Most Touchdowns, Rushing, Game
7 Los Angeles vs. Atlanta, Dec. 4, 1976
6 By many teams

Most Touchdowns, Rushing, Both Teams, Game
8 Los Angeles (6) vs. N.Y. Yanks (2), Nov. 18, 1951
Chi. Bears (5) vs. Green Bay (3), Nov. 6, 1955
Cleveland (6) vs. Los Angeles (2), Nov. 24, 1957
7 In many games

PASSING

ATTEMPTS

Most Passes Attempted, Season
709 Minnesota, 1981
699 New England, 1994
686 New England, 1995

Fewest Passes Attempted, Season
102 Cincinnati, 1933
106 Boston, 1933
120 Detroit, 1937

Most Passes Attempted, Game
70 New England vs. Minnesota, Nov. 13, 1994
68 Houston vs. Buffalo, Nov 1, 1964
66 Atlanta vs. Detroit, Dec. 24, 1989

Fewest Passes Attempted, Game
0 Green Bay vs. Portsmouth, Oct. 8, 1933
Detroit vs. Cleveland, Sept. 10, 1937
Pittsburgh vs. Brooklyn, Nov. 16, 1941
Pittsburgh vs. Los Angeles, Nov. 13, 1949
Cleveland vs. Philadelphia, Dec. 3, 1950

Most Passes Attempted, Both Teams, Game
112 New England (70) vs. Minnesota (42), Nov. 13, 1994
104 Miami (55) vs. N.Y. Jets (49), Oct. 18, 1987 (OT)
N.Y. Jets (58) vs. San Francisco (46), Sept. 6, 1998 (OT)
102 San Francisco (57) vs. Atlanta (45), Oct. 6, 1985

Fewest Passes Attempted, Both Teams, Game
4 Chi. Cardinals (1) vs. Detroit (3), Nov. 3, 1935
Detroit (0) vs. Cleveland (4), Sept. 10, 1937
6 Chi. Cardinals (2) vs. Detroit (4), Sept. 15, 1940
8 Brooklyn (2) vs. Philadelphia (6), Oct. 1, 1939

COMPLETIONS

Most Passes Completed, Season
432 San Francisco, 1995
411 Houston, 1991
409 Minnesota, 1994

Fewest Passes Completed, Season
25 Cincinnati, 1933
33 Boston, 1933
34 Chi. Cardinals, 1934
Detroit, 1934

Most Passes Completed, Game
45 New England vs. Minnesota, Nov. 13, 1994 (OT)
43 Washington vs. Detroit, Nov. 4, 1990 (OT)
42 N.Y. Jets vs. San Francisco, Sept. 21, 1980
N.Y. Jets vs. Seattle, Dec. 6, 1998

Fewest Passes Completed, Game
0 By many teams. Last time: Buffalo vs. N.Y. Jets, Sept. 29, 1974

Most Passes Completed, Both Teams, Game
71 New England (45) vs. Minnesota (26), Nov. 13, 1994
68 San Francisco (37) vs. Atlanta (31), Oct. 6, 1985
66 Cincinnati (40) vs. San Diego (26), Dec. 20, 1982

Fewest Passes Completed, Both Teams, Game
1 Chi. Cardinals (0) vs. Philadelphia (1), Nov. 8, 1936
Detroit (0) vs. Cleveland (1), Sept. 10, 1937
Chi. Cardinals (0) vs. Detroit (1), Sept. 15, 1940
Brooklyn (0) vs. Pittsburgh (1), Nov. 29, 1942
2 Chi. Cardinals (0) vs. Detroit (2), Nov. 3, 1935
Buffalo (0) vs. N.Y. Jets (2), Sept. 29, 1974
Chi. Cardinals (0) vs. Green Bay (2), Nov. 18, 1934
3 In seven games

YARDS GAINED

Most Seasons Leading League, Passing Yardage
10 San Diego, 1965, 1968, 1971, 1978-83, 1985
8 Chi. Bears, 1932, 1939, 1941, 1943, 1945, 1949, 1954, 1964
Washington, 1938, 1940, 1944, 1947-48, 1967, 1974, 1989
7 Houston, 1960-61, 1963-64, 1990-92

Most Consecutive Seasons Leading League, Passing Yardage
6 San Diego, 1978-83
4 Green Bay, 1934-37
3 Miami, 1986-88
Houston, 1990-92

Most Yards Gained, Passing, Season
5,018 Miami, 1984
4,870 San Diego, 1985
4,805 Houston, 1990

Fewest Yards Gained, Passing, Season
302 Chi. Cardinals, 1934
357 Cincinnati, 1933
459 Boston, 1934

ALL-TIME RECORDS

Most Yards Gained, Passing, Game
554 Los Angeles vs. N.Y. Yanks, Sept. 28, 1951
530 Minnesota vs. Baltimore, Sept. 28, 1969
521 Miami vs. N.Y. Jets, Oct. 23, 1988

Fewest Yards Gained, Passing, Game
–53 Denver vs. Oakland, Sept. 10, 1967
–52 Cincinnati vs. Houston, Oct. 31, 1971
–39 Atlanta vs. San Francisco, Oct. 23, 1976

Most Yards Gained, Passing, Both Teams, Game
884 N.Y. Jets (449) vs. Miami (435), Sept. 21, 1986 (OT)
883 San Diego (486) vs. Cincinnati (397), Dec. 20, 1982
874 Miami (456) vs. New England (418), Sept. 4, 1994

Fewest Yards Gained, Passing, Both Teams, Game
–11 Green Bay (–10) vs. Dallas (–1), Oct. 24, 1965
1 Chi. Cardinals (0) vs. Philadelphia (1), Nov. 8, 1936
7 Brooklyn (0) vs. Pittsburgh (7), Nov. 29, 1942

TIMES SACKED

Most Seasons Leading League, Fewest Times Sacked
10 Miami, 1973, 1982-90
4 San Diego, 1963-64, 1967-68
San Francisco, 1964-65, 1970-71
N.Y. Jets, 1965-66, 1968, 1993
3 Houston, 1961-62, 1978
St. Louis, 1974-76
Washington, 1966-67, 1991

Most Consecutive Seasons Leading League, Fewest Times Sacked
9 Miami, 1982-90
3 St. Louis, 1974-76
2 By many teams

Most Times Sacked, Season
104 Philadelphia, 1986
78 Arizona, 1997
72 Philadelphia, 1987

Fewest Times Sacked, Season
7 Miami, 1988
8 San Francisco, 1970
St. Louis, 1975
9 N.Y. Jets, 1966
Washington, 1991

Most Times Sacked, Game
12 Pittsburgh vs. Dallas, Nov. 20, 1966
Baltimore vs. St. Louis, Oct. 26, 1980
Detroit vs. Chicago, Dec. 16, 1984
Houston vs. Dallas, Sept. 29, 1985
11 St. Louis vs. N.Y. Giants, Nov. 1, 1964
Los Angeles vs. Baltimore, Nov. 22, 1964
Denver vs. Buffalo, Dec. 13, 1964
Green Bay vs. Detroit, Nov. 7, 1965
Buffalo vs. Oakland, Oct. 15, 1967
Denver vs. Oakland, Nov. 5, 1967
Atlanta vs. St. Louis, Nov. 24, 1968
Detroit vs. Dallas, Oct. 6, 1975
Philadelphia vs. St. Louis, Dec. 18, 1983
Cleveland vs. Kansas City, Sept. 30, 1984
Minnesota vs. Chicago, Oct. 28, 1984
Atlanta vs. Cleveland, Nov. 18, 1984
Dallas vs. San Diego, Nov. 16, 1986
Philadelphia vs. Detroit, Nov. 16, 1986
Philadelphia vs. L.A. Raiders, Nov. 30, 1986 (OT)
L.A. Raiders vs. Seattle, Dec. 8, 1986
N.Y. Jets vs. Dallas, Oct. 4, 1987
Philadelphia vs. Chicago, Oct. 4, 1987
Dallas vs. Philadelphia, Sept. 15, 1991
Cleveland vs. Indianapolis, Sept. 6, 1992
10 By many teams

Most Times Sacked, Both Teams, Game
18 Green Bay (10) vs. San Diego (8), Sept. 24, 1978
17 Buffalo (10) vs. N.Y. Titans (7), Nov. 23, 1961
Pittsburgh (12) vs. Dallas (5), Nov. 20, 1966
Atlanta (9) vs. Philadelphia (8), Dec. 16, 1984
Philadelphia (11) vs. L.A. Raiders (6), Nov. 30, 1986 (OT)
16 Los Angeles (11) vs. Baltimore (5), Nov. 22, 1964
Buffalo (11) vs. Oakland (5), Oct. 15, 1967

COMPLETION PERCENTAGE

Most Seasons Leading League, Completion Percentage
14 San Francisco, 1952, 1957-58, 1965, 1981, 1983, 1987, 1989, 1992-97
11 Washington, 1937, 1939-40, 1942-45, 1947-48, 1969-70
8 Green Bay, 1936, 1941, 1961-62, 1964, 1966, 1968, 1998

Most Consecutive Seasons Leading League, Completion Percentage
6 San Francisco, 1992-97
4 Washington, 1942-45
Kansas City, 1966-69
3 Cleveland, 1953-55

Highest Completion Percentage, Season
70.65 Cincinnati, 1982 (310-219)
70.25 San Francisco, 1994 (511-359)
70.19 San Francisco, 1989 (483-339)

Lowest Completion Percentage, Season
22.9 Philadelphia, 1936 (170-39)
24.5 Cincinnati, 1933 (102-25)
25.0 Pittsburgh, 1941 (168-42)

TOUCHDOWNS

Most Touchdowns, Passing, Season
49 Miami, 1984
48 Houston, 1961
46 Miami, 1986

Fewest Touchdowns, Passing, Season
0 Cincinnati, 1933
Pittsburgh, 1945
1 Boston, 1932
Boston, 1933
Chi. Cardinals, 1934
Cincinnati/St. Louis, 1934
Detroit, 1942
2 Chi. Cardinals, 1932
Stapleton, 1932
Chi. Cardinals, 1935
Brooklyn, 1936
Pittsburgh, 1942

Most Touchdowns, Passing, Game
7 Chi. Bears vs. N.Y. Giants, Nov. 14, 1943
Philadelphia vs. Washington, Oct. 17, 1954
Houston vs. N.Y. Titans, Nov. 19, 1961
Houston vs. N.Y. Titans, Oct. 14, 1962
N.Y. Giants vs. Washington, Oct. 28, 1962
Minnesota vs. Baltimore, Sept. 28, 1969
San Diego vs. Oakland, Nov. 22, 1981
6 By many teams

Most Touchdowns, Passing, Both Teams, Game
12 New Orleans (6) vs. St. Louis (6), Nov. 2, 1969
11 N.Y. Giants (7) vs. Washington (4), Oct. 28, 1962
Oakland (6) vs. Houston (5), Dec. 22, 1963
10 San Diego (5) vs. Seattle (5), Sept. 15, 1985
Miami (6) vs. N.Y. Jets (4), Sept. 21, 1986 (OT)
San Francisco (6) vs. Atlanta (4), Oct. 14, 1990

PASSES HAD INTERCEPTED

Most Passes Had Intercepted, Season
48 Houston, 1962
45 Denver, 1961
41 Card-Pitt, 1944

Fewest Passes Had Intercepted, Season
5 Cleveland, 1960
Green Bay, 1966
Kansas City, 1990
N.Y. Giants, 1990
6 Green Bay, 1964
St. Louis, 1982
Dallas, 1993
7 Los Angeles, 1969

Most Passes Had Intercepted, Game
9 Detroit vs. Green Bay, Oct. 24, 1943
Pittsburgh vs. Philadelphia, Dec. 12, 1965
8 Green Bay vs. N.Y. Giants, Nov. 21, 1948
Chi. Cardinals vs. Philadelphia, Sept. 24, 1950
N.Y. Yanks vs. N.Y. Giants, Dec. 16, 1951
Denver vs. Houston, Dec. 2, 1962
Chi. Bears vs. Detroit, Sept. 22, 1968
Baltimore vs. N.Y. Jets, Sept. 23, 1973
7 By many teams. Last time:
San Diego vs. Seattle, Dec. 13, 1998

Most Passes Had Intercepted, Both Teams, Game
13 Denver (8) vs. Houston (5), Dec. 2, 1962
11 Philadelphia (7) vs. Boston (4), Nov. 3, 1935
Boston (6) vs. Pittsburgh (5), Dec. 1, 1935
Cleveland (7) vs. Green Bay (4), Oct. 30, 1938
Green Bay (7) vs. Detroit (4), Oct. 20, 1940
Detroit (7) vs. Chi. Bears (4), Nov. 22, 1942
Detroit (7) vs. Cleveland (4), Nov. 26, 1944
Chi. Cardinals (8) vs. Philadelphia (3), Sept. 24, 1950

Washington (7) vs. N.Y. Giants (4), Dec. 8, 1963
Pittsburgh (9) vs. Philadelphia (2), Dec 12, 1965
10 In many games

PUNTING

Most Seasons Leading League (Average Distance)
7 Denver 1962-64, 1966-67, 1982, 1999
6 Washington, 1940-43, 1945, 1958
Kansas City, 1968, 1971-73, 1979, 1984
5 L.A. Rams, 1946, 1949, 1955-56, 1994

Most Consecutive Seasons Leading League (Average Distance)
4 Washington, 1940-43
3 Cleveland, 1950-52
Denver, 1962-64
Kansas City, 1971-73

Most Punts, Season
114 Chicago, 1981
113 Boston, 1934
Brooklyn, 1934
112 Boston, 1935
N.Y. Giants, 1997

Fewest Punts, Season
23 San Diego, 1982
31 Cincinnati, 1982
32 Chi. Bears, 1941

Most Punts, Game
17 Chi. Bears vs. Green Bay, Oct. 22, 1933
Cincinnati vs. Pittsburgh, Oct. 22, 1933
16 Cincinnati vs. Portsmouth, Sept. 17, 1933
Chi. Cardinals vs. Chi. Bears, Nov. 30, 1933
Chi. Cardinals vs. Detroit, Sept. 15, 1940
Oakland vs. San Diego, Oct. 11, 1998
15 N.Y. Giants vs. Chi. Bears, Nov. 17, 1935
Philadelphia vs. N.Y. Giants, Dec. 6, 1987 (OT)

Fewest Punts, Game
0 By many teams. Last time: St. Louis vs. New Orleans, Dec. 12, 1999

Most Punts, Both Teams, Game
31 Chi. Bears (17) vs. Green Bay (14), Oct. 22, 1933
Cincinnati (17), vs. Pittsburgh (14), Oct. 22, 1933
29 Chi. Cardinals (15) vs. Cincinnati (14), Nov. 12, 1933
Chi. Cardinals (16) vs. Chi. Bears (13), Nov. 30, 1933
Chi. Cardinals (16) vs. Detroit (13), Sept. 15, 1940
28 Philadelphia (14) vs. Washington (14), Nov. 5, 1939

Fewest Punts, Both Teams, Game
0 Buffalo vs. San Francisco, Sept. 13, 1992
1 Baltimore (0) vs. Cleveland (1), Nov. 1, 1959
Dall. Cowboys (0) vs. Cleveland (1), Dec. 3, 1961
Chicago (0) vs. Detroit (1), Oct. 1, 1972
San Francisco (0) vs. N.Y. Giants (1), Oct. 15, 1972
Green Bay (0) vs. Buffalo (1), Dec. 5, 1982
Miami (0) vs. Buffalo (1), Oct. 12, 1986
Green Bay (0) vs. Chicago (1), Dec. 17, 1989
Oakland (0) vs. Seattle (1), Dec. 5, 1999
2 In many games

AVERAGE YARDAGE

Highest Average Distance, Punting, Season
47.6 Detroit, 1961 (56-2,664)
47.2 Tennessee, 1998 (69-3,258)
47.0 Pittsburgh, 1961 (73-3,431)

Lowest Average Distance, Punting, Season
32.7 Card-Pitt, 1944 (60-1,964)
33.8 Cincinnati, 1986 (59-1,996)
33.9 Detroit, 1969 (74-2,510)

PUNT RETURNS

Most Seasons Leading League (Average Return)
9 Detroit, 1943-45, 1951-52, 1962, 1966, 1969, 1991
7 Chi. Cardinals/St. Louis, 1948-49, 1955-56, 1959, 1986-87
6 Green Bay, 1950, 1953-54, 1961, 1972, 1996

Most Consecutive Seasons Leading League (Average Return)
3 Detroit, 1943-45
2 By many teams

Most Punt Returns, Season
71 Pittsburgh, 1976
Tampa Bay, 1979
L.A. Raiders, 1985
67 Pittsburgh, 1974
Los Angeles, 1978
L.A. Raiders, 1984
65 San Francisco, 1976

Fewest Punt Returns, Season
12 Baltimore, 1981
San Diego, 1982
14 Los Angeles, 1961
Philadelphia, 1962
Baltimore, 1982
15 Houston, 1960
Washington, 1960
Oakland, 1961
N.Y. Giants, 1969
Philadelphia, 1973
Kansas City, 1982

Most Punt Returns, Game
12 Philadelphia vs. Cleveland, Dec. 3, 1950
11 Chi. Bears vs. Chi. Cardinals, Oct. 8, 1950
Washington vs. Tampa Bay, Oct. 9, 1977
10 Philadelphia vs. N.Y. Giants, Nov. 26, 1950
Philadelphia vs. Tampa Bay, Sept. 18, 1977
Pittsburgh vs. Buffalo, Dec. 16, 1979
Washington vs. New Orleans, Dec. 26, 1982
Philadelphia vs. Seattle, Dec. 13, 1992 (OT)
New England vs. Pittsburgh, Dec. 5, 1993

Most Punt Returns, Both Teams, Game
17 Philadelphia (12) vs. Cleveland (5), Dec. 3, 1950
16 N.Y. Giants (9) vs. Philadelphia (7), Dec. 12, 1954
Washington (11) vs. Tampa Bay (5), Oct. 9, 1977
Oakland (8) vs. San Diego (8), Oct. 11, 1998
15 Detroit (8) vs. Cleveland (7), Sept. 27, 1942
Los Angeles (8) vs. Baltimore (7), Nov. 27, 1966
Pittsburgh (8) vs. Houston (7), Dec. 1, 1974
Philadelphia (10) vs. Tampa Bay (5), Sept. 18, 1977
Baltimore (9) vs. Kansas City (6), Sept. 2, 1979
Washington (10) vs. New Orleans (5), Dec. 26, 1982
L.A. Raiders (8) vs. Cleveland (7), Nov. 16, 1986

FAIR CATCHES

Most Fair Catches, Season
34 Baltimore, 1971
32 San Diego, 1969
31 Minnesota, 1996

Fewest Fair Catches, Season
0 San Diego, 1975
New England, 1976
Tampa Bay, 1976
Pittsburgh, 1977
Dallas, 1982
1 Cleveland, 1974
San Francisco, 1975
Kansas City, 1976
St. Louis, 1976
San Diego, 1976
L.A. Rams, 1982
St. Louis, 1982
Tampa Bay, 1982
2 By many teams

Most Fair Catches, Game
7 Minnesota vs. Dallas, Sept. 25, 1966
Detroit vs. Chicago, Nov. 21, 1976
Philadelphia vs. Buffalo, Dec. 27, 1987
6 By many teams

YARDS GAINED

Most Yards, Punt Returns, Season
875 Green Bay, 1996
785 L.A. Raiders, 1985
781 Chi. Bears, 1948

Fewest Yards, Punt Returns, Season
27 St. Louis, 1965
35 N.Y. Giants, 1965
37 New England, 1972

Most Yards, Punt Returns, Game
231 Detroit vs. San Francisco, Oct. 6, 1963
225 Oakland vs. Buffalo, Sept. 15, 1968
219 Los Angeles vs. Atlanta, Oct. 11, 1981

Fewest Yards, Punt Returns, Game
-28 Washington vs. Dallas, Dec. 11, 1966
-23 N.Y. Giants vs. Buffalo, Oct. 20, 1975
Pittsburgh vs. Houston, Sept. 20, 1970
-20 New Orleans vs. Pittsburgh, Oct. 20, 1968

Most Yards, Punt Returns, Both Teams, Game
282 Los Angeles (219) vs. Atlanta (63), Oct. 11, 1981
245 Detroit (231) vs. San Francisco (14), Oct. 6, 1963
244 Oakland (225) vs. Buffalo (19), Sept. 15, 1968

Fewest Yards, Punt Returns, Both Teams, Game
- -18 Buffalo (-18) vs. Pittsburgh (0), Oct. 29, 1972
- -14 Miami (-14) vs. Boston (0), Nov. 30, 1969
- -13 N.Y. Giants (-13) vs. Cleveland (0), Nov. 14, 1965

AVERAGE YARDS RETURNING PUNTS

Highest Average, Punt Returns, Season
- 20.2 Chi. Bears, 1941 (27-546)
- 19.1 Chi. Cardinals, 1948 (35-669)
- 18.2 Chi. Cardinals, 1949 (30-546)

Lowest Average, Punt Returns, Season
- 1.2 St. Louis, 1965 (23-27)
- 1.5 N.Y. Giants, 1965 (24-35)
- 1.7 Washington, 1970 (27-45)

TOUCHDOWNS RETURNING PUNTS

Most Touchdowns, Punt Returns, Season
- 5 Chi. Cardinals, 1959
- 4 Chi. Cardinals, 1948
  Detroit, 1951
  N.Y. Giants, 1951
  Denver, 1976
- 3 Washington, 1941
  Detroit, 1952
  Pittsburgh, 1952
  Houston, 1975
  Los Angeles, 1981
  Cleveland, 1993
  Green Bay, 1996
  Denver, 1997
  San Diego, 1997

Most Touchdowns, Punt Returns, Game
- 2 Detroit vs. Los Angeles, Oct. 14, 1951
  Detroit vs. Green Bay, Nov. 22, 1951
  Chi. Cardinals vs. Pittsburgh, Nov. 1, 1959
  Chi. Cardinals vs. N.Y. Giants, Nov. 22, 1959
  N.Y. Titans vs. Denver, Sept. 24, 1961
  Denver vs. Cleveland, Sept. 26, 1976
  Los Angeles vs. Atlanta, Oct. 11, 1981
  St. Louis vs. Tampa Bay, Dec. 21, 1986
  L.A. Rams vs. Atlanta, Dec. 27, 1992
  Cleveland vs. Pittsburgh, Oct. 24, 1993
  San Diego vs. Cincinnati, Nov. 2, 1997
  Denver vs. Carolina, Nov. 9, 1997
  Baltimore vs. Seattle, Dec. 7, 1997

Most Touchdowns, Punt Returns, Both Teams, Game
- 2 Philadelphia (1) vs. Washington (1), Nov. 9, 1952
  Kansas City (1) vs. Buffalo (1), Sept. 11, 1966
  Baltimore (1) vs. New England (1), Nov. 18, 1979
  L.A. Raiders (1) vs. Philadelphia (1), Nov. 30, 1986 (OT)
  Cincinnati (1) vs. Green Bay (1), Sept. 20, 1992
  Oakland (1) vs. Seattle (1), Nov. 15, 1998

(Also see previous record)

KICKOFF RETURNS

Most Seasons Leading League (Average Return)
- 8 Washington, 1942, 1947, 1962-63, 1973-74, 1981, 1995
- 6 Chicago Bears, 1943, 1948, 1958, 1966, 1972, 1985
- 5 N.Y. Giants, 1944, 1946, 1949, 1951, 1953

Most Consecutive Seasons Leading League (Average Return)
- 3 Denver, 1965-67
- 2 By many teams

Most Kickoff Returns, Season
- 89 Cleveland, 1999
- 88 New Orleans, 1980
- 87 Atlanta, 1996

Fewest Kickoff Returns, Season
- 17 N.Y. Giants, 1944
- 20 N.Y. Giants, 1941, 1943
  Chi. Bears, 1942
- 23 Washington, 1942

Most Kickoff Returns, Game
- 12 N.Y. Giants vs. Washington, Nov. 27, 1966
- 10 By many teams

Most Kickoff Returns, Both Teams, Game
- 19 N.Y. Giants (12) vs. Washington (7), Nov. 27, 1966
- 18 Houston (10) vs. Oakland (8), Dec. 22, 1963
- 17 Washington (9) vs. Green Bay (8), Oct. 17, 1983
  San Diego (9) vs. Pittsburgh (8), Dec. 8, 1985
  Detroit (9) vs. Green Bay (8), Nov. 27, 1986
  L.A. Raiders (9) vs. Seattle (8), Dec. 18, 1988
  Oakland (10) vs. Seattle (7), Oct. 26, 1997

YARDS GAINED

Most Yards, Kickoff Returns, Season
- 2,020 Cleveland, 1999
- 1,973 New Orleans, 1980
- 1,899 New Orleans, 1996

Fewest Yards, Kickoff Returns, Season
- 282 N.Y. Giants, 1940
- 381 Green Bay, 1940
- 424 Chicago, 1963

Most Yards, Kickoff Returns, Game
- 367 Baltimore vs. Minnesota, Dec. 13, 1998
- 362 Detroit vs. Los Angeles, Oct. 29, 1950
- 304 Chi. Bears vs. Green Bay, Nov. 9, 1952
  New Orleans vs. L.A. Rams, Oct. 23, 1994

Most Yards, Kickoff Returns, Both Teams, Game
- 560 Detroit (362) vs. Los Angeles (198), Oct. 29, 1950
- 511 Baltimore (367) vs. Minnesota (144), Dec. 13, 1998
- 501 New Orleans (304) vs. L.A. Rams (197), Oct. 23, 1994

AVERAGE YARDAGE

Highest Average, Kickoff Returns, Season
- 29.4 Chicago, 1972 (52-1,528)
- 28.9 Pittsburgh, 1952 (39-1,128)
- 28.2 Washington, 1962 (61-1,720)

Lowest Average, Kickoff Returns, Season
- 14.7 N.Y. Jets, 1993 (46-675)
- 15.8 N.Y. Giants, 1993 (32-507)
- 15.9 Tampa Bay, 1993 (58-922)

TOUCHDOWNS

Most Touchdowns, Kickoff Returns, Season
- 4 Green Bay, 1967
  Chicago, 1970
  Detroit, 1994
- 3 Los Angeles, 1950
  Chi. Cardinals, 1954
  San Francisco, 1963
  Denver, 1966
  Chicago, 1967
  New England, 1977
  L.A. Rams, 1985
- 2 By many teams

Most Touchdowns, Kickoff Returns, Game
- 2 Chi. Bears vs. Green Bay, Sept. 22, 1940
  Chi. Bears vs. Green Bay, Nov. 9, 1952
  Philadelphia vs. Dallas, Nov. 6, 1966
  Green Bay vs. Cleveland, Nov. 12, 1967
  L.A. Rams vs. Green Bay, Nov. 24, 1985
  New Orleans vs. L.A. Rams, Oct. 23, 1994
  Baltimore vs. Minnesota, Dec. 13, 1998

Most Touchdowns, Kickoff Returns, Both Teams, Game
- 3 Baltimore (2) vs. Minnesota (1), Dec. 13, 1998
- 2 In many games

FUMBLES

Most Fumbles, Season
- 56 Chi. Bears, 1938
  San Francisco, 1978
- 54 Philadelphia, 1946
- 51 New England, 1973

Fewest Fumbles, Season
- 8 Cleveland, 1959
- 10 Indianapolis, 1998
  Minnesota, 1998
- 11 Green Bay, 1944

Most Fumbles, Game
- 10 Phil-Pitt vs. N.Y. Giants, Oct. 9, 1943
  Detroit vs. Minnesota, Nov. 12, 1967
  Kansas City vs. Houston, Oct. 12, 1969
  San Francisco vs. Detroit, Dec. 17, 1978
- 9 Philadelphia vs. Green Bay, Oct. 13, 1946
  Kansas City vs. San Diego, Nov. 15, 1964
  N.Y. Giants vs. Buffalo, Oct. 20, 1975
  St. Louis vs. Washington, Oct. 25, 1976
  San Diego vs. Green Bay, Sept. 24, 1978
  Pittsburgh vs. Cincinnati, Oct. 14, 1979
  Cleveland vs. Seattle, Dec. 20, 1981
  Cleveland vs. Pittsburgh, Dec. 23, 1990
  Oakland vs. Seattle, Dec. 22, 1996
- 8 By many teams

Most Fumbles, Both Teams, Game
14 Washington (8) vs. Pittsburgh (6), Nov. 14, 1937
Chi. Bears (7) vs. Cleveland (7), Nov. 24, 1940
St. Louis (8) vs. N.Y. Giants (6), Sept. 17, 1961
Kansas City (10) vs. Houston (4), Oct. 12, 1969
13 Washington (8) vs. Pittsburgh (5), Nov. 14, 1937
Philadelphia (7) vs. Boston (6), Dec. 8, 1946
N.Y. Giants (7) vs. Washington (6), Nov. 5, 1950
Kansas City (9) vs. San Diego (4), Nov. 15, 1964
Buffalo (7) vs. Denver (6), Dec. 13, 1964
N.Y. Jets (7) vs. Houston (6), Sept. 12, 1965
Cleveland (7) vs. New Orleans (6), Dec. 12, 1971
Houston (8) vs. Pittsburgh (5), Dec. 9, 1973
St. Louis (9) vs. Washington (4), Oct. 25, 1976
Cleveland (9) vs. Seattle (4), Dec. 20, 1981
Green Bay (7) vs. Detroit (6), Oct. 6, 1985
12 In many games

FUMBLES LOST

Most Fumbles Lost, Season
36 Chi. Cardinals, 1959
31 Green Bay, 1952
29 Chi. Cardinals, 1946
Pittsburgh, 1950
Cleveland, 1978

Fewest Fumbles Lost, Season
3 Philadelphia, 1938
Minnesota, 1980
4 San Francisco, 1960
Kansas City, 1982
Minnesota, 1998
5 Chi. Cardinals, 1943
Detroit, 1943
N.Y. Giants, 1943
Cleveland, 1959
Minnesota, 1982
San Diego, 1993
Detroit, 1996
Indianapolis, 1998

Most Fumbles Lost, Game
8 St. Louis vs. Washington, Oct. 25, 1976
Cleveland vs. Pittsburgh, Dec. 23, 1990
7 Cincinnati vs. Buffalo, Nov. 30, 1969
Pittsburgh vs. Cincinnati, Oct. 14, 1979
Cleveland vs. Seattle, Dec. 20, 1981
6 By many teams

FUMBLES RECOVERED

Most Fumbles Recovered, Season, Own and Opponents'
58 Minnesota, 1963 (27 own, 31 opp)
51 Chi. Bears, 1938 (37 own, 14 opp)
San Francisco, 1978 (24 own, 27 opp)
50 Philadelphia, 1987 (23 own, 27 opp)

Fewest Fumbles Recovered, Season, Own and Opponents'
9 San Francisco, 1982 (5 own, 4 opp)
11 Cincinnati, 1982 (5 own, 6 opp)
12 Washington, 1994 (6 own, 6 opp)
Arizona, 1997 (7 own, 5 opp)

Most Fumbles Recovered, Game, Own and Opponents'
10 Denver vs. Buffalo, Dec. 13, 1964 (5 own, 5 opp)
Pittsburgh vs. Houston, Dec. 9, 1973 (5 own, 5 opp)
Washington vs. St. Louis, Oct. 25, 1976 (2 own, 8 opp)
9 St. Louis vs. N.Y. Giants, Sept. 17, 1961 (6 own, 3 opp)
Houston vs. Cincinnati, Oct. 27, 1974 (4 own, 5 opp)
Kansas City vs. Dallas, Nov. 10, 1975 (4 own, 5 opp)
Green Bay vs. Detroit, Oct. 6, 1985 (5 own, 4 opp)
Pittsburgh vs. Cleveland, Dec. 23, 1990 (1 own, 8 opp)
8 By many teams

Most Own Fumbles Recovered, Season
37 Chi. Bears, 1938
28 Pittsburgh, 1987
27 Philadelphia, 1946
Minnesota, 1963

Fewest Own Fumbles Recovered, Season
2 Washington, 1958
3 Detroit, 1956
Cleveland, 1959
Houston, 1982
4 By many teams

Most Opponents' Fumbles Recovered, Season
31 Minnesota, 1963
29 Cleveland, 1951
28 Green Bay, 1946
Houston, 1977
Seattle, 1983

Fewest Opponents' Fumbles Recovered, Season
3 Los Angeles, 1974
Green Bay, 1995
4 Philadelphia, 1944
San Francisco, 1982
5 Baltimore, 1982
Arizona, 1997
Baltimore, 1998

Most Opponents' Fumbles Recovered, Game
8 Washington vs. St. Louis, Oct. 25, 1976
Pittsburgh vs. Cleveland, Dec. 23, 1990
7 Buffalo vs. Cincinnati, Nov. 30, 1969
Cincinnati vs. Pittsburgh, Oct. 14, 1979
Seattle vs. Cleveland, Dec. 20, 1981
6 By many teams

TOUCHDOWNS

Most Touchdowns, Fumbles Recovered, Season, Own and Opponents'
5 Chi. Bears, 1942 (1 own, 4 opp)
Los Angeles, 1952 (1 own, 4 opp)
San Francisco, 1965 (1 own, 4 opp)
Oakland, 1978 (2 own, 3 opp)
4 Chi. Bears, 1948 (1 own, 3 opp)
Boston, 1948 (4 opp)
Denver, 1979 (1 own, 3 opp)
Atlanta, 1981 (1 own, 3 opp)
Denver, 1984 (4 opp)
St. Louis, 1987 (4 opp)
Minnesota, 1989 (4 opp)
Atlanta, 1991 (4 opp)
Philadelphia, 1995 (4 opp)
Atlanta, 1998 (4 opp)
New Orleans, 1998 (4 opp)
Kansas City, 1999 (4 opp)
3 By many teams

Most Touchdowns, Own Fumbles Recovered, Season
2 Chi. Bears, 1953
New England, 1973
Buffalo, 1974
Denver, 1975
Oakland, 1978
Green Bay, 1982
New Orleans, 1983
Cleveland, 1986
Green Bay, 1989
Miami, 1996

Most Touchdowns, Opponents' Fumbles Recovered, Season
4 Detroit, 1937
Chi. Bears, 1942
Boston, 1948
Los Angeles, 1952
San Francisco, 1965
Denver, 1984
St. Louis, 1987
Minnesota, 1989
Atlanta, 1991
Philadelphia, 1995
Atlanta, 1998
New Orleans, 1998
Kansas City, 1999
3 By many teams

Most Touchdowns, Fumbles Recovered, Game, Own and Opponents'
2 By many teams

Most Touchdowns, Fumbles Recovered, Game, Both Teams, Own and Opponents'
3 Detroit (2) vs. Minnesota (1), Dec. 9, 1962 (2 own, 1 opp)
Green Bay (2) vs. Dallas (1), Nov. 29, 1964 (3 opp)
Oakland (2) vs. Buffalo (1), Dec. 24, 1967 (3 opp)
Oakland (2) vs. Philadelphia (1), Sept. 24, 1995 (3 opp)
Tennessee (2) vs. Pittsburgh (1), Jan. 2, 2000 (3 opp)

Most Touchdowns, Own Fumbles Recovered, Game
2 Miami vs. New England, Sept.1, 1996

Most Touchdowns, Opponents' Fumbles Recovered, Game
2 Detroit vs. Cleveland, Nov. 7, 1937
Philadelphia vs. N.Y. Giants, Sept. 25, 1938
Chi. Bears vs. Washington, Nov. 28, 1948
N.Y. Giants vs. Pittsburgh, Sept. 17, 1950
Cleveland vs. Dall. Cowboys, Dec. 3, 1961
Cleveland vs. N.Y. Giants, Oct. 25, 1964
Green Bay vs. Dallas, Nov. 29, 1964
San Francisco vs. Detroit, Nov. 14, 1965

Oakland vs. Buffalo, Dec. 24, 1967
N.Y. Giants vs. Green Bay, Sept. 19, 1971
Washington vs. San Diego, Sept. 16, 1973
New Orleans vs. San Francisco, Oct. 19, 1975
Cincinnati vs. Pittsburgh, Oct. 14, 1979
Atlanta vs. Detroit, Oct. 5, 1980
Kansas City vs. Oakland, Oct. 5, 1980
New England vs. Baltimore, Nov. 23, 1980
Denver vs. Green Bay, Oct. 15, 1984
Miami vs. Kansas City, Oct. 11, 1987
St. Louis vs. New Orleans, Oct. 11, 1987
Cleveland vs. Pittsburgh, Sept. 10, 1989
Minnesota vs. Atlanta, Dec. 10, 1989
Atlanta vs. Houston, Dec. 9, 1990
Philadelphia vs. Phoenix, Nov. 24, 1991
Cincinnati vs. Seattle, Sept. 6, 1992
Oakland vs. Philadelphia, Sept. 24, 1995
Pittsburgh vs. New England, Dec. 16, 1995
New England vs. San Diego, Dec.1, 1996
Tennessee vs. Pittsburgh, Jan. 2, 2000

Most Touchdowns, Opponents' Fumbles Recovered, Game, Both Teams
3 Green Bay (2) vs. Dallas (1), Nov. 29, 1964
Oakland (2) vs. Buffalo (1), Dec. 24, 1967
Oakland (2) vs. Philadelphia (1), Sept. 24, 1995
Tennessee (2) vs. Pittsburgh (1), Jan. 2, 2000

TURNOVERS

(Number of times losing the ball on interceptions and fumbles.)

Most Turnovers, Season
63 San Francisco, 1978
58 Chi. Bears, 1947
Pittsburgh, 1950
N.Y. Giants, 1983
57 Green Bay, 1950
Houston, 1962, 1963
Pittsburgh, 1965

Fewest Turnovers, Season
12 Kansas City, 1982
14 N.Y. Giants, 1943
Cleveland, 1959
N.Y. Giants, 1990
15 Dallas, 1998

Most Turnovers, Game
12 Detroit vs. Chi. Bears, Nov. 22, 1942
Chi. Cardinals vs. Philadelphia, Sept. 24, 1950
Pittsburgh vs. Philadelphia, Dec. 12, 1965
11 San Diego vs. Green Bay, Sept. 24, 1978
10 Washington vs. N.Y. Giants, Dec. 4, 1938
Pittsburgh vs. Green Bay, Nov. 23, 1941
Detroit vs. Green Bay, Oct. 24, 1943
Chi. Cardinals vs. Green Bay, Nov. 10, 1946
Chi. Cardinals vs. N.Y. Giants, Nov. 2, 1952
Minnesota vs. Detroit, Dec. 9, 1962
Houston vs. Oakland, Sept. 7, 1963
Washington vs. N.Y. Giants, Dec. 8, 1963
Chicago vs. Detroit, Sept. 22, 1968
St. Louis vs. Washington, Oct. 25, 1976
N.Y. Jets vs. New England, Nov. 21, 1976
San Francisco vs. Dallas, Oct. 12, 1980
Cleveland vs. Seattle, Dec. 20, 1981
Detroit vs. Denver, Oct. 7, 1984

Most Turnovers, Both Teams, Game
17 Detroit (12) vs. Chi. Bears (5), Nov. 22, 1942
Boston (9) vs. Philadelphia (8), Dec. 8, 1946
16 Chi. Cardinals (12) vs. Philadelphia (4), Sept. 24, 1950
Chi. Cardinals (8) vs. Chi. Bears (8), Dec. 7, 1958
Minnesota (10) vs. Detroit (6), Dec. 9, 1962
Houston (9) vs. Kansas City (7), Oct. 12, 1969
15 Philadelphia (8) vs. Chi. Cardinals (7), Oct. 3, 1954
Denver (9) vs. Houston (6), Dec. 2, 1962
Washington (10) vs. N.Y. Giants (5), Dec. 8, 1963
St. Louis (9) vs. Kansas City (6), Oct. 2, 1983

PENALTIES

Most Seasons Leading League, Fewest Penalties
13 Miami, 1968, 1976-84, 1986, 1990-91
9 Pittsburgh, 1946-47, 1950-52, 1954, 1963, 1965, 1968
7 Boston/New England, 1962, 1964-65, 1973, 1987, 1989, 1993

Most Consecutive Seasons Leading League, Fewest Penalties
9 Miami, 1976-84
3 Pittsburgh, 1950-52
2 By many teams

Most Seasons Leading League, Most Penalties
16 Chi. Bears, 1941-44, 1946-49, 1951, 1959-61, 1963, 1965, 1968, 1976
12 Oakland/L.A. Raiders, 1963, 1966, 1968-69, 1975, 1982, 1984, 1991, 1993-96
7 L.A./St. Louis Rams, 1950, 1952, 1962, 1969, 1978, 1980, 1997

Most Consecutive Seasons Leading League, Most Penalties
4 Chi. Bears, 1941-44, 1946-49
L.A./Oakland Raiders, 1993-96
3 Chi. Cardinals, 1954-56
Chi. Bears, 1959-61

Fewest Penalties, Season
19 Detroit, 1937
21 Boston, 1935
24 Philadelphia, 1936

Most Penalties, Season
158 Kansas City, 1998
156 L.A. Raiders, 1994
Oakland, 1996
149 Houston, 1989

Fewest Penalties, Game
0 By many teams. Last time:
Indianapolis vs. Cleveland, Dec. 26, 1999

Most Penalties, Game
22 Brooklyn vs. Green Bay, Sept. 17, 1944
Chi. Bears vs. Philadelphia, Nov. 26, 1944
San Francisco vs. Buffalo, Oct. 4, 1998
21 Cleveland vs. Chi. Bears, Nov. 25, 1951
20 Tampa Bay vs. Seattle, Oct. 17, 1976
Oakland vs. Denver, Dec. 15, 1996

Fewest Penalties, Both Teams, Game
0 Brooklyn vs. Pittsburgh, Oct. 28, 1934
Brooklyn vs. Boston, Sept. 28, 1936
Cleveland vs. Chi. Bears, Oct. 9, 1938
Pittsburgh vs. Philadelphia, Nov. 10, 1940

Most Penalties, Both Teams, Game
37 Cleveland (21) vs. Chi. Bears (16), Nov. 25, 1951
35 Tampa Bay (20) vs. Seattle (15), Oct. 17, 1976
34 San Francisco (22) vs. Buffalo (12), Oct. 4, 1998

YARDS PENALIZED

Most Seasons Leading League, Fewest Yards Penalized
13 Miami, 1967-68, 1973, 1977-84, 1990-91
10 Boston/Washington, 1935, 1953-54, 1956-58, 1970, 1985, 1995, 1997
7 Pittsburgh, 1946-47, 1950, 1952, 1962, 1965, 1968
Boston/New England, 1962, 1964-66, 1987, 1989, 1993

Most Consecutive Seasons Leading League, Fewest Yards Penalized
8 Miami, 1977-84
3 Washington, 1956-58
Boston, 1964-66
2 By many teams

Most Seasons Leading League, Most Yards Penalized
15 Chi. Bears, 1935, 1937, 1939-44, 1946-47, 1949, 1951, 1961-62, 1968
11 Oakland/L.A. Raiders, 1963-64, 1968-69, 1975, 1982, 1984, 1991, 1993-94, 1996
6 Buffalo, 1962, 1967, 1970, 1972, 1981, 1983
Houston, 1961, 1985-86, 1988-90

Most Consecutive Seasons Leading League, Most Yards Penalized
6 Chi. Bears, 1939-44
3 Houston, 1988-90
2 By many teams

Fewest Yards Penalized, Season
139 Detroit, 1937
146 Philadelphia, 1937
159 Philadelphia, 1936

Most Yards Penalized, Season
1,304 Kansas City, 1998
1,274 Oakland, 1969
1,266 Oakland, 1996

Fewest Yards Penalized, Game
0 By many teams. Last time:
Indianapolis vs. Cleveland, Dec. 26, 1999

Most Yards Penalized, Game
212 Tennessee vs. Baltimore, Oct. 10, 1999
209 Cleveland vs. Chi. Bears, Nov. 25, 1951
191 Philadelphia vs. Seattle, Dec. 13, 1992 (OT)

Fewest Yards Penalized, Both Teams, Game
0 Brooklyn vs. Pittsburgh, Oct. 28, 1934
Brooklyn vs. Boston, Sept. 28, 1936
Cleveland vs. Chi. Bears, Oct. 9, 1938
Pittsburgh vs. Philadelphia, Nov. 10, 1940

Most Yards Penalized, Both Teams, Game
374 Cleveland (209) vs. Chi. Bears (165), Nov. 25, 1951
310 Tampa Bay (190) vs. Seattle (120), Oct. 17, 1976
309 Green Bay (184) vs. Boston (125), Oct. 21, 1945

DEFENSE

SCORING

Most Seasons Leading League, Fewest Points Allowed
11 N.Y. Giants, 1927, 1935, 1938-39, 1941, 1944, 1958-59, 1961, 1990, 1993
9 Chi. Bears, 1932, 1936-37, 1942, 1948, 1963, 1985-86, 1988
7 Cleveland, 1951, 1953-57, 1994
Green Bay, 1929, 1935, 1947, 1962, 1965-66, 1996

Most Consecutive Seasons Leading League, Fewest Points Allowed
5 Cleveland, 1953-57
3 Buffalo, 1964-66
Minnesota, 1969-71
2 By many teams

Fewest Points Allowed, Season (Since 1932)
44 Chi. Bears, 1932
54 Brooklyn, 1933
59 Detroit, 1934

Most Points Allowed, Season
533 Baltimore, 1981
501 N.Y. Giants, 1966
487 New Orleans, 1980

Fewest Touchdowns Allowed, Season (Since 1932)
6 Chi. Bears, 1932
Brooklyn, 1933
7 Detroit, 1934
8 Green Bay, 1932

Most Touchdowns Allowed, Season
68 Baltimore, 1981
66 N.Y. Giants, 1966
63 Baltimore, 1950

FIRST DOWNS

Fewest First Downs Allowed Season
77 Detroit, 1935
79 Boston, 1935
82 Washington, 1937

Most First Downs Allowed, Season
406 Baltimore, 1981
371 Seattle, 1981
368 Cleveland, 1999

Fewest First Downs Allowed, Rushing, Season
35 Chi. Bears, 1942
40 Green Bay, 1939
41 Brooklyn, 1944

Most First Downs Allowed, Rushing, Season
179 Detroit, 1985
178 New Orleans, 1980
175 Seattle, 1981

Fewest First Downs Allowed, Passing, Season
33 Chi. Bears, 1943
34 Pittsburgh, 1941
Washington, 1943
35 Detroit, 1940
Philadelphia, 1940, 1944

Most First Downs Allowed, Passing, Season
230 Atlanta, 1995
218 San Diego, 1985
216 San Diego, 1981
N.Y. Jets, 1986

Fewest First Downs Allowed, Penalty, Season
1 Boston, 1944
3 Philadelphia, 1940
Pittsburgh, 1945
Washington, 1957
4 Cleveland, 1940
Green Bay, 1943
N.Y. Giants, 1943

Most First Downs Allowed, Penalty, Season
56 Kansas City, 1998
48 Houston, 1985
46 Houston, 1986

NET YARDS ALLOWED RUSHING AND PASSING

Most Seasons Leading League, Fewest Yards Allowed
8 Chi. Bears, 1942-43, 1948, 1958, 1963, 1984-86
6 N.Y. Giants, 1938, 1940-41, 1951, 1956, 1959
Philadelphia, 1944-45, 1949, 1953, 1981, 1991
Minnesota, 1969-70, 1975, 1988-89, 1993
5 Boston/Washington, 1935-37, 1939, 1946

Most Consecutive Seasons Leading League, Fewest Yards Allowed
3 Boston/Washington, 1935-37
Chicago, 1984-86
2 By many teams

Fewest Yards Allowed, Season
1,539 Chi. Cardinals, 1934
1,703 Chi. Bears, 1942
1,789 Brooklyn, 1933

Most Yards Allowed, Season
6,793 Baltimore, 1981
6,403 Green Bay, 1983
6,352 Minnesota, 1984

RUSHING

Most Seasons Leading League, Fewest Yards Allowed
10 Chi. Bears, 1937, 1939, 1942, 1946, 1949, 1963, 1984-85, 1987-88
7 Detroit, 1938, 1950, 1952, 1962, 1970, 1980-81
Philadelphia, 1944-45, 1947-48, 1953, 1990-91
Dallas, 1966-69, 1972, 1978, 1992
5 N.Y. Giants, 1940, 1951, 1956, 1959, 1986
L.A./St. Louis Rams, 1964-65, 1973-74, 1999

Most Consecutive Seasons Leading League, Fewest Yards Allowed
4 Dallas, 1966-69
2 By many teams

Fewest Yards Allowed, Rushing, Season
519 Chi. Bears, 1942
558 Philadelphia, 1944
762 Pittsburgh, 1982

Most Yards Allowed, Rushing, Season
3,228 Buffalo, 1978
3,106 New Orleans, 1980
3,010 Baltimore, 1978

Fewest Touchdowns Allowed, Rushing, Season
2 Detroit, 1934
Dallas, 1968
Minnesota, 1971
3 By many teams

Most Touchdowns Allowed, Rushing, Season
36 Oakland, 1961
31 N.Y. Giants, 1980
Tampa Bay, 1986
30 Baltimore, 1981

PASSING

Most Seasons Leading League, Fewest Yards Allowed
9 Green Bay, 1947-48, 1962, 1964-68, 1996
7 Washington, 1939, 1942, 1945, 1952-53, 1980, 1985
Philadelphia 1934, 1936, 1940, 1949, 1981, 1991, 1998
6 Chi. Bears, 1938, 1943-44, 1958, 1960, 1963
Minnesota, 1969-70, 1972, 1975-76, 1989
Pittsburgh, 1941, 1946, 1951, 1955, 1974, 1990

Most Consecutive Seasons Leading League, Fewest Yards Allowed
5 Green Bay, 1964-68
2 By many teams

Fewest Yards Allowed, Passing, Season
545 Philadelphia, 1934
558 Portsmouth, 1933
585 Chi. Cardinals, 1934

Most Yards Allowed, Passing, Season
4,541 Atlanta, 1995
4,389 N.Y. Jets, 1986
4,311 San Diego, 1981

Fewest Touchdowns Allowed, Passing, Season
1 Portsmouth, 1932
Philadelphia, 1934
2 Brooklyn, 1933
Chi. Bears, 1934
3 Chi. Bears, 1932
Green Bay, 1932
Green Bay, 1934
Chi. Bears, 1936
New York, 1939
New York, 1944

ALL-TIME RECORDS

Most Touchdowns Allowed, Passing, Season
40 Denver, 1963
38 St. Louis, 1969
37 Washington, 1961
Baltimore, 1981

SACKS

Most Seasons Leading League
5 Oakland/L.A. Raiders, 1966-68, 1982, 1986
4 Boston/New England, 1961, 1963, 1977, 1979
Dallas, 1966, 1968-69, 1978
Dallas/Kansas City, 1960, 1965, 1969, 1990
L.A./St. Louis Rams, 1968, 1970, 1988, 1999
3 San Francisco, 1967, 1972, 1976
N.Y. Giants, 1963, 1985, 1998

Most Consecutive Seasons Leading League
3 Oakland, 1966-68
2 Dallas, 1968-69

Most Sacks, Season
72 Chicago, 1984
71 Minnesota, 1989
70 Chicago, 1987

Fewest Sacks, Season
11 Baltimore, 1982
12 Buffalo, 1982
13 Baltimore, 1981

Most Sacks, Game
12 Dallas vs. Pittsburgh, Nov. 20, 1966
St. Louis vs. Baltimore, Oct. 26, 1980
Chicago vs. Detroit, Dec. 16, 1984
Dallas vs. Houston, Sept. 29, 1985
11 N.Y. Giants vs. St. Louis, Nov. 1, 1964
Baltimore vs. Los Angeles, Nov. 22, 1964
Buffalo vs. Denver, Dec. 13, 1964
Detroit vs. Green Bay, Nov. 7, 1965
Oakland vs. Buffalo, Oct. 15, 1967
Oakland vs. Denver, Nov. 5, 1967
St. Louis vs. Atlanta, Nov. 24, 1968
Dallas vs. Detroit, Oct. 6, 1975
St. Louis vs. Philadelphia, Dec. 18, 1983
Kansas City vs. Cleveland, Sept. 30, 1984
Chicago vs. Minnesota, Oct. 28, 1984
Cleveland vs. Atlanta, Nov. 18, 1984
Detroit vs. Philadelphia, Nov. 16, 1986
San Diego vs. Dallas, Nov. 16, 1986
L.A. Raiders vs. Philadelphia, Nov. 30, 1986 (OT)
Seattle vs. L.A. Raiders, Dec. 8, 1986
Chicago vs. Philadelphia, Oct. 4, 1987
Dallas vs. N.Y. Jets, Oct. 4, 1987
Philadelphia vs. Dallas, Sept. 15, 1991
Indianapolis vs. Cleveland, Sept. 6, 1992
10 By many teams

Most Opponents Yards Lost Attempting to Pass, Season
666 Oakland, 1967
583 Chicago, 1984
573 San Francisco, 1976

Fewest Opponents Yards Lost Attempting to Pass, Season
72 Jacksonville, 1995
75 Green Bay, 1956
77 N.Y. Bulldogs, 1949

INTERCEPTIONS BY

Most Seasons Leading League
10 N.Y. Giants, 1933, 1937-39, 1944, 1948, 1951, 1954, 1961, 1997
8 Green Bay, 1940, 1942-43, 1947, 1955, 1957, 1962, 1965
Chi. Bears, 1935-36, 1941-42, 1946, 1963, 1985, 1990
6 Kansas City, 1966-70, 1974

Most Consecutive Seasons Leading League
5 Kansas City, 1966-70
3 N.Y. Giants, 1937-39
2 By many teams

Most Passes Intercepted By, Season
49 San Diego, 1961
42 Green Bay, 1943
41 N.Y. Giants, 1951

Fewest Passes Intercepted By, Season
3 Houston, 1982
5 Baltimore, 1982
6 Houston, 1972
St. Louis, 1982
Atlanta, 1996

Most Passes Intercepted By, Game
9 Green Bay vs. Detroit, Oct. 24, 1943
Philadelphia vs. Pittsburgh, Dec. 12, 1965
8 N.Y. Giants vs. Green Bay, Nov. 21, 1948
Philadelphia vs. Chi. Cardinals, Sept. 24, 1950
N.Y. Giants vs. N.Y. Yanks, Dec. 16, 1951
Houston vs. Denver, Dec. 2, 1962
Detroit vs. Chicago, Sept. 22, 1968
N.Y. Jets vs. Baltimore, Sept. 23, 1973
7 By many teams. Last time:
Seattle vs. San Diego, Dec. 13, 1998

Most Consecutive Games, One or More Interceptions By
46 L.A. Chargers/San Diego, 1960-63
37 Detroit, 1960-63
36 Boston, 1944-47

Most Yards Returning Interceptions, Season
929 San Diego, 1961
712 Los Angeles, 1952
697 Seattle, 1984

Fewest Yards Returning Interceptions, Season
5 Los Angeles, 1959
37 Dallas, 1989
41 Atlanta, 1996

Most Yards Returning Interceptions, Game
325 Seattle vs. Kansas City, Nov. 4, 1984
314 Los Angeles vs. San Francisco, Oct. 18, 1964
245 Houston vs. N.Y. Jets, Oct. 15, 1967

Most Yards Returning Interceptions, Both Teams, Game
356 Seattle (325) vs. Kansas City (31), Nov. 4, 1984
338 Los Angeles (314) vs. San Francisco (24), Oct. 18, 1964
308 Dallas (182) vs. Los Angeles (126), Nov. 2, 1952

Most Touchdowns, Returning Interceptions, Season
9 San Diego, 1961
8 Seattle, 1998
7 Seattle, 1984
St. Louis, 1999

Most Touchdowns Returning Interceptions, Game
4 Seattle vs. Kansas City, Nov. 4, 1984
3 Baltimore vs. Green Bay, Nov. 5, 1950
Cleveland vs. Chicago, Dec. 11, 1960
Philadelphia vs. Pittsburgh, Dec. 12, 1965
Baltimore vs. Pittsburgh, Sept. 29, 1968
Buffalo vs. N.Y. Jets, Sept. 29, 1968
Houston vs. San Diego, Dec. 19, 1971
Cincinnati vs. Houston, Dec. 17, 1972
Tampa Bay vs. New Orleans, Dec. 11, 1977
2 By many teams

Most Touchdown Returning Interceptions, Both Teams, Game
4 Philadelphia (3) vs. Pittsburgh (1), Dec. 12, 1965
Seattle (4) vs. Kansas City (0), Nov. 4, 1984
3 Los Angeles (2) vs. Detroit (1), Nov. 1, 1953
Cleveland (2) vs. N.Y. Giants (1), Dec. 18, 1960
Pittsburgh (2) vs. Cincinnati (1), Oct. 10, 1983
Kansas City (2) vs. San Diego (1), Oct. 19, 1986
(Also see previous record)

PUNT RETURNS

Fewest Opponents Punt Returns, Season
7 Washington, 1962
San Diego, 1982
10 Buffalo, 1982
11 Boston, 1962

Most Opponents Punt Returns, Season
71 Tampa Bay, 1976, 1977
69 N.Y. Giants, 1953
68 Cleveland, 1974
Cleveland, 1999

Fewest Yards Allowed, Punt Returns, Season
22 Green Bay, 1967
30 Buffalo, 1982
34 Washington, 1962

Most Yards Allowed, Punt Returns, Season
932 Green Bay, 1949
913 Boston, 1947
906 New Orleans, 1974

Lowest Average Allowed, Punt Returns, Season
1.20 Chi. Cardinals, 1954 (46-55)
1.22 Cleveland, 1959 (32-39)
1.55 Chi. Cardinals, 1953 (44-68)

Highest Average Allowed, Punt Returns, Season
18.6 Green Bay, 1949 (50-932)
18.0 Cleveland, 1977 (31-558)
17.9 Boston, 1960 (20-357)

Most Touchdowns Allowed, Punt Returns, Season
4 New York, 1959
Atlanta, 1992
3 Green Bay, 1949
Chi. Cardinals, 1951
L.A. Rams, 1951, 1994
Washington, 1952
Dallas, 1952
Pittsburgh, 1959, 1993
N.Y. Jets, 1968
Cleveland, 1977
Atlanta, 1986
Tampa Bay, 1986
2 By many teams

KICKOFF RETURNS

Fewest Opponents Kickoff Returns, Season
10 Brooklyn, 1943
13 Denver, 1992
15 Detroit, 1942
Brooklyn, 1944

Most Opponents Kickoff Returns, Season
91 Washington, 1983
89 New England, 1980
San Francisco, 1994
Denver, 1997
Denver, 1998
88 San Diego, 1981
Pittsburgh, 1995

Fewest Yards Allowed, Kickoff Returns, Season
225 Brooklyn, 1943
254 Denver, 1992
293 Brooklyn, 1944

Most Yards Allowed, Kickoff Returns, Season
2,115 St. Louis, 1999
2,045 Kansas City, 1966
2,008 Minnesota, 1998

Lowest Average Allowed, Kickoff Returns, Season
14.3 Cleveland, 1980 (71-1,018)
14.9 Indianapolis, 1993 (37-551)
15.0 Seattle, 1982 (24-361)

Highest Average Allowed, Kickoff Returns, Season
29.5 N.Y. Jets, 1972 (47-1,386)
29.4 Los Angeles, 1950 (48-1,411)
29.1 New England, 1971 (49-1,427)

Most Touchdowns Allowed, Kickoff Returns, Season
4 Minnesota, 1998
3 Minnesota, 1963, 1970
Dallas, 1966
Detroit, 1980
Pittsburgh, 1986
Buffalo, 1997
2 By many teams

FUMBLES

Fewest Opponents Fumbles, Season
11 Cleveland, 1956
Baltimore, 1982
Tennessee, 1998
12 Green Bay, 1995
Cincinnati, 1998
13 Los Angeles, 1956
Chicago, 1960
Cleveland, 1963
Cleveland, 1965
Detroit, 1967
San Diego, 1969

Most Opponents Fumbles, Season
50 Minnesota, 1963
San Francisco, 1978
48 N.Y. Giants, 1980
N.Y. Jets, 1986
47 N.Y. Giants, 1977
Seattle, 1984

TURNOVERS

(Number of times losing the ball on interceptions and fumbles.)

Fewest Opponents Turnovers, Season
11 Baltimore, 1982
13 San Francisco, 1982
15 St. Louis, 1982

Most Opponents Turnovers, Season
66 San Diego, 1961
63 Seattle, 1984
61 Washington, 1983

Most Opponents Turnovers, Game
12 Chi. Bears vs. Detroit, Nov. 22, 1942
Philadelphia vs. Chi. Cardinals, Sept. 24, 1950
Philadelphia vs. Pittsburgh, Dec. 12, 1965
11 Green Bay vs. San Diego, Sept. 24, 1978
10 By 14 teams

OUTSTANDING PERFORMERS

1,000 YARDS RUSHING IN A SEASON

Year	Player, Team	Att.	Yards	Avg.	Long	TD
1999	*Edgerrin James, Indianapolis	369	1,553	4.2	72	13
	Curtis Martin, N.Y. Jets[5]	367	1,464	4.0	50	5
	Stephen Davis, Washington	290	1,405	4.8	76	17
	Emmitt Smith, Dallas[9]	329	1,397	4.3	63	11
	Marshall Faulk, St. Louis[5]	253	1,381	5.5	58	7
	Eddie George, Tennessee[4]	320	1,304	4.1	40	9
	Duce Staley, Philadelphia[2]	325	1,273	3.9	29	4
	Charlie Garner, San Francisco	241	1,229	5.1	53	4
	Ricky Watters, Seattle[6]	325	1,210	3.7	45	5
	Corey Dillon, Cincinnati[3]	263	1,200	4.6	50	5
	*Olandis Gary, Denver	276	1,159	4.2	71	7
	Jerome Bettis, Pittsburgh[6]	299	1,091	3.7	35	7
	Dorsey Levens, Green Bay[2]	279	1,034	3.7	36	9
	Robert Smith, Minnesota[3]	221	1,015	4.6	70	2
1998	Terrell Davis, Denver[4]	392	2,008	5.1	70	21
	Jamal Anderson, Atlanta[3]	410	1,846	4.5	48	14
	Garrison Hearst, San Francisco[3]	310	1,570	5.1	96	7
	Barry Sanders, Detroit[10]	343	1,491	4.3	73	4
	Emmitt Smith, Dallas[8]	319	1,332	4.2	32	13
	Marshall Faulk, Indianapolis[4]	324	1,319	4.1	68	6
	Eddie George, Tennessee[3]	348	1,294	3.7	37	5
	Curtis Martin, N.Y. Jets[4]	369	1,287	3.5	60	8
	Ricky Watters, Seattle[5]	319	1,239	3.9	39	9
	*Fred Taylor, Jacksonville	264	1,223	4.6	77	14
	Robert Smith, Minnesota[2]	249	1,187	4.8	74	6
	Jerome Bettis, Pittsburgh[5]	316	1,185	3.8	42	3
	Corey Dillon, Cincinnati[2]	262	1,130	4.3	66	4
	Antowain Smith, Buffalo	300	1,124	3.7	30	8
	*Robert Edwards, New England	291	1,115	3.8	53	9
	Duce Staley, Philadelphia	258	1,065	4.1	64	5
	Gary Brown, N.Y. Giants[2]	247	1,063	4.3	45	5
	Adrian Murrell, Arizona[3]	274	1,042	3.8	32	8
	Warrick Dunn, Tampa Bay	245	1,026	4.2	50	2
	Priest Holmes, Baltimore	233	1,008	4.3	56	7
1997	Barry Sanders, Detroit[9]	335	2,053	6.1	82	11
	Terrell Davis, Denver[3]	369	1,750	4.7	50	15
	Jerome Bettis, Pittsburgh[4]	375	1,665	4.4	34	7
	Dorsey Levens, Green Bay	329	1,435	4.4	52	7
	Eddie George, Tennessee[2]	357	1,399	3.9	30	6
	Napoleon Kaufman, Oakland	272	1,294	4.8	83	6
	Robert Smith, Minnesota	232	1,266	5.5	78	6
	Curtis Martin, New England[3]	274	1,160	4.2	70	4
	*Corey Dillon, Cincinnati	233	1,129	4.8	71	10
	Ricky Watters, Philadelphia[4]	285	1,110	3.9	28	7
	Adrian Murrell, N.Y. Jets[2]	300	1,086	3.6	43	7
	Emmitt Smith, Dallas[7]	261	1,074	4.1	44	4
	Marshall Faulk, Indianapolis[3]	264	1,054	4.0	45	7
	Raymont Harris, Chicago	275	1,033	3.8	68	10
	Garrison Hearst, San Francisco[2]	234	1,019	4.4	51	4
	Jamal Anderson, Atlanta[2]	290	1,002	3.5	39	7
1996	Barry Sanders, Detroit[8]	307	1,553	5.1	54	11
	Terrell Davis, Denver[2]	345	1,538	4.5	71	13
	Jerome Bettis, Pittsburgh[3]	320	1,431	4.5	50	11
	Ricky Watters, Philadelphia[3]	353	1,411	4.0	56	13
	*Eddie George, Houston	335	1,368	4.1	76	8
	Terry Allen, Washington[4]	347	1,353	3.9	49	21
	Adrian Murrell, N.Y. Jets	301	1,249	4.1	78	6
	Emmitt Smith, Dallas[6]	327	1,204	3.7	42	12
	Curtis Martin, New England[2]	316	1,152	3.6	57	14
	Anthony Johnson, Carolina	300	1,120	3.7	29	6
	*Karim Abdul-Jabbar, Miami	307	1,116	3.6	29	11
	Jamal Anderson, Atlanta	232	1,055	4.5	32	5
	Thurman Thomas, Buffalo[8]	281	1,033	3.7	36	8
1995	Emmitt Smith, Dallas[5]	377	1,773	4.7	60	25
	Barry Sanders, Detroit[7]	314	1,500	4.8	75	11
	*Curtis Martin, New England	368	1,487	4.0	49	14
	Chris Warren, Seattle[4]	310	1,346	4.3	52	15
	Terry Allen, Washington[3]	338	1,309	3.9	28	10
	Ricky Watters, Philadelphia[2]	337	1,273	3.8	57	11
	Errict Rhett, Tampa Bay[2]	332	1,207	3.6	21	11
	Rodney Hampton, N.Y. Giants[5]	306	1,182	3.9	32	10
	*Terrell Davis, Denver	237	1,117	4.7	60	7
	Harvey Williams, Oakland	255	1,114	4.4	60	9
	Craig Heyward, Atlanta	236	1,083	4.6	31	6
	Marshall Faulk, Indianapolis[2]	289	1,078	3.7	40	11
	*Rashaan Salaam, Chicago	296	1,074	3.6	42	10
	Garrison Hearst, Arizona	284	1,070	3.8	38	1
	Edgar Bennett, Green Bay	316	1,067	3.4	23	3
	Thurman Thomas, Buffalo[7]	267	1,005	3.8	49	6
1994	Barry Sanders, Detroit[6]	331	1,883	5.7	85	7
	Chris Warren, Seattle[3]	333	1,545	4.6	41	9
	Emmitt Smith, Dallas[4]	368	1,484	4.0	46	21
	Natrone Means, San Diego	343	1,350	3.9	25	12
	*Marshall Faulk, Indianapolis	314	1,282	4.1	52	11
	Thurman Thomas, Buffalo[6]	287	1,093	3.8	29	7
	Rodney Hampton, N.Y. Giants[4]	327	1,075	3.3	27	6
	Terry Allen, Minnesota[2]	255	1,031	4.0	45	8
	Jerome Bettis, L.A. Rams[2]	319	1,025	3.2	19	3
	*Errict Rhett, Tampa Bay	284	1,011	3.6	27	7
1993	Emmitt Smith, Dallas[3]	283	1,486	5.3	62	9
	*Jerome Bettis, L.A. Rams	294	1,429	4.9	71	7
	Thurman Thomas, Buffalo[5]	355	1,315	3.7	27	6
	Erric Pegram, Atlanta	292	1,185	4.1	29	3
	Barry Sanders, Detroit[5]	243	1,115	4.6	42	3
	Leonard Russell, New England	300	1,088	3.6	21	7
	Rodney Hampton, N.Y. Giants[3]	292	1,077	3.7	20	5
	Chris Warren, Seattle[2]	273	1,072	3.9	45	7
	*Reggie Brooks, Washington	223	1,063	4.8	85	3
	*Ron Moore, Phoenix	263	1,018	3.9	20	9
	Gary Brown, Houston	195	1,002	5.1	26	6
1992	Emmitt Smith, Dallas[2]	373	1,713	4.6	68	18
	Barry Foster, Pittsburgh	390	1,690	4.3	69	11
	Thurman Thomas, Buffalo[4]	312	1,487	4.8	44	9
	Barry Sanders, Detroit[4]	312	1,352	4.3	55	9
	Lorenzo White, Houston	265	1,226	4.6	44	7
	Terry Allen, Minnesota	266	1,201	4.5	51	13
	Reggie Cobb, Tampa Bay	310	1,171	3.8	25	9
	Harold Green, Cincinnati	265	1,170	4.4	53	2
	Rodney Hampton, N.Y. Giants[2]	257	1,141	4.4	63	14
	Cleveland Gary, L.A. Rams	279	1,125	4.0	63	7
	Herschel Walker, Philadelphia[2]	267	1,070	4.0	38	8
	Chris Warren, Seattle	223	1,017	4.6	52	3
	Ricky Watters, San Francisco	206	1,013	4.9	43	9
1991	Emmitt Smith, Dallas	365	1,563	4.3	75	12
	Barry Sanders, Detroit[3]	342	1,548	4.5	69	16
	Thurman Thomas, Buffalo[3]	288	1,407	4.9	33	7
	Rodney Hampton, N.Y. Giants	256	1,059	4.1	44	10
	Earnest Byner, Washington[3]	274	1,048	3.8	32	5
	Gaston Green, Denver	261	1,037	4.0	63	4
	Christian Okoye, Kansas City[2]	225	1,031	4.6	48	9
1990	Barry Sanders, Detroit[2]	255	1,304	5.1	45	13
	Thurman Thomas, Buffalo[2]	271	1,297	4.8	80	11
	Marion Butts, San Diego	265	1,225	4.6	52	8
	Earnest Byner, Washington[2]	297	1,219	4.1	22	6
	Bobby Humphrey, Denver[2]	288	1,202	4.2	37	7
	Neal Anderson, Chicago[3]	260	1,078	4.1	52	10
	Barry Word, Kansas City	204	1,015	5.0	53	4
	James Brooks, Cincinnati[3]	195	1,004	5.1	56	5
1989	Christian Okoye, Kansas City	370	1,480	4.0	59	12
	*Barry Sanders, Detroit	280	1,470	5.3	34	14
	Eric Dickerson, Indianapolis[7]	314	1,311	4.2	21	7
	Neal Anderson, Chicago[2]	274	1,275	4.7	73	11
	Dalton Hilliard, New Orleans	344	1,262	3.7	40	13
	Thurman Thomas, Buffalo	298	1,244	4.2	38	6
	James Brooks, Cincinnati[2]	221	1,239	5.6	65	7
	*Bobby Humphrey, Denver	294	1,151	3.9	40	7
	Greg Bell, L.A. Rams[3]	272	1,137	4.2	47	15
	Roger Craig, San Francisco[3]	271	1,054	3.9	27	6
	Ottis Anderson, N.Y. Giants[6]	325	1,023	3.1	36	14
1988	Eric Dickerson, Indianapolis[6]	388	1,659	4.3	41	14
	Herschel Walker, Dallas	361	1,514	4.2	38	5
	Roger Craig, San Francisco[2]	310	1,502	4.8	46	9
	Greg Bell, L.A. Rams[2]	288	1,212	4.2	44	16
	*John Stephens, New England	297	1,168	3.9	52	4
	Gary Anderson, San Diego	225	1,119	5.0	36	3
	Neal Anderson, Chicago	249	1,106	4.4	80	12
	Joe Morris, N.Y. Giants[3]	307	1,083	3.5	27	5
	*Ickey Woods, Cincinnati	203	1,066	5.3	56	15
	Curt Warner, Seattle[4]	266	1,025	3.9	29	10
	John Settle, Atlanta	232	1,024	4.4	62	7
	Mike Rozier, Houston	251	1,002	4.0	28	10
1987	Charles White, L.A. Rams	324	1,374	4.2	58	11
	Eric Dickerson, L.A. Rams-Indianapolis[5]	283	1,288	4.6	57	6
1986	Eric Dickerson, L.A. Rams[4]	404	1,821	4.5	42	11
	Joe Morris, N.Y. Giants[2]	341	1,516	4.4	54	14
	Curt Warner, Seattle[3]	319	1,481	4.6	60	13
	*Rueben Mayes, New Orleans	286	1,353	4.7	50	8
	Walter Payton, Chicago[10]	321	1,333	4.2	41	8
	Gerald Riggs, Atlanta[3]	343	1,327	3.9	31	9
	George Rogers, Washington[4]	303	1,203	4.0	42	18
	James Brooks, Cincinnati	205	1,087	5.3	56	5
1985	Marcus Allen, L.A. Raiders[3]	390	1,759	4.6	61	11
	Gerald Riggs, Atlanta[2]	397	1,719	4.3	50	10
	Walter Payton, Chicago[9]	324	1,551	4.8	40	9

	Joe Morris, N.Y. Giants	294	1,336	4.5	65	21
	Freeman McNeil, N.Y. Jets[2]	294	1,331	4.5	69	3
	Tony Dorsett, Dallas[8]	305	1,307	4.3	60	7
	James Wilder, Tampa Bay[2]	365	1,300	3.6	28	10
	Eric Dickerson, L.A. Rams[3]	292	1,234	4.2	43	12
	Craig James, New England	263	1,227	4.7	65	5
	Kevin Mack, Cleveland	222	1,104	5.0	61	7
	Curt Warner, Seattle[2]	291	1,094	3.8	38	8
	George Rogers, Washington[3]	231	1,093	4.7	35	7
	Roger Craig, San Francisco	214	1,050	4.9	62	9
	Earnest Jackson, Philadelphia[2]	282	1,028	3.6	59	5
	Stump Mitchell, St. Louis	183	1,006	5.5	64	7
	Earnest Byner, Cleveland	244	1,002	4.1	36	8
1984	Eric Dickerson, L.A. Rams[2]	379	2,105	5.6	66	14
	Walter Payton, Chicago[8]	381	1,684	4.4	72	11
	James Wilder, Tampa Bay	407	1,544	3.8	37	13
	Gerald Riggs, Atlanta	353	1,486	4.2	57	13
	Wendell Tyler, San Francisco[3]	246	1,262	5.1	40	7
	John Riggins, Washington[5]	327	1,239	3.8	24	14
	Tony Dorsett, Dallas[7]	302	1,189	3.9	31	6
	Earnest Jackson, San Diego	296	1,179	4.0	32	8
	Ottis Anderson, St. Louis[5]	289	1,174	4.1	24	6
	Marcus Allen, L.A. Raiders[2]	275	1,168	4.2	52	13
	Sammy Winder, Denver	296	1,153	3.9	24	4
	*Greg Bell, Buffalo	262	1,100	4.2	85	7
	Freeman McNeil, N.Y. Jets	229	1,070	4.7	53	5
1983	*Eric Dickerson, L.A. Rams	390	1,808	4.6	85	18
	William Andrews, Atlanta[4]	331	1,567	4.7	27	7
	*Curt Warner, Seattle	335	1,449	4.3	60	13
	Walter Payton, Chicago[7]	314	1,421	4.5	49	6
	John Riggins, Washington[4]	375	1,347	3.6	44	24
	Tony Dorsett, Dallas[6]	289	1,321	4.6	77	8
	Earl Campbell, Houston[5]	322	1,301	4.0	42	12
	Ottis Anderson, St. Louis[4]	296	1,270	4.3	43	5
	Mike Pruitt, Cleveland[4]	293	1,184	4.0	27	10
	George Rogers, New Orleans[2]	256	1,144	4.5	76	5
	Joe Cribbs, Buffalo[3]	263	1,131	4.3	45	3
	Curtis Dickey, Baltimore	254	1,122	4.4	56	4
	Tony Collins, New England	219	1,049	4.8	50	10
	Billy Sims, Detroit[3]	220	1,040	4.7	41	7
	Marcus Allen, L.A. Raiders	266	1,014	3.8	19	9
	Franco Harris, Pittsburgh[8]	279	1,007	3.6	19	5
1981	*George Rogers, New Orleans	378	1,674	4.4	79	13
	Tony Dorsett, Dallas[5]	342	1,646	4.8	75	4
	Billy Sims, Detroit[2]	296	1,437	4.9	51	13
	Wilbert Montgomery, Philadelphia[3]	286	1,402	4.9	41	8
	Ottis Anderson, St. Louis[3]	328	1,376	4.2	28	9
	Earl Campbell, Houston[4]	361	1,376	3.8	43	10
	William Andrews, Atlanta[3]	289	1,301	4.5	29	10
	Walter Payton, Chicago[6]	339	1,222	3.6	39	6
	Chuck Muncie, San Diego[2]	251	1,144	4.6	73	19
	*Joe Delaney, Kansas City	234	1,121	4.8	82	3
	Mike Pruitt, Cleveland[3]	247	1,103	4.5	21	7
	Joe Cribbs, Buffalo[2]	257	1,097	4.3	35	3
	Pete Johnson, Cincinnati	274	1,077	3.9	39	12
	Wendell Tyler, Los Angeles[2]	260	1,074	4.1	69	12
	Ted Brown, Minnesota	274	1,063	3.9	34	6
1980	Earl Campbell, Houston[3]	373	1,934	5.2	55	13
	Walter Payton, Chicago[5]	317	1,460	4.6	69	6
	Ottis Anderson, St. Louis[2]	301	1,352	4.5	52	9
	William Andrews, Atlanta[2]	265	1,308	4.9	33	4
	*Billy Sims, Detroit	313	1,303	4.2	52	13
	Tony Dorsett, Dallas[4]	278	1,185	4.3	56	11
	*Joe Cribbs, Buffalo	306	1,185	3.9	48	11
	Mike Pruitt, Cleveland[2]	249	1,034	4.2	56	6
1979	Earl Campbell, Houston[2]	368	1,697	4.6	61	19
	Walter Payton, Chicago[4]	369	1,610	4.4	43	14
	*Ottis Anderson, St. Louis	331	1,605	4.8	76	8
	Wilbert Montgomery, Philadelphia[2]	338	1,512	4.5	62	9
	Mike Pruitt, Cleveland	264	1,294	4.9	77	9
	Ricky Bell, Tampa Bay	283	1,263	4.5	49	7
	Chuck Muncie, New Orleans	238	1,198	5.0	69	11
	Franco Harris, Pittsburgh[7]	267	1,186	4.4	71	11
	John Riggins, Washington[3]	260	1,153	4.4	66	9
	Wendell Tyler, Los Angeles	218	1,109	5.1	63	9
	Tony Dorsett, Dallas[3]	250	1,107	4.4	41	6
	*William Andrews, Atlanta	239	1,023	4.3	23	3
1978	*Earl Campbell, Houston	302	1,450	4.8	81	13
	Walter Payton, Chicago[3]	333	1,395	4.2	76	11
	Tony Dorsett, Dallas[2]	290	1,325	4.6	63	7
	Delvin Williams, Miami[2]	272	1,258	4.6	58	8
	Wilbert Montgomery, Philadelphia	259	1,220	4.7	47	9
	Terdell Middleton, Green Bay	284	1,116	3.9	76	11
	Franco Harris, Pittsburgh[6]	310	1,082	3.5	37	8
	Mark van Eeghen, Oakland[3]	270	1,080	4.0	34	9
	*Terry Miller, Buffalo	238	1,060	4.5	60	7
	Tony Reed, Kansas City	206	1,053	5.1	62	5
	John Riggins, Washington[2]	248	1,014	4.1	31	5
1977	Walter Payton, Chicago[2]	339	1,852	5.5	73	14
	Mark van Eeghen, Oakland[2]	324	1,273	3.9	27	7
	Lawrence McCutcheon, Los Angeles[4]	294	1,238	4.2	48	7
	Franco Harris, Pittsburgh[5]	300	1,162	3.9	61	11
	Lydell Mitchell, Baltimore[3]	301	1,159	3.9	64	3
	Chuck Foreman, Minnesota[3]	270	1,112	4.1	51	6
	Greg Pruitt, Cleveland[3]	236	1,086	4.6	78	3
	Sam Cunningham, New England	270	1,015	3.8	31	4
	*Tony Dorsett, Dallas	208	1,007	4.8	84	12
1976	O.J. Simpson, Buffalo[5]	290	1,503	5.2	75	8
	Walter Payton, Chicago	311	1,390	4.5	60	13
	Delvin Williams, San Francisco	248	1,203	4.9	80	7
	Lydell Mitchell, Baltimore[2]	289	1,200	4.2	43	5
	Lawrence McCutcheon, Los Angeles[3]	291	1,168	4.0	40	9
	Chuck Foreman, Minnesota[2]	278	1,155	4.2	46	13
	Franco Harris, Pittsburgh[4]	289	1,128	3.9	30	14
	Mike Thomas, Washington	254	1,101	4.3	28	5
	Rocky Bleier, Pittsburgh	220	1,036	4.7	28	5
	Mark van Eeghen, Oakland	233	1,012	4.3	21	3
	Otis Armstrong, Denver[2]	247	1,008	4.1	31	5
	Greg Pruitt, Cleveland[2]	209	1,000	4.8	64	4
1975	O.J. Simpson, Buffalo[4]	329	1,817	5.5	88	16
	Franco Harris, Pittsburgh[3]	262	1,246	4.8	36	10
	Lydell Mitchell, Baltimore	289	1,193	4.1	70	11
	Jim Otis, St. Louis	269	1,076	4.0	30	5
	Chuck Foreman, Minnesota	280	1,070	3.8	31	13
	Greg Pruitt, Cleveland	217	1,067	4.9	50	8
	John Riggins, N.Y. Jets	238	1,005	4.2	42	8
	Dave Hampton, Atlanta	250	1,002	4.0	22	5
1974	Otis Armstrong, Denver	263	1,407	5.3	43	9
	*Don Woods, San Diego	227	1,162	5.1	56	7
	O.J. Simpson, Buffalo[3]	270	1,125	4.2	41	3
	Lawrence McCutcheon, Los Angeles[2]	236	1,109	4.7	23	3
	Franco Harris, Pittsburgh[2]	208	1,006	4.8	54	5
1973	O.J. Simpson, Buffalo[2]	332	2,003	6.0	80	12
	John Brockington, Green Bay[3]	265	1,144	4.3	53	3
	Calvin Hill, Dallas[2]	273	1,142	4.2	21	6
	Lawrence McCutcheon, Los Angeles	210	1,097	5.2	37	2
	Larry Csonka, Miami[3]	219	1,003	4.6	25	5
1972	O.J. Simpson, Buffalo	292	1,251	4.3	94	6
	Larry Brown, Washington[2]	285	1,216	4.3	38	8
	Ron Johnson, N.Y. Giants[2]	298	1,182	4.0	35	9
	Larry Csonka, Miami[2]	213	1,117	5.2	45	6
	Marv Hubbard, Oakland	219	1,100	5.0	39	4
	*Franco Harris, Pittsburgh	188	1,055	5.6	75	10
	Calvin Hill, Dallas	245	1,036	4.2	26	6
	Mike Garrett, San Diego[2]	272	1,031	3.8	41	6
	John Brockington, Green Bay[2]	274	1,027	3.7	30	8
	Eugene (Mercury) Morris, Miami	190	1,000	5.3	33	12
1971	Floyd Little, Denver	284	1,133	4.0	40	6
	*John Brockington, Green Bay	216	1,105	5.1	52	4
	Larry Csonka, Miami	195	1,051	5.4	28	7
	Steve Owens, Detroit	246	1,035	4.2	23	8
	Willie Ellison, Los Angeles	211	1,000	4.7	80	4
1970	Larry Brown, Washington	237	1,125	4.7	75	5
	Ron Johnson, N.Y. Giants	263	1,027	3.9	68	8
1969	Gale Sayers, Chicago[2]	236	1,032	4.4	28	8
1968	Leroy Kelly, Cleveland[3]	248	1,239	5.0	65	16
	*Paul Robinson, Cincinnati	238	1,023	4.3	87	8
1967	Jim Nance, Boston[2]	269	1,216	4.5	53	7
	Leroy Kelly, Cleveland[2]	235	1,205	5.1	42	11
	Hoyle Granger, Houston	236	1,194	5.1	67	6
	Mike Garrett, Kansas City	236	1,087	4.6	58	9
1966	Jim Nance, Boston	299	1,458	4.9	65	11
	Gale Sayers, Chicago	229	1,231	5.4	58	8
	Leroy Kelly, Cleveland	209	1,141	5.5	70	15
	Dick Bass, Los Angeles[2]	248	1,090	4.4	50	8
1965	Jim Brown, Cleveland[7]	289	1,544	5.3	67	17
	Paul Lowe, San Diego[2]	222	1,121	5.0	59	7
1964	Jim Brown, Cleveland[6]	280	1,446	5.2	71	7
	Jim Taylor, Green Bay[5]	235	1,169	5.0	84	12
	John Henry Johnson, Pittsburgh[2]	235	1,048	4.5	45	7
1963	Jim Brown, Cleveland[5]	291	1,863	6.4	80	12
	Clem Daniels, Oakland	215	1,099	5.1	74	3
	Jim Taylor, Green Bay[4]	248	1,018	4.1	40	9
	Paul Lowe, San Diego	177	1,010	5.7	66	8
1962	Jim Taylor, Green Bay[3]	272	1,474	5.4	51	19
	John Henry Johnson, Pittsburgh	251	1,141	4.5	40	7

	Cookie Gilchrist, Buffalo	214	1,096	5.1	44	13
	Abner Haynes, Dall. Texans	221	1,049	4.7	71	13
	Dick Bass, Los Angeles	196	1,033	5.3	57	6
	Charlie Tolar, Houston	244	1,012	4.1	25	7
1961	Jim Brown, Cleveland[4]	305	1,408	4.6	38	8
	Jim Taylor, Green Bay[2]	243	1,307	5.4	53	15
1960	Jim Brown, Cleveland[3]	215	1,257	5.8	71	9
	Jim Taylor, Green Bay	230	1,101	4.8	32	11
	John David Crow, St. Louis	183	1,071	5.9	57	6
1959	Jim Brown, Cleveland[2]	290	1,329	4.6	70	14
	J.D. Smith, San Francisco	207	1,036	5.0	73	10
1958	Jim Brown, Cleveland	257	1,527	5.9	65	17
1956	Rick Casares, Chi. Bears	234	1,126	4.8	68	12
1954	Joe Perry, San Francisco[2]	173	1,049	6.1	58	8
1953	Joe Perry, San Francisco	192	1,018	5.3	51	10
1949	Steve Van Buren, Philadelphia[2]	263	1,146	4.4	41	11
	Tony Canadeo, Green Bay	208	1,052	5.1	54	4
1947	Steve Van Buren, Philadelphia	217	1,008	4.6	45	13
1934	*Beattie Feathers, Chi. Bears	119	1,004	8.4	82	8

First season of professional football.

200 YARDS RUSHING IN A GAME

Date	Player, Team, Opponent	Att.	Yards	TD
Nov. 22, 1998	Priest Holmes, Baltimore vs. Cincinnati	36	227	1
Oct. 11, 1998	Terrell Davis, Denver vs Seattle	30	208	1
Dec. 4, 1997	*Corey Dillon, Cincinnati vs. Tennessee	39	246	4
Nov. 23, 1997	Barry Sanders, Detroit vs. Indianapolis	24	216	2
Oct. 26, 1997	Terrell Davis, Denver vs. Buffalo (OT)	42	207	1
Oct. 19, 1997	Napoleon Kaufman, Oakland vs. Denver	28	227	1
Oct. 12, 1997	Barry Sanders, Detroit vs. Tampa Bay	24	215	2
Sept. 21, 1997	Terrell Davis, Denver vs. Cincinnati	27	215	1
Aug. 31, 1997	Eddie George, Tennessee vs. Oakland (OT)	35	216	1
Sept. 22, 1996	LeShon Johnson, Arizona vs. New Orleans	21	214	2
Nov. 13, 1994	Barry Sanders, Detroit vs. Tampa Bay	26	237	0
Dec. 12, 1993	*Jerome Bettis, L.A. Rams vs. New Orleans	28	212	1
Oct. 31, 1993	Emmitt Smith, Dallas vs. Philadelphia	30	237	1
Nov. 24, 1991	Barry Sanders, Detroit vs. Minnesota	23	220	4
Dec. 23, 1990	James Brooks, Cincinnati vs. Houston	20	201	1
Oct. 14, 1990	Barry Word, Kansas City vs. Detroit	18	200	2
Sept. 24, 1990	Thurman Thomas, Buffalo vs. N.Y. Jets	18	214	0
Dec. 24, 1989	Greg Bell, L.A. Rams vs. New England	26	210	1
Sept. 24, 1989	Greg Bell, L.A. Rams vs. Green Bay	28	221	2
Sept. 17, 1989	Gerald Riggs, Washington vs. Philadelphia	29	221	1
Dec. 18, 1988	Gary Anderson, San Diego vs. Kansas City	34	217	1
Nov. 30, 1987	*Bo Jackson, L.A. Raiders vs. Seattle	18	221	2
Nov. 15, 1987	Charles White, L.A. Rams vs. St. Louis	34	213	1
Dec. 7, 1986	Rueben Mayes, New Orleans vs. Miami	28	203	2
Oct. 5, 1986	Eric Dickerson, L.A. Rams vs. Tampa Bay (OT)	30	207	2
Dec. 21, 1985	George Rogers, Washington vs. St. Louis	34	206	1
Dec. 21, 1985	Joe Morris, N.Y. Giants vs. Pittsburgh	36	202	3
Dec. 9, 1984	Eric Dickerson, L.A. Rams vs. Houston	27	215	2
Nov. 18, 1984	*Greg Bell, Buffalo vs. Dallas	27	206	1
Nov. 4, 1984	Eric Dickerson, L.A. Rams vs. St. Louis	21	208	0
Sept. 2, 1984	Gerald Riggs, Atlanta vs. New Orleans	35	202	2
Nov. 27, 1983	*Curt Warner, Seattle vs. Kansas City (OT)	32	207	3
Nov. 6, 1983	James Wilder, Tampa Bay vs. Minnesota	31	219	1
Sept. 18, 1983	Tony Collins, New England vs. N.Y. Jets	23	212	3
Sept. 4, 1983	George Rogers, New Orleans vs. St. Louis	24	206	2
Dec. 21, 1980	Earl Campbell, Houston vs. Minnesota	29	203	1
Nov. 16, 1980	Earl Campbell, Houston vs. Chicago	31	206	0
Oct. 26, 1980	Earl Campbell, Houston vs. Cincinnati	27	202	2
Oct. 19, 1980	Earl Campbell, Houston vs. Tampa Bay	33	203	0
Nov. 26, 1978	*Terry Miller, Buffalo vs. N.Y. Giants	21	208	2
Dec. 4, 1977	*Tony Dorsett, Dallas vs. Philadelphia	23	206	2
Nov. 20, 1977	Walter Payton, Chicago vs. Minnesota	40	275	1
Oct. 30, 1977	Walter Payton, Chicago vs. Green Bay	23	205	2
Dec. 5, 1976	O.J. Simpson, Buffalo vs. Miami	24	203	1
Nov. 25, 1976	O.J. Simpson, Buffalo vs. Detroit	29	273	2
Oct. 24, 1976	Chuck Foreman, Minnesota vs. Philadelphia	28	200	2
Dec. 14, 1975	Greg Pruitt, Cleveland vs. Kansas City	26	214	3
Sept. 28, 1975	O.J. Simpson, Buffalo vs. Pittsburgh	28	227	1
Dec. 16, 1973	O.J. Simpson, Buffalo vs. N.Y. Jets	34	200	1
Dec. 9, 1973	O.J. Simpson, Buffalo vs. New England	22	219	1
Sept. 16, 1973	O.J. Simpson, Buffalo vs. New England	29	250	2
Dec. 5, 1971	Willie Ellison, Los Angeles vs. New Orleans	26	247	1
Dec. 20, 1970	John (Frenchy) Fuqua, Pittsburgh vs. Philadelphia	20	218	2
Nov. 3, 1968	Gale Sayers, Chicago vs. Green Bay	24	205	0
Oct. 30, 1966	Jim Nance, Boston vs. Oakland	38	208	2
Oct. 10, 1964	John Henry Johnson, Pittsburgh vs. Cleveland	30	200	3
Dec. 8, 1963	Cookie Gilchrist, Buffalo vs. N.Y. Jets	36	243	5
Nov. 3, 1963	Jim Brown, Cleveland vs. Philadelphia	28	223	1
Oct. 20, 1963	Clem Daniels, Oakland vs. N.Y. Jets	27	200	2
Sept. 22, 1963	Jim Brown, Cleveland vs. Dallas	20	232	2
Dec. 10, 1961	Billy Cannon, Houston vs. N.Y. Titans	25	216	3
Nov. 19, 1961	Jim Brown, Cleveland vs. Philadelphia	34	237	4
Dec. 18, 1960	John David Crow, St. Louis vs. Pittsburgh	24	203	0
Nov. 15, 1959	Bobby Mitchell, Cleveland vs. Washington	14	232	3
Nov. 24, 1957	*Jim Brown, Cleveland vs. Los Angeles	31	237	4
Dec. 16, 1956	*Tom Wilson, Los Angeles vs. Green Bay	23	223	0
Nov. 22, 1953	Dan Towler, Los Angeles vs. Baltimore	14	205	1
Nov. 12, 1950	Gene Roberts, N.Y. Giants vs. Chi. Cardinals	26	218	2
Nov. 27, 1949	Steve Van Buren, Philadelphia vs. Pittsburgh	27	205	0
Oct. 8, 1933	Cliff Battles, Boston vs. N.Y. Giants	16	215	1

First season of professional football.

TIMES 200 OR MORE

70 times by 47 players...Simpson 6; Brown, Campbell, Sanders 4; Bell, Davis, Dickerson 3; Payton, Riggs, Rogers 2.

4,000 YARDS PASSING IN A SEASON

Year	Player, Team	Att.	Comp.	Pct.	Yards	TD	Int.
1999	Steve Beuerlein, Carolina	571	343	60.1	4,436	36	15
	Kurt Warner, St. Louis	499	325	65.1	4,353	41	13
	Peyton Manning, Indianapolis	533	331	62.1	4,135	26	15
	Brett Favre, Green Bay[3]	595	341	57.3	4,091	22	23
	Brad Johnson, Washington	519	316	60.9	4,005	24	13
1998	Brett Favre, Green Bay[2]	551	347	63.0	4,212	31	23
	Steve Young, San Francisco[2]	517	322	62.3	4,170	36	12
1996	Mark Brunell, Jacksonville	557	353	63.4	4,367	19	20
	Vinny Testaverde, Baltimore	549	325	59.2	4,177	33	19
	Drew Bledsoe, New England[2]	623	373	59.9	4,086	27	15
1995	Brett Favre, Green Bay	570	359	63.0	4,413	38	13
	Scott Mitchell, Detroit	583	346	59.3	4,338	32	12
	Warren Moon, Minnesota[4]	606	377	62.2	4,228	33	14
	Jeff George, Atlanta	557	336	60.3	4,143	24	11
1994	Drew Bledsoe, New England	691	400	57.9	4,555	25	27
	Dan Marino, Miami[6]	615	385	62.6	4,453	30	17
	Warren Moon, Minnesota[3]	601	371	61.7	4,264	18	19
1993	John Elway, Denver	551	348	63.2	4,030	25	10
	Steve Young, San Francisco	462	314	68.0	4,023	29	16
1992	Dan Marino, Miami[5]	554	330	59.6	4,116	24	16
1991	Warren Moon, Houston[2]	655	404	61.7	4,690	23	21
1990	Warren Moon, Houston	584	362	62.0	4,689	33	13
1989	Don Majkowski, Green Bay	599	353	58.9	4,318	27	20
	Jim Everett, L.A. Rams	518	304	58.7	4,310	29	17
1988	Dan Marino, Miami[4]	606	354	58.4	4,434	28	23
1986	Dan Marino, Miami[3]	623	378	60.7	4,746	44	23
	Jay Schroeder, Washington	541	276	51.0	4,109	22	22
1985	Dan Marino, Miami[2]	567	336	59.3	4,137	30	21
1984	Dan Marino, Miami	564	362	64.2	5,084	48	17
	Neil Lomax, St. Louis	560	345	61.6	4,614	28	16
	Phil Simms, N.Y. Giants	533	286	53.7	4,044	22	18
1983	Lynn Dickey, Green Bay	484	289	59.7	4,458	32	29
	Bill Kenney, Kansas City	603	346	57.4	4,348	24	18
1981	Dan Fouts, San Diego[3]	609	360	59.1	4,802	33	17
1980	Dan Fouts, San Diego[2]	589	348	59.1	4,715	30	24
	Brian Sipe, Cleveland	554	337	60.8	4,132	30	14
1979	Dan Fouts, San Diego	530	332	62.6	4,082	24	24
1967	Joe Namath, N.Y. Jets	491	258	52.5	4,007	26	28

400 YARDS PASSING IN A GAME

Date	Player, Team, Opponent	Att.	Comp.	Yards	TD
Dec. 26, 1999	Brad Johnson, Washington vs. San Francisco (OT)	47	32	471	2
Dec. 5, 1999	Jeff Garcia, San Francisco vs. Cincinnati	49	33	437	3
Nov. 28, 1999	Jim Harbaugh, San Diego vs. Minnesota	39	25	404	1
Nov. 14, 1999	Jim Miller, Chicago vs. Minnesota (OT)	48	34	422	3
Sept. 26, 1999	Peyton Manning, Indianapolis vs. San Diego	54	29	404	2
Dec. 6, 1998	Vinny Testaverde, N.Y. Jets vs. Seattle	63	42	418	2
Dec. 6, 1998	John Elway, Denver vs. Kansas City	32	22	400	2
Nov. 26, 1998	Troy Aikman, Dallas vs. Minnesota	57	34	455	1
Nov. 23, 1998	Drew Bledsoe, New England vs. Miami	54	28	423	2
Nov. 15, 1998	Jake Plummer, Arizona vs. Dallas	56	31	465	3
Oct. 5, 1998	Randall Cunningham, Minnesota vs. Green Bay	32	20	442	4
Sept. 6, 1998	Glenn Foley, N.Y. Jets vs. San Francisco (OT)	58	30	415	3
Nov. 2, 1997	Tony Banks, St. Louis vs. Atlanta	34	23	401	2
Oct. 26, 1997	Warren Moon, Seattle vs. Oakland	44	28	409	5
Nov. 10, 1996	Boomer Esiason, Arizona vs. Washington (OT)	59	35	522	3
Nov. 3, 1996	Drew Bledsoe, New England vs. Miami	41	30	419	3
Oct. 27, 1996	Vinny Testaverde, Baltimore vs. St. Louis (OT)	51	31	429	3
Oct. 20, 1996	Mark Brunell, Jacksonville vs. St. Louis	52	37	421	0
Sept. 22, 1996	Mark Brunell, Jacksonville vs. New England (OT)	39	23	432	3
Dec. 18, 1995	Steve Young, San Francisco vs. Minnesota	49	30	425	3
Nov. 26, 1995	Dave Krieg, Arizona vs. Atlanta (OT)	43	27	413	4
Nov. 23, 1995	Scott Mitchell, Detroit vs. Minnesota	45	30	410	4

Oct. 1, 1995	Dan Marino, Miami vs. Cincinnati...48	33	450	2
Nov. 20, 1994	Warren Moon, Minnesota vs. N.Y. Jets...50	33	400	2
Nov. 13, 1994	Drew Bledsoe, New England vs. Minnesota (OT).70	45	426	3
Nov. 6, 1994	Warren Moon, Minnesota vs. New Orleans...57	33	420	3
Sept. 25, 1994	Dan Marino, Miami vs. Minnesota...54	29	431	3
Sept. 4, 1994	Dan Marino, Miami vs. New England (OT)...42	23	473	5
Sept. 4, 1994	Drew Bledsoe, New England vs. Miami (OT)...51	32	421	4
Dec. 19, 1993	Steve Beuerlein, Phoenix vs. Seattle...53	34	431	3
Dec. 5, 1993	Brett Favre, Green Bay vs. Chicago...54	36	402	2
Nov. 28, 1993	Steve Young, San Francisco vs. L.A. Rams...32	26	462	4
Oct. 31, 1993	Jeff Hostetler, L.A. Raiders vs. San Diego...32	20	424	2
Sept. 13, 1992	Steve Young, San Francisco vs. Buffalo...37	26	449	3
Sept. 13, 1992	Jim Kelly, Buffalo vs. San Francisco...33	22	403	3
Nov. 10, 1991	Warren Moon, Houston vs. Dallas (OT)...56	41	432	0
Nov. 10, 1991	Mark Rypien, Washington vs. Atlanta...31	16	442	6
Oct. 13, 1991	Warren Moon, Houston vs. N.Y. Jets...50	35	423	2
Dec. 16, 1990	Warren Moon, Houston vs. Kansas City...45	27	527	3
Nov. 4, 1990	Joe Montana, San Francisco vs. Green Bay..40	25	411	3
Oct. 14, 1990	Joe Montana, San Francisco vs. Atlanta...49	32	476	6
Oct. 7, 1990	Boomer Esiason, Cincinnati vs. L.A. Rams (OT).45	31	490	3
Dec. 23, 1989	Warren Moon, Houston vs. Cleveland...51	32	414	2
Dec. 11, 1989	Joe Montana, San Francisco vs. L.A. Rams...42	30	458	3
Nov. 26, 1989	Jim Everett, L.A. Rams vs. New Orleans (OT).51	29	454	1
Nov. 26, 1989	Mark Rypien, Washington vs. Chicago...47	30	401	4
Oct. 2, 1989	Randall Cunningham, Philadelphia vs. Chicago..62	32	401	1
Sept. 24, 1989	Joe Montana, San Francisco vs. Philadelphia 34	25	428	5
Sept. 24, 1989	Dan Marino, Miami vs. N.Y. Jets...55	33	427	3
Sept. 17, 1989	Randall Cunningham, Phil. vs. Washington...46	34	447	5
Dec. 18, 1988	Dave Krieg, Seattle vs. L.A. Raiders...32	19	410	4
Dec. 12, 1988	Dan Marino, Miami vs. Cleveland...50	30	404	4
Oct. 23, 1988	Dan Marino, Miami vs. N.Y. Jets...60	35	521	3
Oct. 16, 1988	Vinny Testaverde, Tampa Bay vs. Indianapolis..42	25	469	2
Sept. 11, 1988	Doug Williams, Washington vs. Pittsburgh...52	30	430	2
Nov. 29, 1987	Tom Ramsey, New England vs. Philadelphia .53	34	402	3
Nov. 22, 1987	Boomer Esiason, Cincinnati vs. Pittsburgh...53	30	409	0
Sept. 20, 1987	Neil Lomax, St. Louis vs. San Diego...61	32	457	3
Dec. 21, 1986	Boomer Esiason, Cincinnati vs. N.Y. Jets...30	23	425	5
Dec. 14, 1986	Dan Marino, Miami vs. L.A. Rams (OT)...46	29	403	5
Nov. 23, 1986	Bernie Kosar, Cleveland vs. Pittsburgh (OT)..46	28	414	2
Nov. 17, 1986	Joe Montana, San Francisco vs. Washington...60	33	441	0
Nov. 16, 1986	Dan Marino, Miami vs. Buffalo...54	39	404	4
Nov. 10, 1986	Bernie Kosar, Cleveland vs. Miami...50	32	401	0
Nov. 2, 1986	Tommy Kramer, Minnesota vs. Washington (OT).35	20	490	4
Nov. 2, 1986	Ken O'Brien, N.Y. Jets vs. Seattle...32	26	431	4
Oct. 27, 1986	Jay Schroeder, Washington vs. N.Y. Giants...40	22	420	1
Oct. 12, 1986	Steve Grogan, New England vs. N.Y. Jets...42	23	401	3
Sept. 21, 1986	Ken O'Brien, N.Y. Jets vs. Miami (OT)...43	29	479	4
Sept. 21, 1986	Dan Marino, Miami vs. N.Y. Jets (OT)...50	30	448	6
Sept. 21, 1986	Tony Eason, New England vs. Seattle...45	26	414	3
Dec. 20, 1985	John Elway, Denver vs. Seattle...42	24	432	1
Nov. 10, 1985	Dan Fouts, San Diego vs. L.A. Raiders (OT)..41	26	436	4
Oct. 13, 1985	Phil Simms, N.Y. Giants vs. Cincinnati...62	40	513	1
Oct. 13, 1985	Dave Krieg, Seattle vs. Atlanta...51	33	405	4
Oct. 6, 1985	Phil Simms, N.Y. Giants vs. Dallas...36	18	432	3
Oct. 6, 1985	Joe Montana, San Francisco vs. Atlanta...57	37	429	5
Sept. 19, 1985	Tommy Kramer, Minnesota vs. Chicago...55	28	436	3
Sept. 15, 1985	Dan Fouts, San Diego vs. Seattle...43	29	440	4
Dec. 16, 1984	Neil Lomax, St. Louis vs. Washington...46	37	468	2
Dec. 9, 1984	Dan Marino, Miami vs. Indianapolis...41	29	404	4
Dec. 2, 1984	Dan Marino, Miami vs. L.A. Raiders...57	35	470	4
Nov. 25, 1984	Dave Krieg, Seattle vs. Denver...44	30	406	3
Nov. 4, 1984	Dan Marino, Miami vs. N.Y. Jets...42	23	422	2
Oct. 21, 1984	Dan Fouts, San Diego vs. L.A. Raiders...45	24	410	3
Sept. 30, 1984	Dan Marino, Miami vs. St. Louis...36	24	429	3
Sept. 2, 1984	Phil Simms, N.Y. Giants vs. Philadelphia...30	23	409	4
Dec. 11, 1983	Bill Kenney, Kansas City vs. San Diego...41	31	411	4
Nov. 20, 1983	Dave Krieg, Seattle vs. Denver...42	31	418	3
Oct. 9, 1983	Joe Ferguson, Buffalo vs. Miami (OT)...55	38	419	5
Oct. 2, 1983	Joe Theismann, Washington vs. L.A. Raiders.39	23	417	3
Sept. 25, 1983	Richard Todd, N.Y. Jets vs. L.A. Rams (OT)...50	37	446	2
Dec. 26, 1982	Vince Ferragamo, L.A. Rams vs. Chicago...46	30	509	3
Dec. 20, 1982	Dan Fouts, San Diego vs. Cincinnati...40	25	435	1
Dec. 20, 1982	Ken Anderson, Cincinnati vs. San Diego...56	40	416	2
Dec. 11, 1982	Dan Fouts, San Diego vs. San Francisco...48	33	444	5
Nov. 21, 1982	Joe Montana, San Francisco vs. St. Louis...39	26	408	3
Nov. 15, 1981	Steve Bartkowski, Atlanta vs. Pittsburgh...50	33	416	2
Oct. 25, 1981	Brian Sipe, Cleveland vs. Baltimore...41	30	444	4
Oct. 25, 1981	David Woodley, Miami vs. Dallas...37	21	408	3
Oct. 11, 1981	Tommy Kramer, Minnesota vs. San Diego...43	27	444	4
Dec. 14, 1980	Tommy Kramer, Minnesota vs. Cleveland...49	38	456	4
Nov. 16, 1980	Doug Williams, Tampa Bay vs. Minnesota...55	30	486	4
Oct. 19, 1980	Dan Fouts, San Diego vs. N.Y. Giants...41	26	444	3
Oct. 12, 1980	Lynn Dickey, Green Bay vs. Tampa Bay (OT).51	35	418	1
Sept. 21, 1980	Richard Todd, N.Y. Jets vs. San Francisco...60	42	447	3
Oct. 3, 1976	James Harris, Los Angeles vs. Miami...29	17	436	2
Nov. 17, 1975	Ken Anderson, Cincinnati vs. Buffalo...46	30	447	2
Nov. 18, 1974	Charley Johnson, Denver vs. Kansas City...42	28	445	2
Dec. 11, 1972	Joe Namath, N.Y. Jets vs. Oakland...46	25	403	1
Sept. 24, 1972	Joe Namath, N.Y. Jets vs. Baltimore...28	15	496	6
Dec. 21, 1969	Don Horn, Green Bay vs. St. Louis...31	22	410	5
Sept. 28, 1969	Joe Kapp, Minnesota vs. Baltimore...43	28	449	7
Sept. 9, 1968	Pete Beathard, Houston vs. Kansas City...48	23	413	2
Nov. 26, 1967	Sonny Jurgensen, Washington vs. Cleveland .50	32	418	3
Oct. 1, 1967	Joe Namath, N.Y. Jets vs. Miami...39	23	415	3
Sept. 17, 1967	Johnny Unitas, Baltimore vs. Atlanta...32	22	401	2
Nov. 13, 1966	Don Meredith, Dallas vs. Washington...29	21	406	2
Nov. 28, 1965	Sonny Jurgensen, Washington vs. Dallas...43	26	411	3
Oct. 24, 1965	Fran Tarkenton, Minnesota vs. San Francisco .35	21	407	3
Nov. 1, 1964	Len Dawson, Kansas City vs. Denver...38	23	435	6
Oct. 25, 1964	Cotton Davidson, Oakland vs. Denver...36	23	427	5
Oct. 16, 1964	Babe Parilli, Boston vs. Oakland...47	25	422	4
Dec. 22, 1963	Tom Flores, Oakland vs. Houston...29	17	407	6
Nov. 17, 1963	Norm Snead, Washington vs. Pittsburgh...40	23	424	2
Nov. 10, 1963	Don Meredith, Dallas vs. San Francisco...48	30	460	3
Oct. 13, 1963	Charley Johnson, St. Louis vs. Pittsburgh...41	20	428	2
Dec. 16, 1962	Sonny Jurgensen, Philadelphia vs. St. Louis .34	15	419	5
Nov. 18, 1962	Bill Wade, Chicago vs. Dall. Cowboys...46	28	466	2
Oct. 28, 1962	Y.A. Tittle, N.Y. Giants vs. Washington...39	27	505	7
Sept. 15, 1962	Frank Tripucka, Denver vs. Buffalo...56	29	447	2
Dec. 17, 1961	Sonny Jurgensen, Philadelphia vs. Detroit...42	27	403	3
Nov. 19, 1961	George Blanda, Houston vs. N.Y. Titans...32	20	418	7
Oct. 29, 1961	George Blanda, Houston vs. Buffalo...32	18	464	4
Oct. 29, 1961	Sonny Jurgensen, Philadelphia vs. Washington 41	27	436	3
Oct. 13, 1961	Jacky Lee, Houston vs. Boston...41	27	457	2
Dec. 13, 1958	Bobby Layne, Pittsburgh vs. Chi. Cardinals...49	23	409	2
Nov. 8, 1953	Bobby Thomason, Philadelphia vs. N.Y. Giants..44	22	437	4
Oct. 4, 1952	Otto Graham, Cleveland vs. Pittsburgh...49	21	401	3
Sept. 28, 1951	Norm Van Brocklin, Los Angeles vs. N.Y. Yanks.41	27	554	5
Dec. 11, 1949	Johnny Lujack, Chi. Bears vs. Chi. Cardinals.39	24	468	6
Oct. 31, 1948	Sammy Baugh, Washington vs. Boston...24	17	446	4
Oct. 31, 1948	Jim Hardy, Los Angeles vs. Chi. Cardinals...53	28	406	3
Nov. 14, 1943	Sid Luckman, Chi. Bears vs. N.Y. Giants...32	21	433	7

TIMES 400 OR MORE

144 times by 76 players. . .Marino 13; Montana, Moon 7; Fouts 6; Jurgensen, Krieg 5; Bledsoe, Esiason, Kramer 4; Cunningham, Namath, Simms, Testaverde, Young 3; Anderson, Blanda, Brunell, Elway, Johnson, Kosar, Lomax, Meredith, O'Brien, Rypien, Todd, Williams 2.

100 PASS RECEPTIONS IN A SEASON

Year	Player, Team	No.	Yards	Avg.	Long	TD
1999	Jimmy Smith, Jacksonville	116	1,636	14.1	62	6
	Marvin Harrison, Indianapolis	115	1,663	14.5	57	12
1997	Tim Brown, Oakland	104	1,408	13.5	59	5
	Herman Moore, Detroit[3]	104	1,293	12.4	79	8
1996	Jerry Rice, San Francisco[4]	108	1,254	11.6	39	8
	Herman Moore, Detroit[2]	106	1,296	12.2	50	9
	Carl Pickens, Cincinnati	100	1,180	11.8	61	12
1995	Herman Moore, Detroit	123	1,686	13.7	69	14
	Jerry Rice, San Francisco[3]	122	1,848	15.1	81	15
	Cris Carter, Minnesota[2]	122	1,371	11.2	60	17
	Isaac Bruce, St. Louis	119	1,781	15.0	72	13
	Michael Irvin, Dallas	111	1,603	14.4	50	10
	Brett Perriman, Detroit	108	1,488	13.8	91	9
	Eric Metcalf, Atlanta	104	1,189	11.4	62	8
	Robert Brooks, Green Bay	102	1,497	14.7	99	13
	Larry Centers, Arizona	101	962	9.5	32	2
1994	Cris Carter, Minnesota	122	1,256	10.3	65	7
	Jerry Rice, San Francisco[2]	112	1,499	13.4	69	13
	Terance Mathis, Atlanta	111	1,342	12.1	81	11
1993	Sterling Sharpe, Green Bay[2]	112	1,274	11.4	54	11
1992	Sterling Sharpe, Green Bay	108	1,461	13.5	76	13
1991	Haywood Jeffires, Houston	100	1,181	11.8	44	7
1990	Jerry Rice, San Francisco	100	1,502	15.0	64	13
1984	Art Monk, Washington	106	1,372	12.9	72	7
1964	Charley Hennigan, Houston	101	1,546	15.3	53	8
1961	Lionel Taylor, Denver	100	1,176	11.8	52	4

1,000 YARDS PASS RECEIVING IN A SEASON

Year	Player, Team	No.	Yards	Avg.	Long	TD
1999	Marvin Harrison, Indianapolis	115	1,663	14.5	57	12
	Jimmy Smith, Jacksonville[4]	116	1,636	14.1	62	6
	Randy Moss, Minnesota[2]	80	1,413	17.7	67	11
	Marcus Robinson, Chicago	84	1,400	16.7	80	9

	Tim Brown, Oakland[7]	90	1,344	14.9	47	6
	Germane Crowell, Detroit	81	1,338	16.5	77	7
	Muhsin Muhammad, Carolina	96	1,253	13.1	60	8
	Cris Carter, Minnesota[7]	90	1,241	13.8	68	13
	Michael Westbrook, Washington	65	1,191	18.3	65	9
	Amani Toomer, N.Y. Giants	79	1,183	15.0	80	6
	Keyshawn Johnson, N.Y. Jets[2]	89	1,170	13.2	65	8
	Isaac Bruce, St. Louis[3]	77	1,165	15.1	60	12
	Terry Glenn, New England[2]	69	1,147	16.6	67	4
	Albert Connell, Washington	62	1,132	18.3	62	7
	Johnnie Morton, Detroit[3]	80	1,129	14.1	48	5
	Qadry Ismail, Baltimore	68	1,105	16.3	76	6
	Raghib Ismail, Dallas[2]	80	1,097	13.7	76	6
	Patrick Jeffers, Carolina	63	1,082	17.2	88	12
	Antonio Freeman, Green Bay[3]	74	1,074	14.5	51	6
	Bill Schroeder, Green Bay	74	1,051	14.2	51	5
	Marshall Faulk, St. Louis	87	1,048	12.1	57	5
	Tony Martin, Miami[4]	67	1,037	15.5	69	5
	Darnay Scott, Cincinnati	68	1,022	15.0	76	7
	Rod Smith, Denver[3]	79	1,020	12.9	71	4
	Ed McCaffrey, Denver[2]	71	1,018	14.3	78	7
	Terance Mathis, Atlanta[4]	81	1,016	12.5	52	6
1998	Antonio Freeman, Green Bay[2]	84	1,424	17.0	84	14
	Eric Moulds, Buffalo	67	1,368	20.4	84	9
	*Randy Moss, Minnesota	69	1,313	19.0	61	17
	Rod Smith, Denver[2]	86	1,222	14.2	58	6
	Jimmy Smith, Jacksonville[3]	78	1,182	15.2	72	8
	Tony Martin, Atlanta[3]	66	1,181	17.9	62	6
	Jerry Rice, San Francisco[12]	82	1,157	14.1	75	9
	Frank Sanders, Arizona[2]	89	1,145	12.9	42	3
	Terance Mathis, Atlanta[3]	64	1,136	17.8	78	11
	Keyshawn Johnson, N.Y. Jets	83	1,131	13.6	41	10
	Terrell Owens, San Francisco	67	1,097	16.4	79	14
	Wayne Chrebet, N.Y. Jets	75	1,083	14.4	63	8
	Michael Irvin, Dallas[7]	74	1,057	14.3	51	1
	Ed McCaffrey, Denver	64	1,053	16.5	48	10
	O.J. McDuffie, Miami	90	1,050	11.7	61	7
	Joey Galloway, Seattle[3]	65	1,047	16.1	81	10
	Johnnie Morton, Detroit[2]	69	1,028	14.9	98	2
	Raghib Ismail, Carolina	69	1,024	14.8	62	8
	Carl Pickens, Cincinnati[4]	82	1,023	12.5	67	5
	Tim Brown, Oakland[6]	81	1,012	12.5	49	9
	Cris Carter, Minnesota[6]	78	1,011	13.0	54	12
1997	Rob Moore, Arizona[3]	97	1,584	16.3	47	8
	Tim Brown, Oakland[5]	104	1,408	13.5	59	5
	Yancey Thigpen, Pittsburgh[2]	79	1,398	17.7	69	7
	Jimmy Smith, Jacksonville[2]	82	1,324	16.1	75	4
	Irving Fryar, Philadelphia[5]	86	1,316	15.3	72	6
	Herman Moore, Detroit[4]	104	1,293	12.4	79	8
	Antonio Freeman, Green Bay	81	1,243	15.3	58	12
	Michael Irvin, Dallas[6]	75	1,180	15.7	55	9
	Rod Smith, Denver	70	1,180	16.9	78	12
	Keenan McCardell, Jacksonville[2]	85	1,164	13.7	60	5
	Jake Reed, Minnesota[4]	68	1,138	16.7	56	6
	Shannon Sharpe, Denver[3]	72	1,107	15.4	68	3
	Andre Rison, Kansas City[5]	72	1,092	15.2	45	7
	Cris Carter, Minnesota[5]	89	1,069	12.0	43	13
	Johnnie Morton, Detroit	80	1,057	13.2	73	6
	Joey Galloway, Seattle[2]	72	1,049	14.6	53	12
	Frank Sanders, Arizona	75	1,017	13.6	70	4
	Robert Brooks, Green Bay[2]	60	1,010	16.8	48	7
	Derrick Alexander, Baltimore[2]	65	1,009	15.5	92	9
1996	Isaac Bruce, St. Louis[2]	84	1,338	15.9	70	7
	Jake Reed, Minnesota[3]	72	1,320	18.3	82	7
	Herman Moore, Detroit[3]	106	1,296	12.2	50	9
	Jerry Rice, San Francisco[11]	108	1,254	11.6	39	8
	Jimmy Smith, Jacksonville	83	1,244	15.0	62	7
	Michael Jackson, Baltimore	76	1,201	15.8	86	14
	Irving Fryar, Philadelphia[4]	88	1,195	13.6	42	11
	Carl Pickens, Cincinnati[3]	100	1,180	11.8	61	12
	Tony Martin, San Diego[2]	85	1,171	13.8	55	14
	Cris Carter, Minnesota[4]	96	1,163	12.1	43	10
	*Terry Glenn, New England	90	1,132	12.6	37	6
	Keenan McCardell, Jacksonville	85	1,129	13.3	52	3
	Tim Brown, Oakland[4]	90	1,104	12.3	42	9
	Derrick Alexander, Baltimore	62	1,099	17.7	64	9
	Shannon Sharpe, Denver[2]	80	1,062	13.3	51	10
	Curtis Conway, Chicago[2]	81	1,049	13.0	58	7
	Andre Reed, Buffalo[4]	66	1,036	15.7	67	6
	Brett Perriman, Detroit[2]	94	1,021	10.9	44	5
	Rob Moore, Arizona[2]	58	1,016	17.5	69	4
	Henry Ellard, Washington[7]	52	1,014	19.5	51	2
	Charles Johnson, Pittsburgh	60	1,008	16.8	70	3
1995	Jerry Rice, San Francisco[10]	122	1,848	15.1	81	15
	Isaac Bruce, St. Louis	119	1,781	15.0	72	13
	Herman Moore, Detroit[2]	123	1,686	13.7	69	14
	Michael Irvin, Dallas[5]	111	1,603	14.4	50	10
	Robert Brooks, Green Bay	102	1,497	14.7	99	13
	Brett Perriman, Detroit	108	1,488	13.8	91	9
	Cris Carter, Minnesota[3]	122	1,371	11.2	60	17
	Tim Brown, Oakland[3]	89	1,342	15.1	80	10
	Yancey Thigpen, Pittsburgh	85	1,307	15.4	43	5
	Jeff Graham, Chicago	82	1,301	15.9	51	4
	Carl Pickens, Cincinnati[2]	99	1,234	12.5	68	17
	Tony Martin, San Diego	90	1,224	13.6	51	6
	Eric Metcalf, Atlanta	104	1,189	11.4	62	8
	Jake Reed, Minnesota[2]	72	1,167	16.2	55	9
	Quinn Early, New Orleans	81	1,087	13.4	70	8
	Anthony Miller, Denver[5]	59	1,079	18.3	62	14
	Bert Emanuel, Atlanta	74	1,039	14.0	52	5
	*Joey Galloway, Seattle	67	1,039	15.5	59	7
	Terance Mathis, Atlanta[2]	78	1,039	13.3	54	9
	Curtis Conway, Chicago	62	1,037	16.7	76	12
	Henry Ellard, Washington[6]	56	1,005	17.9	59	5
	Mark Carrier, Carolina[2]	66	1,002	15.2	66	3
	Brian Blades, Seattle[4]	77	1,001	13.0	49	4
1994	Jerry Rice, San Francisco[9]	112	1,499	13.4	69	13
	Henry Ellard, Washington[5]	74	1,397	18.9	73	6
	Terance Mathis, Atlanta	111	1,342	12.1	81	11
	Tim Brown, L.A. Raiders[2]	89	1,309	14.7	77	9
	Andre Reed, Buffalo[2]	90	1,303	14.5	83	8
	Irving Fryar, Miami[3]	73	1,270	17.4	54	7
	Cris Carter, Minnesota[2]	122	1,256	10.3	65	7
	Michael Irvin, Dallas[4]	79	1,241	15.7	65	6
	Jake Reed, Minnesota	85	1,175	13.8	59	4
	Ben Coates, New England	96	1,174	12.2	62	7
	Herman Moore, Detroit	72	1,173	16.3	51	11
	Fred Barnett, Philadelphia[2]	78	1,127	14.4	54	5
	Carl Pickens, Cincinnati	71	1,127	15.9	70	11
	Sterling Sharpe, Green Bay[4]	94	1,119	11.9	49	18
	Anthony Miller, Denver[4]	60	1,107	18.5	76	5
	Andre Rison, Atlanta[3]	81	1,088	13.4	69	8
	Brian Blades, Seattle[3]	81	1,088	13.4	45	4
	Rob Moore, N.Y. Jets	78	1,010	12.9	41	6
	Shannon Sharpe, Denver	87	1,010	11.6	44	4
1993	Jerry Rice, San Francisco[8]	98	1,503	15.3	80	15
	Michael Irvin, Dallas[3]	88	1,330	15.1	61	7
	Sterling Sharpe, Green Bay[4]	112	1,274	11.4	54	11
	Andre Rison, Atlanta[3]	86	1,242	14.4	53	15
	Tim Brown, L.A. Raiders	80	1,180	14.8	71	7
	Anthony Miller, San Diego[3]	84	1,162	13.8	66	7
	Cris Carter, Minnesota	86	1,071	12.5	58	9
	Reggie Langhorne, Indianapolis	85	1,038	12.2	72	3
	Irving Fryar, Miami[2]	64	1,010	15.8	65	5
1992	Sterling Sharpe, Green Bay[3]	108	1,461	13.5	76	13
	Michael Irvin, Dallas[2]	78	1,396	17.9	87	7
	Jerry Rice, San Francisco[7]	84	1,201	14.3	80	10
	Andre Rison, Atlanta[2]	93	1,119	12.0	71	11
	Fred Barnett, Philadelphia	67	1,083	16.2	71	6
	Anthony Miller, San Diego[2]	72	1,060	14.7	67	7
	Eric Martin, New Orleans[3]	68	1,041	15.3	52	5
1991	Michael Irvin, Dallas	93	1,523	16.4	66	8
	Gary Clark, Washington[5]	70	1,340	19.1	82	10
	Jerry Rice, San Francisco[6]	80	1,206	15.1	73	14
	Haywood Jeffires, Houston[2]	100	1,181	11.8	44	7
	Michael Haynes, Atlanta	50	1,122	22.4	80	11
	Andre Reed, Buffalo[2]	81	1,113	13.7	55	10
	Drew Hill, Houston[5]	90	1,109	12.3	61	4
	Mark Duper, Miami[4]	70	1,085	15.5	43	5
	James Lofton, Buffalo[6]	57	1,072	18.8	77	8
	Mark Clayton, Miami[5]	70	1,053	15.0	43	12
	Henry Ellard, L.A. Rams[4]	64	1,052	16.4	38	3
	Art Monk, Washington[5]	71	1,049	14.8	64	8
	Irving Fryar, New England	68	1,014	14.9	56	3
	John Taylor, San Francisco[2]	64	1,011	15.8	97	9
	Brian Blades, Seattle[2]	70	1,003	14.3	52	2
1990	Jerry Rice, San Francisco[5]	100	1,502	15.0	64	13
	Henry Ellard, L.A. Rams[3]	76	1,294	17.0	50	4
	Andre Rison, Atlanta	82	1,208	14.7	75	10
	Gary Clark, Washington[4]	75	1,112	14.8	53	8
	Sterling Sharpe, Green Bay[2]	67	1,105	16.5	76	6
	Willie Anderson, L.A. Rams[2]	51	1,097	21.5	55	4
	Haywood Jeffires, Houston	74	1,048	14.2	87	8
	Stephone Paige, Kansas City	65	1,021	15.7	86	5
	Drew Hill, Houston[4]	74	1,019	13.8	57	5
	Anthony Carter, Minnesota[3]	70	1,008	14.4	56	8

1989	Jerry Rice, San Francisco[4]	82	1,483	18.1	68	17
	Sterling Sharpe, Green Bay	90	1,423	15.8	79	12
	Mark Carrier, Tampa Bay	86	1,422	16.5	78	9
	Henry Ellard, L.A. Rams[2]	70	1,382	19.7	53	8
	Andre Reed, Buffalo	88	1,312	14.9	78	9
	Anthony Miller, San Diego	75	1,252	16.7	69	10
	Webster Slaughter, Cleveland	65	1,236	19.0	97	6
	Gary Clark, Washington[3]	79	1,229	15.6	80	9
	Tim McGee, Cincinnati	65	1,211	18.6	74	8
	Art Monk, Washington[4]	86	1,186	13.8	60	8
	Willie Anderson, L.A. Rams	44	1,146	26.0	78	5
	Ricky Sanders, Washington[2]	80	1,138	14.2	68	4
	Vance Johnson, Denver	76	1,095	14.4	69	7
	Richard Johnson, Detroit	70	1,091	15.6	75	8
	Eric Martin, New Orleans[2]	68	1,090	16.0	53	8
	John Taylor, San Francisco	60	1,077	18.0	95	10
	Mervyn Fernandez, L.A. Raiders	57	1,069	18.8	75	9
	Anthony Carter, Minnesota[2]	65	1,066	16.4	50	4
	Brian Blades, Seattle	77	1,063	13.8	60	5
	Mark Clayton, Miami[4]	64	1,011	15.8	78	9
1988	Henry Ellard, L.A. Rams	86	1,414	16.4	68	10
	Jerry Rice, San Francisco[3]	64	1,306	20.4	96	9
	Eddie Brown, Cincinnati	53	1,273	24.0	86	9
	Anthony Carter, Minnesota	72	1,225	17.0	67	6
	Ricky Sanders, Washington	73	1,148	15.7	55	12
	Drew Hill, Houston[3]	72	1,141	15.8	57	10
	Mark Clayton, Miami[3]	86	1,129	13.1	45	14
	Roy Green, Phoenix[3]	68	1,097	16.1	52	7
	Eric Martin, New Orleans	85	1,083	12.7	40	7
	Al Toon, N.Y. Jets[2]	93	1,067	11.5	42	5
	Bruce Hill, Tampa Bay	58	1,040	17.9	42	9
	Lionel Manuel, N.Y. Giants	65	1,029	15.8	46	4
1987	J.T. Smith, St. Louis[2]	91	1,117	12.3	38	8
	Jerry Rice, San Francisco[2]	65	1,078	16.6	57	22
	Gary Clark, Washington[2]	56	1,066	19.0	84	7
	Carlos Carson, Kansas City[3]	55	1,044	19.0	81	7
1986	Jerry Rice, San Francisco	86	1,570	18.3	66	15
	Stanley Morgan, New England[3]	84	1,491	17.8	44	10
	Mark Duper, Miami[3]	67	1,313	19.6	85	11
	Gary Clark, Washington	74	1,265	17.1	55	7
	Al Toon, N.Y. Jets	85	1,176	13.8	62	8
	Todd Christensen, L.A. Raiders[3]	95	1,153	12.1	35	8
	Mark Clayton, Miami[2]	60	1,150	19.2	68	10
	*Bill Brooks, Indianapolis	65	1,131	17.4	84	8
	Drew Hill, Houston[2]	65	1,112	17.1	81	5
	Steve Largent, Seattle[8]	70	1,070	15.3	38	9
	Art Monk, Washington[3]	73	1,068	14.6	69	4
	*Ernest Givins, Houston	61	1,062	17.4	60	3
	Cris Collinsworth, Cincinnati[4]	62	1,024	16.5	46	10
	Wesley Walker, N.Y. Jets[2]	49	1,016	20.7	83	12
	J.T. Smith, St. Louis	80	1,014	12.7	45	6
	Mark Bavaro, N.Y. Giants	66	1,001	15.2	41	4
1985	Steve Largent, Seattle[7]	79	1,287	16.3	43	6
	Mike Quick, Philadelphia[3]	73	1,247	17.1	99	11
	Art Monk, Washington[2]	91	1,226	13.5	53	2
	Wes Chandler, San Diego[4]	67	1,199	17.9	75	10
	Drew Hill, Houston	64	1,169	18.3	57	9
	James Lofton, Green Bay[5]	69	1,153	16.7	56	4
	Louis Lipps, Pittsburgh	59	1,134	19.2	51	12
	Cris Collinsworth, Cincinnati[3]	65	1,125	17.3	71	5
	Tony Hill, Dallas[3]	74	1,113	15.0	53	7
	Lionel James, San Diego	86	1,027	11.9	67	6
	Roger Craig, San Francisco	92	1,016	11.0	73	6
1984	Roy Green, St. Louis[2]	78	1,555	19.9	83	12
	John Stallworth, Pittsburgh[3]	80	1,395	17.4	51	11
	Mark Clayton, Miami	73	1,389	19.0	65	18
	Art Monk, Washington	106	1,372	12.9	72	7
	James Lofton, Green Bay[4]	62	1,361	22.0	79	7
	Mark Duper, Miami[2]	71	1,306	18.4	80	8
	Steve Watson, Denver[3]	69	1,170	17.0	73	7
	Steve Largent, Seattle[6]	74	1,164	15.7	65	12
	Tim Smith, Houston[2]	69	1,141	16.5	75	4
	Stacey Bailey, Atlanta	67	1,138	17.0	61	6
	Carlos Carson, Kansas City[2]	57	1,078	18.9	57	4
	Mike Quick, Philadelphia[2]	61	1,052	17.2	90	9
	Todd Christensen, L.A. Raiders[2]	80	1,007	12.6	38	7
	Kevin House, Tampa Bay[2]	76	1,005	13.2	55	5
	Ozzie Newsome, Cleveland[2]	89	1,001	11.2	52	5
1983	Mike Quick, Philadelphia	69	1,409	20.4	83	13
	Carlos Carson, Kansas City	80	1,351	16.9	50	7
	James Lofton, Green Bay[3]	58	1,300	22.4	74	8
	Todd Christensen, L.A. Raiders	92	1,247	13.6	45	12
	Roy Green, St. Louis	78	1,227	15.7	71	14
	Charlie Brown, Washington	78	1,225	15.7	75	8
	Tim Smith, Houston	83	1,176	14.2	47	6
	Kellen Winslow, San Diego[3]	88	1,172	13.3	46	8
	Earnest Gray, N.Y. Giants	78	1,139	14.6	62	5
	Steve Watson, Denver[2]	59	1,133	19.2	78	5
	Cris Collinsworth, Cincinnati[2]	66	1,130	17.1	63	5
	Steve Largent, Seattle[5]	72	1,074	14.9	46	11
	Mark Duper, Miami	51	1,003	19.7	85	10
1982	Wes Chandler, San Diego[3]	49	1,032	21.1	66	9
1981	Alfred Jenkins, Atlanta[2]	70	1,358	19.4	67	13
	James Lofton, Green Bay[2]	71	1,294	18.2	75	8
	Steve Watson, Denver	60	1,244	20.7	95	13
	Frank Lewis, Buffalo[2]	70	1,244	17.8	33	4
	Steve Largent, Seattle[4]	75	1,224	16.3	57	9
	Charlie Joiner, San Diego[4]	70	1,188	17.0	57	7
	Kevin House, Tampa Bay	56	1,176	21.0	84	9
	Wes Chandler, N.O.-San Diego[2]	69	1,142	16.6	51	6
	Dwight Clark, San Francisco	85	1,105	13.0	78	4
	John Stallworth, Pittsburgh[2]	63	1,098	17.4	55	5
	Kellen Winslow, San Diego[2]	88	1,075	12.2	67	10
	Pat Tilley, St. Louis	66	1,040	15.8	75	3
	Stanley Morgan, New England[2]	44	1,029	23.4	76	6
	Harold Carmichael, Philadelphia[3]	61	1,028	16.9	85	6
	Freddie Scott, Detroit	53	1,022	19.3	48	5
	*Cris Collinsworth, Cincinnati	67	1,009	15.1	74	8
	Joe Senser, Minnesota	79	1,004	12.7	53	8
	Ozzie Newsome, Cleveland	69	1,002	14.5	62	6
	Sammy White, Minnesota	66	1,001	15.2	53	3
1980	John Jefferson, San Diego[3]	82	1,340	16.3	58	13
	Kellen Winslow, San Diego	89	1,290	14.5	65	9
	James Lofton, Green Bay	71	1,226	17.3	47	4
	Charlie Joiner, San Diego[3]	71	1,132	15.9	51	4
	Ahmad Rashad, Minnesota[2]	69	1,095	15.9	76	5
	Steve Largent, Seattle[3]	66	1,064	16.1	67	6
	Tony Hill, Dallas[2]	60	1,055	17.6	58	8
	Alfred Jenkins, Atlanta	57	1,026	18.0	57	6
1979	Steve Largent, Seattle[2]	66	1,237	18.7	55	9
	John Stallworth, Pittsburgh	70	1,183	16.9	65	8
	Ahmad Rashad, Minnesota	80	1,156	14.5	52	9
	John Jefferson, San Diego[2]	61	1,090	17.9	65	10
	Frank Lewis, Buffalo	54	1,082	20.0	55	2
	Wes Chandler, New Orleans	65	1,069	16.4	85	6
	Tony Hill, Dallas	60	1,062	17.7	75	10
	Drew Pearson, Dallas[2]	55	1,026	18.7	56	8
	Wallace Francis, Atlanta	74	1,013	13.7	42	8
	Harold Jackson, New England[3]	45	1,013	22.5	59	7
	Charlie Joiner, San Diego[2]	72	1,008	14.0	39	4
	Stanley Morgan, New England	44	1,002	22.8	63	12
1978	Wesley Walker, N.Y. Jets	48	1,169	24.4	77	8
	Steve Largent, Seattle	71	1,168	16.5	57	8
	Harold Carmichael, Philadelphia[2]	55	1,072	19.5	56	8
	*John Jefferson, San Diego	56	1,001	17.9	46	13
1976	Roger Carr, Baltimore	43	1,112	25.9	79	11
	Cliff Branch, Oakland[2]	46	1,111	24.2	88	12
	Charlie Joiner, San Diego	50	1,056	21.1	81	7
1975	Ken Burrough, Houston	53	1,063	20.1	77	8
1974	Cliff Branch, Oakland	60	1,092	18.2	67	13
	Drew Pearson, Dallas	62	1,087	17.5	50	2
1973	Harold Carmichael, Philadelphia	67	1,116	16.7	73	9
1972	Harold Jackson, Philadelphia[2]	62	1,048	16.9	77	4
	John Gilliam, Minnesota	47	1,035	22.0	66	7
1971	Otis Taylor, Kansas City[2]	57	1,110	19.5	82	7
1970	Gene Washington, San Francisco	53	1,100	20.8	79	12
	Marlin Briscoe, Buffalo	57	1,036	18.2	48	8
	Dick Gordon, Chicago	71	1,026	14.5	69	13
	Gary Garrison, San Diego[2]	44	1,006	22.9	67	12
1969	Warren Wells, Oakland[2]	47	1,260	26.8	80	14
	Harold Jackson, Philadelphia	65	1,116	17.2	65	9
	Roy Jefferson, Pittsburgh[2]	67	1,079	16.1	63	9
	Dan Abramowicz, New Orleans	73	1,015	13.9	49	7
	Lance Alworth, San Diego[7]	64	1,003	15.7	76	4
1968	Lance Alworth, San Diego[6]	68	1,312	19.3	80	10
	Don Maynard, N.Y. Jets[5]	57	1,297	22.8	87	10
	George Sauer, N.Y. Jets[3]	66	1,141	17.3	43	3
	Warren Wells, Oakland	53	1,137	21.5	94	11
	Gary Garrison, San Diego	52	1,103	21.2	84	10
	Roy Jefferson, Pittsburgh	58	1,074	18.5	62	11
	Paul Warfield, Cleveland	50	1,067	21.3	65	12
	Homer Jones, N.Y. Giants[3]	45	1,057	23.5	84	7
	Fred Biletnikoff, Oakland	61	1,037	17.0	82	6
	Lance Rentzel, Dallas	54	1,009	18.7	65	6
1967	Don Maynard, N.Y. Jets[4]	71	1,434	20.2	75	10
	Ben Hawkins, Philadelphia	59	1,265	21.4	87	10

OUTSTANDING PERFORMERS

	Homer Jones, N.Y. Giants[2]	49	1,209	24.7	70	13
	Jackie Smith, St. Louis	56	1,205	21.5	76	9
	George Sauer, N.Y. Jets[2]	75	1,189	15.9	61	6
	Lance Alworth, San Diego[5]	52	1,010	19.4	71	9
1966	Lance Alworth, San Diego[4]	73	1,383	18.9	78	13
	Otis Taylor, Kansas City	58	1,297	22.4	89	8
	Pat Studstill, Detroit	67	1,266	18.9	99	5
	Bob Hayes, Dallas[2]	64	1,232	19.3	95	13
	Charlie Frazier, Houston	57	1,129	19.8	79	12
	Charley Taylor, Washington	72	1,119	15.5	86	12
	George Sauer, N.Y. Jets	63	1,081	17.2	77	5
	Homer Jones, N.Y. Giants	48	1,044	21.8	98	8
	Art Powell, Oakland[5]	53	1,026	19.4	46	11
1965	Lance Alworth, San Diego[3]	69	1,602	23.2	85	14
	Dave Parks, San Francisco	80	1,344	16.8	53	12
	Don Maynard, N.Y. Jets[3]	68	1,218	17.9	56	14
	Pete Retzlaff, Philadelphia	66	1,190	18.0	78	10
	Lionel Taylor, Denver[4]	85	1,131	13.3	63	6
	Tommy McDonald, Los Angeles[3]	67	1,036	15.5	51	9
	*Bob Hayes, Dallas	46	1,003	21.8	82	12
1964	Charley Hennigan, Houston[3]	101	1,546	15.3	53	8
	Art Powell, Oakland[4]	76	1,361	17.9	77	11
	Lance Alworth, San Diego[2]	61	1,235	20.2	82	13
	Johnny Morris, Chicago	93	1,200	12.9	63	10
	Elbert Dubenion, Buffalo	42	1,139	27.1	72	10
	Terry Barr, Detroit[2]	57	1,030	18.1	58	9
1963	Bobby Mitchell, Washington[2]	69	1,436	20.8	99	7
	Art Powell, Oakland[3]	73	1,304	17.9	85	16
	Buddy Dial, Pittsburgh[2]	60	1,295	21.6	83	9
	Lance Alworth, San Diego	61	1,205	19.8	85	11
	Del Shofner, N.Y. Giants[4]	64	1,181	18.5	70	9
	Lionel Taylor, Denver[3]	78	1,101	14.1	72	10
	Terry Barr, Detroit	66	1,086	16.5	75	13
	Charley Hennigan, Houston[2]	61	1,051	17.2	83	10
	Sonny Randle, St. Louis[2]	51	1,014	19.9	68	12
	Bake Turner, N.Y. Jets	71	1,009	14.2	53	6
1962	Bobby Mitchell, Washington	72	1,384	19.2	81	11
	Sonny Randle, St. Louis	63	1,158	18.4	86	7
	Tommy McDonald, Philadelphia[2]	58	1,146	19.8	60	10
	Del Shofner, N.Y. Giants[3]	53	1,133	21.4	69	12
	Art Powell, N.Y. Titans[2]	64	1,130	17.7	80	8
	Frank Clarke, Dall. Cowboys	47	1,043	22.2	66	14
	Don Maynard, N.Y. Titans[2]	56	1,041	18.6	86	8
1961	Charley Hennigan, Houston	82	1,746	21.3	80	12
	Lionel Taylor, Denver[2]	100	1,176	11.8	52	4
	Bill Groman, Houston[2]	50	1,175	23.5	80	17
	Tommy McDonald, Philadelphia	64	1,144	17.9	66	13
	Del Shofner, N.Y. Giants[2]	68	1,125	16.5	46	11
	Jim Phillips, Los Angeles	78	1,092	14.0	69	5
	*Mike Ditka, Chicago	56	1,076	19.2	76	12
	Dave Kocourek, San Diego	55	1,055	19.2	76	4
	Buddy Dial, Pittsburgh	53	1,047	19.8	88	12
	R.C. Owens, San Francisco	55	1,032	18.8	54	5
1960	*Bill Groman, Houston	72	1,473	20.5	92	12
	Raymond Berry, Baltimore	74	1,298	17.5	70	10
	Don Maynard, N.Y. Titans	72	1,265	17.6	65	6
	Lionel Taylor, Denver	92	1,235	13.4	80	12
	Art Powell, N.Y. Titans	69	1,167	16.9	76	14
1958	Del Shofner, Los Angeles	51	1,097	21.5	92	8
1956	Bill Howton, Green Bay[2]	55	1,188	21.6	66	12
	Harlon Hill, Chi. Bears[2]	47	1,128	24.0	79	11
1954	Bob Boyd, Los Angeles	53	1,212	22.9	80	6
	*Harlon Hill, Chi. Bears	45	1,124	25.0	76	12
1953	Pete Pihos, Philadelphia	63	1,049	16.7	59	10
1952	*Bill Howton, Green Bay	53	1,231	23.2	90	13
1951	Elroy (Crazylegs) Hirsch, Los Angeles	66	1,495	22.7	91	17
1950	Tom Fears, Los Angeles[2]	84	1,116	13.3	53	7
	Cloyce Box, Detroit	50	1,009	20.2	82	11
1949	Bob Mann, Detroit	66	1,014	15.4	64	4
	Tom Fears, Los Angeles	77	1,013	13.2	51	9
1945	Jim Benton, Cleveland	45	1,067	23.7	84	8
1942	Don Hutson, Green Bay	74	1,211	16.4	73	17

**First season of professional football.*

250 YARDS PASS RECEIVING IN A GAME

Date	Player, Team, Opponent	No.	Yards	TD
Dec. 12, 1999	Qadry Ismail, Baltimore vs. Pittsburgh	6	258	3
Dec. 18, 1995	Jerry Rice, San Francisco vs. Minnesota	14	289	3
Dec. 11, 1989	John Taylor, San Francisco vs. L.A. Rams	11	286	2
Nov. 26, 1989	Willie Anderson, L.A. Rams vs. New Orleans (OT)	15	336	1
Oct. 18, 1987	Steve Largent, Seattle vs. Detroit	15	261	3
Oct. 4, 1987	Anthony Allen, Washington vs. St. Louis	7	255	3
Dec. 22, 1985	Stephone Paige, Kansas City vs. San Diego	8	309	2
Dec. 20, 1982	Wes Chandler, San Diego vs. Cincinnati	10	260	2
Sept. 23, 1979	*Jerry Butler, Buffalo vs. N.Y. Jets	10	255	4
Nov. 4, 1962	Sonny Randle, St. Louis vs. N.Y. Giants	16	256	1
Oct. 28, 1962	Del Shofner, N.Y. Giants vs. Washington	11	269	1
Oct. 13, 1961	Charley Hennigan, Houston vs. Boston	13	272	1
Oct. 21, 1956	Billy Howton, Green Bay vs. Los Angeles	7	257	2
Dec. 3, 1950	Cloyce Box, Detroit vs. Baltimore	12	302	4
Nov. 22, 1945	Jim Benton, Cleveland vs. Detroit	10	303	1

**First season of professional football.*

2,000 COMBINED NET YARDS GAINED IN A SEASON

Year	Player, Team	Rushing Att.-Yds.	Pass Rec.	Punt Ret.	Kickoff Ret.	Fum. Ret.	Total Yds.
1999	Marshall Faulk, St. Louis	253-1,381	87-1,048	0-0	0-0	0-0	340-2,429
	*Edgerrin James, Indianapolis	369-1,553	62-586	0-0	0-0	2-0	433-2,139
	*Terrence Wilkins, Indianapolis.	1-2	42-565	41-388	51-1,134	1-0	136-2,089
	Glyn Milburn, Chicago	16-102	20-151	30-346	61-1,426	2-0	129-2,025
1998	Brian Mitchell, Washington	39-208	44-306	44-506	59-1,337	0-0	186-2,357
	Marshall Faulk, Indianapolis	324-1,319	86-908	0-0	0-0	2-13	412-2,240
	Terrell Davis, Denver	392-2,008	25-217	0-0	0-0	1-0	418-2,225
	Jamal Anderson, Atlanta	410-1,846	27-319	0-0	0-0	1-0	438-2,165
	Garrison Hearst, San Francisco	310-1,570	39-535	0-0	0-0	1-0	350-2,105
1997	Barry Sanders, Detroit	335-2,053	33-305	0-0	0-0	1-0	369-2,358
	Kevin Williams, Arizona	1-(-2)	20-273	40-462	59-1,458	1-0	121-2,191
	Brian Mitchell, Wash.	23-107	36-438	38-442	47-1,094	0-0	144-2,081
	Terrell Davis, Denver	369-1,750	42-287	0-0	0-0	2-(-7)	413-2,030
	Jermaine Lewis, Balt.	3-35	42-648	28-437	41-905	2-0	116-2,025
1995	Brian Mitchell, Wash.	46-301	38-324	25-315	55-1,408	0-0	164-2,348
	Emmitt Smith, Dallas	377-1,773	62-375	0-0	0-0	0-0	439-2,148
	Glyn Milburn, Denver	49-266	22-191	31-354	47-1,269	0-0	149-2,080
	Ernie Mills, Pittsburgh	5-39	39-679	0-0	54-1,306	0-0	98-2,024
1994	Brian Mitchell, Wash.	78-311	26-236	32-452	58-1,478	0-0	194-2,477
	Barry Sanders, Detroit	331-1,883	44-283	0-0	0-0	0-0	375-2,166
1992	Thurman Thomas, Buffalo	312-1,487	58-626	0-0	0-0	1-0	371-2,113
	Emmitt Smith, Dallas	373-1,713	59-335	0-0	0-0	1-0	433-2,048
	Barry Foster, Pittsburgh	390-1,690	36-344	0-0	0-0	2-(–20)	428-2,014
1991	Thurman Thomas, Buffalo	288-1,407	62-631	0-0	0-0	0-0	350-2,038
1990	Herschel Walker, Minnesota	184-770	35-315	0-0	44-966	4-0	267-2,051
1988	*Tim Brown, L.A. Raiders	14-50	43-725	49-444	41-1,098	7-0	154-2,317
	Roger Craig, San Fran.	310-1,502	76-534	0-0	2-32	2-0	390-2,068
	Eric Dickerson, Indianapolis	388-1,659	36-377	0-0	0-0	1-0	425-2,036
	Herschel Walker, Dallas	361-1,514	53-505	0-0	0-0	3-0	417-2,019
1986	Eric Dickerson, L.A. Rams	404-1,821	26-205	0-0	0-0	2-0	432-2,026
	Gary Anderson, San Diego	127-442	80-871	25-227	24-482	2-0	258-2,022
1985	Lionel James, San Diego	105-516	86-1,027	25-213	36-779	1-0	253-2,535
	Marcus Allen, L.A. Raiders	380-1,759	67-555	0-0	0-0	2-(–6)	449-2,308
	Roger Craig, San Fran.	214-1,050	92-1,016	0-0	0-0	0-0	306-2,066
	Walter Payton, Chicago	324-1,551	49-483	0-0	0-0	1-0	374-2,034
1984	Eric Dickerson, L.A. Rams	379-2,105	21-139	0-0	0-0	4-15	404-2,259
	James Wilder, Tampa Bay	407-1,544	85-685	0-0	0-0	4-0	496-2,229
	Walter Payton, Chicago	381-1,684	45-368	0-0	0-0	1-0	427-2,052
1983	*Eric Dickerson, L.A. Rams	390-1,808	51-404	0-0	0-0	1-0	442-2,212
	William Andrews, Atlanta	331-1,567	59-609	0-0	0-0	2-0	392-2,176
	Walter Payton, Chicago	314-1,421	53-607	0-0	0-0	2-0	369-2,028
1981	*James Brooks, San Diego	109-525	46-329	22-290	40-949	2-0	219-2,093
	William Andrews, Atlanta	289-1,301	81-735	0-0	0-0	0-0	370-2,036
1980	Bruce Harper, N.Y. Jets	45-126	50-634	28-242	49-1,070	3-0	175-2,072
1979	Wilbert Montgomery, Phil.	338-1,512	41-494	0-0	1-6	2-0	382-2,012
1978	Bruce Harper, N.Y. Jets	58-303	13-196	30-378	55-1,280	1-0	157-2,157
1977	Walter Payton, Chicago	339-1,852	27-269	0-0	2-95	5-0	373-2,216
	Terry Metcalf, St. Louis	149-739	34-403	14-108	32-772	1-0	230-2,022
1975	Terry Metcalf, St. Louis	165-816	43-378	23-285	35-960	2-23	268-2,462
	O.J. Simpson, Buffalo	329-1,817	28-426	0-0	0-0	1-0	358-2,243
1974	Mack Herron, New England	231-824	38-474	35-517	28-629	3-0	335-2,444
	Otis Armstrong, Denver	263-1,407	38-405	0-0	16-386	1-0	318-2,198
	Terry Metcalf, St. Louis	152-718	50-377	26-340	20-623	7-0	255-2,058
1973	O.J. Simpson, Buffalo	332-2,003	6-70	0-0	0-0	0-0	338-2,073
1966	Gale Sayers, Chicago	229-1,231	34-447	6-44	23-718	3-0	295-2,440
	Leroy Kelly, Cleveland	209-1,141	32-366	13-104	19-403	0-0	273-2,014
1965	*Gale Sayers, Chicago	166-867	29-507	16-238	21-660	4-0	236-2,272
1963	Timmy Brown, Philadelphia	192-841	36-487	16-152	33-945	2-3	279-2,428
	Jim Brown, Cleveland	291-1,863	24-268	0-0	0-0	0-0	315-2,131
1962	Timmy Brown, Philadelphia	137-545	52-849	6-81	30-831	4-0	229-2,306
	Dick Christy, N.Y. Titans	114-535	62-538	15-250	38-824	2-0	231-2,147
1961	Billy Cannon, Houston	200-948	43-586	9-70	18-439	2-0	272-2,043
1960	*Abner Haynes, Dall. Texans	156-875	55-576	14-215	19-434	4-0	248-2,100

**First season of professional football.*

300 COMBINED NET YARDS GAINED IN A GAME

Date	Player, Team, Opponent	No.	Yards	TD
Dec. 24, 1999	Jason Tucker, Dallas vs. New Orleans	13	331	1
Dec. 7, 1997	Jermaine Lewis, Baltimore vs. Seattle	10	308	3
Dec. 25, 1995	Kevin Williams, Dallas vs. Arizona	16	307	2

Dec. 10, 1995	Glyn Milburn, Denver vs. Seattle	33	404	0
Oct. 23, 1994	Tyrone Hughes, New Orleans vs. L.A. Rams	11	347	2
Dec. 11, 1989	John Taylor, San Francisco vs. L.A. Rams	14	321	2
Nov. 26, 1989	Willie Anderson, L.A. Rams vs. New Orleans (OT)	15	336	1
Nov. 28, 1988	*Tim Brown, L.A. Raiders vs. Seattle	12	308	1
Dec. 22, 1985	Stephone Paige, Kansas City vs. San Diego	8	309	2
Nov. 10, 1985	Lionel James, San Diego vs. L.A. Raiders (OT)	23	345	0
Sept. 22, 1985	Lionel James, San Diego vs. Cincinnati	20	316	2
Dec. 21, 1975	*Walter Payton, Chicago vs. New Orleans	32	300	1
Nov. 23, 1975	Greg Pruitt, Cleveland vs. Cincinnati	28	304	2
Nov. 1, 1970	Eugene (Mercury) Morris, Miami vs. Baltimore	17	302	0
Oct. 4, 1970	O.J. Simpson, Buffalo vs. N.Y. Jets	26	303	2
Dec. 6, 1969	Jerry LeVias, Houston vs. N.Y. Jets	18	329	1
Nov. 2, 1969	Travis Williams, Green Bay vs. Pittsburgh	11	314	3
Dec. 18, 1966	Gale Sayers, Chicago vs. Minnesota	20	339	2
Dec. 12, 1965	*Gale Sayers, Chicago vs. San Francisco	17	336	6
Nov. 17, 1963	Gary Ballman, Pittsburgh vs. Washington	12	320	2
Dec. 16, 1962	Timmy Brown, Philadelphia vs. St. Louis	19	341	2
Dec. 10, 1961	Billy Cannon, Houston vs. N.Y. Titans	32	373	5
Nov. 19, 1961	Jim Brown, Cleveland vs. Philadelphia	38	313	4
Dec. 3, 1950	Cloyce Box, Detroit vs. Baltimore	13	302	4
Oct. 29, 1950	Wally Triplett, Detroit vs. Los Angeles	11	331	1
Nov. 22, 1945	Jim Benton, Cleveland vs. Detroit	10	303	1

First season of professional football.

TOP 20 SCORERS

Player	Years	TD	FG	PAT	TP
George Blanda	26	9	335	943	2,002
Gary Anderson	18	0	439	631	1,948
Morten Andersen	18	0	416	592	1,840
Norm Johnson	18	0	366	638	1,736
Nick Lowery	18	0	383	562	1,711
Jan Stenerud	19	0	373	580	1,699
Eddie Murray	18	0	344	501	1,563
Pat Leahy	18	0	304	558	1,470
Al Del Greco	16	0	320	506	1,466
Jim Turner	16	1	304	521	1,439
Matt Bahr	17	0	300	522	1,422
Mark Moseley	16	0	300	482	1,382
Jim Bakken	17	0	282	534	1,380
Fred Cox	15	0	282	519	1,365
Lou Groza	17	1	234	641	1,349
Jim Breech	14	0	243	517	1,246
Chris Bahr	14	0	241	490	1,213
Kevin Butler	13	0	265	413	1,208
Pete Stoyanovich	11	0	267	394	1,195
Gino Cappelletti	11	42	176	346	1,130

Cappelletti's total includes 4 two-point conversions.

TOP 20 TOUCHDOWN SCORERS

Player	Years	Rush	Rec.	Total Returns	TD
Jerry Rice	15	10	169	1	180
Emmitt Smith	10	136	11	0	147
Marcus Allen	16	123	21	1	145
Jim Brown	9	106	20	0	126
Walter Payton	13	110	15	0	125
John Riggins	14	104	12	0	116
Cris Carter	13	0	114	1	115
Lenny Moore	12	63	48	2	113
Barry Sanders	10	99	10	0	109
Don Hutson	11	3	99	3	105
Steve Largent	14	1	100	0	101
Franco Harris	13	91	9	0	100
Eric Dickerson	11	90	6	0	96
Jim Taylor	10	83	10	0	93
Tony Dorsett	12	77	13	1	91
Bobby Mitchell	11	18	65	8	91
Leroy Kelly	10	74	13	3	90
Charley Taylor	13	11	79	0	90
Don Maynard	15	0	88	0	88
Lance Alworth	11	2	85	0	87
Andre Reed	15	1	86	0	87
Thurman Thomas	12	65	22	0	87

TOP 20 RUSHERS

Player	Years	Att.	Yards	Avg.	Long	TD
Walter Payton	13	3,838	16,726	4.4	76	110
Barry Sanders	10	3,062	15,269	5.0	85	99
Emmitt Smith	10	3,243	13,963	4.3	75	136
Eric Dickerson	11	2,996	13,259	4.4	85	90
Tony Dorsett	12	2,936	12,739	4.3	99	77
Jim Brown	9	2,359	12,312	5.2	80	106
Marcus Allen	16	3,022	12,243	4.1	61	123
Franco Harris	13	2,949	12,120	4.1	75	91
Thurman Thomas	12	2,849	11,938	4.2	80	65
John Riggins	14	2,916	11,352	3.9	66	104
O.J. Simpson	11	2,404	11,236	4.7	94	61
Ottis Anderson	14	2,562	10,273	4.0	76	81
Earl Campbell	8	2,187	9,407	4.3	81	74
Ricky Watters	8	2,272	9,083	4.0	57	70
Jim Taylor	10	1,941	8,597	4.4	84	83
Jerome Bettis	7	2,106	8,463	4.0	71	41
Joe Perry	14	1,737	8,378	4.8	78	53
Earnest Byner	14	2,095	8,261	3.9	54	56
Herschel Walker	12	1,954	8,225	4.2	91	61
Roger Craig	11	1,991	8,189	4.1	71	56

TOP 20 COMBINED YARDS GAINED

	Years	Tot.	Rush.	Rec.	Int. Ret.	Punt Ret.	Kickoff Ret.	Fumble Ret.
Walter Payton	13	21,803	16,726	4,538	0	0	539	0
Jerry Rice	15	19,075	627	18,442	0	0	6	0
Barry Sanders	10	18,308	15,269	2,921	0	0	118	0
Herschel Walker	12	18,168	8,225	4,859	0	0	5,084	0
Marcus Allen	16	17,648	12,243	5,411	0	0	0	-6
Brian Mitchell	10	16,905	1,751	2,087	0	3,476	9,586	5
Eric Metcalf	11	16,727	2,385	5,553	0	3,042	5,747	0
Emmitt Smith	10	16,691	13,963	2,728	0	0	0	0
Tony Dorsett	12	16,326	12,739	3,554	0	0	0	33
Thruman Thomas	12	16,279	11,938	4,341	0	0	0	0
Henry Ellard	16	15,718	50	13,777	0	1,527	364	0
Jim Brown	10	15,459	12,312	2,499	0	0	648	0
Eric Dickerson	11	15,411	13,259	2,137	0	0	0	15
Tim Brown	12	15,408	120	10,944	0	3,106	1,235	3
Irving Fryar	16	15,030	226	12,237	0	2,055	505	7
James Brooks	12	14,910	7,962	3,621	0	565	2,762	0
Franco Harris	13	14,622	12,120	2,287	0	0	233	–18
O.J. Simpson	11	14,368	11,236	2,142	0	0	990	0
James Lofton	16	14,277	246	14,004	0	0	0	27
Bobby Mitchell	11	14,078	2,735	7,954	0	699	2,690	0

TOP 20 PASSERS

Player	Years	Att.	Comp.	Pct. Comp.	Yards	Avg. Gain	TD	Pct. TD	Int.	Pct. Int.	Rating
Steve Young	15	4,149	2,667	64.3	33,124	7.98	232	5.6	107	2.6	96.8
Joe Montana	15	5,391	3,409	63.2	40,551	7.52	273	5.1	139	2.6	92.3
Brett Favre	9	4,352	2,659	61.1	30,894	7.10	235	5.4	141	3.2	87.1
Dan Marino	17	8,358	4,967	59.4	61,361	7.34	420	5.0	252	3.0	86.4
Mark Brunell	6	2,160	1,297	60.0	15,572	7.21	86	4.0	52	2.4	85.4
Jim Kelly	11	4,779	2,874	60.1	35,467	7.42	237	5.0	175	3.7	84.4
Roger Staubach	11	2,958	1,685	57.0	22,700	7.67	153	5.2	109	3.7	83.4
Neil Lomax	8	3,153	1,817	57.6	22,771	7.22	136	4.3	90	2.9	82.7
Troy Aikman	11	4,453	2,742	61.6	31,310	7.03	158	3.5	127	2.9	82.6
Sonny Jurgensen	18	4,262	2,433	57.1	32,224	7.56	255	6.0	189	4.4	82.6
Len Dawson	19	3,741	2,136	57.1	28,711	7.67	239	6.4	183	4.9	82.6
Neil O'Donnell	10	3,057	1,766	57.8	20,408	6.68	114	3.7	62	2.0	82.0
Ken Anderson	16	4,475	2,654	59.3	32,838	7.34	197	4.4	160	3.6	81.9
Bernie Kosar	12	3,365	1,994	59.3	23,301	6.92	124	3.7	87	2.6	81.8
Danny White	13	2,950	1,761	59.7	21,959	7.44	155	5.3	132	4.5	81.7
Dave Krieg	19	5,311	3,105	58.5	38,147	7.18	261	4.9	199	3.7	81.5
Randall Cunningham	14	4,075	2,301	56.5	28,557	7.01	198	4.9	128	3.1	81.4
Chris Chandler	12	2,894	1,668	57.6	20,865	7.21	135	4.7	101	3.5	81.2
Steve Beuerlein	11	2,615	1,469	56.2	19,002	7.27	120	4.6	84	3.2	81.1
Boomer Esiason	14	5,205	2,969	57.0	37,920	7.29	247	4.7	184	3.5	81.1

1,500 or more attempts. The passing ratings are based on performance standards established for completion percentage, interception percentage, touchdown percentage, and average gain. Please consult page 16 for more information.

TOP 20 LEADERS IN PASSES COMPLETED

Dan Marino	4,967
John Elway	4,123
Warren Moon	3,973
Fran Tarkenton	3,686
Joe Montana	3,409
Dan Fouts	3,297
Dave Krieg	3,105
Boomer Esiason	2,969
Steve DeBerg	2,874
Jim Kelly	2,874
Jim Everett	2,841
Johnny Unitas	2,830
Troy Aikman	2,742
Steve Young	2,667
Brett Favre	2,659
Ken Anderson	2,654

Jim Hart 2,593
Phil Simms 2,576
Vinny Testaverde 2,569
John Brodie 2,469

TOP 20 LEADERS IN PASSING YARDS

Dan Marino 61,361
John Elway 51,475
Warren Moon 49,117
Fran Tarkenton 47,003
Dan Fouts 43,040
Joe Montana 40,551
Johnny Unitas 40,239
Dave Krieg 38,147
Boomer Esiason 37,920
Jim Kelly 35,467
Jim Everett 34,837
Jim Hart 34,665
Steve DeBerg 34,241
John Hadl 33,503
Phil Simms 33,462
Steve Young 33,124
Ken Anderson 32,838
Vinny Testaverde 32,575
Sonny Jurgensen 32,224
John Brodie 31,548

TOP 20 LEADERS IN TOUCHDOWN PASSES

Dan Marino 420
Fran Tarkenton 342
John Elway 300
Warren Moon 290
Johnny Unitas 290
Joe Montana 273
Dave Krieg 261
Sonny Jurgensen 255
Dan Fouts 254
Boomer Esiason 247
John Hadl 244
Len Dawson 239
Jim Kelly 237
George Blanda 236
Brett Favre 235
Steve Young 232
John Brodie 214
Terry Bradshaw 212
Y.A. Tittle 212
Jim Hart 209

TOP 20 PASS RECEIVERS

Player	Years	No.	Yards	Avg.	Long	TD
Jerry Rice	15	1,206	18,442	15.3	96	169
Andre Reed	15	941	13,095	13.9	83	86
Art Monk	16	940	12,721	13.5	79	68
Cris Carter	13	924	11,688	12.6	80	114
Steve Largent	14	819	13,089	16.0	74	100
Henry Ellard	16	814	13,777	16.9	81	65
Irving Fryar	16	810	12,237	15.1	80	79
Tim Brown	12	770	10,944	14.2	80	75
James Lofton	16	764	14,004	18.3	80	75
Michael Irvin	12	750	11,904	15.9	87	65
Charlie Joiner	18	750	12,146	16.2	87	65
Andre Rison	11	702	9,599	13.7	80	78
Gary Clark	11	699	10,856	15.5	84	65
Ozzie Newsome	13	662	7,980	12.1	74	47
Charley Taylor	13	649	9,110	14.0	88	79
Drew Hill	14	634	9,831	15.5	81	60
Don Maynard	15	633	11,834	18.7	87	88
Raymond Berry	13	631	9,275	14.7	70	68
Rob Moore	10	628	9,368	14.9	71	49
Herman Moore	9	626	8,664	13.8	93	59

TOP 20 LEADERS IN RECEPTION YARDS

Jerry Rice 18,442
James Lofton 14,004
Henry Ellard 13,777
Andre Reed 13,095
Steve Largent 13,089
Art Monk 12,721
Irving Fryar 12,237
Charlie Joiner 12,146
Michael Irvin 11,904
Don Maynard 11,834
Cris Carter 11,688
Tim Brown 10,944
Gary Clark 10,856
Stanley Morgan 10,716
Harold Jackson 10,372
Lance Alworth 10,266
Drew Hill 9,831
Andre Rison 9,599
Rob Moore 9,368
Raymond Berry 9,275

TOP 20 INTERCEPTORS

Player	Years	No.	Yards	Avg.	Long	TD
Paul Krause	16	81	1,185	14.6	81	3
Emlen Tunnell	14	79	1,282	16.2	55	4
Dick (Night Train) Lane	14	68	1,207	17.8	80	5
Ken Riley	15	65	596	9.2	66	5
Ronnie Lott	14	63	730	11.6	83	5
Dick LeBeau	13	62	762	12.3	70	3
Dave Brown	15	62	698	11.3	90	5
Emmitt Thomas	13	58	937	16.2	73	5
Bobby Boyd	9	57	994	17.4	74	4
Johnny Robinson	12	57	741	13.0	57	1
Mel Blount	14	57	736	12.9	52	2
Everson Walls	13	57	504	8.8	40	1
Lem Barney	11	56	1,077	19.2	71	7
Pat Fischer	17	56	941	16.8	69	4
Eugene Robinson	15	56	762	13.6	49	1
Willie Brown	16	54	472	8.7	45	2
Rod Woodson	13	54	1,163	21.5	66	9
Bobby Dillon	8	52	976	18.8	61	5
Jack Butler	9	52	827	15.9	52	4
Larry Wilson	13	52	800	15.4	96	5
Jim Patton	12	52	712	13.7	51	2
Mel Renfro	14	52	626	12.0	90	3

TOP 20 PUNTERS

Player	Years	No.	Yards	Avg.	Long	Blk.
Sammy Baugh	16	338	15,245	45.1	85	9
Tommy Davis	11	511	22,833	44.7	82	2
Darren Bennett	5	432	19,244	44.5	66	1
Yale Lary	11	503	22,279	44.3	74	4
Tom Rouen	7	470	20,784	44.2	76	3
Bob Scarpitto	8	283	12,408	43.8	87	4
Horace Gillom	7	385	16,872	43.8	80	5
Tom Tupa	11	447	19,583	43.8	73	1
Jerry Norton	11	358	15,671	43.8	78	2
Matt Turk	5	388	16,981	43.8	69	2
David Lewis	4	285	12,447	43.7	63	0
Greg Montgomery	9	524	22,831	43.6	77	8
Don Chandler	12	660	28,678	43.5	90	4
Sean Landeta	15	1,033	44,881	43.4	74	6
Rick Tuten	11	741	32,190	43.4	73	2
Craig Hentrich	6	448	19,437	43.4	78	2
Rohn Stark	16	1,141	49,471	43.4	72	7
Josh Miller	4	284	12,310	43.3	75	0
Reggie Roby	16	992	42,951	43.3	77	5
Jerrel Wilson	16	1,072	46,139	43.0	72	12

250 or more punts.

TOP 20 PUNT RETURNERS

Player	Years	No.	Yards	Avg.	Long	TD
George McAfee	8	112	1,431	12.8	74	2
Jack Christiansen	8	85	1,084	12.8	89	8
Claude Gibson	5	110	1,381	12.6	85	3
Darrien Gordon	6	219	2,726	12.4	94	6
Karl Williams	4	89	1,107	12.4	88	2
Bill Dudley	9	124	1,515	12.2	96	3
Rick Upchurch	9	248	3,008	12.1	92	8
Desmond Howard	8	182	2,189	12.0	92	7
Reggie Barlow	4	117	1,381	11.8	85	2
Billy Johnson	14	282	3,317	11.8	87	6
Mack Herron	3	84	982	11.7	66	0
Billy Thompson	13	157	1,814	11.6	60	0
Henry Ellard	16	135	1,527	11.3	83	4
Rodger Bird	3	94	1,063	11.3	78	0
Bosh Pritchard	6	95	1,072	11.3	81	2
Terry Metcalf	6	84	936	11.1	69	1
Bob Hayes	11	104	1,158	11.1	90	3
Floyd Little	9	81	893	11.0	72	2
Louis Lipps	9	112	1,234	11.0	76	3
Bobby Joe Edmonds	5	134	1,471	11.0	75	1

75 or more returns.

TOP 20 KICKOFF RETURNERS

Player	Years	No.	Yards	Avg.	Long	TD
Gale Sayers	7	91	2,781	30.6	103	6
Lynn Chandnois	7	92	2,720	29.6	93	3
Abe Woodson	9	193	5,538	28.7	105	5
Claude (Buddy) Young	6	90	2,514	27.9	104	2
Travis Williams	5	102	2,801	27.5	105	6
Joe Arenas	7	139	3,798	27.3	96	1
Clarence Davis	8	79	2,140	27.1	76	0
Steve Van Buren	8	76	2,030	26.7	98	3
Lenny Lyles	12	81	2,161	26.7	103	3
Eugene (Mercury) Morris	8	111	2,947	26.5	105	3
Tremain Mack	3	96	2,547	26.5	99	2
Bobby Jancik	6	158	4,185	26.5	61	0
Mel Renfro	14	85	2,246	26.4	100	2
Bobby Mitchell	11	102	2,690	26.4	98	5
Ollie Matson	14	143	3,746	26.2	105	6
Alvin Haymond	10	170	4,438	26.1	98	2
Noland Smith	3	82	2,137	26.1	106	1
Al Nelson	9	101	2,625	26.0	78	0
Timmy Brown	11	184	4,781	26.0	105	5
Vic Washington	6	129	3,341	25.9	98	1

75 or more returns.

TOP 20 LEADERS IN SACKS

Player	*Years	No.
Reggie White	14	192.5
Bruce Smith	15	171.0
Kevin Greene	15	160.0
Chris Doleman	15	150.5
Richard Dent	15	137.5
Leslie O'Neal	13	132.5
Lawrence Taylor	12	132.5
Rickey Jackson	14	128.0
Derrick Thomas	11	126.5
Clyde Simmons	14	121.0
Sean Jones	13	113.0
Greg Townsend	13	109.5
Pat Swilling	12	107.5
John Randle	10	106.0
Neil Smith	12	104.5
Jim Jeffcoat	15	102.5
William Fuller	13	100.5
Charles Haley	12	100.5
Andre Tippett	11	100.0
Simon Fletcher	11	97.5
Jacob Green	11	97.5
Dexter Manley	10	97.5

**Years played since 1982 when sacks became an official statistic.*

POSTSEASON LEADERS

TOP 10 RUSHERS

Player	Att.	Yards	Avg.	Long	TD
Emmitt Smith	349	1,586	4.5	65	19
Franco Harris	400	1,556	3.9	50	16
Thurman Thomas	339	1,442	4.3	40	16
Tony Dorsett	302	1,383	4.6	53	9
Marcus Allen	267	1,347	5.0	74	11
Terrell Davis	204	1,140	5.6	62	12
John Riggins	251	996	4.0	43	12
Larry Csonka	225	891	4.0	49	9
Chuck Foreman	229	860	3.8	62	7
Roger Craig	208	841	4.0	80	7

TOP 10 POSTSEASON PASSERS

Player	Att.	Comp.	Pct. Comp.	Yards	Avg. Gain	TD	Pct. TD	Int.	Pct. Int.	Rating
Bart Starr	213	130	61.0	1,753	8.23	15	7.0	3	1.4	104.8
Joe Montana	734	460	62.7	5,772	7.86	45	6.1	21	2.9	95.6
Ken Anderson	166	110	66.3	1,321	7.96	9	5.4	6	3.6	93.5
Joe Theismann	211	128	60.7	1,782	8.45	11	5.2	7	3.3	91.4
Brett Favre	449	270	60.1	3,390	7.55	25	5.6	12	2.7	91.1
Troy Aikman	502	320	63.8	3,849	7.67	23	4.6	17	3.4	88.3
Steve Young	471	292	62.0	3,326	7.06	20	4.2	13	2.8	85.8
Warren Moon	403	259	64.3	2,870	7.12	17	4.2	14	3.5	84.9
Ken Stabler	351	203	57.8	2,641	7.52	19	5.4	13	3.7	84.2
Bernie Kosar	270	152	56.3	1,953	7.23	16	5.9	10	3.7	83.5

150 or more attempts. The passer ratings are based on performance standards established for completion percentage, interception percentage, touchdown percentage, and average gain. Please consult page 16 for more information.

TOP 10 POSTSEASON PASS RECEIVERS

Player	No.	Yards	Avg.	Long	TD
Jerry Rice	124	1,811	14.6	72	19
Michael Irvin	87	1,315	15.1	53	8
Andre Reed	85	1,229	14.5	72	9
Thurman Thomas	76	672	8.8	27	5
Cliff Branch	73	1,289	17.7	72	5
Fred Biletnikoff	70	1,167	16.7	57	10
Art Monk	69	1,062	15.4	48	7
Drew Pearson	67	1,105	16.5	83	8
Tony Nathan	65	649	10.0	39	2
Roger Craig	63	606	9.6	40	2

TOP 10 POSTSEASON INTERCEPTION LEADERS

Player	Interceptions
Ronnie Lott	9
Bill Simpson	9
Charlie Waters	9
Lester Hayes	8
Willie Brown	7
Dennis Thurman	7
Bobby Bryant	6
Eric Davis	6
Glen Edwards	6
Darrell Green	6
Cliff Harris	6
Vernon Perry	6

TOP 10 POSTSEASON SACK LEADERS

Player	Sacks
Bruce Smith	14.5
Reggie White	12.0
Charles Haley	11.0
Richard Dent	10.5
Charles Mann	10.0
Tony Tolbert	10.0
Neil Smith	9.5
Trace Armstrong	9.0
Jeff Wright	9.0
Kevin Greene	8.5

YEARLY STATISTICAL LEADERS

ANNUAL SCORING LEADERS

Year	Player, Team	TD	FG	PAT	TP
1999	Mike Vanderjagt, Indianapolis, AFC	0	34	43	145
	Jeff Wilkins, St. Louis, NFC	0	20	64	124
1998	Gary Anderson, Minnesota, NFC	0	35	59	164
	Steve Christie, Buffalo, AFC	0	33	41	140
1997	Mike Hollis, Jacksonville, AFC	0	31	41	134
	Richie Cunningham, Dallas, NFC	0	34	24	126
1996	John Kasay, Carolina, NFC	0	37	34	145
	Cary Blanchard, Indianapolis, AFC	0	36	27	135
1995	Emmitt Smith, Dallas, NFC	25	0	0	150
	Norm Johnson, Pittsburgh, AFC	0	34	39	141
1994	John Carney, San Diego, AFC	0	34	33	135
	Fuad Reveiz, Minnesota, NFC	0	34	30	132
1993	Jeff Jaeger, L.A. Raiders, AFC	0	35	27	132
	Jason Hanson, Detroit, NFC	0	34	28	130
1992	Pete Stoyanovich, Miami, AFC	0	30	34	124
	Morten Andersen, New Orleans, NFC	0	29	33	120
	Chip Lohmiller, Washington, NFC	0	30	30	120
1991	Chip Lohmiller, Washington, NFC	0	31	56	149
	Pete Stoyanovich, Miami, AFC	0	31	28	121
1990	Nick Lowery, Kansas City, AFC	0	34	37	139
	Chip Lohmiller, Washington, NFC	0	30	41	131
1989	Mike Cofer, San Francisco, NFC	0	29	49	136
	*David Treadwell, Denver, AFC	0	27	39	120
1988	Scott Norwood, Buffalo, AFC	0	32	33	129
	Mike Cofer, San Francisco, NFC	0	27	40	121
1987	Jerry Rice, San Francisco, NFC	23	0	0	138
	Jim Breech, Cincinnati, AFC	0	24	25	97
1986	Tony Franklin, New England, AFC	0	32	44	140
	Kevin Butler, Chicago, NFC	0	28	36	120
1985	*Kevin Butler, Chicago, NFC	0	31	51	144
	Gary Anderson, Pittsburgh, AFC	0	33	40	139
1984	Ray Wersching, San Francisco, NFC	0	25	56	131
	Gary Anderson, Pittsburgh, AFC	0	24	45	117
1983	Mark Moseley, Washington, NFC	0	33	62	161
	Gary Anderson, Pittsburgh, AFC	0	27	38	119
1982	*Marcus Allen, L.A. Raiders, AFC	14	0	0	84
	Wendell Tyler, L.A. Rams, NFC	13	0	0	78
1981	Ed Murray, Detroit, NFC	0	25	46	121
	Rafael Septien, Dallas, NFC	0	27	40	121
	Jim Breech, Cincinnati, AFC	0	22	49	115
	Nick Lowery, Kansas City, AFC	0	26	37	115
1980	John Smith, New England, AFC	0	26	51	129
	*Ed Murray, Detroit, NFC	0	27	35	116
1979	John Smith, New England, AFC	0	23	46	115
	Mark Moseley, Washington, NFC	0	25	39	114
1978	*Frank Corral, Los Angeles, NFC	0	29	31	118
	Pat Leahy, N.Y. Jets, AFC	0	22	41	107
1977	Errol Mann, Oakland, AFC	0	20	39	99
	Walter Payton, Chicago, NFC	16	0	0	96
1976	Toni Linhart, Baltimore, AFC	0	20	49	109
	Mark Moseley, Washington, NFC	0	22	31	97
1975	O.J. Simpson, Buffalo, AFC	23	0	0	138
	Chuck Foreman, Minnesota, NFC	22	0	0	132
1974	Chester Marcol, Green Bay, NFC	0	25	19	94
	Roy Gerela, Pittsburgh, AFC	0	20	33	93
1973	David Ray, Los Angeles, NFC	0	30	40	130
	Roy Gerela, Pittsburgh, AFC	0	29	36	123
1972	*Chester Marcol, Green Bay, NFC	0	33	29	128
	Bobby Howfield, N.Y. Jets, AFC	0	27	40	121
1971	Garo Yepremian, Miami, AFC	0	28	33	117
	Curt Knight, Washington, NFC	0	29	27	114
1970	Fred Cox, Minnesota, NFC	0	30	35	125
	Jan Stenerud, Kansas City, AFC	0	30	26	116
1969	Jim Turner, N.Y. Jets, AFL	0	32	33	129
	Fred Cox, Minnesota, NFL	0	26	43	121
1968	Jim Turner, N.Y. Jets, AFL	0	34	43	145
	Leroy Kelly, Cleveland, NFL	20	0	0	120
1967	Jim Bakken, St. Louis, NFL	0	27	36	117
	George Blanda, Oakland, AFL	0	20	56	116
1966	Gino Cappelletti, Boston, AFL	6	16	35	119
	Bruce Gossett, Los Angeles, NFL	0	28	29	113
1965	*Gale Sayers, Chicago, NFL	22	0	0	132
	Gino Cappelletti, Boston, AFL	9	17	27	132
1964	Gino Cappelletti, Boston, AFL	7	25	36	#155
	Lenny Moore, Baltimore, NFL	20	0	0	120
1963	Gino Cappelletti, Boston, AFL	2	22	35	113
	Don Chandler, N.Y. Giants, NFL	0	18	52	106
1962	Gene Mingo, Denver, AFL	4	27	32	137
	Jim Taylor, Green Bay, NFL	19	0	0	114
1961	Gino Cappelletti, Boston, AFL	8	17	48	147
	Paul Hornung, Green Bay, NFL	10	15	41	146
1960	Paul Hornung, Green Bay, NFL	15	15	41	176
	*Gene Mingo, Denver, AFL	6	18	33	123
1959	Paul Hornung, Green Bay	7	7	31	94
1958	Jim Brown, Cleveland	18	0	0	108
1957	Sam Baker, Washington	1	14	29	77
	Lou Groza, Cleveland	0	15	32	77
1956	Bobby Layne, Detroit	5	12	33	99
1955	Doak Walker, Detroit	7	9	27	96
1954	Bobby Walston, Philadelphia	11	4	36	114
1953	Gordy Soltau, San Francisco	6	10	48	114
1952	Gordy Soltau, San Francisco	7	6	34	94
1951	Elroy (Crazylegs) Hirsch, Los Angeles	17	0	0	102
1950	*Doak Walker, Detroit	11	8	38	128
1949	Pat Harder, Chi. Cardinals	8	3	45	102
	Gene Roberts, N.Y. Giants	17	0	0	102
1948	Pat Harder, Chi. Cardinals	6	7	53	110
1947	Pat Harder, Chi. Cardinals	7	7	39	102
1946	Ted Fritsch, Green Bay	10	9	13	100
1945	Steve Van Buren, Philadelphia	18	0	2	110
1944	Don Hutson, Green Bay	9	0	31	85
1943	Don Hutson, Green Bay	12	3	36	117
1942	Don Hutson, Green Bay	17	1	33	138
1941	Don Hutson, Green Bay	12	1	20	95
1940	Don Hutson, Green Bay	7	0	15	57
1939	Andy Farkas, Washington	11	0	2	68
1938	Clarke Hinkle, Green Bay	7	3	7	58
1937	Jack Manders, Chi. Bears	5	8	15	69
1936	Earl (Dutch) Clark, Detroit	7	4	19	73
1935	Earl (Dutch) Clark, Detroit	6	1	16	55
1934	Jack Manders, Chi. Bears	3	10	31	79
1933	Ken Strong, N.Y. Giants	6	5	13	64
	Glenn Presnell, Portsmouth	6	6	10	64
1932	Earl (Dutch) Clark, Portsmouth	6	3	10	55

**First season of professional football.*
#Cappelletti's total includes a two-point conversion.

ANNUAL TOUCHDOWN LEADERS

Year	Player, Team	TD	Rush	Pass	Ret.
1999	Stephen Davis, Washington, NFC	17	17	0	0
	*Edgerrin James, Indianapolis, AFC	17	13	4	0
1998	Terrell Davis, Denver, AFC	23	21	2	0
	*Randy Moss, Minnesota, NFC	17	0	17	0
1997	Karim Abdul-Jabbar, Miami, AFC	16	15	1	0
	Barry Sanders, Detroit, NFC	14	11	3	0
1996	Terry Allen, Washington, NFC	21	21	0	0
	Curtis Martin, New England, AFC	17	14	3	0
1995	Emmitt Smith, Dallas, NFC	25	25	0	0
	Carl Pickens, Cincinnati, AFC	17	0	17	0
1994	Emmitt Smith, Dallas, NFC	22	21	1	0
	*Marshall Faulk, Indianapolis, AFC	12	11	1	0
	Natrone Means, San Diego, AFC	12	12	0	0
1993	Jerry Rice, San Francisco, NFC	16	1	15	0
	Marcus Allen, Kansas City, AFC	15	12	3	0
1992	Emmitt Smith, Dallas, NFC	19	18	1	0
	Thurman Thomas, Buffalo, AFC	12	9	3	0
1991	Barry Sanders, Detroit, NFC	17	16	1	0
	Mark Clayton, Miami, AFC	12	0	12	0
	Thurman Thomas, Buffalo, AFC	12	7	5	0
1990	Barry Sanders, Detroit, NFC	16	13	3	0
	Derrick Fenner, Seattle, AFC	15	14	1	0
1989	Dalton Hilliard, New Orleans, NFC	18	13	5	0
	Christian Okoye, Kansas City, AFC	12	12	0	0
	Thurman Thomas, Buffalo, AFC	12	6	6	0
1988	Greg Bell, L.A. Rams, NFC	18	16	2	0
	Eric Dickerson, Indianapolis, AFC	15	14	1	0
	*Ickey Woods, Cincinnati, AFC	15	15	0	0
1987	Jerry Rice, San Francisco, NFC	23	1	22	0
	Johnny Hector, N.Y. Jets, AFC	11	11	0	0
1986	George Rogers, Washington, NFC	18	18	0	0
	Sammy Winder, Denver, AFC	14	9	5	0
1985	Joe Morris, N.Y. Giants, NFC	21	21	0	0
	Louis Lipps, Pittsburgh, AFC	15	1	12	2
1984	Marcus Allen, L.A. Raiders, AFC	18	13	5	0
	Mark Clayton, Miami, AFC	18	0	18	0
	Eric Dickerson, L.A. Rams, NFC	14	14	0	0
	John Riggins, Washington, NFC	14	14	0	0
1983	John Riggins, Washington, NFC	24	24	0	0
	Pete Johnson, Cincinnati, AFC	14	14	0	0
	*Curt Warner, Seattle, AFC	14	13	1	0
1982	*Marcus Allen, L.A. Raiders, AFC	14	11	3	0
	Wendell Tyler, L.A. Rams, NFC	13	9	4	0
1981	Chuck Muncie, San Diego, AFC	19	19	0	0
	Wendell Tyler, Los Angeles, NFC	17	12	5	0

1980	*Billy Sims, Detroit, NFC	16	13	3	0
	Earl Campbell, Houston, AFC	13	13	0	0
	*Curtis Dickey, Baltimore, AFC	13	11	2	0
	John Jefferson, San Diego, AFC	13	0	13	0
1979	Earl Campbell, Houston, AFC	19	19	0	0
	Walter Payton, Chicago, NFC	16	14	2	0
1978	David Sims, Seattle, AFC	15	14	1	0
	Terdell Middleton, Green Bay, NFC	12	11	1	0
1977	Walter Payton, Chicago, NFC	16	14	2	0
	Nat Moore, Miami, AFC	13	1	12	0
1976	Chuck Foreman, Minnesota, NFC	14	13	1	0
	Franco Harris, Pittsburgh, AFC	14	14	0	0
1975	O.J. Simpson, Buffalo, AFC	23	16	7	0
	Chuck Foreman, Minnesota, NFC	22	13	9	0
1974	Chuck Foreman, Minnesota, NFC	15	9	6	0
	Cliff Branch, Oakland, AFC	13	0	13	0
1973	Larry Brown, Washington, NFC	14	8	6	0
	Floyd Little, Denver, AFC	13	12	1	0
1972	Emerson Boozer, N.Y. Jets, AFC	14	11	3	0
	Ron Johnson, N.Y. Giants, NFC	14	9	5	0
1971	Duane Thomas, Dallas, NFC	13	11	2	0
	Leroy Kelly, Cleveland, AFC	12	10	2	0
1970	Dick Gordon, Chicago, NFC	13	0	13	0
	MacArthur Lane, St. Louis, NFC	13	11	2	0
	Gary Garrison, San Diego, AFC	12	0	12	0
1969	Warren Wells, Oakland, AFL	14	0	14	0
	Tom Matte, Baltimore, NFL	13	11	2	0
	Lance Rentzel, Dallas, NFL	13	0	12	1
1968	Leroy Kelly, Cleveland, NFL	20	16	4	0
	Warren Wells, Oakland, AFL	12	1	11	0
1967	Homer Jones, N.Y. Giants, NFL	14	1	13	0
	Emerson Boozer, N.Y. Jets, AFL	13	10	3	0
1966	Leroy Kelly, Cleveland, NFL	16	15	1	0
	Dan Reeves, Dallas, NFL	16	8	8	0
	Lance Alworth, San Diego, AFL	13	0	13	0
1965	*Gale Sayers, Chicago, NFL	22	14	6	2
	Lance Alworth, San Diego, AFL	14	0	14	0
	Don Maynard, N.Y. Jets, AFL	14	0	14	0
1964	Lenny Moore, Baltimore, NFL	20	16	3	1
	Lance Alworth, San Diego, AFL	15	2	13	0
1963	Art Powell, Oakland, AFL	16	0	16	0
	Jim Brown, Cleveland, NFL	15	12	3	0
1962	Abner Haynes, Dallas, AFL	19	13	6	0
	Jim Taylor, Green Bay, NFL	19	19	0	0
1961	Bill Groman, Houston, AFL	18	1	17	0
	Jim Taylor, Green Bay, NFL	16	15	1	0
1960	Paul Hornung, Green Bay, NFL	15	13	2	0
	Sonny Randle, St. Louis, NFL	15	0	15	0
	Art Powell, N.Y. Titans, AFL	14	0	14	0
1959	Raymond Berry, Baltimore	14	0	14	0
	Jim Brown, Cleveland	14	14	0	0
1958	Jim Brown, Cleveland	18	17	1	0
1957	Lenny Moore, Baltimore	11	3	7	1
1956	Rick Casares, Chi. Bears	14	12	2	0
1955	*Alan Ameche, Baltimore	9	9	0	0
	Harlon Hill, Chi. Bears	9	0	9	0
1954	*Harlon Hill, Chi. Bears	12	0	12	0
1953	Joseph Perry, San Francisco	13	10	3	0
1952	Cloyce Box, Detroit	15	0	15	0
1951	Elroy (Crazylegs) Hirsch, Los Angeles	17	0	17	0
1950	Bob Shaw, Chi. Cardinals	12	0	12	0
1949	Gene Roberts, N.Y. Giants	17	9	8	0
1948	Mal Kutner, Chi. Cardinals	15	1	14	0
1947	Steve Van Buren, Philadelphia	14	13	0	1
1946	Ted Fritsch, Green Bay	10	9	1	0
1945	Steve Van Buren, Philadelphia	18	15	2	1
1944	Don Hutson, Green Bay	9	0	9	0
	Bill Paschal, N.Y. Giants	9	9	0	0
1943	Don Hutson, Green Bay	12	0	11	1
	*Bill Paschal, N.Y. Giants	12	10	2	0
1942	Don Hutson, Green Bay	17	0	17	0
1941	Don Hutson, Green Bay	12	2	10	0
	George McAfee, Chi. Bears	12	6	3	3
1940	John Drake, Cleveland	9	9	0	0
	Richard Todd, Washington	9	4	4	1
1939	Andrew Farkas, Washington	11	5	5	1
1938	Don Hutson, Green Bay	9	0	9	0
1937	Cliff Battles, Washington	7	5	1	1
	Clarke Hinkle, Green Bay	7	5	2	0
	Don Hutson, Green Bay	7	0	7	0
1936	Don Hutson, Green Bay	9	0	8	1
1935	*Don Hutson, Green Bay	7	0	6	1
1934	*Beattie Feathers, Chi. Bears	9	8	1	0
1933	*Charlie (Buckets) Goldenberg, Green Bay	7	4	1	2
	John (Shipwreck) Kelly, Brooklyn	7	2	3	2
	*Elvin (Kink) Richards, N.Y. Giants	7	4	3	0
1932	Earl (Dutch) Clark, Portsmouth	6	3	3	0
	Red Grange, Chi. Bears	6	3	3	0

First season of professional football.

ANNUAL LEADERS—MOST FIELD GOALS MADE

Year	Player, Team	Att.	Made	Pct.
1999	Olindo Mare, Miami, AFC	46	39	84.8
	*Martin Gramatica, Tampa Bay, NFC	32	27	84.4
1998	Al Del Greco, Tennessee, AFC	39	36	92.3
	Gary Anderson, Minnesota, NFC	35	35	100.0
1997	Richie Cunningham, Dallas, NFC	37	34	91.9
	Cary Blanchard, Indianapolis, AFC	41	32	78.1
1996	John Kasay, Carolina, NFC	45	37	82.2
	Cary Blanchard, Indianapolis, AFC	40	36	90.0
1995	Norm Johnson, Pittsburgh, AFC	41	34	82.9
	Morten Andersen, Atlanta, NFC	37	31	83.8
1994	John Carney, San Diego, AFC	38	34	89.5
	Fuad Reveiz, Minnesota, NFC	39	34	87.2
1993	Jeff Jaeger, L.A. Raiders, AFC	44	35	79.5
	Jason Hanson, Detroit, NFC	43	34	79.1
1992	Pete Stoyanovich, Miami, AFC	37	30	81.1
	Chip Lohmiller, Washington, NFC	40	30	75.0
1991	Pete Stoyanovich, Miami, AFC	37	31	83.8
	Chip Lohmiller, Washington, NFC	43	31	72.1
1990	Nick Lowery, Kansas City, AFC	37	34	91.9
	Chip Lohmiller, Washington, NFC	40	30	75.0
1989	Rich Karlis, Minnesota, NFC	39	31	79.5
	*David Treadwell, Denver, AFC	33	27	81.8
1988	Scott Norwood, Buffalo, AFC	37	32	86.5
	Mike Cofer, San Francisco, NFC	38	27	71.1
1987	Morten Andersen, New Orleans, NFC	36	28	77.8
	Dean Biasucci, Indianapolis, AFC	27	24	88.9
	Jim Breech, Cincinnati, AFC	30	24	80.0
1986	Tony Franklin, New England, AFC	41	32	78.0
	Kevin Butler, Chicago, NFC	41	28	68.3
1985	Gary Anderson, Pittsburgh, AFC	42	33	78.6
	Morten Andersen, New Orleans, NFC	35	31	88.6
	*Kevin Butler, Chicago, NFC	37	31	83.8
1984	*Paul McFadden, Philadelphia, NFC	37	30	81.1
	Gary Anderson, Pittsburgh, AFC	32	24	75.0
	Matt Bahr, Cleveland, AFC	32	24	75.0
1983	*Ali-Haji-Sheikh, N.Y. Giants, NFC	42	35	83.3
	*Raul Allegre, Baltimore, AFC	35	30	85.7
1982	Mark Moseley, Washington, NFC	21	20	95.2
	Nick Lowery, Kansas City, AFC	24	19	79.2
1981	Rafael Septien, Dallas, NFC	35	27	77.1
	Nick Lowery, Kansas City, AFC	36	26	72.2
1980	*Ed Murray, Detroit, NFC	42	27	64.3
	John Smith, New England, AFC	34	26	76.5
	Fred Steinfort, Denver, AFC	34	26	76.5
1979	Mark Moseley, Washington, NFC	33	25	75.8
	John Smith, New England, AFC	33	23	69.7
1978	*Frank Corral, Los Angeles, NFC	43	29	67.4
	Pat Leahy, N.Y. Jets, AFC	30	22	73.3
1977	Mark Moseley, Washington, NFC	37	21	56.8
	Errol Mann, Oakland, AFC	28	20	71.4
1976	Mark Moseley, Washington, NFC	34	22	64.7
	Jan Stenerud, Kansas City, AFC	38	21	55.3
1975	Jan Stenerud, Kansas City, AFC	32	22	68.8
	Toni Fritsch, Dallas, NFC	35	22	62.9
1974	Chester Marcol, Green Bay, NFC	39	25	64.1
	Roy Gerela, Pittsburgh, AFC	29	20	69.0
1973	David Ray, Los Angeles, NFC	47	30	63.8
	Roy Gerela, Pittsburgh, AFC	43	29	67.4
1972	*Chester Marcol, Green Bay, NFC	48	33	68.8
	Roy Gerela, Pittsburgh, AFC	41	28	68.3
1971	Curt Knight, Washington, NFC	49	29	59.2
	Garo Yepremian, Miami, AFC	40	28	70.0
1970	Jan Stenerud, Kansas City, AFC	42	30	71.4
	Fred Cox, Minnesota, NFC	46	30	65.2
1969	Jim Turner, N.Y. Jets, AFL	47	32	68.1
	Fred Cox, Minnesota, NFL	37	26	70.3
1968	Jim Turner, N.Y. Jets, AFL	46	34	73.9
	Mac Percival, Chicago, NFL	36	25	69.4
1967	Jim Bakken, St. Louis, NFL	39	27	69.2
	Jan Stenerud, Kansas City, AFL	36	21	58.3
1966	Bruce Gossett, Los Angeles, NFL	49	28	57.1
	Mike Mercer, Oakland-Kansas City, AFL	30	21	70.0
1965	Pete Gogolak, Buffalo, AFL	46	28	60.9
	Fred Cox, Minnesota, NFL	35	23	65.7

YEARLY STATISTICAL LEADERS

1964	Jim Bakken, St. Louis, NFL	38	25	65.8
	Gino Cappelletti, Boston, AFL	39	25	64.1
1963	Jim Martin, Baltimore, NFL	39	24	61.5
	Gino Cappelletti, Boston, AFL	38	22	57.9
1962	Gene Mingo, Denver, AFL	39	27	69.2
	Lou Michaels, Pittsburgh, NFL	42	26	61.9
1961	Steve Myhra, Baltimore, NFL	39	21	53.8
	Gino Cappelletti, Boston, AFL	32	17	53.1
1960	Tommy Davis, San Francisco, NFL	32	19	59.4
	*Gene Mingo, Denver, AFL	28	18	64.3
1959	Pat Summerall, N.Y. Giants	29	20	69.0
1958	Paige Cothren, Los Angeles	25	14	56.0
	*Tom Miner, Pittsburgh	28	14	50.0
1957	Lou Groza, Cleveland	22	15	68.2
1956	Sam Baker, Washington	25	17	68.0
1955	Fred Cone, Green Bay	24	16	66.7
1954	Lou Groza, Cleveland	24	16	66.7
1953	Lou Groza, Cleveland	26	23	88.5
1952	Lou Groza, Cleveland	33	19	57.6
1951	Bob Waterfield, Los Angeles	23	13	56.5
1950	Lou Groza, Cleveland	19	13	68.4
1949	Cliff Patton, Philadelphia	18	9	50.0
	Bob Waterfield, Los Angeles	16	9	56.3
1948	Cliff Patton, Philadelphia	12	8	66.7
1947	Ward Cuff, Green Bay	16	7	43.8
	Pat Harder, Chi. Cardinals	10	7	70.0
	Bob Waterfield, Los Angeles	16	7	43.8
1946	Ted Fritsch, Green Bay	17	9	52.9
1945	Joe Aguirre, Washington	13	7	53.8
1944	Ken Strong, N.Y. Giants	12	6	50.0
1943	Ward Cuff, N.Y. Giants	9	3	33.3
	Don Hutson, Green Bay	5	3	60.0
1942	Bill Daddio, Chi. Cardinals	10	5	50.0
1941	Clarke Hinkle, Green Bay	14	6	42.9
1940	Clarke Hinkle, Green Bay	14	9	64.3
1939	Ward Cuff, N.Y. Giants	16	7	43.8
1938	Ward Cuff, N.Y. Giants	9	5	55.6
	Ralph Kercheval, Brooklyn	13	5	38.5
1937	Jack Manders, Chi. Bears		8	
1936	Jack Manders, Chi. Bears		7	
	Armand Niccolai, Pittsburgh		7	
1935	Armand Niccolai, Pittsburgh		6	
	Bill Smith, Chi. Cardinals		6	
1934	Jack Manders, Chi. Bears		10	
1933	*Jack Manders, Chi. Bears		6	
	Glenn Presnell, Portsmouth		6	
1932	Earl (Dutch) Clark, Portsmouth		3	

First season of professional football.

ANNUAL RUSHING LEADERS

Year	Player, Team	Att.	Yards	Avg.	TD
1999	*Edgerrin James, Indianapolis, AFC	369	1,553	4.2	13
	Stephen Davis, Washington, NFC	290	1,405	4.8	17
1998	Terrell Davis, Denver, AFC	392	2,008	5.1	21
	Jamal Anderson, Atlanta, NFC	410	1,846	4.5	14
1997	Barry Sanders, Detroit, NFC	335	2,053	6.1	11
	Terrell Davis, Denver, AFC	369	1,750	4.7	15
1996	Barry Sanders, Detroit, NFC	307	1,553	5.1	11
	Terrell Davis, Denver, AFC	345	1,538	4.5	13
1995	Emmitt Smith, Dallas, NFC	377	1,773	4.7	25
	*Curtis Martin, New England, AFC	368	1,487	4.0	14
1994	Barry Sanders, Detroit, NFC	331	1,883	5.7	7
	Chris Warren, Seattle, AFC	333	1,545	4.6	9
1993	Emmitt Smith, Dallas, NFC	283	1,486	5.3	9
	Thurman Thomas, Buffalo, AFC	355	1,315	3.7	6
1992	Emmitt Smith, Dallas, NFC	373	1,713	4.6	18
	Barry Foster, Pittsburgh, AFC	390	1,690	4.3	11
1991	Emmitt Smith, Dallas, NFC	365	1,563	4.3	12
	Thurman Thomas, Buffalo, AFC	288	1,407	4.9	7
1990	Barry Sanders, Detroit, NFC	255	1,304	5.1	13
	Thurman Thomas, Buffalo, AFC	271	1,297	4.8	11
1989	Christian Okoye, Kansas City, AFC	370	1,480	4.0	12
	*Barry Sanders, Detroit, NFC	280	1,470	5.3	14
1988	Eric Dickerson, Indianapolis, AFC	388	1,659	4.3	14
	Herschel Walker, Dallas, NFC	361	1,514	4.2	5
1987	Charles White, L.A. Rams, NFC	324	1,374	4.2	11
	Eric Dickerson, Indianapolis, AFC	223	1,011	4.5	5
1986	Eric Dickerson, L.A. Rams, NFC	404	1,821	4.5	11
	Curt Warner, Seattle, AFC	319	1,481	4.6	13
1985	Marcus Allen, L.A. Raiders, AFC	380	1,759	4.6	11
	Gerald Riggs, Atlanta, NFC	397	1,719	4.3	10
1984	Eric Dickerson, L.A. Rams, NFC	379	2,105	5.6	14
	Earnest Jackson, San Diego, AFC	296	1,179	4.0	8
1983	*Eric Dickerson, L.A. Rams, NFC	390	1,808	4.6	18
	*Curt Warner, Seattle, AFC	335	1,449	4.3	13
1982	Freeman McNeil, N.Y. Jets, AFC	151	786	5.2	6
	Tony Dorsett, Dallas, NFC	177	745	4.2	5
1981	*George Rogers, New Orleans, NFC	378	1,674	4.4	13
	Earl Campbell, Houston, AFC	361	1,376	3.8	10
1980	Earl Campbell, Houston, AFC	373	1,934	5.2	13
	Walter Payton, Chicago, NFC	317	1,460	4.6	6
1979	Earl Campbell, Houston, AFC	368	1,697	4.6	19
	Walter Payton, Chicago, NFC	369	1,610	4.4	14
1978	*Earl Campbell, Houston, AFC	302	1,450	4.8	13
	Walter Payton, Chicago, NFC	333	1,395	4.2	11
1977	Walter Payton, Chicago, NFC	339	1,852	5.5	14
	Mark van Eeghen, Oakland, AFC	324	1,273	3.9	7
1976	O.J. Simpson, Buffalo, AFC	290	1,503	5.2	8
	Walter Payton, Chicago, NFC	311	1,390	4.5	13
1975	O.J. Simpson, Buffalo, AFC	329	1,817	5.5	16
	Jim Otis, St. Louis, NFC	269	1,076	4.0	5
1974	Otis Armstrong, Denver, AFC	263	1,407	5.3	9
	Lawrence McCutcheon, Los Angeles, NFC	236	1,109	4.7	3
1973	O.J. Simpson, Buffalo, AFC	332	2,003	6.0	12
	John Brockington, Green Bay, NFC	265	1,144	4.3	3
1972	O.J. Simpson, Buffalo, AFC	292	1,251	4.3	6
	Larry Brown, Washington, NFC	285	1,216	4.3	8
1971	Floyd Little, Denver, AFC	284	1,133	4.0	6
	*John Brockington, Green Bay, NFC	216	1,105	5.1	4
1970	Larry Brown, Washington, NFC	237	1,125	4.7	5
	Floyd Little, Denver, AFC	209	901	4.3	3
1969	Gale Sayers, Chicago, NFL	236	1,032	4.4	8
	Dickie Post, San Diego, AFL	182	873	4.8	6
1968	Leroy Kelly, Cleveland, NFL	248	1,239	5.0	16
	*Paul Robinson, Cincinnati, AFL	238	1,023	4.3	8
1967	Jim Nance, Boston, AFL	269	1,216	4.5	7
	Leroy Kelly, Cleveland, NFL	235	1,205	5.1	11
1966	Jim Nance, Boston, AFL	299	1,458	4.9	11
	Gale Sayers, Chicago, NFL	229	1,231	5.4	8
1965	Jim Brown, Cleveland, NFL	289	1,544	5.3	17
	Paul Lowe, San Diego, AFL	222	1,121	5.0	7
1964	Jim Brown, Cleveland, NFL	280	1,446	5.2	7
	Cookie Gilchrist, Buffalo, AFL	230	981	4.3	6
1963	Jim Brown, Cleveland, NFL	291	1,863	6.4	12
	Clem Daniels, Oakland, AFL	215	1,099	5.1	3
1962	Jim Taylor, Green Bay, NFL	272	1,474	5.4	19
	Cookie Gilchrist, Buffalo, AFL	214	1,096	5.1	13
1961	Jim Brown, Cleveland, NFL	305	1,408	4.6	8
	Billy Cannon, Houston, AFL	200	948	4.7	6
1960	Jim Brown, Cleveland, NFL	215	1,257	5.8	9
	*Abner Haynes, Dall. Texans, AFL	156	875	5.6	9
1959	Jim Brown, Cleveland	290	1,329	4.6	14
1958	Jim Brown, Cleveland	257	1,527	5.9	17
1957	*Jim Brown, Cleveland	202	942	4.7	9
1956	Rick Casares, Chi. Bears	234	1,126	4.8	12
1955	*Alan Ameche, Baltimore	213	961	4.5	9
1954	Joe Perry, San Francisco	173	1,049	6.1	8
1953	Joe Perry, San Francisco	192	1,018	5.3	10
1952	Dan Towler, Los Angeles	156	894	5.7	10
1951	Eddie Price, N.Y. Giants	271	971	3.6	7
1950	Marion Motley, Cleveland	140	810	5.8	3
1949	Steve Van Buren, Philadelphia	263	1,146	4.4	11
1948	Steve Van Buren, Philadelphia	201	945	4.7	10
1947	Steve Van Buren, Philadelphia	217	1,008	4.6	13
1946	Bill Dudley, Pittsburgh	146	604	4.1	3
1945	Steve Van Buren, Philadelphia	143	832	5.8	15
1944	Bill Paschal, N.Y. Giants	196	737	3.8	9
1943	*Bill Paschal, N.Y. Giants	147	572	3.9	10
1942	*Bill Dudley, Pittsburgh	162	696	4.3	5
1941	Clarence (Pug) Manders, Brooklyn	111	486	4.4	5
1940	Byron (Whizzer) White, Detroit	146	514	3.5	5
1939	*Bill Osmanski, Chicago	121	699	5.8	7
1938	*Byron (Whizzer) White, Pittsburgh	152	567	3.7	4
1937	Cliff Battles, Washington	216	874	4.0	5
1936	*Alphonse (Tuffy) Leemans, N.Y. Giants	206	830	4.0	2
1935	Doug Russell, Chi. Cardinals	140	499	3.6	0
1934	*Beattie Feathers, Chi. Bears	119	1,004	8.4	8
1933	Jim Musick, Boston	173	809	4.7	5
1932	*Cliff Battles, Boston	148	576	3.9	3

First season of professional football.

ANNUAL PASSING LEADERS

(Current rating system implemented in 1973)

Year	Player, Team	Att.	Comp.	Yards	TD	Int.	Rating
1999	Kurt Warner, St. Louis, NFC	499	325	4,353	41	13	109.2
	Peyton Manning, Indianapolis, AFC	533	331	4,135	26	15	90.7

1998	Randall Cunningham, Minnesota, NFC..425	259	3,704	34	10	106.0
	Vinny Testaverde, NY Jets, AFC......421	259	3,256	29	7	101.6
1997	Steve Young, San Francisco, NFC..356	241	3,029	19	6	104.7
	Mark Brunell, Jacksonville, AFC......435	264	3,281	18	7	91.2
1996	Steve Young, San Francisco, NFC..316	214	2,410	14	6	97.2
	John Elway, Denver, AFC................466	287	3,328	26	14	89.2
1995	Jim Harbaugh, Indianapolis, AFC....314	200	2,575	17	5	100.7
	Brett Favre, Green Bay, NFC...........570	359	4,413	38	13	99.5
1994	Steve Young, San Francisco, NFC..461	324	3,969	35	10	112.8
	Dan Marino, Miami, AFC.................615	385	4,453	30	17	89.2
1993	Steve Young, San Francisco, NFC..462	314	4,023	29	16	101.5
	John Elway, Denver, AFC................551	348	4,030	25	10	92.8
1992	Steve Young, San Francisco, NFC..402	268	3,465	25	7	107.0
	Warren Moon, Houston, AFC..........346	224	2,521	18	12	89.3
1991	Steve Young, San Francisco, NFC..279	180	2,517	17	8	101.8
	Jim Kelly, Buffalo, AFC....................474	304	3,844	33	17	97.6
1990	Jim Kelly, Buffalo, AFC....................346	219	2,829	24	9	101.2
	Phil Simms, N.Y. Giants, NFC..........311	184	2,284	15	4	92.7
1989	Joe Montana, San Francisco, NFC..386	271	3,521	26	8	112.4
	Boomer Esiason, Cincinnati, AFC...455	258	3,525	28	11	92.1
1988	Boomer Esiason, Cincinnati, AFC...388	223	3,572	28	14	97.4
	Wade Wilson, Minnesota, NFC........332	204	2,746	15	9	91.5
1987	Joe Montana, San Francisco, NFC..398	266	3,054	31	13	102.1
	Bernie Kosar, Cleveland, AFC.........389	241	3,033	22	9	95.4
1986	Tommy Kramer, Minnesota, NFC.....372	208	3,000	24	10	92.6
	Dan Marino, Miami, AFC.................623	378	4,746	44	23	92.5
1985	Ken O'Brien, N.Y. Jets, AFC............488	297	3,888	25	8	96.2
	Joe Montana, San Francisco, NFC..494	303	3,653	27	13	91.3
1984	Dan Marino, Miami, AFC.................564	362	5,084	48	17	108.9
	Joe Montana, San Francisco, NFC..432	279	3,630	28	10	102.9
1983	Steve Bartkowski, Atlanta, NFC.......432	274	3,167	22	5	97.6
	*Dan Marino, Miami, AFC.................296	173	2,210	20	6	96.0
1982	Ken Anderson, Cincinnati, AFC.......309	218	2,495	12	9	95.3
	Joe Theismann, Washington, NFC..252	161	2,033	13	9	91.3
1981	Ken Anderson, Cincinnati, AFC.......479	300	3,754	29	10	98.4
	Joe Montana, San Francisco, NFC..488	311	3,565	19	12	88.4
1980	Brian Sipe, Cleveland, AFC............554	337	4,132	30	14	91.4
	Ron Jaworski, Philadelphia, NFC....451	257	3,529	27	12	91.0
1979	Roger Staubach, Dallas, NFC..........461	267	3,586	27	11	92.3
	Dan Fouts, San Diego, AFC............530	332	4,082	24	24	82.6
1978	Roger Staubach, Dallas, NFC..........413	231	3,190	25	16	84.9
	Terry Bradshaw, Pittsburgh, AFC.....368	207	2,915	28	20	84.7
1977	Bob Griese, Miami, AFC..................307	180	2,252	22	13	87.8
	Roger Staubach, Dallas, NFC..........361	210	2,620	18	9	87.0
1976	Ken Stabler, Oakland, AFC.............291	194	2,737	27	17	103.4
	James Harris, Los Angeles, NFC.....158	91	1,460	8	6	89.6
1975	Ken Anderson, Cincinnati, AFC.......377	228	3,169	21	11	93.9
	Fran Tarkenton, Minnesota, NFC.....425	273	2,994	25	13	91.8
1974	Ken Anderson, Cincinnati, AFC.......328	213	2,667	18	10	95.7
	Sonny Jurgensen, Washington, NFC..167	107	1,185	11	5	94.5
1973	Roger Staubach, Dallas, NFC..........286	179	2,428	23	15	94.6
	Ken Stabler, Oakland, AFC.............260	163	1,997	14	10	88.3
1972	Norm Snead, N.Y. Giants, NFC........325	196	2,307	17	12	
	Earl Morrall, Miami, AFC..................150	83	1,360	11	7	
1971	Roger Staubach, Dallas, NFC..........211	126	1,882	15	4	
	Bob Griese, Miami, AFC..................263	145	2,089	19	9	
1970	John Brodie, San Francisco, NFC...378	223	2,941	24	10	
	Daryle Lamonica, Oakland, AFC.....356	179	2,516	22	15	
1969	Sonny Jurgensen, Washington, NFL..442	274	3,102	22	15	
	*Greg Cook, Cincinnati, AFL............197	106	1,854	15	11	
1968	Len Dawson, Kansas City, AFL........224	131	2,109	17	9	
	Earl Morrall, Baltimore, NFL............317	182	2,909	26	17	
1967	Sonny Jurgensen, Washington, NFL..508	288	3,747	31	16	
	Daryle Lamonica, Oakland, AFL......425	220	3,228	30	20	
1966	Bart Starr, Green Bay, NFL..............251	156	2,257	14	3	
	Len Dawson, Kansas City, AFL........284	159	2,527	26	10	
1965	Rudy Bukich, Chicago, NFL...........312	176	2,641	20	9	
	John Hadl, San Diego, AFL............348	174	2,798	20	21	
1964	Len Dawson, Kansas City, AFL........354	199	2,879	30	18	
	Bart Starr, Green Bay, NFL..............272	163	2,144	15	4	
1963	Y.A. Tittle, N.Y. Giants, NFL.............367	221	3,145	36	14	
	Tobin Rote, San Diego, AFL............286	170	2,510	20	17	
1962	Len Dawson, Dall. Texans, AFL.......310	189	2,759	29	17	
	Bart Starr, Green Bay, NFL..............285	178	2,438	12	9	
1961	George Blanda, Houston, AFL........362	187	3,330	36	22	
	Milt Plum, Cleveland, NFL................302	177	2,416	18	10	
1960	Milt Plum, Cleveland, NFL................250	151	2,297	21	5	
	Jack Kemp, L.A. Chargers, AFL......406	211	3,018	20	25	
1959	Charlie Conerly, N.Y. Giants............194	113	1,706	14	4	
1958	Eddie LeBaron, Washington...........145	79	1,365	11	10	
1957	Tommy O'Connell, Cleveland..........110	63	1,229	9	8	
1956	Ed Brown, Chi. Bears.......................168	96	1,667	11	12	
1955	Otto Graham, Cleveland..................185	98	1,721	15	8	
1954	Norm Van Brocklin, Los Angeles.....260	139	2,637	13	21	
1953	Otto Graham, Cleveland..................258	167	2,722	11	9	
1952	Norm Van Brocklin, Los Angeles.....205	113	1,736	14	17	
1951	Bob Waterfield, Los Angeles............176	88	1,566	13	10	
1950	Norm Van Brocklin, Los Angeles.....233	127	2,061	18	14	
1949	Sammy Baugh, Washington............255	145	1,903	18	14	
1948	Tommy Thompson, Philadelphia.....246	141	1,965	25	11	
1947	Sammy Baugh, Washington............354	210	2,938	25	15	
1946	Bob Waterfield, Los Angeles............251	127	1,747	18	17	
1945	Sammy Baugh, Washington............182	128	1,669	11	4	
	Sid Luckman, Chi. Bears.................217	117	1,725	14	10	
1944	Frank Filchock, Washington............147	84	1,139	13	9	
1943	Sammy Baugh, Washington............239	133	1,754	23	19	
1942	Cecil Isbell, Green Bay...................268	146	2,021	24	14	
1941	Cecil Isbell, Green Bay...................206	117	1,479	15	11	
1940	Sammy Baugh, Washington............177	111	1,367	12	10	
1939	*Parker Hall, Cleveland....................208	106	1,227	9	13	
1938	Ed Danowski, N.Y. Giants................129	70	848	7	8	
1937	*Sammy Baugh, Washington...........171	81	1,127	8	14	
1936	Arnie Herber, Green Bay..................173	77	1,239	11	13	
1935	Ed Danowski, N.Y. Giants................113	57	794	10	9	
1934	Arnie Herber, Green Bay..................115	42	799	8	12	
1933	*Harry Newman, N.Y. Giants.............136	53	973	11	17	
1932	Arnie Herber, Green Bay..................101	37	639	9	9	

*First season of professional football.

ANNUAL PASSING TOUCHDOWN LEADERS

Year	Player, Team	TD
1999	Kurt Warner, St. Louis, NFC	41
	Peyton Manning, Indianapolis, AFC	26
1998	Steve Young, San Francisco, NFC	36
	Vinny Testaverde, N.Y. Jets, AFC	29
1997	Brett Favre, Green Bay, NFC	35
	Jeff George, Oakland, AFC	29
1996	Brett Favre, Green Bay, NFC	39
	Vinny Testaverde, Baltimore, AFC	33
1995	Brett Favre, Green Bay, NFC	38
	Jeff Blake, Cincinnati, AFC	28
1994	Steve Young, San Francisco, NFC	35
	Dan Marino, Miami, AFC	30
1993	Steve Young, San Francisco, NFC	29
	John Elway, Denver, AFC	25
1992	Steve Young, San Francisco, NFC	25
	Dan Marino, Miami, AFC	24
1991	Jim Kelly, Buffalo, AFC	33
	Mark Rypien, Washington, NFC	28
1990	Warren Moon, Houston, AFC	33
	Randall Cunningham, Philadelphia, NFC	30
1989	Jim Everett, L.A. Rams, NFC	29
	Boomer Esiason, Cincinnati, AFC	28
1988	Jim Everett, L.A. Rams, NFC	31
	Boomer Esiason, Cincinnati, AFC	28
	Dan Marino, Miami, AFC	28
1987	Joe Montana, San Francisco, NFC	31
	Dan Marino, Miami, AFC	26
1986	Dan Marino, Miami, AFC	44
	Tommy Kramer, Minnesota, NFC	24
1985	Dan Marino, Miami, AFC	30
	Joe Montana, San Francisco, NFC	27
1984	Dan Marino, Miami, AFC	48
	Neil Lomax, St. Louis, NFC	28
	Joe Montana, San Francisco, NFC	28
1983	Lynn Dickey, Green Bay, NFC	32
	Joe Ferguson, Buffalo, AFC	26
	Brian Sipe, Cleveland, AFC	26
1982	Terry Bradshaw, Pittsburgh, AFC	17
	Dan Fouts, San Diego, AFC	17
	Joe Montana, San Francisco, NFC	17
1981	Dan Fouts, San Diego, AFC	33
	Steve Bartkowski, Atlanta, NFC	30
1980	Steve Bartkowski, Atlanta, NFC	31
	Dan Fouts, San Diego, AFC	30
	Brian Sipe, Cleveland, AFC	30
1979	Steve Grogan, New England, AFC	28
	Brian Sipe, Cleveland, AFC	28
	Roger Staubach, Dallas, NFC	27
1978	Terry Bradshaw, Pittsburgh, AFC	28
	Roger Staubach, Dallas, NFC	25
	Fran Tarkenton, Minnesota, NFC	25
1977	Bob Griese, Miami, AFC	22
	Ron Jaworski, Philadelphia, NFC	18
	Roger Staubach, Dallas, NFC	18
1976	Ken Stabler, Oakland, AFC	27

	Jim Hart, St. Louis, NFC	18
1975	Joe Ferguson, Buffalo, AFC	25
	Fran Tarkenton, Minnesota, NFC	25
1974	Ken Stabler, Oakland, AFC	26
	Jim Hart, St. Louis, NFC	20
1973	Roman Gabriel, Philadelphia, NFC	23
	Roger Staubach, Dallas, NFC	23
	Charley Johnson, Denver, AFC	20
1972	Billy Kilmer, Washington, NFC	19
	Joe Namath, N.Y. Jets, AFC	19
1971	John Hadl, San Diego, AFC	21
	John Brodie, San Francisco, NFC	18
1970	John Brodie, San Francisco, NFC	24
	John Hadl, San Diego, AFC	22
	Daryle Lamonica, Oakland, AFC	22
1969	Daryle Lamonica, Oakland, AFL	34
	Roman Gabriel, Los Angeles, NFL	24
1968	John Hadl, San Diego, AFL	27
	Earl Morrall, Baltimore, NFL	26
1967	Sonny Jurgensen, Washington, NFL	31
	Daryle Lamonica, Oakland, AFL	30
1966	Frank Ryan, Cleveland, NFL	29
	Len Dawson, Kansas City, AFL	26
1965	John Brodie, San Francisco, NFL	30
	Len Dawson, Kansas City, AFL	21
1964	Babe Parilli, Boston, AFL	31
	Frank Ryan, Cleveland, NFL	25
1963	Y.A. Tittle, N.Y. Giants, NFL	36
	Len Dawson, Kansas City, AFL	26
1962	Y.A. Tittle, N.Y. Giants, NFL	33
	Len Dawson, Dallas, AFL	29
1961	George Blanda, Houston, AFL	36
	Sonny Jurgensen, Philadelphia, NFL	32
1960	Al Dorow, N.Y. Titans, AFL	26
	Johnny Unitas, Baltimore, NFL	25
1959	Johnny Unitas, Baltimore	32
1958	Johnny Unitas, Baltimore	19
1957	Johnny Unitas, Baltimore	24
1956	Tobin Rote, Green Bay	18
1955	Tobin Rote, Green Bay	17
	Y.A. Tittle, San Francisco	17
1954	Adrian Burk, Philadelphia	23
1953	Robert Thomason, Philadelphia	21
1952	Jim Finks, Pittsburgh	20
	Otto Graham, Cleveland	20
1951	Bobby Layne, Detroit	26
1950	George Ratterman, N.Y. Yanks	22
1949	Johnny Lujack, Chi. Bears	23
1948	Tommy Thompson, Philadelphia	25
1947	Sammy Baugh, Washington	25
1946	Sid Luckman, Chi. Bears	17
	Bob Waterfield, Los Angeles	17
1945	Sid Luckman, Chi. Bears	14
	*Bob Waterfield, Cleveland	14
1944	Frank Filchock, Washington	13
1943	Sid Luckman, Chi. Bears	28
1942	Cecil Isbell, Green Bay	24
1941	Cecil Isbell, Green Bay	15
1940	Sammy Baugh, Washington	12
1939	Frank Filchock, Washington	11
1938	Bob Monnett, Green Bay	9
1937	Bernie Masterson, Chi. Bears	9
1936	Arnie Herber, Green Bay	11
1935	Ed Danowski, N.Y. Giants	10
1934	Arnie Herber, Green Bay	8
1933	*Harry Newman, N.Y. Giants	11
1932	Arnie Herber, Green Bay	9

**First season of professional football.*

ANNUAL PASS RECEIVING LEADERS

Year	Player, Team	No.	Yards	Avg.	TD
1999	Jimmy Smith, Jacksonville, AFC	116	1,636	14.1	6
	Muhsin Muhammad, Carolina, NFC	96	1,253	13.1	8
1998	O.J. McDuffie, Miami, AFC	90	1,050	11.7	7
	Frank Sanders, Arizona, NFC	89	1,145	12.9	3
1997	Tim Brown, Oakland, AFC	104	1,408	13.5	5
	Herman Moore, Detroit, NFC	104	1,293	12.4	8
1996	Jerry Rice, San Francisco, NFC	108	1,254	11.6	8
	Carl Pickens, Cincinnati, AFC	100	1,180	11.8	12
1995	Herman Moore, Detroit, NFC	123	1,686	13.7	14
	Carl Pickens, Cincinnati, AFC	99	1,234	12.5	17
1994	Cris Carter, Minnesota, NFC	122	1,256	10.3	7
	Ben Coates, New England, AFC	96	1,174	12.2	7
1993	Sterling Sharpe, Green Bay, NFC	112	1,274	11.4	11
	Reggie Langhorne, Indianapolis, AFC	85	1,038	12.2	3
1992	Sterling Sharpe, Green Bay, NFC	108	1,461	13.5	13
	Haywood Jeffires, Houston, AFC	90	913	10.1	9
1991	Haywood Jeffires, Houston, AFC	100	1,181	11.8	7
	Michael Irvin, Dallas, NFC	93	1,523	16.4	8
1990	Jerry Rice, San Francisco, NFC	100	1,502	15.0	13
	Haywood Jeffires, Houston, AFC	74	1,048	14.2	8
	Drew Hill, Houston, AFC	74	1,019	13.8	5
1989	Sterling Sharpe, Green Bay, NFC	90	1,423	15.8	12
	Andre Reed, Buffalo, AFC	88	1,312	14.9	9
1988	Al Toon, N.Y. Jets, AFC	93	1,067	11.5	5
	Henry Ellard, L.A. Rams, NFC	86	1,414	16.4	10
1987	J.T. Smith, St. Louis, NFC	91	1,117	12.3	8
	Al Toon, N.Y. Jets, AFC	68	976	14.4	5
1986	Todd Christensen, L.A. Raiders, AFC	95	1,153	12.1	8
	Jerry Rice, San Francisco, NFC	86	1,570	18.3	15
1985	Roger Craig, San Francisco, NFC	92	1,016	11.0	6
	Lionel James, San Diego, AFC	86	1,027	11.9	6
1984	Art Monk, Washington, NFC	106	1,372	12.9	7
	Ozzie Newsome, Cleveland, AFC	89	1,001	11.2	5
1983	Todd Christensen, L.A. Raiders, AFC	92	1,247	13.6	12
	Roy Green, St. Louis, NFC	78	1,227	15.7	14
	Charlie Brown, Washington, NFC	78	1,225	15.7	8
	Earnest Gray, N.Y. Giants, NFC	78	1,139	14.6	5
1982	Dwight Clark, San Francisco, NFC	60	913	15.2	5
	Kellen Winslow, San Diego, AFC	54	721	13.4	6
1981	Kellen Winslow, San Diego, AFC	88	1,075	12.2	10
	Dwight Clark, San Francisco, NFC	85	1,105	13.0	4
1980	Kellen Winslow, San Diego, AFC	89	1,290	14.5	9
	*Earl Cooper, San Francisco, NFC	83	567	6.8	4
1979	Joe Washington, Baltimore, AFC	82	750	9.1	3
	Ahmad Rashad, Minnesota, NFC	80	1,156	14.5	9
1978	Rickey Young, Minnesota, NFC	88	704	8.0	5
	Steve Largent, Seattle, AFC	71	1,168	16.5	8
1977	Lydell Mitchell, Baltimore, AFC	71	620	8.7	4
	Ahmad Rashad, Minnesota, NFC	51	681	13.4	2
1976	MacArthur Lane, Kansas City, AFC	66	686	10.4	1
	Drew Pearson, Dallas, NFC	58	806	13.9	6
1975	Chuck Foreman, Minnesota, NFC	73	691	9.5	9
	Reggie Rucker, Cleveland, AFC	60	770	12.8	3
	Lydell Mitchell, Baltimore, AFC	60	544	9.1	4
1974	Lydell Mitchell, Baltimore, AFC	72	544	7.6	2
	Charles Young, Philadelphia, NFC	63	696	11.0	3
1973	Harold Carmichael, Philadelphia, NFC	67	1,116	16.7	9
	Fred Willis, Houston, AFC	57	371	6.5	1
1972	Harold Jackson, Philadelphia, NFC	62	1,048	16.9	4
	Fred Biletnikoff, Oakland, AFC	58	802	13.8	7
1971	Fred Biletnikoff, Oakland, AFC	61	929	15.2	9
	Bob Tucker, N.Y. Giants, NFC	59	791	13.4	4
1970	Dick Gordon, Chicago, NFC	71	1,026	14.5	13
	Marlin Briscoe, Buffalo, AFC	57	1,036	18.2	8
1969	Dan Abramowicz, New Orleans, NFL	73	1,015	13.9	7
	Lance Alworth, San Diego, AFL	64	1,003	15.7	4
1968	Clifton McNeil, San Francisco, NFL	71	994	14.0	7
	Lance Alworth, San Diego, AFL	68	1,312	19.3	10
1967	George Sauer, N.Y. Jets, AFL	75	1,189	15.9	6
	Charley Taylor, Washington, NFL	70	990	14.1	9
1966	Lance Alworth, San Diego, AFL	73	1,383	18.9	13
	Charley Taylor, Washington, NFL	72	1,119	15.5	12
1965	Lionel Taylor, Denver, AFL	85	1,131	13.3	6
	Dave Parks, San Francisco, NFL	80	1,344	16.8	12
1964	Charley Hennigan, Houston, AFL	101	1,546	15.3	8
	Johnny Morris, Chicago, NFL	93	1,200	12.9	10
1963	Lionel Taylor, Denver, AFL	78	1,101	14.1	10
	Bobby Joe Conrad, St. Louis, NFL	73	967	13.2	10
1962	Lionel Taylor, Denver, AFL	77	908	11.8	4
	Bobby Mitchell, Washington, NFL	72	1,384	19.2	11
1961	Lionel Taylor, Denver, AFL	100	1,176	11.8	4
	Jim (Red) Phillips, Los Angeles, NFL	78	1,092	14.0	5
1960	Lionel Taylor, Denver, AFL	92	1,235	13.4	12
	Raymond Berry, Baltimore, NFL	74	1,298	17.5	10
1959	Raymond Berry, Baltimore	66	959	14.5	14
1958	Raymond Berry, Baltimore	56	794	14.2	9
	Pete Retzlaff, Philadelphia	56	766	13.7	2
1957	Billy Wilson, San Francisco	52	757	14.6	6
1956	Billy Wilson, San Francisco	60	889	14.8	5
1955	Pete Pihos, Philadelphia	62	864	13.9	7
1954	Pete Pihos, Philadelphia	60	872	14.5	10
	Billy Wilson, San Francisco	60	830	13.8	5
1953	Pete Pihos, Philadelphia	63	1,049	16.7	10
1952	Mac Speedie, Cleveland	62	911	14.7	5
1951	Elroy (Crazylegs) Hirsch, Los Angeles	66	1,495	22.7	17

Year	Player, Team	No.	Yards	Avg.	TD
1950	Tom Fears, Los Angeles	84	1,116	13.3	7
1949	Tom Fears, Los Angeles	77	1,013	13.2	9
1948	*Tom Fears, Los Angeles	51	698	13.7	4
1947	Jim Keane, Chi. Bears	64	910	14.2	10
1946	Jim Benton, Los Angeles	63	981	15.6	6
1945	Don Hutson, Green Bay	47	834	17.7	9
1944	Don Hutson, Green Bay	58	866	14.9	9
1943	Don Hutson, Green Bay	47	776	16.5	11
1942	Don Hutson, Green Bay	74	1,211	16.4	17
1941	Don Hutson, Green Bay	58	738	12.7	10
1940	*Don Looney, Philadelphia	58	707	12.2	4
1939	Don Hutson, Green Bay	34	846	24.9	6
1938	Gaynell Tinsley, Chi. Cardinals	41	516	12.6	1
1937	Don Hutson, Green Bay	41	552	13.5	7
1936	Don Hutson, Green Bay	34	536	15.8	8
1935	*Tod Goodwin, N.Y. Giants	26	432	16.6	4
1934	Joe Carter, Philadelphia	16	238	14.9	4
	Morris (Red) Badgro, N.Y. Giants	16	206	12.9	1
1933	John (Shipwreck) Kelly, Brooklyn	22	246	11.2	3
1932	Ray Flaherty, N.Y. Giants	21	350	16.7	3

**First season of professional football.*

ANNUAL PASS RECEIVING LEADERS (YARDS)

Year	Player, Team	No.	Yards	Avg.	TD
1999	Marvin Harrison, Indianapolis, AFC	115	1,663	14.5	12
	Randy Moss, Minnesota, NFC	80	1,413	17.7	11
1998	Antonio Freeman, Green Bay, NFC	84	1,424	17.0	14
	Eric Moulds, Buffalo, AFC	67	1,368	20.4	9
1997	Rob Moore, Arizona, NFC	97	1,584	16.3	8
	Tim Brown, Oakland, AFC	104	1,408	13.5	5
1996	Isaac Bruce, St. Louis, NFC	84	1,338	15.9	7
	Jimmy Smith, Jacksonville, AFC	83	1,244	15.0	7
1995	Jerry Rice, San Francisco, NFC	122	1,848	15.1	15
	Tim Brown, Oakland, AFC	89	1,342	15.1	10
1994	Jerry Rice, San Francisco, NFC	112	1,499	13.4	13
	Tim Brown, L.A. Raiders, AFC	89	1,309	14.7	9
1993	Jerry Rice, San Francisco, NFC	98	1,503	15.3	15
	Tim Brown, L.A. Raiders, AFC	80	1,180	14.8	7
1992	Sterling Sharpe, Green Bay, NFC	108	1,461	13.5	13
	Anthony Miller, San Diego, AFC	72	1,060	14.7	7
1991	Michael Irvin, Dallas, NFC	93	1,523	16.4	8
	Haywood Jeffires, Houston, AFC	100	1,181	11.8	7
1990	Jerry Rice, San Francisco, NFC	100	1,502	15.0	13
	Haywood Jeffires, Houston, AFC	74	1,048	14.2	8
1989	Jerry Rice, San Francisco, NFC	82	1,483	18.1	17
	Andre Reed, Buffalo, AFC	88	1,312	14.9	9
1988	Henry Ellard, L.A. Rams, NFC	86	1,414	16.4	10
	Eddie Brown, Cincinnati, AFC	53	1,273	24.0	9
1987	J.T. Smith, St. Louis, NFC	91	1,117	12.3	8
	Carlos Carson, Kansas City, AFC	55	1,044	19.0	7
1986	Jerry Rice, San Francisco, NFC	86	1,570	18.3	15
	Stanley Morgan, New England, AFC	84	1,491	17.8	10
1985	Steve Largent, Seattle, AFC	79	1,287	16.3	6
	Mike Quick, Philadelphia, NFC	73	1,247	17.1	11
1984	Roy Green, St. Louis, NFC	78	1,555	19.9	12
	John Stallworth, Pittsburgh, AFC	80	1,395	17.4	11
1983	Mike Quick, Philadelphia, NFC	69	1,409	20.4	13
	Carlos Carson, Kansas City, AFC	80	1,351	16.9	7
1982	Wes Chandler, San Diego, AFC	49	1,032	21.1	9
	Dwight Clark, San Francisco, NFC	60	913	15.2	5
1981	Alfred Jenkins, Atlanta, NFC	70	1,358	19.4	13
	Frank Lewis, Buffalo, AFC	70	1,244	17.8	4
	Steve Watson, Denver, AFC	60	1,244	20.7	13
1980	John Jefferson, San Diego, AFC	82	1,340	16.3	13
	James Lofton, Green Bay, NFC	71	1,226	17.3	4
1979	Steve Largent, Seattle, AFC	66	1,237	18.7	9
	Ahmad Rashad, Minnesota, NFC	80	1,156	14.5	9
1978	Wesley Walker, N.Y. Jets, AFC	48	1,169	24.4	8
	Harold Carmichael, Philadelphia, NFC	55	1,072	19.5	8
1977	Drew Pearson, Dallas, NFC	48	870	18.1	2
	Ken Burrough, Houston, AFC	43	816	19.0	8
1976	Roger Carr, Baltimore, AFC	43	1,112	25.9	11
	*Sammy White, Minnesota, NFC	51	906	17.8	10
1975	Ken Burrough, Houston, AFC	53	1,063	20.1	8
	Mel Gray, St. Louis, NFC	48	926	19.3	11
1974	Cliff Branch, Oakland, AFC	60	1,092	18.2	13
	Drew Pearson, Dallas, NFC	62	1,087	17.5	2
1973	Harold Carmichael, Philadelphia, NFC	67	1,116	16.7	9
	*Isaac Curtis, Cincinnati, AFC	45	843	18.7	9
1972	Harold Jackson, Philadelphia, NFC	62	1,048	16.9	4
	Rich Caster, N.Y. Jets, AFC	39	833	21.4	10
1971	Otis Taylor, Kansas City, AFC	57	1,110	19.5	7
	Gene Washington, San Francisco, NFC	46	884	19.2	4
1970	Gene Washington, San Francisco, NFC	53	1,100	20.8	12
	Marlin Briscoe, Buffalo, AFC	57	1,036	18.2	8
1969	Warren Wells, Oakland, AFL	47	1,260	26.8	14
	Harold Jackson, Philadelphia, NFL	65	1,116	17.2	9
1968	Lance Alworth, San Diego, AFL	68	1,312	19.3	10
	Roy Jefferson, Pittsburgh, NFL	58	1,074	18.5	11
1967	Don Maynard, N.Y. Jets, AFL	71	1,434	20.3	10
	Ben Hawkins, Philadelphia, NFL	59	1,265	21.4	10
1966	Lance Alworth, San Diego, AFL	73	1,383	18.9	13
	Pat Studstill, Detroit, NFL	67	1,266	18.9	5
1965	Lance Alworth, San Diego, AFL	69	1,602	23.2	14
	Dave Parks, San Francisco, NFL	80	1,344	16.8	12
1964	Charley Hennigan, Houston, AFL	101	1,546	15.3	8
	Johnny Morris, Chicago, NFL	93	1,200	12.9	10
1963	Bobby Mitchell, Washington, NFL	69	1,436	20.8	7
	Art Powell, Oakland, AFL	73	1,304	17.8	16
1962	Bobby Mitchel, Washington, NFL	72	1,384	19.2	11
	Art Powell, N.Y. Titans, AFL	64	1,130	17.6	8
1961	Charley Hennigan, Houston, AFL	82	1,746	21.3	12
	Tommy McDonald, Philadelphia, NFL	64	1,144	17.9	13
1960	*Bill Groman, Houston, AFL	72	1,473	20.5	12
	Raymond Berry, Baltimore, NFL	74	1,298	17.5	10
1959	Raymond Berry, Baltimore	66	959	14.5	14
1958	Del Shofner, Los Angeles	51	1,097	21.5	8
1957	Raymond Berry, Baltimore	47	800	17.0	6
1956	Billy Howton, Green Bay	55	1,188	21.6	12
1955	Pete Pihos, Philadelphia	62	864	13.9	7
1954	Bob Boyd, Los Angeles	53	1,212	22.9	6
1953	Pete Pihos, Philadelphia	63	1,049	16.7	10
1952	*Bill Howton, Green Bay	53	1,231	23.2	13
1951	Elroy (Crazylegs) Hirsch, Los Angeles	66	1,495	22.7	17
1950	Tom Fears, Los Angeles	84	1,116	13.3	7
1949	Bob Mann, Detroit	66	1,014	15.4	4
1948	Mal Kutner, Chi. Cardinals	41	943	23.0	14
1947	Mal Kutner, Chi. Cardinals	43	944	21.9	7
1946	Jim Benton, Los Angeles	63	981	15.5	6
1945	Jim Benton, Cleveland	45	1,067	23.7	8
1944	Don Hutson, Green Bay	58	866	14.6	9
1943	Don Hutson, Green Bay	47	776	16.5	11
1942	Don Hutson, Green Bay	74	1,211	16.4	17
1941	Don Hutson, Green Bay	58	738	12.7	10
1940	*Don Looney, Philadelphia	58	707	12.2	4
1939	Don Hutson, Green Bay	34	846	24.9	6
1938	Don Hutson, Green Bay	32	548	17.1	9
1937	*Gaynell Tinsley, Chi. Cardinals	36	675	18.8	5
1936	Don Hutson, Green Bay	34	526	15.5	8
1935	Charley Malone, Boston	22	433	19.7	2
1934	Harry Ebding, Detroit	9	257	28.6	2
1933	*Paul Moss, Pittsburgh	18	383	21.3	2
1932	Johnny (Blood) McNally, Green Bay	19	326	17.2	3

**First season of professional football.*

ANNUAL INTERCEPTION LEADERS

Year	Player, Team	No.	Yards	TD
1999	Rod Woodson, Baltimore, AFC	7	195	2
	Sam Madison, Miami, AFC	7	164	1
	James Hasty, Kansas City, AFC	7	98	2
	Donnie Abraham, Tampa Bay, NFC	7	115	2
	Troy Vincent, Philadelphia, NFC	7	91	0
1998	Ty Law, New England, AFC	9	133	1
	Kwamie Lassiter, Arizona, NFC	8	80	0
1997	Ryan McNeil, St. Louis, NFC	9	127	1
	Mark McMillian, Kansas City, AFC	8	274	3
	Darryl Williams, Seattle, AFC	8	172	1
1996	Tyrone Braxton, Denver, AFC	9	128	1
	Keith Lyle, St. Louis, NFC	9	152	0
1995	*Orlando Thomas, Minnesota, NFC	9	108	1
	Willie Williams, Pittsburgh, AFC	7	122	1
1994	Eric Turner, Cleveland, AFC	9	199	1
	Aeneas Williams, Arizona, NFC	9	89	0
1993	Eugene Robinson, Seattle, AFC	9	80	0
	Nate Odomes, Buffalo, AFC	9	65	0
	Deion Sanders, Atlanta, NFC	7	91	0
1992	Henry Jones, Buffalo, AFC	8	263	2
	Audray McMillian, Minnesota, NFC	8	157	2
1991	Ronnie Lott, L.A. Raiders, AFC	8	52	0
	Ray Crockett, Detroit, NFC	6	141	1
	Deion Sanders, Atlanta, NFC	6	119	1
	*Aeneas Williams, Phoenix, NFC	6	60	0
	Tim McKyer, Atlanta, NFC	6	24	0
1990	*Mark Carrier, Chicago, NFC	10	39	0
	Richard Johnson, Houston, AFC	8	100	1
1989	Felix Wright, Cleveland, AFC	9	91	1

Year	Player, Team			
	Eric Allen, Philadelphia, NFC	8	38	0
1988	Scott Case, Atlanta, NFC	10	47	0
	Erik McMillan, N.Y. Jets, AFC	8	168	2
1987	Barry Wilburn, Washington, NFC	9	135	1
	Mike Prior, Indianapolis, AFC	6	57	0
	Mark Kelso, Buffalo, AFC	6	25	0
	Keith Bostic, Houston, AFC	6	-14	0
1986	Ronnie Lott, San Francisco, NFC	10	134	1
	Deron Cherry, Kansas City, AFC	9	150	0
1985	Everson Walls, Dallas, NFC	9	31	0
	Albert Lewis, Kansas City, AFC	8	59	0
	Eugene Daniel, Indianapolis, AFC	8	53	0
1984	Ken Easley, Seattle, AFC	10	126	2
	*Tom Flynn, Green Bay, NFC	9	106	0
1983	Mark Murphy, Washington, NFC	9	127	0
	Ken Riley, Cincinnati, AFC	8	89	2
	Vann McElroy, L.A. Raiders, AFC	8	68	0
1982	Everson Walls, Dallas, NFC	7	61	0
	Ken Riley, Cincinnati, AFC	5	88	1
	Bobby Jackson, N.Y Jets, AFC	5	84	1
	Dwayne Woodruff, Pittsburgh, AFC	5	53	0
	Donnie Shell, Pittsburgh, AFC	5	27	0
1981	*Everson Walls, Dallas, NFC	11	133	0
	John Harris, Seattle, AFC	10	155	2
1980	Lester Hayes, Oakland, AFC	13	273	1
	Nolan Cromwell, Los Angeles, NFC	8	140	1
1979	Mike Reinfeldt, Houston, AFC	12	205	0
	Lemar Parrish, Washington, NFC	9	65	0
1978	Thom Darden, Cleveland, AFC	10	200	0
	Ken Stone, St. Louis, NFC	9	139	0
	Willie Buchanon, Green Bay, NFC	9	93	1
1977	Lyle Blackwood, Baltimore, AFC	10	163	0
	Rolland Lawrence, Atlanta, NFC	7	138	0
1976	Monte Jackson, Los Angeles, NFC	10	173	3
	Ken Riley, Cincinnati, AFC	9	141	1
1975	Mel Blount, Pittsburgh, AFC	11	121	0
	Paul Krause, Minnesota, NFC	10	201	0
1974	Emmitt Thomas, Kansas City, AFC	12	214	2
	Ray Brown, Atlanta, NFC	8	164	1
1973	Dick Anderson, Miami, AFC	8	163	2
	Mike Wagner, Pittsburgh, AFC	8	134	0
	Bobby Bryant, Minnesota, NFC	7	105	1
1972	Bill Bradley, Philadelphia, NFC	9	73	0
	Mike Sensibaugh, Kansas City, AFC	8	65	0
1971	Bill Bradley, Philadelphia, NFC	11	248	0
	Ken Houston, Houston, AFC	9	220	4
1970	Johnny Robinson, Kansas City, AFC	10	155	0
	Dick LeBeau, Detroit, NFC	9	96	0
1969	Mel Renfro, Dallas, NFL	10	118	0
	Emmitt Thomas, Kansas City, AFL	9	146	1
1968	Dave Grayson, Oakland, AFL	10	195	1
	Willie Williams, N.Y. Giants, NFL	10	103	0
1967	Miller Farr, Houston, AFL	10	264	3
	*Lem Barney, Detroit, NFL	10	232	3
	Tom Janik, Buffalo, AFL	10	222	2
	Dave Whitsell, New Orleans, NFL	10	178	2
	Dick Westmoreland, Miami, AFL	10	127	1
1966	Larry Wilson, St. Louis, NFL	10	180	2
	Johnny Robinson, Kansas City, AFL	10	136	1
	Bobby Hunt, Kansas City, AFL	10	113	0
1965	W.K. Hicks, Houston, AFL	9	156	0
	Bobby Boyd, Baltimore, NFL	9	78	1
1964	Dainard Paulson, N.Y. Jets, AFL	12	157	1
	*Paul Krause, Washington, NFL	12	140	1
1963	Fred Glick, Houston, AFL	12	180	1
	Dick Lynch, N.Y. Giants, NFL	9	251	3
	Roosevelt Taylor, Chicago, NFL	9	172	1
1962	Lee Riley, N.Y. Titans, AFL	11	122	0
	Willie Wood, Green Bay, NFL	9	132	0
1961	Billy Atkins, Buffalo, AFL	10	158	0
	Dick Lynch, N.Y. Giants, NFL	9	60	0
1960	*Austin (Goose) Gonsoulin, Denver, AFL	11	98	0
	Dave Baker, San Francisco, NFL	10	96	0
	Jerry Norton, St. Louis, NFL	10	96	0
1959	Dean Derby, Pittsburgh	7	127	0
	Milt Davis, Baltimore	7	119	1
	Don Shinnick, Baltimore	7	70	0
1958	Jim Patton, N.Y. Giants	11	183	0
1957	Milt Davis, Baltimore	10	219	2
	Jack Christiansen, Detroit	10	137	1
	Jack Butler, Pittsburgh	10	85	0
1956	Linden Crow, Chi. Cardinals	11	170	0
1955	Will Sherman, Los Angeles	11	101	0
1954	Dick (Night Train) Lane, Chi. Cardinals	10	181	0
1953	Jack Christiansen, Detroit	12	238	1
1952	*Dick (Night Train) Lane, Los Angeles	14	298	2
1951	Otto Schnellbacher, N.Y. Giants	11	194	2
1950	Orban (Spec) Sanders, N.Y. Yanks	13	199	0
1949	Bob Nussbaumer, Chi. Cardinals	12	157	0
1948	*Dan Sandifer, Washington	13	258	2
1947	Frank Reagan, N.Y. Giants	10	203	0
	Frank Seno, Boston	10	100	0
1946	Bill Dudley, Pittsburgh	10	242	1
1945	Roy Zimmerman, Philadelphia	7	90	0
1944	*Howard Livingston, N.Y. Giants	9	172	1
1943	Sammy Baugh, Washington	11	112	0
1942	Clyde (Bulldog) Turner, Chi. Bears	8	96	1
1941	Marshall Goldberg, Chi. Cardinals	7	54	0
	*Art Jones, Pittsburgh	7	35	0
1940	Clarence (Ace) Parker, Brooklyn	6	146	1
	Kent Ryan, Detroit	6	65	0
	Don Hutson, Green Bay	6	24	0

**First season of professional football.*

ANNUAL PUNTING LEADERS

Year	Player, Team	No.	Avg.	Long
1999	Tom Rouen, Denver, AFC	84	46.5	65
	Mitch Berger, Minnesota, NFC	61	45.4	75
1998	Craig Hentrich, Tennessee, AFC	69	47.2	71
	Mark Royals, New Orleans, NFC	88	45.6	64
1997	Mark Royals, New Orleans, NFC	88	45.9	66
	Tom Tupa, New England, AFC	78	45.8	73
1996	John Kidd, Miami, AFC	78	46.3	63
	Matt Turk, Washington, NFC	75	45.1	63
1995	Rick Tuten, Seattle, AFC	83	45.0	73
	Sean Landeta, St. Louis, NFC	83	44.3	63
1994	Sean Landeta, L.A. Rams, NFC	78	44.8	62
	Jeff Gossett, L.A. Raiders, AFC	77	43.9	65
1993	Greg Montgomery, Houston, AFC	54	45.6	77
	Jim Arnold, Detroit, NFC	72	44.5	68
1992	Greg Montgomery, Houston, AFC	53	46.9	66
	Harry Newsome, Minnesota, NFC	72	45.0	84
1991	Reggie Roby, Miami, AFC	54	45.7	64
	Harry Newsome, Minnesota, AFC	68	45.5	65
1990	Mike Horan, Denver, AFC	58	44.4	67
	Sean Landeta, N.Y. Giants, NFC	75	44.1	67
1989	Rich Camarillo, Phoenix, NFC	76	43.4	58
	Greg Montgomery, Hounton, AFC	56	43.3	63
1988	Harry Newsome, Pittsburgh, AFC	65	45.4	62
	Jim Arnold, Detroit, NFC	97	42.4	69
1987	Rick Donnelly, Atlanta, NFC	61	44.0	62
	Ralf Mojsiejenko, San Diego, AFC	67	42.9	57
1986	Rohn Stark, Indianapolis, AFC	76	45.2	63
	Sean Landeta, N.Y. Giants, NFC	79	44.8	61
1985	Rohn Stark, Indianapolis, AFC	78	45.9	68
	*Rick Donnelly, Atlanta, NFC	59	43.6	68
1984	Jim Arnold, Kansas City, AFC	98	44.9	63
	*Brian Hansen, New Orleans, NFC	69	43.8	66
1983	Rohn Stark, Baltimore, AFC	91	45.3	68
	Frank Garcia, Tampa Bay, NFC	95	42.2	64
1982	Luke Prestridge, Denver, AFC	45	45.0	65
	Carl Birdsong, St. Louis, NFC	54	43.8	65
1981	Pat McInally, Cincinnati, AFC	72	45.4	62
	Tom Skladany, Detroit, NFC	64	43.5	74
1980	Dave Jennings, N.Y. Giants, NFC	94	44.8	63
	Luke Prestridge, Denver, AFC	70	43.9	57
1979	*Bob Grupp, Kansas City, AFC	89	43.6	74
	Dave Jennings, N.Y. Giants, NFC	104	42.7	72
1978	Pat McInally, Cincinnati, AFC	91	43.1	65
	*Tom Skladany, Detroit, NFC	86	42.5	63
1977	Ray Guy, Oakland, AFC	59	43.3	74
	Tom Blanchard, New Orleans, NFC	82	42.4	66
1976	Marv Bateman, Buffalo, AFC	86	42.8	78
	John James, Atlanta, NFC	101	42.1	67
1975	Ray Guy, Oakland, AFC	68	43.8	64
	Herman Weaver, Detroit, NFC	80	42.0	61
1974	Ray Guy, Oakland, AFC	74	42.2	66
	Tom Blanchard, New Orleans, NFC	88	42.1	71
1973	Jerrel Wilson, Kansas City, AFC	80	45.5	68
	*Tom Wittum, San Francisco, NFC	79	43.7	62
1972	Jerrel Wilson, Kansas City, AFC	66	44.8	69
	Dave Chapple, Los Angeles, NFC	53	44.2	70
1971	Dave Lewis, Cincinnati, AFC	72	44.8	56
	Tom McNeill, Philadelphia, NFC	73	42.0	64
1970	Dave Lewis, Cincinnati, AFC	79	46.2	63
	*Julian Fagan, New Orleans, NFC	77	42.5	64

Year	Player, Team	No.	Avg.	Long
1969	David Lee, Baltimore, NFL	57	45.3	66
	Dennis Partee, San Diego, AFL	71	44.6	62
1968	Jerrel Wilson, Kansas City, AFL	63	45.1	70
	Billy Lothridge, Atlanta, NFL	75	44.3	70
1967	Bob Scarpitto, Denver, AFL	105	44.9	73
	Billy Lothridge, Atlanta, NFL	87	43.7	62
1966	Bob Scarpitto, Denver, AFL	76	45.8	70
	*David Lee, Baltimore, NFL	49	45.6	64
1965	Gary Collins, Cleveland, NFL	65	46.7	71
	Jerrel Wilson, Kansas City, AFL	69	45.4	64
1964	Bobby Walden, Minnesota, NFL	72	46.4	73
	Jim Fraser, Denver, AFL	73	44.2	67
1963	Yale Lary, Detroit, NFL	35	48.9	73
	Jim Fraser, Denver, AFL	81	44.4	66
1962	Tommy Davis, San Francisco, NFL	48	45.6	82
	Jim Fraser, Denver, AFL	55	43.6	75
1961	Yale Lary, Detroit, NFL	52	48.4	71
	Billy Atkins, Buffalo, AFL	85	44.5	70
1960	Jerry Norton, St. Louis, NFL	39	45.6	62
	*Paul Maguire, L.A. Chargers, AFL	43	40.5	61
1959	Yale Lary, Detroit	45	47.1	67
1958	Sam Baker, Washington	48	45.4	64
1957	Don Chandler, N.Y. Giants	60	44.6	61
1956	Norm Van Brocklin, Los Angeles	48	43.1	72
1955	Norm Van Brocklin, Los Angeles	60	44.6	61
1954	Pat Brady, Pittsburgh	66	43.2	72
1953	Pat Brady, Pittsburgh	80	46.9	64
1952	Horace Gillom, Cleveland	61	45.7	73
1951	Horace Gillom, Cleveland	73	45.5	66
1950	*Fred (Curly) Morrison, Chi. Bears	57	43.3	65
1949	*Mike Boyda, N.Y. Bulldogs	56	44.2	61
1948	Joe Muha, Philadelphia	57	47.3	82
1947	Jack Jacobs, Green Bay	57	43.5	74
1946	Roy McKay, Green Bay	64	42.7	64
1945	Roy McKay, Green Bay	44	41.2	73
1944	Frank Sinkwich, Detroit	45	41.0	73
1943	Sammy Baugh, Washington	50	45.9	81
1942	Sammy Baugh, Washington	37	48.2	74
1941	Sammy Baugh, Washington	30	48.7	75
1940	Sammy Baugh, Washington	35	51.4	85
1939	*Parker Hall, Cleveland	58	40.8	80

**First season of professional football.*

ANNUAL PUNT RETURN LEADERS

Year	Player, Team	No.	Yards	Avg.	Long	TD
1999	*Charlie Rogers, Seattle, AFC	22	318	14.5	94	1
	*Mac Cody, Arizona, NFC	32	373	11.7	31	0
1998	Deion Sanders, Dallas, NFC	24	375	15.6	69	2
	Reggie Barlow, Jacksonville, AFC	43	555	12.9	85	1
1997	Jermaine Lewis, Baltimore, AFC	28	437	15.6	89	2
	David Palmer, Minnesota, NFC	34	444	13.1	57	0
1996	Desmond Howard, Green Bay, NFC	58	875	15.1	92	3
	Darrien Gordon, San Diego, AFC	36	537	14.9	81	1
1995	David Palmer, Minnesota, NFC	26	342	13.2	74	1
	Andre Coleman, San Diego, AFC	28	326	11.6	88	1
1994	Brian Mitchell, Washington, NFC	32	452	14.1	78	2
	Darrien Gordon, San Diego, AFC	36	475	13.2	90	2
1993	*Tyrone Hughes, New Orleans, NFC	37	503	13.6	83	2
	Eric Metcalf, Cleveland, AFC	36	464	12.9	91	2
1992	Johnny Bailey, Phoenix, NFC	20	263	13.2	65	0
	Rod Woodson, Pittsburgh, AFC	32	364	11.4	80	1
1991	Mel Gray, Detroit, NFC	25	385	15.4	78	1
	Rod Woodson, Pittsburgh, AFC	28	320	11.4	40	0
1990	Clarence Verdin, Indianapolis, AFC	31	396	12.8	36	0
	*Johnny Bailey, Chicago, NFC	36	399	11.1	95	1
1989	Walter Stanley, Detroit, NFC	36	496	13.8	74	0
	Clarence Verdin, Indianapolis, AFC	23	296	12.9	49	1
1988	John Taylor, San Francisco, NFC	44	556	12.6	95	2
	JoJo Townsell, N.Y. Jets, AFC	35	409	11.7	59	1
1987	Mel Gray, New Orleans, NFC	24	352	14.7	80	0
	Bobby Joe Edmonds, Seattle, AFC	20	251	12.6	40	0
1986	*Bobby Joe Edmonds, Seattle, AFC	34	419	12.3	75	1
	*Vai Sikahema, St. Louis, NFC	43	522	12.1	71	2
1985	Irving Fryar, New England, AFC	37	520	14.1	85	2
	Henry Ellard, L.A. Rams, NFC	37	501	13.5	80	1
1984	Mike Martin, Cincinnati, AFC	24	376	15.7	55	0
	Henry Ellard, L.A. Rams, NFC	30	403	13.4	83	2
1983	*Henry Ellard, L.A. Rams, NFC	16	217	13.6	72	1
	Kirk Springs, N.Y. Jets, AFC	23	287	12.5	76	1
1982	Rick Upchurch, Denver, AFC	15	242	16.1	78	2
	Billy Johnson, Atlanta, NFC	24	273	11.4	71	0
1981	LeRoy Irvin, Los Angeles, NFC	46	615	13.4	84	3
	*James Brooks, San Diego, AFC	22	290	13.2	42	0
1980	J.T. Smith, Kansas City, AFC	40	581	14.5	75	2
	*Kenny Johnson, Atlanta, NFC	23	281	12.2	56	0
1979	John Sciarra, Philadelphia, NFC	16	182	11.4	38	0
	*Tony Nathan, Miami, AFC	28	306	10.9	86	1
1978	Rick Upchurch, Denver, AFC	36	493	13.7	75	1
	Jackie Wallace, Los Angeles, NFC	52	618	11.9	58	0
1977	Billy Johnson, Houston, AFC	35	539	15.4	87	2
	Larry Marshall, Philadelphia, NFC	46	489	10.6	48	0
1976	Rick Upchurch, Denver, AFC	39	536	13.7	92	4
	Eddie Brown, Washington, NFC	48	646	13.5	71	1
1975	Billy Johnson, Houston, AFC	40	612	15.3	83	3
	Terry Metcalf, St. Louis, NFC	23	285	12.4	69	1
1974	Lemar Parrish, Cincinnati, AFC	18	338	18.8	90	2
	Dick Jauron, Detroit, NFC	17	286	16.8	58	0
1973	Bruce Taylor, San Francisco, NFC	15	207	13.8	61	0
	Ron Smith, San Diego, AFC	27	352	13.0	84	2
1972	Ken Ellis, Green Bay, NFC	14	215	15.4	80	1
	Chris Farasopoulos, N.Y. Jets, AFC	17	179	10.5	65	1
1971	Les (Speedy) Duncan, Washington, NFC	22	233	10.6	33	0
	Leroy Kelly, Cleveland, AFC	30	292	9.7	74	0
1970	Ed Podolak, Kansas City, AFC	23	311	13.5	60	0
	*Bruce Taylor, San Francisco, NFC	43	516	12.0	76	0
1969	Alvin Haymond, Los Angeles, NFL	33	435	13.2	52	0
	*Bill Thompson, Denver, AFL	25	288	11.5	40	0
1968	Bob Hayes, Dallas, NFL	15	312	20.8	90	2
	Noland Smith, Kansas City, AFL	18	270	15.0	80	1
1967	Floyd Little, Denver, AFL	16	270	16.9	72	1
	Ben Davis, Cleveland, NFL	18	229	12.7	52	1
1966	Les (Speedy) Duncan, San Diego, AFL	18	238	13.2	81	1
	Johnny Roland, St. Louis, NFL	20	221	11.1	86	1
1965	Leroy Kelly, Cleveland, NFL	17	265	15.6	67	2
	Les (Speedy) Duncan, San Diego, AFL	30	464	15.5	66	2
1964	Bobby Jancik, Houston, AFL	12	220	18.3	82	1
	Tommy Watkins, Detroit, NFL	16	238	14.9	68	2
1963	Dick James, Washington, NFL	16	214	13.4	39	0
	Claude (Hoot) Gibson, Oakland, AFL	26	307	11.8	85	2
1962	Dick Christy, N.Y. Titans, AFL	15	250	16.7	73	2
	Pat Studstill, Detroit, NFL	29	457	15.8	44	0
1961	Dick Christy, N.Y. Titans, AFL	18	383	21.3	70	2
	Willie Wood, Green Bay, NFL	14	225	16.1	72	2
1960	*Abner Haynes, Dall. Texans, AFL	14	215	15.4	46	0
	Abe Woodson, San Francisco, NFL	13	174	13.4	48	0
1959	Johnny Morris, Chi. Bears	14	171	12.2	78	1
1958	Jon Arnett, Los Angeles	18	223	12.4	58	0
1957	Bert Zagers, Washington	14	217	15.5	76	2
1956	Ken Konz, Cleveland	13	187	14.4	65	1
1955	Ollie Matson, Chi. Cardinals	13	245	18.8	78	2
1954	*Veryl Switzer, Green Bay	24	306	12.8	93	1
1953	Charley Trippi, Chi. Cardinals	21	239	11.4	38	0
1952	Jack Christiansen, Detroit	15	322	21.5	79	2
1951	Claude (Buddy) Young, N.Y. Yanks	12	231	19.3	79	1
1950	*Herb Rich, Baltimore	12	276	23.0	86	1
1949	Verda (Vitamin T) Smith, Los Angeles	27	427	15.8	85	1
1948	George McAfee, Chi. Bears	30	417	13.9	60	1
1947	*Walt Slater, Pittsburgh	28	435	15.5	33	0
1946	Bill Dudley, Pittsburgh	27	385	14.3	52	0
1945	*Dave Ryan, Detroit	15	220	14.7	56	0
1944	*Steve Van Buren, Philadelphia	15	230	15.3	55	1
1943	Andy Farkas, Washington	15	168	11.2	33	0
1942	Merlyn Condit, Brooklyn	21	210	10.0	23	0
1941	Byron (Whizzer) White, Detroit	19	262	13.8	64	0

**First season of professional football.*

ANNUAL KICKOFF RETURN LEADERS

Year	Player, Team	No.	Yards	Avg.	Long	TD
1999	Tony Horne, St. Louis, NFC	30	892	29.7	101	2
	Tremain Mack, Cincinnati, AFC	51	1,382	27.1	99	1
1998	*Terry Fair, Detroit, NFC	51	1,428	28.0	105	2
	Corey Harris, Baltimore, AFC	35	965	27.6	95	1
1997	Michael Bates, Carolina, NFC	47	1,281	27.3	56	0
	Aaron Glenn, N.Y. Jets, AFC	28	741	26.5	96	1
1996	Michael Bates, Carolina, NFC	33	998	30.2	93	1
	Tamarick Vanover, Kansas City, AFC	33	854	25.9	97	1
1995	Ron Carpenter, N.Y. Jets, AFC	20	553	27.7	58	0
	Brian Mitchell, Washington, NFC	55	1,408	25.6	59	0
1994	Mel Gray, Detroit, NFC	45	1,276	28.4	102	3
	Randy Baldwin, Cleveland, AFC	28	753	26.9	85	1
1993	Robert Brooks, Green Bay, NFC	23	611	26.6	95	1
	*Raghib Ismail, L.A. Raiders, AFC	25	605	24.2	66	0
1992	Jon Vaughn, New England, AFC	20	564	28.2	100	1
	Deion Sanders, Atlanta, NFC	40	1,067	26.7	99	2
1991	Mel Gray, Detroit, NFC	36	929	25.8	71	0
	Nate Lewis, San Diego, AFC	23	578	25.1	95	1

YEARLY STATISTICAL LEADERS

1990	Kevin Clark, Denver, AFC	20	505	25.3	75	0
	David Meggett, N.Y. Giants, NFC	21	492	23.4	58	0
1989	Rod Woodson, Pittsburgh, AFC	36	982	27.3	84	1
	Mel Gray, Detroit, NFC	24	640	26.7	57	0
1988	*Tim Brown, L.A. Raiders, AFC	41	1,098	26.8	97	1
	Donnie Elder, Tampa Bay, NFC	34	772	22.7	51	0
1987	Sylvester Stamps, Atlanta, NFC	24	660	27.5	97	1
	Paul Palmer, Kansas City, AFC	38	923	24.3	95	2
1986	Dennis Gentry, Chicago, NFC	20	576	28.8	91	1
	Lupe Sanchez, Pittsburgh, AFC	25	591	23.6	64	0
1985	Ron Brown, L.A. Rams, NFC	28	918	32.8	98	3
	Glen Young, Cleveland, AFC	35	898	25.7	63	0
1984	*Bobby Humphery, N.Y. Jets, AFC	22	675	30.7	97	1
	Barry Redden, L.A. Rams, NFC	23	530	23.0	40	0
1983	Fulton Walker, Miami, AFC	36	962	26.7	78	0
	Darrin Nelson, Minnesota, NFC	18	445	24.7	50	0
1982	*Mike Mosley, Buffalo, AFC	18	487	27.1	66	0
	Alvin Hall, Detroit, NFC	16	426	26.6	96	1
1981	Mike Nelms, Washington, NFC	37	1,099	29.7	84	0
	Carl Roaches, Houston, AFC	28	769	27.5	96	1
1980	Horace Ivory, New England, AFC	36	992	27.6	98	1
	Rich Mauti, New Orleans, NFC	31	798	25.7	52	0
1979	Larry Brunson, Oakland, AFC	17	441	25.9	89	0
	Jimmy Edwards, Minnesota, NFC	44	1,103	25.1	83	0
1978	Steve Odom, Green Bay, NFC	25	677	27.1	95	1
	*Keith Wright, Cleveland, AFC	30	789	26.3	86	0
1977	*Raymond Clayborn, New England, AFC	28	869	31.0	101	3
	*Wilbert Montgomery, Philadelphia, NFC	23	619	26.9	99	1
1976	*Duriel Harris, Miami, AFC	17	559	32.9	69	0
	Cullen Bryant, Los Angeles, NFC	16	459	28.7	90	1
1975	*Walter Payton, Chicago, NFC	14	444	31.7	70	0
	Harold Hart, Oakland, AFC	17	518	30.5	102	1
1974	Terry Metcalf, St. Louis, NFC	20	623	31.2	94	1
	Greg Pruitt, Cleveland, AFC	22	606	27.5	88	1
1973	Carl Garrett, Chicago, NFC	16	486	30.4	67	0
	*Wallace Francis, Buffalo, AFC	23	687	29.9	101	2
1972	Ron Smith, Chicago, NFC	30	924	30.8	94	1
	*Bruce Laird, Baltimore, AFC	29	843	29.1	73	0
1971	Travis Williams, Los Angeles, NFC	25	743	29.7	105	1
	Eugene (Mercury) Morris, Miami, AFC	15	423	28.2	94	1
1970	Jim Duncan, Baltimore, AFC	20	707	35.4	99	1
	Cecil Turner, Chicago, NFC	23	752	32.7	96	4
1969	Bobby Williams, Detroit, NFL	17	563	33.1	96	1
	*Bill Thompson, Denver, AFL	18	513	28.5	63	0
1968	Preston Pearson, Baltimore, NFL	15	527	35.1	102	2
	*George Atkinson, Oakland, AFL	32	802	25.1	60	0
1967	*Travis Williams, Green Bay, NFL	18	739	41.1	104	4
	*Zeke Moore, Houston, AFL	14	405	28.9	92	1
1966	Gale Sayers, Chicago, NFL	23	718	31.2	93	2
	*Goldie Sellers, Denver, AFL	19	541	28.5	100	2
1965	Tommy Watkins, Detroit, NFL	17	584	34.4	94	0
	Abner Haynes, Denver, AFL	34	901	26.5	60	0
1964	*Clarence Childs, N.Y. Giants, NFL	34	987	29.0	100	1
	Bo Roberson, Oakland, AFL	36	975	27.1	59	0
1963	Abe Woodson, San Francisco, NFL	29	935	32.2	103	3
	Bobby Jancik, Houston, AFL	45	1,317	29.3	53	0
1962	Abe Woodson, San Francisco, NFL	37	1,157	31.3	79	0
	*Bobby Jancik, Houston, AFL	24	826	30.3	61	0
1961	Dick Bass, Los Angeles, NFL	23	698	30.3	64	0
	*Dave Grayson, Dall. Texans, AFL	16	453	28.3	73	0
1960	*Tom Moore, Green Bay, NFL	12	397	33.1	84	0
	Ken Hall, Houston, AFL	19	594	31.3	104	1
1959	Abe Woodson, San Francisco	13	382	29.4	105	1
1958	Ollie Matson, Chi. Cardinals	14	497	35.5	101	2
1957	*Jon Arnett, Los Angeles	18	504	28.0	98	1
1956	*Tom Wilson, Los Angeles	15	477	31.8	103	1
1955	Al Carmichael, Green Bay	14	418	29.9	100	1
1954	Billy Reynolds, Cleveland	14	413	29.5	51	0
1953	Joe Arenas, San Francisco	16	551	34.4	82	0
1952	Lynn Chandnois, Pittsburgh	17	599	35.2	93	2
1951	Lynn Chandnois, Pittsburgh	12	390	32.5	55	0
1950	Verda (Vitamin T) Smith, Los Angeles	22	742	33.7	97	3
1949	*Don Doll, Detroit	21	536	25.5	56	0
1948	*Joe Scott, N.Y. Giants	20	569	28.5	99	1
1947	Eddie Saenz, Washington	29	797	27.5	94	2
1946	Abe Karnofsky, Boston	21	599	28.5	97	1
1945	Steve Van Buren, Philadelphia	13	373	28.7	98	1
1944	Bob Thurbon, Card.-Pitt.	12	291	24.3	55	0
1943	Ken Heineman, Brooklyn	16	444	27.8	69	0
1942	Marshall Goldberg, Chi. Cardinals	15	393	26.2	95	1
1941	Marshall Goldberg, Chi. Cardinals	12	290	24.2	41	0

**First season of professional football.*

ANNUAL LEADERS IN SACKS (SINCE 1982)

Year	Player, Team	Sacks
1999	Kevin Carter, St. Louis, NFC	17
	Jevon Kearse, Tennessee, AFC	14.5
1998	Michael Sinclair, Seattle, AFC	16.5
	Reggie White, Green Bay, NFC	16
1997	John Randle, Minnesota, NFC	15.5
	Bruce Smith, Buffalo, AFC	14
1996	Kevin Greene, Carolina, NFC	14.5
	Michael McCrary, Seattle, AFC	13.5
	Bruce Smith, Buffalo, AFC	13.5
1995	Bryce Paup, Buffalo, AFC	17.5
	William Fuller, Philadelphia, NFC	13
	Wayne Martin, New Orleans, NFC	13
1994	Kevin Greene, Pittsburgh, AFC	14
	Ken Harvey, Washington, NFC	13.5
	John Randle, Minnesota, NFC	13.5
1993	Neil Smith, Kansas City, AFC	15
	Renaldo Turnbull, New Orleans, NFC	13
	Reggie White, Green Bay, NFC	13
1992	Clyde Simmons, Philadelphia, NFC	19
	Leslie O'Neal, San Diego, AFC	17
1991	Pat Swilling, New Orleans, NFC	17
	William Fuller, Houston, AFC	15
1990	Derrick Thomas, Kansas City, AFC	20
	Charles Haley, San Francisco, NFC	16
1989	Chris Doleman, Minnesota, NFC	21
	Lee Williams, San Diego, AFC	14
1988	Reggie White, Philadelphia, NFC	18
	G. Townsend, L.A. Raiders, AFC	11.5
1987	Reggie White, Philadelphia, NFC	21
	Andre Tippett, New England, AFC	12.5
1986	Lawrence Taylor, N.Y. Giants, NFC	20.5
	Sean Jones, L.A. Raiders, AFC	15.5
1985	Richard Dent, Chicago, NFC	17
	Andre Tippett, New England, AFC	16.5
1984	Mark Gastineau, N.Y. Jets, AFC	22
	Richard Dent, Chicago, NFC	17.5
1983	Mark Gastineau, N.Y. Jets, AFC	19
	Fred Dean, San Francisco, NFC	17.5
1982	Doug Martin, Minnesota, NFC	11.5
	Jesse Baker, Houston, AFC	7.5

POINTS SCORED

Year	Team	Points
1999	St. Louis, NFC	526
	Indianapolis, AFC	423
1998	Minnesota, NFC	556
	Denver, AFC	501
1997	Denver, AFC	472
	Green Bay, NFC	422
1996	Green Bay, NFC	456
	New England, AFC	418
1995	San Francisco, NFC	457
	Pittsburgh, AFC	407
1994	San Francisco, NFC	505
	Miami, AFC	389
1993	San Francisco, NFC	473
	Denver, AFC	373
1992	San Francisco, NFC	431
	Buffalo, AFC	381
1991	Washington, NFC	485
	Buffalo, AFC	458
1990	Buffalo, AFC	428
	Philadelphia, NFC	396
1989	San Francisco, NFC	442
	Buffalo, AFC	409
1988	Cincinnati, AFC	448
	L.A. Rams, NFC	407
1987	San Francisco, NFC	459
	Cleveland, AFC	390
1986	Miami, AFC	430
	Minnesota, NFC	398
1985	San Diego, AFC	467
	Chicago, NFC	456
1984	Miami, AFC	513
	San Francisco, NFC	475
1983	Washington, NFC	541
	L.A. Raiders, AFC	442
1982	San Diego, AFC	288
	Dallas, NFC	226
	Green Bay, NFC	226
1981	San Diego, AFC	478
	Atlanta, NFC	426
1980	Dallas, NFC	454
	New England, AFC	441
1979	Pittsburgh, AFC	416
	Dallas, NFC	371
1978	Dallas, NFC	384
	Miami, AFC	372
1977	Oakland, AFC	351
	Dallas, NFC	345
1976	Baltimore, AFC	417
	Los Angeles, NFC	351
1975	Buffalo, AFC	420
	Minnesota, NFC	377
1974	Oakland, AFC	355
	Washington, NFC	320
1973	Los Angeles, NFC	388
	Denver, AFC	354
1972	Miami, AFC	385
	San Francisco, NFC	353
1971	Dallas, NFC	406
	Oakland, AFC	344
1970	San Francisco, NFC	352
	Baltimore, AFC	321
1969	Minnesota, NFL	379
	Oakland, AFL	377
1968	Oakland, AFL	453
	Dallas, NFL	431
1967	Oakland, AFL	468
	Los Angeles, NFL	398
1966	Kansas City, AFL	448
	Dallas, NFL	445
1965	San Francisco, NFL	421
	San Diego, AFL	340
1964	Baltimore, NFL	428
	Buffalo, AFL	400
1963	N.Y. Giants, NFL	448
	San Diego, AFL	399
1962	Green Bay, NFL	415
	Dall. Texans, AFL	389

1961	Houston, AFL	513
	Green Bay, NFL	391
1960	N.Y. Titans, AFL	382
	Cleveland, NFL	362
1959	Baltimore	374
1958	Baltimore	381
1957	Los Angeles	307
1956	Chi. Bears	363
1955	Cleveland	349
1954	Detroit	337
1953	San Francisco	372
1952	Los Angeles	349
1951	Los Angeles	392
1950	Los Angeles	466
1949	Philadelphia	364
1948	Chi. Cardinals	395
1947	Chi. Bears	363
1946	Chi. Bears	289
1945	Philadelphia	272
1944	Philadelphia	267
1943	Chi. Bears	303
1942	Chi. Bears	376
1941	Chi. Bears	396
1940	Washington	245
1939	Chi. Bears	298
1938	Green Bay	223
1937	Green Bay	220
1936	Green Bay	248
1935	Chi. Bears	192
1934	Chi. Bears	286
1933	N.Y. Giants	244
1932	Chicago Bears	160

TOTAL YARDS GAINED

Year	Team	Yards
1999	St. Louis, NFC	6,412
	Indianapolis, AFC	5,726
1998	San Francisco, NFC	6,800
	Denver, AFC	6,092
1997	Denver, AFC	5,872
	Detroit, NFC	5,798
1996	Denver, AFC	5,791
	Philadelphia, NFC	5,627
1995	Detroit, NFC	6,113
	Denver, AFC	6,040
1994	Miami, AFC	6,078
	San Francisco, NFC	6,060
1993	San Francisco, NFC	6,435
	Miami, AFC	5,812
1992	San Francisco, NFC	6,195
	Buffalo, AFC	5,893
1991	Buffalo, AFC	6,252
	San Francisco, NFC	5,858
1990	Houston, AFC	6,222
	San Francisco, NFC	5,895
1989	San Francisco, NFC	6,268
	Cincinnati, AFC	6,101
1988	Cincinnati, AFC	6,057
	San Francisco, NFC	5,900
1987	San Francisco, NFC	5,987
	Denver, AFC	5,624
1986	Cincinnati, AFC	6,490
	San Francisco, NFC	6,082
1985	San Diego, AFC	6,535
	San Francisco, NFC	5,920
1984	Miami, AFC	6,936
	San Francisco, NFC	6,366
1983	San Diego, AFC	6,197
	Green Bay, NFC	6,172
1982	San Diego, AFC	4,048
	San Francisco, NFC	3,242
1981	San Diego, AFC	6,744
	Detroit, NFC	5,933
1980	San Diego, AFC	6,410
	Los Angeles, NFC	6,006
1979	Pittsburgh, AFC	6,258
	Dallas, NFC	5,968
1978	New England, AFC	5,965
	Dallas, NFC	5,959
1977	Dallas, NFC	4,812
	Oakland, AFC	4,736
1976	Baltimore, AFC	5,236
	St. Louis, NFC	5,136
1975	Buffalo, AFC	5,467
	Dallas, NFC	5,025
1974	Dallas, NFC	4,983
	Oakland, AFC	4,718
1973	Los Angeles, NFC	4,906
	Oakland, AFC	4,773
1972	Miami, AFC	5,036
	N.Y. Giants, NFC	4,483
1971	Dallas, NFC	5,035
	San Diego, AFC	4,738
1970	Oakland, AFC	4,829
	San Francisco, NFC	4,503
1969	Dallas, NFL	5,122
	Oakland, AFL	5,036
1968	Oakland, AFL	5,696
	Dallas, NFL	5,117
1967	N.Y. Jets, AFL	5,152
	Baltimore, NFL	5,008
1966	Dallas, NFL	5,145
	Kansas City, AFL	5,114
1965	San Francisco, NFL	5,270
	San Diego, AFL	5,188
1964	Buffalo, AFL	5,206
	Baltimore, NFL	4,779
1963	San Diego, AFL	5,153
	N.Y. Giants, NFL	5,024
1962	N.Y. Giants, NFL	5,005
	Houston, AFL	4,971
1961	Houston, AFL	6,288
	Philadelphia, NFL	5,112
1960	Houston, AFL	4,936
	Baltimore, NFL	4,245
1959	Baltimore	4,458
1958	Baltimore	4,539
1957	Los Angeles	4,143
1956	Chi. Bears	4,537
1955	Chi. Bears	4,316
1954	Los Angeles	5,187
1953	Philadelphia	4,811
1952	Cleveland	4,352
1951	Los Angeles	5,506
1950	Los Angeles	5,420
1949	Chi. Bears	4,873
1948	Chi. Cardinals	4,705
1947	Chi. Bears	5,053
1946	Los Angeles	3,793
1945	Washington	3,549
1944	Chi. Bears	3,239
1943	Chi. Bears	4,045
1942	Chi. Bears	3,900
1941	Chi. Bears	4,265
1940	Green Bay	3,400
1939	Chi. Bears	3,988
1938	Green Bay	3,037
1937	Green Bay	3,201
1936	Detroit	3,703
1935	Chi. Bears	3,454
1934	Chi. Bears	3,900
1933	N.Y. Giants	2,973
1932	Chi. Bears	2,755

YARDS RUSHING

Year	Team	Yards
1999	San Francisco, NFC	2,095
	Jacksonville, AFC	2,091
1998	San Francisco, NFC	2,544
	Denver, AFC	2,468
1997	Pittsburgh, AFC	2,479
	Detroit, NFC	2,464
1996	Denver, AFC	2,362
	Washington, NFC	1,910
1995	Kansas City, AFC	2,222
	Dallas, NFC	2,201
1994	Pittsburgh, AFC	2,180
	Detroit, NFC	2,080
1993	N.Y. Giants, NFC	2,210
	Seattle, AFC	2,015
1992	Buffalo, AFC	2,436
	Philadelphia, NFC	2,388
1991	Buffalo, AFC	2,381
	Minnesota, NFC	2,201
1990	Philadelphia, NFC	2,556
	San Diego, AFC	2,257
1989	Cincinnati, AFC	2,483
	Chicago, NFC	2,287
1988	Cincinnati, AFC	2,710
	San Francisco, NFC	2,523
1987	San Francisco, NFC	2,237
	L.A. Raiders, AFC	2,197
1986	Chicago, NFC	2,700
	Cincinnati, AFC	2,533
1985	Chicago, NFC	2,761
	Indianapolis, AFC	2,439
1984	Chicago, NFC	2,974
	N.Y. Jets, AFC	2,189
1983	Chicago, NFC	2,727
	Baltimore, AFC	2,695
1982	Buffalo, AFC	1,371
	Dallas, NFC	1,313
1981	Detroit, NFC	2,795
	Kansas City, AFC	2,633
1980	Los Angeles, NFC	2,799
	Houston, AFC	2,635
1979	N.Y. Jets, AFC	2,646
	St. Louis, NFC	2,582
1978	New England, AFC	3,165
	Dallas, NFC	2,783
1977	Chicago, NFC	2,811
	Oakland, AFC	2,627
1976	Pittsburgh, AFC	2,971
	Los Angeles, NFC	2,528
1975	Buffalo, AFC	2,974
	Dallas, NFC	2,432
1974	Dallas, NFC	2,454
	Pittsburgh, AFC	2,417
1973	Buffalo, AFC	3,088
	Los Angeles, NFC	2,925
1972	Miami, AFC	2,960
	Chicago, NFC	2,360
1971	Miami, AFC	2,429
	Detroit, NFC	2,376
1970	Dallas, NFC	2,300
	Miami, AFC	2,082
1969	Dallas, NFL	2,276
	Kansas City, AFL	2,220
1968	Chicago, NFL	2,377
	Kansas City, AFL	2,227
1967	Cleveland, NFL	2,139
	Houston, AFL	2,122
1966	Kansas City, AFL	2,274
	Cleveland, NFL	2,166
1965	Cleveland, NFL	2,331
	San Diego, AFL	2,085
1964	Green Bay, NFL	2,276
	Buffalo, AFL	2,040
1963	Cleveland, NFL	2,639
	San Diego, AFL	2,203
1962	Buffalo, AFL	2,480
	Green Bay, NFL	2,460
1961	Green Bay, NFL	2,350
	Dall. Texans, AFL	2,189
1960	St. Louis, NFL	2,356
	Oakland, AFL	2,056
1959	Cleveland	2,149
1958	Cleveland	2,526
1957	Los Angeles	2,142
1956	Chi. Bears	2,468
1955	Chi. Bears	2,388
1954	San Francisco	2,498
1953	San Francisco	2,230
1952	San Francisco	1,905
1951	Chi. Bears	2,408
1950	N.Y. Giants	2,336
1949	Philadelphia	2,607
1948	Chi. Cardinals	2,560
1947	Los Angeles	2,171
1946	Green Bay	1,765
1945	Cleveland	1,714
1944	Philadelphia	1,661
1943	Phil-Pitt	1,730
1942	Chi. Bears	1,881
1941	Chi. Bears	2,263
1940	Chi. Bears	1,818
1939	Chi. Bears	2,043
1938	Detroit	1,893
1937	Detroit	2,074
1936	Detroit	2,885
1935	Chi. Bears	2,096
1934	Chi. Bears	2,847
1933	Boston	2,260
1932	Chi. Bears	1,770

YARDS PASSING

Leadership in this category has been based on net yards since 1952.

Year	Team	Yards
1999	St. Louis, NFC	4,353
	Indianapolis, AFC	4,066
1998	Minnesota, NFC	4,328
	N.Y. Jets, AFC	3,836
1997	Seattle, AFC	3,959
	Green Bay, NFC	3,705
1996	Jacksonville, AFC	4,110
	Philadelphia, NFC	3,745
1995	San Francisco, NFC	4,608
	Miami, AFC	4,210
1994	New England, AFC	4,444
	Minnesota, NFC	4,324
1993	Miami, AFC	4,353
	San Francisco, NFC	4,302
1992	Houston, AFC	4,029
	San Francisco, NFC	3,880
1991	Houston, AFC	4,621
	San Francisco, NFC	3,997
1990	Houston, AFC	4,805
	San Francisco, NFC	4,177
1989	Washington, NFC	4,349
	Miami, AFC	4,216
1988	Miami, AFC	4,516
	Washington, NFC	4,136
1987	Miami, AFC	3,876
	San Francisco, NFC	3,750
1986	Miami, AFC	4,779
	San Francisco, NFC	4,096
1985	San Diego, AFC	4,870
	Dallas, NFC	3,861
1984	Miami, AFC	5,018
	St. Louis, NFC	4,257
1983	San Diego, AFC	4,661
	Green Bay, NFC	4,365
1982	San Diego, AFC	2,927
	San Francisco, NFC	2,502
1981	San Diego, AFC	4,739
	Minnesota, NFC	4,333
1980	San Diego, AFC	4,531
	Minnesota, NFC	3,688
1979	San Diego, AFC	3,915
	San Francisco, NFC	3,641
1978	San Diego, AFC	3,375
	Minnesota, NFC	3,243
1977	Buffalo, AFC	2,530
	St. Louis, NFC	2,499
1976	Baltimore, AFC	2,933
	Minnesota, NFC	2,855
1975	Cincinnati, AFC	3,241
	Washington, NFC	2,917
1974	Washington, NFC	2,978
	Cincinnati, AFC	2,804
1973	Philadelphia, NFC	2,998
	Denver, AFC	2,519
1972	N.Y. Jets, AFC	2,777
	San Francisco, NFC	2,735
1971	San Diego, AFC	3,134
	Dallas, NFC	2,786
1970	San Francisco, NFC	2,923
	Oakland, AFC	2,865
1969	Oakland, AFL	3,271
	San Francisco, NFL	3,158
1968	San Diego, AFL	3,623
	Dallas, NFL	3,026
1967	N.Y. Jets, AFL	3,845
	Washington, NFL	3,730
1966	N.Y. Jets, AFL	3,464
	Dallas, NFL	3,023
1965	San Francisco, NFL	3,487
	San Diego, AFL	3,103
1964	Houston, AFL	3,527
	Chicago, NFL	2,841
1963	Baltimore, NFL	3,296

YEARLY STATISTICAL LEADERS

	Houston, AFL	3,222
1962	Denver, AFL	3,404
	Philadelphia, NFL	3,385
1961	Houston, AFL	4,392
	Philadelphia, NFL	3,605
1960	Houston, AFL	3,203
	Baltimore, NFL	2,956
1959	Baltimore	2,753
1958	Pittsburgh	2,752
1957	Baltimore	2,388
1956	Los Angeles	2,419
1955	Philadelphia	2,472
1954	Chi. Bears	3,104
1953	Philadelphia	3,089
1952	Cleveland	2,566
1951	Los Angeles	3,296
1950	Los Angeles	3,709
1949	Chi. Bears	3,055
1948	Washington	2,861
1947	Washington	3,336
1946	Los Angeles	2,080
1945	Chi. Bears	1,857
1944	Washington	2,021
1943	Chi. Bears	2,310
1942	Green Bay	2,407
1941	Chi. Bears	2,002
1940	Washington	1,887
1939	Chi. Bears	1,965
1938	Washington	1,536
1937	Green Bay	1,398
1936	Green Bay	1,629
1935	Green Bay	1,449
1934	Green Bay	1,165
1933	N.Y. Giants	1,348
1932	Chi. Bears	1,013

FEWEST POINTS ALLOWED

Year	Team	Points
1999	Jacksonville, AFC	217
	Tampa Bay, NFC	235
1998	Miami, AFC	265
	Dallas, NFC	275
1997	Kansas City, AFC	232
	Tampa Bay, NFC	263
1996	Green Bay, NFC	210
	Pittsburgh, AFC	257
1995	Kansas City, AFC	241
	San Francisco, NFC	258
1994	Cleveland, AFC	204
	Dallas, NFC	248
1993	N.Y. Giants, NFC	205
	Houston, AFC	238
1992	New Orleans, NFC	202
	Pittsburgh, AFC	225
1991	New Orleans, NFC	211
	Denver, AFC	235
1990	N.Y. Giants, NFC	211
	Pittsburgh, AFC	240
1989	Denver, AFC	226
	N.Y. Giants, NFC	252
1988	Chicago, NFC	215
	Buffalo, AFC	237
1987	Indianapolis, AFC	238
	San Francisco, NFC	253
1986	Chicago, NFC	187
	Seattle, AFC	293
1985	Chicago, NFC	198
	N.Y. Jets, AFC	264
1984	San Francisco, NFC	227
	Denver, AFC	241
1983	Miami, AFC	250
	Detroit, NFC	286
1982	Washington, NFC	128
	Miami, AFC	131
1981	Philadelphia, NFC	221
	Miami, AFC	275
1980	Philadelphia, NFC	222
	Houston, AFC	251
1979	Tampa Bay, NFC	237
	San Diego, AFC	246
1978	Pittsburgh, AFC	195
	Dallas, NFC	208
1977	Atlanta, NFC	129
	Denver, AFC	148
1976	Pittsburgh, AFC	138
	Minnesota, NFC	176
1975	Los Angeles, NFC	135
	Pittsburgh, AFC	162
1974	Los Angeles, NFC	181
	Pittsburgh, AFC	189
1973	Miami, AFC	150
	Minnesota, NFC	168
1972	Miami, AFC	171
	Washington, NFC	218
1971	Minnesota, NFC	139
	Baltimore, AFC	140
1970	Minnesota, NFC	143
	Miami, AFC	228
1969	Minnesota, NFL	133
	Kansas City, AFL	177
1968	Baltimore, NFL	144
	Kansas City, AFL	170
1967	Los Angeles, NFL	196
	Houston, AFL	199
1966	Green Bay, NFL	163
	Buffalo, AFL	255
1965	Green Bay, NFL	224
	Buffalo, AFL	226
1964	Baltimore, NFL	225
	Buffalo, AFL	242
1963	Chicago, NFL	144
	San Diego, AFL	255
1962	Green Bay, NFL	148
	Dall. Texans, AFL	233
1961	San Diego, AFL	219
	N.Y. Giants, NFL	220
1960	San Francisco, NFL	205
	Dall. Texans, AFL	253
1959	N.Y. Giants	170
1958	N.Y. Giants	183
1957	Cleveland	172
1956	Cleveland	177
1955	Cleveland	218
1954	Cleveland	162
1953	Cleveland	162
1952	Detroit	192
1951	Cleveland	152
1950	Philadelphia	141
1949	Philadelphia	134
1948	Chi. Bears	151
1947	Green Bay	210
1946	Pittsburgh	117
1945	Washington	121
1944	N.Y. Giants	75
1943	Washington	137
1942	Chi. Bears	84
1941	N.Y. Giants	114
1940	Brooklyn	120
1939	N.Y. Giants	85
1938	N.Y. Giants	79
1937	Chi. Bears	100
1936	Chi. Bears	94
1935	Green Bay	96
	N.Y. Giants	96
1934	Detroit	59
1933	Brooklyn	54
1932	Chi. Bears	44

FEWEST TOTAL YARDS ALLOWED

Year	Team	Yards
1999	Buffalo, AFC	4,045
	Tampa Bay, NFC	4,280
1998	San Diego, AFC	4,208
	Tampa Bay, NFC	4,345
1997	San Francisco, NFC	4,013
	Denver, AFC	4,671
1996	Greem Bay, NFC	4,156
	Pittsburgh, AFC	4,362
1995	San Francisco, NFC	4,398
	Kansas City, AFC	4,549
1994	Dallas, NFC	4,313
	Pittsburgh, AFC	4,326
1993	Minnesota, NFC	4,406
	Pittsburgh, AFC	4,531
1992	Dallas, NFC	3,931
	Houston, AFC	4,211
1991	Philadelphia, NFC	3,549
	Denver, AFC	4,549
1990	Pittsburgh, AFC	4,115
	N.Y. Giants, NFC	4,206
1989	Minnesota, NFC	4,184
	Kansas City, AFC	4,293
1988	Minnesota, NFC	4,091
	Buffalo, AFC	4,578
1987	San Francisco, NFC	4,095
	Cleveland, AFC	4,264
1986	Chicago, NFC	4,130
	L.A. Raiders, AFC	4,804
1985	Chicago, NFC	4,135
	L.A. Raiders, AFC	4,603
1984	Chicago, NFC	3,863
	Cleveland, AFC	4,641
1983	Cincinnati, AFC	4,327
	New Orleans, NFC	4,691
1982	Miami, AFC	2,312
	Tampa Bay, NFC	2,442
1981	Philadelphia, NFC	4,447
	N.Y. Jets, AFC	4,871
1980	Buffalo, AFC	4,101
	Philadelphia, NFC	4,443
1979	Tampa Bay, NFC	3,949
	Pittsburgh, AFC	4,270
1978	Los Angeles, NFC	3,893
	Pittsburgh, AFC	4,168
1977	Dallas, NFC	3,213
	New England, AFC	3,638
1976	Pittsburgh, AFC	3,323
	San Francisco, NFC	3,562
1975	Minnesota, NFC	3,153
	Oakland, AFC	3,629
1974	Pittsburgh, AFC	3,074
	Washington, NFC	3,285
1973	Los Angeles, NFC	2,951
	Oakland, AFC	3,160
1972	Miami, AFC	3,297
	Green Bay, NFC	3,474
1971	Baltimore, AFC	2,852
	Minnesota, NFC	3,406
1970	Minnesota, NFC	2,803
	N.Y. Jets, AFC	3,655
1969	Minnesota, NFL	2,720
	Kansas City, AFL	3,163
1968	Los Angeles, NFL	3,118
	N.Y. Jets, AFL	3,363
1967	Oakland, AFL	3,294
	Green Bay, NFL	3,300
1966	St. Louis, NFL	3,492
	Oakland, AFL	3,910
1965	San Diego, AFL	3,262
	Detroit, NFL	3,557
1964	Green Bay, NFL	3,179
	Buffalo, AFL	3,878
1963	Chicago, NFL	3,176
	Boston, AFL	3,834
1962	Detroit, NFL	3,217
	Dall. Texans, AFL	3,951
1961	San Diego, AFL	3,726
	Baltimore, NFL	3,782
1960	St. Louis, NFL	3,029
	Buffalo, AFL	3,866
1959	N.Y. Giants	2,843
1958	Chi. Bears	3,066
1957	Pittsburgh	2,791
1956	N.Y. Giants	3,081
1955	Cleveland	2,841
1954	Cleveland	2,658
1953	Philadelphia	2,998
1952	Cleveland	3,075
1951	N.Y. Giants	3,250
1950	Cleveland	3,154
1949	Philadelphia	2,831
1948	Chi. Bears	2,931
1947	Green Bay	3,396
1946	Washington	2,451
1945	Philadelphia	2,073
1944	Philadelphia	1,943
1943	Chi. Bears	2,262
1942	Chi. Bears	1,703
1941	N.Y. Giants	2,368
1940	N.Y. Giants	2,219
1939	Washington	2,116
1938	N.Y. Giants	2,029
1937	Washington	2,123
1936	Boston	2,181
1935	Boston	1,996
1934	Chi. Cardinals	1,539
1933	Brooklyn	1,789

FEWEST RUSHING YARDS ALLOWED

Year	Team	Yards
1999	St. Louis, NFC	1,189
	Baltimore, AFC	1,231
1998	San Diego, AFC	1,140
	Atlanta, NFC	1,203
1997	Pittsburgh, AFC	1,318
	San Francisco, NFC	1,366
1996	Denver, AFC	1,331
	Green Bay, NFC	1,416
1995	San Francisco, NFC	1,061
	Pittsburgh, AFC	1,321
1994	Minnesota, NFC	1,090
	San Diego, AFC	1,404
1993	Houston, AFC	1,273
	Minnesota, NFC	1,536
1992	Dallas, NFC	1,244
	Buffalo, AFC	1,395
	San Diego, AFC	1,395
1991	Philadelphia, NFC	1,136
	N.Y. Jets, AFC	1,442
1990	Philadelphia, NFC	1,169
	San Diego, AFC	1,515
1989	New Orleans, NFC	1,326
	Denver, AFC	1,580
1988	Chicago, NFC	1,326
	Houston, AFC	1,592
1987	Chicago, NFC	1,413
	Cleveland, AFC	1,433
1986	N.Y. Giants, NFC	1,284
	Denver, AFC	1,651
1985	Chicago, NFC	1,319
	N.Y. Jets, AFC	1,516
1984	Chicago, NFC	1,377
	Pittsburgh, AFC	1,617
1983	Washington, NFC	1,289
	Cincinnati, AFC	1,499
1982	Pittsburgh, AFC	762
	Detroit, NFC	854
1981	Detroit, NFC	1,623
	Kansas City, AFC	1,747
1980	Detroit, NFC	1,599
	Cincinnati, AFC	1,680
1979	Denver, AFC	1,693
	Tampa Bay, NFC	1,873
1978	Dallas, NFC	1,721
	Pittsburgh, AFC	1,774
1977	Denver, AFC	1,531
	Dallas, NFC	1,651
1976	Pittsburgh, AFC	1,457
	Los Angeles, NFC	1,564
1975	Minnesota, NFC	1,532
	Houston, AFC	1,680
1974	Los Angeles, NFC	1,302
	New England, AFC	1,587
1973	Los Angeles, NFC	1,270
	Oakland, AFC	1,470
1972	Dallas, NFC	1,515
	Miami, AFC	1,548
1971	Baltimore, AFC	1,113
	Dallas, NFC	1,144
1970	Detroit, NFC	1,152
	N.Y. Jets, AFC	1,283
1969	Dallas, NFL	1,050
	Kansas City, AFL	1,091
1968	Dallas, NFL	1,195
	N.Y. Jets, AFL	1,195
1967	Dallas, NFL	1,081
	Oakland, AFL	1,129
1966	Buffalo, AFL	1,051
	Dallas, NFL	1,176

Year	Team	Yards
1965	San Diego, AFL	1,094
	Los Angeles, NFL	1,409
1964	Buffalo, AFL	913
	Los Angeles, NFL	1,501
1963	Boston, AFL	1,107
	Chicago, NFL	1,442
1962	Detroit, NFL	1,231
	Dall. Texans, AFL	1,250
1961	Boston, AFL	1,041
	Pittsburgh, NFL	1,463
1960	St. Louis, NFL	1,212
	Dall. Texans, AFL	1,338
1959	N.Y. Giants	1,261
1958	Baltimore	1,291
1957	Baltimore	1,174
1956	N.Y. Giants	1,443
1955	Cleveland	1,189
1954	Cleveland	1,050
1953	Philadelphia	1,117
1952	Detroit	1,145
1951	N.Y. Giants	913
1950	Detroit	1,367
1949	Chi. Bears	1,196
1948	Philadelphia	1,209
1947	Philadelphia	1,329
1946	Chi. Bears	1,060
1945	Philadelphia	817
1944	Philadelphia	558
1943	Phil-Pitt	793
1942	Chi. Bears	519
1941	Washington	1,042
1940	N.Y. Giants	977
1939	Chi. Bears	812
1938	Detroit	1,081
1937	Chi. Bears	933
1936	Boston	1,148
1935	Boston	998
1934	Chi. Cardinals	954
1933	Brooklyn	964

FEWEST PASSING YARDS ALLOWED

Leadership in this category has been based on net yards since 1952.

Year	Team	Yards
1999	Buffalo, AFC	2,675
	Tampa Bay, NFC	2,873
1998	Philadelphia, NFC	2,720
	Oakland, AFC	2,876
1997	Dallas, NFC	2,522
	Indianapolis, AFC	2,820
1996	Green Bay, NFC	2,740
	Pittsburgh, AFC	2,947
1995	N.Y. Jets, AFC	2,740
	Philadelphia, NFC	2,816
1994	Dallas, NFC	2,752
	Houston, AFC	2,795
1993	New Orleans, NFC	2,606
	Cincinnati, AFC	2,798
1992	New Orleans, NFC	2,470
	Kansas City, AFC	2,537
1991	Philadelphia, NFC	2,413
	Denver, AFC	2,755
1990	Pittsburgh, AFC	2,500
	Dallas, NFC	2,639
1989	Minnesota, NFC	2,501
	Kansas City, AFC	2,527
1988	Kansas City, AFC	2,434
	Minnesota, NFC	2,489
1987	San Francisco, NFC	2,484
	L.A. Raiders, AFC	2,727
1986	St. Louis, NFC	2,637
	New England, AFC	2,978
1985	Washington, NFC	2,746
	Pittsburgh, AFC	2,783
1984	New Orleans, NFC	2,453
	Cleveland, AFC	2,696
1983	New Orleans, NFC	2,691
	Cincinnati, AFC	2,828
1982	Miami, AFC	1,027
	Tampa Bay, NFC	1,384
1981	Philadelphia, NFC	2,696
	Buffalo, AFC	2,870
1980	Washington, NFC	2,171
	Buffalo, AFC	2,282
1979	Tampa Bay, NFC	2,076
	Buffalo, AFC	2,530
1978	Buffalo, AFC	1,960
	Los Angeles, NFC	2,048
1977	Atlanta, NFC	1,384
	San Diego, AFC	1,725
1976	Minnesota, NFC	1,575
	Cincinnati, AFC	1,758
1975	Minnesota, NFC	1,621
	Cincinnati, AFC	1,729
1974	Pittsburgh, AFC	1,466
	Atlanta, NFC	1,572
1973	Miami, AFC	1,290
	Atlanta, NFC	1,430
1972	Minnesota, NFC	1,699
	Cleveland, AFC	1,736
1971	Atlanta, NFC	1,638
	Baltimore, AFC	1,739
1970	Minnesota, NFC	1,438
	Kansas City, AFC	2,010
1969	Minnesota, NFL	1,631
	Kansas City, AFL	2,072
1968	Houston, AFL	1,671
	Green Bay, NFL	1,796
1967	Green Bay, NFL	1,377
	Buffalo, AFL	1,825
1966	Green Bay, NFL	1,959
	Oakland, AFL	2,118
1965	Green Bay, NFL	1,981
	San Diego, AFL	2,168
1964	Green Bay, NFL	1,647
	San Diego, AFL	2,518
1963	Chicago, NFL	1,734
	Oakland, AFL	2,589
1962	Green Bay, NFL	1,746
	Oakland, AFL	2,306
1961	Baltimore, NFL	1,913
	San Diego, AFL	2,363
1960	Chicago, NFL	1,388
	Buffalo, AFL	2,124
1959	N.Y. Giants	1,582
1958	Chi. Bears	1,769
1957	Cleveland	1,300
1956	Cleveland	1,103
1955	Pittsburgh	1,295
1954	Cleveland	1,608
1953	Washington	1,751
1952	Washington	1,580
1951	Pittsburgh	1,687
1950	Cleveland	1,581
1949	Philadelphia	1,607
1948	Green Bay	1,626
1947	Green Bay	1,790
1946	Pittsburgh	939
1945	Washington	1,121
1944	Chi. Bears	1,052
1943	Chi. Bears	980
1942	Washington	1,093
1941	Pittsburgh	1,168
1940	Philadelphia	1,012
1939	Washington	1,116
1938	Chi. Bears	897
1937	Detroit	804
1936	Philadelphia	853
1935	Chi. Cardinals	793
1934	Philadelphia	545
1933	Portsmouth	558

SUPER BOWL RECORDS

Compiled by Elias Sports Bureau

1967: Super Bowl I	1979: Super Bowl XIII	1991: Super Bowl XXV
1968: Super Bowl II	1980: Super Bowl XIV	1992: Super Bowl XXVI
1969: Super Bowl III	1981: Super Bowl XV	1993: Super Bowl XXVII
1970: Super Bowl IV	1982: Super Bowl XVI	1994: Super Bowl XXVIII
1971: Super Bowl V	1983: Super Bowl XVII	1995: Super Bowl XXIX
1972: Super Bowl VI	1984: Super Bowl XVIII	1996: Super Bowl XXX
1973: Super Bowl VII	1985: Super Bowl XIX	1997: Super Bowl XXXI
1974: Super Bowl VIII	1986: Super Bowl XX	1998: Super Bowl XXXII
1975: Super Bowl IX	1987: Super Bowl XXI	1999: Super Bowl XXXIII
1976: Super Bowl X	1988: Super Bowl XXII	2000: Super Bowl XXXIV
1977: Super Bowl XI	1989: Super Bowl XXIII	
1978: Super Bowl XII	1990: Super Bowl XXIV	

INDIVIDUAL RECORDS

SERVICE

Most Games

6 Mike Lodish, Buffalo, 1991-94; Denver, 1998-99
5 Marv Fleming, Green Bay, 1967-68; Miami, 1972-74
Larry Cole, Dallas, 1971-72, 1976, 1978-79
Cliff Harris, Dallas, 1971-72, 1976, 1978-79
Charles Haley, San Francisco, 1989-90; Dallas, 1993-94, 1996
D.D. Lewis, Dallas, 1971-72, 1976, 1978-79
Preston Pearson, Baltimore, 1969; Pittsburgh, 1975; Dallas, 1976, 1978-79
Charlie Waters, Dallas, 1971-72, 1976, 1978-79
Rayfield Wright, Dallas, 1971-72, 1976, 1978-79
Cornelius Bennett, Buffalo, 1991-94; Atlanta, 1999
John Elway, Denver, 1987-88, 1990, 1998-99
4 By many players

Most Games, Winning Team

5 Charles Haley, San Francisco, 1989-90; Dallas, 1993-94, 1996
4 By many players

Most Games, Coach

6 Don Shula, Baltimore, 1969; Miami, 1972-74, 1983, 1985
5 Tom Landry, Dallas, 1971-72, 1976, 1978-79
4 Bud Grant, Minnesota, 1970, 1974-75, 1977
Chuck Noll, Pittsburgh, 1975-76, 1979-80
Joe Gibbs, Washington, 1983-84, 1988, 1992
Marv Levy, Buffalo, 1991-94
Dan Reeves, Denver, 1987-88, 1990; Atlanta, 1999

Most Games, Winning Team, Coach

4 Chuck Noll, Pittsburgh, 1975-76, 1979-80
3 Bill Walsh, San Francisco, 1982, 1985, 1989
Joe Gibbs, Washington, 1983, 1988, 1992
2 Vince Lombardi, Green Bay, 1967-68
Tom Landry, Dallas, 1972, 1978
Don Shula, Miami, 1973-74
Tom Flores, Oakland, 1981; L.A. Raiders, 1984
Bill Parcells, N.Y. Giants, 1987, 1991
Jimmy Johnson, Dallas, 1993-94
George Seifert, San Francisco, 1990, 1995
Mike Shanahan, Denver, 1998-99

Most Games, Losing Team, Coach

4 Bud Grant, Minnesota, 1970, 1974-75, 1977
Don Shula, Baltimore, 1969; Miami, 1972, 1983, 1985
Marv Levy, Buffalo, 1991-94
Dan Reeves, Denver, 1987-88, 1990; Atlanta, 1999
3 Tom Landry, Dallas, 1971, 1976, 1979

SCORING

POINTS

Most Points, Career

42 Jerry Rice, San Francisco, 3 games (7-td)
30 Emmitt Smith, Dallas, 3 games (5-td)
24 Franco Harris, Pittsburgh, 4 games (4-td)
Roger Craig, San Francisco, 3 games (4-td)
Thurman Thomas, Buffalo, 4 games (4-td)
John Elway, Denver, 5 games (4-td)

Most Points, Game

18 Roger Craig, San Francisco vs. Miami, 1985 (3-td)
Jerry Rice, San Francisco vs. Denver, 1990 (3-td); vs. San Diego, 1995 (3-td)
Ricky Watters, San Francisco vs. San Diego, 1995 (3-td)
Terrell Davis, Denver vs. Green Bay, 1998 (3-td)
15 Don Chandler, Green Bay vs. Oakland, 1968 (3-pat, 4-fg)
14 Ray Wersching, San Francisco vs. Cincinnati, 1982 (2-pat, 4-fg)
Kevin Butler, Chicago vs. New England, 1986 (5-pat, 3-fg)

TOUCHDOWNS

Most Touchdowns, Career

7 Jerry Rice, San Francisco, 3 games (7-p)
5 Emmitt Smith, Dallas, 3 games (5-r)
4 Franco Harris, Pittsburgh, 4 games (4-r)
Roger Craig, San Francisco, 3 games (2-r, 2-p)
Thurman Thomas, Buffalo, 4 games (4-r)
John Elway, Denver, 5 games (4-r)

Most Touchdowns, Game

3 Roger Craig, San Francisco vs. Miami, 1985 (1-r, 2-p)
Jerry Rice, San Francisco. vs. Denver, 1990 (3-p); vs. San Diego, 1995 (3-p)
Ricky Watters, San Francisco vs. San Diego, 1995 (1-r, 2-p)
Terrell Davis, Denver vs. Green Bay, 1998 (3-r)
2 Max McGee, Green Bay vs. Kansas City, 1967 (2-p)
Elijah Pitts, Green Bay vs. Kansas City, 1967 (2-r)
Bill Miller, Oakland vs. Green Bay, 1968 (2-p)
Larry Csonka, Miami vs. Minnesota, 1974 (2-r)
Pete Banaszak, Oakland vs. Minnesota, 1977 (2-r)
John Stallworth, Pittsburgh vs. Dallas, 1979 (2-p)
Franco Harris, Pittsburgh vs. Los Angeles, 1980 (2-r)
Cliff Branch, Oakland vs. Philadelphia, 1981 (2-p)
Dan Ross, Cincinnati vs. San Francisco, 1982 (2-p)
Marcus Allen, L.A. Raiders vs. Washington, 1984 (2-r)
Jim McMahon, Chicago vs. New England, 1986 (2-r)
Ricky Sanders, Washington vs. Denver, 1988 (2-p)
Timmy Smith, Washington vs. Denver, 1988 (2-r)
Tom Rathman, San Francisco vs. Denver, 1990 (2-r)
Gerald Riggs, Washington vs. Buffalo, 1992 (2-r)
Michael Irvin, Dallas vs. Buffalo, 1993 (2-p)
Emmitt Smith, Dallas vs. Buffalo, 1994 (2-r)
Emmitt Smith, Dallas vs. Pittsburgh, 1996 (2-r)
Antonio Freeman, Green Bay vs. Denver, 1998 (2-p)
Howard Griffith, Denver vs. Atlanta, 1999 (2-r)
Eddie George, Tennessee vs. St. Louis, 2000 (2-r)

POINTS AFTER TOUCHDOWN

Most (One-Point) Points After Touchdown, Career

9 Mike Cofer, San Francisco, 2 games (10 att)
8 Don Chandler, Green Bay, 2 games (8 att)
Roy Gerela, Pittsburgh, 3 games (9 att)
Chris Bahr, Oakland-L.A. Raiders, 2 games (8 att)
Jason Elam, Denver, 2 games (8 att)
7 Ray Wersching, San Francisco, 2 games (7 att)
Lin Elliott, Dallas, 1 game (7 att)
Doug Brien, San Francisco, 1 game (7 att)

Most (One-Point) Points After Touchdown, Game

7 Mike Cofer, San Francisco vs. Denver, 1990 (8 att)
Lin Elliott, Dallas vs. Buffalo, 1993 (7 att)
Doug Brien, San Francisco vs. San Diego, 1995 (7 att)
6 Ali Haji-Sheikh, Washington vs. Denver, 1988 (6 att)
5 Don Chandler, Green Bay vs. Kansas City, 1967 (5 att)
Roy Gerela, Pittsburgh vs. Dallas, 1979 (5 att)
Chris Bahr, L.A. Raiders vs. Washington, 1984 (5 att)
Ray Wersching, San Francisco vs. Miami, 1985 (5 att)
Kevin Butler, Chicago vs. New England, 1986 (5 att)

Most Two-Point Conversions, Game

1 Mark Seay, San Diego vs. San Francisco, 1995
Alfred Pupunu, San Diego vs. San Francisco, 1995
Mark Chmura, Green Bay vs. New England, 1997

FIELD GOALS

Field Goals Attempted, Career

6 Jim Turner, N.Y. Jets-Denver, 2 games
Roy Gerela, Pittsburgh, 3 games
Rich Karlis, Denver, 2 games
5 Efren Herrera, Dallas, 1 game
Ray Wersching, San Francisco, 2 games
Jason Elam, Denver, 2 games

Most Field Goals Attempted, Game

5 Jim Turner, N.Y. Jets vs. Baltimore, 1969
Efren Herrera, Dallas vs. Denver, 1978
4 Don Chandler, Green Bay vs. Oakland, 1968
Roy Gerela, Pittsburgh vs. Dallas, 1976
Ray Wersching, San Francisco vs. Cincinnati, 1982
Rich Karlis, Denver vs. N.Y. Giants, 1987
Mike Cofer, San Francisco vs. Cincinnati, 1989
Jason Elam, Denver vs. Atlanta, 1999
Jeff Wilkins, St. Louis vs. Tennessee, 2000

Most Field Goals, Career
5 Ray Wersching, San Francisco, 2 games (5 att)
4 Don Chandler, Green Bay, 2 games (4 att)
Jim Turner, N.Y. Jets-Denver, 2 games (6 att)
Uwe von Schamann, Miami, 2 games (4 att)
3 Mike Clark, Dallas, 2 games (3 att)
Jan Stenerud, Kansas City, 1 game (3 att)
Chris Bahr, Oakland-L.A. Raiders, 2 games (4 att)
Mark Moseley, Washington, 2 games (4 att)
Kevin Butler, Chicago, 1 game (3 att)
Rich Karlis, Denver, 2 games (6 att)
Jim Breech, Cincinnati, 2 games (3 att)
Matt Bahr, Pittsburgh-N.Y. Giants, 2 games (3 att)
Chip Lohmiller, Washington, 1 game (3 att)
Steve Christie, Buffalo, 2 games (3 att)
Eddie Murray, Dallas, 1 game (3 att)
Jason Elam, Denver, 2 games (5 att)
Jeff Wilkins, St. Louis, 1 game (4 att)

Most Field Goals, Game
4 Don Chandler, Green Bay vs. Oakland, 1968
Ray Wersching, San Francisco vs. Cincinnati, 1982
3 Jim Turner, N.Y. Jets vs. Baltimore, 1969
Jan Stenerud, Kansas City vs. Minnesota, 1970
Uwe von Schamann, Miami vs. San Francisco, 1985
Kevin Butler, Chicago vs. New England, 1986
Jim Breech, Cincinnati vs. San Francisco, 1989
Chip Lohmiller, Washington vs. Buffalo, 1992
Eddie Murray, Dallas vs. Buffalo, 1994
Jeff Wilkins, St. Louis vs. Tennessee, 2000

Longest Field Goal
54 Steve Christie, Buffalo vs. Dallas, 1994
51 Jason Elam, Denver vs. Green Bay, 1998
48 Jan Stenerud, Kansas City vs. Minnesota, 1970
Rich Karlis, Denver vs. N.Y. Giants, 1987

SAFETIES

Most Safeties, Game
1 Dwight White, Pittsburgh vs. Minnesota, 1975
Reggie Harrison, Pittsburgh vs. Dallas, 1976
Henry Waechter, Chicago vs. New England, 1986
George Martin, N.Y. Giants vs. Denver, 1987
Bruce Smith, Buffalo vs. N.Y. Giants, 1991

RUSHING

ATTEMPTS

Most Attempts, Career
101 Franco Harris, Pittsburgh, 4 games
70 Emmitt Smith, Dallas, 3 games
64 John Riggins, Washington, 2 games

Most Attempts, Game
38 John Riggins, Washington vs. Miami, 1983
34 Franco Harris, Pittsburgh vs. Minnesota, 1975
33 Larry Csonka, Miami vs. Minnesota, 1974

YARDS GAINED

Most Yards Gained, Career
354 Franco Harris, Pittsburgh, 4 games
297 Larry Csonka, Miami, 3 games
289 Emmitt Smith, Dallas, 3 games

Most Yards Gained, Game
204 Timmy Smith, Washington vs. Denver, 1988
191 Marcus Allen, L.A. Raiders vs. Washington, 1984
166 John Riggins, Washington vs. Miami, 1983

Longest Run From Scrimmage
74 Marcus Allen, L.A. Raiders vs. Washington, 1984 (TD)
58 Tom Matte, Baltimore vs. N.Y. Jets, 1969
Timmy Smith, Washington vs. Denver, 1988 (TD)
49 Larry Csonka, Miami vs. Washington, 1973

AVERAGE GAIN

Highest Average Gain, Career (20 attempts)
9.6 Marcus Allen, L.A. Raiders, 1 game (20-191)
9.3 Timmy Smith, Washington, 1 game (22-204)
5.3 Walt Garrison, Dallas, 2 games (26-139)

Highest Average Gain, Game (10 attempts)
10.5 Tom Matte, Baltimore vs. N.Y. Jets, 1969 (11-116)
9.6 Marcus Allen, L.A. Raiders vs. Washington, 1984 (20-191)
9.3 Timmy Smith, Washington vs. Denver, 1988 (22-204)

TOUCHDOWNS

Most Touchdowns, Career
5 Emmitt Smith, Dallas, 3 games
4 Franco Harris, Pittsburgh, 4 games
Thurman Thomas, Buffalo, 4 games
John Elway, Denver, 5 games
3 Terrell Davis, Denver, 2 games

Most Touchdowns, Game
3 Terrell Davis, Denver vs. Green Bay, 1998
2 Elijah Pitts, Green Bay vs. Kansas City, 1967
Larry Csonka, Miami vs. Minnesota, 1974
Pete Banaszak, Oakland vs. Minnesota, 1977
Franco Harris, Pittsburgh vs. Los Angeles, 1980
Marcus Allen, L.A. Raiders vs. Washington, 1984
Jim McMahon, Chicago vs. New England, 1986
Timmy Smith, Washington vs. Denver, 1988
Tom Rathman, San Francisco vs. Denver, 1990
Gerald Riggs, Washington vs. Buffalo, 1992
Emmitt Smith, Dallas vs. Buffalo, 1994
Emmitt Smith, Dallas vs. Pittsburgh, 1996
Howard Griffith, Denver vs. Atlanta, 1999
Eddie George, Tennessee vs. St. Louis, 2000

PASSING

PASSER RATING

Highest Passer Rating, Career (40 attempts)
127.8 Joe Montana, San Francisco, 4 games
122.8 Jim Plunkett, Oakland-L.A. Raiders, 2 games
112.8 Terry Bradshaw, Pittsburgh, 4 games

ATTEMPTS

Most Passes Attempted, Career
152 John Elway, Denver, 5 games
145 Jim Kelly, Buffalo, 4 games
122 Joe Montana, San Francisco, 4 games

Most Passes Attempted, Game
58 Jim Kelly, Buffalo vs. Washington, 1992
50 Dan Marino, Miami vs. San Francisco, 1985
Jim Kelly, Buffalo vs. Dallas, 1994
49 Stan Humphries, San Diego vs. San Francisco, 1995
Neil O'Donnell, Pittsburgh vs. Dallas, 1996

COMPLETIONS

Most Passes Completed, Career
83 Joe Montana, San Francisco, 4 games
81 Jim Kelly, Buffalo, 4 games
76 John Elway, Denver, 5 games

Most Passes Completed, Game
31 Jim Kelly, Buffalo vs. Dallas, 1994
29 Dan Marino, Miami vs. San Francisco, 1985
28 Jim Kelly, Buffalo vs. Washington, 1992
Neil O'Donnell, Pittsburgh vs. Dallas, 1996

Most Consecutive Completions, Game
13 Joe Montana, San Francisco vs. Denver, 1990
10 Phil Simms, N.Y. Giants vs. Denver, 1987
Troy Aikman, Dallas vs. Pittsburgh, 1996
9 Jim Kelly, Buffalo vs. Dallas, 1994
Neil O'Donnell, Pittsburgh vs. Dallas, 1996
Steve McNair, Tennessee vs. St. Louis, 2000

COMPLETION PERCENTAGE

Highest Completion Percentage, Career (40 attempts)
70.0 Troy Aikman, Dallas, 3 games, (80-56)
68.0 Joe Montana, San Francisco, 4 games (122-83)
63.6 Len Dawson, Kansas City, 2 games (44-28)

Highest Completion Percentage, Game (20 attempts)
88.0 Phil Simms, N.Y. Giants vs. Denver, 1987 (25-22)
75.9 Joe Montana, San Francisco vs. Denver, 1990 (29-22)
73.5 Ken Anderson, Cincinnati vs. San Francisco, 1982 (34-25)

YARDS GAINED

Most Yards Gained, Career
1,142 Joe Montana, San Francisco, 4 games
1,128 John Elway, Denver, 5 games
932 Terry Bradshaw, Pittsburgh, 4 games

Most Yards Gained, Game
414 Kurt Warner, St. Louis vs. Tennessee, 2000
357 Joe Montana, San Francisco vs. Cincinnati, 1989
340 Doug Williams, Washington vs. Denver, 1988

Longest Pass Completion
81 Brett Favre (to Freeman), Green Bay vs. New England, 1997 (TD)
80 Jim Plunkett (to King), Oakland vs. Philadelphia, 1981 (TD)
Doug Williams (to Sanders), Washington vs. Denver, 1988 (TD)
John Elway (to R. Smith), Denver vs. Atlanta, 1999 (TD)
76 David Woodley (to Cefalo), Miami vs. Washington, 1983 (TD)

SUPER BOWL RECORDS

AVERAGE GAIN

Highest Average Gain, Career (40 attempts)

11.10 Terry Bradshaw, Pittsburgh, 4 games (84-932)
9.62 Bart Starr, Green Bay, 2 games (47-452)
9.41 Jim Plunkett, Oakland-L.A. Raiders, 2 games (46-433)

Highest Average Gain, Game (20 attempts)

14.71 Terry Bradshaw, Pittsburgh vs. Los Angeles, 1980 (21-309)
12.80 Jim McMahon, Chicago vs. New England, 1986 (20-256)
12.43 Jim Plunkett, Oakland vs. Philadelphia, 1981 (21-261)

TOUCHDOWNS

Most Touchdown Passes, Career

11 Joe Montana, San Francisco, 4 games
9 Terry Bradshaw, Pittsburgh, 4 games
8 Roger Staubach, Dallas, 4 games

Most Touchdown Passes, Game

6 Steve Young, San Francisco vs. San Diego, 1995
5 Joe Montana, San Francisco vs. Denver, 1990
4 Terry Bradshaw, Pittsburgh vs. Dallas, 1979
Doug Williams, Washington vs. Denver, 1988
Troy Aikman, Dallas vs. Buffalo, 1993

HAD INTERCEPTED

Lowest Percentage, Passes Had Intercepted, Career (40 attempts)

0.00 Jim Plunkett, Oakland-L.A. Raiders, 2 games (46-0)
Joe Montana, San Francisco, 4 games (122-0)
Kurt Warner, St. Louis, 1 game (45-0)
1.25 Troy Aikman, Dallas, 3 games (80-1)
1.45 Brett Favre, Green Bay, 2 games (69-1)

Most Attempts, Without Interception, Game

45 Kurt Warner, St. Louis vs. Tennessee, 2000
36 Joe Montana, San Francisco vs. Cincinnati, 1989
Steve Young, San Francisco vs. San Diego, 1995
35 Joe Montana, San Francisco vs. Miami, 1985

Most Passes Had Intercepted, Career

8 John Elway, Denver, 5 games
7 Craig Morton, Dallas-Denver, 2 games
Jim Kelly, Buffalo, 4 games
6 Fran Tarkenton, Minnesota, 3 games

Most Passes Had Intercepted, Game

4 Craig Morton, Denver vs. Dallas, 1978
Jim Kelly, Buffalo vs. Washington, 1992
Drew Bledsoe, New England vs. Green Bay, 1997
3 By ten players

PASS RECEIVING

RECEPTIONS

Most Receptions, Career

28 Jerry Rice, San Francisco, 3 games
27 Andre Reed, Buffalo, 4 games
20 Roger Craig, San Francisco, 3 games
Thurman Thomas, Buffalo, 4 games

Most Receptions, Game

11 Dan Ross, Cincinnati vs. San Francisco, 1982
Jerry Rice, San Francisco vs. Cincinnati, 1989
10 Tony Nathan, Miami vs. San Francisco, 1985
Jerry Rice, San Francisco vs. San Diego, 1995
Andre Hastings, Pittsburgh vs. Dallas, 1996
9 Ricky Sanders, Washington vs. Denver, 1988
Antonio Freeman, Green Bay vs. Denver, 1998

YARDS GAINED

Most Yards Gained, Career

512 Jerry Rice, San Francisco, 3 games
364 Lynn Swann, Pittsburgh, 4 games
323 Andre Reed, Buffalo, 4 games

Most Yards Gained, Game

215 Jerry Rice, San Francisco vs. Cincinnati, 1989
193 Ricky Sanders, Washington vs. Denver, 1988
162 Isaac Bruce, St. Louis vs. Tennessee, 2000

Longest Reception

81 Antonio Freeman (from Favre), Green Bay vs. New England, 1997 (TD)
80 Kenny King (from Plunkett), Oakland vs. Philadelphia, 1981 (TD)
Ricky Sanders (from Williams), Washington vs. Denver, 1988 (TD)
Rod Smith (from Elway), Denver vs. Atlanta, 1999
76 Jimmy Cefalo (from Woodley), Miami vs. Washington, 1983 (TD)

AVERAGE GAIN

Highest Average Gain, Career (8 receptions)

24.4 John Stallworth, Pittsburgh, 4 games (11-268)
23.4 Ricky Sanders, Washington, 2 games (10-234)
22.8 Lynn Swann, Pittsburgh, 4 games (16-364)

Highest Average Gain, Game (3 receptions)

40.33 John Stallworth, Pittsburgh vs. Los Angeles, 1980 (3-121)
40.25 Lynn Swann, Pittsburgh vs. Dallas, 1976 (4-161)
38.33 John Stallworth, Pittsburgh vs. Dallas, 1979 (3-115)

TOUCHDOWNS

Most Touchdowns, Career

7 Jerry Rice, San Francisco, 3 games
3 John Stallworth, Pittsburgh, 4 games
Lynn Swann, Pittsburgh, 4 games
Cliff Branch, Oakland-L.A. Raiders, 3 games
Antonio Freeman, Green Bay, 2 games
2 Max McGee, Green Bay, 2 games
Bill Miller, Oakland, 1 game
Butch Johnson, Dallas, 2 games
Dan Ross, Cincinnati, 1 game
Roger Craig, San Francisco, 3 games
Ricky Sanders, Washington, 2 games
John Taylor, San Francisco, 3 games
Gary Clark, Washington, 2 games
Don Beebe, Buffalo-Green Bay, 4 games
Michael Irvin, Dallas, 3 games
Ricky Watters, San Francisco, 1 game
Jay Novacek, Dallas, 3 games

Most Touchdowns, Game

3 Jerry Rice, San Francisco vs. San Diego, 1995; vs. Denver, 1990
2 Max McGee, Green Bay vs. Kansas City, 1967
Bill Miller, Oakland vs. Green Bay, 1968
John Stallworth, Pittsburgh vs. Dallas, 1979
Cliff Branch, Oakland vs. Philadelphia, 1981
Dan Ross, Cincinnati vs. San Francisco, 1982
Roger Craig, San Francisco vs. Miami, 1985
Ricky Sanders, Washington vs. Denver, 1988
Michael Irvin, Dallas vs. Buffalo, 1993
Ricky Watters, San Francisco vs. San Diego, 1995
Antonio Freeman, Green Bay vs. Denver, 1998

INTERCEPTIONS BY

Most Interceptions By, Career

3 Chuck Howley, Dallas, 2 games
Rod Martin, Oakland-L.A. Raiders, 2 games
Larry Brown, Dallas, 3 games
2 Randy Beverly, N.Y. Jets, 1 game
Jake Scott, Miami, 3 games
Mike Wagner, Pittsburgh, 3 games
Mel Blount, Pittsburgh, 4 games
Eric Wright, San Francisco, 4 games
Barry Wilburn, Washington, 1 game
Brad Edwards, Washington, 1 game
Thomas Everett, Dallas, 2 games
James Washington, Dallas, 2 games
Darrien Gordon, San Diego-Denver, 3 games

Most Interceptions By, Game

3 Rod Martin, Oakland vs. Philadelphia, 1981
2 Randy Beverly, N.Y. Jets vs. Baltimore, 1969
Chuck Howley, Dallas vs. Baltimore, 1971
Jake Scott, Miami vs. Washington, 1973
Barry Wilburn, Washington vs. Denver, 1988
Brad Edwards, Washington vs. Buffalo, 1992
Thomas Everett, Dallas vs. Buffalo, 1993
Larry Brown, Dallas vs. Pittsburgh, 1996
Darrien Gordon, Denver vs. Atlanta, 1999

YARDS GAINED

Most Yards Gained, Career

108 Darrien Gordon, San Diego-Denver, 3 games
77 Larry Brown, Dallas, 3 games
75 Willie Brown, Oakland, 2 games

Most Yards Gained, Game

108 Darrien Gordon, Denver vs. Atlanta, 1999
77 Larry Brown, Dallas vs. Pittsburgh, 1996
75 Willie Brown, Oakland vs. Minnesota, 1977

Longest Return

75 Willie Brown, Oakland vs. Minnesota, 1977 (TD)
60 Herb Adderley, Green Bay vs. Oakland, 1968 (TD)
58 Darrien Gordon, Denver vs. Atlanta, 1999

TOUCHDOWNS

Most Touchdowns, Game

1 Herb Adderley, Green Bay vs. Oakland, 1968
Willie Brown, Oakland vs. Minnesota, 1977
Jack Squirek, L.A. Raiders vs. Washington, 1984
Reggie Phillips, Chicago vs. New England, 1986

PUNTING

Most Punts, Career

17 Mike Eischeid, Oakland-Minnesota, 3 games
Mike Horan, Denver-St. Louis, 4 games
15 Larry Seiple, Miami, 3 games
14 Ron Widby, Dallas, 2 games
Ray Guy, Oakland-L.A. Raiders, 3 games
Chris Mohr, Buffalo, 3 games
Craig Hentrich, Green Bay-Tennessee, 3 games

Most Punts, Game

9 Ron Widby, Dallas vs. Baltimore, 1971
8 Tom Tupa, New England vs. Green Bay, 1997
7 By seven players

Longest Punt

63 Lee Johnson, Cincinnati vs. San Francisco, 1989
62 Rich Camarillo, New England vs. Chicago, 1986
61 Jerrel Wilson, Kansas City vs. Green Bay, 1967

AVERAGE YARDAGE

Highest Average, Punting, Career (10 punts)

46.5 Jerrel Wilson, Kansas City, 2 games (11-511)
41.9 Ray Guy, Oakland-L.A. Raiders, 3 games (14-587)
41.3 Larry Seiple, Miami, 3 games (15-620)

Highest Average, Punting, Game (4 punts)

48.8 Bryan Wagner, San Diego vs. San Francisco, 1995 (4-195)
48.5 Jerrel Wilson, Kansas City vs. Minnesota, 1970 (4-194)
46.3 Jim Miller, San Francisco vs. Cincinnati, 1982 (4-185)

PUNT RETURNS

Most Punt Returns, Career

6 Willie Wood, Green Bay, 2 games
Jake Scott, Miami, 3 games
Theo Bell, Pittsburgh, 2 games
Mike Nelms, Washington, 1 game
John Taylor, San Francisco, 3 games
Desmond Howard, Green Bay, 1 game
David Meggett, N.Y. Giants-New England, 2 games
5 Dana McLemore, San Francisco, 1 game
4 By eight players

Most Punt Returns, Game

6 Mike Nelms, Washington vs. Miami, 1983
Desmond Howard, Green Bay vs. New England, 1997
5 Willie Wood, Green Bay vs. Oakland, 1968
Dana McLemore, San Francisco vs. Miami, 1985
4 By seven players

Most Fair Catches, Game

3 Ron Gardin, Baltimore vs. Dallas, 1971
Golden Richards, Dallas vs. Pittsburgh, 1976
Greg Pruitt, L.A. Raiders vs. Washington, 1984
Al Edwards, Buffalo vs. N.Y. Giants, 1991
David Meggett, N.Y. Giants vs. Buffalo, 1991

YARDS GAINED

Most Yards Gained, Career

94 John Taylor, San Francisco, 3 games
90 Desmond Howard, Green Bay, 1 game
67 David Meggett, N.Y. Giants-New England, 2 games

Most Yards Gained, Game

90 Desmond Howard, Green Bay vs. New England, 1997
56 John Taylor, San Francisco vs. Cincinnati, 1989
52 Mike Nelms, Washington vs. Miami, 1983

Longest Return

45 John Taylor, San Francisco vs. Cincinnati, 1989
34 Darrell Green, Washington vs. L.A. Raiders, 1984
Desmond Howard, Green Bay vs. New England, 1997
32 Desmond Howard, Green Bay vs. New England, 1997

AVERAGE YARDAGE

Highest Average, Career (4 returns)

15.7 John Taylor, San Francisco, 3 games (6-94)
15.0 Desmond Howard, Green Bay, 1 game (6-90)
11.2 David Meggett, N.Y. Giants-New England, 2 games (6-67)

Highest Average, Game (3 returns)

18.7 John Taylor, San Francisco vs. Cincinnati, 1989 (3-56)
15.0 Desmond Howard, Green Bay vs. New England, 1997 (6-90)
12.7 John Taylor, San Francisco vs. Denver, 1990 (3-38)

TOUCHDOWNS

Most Touchdowns, Game

None

KICKOFF RETURNS

Most Kickoff Returns, Career

10 Ken Bell, Denver, 3 games
8 Larry Anderson, Pittsburgh, 2 games
Fulton Walker, Miami, 2 games
Andre Coleman, San Diego, 1 game
7 Preston Pearson, Baltimore-Pittsburgh-Dallas, 5 games
Stephen Starring, New England, 1 game
David Meggett, N.Y. Giants-New England, 2 games

Most Kickoff Returns, Game

8 Andre Coleman, San Diego vs. San Francisco, 1995
7 Stephen Starring, New England vs. Chicago, 1986
6 Darren Carrington, Denver vs. San Francisco, 1990
Antonio Freeman, Green Bay vs. Denver, 1998

YARDS GAINED

Most Yards Gained, Career

283 Fulton Walker, Miami, 2 games
244 Andre Coleman, San Diego, 1 game
210 Tim Dwight, Atlanta, 1 game

Most Yards Gained, Game

244 Andre Coleman, San Diego vs. San Francisco, 1995
210 Tim Dwight, Atlanta vs. Denver, 1999
190 Fulton Walker, Miami vs. Washington, 1983

Longest Return

99 Desmond Howard, Green Bay vs. New England, 1997 (TD)
98 Fulton Walker, Miami vs. Washington, 1983 (TD)
Andre Coleman, San Diego vs. San Francisco, 1995 (TD)
94 Tim Dwight, Atlanta vs. Denver, 1999 (TD)

AVERAGE YARDAGE

Highest Average, Career (4 returns)

42.0 Tim Dwight, Atlanta, 1 game (5-210)
38.5 Desmond Howard, Green Bay, 1 game (4-154)
35.4 Fulton Walker, Miami, 2 games (8-283)

Highest Average, Game (3 returns)

47.5 Fulton Walker, Miami vs. Washington, 1983 (4-190)
42.0 Tim Dwight, Atlanta vs. Denver, 1999 (5-210)
38.5 Desmond Howard, Green Bay vs. New England, 1997 (4-154)

TOUCHDOWNS

Most Touchdowns, Game

1 Fulton Walker, Miami vs. Washington, 1983
Stanford Jennings, Cincinnati vs. San Francisco, 1989
Andre Coleman, San Diego vs. San Francisco, 1995
Desmond Howard, Green Bay vs. New England, 1997
Tim Dwight, Atlanta vs. Denver, 1999

FUMBLES

Most Fumbles, Career

5 Roger Staubach, Dallas, 4 games
4 Jim Kelly, Buffalo, 4 games
3 Franco Harris, Pittsburgh, 4 games
Terry Bradshaw, Pittsburgh, 4 games
John Elway, Denver, 5 games
Frank Reich, Buffalo, 4 games
Thurman Thomas, Buffalo, 4 games

Most Fumbles, Game

3 Roger Staubach, Dallas vs. Pittsburgh, 1976
Jim Kelly, Buffalo vs. Washington, 1992
Frank Reich, Buffalo vs. Dallas, 1993
2 Franco Harris, Pittsburgh vs. Minnesota, 1975
Butch Johnson, Dallas vs. Denver, 1978
Terry Bradshaw, Pittsburgh vs. Dallas, 1979
Joe Montana, San Francisco vs. Cincinnati, 1989
John Elway, Denver vs. San Francisco, 1990
Thurman Thomas, Buffalo vs. Dallas, 1994

RECOVERIES

Most Fumbles Recovered, Career

2 Jake Scott, Miami, 3 games (1 own, 1 opp)
Fran Tarkenton, Minnesota, 3 games (2 own)
Franco Harris, Pittsburgh, 4 games (2 own)
Roger Staubach, Dallas, 4 games (2 own)
Bobby Walden, Pittsburgh, 2 games (2 own)
John Fitzgerald, Dallas, 4 games (2 own)
Randy Hughes, Dallas, 3 games (2 opp)
Butch Johnson, Dallas, 2 games (2 own)
Mike Singletary, Chicago, 1 game (2 opp)
John Elway, Denver, 5 games (2 own)
Jimmie Jones, Dallas, 2 games (2 opp)
Kenneth Davis, Buffalo, 4 games (2 own)

Most Fumbles Recovered, Game
2 Jake Scott, Miami vs. Minnesota, 1974 (1 own, 1 opp)
Roger Staubach, Dallas vs. Pittsburgh, 1976 (2 own)
Randy Hughes, Dallas vs. Denver, 1978 (2 opp)
Butch Johnson, Dallas vs. Denver, 1978 (2 own)
Mike Singletary, Chicago vs. New England, 1986 (2 opp)
Jimmie Jones, Dallas vs. Buffalo, 1993 (2 opp)

YARDS GAINED
Most Yards Gained, Game
64 Leon Lett, Dallas vs. Buffalo, 1993 (opp)
49 Mike Bass, Washington vs. Miami, 1973 (opp)
46 James Washington, Dallas vs. Buffalo, 1994 (opp)
Longest Return
64 Leon Lett, Dallas vs. Buffalo, 1993
49 Mike Bass, Washington vs. Miami, 1973 (TD)
46 James Washington, Dallas vs. Buffalo, 1994 (TD)

TOUCHDOWNS
Most Touchdowns, Game
1 Mike Bass, Washington vs. Miami, 1973 (opp 49 yds)
Mike Hegman, Dallas vs. Pittsburgh, 1979 (opp 37 yds)
Jimmie Jones, Dallas vs. Buffalo, 1993 (opp 2 yds)
Ken Norton, Dallas vs. Buffalo, 1993 (opp 9 yds)
James Washington, Dallas vs. Buffalo, 1994 (opp 46 yds)

COMBINED NET YARDS GAINED
(Rushing, receiving, interception returns, punt returns, kickoff returns, and fumble returns)
ATTEMPTS
Most Attempts, Career
108 Franco Harris, Pittsburgh, 4 games
81 Emmitt Smith, Dallas, 3 games
72 Roger Craig, San Francisco, 3 games
Thurman Thomas, Buffalo, 4 games
Most Attempts, Game
39 John Riggins, Washington vs. Miami, 1983
35 Franco Harris, Pittsburgh vs. Minnesota, 1975
34 Matt Snell, N.Y. Jets vs. Baltimore, 1969
Emmitt Smith, Dallas vs. Buffalo, 1994

YARDS GAINED
Most Yards Gained, Career
527 Jerry Rice, San Francisco, 3 games
468 Franco Harris, Pittsburgh, 4 games
410 Roger Craig, San Francisco, 3 games
Most Yards Gained, Game
244 Andre Coleman, San Diego vs. San Francisco, 1995
Desmond Howard, Green Bay vs. New England, 1997
235 Ricky Sanders, Washington vs. Denver, 1988
230 Antonio Freeman, Green Bay vs. Denver, 1998

SACKS
Sacks have been compiled since 1983.
Most Sacks, Career
4.5 Charles Haley, San Francisco-Dallas, 5 games
3 Danny Stubbs, San Francisco, 2 games
Leonard Marshall, N.Y. Giants, 2 games
Jeff Wright, Buffalo, 4 games
Reggie White, Green Bay, 2 games
2.5 Dexter Manley, Washington, 3 games
Most Sacks, Game
3 Reggie White, Green Bay vs. New England, 1997
2 Dwaine Board, San Francisco vs. Miami, 1985
Dennis Owens, New England vs. Chicago, 1986
Otis Wilson, Chicago vs. New England, 1986
Leonard Marshall, N.Y. Giants vs. Denver, 1987
Alvin Walton, Washington vs. Denver, 1988
Charles Haley, San Francisco vs. Cincinnati, 1989
Danny Stubbs, San Francisco vs. Denver, 1990
Jeff Wright, Buffalo vs. Dallas, 1994
Raylee Johnson, San Diego vs. San Francisco, 1995
Chad Hennings, Dallas vs. Pittsburgh, 1996
Tedy Bruschi, New England vs. Green Bay, 1997

TEAM RECORDS

GAMES, VICTORIES, DEFEATS
Most Games
8 Dallas, 1971-72, 1976, 1978-79, 1993-94, 1996
6 Denver, 1978, 1987-88, 1990, 1998-99
5 Miami, 1972-74, 1983, 1985
Washington, 1973, 1983-84, 1988, 1992
San Francisco, 1982, 1985, 1989-90, 1995
Pittsburgh, 1975-76, 1979-80, 1996
Most Consecutive Games
4 Buffalo, 1991-94
3 Miami, 1972-74
2 Green Bay, 1967-68; 1997-98
Dallas, 1971-72; 1978-79; 1993-94
Minnesota, 1974-75
Pittsburgh, 1975-76; 1979-80
Washington, 1983-84
Denver, 1987-88; 1998-99
San Francisco 1989-90
Most Games Won
5 San Francisco, 1982, 1985, 1989-90, 1995
Dallas, 1972, 1978, 1993-94, 1996
4 Pittsburgh, 1975-76, 1979-80
3 Oakland/L.A. Raiders, 1977, 1981, 1984
Washington, 1983, 1988, 1992
Green Bay, 1967-68, 1997
Most Consecutive Games Won
2 Green Bay, 1967-68
Miami, 1973-74
Pittsburgh, 1975-76, 1979-80
San Francisco, 1989-90
Dallas, 1993-94
Denver, 1998-99
Most Games Lost
4 Minnesota, 1970, 1974-75, 1977
Denver, 1978, 1987-88, 1990
Buffalo, 1991-94
3 Dallas, 1971, 1976, 1979
Miami, 1972, 1983, 1985
2 Washington, 1973, 1984
Cincinnati, 1982, 1989
New England, 1986, 1997
Most Consecutive Games Lost
4 Buffalo, 1991-94
2 Minnesota, 1974-75
Denver, 1987-88

SCORING
Most Points, Game
55 San Francisco vs. Denver, 1990
52 Dallas vs. Buffalo, 1993
49 San Francisco vs. San Diego, 1995
Fewest Points, Game
3 Miami vs. Dallas, 1972
6 Minnesota vs. Pittsburgh, 1975
7 By four teams
Most Points, Both Teams, Game
75 San Francisco (49) vs. San Diego (26), 1995
69 Dallas (52) vs. Buffalo (17), 1993
66 Pittsburgh (35) vs. Dallas (31), 1979
Fewest Points, Both Teams, Game
21 Washington (7) vs. Miami (14), 1973
22 Minnesota (6) vs. Pittsburgh (16), 1975
23 Baltimore (7) vs. N.Y. Jets (16), 1969
Largest Margin of Victory, Game
45 San Francisco vs. Denver, 1990 (55-10)
36 Chicago vs. New England, 1986 (46-10)
35 Dallas vs. Buffalo, 1993 (52-17)
Most Points, Each Half
1st: 35 Washington vs. Denver, 1988
2nd: 30 N.Y. Giants vs. Denver, 1987
Most Points, Each Quarter
1st: 14 Miami vs. Minnesota, 1974
Oakland vs. Philadelphia, 1981
Dallas vs. Buffalo, 1993
San Francisco vs. San Diego, 1995
New England vs. Green Bay, 1997
2nd: 35 Washington vs. Denver, 1988
3rd: 21 Chicago vs. New England, 1986
4th: 21 Dallas vs. Buffalo, 1993
Most Points, Both Teams, Each Half
1st: 45 Washington (35) vs. Denver (10), 1988
2nd: 44 Buffalo (24) vs. Washington (20), 1992
Fewest Points, Both Teams, Each Half
1st: 2 Minnesota (0) vs. Pittsburgh (2), 1975
2nd: 7 Miami (0) vs. Washington (7), 1973
Denver (0) vs. Washington (7), 1988
Most Points, Both Teams, Each Quarter
1st: 24 New England (14) vs. Green Bay (10), 1997
2nd: 35 Washington (35) vs. Denver (0), 1988

3rd: 24 Washington (14) vs. Buffalo (10), 1992
4th: 30 Denver (17) vs. Atlanta (13), 1999

TOUCHDOWNS

Most Touchdowns, Game
8 San Francisco vs. Denver, 1990
7 Dallas vs. Buffalo, 1993
San Francisco vs. San Diego, 1995
6 Washington vs. Denver, 1988

Fewest Touchdowns, Game
0 Miami vs. Dallas, 1972
1 By 17 teams

Most Touchdowns, Both Teams, Game
10 San Francisco (7) vs. San Diego (3), 1995
9 Pittsburgh (5) vs. Dallas (4), 1979
San Francisco (8) vs. Denver (1), 1990
Dallas (7) vs. Buffalo (2), 1993
7 N.Y. Giants (5) vs. Denver (2), 1987
Washington (6) vs. Denver (1), 1988
Washington (4) vs. Buffalo (3), 1992
Green Bay (4) vs. New England (3), 1997
Denver (4) vs. Green Bay (3), 1998

Fewest Touchdowns, Both Teams, Game
2 Baltimore (1) vs. N.Y. Jets (1), 1969
3 In six games

POINTS AFTER TOUCHDOWN

Most (One-Point) Points After Touchdown, Game
7 San Francisco vs. Denver, 1990
Dallas vs. Buffalo, 1993
San Francisco vs. San Diego, 1995
6 Washington vs. Denver, 1988
5 Green Bay vs. Kansas City, 1967
Pittsburgh vs. Dallas, 1979
L.A. Raiders vs. Washington, 1984
San Francisco vs. Miami, 1985
Chicago vs. New England, 1986

Most (One-Point) Points After Touchdown, Both Teams, Game
9 Pittsburgh (5) vs. Dallas (4), 1979
Dallas (7) vs. Buffalo (2), 1993
8 San Francisco (7) vs. Denver (1), 1990
San Francisco (7) vs. San Diego (1), 1995
7 Washington (6) vs. Denver (1), 1988
Washington (4) vs. Buffalo (3), 1992
Denver (4) vs. Green Bay (3), 1998

Fewest (One-Point) Points After Touchdown, Both Teams, Game
2 Baltimore (1) vs. N.Y. Jets (1), 1969
Baltimore (1) vs. Dallas (1), 1971
Minnesota (0) vs. Pittsburgh (2), 1975

Most Two-Point Conversions, Game
2 San Diego vs. San Francisco, 1995

Most Two-Point Conversions, Both Teams, Game
2 San Diego (2) vs. San Francisco (0), 1995

FIELD GOALS

Most Field Goals Attempted, Game
5 N.Y. Jets vs. Baltimore, 1969
Dallas vs. Denver, 1978
4 Green Bay vs. Oakland, 1968
Pittsburgh vs. Dallas, 1976
San Francisco vs. Cincinnati, 1982; 1989
Denver vs. N.Y. Giants, 1987
Denver vs. Atlanta, 1999
St. Louis vs. Tennessee, 2000

Most Field Goals Attempted, Both Teams, Game
7 N.Y. Jets (5) vs. Baltimore (2), 1969
San Francisco (4) vs. Cincinnati (3), 1989
St. Louis (4) vs. Tennessee (3), 2000
Denver (4) vs. Atlanta (3), 1999
6 Dallas (5) vs. Denver (1), 1978
5 Green Bay (4) vs. Oakland (1), 1968
Pittsburgh (4) vs. Dallas (1), 1976
Oakland (3) vs. Philadelphia (2), 1981
Denver (4) vs. N.Y. Giants (1), 1987
Dallas (3) vs. Buffalo (2), 1994

Fewest Field Goals Attempted, Both Teams, Game
1 Minnesota (0) vs. Miami (1), 1974
San Francisco (0) vs. Denver (1), 1990
2 Green Bay (0) vs. Kansas City (2), 1967
Miami (1) vs. Washington (1), 1973
Minnesota (1) vs. Pittsburgh (1), 1975
Dallas (1) vs. Pittsburgh (1), 1979
Dallas (1) vs. Buffalo (1), 1993
San Diego (1) vs. San Francisco (1), 1995
Denver (1) vs. Green Bay (1), 1998

Most Field Goals, Game
4 Green Bay vs. Oakland, 1968
San Francisco vs. Cincinnati, 1982
3 N.Y. Jets vs. Baltimore, 1969
Kansas City vs. Minnesota, 1970
Miami vs. San Francisco, 1985
Chicago vs. New England, 1986
Cincinnati vs. San Francisco, 1989
Washington vs. Buffalo, 1992
Dallas vs. Buffalo, 1994
St. Louis vs. Tennessee, 2000

Most Field Goals, Both Teams, Game
5 Cincinnati (3) vs. San Francisco (2), 1989
Dallas (3) vs. Buffalo (2), 1994
4 Green Bay (4) vs. Oakland (0), 1968
San Francisco (4) vs. Cincinnati (0), 1982
Miami (3) vs. San Francisco (1), 1985
Chicago (3) vs. New England (1), 1986
Washington (3) vs. Buffalo (1), 1992
Atlanta (2) vs. Denver (2), 1999
St. Louis (3) vs. Tennessee (1), 2000
3 In eleven games

Fewest Field Goals, Both Teams, Game
0 Miami vs. Washington, 1973
Pittsburgh vs. Minnesota, 1975
1 Green Bay (0) vs. Kansas City (1), 1967
Minnesota (0) vs. Miami (1), 1974
Pittsburgh (0) vs. Dallas (1), 1979
Washington (0) vs. Denver (1), 1988
San Francisco (0) vs. Denver (1), 1990
San Francisco (0) vs. San Diego (1), 1995

SAFETIES

Most Safeties, Game
1 Pittsburgh vs. Minnesota, 1975; vs. Dallas, 1976
Chicago vs. New England, 1986
N.Y. Giants vs. Denver, 1987
Buffalo vs. N.Y. Giants, 1991

FIRST DOWNS

Most First Downs, Game
31 San Francisco vs. Miami, 1985
28 San Francisco vs. Denver, 1990
San Francisco vs. San Diego, 1995
27 Tennessee vs. St. Louis, 2000

Fewest First Downs, Game
9 Minnesota vs. Pittsburgh, 1975
Miami vs. Washington, 1983
10 Dallas vs. Baltimore, 1971
Miami vs. Dallas, 1972
11 Denver vs. Dallas, 1978

Most First Downs, Both Teams, Game
50 San Francisco (31) vs. Miami (19), 1985
Tennessee (27) vs. St. Louis (23), 2000
49 Buffalo (25) vs. Washington (24), 1992
48 San Francisco (28) vs. San Diego (20), 1995

Fewest First Downs, Both Teams, Game
24 Dallas (10) vs. Baltimore (14), 1971
26 Minnesota (9) vs. Pittsburgh (17), 1975
27 Pittsburgh (13) vs. Dallas (14), 1976

RUSHING

Most First Downs, Rushing, Game
16 San Francisco vs. Miami, 1985
15 Dallas vs. Miami, 1972
14 Washington vs. Miami, 1983
San Francisco vs. Denver, 1990
Denver vs. Green Bay, 1998

Fewest First Downs, Rushing, Game
1 New England vs. Chicago, 1986
St. Louis vs. Tennessee, 2000
2 Minnesota vs. Kansas City, 1970; vs. Pittsburgh, 1975; vs. Oakland, 1977
Pittsburgh vs. Dallas, 1979
Miami vs. San Francisco, 1985
3 Miami vs. Dallas, 1972
Philadelphia vs. Oakland, 1981
New England vs. Green Bay, 1997

Most First Downs, Rushing, Both Teams, Game
21 Washington (14) vs. Miami (7), 1983
19 Washington (13) vs. Denver (6), 1988

San Francisco (14) vs. Denver (5), 1990
18 Dallas (15) vs. Miami (3), 1972
Miami (13) vs. Minnesota (5), 1974
San Francisco (16) vs. Miami (2), 1985
N.Y. Giants (10) vs. Buffalo (8), 1991
Denver (14) vs. Green Bay (4), 1998

Fewest First Downs, Rushing, Both Teams, Game
8 Baltimore (4) vs. Dallas (4), 1971
Pittsburgh (2) vs. Dallas (6), 1979
9 Philadelphia (3) vs. Oakland (6), 1981
10 Minnesota (2) vs. Kansas City (8), 1970

PASSING

Most First Downs, Passing, Game
18 Buffalo vs. Washington, 1992
St. Louis vs. Tennessee, 2000
17 Miami vs. San Francisco, 1985
San Francisco vs. San Diego, 1995
16 Denver vs. N.Y. Giants, 1987
San Francisco vs. Cincinnati, 1989

Fewest First Downs, Passing, Game
1 Denver vs. Dallas, 1978
2 Miami vs. Washington, 1983
4 Miami vs. Minnesota, 1974

Most First Downs, Passing, Both Teams, Game
32 Miami (17) vs. San Francisco (15), 1985
31 San Francisco (17) vs. San Diego (14), 1995
St. Louis (18) vs. Tennessee (13), 2000
30 Buffalo (18) vs. Washington (12), 1992

Fewest First Downs, Passing, Both Teams, Game
9 Denver (1) vs. Dallas (8), 1978
10 Minnesota (5) vs. Pittsburgh (5), 1975
11 Dallas (5) vs. Baltimore (6), 1971
Miami (2) vs. Washington (9), 1983

PENALTY

Most First Downs, Penalty, Game
4 Baltimore vs. Dallas, 1971
Miami vs. Minnesota, 1974
Cincinnati vs. San Francisco, 1982
Buffalo vs. Dallas, 1993
St. Louis vs. Tennessee, 2000
3 Kansas City vs. Minnesota, 1970
Minnesota vs. Oakland, 1977
Buffalo vs. Washington, 1992
Green Bay vs. Denver, 1998

Most First Downs, Penalty, Both Teams, Game
6 Cincinnati (4) vs. San Francisco (2), 1982
St. Louis (4) vs. Tennessee, 2000
5 Baltimore (4) vs. Dallas (1), 1971
Miami (4) vs. Minnesota (1), 1974
Buffalo (3) vs. Washington (2), 1992
Green Bay (3) vs. Denver (2), 1998
4 Kansas City (3) vs. Minnesota (1), 1970
Buffalo (4) vs. Dallas (0), 1993

Fewest First Downs, Penalty, Both Teams, Game
0 Dallas vs. Miami, 1972
Miami vs. Washington, 1973
Dallas vs. Pittsburgh, 1976
Miami vs. San Francisco, 1985
1 Green Bay (0) vs. Kansas City (1), 1967
Miami (0) vs. Washington (1), 1983
Cincinnati (0) vs. San Francisco (1), 1989
San Francisco (0) vs. Denver (1), 1990
Dallas (0) vs. Buffalo (1), 1994
Dallas (0) vs. Pittsburgh (1), 1996
Denver (0) vs. Atlanta (1), 1999

NET YARDS GAINED RUSHING AND PASSING

Most Yards Gained, Game
602 Washington vs. Denver, 1988
537 San Francisco vs. Miami, 1985
461 San Francisco vs. Denver, 1990

Fewest Yards Gained, Game
119 Minnesota vs. Pittsburgh, 1975
123 New England vs. Chicago, 1986
156 Denver vs. Dallas, 1978

Most Yards Gained, Both Teams, Game
929 Washington (602) vs. Denver (327), 1988
851 San Francisco (537) vs. Miami (314), 1985
809 San Francisco (455) vs. San Diego (354), 1995

Fewest Yards Gained, Both Teams, Game
452 Minnesota (119) vs. Pittsburgh (333), 1975
481 Washington (228) vs. Miami (253), 1973
Denver (156) vs. Dallas (325), 1978
497 Minnesota (238) vs. Miami (259), 1974

RUSHING

ATTEMPTS

Most Attempts, Game
57 Pittsburgh vs. Minnesota, 1975
53 Miami vs. Minnesota, 1974
52 Oakland vs. Minnesota, 1977
Washington vs. Miami, 1983

Fewest Attempts, Game
9 Miami vs. San Francisco, 1985
11 New England vs. Chicago, 1986
13 New England vs. Green Bay, 1997
St. Louis vs. Tennessee, 2000

Most Attempts, Both Teams, Game
81 Washington (52) vs. Miami (29), 1983
78 Pittsburgh (57) vs. Minnesota (21), 1975
Oakland (52) vs. Minnesota (26), 1977
77 Miami (53) vs. Minnesota (24), 1974
Pittsburgh (46) vs. Dallas (31), 1976

Fewest Attempts, Both Teams, Game
49 Miami (9) vs. San Francisco (40), 1985
New England (13) vs. Green Bay (36), 1997
St. Louis (13) vs. Tennessee (36), 2000
51 San Diego (19) vs. San Francisco (32), 1995
53 Kansas City (19) vs. Green Bay (34), 1967

YARDS GAINED

Most Yards Gained, Game
280 Washington vs. Denver, 1988
276 Washington vs. Miami, 1983
266 Oakland vs. Minnesota, 1977

Fewest Yards Gained, Game
7 New England vs. Chicago, 1986
17 Minnesota vs. Pittsburgh, 1975
25 Miami vs. San Francisco, 1985

Most Yards Gained, Both Teams, Game
377 Washington (280) vs. Denver (97), 1988
372 Washington (276) vs. Miami (96), 1983
338 N.Y. Giants (172) vs. Buffalo (166), 1991

Fewest Yards Gained, Both Teams, Game
158 New England (43) vs. Green Bay (115), 1997
159 Dallas (56) vs. Pittsburgh (103), 1996
168 Buffalo (43) vs. Washington (125), 1992

AVERAGE GAIN

Highest Average Gain, Game
7.00 L.A. Raiders vs. Washington, 1984 (33-231)
Washington vs. Denver, 1988 (40-280)
6.64 Buffalo vs. N.Y. Giants, 1991 (25-166)
6.22 Baltimore vs. N.Y. Jets, 1969 (23-143)

Lowest Average Gain, Game
0.64 New England vs. Chicago, 1986 (11-7)
0.81 Minnesota vs. Pittsburgh, 1975 (21-17)
2.23 Baltimore vs. Dallas, 1971 (31-69)

TOUCHDOWNS

Most Touchdowns, Game
4 Chicago vs. New England, 1986
Denver vs. Green Bay, 1998
3 Green Bay vs. Kansas City, 1967
Miami vs. Minnesota, 1974
San Francisco vs. Denver, 1990
Denver vs. Atlanta, 1999
2 Oakland vs. Minnesota, 1977
Pittsburgh vs. Los Angeles, 1980
L.A. Raiders vs. Washington, 1984
San Francisco vs. Miami, 1985
N.Y. Giants vs. Denver, 1987
Washington vs. Denver, 1988; vs. Buffalo, 1992
Buffalo vs. N.Y. Giants, 1991
Dallas vs. Buffalo, 1994; vs. Pittsburgh, 1996
Tennessee vs. St. Louis, 2000

Fewest Touchdowns, Game
0 By 21 teams

Most Touchdowns, Both Teams, Game
4 Miami (3) vs. Minnesota (1), 1974
Chicago (4) vs. New England (0), 1986
San Francisco (3) vs. Denver (1), 1990
Denver (4) vs. Green Bay (0), 1998
3 In nine games
Fewest Touchdowns, Both Teams, Game
0 Pittsburgh vs. Dallas, 1976
Oakland vs. Philadelphia, 1981
Cincinnati vs. San Francisco, 1989
1 In seven games

PASSING

ATTEMPTS

Most Passes Attempted, Game
59 Buffalo vs. Washington, 1992
55 San Diego vs. San Francisco, 1995
50 Miami vs. San Francisco, 1985
Buffalo vs. Dallas, 1994
Fewest Passes Attempted, Game
7 Miami vs. Minnesota, 1974
11 Miami vs. Washington, 1973
14 Pittsburgh vs. Minnesota, 1975
Most Passes Attempted, Both Teams, Game
93 San Diego (55) vs. San Francisco (38), 1995
92 Buffalo (59) vs. Washington (33), 1992
85 Miami (50) vs. San Francisco (35), 1985
Fewest Passes Attempted, Both Teams, Game
35 Miami (7) vs. Minnesota (28), 1974
39 Miami (11) vs. Washington (28), 1973
40 Pittsburgh (14) vs. Minnesota (26), 1975
Miami (17) vs. Washington (23), 1983

COMPLETIONS

Most Passes Completed, Game
31 Buffalo vs. Dallas, 1994
29 Miami vs. San Francisco, 1985
Buffalo vs. Washington, 1992
28 Pittsburgh vs. Dallas, 1996
Fewest Passes Completed, Game
4 Miami vs. Washington, 1983
6 Miami vs. Minnesota, 1974
8 Miami vs. Washington, 1973
Denver vs. Dallas, 1978
Most Passes Completed, Both Teams, Game
53 Miami (29) vs. San Francisco (24), 1985
52 San Diego (27) vs. San Francisco (25), 1995
50 Buffalo (31) vs. Dallas (19), 1994
Fewest Passes Completed, Both Teams, Game
19 Miami (4) vs. Washington (15), 1983
20 Pittsburgh (9) vs. Minnesota (11), 1975
22 Miami (8) vs. Washington (14), 1973

COMPLETION PERCENTAGE

Highest Completion Percentage, Game (20 attempts)
88.0 N.Y. Giants vs. Denver, 1987 (25-22)
75.0 San Francisco vs. Denver, 1990 (32-24)
73.5 Cincinnati vs. San Francisco, 1982 (34-25)
Lowest Completion Percentage, Game (20 attempts)
32.0 Denver vs. Dallas, 1978 (25-8)
37.9 Denver vs. San Francisco, 1990 (29-11)
38.5 Denver vs. Washington, 1988 (39-15)

YARDS GAINED

Most Yards Gained, Game
407 St. Louis vs. Tennessee, 2000
341 San Francisco vs. Cincinnati, 1989
336 Denver vs. Atlanta, 1999
Fewest Yards Gained, Game
35 Denver vs. Dallas, 1978
63 Miami vs. Minnesota, 1974
69 Miami vs. Washington, 1973
Most Yards Gained, Both Teams, Game
615 San Francisco (326) vs. Miami (289), 1985
St. Louis (407) vs. Tennessee (208), 2000
603 San Francisco (316) vs. San Diego (287), 1995
583 Denver (320) vs. N.Y. Giants (263), 1987
Fewest Yards Gained, Both Teams, Game
156 Miami (69) vs. Washington (87), 1973
186 Pittsburgh (84) vs. Minnesota (102), 1975
204 Miami (80) vs. Washington (124), 1983

TIMES SACKED

Most Times Sacked, Game
7 Dallas vs. Pittsburgh, 1976
New England vs. Chicago, 1986
6 Kansas City vs. Green Bay, 1967
Washington vs. L.A. Raiders, 1984
Denver vs. San Francisco, 1990
5 Dallas vs. Denver, 1978; vs. Pittsburgh, 1979
Cincinnati vs. San Francisco, 1982; 1989
Denver vs. Washington, 1988
Buffalo vs. Washington, 1992
Green Bay vs. New England, 1997
New England vs. Green Bay, 1997
Fewest Times Sacked, Game
0 Baltimore vs. N.Y. Jets, 1969; vs. Dallas, 1971
Minnesota vs. Pittsburgh, 1975
Pittsburgh vs. Los Angeles, 1980
Philadelphia vs. Oakland, 1981
Washington vs. Buffalo, 1992
Denver vs. Green Bay, 1998
Denver vs. Atlanta, 1999
1 By 13 teams
Most Times Sacked, Both Teams, Game
10 New England (7) vs. Chicago (3), 1986
Green Bay (5) vs. New England (5), 1997
9 Kansas City (6) vs. Green Bay (3), 1967
Dallas (7) vs. Pittsburgh (2), 1976
Dallas (5) vs. Denver (4), 1978
Dallas (5) vs. Pittsburgh (4), 1979
Cincinnati (5) vs. San Francisco (4), 1989
8 Washington (6) vs. L.A. Raiders (2), 1984
Fewest Times Sacked, Both Teams, Game
1 Philadelphia (0) vs. Oakland (1), 1981
Denver (0) vs. Green Bay (1), 1998
2 Baltimore (0) vs. N.Y. Jets (2), 1969
Baltimore (0) vs. Dallas (2), 1971
Minnesota (0) vs. Pittsburgh (2), 1975
Denver (0) vs. Atlanta (2), 1999
3 In five games

TOUCHDOWNS

Most Touchdowns, Game
6 San Francisco vs. San Diego, 1995
5 San Francisco vs. Denver, 1990
4 Pittsburgh vs. Dallas, 1979
Washington vs. Denver, 1988
Dallas vs. Buffalo, 1993
Fewest Touchdowns, Game
0 By 18 teams
Most Touchdowns, Both Teams, Game
7 Pittsburgh (4) vs. Dallas (3), 1979
San Francisco (6) vs. San Diego (1), 1995
5 Washington (4) vs. Denver (1), 1988
San Francisco (5) vs. Denver (0), 1990
Dallas (4) vs. Buffalo (1), 1993
4 Dallas (2) vs. Pittsburgh (2), 1976
Oakland (3) vs. Philadelphia (1), 1981
San Francisco (3) vs. Miami (1), 1985
N.Y. Giants (3) vs. Denver (1), 1987
Washington (2) vs. Buffalo (2), 1992
Green Bay (2) vs. New England (2), 1997
Fewest Touchdowns, Both Teams, Game
0 N.Y. Jets vs. Baltimore, 1969
Miami vs. Minnesota, 1974
Buffalo vs. Dallas, 1994
1 In six games

INTERCEPTIONS BY

Most Interceptions By, Game
4 N.Y. Jets vs. Baltimore, 1969
Dallas vs. Denver, 1978
Washington vs. Buffalo, 1992
Dallas vs. Buffalo, 1993
Green Bay vs. New England, 1997
3 By 12 teams
Most Interceptions By, Both Teams, Game
6 Baltimore (3) vs. Dallas (3), 1971
5 Washington (4) vs. Buffalo (1), 1992
4 In nine games

Fewest Interceptions By, Both Teams, Game
0 Buffalo vs. N.Y. Giants, 1991
St. Louis vs. Tennessee, 2000
1 Oakland (0) vs. Green Bay (1), 1968
Miami (0) vs. Dallas (1), 1972
Minnesota (0) vs. Miami (1), 1974
N.Y. Giants (0) vs. Denver (1), 1987
Cincinnati (0) vs. San Francisco (1), 1989

YARDS GAINED

Most Yards Gained, Game
136 Denver vs. Atlanta, 1999
95 Miami vs. Washington, 1973
91 Oakland vs. Minnesota, 1977

Most Yards Gained, Both Teams, Game
137 Denver (136) vs. Atlanta (1), 1999
95 Miami (95) vs. Washington (0), 1973
91 Oakland (91) vs. Minnesota (0), 1977

TOUCHDOWNS

Most Touchdowns, Game
1 Green Bay vs. Oakland, 1968
Oakland vs. Minnesota, 1977
L.A. Raiders vs. Washington, 1984
Chicago vs. New England, 1986

PUNTING

Most Punts, Game
9 Dallas vs. Baltimore, 1971
8 Washington vs. L.A. Raiders, 1984
New England vs. Green Bay, 1997
7 By eight teams

Fewest Punts, Game
1 Atlanta vs. Denver, 1999
Denver vs. Atlanta, 1999
2 Pittsburgh vs. Los Angeles, 1980
Denver vs. N.Y. Giants, 1987
St. Louis vs. Tennessee, 2000
3 By 11 teams

Most Punts, Both Teams, Game
15 Washington (8) vs. L.A. Raiders (7), 1984
New England (8) vs. Green Bay (7), 1997
13 Dallas (9) vs. Baltimore (4), 1971
Pittsburgh (7) vs. Minnesota (6), 1975
12 In three games

Fewest Punts, Both Teams, Game
2 Atlanta (1) vs. Denver (1), 1999
5 Denver (2) vs. N.Y. Giants (3), 1987
St. Louis (2) vs. Tennessee (3), 2000
6 Oakland (3) vs. Philadelphia (3), 1981

AVERAGE YARDAGE

Highest Average, Game (4 punts)
48.75 San Diego vs. San Francisco, 1995 (4-195)
48.50 Kansas City vs. Minnesota, 1970 (4-194)
46.25 San Francisco vs. Cincinnati, 1982 (4-185)

Lowest Average, Game (4 punts)
31.20 Washington vs. Miami, 1973 (5-156)
32.38 Washington vs. L.A. Raiders, 1984 (8-259)
32.40 Oakland vs. Minnesota, 1977 (5-162)

PUNT RETURNS

Most Punt Returns, Game
6 Washington vs. Miami, 1983
Green Bay vs. New England, 1997
5 By five teams

Fewest Punt Returns, Game
0 Minnesota vs. Miami, 1974
Buffalo vs. N.Y. Giants, 1991
Washington vs. Buffalo, 1992
Denver vs. Green Bay, 1998
Green Bay vs. Denver, 1998
Atlanta vs. Denver, 1999
Denver vs. Atlanta, 1999
1 By 16 teams

Most Punt Returns, Both Teams, Game
10 Green Bay (6) vs. New England (4), 1997
9 Pittsburgh (5) vs. Minnesota (4), 1975
8 Green Bay (5) vs. Oakland (3), 1968
Baltimore (5) vs. Dallas (3), 1971
Washington (6) vs. Miami (2), 1983

Fewest Punt Returns, Both Teams, Game
0 Denver vs. Green Bay, 1998
Atlanta vs. Denver, 1999
2 Dallas (1) vs. Miami (1), 1972
Denver (1) vs. N.Y. Giants (1), 1987
Buffalo (0) vs. N.Y. Giants (2), 1991
Buffalo (1) vs. Dallas (1), 1994
3 Kansas City (1) vs. Minnesota (2), 1970
Minnesota (0) vs. Miami (3), 1974
Washington (1) vs. Denver (2), 1988
Washington (0) vs. Buffalo (3), 1992
Dallas (1) vs. Pittsburgh (2), 1996
Tennessee (1) vs. St. Louis (2), 2000

YARDS GAINED

Most Yards Gained, Game
90 Green Bay vs. New England, 1997
56 San Francisco vs. Cincinnati, 1989
52 Washington vs. Miami, 1983

Fewest Yards Gained, Game
–1 Dallas vs. Miami, 1972
Tennessee vs. St. Louis, 2000
0 By 12 teams

Most Yards Gained, Both Teams, Game
120 Green Bay (90) vs. New England (30), 1997
74 Washington (52) vs. Miami (22), 1983
66 San Francisco (51) vs. Miami (15), 1985

Fewest Yards Gained, Both Teams, Game
0 Denver vs. Green Bay, 1998
Atlanta vs. Denver, 1999
7 Tennessee (-1) vs. St. Louis (8), 2000
9 Washington (0) vs. Bufffalo (9), 1992

AVERAGE RETURN

Highest Average, Game (3 returns)
18.7 San Francisco vs. Cincinnati, 1989 (3-56)
15.0 Green Bay vs. New England, 1997 (6-90)
12.7 San Francisco vs. Denver, 1990 (3-38)

TOUCHDOWNS

Most Touchdowns, Game
None

KICKOFF RETURNS

Most Kickoff Returns, Game
9 Denver vs. San Francisco, 1990
8 San Diego vs. San Francisco, 1995
7 By seven teams

Fewest Kickoff Returns, Game
1 N.Y. Jets vs. Baltimore, 1969
L.A. Raiders vs. Washington, 1984
Washington vs. Buffalo, 1992
2 By seven teams

Most Kickoff Returns, Both Teams, Game
12 Denver (9) vs. San Francisco (3), 1990
San Diego (8) vs. San Francisco (4), 1995
11 Los Angeles (6) vs. Pittsburgh (5), 1980
Miami (7) vs. San Francisco (4), 1985
New England (7) vs. Chicago (4), 1986
Green Bay (6) vs. Denver (5), 1998
10 Oakland (7) vs. Green Bay (3), 1968
New England (6) vs. Green Bay (4), 1997
Atlanta (7) vs. Denver (3), 1999

Fewest Kickoff Returns, Both Teams, Game
5 N.Y. Jets (1) vs. Baltimore (4), 1969
Miami (2) vs. Washington (3), 1973
Washington (1) vs. Buffalo (4), 1992
6 In three games

YARDS GAINED

Most Yards Gained, Game
244 San Diego vs. San Francisco, 1995
227 Atlanta vs. Denver, 1999
222 Miami vs. Washington, 1983

Fewest Yards Gained, Game
16 Washington vs. Buffalo, 1992
17 L.A. Raiders vs. Washington, 1984
25 N.Y. Jets vs. Baltimore, 1969

Most Yards Gained, Both Teams, Game
292 San Diego (244) vs. San Francisco (480), 1995
289 Green Bay (154) vs. New England (135), 1997
279 Miami (222) vs. Washington (57), 1983

Fewest Yards Gained, Both Teams, Game
78 Miami (33) vs. Washington (45), 1973
82 Pittsburgh (32) vs. Minnesota (50), 1975
92 San Francisco (40) vs. Cincinnati (52), 1982

AVERAGE GAIN
Highest Average, Game (3 returns)
44.0 Cincinnati vs. San Francisco, 1989 (3-132)
38.5 Green Bay vs. New England, 1997 (4-154)
37.0 Miami vs. Washington, 1983 (6-222)

TOUCHDOWNS
Most Touchdowns, Game
1 Miami vs. Washington, 1983
Cincinnati vs. San Francisco, 1989
San Diego vs. San Francisco, 1995
Green Bay vs. New England, 1997
Atlanta vs. Denver, 1999

PENALTIES
Most Penalties, Game
12 Dallas vs. Denver, 1978
10 Dallas vs. Baltimore, 1971
9 Dallas vs. Pittsburgh, 1979
Green Bay vs. Denver, 1998
Fewest Penalties, Game
0 Miami vs. Dallas, 1972
Pittsburgh vs. Dallas, 1976
Denver vs. San Francisco, 1990
Atlanta vs. Denver, 1999
1 Green Bay vs. Oakland, 1968
Miami vs. Minnesota, 1974; vs. San Francisco, 1985
Buffalo vs. Dallas, 1994
2 By six teams
Most Penalties, Both Teams, Game
20 Dallas (12) vs. Denver (8), 1978
16 Cincinnati (8) vs. San Francisco (8), 1982
Green Bay (9) vs. Denver (7), 1998
15 St. Louis (8) vs. Tennessee (7), 2000
Fewest Penalties, Both Teams, Game
2 Pittsburgh (0) vs. Dallas (2), 1976
3 Miami (0) vs. Dallas (3), 1972
Miami (1) vs. San Francisco (2), 1985
4 Denver (0) vs. San Francisco (4), 1990
Atlanta (0) vs. Denver (4), 1999

YARDS PENALIZED
Most Yards Penalized, Game
133 Dallas vs. Baltimore, 1971
122 Pittsburgh vs. Minnesota, 1975
94 Dallas vs. Denver, 1978
Fewest Yards Penalized, Game
0 Miami vs. Dallas, 1972
Pittsburgh vs. Dallas, 1976
Denver vs. San Francisco, 1990
Atlanta vs. Denver, 1999
4 Miami vs. Minnesota, 1974
10 Miami vs. San Francisco, 1985
San Francisco vs. Miami, 1985
Buffalo vs. Dallas, 1994
Most Yards Penalized, Both Teams, Game
164 Dallas (133) vs. Baltimore (31), 1971
154 Dallas (94) vs. Denver (60), 1978
140 Pittsburgh (122) vs. Minnesota (18), 1975
Fewest Yards Penalized, Both Teams, Game
15 Miami (0) vs. Dallas (15), 1972
20 Pittsburgh (0) vs. Dallas (20), 1976
Miami (10) vs. San Francisco (10), 1985
38 Denver (0) vs. San Francisco (38), 1990

FUMBLES
Most Fumbles, Game
8 Buffalo vs. Dallas, 1993
6 Dallas vs. Denver, 1978
Buffalo vs. Washington, 1992
5 Baltimore vs. Dallas, 1971
Fewest Fumbles, Game
0 By 16 teams
Most Fumbles, Both Teams, Game
12 Buffalo (8) vs. Dallas (4), 1993
10 Dallas (6) vs. Denver (4), 1978
8 Dallas (4) vs. Pittsburgh (4), 1976

Fewest Fumbles, Both Teams, Game
0 Los Angeles vs. Pittsburgh, 1980
Green Bay vs. New England, 1997
1 Oakland (0) vs. Minnesota (1), 1977
Oakland (0) vs. Philadelphia (1), 1981
Denver (0) vs. Washington (1), 1988
N.Y. Giants (0) vs. Buffalo (1), 1991
Denver (0) vs. Atlanta (1), 1999
2 In five games
Most Fumbles Lost, Game
5 Buffalo vs. Dallas, 1993
4 Baltimore vs. Dallas, 1971
Denver vs. Dallas, 1978
New England vs. Chicago, 1986
2 In many games
Most Fumbles Lost, Both Teams, Game
7 Buffalo (5) vs. Dallas (2), 1993
6 Denver (4) vs. Dallas (2), 1978
New England (4) vs. Chicago (2), 1986
5 Baltimore (4) vs. Dallas (1), 1971
Fewest Fumbles Lost, Both Teams, Game
0 Green Bay vs. Kansas City, 1967
Dallas vs. Pittsburgh, 1976
Los Angeles vs. Pittsburgh, 1980
Denver vs. N.Y. Giants, 1987
Denver vs. Washington, 1988
Buffalo vs. N.Y. Giants, 1991
San Diego vs. San Francisco, 1995
Dallas vs. Pittsburgh, 1996
Green Bay vs. New England, 1997
St. Louis vs. Tennessee, 2000
Most Fumbles Recovered, Game
8 Dallas vs. Denver, 1978 (4 own, 4 opp.)
6 Dallas vs. Buffalo, 1993 (1 own, 5 opp.)
5 Chicago vs. New England, 1986 (1 own, 4 opp.)

TURNOVERS
(Number of times losing the ball on interceptions and fumbles.)
Most Turnovers, Game
9 Buffalo vs. Dallas, 1993
8 Denver vs. Dallas, 1978
7 Baltimore vs. Dallas, 1971
Fewest Turnovers, Game
0 Green Bay vs. Oakland, 1968
Miami vs. Minnesota, 1974
Pittsburgh vs. Dallas, 1976
Oakland vs. Minnesota, 1977; vs. Philadelphia, 1981
N.Y. Giants vs. Denver, 1987; vs. Buffalo, 1991
San Francisco vs. Denver, 1990; vs. San Diego, 1995
Buffalo vs. N.Y. Giants, 1991
Dallas vs. Pittsburgh, 1996
Green Bay vs. New England, 1997
St. Louis vs. Tennessee, 2000
Tennessee vs. St. Louis, 2000
1 By many teams
Most Turnovers, Both Teams, Game
11 Baltimore (7) vs. Dallas (4), 1971
Buffalo (9) vs. Dallas (2), 1993
10 Denver (8) vs. Dallas (2), 1978
8 New England (6) vs. Chicago (2), 1986
Fewest Turnovers, Both Teams, Game
0 Buffalo vs. N.Y. Giants, 1991
St. Louis vs. Tennessee, 2000
1 N.Y. Giants (0) vs. Denver (1), 1987
2 Green Bay (1) vs. Kansas City (1), 1967
Miami (0) vs. Minnesota (2), 1974
Cincinnati (1) vs. San Francisco (1), 1989

POSTSEASON GAME RECORDS

Compiled by Elias Sports Bureau

Throughout this all-time postseason record section, the following abbreviations are used to indicate various levels of postseason games:

SB Super Bowl (1966 to date)
AFC AFC Championship Game (1970 to date) or AFL Championship Game (1960-69)
NFC NFC Championship Game (1970 to date) or NFL Championship Game (1933-69)
AFC-D AFC Divisional Playoff Game (1970 to date), AFC Second-Round Playoff Game (1982), AFL Inter-Divisional Playoff Game (1969), or special playoff game to break tie for AFL Division Championship (1963, 1968)
NFC-D NFC Divisional Playoff Game (1970 to date), NFC Second-Round Playoff Game (1982), NFL Conference Championship Game (1967-69), or special playoff game to break tie for NFL Division or Conference Championship (1941, 1943, 1947, 1950, 1952, 1957, 1958, 1965)
AFC-FR AFC First-Round Playoff Game (1978 to date)
NFC-FR NFC First-Round Playoff Game (1978 to date)

POSTSEASON GAME COMPOSITE STANDINGS

	W	L	PCT.	PTS.	OP
Green Bay Packers	22	10	.688	772	558
San Francisco 49ers	24	15	.615	984	759
Dallas Cowboys	32	21	.604	1,271	979
Washington Redskins*	22	15	.595	778	642
Denver Broncos	16	11	.593	613	636
Oakland Raiders**	21	15	.583	855	659
Pittsburgh Steelers	21	15	.583	801	707
Miami Dolphins	19	17	.528	754	784
Chicago Bears	14	14	.500	579	552
Carolina Panthers	1	1	.500	39	47
Jacksonville Jaguars	4	4	.500	208	200
Buffalo Bills	14	15	.483	681	658
Indianapolis Colts***	10	11	.476	376	408
Tennessee Titans†	12	14	.462	461	602
New York Jets	6	7	.462	260	247
Philadelphia Eagles	9	11	.450	359	369
St. Louis Rams††	16	20	.444	584	756
New York Giants	14	19	.424	541	616
Minnesota Vikings	16	22	.421	745	856
Kansas City Chiefs****	8	11	.421	301	384
Cincinnati Bengals	5	7	.417	246	257
Detroit Lions	7	10	.412	365	404
New England Patriots#	7	10	.412	310	357
Atlanta Falcons	4	6	.400	208	260
San Diego Chargers†††	7	11	.389	332	428
Seattle Seahawks	3	5	.375	145	159
Tampa Bay Buccaneers	3	5	.375	88	149
Cleveland Browns	11	19	.367	596	692
Arizona Cardinals††††	2	5	.286	122	182
New Orleans Saints	0	4	.000	56	123

** One game played when franchise was in Boston (lost 21-6).*
*** 12 games played when franchise was in Los Angeles (won 6, lost 6, 268 points scored, 224 points allowed).*
**** 15 games played when franchise was in Baltimore (won 8, lost 7, 264 points scored, 262 points allowed).*
***** One game played when franchise was Dallas Texans (won 20-17).*
 # Two games played when franchise was in Boston (won 26-8, lost 51-10).
† 22 games played when franchise was in Houston and known as the Oilers (won 9, lost 13, 371 points scored, 533 points allowed).
†† One game played when franchise was in Cleveland (won 15-14), 32 games played when franchise was in Los Angeles (won 12, lost 20, 486 points scored, 683 points allowed).
††† One game played when franchise was in Los Angeles (lost 24-16).
†††† Two games played when franchise was in Chicago (won 28-21, lost 7-0), three games played when franchise was in St. Louis (lost 30-14, lost 35-23, lost 41-16).

INDIVIDUAL RECORDS

SERVICE

Most Games, Career
27 D.D. Lewis, Dallas (SB 5, NFC 9, NFC-D 12, NFC-FR 1)
26 Larry Cole, Dallas (SB 5, NFC 8, NFC-D 12, NFC-FR 1)
25 Charlie Waters, Dallas (SB 5, NFC 9, NFC-D 10, NFC-FR 1)

Most Games, Head Coach
36 Tom Landry, Dallas
Don Shula, Baltimore-Miami
24 Chuck Noll, Pittsburgh
22 Bud Grant, Minnesota

Most Games Won, Head Coach
20 Tom Landry, Dallas
19 Don Shula, Baltimore-Miami
16 Chuck Noll, Pittsburgh
Joe Gibbs, Washington

Most Games Lost, Head Coach
17 Don Shula, Baltimore-Miami
16 Tom Landry, Dallas
12 Bud Grant, Minnesota

SCORING

POINTS

Most Points, Career
133 Gary Anderson, Pittsburgh-Philadelphia-San Francisco-Minnesota, 19 games (49-pat, 28-fg)
126 Thurman Thomas, Buffalo, 21 games (21-td)
Emmitt Smith, Dallas, 17 games (21-td)
115 George Blanda, Chi. Bears-Houston-Oakland, 19 games (49-pat, 22-fg)

Most Points, Game
30 Ricky Watters, NFC-D:San Francisco vs. N.Y. Giants, 1993 (5-td)
19 Pat Harder, NFC-D: Detroit vs. Los Angeles, 1952 (2-td, 4-pat, 1-fg)
Paul Hornung, NFC: Green Bay vs. N.Y. Giants, 1961 (1-td, 4-pat, 3-fg)
18 By many players

Most Consecutive Games Scoring
19 George Blanda, Chi. Bears-Houston-Oakland, 1956-75
16 Norm Johnson, Seattle-Atlanta-Pittsburgh, 1983-97 (current)
15 Roy Gerela, Houston-Pittsburgh, 1969-78

TOUCHDOWNS

Most Touchdowns, Career
21 Thurman Thomas, Buffalo, 21 games (16-r, 5-p)
Emmitt Smith, Dallas, 17 games (19-r, 2-p)
19 Jerry Rice, San Francisco, 23 games (0-r, 19-p)
17 Franco Harris, Pittsburgh, 19 games (16-r, 1-p)

Most Touchdowns, Game
5 Ricky Watters, NFC-D:San Francisco vs. N.Y. Giants, 1993 (5-r)
3 Andy Farkas, NFC-D: Washington vs. N.Y. Giants, 1943 (3-r)
Tom Fears, NFC-D: Los Angeles vs. Chi. Bears, 1950 (3-p)
Otto Graham, NFC: Cleveland vs. Detroit, 1954 (3-r)
Gary Collins, NFC: Cleveland vs. Baltimore, 1964 (3-p)
Craig Baynham, NFC-D: Dallas vs. Cleveland, 1967 (2-r, 1-p)
Fred Biletnikoff, AFC-D: Oakland vs. Kansas City, 1968 (3-p)
Tom Matte, NFC: Baltimore vs. Cleveland, 1968 (3-r)
Larry Schreiber, NFC-D: San Francisco vs. Dallas, 1972 (3-r)
Larry Csonka, AFC: Miami vs. Oakland, 1973 (3-r)
Franco Harris, AFC-D: Pittsburgh vs. Buffalo, 1974 (3-r)
Preston Pearson, NFC: Dallas vs. Los Angeles, 1975 (3-p)
Dave Casper, AFC-D: Oakland vs. Baltimore, 1977 (OT) (3-p)
Alvin Garrett, NFC-FR: Washington vs. Detroit, 1982 (3-p)
John Riggins, NFC-D: Washington vs. L.A. Rams, 1983 (3-r)
Roger Craig, SB: San Francisco vs. Miami, 1984 (1-r, 2-p)
Jerry Rice, NFC-D: San Francisco vs. Minnesota, 1988 (3-p)
Jerry Rice, SB: San Francisco vs. Denver, 1989 (3-p)
Kenneth Davis, AFC: Buffalo vs. L.A. Raiders, 1990 (3-r)
Andre Reed, AFC-FR: Buffalo vs. Houston, 1992 (OT) (3-p)
Sterling Sharpe, NFC-FR: Green Bay vs. Detroit, 1993 (3-p)
Napoleon McCallum, AFC-FR: L.A. Raiders vs. Denver, 1993 (3-r)
Thurman Thomas, AFC: Buffalo vs. Kansas City, 1993 (3-r)
William Floyd, NFC-D: San Francisco vs. Chicago, 1994 (3-r)
Ricky Watters, SB: San Francisco vs. San Diego, 1994 (1-r, 2-p)
Jerry Rice, SB: San Francisco vs. San Diego, 1994 (3-p)
Emmitt Smith, NFC: Dallas vs. Green Bay, 1995 (3-r)
Curtis Martin, AFC-D: New England vs. Pittsburgh, 1996 (3-r)
Terrell Davis, SB: Denver vs. Green Bay, 1997 (3-r)
Mario Bates, NFC-D: Arizona vs. Minnesota, 1998 (3-r)
Leroy Hoard, NFC-D: Minnesota vs. Arizona, 1998 (2-r, 1-p)

Most Consecutive Games Scoring Touchdowns
9 Thurman Thomas, Buffalo, 1992-98
8 John Stallworth, Pittsburgh, 1978-83
Emmitt Smith, Dallas, 1993-96
7 John Riggins, Washington, 1982-84
Marcus Allen, L.A. Raiders, 1982-85
Terrell Davis, Denver, 1996-98

POINTS AFTER TOUCHDOWN

Most (One-Point) Points After Touchdown, Career
49 George Blanda, Chi. Bears-Houston-Oakland, 19 games (49 att)
Gary Anderson, Pittsburgh-Philadelphia-San Francisco-Minnesota, 19 games (49 att)
42 Mike Cofer, San Francisco, 12 games (46 att)
41 Rafael Septien, Los Angeles-Dallas, 15 games (41 att)

Most (One-Point) Points After Touchdown, Game
8 Lou Groza, NFC: Cleveland vs. Detroit, 1954 (8 att)
Jim Martin, NFC: Detroit vs. Cleveland, 1957 (8 att)

George Blanda, AFC-D: Oakland vs. Houston, 1969 (8 att)
Mike Hollis, AFC-D: Jacksonville vs. Miami, 1999 (8 att)
7 Danny Villanueva, NFC-D: Dallas vs. Cleveland, 1967 (7 att)
Raul Allegre, NFC-D: N.Y. Giants vs. San Francisco, 1986 (7 att)
Mike Cofer, SB: San Francisco vs. Denver, 1989 (8 att)
Lin Elliott, SB: Dallas vs. Buffalo, 1992 (7 att)
Doug Brien, SB: San Francisco vs. San Diego, 1994 (7 att)
Gary Anderson, NFC-FR: Philadelphia vs. Detroit, 1995 (7 att)
Jeff Wilkins, NFC-D: St. Louis vs. Minnesota, 1999 (7 att)
6 George Blair, AFC: San Diego vs. Boston, 1963 (6 att)
Mark Moseley, NFC-D: Washington vs. L.A. Rams, 1983 (6 att)
Uwe von Schamann, AFC: Miami vs. Pittsburgh, 1984 (6 att)
Ali Haji-Sheikh, SB: Washington vs. Denver, 1987 (6 att)
Scott Norwood, AFC: Buffalo vs. L.A. Raiders, 1990 (7 att)
Jeff Jaeger, AFC-FR: L.A. Raiders vs. Denver, 1993 (6 att)
Jason Elam, AFC-FR: Denver vs. Jacksonville, 1997 (6 att)

Most (Kicking) Points After Touchdown, No Misses, Career
49 George Blanda, Chi. Bears-Houston-Oakland, 19 games
Gary Anderson, Pittsburgh-Philadelphia-San Francisco-Minnesota, 19 games
41 Rafael Septien, L.A. Rams-Dallas, 15 games
40 Matt Bahr, Pittsburgh-Cleveland-N.Y. Giants-New England, 14 games

Most Two-Point Conversions, Career
1 By many players

Most Two-Point Conversions, Game
1 By many players

FIELD GOALS

Most Field Goals Attempted, Career
39 George Blanda, Chi. Bears-Houston-Oakland, 19 games
35 Gary Anderson, Pittsburgh-Philadelphia-San Francisco-Minnesota, 19 games
31 Mark Moseley, Washington-Cleveland, 11 games

Most Field Goals Attempted, Game
6 George Blanda, AFC: Oakland vs. Houston, 1967
David Ray, NFC-D: Los Angeles vs. Dallas, 1973
Mark Moseley, AFC-D: Cleveland vs. N.Y. Jets, 1986 (OT)
Matt Bahr, NFC: N.Y. Giants vs. San Francisco, 1990
Steve Christie, AFC: Buffalo vs. Miami, 1992
5 By many players

Most Field Goals, Career
28 Gary Anderson, Pittsburgh-Philadelphia-San Francisco-Minnesota, 19 games
22 George Blanda, Chi. Bears-Houston-Oakland, 19 games
Steve Christie, Buffalo, 12 games
21 Matt Bahr, Pittsburgh-Cleveland-N.Y. Giants-New England, 14 games

Most Field Goals, Game
5 Chuck Nelson, NFC-D: Minnesota vs. San Francisco, 1987
Matt Bahr, NFC: N.Y. Giants vs. San Francisco, 1990
Steve Christie, AFC: Buffalo vs. Miami, 1992
Brad Daluiso, NFC-FR: N.Y. Giants vs. Minnesota, 1997
4 Gino Cappelletti, AFC-D: Boston vs. Buffalo, 1963
George Blanda, AFC: Oakland vs. Houston, 1967
Don Chandler, SB: Green Bay vs. Oakland, 1967
Curt Knight, NFC: Washington vs. Dallas, 1972
George Blanda, AFC-D: Oakland vs. Pittsburgh, 1973
Ray Wersching, SB: San Francisco vs. Cincinnati, 1981
Tony Franklin, AFC-FR: New England vs. N.Y. Jets, 1985
Jess Atkinson, NFC-FR: Washington vs. L.A. Rams, 1986
Luis Zendejas, NFC-D: Philadelphia vs. Chicago, 1988
Gary Anderson, AFC-FR: Pittsburgh vs. Houston, 1989 (OT)
Norm Johnson, AFC-D: Pittsburgh vs. Buffalo, 1995
Chris Boniol, NFC-FR: Dallas vs. Minnesota, 1996
John Kasay, NFC-D: Carolina vs. Dallas, 1996
Mike Hollis, AFC-D: Jacksonville vs. New England, 1998
Al Del Greco, AFC-D: Tennessee vs. Indianapolis, 1999
3 By many players

Most Consecutive Games Scoring Field Goals
13 Toni Fritsch, Dallas-Houston, 1972-79
9 Kevin Butler, Chicago, 1985-91
Scott Norwood, Buffalo, 1988-91
8 Mark Moseley, Washington-Cleveland, 1982-86
Rich Karlis, Denver-Minnesota, 1984-89
Steve Christie, Buffalo, 1993-95
Gary Anderson, Pittsburgh-Philadelphia, 1989-95
Morten Andersen, New Orleans-Atlanta, 1987-98 (current)
Al Del Greco, Houston-Tennessee, 1991-99 (current)

Most Consecutive Field Goals
16 Gary Anderson, Pittsburgh-Philadelphia, 1989-95
15 Rafael Septien, Dallas, 1978-82
14 Mike Hollis, Jacksonville, 1996-99

Longest Field Goal
58 Pete Stoyanovich, AFC-FR: Miami vs. Kansas City, 1990
54 Ed Murray, NFC-D: Detroit vs. San Francisco, 1983
Steve Christie, SB: Buffalo vs. Dallas, 1993
John Carney, AFC-FR: San Diego vs. Indianapolis, 1995
53 Al Del Greco, AFC-FR: Houston vs. N.Y. Jets, 1991

Highest Field Goal Percentage, Career (10 field goals)
90.9 Chuck Nelson, L.A. Rams-Minnesota, 6 games (11-10)
88.9 Mike Hollis, Jacksonville, 8 games (18-16)
88.0 Steve Christie, Buffalo, 12 games (25-22)

SAFETIES

Most Safeties, Game
1 Bill Willis, NFC-D: Cleveland vs. N.Y. Giants, 1950
Carl Eller, NFC-D: Minnesota vs. Los Angeles, 1969
George Andrie, NFC-D: Dallas vs. Detroit, 1970
Alan Page, NFC-D: Minnesota vs. Dallas, 1971
Dwight White, SB: Pittsburgh vs. Minnesota, 1974
Reggie Harrison, SB: Pittsburgh vs. Dallas, 1975
Jim Jensen, NFC-D: Dallas vs. Los Angeles, 1976
Ted Washington, AFC: Houston vs. Pittsburgh, 1978
Randy White, NFC-D: Dallas vs. Los Angeles, 1979
Henry Waechter, SB: Chicago vs. New England, 1985
Rulon Jones, AFC-FR: Denver vs. New England, 1986
George Martin, SB: N.Y. Giants vs. Denver, 1986
D.D. Hoggard, AFC: Cleveland vs. Denver, 1987
Bruce Smith, SB: Buffalo vs. N.Y. Giants, 1990
Reggie White, NFC-FR: Philadelphia vs. New Orleans, 1992
Willie Clay, NFC-FR: Detroit vs. Green Bay, 1994
Carnell Lake, AFC-D: Pittsburgh vs. Cleveland, 1994
Reuben Davis, AFC-D: San Diego vs. Miami, 1994
Jevon Kearse, AFC-FR: Tennessee vs. Buffalo, 1999

RUSHING

ATTEMPTS

Most Attempts, Career
400 Franco Harris, Pittsburgh, 19 games
349 Emmitt Smith, Dallas, 17 games
339 Thurman Thomas, Buffalo, 21 games

Most Attempts, Game
38 Ricky Bell, NFC-D: Tampa Bay vs. Philadelphia, 1979
John Riggins, SB: Washington vs. Miami, 1982
37 Lawrence McCutcheon, NFC-D: Los Angeles vs. St. Louis, 1975
John Riggins, NFC-D: Washington vs. Minnesota, 1982
36 John Riggins, NFC: Washington vs. Dallas, 1982
John Riggins, NFC: Washington vs. San Francisco, 1983
Curtis Martin, AFC-D: N.Y. Jets vs. Jacksonville, 1998

YARDS GAINED

Most Yards Gained, Career
1,586 Emmitt Smith, Dallas, 17 games
1,556 Franco Harris, Pittsburgh, 19 games
1,442 Thurman Thomas, Buffalo, 21 games

Most Yards Gained, Game
248 Eric Dickerson, NFC-D: L.A. Rams vs. Dallas, 1985
206 Keith Lincoln, AFC: San Diego vs. Boston, 1963
204 Timmy Smith, SB: Washington vs. Denver, 1987

Most Games, 100 or More Yards Rushing, Career
7 Emmitt Smith, Dallas, 17 games
Terrell Davis, Denver, 8 games
6 John Riggins, Washington, 9 games
Thurman Thomas, Buffalo, 21 games
5 Franco Harris, Pittsburgh, 19 games
Marcus Allen, L.A. Raiders-Kansas City, 16 games

Most Consecutive Games, 100 or More Yards Rushing
7 Terrell Davis, Denver, 1997-98 (current)
6 John Riggins, Washington, 1982-83
4 Thurman Thomas, Buffalo, 1990-91

Longest Run From Scrimmage
90 Fred Taylor, AFC-D: Jacksonville vs. Miami, 1999 (TD)
80 Roger Craig, NFC-D: San Francisco vs. Minnesota, 1988 (TD)
78 Curtis Martin, AFC-D: New England vs. Pittsburgh, 1996 (TD)

AVERAGE GAIN

Highest Average Gain, Career (100 attempts)
5.59 Terrell Davis, Denver, 8 games (204-1,140)
5.04 Marcus Allen, L.A. Raiders-Kansas City, 16 games (267-1,347)
4.89 Eric Dickerson, L.A. Rams-Indianapolis, 7 games (148-724)

Highest Average Gain, Game (10 attempts)
15.90 Elmer Angsman, NFC: Chi. Cardinals vs. Philadelphia, 1947 (10-159)
15.85 Keith Lincoln, AFC: San Diego vs. Boston, 1963 (13-206)
11.31 Zack Crockett, AFC-FR: Indianapolis vs. San Diego, 1995 (13-147)

POSTSEASON GAME RECORDS

TOUCHDOWNS

Most Touchdowns, Career

19 Emmitt Smith, Dallas, 17 games
16 Franco Harris, Pittsburgh, 19 games
Thurman Thomas, Buffalo, 21 games
12 John Riggins, Washington, 9 games
Terrell Davis, Denver, 8 games

Most Touchdowns, Game

5 Ricky Watters, NFC-D: San Francisco vs. N.Y. Giants, 1993
3 Andy Farkas, NFC-D: Washington vs. N.Y. Giants, 1943
Otto Graham, NFC: Cleveland vs. Detroit, 1954
Tom Matte, NFC: Baltimore vs. Cleveland, 1968
Larry Schreiber, NFC-D: San Francisco vs. Dallas, 1972
Larry Csonka, AFC: Miami vs. Oakland, 1973
Franco Harris, AFC-D: Pittsburgh vs. Buffalo, 1974
John Riggins, NFC-D: Washington vs. L.A. Rams, 1983
Kenneth Davis, AFC: Buffalo vs. L.A. Raiders, 1990
Napoleon McCallum, AFC-FR: L.A. Raiders vs. Denver, 1993
Thurman Thomas, AFC: Buffalo vs. Kansas City, 1993
William Floyd, NFC-D: San Francisco vs. Chicago, 1994
Emmitt Smith, NFC: Dallas vs. Green Bay, 1995
Curtis Martin, AFC-D: New England vs. Pittsburgh, 1996
Terrell Davis, SB: Denver vs. Green Bay, 1997
Mario Bates, NFC-D: Arizona vs. Minnesota, 1998

Most Consecutive Games Rushing for Touchdowns

8 Emmitt Smith, Dallas, 1993-96
Thurman Thomas, Buffalo, 1992-98
7 John Riggins, Washington, 1982-84
Terrell Davis, Denver, 1996-98
5 Franco Harris, Pittsburgh, 1974-75
Franco Harris, Pittsburgh, 1977-79
Curtis Martin, New England-N.Y. Jets, 1996-98 (current)

PASSING

PASSER RATING

Highest Passer Rating, Career (150 attempts)

104.8 Bart Starr, Green Bay, 10 games
95.6 Joe Montana, San Francisco-Kansas City, 23 games
93.5 Ken Anderson, Cincinnati, 6 games

ATTEMPTS

Most Passes Attempted, Career

734 Joe Montana, San Francisco-Kansas City, 23 games
687 Dan Marino, Miami, 18 games
651 John Elway, Denver, 22 games

Most Passes Attempted, Game

65 Steve Young, NFC-D: San Francisco vs. Green Bay, 1995
64 Bernie Kosar, AFC-D: Cleveland vs. N.Y. Jets, 1986 (OT)
Dan Marino, AFC-FR: Miami vs. Buffalo, 1995
58 Jim Kelly, SB: Buffalo vs. Washington, 1991

COMPLETIONS

Most Passes Completed, Career

460 Joe Montana, San Francisco-Kansas City, 23 games
385 Dan Marino, Miami, 18 games
355 John Elway, Denver, 22 games

Most Passes Completed, Game

36 Warren Moon, AFC-FR: Houston vs. Buffalo, 1992 (OT)
33 Dan Fouts, AFC-D: San Diego vs. Miami, 1981 (OT)
Bernie Kosar, AFC-D: Cleveland vs. N.Y. Jets, 1986 (OT)
Dan Marino, AFC-FR: Miami vs. Buffalo, 1995
32 Neil Lomax, NFC-FR: St. Louis vs. Green Bay, 1982
Danny White, NFC-FR: Dallas vs. L.A. Rams, 1983
Warren Moon, AFC-D: Houston vs. Kansas City, 1993
Neil O'Donnell, AFC: Pittsburgh vs. San Diego, 1994
Steve Young, NFC-D: San Francisco vs. Green Bay, 1995

COMPLETION PERCENTAGE

Highest Completion Percentage, Career (150 attempts)

66.3 Ken Anderson, Cincinnati, 6 games (166-110)
64.3 Warren Moon, Houston-Minnesota, 10 games (403-259)
63.8 Troy Aikman, Dallas, 16 games (502-320)

Highest Completion Percentage, Game (15 completions)

88.0 Phil Simms, SB: N.Y. Giants vs. Denver, 1986 (25-22)
86.7 Joe Montana, NFC: San Francisco vs. L.A. Rams, 1989 (30-26)
84.2 David Woodley, AFC-FR: Miami vs. New England, 1982 (19-16)

YARDS GAINED

Most Yards Gained, Career

5,772 Joe Montana, San Francisco-Kansas City, 23 games
4,964 John Elway, Denver, 22 games
4,510 Dan Marino, Miami, 18 games

Most Yards Gained, Game

489 Bernie Kosar, AFC-D: Cleveland vs. N.Y. Jets, 1986 (OT)
433 Dan Fouts, AFC-D: San Diego vs. Miami, 1981 (OT)
423 Jeff George, NFC-D: Minnesota vs. St. Louis, 1999

Most Games, 300 or More Yards Passing, Career

6 Joe Montana, San Francisco-Kansas City, 23 games
5 Dan Fouts, San Diego, 7 games
4 Warren Moon, Houston-Minnesota, 10 games
Troy Aikman, Dallas, 16 games
Dan Marino, Miami, 18 games
John Elway, Denver, 22 games

Most Consecutive Games, 300 or More Yards Passing

4 Dan Fouts, San Diego, 1979-81
3 Jim Kelly, Buffalo, 1989-90
Warren Moon, Houston, 1991-93
2 Daryle Lamonica, Oakland, 1968
Ken Anderson, Cincinnati, 1981-82
Terry Bradshaw, Pittsburgh, 1979-82
Joe Montana, San Francisco, 1983-84
Dan Marino, Miami, 1984
Troy Aikman, Dallas, 1994
Steve Young, San Francisco, 1994-95

Longest Pass Completion

94 Troy Aikman (to Harper), NFC-D: Dallas vs. Green Bay, 1994 (TD)
93 Daryle Lamonica (to Dubenion), AFC-D: Buffalo vs. Boston, 1963 (TD)
88 George Blanda (to Cannon), AFC: Houston vs. L.A. Chargers, 1960 (TD)

AVERAGE GAIN

Highest Average Gain, Career (150 attempts)

8.45 Joe Theismann, Washington, 10 games (211-1,782)
8.43 Jim Plunkett, Oakland/L.A.Raiders, 10 games (272-2,293)
8.41 Terry Bradshaw, Pittsburgh, 19 games (456-3,833)

Highest Average Gain, Game (20 attempts)

14.71 Terry Bradshaw, SB: Pittsburgh vs. Los Angeles, 1979 (21-309)
13.33 Bob Waterfield, NFC-D: Los Angeles vs. Chi. Bears, 1950 (21-280)
13.16 Dan Marino, AFC: Miami vs. Pittsburgh, 1984 (32-421)

TOUCHDOWNS

Most Touchdown Passes, Career

45 Joe Montana, San Francisco-Kansas City, 23 games
32 Dan Marino, Miami, 18 games
30 Terry Bradshaw, Pittsburgh, 19 games

Most Touchdown Passes, Game

6 Daryle Lamonica, AFC-D: Oakland vs. Houston, 1969
Steve Young, SB: San Francisco vs. San Diego, 1994
5 Sid Luckman, NFC: Chi. Bears vs. Washington, 1943
Daryle Lamonica, AFC-D: Oakland vs. Kansas City, 1968
Joe Montana, SB: San Francisco vs. Denver, 1989
Kurt Warner, NFC-D: St. Louis vs. Minnesota, 1999
4 Otto Graham, NFC: Cleveland vs. Los Angeles, 1950
Tobin Rote, NFC: Detroit vs. Cleveland, 1957
Bart Starr, NFC: Green Bay vs. Dallas, 1966
Ken Stabler, AFC-D: Oakland vs. Miami, 1974
Roger Staubach, NFC: Dallas vs. Los Angeles, 1975
Terry Bradshaw, SB: Pittsburgh vs. Dallas, 1978
Don Strock, AFC-D: Miami vs. San Diego, 1981 (OT)
Lynn Dickey, NFC-FR: Green Bay vs. St. Louis, 1982
Dan Marino, AFC: Miami vs. Pittsburgh, 1984
Phil Simms, NFC-D: N.Y. Giants vs. San Francisco, 1986
Doug Williams, SB: Washington vs. Denver, 1987
Jim Kelly, AFC-D: Buffalo vs. Cleveland, 1989
Joe Montana, NFC-D: San Francisco vs. Minnesota, 1989
Warren Moon, AFC-FR: Houston vs. Buffalo, 1992 (OT)
Frank Reich, AFC-FR: Buffalo vs. Houston, 1992 (OT)
Troy Aikman, SB: Dallas vs. Buffalo, 1992
Jeff George, NFC-D: Minnesota vs. St. Louis, 1999

Most Consecutive Games, Touchdown Passes

13 Dan Marino, Miami, 1983-95
10 Ken Stabler, Oakland, 1973-77
Joe Montana, San Francisco-Kansas City, 1988-93
Brett Favre, Green Bay, 1995-98 (current)
9 John Elway, Denver, 1984-89

HAD INTERCEPTED

Lowest Percentage, Passes Had Intercepted, Career (150 attempts)

1.41 Bart Starr, Green Bay, 10 games (213-3)
2.15 Phil Simms, N.Y. Giants, 10 games (279-6)
2.47 Randall Cunningham, Philadelphia-Minnesota, 12 games (365-9)

Most Attempts Without Interception, Game

54 Neil O'Donnell, AFC: Pittsburgh vs. San Diego, 1994
48 Warren Moon, AFC-FR: Houston vs. Pittsburgh, 1989 (OT)
Randall Cunningham, NFC: Minnesota vs. Atlanta, 1998 (OT)
47 Daryle Lamonica, AFC: Oakland vs. N.Y. Jets, 1968

Most Passes Had Intercepted, Career
28 Jim Kelly, Buffalo, 17 games
26 Terry Bradshaw, Pittsburgh, 19 games
24 Dan Marino, Miami, 18 games

Most Passes Had Intercepted, Game
6 Frank Filchock, NFC: N.Y. Giants vs. Chi. Bears, 1946
Bobby Layne, NFC: Detroit vs. Cleveland, 1954
Norm Van Brocklin, NFC: Los Angeles vs. Cleveland, 1955
5 Frank Filchock, NFC: Washington vs. Chi. Bears, 1940
George Blanda, AFC: Houston vs. San Diego, 1961
George Blanda, AFC: Houston vs. Dall. Texans, 1962 (OT)
Y.A. Tittle, NFC: N.Y. Giants vs. Chicago, 1963
Mike Phipps, AFC-D: Cleveland vs. Miami, 1972
Dan Pastorini, AFC: Houston vs. Pittsburgh, 1978
Dan Fouts, AFC-D: San Diego vs. Houston, 1979
Tommy Kramer, NFC-D: Minnesota vs. Philadelphia, 1980
Dan Fouts, AFC-D: San Diego vs. Miami, 1982
Richard Todd, AFC: N.Y. Jets vs Miami, 1982
Gary Danielson, NFC-D: Detroit vs. San Francisco, 1983
Jay Schroeder, AFC: L.A. Raiders vs. Buffalo, 1990
4 By many players

PASS RECEIVING

RECEPTIONS

Most Receptions, Career
124 Jerry Rice, San Francisco, 23 games
87 Michael Irvin, Dallas, 16 games
85 Andre Reed, Buffalo, 21 games

Most Receptions, Game
13 Kellen Winslow, AFC-D: San Diego vs. Miami, 1981 (OT)
Thurman Thomas, AFC-D: Buffalo vs. Cleveland, 1989
Shannon Sharpe, AFC-FR: Denver vs. L.A. Raiders, 1993
12 Raymond Berry, NFC: Baltimore vs. N.Y. Giants, 1958
Michael Irvin, NFC: Dallas vs. San Francisco, 1994
11 Dante Lavelli, NFC: Cleveland vs. Los Angeles, 1950
Dan Ross, SB: Cincinnati vs. San Francisco, 1981
Franco Harris, AFC-FR: Pittsburgh vs. San Diego, 1982
Steve Watson, AFC-D: Denver vs. Pittsburgh, 1984
John L. Williams, AFC-D: Seattle vs. Cincinnati, 1988
Jerry Rice, SB: San Francisco vs. Cincinnati, 1988
Ernest Givins, AFC-FR: Houston vs. Pittsburgh, 1989 (OT)
Amp Lee, NFC-D: Minnesota vs. Chicago, 1994
Jay Novacek, NFC-D: Dallas vs. Green Bay, 1994
O.J. McDuffie, AFC-FR: Miami vs. Buffalo, 1995
Jerry Rice, NFC-C: San Francisco vs. Green Bay, 1995

Most Consecutive Games, Pass Receptions
23 Jerry Rice, San Francisco, 1985-98 (current)
22 Drew Pearson, Dallas, 1973-83
18 Paul Warfield, Cleveland-Miami, 1964-74
Cliff Branch, Oakland/L.A. Raiders, 1974-83
Thurman Thomas, Buffalo, 1989-98

YARDS GAINED

Most Yards Gained, Career
1,811 Jerry Rice, San Francisco, 23 games
1,315 Michael Irvin, Dallas, 16 games
1,289 Cliff Branch, Oakland/L.A. Raiders, 22 games

Most Yards Gained, Game
240 Eric Moulds, AFC-FR: Buffalo vs. Miami, 1998
227 Anthony Carter, NFC-D: Minnesota vs. San Francisco, 1987
215 Jerry Rice, SB: San Francisco vs. Cincinnati, 1988

Most Games, 100 or More Yards Receiving, Career
7 Jerry Rice, San Francisco, 23 games
6 Michael Irvin, Dallas, 16 games
5 John Stallworth, Pittsburgh, 18 games
Andre Reed, Buffalo, 21 games

Most Consecutive Games, 100 or More Yards Receiving, Career
3 Tom Fears, Los Angeles, 1950-51
Jerry Rice, San Francisco, 1988-89
2 By many players

Longest Reception
94 Alvin Harper (from Aikman), NFC-D: Dallas vs. Green Bay, 1994 (TD)
93 Elbert Dubenion (from Lamonica), AFC-D: Buffalo vs. Boston, 1963 (TD)
88 Billy Cannon (from Blanda), AFC: Houston vs. L.A. Chargers, 1960 (TD)

AVERAGE GAIN

Highest Average Gain, Career (20 receptions)
27.3 Alvin Harper, Dallas, 10 games (24-655)
23.7 Willie Gault, Chicago-L.A. Raiders, 12 games (21-497)
22.8 Harold Jackson, L.A. Rams-New England-Minnesota-Seattle, 14 games (24-548)

Highest Average Gain, Game (3 receptions)
46.3 Harold Jackson, NFC: Los Angeles vs. Minnesota, 1974 (3-139)
42.7 Billy Cannon, AFC: Houston vs. L.A. Chargers, 1960 (3-128)
42.0 Lenny Moore, NFC: Baltimore vs. N.Y. Giants, 1959 (3-126)

TOUCHDOWNS

Most Touchdowns, Career
19 Jerry Rice, San Francisco, 23 games
12 John Stallworth, Pittsburgh, 18 games
10 Fred Biletnikoff, Oakland, 19 games

Most Touchdowns, Game
3 Tom Fears, NFC-D: Los Angeles vs. Chi. Bears, 1950
Gary Collins, NFC: Cleveland vs. Baltimore, 1964
Fred Biletnikoff, AFC-D: Oakland vs. Kansas City, 1968
Preston Pearson, NFC: Dallas vs. Los Angeles, 1975
Dave Casper, AFC-D: Oakland vs. Baltimore, 1977 (OT)
Alvin Garrett, NFC-FR: Washington vs. Detroit, 1982
Jerry Rice, NFC-D: San Francisco vs. Minnesota, 1988
Jerry Rice, SB: San Francisco vs. Denver, 1989
Andre Reed, AFC-FR: Buffalo vs. Houston, 1992 (OT)
Sterling Sharpe, NFC-FR: Green Bay vs. Detroit, 1993
Jerry Rice, SB: San Francisco vs. San Diego, 1994

Most Consecutive Games, Touchdown Passes Caught
8 John Stallworth, Pittsburgh, 1978-83
5 James Lofton, Green Bay-Buffalo, 1982-90
4 Lynn Swann, Pittsburgh, 1978-79
Harold Carmichael, Philadelphia, 1978-80
Fred Solomon, San Francisco, 1983-84
Jerry Rice, San Francisco, 1988-89
John Taylor, San Francisco, 1988-89
Randy Moss, Minnesota, 1998-99 (current)

INTERCEPTIONS BY

Most Interceptions, Career
9 Charlie Waters, Dallas, 25 games
Bill Simpson, Los Angeles-Buffalo, 11 games
Ronnie Lott, San Francisco-L.A. Raiders, 20 games
8 Lester Hayes, Oakland/L.A. Raiders, 13 games
7 Willie Brown, Oakland, 17 games
Dennis Thurman, Dallas, 14 games

Most Interceptions, Game
4 Vernon Perry, AFC-D: Houston vs. San Diego, 1979
3 Joe Laws, NFC: Green Bay vs. N.Y. Giants, 1944
Charlie Waters, NFC-D: Dallas vs. Chicago, 1977
Rod Martin, SB: Oakland vs. Philadelphia, 1980
Dennis Thurman, NFC-D: Dallas vs. Green Bay, 1982
A.J. Duhe, AFC: Miami vs. N.Y. Jets, 1982
2 By many players

Most Consecutive Games, Interceptions
3 Warren Lahr, Cleveland, 1950-51
Ken Gorgal, Cleveland, 1950-53
Joe Schmidt, Detroit, 1954-57
Emmitt Thomas, Kansas City, 1969
Mel Renfro, Dallas, 1970
Rick Volk, Baltimore, 1970-71
Mike Wagner, Pittsburgh, 1975-76
Randy Hughes, Dallas, 1977-78
Vernon Perry, Houston, 1979-80
Lester Hayes, Oakland, 1980
Gerald Small, Miami, 1982
Lester Hayes, L.A. Raiders, 1982-83
Fred Marion, New England, 1985
John Harris, Seattle-Minnesota, 1984-87
Felix Wright, Cleveland, 1987-88
Kurt Gouveia, Washington, 1991
Eric Davis, San Francisco, 1994
Deion Sanders, San Francisco-Dallas, 1994-95
Craig Newsome, Green Bay, 1996
Eugene Robinson, Green Bay-Atlanta, 1997-98

YARDS GAINED

Most Yards Gained, Career
196 Willie Brown, Oakland, 17 games
187 Ronnie Lott, San Francisco-L.A.-Raiders, 20 games
160 George Teague, Green Bay-Dallas-Miami-Dallas, 12 games

Most Yards Gained, Game
108 Darrien Gordon, SB: Denver vs. Atlanta, 1998
101 George Teague, NFC-FR: Green Bay vs. Detroit, 1993
98 Darrol Ray, AFC-FR: N.Y. Jets vs. Cincinnati, 1982

Longest Return
101 George Teague, NFC-FR: Green Bay vs. Detroit, 1993 (TD)
98 Darrol Ray, AFC-FR: N.Y. Jets vs. Cincinnati, 1982 (TD)
94 LeRoy Irvin, NFC-FR: L.A. Rams vs. Dallas, 1983

POSTSEASON GAME RECORDS

TOUCHDOWNS

Most Touchdowns, Career

3 Willie Brown, Oakland, 17 games
2 Lester Hayes, Oakland/L.A. Raiders, 13 games
Ronnie Lott, San Francisco-L.A. Raiders, 20 games
Darrell Green, Washington, 18 games
Melvin Jenkins, Seattle-Detroit, 5 games
George Teague, Green Bay-Dallas-Miami-Dallas, 12 games

Most Touchdowns, Game

1 By many players

PUNTING

Most Punts, Career

111 Ray Guy, Oakland/L.A. Raiders, 22 games
84 Danny White, Dallas, 18 games
72 Mike Eischeid, Oakland-Minnesota, 14 games
Bryan Barker, Kansas City-Jacksonville, 15 games

Most Punts, Game

14 Dave Jennings, AFC-D: N.Y. Jets vs. Cleveland, 1986 (OT)
12 David Lee, AFC-D: Baltimore vs. Oakland, 1977 (OT)
11 Ken Strong, NFC: N.Y. Giants vs. Chi. Bears, 1933
Jim Norton, AFC: Houston vs. Oakland, 1967
Ode Burrell, AFC-D: Houston vs. Oakland, 1969
Dale Hatcher, NFC: L.A. Rams vs. Chicago, 1985

Longest Punt

76 Ed Danowski, NFC: N.Y. Giants vs. Detroit, 1935
Mike Horan, AFC: Denver vs. Buffalo, 1991
72 Charlie Conerly, NFC-D: N.Y. Giants vs. Cleveland, 1950
Yale Lary, NFC: Detroit vs. Cleveland, 1953
71 Ray Guy, AFC: Oakland vs. San Diego, 1980

AVERAGE YARDAGE

Highest Average, Career (25 punts)

44.5 Rich Camarillo, New England, 6 games (35-1,559)
44.4 Lee Johnson, Cleveland-Cincinnati, 7 games (28-1,244)
44.3 Jeff Feagles, Philadelphia-Seattle, 4 games (26-1,151)

Highest Average, Game (4 punts)

56.0 Ray Guy, AFC: Oakland vs. San Diego, 1980 (4-224)
52.5 Sammy Baugh, NFC: Washington vs. Chi. Bears, 1942 (6-315)
52.0 Craig Hentrich, AFC-D: Tennessee vs. Indianapolis, 1999 (5-260)

PUNT RETURNS

Most Punt Returns, Career

34 David Meggett, N.Y. Giants-New England-N.Y. Jets, 13 games
25 Theo Bell, Pittsburgh-Tampa Bay, 10 games
21 Gerald McNeil, Cleveland-Houston, 8 games

Most Punt Returns, Game

7 Ron Gardin, AFC-D: Baltimore vs. Cincinnati, 1970
Carl Roaches, AFC-FR: Houston vs. Oakland, 1980
Gerald McNeil, AFC-D: Cleveland vs. N.Y. Jets, 1986 (OT)
Phil McConkey, NFC-D: N.Y. Giants vs. San Francisco, 1986
David Meggett, AFC-D: New England vs. Pittsburgh, 1996
Reggie Barlow, AFC-FR: Jacksonville vs. New England, 1998
6 George McAfee, NFC-D: Chi. Bears vs. Los Angeles, 1950
Eddie Brown, NFC-D: Washington vs. Minnesota, 1976
Theo Bell, AFC: Pittsburgh vs. Houston, 1978
Eddie Brown, NFC: Los Angeles vs. Tampa Bay, 1979
John Sciarra, NFC: Philadelphia vs. Dallas, 1980
Kurt Sohn, AFC: N.Y. Jets vs. Miami, 1982
Mike Nelms, SB: Washington vs. Miami, 1982
Anthony Carter, NFC-FR: Minnesota vs. New Orleans, 1987
Desmond Howard, SB: Green Bay vs.New England, 1996
Nate Jacquet, AFC-FR: Miami vs. Seattle, 1999
5 By many players

YARDS GAINED

Most Yards Gained, Career

312 David Meggett, N.Y. Giants-New England-N.Y. Jets, 13 games
259 Anthony Carter, Minnesota-Detroit, 9 games
221 Neal Colzie, Oakland-Miami-Tampa Bay, 10 games

Most Yards Gained, Game

143 Anthony Carter, NFC-FR: Minnesota vs. New Orleans, 1987
141 Bob Hayes, NFC-D: Dallas vs. Cleveland, 1967
117 Desmond Howard, NFC-D: Green Bay vs. San Francisco, 1996

Longest Return

84 Anthony Carter, NFC-FR: Minnesota vs. New Orleans, 1987 (TD)
81 Hugh Gallarneau, NFC-D: Chi. Bears vs. Green Bay, 1941 (TD)
79 Bosh Pritchard, NFC-D: Philadelphia vs. Pittsburgh, 1947 (TD)

AVERAGE YARDAGE

Highest Average, Career (10 returns)

15.3 Robert Brooks, Green Bay, 11 games (14-214)
15.2 Anthony Carter, Minnesota-Detroit, 9 games (17-259)
14.3 Antonio Freeman, Green Bay, 10 games (10-143)

Highest Average Gain, Game (3 returns)

47.0 Bob Hayes, NFC-D: Dallas vs. Cleveland, 1967 (3-141)
29.0 George (Butch) Byrd, AFC: Buffalo vs. San Diego, 1965 (3-87)
25.3 Bosh Pritchard, NFC-D: Philadelphia vs. Pittsburgh, 1947 (4-101)

TOUCHDOWNS

Most Touchdowns

1 Hugh Gallarneau, NFC-D: Chicago Bears vs. Green Bay, 1941
Bosh Pritchard, NFC-D: Philadelphia vs. Pittsburgh, 1947
Charley Trippi, NFC: Chicago Cardinals vs. Philadelphia, 1947
Verda (Vitamin T) Smith, NFC-D: Los Angeles vs. Detroit, 1952
George (Butch) Byrd, AFC: Buffalo vs. San Diego, 1965
Golden Richards, NFC: Dallas vs. Minnesota, 1973
Wes Chandler, AFC-D: San Diego vs. Miami, 1981 (OT)
Shaun Gayle, NFC-D: Chicago vs. N.Y. Giants, 1985
Anthony Carter, NFC-FR: Minnesota vs. New Orleans, 1987
Darrell Green, NFC-D: Washington vs. Chicago, 1987
Antonio Freeman, NFC-FR: Green Bay vs. Atlanta, 1995
Desmond Howard, NFC-D: Green Bay vs. San Francisco, 1996

KICKOFF RETURNS

Most Kickoff Returns, Career

31 Kevin Williams, Dallas-Buffalo, 12 games
29 Fulton Walker, Miami-L.A. Raiders, 10 games
25 David Meggett, N.Y. Giants-New England-N.Y. Jets, 13 games
Eric Metcalf, Cleveland-Atlanta-Arizona, 7 games

Most Kickoff Returns, Game

8 Marc Logan, AFC-D: Miami vs. Buffalo, 1990
Andre Coleman, SB: San Diego vs. San Francisco, 1994
7 Don Bingham, NFC: Chi. Bears vs. N.Y. Giants, 1956
Reggie Brown, NFC-FR: Atlanta vs. Minnesota, 1982
David Verser, AFC-FR: Cincinnati vs. N.Y. Jets, 1982
Del Rodgers, NFC-D: Green Bay vs. Dallas, 1982
Henry Ellard, NFC-D: L.A. Rams vs. Washington, 1983
Stephen Starring, SB: New England vs. Chicago, 1985
Darick Holmes, AFC-D: Buffalo vs. Pittsburgh, 1995
Antonio Freeman, NFC: Green Bay vs. Dallas, 1995
Roell Preston, NFC-FR: Green Bay vs. San Francisco, 1998
Robert Tate, NFC-D: Minnesota vs. St. Louis, 1999
6 By many players

YARDS GAINED

Most Yards Gained, Career

677 Fulton Walker, Miami-L.A. Raiders, 10 games
632 Kevin Williams, Dallas-Buffalo, 12 games
565 Eric Metcalf, Cleveland-Atlanta-Arizona, 7 games

Most Yards Gained, Game

244 Andre Coleman, SB: San Diego vs. San Francisco, 1994
210 Tim Dwight, SB: Atlanta vs. Denver, 1998
194 Roell Preston, NFC-FR: Green Bay vs. San Francisco, 1998

Longest Return

100 Brian Mitchell, NFC-D: Washington vs. Tampa Bay, 1999 (TD)
99 Desmond Howard, SB: Green Bay vs. New England, 1996 (TD)
98 Fulton Walker, SB: Miami vs. Washington, 1982 (TD)
Andre Coleman, SB: San Diego vs. San Francisco, 1994 (TD)

AVERAGE YARDAGE

Highest Average, Career (10 returns)

34.3 Tim Dwight, Atlanta, 3 games (10-343)
33.6 Derrick Mason, Tennessee, 4 games (13-437)
30.1 Carl Garrett, Oakland, 5 games (16-481)

Highest Average, Game (3 returns)

56.7 Les (Speedy) Duncan, NFC-D: Washington vs. San Francisco, 1971 (3-170)
51.3 Ed Podolak, AFC-D: Kansas City vs. Miami, 1971 (OT) (3-154)
49.0 Les (Speedy) Duncan, AFC: San Diego vs. Buffalo, 1964 (3-147)

TOUCHDOWNS

Most Touchdowns

1 Vic Washington, NFC-D: San Francisco vs. Dallas, 1972
Nat Moore, AFC-D: Miami vs. Oakland, 1974
Marshall Johnson, AFC-D: Baltimore vs. Oakland, 1977 (OT)
Fulton Walker, SB: Miami vs. Washington, 1982
Stanford Jennings, SB: Cincinnati vs. San Francisco, 1988
Eric Metcalf, AFC-D: Cleveland vs. Buffalo, 1989
Andre Coleman, SB: San Diego vs. San Francisco, 1994
Desmond Howard, SB: Green Bay vs. New England, 1996
Chuck Levy, NFC: San Franisco vs. Green Bay, 1997
Tim Dwight, SB: Atlanta vs. Denver, 1998

Kevin Dyson, AFC-FR: Tennessee vs. Buffalo, 1999
Charlie Rogers, AFC-FR: Seattle vs. Miami, 1999
Brian Mitchell, NFC-D: Washington vs. Tampa Bay, 1999
Tony Horne, NFC-D: St. Louis vs. Minnesota, 1999
Derrick Mason, AFC: Tennessee vs. Jacksonville, 1999

FUMBLES

Most Fumbles, Career
16 Warren Moon, Houston-Minnesota, 10 games
14 John Elway, Denver, 22 games
13 Tony Dorsett, Dallas, 17 games

Most Fumbles, Game
5 Warren Moon, AFC-D: Houston vs. Kansas City, 1993
4 Brian Sipe, AFC-D: Cleveland vs. Oakland, 1980
Randall Cunningham, NFC-FR: Minnesota vs. N.Y. Giants, 1997
3 By many players

RECOVERIES

Most Own Fumbles Recovered, Career
8 Warren Moon, Houston-Minnesota, 10 games
7 John Elway, Denver, 22 games
6 Jim Kelly, Buffalo, 17 games

Most Opponents' Fumbles Recovered, Career
4 Cliff Harris, Dallas, 21 games
Harvey Martin, Dallas, 22 games
Ted Hendricks, Baltimore-Oakland/L.A. Raiders, 21 games
Alvin Walton, Washington, 9 games
Monte Coleman, Washington, 21 games
3 Paul Krause, Minnesota, 19 games
Jack Lambert, Pittsburgh, 18 games
Fred Dryer, Los Angeles, 14 games
Charlie Waters, Dallas, 25 games
Jack Ham, Pittsburgh, 16 games
Mike Hegman, Dallas, 16 games
Tom Jackson, Denver, 10 games
Rich Milot, Washington, 13 games
Mike Singletary, Chicago, 12 games
Darryl Grant, Washington, 16 games
Wes Hopkins, Philadelphia, 3 games
Wilber Marshall, Chicago-Washington, 15 games
Tyrone Braxton, Denver-Miami-Denver, 19 games
Neil Smith, Kansas City-Denver, 16 games
Dave Thomas, Dallas-Jacksonville, 10 games
Tony Brackens, Jacksonville, 7 games
Phil Hansen, Buffalo, 14 games
Carnell Lake, Pittsburgh-Jacksonville, 15 games
2 By many players

Most Fumbles Recovered, Game, Own and Opponents'
3 Jack Lambert, AFC: Pittsburgh vs. Oakland, 1975 (3 opp)
Ron Jaworski, NFC-FR: Philadelphia vs. N.Y. Giants, 1981 (3 own)
2 By many players

YARDS GAINED

Longest Return
93 Andy Russell, AFC-D: Pittsburgh vs. Baltimore, 1975 (opp, TD)
79 Neil Smith, AFC-D: Denver vs. Miami, 1998 (opp, TD)
64 Leon Lett, SB: Dallas vs. Buffalo, 1992 (opp)

TOUCHDOWNS

Most Touchdowns
1 By many players

COMBINED NET YARDS GAINED

Rushing, receiving, interception returns, punt returns, kickoff returns, and fumble returns.

ATTEMPTS

Most Attempts, Career
454 Franco Harris, Pittsburgh, 19 games
417 Thurman Thomas, Buffalo, 21 games
397 Emmitt Smith, Dallas, 17 games

Most Attempts, Game
42 Curtis Martin, AFC-D: N.Y. Jets vs. Jacksonville, 1998
40 Lawrence McCutcheon, NFC-D: Los Angeles vs. St. Louis, 1975
39 John Riggins, SB: Washington vs. Miami, 1982
Rodney Hampton, NFC-FR: N.Y. Giants vs. Minnesota, 1993

YARDS GAINED

Most Yards Gained, Career
2,124 Thurman Thomas, Buffalo, 21 games
2,060 Franco Harris, Pittsburgh, 19 games
1,928 Emmitt Smith, Dallas, 17 games

Most Yards Gained, Game
350 Ed Podolak, AFC-D: Kansas City vs. Miami, 1971 (OT)
329 Keith Lincoln, AFC: San Diego vs. Boston, 1963
285 Bob Hayes, NFC-D: Dallas vs. Cleveland, 1967

SACKS

Sacks have been compiled since 1982.

Most Sacks, Career
14.5 Bruce Smith, Buffalo, 20 games
12 Reggie White, Philadelphia-Green Bay, 19 games
11 Charles Haley, San Francisco-Dallas-San Francisco, 21 games

Most Sacks, Game
3.5 Rich Milot, NFC-D: Washington vs. Chicago, 1984
Richard Dent, NFC-D: Chicago vs. N.Y. Giants, 1985
3 Richard Dent, NFC-D: Chicago vs. Washington, 1984
Garin Veris, AFC-FR: New England vs. N.Y. Jets, 1985
Gary Jeter, NFC-D: L.A. Rams vs. Dallas, 1985
Carl Hairston, AFC-D: Cleveland vs. N.Y. Jets, 1986 (OT)
Charles Mann, NFC-D: Washington vs. Chicago, 1987
Kevin Greene, NFC-FR: L.A. Rams vs. Minnesota, 1988
Greg Townsend, AFC-D: L.A. Raiders vs. Cincinnati, 1990
Wilber Marshall, NFC: Washington vs. Detroit, 1991
Fred Stokes, NFC-FR: Washington vs. Minnesota, 1992
Pierce Holt, NFC-D: San Francisco vs. Washington, 1992
Tony Casillas, NFC: Dallas vs. San Francisco, 1992
Gerald Williams, AFC-FR: Pittsburgh vs. Kansas City, 1993
Chad Brown, AFC-FR: Pittsburgh vs. Indianapolis, 1996
Reggie White, SB: Green Bay vs. New England, 1996
Warren Sapp, NFC-D: Tampa Bay vs. Green Bay, 1997
Trace Armstrong, AFC-FR: Miami vs. Seattle, 1999
2.5 Lyle Alzado, AFC-D: L.A. Raiders vs. Pittsburgh, 1983
Jacob Green, AFC-FR: Seattle vs. L.A. Raiders, 1984
Larry Roberts, NFC-D: San Francisco vs. Minnesota, 1988
Leslie O'Neal, AFC-FR: San Diego vs. Kansas City, 1992
Bruce Smith, AFC-FR: Buffalo vs. Tennessee, 1999

TEAM RECORDS

GAMES, VICTORIES, DEFEATS

Most Seasons Participating in Postseason Games
26 Dallas, 1966-73, 1975-83, 1985, 1991-96, 1998-99
24 N.Y. Giants, 1933-35, 1938-39, 1941, 1943-44, 1946, 1950, 1956, 1958-59,1961-63, 1981, 1984-86, 1989-90, 1993, 1997
23 Cleveland, 1950-55, 1957-58, 1964-65, 1967-69, 1971-72, 1980, 1982, 1985-89, 1994
Cleveland/L.A./St. Louis Rams, 1945, 1949-52, 1955, 1967, 1969, 1973-80, 1983-86, 1988-89, 1999

Most Consecutive Seasons Participating in Postseason Games
9 Dallas, 1975-83
8 Dallas, 1966-73
Pittsburgh, 1972-79
Los Angeles, 1973-80
San Francisco, 1983-90
7 Houston, 1987-93
San Francisco, 1992-98

Most Games
53 Dallas, 1966-73, 1975-83, 1985, 1991-96, 1998-99
39 San Francisco, 1957, 1970-72, 1981, 1983-90, 1992-98
38 Minnesota, 1968-71, 1973-78, 1980, 1982, 1987-89, 1992-94, 1996-99

Most Games Won
32 Dallas, 1967, 1970-73, 1975, 1977-78, 1980-82, 1991-96
24 San Francisco, 1970-71, 1981, 1983-84, 1988-90, 1992-94, 1996-98
22 Green Bay, 1936, 1939, 1944, 1961-62, 1965-67, 1982, 1993-97
Washington, 1937, 1942-43, 1972, 1982-83, 1986-87, 1990-92, 1999

Most Consecutive Games Won
9 Green Bay, 1961-62, 1965-67
7 Pittsburgh, 1974-76
San Francisco, 1988-90
Dallas, 1992-94
Denver, 1997-98 (current)
6 Miami, 1972-73
Pittsburgh, 1978-79
Washington, 1982-83

Most Games Lost
22 Minnesota, 1968-71, 1973-78, 1980, 1982, 1987-89, 1992-94, 1996-99
21 Dallas, 1966-70, 1972-73, 1975-76, 1978-83, 1985, 1991, 1994, 1996, 1998-99
20 L.A. Rams, 1949-50, 1952, 1955, 1967, 1969, 1973-80, 1983-86, 1988-89

Most Consecutive Games Lost
6 N.Y. Giants, 1939, 1941, 1943-44, 1946, 1950
Cleveland, 1969, 1971-72, 1980, 1982, 1985

Minnesota, 1988-89, 1992-94, 1996
Detroit, 1991, 1993-95, 1997, 1999 (current)
5 N.Y. Giants, 1958-59, 1961-63
Los Angeles, 1952, 1955, 1967, 1969, 1973
Denver, 1977-79, 1983-84
Baltimore/Indianapolis, 1971, 1975-77, 1987
Philadelphia, 1980-81, 1988-90
4 Washington, 1972-74, 1976
Miami, 1974, 1978-79, 1981
Chi. Cardinals/St. Louis, 1948, 1974-75, 1982
Boston/New England, 1963, 1976, 1978, 1982
New Orleans, 1987, 1990-92 (current)
Kansas City, 1993-95, 1997 (current)
Seattle, 1984, 1987-88, 1999 (current)
Buffalo, 1995-96, 1998-99 (current)

SCORING

Most Points, Game
73 NFC: Chi. Bears vs. Washington, 1940
62 AFC-D: Jacksonville vs. Miami, 1999
59 NFC: Detroit vs. Cleveland, 1957

Most Points, Both Teams, Game
95 NFC-FR: Philadelphia (58) vs. Detroit (37), 1995
86 NFC-D: St. Louis (49) vs. Minnesota (37), 1999
79 AFC-D: San Diego (41) vs. Miami (38), 1981 (OT)
AFC-FR: Buffalo (41) vs. Houston (38), 1992 (OT)

Fewest Points, Both Teams, Game
5 NFC-D: Detroit (0) vs. Dallas (5), 1970
7 NFC: Chi. Cardinals (0) vs. Philadelphia (7), 1948
9 NFC: Tampa Bay (0) vs. Los Angeles (9), 1979

Largest Margin of Victory, Game
73 NFC: Chi. Bears vs. Washington, 1940 (73-0)
55 AFC-D: Jacksonville vs. Miami, 1999 (62-7)
49 AFC-D: Oakland vs. Houston, 1969 (56-7)

Most Points, Shutout Victory, Game
73 NFC: Chi. Bears vs. Washington, 1940
38 NFC-D: Dallas vs. Tampa Bay, 1981
37 NFC: Green Bay vs. N.Y. Giants, 1961

Most Points Overcome to Win Game
32 AFC-FR: Buffalo vs. Houston, 1992 (trailed 3-35, won 41-38) (OT)
20 NFC-D: Detroit vs. San Francisco, 1957 (trailed 7-27, won 31-27)
18 NFC-D: Dallas vs. San Francisco, 1972 (trailed 3-21, won 30-28)
AFC-D: Miami vs. Cleveland, 1985 (trailed 3-21, won 24-21)

Most Points, Each Half
1st: 41 AFC: Buffalo vs. L.A. Raiders, 1990
AFC-D: Jacksonville vs. Miami, 1999
38 NFC-D: Washington vs. L.A. Rams, 1983
NFC-FR: Philadelphia vs. Detroit, 1995
35 NFC: Cleveland vs. Detroit, 1954
AFC-D: Oakland vs. Houston, 1969
SB: Washington vs. Denver, 1987
2nd: 45 NFC: Chi. Bears vs. Washington, 1940
35 AFC-FR: Buffalo vs. Houston, 1992
NFC-D: St. Louis vs. Minnesota, 1999
30 SB: N.Y. Giants vs. Denver, 1986
AFC: Cleveland vs. Denver, 1987
NFC-FR: Detroit vs. Philadelphia, 1995

Most Points, Each Quarter
1st: 28 AFC-D: Oakland vs. Houston, 1969
24 AFC-D: San Diego vs. Miami, 1981
AFC-D: Jacksonville vs. Miami, 1999
21 NFC: Chi. Bears vs. Washington, 1940
AFC: San Diego vs. Boston, 1963
AFC-D: Oakland vs. Kansas City, 1968
AFC: Oakland vs. San Diego, 1980
AFC: Buffalo vs. L.A. Raiders, 1990
NFC: San Francisco vs. Dallas, 1994
2nd: 35 SB: Washington vs. Denver, 1987
31 NFC-FR: Philadelphia vs. Detroit, 1995
26 AFC-D: Pittsburgh vs. Buffalo, 1974
3rd: 28 AFC-FR: Buffalo vs. Houston, 1992
26 NFC: Chi. Bears vs. Washington, 1940
21 NFC-D: Dallas vs. Cleveland, 1967
NFC-D: Dallas vs. Tampa Bay, 1981
AFC-D: L.A. Raiders vs. Pittsburgh, 1983
SB: Chicago vs. New England, 1985
NFC-D: N.Y. Giants vs. San Francisco, 1986
AFC: Cleveland vs. Denver, 1987
AFC: Cleveland vs. Denver, 1989
NFC-D: St. Louis vs. Minnesota, 1999
4th: 27 NFC: N.Y. Giants vs. Chi. Bears, 1934
26 NFC-FR: Philadelphia vs. New Orleans, 1992
24 NFC: Baltimore vs. N.Y. Giants, 1959
OT: 6 NFC: Baltimore vs. N.Y. Giants, 1958
AFC-D: Oakland vs. Baltimore, 1977
NFC-D: L.A. Rams vs. N.Y. Giants, 1989

TOUCHDOWNS

Most Touchdowns, Game
11 NFC: Chi. Bears vs. Washington, 1940
8 NFC: Cleveland vs. Detroit, 1954
NFC: Detroit vs. Cleveland, 1957
AFC-D: Oakland vs. Houston, 1969
SB: San Francisco vs. Denver, 1989
AFC-D: Jacksonville vs. Miami, 1999
7 AFC: San Diego vs. Boston, 1963
NFC-D: Dallas vs. Cleveland, 1967
NFC-D: N.Y. Giants vs. San Francisco, 1986
AFC: Buffalo vs. L.A. Raiders, 1990
SB: Dallas vs. Buffalo, 1992
SB: San Francisco vs. San Diego, 1994
NFC-FR: Philadelphia vs. Detroit, 1995
NFC-D: St. Louis vs. Minnesota, 1999

Most Touchdowns, Both Teams, Game
12 NFC-FR: Philadelphia (7) vs. Detroit (5), 1995
NFC-D: St. Louis (7) vs. Minnesota (5), 1999
11 NFC: Chi. Bears (11) vs. Washington (0), 1940
10 NFC: Detroit (8) vs. Cleveland (2), 1957
AFC-D: Miami (5) vs. San Diego (5), 1981 (OT)
AFC: Miami (6) vs. Pittsburgh (4), 1984
AFC-FR: Buffalo (5) vs. Houston (5), 1992 (OT)
SB: San Francisco (7) vs. San Diego (3), 1994

Fewest Touchdowns, Both Teams, Game
0 NFC-D: N.Y. Giants vs. Cleveland, 1950
NFC-D: Dallas vs. Detroit, 1970
NFC: Los Angeles vs. Tampa Bay, 1979
1 NFC: Chi. Cardinals (0) vs. Philadelphia (1), 1948
NFC-D: Cleveland (0) vs. N.Y. Giants (1), 1958
AFC: San Diego (0) vs. Houston (1), 1961
AFC-D: N.Y. Jets (0) vs. Kansas City (1), 1969
NFC-D: Green Bay (0) vs. Washington (1), 1972
NFC-FR: New Orleans (0) vs. Chicago (1), 1990
NFC: N.Y. Giants (0) vs. San Francisco (1), 1990
AFC-FR: L.A. Raiders (0) vs. Kansas City (1), 1991
AFC-D: New England (0) vs. Pittsburgh (1), 1997
NFC: Tampa Bay (0) vs. St. Louis (1), 1999
2 In many games

POINTS AFTER TOUCHDOWN

Most (One-Point) Points After Touchdown, Game
8 NFC: Cleveland vs. Detroit, 1954
NFC: Detroit vs. Cleveland, 1957
AFC-D: Oakland vs. Houston, 1969
AFC-D: Jacksonville vs. Miami, 1999
7 NFC: Chi. Bears vs. Washington, 1940
NFC-D: Dallas vs. Cleveland, 1967
NFC-D: N.Y. Giants vs. San Francisco, 1986
SB: San Francisco vs. Denver, 1989
SB: Dallas vs. Buffalo, 1992
SB: San Francisco vs. San Diego, 1994
NFC-FR: Philadelphia vs. Detroit, 1995
NFC-D: St. Louis vs. Minnesota, 1999
6 AFC: San Diego vs. Boston, 1963
NFC-D: Washington vs. L.A. Rams, 1983
AFC: Miami vs. Pittsburgh, 1984
SB: Washington vs. Denver, 1987
AFC: Buffalo vs. L.A. Raiders, 1990
AFC-FR: L.A. Raiders vs. Denver, 1993
AFC-FR: Denver vs. Jacksonville, 1997

Most (One-Point) Points After Touchdown, Both Teams, Game
10 NFC: Detroit (8) vs. Cleveland (2), 1957
AFC-D: Miami (5) vs. San Diego (5), 1981 (OT)
AFC: Miami (6) vs. Pittsburgh (4), 1984
AFC-FR: Buffalo (5) vs. Houston (5), 1992 (OT)
NFC-FR: Philadelphia (7) vs. Detroit (3), 1995
9 In many games

Fewest (One-Point) Points After Touchdown, Both Teams, Game
0 NFC-D: N.Y. Giants vs. Cleveland, 1950
NFC-D: Dallas vs. Detroit, 1970
NFC: Los Angeles vs. Tampa Bay, 1979
NFC: St. Louis vs. Tampa Bay, 1999

Most Two-Point Conversions, Game
2 SB: San Diego vs. San Francisco, 1994
NFC-FR: Detroit vs. Philadelphia, 1995
1 By many teams

FIELD GOALS

Most Field Goals, Game

5 NFC-D: Minnesota vs. San Francisco, 1987
NFC: N.Y. Giants vs. San Francisco, 1990
AFC: Buffalo vs. Miami, 1992
NFC-FR: N.Y. Giants vs. Minnesota, 1997
4 AFC-D: Boston vs. Buffalo, 1963
AFC: Oakland vs. Houston, 1967
SB: Green Bay vs. Oakland, 1967
NFC: Washington vs. Dallas, 1972
AFC-D: Oakland vs. Pittsburgh, 1973
SB: San Francisco vs. Cincinnati, 1981
AFC-FR: New England vs. N.Y. Jets, 1985
NFC-FR: Washington vs. L.A. Rams, 1986
NFC-D: Philadelphia vs. Chicago, 1988
AFC-FR: Pittsburgh vs. Houston, 1989 (OT)
AFC-D: Pittsburgh vs. Buffalo, 1995
NFC-FR: Dallas vs. Minnesota, 1996
NFC-D: Carolina vs. Dallas, 1996
AFC-FR: Jacksonville vs. New England, 1998
AFC-D: Tennessee vs. Indianapolis, 1999
3 By many teams

Most Field Goals, Both Teams, Game

8 NFC-FR: N.Y. Giants (5) vs. Minnesota (3), 1997
7 AFC-FR: Pittsburgh (4) vs. Houston (3), 1989 (OT)
NFC: N.Y. Giants (5) vs. San Francisco (2), 1990
NFC-D: Carolina (4) vs. Dallas (3), 1996
AFC-D: Tennessee (4) vs. Indianapolis (3), 1999
6 NFC-D: Minnesota (5) vs. San Francisco (1), 1987
NFC-D: Philadelphia (4) vs. Chicago (2), 1988
AFC: Buffalo (5) vs. Miami (1), 1992

Most Field Goals Attempted, Game

6 AFC: Oakland vs. Houston, 1967
NFC-D: Los Angeles vs. Dallas, 1973
AFC-D: Cleveland vs. N.Y. Jets, 1986 (OT)
NFC: N.Y. Giants vs. San Francisco, 1990
AFC: Buffalo vs. Miami, 1992
5 By many teams

Most Field Goals Attempted, Both Teams, Game

9 NFC-D: Philadelphia (5) vs. Chicago (4), 1988
NFC-FR: N.Y. Giants (5) vs. Minnesota (4), 1997
8 NFC-D: Los Angeles (6) vs. Dallas (2), 1973
NFC-D: Detroit (5) vs. San Francisco (3), 1983
AFC-D: Cleveland (6) vs. N.Y. Jets (2), 1986 (OT)
NFC-D: Minnesota (5) vs. San Francisco (3), 1987
AFC-FR: Houston (4) vs. Pittsburgh (4), 1989 (OT)
NFC-FR: Chicago (4) vs. New Orleans (4), 1990
NFC: N.Y. Giants (6) vs. San Francisco (2), 1990
7 In many games

SAFETIES

Most Safeties, Game

1 By many teams

Most Safeties, Both Teams, Game

1 In many games

FIRST DOWNS

Most First Downs, Game

34 AFC-D: San Diego vs. Miami, 1981 (OT)
33 AFC-D: Cleveland vs. N.Y. Jets, 1986 (OT)
31 SB: San Francisco vs. Miami, 1984
NFC-D: San Francisco vs. Minnesota, 1997

Fewest First Downs, Game

6 NFC: N.Y. Giants vs. Green Bay, 1961
7 NFC: Green Bay vs. Boston, 1936
NFC-D: Pittsburgh vs. Philadelphia, 1947
NFC: Chi. Cardinals vs. Philadelphia, 1948
NFC: Los Angeles vs. Philadelphia, 1949
NFC-D: Cleveland vs. N.Y. Giants, 1958
AFC-D: Cincinnati vs. Baltimore, 1970
NFC-D: Detroit vs. Dallas, 1970
NFC: Tampa Bay vs. Los Angeles, 1979
8 By many teams

Most First Downs, Both Teams, Game

59 AFC-D: San Diego (34) vs. Miami (25), 1981 (OT)
55 AFC-FR: San Diego (29) vs. Pittsburgh (26), 1982
54 AFC-FR: Buffalo (28) vs. Miami (26), 1995

Fewest First Downs, Both Teams, Game

15 NFC: Green Bay (7) vs. Boston (8), 1936
19 NFC: N.Y. Giants (9) vs. Green Bay (10), 1939
NFC: Washington (9) vs. Chi. Bears (10), 1942
20 NFC-D: Cleveland (9) vs. N.Y. Giants (11), 1950

RUSHING

Most First Downs, Rushing, Game

19 NFC-FR: Dallas vs. Los Angeles, 1980
18 AFC-D: Miami vs. Cincinnati, 1973
AFC: Miami vs. Oakland, 1973
AFC-D: Pittsburgh vs. Buffalo, 1974
AFC-FR: Buffalo vs. Miami, 1995
AFC-FR: Denver vs. Jacksonville, 1997
17 AFC-D: Cincinnati vs. Seattle, 1988
AFC: Buffalo vs. Kansas City, 1993

Fewest First Downs, Rushing, Game

0 NFC: Los Angeles vs. Philadelphia, 1949
AFC-D: Buffalo vs. Boston, 1963
AFC: Oakland vs. Pittsburgh, 1974
NFC-FR: New Orleans vs. Minnesota, 1987
NFC: L.A. Rams vs. San Francisco, 1989
NFC-D: Chicago vs. N.Y. Giants, 1990
AFC-FR: Indianapolis vs. Pittsburgh, 1996
AFC-FR: Seattle vs. Miami, 1999
1 By many teams

Most First Downs, Rushing, Both Teams, Game

26 AFC: Buffalo (14) vs. L.A. Raiders (12), 1990
25 NFC-FR: Dallas (19) vs. Los Angeles (6), 1980
23 NFC: Cleveland (15) vs. Detroit (8), 1952
AFC-D: Miami (18) vs. Cincinnati (5), 1973
AFC-D: Pittsburgh (18) vs. Buffalo (5), 1974
AFC-FR: Buffalo (18) vs. Miami (5), 1995

Fewest First Downs, Rushing, Both Teams, Game

5 AFC-D: Buffalo (0) vs. Boston (5), 1963
NFC-D: Washington (1) vs. Tampa Bay (4), 1999
6 NFC: Green Bay (2) vs. Boston (4), 1936
NFC-D: Baltimore (2) vs. Minnesota (4), 1968
AFC-D: Houston (1) vs. Oakland (5), 1969
AFC-FR: N.Y. Jets (1) vs. Houston (5), 1991
7 NFC-D: Washington (2) vs. N.Y. Giants (5), 1943
NFC: Baltimore (3) vs. N.Y. Giants (4), 1959
NFC: Washington (3) vs. Dallas (4), 1972
AFC-FR: N.Y. Jets (3) vs. Buffalo (4), 1981
NFC-D: Detroit (3) vs. Dallas (4), 1991
AFC-D: Kansas City (3) vs. Houston (4), 1993
NFC-FR: Detroit (1) vs. Green Bay (6), 1994
NFC-FR: Atlanta (1) vs. Green Bay (6), 1995
AFC-FR: New England (1) vs. Pittsburgh (6), 1997
NFC-FR: Arizona (2) vs. Dallas (5), 1998
AFC-FR: Seattle (0) vs. Miami (7), 1999
NFC: St. Louis (3) vs. Tampa Bay (4), 1999

PASSING

Most First Downs, Passing, Game

21 AFC-D: Miami vs. San Diego, 1981 (OT)
AFC-D: San Diego vs. Miami, 1981 (OT)
AFC-D: Cleveland vs. N.Y. Jets, 1986 (OT)
NFC-D: Philadelphia vs. Chicago, 1988
20 NFC-FR: Dallas vs. L.A. Rams, 1983
AFC-D: Buffalo vs. Cleveland, 1989
AFC-FR: Miami vs. Buffalo, 1995
NFC-FR: Detroit vs. Philadelphia, 1995
AFC-FR: San Diego vs. Indianapolis, 1995
NFC-D: Minnesota vs. St. Louis, 1999
19 NFC-FR: St. Louis vs. Green Bay, 1982
NFC-FR: Dallas vs. Tampa Bay, 1982
AFC-FR: Pittsburgh vs. San Diego, 1982
AFC-FR: San Diego vs. Pittsburgh, 1982
NFC: Dallas vs. Washington, 1982
NFC-D: Detroit vs. Dallas, 1991
AFC-FR: Kansas City vs. Pittsburgh, 1993 (OT)
NFC: Minnesota vs. Atlanta, 1998 (OT)

Fewest First Downs, Passing, Game

0 NFC: Philadelphia vs. Chi. Cardinals, 1948
1 NFC-D: N.Y. Giants vs. Washington, 1943
NFC: Cleveland vs. Detroit, 1953
SB: Denver vs. Dallas, 1977
2 By many teams

Most First Downs, Passing, Both Teams, Game

42 AFC-D: Miami (21) vs. San Diego (21), 1981 (OT)
38 AFC-FR: Pittsburgh (19) vs. San Diego (19), 1982
NFC-D: Minnesota (20) vs. St. Louis (18), 1999
36 NFC: Minnesota (19) vs. Atlanta (17), 1998 (OT)

Fewest First Downs, Passing, Both Teams, Game

2 NFC: Philadelphia (0) vs. Chi. Cardinals (2), 1948
4 NFC-D: Cleveland (2) vs. N.Y. Giants (2), 1950
5 NFC: Detroit (2) vs. N.Y. Giants (3), 1935
NFC: Green Bay (2) vs. N.Y. Giants (3), 1939

POSTSEASON GAME RECORDS

PENALTY

Most First Downs, Penalty, Game

7 AFC-D: New England vs. Oakland, 1976
6 AFC-D: Cleveland vs. N.Y. Jets, 1986 (OT)
5 AFC-FR: Cleveland vs. L. A. Raiders, 1982
NFC-D: San Francisco vs. Minnesota, 1997
AFC-FR: Miami vs. Buffalo, 1998
NFC-D: Arizona vs. Minnesota, 1998

Most First Downs, Penalty, Both Teams, Game

9 AFC-D: New England (7) vs. Oakland (2), 1976
8 NFC-FR: Atlanta (4) vs. Minnesota (4), 1982
AFC-FR: Miami (5) vs. Buffalo (3), 1998
7 AFC-D: Baltimore (4) vs. Oakland (3), 1977 (OT)
AFC-FR: Denver (4) vs. L.A. Raiders (3), 1993
NFC-D: Dallas (4) vs. Carolina (3), 1996
AFC-D: Kansas City (4) vs. Denver (3), 1997

NET YARDS GAINED RUSHING AND PASSING

Most Yards Gained, Game

610 AFC: San Diego vs. Boston, 1963
602 SB: Washington vs. Denver, 1987
569 AFC: Miami vs. Pittsburgh, 1984

Fewest Yards Gained, Game

86 NFC-D: Cleveland vs. N.Y. Giants, 1958
99 NFC: Chi. Cardinals vs. Philadelphia, 1948
114 NFC-D: N.Y. Giants vs. Washington, 1943

Most Yards Gained, Both Teams, Game

1,038 AFC-FR: Buffalo (536) vs. Miami (502), 1995
1,036 AFC-D: San Diego (564) vs. Miami (472), 1981 (OT)
1,024 AFC: Miami (569) vs. Pittsburgh (455), 1984

Fewest Yards Gained, Both Teams, Game

331 NFC: Chi. Cardinals (99) vs. Philadelphia (232), 1948
332 NFC-D: N.Y. Giants (150) vs. Cleveland (182), 1950
336 NFC: Boston (116) vs. Green Bay (220), 1936

RUSHING

ATTEMPTS

Most Attempts, Game

65 NFC: Detroit vs. N.Y. Giants, 1935
61 NFC: Philadelphia vs. Los Angeles, 1949
59 AFC: New England vs. Miami, 1985

Fewest Attempts, Game

8 AFC-D: Miami vs. San Diego, 1994
9 SB: Miami vs. San Francisco, 1984
10 NFC: L.A. Rams vs. San Francisco, 1989
NFC-FR: Atlanta vs. Green Bay, 1995
NFC-FR: Detroit vs. Washington, 1999

Most Attempts, Both Teams, Game

109 NFC: Detroit (65) vs. N.Y. Giants (44), 1935
97 AFC-D: Baltimore (50) vs. Oakland (47), 1977 (OT)
91 NFC: Philadelphia (57) vs. Chi. Cardinals (34), 1948

Fewest Attempts, Both Teams, Game

32 AFC-D: Houston (14) vs. Kansas City (18), 1993
38 NFC-D: Detroit (16) vs. Dallas (22), 1991
39 NFC-FR: Atlanta (10) vs. Green Bay (29), 1995

YARDS GAINED

Most Yards Gained, Game

382 NFC: Chi. Bears vs. Washington, 1940
341 AFC-FR: Buffalo vs. Miami, 1995
338 NFC-FR: Dallas vs. Los Angeles, 1980

Fewest Yards Gained, Game

– 4 NFC-FR: Detroit vs. Green Bay, 1994
7 AFC-D: Buffalo vs. Boston, 1963
SB: New England vs. Chicago, 1985
14 AFC-D: Miami vs. Denver, 1998
AFC: N.Y. Jets vs. Denver, 1998

Most Yards Gained, Both Teams, Game

430 NFC-FR: Dallas (338) vs. Los Angeles (92), 1980
426 NFC: Cleveland (227) vs. Detroit (199), 1952
411 AFC-FR: Buffalo (341) vs. Miami (70), 1995

Fewest Yards Gained, Both Teams, Game

77 NFC-FR: Detroit (–4) vs. Green Bay (81), 1994
90 AFC-D: Buffalo (7) vs. Boston (83), 1963
NFC-D: Tampa Bay (44) vs. Washington (46), 1999
106 NFC: Boston (39) vs. Green Bay (67), 1936

AVERAGE GAIN

Highest Average Gain, Game

9.94 AFC: San Diego vs. Boston, 1963 (32-318)
9.29 NFC-D: Green Bay vs. Dallas, 1982 (17-158)
7.35 NFC-FR: Dallas vs. Los Angeles, 1980 (46-338)

Lowest Average Gain, Game

– 0.27 NFC-FR: Detroit vs. Green Bay, 1994 (15-(– 4))
0.58 AFC-D: Buffalo vs. Boston, 1963 (12-7)
0.64 SB: New England vs. Chicago, 1985 (11-7)

TOUCHDOWNS

Most Touchdowns, Game

7 NFC: Chi. Bears vs. Washington, 1940
6 NFC-D: San Francisco vs. N.Y. Giants, 1993
5 NFC: Cleveland vs. Detroit, 1954
NFC-D: San Francisco vs. Chicago, 1994
AFC-FR: Pittsburgh vs. Indianapolis, 1996
AFC-FR: Denver vs. Jacksonville, 1997

Most Touchdowns, Both Teams, Game

7 NFC: Chi. Bears (7) vs. Washington (0), 1940
6 NFC: Cleveland (5) vs. Detroit (1), 1954
NFC-D: San Francisco (6) vs. N.Y. Giants (0), 1993
NFC-D: San Francisco (5) vs. Chicago (1), 1994
AFC-FR: Denver (5) vs. Jacksonville (1), 1997
5 NFC: Chi. Cardinals (3) vs. Philadelphia (2), 1947
AFC: San Diego (4) vs. Boston (1), 1963
AFC-D: Cincinnati (3) vs. Buffalo (2), 1981
AFC-FR: Pittsburgh (5) vs. Indianapolis (0), 1996
NFC-D: Arizona (3) vs. Minnesota (2), 1998

PASSING

ATTEMPTS

Most Attempts, Game

66 AFC-FR: Miami vs. Buffalo, 1995
65 AFC-D: Cleveland vs. N.Y. Jets, 1986 (OT)
NFC-D: San Francisco vs. Green Bay, 1995
61 NFC-FR: Minnesota vs. Chicago, 1994

Fewest Attempts, Game

5 NFC: Detroit vs. N.Y. Giants, 1935
6 AFC: Miami vs. Oakland, 1973
7 SB: Miami vs. Minnesota, 1973

Most Attempts, Both Teams, Game

102 AFC-D: San Diego (54) vs. Miami (48), 1981 (OT)
96 AFC: N.Y. Jets (49) vs. Oakland (47), 1968
95 AFC-D: Cleveland (65) vs. N.Y. Jets (30), 1986 (OT)

Fewest Attempts, Both Teams, Game

18 NFC: Detroit (5) vs. N.Y. Giants (13), 1935
23 NFC: Chi. Cardinals (11) vs. Philadelphia (12), 1948
24 NFC-D: Cleveland (9) vs. N.Y. Giants (15), 1950

COMPLETIONS

Most Completions, Game

36 AFC-FR: Houston vs. Buffalo, 1992 (OT)
34 AFC-D: Cleveland vs. N.Y. Jets, 1986 (OT)
AFC-FR: Miami vs. Buffalo, 1995
33 AFC-D: San Diego vs. Miami, 1981 (OT)
NFC-FR: Minnesota vs. Chicago, 1994

Fewest Completions, Game

2 NFC: Detroit vs. N.Y. Giants, 1935
NFC: Philadelphia vs. Chi. Cardinals, 1948
3 NFC: N.Y. Giants vs. Chi. Bears, 1941
NFC: Green Bay vs. N.Y. Giants, 1944
NFC: Chi. Cardinals vs. Philadelphia, 1947
NFC: Chi. Cardinals vs. Philadelphia, 1948
NFC-D: Cleveland vs. N.Y. Giants, 1950
NFC-D: N.Y. Giants vs. Cleveland, 1950
NFC: Cleveland vs. Detroit, 1953
AFC: Miami vs. Oakland, 1973
4 NFC: N.Y. Giants vs. Detroit, 1935
NFC-D: N.Y. Giants vs. Washington, 1943
NFC-D: Pittsburgh vs. Philadelphia, 1947
NFC-D: Dallas vs. Detroit, 1970
AFC: Miami vs. Baltimore, 1971
SB: Miami vs. Washington, 1982
AFC-FR: Seattle vs. L.A. Raiders, 1984

Most Completions, Both Teams, Game

64 AFC-D: San Diego (33) vs. Miami (31), 1981 (OT)
57 AFC-FR: Houston (36) vs. Buffalo (21), 1992 (OT)
56 NFC-D: Dallas (28) vs. Green Bay (28), 1993
NFC: Minnesota (29) vs. Atlanta (27), 1998 (OT)
NFC-D: Minnesota (29) vs. St. Louis (27), 1999

Fewest Completions, Both Teams, Game

5 NFC: Philadelphia (2) vs. Chi. Cardinals (3), 1948
6 NFC: Detroit (2) vs. N.Y. Giants (4), 1935
NFC-D: Cleveland (3) vs. N.Y. Giants (3), 1950
11 NFC: Green Bay (3) vs. N.Y. Giants (8), 1944
NFC-D: Dallas (4) vs. Detroit (7), 1970

COMPLETION PERCENTAGE

Highest Completion Percentage, Game (20 attempts)
88.0 SB: N.Y. Giants vs. Denver, 1986 (25-22)
87.1 NFC: San Francisco vs. L.A. Rams, 1989 (31-27)
81.8 NFC-D: St. Louis vs. Minnesota (33-27)

Lowest Completion Percentage, Game (20 attempts)
18.5 NFC: Tampa Bay vs. Los Angeles, 1979 (27-5)
20.0 NFC-D: N.Y. Giants vs. Washington, 1943 (20-4)
25.8 NFC: Chi. Bears vs. Washington, 1937 (31-8)

YARDS GAINED

Most Yards Gained, Game
483 AFC-D: Cleveland vs. N.Y. Jets, 1986 (OT)
435 AFC: Miami vs. Pittsburgh, 1984
432 AFC-FR: Miami vs. Buffalo, 1995

Fewest Yards Gained, Game
3 NFC: Chi. Cardinals vs. Philadelphia, 1948
7 NFC: Philadelphia vs. Chi. Cardinals, 1948
9 NFC-D: N.Y. Giants vs. Cleveland, 1950
NFC: Cleveland vs. Detroit, 1953

Most Yards Gained, Both Teams, Game
809 AFC-D: San Diego (415) vs. Miami (394), 1981 (OT)
762 NFC-D: Minnesota (388) vs. St. Louis (374), 1999
747 AFC: Miami (435) vs. Pittsburgh (312), 1984

Fewest Yards Gained, Both Teams, Game
10 NFC: Chi. Cardinals (3) vs. Philadelphia (7), 1948
38 NFC-D: N.Y. Giants (9) vs. Cleveland (29), 1950
102 NFC-D: Dallas (22) vs. Detroit (80), 1970

TIMES SACKED

Most Times Sacked, Game
9 AFC: Kansas City vs. Buffalo, 1966
NFC: Chicago vs. San Francisco, 1984
AFC-D: N.Y. Jets vs. Cleveland, 1986 (OT)
AFC-D: Houston vs. Kansas City, 1993
8 NFC: Green Bay vs. Dallas, 1967
NFC: Minnesota vs. Washington, 1987
7 NFC-D: Dallas vs. Los Angeles, 1973
SB: Dallas vs. Pittsburgh, 1975
AFC-FR: Houston vs. Oakland, 1980
NFC-D: Washington vs. Chicago, 1984
SB: New England vs. Chicago, 1985
AFC-FR: Kansas City vs. San Diego, 1992
AFC-D: Pittsburgh vs. Buffalo, 1992

Most Times Sacked, Both Teams, Game
13 AFC: Kansas City (9) vs. Buffalo (4), 1966
AFC-D: N.Y. Jets (9) vs. Cleveland (4), 1986 (OT)
12 NFC-D: Dallas (7) vs. Los Angeles (5), 1973
NFC-D: Washington (7) vs. Chicago (5), 1984
NFC: Chicago (9) vs. San Francisco (3), 1984
AFC-FR: Kansas City (7) vs. San Diego (5), 1992
11 AFC-D: Houston (9) vs. Kansas City (2), 1993

Fewest Times Sacked, Both Teams, Game
0 AFC-D: Buffalo vs. Pittsburgh, 1974
AFC-FR: Pittsburgh vs. San Diego, 1982
AFC: Miami vs. Pittsburgh, 1984
AFC-D: Buffalo vs. Miami, 1990
AFC-D: Denver vs. Houston, 1991
AFC-FR: Buffalo vs. Miami, 1995
AFC-D: Indianapolis vs. Tennessee, 1999
1 In many games

TOUCHDOWNS

Most Touchdowns, Game
6 AFC-D: Oakland vs. Houston, 1969
SB: San Francisco vs. San Diego, 1994
5 NFC: Chi. Bears vs. Washington, 1943
NFC: Detroit vs. Cleveland, 1957
AFC-D: Oakland vs. Kansas City, 1968
SB: San Francisco vs. Denver, 1989
NFC-D: St. Louis vs. Minnesota, 1999
4 By many teams

Most Touchdowns, Both Teams, Game
9 NFC-D: St. Louis (5) vs. Minnesota (4), 1999
8 AFC-FR: Buffalo (4) vs. Houston (4), 1992 (OT)
7 NFC: Chi. Bears (5) vs. Washington (2), 1943
AFC-D: Oakland (6) vs. Houston (1), 1969
SB: Pittsburgh (4) vs. Dallas (3), 1978
AFC-D: Miami (4) vs. San Diego (3), 1981 (OT)
AFC: Miami (4) vs. Pittsburgh (3), 1984
AFC-D: Buffalo (4) vs. Cleveland (3), 1989
SB: San Francisco (6) vs. San Diego (1), 1994
NFC-FR: Detroit (4) vs. Philadelphia (3), 1995

INTERCEPTIONS BY

Most Interceptions By, Game
8 NFC: Chi. Bears vs. Washington, 1940
7 NFC: Cleveland vs. Los Angeles, 1955
6 NFC: Green Bay vs. N.Y. Giants, 1939
NFC: Chi. Bears vs. N.Y. Giants, 1946
NFC: Cleveland vs. Detroit, 1954
AFC: San Diego vs. Houston, 1961
AFC: Buffalo vs. L.A. Raiders, 1990
NFC-FR: Philadelphia vs. Detroit, 1995

Most Interceptions By, Both Teams, Game
10 NFC: Cleveland (7) vs. Los Angeles (3), 1955
AFC: San Diego (6) vs. Houston (4), 1961
9 NFC: Green Bay (6) vs. N.Y. Giants (3), 1939
8 NFC: Chi. Bears (8) vs. Washington (0), 1940
NFC: Chi. Bears (6) vs. N.Y. Giants (2), 1946
NFC: Cleveland (6) vs. Detroit (2), 1954
AFC-FR: Buffalo (4) vs. N.Y. Jets (4), 1981
AFC: Miami (5) vs. N.Y. Jets (3), 1982

YARDS GAINED

Most Yards Gained, Game
138 AFC-FR: N.Y. Jets vs. Cincinnati, 1982
136 AFC: Dall. Texans vs. Houston, 1962 (OT)
SB: Denver vs. Atlanta, 1998
130 NFC-D: Los Angeles vs. St. Louis, 1975

Most Yards Gained, Both Teams, Game
156 NFC: Green Bay (123) vs. N.Y. Giants (33), 1939
149 NFC: Cleveland (103) vs. Los Angeles (46), 1955
141 AFC-FR: Buffalo (79) vs. N.Y. Jets (62), 1981

TOUCHDOWNS

Most Touchdowns, Game
3 NFC: Chi. Bears vs. Washington, 1940
2 NFC-D: Los Angeles vs. St. Louis, 1975
NFC-FR: Philadelphia vs. Detroit, 1995
1 In many games

Most Touchdowns, Both Teams, Game
3 NFC: Chi. Bears (3) vs. Washington (0), 1940
2 NFC-D: Los Angeles (2) vs. St. Louis(0), 1975
NFC-D: Dallas (1) vs. Green Bay (1), 1982
NFC-D: Minnesota (1) vs. San Francisco (1), 1987
NFC-FR: Detroit (1) vs. Green Bay (1), 1993
NFC-FR: Philadelphia (2) vs. Detroit (0), 1995
AFC-FR: Buffalo (1) vs. Jacksonville (1), 1996
1 In many games

PUNTING

Most Punts, Game
14 AFC-D: N.Y. Jets vs. Cleveland, 1986 (OT)
13 NFC: N.Y. Giants vs. Chi. Bears, 1933
AFC-D: Baltimore vs. Oakland, 1977 (OT)
11 AFC: Houston vs. Oakland, 1967
AFC-D: Houston vs. Oakland, 1969
NFC: L.A. Rams vs. Chicago, 1985

Fewest Punts, Game
0 NFC-FR: St. Louis vs. Green Bay, 1982
AFC-FR: N.Y. Jets vs. Cincinnati, 1982
1 By many teams

Most Punts, Both Teams, Game
23 NFC: N.Y. Giants (13) vs. Chi. Bears (10), 1933
22 AFC-D: N.Y. Jets (14) vs. Cleveland (8), 1986 (OT)
21 AFC-D: Baltimore (13) vs. Oakland (8), 1977 (OT)
NFC: L.A. Rams (11) vs. Chicago (10), 1985

Fewest Punts, Both Teams, Game
1 NFC-FR: St. Louis (0) vs. Green Bay (1), 1982
2 AFC-FR: N.Y. Jets (0) vs. Cincinnati (2), 1982
SB: Atlanta (1) vs. Denver (1), 1998
3 AFC: Miami (1) vs. Oakland (2), 1973
AFC-FR: San Diego (1) vs. Pittsburgh (2), 1982
AFC-D: Buffalo (1) vs. Miami (2), 1990
AFC-FR: L.A. Raiders (1) vs. Kansas City (2), 1991
AFC-D: Houston (1) vs. Denver (2), 1991
NFC-FR: Dallas (1) vs. Minnesota (2), 1996
AFC-FR: Miami (1) vs. Buffalo (2), 1998
NFC-D: Minnesota (1) vs. Arizona (2), 1998

AVERAGE YARDAGE

Highest Average, Punting, Game (4 punts)
56.0 AFC: Oakland vs. San Diego, 1980
52.5 NFC: Washington vs. Chi. Bears, 1942
52.0 AFC-D: Tennessee vs. Indianapolis, 1999

POSTSEASON GAME RECORDS

Lowest Average, Punting, Game (4 punts)
24.9 NFC: Washington vs. Chi. Bears, 1937
25.3 AFC-FR: Pittsburgh vs. Houston, 1989
25.5 NFC: Green Bay vs. N.Y. Giants, 1962

PUNT RETURNS

Most Punt Returns, Game
8 NFC: Green Bay vs. N.Y. Giants, 1944
7 By many teams

Most Punt Returns, Both Teams, Game
13 AFC-FR: Houston (7) vs. Oakland (6), 1980
12 AFC-D: New England (7) vs. Pittsburgh (5), 1996
11 NFC: Green Bay (8) vs. N.Y. Giants (3), 1944
NFC-D: Green Bay (6) vs. Baltimore (5), 1965
AFC-FR: Jacksonville (7) vs. New England (4), 1998

Fewest Punt Returns, Both Teams, Game
0 NFC: Chi. Bears vs. N.Y. Giants, 1941
AFC: Boston vs. San Diego, 1963
NFC-FR: Green Bay vs. St. Louis, 1982
AFC-FR: Houston vs. N.Y. Jets, 1991
AFC-D: Denver vs. Houston, 1991
NFC-D: San Francisco vs. Washington, 1992
SB: Denver vs. Green Bay, 1997
SB: Atlanta vs. Denver, 1998
1 In many games

YARDS GAINED

Most Yards Gained, Game
155 NFC-D: Dallas vs. Cleveland, 1967
150 NFC: Chi. Cardinals vs. Philadelphia, 1947
143 NFC-FR: Minnesota vs. New Orleans, 1987

Fewest Yards Gained, Game
–10 NFC: Green Bay vs. Cleveland, 1965
–9 NFC: Dallas vs. Green Bay, 1966
AFC-D: Kansas City vs. Oakland, 1968
–7 NFC-D: San Francisco vs. Atlanta, 1998

Most Yards Gained, Both Teams, Game
166 NFC-D: Dallas (155) vs. Cleveland (11), 1967
160 NFC: Chi. Cardinals (150) vs. Philadelphia (10), 1947
146 NFC-D: Philadelphia (112) vs. Pittsburgh (34), 1947

Fewest Yards Gained, Both Teams, Game
–9 NFC: Dallas (–9) vs. Green Bay (0), 1966
–6 AFC-D: Miami (–5) vs. Oakland (–1), 1970
–3 NFC-D: San Francisco (–5) vs. Dallas (2), 1972

TOUCHDOWNS

Most Touchdowns, Game
1 By 12 teams

KICKOFF RETURNS

Most Kickoff Returns, Game
10 NFC-D: L.A. Rams vs. Washington, 1983
NFC-FR: Detroit vs. Philadelphia, 1995
9 NFC: Chi. Bears vs. N.Y. Giants, 1956
AFC: Boston vs. San Diego, 1963
AFC: Houston vs. Oakland, 1967
SB: Denver vs. San Francisco, 1989
AFC-D: Miami vs. Buffalo, 1990
AFC: L.A. Raiders vs. Buffalo, 1990
AFC-D: Miami vs. Jacksonville, 1999
8 By many teams

Most Kickoff Returns, Both Teams, Game
15 AFC-D: Miami (9) vs. Buffalo (6), 1990
14 NFC-FR: Detroit (10) vs. Philadelphia (4), 1995
13 NFC-D: Green Bay (7) vs. Dallas (6), 1982
NFC-FR: Green Bay (7) vs. San Francisco (6), 1998

Fewest Kickoff Returns, Both Teams, Game
1 NFC: Green Bay (0) vs. Boston (1), 1936
AFC-FR: San Diego (0) vs. Kansas City (1), 1992
2 NFC-D: Los Angeles (0) vs. Chi. Bears (2), 1950
AFC: Houston (0) vs. San Diego (2), 1961
AFC-D: Oakland (1) vs. Pittsburgh (1), 1972
AFC-D: N.Y. Jets (0) vs. L.A. Raiders (2), 1982
AFC: Miami (1) vs. N.Y. Jets (1), 1982
NFC: N.Y. Giants (0) vs. Washington (2), 1986
3 In many games

YARDS GAINED

Most Yards Gained, Game
244 SB: San Diego vs. San Francisco, 1994
227 SB: Atlanta vs. Denver, 1998
225 NFC: Washington vs. Chi. Bears, 1940

Most Yards Gained, Both Teams, Game
379 AFC-D: Baltimore (193) vs. Oakland (186), 1977 (OT)
348 NFC-D: Minnesota (174) vs. St. Louis (174), 1999
322 NFC-D: Green Bay (194) vs. San Francisco (128), 1998

Fewest Yards Gained, Both Teams, Game
5 AFC-FR: San Diego (0) vs. Kansas City (5), 1992
15 NFC: N.Y. Giants (0) vs. Washington (15), 1986
31 NFC-D: Los Angeles (0) vs. Chi. Bears (31), 1950

TOUCHDOWNS

Most Touchdowns, Game
1 NFC-D: San Francisco vs. Dallas, 1972
AFC-D: Miami vs. Oakland, 1974
AFC-D: Baltimore vs. Oakland, 1977 (OT)
SB: Miami vs. Washington, 1982
SB: Cincinnati vs. San Francisco, 1988
AFC-D: Cleveland vs. Buffalo, 1989
SB: San Diego vs. San Francisco, 1994
SB: Green Bay vs. New England, 1996
NFC: San Francisco vs. Green Bay, 1997
SB: Atlanta vs. Denver, 1998
AFC-FR: Tennessee vs. Buffalo, 1999
AFC-FR: Seattle vs. Miami, 1999
NFC-D: Washington vs. Tampa Bay, 1999
NFC-D: St. Louis vs. Minnesota, 1999
AFC: Tennessee vs. Jacksonville, 1999

PENALTIES

Most Penalties, Game
17 AFC-FR: L.A. Raiders vs. Denver, 1993
14 AFC-FR: Oakland vs. Houston, 1980
NFC-D: San Francisco vs. N.Y. Giants, 1981
13 AFC-FR: Houston vs. Cleveland, 1988
AFC-D: Houston vs. Denver, 1991
NFC-D: Arizona vs. Minnesota, 1998

Fewest Penalties, Game
0 NFC: Philadelphia vs. Green Bay, 1960
NFC-D: Detroit vs. Dallas, 1970
AFC-D: Miami vs. Oakland, 1970
SB: Miami vs. Dallas, 1971
NFC-D: Washington vs. Minnesota, 1973
SB: Pittsburgh vs. Dallas, 1975
NFC: San Francisco vs. Chicago, 1988
SB: Denver vs. San Francisco, 1989
AFC-D: L.A. Raiders vs. Cincinnati, 1990
AFC-D: Miami vs. San Diego, 1992
SB: Atlanta vs. Denver, 1998
1 By many teams

Most Penalties, Both Teams, Game
27 AFC-FR: L.A. Raiders (17) vs. Denver (10), 1993
22 AFC-FR: Oakland (14) vs. Houston (8), 1980
NFC-D: San Francisco (14) vs. N.Y. Giants (8), 1981
AFC-FR: Houston (13) vs. Cleveland (9), 1988
NFC-D: Arizona (13) vs. Minnesota (9), 1998
21 AFC-D: Oakland (11) vs. New England (10), 1976

Fewest Penalties, Both Teams, Game
1 AFC-D: L.A. Raiders (0) vs. Cincinnati (1), 1990
2 NFC: Washington (1) vs. Chi. Bears (1), 1937
NFC-D: Washington (0) vs. Minnesota (2), 1973
SB: Pittsburgh (0) vs. Dallas (2), 1975
3 AFC: Miami (1) vs. Baltimore (2), 1971
NFC: San Francisco (1) vs. Dallas (2), 1971
SB: Miami (0) vs. Dallas (3), 1971
AFC-D: Pittsburgh (1) vs. Oakland (2), 1972
AFC-D: Miami (1) vs. Cincinnati (2), 1973
SB: Miami (1) vs. San Francisco (2), 1984
NFC: San Francisco (0) vs. Chicago (3), 1988

YARDS PENALIZED

Most Yards Penalized, Game
145 NFC-D: San Francisco vs. N.Y. Giants, 1981
133 SB: Dallas vs. Baltimore, 1970
130 AFC-FR: L.A. Raiders vs. Denver, 1993

Fewest Yards Penalized, Game
0 By 11 teams

Most Yards Penalized, Both Teams, Game
227 AFC-FR: L.A. Raiders (130) vs. Denver (97), 1993
206 NFC-D: San Francisco (145) vs. N.Y. Giants (61), 1981
201 NFC-FR: Detroit (126) vs. Washington (75), 1999

Fewest Yards Penalized, Both Teams, Game
5 AFC-D: L.A. Raiders (0) vs. Cincinnati (5), 1990
9 NFC-D: Washington (0) vs. Minnesota (9), 1973
15 SB: Miami (0) vs. Dallas (15), 1971

FUMBLES

Most Fumbles, Game

8 SB: Buffalo vs. Dallas, 1992
7 AFC-D: Houston vs. Kansas City, 1993
6 By 12 teams

Most Fumbles, Both Teams, Game

12 AFC: Houston (6) vs. Pittsburgh (6), 1978
SB: Buffalo (8) vs. Dallas (4), 1992
10 NFC: Chi. Bears (5) vs. N.Y. Giants (5), 1934
SB: Dallas (6) vs. Denver (4), 1977
AFC: Jacksonville (5) vs. Tennessee (5), 1999
9 NFC-D: San Francisco (6) vs. Detroit (3), 1957
NFC-D: San Francisco (5) vs. Dallas (4), 1972
NFC: Dallas (5) vs. Philadelphia (4), 1980

Most Fumbles Lost, Game

5 SB: Buffalo vs. Dallas, 1992
AFC-D: Miami vs. Jacksonville, 1999
4 NFC: N.Y. Giants vs. Baltimore, 1958 (OT)
AFC: Kansas City vs. Oakland, 1969
SB: Baltimore vs. Dallas, 1970
AFC: Pittsburgh vs. Oakland, 1975
SB: Denver vs. Dallas, 1977
AFC: Houston vs. Pittsburgh, 1978
AFC: Miami vs. New England, 1985
SB: New England vs. Chicago, 1985
NFC-FR: L.A. Rams vs. Washington, 1986
NFC-FR: Minnesota vs. Dallas, 1996
AFC-FR: Buffalo vs. Miami, 1998
AFC: N.Y. Jets vs. Denver, 1998
AFC: Jacksonville vs. Tennessee, 1999
3 By many teams

Fewest Fumbles, Both Teams, Game

0 NFC: Green Bay vs. Cleveland, 1965
AFC-D: Houston vs. San Diego, 1979
NFC-D: Dallas vs. Los Angeles, 1979
SB: Los Angeles vs. Pittsburgh, 1979
AFC-D: Buffalo vs. Cincinnati, 1981
NFC: Minnesota vs. Washington, 1987
NFC-D: San Francisco vs. Washington, 1990
NFC: Dallas vs. Green Bay, 1995
AFC-D: New England vs. Pittsburgh, 1996
SB: Green Bay vs. New England, 1996
AFC-FR: Miami vs. Seattle, 1999
1 In many games

RECOVERIES

Most Total Fumbles Recovered, Game

8 SB: Dallas vs. Denver, 1977 (4 own, 4 opp)
7 NFC: Chi. Bears vs. N.Y. Giants, 1934 (5 own, 2 opp)
NFC-D: San Francisco vs. Detroit, 1957 (4 own, 3 opp)
NFC-D: San Francisco vs. Dallas, 1972 (4 own, 3 opp)
AFC: Pittsburgh vs. Houston, 1978 (3 own, 4 opp)
6 AFC: Houston vs. San Diego, 1961 (4 own, 2 opp)
AFC-D: Cleveland vs. Baltimore, 1971 (4 own, 2 opp)
AFC-D: Cleveland vs. Oakland, 1980 (5 own, 1 opp)
NFC: Philadelphia vs. Dallas, 1980 (3 own, 3 opp)
SB: Dallas vs. Buffalo, 1992 (1 own, 5 opp)
NFC-D: Green Bay vs. San Francisco, 1996 (4 own, 2 opp)
AFC: Denver vs. N.Y. Jets, 1998 (2 own, 4 opp)
AFC: Tennessee vs. Jacksonville, 1999 (2 own, 4 opp)

Most Own Fumbles Recovered, Game

5 NFC: Chi. Bears vs. N.Y. Giants, 1934
AFC-D: Cleveland vs. Oakland, 1980
4 By many teams

TOUCHDOWNS

Most Touchdowns, Game

2 SB: Dallas vs. Buffalo, 1992

TURNOVERS

Numbers of times losing the ball on interceptions and fumbles.

Most Turnovers, Game

9 NFC: Washington vs. Chi. Bears, 1940
NFC: Detroit vs. Cleveland, 1954
AFC: Houston vs. Pittsburgh, 1978
SB: Buffalo vs. Dallas, 1992
8 NFC: N.Y. Giants vs. Chi. Bears, 1946
NFC: Los Angeles vs. Cleveland, 1955
NFC: Cleveland vs. Detroit, 1957
SB: Denver vs. Dallas, 1977
NFC-D: Minnesota vs. Philadelphia, 1980
7 In many games

Fewest Turnovers, Game

0 By many teams

Most Turnovers, Both Teams, Game

14 AFC: Houston (9) vs. Pittsburgh (5), 1978
13 NFC: Detroit (9) vs. Cleveland (4), 1954
AFC: Houston (7) vs. San Diego (6), 1961
12 AFC: Pittsburgh (7) vs. Oakland (5), 1975

Fewest Turnovers, Both Teams, Game

0 SB: Buffalo vs. N.Y. Giants, 1990
AFC-FR: Kansas City vs Pittsburgh, 1993 (OT)
NFC-FR: Detroit vs. Green Bay, 1994
AFC-FR: Denver vs. Jacksonville, 1996
SB: St. Louis vs. Tennessee, 1999
1 AFC-D: Baltimore (0) vs. Cincinnati (1), 1970
AFC-D: Pittsburgh (0) vs. Buffalo (1), 1974
AFC: Oakland (0) vs. Pittsburgh (1), 1976
NFC-D: Minnesota (0) vs. Washington (1), 1982
NFC-D: Chicago (0) vs. N.Y. Giants (1), 1985
SB: N.Y. Giants (0) vs. Denver (1), 1986
NFC: Washington (0) vs. Minnesota (1), 1987
AFC-D: Cincinnati (0) vs. L.A. Raiders (1), 1990
NFC: N.Y. Giants (0) vs. San Francisco (1), 1990
NFC-FR: N.Y. Giants (0) vs. Minnesota (1), 1993
AFC-FR: L.A. Raiders (0) vs. Denver (1), 1993
NFC: Dallas (0) vs. San Francisco (1), 1993
AFC: Indianapolis (0) vs. Pittsburgh (1), 1995
NFC-D: San Francisco (0) vs. Minnesota (1), 1997
AFC-D: Indianapolis (0) vs. Tennessee (1), 1999
2 In many games

AFC-NFC PRO BOWL RECORDS

Includes records of AFC-NFC Pro Bowls, 1971-2000
Compiled by Elias Sports Bureau

INDIVIDUAL RECORDS

SERVICE

Most Games

11 ** Reggie White, Philadelphia, 1987-93; Green Bay, 1994, 1996-97, 1999
Randall McDaniel, Minnesota, 1990-2000
10 Lawrence Taylor, N.Y. Giants, 1982-91
Ronnie Lott, San Francisco, 1982-85, 1987-91; L.A. Raiders 1992
Mike Singletary, Chicago, 1984-93
9 * Ken Houston, Houston, 1971-73; Washington, 1974-79
Joe Greene, Pittsburgh, 1971-77, 1979-80
Jack Lambert, Pittsburgh, 1976-84
Walter Payton, Chicago, 1977-81, 1984-87
Harry Carson, N.Y. Giants, 1979-80, 1982-88
Mike Webster, Pittsburgh, 1979-86, 1988
** Anthony Muñoz, Cincinnati, 1982-87, 1989-90, 1992
Warren Moon, Houston, 1989-94; Minnesota 1995-96; Seattle 1998
Derrick Thomas, Kansas City, 1990-98
***Jerry Rice, San Francisco, 1987-88, 1990-94, 1996, 1999
***Bruce Matthews, Houston, 1989-95, 1997; Tennessee, 2000
Junior Seau, San Diego, 1992-2000
**Also selected, but did not play, in one additional game*
***Also selected, but did not play, in two additional games*
****Also selected, but did not play, in three additional games*

SCORING

POINTS

Most Points, Career

45 Morten Andersen, New Orleans, 1986-89, 1991, 1993; Atlanta, 1996 (15-pat, 10-fg)
30 Jan Stenerud, Kansas City, 1971-72, 1976; Minnesota, 1985 (6-pat, 8-fg)
26 Nick Lowery, Kansas City, 1982, 1991, 1993 (5 pat, 7 fg)

Most Points, Game

18 John Brockington, Green Bay, 1973 (3-td)
Mike Alstott, Tampa Bay, 2000 (3-td)
Jimmy Smith, Jacksonville, 2000 (3-td)
15 Garo Yepremian, Miami, 1974 (5-fg)
Jason Hanson, Detroit, 2000 (6-pat, 3-fg)
14 Jan Stenerud, Kansas City, 1972 (2-pat, 4-fg)

TOUCHDOWNS

Most Touchdowns, Career

4 Jimmy Smith, Jacksonville, 1998-2000 (4-p)
3 John Brockington, Green Bay, 1972-74 (2-r, 1-p)
Earl Campbell, Houston, 1979-82, 1984 (3-r)
Chuck Muncie, New Orleans, 1980; San Diego, 1982-83 (3-r)
William Andrews, Atlanta, 1981-84 (1-r, 2-p)
Marcus Allen, L.A. Raiders, 1983, 1985-86, 1988; Kansas City, 1994 (2-r, 1-p)
Cris Carter, Minnesota, 1994-2000 (3-p)
Mike Alstott, Tampa Bay, 1998-2000 (3-r)
2 By 17 players

Most Touchdowns, Game

3 John Brockington, Green Bay, 1973 (2-r, 1-p)
Mike Alstott, Tampa Bay, 2000 (3-r)
Jimmy Smith, Jacksonville, 2000 (3-p)
2 Mel Renfro, Dallas, 1971 (2-ret)
Earl Campbell, Houston, 1980 (2-r)
Chuck Muncie, New Orleans, 1980 (2-r)
William Andrews, Atlanta, 1984 (2-p)
Herschel Walker, Dallas, 1989 (2-r)
Johnny Johnson, Phoenix, 1991 (2-r)
Eric Green, Pittsburgh, 1995 (2-p)

POINTS AFTER TOUCHDOWN

Most Points After Touchdown, Career

15 Morten Andersen, New Orleans, 1986-89, 1991, 1993; Atlanta, 1996 (15 att)
9 Jason Hanson, Detroit, 1998, 2000 (9 att)
6 Chester Marcol, Green Bay, 1973, 1975 (6 att)
Mark Moseley, Washington, 1980, 1983 (7 att)
Ali Haji-Sheikh, N.Y. Giants, 1984 (6 att)
Jan Stenerud, Kansas City, 1971-72, 1976; Green Bay, 1985 (6 att)

Most Points After Touchdown, Game

6 Ali Haji-Sheikh, N.Y. Giants, 1984 (6 att)
Jason Hanson, Detroit, 2000 (6 att)
5 John Carney, San Diego, 1995 (5 att)
4 Chester Marcol, Green Bay, 1973 (4 att)
Mark Moseley, Washington, 1980 (5 att)
Morten Andersen, New Orleans, 1986 (4 att), 1989 (4 att)
Olindo Mare, Miami, 2000 (4 att)

FIELD GOALS

Most Field Goals Attempted, Career

18 Morten Andersen, New Orleans, 1986-89, 1991, 1993; Atlanta, 1996
15 Jan Stenerud, Kansas City, 1971-72, 1976; Minnesota, 1985
10 Nick Lowery, Kansas City, 1982, 1991, 1993

Most Field Goals Attempted, Game

6 Jan Stenerud, Kansas City, 1972
Eddie Murray, Detroit, 1981
Mark Moseley, Washington, 1983
5 Garo Yepremian, Miami, 1974
4 Jan Stenerud, Kansas City, 1976
Nick Lowery, Kansas City, 1991, 1993
Morten Andersen, New Orleans, 1993
Cary Blanchard, Indianapolis, 1997
John Kasay, Carolina, 1997

Most Field Goals, Career

10 Morten Andersen, New Orleans, 1986-89, 1991, 1993; Atlanta, 1996
8 Jan Stenerud, Kansas City, 1971-72, 1976; Minnesota, 1985
7 Nick Lowery, Kansas City, 1982, 1991, 1993

Most Field Goals, Game

5 Garo Yepremian, Miami, 1974 (5 att)
4 Jan Stenerud, Kansas City, 1972 (6 att)
Eddie Murray, Detroit, 1981 (6 att)
3 Nick Lowery, Kansas City, 1991 (4 att)
Nick Lowery, Kansas City, 1993 (4 att)
Jason Elam, Denver, 1999 (3 att)
Jason Hanson, Detroit, 2000 (3 att)

Longest Field Goal

51 Morten Andersen, New Orleans, 1989
Jason Hanson, Detroit, 2000
49 Fuad Reveiz, Minnesota, 1995
48 Jan Stenerud, Kansas City, 1972
Jeff Jaeger, L.A. Raiders, 1992
Mike Hollis, Jacksonville, 1998

SAFETIES

Most Safeties, Game

1 Art Still, Kansas City, 1983
Mark Gastineau, N.Y. Jets, 1985
Greg Townsend, L.A. Raiders, 1992

RUSHING

ATTEMPTS

Most Attempts, Career

81 Walter Payton, Chicago, 1977-81, 1984-87
68 O.J. Simpson, Buffalo, 1973-77
66 Barry Sanders, Detroit, 1990-93, 1995-98

Most Attempts, Game

19 O.J. Simpson, Buffalo, 1974
17 Marv Hubbard, Oakland, 1974
16 O.J. Simpson, Buffalo, 1973
Marcus Allen, L.A. Raiders, 1986

YARDS GAINED

Most Yards Gained, Career

368 Walter Payton, Chicago, 1977-81, 1984-87
356 O.J. Simpson, Buffalo, 1973-77
252 Marshall Faulk, Indianapolis, 1995-96, 1999; St. Louis, 2000

Most Yards Gained, Game

180 Marshall Faulk, Indianapolis, 1995
127 Chris Warren, Seattle, 1995
112 O. J. Simpson, Buffalo, 1973

Longest Run From Scrimmage

49 Marshall Faulk, Indianapolis, 1995 (TD)
41 Lawrence McCutcheon, Los Angeles, 1976
Natrone Means, San Diego, 1995
Marshall Faulk, Indianapolis, 1995
39 Chris Warren, Seattle, 1994

AVERAGE GAIN

Highest Average Gain, Career (20 attempts)

9.36 Chris Warren, Seattle, 1994-96, (25-234)
7.64 Marshall Faulk, Indianapolis, 1995-96, 1999; St. Louis, 2000 (33-252)
5.81 Marv Hubbard, Oakland, 1972-74 (36-209)

Highest Average Gain, Game (10 attempts)
13.85 Marshall Faulk, Indianapolis, 1995 (13-180)
9.07 Chris Warren, Seattle, 1995 (14-127)
7.00 O.J. Simpson, Buffalo, 1973 (16-112)
Ottis Anderson, St. Louis, 1981 (10-70)

TOUCHDOWNS
Most Touchdowns, Career
3 Earl Campbell, Houston, 1979-82, 1984
Chuck Muncie, New Orleans, 1980; San Diego, 1982-83
Mike Alstott, Tampa Bay, 1998-2000
2 John Brockington, Green Bay, 1972-74
O.J. Simpson, Buffalo, 1973-77
Walter Payton, Chicago, 1977-81, 1984-87
Marcus Allen, L.A. Raiders, 1983, 1985-86, 1988; Kansas City, 1994
Herschel Walker, Dallas, 1988-89
Johnny Johnson, Phoenix, 1991
Barry Sanders, Detroit, 1990-93, 1995-98

Most Touchdowns, Game
3 Mike Alstott, Tampa Bay, 2000
2 John Brockington, Green Bay, 1973
Earl Campbell, Houston, 1980
Chuck Muncie, New Orleans, 1980
Herschel Walker, Dallas, 1989
Johnny Johnson, Phoenix, 1991

PASSING
ATTEMPTS
Most Attempts, Career
120 Dan Fouts, San Diego, 1980-84, 1986
101 Steve Young, San Francisco, 1993-96, 1998-99
90 Warren Moon, Houston, 1989-94; Minnesota, 1995-96; Seattle 1998

Most Attempts, Game
32 Bill Kenney, Kansas City, 1984
Steve Young, San Francisco, 1993
30 Dan Fouts, San Diego, 1983
28 Jim Hart, St. Louis, 1976

COMPLETIONS
Most Completions, Career
63 Dan Fouts, San Diego, 1980-84, 1986
48 Steve Young, San Francisco, 1993-96, 1998-99
45 Warren Moon, Houston, 1989-94; Minnesota, 1995-96; Seattle 1998

Most Completions, Game
21 Joe Theismann, Washington, 1984
18 Steve Young, San Francisco, 1993
17 Dan Fouts, San Diego, 1983
Peyton Manning, Indianapolis, 2000

COMPLETION PERCENTAGE
Highest Completion Percentage, Career (40 attempts)
68.9 Joe Theismann, Washington, 1983-84 (45-31)
64.4 Jim Kelly, Buffalo, 1988, 1991-92 (45-29)
58.9 Ken Anderson, Cincinnati, 1976-77, 1982-83 (56-33)

Highest Completion Percentage, Game (10 attempts)
90.0 Archie Manning, New Orleans, 1980 (10-9)
77.8 Joe Theismann, Washington, 1984 (27-21)
72.7 Kurt Warner, St. Louis, 2000 (11-8)

YARDS GAINED
Most Yards Gained, Career
890 Dan Fouts, San Diego, 1980-84, 1986
614 Steve Young, San Francisco, 1993-96, 1998-99
554 Bob Griese, Miami, 1971-72, 1974-75, 1977, 1979

Most Yards Gained, Game
274 Dan Fouts, San Diego, 1983
270 Peyton Manning, Indianapolis, 2000
242 Joe Theismann, Washington, 1984

Longest Completion
93 Jeff Blake, Cincinnati (to Thigpen, Pittsburgh), 1996 (TD)
80 Mark Brunell, Jacksonville (to Brown, Oakland), 1997 (TD)
64 Dan Pastorini, Houston (to Burrough, Houston), 1976 (TD)

AVERAGE GAIN
Highest Average Gain, Career (40 attempts)
8.12 Brett Favre, Green Bay, 1993-94, 1996-97 (57-463)
8.06 Randall Cunningham, Philadelphia, 1989-91; Minnesota, 1999 (52-419)
8.04 Mark Brunell, Jacksonville, 1997-98, 2000 (47-378)

Highest Average Gain, Game (10 attempts)
15.27 Randall Cunningham, Philadelphia, 1991 (11-168)
13.00 Brett Favre, Green Bay, 1997 (11-143)
11.40 Ken Anderson, Cincinnati, 1977 (10-114)

TOUCHDOWNS
Most Touchdowns, Career
4 Steve Young, San Francisco, 1993-96, 1998-99
3 Joe Theismann, Washington, 1983-84
Joe Montana, San Francisco, 1982, 1984-85, 1988
Phil Simms, N.Y. Giants, 1986
Jim Kelly, Buffalo, 1988, 1991-92
John Elway, Denver, 1987-88, 1994-95, 1999
Mark Brunell, Jacksonville, 1997-98, 2000
2 James Harris, Los Angeles, 1975
Mike Boryla, Philadelphia, 1976
Ken Anderson, Cincinnati, 1976-77, 1982-83
Bob Griese, Miami, 1971-72, 1974-75, 1977, 1979
Mark Rypien, Washington, 1990, 1992
Brett Favre, Green Bay, 1993-94, 1996-97
Peyton Manning, Indianapolis, 2000

Most Touchdowns, Game
3 Joe Theismann, Washington, 1984
Phil Simms, N.Y. Giants, 1986
2 James Harris, Los Angeles, 1975
Mike Boryla, Philadelphia, 1976
Ken Anderson, Cincinnati, 1977
Jim Kelly, Buffalo, 1991
Mark Rypien, Washington, 1992
Steve Young, San Francisco, 1998
Peyton Manning, Indianapolis, 2000

HAD INTERCEPTED
Most Passes Had Intercepted, Career
8 Dan Fouts, San Diego, 1980-84, 1986
6 Jim Hart, St. Louis, 1975-78
5 Ken Stabler, Oakland, 1974-75, 1978

Most Passes Had Intercepted, Game
5 Jim Hart, St. Louis, 1977
4 Ken Stabler, Oakland, 1974
3 Dan Fouts, San Diego, 1986
Mark Rypien, Washington, 1990
Steve Young, San Francisco, 1993
Jim Harbaugh, Indianapolis, 1996
Vinny Testaverde, N.Y. Jets, 1999

Most Attempts, Without Interception, Game
27 Joe Theismann, Washington, 1984
Phil Simms, N.Y. Giants, 1986
26 John Brodie, San Francisco, 1971
Danny White, Dallas, 1983
23 Dave Krieg, Seattle, 1990

PERCENTAGE, PASSES HAD INTERCEPTED
Lowest Percentage, Passes Had Intercepted, Career (40 attempts)
0.00 Joe Theismann, Washington, 1983-84 (45-0)
2.13 Dave Krieg, Seattle, 1985, 1989-90 (47-1)
2.22 Jim Kelly, Buffalo, 1988, 1991-92 (45-1)

PASS RECEIVING
RECEPTIONS
Most Receptions, Career
33 Jerry Rice, San Francisco, 1987-88, 1990-94, 1996, 1999
23 Tim Brown, L.A. Raiders, 1989, 1992, 1994-95; Oakland 1996-98
22 Cris Carter, Minnesota, 1994-2000

Most Receptions, Game
9 Randy Moss, Minnesota, 2000
8 Steve Largent, Seattle, 1986
Michael Irvin, Dallas, 1992
Andre Rison, Atlanta, 1993
Jimmy Smith, Jacksonville, 2000
7 John Stallworth, Pittsburgh, 1983
Jerry Rice, San Francisco, 1992
Isaac Bruce, St. Louis, 1997
Keyshawn Johnson, N.Y. Jets, 1999
Randy Moss, Minnesota, 1999

YARDS GAINED
Most Yards Gained, Career
459 Jerry Rice, San Francisco, 1987-88, 1990-94, 1996, 1999
408 Tim Brown, L.A. Raiders, 1989, 1992, 1994-95; Oakland, 1996-98
320 Randy Moss, Minnesota, 1999-2000

Most Yards Gained, Game
212 Randy Moss, Minnesota, 2000
137 Tim Brown, Oakland, 1997
129 Tim Brown, Oakland, 1998

Longest Reception
93 Yancey Thigpen, Pittsburgh (from Blake, Cincinnati), 1996 (TD)
80 Tim Brown, Oakland (from Brunell, Jacksonville), 1997 (TD)
64 Ken Burrough, Houston (from Pastorini, Houston), 1976 (TD)

TOUCHDOWNS
Most Touchdowns, Career
4 Jimmy Smith, Jacksonville, 1998-2000
3 Cris Carter, Minnesota, 1994-2000
2 Mel Gray, St. Louis, 1975-78
Cliff Branch, Oakland, 1975-78
Terry Metcalf, St. Louis, 1975-76, 1978
Tony Hill, Dallas, 1979-80, 1986
William Andrews, Atlanta, 1981-84
James Lofton, Green Bay, 1979, 1981-86; Buffalo 1992
Jimmie Giles, Tampa Bay, 1981-83, 1986
Michael Irvin, Dallas, 1992-95
Eric Green, Pittsburgh, 1994-95
Jerry Rice, San Francisco, 1987-88, 1990-94, 1996, 1999

Most Touchdowns, Game
3 Jimmy Smith, Jacksonville, 2000
2 William Andrews, Atlanta, 1984
Eric Green, Pittsburgh, 1995

INTERCEPTIONS BY
Most Interceptions By, Career
4 Everson Walls, Dallas, 1982-84, 1986
Deion Sanders, Atlanta, 1992-94; San Francisco, 1995; Dallas, 1999
3 Ken Houston, Houston, 1971-73; Washington, 1974-79
Jack Lambert, Pittsburgh, 1976-84
Ted Hendricks, Baltimore, 1972-74; Green Bay, 1975; Oakland, 1981-82; L.A. Raiders, 1983-84
Mike Haynes, New England, 1978-81, 1983; L.A. Raiders, 1985-87
2 By 13 players

Most Interceptions By, Game
2 Mel Blount, Pittsburgh, 1977
Everson Walls, Dallas, 1982, 1983
LeRoy Irvin, L.A. Rams, 1986
David Fulcher, Cincinnati, 1990
Brian Dawkins, Philadelphia, 2000

YARDS GAINED
Most Yards Gained, Career
103 Deion Sanders, Atlanta, 1992-94; San Francisco, 1995; Dallas, 1999
77 Ted Hendricks, Baltimore, 1972-74; Green Bay, 1975; Oakland, 1981-82; L.A. Raiders, 1983-84
73 Rod Woodson, Pittsburgh, 1990-95, 1997; Baltimore, 2000

Most Yards Gained, Game
87 Deion Sanders, Dallas, 1999
73 Rod Woodson, Pittsburgh, 1994
67 Ty Law, New England, 1999

Longest Gain
87 Deion Sanders, Dallas, 1999
73 Rod Woodson, Pittsburgh, 1994 (lateral)
67 Ty Law, New England, 1999 (TD)

TOUCHDOWNS
Most Touchdowns, Game
1 Bobby Bell, Kansas City, 1973
Nolan Cromwell, L.A. Rams, 1984
Joey Browner, Minnesota, 1986
Jerry Gray, L.A. Rams, 1990
Mike Johnson, Cleveland, 1990
Junior Seau, San Diego, 1993
Ken Harvey, Washington, 1996
Ashley Ambrose, Cincinnati, 1997
Ty Law, New England, 1999
Derrick Brooks, Tampa Bay, 2000
Aeneas Williams, Arizona, 2000

PUNTING
Most Punts, Career
33 Ray Guy, Oakland, 1974-79, 1981
23 Rohn Stark, Indianapolis, 1986-87, 1991, 1993
22 Reggie Roby, Miami, 1985, 1990; Washington, 1995

Most Punts, Game
10 Reggie Roby, Miami, 1985
9 Tom Wittum, San Francisco, 1974
Rohn Stark, Indianapolis, 1987
8 Jerrel Wilson, Kansas City, 1971
Tom Skladany, Detroit, 1982
Reggie Roby, Washington, 1995

Longest Punt
64 Tom Wittum, San Francisco, 1974
Darren Bennett, San Diego, 1996
61 Reggie Roby, Miami, 1985
Jeff Feagles, Arizona, 1996
Matt Turk, Washington, 1997
60 Ron Widby, Dallas, 1972
Reggie Roby, Washington, 1995

AVERAGE YARDAGE
Highest Average, Career (10 punts)
46.73 Reggie Roby, Miami, 1985, 1990; Washington, 1995 (22-1,028)
45.27 Matt Turk, Washington, 1997-99 (15-679)
45.25 Jerrel Wilson, Kansas City, 1971-73 (16-724)

Highest Average, Game (4 punts)
55.50 Darren Bennett, San Diego, 1996 (4-222)
52.00 Matt Turk, Washington, 1999 (4-208)
50.13 Reggie Roby, Washington, 1995 (8-401)

PUNT RETURNS
Most Punt Returns, Career
13 Rick Upchurch, Denver, 1977, 1979-80, 1983
11 Vai Sikahema, St. Louis, 1987-88
Eric Metcalf, Cleveland 1994-95; San Diego 1998
10 Mike Nelms, Washington, 1981-83

Most Punt Returns, Game
7 Vai Sikahema, St. Louis, 1987
6 Henry Ellard, L.A. Rams, 1985
Gerald McNeil, Cleveland, 1988
Eric Metcalf, Cleveland, 1995
5 Rick Upchurch, Denver, 1980
Mike Nelms, Washington, 1981
Carl Roaches, Houston, 1982
Johnny Bailey, Phoenix, 1993

Most Fair Catches, Game
2 Jerry Logan, Baltimore, 1971
Dick Anderson, Miami, 1974
Henry Ellard, L.A. Rams, 1985
Isaac Bruce, St. Louis, 1997

YARDS GAINED
Most Yards Gained, Career
183 Billy Johnson, Houston, 1976, 1978; Atlanta, 1984
138 Mel Renfro, Dallas, 1971-72, 1974
Rick Upchurch, Denver, 1977, 1979-80, 1983
135 Eric Metcalf, Cleveland, 1994-95; San Diego 1998

Most Yards Gained, Game
159 Billy Johnson, Houston, 1976
138 Mel Renfro, Dallas, 1971
117 Wally Henry, Philadelphia, 1980

Longest Punt Return
90 Billy Johnson, Houston, 1976 (TD)
86 Wally Henry, Philadelphia, 1980 (TD)
82 Mel Renfro, Dallas, 1971 (TD)

AVERAGE YARDAGE
Highest Average, Career (4 returns)
22.88 Billy Johnson, Houston, 1976, 1978; Atlanta, 1984 (8-183)
21.50 Tony Green, Washington, 1979 (4-86)
15.67 David Meggett, N.Y. Giants, 1990; New England, 1997

Highest Average, Game (3 returns)
39.75 Billy Johnson, Houston, 1976 (4-159)
39.00 Wally Henry, Philadelphia, 1980 (3-117)
21.50 Tony Green, Washington, 1979 (4-86)

TOUCHDOWNS
Most Touchdowns, Game
2 Mel Renfro, Dallas, 1971
1 Billy Johnson, Houston, 1976
Wally Henry, Philadelphia, 1980

KICKOFF RETURNS
Most Kickoff Returns, Career
16 Michael Bates, Carolina, 1997-2000
14 Mel Gray, Detroit, 1991-92, 1995
11 Eric Metcalf, Cleveland, 1994-95; San Diego, 1998

Most Kickoff Returns, Game
7 Mel Gray, Detroit, 1995
6 Greg Pruitt, L.A. Raiders, 1984
David Meggett, New England, 1997
Michael Bates, Carolina, 1998
5 By six players

YARDS GAINED

Most Yards Gained, Career

456 Michael Bates, Carolina, 1997-2000
309 Greg Pruitt, Cleveland, 1974-75, 1977-78; L.A. Raiders, 1984
294 Mel Gray, Detroit, 1991-92, 1995

Most Yards Gained, Game

192 Greg Pruitt, L.A. Raiders, 1984
175 Les (Speedy) Duncan, Washington, 1972
173 David Meggett, New England, 1997

Longest Kickoff Return

66 Michael Bates, Carolina, 2000
62 Greg Pruitt, L.A. Raiders, 1984
61 Eugene (Mercury) Morris, Miami, 1972

AVERAGE YARDAGE

Highest Average, Career (4 returns)

35.00 Les (Speedy) Duncan, Washington, 1972 (5-175)
31.25 Eugene (Mercury) Morris, Miami, 1972-73 (4-125)
30.90 Greg Pruitt, Cleveland, 1974-75, 1977-78; L.A. Raiders, 1984 (10-309)

Highest Average, Game (3 returns)

42.00 Michael Bates, Carolina, 2000 (4-168)
35.00 Les (Speedy) Duncan, Washington, 1972 (5-175)
32.00 Greg Pruitt, L.A. Raiders, 1984 (6-192)

TOUCHDOWNS

Most Touchdowns, Game

None

FUMBLES

Most Fumbles, Career

6 Dan Fouts, San Diego, 1980-84, 1986
4 Lawrence McCutcheon, Los Angeles, 1974-78
Franco Harris, Pittsburgh, 1973-76, 1978-81
Jay Schroeder, Washington, 1987
Vai Sikahema, St. Louis, 1987-88
3 O.J. Simpson, Buffalo, 1973-77
William Andrews, Atlanta, 1981-84
Joe Montana, San Francisco, 1982, 1984-85, 1988
Walter Payton, Chicago, 1977-81, 1984-87
Neil Lomax, St. Louis, 1985, 1988
Jim Kelly, Buffalo, 1988, 1991-92
Chris Chandler, Atlanta, 1998-99

Most Fumbles, Game

4 Jay Schroeder, Washington, 1987
3 Dan Fouts, San Diego, 1982
Vai Sikahema, St. Louis, 1987
2 By 13 players

RECOVERIES

Most Fumbles Recovered, Career

3 Harold Jackson, Philadelphia, 1973; Los Angeles, 1974, 1976, 1978 (3-own)
Dan Fouts, San Diego, 1980-84, 1986 (3-own)
Randy White, Dallas, 1978, 1980-86 (3-opp)
2 By many players

Most Fumbles Recovered, Game

2 Dick Anderson, Miami, 1974 (1-own, 1-opp)
Harold Jackson, Los Angeles, 1974 (2-own)
Dan Fouts, San Diego, 1982 (2-own)
Joey Browner, Minnesota, 1990 (2-opp)
Jessie Armstead, N.Y. Giants, 1999 (1-own, 1-opp)
Steve Beuerlein, Carolina, 2000 (2-own)

YARDAGE

Longest Fumble Return

83 Art Still, Kansas City, 1985 (TD, opp)
51 Phil Villapiano, Oakland, 1974 (opp)
37 Sam Mills, New Orleans, 1988 (opp)

TOUCHDOWNS

Most Touchdowns, Game

1 Art Still, Kansas City, 1985
Keith Millard, Minnesota, 1990

SACKS

Sacks have been compiled since 1983.

Most Sacks, Career

9.5 Reggie White, Philadelphia, 1987-93; Green Bay, 1994, 1996-97, 1999
9 Howie Long, L.A. Raiders, 1984-88, 1990, 1993-1994
7.5 Bruce Smith, Buffalo, 1988-91, 1995-96, 1998-99

Most Sacks, Game

4 Mark Gastineau, N.Y. Jets, 1985
Reggie White, Philadelphia, 1987
3 Richard Dent, Chicago, 1985
Bruce Smith, Buffalo, 1991
2.5 Bruce Smith, Buffalo, 1998

TEAM RECORDS

SCORING

Most Points, Game

51 NFC, 2000

Fewest Points, Game

3 AFC, 1984, 1989, 1994

Most Points, Both Teams, Game

82 NFC (51) vs. AFC (31), 2000

Fewest Points, Both Teams, Game

16 NFC (6) vs. AFC (10), 1987

TOUCHDOWNS

Most Touchdowns, Game

6 NFC, 1984, 2000

Fewest Touchdowns, Game

0 AFC, 1971, 1974, 1984, 1989, 1994
NFC, 1987, 1988

Most Touchdowns, Both Teams, Game

10 NFC (6) vs. AFC (4), 2000

Fewest Touchdowns, Both Teams, Game

1 AFC (0) vs. NFC (1), 1974
NFC (0) vs. AFC (1), 1987
NFC (0) vs. AFC (1), 1988

POINTS AFTER TOUCHDOWN

Most Points After Touchdown, Game

6 NFC, 1984, 2000

Most Points After Touchdown, Both Teams, Game

10 NFC (6) vs. AFC (4), 2000

FIELD GOALS

Most Field Goals Attempted, Game

6 AFC, 1972
NFC, 1981, 1983

Most Field Goals Attempted, Both Teams, Game

9 NFC (6) vs. AFC (3), 1983

Most Field Goals, Game

5 AFC, 1974

Most Field Goals, Both Teams, Game

7 AFC (5) vs. NFC (2), 1974

NET YARDS GAINED RUSHING AND PASSING

Most Yards Gained, Game

552 AFC, 1995

Fewest Yards Gained, Game

114 AFC, 1993

Most Yards Gained, Both Teams, Game

962 NFC (496) vs. AFC (466), 1997

Fewest Yards Gained, Both Teams, Game

424 AFC (202) vs. NFC (222), 1987

RUSHING

ATTEMPTS

Most Attempts, Game

50 AFC, 1974

Fewest Attempts, Game

14 AFC, 1994

Most Attempts, Both Teams, Game

80 AFC (50) vs. NFC (30), 1974

Fewest Attempts, Both Teams, Game

47 NFC (22) vs. AFC (25), 1996

YARDS GAINED

Most Yards Gained, Game

400 AFC, 1995

Fewest Yards Gained, Game

28 NFC, 1992

Most Yards Gained, Both Teams, Game

441 AFC (400) vs. NFC (41), 1995

Fewest Yards Gained, Both Teams, Game

131 NFC (28) vs. AFC (103), 1992

AFC-NFC PRO BOWL RECORDS

TOUCHDOWNS
Most Touchdowns, Game
3 NFC, 1989, 1991, 2000
AFC, 1995
Most Touchdowns, Both Teams, Game
4 AFC (2) vs. NFC (2), 1973
AFC (2) vs. NFC (2), 1980

PASSING
ATTEMPTS
Most Attempts, Game
55 NFC, 1993
Fewest Attempts, Game
17 NFC, 1972
Most Attempts, Both Teams, Game
94 AFC (50) vs. NFC (44), 1983
Fewest Attempts, Both Teams, Game
42 NFC (17) vs. AFC (25), 1972

COMPLETIONS
Most Completions, Game
32 NFC, 1993
Fewest Completions, Game
7 NFC, 1972, 1982
Most Completions, Both Teams, Game
55 AFC (31) vs. NFC (24), 1983
Fewest Completions, Both Teams, Game
18 NFC (7) vs. AFC (11), 1972

YARDS GAINED
Most Yards Gained, Game
387 AFC, 1983
Fewest Yards Gained, Game
42 NFC, 1982
Most Yards Gained, Both Teams, Game
735 AFC (369) vs. NFC (366), 1997
Fewest Yards Gained, Both Teams, Game
215 NFC (89) vs. AFC (126), 1972

TIMES SACKED
Most Times Sacked, Game
9 NFC, 1985
Fewest Times Sacked, Game
0 AFC, 1998, 1999, 2000
NFC, 1971, 1997
Most Times Sacked, Both Teams, Game
17 NFC (9) vs. AFC (8), 1985
Fewest Times Sacked, Both Teams, Game
1 NFC (0) vs. AFC (1), 1997

TOUCHDOWNS
Most Touchdowns, Game
4 NFC, 1984
AFC, 2000
Most Touchdowns, Both Teams, Game
5 NFC (3) vs. AFC (2), 1986
AFC (4) vs. NFC (1), 2000

INTERCEPTIONS BY
Most Interceptions By, Game
6 AFC, 1977
Most Interceptions By, Both Teams, Game
7 AFC (6) vs. NFC (1), 1977

YARDS GAINED
Most Yards Gained, Game
103 AFC, 1994
Most Yards Gained, Both Teams, Game
172 NFC (102) vs. AFC (70), 1999

TOUCHDOWNS
Most Touchdowns, Game
2 NFC, 2000

PUNTING
Most Punts, Game
10 AFC, 1985
Fewest Punts, Game
0 NFC, 1989
Most Punts, Both Teams, Game
16 AFC (10) vs. NFC (6), 1985
Fewest Punts, Both Teams, Game
4 NFC (1) vs. AFC (3), 1992

PUNT RETURNS
Most Punt Returns, Game
7 NFC, 1985, 1987
AFC, 1995
Fewest Punt Returns, Game
0 AFC, 1984, 1989
Most Punt Returns, Both Teams, Game
11 NFC (7) vs. AFC (4), 1985
Fewest Punt Returns, Both Teams, Game
2 AFC (1) vs. NFC (1), 1996

YARDS GAINED
Most Yards Gained, Game
177 AFC, 1976
Fewest Yards Gained, Game
–1 NFC, 1991
Most Yards Gained, Both Teams, Game
263 AFC (177) vs. NFC (86), 1976
Fewest Yards Gained, Both Teams, Game
16 AFC (0) vs. NFC (16), 1984

TOUCHDOWNS
Most Touchdowns, Game
2 NFC, 1971

KICKOFF RETURNS
Most Kickoff Returns, Game
8 NFC, 1995
Fewest Kickoff Returns, Game
1 NFC, 1971, 1984, 1994
AFC, 1988, 1991
Most Kickoff Returns, Both Teams, Game
13 AFC (7) vs. NFC (6), 2000
Fewest Kickoff Returns, Both Teams, Game
5 NFC (2) vs. AFC (3), 1979
AFC (1) vs. NFC (4), 1988
NFC (2) vs. AFC (3), 1992
NFC (1) vs. AFC (4), 1994

YARDS GAINED
Most Yards Gained, Game
232 NFC, 2000
Fewest Yards Gained, Game
6 NFC, 1971
Most Yards Gained, Both Teams, Game
436 NFC (232) vs. AFC (204), 2000
Fewest Yards Gained, Both Teams, Game
99 NFC (48) vs. AFC (51), 1987

TOUCHDOWNS
Most Touchdowns, Game
None

FUMBLES
Most Fumbles, Game
10 NFC, 1974
Most Fumbles, Both Teams, Game
15 NFC (10) vs. AFC (5), 1974

RECOVERIES
Most Fumbles Recovered, Game
10 NFC, 1974 (6 own, 4 opp)
Most Fumbles Lost, Game
4 AFC, 1974, 1988
NFC, 1974

YARDS GAINED
Most Yards Gained, Game
87 AFC, 1985

TOUCHDOWNS
Most Touchdowns, Game
1 AFC, 1985
NFC, 1990

TURNOVERS

(Number of times losing the ball on interceptions and fumbles.)

Most Turnovers, Game

8 AFC, 1974

Fewest Turnovers, Game

0 AFC, 1991, 1997
NFC, 1991, 1995, 1996

Most Turnovers, Both Teams, Game

12 AFC (8) vs. NFC (4), 1974

Fewest Turnovers, Both Teams, Game

0 AFC vs. NFC, 1991

Rules

OFFICIALS

2000 NFL ROSTER OF OFFICIALS

Jerry Seeman, Senior Director of Officiating
Larry Upson, Supervisor of Officials
Al Hynes, Supervisor of Officials
Mike Pereira, Supervisor of Officials
Jim Daopoulos, Supervisor of Officials

No.	Name	Position	College
81	Anderson, Dave	Line Judge	Salem College
66	Anderson, Walt	Line Judge	Sam Houston State
108	Arthur, Gary	Line Judge	Wright State
34	Austin, Gerald	Referee	Western Carolina
22	Baetz, Paul	Field Judge	Heidelberg
91	Baker, Ken	Side Judge	Eastern Illinois
48	Balliet, Brian	Umpire	Lehigh
26	Baltz, Mark	Head Linesman	Ohio University
55	Barnes, Tom	Line Judge	Minnesota
56	Baynes, Ron	Line Judge	Auburn
32	Bergman, Jeff	Line Judge	Robert Morris
7	Blum, Ron	Referee	Marin College
18	Boston, Byron	Line Judge	Austin
110	Botchan, Ron	Umpire	Occidental
31	Brown, Chad	Umpire	East Texas State
134	Camp, Ed	Head Linesman	William Patterson
126	Carey, Don	Back Judge	U.C.-Riverside
94	Carey, Mike	Referee	Santa Clara
39	Carlsen, Don	Side Judge	Cal State-Chico
63	Carollo, Bill	Referee	Wisconsin-Milwaukee
11	Carroll, Duke	Field Judge	Ithaca
41	Cheek, Boris	Field Judge	Morgan State
65	Coleman, Walt	Referee	Arkansas
99	Corrente, Tony	Referee	Cal State-Fullerton
71	Coukart, Ed	Umpire	Northwestern
70	Dawson, Scott	Umpire	Virginia Tech
53	DeFelice, Garth	Umpire	San Diego State
113	Dorkowski, Don	Back Judge	Cal State-Los Angeles
6	Dornan, Kirk	Back Judge	Central Washington
74	Duke, James	Umpire	Howard
89	Dunn, Neely	Side Judge	South Carolina State
3	Edwards, Scott	Field Judge	Alabama
61	Ferguson, Keith	Back Judge	San Jose State
47	Fincken, Tom	Side Judge	Kansas State
111	Frantz, Earnie	Head Linesman	No College
50	Gereb, Neil	Umpire	California
72	Gierke, Terry	Head Linesman	Portland State
19	Green, Scott	Back Judge	Delaware
23	Grier, Johnny	Referee	University of D.C.
104	Hamer, Dale	Head Linesman	California, Pa.
40	Hannah, Charles	Umpire	Middle Tennessee State
105	Hantak, Dick	Referee	Southeast Missouri
125	Hayes, Laird	Side Judge	Princeton
54	Hayward, George	Head Linesman	Missouri Western
97	Hill, Tom	Side Judge	Carson-Newman
28	Hittner, Mark	Head Linesman	Pittsburg State
85	Hochuli, Ed	Referee	Texas-El Paso
82	Horton, Albert	Back Judge	Oregon State
37	Howey, Jim	Back Judge	Erskine College
114	Johnson, Tom	Head Linesman	Miami, Ohio
106	Jury, Al	Field Judge	San Bernardino Valley
86	Kukar, Bernie	Referee	St. John's
120	Lane, Gary	Side Judge	Missouri
17	Lawing, Bob	Back Judge	North Carolina State
127	Leavy, Bill	Back Judge	San Jose State
130	Lewis, Darryll	Line Judge	Dartmouth
76	Liebsack, Ron	Side Judge	Regis
49	Look, Dean	Side Judge	Michigan State
98	Lovett, Bill	Field Judge	Maryland
59	Luckett, Phil	Referee	Texas-El Paso
102	Mack, Keven	Field Judge	Fort Valley State
92	Madsen, Carl	Umpire	Washington
107	Marinucci, Ron	Line Judge	Glassboro State
38	Maurer, Bruce	Line Judge	Ohio State
77	McAulay, Terry	Side Judge	Louisiana State
95	McElwee, Bob	Referee	Navy
35	McGrath, Bob	Field Judge	Western Kentucky
64	McPeters, Lloyd	Field Judge	Oklahoma State
80	Millis, Timmie	Field Judge	Millsaps
117	Montgomery, Ben	Line Judge	Morehouse
60	Moore, Tommy	Side Judge	Stephen F. Austin
135	Morelli, Peter	Field Judge	St. Mary's College
20	Nemmers, Larry	Referee	Upper Iowa
124	Paganelli, Carl	Umpire	Michigan State
46	Paganelli, Perry	Back Judge	Hope College
132	Parry, John	Side Judge	Purdue
15	Patterson, Rick	Side Judge	Wofford
9	Perlman, Mark	Line Judge	Salem
10	Phares, Ron	Line Judge	Virginia Tech
79	Pointer, Aaron	Head Linesman	Pacific Lutheran
5	Quirk, Jim	Umpire	Delaware
83	Reels, Richard	Back Judge	No College
44	Rice, Jeff	Umpire	Northwestern
121	Rivers, Sanford	Head Linesman	Youngstown State
128	Rose, Larry	Side Judge	Florida
58	Saracino, Jim	Field Judge	Northern Colorado
21	Schleyer, John	Head Linesman	Millersville
122	Schmitz, Bill	Back Judge	Colorado State
129	Schuster, Bill	Umpire	Alfred
118	Sifferman, Tom	Field Judge	Seattle
73	Skelton, Bobby	Back Judge	Alabama
30	Slaughter, Gary	Head Linesman	East Texas State
2	Smith, Billy	Back Judge	East Carolina
90	Spanier, Michael	Line Judge	St. Cloud State
119	Spitler, Ron	Back Judge	Panhandle State
12	Spyksma, Bill	Side Judge	South Dakota
24	Stabile, Tom	Head Linesman	Slippery Rock
88	Steenson, Scott	Field Judge	North Texas
84	Steinkerchner, Mark	Line Judge	Akron
112	Steratore, Anthony	Back Judge	California, Pa.
62	Stewart, Charles	Line Judge	Long Beach State
4	Toole, Doug	Side Judge	Utah State
42	Triplette, Jeff	Referee	Wake Forest
36	Veteri, Tony	Head Linesman	Manhattan College
25	Waggoner, Bob	Back Judge	Juniata College
100	Wagner, Bob	Umpire	Penn State
43	Warden, David	Field Judge	Oklahoma State
96	Wash, Undrey	Umpire	Texas-Arlington
87	Weidner, Paul	Head Linesman	Cincinnati
123	White, Tom	Referee	Temple
8	Williams, Dale	Head Linesman	Cal State-Northridge
43	Wilson, James	Head Linesman	Eastern Kentucky
29	Wilson, Steve	Umpire	Whitworth College
14	Winter, Ron	Referee	Michigan State
16	Wyant, David	Side Judge	Virginia
33	Zimmer, Steve	Field Judge	Hofstra

NUMERICAL ROSTER

No.	Name	Position
2	Billy Smith	BJ
3	Scott Edwards	FJ
4	Doug Toole	SJ
5	Jim Quirk	U
6	Kirk Dornan	BJ
7	Ron Blum	R
8	Dale Williams	HL
9	Mark Perlman	LJ
10	Ron Phares	LJ
11	Duke Carroll	FJ
12	Bill Spyksma	SJ
14	Ron Winter	R
15	Rick Patterson	SJ
16	David Wyant	SJ
17	Bob Lawing	BJ
18	Byron Boston	LJ
19	Scott Green	BJ
20	Larry Nemmers	R
21	John Schleyer	HL
22	Paul Baetz	FJ
23	Johnny Grier	R
24	Tom Stabile	HL
25	Bob Waggoner	BJ
26	Mark Baltz	HL
27	David Warden	FJ
28	Mark Hittner	HL
29	Steve Wilson	U
30	Gary Slaughter	HL
31	Chad Brown	U
32	Jeff Bergman	LJ
33	Steve Zimmer	FJ
34	Gerry Austin	R
35	Bob McGrath	FJ
36	Tony Veteri	HL
37	Jim Howey	BJ
38	Bruce Maurer	LJ
39	Don Carlsen	SJ
40	Charles Hannah	U
41	Boris Cheek	FJ
42	Jeff Triplette	R
43	James Wilson	HL
44	Jeff Rice	U
46	Perry Paganelli	BJ
47	Tom Fincken	SJ
48	Brian Balliet	U
49	Dean Look	SJ
50	Neil Gereb	U
53	Garth DeFelice	U
54	George Hayward	HL
55	Tom Barnes	LJ
56	Ron Baynes	LJ
58	Jim Saracino	FJ
59	Phil Luckett	R
60	Tommy Moore	SJ
61	Keith Ferguson	BJ
62	Charles Stewart	LJ
63	Bill Carollo	R
64	Lloyd McPeters	FJ
65	Walt Coleman	R
66	Walt Anderson	LJ
70	Scott Dawson	U
71	Ed Coukart	U
72	Terry Gierke	HL
73	Bobby Skelton	BJ
74	James Duke	U
76	Ron Liebsack	SJ
77	Terry McAulay	SJ
79	Aaron Pointer	HL
80	Timmie Millis	FJ
81	Dave Anderson	LJ
82	Albert Horton	BJ
83	Richard Reels	BJ
84	Mark Steinkerchner	LJ
85	Ed Hochuli	R
86	Bernie Kukar	R
87	Paul Weidner	HL
88	Scott Steenson	FJ
89	Neely Dunn	SJ
90	Michael Spanier	LJ
91	Ken Baker	SJ
92	Carl Madsen	U
94	Mike Carey	R
95	Bob McElwee	R
96	Undrey Wash	U
97	Tom Hill	SJ
98	Bill Lovett	FJ
99	Tony Corrente	R
100	Bob Wagner	U
102	Keven Mack	FJ
104	Dale Hamer	HL
105	Dick Hantak	R
106	Al Jury	FJ
107	Ron Marinucci	LJ
108	Gary Arthur	LJ
110	Ron Botchan	U
111	Earnie Frantz	HL
112	Anthony Steratore	BJ
113	Don Dorkowski	BJ
114	Tom Johnson	HL
117	Ben Montgomery	LJ
118	Tom Sifferman	FJ
119	Ron Spitler	BJ
120	Gary Lane	SJ
121	Sanford Rivers	HL
122	Bill Schmitz	BJ
123	Tom White	R
124	Carl Paganelli	U
125	Laird Hayes	SJ
126	Don Carey	BJ
127	Bill Leavy	BJ
128	Larry Rose	SJ
129	Bill Schuster	U
130	Darryll Lewis	LJ
132	John Parry	SJ
134	Ed Camp	HL
135	Peter Morelli	FJ

2000 OFFICIALS AT A GLANCE

REFEREES

Gerry Austin, No. **34,** Western Carolina, president, leadership development group, 19th year.
Ron Blum, No. **7,** Marin College, professional golfer, 16th year.
Mike Carey, No. **94,** Santa Clara, owner, skiing accessories, 11th year.
Bill Carollo, No. **63,** Wisconsin-Milwaukee, marketing executive, 12th year.
Walt Coleman, No. **65,** Arkansas, president, dairy processor, 12th year.
Tony Corrente, No. **99,** Cal State-Fullerton, educator, 6th year.
Johnny Grier, No. **23,** University of D.C., planning engineer, 20th year.
Dick Hantak, No. **105,** Southeast Missouri, educator, 23rd year.
Ed Hochuli, No. **85,** Texas-El Paso, attorney, 11th year.
Bernie Kukar, No. **86,** St. John's, sales representative, employees benefit plan, 17th year.
Phil Luckett, No. **59,** Texas-El Paso, computer program analyst, federal civil services, 10th year.
Bob McElwee, No. **95,** Navy, owner, heavy construction firm, 25th year.
Larry Nemmers, No. **20,** Upper Iowa, motivational speaker, 16th year.
Jeff Triplette, No. **42,** Wake Forest, assistant treasurer, world-wide energy company, 5th year.
Tom White, No. **123,** Temple, president, athletic sportswear, 12th year.
Ron Winter, No. **14,** Michigan State, university professor, 6th year.

UMPIRES

Brian Balliet, No. **48,** Lehigh, sales engineer, 4th year.
Ron Botchan, No. **110,** Occidental, college professor, former AFL player, 21st year.
Chad Brown, No. **31,** East Texas State, director, intramural/sports clubs, 9th year.
Ed Coukart, No. **71,** Northwestern, vice-president, commercial bank, 12th year.
Scott Dawson, No. **70,** Virginia Tech, president/owner, commercial construction company, 6th year.
Garth Defelice, No. **53,** San Diego State, director of distributing, beverage company, 3rd year.
James Duke, No. **74,** Howard, director of volunteer resources boys and girls clubs, 8th year.
Neil Gereb, No. **50,** California, project manager, aircraft company, 20th year.
Charles Hannah, No. **40,** Middle Tennessee State, federal probation officer, 2nd year.
Carl Madsen, No. **92,** Washington, vice president of operations, 4th year.
Carl Paganelli, No. **124,** Michigan State, federal probation officer, 2nd year.
Jim Quirk, No. **5,** Delaware, consultant, 13th year.
Jeff Rice, No. **44,** Northwestern, attorney, 6th year.
Bill Schuster, No. **129,** Alfred College, insurance broker, 1st year.
Bob Wagner, No. **100,** Penn State, executive director, cardiovascular institute, 16th year.
Undrey Wash, No. **96,** Texas-Arlington, claims manager, 1st year.
Steve Wilson, No. **29,** Whitworth College, church administrator, 1st year.

HEAD LINESMEN

Mark Baltz, No. **26,** Ohio University, sales consultant, 11th year.
Ed Camp, No. **134,** William Peterson, teacher, 1st year.
Earnie Frantz, No. **111,** no college, vice-president and manager, insurance company, 20th year.
Terry Gierke, No. **72,** Portland State, real estate broker, 20th year.
Dale Hamer, No. **104,** California Univ., Pa., consultant, 22nd year.
George Hayward, No. **54,** Missouri Western, vice-president and manager, warehouse company, 10th year.
Mark Hittner, No. **28,** Pittsburg State, insurance sales, 4th year.
Tom Johnson, No. **114,** Miami, Ohio, retired educator, president/owner, security company, 19th year.
Aaron Pointer, No. **79,** Pacific Lutheran, park department administrator, 13th year.
Sanford Rivers, No. **121,** Youngstown State, assistant vice-president, school administration, 12th year.
John Schleyer, No. **21,** Millersville, medical sales, 11th year.
Gary Slaughter, No. **30,** East Texas State, general manager, 5th year.
Tom Stabile, No. **24,** Slippery Rock, secondary educational administrator, 6th year.
Tony Veteri, No. **36,** Manhattan, director of athletics, 9th year.
Paul Weidner, No. **87,** Cincinnati, marketing manager, 15th year.
Dale Williams, No. **8,** Cal State-Northridge, sports official, 21st year.
James Wilson, No. **43,** Eastern Kentucky, area manager, 3rd year.

LINE JUDGES

Dave Anderson, No. **81,** Salem, insurance executive, 17th year.
Walt Anderson, No. **66,** Sam Houston, dentist, orthodontics, 5th year.
Gary Arthur, No. **108,** Wright State, commercial printing sales, 4th year.
Tom Barnes, No. **55,** Minnesota, manufacturing representative, 15th year.
Ron Baynes, No. **56,** Auburn, school administrator, coach, 14th year.
Jeff Bergman, No. **32,** Robert Morris, president and chief executive officer, medical services, 9th year.
Byron Boston, No. **18,** Austin, tax consultant, 6th year.
Darryll Lewis, No. **130,** Dartmouth, associate professor, 3rd year.
Ron Marinucci, No. **107,** Glassboro State, vice president, novelty cone company, 4th year.
Bruce Maurer, No. **38,** Ohio State, administrator/associate director, recreational sports, 14th year.
Ben Montgomery, No. **117,** Morehouse, school administrator, 19th year.
Mark Perlman, No. **9,** Salem, teacher, 1st year.
Ron Phares, No. **10,** Virginia Tech, president, construction company, 16th year.
Michael Spanier, No. **90,** St. Cloud State, middle-school principal, 2nd year.
Mark Steinkerchner, No. **84,** Akron, vice-president, 7th year.
Tom Stephen, No. **68,** Pittsburg State, business broker, 2nd year.
Charles Stewart, No. **62,** Long Beach State, human services administrator, 8th year.

FIELD JUDGES

Paul Baetz, No. **22,** Heidelberg, financial consultant, 23rd year.
Duke Carroll, No. **11,** Ithaca, president, insurance agency, 6th year.
Boris Cheek, No. **41,** Morgan State, director of operations and management, 5th year.
Scott Edwards, No. **3,** Alabama, federal government program analyst, 2nd year.
Al Jury, No. **106,** San Bernardino Valley, state traffic officer, 23rd year.
Bill Lovett, No. **98,** Maryland, managing partner, financial sales, 11th year.
Keven Mack, No. **102,** Ft. Valley State, economic development administrator, 4th year.
Bob McGrath, No. **35,** Western Kentucky, sales representative, fund raiser, 8th year.
Lloyd McPeters, No. **64,** Oklahoma State, business insurance sales, 8th year.
Timmie Millis, No. **80,** Millsaps, financial investigative consultant, 12th year.
Pete Morelli, No. **135,** St. Mary's, high school principal, 4th year.
Jim Saracino, No. **58,** Northern Colorado, secondary educator, 6th year.
Tom Sifferman, No. **118,** Seattle, manufacturer's representative, 15th year.
Scott Steenson, No. **88,** North Texas, commercial real estate broker, 10th year.
David Warden, No. **27,** Oklahoma State, dentist, 3rd year.
Steven Zimmer, No. **33,** Hofstra, attorney, 4th year.

SIDE JUDGES

Ken Baker, No. **91,** Eastern Illinois, college educator, 10th year.
Don Carlsen, No. **39,** Cal State-Chico, assistant superintendent, county school, 12th year.
Neely Dunn, No. **89,** South Carolina State, principal, 6th year.
Tom Fincken, No. **47,** Emporia State, retired educational administrator, 17th year.
Laird Hayes, No. **125,** Princeton, professor, physical education & athletics, 6th year.
Tom Hill, No. **97,** Erskine College, teacher, 2nd year.
Gary Lane, No. **120,** Missouri, owner hunting resort, former NFL player, 19th year.
Ron Liebsack, No. **76,** Regis, manager, telecommunications, 6th year.
Dean Look, No. **49,** Michigan State, consultant, medical manufacturing, former AFL player, 28th year.
Terry McAulay, No. **77,** Louisiana State, senior computer scientist, 3rd year.
Tommy Moore, No. **60,** Stephen F. Austin, marketing, manufacturing representative, 9th year.
John Parry, No. **132,** Purdue, corporate pilot, 1st year.
Rick Patterson, No. **15,** Wofford, banker, 5th year.
Larry Rose, No. **128,** Florida, financial planner, 4th year.
Bill Spyksma, No. **12,** South Dakota, commercial real estate, construction sales, 6th year.
Doug Toole, No. **4,** Utah State, physical therapist, 13th year.
David Wyant, No. **16,** Virginia, systems integration director, 10th year.

BACK JUDGES

Don Carey, No. **126,** California-Riverside, contract manager, 6th year.
Don Dorkowski, No. **113,** Cal State-Los Angeles, work experience coordinator, 15th year.
Kirk Dornan, No. **6,** Central Washington, industrial sales, 7th year.
Keith Ferguson, No. **61,** San Jose State, sales, 1st year.
Scott Green, No. **19,** Delaware, vice-president, government relations, 10th year.
Buddy Horton, No. **82,** Oregon State, water service worker, 2nd year.
Jim Howey, No. **37,** Erskine College, elemenatry school principal, 2nd year.
Bob Lawing, No. **17,** North Carolina State, real estate management, 4th year.
Bill Leavy, No. **127,** San Jose State, supervisor of officials, retired firefighter, 6th year.
Perry Paganelli, No. **46,** Hope College, high school administrator, 3rd year.
Richard Reels, No. **83,** Chicago State, director of security, court services, 8th year.
Bill Schmitz, No. **122,** Colorado State, general sales manager, 12th year.
Bobby Skelton, No. **73,** Alabama, industrial representative, 16th year.
Billy Smith, No. **2,** East Carolina, federal government, 7th year.
Ron Spitler, No. **119,** Panhandle State, owner, service center, 19th year.
Anthony Steratore, No. **112,** California Univ., Pa., president, sanitary supply company, 1st year.
Bob Waggoner, No. **25,** Juniata College, probation officer, 3rd year.

OFFICIAL SIGNALS

1

TOUCHDOWN, FIELD GOAL, or SUCCESSFUL TRY
Both arms extended above head.

2

SAFETY
Palms together above head.

3

FIRST DOWN
Arm pointed toward defensive team's goal.

4

CROWD NOISE, DEAD BALL, or NEUTRAL ZONE ESTABLISHED
One arm above head with an open hand.
With fist closed: **Fourth Down.**

5

BALL ILLEGALLY TOUCHED, KICKED, or BATTED
Fingertips tap both shoulders.

6

TIME OUT
Hands crisscrossed above head.

Same signal followed by placing one hand on top of cap: **Referee's Time Out.**

Same signal followed by arm swung at side: **Touchback.**

7

NO TIME OUT or TIME IN WITH WHISTLE
Full arm circled to simulate moving clock.

8

DELAY OF GAME or EXCESS TIME OUT
Folded arms.

9

FALSE START, ILLEGAL FORMATION, or KICKOFF or SAFETY KICK OUT OF BOUNDS or KICKING TEAM PLAYER VOLUNTARILY OUT OF BOUNDS DURING A PUNT
Forearms rotated over and over in front of body.

10

PERSONAL FOUL
One wrist striking the other above head.

Same signal followed by swinging leg: **Roughing the Kicker.**

Same signal followed by raised arm swinging forward: **Roughing the Passer.**

Same signal followed by grasping face mask: **Major Face Mask.**

11

HOLDING
Grasping one wrist, the fist clenched, in front of chest.

12

ILLEGAL USE OF HANDS, ARMS, or BODY
Grasping one wrist, the hand open and facing forward, in front of chest.

13

PENALTY REFUSED, INCOMPLETE PASS, PLAY OVER, or MISSED FIELD GOAL or EXTRA POINT
Hands shifted in horizontal plane.

14

PASS JUGGLED INBOUNDS AND CAUGHT OUT OF BOUNDS
Hands up and down in front of chest (following incomplete pass signal).

15

ILLEGAL FORWARD PASS
One hand waved behind back followed by loss of down signal (23), when appropriate.

16

INTENTIONAL GROUNDING OF PASS
Parallel arms waved in a diagonal plane across body. Followed by loss of down signal (23).

OFFICIAL SIGNALS

17

INTERFERENCE WITH FORWARD PASS or FAIR CATCH
Hands open and extended forward from shoulders with hands vertical.

18

INVALID FAIR-CATCH SIGNAL
One hand waved above head.

19

INELIGIBLE RECEIVER or INELIGIBLE MEMBER OF KICKING TEAM DOWNFIELD
Right hand touching top of cap.

20

ILLEGAL CONTACT
One open hand extended forward.

21

OFFSIDE, ENCROACHMENT, or NEUTRAL ZONE INFRACTION
Hands on hips.

22

ILLEGAL MOTION AT SNAP
Horizontal arc with one hand.

23

LOSS OF DOWN
Both hands held behind head.

24

INTERLOCKING INTERFERENCE, PUSHING, or HELPING RUNNER
Pushing movement of hands to front with arms downward.

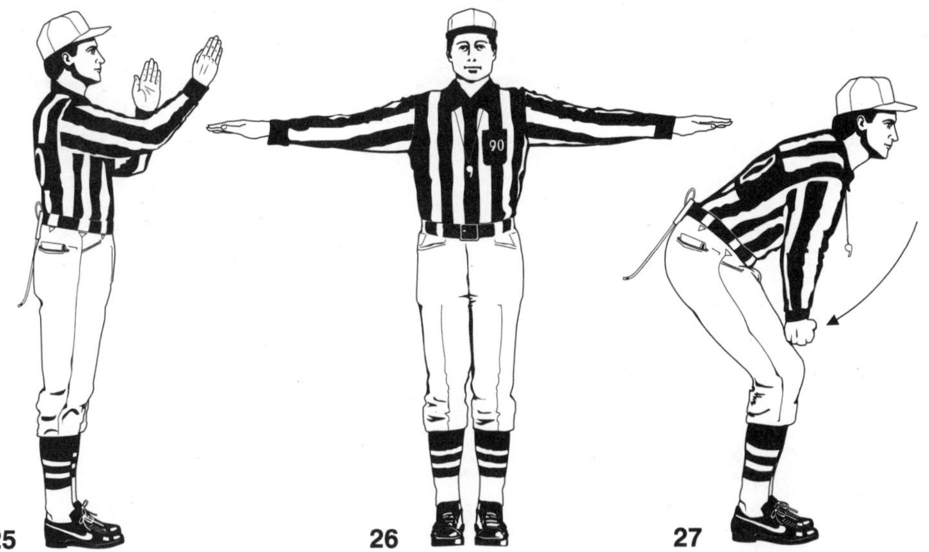

TOUCHING A FORWARD PASS or SCRIMMAGE KICK
Diagonal motion of one hand across another.

UNSPORTSMANLIKE CONDUCT
Arms outstretched, palms down.

ILLEGAL CUT
Hand striking front of thigh.
ILLEGAL BLOCK BELOW THE WAIST
One hand striking front of thigh preceded by personal-foul signal (10).
CHOP BLOCK
Both hands striking side of thighs preceded by personal-foul signal (10).
CLIPPING
One hand striking back of calf preceded by personal-foul signal (10).

ILLEGAL CRACKBACK
Strike of an open right hand against the right mid-thigh preceded by personal foul signal (10).

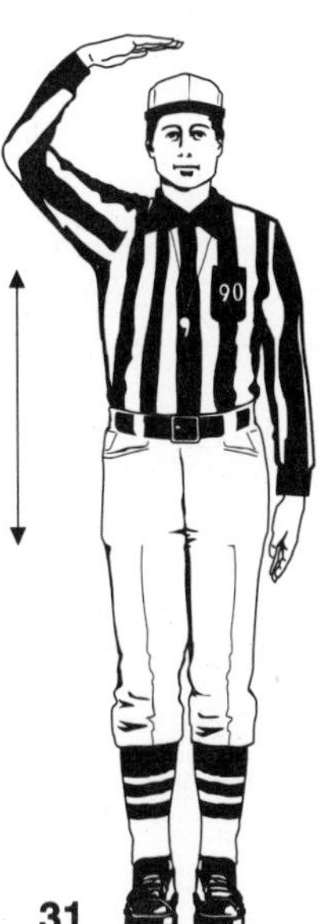

PLAYER DISQUALIFIED
Ejection signal.

TRIPPING
Repeated action of right foot in back of left heel.

UNCATCHABLE FORWARD PASS
Palm of right hand held parallel to ground above head and moved back and forth.

TWELVE MEN IN OFFENSIVE HUDDLE or TOO MANY MEN ON THE FIELD
Both hands on top of head.

33

FACE MASK
Grasping face mask with one hand.

34

ILLEGAL SHIFT
Horizontal arcs with two hands.

35

RESET PLAY CLOCK– 25 SECONDS
Pump one arm vertically.

36

RESET PLAY CLOCK– 40 SECONDS
Pump two arms vertically.

NFL DIGEST OF RULES

This Digest of Rules of the National Football League has been prepared to aid players, fans, and members of the press, radio, and television media in their understanding of the game.

It is not meant to be a substitute for the official rule book. In any case of conflict between these explanations and the official rules, the rules always have precedence.

In order to make it easier to coordinate the information in this digest, the topics discussed generally follow the order of the rule book.

OFFICIALS' JURISDICTIONS, POSITIONS, AND DUTIES

Referee—General oversight and control of game. Gives signals for all fouls and is final authority for rule interpretations. Takes a position in backfield 10 to 12 yards behind line of scrimmage, favors right side (if quarterback is right-handed passer). Determines legality of snap, observes deep back(s) for legal motion. On running play, observes quarterback during and after handoff, remains with him until action has cleared away, then proceeds downfield, checking on runner and contact behind him. When runner is downed, Referee determines forward progress from wing official and, if necessary, adjusts final position of ball.

On pass plays, drops back as quarterback begins to fade back, picks up legality of blocks by near linemen. Changes to complete concentration on quarterback as defenders approach. Primarily responsible to rule on possible roughing action on passer and if ball becomes loose, rules whether ball is free on a fumble or dead on an incomplete pass.

During kicking situations, Referee has primary responsibility to rule on kicker's actions and whether or not any subsequent contact by a defender is legal. The Referee stays wide and parallel on punts and will announce on the microphone when each period has ended.

Umpire—Primary responsibility to rule on players' equipment, as well as their conduct and actions on scrimmage line. Lines up approximately four to five yards downfield, varying position from in front of weakside tackle to strongside guard. Looks for possible false start by offensive linemen. Observes legality of contact by both offensive linemen while blocking and by defensive players while they attempt to ward off blockers. Is prepared to call rule infractions if they occur on offense or defense. Moves forward to line of scrimmage when pass play develops in order to insure that interior linemen do not move illegally downfield. If offensive linemen indicate screen pass is to be attempted, Umpire shifts his attention toward screen side, picks up potential receiver in order to insure that he will legally be permitted to run his pattern and continues to rule on action of blockers. Umpire is to assist in ruling on incomplete or trapped passes when ball is thrown overhead or short. On punt plays, Umpire positions himself opposite Referee in offensive backfield—5 yards from kicker and one yard behind.

Head Linesman—Primarily responsible for ruling on offside, encroachment, and actions pertaining to scrimmage line prior to or at snap. Keys on closest setback on his side of the field. On pass plays, Linesman is responsible to clear his receiver approximately seven yards downfield as he moves to a point five yards beyond the line. Linesman's secondary responsibility is to rule on any illegal action taken by defenders on any delay receiver moving downfield. Has full responsibility for ruling on sideline plays on his side, e.g., pass receiver or runner in or out of bounds. Together with Referee, Linesman is responsible for keeping track of number of downs and is in charge of mechanics of his chain crew in connection with its duties.

Linesman must be prepared to assist in determining forward progress by a runner on play directed toward middle or into his side zone. He, in turn, is to signal Referee or Umpire what forward point ball has reached. Linesman is also responsible to rule on legality of action involving any receiver who approaches his side zone. He is to call pass interference when the infraction occurs and is to rule on legality of blockers and defenders on plays involving ball carriers, whether it is entirely a running play, a combination pass and run, or a play involving a kick. Also assists referee with intentional grounding.

Line Judge—Straddles line of scrimmage on side of field opposite Linesman. Keeps time of game as a backup for clock operator. Along with Linesman is responsible for offside, encroachment, and actions pertaining to scrimmage line prior to or at snap. Line Judge keys on closest setback on his side of field. Line Judge is to observe his receiver until he moves at least seven yards downfield. He then moves toward backfield side, being especially alert to rule on any back in motion and on flight of ball when pass is made (he must rule whether forward or backward). Line Judge has primary responsibility to rule whether or not passer is behind or beyond line of scrimmage when pass is made. He also assists in observing actions by blockers and defenders who are on his side of field. After pass is thrown, Line Judge directs attention toward activities that occur in back of Umpire. During punting situations, Line Judge remains at line of scrimmage to be sure that only the end men move downfield until kick has been made. He also rules whether or not the kick crossed line and then observes action by members of the kicking team who are moving downfield to cover the kick. The Line Judge will advise the Referee when time has expired at the end of each period. Also assists referee with intentional grounding and determines whether pass is forward or backward.

Field Judge—Operates on same side of field as Line Judge, 20 yards deep. Keys on wide receiver on his side. Concentrates on path of end or back, observing legality of his potential block(s) or of actions taken against him. Is prepared to rule from <u>deep</u> position on holding or illegal use of hands by end or back or on defensive infractions committed by player guarding him. Has primary responsibility to make decisions involving sideline on his side of field, e.g., pass receiver or runner in or out of bounds.

Field Judge makes decisions involving catching, recovery, or illegal touching of a loose ball beyond line of scrimmage; rules on plays involving pass receiver, including legality of catch or pass interference; assists in covering actions of runner, including blocks by teammates and that of defenders; calls clipping on punt returns; and, together with Back Judge, rules whether or not field goal attempts are successful.

Side Judge—Operates on same side of field as Linesman, 20 yards deep. Keys on wide receiver on his side. Concentrates on path of end or back, observing legality of his potential block(s) or of actions taken against him. Is prepared to rule from <u>deep</u> position on holding or illegal use of hands by end or back or on defensive infractions committed by player guarding him. Has primary responsibility to make decisions involving sideline on his side of field, e.g., pass receiver or runner in or out of bounds.

Side Judge makes decisions involving catching, recovery, or illegal touching of a loose ball beyond line of scrimmage; rules on plays involving pass receiver, including legality of catch or pass interference; assists in covering actions of runner, including blocks by teammates and that of defenders; and calls clipping on punt returns. On field goals and point after touchdown attempts, he becomes a double umpire.

Back Judge—Takes a position 25 yards downfield. In general, favors the tight end's side of field. Keys on tight end, concentrates on his path and observes legality of tight end's potential block(s) or of actions taken against him. Is prepared to rule from <u>deep</u> position on holding or illegal use of hands by end or back or on defensive infractions committed by player guarding him.

Back Judge times interval between plays on 40/25-second clock plus intermission between two periods of each half; makes decisions involving catching, recovery, or illegal touching of a loose ball beyond line of scrimmage; is responsible to rule on plays involving end line; calls pass interference, fair catch infractions, and clipping on kick returns; together with Field Judge, rules whether or not field goals and conversions are successful; and stays with ball on punts.

DEFINITIONS

1. **Chucking:** Warding off an opponent who is in front of a defender by contacting him with a quick extension of arm or arms, followed by the return of arm(s) to a flexed position, thereby breaking the original contact.
2. **Clipping:** Throwing the body across the back of an opponent's leg or hitting him from the back below the waist while moving up from behind unless the opponent is a runner or the action is in close line play.
3. **Close Line Play:** The area between the positions normally occupied by the offensive tackles, extending three yards on each side of the line of scrimmage. It is legal to clip above the knee.
4. **Crackback:** Eligible receivers who take or move to a position more than two yards outside the tackle may not block an opponent below the waist if they then move back inside to block.
5. **Dead Ball:** Ball not in play.
6. **Double Foul:** A foul by each team during the same down.
7. **Down:** The period of action that starts when the ball is put in play and ends when it is dead.
8. **Encroachment:** When a player enters the neutral zone and makes <u>contact</u> with an opponent before the ball is snapped.
9. **Fair Catch:** An unhindered catch of a kick by a member of the receiving team who must raise one arm a full length above his head and wave his arm from side to side while the kick is in flight.
10. **Foul:** Any violation of a playing rule.
11. **Free Kick:** A kickoff or safety kick. It may be a placekick, dropkick, or punt, except a punt may <u>not</u> be used on a kickoff following a touchdown, successful field goal, or to begin each half or overtime period. A tee cannot be used on a fair-catch or safety kick.
12. **Fumble:** The loss of possession of the ball.
13. **Game Clock:** Scoreboard game clock.
14. **Impetus:** The action of a player that gives momentum to the ball.
15. **Live Ball:** A ball legally free kicked or snapped. It continues in play until the down ends.
16. **Loose Ball:** A live ball not in possession of any player.
17. **Muff:** The touching of a loose ball by a player in an <u>unsuccessful</u> attempt to obtain possession.

DIGEST OF RULES

18. **Neutral Zone:** The space the length of a ball between the two scrimmage lines. The offensive team and defensive team must remain behind their end of the ball.
    Exception: The offensive player who snaps the ball.
19. **Offside:** A player is offside when any part of his body is beyond his scrimmage or free kick line when the ball is snapped.
20. **Own Goal:** The goal a team is guarding.
21. **Play Clock:** 40/25 second clock.
22. **Pocket Area:** Applies from a point two yards outside of either offensive tackle and includes the tight end if he drops off the line of scrimmage to pass protect. Pocket extends longitudinally behind the line back to offensive team's own end line.
23. **Possession:** When a player controls the ball throughout the act of clearly touching both feet, or any other part of his body other than his hand(s), to the ground inbounds.
24. **Post-Possession Foul:** A foul by the receiving team that occurs after a ball is legally kicked from scrimmage prior to possession changing. The ball must cross the line of scrimmage and the receiving team must retain possession of the kicked ball.
25. **Punt:** A kick made when a player drops the ball and kicks it while it is in flight.
26. **Safety:** The situation in which the ball is dead on or behind a team's own goal if the impetus comes from a player on that team. Two points are scored for the opposing team.
27. **Shift:** The movement of two or more offensive players at the same time before the snap.
28. **Striking:** The act of swinging, clubbing, or propelling the arm or forearm in contacting an opponent.
29. **Sudden Death:** The continuation of a tied game into sudden death overtime in which the team scoring first (by safety, field goal, or touchdown) wins.
30. **Touchback:** When a ball is dead on or behind a team's own goal line, provided the impetus came from an opponent and provided it is not a touchdown or a missed field goal.
31. **Touchdown:** When any part of the ball, legally in possession of a player inbounds, breaks the plane of the opponent's goal line, provided it is not a touchback.
32. **Unsportsmanlike Conduct:** Any act contrary to the generally understood principles of sportsmanship.

SUMMARY OF PENALTIES

Automatic First Down

1. Awarded to offensive team on all defensive fouls with these exceptions:
   (a) Offside.
   (b) Encroachment.
   (c) Delay of game.
   (d) Illegal substitution.
   (e) Excessive time out(s).
   (f) Incidental grasp of facemask.
   (g) Neutral zone infraction.
   (h) Running into the kicker.
   (i) More than 11 players on the field at the snap.

Five Yards

1. Defensive holding or illegal use of hands (automatic first down).
2. Delay of game on offense or defense.
3. Delay of kickoff.
4. Encroachment.
5. Excessive time out(s).
6. False start.
7. Illegal formation.
8. Illegal shift.
9. Illegal motion.
10. Illegal substitution.
11. First onside kickoff out of bounds between goal lines and untouched or last touched by kicker.
12. Invalid fair catch signal.
13. More than 11 players on the field at snap for either team.
14. Less than seven men on offensive line at snap.
15. Offside.
16. Failure to pause one second after shift or huddle.
17. Running into kicker.
18. More than one man in motion at snap.
19. Grasping facemask of the ball carrier or quarterback.
20. Player out of bounds at snap.
21. Ineligible member(s) of kicking team going beyond line of scrimmage before ball is kicked.
22. Illegal return.
23. Failure to report change of eligibility.
24. Neutral zone infraction.
25. Loss of team time out(s) or five-yard penalty on the defense for excessive crowd noise.
26. Ineligible player downfield during passing down.
27. Second forward pass behind the line.
28. Forward pass is first touched by eligible receiver who has gone out of bounds and returned.
29. Forward pass touches or is caught by an ineligible receiver on or behind line.
30. Forward pass thrown from behind line of scrimmage after ball once crossed the line.
31. Kicking team player voluntarily out of bounds during a punt.
32. Twelve (12) men in the huddle.

10 Yards

1. Offensive pass interference.
2. Holding, illegal use of hands, arms, or body by offense.
3. Tripping by a member of either team.
4. Helping the runner.
5. Deliberately batting or punching a loose ball.
6. Deliberately kicking a loose ball.
7. Illegal block above the waist.

15 Yards

1. Chop block.
2. Clipping below the waist.
3. Fair catch interference.
4. Illegal crackback block by offense.
5. Piling on.
6. Roughing the kicker.
7. Roughing the passer.
8. Twisting, turning, or pulling an opponent by the facemask.
9. Unnecessary roughness.
10. Unsportsmanlike conduct.
11. Delay of game at start of either half.
12. Illegal low block.
13. A tackler using his helmet to butt, spear, or ram an opponent.
14. Any player who uses the top of his helmet unnecessarily.
15. A punter, placekicker, or holder who simulates being roughed by a defensive player.
16. Leaping.
17. Leverage.
18. Any player who removes his helmet after a play while on the field.

Five Yards and Loss of Down (Combination Penalty)

1. Forward pass thrown from beyond line of scrimmage.

10 Yards and Loss of Down (Combination Penalty)

1. Intentional grounding of forward pass (safety if passer is in own end zone). If foul occurs more than 10 yards behind line, play results in loss of down at spot of foul.

15 Yards and Loss of Coin Toss Option

1. Team's late arrival on the field prior to scheduled kickoff.
2. Captains not appearing for coin toss.

15 Yards (and disqualification if flagrant)

1. Striking opponent with fist.
2. Kicking or kneeing opponent.
3. Striking opponent on head or neck with forearm, elbow, or hands whether or not the initial contact is made below the neck area.
4. Roughing kicker.
5. Roughing passer.
6. Malicious unnecessary roughness.
7. Unsportsmanlike conduct.
8. Palpably unfair act. (Distance penalty determined by the Referee after consultation with other officials.)

15 Yards and Automatic Disqualification

1. Using a helmet (not worn) as a weapon.
2. Striking or purposely shoving a game official.

Suspension From Game For One Down

1. Illegal equipment. (Player may return after one down when legally equipped.)

Touchdown Awarded (Palpably Unfair Act)

1. When Referee determines a palpably unfair act deprived a team of a touchdown. (Example: Player comes off bench and tackles runner apparently en route to touchdown.)

FIELD

1. Sidelines and end lines are out of bounds. The goal line is actually in the end zone. A player with the ball in his possession scores a touchdown when the ball is on, above, or over the goal line.
2. The field is rimmed by a white border, six feet wide, along the sidelines. All of this is out of bounds.

3. The hashmarks (inbound lines) are 70 feet, 9 inches from each sideline.
4. Goal posts must be single-standard type, offset from the end line and painted bright gold. The goal posts must be 18 feet, 6 inches wide and the top face of the crossbar must be 10 feet above the ground. Vertical posts extend at least 30 feet above the crossbar. A ribbon 4 inches by 42 inches long is to be attached to the top of each post. The actual goal is the plane extending indefinitely above the crossbar and between the outer edges of the posts.
5. The field is 360 feet long and 160 feet wide. The end zones are 30 feet deep. The line used in try-for-point plays is two yards out from the goal line.
6. Chain crew members and ball boys must be uniformly identifiable.
7. All clubs must use standardized sideline markers. Pylons must be used for goal line and end line markings.
8. End zone markings and club identification at 50 yard line must be approved by the Commissioner to avoid any confusion as to delineation of goal lines, sidelines, and end lines.

BALL

1. The home club shall have 36 balls for outdoor games and 24 for indoor games available for testing with a pressure gauge by the referee two hours prior to the starting time of the game to meet with League requirements. Twelve (12) new footballs, sealed in a special box and shipped by the manufacturer, will be opened in the officials' locker room two hours prior to the starting time of the game. These balls are to be specially marked with the letter "k" and used exclusively for the kicking game.

COIN TOSS

1. The toss of coin will take place within three minutes of kickoff in center of field. The toss will be called by the visiting captain before the coin is flipped. The winner may choose one of two privileges and the loser gets the other:
   (a) Receive or kick
   (b) Goal his team will defend
2. Immediately prior to the start of the second half, the captains of both teams must inform the officials of their respective choices. The loser of the original coin toss gets first choice.

TIMING

1. The stadium game clock is official. In case it stops or is operating incorrectly, the Line Judge takes over the official timing on the field.
2. Each period is 15 minutes. The intermission between the periods is two minutes. Halftime is 12 minutes, unless otherwise specified.
3. On charged team time outs, the Field Judge starts watch and blows whistle after 1 minute 50 seconds, unless television does not utilize the time for commercial. In this case the length of the time out is reduced to 40 seconds.
4. The Referee will allow necessary time to attend to an injured player, or repair a legal player's equipment.
5. Each team is allowed three time outs each half.
6. Time between plays will be 40 seconds from the end of a given play until the snap of the ball for the next play, or a 25-second interval after certain administrative stoppages and game delays.
7. Clock will start running when ball is snapped following all changes of team possession.
8. With the exception of the last two minutes of the first half and the last five minutes of the second half, the game clock will be restarted following a kickoff return, a player going out of bounds on a play from scrimmage, or after declined penalties when appropriate on the referee's signal.
9. Consecutive team time outs can be taken by opposing teams but the length of the second time out will be reduced to 40 seconds.
10. When, in the judgment of the Referee, the level of crowd noise prevents the offense from hearing its signals, he can institute a series of procedures which can result in a loss of team time outs or a five-yard penalty against the defensive team.

SUDDEN DEATH

1. The sudden death system of determining the winner shall prevail when score is tied at the end of the regulation playing time of all NFL games. The team scoring first during overtime play shall be the winner and the game automatically ends upon any score (by safety, field goal, or touchdown) or when a score is awarded by Referee for a palpably unfair act.
2. At the end of regulation time the Referee will immediately toss coin at center of field in accordance with rules pertaining to the usual pregame toss. The captain of the visiting team will call the toss prior to the coin being flipped.
3. Following a three-minute intermission after the end of the regulation game, play will be continued in 15-minute periods or until there is a score. There is a two-minute intermission between subsequent periods. The teams change goals at the start of each period. Each team has three time outs per half and all general timing provisions apply as during a regular game. Disqualified players are not allowed to return.
   Exception: In preseason and regular season games there shall be a maximum of 15 minutes of sudden death with two time outs instead of three. General provisions that apply for the fourth quarter will prevail. Try not attempted if touchdown scored.

TIMING IN FINAL TWO MINUTES OF EACH HALF

1. On kickoff, clock does not start until the ball has been legally touched by player of either team in the field of play. (In all other cases, clock starts with kickoff.)
2. A team cannot buy an excess time out for a penalty. However, a fourth time out is allowed without penalty for an injured player, who must be removed immediately. A fifth time out or more is allowed for an injury and a five-yard penalty is assessed if the clock was running. Additionally, if the clock was running and the score is tied or the team in possession is losing, the ball cannot be put in play for at least 10 seconds on the fourth or more time out. The half or game can end while those 10 seconds are run off on the clock.
3. If the defensive team is behind in the score and commits a foul when it has no time outs left in the final 40 seconds of either half, the offensive team can decline the penalty for the foul and have the time on the clock expire.
4. Fouls that occur in the last five minutes of the fourth quarter as well as the last two minutes of the first half will result in the clock starting on the snap.

TRY

1. After a touchdown, the scoring team is allowed a try during one scrimmage down. The ball may be spotted anywhere between the inbounds lines, two or more yards from the goal line. The successful conversion counts one point by kick; two points for a successful conversion by touchdown; or one point for a safety.
2. The defensive team never can score on a try. As soon as defense gets possession or the kick is blocked or a touchdown is not scored, the try is over.
3. Any distance penalty for fouls committed by the defense that prevent the try from being attempted can be enforced on the succeeding try or succeeding kickoff. Any foul committed on a successful try will result in a distance penalty being assessed on the ensuing kickoff.
4. Only the fumbling player can recover and advance a fumble during a try.

PLAYERS-SUBSTITUTIONS

1. Each team is permitted 11 men on the field at the snap.
2. Unlimited substitution is permitted. However, players may enter the field only when the ball is dead. Players who have been substituted for are not permitted to linger on the field. Such lingering will be interpreted as unsportsmanlike conduct.
3. Players leaving the game must be out of bounds on their own side, clearing the field between the end lines, before a snap or free kick. If player crosses end line leaving field, it is delay of game (five-yard penalty).
4. Offensive substitutes who remain in the game must move onto the field as far as the inside of the field numerals before moving to a wide position.
5. With the exception of the last two minutes of either half, the offensive team, while in the process of substitution or simulated substitution, is prohibited from rushing quickly to the line and snapping the ball with the obvious attempt to cause a defensive foul; i.e., too many men on the field.

KICKOFF

1. The kickoff shall be from the kicking team's 30-yard line at the start of each half and after a field goal and try. A kickoff is one type of free kick.
2. A one-inch tee may be used (no tee permitted for field goal or try attempt) on a kickoff. The ball is put in play by a placekick.
3. A kickoff may not score a field goal.
4. A kickoff is illegal unless it travels 10 yards OR is touched by the receiving team. Once the ball is touched by the receiving team or has gone 10 yards, it is a free ball. Receivers may recover and advance. Kicking team may recover but NOT advance UNLESS receiver had possession and lost the ball.
5. When a kickoff goes out of bounds between the goal lines without being touched by the receiving team, the ball belongs to the receivers 30 yards from the spot of the kick or at the out-of-bounds spot unless the ball went out-of-bounds the first time an onside kick was attempted. In this case, the kicking team is penalized five yards and the ball must be kicked again.
6. When a kickoff goes out of bounds between the goal lines and is touched last by receiving team, it is receiver's ball at out-of-bounds spot.
7. If the kicking team either illegally kicks off out of bounds or is guilty of a short free kick on two or more consecutive onside kicks, receivers may take pos-

session of the ball at the dead ball spot, out-of-bounds spot, or spot of illegal touch.

SAFETY

1. In addition to a kickoff, the other free kick is a kick after a safety (safety kick). A punt may be used (a punt may not be used on a kickoff).
2. On a safety kick, the team scored upon puts ball in play by a punt, dropkick, or placekick without tee. No score can be made on a free kick following a safety, even if a series of penalties places team in position. (A field goal can be scored only on a play from scrimmage or a free kick after a fair catch.)

FAIR CATCH KICK

1. After a fair catch, the receiving team has the option to put the ball in play by a snap or a fair catch kick (field goal attempt), with fair catch kick lines established ten yards apart. All general rules apply as for a field goal attempt from scrimmage. The clock starts when the ball is kicked. (No tee permitted.)

FIELD GOAL

1. All field goals attempted (kicker) and missed from beyond the 20-yard line will result in the defensive team taking possession of the ball at the spot of the kick. On any field goal attempted and missed where the spot of the kick is on or inside the 20-yard line, ball will revert to defensive team at the 20-yard line.

SAFETY

1. The important factor in a safety is impetus. Two points are scored for the opposing team when the ball is dead on or behind a team's own goal line if the impetus came from a player on that team.

Examples of Safety:

(a) Blocked punt goes out of kicking team's end zone. Impetus was provided by punting team. The block only changes direction of ball, not impetus.
(b) Ball carrier retreats from field of play into his own end zone and is downed. Ball carrier provides impetus.
(c) Offensive team commits a foul and spot of enforcement is behind its own goal line.
(d) Player on receiving team muffs punt and, trying to get ball, forces or illegally kicks (creating new impetus) it into end zone where it goes out of the end zone or is recovered by a member of the receiving team in the end zone.

Examples of Non-Safety:

(a) Player intercepts a pass with both feet inbounds in the field of play and his momentum carries him into his own end zone. Ball is put in play at spot of interception.
(b) Player intercepts a pass in his own end zone and is downed in the end zone, even after recovering in the end zone. Impetus came from passing team, not from defense. (Touchback)
(c) Player passes from behind his own goal line. Opponent bats down ball in end zone. (Incomplete pass)

MEASURING

1. The forward point of the ball is used when measuring.

POSITION OF PLAYERS AT SNAP

1. Offensive team must have at least seven players on line.
2. Offensive players, not on line, must be at least one yard back at snap. **(Exception:** player who takes snap.)
3. No interior lineman may move abruptly after taking or simulating a three-point stance.
4. No player of either team may enter neutral zone before snap.
5. No player of offensive team may charge or move abruptly, after assuming set position, in such manner as to lead defense to believe snap has started. No player of the defensive team within one yard of the line of scrimmage may make an abrupt movement in an attempt to cause the offense to false start.
6. If a player changes his eligibility, the Referee must alert the defensive captain after player has reported to him.
7. All players of offensive team must be stationary at snap, except one back who may be in motion parallel to scrimmage line or backward (not forward).
8. After a shift or huddle all players on offensive team must come to an absolute stop for at least one second with no movement of hands, feet, head, or swaying of body.
9. Quarterbacks can be called for a false start penalty (five yards) if their actions are judged to be an obvious attempt to draw an opponent offside.
10. Offensive linemen are permitted to interlock legs.

USE OF HANDS, ARMS, AND BODY

1. No player on offense may assist a runner except by blocking for him. There shall be no interlocking interference.
2. A runner may ward off opponents with his hands and arms but no other player on offense may use hands or arms to obstruct an opponent by grasping with hands, pushing, or encircling any part of his body during a block. Hands (open or closed) can be thrust forward to initially contact an opponent on or outside the opponent's frame, but the blocker immediately must work to bring his hands on or inside the frame.
   Note: Pass blocking: Hand(s) thrust forward that slip outside the body of the defender will be legal if blocker immediately worked to bring them back inside. Hand(s) or arm(s) that encircle a defender—i.e., hook an opponent—are to be considered illegal and officials are to call a foul for holding.
   Blocker cannot use his hands or arms to push from behind, hang onto, or encircle an opponent in a manner that restricts his movement as the play develops.
3. Hands cannot be thrust forward above the frame to contact an opponent on the neck, face or head.
   Note: The frame is defined as the part of the opponent's body below the neck that is presented to the blocker.
4. A defensive player may not tackle or hold an opponent other than a runner. Otherwise, he may use his hands, arms, or body only:
   (a) To defend or protect himself against an obstructing opponent.
   Exception: An eligible receiver is considered to be an obstructing opponent ONLY to a point five yards beyond the line of scrimmage unless the player who receives the snap clearly demonstrates no further intention to pass the ball. Within this five-yard zone, a defensive player may chuck an eligible player in front of him. A defensive player is allowed to maintain continuous and unbroken contact within the five-yard zone until a point when the receiver is even with the defender. The defensive player cannot use his hands or arms to push from behind, hang onto, or encircle an eligible receiver in a manner that restricts movement as the play develops. Beyond this five-yard limitation, a defender may use his hands or arms ONLY to defend or protect himself against impending contact caused by a receiver. In such reaction, the defender may not contact a receiver who attempts to take a path to evade him.
   (b) To push or pull opponent out of the way on line of scrimmage.
   (c) In actual attempt to get at or tackle runner.
   (d) To push or pull opponent out of the way in a legal attempt to recover a loose ball.
   (e) During a legal block on an opponent who is not an eligible pass receiver.
   (f) When legally blocking an eligible pass receiver above the waist.
   Exception: Eligible receivers lined up within two yards of the tackle, whether on or immediately behind the line, may be blocked below the waist at or behind the line of scrimmage. NO eligible receiver may be blocked below the waist after he goes beyond the line. (Illegal cut)
   Note: Once the quarterback hands off or pitches the ball to a back, or if the quarterback leaves the pocket area, the restrictions (illegal chuck, illegal cut) on the defensive team relative to the offensive receivers will end, provided the ball is not in the air.
5. A defensive player may not contact an opponent above the shoulders with the palm of his hand except to ward him off on the line. This exception is permitted only if it is not a repeated act against the same opponent during any one contact. In all other cases the palms may be used on head, neck, or face only to ward off or push an opponent in legal attempt to get at the ball.
6. Any offensive player who pretends to possess the ball or to whom a teammate pretends to give the ball may be tackled provided he is crossing his scrimmage line between the ends of a normal tight offensive line.
7. An offensive player who lines up more than two yards outside his own tackle or a player who, at the snap, is in a backfield position and subsequently takes a position more than two yards outside a tackle may not clip an opponent anywhere nor may he contact an opponent below the waist if the blocker is moving toward the ball and if contact is made within an area five yards on either side of the line. (crackback)
8. A player of either team may block at any time provided it is not pass interference, fair catch interference, or unnecessary roughness.
9. A player may not bat or punch:
   (a) A loose ball (in field of play) toward his opponent's goal line or in any direction in either end zone.
   (b) A ball in player possession.
   Note: If there is any question as to whether a defender is stripping or batting a ball in player possession, the official(s) will rule the action as a legal act (stripping the ball).
   Exception: A forward or backward pass may be batted, tipped, or deflected in any direction at any time by either the offense or the defense.
   Note: A pass in flight that is controlled or caught may only be thrown back-

ward, if it is thrown forward it is considered an illegal bat.

10. No player may deliberately kick any ball except as a punt, dropkick, or placekick.

FORWARD PASS

1. A forward pass may be touched or caught by any eligible receiver. All members of the defensive team are eligible. Eligible receivers on the offensive team are players on either end of line (other than center, guard, or tackle) or players at least one yard behind the line at the snap. A T-formation quarterback is not eligible to receive a forward pass during a play from scrimmage.
   Exception: T-formation quarterback becomes eligible if pass is previously touched by an eligible receiver.
2. An offensive team may make only one forward pass during each play from scrimmage (Loss of 5 yards).
3. The passer must be behind his line of scrimmage (Loss of down and five yards, enforced from the spot of pass).
4. Any eligible offensive player may catch a forward pass. If a pass is touched by one eligible offensive player and touched or caught by a second offensive player, pass completion is legal. Further, all offensive players become eligible once a pass is touched by an eligible receiver or any defensive player.
5. The rules concerning a forward pass and ineligible receivers:
   (a) If ball is touched accidentally by an ineligible receiver on or behind his line: loss of five yards.
   (b) If ineligible receiver is illegally downfield: loss of five yards.
   (c) If touched or caught (intentionally or accidentally) by ineligible receiver beyond the line: loss of 5 yards.
6. The player who first controls and continues to maintain control of a pass will be awarded the ball even though his opponent later establishes joint control of the ball.
7. Any forward pass becomes incomplete and ball is dead if:
   (a) Pass hits the ground or goes out of bounds.
   (b) Pass hits the goal post or the crossbar of either team.
   (c) Pass is caught by offensive player after touching ineligible receiver.
   (d) An illegal pass is caught by an offensive player.
8. A forward pass is complete when a receiver clearly possesses the pass and touches the ground with both feet inbounds while in possession of the ball. If a receiver would have landed inbounds with both feet but is carried or pushed out of bounds while maintaining possession of the ball, pass is complete at the out-of-bounds spot.
9. If an eligible receiver goes out of bounds accidentally or is legally forced out by a defender and returns to first touch and catch a pass, the play is regarded as an incomplete pass. Loss of 5 yards.
10. On a fourth down pass an incomplete pass results in a loss of down at the line of scrimmage.
11. If a personal foul is committed by the defense prior to the completion of a pass, the penalty is 15 yards from the spot where ball becomes dead.
12. If a personal foul is committed by the offense prior to the completion of a pass, the penalty is 15 yards from the previous line of scrimmage.

INTENTIONAL GROUNDING OF FORWARD PASS

1. Intentional grounding of a forward pass is a foul: loss of down and 10 yards from previous spot if passer is in the field of play or loss of down at the spot of the foul if it occurs more than 10 yards behind the line or safety if passer is in his own end zone when ball is released.
2. Intentional grounding will be called when a passer, facing an imminent loss of yardage due to pressure from the defense, throws a forward pass without a realistic chance of completion.
3. Intentional grounding will not be called when a passer, while out of the pocket and facing an imminent loss of yardage, throws a pass that lands at or beyond the line of scrimmage, even if no offensive player(s) have a realistic chance to catch the ball (including if the ball lands out of bounds over the sideline or end line).
4. Intentional gounding will not be called when a screen pass is developing and the quarterback throws the ball in the vicinity of the screen receiver.

PROTECTION OF PASSER

1. By interpretation, a pass begins when the passer—with possession of ball—starts to bring his hand forward. If ball strikes ground after this action has begun, play is ruled an incomplete pass. If passer loses control of ball prior to his bringing his hand forward, play is ruled a fumble.
2. No defensive player may run into a passer of a legal forward pass after the ball has left his hand (15 yards). The Referee must determine whether opponent had a reasonable chance to stop his momentum during an attempt to block the pass or tackle the passer while he still had the ball.
3. No defensive player who has an unrestricted path to the quarterback may hit him flagrantly in the area of the knee(s) or below when approaching in any direction.
4. Officials are to blow the play dead as soon as the quarterback is clearly in the grasp and control of any tackler, and his safety is in jeopardy.

PASS INTERFERENCE

1. There shall be no interference with a forward pass thrown from behind the line. The restriction for the passing team starts with the snap. The restriction on the defensive team starts when the ball leaves the passer's hand. Both restrictions end when the ball is touched by anyone.
2. The penalty for defensive pass interference is an automatic first down at the spot of the foul. If interference is in the end zone, it is first down for the offense on the defense's 1-yard line. If previous spot was inside the defense's 1-yard line, penalty is half the distance to the goal line.
3. The penalty for offensive pass interference is 10 yards from the previous spot.
4. It is pass interference by either team when any player movement beyond the line of scrimmage significantly hinders the progress of an eligible player of such player's opportunity to catch the ball. Offensive pass interference rules apply from the time the ball is snapped until the ball is touched. Defensive pass interference rules apply from the time the ball is thrown until the ball is touched. Actions that constitute defensive pass interference include but are not limited to:
   (a) Contact by a defender who is not playing the ball and such contact restricts the receiver's opportunity to make the catch.
   (b) Playing through the back of a receiver in an attempt to make a play on the ball.
   (c) Grabbing a receiver's arm(s) in such a manner that restricts his opportunity to catch a pass.
   (d) Extending an arm across the body of a receiver thus restricting his ability to catch a pass, regardless of whether the defender is playing the ball.
   (e) Cutting off the path of a receiver by making contact with him without playing the ball.
   (f) Hooking a receiver in an attempt to get to the ball in such a manner that it causes the receiver's body to turn prior to the ball arriving.

   Actions that do not constitute pass interference include but are not limited to:
   (a) Incidental contact by a defender's hands, arms, or body when both players are competing for the ball, or neither player is looking for the ball. If there is any question whether contact is incidental, the ruling shall be no interference.
   (b) Inadvertent tangling of feet when both players are playing the ball or neither player is playing the ball.
   (c) Contact that would normally be considered pass interference, but the pass is clearly uncatchable by the involved players.
   (d) Laying a hand on a receiver that does not restrict the receiver in an attempt to make a play on the ball.
   (e) Contact by a defender who has gained position on a receiver in an attempt to catch the ball.

   Actions that constitute offensive pass interference include but are not limited to:
   (a) Blocking downfield by an offensive player prior to the ball being touched.
   (b) Initiating contact with a defender by shoving or pushing off thus creating a separation in an attempt to catch a pass.
   (c) Driving through a defender who has established a position on the field.

   Actions that do not constitute offensive pass interference include but are not limited to:
   (a) Incidental contact by a receiver's hands, arms, or body when both players are competing for the ball or neither player is looking for the ball.
   (b) Inadvertent touching of feet when both players are playing the ball or neither player is playing the ball.
   (c) Contact that would normally be considered pass interference, but the ball is *clearly* uncatchable by involved players.

Note 1: If there is any question whether player contact is incidental, the ruling should be no interference.

Note 2: Defensive players have as much right to the path of the ball as eligible offensive players.

Note 3: Pass interference for both teams ends when the pass is touched.

Note 4: There can be no pass interference at or behind the line of scrimmage, but defensive actions such as tackling a receiver can still result in a 5-yard penalty for defensive holding, if accepted.

Note 5: Whenever a team presents an apparent punting formation, defensive pass interference is not to be called for action on the end man on the line of scrimmage, or an eligible receiver behind the line of scrimmage who is aligned or in motion more than one yard outside the end man on the line.

Defensive holding, such as tackling a receiver, still can be called and result in a 5-yard penalty from the previous spot, if accepted. Offensive pass interference rules still apply.

BACKWARD PASS

1. Any pass not forward is regarded as a backward pass. A pass parallel to the line is a backward pass. A runner may pass backward at any time.
2. A backward pass that strikes the ground can be recovered and advanced by either team.
3. A backward pass caught in the air can be advanced by either team.
4. A backward pass in flight may not be batted forward by an offensive player.

FUMBLE

1. The distinction between a fumble and a muff should be kept in mind in considering rules about fumbles. A fumble is the loss of player possession of the ball. A muff is the touching of a loose ball by a player in an unsuccessful attempt to obtain possession.
2. A fumble may be advanced by any player on either team regardless of whether recovered before or after ball hits the ground.
3. A fumble that goes forward and out of bounds will return to the fumbling team at the spot of the fumble unless the ball goes out of bounds in the opponent's end zone. In this case, it is a touchback.
4. On a play from scrimmage, if an offensive player fumbles anywhere on the field during fourth down, only the fumbling player is permitted to recover and/or advance the ball. If any player fumbles after the two-minute warning in a half, only the fumbling player is permitted to recover and/or advance the ball. If recovered by any other offensive player, the ball is dead at the spot of the fumble unless it is recovered behind the spot of the fumble. In that case, the ball is dead at the spot of recovery. Any defensive player may recover and/or advance any fumble at any time.
5. A muffed hand-to-hand snap from center is treated as a fumble.

KICKS FROM SCRIMMAGE

1. Any kick from scrimmage must be made from behind the line to be legal.
2. Any punt or missed field goal that touches a goal post is dead.
3. During a kick from scrimmage, only the end men, as eligible receivers on the line of scrimmage at the time of the snap, are permitted to go beyond the line before the ball is kicked.
   Exception: An eligible receiver who, at the snap, is aligned or in motion behind the line and more than one yard outside the end man on his side of the line, clearly making him the outside receiver, replaces that end man as the player eligible to go downfield after the snap. All other members of the kicking team must remain at the line of scrimmage until the ball has been kicked.
4. Any punt that is blocked and does not cross the line of scrimmage can be recovered and advanced by either team. However, if offensive team recovers it must make the yardage necessary for its first down to retain possession if punt was on fourth down.
5. The kicking team may never advance its own kick even though legal recovery is made beyond the line of scrimmage. Possession only.
6. A member of the receiving team may not run into or rough a kicker who kicks from behind his line unless contact is:
   (a) Incidental to and after he had touched ball in flight.
   (b) Caused by kicker's own motions.
   (c) Occurs during a quick kick, or a kick made after a run behind the line, or after kicker recovers a loose ball on the ground. Ball is loose when kicker muffs snap or snap hits ground.
   (d) Defender is blocked into kicker.
   The penalty for running into the kicker is 5 yards. For roughing the kicker: 15 yards, an automatic first down and disqualification if flagrant.
7. If a member of the kicking team attempting to down the ball on or inside opponent's 5-yard line carries the ball into the end zone, it is a touchback.
8. Fouls during a punt are enforced from the previous spot (line of scrimmage).
   Exception: Illegal touching, fair-catch interference, invalid fair-catch signal, or personal foul (blocking after a fair-catch signal).
9. While the ball is in the air or rolling on the ground following a punt or field goal attempt and receiving team commits a foul only before or after gaining possession, receiving team will retain possession and will be penalized for its foul.
10. It will be illegal for a defensive player to jump or stand on any player, or be picked up by a teammate or to use a hand or hands on a teammate to gain additional height in an attempt to block a kick (Penalty: 15 yards, unsportsmanlike conduct).
11. A punted ball remains a kicked ball until it is declared dead or in possession of either team.
12. Any member of the punting team may down the ball anywhere in the field of play. However, it is illegal touching (Official's time out and receiver's ball at spot of illegal touching). This foul does not offset any foul by receivers during the down.
13. Defensive team may advance all kicks from scrimmage (including unsuccessful field goal) whether or not ball crosses defensive team's goal line. Rules pertaining to kicks from scrimmage apply until defensive team gains possession.
14. When a team presents a punt formation, defensive pass interference is not to be called for actions on the widest player eligible to go beyond line. Defensive holding may be called.

FAIR CATCH

1. The member of the receiving team must raise one arm a full length above his head and wave it from side to side while kick is in flight. (Failure to give proper sign: receivers' ball five yards behind spot of signal.) **Note:** It is legal for the receiver to shield his eyes from the sun by raising one hand no higher than the helmet.
2. No opponent may interfere with the fair catcher, the ball, or his path to the ball. Penalty: 15 yards from spot of foul and fair catch is awarded.
3. A player who signals for a fair catch is not required to catch the ball. However, if a player signals for a fair catch, he may not block or initiate contact with any player on the kicking team until the ball touches a player. Penalty: snap 15 yards.
4. If ball hits ground or is touched by member of kicking team in flight, fair catch signal is off and all rules for a kicked ball apply.
5. Any undue advance by a fair catch receiver is delay of game. No specific distance is specified for undue advance as ball is dead at spot of catch. If player comes to a reasonable stop, no penalty. For violation, five yards.
6. If time expires while ball is in play and a fair catch is awarded, receiving team may choose to extend the period with one fair catch kick down. However, placekicker may not use tee.

FOUL ON LAST PLAY OF HALF OR GAME

1. On a foul by defense on last play of half or game, the down is replayed if penalty is accepted.
2. On a foul by the offense on last play of half or game, the down is not replayed and the play in which the foul is committed is nullified.
   Exception: Fair catch interference, foul following change of possession, illegal touching. No score by offense counts.

SPOT OF ENFORCEMENT OF FOUL

1. There are four basic spots at which a penalty for a foul is enforced:
   (a) Spot of foul: The spot where the foul is committed.
   (b) Previous spot: The spot where the ball was put in play.
   (c) Spot of snap, backward pass or fumble: The spot where the foul occurred or the spot where the penalty is to be enforced.
   (d) Succeeding spot: The spot where the ball next would be put in play if no distance penalty were to be enforced.
   Exception: If foul occurs after a touchdown and before the whistle for a try, succeeding spot is spot of next kickoff.
2. All fouls committed by offensive team behind the line of scrimmage (except in the end zone) shall be penalized from the previous spot. If the foul is in the end zone, it is a safety.
3. When spot of enforcement for fouls involving defensive holding or illegal use of hands by the defense is behind the line of scrimmage, any penalty yardage to be assessed on that play shall be measured from the line if the foul occurred beyond the line.

DOUBLE FOUL

1. If there is a double foul during a down in which there is a change of possession, the team last gaining possession may keep the ball unless its foul was committed prior to the change of possession.
2. If double foul occurs after a change of possession, the defensive team retains the ball at the spot of its foul or dead ball spot.
3. If one of the fouls of a double foul involves disqualification, that player must be removed, but no penalty yardage is to be assessed.
4. If the kickers foul during a kick before possession changes and the receivers foul after possession changes, the receivers will retain the ball after enforcement of its foul.

PENALTY ENFORCED ON FOLLOWING KICKOFF

1. When a team scores by touchdown, field goal, extra point, or safety and either team commits a personal foul, unsportsmanlike conduct, or obvious unfair act during the down, the penalty will be assessed on the following kickoff.

EMERGENCIES AND UNFAIR ACTS

Emergencies—Policy

The National Football League requires all League personnel, including game officials, League office employees, players, coaches, and other club employees to use best effort to see that each game—preseason, regular season, and postseason—is played to its conclusion. The League recognizes, however, that emergencies may arise that make a game's completion impossible or inadvisable. Such circumstances may include, but are not limited to, severely inclement weather, natural or manmade disaster, power failure, and spectator interference. Games should be suspended, cancelled, postponed, or terminated when circumstances exist such that comencement or continuation of play would pose a threat to the safety of participants or spectators.

Authority of Commissioner's Office

1. Authority to cancel, postpone, or terminate games is vested only in the Commissioner and the League President (other League office representatives and referees may suspend play temporarily; see point No. 3 under this section and point No. 1 under "Authority of Referee" below). The following definitions apply:
   - **Cancel.** To cancel a game is to nullify it either before or after it begins and to make no provision for rescheduling it or for including its score or other performance statistics in League records.
   - **Postpone.** To postpone a game is (a) to defer its starting time to a later date, or (b) to suspend it after play has begun and to make provision to resume at a later date with all scores and other performance statistics up to the point of postponement added to those achieved in the resumed portion of the game.
   - **Terminate.** To terminate a game is to end it short of a full 60 minutes of play, to record it officially as a completed game, and to make no provision to resume it at a later date. The Commissioner or League President may terminate a game in an emergency if, in his opinion, it is reasonable to project that its resumption (a) would not change its ultimate result or (b) would not adversely affect any other interteam competitive issue.
   - **Forfeit.** The Commissioner, (except in cases of disciplinary action; see last section on "Removing Team from Field"), League President, and their representatives, including referees, are not authorized unilaterally to declare forfeits. A forfeit occurs only when a game is not played because of the failure or refusal of *one* team to participate. In that event, the other team, if ready and willing to play, is the winner by a score of 2-0.
2. If an emergency arises that may require cancellation, postponement, or termination (see above), the highest ranking representative from the Commissioner's office working the game in a "control" capacity will consult with the Commissioner, League President, or game-day duty officer designated by the League (by telephone, if that person is not in attendance) concerning such decision. If circumstances warrant, the League representative should also attempt to consult with the weather bureau and with appropriate security personnel of the League, club, stadium, and local authorities. If no representative from the Commissioner's office is working the game in a "control" capacity, the referee will be in charge (see "Authority of Referee" below).
3. In circumstances where safety is of immediate concern, the Commissioner's-office representative may, after consulting with the referee, authorize a temporary suspension in play and, if warranted, removal of the participants from the playing field. The representative should be mindful of the safety of spectators, players, game officials, nonplayer personnel in the bench areas, and other field-level personnel such as photographers and cheerleaders.
4. If possible, the League-office representative should consult with authorized representatives of the two participating clubs before any decision involving cancellation, postponement, or termination is made by the Commissioner or League President.
5. If the Commissioner or League President decides to cancel, postpone, or terminate a game, his representative at the game or the game-day duty officer will then determine the method(s) for announcing such decision, e.g., by public-address announcement over referee's wireless microphone, by public-address announcement by home club, or by communication to radio, television, and other news media.

Authority of Referee

1. If a referee determines that an emergency warrants immediate removal of participants from the playing field for safety reasons, he may do so on his own authority. If, however, circumstances allow him the time, he must reach the highest ranking full-time League office representative working at the game in a "control" capacity or the game-day duty officer designated by the League (by telephone, if that person is not in attendance) and discuss the actual or potential emergency with such representative or duty officer. That representative or duty officer then will make the final decision on removal of participants from the field or obtain a decision from the Commissioner or League President.
2. If a referee removes participants from the playing field under No. 1 above, he may order them to their respective bench areas or to their locker rooms, whichever is appropriate in the circumstances.
3. After appropriate consultation under No. 1 above, the referee must advise the two participating head coaches of the nature of the emergency and the action contemplated (if the decision has not yet been reached) or of the final decision.
4. The referee must *not*, before a decision is reached, make an announcement on his microphone concerning the possibility of a cancellation, postponement, or termination unless instructed to do so by an appropriate representative of the Commissioner's office.
5. The referee must *not* discuss a forfeit with head coaches or club personnel and must *not* use that term over the referee's microphone (see definition of *forfeit* under No. 1 of "Authority of Commissioner's Office" above).
6. The referee must *not* assess an unsportsmanlike-conduct penalty on the home team for actions of fans that cause or contribute to an emergency.
7. The referee should be mindful of the safety of not only players and officials, but also of the spectators and other nonparticipants.
8. If an emergency involves spectator interference (for example, nonparticipants on the field or thrown objects), the referee immediately should contact the appropriate club or League representative for additional security assistance, including, if applicable, involvement of the League's security representative(s) assigned to the game.
9. The referee may order the resumption of play when he deems conditions safe for all concerned and, if circumstances warrant, after consultation with appropriate representatives of the Commissioner's office.
10. Under no circumstances is the referee authorized to cancel, postpone, terminate, or declare forfeiture of a game unilaterally.

Procedures for Starting and Resuming Games

Subject to the points of authority listed above, League personnel and referees will be guided by the following procedures for starting and resuming games that are affected by emergencies.

1. If, because of an emergency, a regular-season or postseason game is not started at its scheduled time and cannot be played at any later time that same day, the game nevertheless must be played on a subsequent date to be determined by the Commissioner.
2. If an emergency threatens to occur during the playing of a game (for example, an incoming tropical storm), the starting time of the game will not be moved to an earlier time unless there is clearly sufficient time to make an orderly change.
3. All games that are suspended temporarily and resumed on the same day, and all suspended games that are postponed to a later date, will be resumed at the point of suspension. On suspension, the referee will call timeout and make a record of the following: team possessing the ball, direction in which its offense was headed, position of the ball on the field, down, distance, period, time remaining in the period, and any other pertinent information required for an orderly and equitable resumption of play.
4. For regular-season postponements, the Commissioner will make every effort to set the game for no later than two days after its originally scheduled date and at the same site. If unable to schedule at the same site, he will select an appropriate alternative site. If it is impossible to schedule the game within two days after its original date, the Commissioner will attempt to schedule it on the Tuesday of the next calendar week. The Commissioner will keep in mind the potential for competitive inequities if one or both of the involved clubs has already been scheduled for a game close to the Tuesday of that week (for example, a Thursday game).
5. For postseason postponements, the Commissioner will make every effort to set the game as soon as possible after its originally scheduled date and at the same site. If unable to schedule at the same site, he will select an appropriate alternative site.
6. Whenever postponement is attributable to negligence by a club, the negligent club is responsible for all home club costs and expenses, including, subject to approval by the Commissioner, gate receipts and television-contract income. [See Section 19.11 (C) of the NFL Constitution and Bylaws.]
7. Each home club is strictly responsible for having the playing surface of its stadium well maintained and suitable for NFL play.

UNFAIR ACTS

Commissioner's Authority

The Commissioner has sole authority to investigate and to take appropriate disciplinary or corrective measures if any club action, nonparticipant interference, or emergency occurs in an NFL game which he deems so unfair or outside the accepted tactics encountered in professional football that such action has a major effect on the result of a game.

No Club Protests

The authority and measures provided for in this section (UNFAIR ACTS) do not constitute a protest machinery for NFL clubs to dispute the result of a game. The Commissioner will conduct an investigation under this section only to review an act or occurrence that he deems so unfair that the result of the game in question may be inequitable to one of the participating teams. The Commissioner will not apply his authority under this section when a club registers a complaint concerning judgmental errors or routine errors of omission by game officials. Games involving such complaints will continue to stand as completed.

Penalties for Unfair Acts

The Commissioner's powers under this section (UNFAIR ACTS) include the imposition of monetary fines and draft choice forfeitures, suspension of persons involved, and, if appropriate, the reversal of a game's result or the rescheduling of a game, either from the beginning or from the point at which the extraordinary act occurred. In the event of rescheduling a game, the Commissioner will be guided by the procedures specified above ("Procedures for Starting and Resuming Games" under EMERGENCIES). In all cases, the Commissioner will conduct a full investigation, including the opportunity for hearings, use of game videotape, and any other procedures he deems appropriate.

REMOVING TEAM FROM FIELD

No player, coach, or other person affiliated with a club may remove that club's team from the field during the playing of any game, including preseason, except at the direction of the referee. Any club violating this rule will be subject to disciplinary action by the Commissioner, including possible game forfeiture and sole liability for financial losses suffered by the opposing club and any other affected member clubs of the League. [See Section 9.1 (E) of the NFL Constitution and Bylaws.]

NATIONAL FOOTBALL LEAGUE, 2000

280 Park Avenue, New York, New York 10017 (212) 450-2000

NFL Internet Address: http://nfl.com

Commissioner: Paul Tagliabue

Executive Vice President of Business, Properties & Club Services: Roger Goodell

Executive Vice President-Labor Relations/Chairman NFLMC: Harold Henderson

Executive Vice President, League Counsel & CAO: Jeff Pash

Executive Vice President of New Media/Internet & Enterprises: Tom Spock

Senior Vice President-Football Operations: George Young

NOTES

NOTES

NOTES

NOTES

NOTES

NOTES

NOTES